PAGE 38

ON THE ROAD

YOUR COMPLETE DE[...]
In-depth reviews, detailed listings and insider tips

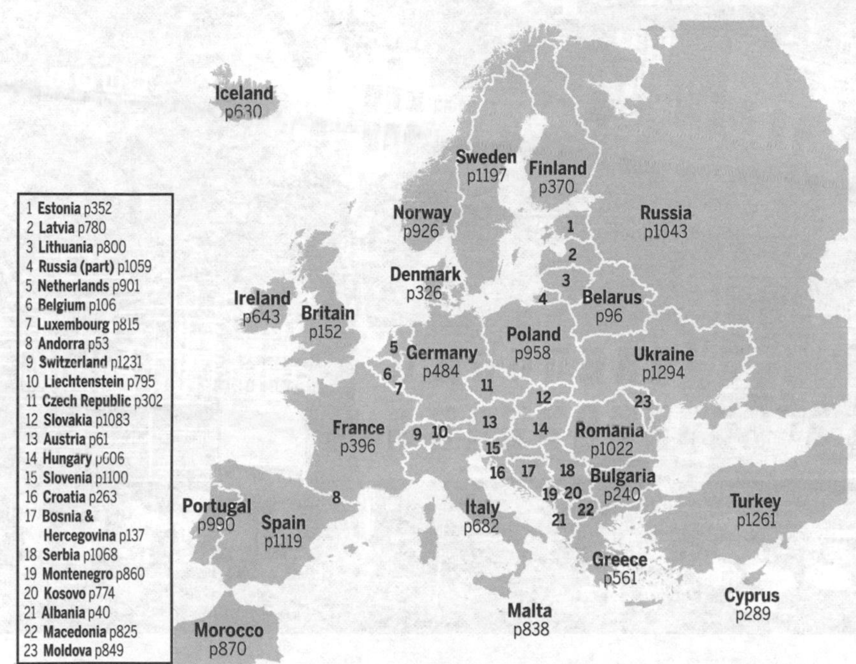

THIS EDITION WRITTEN AND RESEARCHED BY

Tom Masters

Brett Atkinson, Carolyn Bain, James Bainbridge, Mark Baker, Cristian Bonetto, Kerry Christiani, Paul Clammer, Jayne D'Arcy, Chris Deliso, Marc Di Duca, Peter Dragičević, Lisa Dunford, Mark Elliott, David Else, Steve Fallon, Duncan Garwood, Anthony Ham, Anna Kaminski, Craig McLachlan, Anja Mutić, Becky Ohlsen, Fran Parnell, Leif Pettersen, Brandon Presser, Josephine Quintero, Tim Richards, Simon Richmond, Miles Roddis, Tamara Sheward, Caroline Sieg, Regis St Louis, Andy Symington, Ryan Ver Berkmoes, Richard Watkins, Nicola Williams, Neil Wilson

welcome to Europe

Where To Begin?

Overwhelming it can be, confusing for sure – just perusing a map of the crowded Old World will reveal cities, mountain ranges, seas and even countries you may never have even heard of. But the good news is that whatever you decide to do here, you'll leave blown away by the sights, sounds, tastes and other sensations you'll experience: there simply is no way to tour Europe and not be awestruck.

First timers might try a sprinkling of the classics (Britain, France, Germany, Spain) and spice it up with a dash of something classical (Italy, Greece, Turkey), while those who have covered the essentials can try lesser-explored destinations (the Balkans, Scandinavia, Portugal or Poland). For the truly original the sky is the limit – Iceland, Albania, Moldova and Belarus all see few travellers, while for the true eccentric, microstates Andorra, Liechtenstein and Luxembourg might beckon.

Endless Variety

Europe's almost unmanageable wealth of attractions is its biggest single draw. Among its astonishing cultural heritage you'll find everything from the birthplace of democracy in Athens (p563), the Renaissance art of Florence (p733), the graceful canals of Venice (p718) and the Napoleonic splendour of Paris (p400) to less obvious attractions such as the Moorish palaces of

Europe is a patchwork of more than 40 compulsively individualistic countries and is a dazzling and spectacular place to explore. Jump in almost anywhere and join the party.

(left) Aerial view of Bruges (p125), Belgium
(below) Skiing at St Anton am Arlberg, (p90) Austria

Andalucía (p1173), the remains of one of the Seven Wonders of the World in Turkey (p1275) and the majesty of a second Venice in St Petersburg (p1053).

You'll also find glorious scenery (try the Scottish Highlands, volcanic Iceland, the Swiss Alps or Norwegians fjords), world-leading architecture, art, design, fashion and music (see London, Berlin, Paris, Antwerp and Copenhagen) and some of the best nightlife in the world (as well as London, Berlin and Paris, don't miss Moscow, Belgrade, Budapest or Madrid).

Smashing Stereotypes

A trip around Europe's patchwork of nations will inevitably make you rethink what you thought you knew about the place. As with any form of travel, surprises await: nationalities about whom you know little beyond lazy clichés will become humanised, complex and contradictory; you will feel the chill on your spine when you see that iconic work of art in the flesh or find yourself standing right where *that* happened. You will at least once find yourself on a beach, up a mountain, at a cafe or in a club thinking 'these people know how to live'.

Yes, Europe has and offers it all. So don't delay – get planning your own European odyssey as soon as you can. With so many extraordinary destinations offering incredible things to see and do, your only problem will be where to begin...

› Europe

Norwegian Fjords
Take an unforgettable boat trip (p936)
Dublin, Ireland
Enjoy a *craic* at a local pub (p646)
London, Britain
Catch the buzz of the city at night (p156)
Paris, France
Go climb the Eiffel Tower (p400)
Barcelona, Spain
Be humbled by the Sagrada Família (p1146)
Marrakesh, Morocco
Soak up the clamour of the souq (p891)
Swiss Alps
Reach up and touch the sky (p1240)
GREENLAND
ICELAND
Reykjavík
Faxaflói
Greenland Sea
Arctic Circle
Norwegian Sea
Faroe Islands (Denmark)
Shetland Islands
Orkney Islands
Outer Hebrides
SCOTLAND
NORTHERN IRELAND
ATLANTIC OCEAN
Edinburgh
North Sea
Belfast
IRELAND
Dublin
Irish Sea
BRITAIN
ENGLAND
WALES
St George's Channel
Cardiff
London
English Channel
Channel Islands
NORWAY
Oslo
Skagerrak
Copenhagen
DENMARK
Elbe
Berlin
NETHERLANDS
Amsterdam
Brussels
Rhine
GERMANY
BELGIUM
Luxembourg City
LUXEMBOURG
Paris
Seine
FRANCE
Loire
LIECHTENSTEIN
Vaduz
Bern
SWITZERLAND
Mt Blanc (4807m)
ALPS
Venice
Po
San Marino
MONACO
Monaco
ITALY
Rome
Bay of Biscay
PYRENEES
Andorra la Vella
ANDORRA
Golfe du Lion
Corsica (France)
Tyrrhenian Sea
Barcelona
Madrid
Lisbon
SPAIN
PORTUGAL
Sardinia (Italy)
Balearic Islands (Spain)
Mediterranean Sea
Strait of Gibraltar
ALGERIA
TUNISIA
Rabat
MOROCCO
Marrakesh
ATLAS MOUNTAINS
Canary Islands (Spain)
0 800 km
0 500 miles
30°W
20°W
10°W
0° (Greenwich)
10°E
70°N
60°N
50°N
40°N
30°N
40°W

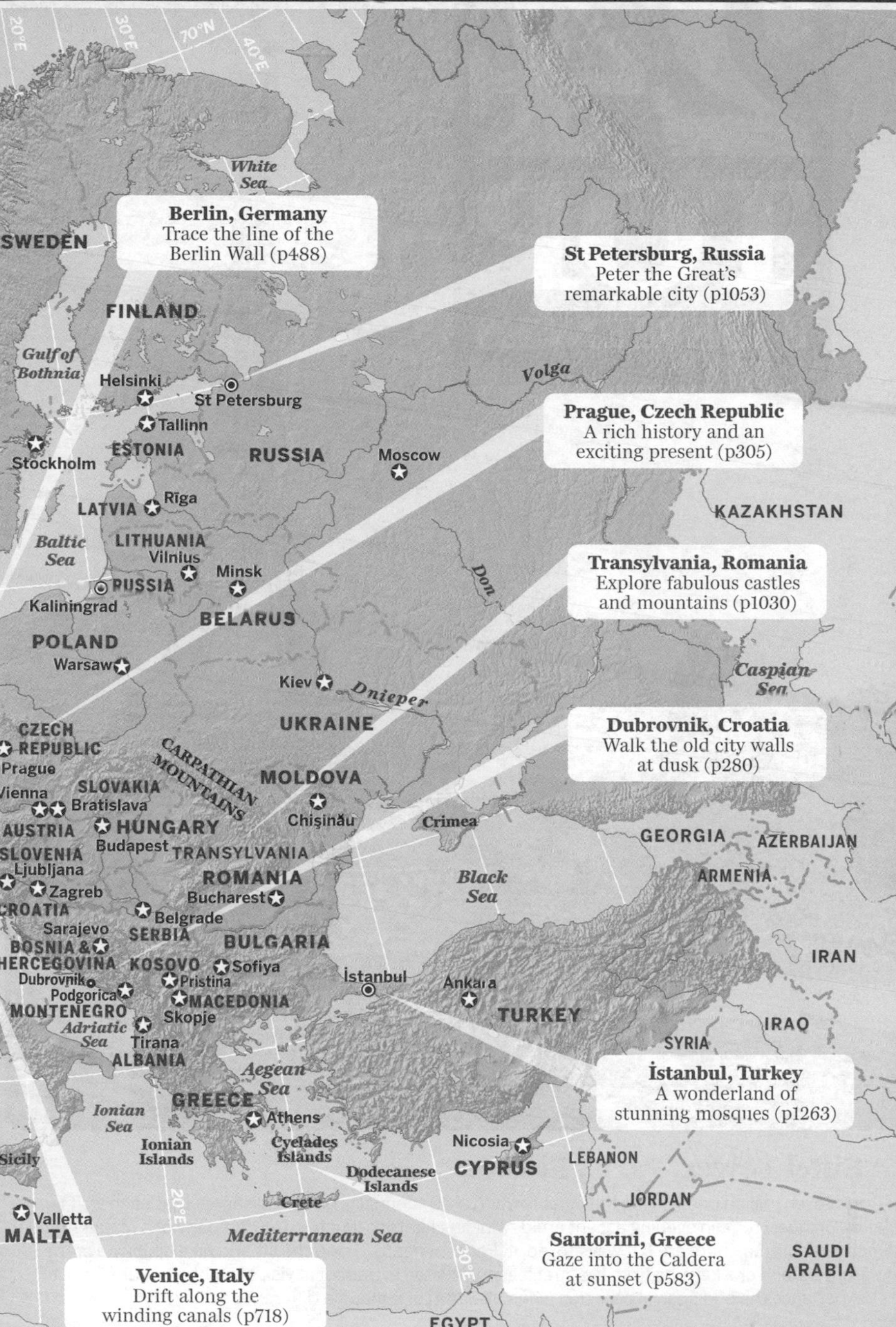

Berlin, Germany
Trace the line of the Berlin Wall (p488)
St Petersburg, Russia
Peter the Great's remarkable city (p1053)
Prague, Czech Republic
A rich history and an exciting present (p305)
Transylvania, Romania
Explore fabulous castles and mountains (p1030)
Dubrovnik, Croatia
Walk the old city walls at dusk (p280)
İstanbul, Turkey
A wonderland of stunning mosques (p1263)
Santorini, Greece
Gaze into the Caldera at sunset (p583)
Venice, Italy
Drift along the winding canals (p718)
White Sea
SWEDEN
FINLAND
Gulf of Bothnia
Helsinki
St Petersburg
Tallinn
Stockholm
ESTONIA
RUSSIA
Moscow
Volga
KAZAKHSTAN
LATVIA
Rīga
Baltic Sea
LITHUANIA
Vilnius
Minsk
RUSSIA
Kaliningrad
BELARUS
Don
POLAND
Warsaw
Kiev
Dnieper
Caspian Sea
CZECH REPUBLIC
Prague
UKRAINE
CARPATHIAN MOUNTAINS
MOLDOVA
Vienna
SLOVAKIA
Bratislava
Chişinău
Crimea
AUSTRIA
HUNGARY
Budapest
TRANSYLVANIA
GEORGIA
AZERBAIJAN
SLOVENIA
Ljubljana
ROMANIA
Black Sea
ARMENIA
Zagreb
Bucharest
CROATIA
Belgrade
Sarajevo
SERBIA
BOSNIA & HERCEGOVINA
BULGARIA
KOSOVO
Sofiya
IRAN
Dubrovnik
Pristina
İstanbul
Ankara
Podgorica
MACEDONIA
MONTENEGRO
Skopje
TURKEY
Adriatic Sea
Tirana
IRAQ
ALBANIA
SYRIA
Aegean Sea
Ionian Sea
GREECE
Athens
Sicily
Ionian Islands
Cyclades Islands
Nicosia
LEBANON
Dodecanese Islands
CYPRUS
JORDAN
Crete
Valletta
MALTA
Mediterranean Sea
SAUDI ARABIA
EGYPT
20°E
30°E
70°N
40°E

24 TOP EXPERIENCES

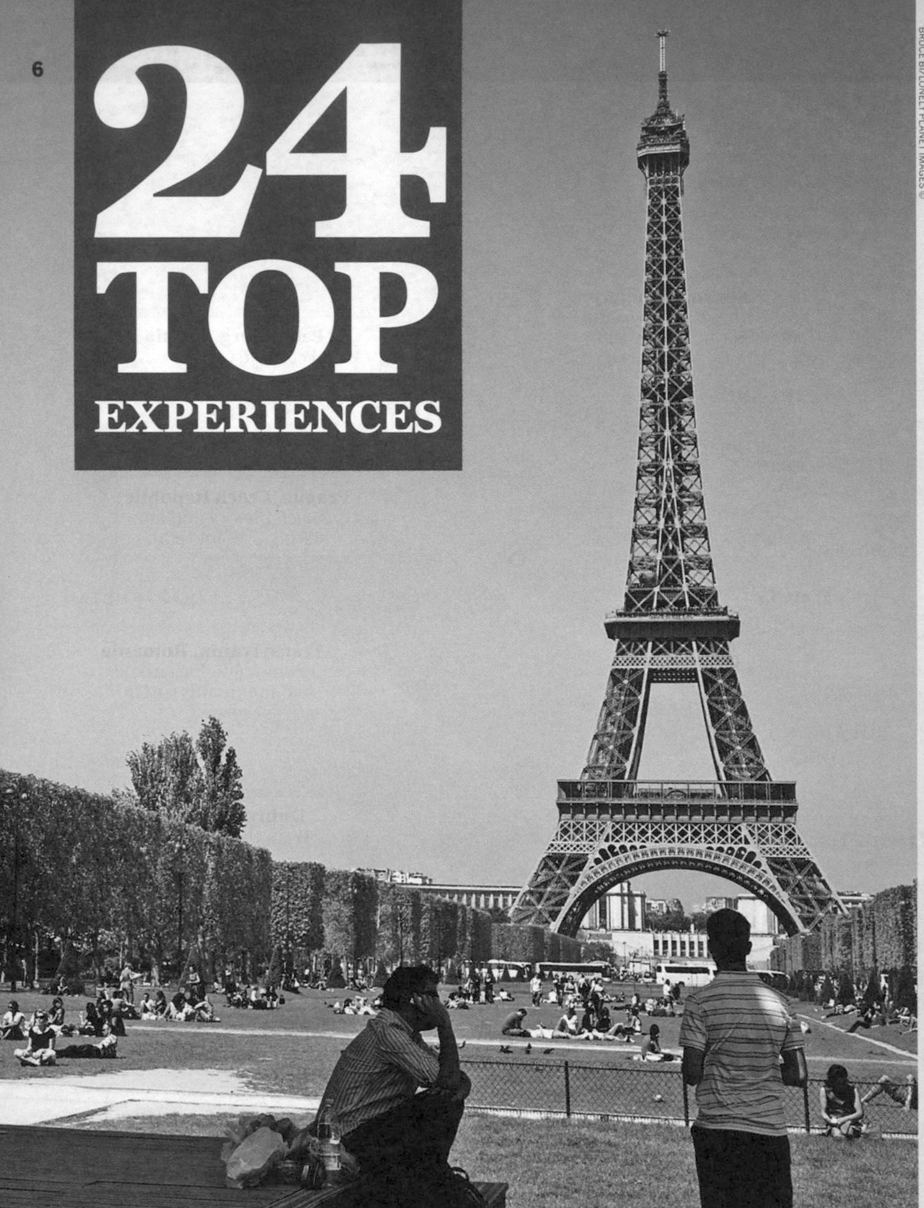

BRUCE BI/LONELY PLANET IMAGES ©

Eiffel Tower, Paris, France

1 Seven million people visit the Eiffel Tower (p400) annually, but few disagree that each visit is unique. From an evening ascent amid twinkling lights to lunch in the company of a staggering city panorama, there are 101 ways to 'do' it. Pedal beneath it, skip the lift and hike up, buy a crêpe from a stand or a key ring from the street, snap yourself in front of it, visit at night or – our favourite – experience the odd special occasion when all 324m of it glows a different colour.

CHRISTER FREDRIKSSON/LONELY PLANET IMAGES ©

Nightlife, London, Britain

2 Can you hear that, music lovers? That's London (p156) calling – from the numerous theatres, concert halls, nightclubs, pubs and even tube stations, where on any given night hundreds, if not thousands, of performers are taking to the stage. Search for your own iconic London experience, whether it's the Proms at the Royal Albert Hall, an East End singalong around a clunky pub piano, a theatre performance in the West End, a superstar DJ set at Fabric or a floppy-fringed guitar band at a Hoxton boozer. Royal Albert Hall

Venice, Italy

3 There's something magical about Venice (p718) on a sunny winter's day. With far fewer tourists around and the light sharp and clear, it's the perfect time to lap up the city's unique and magical atmosphere. Ditch your map and wander Dorsoduro's shadowy backlines while imagining secret assignations and whispered conspiracies at every turn. Then visit two of Venice's top galleries, the Galleria dell'Accademia (p718) and the Collezione Peggy Guggenheim (p719), which houses works by many of the giants of 20th-century art.

GLENN BEANLAND/LONELY PLANET IMAGES ©

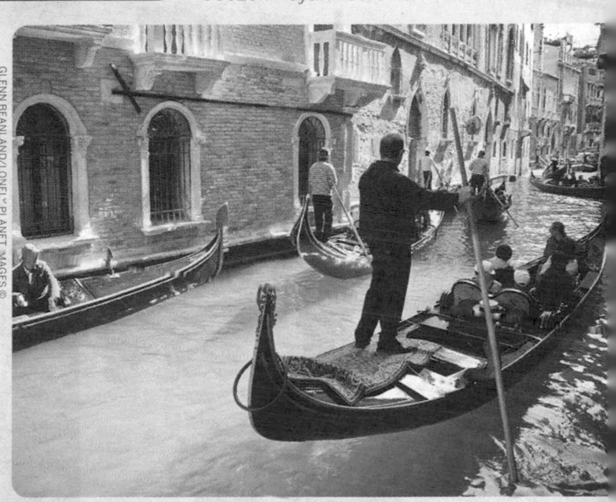

DAVID PEEVERS/LONELY PLANET IMAGES ©

Remembering the Wall, Berlin, Germany

4 Even after 20 years, the sheer magnitude and disbelief that the Berlin Wall really cut through this city doesn't sink in. But the best way to examine its role in Berlin is to make your way – on foot or by bike – along the Berlin Wall Trail (p493). Passing the Brandenburg Gate, analysing graffiti at the East Side Gallery or learning about its history at the Documentation Centre: the path brings it all into context. It's heartbreaking and hopeful and sombre, but integral to trying to understand Germany's capital.

SHANIA SHEGEDYN/LONELY PLANET IMAGES ©

HOLGER LEUE/LONELY PLANET IMAGES ©

Santorini, Greece

5 On first view, startling Santorini (p583) grabs your attention and doesn't let it go. The submerged caldera, surrounded by lava-layered cliffs topped by villages that look like a sprinkling of icing sugar, is one of nature's great wonders, best experienced by a walk along the clifftops from the main town of Fira to the northern village of Oia. The precariousness and impermanence of the place is breathtaking. Recover from your efforts with an ice-cold Mythos beer in Oia as you wait for its famed picture-perfect sunset. Oia

St Petersburg, Russia

6 Marvelling at how many masterpieces there are in the Hermitage; window shopping and people watching along Nevsky Prospekt; gliding down canals past the grand facades of palaces and golden-domed churches; enjoying a ballet at the beautiful Mariinsky Theatre; having a banquet fit for a tsar then dancing till dawn at a dive bar in a crumbling ruin – Russia's imperial capital (p1053) is a visual stunner and hedonist's delight, best visited at the height of summer when the White Nights see the city party around the clock. St Isaac's Cathedral

GRAEME CORNWALLIS/LONELY PLANET IMAGES ©

Norway's Fjords

7 The drama of Norway's fjords (p936) is difficult to overstate. The fjords cut deep gashes into the Norwegian interior, adding texture and depth to the map of northwestern Scandinavia. Sheer rock walls plunge from high, green meadows into water-filled canyons shadowed by pretty fjord-side villages. Sognefjorden, over 200km long, and Hardangerfjord are Norway's most extensive fjord networks, but the quiet, precipitous beauty of Nærøyfjorden (part of Sognefjorden), Lysefjord and – the king of fjords – Geirangerfjord are prime candidates for Scandinavia's most beautiful corner. Sognefjorden

Old City Walls Dubrovnik, Croatia

8 Get up close and personal with the city by walking Dubrovnik's spectacular city walls (p280), as history is unfurled from the battlements. No visit is complete without a leisurely walk along these ramparts, the finest in the world and Dubrovnik's main claim to fame. Built between the 13th and 16th centuries, they are still remarkably intact today and the vistas over the terracotta rooftops and the Adriatic Sea are sublime, especially at dusk when the sundown makes the hues dramatic and the panoramas unforgettable.

WAYNE WALTON/LONELY PLANET IMAGES ©

RACHEL LEWIS/LONELY PLANET IMAGES ©

Prague, Czech Republic

9 Prague's big attractions – Prague Castle and Old Town Square (p305) are highlights of the Czech capital, but for a more insightful look at life two decades after the Velvet Revolution, head to local neighbourhoods around the centre. Working class Žižkov and energetic Smíchov are crammed with pubs, while elegant tree-lined Vinohrady features a diverse menu of cosmopolitan restaurants. Prague showcases many forms of art, from iconic works from the last century to more recent but equally challenging pieces. Staré Město (Old Town)

Kraków, Poland

10 As popular as it is, Poland's former royal capital (p966) never disappoints. It's hard to pinpoint why it's so special, but there's a satisfying aura of history radiating from the sloping stone buttresses of the medieval buildings in the Old Town that makes its streets seem, well, just right. Add to that the extremes of a spectacular castle and the low-key oh-so-cool bar scene within the tiny worn buildings of the Kazimierz back streets, and it's a city you want to seriously get to know. Main Market Square (Rynek Glówny)

BRUCE BI/LONELY PLANET IMAGES ©

Transylvania, Romania

11 The southern swipe of the Carpathian Mountains in Transylvania (p1030) is packed with opportunities. There's cycling in the Bucegi Mountains, day and multiday hikes in the Făgăraş Mountains, driving on the winding Transfăgăraşan Road, declared to be 'the best road in the world' by BBC's *Top Gear*, and skiing in Sinaia and Poiana Braşov. The area also features the vampiric Bran Castle, the ruins of the 13th-century Raşnov Fortress and Peleş Castle. Gothic Castle

CRAIG PERSHOUSE/LONELY PLANET IMAGES ©

Bay of Kotor, Montenegro

12 There's a sense of secrecy and mystery to the Bay of Kotor (p863). Grey mountain walls rise steeply from steely blue waters, getting higher and higher as you progress through their folds to the hidden reaches of the inner bay. Here, ancient stone settlements hug the shoreline, with Kotor's ancient alleyways concealed in its innermost reaches behind hefty stone walls. Talk about drama! But you wouldn't expect anything else of the Balkans, where life is exuberantly Mediterranean and lived full of passion on these ancient streets.

HOLGER LEUE/LONELY PLANET IMAGES ©

HOLGER LEUE/LONELY PLANET IMAGES ©

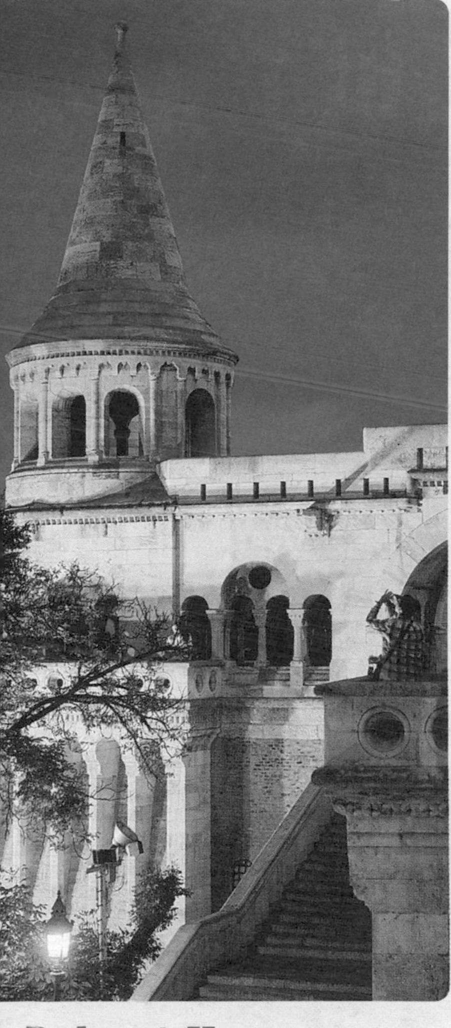

JEAN-PIERRE LESCOURRET/LONELY PLANET IMAGES ©

Budapest, Hungary

13 Hungary's capital (p608) has cleaned up its act in recent years. Gone are those old Soviet-era cars that used to spew their choking blue haze over the flat landscape of Pest. Now, the hills on the Buda side of the city are gleaming, and Pest itself is teeming with energy and life. It's no stretch to say that these days Budapest combines the beauty of Prague and buzz of Berlin into something that's uniquely Hungarian. Fisherman's Bastion

Barcelona's La Sagrada Família, Spain

14 One of Spain's top sights, the Modernista brainchild of Antoni Gaudí remains a work in progress more than 80 years after its creator's death. Fanciful and profound, inspired by nature and barely restrained by a Gothic style, Barcelona's quirky temple (p1147) soars skyward with an almost playful majesty. The improbable angles and departures from architectural convention will have you shaking your head in disbelief, but the detail of the decorative flourishes on the Passion and Nativity Facades are worth studying for hours.

Dublin, Ireland

15 Ireland's capital city (p646) can boast all the attractions and distractions of a major international metropolis, but manages to retain the friendliness, intimacy and atmosphere of a small town. Whether wandering the leafy Georgian terraces of St Stephen's Green or getting up close and personal with the past at Kilmainham Gaol, you're never far from a friendly pub where the beer is grand and the craic is flowing. And, of course, there's the chance to sink a pint of the black stuff at that fountainhead of froth, the original Guinness brewery. Stag's Head pub

OLIVER STREWE/LONELY PLANET IMAGES ©

PAUL BEINSSEN/LONELY PLANET IMAGES ©

Imperial Vienna, Austria

16 Imagine what you could do with unlimited riches and Austria's top architects at your hands for 640 years and you have the Vienna (p63) of the Habsburgs. The graceful Hofburg whisks you back to the age of empires as you marvel at the treasury's imperial crowns, the equine ballet of the Spanish Riding School and Empress Elisabeth's chandelier-lit apartments. The palace is rivalled in grandeur only by Schloss Schönbrunn and also the baroque Schloss Belvedere, both set in exquisite landscaped gardens. Schloss Schönbrunn

Overnight train, Eastern Europe

17 With the windows down, the wind rushing through your hair and the scenery racing past, there are few modes of transport more pleasurable than the overnight sleeper train (p1330), the best way to get about in Eastern Europe. Whether you're in *platzkart* with Bulgarian peasants drinking and playing cards while discussing life under communism or enjoying the more private *kupe,* this is an essential experience and a great way to avoid paying for a hotel. High Tatras Mountains, Slovakia

MARTIN MOOS/LONELY PLANET IMAGES ©

Ancient Greece

18 From the renowned magnificence of Athens' Acropolis to the monastery-crowned rock spires of Meteora, Greece offers some of Europe's most impressive historical sights. Top temples include oracular Delphi, perched above the sparkling Gulf of Corinth, and Olympia, home to the first Olympic Games. The acoustically perfect theatre of Epidavros sits alongside the mystical Sanctuary of Asclepius, an ancient healing centre. Olive and orange groves surround the vast ruins of Mystras, the one-time capital of the Byzantine Empire. The Parthenon in Athens' Acropolis

Alhambra, Granada, Spain

19 The palace complex of the Alhambra (p1179) is close to architectural perfection. It is perhaps the most refined example of Islamic art anywhere in the world, not to mention the most enduring symbol of 800 years of Moorish rule in what was then known as Al-Andalus. From afar, the Alhambra's red fortress towers dominate the Granada skyline, set against a backdrop of the Sierra Nevada's snow-capped peaks. Up close, the Alhambra's perfectly proportioned Generalife gardens complement the exquisite detail of the Palacio Nazariés. Put simply, this is Spain's most beautiful monument.

Amsterdam's Canals, The Netherlands

20 To say Amsterdammers love the water is an understatement. Sure, the city (p904) made its first fortune in maritime trade, but that's ancient history. You can stroll next to the canals and check out some of the city's 3300 houseboats. Or, better, go for a ride. From boat level you'll get to see a whole new set of architectural details, like the ornamentations bedecking the bridges. And when you pass the canalside cafe terraces, you can just look up and wave.

Mostar, Bosnia & Hercegovina

21 If the 1993 bombardment of Mostar's iconic 16th-century stone bridge underlined the heartbreaking pointlessness of Yugoslavia's brutal civil war, its painstaking reconstruction has proved symbolic of a peaceful new era. Although parts of Mostar (p145) are still dotted with shockingly bombed-out buildings, the town continues to dust itself off. Its charming Ottoman quarter has been especially convincingly rebuilt and is once again a delightful patchwork of stone mosques, souvenir peddlers and inviting cafes. Today it's tourists rather than militias that besiege the place.

RICHARD I'ANSON/LONELY PLANET IMAGES ©

WILL SALTER/LONELY PLANET IMAGES ©

SARA-JANE CLELAND/LONELY PLANET IMAGES ©

Marrakesh, Morocco

22 Marrakesh's central square, the Djemaa el-Fna (p891), is the 1001 Nights writ large. By day it's an unassuming place, surrounded with carts selling the freshest squeezed orange juice imaginable, but little else. As the sun dips however, the place comes alive. Noises, smells and actions abound: there's the reedy drone of snake charmers, brightly clad water sellers, crowds gathering around storytellers and acrobats, and the cooking smoke of dozens of open-air food stalls and restaurants everywhere. It's a sensory overload – dive right in. Djemaa el-Fna

İstanbul, Turkey

23 Straddling Europe and Asia, İstanbul's curriculum vitae includes stints as capital of the Byzantine and Ottoman Empires. It's one of the world's great cities. The historical highlights cluster in Sultanahmet (p1263) – the Aya Sofya, Blue Mosque, Topkapı Palace and Grand Bazaar. After marvelling at their ancient domes and glittering interiors, it's time to experience this huge metropolis' vibrant contemporary life. Cross the Galata Bridge, passing ferries and fish kebap stands, to Beyoğlu, where the nightlife thrives from chic rooftop bars to rowdy taverns. Blue Mosque

JEAN-PIERRE LESCOURRET/LONELY PLANET IMAGES ©

SHANIA SHEGEDYN/LONELY PLANET IMAGES ©

Ancient Rome, Italy

24 Rome's famous seven hills (actually, there are nine) offer some superb vantage points. A favourite is the Palatino (p688), a gorgeous green expanse of evocative ruins, towering umbrella pines and unforgettable views over the Roman Forum. This is where it all began, where Romulus supposedly founded the city and where the ancient Roman emperors lived in unimaginable luxury. Nowadays, it's a truly haunting spot; as you walk the gravel paths you can almost sense the ghosts in the air. Roman Forum

need to know

Trains

» Europe's train network is fast and efficient but rarely a bargain unless you book well in advance or use a rail pass wisely.

Buses

» Usually taken for short trips in remoter areas, though long-distance buses can be cheap.

When to Go?

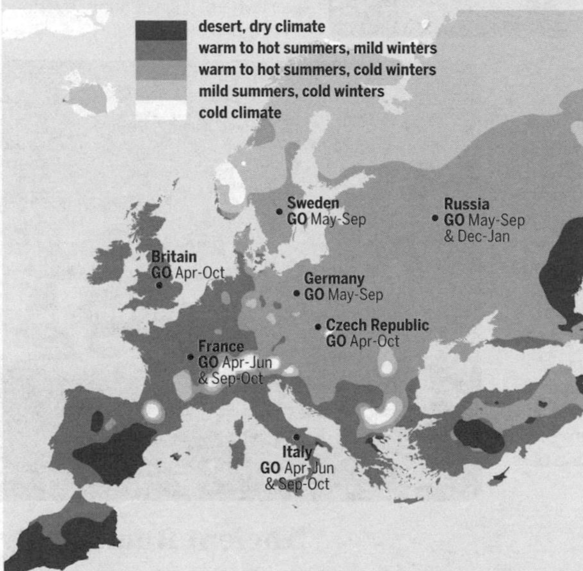

High Season (Jun-Aug)

» Everybody comes to Europe and all of Europe hits the road

» Hotel prices and temperatures are their highest

» Expect the big attractions to be nightmarishly busy

Shoulder Season (Apr-May & Sep-Oct)

» Crowds and prices drop

» Temperatures are generally comfortable – but it can still be hot in southern Europe

» Overall these are the best months to travel in Europe

Low Season (Nov-Mar)

» Outside ski resorts, hotels drop their prices or close down

» The weather can be cold and days short, especially in northern Europe!

» Some places, such as resort towns, are like ghost towns

Your Daily Budget

Budget less than €60

» Dorm beds cost €10-€20

» Grocery stores and markets are great value for self-catering

» Walk around cities and take overnight trains to save costs

Midrange €60-200

» Double room in a small hotel €50-€100

» Stay at small hotels and eat in restaurants at lunchtime

» Meals in good restaurants average around €20 per person

Top end over €200

» Staying at iconic hotels starts at €150

» Car hire starts at around €30 per day

» Enjoy the duty-free refund from an afternoon's stylish shopping

Cars

» You can hire a car or drive your own through Europe. Roads are excellent but petrol is expensive.

Ferries

» Main ferry routes connect Britain and Ireland with mainland Europe, Scandinavia to the Baltic countries, Italy to the Balkans or Greece, and Morocco with Spain.

Bicycles

» Western Europe is best set up for cyclists, but the two-wheeler is a great way to get around just about anywhere.

Planes

» Cheap airfares take you from one end of the continent to the other.

Websites

» **Lonely Planet** (www.lonelyplanet.com/thorntree) Ask other travellers questions

» **Deutsche Bahn** (www.bahn.de) The best online train timetable for Europe

» **Flycheapo** (www.flycheapo.com) Find out which low-cost airlines fly where

» **Michelin** (www.viamichelin.com) Calculates the best route from A to B by vehicle.

» **Tourist Office Directory** (www.towd.com) Links to every tourist office on the continent

Money

See the chapters on individual countries for more information on money and exchange rates. Main currencies:

» **Euro (€)** Andorra, Austria, Belgium, Cyprus, Estonia, Finland, France, Germany, Greece, Ireland, Italy, Kosovo, Liechtenstein, Luxembourg, Malta, Montenegro, Netherlands, Portugal, Slovakia, Slovenia, Spain

» **Pound (£)** Britain, Northern Ireland

» **Swiss franc (Sfr)** Switzerland, Liechtenstein

Visas

Citizens of Australia, Canada, New Zealand and the USA don't need visas for visits of under 90 days to all EU countries and most other countries in this guide.

» EU citizens can stay indefinitely in other member countries. The Schengen Agreement means there are no passport controls at borders between most EU members (see p1317).

» Citizens of Australia, Canada, the EU, New Zealand and the US need a visa to visit Belarus and Russia. Citizens of Australia and New Zealand need a visa to visit Moldova and Ukraine.

Arriving in Europe

» **Schipol Airport, Amsterdam**
Trains to the centre (20min)

» **Heathrow Airport, London**
Trains (15min) and Tube (1hr) to the centre

» **Aeroport Roissy Charles de Gaulle, Paris**
Many buses (1hr) and trains (30min) to centre

» **Frankfurt Airport, Frankfurt**
Trains (15min) to the centre

» **Leonardo da Vinci Airport, Rome**
Buses (1hr) and trains (30min) to centre

What to Take

» **Flip-flops (thongs)** for overnight train rides, in hostel bathrooms and for the beach.

» **Hiking boots** when on Europe's fantastic walks

» **Ear plugs** are helpful anywhere, but especially in hostels

» **Anti-mosquito plugs** are useful in summer, particularly the Baltic and Scandivania

» **European plug adaptors** if you're coming from outside Europe

» **An unlocked mobile phone** for picking up a local SIM card for making cheap calls

» **Smart clothes** to look the part when breaking the budget

if you like...

Castles & Palaces

All corners of Europe have these amazing historical repositories, from ancient bunkers impervious to attack to later showpieces designed to astound rather than to defend.

Leeds Castle, Britain The 'loveliest castle in the world' is no empty PR rhetoric – this absolute stunner set on an island in the middle of a large lake in Kent is perhaps Europe's ultimate medieval castle (p183)

Versailles, France The vast formal palace against which all others are measured includes the Hall of Mirrors and Marie Antoinette's refuge (p422)

Neuschwanstein, Germany So what if it's not even 200 years old? Neuschwanstein, in the heart of the Bavarian Alps, is everybody's (including Disney's) castle fantasy (p522)

Winter Palace, Russia The name alone evokes the brutality of the Russian Revolution, but the golden-green baroque reality is unmatched anywhere for sheer tsarist splendour (p1053)

Beaches

Between the Mediterranean, Aegean, Adriatic, Ionian, Baltic and Black Seas, not to mention the pristine lakes and rivers across the region, definitely plan on being able to take it easy on a beautiful stretch of sand during your trip.

Cyclades, Greece The names Mykonos, Paros and Naxos all conjure up images of perfect golden beaches, and the reality is sure not to disappoint (p578)

Drymades beach, Albania The stuff of legend among backpackers, this white-sand beach on Albania's fast-disappearing undeveloped coastline remains the one to head for (p48)

Menorca, Spain Beaches so beautiful you think they may merely be dreams are tucked away in little coves all around the most beautiful and sandiest of the Balearic Islands (p1172)

Black Sea coast, Bulgaria Bulgaria boasts the best beaches on the Black Sea, but we recommend avoiding the big resort towns and heading instead to smaller Sozopol (p259)

Spectacular Scenery

Criss-crossed by mountain ranges, gentle rolling hills and thick forest, and with hiking of all levels never far away, walkers and mountain lovers will be spoilt rotten in Europe, where the scenery never fails to captivate even the most seasoned explorers.

The Alps, Switzerland There's no competition for the most stunning mountain range in Europe – even its neighbours wouldn't dare suggest that theirs could rival that of beautiful Switzerland (p1231)

Scottish Highlands, Britain Almost certainly the most scenic part of Britain, the wonderful Scottish Highlands are packed full of mountains, misty lochs and spectacular coastline to explore (p225)

Iceland When not disrupting worldwide air travel, this volcanic theme park of towering peaks, waterfalls, geysers and alien landscape thrills anyone lucky enough to get out into its interior (p630)

Fjords, Norway While Norway may scare many off with its high prices, even a short trip along its impossibly beautiful coastline is an unmissable European highlight (p936)

LOU JONES/LONELY PLANET IMAGES ©

» St Petersburg's Hermitage (p1053) is laden with a treasure trove of art and artefacts

Nightlife

Whether it's dancing to cutting-edge international DJs on the dance floors of superclubs in Berlin and London or altogether more traditional live music in pubs, tavernas or jazz clubs, you won't be left wanting.

Berlin, Germany There's nothing quite like arriving at superclub Berghain as the sun comes up, and dancing until sundown in Europe's most serious party city (p499)

London, Britain Whether it's a quiet session down at the local pub or a full-blown night on the tiles of East London, you can be sure to have a good time in the hedonistic bars and clubs of London town (p175 and p176)

Moscow, Russia Once famed for its 'face control' (strict door policies), Moscow is now becoming an essential stop on the clubber's world map with a slew of new democratically run bars and clubs (p1051)

Belgrade, Serbia Lonely Planet readers voted Belgrade the best party city in the world in 2009... come here yourself to see why (p1075)

Great Food

With dozens of rich and varied cuisines competing against each other on the continent, it shouldn't surprise you if you eat some of the best meals of your life on a trip across Europe.

Dining out in London British cuisine may have been the butt of international jokes for decades, but take eating in the country's capital seriously as its fearsome culinary revolution continues to produce new and delightful eating options (p174)

Pizza in Naples The peasant dish that ate the world – or the other way around – is still the best in the city of its birth: accept no imitations! (p751)

Basquing in San Sebastián Spain's Basque powerhouse boasts more Michelin stars per capita than anywhere else in the world (p1162)

Feasting on pork in Lyon Forget Paris, the gastronomic capital of La Belle France is undoubtedly Lyon, a city that runs on pork and will have gourmands swooning (p446)

Kebaps in Turkey This mainstay of Turkish cuisine comes in various forms, from the classic *döner* to the more sophisticated *İskender*.

Outdoor Fun

With its wide-open spaces, innovative tourism industries and endless variety of landscape, Europe literally is your playground.

Bovec and Bled, Slovenia The unrivalled capital of extreme sports in Eastern Europe is tiny Slovenia, where you can do everything from canyoning to hydrospeeding at Bovec and Bled (p1112 and p1108)

Cycling the Loire Valley, France There's a gorgeous chateau around every bend in the river in this beautiful valley (p432)

Skiing year-round, Austria Experience Olympic-sized skiing in Innsbruck, the Austrian Alpine city ringed by famous pistes; if you're passing through in August, head to the glaciers for downhill action (p87)

Rafting and kayaking, Bosnia and Hercegovina Fast-flowing rivers provide world-class rafting and kayaking, especially in the Vrbas Canyons between Jajce and Banja Luka (p148)

If you like... exploring islands
Head for the stunning coast of Croatia, with over 1000 islands to choose from (p263)

If you like... spectacular mountains
Don't miss Bulgaria's seven accessible and largely untouched mountain ranges (p240)

Art Collections

Itself a kind of warehouse of art history featuring works from ancient Greek statues to contemporary pieces that defy description, Europe's great art galleries – or even artfully great cities – are reason enough for a trip.

The Louvre, Paris, France It's not really France's museum, it's the world's; treasures from Europe and all over the planet in exhaustive quantity will simply dazzle you on a day spent exploring (p405)

Florence, Italy It starts with the Duomo, continues through the Uffizi Gallery and crosses the Ponte Vecchio – the entire Renaissance embodied in one city (p733)

Hermitage, St Petersburg, Russia Housed in the Winter Palace, this is quite simply one of the world's greatest art collections, stuffed full of treasures from Egyptian mummies to a superb cache of Picassos (p1053)

Van Gogh Museum, Amsterdam, Netherlands Despite his troubled life and struggles with poverty and madness, Van Gogh's superb creations are gloriously easy to enjoy at this Amsterdam museum (p904)

Music

Classical music of royalty, soulful songs of the masses, pop culture that changed the world: these are just some of the ways the European love of music will get into your beat.

Vienna's Staatsoper The premier venue in a city synonymous with opera and classical music. Wait! Isn't that Mozart I hear? (p71)

The Beatles They sprang – and sang – from Liverpool and now that city does them proud at the Beatles Story, which recounts the lives and work of the Fab Four (p209)

Irish music The Irish love their music and it takes little – sometimes just a pint of beer – to get them singing. The West Coast hums with music pubs, especially in Galway (p664)

Fado Portuguese love the melancholy, nostalgic songs of fado; hear it in Lisbon's Alfama district (p1000)

Cafes & Bars

Whether it's a coffee savoured for an hour or a drink with a roomful of new friends, you'll find plenty of places for liquid joy.

Vienna's coffee houses Unchanged in decades and redolent with the air of refinement; pause for a cup served just so (p71)

Irish pubs Come and join the warm and gregarious crowds of locals in any pub in Ireland for a true cultural experience (p653)

Cafe society, Paris What's more clichéd? The practiced curtness of the Parisian waiter or the studied boredom of the customer? Both are, probably, and we wouldn't miss the show for anything (p400)

Tiny havens, Amsterdam The Dutch call them 'brown cafes' for the stains on the walls from legions of smokers, but they should just call them cosy, for the warm and friendly atmosphere (p922)

month by month

Top Events

1 **Carnevale,** February

2 **Glastonbury Festival,** June

3 **Roskilde Festival,** June

4 **Edinburgh International Festival,** August

5 **Oktoberfest,** September

January

While it's cold across Europe, January is a great time to experience the region's winter-wonderland appearance under blankets of snow. You'll find most towns relatively tourist free and hotel prices are rock bottom.

A Hot Cold New Year, Britain

An enormous, raucous Edinburgh street party sees in the New Year in Scotland. It's replicated Europe-wide as main squares resonate with Champagne corks and fireworks.

Kiruna Snöfestivalen, Sweden

The last weekend in January sees this Lapland snow festival (www.kirunalapland.se), based around a snow-sculpting competition that draws artists from all over Europe. There's also a husky dog competition and a handicrafts fair.

Great-Value Skiing, Eastern Europe

Head to Eastern Europe's ski slopes for wallet-friendly prices. After the first week of January most hotels offer their lowest annual rates, making skiing affordable to all. Bosnia and Bulgaria are your best bets.

Empty Streets, Czech Republic

Wander even the Old Town of Prague unencumbered by huge groups of tourists and have lesser-known sights and cities across the region pretty much to yourself during the least busy time of year.

February

Carnival in all its manic glory sweeps the Catholic regions of the continent. Cold temperatures are forgotten amid masquerades, street festivals and general bacchanalia. Expect to be kissed by a stranger.

Carnaval, Netherlands

Pre-Lent is celebrated with greater vigour in Maastricht than anywhere else in northern Europe. While the rest of the Netherlands hopes the canals will freeze for ice skating, this Dutch corner cuts loose with a celebration that would have done its former Roman residents proud.

Carnevale, Italy

In the period before Ash Wednesday, Venice goes mad for masks. Costume balls, many with traditions centuries old, enliven the social calendar in this storied old city like no other event. Even those without a coveted invite are swept up in the pageantry.

Carnivals, Croatia

For colourful costumes and non-stop revelry head to Rijeka, where Carnival is the pinnacle of the year's calendar. Zadar and Samobor host colourful Carnival celebrations too, with street dancing, concerts and masked balls.

March

Spring arrives in southern Europe, while further north the rest of the continent continues to freeze, though days are often bright.

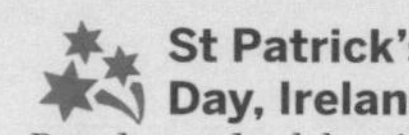

St Patrick's Day, Ireland

Parades and celebrations are held on 17 March in Irish towns big and small to honour the beloved patron saint of Ireland. While elsewhere the day is a commercialised romp of green beer, in his home country it's time for a parade and celebrations with friends and family.

Reindeer Racing, Finland

Held over the last weekend of March or first weekend of April, the King's Cup is the grand finale of Finnish Lapland's reindeer-racing season and a great spectacle.

Drowning of Marzanna, Poland

Head to Poland in March for the quirky rite of the Drowning of Marzanna, a surviving pagan ritual in which the goddess of winter is immersed in water at the advent of spring. The festival is also celebrated as Maslenitsa in Russia, with variants in most other Slavic countries and lots of bliny (pancakes) to boot.

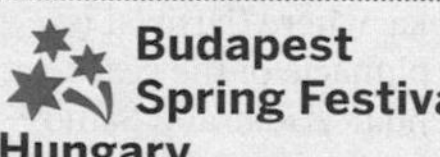

Budapest Spring Festival, Hungary

One of Europe's top classical music events is the two-week Budapest Spring Festival (www.springfestival.hu), which takes place in late March. Concerts are held in a large number of beautiful venues, including several stunning churches, the opera house and national theatre.

April

Spring arrives with a burst of colour, from the glorious bulb fields of Holland to the blooming orchards of Spain. On the most southern beaches it's time to shake the sand out of the umbrellas.

Semana Santa, Spain

Parades of penitents and holy icons in Spain, notably in Seville, during Easter week. Throughout the week thousands of members of religious brotherhoods parade in trad garb before thousands of spectators. Look for the pointed *capirotes* (hoods).

Settimana Santa, Italy

Italy celebrates Holy Week with processions and passion plays. By Holy Thursday Rome is thronged with the faithful and even non-believers are swept up in the emotion and piety of hundreds of thousands thronging the Vatican and St Peter's Basilica.

Greek Easter, Greece

The most important festival in the Greek Orthodox calendar. The emphasis is on the Resurrection so it's a celebratory event and the most significant part is midnight on Easter Saturday, when candles are lit and a fireworks and candlelit procession hits the streets.

Feria de Abril, Spain

Hoods off! A week-long party held in Seville in late April to counterbalance the religious peak of Easter. The many beautiful old squares of this gorgeous city come alive during the long, warm nights for which the nation is known.

Koninginnedag (Queen's Day), Netherlands

The nationwide celebration on 30 April is especially fervent in Amsterdam, which becomes awash in orange costumes and fake afros, beer, dope, leather boys, temporary roller coasters, clogs and general craziness.

May

An excellent time to visit Europe: May is usually sunny and warm and full of things to do, while never too hot or too crowded, though you can still expect the big destinations to feel busy.

Cannes Film Festival, France

The famous, the not-so-famous and the merely topless converge for a year's worth of movies in little more than one week in glamorous Cannes. Those winning awards will be sure to tell you about it in film trailers for years to come.

Beer Festival, Czech Republic

An event dear to many travellers' hearts is the Czech Beer Festival (www.ceskypivnifestival.cz) in Prague, where lots of food, music and – most importantly – around 70 beers from around the country are on offer from mid- to late May.

Brussels Jazz Marathon, Belgium

Around-the-clock jazz performances hit Brussels during the second-last weekend in May (www.brusselsjazzmarathon.be). The saxophone becomes the instrument of choice for this international-flavoured city's most joyous celebration.

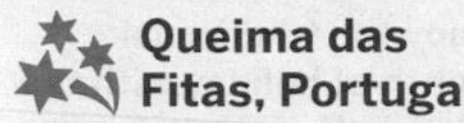

Queima das Fitas, Portugal

Coimbra's annual highlight is this boozy week of fado music and revelry that begins on the first Thursday in May, when students celebrate the end of the academic year. These are clearly honours students as they do it in this Portuguese town better than anywhere.

June

The huge summer travel season hasn't bust out yet, but the sun has broken through the clouds and the weather is gorgeous, from the hot shores in the south to the cool climes of the north.

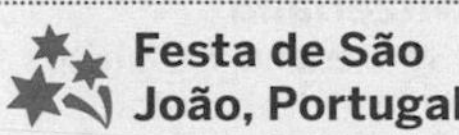

Festa de São João, Portugal

Elaborate processions, live music on Porto's plazas and merrymaking all across Portugal's second city. Squeaky plastic hammers (available for sale everywhere) come out for the unusual custom of whacking one another. Everyone is fair game – expect no mercy.

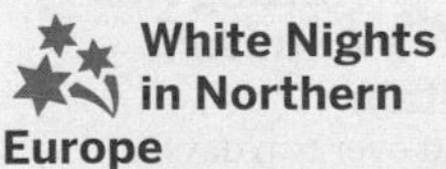

White Nights in Northern Europe

By mid-June the Baltic sun only just sinks behind the horizon at night, leaving the sky a grey-white colour and encouraging locals to forget their routines and party hard. The best place to join the fun is St Petersburg, Russia, where balls, classical-music concerts and other summer events keep spirits high.

Glastonbury Festival, Britain

The town's youthful summer vibe peaks for this long weekend of music, theatre and New Age shenanigans (www.glastonburyfestivals.co.uk). It's one of England's favourite outdoor events and more than 100,000 turn up to writhe around in the grassy fields (or deep mud) at Pilton (Worthy) Farm.

Midsummer, Denmark, Norway, Sweden & Finland

The year's biggest event in continental Nordic Europe sees family feasts, celebration of the summer, bonfires and copious drinking, often at lakeside summer cottages. It takes place on the weekend that falls between 19 and 26 June.

Roskilde Festival, Denmark

Northern Europe's largest music festival (www.roskilde-festival.dk) rocks Roskilde for four consecutive days each summer. It takes place in late June, but advance ticket sales are on offer in December, and the festival usually sells out.

Festa de Santo António, Portugal

In Portugal there's feasting, drinking and dancing in Lisbon's Alfama in honour of St Anthony (12 to 13 June), capping off the even-grander three-week Festas de Lisboa, which features processions and dozens of street parties.

Hellenic Festival, Greece

The ancient theatre at Epidavros and the Theatre of Herodes Atticus are the headline venues of Athens' annual cultural shindig. The festival, which runs from mid-June to August, features music, dance, theatre, and much more besides. For more details, see www.greekfestival.gr.

Oil-wrestling Championship, Turkey

Huge crowds gather in Edirne, north of İstanbul, in late June/early July to cheer greased-up wrestlers as they slap each other around during the Kırkpınar wrestling festival. Dating back to the 14th century, this is the world's oldest wrestling event. See www.kirkpinar.com for more information.

July

Visitors have arrived from around the world and outdoor cafes, beer gardens and outdoor beach clubs are hopping. Expect beautiful – even steamy – weather anywhere you go.

Il Palio, Italy

Siena's great annual event is the Palio (2 July and 16 August), a pageant culminating in a bareback horse race round Il Campo. The city is divided into 17 *contrade* (districts), of which 10 compete for the *palio* (silk banner), with emotions exploding.

Montreux Jazz Festival, Switzerland

It's not all that jazz as big-name rock acts also hit town for this famous festival (www.montreuxjazz.com), held during the first two weeks of July. Glitterati from across the globe gather for a top-end celebration of top-flight music on the shores of Lake Geneva.

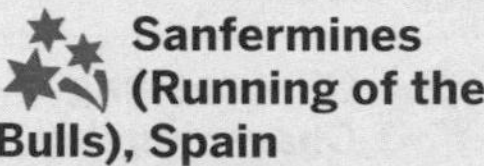

Sanfermines (Running of the Bulls), Spain

Huge male bovines and people who want to be close to them invade Pamplona for the famous festival (6 to 14 July), when the city is overrun with thrill seekers, curious onlookers and, oh yeah, bulls. The Encierro (Running of the Bulls) begins at 8am daily.

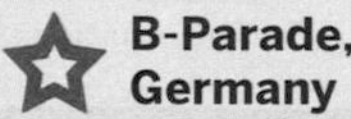

B-Parade, Germany

A huge techno street parade (www.b-parade.de) in Berlin, usually held the second weekend of July. Enormous trucks filled with speakers literally make the earth move for the hundreds of thousands of partiers who line the route, dancing the entire time.

Bastille Day, France

Fireworks, balls, processions and more for France's national day on 14 July. Celebrated in every French town and city: go to the heart of town and get caught up in the patriotic festival that, of course, has good food and wine.

EXIT Festival, Serbia

Eastern Europe's most talked about music festival (www.exitfest.org) takes place each July within the walls of the Petrodvaradin Fortress in Serbia's second city, Novi Sad. Book early for tickets as it attracts music lovers from all over the continent with big international acts headlining.

Marrakesh Popular Arts Festival, Morocco

A jubilant celebration of traditional Moroccan music, this is a hugely popular event, drawing musicians from all over the country, as well as belly dancers, snake charmers and fortune-tellers. Concerts are held at venues across town, including the Palais el-Badi (p671).

De Gentse Feesten, Belgium

Ghent is transformed into a 10-day party of music and theatre, a highlight of which is a vast techno celebration called 10 Days Off (www.gentsefeesten.be). This underappreciated gem of the low country is high on fine bars serving countless kinds of beer.

Medieval Festival of the Arts, Romania

During July the beautiful Romanian city of Sighişoara hosts open-air concerts, parades and ceremonies, all glorifying medieval Transylvania and taking the town back to its fascinating 12th-century origins.

August

Everybody's going someplace as half of Europe shuts down to enjoy the traditional month of holiday with the other half. If it's near the beach, from Germany's Baltic to Spain's Balearics, it's mobbed and the temperatures are hot, hot, hot!

Salzburg Festival, Austria

Austria's most renowned classical-music festival (www.salzburgfestival.at) attracts international stars from late July to the end of August. That urbane person sitting by you having a glass of wine who looks like a famous cellist, probably is.

Zürich Street Parade, Switzerland

In Switzerland, it's Zürich's turn to let its hair down with an enormous techno parade (www.street-parade.ch). All thoughts of numbered accounts are forgotten as bankers, and everybody else in this otherwise staid burg, party to orgasmic, deep-base thump, thump, thump.

Notting Hill Carnival, Britain

Held over two days in August, this is Europe's largest – and London's most vibrant – outdoor carnival, where London's Caribbean community shows the city how to party. Food, frolic and fun are just a part of this vast multicultural celebration.

Edinburgh International Festival, Britain

Three weeks of innovative drama, comedy, dance, music and more from around the globe, held in Edinburgh (www.eif.co.uk). Two weeks overlap with the celebrated Fringe Festival (www.edfringe.com), which draws innovative acts from around the globe. Expect cutting-edge comedy, drama and productions that defy description.

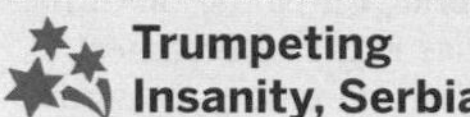

Trumpeting Insanity, Serbia

Guca's Dragačevo Trumpet Assembly (www.guca.rs) is one of the most exciting and bizarre events in all of Eastern Europe. Hundreds of thousands of revellers descend on the small Serbian town to damage their eardrums, livers and sanity in a cacophonous day of revelry.

Sziget Music Festival, Hungary

A week-long, great-value world-music festival (www.sziget.hu) held all over Budapest, Sziget features bands from around the globe playing at more than 60 venues.

September

It's cooling off in every sense, from the northern countries to the romance started on a dance floor in Ibiza. Maybe the best time to visit: the weather's still good and the crowds have thinned.

Venice International Film Festival, Italy

The Mostra del Cinema di Venezia (www.labiennale.org) is Italy's top film fest and one of the world's top indie film fests. The judging here is seen as an early indication of what to look for at the next year's Oscars.

Oktoberfest, Germany

Germany's legendary beer-swilling party (www.oktoberfest.de) starts mid-September in Munich (don't ever tell anyone you turned up for it in October, even if you did). Millions descend for litres of beer and carousing that has no equal. If you didn't plan ahead, you'll sleep in Austria.

Dvořák Autumn, Czech Republic

This festival (www.kso.kso.cz) of classical music honours the work of the Czech Republic's favourite composer, Anton Dvořák. The event is held over three weeks in the spa town of Karlovy Vary.

Festes de la Mercè, Spain

Barcelona knows how to party until dawn and it outdoes itself for the Festes de la Mercè (around 24 September), the city's biggest celebration, with four days of concerts, dancing, *castellers* (human-castle builders), fireworks and *correfocs* – a parade of fireworks-spitting dragons and devils.

October

This is another good month to visit. Almost everything is still open, while prices and visitor numbers are way down. Weather can be unpredictable, though – and even cold in northern Europe.

Iceland Airwaves, Iceland

This five-day event (www.icelandairwaves.is) in Reykjavík is one of the world's most cutting-edge music festivals: don't expect to sleep. It focuses on new musical trends rather than mainstream acts.

Festival at Queen's, Ireland

Belfast hosts the second-largest arts festival (www.belfastfestival.com) in the UK for three weeks in late October/early November in and around Queen's University. It's a time for the city to shed its gritty legacy and celebrate the intellectual and the creative without excessive hype.

Wine Festival, Moldova

Wine-enriched folkloric performances in Moldova draw oenophiles and anyone wanting to profit from the 10-day visa-free regime Moldova introduces during the festival.

November

Leaves have fallen and snow is about to in much of Europe. Even in the temperate zones around the Med it can get chilly, rainy and blustery. Most seasonal attractions have closed for the year.

Aurora Watching, Iceland, Norway, Sweden & Finland

Whether you are blessed with seeing the Northern Lights is largely a matter of luck, but the further north you are, the better the chances. Dark, cloudless nights, patience and a viewing spot away from city lights are other key factors.

Guy Fawkes Night, Britain

Bonfires and fireworks erupt across Britain on 5 November, recalling the foiling of a plot to blow up the Houses of Parliament in the 1600s. Go to high ground in London to see glowing explosions erupt everywhere. It's hard to imagine what might occur if Fawkes had succeeded.

December

December is a magical time to visit Europe: Christmas decorations brighten up the dark streets and, despite the cold across much of the region, prices remain surprisingly low as long as you avoid Christmas and New Year's Eve themselves.

Christmas Markets, Germany & Austria

Christkindlmarkts are held across Germany and Austria. The most famous are in Nuremberg and Vienna, but every town has one. Warm your hands through your mittens holding a hot mug of mulled wine and find that special (or kitsch) present.

Natale, Italy

Italian churches set up intricate cribs or *presepi* (nativity scenes) in the lead-up to Christmas. Some are quite famous, most are works of art and many date back hundreds of years and are venerated for their spiritual ties.

Eastern European Christmas

Christmas is celebrated in different ways in Eastern Europe: most countries celebrate Christmas on Christmas Eve (24 December), with an evening meal and midnight Mass. In Russia, Ukraine and Belarus, Christmas falls in January, as per the Gregorian calendar.

Itineraries

Europe 101 »
Mediterranean Europe »
From London to the Sun »
Scandinavian Highlights »
The Alps to the Rif Mountains »
Eastern Europe Today »

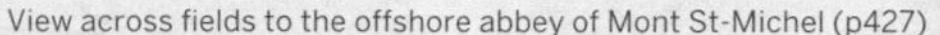

View across fields to the offshore abbey of Mont St-Michel (p427)

Europe 101

Six Weeks

Italy, Switzerland, Germany, the Netherlands, France and Britain are the absolute essentials for any first-time visitor to Europe – all are crammed with world-famous sights, cultural icons and unforgettable experiences.

WITOLD SKRYPCZAK/LONELY PLANET IMAGES ©

DAVID TOMLINSON/LONELY PLANET IMAGES ©

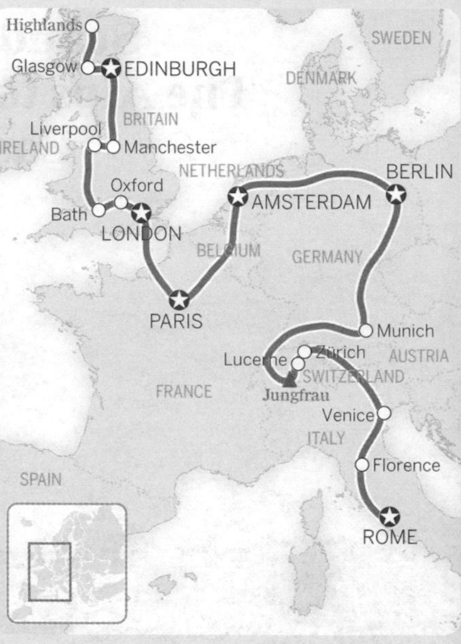

» Begin in **Rome** (p685) and spend several days in this incredible city.

» Go north to heartbreakingly beautiful **Florence** (p733) and then revel in timeless **Venice** (p718).

» Carry on to majestic Switzerland, spend a day in **Zürich** (p1247) and visit lovely **Lucerne** (p1252) and the amazing Swiss Alps by taking the train to the **Jungfrau** (p1255).

» Head to **Munich** (p510) for Oktoberfest if you're there in September.

» Hit **Berlin** (p488) at the weekend to check out Europe's most hedonistic city, see the remains of the wall and dance your nights (and days) away.

» Then go to **Amsterdam** (p904), perfect for a couple of days' exploration, Rembrandt and canal wandering.

» Next up is the train to **Paris** (p400). Spend several days here visiting the Louvre, Versailles and the Eiffel Tower.

» Take the Eurostar to **London** (p156) and see the wealth of great sights and enjoy the city's great eating, drinking and clubbing.

» Travel west to historic **Oxford** (p194) and **Bath** (p187), savouring incredible Stonehenge along the way, and swing north to **Liverpool** (p208).

» End your journey with several days in Scotland – check out magical **Edinburgh** (p214), happening **Glasgow** (p219) and have a walk in the **Highlands** (p225).

Clockwise from top left

1. The Swiss Alps near the Jungfrau **2.** Palazzo Ducale as seen from Piazza San Marco, Venice **3.** Eiffel Tower, Paris **4.** Houses of Parliament, London

2

3

Mediterranean Europe

Four Weeks

Think Europe doesn't do beaches? Think again – it does, but with lashings of culture on the side, as you'll find during this romp along its southern shores, starting in Madrid and ending up in Turkey.

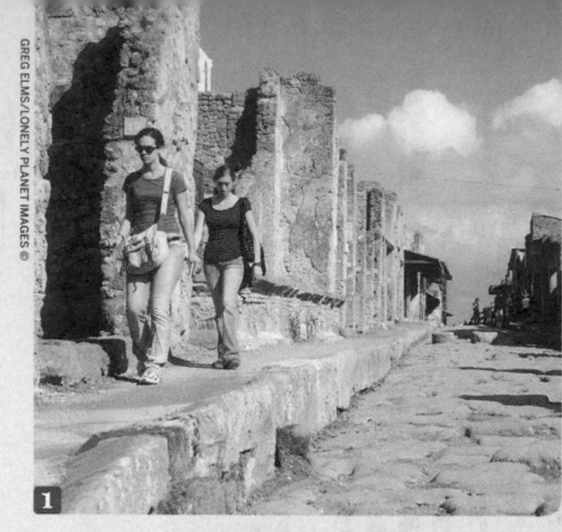

GREG ELMS/LONELY PLANET IMAGES ©

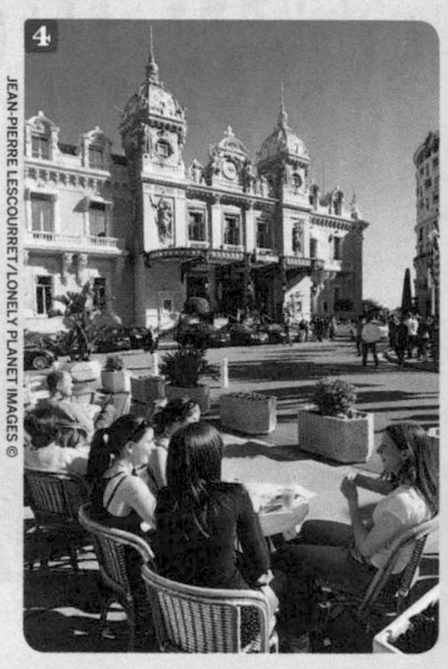

JEAN-PIERRE LESCOURRET/LONELY PLANET IMAGES ©

» Fly into **Madrid** (p1121) and then head directly for the Mediterranean by taking a train to **Barcelona** (p1146) and soak up the seaside ambience of Gaudí's city.

» Head along the Côte d'Azur via **Nice** (p464) and spend time exploring **Monaco** (p470) and the beautiful villages of **Provence** (p458).

» From Nice, take the train to historic **Rome** (p685) and continue south to energetic **Naples** (p747), peer into ill-fated **Pompeii** (p753) and explore the stunning Amalfi Coast.

» Cross Italy to Bari, from where you head across the Adriatic by ferry to the Croatian pearl of **Dubrovnik** (p280).

» Bus it south through Montenegro and Albania – two of Europe's least-known but most-breathtaking gems – and then head to the beautiful Greek island of **Corfu** (p596).

» From Patra, do a loop of the Peloponnese: bus to Byzantine pin-up city **Mystras** (p572), the ancient heavyweight **Mycenae** (p572) and then bus it to venerable **Athens** (p563).

» Go south to Piraeus for an island-hopping expedition to **Mykonos** (p578), **Paros** (p580) and volcanic **Santorini** (p583).

» Continue to island-hop until you've had your fill, then set sail for Turkey from Samos or Lesvos.

» Visit ancient **Ephesus** (p1275) then bus north along the Aegean coast to the ruins of Troy and **Çanakkale** (p1273) and to throbbing, beautiful and chaotic **İstanbul** (p1263).

Clockwise from top left

1. The ruins of Pompeii **2.** Whirling dervish in action in İstanbul **3.** Oia town on Santorini **4.** The Monte Carlo casino at Monaco

From London to the Sun

Four Weeks

Beginning in England, this lovely journey just gets warmer and warmer as you head further south. While you visit just four countries, this is a chance to get to know them all fairly well.

HOLGER LEUE/LONELY PLANET IMAGES ©

KARL BLACKWELL/LONELY PLANET IMAGES ©

» Enjoy **London** (p156) for several days of museums, galleries, world-class shopping and clubbing, then head to **Bath** (p187) by train before returning to London.

» Take the Eurostar to romantic **Paris** (p400) and make side trips to the **D-Day Beaches** (p427) and **Mont St-Michel** (p427).

» Rail south to **Barcelona** (p1146) possibly stopping at Limoges for the **Dordogne Valley** (p449) en route. From Barcelona, it's possible to make a longish round trip to the **Balearic Islands** (p1169) and **Valencia** (p1166).

» Zip up to the Basque seaside resort of **San Sebastián** (p1161) and the Museo Guggenheim in happening **Bilbao** (p1162).

» Next make a beeline for energetic **Madrid** (p1121), making day trips to Moorish **Toledo** (p1143) and enchanting **Segovia** (p1140).

» Then board a bus to the Islamic fortress, the Alhambra in **Granada** (p1179) and see the stunning Mezquita of **Córdoba** (p1177) before dancing the flamenco in **Seville** (p1173).

» Get the bus to **Lisbon** (p993) and relax and eat custard tarts in Portugal's breezy capital and sidestep to **Sintra** (p1001).

» North lies **Porto** (p1010) and the **Parque Nacional da Peneda-Gerês** (p1017), with lots of hiking opportunities.

» The southern **Algarve** (p1003) is touristy, but the train journey along the coast is beautiful.

Above
1. Street scene in Lisbon **2.** Valencia's Ciudad de las Artes y las Ciencias (City of Arts and Sciences), designed by Santiago Calatrava

Scandinavian Highlights

Three Weeks

This is a three-week hop around the classic sights of Scandinavia, though you can easily spend far longer in these fascinating countries: Extra time allows more detailed exploration and side-trips to quieter places.

1

2

» Start in the funky Icelandic capital **Reykjavik** (p632) and spend several days in and around the city – don't miss the Blue Lagoon or the spectacular Gullfoss Falls.

» Fly on to **Copenhagen** (p329), admiring the waterfront and museums and enjoying the lights of Tivoli at night.

» Take a day trip to the cathedral and Viking boat museum at **Roskilde** (p337) and 'Hamlet's' castle at **Helsingør** (p337).

» Next, take the train to **Stockholm** (p1200) and admire the stately, watery centre of town, pehaps stopping along the way at **Göteborg** (p1218) to soak up its bonhomie.

» A ferry-trip from Stockholm could take you to quirky **Helsinki** (p373) or picturesque **Tallinn** (p355).

» An overnight train from Stockholm takes you to **Oslo** (p930), where you can check out much of Munch's work in a stunning setting.

» From Oslo, a long but very scenic day includes the **Norway in a Nutshell rail trip** (p936) to Flåm and a combination boat/bus journey along the Sognefjord to **Bergen** (p937), Norway's prettiest city.

» From here you can take a fjord sidetrip to mighty **Geiranger** (p946) or to **Fjærland** (p937), the gateway to a glacial wonderland.

» Head back to Denmark, stopping at **Århus** (p340) – don't miss the ARoS art museum.

Above
1. Bryggen waterfront in Bergen **2.** Iceland's Blue Lagoon hot springs

The Alps to the Rif Mountains

One to Two Months

If you can't get enough of gorgeous towns on the shores of brilliant-blue lakes surrounded by soaring peaks, then this itinerary is bound to please. Abundant opportunities to hike or ski are available.

KRZYSZTOF DYDYNSKI/LONELY PLANET IMAGES ©

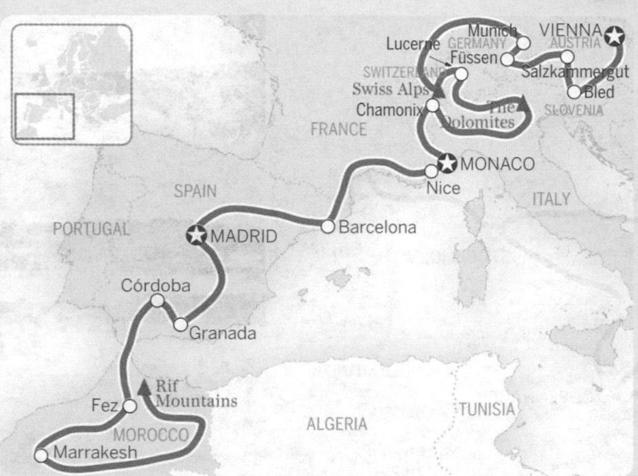

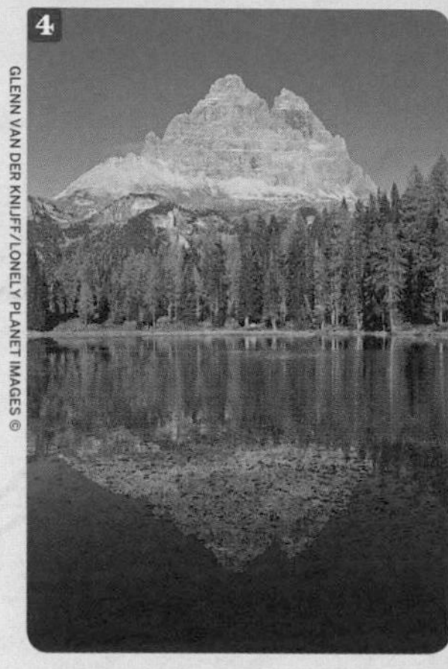

GLENN VAN DER KNIJFF/LONELY PLANET IMAGES ©

» Start with a couple of days on the Danube in elegant **Vienna** (p63) before dropping in to lovely **Bled** (p1108) and perhaps to nearby Bohinj in Slovenia.

» Then it's back to Austria for a couple of days to explore the beautiful **Salzkammergut** (p84) region.

» Detour to fairytale **Neuschwanstein Castle** (p522) near Füssen in Germany. By now you'll be ready to sample some beers in nearby **Munich** (p510).

» Head into Switzerland for a few days in the unbeatable **Swiss Alps** (p1240). Visit lovely **Lucerne** (p1252) and take the train to the top of Jungfrau.

» Head across to Italy to check out the saw-tooth peaks of **The Dolomites** (p732).

» **Chamonix** (p447) in France is a great base to explore around Mt Blanc. Then it's time for some coffee, wine and sun along the Côte d'Azur travelling via **Monaco** (p470) and **Nice** (p464).

» Spain's two most exciting cities, **Barcelona** (p1146) and **Madrid** (p1121) beckon. Head south from here to see the beautiful Alhambra in **Granada** (p1179) and the stunning Mezquita of **Córdoba** (p1177).

» Next, take a ferry across to exotic Morocco. Check out the country's imperial cities of **Fez** (p885) and **Marrakesh** (p891).

» Lastly, chill out in the stunning **Rif Mountains** (p876) dotted by delightful towns and villages.

Clockwise from top left

1. Cafe scene during an evening in Madrid **2.** Delightful Neuschwanstein Castle, near Füssen **3.** Produce at a souq in Marrakesh **4.** A soaring peak in Italy's Dolomites

2

3

Eastern Europe Today

Four Weeks

Forget the stereotypes of the grim and grey 'Eastern Bloc' of the early 1990s – this half of Europe is one of the most dynamic and fast-changing places in the world: come and explore it yourself.

1

4

» Pick a flight to **Berlin** (p488), now a veritable music, art and nightlife mecca.

» Then travel to vibrant **Warsaw** (p961) and **Kraków** (p966), Poland's amazingly preserved royal capital.

» Take in the old town in Lithuania's capital **Vilnius** (p802), wander the streets of gorgeous art nouveau **Rīga** (p783) and party in technophile **Tallinn** (p355).

» Head into Russia and split your time between imperial **St Petersburg** (p1053) and modern-day super-city **Moscow** (p1046).

» Swing into the past by taking a train to **Minsk** (p99) in Belarus to see how things were under communism.

» Continue into Ukraine and spend a few days in its bustling Soviet capital **Kyiv** (p1298), then contrast it with **Lviv** (p1299).

» Entering Romania, you should make a beeline for Transylvania. Sharpen your fangs at 'Dracula's' castle in **Bran** (p1033) and enjoy the gorgeous old towns nearby.

» Romania's capital **Bucharest** (p1024) is next, where urban renewal of the communist kind awaits.

» A train zips you through the mountains to Bulgaria's loveliest town, **Veliko Târnovo** (p252).Travel on to the relaxed capital **Sofia** (p243) and then by train to Serbia's vibrant capital, **Belgrade** (p1071).

» Head back to Berlin via sumptuous **Budapest** (p608) and romantic **Prague** (p305).

Clockwise from top left

1. Art Nouveau decoration in Rīga **2.** St Basil's Cathedral, Moscow **3.** Széchenyi Baths, Budapest **4.** Modern shopping centre, designed by The Jude Partnership, Warsaw

2

3

Look out for these icons:

 Our author's recommendation

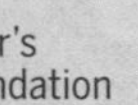 A green or sustainable option

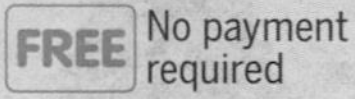 No payment required

See the Index for a full list of destinations covered in this book.

On the Road

Albania

Includes »

Best Places to Eat

» Kujtimi, Gjirokastra (p50)
» Era, Tirana (p45)

Best Places to Stay

» Berat Backpackers (p48)
» Hotel Kalemi, Gjirokastra (p50)

Why Go?

Great peaks sprout in the background, vast plains and lakes surround the central mountain ranges, and coastal areas provide the traveller to Albania with dramatically different cultural and geographical landscapes. People who like city living can down coffee in busy, surprising Tirana before heading out to an exhibition or buzzing nightclub.

August sees quiet seaside spots morph into loud disco-laden towns where every day is a thumping weekend. Head north and you might spot locals in traditional dress, sworn virgins and shepherds guiding flocks in the mountains.

After years of government-enforced isolation, Albanians welcome travellers with sincere hospitality. Upgraded roads swirl past the new houses and bar-restaurant-hotel developments that demonstrate the country's newfound prosperity. The unique sights of Albania are unforgettable: donkeys tethered to concrete bunkers, houses crawling up each other to reach the hilltops in Unesco World Heritage–listed Berat and Gjirokastra, and isolated beaches.

When to Go

Tirana

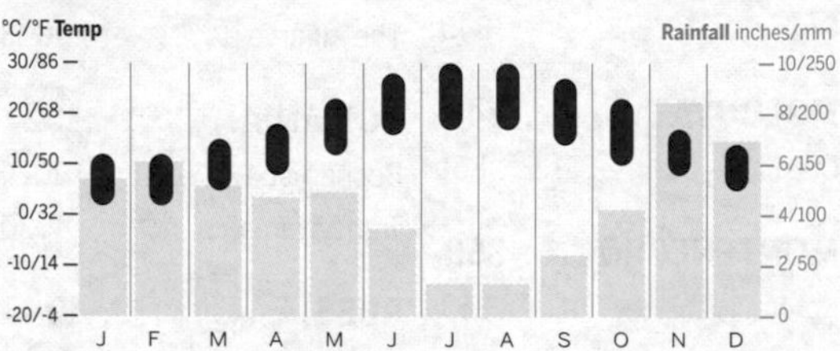

Jun Enjoy the Mediterranean climate and deserted beaches.

Aug Beaches are packed and the mood is bright as overseas-based Albanians return to holiday.

Dec Join a truly adventurous snowshoe expedition to isolated Theth.

Connections

Albania has daily bus connections with Kosovo, Montenegro, Macedonia, Italy (via ferry) and Thessaloniki and Athens in Greece. Albania is a short ferry ride from Greece's Corfu. Travellers heading south from Croatia can pass through Montenegro to Shkodra (via Ulcinj), and can loop the country before heading into Macedonia via Pogradec or Kosovo via the Lake Koman ferry or new superfast Albania–Kosovo highway.

ITINERARIES

Three Days

Drink frappé at Tirana's trendy Blloku cafes, check out the museum and art gallery, then spend the night dancing in packed nightclubs. Make the two-hour trip to the Ottoman-era town of Berat, meander through the castle and stay in authentic accommodation in the town's old quarters. Kruja is a good airport detour; check out one of the country's best ethnographic museums and buy souvenirs in its bazaar.

One Week

Spend a day in Tirana then head south to Berat for a few days. Take on beachside Drymades or Jal before making a pit stop at Saranda to prepare for a stroll around Butrint's ruins. Pause at the Blue Eye Spring before getting lost among the historic slate-roofed houses of Gjirokastra.

Essential Food & Drink

» **Byrek** Pastry with cheese or meat

» **Fergesë** Baked peppers, egg and cheese and occasionally meat

» **Midhje** Wild or farmed mussels, often served fried

» **Paçë koke** Sheep's-head soup, usually served for breakfast

» **Qofta** Flat or cylindrical minced-meat rissoles

» **Sufllaqë** Doner kebab

» **Tavë** Meat baked with cheese and egg

» **Konjak** Local brandy

» **Raki** Popular spirit made from grapes

» **Raki mani** Spirit made from mulberries

AT A GLANCE

» **Currency** Lekë, euro (€)

» **Language** Albanian (some Greek and Italian spoken on the south coast)

» **Money** ATMs in most towns

» **Visas** Nationals of most countries don't need a visa

Fast Facts

» **Area** 28,748 sq km

» **Capital** Tirana

» **Country code** ☎355

» **Emergency** Police ☎129; ambulance ☎127

Exchange Rates

Australia	A$1	103 lekë
Canada	C$1	103 lekë
euro zone	€1	141 lekë
Japan	¥100	118 lekë
New Zealand	NZ$1	76 lekë
UK	UK£1	160 lekë
USA	US$1	99 lekë

Set Your Budget

» **Budget accommodation** €12-15 per person

» **Two-course evening meal** €10

» **Museum entrance** €1-3

» **Beer (bottle)** €1.50

Resources

» **Outdoor Albania** (www.outdooralbania.com)

» **Albania-Hotel** (www.albania-hotel.com)

Albania Highlights

1 Feast your eyes on the wild colour schemes and experience the hip Blloku cafe culture in **Tirana** (p43)

2 Explore the Unesco World Heritage–listed museum cities of calm **Berat** (p47) and slate-roofed **Gjirokastra** (p49)

3 Catch some sun at **Drymades** (p48), just one of the beaches on the south's dramatic Ionian coast

4 Travel back in time to the ruins of **Butrint** (p48), hidden in the depths of a forest in a serene lakeside setting

5 Catch the Lake Koman ferry from Shkodra to near **Valbonë** (p46) and trek the northern Albanian Alps (aka Accursed Mountains) to the village of **Theth** (p46)

TIRANA

☎04 / POP 600,000

Lively, colourful Tirana has changed beyond belief in the last decade from the dull, grey city it once was. It's amazing what a lick of paint can do: it covers one ugly tower block with horizontal orange and red stripes and plants perspective-fooling cubes on its neighbour.

Trendy Blloku buzzes with well-dressed nouvelle bourgeoisie hanging out in bars or zipping between boutiques. Quite where their money comes from is the subject of much speculation, but thankfully you don't need much of it to party in the city's bars and clubs.

Tirana's grand central boulevards are lined with fascinating relics of its Ottoman, Italian and communist past – from delicate minarets to loud socialist murals. Tirana's traffic is unmitigated chaos.

Running north–south through Tirana is Blvd Zogu I, which becomes Blvd Dëshmorët e Kombit as it crosses the Lana River. Sites of interest are on or very close to this large boulevard, including, roughly halfway along, Skanderbeg Sq.

Blloku is an area of some 10 blocks of restaurants, cafes and hotels situated one block west of Dëshmorët and along the Lana River.

Sights

NORTH OF THE RIVER

Skanderbeg Square SQUARE, MONUMENT

Skanderbeg Sq is the best place to start witnessing Tirana's daily goings-on. Until it was pulled down by an angry mob in 1991, a 10m-high bronze statue of former dictator Enver Hoxha stood here, watching over a mainly car-free square. Now only the **equestrian statue of Skanderbeg**, Albania's national hero, remains, deaf to the cacophony of screeching horns as cars four lanes deep try to shove their way through the battlefield below.

Et'hem Bey Mosque MOSQUE

(⌚8am-noon) Stop to examine Skanderbeg's emblematic goat's-head helmet and the minaret of the Et'hem Bey Mosque will catch your eye. The elegant mosque, built between 1789 and 1823, is one of the oldest buildings in the city – it was spared from destruction during the atheism campaign of the late '60s because of its status as a cultural monument.

National History Museum MUSEUM

(Muzeu Historik Kombëtar; Sheshi Skënderbej; admission 200 lekë; ⌚10am-5pm Tue-Sat, 10am-2pm Sun) A mosaic entitled *Albania* adorns the museum's facade and shows Albanians victorious and proud from Illyrian times through to WWII. Don't miss the exhibition of icons by Onufri, the renowned 16th-century master of colour.

National Art Gallery ART GALLERY

(Galeria Kombëtare e Arteve; Blvd Dëshmorët e Kombit; admission 200 lekë; ⌚10am-5pm Tue-Sat, 10am-2pm Sun) This gallery is packed with bright Soviet-realism paintings featuring smiling 'aren't we happy to be here!' workers in their various places of employ.

SOUTH OF THE RIVER

Pyramid NOTABLE BUILDING

(Blvd Dëshmorët e Kombit) Designed by Enver Hoxha's daughter and son-in-law and completed in 1988, this pyramid once housed the Enver Hoxha Museum. It's since had a spell as a convention centre and nightclub but now the white-marble-sided building is falling into disrepair.

Blloku NOTABLE AREA

The once totally forbidden but now totally trendy Blloku area was a former communist party elite hang-out that was opened to the general public for the first time in 1991 and now hosts the coolest coffee drinkers and nightclubbers in town.

Congress Building NOTABLE BUILDING

(Blvd Dëshmorët e Kombit) Another reasonably modern architectural wonder created by Hoxha's daughter and son-in-law is the square, palm tree–fronted Congress Building. Follow Rr Ismail Qemali one block east then two blocks south of Blloku. Security still guards the **former residence of Enver Hoxha** (cnr Rr Dëshmorët e 4 Shkurtit & Rr Ismail Qemali).

Archaeological Museum MUSEUM

(Muzeu Arkeologik; Sheshi Nënë Tereza; admission €1; ⌚10.30am-2.30pm Mon-Fri) This office-like museum houses an extensive collection of antiquities and has information about recent archaeological digs.

Sleeping

Tirana Backpacker Hostel HOSTEL €

(☎068 2167 357; www.tiranahostel.com; Rr Elbasanit 85; dm €12; @) Albania's first hostel opened in 2005 in a 70-year-old villa close to the city centre. Its 25 beds are spread over four rooms and it's blessed with wide balconies, gardens and a cosy outdoor kitchen.

Milingona HOSTEL €
(☎069 2260 775, 069 2049 836; www.milingonahostel.com; Rr Qemal Stafa 277; dm €12; @) Run by uber-enthusiastic and multilingual sisters Zhujeta and Rozana, Milingona (meaning 'ant') is clean and homey, with a 'you'll never want to leave' terrace up top. There's an excellent kitchen for self-caterers.

Hostel Albania HOSTEL €
(☎067 2783 798; www.hostel-albania.com; Rr Beqir Luga 56; dm €11-13; ❄@📶) This hostel has small four- and six-person dorms, with a basement 14-bed dorm that's the coolest spot in summer. There's room for a couple of tents (€7 per person), and a filling breakfast with filter coffee is included.

Pension Andrea PENSION €€
(☎069 2094 915; Rr Anton Harapi 103; s/d €25/30) Grandmother Gina runs this quiet pension with limited English but loads of enthusiasm. From Rr Jeronim de Rada take the first

Tirana

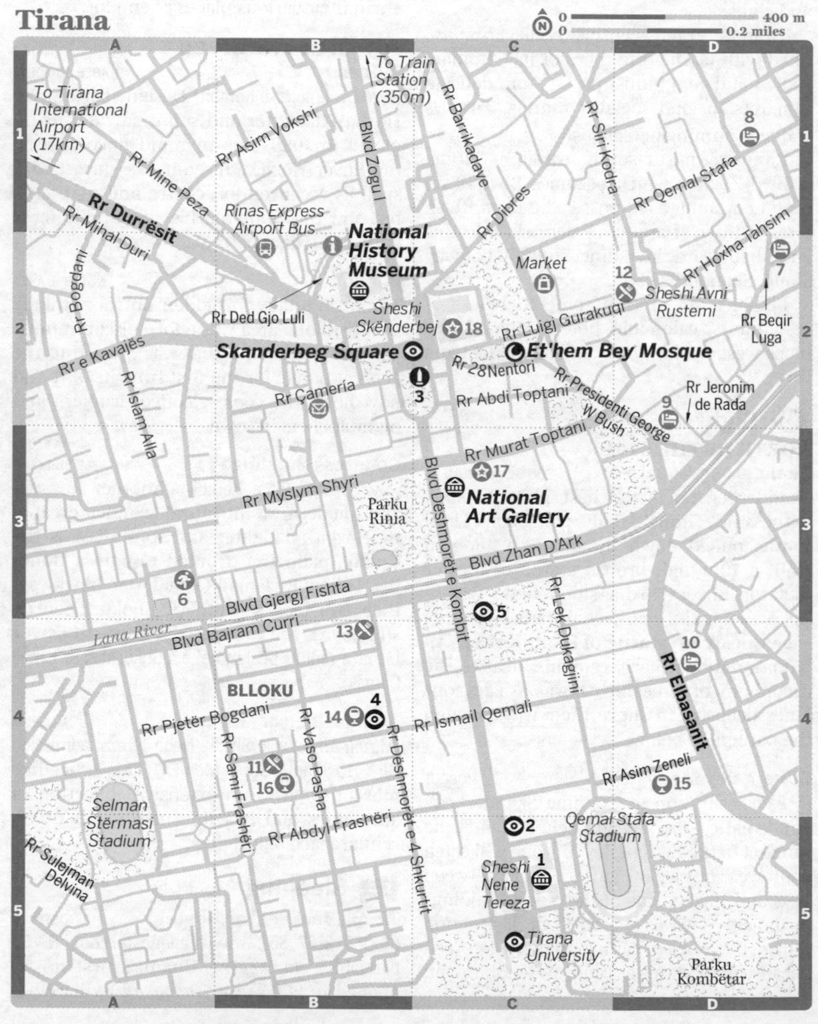

> **SPLURGE**
>
> Get active with **Outdoor Albania** (☎2227 121; www.outdooralbania.com; Metropol Bldg, Rr Sami Frashëri, Tirana; ⏲9am-5pm Mon-Fri). This adventure-tour agency offers rafting, snowshoeing and hikes through the mountains. Day trips start from €50.

right down the court; Gina's through the gate on your right.

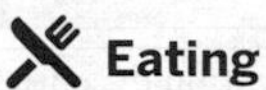

Eating

TOP CHOICE Era — TRADITIONAL ALBANIAN, ITALIAN €

(Rr Ismail Qemali; mains from 200 lekë; ⏲11am-midnight) Generous serves of traditional Albanian and Italian fare in the heart of Blloku. Be warned: it's a very popular place and venturing out to other restaurants will seem a drag after eating here. It's also sometimes quite hard to get a seat.

Oda — TRADITIONAL ALBANIAN €€

(Rr Luigj Gurakuqi; meals 800 lekë) Bright flashing lights guide you to this endearing restaurant down a lane near Sheshi Avni Rustemi. Oda offers diners an authentic vibe, interesting Albanian dishes and restaurant-distilled raki.

Pasticeri Française — BAKERY €

(Rr Dëshmorët e 4 Shkurtit 1; breakfasts from 300 lekë; ⏲8am-10pm; Wi-Fi) It's no wonder this French cafe has a slimming advertisement hanging on its wall; its sweet pastries and macaroons are irresistible.

Drinking

Radio — BAR

(Rr Ismail Qemali 29/1) Set back from the street is this cool understated bar. Check out the owner's collection of antique Albania-made radios while sipping cocktails.

Charl's — BAR

(Rr Pjetër Bogdani 36) Charl's offers live music on the weekends and disco/dance crowd-pleasers the rest of the time.

Kaon Beer Garden — BEER HALL

(Rr Assim Zeneli; ⏲noon-1am) Kaon's 'keg-on-the-table' approach means it can be hard to get a table in the evening, but once you're in, it's a pleasant outdoor bar and restaurant in the fancy villa-filled part of town.

Entertainment

Folie — CLUB

(Rr Murat Toptani) This is where big-name DJs come to play, though the crowd can be more concerned with being seen than actually enjoying itself.

FREE Academy of Film & Multimedia Marubi — CINEMA

(www.afmm.edu.al; Rr Aleksander Moisiu 76; ⏲7pm Thu) Marubi shows free art-house movies (international with subtitles) on Thursday

Tirana

Top Sights

- Et'hem Bey Mosque ... C2
- National Art Gallery ... C3
- National History Museum ... B2
- Skanderbeg Sq ... C2

Sights

1. Archaeological Museum ... C5
2. Congress Building ... C5
3. Equestrian Statue of Skanderbeg Sq ... C2
4. Former Residence of Enver Hoxha ... B4
5. Pyramid ... C3

Activities, Courses & Tours

6. Outdoor Albania ... A3

Sleeping

7. Hostel Albania ... D2
8. Milingona ... D1
9. Pension Andrea ... D2
10. Tirana Backpacker Hostel ... D4

Eating

11. Era ... B4
12. Oda ... D2
13. Pasticeri Française ... B4

Drinking

14. Charl's ... B4
15. Kaon Beer Garden ... D4
16. Radio ... B4

Entertainment

17. Folie ... C3
18. Theater of Opera & Ballet ... C2

DON'T MISS

Theth and **Valbonë** are villages deep in the mountains of Albania, the 'Accursed Mountains', and come summer they're a magnet for those seeking mystery and adventure. Circular hikes are marked out with red and white markers, and the main hike from Theth to Valbonë takes around seven hours. Check www.shkoder-albanian-alps.com for accommodation. *Furgons* (shared minibuses) leave Shkodra at 7am from outside Café Rusi.

during the semester. It's near the last Kino Studio bus stop in the city's northeast.

Theater of Opera & Ballet THEATRE
(☎2224 753; Sheshi Skënderbej; tickets from 300 lekë; ⊙performances from 7pm, from 6pm winter) Check the listings and posters outside the theatre for performance information.

Information

Tirana tourist information centre (☎2223 313; www.tirana.gov.al; Rr Ded Gjo Luli; ⊙9am-7pm Mon-Fri, 9am-4pm Sat & Sun) Friendly staff make getting information easy at this new-to-Tirana government-run initiative.

Getting There & Around

AIR **Tirana International Airport** (www.tirana-airport.com.al) is at Rinas, 17km northwest of Tirana. The Rinas Express airport bus operates an hourly (6am to 6pm) service from Rr Mine Peza for 250 lekë.

BICYCLE Cycling was the main form of transport for Albanians until the early '90s, and it's having a comeback (cyclists make more headway in Tirana's traffic snarls). Bike hire is available from hostels.

BUS & FURGON Buses and *furgons* (shared minibuses) depart from ever-changing places in and around the city; check locally for latest departure points. Domestic buses run to Berat (400 lekë, 2½ hours), Gjirokastra (1000 lekë, seven hours) and Saranda (1200 lekë, eight hours).

Buses for Pristina in Kosovo (€10, five hours, three daily) leave from beside the museum on Blvd Zogu 1. Buses to Skopje in Macedonia leave from the same spot (€20, eight hours). Buses to Ulcinj (€20, three hours) and Budva (€30, four hours) in Montenegro depart from 6am in front of the tourist information centre. Buses to Athens in Greece leave at around 8am and 7pm from travel agents on Blvd Zogu 1 (€35, 15 hours).

TAXI Taxi stands dot the city, and taxis charge 300 to 400 lekë for a ride inside Tirana and 600 lekë at night and to destinations outside the CBD area. Agree on price before setting off.

TRAIN The rundown train station is at the northern end of Blvd Zogu I. Trains are dirt cheap and run to Durrës, Elbasan, Pogradec, Shkodra and Vlora. Check timetables at the station.

NORTHERN ALBANIA

Shkodra

☎022 / POP 91,300

Shkodra (Shkodër), the traditional centre of the Gheg cultural region, is one of the oldest cities in Europe. Rozafa Fortress has stunning views, and the Marubi photography exhibition is small but fascinating. A section of town has benefited from sensitive renovations of its historic buildings, and Shkodra's locals are more likely to ride a bicycle than drive a car. It's also the gateway town to Montenegro and Albania's alpine region.

Sights

Rozafa Fortress CASTLE
(admission 200 lekë; ⊙8am-10pm) This fortress derives its name from a woman named Rozafa, who was allegedly walled into the ramparts as an offering to the gods so that the construction would stand. Municipal buses (30 lekë) stop near the turn-off to the castle; walk up from there.

Marubi Permanent Photo Exhibition ART GALLERY
(Rr Muhamet Gjollesha; admission 100 lekë; ⊙8am-4pm Mon-Fri) Hidden behind a block of shops and flats, the Marubi Permanent Photo Exhibition has fantastic photography taken over three generations by the Marubi family.

Sleeping

Hotel Kaduku HOTEL €
(☎222 42 216; www.hotel-kaduku.com; Sheshi 5 Heronjtë; s/d €23/32) This hotel is behind Raiffeisen Bank near Hotel Rozafa. Owners have access to budget rooms elsewhere and provide good information about accessing Theth.

Getting There & Away

BUS & FURGON Buses and *furgons* depart hourly to Tirana (350 lekë, two hours, from 6am to 4pm). *Furgons* to Ulcinj in Montenegro leave at 9am and 4pm (600 lekë, two hours) from the other side of the park abutting Grand Hotel Europa. From Ulcinj, buses leave for Shkodra at 6am and 12.30pm. Catch the 7am bus to Lake Koman (800 lekë, two hours) in time for the wonderful ferry trip along the lake to Fierza (400 lekë, two hours).

TAXI It costs between €40 and €45 for the trip from Shkodra to Ulcinj in Montenegro.

TRAIN Trains depart Tirana for Shkodra at 1.15pm (145 lekë) and head back at 5.40am.

CENTRAL ALBANIA

Kruja

☎0511 / POP 20,000

From the road below, Kruja's houses appear to sit in the lap of a mountain. An ancient castle juts out to one side, and the massive Skanderbeg Museum erupts out of the castle itself.

Kruja is Skanderbeg's town. Yes, Albania's hero was born here, and although it was over 500 years ago, there's still a great deal of pride in the fact that he and his forces defended Kruja from the Ottomans until his death. As soon as you get off the *furgon* you're face to knee with a statue of him wielding his mighty sword with one hand, and it just gets more Skanderdelic after that.

Sights

Skanderbeg Museum MUSEUM
(admission 200 lekë; ⌚9am-1pm & 4-7pm Tue-Sun) Designed by Enver Hoxha's daughter and son-in-law, this museum's spacious seven-level interior displays replicas of armour and paintings depicting Skanderbeg's struggle against the Ottomans.

Ethnographic Museum MUSEUM
(admission 300 lekë; ⌚9am-1pm & 4-7pm Tue-Sun) Set in an original 19th-century Ottoman house that belonged to the affluent Toptani family, this museum inside the castle walls shows how the household remained self-sufficient. The walls are lined with original frescos from 1764.

Bazaar MARKET
The Ottoman-style bazaar, between the bus station and castle entrance, has quality traditional ware, including beautifully embroidered tablecloths, copper coffee pots and plates.

Getting There & Away

Kruja is 32km from Tirana. Catch a *furgon* from Tirana to Kruja (200 lekë), not just Fush Kruja below. You can reach Tirana International Airport by *furgon* (100 lekë, 15 minutes) or taxi.

Berat

☎032 / POP 45,500

A highlight of any trip to Albania is a visit to beautiful Berat. Its most striking feature is the collection of white Ottoman houses climbing up the hill to its castle, earning it the title of 'town of a thousand windows' and helping it become a Unesco World Heritage site in 2008.

Sights & Activities

Kalasa CASTLE
(admission 100 lekë; ⌚24hr) The neighbourhood inside the castle's walls still lives and breathes; you'll see old Mercedes-Benz cars struggling up the cobblestone roads to return locals home.

Onufri Museum ART GALLERY
(www.beratmuseum.net; admission 200 lekë; ⌚9am-1pm & 4-7pm May-Sep, 9am-4pm Oct-Apr, closed Mon) The Kalasa's biggest church, **Church of the Dormition of St Mary** (Kisha Fjetja e Shën Mërisë), houses this museum, where you can see spectacular 16th-century artworks and beautifully gilded iconostasis.

BUNKER LOVE

On the hillsides, beaches and generally most surfaces in Albania, you will notice small concrete domes (often in groups of three) with rectangular slits. Meet the bunkers: Enver Hoxha's concrete legacy, built from 1950 to 1985. Weighing in at 5 tonnes of concrete and iron, these little mushrooms are almost impossible to destroy. They were built to repel an invasion and can resist full tank assault – a fact proved by their chief engineer, who vouched for his creation's strength by standing inside one while it was bombarded by a tank. The shell-shocked engineer emerged unscathed, and tens of thousands were built. Today, some are creatively painted and one houses a tattoo artist.

Ethnographic Museum MUSEUM
(www.beratmuseum.net; admission 100 lekë; 9am-1pm & 4-7pm May-Sep, 9am-4pm Oct-30 Apr, closed Mon) The ground floor of this 18th-century Ottoman house, down from the castle, displays traditional clothes and tools used by silversmiths and weavers, while the upper storey has rooms decked out in the traditional style.

Chapel of St Michael CHURCH
Perched on a cliff ledge below the citadel is the little chapel of St Michael (Shën Mihell), best viewed from the Gorica quarter.

Mosques MOSQUES
The 16th-century **Sultan's Mosque** (Xhamia e Mbretit) is one of the oldest in Albania. The big mosque on the town square is the 16th-century **Lead Mosque** (Xhamia e Plumbit), so named because of its lead-coated sphere-shaped domes. The 19th-century **Bachelors' Mosque** (Xhamia e Beqarëvet) was built for unmarried shop assistants and junior craftsmen and is perched between Ottoman-era shopfronts along the river.

Sleeping & Eating

TOP CHOICE **Berat Backpackers** HOSTEL €
(069 3064 429; www.beratbackpackers.com; Gorica; dm incl breakfast €12; Apr-Nov) Albania's best backpackers is the brainchild of Englishman Scott: he's transformed a traditional house in the Gorica quarter (across the river from Mangalem) into a vine-clad hostel with a basement bar, an alfresco drinking area and a cheery, relaxed atmosphere. There's a shaded camping area on the terrace (€5 per person).

Hotel Guva HOTEL €
(32 30 014; Mangalem; s/d incl breakfast €15/30) The four rooms of this 'new kid on the block' have tremendous views of Gorica, as does its upstairs terrace bar. One room has four single beds for €10 per person. It's a hike up stairs near St Michael.

Information

Information centre Located in the council building, parallel to the Osumi River.

Getting There & Away

Buses and *furgons* run between Tirana and Berat (400 lekë, 2½ hours) hourly until 3pm. There are also buses to Vlora (300 lekë, 2½ hours), Durrës (400 lekë, 1½ hours) and Saranda via Gjirokastra (1000 lekë, six hours, 8am and 2pm).

SOUTHERN ALBANIA

Drymades

As you zigzag down the mountain from the Llogaraja Pass National Park, the white crescent-shape beaches and azure waters lure you from below. To get to one of the best beaches, turn right just after the beginning of the walk down from the Vlora–Saranda road to Dhërmi beach. After a 20-minute walk you'll be on Drymades' rocky white beach.

TOP CHOICE **Sea Turtle** (069 4016 057; per person 1000 lekë; Jun-Sep) camping ground is created each summer when two brothers turn the family orange orchard into a vibrant tent city. The price includes tent (with mattresses, sheets and pillows), breakfast and dinner. The camping ground is on the left-hand side of the main road just before you reach the beach. It's a 20-minute walk from the main road.

Vuno & Jal

Vuno is a tiny hillside village above the picturesque beach of Jal. **Outdoor Albania** (www.outdooralbania.com) renovated Vuno's primary school and each summer its classrooms are filled with blow-up beds and it becomes **Shkolla Hostel** (068 3133 451; www.tiranahostel.com; dm €7; Jul-Aug). What it lacks in infrastructure and privacy it makes up for with its goat-bell soundtrack and evening campfire. Ask bus or *furgon* drivers on the Vlora–Saranda route to drop you off at Vuno.

Saranda & Around

0852 / POP 32,000

Saranda has grown rapidly in the past few years; skeletal high-rises crowd around its horseshoe shape and hundreds more are being built in the outlying region. Saranda is bustling in summer – buses are crowded with people carrying swimming paraphernalia and the weather means it's almost obligatory to go for a swim.

Sights

Castle of Lëkurësit CASTLE
This former castle is now home to a restaurant with superb views over Saranda and Butrint lagoon, especially at sunset. It's an ideal spot for an evening beer. The castle is a 15-minute walk up from the Saranda–Gjirokastra road.

Butrint ANCIENT RUINS
(www.butrint.org; admission 700 lekë; ⌚8am-dusk) Butrint is an ancient city dating back to before the 6th century BC. Its ruins are spread over the 29-sq-km national park, which is almost 20km south of Saranda. Set aside at least two hours to explore this fascinating place.

Ksamil BEACHES
South of Saranda, off the coastal village of Ksamil, are three small, dreamy islands within swimming distance. Dozens of beachside bars and restaurants open up in summer.

Blue Eye Spring HOT SPRING
(Syri i Kaltër; admission per person/car 50/200 lekë) Blue Eye Spring is a hypnotic pool of deep-blue water surrounded by electric-blue edges like the iris of an eye. If you don't mind a 2km walk, buses travelling between Saranda and Gjirokastra can drop you off at the spring's turn-off (it's 22km from Saranda).

Sleeping & Eating

Hairy Lemon HOSTEL €
(☎069 3559 317; www.hairylemonhostel.com/saranda; dm incl breakfast €12; @📶) With a prime 8th-floor location, a clean beach at its base, and a friendly, helpful atmosphere, this Irish-run backpackers hostel is a good place to chill out. Call for directions.

Bunker Hostel HOSTEL €
(☎069 4345 426; dm incl breakfast €12; 📶) Practically kissing the port, this hostel is run by knowledgeable local Rino. Downsides include a windowless common area and only one bathroom for the 18 beds.

Dropulli TRADITIONAL ALBANIAN €
(cnr Rr Skënderbeu & Rr Mitro Dhmertika; mains 300 lekë) Vegetarians will love the melt-in-your-mouth stuffed peppers with tasty rice.

Beque TRADITIONAL ALBANIAN €
(Sheshi Qendror I Qytetit; mains 300-500 lekë) Listen to the mosque's call to prayer while eating some of Saranda's best Albanian-style food.

Information

Information centre (ZIT; Rr Skënderbeu; ⌚8am-4pm Mon-Fri, 9am-2pm & 4-9pm Sat & Sun)

Getting There & Around

BUS & FURGON The ZIT information centre has up-to-date bus timetables. Municipal buses go to Butrint via Ksamil on the hour from 7am to 5pm (100 lekë, 30 minutes). Buses to Tirana (1200 lekë, seven hours) leave at 5am, 6.30am, 8.30am, 9.30am, 10.30am, 2pm and 10pm. The 5.30am Tirana bus takes the coastal route (1200 lekë, nine hours). Buses and *furgons* to Gjirokastra (300 lekë, 1½ hours) pass the turn-off to the Blue Eye Spring. Buses to Himara leave at 6am, 2pm, 2.30pm and 3pm (600 lekë, two hours) and the daily service to Korça leaves at 5.30am (1200 lekë, eight hours).

FERRY Finikas (☎0852 260 57; finikaslines@yahoo.com; Rr Mithat Hoxha) at the port sells tickets for the **Ionian Cruises** (www.ionian-cruises.com) fast boat, the *Flying Dolphin*, which leaves for Corfu at 10.30am daily except Monday (€19, 45 minutes). A slower boat departs daily at 4.30pm (€19, 1½ hours). In summer a third ferry departs Saranda at 12.45pm Tuesday to Sunday and 10.30am Monday. From Corfu there are three ferries: the *Flying Dolphin* departs at 9am, *Sotiraquis* at 9.30am and *Kaliopi* at 6.30pm. Greek time is one hour ahead of Albanian time.

Gjirokastra

☎084 / POP 35,000

Defined by its castle, roads paved with chunky limestone and shale, imposing slate-roofed houses, and views out to the Drina Valley, Gjirokastra is an intriguing town. Archaeological evidence suggests there's been a settlement here for 2500 years, though these days it's the 600 'monumental' houses in town that attract visitors. Some of these magnificent houses, a blend of Ottoman and local architectural influence, have caved in on themselves.

Sights

Gjirokastra Castle CASTLE
(admission 200 lekë; ⌚8am-8pm) The town's castle hosts an eerie collection of armory (and, occasionally, the Gjirokastra folk festival and Miss Albania).

Zekate House HISTORIC BUILDING
(admission €1) This incredible three-storey house dates from 1811 and has twin towers and a double-arched facade. Check at the information centre for opening hours.

Sleeping & Eating

Guest House Haxhi Kotoni B&B €
(☎084 26 3526, 069 2366 846; www.kotonihouse.com; s/d incl breakfast €20/25; ❄) The fact that these rooms are 220 years old makes up for their small size, and air-con and attached

bathrooms are bonuses. It's wheelchair-friendly.

TOP CHOICE Hotel Kalemi B&B €€
(☎084 26 3724; draguak@yahoo.com; Lagjia Palorto Gjirokastra; r €35; ❄@📶) This delightful, large Ottoman-style hotel has spacious rooms adorned with carved ceilings. The views from the communal balcony are stunning.

TOP CHOICE Kujtimi TRADITIONAL ALBANIAN €
(mains 250-400 lekë; ⏲11am-late) This unassuming outdoor restaurant, run by the Dumi family, has delicious *trofte* (trout, 400 lekë) and *midhje* (fried mussels, 350 lekë).

Information

The new town (no slate roofs here) is on the main Saranda–Tirana road; a taxi up to or back from the old town is 300 lekë.

Information centre (⏲8am-4pm Mon-Fri, 9am-2pm & 4-9pm Sat & Sun Oct-Jun, 8.30am-2pm, 4pm-10pm Jul-Sep) Opposite Cajupi Hotel behind the statue of the partisans.

Getting There & Away

Buses pass through the new town on their way to Tirana, Saranda and Athens. *Furgons* also go to Saranda (400 lekë, one hour).

UNDERSTAND ALBANIA

History

The Illyrians, ancestors of the Albanians, occupied the western Balkans during the 2nd millennium BC. The Greeks arrived in the 7th century BC to establish self-governing colonies at Epidamnos (now Durrës), Apollonia and Butrint. They traded peacefully with the Illyrians, who formed tribal states in the 4th century BC.

Inevitably, the expanding Illyrian kingdom came into conflict with Rome, which sent a fleet of 200 vessels against Queen Teuta in 229 BC. A long war resulted in Roman control over the entire Balkan area by 167 BC.

Under the Romans, Illyria enjoyed peace and prosperity. The main trade route between Rome and Constantinople ran from the port at Durrës. When the Roman Empire was divided in AD 395, Illyria fell within the Byzantine Empire. In 1344 Albania was annexed by Serbia, but after the defeat of Serbia by the Turks in 1389 the region was open to Ottoman attack. The national hero Skanderbeg (Gjergj Kastrioti) led Albanian resistance to the Turks from his castle at Kruja. After Skanderbeg's death the Ottomans took control of the country in 1479. Ottoman rule lasted 400 years.

Uprisings in the late 19th century culminated in a proclamation of independence in 1912. These achievements were severely compromised when Kosovo, roughly one-third of Albania, was ceded to Serbia in 1913. During WWI Albania was occupied in succession by the armies of Greece, Serbia, France, Italy and Austria-Hungary.

In 1920 a republican government under the Orthodox priest Fan Noli helped to stabilise the country, but in 1924 it was overthrown by the interior minister, Ahmed Bey Zogu, who declared himself King Zogu I in 1928. His close collaboration with Italy backfired in April 1939 when Mussolini invaded. On 8 November 1941 the Albanian Communist Party was founded, with Enver Hoxha as first secretary. The communists led the resistance against the Italians and, after 1943, against the Germans.

In September 1948 Albania allied itself with Stalin's USSR until 1960, when it reoriented itself towards the People's Republic of China. From 1966 to 1967 Albania experienced a Chinese-style cultural revolution where administrative workers were transferred to remote areas and younger cadres were placed in leading positions. The collectivisation of agriculture was completed and organised religion banned. It was a dark time for many Albanians.

With the death of Mao Zedong in 1976, Albania's unique relationship with China also came to an end, and the country was left isolated and without allies. The economy was devastated and food shortages became more common.

Hoxha died in April 1985 and his associate Ramiz Alia took over the leadership. Restrictions loosened but the collective farms were neglected, leading to food shortages in the cities. Industries began to fail as spare parts ran out and Tirana's population tripled as people took advantage of free movement within the country. In June 1990 around 4500 Albanians took refuge in Western embassies in Tirana and were granted political asylum in Italy.

The March 1992 elections ended 47 years of communist rule and parliament elected

Sali Berisha president. Albania quickly switched from a tightly controlled communist regime to a rambunctious free-market free-for-all. A huge smuggling racket sprang up, bringing stolen Mercedes-Benzes into the country, and the port of Vlora became a major crossing point for illegal immigrants. In 1996 70% of Albanians lost their savings when private pyramid-investment schemes collapsed. Riots ensued, elections were called, and the victorious Socialist Party under Fatos Nano was able to restore some degree of security.

The general election of 2005 saw a return of Berisha's Democratic Party to government, and in 2009 they narrowly won again. Albania managed to avoid being caught in the crippling economic crisis that struck many countries in 2008 and economic growth has continued. Despite this, infrastructure deficiencies still plague the country. Albania joined NATO in 2009, and EU membership beckons.

People

In July 2010 the population was estimated to be 2,990,000, of which approximately 95% are Albanian, 3% Greek and 2% 'other'. The Ghegs in the north and the Tosks in the south have different dialects, music and dress, and the usual jokes about each other's weaknesses.

Albanians are generally kind, helpful and generous, and shake their heads for yes *(po)* and nod to say no *(jo)*.

Food

Price ranges in this chapter are based on the cost of a main course:

€€€ more than 500 lekë

€€ 200 to 500 lekë

€ less than 200 lekë

Environment

Albania consists of 30% vast interior plains, 362km of coast and a mountainous spine that runs its length. Mt Korab, at 2764m, is Albania's highest peak.

The country's large lakes include the Balkans' biggest, Lake Shkodra, which borders Montenegro in the north, and the ancient Lake Ohrid in the east. Agriculture makes up a small percentage of land use, and citrus and olive trees spice up coastal plains. Most rural householders grow their own food.

There are 15 national parks including Mt Dajti, Llogaraja Pass, Mt Tomorri, Butrint, Valbonë and Theth. The Albanian mountains are home to brown bear, wolf, otter, marten, wild cat, wild boar and deer.

SURVIVAL GUIDE

Directory A–Z

Accommodation

The number of backpacker hostels in Albania has tripled; check www.hostelworld.com for updates. Homestays abound in Theth. A number of camping grounds in coastal towns offer hot showers, on-site restaurants and entertainment.

Price ranges in this chapter are based on the cost of a double room with bathroom:

€€€ more than €100

€€ €30 to €100

€ less than €30

Activities

Hiking and adventure sports are gaining popularity in Albania.

Beach wise, south of Vlora the sandy Adriatic gives it up for its rockier Ionian counterpart, but the swimming is better and the scenery more picturesque.

Business Hours

If opening hours are not listed in reviews they are as follows:

Banks 9am-3.30pm Mon-Fri

Cafes & bars 8am-midnight

Restaurants 8am-midnight

Shops 8am-7pm; siesta time can be any time between noon and 4pm

Gay & Lesbian Travellers

Extensive anti-discrimination legislation became law in 2010, and gay and lesbian life in Albania is alive and well but is not yet organised into gay clubs and nongovernment organisations looking after gay issues. The alternative music and party scene is queer-friendly.

Money

Albania uses both lekë and the euro; accommodation is quoted in euros but can be paid in either currency.

Banknotes come in denominations of 100, 200, 500, 1000, 2000 and 5000 lekë. There are five, 10, 20, 50 and 100 lekë coins. Lekë can't be exchanged outside the country.

Public Holidays

New Year's Day 1 January
Summer Day 16 March
Nevruz 23 March
Catholic Easter March/April
Orthodox Easter March/April
May Day 1 May
Bajram i Madh September
Mother Teresa Day 19 October
Bajram i Vogël November
Independence Day 28 November
Liberation Day 29 November
Christmas Day 25 December

Telephone

It's impossible to miss the extensive advertising by Albania's mobile-phone companies; SIM cards are often available to buy at border crossings and in towns – you usually need to show your passport.

Travellers with Disabilities

High footpaths and hidden potholes make life difficult for mobility-impaired travellers, though Tirana's top hotels do cater to people with disabilities.

Visas

Visas are not required for citizens of EU countries or nationals of Australia, Canada, New Zealand, Japan, South Korea, Norway, South Africa or the USA; otherwise, 90-day visas are issued at the border.

Women Travellers

Albania is a safe country for women travellers, but outside Tirana it is mainly men who go out and sit in bars and cafes in the evenings.

Getting There & Away

Air

Tirana International Airport (Mother Teresa Airport, Rinas Airport, Tirana Airport; www.tirana-airport.com.al) is 17km northwest of Tirana. There are flights to most European countries.

Land

From Tirana, regular buses head to Pristina, Kosovo; to Struga, Tetovo and Skopje in Macedonia; to Budva and Ulcinj in Montenegro; and to Athens and Thessaloniki in Greece. *Furgons* (shared minibuses) and buses leave Shkodra and Tirana for Montenegro, and buses head to Kosovo and Macedonia from Tirana. Buses travel to Greece from Albanian towns on the southern coast and Tirana via Gjirokastra.

Albania is not connected to neighbouring countries by train.

Sea

Two or three ferries a day travel between Saranda and Corfu, in Greece, and many ferry companies connect Italy with Vlora and Durrës.

Getting Around

Cycling in Albania is tough but certainly doable. Expect lousy road conditions including open drains, some abysmal driving from fellow road-users, and roads that barely qualify for the title.

The first bus or *furgon* departure is often at 5am and things slow down around lunchtime. Municipal buses operate in Tirana, Durrës, Shkodra and Vlora, and trips cost 30 lekë.

Though never entirely safe, hitching is a common way to get around in Albania.

Albania's trains are dirt cheap and travelling on them is an adventure. Daily passenger trains leave Tirana for Durrës, Shkodra, Fier, Vlora, Elbasan and Pogradec. Check timetables at the station.

Andorra la Vella

POP 20,400 / ELEV 1030M

Andorra la Vella (pronounced 'vey-yah'; literally 'old') is capital and sole town of this tiny principality. Its main preoccupation is retailing electronic and luxury goods.

Sights & Activities

The tiny **historic quarter** (Barri Antic) was the heart of Andorra la Vella until well after WWII, when the principality's capital remained a village. Within it, **Casa de la Vall** (House of the Valley), built in 1580 as a private home, has been Andorra's parliam[ent] building since 1702.

Sleeping

TOP CHOICE **Hotel Pyrénées** HOTEL €€

(☎879 879; www.hotelpyrenees.com; Avinguda del Príncep Benlloch 20; incl breakfast, s €39-61, d €53-103; P@≋) Built in 1940, this is one of Andorra's very few venerable buildings. Its 70 attractivcly furnished rooms and quality restaurant have plenty of appealing dark woodwork. The €13 *menú* (set meal), with its creative dishes, is excellent value.

Andorra Highlights

1. Slip-slide your way over the snowfields of **Grandvalira** (p57)
2. Steep yourself in the warm mineral waters of space-age **La Caldea** (p57) in Les Escaldes
3. Tramp a sample of the walking trails that thread through the principality, especially above **Ordino** (p58)

Andorra

Includes »

Best Places to Eat

» Ca la Conxita, Andorra la Vella (p55)

» Pampa, Arinsal (p59)

» Pyrénées Department Store, Andorra la Vella (p55)

Best Websites

» **www.andorra.ad** Site of the Ministry of Tourism & Environment

» **www.andorramania.com** Host of worthwhile links

» **www.skiandorra.ad** Snow reports and useful skiing info

Why Go?

Some say Andorra is nothing but skiing and shopping. They may add that Andorra la Vella, its capital and only town, is a fuming traffic jam bordered by palaces of consumerism. (Fact: Andorra has over 2000 shops – that's more than one for every 40 inhabitants.)

They're right to a point, but also way off course. Shake yourself free of Andorra la Vella's tawdry embrace, take one of the state's three secondary roads and you're very soon amid dramatic mountain scenery.

This mini-country wedged between France and Spain offers by far the best ski slopes and resort facilities in all the Pyrenees. Once the snows melt, there's an abundance of great walking, ranging from easy strolls to demanding day hikes in the principality's higher, more remote reaches. Strike out, above the tight valleys, and you can walk for hours, almost alone.

When to Go

Andorra La Vella

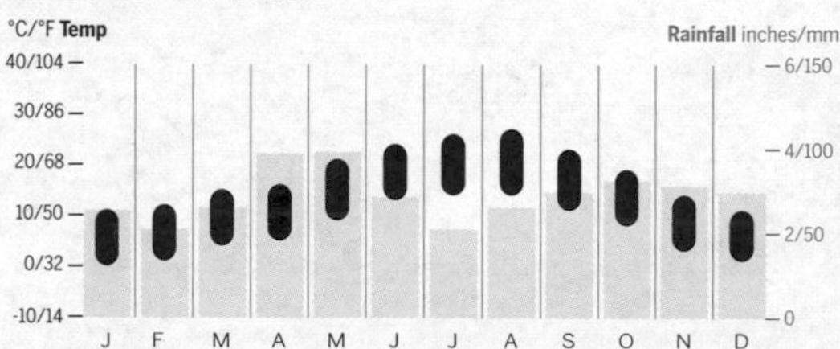

Mid-Jan–mid-Feb Ski slopes quietest after New Year and before French winter school holidays.

Mid-Jun–mid-Jul & Sep Camping and hiking outside summer's holiday peak before snow falls.

8 Sep Every hamlet and village celebrates the Fiesta de Meritxell on Andorra's national day.

For more modest fare, there are tasty *platos combinados* (€4.70 to €8.70).

Hotel Florida HOTEL €€
(☎820 105; www.hotelflorida.ad; Carrer de la Llacuna 15; s/d incl breakfast from €53/58; @☎) This welcoming modern hotel sits on a quiet side street. Ask for one of the larger rooms, which cost no more. After a day's activity, relax in the hotel's sauna – free for guests. The hotel is closed in June and November.

Hotel Residencia Paris HOTEL €
(☎820 843; edumol@andorra.ad; Avinguda de Meritxell 65; s/d €30/40) In a town where most economical lodgings have closed their shutters for good, the Paris still hangs in there. Its 12 rooms, all with bathroom, are fairly bare and clinical.

Pensió La Rosa PENSION €
(☎376 821 810; Antic Carrer Major 18; s/d €19/30) In Andorra's historic quarter, this friendly place has 19 simple rooms with a corridor bathroom. Many are occupied by the month so call ahead to reserve.

Camping Valira CAMPING GROUND €
(☎722 384; campingvalira@andorra.ad; Avinguda de Salou; campsites per person/tent/car €6.50/6.50/6.50;) Just west of town and overlooking the valley, Camping Valira is the town's only camping option. You'll have to hunt to find a space between the resident caravans.

Eating

TOP CHOICE **Ca la Conxita** MEDITERRANEAN €€
(☎829 948; Calle de la Llacuna 12; meals €25-30; Mon-Sat) There's no menu, only the freshest produce of the day; Conxita, your exuberant hostess, will explain. Should her minimal English fail, she'll drag you into her open kitchen and simply show you.

Papanico TAPAS €€
(☎867 333; www.papanico.es; Avinguda del Príncep Benlloch 4; mains €12.50-20.50) At Papanico you can snack on tapas and sandwiches (around €5) or tuck into a full meal. Retreat to the rear restaurant with its vast collection of beer bottles arranged around the walls.

Pyrénées Department Store SELF-SERVICE €
(Avinguda de Meritxell 21) This megastore's top-floor **cafeteria** offers great fare at reasonable prices (salads/mains from €3.85/4.90). One floor down, there's a well-stocked **supermarket** for self-caterers.

Pans y Company SANDWICH BAR €
(Plaça de Rebés 2 & Avinguda de Meritxell 91; baguette, drink & French fries €5.60-7.35) This Spanish chain, with a couple of branches, does crunchy baguettes and salads and combo meals.

Drinking

La Borsa BAR
(Avinguda de Tarragona 36; 11pm-3am Tue-Sun) Like a little flutter while you drink and dance? At the Stock Exchange, the price of each drink varies according to the night's consumption, so keep an eye on the electronic screen.

Cervesería L'Abadia PUB
(Cap del Carrer 2; 6pm-2am Mon-Sat) A place for serious beerophiles, with over eight classics on draught and many more in the bottle.

Shopping

With prices around 25% below those in Spain and France, you can save big time on things such as sports gear, photographic equipment, shoes and clothing. Stock up on rock-bottom-priced booze and cigarettes, too.

ANDORRA FACTS

- **Area** 468 sq km
- **Capital** Andorra la Vella
- **Languages** Catalan (Spanish widely used, French less so)
- **Currency** Euro (€)
- **Exchange rates** A$1 = €0.74; C$1 = €0.74; ¥100 = €0.87; NZ$1 = €0.56; UK£1 = €1.16; US$1 = €0.72
- **Country code** ☎376
- **Emergency** ☎112
- **Money** ATMs abundant
- **Budget hotel room (double)** €40–60
- **Two-course evening meal** €15–30
- **Visas** Follows Schengen rules; see p1319
- **Itinerary** After a day spent pounding the winter ski slopes, drop down to Andorra la Vella for some shopping. In summer, explore Andorra's valleys on day walks. Year-round, steep your weary limbs in the warm and soothing waters of La Caldea spa.

Andorra la Vella

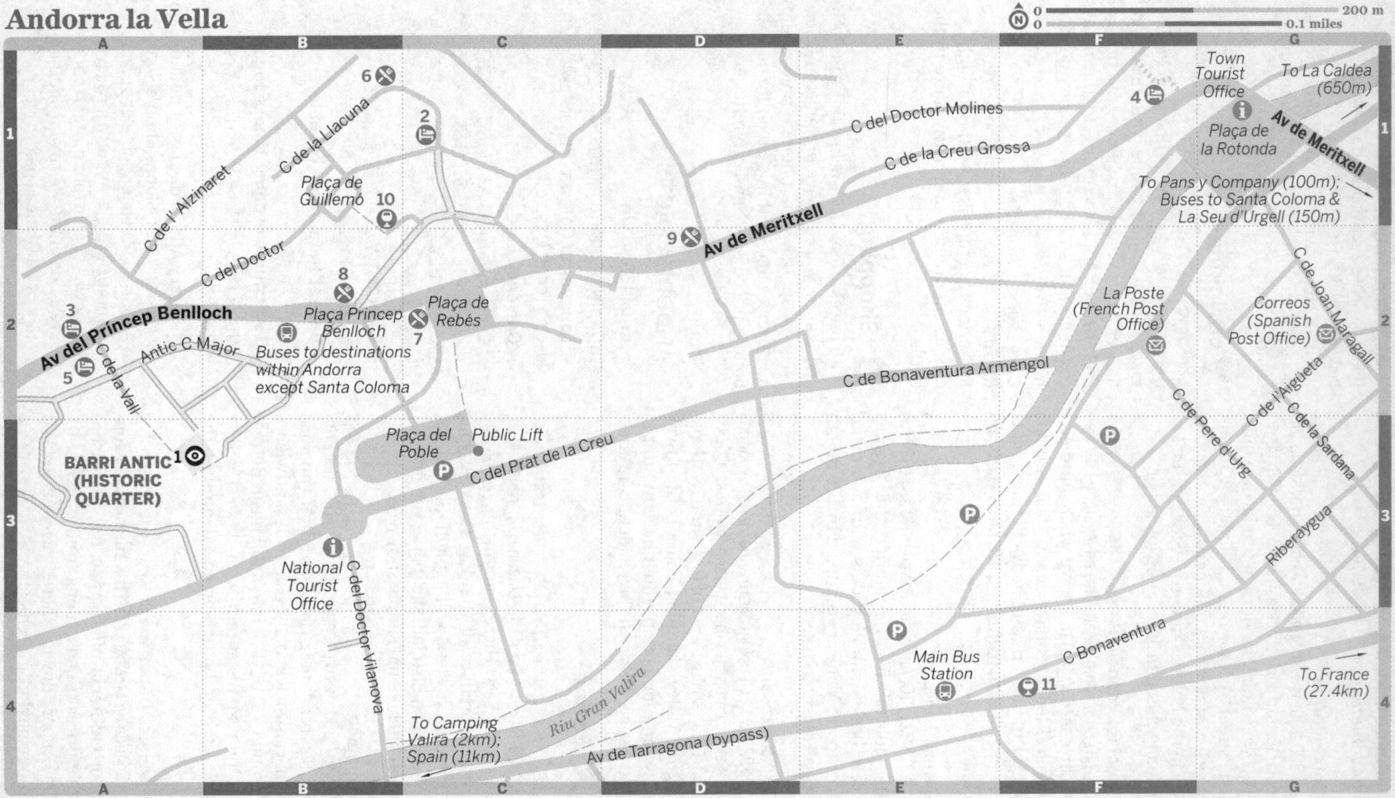

0 200 m
0 0.1 miles
A B C D E F G
1 2 3 4
Town Tourist Office
To La Caldea (650m)
Plaça de la Rotonda
Av de Meritxell
To Pans y Company (100m); Buses to Santa Coloma & La Seu d'Urgell (150m)
4
C del Doctor Molines
C de la Creu Grossa
6
2
C de la Llacuna
Plaça de Guillemó
10
C de l' Alzinaret
C del Doctor
9
Av de Meritxell
8
3
Av del Príncep Benlloch
Plaça Princep Benlloch
Plaça de Rebés
7
Buses to destinations within Andorra except Santa Coloma
5
C de la Vall
Antic C Major
BARRI ANTIC (HISTORIC QUARTER)
1
Plaça del Poble
Public Lift
C del Prat de la Creu
C de Bonaventura Armengol
La Poste (French Post Office)
Correos (Spanish Post Office)
C de Joan Maragall
C de l'Aigüeta
C de la Sardana
C de Pere d'Urg
Riberaygua
National Tourist Office
C del Doctor Vilanova
Riu Gran Valira
To Camping Valira (2km); Spain (11km)
Av de Tarragona (bypass)
Main Bus Station
C Bonaventura
11
To France (27.4km)

SPLURGE

La Caldea (☎800 999; www.caldea.ad; Parc de la Mola 10; admission €34) is a huge spa complex, its lagoons, hot tubs and saunas all fed by thermal springs – it's a great place for a splash and a splurge. Dunk yourself long enough and you can forgo showers for a week! It's in Les Escaldes, just a 10-minute walk upstream from Plaça de la Rotonda. Check the website for opening hours.

Information

Correos (Carrer de Joan Maragall 10) Spanish post office.

La Poste (Carrer de Pere d'Urg 1) French post office.

National tourist office (☎820 214; Edificio Davi, Local C, Carrer del Doctor Vilanova 13; ⏲10am-1.30pm & 3-7pm Mon-Sat)

Town tourist office (☎873 103; Plaça de la Rotonda; ⏲9am-9pm mid-Jun–mid-Sep, shorter hrs rest of yr) Also carries pan-Andorra information.

Getting There & Around

All long-distance buses for France and Spain pull in at the **main bus station** (Avinguda de Tarragona). **La Hispano Andorrana** (☎807 000; www.hispanoandorrana.com, in Spanish) runs hourly buses to La Seu d'Urgell (€2.75, 45 minutes), in Spain, stopping outside Hiper Andorra on Avinguda de Meritxell.

Andorra la Vella is a traffic nightmare. Leave your vehicle in the huge open-air car park north of the bus station.

Andorra la Vella

Sights
1 Casa de la Vall A3

Sleeping
2 Hotel Florida C1
3 Hotel Pyrénées A2
4 Hotel Residencia Paris F1
5 Pensió La Rosa A2

Eating
6 Ca la Conxita B1
7 Pans y Company C2
8 Papanico B2
9 Pyrénées Department Store D2

Drinking
10 Cervesería L'Abadia B1
11 La Borsa F4

Canillo & Soldeu

Canillo (elevation 1500m), 11km northeast of Andorra la Vella, shares a helpful **tourist office** (☎751 090; www.vdc.ad; ⏲9am-1pm & 3-7pm Mon-Sat, 8am-4pm Sun) with **Soldeu**, a further 7km up the valley along the CG2. Grab the comprehensive *Mountain, Nature and Sports Guide* (€2) from the tourist office; it brims with practical information and route descriptions for walkers, climbers, cyclists and canyon clamberers.

Sights & Activities

Museu de les Dues Rodes MUSEUM
(☎853 444; www.m2r.ad; admission €3; ⏲3-7pm Tue-Sat, 10am-1pm Sun) With its vintage Ducatis, BSAs, Triumphs and Harley-Davidsons all restored to pristine, gleaming condition, this museum pays homage to the motorbike and power-assisted cycles.

Grandvalira SKIING
(☎808 900; www.grandvalira.com) Soldeu–El Tarter and Canillo, together with Grau Roig and Pas de la Casa to the southeast, constitute the combined snowfields of Grandvalira. With 193km of runs and a lift system that can shift over 100,000 skiers per hour, it's easily the largest ski area in the Pyrenees.

Palau de Gel ICE SKATING, SWIMMING
(Ice Palace; ☎800 840; www.palaudegel.ad; Carretera General) Canillo's Palau de Gel has an ice rink, an Olympic-size swimming pool, an Italian restaurant and a bar with internet access and free wi-fi.

Sleeping & Eating

Hotel Roc de Sant Miquel HOTEL €
(☎851 079; www.hotel-roc.com; Dec-Apr per person B&B €32-53, half-board €44-65, Jun-Oct s/d €19/30) This friendly Soldeu hotel, run by a young Anglo-Andorran couple, makes a great skiing base. In summer, it hires out mountain bikes to guests and can arrange nature walks and hikes. Half-board is compulsory during most winter months. The hotel is closed in May and November.

Camping Santa Creu CAMPING GROUND €
(☎851 462; camping_santa creu@yahoo.com; per person/tent/car €4/4/4; ⏲Jun-Sep) The greenest,

smallest and quietest of Canillo's five camping grounds.

Fat Albert's BAR, RESTAURANT €€
(☎851 765; pizzas €10, meals around €25; ⏲4-11pm mid-Nov–mid-Apr) In a cosy, converted hay barn, Fat Albert's is a favourite with locals and visitors to Soldeu alike. Drop in just for an après-ski pick-me-up or linger long over a full, satisfying meal.

Cal Lulu CATALAN, FRENCH €€
(☎851 427; pizzas €8.50-13.50, set menu €15, mains €13-18; ⏲closed Mon & Tue except high season) Intimate (it's divided into small booths), Cal Lulu in Canillo is strong on meat dishes, such as grilled rabbit and *pierrade,* three kinds of meat sizzled on a heated stone.

Hotel Bruxelles HOTEL RESTAURANT €
(menus €12-21) On Soldeu's main drag, the Bruxelles does 50 varieties of well-filled sandwiches, whopping burgers and tasty *menús.*

☆ Entertainment

The music pounds on winter nights in Soldeu. **Pussy Cat** rocks until far too late for impressive skiing next day, while **Avalanche** and, three doors away, **Aspen**, have regular live bands.

Getting There & Around

Buses L3 and L4 link Canillo with Andorra la Vella and Soldeu every 20 minutes.

Ordino & Around

Ordino, on highway CG3 8km north of Andorra la Vella, is Andorra's most attractive village. At 1300m, it's a good starting point for summer activity.

Sights & Activities

There are excellent walking trails around Ordino. Pick up *Thirtysix Interesting Itineraries on the Paths of the Vall d'Ordino & the Parish of La Massana* from the tourist office. Walk descriptions are altogether tauter than the title.

Museu d'Areny i Plandolit MANSION, MUSEUM
(☎836 908; admission €3; ⏲10am-2pm & 3-6pm Tue-Sat, 10am-2pm Sun) To sense how the very few rich Andorrans of the time lived, take a half-hour guided visit (in Spanish) around this originally 17th-, mainly 19th-century manor house.

In its grounds, the **Museo Postal de Andorra** (same times and tariffs) is fun, even for the philatelically challenged. There's a 15-minute audiovisual presentation (available in English), and set upon set of stamps issued by France and Spain specifically for Andorra.

Mina de Llorts IRON MINE
(admission €3; ⏲9.30am-1.30pm & 3.30-6.30pm Tue-Sat, 9.30am-1.30pm Sun mid-Jun–mid-Oct) Mina de Llorts recalls the valley's long abandoned iron-mining and charcoal-burning heritage. The **Camino de los Hombres de Hierro** (Iron Miners' Route), a 3km walk with interpretive panels, leads from the mine.

Sleeping & Eating

Camping Borda d'Ansalonga CAMPING GROUND €
(☎850 374; www.campingansalonga.com; per person/tent/car €6.75/4.75/4.75; ⏲mid-Jun–Apr; 🏊) This large, grassy option enjoys an attractive valley site 1.25km from the village.

Casa León BAR, RESTAURANT €
(☎835 977; menus €9-20; ⏲Tue-Sun) French owned, this friendly bar-restaurant offers varied tapas, homemade desserts and plentiful à la carte grilled-meat dishes.

Information

Tourist office (☎878 173; www.ordino.ad; ⏲8am-6pm Mon-Sat, 9am-1pm Sun Jul-Aug, 8.30am-1pm & 3-6.30pm Mon-Sat, 9am-1pm Sun Sep-Jun) Within the Centre Esportiu d'Ordino sports complex beside the CG3.

Getting There & Away

Bus L6 runs to/from Andorra la Vella every half-hour.

Arinsal

Arinsal, 10km northwest of Andorra la Vella, has good skiing and snowboarding and a lively après-ski scene. It's linked with the smaller ski station of **Pal**, in turn part of the **Vallnord complex** (☎878 000; www.vallnord.com). Their combined slopes have 63km of pistes.

In summer the **Vallnord Bike Park** (☎878 000; www.vallnordbikepark.com; per day €21) has a pulse-racing choice of downhill and cross-country mountain-bike tracks.

Arinsal's a good departure point for mountain walks within the scenic **Parc Natural Comunal de les Valls de Comapedrosa**. One popular trail leads to **Estany de les**

Truites (2260m), a natural lake and a staffed mountain hut with beds, refreshments and meals.

Brit-run www.arinsal.co.uk has its finger firmly on the pulse of what's happening in the village.

Sleeping & Eating

TOP CHOICE **Hostal Pobladó** HOSTEL, RESTAURANT €
(835 122; per person incl breakfast €20-25; Dec-Oct; @) Beside the cabin lift, this is a great place to meet other skiers or walkers. There's a small, sunny terrace, a restaurant serving Tex-Mex and à la carte dishes, and a lively bar with free internet for guests.

Hotel Aymà HOTEL €
(835 295; hotelayma@andorra.ad; per person €25) This small, traditional family-run hotel has happily let the 21st century pass it by. The atmosphere's calm, and rooms, all with bathroom, are simple and spruce.

Pampa MAINLY MEAT €€
(839 600; pizzas & pastas around €9, mains €10-14; daily) This newcomer offers bog standard pizzas and pastas. Its juicy, grilled meats, more enticing and scarcely more expensive, are prepared to perfection by the cheery Argentine team.

Vertical Limit Café CAFE-RESTAURANT €
(835 057; Mon-Sat) Snack on salads and crêpes (around €10), cold cuts and cheeses, plus tender grilled meat.

Entertainment

In winter, Arinsal fairly throbs after sunset. In summer, it can be almost mournful. When the snow's around, call by **Surf**, near the base of the cabin lift. It's pub, dance venue and restaurant (sink your teeth into the juicy Argentine grilled-meat dishes) all in one.

Getting There & Away

Bus L5 runs between Andorra la Vella and Arinsal via La Massana every half-hour. There are also at least 12 local buses daily between La Massana and Arinsal.

Sant Julià de Lòria

Occupying a one-time tobacco factory in Sant Julià de Lòria, 6km south of Andorra la Vella, the **Museu del Tabac** (Tobacco Museum; www.museudeltabac.com; Carrer Doctor Palau 17; admission €5; 10am-8pm Tue-Sat, 10am-2.30pm Sun) recalls the pleasurable sins of tobacco and smuggling. Buses run out from Andorra la Vella every 20 minutes.

UNDERSTAND ANDORRA

History & People

From the Middle Ages until 1993, Andorra's sovereignty was vested in two 'princes': the bishop of the Spanish border town of La Seu d'Urgell and the French president (who inherited the job from France's pre-Revolutionary kings). Nowadays, democratic Andorra is styled as a 'parliamentary co-princedom', in which the bishop and president remain joint but nominal heads of state.

The total population is just over 85,000; a mere 36% of Andorra's inhabitants are Andorran nationals, a percentage almost equalled by the number of Spanish residents. The official language is Catalan, closely related to both Spanish and French. Most younger people can manage more than a smattering of English.

Food

Try *escudella*, a thick soup of *albondigas* (meat balls), perhaps with chicken and a lump or two of sausage, chickpeas, carrots and potatoes, which is almost the national dish.

Price ranges in this chapter are based on the cost of a main course:

€€€ more than €20

€€ €10 to €20

€ less than €10

Environment

Andorra is essentially three valleys hugged by steep mountains. It is 25km from north to south and 29km from east to west, with Coma Pedrosa (2942) as its highest point.

SURVIVAL GUIDE

Directory A–Z

Accommodation

Tourist offices stock a free booklet, *Guia d'Allotjaments Turístics* (Guide to Tourist Accommodation).

Outside Andorra la Vella, there are very few budget options for travellers. To compensate, there are plenty of camping grounds, often beautifully situated. During the ski season, many resort hotels won't take independent travellers and may insist upon half-board.

For hikers, Andorra has 27 off-the-beaten-track *refugis* (mountain refuges); all except one are unstaffed and free.

Price ranges in this chapter are based on the cost of a double room with bathroom:

€€€ more than €100

€€ €60 to €100

€ less than €60

Activities

Above the main valleys you'll find attractive lake-dotted mountain country, great for skiing in winter and walking in summer.

SKIING

Andorra has three ski areas: Grandvalira is the largest and best; Vallnord is cheaper but generally colder and windier; Naturlandia is great for cross-country. Ski gear can be rented for €10 to €18 per day; snowboards for €16 to €22. In summer, most resorts rent mountain bikes (around €15 per day).

HIKING

Lonely Planet's *Hiking in Spain* lists a week's worth of hikes within Andorra. The most reliable map for walkers is *Andorra,* published by Editorial Alpina at 1:40,000.

Business Hours

Banks 9am-1pm & 3-5pm Mon-Fri, 9am-noon Sat

Restaurants 1-3.30pm & 8-10.30pm

Shops 10am-1pm & 4-8pm Mon-Sat, 9.30am-1pm Sun; major stores 9.30am-8pm

Post & Telephone

Andorra has no postal system of its own. France and Spain each has its own post boxes and issues its own Andorran stamps (available at tourist offices; you can't use regular French or Spanish stamps).

For international calls, buy a *teletarja* (phonecard; €3 and €6) from tourist offices and kiosks.

Getting There & Away

You can only reach Andorra by road, unless you trek across the mountains (we're not entirely kidding; it's a magnificent way to drop in or out).

All bus services arrive at and leave from Andorra la Vella.

To/From France

Autocars Novatel (☎803 789; www.andorrabybus.com) Up to four minibuses daily (€35) to/from Toulouse's airport (3½ hours) and Gare Matabiau train station.

To/From Spain

Alsa (www.alsa.es) Eight buses daily to/from Barcelona's Estació del Nord (€28.50, three hours).

Autocars Novatel (☎803 789; www.andorrabybus.com) Five minibuses daily (€32) to/from Barcelona's airport (3½ hours).

Direct Bus (☎805 151; www.andorradirectbus.es, in Spanish) Up to eight buses daily to/from Barcelona's airport (€31), via the city's Sants train station.

Viatges Montmantell (☎807 444; www.montmantell.com, in Spanish) Five buses daily (€19, 2¾ hours) to/from Lleida bus and train stations, connecting with the Madrid-bound high-speed AVE train. Services stop outside La Caldea.

Getting Around

Six bus routes radiate from Andorra la Vella along the principality's three main roads. Tourist offices carry *Andorra en Bus,* a free leaflet giving routes and timetables (online, check www.transportpublic.ad).

Austria

Includes »

Best Places to Eat

» Alter Fuchs, Salzburg (p83)

» Zu den Zwei Liesln, Vienna (p69)

» kuk. Hofbäckerei, Linz (p75)

» Chez Nico, Innsbruck (p88)

Best Places to Stay

» Haus Reichl, Salzburg (p82)

» Nepomuks, Innsbruck (p88)

» Pension Hargita, Vienna (p69)

» Hotel Daniel, Graz (p76)

» Snowbunny's Hostel, Kitzbühel (p89)

Why Go?

For such a small country, Austria has made it big. This is, after all, the land where Mozart composed, Strauss taught the world to waltz and Julie Andrews grabbed the spotlight with her twirling entrance in the *Sound of Music*. This is where the Habsburgs built their 600-year empire and where past glories still shine in the resplendent baroque palaces and coffee houses of Vienna, Innsbruck and Salzburg. This is a country of perfectionists and whatever it does – mountains, classical music, new media, castles, cake, you name it – it does exceedingly well.

Beyond its grandiose cities, Austria's allure lies outdoors. Indeed, whether you're schussing down the mythical slopes of Kitzbühel, climbing high in the Alps of Tirol or pedalling along the banks of the sprightly Danube, you'll find the kind of inspiring landscapes that no well-orchestrated symphony, singing nun or camera lens could ever quite do justice.

When to Go?

Vienna

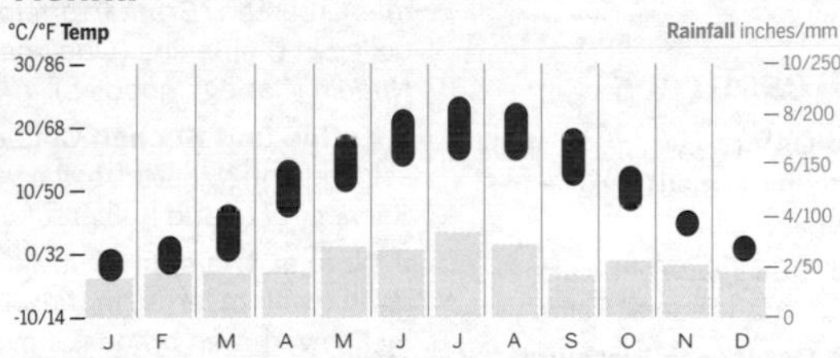

Jul & Aug High-alpine hiking in Tirol, lake swimming in Salzkammergut and a feast of festivals.

Sep & Oct *Sturm* (new wine) in vineyards near Vienna, golden forest strolls and few crowds.

Dec & Jan Christmas markets twinkle, skiers on the Alps and Vienna waltzes into the New Year.

AT A GLANCE

» **Currency** Euro (€)

» **Language** German

» **Money** ATMs widely available

» **Visas** Not required for citizens of the EU, Australia or USA

Fast Facts

» **Area** 83,855 sq km

» **Capital** Vienna

» **Country code** ☎43

» **Emergency** ☎112

Exchange Rates

Australia	A$1	€0.74
Canada	C$1	€0.74
Japan	¥100	€0.87
New Zealand	NZ$1	€0.56
UK	UK£1	€1.16
USA	US$1	€0.72

Set Your Budget

» **Budget hotel room** €50

» **Two-course evening meal** €15

» **Museum entrance** €7

» **Beer (bottle)** €3

» **City transport ticket** €2

Resources

» **ÖAV** (www.alpenverein.at, in German) Austrian Alpine Club

» **ÖBB** (www.oebb.at) Austrian Federal Railways

» **Österreich Werbung** (www.austria.info) National tourism authority

Connections

Bang in the heart of Europe, Austria has speedy connections to its eight neighbouring countries. Trains from Vienna run to many Eastern European destinations, including Bratislava, Budapest, Prague and Warsaw; there are also connections south to Italy via Klagenfurt and north to Berlin. Salzburg is within sight of the Bavarian border, and there are many trains Munich-bound and beyond from the baroque city. Innsbruck is on the main train line connecting Austria to Switzerland, and there are a handful of trains from Bregenz to the bigger Swiss cities.

ITINERARIES

Three Days

Spend two days in Vienna, making sure to visit the Habsburg palaces and Stephansdom before cosying up in a *Kaffeehaus* (coffee house). At night check out the pumping bar scene. Be sure to take in the cutting-edge art collections of the MuseumsQuartier and graze the Naschmarkt for picnic goodies. On day three explore the Salzkammergut lakes or Salzburg.

One Week

Spend two days in Vienna, plus another day exploring the Wachau wine region, a day each in Salzburg and Innsbruck, one day exploring the Salzkammergut lakes, and finally one day in St Anton am Arlberg or Kitzbühel hiking or skiing (depending on the season).

Essential Food & Drink

» **Make it meaty** Go for a classic Wiener schnitzel, *Tafelspitz* (boiled beef with horseradish sauce) or *Schweinebraten* (pork roast). The humble *Wurst* (sausage) comes in various guises.

» **On the side** Lashings of potatoes, either fried (*Pommes*), roasted (*Bratkartoffeln*), in a salad (*Erdapfelsalat*) or boiled in their skins (*Quellmänner*); *Knödel* (dumplings) and *Nudeln* (flat egg noodles).

» **Kaffee und Kuchen** Coffee and cake is Austria's sweetest tradition. Must-trys: flaky apple strudel; rich, chocolatey *Sacher Torte* and *Kaiserschmarrn* (caramelised crepes).

» **Wine at the source** Jovial locals gather in rustic *Heurigen* (wine taverns) in the wine-producing east, identified by an evergreen branch above the door. Sip crisp Grüner Veltliner whites and spicy Blaufränkisch wines.

» **Cheese fest** Dig into gooey *Käsnudeln* (cheese noodles) in Carinthia, *Kaspressknodel* (fried cheese dumplings) in Tirol and *Käsekrainer* (cheesy sausages) in Vienna. The hilly Bregenzerwald is studded with dairies.

VIENNA

☎01 / POP 1.68 MILLION

Few cities in the world glide so effortlessly between the present and the past like Vienna. Its splendid historical face is easily recognised: grand imperial palaces, bombastic baroque interiors, and museums and ornate coffee houses flanking magnificent squares.

But Vienna is also one of Europe's most dynamic urban spaces. A stone's throw from Hofburg, the MuseumsQuartier houses some of the world's most provocative contemporary art behind a striking basalt facade. Outside, a courtyard buzzes on summer evenings with throngs of Viennese drinking and chatting.

Here you can spend your days marvelling at one historical building after the next and evenings clubbing to electronic beats. And that's to mention nothing of the musical history that abounds from this city the Turks once called the 'golden apple'.

Throw in a mass of green space within the confines of the city limits (almost half the city expanse is given over to parkland) and you get a cultured capital with a truly great outdoors.

Sights

Heading into the Innere Stadt (Inner City) will take you to a different age. Designated a Unesco World Heritage site, the heart of the city is blessed with a plethora of architectural wonders that hint at Vienna's long and colourful history.

TOP CHOICE Stephansdom CHURCH

(www.stephanskirche.at; 01, Stephansplatz; admission free; ⏲6am-10pm Mon-Sat, 7am-10pm Sun) Rising high and mighty above Vienna with its dazzling mosaic tiled roof is Stephansdom, or Steffl (little Stephen) as the Viennese call it. The cathedral was built on the site of a 12th-century church but its most distinctive features are Gothic.

The interior is nothing to scoff at either, complete with a 16th-century **stone pulpit** and gigantic baroque **high altar**.

Negotiating 343 steps brings you to a viewing platform for a stunning panorama of Vienna from the 136.7m-high **Südturm** (€3.50; ⏲9am-5.30pm). You can also explore the cathedral's **Katakomben** (catacombs; tours €4; ⏲10-11.30am & 1.30-4.30pm Mon-Sat, 1.30-4.30pm Sun), housing the remains of plague victims and urns containing some of the organs of Habsburg rulers.

MORE FOR YOUR MONEY

The **Wien-Karte** (Vienna Card; €18.50) gives you 72 hours of unlimited travel plus discounts at selected museums, attractions, cafes and shops. It's available from hotels and ticket offices.

The City of Vienna runs some 20 **municipal museums** (www.museum.vienna.at), which are included in a free booklet available at the Rathaus. Permanent exhibitions in all are free on Sunday.

TOP CHOICE Hofburg PALACE

(Imperial Palace; www.hofburg-wien.at) Nothing symbolises the culture and heritage of Austria more than its Hofburg, home base of the Habsburgs from 1273 to 1918. Inside you can tour the opulent **Kaiserappartements** (Imperial Apartments; admission €9.90; ⏲9.30am-5.30pm); the ticket covers entry to the **Sisi Museum**, devoted to the life of Austria's beauty-obsessed Empress Elisabeth. The **Schatzkammer** (Imperial Treasury; 01, Schweizerhof; admission €12; ⏲10am-6pm Wed-Mon) holds all manner of wonders, including the 10th-century Imperial Crown, a 2860-carat Columbian emerald and even a supposed thorn from Christ's crown.

Kaisergruft CHURCH

(01 Neuer Markt; admission €4; ⏲10am-6pm) Not far from the Hofburg is the imperial burial vault, the final resting place of most of the Habsburg elite (their hearts and organs rest elsewhere).

Albertina ART GALLERY

(www.albertina.at; 01, Albertinaplatz 3; admission €9.50; ⏲10am-6pm, to 9pm Wed) Simply reading the highlights should have any art fan lining up for entry into this gallery, harbouring 1.5 million prints and 50,000 drawings. Rembrandt, Dürer (including the famous *Hare*), Raphael, Cézanne, Picasso, Klimt and Michelangelo masterpieces are joined by superbly curated temporary exhibitions.

Schloss Schönbrunn PALACE, MUSEUM

(www.schoenbrunn.at; 13, Schönbrunner Schlossstrasse 47; Imperial Tour with audio guide €9.50; ⏲8.30am-5pm) The Habsburgs' 1441-room summer palace, Schloss Schönbrunn is a grand display of baroque imperialism and a Unesco World Heritage site. Inside is one luxurious apartment after the next, while

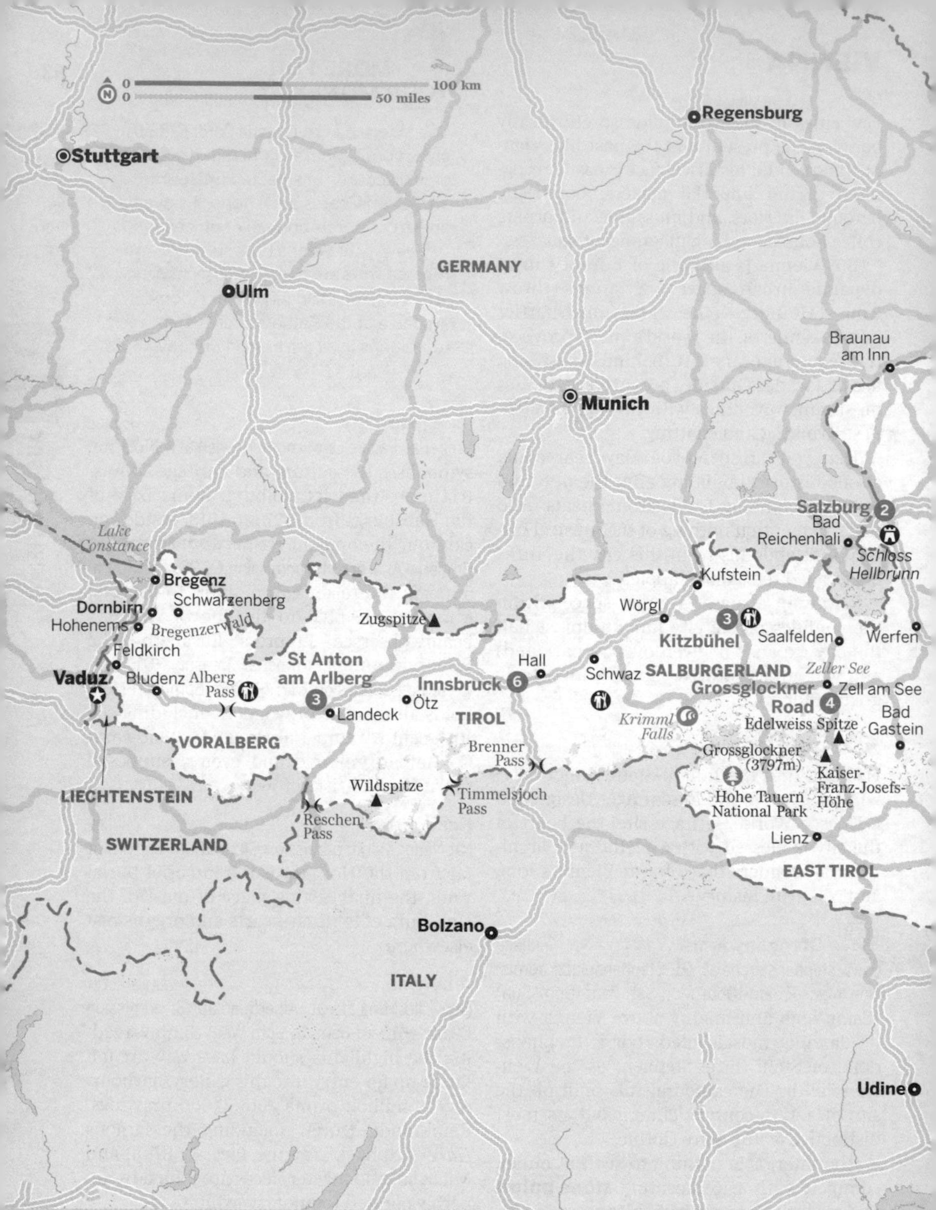

Austria Highlights

1 Discover the opulent Habsburg palaces, coffee houses and cutting-edge galleries of **Vienna** (p63)

2 Survey the baroque cityscape of Salzburg from the giddy height of 900-year-old **Festung Hohensalzburg** (p79)

3 Send your spirits soaring from peak to peak hiking and skiing in **Kitzbühel** (p89) and party-mad **St Anton am Arlberg** (p90)

4 Buckle up for a roller-coaster ride of Alps and glaciers on the **Grossglockner**

Road (p90), one of Austria's greatest drives

5 Dive into the crystal-clear lakes of **Salzkammergut** (p84), Austria's summer playground

6 Whiz up to the Tirolean Alps in Zaha Hadid's space-age **Nordketten Bahnen** (p87) from picture-perfect Innsbruck

7 Explore the romantic Wachau and technology trailblazer Linz in the **Danube Valley** (p73)

Central Vienna

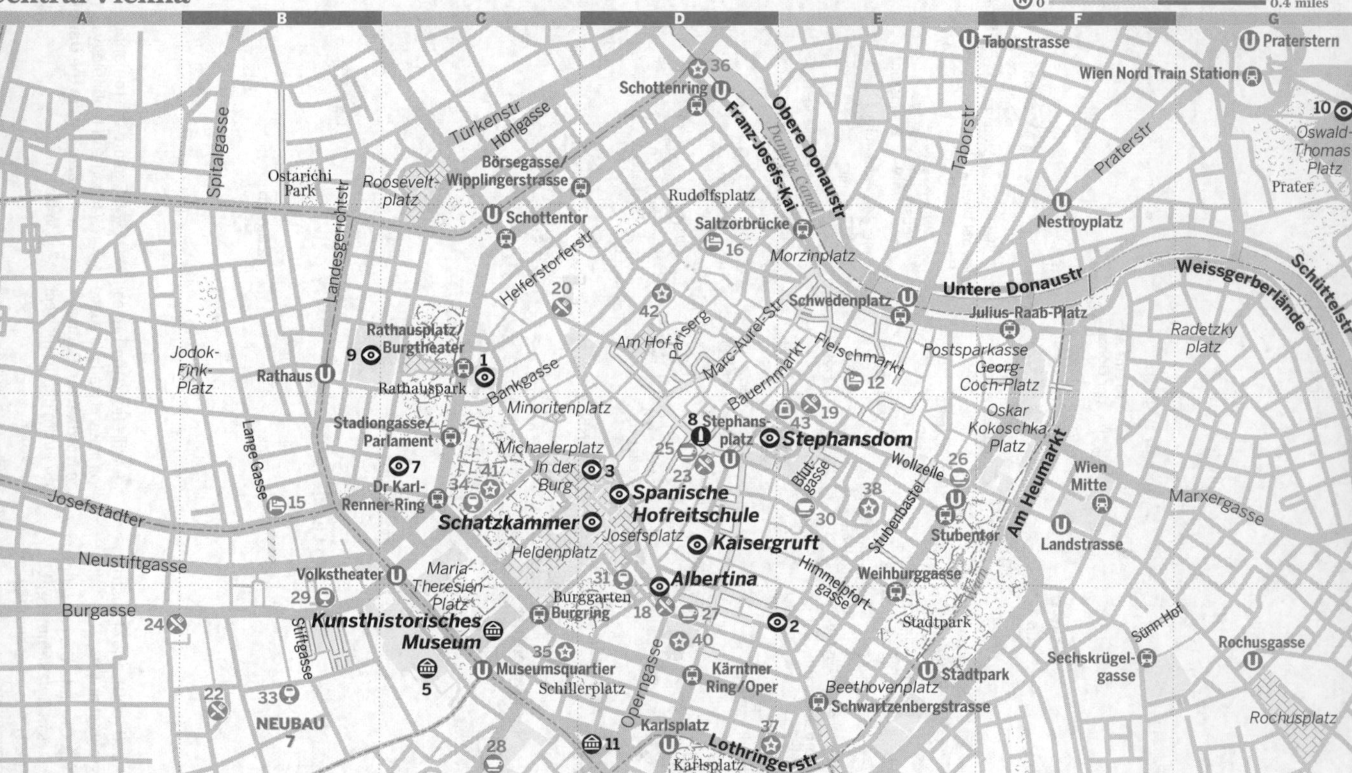

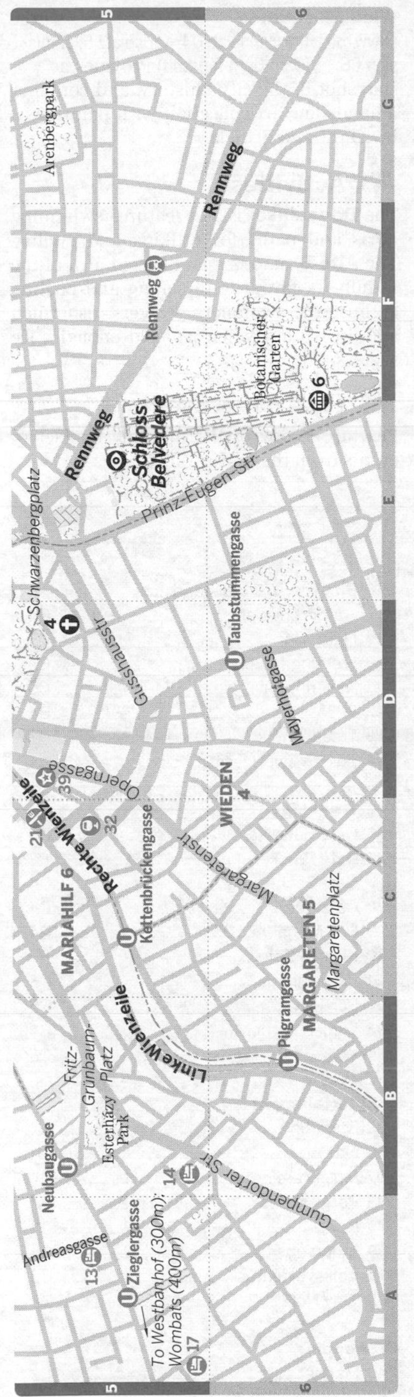

outside are its Versailles-like **gardens** (admission free), containing, among other attractions, the world's oldest zoo, **Tiergarten Schönbrunn** (www.zoovienna.at; admission €14; ⌚9am-6.30pm). The easiest way to reach the zoo is by taking the U4 to Hietzing.

Schloss Belvedere PALACE, ART GALLERY
(www.belvedere.at; combined ticket €13.50) Belvedere is a masterpiece of art and one of the world's finest baroque palaces. The first of the palace's two main buildings is the **Oberes Belvedere** (Upper Belvedere; 03, Prinz-Eugen-Strasse 27; admission €9.50; ⌚10am-6pm), showcasing Gustav Klimt's *The Kiss* (1908) alongside other late-19th- to early-20th-century Austrian works.

The second is the grandiose **Unteres Belvedere** (Lower Belvedere; 03, Rennweg 6; admission €9.50; ⌚10am-6pm Thu-Tue, 10am-9pm Wed), sheltering lavish state apartments such as the richly frescoed Marmorsaal (Marble Hall) and Groteskensaal (Hall of Grotesques). The buildings sit at opposite ends of a manicured garden.

MuseumsQuartier MUSEUM
(Museum Quarter; www.mqw.at; 07, Museumsplatz 1) One of the world's most ambitious cultural spaces, this ensemble of museums, cafes, restaurants and bars contains both contemporary and baroque architectural splendour. Its high point is the **Leopold Museum** (www.leopoldmuseum.org; admission €10; ⌚10am-6pm, to 9pm Thu), which houses the world's largest collection of Egon Schiele paintings, with some fine Klimts and Kokoschkas.

Kunsthistorisches Museum ART GALLERY
(Museum of Fine Arts; www.khm.at; 01, Burgring 5; admission €12; ⌚10am-6pm Tue-Sun, 10am-9pm Thu) When it comes to classical works of art, nothing comes close to the Kunsthistorisches Museum. It houses a huge range of art amassed by the Habsburgs and includes works by Rubens, Van Dyck, Holbein and Caravaggio.

Riesenrad FERRIS WHEEL
(www.wienerriesenrad.com; 02, Prater 90; adult €8.50; ⌚9am-11.45pm) Anyone who's seen *The Third Man* will recognise the Riesenrad in the Prater amusement park; it's where Orson Welles ad-libbed his immortal speech about peace, Switzerland and cuckoo clocks.

Pestsäule MEMORIAL
(Plague Column; 01, Graben) Graben is dominated by the knobbly outline of this memorial, designed by Fischer von Erlach in

1693 to commemorate the 75,000 victims of the Black Death.

Haus der Musik MUSEUM
(www.hdm.at; 01, Seilerstätte 30; admission €10; ⏲10am-10pm) A fun, interactive journey through music; best of all is the room where you can virtually conduct the Vienna Philharmonic.

Secession Building LANDMARK
(www.secession.at; 01, Friedrichstrasse 12; admission exhibition & frieze €8.50; ⏲10am-6pm Tue-Sun) A popular art nouveau 'temple of art', with an intricate gilt dome. The highlight inside is Klimt's 34m-long *Beethoven Frieze.*

Sigmund Freud Museum MUSEUM
(www.freud-museum.at; 09, Berggasse 19; admission €7; ⏲9am-5pm) Former house of the famous psychologist, now housing a small museum featuring some of his personal belongings.

Wien Museum MUSEUM
(www.museum.vienna.at; 04, Karlsplatz 5; admission €6; ⏲10am-6pm Tue-Sun) Provides a snapshot of the city's history, and contains a handsome art collection with paintings by Klimt and Schiele.

Activities

The **Donauinsel** island features swimming areas and paths for walking and cycling. The **Alte Donau** is a landlocked arm of the Danube, a favourite of sailing and boating enthusiasts, swimmers, walkers, fishermen and, in winter (when it's cold enough), ice skaters.

Festivals & Events

Pick up a copy of the monthly booklet of events from the tourist office.

Central Vienna

Top Sights
- Albertina D4
- Kaisergruft D3
- Kunsthistorisches Museum C4
- Schatzkammer D3
- Schloss Belvedere E5
- Spanische Hofreitschule D3
- Stephansdom D3

Sights
- 1 Burgtheater C2
- 2 Haus der Musik E4
- 3 Kaiserappartements D3
- 4 Karlskirche D5
- 5 Leopold Museum C4
- 6 Oberes Belvedere F6
- 7 Parlament C3
- 8 Pestsäule D3
- 9 Rathaus B2
- 10 Riesenrad G1
- 11 Secession Building D4
- Sisi Museum .... (see 3)

Sleeping
- 12 Hotel Kaertnerhof E2
- 13 Pension Hargita A5
- 14 Pension Kraml B5
- 15 Pension Wild B3
- 16 Schweizer Pension D2
- 17 Westend City Hostel A5

Eating
- 18 Bitzinger Würstelstand am Albertinaplatz D4
- 19 Figlmüller E3
- 20 Freyung C2
- 21 Naschmarkt C5
- 22 St Josef B4
- 23 Trzesniewski D3
- 24 Zu den Zwei Liesin A4

Drinking
- 25 Café Hawelka D3
- 26 Café Prückel E3
- 27 Café Sacher D4
- 28 Café Sperl C4
- 29 Das Möbel B4
- 30 Kleines Café E3
- 31 Palmenhaus D3
- 32 Schikaneder C5
- 33 Siebensternbräu B4
- 34 Volksgarten Pavillon C3

Entertainment
- 35 Burg Kino C4
- 36 Flex D1
- 37 Musikverein D4
- 38 Porgy & Bess E3
- 39 Roxy D5
- 40 Staatsoper D4
- 41 Volksgarten C3
- 42 Why Not? D2

Shopping
- 43 Manner E3

Opernball (01, Staatsoper) Of the 300 or so balls held in January and February, the Opernball (Opera Ball) is the ultimate. It's a supremely lavish affair, with the men in tails and women in shining white gowns.

Wiener Festwochen (www.festwochen.or.at) Wide-ranging program of arts from around the world, from May to mid-June.

Donauinselfest Free three-day festival of rock, pop, hardcore, folk and country music on the Donauinsel in June.

Musikfilm Festival (01, Rathausplatz) Screenings of operas, operettas and concerts outside the Rathaus in July and August.

Viennale (www.viennale.at) The country's biggest and best film festival, featuring fringe and independent films from around the world in October.

Christkindlmärkte Vienna's much-loved Christmas-market season runs from mid-November to Christmas Day.

Sleeping

Vienna has its share of budget choices, but rooms fill quickly in the summer, so book ahead.

TOP CHOICE **Pension Hargita** PENSION €
(☎526 19 28; www.hargita.at; 07, Andreasgasse 1; s/d from €57/68;) Ignore the bland exterior – stepping into the wood-panelled lobby is like entering a mountain chalet. This Hungarian-Austrian family-operated space is tasteful simplicity. Fresh colours and flowers decorate the homey rooms, and the breakfast room has a country feel.

Hotel Kaertnerhof HOTEL €€
(☎512 19 23; www.karntnerhof.com; 01, Grashofgasse 4; s/d from €95/140; @) Tucked away from the bustle, this treasure oozes old Vienna charm, from the period paintings to the wood-and-frosted-glass-panelled lift to the roof terrace. Rooms mix a few plain pieces with antiques, chandeliers and elegant curtains. Stephansplatz is less than five minutes away.

Schweizer Pension PENSION €
(☎533 81 56; www.schweizerpension.com; 01, Heinrichsgasse 2; s/d from €48/65) This small, family-run pension is a superb deal, with homely touches and eco credentials. Book in advance, though, as it has only 11 rooms and is popular among those on squeezed budgets. Wi-fi is available in the common areas.

A SPIN OF THE RING

One of the best deals in Vienna is a self-guided tour on tram 1 or 2 of the monumental Ringstrasse boulevard encircling much of the Innere Stadt. For the price of a single ticket you'll take in the neo-Gothic **Rathaus** (city hall), the Greek Revival–style **parliament**, the 19th-century **Burgtheater** and the baroque **Karlskirche** (St Charles' Church), among other sights.

Wombat's HOSTEL €
(☎897 36 23; www.wombats.at; 05, Mariahilferstrasse 137; dm/r €20/56; @) For a relaxed Aussie-hostel vibe in central Vienna, it has to be Wombat's. Interiors are rainbow-bright, dorms modern (with bathrooms), and common areas include a bar and pool tables. Bike rental is available.

Westend City Hostel HOSTEL €
(☎597 67 29; www.westendhostel.at; 06, Fügergasse 3; dm/s/d €20/52/62; @) This independent hostel received a bright and funky head-to-toe revamp in 2009. All of the spacious dorms are en suite and the ivy-clad inner courtyard is superb.

Pension Kraml PENSION €
(☎587 85 88; www.pensionkraml.at; 06, Brauergasse 5; s/d from €35/76, apt from €99;) A quiet and cosy family-run pension, where old-school politeness and comfort are paramount. Rooms are large (if a little dated).

Pension Wild PENSION €
(☎406 51 74; www.pension-wild.com; 08, Lange Gasse 10; s/d from €41/43) One of the few openly gay-friendly pensions in Vienna. Expect a warm welcome and spotlessly clean rooms. Kitchens are available for guests to use and abuse.

Eating

Self-caterers can stock up at the Hofer, Billa and Spar supermarkets in the centre. Some have well-stocked delis that make sandwiches to order – the perfect cheap lunch on the run. The city is also dotted with markets: **Freyung** (01, Freyung; 9am-6pm Fri & Sat 1st & 3rd weekend of month) market exclusively sells fresh organic produce.

TOP CHOICE **Zu den Zwei Liesln** BEISL €
(☎523 32 82; 07, Burggasse 63; lunch menu €4.90-5.30, mains €6-11.90) Six varieties of schnitzel

DON'T MISS

NASCHMARKT NIBBLES

The sprawling **Naschmarkt** (06, Linke & Rechte Wienzeile; ⊙6am-6.30pm Mon-Fri, 6am-5pm Sat) is *the* place to *nasch* (snack) in Vienna. Big and bold, the market is a foodie's dream. The food stalls selling meats, fruits, vegetables, cheeses and spices are perfect for assembling your own picnic. There are also plenty of people-watching cafes, restaurants dishing up good-value lunches, delis and takeaway stands where you can grab a falafel or baguette.

crowd the menu at this classic budget *Beisl* (beer house) of legendary status. The quaint and cosy wood-panelled interior is complemented by a tree-shaded inner courtyard.

Figlmüller BEISL €
(☎512 61 77; 01, Wollzeile 5; mains €7-15; ⊙11am-10.30pm, closed Aug) This famous *Beisl* serves some of the biggest (and best) schnitzels in town. Sure, the rural decor is contrived and beer isn't served (only wine from the owner's own vineyard), but it doesn't get more Viennese than this.

St Josef VEGETARIAN €
(☎526 68 18; 07, Mondscheingasse 10; small/large plates €6.80/8.20; ⊙8am-5pm Mon-Fri, 8am-4pm Sat; ⊘) This canteen-like vegetarian place cooks to a theme each day (Indian, for instance). It has a sparse, industrial character and super-friendly staff.

Kent TURKISH €
(☎405 91 73; 16, Brunnengasse 67; mains €5-10; ⊙6am-2am) Authentic Turkish cuisine and one of the largest gardens in the city make Kent a hugely popular choice. For late-night desserts try the 24-hour Turkish bakery next door.

Bitzinger Würstelstand am Albertinaplatz SAUSAGE STAND €
(01, Albertinaplatz; sausages €2.80-3.50; ⊙24hr) Located behind the Staatsoper, this is one of Vienna's best sausage stands. Watch ladies and gents dressed to the nines while enjoying your *Wurst* and a beer.

Trzesniewski SANDWICHES €
(Dorotheergasse 1; sandwiches from €2.80; ⊙8.30am-7.30pm Mon-Fri, 9am-5pm Sat) Possibly Austria's finest sandwich shop, with 21 delectably thick spreads, from tuna with egg to Swedish herring. Plan on sampling a few; two bites and they're gone.

Drinking

Vienna is riddled with drinking dens, with concentrations of pulsating bars north and south of the Naschmarkt, around Spittelberg (many double as restaurants) and the Gürtel (mainly around the U6 stops of Josefstädter Strasse and Nussdorfer Strasse). The Bermuda Dreieck (Bermuda Triangle), near the Danube Canal in the Innere Stadt, also has many bars, but they're more touristy.

Heurigen (wine taverns) cluster in the wine-growing suburbs to the north, southwest, west and northwest of the city. Opening times are approximately from 4pm to 11pm, and wine costs around €2.50 per *Viertel* (250mL).

TOP CHOICE **Palmenhaus** BAR, CAFE
(01, Burggarten; ⊙10am-2am, closed Mon & Tue Jan & Feb) Housed in a beautifully restored Victorian palm house, the Palmenhaus has a relaxed vibe. In summer, tables spill out onto the pavement overlooking the green of the Burggarten, and there are occasional club nights.

Das Möbel BAR, CAFE
(07, Burggasse 10; ⊙10am-1am; 📶) The interior is never dull at this bar near the MuseumsQuartier. It's remarkable for its funky decor and furniture – cube stools, assorted moulded lamps – and everything is up for sale.

10er Marie STADTHEURIGER
(16, Ottakringerstrasse 222-224; ⊙3pm-midnight Mon-Sat) Vienna's oldest *Heuriger* (wine tavern) has been going strong since 1740 – Schubert, Strauss and Crown Prince Rudolf all kicked back a glass or three here. The usual buffet is available.

Siebensternbräu BREWERY
(www.7stern.at; 07, Siebensterngasse 19; ⊙10am-midnight) Large brewery with all the main varieties, plus hemp beer, chilli beer and smoky beer; its hidden back garden is sublime in summer.

Schikaneder BAR
(04, Margareten Strasse 22-24; ⊙6pm-4am) A grungy bar with a buzzing vibe that attracts students and an arty crowd. Also hosts movie nights.

Volksgarten Pavillon BAR
(01, Burgring 1; ⊙11am-2am Apr–mid-Sep) A lovely 1950s-style pavilion with views of Heldenplatz and an ever-popular garden.

DON'T MISS

SWEET INDULGENCES

The *Kaffeehaus* (coffee house) is an integral part of Viennese life. Most serve light meals alongside a mouth-watering array of cakes and tortes. Expect to pay around €7 for a coffee with a slice of cake. Here are just some of our favourites:

Café Sperl COFFEE HOUSE
(06, Gumpendorfer Strasse 11; 7am-11pm Mon-Sat, 11am-8pm Sun, closed Sun in summer;) This gorgeous Jugendstil coffee house serves the *Sperl Torte* – an almond and chocolate cream dream.

Kleines Café COFFEE HOUSE
(Franziskanerplatz 3; 10am-2am daily) Tiny bohemian cafe with wonderful summer seating on Franziskanerplatz.

Café Hawelka COFFEE HOUSE
(01, Dorotheergasse 6; 8am-2am Mon & Wed-Sat, from 10am Sun) A traditional haunt for artists and writers, this shabby-chic coffee house attracts the gamut of Viennese society.

Café Sacher COFFEE HOUSE
(01, Philharmonikerstrasse 4; 8am-11:30pm) This opulent coffee house is celebrated for its *Sacher Torte* (€4), a rich chocolate cake with apricot jam.

Café Prückel COFFEE HOUSE
(01, Stubenring 24; 8.30am-10pm) Intimate booths, strong coffee and diet-destroying cakes are all attractions at this 1950s gem.

☆ Entertainment

Falter (www.falter.at, in German) has up-to-date listings. Theatres and concert halls often sell cheap standing-room tickets around an hour before performances. Ask the tourist office for details of free concerts at the Rathaus or in churches.

TOP CHOICE **Flex** CLUB
(www.flex.at; 01, Donaukanal, Augartenbrücke; 6pm-4am) One of Vienna's most celebrated clubs, Flex has one of Europe's best sound systems, puts on great shows and features top DJs from Vienna and abroad. 'Messed up' (techno) on Monday and London Calling (alternative and indie) on Wednesday and Friday are always popular.

Staatsoper LIVE MUSIC
(514 44 7880; www.wiener-staatsoper.at; 01, Opernring 2; box office closed Sun) Performances at Vienna's premier opera and classical music venue are lavish, formal affairs, where people dress up.

Musikverein LIVE MUSIC
(505 81 90; www.musikverein.at; 01, Bösendorferstrasse 12; box office closed Sun) The opulent Musikverein, home to the Vienna Philharmonic Orchestra, is celebrated for its acoustics.

Roxy CLUB
(www.sunshine.at; 04, Operngasse 24; 11pm-4am Thu-Sat) Roxy's tiny dance floor reaches bursting point when DJs from the electronic scene guest here, though everything from Brazilian to jazzy grooves can be heard.

Volksgarten CLUB
(01, Burgring 1; Tue-Sat) This club attracts a well-dressed crowd, keen to strut its stuff and scan for talent from the long bar. The quality sound system pumps out an array of music styles.

Burg Kino CINEMA
(www.burgkino.at; 01, Opernring 19) English films; has regular screenings of *The Third Man*.

Porgy & Bess JAZZ CLUB
(www.porgy.at; 01, Riemergasse 11; 7pm-late) Presents a top-drawer line-up of modern jazz acts and DJs fill spots on weekends.

Why Not? CLUB
(www.why-not.at; 01, Tiefer Graben 22; 10pm-4am Fri & Sat) This small, central club fills quickly, mainly with young gay guys on weekends.

Shopping

The Innere Stadt does a brisk trade in designer labels, sweets and jewellery, while most Viennese head to Mariahilfer Strasse for high-street brands. Idiosyncratic local stores cluster in Neubau. Neubaugasse is good for secondhand hunters and collectors, and Josefstädter Strasse is a quaint, old-fashioned shopping experience.

A perfect souvenir from Vienna, which unfortunately won't last long, is the city's favourite sweet, the *Manner Schnitten* (wafers filled with hazelnut cream). Get the real thing from **Manner** (01, Stephansplatz 7; 10am-6.30pm Sun-Fri, 9.30am-8.30pm Sat).

Information

Many cafes and bars have free wi-fi for customers.

Airport information office (6am-11pm) In the arrival hall.

Allgemeines Krankenhaus (404 00; 09, Währinger Gürtel 18-20) Hospital with a 24-hour casualty ward.

Jugendinfo (Vienna Youth Information; 1799; www.jugendinfowien.at; 01, Babenbergerstrasse 1; noon-7pm Mon-Sat) Offers various reduced-price tickets for 14- to 26-year-olds.

Main post office (01, Fleischmarkt 19; 6am-10pm)

Police station (313 10; 01, Deutschmeisterplatz 3)

DON'T MISS

IMPERIAL ENTERTAINMENT

The world-famous **Vienna Boys' Choir** (Wiener Sängerknaben; www.wsk.at) performs on Sunday at 9.15am (October to June) in the Burgkapelle (Royal Chapel) in the Hofburg. **Tickets** (533 99 27) should be booked around six weeks in advance. The group also performs regularly in the Musikverein.

Another throwback to the Habsburg glory days is the **Spanische Hofreitschule** (Spanish Riding School; 533 90 31; www.srs.at; 01, Michaelerplatz 1; performances 11am Sat & Sun mid-Feb–Jun & late Aug-Dec), where Lipizzaner stallions perform equine ballet to classical music. For **morning training** (adult €12; 10am-noon Tue-Sat Feb-Jun & mid-Aug–Dec) sessions, same-day tickets are available at the **visitor centre** (9am-4pm Tue-Fri) on Michaelerplatz.

Tourist Info Wien (211 14-555; www.wien.info; 01, Albertinaplatz; 9am-7pm) Vienna's main tourist office, with a ticket agency, hotel booking service, free maps and every brochure you could ever want.

Getting There & Away

Air

Vienna is a major hub between Western and Eastern Europe, with flight connections to many major European cities. Check with **Austrian Airlines** (www.austrian.com) for domestic schedules.

Boat

Fast hydrofoils travel eastwards along the Danube to Bratislava (€19 to €31, 1¼ hours) daily from April to October and on Saturday and Sunday in March; and to Budapest (one way/return €89/109, 5½ hours) daily. Bookings can be made through **DDSG Blue Danube** (58 880-0; www.ddsg-blue-danube.at; 02, Handelskai 265).

Bus

Vienna currently has no central bus station and national Bundesbuses arrive and depart from several different locations, depending on the destination. Bus lines serving Vienna include **Eurolines** (www.eurolines.com).

Car & Motorcycle

The Gürtel is an outer ring road that joins up with the A22 on the north bank of the Danube and the A23 southeast of town. All the main road routes intersect with this system, including the A1 from Linz and Salzburg, and the A2 from Graz.

Train

Vienna is one of central Europe's man rail hubs. **Österreiche Bundesbahn** (ÖBB, Austrian Federal Railway; www.oebb.at) is the main operator. There are direct services and connections to many European cities. Sample train times include Berlin (nine to 10 hours), Budapest (2¾ to four hours), Munich (four to five hours), Paris (12 to 13 hours), Prague (4½ to 5½ hours) and Venice (eight to nine hours).

Vienna has multiple train stations. At the time of writing, a massive construction project is in progress at Vienna's former Südbahnhof – an eastern section has been set up as a temporary station to serve some regional trains to/from the east, including Bratislava. The complex will reopen as Hauptbahnhof Wien (Vienna Central Station) in late 2012 or early 2013. As a result all long-distance trains are being rerouted among the rest of Vienna's train stations. Additionally, Westbahnhof is undergoing major renovation; at the time of writing a provisional station had been created so that the station could remain in operation – it is slated to reopen in late 2011. Further train stations include Franz-Josefs-Bahnhof

GETTING INTO TOWN

The fastest transport into the centre is **City Airport Train** (CAT; www.cityairporttrain.com; return €18), which takes 16 minutes from the airport to Wien Mitte (every 30 minutes from 5.38am to 11.08pm); book online for a €2 discount. The S-Bahn (S7) does the same journey (one way €3.60, 26 minutes).

(which handles trains to/from the Danube Valley), Wien Mitte, Wien Nord and Meidling.

Getting Around

Vienna has a unified public transport network that encompasses trains, trams, buses, and underground (U-Bahn) and suburban (S-Bahn) trains. Free maps and information pamphlets are available from **Wiener Linien** (www.wienerlinien.at).

All advance-purchase tickets must be slotted into the validation machines at the entrance to U-Bahn stations or on trams and buses. Singles cost €1.80 from automatic machines, or €2.20 on board.

Stunden-Netzkarte (24-hour passes) cost €5.70, 72-hour passes €13.60 and weekly passes (valid Monday to Sunday) €14.

Vienna's public bike scheme is called **Vienna City Bike** (www.citybikewien.at), with more than 60 bicycle stands across the city (first hour free, second hour €1, third hour €2, per hour thereafter €4). A credit card is required to rent bikes – just swipe your card in the machine and follow the instructions (in a number of languages).

THE DANUBE VALLEY

The stretch of Danube between Krems and Melk, known locally as the Wachau, is arguably the loveliest along the entire length of the mighty river. Both banks are dotted with ruined castles and medieval towns and lined with terraced vineyards. Further upstream is the industrial city of Linz, Austria's avant-garde art and new-technology trailblazer.

Krems an der Donau

☎02732 / POP 23,800

Sitting on the northern bank of the Danube against a backdrop of terraced vineyards, Krems marks the beginning of the Wachau. It has an attractive cobbled centre, some good restaurants and the gallery-dotted Kunstmeile (Art Mile). The **tourist office** (☎82 676; www.tiscover.com/krems; Kloster Und, Undstrasse 6; ⏲9am-6pm Mon-Fri, to 5pm Sat, to 4pm Sun) has information on the region. Riverside camping is available at **ÖAMTC Donaupark Camping** (☎844 55; Wiedengasse 7; campsites per person/car/tent €4/3.90/4.60; ⏲closed mid-Oct–Easter; P). The central HI **Jugendherberge** (☎834 52; oejhv.noe.krems@aon.at; Ringstrasse 77; dm €18; ⏲closed Nov-Mar; P) is well geared for cyclists and has a climbing wall.

Frequent daily trains connect Krems with Vienna's Franz Josefs Bahnhof (€13.90, one hour). The quickest way to Melk is by train to Spitz, continuing by bus (€7.30, one hour, five times daily). The boat station is near Donaustrasse, about 2km west of the train station.

Melk

☎02752 / POP 5200

With its sparkling and majestic abbey-fortress, Melk is a highlight of any visit to the Danube Valley. Many visitors cycle here for the day from nearby villages– wearily pushing their bikes through the cobblestone streets.

Sights

TOP CHOICE **Stift Melk** ABBEY

(Benedictine Abbey of Melk; ☎5550; www.stiftmelk.at; Abt Berthold Dietmayr Strasse 1; admission €7.70, with guided tour €9.50; ⏲9am-5.30pm) Rising like a vision on a hill overlooking the town, Stift Melk is Austria's most famous abbey, home to Benedictine monks since the 11th century and redesigned in the 18th century by mastermind Jakob Prandtauer. It's an elaborate example of baroque architecture, most often lauded for its imposing marble hall and beautiful library, but just as unforgettable for the curved terrace connecting these two rooms.

From around November to March, the monastery can only be visited by guided tour (11am and 2pm daily). Always phone ahead to ensure you get an English-language tour.

Sleeping & Eating

Restaurants and cafes with alfresco seating line the Rathausplatz.

Hotel Restaurant zur Post HOTEL €€

(☎523 45; www.post-melk.at, in German; Linzer Strasse 1; s €61-71, d €98-112, apt €155-210; P@) This bright hotel in the heart of town has large, comfortable rooms. There's a sauna, free bike use for guests and a decent restaurant serving Austrian classics.

ON YOUR BIKE

Many towns in the Danube Valley are part of a bike-hire network called **Leihradl**. After registering using a credit card (either by calling the hotline on ☎02742-229 901 or on the German-language website www.leihradl.at), a refunded €1 is deducted and you can begin renting bicycles (per hour/24 hours €1/5).

Jugendherberge HOSTEL €
(☎52 681; www.melk.noejhw.at, in German; Karl Strasse 42; dm/s/d €21/31/52;) This modern HI hostel is 10 minutes' walk from the train station.

Information

The **tourist office** (☎523 07-410; www.niederoesterreich.at/melk; Babenbergerstrasse 1; ⌚9am-noon & 2-6pm Mon-Fri, 10am-noon Sat & Sun) is east of Rathausplatz; it has maps and plenty of useful information.

Getting There & Away

Boats leave from the canal by Pionierstrasse, 400m north of the abbey. There are hourly trains to Vienna (€15.70, 1¼ hours).

Linz

☎0732 / POP 189,000

In Linz beginnt's (it begins in Linz) goes the Austrian saying, and it's spot on. Linz is blessed with a leading-edge cyber centre and world-class contemporary-art gallery, both signs that Upper Austria kick-started the country's technology industry. Beyond the industrial outskirts you'll find plenty of culture, so much so that Linz gained the title of European Capital of Culture 2009.

Sights & Activities

The architecturally eye-catching **Ars Electronica Center** (☎72 72-0; www.aec.at; Hauptstrasse 2; adult/student €6/3; ⌚9am-5pm Wed-Fri, 10am-6pm Sat & Sun) zooms in on tomorrow's technology and science in themed labs where you can interact with robots and (virtually) travel the world.

Across the Danube, and spectacularly lit by night, the riverside **Lentos** (www.lentos.at; Ernst-Koref-Promenade 1; admission €6.50; ⌚10am-6pm Wed & Fri-Mon, to 9pm Thu) guards one of Austria's finest modern-art collections, including works by Warhol, Schiele and Klimt, which sometimes feature in exhibitions.

Other standouts include neo-Gothic giant **Neuer Dom** (New Cathedral; Herrenstrasse 26; ⌚8am-7pm) and the narrow-gauge **Pöstlingbergbahn** (adult €5.60; ⌚every 30min 6am-10pm Mon-Sat, 7.30am-10pm Sun) from Hauptplatz to Pöstlingberg (537m), ranked as the world's steepest mountain railway in the *Guinness Book of Records*.

Festivals & Events

Linz has several famous festivals, held in September:

Ars Electronica Festival TECHNOLOGY FESTIVAL
(www.aec.at) A celebration of weird and wonderful technological art and computer music.

Brucknerfest MUSIC FESTIVAL
(www.brucknerhaus.at) This highbrow classical music festival pays homage to native Linz son Bruckner.

Sleeping & Eating

The tourist office offers a free accommodation-booking service for visitors, but only face-to-face and not over the phone.

Pavement cafes, bistros and lively bars line up on and around Hauptplatz, Landstrasse and the cobbled Altstadt.

Sommerhaus Hotel HOTEL €
(☎24 57 376; www.sommerhaus-hotel.at; Julius-Raab-Strasse 10; s/d €49/74; P@) Sitting between the city and open fields, this revamped uni hotel has simple, comfy rooms and a big indoor pool. Take tram 1 or 2 to Schumpeterstrasse and walk five minutes.

Hotel am Domplatz HOTEL €€
(☎77 30 00; www.hotelamdomplatz.at; Stifterstrasse 4; s €120-140, d €150-180; P❄@) Sidling up to the neo-Gothic Neuer Dom, this glass-and-concrete design hotel sports streamlined interiors and a rooftop spa.

CITY SAVER

The money-saving **Linz Card** (1/3 days €15/25) gives unlimited use of public transport, entry to major museums, and discounts on city tours and river cruises. The card is sold at the tourist office, airport, museums and some hotels.

Herberge Linz HOSTEL €
(☎0699-1180 7003; herberge.linz@aon.at; Kapuzinerstrasse 14; dm/s/d €17/25/40; ⊖) A central hostel with a sociable vibe, well-equipped dorms and a leafy garden.

k.u.k. Hofbäckerei CAFE €
(Pfarrgasse 17; coffee & cake €3-6; ⊙6.30am-6pm Mon-Fri, 7am-12.30pm Sat) The Empire lives on at this gloriously stuck-in-time cafe, where Fritz Rath bakes the richest, spiciest, crumbliest Linzer Torte in town.

Spirali CAFE €
(Graben 32b; mains €5-7; ⊙10am-7pm Mon-Sat) An ethnic-flavoured cafe with good-value lunch specials from pasta to curries. Give the homemade cakes and teas a whirl.

Cubus FUSION €
(Ars-Electronica-Strasse 1; mains €8.50-14.50; ⊙9am-1am Mon-Sat, 9am-6pm Sun; ☎) On the 3rd floor of the Ars Electronica Center, this glass cube has stellar Danube views and does a fab two-course lunch for €7.

Information

Hotspot Linz Free wi-fi at 120 hot spots in the city, including Ars Electronica Center and Lentos; see www.hotspotlinz.at (in German).

Tourist Information Linz (☎7070 2009; www.linz.at; Hauptplatz 1; ⊙9am-7pm Mon-Sat, 10am-7pm Sun, shorter hrs winter) Free city maps and room-reservation service.

Getting There & Around

AIR Ryanair flies to the **Blue Danube Airport** (www.linz-airport.at), 13km southwest of Linz. An hourly shuttle bus (€2.60, 20 minutes) links the airport to the main train station from Monday to Saturday.

TRAIN Linz is halfway between Salzburg and Vienna on the main road and rail routes. Trains to Salzburg (€22, 1¼ hours) and Vienna (€31.20, 1½ hours) leave approximately twice hourly.

PUBLIC TRANSPORT Single bus and tram tickets cost €1.80 and day passes €3.60. Some of the bus services stop early in the evening.

THE SOUTH

Austria's two main southern states, Styria (Steiermark) and Carinthia (Kärnten), often feel worlds apart from the rest of the country, both in climate and attitude. Styria is a blissful amalgamation of genteel architecture, rolling green hills, vine-covered slopes and soaring mountains. Its capital, Graz, is one of Austria's most attractive cities.

A jet-setting, fashion-conscious crowd heads to sun-drenched Carinthia for summer holidays. The region (right on the border with Italy) exudes an atmosphere that's as close to Mediterranean as this staunch country gets.

Graz

☎0316 / POP 257,350

Austria's second-largest city is probably its most relaxed and, after Vienna, its liveliest for after-hours pursuits. It's an attractive place with bristling green parkland, red rooftops and a small, fast-flowing river gushing through its centre. Architecturally it has Renaissance courtyards and provincial baroque palaces complemented by innovative modern designs.

The surrounding countryside, a mixture of vineyards, mountains, forested hills and thermal springs, is within easy striking distance, and Graz has a very beautiful bluff connected to the centre by steps, a funicular and a glass lift. Last but not least, a large student population (some 50,000) propels the nightlife and vibrant arts scene, creating a lovable and liveable city.

Sights

Graz is a city easily enjoyed by simply wandering aimlessly. Admission to all of the major museums with a 24-hour ticket costs €14.

TOP CHOICE **Universalmuseum Joanneum** MUSEUM
(www.museum-joanneum.at; Raubergasse 10) With its 19 locations, this ensemble of museums is the gardener of Graz's rich cultural landscape. Until work is completed, some museums will be closed until late 2011, including **Neue Galerie Graz** (admission €8; ⊙10am-6pm Tue-Sun), Styria's most important historical and contemporary-art collection.

Kunsthaus Graz ART GALLERY
(www.kunsthausgraz.at; Lendkai 1; admission €7; ⊙10am-6pm Tue-Sun) Designed by British architects Peter Cook and Colin Fournier, this world-class contemporary-art space looks something like a space-age sea slug. Exhibitions change every three to four months.

Schloss Eggenberg PALACE
(Eggenberger Allee 90; admission €7; ⊙10am-5pm Tue-Sun, closed Nov-Palm Sunday) A blend of Gothic, Renaissance and baroque styles, this beautiful palace can be reached by tram 1 from Hauptplatz. Admission includes a guided tour (from 10am to 4pm on the hour except at

1pm), taking in 24 astronomy- and mythology-themed *prunkräume* (staterooms).

FREE **Murinsel** BRIDGE

This artificial island-cum-bridge in the River Mur is an open seashell of glass, concrete and steel, by New York artist Vito Acconci. It houses a trendy cafe-bar in aqua blue and a small stage. In summer, a beach bar is set up further downstream.

Schlossberg VIEWPOINT

The wooded slopes of Schlossberg (473m) can be reached on foot, by the funicular **Schlossbergbahn** (Castle Hill Railway; 1hr ticket €1.90) from Kaiser-Franz-Josef-Kai, or by **glass lift** (1hr ticket €1.90) from Schlossbergplatz. Napoleon was hard pressed to raze this fortress, but raze it he did. Today the medieval **Uhrturm** (Clock Tower) and a small **garrison museum** (Schlossberg 5a; admission €1; ⌚10am-4pm Thu-Sun, closed Nov–mid-May) are the legacy.

Landeszeughaus ARMOURY

(www.zeughaus.at; Herrengasse 16; admission €7; ⌚10am-6pm) A must-see for fans of armour and weapons, housing an astounding array of 30,000 gleaming exhibits.

FREE **Burg** CASTLE

(Hofgasse) At the far end of Graz's 15th-century castle is an ingenious double staircase (1499). Adjoining it is the Stadtpark, the city's largest green space.

Sleeping

TOP CHOICE **Hotel Daniel** HOTEL €

(☎711 080; www.hoteldaniel.com; Europaplatz 1; r €59-79, breakfast per person €9; P ❄ @) The Daniel is a design hotel with minimalist-style rooms. You can rent a Vespa (€15 per day) and there's a 24-hour espresso bar.

Hotel Strasser HOTEL €

(☎71 39 77; www.hotel-strasser.at; Eggenberger Gürtel 11; s/d/tr/apt €45/65/93/180; P @ ᯤ) Stras-

Central Graz

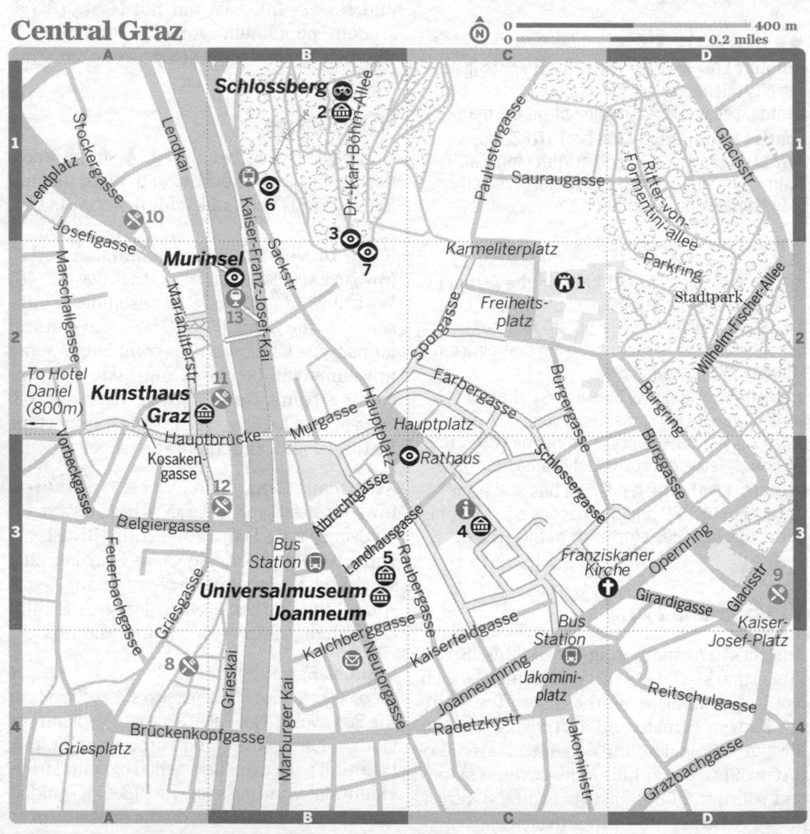

ser has some fascinating pseudo-neoclassical and Mediterranean touches, with Tuscan gold blending with mirrors and cast-iron balustrades. It's handy to the train station.

Camping Central CAMPING GROUND €
(☎0676/378 51 02; Martinhofstrasse 3; campsites per adult/car & tent €8/16; ⏲Apr-Oct; P@≋) Excellent camping ground with pool and playground, 6km from the centre (bus 32 from Jakominiplatz).

Jugend-und Familiengästehaus Graz HOSTEL €
(☎70 83 210; graz@jufa.at; Idlhofgasse 74; dm €22, s €39-46, d €64-77; P@) Take bus 31, 32 or 33 from Jakominiplatz for this HI hostel about 800m south of the main train station.

Eating

Aside from the following listings, there are plenty of cheap eats near Universität Graz, particularly on Halbärthgasse, Zinzendorfgasse and Harrachgasse.

Stock up for a picnic at the **farmers markets** (⏲4.30am-1pm Mon-Sat) on Kaiser-Josef-Platz and Lendplatz. For fast food, head for Hauptplatz and Jakominiplatz.

iku INTERNATIONAL €
(☎8017 9292; www.iku-graz.at, in German; Lendkai 1; lunch menu €7; ⏲9am-1am) This sleek restaurant inside the surrealistic Kunsthaus (p76) does great breakfasts, salads and lunch specials (11.30am to 3pm). Reserve ahead for the Sunday brunch with music.

Mangolds VEGETARIAN €
(www.mangolds.at, in German; Griesgasse 11; meals €5-10; ⏲11am-7pm Mon-Fri, 11am-4pm Sat) Tasty vegetarian patties, rice dishes and over 40 different salads are served at this pay-by-weight vegetarian cafeteria.

Dainadoo INDIAN €
(www.dainadoo.at, in German; Entenplatz 1a; curry of the day €9, lunch menu €7; ⏲Mon-Sat;) This friendly, authentic restaurant serves one delicious vegetarian or meat curry, a dal (lentil curry) and other bites from a small menu.

Drinking

The bar scene in Graz is split between three areas: around the university, adjacent to the Kunsthaus and on Mehlplatz and Prokopigasse (dubbed the Bermuda Triangle).

Insel Café CAFE
(Murinsel; ⏲9.30am-midnight) This cafe on the Murinsel offers a unique experience – here you can sip a drink as the Mur River splashes below your feet.

Orange BAR, CLUB
(www.cafe-bar-orange.at, in German; Elisabethstrasse 30; ⏲8pm-3am) A student crowd flocks to this modern bar and club, with a patio for summer evenings. DJs spin regularly here.

Information

Graztourismus (☎80 75-0; www.graztourismus.at; Herrengasse 16; ⏲10am-6pm) Graz's main

WORTH A TRIP

SPLURGE: HUNDERTWASSER SPA

East Styria is famed for its thermal springs. Fans of Friedensreich Hundertwasser's playful architectural style won't want to miss the surreal **Rogner-Bad Blumau** (☎03383-51 00-0; www.blumau.com; adult €39; ⏲9am-11pm), 50km east of Graz. The spa has all the characteristics of his art, including uneven floors, grass on the roof, colourful ceramics and golden spires. Overnight accommodation includes entry to the spa. Call ahead to book treatments from sound meditation to invigorating Styrian elderberry wraps.

Central Graz

Top Sights

Kunsthaus Graz A2
Murinsel B2
Schlossberg B1
Universalmuseum Joanneum B3

Sights

1 Burg C2
2 Garrison Museum B1
3 Glass Lift B1
4 Landeszeughaus C3
5 Neue Galerie Graz B3
6 Schlossbergbahn B1
7 Uhrturm B2

Eating

8 Dainadoo A4
9 Farmers Market D3
10 Farmers Market A1
11 Iku B2
12 Mangolds B3

Drinking

13 Insel Café B2

tourist office, with loads of free information on the city. Inside the train station is an information stand and terminal and a free hotline to the tourist office.

High Speed Internet-Selfstore (Herrengasse 3; per 30min €1; ⏲7am-10pm) A coin-operated internet space inside the passage.

Getting There & Around

AIR **Ryanair** (www.ryanair.com) has regular flights from London Stansted to **Graz airport** (☎290 20; www.flughafen-graz.at), 10km south of the centre, while **Air Berlin** (www.airberlin.com) connects the city with Berlin.

TRAIN Trains to Vienna depart hourly (€34, 2½ hours) and six daily go to Salzburg (€48, four hours). International train connections from Graz include Ljubljana (€34, 3½ hours) and Budapest (€46, 5½ hours).

PUBLIC TRANSPORT Single tickets (€1.90) for buses, trams and the Schlossbergbahn are valid for one hour, but you're usually better off buying a 24-hour pass (€4.10).

BICYCLE Rentals are available from **Bicycle** (☎68 86 45; Körösistrasse 5; per 24hr €10; ⏲7am-1pm & 2-6pm Mon-Fri).

Klagenfurt

☎0463 / POP 94,000

With its captivating location on Wörthersee and more Renaissance than baroque beauty, Klagenfurt has a distinct Mediterranean feel. Carinthia's capital makes a handy base for exploring Wörthersee's lakeside villages and elegant medieval towns to the north.

Sights & Activities

Boating and swimming are usually possible from May to September.

TOP CHOICE **Wörthersee** LAKE

Owing to its thermal springs, the Wörthersee is one of the region's warmer lakes (an average 21°C in summer) and is great for swimming, lakeshore frolicking and water sports. The 50km **cycle path** around the lake is regarded by many as one of the 'Top 10' in Austria. In summer the tourist office rents bicycles (per 24 hours €10 to €19).

Europapark PARK/BEACH

The green expanse and *Strandbad* (beach) on the shores of Wörthersee are centres for splashy fun, and especially good for kids. The park's biggest draw is **Minimundus** (www.minimundus.at; Villacher Strasse 241; admission €12; ⏲9am-6pm), a 'miniature world' with 140 replicas of the world's architectural icons, downsized to a scale of 1:25. To get there, take bus 10, 11, 12 or 22 from Heiligengeistplatz.

FREE GUIDED WALKS

Tailor your own walking tour by picking up the brochure in English from the Klagenfurt tourist office. It has a map and descriptions of monuments, historic buildings and hidden courtyards. Free guided tours depart from the tourist office at 10am during July and August.

Sleeping & Eating

When you check into accommodation in Klagenfurt, ask for a *Gästekarte* (guest card), entitling you to discounts.

Self-caterers can stock up at the Spar supermarkets on Dr-Hermann-Gasse, Bahnhofstrasse or in the station.

Jugendgästehaus Klagenfurt HOSTEL €

(☎23 00 20; www.oejhv.or.at; Neckheimgasse 6; dm/s/d €20/28/49; P@) This modern HI hostel near Europapark is reached by bus 10, 12, 13 or 22.

Hotel Garni Blumenstöckl HOTEL €

(☎577 93; www.blumenstoeckl.at; 10 Oktober Strasse 11; s/d €47/76) Rooms are arranged around a plant-filled courtyard in this friendly, family-run place in a 400-year-old building.

Firenze ITALIAN €

(Bahnhofstrasse 8; pizza & pasta €6-11, mains €14-17) Large Italian restaurant and pizzeria with continuous kitchen and takeaway.

Information

The **tourist office** (☎53 722 23; www.info.klagenfurt.at; Rathaus, Neuer Platz 1; ⏲8am-6pm Mon-Fri, 10am-5pm Sat, 10am-3pm Sun) books accommodation and sells Kärnten cards, discount cards covering entry to 100 sights in Carinthia (valid mid-April to October). A one-week card costs €34. For full details see www.kaerntencard.at.

Getting There & Around

AIR Klagenfurt's **airport** (www.klagenfurt-airport.com; Flughafenstrasse 60-66) is served by Ryanair from London Stansted and Frankfurt-am-Main, and TUIfly from major German cities.

BUS Bus drivers sell single tickets (€1.80) and 24-hour passes (€4.20). To get to the airport, take bus 40 from the main train station to Annabichl (€1.80, 25 minutes, four times hourly), then change to bus 45 (10 minutes).

TRAIN Two hourly direct trains run from Klagenfurt to Vienna (€48, 3¾ hours) and Salzburg (€35.50, three hours). Trains to Graz depart every two to three hours (€35.50, 2¾ hours). Trains to western Austria, Italy, Slovenia and Germany go via Villach (€7.20, 30 to 40 minutes, two to four per hour).

SALZBURG

0662 / POP 149,000

The joke 'if it's baroque, don't fix it' is a perfect maxim for Salzburg; the tranquil old town, burrowed below steep hills, looks much as it did when Mozart lived here 250 years ago. A Unesco World Heritage site, Salzburg's overwhelmingly baroque old town is entrancing both at ground level and from Hohensalzburg fortress high above. Across the fast-flowing Salzach River rests Schloss Mirabell, surrounded by gorgeous manicured gardens.

If this doesn't whet your appetite, then bypass the grandeur and head straight for kitsch country by joining a tour of *The Sound of Music* film locations.

Sights

Old Town HISTORIC AREA

Presiding over stately Residenzplatz is the **Residenz** (www.residenzgalerie.at; Residenzplatz 1; admission €8.50; 10am-5pm Tue-Sun), once home to the powerful prince-archbishops and worth visiting for its opulently frescoed staterooms and gallery of Old Master paintings.

The mighty baroque **Dom** (cathedral; Domplatz; admission free; 8am-7pm Mon-Sat, 1-7pm Sun), slightly south, has bronze doors symbolising faith, hope and charity, and the **Dommuseum** (admission €6; 10am-5pm Mon-Sat, 11am-6pm Sun), a treasure trove of ecclesiastical art. From here, head west along Franziskanergasse and turn left into a courtyard for **Stiftskirche St Peter** (St Peter Bezirk 1/2; admission free; 8.30am-noon & 2.30-6.30pm), an abbey church founded around AD 700. Among the lovingly tended graves in the grounds you'll find the **Katakomben** (catacombs; adult/student €1/0.60; 10.30am-5pm Tue-Sun). The **Stift Nonnberg** (Nonnberg Convent; admission free; 7am-dusk), where *The Sound of Music* first finds Maria, is back east of Festung Hohensalzburg.

TOP CHOICE **Festung Hohensalzburg** FORTRESS

(www.salzburg-burgen.at; Mönchsberg 34; adult with/without funicular €10.50/7.40, discounts for students; 9am-8pm) Salzburg's most visible icon is this mighty clifftop fortress. Built in 1077 the fortress was home to many prince-archbishops (who ruled Salzburg from 798). Inside are the impressively ornate staterooms, torture chambers and two museums.

It takes 15 minutes to walk up the hill to the fortress, or you can catch the **Festungsbahn funicular** (Festungsgasse 4; 1-way/return €3.60/6; 9am-8pm).

Schloss Mirabell PALACE

(dawn-dusk) Prince-archbishop Wolf Dietrich built this splendid palace in 1606 for his beloved mistress Salome Alt. It's free to visit the fountain-dotted **gardens**, which are less overrun first thing in the morning and in the early evening. The *Tänzerin* (Dancer) sculpture is a great spot to photograph the fortress. *Sound of Music* fans will of course recognise the Pegasus statue where the mini von Trapps practised 'Do-Re-Mi'.

Salzburg Museum MUSEUM

(www.smca.at; Mozartplatz 1; admission €7; 9am-5pm Tue, Wed & Fri-Sun, to 8pm Thu) Housed in the baroque Neue Residenz palace, Salzburg's flagship museum hosts contemporary-art exhibitions and celebrates the city's famous citizens.

Museum der Moderne ART GALLERY

(www.museumdermoderne.at; Mönchsberg 32; admission €8; 10am-6pm, to 8pm Wed) Ultramodern hilltop gallery staging cutting-edge art exhibitions.

Mozarts Geburtshaus MUSEUM

(Mozart's Birthplace; www.mozarteum.at; Getreidegasse 9; admission €7, incl Wohnhaus €12; 9am-5.30pm) A museum paying tribute to famous son Mozart, who was born here in 1756.

Mozart-Wohnhaus MUSEUM

(Mozart's Residence; Makartplatz 8; admission €7, incl Geburtshaus €12; 9am-5.30pm) Mozart's one-time residence showcases family portraits, documents and instruments. There's a film and music archive downstairs.

SALZBURG CARD

The money-saving **Salzburg Card** (1/2/3 days €25/33/38) gets you entry to all the major sights, a free river cruise, unlimited use of public transport (including cable cars) plus numerous discounts on tours and events. The card is €3 cheaper in the low season.

Salzburg

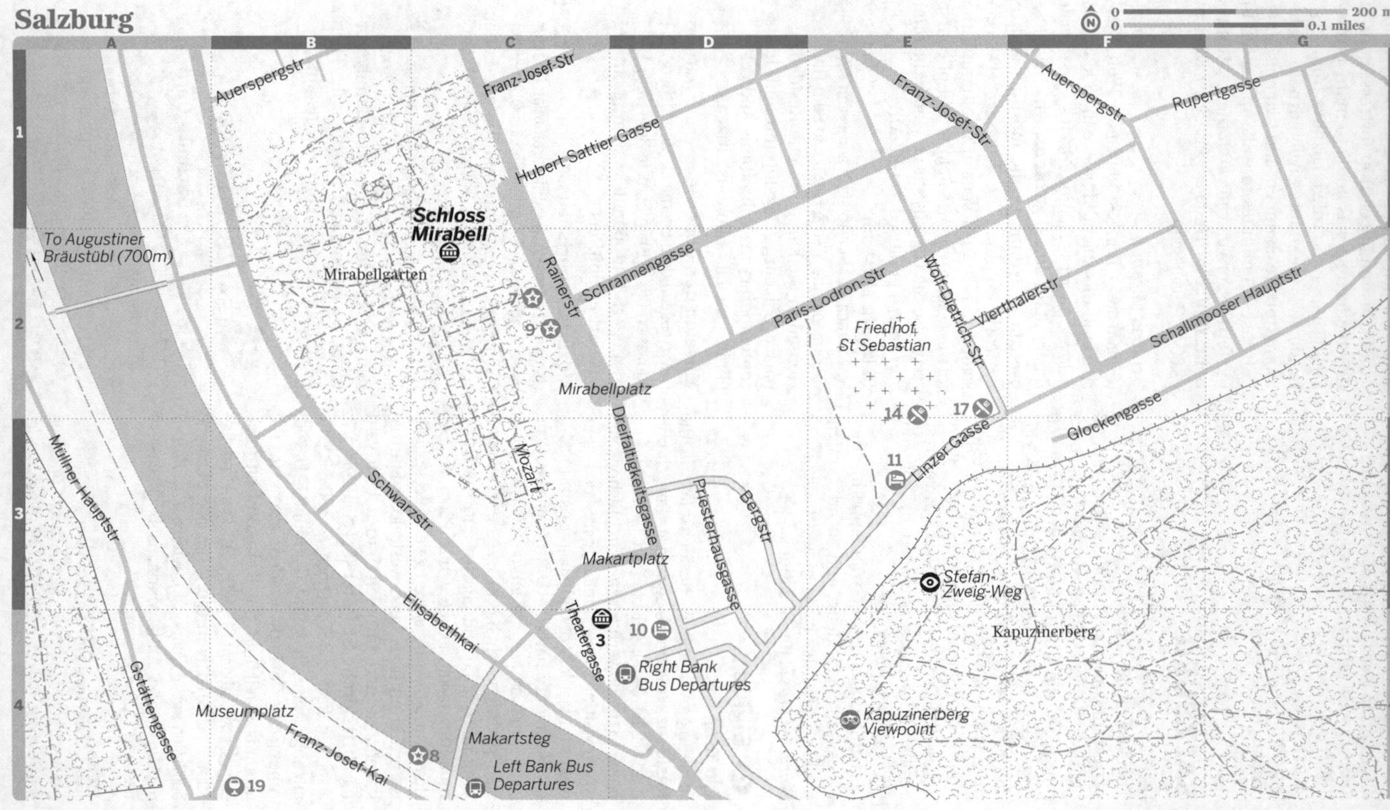
0 200 m
0 0.1 miles
A
B
C
D
E
F
G
1
2
3
4
Auerspergstr
Franz-Josef-Str
Hubert Sattier Gasse
Franz-Josef-Str
Auerspergstr
Rupertgasse
Schloss Mirabell
To Augustiner Bräustübl (700m)
Mirabellgarten
Rainerstr
Schrannengasse
Paris-Lodron-Str
Wolf-Dietrich-Str
Vierthalerstr
Schallmooser Hauptstr
7
9
Friedhof St Sebastian
Mirabellplatz
14
17
Glockengasse
Linzer Gasse
11
Müllner Hauptstr
Mozart
Schwarzstr
Dreifaltigkeitsgasse
Priesterhausgasse
Bergstr
Makartplatz
Stefan-Zweig-Weg
Elisabethkai
Theatergasse
3
10
Kapuzinerberg
Right Bank Bus Departures
Gstättengasse
Museumplatz
Franz-Josef-Kai
8
Makartsteg
Left Bank Bus Departures
Kapuzinerberg Viewpoint
19

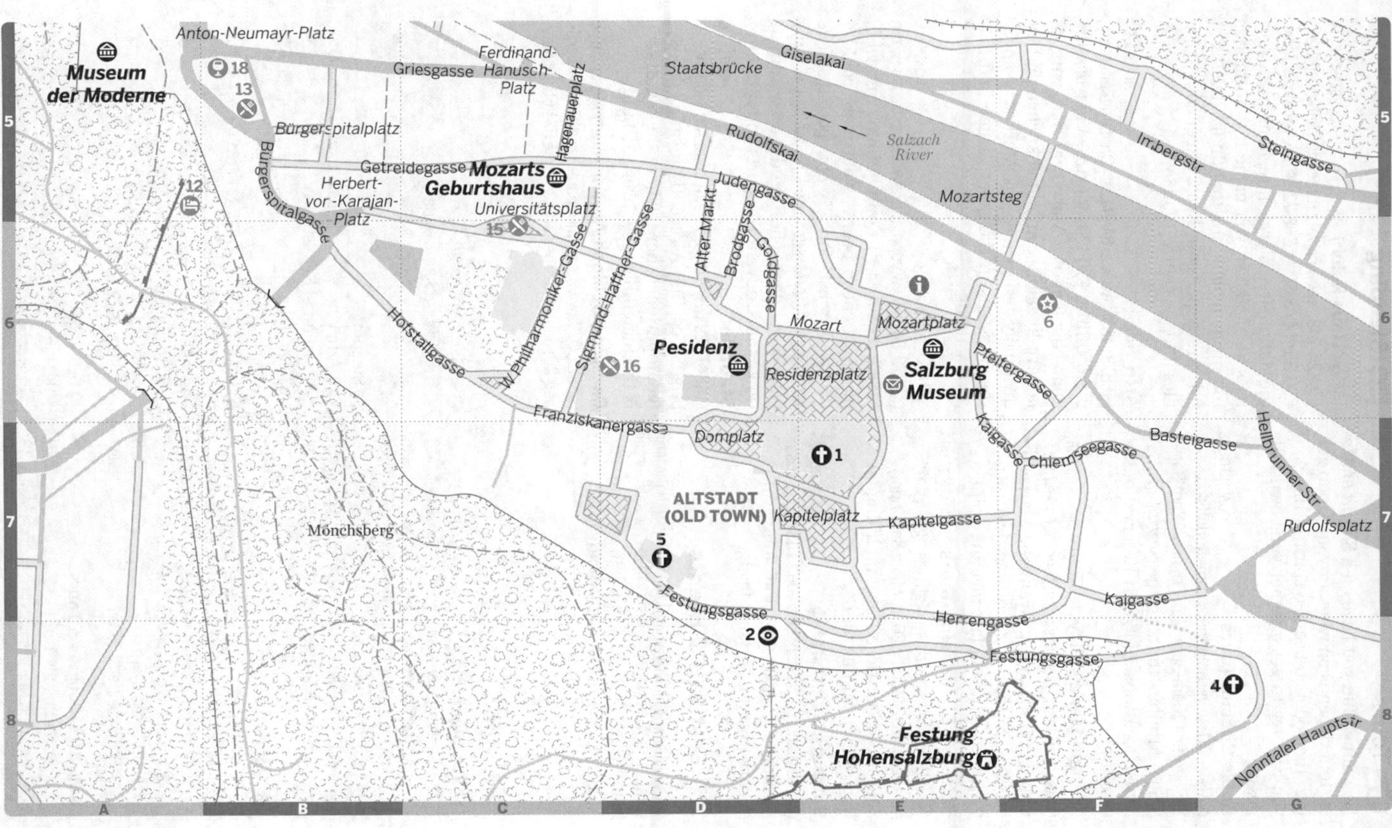
Museum der Moderne
Anton-Neumayr-Platz
18
13
Griesgasse
Ferdinand-Hanusch-Platz
Hagenauerplatz
Staatsbrücke
Giselakai
Bürgerspitalplatz
Bürgerspitalgasse
Getreidegasse
Mozarts Geburtshaus
Herbert-vor-Karajan-Platz
Universitätsplatz
15
12
Rudolfskai
Salzach River
Imbergstr
Steingasse
Judengasse
Mozartsteg
Alter Markt
Brodgasse
Goldgasse
W Philharmoniker-Gasse
Sigmund-Haffner-Gasse
Hofstallgasse
Mozart
Mozartplatz
6
Pesidenz
16
Residenzplatz
Salzburg Museum
Pfeifergasse
Franziskanergasse
Domplatz
1
Kaigasse
Chiemseegasse
Basteigasse
Hellbrunner Str
ALTSTADT (OLD TOWN)
Kapitelplatz
Kapitelgasse
Rudolfsplatz
Mönchsberg
5
Festungsgasse
2
Herrengasse
Kaigasse
Festungsgasse
4
Festung Hohensalzburg
Nonntaler Hauptstr
A
B
C
D
E
F
G
5
6
7
8

Tours

How much fun you have on a *Sound of Music* tour depends on whether your group gets into the yodel-eh-hee-hee spirit of things. If you can, try to get together your own little posse.

Bob's Special Tours COACH TOURS
(☎849 511; www.bobstours.com; Rudolfskai 38; ⊙office 10am-3pm Mon-Fri, noon-2pm Sat & Sun) Minibus tours to the *Sound of Music* locations and Alps. Reservations essential.

Fraülein Maria's Bicycle Tours BICYCLE TOURS
(www.mariasbicycletours.com; tour incl bike hire €24; ⊙9.30am May-Sep) Wannabe Marias on bicycles. No booking required; just turn up at the Mirabellplatz meeting point.

Salzburg Sightseeing Tours COACH TOURS
(☎881 616; www.salzburg-sightseeingtours.at; Mirabellplatz 2; adult €20; ⊙office 8am-6pm) Sells a 24-hour ticket for a multilingual hop-on-hop-off bus tour.

Salzburg Schiffsfahrt RIVER CRUISES
(www.salzburgschifffahrt.at; adult €13, to Schloss Hellbrunn €16; ⊙Apr-Oct) Hour-long cruises depart from Makartsteg bridge.

Festivals & Events

Austria's most renowned classical-music festival, the **Salzburg Festival** (www.salzburgerfestspiele.at), is held from late July to late August. Book online well in advance if you want cheap tickets.

Sleeping

TOP CHOICE **Haus Reichl** GUEST HOUSE €
(☎826 248; www.privatzimmer.at; Reiterweg 52; s €30-35, d €48-52, tr €66-72; P) A pick-up from the station, free bicycle hire, homemade pastries at breakfast, you name it – nothing is too much trouble for the kindly Reichls at this pretty pension. Bus 21 frequently trundles into the centre, 2km away.

Arte Vida GUEST HOUSE €€
(☎873 185; www.artevida.at; Dreifaltigkeitsgasse 9; s €50-110, d €70-120;) Arte Vida has the boho-chic feel of a Marrakchi riad, with its lantern-lit salon, communal kitchen and individually designed rooms. Markus arranges yoga sessions in the quiet garden and outdoor activities.

YOHO Salzburg HOSTEL €
(☎879 649; www.yoho.at; Paracelsusstrasse 9; dm €19-21, d €50; @) Comfy bunks, free wi-fi, plenty of cheap beer – what more could a backpacker ask for? Except, perhaps, *The Sound of Music* screened at 10.30am daily (yes, *every* day). The friendly crew can arrange tours, adventure sports and bike hire.

Stadtalm HOSTEL €
(☎841 729; www.diestadtalm.com; Am Mönchsberg 19c; dm €19) A recently revamped hostel atop Mönchsberg, where the big draw is the incredible view over Salzburg.

Camping Schloss Aigen CAMPING GROUND €
(☎622 079; www.campingparadies.at; Weberbartlweg 20; campsites per adult/tent €5/4.60; ⊙May-

Salzburg

Top Sights
- Festung Hohensalzburg ... E8
- Mozarts Geburtshaus ... C5
- Museum der Moderne ... A5
- Residenz ... D6
- Salzburg Museum ... E6
- Schloss Mirabell ... C2

Sights
- 1 Dom ... E7
- Dommuseum ... (see 1)
- 2 Festungsbahn Funicular ... D8
- 3 Mozart-Wohnhaus ... C4
- 4 Stift Nonnberg ... G8
- 5 Stiftskirche St Peter ... D7

Activities, Courses & Tours
- 6 Bob's Special Tours ... F6
- 7 Fräulein Maria's Bicycle Tours ... C2
- 8 Salzburg Schiffsfahrt ... C4
- 9 Salzburg Sightseeing Tours ... C2

Sleeping
- 10 Arte Vida ... D4
- 11 Institut St Sebastian ... E3
- 12 Stadtalm ... A5

Eating
- 13 Afro Café ... B5
- 14 Alter Fuchs ... E2
- 15 Grüner Markt ... C6
- 16 Mensa Toskana ... D6
- 17 Spicy Spices ... E2

Drinking
- 18 Humboldt Stub'n ... B5
- 19 Republic ... B4

DON'T MISS

DIY SOUND OF MUSIC TOUR

Do a Julie with a free, self-guided *Sound of Music* tour. Let's start at the very beginning:

» **The hills are alive** Cut! Make that *proper* mountains. The opening scenes were filmed around the Salzkammergut lakes (p85).

» **A problem like Maria** The real Maria von Trapp intended to become a nun at Salzburg's Benedictine Stift Nonnberg (p79) before romance struck.

» **So long, farewell** The grand rococo palace of Schloss Leopoldskronn, a 15-minute walk from Festung Hohensalzburg, is where the lake scene was filmed. Its Venetian Room was the blueprint for the Trapps' lavish ballroom, where the children bid their farewells.

» **Do-re-mi** Oh the Pegasus fountain, the steps with fortress views...Schloss Mirabell's garden (p79) might inspire a rendition of 'Do-Re-Mi', especially if there's a drop of golden sun.

» **Sixteen going on seventeen** The loved-up pavilion of the century hides out in Hellbrunn's gardens (p84), where you can act out those 'oh Liesl', 'oh Rolf' fantasies.

Sep) A leafy camping ground overlooking Gaisberg mountain, with playground, minimarket and restaurant. Bus 10 runs into town from the stop 700m away.

Institut St Sebastian GUEST HOUSE €
(☎87 13 86; www.st-sebastian-salzburg.at; Linzer Gasse 41; dm/s/d €21/42/67; wi-fi) Peaceful guest house behind Sebastianskirche with monastic charm. Vaulted corridors lead to well kept dorms and rooms. Ring the bell if reception is unstaffed.

Eating

Look out for good-value lunchtime *Tagesmenü* (fixed menus). The Altstadt's mazy streets are scattered with delis, supermarkets and sausage stands. Self-caterers can find picnic fixings at the **Grüner Markt** (Universitätsplatz; Mon-Sat).

TOP CHOICE **Alter Fuchs** AUSTRIAN €
(☎882 022; Linzer Gasse 47-49; mains €9-16; Mon-Sat) This old fox prides itself on hearty Austrian fare, such as schnitzel fried to golden perfection. Bandana-clad foxes guard the bar in the vaulted interior and there's a courtyard for good-weather dining.

Afro Café AFRICAN €
(☎844 888; Bürgerspitalplatz 5; lunch €6.90, mains €10-14; 10am-midnight Mon-Sat) Hot-pink walls, beach-junk art and *big* hair...this Afro-chic cafe keeps the good vibes and food coming. Fruity cocktails wash down favourites like grilled chicken with honey-lime glaze.

Spicy Spices INDIAN €
(Wolf-Dietrich-Strasse 1; mains €6.50) 'Healthy heart, lovely soul' is the mantra of this tiny eatery, specialising in all-organic, all-veg food from the Indian subcontinent.

Heart of Joy CAFE €
(Franz-Josef-Strasse 3; lunch €6.50, snacks €3-6; 8am-6pm Sun-Fri; wi-fi) Ayurveda-inspired cafe with an all-vegetarian, mostly organic menu. It does great bagels, salads, homemade cakes and juices.

Mensa Toskana INTERNATIONAL €
(Sigmund-Haffner-Gasse 11; lunch €4.20-5.10; lunch Mon-Fri) Atmospheric Mensa (university cafe) in the Altstadt, with a sunny terrace and decent lunches.

Drinking

You'll find the biggest concentration of bars along both banks of the Salzach River and the hippest around Gstättengasse and Anton-Neumayr-Platz.

TOP CHOICE **Augustiner Bräustübl** BREWPUB
(Augustinergasse 4-6; 3-11pm Mon-Fri, 2.30-11pm Sat & Sun) Who says monks can't enjoy themselves? This hillside complex of beer halls and gardens is not to be missed. The local monks' brew keeps the huge crowd of up to 2800 humming.

Republic BAR
(Anton-Neumayr-Platz 2; 8am-1am Sun-Thu, 8am-4am Fri & Sat) One of Salzburg's most happening haunts, with regular DJs and free events from tango on Sunday to salsa on Tuesday.

Humboldt Stub'n BAR
(Gstättengasse 4-6; ⌚10am-4am) A nail-studded Mozart punk guards this upbeat bar opposite Republic. Try a sickly Mozart cocktail (liqueur, cherry juice, cream and chocolate). Beers are €2.50 at Wednesday's student night.

Information

International Telephone Discount (Kaiserschützenstrasse 8; internet per hr €2; ⌚9am-8pm Mon-Sat, 1-8pm Sun) Cheap internet access and calls.

Main tourist office (☎889 87-330; www.salzburg.info; Mozartplatz 5; ⌚9am-7pm) Plenty of information about the city and its immediate surrounds. There's a ticket-booking agency in the same building.

Getting There & Away

AIR Low-cost airlines, including **Ryanair** (www.ryanair.com) and **EasyJet** (www.easyjet.com), serve **Salzburg airport** (www.salzburg-airport.com), 4km west of the city centre.

BUS Buses depart from just outside the Hauptbahnhof on Südtiroler Platz. Hourly buses leave for the Salzkammergut, including Bad Ischl (€9.10, 1½ hours) and St Wolfgang (€8.40, 1¾ hours). For online timetables see www.svv.at (in German).

TRAIN Fast trains leave for Vienna (€47.50, three hours) via Linz (€22, 1¼ hours) hourly. The express service to Klagenfurt (€35.50, three hours) goes via Villach. The quickest way to Innsbruck (€37.80, two hours) is by the 'corridor' train through Germany via Kufstein; trains depart at least every two hours. There are trains every hour or so to Munich (€34).

Getting Around

Bus 2 runs from the Hauptbahnhof to the airport (€2.10, 19 minutes).

Bus drivers sell single tickets for €2.10. Other tickets, including day passes (€5), must be bought from the automatic machines at stops or *Tabak* shops.

Top Bike (2hr/4hr/day €6/10/15, 20% discount with all train tickets) rents bikes from just outside the train station.

AROUND SALZBURG

Schloss Hellbrunn

A prince-archbishop with a wicked sense of humour, Markus Sittikus built Italianate **Schloss Hellbrunn** (www.hellbrunn.at; Fürstenweg 37; admission €9.50; ⌚9am-5.30pm, to 9pm Jul & Aug) as a 17th-century summer palace and an escape from his Residenz functions.

The ingenious trick fountains and water-powered figures are the big draw. When the tour guides set them off, expect to get wet! Admission includes entry to the baroque palace. The rest of the sculpture-dotted gardens are free to visit. Look out for the *Sound of Music* pavilion of 'Sixteen Going on Seventeen' fame.

Bus 25 runs to Hellbrunn, 4.5km south of Salzburg, every 20 minutes from Rudolfskai in the Altstadt.

Werfen

☎06468 / POP 3020

More than 1000m above Werfen in the Tennengebirge mountains is **Eisriesenwelt** (www.eisriesenwelt.at; admission €8.50, with cable car €19; ⌚9am-3.30pm May-Oct). Billed as the world's largest accessible ice caves, this glittering ice empire is a once-seen-never-forgotten experience. Wrap up warm for subzero temperatures. Well below the caves is **Burg Hohenwerfen** (admission €14; ⌚9am-5pm Apr-Oct), a formidable clifftop fortress dating from 1077.

Both the ice caves and fortress can be visited as a day trip from Salzburg if you start early (tour the caves first and be at the castle by 3pm for the falconry show), otherwise consult the **tourist office** (☎53 88; www.werfen.at; Markt 24; ⌚9am-noon & 2-5pm Mon-Fri) for accommodation options.

Werfen can be reached from Salzburg on the A10/E55 motorway or by train (€9.20, 40 minutes). In summer, minibuses (€2.90) run every 25 minutes between Eisriesenstrasse in Werfen and the car park, a 20-minute walk from the cable car to Eisriesenwelt.

SALZKAMMERGUT

The Salzkammergut is Austria's Lake District. An idyllic spot for hiking, water sports and even winter skiing, it boasts salt mines (for which it's named), ice caves, mountains and more than 80 lakes.

Bad Ischl is the region's transport hub, but Hallstatt is its true jewel. For info visit **Salzkammergut Touristik** (☎240 00-0; www.salzkammergut.co.at; Götzstrasse 12, Bad Ischl; ⌚9am-8pm, closed Sun Oct-Mar). The Salzkammergut Card (€4.90, available May to October) provides a 25% discount on sights, ferries, cable cars and some buses.

Hallstatt

06134 / POP 840

With pastel-hued homes and towering mountains on either side of a glassy lake, Hallstatt is like some kind of greeting card for tranquillity. Now a Unesco World Heritage site, Hallstatt was settled 4500 years ago and over 2000 graves haven been discovered in the area.

Sights

Hallstatt's trophy sight is the **Salzbergwerk** (Salt Mine; funicular return & tour €24, tour only €12; 9.30am-4.30pm, closed mid-Oct–Apr), where the fully preserved body of a prehistoric miner was found in 1734 (today he is known as the 'Man in Salt'). A tour revolves around his fate, with an underground railway and miners' slides to an illuminated subterranean salt lake.

Equally unmissable is the macabre yet beautiful **Beinhaus** (Bone House; Kirchenweg 40; admission €1; 10am-6pm May-Oct) behind Hallstatt's parish church. It contains rows of stacked skulls painted with flowery designs and the names of the deceased. The old Celtic pagan custom of mass burial has been practised here since 1600 (mainly due to the lack of graveyard space), and the last skull in the collection was added in 1995.

Sleeping & Eating

Rooms fill quickly in summer, so book ahead, arrive early, or go straight to the tourist office for help finding something, either in Hallstatt or Lahn (the southern part of the village).

Bräugasthof am Hallstätter See GUEST HOUSE **€€**
(8221; www.brauhaus lobisser.com, in German; Seestrasse 120; s €49-55, d €98, tr €130-135) A central, friendly guest house with a lakeside restaurant (mains €14 to €19) serving trout and other local specialities.

Gasthaus Mühle HOSTEL **€**
(8318; www.hallstatturlaub.at, in German; Kirchenweg 36; dm €23; closed Tue & Nov) This hostel with decent (if basic) dorms is handily situated on the way up to the church.

Campingplatz Klausner-Höll CAMPING GROUND **€**
(8322; www.camping.hallstatt.net, in German; Lahnstrasse 7; campsite, per adult/tent/car €7/4/3; mid-Apr–mid-Oct; P) This campsite is conveniently located south of the centre.

Balthazar im Rudolfsturm CAFE, AUSTRIAN **€**
(Rudolfsturm; mains €10-13.50; 9am-6pm May-Oct) Perched at 855m above Hallstatt, and accessible by cable car, this restaurant has the most spectacular terrace for enjoying Austrian cuisine and lake views.

WORTH A TRIP

OBERTRAUN

Near to Hallstatt, Obertraun has the intriguing **Dachstein Rieseneishöhle** (www.dachsteinwelterbe.at; cable car return plus 1 cave €27, 1 cave only €10.80). The caves are millions of years old and extend into the mountain for almost 80km in places.

From Obertraun it's also possible to catch a cable car to **Krippenstein** (return €23; closed mid-Oct–Nov & Easter–mid-May), where you'll find the freaky **5Fingers viewing platform**, which protrudes out over a sheer cliff face – it's not for sufferers of vertigo.

Information

Turn left from the ferry to reach the **tourist office** (8208; www.dachstein-salzkammergut.at; Seestrasse 169; 9am-6pm Mon-Fri, 9am-4pm Sat, 9am-noon Sun, closed Sat & Sun Sep-Jun). It stocks the free leisure map of lakeside towns and hiking and cycling trails.

Getting There & Around

BUS Eight to 10 daily buses connect Hallstatt (Lahn) with Obertraun (€1.90, eight minutes).

BOAT The last ferry connection leaves Hallstatt train station at 6.55pm (€2.20, 10 minutes). Ferry excursions from mid-July to August do the circuit of Hallstatt Lahn via Hallstatt Markt, Obersee, Untersee and Steeg return (€9.50, 1½ hours) three times daily.

TRAIN Hallstatt train station, on a branch line connecting the Salzburg–Linz and Bischofshofen–Graz lines, is across the lake. The boat service from there to the village coincides with train arrivals. About a dozen trains daily connect Hallstatt and Bad Ischl (€3.60, 22 minutes).

TIROL

With converging mountain ranges behind lofty pastures and tranquil meadows, Tirol (also Tyrol) captures a quintessential Alpine panoramic view. Occupying a central position is Innsbruck, the region's jewel, while in the northeast and southwest are superb ski resorts. In the southeast, separated somewhat from the main state since part of south Tirol was ceded to Italy at the end of WWI, lies the protected natural landscape of the Hohe Tauern National Park. The latter is home to 30 peaks over 3000m, including the country's highest, Grossglockner (3797m).

Innsbruck

☎0512 / POP 118,000

Tirol's capital is a sight to behold. The mountains are so close that, within 25 minutes, it's possible to travel from the heart of the city (with an altitude of 574m) to over 2000m above sea level. Summer and winter outdoor activities abound, and it's understandable why some visitors only take a peek at Innsbruck proper before heading for the hills. But to do so is a shame, for Innsbruck has its own share of gems, including an authentic medieval Altstadt (old town), inventive architecture and vibrant, student-driven nightlife.

Sights

Innsbruck's atmospheric, medieval Altstadt is ideal for a lazy stroll. Many of the sights listed below close an hour or two earlier in winter.

Innsbruck Altstadt

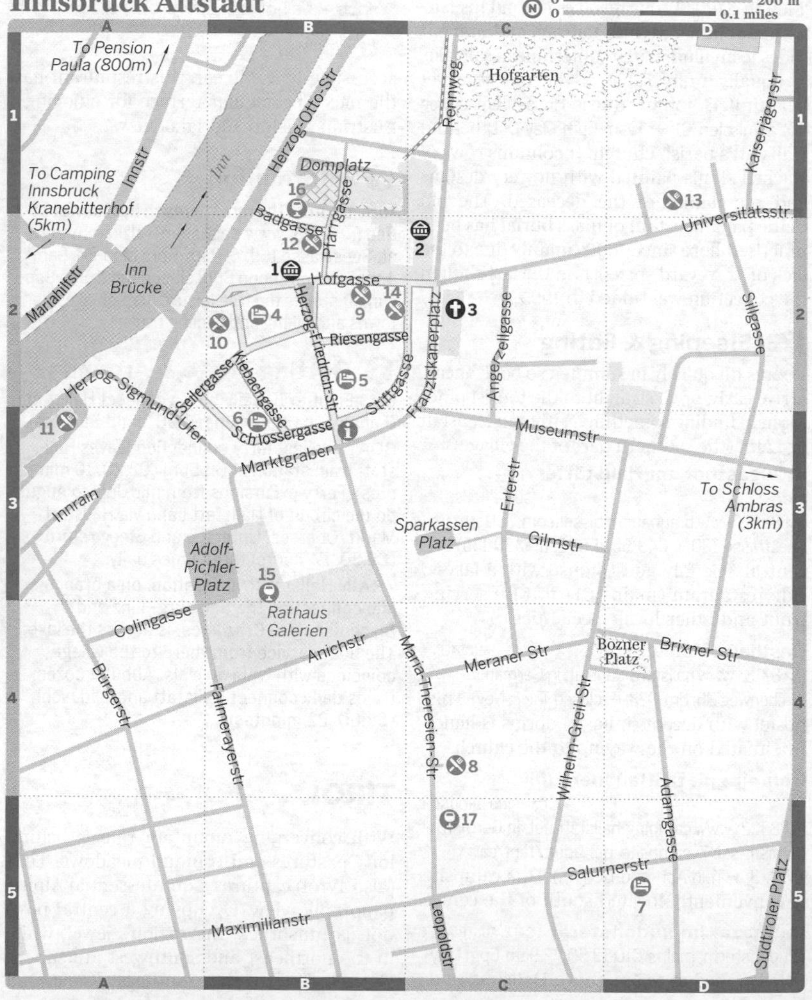

TOP CHOICE **Goldenes Dachl & Museum** MUSEUM

(Golden Roof; Herzog-Friedrich-Strasse 15; admission €4; ⏲10am-5pm, closed Mon Oct-Apr) Innsbruck's golden wonder is this Gothic oriel, built for Emperor Maximilian I and glittering with 2657 fire-gilt copper tiles. An audio guide whizzes you through the history in the museum.

Hofkirche & Volkskunstmuseum CHURCH, MUSEUM

(www.tiroler-landesmuseum.at; Universitätstrasse; combined ticket €8; ⏲Hofkirche 9am-5pm Mon-Sat, 12.30-5pm Sun, Volkskunstmuseum 9am-5pm) The 16th-century Hofkirche is one of Europe's finest royal court churches. Top billing goes to the empty **sarcophagus** of Emperor Maximilian I (1459–1519), guarded by 28 giant bronze figures.

Next door the Volkskunst Museum (Folk Art Museum) houses Tyrolean folk art from hand-carved sleighs to Christmas cribs.

Hofburg PALACE

(Imperial Palace; www.hofburg-innsbruck.at; Rennweg 1; admission €8; ⏲9am-5pm) Empress Maria Theresa gave this Habsburg palace a total baroque makeover in the 16th century. The highlight of the state apartments is the lavishly frescoed **Riesensaal** (Giant's Hall). Tucked behind the palace is the **Hofgarten** (admission free; ⏲daylight hrs), an attractive garden for a botanical stroll.

Bergisel SKI JUMP

(www.bergisel.info; admission €8.50; ⏲10am-6pm) This eye-catching ski jump was designed by much-lauded Iraqi architect Zaha Hadid. It's 455 steps, or a two-minute funicular ride, to the 50m-high **viewing platform**, with a breathtaking panorama of the Nordkette range, Inn Valley and Innsbruck. Bus 4143 and line TS run from the Hauptbahnhof to Bergisel.

Schloss Ambras CASTLE

(www.khm.at/ambras; Schlossstrasse 20; admission €10; ⏲10am-5pm) A grand fortress turned Renaissance palace. Don't miss the dazzling armour collection and the gallery's Velázquez and van Dyck originals. It's free to visit the manicured **gardens** (⏲6am-8pm).

Activities

Anyone who loves the great outdoors will be itching to head up into the Alps in Innsbruck. Zaha Hadid's space-age **Nordketten Bahnen** (www.nordkette.com; ⏲every 15min 8.30am-5.30pm) funicular whizzes you from the Congress Centre to the slopes in just 25 minutes. Tickets cost €14.10/23.40 one way/return to Seegrube and €15.60/26 to Hafelekar. Both afford superb views and appeal to walkers and mountain bikers.

Inntour (www.inntour.com; Leopoldstrasse 4; ⏲9am-6.30pm Mon-Fri, 9am-5pm Sat) is a one-stop adrenalin shop, taking you canyoning (€75), tandem paragliding (€95), white-water rafting (€45) and bungee jumping (€140) from the 192m Europabrücke (Europe Bridge).

Innsbruck is the gateway to the massive **Olympia SkiWorld Innsbruck** (www.ski-innsbruck.at) ski arena, covering nine surrounding resorts and 282km of slopes to test all abilities. The most central place to pound powder is the **Nordpark** (⏲cable cars every 15min 8am-7pm). A three-/seven-day Innsbruck Glacier Ski Pass covering all areas costs €105/200; ski buses are free to anyone with an Innsbruck Card.

Sleeping

The tourist office has lists of private rooms costing between €20 and €40 per person.

Innsbruck

Sights

1 Goldenes Dachl & Museum ... B2
2 Hofburg ... C2
3 Hofkirche ... C2
Volkskunst Museum ... (see 3)

Sleeping

4 Goldener Adler ... B2
5 Hotel Weisses Kreuz ... B2
6 Nepomuks ... B3
7 Pension Stoi ... D5

Eating

Cafe Munding ... (see 6)
8 Chez Nico ... C4
9 Kröll ... B2
10 Mamma Mia ... B2
11 Markthalle ... A3
12 s'Culinarium ... B2
13 Sixty Twenty ... D1
14 s'Speckladele ... B2

Drinking

15 360° ... B3
16 Moustache ... B1
17 Thereisenbräu ... C5

DON'T MISS

FOOTLOOSE FOR FREE

From late May to October, Innsbruck Information arranges daily **guided hikes**, from sunrise walks to lantern-lit strolls, free to those with a complimentary Club Innsbruck Card. Pop into the tourist office to register and browse the program.

TOP CHOICE Nepomuks HOSTEL €
(☎584 118; www.nepomuks.at; Kiebachgasse 16; dm/d €22/54;) Could this be backpacker heaven? Nepomuks sure comes close, with its Altstadt location, well-stocked kitchen and high-ceilinged dorms with homely touches like CD players. The delicious breakfast in attached Café Munding, with home-made pastries, jam and fresh-roasted coffee, gets your day off to a grand start.

Hotel Weisses Kreuz HISTORIC HOTEL €€
(☎594 79; www.weisseskreuz.at; Herzog-Friedrich-Strasse 31; s €36-72, d €100-132; P@) Beneath the Altstadt's arcades, this atmospheric 500-year-old hotel has played host to famous guests, including a 13-year-old Mozart. It remains comfortable to this day.

Pension Paula GUEST HOUSE €
(☎292 262; www.pensionpaula.at; Weiherburggasse 15; s/d €39/62; P) Nestled in the hills above Innsbruck and with great city views, this family-run pension has super-clean, homely rooms (most with balcony). It's 1km north of the Altstadt, near the Alpenzoo.

Goldener Adler HISTORIC HOTEL €€
(☎571 111; www.goldeneradler.com; Herzog-Friedrich-Strasse 6; s/d €92/135; P) Since opening in 1390, the grand Goldener Adler has welcomed kings, queens and Salzburg's two biggest exports: Mozart and Mrs Von Trapp. Rooms are elegant with gold drapes and squeaky-clean marble bathrooms.

Pension Stoi GUEST HOUSE €
(☎585 434; www.pensionstoi.at, in German; Salurnerstrasse 7; s/d/tr/q €44/69/85/98; P) A central, family-run guest house occupying an art nouveau villa with bright, high-ceilinged rooms. Breakfast not included.

Camping Innsbruck Kranebitterhof CAMPING GROUND €
(Herzog-Friedrich-Strasse 21; per person €3; ⊙10am-8pm) Modern camping ground west of town, with Alpine views and a pizzeria. Bus line O stops nearby or you can cycle along the River Inn.

Eating

Self-caterers will find supermarkets such as Hofer and Billa on Museumstrasse. For cheap eats, try student-focused Universitätsstrasse, or pop across the river to Innstrasse for take-aways.

TOP CHOICE Chez Nico VEGETARIAN €€
(☎586 398; www.chez-nico.at; Maria-Theresien-Strasse 49; lunch €12.50, 7-course menu €45; ⊙lunch Tue-Fri, dinner Tue-Sat) Parisian chef Nico cooks seasonal vegetarian delights like chanterelle-apricot goulash and porcini-sage ravioli at this intimate bistro.

Mamma Mia PIZZA €
(☎562 902; Kiebachgasse 2; mains €5-8) This cheerful Italian restaurant serves big helpings of pizza and pasta in the heart of the Altstadt. Its shady terrace is perfect in summer.

Cafe Munding CAFE €
(☎584 118; Kiebachgasse 16; cake €2-4; ⊙8am-8pm) Divine cakes, pastries and home-roasted coffee.

Kröll STRUDEL €
(Hofgasse 6; snacks €3-4.50; ⊙9am-midnight) This hole-in-the-wall cafe's strudels include rhubarb, poppy, feta and plum. The fresh juices pack a vitamin punch.

Drinking

Moustache BAR
(www.cafe-moustache.at, in German; Herzog-Otto-Strasse 8; ⊙11am-2am Tue-Sun) Playing spot-the-moustache (Einstein, Charlie Chaplin and co) is the preferred pastime at this retro newcomer. It has a terrace on Domplatz and Club Aftershave in the basement.

Hofgarten Café BAR
(Rennweg 6a; ⊙11am-2am Tue-Thu, to 4am Fri-Sun) DJs spin at this tree-shaded beer garden and star-studded pavilion, with a happening line-up of events.

Sixty Twenty BAR
(Universitätsstrasse 15; ⊙11am-2am Mon-Thu, 5pm-2am Fri, 7pm-2am Sat & Sun) This retro-chic lounge is student central. Come for half-price drinks on Monday, hip hop on Thursday and vodka-fuelled Saturday.

Theresienbräu PUB
(Maria-Theresien-Strasse 53; ⊙10am-1am Mon-Wed, 10am-2am Thu-Sat, 10am-midnight Sun) A

lively microbrewery with a big beer garden for quaffing a cold one.

360° BAR

(Rathaus Galerien; ⏲10am-1am Mon-Sat) Drink in 360-degree views of the city and Alps from the balcony of this circular bar.

Information

Innsbruck Information (☎535 60; www.innsbruck.info; Burggraben 3; ⏲9am-6pm) Main tourist office with truckloads of info on the city and surrounds. Sells ski passes, public-transport tickets and city maps (€1), and will book accommodation.

International Telephone Discount (Südtirolerplatz 1; internet access per hr €2.50; ⏲9am-9pm Mon-Sat, 10am-9pm Sun) Near the train station. Cheap phone calls as well.

Getting There & Away

AIR EasyJet flies to **Innsbruck Airport** (www.innsbruck-airport.com), 4km west of the city centre.

CAR & MOTORCYCLE Heading south by car through the Brenner Pass to Italy, you'll hit the A13 toll road (€8). Toll-free Hwy 182 follows the same route, although it is less scenic.

TRAIN Fast trains depart every two hours for Bregenz (€31.30, 2¾ hours), Salzburg (€37.80, two hours), Kitzbühel (€17.60, 1¾ hours) and Munich (€37, two hours). Six daily trains head for Lienz (€31.20, three to five hours); some pass through Italy while others take the long way round via Salzburgerland.

Getting Around

Single bus and tram tickets cost €1.80 (from the driver; valid upon issue). A 24-hour ticket is €4.10.

DON'T MISS

PICNIC GOODIES

Innsbruck's glorious parks, promenades and mountains make for some highly scenic picnic spots. Here are our favourite places for assembling a packed lunch:

» **s'Speckladele** (Stiftgasse 4; ⏲9am-1pm & 2-6pm Tue-Fri, 9am-3pm Sat) This hole-in-the-wall shop has been doing a brisk trade in regional sausages, hams and speck made from 'happy pigs' for the past 60 years. Mini *Teufel* sausages with a chilli kick are the must-try.

» **s'Culinarium** (Pfarrgasse 1; ⏲10am-6pm Mon-Fri, 3-6pm Sat) Herby Signor will help you pick an excellent bottle of Austrian wine at his shop-cum-bar.

» **Markthalle** (www.markthalle-innsbruck.at; Innrain; ⏲7am-6.30pm Mon-Fri, 7am-1pm Sat) Fresh-baked bread, Tirolean cheese, organic fruit, smoked ham and salami – it's all under one roof at this riverside covered market.

Kitzbühel

☎05356 / POP 8450

Kitzbühel began life in the 16th century as a silver- and copper- mining town and today continues to preserve a charming medieval centre despite its other persona – as a fashionable and prosperous winter resort.

It's renowned for its excellent slopes and white-knuckle Hahnenkamm downhill ski race in January. A one-day ski pass costs €41.50, though some pensions and hotels offer reductions before mid-December or after mid-March. In summer the **tourist office** (☎666 60; www.kitzbuehel.com; Hinterstadt 18; ⏲8.30am-6pm Mon-Wed, 8.30am-7.30pm Thu-Fri, 9am-6pm Sat, 10am-noon & 4-6pm Sun, closed Sun btwn seasons) offers free guided hiking tours for guests staying in town. It also has loads of info in English and a 24-hour accommodation board.

Snowbunny's Hostel (☎067-6794 0233; www.snowbunnys.co.uk; Bichlstrasse 30; dm/d €25/60; @📶) is a friendly, relaxed hostel with a communal lounge, spacious and bright rooms and DIY breakfast. Family-run **Pension Kometer** (☎622 89; Gerbergasse 7; www.pension-kometer.com; s/d €57/94; Ⓟ) has sparklingly clean rooms, a relaxed lounge and generous breakfasts.

Hosteria (☎753 02; Alf Petzoldweg 2; mains €8-16) does great wood-fired pizzas, while the vaulted **Huberbräu Stüberl** (☎656 77; Vorderstadt 18; mains €7-13) rolls out hearty Austrian fare. For self-caterers, there's a **Spar** (Bichlstrasse 22) supermarket.

The main train station is 1km north of central Vorderstadt. Trains run frequently from Kitzbühel to Innsbruck (€17.60, 1½ hours) and Salzburg (€25.60, 2½ hours). For Kufstein (€9.20, one hour), change at Wörgl.

It's quicker and cheaper to reach Lienz by bus (€13.80, two hours, twice daily).

Lienz

☎04852 / POP 11,950

With the jagged Dolomite mountain ranges crowding its southern skyline, the capital of east Tirol is a scenic staging point for travels through the Hohe Tauern National Park.

Staff at the **tourist office** (☎050-212 400; www.stadt-lienz.at; Europaplatz 1; ⏲8am-6pm Mon-Fri, 9am-noon & 5-7pm Sat) will find rooms free of charge, or you can use the free telephone outside.

Lienz' biggest crowd-puller is medieval fortress **Schloss Bruck** (Schlossberg 1; admission €7.50; ⏲10am-6pm mid-May–late Oct), with a peerless collection of Albin Egger-Lienz paintings. Dip into Lienz's Roman past at archaeological site **Aguntum** (www.aguntum.info, in German; Stribach 97; admission €5; ⏲9.30am-6pm, shorter hrs shoulder season, closed Nov–mid-Apr).

A €36 day pass covers downhill skiing, but the area is more renowned for its cross-country skiing; Lienz fills up for the annual Dolomitenlauf cross-country skiing race in mid-January. The Dolomites make for highly scenic hiking in summer, with cable cars rising to Hochstein (return €13) and Zettersfeld (€10).

A 20-minute walk south of town is well-equipped **Camping Falken** (☎0664-4107973; www.camping-falken.com; Eichholz 7; campsites per adult/tent €6.50/8.50; ⏲mid-Dec–mid-Oct; 📶), affording Dolomite views. Old-world **Altstadthotel Eck** (☎647 85; Hauptplatz 20; s/d €42/74) is a central cheapie. Check with the tourist office for B&B options.

Hearty east Tirolean flavours are served in the vaulted surrounds of hilltop **Kirchenwirt** (☎625 00; Pfarrgasse 7; mains €8.50-16; ⏲9am-1am) and central **Adlerstüberl Restaurant** (☎625 50; Andrä-Kranz-Gasse 7; mains €7.50-13.50). For self-caterers, supermarkets include a **Spar** (Tiroler Strasse 23).

Except for the 'corridor' route through Italy to Innsbruck (€31.20, four hours), trains to the rest of Austria connect via Spittal Millstättersee to the east, including hourly trains to Salzburg (€33.70, 3½ hours). To head south by car, you must first divert west or east along Hwy 100.

Hohe Tauern National Park

The largest national park in the Alps, Hohe Tauern (1786 sq km) is a hiking paradise. The park contains **Grossglockner** (3797m), Austria's highest mountain, which towers over the 8km-long Pasterze Glacier. The best viewing point is **Franz Josefs Höhe** (2369m), reached from Lienz by bus between late June and late September (€10.30, 1½ hours).

WORTH A TRIP

KRIMML FALLS

The thunderous, three-tier **Krimml Falls** (www.wasserfaelle-krimml.at; adult €2, Dec-Apr free; ⏲ticket office 8am-6pm mid-Apr–late Oct) is Europe's highest waterfall at 380m, and one of Austria's most unforgettable sights. The pretty Alpine village of Krimml has a handful of places to sleep and eat – contact the **tourist office** (☎06564 72 39; www.krimml.at; Oberkrimml 37; ⏲8am-noon & 2.30-6pm Mon-Fri, 8.30-10.30am & 4.30-6pm Sat) for more information.

Krimml is on Hwy 168 (which becomes Hwy 165). Buses run year-round from Krimml to Zell am See (€8.40, 1¼ hours, hourly).

Buses go via **Heiligenblut**, famous for its 15th-century pilgrimage church. Here the **tourist office** (☎20 01; www.heiligenblut.at, in German; Hof 4; ⏲9am-6pm Mon-Fri, 9am-noon & 4-6pm Sat) can advise on guided ranger hikes, rock climbing and skiing. The village also has a spick-and-span **Jugendherberge** (☎22 59; www.oejhv.or.at; Hof 36; dm/s/d €20/28/48; 🅿).

The 48km **Grossglockner Road** (Hwy 107; www.grossglockner.at; car/motorcycle €28/18; ⏲May-Oct) through the park is one of Europe's greatest Alpine drives. The road swings giddily around 36 switchbacks, passing jewel-coloured lakes, forested slopes and wondrous glaciers.

VORARLBERG

Alluringly beautiful, Austria's most westerly region is an aesthetic mix of mountains, hills and valleys. Angling down from the Alps to the shores of Lake Constance (Bodensee), it provides a convenient gateway to Germany, Liechtenstein or Switzerland.

Vorarlberg's capital, **Bregenz** (www.bregenz.ws, in German), sits prettily on the shores of Lake Constance and holds the **Bregenzer Festspiele** (www.bregenzerfestspiele.com) in July/August, when opera is performed on a floating stage on the lake. The real action here, though, is in the Arlberg region, shared by Vorarlberg and neighbouring Tirol. Some of the best skiing – not to mention après-ski partying – is in **St Anton am Arlberg**, where challenging medium-to-advanced runs criss-cross the wild Arlberg range. The centrally located **tourist office** (☎05446 226 90; www.stantonamarlberg.com; Arlberg Haus; ⌚8.30am-7pm Mon-Fri, 9am-6pm Sat, 9am-noon & 3-5pm Sun) has information on accommodation, activities and maps.

A ski pass covering all 280km of slopes and 84 ski lifts in the Arlberg region costs €44.50/239 for one/seven days in the winter high season.

Accommodation is mainly in small B&Bs. Many budget places (prices from €30 per person) are booked months in advance.

St Anton is on the main railway route between Bregenz (€16.90, 1½ hours) and Innsbruck (€20, 1¼ hours). It's close to the eastern entrance of the Arlberg Tunnel, the toll road connecting Vorarlberg and Tirol (€8.50).

WORTH A TRIP

BREGENZERWALD

Only a few kilometres southeast of Bregenz, the forests, velvet-green pastures and limestone peaks of the Bregenzerwald unfold. In summer this is a glorious place to spend a few days hiking and filling up on all manner of homemade cheeses in alpine dairies. Winter brings plenty of snow, and the area is noted for its downhill and cross-country skiing.

The **Bregenzerwald tourist office** (☎05512-23 65; www.bregenzerwald.at; Impulszentrum 1135, Egg; ⌚9am-5pm Mon-Fri, 8am-1pm Sat & Sun) has information on the region, and cheese-lovers can consult www.kaesestrasse.at for the low-down on the **Cheese Road**. From Bregenz, buses travel to Bezau (€4.40, one hour), one of the region's main villages, at least every two hours; however, this offbeat region is easier to explore by car.

UNDERSTAND AUSTRIA

History

Austria has been a galvanic force in shaping Europe's history. This little landlocked country of 8.2 million people was once the epicentre of the mighty Habsburg empire and, in the 20th century, a pivotal player in the outbreak of WWI.

Like so many European countries, Austria has experienced invasions and struggles since time immemorial. There are traces of human occupation since the ice age, but it was the Celts who made the first substantial mark on Austria around 450 BC. The Romans followed 400 years later, who in turn were followed by Bavarians, and, in 1278, the House of Habsburg took control of the country by defeating the head of the Bavarian royalty.

For centuries the Habsburgs used strategic marriages to maintain their hold over a territory that encompassed much of central and Eastern Europe and, for a period, even Germany.

The 16th and 17th centuries saw the Ottoman threat reach the gates of Vienna, and in 1805 Napoleon defeated Austria at Austerlitz. Austrian chancellor Metternich cleverly reconsolidated Austria's power in 1815 after Waterloo, but the loss of the 1866 Austro-Prussian War, and the creation of the Austro-Hungarian empire in 1867, diminished the Habsburgs' influence in Europe.

However, these setbacks pale beside Archduke Franz Ferdinand's assassination by Slavic separatists in Sarajevo on 28 June 1914. When his uncle, the Austro-Hungarian emperor Franz Josef, declared war on Serbia in response, the ensuing Great War (WWI) would prove the Habsburgs' downfall. The republic of Austria was formed in 1918.

WWII & Postwar Austria

During the 1930s Nazis began to influence Austrian politics and by 1938 the recession-hit country was ripe for the picking. Invading German troops met little resistance and Hitler was greeted on Heldenplatz as a hero by 200,000 Viennese.

Austria was heavily bombed during WWII, but the country recovered well, largely through the Marshall Plan and sound political and economic decisions (excluding its foray with the far-right Freedom Party and its controversial leader, Jörg Haider, in the '90s). Austria has maintained a neutral stance since 1955, been home to a number of international organisations, including the UN, since 1979 and joined the EU in 1995.

Arts

Beethoven, Brahms, Haydn, Mozart, Schubert and other European composers were drawn to Vienna by the Habsburgs' generous patronage during the 18th and 19th centuries.

BAROQUE MASTERPIECES

Thanks to the Habsburg monarchy and its obsession with pomp and splendour, Austria is packed with high-calibre architecture. It reached giddy heights of opulence during the baroque era of the late 17th and early 18th century. Look out for the Karlskirche (Vienna), Dom (Salzburg), Hofburg (Innsbruck), Schloss Schönbrunn (Vienna) and Stift Melk (Melk).

The waltz originated in this city and was perfected by Johann Strauss junior (1825–99).

In the early 20th century Vienna was also a city of design and painting. The Vienna Secessionist movement, the local equivalent of art nouveau *(Jugendstil),* created such talents as artist Gustav Klimt and architect Otto Wagner. Expressionist painters Egon Schiele and Oskar Kokoschka and modernist architect Adolf Loos followed further into the century.

Today Austria's fine musical tradition has moved in the wholly different direction of chilled, eclectic electronica and dub lounge. Going a bit deeper into the underground, the duo Attwenger (www.attwenger.at) has a large following for its music with flavours of folk, hip hop and trance.

Meanwhile, expert film director Michael Haneke has also been creating a splash with his controversial *Funny Games* (1997 and remade by Haneke in the USA in 2007) and the twisted romance of the much-lauded *The Piano Teacher* (2001).

Food & Drink

Beyond the traditional restaurant, *Gasthaus* or *Gasthof,* you'll find coffee houses serving a handful of light or classic dishes such as goulash, ethnic eat-in and takeaway joints and often corner Italian pizzerias. Solid Austrian fare is on the menu in Vienna's homely, good-value inns called *Beisln* (from the Yiddish word for 'little houses'). In the wine-growing regions rustic *Heurigen* (wine taverns) sell wine directly from their own premises and food is available buffet-style. They open on a roster so pick up the local *Heurigenkalendar* (Heurigen calendar) from the tourist office.

For cheap food, try *Mensen* (university canteens). Another money-saving trick is to make lunch the main meal of the day, as many Austrians do; many restaurants provide a good-value *Tagesteller* or *Tagesmenu* (set meal) at this time. You can assemble your own picnic at local farmers markets, where the freshest of produce is sold.

Price ranges for restaurants listed in this chapter are indicated by the following:

€€€ more than €30

€€ €15 to €30

€ less than €15

Regional & Seasonal

The regional and seasonal delights of the Austrian table go way beyond Wiener schnitzel and *Sacher Torte.* In Lower Austria, fresh game and beef are washed down with quality red and white wines or tangy cider from the Mostviertel. Try healthy, nutty pumpkin oil in Styria, freshwater fish in Carinthia and dumplings *(knödel),* both sweet and savoury, in Upper Austria and Salzburgerland. *Heumilchkäse* (hay-milk cheese) from Vorarlberg and Tirol's hearty *Gröstl* (a fry-up from leftover potatoes, pork and onions) are other regional specialities.

SURVIVAL GUIDE

Directory A–Z

Accommodation

Reservations are recommended at Christmas and Easter, during summer in cities, and winter at alpine resorts.

In mountain resorts, high-season prices can be up to double the prices charged in the low season (May to June and October to November). In other towns, the difference may be 10% or less.

In some resorts (not often in cities) a *Gästekarte* (guest card) is issued if you stay overnight, which offers discounts on things such as cable cars and admission.

Hostels and private rooms generally cost from €15 to €20. If you want a break from dorms, private rooms generally cost €15 to €30 per person. Ask the tourist office or look out for *Zimmer frei* (rooms vacant) signs.

Accommodation prices in this chapter are for the high summer season (April to October), and include breakfast unless otherwise stated. We have used the following price ranges for accommodation.

€€€ more than €200

€€ €80 to €200

€ less than €80

Some useful websites:

Österreichischer Alpenverein (Austrian Alpine Club; www.alpenverein.at, in German) Has a list of mountain huts for overnight stays and details on long-distance hikes.

Österreichischer Camping Club (Austrian Camping Club; www.campingclub.at, in German) Search for campsites by region.

Österreichischer Jugendherbergsverband (www.oejhv.or.at) Find HI hotels online.

Activities

Opportunities for hiking and mountaineering are boundless in Tirol, Salzburgerland and the Hohe Tauern National Park, all of which have extensive alpine-hut networks (see www.alpenverein.at). Names such as St Anton, Kitzbühel and Mayrhofen fire the imagination of serious skiers, but you may find cheaper accommodation and lift passes in little-known resorts; visit www.austria.info for the low-down.

Business Hours

Banks 8am or 9am-3pm Mon-Fri, to 5.30pm Thu

Offices 8am-3.30pm, 4pm or 5pm Mon-Fri

Pubs & Bars Close anywhere between midnight and 4am

Post offices 8am-noon & 2-6pm Mon-Fri, 8am-noon Sat

Restaurants 11am-3pm, 7pm-midnight

Shops 9am-6.30pm Mon-Fri, 9am-5pm Sat

Supermarkets 9am-7pm or 8pm Mon-Sat

Discount Cards

Various regional discount cards are available, many covering a whole region or province. Some are free with an overnight stay. See destinations for details.

International Student Identity Cards (ISIC) and European Youth Cards (Euro<26; check www.euro26.org for discounts) will get you discounts at most museums, galleries and theatres.

See p96 for details of discount rail cards.

Embassies & Consulates

For a complete listing of embassies and consulates, look in the Austrian telephone book under *Botschaften* (embassies) or *Konsulate* (consulates).

Holidays

New Year's Day (Neujahr) 1 January

Epiphany (Heilige Drei Könige) 6 January

Easter Monday (Ostermontag) March/April

Labour Day (Tag der Arbeit) 1 May

Whit Monday (Pfingstmontag) 6th Monday after Easter

Ascension Day (Christi Himmelfahrt) 6th Thursday after Easter

Corpus Christi (Fronleichnam) 2nd Thursday after Whitsunday

Assumption (Maria Himmelfahrt) 15 August

National Day (Nationalfeiertag) 26 October

All Saints' Day (Allerheiligen) 1 November

Immaculate Conception (Mariä Empfängnis) 8 December

Christmas Day (Christfest) 25 December

St Stephen's Day (Stephanitag) 26 December

Language Courses

Many places, including some of Austria's universities, offer German courses, usually with the option of accommodation. Well-known course providers include the following:

Berlitz (www.berlitz.at) Offers intensive courses in Vienna, Klagenfurt, Linz and Graz.

Inlingua Sprachschule (www.inlingua.at) Courses run for a minimum of two weeks and individual tuition is available. Offices in Linz, Graz, Salzburg, Innsbruck, Klagenfurt and Vorarlberg.

Money

Austria's currency is the euro. An approximate 10% tip is expected in restaurants. Pay it directly to the server; don't leave it on the table.

Telephone

Austria's country code is ☎43. Area codes begin with 0 (eg 01 for Vienna). Drop this when calling from outside Austria.

Austrian mobile phones (*Handy*) operate on GSM 900/1800, which is compatible with other European countries and Australia, but not with the North American GSM 1900 system. Roaming can get very expensive if your provider is outside the EU. Phone shops sell pre-paid SIM cards for about €10, which can be refilled at kiosks anywhere.

Public telephones take phonecards or coins; €0.20 is the minimum for a local call. Call centres are also widespread.

For international directory enquiries call ☎0900 11 88 77.

Tourist Information

Tourist offices, which are dispersed far and wide in Austria, tend to adjust their hours from one year to the next, so the hours listed in this chapter are a guide only.

The **Austrian National Tourist Office** (ANTO; www.austria.info) has a number of offices abroad. There is a comprehensive listing on the website.

Visas

Visas for stays of up to three months are not required for citizens of the EU, much of Eastern Europe, Israel, the USA, Canada, the majority of Central and South American nations, Japan, Korea, Malaysia, Singapore, Australia and New Zealand. All other nationalities require a visa; the Ministry of Foreign Affairs website at www.bmaa.gv.at has a list of Austrian embassies.

Getting There & Away

Air

Vienna is the main transport hub for Austria, but Graz, Linz, Klagenfurt, Salzburg and Innsbruck all receive international flights. Flights to these cities are often a cheaper option than those to the capital, as are flights to Airport Letisko (Bratislava Airport), 60km east of Vienna in Slovakia.

Among the low-cost airlines, Ryanair and Air Berlin fly to Graz, Innsbruck, Klagenfurt, Linz, Salzburg and Vienna (Ryanair flies to Bratislava for Vienna).

Following are the key international airports in Austria:

Airport Letisko Bratislava (☎421 2 3303 33 53; www.airportbratislava.sk) Serves Bratislava and has good transport connections to Vienna. Used by Ryanair.

Graz (☎0316-29 02-0; www.flughafen-graz.at)

Innsbruck (☎0512-225 25-0; www.innsbruck-airport.com)

Linz (☎07221-600-0; www.flughafen-linz.at)

Salzburg (☎0662-85800; www.salzburg-airport.com)

Vienna (☎01-7007 22233; www.viennaairport.com)

Bus & Train

Buses depart from Austria for as far afield as England, the Baltic countries, the Netherlands, Germany and Switzerland. Most significantly they provide access to Eastern European cities small and large – from the likes of Sofia and Warsaw to Banja Luka, Mostar and Sarajevo.

Bus services operated by **Eurolines** (www.eurolines.at) leave from Vienna and several regional cities.

The main train services in and out of the country from the west normally pass through Bregenz, Innsbruck or Salzburg en route to Vienna. Trains to Eastern Europe invariably leave from Südbahnhof in Vienna. Express services to Italy go via Innsbruck or Villach; trains to Slovenia are routed through Graz.

Car & Motorcycle

Proof of ownership of a private vehicle and a driver's licence should always be carried while driving. EU licences are accepted in Austria; all other nationalities require a German translation or an International Driving Permit (IDP). Third-party insurance is a minimum requirement and you'll need to carry proof of this in the form of a Green Card.

If you're a member of an automobile association, ask its staff about free reciprocal benefits offered by affiliated organisations in Europe.

River & Lake

Hydrofoils run to Bratislava and Budapest from Vienna. The **Danube Tourist Commission** (www.danube-river.org) has a country-by-country list of operators and agents who can book tours.

Getting Around

Air

Austrian Airlines (www.austrian.com) and **Welcome Air** (www.welcomeair.at) operate regular internal flights, but trains, buses or cars suffice in such a small country and offer wonderful scenery.

Bicycle

Most tourist boards have brochures on cycling facilities and routes. All cities have at least one bike shop that doubles as a rental centre; expect to pay around €10 to €15 per day.

You can take bicycles on any train with a bicycle symbol at the top of its timetable. A day ticket costs €5 for regional, €10 for national (Intercity) and €12 for international trains. You can't take bicycles on buses.

Boat

Services along the Danube are mainly pleasure cruises but provide a leisurely, scenic way of getting from A to B.

Bus

Rail routes are often complemented by Postbus services (the regular bus service in Austria), which usually depart from outside train stations. In remote regions, services are reduced on Saturday and often nonexistent on Sunday. For information call ☎0810 222 333 (6am to 8pm); or visit the website www.postbus.at.

Car & Motorcycle

A *Vignette* (motorway tax) is imposed on all autobahn – charges for cars/motorbikes are €7.90/4.50 for 10 days and €22.90/11.50 for two months. *Vignette* can be purchased at border crossings, petrol stations and *Tabak* shops. There are additional tolls (usually €2.50 to €10) for some mountain tunnels.

Speed limits are 50km/h in built-up areas, 130km/h on motorways and 100km/h on other roads.

All the multinational car-hire firms are here, but local agencies are usually cheaper. The minimum age for renting small cars is 19 years, and 25 for larger 'prestige' cars. Customers must have held a licence for at least a year. Many firms charge an additional fee for taking cars into Eastern Europe.

Crash helmets are compulsory for motorcyclists.

Train

Austria has a clean, efficient rail system, and if you use a discount card it's very inexpensive. The fares quoted in this chapter are for 2nd-class tickets.

ÖBB (☎05 17 17; www.oebb.at) is the main operator, supplemented with a handful of private lines. Tickets and timetables are available online.

RAIL PASSES

Eurail Austria Passes are available to non-EU residents; prices start at €112 for three days' unlimited 1st-class travel within one month. See www.eurail.com for all options that include Austria.

Interrail Passes are for European citizens and include One Country Pass Austria (3/4/6/8 days €172/191/252/290). See www.interrailnet.com for all options.

The Vorteilscard reduces fares by at least 45% and is valid for a year. Bring a photo and your passport or ID. It's available to anyone and costs €100/20/27 for adults 26 and over/adults under 26 years/seniors.

Belarus Беларусь

Includes »

Best Places to Eat

» Jules Verne, Brest (p103)

» Strawnya Talaka, Minsk (p100)

» Gurman, Minsk (p101)

Best Websites

» **Republic of Belarus** (www.belarus.by) Official website

» **Belarus Tourism** (www.eng.belarustourism.by)

» **Belarus Embassy in the UK** (www.uk.belembassy.org)

» **Belarus Tourist Information Portal** (www.belarustourist.minsk.by)

Why Go?

Eastern Europe's outcast, Belarus lies at the edge of the region and seems determined to avoid integration with the rest of the continent at all costs. Taking its lead from the old Soviet Union rather than the European Union, this pint-sized dictatorship may seem like a strange choice for travellers, but its isolation remains at the heart of its appeal.

While the rest of Eastern Europe has charged headlong into capitalism, Belarus allows the chance to visit a Europe with minimal advertising and no litter or graffiti. The country offers two excellent national parks and is home to Europe's largest mammal, the *zoobr* (European bison). While travellers will always be subject to curiosity, they'll also invariably be on the receiving end of extremely warm hospitality and genuine local welcome.

When to Go

Minsk

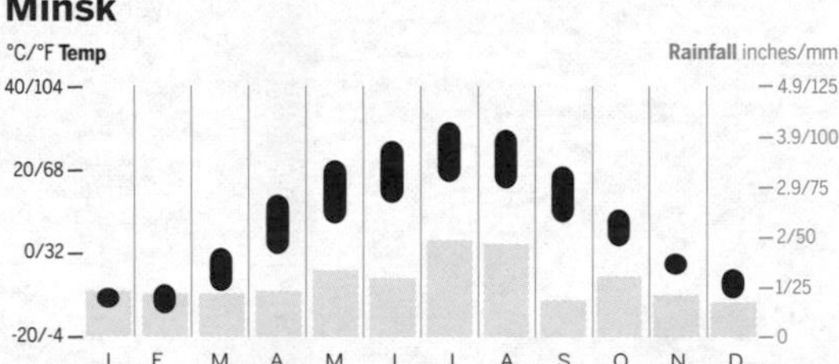

Mid-Jul–Aug Don't worry about high season: come here in summer to escape the crowds elsewhere.

Early–mid-Jul A fine time to enjoy a Belarusian festival or two.

Jun & Sep The weather is fine and there are few tourists.

Connections

Belarus has good overland links to all its neighbouring countries. Daily trains from Minsk serve Moscow, St Petersburg, Vilnius, Warsaw (via Terespol) and Kyiv. Bus services, which tend to be less comfortable, connect Minsk to Moscow, St Petersburg, Kyiv, Warsaw and Vilnius; Vitsebsk to Moscow and St Petersburg; and Brest to Terespol in Poland.

ITINERARIES

Three Days

Spend two days getting to know Minsk, whose Stalinist architecture belies a lively and friendly city, before taking a day trip to the charming Belarusian countryside.

One Week

Begin with two nights in Brest, where the dramatic Brest Fortress and a clutch of museums await, before heading to Minsk for a dose of history and imposing architecture, as well as spending a day or two exploring the countryside around the city.

Essential Food & Drink

» **Belavezhskaya** Bitter herbal alcoholic drink

» **Draniki** Potato pancakes, usually served with *smetana* (sour cream)

» **Kletsky** Dumplings stuffed with mushrooms, cheese or potato

» **Kolduni** Potato dumplings stuffed with meat

» **Manchanka** Pancakes served with a meaty gravy

AT A GLANCE

» **Currency** Belarusian rouble (BR)

» **Languages** Belarusian, Russian

» **Money** ATMs taking international cards widely available

» **Visas** Needed by almost everybody; see p104

Fast Facts

» **Area** 207,600 sq km

» **Capital** Minsk

» **Country code** ☎375

» **Emergency** Police ☎02; ambulance ☎03

Exchange Rates

Australia	A$1	BR3052
Canada	C$1	BR3081
euro zone	€1	BR4274
Japan	¥100	BR3736
New Zealand	NZ$1	BR2235
UK	UK£1	BR4911
USA	US$1	BR3025

Set Your Budget

» **Budget hotel room** BR70,000

» **Two-course evening meal** BR60,000

» **Museum entrance** BR2000

» **Beer (bottle)** BR1000

» **Minsk metro ticket** BR700

Gulf of Rīga
LATVIA
Rīga
Jelgava
Rēzekne
Daugavpils
Panevėžys
LITHUANIA
Kaunas
Vilnius
RUSSIA
Smolensk
Daugava (Zapadnaya Dvina)
Novopolatsk
Polatsk
Vitsebsk
Hlybokoye
Bjarezinski Biosphere Reserve
Orsha
Neris (Vilija)
Khatyn
Maladzechna
Barysau
Mahileu (Mogilev)
Krichev
Minsk
Zaslavl
1
3 Dudutki
Lida
Hrodna
4 Mir
Navahrudak (Novogrudok)
Dnipro (Dnieper)
Babrujsk
5 Nyasvizh
Białystok
Slonim
Baranavichy
Slutsk
Zhlobin
Svetlahorsk
Homel
Rechitsa
POLAND
Belevezhskaya Pushcha National Park
Terespol
Brest
2
Kobryn
Pinsk
Zhytkavichy
Turau
Pripyat
Kalinkavichy
Mazyr
Pripyatsky National Park
Chornobyl Exclusion Zone
Chernihiv
Chornobyl
Desna
UKRAINE
Lutsk
Rivne
Zhytomyr
Kyiv
Kyiv Reservoir
0 160 km
0 100 miles
A6 P133 P46 P18 P46 M3 M8 A141 P45 P28 M3 E30 E28 A101 M6 P11 P68 E28 P43 M8 M10 P43 P31 P136 E30 M10 P17

Belarus Highlights

1 Get under the skin of **Minsk** (p99), the national capital and showpiece of Stalinist architecture, and actually a very friendly and accessible city

2 Stroll through the mellow pedestrian streets of cosmopolitan Brest to the epic WWII memorial that is **Brest Fortress** (p102)

3 Enjoy life at a slow pace while visiting the charming farm-museum in bucolic **Dudutki** (p99)

4 See the fairy-tale 16th-century **Mir Castle** (p99), presiding over the tranquil town of the same name

5 Explore one of the few historical complexes in Belarus to have survived WWII at **Nyasvizh** (p99), amid beautiful lakes and the beautiful Radziwill Palace Fortress

MINSK MIHCK

☎017 / POP 1.73 MILLION

Minsk will almost certainly surprise you. The capital of Belarus is, despite its thoroughly dreary-sounding name, a progressive and modern place quite at odds with its own reputation.

With almost no buildings remaining from the pre-war years, there are relatively few traditional sights in the city. Instead, there are myriad places of interest for anyone fascinated by the Soviet period, and a smattering of cosmopolitan pursuits to keep you entertained come evening.

Sights

Pr Nezalezhnastsi AVENUE

The city's central square is pl Nezalezhnastsi (Independence Sq, also called pl Lenina). Heading northeast from pl Nezalezhnastsi is the main part of pr Nezalezhnastsi and the bustling heart of Minsk. An entire block at No 17 is occupied by the **KGB headquarters**.

Oktyabrskaya Pl SQUARE

This is where opposition groups gather to protest against the president, Alexander Lukashenko, from time to time, most recently in December 2010. Here you'll find the excellent **Museum of the Great Patriotic War** (☎277 5611; pr Nezalezhnastsi 25a; admission BR2000; ⊙10am-6pm Tue & Thu-Sat, 11am-7pm Wed & Sun), where Belarus' horrors and heroism during WWII are exhibited in photographs, huge dioramas and other media.

Tsentralny Skver SQUARE

Across the street is Tsentralny Skver (Central Sq), a small park on the site of a 19th-century marketplace. To one side is the seriously guarded **Presidential Administrative Building**, from where Lukashenko rules.

Traetskae Pradmestse OLD TOWN

In lieu of any real remaining Old Town is Traetskae Pradmestse, a pleasant – if tiny – recreation of Minsk's pre-war buildings on a pretty bend of the river downstream from pl Peramohi. At the end of a little footbridge nearby is evocative Afghan war memorial the **Island of Courage & Sorrow**, more commonly called the Island of Tears.

Zaslavsky Jewish Monument MONUMENT

Another extremely moving sight is the Zaslavsky Jewish Monument, rather hidden away in a sunken gully amid trees off vul Melnikayte. It commemorates the savage murder of 5000 Jews from Minsk at the hands of the Nazis on 2 March 1942.

Sleeping

To rent an apartment try **Belarus Rent** (www.belarusrent.com), where rates range from €40 to €100 per night.

WORTH A TRIP

AROUND MINSK

Heading into the gently appealing Belarusian countryside is a great way to get to know the country and there are several places that can easily be visited on a day trip from Minsk.

The magical old buildings of **Nyasvizh** make it a great place to get in touch with Belarus' past. This green and attractive town 120km southwest of Minsk is also one of the oldest in the country, dating from the 13th century. While here visit the **Farny Polish Roman Catholic Church** and walk the causeway to the beautiful 16th-century **Radziwill Palace Fortress**, the town's main sight. From Minsk's Vostochny bus station there are two daily buses to/from Nyasvizh (BR12,000, 2½ hours).

The charming small town of **Mir**, 85km southwest of Minsk, is dominated by the impossibly romantic 16th-century **Mir Castle** (admission BR10,000; ⊙10am-5pm) that overlooks a small lake at one end of the town. It was once owned by the powerful Radziwill princes and has been under Unesco protection since 1994. The town of Mir itself is a delightful backwater.

Tasting delicious farm-made sausages, cheese and bread is only a small part of the experience of a visit to the **open-air interactive museum** (☎133 0747; www.dudutki.by; admission incl tastings BR25,000; ⊙10am-4pm Tue-Wed, 10am-5pm Thu-Sun) of Dudutki, located 40km south of Minsk.

From Minsk's Vostochny and Tsentralny bus stations there are hourly buses to Navahrudak (Novogrudok in Russian) that stop in Mir (BR10,000 to BR12,000, 2½ hours). There are two daily buses (one hour, BR7,000) to Dudutki from the Vostochny bus station.

Moskovsky Bus Station Dorms DORMITORY €
(☎219 3651; vul Filimonava 63; dm BR24,600) Head to Maskouskaya metro station for these clean, quiet rooms – the cheapest in town. We challenge you to make the serious babushka in charge smile.

40 Let Pobedy HOTEL €
(☎294 7963; vul Azgura 3; s/d from BR64,000/70,000) This slightly out-of-the-way yet central place offers decent, good-value rooms and friendly service. The hotel has made an effort to modernise itself (even if it is with cheap furnishings) and all the bathrooms have been redone. Cheap wi-fi is available throughout.

Hotel Yubileiny HOTEL €€
(☎226 9024; fax 226 9171; pr Peramozhtsau 19; s/d unrenovated BR155,000/190,000, renovated BR228,000/275,000; ❄📶) This centrally located Soviet place is located across the road from Minsk's main athletics stadium and the river. Most of the rooms have been done up, but rooms on the 5th, 7th and 13th floors have not and are cheaper as a result. The staff are friendly and there's cheap lobby wi-fi.

Minsk

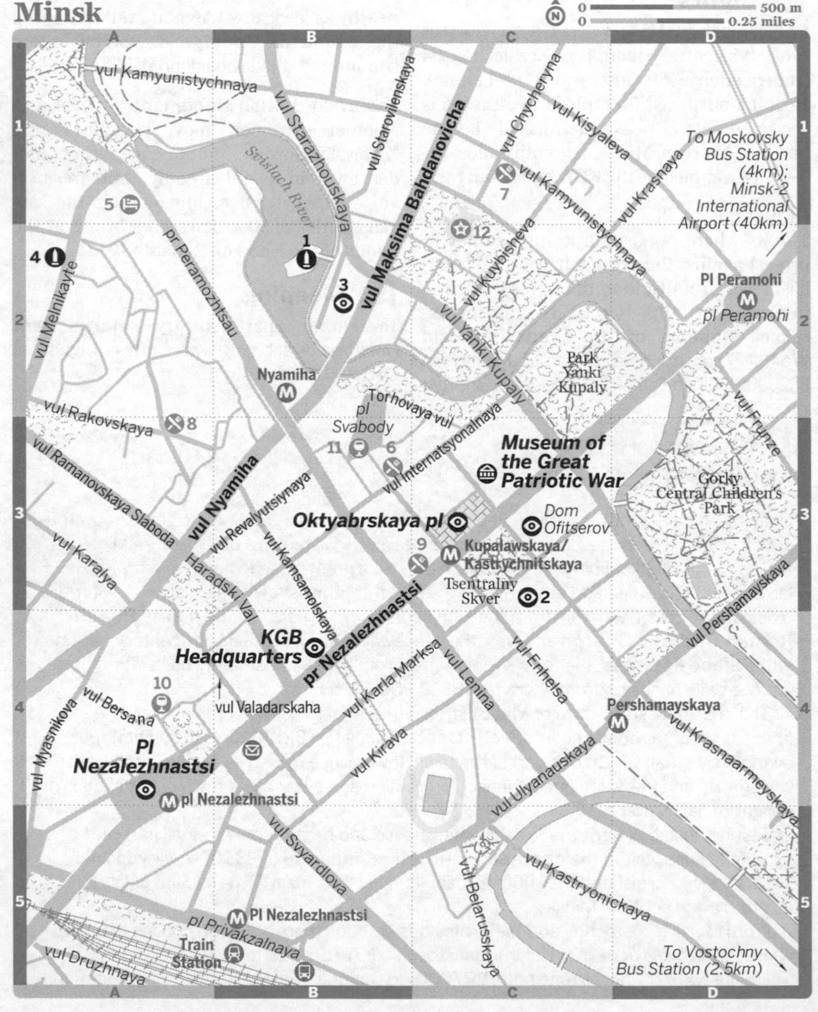

Eating

TOP CHOICE **Strawnya Talaka** TRADITIONAL €€
(vul Rakovskaya 18; mains BR10,000-60,000; ⏲10am-6am) This relaxed and cosy place is the best restaurant in Minsk for an authentic local meal, and it also has very handily long opening hours. Try the hare in bilberry sauce or just have a bowl of ham and bean soup with fabulous *deruni* (potato pancakes).

Gurman RUSSIAN €€
(☎290 6774; vul Kamyunistychnaya 7; mains BR6000-40,000; ⏲8am-11pm) This place specialises in many varieties of delicious, freshly made *pelmeni* (Russian-style ravioli usually stuffed with meat) and also offers a wide selection of pastas and even curries. With light and airy premises and friendly staff, it's worth booking a table for dinner.

Byblos LEBANESE €€
(vul Internatsyanalnaya21; mains BR10,000-25,000; ⏲noon-midnight) What this Lebanese-style place lacks in authenticity it makes up for in value, quick service and an English menu. Great for an easy lunch, the kebabs and hummus are decent enough, given that you're in Belarus, and there's great people-watching from the enclosed terrace.

Tsentralny Magazin SUPERMARKET €
(2nd fl, pr Nezalezhnastsi 23; ⏲9am-11pm) A large, Western-style grocery store with plenty of supplies for self-caterers.

Drinking

U Ratushi PUB
(☎226 0643; vul Gertsena 1; ⏲10am-2am) This pub-style restaurant, across from the *ratusha* (town hall), is packed with a fun-loving crowd on weekends (there is often a small cover charge for live bands). Book ahead if coming on weekends, or arrive at the venue really early.

Drozhzhi United IRISH PUB
(vul Sverdlova 2; ⏲9am-2am) Centrally located, Minsk's Irish pub is instantly recognisable to anyone who has ever been an expat, anywhere. There's good food, Guinness on tap, and a friendly atmosphere.

Graffiti BAR
(www.graffiti.by; pr Kalinina 16; cover BR10,000-20,000; ⏲11am-11pm Sun-Thu, to 2am Fri & Sat) For something more contemporary and underground, Graffiti offers nightly concerts from local bands and big weekend parties popular with an anti-Luka crowd. It's a 10-minute walk from the Park Chelyuskintsev metro station.

Entertainment

Performing arts are good quality and tickets are cheap. Don't miss the highly respected **National Academic Opera & Ballet Theatre** (☎234 8074; pl Parizhskoy Kamunni 1; ⏲ticket office 9am-1pm & 2-6pm Mon-Fri).

Information

24-hour pharmacy (pr Nezalezhnastsi 16)

EcoMedservices (☎207 7474; www.ems.by; vul Tolstoho 4; ⏲8am-9pm) The closest thing to a reliable, Western-style clinic. Dental services are offered here too.

Soyuz Online (2nd fl, vul Krasnaarmeyskaya 3; ⏲24hr) Large internet cafe in the centre of town. Food and drinks available. Go up the steps to the Dom Ofitserov and enter the far door near the tank monument.

BELARUS MINSK

Minsk

Top Sights
- KGB Headquarters ... B4
- Museum of the Great Patriotic War ... C3
- Oktyabrskaya pl ... C3
- Pl Nezalezhnastsi ... A4

Sights
- 1 Island of Courage & Sorrow ... B2
- 2 Presidential Administrative Building ... C3
- 3 Traetskae Pradmestse ... B2
- 4 Zaslavsky Jewish Monument ... A2

Sleeping
- 5 Hotel Yubileiny ... A1

Eating
- 6 Byblos ... B3
- 7 Gurman ... C1
- 8 Strawnya Talaka ... A3
- 9 Tsentralny Magazin ... C3

Drinking
- 10 Drozhzhi United ... A4
- 11 U Ratushi ... B3

Entertainment
- 12 National Academic Opera & Ballet Theatre ... C2

Getting There & Away

Air

International flights entering and departing Belarus do so at the **Minsk-2 international airport** (☎006, 279 1300; www.airport.by), about 40km east of Minsk.

Bus

MinskTrans (www.minsktrans.by) Full timetable information, though it's in Russian only.

Moskovsky bus station (☎219 3622; vul Filimonava 63) Near Maskouskaya metro station, about 5km east of the centre.

Tsentralny bus station (☎227 0473; vul Bobruyskaya 6) By the train station.

Vostochny bus station (☎247 4984; vul Vaneeva 34) To get here from the train station (or metro Pl Lenina), take bus 8 or trolley 20 or 30; get off at 'Avtovokzal Vostochny'.

Train

Domestic train ticket office (☎225 6271; pr Nezalezhnastsi 18; ⏲9am-8pm Mon-Fri, 9am-7pm Sat & Sun) Tickets for domestic and CIS (Commonwealth of Independent States) destinations.

International train ticket office (☎213 1719; vul Bobruyskaya 4; ⏲9am-8pm) Advance tickets for non-CIS destinations; located to the right of the train station.

Minsk train station (☎105, 225 7000; ⏲24hr) Domestic and CIS tickets.

Getting Around

TO/FROM THE AIRPORT From Minsk-2 airport, a 40-minute taxi ride into town should cost anywhere between BR80,000 and BR120,000, depending on your bargaining skills. There are buses and *marshrutky* (shared minibuses; BR5000, 1½ hours, hourly) that bring you to the city centre.

PUBLIC TRANSPORT Minsk's metro is simple: just two lines with one transfer point at the Kastrychnitskaya-Kupalauskaya interchange. One token *(zheton)* costs BR700.

Buses, trams, trolleybuses and the metro operate from 5.30am to 1am. *Marshrutky* cost BR1000 to BR1500.

BREST БРЭСТ

☎0162 / POP 312,000

After visiting Minsk you'd be forgiven for thinking you'd arrived in another country when you get off the train in Brest. This prosperous border town looks far more to the neighbouring EU than to Minsk, and is a pleasant place to spend a couple of days. The city's main sight is the Brest Fortress, a moving WWII memorial.

Sights

FREE **Brest Fortress** MUSEUM COMPLEX

(Brestskaya krepost; pr Masherava) Very little remains of Brest Fortress. Certainly don't come here expecting a medieval turreted affair – this is a Soviet WWII memorial to the devastating battle that resulted when German troops advanced into the Soviet Union in the early days of Operation Barbarossa in 1941. The large complex occupies a beautiful spot at the confluence of the Buh and Mukhavets Rivers, a 20-minute walk from the town centre or a short hop on the hourly bus 17 from outside Hotel Intourist. Of the several museums on site here, head for the **Defence of Brest Museum** (adult/student BR2420/1450; ⏲9am-6pm), whose extensive displays document the plight of the defenders.

Museum of Confiscated Art MUSEUM

(vul Lenina 39; admission BR1500; ⏲10am-5.30pm Tue-Sun) There are a couple of excellent museums in the city centre. The most interesting is the Museum of Confiscated Art, where there's an extraordinary display of icons, paintings, jewellery and other valuables that were seized from smugglers trying to get them across the border to Poland during the 1990s. Items on display are of unknown origin, hence their display in a museum rather than a return to their rightful owners.

Sleeping

TOP CHOICE **Hotel Molodezhnaya** HOTEL €€

(☎21 63 76; vul Kamsamolskaya 6; s/d BR92,300/141,720) This is the newest and least Soviet of Brest's hotels – a small and very centrally located place a short walk from the train station. The rooms are comfortable and clean, all have private facilities and the welcome is almost warm. Cheap lobby wi-fi.

Hotel Buh HOTEL €

(☎23 64 17; vul Lenina 2; s/d BR90,000/146,000, without bathroom BR64,000/96,000) The cheapest and oldest of Brest's hotels is also the best choice for some character – the brightly painted Stalin-era foyer is a highlight and service is friendly. The renovated rooms with private facilities are often booked up in advance though, sometimes leaving the older facility-free rooms as the only option. Cheap lobby wi-fi.

Eating & Drinking

Brest has plenty of takeaway and fast food on offer, particularly around the pedestrianised area of vul Savetskaya. There's also a passable **supermarket** (vul Savetskaya 48; ⌚8am-11pm) in the centre.

TOP CHOICE **Jules Verne** FINE DINING €€
(vul Hoholya 29; mains BR12,000-50,000; ⌚noon-midnight) This gentleman's-club-style restaurant serves up cracking dishes – from mouth-watering curries and a range of French cooking to sumptuous desserts and the best coffee in town. Don't miss it.

Pizzeria PIZZA €
(vul Pushkinskaya 20; pizzas BR10,000-18,000) It's not well signed, but you can pretty much follow your nose into the building through a garish bakery and then down the stairs. Surprisingly good thin-crust pizzas are made to order.

Pub House PUB
(vul Hoholya; ⌚10am-midnight) This friendly and rustic wooden bar offers up a selection of beers from all over Europe.

Information

24-hour pharmacy (vul Hoholya 32)

Cyber Brest (3rd fl, vul Kamsamolskaya 36; por hr BR2000; ⌚9am-midnight) Internet access at your choice of 50 computers; follow the footprints to the top floor.

Getting There & Around

The **train station** (☎005) has on-site customs. Several trains leave for Minsk daily – *platzkart/kupe* (3rd/2nd class) BR15,000/25,000, four hours.

The **bus station** (☎004, 114) is in the centre of town.

UNDERSTAND BELARUS

History

Belarus has an unhappy history. In the 1930s, under Stalin, hundreds of thousands of people were executed in purges here. The savage Nazi occupation during WWII was ended in 1944 by the Red Army, with massive destruction on both sides. At least 25% of the Belarusian population died between 1939 and 1945, most in Nazi concentration camps.

The 1986 nuclear accident at Chornobyl, just over the border in Ukraine, left about a quarter of the country seriously contaminated, and its effects are still felt today.

On 25 August 1991 Belarus declared independence from the USSR. Since 1994, Belarus has been governed by Alexander Lukashenko, whose autocratic presidential style and poor human-rights record has led to Belarus' almost total international isolation.

Belarus Today

President Alexander Lukashenko's relationship with Russia deteriorated sharply in 2007 and 2008, following a spat with Russian energy giant Gazprom over gas price hikes and Russia's war with Georgia, of which the Belarusian government was sharply critical. This was followed by an apparent two-year thaw in relations between the EU and Minsk.

Despite having slapped a travel ban on Lukashenko and having consistently rejected the legitimacy of his electoral victories, the EU, wanting to draw Minsk from Moscow's orbit, waved the carrot of billions of economic aid if the 2010 elections were declared free and fair, and invited Belarus to join the EU's 'Eastern Partnership' program. Lukashenko likewise appeared keen to make new friends in the West and many began to believe that things were slowly changing in Belarus.

Playing Moscow off against the EU has long been a survival mechanism for Lukashenko, but this most audacious display was truly masterful. Fearful of losing one of its very last remaining European allies, Russia agreed to continue providing Belarus with low-cost gas just before the presidential elections in December 2010, alleviating Minsk's need to have the election pronounced fair by EU observers.

After the December 2010 election results, rejected by the Organization for Security and Co-operation in Europe (OSCE) monitors as rigged, protestors on the main square in Minsk were violently dispersed, leaving over 600 people in jail, including several of the opposition candidates, many of whom were allegedly beaten and abducted.

Belarus remains a tightly controlled, repressive police state at the time of writing, and, as a leaked diplomatic cable published by Wikileaks in December 2010 succinctly puts it, 'Lukashenko intends to stay in power indefinitely and sees no reason to change his course'.

People

The Belarusian population of 9.6 million is 81.2% Belarusian, 11.4% Russian, 4% Polish and 2.4% Ukrainian, with the remaining 1% consisting of other groups. Prior to WWII, 10% of the population was Jewish. They now make up less than 1%.

The Belarusian character makes for a refreshing change from that of their Russian cousins. Here, you can usually expect people to be more open and friendly.

Environment

Belarus is, for the most part, completely flat, with marshes and swamps in the south and lakes in the north. The 1986 disaster at Chornobyl in neighbouring Ukraine has been the defining event for the Belarusian environment, if not for the republic as a whole.

Food

Price ranges in this chapter apply to the cost of a meal:

€€€ more than BR12,000

€€ BR5000 to BR12,000

€ less than BR5000

SURVIVAL GUIDE

Directory A–Z

Accommodation

While budget and midrange accommodation standards in Belarus tend to be lower than in Western Europe, they are still generally acceptable and often better than in Russia or Ukraine. Most hotels are fusty old Soviet time warps. Our price ranges are for a double room:

€€€ more than BR300,000

€€ BR100,000 to BR300,000

€ less than BR100,000

Business Hours

Banks 9am-5pm Mon-Fri

Offices 9am-6pm Mon-Fri

Shops 9am or 10am-9pm Mon-Sat, to 6pm Sun if open at all

Embassies & Consulates

Useful embassies and consulates in Belarus:

Moldova (☎017-289 1441; vul Belarusskaya 2, Minsk)

Russia Minsk (☎017-222 4985; vul Novolvilenskaya 1a); Brest (☎0162-23 78 42; vul Pushkinskaya 10)

Ukraine Minsk (☎/fax 017-283 1989/91; vul Staravilenskaya51); Brest (☎0162-22 04 77; vul Vorovskaha 19)

Festivals & Events

The night of 6 July is **Kupalye**, a celebration with pagan roots when young girls gather flowers and throw them into a river as a method of fortune-telling, while everyone else sits by lake or riverside fires drinking beer.

Holidays

New Year's Day 1 January

Orthodox Christmas 7 January

International Women's Day 8 March

Constitution Day 15 March

Catholic & Orthodox Easter March/April

Unity of Peoples of Russia & Belarus Day 2 April

International Labour Day (May Day) 1 May

Victory Day 9 May

Independence Day 3 July

Dzyady (Day of the Dead) 2 November

Catholic Christmas 25 December

Money

The Belarusian rouble (BR) is the national currency, and notes range from BR10 to BR100,000. There are no coins. Ensure you change any remaining roubles before leaving Belarus, as it's almost impossible to exchange the currency outside the country. ATMs and currency-exchange offices are not hard to find in Belarusian cities.

Telephone

To dial a Minsk landline number from a Minsk landline number, just dial the number; from a local mobile phone, dial ☎8 017 or ☎375 17 and then the number.

Visas

Belarusian visa regulations change frequently, so check by telephone with your nearest

Belarusian embassy for the latest details; be aware that embassy websites are not always up to date.

Nearly all visitors require a visa, and arranging one before you arrive is usually essential. Visas on arrival are only issued at the Minsk-2 international airport, but they are expensive and are just as much hassle, so it's well worth getting one in advance (it's rare but not unheard of for people to have problems getting visas at the airport).

If you are passing through Belarus and won't be in the country for more than 48 hours, you can apply for a transit visa, for which no invite or voucher is necessary. Simply show a train or air ticket to prove your need to transit through Belarus.

Visa costs vary depending on the embassy you apply at and your citizenship. Americans pay more, but typically transit visas cost around €65 and single-entry visas cost about €90.

REGISTRATION

If you are staying in Belarus for more than five working days, you must have your visa officially registered. Hotels do this automatically and the service is included in the room price.

If you've received a personal invitation, you'll need to find the nearest *passportnovizovoye upravleniye* (passport and visa department; PVU, formerly OVIR), though this will be time-consuming and your host will need to come with you. The simplest place to register your visa in this case is at Minsk's **PVU main office** (☎017-231 9174; pr Nezalezhnastsi 8).

Getting There & Away

Air

Belarus' two international airports are both in Minsk; most flights are handled at **Minsk-2 international airport** (☎006, 017-279 1300; www.airport.by), about 40km east of the city. Some flights to the former Soviet Union depart from the smaller **Minsk-1 airport** (☎006; vul Chkalova 38), only a few kilometres south of the city centre.

Land

Bus travel is a common and fast way to enter the country, although long queues at border crossings are not uncommon. Immigration and customs control will normally come aboard the bus and check all passengers, and you may be asked to get off for luggage searches.

Trains are usually a more comfortable but slightly slower way to travel than bus. From Minsk there are services to Russia, Lithuania and Poland, plus connections to the rest of Europe via Brest. You can also get to Russia from Vitsebsk.

Getting Around

Bus

Bus services cover much of the country, and are generally a reliable, if crowded, means of transportation. You can always buy tickets on the day, usually before you board, at the bus-station ticket desk. As in Russia, normal bus services are supplemented by *marshrutky* routes.

Car & Motorcycle

It's perfectly possible to hire a car in Minsk, though cars are usually old and badly maintained. Look them over carefully and check the spare tyre before you drive off.

Drivers from the USA or EU can use their own country's driving licence for six months. Cars drive in the right-hand lane, children 12 and under must sit in a back seat, and your blood-alcohol level should be 0%. Fuel is usually not hard to find, but try to keep your tank full, and it would even be wise to keep some spare fuel as well.

You will be instructed by signs to slow down when approaching GAI (road police) stations, and not doing so is a sure-fire way to get a substantial fine. You may see GAI signs in Russian or in Belarusian.

Train

Train is a popular and scenic way to travel between the major towns of Belarus, though the bus network is far more extensive and prices are similar. Travelling by train is an excellent way to meet locals, with whom you'll be sharing compartments. Bring along some food to share and you'll make friends in no time.

Belgium

Includes »

Best Places to Eat

» Den Gouden Harynck, Bruges (p128)

» L'Ogenblik, Brussels (p111)

» De Groote Witte Arend, Antwerp (p120)

» Fin de Siècle, Brussels (p111)

Best Places to Stay

» Hôtel Le Dixseptième, Brussels (p111)

» Relais Bourgondisch Cruyce, Bruges (p128)

» Hotel Julien, Antwerp (p120)

Why Go?

Stereotypes of comic books, remarkable beers and sublime chocolates are just the start in this eccentric little country whose self-deprecating people have quietly spent centuries producing some of Europe's finest art and architecture. Bilingual Brussels is the dynamic yet personable EU capital but also sports what's arguably one of the world's most beautiful city squares. Flat, Dutch-speaking Flanders has many other alluring medieval city cores, all easily linked by regular train hops.

In hilly, French-speaking Wallonia, the attractions are contrastingly rural – castle villages, outdoor activities and extensive cave systems that prove a major draw for Dutch caravaners but are hard to fully appreciate by public transport. War buffs will find Belgium full of moving battlefield sites from many eras. And anyone with a love of the good life will quickly come to appreciate a country where cafe culture is king and fine food is almost a birthright.

When to Go

Brussels

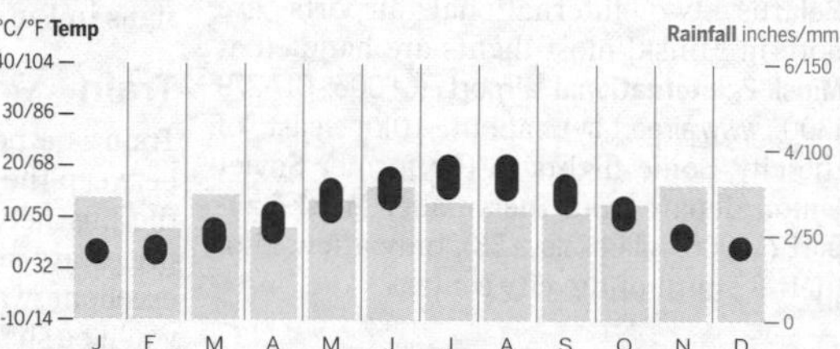

Many weekends before Easter Belgium hosts Mardi Gras and many of Europe's weirdest carnivals.

Mid-Jun Scenes from the Battle of Waterloo recreated on the battlefield.

Mid-Aug, even years Brussels' Grand Place is covered by an ornate 'carpet' of flower petals.

Connections

Amsterdam, Paris, Cologne and London are all under 2½ hours from Brussels by high-speed train. Liège and Antwerp are also on high-speed international routes. Go via Tournai or Ghent to reach France by train if you want to avoid the fast trains and their compulsory reservations. Budget airlines offer cheap deals to numerous European destinations, particularly from Charleroi airport.

ITINERARIES

Four Days

If you've got the energy, four days is just about long enough to get a first taste of Belgium's finest: the glorious canals of Bruges and Ghent, Brussels' magnificent central square and the ancient-modern contrasts of intriguing Antwerp. All are easily accessed by train while you're hopping between Paris and Amsterdam. But once you've discovered all those wonderful cafes you'll wish that you'd budgeted longer.

Ten Days

Add an extra night in each of the above and add Ypres or a jaunt into Wallonia.

Essential Food & Drink

Hearty home-style Belgian cooking, once limited to cheap cafes, has been recently undergoing a degree of gourmet rediscovery.

» **ballekes/bouletten** meatballs

» **chicons au gratin** endive rolled in ham and cooked in cheese/béchamel sauce

» **croquettes de crevettes grises** like fish cakes, but containing tiny, highly flavoured North Sea shrimps

» **filet américain** no, not a succulent American steak but a blob of raw minced beef, typically topped with equally raw egg yolk

» **lambic** a beer-oddity that is spontaneously fermented to make an acidic brew made more palatable by ageing then blended with newer lambic to make *gueuze* or macerated with cherries to produce *kriek*

» **mosselen/moules** steaming cauldrons of in-the-shell mussels, typically cooked in white wine and served with a mountain of *frites* (chips; please don't call the latter 'French' fries here!)

» **stoemp** a mashed-together veg-and-potato dish originally made to use up leftovers

» **Vlaamse stoverij/carbonade flamande** semi-sweet beer-based beef casserole

» **waterzooi** a cream-based chicken or fish stew

AT A GLANCE

» **Currency** Euro (€)

» **Languages** Dutch, French, German

» **Money** ATMs common; credit cards widely accepted

» **Visas** Schengen visa rules apply; see p1319

Fast Facts

» **Area** 30,278 sq km

» **Capital** Brussels

» **Country code** ☎32

» **Emergency** ☎112; ambulance ☎100; police ☎101

Exchange Rates

Australia	A$1	€0.74
Canada	C$1	€0.74
Japan	¥100	€0.87
New Zealand	NZ$1	€0.56
UK	UK£1	€1.16
USA	US$1	€0.72

Set Your Budget

» **Budget hotel room** under €60

» **Two-course evening meal** from €25

» **Museum entrance** €2-8.50

» **Beer (in bar)** €1.90

» **City transport ticket** €1.70

Resources

» **For Flanders** www.visitflanders.com

» **For Wallonia** www.wallonie-tourisme.be, www.belgiumtheplaceto.be

» **For Brussels** http://visitbrussels.be

Belgium Highlights

1 2 Compare classic medieval canalside scenes in **Bruges** (p125) and **Ghent** (p121)

3 Savour the 'world's most beautiful square' then seek out the enticing cafes and chocolate shops of **Brussels** (p110)

4 Follow fashion to hip yet historic **Antwerp** (p117)

5 Explore the castles of **Wallonia** (p131), and also check out the caves near **Rochefort** (p131)

6 7 8 Ponder history's darker moments at battlefields around **Waterloo** (p117), **Ypres** (p128) and **Bastogne** (p130)

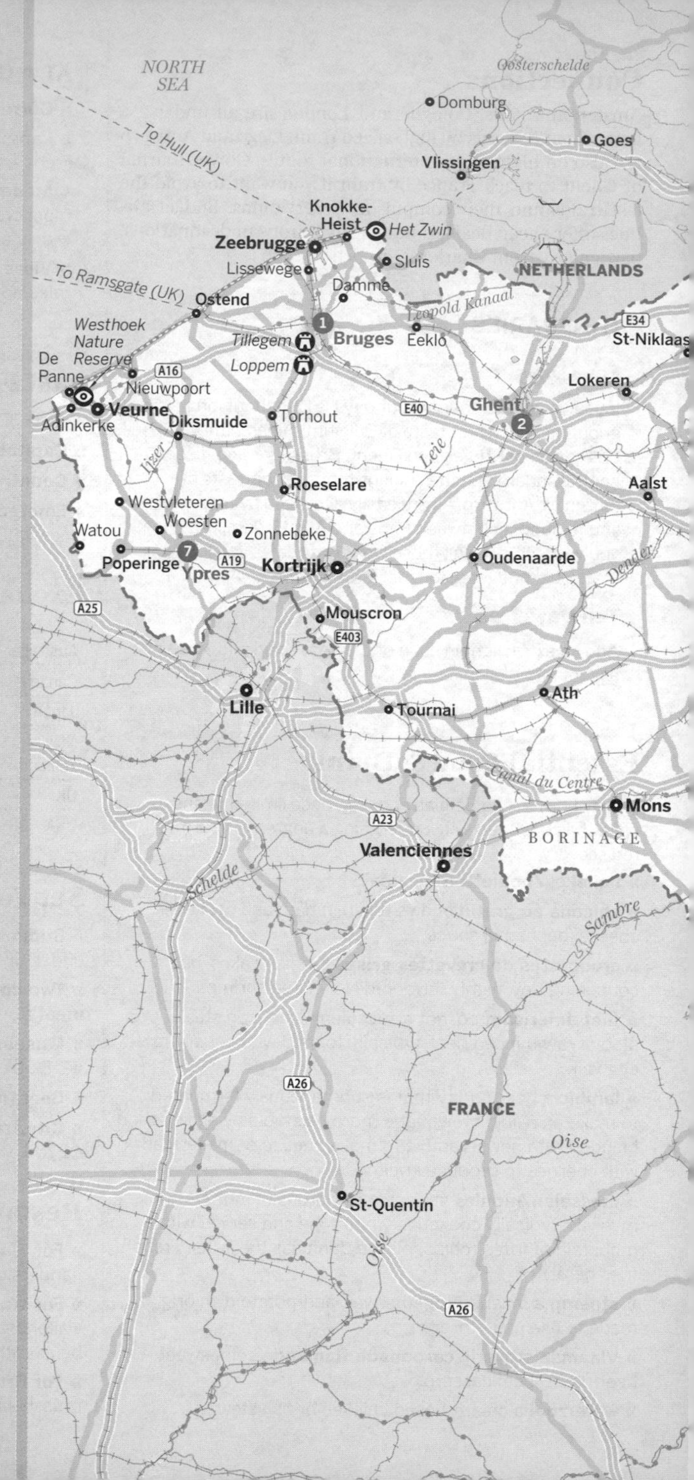

0 30 km
0 20 miles
NETHERLANDS
Tilburg
Roosendaal
Eindhoven
Venlo
A1
N1
Kanaal Antwerpen - Turnhout
Schelde
A12
Turnhout
A21
Maas
Antwerp
4
Antwerp Airport
Herentals
Albert Kanaal
Mol
Neerpelt
Roermond
Lier
Nete
Fort van Breendonk
E313
National Park Hoge Kempen
GERMANY
Mechelen
Diest
A2
Genk
Hasselt
Bokrijk Openluchtmuseum
Brussels Airport
E19
Leuven
Maastricht
3
Brussels
Aachen
E313
A2
Meuse
E19
A3
Waterloo
Louvain-la-Neuve
Braine l'Alleud
6
Ottignies
Waterloo Battlefield
Liège Airport
Liège
Verviers
Hautes Fagnes-Eifel Nature Park
Nivelles
Jehay
Ourthe
Vesdre
Hautes Fagnes
E411
Huy
5
Wallonia's Castles
Remouchamps
Canal Charleroi-Brussels
Charleroi Airport
E42
Meuse
Namur
Modave
Hautes Fagnes Nature Reserve
Coo
Stavelot
Binche
Charleroi
Durbuy
Amblève
Barvaux
Godinne
Melreux
E25
N5
Hotton
Ourthe
E421
Dinant
Marloie
Houyet
Rochefort
La Roche-en-Ardenne
5
Jemelle
Han-sur-Lesse
Botte de Hainaut
Lavaux-Ste-Anne
Champlon
Lesse
E46
Bastogne
8
Chimay
Couvin
E411
Libramont
Semois
E46
Rochehaut
Bouillon
LUXEMBOURG
Charleville-Mezières
Arlon
Findel Airport
Orval
Luxembourg City
Meuse
Virton
Rodange
Aisne

BRUSSELS (BRUSSEL, BRUXELLES)

POP 1.03 MILLION

Like the country it represents, Brussels is a surreal, multilayered place pulling several disparate cultural identities into one enigmatic core. It subtly seduces with great art, tempting chocolate shops and classic cafes. Meanwhile an architectural smorgasbord pits awesome art nouveau and 17th-century masterpieces against shabby suburbanism and the disappointingly soulless glass-faced anonymity of the EU area. Note that Brussels is officially bilingual so all names from streets to train stations have both Dutch and French versions, but for simplicity we use only the French versions in this chapter.

Sights

CENTRAL BRUSSELS

Although Brussels is spread out, most key sights and numerous unmissable cafes are within leisurely walking distance of Grand Pl.

Grand Place NEIGHBOURHOOD

Topping any itinerary is Brussels' magnificent central square, the Grand Pl. Gilt statues and trade symbols adorn the square's elegant **guildhalls** that were rebuilt shortly after the originals were bombarded by French forces in 1695. One older survivor is the splendidly spired Gothic-style **Hôtel de Ville** (city hall) – ironic, as that was the main French target. Opened in 1847, the **Galeries St-Hubert** (www.galeries-saint-hubert.com), to the northeast, were Europe's first covered shopping arcades. South of here, **Rue des Bouchers** is a narrow, colourful dazzle of close-packed seafood eateries and barking hawkers that's undoubtedly photogenic, but beware of scams if you eat here.

Manneken Pis MONUMENT

Making a suitably surreal national symbol, the Manneken Pis is a diminutive fountain in the form of a little boy cheerfully taking a leak into a fountain pool. Sexual equality is ensured by his lesser-known squatting sister to the northeast, the **Jeanneke Pis** (www.jeannekepisofficial.be; Impasse de la Fidélité).

Musées Royaux des Beaux-Arts ART GALLERY

(Royal Museums of Fine Arts; www.fine-arts-museum.be; Rue de la Régence 3; adult/student/BrusselsCard €8/2/free; ⏲10am-5pm Tue-Sun) Belgium's premier art collection is well endowed, notably with works by Flemish Primitives, the Breugel/Breughel family and Rubens. However, many rooms are currently closed for long-term renovation. A €13 combi-ticket includes the Magritte Museum next door.

FREE THRILLS

Once a month, several Belgian cities let you sneak into their municipal museums for free:

» **Brussels** (first Wednesday afternoon of the month)

» **Antwerp** (last Wednesday)

» **Liège and many other towns in Wallonia** (first Sunday)

In Flanders, many offer €1 tickets for those aged under 26.

Magritte Museum ART GALLERY

(www.musee-magritte-museum.be; Pl Royale; adult/youth/BrusselsCard €8/2/free; ⏲10am-5pm Tue-Sun) This state-of-the-art 2009 museum celebrates the life and work of Belgian surrealist artist René Magritte, taking visitors well beyond his stereotypically witty canvases of pipes and bowler hats. Pre-purchasing tickets online can save queuing.

MIM MUSEUM

(Musical Instrument Museum; www.mim.be; Rue Montagne de la Cour 2; adult/concession/BrusselsCard €5/4/free; ⏲10am-5pm Tue-Sun) See and hear one of the world's biggest collections of musical instruments, housed in a showpiece 1899 art nouveau building with unparalleled city views from the top-floor cafe terrace.

BEYOND THE CENTRE

Musée Horta MUSEUM

(www.hortamuseum.be; Rue Américaine 25; adult/concession €7/5; ⏲2-5.30pm Tue-Sun; Ⓜ Horta, 🚊91 or 92) Architect Victor Horta's 1898 house-museum, 2.5km south of the centre, makes a fine introduction to Brussels' art nouveau heritage. For more info, see www.brusselsartnouveau.be or buy the €3 Brussels art nouveau guide pamphlet from tourist offices.

Atomium MONUMENT

(www.atomium.be; Sq de l'Atomium; adult/concession/BrusselsCard €11/8/9; ⏲10am-7pm May-Sep, 10am-6pm Oct-Apr; Ⓜ Heysel, 🚊51) This Brussels icon, 5km north of the city centre, is a space-age leftover from the 1958 World Fair consisting of nine gigantic gleaming balls impressively representing an iron crystal lattice enlarged 165 billion times. Best appreciated from outside.

Musée Bruxellois de la Gueuze MUSEUM
(www.cantillon.be; Rue Gheude 56; admission €5; ⌚9am-5pm Mon-Fri, 10am-5pm Sat; Ⓜ Clemenceau) This fascinating working brewery produces Brussels' unique if startlingly tart *lambic* beers, created through the miracle of spontaneous fermentation. From Bruxelles-Midi station walk 800m north via Pl Bara and Rue Limnander.

Sleeping

At weekends and during July/August, internet deals can get you a discounted top-end hotel room for little more than a basic midrange option, while €69 walk-in deals become possible at several options around the southern entrance of the Galeries St-Hubert. There are various cheap, basic choices around Bruxelles-Midi station, but the area isn't salubrious. **Bed & Brussels** (www.bnb-brussels.be) allows you to filter B&Bs by theme and location.

Downtown-BXL B&B €€
(☎0475 290721; www.downtownbxl.com, Rue du Marché au Charbon 118-120; r €77-109; 📶) Excellent value rooms feature zebra striped cushions and Warhol Marilyn prints in 'Downtown' or Moroccan-Oriental-style decor in the adjacent 'Casa-BXL'. Gay-friendly.

Hostel Jacques Brel HOSTEL €
(☎02 218 0187; brussels.brel@laj.be; Rue de la Sablonnière 30; members dm €16.40-20.50, s/d 34/49.60; 📶@) Neat, presentable and reasonably spacious HI hostel in a quiet, pleasant area less than 15 minutes' walk from Grand Pl. It has a bar. No lockout.

JH Bruegel HOSTEL €
(☎02 511 0436; www.jeugdherbergen.be; Rue du St-Esprit 2; members dm/s/d €21.30/35.50/51.40; @📶) Brussels' most central hostel has a cellar bar, several sitting areas and decent, sex-segregated dorms, but the lock-outs are infuriating: read the HI regulations carefully.

2GO4 HOSTEL €
(☎02 219 3019; www.2G04.be) Hostel (Blvd Émile Jacqmain 99; dm €22-29, s/d/tr/q €55/69/96/116; ⌚reception 7am-1pm & 4-11pm); Grand Place Rooms (Rue des Harengs 6; d €59-70) The well-equipped hostel is toward a slightly sleazier end of town. Check in here even if you're staying in the wonderfully central if haphazardly unpretentious Grand Place Rooms.

Rates include coffee but neither breakfast nor towels (€1). No lockout, no curfew.

Bruxelles Europe à Ciel Ouvert CAMPING GROUND $
(☎02 640 7967; http://cielouvertcamping.wordpress.com; Chaussée de Wavre 203; campsites per adult/tent €6/6, parking €8-12; ⌚7.30am-11pm Jul & Aug; 🚌34 or 80) Modest summer-only camping ground tucked behind a church in the EU area.

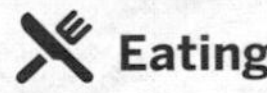

Eating

Several interesting options are dotted along Rue de Flandre with reliable seafood restaurants around nearby Pl Ste-Catherine/Marché aux Poissons. Inexpensive if rarely authentic Asian restaurants line Rue Jules Van Praet between bar-filled Pl St-Géry and the Bourse. See www.resto.be for extensive listings.

Fin de Siècle BELGIAN, ECLECTIC €€
(Rue des Chartreaux 9; mains €10.93-18.97, beer/wine €1.91/2.38; ⌚6pm-1am) No sign on the door, no reservations possible – just join the student-aged throng awaiting a table for giant portions of unsophisticated home cooking chosen from a blackboard menu.

Belga Queen Brussels BRASSERIE €€
(☎02 217 2187; Rue Fossé aux Loups 32; mains €16-25, weekday lunch €16; ⌚noon-2.30pm & 7pm-midnight) Belgian cuisine is given a chic, modern twist within a reverberant 19th-century bank building sporting stained-glass ceilings and unforgettable bathrooms. There's a good wine and beer list.

SPLURGE IN BRUSSELS

Hôtel Le Dixseptième (☎02 502 5744; www.ledixseptieme.be; Rue de la Madeleine 25; s/d/ste from €180/200/270, weekend d/ste from €100/170; ❄) is an alluring boutique hotel that partly occupies a 17th-century ambassadorial mansion where understated opulence reigns in all but the very cheapest rooms.

L'Ogenblik (☎02 511 6151; www.ogenblik.be; Galerie des Princes 1; lunch €11, mains €23-28; ⌚noon-2.30pm & 7pm-midnight), convivially casual yet uncompromising in quality, is an archetypal historic bistro-restaurant with sawdust floors, close-packed tables and fast-witted wait staff.

Central Brussels

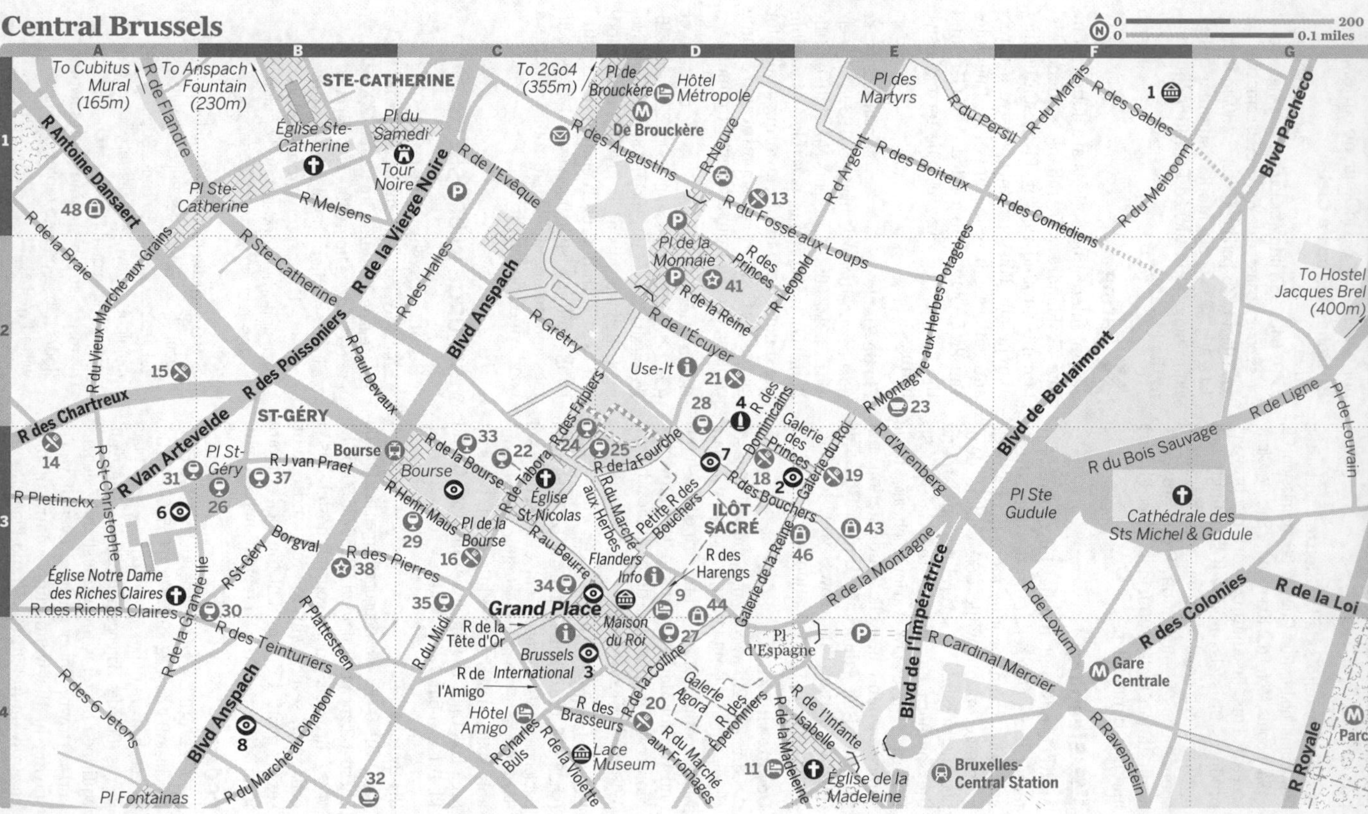

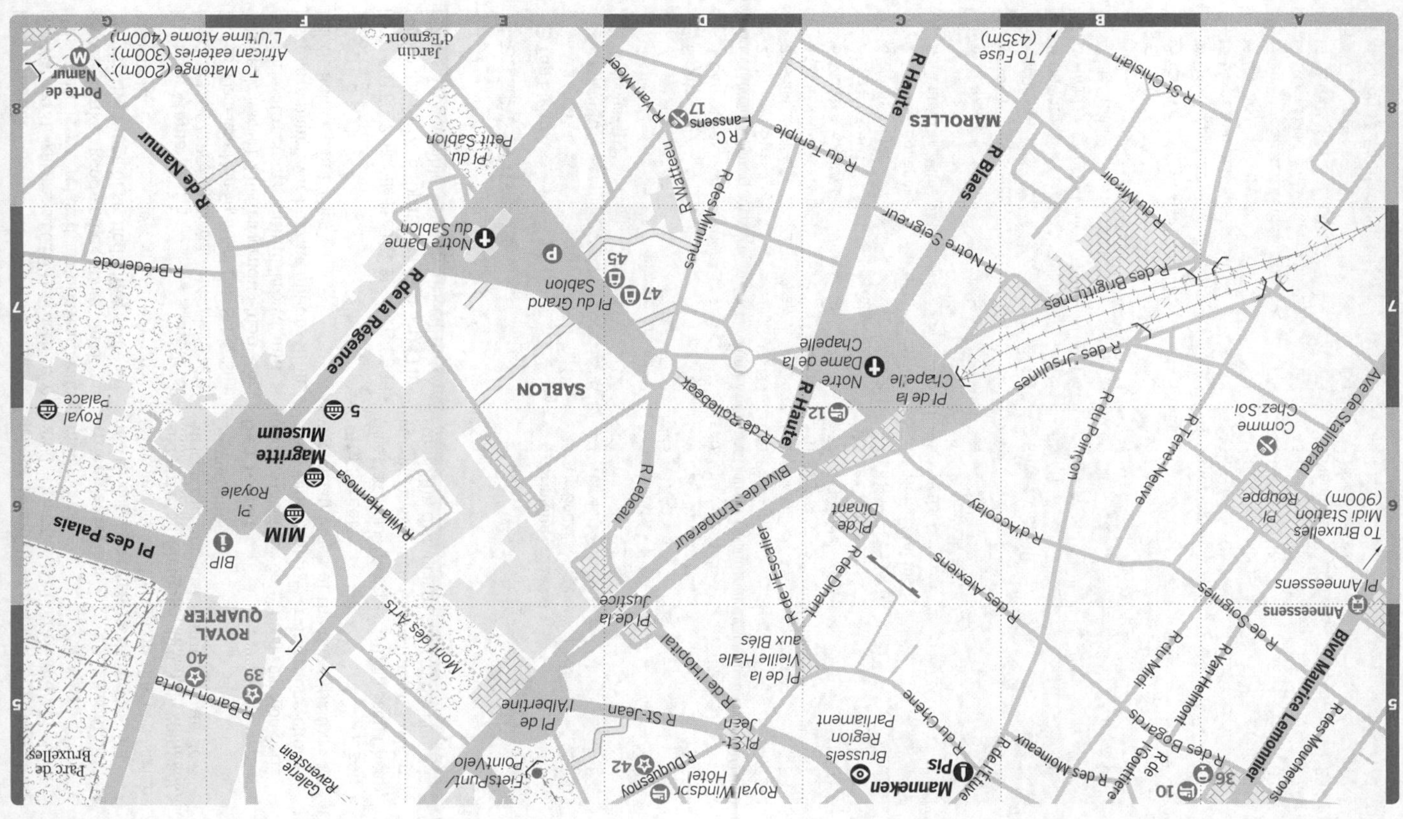
Parc de Bruxelles
Pl des Palais
Royal Palace
R Baron Horta
39
40
ROYAL QUARTER
BIP
Pl Royale
MIM
Magritte Museum
5
Galerie Ravenstein
R Villa Hermosa
Mont des Arts
FietsPunt/ PointVelo
Pl de l'Albertine
R St-Jean
Royal Windsor Hôtel
R Duquesnoy
42
Pl St-Jean
R de l'Hôpital
Pl de la Justice
R Lebeau
SABLON
R de la Régence
R Bréderode
R de Namur
Porte de Namur
To Matonge (200m): African eateries (300m): L'Utime Atome (400m)
Jardin d'Egmont
Notre Dame du Sablon
Pl du Petit Sablon
Pl du Grand Sablon
47
45
R Watteeu
R des Minimes
R Van Moer
R C Fanssens
17
R du Temple
R Haute
MAROLLES
R Blaes
To Fuse (435m)
R St Ghislain
R Notre Seigneur
R du Miroir
R des Brigittines
R des Ursulines
Pl de la Chapelle
Notre Dame de la Chapelle
12
R de Rollebeek
Blvd de l'Empereur
R de l'Escalier
Pl de la Vieille Halle aux Blés
R de Dinant
Pl de Dinant
Manneken Pis
Brussels Region Parliament
R du Chêne
R de l'Etuve
R des Moineaux
R des Alexiens
R d'Accolay
R du Poinçon
R Terre-Neuve
R de l'Gouttière
R des Bogards
10
36
R du Midi
R Van Helmont
R de Soignies
Blvd Maurice Lemonnier
R des Moucherons
Anneessens
Pl Anneessens
To Bruxelles Midi Station (900m)
Pl Rouppe
Comme Chez Soi
Ave de Stalingrad
A
B
C
D
E
F
G
5
6
7
8

Le Perroquet CAFE €
(Rue Watteeu 31; light meals €6.50-11; ⌚noon-1am) This glorious yet relaxed art-nouveau cafe serves drinks, good-value salads and an imaginative range of stuffed pitas; some are vegetarian.

L'Ultime Atome BRASSERIE €€
(☎02 513 1367; Rue St-Boniface 14; mains €11-17; ⌚8.30am-1am Mon-Fri, 10am-1am Sat & Sun; Ⓜ Porte de Namur) This cavernous 'non-stop' brasserie attracts a youthful crowd and is just one of many ever-buzzing options lining Rue St-Boniface in Ixelles.

Ricotta & Parmesan ITALIAN €
(☎02 502 8082; Rue de l'Écuyer 31; mains €9-15; ⌚noon-2.30pm & 6.30pm-11pm Mon-Sat) This place serves reliable, sensibly priced Italian cuisine in a pair of antique buildings decorated with olive-oil bottles and old cooking implements.

African eateries RESTAURANTS €
(Rue Longue Vie; Ⓜ Porte de Namur) Casual Congolese cafes line up on this pedestrianised street in Matonge, Brussels' compact African quarter, just south of Porte de Namur station.

Den Teepot VEGAN €
(rue des Chartreux 66; ⌚noon-2pm Mon-Sat) Macrobiotic eatery serving a one-choice vegetarian lunch of the day (€8.80).

'Pita Street' KEBABS €
(Rue Marché aux Fromages; ⌚11am-3am) Cheap, late-night stomach fillers from €3 within stumbling distance of the Grand Pl.

Central Brussels

Top Sights

Grand Place ... C3
Magritte Museum ... F6
Manneken Pis ... C5
MIM ... F6

Sights

1 Centre Belge de la Bande Dessinée ... F1
2 Galeries St-Hubert ... D3
3 Hôtel de Ville ... C4
4 Jeanneke Pis ... D2
5 Musées Royaux des Beaux-Arts ... F6
6 Néron Mural ... A3
7 Rue des Bouchers ... D3
8 Tibet & Duchâteau Mural ... B4

Sleeping

9 2Go4 Grand Place Rooms ... D3
10 Downtown-BXL ... B5
11 Hôtel Le Dixseptième ... D4
12 JH Bruegel ... C6

Eating

13 Belga Queen Brussels ... D1
14 Den Teepot ... A3
15 Fin de Siècle ... A2
16 Fritland ... C3
17 Le Perroquet ... D8
18 L'Ogenblik ... D3
19 Mokafé ... E3
20 Pita Street ... D4
21 Ricotta & Parmesan ... D2

Drinking

22 À la Bécasse ... C3
23 À la Mort Subite ... E2
24 A l'Image de Nostre-Dame ... C3
25 Au Bon Vieux Temps ... D3
26 Café des Halles ... B3
27 Chaloupe d'Or ... D4
28 Délirium ... D2
29 Falstaff ... C3
30 Floreo ... B3
31 Gecko ... A3
32 Le Cercle des Voyageurs ... B4
33 Le Cirio ... C3
34 Le Roy d'Espagne ... C3
35 L'Homo Erectus ... C3
36 Moeder Lambic Fontainas ... A5
37 Zebra ... B3

Entertainment

38 AB ... B3
39 Bozar ... F5
40 Cinematek ... G5
41 La Monnaie/De Munt ... D2
42 Le You ... D5

Shopping

43 Délices et Caprices ... E3
Galeries St-Hubert ... (see 2)
44 Leonidas ... D3
45 Leonidas ... D7
46 Neuhaus ... E3
47 Pierre Marcolini ... D7
48 Stijl ... A1

COMIC-STRIP CULTURE

Comic strips *(bande dessinée)* are revered here as the 'ninth art' with over 40 comic-murals enlivening Brussels house-ends. Locations are mapped on http://visitbrussels.be. Our favourites include:

» **Tibet & Duchâteau** (Rue du Bon Secours 9)

» **Quick & Flupke** (Rue Haute)

» **Cubitus** (Rue de Flandre) Manneken Pis displaced.

» **Néron** (Pl St-Géry)

Serious comic fans might appreciate Brussels' comprehensive **Centre Belge de la Bande Dessinée** (Belgian Comic Strip Centre; www.comicscenter.net; Rue des Sables 20; adult/concession/BrusselsCard €7.50/6/free; ⌚10am-6pm Tue-Sun), housed in a distinctive Horta-designed art-nouveau building and with a helpfully informative website.

The creator of Belgium's best-known comic-book hero, boy-detective *Tintin*, is celebrated at the superb new **Hergé Museum** (www.museeherge.com; adult/concession €9.50/7; ⌚10.30am-5.30pm Tue-Sun), an hour's train ride southeast of Brussels in the otherwise uninteresting student new-town of Louvain-la-Neuve.

Mokafé WAFFLES €

(Galerie du Roi; ⌚7.30am-11.30pm) Timeless cafe in the awesome Galeries St-Hubert, ideal for coffee or €2.60 waffles.

Fritland CHIPS €

(Rue Henri Maus 49; ⌚11am-1am Sun-Thu, 11am-3am Fri & Sat) Sit-down or takeaway *frites*.

Drinking

Cafe culture is one of Brussels' greatest attractions. The Grand Pl's 300-year-old gems such as **Le Roy d'Espagne** and **Chaloupe d'Or** are alluring but predictably pricey.

Cheaper classics around the Bourse include the sumptuous yet affordable 1866 **Le Cirio** and the art-nouveau **Falstaff** with its festival of century-old stained glass. Venture down shoulder-wide alleys nearby to find medieval **A L'Image de Nostre-Dame**, 1695 Rubenseque **Au Bon Vieux Temps** and Breuglian **À La Bécasse**, which specialises in *lambic* beers.

For a livelier vibe head for Pl St Géry, centred on **Café des Halles** (www.cafedeshalles.be), an 1881 market hall that's now part cafe, part exhibition hall and hosts a free weekend nightclub in its cellars. Surrounding cafes such **Zebra**, **Gecko** or **Floreo** are great for a quiet coffee by day or a musical buffeting on weekend nights.

Around Rue du Marché au Charbon you'll find a dozen gay-oriented bars including **L'Homo Erectus** (www.lhomoerectus.com; Rue des Pierres 57; ⌚4pm-dawn).

Delirium BAR COMPLEX

(www.deliriumcafe.be; Impasse de la Fidélité; ⌚10am-4am, to 2am Sun) Delirium's cellar beer-pub has over 2000 brews. Its **tap house** (www.deliriumtaphouse.be) features copper stills and 25 draft beers, while associated bars (open from 8pm) serve hundreds of *jenevers* (Dutch-style gins), vodkas, rums and absinthes. No wonder the little alley's so lively. Live music at 10.15pm.

Moeder Lambic Fontainas BEER PUB

(Pl Fontainas 8; ⌚10am-4am Mon-Sat, 10am-2am Sun;) A pub with designer decor, it has an incredible 40 brews on draft including *lambics* and gueuze.

Le Cercle des Voyageurs LOUNGE CAFE

(www.lecercledesvoyageurs.be; Rue des Grands Carmes 18; ⌚8am-11pm Wed-Mon;) This calm, high-ceilinged lounge-bar feels like a gentlemen's club and has a library of travel books for browsing.

À la Mort Subite CAFE

(Montagne aux Herbes Potagères 7; ⌚11am-midnight;) Unchanged since 1928 with lined-up wooden tables, mirror-panels and entertainingly brusque service.

☆ Entertainment

AB CONCERT HALL

(Ancienne Belgique; www.abconcerts.be; Blvd Anspach 110) Great venue for international and home-grown bands.

La Monnaie/De Munt OPERA HOUSE

(www.demunt.be; Pl de la Monnaie) Opera, theatre and dance.

USE-IT!

Use-It (www.use-it.be; Rue de la Fourche 50; ⏲10am-1pm & 2-6pm Mon-Sat) creates brilliant info-maps, full of irreverent, spot-on tips from locals. They're available as downloads or free from hostels and tourist offices (ask!). Cities covered by Use-It so far are Brussels, Bruges, Antwerp, Ghent, Leuven, Charleroi and Mechelen.

BoZar ARTS CENTRE
(www.bozar.be; Palais des Beaux-Arts, Rue Ravenstein 23) Music, dance, exhibitions, theatre.

Cinematek CINEMA
(www.cinematek.be; Rue Baron Horta 9; admission €3; ⏲from 5pm) Classic talkies plus silent movies with live piano accompaniment.

NIGHTCLUBS

Leading clubs include the legendary **Fuse** (www.fuse.be; Rue Blaes 208; admission €5-12; ⏲11pm-7am Fri & Sat; Ⓜ Porte de Hal), upstart **K-Nal/Libertine Supersport** (http://libertinesupersport.be; Ave du Port 1; ⏲11pm-6am Sat) and handily central **Le You** (www.leyou.be; Rue Duquesnoy 18; admission €10; ⏲from 11pm Thu-Sat, from 9pm Sun), where Thursday is for under-25s and Sunday is gay night.

Shopping

Tourist-oriented shops selling chocolate, beer, lace and Atomium-baubles stretch between the Grand Pl and Manneken Pis. For better **chocolate shops** in calmer, grander settings peruse the resplendent Galeries St-Hubert or those on and around Pl du Grand Sablon.

Established in 1857, **Neuhaus** (www.neuhaus.be; Galerie de la Reine; per kg €52) is the Brussels choc-classic, **Pierre Marcolini** (www.marcolini.be; per kg €70) is pricey but chic and experimental, while ubiquitous, unfairly maligned **Leonidas** (www.leonidas.com; per kg €20.20) offers an unbeatable price-quality ratio.

Pl du Jeu-de-Balle has a daily **flea market** (⏲6am-2pm). Rue Antoine Dansaert has most of Brussels' **high-fashion boutiques**, with **Stijl** (Rue Antoine Dansaert 74) hosting many cutting-edge collections.

Supermarkets sell a range of **Belgian beers** relatively cheaply, but for advice and specialist purchases visit friendly little **Délices et Caprices** (www.the-belgian-beer-tasting-shop.be; Rue des Bouchers 68; ⏲2-8pm Thu-Mon).

Information

ATMs are widespread. Exchange-agency rates are usually best around the Bourse.

Internet Access

Internet is free at Use-It and upstairs within **Bibliothèque des Riches Claires** (Rue des Riches Claires 24; ⏲12.30-3.30pm Tue, 12.30-5.30pm Wed, 10am-3pm Thu, 10am-5pm Fri, 9.30-11.30am Sat).

Tourist Information

There are info counters at Brussels airport and Bruxelles-Midi train station.

Brussels International (☎02 513 8940; http://visitbrussels.be; Grand Pl; ⏲9am-6pm Mon-Sat plus Sun summer) Cramped and often packed city info office within the Town Hall.

Flanders Info (☎02 504 0390; www.visitflanders.com; Rue du Marché aux Herbes 61; ⏲9am-6pm Mon-Sat, 10am-5pm Sun; 📶)

Use-It Brilliant independent info office (see the boxed text).

Getting There & Away

AIR See p134.

BUS Eurolines (☎02 274 1350; www.eurolines.be; Rue du Progrès 80; ⏲5.45am-8.45pm; 🚊Gare du Nord) International buses depart from Bruxelles-Nord train station.

TRAIN Eurostar, TGV and Thalys high-speed trains stop only at **Bruxelles-Midi** (Brussel-Zuid). If arriving there, jump on any local service for the four-minute hop to more convenient **Bruxelles-Central**. All domestic trains (p135) plus some Amsterdam services stop there anyway. For timetables, see www.b-rail.be.

Getting Around

To/From Brussels Airport

For Brussels–South Charleroi Airport see p134.

TRAIN Four trains run hourly from 5.30am to 11.50pm (€5.10, 16/20 minutes from Bruxelles-Central/Bruxelles-Midi).

TAXI Around €35. Bad idea in rush-hour traffic.

Bicycle

Brussels Bike Tours (www.brusselsbiketours.com; adult/student incl bicycle rental €30/25; ⏲10am & 3pm Apr-Sep, 11am Oct) Has 3½-hour tours, maximum group size 12.

FietsPunt/PointVelo (www.recyclo.org; per day/3 days €7.50/15; ⏲7am-7pm Mon-Fri) Outside Bruxelles-Central's Madeleine exit.

Villo! (www.villo.be; membership per day/week/yr €1.50/7/30; ⏲24hr) Automated rental pick-up/drop-off system is ideal for hops under half an hour. Read conditions carefully.

Public Transport

Services run 6am to midnight daily, though limited 'Noctis' buses (fare €3) run midnight to 3am Friday and Saturday. For general information, see www.stib.be.

Once validated, tickets (€1.70/4.50/9.50 for one hour/one day/three days) can be used on any combination of metros, trams and city buses (but not for reaching the airport). Paying aboard costs more.

AROUND BRUSSELS

Waterloo

POP 31,000

European history changed its course in June 1815 when Napoleon was definitively defeated 5km south of **Waterloo Town** (www.waterloo-tourisme.be). The battlefield is mostly a vast patchwork of rolling fields. Most striking is a steep grassy cone of artificial hill topped with a great bronze **lion**, which you can climb (€6) to survey the scene. Access is through a **visitor centre** (www.waterloo1815.be; ⏲10am-5pm), which offers various paid experiences including diorama, film show, waxworks and guided truck-tours to outer battle sites (€12 for the full experience). A massive annual **battle reconstruction** is held in mid-June.

Instead of arriving at Waterloo's inconvenient train station, get within 800m of the battlefield by TEC bus W from either Ave Fonsny (outside Bruxelles-Midi in Brussels) or from the much closer Braine l'Alleud train station on the Brussels–Charleroi line.

FLANDERS

Belgium's Dutch-speaking northern region is the country's economic powerhouse but also home to the great historic art cities Bruges, Ghent and fashion-conscious Antwerp.

Antwerp (Antwerpen, Anvers)

POP 457,000

Belgium's second-biggest city oozes attitude with a capital A. It's a magnet for fashionistas, foodies and partying club queens but also boasts a fine historical heart, a classic cafe scene and one of Europe's biggest harbours...

WORTH A TRIP

BRUSSELS TO ANTWERP

Train hopping between Brussels and Antwerp? Make a day of it, starting with **Leuven**, to the east, home not only to Stella Artois but also to Flanders' top university and a truly flamboyant 15th-century town hall *(stadhuis)*. Then continue via impressively historic **Mechelen** and very pretty little **Lier** with its canals, begijnhof (see p125) and crazy clock.

Sights

Grote Markt MARKET SQUARE

Antwerp's epicentre is graced by a Renaissance-style **Stadhuis**, photogenically reconstructed guildhalls and the baroque **Brabo Fountain**. The latter features a bronze hero throwing the severed hand of a dastardly giant, illustrating the city's legendary etymology: '*Hand Werpen*' (hand throwing) becoming Antwerpen.

Onze-Lieve-Vrouwekathedraal CATHEDRAL

(www.dekathedraal.be; Handschoenmarkt; adult/concession €5/3; ⏲10am-5pm Mon-Fri, 10am-3pm Sat, 10am-4pm Sun) Belgium's largest Gothic cathedral (built 1352–1521) still dominates the city skyline thanks to a steeple that is arguably the most magnificent in Europe. Priceless artworks inside include two world-famous Rubens tableaux.

Museum Plantin-Moretus HISTORIC BUILDING

(www.museumplantinmoretus.be; Vrijdag Markt 22; adult/youth €6/4; ⏲10am-5pm Tue-Sun) Antwerp has saved numerous historic homes as art-filled museums, but none can compare to this enchanting Unesco-rated medieval building that once housed the world's first industrial printing works.

Rubenshuis HOUSE MUSEUM

(www.museum.antwerpen.be; Wapper 9-11; adult/concession €6/4; ⏲10am-5pm Tue-Sun) The Antwerp home and studio of Pieter Paul Rubens, northern Europe's greatest baroque artist, has been meticulously restored/rebuilt along original lines and is filled with 17th-century artworks, albeit relatively few by the master himself.

Fashion District NEIGHBOURHOOD

Antwerp has emerged as an avant-garde fashion capital thanks to talented alumni

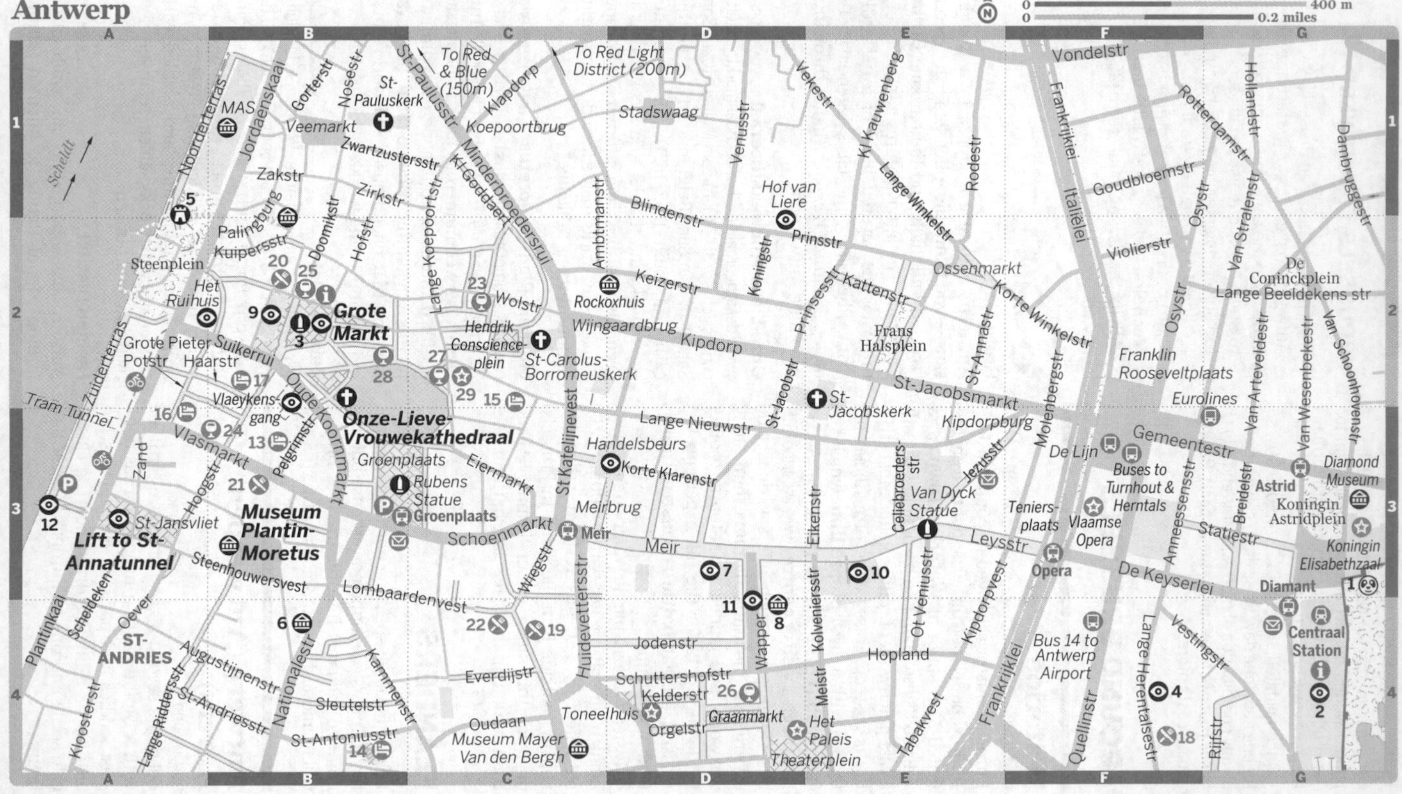
Antwerp
0 400 m
0 0.2 miles
Scheldt
Noorderterras
Jordaenskaal
MAS
Gorterstr
Nosestr
St-Pauluskerk
Veemarkt
Zwartzustersstr
St-Paulusstr
To Red & Blue (150m)
Klapdorp
To Red Light District (200m)
Koepoortbrug
Minderbroedersrui
Kl Goddaert
Stadswaag
Venusstr
Vekestr
Kl Kauwenberg
Lange Winkelstr
Rodestr
Frankrijklei
Italiëlei
Vondelstr
Goudbloemstr
Rotterdamstr
Hollandstr
Dambruggestr
Zakstr
Zirkstr
Palingburg
Kuipersstr
Doornikstr
Hofstr
Lange Koepoortstr
Ambtmanstr
Blindenstr
Hof van Liere
Prinsstr
Koningstr
Violierstr
Osystr
Van Straelenstr
De Coninckplein
Lange Beeldekens str
Steenplein
Het Ruihuis
Grote Markt
Wolstr
Rockoxhuis
Keizerstr
Prinsesstr
Kattenstr
Ossenmarkt
Korte Winkelstr
Grote Pieter Potstr
Haarstr
Suikerrui
Hendrik Conscienceplein
Wijngaardbrug
Kipdorp
St-Carolus-Borromeuskerk
Frans Halsplein
St-Annastr
Franklin Rooseveltplaats
Van Arteveldestr
Van Wesenbekestr
Van Schoonhovenstr
Zuiderterras
Tram Tunnel
Vlaeykensgang
Oude Koornmarkt
Onze-Lieve-Vrouwekathedraal
St-Jacobsmarkt
St-Jacobstr
St-Jacobskerk
Lange Nieuwstr
Kipdorpburg
Molenbergstr
Eurolines
Gemeentestr
Vlasmarkt
Pelgrimstr
Zand
Groenplaats
Eiermarkt
Handelsbeurs
Korte Klarenstr
St Katelijnevest
Cellebroedersstr
Jezusstr
De Lijn
Buses to Turnhout & Herntals
Diamond Museum
Astrid
Koningin Astridplein
Hoogstr
Rubens Statue
Groenplaats
Meirbrug
Van Dyck Statue
Teniersplaats
Vlaamse Opera
Anneessensstr
Breidelstr
Statiestr
Koningin Elisabethzaal
Lift to St-Annatunnel
St-Jansvliet
Museum Plantin-Moretus
Steenhouwersvest
Schoenmarkt
Meir
Wiegstr
Leysstr
Opera
De Keyserlei
Diamant
Lombaardenvest
Huidevettersstr
Eikenstr
Ot Veniusstr
Kipdorpvest
Vestingstr
Centraal Station
Plantinkaai
Scheldeken
Oever
ST-ANDRIES
Augustijnenstr
Nationalestr
Kammenstr
Everdijstr
Jodenstr
Wapper
Kolveniersstr
Hopland
Bus 14 to Antwerp Airport
Lange Herentalsestr
Kloosterstr
Lange Riddersstr
St-Andriesstr
Sleutelstr
St-Antoniusstr
Oudaan
Museum Mayer Van den Bergh
Toneelhuis
Schuttershofstr
Kelderstr
Orgelstr
Graanmarkt
Meistr
Het Paleis
Theaterplein
Tabakvest
Frankrijklei
Quellinstr
Rijfstr
A
B
C
D
E
F
G
1
2
3
4
5
6
7
8
9
10
11
12
13
14
15
16
17
18
19
20
21
22
23
24
25
26
27
28
29

of the **Flanders Fashion Institute** (www.ffi.be), which hosts style museum **MoMu** (www.momu.be; Nationalestraat 28; adult/concession €7/5; ⏲10am-6pm Tue-Sun) featuring regularly changing exhibitions. The boutiques of Antwerp's ever-expanding 'fashion district' spread out from here: the tourist office sells fashion-trail maps.

Scheldt Riverbank NEIGHBOURHOOD

Zuiderterras is a raised promenade following the Scheldt (Schelde) River south from **Het Steen**, Antwerp's partly medieval castle. At the pretty tree-lined square called **St-Jansvliet**, a lift descends to the 1930s **St-Annatunnel** (admission free) allowing pedestrians and cyclists to cross 570m beneath the river to the **Linkeroever** (Left Bank) for a memorable city panorama.

DON'T MISS

STROLLING INTO TOWN

If you're walking from Antwerpen-Centraal to Antwerp's historic centre, follow pedestrianised **Meir/Leystraat,** a splendid shopping street lined with grand, statue-draped architecture. En route, look inside the awesome, gilt-overloaded shopping mall **Stadsfeestzaal** (Meir 76), and watch top-quality chocolates being made at **Chocolate Line** (www.thechocolateline.be; ⏲10.30am-6.30pm) in the mural-overloaded 1745 **Paleis op de Meir** (www.paleisopdemeir.be, in Dutch; Meir 50) embellished by Napoleon.

STATION AREA

The palatial 1905 **Antwerpen-Centraal** train station is an attraction in itself. Antwerp's famous **zoo** (www.zooantwerpen.be) is just outside and nearby, an astounding 80% of all the world's uncut diamonds are traded in the architecturally miserable **Diamond Quarter**. For 'the cost of a smile', see polishers at work at sales-showroom **Diamondland** (www.diamondland.be; Appelmansstraat 33a; admission free; ⏲9.30am-5pm Mon-Sat).

'T ZUID

Around 1km south of the fashion quarter, 't Zuid is a conspicuously prosperous area dotted with century-old architecture, hip bars and fine restaurants. Antwerp's palatial 1890 gallery, **KMSKA** (www.kmska.be; Leopold De Waelplaats, 't Zuid; 🚌1 or 23), has one of northern Europe's finest art collections but is largely closed for renovation until at least 2012. Highlights will be shown across town at Antwerp's brand new city museum, **MAS** (www.mas.be; Hanzestedenplaats).

Antwerp

Top Sights

	Grote Markt	B2
	Lift to St-Anna tunnel	A3
	Museum Plantin-Moretus	B3
	Onze-Lieve-Vrouwekathedraal	B2

Sights

1	Antwerp Zoo	G3
2	Antwerpen Centraal Train Station	G4
3	Brabo Fountain	B2
	Chocolate Line	(see 7)
4	Diamondland	F4
5	Het Steen	A1
6	MoMu	B4
7	Paleis op de Meir	D3
8	Rubenshuis	D4
9	Stadhuis	B2
10	Stadsfeestzaal	E3
11	Ticket Office for Rubenshuis	D4
12	Zuiderterras	A3

Sleeping

13	Den Heksenketel	B3
14	HI Hostel	B4
15	Hotel Julien	C2
16	Katshuis	A3
17	Matelote Hotel	B2

Eating

18	Aahaar	F4
19	Chocolatiers	C4
20	De 7 Schaken	B2
21	De Groote Witte Arend	B3
22	Lombardia	C4

Drinking

23	De Kat	C2
24	De Ware Jacob	B3
25	Den Engel	B2
26	Oud Arsenaal	D4
27	Pelikaan	C2
28	't Elfde Gebod	B2

Entertainment

29	De Muze	C2

SPLURGE

Hotel Julien (☎03 229 0600; www.hotel-julien.com; Korte Nieuwstraat 24; r €170-290; ❄📶@) is a very discreet mansion-hotel that exudes tastefully understated elegance and a subtle modernist style. Many characterful rooms have exposed beams or old brick-tile floors, while reception feels like a designer's office.

Sleeping

Over 40 B&Bs can be sorted by price or map location on www.bedandbreakfast-antwerp.com but relatively few are central.

Matelote Hotel BOUTIQUE HOTEL €€
(☎03 201 8800; www.hotel-matelote.be; Haarstraat 11; r €90-190; @📶) Discreet new design hotel on a pedestrianised backstreet in the heart of the city, with 10 contemporary rooms, tastefully arranged in a 16th-century building.

ABhostel HOSTEL €
(☎0473 570166; www.abhostel.com; Kattenberg 110; dm/d €21/50; ⏲check-in noon-3pm & 6-8pm; 📶) In this adorable family-run hostel, room walls double as chalk-board graffiti spaces and there's lots of little added extras to make it comfy. Its odd inner-suburban setting is 20 minutes' walk east of Antwerpen-Centraal station past inexpensive shops, ethnic restaurants and African wig-shops.

Katshuis GUEST HOUSE €
(☎0476 206947; www.katshuis.be; Grote Pieter Potstraat 18 & 19; s/d/tr €35/50/80) Stairs are steep and rooms vary but while none are overly polished, some have microwave, chandeliers and wooden beams and all are great value. Phone ahead to arrange check-in time (after 4pm).

HI Hostel HOSTEL €
(Jeugdherberg; ☎03 238 0273; antwerpen@vjh.be) A brand new custom-built hostel is due to open during 2011 on helpfully central Bogaardeplein. Most locals haven't a clue where that is so use our map!

Den Heksenketel HOSTEL €
(☎0489 395780; www.denheksenketel.com; Pelgrimstraat 22; dm €20; 📶) Rough-edged but super-central two-dorm backpacker hostel above a decent bar on a buzzing, pedestrianised street with an unbeatable cathedral view. There are only two toilets. New management plans 2011 improvements.

Eating

Find cheap snacks on Hoogstraat (south of Grote Markt); cosy, pricier options in parallel Pelgrimstraat, 'secret' medieval alley Vlaaikeusgang or the picturesque lanes around Rubens' recently fire-damaged St-Carolus-Borromeuskerk. There are several chocolate shops around the cafe Lombardia. A great mix of options both hip and historic are north and west of KMSKA in 't Zuid.

De Groote Witte Arend BELGIAN €€
(☎03 233 5033; www.degrootewittearend.be; Braderijstraat 24; snacks €4-9, mains €12-20; ⏲10.30am-midnight) Well-cooked Belgian classics including *stoemp*, eel, shrimp croquettes and rabbit in Westmalle are served around the open cloister of a former convent with its own preserved chapel. You don't have to dine to sample from its selection of over 80 Belgian beers.

Lombardia ORGANIC, VEGAN €€
(www.lombardia.be; Lombaardenvest 78; sandwiches €7.20-12, vegan/non-veg lunch €13.50/15.50; ⏲7.45am-6pm Mon-Sat) Experience frothy Ginger Love (www.gingerlove.be; €4) at this simple but legendary health-food shop–cafe whose owner has cooked for Sting and Moby.

De 7 Schaken BISTRO €€
(www.de7schaken.be; Braderijstraat 24; snacks €7-10, mains €12-22; ⏲11am-11pm) Entered through a wood-panelled pub just off Grote Markt, this traditionally styled bistro serves sensibly priced Belgian mainstays.

Aahaar INDIAN, VEGAN €
(www.aahaar.com; Lange Herentalsstraat 23; mains/buffet €6.80/9; ⏲noon-3pm & 6-9.30pm) Recommended five-dish budget buffets; it's 100% vegetarian.

Drinking

To sound like a local, stride into a pub and ask for a *bolleke*. Don't worry, that means a 'little bowl' (ie glass) of De Koninck, the city's favourite ale. Atmospheric but good-value places to try one include **Oud Arsenaal** (Pijpelincxstraat 4; ⏲9am-7.30pm Fri-Wed), **De Kat** (Wolstraat 22), **De Ware Jacob** (Vlasmarkt 19) and livelier **Pelikaan** (Melkmarkt 14).

TRAINS FROM ANTWERPEN-CENTRAAL

DESTINATION	FARE	DURATION	SERVICES (PER HR)
Amsterdam	€26.90	190min	1
Bruges	€14.20	70min	1
Brussels	€6.30	35-49min	5
Ghent	€9.90	50min	2
Leuven	€6.60	45min	2
Liège ('Luik')	€14.80	125min	1
Lier	€2.50	15min	2
Mechelen	€2.90	15min	2

Den Engel BAR
(Grote Markt 5; 9am-2am) Historic watering hole whose terrace provides perfect views across the main square.

't Elfde Gebod BAR
(www.kathedraalcafe.be; Torfbrug 10; noon-11pm Mon-Sat, noon-10pm Sun;) Ivy-clad medieval masterpiece decked with angels, saints, pulpits and several deliciously sacrilegious visual jokes.

Bierhuis Kulminator PUB
(Vleminckveld 32; 8pm-midnight Mon, 11am-midnight Tue-Fri, 5pm-late Sat) Classic pub boasting 700 mostly Belgian beers including some rare vintage bottles.

Bar Tabac BAR
(www.bartabac.be; Waalsekaai 43; draft Stella/Westmalle €1.90/2.40; 9pm-7am Wed-Sat) Unpretentious, low-lit one-room bar in 't Zuid that tries hard not to try hard. If you prefer smoother lounges or buzzing music bars, half a dozen are close by (on Waalsekaai and Luikstraat) and crank up insistent music till the wee hours.

Entertainment

For listings consult www.weekup.be/antwerpen/week, www.zva.be in summer or www.gratisinantwerpen.be for free events.

Weekend-only nightclubs include friendly **Café Local** (www.cafelocal.be; Waalsekaai 25; members/nonmembers €9/10, beers/shots €2.50/5; 10pm-late Thu-Sat; 8) in 't Zuid, long-running **Café d'Anvers** (www.cafe-d-anvers.com; Verversrui 15; 7) in the seedy red-light district and nearby **Red & Blue** (www.redandblue.be; Lange Schipperskapelstraat 11), where Fridays are mixed but Saturday nights showcase one of Europe's best-loved gay discos.

De Muze (03 226 0126; Melkmarkt 15; noon-4am) is a two-level cafe that is a bastion of live jazz from 10pm Monday to Saturday. There are other live music alternatives nearby.

Information

Tourism Antwerp (03 232 0103; www.visitantwerpen.be; Grote Markt 13; 9am-5.45pm Mon-Sat, 9am-4.45pm Sun) Central tourist office with a branch at Antwerpen-Centraal train station.

Getting There & Away

BUS Regional **De Lijn** (www.delijn.be) and international **Eurolines** (03 233 8662; Van Stralenstraat 8; 9am-5.45pm Mon-Fri, 9am-3.15pm Sat) buses both start from points near Franklin Rooseveltplaats.

TRAIN Handsome **Antwerpen-Centraal Station** (Diamant) is 1km east of Antwerp's historic centre.

Getting Around

Rooseveltplaats and Koningin Astridplein are hubs for the integrated network of **De Lijn** (www.delijn.be) buses and trams.

Ghent (Gent, Gand)

POP 235,000

Flanders' unsung historic city, Ghent is like a grittier Bruges without the crush of tourists. It nonetheless sports photogenic canals, medieval towers, great cafes and some of Belgium's most inspired museums. Always a lively student city, in mid-July things go crazy during the 10-day **Gentse Feesten** (www.gentsefeesten.be).

Sights

The main sights of the city are within strolling distance of Korenmarkt, the westernmost of three interlinked squares that form the heart of Ghent's historic core.

TOP CHOICE Graslei & Patershol NEIGHBOURHOOD

For one of Belgium's most photogenic views, cross **Grasbrug** bridge and look towards **Graslei**, the city's favoured waterfront promenade, lined with archetypal step-gabled warehouses and townhouses. Tour-

Ghent

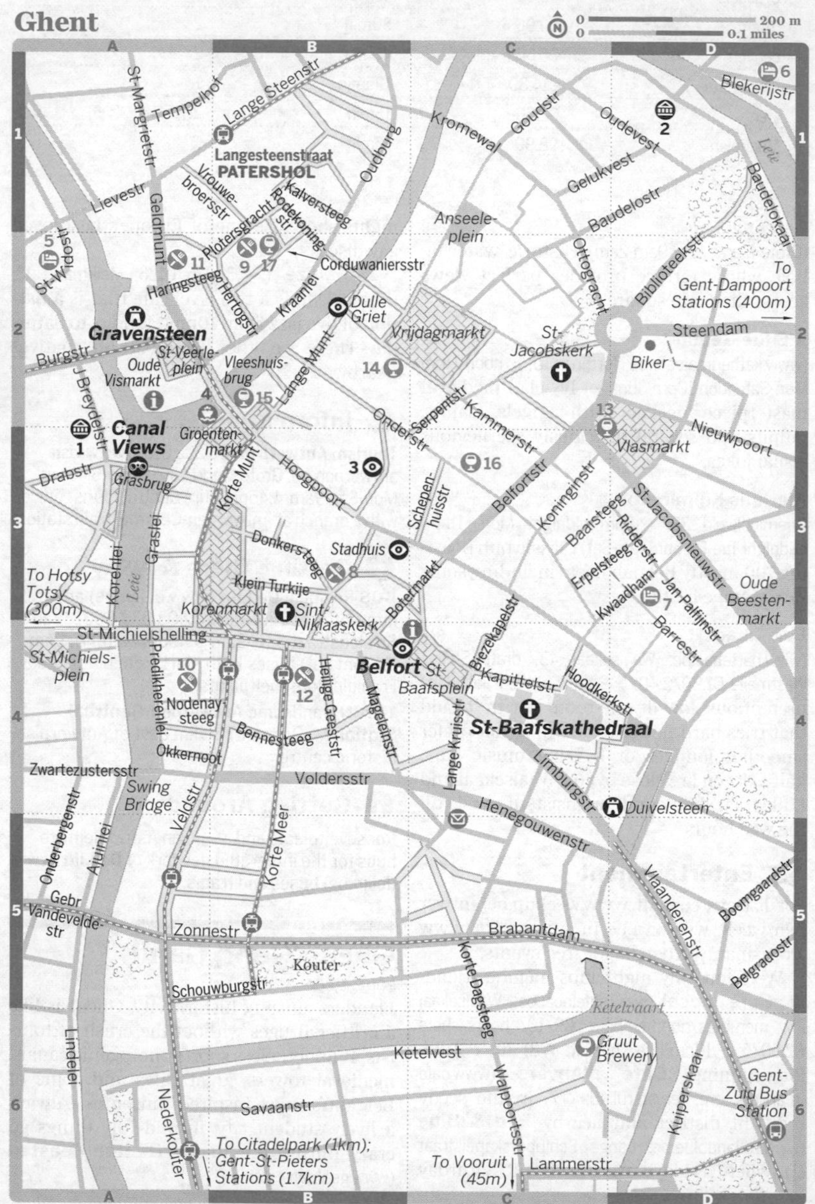

isty **canal-boat rides** (tickets €6; ⏲10am-6pm Mar–mid-Oct, weekends only mid-Oct–Feb) depart regularly from near here or you can stroll aimlessly around the picturesque, restaurant-dotted alleys of the medieval **Patershol district**, north of the bridge.

St-Baafskathedraal CATHEDRAL
(St-Baafsplein; ⏲8.30am-6pm Apr-Oct, 8.30am-5pm Nov-Mar) Massive without majesty, this vast cathedral is an essential stop for fans of Flemish Primitive art who flock to see Jan van Eyck's world-famous 1432 masterpiece the **Adoration of the Mystic Lamb** (admission €3; ⏲9.30am-4.30pm Mon-Sat, 1-4.30pm Sun Apr-Oct, 10.30am-3.30pm Mon-Sat, 1-3.30pm Sun Nov-Mar). To see what the fuss is about without queuing or paying, see the photo-replica in side-chapel 30.

Belfort MEDIEVAL TOWER
(Botermarkt; adult/concession €3/2.50; ⏲10am-5.30pm mid-Mar–mid-Nov) The city's 14th-century belfry affords spectacular views of Ghent while an audioguide provides historical commentary.

Gravensteen CASTLE
(St-Veerleplein; adult/concession €8/6; ⏲9am-5pm Apr-Sep, 9am 4pm Oct-Mar) Lovingly restored, this quintessential 12th-century castle actually spent the 19th century recycled as a factory. An imaginative video story-tour compensates for a relative lack of period furnishings.

Werregarensteeg GRAFFITI ALLEY
Check it out for street art.

Sleeping

For a complete B&B listing see www.bedandbreakfast-gent.be.

Hostel 47 HOSTEL €
(☎0478 712827; www.hostel47.com; Blekerijstraat 47-51; dm €26.50-29.50, d/tr €71/97.50) With white-on-white fashion decor in a refitted high-ceilinged classical house, this is one of Europe's calmest and most stylish hostels. No sign. Phone ahead as reception is often unstaffed.

Hotel Flandria BUDGET HOTEL €€
(☎09 223 0626; www.hotelflandria-gent.be; Barrestraat 3; s/d/tr/q €58/68/100/125, without bathroom s/d €43/53; @📶) Friendly owners are gradually ironing out the dowdier features of this basic but traveller-friendly hotel with comfy beds and a central location on a dark, narrow lane. Reception closes at 10pm.

De Draecke HOSTEL €
(☎09 233 7050; www.vjh.be; St-Widostraat 11; members dm/tw €18.80/46; @) Ideally central if institutionally functional HI hostel behind a traditional step-gabled facade. Breakfast included, towels, lockers and internet extra. No lock-out.

Eating

There's an endlessly tempting selection of eateries in the alleys of Patershol, along Graslei's photogenic canal-side and up Oudburg, where prices fall the further north you walk. Ghent is vegetarian friendly; see www.visitgent.be/Documenten/visit_gent/Veggie/Veggieplan_EN.pdf.

Ghent

Top Sights
- Belfort B4
- Graslei Canal Views A3
- Gravensteen A2
- St-Baafskathedraal C4

Sights
- 1 Design Museum A3
- 2 MIAT D1
- 3 Werregarensteeg (graffiti alley) B3

Activities, Courses & Tours
- 4 Canal Tours A2

Sleeping
- 5 De Draecke A2
- 6 Hostel 47 .... D1
- 7 Hotel Flandria D3

Eating
- 8 Amadeus B3
- 9 Amadeus B2
- 10 Brasserie Pakhuis A4
- 11 Eethuis Avalon A2
- 12 Soup'r B4

Drinking
- 13 Charlatan C2
- 14 Herberg de Dulle Griet B2
- 15 Het Waterhuis aan de Bierkant B2
- Hot Club de Gand .... (see 15)
- 16 Pink Flamingo's C3
- 17 Rococo B2

SEE MORE OF GHENT

Ghent's good-value **Museumpass** (www.visitgent.be; €20) provides three days' free city transport and entrance to all the sights reviewed (except boat tours) plus much more including the dynamic **MIAT** (www.miat.gent.be; Minnemeers 9; adult/youth €5/1; ⏲10am-6pm Tue-Sun) industrial museum, the interesting **Design Museum** (www.designmuseumgent.be; Jan Breydelstraat 5; adult/concession €5/3.75; ⏲10am-6pm Tue-Sun) and less central attractions such as the new **STAM City Museum** (www.stamgent.be; Bijloke Complex; adult/concession €6/4.50; ⏲10am-6pm Tue-Sun; 🚊4), and the spooky **Dr Guislain Mental Health Museum** (www.museumdrguislain.be; Jozef Guislainstraat 43; adult/youth €5/1; ⏲9am-5pm Tue-Fri, 1-5pm Sat & Sun; 🚊1) hidden away in an 1857 neo-Gothic lunatic asylum.

Art galleries covered include **SMAK** (www.smak.be; Citadelpark; adult 26 & over/concession/under 26 €6/4/1, 10am-1pm Sun free; ⏲10am-6pm Tue-Sun; 🚌5) for cutting-edge contemporary exhibitions, and the more classical **Museum voor Schone Kunsten** (www.mskgent.be; Citadelpark; adult 26 & over/under 26 €5/1; ⏲10am-6pm Tue-Sun; 🚌5) in Citadelpark.

Brasserie Pakhuis EUROPEAN, OYSTERS €€
(☎09 223 5555; Schuurkenstraat 4; mains €13.50-29, set lunch €12.90, set dinner €25-42; ⏲noon-11pm Mon-Sat, bar to 1am) This hip if mildly ostentations brasserie-bar-restaurant is set in an elegantly restored former textile warehouse.

Amadeus RIBS €€
(mains €12.50-17; ⏲6.30pm-11pm) Patershol (☎09 225 1385; Plotersgracht 8/10); Botermarkt (☎09 223 3775; Goudenleeuwplein 7) Great-value all-you-can-eat spare ribs (€13.95) served at two equally enticing addresses, both dressed up like Parisian brasseries.

Eethuis Avalon VEGETARIAN €
(☎09 224 3724; Geldmunt 32; meals €9-13; ⏲11.30am-2.30pm Mon-Sat; 🖉) Reliably delicious, organic vegetarian food served in a warren of little rooms or outside on a small, tree-shaded terrace.

Soup'r SOUP €
(Sint-Niklaasstraat 9; small/large soup €3/4.50, sandwiches €2.70-4; ⏲11.30am-5pm Mon-Sat) Attractive modern soup kitchen.

Drinking

For character, variety and eccentricity, Ghent's cafes are world-beaters. Try **Hot Club de Gand** (www.hotclubdegand.be; Schuddevisstraatje; ⏲3pm-late) for live acoustic music, **Hotsy Totsy** (www.hotsytotsy.be; Hoogstraat 1; ⏲6pm-1am) for jazz buzz, **Rococo** (Corduwanierstraat 5; ⏲from 10pm) for candle-lit conversation, **Het Waterhuis aan de Bierkant** (www.waterhuisaandebierkant.be; Groentenmarkt 12; ⏲11am-1am) or **Herberg De Dulle Griet** (Vrijdagmarkt 50; ⏲4.30pm-1am Tue-Sat, noon-7.30pm Mon) for beer choice, **Pink Flamingo's** (www.pinkflamingos.be; Onderstraat 55) for retro-kitsch and **Charlatan** (www.charlatan.be; Vlasmarkt 9; ⏲7pm-late Tue-Sun) for raucous partying.

Information

Tourist office (☎09 266 5232; www.visitgent.be; Botermarkt 17; ⏲9.30am-6.30pm Apr-Oct, 9.30am-4.30pm Nov-Mar) Should move to the old fish-market building on St-Veerleplein during late 2011.

Getting There & Away

Gent-Dampoort, 1km west of the old city, is the handiest train station with useful trains to Antwerp (€8.60, fast/slow 42/64 minutes, three per hour), Bruges (€5.90, 35 minutes, hourly) and Lille, France (€15.20, 68 minutes, hourly) via Kortrijk. Ghent's main station, **Gent-St-Pieters** (2.5km south of centre; 🚊1) has more choice including Brussels (€8.10, 36 minutes, twice hourly) and Bruges (fast/slow 24/42 minutes, five per hour).

Getting Around

BICYCLE Hire bikes from Gent-St-Pieters station **luggage room** (bagagekantoor; per day €9.50, deposit €12.50) or **Biker** (Steendam 16; per half-/full-day €6.50/9; ⏲9am-12.30pm & 1.30-6pm Tue-Sat). ID required.

BUS & TRAM One-hour/all-day tickets cost €1.20/5 if purchased in advance from ticket machines or **De Lijn offices**. Tram 1 picks up within the tunnel to the left as you exit Gent-St-Pieters station then runs to Korenmarkt, Gravensteen and beyond.

Bruges (Brugge)

POP 117,000

Cobblestone lanes, dreamy canals, soaring spires and whitewashed old almshouses combine to make central Bruges (Brugge in Dutch) one of Europe's most picture-perfect historic cities. The only problem is that everyone knows it.

Bruges was one of 14th-century Europe's leading trade centres but the waterway linking the city to the sea silted up, cutting its economic lifeline. Traders abandoned the city, leaving it suspended in time for centuries. The romantic myth of its 19th-century 'rediscovery' adds to its vast tourist appeal.

Sights

The real joy of Bruges is simply wandering the canal-sides soaking up the atmosphere. To avoid the worst crowds explore east of pretty Jan van Eyckplein.

Markt MEDIEVAL SQUARE

Bruges' nerve centre, this large open square is ringed by step-gabled street cafes and dominated by the 84m, 13th-century **Belfort** (adult/concession €8/6; ⏲9.30am-5pm, last tickets 4.15pm), Belgium's most famous belfry. Climbing its 366 steps gets claustrophobic.

Burg MEDIEVAL SQUARE

Bruges' 1420 **Stadhuis** (City Hall; Burg 12) is smothered in statuettes and contains a breathtaking **Gotishe Zaal** (Gothic Hall; adult/concession €2/1; ⏲9.30am-4.30pm). In the easily missed **Basilica of the Holy Blood** (Burg 5; ⏲9.30am-11.50am & 2-5.50pm, to 3.50pm Oct-Mar) is a phial believed to contain a few coagulated drops of Christ's blood. It's venerated daily (usually 2pm).

TOP CHOICE **Groeningemuseum** ART GALLERY

(Dijver 12; adult/concession €8/6; ⏲9.30am-5pm Tue-Sun) This small but extraordinarily valuable collection covers Flemish art from the 14th to 20th centuries, including some priceless Renaissance and Flemish Primitive works.

Onze-Lieve-Vrouwekerk CHURCH

(Mariastraat; ⏲9.30am-4.50pm Mon-Sat, 1.30-4.50pm Sun) This large, sober 13th-century church is best known for Michelangelo's small but serenely contemplative 1504 *Madonna and Child* statue.

Begijnhof CLOISTER GARDEN

(FREE; ⏲6.30am-6.30pm) One of Bruges' quaintest spots, the walled Begijnhof is an area of hushed calm just 10 minutes' walk south of the Markt, close to the romantic **Minnewater** (Lake of Love).

Choco-Story MUSEUM

(www.choco-story.be; Wijnzakstraat 2; adult/concession €6/5; ⏲10am-5pm) This absorbing private museum traces the cocoa bean's crooked path from Aztec currency to dieter's dilemma. Visits culminate in tasting a praline that's made as you watch.

Canal Tours BOAT TOURS

(tickets €6.90; ⏲10am-6pm Easter–early-Nov) Touristy half-hour boat tours depart every 20 minutes from various jetties.

Sleeping

Comprehensive http://hotels.brugge.be/en filters around 250 hotels and B&Bs; nonetheless, all options can still prove oppressively overbooked from Easter to September, over Christmas and especially at weekends. An all-night touch-screen computer outside the main tourist office displays last-minute availability and contact information.

B&B Dieltiens B&B €€

(☎050 334294; www.bedandbreakfastbruges.be; Waalsestraat 40; s/d/tr €70/80/100) Quiet yet central, filled with art old and new, this appealingly real home is run by charming musician hosts.

Tine's Guesthouse B&B €€

(☎050 345018; www.tinesguesthouse.com; Zwaluwenstraat 11; d €65) Homey, super-friendly B&B. It's 1.5km northwest of the belfry, but a great breakfast, a free packed lunch,

WHAT'S A BEGIJNHOF?

Usually enclosed around a central garden, a *begijnhof* (*béguinage* in French) is a pretty cluster of historic houses originally built to house lay sisters. The idea originated in the 12th century, when many such women were left widowed by their crusader-knight husbands. Today 14 of Flanders' historic *begijnhoven* have been declared Unesco World Heritage sites with great examples at **Diest**, **Lier**, **Turnhout**, **Kortrijk** and **Bruges**, which also has dozens of smaller *godshuizen* (almshouses).

free bikes and free station pick-up/drop-off amply compensate.

Hostel Lybeer HOSTEL €
(☎050 334355; www.hostellybeer.com; Korte Vuldersstraat 31; dm from €15, s/d without bathroom €27.50/55; @📶) 'Clean enough to be healthy, dirty enough to be happy', Lybeer has plenty of tatty edges but few hostels have such a homely feeling nor such congenitally good-humoured staff. Large common room, small kitchen, free internet; laundry costs €3.50.

Bruges

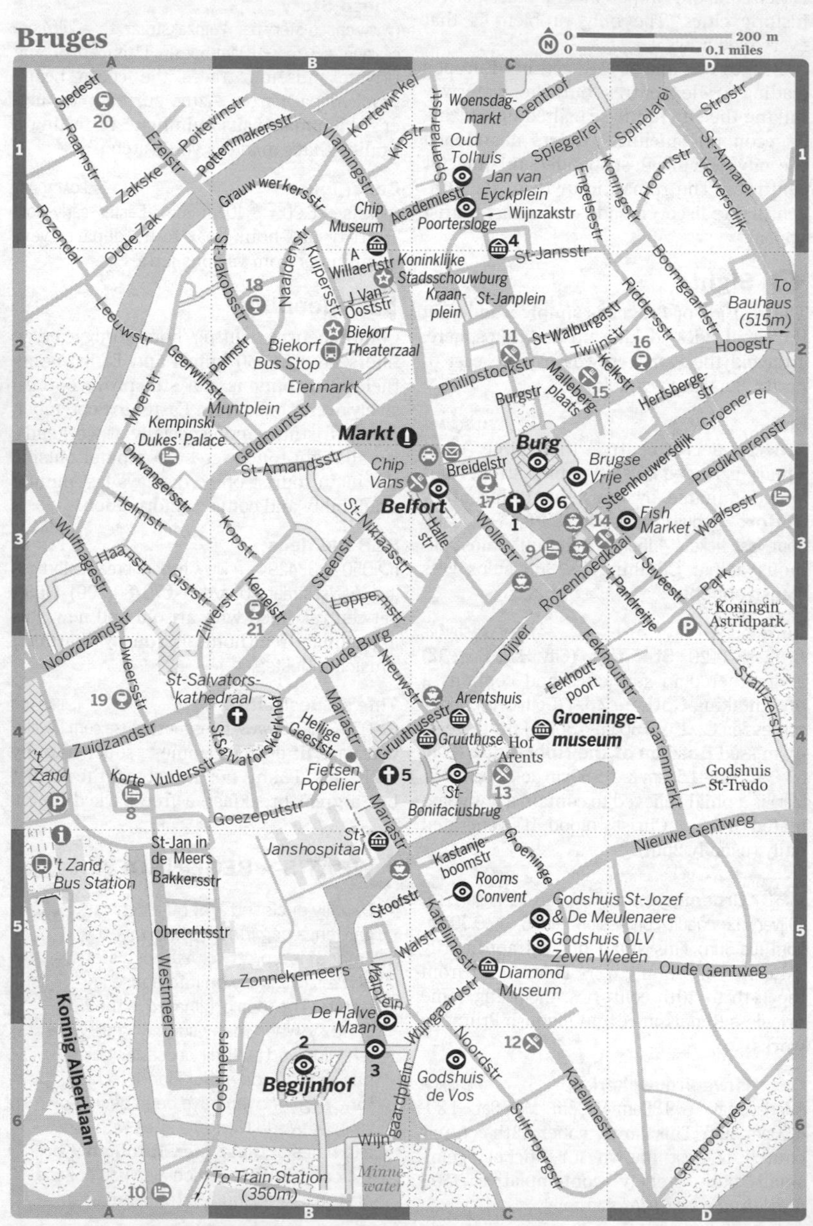

Bauhaus HOSTEL COMPLEX €
(☎050 341093; www.bauhaus.be; Langestraat 135 & 145; dm €15-22, s €30-34, tw €38-50; @📶) This well-run backpacker 'village' incorporates a bustling hostel, apartments, atmospheric bar-restaurant, nightclub, bike hire, internet cafe and a hidden little chill-out room/garden. Take bus 6 or 16 from the train station.

't Keizershof FAMILY HOTEL €
(☎050 338728; www.hotelkeizershof.be; Oostermeers 126; s/d/tr/q without bathroom €25/44/66/80; P) Seven simple but tasteful budget rooms; breakfast and parking included.

Etap Hotel CHAIN HOTEL €
(☎050 405120; www.etaphotel.com; Train Station; tr €49-59) Brand-new budget chain-hotel with retro-style fittings.

Camping Memling CAMPING GROUND €
(☎050 355845; www.camping-memling.be; Veltemweg 109, St Kruis; campsites per 2 people €14; ⏲year-round) A camping ground 3km east of Markt. From the train station take bus 11 to Delhaize.

Eating & Drinking

Est Wijnbar TAPAS €
(☎050 333839; Braambergstraat 7; mains €9.50-12.50, tapas €3.50-9.50; ⏲4pm-midnight Wed-Sun) Tiny two-tiered wine bar with tempting light meals including seven vegetarian options. There's live music on Sunday.

Cambrinus BRASSERIE €€
(Philipstockstraat 19; snacks €7, mains €17-23; ⏲noon-11pm) Pub-style eatery that keeps its kitchen open all day for Belgian favourites including many beer-based meals and offers hundreds of brews to wash them down with.

BRUGES MONEYSAVER

A three-day **Musea Brugge Pass** (adult €15) allows free entry to 16 attractions. Even if you only visit the Beltort and Groeningemuseum you'll already have saved money.

't Gulden Vlies BELGIAN €€
(Mallebergplaats 17; mains €14-22, 2-/3-course set meal €16/27; ⏲7pm-3am Wed-Sun) Intimate late-night restaurant with old-fashioned decor and good value Belgian cuisine.

De Bron VEGETARIAN €
(Katelijnestraat 82; set lunch from €8.50; ⏲11.45am-2pm Mon-Fri) Bright and functional for a one-choice vegetarian lunch-of-the-day.

De Republiek CAFE €
(St Jakobsstraat 36; ⏲from 11am) Congenial cafe with cheap snack-meals available until midnight.

Hostels **Bauhaus**, **Passage** (www.passagebruges.com), **Charlie Rockets** (www.charlierockets.com) and **Snuffel Hostel** (www.snuffel.be) all have pleasant backpacker-oriented pubs, most serving decent yet inexpensive food. For beer choice seek out **'t Brugs Beertje** (Kemelstraat 5; ⏲4pm-1am Thu-Tue) or hidden **De Garre** (Garre 1; ⏲noon-midnight), whose unique Garre Tripel (€3) is an exceptional 11% mind-blower.

Bruges

Top Sights

	Belfort	C3
	Burg	C3
	Groeningemuseum	C4
	Markt	B2

Sights

1	Basilica of the Holy Blood	C3
2	Begijnhof	B6
3	Begijnhof Gateway Bridge	B6
4	Choco-Story	C1
5	Onze-Lieve-Vrouwekerk	B4
6	Stadhuis	C3

Sleeping

7	B&B Dieltiens	D3
8	Hostel Lybeer	A4
9	Relais Bourgondisch Cruyce	C3
10	't Keizershof	A6

Eating

11	Cambrinus	C2
12	De Bron	C6
13	Den Gouden Harynck	C4
14	Est Wijnbar	C3
15	't Gulden Vlies	C2

Drinking

16	Charlie Rockets	D2
17	De Garre	C3
18	De Republiek	B2
19	Passage Hostel & Cafe	A4
20	Snuffel Hostel	A1
21	't Brugs Beertje	B3

BRUGES SPLURGE

Luxury and history intertwine in **Relais Bourgondisch Cruyce** (050 337926; www.relaisbourgondischcruyce.be; Wollestraat 41-47; d €185-375, canal-view r from €285; Mar-Dec), a part-timbered medieval house full of designer fittings, genuine antiques, Persian rugs and even an original Matisse.

Jackets or pearls are appropriate garb in **Den Gouden Harynck** (050 337637; Groeninge 25; mains €38-45, lunch/3-course set lunch €35/74; lunch & dinner Tue-Sat), an uncluttered Michelin-starred restaurant where even the set lunch is a faultless exercise in artistic nouveau cuisine.

Information

Bruggecentraal (www.bruggecentraal.be) has events listings.

Tourist office (050 444646; www.brugge.be) Concertgebouw building ('t Zand 34; 10am-6pm); train station (10am-5pm Mon-Fri, 10am-2pm Sat & Sun) Standard city maps cost €0.50 but the arguably better guide-maps from **Use-It** (www.use-it.be) are free if you ask for one.

Getting There & Away

Bruges' train station is about 1.5km south of Markt, a lovely walk via the Begijnhof. Every hour trains run twice to Brussels (€12.90, one hour), five times to Ghent (€5.60, fast/slow 23/39 minutes), and hourly to Antwerp (€12.90, 70 minutes). For Ypres (Ieper in Dutch), take a train to Roeselare (€4.50, fast/slow 22/33 minutes), then use buses 94 or 95, passing key WWI sites en route.

Getting Around

BICYCLE **Bauhaus** (per half/full day €6/9), **Fietsen Popelier** (Mariastraat 26; per hr/half-/full-day €3.50/7/10; 10am-7pm) and **Rent-a-Bike** (train station; per day/week €12/72; 7.30am-7pm Mon-Fri, 9am-9pm Sat & Sun) hire bikes.

Quasimundo (050 33 07 75; www.quasimundo.eu; adult/student €24/22; mid-Mar–mid-Oct) offers half-day bicycle tours around Bruges and its surroundings, with rental included. Book ahead.

BUS To get from the train station to Markt, take any bus marked 'Centrum'. For the way back, buses stop at Biekorf, just northwest of Markt on Kuiperstraat.

Ypres (Ieper)

POP 35,500

The medieval cloth town of Ypres (Ieper in Dutch) became a last bastion of unoccupied Belgian territory early in WWI. As a key barrier to German advances towards the French coastal ports, the surrounding poppy fields of the Ypres Salient saw hundreds of thousands of pointless combat deaths during four years of merciless fighting. By 1918, bombardments had flattened the city and Flanders' fields had become synonymous with futile killing. A century later, Ypres has been convincingly rebuilt, lovingly tended cemeteries stand witness and numerous widely spread museums and trench-remnants still move floods of visitors.

Sights

CENTRAL YPRES

Grote Markt SQUARE

All the more astonishing for having been meticulously rebuilt post-WWI, Ypres' breathtaking 'medieval' main square is dominated by the vast Gothic **Lakenhallen**. Originally the 13th-century cloth market, it sports a 70m-high belfry reminiscent of London's Big Ben and hosts the gripping museum **In Flanders Fields** (www.inflandersfields.be; Grote Markt 34; admission €8; 10am-5pm, closed for refitting until Apr 2012), a multimedia WWI experience honouring ordinary people's experiences of wartime horrors. The ticket allows free entry to three other minor city museums.

Menin Gate MEMORIAL

This large stone gateway is inscribed with the names of 54,896 'lost' British and Commonwealth WWI troops whose bodies were never found. Every evening at 8pm traffic is halted here while buglers sound the **Last Post** in moving remembrance. It's a block east of Grote Markt, straddling the road beside the city moat. Hefty walkable ramparts lead through parkland to **Rijselpoort war cemetery** and the intriguing little **Ramparts War Museum** ('t Klein Rijsel; Rijselsestraat 208; admission €3; 11am-8pm) displaying WWI mementos through a series of subterranean mannequin scenes.

YPRES SALIENT

Memorial Museum Passchendaele 1917 MUSEUM

(www.passchendaele.be; Ieperstraat 5, Zonnebeke; admission €5; 10am-6pm Feb-Nov; 94) Slick, very informative WWI museum with recreated dugouts and trench-emplacements in the basement of a 1922 'castle'-mansion in Zonnebeke village (6km east of Ypres).

FREE **Tyne Cot** WWI CEMETERY
(24hr; 94) A sparse but movingly well-designed **visitor centre** (9am-6pm Feb-Nov) leads into the world's largest British Commonwealth war cemetery with 11,956 soldiers buried in maudlin straight rows. A further 35,000 'missing' are named on the rear wall. It's 3km beyond Zonnebeke, 500m from the nearest 94 bus stop.

FREE **Deutscher Soldatenfriedhof** WWI CEMETERY
(24hr; 95 to Deits Kerkhof) This small, intensely moving German cemetery, 1km north of Langemark, has up to 10 bodies per grave-slab and is eerily watched over by four shadowy silhouette-statues.

Dozens more WWI sites are accessible nearby by car, bicycle or tour-bus.

Tours

Two WWI specialist bookshops between Grote Markt and Menin Gate sell tickets to twice-daily half-day guided tours of selected war sites. Advance booking is wise.

Over the Top (057 424320; www.overthetoptours.be; Meensestraat 41; 9am-12.30pm, 1.30-5.30pm & 7.30-8.30pm)

British Grenadier (057 214657; www.salienttours.com; Meensestraat 5; 9.30am-1pm, 2-6pm & 7.30-8.30pm)

Sleeping & Eating

Fair-value eateries ring Grote Markt.

B&B Ter Thuyne B&B €€
(057 360042; www.terthuyne.be; Gustave de Stuersstraat 19; s/d €60/75; @) Three comfortable rooms that are luminously bright, scrupulously clean and modern without fashion-consciousness.

Hotel Regina HOTEL €€
(057 218888; www.hotelregina.be; Grote Markt 45; s/d from €70/85) Right on the Markt, the location is ideal. Attempts at 'artistic' decor generally backfire, but the Ensor room is a worthy exception with old-world timber interior and unbeatable views.

B&B Zonneweelde B&B €
(057 202723; Adjudant Masscheleinlaan 18; s/d €28/50) Cheap, basic rooms with a hotchpotch of furniture and scrappy shared bathroom facilities in an old-fashioned suburban home. It faces the canal, three blocks north of Grote Markt.

Jeugdstadion CAMPING GROUND $
(057 217282; www.jeugdstadion.be; Bolwerkstraat 1; campsites per tent/adult €2.50/4; Mar–mid-Nov) Functional camping ground 900m southeast of Grote Markt. You'll need a map.

WWI GRAVE SEARCHES

If your relative died in the region's WWI battles find out at which cemetery or memorial he's commemorated using www.cwgc.org (for UK and Commonwealth soldiers), www.ambc.gov (for Americans) or www.volksbund.de (for Germans).

Information

Toerisme Ieper (057 239220; www.ieper.be; Grote Markt 34; 9am-6pm, to 5pm mid-Nov–Mar) Well-equipped tourist office inside the Lakenhallen.

Getting There & Around

BICYCLE Hire bicycles from **Hotel Ambrosia** (057 366366; www.ambrosiahotel.be; D'Hondtstraat 54; per day €10; 9am-7pm); a credit card is needed as a guarantee.

BUS Services pick up passengers in Grote Markt's northeast corner (check direction carefully!) including Roeselare-bound routes 94 (roughly twice-hourly weekdays, five daily weekends) and 95 (hourly weekdays, five daily weekends).

TRAIN Services run hourly to Ghent (€9.90, one hour) and Brussels (€15.20, 1½ hours) via Kortrijk (€4.50, 30 minutes), where you can change for Bruges or Antwerp.

WALLONIA

Parlez-vous français? You'll need to in hilly Wallonia, Belgium's southern half. Here the main attractions are rural – outdoor activities, fabulous caves and ancient castles looming over tranquil hamlets. To get more than the vaguest hint of these charms you'll really need your own wheels.

Liège (Luik)

POP 189,000

Beneath the disfigured, post-industrial surface, sprawling Liège (Luik in Dutch) is a living architectural onion concealing layer upon layer of history. Fine churches abound, as befits a city that spent 800 years as the capital of an independent principality run by bishops. The proudly free-spirited citizens are disarmingly friendly and no Belgian city bubbles with more *joie-de-vivre*. Love it or loathe it, Liège is quirky and oddly compulsive.

Sights

The historic zone and main museums (free the first Sunday of each month) are a short stroll west of Liége-Palais train station: walk east past the vast, dour former Bishops' Palace (Pl St-Lambert) and through attractive Pl du Marché. Climb the **Montagne de Bueren** stairway for city panoramas.

Allow several hours to do full justice to **Grand Curtius** (www.grandcurtiusliege.be; Féronstrée 136; adult/concession €5/3; 10am-6pm Wed-Mon), an engrossing, ambitious museum interweaving tales of Liège artists and industries with a wide-ranging history of the visual arts. The **Musée de l'Art Wallon** (http://museeartwallon.be; Rue St-Georges; admission €5; 1-6pm Tue-Sat, 11am-4.30pm Sun) displays first-rate paintings by French-speaking Belgians in a disgraceful 1980s architectural travesty. In an adapted convent-cloister building, **Musée de la Vie Wallonne** (www.viewallonne.be; Cour des Mineurs; admission €5; 10am-5pm Tue-Sat, 10am-4pm Sun) has imaginative multimedia experiences examining Wallonia's economic rise and fall.

The **Maison de Tourisme** (04 237 9292; www.liege.be, www.ftpl.be; Pl St-Lambert 32; 9am-5.30pm) can suggest dozens of other city attractions.

Sleeping & Eating

There are terrace restaurants on Pl du Marché, many good-value sandwich shops along Rue Hors Château and an interesting range of little eateries on Rue Roture, hidden away near the youth hostel in Outremeuse. Tread carefully on Rue du Pot d'Or, which has dozens of (overly) lively late-night bars.

Hôtel Hors Château GUEST HOUSE €€
(04 250 6068; www.hors-chateau.be; Rue Hors Château 62; s/d/ste €78/95/125;) Nine stylish new rooms tucked into a half-timbered old building ideally situated in the historic quarter. Call ahead to arrange arrival times. Breakfast costs €12.

DON'T MISS

LIÈGE-GUILLEMINS

Designed by Santiago Calatrava and opened in September 2009, Liège's mainline station is a dazzling showcase of 21st-century architecture that looks like a vast white-concrete manta ray. To connect to the city centre (2km), hop on any local train to much more central **Liège-Palais**.

Auberge de Jeunesse HOSTEL €
(04 344 5689; www.laj.be; Rue Georges Simenon 2; members dm/s/d €18.80/33/46; @) Great HI hostel across the river in the Outremeuse 'republic'.

La Maison du Pékèt/Amon Nanesse PUB, RESTAURANT €€
(www.maisondupeket.be; Rue de l'Épée 4; meals €10.50-18.50; 10am-2am, kitchen noon-2.30 & 6-10.30pm) Just behind Pl du Marché, this rambling antique house with bare brick walls and heavy beams serves satisfying local pub meals and has a lively bar specialising in *pékèt* (Walloon *genièvre/jenever*).

Getting There & Away

Regular trains from **Liège-Palais**:

BRUSSELS (€13.60, 125 minutes, hourly) via Huy (€4.40, 29 minutes)

COO (€7.70, one hour, hourly)

LUXEMBOURG CITY (€38.20, 2½ hours, 18 daily) via Clervaux (€20.60, 1½ hours, every two hours)

Regular trains from **Liège-Guillemins**:

AACHEN (€11.70, 54 minutes, every two hours)

BRUSSELS (€13.60, one hour, hourly) via Leuven (€9.90, 35 minutes)

MAASTRICHT (€4.30, 30 minutes, hourly)

High-speed trains from **Liège-Guillemins** (reservations compulsory):

COLOGNE (standard/pre-booked €33/19, one hour, six daily) via Aachen (€23/14, 23 minutes)

FRANKFURT (€94.60/39, 2½ hours, three daily)

Bastogne

POP 14,200

In late 1944 Allied forces were sweeping east across Europe. But WWII wasn't yet over. Hitler's last gasp was a midwinter counter-attack that devastated the

WORTH A TRIP

ON THE ROAD IN WALLONIA

By car, combining a handful of the following destinations south of Liège can make for a very enjoyable day out. There's a very wide choice of accommodation but much is packed full in summer and closed in winter. For in-depth coverage see Lonely Planet's *Belgium & Luxembourg*.

Kayaking & Outdoor Activities:

» **Durbuy** (www.durbuyinfo.be, www.durbuyadventure.be) The 'world's smallest town' is quaint if touristy and well set up for all manner of sporting fun. Plenty of hotels.

» **La Roche-en-Ardenne** (www.ardenne-aventures.be, www.brandsport.be, www.la-roche-tourisme.com) Watersports and mountain biking from a compact rural town nestled around a medieval castle ruin.

» **Coo** (www.coo-adventure.com) The hamlet's famous 15m 'waterfall' is underwhelming but outdoor options are numerous and there's a family amusement park (www.plopsa.be). Accommodation is limited but more plentiful in nearby Stavelot. Accessible by Liège–Luxembourg trains.

Caves

Belgium's publicly accessible cave systems each have their own character. Visits take over an hour with set departure times that vary seasonally (check websites). There's no 'escape' once you've started so don't forget appropriate footwear, warm clothes and a pre-emptive bathroom stop.

» **Han-sur-Lesse** (www.grotte-de-han.be) Belgium's foremost, stalactite-rich caves are accessed by a little train ride but are often over-stuffed with tourists. There's a hostel (www.gitesdetape.be) and several lacklustre hotels.

» **Rochefort** (www.valdelesse.be) Attractive town, famous for its Trappist beers, where the Grotte de Lorette is remarkable for its depth, not its stalagmites. There's a good choice of accommodation.

» **Hotton** (www.grottesdehotton.com, www.si-hotton.be) Great grottoes and a jaw-dropping vertical subterranean chasm, yet relatively uncommercial.

» **Remouchamps** (www.grottes.be, www.ourthe-ambleve.be) Lacks the drama of the three 'greats' above, but you get to ride an underground river in a boat.

Castles

Wallonia's capital **Namur** (www.namurtourisme.be, www.mtpn.be) is dominated by a massive, sober fortified **citadel** (www.citadelle.namur.be; admission free) but the region has many more romantic castles including the following:

» **Château de Jehay** (www.chateaujehay.be; adult/student €5/2.50, audioguide €1; ⏲2-6pm Tue-Fri, 11am-6pm Sat & Sun Apr-Sep) A 1550 gingerbread fantasy of alternating brick and stone layers rising from a tree-ringed moat between Liège and patchily historic **Huy**, and serviced by bus 85.

» **Château de Modave** (www.modave-castle.be; adult/student €7.50/4; ⏲10am-5pm Tue-Sun Apr–mid-Nov) Palatial chateau with 20 majestically furnished rooms and 17th-century stucco ceilings.

» **Château de Lavaux Sainte-Anne** (www.chateau-lavaux.com; admission €6.50; ⏲9am-5.30pm) Partly furnished 1450 moated fortress visible west of the E411 motorway as you pass junction 22a just 10km west of Han-sur-Lesse.

Ardennes and nearby Luxembourg, creating a 'bulge' in the Allied frontline. During this pivotal 'Battle of the Bulge', plucky Bastogne was surrounded but refused to capitulate. Today the town ain't lovely but it's a must-see for WWII buffs.

The main square – a car park adorned with a tank – has been renamed Pl McAuliffe after the US general whose famous reply to the German call to surrender was one word, 'Nuts!'. Here you'll find the **Maison du Tourisme** (☎061 212711; www.paysdebastogne.be; Pl McAuliffe 60; ⊙9am-6pm mid-Jun–mid-Sep, 9.30am-12.30pm & 1-5.30pm mid-Sep–mid-Jun).

Of numerous WWII museums, Bastogne's best is 800m northeast of the main square; **J'avais 20 ans en '45** (www.bastogne.be/20ansen45; admission €6.50; ⊙10am-6pm, closed Fri Oct-Apr, last entry 5pm) is an imaginative exhibition giving movingly balanced insights into the conflict through dozens of eyewitness video-tales. Keep the entry ticket to get a €1 discount at the **Bastogne Historical Center** (www.bastognehistoricalcenter.be; Colline du Mardasson; admission incl audio guide €8.50; ⊙9.30am-5.30pm Mar-Dec), a much more standard war museum full of uniforms, weapons, a couple of dioramas and a movie. It's located on a gentle hilltop 1.5km further northeast beside the big star-shaped **American War Memorial**.

Friendly **Hôtel Collin** (☎061 214888; www.hotel-collin.com; Pl McAuliffe 8; s/d/tr €67/85/105) is a pleasant family hotel with a pseudo art-nouveau cafe and a Mediterranean styled restaurant.

Bus 163b (€3.80, 45 minutes) runs every two hours to Libramont on the Brussels–Luxembourg train line. Buses also run hourly (except Sunday) to Ettelbrück (one hour) in Luxembourg.

UNDERSTAND BELGIUM

History

Bruges, Ghent and Ypres boomed in the 13th and 14th centuries as northern Europe's foremost cloth-trading cities. Craftspeople established powerful guilds that built elaborate guildhouses around fine market squares typically adorned with a belfry.

In the 16th century, present-day Netherlands, Belgium and Luxembourg embraced Protestantism, much to the chagrin of their fanatical Spanish overlords. The result, from 1568, was a war that lasted 80 years. Eventually Holland expelled the Spaniards, but Belgium and Luxembourg stayed under their strict Catholic rule.

Dynastic squabbles later handed proto-Belgium to the Austrian Habsburgs. They ruled until the 1790s when anti-religious revolutionary French forces invaded and devastated Belgium's monasteries. French rule ended abruptly in 1815 when Napoleon met his Waterloo at, yes, Waterloo near Brussels. Initially the Dutch took power, but following an unexpected 1830 revolution the Catholic Belgians split from protestant Holland and formed their own kingdom.

From the late 19th century Belgium grew rapidly wealthy both through industrialisation and through King Léopold II's disgraceful profiting from the Congo that was brutal even by the colonial standards of that era.

Twentieth Century

When WWI kicked off in 1914, Belgium was officially neutral. The Germans invaded anyway and western Flanders became a blood-soaked killing field. Whole towns, including historic Ypres, were bombarded into the mud, then meticulously rebuilt in the following postwar decades.

During WWII the country was taken over by a surprise German attack in May 1940 and even after an initial 1944 liberation the Ardennes suffered a second devastation during Hitler's last-gasp counter attack.

Despite the wars, for much of the 20th century, Wallonia's mining, glassware and steel industries made it the powerhouse of one of Europe's strongest economies. However, since the 1970s a serious post-industrial decline has affected much of Wallonia, while formerly agricultural Flanders has boomed with new higher-tech businesses. A parallel series of political changes have increasingly emphasised the north–south linguistic divide. With ever less communication between the regions, forming a national consensus has proved ever more difficult in recent years. In 2007 the country was without a government for nearly a year. And the 2010 federal elections saw months more deadlock. At a fundamental level, Flemish politicians want greater autonomy for their wealthy region, while French-speakers fear that further separation of powers will reduce subsidies to the struggling south.

People

Belgium's population of 10.4 million is split north–south by language. In Flanders (Vlaanderen) the language is the Flemish dialect of Dutch. South of the divide in Wallonia (La Wallonie) people speak French with some Belgian peculiarities. A tiny enclave of Wallonia's eastern Ardennes is German speaking. Brussels is officially bilingual though in day-to-day reality, spoken French (and English) predominate. Politically, the two main language communities have long been at loggerheads but they share a low-key form of tolerant Roman Catholicism. Religious-based traditions remain strong, but being 'Catholic' here is often a badge of social status more than a spiritual dogma. Many Belgian cities have large immigrant communities from Italy and France and more conspicuously from Morocco and Turkey.

Arts

In the late Middle Ages, the secularisation of painting was led by sophisticated artists known quite misleadingly as the Flemish 'Primitives'. Notable figures Jan van Eyck and Hans Memling were later followed by Brussels' Breugel/Breughel family, who created some of the 16th century's most memorable art, from peasant scenes to terrifying Bosch-like allegories of hell and damnation. Styles changed radically with the 17th-century Counter Reformation, when the Catholic God's mystical power was emphasised, represented by baroque altarpieces and giant paintings full of angelic awe. That era's foremost artist was Antwerp-based Pieter Paul Rubens.

Belgium owes its independence to an 1830 revolution that started altogether improbably with an opera. Anti-Dutch demonstrations were stoked by crowds who had been stirred into a patriotic fervor by watching Auber's *Muette de Portici* at La Monnae in Brussels. Jazz owes much to Dinant-born Adolphe Sax who invented the saxophone.

In the 19th and early 20th centuries, Victor Horta and other architects put Belgium at the forefront of the sinuously beautiful art-nouveau movement. Belgian art greats of the era include expressionist pioneer James Ensor, Fauvist Rik Wouters, symbolist Fernand Khnopff and surrealist René Magritte.

Among Belgium's best-known contemporary artists are Panamarenko, Luc Tuymans and Jan Fabre, famous for covering a ceiling in Brussels' Palais Royal with 1.4 million iridescent beetle wing cases.

Contemporary names in Belgian music include Arid, Ghinzu, Puggy and dEUS (alternative rock), Soulwax/2manyDJs (electro/mash-up), Axelle Red (pop-chanson) and Hooverphonic (trip-hop).

Food & Drink

Belgian meals are often described as being French in quality, German in quantity. See p107 for local specialities. To save money, order restaurants' weekday lunch deals *(dagmenu/menu du jour)*, eat in cafes or frequent Asian places where the rice is generally included in meal prices. A *belegd broodje/sandwich garni* (filled half-baguette) makes a great, inexpensive snack.

Belgian cafes always serve alcohol as well as coffee and are convivial places to sample the nation's amazing range of beers. Belgium's famous lagers (eg Stella Artois) and white beers (Hoegaarden) are now global brands. But what have connoisseurs really drooling are the robust, rich 'abbey' beers (which were originally brewed in monasteries), and the 'Trappist beers' (that still are). Chimay, Rochefort, Westmalle and Orval are the best known, but for beer maniacs the one that really counts is ultra-rare Westvleteren 12°. See www.belgianstyle.com for more information.

Smoking is banned in restaurants and in cafes that serve meals.

Price ranges for average main courses are as follows:

€€€ more than €25

€€ €14 to €25

€ less than €14

SURVIVAL GUIDE

Directory A–Z

Accommodation

Our reviews refer to double rooms with private bathroom (except in hostels or where otherwise specified) in high season: that's May to September in Bruges, Ypres and the Ardennes, September to June in business cities.

Price ranges used in this chapter for accomodation are as follows:

€€€ more than €150

€€ €60 to €150

€ less than €60

Camping Site listings can be found at www.campingbelgique.be (Wallonia) and www.camping.be (Flanders).

Hostels (*jeugdherbergen* in Dutch, *auberges de jeunesse* in French) Hostels affiliated with **Hostelling International** (HI; www.jeugdherbergen.be, www.laj.be) charge €3 extra for nonmembers, and around €2 less for under 26-year-olds (prices including sheets and a basic breakfast). Be sure to always read the conditions.

B&Bs *(gastenkamers/chambres d'hôtes)* A few are cheap and cheerful (from €35/45 per single/double), but many offer standards equivalent to a boutique hotel (up to €160 double).

Holiday houses *(gîtes)* Easily rented in Wallonia but minimum stays apply and there's a hefty 'cleaning fee' on top of quoted rates. Check out **Belsud** (www.belsud.be).

Activities

In **Flanders** (www.fietsroute.org), **bikes** are a popular means of everyday travel and many roads have dedicated cycle lanes. In **Wallonia** (www.ravel.wallonie.be), the hilly terrain favours mountain bikes (*VTT/vélo tout-terrain* in French). Brussels offers a forward-thinking bike-rental scheme, but its car drivers are notorious for disregarding bicycles – beware!

Canoeing and **kayaking** are best in the Ardennes, but don't expect rapids of any magnitude.

For some onfo on activities in Wallonia, see p131.

Business Hours

Opening hours here are for high season. Many tourism-based businesses reduce their hours in the low season.

Banks 9am-3.30pm Mon-Fri

Clubs 11pm-6am Fri-Sun

Pubs & cafés to 1am or later

Restaurants 11.30am-2.30pm & 6.30-10.30pm

Shops 10am-6pm Mon-Sat, limited opening Sun, some closed lunch

Supermarkets 9am-8pm Mon-Sat, some open Sun

Entertainment

Nightlife listings www.theclubbing.com and www.noctis.com

Cinema listings www.cinenews.be

Concerts and tickets www.fnacagenda.be

Holidays

See http://tinyurl.com/Belhol-f (Francophones) and http://tinyurl.com/Belhol-v (Flemish) for dates of school holidays.

Public holidays:

New Year's Day 1 January

Easter Monday March/April

Labour Day 1 May

Ascension Day Fortieth day after Easter

Whit Monday Seventh Monday after Easter

Flemish Community Festival 11 July (Flanders only)

National Day 21 July

Assumption 15 August

Francophone Community Festival 27 September (Wallonia only)

All Saints' Day 1 November

Armistice Day 11 November

Germanophone Community Festival 15 November (eastern cantons only)

Christmas Day 25 December

Money

ATMs are widespread but often hidden within bank buildings. Banks usually offer better exchange rates than exchange bureaux (*wisselkantoren* in Dutch, *bureaux de change* in French), though sometimes only offer such services to their banking clients.

Tipping is not expected in taxis, bars or restaurants (service and VAT is always included).

Telephone

Mobile phones use the GSM system like most of the world except Japan and North America. Getting a local pre-paid SIM card is generally painless and inexpensive. Major Belgian providers are **Proximus** (www.proximus.be), **Mobistar** (www.mobistar.be) and **Base** (www.base.be).

Getting There & Away

Air

Brussels National Airport (BRU; www.brusselsairport.be) is Belgium's main hub for international flights including for **Brussels Airlines** (SN; www.brusselsairlines.com), which has services to many European and African destinations.

Charleroi (CRL; www.charleroi-airport.com), often confusingly called Brussels-South, is a hub for budget airlines **Ryanair** (www.ryanair), **JetAir** (www.jetairfly.com) and **Wizz Air** (www.wizzair.com). It's 55km south of Brussels and 6km north of the ragged, post-industrial city of Charleroi. **L'Elan** (www.voyages-lelan.be) runs direct buses to/from a stop near Bruxelles-Midi train station roughly every half-hour (single/return €13/22, one hour), last northbound 11.30pm, first southbound 4.30am. Alternatively **'Aeroport' buses** (www.infotec.be; €2.50, 18 minutes) run to Charleroi-Sud train station twice hourly on weekdays, hourly at weekends. A combined bus-rail ticket purchased before leaving the airport is never more than €11 to anywhere on the Belgian train network. Eight mostly generic hotels lie around 2km away including a bare-bones Formule1.

Antwerp airport (ANR; www.antwerpairport.be) has just a few **CityJet** (WX; www.cityjet.com) flights to London City and Manchester.

Boat

Most UK-bound motorists drive to Calais or Dunkirk (Dunkerque) in France but two options leave from Belgium:

Zeebrugge–Hull P&O (www.poferries.com) runs a 14-hour overnight service (from €159). For pedestrians, a connecting Bruges–Zeebrugge bus leaves Bruges train station at 7.30pm (€3.50).

Ostend–Ramsgate TransEuropa Ferries (www.transeuropaferries.com) has four daily services (€55 to €62, four hours); no pedestrians carried.

Bus

International bus companies **Ecolines** (02 279 2057; www.ecolines.net) and **Eurobus** (02 527 5012; www.eurobus.pl) operate from Brussels and Antwerp to various destinations in Eastern Europe.

Eurolines (02 274 1350; www.eurolines.be; telephone bookings 9am-7.30pm Mon-Fri, 9am-5pm Sat) is part of the Europe-wide network. Pre-bookings are compulsory but, although nine Belgian cities are served, only Brussels, Antwerp, Ghent and Liège have ticket offices. Sample standard/'super-promo' fares:

Bruges–London (€41/22, 4¼ hours). Twice weekly, daily in summer.

Brussels–Amsterdam (€17/10, 3¾-4½ hours) Eight daily.

Brussels–Frankfurt (€44/38, six hours) One or two daily.

Brussels–London (€41/22, six to 8½ hours) Five daily.

Brussels–Paris (€29/9, four hours) Twelve daily.

Car & Motorcycle

Border crossings are not usually controlled. **EuroStop** (www.taxistop.be; per 100km €3) matches paying hitchhikers with drivers for long-distance international rides.

Train

For timetables and booking seats, see www.b-rail.be.

HIGH-SPEED TRAINS

International high-speed trains have compulsory pre-booking requirements and charge radically different prices according to availability, so advance booking can save a packet. Operating companies:

Eurostar (www.eurostar.com) Brussels–Lille–London–St-Pancras (two hours) runs up to nine times daily.

Thalys (www.thalys.com) Paris–Brussels–Antwerp–Rotterdam–Schipol–Amsterdam (eight daily); Brussels to Amsterdam takes 113 minutes. Brussels to Paris takes 80 minutes with summer-only connections to Avignon and Marseille (5¾ hours). Brussels–Liège–Aachen–Cologne (108 minutes) runs four times daily.

ICE (www.db.de) Brussels–[Liège]–Aachen–Cologne–Frankfurt airport–Frankfurt (3¼ hours) runs six times daily.

TGV (www.sncf.com) Numerous Belgium–France routes including Brussels–CDG airport (100 minutes, seven daily) but no service to central Paris.

FYRA (www.fyra.com) Brussels–Amsterdam high-speed service (1¾ hours) due to start in 2013.

OTHER INTERNATIONAL TRAINS

NMBS/SNCB trains have fixed fares, accept rail passes without surcharge and don't require advance booking. There's no NMBS/SNCB Brussels–Paris train. Useful international connections:

Antwerp–Ghent–Lille (€23.60, 110 minutes, hourly)

Brussels–Antwerp–Amsterdam (€37.80, 2¾ hours, hourly)

Brussels–Basel (6¾ hours, €82.40, twice daily)
Brussels–Luxembourg (€34.60, 3¼ hours, every two hours)

Getting Around

Bicycle

Bike hire is available from many major train stations from around €6.50/9.50 per half-/full-day. Taking a bike on a train adds €5/8 one-way/all-day to the rail fare(s).

Car & Motorcycle

Speed limits are 30km/h (near schools), 50km/h (in towns), 70km/h to 90km/h (inter-town roads), 120km/h (motorways). Motorways are toll free. The blood-alcohol limit is 0.05%.

Train

NMBS/SNCB (Belgian Railways; www.b-rail.be) trains are nonsmoking. Discount deals:

B-Excursions Good-value one-day excursion fares including return rail ticket plus selected entry fees.

Go Pass/Rail Pass Ten one-way 2nd-class trips to anywhere in Belgium (except frontier points) costing €46/74 for people under/over 26.

Weekend Return Tickets Cost just 20% more than a single; valid from 7pm Friday until Sunday night.

Bosnia & Hercegovina

Includes »

Best Places to Eat

» Bridge-view Restaurants, Mostar (p147)

» Riverside Restaurants on the Una (p149)

Best Places to Stay

» Muslibegović House, Mostar (p145)

» Kostelski Buk, Una Valley (p149)

» Hotel Platani, Trebinje (p148)

Why Go?

This craggily beautiful land retains some lingering scars from the 1990s' heartbreaking civil war. But today visitors will more likely remember Bosnia and Hercegovina (BiH) for its deep, unassuming human warmth and for the intriguing East-meets-West atmosphere born of fascinatingly blended Ottoman and Austro-Hungarian histories.

Major drawcards are the reincarnated antique centres of Sarajevo and Mostar, where rebuilt historic buildings counterpoint fashionable bars and wi-fi-equipped cafes. Elsewhere socialist architectural monstrosities are surprisingly rare blots on predominantly rural landscapes. Many Bosnian towns are lovably small, wrapped around medieval castles and surrounded by mountain ridges or cascading river canyons. There's also world-class rafting, Olympic-quality skiing and a genuine sense of discovery. And it's all great value for money by the standards of 21st-century Europe.

When to Go

Sarajevo

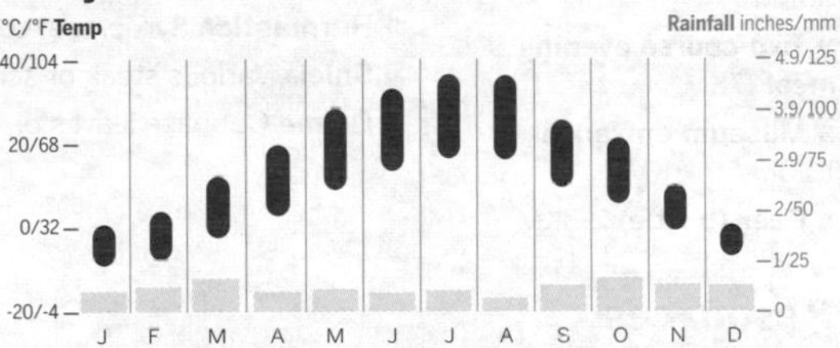

Apr–May Cooler in Hercegovina, blooming flowers in Bosnia and rafting best for professionals.

Jun–Aug Towns are hot and sweaty and accommodation fills up; rafting for beginners is best in July.

Late-Dec–mid-Mar First-class skiing. Prices drop late March when snow cover is more of a gamble.

AT A GLANCE

» **Currency** convertible mark (KM)

» **Languages** Bosnian, Croatian, Serbian

» **Money** ATMs widely available in towns

» **Visas** Not needed for citizens of the EU, USA, Canada, Australia and New Zealand

Fast Facts

» **Area** 51,129 sq km

» **Capital** Sarajevo

» **Country code** ☎387

» **Emergency** Ambulance ☎124, police ☎122

Exchange Rates

Australia	A$1	1.43KM
Canada	C$1	1.42KM
euro zone	€1	1.96KM
Japan	¥100	1.60KM
New Zealand	NZ$1	1.06KM
UK	UK£1	2.21KM
USA	US$1	1.35KM

Set Your Budget

» **Budget hotel room** 60KM

» **Two-course evening meal** 17KM

» **Museum entrance** 1.50KM to 5KM

» **Beer (bottle)** 2-3KM

Resources

» **BiH Tourism** (www.bhtourism.ba)

» **Bosnian Institute** (www.bosnia.org.uk) Cultural.

» **Green Visions** (www.sarajevo-travel.ba)

Connections

Regular buses link the Croatian coast to Mostar and Sarajevo, plus there's a little-publicised Trebinje–Dubrovnik service. Sarajevo, Višegrad and Trebinje all have bus connections to Serbia and Montenegro. Trains connect Sarajevo to Zagreb, Belgrade and Budapest.

ITINERARIES

Five Days

Arriving from coastal Croatia, roam Mostar's Old Town, day trip to surrounding attractions, including Ottoman-era Počitelj and the impressive Kravice Waterfalls, continue to Sarajevo and leave by train to Zagreb, Belgrade or Budapest.

Ten Days

Add Trebinje, ski (winter) or go mountain biking (summer) around Bjelašnica, visit the controversial Visočica Hill pyramid, Travnik and Jajce and consider adding in some high-adrenalin rafting from Banja Luka, Bihać or Foča.

Essential Food

» **Burek** Filo-pastry snack with meat stuffing. Similar equivalents are filled with cheese *(sirnica)*, potato *(krompiruša)* or spinach *(zeljanica)*.

» **Ćevapi** (Ćevapčići) Grilled minced meat formed into small cylinders.

» **Pljeskavica** Like *ćevapi* but flat, patty shaped.

» **Ražnijići** Shish kebab.

» **Ionac** Cabbage and meat hotpot.

» **Uštipci** Bready doughnuts served with sweet or savoury accompaniments.

» **Tufahije** Baked apple stuffed with walnut paste.

» **Hurmastica** Syrup-soaked sponge fingers.

» **Šnicla** Various steak or schnitzels.

» **Dolme** Cabbage leaves or vegetables stuffed with mince.

Bosnia & Hercegovina Highlights

❶ Nose about Mostar's atmospheric Old Town seeking ever-new angles from which to photograph young men throwing themselves off the magnificently rebuilt **Stari Most** (p145)

❷ Potter around the timeless Turkish- and Austrian-era pedestrian lanes of **Sarajevo** (p140), sample its fashionable cafes and eclectic nightlife or gaze down on the mosque-dotted, red-roofed cityscape from Biban restaurant

❸ Raft dramatic canyons down one of BiH's fast-flowing rivers, whether from **Foča** (p148), **Bihać** (p149) or **Karanovac** (p148)

❹ Ski the 1984 Olympic pistes at **Jahorina** (p140) or **Bjelašnica** (p140)

SARAJEVO

033 / POP 737,000

The nation's vibrant capital is folded into steep contours polka-dotted with red-roofed homes, church towers and endless minarets. Distinctive Ottoman-era bazaars along cobblestone lanes date from the city's 16th-century glory days as a Turkic silk-trading entrepôt. After 1878 the Austro-Hungarians added grand central-European buildings. In 1984 Sarajevo hosted the Winter Olympics but just eight years later the city endured an appalling three-year siege. Over 10,500 Sarajevans died and six centuries of heritage was pounded into rubble by Bosnian-Serb shelling. In the southern suburbs some buildings remain bullet-pocked but in the centre, major reconstruction means that today's visitor will be hard-pressed to notice any signs of the conflict in what is now an enticing, low-key city brimming with a very personal warmth and charm.

For Sarajevo listings, see www.sonar.ba.

Sights

CENTRAL SARAJEVO

Baščaršija & Old Sarajevo HISTORIC AREA

Fanning out from the distinctive 1891 **Sebilj Drinking Fountain** (Pigeon Sq) is Baščaršija, old Sarajevo's delightful warren of marble-flagged pedestrian lanes and open courtyards. Cafes, souvenir shops, mosques, copper workshops and charming little restaurants surround Ottoman-era architectural gems, including the one-block covered bazaar and the imposing **Gazi-Husrevbey Mosque** (www.vakuf-gazi.ba; Saraći 18; admission 2KM; 9am-noon, 2.30-4pm & 5.30-7pm May-Sep).

The six-domed 1551 **Bursa Bezistan** (www.muzejsarajeva.ba; Abadžiluk 10; admission 2KM; 10am-6pm Mon-Fri, 10am-3pm Sat), which started life as a silk bazaar, is now a minor museum giving an easily digested introduction to the city's Turkish-era history. The 1740 **Old Orthodox Church** (Mula Mustafe Bašeskije 59; admission 2KM; 8am-3pm Tue-Sun) and 1581 **Sephardic Synagogue** (Mula Mustafe Bašeskije 40; admission 2KM; 10am-6pm Mon-Fri, 10am-1pm Sun) both host interesting, religiously relevant museums.

Ferhadija & Riverbank NEIGHBOURHOOD

To sample Sarajevo's Austro-Hungarian-era architecture, wander cafe-filled Ferhadija and stroll along the riverbank. Facing the **Latin Bridge** and interesting little **Sarajevo 1878-1918 Museum** (Zelenih Beretki 2; admission 2KM; 10am-6pm Mon-Fri, 10am-3pm Sat) is the point where Gavrilo Princip assassinated Austro-Hungary's crown prince Franz Ferdinand in 1914, ultimately triggering WWI.

Inner Hill-Slopes HISTORIC BUILDINGS

For great city views, climb the grassy-topped **Yellow Bastion** (Žuta Tabija; Jekovac) of the once-vast 1720s Vratnik Citadel. For a taste of a traditional Sarajevan home, seek out the brilliantly restored 18th-century **Svrzo House** (Svrzina Kuća; Glođina 8; admission 2KM; 10am-6pm Mon-Fri, 10am-3pm Sat).

NOVO SARAJEVO

Hop off tram 3 just beyond the startling pudding-coloured **Holiday Inn** (wartime home to besieged international journalists) to find the palatial, wide-ranging **National Museum** (www.zemaljskimuzej.ba; Zmaja od Bosne 3; adult/student 5/1KM; 10am-5pm Tue-Fri, 9am-1pm Sat, 10am-2pm Sun). Its archaeological collections are especially impressive. Peep through the locked, high-security glass door of room 37 to glimpse the world-famous **Sarajevo Haggadah**, a priceless 14th-century Jewish codex said to be the world's most valuable book.

Next door, the small but engrossing **History Museum** (Zmaja od Bosne 5; foreigner/local 4/2KM; 11am-7pm Mon-Fri, 10am-2pm Sat & Sun) 'non-ideologically' charts the course of the 1990s conflict with affectingly personal exhibits. Tucked behind is an amusingly tongue-in-cheek Tito-themed **cafe** (www.caffetito.ba).

ILIDŽA AREA

Tunnel Museum MUSEUM

(061 213760; Tuneli 1, Butmir; admission 5KM; 9am-4pm) Way out in Butmir, this unmissable museum gives visitors a glimpse of the makeshift 1m-wide tunnel hand-dug beneath Sarajevo's airport during the 1992–95 siege. Without the food and armaments that passed through it, the besieged city would probably have capitulated. A 20-minute video helps conjure up the wartime tunnel experience. By public transport take tram 3 to the Ilidža terminus (around 35 minutes), switch to the Kotorac bus, then from the end stop, cross the small bridge, turn immediately left and walk 600m.

Activities & Tours

There's superb-value **skiing** (ski pass per half/full day 20/30KM, ski-set rentals 25-40KM) at two 1984 Winter Olympic centres. **Jahorina** (www.oc-jahorina.com) is 13km from Pale (30KM by taxi), while much smaller **Bjelašnica** (www.bjelasnica.ba) is 30km south of Sarajevo, accessible by a 9am bus from the National Museum (ski-season weekends only).

In summer, Bjelašnica's excellent new **Hotel Han** (☎584150; www.hotelhan.ba; s/d summer 70/100KM, winter 105/170KM;) rents bicycles (per hour/day 4/25KM) for back-road explorations.

Tourist offices, travel agents and many hostels run city tours, often fascinatingly accompanied by siege survivors. Ecotourism specialist **Green Visions** (☎717290; www.sarajevo-travel.ba; opposite Radnička 66; ⏲9am-5pm Mon-Fri) offers a wide range of weekend and tailor-made hiking trips into the Bosnian mountains and villages.

Sleeping

Some 'hostels' are essentially homestays with dorm beds. Check if sheets are included and beware that many have far-less-central 'overflow' locations.

Hotel Kovači NEO-TRADITIONAL HOUSE-HOTEL €€
(☎573700; www.hotelkovaci.com; Kovači 12; s/d/tr/apt €50/70/90/100;) This wonderfully central family hotel blends a chic, understated modernism with the basic design of a traditional *doksat* (Turkic home with overhanging upper window boxes) house, its fresh white rooms softened with photos of 19th-century Sarajevo on protruding panels.

Hotel Hecco HOTEL €€
(☎273730; www.hotel-hecco.net; Medresa 1; s/tw/d/tr/apt 80/110/130/150/160KM; @) Twenty-nine bright, airy rooms lead off an artfully designed warren of corridors dotted with armchairs and feeling a little like a Mondrian painting in 3D. Top-floor rooms have air-con. Minibus 58 stops outside.

Residence Rooms HOSTEL €
(☎200157; www.residencerooms.ba; 1st fl, Saliha Muvekita 1; dm/d €15/40; @) Convivial hostel with high ceilings, ample common areas and widely spaced dorm beds, but no lockers.

HCC Sarajevo Hostel HOSTEL €
(☎503294; www.hcc.ba; 3rd fl, Saliha Muvekita 2; dm 25-29KM, s/d 40/65KM; @) Sociable, central hostel with a brilliant kitchen and smaller communal TV lounge/lobby. Don't be put off by the speaker-phone entrance and four flights of ragged access stairs.

Sobe Divan BUDGET ROOMS €
(☎061420254; Brandžiluk 38; s/tw €15/30) Ten twin rooms painted in sunny Provençal colours all come with new, private bathrooms. Check in at the restaurant downstairs.

Haris Hostel HOSTEL €
(☎232563; www.hyh.ba; Vratnik Mejdan 29; dm €15; @) Worth the sweaty 10-minute climb from town for the decent shared kitchen, sitting area and rough concrete-view terrace. Check availability at Kovači 7 (8am to 7pm Monday to Friday and 8am to 4pm Saturday).

Ljubičica ACCOMMODATION AGENCY €
(☎232109, 061131813; www.hostelljubicica.net; Mula Mustafe Bašeskije 65; dm €10, homestay s/d from €15/20; ⏲5.30am-11pm, 8am-10pm winter) This budget tour agency organises widely spread homestay rooms and packed-full, very functional dorms. Several other agencies and minihostels are nearby.

Hotel Telal MINIHOTEL €
(☎525125; www.hotel-telal.ba; Abdesthana 4; s/d/tr/apt €25/35/45/60) Reception feels a little claustrophobic, but the rooms are unexpectedly smart and well tended for the price.

AutoKamp Oaza CAMPING GROUND €
(☎636140; hoteloaza@live.com; per person/tent/car/campervan 10/7/8/12KM) Tree-shaded camping and caravan hook-ups (electricity 3KM extra) tucked behind the Hotel Imzit, 1.5km west of Ilidža tram terminus, itself a 35-minute tram ride from central Sarajevo.

Eating

Close to Pigeon Sq you'll find a Konzum Supermarket, a 24-hour bakery and dozens of street-terrace cafes. For inexpensive snack meals look along Bradžiluk or Kundurdžiluk where the best known (albeit not the sexiest) *ćevabdžinica* is **Željo** (Kundurdžiluk 17 & Kundurdžiluk 20; ćevapi 3-7KM; ⏲8am-10pm).

Dveri BOSNIAN €€
(☎537020; www.dveri.co.ba; Prote Bakovića 10; meals 10-16KM; ⏲10am-11pm;) Charming 'country cottage' hung with garlic loops and corn cobs. Inky risottos or vegie-stuffed eggplants wash down a treat with 6KM glasses of Hercegovinian Blatina (red house wine).

Biban BOSNIAN €€
(☎232026; Hošin Brijeg 95a; mains 7-16KM; ⏲10am-10pm) Way above the city, panoramic views are Biban's key attraction but the meals are perfectly cooked and portions

Central Sarajevo

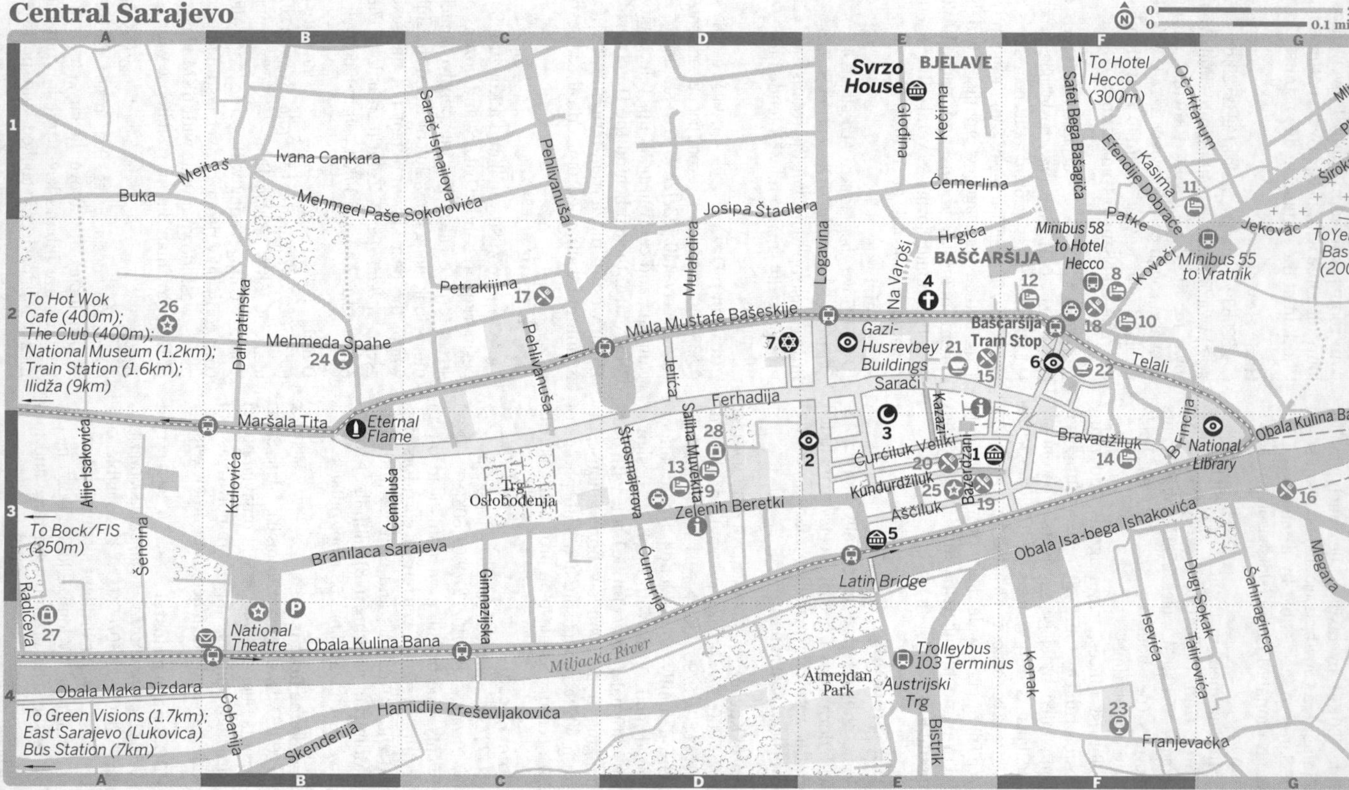

Central Sarajevo

Top Sights
Svrzo House E1

Sights
1 Bursa Bezistan E3
2 Covered Bazaar E3
3 Gazi-Husrevbey Mosque E3
4 Old Orthodox Church E2
5 Sarajevo 1878-1918 Museum E3
6 Sebilj Drinking Fountain F2
7 Sephardic Synagogue D2

Sleeping
8 Haris Hostel Agency F2
9 HCC Sarajevo Hostel D3
10 Hotel Kovaći F2
11 Hotel Telal F1
12 Ljubičica F2
13 Residence Rooms D3
14 Sobe Divan F3

Eating
15 Dveri E2
16 Inat Kuća G3
17 Karuzo C2
18 Konsum Supermarket F2
19 Željo E3
20 Željo E3

Drinking
21 Caffe Divan E2
22 Dibek F2
23 Pivnica HS F4
24 Zlatna Ribica B2

Entertainment
25 Hacienda E3
26 Sloga A2

Shopping
27 BuyBook A4
28 Šahinpašić D3

are generously sized. Take minibus 56 from Latin Bridge and turn left after Nalina 15.

Karuzo VEGETARIAN, SEAFOOD €€
(☎444647; www.karuzorestaurant.com; Dženetića Čikma 2; vegetarian mains 15-18KM; ⊙noon-3pm Mon-Fri & 6-11pm Mon-Sat; ✍) This tiny, friendly, one-man (ie slow-service) restaurant is styled like the interior of a yacht and remarkable in Bosnia for offering an imaginative, meat-free menu.

Inat Kuća BOSNIAN €€
(Spite House; www.inatkuca.ba; Velika Alifakovac 1; mains 12-20KM, snacks 10KM; ⊙11am-10.30pm) This Sarajevo institution occupies a uniquely historic Ottoman house but much of the typical Bosnian food (stews, *dolme*) is pre-prepared and slightly lacklustre.

Hot Wok Café ASIAN FUSION €€
(☎203322; Maršala Tita 12; meals 12-17KM; ⊙11am-11pm Mon-Fri, 11am-1am Sat) Pun-tastic Southeast Asian fusion food in a decor recalling a scene from *Kill Bill*.

Drinking & Entertainment

The cafe choice is joyfully overwhelming, especially as summer warms up and tables overflow onto many old-town streets.

Zlatna Ribica BAR
(Kaptol 5; ⊙10am-2am) Soft jazz serenades this marvellously Gothic cafe-bar that's loaded with eccentricities, including uniquely stocked bathrooms that will have you laughing out loud.

Pivnica HS BREWERY BAR, RESTAURANT
(http://tinyurl.com/PivnicaHS; Franjevačka 15; ⊙10am-1am) If Willy Wonka built a beer hall it would look like this. Come for the excellent Sarajevskaya dark beer, brewed next door. Stay for the superb food (pastas 8KM, mains from 13KM).

The Club CLUB
(www.theclub.ba; Maršala Tita 7; beer 4KM; ⊙10am-4am) This subterranean trio of intimate stone-cavern rooms combines a DJ/concert bar, plush chill-out space and a surprisingly decent late-night restaurant.

Hacienda BAR, RESTAURANT
(www.placetobe.ba; Bazerdzani 3; ⊙10am very late) By 2am the merrily alcoholic ambience is much spicier than the pseudo-Mexican food. Several other bars in the block also buzz.

Bock/FIS CLUB, LIVE MUSIC
(Musala bb; ⊙6pm-2am) Little basement venue with 'urban' party music at weekends, and punk or alternative bands performing midweek.

Sloga CLUBE
(Seljo, Mehmeda Spahe 20; admission weekends 5KM; ⊙8pm-3am) Cavernous, blood-red

club/disco/dance hall with salsa night on Monday.

Dibek BAR

(Laledžina 3; water-pipe 10KM; ⌚8am-11pm) DJ-led bar on a super-quaint little old-town square.

Caffe Divan CAFE

(Morića Han, Saraći 77; ⌚8am-midnight) Wicker chairs within a historic caravanserai courtyard.

Shopping

Wooden-shuttered souvenir shops around Baščaršija flog jewellery, oriental slippers, Bosnian kilims, imported carpets, BiH flags, wooden spoons and metalwork, including archetypal coffee-pot sets and pens made from bullet casings. If you're heading to Mostar you might find prices better there.

Both **BuyBook** (www.buybook.ba; Radićeva 4; ⌚9am-10pm Mon-Sat) and **Šahinpašić** (www.btcsahinpasic.com; Vladislava Skarića 8; ⌚9am-9pm Mon-Sat) are bookshops that are well stocked.

Information

Internet Access

Albatros (Sagradžije 27; per hr 2KM; ⌚10am-midnight)

Internet Caffe Baščaršija (Aščiluk bb; per hr 2KM; ⌚7am-midnight)

Money

There are ATMs outside the bus station, inside the airport and sprinkled all over the city centre. **UniCredit Bank** (Zelenih Beretki 24; ⌚8am-6pm Mon-Fri, 8.30am-1pm Sat) changes travellers cheques.

Tourist Information

The **tourist information centre** (☎220724; www.sarajevo-tourism.com) Baščaršija (Sarači 58; ⌚10am-2pm & 3-8pm Mon-Fri, 10am-4pm Sat & Sun); main office (Zelenih Beretki 22a; ⌚9am-5.30pm Mon-Fri, 9am-3pm Sat) is helpful with maps, brochures and ready answers for many an awkward question. It also organises recommended daily walking and war-era city tours.

Getting There & Away

For information about flying into Sarajevo see p151.

Bus

Sarajevo has two bus stations.

The **main bus station** (☎213100; Put Života 8) is beside the train station. Start here for domestic destinations such as Banja Luka (31KM, five hours, seven daily via Travnik and Jajce), Bihać (42KM, 6½ hours, 7.30am, 1.30pm and 10pm), Mostar (18KM, 2½ hours, 15 daily), Pale (5.40KM, 40 minutes, 7am, 10am and 2pm), Visoko (5.70KM, 50 minutes, hourly).

Services to international destinations also depart from here, including to Dubrovnik (from 44KM, seven hours), Novi Pasar (32KM, 7½ hours, five daily), Split (51KM, 7½ hours, 10am and 9pm), Vienna (100KM, 14½ hours, 11.15am) and Zagreb (54KM, 9½ hours, 6.30am, 9.30am, 12.30pm and 10pm).

East Sarajevo (Lukovica) Bus Station (Автобус Станица Источно Сарајево; ☎057-317377; Nikole Tesle bb) is about 10km south of town, 400m beyond the western terminus of trolleybus 103. Buses run to Foča (9KM, 11.10am and 4.35pm), Belgrade (55KM, eight to 11 hours, five daily), Podgorica (35KM, six hours, 8.15am, 2pm and 10.30pm) and Trebinje (26KM, five hours, 7.45am and 1pm).

Train

Trains run to Mostar (9.90KM, three hours, 7.05am and 6.18pm), Zagreb (58.90KM, 9½ hours, 10.42am and 9.27pm), Budapest (105.90KM, 12 hours, 6.55am) and Belgrade (33KM, nine hours, 11.35am).

Getting Around

Bus, tram and trolleybus tickets cost 1.60/1.80KM from kiosks/drivers. Validate them in the on-board machines. For timetables (in Bosnian) click on 'redove vožnje' on www.gras.co.ba, then select mode of transport.

Tram 1 connects the main bus/train stations to Baščaršija every 15 minutes. More frequent tram 3 runs from Ilidža (6am to 11.45pm), following the north bank past the Holiday Inn then looping anticlockwise around Baščaršija.

Metered taxis, including **Žuti** (Yellow Cab; ☎663555), charge from 2KM, plus around 1KM per kilometre. Rent bicycles from **Rent-A-Bike** (☎062547364; Dženitića Čikma bb; per hr/day/week 3/15/50KM; ⌚9am-2pm & 3.30-9pm Wed-Mon).

To/From the Airport

From Sarajevo Airport or East Sarajevo bus station, the nearest regular public transport is trolleybus 103 running to Austrijski Trg every four to nine minutes from 5.30am to 11pm. From the airport the closest stop is near Mercator Hypermarket (Mimar Sinana 1), around 700m away through an unpromising-looking housing estate: turn right out of the terminal then first left, shimmy right-left-right past the Hotel Octagon, then turn right at the Panda car wash (Brače Mulića 17) and cross over the main road.

AROUND BOSNIA & HERCEGOVINA

Mostar

036 / POP 94,000

Set in a deep valley flanked by arid mountains, Mostar's splendidly rebuilt Ottoman-era core forms one of Eastern Europe's most photogenic scenes.

Sights

Stari Most BRIDGE

Arcing majestically between the Neretva River's rugged banks, Mostar's famous 1566 Stari Most (Old Bridge) was infamously destroyed in the 1990s conflict but has since been meticulously reconstructed as a powerful and very beautiful symbol of BiH's reconciliation.

In summer Mostar's unique breed of **divers** plunge 21m off the bridge's parapet into the icy waters below...at least, once enough photo money has been collected from the watching tourists.

Mostar Old Town NEIGHBOURHOOD

Just east of Stari Most, colourful stone-fronted trinket stores line **Kujundžiluk**, Mostar's very appealing Turkish-era bazaar-lane. Leading north this becomes Mala Tepa then Braće Fejića, Mostar's main commercial thoroughfare, lined with numerous ATMs, eateries and rebuilt historic **mosques**.

Front Line WAR DAMAGE

Back in 1992–95, the **Bulevar** formed an intercommunal **front line** across which Croats and Bosniaks shelled each other almost incessantly. Today it's a fairly ordinary main road but in places shockingly war-ravaged buildings still lie in bullet-peppered ruins awaiting reconstruction. You can learn more across the river at the little **Museum of Hercegovina** (http://muzejhercegovine.com; Bajatova 4; admission 5KM; 8am-2pm Mon-Fri, 10am-noon Sat), which screens a well-paced 10-minute film featuring bridge-diving and showing the very moment that Stari Most was blown apart.

Sleeping

Most budget options are in people's homes with neither reception nor full-time staff, so calling ahead is wise. In low season some are virtually dormant but you might get a whole room for the price of a dorm.

SPLURGE

In summer tourists pay to visit the restored 18th-century Ottoman courtyard **Muslibegović House** (551379; www.muslibegovichouse.com; Osman Dikća 41; s/d/ste €50/85/100;), but it's simultaneously an extremely convivial boutique hotel. Room sizes and styles vary significantly, mixing excellent modern bathrooms with elements of traditional Bosnian, Turkish or even Moroccan design. Doubles cost €70 low season.

Motel Emen OLD-TOWN ROOMS €€

(581120, 061848734; www.motel-emen.com; Oneščukova 32; s/d/tr/q 82/124/154/212KM; @) The term 'Motel' is quite misleading for what are in fact six tastefully appointed new rooms above a restaurant on one of Old Mostar's most popular pedestrian lanes. The decor is understatedly chic.

Kriva Ćuprija MILL-HOUSE ROOMS €€

(550953; www.motel-mostar.ba; s/d/apt from €30/55/65;) Soothe yourself with the sounds of gushing streams in new, impeccably clean (if not necessarily large) rooms ranged above this stone mill-house restaurant overlooking the Crooked Bridge.

Shangri-La B&B €€

(551819; www.shangrila.com.ba; Kalhanska 10; d without/with breakfast €34/44; P) Charming English-speaking hosts are welcoming but not intrusive, while their four rooms are better appointed than those of many Mostar hotels.

Hostel Majdas HOUSE-HOSTEL €

(061382940, 062265324; www.hostelmajdas.com; 1st fl, Franje Milicevica 39; dm/d without bathroom €13/27; @) Although located 600m west of the centre in a very ordinary apartment block, the family's warmth, sharp wit and great-value regional tours have made this a cult house-hostel.

Pansion Oscar GUEST HOUSE €

(580237; Oneščukova 33; s/d €30/40, s/d/tr/q without bathroom €20/30/45/60;) Six presentable rooms in two reconstructed old-town houses, separated by parasol-shaded summer seating. The location is unbeatably close to Stari Most.

Hostel Nina HOUSE-HOSTEL €

(061382743; www.hostelnina.ba; Čelebica 18; dm/s/d without bathroom €10/15/20; @) Popular

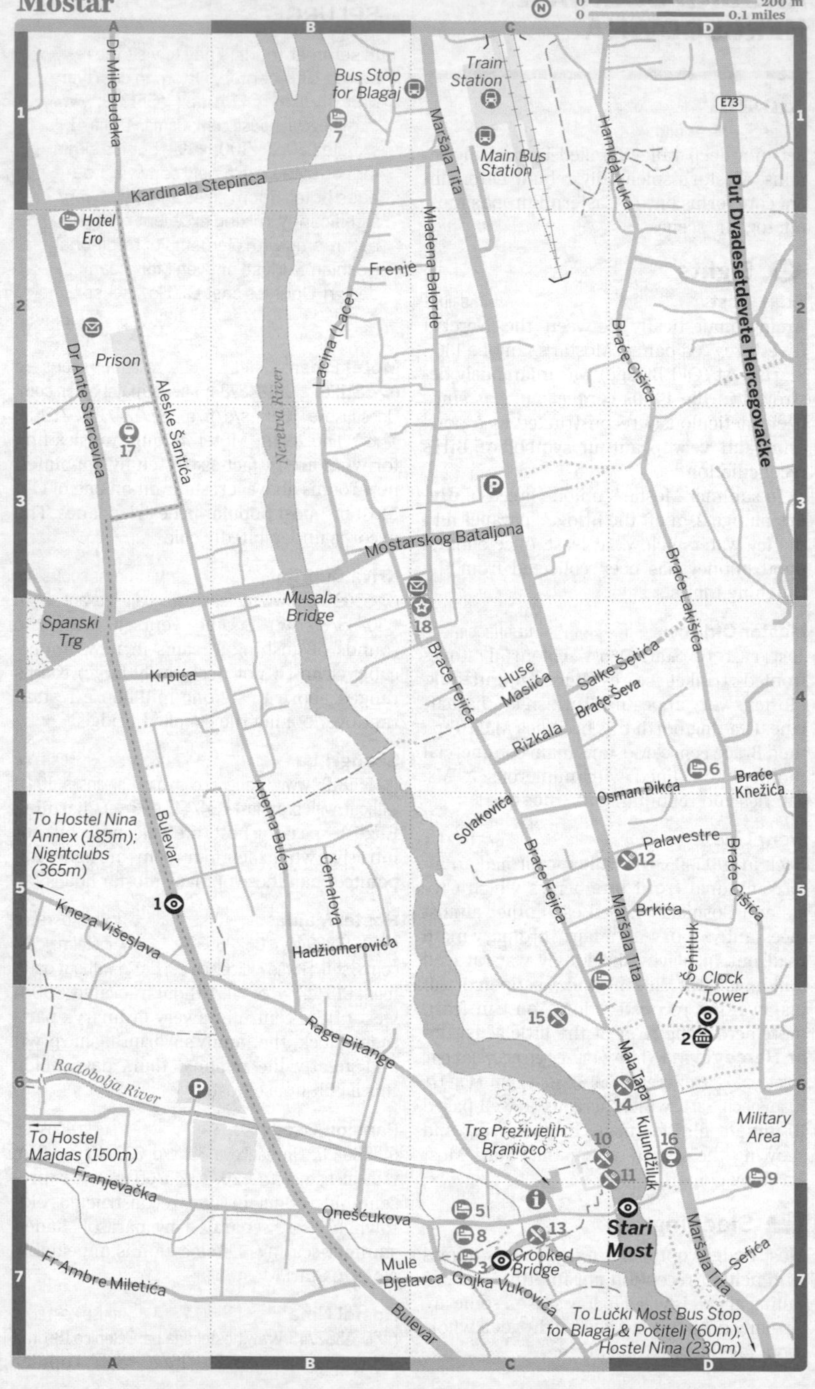

0 200 m
0 0.1 miles
Train Station
Bus Stop for Blagaj
Main Bus Station
Kardinala Stepinca
Hotel Ero
Dr Mile Budaka
Maršala Tita
Hamdija Kreševljakovića
Put Dvadesetdevete Hercegovačke
E73
Mladena Balorde
Frenje
Lacina (Lace)
Neretva River
Prison
Dr Ante Starcevica
Aleske Šantića
Braće Ćišića
Mostarskog Bataljona
Musala Bridge
Spanski Trg
Krpića
Braće Fejića
Huse Maslića
Salke Šetića
Braće Lakišića
Braće Ševa
Rizkala
Solakovića
Osman Đikća
Braće Knežića
Palavestre
To Hostel Nina Annex (185m); Nightclubs (365m)
Bulevar
Aderna Buća
Čermalova
Brkića
Kneza Višeslava
Hadžiomerovića
Šehitluk
Clock Tower
Rage Bitange
Radobolja River
Mala Tapa
Military Area
To Hostel Majdas (150m)
Trg Preživjelih Branioco
Kujundžiluk
Franjevačka
Onešćukova
Stari Most
Mule Bjelavca
Crooked Bridge
Gojka Vukovića
Sefića
Fr Ambre Miletića
To Lučki Most Bus Stop for Blagaj & Počitelj (60m); Hostel Nina (230m)

homestay-hostel running regional tours that often end up at the family's bargain-priced bar in the Tabhana. The overflow annexe is in a dowdy apartment block across town near the Rondo.

Pansion Aldi HOUSE-HOSTEL €
(552185, 061273457; www.pansion-aldi.com; Laćina 69a; dm/d without bathroom €10/20; P❄@) Handy for the bus station, this unsigned family hostel has 17 beds in five large, if simple, rooms. There's a shared kitchenette, three small bathroom cubicles and a riverside garden terrace.

Miturno HOSTEL €
(552408; www.hostel-miturno.ba; Braće Felića 67; dm/d €10/20; ❄) Central minihostel above a main-street shop.

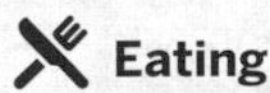

Eating

Although unapologetically tourist-oriented, restaurants with unforgettable Stari Most views are well worth the small extra expense (mains 7KM to 17KM). Try **Restaurant Bella Vista**, **Babilon** or **Teatr**, all tucked behind the Tabhana. Along Mala Tepa/Braće Fejića you'll find a morning vegetable market, supermarkets and several inexpensive places for *ćevapi*.

Konoba Stari Mlin ITALIAN €
(Jusovina bb; meals 5-12KM; 8am-10pm) Down a hidden stairway, this mill-house restaurant serves exceptionally good-value meals, including garlic calf's liver with fries (5KM) and well-cooked trout (10KM).

Urban Grill ĆEVABDŽINICA €
(Mala Tepa; 5/10 ćevapi 3.50/6KM; 8am-11pm) Hip *ćevapi* servery with Stari Most views from the rear terrace.

Eko-Eli BOSNIAN PIES €
(Maršala Tita 115; mains 2-3KM; 7am-11pm) Freshly baked *krompirača, sirnica* and *burek* served up for pennies at sit-and-scoff tables. Tourist free.

Drinking & Entertainment

Unique bar-club **Ali Baba Bar** (24hr summer only) burrows off Kujundžiluk into the cliff face. Hidden, smoky and understatedly intellectual **OKC Abrašević** (www.okcabrasevic.org; Alekse Šantića 25) attracts an alternative crowd. **Club Oxygen** (512244; www.biosphere.ba/biosfere-stranice-oxigen-en.html; Braće Fejića) has DJ nights and Mostar's top live gigs. Other nightclubs are 1km west, around the Rondo.

Shopping

Cute stone-roofed shop-houses found along Kujundžiluk sell colourful and inexpensive souvenirs.

Information

Tourist information centre (397350; Trg Preživjelih Branioco; 9am-9pm Jun-Sep, 10am-6pm Oct, closed Nov-May)

Getting There & Away

BUS From the **main bus station** (552025; Trg Ivana Krndelja) useful services include Dubrovnik (27KM, 3½ hours, three daily), Sarajevo (18KM, three hours, 12 daily), Split (31KM, 4½ hours, four daily) and Trebinje (21KM, three hours, three daily).

Yellow **Mostar Bus** (552250; www.mostarbus.ba/linije.asp) services to Blagaj start from opposite the train station and pick up passengers more conveniently by Lučki Most.

TRAIN Trains to Sarajevo (9.90KM, 2¾ hours) depart at 7.59am and 6.40pm, negotiating switchbacks and 65 tunnels beyond Konjic.

Mostar

Top Sights
Stari Most ... D7

Sights
1 Front Line of Fighting ... A5
2 Museum of Hercegovina ... D6
Tabhana ... (see 11)

Sleeping
3 Kriva Ćuprija ... C7
4 Miturno ... C5
5 Motel Emen ... C7
6 Muslibegović House ... D4
7 Pansion Aldi ... B1
8 Pansion Oscar ... C7
9 Shangri-La ... D6

Eating
10 Babilon ... C6
11 Bella Vista ... D6
12 Eko-Eli ... D5
13 Konoba Stari Mlin ... C7
Teatr ... (see 10)
14 Urban Grill ... D6
15 Vegetable Market ... C6

Drinking
16 Ali Baba Bar ... D6
17 OKC Abrašević ... A3

Entertainment
18 Club Oxygen ... C4

Around Mostar

Rising steeply up a cliffside amphitheatre beside the Mostar–Split road, picturesque **Počitelj** is a half-ruined Ottoman village with photogenic fortification towers. From Mostar take Čapljina-bound buses (6KM, 40 minutes), which run twice hourly except on Sunday. Alternatively, join agency- or hostel-organised tours that also visit **Međugorje** (www.medjugorje.hr), BiH's version of Lourdes, the half-timbered Dervish monastery **Tekija** (admission 3KM; ⏲8am-10pm) at Blagaj and the brilliant but awkward-to-reach **Kravice Waterfalls**, Hercegovina's 25m mini-Niagara.

Eastern Bosnia & Hercegovina

Appealing **Trebinje** (Требиње; www.trebinjeturizam.com) is the most attractive town in the RS (Republika Srpska), with a modest, walled old town (**Stari Grad**), distinctive 1574 **Arslanagić Bridge** (Perovića Most) and eye-catching hilltop church (**Presvete Bogorodice**). On a lovely, tree-shaded central square that feels like southern France, **Hotel Platani** (www.hotelplatani.info; Trg Svobode; old bldg s/d/tr 71/104/126KM, new bldg 82/134/157KM; ❄📶) consists of a pleasant if dated 'old building' and a contrastingly stylish contemporary one behind a traditional facade.

A bus to Dubrovnik (10KM, 40 minutes, Monday to Saturday) leaves Trebinje at 10am, returning at 1.30pm. Three daily buses link to Podgorica in Montenegro via Nikšić (33KM, 3½ hours). Sarajevo buses and the 8am Belgrade bus (48KM, 11 hours) travel via the glorious **Sutjeska National Park** (www.npsutjeska.net) and war-battered **Foča**, a centre for world-class rafting organised through extreme-sports outfit **Encijan** (☎058-211220; www.pkencijan.com; Kraljapetra-I 1, Foča). The Belgrade bus continues via **Višegrad** (www.visegradturizam.com), home to the 1571 'Bridge on the Drina', immortalised by Nobel Prize-winning author Ivo Andrić. Surrounding river gorges are magnificent and a newly reconstructed **narrow-gauge tourist railway** links Višegrad to Mokra Gora in Serbia.

Western Bosnia & Hercegovina

Along the road between Sarajevo and Zagreb are several mildly interesting historic towns.

WORTH A TRIP

THE UNA RIVER VALLEY

In the northwest corner of BiH, the beautiful emerald-green Una Valley is popular for climbing, canyoning, kayaking and a full grade-range of white-water rafting. Useful contacts include **Una Kiro** (☎037-223760, www.una-kiro-rafting.com; Golubić), **Sport Bjeli** (☎037-388555; www.una-rafting.ba; Klokot) and **Limit** (☎061 144248; www.limit.co.ba), based in regional transport hub Bihać. Dining is a delight at several rural mill-house restaurants beside the river banks, while luxurious hotel-restaurant **Kostelski Buk** (☎302340; www.kostelski-buk.com; M14 hwy, Kostela; s/d from 63/96KM, mains 10-18KM; P❄📶) combines fabulous food and some of BiH's best-value rooms. It's 9km from Bihać, towards Banja Luka.

The apparently unremarkable leather-tanning town of **Visoko** was once the capital of medieval Bosnia. Today it draws throngs of visitors intrigued by archaeologist Semir Osmanagic's bold new theory that 250m-high **Visočica Hill** (Sun Pyramid; www.piramidasunca.ba; admission 2KM) might in fact be the world's greatest pyramid.

In **Travnik** (www.tzsbk.com), 1¼ hours further west, Plava Voda restaurants attractively line a gushing stream at the foot of the fortress ruins of **Stari Grad** (adult/student 2/1.50KM; ⏲8am-8pm May-Sep, 9am-6pm Oct & Apr). Nearby **Motel Aba** (☎511462; www.aba.ba; Šumeća 166a; s/d/tr/q 35-40/50/70/80KM; 📶) is a remarkable budget bargain.

Jajce has a compact, picturesque old town topped by a powerful fortress ruin where Bosnia's medieval kings were once crowned. Viewed from the Banja Luka road, the scene is photogenically fronted by a signature 21m **waterfall**. Cute and central, **Hotel Stari Grad** (☎654006; hotel.stari.grad@tel.net.ba; Svetog Luke 3; s/d/apt 55/80/160KM; ❄) is a great accommodation choice. Or continue 5km west to **Plaža Motel** (☎647200; M5 hwy, km 93; s/d 40/70KM) beside **Plivsko Jezero**, a picture-perfect lake. Walk 1km back along the shore to find a quaint collection of 17 miniature **watermills**.

West of Jajce the road passes through canyon valleys. To descend them by raft, visit **Karanovac Rafting Centre** (☎882085,

065420000; www.guidelinebl.com), 8km before **Banja Luka**, the fun-loving but architecturally challenged capital of the Republika Srpska.

UNDERSTAND BOSNIA & HERCEGOVINA

History

Ancient Illyrians, followed by Romans from AD 9 and Slavs from the late 6th century, were Bosnia's early arrivals. The medieval Bosnian kingdom had its own rather mysterious Christian church and reached several cultural zeniths between 1180 and 1463. Thereafter the area was absorbed by the Turkish Ottoman Empire. Islam rapidly became the predominant religion of Bosnia's elite, though much of the peasantry remained Christian.

After 1878 BiH became controlled by predominantly Catholic Austria-Hungary. This alienated Muslim Bosniaks and Orthodox Serbs, and in 1914 a Bosnian Serb assassinated Austria-Hungary's imperial heir, Franz Ferdinand, in Sarajevo. This ultimately ignited WWI, which killed an astonishing 15% of the Bosnian population. Postwar BiH joined proto-Yugoslavia and in WWII its mountains were the scene of numerous battles between Nazi occupiers and Tito's communist Partizans.

In 1991 BiH's Croats and Bosniaks united to declare independence from Serb-dominated Yugoslavia. In reply Bosnian-Serb nationalists started seizing territory and 'ethnic cleansing' Muslims from the north and east. By 1992 a three-way war was raging between Serbs, Croats and Bosniaks. Atrocities were committed by all sides. Most infamously, Croats senselessly destroyed Mostar's Stari Most, while Bosnian Serbs besieged Sarajevo for three years and, in 1995, slaughtered over 7000 Srebrenica Muslims. Eventually NATO air strikes forced the Bosnian Serbs into 1995 peace talks.

The resulting Dayton Accords maintained the existence of BiH under a rotating presidency overseen by the EU's powerful High Representative (www.ohr.int). It also recognised two decentralised 'entities' within BiH: the Federation of Bosnia and Hercegovina (Muslims and Croats, capital Sarajevo), and Republika Srpska (Serbs, capital Banja Luka). Today these entities retain their own administrations, and even separate postal systems, but 'borders' between them have become virtually invisible.

Massive aid has helped rebuild the country's visible scars, but psychological wounds will long remain.

People

The population of BiH is 4.62 million. Bosniaks (Bosnian Muslims, 48% of the population) now live mostly in central BiH, Serbs (Orthodox Christians, 37%) to the north and east in the Republika Srpska, and Croats (Catholics, 14%) mainly in the south and west.

Despite some differences in vocabulary, all three communities speak effectively the same language, though Bosniaks call it 'Bosanski', Croats 'Hrvatski' and Serbs 'Srpski'. The latter is written in Cyrillic script. Useful phrases include *zdravo* (hello), *molim* (please) and *hvala* (thanks).

Food

Price ranges for mains in restaurants listed in this chapter are indicated as follows:

€€€ more than 15KM

€€ 8KM to 15KM

€ less than 8KM

Environment

Almost entirely mountainous, BiH rises from a toe of Adriatic coast at Neum, through stark, arid Hercegovina towards the dramatically canyon-diced central highlands before descending northwards through green rolling hills towards the flat Hungarian plain. BiH's highest peak, Mt Maglić (2387m), crowns the spectacular Sutjeska National Park.

SURVIVAL GUIDE

Directory A–Z

Accommodation

Sarajevo and Mostar offer numerous no-frills house-hotels, which are mostly glorified homestays. In midsummer occupancy and prices rise noticeably but touts helpfully appear at Mostar and Sarajevo stations.

GAY & LESBIAN TRAVELLERS

Although homosexuality was decriminalised per se in 1998 (2000 in the RS), attitudes remain very conservative. Sarajevo's only high-profile LGBT event, the Queer Festival of 2008, was violently attacked by anti-gay protesters. **Association Q** (www.queer.ba) nonetheless attempts to empower the self-reliance of the gay community in BiH and the English-language **Gay Romeo** (www.gayromeo.com) chat site reportedly has several hundred Sarajevo members.

In the provinces decent-value motels and *pansions* are usually less expensive and sometimes better than hotels.

Our price ranges for a double room are as follows:

€€€ more than 190KM

€€ 80KM to 190KM

€ less than 80KM

Activities

Hiking/mountain biking Compromised since the 1990s by the presence of landmines, but many upland areas and national parks now have safe, marked trails. See www.sarajevo-travel.ba.

Rafting Reaches terrifyingly difficult class V in April/May but is more suitable for beginners in summer. Top spots are around Foča, Bihać and Banja Luka.

Skiing Inexpensive yet world-class at Jahorina and Bjelašnica (p150).

Business Hours

Banks 8am-6pm Mon-Fri, 8.30am-1.30pm Sat

Offices 8am-4pm Mon-Fri

Shops 8am-6pm daily

Restaurants 11.30am-10.30pm, often later in summer

Dangers & Annoyances

Landmines and unexploded ordnance still affect around 3% of BiH's area, causing nine recorded deaths in 2009. Stick to asphalt/concrete surfaces or well-worn paths in affected areas and don't enter war-damaged buildings. **BHMAC** (www.bhmac.org) has more information.

Holidays

Some holidays are celebrated only in the Federation or RS.

New Year's Day 1 January

Serbian Orthodox Christmas 7 January (RS)

Independence Day 1 March

Catholic Easter March/April (Federation)

Orthodox Easter April/May (RS)

May Day 1 May

National Statehood Day 25 November

Catholic Christmas 25 December (Federation)

Kurban Bajram Islamic feast of sacrifice (Federation); dates vary each year

Ramazanski Bajram End of Ramadan celebration (Federation); dates vary each year

Money

The currency of BiH, the convertible mark (KM, maraka or BAM) is tied to the euro at around €1 to 1.96KM. Many tourist-oriented places accept euros. Some places in Mostar also take Croatian kuna.

ATMs are widespread. Changing travellers cheques often requires the original purchase receipt. Tipping in restaurants usually means rounding up the bill, or leaving one or two maraka extra.

Post & Telephone

BiH is a philatelic curiosity with three parallel stamp-issuing postal systems (see www.post.ba, www.bhp.ba and www.filatelija.rs.ba) for details.

Republika Srpska and Federation payphones use mutually incompatible prepaid cards, but BiH's three mobile-phone networks have cross-regional coverage.

Visas

Stays of under 90 days require no visa for citizens of most European countries and Australia, Brunei, Canada, Japan, Malaysia, New Zealand, Singapore, South Korea, Turkey and the USA. Other nationals should check out the website www.mfa.ba for more information.

Getting There & Away

Air

Pronounced 'Bay-Ha', **BH Airlines** (JA; ☎033-550125, 768335; www.bhairlines.ba; Branilaca Sarajeva 15; ⏰9am-5pm Mon-Fri, 9am-2pm Sat) is the national carrier, flying from Sarajevo to Belgrade, Copenhagen, Frankfurt, Göteborg, İstanbul, Stockholm, Vienna and Zürich. Thrice weekly the Zürich flight goes via Banja Luka.

The best connected airlines for **Sarajevo airport** (www.sarajevo-airport.ba) are listed here. Alternatively, fly to Dubrovnik, Split or Zagreb (Croatia) and go overland to BiH.

Adria (JP; www.adria.si) Via Ljubljana (also serves Banja Luka).

Austrian (OS; www.austrian.com) Vienna.

Croatia Airlines (OU; www.croatiaairlines.com) Zagreb.

Germanwings (4U; www.germanwings.com) Budget airline for Stuttgart and Köln-Bonn.

JAT (JU; www.jat.com) Belgrade.

Lufthansa (LH; www.lufthansa.com) Munich.

Malév (MA; www.malev.com) Budapest.

Norwegian (DY; www.norwegian.no) Budget weekly flights to Stockholm.

Turkish (TK; www.thy.com) Via İstanbul.

Bus & Train

There are buses to Zagreb and/or Split (Croatia) at least daily from most towns in the Federation, and to Serbia and/or Montenegro from many RS towns. Buses to Vienna and Germany run several times weekly from bigger BiH cities.

The modest train network includes international links from Sarajevo to Belgrade, Zagreb (via Banja Luka), Budapest (via Osijek, Croatia) and Ploče in coastal Croatia (via Mostar).

Car & Motorcycle

Drivers need Green Card insurance and an EU or International Driving Permit. Transiting Neum in a Croatian hire car is usually hassle free.

Getting Around

Bus

BiH's buses are punctual but slow and relatively infrequent. Frequency drops drastically at weekends on shorter-hop routes, some stopping altogether on Sunday. Advance reservations are rarely necessary except for overnight routes.

Fares are around 7KM per hour travelled, plus 2KM per stowed bag.

Car & Motorcycle

Roads are winding, lightly trafficked and almost unanimously beautiful: delightful if you aren't in a hurry. **Hyundai Rent-a-Car** (www.hyundai.ba) in Mostar and Sarajevo includes full insurance, theft protection and CDW in standard rates (per day/week from 75/390KM). For roadside assistance, call ☎1282/1288.

Headlights should be kept on all the time when driving. Speed limits can be infuriatingly slow but are regularly enforced.

Petrol prices are often significantly cheaper in the Republika Srpska than they are in the Federation.

Train

Trains are slower and less frequent than buses but generally around 30% cheaper. **BiH Railways** (www.zfbh.ba) has full, up-to-date rail timetables.

Britain

Includes »

Best Places to Eat

» Smiths of Smithfield, London (p174)

» CB2, Cambridge (p201)

» Gray's Court, York (p204)

» Trof, Manchester (p208)

Best Places to Stay

» Hoxton, London (p170)

» Ethos Hotel, Oxford (p194)

» Ambleside YHA, Lake District (p211)

» Smart City Hostel, Edinburgh (p218)

Why Go?

The Tower of London, Edinburgh Castle, Buckingham Palace, Manchester United, The Beatles. Britain does icons like nowhere else on earth, and this country's astounding range of attractions is a major reason to visit. Cities tempt with bars and restaurants, world-famous clubs and top-class museums. Next day, you're deep in the countryside, high in the hills or enjoying a classic seaside resort.

Along with variety, a journey through Britain is a journey through history. You can marvel at 5000-year-old Stonehenge or walk the Roman remains of Hadrian's Wall, then fast forward to the future and explore the space-age domes of the Eden Project.

And it's all so easy. In this compact nation you're never far from the next scenic national park, the next welcoming pub or the next impressive castle on your hit-list of highlights.

When to Go

London

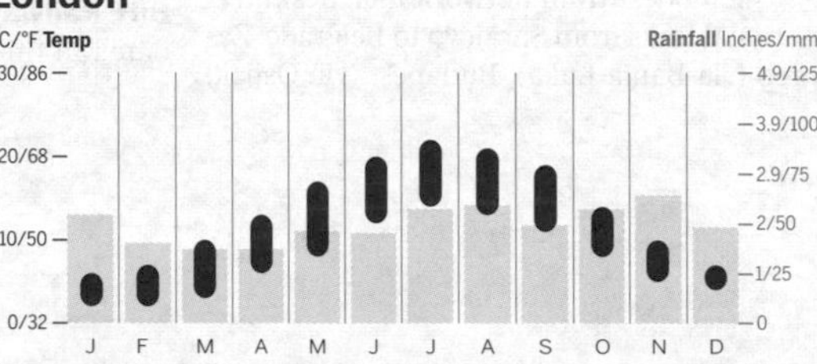

Apr–May Fewer crowds, especially in popular spots such as Bath, York and Edinburgh.

Jun–Aug The weather is at its best but the coast and national parks are busy.

Mid-Sep–Oct Prices drop and the weather is often surprisingly good.

Connections

As an island on the edge of Western Europe, Britain's overland options to neighbouring countries were limited to ferries before the opening of the Channel Tunnel in 1994 brought direct Eurostar rail services to London from Paris and Brussels (for details, see p236). Ferries still sail from southern England across to France in a couple of hours, from eastern England to the Netherlands and Germany, from northern England to Scandinavia, from southwest Scotland to Northern Ireland and from Wales to the Republic of Ireland. For details on ferry routes, see p237.

ITINERARIES

One Week

With just seven days, you're pretty much limited to sights in England. Start with a couple of days in London, then branch out to Canterbury and Brighton, or Salisbury and Stonehenge (or all four). Sample the delights of historic Bath, tootle up to Oxford and Stratford-upon-Avon, then head east to Cambridge, before returning to London.

Two Weeks

Start in London, then do a southeast–southwest loop via the grand cathedral cities of Canterbury, Winchester and Salisbury. Marvel at the iconic menhirs of Stonehenge and nearby Avebury, before enjoying more history in beautiful Bath. Loop over to Cardiff for a taste of Wales, then cruise across the classic English countryside of the Cotswolds to reach Oxford. Not far away is Stratford-upon-Avon, for everything Shakespeare. Strike out north to Scotland's capital, Edinburgh, before crossing the border again down to Durham and York, then Cambridge. Enjoy the last few days of your tour back in London.

Essential Food & Drink

» **Roast beef with Yorkshire pudding** Iconic English dish: beef with baked-batter pudding.

» **Bangers and mash** Another icon: sausages and mashed potato.

» **Fish and chips** Once the nation's most popular takeaway food, though nowadays curry is the favourite.

» **Haggis** Scottish speciality of sheep-offal pudding served with 'tatties and neeps' (potatoes and turnips).

» **Cawl and bara lafwr** Welsh treats: a broth made with lamb and leeks, and savoury scones made with oatmeal and seaweed.

AT A GLANCE

» **Currency** Pound sterling (£)

» **Language** English, Welsh and Scottish Gaelic

» **Money** ATMs are widely available

» **Visas** Not required by most citizens of Europe, Australia, NZ, USA and Canada

Fast Facts

» **Area** 88,500 sq miles (229,000 sq km)

» **Capitals** London (Britain and England), Cardiff (Wales), Edinburgh (Scotland)

» **Country code** ☎44

» **Emergency** ☎999

Exchange Rates

Australia	A$1	UK£0.65
Canada	C$1	UK£0.63
euro zone	€1	UK£0.87
Japan	¥100	UK£0.76
New Zealand	NZ$1	UK£0.49
USA	US$1	UK£0.62

Set Your Budget

» **Hostel dorm bed** £10-25

» **Midrange B&B** £50-100 per double room

» **Cheap meal in cafe or pub** £5-9

» **Beer (pint)** £3

Resources

» **Visit Britain** (www.visitbritain.com)

» **National Traveline** (www.traveline.org.uk)

Britain Highlights

1. Walk the streets of **London** (p156), one of the world's greatest capital cities
2. Take in **Bath** (p187), Britain's belle of the ball
3. Wander Britain's most dramatic Roman ruin, **Hadrian's Wall** (p205)
4. Enjoy mountains, valleys and, of course, lakes in the **Lake District** (p210)
5. Find hiking heritage, medieval city walls and the spectacular cathedral at **York** (p202)
6. See classic chocolate-box countryside at its best in the **Cotswolds** (p195)
7. Marvel at the iconic prehistoric site of **Stonehenge** (p187)

8 Get acquainted with **Edinburgh** (p214), the city of many moods, famous for festivals

9 Experience jaw-dropping moments at every turn in Scotland's **Northwest Highlands** (p225)

10 Discover the best of wild and wonderful West Wales in **Pembrokeshire** (p213)

LONDON

POP 7.51 MILLION

One of the world's greatest cities, London has enough history, vitality and cultural drive to keep you occupied for weeks. This cosmopolitan capital leads international trends in music, fashion and the arts, riding a wave of 21st-century British confidence, breathing new life into established neighbourhoods such as Westminster and Knightsbridge, and reinventing areas such as Southwark and Shoreditch that were formerly off the tourist track. With the Olympic Games rolling into town in 2012, and even despite the little matter of a global economic downturn, London's life and landscape never stands still.

The downside of this renaissance is increasing cost: London is now Europe's most expensive city for visitors – whatever their budget. But with some careful planning and a bit of common sense, you can find great bargains and freebies among the popular attractions.

And don't forget that the greatest show of all is simply wandering the streets, strolling through London's wonderful parks, or admiring the world-famous bridges and buildings from the embankments beside the River Thames – that costs nothing.

No Londoner would be without a pocket-sized *London A-Z* map-book – you can buy them at newsstands and shops everywhere. For getting around the London Underground system ('the tube'), maps are free at underground stations.

History

London first came into being as a Celtic village, possibly called Lundyn, near a ford across the River Thames. In the Roman era the settlement – called Londinium – became properly established, enclosed in protective walls with four main entrances still echoed today in the shape of the City financial district, and the areas of Ludgate, Aldgate, Bishopsgate and Newgate.

By the end of the 3rd century AD, Londinium was home to 30,000 people of many ethnic groups, and was filled with temples dedicated to various cults and religions. But the Romans abandoned Britain in the early 5th century, reducing the city to a sparsely populated backwater.

Then came the Saxons, and the town – now called Lundenwic – prospered again. Perhaps too much, for it caught the eye of Danish Vikings who launched many invasions and razed the city in the 9th century. In 1016 the Saxons finally accepted the Danish ruler Knut (Canute) as King of England,

London

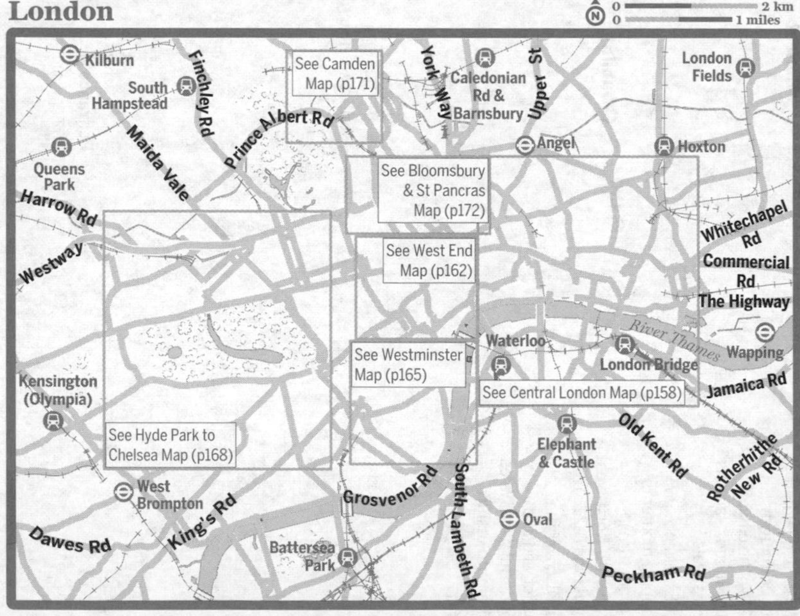

and London became the capital (replacing Winchester).

In 1042 the throne reverted to the Saxon Edward the Confessor, whose main contribution to the city was the building of Westminster Abbey – where British monarchs are still crowned – but the dispute over his successor led to William the Conqueror's landmark invasion and the Battle of Hastings in 1066. William's first moves included ordering the construction of the White Tower (the core of today's Tower of London) and negotiating taxes with the merchants, and affirming the city's right to self-government.

London grew prosperous and increased in global importance throughout the medieval period, surviving devastating challenges such as the 1665 Plague and 1666 Great Fire. Instead, the city simply reinvented itself – many of its landmarks such as St Paul's Cathedral were designed at this time by visionary architect Christopher Wren.

By 1720 London had 750,000 inhabitants and was the centre of a growing world empire. Fuelled by mercantile wealth, the Victorian era was the city's golden age. In contrast, WWII was London's darkest hour, with the city on the edge of destruction after relentless bombing.

The ugly postwar rebuilding phase of the 1950s gave way to the cultural renaissance of the 1960s, when London became the planet's undisputed swinging capital. Things dipped again during the 1970s, while the 1980s heralded a time of plenty for some Londoners and hardship for others. The pendulum swung once more in the 1990s, and London was the focus of the Cool Britannia phenomenon of new politics, arts and music.

In 2000 the modern metropolis of London got its first elected Mayor (as opposed to the largely ceremonial role of Lord Mayor of the City of London).

For every period of success, tragedy has never been far away. In July 2005 four terrorist bombs on underground trains and a bus killed dozens of people around the city. While deep anxiety initially gripped many Londoners, most soon returned to their daily routines – a response mirrored throughout the capital's turbulent history.

Sights

London is teeming with magnificent buildings, world-leading museums and cutting-edge attractions. With so much to see and do, it can be hard to know where to start.

> In this chapter, all admission prices given for sights are the adult rate. At many locations in Britain, 'concessions' (ie discounts) are given for students and under-18s. This may not always be evident at the ticket desk so it's worth asking. You may also get discounts for buying tickets in advance online. Some places – such as churches and museums – are free, but suggest a donation.

Weather will be a determining factor: if it's raining, head for museums and galleries; if the sun shines, make like a Londoner and visit the parks.

WEST END

Westminster may be the brains of the capital, while the parks are the lungs and the City the pockets, but if anywhere is the beating heart of London, it's the West End – a strident mix of culture and consumerism.

Trafalgar Square LANDMARK

(Map p162; ⊖Charing Cross) Trafalgar Square is a great place to start any visit to London. Frequently the venue for rallies and marches (and feverish New Year's festivities), Londoners congregate here to celebrate anything from football victories to the ousting of political leaders. Dominating the square is 43m-high **Nelson's Column**, erected in 1843 to commemorate British hero Admiral Nelson's 1805 victory over Napoleon.

FREE **National Gallery** GALLERY

(Map p162; www.nationalgallery.org.uk; Trafalgar Sq WC2; ⊙10am-6pm Sat-Thu, to 9pm Fri; ⊖Charing Cross) Gazing grandly over Trafalgar Square is Britain's most important art repository. Seminal paintings from every epoch are here, including works by Giotto, Leonardo da Vinci, Michelangelo and Van Gogh.

FREE **National Portrait Gallery** GALLERY

(Map p162; www.npg.org.uk; St Martin's Pl WC2; ⊙10am-6pm Sat-Wed, to 9pm Thu & Fri; ⊖Charing Cross) A visit here is like stepping into a picture book of British history.

Piccadilly Circus LANDMARK

(Map p162; ⊖Piccadilly Circus) Neon-lit, turbo-charged Piccadilly Circus is home to a famous London statue, correctly called the 'angel of Christian charity', and much better (though erroneously) known as **Eros**, the

Central London

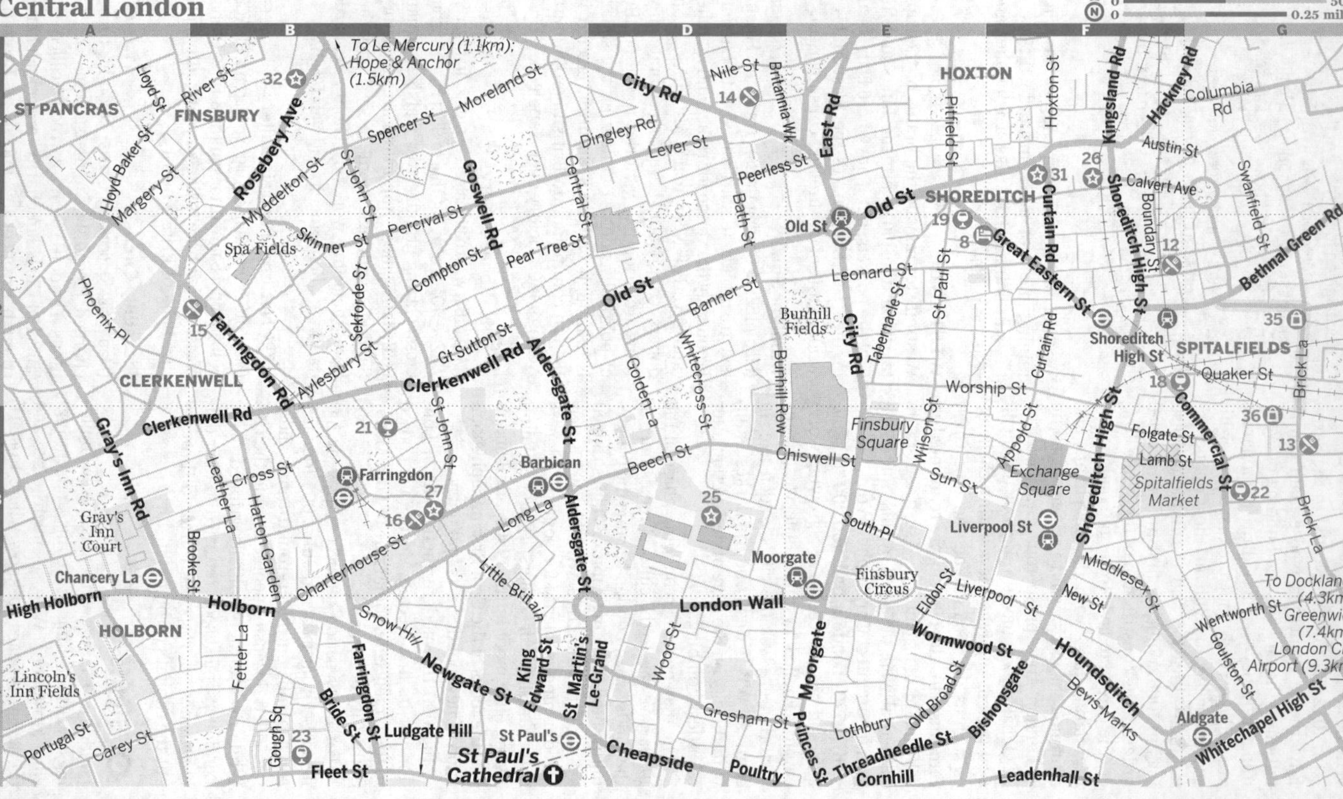

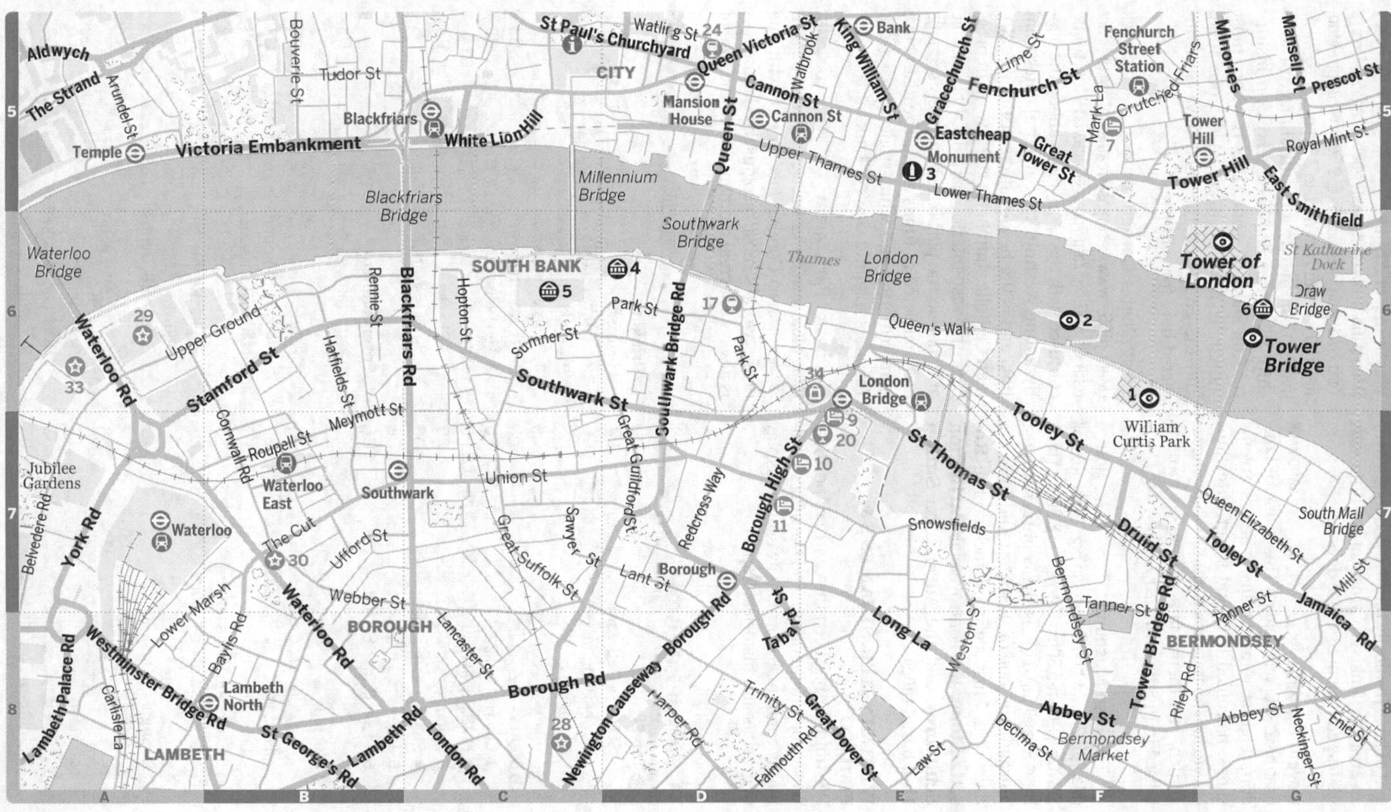
Aldwych
The Strand
Arundel St
Temple
Bouverie St
Tudor St
Blackfriars
White Lion Hill
Victoria Embankment
St Paul's Churchyard
Watling St
CITY
Queen Victoria St
Mansion House
Queen St
Cannon St
Walbrook
King William St
Bank
Gracechurch St
Fenchurch St
Lime St
Fenchurch Street Station
Mark La
Crutched Friars
Minories
Mansell St
Prescot St
Tower Hill
Royal Mint St
Eastcheap
Monument
Great Tower St
Upper Thames St
Lower Thames St
East Smithfield
Millennium Bridge
Blackfriars Bridge
Southwark Bridge
Thames
London Bridge
Tower of London
St Katharine Dock
Draw Bridge
Tower Bridge
Waterloo Bridge
SOUTH BANK
Rennie St
Blackfriars Rd
Hopton St
Park St
Southwark Bridge Rd
Queen's Walk
Upper Ground
Waterloo Rd
Stamford St
Hatfields St
Sumner St
Southwark St
London Bridge
Tooley St
William Curtis Park
St Thomas St
Meymott St
Roupell St
Cornwall Rd
Waterloo East
Jubilee Gardens
Southwark
Union St
Great Guildford St
Redcross Way
Borough High St
Snowsfields
Queen Elizabeth St
South Mall Bridge
Belvedere Rd
York Rd
Waterloo
The Cut
Ufford St
Great Suffolk St
Sawyer St
Lant St
Borough
Druid St
Mill St
Lower Marsh
Webber St
Baylis Rd
BOROUGH
Lancaster St
Borough Rd
Tabard St
Long La
Weston St
Bermondsey St
Tanner St
Tower Bridge Rd
BERMONDSEY
Jamaica Rd
Lambeth Palace Rd
Carlisle La
Westminster Bridge Rd
Lambeth North
LAMBETH
St George's Rd
Lambeth Rd
London Rd
Newington Causeway
Harper Rd
Trinity St
Falmouth Rd
Great Dover St
Law St
Decima St
Abbey St
Bermondsey Market
Riley Rd
Neckinger St
Enid St
A
B
C
D
E
F
G
5
6
7
8

god of love. Ironically the love god looks over an area long linked to prostitution, although it's less conspicuous these days.

Covent Garden LANDMARK
(Map p162; ⊖Covent Garden) This is one of London's biggest tourist traps, where souvenir shops, balconied bars and street entertainers vie for the punter's pound. It *was* once a garden, and then a famous market immortalised in the film *My Fair Lady*.

FREE **British Museum** MUSEUM
(Map p162; www.britishmuseum.org; Great Russell St WC1; ⏲10am-5.30pm Sat-Wed, to 8.30pm Thu & Fri; ⊖Russell Sq) This is the country's largest museum and one of the oldest and finest in the world. Must-see items include the **Rosetta Stone**, the controversial **Parthenon Sculptures**, and the Anglo-Saxon **Sutton Hoo** burial relics.

WESTMINSTER, ST JAMES'S & PIMLICO

Westminster has been the centre of political power for a millennium, and the area's landmarks combine to form an awesome display of gravitas and historical import.

Westminster Abbey CHURCH
(Map p165; www.westminster-abbey.org; 20 Dean's Yard SW1; admission £15; ⏲9.30am-4.30pm Mon, Tue, Thu & Fri, to 7pm Wed, to 2.30pm Sat; ⊖Westminster) Not merely a beautiful place of worship, Westminster Abbey serves up history cold on slabs of stone. This is where most monarchs have been crowned since 1066, and the great and the good have been interred here for centuries.

Westminster Cathedral CHURCH
(Map p165; www.westminstercathedral.org.uk; Victoria St SW1; ⏲7am-7pm; ⊖Victoria) Not to be confused with the eponymous abbey, the neo-Byzantine Westminster Cathedral dates from 1895 and is the headquarters of Britain's Roman Catholic church. It's still a work in progress, the vast interior part dazzling marble and mosaic and part bare brick; new sections are completed as funds allow. The distinctive 83m red-brick and white-stone **tower** (adult £5) offers splendid views of London.

Houses of Parliament LANDMARK
(Map p165; www.parliament.uk; Parliament Sq SW1; ⊖Westminster) Coming face to face with one of the world's most recognisable landmarks is always a surreal moment, but in the case of

Central London

Top Sights

St Paul's Cathedral........C4
Tower Bridge........G6
Tower of London........G6

Sights

1 City Hall........F6
2 HMS Belfast........F6
3 Monument........E5
4 Shakespeare's Globe........D6
5 Tate Modern........C6
6 Tower Bridge Exhibition........G6

Sleeping

7 Apex City of London........F5
8 Hoxton........E2
9 Orient Express........E7
10 St Christopher's Inn........E7
11 St Christopher's Village........D7

Eating

12 Albion........F2
13 Cafe Bangla........G3
14 Fifteen........D1
15 Little Bay........B2
16 Smiths of Smithfield........C3

Drinking

17 Anchor........D6
18 Commercial Tavern........F2
19 Favela Chic........E2
20 George Inn........E7
21 Jerusalem Tavern........B3
22 Ten Bells........G3
23 Ye Olde Cheshire Cheese........B4
24 Ye Olde Watling........D5

Entertainment

25 Barbican Centre........D3
26 Cargo........F1
27 Fabric........C3
28 Ministry of Sound........C8
29 National Theatre........A6
30 Old Vic........B7
31 Plastic People........F1
32 Sadler's Wells........B1
33 Southbank Centre........A6

Shopping

34 Borough Market........E6
35 Brick Lane Market........G2
36 Rough Trade........G3

the Houses of Parliament it's a revelation. Officially called the Palace of Westminster, the oldest part of the interior dates from 1097, but much of the visible building was built in 1840. The palace's most famous feature is its clock tower, known as **Big Ben** – actually the name of the 13-ton bell inside the tower.

FREE **Tate Britain** ART GALLERY

(Map p165; www.tate.org.uk; Millbank SW1; ⏲10am-5.40pm; ⊖Pimlico) Reaching through time from 1500 to the present, this gallery is crammed with British heavyweights such as Blake, Hogarth, Gainsborough, Whistler, Spencer and, especially, Turner, whose 'interrupted visions' – unfinished canvasses of moody skies – wouldn't look out of place in the contemporary section, alongside works by David Hockney, Francis Bacon, Tracey Emin and Damien Hirst. There are free guided tours taking in different sections of the gallery daily at midday and 3pm.

Buckingham Palace PALACE

(Map p165; www.royalcollection.org.uk; Buckingham Palace Rd SW1; admission £17; ⏲late Jul-Sep; ⊖Victoria) With so many imposing buildings in the capital, the Queen's relatively plain city pad can be an anticlimax. A handy way of telling whether she's home is to check whether the 'royal standard' flag is flying on the roof. The gaudily furnished **State Rooms** are open in summer for Royal-loving tourists, but it's more fun – and free – outside watching the **changing of the guard** (11.30am daily May-Jul, alternate days for the rest of the year, weather permitting).

St James's Park & Green Park PARKS

(Map p165; ⊖St James's Park or Green Park) With its manicured flowerbeds and ornamental lake, St James's Park is a wonderful place to stroll and take in the views of Westminster, Buckingham Palace and St James's Palace. The expanse of Green Park links St James's Park to Hyde Park and Kensington Gardens, creating a green corridor from Westminster all the way to Kensington. Although it doesn't have lakes, fountains or formal gardens, it's blanketed with daffodils in spring and sunbathing bodies whenever the sun shines.

THE CITY

For centuries, the City (note the capital C) *was* London. Its boundaries have changed little from the Roman walls built here two millennia ago. Today it's the central business district, so Sunday is a good time to walk around and explore its ancient churches and atmospheric laneways, although you'll miss the smell of fear as the planet's leading bankers cope with global ups and downs.

St Paul's Cathedral CHURCH

(Map p158; www.stpauls.co.uk; admission £12.50; ⏲8.30am-4pm Mon-Sat; ⊖St Paul's) Dominating the City, St Paul's Cathedral was built by 'London's architect' Christopher Wren between 1675 and 1710. The dome is renowned for somehow dodging the bombs in the Blitz and became an icon of the capital's resilience during WWII. Inside, attractions include the **Whispering Gallery** – if you talk close to the wall it carries your words around to the opposite side – and the **Golden Gallery** at the very top, for an unforgettable view of London.

Tower of London CASTLE, PALACE

(Map p158; www.hrp.org.uk; Tower Hill EC3; admission £17; ⏲9am-5.30pm, from 10am Sun & Mon, until 4.30pm Nov-Feb; ⊖Tower Hill) If you only pay one admission fee while you're here, make it the Tower of London, one of the city's three World Heritage Sites. After the obligatory **Crown Jewels** visit, leave plenty of time to explore the walls, dungeons and museum rooms – a window on a gruesome and fascinating history, from the Roman era to the present day.

Tower Bridge LANDMARK

(Map p158) The south bank of the Thames was a thriving port in 1894 when the elegant Tower Bridge was built. The bridge was designed so the roadway could be raised to allow ships to pass and reach the port, and it still goes up most days. Walking across is free. For more insights, the **Tower Bridge Exhibition** (www.towerbridge.org.uk; admission £7; ⏲10am-5.30pm Apr-Sep, 9.30am-5pm Oct-Mar; ⊖Tower Hill), recounts the story with videos and animatronics.

Monument MEMORIAL

(Map p158; www.themonument.info; Monument St; admission £3; ⏲9.30am-5.30pm; ⊖Monument) Designed by Wren to commemorate the Great Fire, the Monument is 60.6m high, the exact distance from its base to the bakery on Pudding Lane where the blaze began. Climb the 311 tight spiral steps for an eye-watering view from beneath the symbolic vase of gold-leaf flames.

SOUTH BANK

Outside the walls (and rules) of the City, Londoners once crossed to the areas south of the river for a wide range of diversions.

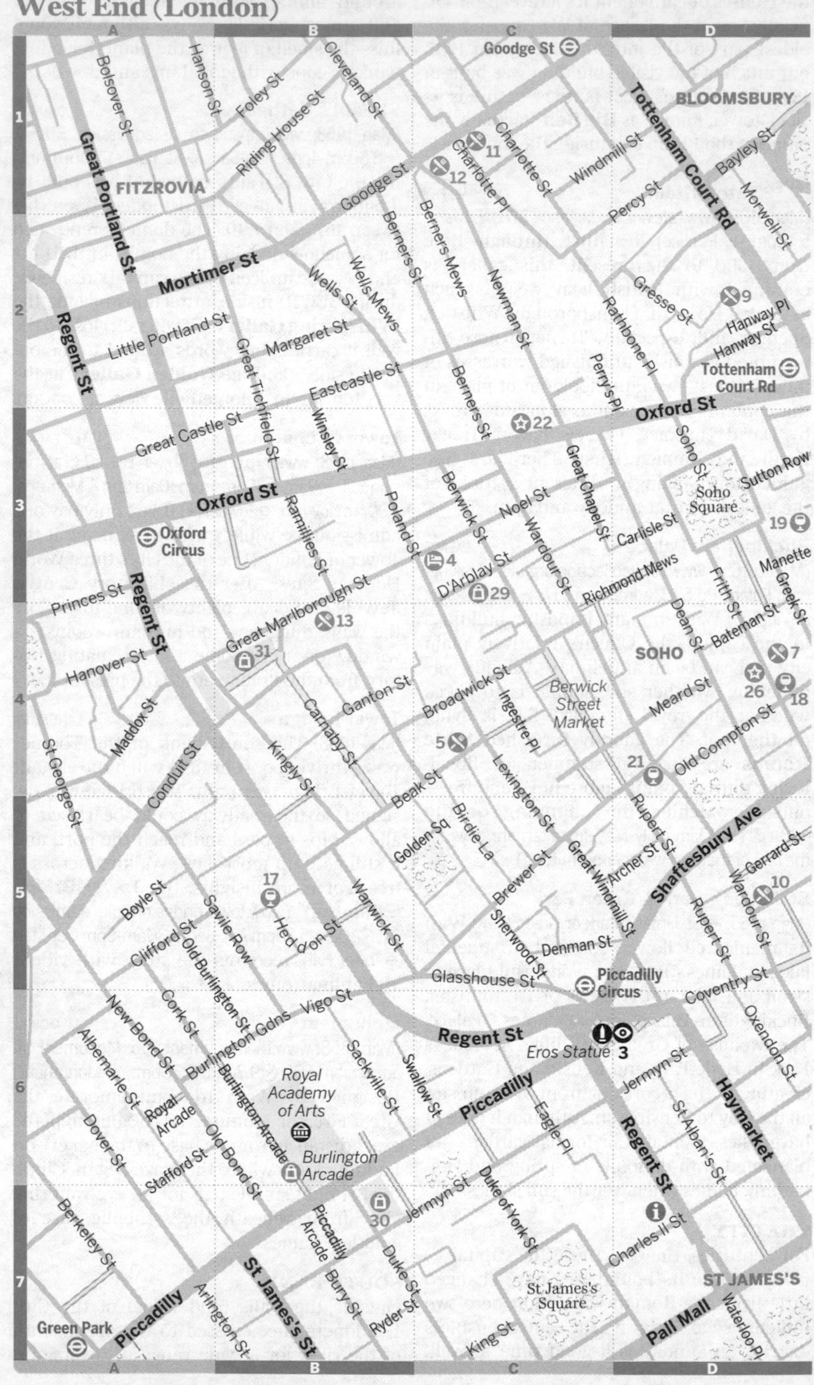

A
B
C
D
1
2
3
4
5
6
7
Goodge St
BLOOMSBURY
FITZROVIA
SOHO
ST JAMES'S
Great Portland St
Regent St
Mortimer St
Oxford St
Tottenham Court Rd
Oxford Circus
Tottenham Court Rd
Piccadilly Circus
Green Park
Bolsover St
Hanson St
Foley St
Cleveland St
Riding House St
Goodge St
Charlotte St
Charlotte Pl
Windmill St
Bayley St
Morwell St
Percy St
Gresse St
Hanway Pl
Hanway St
Rathbone Pl
Perry's Pl
Newman St
Berners Mews
Berners St
Wells St
Wells Mews
Little Portland St
Margaret St
Great Titchfield St
Eastcastle St
Winsley St
Great Castle St
Ramillies St
Poland St
Berwick St
Noel St
Wardour St
Great Chapel St
Carlisle St
Soho St
Soho Square
Sutton Row
Manette
Greek St
Frith St
Dean St
Bateman St
Richmond Mews
D'Arblay St
Princes St
Great Marlborough St
Hanover St
Maddox St
St George St
Conduit St
Carnaby St
Ganton St
Kingly St
Broadwick St
Ingestre Pl
Berwick Street Market
Meard St
Old Compton St
Beak St
Lexington St
Golden Sq
Birdie La
Brewer St
Great Windmill St
Archer St
Rupert St
Shaftesbury Ave
Gerrard St
Boyle St
Clifford St
Savile Row
Heddon St
Warwick St
Sherwood St
Denman St
Glasshouse St
Old Burlington St
Cork St
New Bond St
Vigo St
Burlington Gdns
Coventry St
Oxendon St
Regent St
Eros Statue
Albemarle St
Royal Arcade
Dover St
Burlington Arcade
Royal Academy of Arts
Sackville St
Swallow St
Piccadilly
Eagle Pl
Jermyn St
St Alban's St
Haymarket
Stafford St
Old Bond St
Burlington Arcade
Duke of York St
Charles II St
Berkeley St
Piccadilly Arcade
Duke St
Bury St
Ryder St
St James's St
Arlington St
St James's Square
King St
Pall Mall
Waterloo Pl
Piccadilly
3
4
5
7
9
10
11
12
13
17
18
19
21
22
26
29
30
31

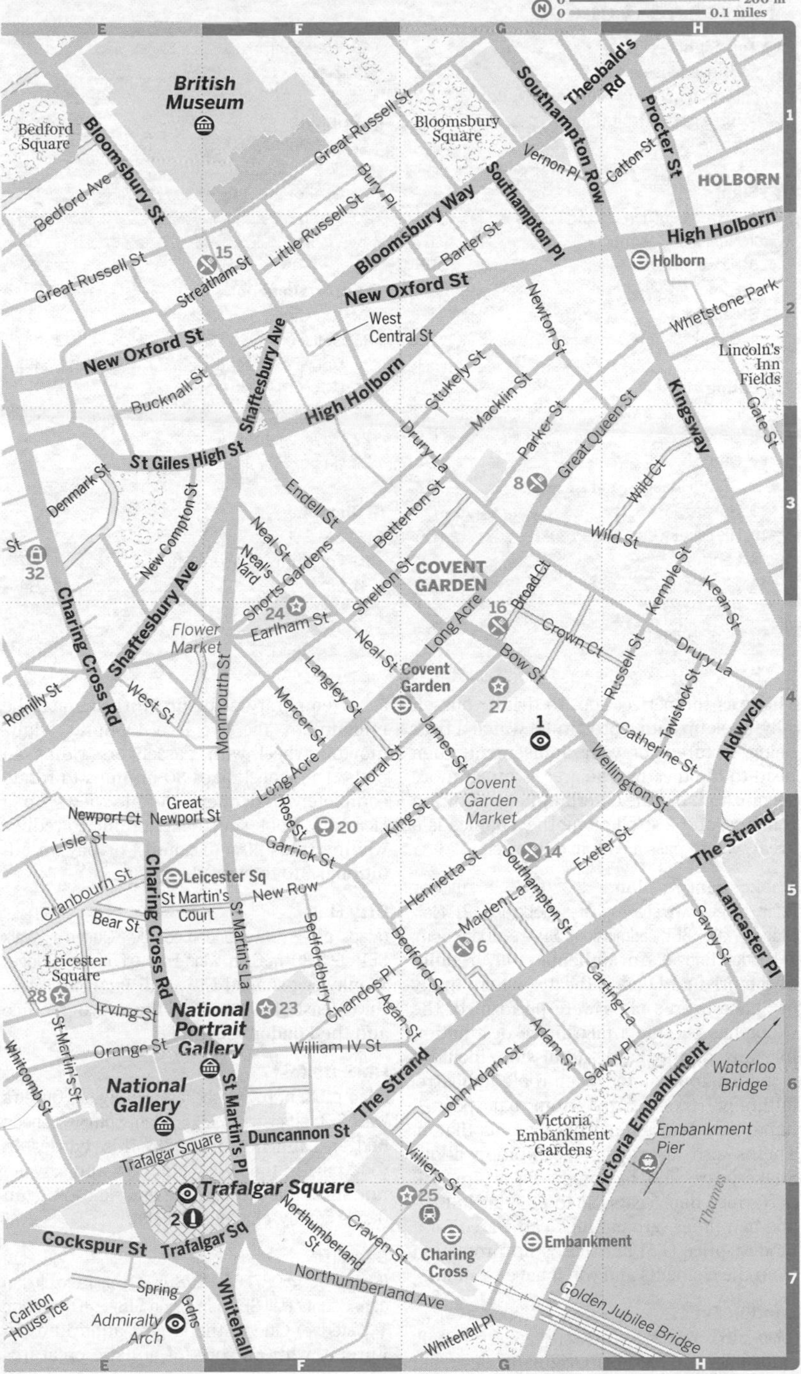
British Museum
Bedford Square
Bloomsbury Square
Bloomsbury St
Great Russell St
Bury Pl
Little Russell St
Bloomsbury Way
Southampton Row
Southampton Pl
Theobald's Rd
Vernon Pl
Catton St
Procter St
HOLBORN
High Holborn
Holborn
Bedford Ave
Streatham St
Barter St
New Oxford St
West Central St
Newton St
Whetstone Park
Lincoln's Inn Fields
Gate St
Shaftesbury Ave
Bucknall St
Stukely St
Macklin St
Parker St
Great Queen St
Kingsway
St Giles High St
Drury La
Denmark St
New Compton St
Endell St
Betterton St
Wild Ct
Wild St
Neal St
Neal's Yard
Shorts Gardens
Shelton St
COVENT GARDEN
Broad Ct
Kemble St
Kean St
Earlham St
Flower Market
Long Acre
Crown Ct
Bow St
Russell St
Charing Cross Rd
Covent Garden
Langley St
Mercer St
James St
Romilly St
West St
Monmouth St
Catherine St
Tavistock St
Aldwych
Wellington St
Floral St
Covent Garden Market
Great Newport St
Newport Ct
Rose St
King St
Lisle St
Garrick St
Southampton St
Exeter St
The Strand
Leicester Sq
Cranbourn St
St Martin's Court
New Row
Henrietta St
Maiden La
Lancaster Pl
Savoy St
Bear St
Bedfordbury
Bedford St
Carting La
Leicester Square
Chandos Pl
Agan St
Irving St
National Portrait Gallery
St Martin's La
Adam St
Savoy Pl
Orange St
William IV St
Waterloo Bridge
Whitcomb St
St Martin's St
National Gallery
John Adam St
Victoria Embankment
Embankment Pier
Victoria Embankment Gardens
Trafalgar Square
Duncannon St
St Martin's Pl
Villiers St
Thames
Trafalgar Square
Northumberland St
Craven St
Embankment
Cockspur St
Trafalgar Sq
Charing Cross
Northumberland Ave
Spring Gdns
Golden Jubilee Bridge
Carlton House Tce
Admiralty Arch
Whitehall
Whitehall Pl
0 200 m
0 0.1 miles
E F G H
1 2 3 4 5 6 7
1 2 6 8 14 15 16 20 23 24 25 27 28 32

West End (London)

Top Sights
British Museum ... F1
National Gallery ... E6
National Portrait Gallery ... F6
Trafalgar Square ... E7

Sights
1 Covent Garden ... G4
2 Nelson's Column ... E7
3 Piccadilly Circus ... D6

Sleeping
4 Oxford St YHA ... C3

Eating
5 Fernandez & Wells ... C4
6 GBK ... G5
7 GBK ... D4
8 Great Queen Street ... G3
9 Hakkasan ... D2
10 HK Diner ... D5
11 Lantana ... C1
12 Ping Pong ... C1
13 Ping Pong ... B4
14 Wagamama ... G5
15 Wagamama ... F2
16 Zizzi ... G4

Drinking
17 Absolut Ice Bar ... B5
18 G-A-Y Bar ... D4
19 G-A-Y Late ... D3
20 Lamb & Flag ... F5
21 Village ... D4

Entertainment
22 100 Club ... C3
23 Coliseum ... F6
24 Donmar Warehouse ... F4
25 G-A-Y Club @ Heaven ... G7
26 Ronnie Scott's ... D4
27 Royal Opera House ... G4
28 tkts ... E6

Shopping
29 BM Soho ... C3
30 Fortnum & Mason ... B7
31 Liberty ... B4
32 Ray's Jazz ... E3

This was the perfect spot to drink yourself silly, hook up with a prostitute, watch a bear being tortured for your amusement, then head to the theatre. The area is much more seemly now, but the entertainment tradition remains, and a stroll along the Thames is a great way to pass a couple of hours.

Shakespeare's Globe THEATRE
(Map p158; www.shakespeares-globe.org; 21 New Globe Walk SE1; admission £11; 10am-5pm; London Bridge) An authentic 1997 rebuild of the original London theatre where many of Shakespeare's plays were performed, the Globe has become a pilgrimage destination for fans of the Bard. Admission includes a guided tour of the open-roofed theatre, faithfully reconstructed from oak beams, handmade bricks, lime plaster and thatch. There's also an extensive exhibition about Shakespeare and his times. Plays are still performed here (seats £15 to £35). As in Elizabethan times, 'groundlings' can watch for a modest price (£5) but there's no protection from the elements and you'll have to stand.

London Eye LANDMARK, VIEWS
(Map p165; www.londoneye.com; admission £18; 10am-8pm; Waterloo) Originally designed as a temporary structure to celebrate the millennium, the Eye is a 135m-tall, slow-moving wheel with passengers riding in pods. The wheel takes 30 minutes to rotate completely and offers 25-mile views on a clear day. Book your ticket online to reduce waiting (plus 20% discount), or pay an additional £10 to jump the queue.

City Hall LANDMARK
(Map p158; www.london.gov.uk; Queen's Walk SE1; 8.30am-6pm Mon-Fri; London Bridge) Wonky-egg-shaped City Hall is an architectural feast and home to the mayor's office and the London Assembly.

HMS Belfast SHIP
(Map p158; http://hmsbelfast.iwm.org.uk; Queen's Walk SE1; admission £13; 10am-5pm; London Bridge) Launched in 1938, this battleship took part in the D-day landings and saw action in Korea. Explore the engine room, gun decks, galley, chapel and cells.

Sea Life AQUARIUM
(Map p165; 0871 663 1678; www.sealife.co.uk/london; County Hall SE1; admission £18; 10am-6pm; Waterloo) One of the largest aquariums in Europe, with all sorts of aquatic creatures

organised into different zones (coral cave, rainforest, River Thames), culminating with the shark walkway.

FREE **Tate Modern** GALLERY

(www.tate.org.uk; Queen's Walk SE1; ⏲10am-6pm Sun-Thu, to 10pm Fri & Sat; ⊖Southwark) This surprisingly elegant former power station is now a tremendous gallery focusing on modern art in all its wonderful permutations, and one of London's most popular attractions.

To get between London's Tate galleries in style, the **Tate Boat** (www.thamesclippers.com) will whisk you from one to the other, via the London Eye. A River Roamer hop-on/hop-off ticket (purchased on board) costs £12 and single tickets are £5.

Westminster (London)

Westminster (London)

Top Sights

Buckingham Palace A2
Houses of Parliament D2
Westminster Abbey C2
Westminster Cathedral B3

Sights

1 Big Ben D2
2 Green Park A1
3 London Eye D1
4 Sea Life D1
5 St James's Park B2
6 Tate Britain C4

Sleeping

7 easyHotel Victoria A4
8 Luna Simone Hotel B4
9 Windermere Hotel A4

THAMES BRIDGES

The River Thames in central London is crossed by several bridges, including the famous Tower Bridge and the surprisingly unremarkable London Bridge. But to get away from the cars and enjoy views up- or down-river, take one of the bridges that are open to walkers only:

The **Millennium Bridge** (Map p158-9; ⊖St Paul's or Blackfriars) is recently built but already iconic. Billed as a 'blade of light', it crosses the Thames and usefully links the key sights of St Paul's Cathedral and the Tate Modern.

On the **Golden Jubilee Bridge** (Map p162-3; ⊖Embankment or Waterloo), two hi-tech, pedestrian walkways straddle the Thames on either side of a rail bridge between Embankment tube station and the South Bank.

CHELSEA, KENSINGTON & KNIGHTSBRIDGE

Knightsbridge is where you'll find some of London's best-known department stores, while Kensington High St has a lively mix of chains and boutiques. Away from mammon, South Kensington boasts some of London's most beautiful and interesting museums.

FREE Victoria & Albert Museum MUSEUM
(V&A; Map p168; www.vam.ac.uk; Cromwell Rd SW7; ⊙10am-5.45pm Sat-Thu, to 10pm Fri; ⊖South Kensington) A vast and wonderful museum of decorative art and design, the V&A is like the nation's attic, comprising four million objects collected from Britain and around the globe. In its 150 galleries you'll see ancient Chinese ceramics, Japanese swords, Asian and Islamic art, Rodin sculptures, Elizabethan gowns, an all-wooden Frank Lloyd Wright study, and a pair of Doc Martens. Yes, you'll need to plan.

FREE Natural History Museum MUSEUM
(Map p168; www.nhm.ac.uk; Cromwell Rd SW7; ⊙10am-5.50pm; ⊖South Kensington) A sure-fire hit with kids of all ages, the Natural History Museum is crammed full of interesting stuff, starting with the giant dinosaur skeleton that greets you in the main hall.

FREE Science Museum MUSEUM
(Map p168; www.sciencemuseum.org.uk; Exhibition Rd SW7; ⊙10am-6pm; ⊖South Kensington) With seven floors of educational exhibits, the Science Museum covers everything from the Industrial Revolution to the exploration of space.

Hyde Park PARK
(Map p168; ⊙5.30am-midnight; ⊖Marble Arch, Hyde Park Corner or Queensway) At 145 hectares, this is central London's largest open space. Henry VIII expropriated it from the Church in 1536, when it became a hunting ground and later a venue for duels and executions. During WWII the park became an enormous potato field. These days, it serves as an occasional concert venue and a full-time green space.

Kensington Gardens PARK
(Map p168; ⊙dawn-dusk; ⊖Queensway) Blending in with Hyde Park, these royal gardens are part of Kensington Palace. In the northwest corner, Diana devotees can visit the **Diana, Princess of Wales Memorial Playground**. In contrast the **Albert Memorial** is a lavish marble, mosaic and gold affair opposite the Royal Albert Hall, built to honour Queen Victoria's husband, Albert (1819–61).

MARYLEBONE

With one of London's best high streets and plenty of green space, increasingly hip Marylebone is a great area to wander.

Regent's Park PARK
(Map p171; ⊖Regent's Park) This is London's finest open space – at once lively and serene, cosmopolitan and local – with football pitches, tennis courts and a boating lake.

Madame Tussauds WAXWORKS
(Map p168; www.madame-tussauds.co.uk; Marylebone Rd NW1; admission £26; ⊙9.30am-5.30pm; ⊖Baker St) With so much fabulous free stuff to do in London, it's a wonder that people still join lengthy queues here. But they do.

CAMDEN TOWN

Once well outside the city limits, the former hamlets of North London have long since been gobbled up by the metropolis, and yet they still maintain a semblance of village atmosphere and a distinct local identity. Of these, the enclave of Camden Town is a lively neighbourhood of pubs, live-music venues, boutiques, technicolour hairstyles, facial furniture, intricate tattoos, ambitious platform shoes and, most famously, **Camden Market**

(Map p171; ⊖Camden Town) There are often some cartoon punks hanging around earning a few bucks for being photographed by tourists, as well as none-too-discreet dope dealers.

GREENWICH

More than any of the former villages swamped by metropolis, Greenwich (*grenitch*) has retained its own sense of identity based on splendid architecture and strong connections with the sea and science. An extraordinary cluster of buildings have earned 'Maritime Greenwich' its place on Unesco's World Heritage list. It's also famous for straddling the hemispheres; this is degree zero, the home of Greenwich Mean Time.

Greenwich is easily reached on the DLR. Or go by boat: **Thames River Services** (www.thamesriverservices.co.uk) departs half-hourly from Westminster Pier (one-way/return £9.50/12.50, one hour). **Thames Clippers** are cheaper.

FREE Old Royal Naval College HISTORIC BUILDINGS
(www.oldroyalnavalcollege.org; 2 Cutty Sark Gardens SE10; ⏲10am-5pm; DLR Cutty Sark) This magnificent example of classical architecture is now partly used by the University of Greenwich and Trinity College of Music, but you can visit the **chapel** and the extraordinary **Painted Hall** that took artist James Thornhill 19 years to complete.

FREE National Maritime Museum & Royal Observatory MUSEUMS
(www.nmm.ac.uk; Romney Rd SE10; ⏲10am-5pm; DLR Cutty Sark) Completing Greenwich's trump hand of historic buildings, exhibits here range from interactive displays to Nelson's uniform, complete with a hole from the bullet that killed him, and the mood changes abruptly between galleries (toy ships to slave trade).

Nearby, idyllic **Greenwich Park** affords great views of London, capped by the **Royal Observatory** (⏲10am-5pm), built in 1675 to help solve the riddle of longitude. Success was confirmed in 1884 and here you can stand with one foot in the western hemisphere and the other foot in the eastern hemisphere.

Tours

One of the best ways to orientate yourself when you first arrive in London is with a 24-hour hop-on/hop-off pass for the double-decker bus tours. The buses loop around interconnecting routes throughout the day, providing a commentary as they go, and the price includes a river cruise and three walking tours. You'll save a couple of pounds by booking online.

Original London Sightseeing Tour BUS TOUR
(☎020-8877 1722; www.theoriginaltour.com; admission £25)

Big Bus Company BUS TOUR
(☎020-7233 9533; www.bigbustours.com; admission £26)

Festivals & Events

University Boat Race BOAT RACE
(www.theboatrace.org) Held annually since 1829 between Oxford and Cambridge universities (late March).

Trooping the Colour ROYAL PARADE
Pomp and pageantry overload to celebrate the Queen's official birthday (June).

Meltdown MUSIC FESTIVAL
(www.southbankcentre.co.uk) Southbank Centre hands over curatorial reins to a legend of contemporary music (such as David Bowie, or Patti Smith) to create a full program of concerts, talks and films (late June).

LONDON FOR FREE

London may be an expensive place to eat, drink and sleep, but when it comes to sights, most of the very best things are free. First off, there are the wonderful parks – you could easily spend a day strolling here. Another great free walk is along the footways and embankments on either side of the River Thames. Anywhere in London you can admire the breathtaking historic buildings from the outside without paying a penny. To go inside, here are a few places where you won't have to put your hand in your pocket: National Gallery (p157), National Portrait Gallery (p157), Tate Britain (p161), Tate Modern (p165), British Museum (p160), Victoria & Albert Museum (p166), Natural History Museum (p166), Science Museum (p166). Several other museums and galleries listed in this London section are also free – plus many more that we haven't got room to mention.

Hyde Park to Chelsea (London)

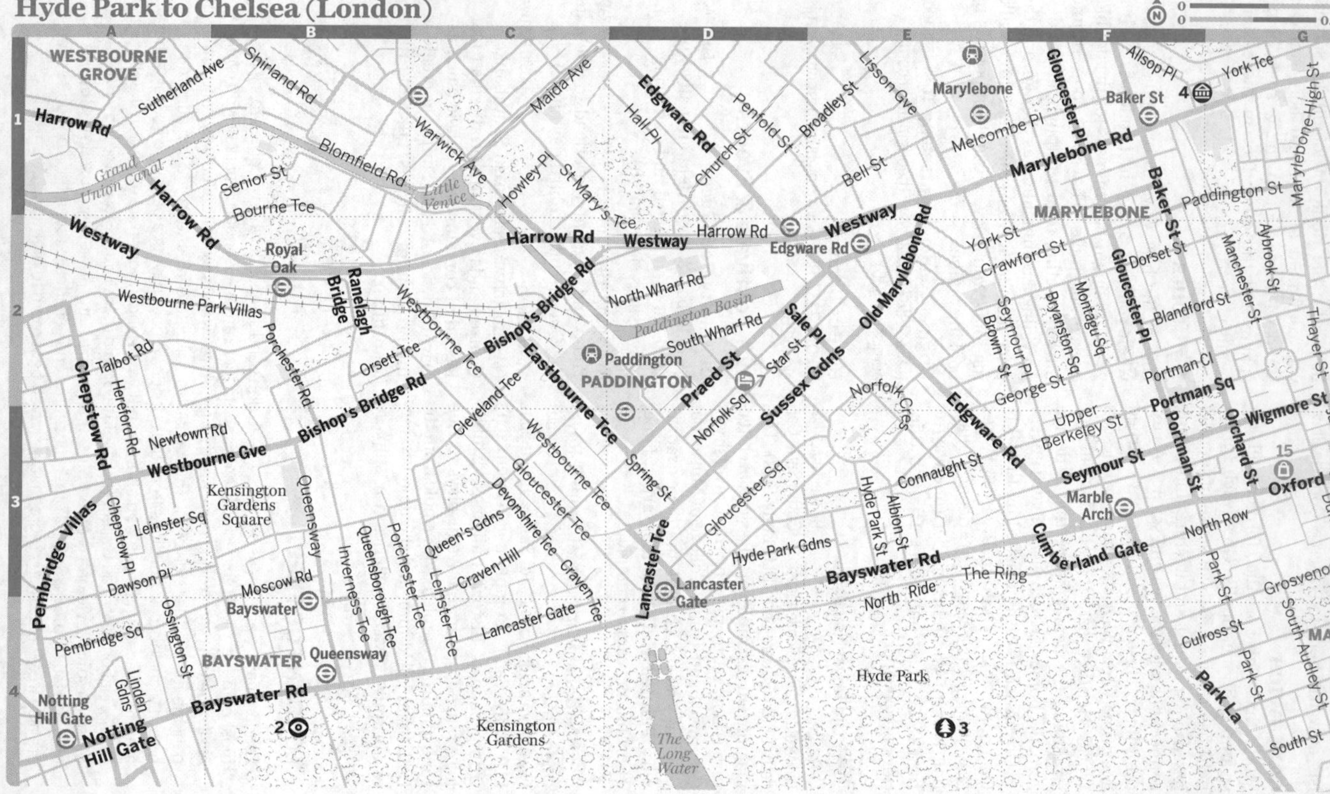

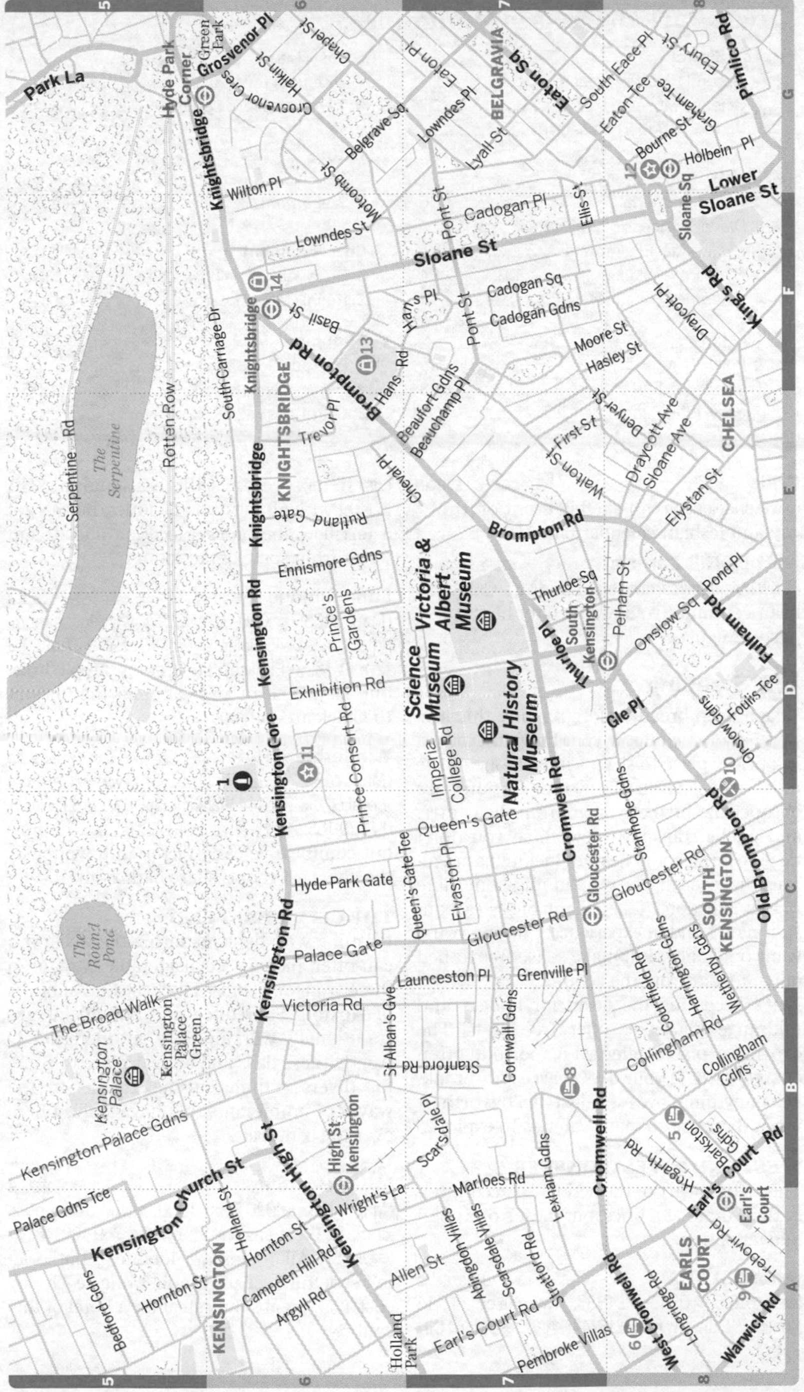
Park La
Hyde Park Corner
Green Park
Grosvenor Pl
Grosvenor Cres
Halkin St
Chapel St
Eaton Pl
BELGRAVIA
Eaton Sq
South Eaton Pl
Ebury St
Pimlico Rd
Eaton Tce
Graham Tce
Bourne St
Holbein Pl
Lower Sloane St
Sloane Sq
Belgrave Sq
Lowndes Pl
Lyall St
Knightsbridge
Wilton Pl
Motcomb St
Lowndes St
Pont St
Cadogan Pl
Ellis St
Sloane St
King's Rd
Cadogan Sq
Cadogan Gdns
Draycott Pl
Basil St
Hans Pl
Hans Rd
Brompton Rd
Moore St
Hasley St
Beaufort Gdns
Beauchamp Pl
Denyer St
First St
Walton St
Draycott Ave
Sloane Ave
CHELSEA
Elystan St
Trevor Pl
Cheval Pl
KNIGHTSBRIDGE
Rutland Gate
Ennismore Gdns
Prince's Gardens
Victoria & Albert Museum
Thurloe Sq
South Kensington
Pelham St
Onslow Sq
Pond Pl
Fulham Rd
Thurloe Pl
Science Museum
Natural History Museum
Exhibition Rd
Kensington Rd
Kensington Gore
Prince Consort Rd
Imperial College Rd
Queen's Gate
Cromwell Rd
Gloucester Rd
Gle Pl
Onslow Gdns
Foulis Tce
Stanhope Gdns
Old Brompton Rd
SOUTH KENSINGTON
Hyde Park Gate
Queen's Gate Tce
Elvaston Pl
Palace Gate
Launceston Pl
Grenville Pl
Courtfield Rd
Harrington Gdns
Wetherby Gdns
Victoria Rd
St Alban's Gve
Cornwall Gdns
Collingham Rd
Collingham Gdns
Stanford Rd
The Serpentine
Serpentine Rd
Rotten Row
South Carriage Dr
The Round Pond
The Broad Walk
Kensington Palace
Kensington Palace Green
Kensington Palace Gdns
Kensington Church St
Kensington High St
High St Kensington
Scarsdale Pl
Wright's La
Marloes Rd
Lexham Gdns
Hogarth Rd
Barkston Gdns
Earl's Court Rd
Earl's Court
Trebovir Rd
EARLS COURT
Longridge Rd
Warwick Rd
West Cromwell Rd
Palace Gdns Tce
Holland St
Hornton St
Campden Hill Rd
KENSINGTON
Bedford Gdns
Argyll Rd
Allen St
Abingdon Villas
Scarsdale Villas
Stafford Rd
Stratford Rd
Pembroke Villas
Holland Park
Earl's Court Rd

Hyde Park to Chelsea (London)

Pride GAY & LESBIAN
(www.pridelondon.org) The big event on the gay and lesbian calendar (June/July).

Notting Hill Carnival STREET PARADE
(www.nottinghillcarnival.biz) London's Caribbean community shows the city how to party (August).

Sleeping

Take a deep breath before reading this section because whatever your budget, London is a pricey place to sleep – in fact, one of the most expensive in the world. Options are cheaper the further you go from the centre, and public transport is good, so you don't need to be sleeping next to Buckingham Palace. However, if you're planning some late nights and don't fancy night buses (a consummate London experience, but one you'll want only once) it'll make sense not to bed down too far from the action.

It's becoming the norm for budget and midrange places to offer free wi-fi. The expensive places offer wi-fi too, but often charge for it. If your digs charges for breakfast, anything over £5 just isn't worth it when there are so many eateries to explore.

WEST END & WESTMINSTER

This is the heart of the action, so accommodation comes at a price, but there's one good budget option.

Oxford St YHA HOSTEL £
(Map p162; ☎0845-371 9133; www.yha.org.uk; 14 Noel St W1; dm/tw from £18/44; @☜; ⊖Oxford Circus) In most respects, this is a standard YHA hostel with all the usual facilities, but it's got a terrific (albeit noisy) location and decent views from some of the rooms.

Luna Simone Hotel B&B ££
(Map p165; ☎020-7834 5897; www.lunasimonehotel.com; 47-49 Belgrave Rd SW1; s £70-75, d £95-120; @☜; ⊖Pimlico) The rooms aren't huge but they're clean and calming; the ones at the back are quieter.

Windermere Hotel B&B ££
(Map p165; ☎020-7834 5163; www.windermere-hotel.co.uk; 142-144 Warwick Way SW1; s £105-155, d £129-165; @☜; ⊖Victoria) This is a chintzy but comfortable early-Victorian townhouse; the cheapest rooms share bathrooms.

THE CITY & EAST END

Bristling with bankers during the week, you can often pick up a considerable bargain in the city at weekends. The East End suburbs of Hoxton, Shoreditch and Spitalfields are traditionally working class but increasingly trendy these days and a great place to come for diverse ethnic cuisine, thanks to the waves of immigrants that have arrived here over the centuries.

TOP CHOICE **Hoxton** HOTEL £
(Map p158; ☎020-7550 1000; www.hoxtonhotels.com; 81 Great Eastern St; d & tw £59-199; @☜; ⊖Old St) All rooms are identical, but pricing structure means the first ones each day cost £59: an absolute steal for a hotel of this calibre.

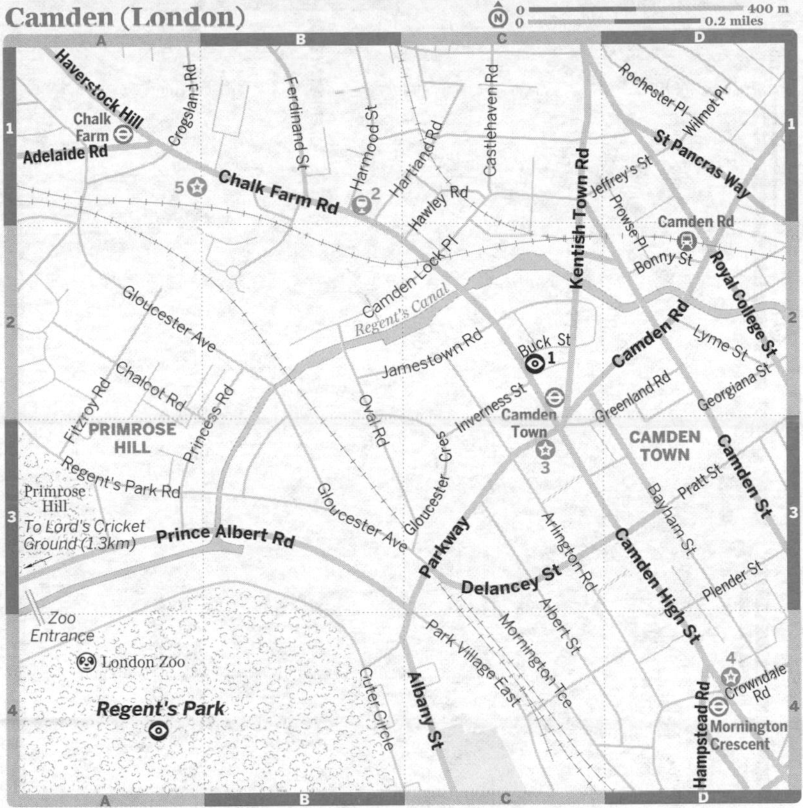

Camden (London)

Top Sights

Regent's Park A4

Sights

1 Camden Market C2

Drinking

2 Lock Tavern B1

Entertainment

3 Jazz Cafe C3

4 Koko D4

5 Roundhouse A1

Shopping

Camden Market .... (see 1)

Apex City of London HOTEL ££

(Map p158; ☎020-7702 2020; www.apexhotels.co.uk; 1 Seething Lane EC3; r from £100; ; Tower Hill) Business focused but close enough to the Tower to hear the heads roll.

SOUTHWARK

Immediately south of the river is good if you want to immerse yourself in workaday London and still be central.

St Christopher's Village HOSTEL £

(Map p158; ☎020-7939 9710; www.st-christophers.co.uk; 163 Borough High St SE1; dm/r from £14/62; @; London Bridge) Huge party hostel, with a club open until 4am at weekends and a roof-terrace bar – either heaven or hell, depending on what you're after. Nearby are two satellites: smaller, quieter **St Christopher's**

Bloomsbury & St Pancras (London)

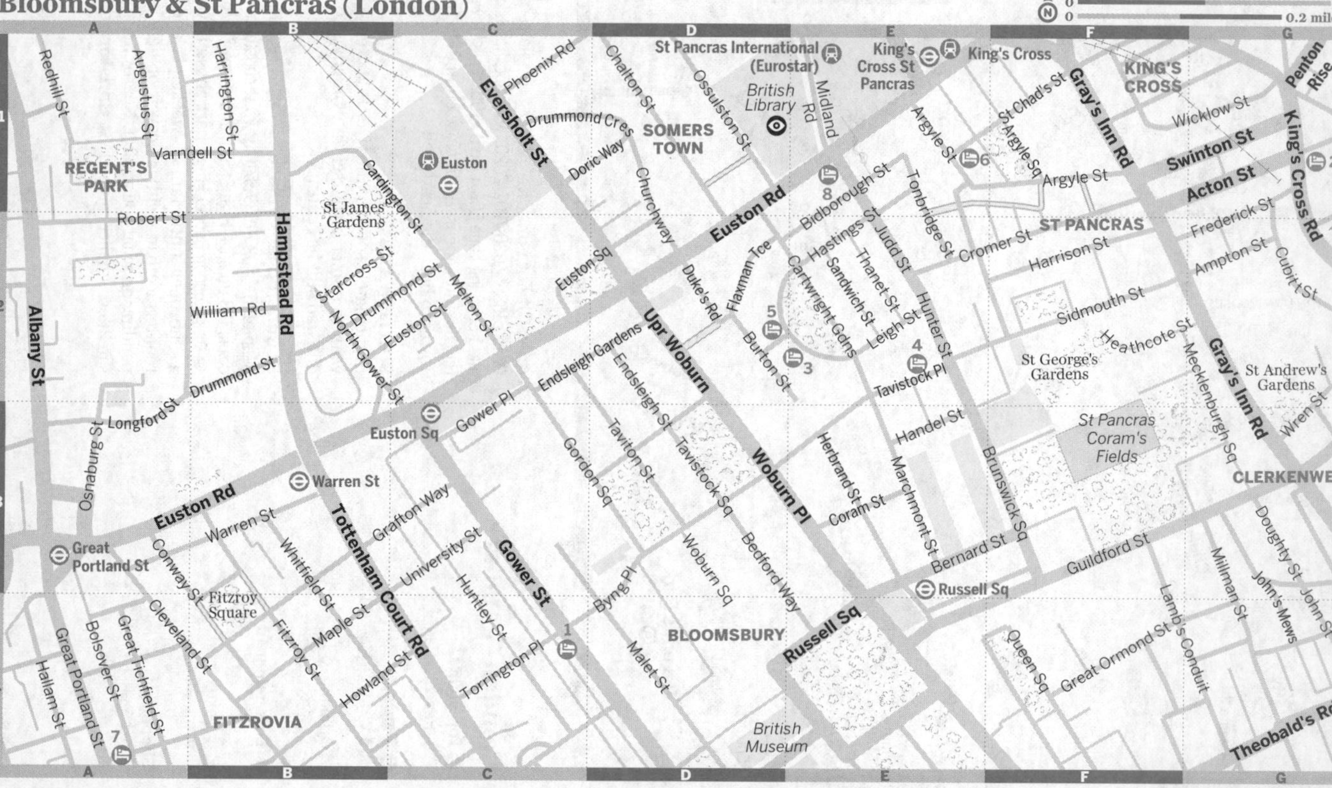

Sleeping

Inn (121 Borough High St); and **Orient Express** (59 Borough High St), a dude-free zone.

BLOOMSBURY & ST PANCRAS

Only one step removed from the West End, the neighbourhoods of Bloomsbury and adjoining Fitzrovia offer good value. You'll find a stretch of lower-priced hotels along Gower St and on pretty Cartwright Gardens. The nearby area of St Pancras is hardly salubrious, but it's handy to absolutely everything and has some excellent budget options.

London Central YHA HOSTEL £
(Map p172; ☎0845-371 9154; www.yha.org.uk; 104-108 Bolsover St W1; dm £21-32, q from £70; @📶; ⊖Great Portland St) One of London's new breed of YHA hostels, most of the four- to six-bed rooms have bathrooms. There's a cafe-bar attached to reception and wheelchair-accessible kitchen downstairs.

Arran House Hotel B&B ££
(Map p172; ☎020-7636 2186; www.arranhotel-london.com; 77-79 Gower St WC1; s/d/tr/q without bathroom £60/80/105/111, with bathroom £70/110/128/132; @📶; ⊖Goodge St) Period features, pretty back garden and a comfy lounge lift this hotel from average to attractive. Squashed private or shared bathrooms are the trade-off for reasonable rates.

Arosfa Hotel B&B ££
(Map p172; ☎020-7636 2115; www.arosfalondon.com; 83 Gower St WC1; s £60-65, d/tr/q £90/102/110; @📶; ⊖Goodge St) Immaculate if unremarkable rooms, blinged up lounge, and bathrooms to all 15 bedrooms – but they're tiny.

Jesmond Dene B&B £
(Map p172; ☎020-7837 4654; www.jesmonddenehotel.co.uk; 27 Argyle St; s/d incl breakfast from £60/65; @📶; ⊖King's Cross St Pancras) A surprisingly pleasant option for a place so close to King's Cross, this modest hotel has clean but small rooms; some share bathrooms.

London St Pancras YHA HOSTEL £
(Map p172; ☎020-7388 9998; www.yha.org.uk; 79 Euston Rd NW1; dm/r from £20/61; @📶; ⊖King's Cross St Pancras) A renovation in 2009 made this 185-bed hostel one of the best in central London. Rooms range from private doubles to six-bed dorms and most have bathrooms. There's a good bar and cafe but no kitchen.

Jenkins Hotel B&B ££
(Map p172; ☎020-7387 2067; www.jenkinshotel.demon.co.uk; 45 Cartwright Gardens WC1; s/d from £52/95; ⊖Russell Sq) This modest hotel has featured in the TV series of Agatha Christie's *Poirot*. Rooms are small but the hotel has charm.

Crescent Hotel B&B ££
(Map p172; ☎020-7387 1515; www.crescenthotelof london.com; 49-50 Cartwright Gardens WC1; s/d from £52/105; @📶; ⊖Russell Sq) One of the cheaper options on Cartwright Gardens, there's a homely feel to this humble hotel, despite the odd saggy bed.

Clink78 HOSTEL £
(Map p172; ☎020-7183 9400; www.clinkhostel.com; 78 King's Cross Rd WC1; dm/r from £12/60; @📶; ⊖King's Cross St Pancras) If anyone can think of a more right-on London place to stay than the courthouse where The Clash went on trial, please let us know.

Generator HOSTEL £
(Map p172; ☎020-7388 7666; www.generatorhostels.com/London; 37 Tavistock Pl WC1; dm/r from £18/55; @📶; ⊖Russell Sq) Lashings of primary colours and shiny metal are the hallmarks of this futuristic 820-bed hostel. The bar stays open until 2am and hosts quizzes, karaoke and DJs. Come to party.

EARLS COURT & FULHAM

Earls Court is so popular with travelling Antipodeans it's nicknamed Kangaroo Valley. There are no real sights, but it has inexpensive digs and an infectious holiday atmosphere.

Barclay House B&B ££
(☎020-7384 3390; www.barclayhouselondon.com; 21 Barclay Rd SW6; s/d £69/89, @📶; ⊖Fulham Broadway) A proper homestay B&B, with just two comfy bedrooms and an exceptionally welcoming hostess.

SPLURGE

A converted meat-packing warehouse, **Smiths of Smithfield** (Map p158; ☎020-7251 7950; www.smithsofsmithfield.co.uk; 67-77 Charterhouse St EC1; mains 1st fl £13-15, top fl £19-30; ⊖Farringdon) is all things to all people. Hit the ground-floor bar for a beer, go upstairs to a relaxed dining space, or continue up for two more floors of feasting, each slightly smarter and pricier than the last.

Twenty Nevern Square HOTEL ££
(Map p168; ☎020-7565 9555; www.20neverns quare.com; 20 Nevern Sq SW5; r from £95; @; ⊖Earl's Court) An Ottoman theme runs through this townhouse hotel, with wooden furniture and luxurious fabrics, while natural light helps maximise space.

base2stay APARTMENT HOTEL ££
(☎020-7244 2255; www.base2stay.com; 25 Courtfield Gardens SW5; s/d from £93/99; @; ⊖Earl's Court) With smart decor, power showers, flat-screen TVs with internet access and artfully concealed kitchenettes, this boutique establishment feels like a four-star hotel without the hefty price tag.

easyHotel BUDGET HOTEL £
(www.easyhotel.com; r from £25; @); Earls Court (Map p168; 44 West Cromwell Rd SW5; ⊖Earl's Court); Paddington (Map p168; 10 Norfolk Pl W2; ⊖Paddington); South Kensington (Map p168; 14 Lexham Gardens W8; ⊖Gloucester Rd); Victoria (Map p165; 36 Belgrave Rd SW1; ⊖Victoria) Run along the same principles as its sibling business easyJet, this no-frills chain has tiny rooms with even tinier bathrooms.

Eating

London has an amazing selection of places to eat, though food and service can vary wildly regardless of price tag. In this section, we steer you towards restaurants and cafes distinguished by location, value for money, unique features, original settings and, of course, good food.

WEST END

Mayfair, Soho and Covent Garden are the gastronomic heart of London, with stacks of restaurants and cuisines at a wide range of budgets.

Great Queen Street BRITISH ££
(Map p162; ☎020-7242 0622; 32 Great Queen St WC2; mains £9-19; ⏲lunch daily, dinner Mon-Sat; ⊖Holborn) There's no tiara on this Great Queen, but the food's still the best of British.

Fernandez & Wells DELICATESSEN CAFE £
(Map p162; www.fernandezandwells.com; 73 Beak St W1; mains £4-5; ⊖Piccadilly Circus) There's no shortage of delicious charcuterie and cheese to fill the fresh baguettes on the counter of this teensy cafe.

HK Diner CHINESE £
(Map p162; 22 Wardour St W1; mains £6-13; ⏲11am-4am; ⊖Piccadilly Circus) For soft-shell crab or barbecued pork in the wee hours of the morning, this Hong Kong–style cafe (delicious food, no-nonsense decor) is the place.

CLERKENWELL & FARRINGDON

Clerkenwell's hidden gems are well worth digging for; Exmouth Market is a good place to start.

Little Bay EUROPEAN £
(Map p158; ☎020-7278 1234; www.littlebay.co.uk; 171 Farringdon Rd EC1; mains before/after 7pm £6.50/8.50; ⊖Farringdon) The crushed-velvet ceiling, handmade twisted lamps and elaborately painted tables are bonkers but fun; the hearty food is very good value.

FITZROVIA

Tucked away behind busy Tottenham Court Rd, Fitzrovia's Charlotte and Goodge Sts form one of central London's most vibrant eating precincts.

Hakkasan CHINESE ££
(Map p162; ☎020-7927 7000; www.hakkasan.com; 8 Hanway Pl W1; mains £11-58; ⊖Tottenham Court Rd) The first Chinese restaurant to get a Michelin star is hidden down a lane – like all fashionable haunts need to be.

Lantana CAFE £
(Map p162; www.lantanacafe.co.uk; 13 Charlotte Pl W1; mains £4-10; ⏲breakfast & lunch Mon-Sat; ⊖Goodge St) Excellent coffee and substantial, inventive brunches induce queues on Saturday mornings outside this Australian-style cafe.

CAMDEN TOWN & ISLINGTON

Camden's great for cheap eats, while neighbouring Chalk Farm and Primrose Hill are salted with gastropubs and upmarket restaurants. Allow at least an evening to explore Islington's Upper St and the lanes leading off it.

TOP CHOICE Le Mercury FRENCH £
(off Map p158; ☎020-7354 4088; www.lemercury.co.uk; 140A Upper St N1; mains £7-10; ⊖Highbury & Islington) A cosy Gallic haunt with great value cuisine. Sunday lunch by the open fire upstairs is a treat.

Regent PIZZA £
(201 Liverpool Rd N1; mains £7-11; ⊖Angel) Loved by the young crowd, with ambience more pub than pizzeria, and a jukebox loaded with indie pop gems.

CITY & EAST END

From the hit-and-miss Bangladeshi restaurants of Brick Lane to the Vietnamese strip on Kingsland Rd, via the Jewish, Spanish, French, Italian and Greek eateries in between, the East End's cuisine is as multicultural as its residents.

Fifteen ITALIAN ££
(Map p158; ☎0871-330 1515; www.fifteen.net; 15 Westland Pl N1; breakfast £2-8.50, trattoria £6-11, restaurant £11-25; ⏲breakfast, lunch & dinner; ⊖Old St) TV chef Jamie Oliver's culinary philanthropy started here. The food is beyond excellent and amazing value.

Albion BRITISH ££
(Map p158; www.albioncaff.co.uk; 2-4 Boundary St E2; mains £9-13; ⊖Old St) Self-consciously retro, serving up top-quality British classics: bangers and mash, steak-and-kidney pies, devilled kidneys and fish and chips.

Cafe Bangla BANGLADESHI £
(Map p158; 128 Brick Lane E1; mains £5-15; ⊖Liverpool St) Among the hordes of interchangeable Brick Lane restaurants, this one stands out for its murals of scantily clad women riding dragons, and a tribute to Princess Di.

Drinking

As long as there's been a city, Londoners have loved to drink – and, as history shows, often immoderately. Soho is undoubtedly the heart of London's bar culture, with enough variety to cater to all tastes. Camden's great for grungy boozers, but is losing ground on the cool front to Hoxton and Shoreditch. Other places with pub-crawl potential include Clerkenwell, Islington, Southwark, Notting Hill, Earls Court…hell, it's just not that difficult. The reviews below are simply to make sure you don't miss out on some of the most historic, unusual, best-positioned or excellent examples of the genre.

WEST END

Lamb & Flag PUB
(Map p162; 33 Rose St WC2; ⊖Covent Garden) Everyone's favourite Covent Garden 'find', this historic pub is often jammed.

Absolut Ice Bar NOVELTY BAR
(Map p162; ☎020-7478 8910; www.belowzerolondon.com; 31-33 Heddon St W1; admission Thu-Sat £16, Sun-Wed £13; ⊖Piccadilly Circus) At -6°C this bar made entirely of ice is literally the coolest in London. It's a gimmick, sure, but a good one.

THE CITY & EAST END

Ye Olde Cheshire Cheese PUB
(Map p158; Wine Office Ct, 145 Fleet St EC4; ⊖Holborn) *Re*built in 1667, this place is a bit touristy but always atmospheric and enjoyable.

TOP CHOICE Commercial Tavern PUB
(Map p158; 142 Commercial St E1; ⊖Liverpool St) The zany decor's a thing of wonder in this reformed East End boozer.

Ye Olde Watling PUB
(Map p158; 29 Watling St; ⊖Mansion House) Another atmospheric olde pub from the 1660s.

Ten Bells PUB
(cnr Commercial & Fournier Sts E1; ⊖Liverpool St) The most famous Jack the Ripper pub; admire the wonderful 18th-century tiles and ponder the past over a pint.

Favela Chic BAR
(Map p158; www.favelachic.com; 91-93 Great Eastern St EC2; entry £5-10 after 8pm; ⊖Old St) Hip young things; crazy theme nights; fun and funky music.

CHAIN GANG

It's an unnerving, but not uncommon, experience to discover an idiosyncratic cafe or pub, then find it again (and again) on completely different streets. But chain eateries shouldn't automatically be sneered at; some offer jolly good food at fair prices. Some of the best include the following:

GBK (www.gbk.co.uk) Gourmet burgers.

Ping Pong (www.pingpongdimsum.com) Dumplings.

Wagamama (www.wagamama.com) Japanese noodles.

Zizzi (www.zizzi.co.uk) Wood-fired pizza.

GAY & LESBIAN LONDON

London's had a thriving scene since at least the 18th century, when 'Mollie houses' were the forerunners of today's gay bars. The West End, particularly Soho, remains the visible centre of gay and lesbian London, with numerous venues clustered around Old Compton St, but there are local gay bars in many other neighbourhoods.

Generally, London's a safe place for lesbians and gays. It's rare to encounter any problem with sharing rooms or holding hands in the inner city, although it pays to keep your wits about you at night.

To find out what's going on, pick up the free press (eg *Pink Paper, Boyz*), but be warned: the ads can be somewhat...confronting. See also www.gaydarnation.com (for men) and www.gingerbeer.co.uk (for women). Here are some venues to get you started:

Village (Map p162; www.village-soho.co.uk; 81 Wardour St W1; ⊖Piccadilly Circus)

G-A-Y (Map p162; www.g-a-y.co.uk) Bar (30 Old Compton St W1; ⊖Leicester Sq) Late (5 Goslett Yard WC2; ⏲11pm-3am; ⊖Tottenham Court Rd); Club @ Heaven (The Arches, Villiers St WC2; ⏲11pm-4am Thu-Sat; ⊖Charing Cross)

CLERKENWELL & FARRINGDON

Jerusalem Tavern PUB

(Map p158; www.stpetersbrewery.co.uk; 55 Britton St; ⊖Farringdon) Pick a wood-panelled cubbyhole at this 1720s coffee-shop-turned-inn, and enjoy St Peter's ales.

SOUTH BANK & SOUTHWARK

George Inn PUB

(Map p158; 77 Borough High St SE1; ⊖London Bridge) London's last surviving galleried coaching inn, dating in its current form from 1677. Dickens and Shakespeare used to prop up the bar here (not together, obviously).

Anchor PUB

(Map p158; 34 Park St SE1; ⊖London Bridge) An 18th-century boozer replacing the 1615 version where Samuel Pepys witnessed the Great Fire, still with superb views across the Thames.

CAMDEN TOWN

Lock Tavern PUB

(Map p171; www.lock-tavern.co.uk; 35 Chalk Farm Rd NW1; ⊖Camden Town) The archetypal Camden pub, with rooftop terrace, garden, interesting crowd and regular live music.

☆ Entertainment

From West End luvvies to East End geezers, Londoners have always loved a spectacle. With bear baiting and public executions no longer an option, they've learnt to make do with having the world's best nightclubs, theatres and live music. For listings see *Time Out* or the free papers at tube stations.

Nightclubs

London's had a lot of practice perfecting the art of clubbing – Samuel Pepys used the term in 1660 – and the variety of venues today is staggering. Admission prices vary widely; it's often cheaper to arrive early or prebook.

Fabric SUPERCLUB

(Map p158; www.fabriclondon.com; 77A Charterhouse St EC1; admission £8-18; ⏲10pm-6am Fri, 11pm-8am Sat; 11pm-6am Sun; ⊖Farringdon) Consistently rated as one of the world's greatest clubs.

Plastic People CLUB

(Map p158; www.plasticpeople.co.uk; 147-149 Curtain Rd EC2; admission £5-10; ⏲10pm-3.30am Fri & Sat, 10pm-2am Sun; ⊖Old St) Low-ceilinged subterranean den of dubsteppy, wonky, funky, no-frills fun times.

Ministry of Sound SUPERCLUB

(Map p158; www.ministryofsound.com; 103 Gaunt St SE1; admission £13-22; ⏲11pm-6.30am Fri & Sat; ⊖Elephant & Castle) London's most famous club, diverse crew, big names.

Cargo CLUB

(Map p158; www.cargo-london.com; 83 Rivington St EC2; admission up to £16; ⊖Old St) Courtyard club where you can enjoy big sounds and the great outdoors. Hosts live bands and gay bingo too.

Live Music

While London may have stopped swinging in the 1960s, every subsequent generation has given birth to a new set of bands in the city's thriving live venues: punk in the 1970s,

New Romantics in the 1980s, Brit pop in the 1990s and the current crop of skinny-jeaned rockers and electro acts thrilling scenesters today. Below are a few of our favourite venues. Big-name gigs sell out quickly, so check www.seetickets.com.

Koko CLUB
(Map p171; www.koko.uk.com; 1A Camden High St NW1; ⊖Mornington Crescent) Occupying the Camden Palace; live bands most nights and Club NME (£5) on Friday.

O2 Academy Brixton CONCERT HALL
(☎0844-477 2000; www.o2academybrixton.co.uk; 211 Stockwell Rd SW9; ⊖Brixton) Always winning awards for 'best live venue'; big-name acts in a relatively intimate setting (5000 capacity).

Jazz Cafe CLUB
(Map p171; www.jazzcafe.co.uk; 5 Parkway NW1; ⊖Camden Town) Intimate club staging a full roster of jazz, rock, pop, hip-hop and dance.

Ronnie Scott's CLUB
(Map p162; www.ronniescotts.co.uk; 47 Frith St W1; ⊖Leicester Sq) London's legendary jazz club, pulling in the hep cats since 1959.

100 Club CLUB
(Map p162; ☎020-7636 0933; www.the100club.co.uk; 100 Oxford St W1; ⊖Oxford Circus) Legendary London venue, now with jazz, rock and even a little swing.

Hope & Anchor LIVE MUSIC
(207 Upper St; ⊖Angel) Live music's still the focus of the pub that hosted the first London gigs of Joy Division and U2.

Roundhouse CONCERT HALL
(Map p171; ☎0844-482 8008; www.roundhouse.org.uk; Chalk Farm Rd NW1; ⊖Chalk Farm) Iconic concert venue. Also used for theatre and comedy.

Theatre

London is a world capital for theatre, with mammoth musicals and more obscure works to tempt you. Big names:

Royal Court Theatre THEATRE
(Map p168;; ☎020-7565 5000; www.royalcourttheatre.com; Sloane Sq SW1; ⊖Sloane Sq) Patron of new British writing.

National Theatre THEATRE
(Map p158; ☎020-7452 3000; www.nationaltheatre.org.uk; South Bank SE1; ⊖Waterloo) Classics and new plays.

> On performance days, you can buy half-price theatre tickets from the official agency **tkts** (Map p162; www.tkts.co.uk; ⊙10am-7pm Mon-Sat, noon-4pm Sun) on Leicester Sq. The booth has a clock tower; beware of touts nearby selling dodgy tickets.

Royal Shakespeare Company THEATRE
(RSC; ☎0844-800 1110; www.rsc.org.uk) Bard's classics and other quality stuff.

Old Vic THEATRE
(Map p158; ☎0844-871 7628; www.oldvictheatre.com; The Cut SE1; ⊖Waterloo) Kevin Spacey continues his run as artistic director (and occasional performer).

Donmar Warehouse THEATRE
(Map p162; ☎0844-871 7624; www.donmarwarehouse.com; 41 Earlham St WC2; ⊖Covent Garden) A not-for-profit company with a West End reputation.

Classical Music, Opera & Dance

With four world-class symphony orchestras, two opera companies, various smaller ensembles, brilliant venues, reasonable prices and high standards of performance, London is a classical capital. Keep an eye out for the free (or cheap) lunchtime concerts held in many of the city's churches.

Royal Albert Hall CONCERT HALL
(Map p168; ☎020-7589 8212; www.royalalberthall.com; Kensington Gore SW7; ⊖South Kensington) Beautiful Victorian arena, hosting classical concerts and contemporary artists.

Barbican Centre ARTS CENTRE
(Map p158; ☎0845-121 6823; www.barbican.org.uk; Silk St EC2; ⊖Barbican) Hulking complex with a full program of film, music, theatre, art and dance.

Southbank Centre CONCERT HALLS
(Map p158; ☎0844-875 0073; www.southbankcentre.co.uk; Belvedere Rd; ⊖Waterloo) Gigantic venue hosting classical, opera, jazz and choral music in three premier venues: the **Royal Festival Hall**, the smaller **Queen Elizabeth Hall** and the **Purcell Room**, plus free recitals in the foyer.

Royal Opera House OPERA, BALLET
(Map p162; ☎020-7304 4000; www.roh.org.uk; Bow St WC2; tickets £5-195; ⊖Covent Garden)

World-famous venue, also the home of the Royal Ballet.

Sadler's Wells DANCE
(Map p158; ☎0844-412 4300; www.sadlers-wells.com; Rosebery Ave EC1; tickets £10-49; ⊖Angel) A glittering venue, bringing modern dance to the mainstream.

Coliseum OPERA
(Map p162; ☎0871-911 0200; www.eno.org; St Martin's Lane WC2; tickets £10-87; ⊖Leicester Sq) Home of the progressive English National Opera; note that all performances are in English.

Shopping

From world-famous department stores to quirky backstreet retail revelations, London is a mecca for shoppers. If you're looking for something distinctly British, eschew the Union Jack-emblazoned kitsch of the tourist thoroughfares and fill your bags with genuine homegrown clothes, music, books and antiques.

Oxford St is the place for everyday fashion, while Regent St cranks it up a notch. Carnaby St is no longer the hip hub that it was in the 1960s, but this area still has good boutiques. The best bargains of all are at the markets, while London's famous department stores are an attraction in themselves, even if you're not buying.

Department Stores

Selfridges DEPARTMENT STORE
(Map p168; www.selfridges.com; 400 Oxford St W1; ⊖Bond St) The funkiest and most vital of London's one-stop shops.

Fortnum & Mason DEPARTMENT STORE
(Map p162; www.fortnumandmason.com; 181 Piccadilly W1; ⊖Piccadilly Circus) The byword for quality and service from a bygone era.

Liberty DEPARTMENT STORE
(Map p162; www.liberty.co.uk; Great Marlborough St W1; ⊖Oxford Circus) An irresistible blend of contemporary styles and indulgent pampering.

Harrods DEPARTMENT STORE
(Map p168; www.harrods.com; 87 Brompton Rd SW1; ⊖Knightsbridge) A pricey but fascinating theme park for fans of Britannia.

Harvey Nichols DEPARTMENT STORE
(Map p168; www.harveynichols.com; 109-125 Knightsbridge SW1; ⊖Knightsbridge) Temple of high fashion, jewellery and perfume.

Music

Befitting a global music capital, London has a wide range of music stores. As well as the big-name main-players, aficionados might like to head for the following:

Ray's Jazz JAZZ, BLUES
(Map p162; www.foyles.co.uk; Foyles, 113-119 Charing Cross Rd WC2; ⊖Tottenham Court Rd) The place to find those elusive back catalogues.

BM Soho DANCE
(Map p162; www.bm-soho.com; 25 D'Arblay St W1; ⊖Oxford Circus) If they haven't got what you're after, they'll know who has.

Rough Trade PUNK, INDIE
(www.roughtrade.com); East (Map p158; Dray Walk, 91 Brick Lane E1; ⊖Liverpool St); West (130 Talbot Rd W11; ⊖Ladbroke Grove) The best place to come for anything alternative.

Markets

London has more than 350 markets selling everything from antiques and curios to flowers and fish. Some, such as Camden and Portobello Rd, are major landmarks and popular with tourists, while others exist just for the locals. Here's a sample:

Borough Market FOOD
(Map p158; www.boroughmarket.org.uk; 8 Southwark St SE1; ⏲11am-5pm Thu, noon-6pm Fri, 8am-5pm Sat; ⊖London Bridge) Sometimes called London's Larder, has everything from organic falafel to boars' heads.

Camden Market ALTERNATIVE ALLSORTS
(Map p171; www.camdenmarkets.org; ⏲10am-5.30pm; ⊖Camden Town) Actually a series of markets. Lock and Stables markets are the place for punk fashion, cheap food, hippy shit and a whole lotta craziness.

Portobello Road Market CLOTHES, ANTIQUES
(www.portobellomarket.org; Portobello Rd W10; ⏲8am-6.30pm Mon-Sat, closes 1pm Thu; ⊖Ladbroke Grove) One of London's most famous (and crowded) street markets; it has new and vintage clothes, antiques and food.

Brick Lane Market ASSORTED
(Map p158; www.visitbricklane.org; Brick Lane E1; ⏲8am-2pm Sun; ⊖Liverpool St) A sprawling East End bazaar featuring everything from fruit to bric-a-brac.

Information

Britain & London Visitor Centre (www.visitbritain.com; 1 Regent St SW1; ⏲9am-6.30pm Mon-Fri, 10am-4pm Sat & Sun; ⊖Piccadilly Circus) Accommodation and theatre bookings, transport tickets, bureau de change, international telephones and internet terminals. Longer hours in summer.

City of London Information Centre (☎020-7332 1456; www.visitthecity.co.uk; ⊙9.30am-5.30pm Mon-Sat, 10am-4pm Sun; St Paul's Churchyard EC4; ⊖St Paul's) Tourist information, fast-track tickets to City attractions and guided walks (admission £6).

Getting There & Away

London is the country's major gateway – for more details see the Transport section at the end of this chapter.

Bus & Coach

The London terminus for long-distance buses (called 'coaches' in Britain) is **Victoria Coach Station** (off Map p165; 164 Buckingham Palace Rd SW1; ⊖Victoria).

Train

London's mainline rail terminals are listed below, with their primary destinations. Most are linked by the Circle line on the Tube.

Charing Cross (Map p162) Canterbury.

Euston (Map p172) Manchester, Liverpool, Scotland.

King's Cross (Map p172) Cambridge, York, Scotland.

Liverpool Street (Map p158) Stansted airport, Cambridge.

London Bridge (Map p158) Gatwick airport, Brighton.

Marylebone (Map p168) Stratford-upon-Avon.

Paddington (Map p168) Heathrow airport, Oxford, Bath, Bristol, Exeter, Plymouth, Cardiff.

St Pancras (Map p172) Gatwick and Luton airports, Brighton, Leeds, Paris (France), Brussels (Belgium).

Victoria (Map p165) Gatwick airport, Brighton, Canterbury.

Waterloo (Map p158) Windsor, Winchester.

Getting Around

To/From the Airports

GATWICK The cheapest option to central London is the mainline train between Gatwick's South Terminal and Victoria (from £12, four per hour, hourly at night, 37 minutes), or to/from St Pancras (from £12, 66 minutes). **Gatwick Express** (www.gatwickexpress.com; one-way/return £16/26, four per hour, 30 minutes) trains run to/from Victoria; the first/last train is 3.30am/12.30am. The **EasyBus** (www.easybus.co.uk; two per hour, about 1¼ hours) minibus service runs between Gatwick and Earls Court; first/last bus is 4.25am/1am; cost £2 to £10, depending on when you book, plus extra if you have more than one carry-on and one check-in bag.

HEATHROW The cheapest option to central London is the Piccadilly line, accessible from every terminal (£4.50, departing every five minutes from around 5am to 11.30pm, one hour). If it's your first time in London, this is a good chance to practise using the tube as it's at the beginning of the line and therefore not too crowded when you get on. If there are vast queues at the ticket office, use the automatic machines instead – some accept credit cards as well as cash. **Heathrow Express** (www.heathrowexpress.co.uk) is a faster train to/from Paddington (one-way/return £16.50/32, every 15 minutes, 5.12am to 11.42pm, 15 minutes); buy tickets online, on board (£5 extra) or from self-service machines at both stations (cash and credit cards accepted).

LONDON CITY The DLR connects London City Airport to the tube network, taking 22 minutes to reach Bank station (£4).

LUTON Mainline trains run between St Pancras (£9.50, 29 to 39 minutes) and Luton Airport Parkway Station, where a shuttle bus (£1) will get you to the airport within 10 minutes. The **easyBus** (www.easybus.co.uk) minibus service between Victoria and Luton Airport (via Baker St) costs from £2 to £10 (about 1½ hours, every 30 minutes).

STANSTED A train service called **Stansted Express** (www.stanstedexpress.com) runs to/from Liverpool St station (one way/return £18/27, 46 minutes, every 15 minutes 6am to 12.30am). The **EasyBus** (www.easybus.co.uk) minibus between Stansted and Baker St costs £2 to £10 (1¼ hours, every 20 minutes). The **Airbus A6** (☎0870 580 8080; www.nationalexpress.com) links with Victoria Coach Station (£11, allow 1¾ hours, at least half-hourly).

Bus

Travelling around London by double-decker bus is an enjoyable way to get a feel for the city. Buses run regularly all day, while less-frequent night buses (prefixed with the letter 'N') start when the tube stops. Single-journey bus tickets (valid for two hours) cost £2 (£1.20 on Oyster ticket card, capped at £3.90 per day). At stops with yellow signs, you have to buy your ticket from the automatic machine (or use an Oyster) *before* boarding. Buses stop on request, so clearly signal the driver with an outstretched arm.

Bicycle

Central London is mostly flat, relatively compact and the traffic moves slowly – though it can get terribly congested, so you'll need your wits about you. Theft is an issue, so lock your bike securely. Bikes can be hired from self-service docking stations (free for the first 30 minutes, thereafter £1/6/15/35/50 for 1/2/3/6/24hrs). For more information go to the Transport for London website (www.tfl.gov.uk) and follow the links to Cycling.

LONDON'S YOUR OYSTER

Although locals love to complain, London's public transport is excellent, with tubes, trains, buses and boats covering the capital. **Transport for London** (TFL; www.tfl.gov.uk) binds it all together; the website also has information on taxis and rental bikes – plus journey planners.

London is divided into concentric transport zones, with almost all places in this book in Zones 1 and 2. You can save money and avoid queues at ticket machines by getting a One Day Travelcard (£7.20 per day for Zones 1 and 2, £5.60 if you avoid peak hours 6.30am to 9.30am and 4pm to 7pm), available from ticket machines or counters at stations. It's valid on bus, tube and most urban trains – and much cheaper than buying two tube tickets or three bus tickets.

If you're in London for a few days, get an Oyster card, a reusable smartcard pre-loaded with credit to give unlimited transport on tube, bus and some rail services. Touch your card to the yellow sensors at the station turnstiles or bus entrance, and the fare is deducted from your card – at a much lower rate than a one-off paper ticket. For four days or less, opt for the daily rate (£7.20 per day for Zones 1 and 2, reduced to £5.60 if you avoid peak hours). If you're here for a week, load up your Oyster card as a weekly ticket (£26). The card itself is £3, fully refundable when you leave.

Car

Don't even think about it. London was recently rated Western Europe's second most congested city (congratulations, Brussels). In addition, you'll pay £8 per day simply to drive into central London from 7am to 6pm on weekdays. Hire a car after sightseeing in London.

Taxi & Minicab

London's famous black cabs are available for hire when the yellow light above the windscreen is lit. To get a licence, cabbies must do 'The Knowledge', which tests them on 25,000 streets and points of interest. Fares are metered, with flag fall of £2.20 and additional rate dependent on time of day, distance travelled and taxi speed. A one-mile trip will cost between £4.60 and £8.60.

Minicabs quote trip fares in advance and are a cheaper alternative to black cabs. They're licensed (recognisable by the ⊖ symbol displayed in the window) but drivers don't do 'The Knowledge', so may not know every street. Minicabs operate via agencies (most busy areas have a walk-in office with drivers waiting).

Train

As well as the tube, London has urban train services – particularly south of the Thames. Oyster cards can be used, but some stations don't have turnstiles so you must tap-in and tap-out at the Oyster reader or you'll be charged extra. You can still buy a paper ticket from machines or counters at train stations.

Underground & DLR

London's underground train network (universally known as the tube) extends its subterranean tentacles across the city and into the surrounding counties, with services running every few minutes from 5.30am to 12.30am (7am to 11.30pm Sunday). It's easy to use: tickets or Travelcards (or Oyster top-ups) can be purchased from counters or machines at stations (cash or credit card). Put your ticket into the slot on the turnstiles (or touch your Oyster card on the yellow reader) and the barrier opens. Once through you can jump on and off different lines as often as needed to reach your destination.

Also included within the tube network are some urban train services, billed as the 'Overground', and the Docklands Light Railway (DLR),which links the City to Docklands, Greenwich and London City Airport. The DLR is worth taking just for the views, especially when it hurtles between the skyscrapers of Canary Wharf; try to get a seat in the driverless front carriage.

The **London Tube Map** is an acclaimed graphic design work, using coloured lines to show 14 different routes. However, it's not remotely to scale. On the map, distances between stations are more or less the same. In reality, central stations can be just 250m apart, while in the outer suburbs it may be miles between one station and the next.

Waterbus

The myriad boats that ply the Thames are a great way to travel, avoiding traffic jams and giving great views. **Thames Clippers** (www.thamesclippers.com; £5.30, one-third off with Travelcard or Oyster) runs regular commuter services between Embankment, Waterloo, Blackfriars, Bankside, London Bridge, Tower, Canary Wharf, Greenwich, North Greenwich and Woolwich from 7am to midnight (from 9.30am weekends).

The classic London bus, the red double-decker 'Routemaster', has been pensioned off and replaced with more modern varieties on most routes. For a taste of history, Routemasters still operate on route 9 (between Aldwych and Royal Albert Hall) and route 15 (Trafalgar Sq and Tower Hill); these are the only buses without wheelchair access.

AROUND LONDON

'When you're tired of London, you're tired of life' opined 18th-century Londoner Samuel Johnson. But he wasn't living in an age when too many days on the Tube can leave you exhausted and grouchy. Luckily, the capital is surprisingly close to some excellent day-trip escapes. Long-time favourites Brighton and Oxford are covered later in the chapter. Two other gems that are an easy train ride from the capital are covered here.

Windsor & Eton

POP 31,000

Dominated by the massive bulk and heavy influence of Windsor Castle, these twin towns have a rather surreal atmosphere, with the morning pomp and ceremony of the changing of the guard in Windsor and the sight of schoolboys dressed in formal tailcoats wandering the streets of Eton.

Windsor Castle CASTLE

(www.royalcollection.org.uk; admission £16; ⌚9.45am-5.15pm) The largest and oldest occupied fortress in the world, Windsor Castle is a majestic vision of battlements and towers used for state occasions and is the Queen's weekend retreat. You can enter large sections of the castle complex, now fully restored after the devastating 1992 fire. Highlights include Queen Mary's giant doll's house, and St George's Chapel containing the tombs of several monarchs, including Henry VIII.

Eton College HISTORIC SCHOOL

(www.etoncollege.com; admission £6.20/5.20; ⌚guided tours 2pm & 3.15pm daily during school holidays, Wed, Fri, Sat & Sun during term). A short walk through Windsor and across the River Thames brings you to this famous public school – which in Britain means a private school – where the sons of royalty from around the world (and, more recently, from the British Royal Family) as well as 19 British prime ministers were educated. Several buildings date from the mid-15th century when Henry VI founded the school. As you wander round you may recognise some of the buildings; *Chariots of Fire, The Madness of King George, Mrs Brown* and *Shakespeare in Love* are just some of the classics filmed here.

Information

Royal Windsor Information Centre (www.windsor.gov.uk; Old Booking Hall, Windsor Royal Shopping Arcade; ⌚9.30am-5pm Mon-Sat, 10am-4pm Sun)

Getting There & Away

TRAIN Trains from London's Paddington run to Windsor Central Station (27 to 43 minutes) and from London Waterloo to Windsor Riverside Station (56 minutes). Services run half-hourly from both stations and tickets cost £8.

SOUTHEAST ENGLAND

Traditionally a day-trip playground for Londoners escaping overcrowded streets, England's southeast offers fascinating historic towns, sweeping greenbelt vistas and some vibrant seaside resorts – many just an hour or so by train from the capital. This section covers the counties of Kent, Sussex and Hampshire, with places listed roughly east to west. For visitor information, see www.visitsoutheastengland.com.

Canterbury

POP 43,000

With its jaw-dropping cathedral surrounded by medieval cobbled streets, this World Heritage city has been a Christian pilgrimage site for several centuries, and a tourist attraction for almost as long. Today, visitors come to immerse themselves in religious and secular history, including Archbishop Thomas Becket's murder and the bawdy works of Chaucer, but this is no mothballed museum: Canterbury is surprisingly vibrant and a good base for exploring the region.

The **Canterbury Attractions Passport** (admission £19) available from the tourist office gives entry to the cathedral and several other local attractions.

Sights

Canterbury Cathedral CHURCH
(www.canterbury-cathedral.org; admission £8; ⏲9am-5pm Mon-Sat, 12.30pm-2.30pm Sun) The Anglican faith could not have a more imposing mother church than this extraordinary early Gothic cathedral. It's an overwhelming edifice filled with striking architecture and an enduring sense of spirituality. The spot where Becket met his grisly end is marked by a flickering candle and striking modern altar.

Museum of Canterbury MUSEUM
(www.canterbury-museums.co.uk; Stour St; admission £3.60; ⏲11am-4pm Mon-Sat, also 1.30-4pm Sun Jun-Sep) A fine 14th-century building now houses the city's absorbing museum with a jumble of exhibits from pre-Roman times to local celeb memorabilia of the modern era.

Sleeping

Kipp's Independent Hostel HOSTEL £
(☎01227-786121; www.kipps-hostel.com; 40 Nunnery Fields; dm/s/d £16/22/36; @) This place is popular for its laid-back, homely atmosphere with lots of communal areas, clean though cramped dorms, bike hire and garden.

White House B&B ££
(☎01227-761836; www.whitehousecanterbury.co.uk; 6 St Peter's Lane; s/d from £60/80; wi-fi) This elegant Regency town house has a friendly welcome, period rooms with modern touches and a grand guest lounge.

Eating & Drinking

The streets of Canterbury are full of coffee bars and sandwich shops, and olde-worlde pubs are satisfyingly plentiful.

THE CANTERBURY TALES

If English literature has a father figure, then it is Geoffrey Chaucer (c1342–1400). Written in the Middle English of the day, his epic *Canterbury Tales* is a series of 24 vivid stories as told by a party of pilgrims on their journey from London to Canterbury. It remains one of the pillars of the literary canon, as well as a collection of rollicking good yarns about adultery, debauchery, crime and edgy romance, all filled with Chaucer's witty observances of human nature.

SPLURGE

Modern rooms at **Canterbury Cathedral Lodge** (☎01227-865350; www.canterburycathedrallodge.org; Canterbury Cathedral precincts; r from £65; @ wi-fi) have excellent facilities but the views and unlimited access to the cathedral make this place really special.

Veg Box Cafe VEGETARIAN CAFE £
(1 Jewry Lane; soups £4.95, specials £6.95; ⏲9am-5pm Mon-Sat) This welcoming, laid-back spot serves organic dishes at stocky timber tables under red paper lanterns.

Thomas Beckett PUB
(21 Best Lane) A classic English pub with quality ales, comfy seating and decent grub.

Information

Tourist office (☎01227-378100; www.canterbury.co.uk; 12 Sun St; ⏲9.30am-5pm Mon-Sat, 9.30am-4.30pm Sun) Situated opposite the cathedral gate.

Getting There & Away

BUS National Express runs buses to London Victoria (£13.40, two hours, hourly) and Dover (£5, 40 minutes, hourly)

TRAIN There are two train stations: Canterbury East for London Victoria (£23, one hour 40 minutes, two to three hourly); and Canterbury West for London St Pancras (high-speed service, £27.80, one hour, hourly). Local services include Dover (£6.50, 25 minutes, every 30 minutes).

Dover

POP 39,100

Dover's shabby town centre is a sad introduction to Britain for travellers arriving by boat, but the town has a couple of stellar attractions to redeem it.

Sights

Dover Castle CASTLE
(admission £13.90; ⏲10am-6pm Apr-Sep) One of the most impressive castles in England, built to defend the shortest sea-crossing to mainland Europe, this site has been in use for 2000 years and commands a tremendous view of the English Channel as far as the French coastline. Highlights include the remains of a **Roman lighthouse**, and a war-

ren of **wartime tunnels** dating from the Napoleonic and WWII eras.

White Cliffs of Dover LANDMARK
Immortalised in song, film and literature, these iconic cliffs are embedded in the national consciousness, a big 'welcome home' sign to generations of travellers and soldiers. The Langdon Cliffs (their proper name) are 2 miles east of town; there's a small information office, from where you can take a bracing walk along the clifftops.

Sleeping & Eating

B&Bs cluster along Castle St, Maison Dieu Rd and Folkestone Rd.

Hubert House B&B ££
(01304-202253; www.huberthouse.co.uk; 9 Castle Hill Rd; s/d from £40/55; @) The comfortable bedrooms may be overly flowery but the welcome is warm, and there's a nice little bistro downstairs.

East Lee Guest House B&B ££
(01304-210176; www.eastlee.co.uk; 108 Maison Dieu Rd; d £60;) Energetic hosts, renovated rooms and excellent breakfasts.

La Salle Verte CAFE £
(14-15 Cannon St; snacks £2-5.50; 9am-5pm Mon-Sat) The funkiest little coffee shop in Dover.

Information

Tourist Office (01304-205108; www.whitecliffscountry.org.uk; Biggin St; 9am-5.30pm daily Jun-Aug, 9am-5.30pm Mon-Fri & 10am-4pm Sat & Sun Apr, May & Sep, closed Sun Oct-Mar)

Getting There & Around

Bus & Coach

Canterbury Bus 15, 45 minutes, twice hourly

London Victoria Coach 007, £13.50, 2¾ hours, 19 daily

Train

The docks and train station are a long walk apart; ferry companies run regular shuttle buses (five minutes).

London Charing Cross £18.50, two hours, twice hourly

London St Pancras High-speed service, £31.70, one hour, hourly

Brighton & Hove

POP 247, 800

While some British seaside resorts are paint-peeled reminders of an earlier era, Brighton and Hove – two towns combined to form a new city in 2000 – has successfully moved on. It's now a cosmopolitan centre with a bohemian spirit, exuberant gay community, dynamic student population and a healthy number of ageing and new-age hippies, as well as traditional fairy-floss fun – although the beach has never been the top attraction, mainly because it has stones, not sand. But Brighton rocks all year round, and really comes to life in summer.

WORTH A TRIP

LEEDS CASTLE

This **castle** (www.leeds-castle.com; admission £17.50; 10am 6pm Apr Sep) is one of the most visited attractions in Britain, an impressive structure on islands amid a large lake transformed from fortress to lavish palace over the centuries. With a vast estate, it is ideal for peaceful walks. Trains run from London Victoria to Bearsted (£17; one hour) near Maidstone, then a shuttle coach to the castle is £5 return.

Sights

Royal Pavilion LANDMARK
(www.royalpavilion.org.uk; admission £9.50; 9.30am-5.45pm Apr-Sep, 10am-5.15pm Oct-Mar) The city's must-see attraction is the glittering palace and party pad of the Prince Regent (later King George IV), still an apt symbol of Brighton's reputation for hedonism. The domes and minarets outside are only a prelude to the palace's lavish oriental-themed interior.

Brighton Pier PIER
(www.brightonpier.co.uk) This grand old centenarian pier has plenty of fairground rides and dingy amusement arcades, plus fairy floss and Brighton rock to chomp.

Lanes SHOPPING PRECINCT
Brighton's original fishing-village heart, a cobblestone web of 17th-century cottages, is now a gentrified cornucopia of independent shops, pubs and one-of-a-kind eateries. Adjacent **North Laine** has a funkier vibe with multicoloured boutiques, used record stores and vegetarian cafes.

Sleeping & Eating

Traditional B&Bs line the streets radiating from Brighton Pier, and there's a good

Brighton & Hove

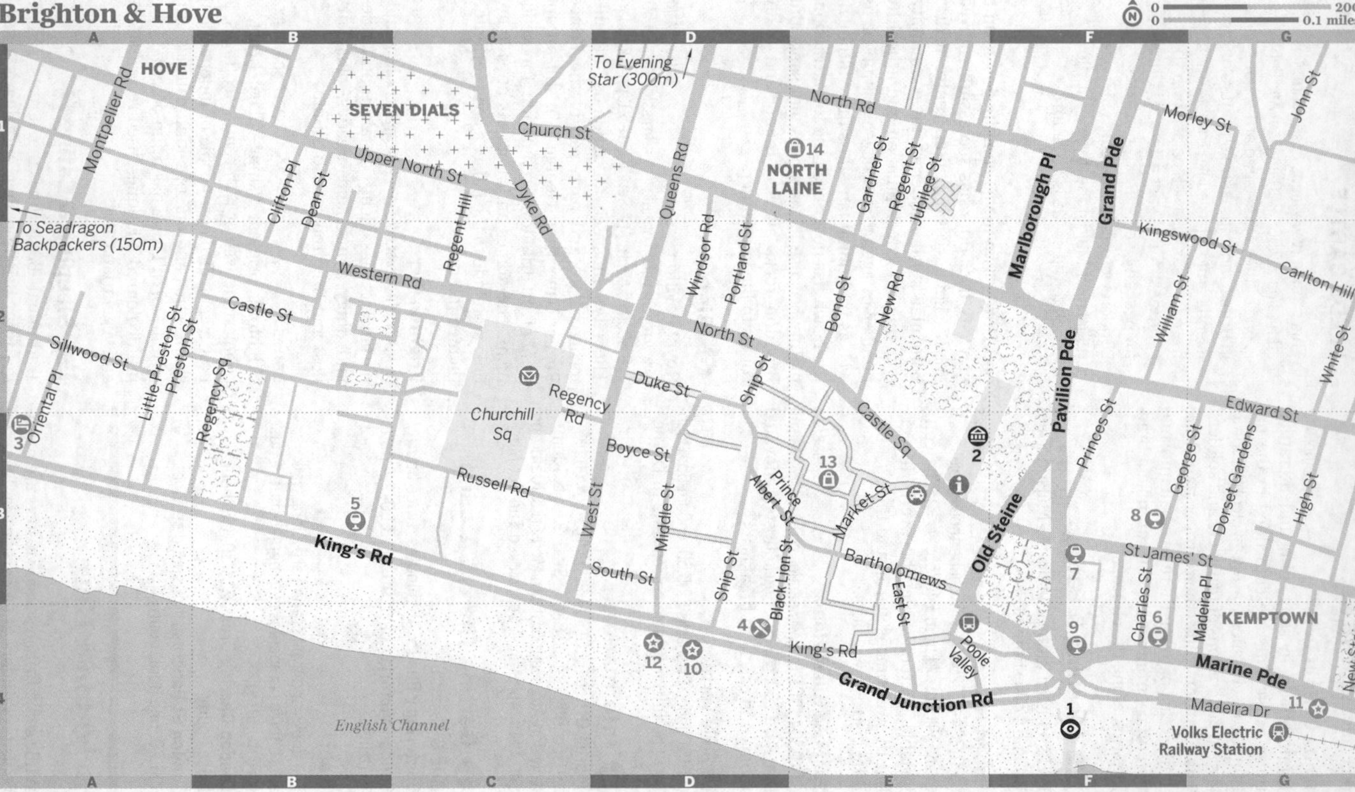

Brighton & Hove

Sights
1 Brighton Pier F4
2 Royal Pavilion E3

Sleeping
3 Baggies Backpackers A3

Eating
4 JB's American Diner D4

Drinking
5 106 Bar & Brasserie B3
6 Amsterdam F4
7 Candy Bar F3
8 Queen's Arms F3
9 Revenge F4

Entertainment
10 Coalition D4
11 Concorde 2 G4
12 Funky Buddha D4

Shopping
13 Lanes E3
14 North Laine E1

selection of backpacker joints too – several catering to raucous stag and hen nights, while others are more traditional and homely, so choose wisely! Brighton also has the best choice on the south coast, with cafes, restaurants, pubs and bars to fulfil every whim; the Lanes is a particularly good area to explore.

Baggies Backpackers HOSTEL £
(☎01273-733740; www.baggiesbackpackers.com; 33 Oriental Pl; dm/d £13/35; 📶) A warm atmosphere, onsite owners and clean dorms have made this long-established hostel something of an institution.

Seadragon Backpackers HOSTEL £
(☎01273-711854; www.seadragonbackpackers.co.uk; 36 Waterloo St; dm/tw £20/50; 📶) Perched on the edge of Hove, this simple and well-equipped hostel lacks vibe but is ideal for budget nomads who like to party elsewhere then snooze in peace.

JB's American Diner US DINER £
(31 King's Rd; burgers £7, other mains £6.50-12; ⏰lunch & dinner) Shiny red-leather booths, stars and stripes, and a '50s soundtrack provide the background for colossal portions of burgers, fries and milkshakes.

Evening Star PUB
(www.eveningstarbrighton.co.uk; 55-56 Surrey St) This cosy pub is a beer-drinker's nirvana, with a wonderful selection of award-winning real ales.

106 Bar & Brasserie BAR
(www.106brasseries.com; Kings Rd; ⏰Fri 3-11pm, Sat noon-11pm, Sun 11am-5pm) Huge sea-view windows drench this weekend venue in light as you sip a pre-club cocktail and watch the sun go down.

☆ Entertainment

When Britain's top DJs aren't plying their trade in London, Ibiza or Aya Napa, chances are you'll spy them here.

Coalition BAR, CLUB
(171-181 Kings Rd Arches) All sorts happen here: comedy, live music, club nights.

Funky Buddha NIGHTCLUB
(Kings Rd Arches) Funky house, '70s, R&B and disco please a stylish and attitude-free crowd.

Concorde 2 NIGHTCLUB
(www.concorde2.co.uk; Madeira Dr, Kemptown) Brighton's best-loved club, where Fatboy Slim still occasionally graces the decks.

Information

Tourist office (☎0300-300 0088; www.visitbrighton.com; Royal Pavilion Shop, Royal Pavilion; ⏰10am-5.30pm)

GAY & LESBIAN BRIGHTON

For more than 100 years Brighton has been a queer haven, with Kemptown (aka Camptown) the centre of the action. Venues include the following:

Amsterdam (www.amsterdam.uk.com; 11-12 Marine Pde; ⏰noon-2am) Hotel, sauna, restaurant and extremely hip bar.

Candy Bar (www.thecandybar.co.uk; 129 St James' St; ⏰9pm-2am) Slick cafe-bar-club for the girls.

Queen's Arms (www.queensarmsbrighton.com; 7 George St; ⏰3pm-late) Plenty of camp cabaret and karaoke.

Revenge (www.revenge.co.uk; 32-34 Old Steine; ⏰10.30pm-3am) Nightly disco with occasional cabaret.

Getting There & Away

BUS National Express runs buses to London Victoria (£11.80, two hours, hourly)

TRAIN All London-bound train services pass through Gatwick Airport.

London St Pancras £16.90, 1¼ hours, half hourly

London Victoria £13.90, 50-70 minutes, half hourly

Winchester

POP 41,420

Calm, collegiate Winchester is a mellow must-see for all visitors. The past still echoes around the flint-flecked walls of this ancient cathedral city. It was the capital of Saxon kings, and its statues and sights evoke two of England's mightiest myth-makers: Alfred the Great and King Arthur (yes, he of the round table).

Sights

Winchester Cathedral CHURCH
(www.winchester-cathedral.org.uk; admission £6, combined admission & tower tour £9; 9am-5pm Sat, 12.30-3pm Sun) Almost 1000 years of history are crammed into Winchester's glorious cathedral. The exterior isn't at first glance appealing, but the interior is awe inspiring, with one of the longest medieval naves (164m) in Europe, and a fascinating collection of features from all eras. Jane Austen, one of England's best-loved authors, is buried near the entrance in the northern aisle.

Great Hall & Round Table HISTORIC ARTEFACT
(Castle Ave; donation £1; 10am-5pm) The cavernous Great Hall is the only part of 11th-century Winchester Castle that Oliver Cromwell spared from destruction. Crowning the wall is King Arthur's Round Table. It's actually a 700-year-old fake, but it is fascinating nonetheless.

Sleeping & Eating

There's no hostel in town, and the cheaper B&B are out in the suburbs. For food and drink, there are plenty of options along the main street.

Dolphin House B&B ££
(01962-853284; www.dolphinhousestudios.co.uk; 3 Compton Rd; s/d £55/70; wi-fi) At this place your Continental breakfast is delivered to a compact kitchen – perfect for lazy lie-ins – while the terrace overlooks a gently sloping lawn.

No 21 B&B ££
(01962-852989; St Johns St; s/d £45/90) Gorgeous cathedral views, a flower-filled cottage garden and rustic-chic rooms (think painted wicker and woven bedspreads) make this art-packed house a tranquil city bolthole.

Black Boy PUB
(www.theblackboypub.com; 1 Wharf Hill; noon-11pm, to midnight Fri & Sat) This adorable old pub serves up good food and drink in rooms filled with freaky collections from pocket watches to bear traps.

Information

Tourist office (01962-840500; www.visitwinchester.co.uk; High St; 10am-5pm Mon-Sat, also 11am-4pm Sun May-Sep)

Getting There & Away

BUS National Express has coaches to/from London Victoria (£14, two hours).

TRAIN Trains run to London Waterloo (£26, every 30 minutes, 1¼ hours).

SOUTHWEST ENGLAND

Southwest England offers the pick of Britain's cities and countryside – all on one sea-fringed platter. Here you'll find Cornwall's golden sands and surging waves, Dorset's fossil-ridden Jurassic Coast, Wiltshire's prehistoric sites, Bath's exquisite cityscape, Bristol's buzzing nightlife, Somerset's hippy-chic ambience and Devon's beguiling blend of moors and shores.

The places in this section are listed roughly east to west. For information, see www.visitsouthwest.com.

Salisbury

POP 43,300

Centred on a majestic cathedral topped by the tallest spire in England, the gracious city of Salisbury has been important for more than 1000 years, and its streets form an architectural timeline from medieval walls and half-timbered Tudor houses to Georgian mansions and Victorian villas.

Sights

England is endowed with countless stunning churches, but few can hold a candle to the grandeur and sheer spectacle of **Salisbury Cathedral** (www.salisburycathedral.org.uk;

donation £5; ⏲7.15am-6.15pm). Tours illuminate the intricate interior of flying buttresses and vaulted ceilings. Restore the crick in your neck in the octagonal **chapter house**, where one of only four original Magna Carta documents is displayed, before heading into **Cathedral Close**, an impressive medieval perimeter of small museums and restored period houses.

Sleeping & Eating

There's a wide choice of places to stay, with eateries around the main square and the streets near the Cathedral.

Salisbury YHA HOSTEL £
(☎0845-371 9537; www.yha.org.uk; Milford Hill; dm £18; @) A real gem: neat rooms in a rambling Victorian building. Choose from doubles or dorms. A cafe-bar, laundry and dappled gardens add to the appeal.

Rokeby Guesthouse B&B ££
(☎01722-329800; www.rokebyguesthouse.co.uk; 3 Wain-a-long Rd; s/d from £50/60; @ 📶) Fancy furnishings, free-standing baths and lovely bay windows make this place stand out from the crowd. The decking overlooking the lawn helps too.

Haunch of Venison PUB
(www.haunchofvenison.uk.com; 1 Minster St; mains from £10) Featuring wood-panelled snugs and wonky ceilings, this 14th-century drinking den is packed with atmosphere.

Information

Tourist office (☎01722-334956; www.visitwiltshire.co.uk/salisbury; Fish Row, Market Sq; ⏲9.30am-6pm Mon-Sat 10am-4pm Sun Jun-Sep, 9.30am-5pm Mon-Sat Oct-Apr).

Getting There & Away

BUS National Express coaches to/from London via Heathrow (£16, three hours, three daily). Also to/from Bath (£10, 1¼ hours, one daily) and Bristol (£10, 2¼ hours, one daily). Regular buses serve Avebury.

TRAIN To/from London Waterloo (£32, 2 per hour, 1½ hours) and Exeter (£27, hourly, two hours). Another line provides hourly connections to Bath (£8, one hour) and Bristol (£9, 1¼ hours).

Stonehenge

Britain's most iconic archaeological site, **Stonehenge** (www.english-heritage.org.uk; admission £6.90; ⏲9am-7pm Jun-Aug, reduced hours rest of year) is a compelling ring of monoliths attracting a stream of pilgrims, poets and philosophers for the past 5000 years. Despite the huge numbers of visitors that traipse around the perimeter on a daily basis, and the traffic on the road nearby, Stonehenge still manages to be a mystical place – a haunting echo of Britain's forgotten past.

Visitors to Stonehenge normally have to stay outside the stone circle, but on **Stone Circle Access Visits** (☎01722-343830; www.english-heritage.org.uk; admission £14.50) you can wander around the core of the site, getting up-close views of the iconic menhirs. The walks take place in the evening or early morning so the quiet atmosphere and slanting sunlight add to the effect. Each visit only takes 26 people; advance booking is required.

DON'T MISS

AVEBURY

While the tour buses usually head straight to Stonehenge, prehistoric purists make for Avebury Stone Circle. Though it lacks the dramatic trilithons ('gateways') of its sister site across the plain, Avebury is the largest stone circle in the world and a more rewarding place to visit simply because you can get closer to the giant boulders. A large section of Avebury village is actually inside the circle, meaning you can sleep, or at least have lunch and a pint, inside the mystic ring. To get here, bus 5/6/96 runs from Salisbury (1¾ hours, hourly Monday to Saturday, five on Sunday).

Getting There & Around

No regular buses go to the site. The **Stonehenge Tour** (☎01722-336855; www.thestonehengetour.info; return admission £11/5) leaves Salisbury's train and bus stations half-hourly in June and August, and hourly between September and May.

Bath

POP 90,150

A cultural trendsetter and fashionable haunt for the past three hundred years, the honey-stoned city of Bath is especially renowned for its architecture. Along its stately streets you'll find Roman bathhouses, a medieval abbey and grand Georgian terraces. In fact, Bath has so many listed buildings the entire place has been named a World Heritage Site.

History

Bath's existence is based upon geological luck. Hot springs bubble to the surface here, and legend has it King Bladud, father of King Lear, founded the city some 2800 years ago when his pigs were cured of leprosy by a dip in the warm swampy water. In AD 44, along came the Romans; they established the town of Aquae Sulis and built an extensive baths complex and a temple to the goddess Sulis-Minerva. Through the Middle Ages, Bath was wool-trading town, then in the early 18th century the celebrated dandy Richard 'Beau' Nash made it the centre of fashionable society, and the present-day city owes much of its appearance to this golden age.

Sights

Roman Baths LANDMARK, MUSEUM

(www.romanbaths.co.uk; Abbey Churchyard; admission £12; ⏲9am-8pm Jul & Aug, 9am-6pm Mar, Jun, Sep & Oct, 9.30am-5.30pm Jan, Feb, Nov & Dec). In typically ostentatious style, the Romans constructed a glorious complex of bath-houses above the thermal waters, and 2000 years later this is one of the best-preserved Roman spas in the world. The site gets very busy in summer; you can usually dodge the

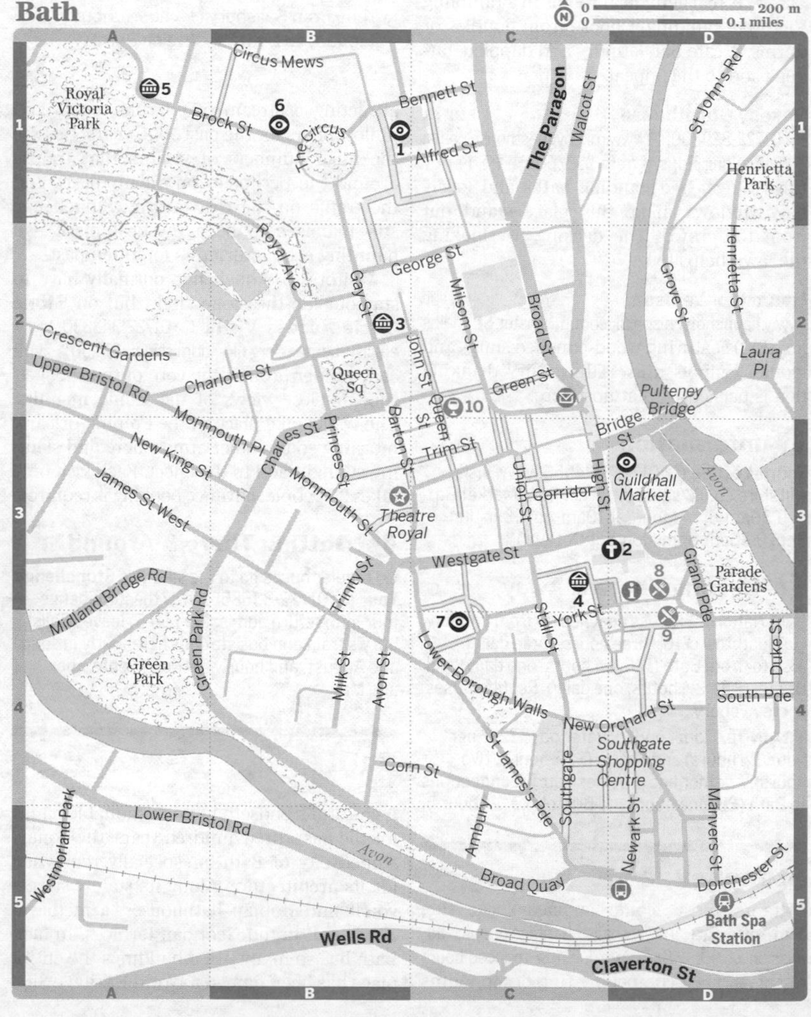

worst crowds by visiting early on a midweek morning.

Bath Abbey CHURCH
(www.bathabbey.org; donation £2.50; ⏲9am-6pm Mon-Sat Easter-Oct, to 4.30pm Nov-Easter, 1-2.30pm & 4.30-5.30pm Sun year-round) Constructed between 1499 and 1616, this is the last great medieval church built in England. Inside, the nave's wonderful fan vaulting was erected in the 19th century. Outside, the most striking feature is the west facade, where angels climb up and down stone ladders.

Royal Crescent & the Circus ARCHITECTURE
Bath's crowning glory is the Royal Crescent, a semicircular terrace of majestic houses originally built for wealthy socialites overlooking the green sweep of Royal Victoria Park. Nearby is the Circus, a ring of 30 houses divided into three terraces; plaques commemorate its famous former residents such as Thomas Gainsborough, Clive of India and David Livingstone.

FREE **Assembly Rooms** ARCHITECTURE
(Bennett St; ⏲10.30am-5pm Mar-Oct, 10.30am-4pm Nov-Feb) Opened in 1771, this was where fashionable Bath socialites gathered to play cards and listen to the latest chamber music. Most days, you're free to wander around the rooms, all lit by original 18th-century chandeliers.

Jane Austen Centre MUSEUM
(www.janeausten.co.uk; 40 Gay St; admission £6.50; ⏲9.45am-5.30pm Apr-Sep, 11am-4.30pm Oct-Mar) Bath is a location in Jane Austen novels including *Persuasion* and *Northanger Abbey,* and the author's connections with the city are celebrated here. Other displays include period costumes.

Bath

Sights

1 Assembly Rooms ... B1
2 Bath Abbey ... D3
3 Jane Austen Centre ... B2
4 Roman Baths ... C3
5 Royal Crescent ... A1
6 The Circus ... B1
7 Thermae Bath Spa ... C4

Eating

8 Café Retro ... D3
9 Sally Lunn's ... D4

Drinking

10 Raven ... C2

SPLURGE

Splashing about in the ancient Roman Baths might be off the agenda, but you can still sample the city's famous curative waters at **Thermae Bath Spa** (☎0844-888 0844; www.thermaebathspa.com; Hot Bath St; spa session per 2hr/4hr/day £24/34/54; ⏲9am-10pm). Attractions include steam rooms, waterfall shower and a choice of bathing venues – including the open-air rooftop pool, where you can swim in the thermal waters with a backdrop of Bath's stunning cityscape.

Sleeping & Eating

Bath is full of eating options. The narrow lanes off Milsom St and the area around Walcot St are good places to start exploring.

Bath YHA HOSTEL £
(☎08453-719303; www.yha.org.uk; dm £14, d from £35; @) Hostels don't come much grander than this Italianate mansion, a steep climb (or a short hop on bus 18) from the city centre.

Appletree Guest House B&B ££
(☎01225-337642; www.appletreeguesthouse.co.uk; 7 Pulteney Gardens; s £55-66, d £85-110, f £120-132;) It's absolutely tiny, but recommended for the sunny disposition of its owners.

Café Retro CAFE £
(18 York St; mains £5-11; ⏲breakfast, lunch & dinner Tue-Sat, breakfast & lunch Mon) The paint-job's scruffy, the crockery's ancient, but that's all part of the charm, and there's nowhere better for a stonking burger or a good mug of tea.

Sally Lunn's TEAROOM £
(4 North Parade Passage; lunch mains £5-6, dinner mains from £8; ⏲lunch & dinner) Classic chintzy tearoom serving the trademark Sally Lunn's bun.

Raven PUB
(Queen St) Highly respected by real ale aficionados, this fine city drinking den commands a devoted following for its well-kept beer and traditional atmosphere.

Information

Tourist office (enquiries ☎0906-711 2000, accommodation ☎0844-847 5256; www.visitbath.co.uk; Abbey Churchyard; ⏲9.30am-6pm Mon-Sat & 10-4pm Sun Jun-Sep, 9.30am-5pm Mon-Sat & 10-4pm Sun Oct-May)

Getting There & Away

BUS Bath's new bus and coach station is near the train station. National Express coaches run to/from London (£21.25, 3½ hours, 10 daily) via Heathrow (£17.50, 2¾ hours), and to Bristol (45 minutes, every 30 minutes).

TRAIN Direct trains go to/from London Paddington (£22 to £39, 1½ hours, at least hourly) and Bristol (£5.80, 11 minutes, four per hour), which has connections to most major British cities.

Bristol

POP 393,300

Bristol's buzzing. After decades of neglect, there's change happening everywhere in the southwest's biggest city: the historic docks have been redeveloped, the harbourside is crammed with galleries and urban pieds-à-terre, and the tired old city centre is now almost unrecognisable thanks to the addition of one of Britain's largest new shopping centres at Cabot's Circus. Recently Bristol has garnered a reputation as one of the southwest's most creative corners, thanks to its thriving media industry and its lively music, theatre and art scenes.

As in any big city, it pays to keep your wits about you after dark, especially around the suburb of St Paul's, just northeast of the centre.

Sights

TOP CHOICE SS Great Britain MUSEUM
(www.ssgreatbritain.org; Great Western Dock, Gas Ferry Rd; admission £11.95; ⏲10am-5.30pm Apr-Oct, 10am-4.30pm Nov-Mar; 📶) In 1843 Bristol's favourite engineer Isambard Kingdom Brunel designed the mighty SS Great Britain, the first transatlantic steamship to be driven by a screw propeller. A massive 30-year restoration program has brought the ship back to stunning life.

Clifton Suspension Bridge BRIDGE
(www.clifton-suspension-bridge.org.uk) Bristol's most famous landmark is another Brunel masterpiece, spanning the Avon Gorge on the edge of the city centre. It's free to walk or cycle across the bridge; car drivers pay a £0.50 toll.

FREE Arnolfini Arts Centre GALLERY
(www.arnolfini.org.uk; 16 Narrow Quay; ⏲10am-6pm Tue-Sun) The city's avant-garde gallery remains the top venue in town for modern art, as well as occasional exhibitions of dance, film and photography.

Sleeping

Bristol YHA HOSTEL £
(☎0845-371 9726; www.yha.org.uk; 14 Narrow Quay; dm £20, s £25-35, d £40-45; @) This hostel has one of the best locations in town, overlooking the harbour. Facilities are superb, including modern four-bed dorms and doubles, and an excellent coffee lounge.

Premier Inn, King St HOTEL ££
(☎0117-910 0619; www.premiertravelinn.com; The Haymarket; r £59-79; ❄📶) Swallow those preconceptions. In the absence of any decent B&Bs near the city centre, this budget chain is a real find, literally steps from the harbour.

Eating & Drinking

Eating and drinking in Bristol is a real highlight – the city is jammed with restaurants, bars and pubs of every description. The areas around Park St and the waterfront are good options if you want to stroll and see what takes your fancy.

BANKSY

Bristol brings you closer to the guerilla graffiti artist Banksy. Acknowledged as a local boy, his true identity is a secret, though his work is well known. Headline-grabbing works include issuing spoof British £10 notes (with Princess Diana's head instead of the Queen's); replacing 500 copies of Paris Hilton's debut album in record shops with remixes (featuring tracks titled 'Why Am I Famous?' and 'What Have I Done?'); painting an image of a ladder going up and over the Israeli West Bank Barrier; and covertly inserting his own version of a primitive cave painting (with a human hunter-gatherer pushing a shopping trolley) into the British Museum in London.

Around Bristol, a few of his early works survive. Look out for his notorious love triangle (featuring an angry husband, a two-timing wife and a naked man dangling from a window) at the bottom of Park St, and there's a large mural called *Mild Mild West* featuring a Molotov cocktail-wielding teddy bear on Cheltenham Rd opposite the junction with Jamaica St. For more, see www.banksy.co.uk.

Information

Bristol Visitor Information Centre (0333-321 0101; www.visitbristol.co.uk; E-Shed, 1 Canons Rd; 10am-6pm)

Getting There & Away

BUS National Express coaches serve London (£18, 2½ hours, at least hourly).

TRAIN Bristol is an important rail hub. Services include London Paddington (£34, 1¾ hours, hourly), via Bath, and Edinburgh (£80, 6½ hours, four daily).

Glastonbury

POP 8430

If you suddenly feel the need to get your third eye cleansed or your chakras realigned, there's really only one place in Britain that fits the bill: good old Glastonbury, a long-time bohemian haven and still a favourite hangout for mystics and counter-cultural types. The main street is lined with crystal sellers, vegie cafes and bong emporiums, but Glastonbury has been a spiritual centre since long before the hippies arrived; it's supposedly the birthplace of Christianity in England, and the gravesite of mythical King Arthur. The town is also famous for June's **Glastonbury Festival** (www.glastonburyfestivals.co.uk), a massive, often mud-soaked extravaganza of music, dance, good times and all-round weirdness.

Sights

Glastonbury Abbey ABBEY
(www.glastonburyabbey.com; Magdalene St; admission £5.50; 9.30am-6pm or dusk Sep-May, from 9am Jun-Aug) Legend has it that after the death of Jesus, his great-uncle, Joseph of Arimathea, came here with the Holy Grail, founding England's first church, now occupied by the ruined abbey dating from 1184. The grounds also contain the Holy Thorn tree, supposedly sprung from Joseph's staff, which mysteriously blooms twice a year, at Christmas and Easter.

FREE **Glastonbury Tor** LANDMARK
This grassy hill looms up from flat fields northwest of town, providing glorious views. It's also the focal point for a bewildering array of myths, being variously the home of a faery king, the stronghold of Gwyn ap Nudd (ruler of the Underworld), and the mythic Isle of Avalon where King Arthur sleeps until his country calls again.

Sleeping & Eating

Glastonbury Backpackers HOSTEL £
(01458-833353; www.glastonburybackpackers.com; 4 Market Pl; dm £14-16, tw £35-45, d £45-50; @) Pretty basic, but very friendly, with lounge, kitchen and cafe-bar.

Parsnips B&B ££
(01458-835599; www.parsnips-glastonbury.co.uk; 99 Bere Lane; s/d £50/65; @) If you need an escape from tie-dye and crystals, this modern place is a decent bet.

Rainbow's End CAFE £
(17A High St; mains £4-7; 10am-4pm) A Glasto classic, serving up generous portions in a cheery dining room.

Who'd A Thought It Inn PUB ££
(17 Northload St; mains £8.25-16.95; lunch & dinner) In keeping with Glastonbury's spirit, this pub brims with wacky character, from the bike on the ceiling to the red telephone box in one corner.

Information

Glastonbury tourist office (01458-832954; www.glastonburytic.co.uk; The Tribunal, 9 High St; 10am-5pm Apr-Sep, to 4pm Oct-Mar)

Getting There & Away

There is no train station in Glastonbury. Bus 376/377 travels to/from Bristol (1¼ hours, hourly Monday to Saturday, seven on Sundays).

Dartmoor National Park

Devon's best-known national park is a compelling landscape of exposed granite hills (called 'tors'), linked by swathes of moody moorland. On the fringes, streams tumble over boulders in woods of twisted trees. Naturally, Dartmoor's charms include outdoor activities and rustic pubs – perfect boltholes when the mist rolls in. We've listed a few favourites below. For information see www.dartmoor.co.uk

POSTBRIDGE

A good base for exploring the park, this quaint village has a couple of shops and pubs and is best known for its 13th-century **clapper bridge**.

Bellever YHA (0845-371 9622; www.yha.org.uk; dm £14; Mar-Oct) is a former farm that's full of character, a mile south of Postbridge, with a huge kitchen, lots of rustic stone walls and cosy dorms.

WORTH A TRIP

EDEN PROJECT

If any one thing is emblematic of Cornwall's regeneration, it's the **Eden Project** (☎01726-811911; www.eden project.com; Bodelva; admission £15/5; ⏰10am-6pm Apr-Oct, 10am-4.30pm Nov-Mar). Ten years ago the site was an exhausted clay pit, a symbol of the county's industrial decline. Now it's home to the largest greenhouses in the world – a monumental education project about the natural world. Tropical, temperate and desert environments have been re-created inside the massive biomes, so a single visit carries you from the steaming rainforests of South America to the dry deserts of North Africa.

WIDECOMBE-IN-THE-MOOR

This is archetypal Dartmoor, down to the ponies grazing on the village green. Widecombe's honey-grey, 15th-century buildings circle a church whose 40m tower has seen it dubbed the Cathedral of the Moor.

Higher Venton Farm B&B ££
(☎01364-621235; www.ventonfarm.com; Widecombe; d £50-60) This 16th-century farmhouse defines the 'picture-postcard thatch' architectural style.

Rugglestone Inn PUB £
(www.rugglestoneinn.co.uk; mains £4-9; ⏰lunch & dinner) You'll find plenty of locals in front of this intimate old pub's wood-burning stove.

Newquay

POP 19,400

Bright, breezy and unashamedly brash, Newquay in Cornwall is the undisputed capital of British surfing, with a non-stop parade of beach lovers and boozed-up clubbers creating a drink-till-dawn party atmosphere. If you've come to catch the waves, the best-known beach is **Fistral** – the venue for the annual Boardmasters surfing festival. Below town are **Great Western** and **Towan**; a little further up the coast you'll find **Tolcarne**, **Lusty Glaze**, **Porth** and **Watergate Bay**. All these beaches are good for swimming and supervised by lifeguards in summer.

Sleeping & Eating

Newquay has stacks of surf-lodges, and a good selection of cafes and bars.

Goofys HOSTEL £
(☎01637-872684; www.goofys.co.uk; 5 Headland Rd; r £32.50-40 per person; @) The town's top surf lodge bills itself as a 'boutique hostel'. All the dorms are nicely furnished, and there are doubles too.

Carlton Hotel B&B ££
(☎01637-872658; www.carltonhotelnewquay.co.uk; 6 Dane Rd; s £45, d £68-94) Swanky rooms, frilly edged beds, DVD players and country-cream furnishings run throughout this upmarket B&B.

Café Irie CAFE £
(☎01637-859200; www.cafeirie.co.uk; 38 Fore St; lunch £3-8; ⏰9am-5.30pm Mon-Sat) Run by surfers for surfers, with vintage vinyl on the walls, multi-coloured plates and chalkboards scrawled with specials.

Chy BAR
(www.thekoola.com/the-chy-bar; 12 Beach Rd) Chrome, wood and leather dominate this stylish cafe-bar overlooking Towan Beach. The patio is perfect for a gourmet breakfast or lunchtime salad. Later, DJs take to the decks and the beers start to flow.

Information

Tourist office (☎01637-854020; www.newquay.co.uk; Marcus Hill; ⏰9.30am-5.30pm Mon-Sat, 9.30am-12.30pm Sun)

Getting There & Away

BUS The 585/586 is the fastest service to Truro (50 minutes, twice hourly Monday to Saturday), where you can connect with other services.

TRAIN There are trains every couple of hours along the branch line between Newquay and Par (£3.80, 45 minutes). Par is on the mainline between London, Paddington and Penzance.

St Ives

POP 9870

Sitting on the fringes of a glittering arc-shaped bay, St Ives was once a pilchard-fishing harbour, but it's better known today as a centre of the arts. Cobbled alleyways lead through a jumble of galleries, cafes and brasseries that cater for thousands of summer visitors – an intriguing mix of boutique chic and traditional seaside.

The landmark **Tate St Ives** (☎01736-796226; www.tate.org.uk/stives; Porthmeor Beach; admission £5.75; ⏲10am-5pm Mar-Oct, 10am-4pm Tue-Sun Nov-Feb) gallery contains work by celebrated local artists, including Terry Frost, Patrick Heron and Barbara Hepworth, and hosts regular special exhibitions.

Sleeping & Eating

Treliska B&B ££
(☎01736-797678; www.treliska.com; 3 Bedford Rd; d £60-80; 📶) The smooth decor is attractive – chrome taps, wooden furniture, cool sinks – but what really sells it is the fantastic position, literally steps from St Ives' centre.

Blas Burgerworks CAFE £
(The Warren; burgers £5-10; ⏲dinner Tue-Sun) This pocket-sized joint offers lots of wacky burger variations, earning it a loyal following.

Sloop Inn PUB
(The Wharf) A classic fishermen's boozer, complete with low ceilings, tankards behind the bar and a comprehensive selection of Cornish ales.

Information

Tourist office (☎01736-796297; Street-an-Pol; ⏲9am-5.30pm Mon-Fri, 9am-5pm Sat, 10am-4pm Sun)

Getting There & Away

BUS Quickest bus to Penzance is the 17 (30 minutes, twice hourly Mon-Sat, hourly Sun). In summer the open-top 300 takes the scenic route to Land's End.

TRAIN Worth taking just for the coastal views is the branch line between St Ives and St Erth (£3, 14 minutes, half-hourly) on the Penzance–London Paddington mainline.

Penzance

POP 21,200

The historic harbour town of Penzance is a hotchpotch of winding streets, old shopping arcades and a grand seafront promenade. It's much more, er, authentic than prettified St Ives, and makes an excellent base for exploring the rest of west Cornwall.

Sights

St Michael's Mount LANDMARK
(☎01736-710507; admission £8.75; ⏲10.30am-5.30pm Sun-Fri late-Mar-Oct) Looming up from the waters of Mount's Bay is the unmistakeable silhouette of St Michael's Mount, a craggy island topped by an ancient monastery – one of Cornwall's most iconic landmarks. Highlights include the original armoury, the 14th-century priory church and the abbey's subtropical gardens teetering dramatically above the sea. The island is reached from the little town of Marazion, three miles from Penzance; you can walk across the causeway at low tide, or catch a ferry at high tide in the summer.

Sleeping & Eating

Penzance YHA HOSTEL £
(www.yha.org.uk; Castle Horneck, Alverton; dm £14; @) An 18th-century manor house on the outskirts of town, this hostel has an on-site cafe, laundry and four- to 10-bed dorms.

Archie Brown's CAFE £
(☎01736-362828; Bread St; mains £3-10; ⏲9.30am-5pm Mon-Sat) A cosier wholefood caff you couldn't hope to find.

Turk's Head PUB
(Chapel St) The oldest pub in town, covered in maritime memorabilia.

Information

Tourist office (☎01736-362207; penzancetic@cornwall.gov.uk; Station Approach; ⏲9am-5pm Mon-Sat, 10am-1pm Sun)

Getting There & Away

BUS Bus 17/17A/17B runs to/from St Ives (30 minutes, twice hourly Monday to Saturday, hourly on Sunday).

TRAIN Destinations include: Exeter (£11, three hours), Bristol (£37, four hours) and London Paddington (£57, 5½ hours).

Land's End

Just 9 miles from Penzance, Land's End is the most westerly point of mainland England, where cliffs plunge dramatically into the pounding Atlantic surf. It's worth skipping the **Legendary Land's End** (☎0870 458 0099; www.landsend-landmark.co.uk; admission £11; ⏲10am-5pm summer, til 3pm winter) theme park and opting instead for an exhilarating clifftop stroll – it's free too. To get here, bus 1/1A travels to/from Penzance (eight daily, five on Saturday).

CENTRAL ENGLAND

The geographic heartland of England is a mix of wildly differing scenes, from historic towns like Oxford and Stratford-upon-Avon to flower-decked villages and rolling countryside in the Cotswolds. In this section we also cover the lush dales and peaty moors of the Peak District. Places are listed roughly south to north. For information, see www.visitheartofengland.com and www.oxfordshirecotswolds.org.

Oxford

POP 134,300

Renowned as one of the world's most famous university towns, Oxford lives up to its advance billing as a busy, history-soaked place. The first of the 39 separate colleges dates from the 13th century, while the 14th century saw a riot over the quality of a local innkeeper's wine – suggesting that students have changed little over the years.

For visitors short on time, 'Oxford or Cambridge?' is a common conundrum. If we're blunt we'd say Oxford is not quite as quaint or pretty as Cambridge, but it more than makes up for this by being far more vibrant, with a wider array of attractions.

Sights

Oxford's graceful university buildings are individual in appearance and academic specialities. Not all are open to the public; to check the hours of those that are see www.ox.ac.uk/colleges.

Christ Church College COLLEGE
(www.chch.ox.ac.uk; St Aldate's; admission £6; 9am-5pm Mon-Sat, 2-5pm Sun) The largest and grandest of all of Oxford's colleges; also the most popular thanks to the magnificent buildings and latter-day fame as a location used in the Harry Potter films.

Magdalen College COLLEGE
(www.magd.ox.ac.uk; High St; admission £4.50; 1-6pm) Set amid lawns and river walks, **Magdalen** (pronounced *mawd-len*) is one of the wealthiest and most beautiful colleges.

Bodleian Library LIBRARY
(www.bodley.ox.ac.uk; Broad St; 9am-5pm Mon-Fri, 9am-4.30pm Sat, 11am-5pm Sun) Among the oldest public libraries in the world, this historic building holds more than seven million items on 118 miles of shelving.

Radcliffe Camera LIBRARY
(Radcliffe Sq; no public access) Another library and quintessential Oxford landmark – and one of the city's most photographed buildings.

Merton College COLLEGE
(www.merton.ox.ac.uk; Merton St; admission £2; 2-5pm Mon-Fri, 10am-5pm Sat & Sun) One of Oxford's original three colleges, founded in 1264.

Sleeping

There are strings of B&Bs along Iffley, Abingdon, Banbury and Headington roads. The following places stand out for their value for money.

Oxford YHA HOSTEL £
(01865-727275; www.yha.org.uk; 2a Botley Rd; dm/d from £18/46; @) Bright, clean and tidy, with comfortable dorm accommodation, private rooms and loads of facilities.

Central Backpackers HOSTEL £
(01865-242288; www.central backpackers.co.uk; 13 Park End St; dm £17-20; @) A good budget option in the centre of town, with rooms sleeping four to 12 people, a decent lounge, a rooftop terrace and free internet.

Oxford Rooms STUDENT ROOMS ££
(www.oxfordrooms.co.uk; r from £40) Didn't quite make the cut for a place at uni here? At least you can experience life inside the hallowed college grounds and breakfast in a grand college hall by staying overnight in one of their student rooms.

Ethos Hotel HOTEL ££
(01865-245800; www.ethoshotels.co.uk; 59 Western Rd; d from £80; @) This funky new hotel has spacious rooms, marble bathrooms, mini kitchen, breakfast basket and

Oxford

Top Sights
Bodleian Library ... D2
Christ Church College ... D4
Magdalen College ... F3
Radcliffe Camera ... D3

Sights
1 Merton College ... E4

Sleeping
2 Central Backpackers ... A3

Eating
3 Café Coco ... G4
4 Georgina's ... D3

Drinking
5 Eagle & Child ... C1
6 Turf Tavern ... E2

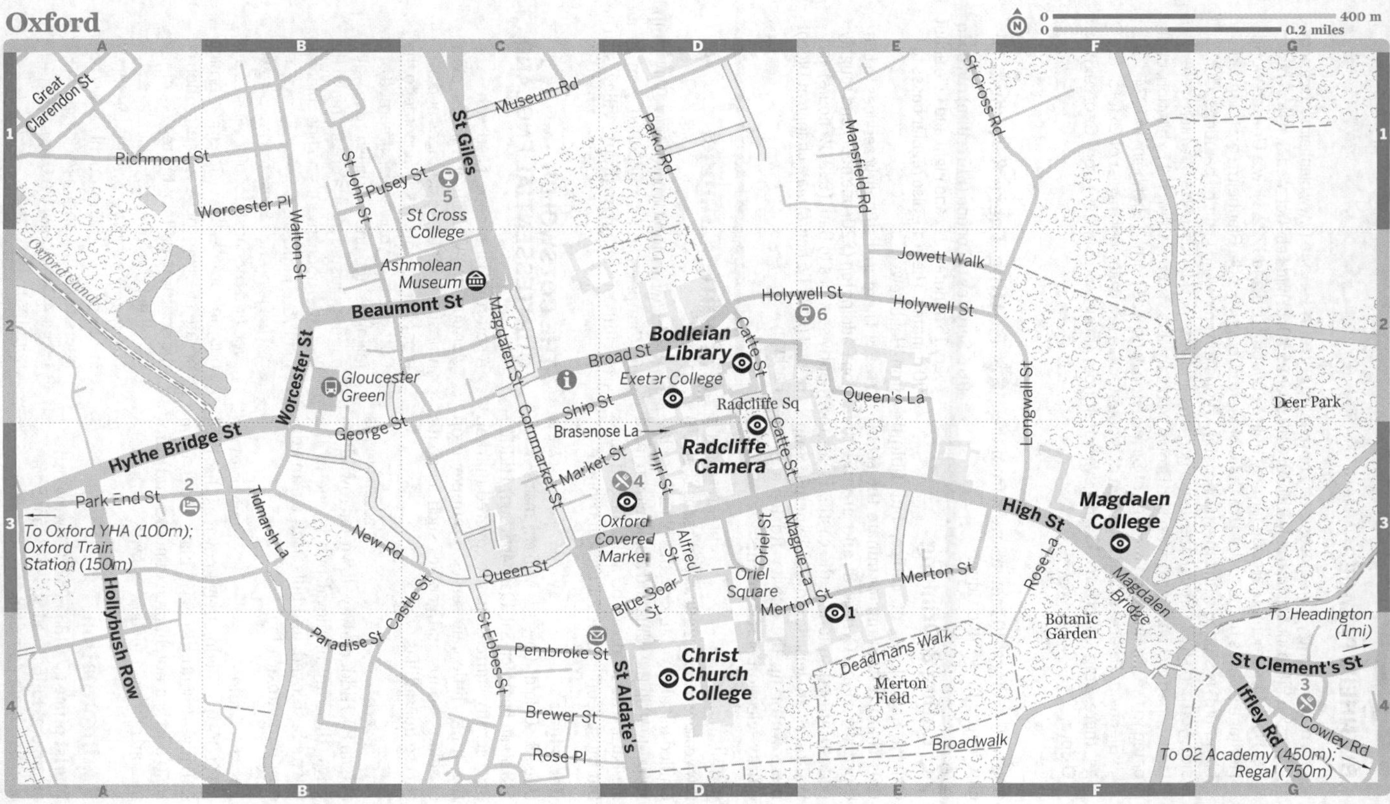
Oxford
0 400 m
0 0.2 miles
Great Clarendon St
Richmond St
Worcester Pl
Walton St
St John St
Pusey St
5
St Cross College
St Giles
Museum Rd
Parks Rd
Mansfield Rd
St Cross Rd
Jowett Walk
Oxford Canal
Ashmolean Museum
Beaumont St
Worcester St
Gloucester Green
Magdalen St
Broad St
Bodleian Library
Catte St
Holywell St
6
Exeter College
Ship St
Radcliffe Sq
Queen's La
Longwall St
Deer Park
Hythe Bridge St
George St
Cornmarket St
Brasenose La
Radcliffe Camera
Market St
Turl St
4
2
Park End St
To Oxford YHA (100m); Oxford Train Station (150m)
Tidmarsh La
New Rd
Oxford Covered Market
Alfred St
Oriel St
Magpie La
High St
Magdalen College
Queen St
Oriel Square
Merton St
Rose La
Magdalen Bridge
Blue Boar St
1
Botanic Garden
To Headington (1mi)
Hollybush Row
Paradise St
Castle St
St Ebbes St
Pembroke St
St Aldate's
Christ Church College
Deadmans Walk
Merton Field
St Clement's St
3
Iffley Rd
Cowley Rd
Brewer St
Rose Pl
Broadwalk
To O2 Academy (450m); Regal (750m)

DON'T MISS

BLENHEIM PALACE

One of the country's greatest stately homes, **Blenheim Palace** (www.blenheimpalace.com; admission £18, park & garden only £10.30; ⏲10.30am-5.30pm mid-Feb–Oct, Wed-Sun Nov–mid-Dec) is a monumental baroque fantasy built between 1705 and 1722. Now a Unesco World Heritage site, it's home to the 11th Duke of Marlborough. Inside, Blenheim (pronounced blen-num) is stuffed with tapestries, ostentatious furniture and giant oil paintings. Outside, you can stroll through the lavish gardens and vast parklands, parts of which were landscaped by Lancelot 'Capability' Brown. You can also visit the Churchill Exhibition, dedicated to the life, work and writings of Sir Winston, who was born at Blenheim in 1874.

Blenheim Palace is near the town of Woodstock, a few miles northwest of Oxford. To get there, Stagecoach bus S3 runs every half-hour (hourly on Sunday) from George St in Oxford.

free wi-fi – all just 10 minutes walk from the city centre. Incredible value.

Eating & Drinking

Oxford has plenty of choice, but ubiquitous chain restaurants dominate the scene, especially along George St and around the pedestrianised square at the castle. Head to Walton St in Jericho, to St Clements, Summertown or up the Cowley Rd for a more quirky selection of restaurants.

Cafe Coco MEDITERRANEAN £
(www.cafe-coco.co.uk; 23 Cowley Rd; mains £6-10.50) Chilled but always buzzing, this place has classic posters on the walls and a bald clown in an ice bath. The food can be a bit hit and miss but most people come for the atmosphere.

Georgina's CAFE £
(Ave 3, Oxford Covered Market; mains £3-6; ⏲8.30am-5pm Mon-Sat, 10am-4pm Sun) Hidden up a scruffy staircase in the covered market, this funky little cafe serves a bumper crop of salads, soups and goodies such as goat's cheese quesadillas.

Turf Tavern TRADITIONAL PUB
(4 Bath Pl) Hidden away down narrow alleyways, this tiny medieval pub is one of the town's best-loved, and bills itself as 'an education in intoxication'.

Eagle & Child TRADITIONAL PUB
(49 St Giles) Affectionately known as the 'Bird & Baby', this atmospheric place dates from 1650 and is a hotchpotch of nooks and crannies attracting a mellow crowd.

Information

Tourist office (☎01865-252200; www.visitoxford.org; 15-16 Broad St; ⏲9.30am-5pm Mon-Sat, 10am-4pm Sun)

Getting There & Away

BUS Services to London (£16 return) run up to every 15 minutes, day and night and take about 90 minutes. There are also regular buses to/from Heathrow.

TRAIN There are half-hourly services to London Paddington (£20, one hour) and roughly hourly services to Bath (£22, 1¼ hours) and Bristol (£24, 1½ hours) via a change at Didcot Parkway.

Chipping Campden

POP 2200

In the heart of the Cotswolds region, Chipping Campden is an unspoiled gem in an area full of achingly pretty villages. The

THE COTSWOLDS – QUINTESSENTIAL ENGLAND

A soft rural landscape, filled with glorious honey-coloured villages, old mansions, thatched cottages and atmospheric churches – welcome to the Cotswolds. If you've ever dreamed of falling asleep under English-rose wallpaper or lusted after a cream tea in the mid-afternoon, there's no finer place to fulfil your fantasies.

This is prime tourist territory, however, and the most popular villages are busy in summer. So visit early morning or late evening, focus your attention on the southern parts of the region, or take to the hills on foot or by bike.

A handy gateway town is Moreton-in-Marsh: with trains roughly every two hours to/from London Paddington (£27, 1 hour 40 minutes) via Oxford (£8, 40 minutes).

graceful curving main street is flanked by a wonderful array of wayward stone cottages, fine terraced houses, ancient inns and historic homes, liberally sprinkled with chichi boutiques and upmarket shops.

Sleeping & Eating

Chance B&B ££
(☎01386-849079; www.the-chance.co.uk; 1 Aston Rd; d £75; 📶) Two pretty rooms with floral bedspreads and fresh flowers make this a good choice. The owners are helpful and we love the little extras, such as dressing gowns and hot water bottles.

Eight Bells PUB ££
(☎01386-840371; www.eightbellsinn.co.uk; Church St; mains £13-17) Dripping with old-world character, but also decidedly modern, this 14th-century inn serves real ales and a fine selection of modern British and Continental dishes in rustic settings.

Getting There & Away

Buses 21/22 run (almost hourly Mon-Sat) to Moreton-in-Marsh and Stratford-upon-Avon.

Stow-On-The-Wold

POP 2800

A popular stop on a tour of the Cotswolds, Stow is anchored by a large market square surrounded by handsome buildings and a good number of antique shops, boutiques, tearooms and delis. It can be a little too busy if you're looking for true Cotswold charm, but on a quiet day it's a wonderful place.

Slap bang on the market square, the **Stow-on-the-Wold YHA** (☎0845 371 9540; www.yha.org.uk; The Square; dm £15.95; @) is in a wonderful 16th-century town house with small dorms and a warm welcome for families.

Getting There & Away

Buses 855/801 link Stow with Moreton-in-Marsh (at least eight daily Mon-Sat).

Winchcombe

POP 4380

Winchcombe is a sleepy Cotswold town, with butchers, bakers and small independent shops giving it a very authentic feel. It was capital of the Saxon kingdom of Mercia and important until the Middle Ages. Today the remnants of its illustrious past can still be seen. Among the sleeping and eating options, the **White Hart Inn** (☎01242-602359; www.wineandsausage.co.uk; r £40-115) is excellent.

Stratford-Upon-Avon

POP 22,200

The author of some of the most quoted lines in the English language, William Shakespeare was born in Stratford in 1564 and died here in 1616, and the town is now a tourist attraction that verges on a cult of personality. Experiences range from the tacky (Bard-themed tearooms) to the sublime (a play by the Royal Shakespeare Company). If you can leave without buying at least a Shakespeare novelty pencil, you'll have resisted one of the most keenly honed marketing machines in the nation.

Sights & Activities

Shakespeare Houses HISTORIC BUILDINGS
(☎01789-204016; www.shakespeare.org.uk; all five properties £19, three in-town houses £12.50; ⏲9am-5pm Apr-Oct) Five important buildings associated with Shakespeare are together called the Shakespeare Houses. You can buy individual tickets, but it's more cost effective to buy a combination ticket.

Shakespeare's Birthplace
(Henley St) Start your Shakespeare tour at the house where the world's most famous playwright supposedly spent his childhood days.

Nash's House & New Place
(☎01789-292325; cnr Chapel St & Chapel Lane) When Shakespeare retired, he swapped the bright lights of London for a comfortable town house on New Place.

Hall's Croft
(☎01789-292107, Old Town) Shakespeare's daughter Susanna married Dr John Hall, and this is their fine Elizabethan residence.

Anne Hathaway's Cottage
(☎01789-292100, Cottage La, Shottery) Before marrying Shakespeare, Anne Hathaway lived in this pretty thatched farmhouse, a mile from town.

Mary Arden's Farm
(☎01789-293455; Station Rd, Wilmcote) The childhood home of Shakespeare's mum, three miles west of Stratford. Aimed at families, exhibits trace country life over the

DON'T MISS

ROYAL SHAKESPEARE COMPANY

You just can't come to Stratford without seeing one of the Bard's plays performed by the **Royal Shakespeare Company** (RSC; ☎0844 800 1110; www.rsc.org.uk; tickets £8-38). There are often special deals for under-25s and students, and a few tickets are held back for sale on the day of performance.

centuries, with nature trails and rare-breed farm animals.

Holy Trinity Church CHURCH
(☎01789-266316; www.stratford-upon-avon.org; Old Town; admission to church free, Shakespeare's grave £1.50; ⏲8.30am-6pm Mon-Sat, 12.30-5pm Sun Apr-Sep, shorter winter hours) The final resting place of the Bard is said to be the most visited parish church in England, with the grave of the man himself marked with its ominous epitaph: 'cvrst be he yt moves my bones'.

Sleeping

Stratford-upon-Avon YHA HOSTEL £
(☎0845 371 9661; www.yha.org.uk; Hemmingford House, Alveston; dm from £16; @) Set in a large, 200-year-old mansion 1½ miles east of the town centre, this superior hostel attracts travellers of all ages.

B&Bs are also plentiful along Grove Rd and Evesham Pl, including the following:

Ambleside Guest House B&B ££
(☎01789-297239; www.amblesideguesthouse.co.uk; 41 Grove Rd; s/d from £25/50; @) Lovely B&B, with spotless rooms, well-informed hosts and big organic breakfasts.

Ashgrove Guest House B&B ££
(☎01789-297278; www.ashgrovehousestratford.co.uk; 37 Grove Rd; s/d from £25/50) Tidy rooms in varying degrees of burgundy. Look for the wooden bear sculpture outside.

Broadlands Guest House B&B ££
(☎01789-299181; www.broadlandsguesthouse.co.uk; 23 Evesham Pl; s/d from £48/80) Prim and blue, with classic rooms and filling breakfasts.

Eating & Drinking

Sheep St is clustered with eating options, mostly aimed at theatregoers (look out for good-value pre-theatre menus).

Oscar's CAFE £
(13-14 Meer St; sandwiches & lunches £4-7; ⏲11.30am-late) A casual cafe serving appetising breakfasts, lunches and afternoon tea; it turns into a bar after hours.

Dirty Duck PUB
(Waterside) Officially called the 'Black Swan', this enchanting riverside alehouse is a favourite thespian watering hole.

Information

Tourist office (☎0870-160 7930; www.shakespeare-country.co.uk; Bridgefoot; ⏲call for opening times)

Getting There & Around

BUS Destinations served include Oxford (National Express £10, one hour, twice daily), London Victoria (National Express, £17, three to four hours, five daily) and Moreton-in-Marsh (Bus 21/22, one hour, hourly).

TRAIN Mainline trains go to/from London Marylebone (£50, 2¼ hours, four daily).

BICYLE A bicycle is handy for getting to the outlying Shakespeare properties; **Stratford Bike Hire** (☎07711-776340; www.stratfordbikehire.com; 7 Seven Meadows Rd; per half/full day from £7/13) will deliver to your accommodation.

Peak District National Park

Surrounded by industrial cities, the surprisingly rural Peak District is one of the finest areas in England for walking, cycling and other outdoor activities. Don't be misled by the name; there are few peaks, but plenty of wild moors, rolling farmland and deep valleys – plus hardy villages, prehistoric sites and limestone caves. It's one of England's best-loved national parks, but escaping the crowds is no problem if you avoid summer weekends.

The region is divided into the wilder scenery of the Dark Peak in the north and the gentler meadows and dales of the White Peak in the south. The town of Buxton makes a good gateway, or you can stay right in the centre at Edale or Bakewell.

Sights

Chatsworth House STATELY HOME
(☎01246-582204; www.chatsworth.org; admission £11.25; ⏲11am-5.30pm Mar-Dec) Known as the 'Palace of the Peak', this vast edifice has been occupied by the dukes of Devonshire for centuries. Among the prime attractions in the house are magnificent artworks, deco-

rated ceilings and a treasure trove of splendid furniture.

The house sits in vast **gardens** (admission £7.50), with grottoes, fountains, a maze and changing collections of modern sculptures. Beyond that is another 400 hectares of **park** (admission free), open for walking and picnicking.

Chatsworth is 3 miles northeast of Bakewell. Buses 170 and 218 run several times a day (15 minutes), plus bus 215 on Sunday. Another option is to walk from Bakewell (about 2 miles each way), following a quiet lane then footpaths through Chatsworth Park down to the house.

Sleeping

The Peak District has a great selection of B&Bs. We've picked just a few favourites here. For more ideas, see www.visitpeakdistrict.com.

BUXTON

Buxton is a picturesque sprawl of Georgian terraces, Victorian amusements and pretty parks.

Roseleigh Guest House (01298-24904; www.roseleighhotel.co.uk; 19 Broad Walk; s/d incl breakfast from £38/72) is a gorgeous B&B with excellent rooms and a great location. The owners are seasoned travellers, with plenty of tales to tell.

EDALE

Surrounded by majestic countryside, this tiny cluster of cottages is an enchanting spot. Despite the remote location, the Manchester–Sheffield train line passes nearby, meaning easy access.

Stonecroft (01433-670262; www.stonecroftguesthouse.co.uk; Grindsbrook; r from £75) is a handsome house with two comfortable bedrooms. Vegetarians and vegans are well catered for.

BAKEWELL

The second largest town in the Peak District, Bakewell is probably best known for its eponymous pudding (and woe betide anyone asking for a Bakewell *tart*).

Melbourne House (01629-815357; Buxton Rd; r from £55) is in a picturesque building dating back more than three centuries.

Information

Bakewell (01629-813227; Bridge St; 9.30am-5pm, from 10am Nov-Mar)

Buxton (01298-25106; Pavilion Gardens; 9.30-5pm daily Oct-Mar, 10am-4pm Apr-Sep)

Castleton (01433-620679; Buxton Rd; 9.30am-5.30pm Mar-Oct, 10am-5pm Nov-Feb)

Getting There & Around

BUS National Express coaches run from London Victoria to Manchester and Buxton, from where you can switch to a local bus.

By far the handiest local bus is the hourly **Transpeak** (www.transpeak.co.uk) service that cuts across the Peak District from Derby to Manchester, via Bakewell and Buxton.

TRAIN Trains also run between Sheffield and Manchester via Edale and several other Peak villages.

PEAK HOSTELS

Outdoors types and shoestring travellers can take advantage of some useful YHA hostels, including popular **Castleton YHA Hostel** (0870 770 5758; www.yha.org.uk; Castle St; dm £14) and **Edale YHA Hostel** (0870 770 5808; www.yha.org.uk; dm from £11.95). There's also a series of rudimentary **'bunk barns'** (beds per person from £6) in remote locations. For details see www.yha.org.uk.

EASTERN ENGLAND

The vast flatland of Eastern England (or East Anglia, as it's usually called) is a mix of lush farms, melancholy fens and big skies, while the meandering coast is lined with pretty fishing villages and bucket-and-spade resorts. For information see www.visiteastofengland.com.

Cambridge

POP 108,900

Drowning in exquisite architecture, steeped in history and renowned for its quirky rituals, Cambridge is a university town extraordinaire. The tightly packed core of ancient colleges, the picturesque riversides and the leafy green meadows give it a far more tranquil appeal than rival Oxford.

Sights

Cambridge University comprises 31 colleges, though not all are open to the public.

Opening hours vary from day to day, so contact the colleges or the tourist office for information as hours given here are only a rough guide.

Trinity College COLLEGE

(www.trin.cam.ac.uk; Trinity St; admission £1; ⏲9am-4pm) The largest of Cambridge's colleges is entered via an impressive gateway. Don't miss the statue of the founder, Henry VIII; his right hand grips not a sceptre but a table leg, put there by student pranksters and never replaced.

Corpus Christi College COLLEGE

(www.corpus.cam.ac.uk; Trumpington St) Entry to this illustrious college is via the so-called New Court that dates back a mere 200 years.

King's College Chapel CHAPEL

(www.kings.cam.ac.uk/chapel; King's Pde; admission £5; ⏲9.30am-4.30pm Mon-Sat, 10am-5pm Sun) In a city crammed with glorious architecture, this is the show-stealer; one of the most extraordinary examples of Gothic architecture in England – most famous for its **fan-vaulted ceiling**, with intricate tracery soaring upwards before exploding into a series of stone fireworks.

Backs PARKLANDS

Behind the stately courts and manicured lawns of the city's central colleges lies a series of riverside gardens collectively known as the Backs. These tranquil green spaces and shimmering waters offer unparalleled views of the colleges and are often the most enduring image of Cambridge for visitors.

FREE **Fitzwilliam Museum** MUSEUM

(www.fitzmuseum.cam.ac.uk; Trumpington St; ⏲10am-5pm Tue-Sat, noon-5pm Sun) This museum is filled with priceless treasures from ancient Egyptian sarcophagi to Greek and Roman art, Chinese ceramics to English glass, as well as some dazzling illuminated manuscripts.

Cambridge

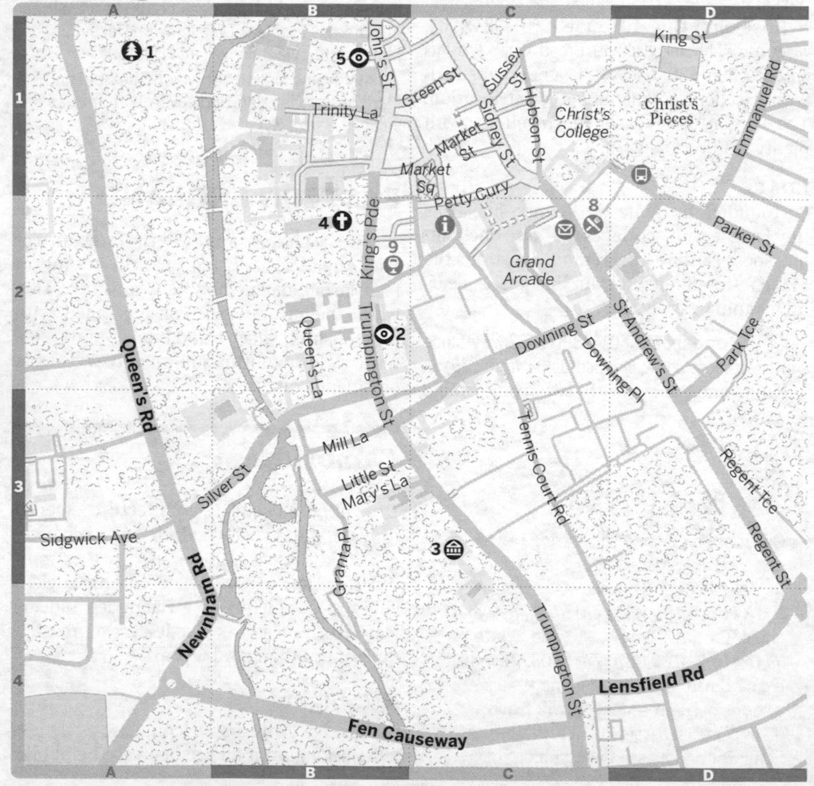

Sleeping

Cambridge has many B&Bs; some of the best-value options are a bit of a hike from town but well worth the effort.

Cambridge YHA HOSTEL £
(☎0845 371 9728; www.yha.org.uk; 97 Tenison Rd; dm/tw £16/40; @) Within walking distance of the city centre, the dorms at this cheap and cheerful hostel are small and basic, and with lots of groups it can be noisy.

Cambridge Rooms COLLEGE ROOMS ££
(www.cambridgerooms.co.uk; r £35-120) For a taste of life inside the hallowed college grounds, varying from traditional singles (with shared bathroom) overlooking college quads to modern en suite rooms in nearby annexes.

Tenison Towers B&B ££
(☎01223-363924; www.cambridgecitytenisontowers.com; 148 Tenison Rd; s/d from £40/60) This exceptionally friendly and homely place is really handy if you're arriving by train. The rooms are bright and simple with pale colours and fresh flowers.

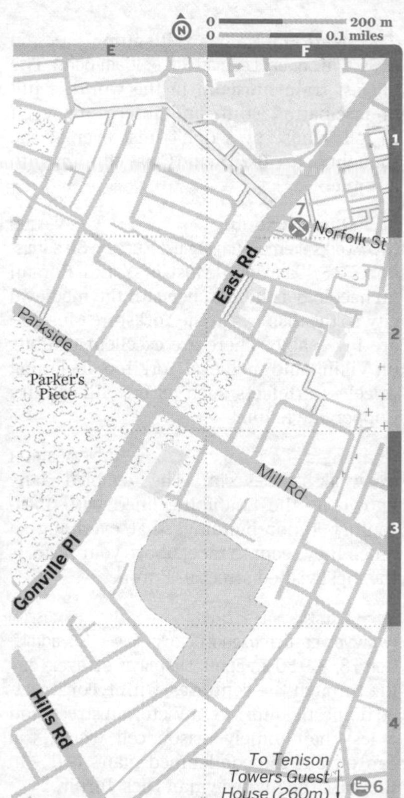

Eating & Drinking

There are plenty of restaurants around the city centre and a good selection of Asian eateries on Regent St, and the city is awash with historic pubs.

Origin8 DELI CAFE £
(www.origin8delicafes.com; 62 St Andrew's St; mains £4-6.50; ⏲8am-6pm Mon-Sat, 11am-5.30pm Sun) Bright and airy, this cafe-deli prides itself on its local organic ingredients.

CB2 BISTRO, VENUE ££
(www.cb2bistro.com; 5-7 Norfolk St; mains £6-13; @) Internet cafe, bistro, music venue and cinema all rolled into one, this lively place dishes up a great range of rustic cuisine in a relaxed and friendly atmosphere.

Eagle PUB
(Bene't St) Cambridge's most famous pub has loosened the tongues and pickled the grey cells of many illustrious academics.

Kingston Arms PUB
(33 Kingston St; mains £8.50-13.50; wi-fi) Down to earth and friendly, with real ales, decent grub, garden and free wi-fi.

Information

Tourist office (☎0871 266 8006; www.visitcambridge.org; Old Library, Wheeler St; ⏲10am-5.30pm Mon-Fri, to 5pm Sat, 11am-3pm Sun)

Getting There & Away

There are regular buses to/from Britain's main airports: Stansted (£12, 50 minutes), Heathrow

Cambridge

Sights

1	Backs	A1
2	Corpus Christi College	B2
3	Fitzwilliam Museum	C3
4	King's College Chapel	B2
5	Trinity College	B1

Sleeping

6	Cambridge YHA Youth Hostel	F4

Eating

7	CB2	F1
8	Origin8	C2

Drinking

9	Eagle	B2

PUNTING

Gliding a punt along the Backs is a blissful experience once you've got the knack, though it can also be a challenge to begin. Renting costs £14 to £16 per hour, while safer and more relaxing chauffeured trips cost £10 to £12 (a return trip to Grantchester £20 to £30).

(£30, 2½ to three hours) and Gatwick (£31, four hours). Trains run at least every 30 minutes to/from London King's Cross (£19, 45 minutes to 1¼ hours).

NORTHEAST ENGLAND

By turns rural and urban, modern and ancient, Northeast England contains the counties of Yorkshire and Northumberland, with the historic cities of York and Durham, wild national parks with excellent walking and other outdoor activities, great expanses of empty beach, plus a hoard of world-class relics and ruins.

Places in this section are described roughly south to north. For general information, see www.yorkshirevisitor.com and www.visitnortheastengland.com.

York

POP 181,100

Nowhere in northern England says 'medieval' quite like York, a city of extraordinary historical wealth. Its web of narrow streets is enclosed by a magnificent circuit of 13th-century walls and the city's rich heritage is woven into virtually every brick, while the modern city of York – with its museums, restaurants and pubs – is a carefully maintained heir to that heritage.

Sights

York Minster CHURCH

(www.yorkminster.org; admission £8; 9am-5.30pm Mon-Sat, noon-3.45pm Sun Apr-Oct, 9.30am-5.30pm Mon-Sat, noon-3.45pm Sun Nov-Mar) The awe-inspiring York Minster is the largest medieval cathedral in Northern Europe, and if this is the only cathedral you visit in Britain, you'll still walk away satisfied. Built mainly between 1220 and 1480, it encompasses all the major stages of Gothic architecture, with highlights including the west front, octagonal chapter house, the towers, and the fabulous stained-glass windows.

Jorvik MUSEUM

(www.vikingjorvik.com; Coppergate; admission £9; 10am-5pm Apr-Oct, to 4pm Nov-Mar) Interactive multimedia exhibits aimed at 'bringing history to life' often achieve just the opposite, but the much-hyped Jorvik – the most visited attraction in town after the Minster – pulls it off with aplomb. It's a smells-and-all reconstruction of the original Viking settlement that gave York its name.

FREE **City Walls** CITY WALLS

(8am-dusk) Walking the ramparts of the City Walls gives a whole new perspective on the city. The full circuit is 4½ miles (allow two hours); if you're pushed for time, do the short stretch from Bootham Bar to Monk Bar (and note, in York, a 'bar' is a gateway).

FREE **National Railway Museum** MUSEUM

(www.nrm.org.uk; Leeman Rd; 10am-6pm) The biggest train museum in the world is full of fascinating stuff, and interesting even to folk whose eyes don't mist over at the thought of a 4-6-2 Pacific Class chuffing into a tunnel.

Yorkshire Museum MUSEUM

(www.yorkshiremuseum.org.uk; Museum St; admission £7; 10am-5pm) Most of York's Roman archaeology is hidden beneath the medieval city, so the displays in the Yorkshire Museum are invaluable. There are excellent exhibits on Viking and medieval York too, including priceless artefacts such as the 8th-century Coppergate helmet.

Shambles MEDIEVAL STREET

(www.yorkshambles.com) The cobbled lane known as the Shambles, lined with 15th-century Tudor buildings that overhang so much they seem to meet above your head, is the most visited street in Europe.

York Castle Museum MUSEUM

(www.yorkcastlemuseum.org.uk; Tower St; admission £8; 9.30am-5pm) Displays of everyday life through the centuries, with reconstructed domestic interiors, a Victorian street, and a less-than-homely prison cell where you can try out the condemned man's bed – in this case the highwayman Dick Turpin.

York

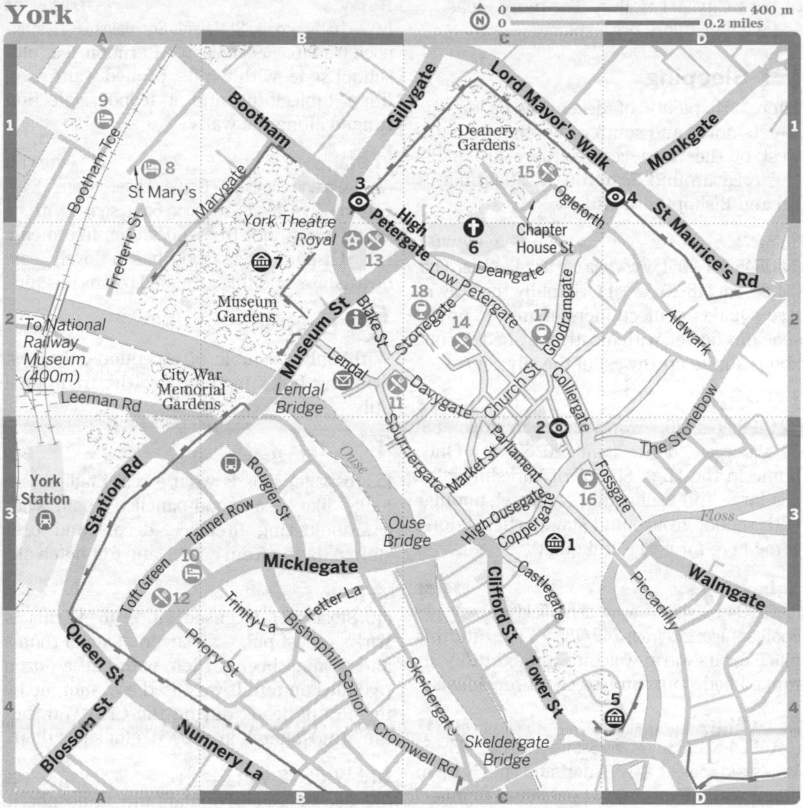

York

Sights

1 Jorvik ... C3
2 Shambles ... C3
3 Steps to City Walls ... B1
4 Steps to City Walls ... D1
5 York Castle Museum ... D4
6 York Minster ... C2
7 Yorkshire Museum ... B2

Sleeping

8 23 St Mary's ... A1
9 Abbeyfields ... A1
10 Ace Hotel ... A3

Eating

11 Betty's ... B2
12 Blake Head ... A3
13 Café Concerto ... B2
14 El Piano ... C2
15 Gray's Court ... C1

Drinking

16 Blue Bell ... C3
17 Old White Swan ... C2
18 Ye Olde Starre ... C2

Tours

There's a bewildering range of organised tours on offer, including a host of ever-more-competitive night-time ghost tours – York is reputed to be England's most haunted city. Most cost around £5. York's **Association of Voluntary Guides** offer two-hour walking tours (three per day in summer, free) from Exhibition Sq in front of York City Art Gallery. For more ideas, see www.visityork.org/explore.

Sleeping

There are plenty of decent B&Bs on the streets north and south of Bootham. Southwest of the town centre, there are B&Bs clustered around Scarcroft Rd, Southlands Rd and Bishopthorpe Rd.

York YHA HOSTEL £
(0845-371 9051; www.yha.org.uk; 42 Water End, Clifton; dm £18-20; @) Originally the Rowntree (Quaker confectioners) mansion, now a spacious hostel, with mostly four-bed dorms, about a mile northwest of the city centre.

Ace Hotel HOSTEL £
(01904-627720; www.acehotelyork.co.uk; 88-90 Micklegate; dm/tw from £20/60; @) Once home to the High Sheriff of Yorkshire, this is a large and well-equipped hostel, popular with school groups and stag parties – don't come here for peace and quiet!

Abbeyfields B&B ££
(01904-636471; www.abbeyfields.co.uk; 19 Bootham Tce; s/d from £49/78;) We rate this place for its warm welcome, thoughtfully arranged bedrooms and excellent breakfasts.

23 St Mary's B&B ££
(01904-622738; www.23stmarys.co.uk; 23 St Mary's; s/d £55/90; @) A smart and stately town house with nine country house-style rooms.

Eating

York has a wide range of eating options to suit all budgets.

Gray's Court CAFE ££
(http://grayscourtyork.com; Chapter House St; mains £6-7; 10am-6pm) A gem in the very heart of York, this place has a historic atmosphere, a sunny garden and gourmet coffee and cake.

Blake Head VEGETARIAN CAFE £
(104 Micklegate; mains £5-7; 9.30am-5pm Mon-Sat, 10am-5pm Sun) A bright and airy space at the back of a bookshop, filled with modern oak furniture and funky art.

Café Concerto CAFE/BISTRO ££
(01904-610478; www.cafeconcerto.biz; 21 High Petergate; snacks £3-8, mains £10-17; 8.30am-10pm) Walls papered with sheet music and chilled jazz on the stereo set the bohemian tone in this comforting coffee shop by day, which is a sophisticated bistro in the evening.

Betty's TEAROOM ££
(www.bettys.co.uk; St Helen's Sq; mains £6-11, afternoon tea £16; 9am-9pm) Afternoon tea, old-school style, with white-aproned waitresses, linen tablecloths and a teapot collection ranged along the walls.

El Piano VEGAN £
(www.elpiano.com; 15 Grape Lane; mains £4-7; 11am-11pm Mon-Sat, noon-6pm sun) With a 100% vegan, nut-free and gluten-free menu, this Hispanic-style spot has a lovely cafe downstairs and three themed rooms upstairs.

Drinking

With only a couple of exceptions, the best drinking holes in town are the traditional pubs.

TOP CHOICE **Blue Bell** PUB
(53 Fossgate) This is what a real English pub looks like – a wood-panelled room with a smouldering fireplace, decor (and beer stains) dating from c 1798, and top-notch ale.

Ye Olde Starre PUB
(40 Stonegate) Licensed since 1644, this is York's oldest pub – a warren of small rooms and a small beer garden, with half a dozen real ales on tap. It was used as a morgue by the Roundheads during the Civil War, but the atmosphere's improved a lot since then.

Old White Swan PUB
(80 Goodramgate) Popular and atmospheric old pub with small beer garden and good beer. And it's haunted…

Information

York Visitor Centre (01904-550099; www.visityork.org; 1 Museum St; 9am-6pm Mon-Sat, 10am-5pm Sun Apr-Sep, shorter hrs Oct-Mar)

Getting There & Away

BUS There are National Express coaches to/from London (£26, 5½ hours, four daily).

TRAIN York is a major train hub with frequent direct services to/from London King's Cross (£80, two hours), and Manchester (£15, 1½ hours).

Durham

POP 42,900

The grand city of Durham is crowned by a magnificent castle and Britain's finest Norman cathedral, together a Unesco World Heritage site. Surrounding them both is a

WORTH A TRIP

CASTLE HOWARD

Stately homes may be two a penny in Britain, but you'll have to try hard to find one as breathtakingly stately as **Castle Howard** (www.castlehoward.co.uk; admission house & grounds £12.50, grounds only £8.50; ⌚house 11am-4.30pm, grounds 10am-6.30pm Mar-Oct & 1st three weeks of Dec), a work of theatrical grandeur and audacity, and one of the world's most beautiful buildings, instantly recognisable from its starring role in the 1980s TV miniseries *Brideshead Revisited* and more recently in the 2008 film of the same name (both based on Evelyn Waugh's 1945 novel of nostalgia for the English aristocracy).

If you can, try to visit on a weekday, when it's easier to find the space to appreciate this hedonistic combination of art, architecture, landscaping and natural beauty. Castle Howard is 15 miles northeast of York. There are several organised tours from York – check with the tourist office. By public transport, catch Yorkshire Coastliner bus 840 (40 minutes from York, one daily).

maze of cobbled streets usually full of upper-crust students attending Durham's prestigious university. It's a place rich in history, and (thanks to those students) also packed with busy pubs and bars.

Sights

Durham Cathedral CHURCH
(www.durhamcathedral.co.uk; donation requested; ⌚7.30am-6pm, to 5.30pm Sun) Durham's most famous building has earned superlative praise for centuries. This is, quite simply, the definitive structure of the Anglo-Norman Romanesque style, and one of the world's greatest places of worship. There are **guided tours** (admission £4; ⌚10.30am, 11am & 2pm Mon & Sat) and **evensong** is at 5.15pm from Monday to Saturday and at 3.30pm on Sunday.

Durham Castle CASTLE
(www.dur.ac.uk; admission £5; ⌚tours 2pm, 3pm, 4pm term time, 10am, 11am & noon university vacations) Built in 1072, Durham Castle is now part of the university. Highlights of the 45-minute tour include the groaning 17th-century Black Staircase, the 16th-century chapel and the beautifully preserved Norman chapel.

Sleeping & Eating

Durham is surprisingly thin on budget accommodation so this could be a place to push the boat out. Cheap eats aren't a problem, though, thanks to the students, and some pubs do good bar food.

Cathedral View B&B ££
(☎0191-3869566; www.cathedralview.com; 212 Gilesgate; s/d from £60/80) Does exactly what it says: six large rooms, with the two at the back offering fantastic views of the cathedral. Breakfast is served on the vista-rich terrace.

Shakespeare PUB
(63 Saddler St) The perfect locals' boozer, complete with dartboard, cosy snugs and a small TV to show the racing.

Swan & Three Cygnets PUB
(Elvet Bridge; mains around £8) Riverside pub with courtyard tables overlooking the river, with good food.

Information

Tourist office (☎0191-3843720; www.thisisdurham.com; 2 Millennium Pl; ⌚9.30am-5.30pm Mon-Sat, 10am-4pm Sun)

Getting There & Away

National Express coaches run to London (£30, 6½ hours, four daily). Trains run to Edinburgh (£50, two hours, hourly) and York (£22, one hour, four hourly).

Hadrian's Wall

Built in AD 122 to mark the edge of the Roman Empire, this 73-mile coast-to-coast barrier across England remains a major feature on the landscape nearly 2000 years later. Although some parts of the wall have virtually disappeared, other stretches are remarkably well preserved and utterly spectacular.

The best area to visit is just to the north of the modern towns of Hexham and Brampton. Good gateways include the tiny twin settlements of Once Brewed and Twice Brewed, and the small towns of Haltwhistle and Greenhead, all with accommodation (ranging from YHA hostels to pubs

WORTH A TRIP

ANGEL OF THE NORTH

This extraordinary, gigantic, apocalyptic statue of a human frame with wings looms over the main A1 highway 5 miles south of Newcastle and north of Durham. At 20m high, 200 tonnes and with a wingspan wider than a Boeing 767, it's Antony Gormley's best-known sculpture and – thanks to all those passing cars – the most viewed piece of public art in the country (though Mark Wallinger's White Horse in Kent may pinch the title over the next decade).

and B&Bs) and tourist information centres (TICs) packed with maps, leaflets and information about the wall and surrounding area. The best portal site for information is www.hadrians-wall.org.

Walkers and cyclists can follow the entire length of the Wall – or just bits of it – on the **Hadrian's Wall Path** (www.nationaltrail.co.uk/hadrianswall) or **Hadrian's Wall Cycleway** (www.cycle-routes.org/hadrianscycleway).

You can also marvel at the Roman forts and castles along the wall's length.

Chesters ROMAN FORT
(Chollerford; admission £4.80; ⏲10am-6pm Apr-Sep) Situated near Chollerford, this well-preserved fortification has an impressive bathhouse, while its museum displays a fascinating array of Roman sculptures and drawings unearthed in the area.

Vindolanda Roman Fort & Museum ROMAN FORT
(www.vindolanda.com; admission £5.90, with Roman Army Museum £9/5; ⏲10am-6pm Apr-Sep, to 5pm Feb-Mar & Oct) About 1 mile from Once Brewed, this extensive site offers a fascinating glimpse into the daily life of a Roman garrison town.

Housesteads Roman Fort & Museum ROMAN FORT
(admission £4.80; ⏲10am-6pm Apr-Sep) This is the best-preserved Roman fort in the whole country, and the area's most dramatic and popular ruin. The carefully preserved foundations include a public latrine, and a gateway overlooking the wild Northumbrian countryside that is little changed since the legionaries pulled out in AD 410. It's 2½ miles north of Bardon Mill, or a spectacular walk (3 miles) along the Wall itself from Once Brewed.

 Getting There & Around

Reaching Hadrian's Wall is straightforward. The Newcastle–Carlisle train line runs parallel to the Wall a mile or two to the south, with stations at Hexham, Haydon Bridge, Bardon Mill, Haltwhistle and Brampton. There are hourly buses between Carlisle and Newcastle via most of the same towns. From June to September the hail-and-ride Hadrian's Wall Bus (number AD 122 – geddit?) shuttles between all the major sites, towns and villages along the way.

NORTHWEST ENGLAND

A place of two halves, Northwest England offers two very contrasting experiences: culture, music and big nights out in the world-famous cities of Manchester and Liverpool; peace, quiet, fresh air and high peaks in the mountainous Lake District. So pack your dancing shoes and your hiking boots, and come on over.

Manchester

POP 394,300

'Manchester has everything but a beach.' Former Stone Roses' frontman Ian Brown's description of his native city has become the city's unofficial motto – and even accounting for a bit of northern bluster, Brown isn't far wrong. This is the uncrowned capital of the north – as well as the birthplace of capitalism and the crucible of the Industrial Revolution.

Manchester was raised on lofty ambition, and its world-class museums and heavyweight art galleries are a fitting legacy, but what makes this city truly special are its distractions of pure pleasure. This is the best place to dine, drink and dance outside London – and at a much more reasonable price.

Sights

CITY CENTRE

FREE **Museum of Science & Industry** MUSEUM
(MOSI; ☎0161-832 1830; www.msim.org.uk; Liverpool Rd; ⏲10am-5pm) If there's anything you want to know about the Industrial (and post-Industrial) Revolution, you'll find the answers here.

HADRIAN'S HISTORY

Hadrian's Wall is named in honour of the emperor who ordered it built, and is one of the Roman Empire's greatest engineering projects – a spectacular testament to ambition and the practical Roman mind. Even today, almost 2000 years after the first stone was laid, the sections that still stand remain an awe-inspiring sight, proof that when the Romans wanted something done, they just knuckled down and did it.

When completed, the mammoth structure ran from the Solway Firth (west of Carlisle) to the mouth of the Tyne (east of Newcastle). Every Roman mile (about 1500m, slightly shorter than a modern mile) there was a gateway guarded by a small fort (milecastle) and between each milecastle were two observation turrets. Milecastles are numbered right across the country, starting with Milecastle 0 in the appropriately named Newcastle suburb of Wallsend, and ending with Milecastle 80 at Bowness-on-Solway.

A series of forts were developed as bases some distance south (and may pre-date the wall), and 16 lie astride the wall. The prime remaining forts on the wall are Cilurnum (Chesters), Vercovicium (Housesteads) and Banna (Birdoswald). The best forts behind the wall are Corstopitum at Corbridge, and Vindolanda, north of Bardon Mill.

FREE People's History Museum MUSEUM
(0161-839 6061; www.phm.org.uk; Left Bank, Bridge St) One of the city's best museums, devoted to British social history and the labour movement. Compelling stuff.

National Football Museum MUSEUM
(0161-907 9099; www.nationalfootballmuseum.com; Urbis, Cathedral Gardens, Corporation St) It's the world's most popular game and Manchester is home to the world's most popular team, so naturally this will be a major stop on any fan's itinerary.

SALFORD QUAYS

Get here from the city centre via Metrolink tram (£2). For the Imperial War Museum North and the Lowry, get off at Harbour City; get off at Old Trafford for the eponymous stadium.

FREE Imperial War Museum North MUSEUM
(0161-836 4000; www.iwm.org.uk/north; Trafford Wharf Rd; 10am-6pm Mar-Oct, 10am-5pm Nov-Feb) War museums generally appeal to those with a fascination for military hardware but this place takes a radically different approach: war is hell, it tells us, but it's a hell we revisit with tragic regularity.

FREE Lowry ARTS CENTRE
(0161-876 2020; www.thelowry.com; Pier 8, Salford Quays; 11am-8pm Tue-Fri, 10am-8pm Sat, 11am-6pm Sun & Mon) Attracts more than one million visitors a year to its many functions – everything from exhibitions and performances to bars, restaurants and, inevitably, shops – this complex is also home to more than 300 paintings and drawings by northern England's favourite artist, LS Lowry (1887–1976).

Old Trafford (Manchester United Museum & Tour) STADIUM
(0870-442 1994; www.manutd.com; Sir Matt Busby Way; tour £12.50; 9.30am-5pm) Home of the world's most famous club, the Old Trafford stadium is both a theatre and a temple for its millions of fans worldwide, many of whom come in pilgrimage to pay tribute to the minor deities that others may know only as highly paid footballers.

Sleeping

Hatters HOSTEL £
(0161-236 9500; www.hattersgroup.com; 50 Newton St; dm/s/d/tr from £14.50/27.50/50/67.50; @) One of the best hostels in town, with a location to match.

Manchester YHA HOSTEL £
(0845-371 9647; www.yha.org.uk; Potato Wharf; dm incl breakfast from £16; @) This purpose-built hostel in the Castlefield area is one of the best in the country, with four- and six-bed dorms and a host of good facilities.

Palace Hotel BOUTIQUE HOTEL ££
(0161-288 1111; www.principal-hotels.com; Oxford St; s/d from £85/105;) An elegant refurbishment of one of Manchester's most magnificent Victorian palaces has resulted in this good-value boutique hotel.

Eating

Manchester has something for every budget, including a superb selection in Chinatown and the organic havens of the Northern Quarter.

Earth Cafe VEGETARIAN £
(☎0161-834 1996; www.earthcafe.co.uk; 16-20 Turner St; chef's special £3.20; ⊙10am-5pm Tue-Sat) Below the Manchester Buddhist Centre, this gourmet vegetarian cafe's motto is 'right food, right place, right time'. The result is wonderful.

Love Saves the Day CAFE £
(☎0161-832 0777; Tib St; lunch £6-8; ⊙8am-7pm Mon-Wed, to 9pm Thu, to 8pm Fri, 10-6pm Sat, 10am-4pm Sun) The Northern Quarter's most popular cafe is a New York-style deli, small supermarket and sit-down eatery in one large, airy room.

Trof CAFE £
(☎0161-832 1870; 5-8 Thomas St; sandwiches £4, mains around £8; ⊙) Great music, top staff and a fab menu, plus a broad selection of beers and tunes (Tuesday night is acoustic night), make this hangout a firm favourite with students.

Drinking

There's every kind of drinking hole in Manchester. Here's a few to get you going:

Bluu BAR
(☎0161-839 7740; www.bluu.co.uk; Unit 1, Smithfield Market, Thomas St; ⊙noon-midnight Sun-Mon, to 1am Tue-Thu, to 2am Fri & Sat) Our favourite of the Northern Quarter's collection of great bars; cool, comfortable and with a great terrace.

Lass O'Gowrie TRADITIONAL PUB
(☎0161-273 6932; 36 Charles St; mains around £6) A Victorian classic and a favourite with students, old-timers and BBC employees.

Odd DJ BAR
(☎0161-833 0070; www.oddbar.co.uk; 30-32 Thomas St; ⊙11am-11pm Mon-Sat, to 10.30pm Sun) This eclectic little bar – with its oddball furnishings, wacky tunes and anti-establishment crew of customers – is a slice of Mancuniana to be treasured.

Peveril of the Peak PUB
(☎0161-236 6364; 127 Great Bridgewater St) An unpretentious pub with wonderful Victorian glazed tilework outside.

Entertainment

With a terrific club scene, Manchester remains at the vanguard of dance-floor culture. Below are some of our favourite places. Before going out, here's a handy tip: drop all mention of 'Madchester' and keep talk of being 'up for it' to strict irony.

TOP CHOICE **Sankey's** CLUB
(☎0161-950 4201; www.sankeys.info; Radium St, Ancoats; ⊙10pm-3am Thu & Fri, 10pm-4am Sat) Pioneer of dance music, and still with an unwavering commitment to top-class DJs. Choon!

AC 251: The Factory CLUB
(☎0161-272 7251; www.factorymanchester.com; 112-118 Princess St; admission £3-6; ⊙9.30pm-3am Mon-Sat) Tony Wilson's legendary Factory Records label HQ has been converted into a brand new club and live music venue.

Band on the Wall BAR
(☎0161-834 1786; www.bandonthewall.org; 25 Swan St) A top-notch venue that hosts everything from rock to world music.

Information

Tourist office (☎0871 222 8223; www.visitmanchester.com; Piccadilly Plaza, Portland St; ⊙10am-5.15pm Mon-Sat, 10am-4.30pm Sun)

Getting There & Away

BUS National Express coaches serve Liverpool (£6, 1¼ hours, hourly), and London (£24, 3¾ hours, hourly).

TRAIN Manchester Piccadilly is the main station for trains to and from the rest of the country, including Liverpool (£9, 45 minutes, half-hourly) and London (£60, three hours, seven daily).

LIVERPOOL

POP 469,000

Beleaguered by a history of hard times and chronic misfortune, Liverpool's luck has changed dramatically in recent years. The centre is being transformed, while the city's magnificent cultural heritage is celebrated on the waterfront around Albert Dock.

Sights

CITY CENTRE

FREE **World Museum** MUSEUM
(☎0151-478 4399; www.liverpoolmuseums.org.uk/wml; William Brown St; ⊙10am-5pm) Natural history, science and technology are the themes of this sprawling museum. It also includes the country's only free planetarium.

FREE **St George's Hall** CULTURAL CENTRE
(☎0151-707 2391; www.stgeorgesliverpool.co.uk; William Brown St; ⊙Tue-Sat 10am-5pm, 1-5pm Sun) Liverpool's most impressive building – a magnificent example of neoclassical architecture. Curiously, it was built as law courts *and* as a concert hall – presumably a judge could pass sentence, then relax to a string quartet.

Liverpool Cathedral CHURCH
(☎0151-709 6271; www.liverpoolcathedral.org.uk; Hope St; ⊙8am-6pm) A building of superlatives: Britain's largest church; the world's largest Anglican cathedral; the world's third-largest bell (with the world's heaviest peal); even the world's largest organ.

Metropolitan Cathedral of Christ the King CHURCH
(☎0151-709 9222; www.liverpoolmetrocathedral.org.uk; Mt Pleasant; ⊙8am-6pm Mon-Sat, 8am-5pm Sun Oct-Mar) Liverpool's Catholic cathedral is a mightily impressive modern building, completed in 1967. The central tower frames the world's largest stained-glass window.

ALBERT DOCK & AROUND

Liverpool's biggest tourist attraction is **Albert Dock** (www.albertdock.com; admission free). This former port and its surrounding buildings is now a World Heritage site.

TOP CHOICE **International Slavery Museum** MUSEUM
(☎0151-478 4499; www.liverpoolmuseums.org.uk/ism; Albert Dock; admission free; ⊙10am-5pm) This magnificent museum reveals slavery's unimaginable horrors – including Liverpool's own role in the slave trade – and it doesn't baulk at confronting racism.

Beatles Story MUSEUM
(☎0151-709 1963; www.beatlesstory.com; Albert Dock; admission £12.95; ⊙9am-7pm, last admission 5pm) Liverpool's most popular museum tells the story most famous foursome, with plenty of genuine memorabilia – and hardly a mention of internal discord, drugs or Yoko Ono.

FREE **Merseyside Maritime Museum** MUSEUM
(☎0151-478 4499; www.liverpoolmuseums.org.uk/maritime; Albert Dock; ⊙10am-5pm) A graphic celebration of one of the world's great ports.

The area to the north of Albert Dock is known as Pier Head, still the departure point for ferries across the River Mersey. The story of the millions of migrants that sailed from Liverpool is told at the eye-catching **Museum of Liverpool** (☎0151 478 4499; www.liverpoolmuseums.org.uk/mol; Pier Head; admission free). This area is dominated by a trio of buildings known as the 'Three Graces': the domed **Port of Liverpool Building**, the **Cunard Building**, in the style of an Italian palazzo; and the **Royal Liver Building** (pronounced *lie*-ver) crowned by the city's symbol, the famous copper Liver Bird.

Sleeping

International Inn HOSTEL £
(☎0151-709 8135; www.internationalinn.co.uk; 4 South Hunter St; dm/d from £15/36; 📶) A superb converted warehouse in the middle of uni-land: heated rooms with tidy wooden beds and bunks accommodate from two to 10 people.

Liverpool YHA HOSTEL £
(☎0845-371 9527; www.yha.org.uk; 25 Tabley St; dm from £16; 📶) It may look like an Eastern European apartment complex, but this award-winning hostel in Albert Dock is very comfortable. The dorms have attached bathrooms and even heated towel rails.

Eating & Drinking

Liverpool has plenty of choices to satisfy every taste. The best areas include Ropewalks, along Hardman St and Hope St or along Nelson St in the heart of Chinatown.

Everyman Bistro CAFE £
(☎0151-708 9545; www.everyman.co.uk; 13 Hope St; mains £5-8; ⊙noon-2am Mon-Fri, 11am-2am Sat, 7-10.30pm Sun) Out-of-work actors and other creative types make this place (located beneath the Everyman Theatre) their second home – with good reason. It has great tucker and a terrific atmosphere.

Philharmonic TRADITIONAL PUB
(☎0151-707 2837; 36 Hope St; ⊙to 11.30pm) This extraordinary pub, designed by the

SPLURGE

You don't have to be a Beatles fan to stay at **Hard Days Night Hotel** (☎0151-236 1964; www.harddaysnighthotel.com; Central Bldgs, North John St; r £110-160; @📶), but it helps: the 110 ultramodern rooms are decorated with specially commissioned drawings of the band.

DOING THE BEATLES TO DEATH

It doesn't matter that two of them are dead, that the much-visited Cavern Club is an unfaithful reconstruction of the original, nor that, if he were alive, John Lennon would have devoted much of his cynical energy to mocking the 'Cavern Quarter' that has grown up around Mathew St. No, it doesn't matter at all, because the Beatles phenomenon lives on, and a huge chunk of the city's visitors come to visit, see and touch anything – and we mean anything – even vaguely associated with the Fab Four. Which isn't to say that a wander around Mathew St isn't fun: from shucking shellfish in the Rubber Soul Oyster Bar to buying a Ringo pillowcase in the From Me to You shop, virtually all of your Beatles needs can be taken care of.

True fans will also undoubtedly want to visit the National Trust-owned **Mendips**, the home where John lived with his Aunt Mimi from 1945 to 1963 and **20 Forthlin Rd**, where Paul grew up; you can only do so by prebooked **tour** (0151-427 7231; admission £16.80; 10.30am & 11.20am Wed-Sun, Easter-Oct) from outside the National Conservation Centre.

shipwrights who built the *Lusitania,* is one of the most beautiful in all of England.

Hannah's BAR
(0151-708 5959; 2 Leece St) One of the top student bars in town, with an easygoing crowd and some pretty decent music.

Entertainment

Most of the city's clubs and late-night bars are concentrated in the area of Ropewalks.

Masque CLUB
(0151-707 6171; 90 Seel St; admission £4-11; Mon-Sat) This converted theatre is home to our favourite club in town.

Le Bateau CLUB
(0151-709 6508; 62 Duke St; admission £3-8; Thu-Sat) In this superb indie club 500 punters cram the dancefloor and hear everything from techno to hard rock.

Information

Albert Dock tourist office (0151-478 4599) Anchor Courtyard (10am-6pm) Merseyside Maritime Museum (10am-6pm)
08 Place tourist office (0151-233 2008; Whitechapel; 9am-8pm Mon-Sat, 11am-4pm Sun Apr-Sep, 9am-6pm Mon-Sat, 11am-4pm Sun Oct-Mar) The main branch of the tourist office.

Getting There & Away

BUS There are National Express coaches to/from most major towns, including Manchester (£6.30, 1¼ hours, hourly), and London (£25.60, five to six hours, six daily).

TRAIN Liverpool's main station is Lime St, with hourly services to London (£65, 3¼ hours) and Manchester (£9, 45 minutes).

Lake District National Park

A dramatic landscape of high peaks, dizzying ridges and huge lakes gouged by the march of Ice Age glaciers, the Lake District is a beautiful corner of Britain. It may not be the wildest place on earth, and there are much bigger mountains in Wales and Scotland, but for England it's as extreme as it gets. Not surprisingly, the awe-inspiring geography here shaped the literary persona of one of Britain's best-known poets, William Wordsworth. Principal gateways include the twin towns of Windermere and Bowness in the south, Ambleside slightly nearer the centre.

The Lake District is home to England's highest peak (Scafell; 978m), the wettest inhabited place (Seathwaite; over 3m of rain a year), and notoriously changeable weather conditions – which prove fatal to a few unready souls each year – so make sure you're prepared if you're heading for the hills

Sleeping & Eating

There's a host of B&Bs in the area, plus more than 20 YHA hostels, many of which can be linked by foot. The following is just the tip of the mountain.

WINDERMERE & BOWNESS

POP 8430

Windermere – the lake and the town of the same name – has been a centre for Lakeland tourism since the first steam trains arrived in 1847. The town of Windermere is 1½ miles uphill from the lake, and bustling Bowness is on the shore, where a bevy of boat trips and teashops jostle for space. Here is a selection of places to stay:

Lake District Backpackers Lodge HOSTEL £
(☎015394-46374; www.lakedistrictbackpackers.co.uk; High St; dm £15-17; @) A little underwhelming, with cramped dorms, but it's cheap, near Windermere train station and the managers organise local biking/hiking trips.

Number 80 Bed Then Breakfast B&B ££
(☎015394-43584; www.number80bed.co.uk; 80 Craig Walk; d £80-90; 📶) A lovely little bolthole in Bowness.

AMBLESIDE

POP 3380

Windermere and Bowness are tourist towns, but Ambleside is for walkers and outdoor types, and the start-point of several classic hikes on the surrounding hills.

TOP CHOICE **Ambleside YHA** HOSTEL £
(☎0845-371 9620; www.yha.org.uk; Windermere Rd; dm from £14; 📶) Thanks to a recent refit, this place has excellent rooms and facilities, plus top lake views and a host of organised activities.

Ambleside Backpackers HOSTEL £
(☎015394-32340; www.englishlakesbackpackers.co.uk; Old Lake Rd; dm £16; @) Cottage hostel a short walk south from town.

Gables B&B ££
(☎015394-33272; www.thegables-ambleside.co.uk; Church Walk; s £40-50, d £60-80) This double-fronted house is in a quiet spot overlooking the recreation ground.

Information

Ambleside (☎015394-32582; tic@thehubofambleside.com; Central Buildings, Market Cross; ⌚9am-5pm)

Bowness (☎015394-42895; bownesstic@lake-district.gov.uk; Glebe Rd; ⌚9.30am-5.30pm Easter-Oct, 10am-4pm Fri-Sun Nov-Mar)

Windermere (☎015394-46499; windermeretic@southlakeland.gov.uk; Victoria St; ⌚9am-5.30pm Mon-Sat, 9.30am-5.30pm Sun Apr-Oct)

Getting There & Around

TRAIN To reach the Lakes by rail, take any stopping train on the main line between London and Glasgow, change at Oxenholme, from where regular trains run to Windermere.

BUS National Express coaches run direct from London and Glasgow (and various other towns around Britain) to Windermere.

For getting around the Lakes, the most useful bus routes include 555 (Lakeslink) between Lancaster and Carlisle, across the heart of the Lakes via all the main towns.

SOUTH & WEST WALES

Lying to the west of England, the nation of Wales is a separate country within the state of Great Britain. It's a nation with Celtic roots, its own language and a rich historic legacy. While some areas in the south are undeniably scarred by coal mining, overall Wales boasts a landscape of wild mountains, rolling hills, rich farmland and some beautiful beaches. If you're on a long tour, South Wales is most easily reached from southern or central England, and is well worth the diversion.

Cardiff

The capital of Wales since only 1955, Cardiff has embraced its new role with vigour, emerging as one of Britain's leading urban centres. Caught between its ancient castle and its ultramodern waterfront, this compact city has entered the new millennium with confidence, flexing its architectural muscles as if it's still astonished to have them. Day or night, a definite buzz reverberates through the streets.

Sights

CENTRAL CARDIFF

Cardiff Castle CASTLE
(www.cardiffcastle.com; Castle St; admission £8.95; ⌚9am-6pm Mar-Oct, 9am-5pm Nov-Feb) Victorian mock-Gothic extravagance and genuine Norman relics makes Cardiff Castle a leading attraction. It's far from a traditional Welsh castle but it neatly encompasses the city's history.

Millennium Stadium STADIUM
(☎029-2082 2228; www.millenniumstadium.com; Westgate St; admission & tour £6.50; ⌚10am-5pm Mon-Sat, 10am-4pm Sun) This spectacular stadium squats like a stranded spaceship in the heart of the city – and in this rugby mad nation somehow gets away with it.

CARDIFF BAY

The redeveloped dockland of Cardiff Bay is about 2 miles from the city centre, lined with bars, restaurants and shops – and a collection of stunning buildings

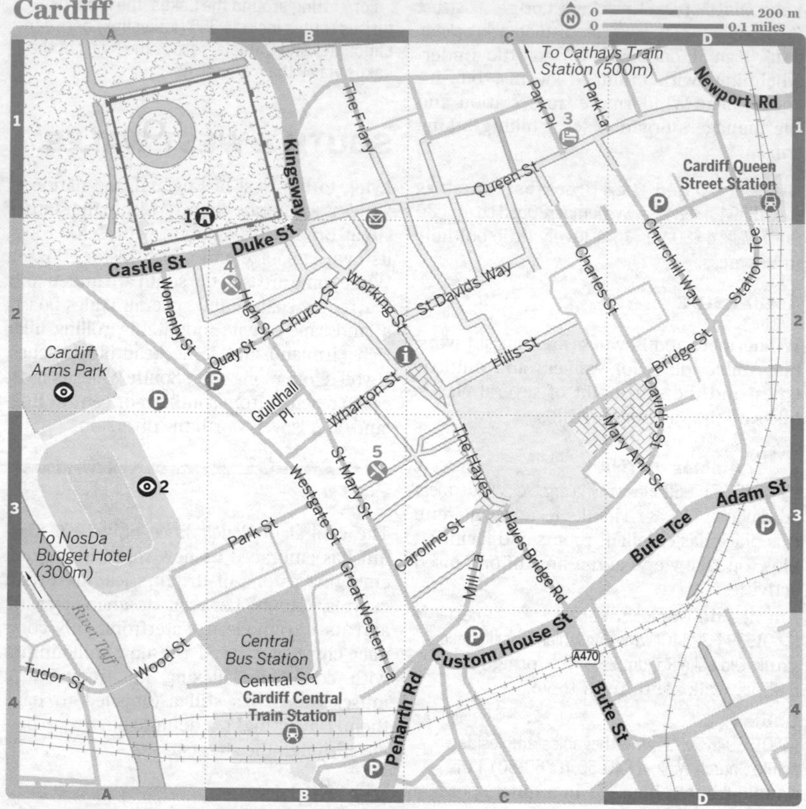

BRITAIN SOUTH & WEST WALES

Cardiff

Sights

1 Cardiff Castle A1
2 Millennium Stadium A3

Sleeping

3 Parc Hotel C1

Eating

4 Goat Major B2
5 Plan B3

FREE Wales Millennium Centre ARTS CENTRE
(029-2063 6464; www.wmc.org.uk) This architectural masterpiece of slate and bronze is the premier arts complex of Wales.

FREE Senedd (National Assembly Building) NOTABLE BUILDING
(0845-010 5500; www.assemblywales.org/sen-home; 10.30am-4.30pm) This striking structure is home to the Welsh National Assembly. The lobby and surrounding area is littered with public artworks.

FREE Pierhead MUSEUM
(0845-010 5500; www.pierhead.org; 10.30am-4.30pm Mon-Fri & most weekends) One of the area's few Victorian remnants, this red-brick building with its famous clock tower is a long-time Cardiff icon.

Sleeping & Eating

TOP CHOICE NosDa Budget Hotel HOSTEL £
(029-2037 8866; www.nosda.co.uk; 53-59 Despenser St; dm/tw from £19/43; @) You won't find a better budget bed any closer to the city centre than this hostel right across the river from the Millennium Stadium.

Parc Hotel HOTEL ££
(0871-376 9011; www.thistle.com/theparchotel; Park Place; r from £99; @) A smart contem-

porary hotel located right at the heart of the main shopping area, with tasteful rooms, good facilities and helpful staff.

Plan CAFE £
(28 Morgan Arcade; mains £5-8; 9am-5pm) Serving quite possibly Wales' best coffee, and specialises in healthy, organic, locally sourced food.

Goat Major PUB £
(33 High St; mains £7-8; food noon-6pm Mon-Sat, noon-4pm Sun) A solidly traditional pub with local ale and a fine selection of homemade pies.

Information

Cardiff Bay Visitor Centre (029-2087 7927; 10am-6pm)
Tourist office (029-2087 3573; www.visitcardiff.com; The Hayes; 9.30am-5.30pm Mon-Sat, 10am-4pm Sun; @)

Getting There & Away

BUS National Express coach destinations include Fishguard (£10, three hours), Brecon (£4.10, 1¼ hours) and London (£22, 3¼ hours).

TRAIN Direct services from Cardiff include London Paddington (£43, 2¾ hours) and Fishguard Harbour (£20, 2¼ hours).

Pembrokeshire Coast National Park

At the far southwest tip of Wales sits the beautiful Pembrokeshire Coast National Park (Parc Cenedlaethol Arfordir Sir Benfro), covering the cliffs and beaches of the coast and its offshore islands, as well as the Preseli Hills and Daugleddau waterway inland. Good bases include St Davids. For wider travels, ferries leave the port of Goodwick near Fishguard bound for Ireland.

ST DAVIDS

POP 1800

St Davids (yes, it has dropped the apostrophe from its name) is Britain's smallest city, its status ensured by the magnificent 12th-century cathedral named for the nation's patron saint – a place of pilgrimage for centuries. Today, St Davids is known for a laid-back vibe and the excellent hiking, surfing and wildlife-watching in the surrounding area. Our favourite places to eat and drink include the following.

TOP CHOICE **Ramsey House** B&B ££
(01437-720321; www.ramseyhouse.co.uk; Lower Moor; r £100;) Friendly and fresh B&B on the outskirts of town.

St Davids YHA HOSTEL £
(0845-371 9141; www.yha.org.uk; Llaethdy, Whitesands Bay) Former farmhouse tucked beneath Carn Llidi, 2 miles northwest of town, with snug dorms in the cow sheds.

Bench CAFE, BISTRO £
(www.bench-bar.co.uk; 11 High St; mains £5-17; 9am-late; @) Serving snacks, ice-cream and coffee during the day, and by night a bustling bar-bistro with a strong Mediterranean motif.

Farmer's Arms PUB
(14 Goat St) Authentic country pub, with a garden out back to watch the sun go down on a summer's evening.

Information

Fishguard (01437-776636; Town Hall, Market Sq; 10am-4pm Mon-Sat; @)
Goodwick (01348-874737; Ocean Lab; 10am-4pm; @)
St Davids (01437-720392; www.orielyparc.co.uk; 10am-4.30pm)

MID- & NORTH WALES

Mid-Wales is rural region with epic scenery and sturdy little market towns, while the landscape of North Wales is more mountainous and surrounded by a beautiful coastline – which makes it the more visited of the two regions (whereas Mid-Wales is way off the

MACHYNLLETH

Machynlleth (pronounced (ma-hun-khleth) is a small country town that punches well above its weight. It's rich in historical importance as the spot where nationalist hero Owain Glyndŵr defied the English to establish Wales's first parliament in 1404, and more recently the town has reinvented itself as a green capital and home to the **Centre for Alternative Technology** (www.cat.org.uk). The town boasts several good eating and sleeping options, and makes a good base for exploring the area; heading south from Machynlleth into Mid-Wales proper can be especially rewarding.

beaten track for most visitors). In many ways, North Wales distils the very essence of Welshness – you'll hear the language on the street, and see the Celtic legacy in the landscape – just don't mention that to the folks in Cardiff.

Snowdonia National Park

The jagged peaks of Snowdonia National Park (Parc Cenedlaethol Eryri) offer the most spectacular mountain scenery in Wales, and the most popular area is in the north around Snowdon (at 1085m the highest peak in Britain south of the Scottish Highlands) although the park extends all the way south to Machynlleth. For outdoor types, walking on the mountains is the main activity. For mountain bikers there are excellent trails in the surrounding forests. For more information see www.visit snowdonia.info.

Good bases and gateways include the busy village of Betws-y-Coed on the eastern side of the park. Most convenient for Snowdon itself is the town of Llanberis – less attractive, but with all the facilities you need.

BETWS-Y-COED

POP 950

This busy tourist town has a bit of an Alpine feel and plenty of accommodation options:

Betws-y-Coed YHA HOSTEL £
(01690-710796; www.yha.org.uk; Swallow Falls; dm from £16) A functional hostel and bustling traveller hub.

Maes-y-Garth B&B ££
(01690-710441; www.maes-y-garth.co.uk; Lon Muriau, off A470; r £66-70;) Just outside town, this new place has earned itself many fans, thanks to its warm welcome and quietly stylish rooms.

LLANBERIS & PEN-Y-PASS

POP 1900

Llanberis is a major hub for walkers and climbers, and the terminus for the Snowdon Mountain Railway. Yes, you can get to the top of the country's highest summit by *train*.

Pen-y-pass is no more than a car park, information centre and YHA hostel at the highest point on the road between Betws-y-Coed and Llanberis, but it's a popular start-point for walkers heading up Snowdon. At **Pen-y-Pass YHA**, (0845-371 9534; www.yha.org.uk; dm from £16), superbly situated on the slopes of Snowdon, guests can walk out the door and up the mountain.

DON'T MISS

CONWY

On the north coast of Wales, the historic town of Conwy is utterly dominated by the cultural treasure of **Conwy Castle** (Cadw; admission £4.60; 9am-5pm high season, 9.30am-4pm Mon-Sat & 11am-4pm Sun low season), the most stunning of all Edward I's Welsh fortresses, built between 1277 and 1307. Exploring the castle's nooks and crannies is great fun, before heading to the battlements for panoramic views. The 1200m-long town wall was built with the castle to guard Conwy's residents at night. Today you can walk part way round the wall for more excellent views; the best are to be had from Upper Gate.

Dolafon B&B, TEAROOMS ££
(01286-870993; www.dolafon.com; High St, Llanberis; s/d from £30/60) Set back from the road, this imposing 19th-century house has good traditional rooms.

Llanberis YHA HOSTEL £
(0845-371 9645; dm from £18) Former quarry manager's house on the slopes above the town.

Pete's Eats CAFE, BUNKHOUSE £
(01286-870117; www.petes-eats.co.uk; 40 High St, Llanberis; meals £4-6; @) A classic cafe and bunkhouse where hikers swap tips over monster portions in a hostel environment.

Information

Betws-y-Coed (01690-710426; www.betws-y-coed.co.uk; 9.30am-4.30pm)
Llanberis (01286-870765; 9.30am-4.30pm Apr-Oct, 9.30am-3pm Fri-Mon Nov-Mar)

Getting There & Around

The handiest train line runs along the North Wales coast between Chester and Holyhead, via Bangor (from where you can get buses into the park). An excellent local bus network called the **Snowdon Sherpa** serves the park, with connections to Betws-y-Coed, Bangor and Llanberis.

EDINBURGH & GLASGOW

The Scottish capital, Edinburgh, and neighbouring Glasgow, with several nearby towns, together make up the 'Central Belt'. For many years, visitors tended to favour Edinburgh and overlook Glasgow, but recently Scotland's second city has enjoyed a cultural and architectural renaissance. Rather than weighing up which of the two cities to see, it's well worth making the effort to fit them both on your itinerary.

Edinburgh

POP 440,000

Scotland's historic capital city is a visual delight, built on a grand scale around two hills – one topped by its impressive castle, the other a big chunk of undeveloped mountain seemingly helicoptered in for effect. Among the well-proportioned buildings and the tangle of walkways you'll find a rich haul of excellent museums, galleries, pubs, and entertainment options to suit every taste and budget. History jumps out at you at every turn, and every house seems to have its own ghost story. And with the UK's most popular and comprehensive summer festival scene, visitors who plan a brief stopover often end up staying longer.

Sights

Edinburgh's city centre is divided into two parts – Old Town and New Town – and most of the sights are here. A major exception is the Royal Yacht *Britannia*, in the redeveloped docklands district of Leith, 2 miles northeast of the centre.

Edinburgh Castle CASTLE
(www.edinburghcastle.gov.uk; Castle Hill; admission £14; 9.30am-6pm Apr-Sep, 9.30am-5pm Oct-Mar) Dominating the skyline like a city in the clouds, this historic hilltop fortress should be the first stop for any visitor. It's a mix of architectural styles, representing centuries of use. Highlights include **St Margaret's Chapel** (the oldest building in Edinburgh) and the **Royal Palace** (including the Stone of Destiny and the Scottish Crown Jewels).

If you're pushed for time, here's a hit list of the top things to see at Edinburgh Castle:

» Views from Argyle Battery
» One O'Clock Gun
» Great Hall
» Honours of Scotland
» Prisons of War

Real Mary King's Close HISTORIC BUILDING
(0845-070 6255; www.realmarykingsclose.com; 2 Warriston's Close, High St; admission £11; 10am-9pm Apr-Oct, to 11pm Aug, 10am-5pm Sun-Thu & 10am-9pm Fri & Sat Nov-Mar) This medieval Old Town alley survived untouched for 250 years, and now gives visitors a fascinating insight into 16th- and 17th-century daily life.

FREE **Scottish Parliament Building** LANDMARK
(0131-348 5200; www.scottish.parliament.uk; 9am-6.30pm Tue-Thu, 10am-5.30pm Mon & Fri in session, 10am-6pm Mon-Fri in recess Apr-Oct, 10am-4pm in recess Nov-Mar;) Scotland's own parliament opened in October 2005, and you can visit the public areas or take a free guided tour. The strange forms of the exterior are all symbolic, including the ground plan of the whole complex, which represents a 'flower of democracy rooted in Scottish soil'.

Palace of Holyroodhouse ROYAL PALACE
(www.royalcollection.org.uk; Canongate; admission £10.25; 9.30am-6pm Apr-Oct, 9.30am-4.30pm Nov-Mar) The royal family's official residence in Scotland, and most famous as the 16th-century home of the ill-fated Mary, Queen of Scots.

Holyrood Park PARK
The former hunting ground of Scottish monarchs – including crags, moorland and loch – bang in the heart of the city. The highest point is **Arthur's Seat**, giving an excellent view over Edinburgh.

Royal Yacht Britannia HISTORIC SHIP
(www.royalyachtbritannia.co.uk; Ocean Terminal, Leith; admission £10.50; 9.30am-6pm Jul-Sep, 10am-5.30pm Apr-Jun & Oct, 10am-5pm Nov-Mar) Two miles northeast of the city centre, Leith has been Edinburgh's seaport since the 14th century. Like many of Britain's dockland areas, it fell into decay but since the late 1980s has been undergoing a revival. This is where you will find one of Scotland's biggest tourist attractions: the former Royal Yacht *Britannia*, the British

FESTIVAL CITY

Edinburgh boasts a frenzy of festivals, especially in August with several world-class events running at the same time, including the Edinburgh International Festival, Edinburgh Festival Fringe, Edinburgh Military Tattoo and Edinburgh International Book Festival. For more see www.edinburghfestivals.co.uk.

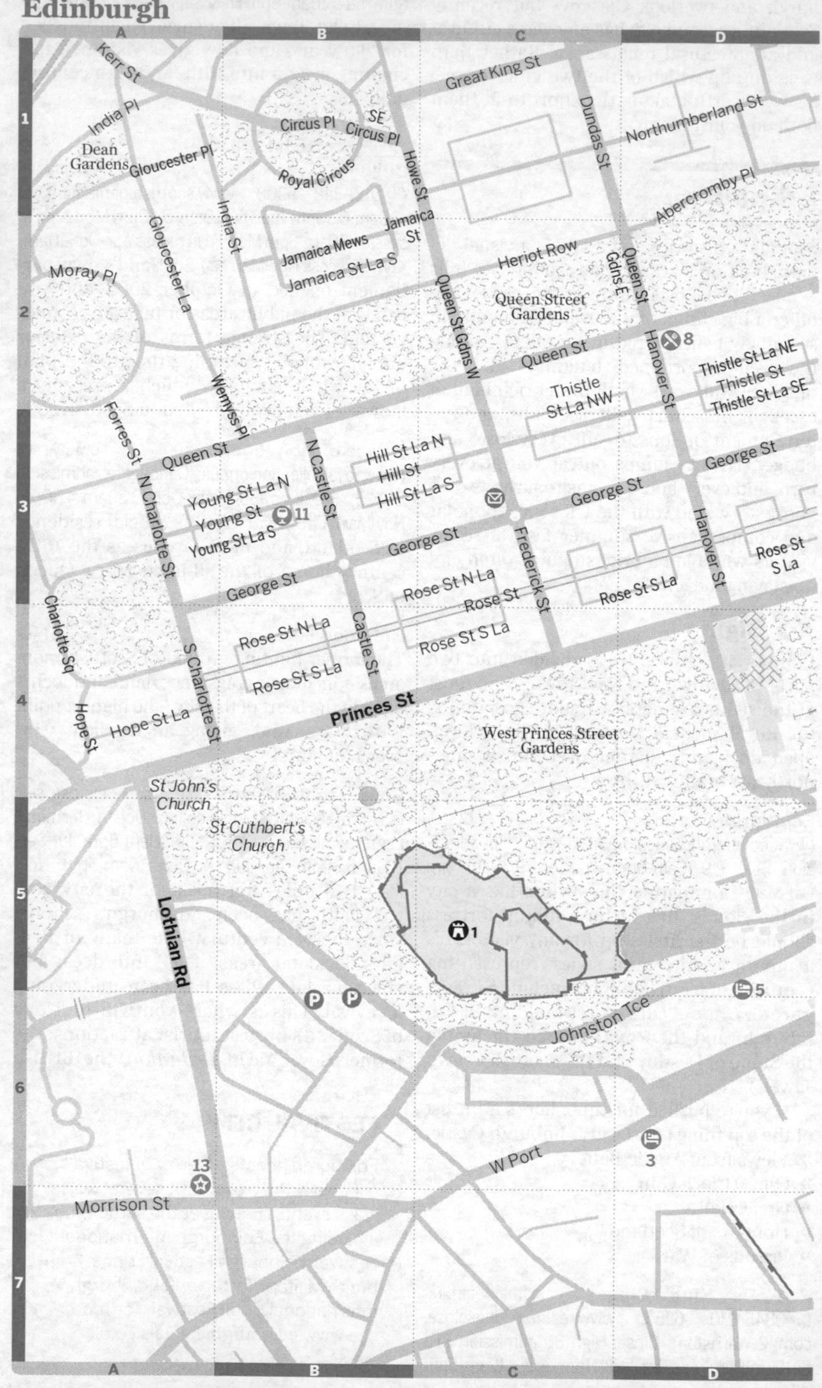

A
B
C
D
1
2
3
4
5
6
7
Kerr St
India Pl
Dean Gardens
Gloucester Pl
Circus Pl
SE Circus Pl
Royal Circus
Great King St
Howe St
Dundas St
Northumberland St
India St
Gloucester La
Jamaica St
Jamaica Mews
Jamaica St La S
Heriot Row
Abercromby Pl
Queen St Gdns E
Queen St
Moray Pl
Queen St Gdns W
Queen Street Gardens
8
Hanover St
Queen St
Thistle St La NE
Thistle St
Thistle St La SE
Thistle St La NW
Wemyss Pl
Forres St
Queen St
N Castle St
Hill St La N
Hill St
Hill St La S
George St
N Charlotte St
Young St La N
Young St
Young St La S
11
George St
Frederick St
George St
Rose St S La
George St
Charlotte Sq
Rose St N La
Rose St
Rose St S La
Castle St
Rose St N La
Rose St S La
S Charlotte St
Hope St
Hope St La
Princes St
West Princes Street Gardens
St John's Church
St Cuthbert's Church
1
Lothian Rd
5
P
P
Johnston Tce
3
13
W Port
Morrison St
A
B
C
D

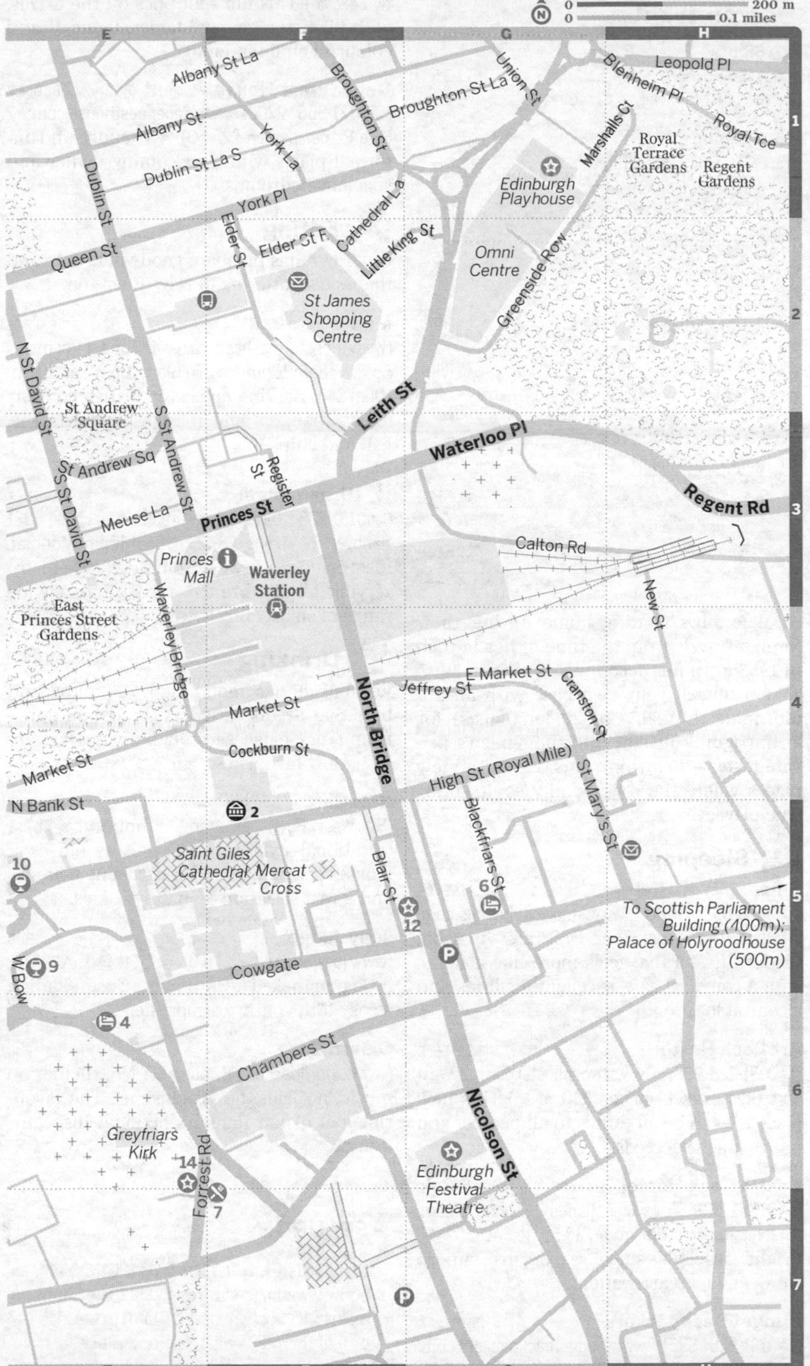

0 200 m
0 0.1 miles
E
F
G
H
Albany St La
Broughton St
Union St
Blenheim Pl
Leopold Pl
Broughton St La
Albany St
York La
Marshalls Ct
Royal Tce
Royal Terrace Gardens
Regent Gardens
Dublin St La S
Dublin St
Edinburgh Playhouse
York Pl
Cathedral La
Elder St
Elder St
Little King St
Omni Centre
Queen St
Greenside Row
St James Shopping Centre
N St David St
Leith St
St Andrew Square
S St Andrew St
Waterloo Pl
St Andrew Sq
Register St
S St David St
Meuse La
Princes St
Regent Rd
Calton Rd
Princes Mall
Waverley Station
New St
East Princes Street Gardens
Waverley Bridge
E Market St
Jeffrey St
Cranston St
North Bridge
Market St
Cockburn St
Market St
High St (Royal Mile)
St Mary's St
N Bank St
2
Blackfriars St
Saint Giles Cathedral
Mercat Cross
10
Blair St
6
To Scottish Parliament Building (400m); Palace of Holyroodhouse (500m)
12
Cowgate
W Bow
9
4
Chambers St
Nicolson St
Greyfriars Kirk
Forrest Rd
14
7
Edinburgh Festival Theatre
1
2
3
4
5
6
7

Edinburgh

Sights
1 Edinburgh Castle C5
2 Real Mary King's Close F5

Sleeping
3 Art Roch Hostel D6
4 Budget Backpackers E6
5 Castle Rock Hostel D5
6 Smart City Hostel G5

Eating
7 Mums F7
8 Urban Angel D2

Drinking
9 Bow Bar E5
10 Jolly Judge E5
11 Oxford Bar B3

Entertainment
12 Cabaret Voltaire G5
13 Henry's Cellar A6
14 Sandy Bell's E6

royal family's floating home during their foreign travels from the time of her launch in 1953 until her decommissioning in 1997. Take a tour at your own pace with an audio guide (available in 20 languages) for an intriguing insight into the Queen's private tastes – *Britannia* was one of the few places where the royal family could enjoy true privacy.

Sleeping

Smart City Hostel HOSTEL ££
(☎0870-892 3000; www.smartcityhostels.com; 50 Blackfriars St; dm £9-22, tw £80; @) A big modern hostel that feels more like a hotel, with a convivial cafe, excellent facilities and a central location.

Art Roch Hostel HOSTEL £
(☎0131-228 9981; www.artrochhostel.com; 2 West Port, Grassmarket; dm from £10; @) This new place tries to be all things to all people, and pretty much succeeds.

Castle Rock Hostel HOSTEL £
(☎0131-225 9666; www.scotlands-top-hostels.com; 15 Johnston Tce; dm from £13.50, d £40-55; @) Bright, spacious, single-sex dorms, superb views and a great location.

Budget Backpackers HOSTEL £
(☎0131-226 6351; www.budgetbackpackers.com; 39 Cowgate, The Grassmarket; dm from £12.50-16, tw £48; @) This fun spot piles on the extras, with bike storage, pool tables, laundry, and colourful chill-out lounge.

Dene Guest House B&B ££
(☎0131-556 2700; www.deneguesthouse.com; 7 Eyre Pl; per person £25-50) A friendly and informal place, with a welcoming owner and spacious bedrooms.

Eating

Old Town has plenty of good-value eats and there's a smattering in New Town too.

Mums CAFE £
(www.monstermashcafe.co.uk; 4a Forrest Rd; mains £6-8; ⊙8am-10pm Mon-Fri, 9am-10pm Sat, 10am-10pm Sun) Serving up classic British comfort food – bangers and mash, shepherd's pie, fish and chips.

Urban Angel CAFE £
(☎0131-225 6215; www.urban-angel.co.uk; 121 Hanover St; mains £8-12; ⊙9am-10pm Mon-Sat, 10am-5pm Sun) A wholesome deli-cafe-bistro serving all-day brunch, tapas, and a wide range of snacky meals.

Drinking

Edinburgh has more than 700 pubs and bars that are as varied as the population – from fancy palaces to rough dives. Here are just a few favourites:

Bow Bar PUB
(80 West Bow) One of Edinburgh's best traditional-style pubs (it's not as old as it looks) serving a range of excellent real ales and a vast selection of malt whiskies.

Jolly Judge PUB
(www.jollyjudge.co.uk; 7a James Ct;) A snug little pub tucked away down a close, exuding a cosy 17th-century atmosphere.

Oxford Bar PUB
(www.oxfordbar.com; 8 Young St) No 'theme', no music, no frills, no pretensions. The favourite spot of Ian Rankin's fictional Inspector Rebus.

SPLURGE

Cosy little **Fishers Bistro** (☎0131-554 5666; www.fishersbistros.co.uk; 1 The Shore; mains £10-35; ⊙noon-10.30pm) in Leith is one of the city's best seafood places.

✩ Entertainment

To see what's on, get a copy of *The List* – covering both Edinburgh and Glasgow – or check out www.list.co.uk.

Henry's Cellar LIVE MUSIC
(www.theraft.org.uk; 8a Morrison St) One of Edinburgh's most eclectic live-music venues.

Sandy Bell's LIVE MUSIC
(25 Forrest Rd) This unassuming bar has been a stalwart of the traditional-music scene for decades.

Cabaret Voltaire CLUB
(www.thecabaretvoltaire.com; 36 Blair St) Edinburgh's most alternative club, eschewing huge dance floors in favour of a 'creative crucible' of DJs, live acts, comedy, theatre and visual arts.

Information

Edinburgh & Scotland Information Centre
(ESIC; ☎0845-225 5121; www.edinburgh.org; Princes Mall, 3 Princes St; ⊙9am-9pm Mon-Sat, 10am-8pm Sun Jul & Aug, reduced hours rest of year)

Getting There & Away

Air

Edinburgh Airport (☎0131-333 1000; www.edinburghairport.com), 8 miles west of the city, has numerous flights to other parts of Britain, Ireland and mainland Europe.

Bus

Scottish Citylink (☎0871 266 3333; www.citylink.co.uk) coaches connect Edinburgh with all Scotland's cities and major towns. The following are sample one-way fares:

Fort William £30, four to five hours, eight daily
Glasgow £6, 1¼ hours, every 15 minutes
Inverness £26, four hours, hourly
Stirling £7, one hour, hourly

Megabus (☎0900 160 0900; www.megabus.com) offers intercity coaches from as little as £3, including Edinburgh to Glasgow and Inverness.

Train

The main terminus is Waverley train station, located in the heart of the city. Trains arriving from, and departing for, the west also stop at Haymarket station.

First ScotRail operates a regular shuttle service between Edinburgh and Glasgow (£11, 50 minutes, every 15 minutes), and frequent daily services to all Scottish cities including Aberdeen (£40, 2½ hours), Dundee (£20, 1¼ hours) and Inverness (£55, 3¼ hours).

Glasgow

POP 634,700

Unpretentious and gregarious, Glasgow defines urban renewal. Gone are the rusting relics of a moribund shipbuilding industry, to be replaced by absorbing attractions that celebrate that very heritage. Add to this Scotland's premier eating scene, northern Britain's best range of live music, cutting-edge nightclubs, a vibrant gay culture, and an amazing collection of pubs and bars, and a night or two in Glasgow could be a highlight of your trip.

Sights

Glasgow's main square in the city centre is grand **George Sq**, built in the Victorian era to show off the city's wealth – dignified by statues of notable Scots, including Robert Burns, James Watt and Sir Walter Scott. The prosperity of Glasgow's 18th-century 'tobacco lords' is reflected in the grand buildings southeast of George Sq, now known as the **Merchant City**; many renewed as stylish apartments, bars and restaurants.

Glasgow School of Art NOTABLE BUILDING
(☎0141-353 4526; www.gsa.ac.uk/tours; 167 Renfrew St; admission £8.75; ⊙9.30am-6.30pm Apr-Sep, 10am-5pm Oct-Mar) The architect and designer Charles Rennie Mackintosh is a Glasgow icon, and this is one of his greatest buildings, still fulfilling its original function.

FREE **Kelvingrove Art Gallery & Museum** MUSEUM
(www.glasgowmuseums.com; Argyle St; 10am-5pm Mon-Thu & Sat, 11am-5pm Fri & Sun) In Glasgow's West End, this magnificent cathedral of culture has been revamped into an unusual museum with an amazing variety of exhibits.

Glasgow Science Centre MUSEUM
(www.glasgowsciencecentre.org; 50 Pacific Quay; admission £10; ⊙10am-5pm) Once a thriving ship-building area, the River Clyde sank into dereliction in the 1980s. Its rejuvenation has been spearheaded by projects such as this, bringing science and technology alive through hundreds of interactive exhibits.

Sleeping

Euro Hostel HOSTEL £
(☎0141-222 2828; www.euro-hostels.co.uk; 318 Clyde St; dm £15-25, s £35-50, d £40-70; @☜)

With hundreds of beds, this mammoth hostel is handily close to the station and centre. While it feels a bit institutional, it has excellent facilities.

McLay's Guesthouse B&B ££
(☎0141-332 4796; www.mclays.com; 260 Renfrew St; s/d £36/56, without bathroom £28/48, @📶) The string of cheapish guest houses along the western end of Renfrew St are a mixed bag but this is among the best of them.

Glasgow SYHA HOSTEL £
(☎0141-332 3004; www.syha.org.uk; 8 Park Tce; dm/tw £23/62; @📶) Perched on a hill overlooking Kelvingrove Park in a charming town house, this place is simply fabulous and one of Scotland's best official hostels. Dorms are mostly four to six beds with padlock lockers and all have their own bathroom – very posh.

Alamo Guest House B&B ££
(☎0141-339 2395; www.alamoguesthouse.com; 46 Gray St; d £84, s/d/tw without bathroom £42/64/68; 📶) The Alamo may not sound like a peaceful spot, but it feels miles from the hustle of the city, with the city centre and West End still a walkable distance. The decor is an enchanting mixture of antique and

Glasgow

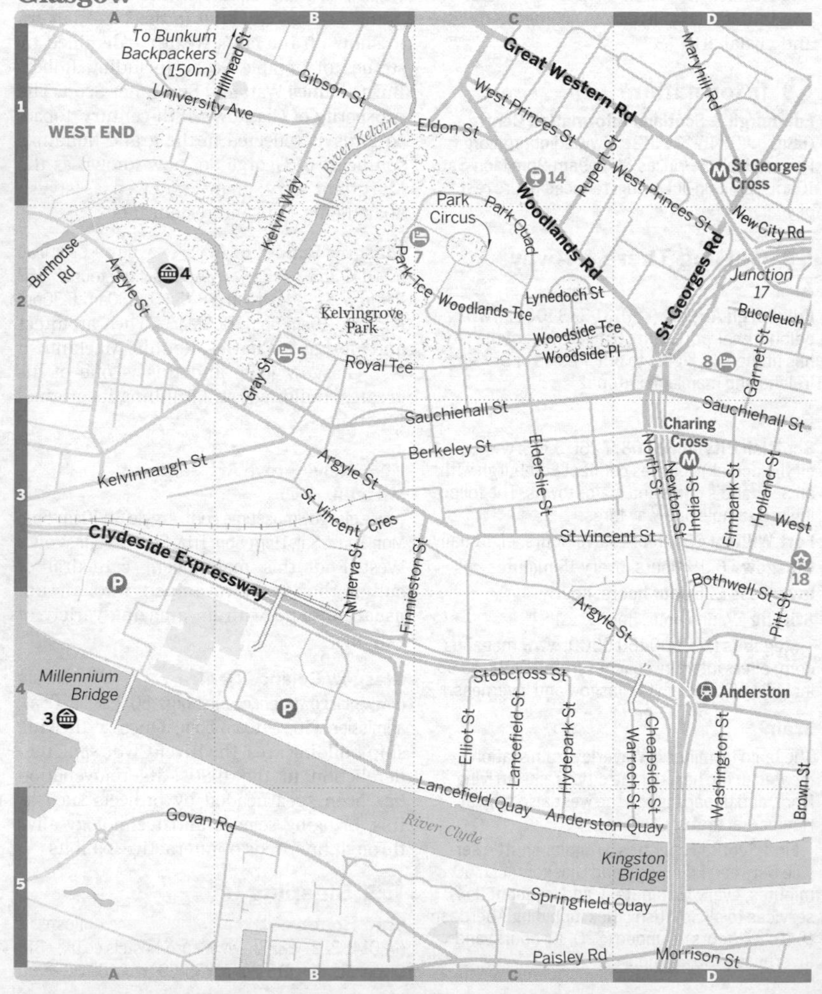

modern, and the breezy owners will make you very welcome.

Bunkum Backpackers HOSTEL ££
(☎0141-581 4481; www.bunkumglasgow.co.uk; 26 Hillhead St; dm/tw £14/36; 📶) A tempting budget headquarters for assaults on the eateries and pubs of the West End. There's no curfew, but it's not a party hostel.

Eating & Drinking

The West End is the culinary centre of the city, with Merchant City also boasting an incredible concentration of restaurants, cafes, pubs and bars.

Where the Monkey Sleeps CAFE £
(www.monkeysleeps.com; 182 West Regent St; dishes £5-7; ⏰7am-5pm Mon-Fri, 10am-5pm Sat) This funky little number in the city centre is just what you need to get away from the ubiquitous coffee chains.

Mono VEGETARIAN £
(www.myspace.com/monoglasgow; 12 Kings Ct, King St; mains £3-8; ⏰lunch, dinner) Combining food with music, Mono is one of Glasgow's best vegetarian-vegan eateries.

Café Gandolfi CAFE-BISTRO ££
(☎0141-552 6813; 64 Albion St; mains £8-14; ⏰9am-11.30pm Mon-Sat, noon-11.30pm Sun) In

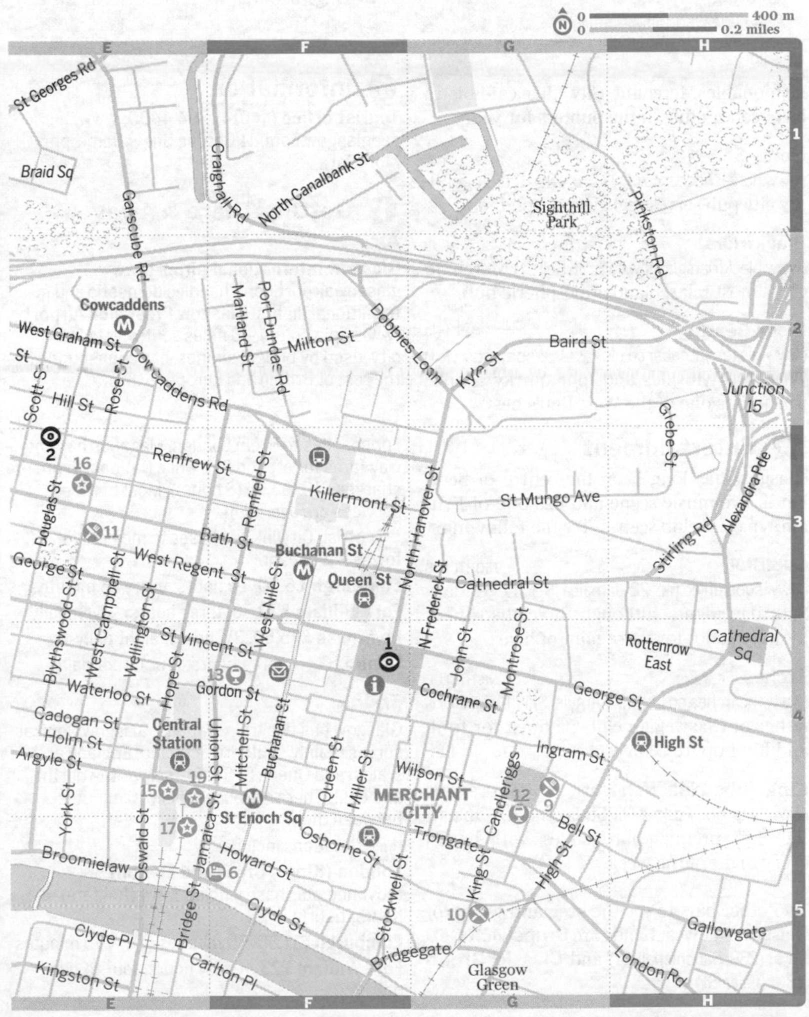

Glasgow

Sights
1 George Square F4
2 Glasgow School of Art E3
3 Glasgow Science Centre A4
4 Kelvingrove Art Gallery & Museum A2

Sleeping
5 Alamo Guest House B2
6 Euro Hostel F5
7 Glasgow SYHA C2
8 McLay's Guest House D2

Eating
9 Café Gandolfi G4
10 Mono G5
11 Where the Monkey Sleeps E3

Drinking
12 Blackfriars G4
13 Horse Shoe F4
14 Uisge Beatha C1

Entertainment
15 Arches E4
16 Brunswick Cellars E3
17 Classic Grand E5
18 King Tut's Wah Wah Hut D3
19 Sub Club E4

fashionable Merchant City, this cafe-bistro has been pulling in the punters for years.

Horse Shoe PUB
(www.horseshoebar.co.uk; 17 Drury St) This legendary city pub serves real ale and good food.

Blackfriars PUB
(www.blackfriarsglasgow.com; 36 Bell St) Merchant City's most relaxed and atmospheric pub.

Uisge Beatha PUB
(www.uisgebeathabar.co.uk; 232 Woodlands Rd) With 100 whiskies and four quirky rooms, this pub is one of the West End's best.

Entertainment

Glasgow has long been the centre of Scotland's live-music scene and has one of Britain's biggest club scenes. Try the following:

Sub Club NIGHTCLUB
(www.subclub.co.uk; 22 Jamaica St) Legendary Saturday nights, although the claustrophobic vibe is not for those faint of heart.

Arches NIGHTCLUB
(www.thearches.co.uk; 253 Argyle St) The Godfather of Glaswegian clubs; a must for funk and hip-hop freaks.

King Tut's Wah Wah Hut LIVE MUSIC
(www.kingtuts.co.uk; 272a St Vincent St) One of the city's premier pub venues, with bands every night of the week.

Two other bars to see the best, and worst, of Glasgow's newest bands are **Brunswick Cellars** (239 Sauchiehall St) and **Classic Grand** (18 Jamaica St).

Information

Tourist office (☎0141-204 4400; www.seeglasgow.com; 11 George Sq; ⊙9am-5pm Mon-Sat)

Getting There & Away

Air

Glasgow International Airport (www.glasgowairport.com) handles domestic and international flights. **Glasgow Prestwick Airport** (www.gpia.co.uk), 30 miles southwest of the city, used by budget airlines, has connections to the rest of Britain and Europe.

Bus

For coaches to/from London, Megabus has one-way fares for around £11; while National Express charges £10 to £35 (8 hours). Most of these services are overnight.

Scottish Citylink has buses to most major towns in Scotland.

Edinburgh £6.30, 1¼ hours, every 15 minutes
Fort William £20.50, three hours, seven daily
Inverness £25.50, 3½ hours, eight daily
Oban £16.40, three hours, four direct daily

Train

Glasgow has two train stations: Glasgow Central serves mainly southern Scotland, England and Wales, and Queen St Station serves the north and east. There are buses every 10 minutes between them.

Destinations include:

London (King's Cross and Euston) £60 (advance purchase single), £144 (full fare), 4½ hours, hourly
Edinburgh £11.50, 50 minutes, every 15 minutes
Fort William £23.40, 3¾ hours, four to five daily

Inverness £70.40, 3½ hours, 10 daily, four on Sundays

Oban £19.30, three hours, three to four daily

CENTRAL SCOTLAND

Central Scotland is less a geographical region, more a catch-all term for everything between the Glasgow–Edinburgh conurbation and the northwest Highlands. Anything you ever dreamed about Scotland you can find here: lochs, hills, castles, whisky distilleries and some truly beautiful islands.

Loch Lomond

The 'bonnie banks' and 'bonnie braes' of Loch Lomond have long been Glasgow's rural retreat, and today the loch's popularity shows no sign of decreasing. The main tourist focus is on the loch's western shore, along the A82. The southern end, around Balloch, is busy. The eastern shore, followed by the West Highland Way long-distance footpath, is a little quieter. The region's importance was recognised in 2002 when it became the heart of **Loch Lomond & the Trossachs National Park** (www.lochlomond-trossachs.org).

Sleeping

Loch Lomond SYHA HOSTEL £
(01389-850226; www.syha.org.uk; Arden; dm £18; Mar-Oct; @) Forget about roughing it, this is one of the most impressive hostels in the country – an imposing 19th-century country house set in beautiful grounds overlooking the loch. It's 2 miles north of Balloch and very popular, so book in advance in summer. And yes, it *is* haunted.

Information

National Park Gateway Centre (01389-751035; www.lochlomondshores.com; Loch Lomond Shores, Balloch; 10am-6pm Apr-Sep, 10am-5pm Nov-Mar; @)

Getting There & Away

BUS First Glasgow buses 204 and 215 run from Argyle St in central Glasgow to Balloch and Loch Lomond Shores (1½ hours, at least two per hour). Scottish Citylink coaches from Glasgow to Oban and Fort William stop at Luss on the loch's western shore (£8, 55 minutes, six daily).

TRAIN There are frequent trains from Glasgow to Balloch (£4.15, 45 minutes, every 30 minutes).

Stirling

POP 32,700

With an utterly impregnable position atop a mighty crag, Stirling's beautifully preserved old town is a treasure of noble buildings and cobbled streets winding up to the ramparts of its dominant castle. Also here is the brooding Wallace Monument, honouring the giant freedom fighter of *Braveheart* fame.

Sights

Stirling Castle CASTLE
(www.historic-scotland.gov.uk; 9.30am-6pm Apr-Sep, to 5pm Oct-Mar) Hold Stirling and you control Scotland. This maxim has ensured that a fortress of some kind has existed here since prehistoric times. Commanding superb views, you cannot help drawing parallels with Edinburgh Castle, but many find Stirling's fortress more atmospheric; the location, architecture and historical significance combine to make it a grand and memorable visit.

Sleeping

Willy Wallace Backpackers Hostel HOSTEL £
(01786-446773; www.willywallacehostel.com; 77 Murray Pl; dm/tw £17/36; @) This highly convenient hostel is friendly, spacious and sociable, with colourful dorms, free tea and coffee, a good kitchen and a laissez-faire atmosphere.

Stirling SYHA HOSTEL £
(01786-473442; www.syha.org.uk; St John St; dm/tw £17.25/45; @) Right in the old town, this hostel has an unbeatable location and great facilities.

Information

Tourist office (01786-475019; stirling@visitscotland.com; 41 Dumbarton Rd; 10am-5pm Mon-Sat year-round, plus Sun Jun–mid-Sep; @)

Getting There & Away

BUS Citylink offers services to/from Edinburgh (£7, one hour, hourly) and Glasgow (£6.50, 45 minutes, hourly).

TRAIN ScotRail has services to/from Edinburgh (£6.90, 55 minutes, at least hourly) and Glasgow (£7.10, 40 minutes, at least hourly).

Oban

POP 8120

Oban is a peaceful waterfront town on a delightful bay, and the main gateway to the western islands – especially Mull. As befits a ferry town, Oban has lots of B&B accommodation. Our recommendations include the following.

Oban Backpackers Lodge HOSTEL £
(☎01631-562107; www.obanbackpackers.com; Breadalbane St; dm £12.50-13.50; @☎) A friendly place with nice atmosphere, good facilities and a large lounge with lots of sofas.

Barriemore Hotel B&B ££
(☎01631-566356; www.barriemore-hotel.co.uk; Corran Esplanade; s/d from £65/92) With a grand location overlooking Oban Bay and spacious rooms (ask for a sea view).

Information

Tourist office (☎01631-563122; www.oban.org.uk; Argyll Sq; ⊙9am-7pm daily Jul & Aug, 9am-5.30pm Mon-Sat & 10am-5pm Sun May, Jun & Sep, 9am-5.30pm Mon-Sat Oct-Apr)

Getting There & Away

The bus, train and ferry terminals are all grouped conveniently together next to the harbour on the southern edge of the bay.

BOAT **CalMac** (www.calmac.co.uk) ferries link Oban with the islands of Mull, Coll, Tiree, and others.

BUS Scottish Citylink buses run to/from Glasgow (£17, three hours, four daily).

TRAIN Oban is at the terminus of a scenic route that branches off the West Highland line at Crianlarich. There are up to three trains daily to/from Glasgow (£19, three hours). If you're heading north, the train to Fort William takes a very roundabout route. You're better off travelling by bus.

Isle of Mull

POP 2600

The lovely island of Mull has beautiful and varied scenery. Add in two impressive castles, and easy access from Oban and it's a gem. Tobermory, the island's main town, is a picturesque little fishing port with brightly painted houses that are the setting for a children's TV program. Places to sleep include the following.

2 Victoria St B&B £
(☎01688-302263; 2 Victoria St; s/d without bathroom £25/40; ⊙Easter-Oct) Traditional, old-school B&B with simple, homely bedrooms and a friendly and hospitable owner.

Tobermory SYHA Hostel HOSTEL £
(☎01688-302481; www.syha.org.uk; Main St; dm £15; ⊙Mar-Oct; @) Great location in a Victorian house right on the waterfront. Bookings recommended.

> **THAR SHE BLOWS!**
>
> The North Atlantic Drift – a swirling tendril of the Gulf Stream – carries warm water into the nutrient-rich seas off the Scottish coast, resulting in huge blooms of plankton. Small fish feed on the plankton, and bigger fish feed on the smaller fish. And this seafood smorgasbord attracts large numbers of marine mammals: porpoises, dolphins, minke whales and even – though sightings are rare – humpback and sperm whales. Scotland has embraced the cetations, and dozens of operators around the coast offer boat trips. While seals, porpoises and dolphins can be seen year-round, minke whales are migratory. The best time to see them is from June to August, with August being the peak month for sightings. For more details see the website of the Hebridean Whale & Dolphin Trust (www.whaledolphintrust.co.uk).

Information

Tobermory tourist office (☎01688-302182; ⊙9am-6pm Mon-Sat & 10am-5pm Sun Jul & Aug, 9am-5pm Mon-Sat & 11am-5pm Sun May & Jun, shorter hours rest of year)

Getting There & Around

FERRY CalMac car ferries sail from Oban to Craignure, the island's main port (passenger/car £4/41, 40 minutes, every two hours).

BICYCLE You can hire bikes for £10 to £15 a day from:

Brown's Hardware Shop (☎01688-302020; www.brownstobermory.co.uk; Main St, Tobermory)

On Yer Bike (☎01680-300501; Inverinate, Salen) Also has an outlet by the ferry terminal at Craignure.

BUS **Bowman's Tours** (☎01680-812313; www.bowmanstours.co.uk) bus 495 runs from Craignure to Tobermory (£7 return, one hour, six daily Monday to Friday, four or five Saturday and Sunday).

St Andrews

POP 14,200

For a small place, St Andrews has made a big name for itself, firstly as a religious centre, then as Scotland's oldest university town, and then as the home of golf. But it's a lovely place to visit even if you've no interest in the game, with impressive medieval ruins, stately buildings, idyllic white sands, and excellent accommodation and eating options.

Sights

British Golf Museum MUSEUM
(www.britishgolfmuseum.co.uk; Bruce Embankment; admission £6; 9.30am-5pm Mon-Sat & 10am-5pm Sun Apr-Oct, 10am-4pm Nov-Mar) An extraordinarily comprehensive overview of the history and development of the game, and the role of St Andrews in that development, plus a large collection of memorabilia. Opposite the museum is the **Royal & Ancient Golf Club**, which stands proudly at the head of the **Old Course**, which you can stroll on once play is finished for the day.

St Andrews Cathedral CATHEDRAL RUINS
You can wander freely around the atmospheric ruins of one of Britain's most magnificent medieval buildings, and still appreciate the scale and majesty.

St Andrews Castle CASTLE
(www.historic-scotland.gov.uk; admission £5; 9.30am-5.30pm Apr-Sep, to 4.30pm Oct-Mar) With dramatic coastline views, this ruined castle is very evocative.

Sleeping

TOP CHOICE **Abbey Cottage** B&B ££
(01334-473727; www.abbeycottage.co.uk; Abbey Walk; s £40, d £59-64) This engaging spot sits below the town, with a rambling garden. It feels like you are staying in the country.

St Andrews Tourist Hostel HOSTEL £
(01334-479911; www.standrewshostel.com; St Marys Pl; dm £13-14; wi-fi) Laid-back and central, this hostel is located in a stately old building and has a laissez-faire approach.

Eating

Grill House BISTRO £
(www.grillhouserestaurant.co.uk; St Mary's Pl; mains £6-15; lunch & dinner) This sometimes boisterous restaurant offers something for every taste and budget.

The Tailend BISTRO £
(130 Market St; mains £6-10; 9am-late) Delicious local fresh fish puts this place in a class above most chippies.

Information

Tourist office (01334-472021; www.visit-standrews.co.uk; 70 Market St; 9.15am-6.30pm Mon-Sat, 9.30am-5pm Sun Jul-Sep, reduced hours rest of year; @)

Getting There & Away

BUS There are frequent services to/from:

Edinburgh via Kirkcaldy £9.40, two hours, hourly

Glasgow £9.40, 2½ hours, hourly

Stirling £7.30, two hours, six to seven services Monday to Saturday

TRAIN There is no train station in St Andrews itself, but you can take a train from Edinburgh (grab a seat on the right-hand side of the carriage for great firth views) to Leuchars, 5 miles to the northwest (£11.20, one hour, hourly). From here, buses leave very regularly for St Andrews.

NORTHERN & WESTERN SCOTLAND

This area is a long way north and takes effort to reach, but is by far the best bit of Scotland, and one of the best bits of the whole of Britain too. Some folks (well, those that love mountains and wild places) would even say that it's one of the finest regions in the whole of Europe. It's easy to underestimate the scale of this part of Scotland, so give yourself extra time to explore. See www.visithighlands.com for transport and accommodation advice.

Inverness

POP 55,000

Inverness is the capital of the Highlands, a transport hub and jumping-off point, and one of the fastest growing towns in Britain. In summer it overflows with visitors from monster-hunting trips at nearby Loch Ness, but it's worth a visit for a stroll along the picturesque river or for a dolphin-spotting cruise on the Moray Firth.

Sleeping

There are lots of B&Bs along Old Edinburgh Rd and Ardconnel St on the east side of the river, and on Kenneth St and Fairfield Rd on the west side.

Bazpackers Backpackers Hotel HOSTEL £
(01463-717663; 4 Culduthel Rd; dm/tw £14/38; @) A quiet, friendly and hugely popular

place with a convivial lounge, a small garden and great views.

Inverness Millburn SYHA HOSTEL £
(☎01463-231771; www.syha.org.uk; Victoria Dr; dm £18.50; ⊙Apr-Dec; @📶) This modern 166-bed hostel is 10 minutes' walk northeast of the city centre. With its comfy beds and flashy stainless-steel kitchen, some reckon it's the best hostel in the country.

Ardconnel House B&B ££
(☎01463-240455; www.ardconnel-inverness.co.uk; 21 Ardconnel St; per person from £35; 📶) Comfortable en-suite rooms, a dining room with crisp white table linen, and a breakfast menu that includes Vegemite.

Eating & Drinking

TOP CHOICE **Clachnaharry Inn** PUB £
(www.clachnaharryinn.co.uk; 17-19 High St; Clachnaharry) Just over a mile northwest of the centre, on the bank of the Caledonian Canal, this delightful old coaching inn (with beer garden out back) serves an excellent range of real ales and good grub.

Café 1 BISTRO ££
(☎01463-226200; www.cafe1.net; 75 Castle St; mains £10-20; ⊙noon-2pm & 5.30-9.30pm Mon-Sat) This friendly and appealing little bistro has candlelit tables and an international menu based on quality Scottish produce.

Leakey's CAFE £
(Greyfriars Hall, Church St; ⊙10am-5.30pm Mon-Sat) Cafe in secondhand bookshop.

Information

Tourist office (☎01436-234353; www.visithighlands.com; Castle Wynd; ⊙9am-6pm Mon-Sat, 9.30am-5pm Sun Jul & Aug, reduced hours rest of year)

Getting There & Away

AIR Inverness Airport (www.hial.co.uk/inverness-airport) is at Dalcross, 10 miles east of the city. There are scheduled flights to London, Belfast, several Scottish islands and other parts of Britain.

BUS National Express operates a direct overnight bus to/from London (£45, 13 hours, one daily). Citylink has connections to Glasgow (£26, 3½ to 4½ hours, hourly), Edinburgh (£26, 3½ to 4½ hours, hourly), Fort William (£11, two hours, five daily), and Portree on the Isle of Skye (£17, 3½ hours, five daily).

TRAIN There are several trains a day to/from Glasgow (£55, 3½ hours) and Edinburgh (£55, 3¼ hours) and Aberdeen (£25, 2¼ hours). The line from Inverness to Kyle of Lochalsh, for the Isle of Skye, is one of Britain's great scenic train journeys (£18, 2½ hours, four daily Monday to Saturday, two Sunday).

Loch Ness

Deep, dark and narrow, Loch Ness stretches for 23 miles between Inverness and Fort Augustus. Its bitterly cold waters have been extensively explored in search of the elusive Loch Ness monster, but most visitors see her only in cardboard-cutout form at the monster exhibitions. The village of Drumnadrochit is a hotbed of beastie fever, with two monster exhibitions battling it out for the tourist dollar. The **Loch Ness Exhibition Centre** (www.loch-ness-scotland.com; admission £6.50/4.50; ⊙9am-6.30pm Jul & Aug, to 6pm Jun & Sep, 9.30am-5pm Feb-May & Oct, 10am-3.30pm Nov-Jan; 📶) is the better of the two Nessie-themed attractions, with a scientific approach that allows you to weigh up the evidence for yourself.

Getting There & Away

Scottish Citylink and Stagecoach buses from Inverness towards Fort William run along the shores of Loch Ness (six to eight daily, five on Sunday). The bus stops at Drumnadrochit (£6.20, 30 minutes) and Loch Ness Youth Hostel (£10, 45 minutes).

Fort William

POP 9910

Basking on the shores of Loch Linnhe amid magnificent mountain scenery, Fort William has one of the most enviable settings in the whole of Scotland. If it wasn't for the busy dual carriageway crammed between the town centre and the loch, and one of the highest rainfall records in the country, it would be almost idyllic. Even so, the self-proclaimed 'Outdoor Capital of the UK' (www.outdoorcapital.co.uk) is easy to reach by rail and bus, making it a good launch-pad for Highland exploration.

Sleeping &Eating

Fort William Backpackers HOSTEL £
(☎01397-700711; www.scotlands-top-hostels.com; Alma Rd; dm/tw from £14/38; @) A 10-minute walk from the bus and train stations, this lively and welcoming hostel is perched on a hillside with great views over Loch Linnhe.

Bank Street Lodge HOSTEL £
(☎01397-700070; www.bankstreet lodge.co.uk; Bank St; dm/tw £14.50/48) Part of a modern hotel-restaurant complex, this is the most central budget option.

Grange B&B ££
(☎01397-705516; www.grangefortwilliam.com; Grange Rd; r per person £56-59) An exceptional 19th-century villa set in landscaped grounds, crammed with antiques and fitted with log fires, chaise longues and Victorian roll-top baths.

Grog & Gruel PUB/RESTAURANT ££
(www.grogandgruel.co.uk; 66 High St; mains £9-12; ⏲bar meals noon-9pm, restaurant 5-9pm) A traditional pub with an excellent range of ales and a lively Tex-Mex restaurant upstairs.

Information

Tourist office (☎01397-703781; www.visithighlands.com; 15 High St; ⏲9am-6pm Mon-Sat, 10am-5pm Sun Apr-Sep, limited hours Oct-Mar)

Getting There & Away

BUS Scottish Citylink buses link Fort William with Glasgow (£21, three hours, eight daily), Edinburgh (£30, 4½ hours, one daily direct, seven with a change at Glasgow), Oban (£9, 1½ hours, three daily), Inverness (£11, two hours, five daily) and Portree on the Isle of Skye (£28, three hours, four daily).

TRAIN The spectacular West Highland line runs from Glasgow to Mallaig via Fort William. There are three trains daily (two on Sunday) from Glasgow to Fort William (£24, 3¾ hours), and four daily (three on Sunday) between Fort William and Mallaig (£10, 1½ hours). For long-haul adventures, the overnight **Caledonian Sleeper** service connects Fort William and London Euston (£30–60 per person one-way advance booking, from £110 standard single, 13 hours).

Isle of Skye

POP 9900

The Isle of Skye is the biggest of Scotland's islands, a 50-mile-long smorgasbord of velvet moors, jagged mountains, sparkling lochs and towering sea cliffs. It takes its name from the old Norse *sky-a*, meaning 'cloud island', a Viking reference to the often mist-enshrouded Cuillin Hills. The stunning scenery is the main attraction, but there are plenty of cosy pubs to retire to when the mist closes in.

Sleeping

Portree, the island's capital, has the largest selection of accommodation, places to eat and other services. A small selection of favourites is listed here, but there are many more hostels and B&Bs dotted around the island.

Bayfield Backpackers HOSTEL £
(☎01478-612231; www.skyehostel.co.uk; Bayfield; dm from £13; @📶) Clean, central and

CLIMBING BEN NEVIS

Looming over Fort William is Ben Nevis (1344m). As the highest peak in the British Isles, it attracts thousands of people who would not normally go anywhere near the summit of a Scottish mountain. Many get to the top with no trouble, but every year a surprisingly large number of people have to be rescued. Even if you're climbing 'the Ben' on a fine summer's day, the ascent should not be undertaken lightly. You will need proper walking boots (the path is rough and stony, and there may be wet snowfields on the summit), warm clothing, waterproofs, a map and compass, and plenty of food and water. And don't forget to check the weather forecast (see www.bennevisweather.co.uk). In thick cloud, visibility at the summit can be 10m or less; in such conditions the only safe way off the mountain requires careful use of a map and compass to avoid walking over 700m cliffs.

There are three possible starting points for the tourist track ascent (the easiest route to the top) – Achintee Farm; the footbridge at Glen Nevis Youth Hostel; and the car park at Glen Nevis Visitor Centre. The path climbs gradually to the shoulder at Lochan Meall an t-Suidhe (known as the Halfway Lochan), then zigzags steeply up beside the Red Burn to the summit plateau. The total distance to the summit and back is 8 miles; allow at least four or five hours to reach the top, and another 2½ to three hours for the descent. Afterwards, as you celebrate in the pub with a pint, consider the fact that the record time for the annual Ben Nevis Hill Race is just under 1½ hours – up *and* down. Then have another pint.

modern, this hostel provides the best backpacker accommodation in town. The friendly owner is a font of advice on what to do and where to go in Skye.

Bayview House B&B £
(☎01478-613340; www.bayviewhouse.co.uk; Bayfield; r per person from £23; 📶) This is a modern house with spartan but clean rooms. At this price and location, it's a bargain.

Ben Tianavaig B&B B&B ££
(☎01478-612152; www.ben-tianavaig.co.uk; 5 Bosville Tce; r £65-75; 📶) You'll get a warm welcome at this appealing B&B bang in the centre of town. All four bedrooms have a view across the harbour to the hill that gives the house its name.

Eating & Drinking

TOP CHOICE **Café Arriba** CAFE £
(www.cafearriba.co.uk; Quay Brae; dinner mains £10-13; 🕗7am-10pm May-Sep, 8am-5.30pm Oct-Apr) This funky little cafe has the best selection of vegetarian and carnivorous treats, plus excellent coffee.

Granary Bakery CAFE £
(Somerled Sq; light mains £5-8; 🕗8am-5pm Mon-Sat) Most of Portree seems to congregate at this cosy coffee shop to snack on tasty sandwiches, pies, cakes and pastries.

Information

Portree tourist office (☎01478-612137; Bayfield Rd, Portree; 🕗9am-6pm Mon-Sat & 10am-4pm Sun Jun-Aug, 9am-5pm Mon-Fri & 10am-4pm Sat Apr, May & Sep, limited opening Oct-Mar)

Getting There & Away

BOAT The island became permanently tethered to the Scottish mainland when the Skye Bridge opened in 1995. However, there's still a couple of ferry links; the main one is between Mallaig and Armadale (www.calmac.co.uk,driver or passenger £4, car £20, 30 minutes, five to eight sailings daily).

BUS Scottish Citylink runs buses from Glasgow to Portree (£38, seven hours, four daily) via Fort William. Buses also run from Inverness to Portree (£17, 3½ hours, five daily).

John O'Groats

POP 500

Mainland Britain's northeasterly extreme, John O'Groats is no more than a car park surrounded by tourist shops, and offers little to the visitor beyond a means to get across to Orkney. Even the famous pub has been shut for a while now (although there are a couple of cafes). John O'Groats is best known as the endpoint of the 874-mile trek from Land's End in Cornwall, a popular if arduous challenge for cyclists and walkers, many of whom raise money for charitable causes. If you see someone stagger in, give them a round of applause.

UNDERSTAND BRITAIN

History

It may be a small island on the edge of Western Europe, but Britain has never been on the sidelines of history. For thousands of years, invaders and incomers have arrived, settled and made their mark. The result is Britain's fascinating mix of landscape and culture – a dynamic pattern that shaped the nation and continues to evolve today.

In prehistoric times, the island now called Britain was populated by bands of hunter-gatherers, and changed significantly around 4000 BC when a group of migrants wielding new-fangled stone tools crossed the land-bridge from the European mainland. (Sea levels were lower then – and it was long before the Channel Tunnel). Perhaps the most enduring legacy left by these nascent Britons are the great stone circles of Avebury and Stonehenge, still visible today.

The next important migration was the Celts from central Europe, whose smelting skills launched a mini cultural revolution.

The main Roman invasion was in AD 43, and the legions quickly overcame local resistance to rule much of the province they called Britannia for the next 350 years. The Romans built temples, spas and forts that can still be seen in cities such as Bath and at Hadrian's Wall.

The Dark Ages

The Romans abandoned Britain in AD 410, and the province entered a period often called the Dark Ages. Local warlords fought over fiefdoms, but the vacuum didn't go unnoticed and once again invaders crossed from the European mainland – this time Germanic tribes called Angles and Saxons.

By the late 6th century much of southern and central Britain was predominantly Anglo-Saxon, divided into separate kingdoms dominated by Wessex (today's southern England), Mercia (central England) and Northumbria (northern England and southern Scotland), with the Celts pushed to the western and northern edges (today's Wales and northern Scotland).

Anglo-Saxon expansion forced the disparate tribes of Wales to band together and sow the seeds of nationhood. They called themselves cymry (fellow countrymen), and today Cymru is the Welsh word for Wales. Meanwhile, in the north of Britain, the local people, called the Picts, were invaded from the south by the Anglo-Saxons, and from the west by the Scotti tribe from Ireland – the latter group eventually became dominant and gave their name to the region we call Scotland.

Then yet again the island was invaded, by the Vikings (from modern-day Scandinavia) – and by the end of the first millennium they occupied large parts of northern and eastern England, making York their capital.

In the 9th century, the king of the Scotti declared himself ruler of all Scotland. The Stone of Destiny, now at Edinburgh Castle, was launched into legend as a symbol of nascent Scottish nationhood.

1066 & All That

Back in England things remained unsettled until the Battle of Hastings in 1066, when King William of Normandy landed his army on England's southern coast, and defeated the Saxons. Their king, Harold, was killed – according to legend by an arrow in the eye.

England's Norman rulers built an imposing network of hulking castles and astonishing cathedrals. Many architectural landmarks you'll see on your travels in Britain date from this period, such as Windsor Castle and Durham Cathedral, although of course they've undergone additions over the centuries.

After the Norman invasion England was racked with conspiracy as aristocratic families competed to influence the royal succession, and the era also introduced an enduring tendency of bickering between royalty and the church. This was epitomised in 1170 when King Henry II had 'turbulent priest' Thomas Becket murdered in Canterbury Cathedral.

In the 1270s King Edward I led a bloody invasion of Wales that ended with the defeat of Welsh Prince Llewellyn and with Wales becoming a dependent principality. But Edward had less luck in Scotland; in 1297, his army was routed by the Scots under William Wallace – still remembered today as the epitome of Scottish patriots.

Great Dynasties

By 1485 King Henry VII had been crowned, the first of the Tudor dynasty – a period characterised by the timber-framed buildings of towns such as Stratford-upon-Avon. For the next king, Henry VIII, fathering a male heir was a major problem (hence the famous six wives), but the Pope's disapproval of the king's intended divorce led to a split with the Roman Catholic Church.

Henry's daughter, Elizabeth I, had to overcome a nasty mess of religious strife and divided loyalties, but after an uncertain start she turned the country around. Highlights of her 45-year reign included the naval defeat of the Spanish Armada, the far-flung explorations of English seafarers Walter Raleigh and Francis Drake, the expansion of England's increasingly global trading network, and a cultural flourishing thanks to writers such as William Shakespeare.

Britain United

When Elizabeth I died in 1603, she was succeeded by the Scottish (and Protestant) King James. He became James I of England and VI of Scotland, uniting England, Wales and Scotland into one kingdom. The next step came in 1707, when the Act of Union was passed, bringing an end to the independent Scottish Parliament, and finally linking England, Wales and Scotland under one parliament (based in London) for the first time in history.

Scotland's cultural and intellectual life flourished throughout the 18th century, and Edinburgh in particular became an important centre of Enlightenment thinking. The philosopher Adam Smith and poet Robert Burns influenced generations of thinkers.

The Industrial Age

By the 19th century, Britain had become the crucible of the Industrial Revolution. The towns of the English Midlands became the first industrial cities, and millions of former country-dwellers migrated in search of work. From about 1750 onwards, much of the Scottish Highlands region had been emptied of people, as landowners expelled entire villages to make way for sheep farming, a seminal event known as the Clearances. Industrialisation just about finished off the job. Many of the dispossessed came from the glens to the burgeoning Lanarkshire mills and Glasgow shipyards.

The same happened in Wales. By the early 19th century iron and slate were being extracted. The 1860s saw the Rhondda valleys opened up for mining, and Wales became a major exporter of coal. The rapid change from rural to urban society caused great dislocation, so for many people the side effects of Britain's economic blossoming were poverty and deprivation.

Nevertheless, by the time Queen Victoria took the throne in 1837, Britain's factories dominated world trade and Britain's fleets dominated the oceans. The rest of the 19th century was seen as Britain's Golden Age – and the lasting cultural impact of the Victorian era is still evident in the great red-brick factories, enormous glass-roofed train stations and magnificent public buildings in cities such as London, Liverpool, Manchester and Glasgow.

The Modern Era

Most of Britain's 20th century was a period of conflict and decline. Two world wars brought the nation almost to its knees, although many still recall the 1940 Battle of Britain – when the country resisted a three-month air attack from Germany – as its finest hour. In the 1950s and '60s, many former British colonies gained independence while at home the once-great manufacturing industries started to falter and die.

By the 1990s, though, Britain had bounced back, and it entered the new millennium with a strong economy and a cultural scene dubbed (briefly) 'Cool Britannia'. In the general election of 1997, after nearly 18 years of Conservative rule, 'New' Labour swept to power under a fresh-faced leader called Tony Blair.

Britain's role on the world stage was exemplified by its relationship with the USA and military campaigns in Afghanistan and Iraq – not that everyone agreed with such moves. Meanwhile, on the home front, history turned full circle as the state of Britain began to devolve into its three constituent nations. The new Scottish Parliament came into being in 1999. Concurrently, the people of Wales voted for a Welsh Assembly.

In June 2007 Tony Blair resigned, and Gordon Brown stepped into the top job. His first year in office garnered criticism, but his handling of the global economic crisis towards the end of 2008 earned many plaudits.

But it wasn't enough. In 2010, a record 14 years of Labour rule came to an end, and a new coalition between the Conservative and Liberal-Democrat parties became the government, with David Cameron as the new Prime Minister. Despite coming from opposite sides of the centre ground, the 'Con-Lib' alignment impressed many observers with their displays of collaboration. Crunch time came in October 2010, when Chancellor George Osborne set out his money-saving plans for Britain. For the people of Britain, it remains to be seen exactly what gets cut, and what gets spared.

People

Britain's population is 58 million (England around 50 million, Wales around three million and Scotland around five million), making it one of the world's most densely populated countries.

Several British towns and cities – particularly London, Glasgow and Manchester – have large South Asian and Afro-Caribbean communities, many established for three or more generations. In recent years large numbers of people from eastern Europe have also come to Britain for work.

In the 2001 national census, around 35 million people in Britain stated their religion as Christian although far fewer attend Sunday services. The census also recorded around 1.5 million Muslims in Britain (about 3% of the population). Other faiths include Hinduism (1%), Sikhism (0.7%), Judaism (0.5%) and Buddhism (0.3%). Nowadays more non-Christians regularly visit their places of worship than do all the Anglicans, Catholics, Methodists and Baptists combined – especially if you include the druids at Stonehenge.

Historically the three nations that make up Britain have been dominated by England, which is why many visitors confuse 'Britain' with 'England', and 'British' with 'English', but you should take care to use the right term, especially when in Wales and Scotland. Calling a Scot 'English' is like calling a New Zealander 'Australian' or a Canadian 'American'.

Language

The dominant language of Britain is English. In Wales about 600,000 people (20% of its population) speak Welsh as a first lan-

READING UP

To get under the skin of Britain, and to while away the waiting time at dreary bus stations, nothing beats losing yourself in a novel. Britain's best-known contemporary writer is probably JK Rowling, author of the Harry Potter stories, closely followed in a similar genre by Philip Pullman's *His Dark Materials* trilogy. But away from parallel worlds, some novels based in Britain to sample might include Muriel Spark's *The Prime of Miss Jean Brodie*, Irvine Welsh's *Trainspotting*, Zadie Smith's *White Teeth*, Monica Ali's *Brick Lane* or Nick Hornby's *Fever Pitch* and *High Fidelity*. In the travelogue genre, try Bill Bryson's classic but still-on-the-button *Notes from a Small Island*, or Josie Dew's *Slow Coast Home*.

guage, and many more as a strong second tongue, especially in the north – although everyone speaks English as well. Welsh is a Celtic language, entirely different to English. It almost died out in the 1960s, but today Welsh-language TV, radio and literature is increasingly popular, and all signs on roads and in public places are in both languages. In Scotland, Gaelic – another Celtic language – is spoken by about 80,000 people, mainly in the Highlands and islands, while Lallans (or Lowland Scots) is much closer to English.

Arts

Britain has a rich artistic history – notably in the realms of theatre and literature – that stretches back centuries, while its modern popular culture – especially pop and rock music – resonates throughout the world.

Literature

Travelling in the footsteps of English, Scottish or Welsh writers can be the highlight of any trip to Britain. Ambling through the cobbled streets of Canterbury recalls Chaucer's ribald comedy, a trip to Bath evokes Jane Austen, while strolling in the Scottish glens might summon the spirit of Robbie Burns. Spirits of a different variety should be sampled in the pubs of Wales, some of which inspired the poetry of Dylan Thomas.

Cinema

Britain's home-grown film industry's worldwide hits include *Shakespeare in Love* and *Bend it Like Beckham*. For more grit, try *The Full Monty, Secrets and Lies, Billy Elliot, East is East* or *Atonement*. For a great laugh, go for *Hot Fuzz*.

Visual Arts

Cities like Glasgow, Cardiff, Manchester and London boast some of Europe's finest galleries, with works by well-known British artists such as Turner, Constable, Francis Bacon and Lucian Freud.

In recent years, contemporary art has undergone a transformation, with new galleries such as the capital's Tate Modern.

Music

There's a great depth of classical music performance in Britain, with several cities hosting their own renowned symphony orchestras, but the music this country is best known for is pop and rock, with venerable juggernauts like Elton John and the Rolling Stones still routinely topping lists of high-grossing concert tours around the world.

In recent decades, the '90s was notable for the rise of British 'indie' bands, with the likes of Blur, Elastica, Suede, Supergrass, Ocean Colour Scene, Manic Street Preachers, the Verve, Pulp, Travis, Feeder, Super Furry Animals, Stereophonics, Catatonia, Radiohead and, above all, Oasis, reviving the guitar-based format. Heralded as the 'Britpop' revolution, part of the even bigger Cool Britannia phenomenon that combined new music, new art, new fashion and New Labour politics, it was over almost as soon as it started, but a host of bands such as Coldplay, Badly Drawn Boy, Snow Patrol and Razorlight played on, and in the following years were joined by a wave of imitators.

By 2010, British pop music was as fast-moving and varied as ever, divided into a host of genres mixing a wide range of influences including glam, punk, electronica and folk. Recent big names at the summer festivals include Muse, Dizzee Rascal and Franz Ferdinand, along with current favourites like Mumford & Sons, Bombay Bicycle Club, Foals and The XX. Meanwhile, British folk music, thanks largely to the rise of world music, is enjoying its biggest revival since the 1960s.

Beyond the festivals, Britain's live music scene continues to thrive; a vital opportunity for bands to make money in a business squeezed by free file-sharing. At the other end of the scale, big-selling commercial pop acts like Leona Lewis and Diana Vickers are spawned by endless – and obsessively followed – reality TV talent shows.

Sport

If you want to take a shortcut into the heart of British culture, watch the British at play. They're fierce and proud about their sport, whether participating or spectating, and the mood of the nation is more closely aligned to the success of its international teams than budget announcements from the government, or even the weather – no more clearly evidenced than by the massive support for Team GB, especially the phenomenal cyclists and swimmers, in the 2008 Beijing Olympics.

Sometimes, though, it's the success of the nations that matters; the separate rugby teams of England, Wales and Scotland, and the English and Scottish national football sides have supporters with passion that borders on the insane. This passion is also evident in the support of football clubs throughout the country.

Elsewhere, sporting highlights such as tennis at Wimbledon or the Grand National horse race keep everyone enthralled. And Team GB will have a chance to shine again, this time on home soil, at the 2012 London Olympics.

Food & Drink

The words 'British' and 'cuisine' never used to be uttered in the same sentence without a nervous laugh or gagging reflex. Those days are long gone and there's now a rich variety of well-prepared regional dishes alongside an impressive array of cosmopolitan options, that reflect the nation's burgeoning ethnic diversity.

You'll find a good variety of eateries in most British towns and cities – whether you're vegetarian, vegan or carnivore.

As well as restaurants and cafes, in country areas you'll find teashops (essentially a smart cafe), and across Britain pubs are often a good option for good-value, no-nonsense food. Look out for the ploughman's lunch, a plate of bread, cheese and pickles that goes down well with a pint or two of traditional beer.

Prices ranges for eateries in this chapter are for a main meal and are presented as follows:

£££ more than £18

££ £9 to £18

£ less than £9

REAL ALE

For many foreigners, traditional British beer (often called 'real ale') can be a bit of a shock – a warm, flat and expensive shock – but that's because taste is the key; the beer doesn't need to be cold or pressurised to make it palatable. Once you've got used to that idea you can start experimenting with the many different regional tastes and textures.

Staples & Specialities

Britain's traditional meals include fish and chips, roast beef, bangers and mash, and steak and kidney pie. Many of these revered dishes have been reinvented for foodies at some of the nation's finest restaurants, as well as in more straightforward restaurants and cafes.

Another British speciality – especially if you're staying at B&Bs – is the big fry-up breakfast, containing bacon, sausage, egg, beans, mushrooms, toast and more, often called the 'full English' (in England). In Scotland you may get offered haggis or black pudding, and oatcakes instead of toast.

Alongside the home-grown favourites, most Brits have also embraced a huge variety of ethnic cuisines, with Chinese and Indian restaurants now more common than traditional fish-and-chip shops.

Environment

The island of Britain sits on the eastern edge of the North Atlantic and consists of three nations: England in the south and centre, Scotland to the north and Wales to the west – together making up the state of Great Britain. Further west lies the island of Ireland. Looking southeast, France is just 20 miles away, while to the northeast lie the countries of Scandinavia.

Measuring around 600 miles (around 1000km) north to south, and about half that at its widest point, Britain is roughly the same size as New Zealand and half the size of France. When it comes to topology, Britain is not a place of extremes – there are no

Himalayas or Lake Baikals – but even a short journey can take you through a surprising mix of landscapes, from the flatlands of eastern England or rolling moors of Devon to the craggy peaks of Snowdonia and windswept islands off the west coast of Scotland.

SURVIVAL GUIDE

Directory

Accommodation

Accommodation in Britain is as varied as the sights you visit. From hip hotels to basic barns, the wide choice is all part of the attraction. Across Britain, whatever the budget level, rates tend to drop in low season. In summer, popular spots (York, Canterbury, Bath etc) get very crowded, so booking ahead is often essential. Prices for B&Bs and hotels are generally for rooms with private bathroom – either en suite or across the landing from the room.

Our reviews refer to double rooms with a private bathroom, except in hostels or where otherwise specified. Quoted rates are for high season, which is May to September.

£££ more than £130

££ £50 to £130

£ less than £50

B&BS AND GUEST HOUSES

The B&B ('bed and breakfast') is a great British institution. Smaller places may have just one room, and you'll feel like part of the family. Larger B&Bs may have around 10 rooms and more facilities. 'Guest house' is sometimes just another name for a B&B, or something in between B&B and hotel. Room rates are nearly always quoted per person, but are based on two people sharing. Single rooms cost more. At the bottom end you'll pay around £20 per person; in the midrange you're looking at around £35 or £40. Most B&Bs serve enormous breakfasts, included in the rate, and some also offer packed lunches (around £5) and evening meals (around £10 to £15).

CAMPING

Free camping is rare in Britain, but there are many camping grounds, on the edge of towns and in the countryside. Rates range from £5 to £10 per person, depending on location, season and facilities.

Most towns ands cities have a local tourist information centre (TIC) that can help you find and book accommodation on the spot, or ahead of your arrival if you tell them what you're looking for. This service is sometimes free but usually a fee (around £4) is charged. It's often worth the money as it saves you hiking around or phoning loads of places. Sometimes the fee is deducted from your accommodation cost, meaning no extra charge to you.

HOSTELS

Britain has two national hostelling organisations: **Youth Hostels Association** (YHA; www.yha.org.uk), covering England and Wales, and **Scottish Youth Hostels Association** (SYHA; www.syha.org.uk). Dorm beds range from £9 to £20 per night, and many hostels also have double and four-bed rooms. You don't *have* to be a member of YHA or SHYA (or another Hostelling International – HI – organisation) to stay at YHA/SYHA hostels, but nonmembers pay extra: £3 extra per person per night in England and Wales; £1 extra per person per night in Scotland. Annual YHA membership costs £16; SYHA costs £10. Under 16s, under 26s, seniors and families get discounts.

Most hostel prices vary according to demand and season. Book early for an off-peak Tuesday night in May and you'll get a cheap rate. Book late for a weekend in August and you'll pay top whack – if there's space at all. Throughout this chapter, we've generally quoted the cheaper rates (in line with those on YHA's and SYHA's websites); you may pay more. Some hostels also have varying opening times and days, especially in remote locations or out of the tourist season, so check before turning up.

There's a growing array of independent and backpacker hostels across Britain, varying widely in quality, facilities and price (typically from £10 to £25). Some are quiet and cosy, while others are for serious party travellers. The print and online **Independent Hostel Guide** (www.independenthostelguide.co.uk) is the best listing. North of the border, an excellent site is www.hostel-scotland.co.uk.

PUBS & INNS

As well as selling drinks, many pubs and inns offer lodging, particularly in country areas. Staying in a pub can be good fun – you're automatically at the centre of the community – although accommodation varies enormously. Expect to pay around £20 per person at the cheap end, and around £30 to £35 for something better. An advantage for solo tourists is that pubs are more likely to have single rooms, and if a pub does B&B, it normally does evening meals too.

UNIVERSITY ACCOMMODATION

Many universities offer student accommodation to visitors during vacations. You usually get a functional single bedroom with private bathroom, and self-catering flats are also available. Prices range from £15 to £30 per person. A handy portal is www.universityrooms.co.uk.

Activities

Britain is a great destination for outdoor enthusiasts. Walking (hiking) and cycling are the most popular activities – you can do them on a whim, and they're the perfect way to open up some beautiful corners of the country. Britain supplies the goods for thrill-seekers, too: the coast has excellent spots for surfing and the wacky sport of coasteering. A good site for inspiration is www.visitbritain.com – follow links to Holiday Ideas and Outdoor Activities.

Cycling

Compact Britain is an excellent destination to explore by bike, whether you're pottering around a cycle-friendly city such as Oxford or heading into the countryside. Popular regions to tour include southwest England, the Peak District, Mid-Wales and the Scottish Borders. There are cycle-hire outlets in most tourist centres; rates range from £6 per half-day to £60 per week.

Walking & Hiking

Britain's picturesque terrain is great for walking – whether you want an easy stroll or an energetic hike. Every country town is surrounded by a network of footpaths, with even more choice in the national parks and mountain areas such as Dartmoor, the Lake District, North Wales and the Highlands of Scotland. Some long-distance routes in Britain are designated National Trails (www.nationaltrails.co.uk) but you don't have to do the whole thing; many people follow sections for a day or two, or a just few hours. It still makes for a great walk.

Other Activities

As long as you've got a wetsuit, Britain offers many excellent **surfing** opportunities, including Pembrokeshire, Cornwall and Devon; for info see www.britsurf.co.uk. You could also try your hand at **coasteering**. It's like mountaineering, although instead of going up a mountain, you go along the coast – a steep rocky coast, often with waves breaking around your feet. And if the rock gets too steep, you jump in and start swimming. Outdoor centres – notably in Cornwall and Pembrokeshire – provide guides and all the gear. You provide the sense of adventure. See www.coasteering.org.

ROOM RATES

In Britain there's often no such thing as a 'standard' hotel rate. Many hotels, especially larger places or chains, vary prices according to demand. So if you book early for a night when the hotel is likely to be quiet, rates are cheap. Try to book late, or aim for a public holiday weekend, and you'll pay a lot. However, if you're prepared to be flexible and leave booking to the very last minute you can sometimes get a bargain as drop rates again. The end result: you can pay anything from £19 to £190 for the very same hotel room. With that in mind, the hotel rates we quote throughout this book are often guide prices only. (B&B prices tend to be much more consistent.)

Business Hours

Banks 9.30am-5pm Mon-Fri; larger branches also open Sat morning

Post Offices 9.30am-5pm Mon-Sat

Pubs 11am-11pm Mon-Sat, to 10.30pm Sun; some pubs – and many bars, particularly in the cities – stay open later, especially on weekends

Restaurants lunch 11am-3pm, dinner 6pm-10pm; specific hours vary widely

Shops 9am-5pm Mon-Sat, 10am-4pm Sun

Heritage Organisations

A highlight of a journey through Britain is visiting the numerous castles and historic sites that pepper the country. Membership of a heritage organisation gets you free admission (usually a good saving) as well as information handbooks and so on. If you join an English heritage organisation, it covers you for Wales and Scotland, and vice versa.

National Trust (NT; www.nationaltrust.org.uk) A Touring Pass allows free entry to NT properties for one/two weeks (£21/26 per person). The **National Trust for Scotland** (NTS; www.nts.org.uk) is similar.

English Heritage (EH; www.english-heritage.org.uk) An Overseas Visitors Pass allows free entry to most sites for seven/14 days for £20/25. In Wales and Scotland the equivalent organisations are: **Cadw** (www.cadw.wales.gov.uk) and **Historic Scotland** (HS; www.historic-scotland.gov.uk).

Holidays

Holidays for the whole of Britain are:

New Year's Day 1 January

Easter March/April (Good Friday to Easter Monday inclusive)

May Day First Monday in May

Spring Bank Holiday Last Monday in May

Summer Bank Holiday Last Monday in August

Christmas Day 25 December

Boxing Day 26 December

If a public holiday falls on a weekend, the nearest Monday is usually taken instead.

In England and Wales, most businesses and banks close on official public holidays (hence the quaint term 'bank holiday').

In Scotland, bank holidays are just for the banks, and many businesses stay open.

Many Scottish towns have an additional spring and autumn holiday, but dates vary.

Money

The currency of Britain is the pound sterling (£). Paper money ('notes') comes in £5, £10, £20 and £50 denominations, although some shops don't accept £50 notes because fakes circulate.

ATMs (often called 'cash machines') are easy to find in cities and small towns.

Watch out for ATMs that might have been tampered with – a common ruse is to attach a card-reader to the slot.

Cities and larger towns have banks and bureaus for changing your money (cash or travellers cheques) into pounds. Check rates first; some bureaus may claim 'no commission' but they change at poor rates. You can change money at some post offices – very handy in country areas, and exchange rates are fair.

Credit & Debit Cards

Visa and MasterCard credit and debit cards are widely accepted in Britain. Smaller businesses, such as pubs or B&Bs, prefer debit cards and some take cash only.

Nearly all credit and debit cards use a 'Chip and PIN' system (instead of signing). This usually does not apply to cards issued overseas: you should be able to sign, but some places may decline your card.

Tipping

In Britain, you're not obliged to tip if service or food was unsatisfactory (even if it's been added to your bill as a 'service charge'). In restaurants, tip around 10%; do the same in teashops and smarter cafes with full table service.

In pubs, also tip around 10% if you order food at the table and your meal is brought to you. If you order and pay at the bar (food or drinks), tips are not expected.

Telephone

In this Britain chapter, area codes and individual numbers are listed together, separated by a hyphen.

Area codes in Britain do not have a standard format or length, eg ☎020 for London, ☎0161 for Manchester, ☎01225 for Bath, ☎015394 for Ambleside, followed as usual by the individual number.

Other phone codes:

☎0500 or ☎0800 – free calls

☎0845 – calls at local rate, wherever you're dialling from within the UK.

☎087 – calls at national rate

☎089 or ☎09 – premium rate

☎07 – mobile phones, more expensive than calling a landline

To call outside the UK dial ☎00, then the country code (☎1 for USA, ☎61 for Australia

Scotland issues its own currency (including a £1 note), interchangeable with the money used in the rest of the UK. However, you'll find shops more readily accept Scottish money in the north of England than in the south. Banks will always change them.

etc), the area code (you usually drop the initial zero) and the number.

To get the operator dial ☎100; ☎155 for the international operator and also for reverse-charge (collect) calls.

For directory inquiries, a host of agencies compete for your business and charge from 10p to 40p; numbers include ☎118 192, ☎118 118, ☎118 500 and ☎118 811.

Tourist Offices

All British cities and towns, and some villages, have a tourist information centre (TIC) with helpful staff, books and maps, free leaflets, and loads of advice on things to see or do. They can also assist with booking accommodation. Most tourist offices keep regular business hours; in quiet areas they close from October to March, while in popular areas they open daily year-round. For a list see www.visitmap.info/tic.

Visas

If you're a European Economic Area (EEA) national, you don't need a visa to visit (or work in) Britain. Citizens of Australia, Canada, New Zealand, South Africa and the USA are given leave to enter the UK at their point of arrival for up to six months (three months for some nationalities), but are prohibited from working. For more info see www.ukvisas.gov.uk or www.ukba.homeoffice.gov.uk.

Getting There & Away

Air

You can easily fly to Britain from just about anywhere in the world. London is a global hub, but major regional airports such as Manchester and Glasgow also handle international flights. In recent years other regional airports around Britain have massively increased their offerings – especially on budget ('no-frills') airlines to/from mainland Europe – very handy for travels around the continent.

LONDON AIRPORTS

London is served by five airports – Heathrow and Gatwick are the busiest.

London City (LCY; www.londoncityairport.com)

London Gatwick (LGW; www.gatwickairport.com)

London Heathrow (LHR; www.heathrowairport.com)

Luton (LTN; www.london-luton.co.uk)

Stansted (STN; www.stanstedairport.com)

REGIONAL AIRPORTS

Regional airports with international flights:

Birmingham (BHM; www.bhx.co.uk)

Bristol (BRS; www.bristolairport.co.uk)

Cardiff (CWL; www.cwlfly.com)

Edinburgh (EDI; www.edinburghairport.com)

Glasgow (GGW; www.glasgowairport.com)

Liverpool (LPL; www.liverpooljohnlennonairport.com)

Manchester (MAN; www.manchesterairport.co.uk)

Newcastle (NCL; www.newcastleairport.com)

Southampton (SOU; www.southamptonairport.com)

Bus & Coach

Most long-distance services to/from Britain are operated by **National Express** (www.nationalexpress.com) or another operator in the **Eurolines** network (www.eurolines.com). Some sample journey times to/from London include Amsterdam (12 hours), Paris (eight hours), Dublin (12 hours) and Barcelona (24 hours).

If you're flexible with timings (ie travel when few other people want to) and book early, you can get some very good deals – for example, London to Paris or Amsterdam one-way starts at just £18, although paying nearer £25 is more usual.

Train

The Channel Tunnel makes direct train travel between Britain and continental Europe a fast and enjoyable option.

High-speed **Eurostar** (www.eurostar.com) passenger services hurtle at least 10 times daily between London and Paris (2½ hours) or Brussels (two hours). You can buy tickets from travel agencies, major train stations or direct from the Eurostar website – the latter is invariably the cheapest option. The normal single fare between London and Paris/Brussels is around £150, but if you buy in advance and travel at a less busy period, deals drop to around £90 return or even less. You can also buy 'through fare' tickets from many cities in Britain – for example York to Paris, or Manchester to Brussels. You can also get very good train and hotel combination deals – bizarrely sometimes cheaper than train fare only.

Drivers use **Eurotunnel** (www.eurotunnel.com). The one-way cost for a car and passengers is around £90 to £150 depending on the time of day (less busy times are cheaper); promotional fares bring it nearer to £50.

As well as Eurostar, many 'normal' trains run between Britain and mainland Europe. You buy one ticket, but get off the train at the port, walk onto a ferry, then get another train on the other side. Routes include Amsterdam-London (via Hook of Holland and Harwich).

Travelling between Ireland and Britain, the main train ferry-train route is Dublin to London, via Dun Laoghaire and Holyhead. Ferries also run between Rosslare and Fishguard (Wales), with train connections on either side.

Sea

The main ferry routes between Britain and mainland Europe include Dover to Calais or Boulogne (France), Harwich to Hook of Holland (Netherlands), Hull to Zeebrugge (Belgium) or Rotterdam (Netherlands), Rosyth to Zeebrugge, Portsmouth to Santander or Bilbao (Spain), Newcastle to Bergen (Norway) or Gothenberg (Sweden). Routes to/from Ireland include Holyhead to Dun Laoghaire.

Competition from Eurotunnel and budget airlines means ferry operators discount heavily and offer flexible fares, meaning great bargains at quiet times of day or year. For example, the short cross-channel routes such as Dover to Calais or Boulogne can be as low as £20 for a car plus up to five passengers, although around £50 is more likely. If you're a foot passenger, or cycling, there's often less need to book ahead, and cheap fares on the short crossings start from about £10 each way.

Main operators include the following.

Brittany Ferries (www.brittany-ferries.com)

DFDS Seaways (www.dfds.co.uk)

Irish Ferries (www.irishferries.com)

Norfolkline (www.irishferries.com)

P&O Ferries (www.poferries.com)

Speedferries (www.speedferries.com)

Stena Line (www.stenaline.com)

Transmanche (www.transmancheferries.com)

Broker sites covering all routes and options include www.ferrybooker.com and www.directferries.co.uk.

Getting Around

For getting around Britain your first main choice is going by car or public transport. Having your own car makes the best use of time and helps you reach remote places, but rental and fuel costs can be expensive for budget travellers – while the hassles of parking and traffic jams in major cities hit everyone – so public transport is often the better way to go.

Your main public transport options are train and long-distance bus (called coach in Britain). Services between major towns and cities are good and if you book ahead early or travel at off-peak periods, train and coach tickets can be very cheap.

Traveline (www.traveline.org.uk) is a very useful information service covering bus, coach, taxi and train services nationwide.

Air

If you're pushed for time, flights on longer routes across Britain (eg Newquay to Edinburgh) are handy. With advance booking, fares start as low as £20 one way, but up to £100 is more likely.

AIRLINES IN BRITAIN

Airlines operating domestic flights within Britain include:

Air Southwest (www.airsouthwest.com) Serving Bristol, Cardiff, Leeds-Bradford, Gatwick, Manchester, Newquay, Plymouth.

bmiBaby (www.bmibaby.com) Birmingham, East Midlands, Cardiff, Edinburgh, Glasgow, Manchester, Newquay.

Eastern Airways (www.easternairways.com) Aberdeen, Newcastle, Norwich, Cardiff, Southampton and more.

easyJet (www.easyjet.com) Aberdeen, Bristol, Edinburgh, Glasgow, Inverness, Liverpool, Luton, Stansted, Newcastle.

Flybe (www.flybe.com) Airports served include Aberdeen, Bristol, Edinburgh, Exeter, Glasgow, Liverpool, Manchester, Newcastle, Newquay, Southampton and many Scottish islands.

Ryanair (www.ryanair.com) Aberdeen, Birmingham, Bournemouth, Edinburgh, Glasgow, Inverness, Liverpool, Stansted and Newquay.

Bus

If you're on a tight budget, long-distance buses nearly always offer the cheapest way to get around, although also the slowest. Many towns have separate stations for local bus and long-distance coach; make sure you go to the right place!

National Express (☎08717-818181; www.nationalexpress.com) is the main coach operator, with a wide network and frequent services between main centres. North of the border, **Scottish Citylink** (☎08705-505050; www.citylink.co.uk) is the leading coach company. Fares vary: they're cheaper if you book in advance and travel at quieter times (special off-peak fares cost as low as £1). As a guide, a 200-mile trip (eg London to York) will cost around £10 to £20 if you book in advance, and a lot more if booking's left to the last minute.

Also offering fares from £1 is **Megabus** (www.megabus.com), a budget coach service serving about 30 destinations in Britain.

BUS PASSES

National Express offers discount passes to full-time students and under-26s, called Young Persons Coachcards. They cost £10 and get you 30% off standard adult fares.

For touring the country, National Express offers Brit Xplorer passes, allowing unlimited travel for seven days (£79), 14 days (£139) and 28 days (£219). You don't need to book journeys in advance; if the coach has a spare seat, you can take it.

Car & Motorcycle

Most overseas driving licences are valid in Britain for up to 12 months from the date of entry.

RENTAL

Compared to many countries (especially the USA), car rental is expensive in Britain; you'll pay around £250 per week for a small car (including insurance and unlimited mileage) but rates rise at busy times and drop at quiet times. See p1325 for a list of the main European car-rental firms.

Another option is to look online for small local car-hire companies in Britain who can undercut the international franchises. Generally those in cities are cheaper than in rural areas. Rental-broker sites include **UK Car Hire** (www.ukcarhire.net).

ROAD RULES

The *Highway Code,* available in bookshops (or at www.direct.gov.uk/en/TravelAndTransport/Highwaycode), contains everything you need to know about Britain's road rules. The main ones:

- » drive on the left
- » wear fitted seat belts in cars
- » wear crash helmets on motorcycles
- » give way to your right at junctions and roundabouts
- » always use the left-side lane on motorways and dual-carriageways, unless overtaking
- » don't use a mobile phone while driving unless it's fully hands-free.

Speed limits are 30mph in built-up areas, 60mph on main roads and 70mph on motorways and most (but not all) dual carriageways. Drinking and driving is taken very seriously; the maximum blood-alcohol level allowed is 80mg/100mL.

Train

For long-distance travel around Britain, trains are faster and more comfortable than coaches but can be more expensive – although with discount tickets they're competitive – and often very scenic.

About 20 companies operate train services in Britain (for example, First Great Western runs from London to Bristol; National Express East Coast runs from London to Edinburgh, First ScotRail operates trains in Scotland) while Network Rail operates tracks and stations. This system can seem confusing, but information and ticket-buying are mostly centralised. If you have to change trains, or use two train operators, you usually still buy one ticket valid for the whole journey. The main railcards are also accepted by all operators.

Your first stop should be **National Rail Enquiries** (☎08457-484950; www.nationalrail.co.uk), Britain's service for timetable and fare information. Punch in your start and end destinations, and the site will offer a range of routes, times and fares. In Scotland you can also use **First ScotRail** (☎08457-550033; www.scotrail.co.uk).

Once you've found the journey you need, links take you to the relevant train operator or centralised ticketing services (www.thetrainline.com, www.qjump.co.uk and www.raileasy.co.uk) to buy the ticket. Train-travel websites can be confusing at first (you always have to state an approximate preferred time and day of travel, even if you don't mind *when* you go), but with a little delving they offer some real bargains.

CLASSES, COSTS & RESERVATIONS

There are two classes of train travel: first and standard. Travelling first class costs around 50% more than standard and, except on crowded trains, is not worth it.

HOW MUCH TO...?

When travelling long-distance by train or bus/coach in Britain, it's important to realise that there's no such thing as a standard fare. Prices vary according to demand and when you buy your ticket. Book long in advance and travel on Tuesday mid-morning, and it's cheap. Buy your ticket on the spot late Friday afternoon, and it'll be a lot more expensive. Ferries use similar systems. Throughout this book, we have generally quoted sample fares somewhere in between the very cheapest and most expensive options. The price you pay will almost certainly be different.

For short journeys (under about 50 miles) it's usually best to buy tickets on the spot at rail stations. For longer journeys, on-the-spot fares are always available, but tickets are much cheaper if bought in advance. Essentially, the earlier you book, the cheaper it gets. You can also save if you travel 'off-peak' (ie the days and times that aren't busy). Advance purchase usually gets a reserved seat too. The cheapest fares are nonrefundable.

If you buy online, you can have the ticket posted (UK addresses only), or collect it at the station on the day of travel from automatic machines.

Whichever operator you travel with and wherever you buy tickets, these are the three main fare types:

Anytime Buy anytime, travel anytime – usually the most expensive option

Off-peak Buy ticket any time, travel off-peak

Advance Buy ticket in advance, travel only on specific trains – usually the cheapest option

If train doesn't get you all the way to your destination, a PlusBus supplement (usually around £2) validates your train ticket for onwards travel by bus – more convenient, and usually cheaper, than buying a separate bus ticket. For details see www.plusbus.info.

TRAIN PASSES

If you're staying in Britain for a while, passes known as 'railcards' are available (www.railcard.co.uk) including the **16-25 Railcard** for those aged 16 to 25. It costs £26 (valid for one year, available from major stations or online) and gets you a 33% discount on most train fares, except those already heavily discounted.

For country-wide travel, **BritRail** (www.britrail.com) passes are available for visitors from overseas. They must be bought in your country of origin (not in Britain). They're available in three different versions (England only; all Britain; UK and Ireland) and for periods from four to 30 days

Of the other international passes, **Eurail** cards are not accepted in Britain, and **InterRail** cards are only valid if bought in another mainland European country.

Bulgaria България

Includes »

Best Places to Eat

- » Pri Yafata, Sofia (p247)
- » Malâk Bunardzhik, Plovdiv (p251)
- » Dream House, Sofia (p247)
- » Ego Pizza, Veliko Târnovo (VT; p253)

Best Places to Stay

- » Hotel Romantica,Plovdiv (p250)
- » Hotel California, Nesebâr (p258)
- » Red House, Sofia (p246)
- » Phoenix Hostel, VT (p253)
- » X Hostel, Varna (p255)

Why Go?

Bulgaria may be best known for its long, sandy Black Sea beaches, but there's much more to see. Bulgaria boasts no fewer than seven mountain ranges and varied landscapes ideal for hiking, cycling, climbing and wildlife watching, as well as modern ski resorts.

You'll find churches and monasteries full of vibrant icons, picturesque villages of timber-framed houses and cobbled lanes, and dramatic reminders of the country's ancient heritage, from Thracian tombs and Roman ruins to medieval fortresses, Ottoman mosques and communist monuments slowly crumbling away into history.

Bulgaria's cities, too, reward visitors, with treasure-filled museums and galleries and cafe-sprinkled parks. Getting around is easy and still remarkably cheap so brush up on your Cyrillic, buy a bus ticket and get ready to explore.

When to Go

Sofia

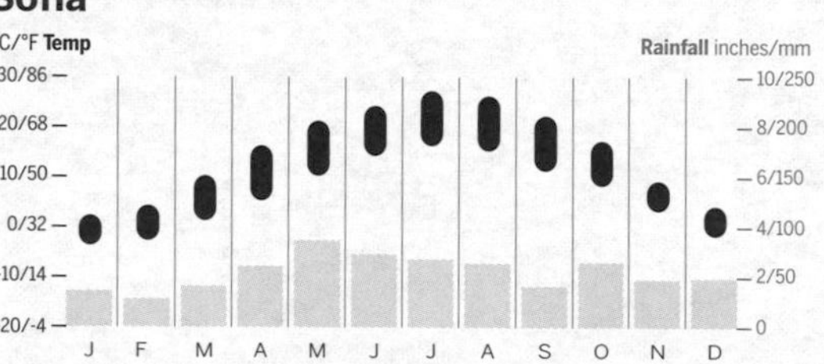

Jan Skiing or snowboarding down Mt Vitosha is just the thing.

Mar–May The fine spring weather welcomes folk and music festivals across the country.

Jun–Sep Spend lazy days on Black Sea beaches and nights at Bulgaria's best clubs.

Connections

Although Sofia has international bus and train connections, it's not necessary to backtrack to the capital if you're heading to Bucharest (Romania) or İstanbul (Turkey). From central Veliko Târnovo, for example, there are daily trains both ways – and several cities offer overnight buses to İstanbul. Heading to Greece or Belgrade (Serbia) by train means going through Sofia; for Skopje (Macedonia), you'll need to catch a bus from Sofia, too.

ITINERARIES

One Week

Start off with a full day in Sofia, visiting the Archaeological Museum and Aleksander Nevski church, then take the bus to Veliko Târnovo for a few days of sightseeing and hiking. For the rest of the week, head to Varna for some sea and sand.

Two Weeks

After a couple of days in Sofia, catch a bus to Plovdiv and wander the cobbled lanes of the Old Town. From there, take a day trip to visit the Roman spa town of Hisar. After a few days in Plovdiv, make for the coast, staying a couple of nights in ancient Sozopol. Head north to overnight in Varna, then hop on a bus to Veliko Târnovo.

Essential Food & Drink

» **Banitsa** The ultimate Bulgarian street snack, the *banitsa* is a flaky cheese pastry, often served fresh and hot.

» **Kebabche** There's no escaping this thin, grilled pork sausage, a staple of every *mehana* (tavern) in the country. *Kyufte* is a round, flat, burger-like variation of the same, sometimes filled with cheese.

» **Tarator** On a hot day there's nothing better than this delicious chilled cucumber and yoghurt soup, served with garlic, dill and crushed walnuts.

» **Beer** You're never far from a cold beer in Bulgaria. Zagorka, Kamenitza and Shumensko are the most popular nationwide brands, but look for regional brews, too.

» **Wine** They've been producing wine here since Thracian times, and there are some excellent varieties to try, including the unique, blood-red Melnik.

AT A GLANCE

» **Currency** Lev (lv)

» **Language** Bulgarian

» **Money** ATMs are everywhere

» **Visas** Visas not required for citizens of the EU, UK, US, Canada, Australia and New Zealand

Fast Facts

» **Area** 110,910 sq km

» **Capital** Sofia

» **Country code** ☎359

» **Emergency** ☎112

Exchange Rates

Australia	A$1	1.44lv
Canada	C$1	1.41lv
euro zone	€1	1.96lv
Japan	¥100	1.63lv
New Zealand	NZ$1	1.08lv
UK	UK£1	2.22lv
USA	US$1	1.34lv

Set Your Budget

» **Budget hotel room** 40lv

» **Two-course evening meal** 10lv

» **Museum entrance** 4–10lv

» **Beer (bottle)** 1.80lv

» **City transport ticket** 1lv

Resources

» **Bulgaria Travel** (www.bulgariatravel.org)

» **City Info Guide** (www.cityinfoguide.net)

» **Novinite** (www.novinite.com)

» **Sofia Life** (www.sofia-life.com)

Bulgaria Highlights

1. Explore the luminous artistic and religious treasures of Bulgaria's most revered monastery at **Rila** (p249)
2. Relax on the sands or take a dip in the Black Sea at historic **Sozopol** (p259)
3. Go clubbing, take in the Summer International Festival and stroll through leafy Primorski Park in cosmopolitan seaside **Varna** (p255)
4. Visit the tsars' medieval stronghold in **Veliko Târnovo** (p252) and use the town as a base to explore nearby churches, monasteries and pretty villages
5. Take the waters in the peaceful spa town of **Hisar** (p251) and investigate its monumental Roman ruins

SOFIA СОФИЯ

☎02 / POP 1.4 MILLION

Don't expect to uncover the 'new Prague' here in this mostly modern city at the base of towering Mt Vitosha. There's a lingering Soviet tinge to the Bulgarian capital, with blocky architecture and a scattering of stubborn Red Army monuments, but there are also some fine museums and parks, beautiful churches and a buzzing nightlife scene.

Settled some 7000 years ago by the Thracians, and named Serdica by the Romans, Sofia was a backwater market town of 1200 residents when it became the nation's unlikely fourth capital in 1879.

Sofia's neighbouring main bus and train stations are on bul Maria Luisa, about 500m north of the city centre; take trams 1 or 7 to central pl Sveta Nedelya.

Sights & Activities

PLOSHTAD ALEKSANDER NEVSKI

Aleksander Nevski Memorial Church CHURCH

(pl Aleksander Nevski; ⏲7am-7pm) Constructed between 1882 and 1912, this awe-inspiring, gold-domed church was built as a memorial to the 200,000 Russian soldiers who died fighting for Bulgarian independence in the Russo-Turkish War (1877–78). Naturalistic and faded murals of saints adorn the walls.

To the left of the main church entrance, a door leads down to the **Aleksander Nevski Crypt** (adult/student 6/3lv; ⏲10.30am-5.30pm Wed & Fri-Sun, 10am-6.30pm Tue & Thu), now displaying a vast collection of icons dating from the 5th century onwards.

Sveta Sofia Church CHURCH

(ul Parizh; ⏲7am-6pm or 7pm) The capital's oldest church gave the city its name. It's been restored many times over the centuries, and sections of older structures can be seen through glass floor panels. The **Tomb of the Unknown Soldier** is outside.

AROUND SOFIA CITY GARDEN

Archaeological Museum MUSEUM

(pl Nezavisimost; adult/student 10/2lv; ⏲10am-6pm daily May-Oct, 10am-5pm Tue-Sun Nov-Apr) Housed in a former mosque, this excellent museum is a treasure trove of Thracian and Roman artefacts, including the lifelike bronze head of a 4th century BC Thracian king, with coloured glass eyes and fine copper eyelashes, found near Shipka in 2004.

Across the street is the **President's Building** (closed to the public), the site of the theatrical **changing of the guards** ceremony, staged on the hour during daylight hours.

Royal Palace ART GALLERY, MUSEUM

(ul Tsar Osvoboditel) Facing the City Garden, the former Royal Palace is now home to the **National Art Gallery** (adult/student 6/3lv; ⏲10am-6pm Tue-Sun), with a large collection of 19th- and 20th-century Bulgarian paintings and sculpture, and the **Ethnographical Museum** (adult/student 3/1lv; ⏲10am-6pm Tue-Sun), displaying folk art.

FREE **Sofia City Art Gallery** ART GALLERY

(ul General Gurko 1; ⏲10am-7pm Tue-Sat, 11am-6pm Sun) Temporary themed exhibitions, mainly of contemporary art, are on show here.

AROUND PLOSHTAD SVETA NEDELYA

Sveta Nedelya Cathedral CHURCH

(pl Sveta Nedelya; ⏲7am-7pm) Sofia's cathedral, completed in 1863, is filled with colourful saintly murals and contains the supposedly miracle-working relics of a medieval Serbian king.

Banya Bashi Mosque MOSQUE

(bul Maria Luisa; ⏲dawn-dusk) Built in 1576, this is Sofia's only working mosque, with a distinctive red-brick minaret.

Mineral Baths NOTABLE BUILDING

(pl Banski) Also known as the Turkish Baths, this elegant building with its striped facade, behind the mosque, dates from 1913. It's been under renovation for *many* years, and looks unlikely to open again any time soon. Across the street, locals fill bottles with hot mineral water at the modern **drinking-fountain complex**.

Ploshtad Bulgaria PARK

Around 1km south of pl Sveta Nedelya, via the main shopping street of bul Vitosha, is this elongated, tree-lined plaza with outdoor bars and popcorn and ice-cream vendors, watched over by the brooding **National Palace of Culture** (NDK) complex, the city's main concert and trade-fair venue.

MT VITOSHA & BOYANA

At the southern edge of town, Mt Vitosha is popular for summer hikes and winter skiing that's cheaper than ski resorts (about 30lv for a lift ticket). Get the trail map *Vitosha Turisticheska Karta* (1:50,000) in Sofia.

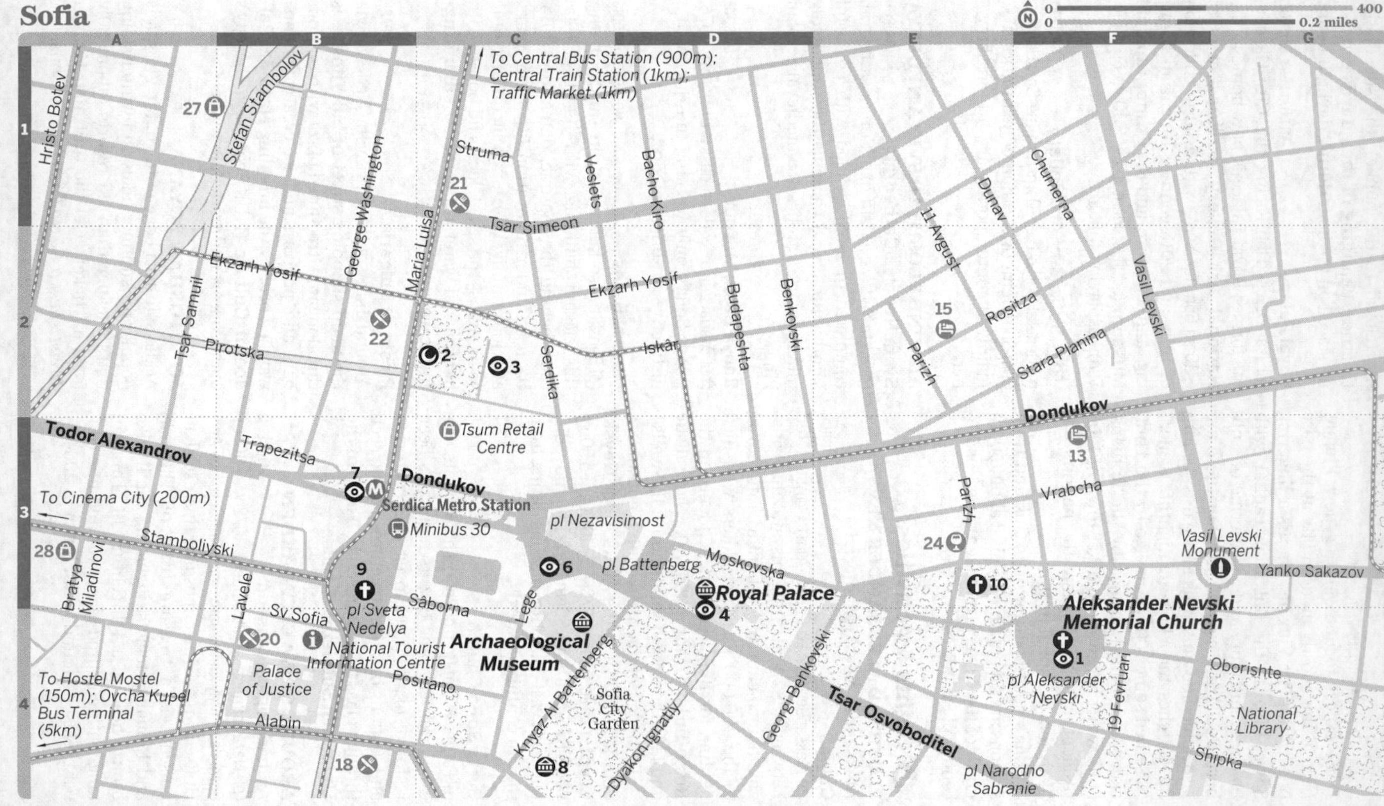
Sofia
0 400 m
0 0.2 miles
A
B
C
D
E
F
G
1
2
3
4
To Central Bus Station (900m); Central Train Station (1km); Traffic Market (1km)
Hristo Botev
27
Stefan Stambolov
Struma
21
Tsar Simeon
Veslets
Bacho Kiro
11 Avgust
Dunav
Chumerna
Vasil Levski
George Washington
Maria Luisa
Ekzarh Yosif
Ekzarh Yosif
Tsar Samuil
Pirotska
22
2
3
Serdika
Iskâr
Budapeshta
Benkovski
15
Rositza
Parizh
Stara Planina
Dondukov
13
Tsum Retail Centre
Todor Alexandrov
Trapezitsa
7
Dondukov
Serdica Metro Station
To Cinema City (200m)
Minibus 30
pl Nezavisimost
Vrabcha
Parizh
24
Vasil Levski Monument
Yanko Sakazov
28
Stamboliyski
Bratya Miladinovi
9
pl Sveta Nedelya
6
pl Battenberg
Moskovska
Royal Palace
4
10
Aleksander Nevski Memorial Church
1
Lavele
Sv Sofia
Sâborna
Lege
20
National Tourist Information Centre
Archaeological Museum
Palace of Justice
Positano
Knyaz Al Battenberg
Sofia City Garden
Dyakon Ignatiy
Georgi Benkovski
Tsar Osvoboditel
pl Aleksander Nevski
19 Fevruari
Oborishte
National Library
Shipka
To Hostel Mostel (150m); Ovcha Kupel Bus Terminal (5km)
Alabin
18
8
pl Narodno Sabranie

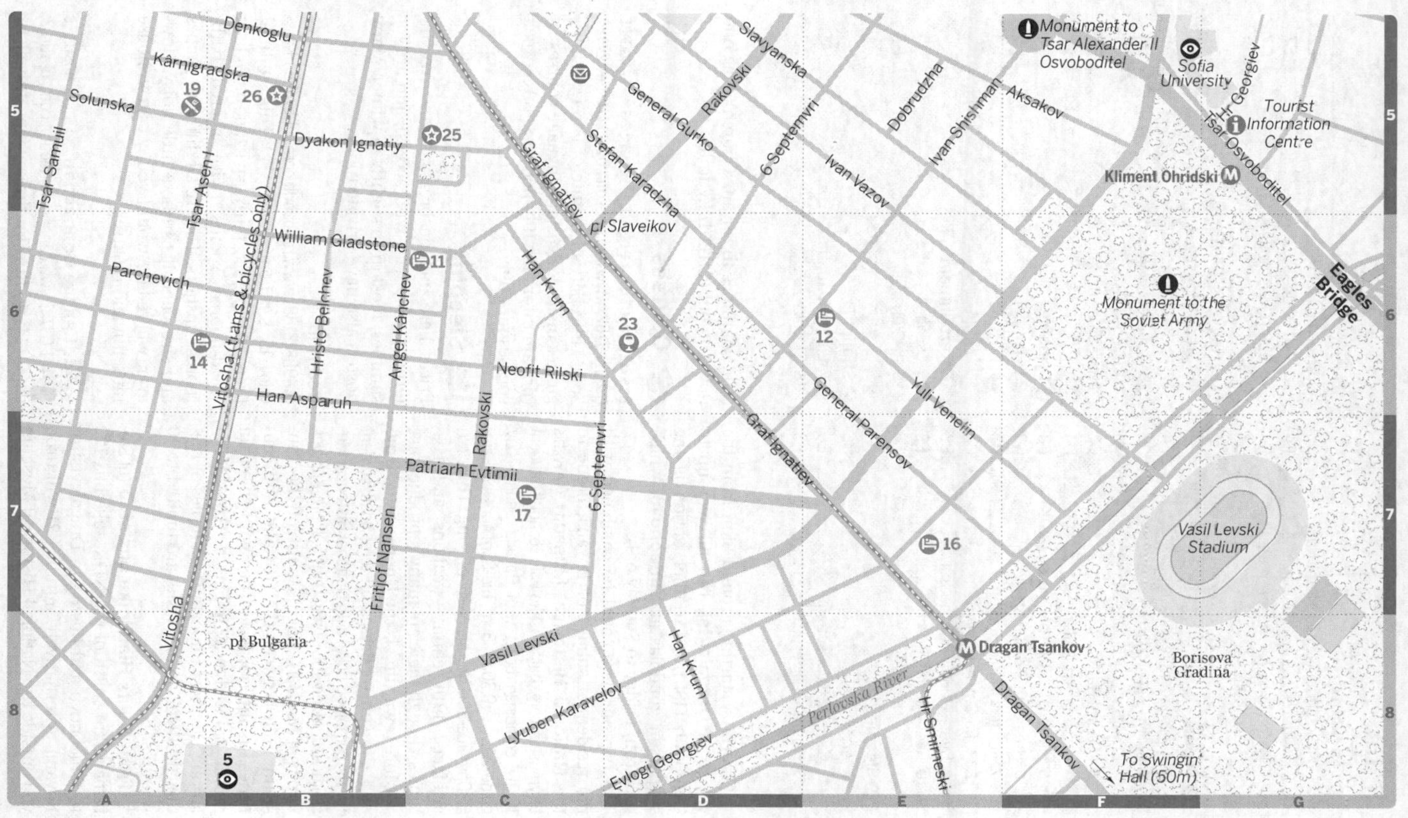

Denkoglu
Kârnigradska
Solunska
Tsar Samuil
Tsar Asen I
Vitosha (trams & bicycles only)
Dyakon Ignatiy
William Gladstone
Parchevich
Hristo Belchev
Angel Kânchev
Han Asparuh
Neofit Rilski
Rakovski
Patriarh Evtimii
6 Septemvri
Fritjof Nansen
Vitosha
pl Bulgaria
Vasil Levski
Lyuben Karavelov
Evlogi Georgiev
Han Krum
Perlovska River
Hr Smirneski
Dragan Tsankov
To Swingin' Hall (50m)
Borisova Gradina
Vasil Levski Stadium
Graf Ignatiev
pl Slaveikov
Stefan Karadzha
General Gurko
Rakovski
Slavyanska
6 Septemvri
Ivan Vazov
Dobrudzha
Ivan Shishman
Aksakov
General Parensov
Yuli Venelin
Monument to Tsar Alexander II Osvoboditel
Sofia University
Hr Georgiev
Tourist Information Centre
Tsar Osvoboditel
Kliment Ohridski
Monument to the Soviet Army
Eagles Bridge
Dragan Tsankov
5
11
12
14
16
17
19
23
25
26

Sofia

Top Sights

- Aleksander Nevski Memorial Church ... F4
- Archaeological Museum ... C4
- Royal Palace ... D3

Sights

- 1 Aleksander Nevski Crypt ... F4
- 2 Banya Bashi Mosque ... C2
- Ethnographical Museum ... (see 4)
- 3 Mineral Baths ... C2
- 4 National Art Gallery ... D4
- 5 National Palace of Culture (NDK) ... B8
- 6 President's Building ... C3
- 7 Serdica Metro Station ... B3
- 8 Sofia City Art Gallery ... C4
- 9 Sveta Nedelya Cathedral ... B3
- 10 Sveta Sofia Church ... E3

Sleeping

- 11 Art Hostel ... C6
- 12 Canapé Connection ... E6
- 13 Hostel Gulliver ... F3
- 14 Hotel Niky ... A6
- 15 Kervan Hostel ... E2
- 16 Red House ... E7
- 17 Sofia Guesthouse ... C7

Eating

- 18 Dream House ... B4
- 19 Pri Yafata ... A5
- 20 Sofiiska Banitsa ... B4
- 21 Trops Kâshta ... C1
- 22 Tsentralni Hali ... B2

Drinking

- 23 Hambara ... D6
- 24 Pri Kmeta ... E3

Entertainment

- 25 Escape ... C5
- 26 ID Club ... B5

Shopping

- 27 Ladies Market ... A1
- 28 Stenata ... A3

Chairlifts, starting around 3km from the village of **Dragalevtsi**, run all year up to Goli Vrâh (1837m). Another option is the six-person gondolas at **Simeonovo**, which runsfrom Friday to Sunday only.

A trip out here could be combined with the residential suburb of Boyana, home to the **National Historical Museum** (www.historymuseum.org; bul Vitoshko Lale 16; adult/student 10/1lv, combined ticket with Boyana Church 12lv, guide 20lv; ⌚9.30am-6pm Tue-Sun Apr-Oct, 9am-5.30pm Tue-Sun Nov-Mar), displaying Thracian artefacts, 19th-century weapons and costumes, though there are many reproductions.

More rewarding is the Unesco-listed **Boyana Church** (ul Boyansko Ezero; adult/student 10/1lv, combined ticket with National Historical Museum 12lv, guide 10lv; ⌚9.30am-5.30pm Apr-Oct, 9am-5pm Nov-Mar), 1.5km south of the museum, built between the 11th and 19th centuries. Its interior is adorned with colourful murals painted in 1259. They are considered among the most important examples of medieval Bulgarian art. Visits are limited to 10 minutes.

From Sofia's **Hladilnika bus stop** (ul Srebârna), 2km south of the NDK, take bus 122 to Simeonovo and bus 64 to Dragalevtsi or Boyana. Alternatively, minibus 21 will drop you outside the National Historical Museum (and continues to Boyana Church). Flag one down on bul Patriarh Evtimii.

Courses

Institute of Foreign Languages LANGUAGE
(☎971 7162; www.deo.uni-sofia.bg; ul Lulchev 27) Sofia University's Institute of Foreign Languages offers Bulgarian-language courses (private tutors for 19lv per hour, three-week courses for 599lv).

Sleeping

Prices here include breakfast and free internet (many with wi-fi access), and are for summer; most drop slightly in winter. Many hostels also have private rooms.

Red House B&B €€
(☎988 8188; www.redbandb.com; ul Lyuben Karavelov 15; s/d from €25/40; @) This cultural house keeps six fairly spartan but clean wood-floored rooms (with shared bathrooms) upstairs. They're all different shapes and sizes, and it can be a little noisy. However, where else would you get an in-house museum and theatre?

TOP CHOICE **Canapé Connection** HOSTEL €
(☎441 6373; www.canapeconnection.com; ul Yuri 2; dm €11-14; @) Run by three young travellers,

Canapé is a newish place with eight- and four-bed dorms (one en suite) with smart wooden bunks and wooden floors. Homemade breakfast includes *banitsa,* pancakes and croissants.

Ethno Hostel HOSTEL €
(☎0878 345 845; www.ethnohostel.com; ul Tsar Ivan Assen II 33; dm €11; @) East of the city centre, Ethno has a relaxed, friendly, hippyish vibe, with a cosy lounge, a log fire, colourful wall paintings, bongos, guitars and even a double bass for some late-night jamming.

Hostel Gulliver HOSTEL €
(☎987 5210; www.gulliver1947-bg.com; bul Dondukov 48; dm/s/d 18/38/48lv; @) Conveniently located just a couple of blocks north of pl Aleksander Nevski, Gulliver is a clean and brightly furnished little hostel with a couple of five-bed dorms and four doubles, one en-suite. All rooms have TVs and fridges. Laundry costs 6lv per load.

Hotel Niky HOTEL €€€
(☎952 3058; www.hotel-niky.com; ul Neofit Rilski 16; s/d from €40/45; ❄@) Niky offers 23 smart rooms and suites, all with tiny kitchenettes. The central location and reasonable prices mean it's often full, so book ahead. There's also a good restaurant.

Sofia Guesthouse HOSTEL €€
(☎403 0100; www.sofiaguest.com; ul Patriarh Evtimii 27; dm/d €9/30; ❄@) In a private garden just off the busy street, this hostel has a travel agent and bright but rather small dorms, plus private rooms with en-suite facilities.

Hostel Mostel HOSTEL €€
(☎0889 223 296; www.hostelmostel.com; ul Makedoniya 2; dm €8-13, s €22, d €30-39; @) One of Sofia's most popular hostels, Mostel fills the 1st floor of an old tavern with a choice of six- and eight-bed dorms as well as doubles, triples and one single, some en suite. There are comfy sofas, a pool table, a wooden verandah and a 107cm plasma TV.

Kervan Hostel HOSTEL €€
(☎983 9428; www.kervanhostel.com; ul Rositza 3; dm/d €10/30; 📶) Clean and friendly, the Kervan has an entry lined with antique radios and a 'Spanish' tiled kitchen. Free tea and coffee is on hand and bikes are available to hire for €10 per day.

Hotel Enny HOTEL €
(☎983 4395; www.enyhotel.com; ul Pop Bogomil 46; s/d from 25/40lv) A back-up accommodation option in the centre, the Enny has simple rooms (some small, all without air-con or fan) that can get you to the next day OK, but there's no breakfast. Most rooms have shared bathrooms.

TAXI SCAM

Bulgaria (and especially Sofia) has an abundance of crooked taxi drivers waiting to overcharge unwary foreign visitors. In the capital, the **OK Supertrans** (☎973 2121) taxi company is reliable, but there are also 'fake' OK Taxi taxis around; even Bulgarians get caught. Have your hostel or restaurant call your cab, and check that the meter's on and that the taxi's posted rates aren't exorbitant; 0.56lv to 0.79lv per km is normal.

Art Hostel HOSTEL €€
(☎987 0545; www.art-hostel.com; ul Angel Kânchev 21a; dm/s/d incl breakfast €11/28/38; @) They claim it's 'like joining a family for a few days'; this boho hang-out has plenty of character, with a back garden and a cool basement bar. The dorms are a bit cramped, though, with triple bunks.

Eating

There are snack bars selling kebabs, sandwiches, coffee and *banitsa* everywhere.

Pri Yafata BULGARIAN €€
(ul Solunska 28; mains 5-15lv) Better-quality Bulgarian cuisine is served at this faux-folksy restaurant with a huge menu of traditional favourites and occasional live music.

TOP CHOICE **Dream House** VEGETARIAN €
(ul Alabin 50a; mains 3-8lv; ✍) Offering Sofia's best meatless dining, this relaxed place serves an inspired menu of vegie and vegan dishes such as stir-fries, buckwheat pancakes and soups.

Sofiiska Banitsa STREET FOOD €
(cnr ul Positano & ul Lavele; banitsa 1lv; ⏲7am-7.30pm Mon-Sat) It's a typical street-corner bakery selling fresh hot *banitsa* and other savoury snacks.

Tsentralni Hali MARKET €
(bul Maria Luisa 25; ⏲7am-10pm) This refurbished covered market sells fresh fruit and vegetables, cheese, bread, cakes and wine, and has a small food court upstairs.

Trops Kâshta BULGARIAN €
(bul Maria Luisa 26; mains from 3lv; ⏲8am-8.30pm) For cheap, fast, fresh cafeteria-style food, like *kebabche* and moussaka (plus beer), this busy place doesn't disappoint. Other branches are at ul General Gurko 38 and in the basement of Tsentralni Hali.

Drinking

Several English-language publications list bars; see the free monthly *Sofia City Guide*.

Hambara PUB
(ul 6 Septemvri 22; ⏲8pm-late) Located in a two-level cellar lit only by candles, this rather secretive place is unsigned, and down a dark and dingy path; you might have to knock on the door to be let in.

Pri Kmeta PUB
(ul Parizh 2; ⏲noon-4am) In a big cellar behind the Sveta Sofia Church, this is Sofia's only microbrewery, complete with gleaming copper vats in the corner. It produces four home brews (500mL from 2.60lv) including a cloudy wheat beer and a strong dark beer.

Studentski Grad BARS, CLUBS
The college-student enclave of Studentski Grad (Student Town) comprises drab communist-era apartment blocks with numerous bars and clubs. **Strozha** (Block 23B) is an indie-rock dive designed to look like a construction site, while **Avenue** (ul Manchev 1A) is the place for some hip-shaking *chalga* (traditional folk-pop). Get there by minibus 7 from bul Maria Luisa or minibus 8 along ul Rakovski (one way 1.50lv).

☆ Entertainment

Escape NIGHTCLUB
(ul Angel Kânchev 1; cover 10lv; ⏲10pm-late Thu-Sun) Popular central disco with theme nights such as Britpop party and hip-hop night.

ID Club GAY & LESBIAN CLUB
(bul Vitosha 18; ⏲9pm-5am Tue-Sat) Glitzy gay club with cabaret nights and varied playlist.

Swingin' Hall LIVE MUSIC
(bul Dragan Tsankov 8; ⏲Tue-Sun) The coolest cellar-fashioned live-music venue featuring rock, blues and jazz.

Cinema City CINEMA
(bul Stamboliyski 101; tickets 5-9lv) On the top floor of the Mall of Sofia shopping centre, this multiscreen cinema shows the latest Hollywood offerings.

Shopping

Stenata OUTDOOR GEAR
(ul Bratya Miladinovi 5; ⏲10am-8pm Mon-Fri, 10am-6pm Sat) Bulgaria's best outfitter for the outdoors-bound and active.

Ladies Market MARKET
(ul Stefan Stambolov; ⏲dawn-dusk) A busy daily market selling food and clothes.

Information

Garibaldi (ul Graf Ignatiev 6; per hr 3.30lv; ⏲8.30am-midnight) Central internet cafe.

Immigration office (☎982 3316; bul Maria Luisa 48; ⏲foreigner services 12.15-1.30pm Mon-Fri) This hectic office can extend visas and entry stamps beyond 90 days.

Poliklinika Torax (☎91285; www.thorax.bg; bul Stamboliyski 57; ⏲24hr) Good private clinic west of the centre.

Tourist Information Centre (☎491 8345; Sofia University underpass; ⏲8am-8pm) Hands out free leaflets and city maps.

Unicredit Bulbank (ul Lavele & ul Todor Aleksandrov; ⏲8.30am-6pm Mon-Fri) Changes travellers cheques for 4% commission.

Usit Colours (☎981 1900; www.usitcolours.bg; ul Vasil Levski 35; ⏲9.30am-6.30pm Mon-Fri, 10.30am-6pm Sat) Sells ISIC cards (10lv) and offers discounted air fares for students.

Zig Zag/Odysseia-In (☎980 5102; www.zigzagbg.com; bul Stamboliyski 20V; ⏲9.30am-6.30pm Mon-Fri) Helpful English-language staff charge 12lv for a 30-minute consultation on priceless hiking tips. Also books rooms, sells maps and offers a host of day trips and multiday activities such as guided climbing and caving trips. Enter from ul Lavele.

Getting There & Away

Air

Sofia airport has two terminals; most flights land at terminal two, where there's a taxi stand, an ATM and an **information booth** (☎937 2211; www.sofia-airport.bg). Minibus 30 runs between the airport and central pl Nezavisimost (1.50lv).

Bus

DOMESTIC BUSES Sofia's **Central Bus Station** (www.centralnaavtogara.bg; bul Maria Luisa; ⏲24hr) is 100m south of the train station, with numerous stands (serving some international destinations) in the Traffic Market in between. The following routes have frequent services:

Bansko 13lv, three hours.

Burgas 20lv to 24lv, six hours.

Nesebâr 28lv, seven hours.

Plovdiv 13lv, two hours.

Ruse 15lv, 4½ hours.

READING UP

Ivan Ilchev's *The Rose of the Balkans* is a recent historical overview of Bulgaria translated into English, while Ivan Vazov's *Under the Yoke*, also available in translation, is Bulgaria's best-loved novel, based around the 1876 April Uprising. Lonely Planet's *Bulgaria* offers comprehensive coverage of the country.

Varna 28lv, six hours.
Veliko Târnovo 18lv, 3½ hours.

Two buses connect Sofia with Rila monastery (10lv, 2½ hours), leaving at 10.20am and 6.20pm from the **Ovcha Kupel Bus Terminal** (Zapad; bul Tsar Boris III). Tram 5 from pl Makedoniya goes to the station.

INTERNATIONAL BUSES Most international buses go from the Traffic Market. **Matpu** (www.matpu.com) sells tickets for Skopje (Macedonia; 32lv, six hours, five daily), Belgrade (Serbia; 54lv, eight hours, two daily) and Zagreb (Croatia; 110lv, 10 hours, one daily). Other stands sell tickets for Budapest (Hungary), Bratislava (Slovakia) and Prague (Czech Republic).

South a couple of hundred metres, **MTT** (bul Maria Luisa 84) sends regular buses to Thessaloniki (48lv, 6½ hours) and Athens (108lv, 12 to 13 hours) and a weekly bus to Patras (123lv, 14 hours), in Greece.

Several companies go daily to İstanbul (Turkey; 40lv to 50lv, eight to 10 hours) from the central station.

Train

At Sofia's **Central Train Station** (bul Maria Luisa) buy same-day tickets for Vidin, Ruse and Varna on the main floor; all other domestic destinations are downstairs.

International tickets can be purchased at the **Rila Bureau** (⌚24hr) in the northern part of the main floor, or at its **centre office** (ul General Gurko 5; ⌚7am-7.30pm Mon-Fri, 7am-6.30pm Sat).

Sample train routes (sleeper rates for international trains):

Athens 95lv, 15 hours, one daily.
Belgrade 60lv, 7½ hours, two daily.
Bucharest 57lv, 10½ hours, two daily.
Burgas 21.50lv, 6½ to 7½ hours, six daily.
Gorna Oryahovitsa (near Veliko Târnovo) 15.50lv, 4½ hours, 10 daily.
İstanbul 90lv, 12 to 14 hours, one daily.
Plovdiv 10.20lv, 2½ hours, 12 daily.
Ruse 20.40lv, 6½ hours, four daily.
Varna 25.20lv, eight to nine hours, six daily.

Getting Around

CAR & MOTORCYCLE Bulgaria Car Rental (☎400 1060; www.bulgariacarrent.com; ul Orfei 9) rents cars from €19/29 per day for September to June/July and August.

PUBLIC TRANSPORT Sofia's trams, buses and metro line run from 5.30am to 11pm and share a ticket system. A single ride is 1lv, a day pass is 4lv. There are no transfers. Blue ticket booths are near most stops and many newsstands sell tickets, too. Single-ride tickets must be validated once you board. Note that you must buy an additional bus or tram ticket for any large bag (60cm x 40cm x 40cm or bigger) unless you want to risk a 10lv fine.

Minibuses *(marshrutki)* ply many useful city routes at 1.50lv per ride.

TAXI The dependable **OK Supertrans Taxi** (☎973 2121) uses the meter.

SOUTHERN BULGARIA

Many of Bulgaria's most popular hiking trails and ski runs are in the mountainous southwest. The **Rila Mountains** (www.rilanationalpark.org) are south of Sofia, the **Pirin Mountains** (www.pirin-np.com) are further south towards the Greek border, and the **Rodopi Mountains** are just east and south of Plovdiv.

Check www.bulgariaski.com for ski information on the three main resorts: Borovets, Bansko and Pamporovo.

Drop by Zig Zag/Odysseia-In in Sofia for tips on activities.

Rila Monastery Рилски Манастир

Many Bulgarians say you haven't been to Bulgaria without paying your respects to this Unesco-protected **monastery** (admission free; ⌚6am-9pm or 10pm) 120km south of Sofia. Set in a forested valley offering excellent hikes, it's famed for its mural-filled **Nativity Church**, dating from the 1830s.

Built in 927, and heavily restored in 1469, the monastery helped keep Bulgarian culture and language alive during Ottoman rule.

If you have time, you can hike up the **Tomb of St Ivan**. The 15-minute hike begins along the road 3.7km east behind the monastery.

There are hotels and camping grounds nearby. You can also sleep in the monastery's simple **rooms** (☎07054-2208; r 30-60lv).

Two daily direct buses run to the monastery from Sofia's Ovcha Kupel Bus Terminal (10lv, 2½ hours), with one returning at 3pm.

Five daily buses reach nearby Rila village (2lv, 30 minutes), where hourly buses go south to Blagoevgrad (1.80lv, 25 minutes) for more connections.

Plovdiv Пловдив

☎032 / POP 375,000

Bulgaria's second city, and one of its oldest, has a rich cultural heritage and an impressive roll-call of attractions, including the still-functioning Roman theatre, several art galleries, and ancient churches. The cobbled lanes of the hilltop Old Town are especially rewarding, with a number of restored National Revival–era houses to visit.

Plovdiv was settled by Thracians as early as 5000 BC, and was named Philipopolis by the conquering 4th-century-BC Macedonians, in honour of Philip II (Alexander the Great's father). It was renamed Trimontium by the Romans who swung by later.

Plovdiv's train station and (main) Yug Bus Terminal are about 600m southwest of the central pl Tsentralen. From the square, the main pedestrian thoroughfare, ul Knyaz Aleksandâr, stretches 500m north to pl Dzhumaya.

On arrival, take bus 7, 20 or 26 in front of the train station (1lv, buy on board) and exit on ul Tsar Boris III Obedinitel past the tunnel to reach the Old Town.

Sights

Most of Plovdiv's main sights are in or around the Old Town.

Old Town HISTORIC AREA

The charming Old Town is the pride of Plovdiv. Wander the cobbled lanes, and you can visit art galleries, about a dozen National Revival houses *(kâshta)*, a couple of museums and some interesting churches.

Ethnographical Museum MUSEUM

(ul Dr Chomakov 2; adult/student 5/1lv; ⌚9am-noon & 2-5.30pm) Occupying a restored 1847 home with beautifully carved wooden ceilings, this museum has a fascinating array of traditional costumes and crafts, including vintage apparatus for distilling attar of roses.

Hindlyian Kâshta HISTORIC BUILDING

(ul Artin Gidilov 4; adult/student 5/1lv; ⌚8.30am-4.30pm) This is the best of the Old Town house-museums, dating from 1835 and filled with period furniture and exotic murals.

Roman Theatre HISTORIC SITE

(ul Hemus; admission 3lv; ⌚10am-5pm) The Roman theatre is easily seen from the cafe outside the gates, but entry lets you tread on worn steps approaching their 2000th birthday. The theatre holds music events from June to August.

State Gallery of Fine Arts ART GALLERY

(ul Sâborna 14; admission 3lv, Thu free; ⌚9.30am-12.30pm & 1-5.30pm, from 10am Sat & Sun) This gallery holds an absorbing collection of works by major 19th- and 20th-century Bulgarian artists, as well as exhibitions of contemporary art.

Dzhumaya Mosque MOSQUE

(pl Dzhumaya; ⌚dawn-dusk) Dating back to 1368 (though rebuilt in 1784), the 'Friday Mosque' is one of the oldest in the Balkans, with an elegant 23m-high minaret.

Sleeping

For private rooms, try **Esperansa** (☎office 260 653, 24hr mobile phone 0897 944 951; travel_plovdiv@abv.bg; ul Ivan Vazov 14; s/d 25/50lv, apt from 80lv; ⌚approx 10am-8pm), a 10-minute walk from the main stations.

Hotel Romantica BOUTIQUE HOTEL €€

(☎622 675; www.hotelromantica.net; ul Gurko 17; r incl breakfast from 70lv; ❄📶) Just off the main drag, the Romantica offers six large and tastefully furnished rooms, most with small kitchen areas as well as TVs. The English-speaking staff are super-friendly.

TOP CHOICE **Raisky Kat Hostel** HOSTEL €

(☎268 849; www.raiskykat.hostel.com; ul Slaveikov 6; dm/d incl breakfast €10/24; @) With just five rooms, with between two and three single beds each, this peaceful, family-run Old Town hostel is more like a cosy little hotel, and is well placed for sightseeing.

Hiker's Hostel HOSTEL €

(☎0885 194 553; www.hikers-hostel.org/pd; ul Sâborna 53; dm €7-10lv, d €25; 📶) This cosy backpacker stop occupies a little house in the Old Town, with clean dorms and comfy communal areas. The laid-back staff can arrange excursions. Breakast is 2lv extra.

Plovdiv Guesthouse HOSTEL €€

(☎622 432; www.plovdivguest.com; ul Sâborna 20; dm/s/d incl breakfast May-Sep €10/28/36, Oct-Apr €10/20/23; ❄@🚭) Home to a travel agency, this clean pink house in the Old Town has large dorms and twin rooms. No alcohol or smoking allowed inside.

Hostel Bell HOSTEL €
(☎649 185; www.hostel-bell.com; ul Radetski 18; dm €12;) Around 400m north of the train station, the Bell has 12-bed dorms, most with single beds, balcony, fridge and TV. It's a bit cramped, though.

Hotel Elite HOTEL €€
(☎624 537; www.hotel-elite.eu; ul Raiko Daskalov 53; s/d from 49/59lv; @) Rooms (all with TVs) vary, but are clean, with views of Imaret Mosque. There's cheap internet access downstairs, but no breakfast.

Eating

TOP CHOICE **Malâk Bunardzhik** BULGARIAN €
(ul Volga 1; mains 4-11lv; ⏰9am-midnight) With tables set in a quiet, leafy courtyard, this is a great place for traditional Bulgarian food like *kebabche* and *tarator* soup. There's occasional live music in the evenings.

Gusto PIZZA €€
(ul Otets Paisii 26; mains 6-15lv; ⏰9am-1am) Pizzas and pasta dishes (both very good) are mainstays at this busy place. Alternatives include steaks, chicken, duck and fish. The outdoor seats fill up quickly in the evenings so get in early.

Chilli CAFE €
(Maritsa Bridge; mains 3-6lv; ⏰11am-8pm) On the pedestrian bridge over the Maritsa, this simple cafeteria offers cheap dishes like sausages, soups and fish, with great river views. It's best for lunch, as things tend to dry up later in the day.

Banicharnitsa BAKERY €
(banitsas 0.90lv, pizzas 1-1.50lv; ⏰6am-6pm Mon-Sat) In the underpass off pl Tsentralen; a popular take-away bakery.

Drinking & Entertainment

Vinalia WINE BAR
(cnr ul Knyaz Aleksândar & ul Gurko; wine per glass 3lv; ⏰10am-midnight) This central wine bar offers a huge list of Bulgarian wines to sip while munching your way through various tapas dishes (from 3.90lv).

Chocolate CAFE
(ul Daskalov 48; cocktails 3-3.50lv; ⏰7am-11pm Mon-Fri, 9am-11pm Sat & Sun) With outdoor seating on both sides of the road, this place serves a colourful range of both alcoholic and nonalcoholic cocktails.

WORTH A TRIP

HISAR (ХИСАР)

If Plovdiv's Roman remnants have whetted your appetite for archaeology, the peaceful Roman spa town of **Hisar** is an easy day trip north of town. Here you can explore Bulgaria's most extensive, and impressive, Roman ruins; you'll see a picture of the gigantic town gate on bottles of the eponymous Hisar mineral water sold all over Bulgaria. Lengthy stretches of monumental walls (many over 5m high), bathhouses, theatres and more are still standing, set in and around peaceful parks. There are also 22 continually gushing mineral springs, whose waters are said to cure all kinds of ailments, and if you want to stay to unwind, there are plenty of midrange hotels offering spa therapies. Hisar is roughly 40km, and a one-hour bus ride, north of Plovdiv.

Petnoto NIGHTCLUB
(ul Yoakim Gruev 36) Local bands and DJs mixing things up, plus jazz on Monday and rock on Thursday.

Caligula GAY & LESBIAN CLUB
(ul Knyaz Aleksandâr 30) Plovdiv's only gay club attracts a mixed crowd.

Information

Left luggage The train station has 24-hour luggage storage (3lv per piece per day); the Yug and Rodopi Bus Terminals both hold bags for 1lv per day.

Tourist Information Centre (☎656 794; www.plovdiv-tour.info; pl Tsentralen; ⏰9am-6pm Mon-Fri, 10am-2pm Sat & Sun) Staff can find private accommodation.

Unicredit Bulbank (ul Ivan Vazov 4; ⏰8am-6pm Mon-Fri)

Getting There & Away

BUS **Yug Bus Terminal** (bul Hristo Botev), 100m northeast of the train station, sends frequent buses to Sofia (13lv, two hours) every half-hour or hour, plus a few daily buses to Varna (26lv, seven hours), Burgas (20lv, four hours) and Hisar (3.20lv, one hour). Around half a dozen buses go to İstanbul (40lv, six hours).

More than 1km north of the river, Sever Bus Terminal has four daily buses to Veliko Târnovo (15lv, 4½ hours). Get there by minibus 4 from ul Tsar Boris III Obedinitel.

About 100m south of Yug Bus Terminal, Rodopi Bus Terminal, accessible by underpass from the train station, sends buses into the Rodopi Mountains and İstanbul.

TRAIN Daily direct services from the **train station** (bul Hristo Botev) include the following: Burgas (13.40lv, five hours, five daily), İstanbul (49lv, 11 hours, one daily), Sofia (8.10lv to 10.20lv, 2½ hours, frequent), Varna (16.70lv, six hours, four daily) and Veliko Târnovo (11lv, five hours, one daily).

For international tickets, go to **Rila Bureau** (☎643 120; bul Hristo Botev 31a; ⏰7.30am-7.30pm Mon-Fri, 8am-6pm Sat summer, shorter hr in winter).

CENTRAL BULGARIA

Bulgaria is bisected by the long **Stara Planina** (www.staraplanina.org) range, the local name for the Balkans. Some appealing towns line the south side of the range – like **Kazanlâk**, handy for visiting the tombs in the 'Valley of the Thracian Kings', and the lovely museum-village of **Koprivshtitsa**, famed for its National Revival houses. Most visitors head to Central Bulgaria's main hub, the medieval capital of Veliko Târnovo.

Veliko Târnovo Велико Търново

☎062 / POP 72,000

Clinging to a sharp S-shaped gorge carved by the snaking Yantra River, Veliko Târnovo is one of Bulgaria's real highlights. The medieval capital (1185–1393) and important university town is a pleasure to explore and filled with days of potential.

From the train platform, a walkway heads northwest towards an underpass that leads to ul Hristo Botev, near the Yug Bus Terminal. Alternatively, there are several buses to the centre from in front of the train station; taxis cost 3lv to 4lv to the centre. From the bus station, it's an uphill walk of around 15 minutes to the town centre.

Sights

As well as the legendary Tsarevets Fortress, there are a handful of museums, plus a few Byzantine-influenced churches open for (fee-paying) visits in the **Asenova quarter** below Tsarevets Hill. For great views of the gorge, walk along cobbled **ul Gurko**, Veliko Târnovo's oldest street.

Tsarevets Fortress FORTRESS
(adult/student 6/2lv; ⏰8am-7pm Apr-Sep, 9am-5pm Oct-Mar) About 1km east of the centre, this huge citadel and former seat of the medieval tsars sprawls over a vast and commanding site. Today you can see the remains of more than 400 houses, 18 churches, the royal palace, execution rock and several towers. Watch your step though, as there are lots of holes, broken steps and unfenced drops.

Archaeological Museum MUSEUM
(ul Ivan Vazov; adult/student 6/2lv; ⏰9am-6pm Tue-Sun) Prehistoric flint tools, Roman pottery and fearsome-looking medieval weaponry are among the exhibits at this musty museum, down steps from ul Ivan Vazov.

Sarafkina Kâshta MUSEUM
(ul Gurko 88; adult/student 6/2lv; ⏰9am-6pm Mon-Fri) This two-storey former banker's home built in 1861 displays period furnishings, traditional costumes and photographs of the old town.

State Art Gallery ART GALLERY
(Asenovtsi Park; adult/student 3/1lv, Thu free; ⏰10am-6pm Tue-Sun) Set dramatically on the little finger of land poking into the Yantra, this gallery has two floors of Bulgarian paintings. In front stands the huge 1985 **Asenevs Monument** depicting medieval Bulgarian tsars on horseback.

Activities

Trapezitsa ROCK CLIMBING, HIKING
(☎635 823; www.trapezitca1902.com; ul Stefan Stambolov 79; ⏰9am-6pm Mon-Fri) Trapezitsa can help arrange rock-climbing and hiking trips.

Gorgona CYCLING
(☎601 400; www.gorgona-shop.com, in Bulgarian; ul Zelenka 2; ⏰10am-1pm & 2-7pm Mon-Fri, 10am-2pm Sat) For cycling options, Gorgona rents out mountain bikes (10lv per day).

Hiking

Veliko Târnovo is surrounded by stunning countryside. From town, you can walk 6km to medieval **Preobrazhenski Monastery**, with its mural-bedecked **church** (admission 2lv). The path there begins near Hikers Hostel – up from the centre.

Another great hike is to the hilltop village of **Arbanasi**, 4km northeast. The 16th-century **Nativity Church** (adult/student 6/2lv; ⏰9am-5pm), 200m west of the bus stop, is worth a look. It's unremarkable outside but the interior is covered with fabulous murals. The hike begins across a small bridge behind the Tsaravets (go around to the left side); you can also catch the bus up.

Sleeping

Be wary of touts at the bus and train stations offering private rooms (around 15lv per person) – these are often far from the centre.

TOP CHOICE Phoenix Hostel HOSTEL €
(603 112; www.phoenixhostel.com; ul Daskalov 12; dm/d incl breakfast 20/50lv; @) This British-run hostel occupies a lovely old timber-framed house in the Varosha district, with a peaceful common room (pointedly with no TV) and kitchen. Various day trips can be arranged.

Nomads Hostel HOSTEL €
(603 092; www.nomadshostel.com; ul Gurko 27; dm incl breakfast 20-22lv, s 40lv, d 50-54lv; @) Veliko Târnovo's only air-conditioned hostel, Nomads enjoys a peaceful location on historic ul Gurko. All rooms look over the river.

Hostel Mostel HOSTEL €€
(0897 859 359; www.hostelmostel.com; ul Iordan Indjeto 10; campsites/dm/s/d 18/20/46/60lv; @) Just 150m from Tsarevets Fortress, Mostel has bright dorms and a few en-suite doubles. There's a BBQ in the garden, plus a bar and lounge.

Ivan's House PENSION €
(0886 438 370; www.ivanovata-kashta.com; ul Vastanicheska 5; s/d/apt 25/40/50lv;) On a cobbled side street in the town centre, Ivan's feels like staying in a private home, with small, simple but bright rooms, all with private bathrooms and TVs, plus a communal kitchen.

Hotel Kiev HOTEL €€
(600 572; www.hotelkiev.eu; ul Velchova Zavera 4; s/d 40/55lv;) The Kiev occupies a stately 1930s building in the town centre and offers plain but big rooms which are quite good value.

Hikers Hostel HOSTEL €€
(0889 691 661; www.hikers-hostel.org; ul Rezevoarska 91; campsites/dm/d incl breakfast 14/20/52lv;) Way up a steep cobbled path, this small hostel is a hike to reach but has superb views.

Eating & Drinking

Ego Pizza PIZZA €
(ul Nezavisimost 17; pizzas 5-10lv) A busy spot for pizzas, with an outdoor terrace overlooking the river. Service is quick and pizzas are huge. Alternatives include chicken and pork dishes.

Martin McNamara PUB
(ul Nezavisimost 25; noon-late) This buzzing basement Irish pub has regular live music on Friday and Saturday, as well as jam sessions and party nights.

Entertainment

Follow students to popular clubs such as **Spider** (ul Hristo Botev; cover 2-3lv), a two-floor dance club near the Etap bus stand.

Information

Era Internet (off ul Hristo Botev; per hr 1.20-1.40lv; 24hr)
Postbank (ul Hristo Botev)
Tourist information centre (622 148; www.velikoturnovo.info; ul Hristo Botev 5; 9am-6pm Mon-Fri, plus 9am-6pm Sat in summer) Staff can arrange accommodation and rental cars (from 30lv per day).
USIT Colours (601 751; pl Slaveikov 7; 9.30am-6.30pm Mon-Fri, 10.30am-4pm Sat) Sells ISIC cards for 10lv.

Getting There & Away

BUS For buses to Sofia (18lv, 3½ hours) or Varna (16lv, 3½ hours), it's easiest to catch one of the 10 daily stopping at **Etap Adress** (ul Ivailo, Hotel Etâr), 100m south of the information centre.

Yug Bus Terminal (ul Hristo Botev), a few hundred metres farther downhill from the centre, also serves Sofia and Varna, plus Plovdiv (13lv, four hours, one daily), Burgas (20lv, four hours, four daily), Bucharest (28lv; midday bus with a quick transfer in Ruse) and İstanbul (40lv, seven hours; night bus).

Regional buses, plus more to Plovdiv, leave from the Zapad Bus Terminal, 4km west of the centre.

TRAIN Veliko Târnovo's small train station sends about one direct train a day to Plovdiv (11lv, five hours). Five daily trains to Sofia (16.20lv, five to six hours) and four to Varna (12.50lv, four or five hours) require a change at the busier Gorna Oryahovitsa train station, 13km north of town. Minibuses along ul Vasil Levski, or bus 10 east from the centre, head there every 10 or 15 minutes.

An overnight train to İstanbul (couchette/sleeper 55/79lv, 13¾ hours) and a mid-morning train to Bucharest (29lv, six hours) stop in Veliko Târnovo. Buy international tickets at **Rila Bureau** (622 130; ul Tsar Kolyan; 8am-noon & 1-6.30pm Mon-Fri), behind the information centre.

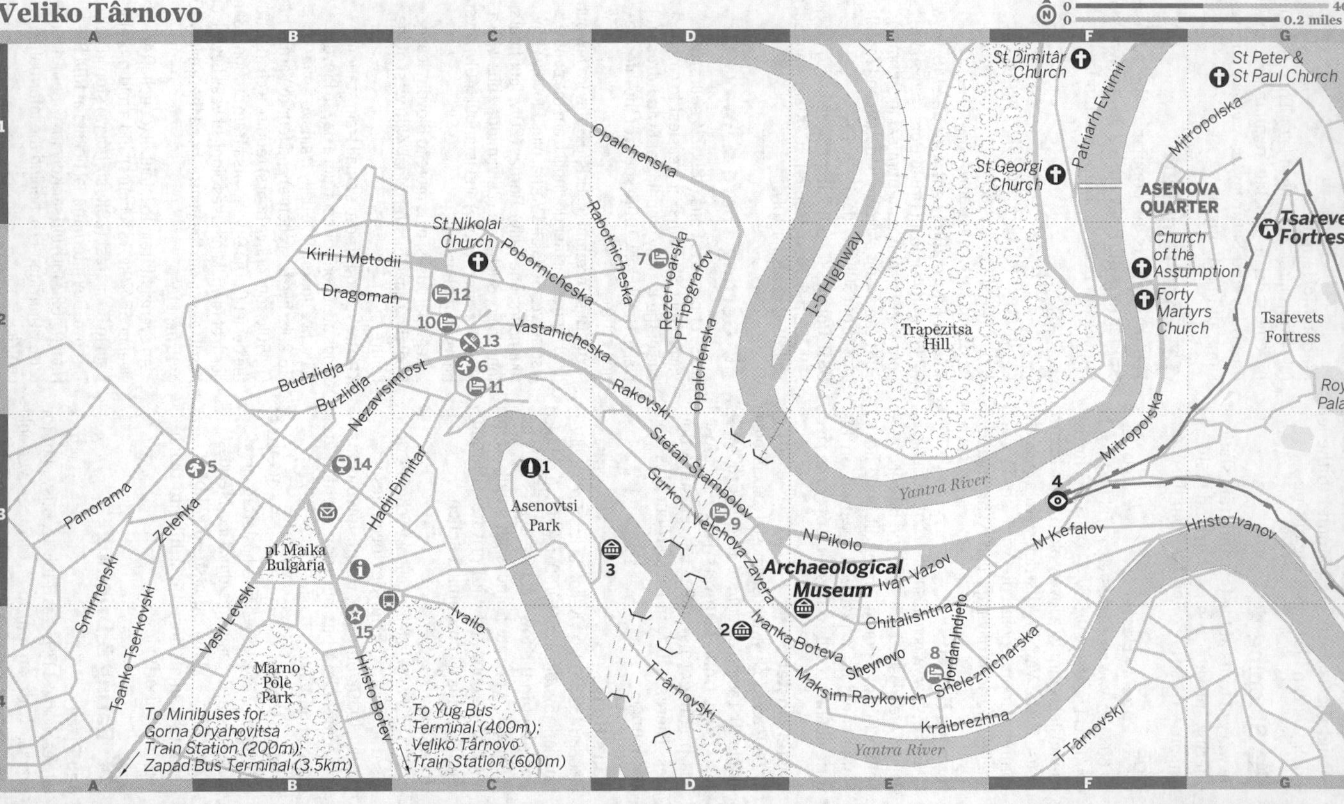
Veliko Târnovo
0 400 m
0 0.2 miles
St Dimitâr Church
St Peter & St Paul Church
Patriarh Evtimii
Mitropolska
St Georgi Church
ASENOVA QUARTER
Tsarevets Fortress
Church of the Assumption
Forty Martyrs Church
Tsarevets Fortress
Royal Palace
Opalchenska
Rabotnicheska
Rezervoarska
P Tipografov
I-5 Highway
Trapezitsa Hill
St Nikolai Church
Kiril i Metodii
Pobornicheska
Dragoman
Vastanicheska
Opalchenska
Budzlidja
Buzlidja
Nezavisimost
Rakovski
Stefan Stambolov
Gurko
Velchova Zavera
Yantra River
Mitropolska
Panorama
Zelenka
Hadji Dimitar
Asenovtsi Park
N Pikolo
M Kefalov
Hristo Ivanov
pl Maika Bulgaria
Archaeological Museum
Ivan Vazov
Smirnenski
Tsanko Tserkovski
Vasil Levski
Ivailo
Chitalishtna
Iordan Indjeto
Ivanka Boteva
Sheynovo
Shelesnicharska
Marno Pole Park
Hristo Botev
T Târnovski
Maksim Raykovich
Kraibrezhna
To Minibuses for Gorna Oryahovitsa Train Station (200m); Zapad Bus Terminal (3.5km)
To Yug Bus Terminal (400m); Veliko Târnovo Train Station (600m)
Yantra River
T Târnovski

Veliko Târnovo

Top Sights

- Archaeological Museum E4
- Tsarevets Fortress G2

Sights

1 Asenevs Monument C3
2 Sarafkina Kâshta D4
3 State Art Gallery D3
4 Tsarevets Fortress Entrance F3

Activities, Courses & Tours

5 Gorgona B3
6 Trapezitsa C2

Sleeping

7 Hikers Hostel D2
8 Hostel Mostel E4
9 Hotel Kiev D3
10 Ivan's House C2
11 Nomads Hostel C2
12 Phoenix Hostel C2

Eating

13 Ego Pizza C2

Drinking

14 Martin McNamara B3

Entertainment

15 Spider B4

BLACK SEA COAST

Every summer, hordes of international package holidaymakers head to bland, overdeveloped resorts like Sunny Beach and Golden Sands. Neither are very user-friendly for independent travellers, and there are far more interesting places to enjoy the Bulgarian seaside. Varna is a lively, beachfront city, but the best stretches of sand are to the south.

Hotel rates are most expensive in July and August, a bit less in June and September.

Varna Варна

052 / POP 353,000

Cosmopolitan Varna, with its long sandy beaches, Roman ruins, museums and legendary nightlife, was established as Bulgaria's first seaside resort in 1921, with the still-going **Summer International Festival**, held between May and October, following a few years later. Briefly called 'Stalin' after WWII, Varna's origins stretch back 6000 years or so to the Thracians. Greek colonists founded the city of Odessos here in the 6th century BC, while the name Varna first appeared under Byzantine rule in the 6th century AD.

The train station is 650m south of central pl Nezavisimost, where pedestrian ul Knyaz Boris I heads east to ul Slivnitsa, which runs southeast to seaside Primorski Park. The bus station is 2km north of the centre.

Sights & Activities

The beach is a big part of why people come here, but there's a lot more to Varna.

Beach BEACH

Starting just steps from the train station, **Varna city beach** is 8km long. The southernmost section (with pool complex and water slides) is very popular (and crowded); the thinner central beach is dominated by clubs; further north there are some wider stretches of sand and a **thermal pool** with year-round hot water.

Inland from the beach is **Primorski Park**, a vast expanse of greenery and flower beds with open-air cafes, a communist monument and little old ladies selling homemade lace.

Archaeological Museum MUSEUM

(ul Maria Luisa 41; adult/student 10/2lv; 10am-5pm Tue-Sun Apr-Sep, 10am-5pm Tue-Sat Oct-Mar) One of Bulgaria's best museums, filled with more than 100,000 artefacts ranging from 6500-year-old gold jewellery (apparently the oldest worked gold in the world) to Roman statues and Thracian tombstones.

Roman Thermae RUINS

(ul Khan Krum; adult/student 4/2lv; 10am-5pm daily May-Oct, 10am-5pm Tue-Sat Nov-Apr) The ruins of the 2nd-century-AD Roman baths are the biggest in Bulgaria, but there's not much information inside. You can just about make out the various bathing areas, and peer into the furnaces, where slaves kept the whole enterprise going.

Ethnographic Museum MUSEUM

(ul Panagyurishte 22; adult/student 4/2lv; 10am-5pm Tue-Sun Apr-Sep, 10am-5pm Tue-Fri Oct-Mar) Housed in an 1860 National Revival building, this museum's collection includes colourful folk costumes and traditional fishing and wine-making equipment.

Sleeping

Summer-only accommodation bureaux in the train station offer private rooms from 12lv to 30lv. Across from the train station, **Victorina** (603 541; Tsar Simeon 36; s/d apt from 25/35lv; ⌚9am-6pm Mon-Sat, 10am-3pm Sun) arranges rooms year-round.

TOP CHOICE **X Hostel** HOSTEL €€
(☎0885 049 084; www.xhostel.eu; Evksinograd 19, 16th Rd, Sveti Konstantin; dm/s/d €11/14/28; @✈) About 10km north of Varna, on the edge of the Sveti Konstantin resort, the X has a garden, a restaurant and movie nights. Follow the 'Villa Waikiki' signs.

Hotel Acropolis HOTEL €€
(☎603 108; www.hotelacropolis.net; ul Tsar Ivan Shishman 13; s incl breakfast 40-50lv, d incl break-

Varna

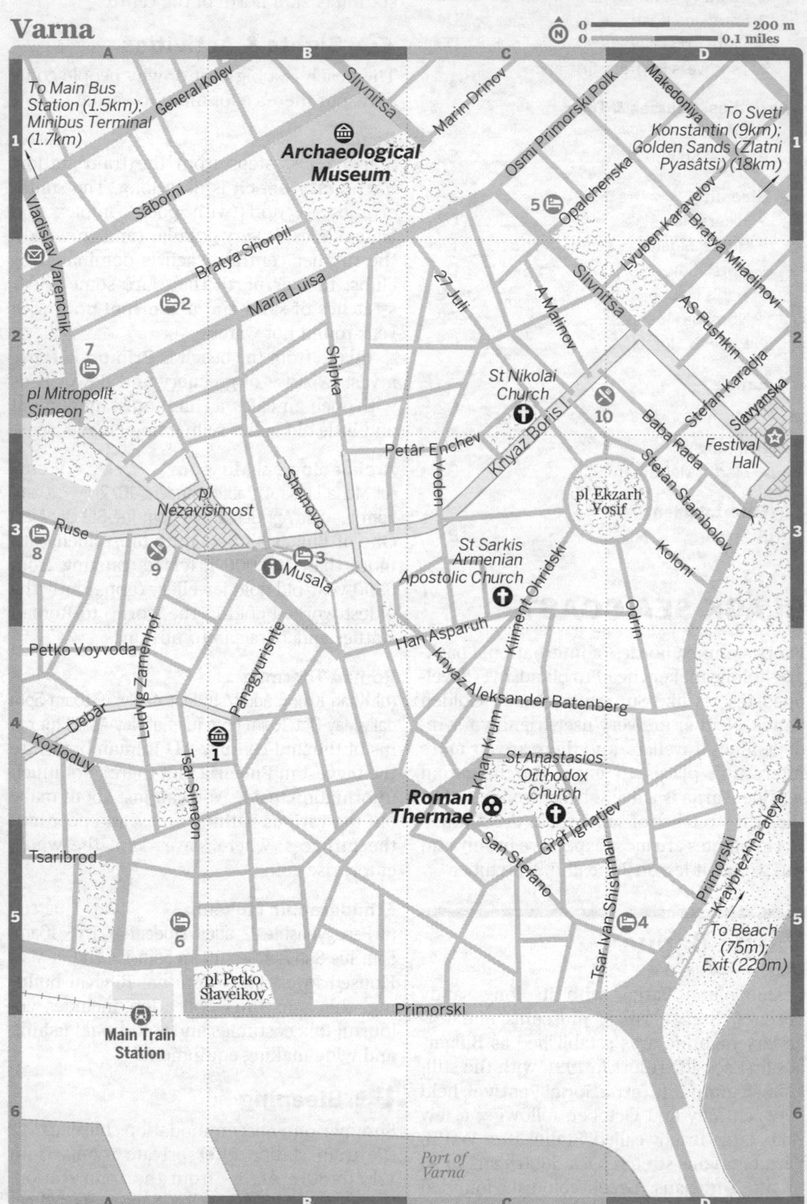

fast 50-60lv; ❄📶) On a residential street across the road from the beach, the Acropolis is a family-run hotel with simple but clean rooms with modern bathrooms.

Hotel Astra HOTEL €€
(☎630 524; hotel_astra@abv.bg; ul Opalchenska 9; s/d from 40/50lv; ❄📶) The Astra is a peaceful family hotel with 10 decent-sized rooms with polished wood floors, TVs and fridges on a leafy central street. Some rooms have balconies.

Flag Hostel HOSTEL €
(☎0897 408 115; www.varnahostel.com; ul Bratya Shkorpil 13a; dm incl breakfast €9; 📶) The Flag is a popular choice, offering bright, clean dorms with single beds (no bunks), free beer on arrival, and shared bathrooms.

Yo Ho Hostel HOSTEL €
(☎0886 382 905; www.yohohostel.com; ul Ruse 23; dm/d €11/15; @) With a vaguely piratey theme, this laid-back hostel is run by four local guys who organise day trips.

Voennomorski Club HOTEL €€
(☎617 965; ul Vladislav Varenchik 2; s 25-48lv, d 72lv; ❄) Filling the top two floors of the 'Naval Club', rooms here are a bit dated and cheerless, but the location is convenient.

Eating

Trops Kâshta BULGARIAN €
(bul Knyaz Boris I 48; dishes 3-5lv) This bright cafeteria chain offers fresh and cheap Bulgarian staples.

Varna

Top Sights

Sights

Sleeping

Eating

SPLURGE

Varna's oldest hotel, the **Grand Hotel London** (☎664 100; www.londonhotel.bg; ul Musala 3; s/d from €120/140; ❄📶) dates back to 1912 and has recently undergone a refit, bringing back a touch of belle époque style to the seaside. Plush carpets, swaggy drapes, potted ferns and antique-style furnishings create an old-world ambience, while you can dine on fine French cuisine in the award-winning restaurant and relax with a massage in the wellness centre.

Morsko Konche PIZZA €
(pl Nezavisimost; pizzas 5-10lv) The 'Seahorse' is a friendly place with outdoor seating, serving pizzas, salads and beer.

Drinking & Entertainment

In summer, there are plenty of lively open-air bars along the beachfront path known as Kraybrezhna aleya; many change names from one season to the next. You'll also find several clubs along here, such as **Exit** (⌚10pm-4am).

Information

Find entertainment listings in the free monthly *Varna City Guide* (www.cityinfoguide.net).

Global Tours (☎601 085; www.globaltours-bg.com; ul Kynaz Boris I 67; ⌚8am-8pm Mon-Fri, 10am-6pm Sat Jun-Sep, 9am-6pm Mon-Fri Oct-May) This travel agent books private apartments (from €20 in summer), rents cars, and runs bus tours to Balchik and Kaliakra Cape (€22) and fishing trips (€23).

Internet Doom (ul 27 Yuli 13; per hr 1.60lv; ⌚24hr) Internet access.

Left luggage (per day 2lv; ⌚7am-12.30pm & 1-9.50pm) At the train station.

Municipal tourist information centre (☎602 907; pl Musala; ⌚9am-7pm Mon-Sat May-Sep, 9am-6pm Mon-Sat Oct-Apr)

Unicredit Bulbank (ul Slivnitsa)

Getting There & Away

AIR **Varna airport** (www.varna-airport.bg) is 8km northwest of town; catch bus 409.

BUS The **main bus station** (bul Vladislav Varenchik 158) is 2km north of the city centre (take bus 409 or 148). Services include the following:

Athens 125lv, 26 hours, three weekly in summer.

Bucharest 50lv, seven hours, daily in summer.

Burgas 12lv, 2½ hours, frequent.

İstanbul 55lv, 10 hours, twice daily.
Odesa (Ukraine) 79lv, 20 hours, five weekly.
Plovdiv 26lv, six hours, two daily.
Ruse 15lv, four hours, three daily.
Sofia 30lv, seven to eight hours, half-hourly.
Veliko Târnovo 17lv, four hours, half-hourly.

MINIBUS The **minibus terminal** (Avtogara Mladost; ul Dobrovoltsi), 200m west of the bus station (cross the street via an underpass and go left 50m, then right past the next block), sends minibuses hourly to Burgas (12lv) from 7am to 7pm. Less-frequent services go to Nesebâr (via Sunny Beach; 10v).

TRAIN Direct train services from the **main train station** (bul Primorski) link Varna to Sofia (21.90lv, eight to nine hours, six daily), Plovdiv (16.70lv, 6½ to 7½ hours, four daily), Ruse (11lv, 3¾ hours, two daily) and Gorna Oryahovitsa (for Veliko Târnovo; 11.80lv, 3½ hours, five daily).

There are two daily trains to Bucharest (30lv, 13 hours), both requiring a change in Ruse. International tickets must be purchased at **Rila Bureau** (ul Preslav 13; ⊙8.30am-5.30pm Mon-Fri, 8am-3.30pm Sat), a few minutes' walk from the station.

North Coast

As well as pricier package resorts north of Varna such as **Sveti Konstantin** and **Golden Sands**, **Balchik** is a possible day trip. There's not much of a beach – most of the far-north coast is rocky – but the **Summer Palace of Queen Marie & Botanical Gardens** (Dvorets; admission 10lv; ⊙8am-8pm May–mid-Oct, 8.30am-6.30pm mid-Oct–Apr), the eccentric former holiday home of the Queen of Romania, is worth a look. The **Irish Rover** (☎0888 510 530; www.balchikirish.com; ul Primorska 27; s/d Jul & Aug €15/30, Sep-Jun €10/20; @) has cosy rooms above a town-centre pub.

From Balchik you can bus 30km northeast once daily to lovely Kaliakra Cape (5lv, 45 minutes), where the 2km-long **Kaliakra Nature Reserve** (admission 3lv; ⊙24hr) pokes out into the Black Sea and features Thracian ruins dating from the 4th century BC.

Nesebâr Несебър

☎0554 / POP 10,000

Around 40km northeast of Burgas, historic but very commercialised Nesebâr occupies a small rocky isthmus on the south end of a wide bay, facing the megaresort of **Sunny Beach** (Slânchev Bryag), with its 8km-long beach.

Nesebâr was settled by Greek colonists in 512 BC and named Messembria, but today it's more famous for its (mostly ruined) medieval **churches**, including the vast shell of the 6th-century **Old Metropolitan Church** (ul Mitropolitska).

The **Archaeological Museum** (ul Mesembria 2; adult/student 4/2lv; ⊙9am-7pm Mon-Fri, 9am-6pm Sat & Sun summer, 9am-1.30pm & 2-6pm Mon-Sat winter) has an interesting collection of local Greek and Roman finds.

At the north end of town, **Hotel Toni** (☎42 403, 0889 268 004; ul Kraybrezhna 20; r from 40lv; ❄) is a family-run hotel with balconies facing Sunny Beach.

Most Varna–Burgas buses stop on the main highway, 2km west of town. Nesebâr's bus stand is at the Old Town gate, where you can catch buses to Burgas (5lv, 40 minutes) every 40 minutes, or to Varna (10lv, two hours) five times a day. There are also a few daily buses to Sofia (28lv, seven hours).

Burgas Бургас

☎056 / POP 189,500

Burgas may not have Varna's big-city buzz, but it has a laid-back, un-touristy charm, a perfectly good, 2km-long sandy beach, and a pleasant seaside park dotted with statues, fountains and cafes. It also makes a good base for exploring nearby attractions like Sozopol and Nesebâr. The lively, pedestrianised ul Aleksandrovska runs north from the train station and Yug Bus Terminal. At pl Svoboda it meets cafe-lined ul Bogoridi, which extends eastwards to the beach.

Sleeping

TOP CHOICE **Hotel California** HOTEL €€
(☎531 000; www.burgashotel.com; ul Lyuben Karavelov 36; s/d incl breakfast 60/70lv; ❄📶) Five minutes' walk west of the centre, the California is a charming boutique hotel with very soft mattresses and an excellent restaurant.

Burgas Hostel HOSTEL €
(☎825 854; elanbase@gmail.com; ul Slavyanska 14; dm/d incl breakfast €10/25; @) This central hostel has basic but clean dorms, an en-suite double and a communal kitchen.

Getting There & Away

AIR Wizz Air (www.wizzair.com) connects London's Luton with Burgas airport (8km north); take bus 15 to the centre.

BUS From **Yug Bus Terminal** (cnr ul Aleksandrovska & ul Bulair), buses go to Varna (12lv, 2½ hours, half-hourly), Nesebâr (5lv, 45 minutes, frequent), Sozopol (4lv, 40 minutes, frequent), Sofia (22lv to 28lv, 6¼ hours, eight daily), Plovdiv (18lv to 20lv, four hours, several daily) and Veliko Târnovo (26lv, 4½ hours, two daily).

Enturtrans/Istanbul Seyahat (ul Bulair 22) sells tickets for İstanbul (50lv, seven hours).

TRAIN The **train station** (ul Ivan Vazov) has direct trains to Sofia (18.30lv, 7½ hours, seven daily) and Plovdiv (13.40lv, four to five hours, three daily). Trains to Bucharest (55lv, 11 hours, twice weekly) leave June through August only and require a transfer in Ruse. Buy international tickets at **Rila Bureau** (⌚8am-4pm Mon-Fri, 8am-2.30pm Sat) in the station.

South Coast

Fine sandy beaches dot the coast south from Sozopol to Turkey, including at unexciting modern resorts like **Primorsko** and **Kiten** that cater mostly to Bulgarians.

SOZOPOL СОЗОПОЛ

☎0550 / POP 4650

A curling peninsula of cobbled streets, sandy beaches and ancient Greek heritage, Sozopol is a favourite Bulgarian summer destination.

There are two good beaches in town, and a small **Archaeological Museum** (ul Han Krum 2; admission 4lv; ⌚8.30am-6pm daily, closed Sat & Sun Nov-Mar).

Sasha Khristov's Private Rooms (☎23 434; ul Venets 17; r with shared bathroom 25lv) offers four rooms in the Old Town. Agents like **Enigma Tours** (☎0888 338 089; ul Kulata 5) find private accommodation from 35lv. The New Town has plenty of hotels with doubles for 40lv or 50lv. There are cheap fish restaurants along harbour front ul Kraybrezhna in the Old Town.

The **bus terminal** (ul Han Krum) is about halfway between the Old Town and inland New Town (Harmanite). Buses and minibuses leave for Burgas (5lv, 40 minutes, half-hourly from 6am to 9pm) all year.

UNDERSTAND BULGARIA

History

Thracians moved into the area of modern Bulgaria by around 5000 BC, and Greeks founded cities on the Black Sea coast from the 7th century BC on. By AD 100 Bulgaria was part of the Roman Empire. The first Slavs migrated here from the north in the 5th century AD, and the first Bulgarian state was formed in 681.

The Byzantine Empire conquered Bulgaria in 1014. Bulgaria gained independence from Constantinople in 1185, and this second kingdom, based in Veliko Târnovo, lasted until the Ottoman takeover in 1396.

During the 18th and 19th centuries, many 'awakeners' are credited with reviving Bulgarian culture. By the 1860s several revolutionaries (including Vasil Levski; see p260) organised *cheti* (rebel) bands for the unsuccessful April Uprising of 1876. With Russia stepping in, the Turks were defeated in 1878, and Bulgaria regained its independence.

Hoping to annex Macedonia, Bulgaria aligned with Germany in WWII, but after the war, Bulgaria embraced communism wholeheartedly (even proposing in 1973 to join the USSR).

Since 1989, Bulgaria has stumbled slightly as a new democracy. It joined NATO in 2004 and the EU in 2007, but low wages, organised crime and corruption are sources of continual complaint and anguish.

People

Of Bulgaria's 7.2 million people, Bulgarians constitute 85%. The largest minorities are Turks (9%) and Roma (4.5%), with smaller populations of Russians, Jews and Greeks.

During the communist era Bulgaria was officially atheist. These days, about 83% of the population are Orthodox Christian and 12% are Muslim (almost all of these are Sunni).

Art & Architecture

Bulgaria has an impressive musical tradition, stretching back more than a thousand years. Bulgarian ecclesiastical music is powerfully evocative, especially Orthodox chants and choral music.

One very popular form of modern music is *chalga*, a vaguely Oriental-sounding, warbling folk-pop, often with a scantily clad female vocalist. It's considered pretty lowbrow, and many Bulgarians will visibly cringe at the mention of it. However, the success of *chalga* clubs suggests many Bulgarians *do* quite like it, even if they'd rather not admit it.

Bulgaria's most treasured art graces the walls of medieval monasteries and churches, such as Boyana Church (p246) near Sofia, Arbanasi's Nativity Church (p254) and the

VASIL LEVSKI

It's a name you'll see on street signs in every Bulgarian town, and the matinee-idol looks will soon become familiar from the countless moustachioed, gazing-into-the-distance statues across the country; a bit like Che Guevara but with neater hair. It's Vasil Levski, Bulgaria's undisputed national hero.

Born in Karlovo in 1837, Levski (a nickname meaning 'Lion') originally trained as a monk, but in 1862 fled to Belgrade to join the revolutionary fight against the Turks. A few years later he was back, setting up a network of revolutionary committees. Levski, who believed in the ideals of the French Revolution, was a charismatic and able leader of the independence movement, but he was captured in Lovech in December 1872, and was hanged in Sofia in February 1873; the Vasil Levski Monument marks the spot where he died.

paintings by Zahari Zograf (1810–53) at Rila Monastery (p249).

Bulgaria's 19th-century National Revival saw many town makeovers, with traditionally styled *kâshta* buildings with whitewashed walls and wood-carved ceilings.

Food

Price ranges in this chapter are based on the cost of a main course:

€€€ more than 20lv

€€ 10lv to 20lv

€ less than 10lv

Environment

Bulgaria lies in the heart of the Balkan Peninsula, stretching 502km from the Serbian border to the 378km-long Black Sea coast.

The Stara Planina (Balkan Mountain) range stretches across central Bulgaria. In the southwest are three higher ranges – the Rila Mountains (home to Mt Musala, Bulgaria's highest point at 2925m), Pirin Mountains and Rodopi Mountains.

Bulgaria has some 56,000 kinds of living creatures, including bears, wild goats and deer. It maintains three national parks (Rila, Pirin and Central Balkans) and 10 nature parks.

SURVIVAL GUIDE

Directory A–Z

Accommodation

Sofia, Plovdiv, Veliko Târnovo, Varna and Burgas all have hostels, with beds from 18lv.

Private homestays are another cheap option in summer, available from bus- and train-station touts, accommodation agencies or by posted *'stai pod naem'* (rooms for rent) signs. Rates are 10lv to 25lv per person.

Average rates for budget hotels (which usually have private bathrooms, TVs and air-con) are around 40lv for a single, 50lv for a double.

Camping for most Bulgarians means an area with side-by-side basic bungalows and a couple of spots to pitch a tent. Up in the mountains there are many *hizhas* (mountain huts) in varying condition.

Price ranges in this chapter are based on the cost of a double room with bathroom:

€€€ more than 80lv

€€ 50lv to 80lv

€ less than 50lv

Activities

Bulgaria's mountains have more than 37,000km of hiking trails, some of which can be cross-country skied or cycled; nearly all lead to *hizhas* with dorms or private rooms. There are excellent opportunities for climbing, caving, skiing and snowboarding.

Before setting out, drop by the expert consultants at Zig Zag/Odysseia-In (p248) in Sofia for tips and maps. They also offer caving, climbing, hiking, cycling and snowshoeing excursions.

Other companies offering interesting activities include the following:

Crazy Sharks (www.dive-bg.com) Certified PADI diving courses.

Cycling Bulgaria (www.cycling.bg) Multiday mountain-bike tours.

Horse Riding Holidays (www.horseridingholidaysbulgaria.com) Day rides in the Stara Planina region.

Neophron (www.birdwatchingbulgaria.net) Birdwatching, botany, bear-viewing and wildlife photography tours.

Business Hours

Banks 8.30am-5.30pm Mon-Fri

Shops 9am-6pm daily

Post offices 8.30am-5pm Mon-Sat

Restaurants 10am-11pm

Dangers & Annoyances

You're unlikely to face major problems in Bulgaria. Pickpocketing can happen in summer, particularly on Varna's beach. There are plenty of rogue taxi drivers waiting to rip off foreigners; always use a reputable firm, and, if possible, ask your hostel to call your cab. If you're a nonsmoker, there's bad news: chain-smoking seems to be Bulgaria's top pastime, and smoking is allowed in most places.

Discount Cards

Most museums offer discounts up to 75% for students with valid ID, and some travel agents offer discounted air fares.

Gay & Lesbian Travellers

Homosexuality is legal in Bulgaria, but Bulgaria is far from openly tolerant. There are a few gay clubs in big cities listed in this chapter. Gay events include Sofia's **Gay Pride** parade in June and Varna's **Gay Week** in September. Useful websites include the following:

Bulgarian Gay Organization Gemini (www.bgogemini.org)

Bulgayria (www.gay.bg)

Sofia Gay Guide (http://sofia.gayguide.net)

Holidays

New Year's Day 1 January

Liberation Day (National Day) 3 March

Orthodox Easter Sunday & Monday March/April; one week after Catholic/Protestant Easter

St George's Day 6 May

Cyrillic Alphabet Day 24 May

Unification Day (National Day) 6 September

Bulgarian Independence Day 22 September

National Revival Day 1 November

Christmas 25 & 26 December

Money

The lev (lv) comprises 100 stotinki. It's pegged to the euro (roughly 2lv to €1). Prices in this chapter conform to local usage (alternating between euro and leva). Banknotes come in denominations of two, five, 10, 20 and 50 leva and coins in one, two, five, 10, 20 and 50 stotinki and one lev. Bulgaria won't adopt the euro during the life of this book.

ATMs and foreign-exchange offices are found in all towns listed in this chapter. American Express and Thomas Cook travllers cheques can be cashed at most banks (for approximately 4% commission).

Telephone

Nearly all Mobika and BulFon telephone booths use phonecards *(fonkarta)*, available at newsstands for 5lv to 25lv, for local or international calls.

GSM mobile phones can be used in nearly all places in Bulgaria. M-tel, Globul and Vivatel are the three operators.

To ring Bulgaria from abroad, dial the international access code then ☎359, followed by the area code (minus the first zero) then the number.

To call direct from Bulgaria, dial ☎00 followed by the country code.

Getting There & Away

Air

Bulgaria's main airports are Sofia and (in summer) Varna and Burgas. There is no additional departure tax levied at the airport.

Airlines flying to/from Bulgaria: **Aeroflot** (SU; www.aeroflot.ru)

British Airways (www.britishairways.com)

Bulgaria Air (www.air.bg)

ČSA (www.czechairlines.com)

easyJet (www.easyjet.com)

Lufthansa (www.lufthansa.com)

Wizz Air (www.wizzair.com)

Bus

International tickets to the region are available at practically any bus station in the country. Prices aren't set, so it's worth checking a couple of companies to find the cheapest fare. You will need to get off the bus at international borders for passport checks. The cost of visas is not included in the price of the bus ticket; check before you go if you need to buy in advance or whether you can purchase a visa, if needed, at the border crossing.

Car & Motorcycle

Drivers bringing a car into Bulgaria pay a weekly €5 road tax.

Train

Tickets for international trains can be bought at any government-run **Rila Bureau** (www.bdz-rila.com; ⊙most closed Sun) or at dedicated ticket offices (most open daily) at larger stations with international connections.

The daily *Trans-Balkan Express* (between Budapest and Thessaloniki, Greece) stops at Ruse, Gorna Oryahovitsa (near Veliko Târnovo) and Sofia.

The *Balkan Express* normally goes daily between Belgrade and İstanbul, with stops in Sofia and Plovdiv. The *Bulgaria Express* to Bucharest leaves from Sofia.

Getting Around

Air

Bulgaria Air (www.air.bg) flies between Sofia and Varna daily; it also flies to Burgas. **Wizz Air** (www.wizzair.com) also flies between Sofia and Varna.

Bus

This chapter lists the price and duration of trips and number of buses daily – *use these as a gauge only.* Buses connect all cities and major towns, and there are numerous private companies. The website of **Sofia Central Bus Station** (www.centralnaavtogara.bg) has comprehensive information (in English) on domestic bus routes. Intercity buses are normally modern and comfortable. Local buses are usually older but fine for shorter trips.

Car & Motorcycle

You must be 21 and have a driver's licence from your country to rent a car. The cheapest place to rent is Veliko Târnovo, where hostels find cars from 30lv per day. Speed limits are usually 130km/h on main highways and 90km/h on smaller ones. Town speed limits are 50km/h unless otherwise noted.

To drive on Bulgarian roads you need to purchase and display a 'vignette', available at border crossings and post offices. It costs from €5 per week.

Train

Trains, run by the **Bulgarian State Railways** (BDZh; www.bdz.bg), are normally cheaper than buses, but slower. *Ekspresen* (express) and *bârz* (fast) trains way outspeed the slow *pâtnicheski* (passenger).

Listings in this chapter are for 2nd-class seats. First-class seats – usually costing an extra 20% to 30%, are marginally more comfortable. It's worth paying for 1st class on longer journeys. Check updated schedules online.

Europe-wide rail passes are not good value in Bulgaria.

Bring food and water on board with you. Most train stations are poorly signposted and in Cyrillic only.

Croatia

Includes »

Best Places to Eat

» Vinodol, Zagreb (p271)

» Vodnjanka, Pula (p274)

» Kod Fife, Split (p277)

» Konoba Menego, Hvar (p278)

Best Places to Stay

» Hobo Bear Hostel, Zagreb (p270)

» Silver Central Hostel, Split (p276)

» Luka's Lodge, Hvar (p278)

» Fresh Sheets, Dubrovnik (p282)

Why Go?

Touted as the 'new this' and the 'new that' for years since its re-emergence on the tourism scene, Croatia has become a unique destination that holds its own and then some: this is a country with a glorious 1778km-long coast and a staggering 1244 islands. The Adriatic coast is a knockout: its sapphirine waters draw visitors to remote islands, hidden coves and traditional fishing villages, all while touting a glitzy beach and yacht scene. Istria captivates with its gastronomic delights and wines; the bars, clubs and festivals of Zagreb and Split remain little-explored gems. Eight national parks showcase primeval beauty with their forests, mountains, rivers, lakes and waterfalls.

Punctuate all this with dazzling Dubrovnik in the south – just the right finale. Best of all, Croatia hasn't given in to mass tourism: there are pockets of authentic culture and plenty to discover off the grid.

When to Go

Zagreb

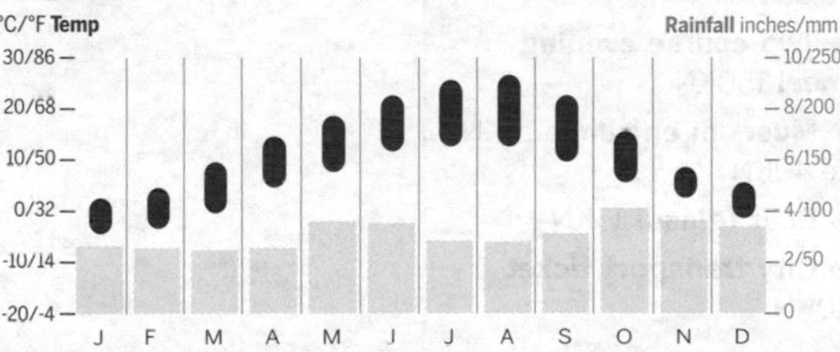

Jul & Aug Lots of sunshine, warm sea and festivals; many tourists and high prices.

Jun Best time to visit: beautiful weather, fewer people, lower prices, the festival season kicks off.

May & Sep Reliable weather, lack of tourists, full events calendar, wonderful for hiking.

AT A GLANCE

» **Currency** Kuna (KN)

» **Language** Croatian

» **Money** ATMs widely available; credit cards accepted in most hotels and larger restaurants

» **Visas** Generally not required for stays of up to 90 days; see p287

Fast Facts

» **Area** 56,538 sq km

» **Capital** Zagreb

» **Country code** ☎385

» **Emergency** Ambulance ☎194; Police ☎192

Exchange Rates

Australia	A$1	KN5.55
Canada	C$1	KN5.39
Euro Zone	€1	KN7.44
Japan	¥100	KN6.43
New Zealand	NZ$1	KN4.20
UK	UK£1	KN8.60
USA	US$1	KN5.28

Set Your Budget

» **Budget hotel room** up to 350KN

» **Two-course evening meal** 150KN

» **Museum entrance** 10KN to 40KN

» **Beer (glass)** 15KN

» **City transport ticket** 10KN

Resources

» **Croatian National Tourist Board** (www.croatia.hr)

» **Adriatica.net** (www.adriatica.net)

Connections

Croatia is a convenient transport hub for southeastern Europe and the Adriatic. Zagreb is connected by train and/or bus to Venice, Budapest, Belgrade, Ljubljana and Sarajevo. Down south there are easy bus connections from Dubrovnik to Mostar and Sarajevo, and to Kotor. There are a number of ferries linking Croatia with Italy, including from Dubrovnik to Bari, and Split to Ancona.

ITINERARIES

One Week

After a day in dynamic Zagreb, delving into its simmering nightlife, fine restaurants and choice museums, head down to Split for a day and night at Diocletian's Palace, a living part of this exuberant seafront city. Then hop over to chic Hvar for its beaches and nightlife. Next take it easy down the winding coastal road to magnificent Dubrovnik, for the final two days.

Essential Food & Drink

» **Ćevapčići** Small spicy sausages of minced beef, lamb or pork

» **Pljeskavica** An ex-Yugo version of a hamburger

» **Ražnjići** Small chunks of pork grilled on a skewer

» **Burek** Pastry stuffed with ground meat, spinach or cheese

» **Rakija** Strong Croatian brandy comes in different flavours, from plum to honey

» **Beer** Two top types of Croatian *pivo* (beer) are Zagreb's Ožujsko and Karlovačko from Karlovac

ZAGREB

☎01 / POP 779,145

Everyone knows about Croatia's coast and islands, but a mention of the country's capital still draws questions: 'Is it worth going to?' Here is the answer: Zagreb is a great destination, with lots of culture, arts, music, architecture, good food and all the other things that make a quality capital.

Visually, Zagreb is a mixture of straight-laced Austro-Hungarian architecture and rough-around-the-edges socialist structures; its character sometimes an uneasy combination of the two. This city is made for strolling the streets, drinking coffee in the often full cafes, popping into museums and galleries, and enjoying the theatres, concerts and cinema. It's a year-round outdoor city: in spring and summer everyone scurries to Jarun Lake in the southwest to swim, boat or dance the night away at lakeside discos, while in autumn and winter Zagrebians go skiing at Mt Medvednica, only a tram ride away, or hiking in nearby Samobor.

Sights

As the oldest part of Zagreb, the Upper Town (Gornji Grad) offers landmark buildings and churches from the earlier centuries of Zagreb's history. The Lower Town (Donji Grad) has the city's most interesting art museums and fine examples of 19th- and 20th-century architecture.

UPPER TOWN

Cathedral of the Assumption of the Blessed Virgin Mary CHURCH

(Katedrala Marijina Uznešenja; Kaptol; ⏲10am-5pm Mon-Sat, 1-5pm Sun) Kaptol Sq is dominated by the twin neo-Gothic spires of this 1899 cathedral, with an interior containing 13th-century frescos, Renaissance pews, marble altars and a baroque pulpit.

Dolac Market MARKET

(⏲6am-3pm Mon-Sat, 6am-1pm Sun) Zagreb's colourful Dolac is just north of Trg Josipa Jelačića. Since the 1930s, this buzzing centre of Zagreb's daily activity has drawn in traders from all over Croatia who flog their products here.

Lotrščak Tower HISTORIC BUILDING

(Kula Lotrščak; Strossmayerovo Šetalište 9; adult/concession 10/5KN; ⏲10am-8pm) Climb this medieval tower for a sweeping 360-degree view of the city. The nearby **funicular railway** (4KN), constructed in 1888, connects the Lower and Upper Towns.

St Mark's Church CHURCH

(Crkva Svetog Marka; Markov Trg; ⏲7.30am-6.30pm) Its colourful tiled roof makes this Gothic church one of Zagreb's most emblematic buildings. Inside are works by Ivan Meštrović, Croatia's most famous modern sculptor.

Meštrović Atelier ART GALLERY

(Mletačka 8; adult/concession 30/15KN; ⏲10am-6pm Tue-Fri, to 2pm Sat & Sun) The former home of Croatia's most recognised artist, Ivan Meštrović, houses an excellent collection of some 100 sculptures, drawings, lithographs and furniture created by the artist.

Galerija Klovićevi Dvori ART GALLERY

(www.galerijaklovic.hr; Jezuitski Trg 4; adult/concession 30/20KN; ⏲11am-7pm Tue-Sun) Housed in a former Jesuit monastery, this is the city's most prestigious space for exhibiting modern Croatian and international art.

Stone Gate LANDMARK

This eastern gate to medieval Gradec Town is now a shrine. According to legend, a great fire in 1731 destroyed every part of the wooden gate except for the painting of the Virgin and Child, produced by an unknown 17th-century artist.

LOWER TOWN

Trg Josipa Jelačića SQUARE

This is Zagreb's main orientation point and its geographic heart. It has an **equestrian statue** of Jelačić, the 19th-century *ban* (viceroy).

Museum Mimara MUSEUM

(Muzej Mimara; Roosveltov Trg 5; adult/concession 40/30KN; ⏲10am-7pm Tue-Fri, to 5pm Sat, to 2pm Sun Jul-Sep, shorter hr rest of year) Housed in a neo-Renaissance palace, this diverse collection includes icons, glassware, sculpture, Oriental art, and works by renowned painters such as Rembrandt, Velázquez, Raphael and Degas.

Strossmayer Gallery of Old Masters MUSEUM

(Strossmayerova Galerija Starih Majstora; www.mdc.hr/strossmayer; Trg Nikole Šubića Zrinskog 11; adult/concession 10/5KN; ⏲10am-7pm Tue, to 4pm Wed-Fri, to 1pm Sat & Sun) Check out the impressive fine-art collection donated to Zagreb by Bishop Strossmayer in 1884.

Croatia Highlights

1. Gape at the Old Town wall of **Dubrovnik** (p280), which surrounds luminous marble streets and finely ornamented buildings
2. Admire the Venetian architecture and vibrant nightlife of **Hvar Town** (p278)
3. Indulge in the lively and historic delights of Diocletian's Palace in **Split** (p274)

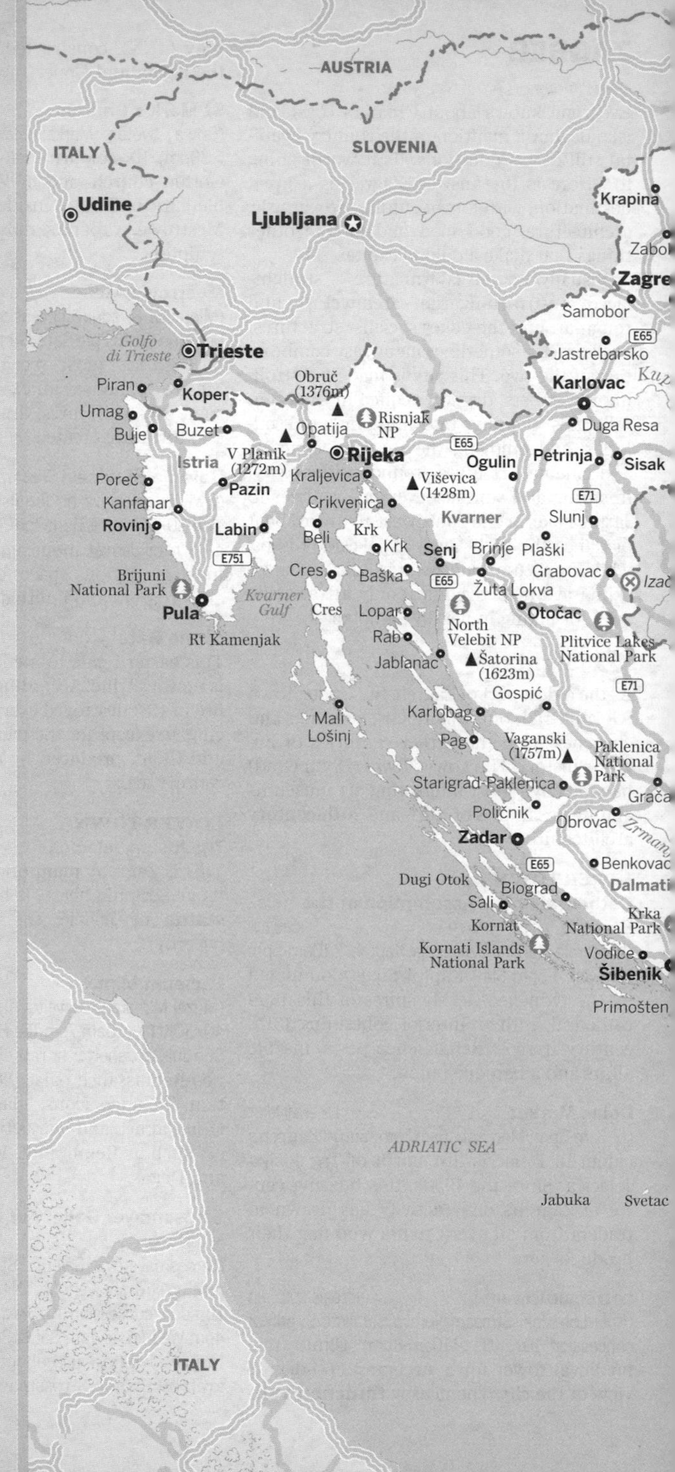

0 100 km
0 50 miles
HUNGARY
SERBIA
BOSNIA AND HERCEGOVINA
MONTENEGRO
ALBANIA
Čakovec
Goričan
Varaždin
Varaždinske Toplice
Koprivnica
Gola
Drava
Đurđevac
Križevci
Pecs
Terezino Polje
Pitomača
Bjelovar
Virovitica
Zagreb Airport
Čazma
Slatina
Donji Miholjac
Beli Manastir
Kopački Rit National Park
Backi Breg
Bezdan
Bogojevo
Daruvar
Kapovac (790m)
Našice
Osijek
Dalj
Kutina
Sisak
Petrinja
Pakrac
Slavonska Požega
Nova Gradiška
Novska
Glina
Borovo
Vukovar
Danube
Novi Sad
Đakovo
Đakovačka Breznica
Vinkovci
Bačka Palanka
Otok
Hrvatska Kostjanica
Slavonski Brod
Bosanska Dubica
Kozara National Park
Sava
Davor
Županja
Batrovci
Una
Brčko
Banja Luka
Knin
Cikola
Sinj
Sarajevo
Trogir
Split
Omiš
Imotski
Gorica-Vinjani Donji
Supetar
Brela
Šolta
Makarska
Brač
Bol
Hvar Town
Stari Grad
Hvar
Drvenik
Ploče
Metković
Metković-Doljani
Vis
Vis Town
Komiža
Orebić
Vela Luka
Korčula
Polače
Sobra
Pomena
Mljet
Lastovo
Mljet National Park
Dubrovnik
Ivanica
Cavtat
Piva
Podgorica
A4
E661
E70
E73
E71
E65

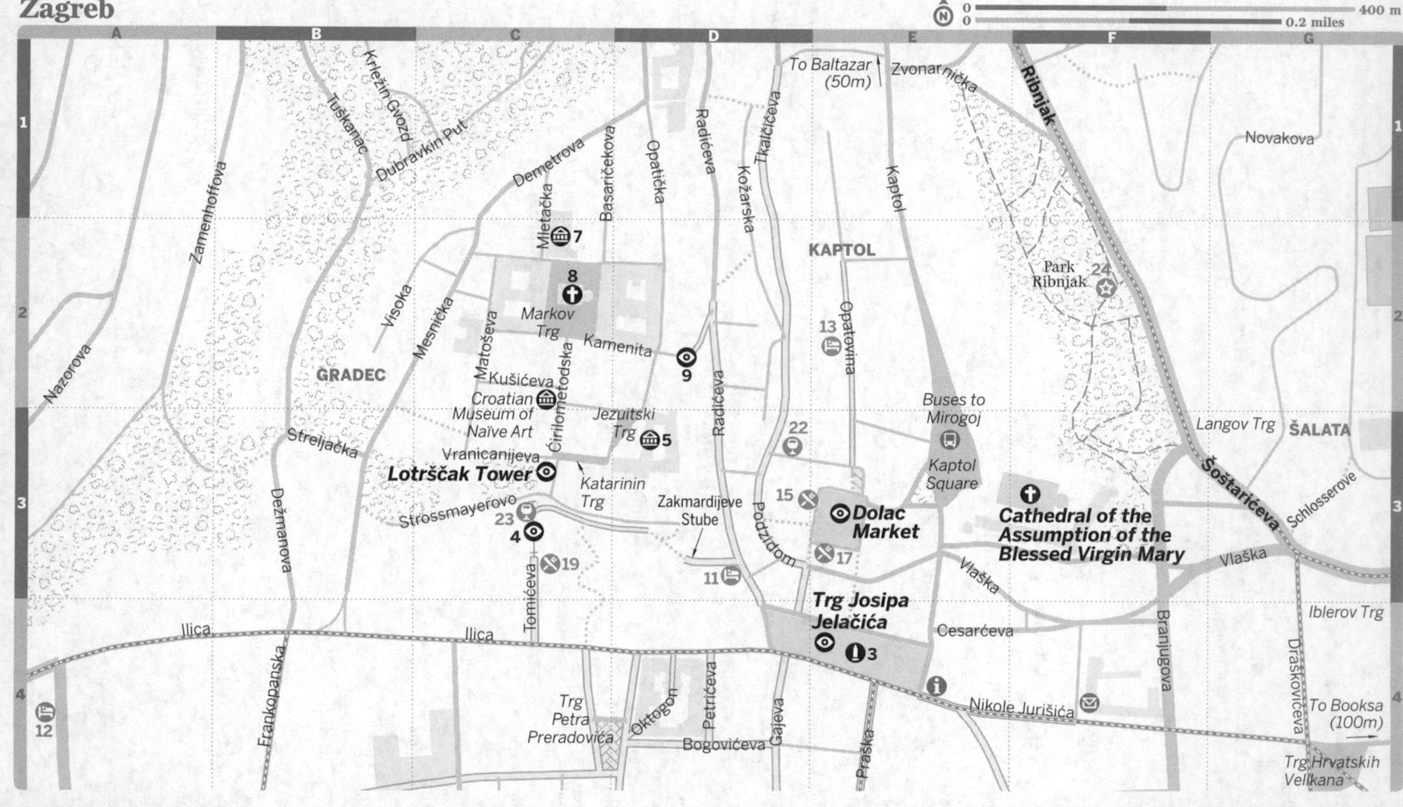
Zagreb
0
400 m
0
0.2 miles
A
B
C
D
E
F
G
1
2
3
4
Zamenhoffova
Nazorova
Tuškanac
Krležin Gvozd
Dubravkin Put
Demetrova
Mletačka
7
Basaričekova
Opatička
Radićeva
Tkalčićeva
Kožarska
To Baltazar (50m)
Zvonarnička
Kaptol
Ribnjak
Novakova
KAPTOL
Park Ribnjak
24
8
Markov Trg
Kamenita
9
Visoka
Mesnička
GRADEC
Matoševa
Kušićeva
Croatian Museum of Naïve Art
Ćirilometodska
Jezuitski Trg
5
13
Opatovina
Buses to Mirogoj
Kaptol Square
22
Langov Trg
ŠALATA
Streljačka
Vranicanijeva
Lotrščak Tower
Katarinin Trg
Zakmardijeve Stube
15
Dolac Market
Cathedral of the Assumption of the Blessed Virgin Mary
Šoštarićeva
Schlosserove
Dežmanova
Strossmayerovo
23
4
19
Tomićeva
11
Podzidom
17
Vlaška
Trg Josipa Jelačića
3
Cesarćeva
Branjugova
Iblerov Trg
Draškovićeva
Ilica
Frankopanska
12
Trg Petra Preradovića
Oktogon
Petrićeva
Bogovićeva
Gajeva
Praška
Nikole Jurišića
To Booksa (100m)
Trg Hrvatskih Velikana

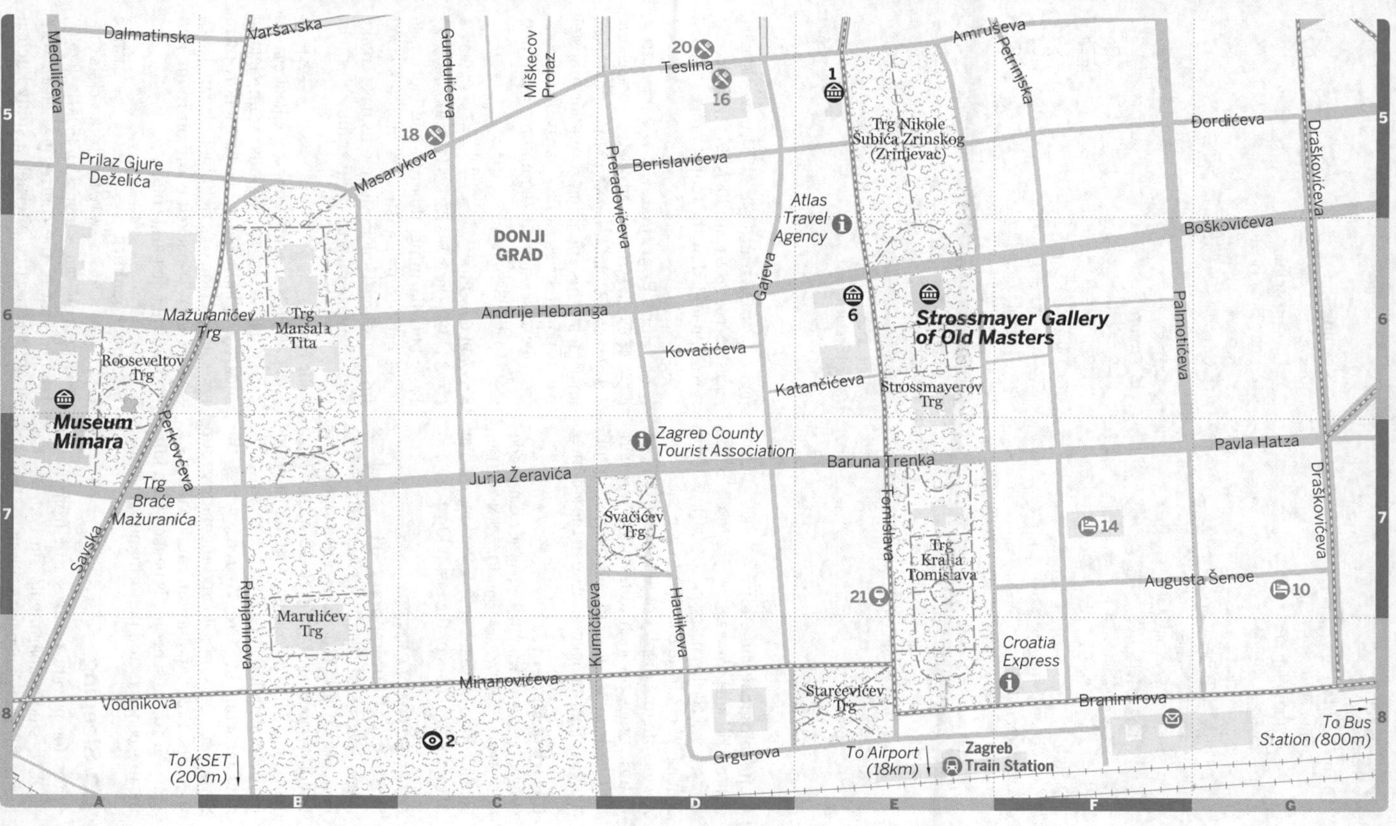
Dalmatinska
Varšavska
Medulićeva
Gundulićeva
Miškecov Prolaz
20
Teslina
16
1
Amruševa
Petrinjska
18
Trg Nikole Šubića Zrinskog (Zrinjevac)
Đorđićeva
Draškovićeva
Prilaz Gjure Deželića
Masarykova
Preradovićeva
Berislavićeva
Atlas Travel Agency
Boškovićeva
DONJI GRAD
Gajeva
6
Strossmayer Gallery of Old Masters
Palmotićeva
Mažuranićev Trg
Trg Maršala Tita
Andrije Hebranga
Kovačićeva
Rooseveltov Trg
Katančićeva
Strossmayerov Trg
Museum Mimara
Perkovčeva
Zagreb County Tourist Association
Pavla Hatza
Baruna Trenka
Jurja Žeravića
Trg Braće Mažuranića
Svačićev Trg
Tomislava
14
Savska
Trg Kralja Tomislava
Augusta Šenoe
10
21
Runjaninova
Marulićev Trg
Kumičićeva
Haulikova
Croatia Express
Minanovićeva
Vodnikova
Starčevićev Trg
Branimirova
2
To KSET (200m)
Grgurova
To Airport (18km)
Zagreb Train Station
To Bus Station (800m)

Zagreb

Top Sights

	Cathedral of the Assumption of the Blessed Virgin Mary	F3
	Dolac Market	E3
	Lotrščak Tower	C3
	Museum Mimara	A6
	Strossmayer Gallery of Old Masters	E6
	Trg Josipa Jelačića	E4

Sights

1	Archaeological Museum	E5
2	Botanical Garden	C8
3	Equestrian Statue	E4
4	Funicular Railway	C3
5	Galerija Klovićevi Dvori	D3
6	Gallery of Modern Art	E6
7	Meštrović Atelier	C2
8	St Mark's Church	C2
9	Stone Gate	D2

Sleeping

10	Evistas	G7
11	Fulir Hostel	D3
12	Hobo Bear Hostel	A4
13	Krovovi Grada	E2
14	Omladinski Hotel	F7

Eating

15	Amfora	D3
16	Pingvin	D5
17	Rubelj	E3
18	Tip Top	C5
19	Vallis Aurea	C3
20	Vinodol	D5

Drinking

21	Bacchus	E7
22	Cica	D3
23	Stross	C3

Entertainment

24	Purgeraj	F2

Archaeological Museum MUSEUM
(Arheološki Muzej; www.amz.hr; Trg Nikole Šubića Zrinskog 19; adult/concession 20/10KN; ⊙10am-5pm Tue, Wed & Fri, to 8pm Thu, to 1pm Sat & Sun) A wide-ranging display of artefacts from prehistoric times through to the medieval period. Check out the garden of Roman sculpture that becomes an open-air cafe in the summer.

Gallery of Modern Art ART GALLERY
(Moderna Galerija; www.moderna-galerija.hr; Andrije Hebranga 1; adult/concession 40/20KN; ⊙10am-6pm Tue-Fri, to 1pm Sat & Sun) A glorious display of Croatian artists of the last 200 years.

OUT OF TOWN CENTRE

Museum of Contemporary Art MUSEUM
(Muzej Suvremene Umjetnosti; www.msu.hr; Avenija Dubrovnik 17; adult/concession 30/15KN, free first Wed of the month; ⊙11am-7pm Tue-Sun, 11am-10pm Thu) Housed in a dazzling functionalist building by local architect Igor Franić, this swanky new museum in Novi Zagreb, across the Sava River, puts on solo and thematic group shows by Croatian and international artists. The year-round schedule is packed with film, theatre, concerts and performance art.

Sleeping

Prices for private doubles run from about 300KN; studio apartments start at 400KN per night. There's usually a surcharge for one-night stays. **Evistas** (☎48 39 554; www.evistas.hr; Augusta Šenoe 28; s from 210KN, d/apt 295/360KN) is recommended by the tourist office.

TOP CHOICE **Hobo Bear Hostel** HOSTEL €
(☎48 46 636; www.hobobearhostel.com; Medulićeva 4; dm/d from 122/400KN; ❄@☜) Inside a duplex apartment, this sparkling seven-dorm hostel has exposed brick walls, hardwood floors, free lockers, kitchen, common room and book exchange.

Krovovi Grada PENSION €
(☎48 14 189; Opatovina 33; s/d 200/300KN; @☜) Basic but charming, this restored old house is set back from the street a minute's stroll from bustling Tkalčićeva. Rooms have creaky floors, vintage furniture and granny blankets.

Fulir Hostel HOSTEL €
(☎48 30 882; www.fulir-hostel.com; Radićeva 3a; dm 130-140KN; @☜) Seconds from Jelačić square, the Fulir has 28 beds, friendly owners, self-catering (it's right by Dolac market), lockers, a DVD-packed common room, and free internet, tea and coffee.

Buzzbackpackers HOSTEL €
(☎23 20 267; www.buzzbackpackers.com; Babukićeva 1b; dm/d from 130/450KN; ❄@☜) Located east of the centre, it is clean with bright rooms, free internet, a shiny kitchen

and a BBQ area. Take tram 4 or 9 from the train station to the Heinzelova stop.

Omladinski Hostel HOSTEL €
(☎48 41 261; www.hfhs.hr; Petrinjska 77, G-/3 bcd dm 113KN, s/d 203/286KN;) The rooms are sparse and gloomy but it's fairly central, clean and the cheapest in town.

Eating

Tip Top SEAFOOD €€
(Gundulićeva 18; mains from 55KN; Mon-Sat) The excellent Dalmatian food is served by wait staff sporting old socialist uniforms. Every day has its own set menu of mainstays; the Thursday octopus goulash is particularly tasty.

TOP CHOICE **Amfora** SEAFOOD €
(Dolac 2; mains from 40KN; to 3pm Mon-Sat, to 1pm Sun) This locals' lunch fave serves super-fresh seafood straight from the market across the way, paired with off-the-stalls veggies. The hole-in-the-wall has a few tables outside and an upstairs gallery.

Vallis Aurea CROATIAN €
(Tomićeva 4; mains from 37KN; Mon-Sat) This true local eatery has some of the best home cooking you'll find in town, so it's no wonder it gets chock-a-block at lunchtime for its *gableci* (traditional lunches). It's right by the lower end of the funicular.

Vinodol CROATIAN €€
(Teslina 10; mains from 70KN) Serves excellently prepared Central European fare.

ZAGREB FOR FREE

There are some gorgeous parks and markets in Zagreb to be enjoyed for nowt. For a free day of relaxing, check out **Dolac Market** where you can taste bits of food for free (but don't be too cheeky!), smell the herbs at the **Botanical Garden** (Mihanovićeva bb; 9am-2.30pm Mon & Tue, 9am-7pm Wed-Sun Apr-Oct), enjoy the long walks around **Maksimir Park** (Maksimirska bb; www.park-maksimir.hr; 9am-dusk) and see the magnificent **Mirogoj cemetery** (6am-8pm Apr-Sep, 7.30am-6pm Oct-Mar), north of the centre.

Maksimir Park is accessible by trams 4, 7, 11 and 12, while the Mirogoj is reached by a 10-minute ride north of the city centre on bus 106 from the cathedral.

Pingvin SANDWICH STAND €
(Teslina 7; 9am-4am Mon-Sat, 6pm-2am Sun) This quick-bite institution, around since 1987, offers tasty designer sandwiches and salads, which locals savour on a handful of bar stools.

Rubelj FAST FOOD €
(Dolac 2; mains from 25KN) One of the many Rubeljs across town, this Dolac branch is a great place for a quick portion of *ćevapi* (small spicy sausage of minced beef, lamb or pork).

Drinking

In the Upper Town, the chic Tkalčićeva is throbbing with bars. In the Lower Town, Trg Petra Preradovića (known locally as Cvjetni Trg) is the most popular spot for street performers and occasional bands in mild weather.

Booksa COFFEE HOUSE
(www.booksa.hr; Martićeva 14d; 11am-8pm Tue-Sun, closes for 3 weeks from late Jul) Bookworms and poets, writers and performers, oddballs and artists, and other creative types come to chat over coffee, buy books and hear readings at this lovely bookshop.

TOP CHOICE **Bacchus** BAR
(www.bacchusjazzbar.hr; Trg Kralja Tomislava 16) You'll be lucky if you score a table at Zagreb's funkiest courtyard garden – lush and hidden into a passageway. After 10pm, the action moves indoors, inside the artsy subterranean space, which hosts jazz concerts, poetry readings and oldies' nights.

Stross BAR
(Strossmayerovo Šetalište) From June to September, a makeshift bar is set up at the Strossmayer promenade in the Upper Town, with cheap drinks and live music most nights. Come for the mixed-bag crowd, great city views and leafy ambience.

Cica BAR
(Tkalčićeva 18) This tiny storefront bar is as underground as it gets on Tkalčićeva. Sample one or – if you dare – all 15 kinds of *rakija* (home-made brandy) that the place is famous for.

Clubbing

Nightclub entry ranges from 20KN to 100KN. It doesn't get lively until around midnight.

INTERNATIONAL TRAINS FROM ZAGREB

DESTINATION	FARE (KN)	DURATION (HR)	DAILY SERVICES
Belgrade	159	6½	4
Ljubljana	100	2½	7
Sarajevo	222	9½	2
Vienna	446	5½-6½	2

Aquarius CLUB
(www.aquarius.hr; Jarun Lake) A truly fab place to party, this enormously popular spot opens onto a huge terrace on the lake.

Močvara CLUB
(www.mochvara.hr, in Croatian; Trnjanski Nasip bb) In a former factory on the banks of the Sava River, 'Swamp' is one of the best venues in town for the cream of alternative music and attractively dingy charm.

KSET CLUB
(www.kset.org, in Croatian; Unska 3) Zagreb's best music venue, with anyone who's anyone performing here – from ethno to hip-hop acts.

Purgeraj CLUB
(www.purgeraj.hr; Park Ribnjak 1) Live rock, blues and avant-garde jazz is on the music menu at this funky space.

Information

The **Zagreb Card** (www.zagrebcard.fivestars.hr; 24/72hr 60/90KN) provides free travel on all public transport, a 50% discount on museum and gallery entries, plus discounts in some bars and restaurants, car rental etc. It's sold at the tourist office and many hostels, hotels, bars and shops.

There are ATMs at the bus and train stations, the airport, and at numerous locations around town. Some banks in the train and bus stations accept travellers cheques.

Atlas Travel Agency (☎48 07 300; www.atlas-croatia.com; Zrinjevac 17) Tours around Croatia.

Croatia Express (☎49 22 237; Trg Kralja Tomislava 17) Train reservations, car rental, air and ferry tickets, hotels and excursions.

KBC Rebro (☎23 88 888; Kišpatićeva 12; ⏲24hr) East of the city, it provides emergency medical aid.

Sublink (www.sublink.hr; Teslina 12; per hr 15KN; ⏲9am-10pm Mon-Sat, 3-10pm Sun) The city's first cybercafe remains its best.

Tourist office (☎48 14 051; www.zagreb-touristinfo.hr; Trg Josipa Jelačića 11; ⏲8.30am-9pm Mon-Fri, 9am-6pm Sat & Sun Jun-Sep, less hrs rest of year) City maps and leaflets.

Getting There & Away

For information about international flights to and from Croatia, see p288.

Bus

Zagreb's **bus station** (☎060 313 333; www.akz.hr; Avenija M Držića 4) is 1km east of the train station. Trams 2, 3 and 6 run from the bus station to the train station. Tram 6 goes to Trg Josipa Jelačića. Some domestic buses that depart from Zagreb (schedules reduced outside high season):

DUBROVNIK (215KN to 228KN, 9½ to 11 hours, 10 daily)

PULA (162KN to 185KN, 3½ to 5½ hours, 14 to 17 daily)

SPLIT (165KN to 181KN, five to 8½ hours, 32 to 34 daily)

Some International buses departing from Zagreb:

BELGRADE (199KN to 204KN, six hours, six daily)

SARAJEVO (188KN to 244KN, seven to eight hours, five daily)

VIENNA (250KN, five to six hours, two daily)

Train

The **train station** (☎060 333 444; www.hznet.hr) is in the southern part of the city. It's advisable to book train tickets in advance because of limited seating. Five trains daily depart from Zagreb to Split (166KN, 5½ to eight hours).

Getting Around

Public transport is based on an efficient network of trams, although the city centre is compact enough to make them unnecessary.

Buy tickets at newspaper kiosks for 8KN. Tickets can be used for transfers within 90 minutes, but only in one direction. You can ride the tram for free two stations in each direction from Trg Josipa Jelacica.

A *dnevna karta* (day ticket), valid on all public transport until 4am the next morning, is available for 25KN at most newspaper kiosks.

Validate your ticket when you get on the tram.

Zagreb's taxis have meters, which begin at 19KN and then ring up 7KN per kilometre. On Sunday and at night there's a 20% surcharge.

The Croatia Airlines bus to/from the airport (30KN) leaves from the bus station or airport every half-hour or hour from about 5am to 8pm. Taxis cost between 150KN and 300KN.

ISTRIA

☎052

Continental Croatia meets the Adriatic in Istria (Istra to Croats), the heart-shaped 3600-sq-km peninsula just south of Trieste in Italy. While the bucolic interior of rolling hills and fertile plains attracts artsy visitors to its hilltop villages, rural hotels and farmhouse restaurants, the verdant indented coastline is enormously popular with the sun-'n'-sea set. Vast hotel complexes line much of the coast (or 'Blue Istria', as the tourist board calls it) and its rocky beaches are not Croatia's best, but the facilities are wide-ranging, the sea is clean and secluded spots still aplenty.

The coast gets flooded with tourists in summer, but you can still feel alone and undisturbed in 'Green Istria' (the interior), even in mid-August. Add acclaimed gastronomy (starring fresh seafood, prime white truffles, wild asparagus, top-rated olive oils and award-winning wines) sprinkle it with historical charm and you have a little slice of heaven.

Pula

POP 60,000

The wealth of Roman architecture makes the otherwise workaday Pula (ancient Polensium) a standout among Croatia's larger cities. The star of the Roman show is the remarkably well-preserved Roman amphitheatre, which dominates the streetscape and doubles as a venue for summer concerts and performances. Historical attractions aside, Pula is a busy commercial city on the sea that has managed to retain a friendly small-town appeal.

A series of beaches and good nightlife are just a short bus ride away at the resorts that occupy the Verudela Peninsula to the south. Further south along the indented shoreline, the Premantura Peninsula hides a spectacular nature area, the protected cape of Kamenjak.

Sights

Most sights and businesses are clustered in and around the Old Town.

Roman Amphitheatre ANCIENT SITE
(Arena; Flavijevska bb; adult/concession 40/20KN; 8am-9pm summer, 9am-8pm spring & autumn, 9am-5pm winter) Pula's most imposing sight, this 1st-century amphitheatre overlooks the harbour northeast of the Old Town. Built entirely from local limestone, the amphitheatre with seating for up to 20,000 spectators was designed to host gladiatorial contests. Every summer the **Pula Film Festival** is held here, as are pop and classical concerts.

Temple of Augustus ANCIENT RUINS
(Forum; adult/concession 10/5KN; 9am-8pm Mon-Fri, 10am-3pm Sat & Sun summer, by appointment other times) This Roman temple, erected from 2 BC to AD 14, now houses a small historical museum with captions in English.

Archaeological Museum MUSEUM
(Arheološki Muzej; Carrarina 3; adult/concession 20/10KN; 9am-8pm Mon-Sat, 10am-3pm Sun May-Sep, 9am-2pm Mon-Fri Oct-Apr) This museum presents archaeological finds from all over Istria. Visit the large **sculpture garden** around it, and the **Roman theatre** behind.

Museum of History MUSEUM
(Povijesni Muzej Istre; Gradinski Uspon 6; adult/concession 15/7KN; 8am-9pm Jun-Sep, 9am-5pm Oct-May) In a 17th-century Venetian fortress on a hill above the Old Town's centre, it has meagre exhibits, but has great views from the citadel walls.

Beaches

The most tourist-packed beaches are undoubtedly those surrounding the hotel complex on the **Verudela Peninsula**, although some locals will dare to be seen at the small turquoise-coloured **Hawaii Beach** near Hotel Park.

For more seclusion, head out to the wild **Rt Kamenjak** (www.kamenjak.hr, in Croatian; pedestrians & cyclists free, cars/scooters 25/15KN; 7am-10pm) on the Premantura Peninsula, 10km south of town.

Sleeping & Eating

Any travel agency can give you information and book you into one of the hotels, or you can contact **Arenaturist** (☎529 400; www.arenaturist.hr; Splitska 1a). The travel agencies in Pula can find you private accommodation, but there is little available in the town centre. Count on paying from 250KN to 490KN for a double (up to 535KN for a two-person apartment). Browse the list of private accommodation at www.pulainfo.hr.

Hotel Scaletta HOTEL €€
(☎541 599; www.hotel-scaletta.com; Flavijevska 26; s/d 505/732KN; ❄🅿📶) There's a friendly family vibe here, the recently spruced up rooms have tasteful decor and a bagful of trimmings (such as minibars). Plus it's just a hop and a skip from town.

Hotel Omir HOTEL €
(☎218 186; www.hotel-omir.com; Dobricheva 6; s/d 450/600KN; ❄📶) The best budget option smack in the heart of town, Hotel Omir has modest but clean and quiet rooms with TV. The more expensive units have air-con. There's no elevator.

Youth Hostel HOSTEL €
(☎391 133; www.hfhs.hr; Valsaline 4; dm 117KN, caravan 137KN; @) This hostel overlooks a beach in Valsaline Bay, 3km south of central Pula. There are dorms and caravans split into two tiny four-bed units, each with bathroom. To get here, take bus 2A or 3A to the 'Piramida' stop, walk back towards the city to the first street, turn left and look for the hostel sign.

Camping Stoja CAMPING GROUND €
(☎387 144; www.arenacamps.com; Stoja 37; per person/tent 57/34KN; ⊙Apr-Oct) The closest camping ground to Pula, 3km southwest of the centre, has lots of space on the shady promontory, with a restaurant and diving centre. Take bus 1 to Stoja.

Vodnjanka ISTRIAN €
(Vitezića 4; mains from 40KN; ⊙closed Sat dinner & Sun) Locals swear by the real-deal home cooking at this cash-only no-frills spot. Its small menu concentrates on simple Istrian dishes. To get here, walk south on Radićeva to Vitezića.

Jupiter PIZZERIA €
(Castropola 42; pizzas 25-84KN) The pizza here would make any Italian mama proud; the pasta is yummy, too. There's a terrace upstairs and a 20% discount on Wednesday.

Drinking & Entertainment

Cabahia BAR
(Širolina 4) This artsy hideaway in the Veruda neighbourhood has a cosy wood-beamed interior, eclectic decor of old objects, dim lighting, South American flair and a great garden terrace out the back.

TOP CHOICE **Scandal Express** CAFE-BAR
(Ciscuttijeva 15) Mingle with a mixed-bag crowd of locals at this popular gathering spot with a cool train carriage vibe and lots of posters; smoking is allowed.

Information

You can exchange money in travel agencies, banks or at the post offices. There are numerous ATMs around town.

Tourist information centre (☎212 987; www.pulainfo.hr; Forum 3; ⊙8am-9pm Mon-Fri, 9am-9pm Sat & Sun summer, less hr rest of year) Knowledgeable staff provide maps, brochures and schedules of events in Pula and around Istria. Pick up *Domus Bonus*, a booklet listing the best private accommodation in Istria.

Getting There & Away

From the Pula **bus station** (☎500 012; Trg 1 Istarske Brigade bb), 500m northeast of the city centre, there are buses heading to Zagreb (170KN to 216KN, four to 5½ hours, 15 daily), Split (387KN to 392KN, 10 hours, three daily) and Dubrovnik (557KN, 15 hours, one daily).

There are three daily trains to Zagreb (140KN, nine hours), but you must board a bus for part of the trip, from Lupoglav to Rijeka.

Getting Around

Bus 1 runs to Camping Stoja, and 2A and 3A to Verudela. Tickets are sold at *tisak* (newsstands) for 6KN, or 11KN from the driver.

DALMATIA

Roman ruins, spectacular beaches, old fishing ports, medieval architecture and unspoilt offshore islands make a trip to Dalmatia (Dalmacija) unforgettable. Occupying the central 375km of Croatia's Adriatic coast, Dalmatia offers a matchless combination of hedonism and historical discovery. The jagged coast is speckled with lush offshore islands and dotted with historic cities.

Split

☎021 / POP 188,700

The second-largest city in Croatia, Split (Spalato in Italian) is a great place to see Dalmatian life as it's really lived. Free of mass tourism, this always-buzzing city has arguably just the right balance of tradition and modernity. Step inside Diocletian's Palace – a Unesco World Heritage Site and one of the world's most impressive Roman monuments – and you'll see dozens of bars, restaurants and shops thriving amid the atmospheric old walls. Split's unique setting

Central Split

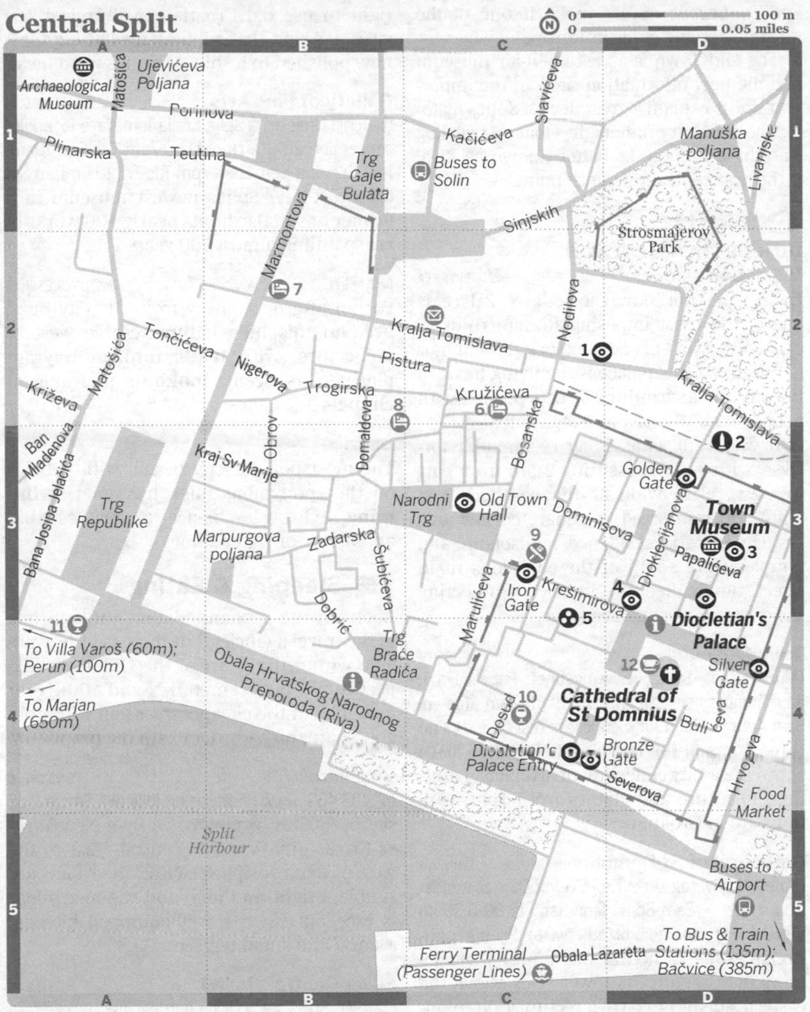

Central Split

Top Sights

Cathedral of St Domnius	D4
Diocletian's Palace	D3
Town Museum	D3

Sights

1	Gallery of Fine Arts	C2
2	Gregorius of Nin	D3
3	Papalić Palace	D3
4	Peristil	D3
5	Temple of Jupiter	C4
	Vestibule	(see 4)

Sleeping

6	Fiesta Siesta	C2
7	Silver Central Hostel	B2
8	Split Hostel Booze & Snooze	B2

Eating

9	Konoba Trattoria Bajamont	C3

Drinking

10	Ghetto Club	C4
11	Libar	A4
12	Luxor	D4

and exuberant nature make it one of the most delectable cities in Europe.

The Old Town is a vast open-air museum and the new information signs at the important sights explain a great deal of Split's history. The seafront promenade, Obala Hrvatskog Narodnog Preporoda, better known as Riva, is the best central reference point.

Sights

DIOCLETIAN'S PALACE

Diocletian's Palace HISTORIC AREA

Facing the harbour, Diocletian's Palace is one of the most imposing Roman ruins in existence. Don't expect a palace though, nor a museum – this palace is the living heart of the city, its labyrinthine streets packed with people, bars, shops and restaurants.

It was built as a strong rectangular fortress, with walls measuring 215m from east to west, 181m wide at the southernmost point and reinforced by square corner towers. The imperial residence, mausoleum and temples were south of the complex's main street, now called Krešimirova, connecting the east and west palace gates.

Town Museum MUSEUM

(Muzej Grada Splita; www.mgst.net; Papalićeva 1; adult/concession 10/5KN; ⌚9am-9pm Tue-Fri, 9am-4pm Sat-Mon Jun-Sep, less hr rest of year) The three floors of the late-Gothic Papalić Palace showcase a tidy collection of artefacts, paintings, furniture and clothes from Split; captions are in Croatian.

Cathedral of St Domnius CHURCH

(Katedrala Svetog Duje; Kraj Svetog Duje 5; admission free; ⌚8am-8pm Mon-Sat, 12.30-6.30pm Sun Jun-Sep, sporadic hr otherwise) Split's neo-Romanesque cathedral was built as Diocletian's mausoleum. Its tower rises above the eastern side of **Peristil**, a picturesque colonnaded square, which is a great place for a break in the sun. The **vestibule** at the southern end of Peristil is an open dome above the ground-floor passageway; it is overpoweringly grand and cavernous.

Temple of Jupiter RUINS

(admission 5KN; ⌚8am-8pm Jun-Sep) The one column you see here dates from the 5th century. Below the temple is a crypt, which was once used as a church.

OUTSIDE THE PALACE WALLS

Gregorius of Nin LANDMARK

This statue is of a 10th-century Croatian bishop (Grgur Ninski) who fought for the right to use old Croatian in liturgical services. It's said that rubbing his left big toe – now polished to a shine – brings good luck.

Gallery of Fine Arts MUSEUM

(Galerija Umjetnina Split; Kralja Tomislava 15; adult/concession 20/10KN; ⌚11am-7pm Tue-Sat, 10am-1pm Sun Jun-Sep, 11am-7pm Tue-Fri, 10am-1pm Sat & Sun Oct-May) Split's newest museum in a former hospital exhibits nearly 400 works of art spanning almost 700 years.

Marjan NATURE RESERVE

For an afternoon away from the city buzz, head to this hilly nature reserve west of the centre, with **trails** through fragrant pine forests, scenic **lookouts** and ancient **chapels**.

Bačvice BEACH

The most popular city beach, with pebbles on the eponymous inlet, has good **swimming**, a lively ambience, a great cafe-bar and plenty of water games.

Sleeping & Eating

Book private accommodation through one of the travel agencies, but there is little available within the heart of the Old Town. Expect to pay between 200KN and 400KN for a double; in the cheaper ones you will probably share the bathroom with the proprietor.

Villa Varoš PENSION €

(☎483 469; www.villavaros.hr; Miljenka Smoje 1; d/ste 500/800KN; ❄📶) Owned by a New Yorker Croat, Villa Varoš is central (just to the west of Bana Josipa Jelačića), the rooms are simple, bright and airy, and the apartment is excellent (with a well-equipped kitchen, Jacuzzi and small terrace).

Silver Central Hostel HOSTEL €

(☎490 805; www.silvercentralhostel.com; Kralja Tomislava 1; dm 150-180KN; ❄@📶) In an upstairs apartment, this light yellow-coloured boutique hostel has four dorm rooms, free internet and cable TV in the pleasant lounge. Its sister hostel, **Silver Gate** (☎322 857; www.silvergatehostel.com; Hrvojeva 6; dm 165KN), northeast of the Old Torwn's Silver Gate and near the food market, has the same facilities.

Split Hostel Booze & Snooze HOSTEL €

(☎342 787; www.splithostel.com; Narodni Trg 8; dm 150-180KN; ❄@📶) Run by a pair of Aussie Croat women, this party place at the heart of town has four dorms, a terrace, book swap and free internet. Their brand-new outpost,

Fiesta Siesta (Kružićeva 5; dm 150-180KN, d 440-500KN; ❄@☎) has five sparkling dorms and one double above the popular Charlie's Backpacker Bar.

Konoba Trattoria Bajamont DALMATIAN €€
(Bajamontijeva 3; mains from 60KN; ⊙closed Sun dinner) At this one-room joint with a handful of tables, the menu features excellent Dalmatian mainstays, such as small fried fish, squid-ink risotto and *brujet* (seafood stew with wine, onions and herbs, served with polenta).

TOP CHOICE **Kod Fife** DALMATIAN €
(Trumbićeva Obala 11; mains from 40KN) Dragan presides over a motley crew of sailors, artists and misfits who drop in for his simple, Dalmatian home cooking (especially the *pašticada*), and his own brand of grumpy slow but loving hospitality. Go west of the Riva, which turns into Trumbićeva Obala.

Perun DALMATIAN €€
(Senjska 9; mains from 70KN) This adorable spot in Varoš has a leafy terrace amid ancient stone, a rustic low-key vibe and seafood (and meat) done *na gradele* (on the grill), depending on what's fresh that day.

Drinking & Entertainment

Split is great for nightlife, especially during spring and summer. The palace walls are generally throbbing with loud music on Friday and Saturday nights.

Žbirac CAFE
(Bačvice bb) This beachfront cafe in Bačvice is like the locals' open-air living room; it's a cult hang-out with great sea views, swimming day and night, and occasional concerts.

Ghetto Club BAR
(Dosud 10) Head for Split's most bohemian bar in an intimate courtyard amid flowerbeds, a trickling fountain, great music and a friendly atmosphere.

Luxor CAFE-BAR
(Kraj Sv Ivana 11) Touristy, yes, but having coffee in the courtyard of the cathedral is great: cushions are laid out on the steps and you can watch the locals go by.

Libar CAFE-BAR
(Trg Franje Tuđmana 3) A relaxed place away from the palace buzz, this little spot has a lovely upper terrace, great breakfasts and tapas all day.

Information

Get the Split Card for 35KN for one day and you can use it for three days without paying anything extra. You get free access to most of the city museums and discounts to many galleries.

Change money at travel agencies or the **post office** (Kralja Tomislava 9). You'll find ATMs all around the city, as well as around the bus and train stations.

Atlas Airtours (☎343 055; www.atlasairtours.com; Bosanska 11) Tours, private accommodation and money exchange.

Backpackers Cafe (☎338 548; Obala Kneza Domagoja 3; per hr 30KN; ⊙7am-9pm; ☎) Offers wi-fi, sells used books and provides information for backpackers. Between 3pm and 5pm internet is 50% cheaper.

Croatian Youth Hostel Association (☎396 031; www.hfhs.hr; Domilijina 8; ⊙8am-4pm Mon-Fri) Sells HI cards and has information about youth hostels all over Croatia.

Tourist office (☎345 606; www.visitsplit.com; Peristil; ⊙8am-8.30pm Jul & Aug, less hr and days rest of the year) Has information on Split and sells the Split Card.

Turist Biro (☎347 100; www.turistbiro-split.hr; Obala Hrvatskog Narodnog Preporoda 12) Its forte is private accommodation.

Getting There & Away

Air

Croatia Airlines (☎362 997; www.croatiaairlines.hr; Obala Hrvatskog Narodnog Preporoda 9; ⊙8am-8pm Mon-Fri, 9am-noon Sat) operates one-hour flights to Zagreb several times a day and a weekly flight to Dubrovnik.

A couple of low-cost international airlines fly to Split, including **Easyjet** (www.easyjet.com) and **Germanwings** (www.germanwings.com).

Boat

Jadrolinija (☎338 333; Gat Sv Duje bb), in the large ferry terminal opposite the bus station, handles most of the coastal ferry lines and catamaran boats that operate between Split and the islands.

There is also a fast passenger boat, the **Krilo** (www.krilo.hr), that goes to Hvar Town (22KN, one hour) daily and on to Korčula (55KN, 2¾ hours).

SNAV (☎322 252; www.snav.it) and **BlueLine** (www.blueline-ferries.com) have ferries to Ancona.

Note that passenger services leave from Obala Lazareta and car ferries from Gat Sv Duje. You can buy tickets from either the main Jadrolinija office, or one of the two stalls near the docks. In summer, reserve at least a day in advance for a car ferry.

Bus

Advance reservations are recommended. There are buses from the main **bus station** (☎060 327 777; www.ak-split.hr) beside the harbour to the following destinations, among others:

DUBROVNIK (105KN to 157KN, 4½ hours, 20 daily)

PULA (397KN, 10 to 11 hours, three daily)

ZAGREB (185KN, five to eight hours, 29 daily)

Train

There are five daily trains between Split **train station** (☎338 525; www.hznet.hr; Obala Kneza Domagoja 9) and Zagreb (179KN to 189KN, 5½ to eight hours), two of which are overnight.

Hvar Island

☎021 / POP 11,459

Hvar is the number one-carrier of Croatia's superlatives: it's the most luxurious island, the sunniest place in the country, and, along with Dubrovnik, the most popular tourist destination. Hvar is also famed for its verdancy and its lilac lavender fields.

The island's hub and busiest destination is Hvar Town, which draws around 30,000 people a day in the high season. It's odd that they can all fit in the small bay town, but fit they do. Visitors wander along the main square, explore the sights on the winding stone streets, swim on the numerous beaches or pop off to get into their birthday suits on the Pakleni Islands, but most of all they party at night. There are several good restaurants and a number of top hotels, as well as a couple of hostels.

Car ferries from Split deposit you in Stari Grad but local buses meet most ferries in summer for the trip to Hvar Town. The town centre is Trg Sv Stjepana, 100m west of the bus station. Passenger ferries tie up on Riva (seafront promenade), the eastern quay.

Sights & Activities

Franciscan Monastery & Museum MONASTERY

(admission 20KN; 9am-1pm & 5-7pm Mon-Sat) At the southeastern end of Hvar you'll find this 15th-century Renaissance monastery, with a collection of Venetian paintings in the adjoining **church** and a **cloister garden**, with a cypress tree said to be more than 300 years old.

Arsenal HISTORIC BUILDING

(Trg Svetog Stjepana; admission 20KN for arsenal & theatre; 9am-9pm) Smack in the middle of Hvar Town is the imposing Gothic arsenal, and upstairs is Hvar's prize, the **Renaissance theatre** built in 1612 – reported to be the first theatre in Europe open to plebeians and aristocrats alike.

Cathedral of St Stephen CHURCH

(Katedrala Svetog Stjepana; Trg Svetog Stjepana; 30min before twice-daily Mass) Forming a stunning backdrop to Trg Sv Stjepana, the cathedral was built in the 16th and 17th centuries at the height of the Dalmatian Renaissance.

Fortica FORTRESS

(admission 20KN; 8am-9pm Jun-Sep) On the hill high above Hvar Town, this Venetian fortress (1551) is worth the climb up to appreciate the sweeping panoramic views. There's a cafe at the top.

Sleeping & Eating

Accommodation in Hvar Town is extremely tight in July and August: a reservation is highly recommended. Try the travel agencies for help. Expect to pay anywhere from 150KN to 300KN per person for a room with a private bathroom in the town centre. Prices are more negotiable outside high season.

Luka's Lodge HOSTEL €

(☎742 118; www.lukalodgehvar.hostel.com; Lučica bb; dm 140KN, d 240-350KN; @ 🛜 ❄) Friendly owner Luka takes good care of his guests at this homey hostel, a five-minute walk from town, with a living room, two terraces and a kitchen. All rooms come with fridges, some with balconies.

Green Lizard HOSTEL €

(☎742 560; www.greenlizard.hr; Ulica Domovinskog Rata 13; dm 140KN, d 240-350KN; Apr-Oct; @ 🛜) This private hostel is a friendly and cheerful budget option, a short walk from the ferry. Dorms are simple and clean, there's a communal kitchen, laundry service, and a few doubles with private and shared facilities.

Camping Vira CAMPING GROUND €

(☎741 803; www.campingvira.com; per adult/site 50/87KN; May–mid-Oct; 🛜) This four-star camping ground on a wooded bay 4km from town is one of the best in Dalmatia. There's a gorgeous beach, a lovely cafe and restaurant, and a volleyball pitch.

Konoba Menego DALMATIAN €€

(Put Grode bb; tapas-style dishes 45-70KN) At this rustic old house, everything is decked out in Hvar antiques and the staff wear traditional outfits. Try the marinated cheeses and vegetables, prepared the old-fashioned Dalmatian way.

The **pizzerias** along the harbour offer predictable but inexpensive eating. Self-caterers can head to the **supermarket** next to the bus station, or pick up fresh supplies at the next-door **vegetable market**.

Drinking

Hvar has some of the best nightlife on the Adriatic coast.

Falko Bar BEACH BAR
(⏲10am-10pm mid-May–mid-Sep) A 20-minute seafront walk from the town centre brings you to this adorable hideaway in a pine forest just above the beach. Think low-key artsy vibe, homemade *rakija,* hammocks, and occasional concerts and exhibits.

Carpe Diem BAR-CLUB
(www.carpe-diem-hvar.com; Riva) This swanky harbourfront spot is the mother of Croatia's coastal clubs, with house music spun nightly by resident DJs. The new **Carpe Diem Beach** on the nearby island of Stipanska is the hottest place to party.

Information

Del Primi (☎095 998 1235; www.delprimi-hvar.com; Burak 23) Travel agency specialising in private accommodation.

Pelegrini Tours (☎742 743; www.pelegrini-hvar.hr; Riva bb) Private accommodation, boat tickets to Italy, excursions (daily trip to Pakleni Otoci), and bike, scooter and boat rental.

Secret Hvar (☎717 615; www.secrethvar.com) Great offroad tours of the island's scenic interior, with abandoned villages, dramatic canyons and endless lavender fields.

Tourist office (☎742 977; www.tzhvar.hr; ⏲8am-2pm & 3-9pm Jun & Sep, 8am-2pm & 3-10pm Jul-Aug, 8am-2pm Mon-Sat Sep-May) On Trg Svetog Stjepana.

Getting There & Away

The Jadrolinija car ferry from Split calls at Stari Grad (47KN, two hours) six times a day in summer months. Jadrolinija also has a daily catamaran to Hvar Town (22KN, one hour). **Krilo** (www.krilo.hr), the fast passenger boat, travels once a day between Split and Hvar Town (22KN, one hour) in summer. You can buy tickets at Pelegrini Tours. The **Jadrolinija agency** (☎741 132; www.jadrolinija.hr) is beside the landing in Stari Grad.

There are at least 10 car ferries (fewer in the low-season) running from Drvenik, on the mainland, to Sućuraj (16KN, 35 minutes) on the eastern tip of Hvar Island.

Buses meet most ferries that dock at Stari Grad and go to Hvar Town (25KN, 50 minutes). A taxi costs from 150KN to 350KN. **Radio Taxi Tihi** (☎098 338 824) is cheaper if there are a number of passengers to fill up the minivan.

Korčula Island

☎020 / POP 16,200

Rich in vineyards and olive trees, the island of Korčula was named Korkyra Melaina (Black Korčula) by the original Greek settlers because of its dense woods and plant life. The largest island in an archipelago of 48, it provides plenty of opportunities for scenic drives, particularly along the southern coast.

Swimming opportunities abound in the many quiet coves and secluded beaches, while the interior produces some of Croatia's finest wine, especially dessert wines made from the *grk* grape cultivated around Lumbarda.

On a hilly peninsula jutting into the Adriatic sits **Korčula Town**, a striking walled town of round defensive towers and red-roofed houses. Resembling a miniature Dubrovnik, the gated, walled Old Town is criss-crossed by narrow stone streets designed to protect its inhabitants from winds.

The big Jadrolinija car ferry drops you off either in the west harbour next to Hotel Korčula or the east harbour next to Marko Polo Tours. The Old Town lies between the two harbours. The large hotels and main beach lie south of the east harbour. The town bus station is 100m south of the Old Town centre.

Sights

Other than following the circuit of the city walls or walking along the shore, sightseeing in Korčula centres on Trg Sv Marka.

St Mark's Cathedral CHURCH
(Katedrala Svetog Marka; Statuta 1214; ⏲9am-9pm Jul & Aug, Mass only Sep-Jun) Dominating Trg Sv Marka, the 15th-century Gothic-Renaissance cathedral features two paintings by Tintoretto. Close by is the **Town Museum** (Gradski Muzej; ☎711 420; Statuta 1214; admission 15KN; ⏲9am-9pm Jun-Aug, 9am-1pm Mon-Sat Sep-May), in the 16th-century Gabriellis Palace, with exhibits of Greek pottery, Roman ceramics and home furnishings, all with English captions.

Marco Polo Museum MUSEUM
(Ulica De Polo; admission 15KN; ⏲9am-7pm Jun-Sep, 10am-4pm May & Oct) It's said that Marco Polo was born in Korčula in 1254; visit what is believed to have been his house and climb

the tower for an eagle's eye vista over the Korčula peninsula.

Sleeping & Eating

If you don't fancy staying in any of the big hotels, a more personal option is a guest house. Atlas Travel Agency and Marko Polo Tours arrange private rooms (from 250KN in high season).

Villa DePolo APARTMENTS €
(☎711 621; tereza.depolo@du.t-com.hr; Svetog Nikole bb; d 330KN; ❄📶) The small, simple but attractive modern rooms (and one apartment) come with comfortable beds; one has a terrace with amazing views. It's a short walk from the Old Town.

Pansion Hajduk PENSION €
(☎711 267; olga.zec@du.t-com.hr; d from 430KN; ❄🏊) It's a couple of kilometres from town on the road to Lumbarda, but you get a warm welcome, rooms with air-con and TVs, and there's a swimming pool.

Autocamp Kalac CAMPING GROUND €
(☎711 182; www.korculahotels.com; per person/site 54/48KN; ⌚May-Oct) This attractive camping ground with tennis courts is a 30-minute walk from the Old Town, in a dense pine grove near the beach.

TOP CHOICE **Konoba Komin** DALMATIAN €€
(☎716 508; Don Iva Matijace; mains from 45KN) This family-run *konoba* (traditional tavern) looks almost medieval, with its *komin* (roaring fire), roasting meat, ancient stone walls and solid wooden tables. The menu is simple and delicious. Book ahead.

Buffet-Pizzeria Doris RESTAURANT $
(Tri Sulara; mains from 40KN) Simple place that serves a bit of everything, including pasta and pizza, seafood and steaks and tasty grilled veggie platters.

Information

There are several ATMs around town, including one at HVB Splitska Banka. You can also change money at the post office or at any of the travel agencies.

Atlas Travel Agency (☎711 231; atlas -korcula@du.htnet.hr; Trg 19 Travnja bb) Represents American Express, runs excursions and finds private accommodation.

Kantun Tours (☎715 622; www.kantun-tours.com; Plokata 19 Travnja bb) Probably the best organised and largest agency, it offers private accommodation, excursions, car hire, luggage storage and boat tickets.

PC Centrar Doom (Obvjeknik Vladimir DePolo) Internet access (25KN per hr) and cheapish international phone calls.

Tourist office (☎715 701; www.korcula.net; Obala Franje Tuđmana 4; ⌚8am-3pm & 5-8pm Mon-Sat, 9am-1pm Sun Jul & Aug, 8am-2pm Mon-Sat Sep-Jun) On the west harbour; an excellent source of information.

Getting There & Away

There are buses to Dubrovnik (85KN, three hours, one to three daily) and one to Zagreb (239KN, 11 hours). Book ahead in summer.

The island has two major entry ports by boat – Korčula Town and Vela Luka. All the Jadrolinija ferries between Split and Dubrovnik stop in Korčula Town. There's a **Jadrolinija office** (☎715 410) about 25m down from the west harbour.

Dubrovnik

☎020 / POP 29,995

No matter whether you are visiting Dubrovnik for the first time or if you're returning to this marvellous city, the sense of awe and beauty when you set eyes on the Old Town's Stradun (Placa) never fades. It's hard to imagine anyone becoming jaded by its marble streets and baroque buildings, or failing to be inspired by a walk along the ancient city walls that once protected a civilised, sophisticated republic for five centuries and that now look out onto the endless shimmer of the peaceful Adriatic.

The leafy promontory of Lapad in the northwest of the city contains many of the town's hotels. All the sights are in the Old Town, which is closed to cars. Looming above the city is Srđ Hill, which is connected by cable car to Dubrovnik.

Sights

THE OLD TOWN & AROUND

The City Walls & Forts LANDMARK
(Gradske Zidine; adult/concession 70/30KN; ⌚9am-6.30pm Apr-Oct, 10am-3pm Nov-Mar) No visit to Dubrovnik would be complete without a leisurely walk around the spectacular **city walls**, Dubrovnik's main claim to fame. Built between the 13th and 16th centuries, they are still intact today. The main entrance and ticket office to the walls is by the Pile Gate. You can also enter at the Ploče gate in the east (a wise move at really busy times of day).

War Photo Limited PHOTO GALLERY
(www.warphotoltd.com; Antuninska 6; admission 30KN; ⏲9am-9pm Jun-Sep, 9am-3pm Tue-Sat, to 1pm Sun May & Oct) This state-of-the-art photographic gallery has changing exhibitions curated by the gallery owner and former photojournalist Wade Goddard.

Franciscan Monastery & Museum MONASTERY
(Muzej Franjevačkog Samostana; Placa 2; adult/concession 30/15KN; ⏲9am-6pm) Inside the monastery complex is a splendid mid-14th-century **cloister**, the third-oldest functioning **pharmacy** in Europe (in business since 1391) and a small **museum** with a collection of relics, liturgical objects and pharmacy items. Opposite the monastery is the **Onofrio Fountain**, built in 1438 as part of a water-supply system that involved bringing water from a well 12km away.

Dominican Monastery & Museum MONASTERY
(Muzej Dominikanskog Samostana; off Ulica Svetog Dominika 4; adult/concession 20/10KN; ⏲9am-6pm May-Oct, till 5pm rest of yr) This imposing 14th-century structure in the city's north-eastern corner is a real architectural highlight, with a forbidding fortress-like exterior that shelters a rich trove of paintings from Dubrovnik's finest 15th- and 16th-century artists.

Rector's Palace PALACE
(Pred Dvorom 3; adult/concession 35/15KN, audio guide 30KN; ⏲9am-6pm May-Oct, till 4pm rest of yr) This Gothic-Renaissance palace built in the late 15th century houses a museum with furnished rooms, baroque paintings and historical exhibits.

Cathedral of the Assumption of the Virgin CHURCH
(Stolna Crkva Velike Gospe; Poljana M Držića; ⏲morning & late-afternoon Mass) Completed in 1713 in baroque style, the cathedral is notable for its fine altars and its **treasury** (Riznica; adult/concession 10/5KN; ⏲8am-5.30pm Mon-Sat, 11am-5.30pm Sun May-Oct, 10am-noon & 3-5pm rest of yr).

Sponza Palace PALACE
The 16th-century Sponza Palace houses the **Memorial Room of the Defenders of Dubrovnik** (⏲10am-10pm Mon-Fri, 8am-1pm Sat), a heartbreaking collection of portraits of young people who perished between 1991 and 1995.

DON'T MISS

CABLE CAR

Reopened after 19 years, the **cable car** (Petra Krešimira IV; www.dubrovnikcablecar.com; adult/concession 40/20KN; ⏲9am-10pm Tue-Sun May-Oct, shorter hr rest of year) whisks you from just north of the city walls up to Mt Srđ in under four minutes, for a stupendous perspective from a lofty 405m.

St Blaise's Church CHURCH
(Crkva Svetog Vlahe; Luža Sq; ⏲morning & late-afternoon Mass Mon-Sat) This imposing church was built in 1715 in baroque style. Its ornate exterior contrasts strongly with the sober residences surrounding it. The **Orlando Column** in Luža Sq is a popular meeting place where edicts, festivities and public verdicts used to be announced.

Serbian Orthodox Church & Museum CHURCH
(Muzej Pravoslavne Crkve; Od Puča 8; adult/concession 10/5KN; ⏲9am-2pm Mon-Sat) This 1877 Orthodox church has a fascinating collection of icons dating from the 15th to 19th century.

Synagogue SYNAGOGUE
(Sinagoga; Žudioska 5; admission 10KN; ⏲10am-8pm May-Oct Mon-Fri, till 3pm Nov-Apr) The oldest Sephardic and second-oldest synagogue in the Balkans, dating back to the 15th century, has a small museum inside.

BEACHES

Banje Beach, 500m east of Ploče Gate, used to be the most popular city beach, though it's less popular now a section has been roped off for the exclusive EastWest Club. Just southeast is **Sveti Jakov**, a good local beach that doesn't get rowdy. **Lapad Bay** brims with hotel beaches.

A better option is to take the ferry that shuttles hourly in summer to lush **Lokrum Island** (return 40KN, last boat back at 6pm), a national park with a rocky nudist beach (marked FKK), a botanical garden and the ruins of a medieval Benedictine monastery. The ferry landing is south of Ploče Gate.

Festivals & Events

Dubrovnik Summer Festival (www.dubrovnik-festival.hr) takes place over five weeks in July and August, with theatre, music and dance performances at different venues in the Old Town.

Sleeping

Private accommodation is generally the best option in Dubrovnik, which is the most expensive destination in Croatia. Beware the scramble of private owners at the bus station and ferry terminal: some are scamming. Expect to pay from 300/500KN for a double/apartment in high season.

Fresh Sheets HOSTEL €
(☎091 79 92 086; www.igotfresh.com; Sv Šimuna 15; dm/d 210/554KN;) The only hostel in the Old Town is a warm, welcoming place right by the city walls, with rooms and reception areas painted in zany colours and space for socialising downstairs. It's run by a party-hard crew who organise legendary booze-ups.

Begović Boarding House PENSION €
(☎435 191; www.begovic-boarding-house.com; Primorska 17; dm/r/apt 146/292/364KN;) A steep walk uphill from Lapad harbourfront, this family-run place has smallish but clean pine-trimmed rooms, some opening out onto a communal garden with amazing views. There's free pick-up from the bus or ferry, free internet, a kitchen and excursions.

Dubrovnik

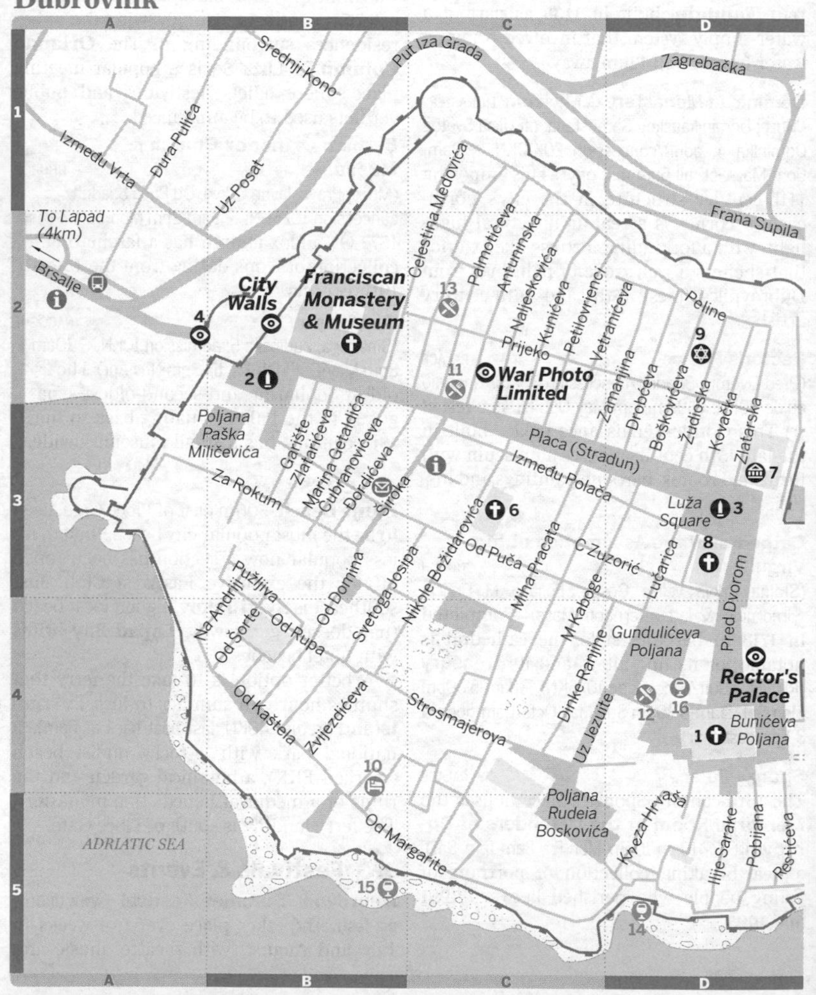

YHA Hostel
HOSTEL €

(☎423 241; dubrovnik@hfhs.hr; Vinka Sagrestana 3; dm 148KN; @) Its location is pretty good, in a quiet area 1km west of the Old Town. This mid-sized hostel has decent, spacious if plain dorms (and one double) and a rooftop terrace. Rates include breakfast. Book ahead.

Solitudo
CAMPING GROUND €

(☎448 200; www.camping-adriatic.com; per person/campsite 52/80KN; ⏲Apr-Nov) Just west of Lapad harbour, this camping ground is about 5km from the Old Town and close to the beach. The shower blocks are bright and modern, and there's a cafe-bar.

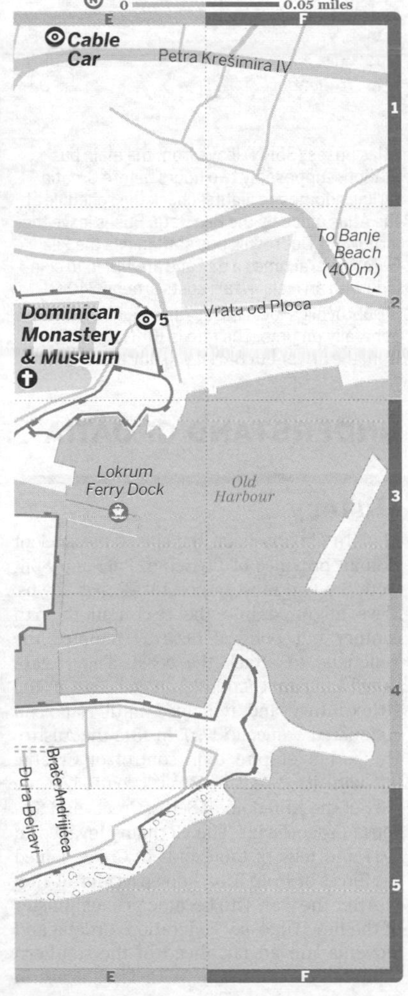

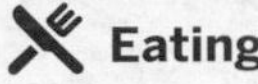

Eating

Taj Mahal
BOSNIAN INTERNATIONAL €

(Nikole Gučetića 2; mains from 40KN) It's like an Aladdin's cave, with oriental decorations and subdued lighting. Order the *džingis kan* and get a taste of everything Bosnian or feast on spicy *sudžukice* (beef sausage).

Nishta
VEGETARIAN €

(www.nishtarestaurant.com; Prijeko bb; mains from 59KN; ⏲closed Mon) A casual enjoyable vegetarian restaurant, Nishta raids the globe for dishes so you'll find miso soup, nachos, Indian food, Thai curries and chow mein.

Buffet Skola
CAFE €

(Antuninska 1; snacks from 17KN) For a quick bite between sightseeing, you can't do better. The ham and cheese sandwich is the thing to order.

Kamenice
BUDGET SEAFOOD €

(Gundulićeva Poljana 8; mains from 40KN) Looks vaguely like a socialist-style canteen, with prices to match. Order the squid, griddled anchovies or *kamenice* (oysters).

Drinking

Buža
BAR

(Ilije Sarake) Duck and dive around the city walls to find the entrance tunnel to this isolated bar on a cliff. It showcases tasteful music and a mellow crowd soaking up the vibes and views. Check out **Buža II** lower on the rocks to the west.

Troubadur
BAR

(Bunićeva Poljana 2) Come to this corner bar, a legendary Dubrovnik venue, for live jazz concerts in the summer.

EastWest Club
BAR-CLUB

(www.ew-dubrovnik.com; Frana Supila bb) By day this outfit on Banje Beach rents out beach chairs and umbrellas and serves drinks to the bathers. At night, it functions as a cocktail bar.

Information

There are numerous ATMs in town, in Lapad, and at the ferry terminal and bus station. Travel agencies and the post office will also exchange cash.

Atlas Travel Agency (www.atlas-croatia.com) Gruž Harbour (☎418 001; Obala Papa Ivana Pavla II 1); Pile Gate (☎442 574; Sv Đurđa 1) Organises excursions within Croatia and to Mostar and Montenegro. Also finds private accommodation.

Netcafé (www.netcafe.hr; Prijeko 21; per hr 30KN; 📶) Cybercafe with fast connections, CD/DVD burning, wi-fi, photo printing and scanning.

Dubrovnik

Top Sights

Cable Car ... E1
City Walls ... B2
Dominican Monastery & Museum ... E2
Franciscan Monastery & Museum ... B2
Rector's Palace ... D4
War Photo Limited ... C2

Sights

1 Cathedral of the Assumption of the Virgin ... D4
Memorial Room of the Defenders of Dubrovnik ... (see 7)
2 Onofrio Fountain ... B2
3 Orlando Column ... D3
4 Pile Gate ... A2
5 Ploče Gate ... E2
6 Serbian Orthordox Church & Museum ... C3
7 Sponza Palace ... D3
8 St Blaise's Church ... D3
9 Synagogue ... D2
Treasury ... (see 1)

Sleeping

10 Fresh Sheets ... B4

Eating

11 Buffet Skola ... C2
12 Kamenice ... D4
13 Nishta ... C2

Drinking

14 Buža ... D5
15 Buža II ... B5
16 Troubadur ... D4

Tourist office (www.tzdubrovnik.hr; 8am-8pm Jun-Sep, 8am-3pm Mon-Fri, 9am-2pm Sat Oct-May) Lapad (437 460; Šetalište Kralja Zvonimira 25); Old Town (323 587; Široka 1); Old Town 2 (323 887; Ulica Svetog Dominika 7) Maps, information and the indispensable *Dubrovnik Riviera* guide. The smart new head office that's under construction just west of the Pile Gate should open by the time you read this. There are also branch offices in the bus station and Gruž Harbour.

Getting There & Away

Daily flights to/from Zagreb are operated by **Croatia Airlines** (01-66 76 555; www.croatia airlines.hr).

A twice-weekly **Jadrolinija** (418 000; www.jadrolinija.hr; Gruž Harbour) coastal ferry heads north to Korčula, Hvar and Split. Ferries also go from Dubrovnik to Bari, in southern Italy. **Jadroagent** (419 000; Obala Stjepana Radića 32) books ferry tickets and has information.

The Jadrolinija ferry terminal and the bus station are next to each other at Gruž, several kilometres northwest of the Old Town. Buses go daily to Korčula (95KN, three hours, two daily), Split (122KN, 4½ hours, 19 daily) and Zagreb (250KN, 11 hours, seven daily).

Buses out of Dubrovnik **bus station** (060 305 070; Obala Pape Ivana Pavla II 44a) can be crowded, so book tickets ahead in summer. For bus schedules see www.libertasdubrovnik.hr.

Getting Around

Čilipi international airport (www.airport-dubrovnik.hr) is 24km southeast of Dubrovnik. Atlas buses (35KN) leave from the main bus station, supposedly two hours before Croatia Airlines domestic flights; check the schedule at the Atlas office by the Pile Gate. Buses leave the airport for Dubrovnik bus station (via the Pile Gate) several times a day and are timed to coincide with arrivals. A taxi costs around 240KN.

Dubrovnik's local buses run frequently and generally on time. The fare is 10KN if you buy from the driver but 8KN if you buy it at a kiosk.

UNDERSTAND CROATIA

History

Modern Croatia is on the site of the ancient Roman province of Illyricum. Pula and Split were the two most important Roman towns. Slavs migrated into the region in the 7th century but political disarray tempted the Venetians to attack the coast. They established their first foothold on the coast in the 11th century and remained until Napoleon conquered Venice in 1797. In 1815 the Austro-Hungarian empire took control of Croatia, but with its defeat in WWI, Croatia became part of the Kingdom of Serbs, Croats and Slovenes (Yugoslavia). The Germans invaded in 1941 and tens of thousands of Croats joined the forces of Josip Broz, known as Maršal Tito.

After the war, Tito became prime minister of the new Yugoslav Federation. Croatia and Slovenia moved far ahead of the southern republics economically. With Tito's death in

1980, many Croats wanted autonomy. When Slobodan Milošević rose to power in Yugoslavia on a wave of Serbian nationalism, Croatia moved towards independence. Under the leadership of Franjo Tuđman, Croatia declared independence on 25 June 1991.

Heavy fighting broke out in Serbian areas in eastern Croatia and in the Serbian enclave of Krajina (from northeast to east of Zadar). In six months of fighting, 10,000 people died, hundreds of thousands fled and tens of thousands of homes were destroyed.

A series of international peace plans halted the fighting until, in January 1993, the Croatian army suddenly launched an offensive in southern Krajina, recapturing much land. Their hold was consolidated in a new offensive launched on 1 May 1995, which essentially set Croatia's new borders. The Dayton Agreement of December 1995 established borders and finally brought lasting peace to Croatia and a tenuous peace to the rest of the region.

Franjo Tuđman became Croatia's first president and presided over a regime that became increasingly authoritarian. Tuđman succumbed to cancer in 1999 and the 2000 election brought a centre-left coalition to power with Stipe Mesić elected president. He held the presidential throne for 10 years, until January 2010, when Ivo Josipović of the Social Democratic Party of Croatia (SDP) won the presidential election. Many Croats see Josipović as ineffective, a puppet of a corrupt regime. Others regard him as pro-European, in his (some say weak) attempts to employ zero tolerance policy towards corruption and inspire foreign investment.

Membership negotiations with the EU continue, as Croatia deals with the repercussions of global recession on its home turf as well as widespread government corruption and elements of rabid nationalism. It aims to join the EU in 2012.

People

According to the most recent census (2001), Croatia had a population of 4.5 million people, a decline from the pre-civil war population of nearly five million. About 280,000 Serbs (50% of the Serbian population) departed in the early 1990s; an estimated 110,000 have returned. The next largest ethnic group is Bosnians. Italians are concentrated in Istria, while Albanians, Bosniaks and Roma can be found in Zagreb, Istria and some Dalmatian towns.

About 87.8% of the population identified itself as Catholic, 4.4% Orthodox, 1.3% Muslim, 0.3% Protestant, and 6.2% others and unknown. Croats are overwhelmingly Roman Catholic

READING UP

Marcus Tanner's *Croatia: A Nation Forged in War* is the most comprehensive recent account of Croatian history. From the Roman era to President Tuđman, the complicated struggles of Croatia are presented in a lively, readable style. For insight into the changes sweeping through Croatian culture, read Slavenka Drakulić's nonfiction: *How We Survived Communism and Even Laughed*, *Café Europa* and *They Wouldn't Hurt a Fly*.

Arts

Croatia's most famous artist is the sculptor Ivan Meštrović (1883–1962), whose work is seen in town squares throughout Croatia. Besides creating public monuments, Meštrović designed imposing buildings, such as the circular Croatian History Museum in Zagreb. Another notable sculptor was Antun Augustinčić (1900–79), who created the Monument to Peace in front of the UN building in New York.

Croatia's towering literary figure is novelist and playwright Miroslav Krleža (1893–1981). His most popular novels include *The Return of Philip Latinovicz* (1932).

Food

In this chapter the following price indicators for mains apply:

€€€ more than 80KN

€€ 50KN to 80N

€ less than 50KN

Environment

Croatia is shaped like a boomerang: from the Pannonian plains of Slavonia between the Sava, Drava and Danube Rivers, across hilly central Croatia to the Istrian Peninsula, then south through Dalmatia along the rugged Adriatic coast.

Croatia has 1244 islands and islets along the Adriatic coastline, 50 of them inhabited.

There are eight national parks, covering an area of 96,135 sq km. The lack of heavy industry in Croatia has had the happy effect of leaving its forests, coasts, rivers and air generally fresh and unpolluted.

SURVIVAL GUIDE

Directory A-Z

Accommodation

Reviews are listed in the order of preference. In this chapter the following price indicators apply (for a high-season double room):

€€€ more than 800KN

€€ 350KN to 800KN

€ less than 350KN

Note that private accommodation is a lot more affordable in Croatia, very often providing great value if you don't mind foregoing hotel facilities.

Along the coast, accommodation is priced according to four seasons, which vary from place to place. During July and August, count on paying top price; book in advance. November to March are the cheapest months.

Note that many establishments add a 30% charge for less than three-night stays and include 'residence tax', which is around 7KN per person per day. Prices in this book do not include the residence tax.

CAMPING

Nearly 100 camping grounds are scattered along the Croatian coast. They generally operate from mid-April to mid-September. Call in advance if you're arriving at either end of the season. A good site for camping information is www.camping.hr.

HOSTELS

The **Croatian YHA** (☎01-48 29 291; www.hfhs.hr; Savska 5/1, Zagreb) operates youth hostels in Dubrovnik, Zagreb and Pula. Nonmembers pay an additional 10KN per person per day for a stamp on a welcome card; six stamps entitle you to membership.

HOTELS

Hotels are ranked from one to five stars with the most being in the two- and three-star range. In August some hotels may demand a surcharge for stays of less than three to four nights but this surcharge is usually waived during the rest of the year, when prices drop steeply. Breakfast is included in hotel prices.

PRIVATE ROOMS

Private rooms or apartments are the best-value accommodation in Croatia. Service is excellent and the rooms are usually well kept. You may very well be greeted by offers of *sobe* (rooms) or *apartmani* (apartments) as you step off your bus and boat, but rooms are most often arranged by travel agencies or the local tourist office. Booking through an agency will ensure that the place you're staying in is officially registered.

Prices are fixed by the local tourist association. You'll pay a 30% surcharge for stays of less than four or three nights and sometimes 50% or even 100% more for a one-night stay, although you may be able to get them to waive the surcharge if you arrive in the low season.

Don't hesitate to bargain, especially for longer stays.

Activities

There are numerous outdoorsy activities in Croatia.

Diving Most of the coastal and island resorts have dive shops. For further information, see **Croatian Association of Diving Tourism** (www.croprodive.info), **Croatian Diving Federation** (www.diving-hrs.hr, in Croatian) and **Pro Diving Croatia** (www.diving.hr).

Cycling Croatia has become a popular destination for cycle enthusiasts. See www.bicikl.hr and www.pedala.com.hr.

Hiking For info about hiking in Croatia, check out the **Croatian Mountaineering Association** (www.plsavez.hr).

Kayaking & rafting Zagreb-based **Huck Finn** (www.huck-finn.hr) is a good contact for sea and river kayaking packages as well as rafting.

Business Hours

Banks 9am-7pm Mon-Fri, 8am-1pm or 9am-2pm Sat

Bars 9am-midnight

Offices 8am-4pm or 9am-5pm Mon-Fri, 8am-1pm or 9am-2pm Sat

Restaurants noon-11pm or midnight, closed Sun out of peak season

Shops 8am-8pm Mon-Fri, to 2pm Sat

Festivals & Events

In July and August there are summer festivals in Dubrovnik, Split, Pula and Zagreb. **Mardi Gras** celebrations have recently been revived in many towns with attendant parades and festivities; nowhere is it celebrated with more verve than in Rijeka.

Holidays

New Year's Day 1 January

Epiphany 6 January

Easter Monday March/April

Labour Day 1 May

Corpus Christi 10 June

Day of Antifascist Resistance 22 June; marks the outbreak of resistance in 1941

Statehood Day 25 June

Homeland Thanksgiving Day 5 August

Feast of the Assumption 15 August

Independence Day 8 October

All Saints' Day 1 November

Christmas 25 & 26 December

Money

Croatia uses the kuna (KN). Commonly circulated banknotes come in denominations of 500, 200, 100, 50, 20, 10 and five kuna. Each kuna is divided into 100 lipa. You'll find silver-coloured 50- and 20-lipa coins, and bronze-coloured 10-lipa coins.

Although they are widely accepted in upmarket places, don't count on credit cards to pay for private accommodation or meals in small restaurants. ATMs are available in most bus and train stations, airports, all major cities and most small towns.

Telephone

PHONE CODES

To call Croatia from abroad, dial your international access code, then ☎385 (the country code for Croatia), then the area code (without the initial 0) and the local number.

To call from region to region within Croatia, start with the area code (with the initial zero); drop the zero when dialling within the same code.

Phone numbers that begin with ☎09 are mobile phone numbers, which are billed at a much higher rate than regular numbers. If your phone is unlocked, local SIM cards are easy to buy. Otherwise you'll be roaming.

Phone numbers with the prefix ☎060 are either free or charged at a premium rate, so watch out for the small print.

To make a phone call from Croatia, go to the town's main post office. You'll need a phonecard to use public telephones. Phonecards are sold according to *impulsa* (units), and you can buy cards of 25 (15KN), 50 (30KN), 100 (50KN) and 200 (100KN) units. These can be purchased at any post office and most tobacco shops and newspaper kiosks.

Tourist Information

The **Croatian National Tourist Board** (www.croatia.hr) is a good source of information. There are regional tourist offices that supervise tourist development, and municipal tourist offices that have free brochures and information on local events.

Visas

Citizens of the EU, USA, Canada, Australia, New Zealand, Israel, Ireland, Singapore and the UK do not need a visa for stays of up to 90 days. South Africans must apply for a 90-day visa in Pretoria.

Getting There & Away

Air

There are direct flights to Croatia from a variety of European cities; however, there are no nonstop flights from North America to Croatia.

The major airports in Croatia.

Dubrovnik (www.airport-dubrovnik.hr) Nonstop flights from Brussels, London (Gatwick), Manchester, Hannover, Frankfurt, Cologne, Stuttgart and Munich

Pula (www.airport-pula.com) Nonstop flights from Manchester and London (Gatwick).

Split (www.split-airport.hr) Nonstop flights from London, Frankfurt, Munich, Cologne, Prague and Rome.

Zagreb (www.zagreb-airport.hr) Direct flights from all European capitals, plus Hamburg, Stuttgart and Cologne.

Boat

Regular boats from the following companies connect Croatia with Italy:

Blue Line (www.blueline-ferries.com)

Commodore Cruises (www.commodore-cruises.hr)

Emilia Romagna Lines (www.emiliaromagnalines.it)

Jadrolinija (www.jadrolinija.hr)

Split Tours (www.splittours.hr)

SNAV (www.snav.com)

Termoli Jet (www.termolijet.it)

Ustica Lines (www.usticalines.it)

Venezia Lines (www.venezialines.com)

Bus & Train

The border between Montenegro and Croatia is open to visitors, allowing Americans, Australians, Canadians and Brits to enter visa free.

For specific details on international bus and train trips, see the relevant towns.

Getting Around

Air

Croatia Airlines (☎01-66 76 555; www.croatiaairlines.hr) is the one and only carrier for flights within Croatia. There are daily flights between Zagreb and Dubrovnik, Pula, Split and Zadar.

Boat

Jadrolinija Ferries (www.jadrolinija.hr) operates an extensive network of car ferries and catamarans along the Adriatic coast. Ferries are a lot more comfortable than buses, though somewhat more expensive.

Ferries operate year-round, though services are less frequent in winter. Cabins should be booked a week ahead, while deck space is usually always available. You must buy tickets in advance at an agency or a Jadrolinija office; tickets are not sold on board. In summer months, check in two hours in advance if you bring a car.

Bus

At large stations bus tickets must be purchased at the office; book ahead to be sure of a seat. Tickets for buses that arrive from somewhere else are usually purchased from the conductor. Buy a one-way ticket only or you'll be locked into one company's schedule for the return.

On schedules, *vozi svaki dan* means 'every day' and *ne vozi nedjeljom ni praznikom* means 'not Sunday and public holidays'. Check www.akz.hr (in Croatian) for information on schedules and fares to and from Zagreb.

Luggage stowed in the baggage compartment under the bus costs extra (7KN a piece, including insurance).

Car & Motorcycle

Any valid driving licence is sufficient to drive legally and rent a car.

Motorists require vehicle registration papers and Green Card insurance (which proves drivers travelling through Europe have sufficient insurance) to enter Croatia.

A new motorway connects Zagreb with Split and will eventually reach Dubrovnik.

The **Hrvatski Autoklub** (HAK; Croatian Auto Club; ☎01-46 40 800; www.hak.hr; Avenija Dubrovnik 44, Zagreb) offers help and advice. For help on the road, contact the nationwide **HAK road assistance** (Vučna Služba; ☎1987).

The large car-rental chains represented are Avis, Budget, Europcar and Hertz.

Local Transport

The main form of local transport is buses (although Zagreb also has well-developed tram systems).

Buses in major cities such as Dubrovnik, Zagreb and Split run about once every 20 minutes, less on Sunday. Bus transport within the islands is infrequent since most people have their own cars.

Train

Trains are less frequent than buses but more comfortable. For information contact **Croatian Railways** (Hrvatske Željeznice; ☎060-333 444; www.hznet.hr).

Zagreb is the hub for Croatia's less-than-extensive train system. The main lines run from Zagreb to Rijeka, Zadar and Split and east to Osijek. There are no trains travelling along the coast.

On posted timetables in Croatia, the word for arrivals is *dolazak* and for departures it's *odlazak* or *polazak*.

Cyprus Κύπρος

Includes »

Best Places to Eat

» Inga's Veggie Heaven, Lefkosia (p291)

» 1900 Art Café, Larnaka (p295)

» Sabor, Lefkoşa (p298)

Best Historical Sites

» Kykkos Monastery (p296)

» Kourion (p295)

» Pafos Archeological Sites (p297)

Why Go?

Cyprus captures the imagination. This is not your standard Mediterranean island cliché; Cyprus reflects its proximity to Asia and the Middle East in its culture, cuisine and history. Similarly evocative is the contrast between old and new, particularly evident in the capital, Lefkosia (Nicosia). Here you can see the merging of traditional and modern Cyprus, with dusty dilapidated buildings lying round the corner from smart boutiques and arty bars. The flip side of this are the tourist driven areas of Kato Pafos and Agia Napa although, thankfully, development has remained relatively low rise.

Get away from the coastal clamour and head for the Troodos Massif, or the iconic northern Cyprus resort of Kyrenia (Girne). Most importantly, visit both the Turkish and Greek sides of the divided island – you'll get a fuller picture of the complex and fractured Cypriot identity. Talks on peace and unification continue: watch this space.

When to Go

Lefkosia (Nicosia)

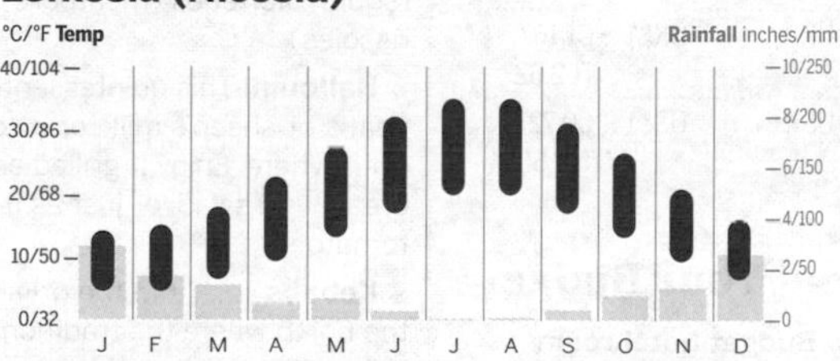

Mar–Apr Enjoy superb weather and that top religious festival for Greek Cypriots: Easter Week.

Jun–Aug Culture, art and music festivals such as the International Music Festival in Lemesos in July.

Sep–Oct An impressionist's palette of autumn colours; hike the trails in the Troodos mountains.

AT A GLANCE

» **Currency** Republic: euro (€); North Cyprus: Turkish lira (TL)

» **Languages** Republic: Greek; North Cyprus: Turkish

» **Money** ATMs are plentiful

» **Visas** Nationals of the USA, Canada, Australia and New Zealand can stay for up to three months without a visa; visas are not needed for EU citizens

Fast Facts

» **Area** 9250 sq km

» **Capital** Lefkosia (Republic); Lefkoşa (North Cyprus)

» **Country codes** Republic ☎357, North Cyprus ☎90 392

» **Emergency** ☎112

Exchange Rates

Australia	A$1	€0.74/ TL1.69
Canada	C$1	€0.74/ TL1.64
Euro Zone	€1	–/TL2.27
Japan	¥100	€0.87/ TL1.96
UK	UK£1	€1.16/ TL2.62
USA	US$1	€0.72/ TL1.60

Set Your Budget

» **Budget hotel room** Republic: €45; North Cyprus: €35 (hotels in North Cyprus commonly quote prices in euros)

» **Two course evening meal** Republic: €15; North Cyprus: TL25

Connections

The main place to get to and from Cyprus by boat is Turkey – go between Girne (in Turkish North Cyprus) and Taşucu or Alanya in summer, and Gazimağusa to Mersin overnight (for details, see p301). Ferries to the (Greek) Republic of Cyprus were suspended in the 1990s but are expected to resume soon, with a route opening between Lemesos and Laurion in Greece. Meanwhile mini three-day cruises between Lemesos and Egypt are one option for those wanting to take to the seas (see p301). Most visitors arrive in Cyprus via air to Pafos or Larnaka airports in the (Greek) Republic, and to Ercan airport in the (Turkish) North. Note that the latter is not recognised by the international airline authorities so flights there are via Turkey.

ITINERARIES

One Week

With just a week in Cyprus, head to the capital to explore north and south Lefkosia. Cross the border for an overnight trip to Girne, then head south to Lemesos and Pafos for the island's best Graeco-Roman ruins, with a stop in the scenic Troodos Massif.

Two Weeks

With the extra week, hire a car and explore Frankish ruins in Gazimağusa (Famagusta), then drive up to the wild Karpas region. If you're up for some more untamed nature, head to the rugged Akamas Peninsula. Then visit Larnaka to pay your respects at the grave of Lazarus.

Essential Food & Drink

» **Meze** A healthy and sociable way to enjoy a wide variety of different foods and flavours, a meze comprises around 30 small plates of food, including dips, vegetables, and a wide range of traditional fish and meat dishes, like *calamare* (squid), *keftedes* (meatballs) and *sheftalia* (pork and lamb rissoles)

» **Halloumi** This quintessential Cypriot cheese made from goat's or sheep's milk, or a combination of both, appears everywhere. Enjoy it grilled as a side dish or stuffed in pita bread with salad, or just as it comes with cucumbers and tomatoes

» **Kebabs** Tuck into the original doner kebab, especially in the north where the traditional shredded lamb is usually wrapped in flat bread and served with salad. *Urfa* kebab comes with onions and black pepper, while *adana* is slightly hot with spicy red pepper

For Cyprus' internet resources, see p300

REPUBLIC OF CYPRUS

Covering the southern 63% of the island, the Greek-speaking Republic of Cyprus has the lion's share of the beaches and historical treasures. Development is rampant at the main beach resorts, but inland are quiet stone villages that have hardly changed in centuries.

Lefkosia (South Nicosia) ΛΕΦΚΩΣΙΑ

POP 213,500

Lefkosia is an enticing city and ideal for experiencing what modern Cyprus is all about. The ancient walls, traditional eateries and a growing multicultural core effectively showcase the city's basic make-up. Almost everything of interest lies within the city's walls, with its labyrinth of narrow streets hiding churches, mosques and evocative, often crumbling, colonial houses. The city has been labelled 'the last divided capital', a reality that, although still present, is slowly changing thanks to 24-hour checkpoint crossings into its northern half, Lefkoşa. It's now possible to see Lefkosia as one city, though it may still be years until it's truly that way.

See p297 for details on Lefkoşa (Nicosia) in North Cyprus.

Sights

TOP CHOICE **Cyprus Museum** ARCHAEOLOGICAL MUSEUM
(Leoforos Mouseiou 1; admission €4; 9am-5pm Mon-Sat, 10am-1pm Sun) Located near the old Pafos Gate, this is the best archaeological museum on the island. Covering the Neolithic to Byzantine periods, exhibits include the famous Aphrodite statue from Soloi.

Archbishop's Palace MUSEUMS
There are three museums within the palace's compound. **St John's Cathedral** (9am-1pm Mon-Sat, 2-4pm Mon-Fri) has stunning frescoes dating from 1662; the **Ethnographic Museum** (Plateia Archiepiskopou Kyprianou; admission €1.70; 9am-5pm Mon-Fri, 10am-1pm Sat) displays traditional Cypriot folk art; and the **Byzantine Museum** (Plateia Archiepiskopou Kyprianou; admission €1.70; 9am-4.30pm Mon-Fri, to 1pm Sat) has ancient icons and frescoes.

Shacolas Tower Observatory OBSERVATORY
(11th fl, Shakolas Tower, cnr Ledra & Arsinois; admission €0.85; 10am-6.30pm) Take the lift to the 11th floor where the observatory offers sweeping city views, including across the Green Line.

Hamam Omerye TURKISH BATHS
(www.hamambaths.com; Plateia Tyllirias 8; admission & Turkish bath 2hr €20; men 9am-9pm Tue, Thu & Sat, women 9am-9pm Wed, Fri & Sun, couples 11am-7pm Mon)

House of Hatzigeorgakis Kornesios OTTOMAN MUSEUM
(Patriarchou Grigoriou 20; admission €1.70; 8am-2pm Mon-Fri, 9am-1pm Sat) Rooms in this 18th-century house are extravagantly decked out with original Ottoman furnishings.

Sleeping & Eating

Sky Hotel SMALL HOTEL €
(2266 6880; www.skyhotel.ws; Solonos 7c; s/d €49/60;) Best budget place in Lefkosia, Sky is bang in the centre of the Old Town surrounded by souvenir shops and cafes frequented by the hubble bubble aficionados.

Shiantris HOMESTYLE CYPRIOT €
(Pericleous 21; mains from €7; lunch) Head here for a really good, simple, home-made Cypriot lunch, including a fantastic array of seasonal beans with lemon, parsley and olive oil and, for the carnivores, baked lamb.

Inga's Veggie Heaven VEGETARIAN €
(2 Dimonaktos, Chrisaliniotissa Crafts Centre; mains €8-10; 9am 5pm) Inga is a friendly Icelandic chef who prepares several fresh dishes of the day, such as almond stuffed peppers or a delicious lentil burger, always served with a salad and home-made bread.

Fanous LEBANESE €
(Solonos 7; mains from €7;) Lebanese specialities.

Drinking & Entertainment

Explore the bar scene in the Old Town for the top spots.

Hammam COCKTAIL BAR
(Soutsou 9) Right behind Hamam Omerye, this atmospheric colonial house, with its arched door and beautifully tiled floors, is perfect for sitting under the stars and sipping a cocktail underneath the fig tree.

TOP CHOICE **Oktana** CAFE, BAR
(Aristidou 6) Decorated with edgy art deco posters, there are regular art exhibitions and poetry readings, plus a delightful sunken patio out the back. The rambling interior includes a bookshop and various rooms, including a basement space favoured by the *nargileh* smokers.

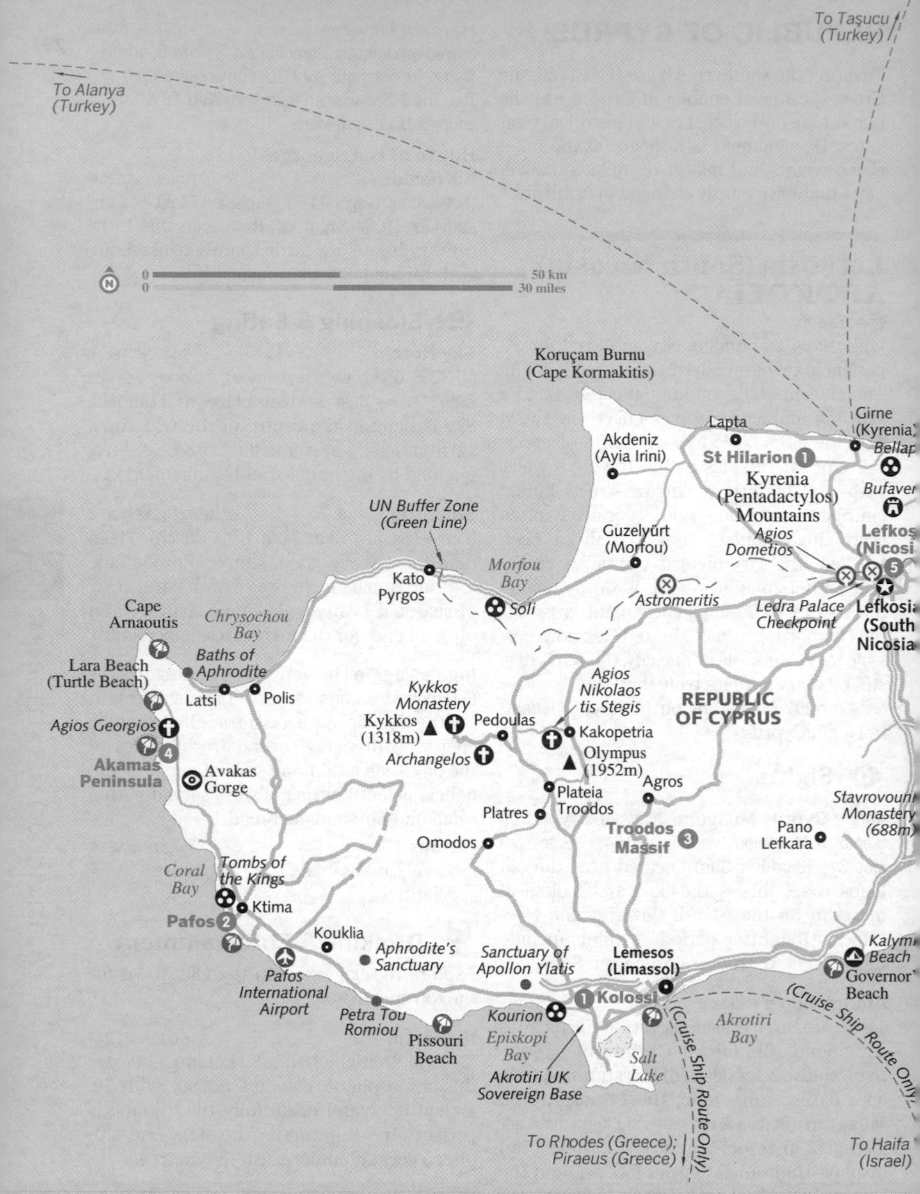

Cyprus Highlights

1. Be king of the castle at the Crusader fortresses of **Kolossi** (p295), **Kantara** (p299) and **St Hilarion** (p299)
2. Bring history to life at the fabulous Graeco-Roman ruins of **Pafos** (p296)
3. Step back to Byzantine times in the **Troodos Massif** (p296)

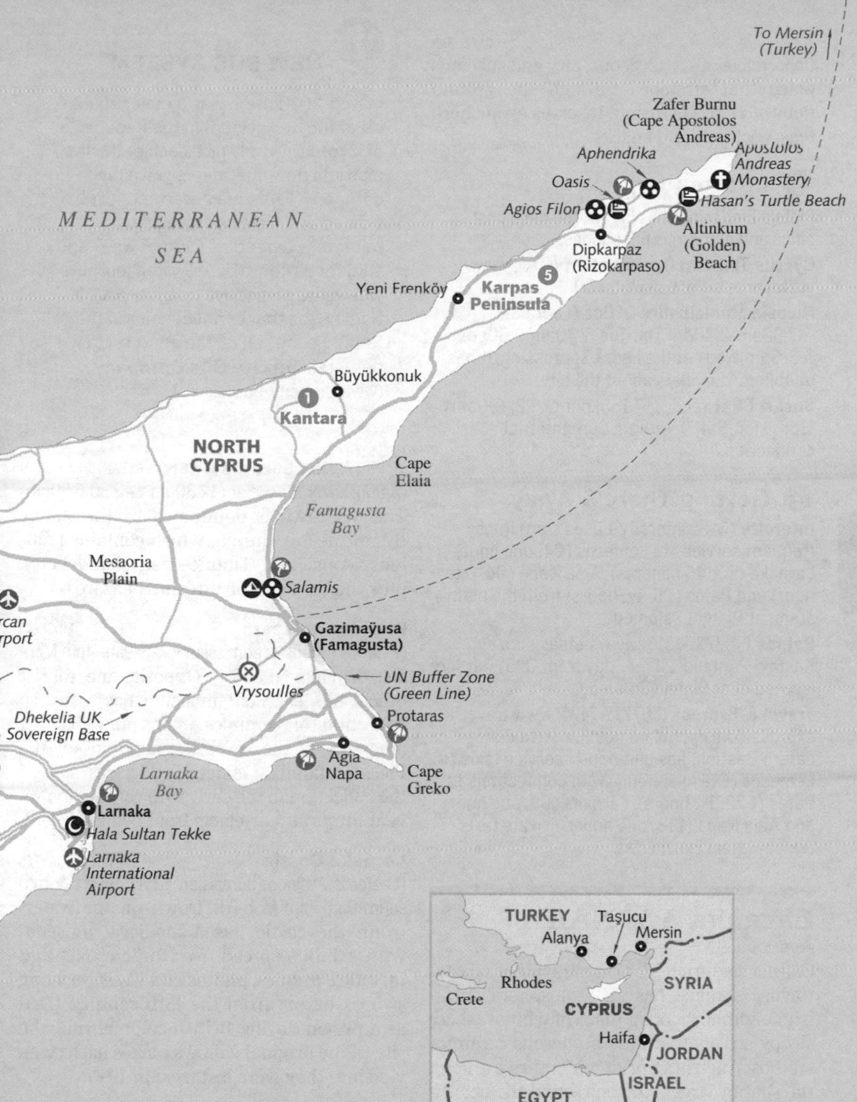

4 Hike the wild trails of the **Akamas Peninsula** (p297)

5 Taste a fantastic kebab at one of the eateries in **Lefkoşa** (p298)

Brew CAFE, BAR
(Ippocratous 30) A gorgeous, airy and spacious place that stretches through the ground floor of an old mansion. It serves exotic herb teas, cocktails and snacks.

 Information

Plateia Eleftherias has banks, the main post office and numerous payphones.

Cyprus Tourism Organisation (CTO; www.visitcyprus.com; Laïki Yitonia)

Nicosia Municipality Office (Ledra St; ⏲7.30am-2.30pm Thu-Tue, 7.30am-2.30pm & 3-6pm Wed) At the Ledra St crossing, it has multilingual leaflets about the city.

Surf & Chat (Ledra St 156; per hr €2; ⏲9am-11pm Mon-Sat, 9am-8pm Sun) Internet connection.

 Getting There & Away

Intercity (www.intercity-buses.com) Runs frequent services to Lemesos (€4, one hour), Larnaka (€3, 45 minutes), Agia Napa (€4, one hour) and Pafos (€5, 1½ hours) from the main stand at Plateia Solomou.

Petsas (☎7777 1515; www.petsas.com.cy; Kostaki Pantelidi 24; per day from €25) Car hire located near Plateia Solomou.

Travel & Express (☎7777 7474; www.travelexpress.com.cy; Salaminos) Close to Podocataro Bastion, has half-hourly service taxis to Lemesos (€12, one hour), with connections to Pafos (€22, 1½ hours), Larnaka (€9, one hour) and Agia Napa (€18, one hour). Private taxis are at Plateia Eleftherias.

Larnaka ΛΑΡΝΑΚΑ

POP 71,740

Calmer and friendlier than the other coastal towns, Larnaka has an atmospheric Turkish neighbourhood; a maze of whitewashed, sleepy streets that hide numerous ceramics studios. Ancient Cypriot crafts thrive among the shabby streets that surround the beautiful Agios Lazaros church.

Back from the seafront are the CTO (Plateia Vasileos Pavlou), the post office and several banks. For internet access, try **Replay** (Leoforos Athinon; per hr €3) on the main promenade.

 Sights

Aside from the listings following, Larnaka also has an **archaeological museum** and several **mosques**; the tourist office has all the details.

NEW BUS SYSTEM

In mid-2010 there was a major shake-up of the bus system in the Republic of Cyprus. Simply put, each of the five districts now operates its own bus company. Fares are government subsidised and have been pegged at €1 per ride, €2 per day, €10 per week and €30 for a month of unlimited journeys within the respective district. In addition, buses that connect cities in the Republic are run by the appropriately named **Intercity Bus Company** (www.intercity-buses.com).

FREE **Agios Lazaros Church** BYZANTINE CHURCH
(Agiou Lazarou; ⏲8am-12.30pm & 3.30-6.30pm) The old town is dominated by the stately Byzantine-era church, which contains fabulous icons (and Titanic-sized chandeliers), plus the tomb of the esteemed Lazaros.

Pierides Museum MUSEUM
(Zinonos Kitieos 4; admission €2; ⏲9am-4pm Mon-Thu, 9am-1pm Fri & Sat) Opposite the tourist office, this excellent museum has a superb collection of ceramics, maps and folk art amassed by the several generations of the Pierides family. Demetrios Pierides started the collection in the early 19th century to prevent important artefacts from being pillaged.

Larnaka Castle CASTLE
(Leoforos Athinon; admission €1.70; ⏲fort & museum 9am-7pm Mon-Fri) Down on the waterfront, the castle has a medieval museum with exhibits spread over three rooms that include ceramics, photos and swashbuckling swords dating from the 15th century. Used as a prison during British colonial rule, the site of the original gallows makes harrowing viewing; they were last used in 1945.

Sleeping & Eating

Petrou Bros APARTMENT HOTEL €
(☎2465 0600; www.petrou.com.cy; Armenikis Eklisias; 2-bed apt €45-60; P❄@☜) Good value and central with sizeable, if starkly lit, kitchenettes with a fridge, two hotplates and plenty of pots and pans. The bedrooms are small by comparison, but pleasantly furnished with private terraces.

Prasino Amaxoudi KEBABS €
(Agias Faneromenis; mains €5-8) This diner-style restaurant is the top place in Larnaka for

kebabs. Go with friendly owner Dimitris' recommendations such as tender chicken kebabs. It's by the Grand Mosque in the old Turkish quarter

1900 Art Café HOMESTYLE €€
(Stasinou 6; mains from €8; 6-11pm Wed-Mon;) Atmospheric rooms with high ceilings and walls papered with posters, black-and-white prints and paintings. Don't expect art on a plate though; the food is filling homestyle cooking with hearty vegetable soups and a choice of meat, fish and vegetarian dishes.

Getting There & Away

Intercity (www.intercity-buses.com) Has regular daily buses to Lemesos (€3, 45 minutes), Lefkosia (€3, 45 minutes) and Agia Napa (€3, one hour). From the airport to central Larnaka, take local buses 431 and 440 (€1, 30 minutes, Monday to Saturday).

Travel & Express (7777 7474; www.travelexpress.com.cy; Papakyriakou) Operates service taxis every half-hour to Lemesos (€11, one hour) and Lefkosia (€9, one hour).

Lemesos (Limasol) ΛΕΜΕΣΟΣ

POP 160,730

Part beach resort, part economic hub, Lemesos is the second-largest city in Cyprus. It is becoming increasingly sophisticated with a long-awaited luxurious new marina due to open in 2014, after suffering innumerable delays. The historic centre has plenty of atmosphere with pedestrian shopping streets that are only truly busy when the cruise ships disgorge their passengers. The **CTO** (cnr Spyros Araouzou & Dimitriou Nikolaidi) is on the waterfront. **CyberNet** (Eleftherias 79; per hr €2.50) offers internet access in the historic quarter.

Sights & Activities

Beach lovers will have to head west out of town. Kourion Beach is best for wind- and kitesurfers.

FREE **Lemesos Castle Medieval Museum** CASTLE MUSEUM
(Eirinis; 9am-5pm Mon-Sat, 10am-1pm Sun) The main attraction in Lemesos is the solid-looking castle. Inside there are lovely shady gardens and a museum where exhibits include Crusader gravestones, Ottoman pottery, suits of armour and an interesting display of black-and-white photos of Byzantine sites all over Cyprus.

Kourion & Castle HISTORICAL SITES
(Kourion; admission €1.70; 8am-7.30pm) A few kilometres west, the Graeco-Roman site at Kourion has Roman baths, an *agora* (public forum) and a famous amphitheatre backed by the setting sun. Get here before 10am to beat the crowds, or arrive in the afternoon to appreciate the sunset. Just northeast of here is the robust keep of **Kolossi Castle** (admission €1.70; 9am-7.30pm), built in Crusader times.

Sanctuary of Apollon Ylatis SANCTUARY
(Episkopi; admission €1.70; 9am-7.30pm) About 5km due west from Kourion are the partly restored remains of this sacred sanctuary created by a cult of Apollo worshippers.

FREE **Grand Mosque** MOSQUE
(Genethliou Mitella) Surrounded by palms, the mosque is open to visitors, outside of prayer time. Nearby is the tiny mixed-sex **Hammam** (Loutron 3; steam bath & sauna/massage €18; 2-10pm).

Sleeping & Eating

TOP CHOICE **Luxor Guest House** GUEST HOUSE €
(2536 2265; www.luxorlimassol.com; Agiou Andreou 101; dm €12, d €35; @) The Luxor has a rare backpacking atmosphere – in a positive sense. The rooms are airy, with painted wood-board ceilings and small balconies overlooking this bustling pedestrian street There is one double with bathroom.

127 INTERNATIONAL €
(Elenis Paleologinas 5; salad/sandwiches from €7.50) This place has a late-night lounge atmosphere with its edgy artwork, black sofas and elegant terrace out the back. There is a choice of 10 innovative salads, as well as hot dishes – and cool cocktails.

There's a cluster of excellent open-air **kebab restaurants** near the municipal market on Saripolou.

Getting There & Away

Intercity (www.intercity-buses.com) has regular daily buses to Lefkosia (€4, one hour), Larnaka (€3, 45 minutes) and Pafos (€3, one hour) from its bus stop north of the castle.

Limassol Buses (www.limassolbuses.com) operates buses to the Troodos.

Travel & Express (7777 7474; www.travelexpress.com.cy; Thessalonikis 21) has regular service taxis to Lefkosia (€12, 1½ hours), Larnaka (€11, one hour) and Pafos (€10.50, one hour). Will also drop you off at Larnaka airport (€13.50) and Pafos airport (€12.50). Another

WORTH A TRIP

TIMIOS STAVROS MONASTERY

About 30km south of Pedoulas, **Omodos** is a pretty village of stone houses, cobbled streets and stalls selling everything from lacework to honey – all centred around the magnificent **Timios Stavros Monastery** (8am-4pm). The monastery has a lavish altar with colourful icons, plus three small museums off the rear courtyard, including the quaintly named EOKA Straggle Museum (sic) with its harrowing photos and text about the 1955–59 EOKA (Ethniki Organosis Kyprion Agoniston; National Organisation of Cypriot Fighters) independence struggle.

taxi option is **Acropolis Service Taxis** (2536 6766; Spyrou Araouzou 65), which departs regularly for the same destinations.

Troodos Massif ΤΡΟΟΔΟΣ

Wild and rugged, the Troodos Massif is a haven for walkers and nature buffs. Dotted among the black pines are waterfalls, winemaking villages and World Heritage–listed Byzantine churches and monasteries.

The village of Platres has a **CTO** (8.30am-4pm Mon-Fri). Just south of Troodos town is the **Troodos Visitor Centre** (admission €0.85; 10am-4pm), with a museum, video show and nature leaflets. For skiing information, contact the **Cyprus Ski Federation** (www.cyprusski.com).

Sights & Activities

FREE **Kykkos Monastery** MONASTERY
(www.kykkos-museum.cy.net; 10am-dusk) Located about 20km northwest of Pedoulas, this monastery is the most famous in the Troodos. The walls of the cloisters on several floors are faced with early 19th-century vivid mosaics and frescoes. There's also a distillery here that produces *komandaria* and *zivania*, available for purchase.

FREE **Byzantine museum** ICONS FRESCOES
(Pedoulas; 10am-1pm & 2.30-5pm) This small icon museum is in the lower part of the village. Ask for the key to the small stone **Church of Archangelos** opposite which contains hellfire-and-brimstone frescoes dating from 1474.

FREE **Agios Nikolaos tis Stegis** FRESCOES
(9am-4pm Tue-Sat, 11am-4pm Sun) Located near Kakopetria, this church has even older 12th-century frescoes.

Sleeping & Eating

There are some choice places to stay and eat in the mountains.

Two Flowers GUEST HOUSE €
(2295 2372; d €50, August full board only €100) A lovely little B&B with 19 simple, clean and bright rooms, five of which sit in an old house around 300m down the road that overlooks the valley. The rest of the rooms are in the main building. Outside of the more expensive month of August, it's great value.

Troodos camping ground CAMPING GROUND €
(2242 1624; camp sites €4; May-Oct) Below town on the Lefkosia road, the camping ground has plenty of pines for shade, plus a small cafe.

TOP CHOICE **Platanos** HOMESTYLE €
(mains €8) Platanos offers a real slice of rural life – there's often an intense backgammon game going on in the corner and the shade of the *platanos* (plane trees) provides atmospheric seating. Enjoy good moussaka and *afelia*, as well as some juicy kebabs.

Getting There & Away

Villages in the Troodos are widely spaced so a rental car is the best way to get around.
Limassol Buses (www.limassolbuses.com); has daily buses from Lemesos to Troodos and Platres (1¾ hours).

Pafos ΠΑΦΟΣ

POP 47,200

The former capital of Cyprus, Pafos is packed with historical relics...and tourists. Pafos consists of beachside, and busier, Kato Pafos (Lower Pafos) and quieter Ktima (Upper Pafos) up the hill.

A private taxi to/from the airport, 8km southeast of town, costs from €30 – you're better off getting a service taxi.

The main **CTO** (Gladstonos 3) is just down from Ktima's main square. Check your emails at **Maroushia Internet** (Plateia Kennedy 6, Ktima; per hr €3).

Sights

Aside from the following must-see sights, Pafos has a **castle**, **Roman basilica** and several **museums**.

Tombs of the Kings ANCIENT TOMBS
(admission €2; 8.30am-7.30pm) A Unesco World Heritage site and Pafos' main attraction, the site contains a set of well-preserved underground tombs and chambers used by residents of Nea Pafos from the 3rd century BC to the 3rd century AD, during the Hellenistic and Roman periods. It's about 2km north of Kato Pafos.

TOP CHOICE **Pafos Archaeological Sites** ARCHAEOLOGICAL SITES
(admission €3.60; 8am-7.30pm) It's worth braving the crowds to see this site with its astounding Roman mosaics, many featuring the rambunctious exploits of Dionysos, the god of wine. Within the same compound are the ruins of a castle and an amphitheatre. There's another castle on the harbour and more impressive Roman ruins, **Hrysopolitissa Basilica** (dawn-dusk), just up the hill near the Pyramos Hotel.

Sleeping & Eating

TOP CHOICE **Pyramos Hotel** HOTEL €
(2693 0222; www.pyramos-hotel.com; Agias Anastasias 4, Kato Pafos; s/d incl breakfast €35/45;) For something different, grab a room overlooking the adjacent archaeological site of Hrysopolitissa Basilica. Soothingly decked out and with classy mosaic-tiled bathrooms, this is a good bet in Kato Pafos.

Kiniras HOTEL €€
(2694 1604; www.kiniras.cy.net; Archiepiskopou Makariou III 91, Ktima; s/d €60/70;) Bang in the centre of Ktima, Kiniras is passionately run by its house-proud owner. The rooms are decorated with colourful frescoes, and have telephone, radio, TV, fridge and safe box.

Muse INTERNATIONAL €
(Mousallas, Ktima; snacks from €7; 9am-2am) A hip new place with sweeping views for a mid-morning frappé, midday light lunch or an evening cocktail when the place morphs into a fashionable lounge bar. Menu choices include *quesadillas*, sushi, salads and sandwiches.

Getting There & Away

Intercity (www.intercity-buses.com) hasregular daily buses to Lefkosia (€5, 1½ hours) and Lemesos (€3, 45 minutes).

Travel & Express (0777 7474; www.travelexpress.com.cy; Leoforos Evagora Pallikaridi 9, Ktima) Operates service taxis to Lemesos (€10, one hour), Larnaka (change at Lemesos; €20, 1½ hours) and Lefkosia (change at Lemesos; €22, 1½ hours).

Dozens of hire places in Kato Pafos rent bikes, mopeds and cars.

> WORTH A TRIP
>
> **POLIS & THE AKAMAS**
>
> Built over the ruins of ancient Marion in the northwest of the Republic, pretty **Polis** makes a great base for hiking or mountain biking in the Akamas. This stunning natural wilderness is protected as a national park and the hills are criss-crossed by dirt tracks and walking trails – pick up CTO's *European Long Distance Path* brochure. **Avakas Gorge** on the west side of the cape is a particularly rewarding hike.
>
> There are also some wild, isolated beaches near here – **Lara Beach** has a turtle research station operating from June to September, accessible by car from Agios Georgios.

NORTH CYPRUS

Increasing numbers of tourists are beginning to explore the Turkish Republic of Northern Cyprus (TRNC). Historic ruins abound and beaches are breathtaking, but the legacy of of the country's split in 1974 (see p299) casts a long shadow in the form of looted churches and neglected national treasures.

Lefkoşa (North Nicosia)

POP 39,180

The northern half of Lefkosia is another world. Approaching from the smart boutiques in Ledra St, the avenue fractures into a medina-style market of stalls and kebab houses. Thankfully many of the historic buildings are gradually being restored and the area around the Selimiye Mosque has a real sense of heritage. With the relaxing of border restrictions, many people take a day trip across from the Republic (and vice versa) via the Ledra Palace or Ledra St checkpoints.

CROSSING THE LINE

Border restrictions in Cyprus were relaxed in December 2003, allowing overnight trips across the Green Line. In theory, foreign tourists are permitted to cross from south to north (or vice versa) and stay for up to three months, but it's not currently possible to enter Cyprus on one side of the line and leave from the other. Pedestrian crossings are at Ledra St and Ledra Palace Hotel in Lefkosia. There are seven access points linking the Greek Cypriot and Turkish Cypriot sides. Hire cars can only be taken from south to north; not the other way.

Sights

Pick up a copy of the *Nicosia Trail* brochure from the tourist office, which details the renovations taking place here.

Mevlevi Museum CULTURAL MUSEUM
(Mevlevi Tekke Müzesi; Girne Caddesi; admission TL5; ⌚9am-12.30pm & 1.30-4.45pm) Just inside the walls, the museum is dedicated to the whirling Sufi dervishes (Muslim mystics), based here until the 1950s. Traditional devotional dances take place during the Shebu Arus celebrations in December.

FREE **Selimiye Mosque** MOSQUE
(Selimiye Camii; Selimiye Meydani) The Selimiye quarter is dominated by this imposing mosque, originally built as a cathedral between 1209 and 1326.

Sleeping & Eating

Accommodation is limited in Lefkoşa, especially in the budget category.

City Royal HOTEL €€
(☎228 7621; www.city-royal.com; Gazeteci Kemal Aşik Caddesi; r from TL130; ❄📶🏊) Rooms are carpeted and spacious with minibar, phone, satellite TV and even a phone in the bathroom. There is also a swimming pool and a gym. To reach here, head northeast of the Kyrenia Gate for about 300m.

TOP CHOICE **Sabor** MEDITERRANEAN €€
(Selimiye Meydanı 29; mains around TL15) Right next to Selimiye Mosque, this is Lefkoşa's best choice for those who can't take another kebab. The menu specialises on Italian and Spanish food, with some Asian noodle dishes.

Bereket STREET FOOD €
(Irfan Bey Sokak; pide & lahmacun TL7-10; ⌚4am-1.30pm) A rough and ready kiosk a few metres away from the grand Büyük Han with the best pide and *lahmacun* (Turkish-style pizza, topped with minced lamb and parsley) in town. There are a couple of chairs outside or you can munch on the go.

Information

Tourist office (Kyrenia Gate; ⌚8am-5pm Mon-Fri, to 3pm Sat & Sun) Has free maps and brochures.

Tourist kiosk (Ledra St crossing; ⌚8am-5pm Mon-Fri, to 3pm Sat & Sun)

Watch & Watch (Girne Caddesi; per hr TL1; ⌚24hr) Internet connection.

Getting There & Around

Girneliler Seyahat has regular minibuses to Girne (TL4, 30 minutes), while Akva/Ulusoy goes frequently to Güzelyurt (TL5.50, 45 minutes). Virgo Trans minibuses to Gazimağusa (TL4, one hour) leave half-hourly from Kaymakli Yolu Sokak, just east of Kyrenia Gate.

Kombos service taxis that take up to seven people run to Girne (TL5, 30 minutes) from Mevlevi Tekke Sokak near the Kyrenia Gate. A private taxi (departing from the charter taxi stand) to Ercan airport will cost TL35 (40 minutes).

Sun Rent-a-Car (☎227 2303; www.sunrentacar.com; Abdi Ipekci Caddesi 10; per day from TL45) is a reliable car-rental outfit located 500m north of Kyrenia Gate. Note that all car-rental agencies in Northern Cyprus have a minimum of three-day rental.

Girne (Kyrenia)

POP 14,200

Girne's picturesque stone harbour ends abruptly at a looming Byzantine castle. The **tourist office** (⌚9am-5pm) is at the west end of the harbour.

Kyrenia Castle & Shipwreck Museum CASTLE MUSEUM
(Girne Kalesi; admission TL13; ⌚9am-12.30pm & 1.30-4.45pm) Dominating the harbour is this magnificent castle with archaeological displays, gloomy dungeons, and the remains of the world's oldest shipwreck to be brought to the surface, dating from 300 BC.

St Hilarion Castle CASTLES
(admission TL7; ⌚9am-12.30pm & 1.30-4.45pm) This archetypal Crusader castle is draped along the highest, rockiest ridge above Kyrenia. On a 4WD track off the Girne-Gazimağusa road, the remote Crusader castle of **Buffavento** offers more breathtaking views.

Bellapais ABBEY RUINS
(admission TL9; ⌚9am-12.30pm & 1.30-4.45pm) A TL50 return taxi ride from Girne (the driver will wait for you for an hour) gets you to the late-Byzantine abbey ruins at Bellapais, the setting for Lawrence Durrell's *Bitter Lemons*.

Sleeping & Eating

There is a good choice of accommodation and restaurants in town. Avoid the overpriced waterfront tourist restaurants and head for the cheaper kebab houses west of Ramadan Cemil Meydanı

Sidelya Hotel HOTEL €
(☎815 6051; Nasır Güneş Sokak 7; s/d TL32/54; ❄) A good budget option having a total makeover at time of research. The rooms are spacious with sea views.

TOP CHOICE **White Pearl Hotel** HOTEL €€
(☎815 4677; www.whitepearlhotel.com; Girne Limanı; s/d with breakfast TL100/136; ❄) Overlooking the harbour, the nine rooms exude cleanliness and understated style, and are very good value. Those at the front are smaller, but preferable, as they have balconies with fabulous views of the harbour.

Cyprus Dorms BUDGET HOTEL €
(☎887 2007; www.cyprusdorms.com; Bozaklar Sok 6; dm TL16, d TL50) A sparkling-clean new *hostal* near the harbour.

Getting There & Around

Buses and service taxis stop near the main roundabout.

Girneliler Seyahat has regular minibuses to Lefkoşa (TL4, 30 minutes). Hourly Virgo Trans minibuses to Gazimağusa (TL7, one hour) leave from an office on the south side of Ramadan Cemil Meydani. Kibhas has six daily buses to the airport at Ercan (TL10, one hour).

Kombos (Ramadan Cemil Meydani) has service taxis to Lefkoşa (TL5, 30 minutes) and Gazimağusa (TL8, one hour).

The ferry terminal is a TL6 taxi ride from town – see p301 for information on boats to and from Turkey.

Around North Cyprus

In the island's northwest, the ancient walled city of **Gazimağusa** (Famagusta) is dotted with ruined Frankish churches. There's a **tourist office** (Akkule Bastion, İstiklal Caddesi; ⌚7.30am-4pm Mon-Fri, 9am-6pm Sat & Sun) and several cheap (albeit shabby) hotels.

The overgrown Graeco-Roman ruins of **Salamis** (admission TL12; ⌚8am-6pm), about 9km north, overlook a sandy beach with interesting snorkelling – a return taxi from Gazimağusa costs TL35.

A reminder of what Cyprus was like before partition, the remote Karpas Peninsula has incredible beaches, Byzantine basilicas, a handful of Greek Orthodox monasteries and the romantic Crusader castle of **Kantara** (admission TL6; ⌚9am-5pm). Altinkum (Golden Beach) has nesting turtles from June to August.

UNDERSTAND CYPRUS

History

Greek culture in Cyprus dates back to 2500 BC, but the island was taken over by the Romans and then the Byzantines, who built churches and monasteries across the island.

Next came the Crusaders, who constructed numerous castles; the Franks, who erected Gothic cathedrals; and the Venetians, who built huge walls around Lefkosia and Gazimağusa. This didn't stop the Ottomans invading in 1571 and dominating Cyprus for the next 300 years.

In 1878 Turkey sold Cyprus to Britain but the majority Greek Cypriot population demanded independence from foreign rule and union with Greece. In response, Britain appointed a Turkish Cypriot police force to subdue the Greeks, triggering decades of intercommunal violence. Britain finally granted independence to Cyprus in August 1960.

On 15 July 1974, Greek forces launched a coup against the Cypriot government and Turkey invaded the northern third of the island, driving 180,000 Greek Cypriots from their homes and killing thousands. The UN later interceded and partitioned the island into Turkish and Greek states.

Despite a series of UN resolutions, Cyprus remains a divided island. As a result, the southern (Greek) Republic of Cyprus entered the EU alone in May 2004. Since then, border restrictions have eased, but wounds are still fresh and the most recent elections of April 2010 in North Cyprus of the 72-year-old veteran politician and hardliner Dervis Eroglu has concerned some analysts. As before, the most difficult, pressing and perennial issues for the two leaders to resolve remain power-sharing, land ownership – and compensation.

People

The population of the Republic of Cyprus is 789,300, while in North Cyprus it is 265,100. Since partition, most Greek Cypriots live in the south. In the north, the Turkish Cypriot population is heavily outnumbered by settlers from the Turkish mainland. More than 99% of the North Cyprus population is Sunni Muslim, while the south is 94% Greek Orthodox, with Roman Catholic, Maronite and Muslim minorities.

The definitive art of Cyprus is the production of icons and frescoes; you can see examples dating back to the 12th century in churches and monasteries across Cyprus.

Food

The price ranges used in this book are based on the cost of a main course for the Republic/North Cyprus, and listings are ordered by preference.

€€€ more than €12/TL20

€€ €7 to €12/TL10 to TL20

€ less than €7/TL10

Environment

Cyprus is divided by the Kyrenia (Pentadactylos) Mountains in North Cyprus and the Troodos Massif in the centre of the Republic. A less tangible divide is the Green Line – the UN-patrolled buffer zone that divides the Republic of Cyprus from the North.

SURVIVAL GUIDE

Directory A-Z

Accommodation

There are inexpensive choices in most towns, plus a few camping grounds. Prices increase by 20% to 30% from June to August. The price ranges used in this chapter are based on the cost of a double room with a private bathroom and breakfast included in the Republic/North Cyprus, during the high season.

€€€ More than €90/€70

€€ €60 to €90/€40 to €70

€ Up to €60/€40

Activities

All the seaside resorts offer watersports. The Akamas and Karpas Peninsulas and the Troodos Massif and Pentadaktylos Mountains are fantastic for hiking and mountain biking.

Business Hours

Usual opening times in Cyprus:

Banks 8.30am-2.30pm Mon-Fri, plus Mon afternoon in the Republic

Offices 7.30am-2.30pm Mon-Fri & 3-6pm Thu (in the Republic) or Mon (in the North)

Restaurants 11am-2pm & 7pm-11pm

Shops 8.30am-7.30pm Mon-Sat Jun–mid-Sep, less hr rest of year. Shops close early on Wed & Sat & also at lunchtime

Internet Resources

» **Tourism in North Cyprus** (www.northcyprus.cc)

» **Republic of Cyprus website** (www.visitcyprus.com)

» **Environmental tourism** (www.cypenv.info)

Money

The Republic's currency is the euro (€). The unit of currency in North Cyprus is the revalued Turkish lira (TL), but euros and UK pounds are widely accepted.

Telephone

There are no area codes in Cyprus.Roaming-enabled GSM mobile phones can be used all over Cyprus. Payphones take phonecards, available from shops and kiosks. Prepay SIM cards cost around €30.

Visas

In both the Republic and North Cyprus, nationals of Australia, New Zealand, USA, Canada and EU countries can stay for up to three months without a visa.

Getting There & Away

Most travellers arrive by air, but there are also ferries to the North from Turkey.

Air

The Republic's international airports are at Larnaka and Pafos. There are regular scheduled and charter flights from Europe and the Middle East with **Cyprus Airways** (CY; www.cyprusairways.com) and other carriers. Flights to Ercan airport in North Cyprus start in Turkey.

Scheduled airlines flying to North Cyprus:

Turkish Airlines (TK; www.turkishairlines.com)

Cyprus Turkish Airlines (YK; www.kthy.net)

Discount airlines flying to Cyprus:

EasyJet (U2; www.easyjet.com)

Aegean Airlines (A3; www.aegeanair.com)

Monarch (ZB; http://flights.monarch.co.uk)

Sea

Services from Greece to the Republic's main port at Lemesos are currently suspended. However, they may restart any time. Check with **Salamis Shipping** (www.salamisinternational.com) and **Louis Cruise Lines** (www.louiscruises.com). Short cruises between Egypt and Lemesos are available from **Lefkothea** (lefkothea.travel@cytanet.com.cy), which is a reliable agent.

Fergün Denizcilikik (www.fergun.net) operates a daily express boat and a slower car ferry between Girne and Taşucu (TL69 to T150, 2½ to 7½ hours). In summer there are additional ferries between Girne and Alanya, Antalya and Anamur. There are also sailings from Gazimağusa to Mersin (TL80, 10 hours) three times a week operated by **Cyprus Turkish Shipping** (cypship@superonline.com).

Getting Around

Inexpensive buses link the major cities, except on Sunday. Shared service-taxis cover similar routes for similar prices.

Cheap car and motorbike rental is available in most towns. Most national driving licences are valid in the Republic, but only British and International Driving Permits are accepted in North Cyprus. The boxed text, p298, has information on crossing the border.

Czech Republic

Includes »

Best Places to Eat

» Pivovarský Klub, Prague (p312)

» U kašny, Olomouc (p322)

» Laibon, Český Krumlov (p320)

» Rebio, Brno (p321)

Best Places to Stay

» Dahlia Inn, Prague (p309)

» Little Town Budget Hotel, Prague (p309)

» Poet's Corner, Olomouc (p322)

Why Go?

Located in the centre of Europe, the Czech Republic is likely to feature as a through road in your travels. Try not to rush your visit though, and be sure to venture beyond the obvious attractions. Definitely spend time exploring the beauty, culture and energy of Prague, and a lazy sojourn on the Vltava River around Český Krumlov is also mandatory.

But once you've ticked off these 'Must Do' destinations, venture off the beaten path to fully understand the Czech Republic's thrilling history. Castles and palaces abound, bringing the past to life and illuminating the stories of families and individuals whose influence was felt well beyond the nation's current borders. The pristine Old Towns of Loket, Telč and Olomouc provide your best chance to ease off the travel accelerator, and in quickly changing cities such as Plzeň, Brno and České Budějovice you'll soon discover 21st-century Czech life beyond Prague's tourist bustle.

When to Go

Prague

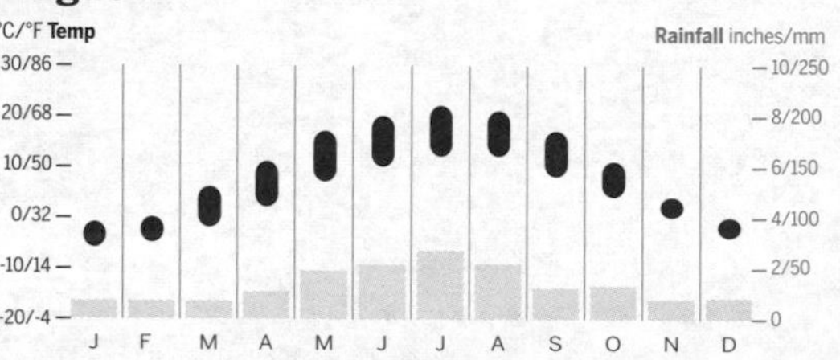

May Prague comes alive with festivals from classical music to fringe arts and beer.

Jul The sleepy spa town of Karlovy Vary is energised during its annual film festival.

May & Sep Enjoy a (relative) lack of tourists and cheaper accommodation.

Connections

The Czech Republic is a convenient hub for exploring neighbouring countries. Prague is well connected to Berlin, Dresden, Nuremberg and Hamburg, and Plzeň is on the main train line from Nuremberg to Munich. From Český Krumlov it's a short distance to Linz or Salzburg in Austria, with connections to Vienna and to Budapest in Hungary. For travel to Poland, Olomouc is a key transit point for trains to Warsaw and Kraków, and the eastern Czech city of Brno has regular bus and train services to Vienna and the Slovakian capital, Bratislava.

ITINERARIES

One Week

Experience Prague's exciting combination of a tumultuous past and an energetic present. Invest in day trips to Karlštejn and Kutná Hora, and then head south to Český Krumlov for a few days of riverside R&R.

Two Weeks

Begin in Prague before heading west for the spa scene at Karlovy Vary. Balance the virtue-and-vice ledger with a few Bohemian brews in Plzeň before heading south for relaxation and rigour around Český Krumlov. Head east through České Budějovice en route to the Renaissance grandeur of Telč and Brno's cosmopolitan galleries and museums. Continue to Olomouc to admire the Holy Trinity Column. From Olomouc it's an easy trip back to Prague or on to Poland.

Essential Food & Drink

» **Beer** Make it your mission to search out excellent *pivo* (beer) from smaller, local microbreweries. Look for the hand-drawn blackboards outside pubs

» **The perfect bramboráčky** Forget French fries – always order authentic Czech fried potato pancakes as a side dish

» **Meaty treats** *Pečená kachna* (roast duck) in a restaurant setting or *klobása* (sausage) as a boozy late night/early morning option in Prague's Wenceslas Sq

» **Cola meets cough medicine** The uniquely Czech soft drink Kofola is worth sampling; you may even grow to like it

AT A GLANCE

» **Currency** Crown (Kč)

» **Language** Czech

» **Money** ATMs are all over

» **Visas** Schengen rules apply; see p1319

Fast Facts

» **Area** 78,864 sq km

» **Capital** Prague

» **Country code** ☎420

» **Emergency** ☎112; Ambulance ☎155; Municipal Police ☎156

Exchange Rates

Australia	A$1	17.73Kč
Canada	C$1	17.49Kč
Euro Zone	€1	24.22Kč
Japan	¥100	20.19Kč
New Zealand	NZ$1	13.42Kč
UK	UK£1	27.40Kč
USA	US$1	16.78Kč

Set Your Budget

» **Budget hotel room** 1300Kč

» **Two-course evening meal** 200Kč

» **Museum entrance** 150Kč

» **Beer** (glass) 40Kč

» **Prague metro/tram ticket** 26Kč

Resources

» **Czech Tourism** (www.czechtourism.com) Official tourist information.

» **Prague Information Service** (www.praguewelcome.cz) Prague.

» **IDOS** (www.idos.cz) Train and bus timetables.

Czech Republic Highlights

1 Experience Europe's past, present and future in **Prague's** (p305) vibrant mix of history, art and architecture, and nightlife

2 Enjoy lazy days on the Vltava River and energetic nights in riverside cafes in **Český Krumlov** (p319)

3 Discover sleepy **Loket** (p316), topped by a brooding castle and winding around a serpentine river

4 Unearth the easygoing and cosmopolitan student scene in **Olomouc** (p322)

5 Create your own beer taste test in the 'Big Two' of Bohemian brewing – **Plzeň** (p317) and **České Budějovice** (p318)

PRAGUE

POP 1.22 MILLION

It's Prague's perfect irony. You are lured by the past, but compelled to linger by the present and the future. Fill your days with Prague's artistic and architectural heritage, but after dark move your focus to lively restaurants, bars and clubs in emerging neighbourhoods like Vinohrady and Žižkov.

If Prague's seasonal legions of tourists sometimes wear you down, just drink a glass of Bohemian lager, relax and be reassured that quiet moments still exist: enjoying a private dawn on Charles Bridge; sipping a chilled beer in Letná above the improbable cityscape of Staré Město; or getting reassuringly lost in the intimate lanes of Malá Strana or Josefov.

Every day you'll uncover more reasons to support Prague's enduring reputation as one of Europe's most exciting cities.

Sights

Prague Castle CASTLE

(Map p310; www.hrad.cz; ⌚castle 9am-6pm Apr-Oct, 9am-4pm Nov-Mar, grounds 5am-midnight Apr-Oct, 9am-11pm Nov-Mar, gardens closed Nov-Mar; 🚊22, 23 to Pražský hrad) Located on the western bank of the Vltava River, Prague Castle is the city's number-one attraction. Highlights include the jewel-studded **St Wenceslas Chapel** in **St Vitus Cathedral**; the view from the **cathedral tower**; the spectacular **Vladislav Hall** in the Old Royal Palace; and the **Basilica of St George**, Prague's finest Romanesque church. The **Long Tour** (adult/concession 350/175Kč) includes the Old Royal Palace, St Vitus Cathedral, the Story of Prague Castle exhibit, the Basilica of St George, the Convent of St George, the Prague Castle Picture Gallery and Golden Lane with Daliborka Tower. The **Short Tour** (250/125Kč) focuses only on the Old Royal Palace, St Vitus Cathedral, the Basilica of St George, Golden Lane and the Story of Prague Castle exhibit.

It's free to wander around the castle courtyards and gardens. Also free is the **Changing of the Guard**, which takes place every hour, with fanfare and a flag ceremony at noon daily. Tickets to the various attractions are valid for two days, but you can only visit each attraction once.

The **Convent of St George** (Map p310; www.ngprague.cz; admission on long tour or adult/concession 150/80Kč; ⌚10am-6pm Tue-Sun) was Bohemia's first convent, established in 973 by Boleslav II. It now showcases 19th-century Bohemian art.

On the right, before the castle's exit, is the **Lobkowicz Palace** (Map p310; www.lobkowiczevents.cz/palace; Jiřská 3; adult/concession 275/175Kč; ⌚10.30am-6pm). Built in the 1570s, this palace was home to the aristocratic Lobkowicz family until WWII when it was co-opted by the Nazis. The communists confiscated it in 1948, and it was only returned to the family in 2002. Now it is a private museum focused on the **Princely Collections**, with highlights including paintings by Canaletto and music by Mozart, Beethoven and Hadyn.

Other sights are listed on the map of the castle. Outside the castle entrance is the 18th-century **Šternberg Palace** (Map p310; www.ngprague.cz; adult/concession 150/80Kč; ⌚10am-6pm Tue-Sun; 🚊22, 23 to Pražský hrad), with the country's principal collection of 14th- to 18th-century European art.

Malá Strana HISTORIC AREA

Head downhill from the castle to the baroque backstreets of Malá Strana (Little Quarter). Close to the cafe-crowded main square, Malostranské nám, is **St Nicholas Church** (www.psalterium.cz; adult/student 70/35Kč; ⌚9am-5pm Mar-Oct, to 4pm Nov-Feb; 🚊12, 20, 22, 23 to Malostranské nam), one of the city's greatest baroque buildings.

To escape Malá Strana's tourist throng, head for **Kampa**, a broad park beside the river. Nearby, the innovative **Franz Kafka Museum** (www.kafkamuseum.cz; Cihelná 2b; adult/child 120/60Kč; ⌚10am-6pm; Ⓜ Malostranská) proves the writer was much more than the T-shirt logo he's become.

At the northern end of Kampa is the elegant **Charles Bridge**, built in 1357 and graced by 30 statues dating from the 18th century. Try and visit at dawn before the tourist hordes arrive.

Across the river, the **Charles Bridge Museum** (Map p306; www.muzeumkarlovamostu.cz; Křížovnické nám; adult/student 180/120Kč; ⌚10am-8pm, to 6pm Oct-Apr; 🚊17, 18 to Karlovy lávně) showcases 650 years of turbulent history.

Staré Město HISTORIC AREA

On the Staré Město (Old Town) side of Charles Bridge, narrow and crowded Karlova leads east to **Staroměstské nám** (Map p306; Old Town Sq; Ⓜ Staroměstská), dominated by the Gothic steeples of **Týn Church** (1365) and **St Nicholas Church** (1730s), and the clock tower of the **Old Town Hall**, where the **astronomical clock** (1410) entertains

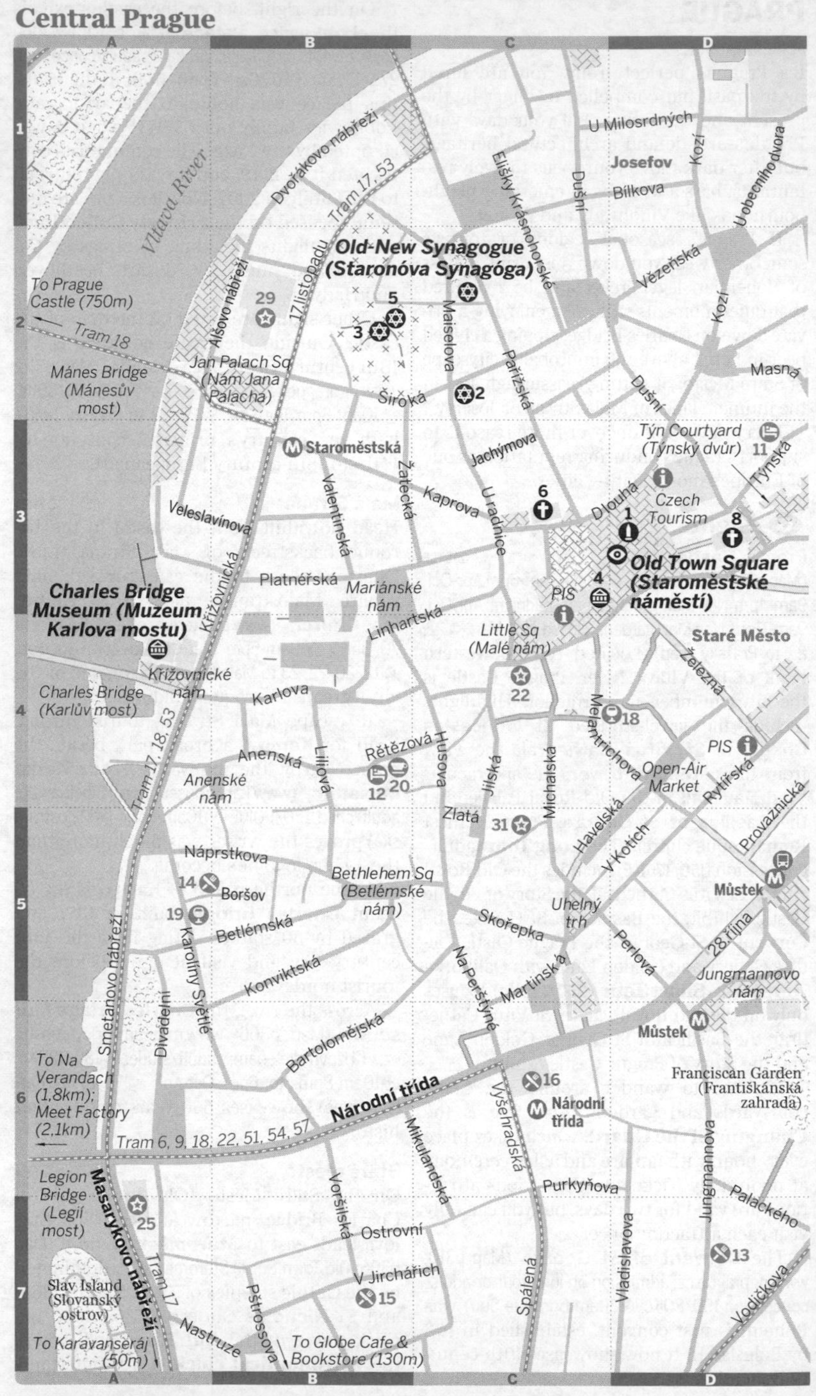
Vltava River
Dvořákovo nábřeží
Tram 17, 53
17 listopadu
Old-New Synagogue (Staronóva Synagóga)
To Prague Castle (750m)
Tram 18
Alšovo nábřeží
Jan Palach Sq (Nám Jana Palacha)
Mánes Bridge (Mánesův most)
Široká
Maiselova
Pařížská
Eliśky Krásnohorské
Dušní
Josefov
U Milosrdných
Bílkova
Kozí
U obecního dvora
Vězeňská
Masná
Staroměstská
Jachýmova
Týn Courtyard (Týnský dvůr)
Týnská
Kaprova
U radnice
Dlouhá
Czech Tourism
Old Town Square (Staroměstské náměstí)
PIS
Staré Město
Veleslavínova
Valentinská
Žatecká
Křižovnická
Platnéřská
Mariánské nám
Linhartská
Charles Bridge Museum (Muzeum Karlova mostu)
Little Sq (Malé nám)
Železná
Křižovnické nám
Charles Bridge (Karlův most)
Karlova
Tram 17, 18, 53
Melantrichova
Anenská
Řetězová
Husova
Jilská
Michalská
Open-Air Market
Rytířská
Anenské nám
Lilijová
Zlatá
Havelská
V Kotcích
Provaznická
Náprstkova
Bethlehem Sq (Betlémské nám)
Boršov
Můstek
Betlémská
Uhelný trh
Skořepka
Perlová
28.října
Karoliny Světlé
Konviktská
Na Perštýně
Martinská
Jungmannovo nám
Smetanovo nábřeží
Divadelní
Bartolomějská
To Na Verandach (1,8km); Meet Factory (2,1km)
Národní třída
Vyšehradská
Franciscan Garden (Františkánská zahrada)
Tram 6, 9, 18, 22, 51, 54, 57
Mikulandská
Legion Bridge (Legií most)
Masarykovo nábřeží
Voršilská
Purkyňova
Jungmannova
Palackého
Ostrovní
Vladislavova
Slav Island (Slovanský ostrov)
Tram 17
V Jirchářích
Spálená
Vodičkova
Pštrossova
Nastruze
To Karavanserái (50m)
To Globe Cafe & Bookstore (130m)

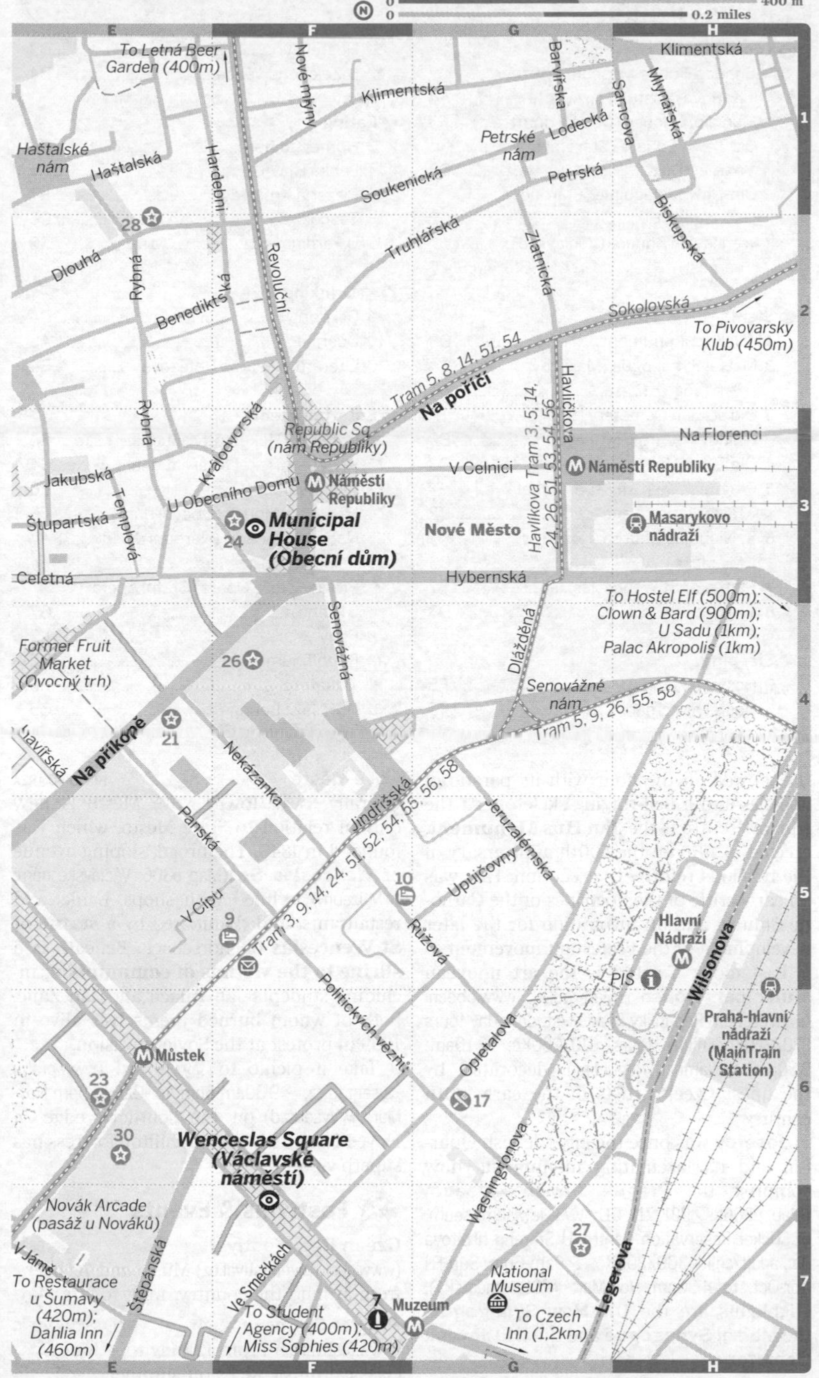
0 400 m
0 0.2 miles
To Letná Beer Garden (400m)
Klimentská
Nové mlýny
Haštalské nám
Haštalská
Hardební
Petrské nám
Lodecká
Samcova
Mlynářská
Barvířská
Petrská
Soukenická
Biskupská
Truhlářská
Zlatnická
Dlouhá
Rybná
Revoluční
Benediktská
Sokolovská
To Pivovarsky Klub (450m)
Tram 5, 8, 14, 51, 54
Na poříčí
Havlíčkova
Havlíčkova Tram 3, 5, 14, 24, 26, 51, 53, 54, 56
Králodvorská
Republic Sq (nám Republiky)
Na Florenci
V Celnici
Náměstí Republiky
Jakubská
U Obecního Domu
Templová
Štupartská
Municipal House (Obecní dům)
Masarykovo nádraží
Nové Město
Celetná
Hybernská
Senovážná
To Hostel Elf (500m); Clown & Bard (900m); U Sadu (1km); Palac Akropolis (1km)
Former Fruit Market (Ovocný trh)
Dlážděná
Senovážné nám
Tram 5, 9, 26, 55, 58
Na příkopě
Havířská
Nekázanka
Panská
Jindřišská
Tram 3, 9, 14, 24, 51, 52, 54, 55, 56, 58
Jeruzalémská
Opletalova
V Cípu
Růžová
Politických vězňů
Hlavní Nádraží
PIS
Wilsonova
Praha-hlavní nádraží (Main Train Station)
Můstek
Washingtonova
Wenceslas Square (Václavské náměstí)
Novák Arcade (pasáž u Nováků)
V Jámě
To Restaurace u Šumavy (420m); Dahlia Inn (460m)
Štěpánská
Ve Smečkách
To Student Agency (400m); Miss Sophies (420m)
Muzeum
National Museum
To Czech Inn (1,2km)
Legerova
28
24
26
21
10
9
23
30
17
27
7
E
F
G
H
1
2
3
4
5
6
7

Central Prague

Top Sights
Charles Bridge Museum (Muzeum Karlova mostu) ... A4
Municipal House (Obecní dům) ... F3
Old Town Square (Staroměstské náměstí) ... D3
Old-New Synagogue (Staronóva Synagóga) ... C2
Wenceslas Square (Václavské náměstí) ... F7

Sights
1 Jan Hus Monument ... D3
2 Maisel Synagogue (Maiselova Synagóga) ... C2
3 Old Jewish Cemetery (Starý Židovský Hřbitov) ... B2
4 Old Town Hall ... C3
5 Prague Jewish Museum Ticket Reservation Centre ... B2
6 St Nicholas Church (Kostel sv Mikuláše) ... C3
7 Statue of St Wenceslas ... F7
8 Týn Church ... D3

Sleeping
9 Hostel AZ ... F5
10 Hostel Rosemary ... F5
11 Hostel Týn ... D3
12 U Zeleného věnce ... B4

Eating
13 Home Kitchen ... D7
14 Lehká Hlava ... A5
15 Pizzeria Kmotra ... B7
16 Tesco ... C6
17 U Ferdinanda ... G6

Drinking
18 Čili Bar ... D4
19 Duende ... A5
20 Literární Kavárna Řetězová ... B4

Entertainment
21 Bohemia Ticket International ... E4
22 Bohemia Ticket International ... C4
23 Kino Světozor ... E6
24 Municipal House (Obecní dům) ... F3
25 National Theatre (Národni divadlo) ... A7
26 Palace Cinemas ... F4
27 Prague State Opera (Státní opera Praha) ... G7
28 Roxy ... E2
29 Rudolfinum ... B2
30 Ticketpro ... E6
31 USP Jazz Lounge ... C5

the crowds on the hour with its parade of apostles and a bell-ringing skeleton. At the square's centre is the **Jan Hus Monument**, erected in 1915 on the 500th anniversary of the religious reformer's execution. Hus was an early critic of the doctrines of the Catholic Church, and an inspiration for the later development of the Protestant movement.

East along Celetná is the art nouveau **Municipal House** (Map p306; www.obecni-dum.cz; nám Republiky 5; adult/student day tours 270/220Kč, night tours 310/260Kč; ⊙10am-9.30pm; Ⓜ Náměstí Republiky), decorated by the finest Czech artists of the early 20th century.

Josefov was once the city's Jewish Quarter, and its fascinating monuments now comprise the **Prague Jewish Museum** (Map p306; ☎221 711 511; www.jewishmuseum.cz; Ticket Reservation Centre, U Starého hřbitova 3a; adult/child 300/200Kč; ⊙9am-6pm Sun-Fri Apr-Oct, to 4.30pm Nov-Mar; Ⓜ Staroměstská). Highlights are the **Old-New Synagogue**, the **Maisel Synagogue** and the **Old Jewish Cemetery**.

Nové Město HISTORIC AREA

Literally 'New Town', Nové Město is new only in relation to Staré Město, which was founded in 1348. The broad, sloping avenue of **Wenceslas Sq** (Map p306; Václavské nám; Ⓜ Muzeum) is lined with shops, banks and restaurants, and dominated by a **statue of St Wenceslas** on horseback. Beneath is a **shrine to the victims of communism**, including students Jan Palach and Jan Zajíc, both of whom burned themselves alive in 1969 in protest at the Soviet invasion.

Take a picnic to **Vyšehrad** (www.praha-vysehrad.cz; ⊙9.30am-6pm Apr-Oct, to 5pm Nov-Mar; Ⓜ Vyšehrad) on the southern edge of Nové Město. This ancient hilltop fortress has superb views.

Festivals & Events

Czech Beer Festival BEER

(www.ceskypivnifestival.cz) Music and 70 beers from around the country; mid- to late May.

Prague Spring CLASSICAL MUSIC

(www.festival.cz) From 12 May to 4 June, classical music kicks off summer.

Prague Fringe Festival ARTS
(www.praguefringe.com) Eclectic action in late May and early June.

United Islands MUSIC
(www.unitedislands.cz) World music in mid-June.

Sleeping

For Christmas and Easter, or from May to September, book ahead. High-season prices, charged from April to October, are quoted in the following reviews. These rates can increase around 15% at Christmas, New Year and Easter, and in May during the Prague Spring festival. Some hotels have slightly lower rates in July and August, and from November to March rates drop further.

Hostel.cz (☎415 658 580; www.hostel.cz) offers around 60 hostels with online booking. **Prague City Apartments** (☎800 800 722; www.prague-city-apartments.cz) specialises in holiday apartments near the city centre.

TOP CHOICE **Dahlia Inn** BOUTIQUE HOTEL €€
(off Map p306; ☎222 517 518; www.dahliainn.com; Lípová 1444/20 16, Nové Město; s/d €49/59; ; MKarlovo Náměstí) From the outside the building is nondescript, but concealed inside is a relaxed and friendly hotel with spacious, designer-decorated rooms, flat-screen TVs, and cool and classy bathrooms. The well-travelled British-Czech owner is a wealth of information on local restaurants, bars and clubs. Rates exclude breakfast.

U Zeleného věnce PENSION €€
(Green Garland; Map p306; ☎222 220 178; www.uzv.cz; Řetězová 10, Staré Město; s/d/tr 1700/2200/2800Kč; @; MStaroměstská) Just a few minutes' amble from Old Town Sq, the Green Garland is very peaceful for somewhere so central. The simply furnished bedrooms vary in size – have a look first – but all are spotlessly clean and the attic rooms have exposed medieval roof beams.

Little Town Budget Hotel HOSTEL, HOTEL €
(☎242 406 965; www.littletownhotel.cz; Malostranské nám 11/260, Malá Strana; dm 500-600Kč, s/d/tr from 1000/1400/1650Kč; @; 12, 20, 22, 23 to Malostranské nám;) With a brilliant location in Malá Strana, this hostel frames a quiet, central courtyard. Rooms are simply furnished with whitewashed walls and have a relaxed ambience verging on monastic. The more expensive three- and four-person self-contained rooms/apartments (1850Kč to 2400Kč) with kitchen and bathroom are excellent value for groups.

Hotel Leon HOTEL €
(☎220 941 351; www.leonhotel.eu; Ortenovo náměstí 26, Holešovice; s/d/tr/q from 810/1380/1770/2000Kč; @; MNádraží Holešovice or 5, 12 to Ortenovo nám; Bridging the gap between small hotel and hostel, the Leon has simply-furnished compact rooms, some with private bathrooms, and a super-convenient tram stop just outside. The Nádraží Holešovice metro station is just a short walk away; some 3.5km from the city centre. If you're travelling in a group of three of four, consider this spot rather than a crowded hostel dorm.

Czech Inn HOSTEL, BOUTIQUE HOTEL €€
(☎267 267 600; www.czech-inn.com; Francouzská 76, Vinohrady; dm 300-400Kč, d/tw/tr from 1400/1400/2100Kč; @; 5, 9, 26 to Husinecká) From dorms to private apartments, everything's covered at this designer hostel-hotel with good transport links. There are no kitchen facilities, but Vinohrady's restaurants and cheap eats are minutes away. There's a cool on-site bar downstairs.

Sir Toby's Hostel HOSTEL €
(☎283 870 635; www.sirtobys.com; Dělnická 24, Holešovice; dm 350-500Kč, s/d/tw/tr 1150/1400/1600/1800Kč; @; 1, 3, 5, 25 to Dělnická) In an up-and-coming suburb a 10-minute tram ride north of the city centre, Sir Toby's is in a refurbished apartment building on a quiet street. The staff are friendly and knowledgeable, and there is a shared kitchen and lounge.

Prague's Heaven HOSTEL €
(☎603 153 617; www.hostelpraha.eu; Jaromírova 20, Vyšehrad; dm 320-350Kč, s/d/tr/q from 850/1300/1500/1980Kč; @; 17, 18, 24 to Svatoplukova) This quieter spot in Vyšehrad is ideal for travellers not interested in Prague's reputation as a party town. Apartment-style

SPLURGE

In a quiet, atmospheric corner of Malá Strana, the eclectically furnished **Hotel Sax** (☎257 531 268; www.hotelsax.cz; Jánský vršek 328/3, Malá Strana; d from €120; @; 12, 20, 22, 23 to Malostranské nám) has huge bathtubs, big flat-screen TVs, primary-coloured leather couches and striking abstract photography; all tinged with a thoroughly retro 1960s design aesthetic.

Prague Castle

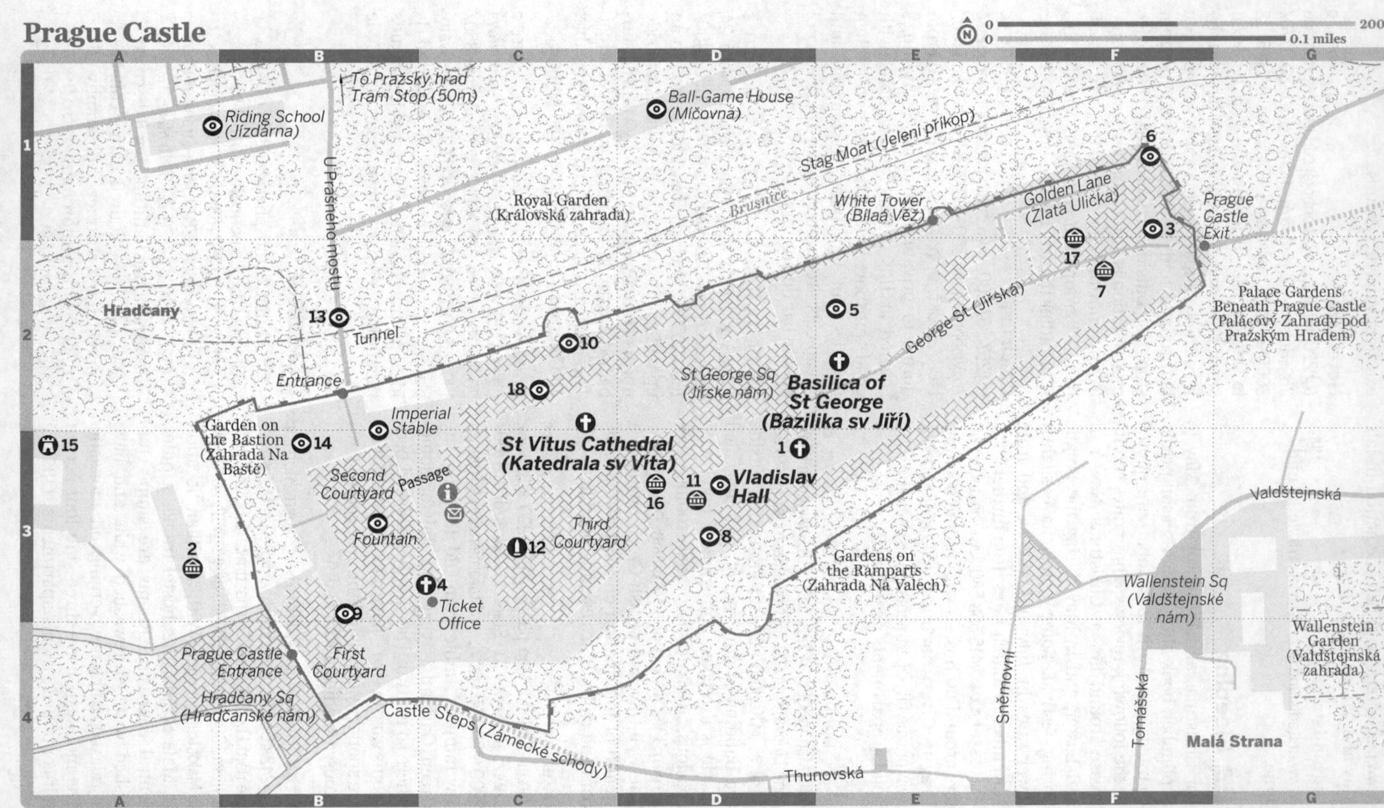

rooms and shiny new bathrooms huddle around a central lounge.

Miss Sophie's HOSTEL, BOUTIQUE HOTEL €€
(☎296 303 530; www.miss-sophies.com; Melounova 3, Nové Město; dm 450Kč, s/d/apt from 1750/2050/3000Kč; @☜; ⓂIP Pavlova) 'Boutique hostel' sums up this converted apartment building. Polished concrete blends with oak flooring, and the basement lounge is all bricks and black leather. Good restaurants await outside.

Clown & Bard Hostel HOSTEL €
(☎222 716 453; www.clownandbard.com; Bořivojova 102, Žižkov; dm 300-380Kč, d/tw/tr 1000/1400/2100Kč; @☜; 🚊5, 9, 26 to Husinecká) The party crowd gravitates towards the thumping basement bar that stays open till midnight. Recharge at the all-veggie, all-you-can-eat breakfast (not included in the price) any time until 2pm.

Hostel Rosemary HOSTEL €
(Map p306; ☎222 211 124; www.praguecityhostel.cz; Růžová 5, Nové Město; dm 400-500Kč, s/tw/tr from 900/1300/1650Kč; @☜; ⓂMůstek) Hostel Rosemary enjoys a quiet location near Wenceslas Sq and Prague's main train station. Rooms are light and airy with high ceilings; some include a private bathroom and kitchen.

Hostel Týn HOSTEL €
(Map p306; ☎224 808 333; www.hosteltyn,com; Týnská 19, Staré Město; dm/s/d/tr 420/1300/1300/1440Kč; @☜; ⓂStaroměstská) You'll struggle to find better-value central accommodation than this hostel located in a quiet lane metres from Old Town Sq. Look forward to occasional church bells. Cash only.

Hostel Elf HOSTEL €
(☎222 540 963; www.hostelelf.com; Husitská 11, Žižkov; dm 340-420Kč, s/d/tr from 980/1260/1440Kč; @☜; ⓂFlorenc) Have the best of both worlds at this hip hostel, a shortish walk downhill from Žižkov's bars. Swap tales in the beer garden or grab quiet time in the hidden nooks and crannies. More expensive rooms have private bathrooms.

Hostel AZ HOSTEL €
(Map p306; ☎246 052 409; www.hostel-az.com; Jindřišská 5, Nové Město; dm 320-350Kč, s/d/tr/q 950/1000/1450/1600Kč; @☜; ⓂMůstek) This smaller, homey hostel enjoys a central location near Wenceslas Sq, an in-house laundromat and seven-bed dorms.

Autocamp Trojská CAMPING GROUND €
(☎283 850 487; www.autocamp-trojska.cz; Trojská 157; campsite per person 100Kč, plus tent/car 150/90Kč; ⓂNádraží Holešovice then bus 112 to Kazanka) The most comfortable and secure of half a dozen camping grounds in the quiet northern suburb of Trojská.

Eating

U Ferdinanda CZECH €
(Map p306; cnr Opletalova & Politických vězňů, Nové Město; mains 100-180Kč; ⓂMuzeum) Welcome to a thoroughly modern spin on a classic Czech pub with beer courtesy of the Ferdinand brewery from nearby Benešov. Quirky gardening implements and corrugated iron decorate the raucous interior, and a younger local clientele crowds in for well-priced Czech food.

Prague Castle

Top Sights
- Basilica of St George (Bazilika sv Jiří) ... E2
- St Vitus Cathedral (Katedrala sv Víta) ... C2
- Vladislav Hall ... D3

Sights
1. All Saints' Chapel (Kaple Všech Svatých) ... D3
2. Archbishop's Palace (Arcibiskupský Palác) ... A3
3. Black Tower ... F1
4. Chapel of the Holy Cross (Kaple sv Kríže) ... C3
5. Convent of St George (Klášter sv Jiří) ... E2
6. Daliborka Tower ... F1
7. Lobkowicz Palace ... F2
8. Ludwík Wing ... D3
9. Matthias Gate (Matyášova Brána) ... B3
10. Mihulka (Powder Tower) ... C2
11. Old Royal Palace (Starý Královský Palác) ... D3
12. Plečník Monolith ... C3
13. Powder Bridge (Prašná most) ... B2
14. Prague Castle Picture Gallery ... B3
15. Šternberg Palace ... A3
16. Story of Prague Castle Exhibit ... D3
17. Toy Museum (Muzeum Hraček) ... F2
18. Vikářská ... C2

Karavanseráj MIDDLE EASTERN €
(Map p306; Masarykovo nábřeží 22, Nové Město; mains 130-250Kč; 6, 9, 17, 18, 21 to Národní divadlo) Lebanese flavours dominate at this relaxed spot that's part ethnic eatery and part travellers cafe, but the menu also touches down in India and Morocco. There's an ever-changing array of large-format travel photography on the walls.

Restaurace u Šumavy CZECH €
(off Map p306; Štěpánská 3, Nové Město; mains 100-150Kč; IP Pavlova) Here's emphatic and tasty proof that good-value Bohemian food still exists in central Prague. Canny locals crowd in, ensconcing themselves in country-cottage decor for lunch specials that remind them of their grandmother's cooking.

Lehká Hlava VEGETARIAN €€
(Map p306; Boršov 2, Staré Město; mains 120-210Kč; 17, 18 to Karlovy lázně) Lehká Hlava means 'clear head', and the emphasis here is on healthy, freshly prepared vegetarian and vegan dishes, ranging from hummus and roast vegetables to spinach burritos and a spicy stir-fry.

Na Verandách CZECH €€
(Nádražní 84, Smíchov; mains 150-300Kč; 6, 12, 14 to Na Knížeci) Across the river in Smíchov, the Staropramen brewery's restaurant is a modern spot crowded with locals enjoying superior versions of favourite Czech dishes and an 'it could be a long night' selection of different brews.

Home Kitchen CAFE €
(Map p306; Jungmannova 8, Nové Město; mains 65-120Kč; 7.30am-7pm Mon-Fri, 8.30am-3pm Sat; 3, 9, 14, 24 to Lazarská) With organic soups, salads and homestyle daily specials, this cosy brick-lined spot away from the tourist sprawl of Old Town Sq provides the perfect escape for lunch. The daily soup special (65Kč including bread) is always good.

Pizzeria Kmotra PIZZA €
(Map p306; www.kmotra.cz; V Jirchářích 12, Nové Město; pizza 100-180Kč; 6, 9, 17, 18, 21 to Národní divadlo) More than 30 varieties feature at this cellar pizzeria that gets superbusy after 8pm.

Tesco SUPERMARKET €
(Map p306; Národní třída 26, Nové Město; 7am-10pm Mon-Fri, 8am-8pm Sat, 9am-8pm Sun) Prague's best-stocked supermarket.

Drinking

The most famous Czech beer brands are Budvar, Plzeňský Prazdroj (Pilsner Urquell) and Prague's own Staropramen. Independent microbreweries and regional Czech beers are also popular in Prague. Look out for blackboards advertising weekly specials.

TOP CHOICE **Literární Kavárna Řetězová** CAFE
(Map p306; Řetězová, Staré Město; 17, 21 to Karlovy lázně) This is where you would have headed post-1989 to become the next great expat novelist. Two decades on, leave your netbook and notebook at home, take in the vintage black-and-white pics of famous Czech writers, and treat yourself to a coffee or a beer. When someone asks you, 'So what was the best cafe you went to in Prague?' this is the correct answer.

Pivovarský Klub BEER HALL
(Křižíkova 17, Karlín; Florenc;) Submit to your inner hophead at this pub-restaurant-beer-shop with interesting limited-volume draught beers and bottled brews from around the Czech Republic. Come for lunch, as it gets full of loyal regulars later on.

TOP CHOICE **Duende** BAR
(Map p306; Karolíny Světlé 30, Staré Město; 1pm-midnight Mon-Fri, 3pm-midnight Sat, 4pm-midnight Sun; Národní třída) Barely five minutes' walk from the tourist hubbub of Charles Bridge, this bohemian drinking den pulls in an arty mixed-age crowd of locals. Peruse the quirky art on the walls or listen to occasional live music.

Čili Bar BAR
(Map p306; Kozná 10, Staré Město; from 5pm; Můstek) This raffish bar is more Žižkov than Staré Město, with cool cocktails and a grungy tinge in welcome contrast to the crystal shops and Russian dolls around the corner.

U Sadu PUB
(Škroupovo nám, Žižkov; Jiřího z Poděbrad) Escape the overpriced tyranny of central Prague at this neighbourhood pub in grungy Žižkov. With its ragtag collection of memorabilia, including communist-era posters of forgotten politicians, nothing's really changed here in a few decades.

Letná Beer Garden BEER GARDEN
(off Map p306; Letná Gardens, Bubeneč; 12, 17 to Čechův most) This garden bar has views across the river of the Old Town and south-

west to the castle. In summer it's packed with a young crowd enjoying cheap beer and grilled sausages.

Entertainment

From clubbing to classical music, puppetry to performance art, Prague offers plenty of entertainment. It's an established centre of classical music and jazz. For current listings see www.prague.tv or www.praguewelcome.cz.

Try the following ticket agencies:

Bohemia Ticket International (Map p306; www.ticketsbti.cz) Nové Město (Na příkopě 16; Ⓜ Náměstí Republiky); Staré Město (Malé nám 13; Ⓜ Staroměstská)

Ticketpro (Map p306; www.ticketpro.cz; Lucerna pasáž, Štěpánská 61, Nové Město; Ⓜ Můstek) Also at branches of the Prague Information Service.

Ticketstream (www.ticketstream.cz) Online bookings for events in Prague and the Czech Republic.

Nightclubs

Palác Akropolis CLUB
(www.palacakropolis.cz; Kubelikova 27, Žižkov; club 7pm-5am; 5, 9, 26 to Lipanska) Get lost in the labyrinth of theatre, live music, clubbing, drinking and eating that makes up Prague's coolest venue. Hip-hop, house, reggae, or rocking Roma bands from Romania – anything goes. Kick your night off nearby at the quirky U Sadu pub.

MeetFactory ALTERNATIVE
(www.meetfactory.cz; Ke Sklárně 3213/15, Smíchov; 12, 14, 20 to Lihovar) The MeetFactory is a multifaceted workspace for visiting artists, and a gallery and entertainment venue. It's very much a fluid work-in-progress and hosts everything from film screenings to concerts and DJ events. Get off at the Lihovar stop, look for the two giant red cars, and be careful crossing the five sets (!) of railway tracks.

Cross Club ALTERNATIVE
(www.crossclub.cz; Plynární 23, Holešovice; admission 50-120Kč; 4pm-late; Ⓜ Nádraží Holešovice) It's worth visiting this place for the ever-changing sci-fi industrial decor alone, but the mix of eclectic mix of live music including dub, techno and reggae is another reason to jump on the metro for a 3km trip to the grungier, northern side of the river.

Roxy ALTERNATIVE
(Map p306; www.roxy.cz; Dlouhá 33, Staré Město; admission 150-300Kč; 10pm-6am; 5, 8, 14 to Dlouhá třída) In a resurrected old cinema, the Roxy presents innovative DJs and the occasional global act. 'Free Mondays' will give you more money for beer.

USP Jazz Lounge JAZZ
(Map p306; www.jazzlounge.cz; Michalská 9, Staré Město; 8pm-3am; Ⓜ Staroměstská) A less traditional venue with modern jazz from 10pm. DJs kick on from midnight.

Cinemas

Most films are screened in their original language with Czech subtitles *(české titulky)*, but Hollywood blockbusters are sometimes dubbed into Czech *(dabing)*; look for the labels 'tit.' or 'dab.' on listings. Tickets are around 180Kč.

Kino Světozor ART HOUSE
(Map p306; www.kinosvetozor.cz; Vodičkova 41, Nové Město; Ⓜ Můstek) An art-house cinema with themed weeks and retrospectives, often with English subtitles; also has a DVD shop with lots of Czech movies.

Palace Cinemas MAINSTREAM
(Map p306; www.palacecinemas.cz; Slovanský dům, Na příkopě 22, Nové Město; Ⓜ Náměstí Republiky) Multiplex showing current Hollywood films.

Classical Music & Performance Arts

Prague's main venues are the **Rudolfinum** (Map p306; nám Jana Palacha, Staré Město; Ⓜ Staroměstská) and the art nouveau **Municipal House** (Map p306; Obecní dům, nám Republiky 5, Staré Město; Ⓜ Náměstí Republiky).

Opera and ballet is performed at the **Prague State Opera** (Map p306; www.opera.cz; Legerova 75, Nové Město; Ⓜ Muzeum) and **National Theatre** (Map p306; www.narodni-divadlo.cz; Národní třída 2, Nové Město; Ⓜ Národní třída).

Information

Internet Access

Globe Café & Bookstore (www.globebookstore.cz; Pštrossova 6, Nové Město; per min 1.50Kč; 9.30am-midnight; Ⓜ Karlovo Náměstí)

Mobilarium (Rathova pasaž, Na příkopě 23, Nové Město; per min 1.50Kč; 10am-7pm Mon-Fri, 11am-6pm Sat; Ⓜ Náměstí Republiky)

Medical Services

Na Homolce Hospital (257 271 111, after-hours 257 272 527; www.homolka.cz; 5th fl, Foreign Pavilion, Roentgenova 2, Motol; 167 from Ⓜ Anděl) Prague's main casualty department.

Polyclinic at Národní (222 075 120, 24hr emergency 720 427 634; www.poliklinika.narodni.cz; Národní třída 9, Nové Město;

⌚8.30am-5pm Mon-Fri; Ⓜ Národní Třída) English-, French- and German-speaking staff.

Praha lékárna (☎224 946 982; Palackého 5, Nové Město; ⌚24hr; Ⓜ Můstek;) Pharmacy.

Money

The major banks are best for changing cash, but using a debit card in an ATM gives a better rate of exchange. Avoid *směnárna* (private exchange booths), which advertise misleading rates and have exorbitant charges.

Tourist Information

Czech Tourism (Map p306; www.czechtourism.com; Staroměstské nám, Staré Město; ⌚9am-5pm Mon-Fri; Ⓜ Staroměstská) Information if you're venturing beyond Prague; in Old Town Sq.

Prague Information Service (PIS; ☎12 444, in English & German; www.praguewelcome.cz); main train station (Map p306; Wilsonova 2, Nové Město; ⌚9am-7pm Mon-Fri, to 6pm Sat & Sun; Ⓜ Hlavní nádraží); Malá Strana Bridge Tower (Charles Bridge; ⌚10am-6pm Apr-Oct; 🚋12, 20, 22, 23 to Malostranské nám); Old Town Hall (Map p306; Staroměstské nám 5, Staré Město; ⌚9am-7pm Mon-Fri, to 6pm Sat & Sun Apr-Oct, to 6pm Mon-Fri, to 5pm Sat & Sun Nov-Mar; Ⓜ Staroměstská); Rytířská (Map p306; Rytířská 31; ⌚9am-7pm Apr-Oct, 9am-6pm Nov-Mar; Ⓜ Můstek) Provides free tourist information with good maps; the Old Town Hall branch is the main one.

Travel Agencies

Čedok (☎800 112 112; www.cedok.cz; Na příkopě 18, Nové Město; ⌚9am-7pm Mon-Fri, 9.30am-1pm Sat; Ⓜ Můstek) Travel agency; also books accommodation, concert and theatre tickets, and rental cars.

Student Agency (☎800 100 1300; www.studentagency.eu; Ječná 37, Vinohrady; ⌚9am-6pm Mon-Fri, to 1pm Sat; Ⓜ IP Pavlova) Air and bus tickets. Office at Florenc bus station also.

ℹ Getting There & Away

See p324 for details of main overland and air routes to Prague and the Czech Republic.

ℹ Getting Around

To/From the Airport

Prague-Ruzyně Airport (www.prg.aero) is 17km west of the city centre. Buy a ticket from the public transport (DPP) desk in arrivals and take bus 119 (26Kč, 20 minutes, every 15 minutes) to the end of the line (Dejvická), then continue by metro into the city centre (another 10 minutes; no new ticket needed). You'll also need a half-fare ticket (13Kč) for your bag. Alternatively, the **Airport Express** (50Kč; ⌚5am-10pm) goes direct to the main train station. Luggage is free; buy your ticket from the driver.

Public Transport

Buy a ticket before you enter a tram, bus or metro – available from metro stations, vending machines, newsstands, tobacco kiosks, hotels and tourist information offices.

Validate your ticket in the yellow machine in the metro station or on the bus or tram. Once validated, a 26Kč *jízdenka* (ticket) remains valid for 75 minutes from the time of stamping (90 minutes if stamped between 8pm and 5am weekdays, or at any time on weekends). Within this period, unlimited transfers between tram, metro and bus are allowed. You also need a half-fare ticket (13Kč) for large backpacks.

There's also an 18Kč ticket, valid for 20 minutes on buses and trams, or for up to five metro stations. No transfers are allowed, and they're not valid on night trams or night buses.

The metro operates from 5am to midnight daily. Night trams and buses traverse the city every 40 minutes.

If you've arrived in Prague at the Praha Florenc bus station, Prague's main international bus terminal, take Line B (yellow) two stops west to Můstek for the city centre.

Taxi

Avoid getting a taxi in tourist areas. To avoid being ripped off, phone a reliable company such as **AAA** (☎14 014; www.aaa.radio taxi.cz) or **City Taxi** (☎257 257 257; www.citytaxi.cz); both offer online bookings also.

Prague has the 'Taxi Fair Place' scheme with authorised taxis. Drivers can charge a maximum of 28Kč per kilometre and must announce the estimated price in advance. Look for the yellow and red signs.

AROUND PRAGUE

The following are easy day trips from Prague.

Karlštejn

Erected by Emperor Charles IV in the mid-14th century, **Karlštejn Castle** (☎274 008 154; www.hradkarlstejn.cz; Karlštejn; ⌚9am-6pm Tue-Sun Jul & Aug, to 5pm May, Jun & Sep, to 4pm Apr & Oct) crowns a ridge above Karlštejn village. It's a 20-minute walk from the train station.

The **Chapel of the Holy Rood** is where the Bohemian crown jewels were kept until 1420. Guided tours on Route I cost 250/150Kč for adult/concession tickets. Route II, which includes the chapel (June to October only), is 300/200Kč and must be prebooked.

Trains from Prague's main train station to Beroun stop at Karlštejn (49Kč, 45 minutes, hourly).

Kutná Hora

POP 22,000

In the 14th century, Kutná Hora rivalled Prague as the most important town in Bohemia, growing rich on the silver ore lacing the rocks beneath it. Today it's an delightful medieval town with historical attractions.

The **information centre** (☎327 512 378; www.kutnahora.cz; Palackého nám 377; ⏰8am-6pm daily Apr-Sep, 9am-5pm Mon-Fri, 10am-4pm Sat & Sun Oct-Mar) books accommodation, has internet access and rents out bicycles.

Walk 10 minutes south from Kutná Hora's main train station to the remarkable **Sedlec Ossuary** (www.kostnice.cz; adult/concession 50/30Kč; ⏰8am-6pm Apr-Sep, 9am-noon & 1-5pm Oct & Mar, 9am-noon & 1-4pm Nov-Feb). When the Schwarzenberg family purchased Sedlec monastery in 1870, a local woodcarver got creative with the bones of 40,000 people from the centuries-old crypt. From the Kutná Hora bus station, catch bus 1B and get off at the 'Tabak' stop.

In the town centre is the **Hrádek** (Little Castle), a 15th-century palace housing the **Czech Silver Museum** (www.cms-kh.cz; adult/student 70/40Kč; ⏰10am-6pm Tue-Sun Jul & Aug, 9am-5pm Tue-Sun Apr-May & Sep-Oct). Don a miner's helmet to join the 1½-hour **Way of Silver tour** (adult/student 120/80Kč) through 500m of medieval mine shaft. A combination ticket for the museum and the mine tour is 140Kč.

Rivaling Prague's St Vitus in magnificence, the Gothic **Cathedral of St Barbara** (www.chramsvatebarbory.cz; adult/student 50/30Kč; ⏰9am-6pm Apr-Oct, 10am-4pm Nov-Mar) has a soaring nave culminating in elegant, ribbed vaulting.

There are direct trains from Prague's main train station to Kutná Hora's main train station (98Kč, 55 minutes, seven daily).

Buses to Kutná Hora from Prague (62Kč, 1¼ hours, hourly) depart from Florenc bus station; services are less frequent at weekends. A weekday bus leaves Prague Florenc at 8.10am for an early start.

During summer, a special tourist minibus (40Kč per person) travels a loop including the train station, the Sedlec Ossuary and the Cathedral of St Barbara.

Karlovy Vary

POP 60,000

According to legend, Emperor Charles IV discovered Karlovy Vary's hot springs accidentally in 1350 when one of his hunting dogs fell into the waters. Now the well heeled from Germany, Austria and (especially) Russia make the pilgrimage for courses of lymphatic drainage, hydrocolonotherapy and other dodgy-sounding treatments. The preferred form is to sip the mineral-laden waters from a dainty porcelain cup, but the caffeine-enriched offerings from the town's cafes are actually much tastier.

Sights & Activities

At the heart of the old spa district, on the west bank of the river, is the neoclassical **Mlýnská Kolonáda** (Mill Colonnade), where bands play in summer. Other elegant colonnades and imposing 19th-century spa centres punctuate the Teplá River, though the ugly 1970's **Hotel Thermal** and the **Vřídelní Kolonáda** (Geyser Colonnade) spoil the effect slightly.

Pretend to be a spa patient by purchasing a *lázenské pohár* (spa cup) and a box of *oplátky* (spa wafers), and sampling the various hot springs (free). There are 12 springs in the 'drinking cure', ranging from the **Skalní Pramen** (Rock Spring), which dribbles a measly 1.3L per minute, to the **Vřídlo** (Geyser), which spurts 2000L per minute in a steaming, 14m-high jet.

Festivals & Events

Karlovy Vary International Film Festival FILM

(www.kviff.com) This early July festival gives the sleepy town a much-needed energy transfusion.

Sleeping

Accommodation is pricey, especially during weekends and festivals; book ahead. Infocentrum can find hostel, *pension* (guesthouse) and hotel rooms. Consider staying in nearby Loket and visiting Karlovy Vary as a day trip.

Hotel Maltézsky Kříž HOTEL €€

(☎353 169 011; www.maltezskykriz.cz; Stará Louka 50; s/d/apt €69/117/133; @☎) Oriental rugs and wooden floors combine at this spiffy, recently opened hotel with cosy rooms and a more spacious double-storied apartment.

WORTH A TRIP

LOKET – A QUIET & AFFORDABLE GEM

Avoid Karlovy Vary's high prices by staying in the nearby riverside village of Loket. **Loket Castle** (www.hradloket.cz; Zámecká 67; adult/student guided tours 90/75Kč; ⊙9am-4.30pm Apr-Oct, to 3.30pm Nov-Mar) is one of the Czech Republic's most dramatic structures, and the sleepy village also makes a good alternative to Český Krumlov for river rafting.

The **Lazy River Hostel** (☎776 235 417; www.lazyriver-hostel.com; Kostelní 61; dm/d/tr 300/800/1200Kč; @☜) is an easygoing place crammed with ideas for day trips. Spacious and romantic rooms feature at **Penzion Ve Skalé** (☎352 624 936; www.penzionveskale.cz; Nádražní 232; s/d 650/1200Kč; ☜), just up the hill from the train station.

A few enthusiastic locals brew what could be Bohemia's best beer at **Pivovar Sv Florian** (☎352 225 959; TG Masaryka 81). Ask about the nightly terrace barbecues during summer.

Buses to Karlovy Vary run throughout the day, or you can walk via a pretty 17km (four hours) track.

Bathrooms are decked out in warm earth tones.

Hotel Kavalerie HOTEL €
(☎353 229 613; www.kavalerie.cz; TG Masaryka 43; s/d from 950/1225Kč) Friendly staff abound in this cosy spot above a cafe. It's located near the bus and train stations, and nearby eateries can help you avoid the spa district's high restaurant prices. Rooms are starting to look a bit worn, but it's still OK value in an expensive destination.

Eating

Tandoor INDIAN €
(IP Pavlova 25; mains 120-180Kč) Located under a block of flats, Tandoor turns out the winning combo of authentic Indian flavours, smooth, creamy lassis, and Gambrinus beer for just 28Kč. Vegetarian options abound, and if you're after a serious chilli hit, order the Chicken Phall (140Kcv).

Kus CAFE €
(Bělehradská 8; snacks 50-70Kč; ⊙7am-5pm Mon-Fri) This cosy cafe-bakery serves salads, pasta and home-made desserts with an organic and vegetarian tinge.

Café Elefant CAFE €
(Stará Louka 30; coffee 50Kč) Classy old-school spot for coffee and cake. A tad touristy, but still elegant and refined.

Albert SUPERMARKET €
(Horova 1223/1) Near the Tržnice bus station.

Information

Infocentrum (www.karlovyvary.cz) Dolni nádraží (☎353 232 838; Západni; ⊙9am-6pm Mon-Fri, 10am-5pm Sat & Sun); Spa No 3 (☎353 321 176; Spa No 3; ⊙10am-5pm) Loads of information on the town, plus maps, accommodation help and internet access (per minute 2Kč).

Moonstorm Internet (TG Masaryka 31; per min 2Kč; ⊙9am-9pm) Internet access.

Getting There & Away

BUS **Student Agency** (www.studentagency.eu) and **Megabus** (www.megabus.cz) run buses to/from Prague Florenc (from 100Kč, 2¼ hours, eight daily). There are direct buses to Plzeň (92Kč, 1½ hours, hourly), and buses to Loket run throughout the day (28Kč, 20 minutes).

TRAIN There are direct (but slow) trains from Karlovy Vary to Prague Holešovice (294Kč, three hours). The train journey to Mariánské Lázně (60Kč, 1¾ hours) is slow but scenic.

Getting Around

Karlovy Vary has two train stations: Dolní nádraží (Lower Station), beside the main bus station, and Horní nádraží (Upper Station), across the Ohře River to the north.

Prague trains arrive at Horní nádraží. Take bus 11, 12 or 13 (12Kč) from across the road to the Tržnice bus stop; bus 11 continues to Divadelni nám in the spa district. Alternatively, it's 10 minutes on foot: cross the road outside the station and go right, then first left on a footpath that leads downhill under the highway. At its foot, turn right on U Spořitelny, then left at the far end of the big building and head for the bridge over the river.

The Tržnice bus stop is three blocks east of Dolní nádraží and the main bus station, in the middle of the town's modern commercial district. Pedestrianised TG Masaryka leads east to the Teplá River; from here the old spa district stretches upstream for 2km along a steep-sided valley.

Plzeň

POP 175,000

Brew aficionados flock to this city where lager was invented in 1842. Plzeň (Pilsen in German) is the hometown of Pilsner Urquell (Plzeňský prazdroj), the world's first lager beer, and now imitated around the world. Pilsner Urquell is today owned by international conglomerate SAB-Miller, and some beer buffs claim the brew is not as good as before. One sip of the town's tasty *nefiltrované pivo* (unfiltered beer) will have you disputing that claim, and the original brewery is still an essential stop for beer fans.

Plzeň is an easy day trip from Prague, but the city's pubs and other smaller breweries reward an overnight stay.

Sights

Brewery Museum MUSEUM
(www.prazdroj.cz; Veleslavínova 6; adult/student guided tours 120/90Kč, with English text 90/60Kč; ⏲10am-5pm) The Brewery Museum is in a medieval malt house and showcases the history of beer and brewing. A **combined entry ticket** (adult/student 250/130Kč) including the Pilsner Urquell Brewery is also available.

Pilsner Urquell Brewery BREWERY
(www.prazdroj.cz; adult/student guided tour 150/80Kč; ⏲10am-5pm) Beer fans should make the pilgrimage east across the river to the famous Pilsner Urquell Brewery.

Plzeň Historical Underground HISTORIC AREA
(www.plzenskepodzemi.cz; Veleslavínova 6; adult/student 90/60Kč; ⏲10am-5pm) In previous centuries beer was brewed and stored in the tunnels beneath the Old Town. Take a 30-minute guided tour through 500m of tunnels at the Plzeň Historical Underground. The temperature is a chilly 10°C, so wrap up and bring a torch (flashlight). Tours begin at the Brewery Museum.

Sleeping

Pension Stará Plzeň PENSION €
(☎377 259 901; www.pension-sp.cz; Na Roudné 12; s/d from 875/1250Kč; @📶) Rooms are light and sunny, with skylights, wooden floors and huge beds. A newly completed addition has transformed old stables into spacious accommodation with high ceilings. Cross the river north on Rooseveltova, veer right into Luční and turn left into Na Roudné.

Euro Hostel HOSTEL €
(☎377 259 926; www.eurohostel.cz; Na Roudné 13; dm 350-400Kč; 📶) In newly renovated rooms in the associated Hotel Roudna, the Euro Hostel offers Plzeň's best budget accommodation. It's about a five-minute walk from the main square; cross the river north on Rooseveltova, veer right into Luční and turn left into Na Roudné.

Eating & Drinking

Na Parkanu PUB €
(Veleslavínova 4; mains 100-150Kč) Attached to the Brewery Museum, Na Parkanu lures tourists and locals with good-value meals and a garden bar. Don't leave without trying the *nefiltrované pivo*. It's not our fault if you stay for another.

Dominik Rock Cafe CAFE €
(Dominikánská 3; mains 130Kč; ⏲10am-11pm Mon-Wed, to 2am Thu & 4am Fri, 1pm-2am Sat, 1pm-10pm Sun) Get lost in the nooks and crannies of this vast student hang-out. There are cool beats all day, every day, and excellent beer, pizza and sandwiches are served in the nicely grungy beer garden.

PLZEŇ'S OTHER BEERS

Pilsner Urquell may enjoy the international reputation, but beer fans should also seek out these other examples of hoppy west Bohemian goodness.

Groll Pivovar (Truhlářska 10; mains 100-200Kč) Enjoy a beer-garden lunch at this recently opened microbrewery. Its own LOTR beers are complemented by well-priced steaks and salads. From Sady 5 kvetna cross over busy Tyršova to Truhlářska.

Caffe Emily (Hotel Rous, Zbrojnicka 113/7; mains 120-200Kč) Another beer garden – this time tucked into the Old Town walls – and another couple of local brews to try.

Restaurace Gondola (Hotel Gondola, Pallova 12; mains 115-220Kč) Plzeň's Purkmistr brewery (www.purkmistr.cz) has a suburban location, so the best bet for visitors is to try its beers at the centrally located restaurant at the Hotel Gondola. Ask about the seasonal brews.

TOP PLACES FOR CZECH BEER

» Pivovarský Klub, Prague
» Groll Pivovar, Plzeň
» Pivovar Sv Florian, Loket
» Pivnice Pegas, Brno
» Moritz, Olomouc

Slunečnice VEGETARIAN €
(Jungmanova 10; baguettes 70Kč; ⊙11am-10pm) Fresh sandwiches, self-service salads and vegetarian dishes. For around 120Kč you can buy a heaped plateful. The fresh juice and smoothie bar is another tasty distraction.

Albert SUPERMARKET €
(Plzeň Plaza Shopping Centre) Catch tram 2 en route to the bus station.

Information

American Center Plzeň (Dominikánská 9; per hr 60Kč; ⊙10am-10pm) Internet access.

City Information Centre (www.plzen.eu) nám Republiky (městské informační středisko; ☎378 035 330; nám Republiky 41; ⊙9am-6pm); train station (☎972 524 313; ⊙9am-7pm Apr-Sep, to 6pm Oct-Mar)

Getting There & Away

BUS Express buses run to/from Prague Florenc (110Kč, 1½ hours, hourly). Buses also link Plzeň to Karlovy Vary (84Kč, 1¾ hours, five daily) and Mariánské Lázně (80Kč, 1¼ hours, four daily).

TRAIN Fast trains link Plzeň with Prague's main train station (147Kč, 1½ hours, eight daily), České Budějovice (174Kč, two hours, five daily) and Mariánské Lázně (101Kč, 1½ hours, eight daily).

Getting Around

The main bus station is west of the centre on Husova. Plzeň-hlavní nádraží, the main train station, is on the eastern side of town, 10 minutes' walk from nám Republiky, the Old Town square. Tram 2 (12Kč) goes from the train station through the centre of town and on to the bus station.

České Budějovice

POP 100,000

Post Plzeň, you can conduct the ultimate Bohemian beer taste test at České Budějovice (Budweis in German), the home of Budvar lager. The regional capital of south Bohemia, it's a picturesque medieval city with one of Europe's largest Old Town squares.

Sights

Budweiser Budvar Brewery BREWERY
(www.budweiser-budvar.cz; cnr Pražská & K Světlé; adult/student 100/50Kč; ⊙9am-5pm daily Mar-Dec, 9am-5pm Tue-Sat Jan-Feb) The Budweiser Budvar Brewery is 3km north of the main square. Group tours run every day and the 2pm tour (Monday to Friday only) is open to individual travellers. The highlight is a glass of real-deal Budvar deep in the brewery's chilly cellars. Catch bus 2 to the Budvar stop (12Kč).

Sleeping

Penzión Centrum PENSION €
(☎387 311 801; www.penzioncentrum.cz; Biskupská 130/3; s/d 1000/1400Kč; 📶) Huge rooms with queen-size beds and crisp linen make this an excellent reader-recommended spot near the main square. Right next door there's a good vegetarian restaurant.

Cafe Hostel HOSTEL €
(☎387 204 203; Panská 13; www.cafehostel.cz; dm 350Kč; 📶) Simple and central dorm accommodation above a buzzy cafe-bar. Look forward to regular live music in the evenings.

Eating & Drinking

Masné kramy BEER HALL €€
(Krajinská 13; mains 140-240Kč) The best place in town for a cold Budvar is this beer hall in České Budějovice's 16th-century meat markets. Try the hard-to-find Budvar Super Strong, or the superb unfiltered yeast beer, *kroužkovaný ležák*. Tuck yourself away in one of the cosy booths and enjoy the hoppy goodness with hearty Czech food.

Greenhouse VEGETARIAN €
(Biskupská 130/3; mains 120Kč; ⊙8am-5pm Mon-Fri; ✎) České Budějovice's best vegetarian flavours are found at this modern self-service cafe. The healthy array of soups, salads and casseroles changes daily, with wraps and baguettes for smaller appetites. Here's your best chance to try organic beer as well.

CK Solnice CAFE €
(www.bazilika.cz; Česká 141/66) This cafe and versatile performance space could be the most bohemian venue in all of south Bohemia. It's got an arty, student vibe, České Budějovice's best espresso, cold beer, and an eclectic program of art, music and dance throughout the year. Check the website for what's on.

Albert SUPERMARKET €
(Lannova 22) East of the main square.

Getting There & Around

BUS The bus to Brno (220Kč, 3½ hours) travels via Telč (92Kč, two hours). Buses regularly shuttle south to Český Krumlov (32Kč, 45 minutes), and north to Prague's Na Knížecí metro station (152Kc, 2¼ hours). České Budějovice's bus station is 300m southeast of the train station above the Mercury Central shopping centre on Dvořákova.

TRAIN There are trains from České Budějovice to Prague (213Kč, 2½ hours, hourly) and Plzeň (174Kč, two hours, five daily). Frequent trains trundle to Český Krumlov (46Kč, 45 minutes). From the train station it's a 10-minute walk west down Lannova třída, then Kanovnická, to nám Přemysla Otakara II, the main square.

Český Krumlov

POP 14,600

Crowned by a stunning castle, and centred on an elegant Old Town square, Český Krumlov's Renaissance and baroque buildings enclose a meandering arc of the Vltava River.

During summer, pigeons dart through busloads of day-trippers exploring the town's narrow lanes and footbridges. Either side of July and August the town is (slightly) more subdued and secluded. Come in winter to experience the castle blanketed in snow.

For too many travellers, Český Krumlov is just a hurried day trip, but its combination of glorious architecture and waterborne fun deserves more attention. Add in the rugged attractions of the nearby Newcastle mountains region, and you can easily fill three days.

Sights & Activities

TOP CHOICE **Český Krumlov Castle** CASTLE
(www.castle.ckrumlov.cz; 9am-6pm Tue-Sun Jun-Aug, to 5pm Apr-May & Sep-Oct) The Old Town, almost encircled by the Vltava River, is watched over by Český Krumlov Castle and its ornately decorated **Round Tower** (adult/student 50/30Kč). Three guided tours are on offer: **Tour I** (adult/student 240/140Kč) takes in the Renaissance and baroque apartments that the aristocratic Rožmberk and Schwarzenberg families called home; **Tour II** (adult/student 180/110Kč) visits the Schwarzenberg apartments used in the 19th century; and the **Theatre Tour** (adult/student 380/220Kč; from 10am to 4pm Tuesday to Sunday; tours run May to October) explores the chateau's remarkable rococo theatre, complete with original stage machinery. Wandering through the courtyards and gardns is free.

Maleček RAFTING
(www.en.malecek.cz; Rooseveltova 28; 9am-5pm) Rents canoes, rafts and rubber rings. A one-hour splash in a two-person canoe costs 400Kč, or you can rent a canoe for a full-day trip down the river from Rožmberk (850Kč, six to eight hours).

Expedicion OUTDOORS ACTIVITIES
(607 963 868; www.expedicion.cz; Soukenická 33; 9am-6.30pm) Rents bikes (280Kč a day), arranges horse riding (300Kč an hour) and operates action-packed day trips (1680Kč, including lunch) incorporating horse riding, fishing, mountain biking and rafting in the nearby Newcastle mountains region.

Sleeping

Pension Sebastian PENSION €
(608 357 581; www.sebastianck.com; 5 Května Ul, Plešivec; s/d/tr incl breakfast 1090/1250/1590Kč; Apr-Oct;) An excellent option just 10 minutes' walk from the Old Town, and therefore slightly cheaper. Larger four-bed rooms (1780Kč) are good for families and there's a garden gazebo for end-of-day drinks and diary writing.

Hostel Postel HOSTEL €
(776 720 722; www.hostelpostel.cz; Rybářská 35; dm/d from 300/700Kč;) Conveniently situated near good bars in Rybářská, Hostel Postel has a sunny courtyard with shady umbrellas to wake you up slowly after a big night.

Krumlov House HOSTEL €
(380 711 935; www.krumlovhostel.com; Rooseveltova 68; dm/d/tr 300/750/1350Kč; @) Perched above the river, Krumlov House is friendly and comfortable and has plenty of books, DVDs and local info to feed your inner backpacker. Look forward to lots of suggestions for day trips.

Pension Kapr PENSION €
(602 409 360; www.penzionkapr.cz; Rybářská 28; s 1000Kč, d 1220-1600Kč; @) This riverside *pension* with exposed bricks and 500 years of history has a quiet location and Old Town views. The lovely rooms with whitewashed walls and wooden floors are all named after the owners' children.

Kemp Nové Spolí CAMPING GROUND €
(☎380 728 305; www.kempkrumlov.cz; campsites per person 50Kč; ⊙Jun-Aug; 📶) Located on the Vltava River about 2km south of town, with basic facilities but an idyllic location. Take bus 3 from the train or bus station to the Spolí mat šk stop, otherwise it's a half-hour walk from the Old Town.

Eating & Drinking

TOP CHOICE **Laibon** VEGETARIAN €
(Parkán 105; mains 100-180Kč; 🍴) Candles and vaulted ceilings create a great boho ambience in the best little vegetarian teahouse in Bohemia. The riverside setting's pretty fine as well. Order the blueberry dumplings for dessert and don't miss the special 'yeast beer' from the Bernard brewery. Ask David the owner where he's travelling next.

Láb PUB €
(náměstí Svornosti; mains 110-160Kč) Český Krumlov's best pub is hidden away on the edge of the main square. The kitchen also serves other more touristy eateries, but you're guaranteed a cheaper, and more local, experience here.

Divadelní Klub Ántré CAFE
(Horní Braná 2; ⊙11am-11pm; 🚭📶) This non-smoking arty cafe-bar in the town theatre has a sprawling terrace overlooking the river. There's free wi-fi and it's always worth dropping by to see if any music gigs are scheduled.

Deli 99 CAFE €
(Latrán 106; snacks 60-90Kč; ⊙7am-7pm Mon-Sat, 8am-5pm Sun; 📶) Bagels, sandwiches, organic juices and wi-fi all tick the box 'Slightly Homesick Traveller'.

Potraviny SUPERMARKET €
(Latrán 55) Self-catering central.

Information

Infocentrum (☎380 704 622; www.ckrumlov.cz; nám Svornosti 1; ⊙9am-6pm) Transport and accommodation info, maps, internet access (5Kč per five minutes) and audio guides (100Kč per hour). A guide for disabled visitors is available.

Krumlov Tours (☎723 069 561; www.krumlovtours.com; nám Svornosti; tours per person 200-250Kč) Has walking tours with regular departure times; good for solo travellers.

Oldřiška Baloušková (oldriskab@gmail.com) Offers tailored walking tours (per hour 450Kč).

Getting There & Away

BUS Student Agency (www.studentagency.eu) buses depart frequently from Prague Ná Knížecí metro (180Kč, three hours) via České Budějovice. In July and August this route is very popular and booking a couple of days ahead is recommended.

The main bus station is east of the town centre, but if you're arriving from České Budějovice or Prague get off at the Špičák bus stop (the first in the town centre, just after you pass beneath a road bridge). Local buses (32Kč, 50 minutes, seven daily) run to České Budějovice, for onward travel to Brno or Plzeň.

SHUTTLE BUS Several companies offer direct shuttle buses to Austria – to Vienna (1100Kč), Salzburg (1100Kč) and Linz (450Kč).

TRAIN For a train, you'll need to first head to České Budějovice, where trains go to Linz (Austria; two hours). From Linz there are regular trains to Vienna, Salzburg and Munich.

MORAVIA

Brno

POP 387,200

Brno's attractions aren't obvious after Prague's showy buzz, but you'll soon see the traditional Moravian reserve melting away in the Old Town's bars and restaurants. Leave the touristy commotion in the capital, and have Brno's stellar array of museums and galleries almost to yourself.

Sights & Activities

Ask at the tourist information office about Brno's many excellent galleries and museums.

Špilberk Castle CASTLE
(www.spilberk.cz; ⊙9am-6pm May-Sep, to 5pm Oct-Apr, closed Mon Sep-Jun) Špilberk Castle looms above the Old Town. Founded in the 13th century and converted into a citadel during the 17th century, it imprisoned opponents of the Habsburgs until 1855. The underground **Casemates** (adult/concession 70/35Kč) house a creepy prison museum, and the main building houses the **Brno City Museum** (adult/concession 120/60Kč).

Capuchin Monastery MONASTERY
(Kapucínské nám 5; adult/concession 60/30Kč; ⊙9am-noon & 2-4.30pm Mon-Sat, 11-11.45am & 2-4.30pm Sun May-Sep, closed Mon Oct-Apr) This gruesome monastery displays the desiccated

corpses of 18th-century monks and local aristocrats.

Sleeping

Hotel Omega HOTEL €
(☎543 213 876; www.hotelomega.eu; Křídlovická 19b; s/d 950/1450Kč;) In a quiet neighbourhood 1km from the centre, the Omega has spacious rooms with modern pine furniture, and breakfast comes complete with castle views. Catch tram 1 from the train station to the Václavská stop.

Hostel Fléda HOSTEL €
(☎533 433 638; www.hostelfleda.com; Štefánikova 24; dm/tw from €12/32; @) One of Brno's best music clubs also offers funky and colourful rooms a quick tram ride from the centre. A good bar reinforces a social vibe. Catch tram 1 or 6 to the Hrnčirská stop. Fléda is not recommended if you're looking for a quiet night.

Travellers' Hostel HOSTEL €
(☎542 213 573; www.travellers.cz; Jánská 22; dm 320Kč; Jul & Aug) Set in the heart of the Old Town, this place provides the most central cheap beds in the city – for July and August anyway.

Eating & Drinking

Zelená Kočka CZECH €
(Solniční 1;) Tasty beers from the tiny Dalešice brewery are the main drawcard at this relaxed spot in central Brno, but the food is damn good too and it's all nonsmoking. And no, we don't know why it's called the 'Green Cat'.

Rebio VEGETARIAN €
(Orli 16; mains 80-120Kč; 8am-7pm Mon-Fri, 10am-3pm Sat) Healthy risottos and veggie pies stand out in this self-service spot that changes its tasty menu every day. Organic beer and wine is available, and there's another all-veggie **branch** (Mečova 2; 9am-9pm Mon-Fri, 11am-8pm Sat & Sun) on the 1st floor of the Velký Spalicek shopping centre.

Minach CAFE €
(Poštovská 6; per chocolate 13Kč; 10am-7pm Mon-Sat, from 2pm Sun) More than 50 kinds of handmade chocolates and bracing coffee make this an essential mid-morning or mid-afternoon detour.

Tesco SUPERMARKET €
(cnr Úzká & Uhelná, 24hr) Tesco is 300m south of the train station through the pedestrian tunnel.

Pivnice Pegas BEER HALL
(Jakubská 4) *Pivo* melts that old Moravian reserve as the locals become pleasantly noisy. Try the zingy *Pšeničné pivo* (unfiltered wheat beer) with a slice of lemon.

Klub Desert CLUB
(www.dodesertu.com; Rooseveltova 24; 5pm-3am Mon-Thu, 10am-3am Fri, 5pm-2am Sat & Sun) Part cool bar-cafe and part intimate performance venue, Klub Desert features Brno's most eclectic live late-night lineup. Gypsy bands, neo-folk – anything goes.

Information

Cyber Cafe (Velký Spalicek shopping centre, Mečova 2; per hr 60Kč; 9am-11pm) There's a wi-fi hot spot throughout the surrounding shopping centre.

Tourist information office (☎542 211 090; www.ticbrno.cz; Radnická 8; 8am-6pm Mon-Fri, 9am-5.30pm Sat & Sun Apr-Sep, 9am-5pm Sat, 9am-3pm Sun Oct-Mar) Sells maps and books accommodation. Free internet up to 15 minutes.

Getting There & Away

BUS There are frequent buses from Brno to Prague (165Kč, 2½ hours, hourly), Bratislava (135Kč, 2¼ hours, hourly) and Vienna (180Kč, two hours, five daily). The departure point is either the bus station or near the train station opposite the Grand Hotel; check your ticket. Private companies **Student Agency** (☎841 101 101; www.studentagency.eu) and **Megabus** (☎234 704 977; www.megabus.cz) both leave from their ticket booths near the train station. The main bus station (Brno ÚAN Zvonařka) is 800m south of the train station through the Galerie Vaňkovka shopping centre.

TRAIN Trains run to Prague (319Kč, three hours) every two hours. Direct Eurocity trains run from Brno to Vienna (229Kč, 1¾ hours, five daily). There are frequent trains to Bratislava (300Kč, two hours), and direct trains to Berlin (991Kč, 7½ hours), Dresden (737Kč, five hours) and Hamburg (1245Kč, 10 hours). The train station (Brno-hlavní nádraží) is at the southern edge of the Old Town.

Telč

POP 6000

Telč's gorgeous old centre is ringed by medieval fish ponds and unspoilt by modern buildings. Unwind with a glass of Moravian wine at one of the local cafes.

WORTH A TRIP

OLOMOUC

Olomouc (olla-moats) is one of the Czech Republic's most underrated destinations. There's great nightlife fuelled by a cosmopolitan student population, and two essential sights worthy of any European city.

Olomouc's Unesco World Heritage–listed **Holy Trinity Column** was built between 1716 and 1754; the exquisite baroque structure is reminiscent of the Buddhist stupa. The surrounding square is ringed by historic facades and features two of the city's six baroque fountains.

The superb **Archdiocesan Museum** (www.olumart.cz; Václavské nám 3; adult/concession 50/25Kč; ⏲10am-6pm Tue-Sun) includes treasures from the 12th to 18th centuries, when Olomouc was the Moravian capital.

Stay at **Poet's Corner** (☎777 570 730; www.hostelolomouc.com; 3rd fl, Sokolská 1; dm/s/tw/tr/q 350/650/900/1200/1600Kč;), a friendly and well-run hostel. In summer there's a two-night minimum stay. Aussie owners Greg and Francie have loads of ideas for interesting day trips.

With a cosy cellar bar and a breezy beer garden, **U kašny** (Dolní nám 43; mains 120-250Kč) is the kind of place you'll return to on consecutive nights. There's a rotating mix of excellent beers from smaller regional breweries, and U kašny's deliciously meaty meals go well with Moravia's best *bramboráčky* (fried potato pancakes). There's also great microbrewery beer and good food at **Moritz** (Nešverova 2; mains 100-180Kč;). In summer, the beer garden's the only place to be.

The **Olomouc Beer Festival** (www.beerfest.cz), in June, is one of the Czech Republic's biggest. With around 20 different breweries and live music, it's Beervana for curious hopheads.

Frequent buses link Olomouc with Brno (92Kč, 1¼ hours) and Prague's Florenc bus station (220Kč, 3¾ hours). Five direct fast trains (130Kč, 1½ hours) link Brno and Olomouc daily. Trains from Prague (3210Kč, 3¼ hours) leave from the main train station (Praha-hlavní nádraží).

From Olomouc to Poland there are two direct trains to Warsaw at 12.37am and 12.54pm daily (750Kč, six hours), and one to Krakow at 12.37am (430Kč, 4½ hours).

The **information office** (☎567 243 145; www.telc-etc.cz; nám Zachariáše z Hradce 10; ⏲8am-5pm Mon-Fri, 10am-5pm Sat & Sun) books accommodation in private homes (350Kč to 400Kč per person). Internet access is 1Kč per minute.

Telč's pristine Old Town square, ringed with Gothic arcades and elegant Renaissance facades, is a Unesco World Heritage Site. At the square's northwestern end is the **Water Chateau** (www.zamek-telc.cz). The one-hour **Tour A** (adult/concession 110/70Kč; 9am to 5pm Tuesday to Sunday from May to September; to 4pm April & October) visits the Renaissance halls, while the 45-minute **Tour B** (adult/concession 80/50Kč; 9am to 5pm Tuesday to Sunday from May to September only) visits the private apartments, inhabited by the aristocratic owners until 1945.

Lots of brick, exposed beams and warm wooden floors make **Penzion Kamenné Slunce** (☎732 193 510; www.kamenne-slunce.cz; Palackého 2; s/d/apt 600/900/2000Kč;) a very welcoming spot just off the main square. Telč's hipper younger citizens crowd the buzzy **U Marušky** (Palackého) for cool jazz and tasty eats.

Five buses travel daily from Prague Florenc to Telč (150Kč, 2½ hours). Buses between České Budějovice and Brno also stop at Telč (100Kč, two hours, two daily).

The bus and train stations are a few hundred metres apart on the eastern side of town. A 10-minute walk along Masarykova leads to nám Zachariáše z Hradce, the Old Town square.

UNDERSTAND CZECH REPUBLIC

History

The Good King Wenceslas of Christmas carol fame was actually a prince, and the land he looked out over was the ancient territory of Bohemia. Beatified as St Wenceslas (svatý Václav in Czech), he remains the country's patron saint.

The tides of war and imperial domination have washed through Bohemia and Moravia for centuries. Events in Czech history have impacted throughout Europe. Two Habsburg councillors were thrown from a Prague Castle window in 1618 (the famous Defenestration of Prague), igniting the Thirty Years War. Hitler's 1938 annexation of the Sudetenland (the western borderlands of Czechoslovakia) triggered the final slide towards WWII.

The two 'Golden Ages' of Czech history were the rule of Charles IV (1346–78), who founded Prague's St Vitus Cathedral, built Charles Bridge and established Charles University, and the reign of Rudolf II (1576–1612), who made Prague the capital of the Habsburg empire and drew many great artists, scholars and scientists to his court.

The 20th century was notable for the 'years of eight'. Czechoslovakia was created after the fall of the Habsburg empire in 1918, was occupied by the Nazis in 1938 and fell to a communist coup in 1948. The hopeful 'Prague Spring', when censorship was relaxed and political prisoners were released, was crushed by the Soviet invasion of 1968.

The Velvet Revolution – the bloodless overthrow of the communist regime – didn't happen until 1989. It was soon followed by the Velvet Divorce of 1993, when Czechoslovakia split into separate Czech and Slovak republics, the former led by famous playwright and former political prisoner Václav Havel.

The Czech Republic joined the EU on 1 May 2004, and the country is currently scheduled to adopt the euro in 2012.

People

Ninety-five percent of the population of 10.2 million are Czech and 3% are Slovak. A significant Roma population (0.3%) is subject to hostility and racism, and suffers from poverty and unemployment.

Arts

Famous Czech writers include Franz Kafka (1883–1924; *The Trial, Metamorphosis*), Milan Kundera (b 1929; *The Book of Laughter and Forgetting, The Unbearable Lightness of Being*) and Bohumil Hrabal (1914–97; *I Served The King of England*).

Antonín Dvořák (1841–1904; *New World Symphony*) is the country's best-known composer, and painter Alfons Mucha (1860–1939) is famous for his art nouveau posters.

The films of Jan Hrebejk (b 1967), *Musíme si pomáhat* (Divided We Fall; 2000), *Pupendo* (2003) and *Horem pádem* (Up and Down; 2004), all cover different times in the country's tumultuous 20th-century history.

Občan Havel (Citizen Havel; 2008) is a fascinating documentary about Václav Havel. A recent box-office hit was *Kajinek* (2010), a thriller about the Czech Republic's most notorious hitman.

Food

Traditional Czech cuisine is strong on meat, dumplings and gravy. Try *knedlo-zelo-vepřo* (bread dumplings, sauerkraut and roast pork), *cesneková* (garlic soup) or *kapr na kmíní* (carp with caraway seed).

In this chapter, the following price indicators apply (for a main meal):

€€€ more than 500Kč

€€ 200Kč to 500Kč

€ less than 200Kč

SURVIVAL GUIDE

Directory A–Z

Accommodation

Unless otherwise stated, prices include a private bathroom and a simple breakfast. Outside of the peak summer season hotel rates can fall by up to 40% from these prices. Booking ahead – especially in Prague – is recommended for summer and around Christmas and Easter.

The following price indicators apply for this chapter (for a high-season double room):

€€€ more than 3700Kč

€€ 1600Kč to 3700Kč

€ less than 1600Kč

CAMPING

Most camping grounds are open from May to September and charge around 100Kč per person. Camping on public land is prohibited.

Czech Camping (www.czechcamping.com)

Do Kempu (www.czech-camping.com)

HOSTELS

Prague and Český Krumlov are the only places with a choice of backpacker-oriented hostels. Dorm beds cost around 450Kč in Prague and 350Kč to 400Kč elsewhere. Booking ahead is recommended.

Czech Youth Hostel Association (www.czechhostels.com) Information and booking for Hostelling International (HI) hostels.

HOTELS

Hotels in central Prague, Český Krumlov and Brno can be expensive, but in smaller towns are usually cheaper. Two-star hotels offer reasonable comfort for 1000Kč to 1200Kč for a double, or 1200Kč to 1500Kč with private bathroom (around 50% higher in Prague).

Czech Hotels (www.czechhotels.net)

Czech Hotels.cz (ww.czechhotels.cz)

PENSIONS

Pensions *(penzióny)* are small, often family-run, accommodation offering rooms with private bathroom and breakfast. Rates range from 1000Kč to 1500Kč for a double room (1900Kč to 2500Kč in Prague). Check out **Czech Pensions** (www.czechpension.cz).

PRIVATE ROOMS

Look for signs advertising private rooms *(privát* or *Zimmer frei)*. Most tourist information offices book these. Expect to pay from 450Kč to 550Kč per person outside Prague.

Business Hours

Castles, chateaux and museums are usually closed Mondays year-round.

Banks 8.30am-4.30pm Mon-Fri

Bars 11am-midnight

Post offices 8.30am-6pm Mon-Fri, to noon Sat

Restaurants 11am-11pm

Shops 8.30am-6pm Mon-Fri, to noon Sat

Gay & Lesbian Travellers

Homosexuality is legal in the Czech Republic. Look at **Prague Gay Guide** (www.prague.gayguide.net) and **Prague Saints** (www.praguesaints.cz).

Holidays

New Year's Day 1 January; also anniversary of the founding of the Czech Republic

Easter Monday March/April

Labour Day 1 May

Liberation Day 8 May

SS Cyril and Methodius Day 5 July

Jan Hus Day 6 July

Czech Statehood Day 28 September

Republic Day 28 October

Struggle for Freedom and Democracy Day 17 November

Christmas 24 to 26 December

Money

Use ATMs or use the main banks to change cash or get a cash advance on credit cards. Beware of *směnárna* (private exchange offices), especially in Prague – they advertise misleading rates and often charge exorbitant commissions. There is no black market, and anyone who offers to change money in the street is probably a thief.

Tipping is optional in restaurants and taxis, but increasingly expected in Prague. Round the bill/fare up to the next 20Kč or 30Kč (5% to 10%). Leave small change as a tip in bars.

Telephone

All Czech phone numbers have nine digits; dial all nine for any call, local or long distance.

Mobile phone coverage (GSM 900) is excellent. If you're from Europe, Australia or New Zealand, your mobile phone should work. Local mobile phone numbers start with digits from 601 to 608 and 720 to 779.

Visas

The Czech Republic is part of the Schengen Agreement, and citizens of most countries can spend up to 90 days in the country in a six-month period without a visa. For travellers from some other countries, a Schengen Visa is required; you can only get this from your country of residence. Check www.czech.cz for the latest information.

Getting There & Away

Located in the geographic heart of Europe, the Czech Republic is easily reached by air from key European hubs or overland by road or train from neighbouring countries.

With an economy that depends heavily on tourism, the Czech Republic has wisely kept red tape to a minimum for foreign visitors. If you're travelling overland into the Czech Republic, or have already flown into a European hub like Frankfurt or Amsterdam, note that under the Schengen Agreement there's no border control between the Czech Republic and other member countries.

Air

Most international flights arrive in Prague, with Frankfurt, Amsterdam or Munich being the most convenient European hubs.

Prague-Ruzyně Airport (www.prg.aero)

Brno-Tuřany Airport (www.airport-brno.cz)

Land

The Czech Republic has border crossings with Austria, Germany, Poland and Slovakia.

BUS

Prague's main international bus terminal is Florenc bus station. The peak season for bus travel is mid-June to the end of September, with daily buses to major European cities. Outside this season frequency falls to two or three services a week.

See **Student Agency** (www.studentagency.eu), **Eurolines** (www.elines.cz) and **Tourbus** (www.tourbus.cz) for international bus travel. Services to neighbouring countries:

Austria Several daily services run from Prague (€24, 4½ hours) and Brno (€8, two hours) to Vienna. Private shuttle buses also link Český Krumlov with Vienna, Linz and Salzburg.

Germany Daily services run from Prague to German cities: Berlin (€29, 4½ hours), Dresden (€23, 2¼ hours), Frankfurt (€60, 7½ hours) and Munich (€35, 5¼ hours).

Poland Weekly services link Brno with Krakow (€29, five hours) and Warsaw (€42, 10 hours). Three weekly services link Prague with Warsaw (€37, 12 hours).

Slovakia Several daily services link Prague with Bratislava (€14, 4¼ hours) and Košice (€19.50, 10 hours), and Brno with Bratislava (€10, two hours) and Košice (€15.50, seven hours).

TRAIN

International trains arrive at Prague's main train station (Praha-hlavní nádraží, or Praha hl n) or the outlying Holešovice (Praha Hol) and Smíchov (Praha Smv) stations. InterRail (Zone D) passes are valid in the Czech Republic, and in 2009 the country became part of the Eurail network.

International train tickets can be purchased online with **Czech Railways** (České Dráhy; www.cd.cz). Services to neighbouring countries:

Austria Several daily trains run from Brno (229Kč, two hours) and Prague (483Kč, five hours) to Vienna, and from České Budějovice to Linz (250Kč, two hours).

Germany Services run from Prague to German cities: Berlin (737Kč, five hours, daily), Dresden (483Kč, 2¼ hours, several daily), Frankfurt (1245Kč, seven hours, two daily) and Munich (€35, six hours, two daily).

Poland Services link Prague to Warsaw (477Kč, 8½ hours, two daily), and Olomouc to Warsaw (380Kč, 5½ hours, daily) and Krakow (400Kč, six hours, daily).

Slovakia Several daily services run from Brno (210Kč, 1½ hours) and Prague (500Kč, 4¼ hours) to Bratislava.

Getting Around

Bus

Within the Czech Republic buses are often faster, cheaper and more convenient than trains. Many bus routes have reduced frequency at weekends. Bus companies:

CŠAD (☎information line 900 144 444) The national bus company, linking cities and smaller towns.

Megabus (www.megabus.cz) Linking Prague with Karlovy Vary, Brno and Plzeň.

Student Agency (www.studentagency.eu) With destinations including Prague, Brno, České Budějovice, Český Krumlov, Karlovy Vary and Plzeň.

Car & Motorcycle

For motoring assistance, call ☎1230. Foreign driving licences are valid for up to 90 days. Typical hire rates for a Škoda Fabia are around 700Kč a day including unlimited kilometres, collision-damage waiver and value-added tax (VAT). Car-hire companies in Prague:

Secco Car (☎220 802 361; www.seccocar.cz; Přístavní 39, Holešovice)

Vecar (☎224 314 361; www.vecar.org; Svatovítská 7, Dejvice)

Train

Czech Railways (České Dráhy; www.cd.cz) has trains to almost every bit of the country. If you're paying by credit card, advise this *before* staff issue tickets. See www.cd.cz and www.idos.cz for fares and timetables.

Denmark

Includes »

Best Places to Eat

» Shønnemann, Copenhagen (p334)

» Restaurant Kadeau, Bornholm (p339)

» Mielcke & Hurtigkarl, Copenhagen (p335)

» Nordisk Spisehus, Århus (p343)

Best Places to Be Inspired

» Louisiana Museum (p336)

» Bornholm (p338)

» ARoS, Århus (p340)

» Skagen (p345)

Why Go?

Denmark is the bridge between Scandinavia and northern Europe. To the rest of Scandinavia, the Danes are fun-loving, frivolous party animals, with relatively liberal, progressive attitudes. Their culture, food, architecture and appetite for conspicuous consumption owe as much, if not more, to their German neighbours to the south than to their former colonies – Sweden, Norway and Iceland – to the north.

Denmark's capital, Copenhagen, is one of the most charming and accessible cities in northern Europe, with top-notch museums, shops, bars, nightlife and, in particular, restaurants. Elsewhere, though there are other cities of interest such as Odense and Århus. Denmark's chief appeal lies in its gently idyllic countryside, coastline and historic sights such as Neolithic burial chambers; the bodies of well-preserved Iron Age people exhumed from their slumber in peat bogs; and atmospheric Viking ruins and treasures.

When to Go

Copenhagen

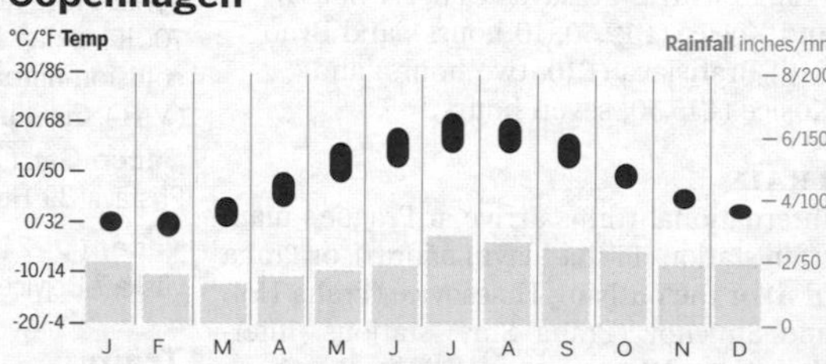

Jun & Jul Long days, buzzing beachside towns, Copenhagen Jazz and A-list rock fest Roskilde.

Sep & Oct Fewer crowds, golden landscapes and cosy nights by crackling open fires.

Dec Twinkling Christmas lights, ice-skating rinks and gallons of warming *glögg* (mulled wine).

Connections

Denmark's modern, efficient transport network is well connected to the region and the rest of the world. Located in Copenhagen, its main airport, Kastrup, offers excellent long- and short-haul connections, while regional airports Billund and Århus in Jutland offer numerous European short-haul options. Good road and rail connections link Sweden and Germany to Denmark. Plentiful ferries link Denmark with all major Baltic destinations and also with Atlantic coast destinations in Norway, Faroe, Iceland and the UK.

ITINERARIES

One Week

You could comfortably spend three days in Copenhagen exploring the museums and galleries, bar hopping and shopping. A trip north along the coast to the magnificent modern-art museum, Louisiana, and then further north still to Helsingborg Slot, before returning south would be a great way to spend two days. If the weather is on your side, spend an extra day exploring north Zealand's historic fishing villages and sandy beaches. Otherwise, delve into Danish history in Roskilde.

Two Weeks

After time in Copenhagen, a quick catamaran ride will take you to the Baltic island of Bornholm, reputedly the sunniest slice of Denmark and famed for cycling, beaches and tasty smokehouses. Alternatively, head west, stopping off on the island of Funen to see Hans Christian Andersen's birthplace in Odense. Continue west to the Jutland Peninsula for the bustling city of Århus and magnificent Skagen, where the Baltic and North seas clash.

Essential Food & Drink

» **Smørrebrød** Rye bread topped with anything from beef tartare to egg and prawns (shrimp); the open sandwich is Denmark's most famous culinary export

» **Sild** Smoked, cured, pickled or fried, herring is a local staple and best washed down with generous serves of akvavit (schnapps)

» **Kanelsnegle** A calorific delight, 'cinnamon snails' are sweet, buttery scrolls, sometimes laced with chocolate

» **Akvavit** Denmark's best-loved spirit is caraway-spiced akvavit from Aalborg, drunk straight down as a shot, followed by a chaser of *öl* (beer)

» **Lashings of beer** Carlsberg may dominate, but Denmark's expanding battalion of microbreweries includes Ølfabriken, Bröckhouse and Grauballe

AT A GLANCE

» **Currency** Danish krone (Dkr)

» **Language** Danish

» **Money** ATMs readily available

» **Visas** Not required for citizens of EU, USA, Canada, Australia and New Zealand

Fast Facts

» **Area** 43,094 sq km

» **Capital** Copenhagen

» **Country code** ☎45

» **Emergency** ☎112

Exchange Rates

Australia	A$1	Dkr5.40
Canada	C$1	Dkr5.40
Euro Zone	€1	Dkr7.46
Japan	¥100	Dkr6.75
New Zealand	NZ$1	Dkr3.85
UK	UK£1	Dkr8.60
USA	US$1	Dkr5.33

Set Your Budget

» **Budget hotel room** Dkr500

» **Two-course evening meal** Dkr350

» **Museum entrance** free to Dkr75

» **Beer** (glass) Dkr45

Resources

» **Visit Denmark** (www.visitdenmark.com) Comprehensive tourist information

» **Visit Copenhagen** (www.visitcopenhagen.com) Info on Copenhagen

» **AOK** (www.aok.dk) What's hot in the Danish capital

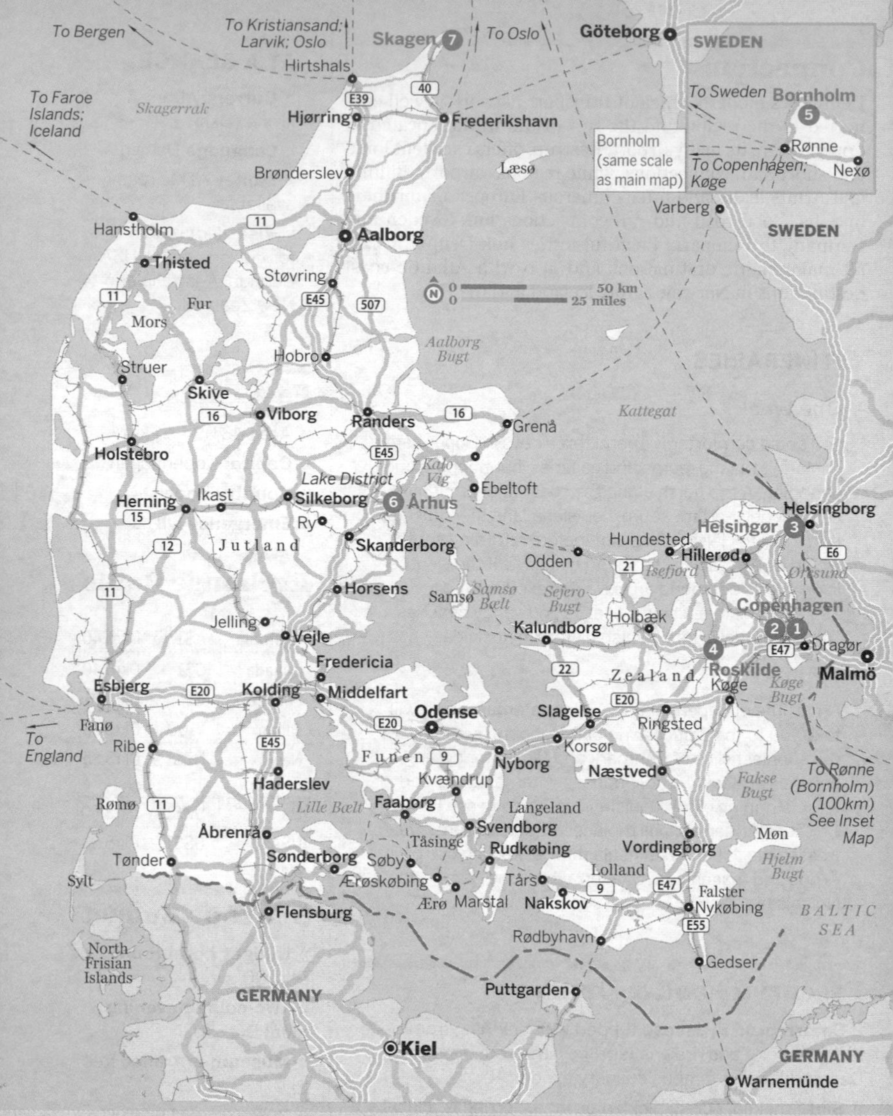

Denmark Highlights

1 Shop, nosh and chill in Scandinavia's capital of cool, **Copenhagen** (p329)

2 Be inspired by the art and the views at the sublime **Louisiana Museum of Modern Art** (p336)

3 Snoop around **Kronborg Slot** (p337), Hamlet's epic home in Helsingør

4 Check out the impressive cathedral and Viking boat musem in **Roskilde** (p337)

5 Lose yourself in nature and smoked fish on the Baltic island of **Bornholm** (p338)

6 See Århus through Technicolour glass at top-notch art museum **ARoS** (p340)

7 Watch angry seas collide above luminous, northern **Skagen** (p345)

COPENHAGEN

POP 1.8 MILLION

Stockholm might be more grandiose and Oslo more spectacularly located, but there is no more charming, exciting and stimulating city in Scandinavia than Copenhagen.

This 1000-year-old harbour town has managed to retain much of its historic charm – its copper spires, cobbled squares and pastel-coloured gabled town houses – while at the same time being everything a modern metropolis should be: home to cutting-edge designers, a super-efficient transport system and an impressive environmental conscience. It has intriguing, independent shops galore; excellent restaurants and bars; world-class museums and art collections; and brave new architecture. This is also a royal city, home to the beloved Queen Margrethe II and her family. Copenhagen is proud of its regal past and the architectural legacy of one king in particular: Christian IV, to whose reign in the 17th century we can credit some of the city's most picturesque buildings.

Sights

Tivoli AMUSEMENT PARK

(www.tivoli.dk; adult Dkr95; 11am-11pm Sun-Thu, to 12.30am Fri, to midnight Sat mid-Jun–mid-Aug, less hr rest of year, closed mid-Sep–late Oct & Jan-mid-Apr) Copenhagen's historic amusement park has been Denmark's number-one tourist attraction pretty much since the day it opened over 160 years ago. At first glance, visitors used to the scale and glitz of Disneyland might wonder what the fuss is about, but Tivoli Gardens has a unique atmosphere and no one can deny its appeal, particularly after dark when its wonderful illuminations work their magic. The gardens have an innocent, old-fashioned charm, with food pavilions, amusement rides, carnival games and various stage shows.

Nationalmuseet MUSEUM

(National Museum; www.natmus.dk; Ny Vestergade 10; admission free; 10am-5pm Tue-Sun) For a whistle-stop tour through the history of Denmark, nothing can beat the Nationalmuseet. Here you will find the world's most extensive collection of Danish artefacts from the Palaeolithic period to the 19th century. Naturally, the stars of the show are the Vikings, those much maligned, yet remarkably sophisticated, marauders. Highlights include Bronze Age burial remains in oak coffins and various examples of *lur* (musical horns) that were used for ceremonies and communication, ancient rune stones, a golden sun chariot and the silver Gundestrip cauldron. But the displays don't stop with the Vikings; there are excellent collections covering the Middle Ages and the Renaissance period, plus delightful Egyptian and classical antiquities, as well as frequently changing special exhibitions.

TOP CHOICE **Ny Carlsberg Glyptotek** MUSEUM

(www.glyptoteket.dk; Dantes Plads 7, HC Andersens Blvd; admission Dkr60, free Sun; 10am-5pm Tue-Sun) This splendid museum, occupying a grand period building near Tivoli Gardens, features Etruscan art, 18th- and 19th-century paintings from France and Denmark (the Gauguins are particularly notable) and sculpture spanning five millennia (including over 30 works by Rodin). At its heart is a beautiful tropical winter garden with a cafe.

Rosenborg Slot CASTLE

(www.rosenborgslot.dk; admission Dkr75, combined ticket incl Amalienborg Slot Dkr100; castle & treasury 10am-5pm Jun-Aug, 11am-4pm mid-late Feb, May, Sep, Oct & late Dec, 11am-4pm Tue-Sun Mar & Apr, castle 11am-2pm & treasury 11am-4pm Tue-Sun Jan–mid-Feb, closed early-late Dec) This early 17th-century castle, built by Christian IV in the Dutch Renaissance style, stands at the edge of **Kongens Have** (King's Gardens; admission free). It is a fairy-tale castle and one of Copenhagen's great landmarks. Inside you'll find glorious marbled and painted ceilings, gilded mirrors, priceless Dutch tapestries, solid silver lions, gold and enamelware. The Royal Treasury, in the castle basement, is home to the Danish crown jewels.

Statens Museum for Kunst MUSEUM

(www.smk.dk; Sølvgade 48-50; admission free; 10am-5pm Tue & Thu-Sun, to 8pm Wed) Occupying a grand 19th-century building and a dramatic glass extension, Denmark's national gallery houses an impressive collection of works from Danish artists, particularly those of the 19th-century 'Golden Age' such as Hammershöj and Eckersberg. Modern works include creations by international A-listers like Picasso and Munch, as well as more contemporary Danish artists such as Per Kirkeby, Sören Jensen, Michael Ancher and Richard Mortensen.

Slotsholmen PALACE, MUSEUMS & LIBRARY

An island separated from the city centre by a moatlike canal on three sides and the harbour on the other side, Slotsholmen is the site of **Christiansborg Palace** (33 92 64 92), home

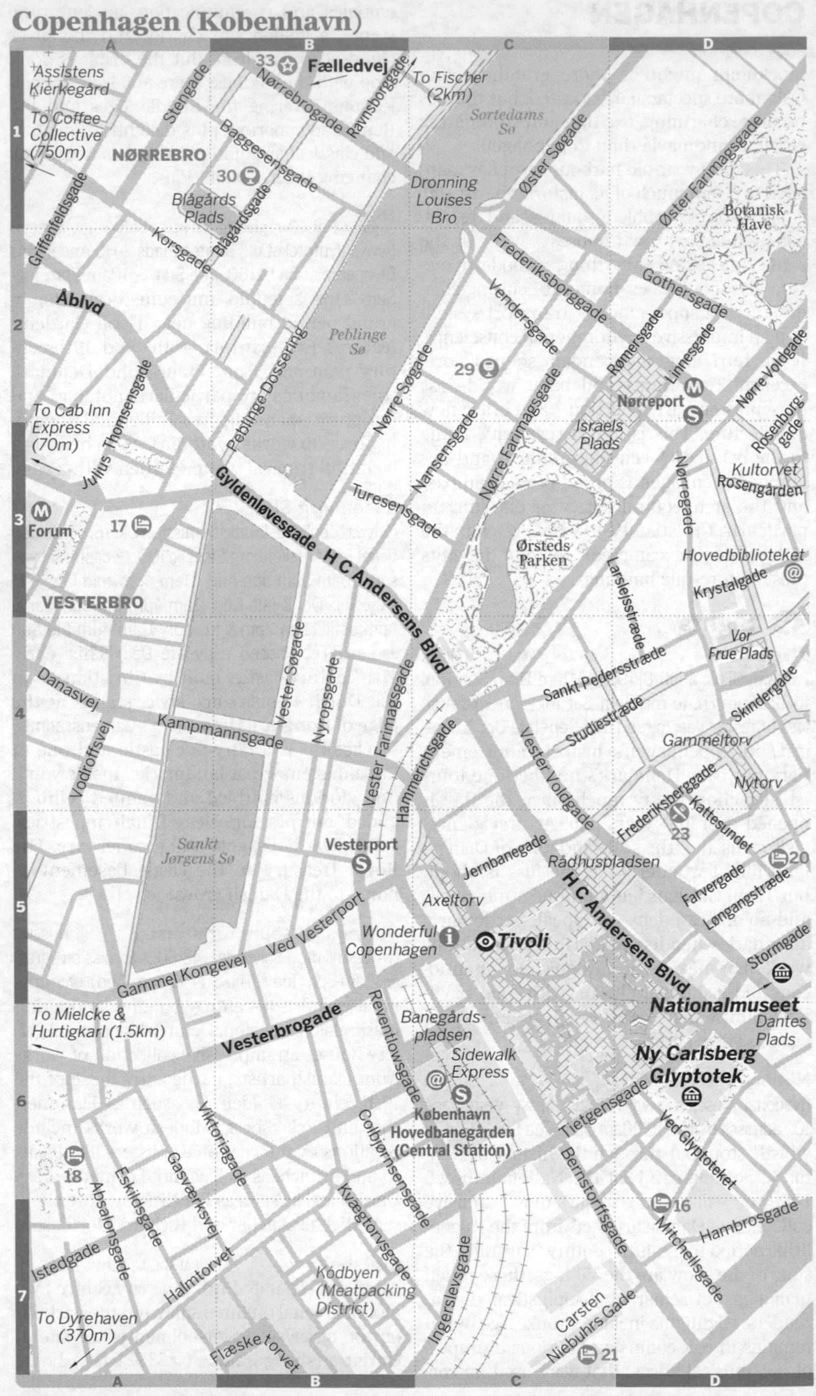

A
B
C
D
1
2
3
4
5
6
7
Assistens Kierkegård
To Coffee Collective (750m)
NØRREBRO
33 Fælledvej
To Fischer (2km)
Sortedams Sø
Stengade
Nørrebrogade
Ravnsborggade
Baggesensgade
30
Blågårds Plads
Blågårdsgade
Korsgade
Griffenfeldsgade
Åblvd
Dronning Louises Bro
Øster Søgade
Øster Farimagsgade
Botanisk Have
Gothersgade
Frederiksborggade
Vendersgade
Peblinge Sø
Peblinge Dossering
Nørre Søgade
29
Rømersgade
Linnésgade
Nørre Voldgade
Nørreport
Israels Plads
Rosenborggade
To Cab Inn Express (70m)
Julius Thomsensgade
Nansensgade
Nørre Farimagsgade
Nørregade
Kultorvet
Rosengården
Forum
17
Gyldenløvesgade
H C Andersens Blvd
Turesensgade
Ørsteds Parken
Larslejsstræde
Hovedbiblioteket
Krystalgade
VESTERBRO
Vor Frue Plads
Vester Søgade
Nyropsgade
Vester Farimagsgade
Sankt Pedersstræde
Skindergade
Danasvej
Kampmannsgade
Studiestræde
Gammeltorv
Vodroffsvej
Hammerichsgade
Vester Voldgade
Nytorv
Frederiksberggade
Kattesundet
23
Sankt Jørgens Sø
Vesterport
Jernbanegade
Rådhuspladsen
20
Farvergade
Løngangstræde
Axeltorv
Ved Vesterport
Wonderful Copenhagen
Tivoli
Stormgade
Gammel Kongevej
Nationalmuseet
Dantes Plads
To Mielcke & Hurtigkarl (1.5km)
Vesterbrogade
Reventlowsgade
Banegårds-pladsen
Sidewalk Express
Ny Carlsberg Glyptotek
København Hovedbanegården (Central Station)
Tietgensgade
Ved Glyptoteket
Viktoriagade
Colbjørnsensgade
18
Gasværksvej
Eskildsgade
Absalonsgade
Istedgade
Kvægtorvsgade
Bernstorffsgade
16
Mitchellsgade
Hambrosgade
Halmtorvet
Kødbyen (Meatpacking District)
Ingerslevsgade
Carsten Niebuhrs Gade
To Dyrehaven (370m)
Flæsketorvet
21

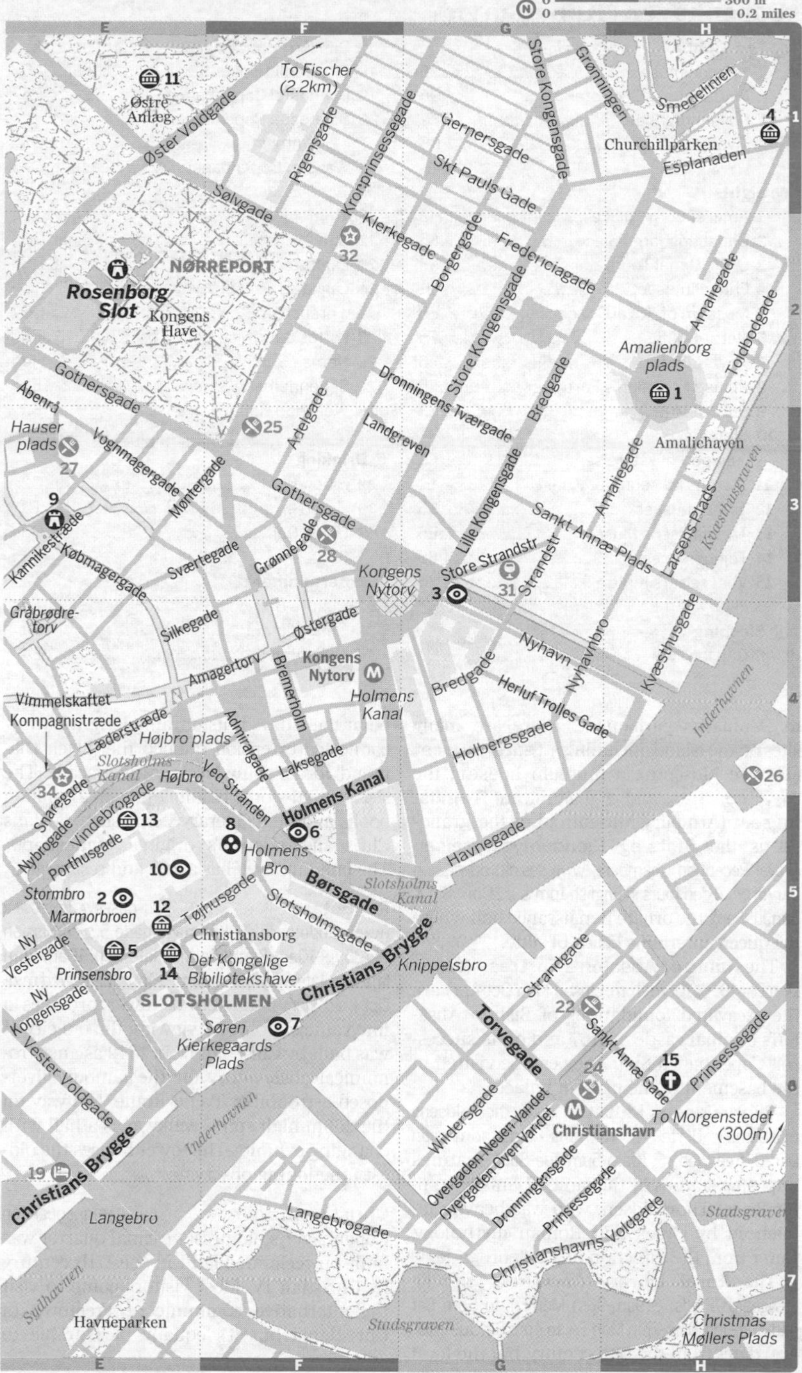

0 300 m
0 0.2 miles
To Fischer (2.2km)
Østre Anlæg
Øster Voldgade
Rigensgade
Kronprinsessegade
Gernersgade
Skt Pauls Gade
Store Kongensgade
Grønningen
Smedelinien
Churchillparken
Esplanaden
Sølvgade
Klerkegade
Borgergade
Fredericiagade
NØRREPORT
Rosenborg Slot
Kongens Have
Amaliegade
Toldbodgade
Amalienborg plads
Gothersgade
Åbenrå
Hauser plads
Vognmagergade
Adelgade
Dronningens Tværgade
Landgreven
Bredgade
Amalichaven
Møntergade
Lille Kongensgade
Sankt Annæ Plads
Larsens Plads
Kvæsthusgraven
Kannikestræde
Købmagergade
Sværtegade
Grønnegade
Kongens Nytorv
Store Strandstr
Strandstr
Gråbrødretorv
Silkegade
Østergade
Nyhavn
Nyhavnbro
Kvæsthusgade
Amagertorv
Bremerholm
Holmens Kanal
Herluf Trolles Gade
Vimmelskaftet
Kompagnistræde
Læderstræde
Højbro plads
Admiralgade
Laksegade
Holbergsgade
Inderhavnen
Slotsholms Kanal
Højbro
Ved Stranden
Snaregade
Nybrogade
Vindebrogade
Porthusgade
Holmens Bro
Havnegade
Stormbro
Marmorbroen
Tøjhusgade
Børsgade
Slotsholmsgade
Christiansborg
Ny Vestergade
Prinsensbro
Det Kongelige Bibiliotekshave
Knippelsbro
Christians Brygge
Ny Kongensgade
SLOTSHOLMEN
Strandgade
Søren Kierkegaards Plads
Torvegade
Sankt Annæ Gade
Prinsessegade
Vester Voldgade
Wildersgade
Overgaden Neden Vandet
Overgaden Oven Vandet
Christianshavn
To Morgenstedet (300m)
Dronningensgade
Prinsessegade
Stadsgraven
Langebro
Langebrogade
Christianshavns Voldgade
Sydhavnen
Havneparken
Christmas Møllers Plads

Copenhagen (Kobenhavn)

Top Sights

Nationalmuseet ... D5
Ny Carlsberg Glyptotek ... D6
Rosenborg Slot ... E2
Tivoli ... C5

Sights

1 Amalienborg Palace ... H2
2 Christiansborg Palace ... E5
3 DFDS Canal Tours ... G3
4 Frihedsmuseet ... H1
5 Museum of Royal Coaches ... E5
6 Netto-Boats ... F5
7 Royal Library ... F6
8 Ruins of Absalon's Fortress ... F5
9 Rundetårn ... E3
10 Slots-og Ejendomysstyrelsen ... E5
11 Statens Museum for Kunst ... E1
12 Teatermuseet ... E5
13 Thorvaldsens Museum ... E5
14 Tøjhusmuseet ... E5
15 Vor Frelsers Kirke ... H6

Sleeping

16 Cab Inn City ... D7
17 Cab Inn Scandinavia ... A3
18 City Public Hostel ... A6
19 Danhostel Copenhagen City ... E6
20 Danhostel Copenhagen Downtown ... D5
21 Wakeup Copenhagen ... C7

Eating

22 Café Wilder ... G6
23 Lagkagehuset ... D5
24 Lagkagehuset (Torvegade branch) ... G6
25 Lottes Sandwich Bar ... F3
26 Noma ... H4
27 Schønnemann ... E3
28 Wokshop Cantina ... F3

Drinking

29 Bibendum ... C2
30 Harbo ... B1
31 Union Bar ... G3

Entertainment

32 Culture Box ... F2
33 Gefährlich ... B1
34 La Fontaine ... E4

to Denmark's parliament. There are many sites on the island, including a **Teatermuseet** (Theatre Museum), a museum housing the **royal coaches**, and a magnificent **Tøjhusmuseet** (Armoury Museum), but the grandest is the **Slots-og Ejendomysstyrelsen** (Royal Reception Chambers; www.ses.dk; admission Dkr75; guided tours in English 1pm & 2.30pm Sat & Sun Jul-Sep), the ornate Renaissance hall where the queen entertains heads of state.

The **Ruins of Absalon's Fortress** (admission Dkr40; 10am-4pm, closed Mon Oct-Apr) are the excavated foundations of Bishop Absalon's original castle of 1167 and of its successor, Copenhagen Slot. They can be visited in the basement of the present palace.

Thorvaldsens Museum (www.thorvaldsensmuseum.dk; Bertel Thorvaldsens Plads; admission Dkr20, free Wed; 10am-5pm Tue-Sun) features imposing statues by the famed Danish sculptor Bertel Thorvaldsen, who was heavily influenced by Greek and Roman mythology. Enter from the direction of Vindebrogade.

The **Royal Library** (www.kb.dk; Søren Kierkegaards Plads; 9am-9pm Mon-Fri, to 5pm Sat mid-Aug–Jun, 9am-7pm Mon-Fri, to 4pm Sat Jul–mid-Aug) dates from the 17th century, but the focal point these days is its ultramodern, walkway-connected extension dubbed the 'Black Diamond' for its shiny black granite facade. The sleek, seven-storey building houses 21 million books and other literary items such as Hans Christian Andersen's original manuscripts. The building itself has a cafe and restaurant.

Rundetårn OBSERVATION TOWER
(www.rundetaarn.dk; Købmagergade 52; admission Dkr25; 10am-8pm late May-late Sep, 10am-5pm late Sep-late May, also open 7-10pm Tue & Wed mid-Oct–mid-Mar) The Round Tower provides a fine vantage point for viewing the old city. It was built by Christian IV in 1642 as an astronomical observatory for the famous silver-nosed astronomer Tycho Brahe. Halfway up the 209m-high spiral walkway is a hall with changing exhibits. The tower houses the oldest functioning observatory.

Christianshavn NEIGHBOURHOOD
Copenhagen's picturesque canal quarter was built on reclaimed land in the 17th century by Christian IV. Most visitors come to visit the alternative commune at Freetown of Christiania but it's equally pleasurable to

wander beside the canals and visit the quarter's pleasant cafes.

To get there, walk over the bridge from the southeastern side of Slotsholmen, or you can take the Metro from Kongens Nytorv or Nörreport direct to Christianshavnstorv.

Close to Freetown of Christiania is the 17th-century **Vor Frelsers Kirke** (www.vorfrelserskirke.dk; Sankt Annæ Gade 29; church/tower admission free/Dkr25; ⏲11am-4pm Apr-Aug, to 3.30pm Sep-Mar, closed during services, tower closed Nov-Mar). For a panoramic view of the city and across to Sweden, climb the 400 steps of the church's 95m-high spiral tower. The last 160 steps run spectacularly and dizzyingly along the outside rim.

Waterfront PALACE, MUSEUM & SCULPTURE

The home of the royal family since 1794, **Amalienborg Palace** (admission Dkr60, combined ticket incl Rosenborg Slot Dkr100; ⏲10am-4pm May-Oct & mid-late Dec, 11am-4pm Tue-Sun Jan-Apr & Nov–mid-Dec) comprises four austere mansions surrounding the central square and is guarded by sentries, who are relieved at noon in a ceremonial **changing of the guard**. You can view the interior of the northwestern mansion, with its royal memorabilia and the study rooms of three kings.

Back on Amalienborg Plads, and 500m north along Amaliegade, is Churchillparken, where you'll find **Frihedsmuseet** (admission free; ⏲10am-5pm Tue-Sun May-Sep, 10am-3pm Tue-Sat Oct-Apr), with moving relics from the time of the Danish Resistance against Nazi occupation.

About 150m north of the Frihedsmuseet you pass the spectacular **Gefion Fountain**, which features the goddess Gefion, ploughing the island of Zealand with her four sons yoked as oxen. Another 400m north along the waterfront is the statue of the unjustly famed **Little Mermaid** (Den Lille Havfrue) – a rather forlorn statue that is actually one of the least interesting of Copenhagen's many sights.

Festivals

The **Copenhagen Jazz Festival** (www.jazzfestival.dk) is the city's largest music event, invigorating the whole city with 10 days of music in early July. The festival presents a wide range of Danish and international jazz, blues and fusion music, with music wafting out of practically every public square, park, pub and cafe from Strøget to Tivoli Gardens.

Usually held on the second Friday in October, **Kulturnatten** (Culture Night; www.kulturnatten.dk) sees more than 200 of the city's museums, galleries, theatres and libraries throw open their doors through the night, with a wide range of special events. Public transport is free with the Kulturnatten Pass (Dkr85).

DON'T MISS

CANAL TOURS

The best way to see Copenhagen is from the water. There are several ways to take a boat tour around the city's canals and harbour. **DFDS Canal Tours** (www.canaltours.dk; adult Dkr60) leave from the head of Nyhavn or the Marriott Hotel. Tours take 50 minutes, passing by the Little Mermaid, Christianshavn and Christiansborg Palace, and leave up to every 15 minutes between 9.15am and 5.30pm. **Netto-Boats** (www.netto-baadene.dk; adult Dkr30) are cheaper, run the same times and depart from Holmens Kirke and from Nyhavn.

Sleeping

Danhostel Copenhagen City HOSTEL €

(☎33 11 85 85; www.danhostel.dk; HC Andersens Blvd 50; dm Dkr130-195) The best of Copenhagen's hostels occupies a modern high-rise overlooking the harbour a short walk from Central Station. With a reception that resembles a boutique hotel, a great cafe and a 25% discount on the facilities at the DGI-Byen swimming pool and sports centre included in the price, it's wise to book ahead.

Wakeup Copenhagen HOTEL €€

(☎44 80 00 10; www.wakeupcopenhagen.com; Carsten Niebuhrs Gade 11; s Dkr400-900, d Dkr500-1000; @) Cheap meets chic at this new 510-room budget hotel, complete with designer Danish furniture, free internet access and podlike showers in each room. Close to Central Station, its top floors offers spectacular views while three of its floors feature wooden flooring for the allergy inclined. Book online for the best rates.

Danhostel Copenhagen Downtown HOSTEL €

(☎70 23 21 10; www.copenhagendowntown.com; Vandkunsten 5; dm/d from Dkr130/499) This characterful, buzzing hostel could not be more centrally located, right beside the main pedestrian shopping street, Strøget, and prides itself on its cultural dynamism, with several artists in residence.

Cab Inn City HOTEL €
(☎33 46 16 16; www.cabinn.com; Mitchellsgade 14; s/d/tr Dkr545/675/805) Cab Inns are modern and rather clinical but boast good facilities (including kettle and TV) and reliable levels of comfort, although the ship-cabin (cab-in, geddit?) style means small rooms and rather narrow bunk-style beds. This is the best located of all Copenhagen's Cab Inns, a short walk south of Tivoli Gardens. Book ahead. Its sister hotels are **Cab Inn Scandinavia** (☎35 36 11 11; www.cabinn.com; Vodroffsvej 57; s/d/tr/q Dkr545/675/805/935; P) and **Cab Inn Express** (☎33 21 04 00; www.cabinn.com; Danasvej 32-34; s/d/tr/q Dkr485/615/745/935; P).

City Public Hostel HOSTEL €
(☎33 31 20 70; www.citypublichostel.dk; Absalonsgade 8; dm Dkr125-170; ⊙early May-late Aug) A central, well-run hostel with dorms sleeping six to 66; they are both mixed and separate gender. Breakfast costs Dkr40. There is an outdoor barbecue area.

Camping Charlottenlund Fort CAMPING GROUND €
(☎39 62 36 88; www.campingcopenhagen.dk; Strandvejen 144, Charlottenlund; campsite per adult/tent Dkr95/40) This is 6km north of the city centre, beside a delightful sandy beach overlooking the Øresund sea. Take bus 14 for a half-hour trip.

Eating

Schønnemann DANISH €€
(☎33 12 07 85; www.restaurantschonnemann.dk; Hauser Plads 16; meals Dkr59-148; ⊙11.30am-5pm Mon-Sat) Schønnemann has been filling bellies with smørrebrød (open sandwiches) and schnapps since 1877. Not much has changed, from the sawdust-sprinkled floor to the stoic Danish grub. It's an institution – book ahead.

Fischer ITALIAN €€
(www.hosfischer.dk, in Danish; Victor Borges Plads 12; dinner mains Dkr135-195; ⊙lunch & dinner Mon-Sat, brunch & lunch Sun) Cosy Fischer serves authentic Italian soul food in a converted working-man's bar. That it's all seriously good isn't surprising given owner and head chef David Fischer worked at Rome's Michelin-starred La Pergola.

Café Wilder CAFE €€
(Wildersgade 56; mains Dkr85-185) The archetypal Christianshavn cafe serves simple, beautiful dishes like goat cheese au gratin on bruschetta, or roasted cockerel breast with butter-sauteed asparagus, pak choi and baby carrots.

Morgenstedet VEGETARIAN €
(www.morgenstedet.dk; Langgaden; mains Dkr70; ⊙noon-9pm Tue-Sun) This long-established vegetarian and vegan place has a pretty garden in the heart of Christiania. Its dish of the day – usually a curry – is Dkr70.

Lagkagehuset BAKERY €
(www.lagkagehuset.dk; Torvegade 45; sandwiches & salads Dkr45; ⊙6am-7pm Mon-Fri, to 6pm Sat & Sun) One of the best bakeries in town lies right in the heart of Christianshavn and is highly recommended for sandwiches and salads.

Wokshop Cantina THAI & VIETNAMESE €€
(www.wokshop.dk; Ny Adelgade 6; curry Dkr119-140; ⊙lunch & dinner Mon-Fri, dinner Sat) This basement canteen in a street just off Kongens Nytorv serves excellent, cheap Thai and Vietnamese staples.

Lottes Sandwich Bar CAFE €
(www.lottessandwichbar.dk, in Danish; Kronprinsessegade 10; sandwiches Dkr45-55, wraps Dkr50, salads Dkr40-60; ⊙8am-6pm Mon-Fri, 10am-4pm Sat) Huge, tasty sandwiches and wraps are the main drawcard at this popular takeaway. If the weather is on your side, devour the goodness in leafy Kongens Have across the street.

Drinking

Drinking is one of the Danes' chief pastimes and Copenhagen is packed with a huge range of places, from cosy, old-school cellar bars or bodegas, to indie hipster cafes and secretive cocktail bars. Many places change from one role to another as the day progresses.

Union Bar BAR
(www.theunionbar.dk; Store Strandstræde 19; ⊙Wed-Sat) Inspired by the speakeasy bars of old New York (even the cocktails are named after 1920s slang), this sneaky hotspot hides behind an unmarked black door. Ring the buzzer and get set for some seriously smooth libations.

Bibendum BAR
(www.vincafeen.dk; Nansensgade 45; ⊙Mon-Sat) Cosy Bibendum is run by an exceptionally knowledgeable and snobbery-free crowd of wine enthusiasts serving a broad range of Old and New World wines by the glass.

TOP CHOICE **Coffee Collective** CAFE
(www.coffeecollective.dk; Jægersborggade 10; ⊙7.30am-8pm Mon-Fri, 9am-6pm Sat, 10am-6pm Sun) On up-and-coming Jægersborggade in the Nørrebro district, this cafe roaster

SPLURGE

Arguably the most enchanting Modern Scandinavian restaurant in Copenhagen, **Mielcke & Hurtigkarl** (☎38 34 84 36; www.mielcke-hurtigkarl.dk; Frederiksberg Runddel 1; 4-/8-course dinner Dkr595/850; ⏲lunch & dinner Wed-Sun Apr-Sep, dinner Thu-Sat Oct-Mar, closed mid-Dec–mid-Jan) occupies a former royal summer house in leafy Frederiksberg Have, one of the city's most beautiful parks. Adorned with botanical murals and forest-inspired sound and lighting, it's the domain of A-list chef Jakob Mielcke and his culinary creations (think Norwegian lobster jelly with salty plum ice cream). While the set menu offers simpler, cheaper fare, the evening degustation menu is the real drawcard. Topping it off are friendly, knowledgeable staff with a genuine passion for the food and wine they serve. Book ahead.

peddles complex, flavoursome coffee to in-the-know locals.

Harbo BAR
(Blågårdsgade 2d; ⏲8.30am-midnight Mon-Thu, 8.30am-2am Fri, 9.30am-2am Sat, 9.30am-11pm Sun) Recycled interiors, affordable drinks and the odd exhibition/performance make this lo-fi bar a new favourite in arty, edgy Nørrebro.

Dyrehaven CAFE,BAR
(www.dyrehavenkbh.dk; Sønder Blvd 72; ⏲9am-midnight Mon-Wed, 9am-2am Thu & Fri, 10am-2am Sat, 10am-6pm Sun) Gloriously retro Dyrehaven is a hit with the cool, young bohemians of Copenhagen's Vesterbro district. Join them for cheap drinks, simple tasty grub like smørrebrød, and late-night camaraderie.

☆ Entertainment

Copenhagen really revs into gear from Thursday to Saturday when it turns into a genuine 24-hour party city. Club admission is usually around Dkr70, but you can often get in for free if you arrive early. Major international rock acts often play the national stadium. Visit www.aok.dk for full listings.

Culture Box NIGHTCLUB
(www.culture-box.com; Kronprinsessegade 54; ⏲bar 8pm-late Fri & Sat, club usually midnight-6am Fri & Sat) This iconic, two-level nightclub pumps out innovative, noncommercial beats spanning anything from electro and techno to house, dubstep and electronic jazz. Next door you'll find Cocktail Box, handy for a preclub swill.

TOP CHOICE **La Fontaine** LIVE MUSIC
(www.lafontaine.dk, in Danish; Kompagnistræde 11, Strædet; ⏲7pm-5am, live music 11pm-3am Fri & Sat & 9pm-1am Sun) Cosy La Fontaine is a stalwart of the city's thriving jazz scene. It offers live gigs from Friday to Sunday and legendary late-night jam sessions.

Gefährlich BAR, CULTURAL CENTRE
(www.gefarlich.dk; Fælledvej 7, Nørrebro; admission usually free; ⏲11am-midnight Tue, 11am-2am Wed, 11am-3am Thu, 11am-3.30am Fri, 10am-3.30am Sat) This deeply groovy bar-club-restaurant-lounge-cafe-hairdresser-art space (really) gets packed on weekends, with the incriminating evidence usually posted on MySpace by midweek.

ⓘ Information

Internet Access

Hovedbiblioteket (Krystalgade 15; ⏲10am-7pm Mon-Fri, 10am-2pm Sat, to 4pm Sat Oct-Mar) A public library offering free internet access on nine computers.

Sidewalk Express (www.sidewalkexpress.com; Central Station; per 90 min Dkr29; ⏲24hr) Internet cafe inside Central Station.

Left Luggage

Central Station (per 24hr small/large locker Dkr40/50, maximum 72hr; ⏲5.30am-1am Mon-Sat, 6am-1am Sun) Lockers are in the lower level, near the Reventlowsgade exit.

Medical Services

Frederiksberg Hospital (☎38 16 35 22; Nordre Fasanvej 57) West of the city centre, with a 24-hour emergency ward.

Steno Apotek (Vesterbrogade 6c; ⏲24hr) Pharmacy opposite Central Station.

Money

Banks, all of which charge transaction fees, are found throughout the city centre. Banks in the airport arrival and transit halls are open 6am to 10pm daily. The **Forex exchange booth** (Central Station; ⏲8am-9pm) has the lowest fees but you will find other exchange shops all along Strøget.

Tourist Information

Wonderful Copenhagen (www.visitcopenhagen.dk; Vesterbrogade 4a; ⏲9am-8pm Mon-Sat, 10am-6pm Sun Jul & Aug, less hr rest of year) A tourist information centre that distributes the informative *Tourist in Copenhagen*, a free city map and brochures covering all the regions of Denmark.

Travel Agencies

Kilroy Travels (www.kilroytravels.com; Skindergade 28; ⌚11am-5.30pm Mon-Fri, 10am-2pm Sat)

 Getting There & Away

Air

Copenhagen's modern international airport is in Kastrup, 10km southeast of the city centre. Flights connect frequently with most major Danish and Scandinavian destinations. Many airline offices are north of Central Station, near the intersection of Vester Farimagsgade and Vesterbrogade.

Boat

The ferry to Oslo, operated by **DFDS Seaways** (www.dfdsseaways.co.uk; Dampfærgevej 30), departs from the Nordhavn area, north of the city (past Kastellet).

Bus

International buses leave from Central Station; advance reservations on most routes can be made at **Eurolines** (www.eurolines.dk; Reventlowsgade 8).

Car

Close to Copenhagen airport, **Autorental** (www.bilbooking.dk; Amagerstrandvej 418) hires out cars (actually not that old, but usually quite used) from as little as Dkr319 per day. Rates are even more competitive on longer hires.

Train

Long-distance trains arrive and depart from Central Station (Hovedbanegården), a huge complex with numerous eateries and services. Public showers (Dkr20, towel hire Dkr10) are located at the underground toilets opposite the police office.

TRAIN TICKETS

There are three ways of buying a train ticket. **Billetautomats** are coin-operated machines and are the quickest, but only if you've mastered the zone-system prices. They are best for S-Train tickets. If you're not rushed, then **DSB Billetsalg** (⌚5.45am-11.30pm, international ticket sales 9.30am-6pm) is best for reservations and for purchasing international train tickets. Alternatively you can make reservations at **www.dsb.dk**, which has an English-language option.

 Getting Around

Copenhagen boasts a large, efficient public-transport system. Buses, metro and trains use a common fare system based on the number of zones you pass through. The basic fare of Dkr24 for up to two zones covers most city runs and allows transfers between buses and trains on a single ticket as long as they're made within an hour. A 24-hour pass permits unlimited travel in all zones for Dk130.

Bicycle

Köbenhavns Cykler (per day Dkr75) rents out bikes beneath platform 12 at Central Station. City Bikes offers free-use bikes from April to November at 110 bike racks throughout central Copenhagen. Deposit a Dkr20 coin in the stand to release the bike. You can return the bicycle into any rack to get your money back.

Bus

Rådhuspladsen is the main terminus for Copenhagen's vast bus network. Night buses (12.30am to 5am) run on a few major routes.

Metro

The driverless, round-the-clock **metro** (www.m.dk) operates two lines (M1 and M2). Trains run a minimum of every three minutes.

Taxi

Taxis with signs saying '*fri*' (free) can be flagged down. Alternatively, call ☎35 35 35 35.

Train

Seven lines make up the **S-Tog** (S-Train; www.dsb.dk) metropolitan network. All lines pass through Central Station (København H).

AROUND COPENHAGEN

Louisiana Museum of Modern Art

Atmospherically perched beside the Øresund Sea, Denmark's foremost **modern art museum** (www.louisiana.dk; Gl Strandvej 13; adult/child Dkr95/free; ⌚11am-11pm Tue-Fri, 11am-6pm Sat & Sun) features works by Giacometti, Picasso, Warhol, Rauschenberg and many more, as well as outstanding temporary exhibitions. It's a terrific spot even if you're not passionate about modern art, with sculpture-studded gardens, a top-notch cafe and restaurant, and views across to Sweden.

The museum is about a 10-minute walk north on Strandvej from Humlebæk station, which is 36 minutes on the S-train's line C

GETTING INTO TOWN

A train links the airport with Central Station (Dkr36, 12 minutes, every 10 minutes). The airport is 15 minutes and about Dkr250 from the city centre by taxi. The **metro** (www.m.dk) links the airport to the eastern side of the city, stopping at Christianshavn Torv, Kongens Nytorv and Nørreport stations (Dkr48, 13 minutes, every five minutes).

from Copenhagen. If you're day tripping from Copenhagen, it's cheapest to buy a 24-hour public transport pass (Dkr130) from ticket vending machines.

ZEALAND

Though Copenhagen is the centre of gravity for most visitors to Denmark's eastern island, there is plenty to make it worth your while exploring beyond the city limits. This is an island with a rich history, a beautiful coastline and plenty of gentle rolling countryside – it's hardly surprising that many Copenhageners choose to holiday on their home island in summer houses rather than head abroad.

Helsingør (Elsinore)

POP 46,200

Helsingør's top sight is **Kronborg Slot** (www.kronborg.dk; admission Dkr75; ⌚11am-3pm Tue-Sun Jan-Mar, Nov & Dec, to 4pm Tue-Sun Apr & Oct, 10.30am-5pm May-Sep), made famous as the Elsinore Castle of Shakespeare's *Hamlet*. Kronborg's primary function was not as a royal residence, but rather as a grandiose tollhouse, wresting taxes (the infamous and lucrative 'Sound Dues') for more than 400 years from ships passing through the narrow Øresund. The castle is on the northern side of the harbour, within easy walking distance of the train station.

The **tourist office** (www.visitnordsjaelland.com; Havnepladsen 3; ⌚10am-5pm Mon-Fri, to 2pm Sat late Jun-early Aug, reduced hr rest of year) is opposite the train station.

Sleeping & Eating

Danhostel Helsingør HOSTEL €
(☎49 28 49 49; www.helsingorhostel.dk; Nordre Strandvej 24; dm Dkr175, r Dkr475-850; ⌚Feb-Nov) The hostel, housed in the imposing, red-brick Villa Moltke, is 2km northwest of the centre, and is right by the water with its own beach. Rooms are clean and simple.

Helsingør Camping Grønnehave CAMPING GROUND €
(☎49 28 49 50; www.helsingorcamping.dk; Strandalleen 2; campsite per adult Dkr60, cabin Dkr350) A well-spaced beachside camping ground, east of the hostel and close to one of the area's best beaches.

Madam Sprunck CAFE, RESTAURANT €€€
(www.madamsprunck.dk; Stengade 48; salads Dkr92-96, mains Dkr198-225) Housed in a building dating back to 1781, this local institution serves tasty bistro grub, a lavish brunch (Dkr135) and a two-course lunch for Dkr160.

Gæstgivergaarden PUB €€
(Kampergade 11; open sandwiches Dkr59-69, mains Dkr89-149) This traditional Danish pub offers a good-value lunch menu.

Getting There & Away

BOAT Scandlines (www.scandlines.dk) sails around 75 times daily from Helsingør to Helsingborg, in Sweden (return adult/car including 9 passengers from Dkr48/355).

TRAIN Trains from Copenhagen run a few times hourly (Dkr108, 45 minutes). If you're day tripping from Copenhagen, it's cheapest to buy a 24-hour transport pass (Dkr130). Trains departing from Hillerød (Dkr69, 30 minutes) run at least hourly.

Roskilde

POP 46,700

Home to one of northern Europe's best outdoor music festivals, resting place of a millennia of Danish royalty, and the site of several remarkable Viking ship finds, Roskilde is worth the day trip. For information, see the **tourist office** (www.visitroskilde.com; Stændertorvet 1; ⌚10am-5pm Mon-Fri, to 1pm Sat Apr-Jun, to 2pm Sat Jul & Aug, 10am-5pm Mon-Thu, to 4pm Fri, to 1pm Sat Sep-Mar).

Though most of Roskilde's medieval buildings have vanished in fires over the centuries, the imposing, twin-spired **Roskilde Domkirke** (www.roskildedomkirke.dk; Domkirkepladsen; admission Dkr25; ⌚10am-5pm Mon-Fri, to 2pm Sat Jul & Aug, reduced hr rest of year) still dominates the city centre. Started by Bishop Absalon in 1170, its **crypts** contain the sarcophagi of 39 Danish kings and queens. Some are lavishly embellished and guarded by marble statues of knights and women in mourning. Others are simple and unadorned.

Don't miss the excellent, purpose-built **Viking Ship Museum** (www.vikingskibesmuseet.dk; Vindeboder 12; admission May-Sep Dkr100, Oct-Apr Dkr70; ⏲10am-5pm), which contains five reconstructed Viking longboats.

Harbourside **Danhostel Roskilde** (☎46 35 21 84; www.danhostel.dk/roskilde; Vindeboder 7; dm Dkr180-200, r Dkr400-600) is an especially smart and modern hostel, even by Danish standards. Though made up of small three- to eight-bed dorms, most are offered as private rooms. It's adjacent to the Viking Ship Museum.

Trains from Copenhagen to Roskilde are frequent (Dkr92, 25 minutes). From Copenhagen by car, Rte 21 leads to Roskilde; upon approaching the city, exit onto Rte 156, which leads into the centre.

BORNHOLM

POP 42,200

Bornholm is a little Baltic pearl. Though a Danish island, it lies some 200km east of the mainland, north of Poland, and boasts more hours of sunshine than any other part of the country. It also has gorgeous sandy beaches, idyllic fishing villages, numerous historic sights, endless cycle paths, and a burgeoning reputation for culinary curiosities, ceramic artists and glass makers.

The **tourist office** (Bornholms Velkomstcenter; www.bornholm.info; Nordre Kystvej 3, Rønne; ⏲9am-5.30pm end Jun–mid-Aug, reduced hr rest of year) with information on accommodation, activities, events and transport, is a few minutes' walk from the harbour and has masses of information on all of Bornholm. There's free internet access at the **public library** (Pingels Allé; ⏲10am-7pm Mon-Tue, to 6pm Wed-Fri, to 2pm Sat), for which you must book a slot first.

BORNHOLM BY BIKE

Cycling is a great way to explore Bornholm. The island is criss-crossed by more than 200km of bike trails, many built over former rail routes. You can download bicycle routes across the island for free at www.cykel.bornholm.info. In Rønne, **Bornholms Cykeludlejning** (www.bornholms-cykeludlejning.dk, in Danish; Nordre Kystvej 5; per day/week Dkr70/360), next to the tourist office, has a large fleet of bikes for hire. Bicycles can usually be rented from hostels and camping grounds around the island for about Dkr60 a day.

Sights & Activities

The harbour town of **Svaneke** has award-winning historic buildings, especially those near the village church, a few minutes' walk south of the centre. The **tourist office** (Peter F Heerings Gade 7; ⏲10am-4pm Mon-Fri Jun-Aug) is only open in the summer.

Gudhjem is the perfect Danish seaside holiday village, with plenty of places to eat and stay, and excellent beaches within 1km or so. Its charming half-timbered houses and sloping streets rolling down to the pleasant harbour make it one of the island's most attractive towns. The **tourist office** (Åbogade 7; ⏲8.30am-noon & 12.30-3.15pm) is a block inland from the harbour, alongside the library. Gudhjem has narrow streets and parking can be difficult. There's a public car park northwest of the harbour.

Sleeping & Eating

Fifty metres from the harbourside bus stop, **Danhostel Gudhjem** (☎56 48 50 35; www.danhostel-gudhjem.dk; dm/s/d Dkr195/340/440) is in an attractive spot right by the harbour, with small cosy, bright-white six-bed dorms. The management also handles the pleasant **Therns Hotel** (☎56 48 50 35; www.therns-hotel.dk; Brøddegade 31; s Dkr750, d Dkr850-1050).

Further along is the waterfront smokehouse **Gudhjem Rogeri** (buffet Dkr98), the oldest on the island (dating from 1910), with an all-you-can-eat buffet and some challenging seating, including on the upper floor, which is reached by rope ladder. It has live folk, country and rock music most nights in summer.

Getting There & Around

From Copenhagen, **DSB** (www.dsb.dk) offers a combined train/catamaran ticket (one way Dkr294, three hours), which includes train travel to Ystad (Sweden) and high-speed catamaran from Ystad to Rønne on Bornholm. This is the most cost- and time-efficient way to get to Bornholm from Copenhagen.

Bornholmer Færgen (www.bornholmerfaergen.dk; adult Dkr266, car Dkr1532-1550) operates an overnight ferry service from Køge, around 30 minutes south of Copenhagen by train, to Bornholm. The ferry departs daily at 12.30am and arrives at 6am.

A good, inexpensive bus service around the island is operated by **Bornholms Amts Trafikselskab** (BAT; www.bat.dk; day/weekly pass

RESTAURANT KADEAU

A short drive west of Dueodde lies **Restaurant Kadeau** (☎56 97 82 50; www.kadeau.dk, in Danish; Baunevej 18; lunch mains Dkr120-240, 2-/3-/4-course dinner Dkr395/425/465; ⊙lunch & dinner daily Jul & Aug, lunch & dinner Wed-Sun May, Jun & Sep). Overlooking lapping waves and sand dunes, this tucked-away restaurant is Bornholm's best. The staff often hit the island's coast and forests foraging for native ingredients to use in ambitious, modern dishes such as salt-and-sugar cured salmon with smoked cheese and seasonal vegetables, or pork belly with pickled and raw beets, malt crumble and sorrel. Despite its A-list rep, service is genuine and relaxed... And did we mention the view? Book ahead.

Dkr150/500). Fares are based on a zone system and cost Dkr12 per zone; the maximum fare is for five zones.

FUNEN

POP 454,300

As a stepping stone from Zealand to the Jutland Peninsula, the rural island of Funen is often overlooked by visitors who, at most, make a whistle-stop visit to Hans Christian Andersen's birthplace and museum in the island's capital, Odense. But there is more to Funen ('Fyn' in Danish) than this: the towns of Svendborg and Faaborg have a gentle charm, particularly in summer, and there are excellent, clean beaches all around the island.

Odense

POP 166,300

There's plenty more to Odense than the legacy of Denmark's most famous son, the writer and traveller Hans Christian Andersen. Nevertheless, HCA's birthplace and adjoining museum are the number-one draw, even if there is no concrete evidence to show he ever lived in the house in question.

The **tourist office** (www.visitodense.com; ⊙9.30am-6pm Mon-Fri, 10am-3pm Sat, 11am-2pm Sun Jul & Aug, reduced hr rest of year) is at Rådhus, a 15-minute walk from the train station.

Sights

The **HC Andersens Museum** (www.museum.odense.dk; Bangs Boder 29; admission Dkr60; ⊙10am-4pm Tue-Sun Jan-late Jun & Sep-Dec, 10am-5pm late Jun-Aug) lies amid the picturesque houses of the old, working-class part of Odense, now often referred to as the 'HCA Quarter'. The museum puts Andersen's life into an interesting historical context and is leavened by some good audiovisual material.

Odense's 13th-century Gothic cathedral, **Sankt Knuds Kirke** (Flakhaven; admission free; ⊙10am-4pm Mon-Sat, noon-4pm Sun, to 5pm Sat Apr-Oct), reflects the city's medieval wealth and stature. The stark white interior has a handsome rococo pulpit, a dazzling 16th-century altarpiece and a gilded wooden triptych crowded with over 300 carved figures, and is said to be one of the finest pieces of religious art in northern Europe.

Sleeping

Cab Inn HOTEL €€
(☎63 14 57 00; www.cabinn.com; Østre Stationsvej 7; s Dkr485, d Dkr675-805) The reliably cheap and modern bargain hotel chain has arrived in Odense with a 200-plus-room place right beside the train station.

DCU Camping CAMPING GROUND €
(☎66 11 47 02; www.camping-odense.dk; Odensevej 102; adult/tent Dkr74/45;) Just under 4km from the city centre, this camping ground is top notch, with an open-air pool, various sports facilities and 13 chalets for rent. Prices drop in the low season.

Danhostel Odense City HOSTEL €
(☎63 11 04 25; www.cityhostel.dk; Østre Stationsvej 31; dm/s/d/tr incl breakfast from Dkr200/400/500/500) An excellent, modern, 139-bed place with four- and six-bed dorms, a kitchen and laundry facilities located alongside the train and bus stations.

Eating & Drinking

There are numerous fast-food places along Kongensgade. Odense Banegård Center, which incorporates the train and bus stations, has low-priced options, including a **bakery** (⊙5.45am-6.30pm Mon-Fri, 7am-5.30pm Sat & Sun), a supermarket and a pub.

Cuckoos Nest RESTAURANT, BAR €€
(www.cuckoos.dk; Vestergade 73; mains Dkr159-169) A great stalwart of Odense's nightlife scene is this cavernous bar and restaurant on the corner of the main shopping street and Brandts

Passage. A lengthy, wide-ranging menu includes everything from nachos and burgers to *confit de canard* (duck confit).

Joe & The Juice CAFE €
(Vestergade 20; juices Dkr38, sandwiches Dkr45; ⌚10am-6pm Mon-Thu, to 8pm Fri, to 5pm Sat) Attached to the Magasin department store, this hip chain peddles freshly squeezed juices with names like 'Total Rehab', decent coffee and freshly made sandwiches.

Getting There & Around

Odense is on the main railway line between Copenhagen (Dkr244, 1½ hours, at least twice hourly), Århus (Dkr212, 1¾ hours, twice hourly), Aalborg (Dkr327, three hours, once or twice hourly) and Esbjerg (Dkr193, 1¾ hours, one to three times hourly). Buses leave from the rear of the train station.

Bikes can be rented at the tourist office (per day/week Dkr100/500).

JUTLAND

Jutland (Jylland) is Denmark's largest land mass by far. The area where the borders meet is a rather monotonous procession of moor and marsh but further north things improve as you hit the pretty, forested lake district. Cosmopolitan Århus, Denmark's second city, hugs the eastern coast. Further north still, there's the windswept western and northern coasts (a windsurfer's dream) lined with vast sandy beaches and an incredible, constantly shifting landscape of mammoth, grassy dunes. Then there's Grenen, a bracing, epic sandy spit where the currents collide in a maelstrom of white water.

Århus

POP 242,900

Århus (the second-largest city in Denmark) has tended to labour in the cultural shadows of Copenhagen, but all the same it is a terrific city in which to spend a day or two. It is the cultural and commercial heart of Jutland and has one of Denmark's best music and entertainment scenes (there is a very large student population on account of the city's university), a well-preserved historic quarter and plenty to see and do.

Århus is fairly compact and easy to get around. The train station is on the southern side of the city centre. The pedestrian shopping streets of Ryesgade, Søndergade and Sankt Clements Torv extend around 1km from the station to the cathedral at the heart of the old city.

Sights & Activities

TOP CHOICE **ARoS** MUSEUM
(www.aros.dk; Aros Allé 2; admission Dkr95; ⌚10am-5pm Thu-Sun & Tue, to 10pm Wed) Århus' showpiece art museum may look rather mundane from the outside but inside it's all sweeping curves, soaring spaces and white walls. One of the top three art galleries in Denmark, it is home to a comprehensive collection of 19th- and 20th-century Danish art and a wide range of arresting and vivid contemporary art. Hard to miss is Ron Mueck's startlingly lifelike giant *Boy* and Olafur Eliasson's whimsical *Your Rainbow Panorama,* a 360-degree rooftop walkway offering technicolour views of the city.

Den Gamle By MUSEUM
(The Old Town; www.dengamleby.dk; Viborgvej 2; admission Dkr125; ⌚9am-6pm late Jun-early Sep, reduced hr low season) The Danes' seemingly limitless enthusiasm for dressing up and re-creating history reaches its zenith at this engaging open-air museum. On display are 75 half-timbered houses brought here from around Denmark and reconstructed as a provincial town, complete with a functioning bakery, silversmith and bookbinder. It's a 20-minute walk from the city centre. Buses 3, 14, 25 and 55 will take you there.

Århus Domkirke CHURCH
(Bispetorvet; admission free; ⌚9.30am-4pm Mon & Wed-Sat, 10.30am-4pm Tue) Århus' impressive cathedral is Denmark's longest, with a lofty nave that spans nearly 100m. The original Romanesque chapel at the eastern end dates from the 12th century, while most of the rest of the church is 15th-century Gothic.

Moesgård PARK, MUSEUM
Visit Moesgård, 5km south of the city centre, for its glorious beech woods and the trails threading through them towards sandy beaches. Visit for the well-presented history exhibits from the Stone Age to the Viking Age at **Moesgård Museum of Prehistory** (admission Dkr60; ⌚10am-5pm Apr-Sep, to 4pm Tue-Sun Oct-Mar). But above all else, visit Moesgård for the museum's most dramatic exhibit: the 2000-year-old **Grauballe Man**, or Grauballemanden, whose astonishingly well-preserved body was found in 1952 at the village of Grauballe, 35km west of Århus.

Århus

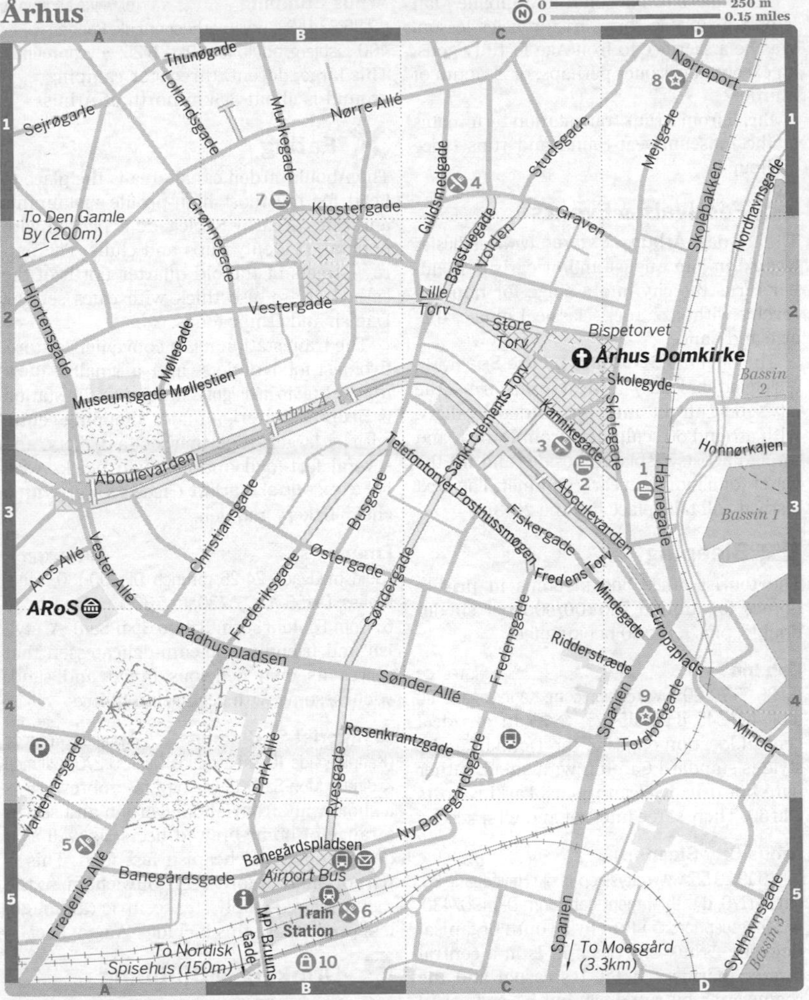

Århus

Top Sights

Århus Domkirke ... C2
ARoS ... A3

Sleeping

1 Århus City Sleep-In ... D3
2 Cab Inn Århus ... C3

Eating

3 Bryggeriet St Clemens ... C3
4 Emmery's ... C1
5 Føtex Supermarket ... A5
6 Supermarket ... B5

Drinking

7 Café Gemmestedet ... B1

Entertainment

8 Musikcaféen ... D1
9 Train ... D4

Shopping

10 Bruuns Galleri ... B5

The superb display on the Grauballe Man is part history lesson, part forensics lesson. Was he a sacrifice to Iron Age fertility gods, an executed prisoner perhaps, or a victim of murder?

Bus 6 from Århus train station terminates at the museum year-round and runs twice an hour.

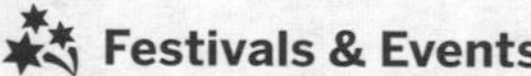

Festivals & Events

The 10-day **Århus Festival** (www.aarhusfestuge.dk) in late August and/or early September turns the city into a stage for nonstop revelry with jazz, rock, classical music, theatre and dance.

The biennial **Sculpture by the Sea** (www.sculpturebythesea.dk) festival transforms the city's beachfront into an outdoor gallery, with around 60 sculptures from Danish and foreign artists displayed beside (and in) the water for a month in early summer. The next festival will take place in June 2013.

Sleeping

The tourist office books rooms in private homes for around Dkr400/500 per single/double, plus a Dkr50 booking fee.

Cab Inn Århus HOTEL €€

(86 75 70 00; www.cabinn.com; Kannikegade 14; s Dkr485-545, d Dkr615-675;) In an ideal central location opposite the Domkirke, the style is standard Cab Inn with small, rather bare but usually clean rooms. Parking costs Dkr60. There's free internet and wi-fi access.

Århus City Sleep-In HOSTEL €

(86 19 20 55; www.citysleep-in.dk; Havnegade 20; dm Dkr170, d with/without bathroom Dkr490/430; 24hr reception;) Run by a youth organisation, the Århus City Sleep-In is in a central former mariners' hotel. It's casual and the rooms are a bit run-down but it's a cheerful place and by far the best budget option in the centre. Sheet hire costs Dkr50 and padlocks are Dkr25 if you don't have your own. There's a TV, pool table, guest kitchen and laundry facilities.

Danhostel Århus HOSTEL €

(86 21 21 20; www.aarhus-danhostel.dk; Marienlundsvej 10; dm Dkr165, r Dkr570-810; Jan–mid-Dec) It's 4km north of the city centre but well worth considering for the lovely parkland setting in a renovated 1850s dance hall. It's at the edge of the Risskov Woods and not far from the beach. Buses 6 and 9 pass nearby.

Århus Camping CAMPING GROUND €

(86 23 11 33; www.aarhusnord.dk; Randersvej 400, Lisbjerg; adult/tent Dkr81/25; year-round) This large, decent, three-star camping ground is about 3.5km north of Århus.

Eating

The Åboulevarden canal area is the place to head for the most high-profile restaurants and cafes. Nearby Skolegade is packed with popular, studenty pubs and clubs. The narrow streets of the old quarter north of the cathedral are also thick with cafes serving Danish and ethnic foods.

The train station has a convenience store, two fast-food outlets, and a small **supermarket** (to midnight). Adjoining the station is **Bruuns Galleri**, a major shopping centre with a larger supermarket, a bakery and several fast-food options. Two blocks west is **Føtex supermarket** (Frederiks Allé), with a cheap bakery and deli.

Emmery's CAFE, BAKERY €

(Guldsmedgade 24-26; brunch Dkr100-130, sandwiches Dkr55-70; 7.30am-5.30pm Mon-Thu, to 6.30pm Fri, to 3.30pm Sat, to 3pm Sun) A stylish and friendly cafe-cum-delicatessen that serves its own delicious bread and sandwiches, some with vegetarian fillings.

Bryggeriet St Clemens MICROBREWERY €€

(Kannikegade 10 & 12; mains Dkr100-270; lunch & dinner Mon-Sat) This cosy microbrewery is a short walk from Åboulevarden and serves a range of home-brewed beers, as well as a decent range of cheapish fast food. This is part of the Hereford Beefstouw chain, so the menu is predictably steakcentric (although, less predictably, this includes Wagyu beef).

Drinking & Clubbing

Århus has a vibrant music scene with something for all ages and tastes. For the lowdown on what's happening, click onto www.visitaarhus.com.

Café Gemmestedet CAFE

(www.cafegemmestedet.dk, in Danish; Gammel Munkegade 1) This cosy, bohemian-spirited cafe-cum-bar is known for its kookily named cocktails, interesting beers and laid-back, convivial vibe.

Train LIVE MUSIC & CLUB

(www.train.dk, in Danish; Toldbodgade 6; until 5am Thu-Sat) One of the biggest venues in Denmark stages concerts by international rock,

NORDISK SPISEHUS

Nordisk Spisehus (☎86 17 70 99; www.nordiskspisehus.dk; MP Bruunsgade 31; mains Dkr180-255, 3 courses Dkr350, weekend brunch Dkr149) is a must for kronor-conscious gourmands. Dubbed a 'budget' version of Copenhagen's Noma – arguably the world's most famous Modern Scandinavian restaurant – it serves clean, seasonal dishes using regional delicacies such as free-range veal, Nordic cheeses and fjord prawns (shrimp). Don't miss the home-smoked salmon, given an extra last-minute hay smoking beneath a glass cloche at your table. It is served with a dazzlingly fresh salad with salt-cured apples, radish and cucumber (Dkr98). Service is friendly and knowledgeable.

pop and country stars, and there's a late-night disco.

Musikcaféen LIVE MUSIC
(www.musikcafeen.dk, in Danish; Mejlgade 53; ⏱8.30pm-2am Mon-Sat) Along with the adjacent Gyngen, this place is an alternative and often vibrant venue with rock, jazz and world music. Both are a showcase for hopefuls and up-and-coming acts.

Information

Bus station lockers cost Dkr10 for 24 hours. Train station lockers cost Dkr20 to Dkr40 for the same period.

From September 2011, numerous information booths are set to replace the current tourist office. Check www.visitaarhus.com for updates and locations.

Getting There & Away

Air

The airport, in Tirstrup, is 44km northeast of Århus. SAS flies one way from Copenhagen for around Dkr300. Budget carrier Ryanair flies once daily between London Stansted and Århus.

Boat

Mols-Linien (www.mols-linien.dk) runs car ferries from Århus to Odden in northwest Zealand (adult Dkr325, car and five passengers Dkr725, 65 minutes).

Bus

The **bus station** (Fredensgade) has a DSB cafe and small supermarket. **Abildskou** (www.abildskou.dk) buses run a few times daily between Århus and Copenhagen's Valby station (Dkr290, three hours) and the airport, also stopping in Odense. For info on travel to other destinations in Jutland, see www.dsb.dk.

Train

Trains to Århus, via Odense, leave Copenhagen twice hourly (Dkr339, three hours). There are regular trains to Aalborg (Dkr171, 1½ hours) and Esbjerg (Dkr235, 2½ hours). Take a ticket and wait your turn to be served at the counter.

Getting Around

The airport bus to Århus train station costs Dkr95 and takes approximately 45 minutes. Check times to the airport at the stands outside the train station. The taxi fare to the airport is about Dkr750.

Most in-town buses stop in front of the train station or around the corner on Park Allé.

Aalborg

POP 123,400

Aalborg has a vibrant nightlife, thanks to a large student population, and several worthwhile sights, not least the remarkable Lindholm Høje, Denmark's largest Viking burial ground.

The town centre is a 10-minute walk north on Boulevarden from the train and bus stations. The **tourist office** (www.visitaalborg.com; Østerågade 8; ⏱11am-8pm Mon-Fri, 10am-2pm Sat) has friendly and helpful staff, with masses of information, including a diary of events, *What's on in Aalborg*. **Hovedbiblioteket** (City library; Rendsburggade 2; ⏱10am-7pm Mon-Thu, to 6pm Fri, to 2pm Sat) offers free internet access.

Sights

The whitewashed **Buldolfi Domkirke** marks the centre of the old town and has colourful frescoes in the foyer. About 75m east of the cathedral is the **Nordjyllands Historiske Museum** (www.nordmus.dk, in Danish; Algade 48; admission Dkr30; ⏱10am-5pm Tue-Sun), with artefacts from prehistory to the present, and furnishings and interiors that hint at the wealth Aalborg's merchants enjoyed during the Renaissance.

TOP CHOICE **Lindholm Høje** (admission free; ⏱dawn-dusk) is a wonderfully atmospheric Viking burial ground where nearly 700 graves from the Iron Age and Viking Age are strewn around a hilltop pasture ringed by a wall of tall beech trees. The **museum**

(☎99 31 74 40; admission Dkr60; ⏲10am-5pm Apr-Oct, 10am-4pm Tue-Sun Nov-Mar), adjacent to the field, depicts the site's history, while huge murals behind the exhibits speculate on what the people of Lindholm looked like and how they lived. Lindholm Høje is 15 minutes from Aalborg centre on bus 2.

Lindholm Høje is located on the north side of Limfjorden (Chalk Fjord), which was a kind of Viking motorway providing easy and speedy access to the Atlantic for longboat raiding parties. It's perhaps not surprising then that by far the most important piece of Aalborg's historical heritage is the Viking one.

Sleeping

Accommodation options are pretty good in town, inexpensive compared to other Danish destinations and not generally in massive demand.

Cab Inn Aalborg HOTEL €€
(☎96 20 30 00; www.cabinn.com; Fjordgade 20; s/d/tr Dkr485/615/805) The cheap and reliable Cab Inn chain recently added Aalborg to its portfolio with this modern, centrally located hotel. All 239 rooms have TV and bathroom.

Danhostel Aalborg HOSTEL €
(☎98 11 60 44; www.danhostelaalborg.dk; Skydebanevej 50; dm/s/d Dkr288/460/530; @) Handy for boating activities on the fjord but hardly central, the hostel is at the marina 4km west of the centre. It also runs an adjacent camping ground with cabins. Otherwise, the facilities are rather basic.

Aalborg Camping CAMPING GROUND €
(☎98 11 60 44; www.aalborgcamping.dk; Skydebanevej 50; adult/tent Dkr50/45) This pleasant two-star camping ground is popular with naturists.

Eating & Drinking

Eating out in Aalborg is very much about quantity rather than quality. If it's just ballast you want with your alcohol, then Jomfru Ane Gade, a lively, pedestrian street jammed solid with fast-food-style restaurants and bars, is the place to go.

Penny Lane CAFE €
(Boulevarden 10; ⏲10am-6pm Mon-Fri, 9.30am-2pm Sat) This is one of the most charming cafes in Jutland, featuring a well-stocked delicatessen and terrific cakes and pastries.

Studenterhuset BAR
(Student Union; Gammeltorv 10; ⏲Mon-Sat, closed mid-Jul–mid-Aug) A convivial budget drinking and entertainment option. Lined with bookshelves, it's surprisingly upmarket and, well, studious for a student union. There's inexpensive beer, regular live bands and DJ nights.

Getting There & Around

Trains run to Århus (Dkr171, 1½ hours, at least hourly) and Frederikshavn (Dkr99, one hour, hourly). **Abildskou** (www.abildskou.dk) buses run to Copenhagen (Dkr330, 5½ hours) once or twice daily.

City buses leave from the intersection of Østerågade and Nytorv. The bus fare is Dkr18 to any place in greater Aalborg.

Frederikshavn

POP 23,300

A transport hub rather than a compelling destination, this bustling port town is pleasant enough but not one to linger in.

An overhead walkway leads from the ferry terminal to the **tourist office** (www.visitfrederikshavn.dk; Skandiatorv 1; ⏲9am-4pm Mon-Sat, 10am-1pm Sun late Jun–early Aug, reduced hr rest of year). The train station and adjacent bus terminal are a 10-minute walk to the north.

Danhostel Frederikshavn (☎98 42 14 75; www.danhostel.dk/frederikshavn; Buhlsvej 6; dm/s/d Dkr100/350/400; ⏲Feb-Nov) is a pleasant place, 2km north of the ferry terminal, with chalet-style, six-bed dorms.

Super Best (Læsøgade 16) supermarket, located next to the tourist office, is a good place to pick up provisions, especially if you're catching a ferry to expensive Norway.

Getting There & Away

From Frederikshavn, **Stena Line** (www.stenaline.co.uk) runs ferries four to eight times daily to Göteborg, Sweden (adult/car including five passengers from Dkr100/460, two to 3½ hours). It also runs to Oslo six to seven times weekly (8½ hours). Prices vary by season.

Frederikshavn is the northern terminus of the DSB train line. Trains run about hourly south to Aalborg (Dkr99) and then onto Copenhagen (Dkr393). **Nordjyske Jernbaner** (www.njba.dk, in Danish) runs trains to Skagen (Dkr54) hourly on weekdays and around every two hours on weekends. Trains to Hirtshals (Dkr63) run roughly every hour.

Skagen

POP 8600

Skagen is a magical place, both bracing and beautiful. Artists discovered its luminous light and its colourful, wind-blasted, heath-and-dune landscape in the mid-19th century.

Today Skagen is a very popular tourist resort, packed in high summer. But the sense of a more picturesque Skagen survives and the town's older neighbourhood, Gammel Skagen, 5km west, is filled with distinctive, single-storey, yellow-walled, red-roofed houses. The peninsula is lined with fine beaches, including a sandy stretch on the eastern end of Østre Strandvej, a 15-minute walk from the town centre.

Sankt Laurentii Vej, Skagen's main street, runs almost the entire length of this long, thin town, and is never more than five minutes from the waterfront. The **tourist office** (www.skagen-tourist.dk; Vestre Strandvej 10; ⏲9am-4pm Mon-Sat, 10am-2pm Sun late Jun–late Aug, reduced hr rest of year) is by the harbour.

Sleeping & Eating

Grenen Camping CAMPING GROUND €

(☎98 44 25 46; www.grenencamping.dk; Fyrvej 16; adult Dkr85) A fine seaside location with semi-private tent sites and pleasant four-bunk huts, 1.5km northeast of Skagen centre. The only downside is the rather tightly bunched sites.

Danhostel Skagen HOSTEL €

(☎98 44 22 00; www.danhostel.dk/skagen; Rolighedsvej 2; dm Dkr150, s/d Dkr500/600; ⏲mid-Feb–Nov) Danhostel is well kept, very popular and 1km from the centre, so book ahead in summer. Rates drop sharply in low season.

Around half-a-dozen shacks line the harbour selling good seafood to eat inside, outside or takeaway. Freshly caught prawns are the favourite fare, costing around Dkr95 for a generous helping. You'll find a couple of pizzerias, Mexican restaurants, a burger joint and an ice-cream shop clustered near each other on Havnevej. The supermarket **Super Brugsen** (Sankt Laurentii Vej 28) has a bakery.

Getting There & Around

Nordjyske Jernbaner (www.njba.dk, in Danish) runs trains to Frederikshavn (Dkr54, 35 minutes) once or twice hourly on weekdays and every two hours on weekends. The seasonal Skagerakkeren bus 99 runs between Hirtshals and Skagen (Dkr45, 1½ hours, two to four daily late June to early August). The same bus continues to Hjørring and Løkken.

Cycling is an excellent way of exploring Skagen and the surrounding area. Close to the tourist office, **Cykelhandler** (Vestre Strandvej 4; per day Dkr70) rents out bicycles through the liquor store next door.

Skagen is very busy with traffic in high season. You will find convenient car parks (Dkr12 per hour, free between 6pm and 9am) near the harbour: one between the tourist office and the waterfront; the other, one block west of the tourist office.

Hirtshals

POP 6300

A busy, modern little town, thanks to a large commercial fishing harbour and ferry terminal, Hirtshals has an easy, friendly character, an excellent aquarium and some fine stretches of beach. For information, pop in to the **tourist office** (www.visithirtshals.com; Nörregade 40; ⏲9am-4pm Mon-Sat Jul & Aug, reduced hr rest of the year).

Hirtshals' big draw is the **Nordsøen Oceanarium** (www.nordsoenoceanarium.dk; Willemoesvej 2; admission Dkr145; ⏲9am-6pm Jul-Aug, to 5pm Apr-Jun, Sep & Oct, 9am-4pm Mon-Fri, to 5pm Sat & Sun Feb, Mar, Nov, Dec, closed Jan), an impressive aquarium that re-creates a slice of the North Sea in a massive four-storey tank containing elegantly balletic schools of thousands of fish. Divers feed the fish at 1pm and the seals at 11am and 3pm.

Hirtshals Hostel (☎98 94 12 48; www.danhostelnord.dk/hirtshals; Kystvejen 53; dm/s/d Dkr150/400/520; ⏲Mar-Oct) occupies a bland building and offers basic facilities about 1km from the centre. The saving grace is its location a bucket-and-spade's throw from the beach.

Getting There & Away

Ferry company **Color Line** (www.colorline.com) runs year-round services to the Norwegian ports of Larvik (3¾ hours, once or twice daily) and Kristiansand (three to four hours, once or twice daily). Fares on both routes range from Dkr200 per adult midweek in the low season to Dkr500 on summer weekends for passengers, and Dkr310 to Dkr660 for cars. **Fjord Line** (www.fjordline.dk) goes to Stavanger and Bergen in Norway (car to Stavanger from Dkr765; to Bergen from Dkr1232).

Hirtshals' main train station, 500m south of the ferry harbour, connects Hirtshals with Hjørring (Dkr24), 20 minutes to the south. Trains run at least hourly. From Hjørring you can take a DSB train to Aalborg (Dkr81) or Frederikshavn (Dkr54).

Ribe

POP 8200

The charming, crooked cobblestone streets of Ribe date from 869, making it one of Scandinavia's oldest and Denmark's most attractive towns. It is a delightful chocolate-box confection of half-timbered, 16th-century houses, clear-flowing streams and water meadows.

There's a **tourist office** (www.visitribe.dk; Torvet 3; ⌚9am-6pm Mon-Fri, 10am-5pm Sat, 10am-2pm Sun Jul & Aug, reduced hr rest of year).

Dominating the heart of the town, **Ribe Domkirke** (Torvet; admission cathedral/steeple free/Dkr10) boasts a variety of styles from Romanesque to Gothic. The highlight is the climb up the steeple for breathtaking views.

Ribes Vikinger (www.ribesvikinger.dk; Odins Plads 1; admission Dkr60; ⌚10am-6pm Jul & Aug, to 4pm Apr-Jun, Sep & Oct, to 4pm Tue-Sun Nov-Mar) is a substantial museum opposite the train station. It has archaeological displays of Ribe's Viking past, including a reconstructed marketplace and Viking ship, with lots of hands-on features.

The tourist office maintains a list of singles/doubles in private homes from around Dkr300/400.

Danhostel Ribe (☎75 42 06 20; www.danhostel-ribe.dk; Sankt Pedersgade 16; dm Dkr170, s Dkr340-580, d Dkr380-580; ⌚mid-Feb–mid-Dec) is a modern, 170-bed hostel with friendly staff and a good, uncrowded location. The rooms at the top are especially appealing and worth the extra cost. In July, a bed in one of the larger dorms costs Dkr120.

Trains run once or twice hourly between Esbjerg and Ribe (Dkr60, 40 minutes).

UNDERSTAND DENMARK

History

The Mighty Vikings

The Danes are thought to have migrated south from Sweden around AD 500. What we think of as modern Denmark was an important trading centre within the Viking empire. In the late 9th century, warriors led by the Viking chieftain Hardegon conquered the Jutland Peninsula. The Danish monarchy, Europe's oldest, dates back to Hardegon's son, Gorm the Old. Gorm's son, Harald Bluetooth, completed the conquest of Denmark and spearheaded the conversion of the Danes to Christianity. Successive Danish kings sent their subjects to row their longboats to England and to conquer most of the Baltic region.

War & Wonder

In 1397 Margrethe I of Denmark established a union between Denmark, Norway and Sweden to counter the influence of the powerful Hanseatic League. Sweden withdrew from the union in 1523 and over the next few hundred years Denmark and Sweden fought numerous border skirmishes and a few fully fledged wars, largely over control of the Baltic Sea. Norway remained under Danish rule until 1814.

In the 16th century the Reformation swept through the country, accompanied by church burnings and civil warfare. The fighting ended in 1536, the Catholic Church was ousted and the Danish Lutheran Church, headed by the monarchy, was established.

Denmark's 'Golden Age' was under Christian IV (1588–1648), with Renaissance cities, castles and fortresses flourishing throughout his kingdom. In 1625 Christian IV, hoping to neutralise Swedish expansion, entered an ill-advised and protracted struggle known as the Thirty Years War. The Swedes triumphed and won large chunks of Danish territory.

The Modern Nation

Denmark remained neutral throughout WWI and also declared its neutrality at the outbreak of WWII. Nevertheless, on 9 April 1940, the Germans invaded, initially allowing the Danes a degree of autonomy. However, in August 1943 the Germans took outright control. The Danish Resistance movement mushroomed and 7000 Jewish Danes were smuggled into neutral Sweden.

Denmark joined NATO in 1949, and the European Community, now the EU, in 1973. In 1993 Denmark narrowly voted to accept the Maastricht Treaty, which established the terms of a European economic and political union, but only after being granted exemptions from common-defence and single-currency provisions. They also voted not to adopt the euro in 2000.

In 2004 the country's most eligible bachelor Crown Prince Frederik married Australian Mary Donaldson in a hugely popular storybook wedding. It has not all been fairy tales, though. Critics say Denmark's increasingly tough immigration laws are proof of creeping xenophobia and racism, earning it a rebuke from the European Council.

Meanwhile, in 2006 the Danes were deeply traumatised when the national newspaper *Jyllands Posten* printed controversial cartoon depictions of the prophet Mohammed, leading to outrage and violence against Danish embassies in the Middle East. This seemed to have little impact on the popularity of their long-serving Prime Minister Anders Fogh Rasmussen, who was returned to power in 2007, after which he handed over the post to his cabinet colleague Lars Løkke Rasmussen to take up a new job as NATO Secretary General.

People

The Danes are tolerant and modest yet confident in their country and its achievements. They are an outwardly serious people, yet with an ironic sense of humour closely akin to the English. They have a strong sense of family and an admirable environmental sensitivity. Above all, they are the most egalitarian of people – they officially have the smallest gap between rich and poor in the world – proud of their social equality, although this can lead to a sense that they are somewhat homogenous. Of Denmark's 5.5 million inhabitants, 10.1% are of non-Danish origin.

Food

Throughout this chapter, the following price indicators have been used (prices refer to the cost of a main course):

€€€ more than Dkr190

€€ Dkr100 to Dkr190

€ less than Dkr100

Arts

By far the most famous Danish author is fairy-tale master Hans Christian Andersen. Other prominent Danish scribes include religious philosopher Søren Kierkegaard, whose writings were a forerunner of existentialism, and Karen Blixen, who penned *Out of Africa* and *Babette's Feast,* both made into acclaimed movies in the 1980s.

For a small country Denmark has had a massive global impact in the fields of architecture and design. Arne Jacobsen, Verner Panton, Jörn Utzon and Hans J Wegner are now considered among the foremost designers of the 20th century.

The last decade or so has seen director Lars von Trier stir up repeated controversy – and win numerous international film prizes – with his challenging films such as *Breaking the Waves, Dancer in the Dark* and *Dogville.*

Before the 19th century, Danish art had consisted mainly of formal portraiture. Late in that century, though, the 'Skagen School' evolved towards outdoor painting of scenes from working life, especially of fishing communities on the northern coasts of Jutland and Zealand. Stars of the contemporary Danish art scene include conceptual artists Jeppe Hein and Olafur Eliasson.

Environment

If you arrive in Denmark at Copenhagen airport you will see the country's major contribution to improving the global environment: a row of wind turbines. Turbines such as these provide the country with around 20% of its energy requirements and the company that makes them, Vestas, is the world leader in wind-turbine technology. Danes also lead the way in the consumption of organic produce, recycling and environmentally friendly transport: more Danes commute by bicycle than any other European nationality.

Still commonly seen in Denmark are wild hare, deer and many species of birds, including magpies, coots, swans and ducks. Restoration programs have brought some wetland habitats back from the brink, helping endangered species such as the freshwater otter as well as beavers, which have been reintroduced to Denmark. The Danes are particularly proud of their eagles – they have two pairs of golden eagles that live in Lille Vildemose, close to Aalborg on Jutland, and are national celebrities.

SURVIVAL GUIDE

Directory A-Z

Accommodation

In this chapter prices quoted are the minimum-maximum for rooms with a private bathroom, and unless otherwise stated include breakfast. The following price indicators apply (for a high-season double room):

€€€ more than €200

€€ €110 to €200

€ less than €110

CAMPING & CABINS

Denmark's 478 camping grounds typically charge from Dkr70 to Dkr85 per person to pitch a tent. Many places add about Dkr25 for the tent. A camping pass (available at any camping ground) is required (Dkr100). If you do not have a seasonal pass you pay an extra Dkr35 a night for a temporary pass.

The **Danish Camping Association** (www.campingraadet.dk; Campingrådet, Mosedalvej 15, Valby) inspects and grades Danish camping grounds using a star system and carries a full list on its website.

HOSTELS

The national Hostelling International office is **Danhostel** (www.danhostel.dk; Vesterbrogade 39, 1620 Copenhagen V).

Most of Denmark's 95 *vandrerhjem* (hostels) in the Danhostel association have private rooms in addition to dorms, making hostels an affordable and popular alternative to hotels (so book ahead from June to August). Dorm beds cost from about Dkr150, while private rooms range from Dkr300 to Dkr500 for singles, and Dkr400 to Dkr500 for doubles.

A Hostelling International Card costs Dkr160. Without one you pay Dkr35 extra a night. You can buy one at all Danhostels.

HOTELS

Budget hotels start at around Dkr500/650 for singles/doubles. *Kro*, a name that implies country inn but is more often the Danish version of a motel, are generally cheaper, often in period houses, and usually more homey than chain hotels. Both hotels and *kros* usually include an all-you-can-eat breakfast. You can find and book a number of inns online at www.krohotel.dk (note that those listed pay to be included).

Activities

Cycling is a popular holiday activity and there are thousands of kilometres of established cycling routes. Those around Bornholm, Funen and Møn, as well as the 440km Old Military Rd (Hærvejen) through central Jutland, are among the most popular.

Dansk Cyklist Forbund (DCF; www.dcf.dk; Rømersgade 5, 1362 Copenhagen K) publishes *Cykelferiekort,* a 1:500,000-scale cycling map of the entire country (Dkr25), as well as more detailed regional cycling maps.

DCF also publishes *Overnatning i det fri* (Dkr129), which lists hundreds of farmers who provide cyclists with a place to pitch a tent for Dkr20 a night.

Canoeing possibilities on Denmark's lakes, such as canoe touring between lakeside camping grounds in Jutland's Lake District, are superb. You can hire canoes and equipment at many camping grounds or in main centres.

Denmark's coastline offers terrific windsurfing and kitesurfing. Good areas are along the northern coast of Zealand at places such as Smidstrup Strand, and in northwest Jutland. The Limfjord area of northwest Jutland is particularly suitable.

Business Hours

Standard business hours are as follows. Opening hours that differ from these are listed under the specific point of interest.

Banks 9.30am-4pm Mon-Fri, to 5pm or 6pm Thu

Bars 4pm-1am, 2am, 3am, 4am or 5am

Post offices 9am or 10am-5pm or 6pm Mon-Fri, to noon or 2pm Sat

Restaurants 11am-2.30pm & 5-10pm

Stores 9.30am-5.30pm Mon-Thu, to 7pm Fri, to 2pm Sat

Supermarkets 9am-7pm or 8pm Mon-Fri, 8am or 9am-5pm Sat

Festivals & Events

Midsummer's Eve Starting with bonfires in late June, Denmark buzzes with outdoor activity throughout the summer. Main attractions are the 180 music festivals that run throughout the country, covering a broad spectrum of music from jazz, rock and blues to gospel, folk, classical, country, Cajun and much more.

Roskilde Rock Festival (www.roskilde-festival.dk) Last weekend of June; a single admission fee includes camping space and entry to all concerts.

Copenhagen Jazz Festival (www.jazz.dk) A 10-day festival held in early July, with outdoor concerts and numerous performances in clubs around the city.

Smukkeste Festival (www.smukfest.dk) An August rock and pop festival said to be Denmark's most beautiful.

Århus Festival Early September, featuring music and multicultural events.

Gay & Lesbian Travellers

Denmark is a popular destination for gay and lesbian travellers. Copenhagen, in particular, has an active, open gay community and lots of nightlife options. A good English-language website is www.copenhagen-gay-life.dk.

Holidays

Summer holidays for schoolchildren begin around 20 June and end around 10 August. Many Danes go on holiday during the first three weeks of July. The following public holidays are observed in Denmark:

New Year's Day 1 January

Maundy Thursday Thursday before Easter

Good Friday to Easter Monday March/April

Common Prayer Day Fourth Friday after Easter

Ascension Day Fifth Thursday after Easter

Whit Sunday Fifth Sunday after Easter

Whit Monday Fifth Monday after Easter

Constitution Day 5 June

Christmas Eve 24 December from noon

Christmas Day 25 December

Legal Matters

Denmark is taking a much harder line on even the 'softest' drugs these days. All forms of cannabis and harder drugs are illegal.

Money

Although Denmark remains outside the euro zone, acceptance of euros is commonplace. Most hotels and restaurants will take euros, as do many bars, cafes and shops, although you may find reluctance in more remote areas or from very small businesses. Government institutions do not accept euros.

ATMS

Major banks have ATMs, which accept Visa, MasterCard and the Cirrus and Plus bank cards. All major credit and debit cards are widely accepted throughout Denmark. A surcharge of up to 3.75% is imposed on foreign credit-card transactions in some restaurants, shops and hotels.

TIPPING

Restaurant bills and taxi fares include service charges in the quoted prices, and further tipping is not expected.

Telephone

Local calls at coin phones cost Dkr5. Domestic calls are cheapest between 7.30pm and 8am daily and all day on Sunday. Phonecards (Dkr50 to Dkr100) can be bought at post offices and newspaper kiosks.

Prepay SIM cards cost around Dkr100.

Visas

Citizens of the EU, USA, Canada, Australia and New Zealand need a valid passport to enter Denmark, but don't need a visa for stays of less than three months. If you wish to apply for a visa, do so at least three months in advance of your planned arrival.

Getting There & Away

Air

The profusion of budget carriers and flights into Denmark from elsewhere on the Continent, Ireland and the UK makes flying here very affordable. If you're coming from European destinations, consider flying into an airport other than **Copenhagen** (www.cph.dk), such as **Århus** (www.aar.dk) or **Billund** (www.bll.dk); air fares can be competitive and the airports are well connected by bus with neighbouring towns, affording fast access to some great parts of northern and central Jutland. The budget carrier Ryanair, for instance, has regular, cheap flights from Stansted Airport in England to Århus and Billund airports.

Boat

TO/FROM GERMANY

Scandlines (www.scandlines.dk) operates a Rødbyhavn–Puttgarden ferry service (car including nine passengers Dkr450, 45 minutes, every 30 minutes). Advanced online bookings can be significantly cheaper than the price listed here. The cost is included in train tickets for those travelling by rail.

BornholmerFærgen (www.bornholmerfaergen.dk) operates a ferry service between Rønne and Sassnitz (car including five passengers Dkr797 to Dkr1585, 3½ hours, three to eight times daily).

TO/FROM NORWAY

DFDS (www.dfdsseaways.com) operates a daily overnight ferry between Copenhagen and Oslo (from Dkr895, 16½ hours). **Colorline** (www.colorline.dk) sails from Hirtshals to Larvik and Kristiansand. **Stena Line** (www.stenaline.co.uk) sails between Frederikshavn and

BUSES FROM COPENHAGEN

DESTINATION	STANDARD FARE (DKR)	DURATION (HR)	WEEKLY SERVICES
Berlin	282	7	11
Frankfurt (via Hamburg)	734	13	7
Göteborg	275	4½	3
Oslo (via Göteborg)	385	9	3 to 4
Stockholm	385	9¾	3

Oslo. See the relevant Getting There & Away sections of the towns for details.

TO/FROM POLAND

Polferries (www.polferries.pl) operates ferries to Świnoujście from both Copenhagen (from Dkr470, 10 hours, three times weekly) and Rønne (from Dkr300, three to four hours, Saturday).

TO/FROM SWEDEN

Scandlines (www.scandlines.dk) sails 75 times daily from Helsingør to Helsingborg. Prices vary, but are roughly Dkr48 return per adult or from Dkr530 return if you are taking a car with nine passengers. Book online for the cheapest fares.

Other ferries go from Frederikshavn to Göteborg and Oslo, and Rønne to Ystad. See the relevant Getting There & Away sections in this chapter.

TO/FROM UK

DFDS Seaways (www.dfdsseaways.co.uk) sails from Esbjerg to Harwich (cabin from UK£142 per person, 19 hours, three to four times weekly).

Bus

Eurolines (www.eurolines.dk) runs buses to Sweden, Norway and Germany, as well as most other European countries several times a week.

Car & Motorcycle

For those travelling by road, there's a Dkr295/160 toll per car/motorcycle for the bridge crossing to Sweden.

Train

Reliable, regular train services link Denmark to Sweden, Germany and Norway. Tickets booked online in advance can be cheaper. Visit www.dsb.dk for details. The fares in the table below are approximations.

Getting Around

Air

Most internal flights cost around Dkr500 for a standard ticket and can be much cheaper if you book in advance.

Denmark's domestic air routes are operated by the following airlines.

Cimber Air (www.cimber.dk) Services from Copenhagen include Aalborg (50 minutes, at least five daily), Rønne (35 minutes, at least four daily), Billund (45 minutes, six daily on weekdays, at least three daily on weekends) and Karup in central Jutland (50 minutes, 11 daily on weekdays, at least four daily on weekends).

TRAINS FROM COPENHAGEN

DESTINATION	2ND CLASS FARE (DKR)	DURATION (HR)	DAILY DIRECT SERVICES
Berlin	1010	6¾	1
Göteborg	395	3½	20
Malmö	90	¾	every 20 mins
Oslo (via Sweden)	830	8	1
Stockholm	975	5	16

SAS (www.flysas.com) Links Copenhagen with Aalborg (at least five daily) and Århus (at least four daily), among other domestic and international routes.

Bicycle

Denmark has extensive bike paths linking towns, and bike lanes through most city centres. You can rent bikes in most towns for around Dkr75 a day, plus a deposit of about Dkr250. Bikes can be taken on ferries and most trains for a modest cost. From May to August you must make a reservation to carry a bicycle on InterCity and InterCity-Lyn trains, either at the station or by calling ☎70 13 14 15. Bikes can be carried for free on Copenhagen's S-trains outside the morning and evening rush hours.

Boat

A network of ferries links virtually all of Denmark's populated islands. Where there's not a bridge, there's usually a ferry, most of which take cars.

Bus

All large cities and towns have a local bus system and most places are also served by regional buses, many of which connect with trains. There are also a few long-distance bus routes, including from Copenhagen to Aalborg or Århus. Travelling by bus on long-distance routes costs about 20% less than travel by train, although it's usually a bit slower.

Car & Motorcycle

Denmark is perfect for touring by car. Roads are in good condition and well signposted. Traffic is manageable, even in major cities such as Copenhagen (rush hours excepted).

Access to and from motorways is made easy since roads leading out of city and town centres are sensibly named after the main city to which they're routed. For instance, the road leading to Nyborg is Nyborgvej, and so on.

Denmark's extensive network of ferries carries motor vehicles for reasonable rates. It's always a good idea to call ahead and make reservations.

Train

With the exception of a few short private lines, the **Danish State Railways** (DSB; www.dsb.dk) runs all Danish train services. There are two types of long-distance trains: sleek intercity (IC) trains that generally require reservations (Dkr30) and slower interregional (IR) trains that make more stops and don't require reservations. Both cost the same, apart from the InterCityLyn, a cushy, pricier express train aimed at business people. Rail passes don't cover reservation fees or surcharges.

Overall, train travel in Denmark is not expensive, in large part because the distances are short. Scanrail, Eurail and other rail passes are valid on DSB ferries and trains, but not on the private lines.

Estonia

Includes »

Best Places to Eat

» Altja Kõrts, Lahemaa National Park (p363)

» Genialistide Klubi, Tartu (p363)

» Supelsaksad, Pärnu (p366)

» Olde Hansa, Talinn (p360)

» Tsink Plekk Pang, Tartu (p364)

Best Places to Stay

» Tallinn Backpackers (p359)

» Terviseks Backpackers, Tartu (p364)

» Toomarahva Turismitalu, Lahemaa National Park (p362)

» Hommiku Hostel, Pärnu (p366)

Why Go?

The 20th century was full of twists and turns for Estonia, but it's now primped and primed and waiting to shine in the spotlight.

In only one generation this diminutive country has shaken off the dead weight of the Soviet era and turned its focus to the West, and to promises of a richer, shinier future. In recent years it's claimed EU membership and coveted membership of the euro zone, and the country is celebrating its return to the world stage – proud, independent, economically robust and tech-savvy.

And the world is tuning in to the low-key, lovely Estonian charms, an irresistible blend of Eastern European and Nordic. Soaking up Tallinn's long white nights and medieval history, and exploring the country's coastline, studded with islands, are joys to be savoured. National parks provide plenty of elbow room, quaint villages evoke a timeless sense of history and uplifting song festivals celebrate age-old traditions.

When to Go

Tallinn

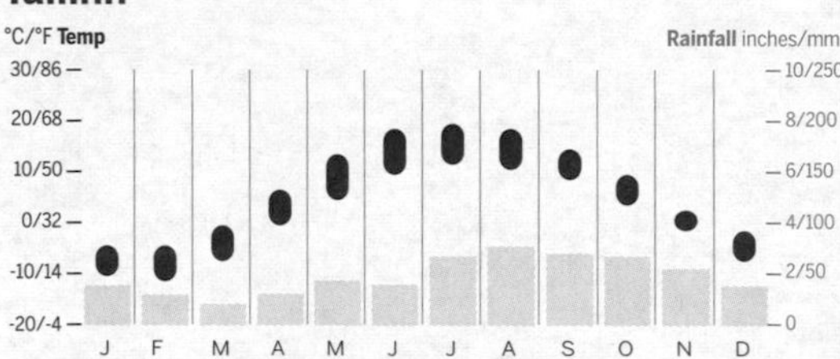

Apr & May Beat the summer crowds and see spring sunshine shake off winter's gloom.

Jun–Aug White nights, beach parties and loads of summer festivals.

Dec Christmas markets, mulled wine and long cosy nights.

Connections

Estonia is well connected for visiting the neighbours. It's an easy northern addition to Eastern European roaming, as plenty of daily buses connect with the Latvian and Lithuanian capitals. There's the option of following the white nights to Scandinavia – Tallinn has daily ferry connections to/from Stockholm and Helsinki. If you're hearing the siren call of Russia, nightly trains connect Tallinn and Moscow, and daily buses run between Tallinn/Tartu and St Petersburg.

ITINERARIES

Three Days

Hit Tallinn on a weekend to get in your sightseeing and partying, then join a day trip east to Lahemaa National Park – a bike tour will help blow away the cobwebs.

One Week

There'll be time to explore Tallinn more deeply, then Altja in Lahemaa National Park offers the perfect rustic retreat. If the weather's fine, opt for fun in the sun in Pärnu; finish with a pub crawl with local students in Tartu.

Essential Food & Drink

» **Vana Tallinn** A syrupy, sweet liqueur of indeterminate origin, best served in coffee, over ice or in champagne. There's also a cream version

» **Pork & potatoes** Prepared in 100 different ways

» **Verivorst (blood sausage)** Call it black pudding and it might sound more palatable

» **Berries & mushrooms** Seasonal delights freshly picked from the forests – in summer and autumn, respectively

» **Coffee & handmade chocolates** In one of Tallinn's cosy old-town cafes

AT A GLANCE

» **Currency** euro (€)

» **Language** Estonian

» **Money** ATMs are all over

» **Visas** Not required for 90-day stays for citizens of the EU, UK, USA, Canada, New Zealand and Australia

Fast Facts

» **Area** 45,226 sq km

» **Capital** Tallinn

» **Country code** ☎372

» **Emergency** Ambulance & Fire ☎112, Police ☎110

Exchange Rates

Australia	A$1	€0.74
Canada	C$1	€0.74
Japan	¥100	€0.87
New Zealand	NZ$1	€0.56
UK	UK£1	€1.16
USA	US$1	€0.72

Set Your Budget

» **Budget hotel room** €40

» **Two-course evening meal** €10 to €15

» **Museum entrance** €3 to €5

» **Beer** €2.50 to €3 for 500mL

» **Tallinn transport ticket** €1

Resources

» **VisitEstonia.com** (www.visitestonia.com)

» **Tallinn Tourism** (www.tourism.tallinn.ee)

» **Estonia Public Broadcasting News** (http://news.err.ee/)

Estonia Highlights

1 Find medieval bliss exploring **Tallinn's Old Town** (p355), then unwind at leafy, lovely Kadriorg Park

2 Get sand in your shorts in **Pärnu** (p365), Estonia's summertime mecca

3 Further your local education among the bars and cafes of **Tartu** (p363), Estonia's second city

4 Look for shy beavers, go cycling and discover your own slice of deserted coast in **Lahemaa National Park** (p362)

TALLINN

POP 400,000

Tallinn fuses medieval and cutting-edge to come up with an energetic mood all of its own – an intoxicating mix of ancient church spires, glass-and-chrome skyscrapers, cosy wine cellars inside 15th-century basements, lazy afternoons spent people-watching on Raekoja plats, and bike paths to beaches and forests – with a few Soviet throwbacks in the mix, for added spice.

The jewel in Tallinn's crown remains the two-tiered Old Town, a compact 14th- and 15th-century jumble of turrets, spires and winding streets. Most tourists see nothing other than this cobblestoned labyrinth of intertwining alleys and picturesque courtyards. Tallinn's modern dimension – its growing skyline, shiny shopping malls, cutting-edge art museum, the wi-fi that bathes much of the city – is a cool surprise.

GOODBYE KROON, HELLO EURO

On 1 January 2011 Estonia bid a very fond farewell to its national currency, the kroon (EEK; introduced in 1992 to replace the Soviet rouble). The official currency of Estonia is now the euro.

Prices in this chapter were researched when the kroon was still in place, and have been converted at the official exchange rate (€1 = EEK15.65). Visitors to Estonia should expect some changes to listed prices as the euro settles in.

Sights

The medieval Old Town comprises Toompea (the upper town) and the lower town, which is still surrounded by much of its 2.5km defensive wall. Its centre is Raekoja plats (Town Hall Sq). Immediately east of Old Town is the modern city centre.

Raekoja plats TOWN SQUARE

Raekoja plats has been the heart of Tallinn life since the 11th century; bathed in sunlight or sprinkled with snow, it's always a photogenic spot. It's dominated by northern Europe's only surviving Gothic **town hall** (www.tallinn.ee/raekoda; Raekoja plats; adult/student €4/2; ⏲10am-4pm Mon-Sat Jul & Aug), built between 1371 and 1404. Climb the **tower** (adult/student €3/1; ⏲11am-6pm May–mid-Sep) for fine Old Town views.

The nearby **Town Council Pharmacy** (Raeapteek; Raekoja plats 11) is another ancient Tallinn institution; there's been a pharmacy or apothecary here since 1422. An arch beside it leads into narrow Saiakang (White Bread Passage), at the far end of which is the striking 14th-century Gothic **Holy Spirit Church** (adult/concession €1/0.50; ⏲9am-5pm Mon-Sat May-Sep, 10am-3pm Mon-Fri Oct-Apr).

Lower Old Town HISTORIC NEIGHBOURHOOD

From the Holy Spirit Church, stroll along **Pikk** (Long St), which runs north to the **Great Coast Gate** – the medieval exit to Tallinn's port. Pikk is lined with the 15th-century houses of merchants and gentry (check out the fabulous sculpted facade of the art gallery at number 18).

At the northern end of Pikk stands a chief Tallinn landmark, the gargantuan **St Olaf's Church** (entry at Lai 50). View-seekers unafraid of a bit of sweat should head up to the **observation tower** (adult/student €2/1; ⏲10am-6pm Apr-Oct). Just south of the church is the **former KGB headquarters** (Pikk 59), where the basement windows were sealed to conceal the sounds of cruel interrogations.

A medieval merchant's home houses the **City Museum** (www.linnamuuseum.ee; Vene 17; adult/student €3.20/1.90; ⏲10.30am-5pm or 6pm Wed-Mon), which traces Tallinn's development from its beginnings through to 1940 with some quirky displays and curious artefacts.

The street of **Vene** is home to some photogenic passageways and courtyards – check out **Katariina käik** (Vene 12), housing artisans' studios, and **Masters' Courtyard** (Vene 6), a cobblestoned charmer, some of it dating from the 13th century. It's full of craft stores and a sweet cafe-chocolaterie.

The majestic St Nicholas' Church (Niguliste Kirik), now known as the **Niguliste Museum** (www.ekm.ee; Niguliste 3; adult/student €3.20/1.90; ⏲10am-5pm Wed-Sun), stages concerts and serves as a museum of medieval church art.

Toompea HISTORIC NEIGHBOURHOOD

A regal approach to Toompea is through the red-roofed 1380 **Pikk jalg gate tower** at the western end of Pikk in the lower town, and then uphill along Pikk jalg (Long Leg). Alternatively, a winding stairway connects Lühike jalg (Short Leg), off Rataskaevu, to Toompea.

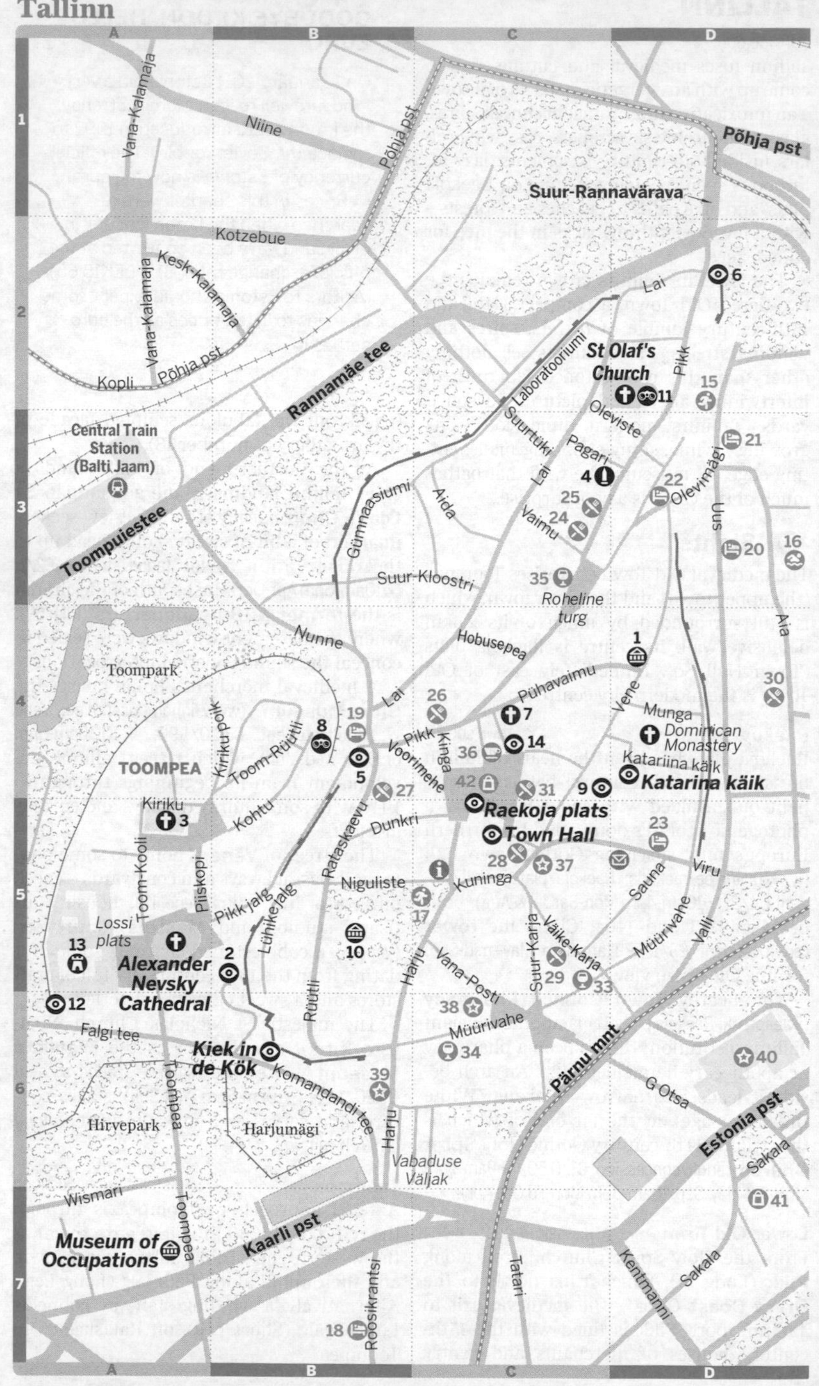
Niine
Põhja pst
Vana-Kalamaja
Kotzebue
Kesk-Kalamaja
Kopli
Suur-Rannavärava
Lai
Pikk
St Olaf's Church
Laboratooriumi
Rannamäe tee
Central Train Station (Balti Jaam)
Toompuiestee
Oleviste
Suurtüki
Pagari
Olevimägi
Uus
Gümnaasiumi
Aida
Vaimu
Suur-Kloostri
Roheline turg
Hobusepea
Nunne
Toompark
Pühavaimu
Vene
Munga
Dominican Monastery
Katariina käik
Aia
Toom-Rüütli
Kiriku põik
TOOMPEA
Kiriku
Kohtu
Voorimehe
Kinga
Raekoja plats
Town Hall
Dunkri
Rataskaevu
Niguliste
Kuninga
Viru
Sauna
Toom-Kooli
Piiskopi
Pikk jalg
Lühikejalg
Lossi plats
Alexander Nevsky Cathedral
Rüütli
Harju
Vana-Posti
Suur-Karja
Väike-Karja
Müürivahe
Valli
Falgi tee
Kiek in de Kök
Komandandi tee
Pärnu mnt
G Otsa
Estonia pst
Sakala
Hirvepark
Toompea
Harjumägi
Vabaduse Väljak
Wismari
Kaarli pst
Museum of Occupations
Tatari
Kentmanni
Roosikrantsi
ESTONIA TALLINN

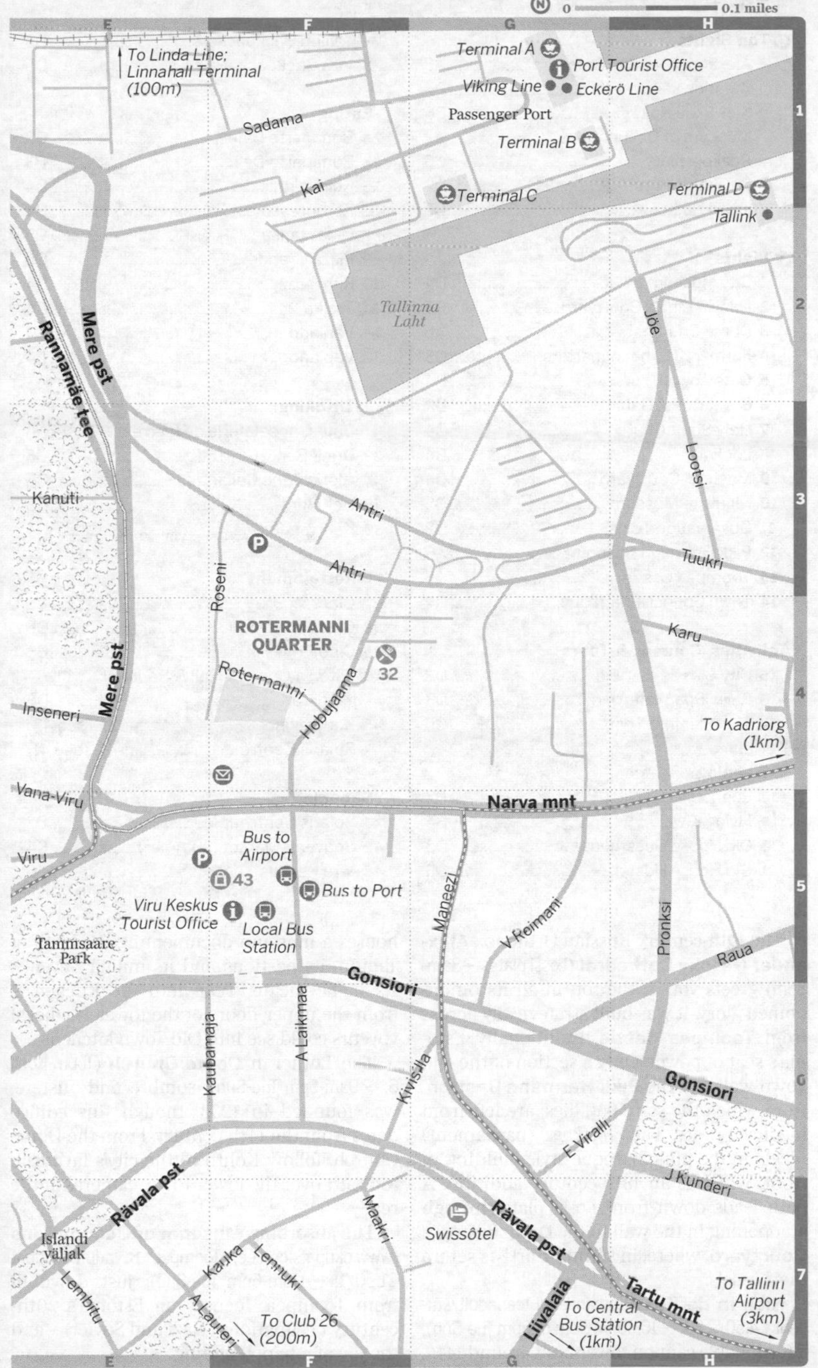
0 200 m
0 0.1 miles
E
F
G
H
1
2
3
4
5
6
7
To Linda Line; Linnahall Terminal (100m)
Terminal A
Port Tourist Office
Viking Line
Eckerö Line
Passenger Port
Terminal B
Terminal C
Terminal D
Tallink
Sadama
Kai
Tallinna Laht
Mere pst
Rannamäe tee
Jõe
Lootsi
Kanuti
Ahtri
Tuukri
Roseni
ROTERMANNI QUARTER
Karu
Rotermanni
Hobujaama
32
Inseneri
To Kadriorg (1km)
Vana-Viru
Narva mnt
Viru
Bus to Airport
43
Bus to Port
Viru Keskus Tourist Office
Local Bus Station
Maneeži
V Reimani
Pronksi
Raua
Tammsaare Park
Gonsiori
Kaubamaja
A Laikmaa
Kivisilla
E Vilde
J Kunderi
Rävala pst
Maakri
Swissôtel
Islandi väljak
Lembitu
Kaika
Lennuki
A Lauteri
To Club 26 (200m)
Liivalaia
To Central Bus Station (1km)
Tartu mnt
To Tallinn Airport (3km)

Tallinn

Top Sights

- Alexander Nevsky Cathedral A5
- Katarina käik D4
- Kiek in de Kök B6
- Museum of Occupations A7
- Raekoja plats C5
- St Olaf's Church D2
- Town Hall C5

Sights

1 City Museum D4
2 Danish King's Courtyard B5
3 Dome Church A5
4 Former KGB headquarters C3
5 Gate Tower B4
6 Great Coast Gate D2
7 Holy Spirit Church C4
8 Lookout B4
9 Masters' Courtyard C4
10 Niguliste Museum B5
11 Observation Tower D2
12 Pikk Hermann Bastion A6
13 Toompea Castle A5
14 Town Council Pharmacy C4

Activities, Courses & Tours

15 City Bike D2
16 Kalev Spa Waterpark D3
17 Traveller Info Tent C5

Sleeping

18 Euphoria B7
19 Flying Kiwi B4
20 Old House Guesthouse D3
21 Old House Hostel D3
22 Tallinn Backpackers D3
23 Viru Backpackers D5

Eating

24 Bonaparte Café C3
25 Bonaparte Deli C3
26 Kolmjalg C4
27 Kompressor B4
28 Olde Hansa C5
29 Pizza Grande C5
30 Rimi D4
31 Troika C4
Vapiano .... (see 41)
32 Vapiano F4

Drinking

Café-Chocolaterie de Pierre .... (see 9)
33 Drink Bar & Grill C5
34 Gloria Wine Cellar C6
35 Hell Hunt C3
36 Kehrwieder C4

Entertainment

37 Clazz C5
38 Club Hollywood C6
39 Club Privé B6
40 Estonia Concert Hall & National Opera D6
Katusekino .... (see 43)
Solaris Centre .... (see 41)

Shopping

41 Solaris Centre D7
42 Souvenir Market (summer) C4
43 Viru Keskus F5

The 19th-century Russian Orthodox **Alexander Nevsky Cathedral** (Lossi plats; ⌚8am-8pm) greets you at the top in all its onion-domed glory. It was built strategically across from **Toompea Castle**, traditionally Estonia's seat of power. Only a section of the Old Town wall and the **Pikk Hermann Bastion**, from which the state flag flies, are left from medieval times. The *riigikogu* (parliament) meets in the pink, baroque-style building in front, which is an 18th-century addition. A path leads down from Lossi plats through an opening in the wall to the **Danish King's Courtyard**, where, in summer, artists set up their easels.

Kiek in de Kök (Komandandi tee; adult/student €4.50/2.60; ⌚10.30am-5pm or 6pm Tue-Sun), a formidable cannon tower built around 1475, houses a museum documenting the birth of Tallinn, its bastions and its military events. Its name means 'Peep into the Kitchen' – from the upper floors of the tower, medieval voyeurs could see into Old Town kitchens.

The Lutheran **Dome Church** (Toom-Kooli 6; ⌚9am-5pm Tue-Sun), sombre and austere, was founded in 1233, though this edifice dates from the 14th century. From the Dome Church, follow Kohtu to the city's favourite **lookout** over the lower town, cameras at the ready.

The absorbing **Museum of Occupations** (www.okupatsioon.ee; Toompea 8; adult/student €1.90/1; ⌚11am-6pm Tue-Sun), just downhill from Toompea, focuses on Estonia's 20th-century occupations (Nazi and Soviet) – and the joy of a happy ending.

Kadriorg PARK, MUSEUMS

To reach **Kadriorg Park**, 2km east of Old Town along Narva maantee, take tram 1 or 3 to the last stop.

This lovely, wooded park and its palace were designed for Peter the Great for his wife Catherine I. The park's original centrepiece is **Kadriorg Palace** (1718–36), now home to the **Kadriorg Art Museum** (www.ekm.ee; Weizenbergi 37; adult/student €4.15/2.25; ⏲10am-5pm Tue-Sun May-Sep, 10am-5pm Wed-Sun Oct-Apr). The 17th- and 18th-century foreign art is mainly unabashedly romantic, and the palace unashamedly splendid.

The grand new showpiece of Kadriorg is **KUMU** (www.ekm.ee; Weizenbergi 34; adult/student €5.75/3.20; ⏲11am-6pm Tue-Sun May-Sep, 11am-6pm Wed-Sun Oct-Apr), also known as the Art Museum of Estonia. It's a spectacular modern structure of limestone, glass and copper, and contains the largest repository of Estonian art, plus constantly changing contemporary exhibits.

Activities & Tours

Water parks are all the rage in Estonia; the biggest in Tallinn is the **Kalev Spa Waterpark** (www.kalevspa.ee; Aia 18; 2½hr visit €9.60), offering plenty of ways to wrinkle your skin. There's also a gym and day spa.

For a steamy sauna experience with outstanding city views, splurge at **Club 26** (☎631 5585; www.club26.ee; Liivalaia 33; per hr before/after 3pm €19.20/38.40; ⏲7am-10pm), on the 26th floor of the Radisson Blu Hotel Olümpia.

The most popular **beaches** are at Pirita (northeast of the centre; bus 1A, 8, 34A and 38) and Stroomi (4km due west of the centre; bus 40).

From June to August, **360° Adventures** (☎5555 8785; www.360.ee) offers twice-weekly guided kayaking trips, giving you four hours out on Tallinn Bay (€30) and a new perspective on Tallinn's sights.

City Bike (☎511 1819; www.citybike.ee; Uus 33) rents bikes for city- or country-wide exploring, and has a range of Tallinn tours, as well as tours (cycling or bus) to Lahemaa National Park. The guys behind the excellent **Traveller Info Tent** (☎5554 2111; www.traveller.ee; Niguliste) run entertaining, good-value walking or cycling city tours (and a pub crawl). Their finest offering to tightwads is a free, two-hour walking tour of the capital. From June to August the tours run daily from the tent itself; the rest of the year they need to be booked in advance via email or phone (minimum three participants).

TALLINN FOR FREE

» Absorb the medieval magic wandering **Old Town** – on your own or on a free tour

» Get a breath of fresh air at **Kadriorg Park**

» Hit the beach at **Pirita** or retro-Soviet **Stroomi**

» Browse the artisans' studios of **Katariina käik** and **Masters' Courtyard**

Festivals & Events

For a complete list of Tallinn's festivals, visit **culture.ee** (www.culture.ee) and the 'Experience' pages of **Tallinn** (www.tourism.tallinn.ee).

Jazzkaar JAZZ FESTIVAL

(www.jazzkaar.ee) Jazz greats from around the world converge in mid-April.

Old Town Days HISTORY

(www.vanalinnapaevad.ee) Week-long fest in early June featuring dancing, concerts and plenty of medieval merrymaking.

Õllesummer MUSIC

(Beer Summer; www.ollesummer.ee) Popular ale-guzzling, rock-music extravaganza over four days in early July.

Black Nights Film Festival FILM FESTIVAL

(www.poff.ee) Films and animations from all over the world, bringing life to cold nights from mid-November to mid-December.

Sleeping

TOP CHOICE **Tallinn Backpackers** HOSTEL €

(☎644 0298; www.tallinnbackpackers.com; Olevimägi 11; dm €9-13; @📶) In a perfect Old Town location, this 26-bed place has a global feel and a roll-call of traveller-friendly features: happy hours, cheap dinners, free wi-fi and internet, lockers, free sauna, snazzy bathrooms, bike rental and day trips to nearby attractions. Staff organise pub crawls and city tours that anyone can join, and a shuttle bus to Rīga. Private rooms are available at the offshoot **Viru Backpackers** (☎644 6050; 3rd fl, Viru 5; s/d/tw/q €25/36/36/48), which has less atmosphere but a good central location; its only downside is the shortage of bathrooms.

GETTING INTO TOWN

From Tallinn's airport, 4km from the centre, take bus 2 to the city centre; taxis shouldn't charge more than €7.50 to €8 for the same journey. From the bus station (Autobussijaam), walk one block east to Tartu maantee, cross the street and hop on any tram into the centre. The train station is directly across the street, to the northwest, from Old Town and is served by trams 1 and 2, which take you to the city centre in three or four stops. The main ferry terminals are just 350m from the northeastern edge of Old Town – from these it's best to walk, though bus 2 also services the port.

Old House Hostel & Guesthouse GUEST HOUSES €
(☎641 1464; www.oldhouse.ee; Uus 22 & Uus 26; dm/s/tw/tr/q without bathroom from €19/29/42/63/83; P @ wi-fi) Although one is called a hostel, these twin establishments feel much more like cosy guest houses, and they're a long way from earning the party-hostel tag. Instead they offer homey, old-world decor (antiques, plants, lamps and bedspreads, with minimal bunks) to appeal to the more mature budgeteer. Dorms and private rooms are available at both (all bathrooms are shared); guest kitchen, free wi-fi and parking are quality extras. It also rents fantastic Old Town apartments at reasonable prices (see the website).

Euphoria HOSTEL €
(☎5837 3602; www.euphoria.ee; Roosikrantsi 4; dm €9-15, d without bathroom €35; P @ wi-fi) So laid-back it's almost horizontal, this hostel, just south of Old Town, has adopted some very '60s hippie vibes and given them a modern twist. It's a fun place to stay, with a sense of traveller community – especially if you like hookah pipes, bongo drums, jugglers, musos, artists and impromptu late-night jam sessions (pack earplugs if you don't).

The Flying Kiwi HOSTEL €
(☎5821 3292; www.flyingkiwitallinn.com; Nunne 1; dm €9-14, tw & d €23-40, tr with bathroom €40-51; @ wi-fi) Not far from the train station is this relaxed, friendly hostel, newly purchased by a Kiwi couple.

Tallinn City Camping CAMPING GROUND €
(☎605 2044; www.tallinn-city-camping.ee; Pirita tee 28; campsite/car/adult €12.80/6.40/3.20; ⏲late May–mid-Sep; @) Basic site an amble away from Pirita beach and Kadriorg Park, and a bus ride into town (bus 1A, 8, 34A and 38 to Lauluväljak stop), or you can rent bikes here.

Eating

See the options listed under Drinking for more good eating choices.

Olde Hansa MEDIEVAL €€
(www.oldehansa.ee; Vana turg 1; mains €10-23) Candlelit Olde Hansa is the place to indulge in a gluttonous feast. And if the medieval music, communal wooden tables and aromas of red wine and roast meats sound a bit much, take heart – the chefs have done their research in producing historically authentic fare. It may sound a bit cheesy and touristy, but even the locals rate this place.

Kompressor PANCAKES €
(Rataskaevu 3; pancakes €2.60-3.70) Under an industrial ceiling you can plug any holes in your stomach with cheap pancakes of the sweet or savoury persuasion. The smoked cheese and bacon is a treat, but don't go thinking you'll have room for dessert. By night, this is a decent detour for a budget drink. It's low on aesthetics but high on value.

Vapiano ITALIAN €
(Hobujaama 10; pizza & pasta €4-8) Choose your pasta or salad from the appropriate counter and watch as it's prepared in front of you. If it's pizza you're after, you'll receive a pager to notify you when it's ready. This is 'fast' food done healthy, fresh and cheap, in a bright, buzzing spot. There's a second branch inside the Solaris Centre.

Troika RUSSIAN €€
(Raekoja plats 15; soup or pelmeni €5-6.30, mains €8.80-16.80) Head to Troika's *trahter,* the cheerfully folksy country tavern (at ground level), for a plate of delicious *pelmeni* (Russian-style ravioli stuffed with meat), bliny or a bowl of borsch, or stop in for an ice-cold shot of vodka poured from on high.

Bonaparte Café CAFE €
(Pikk 45; pastries €1, meals €2.90-8.30) Flaky pastries and French-flavoured cafe fare.

Pizza Grande PIZZA €
(Väike-Karja 6; small pizzas & pasta €3.10-4.40) Popular student haunt proffering cheap pizza and pasta.

There's a small, 24-hour grocery store, **Kolmjalg** (Pikk 11), situated in Old Town. For first-rate picnic fodder, stock up at **Bonaparte Deli** (Pikk 47). Otherwise, try **Rimi** (Aia 7) supermarket, on the outskirts of Old Town.

Drinking

Hell Hunt PUB
(Pikk 39) See if you can score a few of the comfy armchairs out the back of this trouper of the pub circuit. It boasts an amiable air and reasonable prices for local-brewed beer and cider, plus decent pub grub. Don't let the menacing-sounding name put you off – it means 'Gentle Wolf'.

Kehrwieder CAFE
(Saiakang 1) Sure there's seating on Raekoja plats, but inside the city's cosiest cafe is where ambience is found in spades – you can stretch out on a couch, read by lamplight and bump your head on the arched ceilings. Open until midnight.

Café-Chocolaterie de Pierre CAFE
(Masters' Courtyard, Vene 6; ⊙9am-10pm) Nestled inside the picturesque Masters' Courtyard, this snug, antique-filled cafe feels like you're hiding away at your granny's place. It's renowned for its delectable handmade chocolates.

Drink Bar & Grill PUB
(Väike-Karja 8) You know a bar means business when it calls itself Drink. This place takes its beer seriously and offers plenty of beer-friendly accompaniments: traditional pub grub, happy hour from 5pm to 7pm, big-screen sports and quiz nights.

Gloria Wine Cellar WINE BAR
(Müürivahe 2) This maze-like cellar has a number of nooks and crannies where you can secrete yourself with a date and/or a good bottle of shiraz. The dark wood, antique furnishings and flickering candles add to the allure.

☆ Entertainment

Clazz BAR
(www.clazz.ee; Vana turg 2) Behind the cheesy name (a contraction of 'classy jazz') is an increasingly popular restaurant-bar featuring live music almost every night (admission varies) and food served into the wee hours. Sunday is salsa night (with free classes starting at 8pm). On other nights it could be DJs or bands – jazz, blues, Brazilian etc (check the website).

Club Hollywood CLUB
(www.club-hollywood.ee; Vana-Posti 8; ⊙from 11pm Wed-Sat) A multilevel emporium of mayhem, this is the nightclub that draws the largest crowds. Plenty of tourists and Tallinn's young party crowd mix it up to international and local DJs. Wednesday night is ladies' night (free entry for women), so expect to see loads of guys looking to get lucky.

Club Privé CLUB
(www.clubprive.ee; Harju 6; ⊙11pm-6am Wed-Sat) Global DJs attract a club-savvy local and foreign crowd after something more cutting-edge than the likes of Club Hollywood. Minimum age is 20 on Friday and Saturday.

Katusekino OUTDOOR CINEMA
(www.katusekino.ee; rooftop of Viru Keskus, Viru väljak 4; ⊙May-Sep) In the warmer months, an outdoor cinema is set up on the rooftop of Viru Keskus. It screens an eclectic list (cult classics as well as interesting new releases). Screen times depend on sunset – anything from 9pm (September) to 11pm (July), but food and drinks are available from 6pm.

Solaris Centre CINEMAS
(www.solaris.ee; Estonia puiestee 9) Home to both the Artis art-house cinema and Solaris Kino, screening Hollywood releases.

Shopping

You'll be tripping over handicraft stores – look for signs for *käsitöö*. Dozens of small shops sell Estonian-made handicrafts, linen, leather-bound books, ceramics, jewellery, silverware, stained glass and objects carved from juniper wood. These are all traditional Estonian souvenirs – and a bottle of Vana Tallinn liqueur, of course. In summer a **souvenir market** sets up daily on Raekoja plats.

Tallinn's showpiece shopping mall, **Viru Keskus** (www.virukeskus.com; Viru väljak 4; ⊙9am-9pm), aka Viru Centre, lies just outside Old Town. Newcomer **Solaris Centre** (www.solaris.ee; Estonia puiestee 9; ⊙9am-11pm) is also worth a look.

Information

Discount Cards

Tallinn Card (www.tallinncard.ee; per person €24-32) offers free rides on public transport, admission to museums, free excursions and discounts at restaurants; valid for six to 72 hours.

Internet Access

Metro Internet (Basement, Viru Keskus, Viru väljak 4; per hr €1.60) is by the bus terminal under Viru Keskus shopping centre.

Medical Services

Apteek 1 (Aia 7) One of many well-stocked pharmacies in town; open daily.

East Tallinn Central Hospital (☎622 7070, emergency department 620 7040; Ravi 18) Has a full range of services and a 24-hour emergency room.

First-aid hotline (☎697 1145) English-language advice on treatment, hospitals and pharmacies.

Money

Tavid (Aia 5; ⏲24hr) has reliably good exchange rates, though night-time rates aren't as good.

Post & Telephone

You can buy chip cards from newsstands to use for local and international calls at any of the blue phone boxes scattered around town. Post offices, supermarkets, phone-company stores (in the shopping centres) and some kiosks sell cheap mobile-phone starter kits with prepaid SIM cards (from €3.20).

Central post office (Narva mnt 1)

Tourist Information

Tallinn In Your Pocket (www.inyourpocket.com) The king of the region's listings. Its booklets are on sale at bookshops, or can be downloaded free from its website.

Tallinn tourist information centre (☎645 7777; www.tourism.tallinn.ee; cnr Kullassepa & Niguliste; ⏲9am-5pm Mon-Fri, 10am-3pm Sat Oct-Apr, 9am-6pm or later Mon-Fri, 10am-5pm Sat & Sun May-Sep) A block south of Raekoja plats. There are also information desks at the port (Terminal A) and inside Viru Keskus shopping centre. None of these centres book accommodation.

Traveller Info Tent (www.traveller.ee; Niguliste; ⏲9am-9pm or 10pm Jun-Aug) Fabulous source of information, set up by young locals in a tent opposite the official tourist info centre. It produces an invaluable map of Tallinn with recommended places, dispenses lots of local tips, keeps a 'what's on' board, and operates entertaining, well-priced walking and cycling tours (see p362).

Travel Agencies

Bookingestonia.com (☎5618 3909; www.bookingestonia.com; 2nd fl Voorimehe 1) Books bus, train and ferry tickets (no commission) and helps arrange accommodation and car rental.

Union Travel (☎627 0621; Lembitu 14) Can help arrange visas to Russia.

ℹ Getting There & Away

See p368 for details on getting to Tallinn.

ℹ Getting Around

Tallinn has an excellent network of buses, trolleybuses and trams, running from 6am to midnight; all three modes of transport use the same ticket system. Buy *piletid* (tickets) from street kiosks (€1, or a book of 10 single tickets for €6.40) or from the driver (€1.60). Validate your ticket using the machine or hole-puncher inside the vehicle – watch a local to see how it's done.

The major bus terminal for local buses is at the basement level of Viru Keskus shopping centre or the surrounding streets (just east of Old Town). Public transport timetables are at www.tallinn.ee.

City Bike (☎511 1819; www.citybike.ee; Uus 33; rental per hr/day/week €2.30/13/51) can help you get around by bike, within Tallinn and around Estonia.

Taxis are plentiful, but it's best to order one by phone: **Krooni Takso** (☎1212, 638 1212) and **Reval Takso** (☎621 2111).

AROUND ESTONIA

Lahemaa National Park

The perfect country retreat from the capital, Lahemaa takes in a stretch of deeply indented coast with several peninsulas and bays, plus 475 sq km of pine-fresh forested hinterland. Visitors are well looked after with cosy guest houses, restored manor houses, remote seaside campsites, and an extensive network of nature trails and cycling paths.

A good first stop is the **visitor centre** (☎329 5555; www.lahemaa.ee; ⏲9am-6pm or 7pm daily mid-Apr–mid-Oct, 9am-5pm Mon-Fri mid-Oct–mid-Apr) in Palmse, 7km north of Viitna (71km east of Tallinn) in the park's southeast. Next door is park showpiece **Palmse Manor** (www.palmse.ee; adult/concession €4.80/3.20; ⏲10am-6pm or 7pm), once a wholly self-contained Baltic-German estate. The small coastal towns of **Võsu**, **Käsmu** and (to a lesser extent) **Loksa** are popular seaside spots in summer. Käsmu is particularly lovely.

TOP CHOICE **Toomarahva Turismitalu** (☎325 2511; http://web.zone.ee/toomarahva/; Altja; campsites per person €3, r without bathroom €40, apt €60; wi-fi) is a gem, offering a gorgeous taste of rural Estonia – a farmstead with thatch-roofed wooden outhouses and a garden full of flowers and sculptures. There's a rustic sauna, and bikes for rent; Ülle, the friendly owner, also offers meals. Signage is minimal – look for it opposite the yard of the farmhouse tavern, **Altja Kõrts** (mains €4-12), itself well worth a visit for its rustic interior and traditional dishes.

Hiring a car is a good way to reach and explore the park, or take a tour from Tallinn – **City Bike** (☎511 1819; www.citybike.ee; Uus 33, Tallinn) offers tours by bus or bike. Otherwise, for public-transport exploration, you'll need patience and plenty of time up your sleeve. The best starting point for buses is the town of Rakvere, about halfway between Tallinn and Narva.

Tartu

POP 102,000

If Tallinn is Estonia's head, Tartu may well be its heart (and its university-educated brain, too). Small and provincial, Tartu is Estonia's premier university town, with students making up nearly one-fifth of the population. This injects a boisterous vitality into the leafy, historic setting and grants it a surprising sophistication for a city of its size.

Tartu was the cradle of Estonia's 19th-century national revival and it escaped Sovietisation to a greater degree than Tallinn. Today visitors to Estonia's second city can get a more authentic depiction of the rhythm of Estonian life than in its bigger, brasher cousin to the north.

Sights & Activities

Raekoja plats SQUARE

At the town centre on Raekoja plats is the **town hall** (1782–9), fronted by a statue of students kissing under an umbrella. At the other end of the square is the wonderfully skew-whiff building housing the **Tartu Art Museum** (Raekoja plats 18; adult/student €2.20/1; ⏰noon-6pm Wed-Sun). In between are loads of cafes and al fresco tables.

A little north, Tartu University was founded in 1632; the main **university building** (www.ut.ee; Ülikooli 18) dates from 1804. It houses the **University Art Museum** (admission €1.30; ⏰11am-5pm Mon-Fri) and entertaining **Student's Lock-Up** (admission €0.65; ⏰11am-5pm Mon-Fri), where 19th-century students were held for their misdeeds.

Other Sights OTHER SIGHTS

North of the university stands the magnificent Gothic **St John's Church** (Jaani 5; ⏰10am-6pm Tue-Sat), dating back to at least 1323. Climb the 135 steps of the 30m-high **observation tower** (admission €1.60) for a bird's-eye view of Tartu.

STUDENT LIFE IN TARTU

The world over, students gravitate to cheap meals and booze, and in Tartu it's no different. Many of the cafes on Raekoja plats cater to impoverished students with weekday lunch deals for around €2.50 (check out **Sõprade Juures** at number 12).

Of an evening, down cheap beer (500mL for around €1.60) alongside students at dive bars like tiny basement **Möku** (Rüütli 18) and industrial-chic **Zavood** (Lai 30). Other popular drinking spots include **Illegaard** (Ülikooli 5), a laid-back pub where you're likely to encounter foreign students, and the incomparable **Genialistide Klubi** (www.genklubi.ee; behind Lai 37, enter from Magasini), an all-purpose 'subcultural establishment' that encompasses music, a cinema, theatre, cafe, library and stores; be sure to check it out.

Rising to the west of Raekoja plats is the splendid **Toomemägi** (Cathedral Hill), landscaped in the manner of a 19th-century English park and perfect for a stroll. The 13th-century Gothic **Tartu cathedral** (Toomkirik) at the top was rebuilt in the 15th century, despoiled during the Reformation in 1525, and partly rebuilt in 1804–07 to accommodate the university library, which is now the **Museum of University History** (adult/student €1.60/1; ⏰11am-5pm Wed-Sun).

Tartu, as the major repository of Estonia's cultural heritage, has an abundance of first-rate museums. Among them is the absorbing **Estonian National Museum** (www.erm.ee; Kuperjanovi 9; adult/student €1.30/1, free Fri; ⏰11am-6pm Tue-Sun), which traces the history, life and traditions of the Estonian people. The former KGB headquarters now houses the sombre and highly worthwhile **KGB Cells Museum** (Riia mnt 15b; adult/student €1.30/0.65; ⏰11am-4pm Tue-Sat). Chilling in parts, it gives a fascinating rundown of deportations during the Soviet era. Entrance is on Pepleri.

The best place to pass a few rainy hours is the enchanting **Toy Museum** (www.mm.ee; Lutsu 8; admission €1.90; ⏰11am-6pm Wed-Sun), showcasing dolls, model trains, rocking horses, toy soldiers and lots of other desirables dating back a century or so.

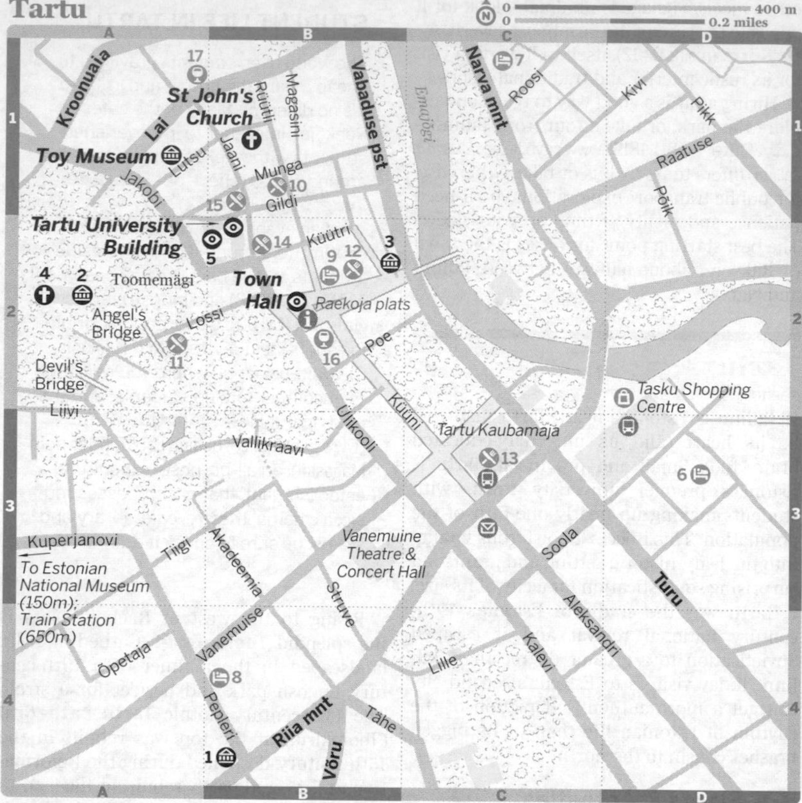

Sleeping

Terviseks Backpackers HOSTEL €
(☎565 5385; terviseksbackpackers@gmail.com; top fl, Raekoja plats 10; dm/r from €15/30; @ wi-fi) In a brand-new, fully renovated location smack in the heart of town, this true backpackers' refuge (run by a Brit and a Canadian) offers dorms, private rooms, shiny new facilities and lots of switched-on info about the cool places in town.

Tartu Student Village Hostels STUDENT RESIDENCES €
(☎742 7608; www.tartuhostel.eu; s/d €22/32; wi-fi) Narva dorm (Narva mnt 27); Pepleri dorm (Pepleri 14) These student residences offer outstanding value in prime central locations – Pepleri south of the river; Narva opposite parklands north of the city centre. The Narva option has five two-room apartments, each with its own living room, bathroom and kitchenette. Pepleri's standard rooms are smaller, minus the living room, but larger apartments are available (for €51). Reservations are a must.

Hotel Tartu HOTEL €€
(☎731 7728; www.tartuhotell.ee; Soola 3; budget s/d/tr €32/32/48, s/d €48/74; @ wi-fi) In a handy location across from the bus station and new Tasku shopping centre, this hotel offers fine modern rooms from the IKEA school of decoration. The on-site 'hostel' is actually six spotless, older-style hotel rooms (shared bathrooms in the corridor) sleeping three.

Eating & Drinking

TOP CHOICE **Tsink Plekk Pang** ASIAN €€
(Küütri 6; dishes €4-19) Behind Tartu's funkiest facade (look for the stripy paintwork) and set over three floors is this cool Chinese-flavoured restaurant-lounge. You'll need time to peruse the huge, veg-friendly menu – plenty of well-priced noodles and soups, plus a decent Indian selection and

Tartu

Top Sights

- St John's Church ... B1
- Town Hall ... B2
- Toy Museum ... A1
- University Building ... B2

Sights

1. KGB Cells Museum ... B4
2. Museum of University History ... A2
   Student's Lock-Up ... (see 5)
3. Tartu Art Museum ... B2
4. Tartu Cathedral ... A2
5. University Art Museum ... B2

Sleeping

6. Hotel Tartu ... D3
7. Tartu Student Village Hostel (Narva) ... C1
8. Tartu Student Village Hostel (Pepleri) ... B4
9. Terviseks Backpackers ... B2

Eating

10. Crepp ... B1
11. Püssirohukelder ... A2
12. Sõprade Juures ... B2
13. Supermarket ... C3
    Trepp ... (see 10)
14. Tsink Plekk Pang ... B2
15. University Café ... B1

Drinking

16. Illegaard ... B2
    Möku ... (see 10)
17. Zavood ... A1

even a handful of Japanese dishes. Or simply stop by to enjoy drinks with a DJ-spun soundtrack on weekends.

Crepp CAFE €
(Rüütli 16; crêpes €2.60-3.20) Locals love this place, and its warm, stylish decor belies its bargain-priced crêpes (sweet or savoury, with tempting combos like cherry-choc and almonds). Upstairs and open of an evening, **Trepp** is a popular watering hole, also offering good-value meals (and the all-important happy hour from 7pm to 9pm).

University Café CAFE €
(Ülikooli Kohvik; Ülikooli 20; mains €3.50-12.50; cafeteria 8am-7pm Mon-Fri, 10am-4pm Sat & Sun, cafe noon-11pm Mon-Thu, noon-1am Fri & Sat, noon-8pm Sun) Some of the most economical meals in town are waiting at the ground-floor cafeteria, which serves up decent breakfasts and a simple daytime buffet (per 100g €0.60 to €0.75). Upstairs is a labyrinth of elegantly decorated rooms, both old-world grand and embracingly cosy.

Püssirohukelder PUB €€
(Lossi 28; mains €4-17) Set in a cavernous old gunpowder cellar under a soaring, 10m-high vaulted ceiling, this is both a boisterous pub and a good choice for meaty meals (lots of pork options). Regular live music kicks in later in the night.

The most central **supermarket** (Riia 1; 9am-10pm Mon-Sat, 9am-7pm Sun) is in the basement of the Tartu Kaubamaja shopping centre.

Information

Tartu in Your Pocket (www.inyourpocket.com) More great info from this listings guide; available in bookshops or online.

Tartu tourist office (744 2111; www.visittartu.com; town hall, Raekoja plats; 9am-6pm Mon-Fri, 10am-5pm Sat, 10am-3pm Sun mid-May–mid-Sep, 9am-5pm Mon-Fri, 10am-2pm Sat mid-Sep–mid-May) Has local maps and brochures and loads of city info. Can also book accommodation and get you online (free internet access available).

Getting There & Away

From the **bus station** (12550; Turu 2) buses run to/from Tallinn (€8 to €10, 2½ to 3½ hours) about every 15 to 30 minutes from 6am to 9pm. Four or five daily trains also make the journey (€6.70, 2½ to three hours). Around nine buses a day serve Pärnu (€9 to €10, 2½ to 3½ hours).

Pärnu

POP 44,000

Local families, young partygoers and German and Finnish holiday makers join together in a collective prayer for sunny weather while strolling the golden-sand beaches, sprawling parks and picturesque historic centre of Pärnu (*pair*-nu), Estonia's premier seaside resort, 130km south of Tallinn on the main road to Rīga.

Sights & Activities

The wide, golden-sand **beach** and **Ranna puiestee**, the beachside avenue with its buildings dating from the early 20th century, are Pärnu's prime attractions. The handsome 1927 neoclassical **Mudaravila** is a symbol of the town's history; the legendary mud baths that once operated here are closed, awaiting restoration.

A curving path stretching along the sand is lined with fountains and benches perfect for people-watching. The beach itself is littered with volleyball courts and tiny changing cubicles. Back from the sand, a park holds plenty of picnic tables, and in summer you can rent bikes here.

At the beach's far end is Estonia's largest water park (part of the huge Tervise Paradiis hotel complex). **Veekeskus** (☎445 1166; www.terviseparadiis.ee; Side 14; day ticket adult/concession €19/13; ⏲10am-10pm) beckons with pools, slides, tubes etc – it holds special appeal when bad weather ruins beach plans.

Sleeping

In summer it's worth booking ahead. Prices listed below are for high season (websites list low-season rates, which can be up to 40% lower).

Hommiku Hostel GUEST HOUSE €€
(☎445 1122; www.hommikuhostel.ee; Hommiku 17; dm/s/d/tr/q €19/38/57/77/89; wi-fi) Hommiku is far more like a hotel than a hostel (except for its prices). This modern place has handsome rooms with private bathrooms, TV and kitchenettes; some also have old beamed ceilings. It's in a prime in-town position.

Camping Konse CAMPING GROUND, GUEST HOUSE €
(☎5343 5092; www.konse.ee; Suur-Jõe 44a; campsites €4 plus per person €4, r with/without bathroom €55/39; @ wi-fi) Perched on a spot by the river, 1km from Pärnu's Old Town, Konse offers campsites and a variety of rooms (half with private bathroom, half with shared facilities, all with kitchen access). It's not an especially charming spot but there is a sauna, and bike and rowboat rental. Open year-round.

Eating & Drinking

Supelsaksad CAFE €
(cnr Supeluse & Nikolai; meals €5-11) The street of Supeluse is lined with old wooden villas, and this one houses a gorgeously colourful cafe – what your granny's place might have looked like if she was prone to bold colours. The menu holds an appealing mix of wraps, salads and pastas, and there's a bountiful cake display.

Steffani Pizzeria PIZZA €
(Nikolai 24; pizzas €4.80-7) The queue out the front should alert you – this is a top choice for pizza, particularly in summer when you can dine al fresco on the big, flower-filled terrace. In a smart business move, a second **summertime branch** (Ranna puiestee 1) opens near the beach.

Veerev Õlu PUB
(Uus 3a) The 'Rolling Beer' (named after the Rolling Stones) wins friendliest and cosiest pub – it's a tiny space with lots of good vibes, cheap beer and the occasional live rock-folk band (with compulsory dancing on tables, it would seem).

A central supermarket is **Port Artur Toidukaubad** (⏲9am-10pm), inside Port Artur 2 complex, off Pikk (opposite the bus station).

Information

Pärnu in Your Pocket (www.inyourpocket.com) More great info from this listings guide; available in bookshops or online.

Pärnu tourist office (☎447 3000; www.visitparnu.com; Uus 4; ⏲9am-6pm daily mid-May–mid-Sep, 9am-5pm Mon-Fri, 10am-2pm Sat & Sun mid-Sep–mid-May) Pick up maps and brochures, or use the internet (free for first 15 minutes). Staff will book accommodation or car hire for €2.

Getting There & Away

About 25 daily buses connect Pärnu with Tallinn (€5.75 to €8, two hours), and nine services connect Pärnu with Tartu (€9 to €9.60, 2½ to three hours). Tickets for other destinations, including Rīga (Latvia) and beyond, are available at the **bus station ticket office** (☎12550; Ringi), across from the bus station.

There are also two daily Tallinn–Pärnu trains (€5.40, 2¾ hours), though the train station is an inconvenient 5km east of the town centre.

UNDERSTAND ESTONIA

History

Most of Estonia's history has been one of occupation and domination. Bandied about between European major powers, it has enjoyed only sparse periods of independence, notably in the 20th century, between the world wars and since 1991.

In the 3rd millennium BC Finno-Ugric tribes from the east mixed with the Baltic tribes already there. The Germanic Teutonic Order took control in 1346, placing Estonians under servitude to a German nobility that would last until the early 20th century, despite Danish, Swedish and Russian rulers.

After the Great Northern War (1700–21) Estonia became part of the Russian empire. During WWI, the Soviet government relinquished Estonia. Until 1940 Estonia was ruled by benevolent dictator Konstantin Päts, who was forced to accept Soviet occupation. Estonia was 'accepted' into the USSR after fabricated elections and, within a year, over 10,000 people in Estonia were killed or deported before the German occupation. Between 1945 and 1949 a further 60,000 Estonians were killed or deported.

Estonia declared independence from the USSR on 20 August 1991. It is an independent parliamentary republic led by Prime Minister Andrus Ansip; the head of state is President Toomas Ilves. It's now a member of NATO and the EU. The country has come to be seen as *the* post-Soviet economic miracle, and in 2011 took the euro as its national currency. Business is recovering after the country was hit hard by the global financial crisis. The new currency highlights Estonia's resolve to look West, catch up with its Nordic neighbours and to not look back (or east).

People

Estonia's population of 1.3 million is 69% Estonian, 26% Russian, and 3% Ukrainian and Belarusian. The Russian speakers are concentrated in Tallinn and in the industrial northeast, forming around 39% and up to 95% of the respective populations.

Estonians are historically a rural people cautious of outsiders and stereotypically shy and reticent. They are nature lovers who enjoy a sauna with friends by a lake, and are emotionally connected to their history, folklore and national song tradition.

Food

Eating options are listed in order of preference; prices indicate the cost of a main meal.

€ below €10

€€ €10 to €20

€€€ more than €20

Environment

Estonia is a low-lying land whose highest peak (Suur Munamägi) stands at just 318m. Despite its tiny size, it boasts some 1500 islands and 3794km of heavily indented coastline.

SURVIVAL GUIDE

Directory A-Z

Accommodation

Finding a decent place to lay your head in Estonia is not a problem. Peak tourist season is June through August – if you visit then, book your accommodation in advance.

There are a few *kämpingud* (camping grounds; open from mid-May to September) that allow you to pitch a tent, though most consist mainly of permanent wooden cabins, with communal showers and toilets. Farms and homestays offer more than a choice of rooms – in many cases meals, sauna and a range of activities are on offer.

There's a search engine at **VisitEstonia** (www.visitestonia.com) for all types of accommodation throughout the country.

All prices listed in this chapter are high-season prices and for rooms that have private bathroom, unless otherwise stated. Price ranges are as follows:

€€€ more than €130

€€ from €40 to €130

€ less than €40

Activities

A list of companies keeping tourists active can be found at www.turismiweb.ee.

For ecofriendly activities, contact **Reimann Retked** (☎511 4099; www.retked.ee). The company offers a wide range of sea-kayaking excursions, including overnight trips and four-hour paddles out to Aegna island, 14km offshore from Tallinn (€28.80). Other possibilities include diving, rafting, bog-walking and snowshoeing, as well as kicksledding on sea ice, frozen lakes or in snowy forest; most arrangements need a minimum of eight to 10 people, but smaller groups should enquire as you may be able to tag along with another group.

City Bike (☎511 1819; www.citybike.ee; Uus 33, Tallinn) can take care of all you need to get around by bike, within Tallinn, around Estonia or throughout the Baltic region.

Embassies & Consulates

For up-to-date contact details of Estonian diplomatic organisations, as well as foreign embassies and consulates in Estonia, check the website of the **Estonian Ministry of Foreign Affairs** (www.vm.ee).

Festivals & Events

Estonia has a packed festival calendar that hits its peak in summer. A list of upcoming major events can be found at www.culture.ee.

Jaanipäev (St John's Eve; 24 June) A celebration of the pagan midsummer or summer solstice, this is the biggest occasion in Estonia. Celebrations peak on the evening of 23 June, and are best experienced far from the city along a stretch of beach, where huge bonfires are lit for all-night parties.

Estonian Song & Dance Celebration (www.laulupidu.ee) Convenes every five years and culminates in a 30,000-strong traditional choir. It's due in Tallinn in 2014.

Baltica International Folk Festival (www.cioff.org) A week in June of music, dance and displays focusing on Baltic and other folk traditions, this festival is shared between Rīga, Vilnius and Tallinn; it's Tallinn's turn to play host again in 2013.

Holidays

New Year's Day 1 January

Independence Day 24 February

Good Friday March/April

Spring Day 1 May

Whitsunday Seventh Sunday after Easter; May/June

Victory Day (1919; Battle of Võnnu) 23 June

Jaanipäev (St John's Day or Midsummer Day) 24 June

Day of Restoration of Independence (1991) 20 August

Christmas Day 25 December

Boxing Day 26 December

Money

On 1 January 2011, Estonia joined the euro zone; see the boxed text, p358. Credit cards are widely accepted. Tipping in service industries has become the norm, but generally no more than 10% is expected.

Post & Telephone

Mail service in/out of Estonia is highly efficient. To post a letter up to 50g anywhere in the world costs €0.58.

There are no area codes in Estonia. All land-line numbers have seven digits; mobile numbers have seven or eight digits, and begin with ☎5. Prepaid SIM cards are available for €3.20

Visas

EU citizens can spend unlimited time in Estonia, while citizens of Australia, Canada, Japan, New Zealand, the USA and many other countries can enter visa-free for a maximum 90-day stay over a six-month period. Travellers holding a Schengen visa (see p1319) do not need an additional Estonian visa. For more info, see the website of the **Estonian Ministry of Foreign Affairs** (www.vm.ee).

Getting There & Away

Air

The national carrier **Estonian Air** (OV; ☎640 1163; www.estonian-air.ee) links Tallinn with 15 cities in Europe and Russia. Other airlines serving **Tallinn airport** (www.tallinn-airport.ee) include **airBaltic** (BT; ☎17107; www.airbaltic.com), with flights to Vilnius and Rīga, and **Finnair** (AY; ☎626 6309; www.finnair.com), with flights to Helsinki. Budget airlines serving Tallinn include **Ryanair** (FR; www.ryanair.com) and **easyJet** (U2; www.easyjet.com).

Boat

TO/FROM FINLAND

Oodles of daily ferries ply the 85km separating Helsinki and Tallinn (ships take two to 3½ hours, hydrofoils approximately 1½ hours). In high winds or bad weather, hydrofoils are often cancelled; they operate only when the sea is free from ice, while larger ferries sail year-round.

All companies provide concessions. Prices are cheaper on weekdays and outside summer. There's lots of competition, so shop around.

Eckerö Line (☎664 6000; www.eckeroline.ee; Terminal A) Sails once daily back and forth year-round (adult one way €19 to €23, three to 3½ hours).

Linda Line (☎699 9333; www.lindaliini.ee; Linnahall Terminal) Small, passenger-only hydrofoils up to seven times daily late March to late December (€19 to €45, 1½ hours).

Tallink (☎640 9808; www.tallinksilja.com; Terminal D) At least five services daily in each direction, year-round. The huge *Baltic Princess* takes 3½ hours; newer high-speed ferries take two hours. Adult prices from €26 to €44.

Viking Line (☎666 3966; www.vikingline.ee; Terminal A) Operates a giant car ferry, with two departures daily (adult €22 to €39, 2½ hours).

TO/FROM SWEDEN

Tallink (☎640 9808; www.tallinksilja.com) sails every night between Tallinn's Terminal D and Stockholm, via the Åland islands (cabin berth from €144, 16 hours). Book ahead.

Bus

Ecolines (☎614 3600; www.ecolines.net) connects Tallinn with several cities in central and Eastern Europe. **Lux Express** (☎680 0909; www.luxexpress.eu), the Eurolines operator within the Baltic countries, has direct services connecting Tallinn with Rīga (from €10.50, 4½ hours, eight or nine daily) and Vilnius (from €26.40, nine to 11 hours, seven daily via Rīga). Buses leave Tallinn for St Petersburg eight or nine times daily (from €22, seven to nine hours). Two daily buses connect Tartu with St Pete (from €21.40, 7½ hours).

Train

There are no rail connections to Rīga, Vilnius or St Petersburg; however, an overnight train runs every evening in either direction between Moscow and Tallinn (€121 in a four-berth compartment, 15 hours), operated by **GO Rail** (☎631 0044; http://tickets.gorail.ee).

Getting Around

Bicycle

The flatness and small scale of Estonia, and the light traffic on most roads, make it excellent cycling territory. Plenty of places rent bikes, including Tallinn's **City Bike** (☎511 1819; www.citybike.ee; Uus 33), which also offers plenty of useful advice.

Bus & Train

Buses are the best option, as they're more frequent and faster than trains and cover destinations not serviced by the limited rail network. For bus information and advance tickets, contact Tallinn's **Central Bus Station** (Autobussijaam; ☎12550; Lastekodu 46). The website **BussiReisid** (www.bussireisid.ee) has schedules and prices for all national bus services.

Regional train schedules are listed at **Edelaraudtee** (www.edel.ee).

Finland

Includes »

Best Places to Eat

» Tuulensuu, Tampere (p384)

» Kosmos, Helsinki (p376)

» Indigo, Mariehamn (p382)

» Kummisetä, Kuopio (p386)

Best Places to Stay

» Lossiranta Lodge, Savonlinna (p385)

» Dream Hostel, Tampere (p383)

» Hostel Academica, Helsinki (p375)

Why Go?

There's something pure in the Finnish air and spirit that's incredibly vital and exciting. It's an invitation to get out and be active year-round. A post-sauna dip in an ice hole under the majestic aurora borealis after whooshing across the snow behind a team of huskies isn't a typical winter day just anywhere. And hiking or canoeing under the midnight sun through pine forests populated by wolves and bears isn't your typical tanning-oil summer either.

Although socially and economically in the vanguard of nations, large parts of Finland remain gloriously remote, with trendsetting, modern Helsinki counterbalanced by vast pine- and birch-forested wildernesses in the north and east.

Nordic peace in a lakeside cottage, summer sunshine on convivial beer terraces, avant-garde Helsinki design, dark, melodic music and cafes warm with baking cinnamon aromas are other facets of Suomi seduction. As are the independent, loyal, warm and welcoming Finns, who tend to do their own thing and are much the better for it.

When to Go

Helsinki

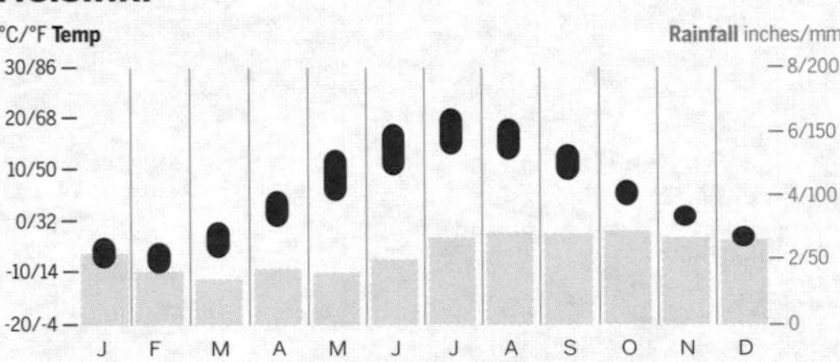

Mar There's snow, and enough daylight to enjoy winter sports.

Jul Everlasting daylight, festivals and discounted accommodation make this a top time to explore.

Sep The stunning colours of the autumn *ruska* season make this prime hiking time up north.

Connections

Road connections with Norway and Sweden are way up in the north, but ferries (p395) are big on the Baltic; an overnight boat can take you to Stockholm or even as far as Germany. Helsinki's harbour also offers quick and easy boat connections to Tallinn in Estonia, launch pad for the Baltic states and Eastern Europe. Finland's also a springboard for Russia, with boat (p395), bus (p395) and train (p395) services available, some visa free.

ITINERARIES

One Week

Helsinki demands at least a couple of days. In summer, head to the eastern Lakeland and explore Savonlinna and Kuopio (catch a lake ferry between the latter towns). Take an overnight train or budget flight to Lapland (Rovaniemi) for a few days, visiting Santa, exploring Sàmi culture and getting active.

Two Weeks

Spend a few days in Helsinki and Porvoo, then visit the harbour town of Turku and lively Tampere. Next stops are Savonlinna and Kuopio in the beautiful eastern Lakeland. Head up to Rovaniemi, and perhaps as far north as Inari. You could also fit in a summer festival, some hiking in Lapland or North Karelia or a quick cycling trip to Åland.

Essential Food & Drink

» **Offbeat eats** Unusual meats appear on menus: reindeer is a staple up north, elk is commonly eaten and bear is also seasonally available.

» **Markets** The *kauppahalli* (market hall) is the place to go for a stunning array of produce.

» **Pubs** Beer is a staple. Finns also love dissolving things in vodka; try a shot of *salmiakkikossu* (salty-liquorice flavoured) or *fisu* (Fisherman's Friend–flavoured).

» **Coffee** Finns are the world's biggest coffee drinkers. To fit in, eight or nine cups a day is about right, best accompanied with a cinnamon-flavoured pastry.

AT A GLANCE

» **Currency** Euro (€)

» **Languages** Finnish, Swedish, Sámi languages

» **Money** ATMs are widespread

» **Visas** Schengen rules apply; see p1319; visas not required by most other visitors for stays of up to 90 days

Fast Facts

» **Area** 338,145 sq km

» **Capital** Helsinki

» **Country code** ☎358

» **Emergency** ☎112

Exchange Rates

Australia	A$1	€0.74
Canada	C$1	€0.74
Japan	¥100	€0.87
New Zealand	NZ$1	€0.56
UK	UK£1	€1.16
USA	US$1	€0.72

Set Your Budget

» **Budget hotel room** €60

» **Two-course evening meal** €40

» **Museum entrance** €6

» **Beer** €5.50

» **City transport ticket** €3

Resources

» **Finnish Tourist Board** (www.visitfinland.com)

» **Metsähallitus** (www.outdoors.fi) Great hiking resource

» **This Is Finland** (www.finland.fi) Informative and entertaining

Finland Highlights

1 Immerse yourself in harbourside **Helsinki** (p373) for the latest in Finnish design and nightlife

2 Marvel at the shimmering lakescapes of handsome **Savonlinna** (p385)

3 Cross the Arctic Circle, hit the awesome Arktikum museum and visit Santa in his official grotto at **Rovaniemi** (p389)

4 Learn about Sámi culture and reindeer at **Inari** (p391)

5 Grab a bike and explore the picturesque archipelago of **Åland** (p381)

HELSINKI

☎09 / POP 583,350

It's fitting that harbourside Helsinki, capital of a country with such a watery geography, melds so graciously into the Baltic Sea. Half the city seems to be liquid, and the tortured writhing of the complex coastline includes any number of bays and inlets, and a speckling of islands.

Though Helsinki can seem like a younger sibling of other Scandinavian capitals, it's the one that went to art school, scorns pop music, is working in a cutting-edge design studio and hangs out with friends who like black and plenty of piercings. The city's design shops are legendary, and its music and pub scene is kicking.

History

Helsinki (Swedish: Helsingfors) was founded in 1550 by the Swedish king Gustav Vasa, who hoped to compete with the Hanseatic trading port of Tallinn across the water. Once the Russians were in control of Finland, they needed a capital a bit closer to home than current top dog Turku, on the Swedish-influenced west coast. Helsinki was it, and grew rapidly, with German architect CL Engel responsible for many noble central buildings. In the bitter postwar years, the 1952 Olympic Games symbolised the city's, and Finland's, gradual revival from the devastating Winter and Continuation Wars.

Sights

Historic Helsinki HISTORIC BUILDINGS

Helsinki's **kauppatori** (market square) sits right by the passenger harbour in the old part of town. Just north of it, chalk-white **Tuomiokirkko** (Lutheran Cathedral; Unioninkatu 29; 9am-6pm Sep-May, 9am-midnight Jun-Aug) presides over Senate Sq. Its interior is fairly unadorned, unlike that of red-brick **Uspenskin Katedraali** (Uspenski Cathedral; Kanavakatu 1; 9.30am-4pm Mon-Sat, noon-3pm Sun May-Sep, 9.30am-4pm Tue-Fri, 9.30am-2pm Sat, noon-3pm Sun Oct-Apr), the lavishly decorated Orthodox cathedral topped with onion domes on nearby Katajanokka island.

Suomenlinna ISLAND FORTRESS

From the *kauppatori* it's an entertaining day or half-day boat trip to the islands of **Suomenlinna** (Sveaborg), the 'fortress of Finland', founded by the Swedes in 1748 to protect the eastern part of the empire from the Russians. At the bridge connecting the two main islands is the **Inventory Chamber visitor centre** (www.suomenlinna.fi; walking tours €7, with Helsinki Card free; 10am-6pm May-Sep, 10.30am-4.30pm Oct-Apr), which has tourist information, maps and guided walking tours, daily in summer and weekends only in winter. Ramble around the various fortifications to your heart's content. The main attractions include several naval and military-themed museums. Join the locals and grab a picnic from the supermarket here. At around 5.15pm it's worth finding a spot to watch the enormous Baltic ferries pass through the narrow gap. HKL ferries run from the passenger quay at the *kauppatori* (return €3.80, 15 minutes, three times hourly 6.20am to 2.20am).

Museums & Galleries MUSEUMS/GALLERIES

Curvaceous, metallic **Kiasma** (www.kiasma.fi; Mannerheiminaukio 2; adult/under 18yr €8/free; 10am-5pm Tue, 10am-8.30pm Wed-Fri, 10am-6pm Sat & Sun) exhibits an eclectic collection of Finnish and international modern art but is more than just a gallery; its cafe and terrace are hugely popular, locals sunbathe on the grassy fringes and skateboarders perform aerobatics under the stern gaze of Mannerheim's statue outside.

The impressive **Kansallismuseo** (National Museum; www.kansallismuseo.fi; Mannerheimintie 34; adult/child €7/free; 11am-8pm Tue, 11am-6pm Wed-Sun) is Finland's top historical museum, with displays on prehistory and archaeological finds, church relics, Sámi history and cultural exhibitions. Check out the *Kalevala* frescoes on the ceiling.

Visit the **Ateneum** (www.ateneum.fi; Kaivokatu 2; adult/child €8/free; 10am-6pm Tue & Fri, 10am-8pm Wed & Thu, 11am-5pm Sat & Sun) for a course in the who's who of Finnish art. Pride of place goes to the prolific Akseli Gallen-Kallela's triptych from the *Kalevala* epic.

There are numerous other museums in town: browse a full list at the tourist office.

Activities

Kotiharjun Sauna SAUNA

(www.kotiharjunsauna.fi; Harjutorinkatu 1; adult/child €10/5; 2-8pm Tue-Fri, 1-7pm Sat, sauna time until 10pm) A traditional public wood-fired sauna dating back to 1928. It's a classic experience, where you can also get a scrub down and massage. There are separate saunas for men and women. It's a short stroll from Sörnäinen metro station.

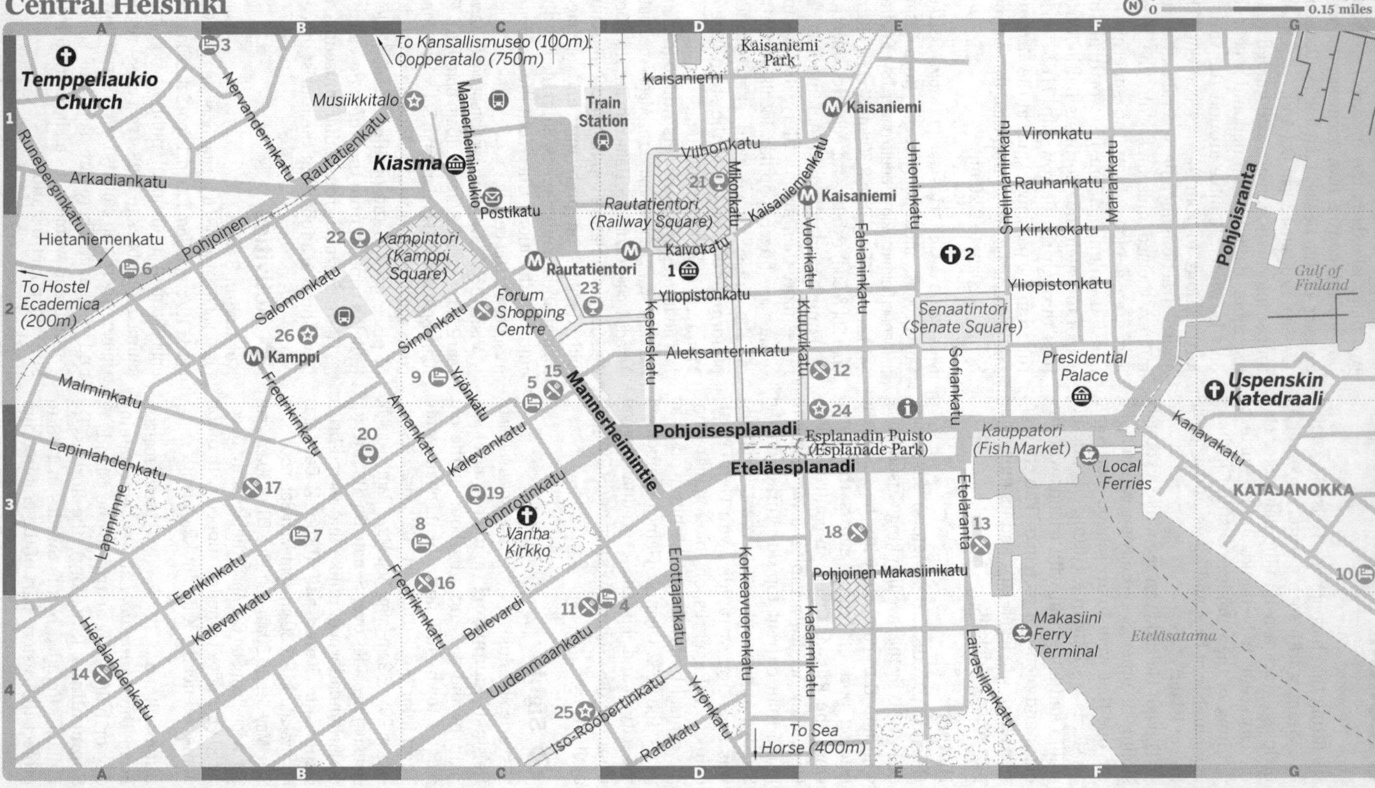
Central Helsinki
0
0
300 m
0.15 miles
Temppeliaukio Church
To Kansallismuseo (100m); Oopperatalo (750m)
Kaisaniemi Park
Kaisaniemi
Musiikkitalo
Train Station
Nervanderinkatu
Mannerheiminaukio
Kiasma
Rautatienkatu
Runeberginkatu
Arkadiankatu
Postikatu
Vilhonkatu
Mikonkatu
Kaisaniemenkatu
Unioninkatu
Snellmaninkatu
Vironkatu
Rauhankatu
Mariankatu
Kirkkokatu
Pohjoisranta
Gulf of Finland
Rautatientori (Railway Square)
Hietaniemenkatu
Pohjoinen
Kampintori (Kamppi Square)
Kaivokatu
Rautatientori
Vuorikatu
Fabianinkatu
Yliopistonkatu
To Hostel Ecademica (200m)
Salomonkatu
Forum Shopping Centre
Keskuskatu
Kluuvikatu
Senaatintori (Senate Square)
Kamppi
Simonkatu
Aleksanterinkatu
Presidential Palace
Uspenskin Katedraali
Malminkatu
Yrjönkatu
Fredrikinkatu
Annankatu
Mannerheimintie
Sofiankatu
Pohjoisesplanadi
Esplanadin Puisto (Esplanade Park)
Kauppatori (Fish Market)
Kanavakatu
Lapinlahdenkatu
Kalevankatu
Eteläesplanadi
Local Ferries
KATAJANOKKA
Lapinrinne
Lönnrotinkatu
Vanha Kirkko
Eteläranta
Erottajankatu
Korkeavuorenkatu
Pohjoinen Makasiinikatu
Eerikinkatu
Kalevankatu
Fredrikinkatu
Bulevardi
Kasarmikatu
Laivasillankatu
Makasiini Ferry Terminal
Eteläsatama
Hietalahdenkatu
Uudenmaankatu
Iso-Roobertinkatu
Yrjönkatu
Ratakatu
To Sea Horse (400m)

There are several cruise companies departing hourly on harbour jaunts from the *kauppatori* in summer.

An excellent budget city tour is to catch the 3T/3B tram, with the free *Sightseeing on 3T/3B* brochure as your guide around the city centre.

Festivals & Events

There's something going on in Helsinki year-round. Some of the biggies include the following:

Vappu GRADUATION
Held on May Day, this student graduation festival is celebrated by gathering around the Havis Amanda statue, which receives a white 'student cap'.

Helsinki Day CITY ANNIVERSARY
Free events celebrating the city's anniversary on 12 June.

Helsinki Festival ARTS
(Helsingin Juhlaviikot; www.helsinginjuhlaviikot.fi; tickets €10-50) From late August to early September, this arts festival features chamber music, jazz, theatre, opera and more.

Sleeping

Bookings are advisable from mid-May to mid-August (and essential for Helsinki Day).

TOP CHOICE **Hostel Academica** HOSTEL €
(☎1311 4334; www.hostelacademica.fi; Hietaniemenkatu 14; dm/s/d €24/56/69; ⊙Jun-Aug; @) Finnish students live well, so in summer take advantage of this residence, a super-clean spot packed with features (pool and sauna) and cheery staff. HI discount.

TOP CHOICE **Hotelli Helka** HOTEL €€€
(☎613 580; www.helka.fi; Pohjoinen Rautatiekatu 23A; s/d €151/189, weekends & summer €100/124; @) One of the centre's best midrange hotels – you can nearly always bag it cheaper than the listed price – the Helka has competent, friendly staff and excellent facilities.

Hotelli Finn HOTEL €€
(☎684 4360; www.hotellifinn.fi; Kalevankatu 3b; s/d with toilet €65/75, with toilet & shower €75/90) High in a central city building, and offering top value for Helsinki, this small, friendly hotel was under gradual refurbishment when we last passed by. The decor and rates may change but it'll remain a great choice.

Rastila Camping CAMPING GROUND €
(☎0310 78517; www.rastilacamping.fi; Karavaanikatu 4; campsites per adult/tent €5/10, hostel dm/s/d €19/30/55, modern/traditional 2-4 person cabins €70/45, cottages with/without sauna €167/124; @) Only 20 minutes on the metro (Rastila station) from the heart of town, in a pretty, waterside location, this camping ground has

Central Helsinki

Top Sights
- Kiasma ... C1
- Temppeliaukio Church ... A1
- Uspenskin Katedraali ... G2

Sights
1. Ateneum ... D2
2. Tuomiokirkko ... E2

Sleeping
3. Hellsten Helsinki Parliament ... B1
4. Hostel Erottajanpuisto ... D4
5. Hotelli Finn ... C3
6. Hotelli Helka ... A2
7. Omenahotelli Eerikinkatu ... B3
8. Omenahotelli Lönnrotinkatu ... C3
9. Omenahotelli Yrjönkatu ... C2
10. Scandic Grand Marina ... G3

Eating
11. Café Bar 9 ... C4
12. Karl Fazer ... E2
13. Vanha Kauppahalli ... E3
14. Konstan Möljä ... A4
15. Kosmos ... C2
16. Koto ... C3
17. Ravintola Martta ... B3
18. Zucchini ... E3

Drinking
19. Bar Loose ... C3
20. Corona Bar & Kafe Moskova ... B3
21. Pub Tram Spårakoff ... D1
22. Teerenpeli ... B2
23. Zetor ... C2

Entertainment
24. FinnKino Maxim ... E3
25. Lost & Found ... C4
26. The Tiger ... B2

WIRELESS INTERNET

In Finland wi-fi is available in just about every accommodation option and a good proportion of cafes and bars. Many cities have a free public network. It's all so easy to access that we haven't used the wi-fi icon in this chapter.

tent and van sites, wooden cabins and more upmarket log cottages, as well as a summer hostel (open July and August).

Hostel Erottajanpuisto HOSTEL €
(☎642 169; www.erottajanpuisto.com; Uudenmaankatu 9; dm/s/d €26/49/65; @) Helsinki's smallest and most laid-back hostel occupies the top floor of a building in a lively street of bars and restaurants close to the heart of the city. Forget curfews, lockouts, school kids and bringing your own sleeping sheet – this is more like a guest house with (crowded) dormitories.

Eurohostel HOSTEL €
(☎622 0470; www.eurohostel.fi; Linnankatu 9; s €43-48, d €51-58; @) On Katajanokka island, less than 500m from the Viking Line terminal, this HI affiliate is busy but a bit soulless and offers both backpacker and 'hotel' rooms. Both share common bathrooms. Tram 4 stops right alongside.

Omenahotelli HOTEL €€
(☎0600 18018; www.omena.com; r €80-95) This good-value staffless hotel chain has three handy Helsinki locations: Eerikinkatu 24, Lönnrotinkatu 13 and Yrjönkatu 30. As well as a double bed, rooms have a fold-out sofa that can sleep two more, plus there's a microwave and minifridge. Book online or via a terminal in the lobby.

Hostel Stadion HOSTEL €
(☎477 8480; www.stadionhostel.fi; Pohjoinen Stadiontie 3; dm/s/d €20/38/47; @) An easy tram ride from town, this well-equipped hostel is actually part of the Olympic Stadium. There are no views though, and it feels old-style with big dorms and not much light-heartedness. It's the cheapest bed in town, so sometimes there's the odd curious character about. HI discount.

Eating

Helsinki has by far Finland's best range of Finnish and international cafes and restaurants.

TOP CHOICE **Kosmos** FINNISH €€
(☎647 255; www.kosmos.fi; Kalevankatu 3; mains €17-26; ⏲11.30am-1am Mon-Fri, 4pm-1am Sat, closed Jul) Designed by Alvar Aalto, this classical place could qualify as an institution on that fact alone, but the great formal service and reliably excellent food make it a real Helsinki redoubt.

Sea Horse FINNISH €€
(☎010-837 5700; www.seahorse.fi; Kapteeninkatu 11; mains €14-24; ⏲10.30am-midnight) Seahorse dates back to the 1930s and is as traditional a Finnish restaurant as you'll find anywhere. Locals gather in the gloriously unchanged interior to meet and drink over hefty dishes of Baltic herring, Finnish meatballs and cabbage rolls.

Zucchini VEGETARIAN €
(Fabianinkatu 4; lunch €7-10; ⏲lunch Mon-Fri) One of the city's few vegetarian eateries, covering a lot of bases with friendliness and fresh-baked quiches and piping-hot soups. The sunny terrace out the back is stunning in summer.

Café Bar 9 CAFE €
(www.bar9.net; Uudenmaankatu 9; mains €8-10) It's tough to find low-priced food at dinnertime in Helsinki that's not shaved off a spinning stick, so this place stands out. Plates vary, with some solid Finnish fare backed up by big sandwiches, Thai-inspired stir-fries and pastas.

Konstan Möljä FINNISH €
(☎694 7504; www.konstanmolja.fi; Hietalahdenkatu 14; lunch/dinner buffet €8/18; ⏲lunch Tue-Fri, dinner Tue-Sat) The maritime interior of this old sailors' eatery hosts an impressive husband-and-wife team who turn out a great-value Finnish buffet for lunch and dinner.

Karl Fazer CAFE €
(www.fazer.fi; Kluuvikatu 3; lunch €8-12; ⏲7.30am-10pm Mon-Fri, 9am-10pm Sat) A historical cafe worth delving into, this is a huge space with plenty of character, classic decor and a small terrace. It does amazing ice-cream sundaes and also sells cakes and tea to take away.

Ravintola Martta FINNISH €
(www.ravintolamartta.fi; Lapinlahdenkatu 3; lunches €7-9; ⏲lunch Mon-Sat, dinner Tue-Sat) One of the best-value lunch stops around, Martta is run by a historic women's organisation. The light, bright dining room is matched by the tasty, wholesome food.

Koto JAPANESE €
(www.ravintola-koto.fi; Lönnrotinkatu 22; mains €10-16, lunch €9-15; ⌚lunch & dinner Mon-Sat) It's blonde-wood Zen at this Japanese joint that does sashimi, yakitori and brilliant sushi.

Quick Eats & Self-Catering

In summer there are food stalls, fresh produce and expensive berries at the *kauppatori*, but the real picnic treats are in the **Vanha Kauppahalli** (Old Market Hall; Eteläranta 1; ⌚8am-6pm Mon-Fri, 8am-4pm Sat, 10am-4pm Sun summer only) nearby, where you can get filled rolls, cheese, bread, fish and an array of Finnish snacks and delicacies (plus there's a small Alko).

 Drinking

The centre's full of bars and clubs, with the Punavuori area around Iso-Roobertinkatu one of the most worthwhile for trendy alternative choices. For the cheapest beer in Helsinki (under €3 a pint during the seemingly perpetual happy hours), hit working-class Kallio (near Sörnäinen metro station), north of the centre. There's a string of earthy local pubs along Helsinginkatu, such as grungy local favourite **Roskapankki** (Helsinginkatu 20; ⌚9am-2am), whose name means 'trash bank'.

Teerenpeli PUB
(www.teerenpeli.com; Olavinkatu 2) Get away from the Finnish lager mainstream with this excellent pub right by the bus station. It serves very tasty ales, stouts and berry ciders from a microbrewery in Lahti in a long, split-level area with romantically low lighting and intimate tables. A top spot.

Corona Bar & Kafe Moskova BAR
(www.andorra.fi; Eerikinkatu 11-15; ⌚bar 11am-2am daily, cafe 6pm-2am Mon-Sat) Those offbeat film-making Kaurismäki brothers are up to their old tricks with this pair of conjoined drinking dens. Corona plays the relative straight man with pool tables and cheap beer, while Moskova is back in the USSR with a bubbling samovar and Soviet vinyl.

Bar Loose BAR
(www.barloose.com; Annankatu 21; ⌚4pm-2am Mon-Tue, 4pm-4am Wed-Sat, 6pm-4am Sun) The opulent blood-red interior and comfortably cosy seating seem too stylish for a rock bar, but that's what this is, with portraits of guitar heroes lining one wall and an eclectic mix of people filling the upstairs, served by two bars. Downstairs is a club area, with live music more nights than not.

Zetor PUB
(www.ravintolazetor.fi; Mannerheimintie 3-5; mains €12-22; ⌚11.30am-4am Tue-Sat, noon-midnight Sun & Mon) A fun Finnish restaurant and pub with deeply ironic tractor decor. It's owned by film-maker Aki Kaurismäki and designed by the Leningrad Cowboys. It's worth going in just for a drink and a ride on a tractor, but the food is decent value too, and served until very late.

Pub Tram Spårakoff PUB TRAM
(www.koff.net; tickets €8; ⌚departs hourly 2-3pm & 5-8pm Tue-Sat late May-late Aug) Not sure whether to go sightseeing or booze the day away? Do both in this bright-red pub tram, the tipsy alternative to traditional tours around town. Departs from Mikonkatu, east of train station.

☆ Entertainment

Cinemas in Helsinki show original-version films with Finnish and Swedish subtitles. Various bars and clubs around Helsinki host live bands, while the city also has a dynamic club scene; some nights have age limits.

For upcoming theatre and concert performances, see *Helsinki This Week*, enquire at the tourist office or check the website of ticket outlet **Lippupiste** (☎0600 900 900; www.lippu.fi).

Finnkino CINEMA
(☎06000 07007; www.finnkino.fi; adult €7-11.50) Operates several Helsinki cinemas with big-name films. Handy branches include Tennispalatsi (Salomonkatu 15) and Maxim (Kluuvikatu 1).

Tavastia BAR./LIVE MUSIC
(www.tavastiaklubi.fi; Urho Kekkosenkatu 4; tickets from €15; ⌚9pm-late) One of Helsinki's legendary rock venues, this attracts both up-and-coming local acts and bigger international groups. There's a band every night of the week. Also check out what's on at **Semifinal**, the smaller venue next door (tickets €6 to €8).

The Tiger CLUB
(www.thetiger.fi; Urho Kekkosen katu 1A; door charge €10; ⌚10pm-4am Fri-Sun) Ascend into clubbing heaven at this super-slick club with stellar lighting and high-altitude cocktails. Music runs from chart hits to R&B; drinks are expensive but the view from the terrace is stunning. Entrance via Kamppi Sq.

Kuudes Linja CLUB
(www.kuudeslinja.com; Hämeentie 13; tickets €8-12; ⌚9pm-3am Sun & Tue-Thu, 10pm-4am Fri & Sat)

GAY & LESBIAN VENUES

Check out www.gayfinland.fi for listings of gay and lesbian venues.

Lost & Found (www.lostandfound.fi; Annankatu 6; ⌚10pm-4am) is a sophisticated mixed bar that is still a hugely popular late-night hang-out with people of all persuasions. Head downstairs to the grotto-like dance floor and wait for your favourite chart hits to spin.

DTM (www.dtm.fi; Iso Roobertinkatu 28; admission €2-10, cafe free; ⌚9am-4am Mon-Sat, noon-4am Sun; @), Scandinavia's biggest gay club (Don't Tell Mum), is a multilevel complex with an early-opening cafe-bar. There are a couple of dance floors with regular club nights as well as drag shows or women-only sessions.

Between Hakaniemi and Sörnäinen metro stops, this is the place to find Helsinki's more experimental beats from top visiting DJs playing techno, industrial, post-rock and electro. There are also live gigs.

Shopping

Known for design and art, Helsinki is an epicentre of Nordic cool, from fashion to the latest furniture and homewares. The central but touristy Esplanadi has the chic boutiques of Finnish classics like Marimekko, Stockmann, Aarikka and Artek. The hippest area is definitely Punavuori, which has several good boutiques and art galleries to explore.

Information

Discount Cards

If you plan to see a lot of sights, the **Helsinki Card** (www.helsinkicard.fi; adult 24/48/72hr €34/45/55, child €13/16/19) gives you free travel, entry to more than 50 attractions in and around Helsinki, and discounts on day tours to Porvoo and Tallinn. It's cheapest to buy it online.

Internet Access

Kirjasto 10 (Elielinkatu 2; access free; ⌚10am-10pm Mon-Thu, 10am-6pm Fri, noon-6pm Sat & Sun, shorter hrs summer) On the 1st floor of the main post office. Several half-hour terminals and others bookable.

Sidewalk Express (www.sidewalkexpress.com; per hr €2) There are several of these unstaffed, stand-up access points around town. Buy your ticket from the machine; it's valid for all of them. Handy locations include the central train station (far left as you look at the trains) and Kamppi bus station (outside the ticket office).

Left Luggage

Small/large lockers cost €2/4 per 24 hours at the bus and train station. There are similar lockers and left-luggage counters at the ferry terminals.

Medical Services

Haartman Hospital (☎3106 3231; Haartmaninkatu 4; ⌚24hr) For emergency medical assistance.

Money

Forex (www.forex.fi; ⌚8am-9pm Mon-Fri, 9am-7pm Sat & Sun) At Pohjoisesplanadi 27 and at the train station; the best place to change cash or travellers cheques.

Tourist Information

Helsinki City tourist office (☎3101 3300; www.visithelsinki.fi; Pohjoisesplanadi 19; ⌚9am-8pm Mon-Fri, 9am-6pm Sat & Sun May-Sep, shorter hrs rest of yr) Busy multilingual office with booking desk.

Getting There & Away

Air

There are direct flights to Helsinki from many major European cities and several intercontinental ones. The airport is at Vantaa, 19km north of Helsinki.

Finnair (☎0600 140140; www.finnair.fi) and cheaper **Finncomm** (www.fc.fi) fly to 20 Finnish cities, usually at least once a day. **Blue1** (☎06000 25831; www.blue1.com) has budget flights to a handful of Finnish destinations.

Boat

International ferries travel the Baltic from Helsinki; see p395.

There are five main terminals, three close to the centre: Katajanokka terminal is served by bus 13 and trams 2, 2V and 4, and Olympia and Makasiini terminals by trams 3B and 3T. Länsiterminaali (West Terminal), is served by bus 15, while further-afield Hansaterminaali (Vuosaari) can be reached on bus 90A.

Bus

Regional and long-distance buses dock at underground **Kamppi bus station** (www.matkahuolto.fi). There are services to all major towns in Finland.

Train

Helsinki's **train station** (Rautatieasema; www.vr.fi; ⌚tickets 6.30am-9.30pm) is central. It's linked to the metro (Rautatientori stop), and is a short walk from the bus station.

The train is the fastest and cheapest way to get from Helsinki to major centres. There are also daily trains to Russia (p395).

Getting Around

To/From the Airport

Bus 615 (€3.40, 45 minutes) shuttles between Vantaa airport and Rautatientori, by the train station. Faster Finnair buses (€5.90, 30 minutes, every 20 minutes) also depart from the railway station.

Local Transport

The city's public transport system, **HKL** (www.hkl.fi), operates buses, metro and local trains, trams and the Suomenlinna ferry. A one-hour ticket for any HKL transport costs €2.50 when purchased on board, and €2 when purchased in advance. The ticket allows unlimited transfers but must be validated in the stamping machine on board when you first use it. Day or multiday tickets (€6.80/10.20/13.60 for 24/48/72 hours) are the best option if you're in town for a short period of time.

HKL offices (7.30am-7pm Mon-Thu, 7.30am-5pm Fri, 10am-3pm Sat) at the Kamppi bus station and the Rautatientori metro station sell tickets and passes, as do many of the city's R-kioskis and the tourist office.

AROUND HELSINKI

Porvoo

019 / POP 47,832

A great day trip from Helsinki, charming medieval Porvoo is Finland's second-oldest town (founded in 1346). The **old town**, with its tightly clustered wooden houses, cobbled streets and riverfront setting, is one of the most picturesque in Finland. During the day, its craft shops are bustling with visitors; if you can stay the night you'll have it more or less to yourself. The old painted buildings are spectacular in the setting sun. The **tourist office** (520 2316; www.porvoo.fi; Rihkamakatu 4; 9am-6pm Mon-Fri, 10am-4pm Sat & Sun early Jun-Aug, 9am-4.30pm Mon-Fri, 10am-2pm Sat Sep-early Jun; @) is at the southern edge of the old town.

Cosy, family-run **Gasthaus Werneri** (0400 494 876; www.werneri.net; Adlercreutzinkatu 29; s/d/tr €45/60/90), in an apartment block 10 minutes' walk from the old town, is decent value with just five rooms (with shared bathrooms).

A 10-minute walk southeast of the old town, a historic wooden house holds a well-kept hostel, **Porvoon Retkeilymaja** (523 0012; www.porvoohostel.fi; Linnankoskenkatu 1-3; dm/s/d €18/33/44; check-in 4-7pm) in a grassy garden. It has HI discount.

Porvoo's most atmospheric cafes, restaurants and bars are in the old town. Porvoo is famous for its sweets; **Brunberg** (www.brunberg.fi; Välikatu 4) does legendary chocolate and liquorice.

TOP CHOICE **Porvoon Paahtimo** (www.porvoonpaahtimo.fi; Mannerheiminkatu 2; 10am-11pm) is right at the main bridge and is a cosy, romantic spot for drinks of any kind: it roasts its own coffee and has tap beer and several wines by the glass.

Getting There & Away

The bus station is on the *kauppatori*; buses run every half-hour between Porvoo and Helsinki's bus station (€11, one hour).

SOUTHWESTERN FINLAND

Finland's southwestern corner is an archipelago of numerous islands clustered around the harbour town of Turku and stretching right out to the semi-independent Åland islands. Turku is the natural base but, if you have time, you could explore this coastline by local ferry or even canoe.

Turku

02 / POP 176,087

Turku is Finland's oldest town, but today it's a modern maritime city, brimming with museums and boasting a robust harbourside castle and magnificent cathedral. Once the capital under the Swedes, Turku (Swedish: Åbo) was founded in 1229 and grew into an important trading centre despite being ravaged by fire many times. In 2011 it shone again as one of the EU's Capitals of Culture.

Sights

Turun Linna CASTLE

(Turku Castle; www.museumcentreturku.fi; admission €7, guided tour €2; 10am-6pm Tue-Sun May-mid-Sep, 10am-6pm Tue & Thu-Sun, noon-8pm Wed mid-Sep–Apr) A visit to lofty Turku Castle, near the harbour, should be your first stop. Founded in 1280 at the mouth of the Aurajoki, the castle has been rebuilt a number of times since.

Aboa Vetus & Ars Nova MUSEUM, ART GALLERY
(☎250 0552; www.aboavetusarsnova.fi; Itäinen Rantakatu 4-6; admission €8; ⏲11am-7pm, closed Mon mid-Sep–Mar, English-language tour 11.30am daily Jul & Aug) Two museums under one roof. Aboa Vetus is live archaeology: you descend into the comprehensively excavated remains of medieval Turku. Ars Nova is a museum of contemporary art with temporary exhibitions, the highlight of which is the Turku Biennaali, held in summer in odd years.

Luostarimäen Käsityöläismuseo MUSEUM
(www.museumcentreturku.fi; Vartiovuorenkatu 2; admission €6; ⏲10am-6pm Tue-Sun Feb–mid-Sep) The open-air Luostarinmäki Handicrafts Museum, in the only surviving 18th-century area of this medieval town, is one of the best of its kind in Finland and much more intriguing than the name suggests – it's a Turku must-see.

Forum Marinum MUSEUM
(www.forum-marinum.fi; Linnankatu 72; admission €7, plus museum ships €5; ⏲11am-7pm daily May-Sep, 11am-6pm Tue-Sun Oct-Apr) Forum Marinum is an impressive maritime museum near Turku Castle. As well as a nautically crammed exhibition space devoted to Turku's shipping background, it incorporates a fleet of **museum ships**.

FREE **Turun Tuomiokirkko** CATHEDRAL
(www.turunseurakunnat.fi; ⏲9am-7pm) Commanding Turku Cathedral, dating from the 13th century, is the national shrine and 'mother church' of the Lutheran Church of Finland.

Festivals & Events

Big events on the Turku calendar include the **Turku Music Festival** (www.tmj.fi) in the second week in August, and **Ruisrock** (www.ruisrock.fi), a major music festival held on Ruissalo island in early July.

Sleeping

Bed & Breakfast Tuure B&B €
(☎233 0230; www.tuure.fi; Tuureporinkatu 17c; s/d/tr €38/52/75; @) Very handy for the bus station, and close to the market square, this tidy and friendly guest house makes an excellent place to stay. The rooms are bright and thoughtfully decorated, you get your own keys, and there's a microwave, a fridge and free internet use for guests.

Centro Hotel HOTEL €€
(☎211 8100; www.centrohotel.com; Yliopistonkatu 12; s/d €98/108, Sat, Sun & summer €75/90; @) This place has a good balance: attentive service always feels friendly, and blonde-wood rooms are a good compromise between size and price, with superiors that have a more designer feel. The breakfast buffet has fresh pastries and a varied spread that's worth getting out of bed for.

Turku Hostel HOSTEL €
(☎262 7680; www.turku.fi/hostelturku; Linnankatu 39; dm/s/tw €18/38/45; @) Well located on the river, close to the town centre, this is a neat place with good lockers, spacious dorms, key-card security and a minifridge in each private room. There's also bike hire and an internet cafe. There's a 2am curfew if you're dorming it. HI discount.

Eating

There are plenty of cheap eateries on and around Turku's bustling central *kauppatori*. The **kauppahalli** (Eerikinkatu 16; ⏲7am-5.30pm Mon-Fri, 7am-3pm Sat) is packed with produce, a sushi bar and a cool cafe in a converted train carriage.

TOP CHOICE **Bossa** BRAZILIAN €€
(☎251 5880; www.bossa.fi; Kauppiaskatu 12; mains €19-25; ⏲4pm-10pm or 11pm Mon-Fri, 2-11pm Sat, 3-9pm Sun) Buzzy and inviting, this L-shaped Brazilian restaurant is decorated with arty photos of the carnival capital. There's excellent, authentic eating to be done her.e Portions are generous and service is excellent. Live music Tuesday.

Trattoria Romana ITALIAN €
(Hämeenkatu 9; pizza & pasta €10-15) With that reliably comfortable trattoria decoration, this intimate spot adds to the tried-and-tested favourites with some more interesting combinations, including a changing list of daily specials. Get the waiter to translate them for you, as they're very worthwhile, and better value than the à la carte meat dishes. Delicious salads are available here too.

Vaakahuoneen Paviljonki FINNISH, ASIAN €
(www.vaakahuone.fi; Linnankatu 38; mains €11-24, fish buffet €10; ⏲food served 11am-10pm May-Aug) This riverfront jazz restaurant is the place to go for great-value food and entertainment in summer. As well as an à la carte menu there's a daily 'archipelago fish buffet' (June

to August), plus a changing Asian buffet, all served to foot tapping live trad-jazz bands.

 Drinking & Entertainment

Summer drinking begins on the decks of boats lining the south bank of the river. If the beer prices make you wince, join locals gathering on the grassy riverbank drinking takeaway alcohol.

Turku also has some of Finland's most eccentric bars that make for an offbeat pub crawl.

Panimoravintola Koulu PUB
(www.panimoravintolakoulu.fi; Eerikinkatu 18; 11am-2am or 3am) They've done their homework at this brewery pub, set in a former school, with nine of its own beers and ciders. As well as inkwells and school desks, there's a rowboat on the roof.

Puutorin Vessa PUB
(www.puutorinvessa.fi; Puutori; noon-midnight) In the middle of a small square near the bus terminal, this novel bar was a public toilet in a former life. Toilet humour and memorabilia adorn the walls and you can even have your drink in a tin potty.

Uusi Apteeki PUB
(www.uusiapteeki.fi; Kaskenkatu 1; 10am-2am) This characterful bar was once a pharmacy; the antique shelving and desks have been retained, but they are filled with hundreds of old beer bottles.

Information

Library (262 3611; Linnankatu 2; 11am-8pm Mon-Thu, 11am-6pm Fri, 11am-4pm Sat) Free Internet terminals (15-minute maximum).

Turku Card (www.turkutouring.fi; 24/48hr €21/28) Gives free admission to most museums and attractions in the region, free public transport and various other discounts. Available from the tourist office or any participating attraction.

Tourist office (262 7444; www.turkutouring.fi; Aurakatu 4; 8.30am-6pm Mon-Fri, 9am-4pm Sat & Sun, 10am-3pm winter weekends; @) Busy, very helpful and with information on the entire region.

Getting There & Around

Turku airport is 8km north of the city. **Blue1** (06000 25831; www.blue1.com) has cheap flights to Copenhagen and Stockholm. Wizzair and AirBaltic service various Eastern European cities.

From the **bus terminal** (Aninkaistenkatu 20) there are hourly express buses to Helsinki (€28.50, 2¼ hours) and frequent services to Tampere (€23.20, three hours).

The train station is a short walk northwest of the centre; express trains run frequently to and from Helsinki (from €26.50, two hours), Tampere (from €23.90, 1¾ hours) and beyond.

The harbour, southwest of the centre, has terminals for **Tallink/Silja Line** (0600 15700; www.tallinksilja.fi) and **Viking Line** (0600 41577; www.vikingline.fi). Both companies sail to Stockholm (11 hours) and Mariehamn (six hours).

Bus 1 runs between the *kauppatori* and the airport (€2.50, 25 minutes). This same bus also goes from the *kauppatori* to the harbour.

Åland

018 / POP 27,700

Little known beyond the Baltic, this archipelago spattered between Finland and Sweden is a curious geopolitical entity that belongs to Finland, speaks Swedish, but has its own parliament, flies its own flag proudly from every pole and issues its own national stamps.

Getting There & Around

Eckerö Linjen (28000; www.eckerolinjen.ax; Torggatan 2, Mariehamn) Sails to Grisslehamn, Sweden (€10, three hours), from Eckerö.

Tallink/Silja Lines (0600 15700; www.tallinksilja.com, Torggatan 14, Mariehamn) Runs direct services to Mariehamn from Turku (€16-27, five hours), Helsinki (€29, 11½ hours) and Stockholm (€39, 5½ hours).

Viking Line (26211; www.vikingline.fi; Storagatan 2, Mariehamn) Runs to Turku (€16, 5½ hours), Helsinki (€45, 11 hours) and Stockholm (€16, six hours). Also runs to Kapellskär, a quicker crossing to Sweden with bus connection to Stockholm.

There's an island bus service, but a bike is the way to go. **Ro-No Rent** (12820; www.visitaland.com/rono; bicycles per day/week from €8/40; Jun–mid-Aug) has offices at Mariehamn and Eckerö harbours.

MARIEHAMN

POP 11,161

Villagey Mariehamn is Åland's main port and capital, a pretty place lined with linden trees and timber houses set between two large harbours. Compared to the rest of the archipelago, it's a metropolis, and gets quite busy in summer with tourists off the ferries, and yachts stocking the marinas. Outside the season you could safely fire a cannon through the town.

SELF-CATERING ACCOMMODATION

There's a wealth of cottages for rent on Åland. Both Eckerö (p381) and Viking (p395) ferry lines have a comprehensive list of places that can be booked, as does **Destination Åland** (☎0400 108 800; www.destinationaland.com; Östra Esplanadgatan 7, Mariehamn).

Sights

Ålands Museum & Ålands Konstmuseum MUSEUM, ART GALLERY
(www.regeringen.ax; Stadhusparken; admission €4, Oct-Apr free; ⌚10am-5pm Jun-Aug, 10am-4pm Wed & Fri, 10am-8pm Tue & Thu, noon-4pm Sat & Sun Sep-May) In the centre of town, near the East Harbour, the Ålands Museum & Ålands Konstmuseum, housed together in the same building, give an account of Åland's history, culture and art. There's little info in English.

Sjöfartsmuseum & Pommern MUSEUMS
The stalwarts of Åland are mariners and the best place to get a feel for their exploits is down at the West Harbour. The **Sjöfartsmuseum** (Maritime Museum; www.sjofartsmuseum.ax; Hamngatan 2) was undergoing a major renovation when we last visited, and was closed until 2012. You could still visit, anchored outside, the museum ship **Pommern** (www.mariehamn.ax/pommern; admission €5; ⌚9am-5pm May-Aug, 10am-4pm Sep), a beautifully preserved four-masted barque built in Glasgow in 1903.

Sleeping

Pensionat Solhem GUEST HOUSE €
(☎16322; www.visitaland.com/solhem; Lökskärsvägen; s/d €50/69; ⌚May-Oct) Although it's 3km south of the centre, it's only 2km from the ferries to this delightful seaside spot that can feel like your very own villa. Rooms are basic with shared bathrooms, but cheerful staff keep the place running like clockwork. The local bus (routes B and D) stops nearby.

Gröna Udden Camping CAMPING GROUND €
(☎21121; www.gronaudden.com; campsite €7 plus per adult €7, 2-/4-person cabins €80/105, r €80;⌚May–mid-Sep) A kilometre south of the centre, this camping ground is a family favourite with a safe swimming beach, minigolf course, bike hire and sauna. If the tent plots are a little small, opt for the spruce-red cabins that are fully equipped.

Gästhem Kronan GUEST HOUSE €
(☎12617; www.visitaland.com/kronan; Neptunigatan 52; s/d €49/71) Mariehamn has no hostels, but Kronan is a good-value guest house with basic but spotless, renovated rooms with shared bathroom. It's in a quiet street a short walk from the ferry terminal.

Eating & Drinking

Mariehamn's many cafes serve the local speciality, *Ålandspannkaka* (Åland pancakes), a fluffy square pudding made with semolina and served with stewed prunes.

Indigo SCANDINAVIAN €€
(☎16550; www.indigo.ax; Nygatan 1; mains €22-27; ⌚lunch & dinner Mon-Fri, dinner Sat, bar to 3am weekends) Attractive and upmarket, this stylish restaurant is in a historic brick-and-timber building but the menu is contemporary Scandinavian. Upstairs, in a beautiful loft space, it serves a good-value bistro menu in the evenings (dishes €12 to €18).

Café Bönan CAFE €
(www.cafebonan.ax; Sjökvarteret; lunch buffet €8; ⌚10.30am-1.30pm Mon-Fri) This vegetarian place does healthy salad buffets all sourced from ethical producers so it's total guilt-free lunching. Opens weekends in summer.

Dino's Bar & Grill BAR, BISTRO €€
(www.dinosbar.com; Strandgatan 12; mains €12-20; ⌚lunch Mon-Sat, dinner daily) Popular as a meeting spot, this bar does thick burgers and creative pastas and steaks, best eaten on its great outdoor deck. It's a good place to hang around for a few beers, especially when the house band is playing.

Information

Library (Strandgatan 8; ⌚10am-8pm Mon-Fri, 11am-4pm Sat, noon-4pm Sun) Free internet access.

Tourist office (☎24000; www.visitaland.com; Storagatan 8; ⌚9am-4pm Mon-Fri Sep-May, plus Sat 10am-3pm Apr-May & Sep, 9am-5pm Mon-Fri, 9am-4pm Sat & Sun Jun-Aug; @) Plenty of island info. Books tours.

THE ISLANDS

You can explore most of the main islands in a few days' cycling. The central group comprises **Jomala** and **Sund**, north of Mariehamn, and **Eckerö** to the west. Pick up a copy of the *Visit Åland* brochure and the camping guide from the Mariehamn tourist office for details of places to stay.

Åland's most striking attraction is the medieval castle **Kastelholm** (admission €5; ⏲10am-5pm May–mid-Sep, to 6pm Jul, English tours 2pm late Jun-early Aug) in Sund, about 25km northeast of Mariehamn. Catch bus 4 from Mariehamn or go by bike.

Tampere

☎03 / POP 211,507

For many visitors, Tampere is Finland's number-one city, and it's easy to see why. It combines Nordic sophistication with urban vitality and a most scenic location between two vast lakes. Through its centre churn the Tammerkoski rapids, its grassy banks contrasting with the red brick of the imposing but picturesque chimneys of the fabric mills that once gave the city the moniker 'Manchester of Finland'.

Sights

FREE **Tuomiokirkko** CATHEDRAL

(Tuomiokirkonkatu 3; ⏲10am-5pm Jun-Aug, 11am-3pm Sep-Apr) Intriguing Tampere Cathedral is one of the most notable examples of National Romantic architecture in Finland. The famous artist Hugo Simberg was responsible for the frescoes and stained glass; once you've seen them you'll appreciate that they were controversial at the time.

Vakoilumuseo MUSEUM

(Spy Museum; www.vakoilumuseo.fi; Satakunnankatu 18; adult/child €7/5.50; ⏲10am-6pm Mon-Sat, 11am-5pm Sun Jun-Aug, 11am-5pm daily Sep-May) Tampere's era as industrial city began with the arrival of Scot James Finlayson, who erected a huge cotton mill, now sensitively converted into a mall of cafes and shops called the Finlayson Centre. You'll also find a cinema here, as well as a great brewery-pub and the offbeat Vakoilumuseo, with espionage history, numerous Bond-style gadgets and some interactive displays.

Activities

Traditional **Rajaportin Sauna** (www.rajaportinsauna.fi; Pispalan Valtatie 9; adult/child €6/1; ⏲6-10pm Mon & Wed, 3-9pm Fri, 2-10pm Sat) is Finland's oldest operating public sauna. It's a couple of kilometres west of the centre; buses 1, 13 and 22, among others, head out there.

Festivals & Events

There are events in Tampere almost year-round. Usually held in early March, the **Tampere Film Festival** (www.tamperefilmfestival.fi) is a respected international festival of short films. **Tammerfest** (www.tammerfest.fi) is the city's premier rock-music festival, held over four days in mid-July with concerts at various stages around town.

Sleeping

TOP CHOICE **Dream Hostel** HOSTEL €

(☎045 236 0517; www.dreamhostel.fi; Åkerlundinkatu 2; dm €22.50-27.50, tw/q €65/110; @) Sparky and spacious, this new arrival is just about Finland's best hostel. Helpful staff, super-comfortable wide-berth dorms in various sizes (both unisex and female are available), a heap of facilities, original decor and the right attitude about everything make it a real winner.

Hotelli Victoria HOTEL €€

(☎242 5111; www.hotellivictoria.fi; Itsenäisyydenkatu 1; s/d around €109/142, weekends & summer €89/99; @≋) Just the other side of the railway station from the centre, this friendly hotel offers sound summer value with its spruce rooms, free internet and a commendable breakfast spread that includes waffles, sausage omelette and berry pudding options.

Hostel Sofia HOSTEL €

(☎254 4020; www.hostelsofia.fi; Tuomiokirkonkatu 12A; dm/s/d €28/59/75; @) This comfortable hostel is right opposite the cathedral and fills up fast. A recent refit has left it looking very spruce, offering rooms with comfortable beds (no bunks), large windows and stepladder shelves, as well as good showers and a kitchenette on every floor. HI discount and bike rental.

Omenahotelli HOTEL €

(☎0600 18018; www.omena.com; Hämeenkatu 7 & Hämeenkatu 28; r to €65; @) With two locations at the western and eastern ends of the main drag – the latter very handy for the train station – this receptionless hotel offers the usual comfortable rooms with twin beds, microwave, kettle and fold-out couch. Book online or via the terminal at the entrance.

Eating

Tampere's speciality, *mustamakkara,* is a mild sausage made with cow's blood, black-pudding style. It's normally eaten with lingonberry jam and is tastier than it sounds. You can get it at the *kauppahalli* or a summer kiosk at Laukontori market.

TOP CHOICE **Tuulensuu** GASTRO-PUB €€
(www.gastropub.net/tuulensuu; Hämeenpuisto 23; mains €13-20; ⏲food 4pm-midnight Mon-Fri, noon-midnight Sat, 5pm-midnight Sun) The best of an array of gastro-pubs that have recently sprouted, this corner spot has a fine range of beers and wines, as well as a lengthy port and cigar menu. The food is lovingly prepared and features staples such as liver and schnitzel, as well as more elaborate plates like duck confit and an excellent cassoulet (vegie version available too).

Neljä Vuodenaikaa BISTRO €
(www.4vuodenaikaa.fi; Kauppahalli; dishes €8-18; ⏲breakfast Tue-Fri, lunch Mon-Sat) Tucked into a corner of the *kauppahalli*, this recommended spot brings a Gallic flair to the Finnish lunch hour with delicious plates such as bouillabaisse and French country salad, augmented by excellent daily specials and wines by the glass.

Vohvelikahvila CAFE €
(www.vohvelikahvila.com; Ojakatu 2; waffles €4-6.50; ⏲10am-8pm Mon-Sat, 11am-7pm Sun) This cosy and quaint little place does a range of sweet delights, but specialises above all in fresh waffles, which come laden with cream and chocolate.

Panimoravintola Plevna BEER HALL €€
(www.plevna.fi; Itäinenkatu 8; mains €10-19; ⏲food served 11am-10pm) Inside the old Finlayson textile mill, this big barn of a place offers a wide range of delicious beer, cider and perry brewed on the premises, including an excellent strong stout. Meals are large and designed for soaking it all up.

Quick Eats

Kauppahalli MARKET HALL €
(Hämeenkatu 19; ⏲8am-6pm Mon-Fri, 8am-3pm Sat) This intriguing indoor market is one of Finland's best, with picturesque wooden stalls serving a dazzling array of wonderful meat, fruit, baked goodies and fish.

Drinking

Café Europa PUB, CAFE
(Aleksanterinkatu 29; ⏲noon-late) Furnished with 1930s-style horsehair couches and chairs, this is a romantic, old-world-European type of place complete with Belgian and German beers, board games, ornate mirrors and chandeliers and an excellent summer terrace.

O'Connell's PUB
(www.oconnells.fi; Rautatienkatu 24; ⏲4pm-1am or 2am) Popular with both Finns and expats, this rambling Irish pub is handy for the train station and has plenty of time-worn, comfortable seating and an air of bonhomie. Its best feature is the range of interesting beers on tap and carefully selected bottled imports.

Suvi BOAT BAR
(www.laivaravintolasuvi.fi; Laukontori; ⏲10am-late Jun-Sep) Moored alongside the Laukontori quay, this is a typical Finnish boat bar offering no-nonsense deck-top drinking. Prepare a boarding party and lap up the afternoon sun.

Information

GoTampere Oy (☎5656 6800; www.gotampere.fi; Rautatienkatu 25; ⏲9am-5pm Mon-Fri Nov-Mar, plus 11am-3pm Sat & Sun Apr-May, Sep & Oct, 9am-8pm Mon-Fri, 9.30am-5pm Sat & Sun Jun-Aug; @) Tourist office, in the railway station. Has a booking desk.

Library (Metso; Pirkankatu 2; ⏲10am-8pm Mon-Fri, 10am-4pm Sat, 11am-5pm Sun, 10am-7pm weekdays only Jun-Aug) Several internet terminals.

Getting There & Away

Finnair serves major Finnish cities. **AirBaltic** (www.airbaltic.com) connects Tampere with Rovaniemi as well as Riga. **Blue 1** (☎06000 25831; www.blue1.com) flies direct to Stockholm. **Ryanair** (☎0200 39000; www.ryanair.com) has daily services to several European destinations, including London Stansted.

The **bus station** (Hatanpään valtatie 7) is in the south of town. Most major towns in Finland are served from here; services include express buses to Helsinki (€24.60, 2½ hours) and Turku (€23.20, two to three hours).

The **train station** (www.vr.fi; Rautatienkatu 25) is in the centre, at the eastern end of Hämeenkatu. Express trains run hourly to/from Helsinki (€26.30, two hours). There are direct trains to Turku (€23.90, 1¾ hours), Oulu (€57 to €67, 4½ to seven hours) and other Finnish cities.

Getting Around

Tampere's bus service is extensive and a one-hour ticket costs €2. A 24-hour Tourist Ticket costs €6. Buses (€2) run between the airport and centre. A separate company serves Ryanair flights (€6).

SOUTHEASTERN FINLAND

Most of southern Finland could be dubbed Lakeland, but this spectacular area takes it to extremes. It often seems there's more water than land here, and what water it is – sublime, sparkling and clean, reflecting sky and forests as clearly as a mirror. It's a land that leaves an indelible impression on every visitor. If you've only got the time or money to visit one part of Finland outside Helsinki in summer, make this the place.

Savonlinna

☎015 / POP 27,726

Often considered Finland's prettiest town, Savonlinna shimmers on a sunny day as the water ripples around its centre. One of Europe's most visually dramatic castles lords it over the picturesque centre and hosts July's world-famous opera festival in a spectacular setting.

Sights & Activities

Olavinlinna CASTLE

(www.olavinlinna.fi; adult/child €5/3.50; ⏰10am-6pm Jun–mid-Aug, 10am-4pm Mon-Fri, 11am-4pm Sat & Sun mid-Aug–May, last tour leaves 1hr before close) Standing immense and haughty on a rock in the lake, 15th-century Olavinlinna is one of the most spectacular castles in northern Europe and, as well as being an imposing fortification, is also the spectacular venue for the month-long Savonlinna Opera Festival. To visit the interior, including original towers, bastions and chambers, you must join a guided tour (around 45 minutes). Tours are multilingual and depart on the hour. Guides are good at bringing the castle to life.

Cruises BOAT TRIPS

(cruises €10-15) Dozens of 1½-hour scenic cruises leave from the harbour near the *kauppatori* daily in summer.

Festivals

The **Savonlinna Opera Festival** (☎476 750; www.operafestival.fi; Olavinkatu 27) is Finland's most famous festival, with an enviably dramatic setting: the covered courtyard of Olavinlinna castle. It offers four weeks of high-class opera performances from early July to early August. Buy tickets up to a year in advance from **Lippupalvelu** (☎0600 10800; www.lippupalvelu.fi) or from Savonlinna Travel.

Sleeping

Prices rise sharply during the opera festival, when hotel beds are scarce. Fortunately, students are out of town and their residences are converted to summer hotels and hostels. Book accommodation well in advance if you plan to visit during July.

TOP CHOICE **Lossiranta Lodge** HOTEL €€

(☎044 511 2323; www.lossiranta.net; Aino Acktén Puistotie; r €110-160, during opera festival €170-220) This beautifully designed boutique villa boasts a stunning lakeside location and the closest possible view of Olavinlinna. The five unique rooms are impossibly cute, lovingly designed and surprisingly functional.

Vuorilinna HOTEL, HOSTEL €

(☎73950; www.fontana.fi; Kylpylaitoksentie; dm/s/d €30/65/85; ⏰Jun-Aug;) Set in several buildings mostly used by students, this friendly complex offers an appealing location across a footbridge from the centre. Rooms are clean and comfortable; the cheaper ones share bathrooms and kitchen between two. Dorm rates get you the same deal, and there's an HI discount.

Vuohimäki CAMPING GROUND €

(☎537 353; www.fontana.fi; per tent/person €13.50/4, 4-person r €58-76, 4-/6-person cabins €76/84; ⏰early Jun-late Aug) Located 7km southwest of town, this has good facilities but fills quickly in July. Prices for rooms and cabins are cheaper in June and August. It hires canoes, bikes and rowboats.

S Heinävesi BOAT HOTEL €€

(☎533 120; www.savonlinnanlaivat.fi; cabins upper/lower deck per person €33/28) During summer this steamer offers cramped but cute two-bunk cabins after the last cruise every afternoon/evening. It's moored right in the centre of things. Nearby, *Lake Star* and *Lake Seal* also offer **cabins** (☎0400-200 117; www.lakestar.info; d €40).

Eating & Drinking

The lively lakeside *kauppatori* is the place for casual snacking. A *lörtsy* (turnover) is typical and comes savoury with meat *(lihalörtsy)* or sweet with apple *(omenalörtsy)* or cloudberry *(lakkalörtsy)*. Savonlinna is also famous for fried *muikku* (vendace, tiny lake fish).

Majakka FINNISH €€

(☎206 2825; www.ravintolamajakka.fi; Satamakatu 11; mains €12-20) This restaurant has a deck-like terrace fitting the nautical theme (the name means 'lighthouse'). Local meat and fish specialities are tasty, generously sized and fairly priced and the select-your-own appetiser plate is a nice touch.

Olutravintola Sillansuu PUB
(Verkkosaarenkatu 1; ⏲2pm-late) Savonlinna's best pub by some distance is compact and cosy, offering an excellent variety of international bottled beers, a decent whisky selection and friendly service.

Information

Library (Tottinkatu 6; ⏲11am-7pm Mon-Thu, 10am-4pm Fri) Free internet access.

Savonlinna Travel (☎517 510; www.savonlinna.travel; Puistokatu 1; ⏲9am-5pm Mon-Fri Aug-Jun, 9am-7pm daily Jul) Tourist information, including accommodation reservations, farm stays, festival tickets and tours. Free internet.

Getting There & Away

Boat

From mid-June to mid-August, **MS Puijo** (www.mspuijo.fi) travels to Kuopio on Monday, Wednesday and Friday at 9am (€79, 10½ hours), returning on Tuesday, Thursday and Saturday.

Bus

Savonlinna is off major routes, but there are several express buses a day from Helsinki (€48.40, 4½ to 5½ hours), and buses run almost hourly from Mikkeli (€21.70, 1½ hours).

Train

Trains departing from Helsinki (€55.60, five hours) require a change in Parikkala. For Kuopio and Tampere, rail buses will shuttle you for the two-hour trip to Pieksämäki to connect with trains. The main train station is a walk from the centre of Savonlinna; board and alight at the Kauppatori station instead.

Kuopio

☎017 / POP 92,626

Most things a reasonable person could desire from a summery lakeside town are in Kuopio, with pleasure cruises on the azure water, spruce forests to stroll in, wooden waterside pubs and local fish specialities to taste.

Sights & Activities

Jätkänkämppä Savusauna SAUNA
(☎030-60830; www.rauhalahti.fi; adult/child €12/6; ⏲4-10pm Tue, also Thu from Jun-Aug) Time your Kuopio visit so you can sweat in Jätkänkämppä smoke sauna, a memorable and sociable experience that draws locals and visitors. This giant *savusauna* (smoke sauna) seats 60; it's mixed and guests are given towels to wear. Bring a swimsuit for a dip in the lake. Bus 7 goes from the *kauppatori* to the Rauhalahti hotel complex, from where it's a 600m walk to the sauna, or take the lake boat from the passenger harbour in summer.

Lake cruises BOAT TRIPS
In summer there are regular lake and canal cruises from the harbour. Ninety-minute jaunts cost €11 (half price for children) and depart hourly from 11am to 6pm.

Sleeping

Matkustajakoti Rautatie GUEST HOUSE €
(☎580 0569; www.kuopionasemagrilli.com; Asemakatu 1; s/d with bathroom €55/79, without bathroom €45/60) This friendly place, run out of the *grilli* (Finnish fast-food outlet) at the railway station, actually offers ensuite rooms in the station itself, which are very comfortable, exceedingly spacious and surprisingly peaceful. Across the road, it has some cheaper, but also most acceptable rooms, this time with shared bathroom.

Hostelli Hermanni HOSTEL €
(☎040 910 9083; www.hostellihermanni.fi; Hermanninaukio 3e; dm/s/d €25/40/50; @) Tucked away in a quiet area 1.5km south of the *kauppatori* (follow Haapaniemenkatu and bear left when you can; the hostel's in the Metsähallitus building), this is a well-run little hostel with comfy wooden bunks and beds, high ceilings and decent shared bathrooms and kitchen.

Eating

The **kauppahalli** (⏲8am-5pm Mon-Fri, 8am-3pm Sat), at the southern end of the *kauppatori*, is a classic Finnish indoor market hall. Here stalls sell local speciality *kalakukko*, a large rye loaf stuffed with whitefish and then baked. The bakery by the western door sells mini ones for €2 if you just want a taste.

Kummisetä FINNISH €€
(www.kummiseta.com; Minna Canthinkatu 44; mains €14-21; ⏲dinner daily, lunch Sat) The sober brown colours of the 'Godfather' restaurant give it a traditional and romantic feel that's replicated on the menu, with country pâté, pike-perch, chanterelle sauces and berries all making welcome appearances alongside chunky steaks. Food and service are both excellent.

THE SAUNA

Nothing is more traditionally or culturally Finnish than the sauna. For centuries it has been a place to bathe, meditate, warm up during cold winters and even give birth, and most Finns still use the sauna at least once a week. An invitation to bathe in a family's sauna is an honour.

Bathing is done in the nude (there are some exceptions in public saunas, which are almost always sex-segregated anyway) and Finns are quite strict about the nonsexual – even sacred – nature of the sauna.

According to sauna etiquette you should wash or shower first. Once inside the sauna (with a temperature of 80°C to 100°C), water is thrown onto the stove using a *kauhu* (ladle), producing steam *(löyly)*. A whisk of birch twigs and leaves *(vihta)* is sometimes used to lightly strike the skin, improving circulation. Once you're hot enough, go outside and cool off with a cold shower or, preferably, by jumping into a lake or pool – enthusiastic Finns do so even in winter by cutting a hole in the ice. Repeat the process. The sauna beer afterwards is also traditional.

Vapaasatama Sampo FINNISH €
(www.wanhamestari.fi; Kauppakatu 13; muikku dishes €9-14) Have it stewed, fried, smoked or in a soup, but it's all about *muikku* (vendace) here. This is one of Finland's most famous spots to try the small lake fish that drive Savo stomachs.

Kaneli CAFE €
(www.kahvilakaneli.net; Kauppakatu 22; ⏱noon-6pm Mon-Fri, 11am-4pm Sat, noon-4pm Sun) This cracking cafe, just off the *kauppatori*, evokes a bygone age with much of its decor but offers modern comfort in its shiny espresso machine, as well as many other flavoured coffees to accompany your toothsome and sticky *pulla*. Opens longer hours in summer.

Drinking & Entertainment

Kuopio's nightlife area is around Kauppakatu, east of the *kauppatori*. There are many options in this block, some with summer terraces. Nearby, **Henry's Pub** (www.henryspub.net; Käsityökatu 17; ⏱9pm-4am) is an atmospheric underworld with bands playing several times a week.

Information

Kuopio Tourist Service (☎182 585; www.kuopioinfo.fi; Haapaniemenkatu 17; ⏱9.30am-4.30pm Mon-Fri Sep-May, to 5pm Jun-Aug, also 9.30am-3pm Sat Jul) By the *kauppatori*, with information on regional attractions and accommodation.

Library (Maaherrankatu 12; ⏱10am-7pm Mon-Fri, 10am-3pm Sat) Free internet access.

Getting There & Away

The train station is 400m north of the centre on Asemakatu. There are direct services to Helsinki (€58.10, 4½ hours), Kajaani (€23.90, 1¾ hours) and Oulu (€45.30, four hours).

The bus terminal is just north of the train station. Regular express services to/from Kuopio include Helsinki (€60.20, 6½ hours), Kajaani (€31.50, 2¾ hours), Jyväskylä (€23.20, 2¼ hours) and Savonlinna (€29.70, three hours).

NORTHERN FINLAND

Northern Finland is a true wilderness and place of extremes: continuous daylight in summer and continuous night in winter. October, February and March are ideal times to see the stunning aurora borealis. September brings exceptional autumn colours *(ruska)*. The region includes pristine national parks, ski resorts, dog-sledding opportunities, reindeer, Santa Claus and other wintry wonders.

The northernmost part, Finnish Lapland, is a mysterious land of clear Arctic air and unpopulated vastness. It's home to the Sámi, who have traditionally made their living from their domesticated reindeer herds, which number some 200,000 antlered beasts.

Oulu

☎08 / POP 139,133

Prosperous Oulu is spread across several islands, elegantly connected by pedestrian bridges, and water never seems far away. In summer, the angled sun bathes the *kauppatori* in light and all seems well with the world. Locals, who appreciate daylight when

SHE AIN'T HEAVY, SHE'S MY WIFE

If the thought of grabbing your wife by the legs, hurling her over your shoulder and running for your life sounds appealing, make sure you're in Sonkajärvi, 100km north of Kuopio, near the town of Iisalmi, in early July for the **Wife-Carrying World Championships** (www.eukonkanto.fi). What began as a heathenish medieval habit of pillaging neighbouring villages in search of nubile women has become one of Finland's oddest – and most publicised – events. The winners get the wife's weight in beer.

Buses and trains connect Kuopio with Iisalmi, from where buses run to Sonkajärvi, 18km northeast.

they get it, crowd the terraces, and stalls groan under the weight of Arctic berries.

The **Air Guitar World Championships** (www.airguitarworldchampionships.com) are part of the **Oulu Music Video Festival** (www.omvf.net) in late August. Contestants from all over the world take the stage to show what they can do with their imaginary instruments.

Sights & Activities

Kauppatori MARKET SQUARE
By the waterside, this is one of the liveliest and most colourful market squares in Finland, with its red wooden storehouses (now housing restaurants, bars and craft shops), market stalls, bursting summer terraces and the rotund *Toripolliisi* statue, a humorous representation of the local police.

Bicycle Paths CYCLING
Oulu's extensive network of wonderful bicycle paths is among the best in Finland and nowhere is the Finns' love of two-wheeled transport more obvious than here in summer. Bikes (per hour/day €2/15) can be hired from Kiikeli **hire shed** (0440 552 808; 9am-6pm May-Sep) near the *kauppatori*, and from Nallikari camping ground. The tourist office has a free cycle-route map.

Sleeping

There's precious little budget accommodation in Oulu.

As this book went to press, a new hotel, **Forenom Hotel Oulu** (020-1983 420; www.forenom.fi; Rautatienkatu 9; s/d €75/85; P @) was opening opposite the train station. Reception is only open 9am to 5pm weekdays, but staff can give you a door code if you'll be arriving at other times.

TOP CHOICE **Hotel Lasaretti** HOTEL €€
(020 757 4700; www.lasaretti.com; Kasarmintie 13; s/d €127/148, summer €70/82; @) Bright, modern and optimistic, this inviting hotel sits in a group of renovated brick buildings, once a hospital. It's close to town but the parkside location by the bubbling-bright stream makes it feel rural.

Nallikari CAMPING GROUND €
(044 703 1353; www.nallikari.fi; Hietasaari; campsites €13-16 plus per adult/child €4/1, cabins €36-42, cottages €98-139; @) Resembling a small town, this excellent camping ground offers all sorts of options in a location close to the beach on Hietasaari, a 40-minute walk to town via pedestrian bridges. Bus 17 gets you there from the *kauppatori*.

Eating

Local specialities can be found in and around the lively *kauppatori*. On the square is the **kauppahalli** (8am-6pm Mon-Fri, 8am-3pm Sat), with plenty of spots to snack on anything from cloudberries to sushi.

Café Bisketti CAFE €
(www.cafebisketti.fi; Kirkkokatu 8; lunches €5-8; 8am-9.30pm Mon-Thu, 8am-11.30pm Fri & Sat, 11am-9.30pm Sun) Think twice before getting that pastry with your morning coffee; they're enormous and might not leave room for lunch, with cheap deals on soup, salad, coffee and a pastry, and hot dishes for not much extra. In the evenings, the terrace is a decent spot for a people-watching beer.

Crecian GREEK €€
(www.crecian.fi; Kirkkokatu 55; mains €20-27) It's worth the short stroll from the centre to this popular neighbourhood restaurant, predictably decked out in blue and white, though the owner's actually Cypriot. The dishes are tasty and generously proportioned, and service is welcoming.

Drinking & Entertainment

There's plenty going on in Oulu at night. The *kauppatori* is the spot to start in summer.

TOP CHOICE **Never Grow Old** BAR
(www.ngo.fi; Hallituskatu 17; 6pm-2am or 3am) This enduringly popular bar hits its stride

after 10pm, with plenty of dancing, DJs and revelry in the tightly packed interior. The goofy decor includes some seriously comfortable and extremely uncomfortable places to sit, and a log-palisade bar that seems designed to get you to wear your drink.

Kaarlenholvi Jumpru Pub PUB
(www.jumpru.fi; Kauppurienkatu 6; ⏲11am-2am Mon & Tue, 11am-4am Wed-Sat, noon-2am Sun) This Oulu institution is a great place for meeting locals and its enclosed outdoor area always seems to be humming with cheerfully sauced-up folk. There's a warren of cosy rooms inside, as well as a nightclub opening from 10pm Wednesday to Saturday.

Information

Wi-fi is available throughout the city centre on the PanOulu network.

Library (☎558 410; Kaarlenväylä; ⏲10am-8pm Mon-Fri, 10am-3pm Sat, noon-4pm Sun) On the waterfront, opposite the Oulu Theatre. Several internet terminals.

Tourist office (☎044 703 1330; www.oulutourism.fi; Torikatu 10; ⏲9am-5pm Mon-Thu, 9am-4pm Fri) Publishes the useful guide *Look at Oulu*.

Getting There & Away

Air

There are several daily direct flights from Helsinki, operated by Finnair and Blue1. AirBaltic flies to Turku, Riga and Stockholm and probably more places by the time you read this. Bus 19 runs between the centre and the airport (€3.60, 25 minutes, every 20 minutes).

Bus

The bus station, near the train station, has services connecting Oulu with all the main centres. These include Rovaniemi (€39.80, 3½ hours), Tornio (€22.80, 2½ hours), Kajaani (€28.50, 2½ hours) and Helsinki (€89.10, 10 hours).

Train

The station is just east of the centre. Six to 10 trains a day run from Helsinki to Oulu (€71.50, seven to nine hours); the Pendolino service takes only six hours (€77.20). There are also trains via Kajaani, and trains north to Rovaniemi.

Rovaniemi

☎016 / POP 59,848

Expanding rapidly on the back of a tourism boom, the 'official' terrestrial residence of Santa Claus is the capital of Finnish Lapland and a more-or-less obligatory northern stop. Its wonderful Arktikum museum is the perfect introduction to the mysteries of these latitudes, and Rovaniemi is a good place from which to organise activities.

Sights

TOP CHOICE **Arktikum** MUSEUM
(www.arktikum.fi; Pohjoisranta 4; adult/student €12/8; ⏲9am-7pm mid-Jun–mid-Aug, 10am-6pm Tue-Sun rest of yr, also Mon early Jun, late Aug & Dec) With its beautifully designed glass tunnel stretching out to the Ounasjoki, Arktikum is one of Finland's best museums. There are two main exhibitions. One side deals with Lapland, with some information on Sámi culture. The highlight, though, is the other side, with a wide-ranging display on the Arctic itself, with superb static and interactive displays focusing on Arctic peoples, flora and fauna.

Napapiiri & Santa Claus Village TOURIST COMPLEX
The **Arctic Circle**, called Napapiiri in Finland, crosses the road 8km north of Rovaniemi – and built right on top of it is the 'official' **Santa Claus Village** (www.santaclausvillage.info; admission free; ⏲10am-5pm Sep-May, 9am-6pm Jun-Aug, 9am-7pm Dec-early Jan), a touristy complex of shops. Here too is **Santa Claus Post Office** (www.santaclaus.posti.fi; FIN-96930 Arctic Circle), which receives nearly 750,000 letters each year from children all over the world.

But the big attraction is, of course, **Santa** himself, who sees visitors year-round in a rather impressive **grotto** (www.santaclauslive.com; admission free; ⏲9am-6pm Jun-Aug, 10am-5pm Sep-May). The portly saint is quite a linguist, and an old hand at chatting with kids and adults alike. A private chinwag is absolutely free, but you can't photograph the moment…and official photos of your visit start at an outrageous €25.

LAPLAND SEASONS

It's important to pick your time in Lapland carefully. In the far north there's no sun for 50 days of the year, and no night for 70-odd days. In June it's very muddy, and in July insects can be hard to deal with. If you're here to walk, August is great and in September the *ruska* autumn colours can be seen. There's thick snow cover from mid-October to May; the best time for skiing and husky/reindeer/snowmobile safaris is March and April, when you get a decent amount of daylight and less extreme temperatures.

Bus 8 heads to Napapiiri (adult/child return €6.60/3.80) from the train station, passing through the centre.

Tours

Rovaniemi is Lapland's most popular base for winter and summer activities, offering the convenience of frequent departures and professional trips with multilingual guides. The tourist office has a full weekly list of activities, and can book them for you.

Sleeping

TOP CHOICE City Hotel HOTEL €€
(☎330 0111; www.cityhotel.fi; Pekankatu 9; s/d €107/124, Jun-Sep €70/75; @) There's something pleasing about this warm and welcoming place a block off the main drag. It's worth the small upgrade to the recently refurbished 'comfort' rooms with their new beds and plush maroon-and-brown fabrics.

Hostel Rudolf HOSTEL €
(☎321 321; www.rudolf.fi; Koskikatu 41; dm/s/d winter €46/60/85, summer €35/44/56) Run by Hotel Santa Claus (Korkalonkatu 29), where you inconveniently have to go to check in, this staffless place is Rovaniemi's only hostel and can fill up fast. Dorms are comfortable and the private rooms good for the price, with spotless bathrooms, solid desks and bedside lamps; there's also a kitchen available but no wi-fi. HI discount.

Guesthouse Borealis GUEST HOUSE €
(☎342 0130; www.guesthouseborealis.com; Asemieskatu 1; s/d/tr €45/56/81; @) The cordial hospitality and proximity to the train station make this family-run spot a winner. The rooms have no frills but are bright and clean; some have a balcony.

Eating

Kauppayhtiö CAFE, BAR €
(Valtakatu 24; light meals €4-7; ⌚10.30am-8pm Mon-Thu, 10.30am-2am Fri & Sat; @) Rovaniemi's best cafe, this is an oddball collection of retro curios with a coffee-bean and gasoline theme and colourful plastic tables.

Mariza LUNCH BUFFET €
(www.ruokahuonemariza.fi; Ruokasenkatu 2; lunch €8.20; ⌚lunch Mon-Fri) A couple of blocks from the centre, in untouristed territory, this simple lunch place is a real find and offers a buffet of home-cooked Finnish food, including daily changing hot dishes, soup and salad. Authentic and excellent.

Drinking & Entertainment

Excluding ski resorts, Rovaniemi is the only place north of Oulu with a half-decent nightlife.

ZoomIt CAFE, BAR
(www.hotelsantaclaus.fi; Koskikatu; ⌚11am-11pm, later on weekends) Large, light, modern ZoomIt is a popular, buzzy central bar and cafe. Right in the heart of town, its terrace is the spot to be on a sunny afternoon and its spacious interior gives room to stretch out with a book if it's snowing.

Roy Club BAR, CLUB
(www.royclub.fi; Maakuntakatu 24; ⌚9pm-4am) This friendly bar has a sedate, comfortable top half with cosy seating, a very cheap happy hour until 1am nightly and well-attended Tuesday karaoke. There's also a downstairs nightclub that gets cheerily boisterous with students and goes late.

Information

Library (Hallituskatu 9; ⌚11am-7pm Mon-Fri, 11am-5pm Sat) Aalto-designed; has free internet access.

Tourist information (☎346 270; www.visitrovaniemi.fi; Maakuntakatu 29; ⌚9am-5pm Mon-Fri) On the square in the middle of town. Free internet.

Getting There & Away

Air

Finnair flies daily from Helsinki and Oulu. The budget carrier Blue1 also flies to Helsinki, and AirBaltic flies to Riga and Tampere. Buses meet each arriving flight (€7, 15 minutes).

Bus

Frequent express buses go south to Kemi (€23.20, 1½ hours) and Oulu (€39.80, 3½ hours) and there are night buses to Helsinki (€118, 12½ hours). Daily connections serve just about everywhere else in Lapland.

Train

The train to Helsinki (€79 to €83, 10 to 12 hours) is quicker, cheaper and more commodious than the bus.

Saariselkä

☎016

Between Sodankylä and Inari, this collection of enormous hotels and holiday cottages makes a great stop for the active. It's on the edge of one of Europe's great wilderness areas, much of which is covered by the

UKK National Park. You could hike for weeks here; there's a good network of huts and a few marked trails. In winter this is a ski resort and a very popular base for snowmobiling and husky trips. In the Siula centre there's tourist information and a **national parks office** (☎020 564 7200; www.outdoors.fi; ⊙9am-5pm Mon-Fri, also 9am-3pm Sat & Sun summer & winter high seasons) that sells maps and reserves wilderness cabins.

Hit the website www.saariselka.fi for cottage accommodation; the cheapest place to stay is **Saariselän Panimo** (☎675 6500; www.saariselanpanimo.fi; s/d €44/58), a cosy brewpub with spacious, clean rooms that are a real bargain. Buses run regularly north to Ivalo and south to Rovaniemi.

Inari

☎016 / POP 550

Finland's most significant Sámi centre, this tiny village on the shores of spectacular Inarijärvi, Lapland's largest lake, is the place to learn something of their culture, with authentic handicraft shops and a brilliant museum.

An excellent year-round activities program is operated by **Inari Event** (☎040-777 4339; www.visitinari.fi), based at the Inarin Kultahovi hotel.

TOP CHOICE **Siida** (www.siida.fi, adult/student €8/6.50; ⊙9am-8pm Jun-Sep, 10am-5pm Tue-Sun Oct-May) is one of Finland's finest museums. It's a comprehensive overview of the Sámi and their Arctic environment that's actually two museums skilfully interwoven. Outside is the original museum, a complex of open-air buildings that reflect post-nomadic Sámi life.

Lomakylä Inari (☎671 108; www.saariselka.fi/lomakylainari; campsites for 1/2/4 people €10/15/18, 2-/4-person cabins without bathroom €43/48, with bathroom €65/75, cottages with sauna €80-170; ⊙Jun-Sep; @) Provides the closest cabin accommodation to town (500m south of the centre) and is a good option. Some cottages are available in winter.

ℹ Information

Inari's **tourist office** (☎040 168 9668; www.inari.fi) is in the Siida museum and open the same hours. There's also a nature information point here.

ℹ Getting There & Away

Two daily buses hit Inari from Rovaniemi (€54.50, 5¼ hours) and continue to Norway.

UNDERSTAND FINLAND

History

Finland's story is that of a wrestling match between heavyweights Sweden and Russia, and the country's eventful emergence from between their grip to become one of the world's most progressive and prosperous nations.

Though evidence of pre–ice age habitation exists, it wasn't until around 9000 years ago that settlement was re-established after the big chill. Things are hazy, but the likeliest scenario seems to be that the Finns' ancestors moved into the south and drove the nomadic ancestors of the Sámi north towards Lapland.

The 12th and 13th centuries saw the Swedes begin to move in, Christianising the Finns in the south and establishing settlements and fortifications. The Russians were never far away, though. There were constant skirmishes with the power of Novgorod, and in the early 18th century Peter the Great attacked and occupied much of Finland. By 1809 Sweden was in no state to resist and Finland became a duchy of the Russian Empire. The capital was moved to Helsinki from Turku, but the communist revolution of October 1917 brought the downfall of the Russian tsar and enabled Finland to declare independence.

Stalin's aggressive territorial demands in 1939 led to the Winter War between Finland and the Soviet Union, conducted in horribly low temperatures. Little Finland resisted heroically but was defeated and forced to cede 10% of its territory. When pressured for more, Finland accepted assistance from Germany. This Continuation War against the Russians cost Finland almost 100,000 lives. Eventually Finland negotiated an armistice with the Russians, ceding more land, and then waged a bitter war in Lapland to oust the Germans. Against the odds, Finland remained independent, but at a heavy price.

Recent Times

Finland managed to take a neutral stance during the Cold War and, once the USSR collapsed, it joined the EU in 1995, adopting the euro in 2002.

In the new millennium, Finland has boomed, on the back of a strong technology sector, the traditionally important forestry industry, design and manufacturing and, increasingly, tourism. It's a major success story of the new Europe, with a strong economy, robust social values and superlow crime and corruption.

People

With a population of 5.4 million, Finland is one of Europe's most sparsely populated countries, having 17 people per sq km, falling to less than one per sq km in parts of Lapland. Both Finnish and Swedish are official languages, with some 5.5% of Finns having Swedish as their mother tongue, especially on the west coast and the Åland archipelago. Just over 2% of all Finnish residents are immigrants.

Finland's minorities include around 6000 Roma in the south and, in the north, the Sámi, from several distinct groups.

A capacity for silence and reflection are the traits that best sum up the Finnish character, though this seems odd when weighed against their global gold medal in coffee consumption, their production line of successful heavy bands and their propensity for a tipple. The image of a log cabin with a sauna by a lake tells much about Finnish culture: independence, endurance (*sisu* or guts) and a deep love of nature.

Food & Drink

Typical Finnish food features lots of fish, such as Baltic herring, salmon and whitefish, along with solid stuff like potatoes, meatballs, sausages, soups, stews and dark rye bread. Big towns all have a *kauppahalli* (market hall), the place to head for all sorts of Finnish specialities. The summer *kauppatori* (market square) also has food stalls and market produce.

Meals in a restaurant *(ravintola)* can be expensive, but many put on a generous lunch *(lounas)* buffet for between €7 and €10. These include all-you-can-eat salad, bread, coffee and dessert, plus big helpings of hearty fare.

Finns are the world's biggest coffee drinkers, so cafes are everywhere.

Price ranges for a main course in this chapter have been categorised as follows:

€€€ more than €25

€€ €15 to €25

€ less than €15

Arts

Jean Sibelius (1865–1957) was at the forefront of the Finnish nationalist movement. His stirring *Finlandia* has been raised to the status of national hymn. Sibelius and nationalistic painter Akseli Gallen-Kallela fell under the spell of Karelianism, a movement that drew its inspiration from the folk songs collected in the 1830s by Elias Lönnrot to form the national epic *Kalevala*.

Other famed Finnish writers include Tove Jansson, creator of the Moomintrolls, and novelist Arto Paasilinna. Finland's pre-eminence in architecture and design owes much to Alvar Aalto, who designed everything from public buildings to furniture and vases.

The best-known Finnish film-maker is Aki Kaurismäki, director of films like the 2002 success *Man Without a Past,* while director Renny Harlin has established himself in Hollywood.

Classical music is thriving in Finland, which is an assembly line of orchestral and operatic talent: see a performance if you can. Finnish bands have also made a big impact on the heavier, darker side of the music scale in recent years. The Rasmus, Nightwish, HIM, The 69 Eyes and Apocalyptica are huge around the world. But there is lighter music, such as emo-punks Poets of the Fall and melodic Husky Rescue.

Environment

Finland is a country of forests and lakes. Some 10% of the country is taken up by bodies of water, and nearly 70% is forested with birch, spruce and pine. It's a fairly flat expanse of territory – though the fells of Lapland add a little height to the picture, they are small change compared to mountainous Norway.

Weighing in as Europe's seventh-largest nation, Finland hits remarkable latitudes: even its southernmost point is comparable with southern Alaska or Greenland.

Finland's excellent network of national parks and other protected areas is maintained by **Metsähallitus** (www.outdoors.fi), the Finnish Forest and Park Service. In total, over 30,000 sq km – some 9% of the total area – is in some way protected land.

Elk, lynx, wolverines, brown bears and wolves are native to Finland, although sightings are rare. In Lapland, the Sámi keep commercial herds of around 200,000 reindeer.

SURVIVAL GUIDE

Directory A–Z

Accommodation

Most camping grounds are open only from June to August. Sites usually cost around €10 plus €4 per person. Almost all camping grounds have cabins or cottages for rent, which are usually excellent value (from €35 for a basic double cabin).

Finnish hostels are invariably clean, comfortable and very well equipped, if sometimes short on atmosphere. It's worth being a member of **HI** (www.hihostels.com), as members save €2.50 per night at affiliated places. You'll save money with a sleeping sheet or your own linen, as hostels tend to charge €4 to €8 for this.

From June to August, many student residences function as hostels and hotels. These can be great value. In summer and on weekends, the big hotels lower their prices, so that a double that would normally cost €110 might be €70.

Sleeping listings in this chapter are divided into three price categories, based on the cost of a standard double room during high season:

€€€ more than €150

€€ €70 to €150

€ less than €70

Activities

BOATING, CANOEING & KAYAKING

Every waterside town has a place (most frequently the camping ground) where you can rent a canoe, kayak or rowboat by the hour or day.

HIKING

Hiking is best from June to September, although in July mosquitoes and other biting insects can be a big problem in Lapland. Wilderness huts line the northern trails (both free shared ones and private bookable ones). According to the law, a principle of common access to nature applies, so you are generally allowed to hike in any forested or wilderness area. The website www.outdoors.fi provides comprehensive information on trekking routes and huts in national parks.

SKIING

Finns love to ski; slopes are generally quite low and so are well suited to beginners and families. The ski season in Finland runs from late November to early May and slightly longer in the north, where it's possible to ski from October to May.

SWIMMING & SAUNAS

Many hotels, hostels and camping grounds have saunas that are free with a night's stay. See the boxed text, p387, for more sauna information.

Business Hours

Following are usual business hours in Finland. Opening hours aren't given in the book unless they differ significantly from these.

Alko (state alcohol store) 9am-8pm Mon-Fri, 9am-6pm Sat

Banks 9am-4.15pm Mon-Fri

Nightclubs As late as 4am

Post offices 9am-6pm Mon-Fri

Pubs 11am-1am (often later Fri & Sat)

Restaurants 11am-10pm, lunch 11am-3pm

Businesses & Shops 9am-6pm Mon-Fri, to 3pm Sat

Holidays

Finland grinds to a halt twice a year: around Christmas and New Year and during the Midsummer weekend. National public holidays:

New Year's Day 1 January

Epiphany 6 January

Good Friday March/April

Easter Sunday & Monday March/April

May Day 1 May

Ascension Day May (fifth Thursday after Easter)

Whit Sunday Late May or early June (seventh Sunday after Easter)

Midsummer Eve & Day Weekend closest to 24 June

All Saints Day First Saturday in November

Independence Day 6 December

Christmas Eve 24 December

Christmas Day 25 December

Boxing Day 26 December

Internet Access

Public libraries always have at least one free internet terminal. Many tourist offices have an internet terminal that you can use for free (usually 15 minutes).

Money

Credit cards are widely accepted and Finns are dedicated users of the plastic, even to buy a beer or cup of coffee

Using ATMs with a credit or debit card is by far the easiest way of getting cash in Finland. ATMs have a name, Otto, and can be found even in small villages.

Travellers cheques and cash can be exchanged at banks and, in the big cities, independent exchange facilities such as **Forex** (www.forex.fi), which usually offer better rates.

Service is considered to be included in bills, so there's no need to tip, unless you want to reward exceptional service.

Telephone

Public telephones basically no longer exist on the street in Finland.

The cheapest and most practical solution is to purchase a Finnish SIM card (at any R-kioski shop) and pop it in your own mobile phone. There are always deals and you might be able to pick up a card for as little as €10, including some call credit.

The country code for Finland is ☎358. To dial abroad it's ☎00. The number for the international operator is ☎020208.

Toilets

Public toilets are widespread but expensive – often €1 a time.

Visas

A valid passport or EU identity card is required to enter Finland. Most Western nationals don't need a tourist visa for stays of less than three months.

South Africans, Indians and Chinese, however, are among those who need a Schengen visa (see p1319). For more details contact the nearest Finnish embassy or consulate, or check the website www.formin.finland.fi.

Getting There & Away

Air

Finland is easily reached, with direct flights to Helsinki from all over the world. It's also served by budget carriers from European countries; check www.whichbudget.com for a list. Most other flights are with Finnair or Scandinavian Airlines (SAS). Most flights to Finland arrive at **Helsinki-Vantaa airport** (HEL; ☎0200 14636; www.helsinki-vantaa.fi), 19km north of the capital.

Bus

SWEDEN

The only bus route between Finland and Sweden is between the linked towns of Tornio (Finland) and Haparanda (Sweden), from where you can get onward transport into their respective countries.

NORWAY

There are five daily routes linking Finnish Lapland with northern Norway, some running only in summer. These are operated by **Eskelisen Lapin Linjat** (www.eskelisen-lapinlinjat.com). Its website has detailed maps and timetables, as does the Finnish bus website for **Matkahuolto** (www.matkahuolto.fi).

RUSSIA

There are daily express buses to Vyborg and St Petersburg from Helsinki (one originates in Turku). These services appear on the website of **Matkahuolto** (www.matkahuolto.fi).

Sea

Arriving in Finland by ferry is a memorable way to begin your visit, especially if you dock in Helsinki. Ferry companies have detailed timetables and fares on their websites. Fares vary according to season.

Eckerö Line (☎06000 4300) Tallinn (www.eckeroline.fi); Åland (www.eckerolinjen.fi)

Finnlines (☎010-343 4500; www.finnlines.com)

Linda Line (☎06000 668 970; www.lindaliini.ee)

St Peter Line (☎010-346 7820; www.stpeterline.com)

Tallink/Silja Line (☎0600 15700; www.tallinksilja.com)

Viking Line (☎0600 41577; www.vikingline.fi)

ESTONIA

Several ferry companies ply the Gulf of Finland between Helsinki and Tallinn in Estonia. Car ferries cross in 3½ hours, catamarans and hydrofoils in about 1½ hours. Ferries are cheapest: Tallink, Viking Line and Silja Line have several daily departures (€22 to €38). Eckerö Line has fewer departures but is the cheapest.

GERMANY & POLAND

Finnlines runs from Helsinki to Travemünde in Germany (from €196 June to August, 28 hours) and to Gdynia in Poland (€62 to €83, from 21 hours).

Tallink/Silja also runs a fast ferry from Helsinki to Rostock in Germany (27 hours), with seats costing between €73 and €98 and berths starting at €127.

RUSSIA

St Peter Line connects Helsinki with St Petersburg three times weekly, an overnight trip of 14 hours that costs €38 to €61 per passenger. A significant added benefit of arriving in Russia this way is a visa-free stay of up to three days in St Petersburg. You'll need to be travelling as a group of two or more and have confirmation of a hotel reservation.

SWEDEN

The daily Stockholm–Helsinki, Stockholm–Turku and Kapellskär–Mariehamn (Åland) routes are dominated by Tallink/Silja and Viking Lines. Viking Line is the cheaper, with a passenger ticket between Stockholm and Helsinki costing from €36 to €62. It's cheaper to cross to Turku (11 to 12 hours), with tickets costing €20 in summer on the day ferries. Eckerö Linjen sails from Grisslehamn, north of Stockholm, to Eckerö in Åland. It's by far the quickest, at just two hours, and, with prices around €6 to €10 return, it's a bargain.

Train

International train links with Finland are to/from Moscow and St Petersburg in Russia.

There are two high-speed *Allegro* train services daily from Helsinki to the Finland Station in St Petersburg (2nd/1st class €84/134, 3½ hours). The *Tolstoi* sleeper runs from Helsinki via St Petersburg (Ladozhki station) to Moscow (2nd/1st class €103/155, 13 hours). The fare includes a sleeper berth.

You must have a valid Russian visa; passport checks are carried out on board.

There are significant discounts for families and groups. See www.vr.fi for details.

Getting Around

Air

Major airlines flying domestically are the following:

AirBaltic (☎0600 18181; www.airbaltic.com) Offers several budget domestic routes.

Blue1 (☎06000 25831; www.blue1.com) Budget flights from Helsinki to Kuopio, Oulu, Rovaniemi and Vaasa.

Finnair (☎81881; www.finnair.com) Extensive domestic network.

FinnComm (☎09-4243 2000; www.fc.fi) Finnair affiliate offering budget fares.

Bicycle

Finland is flat and as bicycle friendly as any country, with many kilometres of bike paths. Bikes can be carried on most trains, buses and ferries. The Åland islands are particularly good cycling country.

Daily/weekly hire from €15/70 is possible in most cities. Camping grounds, hotels and hostels often have cheap bikes available for local exploration.

Boat

Lake and river passenger services were once important means of summer transport in Finland. These services are now largely kept on as cruises and make a great, leisurely way to journey between towns. The most popular routes are Tampere–Hämeenlinna, Savonlinna–Kuopio, Lahti–Jyväskylä and Joensuu–Koli–Lieksa.

Bus

Long-distance bus ticketing is handled by **Matkahuolto** (☎0200 4000; www.matkahuolto.fi); its excellent website has all timetables. Buy tickets at the bus station (*linja-autoasema*) or from the driver.

Buses may be express *(pikavuoro)* or regular *(vakiovuoro)*. Fares are based on distance travelled. The one-way fare for a 100km trip is €16.90/19.90 for normal/express.

If booking three or more adult tickets together, a 25% discount applies.

Car & Motorcycle

Car rental is expensive, but between a group of three or four it can work out at a reasonable cost. From the major rental companies a small car costs from €60/280 per day/week with 300km free per day. As ever, the cheapest deals are online.

While the daily rate is high, the weekly rate offers some respite. Best of all, though, are the weekend rates. One of the cheapest operators is **Sixt** (☎0200 111 222; www.sixt.fi).

Train

Finnish trains are run by the state-owned **Valtion Rautatiet** (VR; ☎0600 41900; www.vr.fi) and are an excellent service: they are fast, efficient and cheaper than the bus. VR's website has comprehensive timetable information and some ticket sales.

International rail passes accepted in Finland include the Eurail Scandinavia Pass, Eurail Global Pass and InterRail Global Pass.

France

Includes »

Best Places to Eat

» Pink Flamingo, Paris (p416)

» La Crèmerie du Glacier, Chamonix (p449)

» La Cave à Champagne, Épernay (p436)

» La Tupina, Bordeaux (p452)

Best Places to Stay

» St Christopher's Inn, Paris (p410)

» Family Home, Bayeux (p427)

» Ecolodge des Chartrons, Bordeaux (p451)

» Villa St-Exupéry, Nice (p465)

Why Go?

Few countries provoke such passion as La Belle France. Love it or loathe it, everyone has their own opinion about this Gallic goliath. Snooty, sexy, superior, chic, fascinating, infuriating, arrogant, officious and inspired in equal measures, the French have long lived according to their own idiosyncratic rules, and if the rest of the world doesn't always see eye to eye with them, well, *tant pis* (too bad) – that's the price you pay for being a culinary trendsetter, artistic pioneer and cultural icon.

If ever there was a country of contradictions, this is it: France is a deeply traditional place: castles, châteaux and ancient churches litter the landscape while centuries-old principles of rich food, fine wine and joie de vivre underpin everyday life. Yet it is also a country that has one of Europe's most multicultural make-ups, not to mention a well-deserved reputation for artistic experimentation and architectural invention. Enjoy.

When to Go

Paris

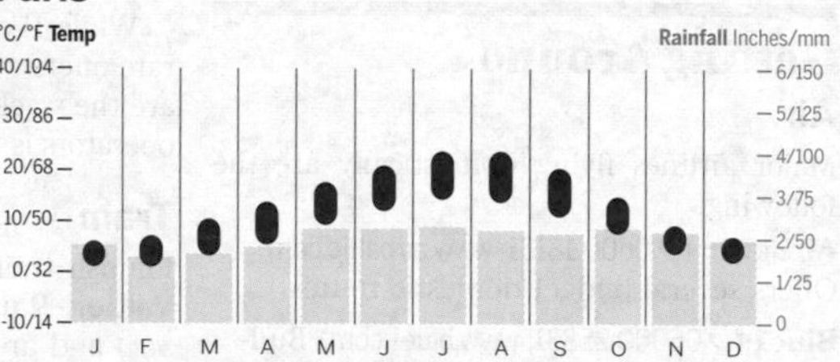

Dec–Mar Don your helmet, grab skis or board and hit the Alps for some serious ski action.

Apr–Jun France at its springtime best; the Fête de la Musique (21 June) means free concerts.

Sep Cooling temperatures, abundant local produce and the *vendange* (grape harvest).

Connections

High-speed trains link Paris' Gare du Nord with London St Pancras (with Eurostar) in just over two hours; Gare du Nord is also the point of departure for speedy trains to Brussels, Amsterdam and Cologne. Many more trains make travelling between the French capital and pretty much any city in every neighbouring country a real pleasure. Ferry links from Cherbourg, St-Malo, Calais and other north-coast ports travel to England and Ireland; and ferries from Marseille and Nice provide regular links with seaside towns in Corsica, Italy and North Africa.

Regular bus and rail links cross the French–Spanish border via the Pyrenees, and the French–Italian border via the Alps and the southern Mediterranean coast. For more see p481.

ITINERARIES

One Week

Start with a few days exploring Paris, taking in the Louvre, Eiffel Tower, Musée d'Orsay, Notre Dame, Montmartre and a boat trip along the Seine. Then head out to Versailles or Monet's garden at Giverny; or throw yourself into the Renaissance high life at châteaux in the Loire Valley.

Two Weeks

For the second week explore one or two regions rather than trying to do too much in a whistlestop dash. High-speed TGV trains zip from Paris to practically every province: for prehistoric interest go to the Dordogne; for architectural splendour, you can't top the Loire Valley; for typical French atmosphere, try the hilltop villages of Provence; and for sunshine and seafood, the French Riviera on the sparkling Med is the only place to be.

Essential Food & Drink

» **Fondue & Raclette** Cockle-warming, cheese dishes in the snowy French Alps.

» **Oysters & White Wine** Everywhere on the Atlantic Coast, although we love culinary Cancale and Saturday morning at Bordeaux market.

» **Bouillabaisse** Marseille's signature two-part fish stew – saffron-scented broth with croutons and *rouille* (garlic chilli-fired mayonnaise) as starter, fish as main.

» **Niçois tapas** Only in Riviera queen Nice and best consumed with drink in hand.

» **Piggy-part cuisine** Big fat *andouillette* (pig-intestine sausage), Côtes du Rhône red, lace-curtained *bouchon* (traditional Lyonnais bistro): the gastronomic capital Lyon.

» **Champagne** Pedalling between vines and tasting in century-old cellars is an essential part of Champagne's bubbly experience.

AT A GLANCE

» **Currency** euro

» **Language** French

» **Money** ATMs are everywhere

» **Visas** Schengen rules apply; see p1319

Fast Facts

» **Area** 551,000 sq km

» **Capital** Paris

» **Country code** ☎33

» **Emergency** ☎112

Exchange Rates

Australia	A$1	€0.74
Canada	C$1	€0.74
Japan	¥100	€0.87
New Zealand	NZ$1	€0.56
UK	UK£1	€1.16
USA	US$1	€0.72

Set Your Budget

» **Budget hotel room** up to €70

» **Two-course evening meal** €15 to €50

» **Museum entrance** €4 to €8

» **Glass of wine** €2 to €5

» **Paris metro ticket** €1.60

Resources

» **Paris by Mouth** (http://parisbymouth.com) Capital dining and drinking.

» **France 24** (www.france24.com/en/france) French news in English.

» **France.fr** (www.france.fr) Official country website.

France Highlights

1. Gorge on the iconic sights and sophistication of Europe's most hopelessly romantic city, **Paris** (p400)
2. Relive the French Renaissance with extraordinary châteaux built by kings and queens in the **Loire Valley** (p431)
3. Tuck into France's halest, piggy-driven cuisine in a traditional eatery at **Lyon** (p446)
4. Dodge tides, stroll moonlit sand and immerse yourself in legend at island abbey **Mont St-Michel** (p427)
5. Savour ancient Rome, modern art, markets, lavender and hilltop villages in slow-paced **Provence** (p458)
6. Romp around **Nice** (p464), slap-bang in the heart of the French Riviera and *the* French beach destination for well over a century.
7. Soak up the mystery of the world's best megaliths from the back of a Breton bicycle around **Carnac** (p430)

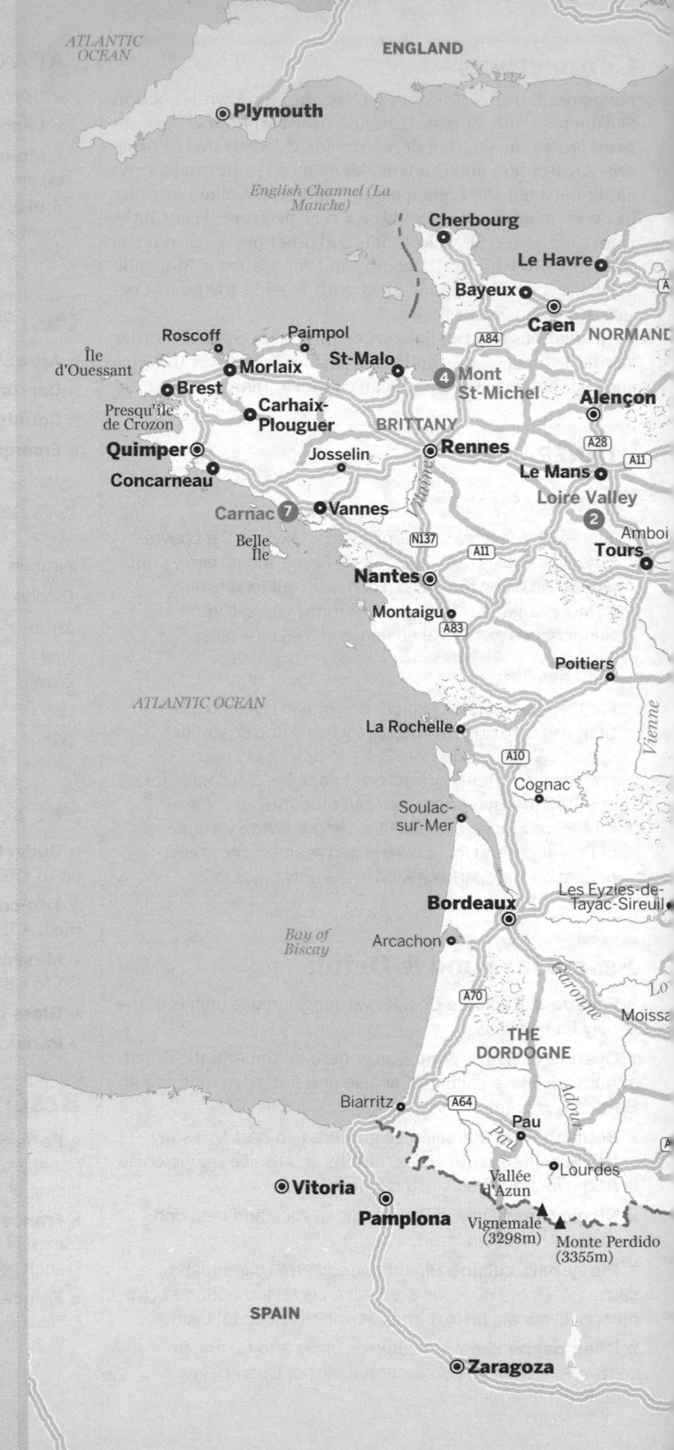

Folkestone
Dunkirk
Calais
Boulogne-sur-Mer
Brussels
NETHERLANDS
BELGIUM
Lille
Meuse
GERMANY
A28
Authie
Somme
SOMME
Mainz
LUXEMBOURG
Luxembourg
Rouen
A1
Oise
Aisne
Reims
Vernon
A4
Marne
Épernay
Metz
Paris
Versailles
ALSACE
Stuttgart
Dreux
Nancy
Strasbourg
CHAMPAGNE
Seine
Marne
A5
Moselle
Chartres
Troyes
Sélestat
Schnellenbuhl
A10
LORRAINE
A6
BURGUNDY
A31
Katzenthal
Orléans
Auxerre
Beaugency
Blois
Chambord
Saône
Cheverny
Basel
LA SOLOGNE
Dijon
Besançon
Doubs
AUSTRIA
CÔTE D'OR
A86
Beaune
Arc-et-Senans
Arbois
Cher
Métabief Mont d'Or
SWITZERLAND
Loire
Le Creusot
JURA
Les Rousses
Lausanne
Lake Geneva
A20
A6
Les Portes du Soleil
A71
Gueret
Chamonix
Annecy
Lyon
Mont Blanc (4810m)
A72
Limoges
Clermont-Ferrand
Rhône
LIMOUSIN
Chambéry
Dordogne
St-Étienne
A48
FRENCH ALPS
ITALY
Grenoble
Drac
A49
Allier
Puy Mary (1787m)
Sarlat-la-Canéda
Valence
Sestriere
Rhône
D921
A7
Vaison la Romaine
Mt Lozère (1699m)
Durance
Cahors
Mt Ventoux (1912m)
THE LOT
Pont du Gard
Tarn
A75
Avignon
Nîmes
Monaco
Ligurian Sea
Les Baux de Provence
Grasse
Arles
Provence
Nice
Toulouse
Montpellier
Cannes
LANGUEDOC
Aix-en-Provence
A61
Marseille
St-Tropez
Carcassonne
ROUSILLON
A9
Golfe de Beauduc
Île Rousse
Bastia
Perpignan
ANDORRA
Calvi
Monte Cinto (2706m)
Andorra la Vella
Puig Neulós
Mediterranean Sea
CORSICA
SPAIN
Ajaccio
Bonifacio
Barcelona
ITALY
0 200 km
0 100 miles
N
1
3
5
6

PARIS

POP 2.21 MILLION

What can we say about the sexy, sophisticated City of Lights that hasn't already been said countless times over? Quite simply, this is one of the world's great metropolises, a trendsetter, market leader and cultural capital for over a thousand years and still going strong. This is the place that gave the world the cancan and the cinematograph, a city that reinvented itself during the Renaissance, bopped to the beat of the Jazz Age and positively glittered during the *belle époque* (beautiful era).

As you might expect, Paris is strewn with historic architecture, glorious galleries and cultural treasures. But the modern-day city is much more than just a museum piece. It's a heady hotchpotch of cultures and ideas – a place to stroll the boulevards, shop till you drop, flop riverside or just do as the Parisians do and watch the world buzz by from a streetside cafe. Savour every moment.

Sights

LEFT BANK

Eiffel Tower LANDMARK

(Map p402; www.tour-eiffel.fr; lifts to 2nd fl €8.10, to 3rd fl €13.10, stairs to 2nd fl €4.50; ⏲lifts & stairs 9am-midnight mid-Jun–Aug, lifts 9.30am-11pm, stairs 9.30am-6pm Sep–mid-Jun; Ⓜ Champ de Mars-Tour Eiffel or Bir Hakeim) It's impossible to imagine Paris without the Tour Eiffel, but the 'metal asparagus' faced fierce opposition from Paris' artistic elite when it was built for the 1889 World Fair. The tower was almost torn down in 1909, and was only saved by the new science of radiotelegraphy. Named after its designer, Gustave Eiffel, the tower is 324m high, including the TV antenna at the tip, and contains 7300 tonnes of iron. The views are superb.

The three levels are open to the public (entrance to the 1st level is included in all admission tickets), though the top level closes in heavy wind. Take the lifts or – don't blame us if you run out of steam half-way up – the stairs in the south pillar up to the 2nd platform. Buy tickets in advance online to avoid monumental queues at the ticket office.

Spreading out around the Eiffel Tower are the **Jardins du Trocadéro** (Ⓜ Trocadéro), whose fountains and statue garden are grandly illuminated at night.

Musée d'Orsay ART GALLERY

(Map p402; www.musee-orsay.fr; 62 rue de Lille, 7e; admision €8; ⏲9.30am-6pm Tue, Wed & Fri-Sun, 9.30am-9.45pm Thu; Ⓜ Musée d'Orsay or Solférino) This museum, housed in a turn-of-the-century train station overlooking the Seine, displays France's national collection of paintings, sculptures and artwork produced between the 1840s and 1914. It is especially renowned for its impressionist and art-nouveau collections, with works by Monet, Renoir, Sisley, Degas, Manet, Cézanne, Van Gogh, Seurat and Matisse.

Musée du Quai Branly MUSEUM

(Map p402; www.quaibranly.fr; 37 quai Branly, 7e; admission €8.50; ⏲11am-7pm Tue, Wed & Sun, to 9pm Thu-Sat; Ⓜ Pont de l'Alma or Alma-Marceau) This unimaginatively named museum, in an architecturally impressive building designed by architect Jean Nouvel, explores the cultures of Africa, Oceania, Asia and the Americas through a range of multimedia exhibits. Anthropological explanations are kept to a minimum; what is displayed here is meant to be viewed as art.

TOP CHOICE **Jardin du Luxembourg** CITY PARK

(Map p406; ⏲7.30am to 8.15am-5pm to 10pm according to the season; Ⓜ Luxembourg) Parisians of all ages flock to the formal terraces and chestnut groves of this 23-hectare city park to read, relax, stroll through urban **orchards** and visit the honey-producing **Rucher du Luxembourg** (Luxembourg Apiary). **Palais du Luxembourg** (rue de Vaugirard, 6e), built for Marie de Médicis, Henri IV's consort, at the garden's northern end, houses the Senate (upper house of the French parliament).

Top spot for sun soaking – always loads of chairs here – is the southern side of the palace's 19th-century **Orangery** (1834) where lemon and orange trees, palms, grenadiers and oleanders shelter from the cold.

TOP CHOICE **Musée Rodin** GARDEN, ART MUSEUM

(Map p402; www.musee-rodin.fr; 79 rue de Varenne, 7e; admission incl garden €7-10, garden only €1; ⏲10am-5.45pm Tue-Sun; Ⓜ Varenne) This sublime museum with lovely sculpture garden displays some of Rodin's most famous works, including *The Burghers of Calais (Les Bourgeois de Calais), Cathedral, The Thinker (Le Penseur)* and *The Kiss (Le Baiser)*. Nearby, **Hôtel des Invalides** was built in the 1670s as housing for *invalides* (disabled war veterans). On 14 July 1789, a mob forced its way into the building and seized 28,000 rifles before heading to the prison at Bastille, starting the French Revolution.

MUSEUM BASICS

Most Paris museums close Monday, but a dozen-odd including the Louvre and Centre Pompidou close Tuesdays instead.

Paris' national museums are a bargain: admission is reduced for those aged over 60 and from 18 to 25; and completely free for EU residents under 26 years of age, anyone under 18 years, and everyone on the first Sunday of each month. These include: the Louvre, Musée National d'Art Moderne in the Pompidou, Musée du Quai Branly, Musée d'Orsay and Musée Rodin.

Ditto for the following except they're only free the first Sunday of the month from November to March: Arc de Triomphe, Conciergerie, Panthéon, Ste-Chapelle and the Tours de Notre Dame.

The **Paris Museum Pass** (www.parismuseumpass.fr; 2/4/6 days €32/48/64) is valid for some 38 sights including the Louvre, Centre Pompidou, Musée d'Orsay, St-Denis basilica, parts of Versailles and Fontainebleau. Buy it online, from the Paris Convention & Visitors Bureau (p420), Fnac outlets, major metro stations and all participating venues.

Les Catacombes OSSUARY

(Map p402; www.catacombes.paris.fr, in French; 1 av Colonel Henri Roi-Tanguy, 14e; admission €8; ⏲10am-5pm Tue-Sun; Ⓜ Denfert Rochereau) There are few spookier sights in Paris than the Catacombes, one of three underground cemeteries created in the late 18th century to solve the problems posed by Paris' overflowing cemeteries. Winding tunnels, 1.7km long, are stacked floor to ceiling with bones and skulls – guaranteed to send a shiver down your spine.

Panthéon MONUMENT

(Map p406; place du Panthéon, 5e; admisiosn €8; ⏲10am-6.30pm Apr-Sep, to 6pm Oct-Mar; Ⓜ Luxembourg) This domed landmark was completed in 1789 and houses the tombs of Voltaire, Jean-Jacques Rousseau, Victor Hugo, Émile Zola, Jean Moulin and Nobel Prize winner Marie Curie, among many others, in its crypt.

Musée des Égouts de Paris MUSEUM

(Map p402; place de la Résistance, 7e; admission €4.20; ⏲11am-5pm Sat-Wed May-Sep, til 4pm Sat-Wed Oct-Dec & Feb-Apr; Ⓜ Pont de l'Alma) This is a working museum whose entrance – a rectangular maintenance hole topped with a kiosk – is across the street from 93 quai d'Orsay. Raw sewage flows beneath your feet as you walk through 480m of odoriferous tunnels, passing artefacts illustrating the development of Paris' waste-water disposal system. A visit here quite takes your breath away.

Église St-Germain des Prés CHURCH

(Map p406; 3 place St-Germain des Prés, 6e; ⏲8am-7pm Mon-Sat, 9am-8pm Sun; Ⓜ St-Germain des Prés) Paris' oldest church, this 11th-century Romanesque Église St-Germain des Prés, was the dominant church in Paris until the arrival of Notre Dame.

Église St-Sulpice CHURCH

(Map p406; place St-Sulpice, 6e; ⏲7.30am-7.30pm; Ⓜ St-Sulpice) Lined with 21 side chapels, this beautiful Italianate church was built between 1646 and 1780. The facade, designed by a Florentine architect, has two rows of superimposed columns and is topped by two towers.

THE ISLANDS

Paris' twin set of islands could not be more different: **Île de la Cité**, site of the Roman town of Lutèce (Lutetia), is bigger, full of sights and very touristed (few people live here). The seven decorated arches of Paris' oldest bridge, **Pont Neuf** (Ⓜ Pont Neuf), have linked the island with both banks of the Seine since 1607.

Smaller **Île St-Louis** is residential with just enough boutiques, restaurants and a legendary ice-cream maker to lure visitors. The area around **Pont St-Louis**, the bridge across to Île de la Cité, and **Pont Louis Philippe**, the bridge to the Marais, is one of the most romantic spots in Paris.

Cathédrale de Notre Dame de Paris CATHEDRAL

(Map p406; www.cathedraledeparis.com; 6 place du Parvis Notre Dame, 4e; audio guide €5; ⏲8am-6.45pm Mon-Fri, 8am-7.15pm Sat & Sun; Ⓜ Cité) Notre Dame is the true heart of Paris: distances from Paris to all parts of metropolitan France are measured from **place du Parvis Notre Dame**, the square in front of this masterpiece of French Gothic architecture.

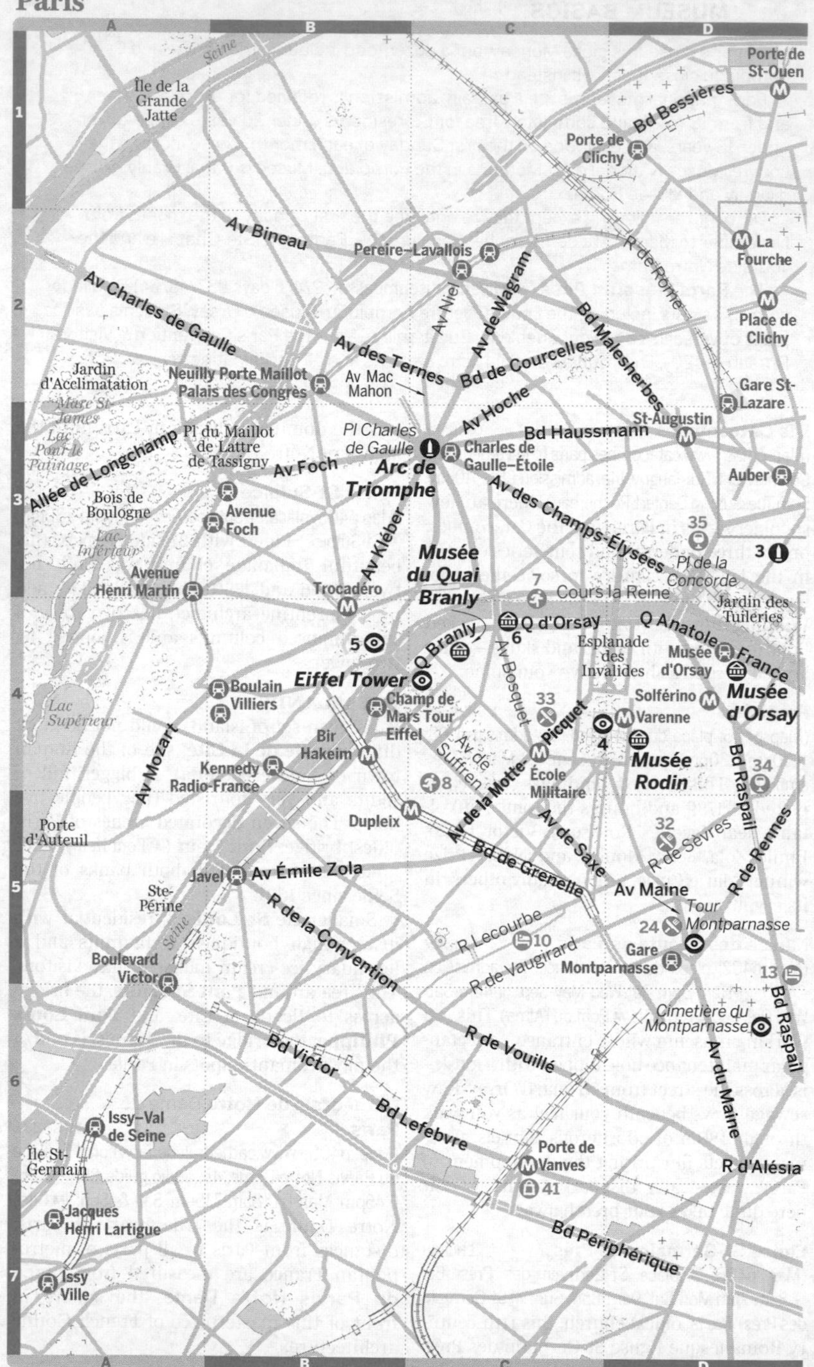
Île de la Grande Jatte
Seine
Porte de St-Ouen
Bd Bessières
Porte de Clichy
Av Bineau
Pereire–Lavallois
R de Rome
La Fourche
Av Charles de Gaulle
Av Niel
Av de Wagram
Bd Malesherbes
Place de Clichy
Av des Ternes
Bd de Courcelles
Jardin d'Aclimatation
Neuilly Porte Maillot Palais des Congrès
Av Mac Mahon
Gare St-Lazare
Mare St-James
Av Hoche
St-Augustin
Lac Pour le Patinage
Pl du Maillot de Lattre de Tassigny
Pl Charles de Gaulle
Charles de Gaulle–Étoile
Bd Haussmann
Allée de Longchamp
Av Foch
Arc de Triomphe
Auber
Bois de Boulogne
Avenue Foch
Av des Champs-Élysées
Lac Inférieur
Av Kléber
Musée du Quai Branly
35
3
Pl de la Concorde
Avenue Henri Martin
Trocadéro
7
Cours la Reine
Jardin des Tuileries
Q d'Orsay
6
Q Anatole France
Q Branly
Av Bosquet
Esplanade des Invalides
Musée d'Orsay
5
Eiffel Tower
Boulain Villiers
Champ de Mars Tour Eiffel
33
Solférino
Musée d'Orsay
Lac Supérieur
Varenne
Picquet
4
Bir Hakeim
Av de Suffren
Musée Rodin
Bd Raspail
34
Av Mozart
Kennedy Radio-France
8
École Militaire
Av de la Motte-
Dupleix
32
R de Sèvres
R de Rennes
Porte d'Auteuil
Av de Saxe
Bd de Grenelle
Javel
Av Émile Zola
Av Maine
Ste-Périne
R de la Convention
Tour Montparnasse
R Lecourbe
24
10
Gare Montparnasse
R de Vaugirard
Boulevard Victor
13
Cimetière du Montparnasse
Bd Raspail
R de Vouillé
Bd Victor
Av du Maine
Issy–Val de Seine
Bd Lefebvre
Île St-Germain
Porte de Vanves
41
R d'Alésia
Jacques Henri Lartigue
Bd Périphérique
Issy Ville
A
B
C
D
1
2
3
4
5
6
7

FRANCE

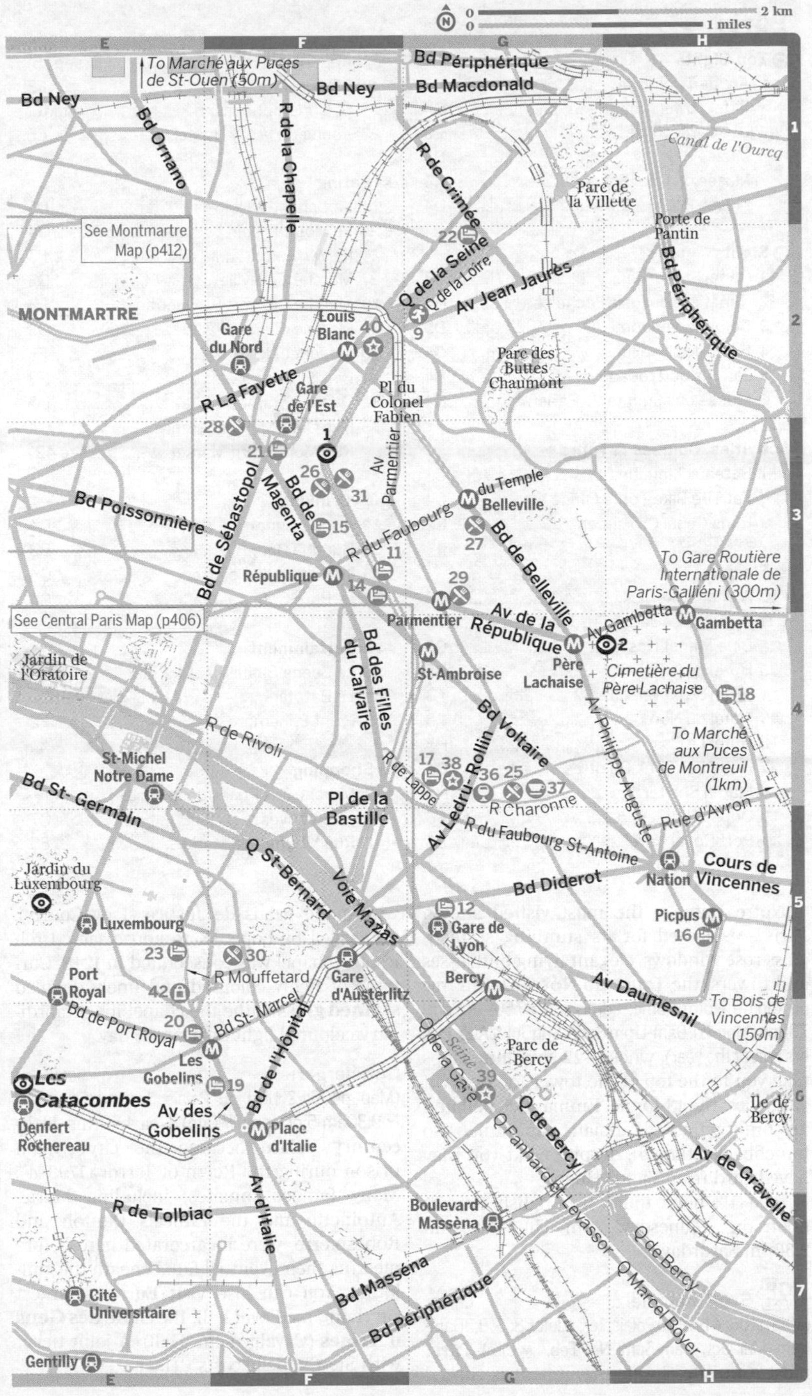

0 2 km
0 1 miles
E
F
G
H
To Marché aux Puces de St-Ouen (50m)
Bd Périphérique
Bd Ney
Bd Macdonald
Bd Ney
Bd Ornano
R de la Chapelle
R de Crimée
Canal de l'Ourcq
Parc de la Villette
Porte de Pantin
See Montmartre Map (p412)
22
Q de la Seine
Q de la Loire
Av Jean Jaurès
Bd Périphérique
MONTMARTRE
Gare du Nord
Louis Blanc
40
9
Parc des Buttes Chaumont
R La Fayette
Gare de l'Est
Pl du Colonel Fabien
28
21
1
Av Parmentier
26
31
Bd Poissonnière
Bd de Sébastopol
Bd de Magenta
15
R du Faubourg du Temple
Belleville
27
Bd de Belleville
11
To Gare Routière Internationale de Paris-Galliéni (300m)
République
14
29
Parmentier
Av de la République
Av Gambetta
Gambetta
2
See Central Paris Map (p406)
Jardin de l'Oratoire
Bd des Filles du Calvaire
St-Ambroise
Père Lachaise
Cimetière du Père Lachaise
18
R de Rivoli
Bd Voltaire
Av Philippe Auguste
To Marché aux Puces de Montreuil (1km)
St-Michel Notre Dame
R de Lappe
17
38
36
25
37
Av Ledru-Rollin
R Charonne
Bd St-Germain
Pl de la Bastille
Rue d'Avron
R du Faubourg St-Antoine
Q St-Bernard
Nation
Cours de Vincennes
Jardin du Luxembourg
Voie Mazas
Bd Diderot
12
Gare de Lyon
Picpus
16
Luxembourg
23
30
R Mouffetard
Gare d'Austerlitz
Bercy
Av Daumesnil
Port Royal
42
To Bois de Vincennes (150m)
Bd de Port Royal
Bd St-Marcel
20
Bd de l'Hôpital
Q de la Gare
Seine
Parc de Bercy
Les Gobelins
19
39
Les Catacombes
Av des Gobelins
Q de Bercy
Ile de Bercy
Denfert Rochereau
Place d'Italie
Q Fanhard et Levassor
Av de Gravelle
Av d'Italie
R de Tolbiac
Boulevard Massèna
Q de Bercy
Bd Masséna
Q Marcel Boyer
Cité Universitaire
Bd Périphérique
Gentilly
1
2
3
4
5
6
7
FRANCE

Paris

Notre Dame – the most visited site in Paris – is famed for its stunning stained-glass rose windows, elegant flying buttresses and towers, the **Tours de Notre Dame** (rue du Cloître Notre Dame; admission €7.50; 9am-7.30pm Mon-Fri, 9am-11pm Sat & Sun Jul & Aug, less hrs rest of the year), whose 422 spiralling steps take you to the top of the tower for views of gargoyles, the 13-tonne 'Emmanuel' bell and an unforgettable Parisian panorama. No hunchbacks, though, despite what you may have heard from Victor Hugo.

Free 1½-hour tours in English run at noon on Wednesday, 2pm Thursday and 2.30pm Saturday.

TOP CHOICE Ste-Chapelle CHAPEL
(Map p406; 4 blvd du Palais, 1er; adult €8; 9.30am-6pm Mar-Oct, 9am-5pm Nov-Feb; M Cité) Paris' most exquisite Gothic monument is tucked within the Palais de Justice (Law Courts). Conceived by Louis IX to house sacred relics, the chapel was consecrated in 1248. Curtains of richly coloured and finely detailed **stained glass** bathe the chapel in extraordinary coloured light on a sunny day.

Conciergerie MONUMENT
(Map p406; 2 blvd du Palais, 1er; admision €7; 9.30am-5 or 6pm; M Cité) Nearby, this 14th-century palace became the city's main prison during the Reign of Terror (1793–4). Many famous inmates, including Marie-Antoinette and the radicals Danton and Robespierre, were incarcerated here before meeting their eventual fate beneath the guillotine. You can also visit Europe's largest surviving medieval hall, the **Salle des Gens d'Armes** (Cavalrymen's Hall). A joint ticket with Ste-Chapelle costs €11.

RIGHT BANK

Musée du Louvre ART MUSEUM

(www.louvre.fr; permanent collections/permanent collections & temporary exhibits €9.50/14, after 6pm Wed & Fri €6/12; 9am-6pm Mon, Thu, Sat & Sun, 9am-10pm Wed & Fri; M Palais Royal-Musée du Louvre) The vast Palais du Louvre, overlooking the fashionable **Jardin des Tuileries** gardens, was constructed as a fortress by Philippe-Auguste in the 13th century and rebuilt in the mid-16th century for use as a royal residence. In 1793 the Revolutionary Convention transformed it into the nation's first national museum.

The Louvre's top attraction is da Vinci's mischievous *Mona Lisa,* but there's much, much more to see. Take the glorious collection of Greek and Roman antiquities (including the *Venus de Milo* and the *Winged Victory of Samothrace*); masterpieces by Raphael, Botticelli, Delacroix and Titian; Louis XV's dazzling crown jewels; or the lavish apartments of Napoleon III's Minister of State. Tickets remain valid for the whole day, so take your time – you'll enjoy it more if you don't try and pack too much into one day.

The museum's main entrance and ticket windows in the Cour Napoléon are covered by the iconic 21m-high **Pyramide du Louvre**, a glass pyramid designed by the Chinese-American architect IM Pei. Skip the pyramid-entrance queue by entering via the Porte des Lions entrance or the **Carrousel du Louvre** shopping centre.

Arc de Triomphe LANDMARK

(Map p402; viewing platform €9; 10am-10.30 or 11pm; M Charles de Gaulle-Étoile) The Arc de Triomphe stands in the middle of the world's largest traffic roundabout, **place de l'Étoile**, officially known as place Charles de Gaulle. The 'triumphal arch' was commissioned in 1806 by Napoleon to commemorate his victories, but remained unfinished when he started losing battles, and wasn't completed until 1836. Since 1920, the body of an **unknown soldier** from WWI has lain beneath the arch; a memorial flame is rekindled each evening around 6.30pm.

The **viewing platform** affords wonderful views of the dozen avenues that radiate out from the arch. **Av Foch** is Paris' widest boulevard, while **av des Champs Élysées** leads southeast to **place de la Concorde** and its famous 3300-year-old pink granite obelisk from Egypt.

Centre Pompidou MUSEUM

(Map p406; www.centrepompidou.fr; place Georges Pompidou, 4e; M Rambuteau) Opened in 1977, this 'insides' turned-out building is one of central Paris' most iconic. Inside, the **Musée National d'Art Moderne** (admission €10-12, 11am-9pm Wed-Mon) showcases France's national collection of post-1905 art.

Outside, buskers and street artists congregate around lively **place Georges Pompidou**. Nearby **place Igor Stravinsky** delights with its fanciful mechanical fountains of skeletons, treble clef and pair of ruby-red lips.

Place des Vosges SQUARE

(Map p406; M St-Paul or Bastille) The Marais, the area of the Right Bank north of Île St-Louis in the 3e and 4e, was transformed into one of the city's most fashionable districts by Henri IV, who constructed the elegant *hôtels particuliers* around place Royale – today known as the place des Vosges.

Novelist Victor Hugo lived here from 1832 to 1848; his home is now the **Maison de Victor Hugo** (www.musee-hugo.paris.fr, in French; admision €7; 10am-6pm Tue-Sun) with drawings and memorabilia relating to the author.

Musée Picasso MUSEUM

(Map p406; www.musee-picasso.fr, in French; 5 rue de Thorigny, 3e; 9.30am-6pm Wed-Mon; M St-Paul or Chemin Vert) The Picasso Museum contains more than 3500 of the *grand maître*'s engravings, paintings, ceramics and sculptures. It will reopen after extensive renovations in 2012.

PARIS FOR FREE

Paris sure ain't cheap, but a visit to the City of Lights doesn't have to blow your budget. Here are a few of our favourite free treats:

» Turn up some treasures at the **Marché aux Puces de St-Ouen** (p419)

» Pack a picnic for the **Jardin du Luxembourg** (p398)

» Wander the celebrity gravestones at the **Cimetière du Père Lachaise** (p407)

» Marvel at the architectural ambition of **Cathédrale de Notre Dame de Paris** (p401)

» Watch the painters and portraitists at work on **place du Tertre** (p407) in Montmartre

Central Paris

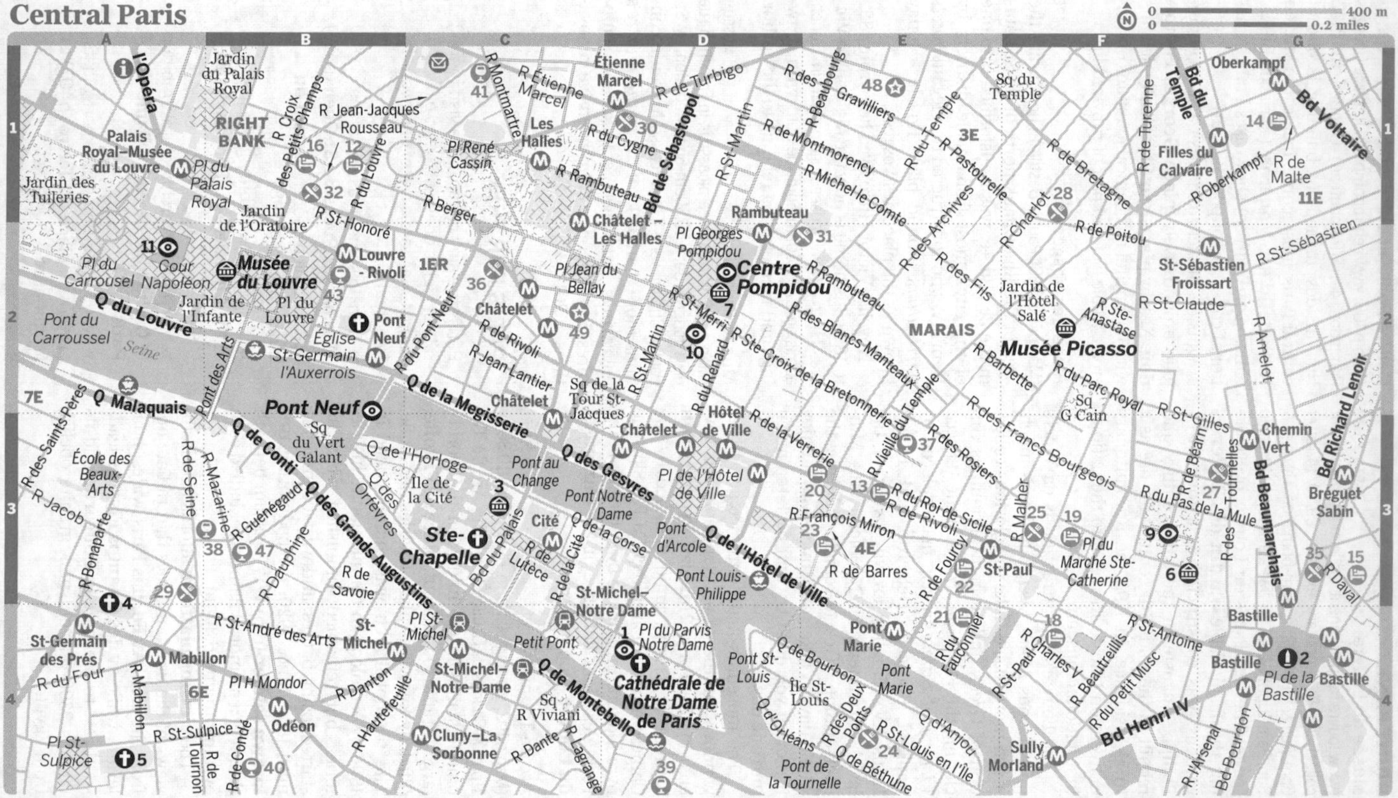

0 — 400 m
0 — 0.2 miles

A B C D E F G
1 2 3 4

l'Opéra
Jardin du Palais Royal
RIGHT BANK
R Croix des Petits Champs
R Jean-Jacques Rousseau
R Montmartre
R Étienne Marcel
Étienne Marcel
R de Turbigo
R Beaubourg
R des Gravilliers
48
Sq du Temple
R de Turenne
Bd du Temple
Oberkampf
Bd Voltaire
14
Palais Royal–Musée du Louvre
Pl du Palais Royal
Jardin des Tuileries
16
12
32
R du Louvre
41
Pl René Cassin
Les Halles
R du Cygne
30
Bd de Sébastopol
R St-Martin
R de Montmorency
R du Temple
3E
R Pastourelle
R de Bretagne
Filles du Calvaire
R Oberkampf
R de Malte
11E
Jardin de l'Oratoire
R St-Honoré
R Berger
R Rambuteau
Châtelet – Les Halles
Rambuteau
Pl Georges Pompidou
31
R Michel le Comte
R des Archives
R Charlot
28
R de Poitou
St-Sébastien Froissart
R St-Sébastien
11
Cour Napoléon
Pl du Carrousel
Musée du Louvre
Louvre - Rivoli
1ER
36
Pl Jean du Bellay
Centre Pompidou
R Rambuteau
R des Fils
Jardin de l'Hôtel Salé
R Ste-Anastase
R St-Claude
R Amelot
43
Jardin de l'Infante
Pl du Louvre
Pont du Carrousel
Q du Louvre
Seine
Pont Neuf
Église St-Germain l'Auxerrois
R du Pont Neuf
Châtelet
R de Rivoli
49
R St-Merri
7
10
R des Blancs Manteaux
MARAIS
Musée Picasso
R Jean Lantier
Pont des Arts
7E
Q Malaquais
Pont Neuf
Q de la Megisserie
Sq de la Tour St-Jacques
R St-Martin
R du Renard
R Ste-Croix de la Bretonnerie
R Vieille du Temple
R Barbette
R du Parc Royal
Sq G Cain
R St-Gilles
Chemin Vert
Bd Richard Lenoir
R des Saints Pères
École des Beaux-Arts
R de Seine
R Mazarine
Q de Conti
Sq du Vert Galant
Q de l'Horloge
Pont au Change
Q des Gesvres
Hôtel de Ville
R de la Verrerie
37
R des Rosiers
R des Francs Bourgeois
R de Béarn
27
R des Tournelles
Bréguet Sabin
R Jacob
38
47
R Guénégaud
Q des Grands Augustins
Q des Orfèvres
Île de la Cité
3
Pont Notre Dame
Pl de l'Hôtel de Ville
20
13
R du Roi de Sicile
R de Rivoli
R Malher
25
19
R du Pas de la Mule
9
Bd Beaumarchais
R Bonaparte
R Dauphine
Ste-Chapelle
Bd du Palais
R de Lutèce
Cité
R de la Cité
Q de la Corse
Pont d'Arcole
R François Miron
23
4E
R de Barres
R de Fourcy
St-Paul
22
Pl du Marché Ste-Catherine
6
35
15
R Daval
29
4
R de Savoie
R St-André des Arts
St-Michel
Pl St-Michel
St-Michel–Notre Dame
Q de l'Hôtel de Ville
Pont Louis-Philippe
21
R du Fauconnier
18
R St-Antoine
Bastille
St-Germain des Prés
Mabillon
6E
R du Four
R Mabillon
Pl H Mondor
R Danton
R Hautefeuille
Petit Pont
1
Pl du Parvis Notre Dame
Cathédrale de Notre Dame de Paris
Pont St-Louis
Q de Bourbon
Île St-Louis
Pont Marie
R St-Paul
R Charles V
R Beautreillis
R du Petit Musc
2
Pl de la Bastille
Odéon
R St-Sulpice
Pl St-Sulpice
5
R de Tournon
R de Condé
40
Cluny–La Sorbonne
Sq R Viviani
R Dante
R Lagrange
Q de Montebello
39
Q d'Orléans
R des Deux Ponts
24
R St-Louis en l'Île
Q d'Anjou
Q de Béthune
Pont de la Tournelle
Sully Morland
Bd Henri IV
R l'Arsenal
Bd Bourdon

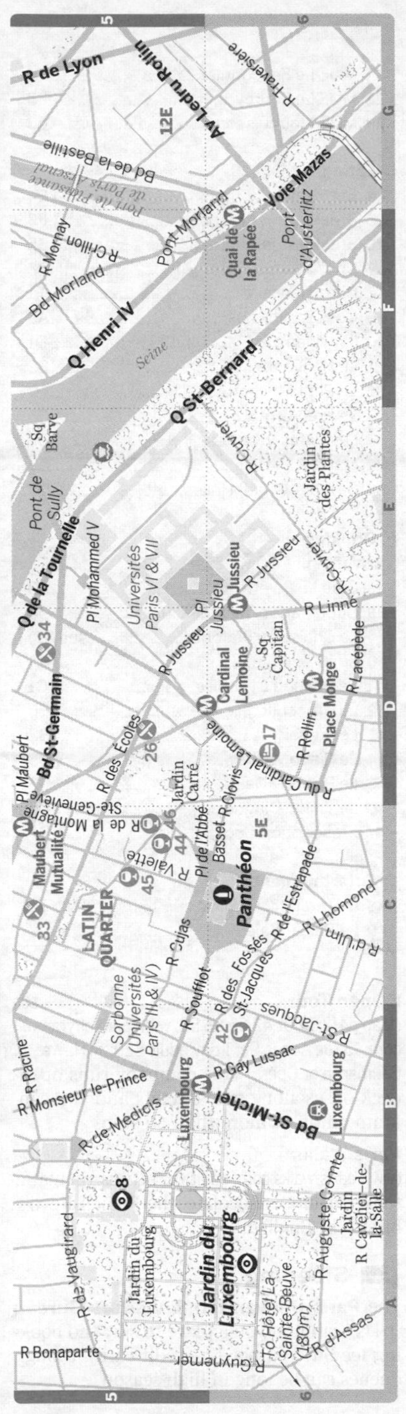

Place de la Bastille — SQUARE

(Map p406; Ⓜ Bastille) The Bastille is the most famous monument in Paris that no longer exists; the notorious prison was demolished by a Revolutionary mob on 14 July 1789, and the place de la Bastille where the prison once stood is now a busy traffic roundabout. The 52m-high **Colonne de Juillet** (July Column) was erected in memory of Parisians killed during the July Revolution of 1830.

MONTMARTRE & PIGALLE

During the late 19th and early 20th centuries, artsy bohemian **Montmartre** attracted writers and artists, including Picasso who lived at the studio **Bateau Lavoir** (Map p412; 11bis Émile Goudeau; Ⓜ Abbesses) from 1908 to 1912. Cafes, restaurants, tourists, caricaturists and painters fill the main square, **place du Tertre** (Map p412).

A few blocks southwest is lively, neon-lit **Pigalle** (9e and 18e), one of Paris' two main sex districts. A funicular connects it to the top of Butte de Montmartre (Montmartre Hill).

Basilique du Sacré Cœur — CHURCH

(Map p412; www.sacre-coeur-montmartre.com; place du Parvis du Sacré Cœur, 18e; 6am-10.30pm; Ⓜ Anvers) The gleaming white **dome** (admission €5; 9am-7pm Apr-Sep, to 6pm Oct-Mar) of this iconic basilica has one of Paris' most spectacular city panoramas.

TOP CHOICE Cimetière du Père Lachaise — CEMETERY

(Map p402; www.pere-lachaise.com; 8am-6pm Mon-Fri, from 8.30am Sat, from 9am Sun; Ⓜ Philippe Auguste, Gambetta or Père Lachaise) Its one-way doors opened in 1804 and since then 800,000 people have been buried here, among them Chopin, Molière, Balzac, Proust, Gertrude Stein, Colette, Pissarro, Seurat, Modigliani, Sarah Bernhardt, Yves Montand, Delacroix and Édith Piaf. In 1817 the remains of 12th-century lovers Abélard and Héloïse were disinterred and reburied here beneath a neo-Gothic tombstone. Then, of course, there are the perennially popular graves of **Oscar Wilde** (Division 89) and **Jim Morrison** (Division 6).

Tours

Fat Tire Bike Tours — BICYCLE

(Map p402; 01 56 58 10 54; www.fattirebiketours.com; 24 rue Edgar Faure, 15e; Ⓜ Dupleix) Bike tours by day (€28; four hours) and night; to Versailles, Monet's garden (Giverny) and the Normandy beaches. Participants generally meet opposite the Eiffel Tower's South Pillar at the start of the Champ de Mars.

Central Paris

Top Sights

Cathédrale de Notre Dame de Paris D4
Centre Pompidou D2
Jardin du Luxembourg A6
Musée du Louvre B2
Musée Picasso F2
Panthéon C6
Pont Neuf B2
Ste-Chapelle C3

Sights

1 Cathédrale de Notre Dame de Paris North Tower (Entrance to Tours de Notre Dame) D4
2 Colonne de Juillet G4
3 Conciergerie C3
4 Église St-Germain des Prés A3
5 Église St-Sulpice A4
6 Maison de Victor Hugo F3
7 Musée National d'Art Moderne D2
8 Palais du Luxembourg B5
9 Place des Vosges F3
10 Place Igor Stravinsky D2
11 Pyramide du Louvre (Main Entrance to Musée du Louvre) A2

Sleeping

12 BVJ Paris-Louvre B1
13 Hôtel Caron de Beaumarchais E3
14 Hôtel Croix de Malte G1
15 Hôtel Daval G3
16 Hôtel de Lille B1
17 Hôtel des Grandes Écoles D6
18 Hôtel du 7e Art F4
19 Hôtel Jeanne d'Arc F3
20 Hôtel Rivoli E3
21 MIJE Le Fauconnier E4
22 MIJE Le Fourcy E3
23 MIJE Maubuisson E3

Eating

24 Berthillon E4
25 Breakfast in America F3
26 Breakfast in America D5
27 Chez Janou G3
28 Chez Nénesse F1
29 Cosi A3
30 Joe Allen D1
31 Le Hangar E2
32 Le Petit Mâchon B1
33 Le Pré Verre C5
34 Les Pâtes Vivantes D5
35 Marché Bastille G3
36 Saveurs Végét' Halles C2

Drinking

37 Au Petit Fer à Cheval E3
38 Café La Palette B3
39 Curio Parlor Cocktail Club D4
La Chaise au Plafond .... (see 37)
40 Le 10 .... B4
41 Le Cochon à l'Oreille C1
42 Le Crocodile B6
43 Le Fumoir B2
44 Le Piano Vache C5
45 Le Pub St-Hilaire C5
46 Le Violon Dingue C5
47 Prescription Cocktail Club B3

Entertainment

48 L'Attirail E1
49 Le Baiser Salé C2

Costs include the bicycle and rain gear. Reserve in advance.

Bateaux Mouches BOAT
(Map p402; ☎01 42 25 9610; www.bateauxmouches.com; Port de la Conférence, 8e; adult €10; ⏲Mar-Nov; Ⓜ Alma Marceau) Paris' most famous riverboat company runs 1000-seat tour boats.

Paris Canal Croisières BOAT
(Map p402; ☎01 42 40 96 97; www.pariscanal.com; Bassin de la Villette, 19-21 quai de la Loire, 19e; adult €17; ⏲Mar-Nov; Ⓜ Jaurès or Musée d'Orsay) Daily 2½-hour cruises departing from near the Musée d'Orsay (quai Anatole France) for Bassin de la Villette, 19e, via the charming Canal St-Martin and Canal de l'Ourcq.

L'Open Tour BUS
(Map p412; ☎01 42 66 56 56; www.pariscityrama.com; 13 rue Auber, 9e; 1 day adult €29; Ⓜ Havre Caumartin or Opéra) This company runs open-deck buses along four circuits and you can jump on/off at more than 50 stops.

Paris Walks WALKING
(www.paris-walks.com; adult €12) Runs thematic tours (fashion, chocolate, the French Revolution) in English.

Sleeping

The **Paris Convention & Visitors Bureau** (p419) can find you a place to stay (no booking fee but you need a credit card), though queues can be long in high season.

For B&B accommodation try **Alcôve & Agapes** (www.bed-and-breakfast-in-paris.com), **Good Morning Paris** (www.goodmorningparis.fr) and **B&B Paris** (www.2binparis.com).

LOUVRE & LES HALLES

Hôtel de Lille HOTEL €
(Map p406; ☎01 42 33 33 42; 8 rue du Pélican, 1er; s €39-43, d €50-55, tr €85; Ⓜ Palais Royal-Musée du Louvre;) This old-fashioned but spotlessly clean 13-room hotel is down a quiet side street from the Louvre in a 17th-century building.

BVJ Paris-Louvre HOSTEL €
(Map p406; ☎01 53 00 90 90; www.bvjhotel.com; 20 rue Jean-Jacques Rousseau, 1er; dm/d €29/70; @; Ⓜ Louvre-Rivoli) This modern, 200-bed hostel has doubles and bunks in a single-sex room for four to 10 people with showers down the corridor. Guests must be aged 18 to 35. Rooms are accessible from 2.30pm on the day you arrive and all day after that. No kitchen.

MARAIS & BASTILLE

Budget accomodation is a forte of the Marais. East of Bastille, the untouristed 11e provides a glimpse up close of working-class Paris.

Hôtel Daval HOTEL €
(Map p406; ☎01 47 00 51 23; www.hoteldaval.com; 21 rue Daval, 11e; s €81, d €89-98, tr/q €109/127; Ⓜ Bastille) Always a favourite, this 23-room property is a very central option if you're looking for almost budget accommodation just off place de la Bastille. If you're looking for peace and quiet, choose a back room (eg room 13).

Hôtel du 7e Art THEMED HOTEL €€
(Map p406; ☎01 44 54 85 00; www.paris-hotel-7art.com; 20 rue St-Paul, 4e; s €75-150, d €95-155; Ⓜ St-Paul) Film buffs; this fun 23-room place with black-and-white-movie theme throughout its 23 rooms is for you.

Hôtel Croix de Malte HOTEL €
(Map p406; ☎01 48 05 09 36; www.hotelcroixdemalte-paris.com; 5 rue de Malte, 11e; s €60-90, d €65-97; Ⓜ Oberkampf) This cheery hotel will have you thinking you're in the tropics. The breakfast room just off the lobby is bathed in light and looks out onto a tiny glassed-in courtyard with greenery and a giant jungle mural; Walasse Ting prints of jungles and parrots complete the picture.

Auberge de Jeunesse Jules Ferry HI HOSTEL €
(Map p402; ☎01 43 57 55 60; www.fuaj.fr; 8 blvd Jules Ferry, 11e; dm/d €23/46; Ⓜ République or Goncourt; @) This hostel three blocks east of place de la République is somewhat institutional and the rooms could use a refit, but the atmosphere is relaxed. Beds are in two- to six-person rooms, locked between 10.30am and 2pm for housekeeping; there's no curfew. Pay €2.90 extra per night if you don't have an HI card or equivalent.

Hôtel Rivoli HOTEL €
(Map p406; ☎01 42 72 08 41; 44 rue de Rivoli or 2 rue des Mauvais Garçons, 4e; €35-55, d €44-55, tr €70; Ⓜ Hôtel de Ville) Long a favourite, the Rivoli is forever cheery with 20 basic, noisy rooms. Cheaper singles and doubles have washbasins only, but the hallway showers are free. The front door is locked from 2am to 7am.

Hôtel de Nevers HOTEL €
(Map p402; ☎01 47 00 56 18; www.hoteldenevers.com; 53 rue de Malte, 11e; s/d/tr/q €62/69/93/103; Ⓜ Oberkampf) This 32-room budget hotel, a family affair, is handy for the Marais nightlife. If you like cats you'll be happy here – there are three inhouse moggies to greet prospective guests.

Hôtel Jeanne d'Arc HOTEL €
(Map p406; ☎01 48 87 62 11; www.hoteljeannedarc.com; 3 rue de Jarente, 4e; s €62-90, d €90-116, tr/q €146/160; Ⓜ St-Paul) Near place du Marché Ste-Catherine, this cosy, 35-room hotel almost has a country feel and is a great little

THE LOUVRE: TICKETS & TOURS

Buy tickets in advance from ticket machines in the **Carrousel du Louvre shopping centre** (99 rue de Rivoli) or, for an extra €1 to €1.60, from Fnac or Virgin Megsatores *billetteries*, and walk straight in without queuing. Also, buy tickets direct on www.louvre.fr.

Before hitting the collections, pick up a free English-language *plan* (map) of the labyrinthine Louvre from the information desk in the centre of the Hall Napoléon. At the entrance to each wing rent a self-paced audio guide (€6).

English-language **guided tours** (☎01 40 20 52 63) depart at 11am, 2pm and (sometimes) 3.45pm Monday and Wednesday to Saturday. Tickets cost €5 in addition to the cost of admission. Sign up at least 30 minutes before departure time.

CENTRAL PARIS SPLURGE

Decorated as an 18th-century private house, **Hôtel Caron de Beaumarchais** (Map p406; ☎01 42 72 34 12; www.carondebeaumarchais.com; 12 rue Vieille du Temple, 4e; r €125-162; ❄📶; Ⓜ St-Paul) is an ostentatious little gem that has to be seen to be believed. In the palatial lobby an 18th-century pianoforte, gaming tables, gilded mirrors and candelabras set the tone for a stay that promises to be unique.

base for exploring the Marais. About the only thing wrong with it is that everyone knows about it, so you'll have to book well in advance.

Hôtel Les Sans Culottes HOTEL €
(Map p402; ☎01 48 05 42 92; www.lessansculottesfr.com; 27 rue de Lappe, 11e; s/d from €60/75; Ⓜ Bastille) The nine rooms of this hotel above a nice little bistro of the same name are small but clean, bright and floral. Best of all, the place is very central to restaurants and nightlife of the Bastille.

Maison Internationale de la Jeunesse et des Étudiants HOSTEL €
(MIJE; ☎01 42 74 23 45; www.mije.com; dm/s/d/tr €30/49/72/96; @) The MIJE runs three hostels in attractively renovated 17th- and 18th-century *hôtels particuliers* in the heart of the Marais, and it's difficult to think of a better budget deal in Paris. Rooms are closed from noon to 3pm, and the curfew is 1am to 7am. Annual membership €2.50. **MIJE Le Fourcy** (Map p406; 6 rue de Fourcy, 4e; Ⓜ St-Paul), with 200 beds, is the largest of the three and has a cheap eatery serving a three-course fixed-price *menu* including a drink for €10.50. **MIJE Le Fauconnier** (Map p406; 11 rue du Fauconnier, 4e; Ⓜ St-Paul or Pont Marie), two blocks south, sleeps 125. **MIJE Maubuisson** (Map p406; 12 rue des Barres, 4e; Ⓜ Hôtel de Ville or Pont Marie) – the pick of the three – is half a block south of the *mairie* (town hall) of the 4e and has 99 beds.

LATIN QUARTER

Oops DESIGN HOSTEL €
(Map p402; ☎01 47 07 47 00; www.oops-paris.com; 50 av des Gobelins, 13e; dm €28-35; @📶; Ⓜ Les Gobelins) It might be discretely wedged between cafe terraces and shop fronts but inside there is nothing discrete about this address. A lurid candyfloss-pink lift scales its six floors. Doubles (book in advance) are well sized and stylish dorms max out at four to six beds. Breakfast is a generous affair and in keeping with that true hostel spirit, guests must evacuate their room between 11am and 5pm. Reserve online.

Port Royal Hôtel HOTEL €
(Map p402; ☎01 43 31 70 06; www.hotelportroyal.fr; 8 blvd de Port Royal, 5e; s €41-89, d €52.50-89; Ⓜ Les Gobelins) This 46-room hotel has been run by the same family since 1931. Its six floors are served by a lift, but the cheapest (washbasin-clad) rooms share a toilet and shower (buy a €2.50 token at reception). Predictably, this value-for-money place is no secret, so book ahead. No credit cards.

Hôtel des Grandes Écoles GARDEN HOTEL €€
(Map p406; ☎01 43 26 79 23; www.hotel-grandes-ecoles.com; 75 rue du Cardinal Lemoine, 5e; d €115-140; @📶; Ⓜ Cardinal Lemoine or Place Monge) This wonderful 51-room hotel is tucked in a courtyard off a medieval street with its own garden. Choose a room in one of three buildings: our favourites are rooms 29 to 33 with direct garden access.

Young & Happy Hostel HOSTEL €
(Map p402; ☎01 47 07 47 07; www.youngandhappy.fr; 80 rue Mouffetard, 5e; dm €26-28, d €60; @📶; Ⓜ Place Monge) Check in after 4pm, out before 11am at this frayed place in the heart of the Latin Quarter. Beds are in cramped rooms with washbasins, and accommodate three to 10 people – double rooms can be reserved in advance so get in quick! Rates include breakfast in the dark stone-vaulted cellar, sheets and towels (you need a €5 and €1 deposit respectively for the latter two). Happy-go-lucky is the general mood of this busy hostel.

GARE DU NORD & GARE DE L'EST

This area is far from Paris' prettiest, but decent-value accommodation is rife.

TOP CHOICE **St Christopher's Inn** HOSTEL €
(Map p402; ☎01 40 34 34 40; www.st-christophers.co.uk; 68-74 quai de la Seine, 19e; dm €15-38, d from €35; @📶; Ⓜ Riquet or Jaurès) This is one of Paris' best, biggest (300 beds) and up-to-date hostels – think modern design, dorms plus doubles with or without bathrooms, canal-side cafe, free wi-fi (temperamental) and breakfast, internet cafe, female-only floor and bar. Seasonal prices vary wildly; check the website. There is no kitchen.

Hôtel du Nord HOTEL €
(Map p402; ☎01 42 01 66 00; www.hoteldunord-leparivelo.com; 47 rue Albert Thomas, 10e; r/q €69/105; 📶; Ⓜ République) A cosy place with 23 personalised rooms decorated with flea-market antiques, Hôtel du Nord's other winning attribute is its prized location near place République. Borrow a bike from reception.

République Hôtel THEMED HOTEL €€
(Map p402; ☎01 42 39 19 03; www.republiquehotel.com; 31 rue Albert Thomas, 10e; s/d/tr/q €75/88/108/159; 📶; Ⓜ République) This hip spot is heavy on the pop art and UK paraphernalia – the Union Jack and the Beatles turn up an awful lot – but you cannot fault the inexpensive rates and fantastic location off place République.

Sibour Hôtel HOTEL €
(Map p402; ☎01 46 07 20 74; www.hotel-sibour.com, in French; 4 rue Sibour, 10e; s €40-60, d €45-68, tr/q €80/110; 📶; Ⓜ Gare de l'Est) This friendly place has 45 well-kept rooms, including some old-fashioned ones (the cheapest singles and doubles) with washbasins only. Communal showers cost €3. Some of the rooms look down on pretty Église de St-Laurent.

GARE DE LYON & NATION

Blue Planet Hostel HOSTEL €
(Map p402; ☎01 43 42 06 18; www.hostelblueplanet.com; 5 rue Hector Malot, 12e; dm €25; Ⓜ Gare de Lyon; @) This 43-room hostel is very close to Gare de Lyon – convenient if you're heading south or west at the crack of dawn. Dorm beds are in rooms for two to four people, and the hostel closes between 11am and 3pm (no curfew).

Hôtel Le Cosy HOTEL €
(Map p402; ☎01 43 43 10 02; www.hotel-cosy.com; 50 av de St-Mandé, 12e; s €45-65, d €55-100; ❄📶; Ⓜ Picpus) This slightly eccentric hotel oozes charm. The 28 rooms, though basic, are decorated in warm pastels and hardwood floors; for extra luxury there are four 'VIP' rooms in the courtyard annexe.

MONTMARTRE & AROUND

TOP CHOICE **Hôtel Eldorado** QUIRKY HOTEL €
(Map p412; ☎01 45 22 35 21; www.eldoradohotel.fr; 18 rue des Dames, 17e; s €35-60, d €70-80, tr €80-90; 📶; Ⓜ Place de Clichy) This bohemian place is one of Paris' greatest finds: a welcoming, well-run place with 23 colourfully decorated and (often) ethnically themed rooms. We love the garden annexe. Cheaper-category singles have washbasin only. The hotel's excellent **Bistro des Dames** is a bonus.

Hôtel Bonséjour Montmartre HOTEL €
(Map p412; ☎01 42 54 22 53; www.hotel-bonsejourmontmartre.fr; 11 rue Burq, 18e; s/d from €33/56; @; Ⓜ Abbesses) At the top of a quiet street, the 'Good Stay' is a perennial favourite. It's simple, welcoming, comfortable and very clean. Some rooms have balconies and Room 55 glimpses Sacré Cœur. Hall showers are €2.

Le Village Hostel HOSTEL €
(Map p412; ☎01 42 64 22 02; www.villagehostel.fr; 20 rue d'Orsel, 18e; dm €28-38, d €70-90, tr €96-115, q €112-140; @📶; Ⓜ Anvers) A fine address with beamed ceilings, lovely terrace and Sacré Cœur views. Has a kitchen and popular bar too; rooms closed between 11am and 4pm but no curfew.

Plug-inn Hostel HOSTEL €
(Map p412; ☎01 42 58 42 58; www.plug-inn.fr; 7 rue Aristide Bruant, 18e; dm €20-30, d €60-80, tr €90; @📶; Ⓜ Abbesses or Blanche) This 2010 hostel has several things going for it, central Montmartre location for starters. Lockout by day; no curfew by night.

Hotel Caulaincourt Square HOTEL €
(Map p412; ☎01 46 06 46 06; www.caulaincourt.com; 2 square Caulaincourt, 18e; dm €25, s €50-60, d & tw €63-76, tr €89; @📶; Ⓜ Lamarck Caulaincourt) This hotel with dorms is perched on the backside of Montmartre, beyond the tourist hoopla in a real Parisian neighbourhood.

MONTPARNASSE & THE 15E

Aloha Hostel HOSTEL €
(Map p402; ☎01 42 73 03 03; www.aloha.fr; 1 rue Borromée, 15e; dm/d €25/56 incl breakfast; @📶; Ⓜ Volontaires) Flags flutter outside this laid-back crash pad with a rainbow of colours

PARIS SPLURGE

Was Mick J thinking of the hip **Mama Shelter** (Map p402; ☎01 43 48 47 40; www.mamashelter.com; 109 rue de Bagnolet, 20e; s €89-99, d €99-109, ste €299-399; ❄📶; Ⓜ Alexandre Dumas or Gambetta) when he lipped 'If I don't get some shelter/I'm gonna fade away'? Coaxed into its zany new incarnation by über-designer Philippe Starck, this former car park southeast of Cimetière du Père Lachaise boasts 170 super comfortable (though smallish) rooms, 7th-floor terrace and candle-lit **pizzeria**. Only drawback: Mama Shelter is a hike to the nearest metro stop.

as paint job. Opera music adds funk to the reception-lounge, dorms have four to eight beds and the cream of the crop is its rooms for two (no advance reservations). Rooms are locked from 11am to 5pm (curfew from 2am).

Hôtel de la Paix BOUTIQUE HOTEL **€€**
(Map p402; ☎01 43 20 35 82; www.paris-montparnasse-hotel.com; 225 blvd Raspail, 14e; d €93-165; ❄@📶; Ⓜ Montparnasse Bienvenüe) Stunningly good value, this restyled hotel stacked in a 1970s building is a charm. A hip mix of industrial workshop and *côte maison* (home-like), rooms mix modern with vintage.

Eating

As culinary centre of the most aggressively gastronomic country in the world, Paris has more 'generic French', regional and ethnic restaurants than anywhere else in France. In pricier restaurants, ordering a *menu* (set two- or three-course meal at a fixed price) at lunchtime is invariably extraordinary good value.

LOUVRE & LES HALLES

This area is filled with trendy restaurants, though few are outstanding – most cater to tourists. Streets lined with places to eat include rue des Lombards, the narrow streets north and east of Forum des Halles, and food-

Montmartre

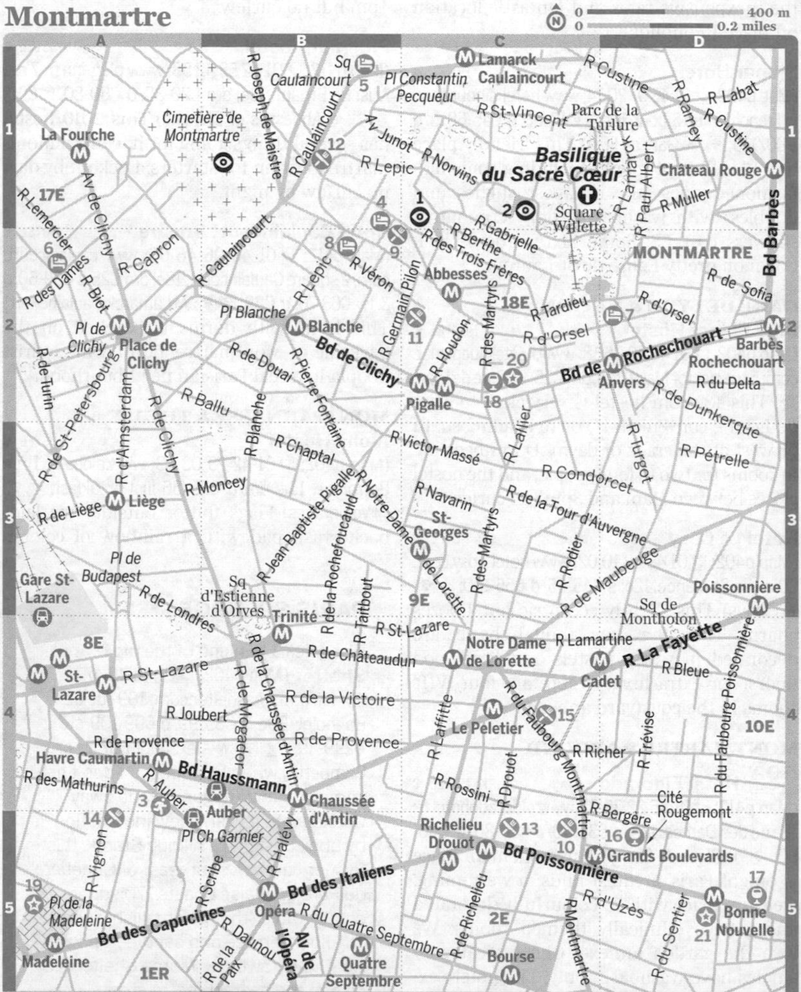

0 — 400 m
0 — 0.2 miles

ie streets rue Montorgueil and rue Ste-Anne. Find supermarkets around Forum des Halles.

Saveurs Végét' Halles VEGETARIAN €
(Map p406; ☎01 40 41 93 95; 41 rue des Bourdonnais, 1er; menus €9.90-18.90; ⊙Mon-Sat; ✍; MChâtelet) This strictly vegan eatery is egg-free and serves a fair few mock-meat dishes such as *poulet végétal aux champignons* ('chicken' with mushrooms) and *escalope de seitan* (wheat gluten 'escalope'). No booze.

Le Petit Mâchon LYONNAIS €€
(Map p406; ☎01 42 60 08 06; 158 rue St-Honoré, 1er; mains €14-22; ⊙Tue-Sun; MPalais Royal-Musée du Louvre) Close to the Louvre, this upbeat bistro serves some of the best Lyonnais specialities in town.

Joe Allen AMERICAN €€
(Map p406; ☎01 42 36 70 13; 30 rue Pierre Lescot, 1er; lunch menu €14, dinner menu €18.10 & €22.50; ⊙noon-1am; MÉtienne Marcel) An institution since 1972, Joe Allen is a little bit of New York in Paris. The ribs are particularly recommended.

MARAIS & BASTILLE

These are premier dining neighbourhoods: book ahead at weekends. Hunt down decent ethnic cuisine towards République: Chinese noodle shops and restaurants on rue Au Maire (MArts et Métiers), and takeaway falafel et al on rue des Rosiers (MSt-Paul).

TOP CHOICE **Le Mouton Noir** FRENCH €€
(Map p402; ☎01 48 07 05 45; 65 rue de Charonne, 11e; menu €29; ⊙dinner Tue-Sat, lunch Sat & Sun; MCharonne) Tiny, but practically perfect, this is no *mouton noir* (black sheep). Fabulously unique, this dining address with a mere two-dozen covers west of Bastille is a neighbourhood secret we've just blown. The idea is to use unusual products in traditional French cooking – *cuisine hippy groove* the chef calls it. Try crab bisque with red curry and lentils, sea bass with cheese or eggplant with thyme. Brunch (€19) is a fine weekend tradition.

TOP CHOICE **Chez Janou** PROVENCAL €€
(Map p406; ☎01 42 72 28 41; 2 rue Roger Verlomme, 3e; mains €14.50-19; MChemin Vert) This lovely little spot just northeast of place des Vosges attracts celebs (last seen: John Malkovich) with its inspired cooking from the south of France, 80 types of pastis and great service.

DON'T MISS

CANAL ST-MARTIN

The shaded towpaths of the tranquil, 4.5km-long **Canal St-Martin** (Map p402; MRépublique, Jaurès or Jacques Bonsergent) in Paris' eastern suburbs are a wonderful place for a romantic stroll or a bike ride past nine locks, metal bridges and ordinary Parisian neighbourhoods. The waterbanks here have undergone a real urban renaissance, and the southern stretch in particular is a hip spot for cafe lounging, bistro dining, quay-side summer picnics and late-night drinks.

Montmartre

Top Sights
Basilique du Sacré Cœur C1

Sights
1 Bateau Lavoir C1
2 Place du Tertre C1

Activities, Courses & Tours
3 L'Open Tour A4

Sleeping
4 Hôtel Bonséjour Montmartre B1
5 Hôtel Caulaincourt Square B1
6 Hôtel Eldorado A2
7 Le Village Hostel D2
8 Plug-inn Hostel B2

Eating
9 Café Burq B2
10 Chartier C5
11 Chez Toinette C2
12 Le Café qui Parle B1
13 Le J'Go C5
14 Le Roi du Pot au Feu A5
15 Les Pâtes Vivantes C4

Drinking
16 Au Limonaire D5
17 DeLaVille Café D5
18 La Fourmi C2

Entertainment
19 Kiosque Théâtre Madeleine A5
20 La Cigale C2
21 Le Rex Club D5

PARISIAN EAT STREETS

» **Av de Choisy, av d'Ivry & rue Baudricourt** Chinatown: Cheap Chinese and Southeast Asian (especially Vietnamese) eateries (Ⓜ Tolbiac).

» **Blvd de Belleville** Middle Eastern (Algerian, Tunisian) food, especially couscous (Ⓜ Belleville).

» **Passage Brady** Magnet for Indian, Pakistani and Bangladeshi dishes (Ⓜ Château d'Eau).

» **Rue Cadet, rue Richer & rue Geoffroy Marie** Triangle of streets Jewish (mostly Sephardic) and kosher food (Ⓜ Cadet).

» **Rue de Belleville** Asian, especially Thai and Vietnamese (Ⓜ Belleville).

» **Rue des Rosiers** Specialities from Central Europe, North Africa and Israel, including Ashkenazic Jewish kosher food, especially felafel and *shawarma* (kebabs) (Ⓜ St-Paul).

» **Rue du Faubourg St-Denis** Indian, Pakistani and Bangladeshi (Ⓜ Strasbourg St-Dennis).

» **Rue Montorgueil** Pedestrian market street packed with tiptop quality, quick eats (Ⓜ Les Halles).

» **Rue Ste-Anne** The heart of Paris' Japantown (Ⓜ Quatre Septembre).

Le Hangar FRENCH, BISTRO €€
(Map p406; ☎01 42 74 55 44; 12 impasse Berthaud, 3e; mains €16-20; ⏰Tue-Sat; Ⓜ Rambuteau) Unusual for big mouths like us, we almost baulk at revealing details of this perfect little restaurant. It serves all the bistro favourites – rillettes, foie gras, steak tartare – in relaxing surrounds. The terrace is a delight in fine weather.

Chez Nénesse FRENCH, BISTRO €
(Map p406; ☎01 42 78 46 49; 17 rue Saintonge, 3e; mains €18; ⏰Mon-Fri; Ⓜ Filles du Calvaire) The atmosphere here is charmingly 'old Parisian' and unpretentious. Dishes are prepared with fresh, high-quality ingredients and pose good value for money.

Marche ou Crêpe FRENCH, BRETON €
(Map p402; ☎01 43 57 04 78; 88 rue Oberkampf, 11e; crepes & galettes €2.20-7.80; ⏰6pm-midnight Tue-Thu, 6pm-2am Fri & Sat, 5pm-midnight Sun; Ⓜ Parmentier) This little outlet near nightlife-busy rue Jean-Pierre Timbaud serves delicious savoury galettes, sweet crêpes, homemade soups and salads – until late late late.

Breakfast in America AMERICAN €
(Map p406; 4 rue Malher, 4e; meals €6.95-11.50; ⏰8.30am-11.30pm; Ⓜ St-Paul) US-style diner, complete with red banquettes and Formica surfaces. Breakfast, served all day and with free coffee refills, starts at just under €7, and there are generous burgers, chicken wings and fish and chips. Its **Latin Quarter branch** (Map p406; 17 rue des Écoles, 5e; Ⓜ Cardinal Lemoine) opens the same hours.

LATIN QUARTER

Cheap-eat student haunt to chandelier-lit palace – the Latin Quarter suits all tastes. Hit rue Mouffetard for its food market and its side streets, especially pedestrianised rue du Pot au Fer, for fine budget dines.

TOP CHOICE **Le Pré Verre** FRENCH, BISTRO €€
(Map p406; ☎01 43 54 59 47; 25 rue Thénard, 5e; 2-/3-course menu €13.50/28; ⏰Tue-Sat; Ⓜ Maubert Mutualité) Noisy, busy and buzzing, this jovial bistro plunges diners into the heart of a Parisian's Paris. At lunchtime join the flock and go for the fabulous-value *formule dejeuner* (€13). The wine list features France's small independent *vignerons* (wine producers).

La Mosquée de Paris NORTH AFRICAN €€
(Map p406; ☎01 43 31 38 20; 39 rue Geoffroy St-Hilaire, 5e; mains €15-20; Ⓜ Censier Daubenton or Place Monge) Dig into a couscous, *tajine* or meaty grill within the walls of the city's **central mosque**. Or spoil yourself with a peppermint tea and oriental pastry in its **tearoom** (⏰9am-11.30pm) or lunch, body scrub and massage in its *hammam* (Turkish bath).

ST-GERMAIN & LUXEMBOURG

There's far more to this fabled pocket of Paris than the literary cafes of Sartre or picnicking turf of **Jardin de Luxembourg**. Rue St-André des Arts (Ⓜ St-Michel or Odéon) is lined with eating joints, as is the stretch

TOP FIVE FOOD MARKETS

» **Marché Bastille** (Map p406; blvd Richard Lenoir, 11e; ⏱7am-2.30pm Thu & Sun; Ⓜ Bastille or Richard Lenoir) Paris' best outdoor food market.

» **Marché Belleville** (Map p402; blvd de Belleville btwn rue Jean-Pierre Timbaud & rue du Faubourg du Temple, 11e & 20e; ⏱7am-2.30pm Tue & Fri; Ⓜ Belleville or Couronnes) Fascinating entry into the large, vibrant communities of the eastern neighbourhoods, home to artists, students and immigrants from Africa, Asia and the Middle East.

» **Marché Couvert St-Quentin** (Map p402; 85 blvd de Magenta, 10e; ⏱8am-1pm & 3.30-7.30pm Tue-Sat, 8.30am-1pm Sun; Ⓜ Gare de l'Est) Iron-and-glass-covered market built in 1866, lined with gourmet food stalls.

» **Rue Cler** (Map p402; rue Cler, 7e; ⏱8am-7pm Tue-Sat, 8am-noon Sun; Ⓜ École Militaire) Commercial street market with an almost party-like atmosphere at weekends.

» **Rue Mouffetard** (Map p402; rue Mouffetard; ⏱8am-7.30pm Tue-Sat, 8am-noon Sun; Ⓜ Censier Daubenton) The city's most photogenic market street.

between Église St-Sulpice and Église St-Germain des Prés (especially rue des Canettes, rue Princesse and rue Guisarde).

Cosi SANDWICH BAR €
(Map p406; 54 rue de Seine, 6e; sandwich menus €10-15; ⏱noon-11pm; Ⓜ Odéon) With sandwich names like Stonker, Tom Dooley and Naked Willi, Kiwi-owned Cosi could easily run for Paris' most imaginative sandwich maker.

TOP CHOICE **Quatrehommes** CHEESE SHOP €
(Map p402; 62 rue de Sèvres, 6e; Ⓜ Vanneau) Buy the best of every French cheese at this king of *fromageries*, well worth a visit for the smell alone.

OPÉRA & GRANDS BOULEVARDS

The neon-lit area around blvd Montmartre forms one of the Right Bank's most animated cafe and dining districts.

TOP CHOICE **La Cabane à Huîtres** FRENCH, OYSTERS €
(Map p402; ☎01 45 49 47 27; 4 rue Antoine Bourdelle, 14e; menus €18; ⏱Wed-Sat; Ⓜ Montparnasse-Bienvenüe) One of Paris' best oyster addresses, this earthy wooden-styled *cabane* (cabin) with just nine tables is the pride and joy of fifth-generation oyster-farmer Françis Dubourg, who splits his week between the capital and his oyster farm in Arcachon on the Atlantic coast.

TOP CHOICE **Les Pâtes Vivantes** CHINESE €
(Map p412; 46 rue du Faubourg Montmartre, 9e; noodles €9.50-12; ⏱Mon-Sat; Ⓜ Le Peletier) This is one of the few spots in Paris for hand-pulled noodles *(là miàn)* made to order in the age-old northern Chinese tradition. There's also a **Latin Quarter branch** (Map p406; ☎01 40 46 84 33; 22 blvd St-Germain, 5e; Ⓜ Cardinal Lemoine).

Chartier FRENCH, BISTRO €
(Map p412; 7 rue du Faubourg Montmartre, 9e; menu with wine €19.40; Ⓜ Grands Boulevards) Chartier started life as a *bouillon* (soup kitchen) in 1896 and is a real *belle époque* gem. For a taste of old-fashioned Paris, it's unbeatable. No reservations.

Le J'Go SOUTHWEST FRENCH €€
(Map p412; ☎01 40 22 09 09; 4 rue Drouot, 9e; menus €15-20; ⏱lunch Mon-Fri, dinner Mon-Sat; Ⓜ Richelieu Druot) This contemporary, Toulouse-style bistro magics diners away to southwestern France. Flavourful regional cooking revolves around a *rôtissoire* (meat on a spit) – minimum 20 minutes roasting.

Le Roi du Pot au Feu FRENCH, BISTRO €€
(Map p412; 34 rue Vignon, 9e; menus €24-29; ⏱noon-10.30pm Mon-Sat; Ⓜ Havre Caumartin)

THE GOURMET GLACIER

Berthillon (Map p406; 31 rue St-Louis en l'Île, 4e; ice cream €2.10-5.40; ⏱10am-8pm Wed-Sun; Ⓜ Pont Marie), on Île St-Louis, is the place to head to for Paris' finest ice cream. There are 70 flavours to choose from, ranging from fruity cassis to chocolate, coffee, *marrons glacés* (candied chestnuts), *Agenaise* (Armagnac and prunes), *noisette* (hazelnut) and *nougat au miel* (honey nougat). One just won't be enough...

The typical Parisian bistro atmosphere adds to the charm of the 'King of Hotpots', but what you really come here for is its *pot au feu* (beef, root vegetable and herb stew), the stock as entrée and the meat 'n veg as main. No bookings.

MONTMARTRE & PIGALLE

Beware tourist traps; try side streets off blvd de Clichy such as rue Lepic. Towards place Pigalle there grocery stores galore, many open until late

Chez Toinette FRENCH €€
(Map p412; ☎01 42 54 44 36; 20 rue Germain Pilon, 18e; mains €17-22; ⌚dinner Mon-Sat; MAbbesses) Chez Toinette keeps alive the tradition of old Montmartre with its simplicity and culinary expertise. Partridge, doe and duck are house specialities.

Café Burq FRENCH, BISTRO €€
(Map p412; ☎01 42 52 81 27; 6 rue Burq, 18e; menus €26 & €30; ⌚7pm-2am Tue-Sat; MAbbesses) This convivial, retro bistro is always buzzing; book ahead. But don't come for the decor or space – both are nonexistent.

Le Café qui Parle FRENCH €€
(Map p412; ☎01 46 06 06 88; 24 rue Caulaincourt, 18e; menus €12.50 & €17; ⌚Mon-Sat, lunch Sun; Wi-Fi; MLamarck Caulaincourt or Blanche) We love The Talking Café's wall art and ancient safes below (the building was once a bank), but not as much as we love its weekend brunch (€17).

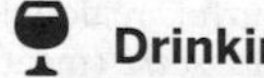

Drinking

Drinking in Paris means paying the rent for the space you are occupying – it costs more sitting at tables than standing, more on a fancy square than a backstreet, more in the 8e than the 18e.

LOUVRE & LES HALLES

Le Fumoir COCKTAIL BAR
(Map p406; 6 rue de l'Amiral Coligny, 1er; ⌚11am-2am; MLouvre-Rivoli) The 'Smoking Room' is a huge, stylish colonial-style bar-cafe opposite the Louvre – a fine place to sip top-notch gin while nibbling on olives.

Le Cochon à l'Oreille BAR, CAFÉ
(Map p406; 15 rue Montmartre, 1er; ⌚10am-11pm Tue-Sat; MLes Halles or Étienne Marcel) A Parisian jewel, this heritage-listed hole-in-the wall retains its *belle époque* tiles with market scenes of Les Halles and just eight tiny tables.

MARAIS & BASTILLE

Le Pure Café CAFE
(Map p402; 14 rue Jean Macé, 11e; ⌚7am-2am; MCharonne) This old cafe moonlights as a restaurant, but we like it as it was intended to be, especially over a *grand crème* (large white coffee) and the papers on Sunday morning.

Le Bistrot du Peintre WINE BAR
(Map p402; 116 av Ledru-Rollin, 11e; ⌚8am-2am; MBastille) Lovely *belle époque* bistro and wine bar, with 1902 art nouveau bar, elegant terrace and spot-on service.

Au Petit Fer à Cheval BAR
(Map p406; 30 rue Vieille du Temple, 4e; ⌚8am-2am; MHôtel de Ville or St-Paul) The original horseshoe-shaped zinc counter (1903) leaves little room for much else at this genial bar, but nobody seems to mind.

La Chaise Au Plafond BAR
(Map p406; 10 Rue du Trésor, 4e; ⌚10am-2am; ⌚Hôtel de Ville or St-Paul) The Chair on the Ceiling is a peaceful, warm place with terrace – a real oasis from the frenzy of the Marais and worth knowing about in summer.

DON'T MISS

CANAL ST-MARTIN: A PARISIAN-PERFECT PICNIC

Pink Flamingo (Map p402; ☎01 42 02 31 70; 67 rue Bichat, 10e; pizzas €10.50-16; ⌚until 11pm Tue-Sat, 1-11pm Sun; MJacques Bonsergent) is not just another pizza place. *Mais non, chérie!* Once the weather warms up, the Flamingo unveils its secret weapon – pink helium balloons that the delivery guy uses to locate you and your perfect canal-side picnic spot. Nip inside to order Paris' most inventive pizza (duck, apple and chèvre perhaps, or what about gorgonzola, figs and cured ham?), grab a balloon and stroll off along the canal to your perfect picnic spot.

To make your picnic Parisian perfect, buy a bottle of wine from nearby **Le Verre Volé** (Map p402; 67 rue de Lancry, 10e; mains €12; MJacques Bonsergent), a wine shop with a few tables, excellent wines (€5 to €60 per bottle, €4.50 per glass) and expert advice.

LATIN QUARTER

Curio Parlor Cocktail Club COCKTAIL BAR
(Map p406; 16 rue des Bernardins, 5e; ⏲7pm-2am Tue-Thu, 7pm-4am Fri & Sat; Ⓜ Maubert Mutualité) This hybrid bar-club looks to the *années folles* (crazy years) of 1920s Paris, London and New York for inspiration. Go to its Facebook page to track the next party.

Le Crocodile BAR
(Map p406; 6 rue Royer Collard, 5e; ⏲10pm-6am Mon-Sat; Ⓜ Luxembourg) The Crocodile has been dispensing cocktails (more than 200 on the list) since 1966. Arrive late for a truly eclectic crowd, very studenty, and an atmosphere that goes from quiet tippling to raucous revelry.

Le Piano Vache BAR
(Map p406; 8 rue Laplace, 5e; ⏲noon-2am Mon-Fri, 9pm-2am Sat & Sun; Ⓜ Maubert Mutualité) Just downhill from the Panthéon, the 'Mean Piano' is effortlessly underground – a huge student favourite. Bands and DJs play mainly rock, plus some Goth, reggae and pop.

Le Violon Dingue PUB
(Map p406; 46 rue de la Montagne Ste-Geneviève, 5e; ⏲8pm-5am Tue-Sat; Ⓜ Maubert Mutualité) A loud, lively bar adopted by revolving generations of students, the 'Crazy Violin' attracts lots of young Englishspeakers with big-screen sports shown upstairs and the flirty 'Dingue Lounge' downstairs.

Le Pub St-Hilaire PUB
(Map p406; www.pubsthilaire.com; 2 rue Valette, 5e; ⏲11am-2am Mon-Thu, 11am-4am Fri, 4pm-4am Sat, 3pm-midnight Sun; Ⓜ Maubert Mutualité) 'Buzzing' fails to do justice to this student-loved pub. Happy hours last forever, while pool tables, board games, and music on two floors keep the punters happy.

ST-GERMAIN & LUXEMBOURG

TOP CHOICE **Au Sauvignon** WINE BAR
(Map p402; 80 rue des Sts-Pères, 7e; ⏲8am-midnight; Ⓜ Sèvres-Babylone) To savour the full flavour of this 1950s wine bar, order a plate of *casse-croûtes au pain Poilâne* – sandwiches made with the city's most famous bread.

TOP CHOICE **Prescription Cocktail Club** COCKTAIL CLUB
(Map p406; 23 rue Mazarine, 6e; ⏲7pm-2am Mon-Thu, 7pm-4am Fri & Sat; Ⓜ Odéon) With bowler and flat-top hats as lampshades and a 1930s speakeasy New York air to the place, this cocktail club is Parisian-cool. Watch Facebook for events.

BAR-HOPPING STREETS

Prime Parisian drinking spots, perfect for evening meandering to soak up the scene:

» **Rue Vieille du Temple & surrounding streets, 4e** Marais cocktail of gay bars and chic cafes (Ⓜ Hôtel de Ville).

» **Rue Oberkampf & rue Jean-Pierre Timbaud, 11e** Hip bars, bohemian hang-outs and atmospheric cafes (Ⓜ Oberkampf).

» **Rue de la Roquette, rue Keller & rue de Lappe, 11e** Whatever you fancy, Bastille has the lot (Ⓜ Bastille).

» **Rue Montmartre, 2e** Modern, slick bars and pubs.

» **Canal St-Martin, 10e** Heady summer nights in casual canal-side cafes (Ⓜ République).

» **Rue Princesse & rue des Canettes, 6e** Pedestrian duo of student, sports 'n' tapas bars and pubs on the Left Bank (Ⓜ Mabillon).

Le 10 CELLAR PUB
(Map p406; 10 rue de l'Odéon, 6e; ⏲5.30pm-2am; Ⓜ Odéon) Plot the next revolution or conquer a lonely heart at this local institution that groans with students, smoky ambience and cheap sangria.

Café La Palette HISTORIC CAFE
(Map p406; 43 rue de Seine, 6e; ⏲8am-2am Mon-Sat; Ⓜ Mabillon) In the heart of gallery land, this cafe where Cézanne and Braque drank, attracts fashionable people and art dealers. Its summer terrace is as beautiful.

MONTMARTRE & AROUND

TOP CHOICE **Au Limonaire** WINE BAR
(Map p412; ☎01 45 23 33 33; http://limonaire.free.fr; 18 cité Bergère, 9e; ⏲7pm-midnight Mon, 6pm-midnight Tue-Sun; Ⓜ Grands Boulevards) This little wine bar is one of the best places to listen to traditional French *chansons* and local singer-songwriters. Reservations recommended.

DeLaVille Café BAR, CAFE
(Map p412; 34 blvd de Bonne Nouvelle, 10e; ⏲11am-2.30am; 📶; Ⓜ Bonne Nouvelle) This erstwhile brothel fuses history (original mosaic tiles, distressed walls) with industrial chic. DJs

play Thursday to Saturday, making it a hot 'before' venue for clubbers.

Buddha Bar COCKTAIL BAR
(Map p402; 8-12 rue Boissy d'Anglas, 8e; ⌚noon-2am Sun-Thu, 4pm-3am Fri & Sat; Ⓜ Concorde) The decor is spectacular, with a two-storey golden Buddha and millions of candles, at this A-list cocktail bar known for its Zen lounge music.

La Fourmi BAR
(Map p412; 74 rue des Martyrs, 18e; ⌚8am-2am Mon-Thu, to 4am Fri & Sat, 10am-2am Sun; Ⓜ Pigalle) A Pigalle stayer, 'The Ant' always hits the mark: hip but not snobby, with a laid-back crowd and a rock-orientated playlist.

☆ Entertainment

To find out what's on, surf **Figaroscope** (www.figaroscope.fr) or buy *Pariscope* (€0.40) and *Officiel des Spectacles* (€0.35; www.offi.fr, in French) at Parisian newskiosks. *Billeteries* (ticket offices) in **Fnac** (www.fnacspectacles.com, in French) or **Virgin Megastores** (www.virginmega.fr, in French) sell tickets.

The same day of a performance, snag a half-price ticket (plus €3 commission) for ballet, theatre, opera etc at discount-ticket outlet **Kiosque Théâtre Madeleine** (Map p412; www.kiosquetheatre.com; opposite 15 place de la Madeleine, 8e; ⌚12.30-8pm Tue-Sat, to 4pm Sun; Ⓜ Madeleine). Online, get discount tickets at www.billetreduc.com, www.ticketac.com and www.webguichet.com.

Live Music

La Cigale ROCK, JAZZ
(Map p412; ☎01 49 25 81 75; www.lacigale.fr; 120 blvd de Rochechouart, 18e; admission €25-60; Ⓜ Anvers or Pigalle) A music hall dating from 1887 and redecorated 100 years later by Philippe Starck; has an avant-garde musical program.

Point Éphemère ROCK, INDIE
(Map p402; ☎01 40 34 02 48; www.pointephemere.org; 200 quai de Valmy, 10e; admission free-€21; ⌚bar noon-2am Mon-Sat, 1-9pm Sun; Ⓜ Louis Blanc) Great location by Canal St-Martin, with indie concerts and the odd electro dance night. Has a bar, restaurant and exhibit area too.

L'Attirail WORLD, LATINO
(Map p406; ☎01 42 72 44 42; www.lattirail.com; 9 rue au Maire, 3e; admission free; ⌚10.30am-1.30am Mon-Sat, 3pm-1.30am Sun; Ⓜ Arts et Métiers) Concerts of *chansons françaises* and world music almost every night. Manic but friendly customers crowd the Formica bar with its cheap *pots* (460mL bottle) of wine.

Le Baiser Salé JAZZ
(Map p406; www.lebaisersale.com, in French; 58 rue des Lombards, 1er; admission free-€20; ⌚5pm-6am; Ⓜ Châtelet) One of several jazz clubs on this street, the Salty Kiss hosts concerts of jazz, Afro and Latin jazz and jazz fusion. Monday's jam session is free.

Clubbing

Paris' clubbing scene changes fast – online is the best place to keep on top of it. Check out:

» www.gogoparis.com (in English)
» www.lemonsound.com
» www.novaplanet.com
» www.parisbouge.com
» www.parissi.com
» www.tribudenuit.com

TOP CHOICE **La Scène Bastille** CLUB
(Map p402; www.scenebastille.com; admission €12-15; 2bis rue des Taillandiers, 11e; ⌚Mon-Sat; Ⓜ Bastille or Ledru Rollin) The unpretentious

DON'T MISS

FREE SHOWS

Top-notch musicians perform in the long echo-filled corridors of the Paris metro, a privilege artists have to audition for. Outside, you can guarantee a good street show – think clowns, mime artists, living statues, acrobats, rollerbladers, buskers et al – at:

» **Place Georges Pompidou, 4e** In front of the Centre Pompidou (Ⓜ Rambuteau).

» **Pont St-Louis, 4e** Bridge linking Paris' two islands (best enjoyed with Berthillon ice-cream in hand, see p415) (Ⓜ Pont Marie).

» **Pont au Double, 4e** Pedestrian bridge linking Notre Dame and the Left Bank (ice-cream ditto)(Ⓜ St-Michel).

» **Place Jean du Bellay, 1er** Musicians and fire-eaters near the Fontaine des Innocents (Ⓜ Hôtel de Ville).

» **Parc de la Villette, 19e** African drummers at the weekend (Ⓜ Porte de la Villete).

» **Place du Tertre, Montmartre, 18e** Montmartre's original main square wins hands down as Paris' busiest street-artist stage (Ⓜ Abbesses).

Bastille Scene is the kind of place where local DJs go to relax and listen to music.

TOP CHOICE **Le Batofar** TUG BOAT

(Map p402; www.batofar.org, in French; opp 11 quai François Mauriac, 13e; admission free-€15; ⏲9pm-midnight Mon & Tue, to 4am or later Wed-Sun; Ⓜ Quai de la Gare or Bibliothèque) This much-loved tugboat has a rooftop bar that's great in summer, while the club underneath provides memorable underwater acoustics between its metal walls and portholes.

Le Rex Club CLUB

(Map p412; www.rexclub.com; 5 blvd Poissonnière, 2e; admission free-€12; ⏲11.30pm-6am Wed-Sat; Ⓜ Bonne Nouvelle) The Rex reigns majestic in the House and techno scene – always has, always will.

Information

Dangers & Annoyances

Paris is generally safe. Metro stations best avoided late at night include: Châtelet-Les Halles and its seemingly endless corridors; Château Rouge in Montmartre; Gare du Nord; Strasbourg St-Denis; Réaumur Sébastopol; and Montparnasse Bienvenüe.

Pickpocketing and theft from handbags and packs is a problem wherever there are crowds (especially of tourists). Be careful around Montmartre's Sacré Cœur, Pigalle, the areas around Forum des Halles and Centre Pompidou, the Latin Quarter, below the Eiffel Tower and on the metro during rush hour.

Internet Resources

Mairie de Paris (www.paris.fr)

My Little Paris (www.mylittleparis.com)

Paris by Mouth (www.parisbymouth.com)

Paris Convention & Visitors Bureau (www.parisinfo.com)

Medical Services

American Hospital of Paris (☎01 46 41 25 25; www.american-hospital.org; 63 blvd Victor Hugo, 92200 Neuilly-sur-Seine; Ⓜ Pont de Levallois Bécon)

Hôpital Hôtel Dieu (☎01 42 34 82 34; www.aphp.fr; 1 place du Parvis Notre Dame, 4e; Ⓜ Cité) One of the city's main government-run public hospitals; after 8pm use the emergency entrance on rue de la Cité, 4e.

Pharmacie Les Champs (☎01 45 62 02 41; Galerie des Champs, 84 av des Champs-Élysées, 8e; ⏲24hr; Ⓜ George V)

Tourist Information

Paris Convention & Visitors Bureau (Map p406; www.parisinfo.com; 25-27 rue des Pyramides, 1er; Ⓜ Pyramides; ⏲9am-7pm Jun-Oct, 10am-7pm Mon-Sat & 11am-7pm Sun Nov-May) Main tourist office, northwest of the Louvre, with a clutch of smaller centres elsewhere in the city.

Getting There & Away

Air

Aéroport d'Orly (ORY; ☎39 50, 01 70 36 39 50; www.aeroportsdeparis.fr) Older and smaller of Paris' two major airports, 18km south of the city.

Aéroport Roissy Charles de Gaulle (CDG; ☎39 50, 01 70 36 39 50; www.aeroportsdeparis.fr) Three terminal complexes – Aérogare 1, 2 and 3 – 30km northeast of Paris in the suburb of Roissy.

Aéroport Paris-Beauvais (BVA; ☎08 92 68 20 66; www.aeroportbeauvais.com) About 80km north of Paris, used by charter and budget airlines.

Bus

Eurolines (☎01 43 54 11 99; www.eurolines.fr; 55 rue St-Jacques, 5e; Ⓜ Cluny-La Sorbonne) Reservations and tickets for international buses to Western and Central Europe, Scandinavia and Morocco.

Gare Routière Internationale de Paris-Galliéni (off Map p402; ☎08 92 89 90 91; 28 av du Général de Gaulle; Ⓜ Galliéni) Paris' international bus terminal in the eastern suburb of Bagnolet.

Train

Paris has six major train stations. For 24-hour mainline train information contact **SNCF** (☎08 91 36 20 20, timetables 08 91 67 68 69; www.sncf.fr).

DON'T MISS

FLEA MARKETS

» **Marché aux Puces de Montreuil** (off Map p402; av du Professeur André Lemière, 20e; ⏲8am-7.30pm Sat-Mon; Ⓜ Porte de Montreuil) Particularly known for its second-hand clothing, designer seconds, engravings, jewellery, linen, crockery and old furniture.

» **Marché aux Puces de St-Ouen** (off Map p402; rue des Rosiers, av Michelet, rue Voltaire, rue Paul Bert & rue Jean-Henri Fabre, 18e; ⏲9am-6pm Sat, 10am-6pm Sun, 11am-5pm Mon; Ⓜ Porte de Clignancourt) Around since the late 19th century, said to be Europe's largest.

» **Marché aux Puces de la Porte de Vanves** (Map p402; av Georges Lafenestre & av Marc Sangnier, 14e; ⏲7am-6pm or later Sat & Sun; Ⓜ Porte de Vanves) The smallest and, some say, friendliest of the trio.

Gare d'Austerlitz (Map p406; blvd de l'Hôpital, 13e; Ⓜ Gare d'Austerlitz) Trains to/from Spain and Portugal; Loire Valley and non-TGV trains to southwestern France (eg Bordeaux and Basque Country).

Gare de l'Est (Map p402; blvd de Strasbourg, 10e; Ⓜ Gare de l'Est) Luxembourg, parts of Switzerland (Basel, Lucerne, Zurich), southern Germany (Frankfurt, Munich) and points further east; regular and TGV Est trains to areas of France east of Paris (Champagne, Alsace and Lorraine).

Gare de Lyon (Map p402; blvd Diderot, 12e; Ⓜ Gare de Lyon) Parts of Switzerland (eg Bern, Geneva, Lausanne), Italy and points beyond; regular and TGV Sud-Est and TGV Midi-Méditerranée trains to areas southeast of Paris, including Dijon, Lyon, Provence, the Côte d'Azur and the Alps.

Gare du Nord (Map p402; rue de Dunkerque, 10e; Ⓜ Gare du Nord) UK, Belgium, northern Germany, Scandinavia, Moscow etc (terminus of the high-speed Thalys trains to/from Amsterdam, Brussels, Cologne and Geneva and Eurostar to London); trains to the northern suburbs of Paris and northern France, including TGV Nord trains to Lille and Calais.

Gare Montparnasse (Map p402; av du Maine & blvd de Vaugirard, 15e; Ⓜ Montparnasse Bienvenüe) Brittany and places en route (eg Chartres, Angers, Nantes); TGV Atlantique Ouest and TGV Atlantique Sud-Ouest trains to Tours, Nantes, Bordeaux and other destinations in southwestern France.

Gare St-Lazare (Map p402; rue St-Lazare & rue d'Amsterdam, 8e; Ⓜ St-Lazare) Normandy (eg Dieppe, Le Havre, Cherbourg).

ℹ Getting Around

To/From the Airports

Getting into town is straightforward and inexpensive thanks to a fleet of public-transport options. Bus drivers sell tickets.

AÉROPORT D'ORLY

From about 12.30am to 5.30am, the Noctilien bus 31 service is the only option.

Air France bus 1 (☎0 892 350 820; http://videocdn.airfrance.com/cars-airfrance; single/return €11.50/18.50) This *navette* (shuttle bus) runs every 30 minutes to/from **Gare Montparnasse** (rue du Commandant René Mouchotte, 15e; Ⓜ Montparnasse Bienvenüe) and **Aérogare des Invalides** (Ⓜ Invalides) in the 7e.

Noctilien bus 31 (☎32 46; www.noctilien.fr; adult €6.40 or 4 metro tickets; ⌚12.30am-5.30pm) Part of the RATP night service, links Orly-Sud hourly with Gare de Lyon, Place d'Italie and Gare d'Austerlitz (45 minutes).

Orlybus (☎32 46; www.ratp.fr; adult €6.40) RATP bus every 15 to 20 minutes until 11pm to/from metro Denfert Rochereau (20 to 30 minutes) in the 14e.

Orlyval (☎32 46; www.ratp.fr; adult €9.85) This RATP service links Orly with the city centre via a shuttle train and the RER (p421). Automatic rail (€7.60) to the RER B station Antony, then RER B4 north (€2.25, 35 to 40 minutes to Châtelet, every four to 12 minutes). Orlyval tickets are valid for the subsequent RER and metro journey.

RATP bus 183 (☎32 46; www.ratp.fr; adult €1.60 or 1 metro/bus ticket) Cheapest and slowest (one hour) way of getting between Orly Sud and metro Porte de Choisy; every 30 minutes until 8.35pm.

RATP bus 285 (☎32 46; www.ratp.fr; adult €6.40 or 4 metro tickets) Every 10 to 30 minutes to/from metro Villejuif Louis Aragon (55 minutes).

RER C & shuttle (☎32 46; www.ratp.fr; adult €6.20) Shuttle bus every 15 to 30 minutes to RER line C station, Pont de Rungis-Aéroport d'Orly RER station, then RER C2 train to Paris' Gare d'Austerlitz (50 minutes).

AÉROPORT ROISSY CHARLES DE GAULLE

From about 12.30am to 5.30am, Noctilien buses 140 and 143 are your only option.

Air France bus 2 (☎0 892 350 820; http://videocdn.airfrance.com/cars-airfrance; one way/return €15/24) Links airport every 30 minutes until 11pm with the Arc de Triomphe outside 1 av Carnot, 17e, and metro Porte Maillot metro, 17e.

Air France bus 4 (☎0 892 350 820; http://videocdn.airfrance.com/cars-airfrance; adult one way/return €16.50/27) Links airport every 30 minutes until 9pm with **Gare de Lyon** (20bis blvd Diderot, 12e; Ⓜ Gare de Lyon) and **Gare Montparnasse** (rue du Commandant René Mouchotte, 15e; Ⓜ Montparnasse Bienvenüe); journey time 55 minutes.

Noctilien buses 140 & 143 (☎32 46; www.noctilien.fr; adult €4.80 or 3 metro tickets; ⌚12.30am-5.30pm) Hourly nght buses to/from Gare de l'Est (140 & 143) and Gare de Nord (143).

RATP bus 350 (☎32 46; www.ratp.fr; adult €4.80 or 3 metro tickets) Every 30 minutes until 11pm to/from Gare de l'Est and Gare du Nord (both one hour).

RER B (☎32 46; www.ratp.fr; adult €8.50) Under renovation at the time of research, with replacement buses on duty; this line usually links CDG1 and CDG2 with the city every 30 minutes (10 to 15 minutes).

Roissybus (☎32 46; www.ratp.fr; adult €9.10) Direct bus every 15 minutes until 11pm to/from **Opéra** (cnr rue Scribe & rue Auber, 9e).

BETWEEN ORLY & CHARLES DE GAULLE

Air France shuttle bus 3 (www.cars-airfrance.com, in French; adult €19; ⏲6am-10.30pm) Every 30 minutes; free for connecting Air France passengers; journey time one hour.

Orlyval (☎32 46; www.ratp.fr; adult €17.60; ⏲6am-11pm) RER line B3 from Charles de Gaulle to the Antony station, then Orlyval automatic metro to Orly.

AÉROPORT PARIS-BEAUVAIS

Navette Officielle (☎08 92 68 20 64, airport 08 92 68 20 66; adult €14) Leaves Parking Pershing, west of the Palais des Congrès de Paris, 3¼ hours before flight departures (board 15 minutes before) and leaves the airport 20 minutes after arrivals, dropping passengers south of the Palais des Congrès on place de la Porte Maillot. Journey time 1¼ hours; buy tickets just outside the terminal and from a kiosk in the car park.

Bicycle

Vélib' (www.velib.paris.fr; day/week subscription €1/5, bike hire per 1st/2nd/additional 30min free/€2/4) With this self-service bike scheme you can pick up a pearly grey bike for peanuts from one roadside Vélib' station and drop it off at any of its almost 1500 bike *stations* accessible around-the-clock. IPhone users can download the Vélib' application. To get a bike, open a Vélib' account: subscriptions can be done at any station with any credit card that has a microchip. If the station you want to return your bike to is full, swipe your card across the multilingual terminal to get 15 minutes for free to find another station. Bikes are geared to cyclists aged 14 and over, and are fitted with gears, antitheft lock with key, reflective strips and front/rear lights.

Boat

Batobus (☎08 25 05 01 01; www.batobus.com; adult 1-/2-/3-day pass €13/17/20; ⏲10am-9.30pm May-Aug, shorter hrs rest of year) Fleet of glassed-in trimarans dock at eight small piers along the Seine every 15 to 30 minutes; buy tickets at each stop or tourist offices and jump on and off as you like.

Public Transport

Paris' public transit system is operated by **RATP** (www.ratp.fr). RATP tickets are valid on the metro, RER, buses, trams and Montmartre funicular. A single ticket/carnet of 10 costs €1.60/11.60.

One ticket covers travel (no return journeys) for 1½ hours. Keep your ticket until you exit the station; ticket inspectors fine you if you can't produce a valid ticket.

BUS Paris' bus system runs from 5.30am to 8.30pm Monday to Saturday, after which certain *service en soirée* (evening service) lines continue until midnight or 12.30am when **Noctilien** (www.noctilien.fr) night buses, departing every hour between 12.30am and 5.30am, kick in. Two circular lines (the N01 and N02) link the four main train stations – St-Lazare, Gare de l'Est, Gare de Lyon and Montparnasse – plus popular nightspots such as Bastille, the Champs-Élysées, Pigalle and St-Germain. Look for blue *N* or 'Noctilien' signs.

Short bus rides (ie rides in one or two bus zones) cost one metro/bus ticket (€1.60 or €1.70 direct from the driver); longer rides require two. Cancel *(oblitérer)* single-journey tickets in the *composteur* (cancelling machine) next to the driver.

METRO & RER Paris' underground network consists of the 14-line metro and the RER, a network of suburban train lines. The last metro on each line begins sometime between 12.35am and 1.04am, before starting up again around 5.30am.

TOURIST PASSES The Mobilis card allows unlimited travel for one day in two to six zones (€5.90 to €16.70) on the metro, RER, buses, trams and the Montmartre funicular. The Paris Visite pass allows unlimited travel (including to/from airports) plus discounted entry to museums and activities; it costs €8.80/14.40/19.60 for one to three zones for one/two/three/five days.

TRAVEL PASSES **Navigo** (www.navigo.fr, in French) consists of a weekly, monthly or yearly unlimited pass that can be recharged at Navigo machines in most metro stations; swipe the card across the electronic panel to go through turnstiles. Standard Navigo passes, available to anyone with an address in Île de France, are free but take up to three weeks to be issued. Otherwise pay €5 for a rechargable Nagivo Découverte (Navigo Discovery) card, issued on the spot. Both require a passport photo.

Otherwise, weekly tickets *(coupon hebdomadaire)* cost €17.20 for zones 1 and 2, valid Monday to Sunday, monthly tickets (*coupon mensuel;* €56.60 for zones 1 and 2) run from the first day of the month.

Taxi

The flag fall is €2.10, plus €0.89 per kilometre within the city limits from 10am and 5pm Monday to Saturday (Tarif A; white light on meter), and €1.14 per kilometre from 5pm to 10am, all day Sunday, and public holidays (Tarif B; orange light on meter).

Alpha Taxis (☎01 45 85 85 85; www.alphataxis.com)

Central taxi switchboard (☎01 45 30 30 30).

Taxis Bleus (☎01 49 36 29 48, 08 91 70 10 10; www.taxis-bleus.com)

Taxis G7 (☎01 47 39 47 39; www.taxisg7.fr, in French)

DON'T MISS

SUMMER MAGIC

The largest fountains of Château de Versailles' gardens are the 17th-century **Bassin de Neptune** (Neptune's Fountain), a dazzling mirage of 99 spouting gushers 300m north of the palace. Watch them 'dance' in all their glory during summer's **Grandes Eaux Musicales** (adult €8; 11am-noon & 3.30-5pm Tue, Sat & Sun Apr-Sep) or after-dark **Grandes Eaux Nocturnes** (adult €21; 9-11.30pm Sat & Sun mid-Jun–Aug). Both 'dancing water' displays, set to baroque and other classical music of the era, are nothing sort of magical.

AROUND PARIS

Versailles

POP 88,930

This leafy, bourgeois suburb, 21km southwest of Paris, is the site of France's grandest and most famous royal residence, **Château de Versailles** (www.chateauversailles.fr; adult/EU resident under 26yr €15/free; 9am-6.30pm Tue-Sun summer, 9am-5.30pm Tue-Sun winter), built in the mid-17th century by Louis XIV – the Roi Soleil (Sun King) – to project the power of the French monarchy. The 580m-long palace itself is split into several wings, each with its own astonishing array of grand halls, wood-panelled corridors and sumptuous bedchambers, including the **Grand Appartement du Roi** (King's Suite) and the **Galerie des Glaces** (Hall of Mirrors), a fabulous 75m-long mirrored ballroom. Outside, the **landscaped gardens** are filled with canals, pools, fountains and neatly trimmed hedges, and two outbuildings, the **Grand Trianon** and the **Petit Trianon**.

The current €400 million restoration project is Versailles' most ambitious yet; until 2020 part of the palace is likely to be clad in scaffolding.

Getting There & Away

RER line C5 (€2.95, every 15 minutes) goes from Paris' Left Bank RER stations to Versailles-Rive Gauche, 700m southeast of the château.

SNCF operates up to 70 trains daily from Paris' Gare St-Lazare (€3.70) to Versailles-Rive Droite, 1.2km from the château. Versailles-Chantiers is served by half-hourly SNCF trains daily from Gare Montparnasse (€2.95); trains continue to Chartres (€11.50, 30 to 60 minutes).

Chartres

POP 45,600

Medieval Chartres is famous for its stunning cathedral, the **Cathédrale Notre Dame de Chartres** (www.diocese-chartres.com, in French; place de la Cathédrale; 8.30am-7.30pm, till 10pm Tue, Fri & Sun summer). The original Romanesque cathedral was devastated in a fire in 1194, but remnants of it remain in the **Portail Royal** (Royal Portal) and the 103m-high **Clocher Vieux** (Old Bell Tower, also known as the South Tower). The rest of the cathedral dates mainly from the 13th century, including many of the 172 glorious stained-glass windows, which are renowned for their intense 'Chartre blue' tones.

To study the extraordinary detail of Chartres' cathedral close-up, rent binoculars (€2) from Chartre's **tourist office** (02 37 18 26 26; www.chartres-tourisme.com; place de la Cathédrale; 9am-7pm Mon-Sat, 9.30am-5.30pm Sun summer, shorter hrs rest of the year), across the square from the cathedral.

A visit up the lacy Flamboyant Gothic, 112m **Clocher Neuf** (New Bell Tower; adult €7, free to all 1st Sun of certain months; 9.30am-12.30pm & 2-6pm Mon-Sat, 2-6pm Sun summer, to 5pm winter) rewards with superb views of the three-tiered flying buttresses and the 19th-century copper roof, turned green by verdigris.

Getting There & Away

Some three dozen SNCF trains a day link Paris' Gare Montparnasse (€13.60, 55 to 70 minutes) with Chartres via Versailles-Chantiers (€11.50, 45 minutes to one hour).

LILLE, FLANDERS & THE SOMME

It's grim up north – or so the stereotype goes. But while France's northernmost corner is one of the most densely populated and heavily industrialised areas of the country, there's bags to enjoy: the Flemish-style city of Lille for starters, the cross-channel shopping centre of Calais, moving battlefields of WWI...and great beer.

Lille

POP 232,000

Lille (Rijsel in Flemish) may be France's most underrated major city. In recent decades this once-grimy industrial metropolis has transformed itself into a glittering and self-confident cultural and commercial hub. Highlights include an attractive old town with a strong Flemish accent, renowned art museums, stylish shopping and a cutting-edge, student-driven nightlife.

Sights

Vieux Lille (Old Lille), which begins just north of place du Général de Gaulle, is justly proud of its restored 17th- and 18th-century houses. The old brick residences along **rue de la Monnaie** house the city's chicest boutiques and the **Hospice Comtesse Museum** (32 rue de la Monnaie; admission €3.50; 10am-12.30pm & 2-6pm, closed Mon morning & Tue), packed with religious art.

Lille's world-renowned **Palais des Beaux Arts** (Fine Arts Museum; www.pba-lille.fr; place de la République; adult €5.50; 2-6pm Mon, 10am-6pm Wed-Sun; M République Beaux Arts) has a first-rate collection of 15th- to 20th-century paintings, including works by Rubens, Van Dyck and Manet.

Housed in an art-deco swimming pool (built 1927–32), **La Piscine Musée d'Art et d'Industrie** (www.roubaix-lapiscine.com; 23 rue de l'Espérance, Roubaix; admission €4.50; 11am-6pm Tue-Thu, 11am-8pm Fri, 1-6pm Sat & Sun; M Gare Jean Lebas), 12km northeast of Gare Lille-Europe, showcases fine arts and sculpture in an unexpected setting.

Sleeping

Auberge de Jeunesse HOSTEL €
(03 20 57 08 94; www.hihostels.com; 12 rue Malpart; dm incl breakfast €18, d €37; Feb–mid-Dec; @; M Mairie de Lille) This old former maternity hospital has 163 beds (two to eight per room), kitchen facilities and a rather spartan air. A few of the doubles have en-suite showers.

Hôtel du Moulin d'Or HOTEL €€
(03 20 06 12 67; www.hotelmoulindor.com, in French; 15 rue du Molinel; d/tr €87/98; ; M Gare Lille-Flandres) Rich yellow and blue tones welcome you warmly to this family-run establishment with 14 rooms, some flowery, others striped. The cute little breakfast rooms feels like a B&B.

DON'T MISS

WORLD'S LARGEST FLEA MARKET

On the first weekend in September, Lille's city centre is consumed by the world's largest flea market, the **Braderie de Lille**. The extravaganza, with stands selling antiques, local delicacies, handicrafts and more, dates to the Middle Ages when Lillois servants were permitted to hawk their employers' old garments for some extra cash.

The Braderie runs nonstop (yes, all night) from 2pm on Saturday to 11pm on Sunday, when street sweepers emerge to tackle the mounds of mussel shells and old *frites* (French fries) left behind by the merrymakers.

Eating

Keep an eye out for *estaminets* (traditional eateries serving Flemish specialities such as *carbonnade* – beef braised with Flemish beer, spice bread and brown sugar).

Eat streets in the Old Town include rue de Gand Small, for moderately-priced French and Flemish restaurants; rue de la Monnaie, which has quirky restaurants, and on neighbouring side streets, rue Royale Ethnic cuisine, for couscous, Japanese etc; and rues Solférino and Masséna, which have lively, student-dominated cheap eats near the Palais des Beaux-Arts.

TOP CHOICE **Marché de Wazemmes** FOOD MARKET €
(place de la Nouvelle Aventure; 8am-2pm Tue-Thu, 8am-8pm Fri & Sat, 8am-3pm Sun & holidays; M Gambetta) Beloved foodie space, 1.7km southwest of the tourist office in Lille's working-class quarter of Wazemmes.

Chez la Vieille TRADITIONAL €
(03 28 36 40 06; 60 rue de Gand; mains €9.50-12; Tue-Sat) One of the best places in Lille to tuck into Flemish specialities. Old-time prints, antiques and fresh hops hanging from the rafters create the ambience of a Flemish village c 1900. The vibe is informal but it's a good idea to call ahead.

Meert TEAROOM €
(www.meert.fr; 27 rue Esquermoise; 9.30am-7.30pm Tue-Fri, 9am-7.30pm Sat, 9am-1pm & 3-7pm Sun; M Rihour) Vanilla-flavoured *gaufres* (waffles; €2.30) are the speciality of this luxury tearoom-cum-pastry-and-

DON'T MISS

NORTHERN BREWS

French Flanders brews some truly excellent *bière blonde* (lager) and *bière ambrée* (amber beer) with an alcohol content of up to 8.5%. Brands that give the Belgian brewers a run for their money include 3 Monts, Amadeus, Ambre des Flandres, Brasserie des 2 Caps, Ch'ti, Enfants de Gayant, Grain d'Orge, Hellemus, Jenlain, L'Angellus, La Wambrechies, Moulins d'Ascq, Raoul, Septante 5, St-Landelin, Triple Secret des Moines and Vieux Lille.

sweets-shop, in the biz since 1761. Its adjacent **chocolate shop** (per kg €89) transports you to 1839.

Drinking

Two key nightlife zones are Vieux Lille's small, chic bars and the student-orientated bars around rue Masséna and rue Solférino. In summer cafe terraces render place de la Théâtre a prime beer-sipping terrain.

L'Illustration Café BAR, CAFE
(www.bar-lillustration.com, in French; 18 rue Royale; ⏲12.30pm-3am Mon-Sat, 2pm-3am Sun) Adorned with art-nouveau woodwork and changing exhibits by local painters, this laid-back bar attracts artists, musicians, budding intellectuals and teachers. A mellow soundtrack mixes Western classical with jazz, French *chansons* and African.

Information

Tourist office (☎08 91 56 20 04; www.lilletourism.com; place Rihour; ⏲9.30am-6.30pm Mon-Sat, 10am-noon & 2-5pm Sun; Ⓜ Rihr) Sells the Lille City Pass (one-/two-/three-day €20/30/45) covering Lille's museums and public transport.

Getting There & Away

Eurolines (☎08 92 89 90 91; 23 parvis St-Maurice; Ⓜ Gare Lille-Flandres) serves cities such as Brussels (€17, 1½ hours), Amsterdam (€42, five hours) and London (€35, 5½ hours; by day via the Channel Tunnel, at night by ferry). Buses depart from blvd de Leeds near Gare Lille-Europe.

Lille has two train stations: Gare Lille-Flandres for regional services and Paris' Gare du Nord (€40 to €55, one hour, 14 to 18 daily), and ultramodern Gare Lille-Europe for all other trains, including Eurostar to London and TGVs/Eurostar to Brussels-Nord (€18 to €26, 35 minutes, 12 daily).

Calais

POP 76,200

Over 15 million people pass through Calais en route to the cross-Channel ferries, but few explore the town itself – it's worth it, if only to ogle Rodin-style.

Sights

By the time you read this, it should be possible to ride a lift up to the top of the Unesco World Heritage–listed **belfry** crowning Calais' Flemish Renaissance-style **town hall** (1911–25). Inside is Calais' main sight: Rodin's *Les Bourgeois de Calais* (The Burghers of Calais; 1895), honouring six local citizens who, in 1347, held off the besieging English forces for more than eight months. Edward III was so impressed by their efforts he ultimately spared the Calaisiens and their six leaders.

Watch a century-old mechanical loom with 3500 vertical threads and 11,000 horizontal ones bang, clatter and clunk according to instructions given by perforated Jacquard cards at the **Musée de la Dentelle et de la Mode** (www.cite-dentelle.fr; 135 quai du Commerce; admission €5; ⏲10am-5pm or 6pm Wed-Mon), Calais' cutting-edge Lace and Fashion Museum.

Sleeping & Eating

TOP CHOICE **Hôtel Meurice** HOTEL €€
(☎03 21 34 57 03; www.hotel-meurice.fr; 5-7 rue Edmond Roche; d €85-150; @ 📶) Meurice is a veteran hotel with 39 rooms and plenty of atmosphere thanks to its grand lobby staircase, antique furnishings, Hemingwayesque bar and breakfast room with garden views.

Auberge de Jeunesse HOSTEL €
(☎03 21 34 70 20; www.auberge-jeunesse-calais.com; av Maréchal de Lattre de Tassigny; s/d incl breakfast €26/38; 📶) Modern, well equipped and just 200m from the beach is what Calais' hostel is all about. Arrive with bus 3, 5 or 9.

Histoire Ancienne BISTRO €
(☎03 21 34 11 20; 20 rue Royale; lunch/dinner menus from €13/19; ⏲Tue-Sat, lunch Mon) Specialising in French and regional dishes, some grilled over an open wood fire, this 1930s Paris-style bistro has treats such as *escargots à l'ail* (garlic snails).

Information

Tourist Office (☎03 21 96 62 40; www.calais-cotedopale.com; 12 blvd Georges Clemenceau;

⌚9am or 10am-6pm or 7pm, closed Sun mid-Sep–Mar)

Getting There & Around

Boat

Some 40-odd car and passenger ferries from Dover dock daily at Calais' bustling car-ferry terminal, 1.5km northeast of place d'Armes. For details see p481.

Car & Motorcycle

To reach the Channel Tunnel's vehicle-loading area at Coquelles, 6km southwest of the town centre, follow the road signs on the A16 to 'Tunnel Sous La Manche' (exit 42).

Train

Calais has two train stations: **Gare Calais-Ville**, 650m south of the main square, place d'Armes; and TGV station **Gare Calais-Fréthun**, 10km southwest near the Channel Tunnel entrance. Trains and shuttle buses (€2, free with train ticket) link the two.

Gare Calais-Ville serves Amiens (€24, 2½ to 3½ hours, six to eight daily), Boulogne (€7.50, 30 minutes, up to 19 daily), Dunkirk (€8, 50 minutes, two to five Monday to Saturday) and Lille-Flandres (€16, 1¼ hours, eight to 19 daily).

Gare Calais-Fréthun is served by TGVs to Paris' Gare du Nord (€41 to €62, 1½ hours, three to six daily) and Eurostar to London St-Pancras (€149, one hour, three daily).

NORMANDY

Famous for cows, cider and Camembert, this largely rural region (www.normandie-tourisme.fr) is one of France's most traditional – and visited thanks to big sights such as historic D-Day beaches, Monet's garden at Giverny, the otherworldly spires of Mont St-Michel and the world's largest comic-strip aka the Bayeux Tapestry.

Rouen

POP 120,000

With its elegant spires, beautifully restored medieval quarter and soaring Gothic cathedral, the ancient city of Rouen is a Normandy highlight. Devastated several times during the Middle Ages by fire and plague, the city was later badly damaged by WWII bombing raids, but has since been meticulously rebuilt. The city makes an ideal base for exploring the northern Normandy coast.

Sights

The old city's main thoroughfare, rue du Gros Horloge, runs from the cathedral west to **place du Vieux Marché**. Dedicated in 1979, the thrillingly bizarre **Église Jeanne d'Arc** (place du Vieux Marché), with its fish-scale exterior, marks the spot where 19-year-old Joan of Arc was burned at the stake in 1431.

Rouen's stunning Gothic **Cathédrale Notre Dame** (⌚2-7pm Mon, 7.30am-7pm Tue-Sat, 8am-6pm Sun), with polished, brilliant-white facade, is the famous subject of a series of paintings by Monet. Its 75m-tall **Tour de Beurre** (Butter Tower) was financed by locals in return for being allowed to eat butter during Lent – or so the story goes.

The **Musée des Beaux-Arts** (esplanade Marcel Duchamp; adult/child €5/free; ⌚10am-6pm Wed-Mon), housed in a grand structure erected in 1870, features canvases by Caravaggio, Rubens, Modigliani, Pissarro, Renoir, Sisley (lots) and (of course) several works by Monet.

Inside a desanctified 16th-century church, the riveting **Musée Le Secq des Tournelles** (☎02 35 88 42 92; 2 rue Jacques Villon; admission €3; ⌚10am-1pm & 2-6pm Wed-Mon) examines the blacksmith's craft.

Sleeping

Hôtel de la Cathédrale HOTEL €
(☎02 35 71 57 95; www.hotel-de-la-cathedrale.fr; 12 rue St-Romain; s €56-79, d €66-96, q €119; 📶) Hiding behind a 17th-century half-timbered facade, this atmospheric hotel has 27 stylish rooms, mostly overlooking a plant-filled courtyard.

DON'T MISS

THE CIDER ROAD

Normandy's signposted 40km **Route du Cidre**, about 20km east of Caen, wends its way through the Pays d'Auge, a rural area of orchards, pastures, hedgerows, half-timbered farmhouses and stud farms, and through picturesque villages such as Cambremer and Beuvron-en-Auge. Along the way, signs reading 'Cru de Cambremer' indicate the way to about 20 small-scale, traditional producers who are happy to show you their facilities and sell you their home-grown cider (€3 a bottle) and Calvados .

Hôtel Dandy HOTEL €€
(☎02 35 07 32 00; www.hotels-rouen.net; 93 rue Cauchoise; d €80-105; 📶) Decorated in a grand Louis XV style, this charming place has individually designed rooms brimming with character, and is passionately run by a friendly family.

Hôtel des Carmes HOTEL €
(☎02 35 71 92 31; www.hoteldescarmes.com, in French; 33 place des Carmes; d €49-65, tr €67-77; @📶) This sweet little number has a dozen rooms with a bright, quirky decor; some have cerulean-blue cloudscapes painted on the ceilings. Burn off some Camembert calories by taking one of the cheaper, 4th-floor rooms.

Eating

Little eateries crowd rue Martainville. For ethnic cuisine head two blocks south to rue des Augustins.

Le P'tit Bec BISTRO €
(☎02 35 07 63 33; www.leptitbec.com, in French; 182 rue Eau de Robec; menus €13-15.50; ⏱lunch Mon-Sat, dinner Fri & Sat, also dinner Tue-Thu Jun-Aug) The down-to-earth menu here is stuffed with pasta, salads, *œufs cocottes* (eggs with grated cheese baked in cream), several vegetarian options and home-made desserts. Its summer terrace sits on one of Rouen's most picturesque side streets.

Pascaline BISTRO €
(☎02 35 89 67 44; 5 rue de la Poterne; mains €10-20) A top spot for a great-value lunch, this bustling bistro serves up traditional French cuisine in typically Parisian surroundings. There's live piano nightly and jazz on Thursdays.

Information

Tourist Office (☎02 32 08 32 40; www.rouentourisme.com; 25 place de la Cathédrale; ⏱9am-7pm Mon-Sat, 9.30am-12.30pm & 2-6pm Sun) Hotel reservations cost €3; audioguides €5.

Getting There & Away

From **Gare Rouen-Rive Droite** (rue Jeanne d'Arc), direct train services include:

AMIENS €18.20, 1¼ hours, four or five daily

CAEN €23.30, 1½ hours, eight to 10 daily

DIEPPE €10.40, 45 minutes, up to 16 daily

LE HAVRE €13.60, 50 minutes, 10 to 18 daily

PARIS ST-LAZARE €20.50, 1¼ hours, up to 25 daily

Bayeux

POP 14,350

Bayeux is world-famous for a 68m-long piece of painstakingly embroidered cloth: the 11th-century Bayeux Tapestry. The town is also one of the few in Normandy to have survived WWII practically unscathed, with a centre crammed with 13th- to 18th-century buildings, wooden-framed Norman-style houses and a spectacular Norman Gothic cathedral.

Sights

TOP CHOICE **Bayeux Tapestry** TAPESTRY
(www.tapisserie-bayeux.fr; rue de Nesmond; admission incl audioguide €7.80; ⏱9am-7pm May-Aug, shorter hrs rest of the year) The world's most celebrated embroidery vividly recounts William the Conqueror's 1066 conquest of England in 58 remarkable (and sometimes graphic) scenes (plenty of lopped-off heads and severed limbs). For an animated version, check out David Newton's creative short film on YouTube.

Musée Mémorial de la Bataille de Normandie WAR MUSEUM
(Battle of Normandy Memorial Museum; blvd Fabien Ware; admission €6.50; ⏱9.30am-6.30pm May-Sep, 10am-12.30pm & 2-6pm Oct-Apr) Using well-chosen photos, personal accounts, dioramas and wartime objects, this first-rate museum offers an excellent introduction to WWII in

DON'T MISS

MAISON DE CLAUDE MONET

Monet's home for the last 43 years of his life is now the delightful **Maison et Jardins de Claude Monet** (☎02 32 51 28 21; www.fondation-monet.com; admission €6; ⏱9.30am-6pm Apr-Oct), where you can view the impressionist's pastel-pink house and famous gardens with lily pond, Japanese bridge draped in purple wisteria and so on. The gardens are in **Giverny**, 66km southeast of Rouen. Several trains (€10.10, 40 minutes) leave Rouen before noon; with hourly return trains between 5pm and 10pm (9pm Sat). From Paris' Gare St-Lazare two early-morning trains run to Vernon (€12.50, 50 minutes) from where **shuttle buses** (☎08 25 07 60 27; www.mobiregion.net; €4 return) shunt passengers the 7km east to Giverny.

Normandy. Don't miss the 25-minute film on the Battle of Normandy. Nearby, the **Bayeux war cemetery** (blvd Fabien Ware) contains the graves of 4848 soldiers from the UK and 10 other countries (including Germany).

Sleeping & Eating

TOP CHOICE **Family Home** HOSTEL €
(☎02 31 92 15 22; 39 rue Général de Dais; dm/s €19/30) One of France's most charming hostels, this place sports a 17th-century dining room, 16th-century courtyard and 80 beds in rooms for one to four people. Check-in any time of day – phone if no one's there and someone will pop by.

Hôtel Reine Mathilde HOTEL €
(☎02 31 92 08 13; www.hotel-bayeux-reinemathilde.fr; 23 rue Larcher; d €60-63, tr/q €73/85;) Above a bustling cafe, this charming little hotel is an excellent bet. Rooms, smallish but comfortable, are named after Norman folk of yore.

La Rapière NORMAN €€
(☎02 31 21 05 45; 53 rue St-Jean; menus €15-33.50; ⊙Fri-Tue) In a 15th-century mansion held together by original oak beams, this restaurant cooks up hearty home cooking – the *timbale de pêcheur* (fisherman's stew) is served up piping hot in a cast-iron pan. Dessert has to be *trou normand* (apple sorbet with a dash of Calvados).

Information

Tourist Office (☎02 31 51 28 28; www.bayeux-bessin-tourism.com; pont St-Jean; ⊙9.30am-12.30pm & 2-6pm)

Getting There & Away

Trains link Bayeux with Caen (€5.80, 20 minutes, up to 13 daily), from where there are connections to Paris' Gare St-Lazare (€31.20, two hours) and Rouen (€22.70, 1½ hours).

Mont St-Michel

On a rocky island opposite the coastal town of Pontorson, connected to the mainland by a narrow causeway, the sky-scraping turrets of the abbey of **Mont St-Michel** (☎02 33 89 80 00; www.monuments-nationaux.fr; admission incl guided tour €8.50; ⊙9am-7pm May-Aug, 9.30am-6pm Sep-Apr, last entry 1hr before closing) provide one of France's iconic sights. The surrounding bay is notorious for its fast-rising tides: at low tide the Mont is surrounded by bare sand for kilometres around, but at high tide, barely six hours later, the bay, causeway and nearby car parks can be submerged.

When the tide is out, you can walk all the way around Mont St-Michel, a distance of about 1km. Stray too far from the Mont and you risky getting stuck in wet sand – from which Norman soldiers are depicted being

WORTH A TRIP

D-DAY BEACHES

On 6 June 1944, Allied troops stormed 80km of beaches north of Bayeux, code-named (from west to east) Utah, Omaha, Gold, Juno and Sword. The audacious invasion of D-Day – known as Jour J in French – ultimately liberated the European mainland from Nazi occupation. For context, see www.normandiememoire.com and www.6juin1944.com.

The most brutal fighting took place 15km northwest of Bayeux at **Omaha Beach**, home to the huge **Normandy American Cemetery & Memorial** (www.abmc.gov; Colleville-sur-Mer; ⊙9am-5pm). Featured in the opening scenes of Steven Spielberg's *Saving Private Ryan*, this is the largest American cemetery in Europe. Nearby **Juno Beach**, 12km east of Arromanches, was stormed by Canadian troops, while bomb craters and German gun emplacements dot the **Pointe du Hoc Ranger Memorial**. One of the Allies' prefabricated 'Mulberry Harbours' can be seen at low tide at **Arromanches**, 10km northeast of Bayeux.

Caen's hi-tech museum, **Mémorial – Un Musée pour la Paix** (Memorial – A Museum for Peace; www.memorial-caen.fr; esplanade Général Eisenhower; adult €17.50; ⊙9am-7pm Mar-Oct, 9.30am-6pm Tue-Sun Nov-Feb), uses sound, film and animation to explore the events of WWII, D-Day and the Cold War.

For guided tours check out:

Mémorial (www.memorial-caen.fr; tours €69) Excellent year-round minibus tours (four to five hrs); rates include entry to Mémorial. Book online.

Normandy Sightseeing Tours (www.normandywebguide.com) Half-/full-day walking, cycling or minibus tours (€40/75) of various beaches and cemeteries.

rescued in one scene of the Bayeux Tapestry – or being overtaken by the incoming tide, providing your next of kin with a great cocktail-party story.

Check the *horaire des marées* (tide table) at the **tourist office** (☎02 33 60 14 30; www.ot-montsaintmichel.com; ⊙9am-7pm Jul & Aug, shorter hrs rest of year), at the base of the mount, a cobbled street winds up to the **Église Abbatiale** (Abbey Church), incorporating elements of both Norman and Gothic architecture. Other notable sights include the arched **cloître** (cloister), the barrel-roofed **réfectoire** (dining hall) and the Gothic **Salle des Hôtes** (Guest Hall), dating from 1213. A one-hour tour is included in the ticket price: English tours run hourly in summer, twice daily (11am and 3pm) in winter. In July and August, Monday to Saturday, there are illuminated *nocturnes* (night-time visits) with music from 7pm to 10pm.

Getting There & Away

Bus 6 (☎08 00 15 00 50; www.mobi50.com, in French) links Mont St-Michel with Pontorson (€2, 13 minutes), from where there are two to three daily trains to/from Bayeux (€20.80, 1¾ hours) and Cherbourg (€25.90, three hours).

BRITTANY

Brittany is for explorers. Its wild dramatic coastline, medieval towns, thick forests and eeriest stone circles this side of Stonehenge make a trip here well worth the detour from the beaten track. This is a land of prehistoric mysticism, proud tradition and culinary wealth, where locals still remain fiercely independent, where Breton culture (and cider) is celebrated and where Paris feels a very long way away indeed.

St-Malo

POP 50,200

The mast-filled port of fortified St-Malo is inextricably tied up with the briny blue: the town became a key harbour during the 17th and 18th centuries as a base for merchant ships and government-sanctioned privateers, and these days it's a busy cross-Channel ferry-port and summertime getaway.

The old walled city of St-Malo, called Intra-Muros (within the walls) or Ville Close, is a 15-minute walk from the train station along av Louis Martin.

Sights

The city's sturdy ramparts were constructed at the end of the 17th century by the military architect Vauban, and afford fine views of the old walled city – you can access them from all of the main city *portes* (gates). From their northern stretch, you'll see the remains of the former prison, **Fort National** (www.fortnational.com; adult €5; ⊙Easter & Jun-Sep), and the rocky islet of **Île du Grand Bé** where the great St-Malo–born 18th-century writer Chateaubriand is buried. You can walk across at low tide, but check the tide times with the tourist office.

The battle to liberate St-Malo destroyed around 80% of the old city during August 1944; damage to **Cathédrale St-Vincent** (place Jean de Châtillon; ⊙9.30am-6pm) was particularly severe.

Within **Château de St-Malo**, built by the dukes of Brittany in the 15th and 16th centuries, is the **Musée du Château** (admission €5; ⊙10am-noon & 2-6pm Apr-Sep, Tue-Sun Oct-Mar), a history museum that looks at local cod fishing and photos of St-Malo after WWII.

The attractions at St-Malo's excellent **Aquarium** (www.aquarium-st-malo.com; av Général Patton; adult €15.50; ⊙10am-6pm Feb-Oct & Dec, to 8pm Jul & Aug), 4km south of the city centre, include a minisubmarine descent and *bassin tactile* (touch pool). Bus C1 travels from the train station every half-hour.

If you're hardy enough to brave the Atlantic swells, there are several pleasant **beaches** around St-Malo.

Sleeping

Hôtel San Pedro HOTEL €
(☎02 99 40 88 57; www.sanpedro-hotel.com; 1 rue Ste-Anne; s €52-54, d €63-73;) Tucked at the back of the old city, the San Pedro has cool, crisp, neutral-toned decor with subtle splashes of colour, friendly service and superb sea views.

Camping Aleth CAMPING GROUND €
(☎06 78 96 10 62; www.camping-aleth.com; allée Gaston Buy, St-Servan; 2-person tent €13.40; ⊙May-Sep) Perched on a peninsula, Camping Aleth has panoramic 360-degree views and is close to beaches and some lively bars.

Auberge de Jeunesse Éthic Étapes HOSTEL €
(☎02 99 40 29 80; www.centrevarangot.com; 37 av du Père Umbricht; dm incl breakfast €17.50-19.80; @) This efficient place has a self-catering kitchen and free sports facilities. Take bus C1 from the train station.

Eating

Restaurants abound between Porte St-Vincent, the cathedral and the Grande Porte.

TOP CHOICE **Restaurant Delaunay** GASTRONOMIC €€
(☎02 99 40 92 46; 6 rue Ste-Barbe; menus €28-65; ⏲dinner Mon-Sat, closed Mon in winter) Chef Didier Delaunay creates standout gastronomic cuisine within aubergine-painted walls at this superb address for both surf (Breton lobster is a speciality) and turf (tender lamb).

Le Chalut SEAFOOD €€
(☎02 99 56 71 58; 8 rue de la Corne-du-Cerf; menus €25-68; ⏲Wed-Sun) This unremarkable-looking establishment is, in fact, St-Malo's most celebrated restaurant. Its kitchen overflows with the best the Breton coastline has to offer – buttered turbot, line-caught sea bass and scallops in champagne sauce.

La Bouche en Folie FRENCH, MODERN €
(☎06 72 49 08 89; 14 rue du Boyer; menus €12.90-29; ⏲Wed-Sun) Well off the tourist trail, this sleek joint oozes Gallic gorgeousness and casts a modern spin on French staples – lamb is fricasséed with garlic and artichokes, monkfish is partnered by peas, black olives and asparagus.

Information

Tourist office (☎08 25 13 52 00, 02 99 56 64 43; www.saint-malo-tourisme.com; esplanade St-Vincent; ⏲9am-7.30pm Mon-Sat, 10am-6pm Sun Jul & Aug, shorter hrs rest of year).

Getting There & Away

Brittany Ferries (www.brittany-ferries.com) sails between St-Malo and Portsmouth; **Condor Ferries** (www.condorferries.co.uk) runs to/from Poole and Weymouth via Jersey or Guernsey.

Keolis Emeraude (www.keolis-emeraude.com) has buses to/from Mont St-Michel (€3.30, 1½ hours, three to four daily). **Illenoo** (www.illenoo-services.fr) has buses to Dinard (€1.70, 30 minutes, hourly) and Rennes (€3, one to 1½ hours, up to six daily).

TGV train services include to/from Rennes (€11.60, one hour) and Paris' Gare Montparnasse (€62.40, three hours, up to 10 daily).

WORTH A TRIP

CULINARY CANCALE

No day trip from St-Malo is tastier than **Cancale** (www.cancale-tourisme.fr), an idyllic Breton fishing port 14km to the east and which is famed for its offshore *parcs à huîtres* (oyster beds).

Learn all about oyster farming at the **Ferme Marine** (www.ferme-marine.com; corniche de l'Aurore; adult €6.80; ⏲mid-Feb–Oct, tours in English 2pm Jul–mid-Sep) and shop for oysters fresh from their beds at the **Marché aux Huîtres** (dozen oysters from €3.50, lunch platters €20; ⏲9am-6pm), the local oyster market atmospherically clustered around the Pointe des Crolles lighthouse.

Buses from St-Malo (www.keolis-emeraude.com; €2, 30 minutes) stop in Cancale at Port de la Houle, next to the pungent fish market.

Quimper

POP 67,250

Small enough to feel like a village – with its slanted half-timbered houses and narrow cobbled streets – and large enough to buzz as the troubadour of Breton culture, Quimper (*kam-pair*) is the Finistère region's thriving capital.

Sights

Most of Quimper's historic architecture is concentrated in a tight triangle formed by place Médard, rue Kereon, rue des Gentilhommes and its continuation, rue du Sallé, to place au Beurre. At the centre of the city is **Cathédrale St-Corentin** (⏲9.30am-noon & 1.30-6.30pm) with its distinctive kink, said to symbolise Christ's inclined head as he was dying on the cross. Construction began in 1239 but the cathedral's dramatic twin spires weren't added until the 19th century. High on the west facade, look out for an equestrian statue of King Gradlon, the city's mythical 5th-century founder.

Beside the cathedral, recessed behind a magnificent stone courtyard, the **Musée Départemental Breton** (1 rue du Roi Gradlon; admission €4; ⏲9am-6pm) showcases Breton history, furniture, costumes, crafts and archaeology in a former bishop's palace. Adjoining the museum is the **Jardin de l'Évêché** (Bishop's Palace Garden; admission free; ⏲9am-5pm or 6pm).

Sleeping

Hôtel de la Gare HOTEL €
(☎02 98 90 00 81; www.hoteldelagarequimper.com; 17 av de la Gare; s/d €49/54; 📶) This cheap

QUIMPER SPLURGE!

Hôtel Manoir des Indes (02 98 55 48 40; www.manoir-hoteldesindes.com; 1 allée de Prad ar C'hras; s €105-150, d €150-170;), a short drive from the centre of Quimper, is a manor house that has undergone a stunning hotel conversion. It has been restored with the original world-traveller owner in mind, and decor is minimalist and modern with Asian objets d'art and lots of exposed wood.

friendly place opposite the train station is the best deal in town. There's a pleasant cafe feel to the lobby, free parking and a small courtyard garden.

Auberge de Jeunesse HOSTEL €
(02 98 64 97 97; www.fuaj.org/quimper; 6 av des Oiseaux; campsite €6, dm incl breakfast from €12.70, sheets €3; Apr-Sep) Seasonal hostel with self-catering facilities.

Eating

TOP CHOICE **Le Cosy Restaurant** REGIONAL CUISINE €
(02 98 95 23 65; 2 rue du Sallé; mains €10-14.50; lunch Tue-Sat, dinner Wed, Fri & Sat) Make your way through the *épicerie* (specialist grocer) crammed with locally canned sardines, ciders and other Breton specialities to this eclectic dining room where you can tuck into top-quality gratins and *tartines* (toasts and open sandwiches with various toppings).

Crêperie La Krampouzerie CRÊPERIE €
(9 rue du Sallé; galettes €2-7; Tue-Sat, dinner Sun) Crêpes and galettes made from organic flours and regional ingredients such as *algues d'Ouessant* (seaweed), Roscoff onions and home-made ginger caramel are king here. Tables on the square out the front create a real street-party atmosphere.

Le Petit Gaveau BISTRO €
(02 98 64 29 86; 16 rue des Boucheries; mains €8-15 lunch Mon-Sat, dinner Wed-Sat) This sleek conversion of an old stone house plays host to simple yet excellent food. There's live jazz Thursday to Saturday (€3 supplement).

Information

Tourist office (02 98 53 04 05; www.quimper-tourisme.com, in French; place de la Résistance; 9.30am-12.30pm & 1.30-6.30pm)

Getting There & Away

CAT/Viaoo (www.viaoo29.fr) bus destinations include Brest (€6.50, 1¼ hours); **Le Coeur** (02 98 54 40 15) runs to Concarneau (€2, 45 minutes, seven to 10 daily).

WORTH A TRIP

THE MORBIHAN MEGALITHS

Predating Stonehenge by 100 years, **Carnac** comprises the world's greatest concentration of megalithic sites. There are more than 3000 of these upright stones scattered across the countryside between **Carnac-Ville** and **Locmariaquer** village, mostly erected between 5000 BC and 3500 BC. No one's quite sure what purpose these sites served, although theories abound. A sacred site? Phallic fertility cult? Or maybe a celestial calendar? Even more mysterious is the question of their construction – no one really has the foggiest idea how the builders hacked and hauled these vast granite blocks several millennia before the wheel arrived in Brittany, let alone mechanical diggers.

Because of severe erosion, the sites are usually fenced off to allow vegetation to regrow. **Guided tours** (€4) run in French year-round and in English at 3pm Wednesday, Thursday and Friday early July to late August. Sign up at the **Maison des Mégalithes** (02 97 52 89 99; route des Alignements; 9am-8pm Jul & Aug, to 7pm May & Jun, to 5.15pm Sep-Apr). Opposite, the largest menhir field – with no less than 1099 stones – is the **Alignements du Ménec**, 1km north of Carnac-Ville. From here, the D196 heads northeast for about 1.5km to the **Alignements de Kermario**. Climb the stone observation tower midway along the site to see the alignment from above. Another 500m further on are the **Alignements de Kerlescan**, while the **Tumulus St-Michel**, 400m northeast of the Carnac-Ville tourist office, dates back to at least 5000 BC.

For background, Carnac's **Musée de Préhistoire** (10 place de la Chapelle, Carnac-Ville; admission €5; 10am-6pm) chronicles life in and around Carnac from the Palaeolithic and neolithic eras to the Middle Ages.

Frequent trains serve Brest (€15.40, 1¼ hours), Rennes (€38, 2½ hours) and Paris' Gare Montparnasse (€74.80, 4¾ hours).

LOIRE VALLEY

One step removed from the French capital and poised on the frontier between northern and southern France, the Loire was historically the place where princes, dukes and notable nobles established their country getaways, and the countryside is littered with some of the most extravagant architecture outside Versailles.

Blois

POP 40,057

Blois' historic château was the feudal seat of the powerful counts of Blois, and its grand halls, spiral staircases and sweeping courtyards provide a whistle-stop tour through the key periods of French architecture.

Sights

Château Royal de Blois (www.chateaudeblois.fr; place du Château; admission €8; 9am-7pm Jul & Aug, shorter hrs rest of year) makes an excellent introduction to the châteaux of the Loire Valley, with elements of Gothic (13th century), Flamboyant Gothic (1498–1503), early Renaissance (1515–24) and classical (1630s) architecture in its four grand wings.

Opposite is the former home of watchmaker, inventor and conjurer Jean Eugène Robert-Houdin (1805–71), after whom the great Houdini named himself. It's now the **Maison de la Magie** (www.maisondelamagie.fr, in French; 1 place du Château; adult €9; 10am-12.30pm & 2-6.30pm, closed mornings Mon-Fri Sep).

The eye-catching **Musée de l'Objet** (www.museedelobjet.org, in French; 6 rue Franciade; admission €4; 1.30-6.30pm Wed-Sun late Jun-Aug, Fri-Sun Mar-late Jun & Sep-Oct, closed Dec-Feb) is a treasure trove of modern art based around everyday materials – look out for works by Dali and Man Ray.

CHÂTEAUX TOURS

Several big-name châteaux are covered by the **Pass'-Châteaux**, which offers savings of between €1.20 and €5.30 depending on which châteaux you visit; contact tourist offices in Blois, Cheverny and Chambord. Blois tourist office and **TLC** (02 54 58 55 44; www.tlcinfo.net, in French; 3 morning departures Apr-Aug) run a shuttle (€6) from Blois to Chambord and Cheverny.

If you don't have your own wheels, a minibus tour can be the most time-efficient way of taking in the Loire Valley biggies. Half-day trips cost €18 to €33; full-day trips €43 to €50. Reserve at the tourist office in Tours:

Acco-Dispo (www.accodispo-tours.com)

Alienor (www.alienor.com)

Loire Valley Tours (www.loire-valley-tours.com)

Quart de Tours (www.quartdetours.com)

St-Eloi Excursions (www.saint-eloi.com)

Touraine Evasion (www.tourevasion.com)

Sleeping & Eating

Côté Loire HOTEL €
(02 54 78 07 86; www.coteloire.com; 2 place de la Grève; d €55-76;) If it's charm and colours you want, head for the Loire Coast. Rooms come in cheery checks, bright pastels and the odd bit of exposed brick; and breakfast is served on a wooden-decking patio.

Hôtel Anne de Bretagne HOTEL €
(02 54 78 05 38; http://annedebretagne.free.fr; 31 av du Dr Jean Laigret; s €45-51, d €54-56, tr €60-72;) This creeper-covered hotel has friendly staff and a bar full of polished wood and vintage pictures. Modern rooms are finished in flowery wallpaper and stripy bedspreads.

Les Banquettes Rouges TRADITIONAL, FRENCH €€
(02 54 78 74 92; 16 rue des Trois Marchands; menus €14.50-32; Tue-Sat) Handwritten slate menus and wholesome food distinguish the Red Benches: rabbit with marmalade, duck with lentils and salmon with apple vinaigrette, all done with a spicy twist and a smile.

Le Castelet TRADITIONAL, FRENCH €€
(02 54 74 66 09; 40 rue St-Lubin; menus €15-32; Mon-Sat) Rusticana and rural frescoes cover the walls of this country restaurant that emphasises seasonal ingredients, organics and vegetarian options.

Information

Tourist office (02 54 90 41 41; www.bloispaysdechambord.com; 23 place du Château; 9am-7pm)

Getting There & Away

BUS TLC (☎02 54 58 55 44; www.tlcinfo.net) runs a château shuttle (see p431) and buses from Blois' train station (tickets €2 on board) to Chambord (Line 3; 40 minutes, up to four daily), Beaugency (Line 16; 55 minutes, up to four daily) and Cheverny (Line 4; 45 minutes, six to eight Monday to Friday, two Saturday, one Sunday).

TRAIN Services go to Amboise (€11, 20 minutes, 10 daily), Orléans (€13 to €20, 45 minutes, hourly), Tours (€13 to €19, 40 minutes, 13 daily) and Paris' Gares d'Austerlitz & Montparnasse (€34 to €57, two hours, 26 daily).

Around Blois

CHÂTEAU DE CHAMBORD

For full-blown château splendour, you can't top **Chambord** (☎02 54 50 50 20; www.chambord.org; adult €9.50; ⏲9am-7.30pm mid-Jul–mid-Aug, less hrs rest of year).

The château's most famous feature is the double-helix staircase, attributed by some to Leonardo da Vinci, who lived in Amboise (34km southwest) from 1516 until his death three years later. The Italianate rooftop terrace, surrounded by cupolas, domes, chimneys and slate roofs, was where the royal court assembled to watch military exercises and hunting parties returning at the end of the day.

Several times daily there are 1½-hour **guided tours** (€4) in English. The *son et lumière* (sound and light) show, **Chambord, Rêve de Lumières** (adult €12; ⏲Jul–mid-Sep), projected on the château's facade nightly, is a summer stunner, as is the daily **equestrian show** (☎02 54 20 31 01; www.ecuries-chambord.com, in French; adult €9.50; ⏲May-Sep).

Chambord is 16km east of Blois and 45km southwest of Orléans. For public transport options, see p432.

THE LOIRE BY BIKE

The flat Loire Valley is excellent cycling country. **Loire à Vélo** (www.loireavelo.fr) maintains 800km of signposted routes. Pick up info from tourist offices, or download route maps, audio guides and bike-hire details online.

Les Châteaux à Vélo (www.chateauxavelo.com) has a bike-rental circuit between Blois, Chambord and Cheverny, 300km of marked trails, and can shuttle you by minibus. Free route maps online (also downloadable MP3 guides).

Détours de Loire (www.locationdevelos.com) has bike-rental shops in Tours and Blois (☎02 54 56 07 73; train station); delivers bikes; and allows you to collect/return bikes along the route for a small surcharge. Bikes cost €14/59 per day/week; tandems €45 per day.

CHÂTEAU DE CHEVERNY

Thought by many to be the most perfectly proportioned château, **Cheverny** (☎02 54 79 96 29; www.chateau-cheverny.fr; admission €7.50; ⏲9.15am-6.45pm Jul & Aug, less hrs rest of year) has hardly been altered since its construction between 1625 and 1634. Inside you'll find a formal dining room, bridal chamber and children's playroom (complete with Napoléon III–era toys), as well as a guards' room full of pikestaffs, claymores and suits of armour. Many priceless artworks (including the *Mona Lisa*) were stashed in the 18th-century **Orangerie** during WWII.

Tucked at the foot of Cheverny's driveway amid grassland, the renovated 19th-century farmhouse **La Levraudière** (☎02 54 79 81 99; http://lalevraudiere.free.fr; 1 chemin de la Levraudière; s incl breakfast €55, d €59-65, tr €75-83) is a perfect blend of tradition and modernity. Breakfast is around a slablike wooden table laden with fabulous home-made jams, while rooms are all about crisp linens and meticulous presentation.

Cheverny is 16km southeast of Blois and 17km southwest of Chambord. For information on the bus from Blois, see p432.

CHÂTEAU DE CHAUMONT

It's a brisk climb up to **Château de Chaumont-sur-Loire** (www.domaine-chaumont.fr, in French; admission €9; ⏲10am-6.30pm Apr-Sep, to 5pm or 6pm Oct-Mar), on a bluff overlooking the Loire. The entrance, across a wooden drawbridge between two wide towers, opens onto an inner courtyard from where there are stunning views. Opposite the main entrance are luxurious stables, built in 1877.

Chaumont-sur-Loire is 17km southwest of Blois. Onzain, a 2.5km walk from Chaumont across the Loire, has trains to Blois (€11, 10 minutes, 13 daily) and Tours (€11 to €15, 35 minutes, 10 daily).

Tours

POP 298,000

Hovering somewhere between the style of Paris and the conservative sturdiness of central France, Tours is one of the principal cities of the Loire Valley. It's a smart, solidly bourgeois kind of place, filled with wide 18th-century boulevards, parks and imposing public buildings, as well as a busy university.

Sights

Arranged around the courtyard of the former archbishop's palace, the **Musée des Beaux-Arts** (18 place François Sicard; admission €4; 9am-12.45pm & 2-6pm Wed-Mon) is a fine example of a French provincial arts museum.

With its twin west towers and Gothic arches and gargoyles, **Cathédrale St-Gatien** (place de la Cathédrale; 9am-7pm) is a showstopper. It's particularly known for its stained glass; the interior dates from the 13th to 16th centuries, and the domed tops of the 70m-high towers date from the Renaissance.

France's skilled labourers, including pastry chefs, coopers and locksmiths, are celebrated at the **Musée du Compagnonnage** (8 rue Nationale, in Cloître St-Julien; adult/child €5/3.30; 9am-noon & 2-6pm, closed Tue mid-Sep–mid-Jun).

Sleeping & Eating

Hôtel Ronsard BOUTIQUE HOTEL €
(02 47 05 25 36; www.hotel-ronsard.com; 2 rue Pimbert; s €53-67, d €59-72;) This hotel translates as centrally located and comfortable value. Think sleek modern rooms dressed in slate grey and sparkling white linen.

TOP CHOICE **L'Adresse** BOUTIQUE HOTEL €€
(02 47 20 85 76; www.hotel-ladresse.com; 12 rue de la Rôtisserie; s €50, d €70-100;) Looking for Parisian style in provincial Tours? Then you're in luck – 'The Address' is a boutique bonanza, with rooms finished in sleek slates and ochres, topped off with wi-fi, flat-screen TVs and designer sinks.

Auberge de Jeunesse du Vieux Tours HOSTEL €
(02 47 37 81 58; www.ajtours.org; 5 rue Bretonneau; dm €19.50; reception 8am-noon & 5-11pm;) Friendly, bustling Hostelling International hostel; shared bathrooms are a bit rough. Rents bikes.

In the old city, place Plumereau, rue du Grand Marché and rue de la Rôtisserie are crammed with cheap eats of variable quality.

TOP CHOICE **Cap Sud** GASTRO BISTRO €€
(02 47 05 24 81; 88 rue Colbert; menus €14.50-36; Tue-Sat) A hot-mod red interior combines nicely with genial service, and the food! The food! Sensitive, refined creations are made from the freshest ingredients presented in style. Reserve in advance.

Tartines & Co GOURMET SANDWICHES €
(6 rue des Fusillés; mains €9-12; lunch Tue-Sat, dinner Wed-Fri) This snazzy little bistro reinvents the traditional *croque* (toasted sandwich) amid jazz and friendly chatter. Choose your topping and it's served up quick-as-a-flash on toasted artisanal bread.

Information

Tourist office (02 47 70 37 37; www.ligeris.com; 78-82 rue Bernard Palissy; 8.30am-7pm Mon-Sat, 10am-12.30pm & 2.30-5pm Sun)

Getting There & Away

Air

Tours-Val de Loire Airport (www.tours-aeroport.fr), 5km northeast, is linked to London's Stansted, Dublin, Marseille and Porto by Ryanair.

Bus

The **information desk** (8am-6.30pm Mon-Fri, 8.30am-12.30pm & 1.30-6.30pm Sat) for **Touraine Fil Vert** (02 47 31 14 00; www.touraine-filvert.com, in French) is at the bus station, next to the train station. Line C links Tours with Amboise (€1.60, 35 minutes, 12 daily Monday to Saturday) and Chenonceau (€1.60, 1¼ hours, two daily).

Train

Tours is the Loire's main rail hub. The train station is linked to St-Pierre-des-Corps, Tours' TGV train station, by frequent shuttle trains. Services go to:

AMBOISE €11, 20 minutes, 12 daily
BLOIS €9.10, 40 minutes, 12 daily
BORDEAUX €40 to €62, 2¾ hours
CHENONCEAU €11, 30 minutes, eight daily
NANTES €28 to €55, 1½ hours
ORLÉANS €24 to €35, 1½ hours, hourly
PARIS' GARE D'AUSTERLITZ €41 to €62, two to 2¾ hours, five daily. Slow trains
PARIS' GARE MONTPARNASSE €44 to €83, 1¼ hours, 30 daily. High-speed TGVs

Amboise

POP 12,900

The childhood home of Charles VIII and the final resting place of Leonardo da Vinci, upmarket Amboise is an elegant provincial town, perched along the Loire and overlooked by its fortified 15th-century château. Da Vinci whiled away his last three years here under the patronage of François I.

WORTH A TRIP

CHÂTEAUX TRIPS NEAR TOURS

Tours is an excellent base for exploring nearby châteaux:

» **Chenonceau** (www.chenonceau.com; adult €10.50; 9am-8pm Jul & Aug, shorter hrs rest of year) Framed by a glassy moat and sweeping gardens, and topped by turrets and towers, this 16th-century castle is straight out of a fairy tale. Don't miss the yew-tree labyrinth or the 60m-long Grande Gallerie spanning the Cher River.

» **Azay-le-Rideau** (02 47 45 42 04; adult €7.50; 9.30am-6pm, to 7pm Jul & Aug, 10am-12.30pm & 2-5.30pm Oct-Mar) Built in the 1500s on an island in the River Indre, this romantic, moat-ringed wonder flouts geometric windows, ordered turrets and decorative stonework. Don't miss its famous loggia staircase and summertime *son et lumière*.

» **Villandry** (www.chateauvillandry.com; adult €9, gardens only €6; château 9am-6pm, to 5.30pm Mar, to 5pm Feb & early Nov, gardens 9am-5pm to 7.30pm year-round) This major Renaissance château is more famous for what's outside than in. Its gardens are glorious. Don't miss love in the Ornamental Garden or the *potager* (kitchen garden).

Sights

Château Royal d'Amboise (place Michel Debré; adult €9.70; 9am-6pm Apr–mid-Nov, shorter hrs rest of year) sprawls on a rocky bluff above town. Charles VIII (r 1483–98) was responsible for the château's Italianate remodelling in 1492. Today, just a few of the original 15th- and 16th-century structures survive, notably the **Flamboyant Gothic wing** and the **Chapelle St-Hubert**, believed to be the final resting place of da Vinci.

Leonardo da Vinci moved into nearby **Clos Lucé** (www.vinci-closluce.com; 2 rue du Clos Lucé; admission €12.50; 9am-7pm Feb-Oct, 9am-6pm Nov & Dec, 10am-6pm Jan) in 1516, and the house and grounds feature scale models of his inventions, including a protoautomobile, tank, parachute, hydraulic turbine and even a primitive helicopter.

Sleeping & Eating

Centre Charles Péguy-Auberge de Jeunesse HOSTEL €
(02 47 30 60 90; www.mjcamboise.fr; Île d'Or; dm €12; reception 2-8pm Mon-Fri, 5-8pm Sat & Sun; @) Efficient boarding school–style hostel on Île d'Or, with 72 beds mostly in three- or four-bed dorms. Has table tennis and bike hire.

Hôtel Le Blason HOTEL €
(02 47 23 22 41; www.leblason.fr; 11 place Richelieu; s/d/tr €45/55/70; @) Quirky creaky budget hotel on a quiet square with 25 higgledy-piggledy rooms, wedged in around corridors: most are titchy, flowery and timber beamed.

Chez Bruno REGIONAL CUISINE €
(02 47 57 73 49; place Michel Debré; menus from €12; lunch Tue-Sun, dinner Tue-Sat) Uncork a host of local vintages in a coolly contemporary setting, accompanied by honest regional cooking.

Bigot TEAROOM €
(2 rue Nationale; 9am-7.30pm Tue-Fri, 8.30am-7.30pm Sat & Sun) This award-winning chocolatier and cake shop has been whipping up some of the Loire's creamiest cakes and gooiest treats since 1913.

Information

Tourist office (02 47 57 09 28; www.amboise-valdeloire.com; 9am-7pm Mon-Sat, 10am-1pm & 2-6pm Sun) In a riverside building opposite 7 quai du Général de Gaulle.

Getting There & Around

Bicycle

Cycles Richard (02 47 57 01 79; 2 rue de Nazelles; €15 per day; 9am-noon & 2.30-7pm Tue-Sat)

Bus

Touraine Fil Vert's (02 47 31 14 00) Line C links Amboise's post office with Tours' bus terminal (€1.60, 45 minutes, 12 daily Monday to Saturday). Two go to Chenonceaux (15 minutes, Monday to Saturday).

Train

Services run to Blois (€11, 20 minutes, 14 daily), Tours (€11, 20 minutes, 10 daily), Paris' Gare d'Austerlitz (€38 to €56, 2¼ hours, 14 daily) and Paris' Gare Montparnasse (TGV; €107, 1¼ hours, 10 daily).

CHAMPAGNE

Known in Roman times as Campania (meaning 'plain'), the agricultural region of Champagne is synonymous with bubbly – a multimillion dollar industry strictly protected under French law meaning only grapes grown in designated Champagne vineyards can truly lay a claim to the hallowed title.

Reims

POP 187,650

Over the course of a millennium some 34 sovereigns began their reigns in Reims' famed cathedral. Meticulously reconstructed after WWI and again following WWII, the city – whose name is pronounced something like 'rance' – is endowed with handsome pedestrian zones, lovely parks and lively nightlife.

The **Reims City Card** (€15), sold at the tourist office, gets you a tour of a Champagne house, a DIY audio-guide tour of the cathedral and admission into Reims' municipal museums.

Sights

Cathédrale Notre Dame CATHEDRAL
(www.cathedrale-reims.com, in French; place du Cardinal Luçon; 7.30am-7.30pm) Begun in 1211, for centuries this cathedral served as the venue for all French royal coronations – including that of Charles VII, who was crowned here on 17 July 1429, with Joan of Arc at his side. Heavily restored since WWI, the 139m-long cathedral is a Unesco World Heritage Site. Its most famous features include the western facade's 12-petalled **great rose window**, a 15th-century wooden **astronomical clock** and several decorative windows by painter Marc Chagall. Climb the 250 steps (guided tour only) of the **cathedral tower** (adult €7; at least hourly 10am-4pm or 5pm Tue-Sat & Sun morning mid-Mar–Oct) for a stunning 360° view across France's flattest region; book tours next door at Palais du Tau.

Palais du Tau PALACE MUSEUM
(www.palais-du-tau.fr; 2 place du Cardinal Luçon; admission €7; 9.30am-12.30pm & 2-5.30pm Tue-Sun) This former archbishop's residence is now a museum displaying exceptional statuary, liturgical objects and tapestries from the cathedral.

TOP CHOICE **Basilique St-Rémi** BASILICA
(place du Chanoine Ladame) This Benedictine abbey church, a Unesco World Heritage Site, mixes Romanesque elements with early Gothic. It honours Bishop Remigius who baptised Clovis and 3000 Frankish warriors in 498. The 12th-century-style chandelier has 96 candles, one for each year of the life of St Rémi, whose tomb lies in the choir. Take the Citadine 1 or 2 or bus A or F to the St-Rémi stop.

Tours

The bottle-filled cellars (10°C to 12°C – bring a sweater!) of eight Reims-area *maisons de champagne* (Champagne houses) can be visited by guided tour which ends, *naturellement*, with a tasting session.

Mumm CHAMPAGNE HOUSE
(www.mumm.com; 34 rue du Champ de Mars; adult €10; 9am-11am & 2-5pm Mar-Oct, Sat Nov-Feb) Mumm is the world's third-largest Champagne producer. Engaging and edifying one-hour tours take you through cellars filled with 25 million bottles of bubbly.

Taittinger CHAMPAGNE HOUSE
(www.taittinger.com; 9 place St-Niçaise; adult €10; 9.30-11.50am & 2-4.20pm, closed Sat & Sun mid-Nov–mid-Mar) Parts of these cellars, 1.5km southeast of the cathedral, occupy 4th-century Roman stone quarries.

Sleeping & Eating

Hôtel de la Cathédrale HOTEL €
(03 26 47 28 46; www.hotel-cathedrale-reims.fr; 20 rue Libergier; s/d/q from €56/59/79;) Graciousness and a resident Yorkshire terrier greet guests at this hostelry, run by a music-loving couple.

Latino Hôtel HOTEL €
(03 26 47 48 89; www.latinocafe.fr, in French; 33 place Drouet d'Erlon; d €58-79, ste €130;) Above a buzzy cafe with a Latin beat, this almost-boutique hotel has fun furnishings, a warm welcome and great quotes sgraffitoed on the walls.

Place Drouet d'Erlon is lined with inexpensive restaurants and pub-cafes. More discerning diners head to rue de Mars, adjacent rue du Temple and place du Forum.

Brasserie Le Boulingrin BRASSERIE €€
(03 26 40 96 22; www.boulingrin.fr; 48 rue de Mars; menus €18-28; Mon-Sat) An old-time brasserie – the decor and zinc bar date to 1925 – whose ambience and cuisine make it an enduring favourite. From September to June, the culinary focus is *fruits de mer* (seafood).

Côté Cuisine TRADITIONAL, FRENCH €
(03 26 83 93 68; 43 blvd Foch; mains €11.80-22.50; Mon-Sat) A spacious, modern place with well-regarded traditional French cuisine – great value for lunch.

Information

Tourist office (www.reims-tourisme.com; 2 rue Guillaume de Machault; 9am-7pm Mon-Sat, 10am-6pm Sun)

Getting There & Away

Direct trains link Reims with Épernay (€6, 20 to 36 minutes, at least 14 daily) and Paris' Gare de l'Est (€24, 1¾ hours, 10 to 15 daily), half of which are speedy TGVs (€32 to €41, 45 minutes).

Épernay

POP 25,225

Beneath the streets of Épernay, 25km south of Reims,, some 200 million of bottles of Champagne are slowly being aged, just waiting around to be popped open for some fizz-fuelled celebration.

Activities & Tours

Many of Épernay's Champagne houses are based along the handsome and eminently strollable av de Champagne. Cellar tours end with tasting and a visit to the factory-outlet bubbly shop.

Moët & Chandon CHAMPAGNE HOUSE
(03 26 51 20 20; www.moet.com; adult €14.50; 20 av de Champagne; 9.30-noon & 2-4.30pm, closed Sat & Sun mid-Nov–mid-Mar, also closed Jan) Among the region's best cellar tours.

Mercier CHAMPAGNE HOUSE
(03 26 51 22 22; www.champagnemercier.com; 68-70 av de Champagne; adult €9; 9.30-11.30am & 2-4.30pm, closed mid-Dec–mid-Feb) Flashy: think lift that transports visitors 30m underground, and laser-guided touring train.

De Castellane CHAMPAGNE HOUSE
(03 26 51 19 11; www.castellane.com, in French; 64 av de Champagne; adult €8.50; 10-11am & 2-5pm mid-Mar–Dec, closed Jan–mid-Mar) Informative bubbly museum and 66m-high tower (1905) with fine panorama.

Sleeping & Eating

Épernay's main dining area is rue Gambetta and adjacent place de la République.

TOP CHOICE **La Cave à Champagne** FRENCH, REGIONAL €€
(03 26 55 50 70; www.la-cave-a-champagne.com, in French; 16 rue Gambetta; menus €17-32; Thu-Mon, lunch Tue) 'The Champagne Cellar' is well regarded by locals for its *champenoise* cuisine, served in a warm, traditional, bourgeois atmosphere. Taste three different Champagnes for €21.

La Villa St-Pierre HOTEL €
(03 26 54 40 80; www.villasaintpierre.fr; 14 av Paul Chandon; d €45-50;) In an early-20th-century mansion, this homey hotel with 11 simple rooms retains much of the charm of yesteryear.

Information

Tourist office (03 26 53 33 00; www.ot-epernay.fr; 7 av de Champagne; 9.30am-12.30pm & 1.30-7pm Mon-Sat, 11am-4pm Sun, closed Sun mid-Oct–mid-Apr) Details on cellar visits, car touring, and walking/cycling options.

Getting There & Away

Direct trains go to Reims (€6.20, 20 to 36 minutes, 11 to 18 daily) and Paris' Gare de l'Est (€21, 1¼ hours, five to 10 daily).

ALSACE & LORRAINE

Teetering on the tempestuous frontier between France and Germany, the neighbouring regions of Alsace and Lorraine are where the worlds of Gallic and Germanic culture collide. Half-timbered houses, lush vineyards and forest-clad mountains hint at Alsace's Teutonic leanings, while Lorraine is indisputably Francophile.

Strasbourg

POP 276,000

Prosperous, cosmopolitan Strasbourg (City of the Roads) is the intellectual and cultural capital of Alsace, and the unofficial seat of European power – the European Parliament, the Council of Europe and the European Court of Human Rights are all here. The city's most famous landmark is its pink sandstone cathedral, towering above the restaurants, *winstubs* (traditional Alsatian eateries) and pubs of the lively Old Town.

Mulled wine and spicy *bredele* (biscuits) make a trip to Strasbourg's sparkly **Marché de Noël** (Christmas Market; www.noel.strasbourg.eu)

a must; it runs from the last Saturday in November until 24 December.

Raise a glass to Alsatian beer at October's **Mondial de la Bière** (www.mondialbierestrasbourg.com) or of wine at March's **Riesling du Monde** (www.riesling-du-monde.com).

Sights & Activities

With its bustling squares, narrow streets and upmarket shopping, Unesco-listed **Grande Île** is enchanting. The half-timbered buildings and flowery canals around **Petite France** are fairy-tale pretty.

Strasbourg's lacy, candy-coloured Gothic **Cathédrale Notre Dame** (place de la Cathédrale; ⌚7am-7pm) is one of the marvels of European architecture. Inside, a stunning 16th-century *horloge astronomique* (astronomical clock) strikes solar noon at 12.30pm. Hike up to the 66m-high **platform** (adult €4.70; ⌚9am-7.15pm) for a stork's-eye view of Strasbourg.

Discover every major art movement from impressionism to cubism and surrealism at the **Musée d'Art Moderne et Contemporain** (place Hans Jean Arp; adult/child €6/free; ⌚noon-7pm Tue, Wed & Fri, noon-9pm Thu, 10am-6pm Sat & Sun).

Tours

Batorama BOAT TRIPS
(www.batorama.fr, in French; adult/child €8.50/4.50; ⌚half-hourly 9.30am-9pm) Scenic boat trips along the storybook canals of Petite France, taking in the Vauban Dam and the glinting EU institutions. Tours depart from in front of Palais Rohan.

Brasseries Heineken BREWERY
(☎03 88 19 57 55; 4 rue St-Charles; ⌚hourly 9am-4pm Mon-Fri) Free two-hour tours of the Heineken brewery (some in English; reserve ahead), 2.5km north of Grande Île; take bus 4 to the Schiltigheim Mairie stop in Schiltigheim.

Cave des Hospices de Strasbourg WINERY
(www.vins-des-hospices-de-strasbourg.fr, in French; 1 place de l'Hôpital; ⌚8.30am-noon & 1.30-5.30pm Mon-Fri, 9am-12.30pm Sat) First-rate Alsatian wines deep in the brick-vaulted bowels of Strasbourg's hospital; just south of Grande Île.

Sleeping

Hôtel du Dragon HOTEL €€
(☎03 88 35 79 80; www.dragon.fr; 12 rue du Dragon; s €79-112, d €89-124; @📶) Step through a tree-shaded courtyard into the blissful calm of this bijou hotel near Petite France.

Camping de la Montagne Verte CAMPING GROUND €
(☎03 88 30 25 46; www.camping-montagne-verte-strasbourg.com; 2 rue Robert Forrer; campsites €14-18.50) Pitch up at this quiet camping ground, a 10-minute stroll from Montagne Verte tram stop, 3km west of Petite France. It's right next to the cycling lane leading into town.

Eating & Drinking

Try canalside Petite France for Alsatian fare and half-timbered romance; Grand' Rue for curbside kebabs and *tarte flambée;* and rue des Veaux or rue des Pucelles (both east of the cathedral) for hole-in-the-wall eateries.

TOP CHOICE **La Choucrouterie** ALSATIAN €€
(☎03 88 36 52 87; www.choucrouterie.com, in French; 20 rue St Louis; choucroute €12-16; ⌚lunch Mon-Fri, dinner daily) Naked ladies straddling giant sausages (on the menu, we hasten to add) and eccentric chefs juggling plates of steaming *choucroute garnie* are the tip of the theatrical iceberg at this bistro-playhouse double act.

Bistrot et Chocolat CAFE €
(www.bistrotetchocolat.net, in French; 8 rue de la Râpe; snacks €4-8, brunch €10-19; ⌚10.30am-7pm Tue-Sun) Chocolate fondue, organic hot chocolate with ginger, chocolate soup sprinkled with gingerbread croutons…this boho-chic bistro is an ode to the cocoa bean. Weekend brunches are a treat.

DON'T MISS

WHEN HELL WAS HELL

Hollywood gore is tame compared to the tortures back when Hell really was hell. Sure to scare you into a life of chastity is *Les Amants Trépassés* (the Deceased Lovers), painted in 1470, showing a grotesque couple being punished for their illicit lust: their entrails are being devoured by dragon-headed snakes. Track it down in room 23 of Strasbourg's world-renowned ecclesiastical museum, **Musée de l'Œuvre Notre Dame** (3 place du Château; admission €4; ⌚noon-6pm Tue-Fri, 10am-6pm Sat & Sun), showcasing one of Europe's premier collections of Romanesque, Gothic and Renaissance sculptures, 15th-century paintings and stained glass.

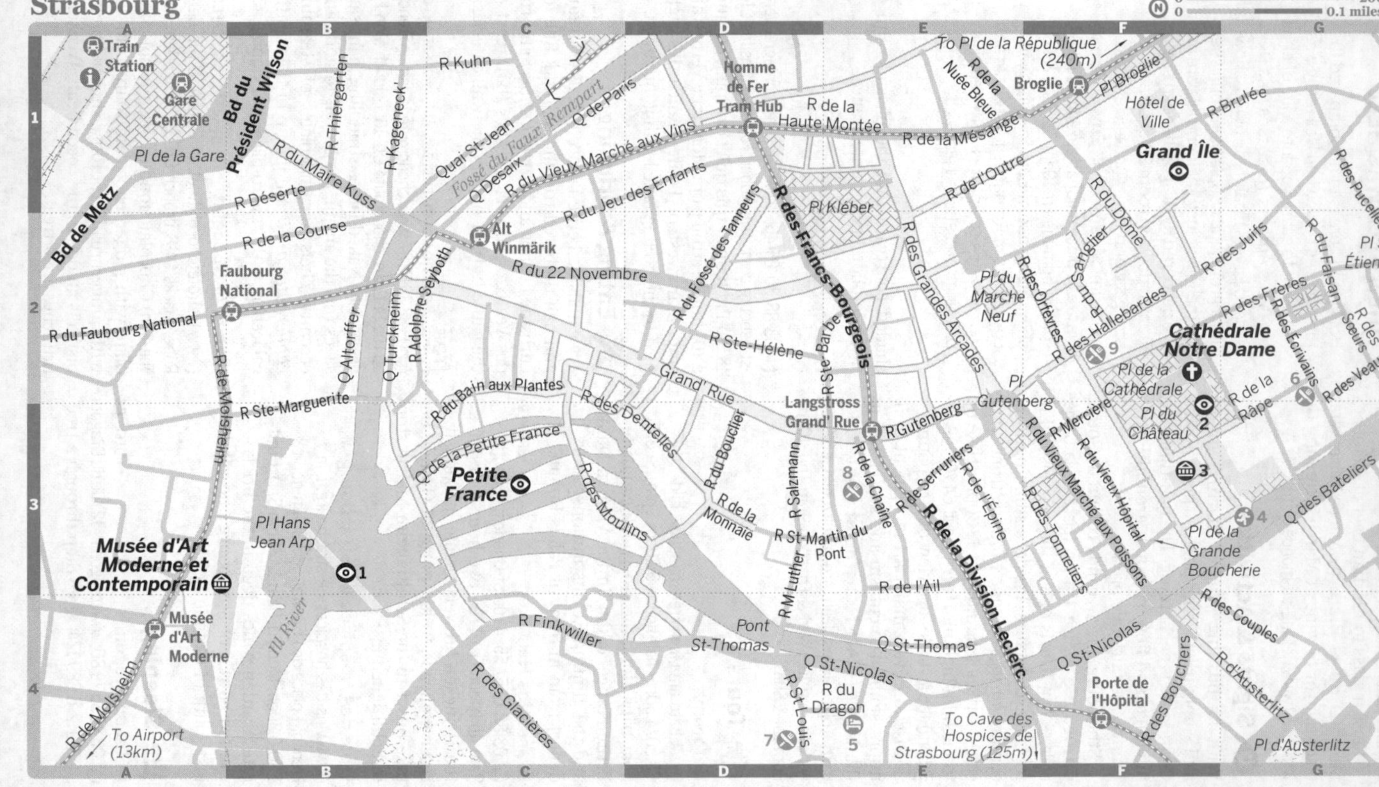
Strasbourg
0 200 m
0 0.1 miles
Train Station
Gare Centrale
Bd du Président Wilson
Pl de la Gare
Bd de Metz
R Thiergarten
R Kageneck
R Kuhn
Quai St-Jean
Fossé du Faux Rempart
Q de Paris
Q Desaix
R du Vieux Marché aux Vins
R du Maire Kuss
R Déserte
R de la Course
R du Jeu des Enfants
Alt Winmärik
R du 22 Novembre
Faubourg National
R du Faubourg National
R de Molsheim
Q Altorffer
Q Turckheim
R Adolphe Seyboth
R Ste-Marguerite
R du Bain aux Plantes
Q de la Petite France
Petite France
R des Moulins
Pl Hans Jean Arp
Musée d'Art Moderne et Contemporain
Musée d'Art Moderne
Ill River
To Airport (13km)
R Finkwiller
R des Glacières
Homme de Fer Tram Hub
R de la Haute Montée
R du Fossé des Tanneurs
R des Francs-Bourgeois
Pl Kléber
R Ste-Hélène
Grand' Rue
R des Dentelles
R du Bouclier
R de la Monnaie
Langstross Grand' Rue
R Ste-Barbe
R Salzmann
R de la Chaîne
R St-Martin du Pont
R M Luther
Pont St-Thomas
Q St-Nicolas
R du Dragon
R St Louis
To Pl de la République (240m)
R de la Nuée Bleue
Broglie
Pl Broglie
R de la Mésange
R de l'Outre
R des Grandes Arcades
Pl du Marche Neuf
R des Orfèvres
R du Sanglier
R du Dôme
Pl Gutenberg
R Gutenberg
R de la Division Leclerc
R des Serruriers
R de l'Épine
R de l'Ail
Q St-Thomas
R des Tonneliers
R du Vieux Marché aux Poissons
R du Vieux Hôpital
R Mercière
To Cave des Hospices de Strasbourg (125m)
Porte de l'Hôpital
Hôtel de Ville
R Brulée
Grand Île
R des Hallebardes
R des Juifs
R des Pucelles
R du Faisan
Pl St-Étienne
R des Frères
R des Écrivains
R des Sœurs
R des Veaux
Cathédrale Notre Dame
Pl de la Cathédrale
Pl du Château
R de la Râpe
Pl de la Grande Boucherie
Q des Bateliers
R des Couples
R des Bouchers
R d'Austerlitz
Pl d'Austerlitz
A
B
C
D
E
F
G
1
2
3
4
5
6
7
8
9

Strasbourg

Top Sights

Cathédrale Notre Dame F2
Grand Île F1
Musée d'Art Moderne et Contemporain A3
Petite France C3

Sights

1 Barrage Vauban B3
2 Cathedral's South Entrance F3
Maison Kammerzell .... (see 9)
3 Musée de l'Œuvre Notre Dame F3

Activities, Courses & Tours

4 Batorama G3

Sleeping

5 Hôtel du Dragon E4

Eating

6 Bistrot et Chocolat G2
7 La Choucrouterie D4
8 L'Assiette du Vin E3
9 Maison Kammerzell F2

L'Assiette du Vin BISTRO €€
(☎03 88 32 00 92; www.assietteduvin.fr, in French; 5 rue de la Chaîne; lunch menu €19, dinner menu €32-55; ⏲Tue-Fri, dinner only Sat-Mon) Market-fresh cuisine with a twist, discreet service and an award-winning wine list lure discerning foodies to this rustic-chic bistro in the Old Town. The *plat du jour* is a snip at €8.50.

Information

Tourist office (☎03 88 52 28 28; www.otstrasbourg.fr; 17 place de la Cathédrale; ⏲9am-7pm) Also an annexe at Strasbourg train station.

Getting There & Away

Air

Strasbourg's international **airport** (www.strasbourg.aeroport.fr) is 17km southwest of the city centre (towards Molsheim), near Entzheim.

Ryanair links London Stansted with **Karlsruhe/Baden Baden airport** (www.badenairpark.de), 58km northeast of Strasbourg, across the Rhine in Germany.

Train

PARIS' GARE DE L'EST (€67, 2¼ hours, 17 daily)
LILLE (€94, four hours, 13 daily)
LYON (€52, six hours, five daily)
MARSEILLE (€87, eight hours, five daily)
METZ (€23, two hours, 20 daily)

Metz

POP 125,720

Straddling the confluence of the Moselle and Seille Rivers, Metz is Lorraine's graceful capital. Its Gothic marvel of a cathedral, yellow-stone old town and regal Quartier Impérial that's up for Unesco World Heritage status has somehow managed to sidestep the world spotlight. But no more: the show-stopping Centre Pompidou-Metz has arrived.

Sights

Cathédrale St-Étienne CATHEDRAL
(place St-Étienne; ⏲8am-6pm) The delicate golden spires of this Gothic cathedral, nicknamed 'God's lantern' because of its stained glass, crown the town's skyline.

Quartier Impérial HISTORICAL QUARTER
The stately boulevards and bourgeois villas of the German Imperial Quarter, including rue Gambetta and av Foch, are the brain-

WORTH A TRIP

KATZENTHAL

Tiptoe off the tourist trail to Alsatian village of **Katzenthal** (population 550), 80km south of Strasbourg. *Grand cru* vines ensnare the hillside, topped by the medieval ruins of Château du Wineck from where walking trails into forest and vineyard begin.

Then there is the fabulous, family-run **Vignoble Klur** (☎03 89 80 94 29; www.klur.net; 105 rue des Trois Epis; d €80-110), an organic winery and guesthouse, which hosts wine tastings, Alsatian cookery classes, herb walks in the vineyards, creative workshops and tandems to pedal through the vines *á deux*. Make yourself at home in a sunny apartment with kitchenette, read a book by an open fire in the salon, or unwind in the organic sauna. Oh, and don't miss Jean-Louis Frick's hilarious mural of hedonistic wine lovers above the entrance – it has raised a few local eyebrows, apparently.

child of Kaiser Wilhelm II. Built to trumpet the triumph of Metz' post-1871 status as part of the Second Reich, the architecture is a whimsical mix of art deco, neo-Romanesque and neo-Renaissance influences. Philippe Starck lampposts juxtapose Teutonic sculptures.

Sleeping & Eating

TOP CHOICE **Péniche Alclair** HOUSEBOAT €
(06 37 67 16 18; www.chambrespenichemetz.com; allée St Symphorien; r incl breakfast €65;) Cécile and Xavier Bonfils have transformed an old barge into this stylish blue houseboat with snazzy bathrooms and watery views. Find it moored a pleasant 15-minute riverside stroll south of the centre.

La Voile Blanche MODERN FRENCH €€
(03 87 20 66 66; 1 parvis des Droits de l'Homme; menus €25-35; Wed-Mon, lunch Sun) Art on a plate is the aim at Centre Pompidou-Metz' kaleidoscope-inspired restaurant, which was designed by architects Patrick Jouin and Sanjit Manku.

Marché Couvert FOOD MARKET
(Covered Market; place de la Cathédrale; 8am-6.30pm Tue-Sat) If only every market were like Metz' grand market. Once a bishop's palace, now a temple to fresh local produce, this is the kind of place where you pop in for a baguette and struggle out an hour later with bags overflowing with charcuterie, ripe fruit and five different sorts of fromage. Make a morning of it, stopping for an early, inexpensive lunch and a chat with the market's larger-than-life characters. At **Chez Mauricette** (sandwiches €2-4.50, antipasti plate €5-7), Mauricette tempts with Lorraine goodies from herby saucisson to local charcuterie and *mirabelle* (plum) pâté. Her neighbour is **Soupes á Soups** (soups €2.80-5.50), where Patrick ladles out home-made soups, from mussel to creamy mushroom varieties.

DON'T MISS

CENTRE POMPIDOU-METZ

(www.centrepompidou-metz.fr; 1 parvis des Droits de l'Homme; admission €7; 11am-6pm Mon, Wed & Sun, 11am-8pm Thu, Fri & Sat) This architecturally innovative museum, dazzling white and sinuous, is the satellite branch of Paris' Centre Pompidou. Its gallery draws on Europe's largest collection of modern art to stage ambitious temporary exhibitions. The dynamic space also hosts top-drawer cultural events.

Information

Tourist Office (03 87 55 53 76; http://tourisme.mairie-metz.fr; 2 place d'Armes; 9am-7pm Mon-Sat, 10am-5pm Sun)

Getting There & Away

Train it from Metz' ornate early 20th-century **train station** (pl du Général de Gaulle) to Paris' Gare de l'Est (€53, 80 minutes, 13 daily) and Strasbourg (€23, 1¾ hours, 14 daily).

BURGUNDY & THE RHÔNE VALLEY

If there's one place in France where you're really going to find out what makes the nation tick, it's Burgundy. Two of the country's enduring passions – food and wine – come together in this gorgeously rural region, and if you're a sucker for hearty food and the fruits of the vine, you'll be in seventh heaven.

Dijon

POP 250,000

This is one of France's most appealing cities. Filled with elegant medieval and Renaissance buildings, dashing Dijon is Burgundy's lively capital and spiritual home of French mustard. Its lively Old Town is great for strolling and shopping interspersed with some snappy, student-fuelled dining and drinking.

Sights & Activities

Once home to the region's rulers, the elaborate **Palais des Ducs et des États de Bourgogne** complex lies at the heart of old Dijon. The palace's eastern wing houses the outstanding **Musée des Beaux-Arts**, whose entrance is next to the **Tour de Bar**, a squat 14th-century tower that once served as a prison. The 15th-century **Tour Philippe le Bon** (adult €2.30; guided tour every 45min 9am-noon & 1.45-5.30pm, closed Mon-Tue & morning Wed, also Thu-Fri late Nov-Easter) affords fantastic views.

The **Musée de la Vie Bourguignonne** (17 rue Ste-Anne; 9am-noon & 2-6pm Wed-Mon) explores rural Burgundian life.

WORTH A TRIP

A TRIP BETWEEN VINES

Burgundy's most renowned vintages come from the **Côte d'Or** (Golden Hillside), a range of hills made of limestone, flint and clay that runs south from Dijon for about 60km. The northern section, the **Côte de Nuits**, stretches from Marsannay-la-Côte south to Corgoloin and produces reds known for their robust, full-bodied character. The southern section, the **Côte de Beaune**, lies between Ladoix-Serrigny and Santenay and produces great reds and whites.

Tourist offices can provide local brochures: *The Burgundy Wine Road*, an excellent free booklet published by the **Burgundy Tourist Board** (www.bourgogne-tourisme.com); and a useful map, *Roadmap to the Wines of Burgundy* (€0.50). There's also the **Route des Grands Crus** (www.road-of-the-fine-burgundy-wines.com), a signposted road route of some of the most celebrated Côte de Nuits vineyards.

Wine & Voyages (www.wineandvoyages.com; adult €48-58) and **Alter & Go** (www.alterandgo.fr; adult €60-80), with an emphasis on history and winemaking methods, run minibus tours in English; reserve online or at the Dijon tourist office.

Sleeping

Hôtel Le Jacquemart HOTEL €
(03 80 60 09 60; www.hotel-lejacquemart.fr; 32 rue Verrerie; d €49-65; @) In the heart of old Dijon, this two-star hotel has tidy, comfortable rooms; the pricier ones come with marble fireplaces.

Hôtel Chambellan HOTEL €
(03 80 67 12 67; www.hotel-chambellan.com; 92 rue Vannerie; s/d from €45/50) Built in 1730, this Old-Town address has a vaguely medieval feel. Rooms come in cheerful tones of red, orange, pink and white; some with a courtyard view.

Hôtel Le Sauvage HOTEL €
(03 80 41 31 21; www.hotellesauvage.com, in French; 64 rue Monge; s €46-55, d €51-61, tr €80;) In a 15th-century post-relay house set around a cobbled vine-shaded courtyard, this hotel just off lively rue Monge is good value.

Eating & Drinking

Eat streets loaded with restaurants include buzzy rue Berbisey, place Émile Zola, rue Amiral Roussin and around the perimeter of the covered market. Outdoor cafes fill place de la Libération.

Café Chez Nous CAFE €
(Impasse Quentin; lunch menu €8; lunch noon-2pm, bar 10am-2am, 11am-2pm Sun, closed Mon) This quintessentially French *bar du coin* (neighbourhood bar), often crowded, hides down an alleyway near the covered market. Lunches are generally organic and wine by the glass is a bargain (€1.20 to €2.40). Check the chalkboard for live music.

TOP CHOICE **Le Petit Roi de la Lune** BISTRO €€
(03 80 49 89 93; 28 rue Amiral Roussin; lunch menu €10, mains €15-18; lunch Tue-Sat, dinner Mon-Sat) A hip, younger crowd comes for French cuisine that, explains the chef, has been *revisitée, rearrangée et decalée* (revisited, rearranged and shifted). Breaded and fried Camembert served with blackberry jam tops the list.

Information

Tourist Office (08 92 70 05 58; www.visitdijon.com; 11 rue des Forges; 9am-6.30pm Mon-Sat, 10am-6pm Sun) Also an annexe at the train station.

Getting There & Away

BUS Transco (08 00 10 20 04; www.mobigo-bourgogne.com) buses stop in front of the train station. Bus 60 (€1.50) links Dijon with the northern Côte de Nuits wine villages of Marsannay-la-Côte, Couchey, Fixin and Gevrey-Chambertin (30 minutes). **Eurolines** (03 80 68 20 44; 53 rue Guillaume Tell) has international buses.

TRAIN Services go to Paris' Gare de Lyon (€52 to €136, 1¾ hours by TGV, three hours regular train, 20 daily), Lyon-Part Dieu (€36 to €90, two hours, 25 daily), Nice (€106 to €213, 6¼ hours by TGV, two direct daily) and Strasbourg (€55 to €126, 3½ hours, nine daily).

Beaune

POP 22,720

Beaune (pronounced 'bone'), 44km south of Dijon, is the unofficial capital of the Côte d'Or wine region. This thriving town's *raison d'être* is wine: making it, tasting it, selling it, but most of all, drinking it.

Sights & Activities

TOP CHOICE Hôtel-Dieu des Hospices de Beaune GOTHIC HOSPITAL

(rue de l'Hôtel-Dieu; adult €6.50; 9am-6.30pm) The jewel of Beaune's old town is the magnificent Hôtel-Dieu, France's most splendiferous medieval charity hospital (1443) famously topped by stunning turrets and pitched rooftops covered in multicoloured tiles. Interior highlights include the barrel-vaulted **Grande Salle** (look for the dragons and peasant heads up on the roof beams); the mural-covered **St-Hughes Room**; an 18th-century **pharmacy**; and the multi-panelled masterpiece *Polyptych of the Last Judgement* by 15th-century Flemish painter Rogier van der Weyden.

Cellar Visits WINE TASTING

Millions of bottles of wine age to perfection in cool dark cellars beneath Beaune's streets. Tasting opportunities abound and dozens of cellars can be visited by guided tour. Our favourites include the candle-lit cellars of the former Église des Cordeliers, **Marché aux Vins** (www.marcheauxvins.com, in French; 2 rue Nicolas Rolin; admission €10; 9.30-11.45am & 2-5.45pm, no midday closure mid-Jun–Aug); and **Cellier de la Vieille Grange** (www.bourgogne-cellier.com, in French; 27 blvd Georges Clemenceau; 9am-noon & 2-7pm Wed-Sat, by appointment Sun-Tue) where locals buy Burgundy wines for as little as €1.25 per litre (from €3.40 per litre for AOC). Tasting is done direct from barrels using a pipette. Bring your own jerrycan or buy a vinibag. **Patriarche Père et Fils** (www.patriarche.com; 5 rue du Collège; audio guide tour €10; 9.30-11.30am & 2-5.30pm), lined with about five million bottles of wine, are Burgundy's largest cellars.

Sleeping & Eating

Hôtel Rousseau HOTEL €

(03 80 22 13 59; 11 place Madeleine; d incl breakfast €58, s/d with washbasin only from €40, hall shower €3) An endearingly old-fashioned, 12-room hotel where the lady who has run the place since 1959 occasionally shuts reception without warning so she can go shopping.

Caves Madeleine BURGUNDIAN €€

(03 80 22 93 30; 8 rue du Faubourg Madeleine; menus €14-24; Mon-Wed & Sat, dinner Fri) This is a convivial Burgundian restaurant where locals tuck into regional classics such as *boeuf bourguignon* and *cassolette d'escargots* at long shared tables surrounded by wine racks.

Le Bistrot Bourguignon BURGUNDIAN €€

(03 80 22 23 24; 8 rue Monge; mains €16-19; Tue-Sat) This lively bistro and wine bar serves hearty regional cuisine and 17 Burgundy wines by the glass (€3 to €9). Hosts live jazz at least once a month.

Information

Tourist office (03 80 26 21 30; www.beaune-burgundy.com; 6 blvd Perpreuil; 9am-7pm Mon-Sat, 9am-6pm Sun)

Getting There & Away

BUS Bus 44 links Beaune with Dijon (€1.50, 1½hr, up to seven daily), stopping at Côte d'Or villages such as Vougeot and Nuits-St-Georges.

TRAIN Services go to Dijon (€11, 25 minutes, 40 daily), Lyon-Part Dieu (€31 to €46, 1¾ hours, 16 daily), Nuits-St-Georges (€11, 10 minutes, 40 daily) and Paris' Gare de Lyon (€64 to €118, 2¼ hours by TGV, 20 daily, two direct TGVs daily).

Lyon

POP 480,660

Gourmets, eat your heart out: Lyon is *the* gastronomic capital of France, with a lavish table of piggy-driven dishes and delicacies to savour. The city has been a commercial, industrial and banking powerhouse for the past 500 years, and is still France's second-largest conurbation, with outstanding art museums, a dynamic nightlife, green parks and a Unesco-listed Old Town.

Sights

Vieux Lyon OLD TOWN

Old Lyon (M Vieux Lyon) is divided into three quarters: St-Paul at the northern end, St-Jean in the middle and St-Georges in the south. Lovely old buildings languish on **rue du Bœuf**, **rue St-Jean** and **rue des Trois Maries**. The part-Romanesque **Cathédrale St-Jean** (place St-Jean, 5e; 8am-noon & 2-7.30pm Mon-Fri, 8am-noon & 2-7pm Sat & Sun) was built from the late 11th to the early 16th centuries. Its **astronomical clock** chimes at noon, 2pm, 3pm and 4pm.

Fourvière HILL, VIEWPOINT

Over two millennia ago, the Romans built the city of Lugdunum on the slopes of Fourvière. Today, Lyon's 'hill of prayer' is topped by the iconic **Basilique Notre Dame de Fourvière** (www.fourviere.org; 8am-7pm), a superb example of exaggerated 19th-century ecclesiastical architecture, and the Eiffel

Tower-like **Tour Métallique** (1893) – in fact a TV transmitter. The hill affords spectacular views of the city. Footpaths wind uphill but the **funicular** (place Édouard Commette; €2.40 return) is the least taxing way up.

Presqu'île CITY CENTRE

The centrepiece of **place des Terreaux** (MHôtel de Ville) is the 19th-century fountain sculpted by Frédéric-Auguste Bartholdi, creator of the Statue of Liberty. The **Musée des Beaux-Arts** (www.mba-lyon.fr; 20 place des Terreaux, 1er; admission €7; 10am-6pm Wed, Thu & Sat-Mon, 10.30am-6pm Fri; MHôtel de Ville) showcases France's finest collection of sculptures and paintings outside Paris.

North of here, the charmful hilltop quarter of **Croix Rousse** (MCroix Rousse) is famed for its bohemian inhabitants, outdoor food market and silk- weaving tradition, illustrated by the **Maison des Canuts** (www.maisondescanuts.com; 10-12 rue d'Ivry, 4e; admission €6; 10am-6pm Tue-Sat, guided tours 11am & 3.30pm; MCroix Rousse).

Laid out in the 17th century, **place Bellecour** (MBellecour) – one of Europe's largest public squares – is pierced by an equestrian **statue of Louis XIV**.

A fair trek south of place Bellecour, past **Gare de Perrache**, lies the once-downtrodden industrial area of **Lyon Confluence** (www.lyon-confluence.fr) where the Rhône and Saône Rivers meet. Trendy restaurants now line its quays.

Rive Gauche LEFT BANK, NEIGHBOURHOOD

Lyon's lovely **Parc de la Tête d'Or** (blvd des Belges, 6e; MMasséna), landscaped in the 1860s, is graced by a lake, botanic garden with greenhouses, rose garden and zoo. Its northern fringe is ensnared by the post-1960 art of the **Musée d'Art Contemporain** (www.moca-lyon.org; 81 quai Charles de Gaulle, 6e; admission €8; noon-7pm Wed-Fri, 10am-7pm Sat & Sun). Buses 41 and 47 link the park with metro Part-Dieu.

Cinema's glorious beginnings are showcased at the **Musée Lumière** (www.institut-lumiere.org; 25 rue du Premier Film, 8e; admission €6; 11am-6.30pm Tue-Sun; MMonplaisir-Lumière), the art-nouveau home of Antoine Lumière who moved to Lyon with sons Auguste and Louis in 1870. The brothers shot the world's first motion picture, *La Sortie des Usines Lumières* (Exit of the Lumières Factories), here in 19 March 1895. The factory is the Hangar du Premier Film cinema today.

Sleeping

Auberge de Jeunesse du Vieux Lyon HOSTEL €

(04 78 15 05 50; lyon@fuaj.org; 41-45 montée du Chemin Neuf, 5e; dm incl breakfast €18; reception 7am-1pm, 2-8pm & 9pm-1am; @; MVieux Lyon) Stunning city views unfold from the terrace of Lyon's only hostel, and from many of the (mostly six-share) dorms.

Hôtel de Paris HOTEL €€

(04 78 28 00 95; www.hoteldeparis-lyon.com; 16 rue de la Platière, 1er; s €49-59, d €65-90; @; MHôtel de Ville) At this fantastic-value hotel in a 19th-century bourgeois building, the funkiest rooms' retro '70s decor incorporates a palette of chocolate-and-turquoise or candyfloss-pink.

Hôtel Le Boulevardier HOTEL €

(04 78 28 48 22; www.leboulevardier.fr; 5 rue de la Fromagerie, 1er; s €45-51, d €47-53; ; MHôtel de Ville) Sporting quirky touches such as old skis and tennis racquets adorning the hallways, Le Boulevardier is a bargain 11-room hotel with snug, spotless rooms. It's up a steep spiral staircase above a cool little bistro and jazz club of the same name, which doubles as reception.

Hôtel Iris HOTEL €

(04 78 39 93 80; www.hoteliris.fr; 36 rue de l'Arbre Sec, 1er; s €43-55, d €56-80; MHôtel de Ville) This basic but colourful dame in a centuries-old convent couldn't be better placed: its street brims with hip places to eat and drink.

Hotelo HOTEL €€

(04 78 37 39 03; www.hotelo-lyon.com; 37 cours de Verdun, 2e; d from €70; MPerrache) Our hot choice around Gare de Perrache, this one stands out for its crisp contemporary design. Studios have a kitchenette and one room is perfectly fitted out for travellers with disabilities.

LYON SPLURGE!

Moored on the Rhône between Pont Morand and the Passerelle du Collège footbridge, **Péniche Barnum** (06 63 64 37 39; www.peniche-barnum.com; 3 quai du Général Sarrail, 6e; d €120-150; ; MFoch), Lyon's most unique B&B is a navy-and-timber barge with two smart guest rooms with en suite, a book-filled lounge, and shaded terrace on deck. Organic breakfast is €10.

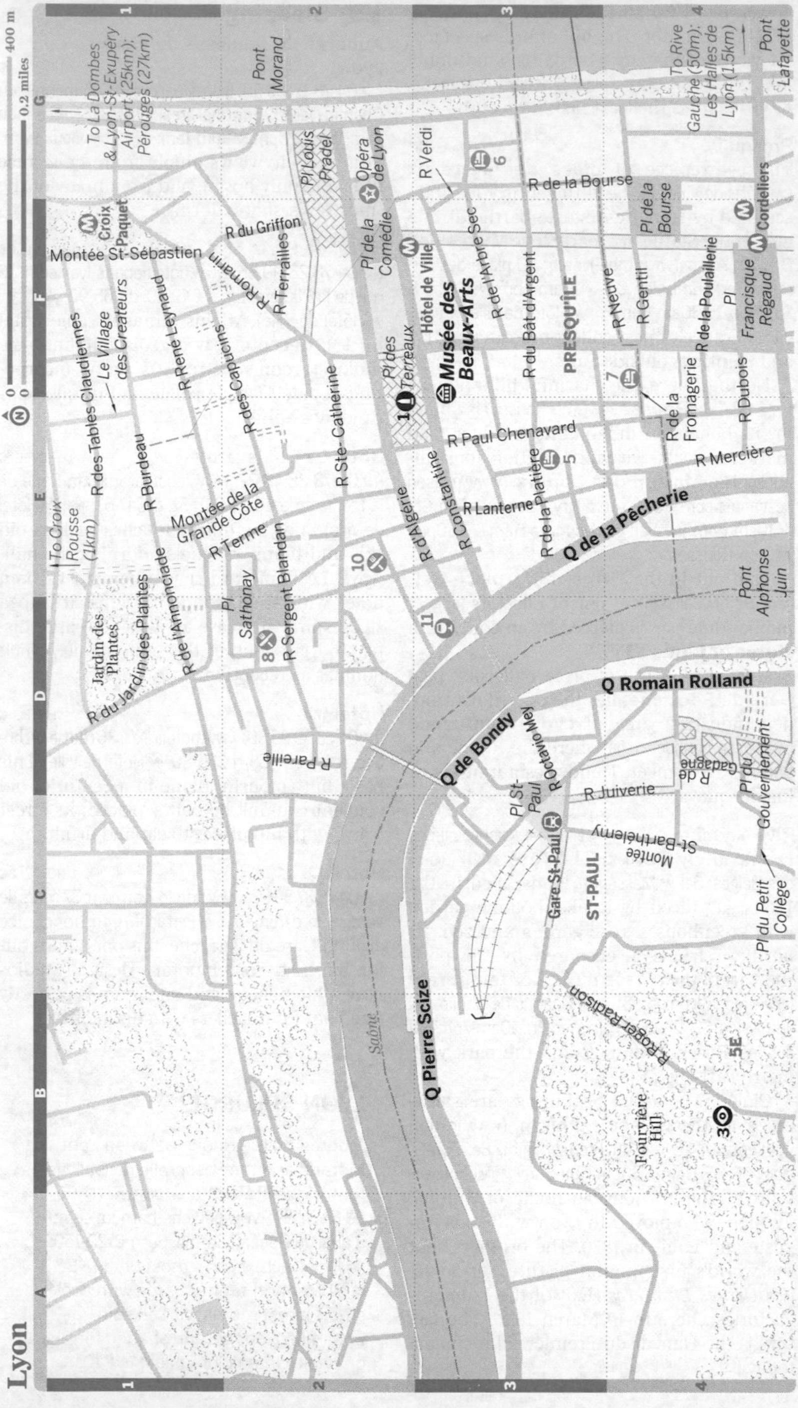

Lyon

0 400 m
0 0.2 miles

A B C D E F G
1 2 3 4

To Croix Rousse (1km)
Jardin des Plantes
R du Jardin des Plantes
R des Tables Claudiennes
Le Village des Createurs
Montée St-Sébastien
Croix Paquet
To La Dombes & Lyon-St-Exupéry Airport (25km); Pérouges (27km)
R de l'Annonciade
R Burdeau
R René Leynaud
Montée de la Grande Côte
R Terme
Pl Sathonay
8
R Sergent Blandan
R des Capucins
R Romarin
R du Griffon
R Terrailles
Pont Morand
Pl Louis Pradel
R Pareille
R Ste- Catherine
10
Saône
Pl de la Comédie
Opéra de Lyon
1
Pl des Terreaux
Hôtel de Ville
Musée des Beaux-Arts
R Verdi
Q Pierre Scize
11
R d'Algérie
R Constantine
R Lanterne
R Paul Chenavard
R de l'Arbre Sec
6
Q de Bondy
Pl St-Paul
R Octavio Mey
Gare St-Paul
R de la Platière
5
R du Bât d'Argent
PRESQU'ÎLE
R de la Bourse
ST-PAUL
R Juiverie
Q Romain Rolland
Q de la Pêcherie
7
R Neuve
R Gentil
Pl de la Bourse
Fourvière Hill
R Roger Radison
Montée St-Barthélemy
R de Gadagne
R de la Fromagerie
R de la Poulaillerie
To Rive Gauche (50m); Les Halles de Lyon (1.5km)
3
5E
Pl du Gouvernement
Pl du Petit Collège
Pont Alphonse Juin
R Mercière
R Dubois
Pl Francisque Régaud
Cordeliers
Pont Lafayette

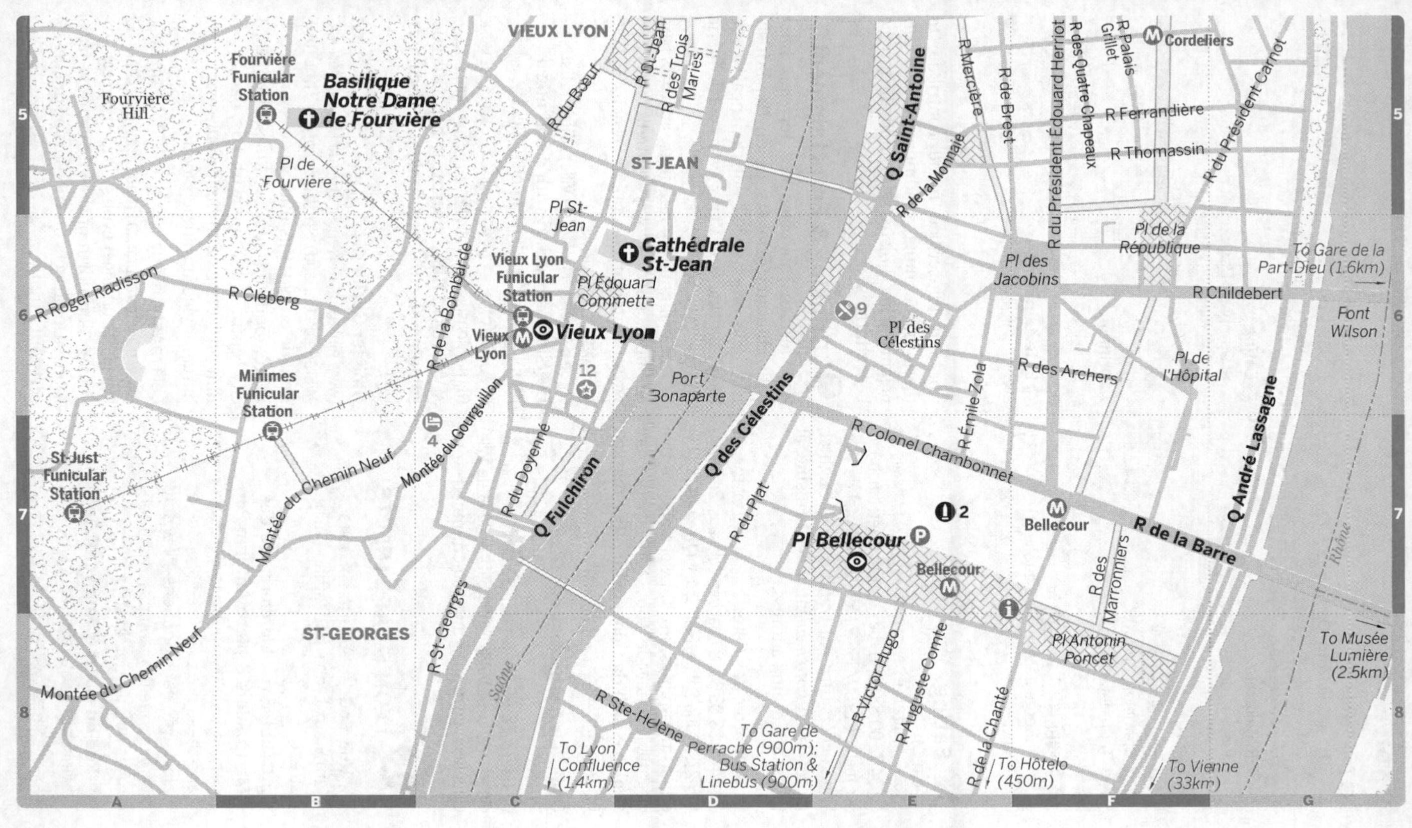

VIEUX LYON
Fourvière Hill
Fourvière Funicular Station
Basilique Notre Dame de Fourvière
Pl de Fourvière
R du Bœuf
R St-Jean
R des Trois Maries
ST-JEAN
Pl St-Jean
Cathédrale St-Jean
Vieux Lyon Funicular Station
Pl Édouard Commette
R Roger Radisson
R Cléberg
R de la Bombarde
Vieux Lyon
Vieux Lyon
12
Minimes Funicular Station
4
Montée du Gourguillon
St-Just Funicular Station
Montée du Chemin Neuf
R du Doyenné
Q Fulchiron
ST-GEORGES
R St-Georges
Saône
Montée du Chemin Neuf
Q Saint-Antoine
R de la Monnaie
R Mercière
R de Brest
R du Président Édouard Herriot
R des Quatre Chapeaux
R Palais Grillet
Cordeliers
R Ferrandière
R Thomassin
R du Président Carnot
Pl de la République
Pl des Jacobins
To Gare de la Part-Dieu (1.6km)
R Childebert
9
Pl des Célestins
Font Wilson
R des Archers
Pl de l'Hôpital
Port Bonaparte
Q des Célestins
R Émile Zola
R Colonel Chambonnet
Q André Lassagne
2
Bellecour
R de la Barre
R du Plat
Pl Bellecour
Bellecour
R des Marronniers
Rhône
Pl Antonin Poncet
To Musée Lumière (2.5km)
R Ste-Hélène
R Victor Hugo
R Auguste Comte
R de la Chanté
To Lyon Confluence (1.4km)
To Gare de Perrache (900m); Bus Station & Linebus (900m)
To Hôtelo (450m)
To Vienne (33km)

Lyon

Top Sights

- Basilique Notre Dame de Fourvière B5
- Cathédrale St-Jean D6
- Musée des Beaux-Arts F3
- Pl Bellecour E7
- Vieux Lyon C6

Sights

1 Bartholdi's Fountain E2
2 Statue of Louis XIV E7
3 Tour Métallique B4

Sleeping

4 Auberge de Jeunesse du Vieux Lyon C7
5 Hôtel de Paris E3
6 Hôtel Iris G3
7 Hôtel Le Boulevardier F4

Eating

8 Comptoir-Restaurant des Deux Places D2
9 Le Comptoir des Filles E6
10 Magali et Martin E2

Drinking

11 Le Voxx D3

Entertainment

12 (L'A)Kroche C6

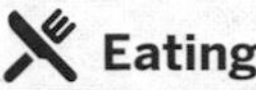

Eating

TOP CHOICE **Magali et Martin** LYONNAIS €€

(☎04 72 00 88 01; 11 rue Augustins, 1er; lunch/dinner menu €19.60/35; ⊙Mon-Fri; Ⓜ Hôtel de Ville) Watch chefs turn out traditional but lighter, more varied *bouchon*-influenced cuisine, at this sharp dining address.

Le Comptoir des Filles LYONNAIS €€

(☎04 78 38 03 30; 8 quai des Celestins, 2e; mains €15-23; ⊙Tue-Sat; Ⓜ Bellecour) *Quenelles* (Lyonnais dumplings) are the speciality of this elegant, Saône-side spot. Six varieties are available each day along with other market-prepared dishes.

Comptoir-Restaurant des Deux Places BOUCHON €€

(☎04 78 28 95 10; 5 place Fernand Rey; lunch/dinner menu €13/28; ⊙Tue-Sat; Ⓜ Hôtel de Ville) Checked curtains, antique-crammed interior and ink-scribed menu contribute to the overwhelmingly traditional feel of this neighbourhood bistro with an idyllic terrace beneath trees.

LYON'S EAT STREETS

» **Rue St-Jean** A surfeit of restaurants jam Vieux Lyon's pedestrian main street.

» **Cobbled rue Mercière, rue des Marronniers & place Antonin Poncet, 2e** Ride the metro to Bellecour and these buzzing streets, chock-a-block with eating options (of widely varying quality), and pavement terraces overflowing in summer.

» **Rue du Garet & Rue Verdi, 1er** This twinset of parrallel streets sits snug by Lyon's opera house.

Drinking & Entertainment

Cafe terraces on place des Terreaux buzz with all-hours drinkers, as do the British, Irish and other-styled pubs on nearby rue Ste-Catherine, and Vieux Lyon's rue Lainerie and rue St-Jean.

Track nightclub offerings at www.lyonclubbing.com, www.lyon2night.com and www.night4lyon.com (all in French).

Le Voxx BAR

(1 rue d'Algérie; Ⓜ Hôtel de Ville) Minimalist riverside bar packed with a real mix of people, from student to city slicker.

(L'A)Kroche LIVE MUSIC

(8 rue Monseigneur Lavarenne; ⊙Tue-Sun; Ⓜ Vieux Lyon) Hip concert cafe-bar with DJs spinning electro, soul, funk and disco; has bands too.

Ninkasi Gerland LIVE MUSIC

(www.ninkasi.fr, in French; 267 rue Marcel Mérieux; Ⓜ Stade de Gerland) Spilling over with a fun, frenetic crowd, this microbrewery near Lyon's football stadium, 4km south of the city centre, entertains with DJs, bands, film projections and build-your-own burger-styled un-French food.

Le Transbordeur LIVE MUSIC

(www.transbordeur.fr, in French; 3 blvd de Stalingrad, Villeurbanne) Lyon's prime concert venue, 3km north of the city centre, draws international acts on the European concert-tour circuit.

DON'T MISS

DRINKS AFLOAT

Floating bars with DJs and live bands rock until around 3am aboard the string of *péniches* (river barges) moored along the Rhône's left bank. Our favourites: laidback **Passagère** (21 quai Victor Augagneur, 7e; daily); classy **La Pie** (http://lapieresto.com, in French; 2 quai Victor Augagneur, 3e; Wed-Sat); party-hard **Le Sirius** (www.lesirius.com, in French; 4 quai Victor Augagneur, 3e; daily; wi-fi); and electro-oriented **La Marquise** (www.marquise.net, in French; 20 quai Victor Augagneur, 3e; Tue-Sun).

Information

Tourist Office (04 72 77 69 69; www.lyon-france.com; place Bellecour, 2e; 9am-6pm; M Bellecour)

Getting There & Away

Air

Lyon-St-Exupéry Airport (www.lyon.aeroport.fr), 25km east of the city, serves 120 direct destinations across Europe and beyond, including many budget carriers.

Tramway **Rhonexpress** (www.rhonexpress.net, in French) links the airport with Part-Dieu train station in under 30 minutes. Trams depart about every 15 minutes between 6am and 9pm, and every 30 minutes from 5am to 6am and 9pm to midnight. A one-way/return ticket costs €13/23.

Bus

Eurolines (04 72 56 95 30; www.eurolines.fr; Gare de Perrache)

Linebús (04 72 41 72 27; www.linebus.com, in Spanish; Gare de Perrache)

Train

Lyon has two main-line train stations: **Gare de la Part-Dieu** (M Part-Dieu) and **Gare de Perrache** (M Perrache). Destinations by direct TGV include:

BEAUNE €23.10, 2¼ hours, up to nine daily

DIJON €30.20, two hours, at least 12 daily

LILLE-EUROPE €92, 3¼ hours, nine daily

MARSEILLE €58.60, 1¾ hours, every 30 to 60 minutes

PARIS GARE DE LYON €64.30, two hours, every 30 to 60 minutes

STRASBOURG €55.90, 4¾ hours, five daily

Getting Around

Buses, trams, a four-line metro and two funiculars linking Vieux Lyon to Fourvière hill are run by **TCL** (www.tcl.fr). Public transport runs from around 5am to midnight. Tickets cost €1.60/13.70 for one/carnet of 10; bring coins as machines don't accept notes (or some international credit cards). Time-stamp tickets on all forms of public transport or risk a fine.

Bikes are available from 200-odd bike stations thanks to **vélo'v** (www.velov.grandlyon.com; first 30min free, first/subsequent hr €1/2).

THE FRENCH ALPS

The French Alps is the undisputed centre of adventure sports in France, whether it's paragliding among the peaks, hiking beneath Mont Blanc's 4810m of raw wilderness or hurtling down a mountainside on a pair of glorified toothpicks.

Chamonix

POP 9400 / ELEV 1037M

With the pearly white peaks of the Mont Blanc massif as sensational backdrop, being an icon comes naturally to Chamonix as a mecca of mountaineering. Its knife-edge peaks, plunging slopes and massive glaciers have enthralled generations of adventurers and thrill-seekers. Its après-ski scene (and the world's highest, most terrifying cable car) is equally pumping.

Sights & Activities

Aiguille du Midi MOUNTAIN, CABLE CAR

A jagged pinnacle of rock 8km from the domed summit of Mont Blanc, the Aiguille du Midi (3842m) is one of Chamonix' iconic landmarks. If you can handle the height, the 360° panorama from the summit is unforgettable.

The vertiginous **Téléphérique du l'Aiguille du Midi** (04 50 53 30 80, reservations 24hr 04 50 53 22 75; 100 place de l'Aiguille du Midi; adult return Aiguille du Midi €41, Plan de l'Aiguille €24; 8.30am-4.30pm) links Chamonix with the Aiguille du Midi. In summer you need a boarding card (marked with the number of your departing *and* returning cable car) as well as ticket. Bring warm clothes as even in summer the temperature rarely rises above -10°C at the top.

Mid-May to mid-September, the unrepentant can continue for a further 30 minutes of mind-blowing scenery – think suspended glaciers and spurs, seracs and shimmering ice fields – in the smaller bubbles of the **Télécabine Panoramic Mont Blanc** (adult return from Chamonix €65; 8.30am-3.45pm)

to **Pointe Helbronner** (3466m) on the French–Italian border. From here another cable car descends to the Italian ski resort of Courmayeur.

Mer de Glace GLACIER

The glistening **Mer de Glace** (Sea of Ice) is the second-largest glacier in the Alps, 14km long, 1800m wide and up to 400m deep. A quaint red mountain train links **Gare du Montenvers** (35 place de la Mer de Glace; adult €24; ⊙10am-4.30pm) in Chamonix with Montenvers (1913m), from where a cable car transports tourists in summer down to the glacier and the **Grotte de la Mer de Glace** (⊙Dec-May & mid-Jun–Sep), an ice cave where frozen tunnels and ice sculptures – carved anew every year since 1946 – change colour like mood rings.

The **Maison de la Montagne** (190 place de l'Église; ⊙8.30am-noon & 3-7pm), across the square from the tourist office, supplies comprehensive details on hiking, skiing and every other imaginable pastime in the Mont Blanc area.

Sleeping

Le Vert Hôtel PARTY HOTEL €€

(☎04 50 53 13 58; www.verthotel.com; 964 rte des Gaillands; s/d/tr/q €75/96/120/140, minimum 3-night stay) The self-proclaimed 'Chamonix' house of sports and creativity', this party house 1km south of town has no-frills rooms, some with microscopic bathrooms. But what people really come for is the hotel's all-happening, ultrahip bar, a regular venue for top DJs and live music.

Hôtel El Paso PARTY HOTEL €

(☎04 50 53 64 20; www.cantina.fr; 37 impasse des Rhododendrons; s/d/tr/q €49/64/75/90) What you'll get is a threadbare mattress and four scuffed walls reminiscent of good times – small sacrifices given El Paso is cheap, central and *the* place to party, dude. Tex-Mex feasts and DJs downstairs keep the place rocking.

Les Deux Glaciers CAMPING GROUND €

(☎04 50 53 15 84; http://les2glaciers.com; 80 rte des Tissières; campsites €14.50; ⊙mid-Dec–mid-Nov; 📶) Oh, what a beautiful morning! Draw back your tent flap and be dazzled by Mont Blanc and glaciated peaks at this almost year-round camping ground in Les Bossons, 3km south of Chamonix. Take the train to Les Bossons, or the Chamonix bus to Tremplin-le-Mont.

CHAMONIX SPLURGE!

A beautifully converted farmhouse, ablaze with geraniums in summer, **Auberge du Manoir** (☎04 50 53 10 77; http://aubergedumanoir.com, in French; 8 rte du Bouchet; s €94-108, d €104-150, q €165; 📶) ticks all the perfect Alpine chalet boxes: pristine mountain views, pine-panelled rooms and an inviting bar where an open fire keeps things cosy.

Eating

Munchie FUSION €€

(☎04 50 53 45 41; www.munchie.eu; 87 rue des Moulins; mains €18-24; ⊙dinner) Think pan-Asian fusion at this trendy Swedish-run hang-out where sittings go faster than musical chairs (making it worth a try even without a reservation).

TOP CHOICE **Les Vieilles Luges** TRADITIONAL FRENCH €€

(www.lesvieillesluges.com; Les Houches; menus €20-35) Like a scene from a snow globe, this childhood dream of a 250-year-old farmhouse can only be reached by slipping on skis or taking a scenic 20-minute hike from the Maison Neuve chairlift.

Le GouThé TEA ROOM €

(95 rue des Moulins; menus €9; ⊙9am-6.30pm Fri-Mon) Philippe's hot chocolates with pistachio and gingerbread infusions, startlingly bright macaroons and crumbly home-made tarts are just the sugar fix needed for the slopes. He's a dab hand with *galettes* (buckwheat crêpes), too.

Drinking & Entertainment

Nightlife rocks. In the centre, riverside rue des Moulins touts a line-up of drinking holes. Most après-ski joints serve food as well as booze.

Chambre Neuf BAR

(272 av Michel Croz; 📶) Cover bands, raucous après-ski drinking and Swedes dancing on the tables make Room Nine one of Chamonix' liveliest party haunts. Conversations about epic off-pistes and monster jumps that are, like, totally mental, man, dominate at every table.

MBC MICROBREWERY

(www.mbchx.com; 350 rte du Bouchet; ⊙4pm-2am) Be it with burgers, cheesecake, live

DON'T MISS

A LOFTY LUNCH

Feast on fondue and even finer mountain views at these high-altitude faves:

La Crémerie du Glacier (☎04 50 54 07 52; www.lacremerieduglacier.fr, in French; 766 chemin de la Glacière; mains €10-19; ⏲closed Wed) Crazy as it sounds for a piste restaurant, you might have to book to get a chance to bite into La Crémerie's world-famous *croûtes au fromage* (chunky slices of toasted bread topped with melted cheese). Ski here with the red Pierre à Ric piste in Les Grands Montets.

Le 3842 (☎04 50 55 82 23; Aiguille du Midi; mains €12-21; ⏲restaurant mid-Jun–mid-Sep, snack bar all year) Stylish summit dining and drinking with knockout views at the top of the Aiguille du Midi in what is claimed to be Europe's highest cafe.

Le Panoramic (☎04 50 53 44 11; Le Brévent; menus from €15; ⏲mid-Dec–Apr & late Jun-Sep) Views of Mont Blanc are included in the menu of cheeses, cured meats and BBQ fare. A *vin chaud* (hot mulled wine) on the terrace will also do just fine.

music or amazing locally brewed beers, this trendy microbrewery delivers.

Monkey Bar MUSIC BAR

(81 place Edmond Desailloud; ⏲1pm-2am; 📶) Slightly grungy, very cool, this party hotspot has live gigs and DJs several times a week. There's a mad rush to the bar at 4.45pm when pints are €1.50 for 15 minutes!

Information

Tourist Office (☎04 50 53 00 24; www.chamonix.com; 85 place du Triangle de l'Amitié; ⏲8.30am-7pm)

Getting There & Away

Bus

From **Chamonix bus station** (www.sat-montblanc.com; place de la Gare), next to the train station, two to three buses run daily to/from Geneva airport (€33, 1½ to two hours) and Courmayeur (one way/return €13/20, 45 minutes). Advanced booking only.

Train

From Chamonix-Mont Blanc **train station** (place de la Gare) the Mont Blanc Express narrow-gauge train trundles to/from St-Gervais-Le Fayet (€9.50, 40 minutes, nine to 12 daily), from where there are trains to most major French cities.

THE DORDOGNE & LOT

If it's French heart and soul you're after, look no further. Tucked in the country's south-western corner, the neighbouring regions of the Dordogne and Lot combine history, culture and culinary sophistication in one unforgettably scenic package. The Dordogne is best known for its sturdy *bastides* (fortified towns), clifftop châteaux and spectacular prehistoric cave paintings, while the Mediterranean-tinged region of the Lot is home to endless vintage vineyards and the historic city of Cahors.

Sarlat-La-Canéda

POP 9950

A gorgeous tangle of honey-coloured buildings, alleyways and secret squares make up this unmissable Dordogne village – a natural if touristy launch pad into the Vézère Valley.

Part of the fun of Sarlat is getting lost in its twisting alleyways and backstreets. **Rue Jean-Jacques Rousseau** or the area around **Le Présidial** are good starting points, but for the grandest buildings and *hôtels particuliers* you'll want to explore **rue des Consuls**.

Whichever street you take, sooner or later you'll hit the **Cathédrale St-Sacerdos** (place du Peyrou), a real mix of architectural styles and periods: the belfry and western facade are the oldest parts.

Nearby, the former **Église Ste-Marie** (place de la Liberté) houses Sarlat's mouthwatering **Marché Couvert** (Covered Market) and a state-of-the-art **panoramic lift** (elevator) in its belltower. It was designed by top French architect Jean Nouvel (whose parents live in Sarlat).

The **tourist office** (☎05 53 31 45 45; www.sarlat-tourisme.com; rue Tourny; ⏲9am-6pm Mon-Sat, 10am-1pm & 2-5pm Sun) neighbours the cathedral.

WORTH A TRIP

PREHISTORIC PAINTINGS

Fantastic prehistoric **caves** with some of the world's finest cave art is what makes the **Vézère Valley** so very special. Most of the caves are closed in winter, and get very busy in summer. Visitor numbers are strictly limited, so you'll need to reserve well ahead.

Of the valley's 175 known sites, the most famous include **Grotte de Font de Gaume** (http://eyzies.monuments-nationaux.fr; adult €7; ⌚9.30am-12.30 & 2-5.30pm Sun-Fri), 1km northeast of Les Eyzies-de-Toyac-Sireuil. About 14,000 years ago, the prehistoric artists created the gallery of over 230 figures, including bison, reindeer, horses, mammoths, bears and wolves, of which 25 are on permanent display.

About 7km east of Les Eyzies, **Abri du Cap Blanc** (http://eyzies.monuments-nationaux.fr; adult €7; ⌚9.30am-12.30 & 2-5.30pm Sun-Fri) showcases an unusual sculpture gallery of horses, bison and deer.

Then there is **Grotte de Rouffignac** (www.grottederouffignac.fr; adult/child €6.30/4; tours in French ⌚10-11.30am & 2-5pm), sometimes known as the 'Cave of 100 Mammoths' because of its painted mammoths. Access to the caves, hidden in woodland 15km north of Les Eyzies, is aboard a trundling electric train.

Star of the show goes hands down to **Grotte de Lascaux** (Lascaux II: ☎05 53 51 95 03; www.semitour.com; adult €8.80; ⌚9.30am-6pm), 2km southeast of Montignac, featuring an astonishing menagerie including oxen, deer, horses, reindeer and mammoth, as well as an amazing 5.5m bull, the largest cave drawing ever found. The original cave was closed to the public in 1963 to prevent damage to the paintings, but the most famous sections have been meticulously re-created in a second cave nearby – a massive undertaking that required some 20 artists and took 11 years.

Sleeping & Eating

Hôtel Les Récollets HOTEL €
(☎05 53 31 36 00; www.hotel-recollets-sarlat.com; 4 rue Jean-Jacques Rousseau; d €45-69; ❄📶) Lost in the old town's medieval maze, the Récollets is a budget beauty. Nineteen topsy-turvy rooms and a charming vaulted breakfast room are rammed in around the medieval *maison*.

Bistro de l'Octroi REGIONAL CUISINE €€
(☎05 53 30 83 40; www.lebistrodeloctroi.fr, in French; 111 av de Selves; menus €18-26) This local's tip is a little way out of town, but don't let that dissuade you. Sarladais pack into this cosy townhouse for the artistically presented, accomplished cooking that doesn't sacrifice substance for style.

Le Bistrot REGIONAL CUISINE €€
(☎05 53 28 28 40; place du Peyrou; menus €18.50-24.50; ⌚Mon-Sat) Red-check tablecloths and twinkling fairy lights create an intimate atmosphere at this diminutive bistro. Don't miss the *pommes sarlardaises* (potatoes cooked in duck fat).

Getting There & Away

From the **train station** (ave de la Gare), 1.3km south of the old town, services go to Les Eyzies (change at Le Buisson; €8.60, 50 minutes to 2½ hours, three daily).

ATLANTIC COAST & FRENCH BASQUE COUNTRY

Though the Côte d'Azur is the most popular beach spot in France, the many seaside resorts along the Atlantic Coast are fast catching up. If you're a surf nut or a beach bum, the sandy bays around Biarritz will be right up your alley, while oenophiles can sample the fruits of the vine in the capital of French winemaking, Bordeaux. Towards the Pyrenees you'll find the Basque Country, which feels closer to northern Spain than to the rest of France.

Bordeaux

POP 238,900

The new millennium was a turning point for the city long nicknamed *La Belle au Bois Dormant* (Sleeping Beauty), when the mayor, ex-Prime Minister Alain Juppé, roused Bordeaux, pedestrianising its boulevards, restoring its neoclassical architecture and implementing a hi-tech public-transport system. Today the city is a Unesco World Heritage Site and, with its merry student population and 2.5 million-odd annual tourists, scarcely sleeps at all.

Sights

The Unesco-listed **Cathédrale St-André** is almost overshadowed by the gargoyled, 50m-high Gothic belfry, **Tour Pey-Berland** (adult €5; ⏲10am-1.15pm & 2-6pm Jun-Sep, shorter hrs rest year). Erected between 1440 and 1466, its spire was later topped off with the statue of Notre Dame de l'Aquitaine. Scaling the tower's 232 narrow steps rewards you with a spectacular panorama of the city.

Bordeaux's museums have free entry for permanent collections. Gallo-Roman statues and relics dating back 25,000 years are among the highlights at the impressive **Musée d'Aquitaine** (20 cours Pasteur; temporary exhibitions €3; ⏲11am-6pm Tue-Sun), while more than 700 post-1960s works by 140 European and American artists are on display at the **CAPC Musée d'Art Contemporain** (Entrepôt 7, rue Ferrére; ⏲11am-6pm Tue, Thu-Sun, to 8pm Wed, closed Mon).

The evolution of Occidental art from the Renaissance to the mid-20th century is on view at Bordeaux's **Musée des Beaux-Arts** (20 cours d'Albret; ⏲11am-6pm Wed-Mon), while *faïence* pottery, porcelain, gold, iron, glasswork and furniture are displayed at the **Musée des Arts Décoratifs** (39 rue Bouffard; ⏲museum 2-6pm Wed-Mon, temporary exhibits from 11am Mon-Fri).

The only remains of the Roman city of Burdigala are the crumbling ruins of the 3rd-century amphitheatre, **Palais Gallien** (rue du Docteur Albert Barraud; adult €3; ⏲2-7pm Jun-Sep).

Sleeping

Auberge de Jeunesse HOSTEL €
(☎05 56 33 00 70; www.auberge-jeunesse-bordeaux.com; 22 cours Barbey; dm incl sheets & breakfast €22; ⏲reception 7.30am-1.30pm & 3.30-9.30pm; 📶) Bordeaux's hostel is in an ultramodern building. From the train station, follow cours de la Marne for 300m and turn left opposite the park; the hostel is about 250m further.

TOP CHOICE **Ecolodge des Chartrons** B&B €€
(☎05 56 81 49 13; www.ecolodgedeschartrons.com; 23 rue Raze; s/d incl breakfast €98/110) Hidden on a side street off the quays in Bordeaux's Chartrons wine merchants district, this *chambre d'hôte* spearheads ecofriendly sleeping in the city: think solar-heated water, hemp-based soundproofing and recycled antique furniture.

Une Chambre en Ville BOUTIQUE HOTEL €€
(☎05 56 81 34 53; www.bandb-bx.com; 35 rue Bouffard; s/d €103/115) A Room In Town blends in well with the antique and art shops on the same street. Each of the five rooms is a work of art.

Eating

A classic Saturday-morning Bordeaux experience is slurping oysters and white wine from one of the seafood stands at the market, **Marché des Capucins** (6 oysters & glass of wine €6; ⏲7am-noon).

Place du Parlement, rue du Pas St-Georges, rue des Faussets and place de la Victoire are loaded with dining addresses, as is the old waterfront warehouse district around quai des Marques – great for a sunset meal or drink.

TOP CHOICE **Le Cheverus Café** BISTRO €
(☎05 56 48 29 73; 81-83 rue du Loup; menu from €10.50; ⏲Mon-Sat) Friendly, cosy and chaotically busy (be prepared to wait for a table

ON THE WINE TRAIL

Thirsty? The 1000-sq-km wine-growing area around Bordeaux is, along with Burgundy, France's most important producer of top-quality wines. Whet your palate with Bordeaux tourist office's introduction wine-and-cheese courses (€24) or a tasting course at the **Maison du Vin de Bordeaux** (3 cours du 30 Juillet).

Bordeaux has over 5000 wine-producing estates. One of the easiest to visit is **Château Lanessan** (☎05 56 58 94 80; www.lanessan.com; Cussac-Fort-Medoc; adult €8; ⏲advance reservation).

Favourite vine-framed villages nearby brimming with charm and tasting/buying opportunities include medieval **St-Émilion** (www.saint-emilion-tourisme.com), port town **Pauillac** (www.pauillac-medoc.com) and **Listrac-Médoc**. In **Arsac-en-Médoc**, Philippe Raoux's vast glass-and-steel wine centre, **La Winery** (☎05 56 39 04 90; www.lawinery.fr, in French; Rond-point des Vendangeurs, D1), stuns with concerts and contemporary art exhibitions alongside tastings to determine your *signe œnologique* ('wine sign'; booking required).

Many wine châteaux close during October's *vendange* (grape harvest).

at lunchtime) best describes this neighbourhood bistro. Lunch in particular is an all-out bargain.

La Boîte à Huîtres OYSTERS €
(☎05 56 81 64 97; 36 cours du Chapeau Rouge; mains €8) This rickety wood-panelled little place is the best spot in Bordeaux to slurp fresh Aracachon oysters, traditionally served with sausage.

TOP CHOICE **La Tupina** REGIONAL CUISINE €€
(☎05 56 91 56 37; 6 rue Porte de la Monnaie; mains €18-40) Filled with the smell of soup simmering in an old *tupina* ('kettle' in Basque) over an open fire, this white-tableclothed place is feted far and wide for its seasonal regional specialities: minicasserole of foie gras and eggs, milk-fed lamb or goose wings with potatoes and parsley. Lunch here weekdays for €16.

Information

Tourist office (☎05 56 00 66 00; www.bordeaux-tourisme.com; 12 cours du 30 Juillet; ⊙9am-7.30pm Mon-Sat, 9.30am-6.30pm Sun Jul & Aug, shorter hrs rest of year) Runs a smaller but helpful branch by the train station.

Getting There & Away

Air

Bordeaux airport (www.bordeaux.aeroport.fr) is in Mérignac, 10km west of the city centre, with domestic and some international services.

Jet'Bus (☎05 56 34 50 50; €7, 45 minutes, every 45 minutes) shuttle buses link it with the train station, place Gambetta and main tourist office in town.

Bus

Citram Aquitaine (www.citram.fr, in French) Regional buses.

Eurolines (☎05 56 92 50 42; 32 rue Charles Domercq) International lines.

Train

From Bordeaux's Gare St-Jean, 3km from the centre:

PARIS' GARE MONTPARNASSE €69.80, three hours, at least 16 daily

TOULOUSE €33, 2¼ hours

Biarritz

POP 27,500

Edge your way along the coast towards Spain and you arrive in stylish Biarritz, as ritzy as its name suggests. The resort took off in the mid-19th century when Napoleon III visited and it still shimmers with architectural treasures from the *belle époque* and art-deco eras. Big waves – some of Europe's best – and a beachy lifestyle meanwhile are a magnet for Europe's hip surfing set.

Sights & Activities

Biarritz' fashionable beaches, particularly **Grande Plage** and **Plage Miramar**, are end-to-end bodies on hot summer days. Rent a stripey 1920s-style beach tent for €9.50 per day. North of Pointe St-Martin, the adrenaline-pumping surfing beaches of **Anglet** continue northwards for over 4km. Ride eastbound bus 9 from av Verdun (just near av Édouard VII).

Beyond long, exposed **Plage de la Côte des Basques**, some 500m south of Port Vieux, are **Plage de Marbella** and **Plage de la Milady**. Take westbound bus 9 from rue Gambetta where it crosses rue Broquedis.

Biarritz' history as a fishing and whaling marine is explored at the **Musée de la Mer** (www.museedelamer.com; Esplanade du Rocher de la Vierge; adult €8; ⊙9.30am-midnight Jul & Aug, shorter hrs rest of year) alongside underwater life collected from the Bay of Biscay (Golfe de Gascogne).

Sleeping

Hôtel Les Alizès BOUTIQUE HOTEL €
(☎05 59 24 11 74; www.alizes-biarritz.com; 13 rue du Port Vieux; s/d €62/90; 📶) With its brash and blushing shades clashing brilliantly with old-fashioned desks and wardrobes, this funky family-run hotel is one of the town's most memorable cheapies. Its beach-facing location is spot-on.

Auberge de Jeunesse de Biarritz HOSTEL €
(☎05 59 41 76 00; www.hibiarritz.org; 8 rue Chiquito de Cambo; dm incl sheets & breakfast €19.50; ⊙reception 8.30-11.30am & 6-9pm, to noon & 10pm May-Sep, closed mid-Dec–early Jan; @📶) This popular place offers outdoor activities including surfing. Rooms for two to four hostellers have a private bathroom. From the train station, follow the railway westwards for 800m.

Eating

See-and-be-seen cafes and restaurants line Biarritz' beachfront. Anglet is also becoming increasingly trendy, with cafes strung along the waterfront.

DON'T MISS

EUROPE'S LARGEST SAND DUNE

Between oyster beds and pine forest, the **Dune de Pilat** quite literally takes your breath away. From its magnificent top, you can see **Cap Ferret** and the sandy shoals at the mouth of the **Bassin d'Arcachon** (www.bassin-arcachon.com) to the west, and dense dark-green pine forests eastwards almost as far as the eye can see.

Sometimes called Dune de Pyla after the neighbouring resort town of **Pyla-sur-Mer**, 8km south of Arcachon, this colossal mountain of golden sand stretches south from the Bassin d'Arcachon for almost 3km. Europe's largest, it spreads 4.5m eastwards a year – swallowing trees, a road junction and a hotel in the process.

Easily the most atmospheric way of getting to the dune is by bicycle. A cycling path links it with **Arcachon** (www.arcachon.com), a 19th-century hideaway for bourgeois Bordelaise that retains its seaside charm with gorgeous *belle époque* villas and four little quarters romantically named after the seasons. Lunch on oysters harvested fresh from the bay and traditional *crepinettes* (local small, flat sausages), and afterwards sail with **Les Bateliers Arcachonnais** (www.bateliers-arcachon.com, in French) to **Île aux Oiseaux**, the uninhabited 'bird island' in the middle of the bay, perhaps, or **Banc d'Arguin**, the sand bank off the Dune du Pilat.

Frequent trains link Arcachon and Bordeaux (€9.80, 50 minutes).

TOP CHOICE **Casa Juan Pedro** SEAFOOD €
(☎05 59 24 00 86; Port des Pêcheurs; mains €5-15) Down by the old port – something of a hidden village of wooden fishing cottages – this cute shack restaurant cooks up tuna, sardines and squid with bags of friendly banter. There are several similar neighbouring places.

Le Crabe-Tambour SEAFOOD €€
(☎05 59 23 24 53; 49 rue d'Espagne; menus €13-18) Named after a 1977 film (the owner was the cook for the film set) this local address serves great seafood at a price that is hard to fault.

Bistrot des Halles BASQUE €€
(☎05 59 24 21 22; 1 rue du Centre; mains €14.50-17) One of several decent restaurants on rue du Centre that get their produce fresh from the nearby covered market, this bustling place serves excellent fish and other fresh fare in an interior adorned with old metallic advertising posters.

Le Clos Basque BASQUE €€
(☎05 59 24 24 96; 12 rue Louis Barthou; menus €24; ⏲lunch Tue-Sun, dinner Tue-Sat) Basque cuisine with a contemporary twist and fab terrace.

Drinking

Great bars stud rue du Port Vieux, place Clemenceau and the central food-market area.

Ventilo Caffé BAR €
(rue du Port Vieux; ⏲closed Tue out of season) Dressed up like a tart's boudoir, this fun and funky place continues its domination of the Biarritz bar scene.

Arena Café Bar BAR €
(Plage du Port Vieux; ⏲9am-2am Apr-Sep, 10am-2am Wed-Sun Oct-Mar) Tucked in a tiny cove, this beachfront hang-out combines a style-conscious restaurant (mains €15 to €22) with fuchsia- and violet-tinged bar and DJs.

Milk Bar BAR €
(17 blvd du Géneral de Gaulle; ⏲Tue-Sun) If you want to hang out with surfers, then this bar, just back from the beach, is the place to go.

Information

Tourist office (☎05 59 22 37 00; www.biarritz.fr; square d'Ixelles; ⏲9am-7pm Jul & Aug, 9am-6pm Mon-Sat, 10am-5pm Sun Sep-Jun)

Getting There & Away

Air

Biarritz-Anglet-Bayonne Airport (www.biarritz.aeroport.fr), 3km southeast of Biarritz, is served by EasyJet, Ryanair and other low-cost carriers. STAB bus No 6 (line C on Sunday) links it once or twice hourly with Biarritz.

Bus

ATCRB (www.transdev-atcrb.com) buses head down the coast to the Spanish border.

Train

Biarritz-La Négresse train station, 3km south of town, is linked to the centre by buses 2 and 9 (B and C on Sundays).

LANGUEDOC-ROUSSILLON

Languedoc-Roussillon comes in three distinct flavours. Bas-Languedoc (Lower Languedoc), land of bullfighting, rugby and robust red wines, sun-baked Nîmes with its fine Roman amphitheatre, and the fairy-tale walled fortress of Carcassonne.

Inland is mountainous Haut Languedoc (Upper Languedoc), a sparsely populated terrain made for outdoor enthusiasts; while south sits Roussillon, snug against the rugged Pyrenees.

Languedoc's traditional centre, Toulouse, was hived off when regional boundaries were redrawn almost half a century ago, but we've chosen to include it in this section.

Toulouse

POP 446,200

Often known as *la ville rose* (the pink city), funky Toulouse is one of the nation's liveliest and fastest-growing metropolises. Sliced through by the twin rivers of Canal du Midi and River Garonne, it's a city with a long history and forward-looking attitude: medieval streets and old churches fill the old town, while buzzy bars, grungy gig venues and over 100,000 students give the place a youthful kick.

Sights

Bustling **place du Capitole** is the city's main square.

The predominantly 18th-century **Vieux Quartier** is a tiny web of narrow lanes and squares. The vast **Basilique St-Sernin** (place St-Sernin; ⌚8.30am-noon & 2-6pm Mon-Sat, 8.30am-12.30pm & 2-7.30pm Sun) is France's largest Romanesque structure, topped by an octagonal 13th-century tower and 15th-century spire.

Inside an old Augustinian monastery, the **Musée des Augustins** (www.augustins.org; 21 rue de Metz; adult €3, temporary exhibitions €6; ⌚10am-6pm Thu-Tue, 10am-9pm Wed) houses everything from Roman artefacts to paintings by Rubens, Delacroix and Toulouse-Lautrec.

The **Cathédrale St-Étienne** (place St-Étienne) is a hotchpotch of styles: highlights include a glorious 13th-century rose window and the choir.

Red-brick **Les Abattoirs** (www.lesabattoirs.org; 76 allées Charles de Fitte; admission €3-10; ⌚11am-7pm Sat & Sun, 10-6pm Wed-Fri), the city's main abattoir, has since been reinvented as

WORTH A TRIP

LOURDES

Lourdes (pop 15,700; www.lourdes-infotourisme.com); in the heart of the Pyrenees, has been one of the world's most important pilgrimage sites since 1858, when 14-year-old Bernadette Soubirous (1844–79) saw the Virgin Mary in a series of 18 visions. The town now feels dangerously close to a religious theme park, but the commercialism doesn't extend to the *sanctuaires* (sanctuaries) themselves, mercifully souvenir-free.

Grotte de Massabielle (Massabielle Cave) is the most revered site. Esplanade des Processions, lined with enormous flickering candles left by previous pilgrims, leads along a river to the grotto's entrance where people queue to enter the cave or dip in one of the 19 holy **baths** (⌚generally 9-11am & 2.30-4pm Mon-Sat, 2-4pm Sun & holy days). Not for wallflowers, once you're behind the curtain, you're expected to strip off before being swaddled in a sheet and plunged backwards into the icy water.

The main 19th-century section of the sanctuaries is divided between the neo-Byzantine **Basilique du Rosaire**, the **crypt** and spire-topped **Basilique Supérieure** (Upper Basilica). From Palm Sunday to mid-October, nightly torchlight processions start from the Massabielle Grotto at 9pm, while at 5pm there's the **Procession Eucharistique** (Blessed Sacrament Procession) along Esplanade des Processions.

When the crowds of pilgrims gets too much, seek refuge on the rocky 94m-high pinnacle of **Pic du Jer** – the panorama of Lourdes and the Pyrenees is inspiring. Walk three hours along a marked trail or ride six minutes in the century-old **funicular** (www.picdujer.info; blvd d'Espagne; adult €9.50; ⌚9.30am-6pm or 7pm Mar-Nov). The summit is a superb picnic spot.

Lourdes is well connected by train; destinations include Bayonne (€21, 1¾ hours, up to four daily), Toulouse (€25.10, 1¾ hours, six daily) and Paris' Gare Montparnasse (€89.30, 6½ hours, four daily).

a cutting-edge art gallery and venue for concerts and exhibitions.

Sleeping

TOP CHOICE **Hôtel St-Sernin** BOUTIQUE HOTEL €€
(☎05 61 21 73 08; www.hotelstsernin.com; 2 rue St-Bernard; d €111-131;) A swish little number in the shade of Basilique St-Sernin, this hotel is beautifully finished with slate-grey walls, crisp white sheets and splashes of zesty colour.

Le Clos des Potiers HOTEL €€
(☎05 61 47 15 15; www.le-clos-des-potiers.com; 12 rue des Potiers; d €100-125;) This little-known hideaway near the cathedral is one of Toulouse's best-kept secrets. Rooms blend the bespoke feel of an upmarket B&B (antique rugs, characterful furniture, original mantelpieces) with the comfort and efficiency of a smart hotel (private garden, lovely lounge, treat tray).

Hôtel La Chartreuse HOTEL €
(☎05 61 62 93 39; www.chartreusehotel.com; 4bis blvd de Bonrepos; s/d/tr €41/47/57) This super, family-run establishment by the station is a welcome surprise: clean, friendly and surprisingly quiet, with a lovely little breakfast room and back garden patio.

Eating

Blvd de Strasbourg, place St-Georges and place du Capitole are perfect spots for dining al fresco. Try rue Pargaminières for kebabs, burgers and late-night student grub.

TOP CHOICE **Chez Navarre** REGIONAL CUISINE €€
(☎05 62 26 43 06; 49 Grande Rue Nazareth; menus €13-20; Mon-Fri) Wanna' dine with locals? Then come to this wonderful *table d'hôtes* where honest Gascon cuisine is dished up beneath a hefty beamed ceiling. Dining is around communal, candlelit tables.

Au Jardins des Thés CAFE €€
(16 pl St-Georges; menus €12.50-15.50) A perennially packed terrace on one of the city's smartest squares testifies to just how good its salads, *tartes salées* (savoury tarts) and other lunchy treats are.

Les Halles Victor Hugo BISTRO €
(place Victor Hugo; menus €10-20; lunch Tue-Sun) For a quintessentially French experience, join the punters at the string of tiny restaurants on the 1st floor of the Victor-Hugo food market. Food is simple, unfussy and full of character.

DON'T MISS

ALL AFLOAT

Toulouse is a river city, and you couldn't possibly leave without venturing out onto the water. From March to November, several operators run scenic hour-long boat trips (adult €8) along the Garonne from quai de la Daurade; in summer trips also pass through the St-Pierre lock onto the Canal du Midi and Canal de Brienne.

Buy tickets on the boat, up to 10 minutes before departure, from **Les Bateaux Toulousains** (www.bateaux-toulousains.com), **Toulouses Croisières** (www.toulouse-croisieres.com) or **L'Occitania** (www.loccitania.fr).

Faim des Haricots VEGETARIAN €
(www.lafaimdesharicots.fr; 3 rue du Puits Vert; Mon-Sat) Everything's served *á volonte* (all you can eat) at this 100% veggie/wholefood restaurant where €15.50 buys you a savoury tart, salad, hot dishes, dessert and a pichet of wine.

Drinking & Entertainment

Almost every square in the Vieux Quartier has at least one cafe, busy day and night. Other after-dark hot spots include rue Castellane, rue Gabriel Péri and near the river around place St-Pierre. Tune into Toulouse's live-music and clubbing scene at http://toulouse.sortir.eu.

Bodega Bodega TAPAS BAR
(1 rue Gabriel Péri; tapas €4.50-10; 7pm-2am Mon-Fri, 7pm-6am Sat, 8pm-2am Sun) Revel in all the fun of the *feria* in a historic building where the tax authority once was. There's tip-top tapas, and it has live music at weekends.

La Maison BAR
(9 rue Gabriel Péri; 5pm-2am Sun-Fri, 5pm-5am Sat) The House is a hip, shabby-chic hangout for students and trendies, with plenty of vintage fireplace, scruffy sofas and second-hand chairs dotted around the living room.

Au Père Louis HISTORIC BAR
(45 rue des Tourneurs; 8.30am-3pm & 5-10.30pm Mon-Sat) Top of our list for irresistible old-fashioned charm, 'Father Louis' is Toulouse's oldest bar (franked 1889).

Opus Café CLUB
(24 rue Bachelier; admission free; midnight-5am Mon-Wed, 11pm-6am Thu-Sat) Dance until

dawn at this much-loved venue for seasoned clubbers.

Le Bikini MUSIC CLUB
(www.lebikini.com; rue Hermès, Ramonville St-Agne) The stuff of Toulousien legend, at the end of metro line B (Ramonville).

Information

Tourist office (☎05 61 11 02 22; www.toulouse-tourisme.com; square Charles de Gaulle; ⏰9am-7pm Mon-Sat, 10.30am-5.15pm Sun Jun-Sep; shorter hrs rest of year)

Getting There & Away

AIR **Toulouse-Blagnac Airport** (www.toulouse.aeroport.fr/en), 8km northwest of the centre, has flights to Paris and other large French and European cities. Easyjet, BmiBaby, Ryanair, KLM, Flybe and Germanwings fly here. A **shuttle bus** (www.tisseo.fr; €5, 20 minutes, every 20 minutes) links it with town.

TRAIN **Gare Matabiau** (blvd Pierre Sémard), 1km northeast of the centre, is served by TGVs west to Bordeaux (€36.90; two hours; connections to Bayonne and the southwest, plus Paris), and east to Carcassonne (€12, one hour) and beyond.

Carcassonne

POP 49,100

With its witch's hat turrets and walled city, Carcassonne looks like some fairy-tale fortress from afar – but the medieval magic's more than a little tarnished by an annual influx of over four million visitors. It can be a tourist hell in high summer, so pitch up out of season to see the town at its best (and quietest).

Pick up an audio guide (€3 for two hours) to **La Cité** (the Old City) at the **tourist office** (☎04 68 10 24 30; www.carcassonne-tourisme.com; 28 rue de Verdun; ⏰9am-6pm or 7pm Mon-Sat, 9am-noon or 1pm Sun) or its **annexe** (Porte Narbonnaise).

The old city is dramatically illuminated at night and enclosed by two **rampart walls** punctuated by 52 stone towers, Europe's largest city fortifications. Successive generations of Gauls, Romans, Visigoths, Moors, Franks and Cathars reinforced the walls, but only the lower sections are original; the rest, including the turrets, were stuck on by the 19th-century architect Viollet-le-Duc.

A drawbridge leads to the old gate of **Porte Narbonnaise** and rue Cros Mayrevieille en route to place Château and the 12th-century **Château Comtal** (adult €8.50; ⏰10am-6.30pm Apr-Sep). Admission includes a castle meander, a short film and an optional 30- to 40-minute guided tour of the ramparts (tours in English July and August). South is **Basilique St-Nazaire** (⏰9-11.45am & 1.45-5pm or 5.30pm), illuminated by delicate medieval rose windows.

Carcassonne is on the main rail line to/from Toulouse (€14, 50 minutes).

Nîmes

POP 146,500

This buzzy city boasts some of France's best-preserved classical buildings, including a famous Roman amphitheatre, although the city is most famous for its sartorial export, *serge de Nîmes* – better-known to cowboys, clubbers and couturiers as denim.

Buy a **combination ticket** (adult €9.90), valid for three days, covering all three of Nîmes major sights. Buy one at the first sight you visit.

Sights

Nîmes' magnificent Roman amphitheatre, **Les Arènes** (adult €7.80; ⏰9am-6.30pm), the best preserved in the Roman Empire, was built around AD 100 to seat up to 24,000 spectators.

The **Maison Carrée** (Square House; place de la Maison Carrée; admission €4.50; ⏰10am-6.30pm) is a rectangular Roman temple, constructed around AD 5 to honour Emperor Augustus' two adopted sons. Opposite, the striking glass-and-steel facade of contemporary art museum **Carré d'Art** (www.carreeartmusee.com, in French; place de la Maison Carrée; permanent collection free, temporary exhibitions

DON'T MISS

FESTIVE NÎMES

Nîmes becomes more Spanish than French during its two *férias* (bullfighting festivals): the five-day **Féria de Pentecôte** (Whitsuntide Festival) in June, and the three-day **Féria des Vendanges** celebrating the grape harvest on the third weekend in September. Each is marked by daily *corridas* (bullfights). Buy tickets at the **Billeterie des Arènes** (www.arenesdenimes.com; 2 rue de la Violette).

WORTH A TRIP

PONT DU GARD

A Unesco World Heritage Site, this three-tiered Roman aqueduct is exceptionally well preserved. It's part of a 50km-long system of canals built about 19 BC by the Romans to bring water from near Uzès to Nîmes. The scale is huge: the 35 arches of the 275m-long upper tier, running 50m above the Gard River, contain a watercourse designed to carry 20,000 cubic metres of water per day and the largest construction blocks weigh over five tonnes.

Pick up an auduo guide (€6) from the **visitors centre** (www.pontdugard.fr; ⌚9.30am-7pm May-Sep, to 5pm or 6pm Oct-Apr) on the left, northern bank and allow around 1½ hours to take in the vast, hugely informative and innovative **Musée de la Romanité** inside. Afterwards, walk the **Mémoires de Garrigue**, a 1.4km trail with explanatory panels through typical Mediterranean bush and scrubland.

A day ticket covering the above plus parking in one of the car parks by the Gard River is €15 for up to five passengers (€10 November to March). In July and August pay an extra €2 to teeter along the aqueduct's top tier with a guide (every half-hour 10am to 11.30am and 2pm to 5.30pm). Admission to the site is free once the museum has closed.

The best view of the Pont du Gard is from upstream, beside the river, where you can swim on hot days.

adult €5; ⌚10am-6pm Tue-Sun) provides a dramatic contrast.

Sleeping

Hôtel Amphithéâtre HOTEL €
(☎04 66 67 28 51; http://perso.wanadoo.fr/hotel-amphitheatre; 4 rue des Arènes; s €41-45, d €53-70) A pair of 18th-century mansions, the Amphitheatre Hotel just down the road from its namesake has 15 rooms, each named after a writer or painter. Montesquieu and Arrabal have a balcony.

Auberge de Jeunesse HOSTEL €
(☎04 66 68 03 20; www.hinimes.com; 257 chemin de l'Auberge de Jeunesse, La Cigale; dm/d €13.50/34; ⌚Feb-Dec) This sterling, well-equipped hostel with self-catering facilities has houses for two to six in its extensive grounds as well as regular dorms. Find it 3.5km northwest of the train station; take bus I, direction Alès or Villeverte, to the Stade stop.

Eating

Nîmes' gastronomy owes as much to Provence as to Languedoc. Look out for *cassoulet* (pork, sausage and white-bean stew, sometimes served with duck), aïoli and *rouille* (a spicy chilli mayonnaise).

Au Plaisir des Halles FRENCH €€
(☎04 66 36 01 02; 4 rue Littré; mains €24-30; ⌚Tue-Sat) Near the covered market, ingredients here are locally sourced and the lunchtime three-course *menu* (€20) is excellent value. Local winegrowers feature both on the walls and in the wine racks.

Le Marché sur la Table FRENCH €€
(☎04 66 67 22 50; 10 rue Littré; mains €17-19; ⌚Wed-Sun) You *could* just pop in for a glass of wine at this first-class bistro, but you'd be missing out on Éric Vidal's market-fuelled food. Dining in the quiet rear courtyard is delightful.

Le 9 FRENCH €€
(☎04 66 21 80 77; 9 rue de l'Étoile; mains €15-18; ⌚Mon-Sat & lunch Sun May-Sep) Have a meal or drop in for a drink at this mildly eccentric place, tucked behind high green doors. Eat in vast, arched former stables or in the leafy, vine-clad courtyard.

Information

Tourist office (☎04 66 58 38 00; www.ot-nimes.fr; 6 rue Auguste; ⌚8.30am-6.30pm Mon-Fri, 9am-6.30pm Sat, 10am-5pm Sun)

Getting There & Away

Air

Ryanair is the only airline to use Nîmes' **airport** (☎04 66 70 49 49), 10km southeast of the city on the A54.

Bus

Bus station (☎04 66 38 59 43; rue Ste-Félicité) Has services to Pont du Gard (€1.50, 30 minutes, two to seven daily) and Uzès (€1.50, 45 minutes, four to 10 daily).

Train

Services go to Avignon (€8.50, 30 minutes), Marseille (€19, 1¼ hours) and Paris' Gare de Lyon (€52 to €99.70, three hours).

PROVENCE

Provence conjures up images of rolling lavender fields, blue skies, gorgeous villages, wonderful food and superb wine. It certainly delivers on all those fronts, but dig deeper and discover multicultural Marseille, artistic Aix-en-Provence and Roman Arles.

Marseille

POP 860,350

There was a time when Marseille was the butt of French jokes. No more. The *cité phocéenne* has undergone a vast makeover. Marseillais will tell you that the city's rough-and-tumble edginess is part of its charm and that, for all its flaws, it is a very endearing place. They're right: Marseille grows on you with its unique history, souqlike markets, millennia-old port and spectacular *corniches* (coastal roads) – good reasons indeed why Marseille was chosen as European Capital of Culture in 2013.

Sights

The **Marseille City Pass** (1-/2-day pass €22/29) gets you admission to Marseille's museums, a guided tour of town, unlimited public transport travel, a boat trip, entrance to Château d'If and a load of discounts. Buy it at the tourist office.

Vieux Port OLD PORT

Ships have docked for more than 26 centuries at Marseille's colourful Vieux Port (Old Port). Although the main commercial docks were transferred to the Joliette area on the coast north of here in the 1840s, it still overflows with fishing craft, yachts and local ferries. Wedged between restaurants on the cafe-lined quays is the **La Maison du Pastis** (108 quai du Port), a distillery where you can sample 90 varieties of the local aniseed-flavoured firewater, pastis.

Basilique Notre Dame de la Garde BASILICA

(Montée de la Bonne Mère; 7am-7pm, longer hrs summer) Be blown away by the celestial views and knock-out 19th-century architecture at this hilltop Romano-Byzantine basilica dominating Marseille's skyline. Built between 1853 and 1864 it is ornamented with coloured marble, murals and mosaics. From the Vixu Port, ride bus 60 1km south or walk up (30 minutes).

Château d'If CASTLE

(adult/child €5/free; 9.30am-6.30pm, shorter hrs & closed Mon winter) Immortalised in Alexandre Dumas' 1840s novel *Le Comte de Monte Cristo* (The Count of Monte Cristo), the 16th-century island prison of Château d'If played host to political prisoners of all persuasions, along with Protestants, the Revolutionary hero Mirabeau and the Communards of 1871. **Frioul If Express** (www.frioul-if-express.com; 1 quai des Belges, 1er; €10, 20 minutes) boats sail from the corner of quai de la Fraternité and quai de Rive Neuve at the Vieux Port.

TOP CHOICE **Le Panier** HISTORIC QUARTER

North of the Vieux Port, Le Panier (The Basket) was the site of the Greek *agora* (marketplace). Today, its narrow streets are a jumble of old stone houses, candy-coloured wooden shutters and artisans' shops. Be prepared to get lost and don't miss the stunning **Centre de la Vieille Charité** (2 rue de la Charité, 2e; M Joliette), a former charity shelter home to a twinset of museums covering Mediterranean archeology and African, Oceanic and American indigenous art. Later, hang out at a cafe on people-watching **place de Lenche**.

Sleeping

Vertigo BOUTIQUE HOSTEL €

(04 91 91 07 11; www.hotelvertigo.fr; 42 rue des Petites Maries, 1er; dm €25-27, d €60-70; @; M Gare St-Charles SNCF) This snappy boutique hostel kisses goodbye to dodgy bunks and hospital-like decor, and says 'hello' to vintage posters, designer chrome kitchen, groovy communal spaces and polite multilingual staff.

Hôtel Saint-Ferréol HOTEL €€

(04 91 33 12 21; www.hotelsaintferreol.com; 19 rue Pisançon, 1er; d €99-120; @; M Vieux Port) On the corner of the city's prettiest pedestrianised street, this plush hotel has individually decorated rooms inspired by artists. Service is exceptional.

Hôtel Le Richelieu BEACH HOTEL €€

(04 91 31 01 92; www.lerichelieu-marseille.com; 52 corniche Président John F Kennedy, 7e; d €53-88, tr €91-110; @) The best rooms at this economical seaside place face the sea, lending the place a beach-house feel. Breakfast on the water-view terrace is idyllic.

WORTH A TRIP

LES CALANQUES

Marseille abuts the wild and spectacular Les Calanques, a protected 20km stretch of high, rocky promontories rising from the bright turquoise sea. Sheer cliffs are occasionally interrupted by idyllic beach-fringed coves, many only possible to reach with kayak. The area has been protected since 1975 and is slated to become a national park by 2011.

Calanque de Sormiou is the largest rocky inlet with two seasonal restaurants cooking up fabulous views: **Le Château** (☎04 91 25 08 69; mains €18-24; ⏰Apr–mid-Oct) – with better food – and **Le Lunch** (☎04 91 25 05 39, 04 91 25 05 37; http://wp.resto.fr/lelunch; mains €16-28; ⏰Apr–mid-Oct) – nearer the water – both require advance reservation. By bus, take No 23 from the Rond Point du Prado metro stop in Marseille to La Cayolle, from where it's a 3km walk (note diners with a table reservation can drive through; otherwise, the road is open to cars weekdays only September to June).

Marseille's tourist office leads guided hikes in Les Calanques and has information on walking trails (shut July and August due to forest-fire risk). For great views from out at sea hop aboard a boat trip to the wine-producing port of **Cassis** (www.ot-cassis.com), 30km east along the coast, with **Croisières Marseille Calanques** (www.croisieres-marseille-calanques.com, in French; 74 quai du Port).

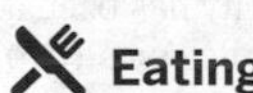

Eating

The Vieux Port overflows with restaurants, but choose carefully. Head to Cours Julien and its surrounding streets for world cuisine; and to the near Marché des Capucins area for cheap-eat pizza and couscous (under €10).

The small but enthralling **fish market** (quai des Belges; ⏰8am-1pm; Ⓜ Vieux Port) is a daily fixture at the Vieux Port. **Cours Julien** hosts a Wednesday-morning organic fruit and vegetable market, and **Prado Market** (av du Prado; ⏰8am-1pm; Ⓜ Castellane or Périer) is the place to go for anything and everything other than food.

When in Marseille eat *bouillabaisse* (fish stew) and *supions* (squid pan-fried with garlic, parsley and lemon).

Jardin des Vestiges ARMENIAN-MEDITERRANEAN €
(15 rue Reine Elizabeth, 1er; mains €7-13; ⏰9am-6pm Mon-Sat; Ⓜ Vieux Port) Our favourite budget choice draws on Armenian, Greek and Lebanese kitchens to create dishes such as kebabs, stuffed eggplant, moussaka and tabbouleh. Buy to-go sandwiches here (€4 to €6) before boarding an island ferry.

Pizzaria Chez Étienne MARSEILLAIS, ITALIAN €€
(43 rue de Lorette, 2e; mains €12-15; ⏰Mon-Sat; Ⓜ Colbert) This family-style neighbourhood haunt serves Marseille's best wood-fired pizza, beef steak and *supions* (pan-fried squid). Pop in beforehand to reserve in person (no phone). No credit cards.

La Cantinetta ITALIAN €€
(☎04 91 48 10 48; 24 cours Julien; mains €9-19; ⏰Tue-Sat; Ⓜ Notre Dame du Mont-Cours Julien) Our top choice on cours Julien serves perfectly *al dente* housemade pasta and other Italian goodies. Tables inside are cheek-by-jowl; we prefer the sun-dappled, tiled patio garden.

DON'T MISS

MARSEILLE SPLURGE!

Chez Madie Les Galinettes (☎04 91 90 40 87; 138 quai du Port, 2e; menus €25-35; ⏰Mon-Sat, closed Sat lunch in summer; Ⓜ Vieux Port) is a port-side terrace that's always packed, as is the arty interior when the weather isn't cooperating. *Bouillabaisse* needs to be ordered 48 hours ahead.

Drinking & Entertainment

Options for a coffee and something stronger abound on both Vieux Port quays, cours Honoré d'Estienne d'Orves and place de la Préfecture.

La Caravelle BAR
(34 quai du Port, 2e; ⏰7am-2am; Ⓜ Vieux Port) Look up or miss this upstairs hideaway with miniature portside terrace. Live jazz Friday from 9pm.

TOP CHOICE **La Part des Anges** WINE BAR
(33 rue Sainte; mains €15, ⏰lunch Mon-Sat, dinner daily) The wine list at this happening wine bar and restaurant is an oenologist's dream.

Dame Noir BAR

(30 place Notre Dame de Mont, 6e; 5pm-2am Tue-Sat; Notre Dame du Mont-Cours Julien) Hip cats spill onto the pavement from this neighbourhood bar. DJs spin Thursday to Saturday. No sign; look for the red lights by the door.

Information

Dangers & Annoyances

Petty crimes and muggings are common. Avoid the Belsunce area (southwest of the train station, bounded by La Canebière, cours Belsunce and rue d'Aix, rue Bernard du Bois and blvd d'Athènes) at night. Walking La Canebiére is annoying (expect to encounter kids peddling hash), but generally not dangerous.

Tourist information

Tourist Office (04 91 13 89 00; www.marseille-tourisme.com; 4 La Canebière, 1er; 9am-7pm Mon-Sat, 10am-5pm Sun; Vieux Port)

Getting There & Away

Air

Aéroport Marseille-Provence (www.marseille.aeroport.fr), 25km northwest in Marignane, has numerous budget flights to various European destinations. **Shuttle buses** (Marseille 04 91 50 59 34; airport 04 42 14 31 27; www.lepilote.com; €8.50; 25 minutes, every 20 minutes 5am-11.30pm) link the airport with Marseille train station.

Boat

Gare Maritime (passenger ferry terminal; www.marseille-port.fr; Joliette)

SNCM (www.sncm.fr; 61 blvd des Dames, 2e; Joliette) Ferries to/from Corsica, Sardinia, Algeria and Tunisia.

Bus

The **bus station** (3 rue Honnorat, 3e; Gare St-Charles) is behind the train station.

AIX-EN-PROVENCE €4.90, 35 to 60 minutes, every five to 10 minutes

AVIGNON €18.50, two hours, one daily

CANNES €25, two hours, up to three daily

NICE €26.50, three hours, up to three daily

Train

From Marseille's **Gare St-Charles** trains serve France and Europe:

AVIGNON €22.80, 35 minutes, 27 daily

LYON €47.30, 1¾ hours, 16 daily

NICE €29.70, 2½ hours, 21 daily

PARIS' GARE DE LYON €84.20, three hours, 21 daily

Getting Around

Pick up a bicycle from more than 100 bike stations across the city with **Le Vélo** (www.levelo-mpm.fr); the first 30 minutes are free, then pay €1/1 for the next 30 minutes/per hour after that.

Marseille has two metro lines, two tram lines and an extensive bus network, all run by **RTM** (6 rue des Fabres, 1er; 8.30am-6pm Mon-Fri, 9am-12.30pm & 2-5.30pm Sat; Vieux Port) where you can obtain information and transport tickets (€1.50).

Aix-en-Provence

POP 146,700

Aix-en-Provence is to Provence what the Left Bank is to Paris: a pocket of bohemian chic with an edgy student crowd. It's hard to believe Aix (pronounced 'ex') is just 25km from chaotic, exotic Marseille. The city has been a cultural centre since the Middle Ages (two of the town's most famous sons are painter Paul Cézanne and novelist Émile Zola) but for all its polish, it's a laid-back Provençal town at heart.

Aix's annual **Festival d'Aix-en-Provence** (www.festival-aix.com), held late June to mid-July, lures some of the world's best classical music, opera, ballet and buskers.

Sights

Circuit de Cézanne ARTIST TRAIL

Art, culture, and architecture abound in Aix thanks to local lad Paul Cézanne (1839–1906). See where he ate, drank, studied and painted along this walking trail, marked by footpath-embedded bronze plaques inscribed with the letter C. Grab the explanatory brochure at the tourist office.

The trail takes in Cézanne's last studio, **Atelier Paul Cézanne** (www.atelier-cezanne.com; 9 av Paul Cézanne; adult €5.50; 10am-noon & 2-6pm, closed Sun winter), 1.5km north of the tourist office; family home, **Bastide du Jas de Bouffan**, where Cézanne started painting; and the **Bibémus quarries**, where he did most of his Montagne Ste-Victoire paintings. Book at the tourist office.

Musée Granet ART GALLERY

(www.museegranet-aixenprovence.fr, in French; place St-Jean de Malte; adult €4; 11am-7pm Tue-Sun) In a 17th-century priory, this gallery's pride and joy is its Cézanne collection and works by Picasso, Léger, Matisse, Tal Coat and Giacometti.

AIX SPLURGE!

Fancy a haddock milkshake, duck sushi, or thyme-and-cinnamon apple tart with Baileys whipped cream? Try **Le Poivre d'Ane** (☎04 42 21 32 66; www.restaurantlepoivredane.com; 40 place des Cardeurs; menus €28-45; ⊙dinner Thu-Tue), with summer tables smack dab on one of Aix's loveliest pedestrian squares; reservations essential.

Sleeping

Book accommodation through the **Centrale de Réservation** (☎04 42 16 11 84; www.aixenprovencetourism.com).

Auberge de Jeunesse du Jas de Bouffan HOSTEL €
(☎04 42 20 15 99; www.auberge-jeunesse-aix.fr; 3 av Marcel Pagnol; dm incl breakfast & sheets €19-22; ⊙reception 7am-2.30pm & 4.30pm-midnight, closed mid-Dec–Jan) Shiny new with a bar, tennis courts, bike shed and massive summer BBQs, this HI hostel is 2km west of the centre; shame about the motorway. Take bus 4 from La Rotonde to the Vasarely stop.

Hôtel Cardinal HOTEL €
(☎04 42 38 32 30; www.hotel-cardinal-aix.com; 24 rue Cardinale; s/d €60/70) Beneath stratospheric ceilings, Hôtel Cardinal's 29 romantic rooms are beautifully furnished with antiques, tasselled curtains, and newly tiled bathrooms.

Eating & Drinking

Aix' sweet treat is marzipan-like *calisson d'Aix*. Daily **produce market** (place Richelme) sells olives, goat's cheese, garlic, lavender, honey, peaches, melons and other sun-kissed products.

Le Petit Verdot FRENCH €€
(☎04 42 27 30 12; www.lepetitverdot.fr; 7 rue Entrecasteaux; mains €15-25; ⊙dinner Mon-Sat, lunch Sat) Wine is the focus at this earthy restaurant, where tabletops are cast-off wine crates. Fun when you're feeling festive.

La Chimère Café SUPPER CLUB €€
(☎04 42 38 30 00; www.lachimerecafe.com; 15 rue Brueys; menus €28-32) Aix's party crowd laps up the cabaret atmosphere of this former nightclub: starry-night vaulted ceiling in the underground room; grand chandeliers with crimson, velvety furnishings on the main floor. Food is classic French.

Information

Tourist office (www.aixenprovencetourism.com; 2 place du Général de Gaulle; ⊙8.30am-7pm Mon-Sat, 10am-1pm & 2-6pm Sun, longer hrs summer)

Getting There & Away

BUS From Aix' **bus station** (av de l'Europe), a 10-minute walk southwest from La Rotonde, destinations include Marseille (€4.90, 35 minutes via the autoroute or one hour via the D8), Arles (€9, 1½ hours) and Avignon (€14.70, 1¼ hours).

Half-hourly shuttle buses go to/from Aix TGV station and Aéroport Marseille-Provence.

TRAIN The only useful train from Aix' **city centre train station** (av Victor Hugo) is to/from Marseille (€7, 50 minutes). Other services use **Aix TGV station**, 15km away.

Avignon

POP 93,560

Hooped by 4.3km of superbly preserved, 14th-century stone ramparts, this graceful city is the belle of Provence's ball. Famed for its annual performing-arts festival and its fabled bridge, the Pont St-Bénezet (aka the Pont d'Avignon), Avignon is an ideal spot from which to step out into the surrounding region.

Early July to early August is the time to hit Avignon when hundreds of artists take to the stage and streets during its world-famous **Festival d'Avignon** (www.festival-avignon.com) and fringe **Festival Off** (☎04 90 85 13 08; www.avignonleoff.com, in French).

Sights

Pont St-Bénezet BRIDGE
(adult €4.50; ⊙9am-8pm Apr-Oct, 9.30am-5.45pm Nov-Mar) This fabled bridge, immortalised in the French nursery rhyme *Sur le Pont d'Avignon,* was completed in 1185. The 900m-long wooden bridge was repaired and rebuilt several times before all but four of its 22 spans were washed away in the 1600s. View it for free from the Rocher des Doms park, Pont Édouard Daladier or from across the river on Île de la Barthelasse.

Palais des Papes PAPAL PALACE
(www.palais-des-papes.com; place du Palais; admission €6; ⊙9am-9pm Aug, less hrs rest of the year) This Unesco World Heritage Site, the world's largest Gothic palace, was built when Pope Clement V abandoned Rome in 1309 and settled in Avignon.

Musée Angladon ART GALLERY
(www.angladon.com; 5 rue Laboureur; admission €6; ⌚1-6pm Tue-Sun Apr-Nov, 1-6pm Wed-Sun Jan-Mar, closed Dec) This charming museum harbours impressionist treasures, including the only Van Gogh painting in Provence *(Railway Wagons)*, and works by Cézanne, Manet, Degas and Picasso.

Sleeping

YMCA-UCJG HOSTEL €
(☎04 90 25 46 20; www.ymca-avignon.com; 7bis chemin de la Justice; dm with/without bathroom

Avignon

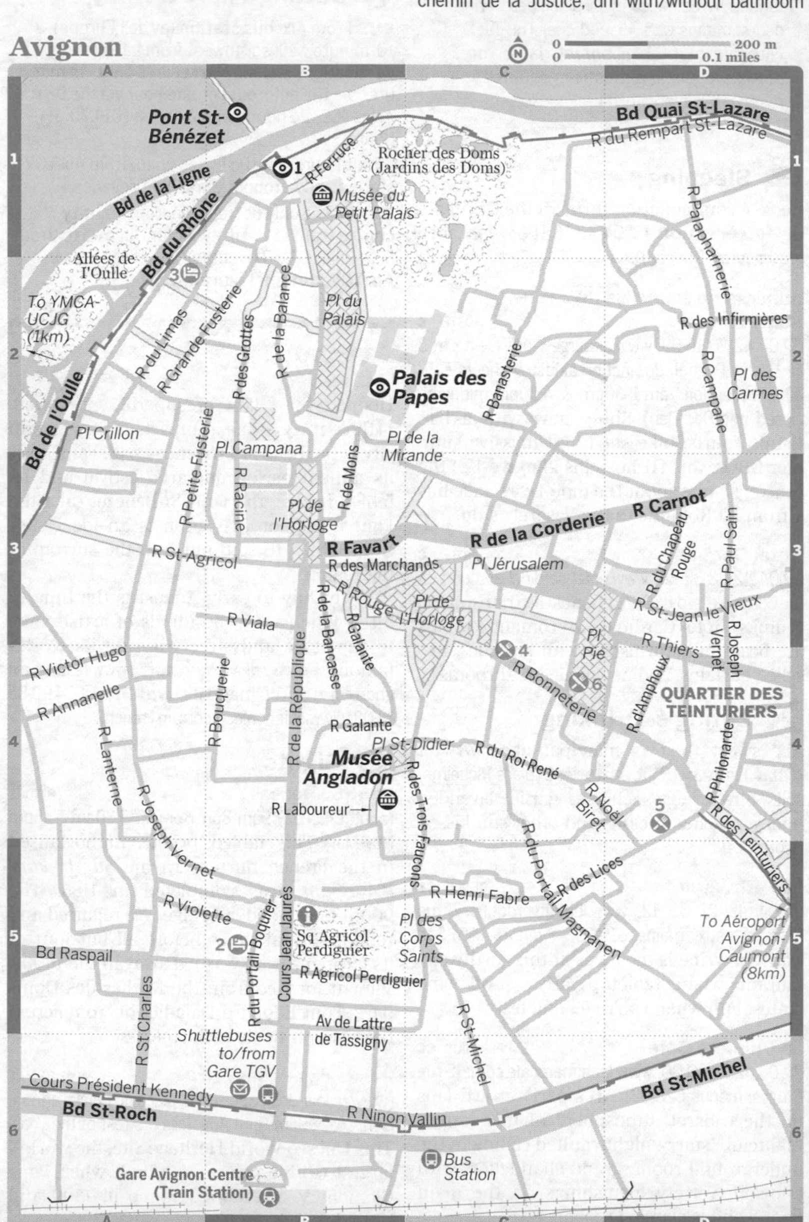

€36/25; ⏲reception 8.30am-6pm, closed Dec-early Jan; 📶🏊) This spotless hostel across the river has some private rooms and a swimming pool and terrace with panoramic views of the city. Take bus 10 to the Monteau stop.

Hôtel Boquier HOTEL €
(☎04 90 82 34 43; www.hotel-boquier.com, in French; 6 rue du Portail Boquier; d €50-70; ❄📶) The infectious enthusiasm of owners Sylvie and Pascal Sendra sweeps through this central little place that's bright, airy and spacious.

Le Limas B&B €€
(☎04 90 14 67 19; www.le-limas-avignon.com; 51 rue du Limas; d/tr incl breakfast from €120/200; ❄@) Behind its discreet lavender door, this chic address in an 18th-century town house is everything interior designers strive for when mixing old and new. Breakfast is by the fireplace or on a sun-drenched terrace!

Eating

Cuisine du Dimanche PROVENÇAL €€
(☎04 90 82 99 10; 31 rue Bonneterie; mains €15-25; ⏲closed Sun & Mon Oct-May) Spitfire chef Marie shops every morning at Les Halles (p463) to find the freshest ingredients for her earthy flavour-packed cooking. Specialities include scallops and simple roast chicken with pan gravy.

L'Epice and Love FRENCH €
(☎04 90 82 45 96; 30 rue des Lices; mains €11-12; ⏲dinner Mon-Sat) Stews, roasts and other home-style French dishes is what make this tiny bohemian restaurant, decorated with antique kitchenware and mismatched chairs, so appealing. No credit cards.

Avignon

Top Sights
- Musée Angladon B4
- Palais des Papes B2
- Pont St-Bénézet B1

Sights
- 1 Pont St-Bénézet Entrance B1

Sleeping
- 2 Hôtel Boquier B5
- 3 Le Limas A2

Eating
- 4 Cuisine du Dimanche C4
- 5 L'Epice and Love D4
- 6 Les Halles C4

DON'T MISS

LES HALLES

There is no better spot to shop for that perfect Provence picnic to scoff atop bluff-top park **Rocher des Doms** (with tasty views of the Rhône, Avignon and and Mont Ventoux) than at the market. Bursting with local life and an artsy vegetal wall by green designer Patrick Blanc (of Paris' Musée du Quai Branly fame), **Les Halles** (place Pie; ⏲7am-1pm Tue-Sun) is a gourmand paradise of local seasonal produce. Learn how to cook at 11am each Saturday with **La Petite Cuisine des Halles**; details online.

Information

Tourist office (www.avignon-tourisme.com; 41 cours Jean Jaurès; ⏲9am-5pm Mon-Sat, 9.45am-5pm Sun)

Getting There & Away

Air

Aéroport Avignon-Caumont (www.avignon.aeroport.fr), 8km southeast, has seasonal flights to/from Britain and Ireland.

Bus

Services from the **bus station** (blvd St-Roch), down the ramp to the right as you exit the train station include Aix-en-Provence (€14, 1¼ hours), Arles (€7.70, 1½ hours), Marseille (€20, two hours) and Nîmes (€8.10, 1¼ hours).

Train

Avignon has two stations: **Gare Avignon TGV**, 4km southwest in Courtine; and central **Gare Avignon Centre** (blvd St-Roch) with trains to/from Arles (€6.70, 20 minutes) and Nîmes (€8.70, 30 minutes).

Some TGVs to/from Paris stop at Gare Avignon Centre, but TGVs for Marseille (€22.80, 35 minutes) and Nice (€54.40, three hours) only use Gare Avignon TGV.

FRENCH RIVIERA & MONACO

With its glistening seas, idyllic beaches and lush hills, the French Riviera (Côte d'Azur in French) screams exclusivity, extravagance and excess. It's long been a favourite getaway for the European jetset, and there is nowhere more chichi or glam in France than St-Tropez, Cannes and super-rich, sovereign Monaco.

DON'T MISS

THE CORNICHES

Some of the Riviera's most spectacular scenery stretches from Nice to Monaco. A trio of *corniches* (coastal roads) hugs the cliffs between the two seaside cities, each higher up the hill than the last. The middle corniche ends in Monaco; the upper and lower continue to Menton near the French–Italian border.

But it's not just a high-roller's playground. Every year millions of visitors descend on the southern French coast to bronze their bodies, smell the lavender and soak up that hip Mediterranean vibe.

Nice

POP 352,400

Riviera queen Nice is what good living is all about – shimmering shores, the very best of Mediterranean food, a unique historical heritage, free museums, a charming old town, exceptional art and Alpine wilderness within an hour's drive. No wonder so many young French people aspire to live here while the tourists just keep flooding in.

To get stuck in straight away, make a beeline upon arrival for Promenade des Anglais, Nice's curvacious palm-lined seafront that follows its busy pebble beach for 6km from the city centre to airport.

Nice's exuberant **Carnaval de Nice** (www.nicecarnaval.com) in February is France's largest street carnival.

Sights

Vieux Nice OLD TOWN

Ditch the map and lose yourself in the old town's tangle of 18th-century pedestrian passages and alleyways, historic churches and hole-in-the-wall joints selling Niçois tapas. Cours Saleya, running parallel to the seafront, hosts one of France's most vibrant, vividly hued **food markets** (6am-1.30pm Tue-Sun). Baroque **Cathédrale Ste-Réparate** (place Rossetti) with its glazed terracotta dome (1650), and **Chapelle de la Miséricorde** (cours Saleya) are equally exuberant. At the eastern end of quai des États-Unis, steep steps and a **cliffside lift** (€1.10; 9am-7pm Apr-Sep, shorter hrs rest year) climb to **Parc du Château**, a hilltop park with great views over Old Nice and the beachfront.

Musée Matisse MUSEUM

(www.musee-matisse-nice.org; 164 av des Arènes de Cimiez; 10am-6pm Wed-Mon) Housed in a 17th-century Genoese mansion, this small museum reveals Matisse's evolution as an artist rather than wowing the crowds with masterpieces. Take bus 17 from the bus station or bus 22 from place Masséna to the Arènes stop.

MAMAC MODERN ART GALLERY

(www.mamac-nice.org; promenade des Arts; 10am-6pm Tue-Sun) This one is worth it for its stunning architecture alone. Inside, enjoy Roy Lichtenstein, Andy Warhol's 1965 *Campbell's Soup Can* and other avant-garde art from the 1960s to the present. End on the fab rooftop garden-gallery.

Musée National Message Biblique Marc Chagall ART GALLERY

(www.musee-chagall.fr, in French; 4 av Dr Ménard; admission €7.50; 10am-5pm Wed-Mon Oct-Jun, to 6pm Jul-Sep) This small museum houses the largest public collection of the Russian-born artist's seminal paintings of *Old Testament* scenes.

Beaches BEACH

Free sections of pebble beach alternate with 15 sunlounge-lined **private beaches** (www.plagesdenice.com, in French; May-Sep) where you pay to rent a sunlounger (around €15 per day). On the beach, operators rent catamarans, paddleboats and jet skis; you can also parascend, waterski or paraglide.

WORTH A TRIP

THE PINE CONE TRAIN

Chugging between mountains and the sea, narrow-gauge railway **Train des Pignes** (Pine Cone Train; www.trainprovence.com) is one of France's most picturesque train rides. Rising to 1000m, with breathtaking views, the 151km-long track between Nice and **Digne-les-Bains** passes through the scarcely populated back country of little known Haute Provence. The train departs from **Nice CP** (Chemins de Fer de Provence; 4bis rue Alfred Binet).

Day trip suggestion: a picnic and meander around the historical centre and citadel of the beautiful medieval village of **Entrevaux** (€18 return, 1½ hours).

Tramway Art ART
From original soundbites at tram stops to futuristic art installations and local artist Ben's stop-name calligraphy, Nice's tramway is one big work of art. Of the 13 world artists who made it happen, Barcelona artist Jaume Plensa's *The Conversation* stands out the most. But don't mistake his seven glowing figures squatting overhead on lamp posts on place Masséna (av Jean Jaurès) as Buddhas. Each represents the earth's continents, changing colours in time with each other to symbolise world dialogue.

Sleeping

TOP CHOICE **Villa Saint-Exupéry** HOSTEL €
(04 93 84 42 83; www.villahostels.com; 22 av Gravier; dm €25-30, s/d €45/90; @) Why can't all hostels be like this? Set in a converted monastery 4km northwest of the city centre, this backpacker's palace features a 24-hour common room, state-of-the-art-kitchens, BBQ terraces and lovely dorms; staff even pick up guests from the nearby Comte de Falicon tram stop or St Maurice stop for bus 23 (from the airport).

TOP CHOICE **Hôtel Wilson** BOUTIQUE HOTEL €
(04 93 85 47 79; www.hotel-wilson-nice.com; 39 rue de l'Hôtel des Postes; s/d €50/55;) Many years of travelling, an experimental nature and exquisite taste have turned Jean-Marie's rambling flat into a compelling place to stay. Mind the two resident tortoises as you sit down for breakfast.

Hôtel Armenonville HOTEL €€
(04 93 96 86 00; www.hotel-armenonville.com; 20 av des Fleurs; d €86-105; @) Shielded by its large garden, this grand early-20th-century mansion has sober rooms, three (12, 13 and 14) with huge terrace overlooking the garden.

NICE SPLURGE

Hôtel Windsor BOUTIQUE HOTEL €€
(04 93 88 59 35; www.hotelwindsor nice.com; 11 rue Dalpozzo; d €120-175; @) Graffiti casts aggressive splashes of colour on the edgy, oversize rooms of the Windsor – a real nod to contemporary art. Rooms overlooking the backyard tropical garden have a particularly lush view.

Belle Meunière HOSTEL €
(04 93 88 66 15; www.bellemeuniere.com; 21 av Durante; dm €18-24, d €55-62;) Great for unfussy guests, but the street outside is loud and there's no double glazing.

Auberge de Jeunesse Les Camélias HOSTEL €
(04 93 62 15 54; www.fuaj.org, in French; 3 rue Spitaleri; dm incl breakfast & sheets €23; @) Clean, spacious dorms, a bar, a self-catering kitchen and a laundry; midday lockout (11am to 3pm) but no night curfew.

Eating

Traditional Niçois tapas-styled nibbles include *socca* (a thin layer of chickpea flour and olive oil batter), *salade niçoise* and *farcis* (stuffed vegetables). Restaurants in Vieux Nice are a mixed bag.

For locals a quick bite is a *pan bagnat* (loosely translated as sopped bread), the local version of a tuna sandwich made with crusty round bread, chunks of cold tuna, lettuce, tomatoes, onions, radish and egg, all drizzled with loads' olive oil. The best come from port-side snack-bar **La Gratta** (2 blvd Franck Pilatte; sandwiches €4.50; lunch). Dangle your feet over the quay and watch masts bob in the harbour while olive oil drips down your chin...

Chez René Socca NIÇOIS €
(2 rue Miralhéti; dishes from €2; 9am-9pm Tue-Sun, to 10.30pm Jul & Aug, closed Nov) This address is about taste, not presentation or even manners. Grab some *socca* or *petits farçis* and head across the street to the bar for a *grand pointu* (glass) of red, white or rosé as the perfect accompaniment.

Zucca Magica VEGETARIAN €€
(04 93 56 25 27; www.lazuccamagica.com; 4bis quai Papacino; menus €30; Tue-Sat) The 'Magic Pumpkin' is a rarity in France – a vegetarian restaurant that nonvegetarians like! Bring an appetite: fixed-price meals comprise four set dishes (five for dinner) plus dessert, all sourced from the market.

La Table Alziari NIÇOIS €
(04 93 80 34 03, 4 rue François Zanin; mains €9-15, Tue-Sat) Run by the grandson of the famous Alziari olive oil family, this citrus-coloured restaurant chalks up local specialities such as *morue à la niçoise* (cod served with potatoes, olives and a tomato sauce) and *daube* (stew) on its blackboard.

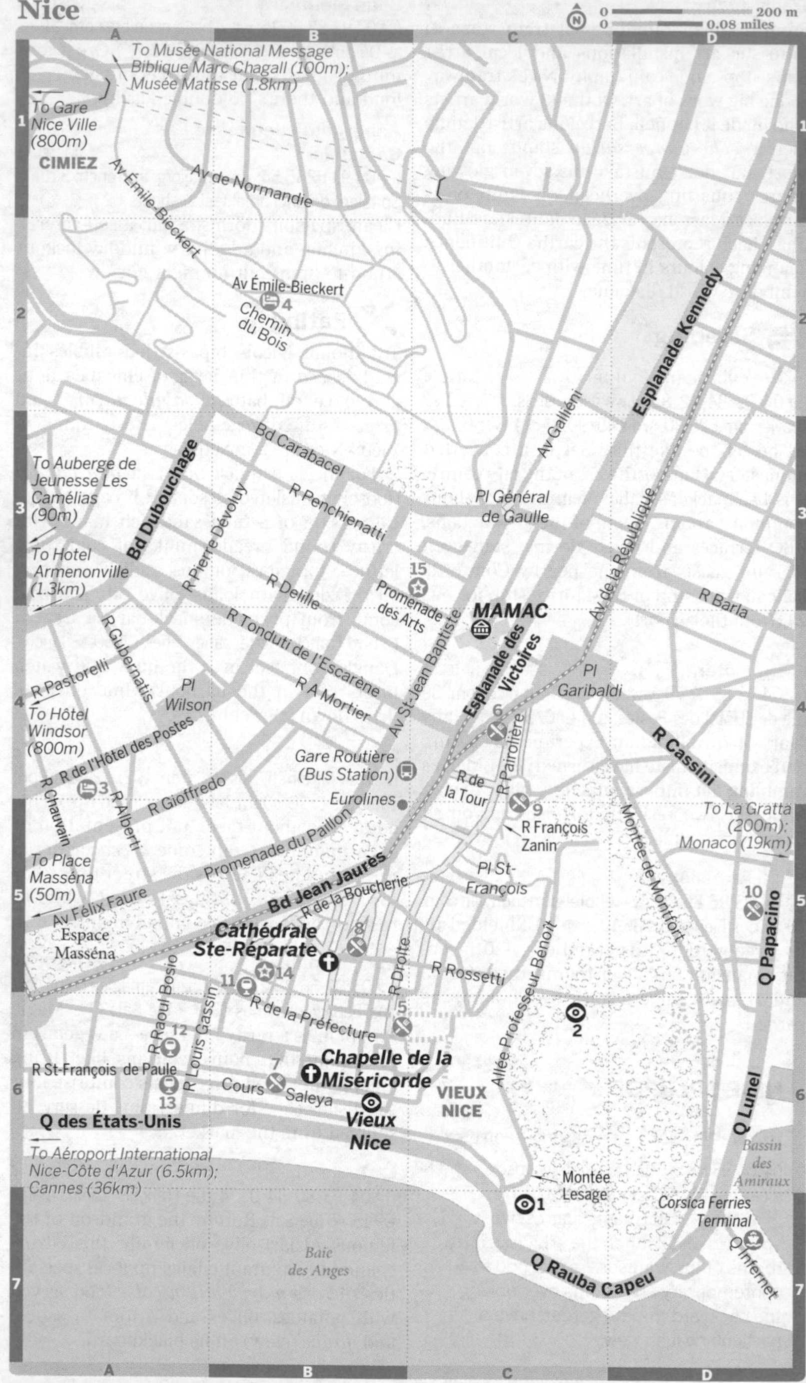

0 200 m
0 0.08 miles
To Musée National Message Biblique Marc Chagall (100m); Musée Matisse (1.8km)
To Gare Nice Ville (800m)
CIMIEZ
Av Émile-Bieckert
Av de Normandie
Av Émile-Bieckert
4
Chemin du Bois
Esplanade Kennedy
Av Gallieni
Bd Carabacel
To Auberge de Jeunesse Les Camélias (90m)
Bd Dubouchage
R Penchienatti
R Pierre Devoluy
Pl Général de Gaulle
Av de la République
To Hotel Armenonville (1.3km)
15
Promenade des Arts
R Delille
MAMAC
R Barla
R Gubernatis
R Tonduti de l'Escarène
Av St-Jean Baptiste
Esplanade des Victoires
R Pastorelli
Pl Wilson
R A Mortier
Pl Garibaldi
To Hôtel Windsor (800m)
6
R Cassini
R de l'Hôtel des Postes
R Pairolière
Gare Routière (Bus Station)
R de la Tour
R Chauvain
3
R Gioffredo
R Alberti
Eurolines
9
R François Zanin
To La Gratta (200m); Monaco (19km)
Promenade du Paillon
Montée de Montfort
To Place Masséna (50m)
Bd Jean Jaurès
Pl St-François
Av Félix Faure
R de la Boucherie
10
Q Papacino
Espace Masséna
Cathédrale Ste-Réparate
8
R Droite
R Rossetti
Allée Professeur Benoit
14
11
R Raoul Bosio
R Louis Gassin
R de la Préfecture
5
2
12
Chapelle de la Miséricorde
R St-François de Paule
7
Cours Saleya
VIEUX NICE
13
Q des États-Unis
Vieux Nice
Q Lunel
Bassin des Amiraux
To Aéroport International Nice-Côte d'Azur (6.5km); Cannes (36km)
Montée Lesage
1
Corsica Ferries Terminal
Baie des Anges
Q Rauba Capeu
Q Infernet
FRANCE

Acchiardo BISTRO €
(38 rue Droite; mains €14-20; ⌚Mon-Fri) Going strong since 1927, locals flock to Acchiardo for the *plat du jour* (daily special), a glass of wine and a load of gossip served straight up on the counter.

Drinking & Entertainment

Vieux Nice is stuffed with a host of bars and cafes.

Smarties LOUNGE BAR
(http://nicesmarties.free.fr; 10 rue Defly; ⌚6pm-2am Tue-Sat) We love Smarties' sexy-'70s swirly orange style, free buffet with happy hour (6pm to 9pm) and weekend DJs. It attracts a hot-looking straight-gay crowd.

Ma Nolan's PUB
(www.ma-nolans.com; 2 rue St François de Paule; ⌚noon-2am Mon-Fri, 11pm-2am Sat & Sun) Irish pub.

Le Six GAY BAR
(www.le6.fr; 6 rue Raoul Bosio; ⌚Tue-Sun 10pm-4:30am) Primped and pretty A-gays crowd in at Nice's compact, perennially popular 'mo bar. Climb the ladder to the mezzanine.

Chez Wayne's BAR
(www.waynes.fr; 15 rue de la Préfecture; ⌚2.30pm-12.30am) Raucous watering hole with live bands every night.

Le Bar des Oiseaux CABARET
(www.bardesoiseaux.com, in French; 5 rue St-Vincent; ⌚lunch Mon-Sat, dinner Tue-Sat) Artists dig this bohemian bar for live jazz, *chanson française* (French songs) and cabaret nights.

DON'T MISS

FENOCCHIO

Beat the summer heat with Nice's most fabulous *glacier* (ice-cream maker), **Fenocchio** (2 place Rossetti; from €2; ⌚9am-midnight Feb-Oct). Eschew predictable favourites and indulge in a new taste sensation: black olive, tomato-basil, rhubarb, avocado, rosemary, *calisson* (almond biscuit frosted with icing sugar), lavender, ginger or liquorice.

Information

Tourist Office (☎08 92 70 74 07; 5 promenade des Anglais; ⌚8am-8pm Mon-Sat, 9am-7pm Sun Jun-Sep, 9am-6pm Mon-Sat Oct-May) Right by the beach with an annexe at the train station.

Getting There & Away

Air

Aéroport International Nice-Côte d'Azur (www.nice.aeroport.fr), 6km west of the centre, is served by numerous carriers, including several low-cost ones.

Ligne d'Azur runs two airport buses (€4). Route 99 shuttles about every 30 minutes direct between Gare Nice Ville and both airport terminals from around 8am to 9pm daily. Route 98 takes the slow route and departs from the bus station every 20 minutes (30 minutes Sunday) from around 6am to around 9pm.

A second tram line is planned to connect Nice's centre with the airport.

Nice

Top Sights
- Cathédrale Ste-Réparate ... B5
- Chapelle de la Miséricorde ... B6
- MAMAC ... C4
- Vieux Nice ... B6

Sights
1 Cliffside Lift ... C7
2 Parc du Château ... C6

Sleeping
3 Hôtel Wilson ... A4
4 Le Petit Palais ... B2

Eating
5 Acchiardo ... B6
6 Chez René Socca ... C4
7 Cours Saleya Food Market ... B6
8 Fenocchio ... B5
9 La Table Alziari ... C5
10 Zucca Magica ... D5

Drinking
11 Chez Wayne's ... B5
12 Le Six ... A6
13 Ma Nolan's ... A6

Entertainment
14 Le Bar des Oiseaux ... B5
15 Smarties ... C3

Boat

The fastest, cheapest ferries to Corsica depart from Nice. Try **SNCM** (www.sncm.fr; ferry terminal, quai du Commerce) or **Corsica Ferries** (www.corsicaferries.com; quai Lunel).

Bus

From the **bus station** (5 blvd Jean Jaurès) a €1 fare takes you anywhere in the Alpes-Maritimes *département* (with a few exceptions, such as the airport) and includes one connection, within 74 minutes. Buses run daily to Cannes (1½ hours), Monaco (45 minutes) and Vence (one hour).

Eurolines (www.eurolines.com) operates from the bus station.

Train

From **Gare Nice Ville** (av Thiers), 1.2km north of the beach, frequent services include Cannes (€6.10, 40 minutes) and Monaco (€3.40, 20 minutes). Direct TGV trains serve with Paris' Gare de Lyon (€115, 5½ hours).

Between July and September, the SNCF's Carte Isabelle (€14) covers unlimited train trips in a single day (except TGV trains) from Fréjus to Ventimiglia in Italy, and from Nice inland to Tende.

Cannes

POP 71,800

Everyone's heard of Cannes and its celebrity two-week film festival in May. But the buzz and glitz linger all year thanks to celebrities who come here year-round to indulge in designer shopping, beaches and the palace hotels of the Riviera's glammest seafront, blvd de la Croisette.

Sights & Activities

The best public beaches are **Plages du Midi** and **Plages de la Bocca**, west from the Vieux Port along blvd Jean Hibert and blvd du Midi.

The **Musée de la Castre** (place de la Castre; adult €3.20; 10am-7pm Jul & Aug, 10am-1pm & 2-5pm Tue-Sun Sep-Jun) houses ethnographic exhibits in a castle at the top of Cannes' old town.

Twenty minutes away by boat are the idyllic islands, **Îles de Lérins**. The closest is **Île Ste-Marguerite**, where the mysterious Man in the Iron Mask was incarcerated during the late 17th century; it's now better known for its bone-white beaches, eucalyptus groves and small marine museum. Smaller still is **Île St-Honorat**, which has been a monastery since the 5th century.

Boats sail from quai des Îles on the western side of the harbour. **Riviera Lines** (ww.riviera-lines.com) runs ferries to Île Ste-Marguerite (adult €11.50 return) and **Compagnie Planaria** (www.cannes-ilesdelerins.com) covers Île St-Honorat (adult €12).

Sleeping

TOP CHOICE **Hôtel 7e Art** BOUTIQUE HOTEL €

(04 93 68 66 66; www.7arthotel.com; 23 rue Maréchal Joffre; s €68, d €60-98;) Cannes' newest star puts boutique style within reach of budgeteers. The owners schooled in Switzerland and their snappy design of putty-coloured walls, padded headboards and pop art far exceeds what you'd expect at this price.

Hôtel Le Mistral BOUTIQUE HOTEL €€

(04 93 39 91 46; www.mistral-hotel.com; 13 rue des Belges; d from €89;) This small hotel, a mere 50m from La Croisette, wins the *palme d'or* for best value in town: rooms are in red and plum tones and bathrooms feature designer fittings.

Eating

Find the cheapest restaurants around rue du Marché Forville, the trendiest in Le Suquet and the 'Carré d'Or' (the 'golden square' streets between La Croisette and rue d'Antibes). Picnic on square Lord Brougham, next to the Vieux Port.

WORTH A TRIP

THE SCENT OF THE CÔTE D'AZUR

Mosey 11km west of Nice to inhale the sweet smell of lavender, jasmine, mimosa and orange blossom fields. In **Grasse**, one of France's leading perfume producers, dozens of perfumeries create essences to sell to factories (for aromatically enhanced foodstuffs and soaps) as well as to prestigious couture houses – the highly trained noses of local perfume-makers can identify 3000 scents in a single whiff.

Fragonard (www.fragonard.com; 20 blvd Fragonard; 9am-6pm Feb-Oct, 9am-12.30pm & 2-6pm Nov-Jan) is the easiest perfumery to reach by foot. The tourist office has information on other perfumeries and field trips to local flower farms, including the flower-strewn **Domaine de Manon** (04 93 60 12 76; www.domaine-manon.com; admission €6). Roses are picked mid-May to mid-June, jasmine July to late October.

CANNES SPLURGE!

The Italian maître d' at **Mantel** (☎04 93 39 13 10; www.restaurantmantel.com; 22 rue St-Antoine; menus €25-38; ⏰Fri-Mon, dinner Tue & Thu) will make you feel like a million dollars and you'll melt for Noël Mantel's divine modern European cuisine and great-value prices. Best of all, you get not one but two desserts with your *menu* (oh, the pannacotta…).

Coquillages Brun SEAFOOD €€
(☎04 93 39 21 87; www.astouxbrun.com; 27 rue Félix Faure; menus from €28; ⏰noon-1am) Cannes' most famous brasserie is *the* place to indulge in oysters, mussels, prawns, crayfish and other delightfully fresh shells with a glass of crisp white wine.

Aux Bons Enfants TRADITIONAL FRENCH €€
(80 rue Meynadier; menu €23; ⏰Tue-Sat) This familial little place, where you can feast on top-notch regional dishes, buzzes. The lucky ones get a table (arrive early or late).

Information

Tourist office (☎04 92 99 84 22; www.cannes.travel; blvd de la Croisette; ⏰9am-8pm Jul & Aug, 9am-7pm Mon-Sat Sep-Jun) On the ground floor of Palais des Festivals; runs an annexe next to the train station.

Getting There & Away

BUS From the **bus station** (place Bernard Cornut Gentille) buses serve Nice (bus 200; €1, 1½ hours) and Nice airport (bus 210; €15, 50 minutes, half-hourly)

TRAIN Services go to Nice (€6.10, 40 minutes) and Marseille (€22, two hours).

St-Tropez

POP 5700

In the soft autumn or winter light, it's hard to believe the pretty terracotta fishing village of St-Tropez is a stop on the Riviera celebrity circuit. It seems far removed from its glitzy siblings further up the coast, but come spring or summer, it's a different world: the population increases tenfold, prices triple, and fun-seekers pile in to party till dawn, strut around the luxury yacht-packed Vieux Port and enjoy the creature comforts of exclusive A-listers beaches in the Baie de Pampelonne.

If you can at all avoid visiting in July and August, do. But if not, take heart: it's always fun to play 'I spy...' (a celebrity).

Sights & Activities

Musée de l'Annonciade ART GALLERY
(place Grammont, Vieux Port; admission €6; ⏰10am-noon & 2-6pm Wed-Mon Oct & Dec-May, longer hrs in summer) Displayed in a disused chapel at the Vieux Port, this small water-facing museum displays works by Matisse, Bonnard, Dufy and pointalist Signac, who set up his home and studio in St-Tropez.

Citadelle CITADEL
(admission €2.50; ⏰10am-6.30pm Apr-Sep, 10am-12.30pm & 1.30-5.30pm Oct-Mar) The panoramas of St-Tropez' iconic church tower and glistening bay from this lofty 17th-century fortress are worth the climb.

Plage de Pampelonne BEACH
The golden sands of **Plage de Tahiti**, 4km southeast of town, morph into the 5km-long, celebrity-studded **Plage de Pampelonne**, which sports a line-up of exclusive beach restaurants and clubs in summer. The bus to Ramatuelle stops at various points along a road, 1km inland from the beach.

DON'T MISS

TOP BEACH EATS & DRINKS

Book lunch (mains €15 to €40) at the following, open May to September:

» **Club 55** (www.leclub55.fr; 43 blvd Path) St-Tropez's oldest-running beach club, this 1950s address was the crew canteen for the filming of *And God Created Woman* with Brigitte Bardot. Celebs flock here to be seen, but the food is nothing special.

» **Liberty Plage** (www.plagelibcrty.com; chemin des Tamaris; ⏰year-round) Clothing optional – eat naked.

» **Moorea Plage** (www.moorea-plage-st-tropez.com; route des Plages) Ideal for conversation and backgammon (they have); tops for steak.

» **Nikki Beach** (www.nikkibeach.com/sttropez; route de l'Epi) Dance-on-the-bar celebs such as Paris Hilton and Pamela Anderson love this place; the deafening scene ends at midnight.

Sleeping

St-Tropez is no shoestring destination, but multistar camping grounds abound on the road to Plage de Pampelonne.

TOP CHOICE **Lou Cagnard** HOTEL €€
(04 94 97 04 24; www.hotel-lou-cagnard.com; 18 av Paul-Roussel; d €69-140, tr €160;) Book well ahead for this great-value courtyard charmer, shaded by lemon and fig trees. Rooms are spotlessly kept and five have garden terraces.

Les Palmiers BOUTIQUE HOTEL €€
(04 94 97 01 61; www.hotel-les-palmiers.com; 26 blvd Vasserot; d €89-189;) In an old villa with courtyard garden overlooking place des Lices, Les Palmiers has friendly service and simple rooms. Skip the annexe for the main building.

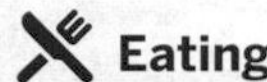

Eating

Quai Jean Jaurès at the Vieux Port is littered with restaurants and cafes.

Le Sporting BRASSERIE €€
(04 94 97 00 65; place des Lices; mains €14-24; 8am-1am) There's a bit of everything on the menu at always-packed Le Sporting, but the speciality is hamburger topped with foie gras and creamy morel sauce. Reservations essential.

Brasserie des Arts MODERN FRENCH €€
(04 94 40 27 37; www.brasseriedesarts.com; 5 place des Lices; mains €20) Wedged in a line-up of eating/drinking terraces jockeying for attention on St-Tropez's people-watching square, BA, as it is known, is where the locals go. Its fixed three-course menu is gourmet and excellent value.

Information

Tourist office (04 94 97 45 21; www.ot-saint-tropez.com; quai Jean Jaurès; 9.30am-8pm Jul & Aug, shorter hrs rest of year)

Getting There & Away

BOAT **Trans Côte d'Azur** (www.trans-cote-azur.com) runs day trips from Nice and Cannes, Easter to September.

BUS From the **bus station** (av Général de Gaulle), services run by **VarLib** (www.varlib.fr, in French) serve Ramatuelle (€2, 35 minutes) and St-Raphaël train station (€2, 1¼ hours) via Grimaud, Port Grimaud and Fréjus. There are four daily buses to Toulon-Hyères airport (€15, 1½ hours).

DON'T MISS

THE MARKET

One of southern France's busiest and best, St-Trop's **place des Lices market** (mornings Tue & Sat) is a highlight of local life, with colourful stalls groaning under the weight of plump fruit and veg, mounds of olives, local cheeses, chestnut purée and fragrant herbs. Afterwards meander to the port and duck beneath the stone arch to the bijou **fish market** (mornings Tue-Sun, daily summer), hidden between stone walls on place aux Herbes.

Monaco

377 / POP 32,000

This beguiling principality, the world's second-smallest state (the Vatican is a smidgen smaller), has long been a favourite haunt of super-rich celebs, high-rolling gamblers and tax exiles. Even the prices for a humble morning *café* will make your heart sink, but it's worth a day trip from Nice for its legendary casino, sparkling harbour, luxury yachts and cruisers, and a fantastic aquarium in hilltop Monaco Ville.

Since 1297, Monaco has been ruled by the Grimaldi family and has its own flag, national holiday (19 November), postal system and telephone code. Prince Rainier was famous for marrying Hollywood starlet Grace Kelly; since his death in 2005, his son Prince Albert (b 1958) has been in charge.

Brazilian triple-world champion Nelson Piquet famously likened driving Monaco's annual **Formula One Grand Prix** that tears acround the streets of Monaco each May to riding a bike around your living room.

Sights & Activities

At 11.55am every day, guards are changed at Monaco's **Palais du Prince** (Prince's Palace) in Monaco Ville. For a glimpse at royal life, tour the **state apartments** (www.palais.mc; adult €8; 10am-6pm Apr-Sep) with an audio guide.

The graceful 1910 **Musée Océanographique de Monaco** (www.oceano.org; av St-Martin; adult €13; 9.30am-7pm) houses an aquarium stocked with sharks, tropical fish and other local sea creatures. Don't miss the spectacular views from the rooftop terrace.

DON'T MISS

MONTE CARLO CASINO

(www.casinomontecarlo.com; place du Casino; ⏲European Rooms from noon Sat & Sun, from 2pm Mon-Fri) Living out your James Bond fantasies just doesn't get any better than Monte Carlo's monumental, richly decorated showstopper built in 1910. Admission is €10 for the European Rooms, with poker/slot machines, French roulette and *trente et quarante* (a card game), and €20 for the Private Rooms, which offer baccarat, blackjack, craps and American roulette. Jacket-and-tie dress code kicks in after 10pm. Minimum entry age is 18; bring photo ID.

Information

Tourist Office (www.visitmonaco.com; 2a blvd des Moulins; ⏲9am-7pm Mon-Sat, 11am-1pm Sun) From mid-June to late September additional tourist info kiosks mushroom around the harbour and train station.

Getting There & Away

Monaco's **train station** (av Prince Pierre) has frequent trains to Nice (€3.40, 20 minutes), and east to Menton (€1.90, 10 minutes) and beyond into Italy.

CORSICA

This rugged island (Corse in French) is officially a part of France, but remains fiercely proud of its own culture, history and language. It's one of the Med's most dramatic islands, with a bevy of beautiful beaches, glitzy ports and a mountainous, maquis-covered interior to explore, as well as a wild, independent spirit all of its own.

DON'T MISS

BACKPACKER PARADISE

If you're not up for the Nice–Monaco train trip, check into **Relais International de la Jeunesse Thalassa** (☎04 93 81 27 63; www.clajsud.fr; 2 av Gramaglia, Cap d'Ail; dm incl sheets & breakfast €18; ⏲Apr-Oct), Monaco's closest hostel right on the seashore in a beautiful spot on Cap d'Ail.

Ajaccio

POP 52,880

Ajaccio, Corsica's main metropolis, is all class and seduction with its sweeping bay and buzzing centre replete with mellow-toned buildings, cafes and yacht-packed marina. Looming over this elegant port city is the spectre of Corsica's great general: Napoleon Bonaparte was born here in 1769 and the city is dotted with statues and museums relating to the diminutive dictator.

Sights

The Napoleonic saga begins at the **Musée National de la Maison Bonaparte** (rue St-Charles; adult €5; ⏲2-5.50pm Mon, 9-11.30am & 2-5.30pm Tue-Sun Apr-Sep, less hrs rest of year), where Napoleon was born and spent the first nine years of his childhood.

Established by Napoléon's uncle, **Palais Fesch – Musée des Beaux-Arts** (www.musee-fesch.com; 50-52 rue du Cardinal Fesch; adult €8; ⏲10.30-5pm Mon, Wed & Sat, noon-5pm Thu, Fri & Sun) has France's largest collection of Italian paintings outside the Louvre.

Boat trips around the **Golfe d'Ajaccio** and **Îles Sanguinaires** (€27), and excursions to the Scandola Nature Reserve (see p472; adult €50) depart daily from the quay opposite place Foch.

Sleeping & Eating

Hôtel Marengo HOTEL €
(☎04 95 21 43 66; www.hotel-marengo.com; 2 rue Marengo; d €61-83; ⏲Apr-Oct; ❄) Expect pastel rooms (all with balconies) and a quiet courtyard, all a stroll from the beach, at this jolly, hospitably run little bolthole.

U Pampasgiolu TRADITIONAL CORSICAN €€
(☎06 09 39 26 92; 15 rue de la Porta; mains €14-28; ⏲dinner Mon-Sat) This rustic arch-vaulted dining room is always packed thanks to first-rate Corsican food. Try the *planche spuntinu* (snack selection) or *planche de la mer* (fish and seafood selection).

Le 20123 TRADITIONAL CORSICAN €€
(☎04 95 21 50 05; www.20123.fr; 2 rue du Roi de Rome; menu €32; ⏲dinner Tue-Sun) Decked out like a traditional village, this is another good bet for authentic Corsican fare. It has one single *menu*, presented orally!

Information

Tourist office (www.ajaccio-tourisme.com; 3 blvd du Roi Jérôme; ⏲9am-6pm Mon-Sat,

WORTH A TRIP

RÉSERVE NATURELLE DE SCANDOLA

There's no vehicle access or footpath into this magnificent **reserve** – Corsica's only Unesco-protected marine reserve midway between Ajaccio and the coastal town of **Porto** – so the only way to get up close is by sea. April to October several companies based on the quayside at Porto's marina sail through its shimmering sapphire waters to the base of its cliffs. Expect to pay around €40 for the privilege.

Predictably this is paradise for divers and snorkellers, and several companies organise introductory dives for beginners (from €45) and snorkelling trips (€15) to the fringe of Scandola. At Porto's quay try diving oufits **Centre de Plongée du Golfe de Porto** (www.plongeeporto.com), **Génération Bleue** (www.generation-bleue.com) or **Méditerranée Porto Sub** (www.plongeecose.fr)

9am-1pm Sun Jun-Sep, 8.30am-12.30pm & 2-5pm Mon-Fri Oct-May)

Getting There & Away

Air

Bus 8 links **Aéroport d'Ajaccio-Campo dell'Oro** (www.ajaccio.aeroport.fr), 8km east, to Ajaccio's train and bus stations (€4.50, 20 minutes).

Boat

Boats to/from Toulon, Nice and Marseille from **Terminal Maritime et Routier** (quai l'Herminier):

La Méridionale (www.lameridionale.fr)

Corsica Ferries (www.corsicaferries.com)

SNCM (www.sncm.fr, quai L'Herminier)

Bus

Local bus companies have kiosks inside the ferry terminal.

Autocars Ceccaldi (☎04 95 22 41 99) Travels to Porto (2½ hours, two daily, no Sunday buses September to June) via Piana (1½ hours).

Eurocorse (☎04 95 21 06 30) Travels to Bastia (three hours, two daily) via Corte (two hours), and Bonifacio (four hours, one or two daily)

Train

From the **train station** (place de la Gare) services go to Bastia (four hours, three to four daily), Calvi (five hours, two daily; change at Ponte Leccia) and Corte (two hours, three to four daily).

Bonifacio

POP 2700

With its glittering harbour, creamy cliffs and stout citadel, this dazzling port has a distinctly Italianate feel: sun-bleached townhouses, washing lines and murky chapels cram the old citadel, while brasseries and boat-kiosks tout their wares at the harbour.

A steep staircase links the harbour with the citadel's old gateway, **Porte de Gênes**, complete with its original 16th-century drawbridge. Inside the gateway is the 13th-century **Bastion l'Étendard**, which houses a small historical museum exploring Bonifacio's past. Along the ramparts, fabulous panoramic views unfold from **place du Marché** and **place Manichella**. From the citadel, the **Escalier du Roi d'Aragon** (admission €2.50; ⌚9am-7pm Apr-Oct) staggers down the cliff.

Boat trips to the remote beaches and gin-clear waters of the offshore **Îles Lavezzi** (Lavezzi Islands) run from the quayside. Bonifacio is surrounded by beaches, including **Piantarella** (popular with windsurfers) and shingly **Calalonga**.

Sleeping & Eating

Hôtel des Étrangers HOTEL €

(☎04 95 73 01 09; hoteldesetrangers.ifrance.com; av Sylvère Bohn; d €46-65; ⌚Apr–mid-Oct; ❄📶) Bonifacio's only budget option is the 'Foreigners' Hotel'. Spick-and-span rooms, all with tiled floors, clean bathrooms and simple colour schemes almost make up for the road racket.

TOP CHOICE **Domaine de Licetto** TRADITIONAL CORSICAN €€

(☎04 95 73 03 59; route du Phare; menus €36; ⌚dinner Mon-Sat Apr-Jul & Sep–mid-Oct, dinner daily Aug) For the authentic Corsican experience this address is hard to beat. The five-course *menu* is a culinary feast of local ingredients (suckling lamb, cheese-stuffed eggplant…) produced by small-scale farmers. Find it in the *maquis* (scrubland) on the way to Phare de Pertusato.

Cantina Doria CORSICAN €

(☎04 95 73 50 49; 27 rue Doria; mains €10-14; ⌚Apr-Oct) *The* place for Corsican country food, served at wooden benches amid copper pots, rustic tools and dented signs.

DON'T MISS

THE PERFECT SNAPSHOT

If you're after that perfect picture, don't miss the fantastic, three-hour return walk along cliffs from Bonifacio to **Phare de Pertusato** (Pertusato Lighthouse), which offers seamless views of the cliffs, Îles Lavezzi, Bonifacio and Sardinia that will sweep you off your feet. The starting point (signposted) is just to the left of the sharp bend on the hill up to Bonifacio's citadel. Complete the experience with lunch at Domaine de Licetto (p472).

Information

Tourist office (www.bonifacio.fr; 2 rue Fred Scamaroni; 9am-8pm May–mid-Oct, 9am-noon & 2-6pm Mon-Fri mid-October to April).

Getting There & Away

Air

A taxi into town from **Aéroport de Figari** (www.figari.aeroport.fr), 21km north, costs costs about €40 (there's no public transport).

Boat

Saremar (www.saremar.it, in Italian) and **Moby Lines** (www.mobylines.it) sail between Bonifacio and Santa Teresa di Gallura (on neighbouring Sardinia) in summer.

Bus

Eurocorse (04 95 70 13 83) runs buses to Porto-Vecchio (30 minutes), with onward connections to Ajaccio (four hours).

Bastia

POP 44,000

Ramshackle Bastia might not measure up to the sexy style of Ajaccio or the architectural appeal of Bonifacio, but in many ways it's a more authentic snapshot of modern-day Corsica – a lived-in, well-loved city that's resisted the urge to polish up its image just to please the tourists.

Sights & Activities

Even by Corsican standards Bastia is pocket-sized. The 19th-century **place St-Nicholas** sprawls along the seafront between the ferry port and harbour. The square is lined with plane trees, cafes and a **statue of Napoléon Bonaparte**, Corsica's most famous son.

A network of lanes leads south towards the attractive neighbourhood of **Terra Vecchia**. Further south is the Vieux Port (Old Port), ringed by pastel-coloured tenements and buzzy brasseries, as well as the twin-towered **Église St-Jean Baptiste**. Behind the port looms Bastia's sunbaked **citadel**, built from the 15th to 17th centuries by the city's Genoese masters. Inside one of the citadel's landmarks, the **Palais des Gouverneurs** (Governors' Palace; place du Donjon) is Bastia's top-notch local history museum, **Musée d'Histoire de Bastia** (admission €5; 10am-6pm Tue-Sun).

Sleeping & Eating

Hôtel Central HOTEL €€

(04 95 31 71 12; www.centralhotel.fr; 3 rue Miot; d €85-100;) This family-run number in a stately 19th-century building has 21 rooms wrapped with a retro feel.

A Casarella MODERN CORSICAN €€

(04 95 32 02 32; 6 rue Ste-Croix; mains €15-28; Tue-Sun) Tuck into innovative organic dishes on Bastia's loveliest terrace, poised above the port in the citadel, with twinkling harbour lights below.

Chez Vincent TRADITIONAL CORSICAN €€

(04 95 31 62 50; 12 rue St-Michel; mains €9-22; Mon-Fri, dinner Sat) Corsican staples and wood-fired pizzas are what beckons. The *assiette du bandit Corse* (€18.50) features a smorgasbord of local nosh, including stewed veal chestnuts, cured meats, ewe's-milk cheese, wild boar pâté and roast *figatellu* (liver sausage).

Information

Tourist office (www.bastia-tourisme.com; place St-Nicolas; 8.30am-8pm Apr-Sep, shorter hrs rest year)

Getting There & Away

Air

Aéroport Bastia-Poretta (www.bastia.aeroport.fr) is 24km south of the city. Buses (€8.50, 30 minutes, 10 daily) depart from outside the Préfecture building; timetables are posted at the stop.

Boat

Bastia's two ferry terminals are connected by a free shuttle bus. Ferries sail to/from Marseille, Toulon and Nice on mainland France, and several ports in Italy.

Corsica Ferries (www.corsicaferries.com; 15bis rue Chanoine Leschi)

La Méridionale (www.lameridionale.fr)

Moby Lines (www.moby.it; 4 rue du Commandant Luce de Casabianca)

SNCM (www.sncm.fr; inside Southern Terminal)

Bus

Beaux Voyages (☎04 95 65 11 35) Buses to Île Rousse (€13, 90 minutes) and Calvi (€16, 2½ hours) daily except Sunday. Buses leave from the train station.

Eurocorse (☎04 95 31 73 76) Buses to Ajaccio (€21, three hours, twice daily except on Sunday) from Bastia's 'bus station', a car park north of place St-Nicholas.

Les Rapides Bleus (☎04 95 31 03 79; 1 av Maréchal Sébastiani) Buses leave from in front the post office to Porto-Vecchio (€22, three hours) twice daily except Sunday and holidays.

Train

From the **train station** (av Maréchal Sébastiani) main destinations include Ajaccio (€25, 3¾ hours, four daily) and Calvi (three hours, three or four daily) via Île Rousse.

UNDERSTAND FRANCE

History

France's early history is encapsulated in the *Astérix* comic books: the Celtic Gauls arrived between 1500 and 500 BC, and were under Roman rule from 52 BC until the 5th century. After the Roman Empire's decline, France was governed by monarchs including Charlemagne (from 800). William the Conqueror extended French rule to England in 1066.

During the Reformation, fighting between Catholics and Protestants brought France close to disintegration. However, that paled beside the seismic events of the 1780s, when the population rose up against Louis XVI and his queen, Marie Antoinette. On 14 July 1789, a Parisian mob stormed the Bastille, unleashing the French Revolution. The vicious Reign of Terror followed; thousands of aristocrats were guillotined, including Louis XVI and his queen in 1793.

A young Corsican general by the name of Napoleon Bonaparte assumed power in 1799 and embarked on European conquest. Initially defeated and exiled to the island of Elba, he staged a short comeback before meeting his final defeat at Waterloo in 1815.

The subsequent years were marked by civil strife, with monarchists and revolutionaries vying for power. Napoleon's nephew Louis-Napoleon Bonaparte seized power in 1851, declaring himself Emperor Napoleon III, but proved no match for his uncle in terms of military prowess: he embroiled France in various catastrophic conflicts, including the Crimean War (1853-56) and the Franco-Prussian War (1870-71).

Central to France's entry into WWI was the desire to regain Alsace and Lorraine, lost to Germany in 1871. This was achieved but at immense cost: 1.3 million killed and almost one million crippled. The Treaty of Versailles, signed in 1919, demanded punitive reparations from Germany, causing long-lasting bitterness – a fact that was later ruthlessly exploited by an Austrian house painter called Adolf Hitler.

Following the outbreak of WWII, the German *blitzkrieg* swept west with astonishing speed; by 1940 France had capitulated and the country was divided into an occupied zone in the north and the collaborationist Vichy regime in the south.

France had to wait four years for liberation. On 6 June 1944, US, British and Canadian troops stormed the beaches of Normandy and pushed east towards Paris. General Charles de Gaulle, leader of the French government-in-exile, returned to France and established a provisional government.

Political power see-sawed over the next 50 years, a period that saw the end of French colonies in Vietnam and Algeria and the elections of several important French presidents, including Georges Pompidou (president from 1969–74) and François Mitterrand (1981-95) and Jacques Chirac (1995–2007).

France Today

Presidential elections in 2007 ushered in big change for France in the shape of Nicolas Sarkozy (b 1955) of Chirac's centre-right party UMP *(Union pour un Mouvement Populaire)*. Dynamic, ambitious and far from mediashy, Sarko (as he was quickly dubbed by the popular press) wooed voters with big talk of job creation, lower taxes, crime crackdown and help for France's substantial immigrant population. Yet controversy dogged Sarko's first period in office, infamously marked by him splitting with his second wife and swiftly wedding Italian chanteuse and multimillionaire supermodel Carla Bruni.

Beyond Sarkozy's high-profile private life, there have been major political developments too, including the banning of smoking in public places (2007) and the ratification of a new EU treaty (2008). More controversially the wearing of crucifixes, the Islamic headscarf and other overtly religious symbols has been banned in state schools since 2004 and the wearing of face-covering veils in public since 2010 – much to the consternation of France's notable Muslim community (around 10% of the population of 64.4 milion).

For a few fleeting months in 2009 France joined much of the rest of Europe in recession and by mid-2010 unemployment was hovering at a disconcerting 10%. Pension reforms the same year saw France's retirement age upped from 60 to 62 and full state pension age from 65 to 67, much to the horror of most French who joined forces in a series of national strikes and protests.

Arts

Literature

The philosophical work of Voltaire (1694–1778) and Jean-Jacques Rousseau (1712–78) dominated the 18th century. A century on, the poems and novels of Victor Hugo – *Les Misérables* and *Notre Dame de Paris* (The Hunchback of Notre Dame) among them – became landmarks of French Romanticism.

In 1857 two literary landmarks were published: *Madame Bovary* by Gustave Flaubert (1821–80) and a collection of poems by Charles Baudelaire (1821–67), *Les Fleurs du Mal* (The Flowers of Evil). Émile Zola (1840–1902) meanwhile strove to convert novel writing from an art to a science.

The expression of mental states was the aim of symbolists such as Paul Verlaine (1844-96). Verlaine's poems, alongside those of Arthur Rimbaud (1854–91), are seen as French literature's first modern poems.

After WWII, existentialism developed around the lively debates of Jean-Paul Sartre (1905–80), Simone de Beauvoir (1908–86) and Albert Camus (1913–60) in Paris' Left Bank cafes.

Contemporary authors include Françoise Sagan, Pascal Quignard, Anna Gavalda, Emmanuel Carrère, Stéphane Bourguignon and Martin Page, whose novel *Comment Je Suis Devenu Stupide* (How I Became Stupid) explores a 25-year-old Sorbonne student's methodical attempt to become stupid. No French writer better delves into the mind, mood and politics of the country's ethnic population than Faïza Guène (b 1985), born and bred on a ghetto housing estate outside Paris.

Then there is 'bestseller, troublemaker' and winner of the Prix Goncourt in 2010, Michel Houellebecq (www.houellebecq.info).

Cinema

Cinematographic pioneers the Lumière brothers shot the world's first-ever motion picture in March 1895 and French film flourished in the following decades. The post-WWII *nouvelle vague* (new wave) filmmakers, such as Claude Chabrol, Jean-Luc Godard and François Truffaut, pioneered the advent of modern cinema, using fractured narratives, documentary camerawork and highly personal subjects.

Big-name stars, slick production values and nostalgia were the dominant motifs in the 1980s. Claude Berri's depiction of prewar Provence in *Jean de Florette* (1986), Jean-Paul Rappeneau's *Cyrano de Bergerac* (1990) and *Bon Voyage* (2003), set in 1940s Paris – all starring France's best-known (and biggest-nosed) actor, Gérard Depardieu – found huge audiences in France and abroad.

La Haine (1995), directed by Mathieu Kassovitz, documents the bleak reality of life in the Parisian suburbs. At the other end of the spectrum, massive international hit *Le Fabuleux Destin de Amélie Poulain* (*Amélie;* 2001) is a feel-good story about a Parisian do-gooder. Or watch *Bienvenue chez les Ch'tis* (2008), another big box-office hit of recent years which debunks grim stereotypes about the industrialised regions of the north of France with high jinks and hilarity.

Music

France produced a string of great composers in the 19th century, including Georges Bizet (1838–75) who created *Carmen* and Claude Debussy (1862–1918). Jazz hit 1920s Paris, while the *chanson française* (French song) was revived in the 1930s by Édith Piaf and Charles Trenet. In the 1950s the Left Bank cabarets nurtured *chansonniers* (cabaret singers) such as Léo Ferré, Georges Brassens, Claude Nougaro, Jacques Brel and Serge Gainsbourg.

French pop music has evolved massively since the 1960s *yéyé* (imitative rock) days of Johnny Halliday. There's a strong tradition of world music, ranging from Senegalese *mbalax* (Youssou N'Dour) to West Indian *zouk* (Zouk Machine); one of the most popular figures is Paris-born Manu Chao. Electronic music (Daft Punk, Air) has found a global following, while French rap continues to break

DON'T MISS

WORLD SOUND

No artist has cemented France's reputation in world music more than Paris-born, Franco-Congolese rapper, slam poet and three-time Victoire de la Musique–award winner, Abd al Malik (www.abdalmalik.fr). Hot on the heels of his first two albums, albums *Gibraltar* (2006) and *Dante* (2008) – both classics – is his fabulous *Château Rouge* (2010).

new ground: pioneered in the 1990s by MC Solaar and continued by young French rappers such as Disiz La Peste, Monsieur R, Rohff and Marseille's IAM (www.iam.tm.fr).

Architecture

Southern France is the place to find France's Gallo-Roman legacy, especially in and around Nîmes.

Several centuries later, architects adopted Gallo-Roman motifs in roman (Romanesque) masterpieces such as the original portions of the cathedral in Chartres, as well as Toulouse's huge Basilique St-Sernin and Paris' lovely Église St-Germain des Prés.

Impressive 12th-century Gothic structures include Avignon's pontifical palace, Chartres' cathedral and, of course, Notre Dame in Paris.

Art nouveau (1850–1910) combined iron, brick, glass and ceramics in new ways. See it for yourself at Paris' metro entrances and in the Musée d'Orsay.

Contemporary buildings to look out for include the once-reviled (now much-revered) Centre Pompidou and IM Pei's glass pyramid at the Louvre. In the provinces, notable buildings include Strasbourg's European Parliament, a 1920s art deco swimming pool-turned-art museum in Lille and the stunning new Centre Pompidou in Metz.

Painting

An extraordinary flowering of artistic talent occurred in 19th- and 20th-century France. The Impressionists, who endeavoured to capture the ever-changing aspects of reflected light, included Edouard Manet, Claude Monet, Edgar Degas, Camille Pisarro and Pierre-Auguste Renoir. They were followed by the likes of Paul Cézanne (who lived in Aix-en-Provence) and Paul Gauguin, as well as the fauvist Henry Matisse (a resident of Nice) and cubists including Spanish-born Pablo Picasso and Georges Braque (1882–1963).

Food

Price ranges in this chapter for a two-course evening meal:

€€€ more than €50

€€ €15 to €50

€ below €15

Environment

France is the third-largest country in Europe. Mont Blanc (4810m) crowns the French Alps along France's eastern border, while the rugged Pyrenees define France's 450km-long border with Spain, peaking at 3404m. The country's major river systems include the Garonne, Rhône, Seine and France's longest river, the Loire.

France has more mammals (around 110) than any other country in Europe, as well as 363 bird species, 30 types of amphibian, 36 varieties of reptile and 72 kinds of fish. Around 80% of its electricity comes from nuclear power stations – the highest ratio in the world.

France is lagging behind many other European countries on the sustainable-travel front, although it does boast one of the finest and most efficient train systems in Europe – so there's little excuse not to use public transport. Shopping at local markets rather than supermarkets is an excellent way of cutting down on food miles, and *restaurants bios* (organic restaurants) are gaining ground.

SURVIVAL GUIDE

Directory A-Z

Accommodation

Many tourist offices make room reservations, often for a fee of €5, but many only do so if you stop by in person. In the French Alps, ski resort tourist offices operate a central reservation service.

Prices ranges in this chapter refer to the cost of a double room with private bathroom in high season. Prices exclude breakfast unless otherwise noted.

€€€ more than €175 (€180 in Paris)

€€ €70 to €175 (€80 to €180)

€ less than €70 (€80 in Paris)

B&B

For charm, a heartfelt *bienvenue* (welcome) and home cooking, it's hard to beat a *chambre d'hôtes* (B&B). Pick up lists at local tourist offices or online:

Bienvenue à la Ferme (www.bienvenue-a-la-ferme.com) Sleep on a farm.

Chambres d'Hôtes France (www.chambresdhotesfrance.com)

Fleurs de Soleil (http://fleursdesoleil.fr, in French)

Gîtes de France (www.gites-de-france.fr) Umbrella organisation for B&Bs and self-catering properties *(gîtes);* check *Gîtes de Charme* (www.gites-de-france-charme.com).

Samedi Midi Éditions (www.samedimidi.com)

CAMPING

Camping has never been more en vogue. Gîtes de France and Bienvenue à la Ferme (see earlier) coordinate camping on farms. Most camping grounds open March or April to October.

Euro-economisers should look for good-value but no-frills *campings municipaux* (municipal camping grounds). Camping in nondesignated spots *(camping sauvage)* is illegal in France.

Easy-to-navigate websites with campsites:

Camping en France (www.camping.fr)

Camping France (www.campingfrance.com)

Guide du Camping (www.guideducamping.com)

HPA Guide (http://camping.hpaguide.com)

Les Cabanes de France (www.cabanes-de-france.com, in French) Tree houses

HOSTELS

Hostels range from funky to threadbare. A dorm bed in an *auberge de jeunesse* (youth hostel) costs about €25 in Paris, and anything from €10 to €28 in the provinces; sheets are always included and often breakfast too.

To prevent outbreaks of bed bugs, sleeping bags are no longer permitted. All hostels are nonsmoking.

HOTELS

French hotels range from low-budget no-star pads to full-blown pleasure palaces. They almost never include breakfast in their advertised nightly rates.

Hotels are rated with one to five stars; ratings are based on objective criteria (eg size of entry hall), not service, decor or cleanliness. A double room has one double bed (or two singles pushed together); a room with twin beds is more expensive, as is a room with bathtub instead of shower.

Activities

From glaciers, rivers and canyons in the Alps to porcelain-smooth cycling trails in the Dordogne and Loire Valley – not to mention 3200km of coastline – France's landscapes beg exhilarating outdoor escapes.

The French countryside is criss-crossed by a staggering 120,000km of *sentiers balisés* (marked walking paths), which pass through every imaginable terrain in every region of the country. No permit is needed to hike. Probably the best-known trails are the *sentiers de grande randonnée* (GR), long-distance paths marked by red-and-white-striped track indicators.

France – a great place to cycle – sports loads of urban and rural *pistes cyclables* (bike paths and lanes; www.voiesvertes.com, in French) and an extensive network of secondary and tertiary roads with relatively light traffic.

For details on regional activities, courses, equipment rental, clubs and companies, see this book's destination listings and contact local tourist offices.

ORGANISATIONS

Whether you are a peak bagger, surfer dude or thrill-seeking mountain biker, the following organisations can help you plan your petit adventure:

Club Alpin Français (French Alpine Club; www.ffcam.fr, in French) Groups 280 mountain-sports clubs and arranges professional guides for escapades in *alpinisme* (mountaineering), *escalade* (rock climbing), *escalade de glace* (ice climbing) and other highland activities. Runs *refuges* (mountain huts) in the French Alps too.

École du Ski Français (ESF; www.esf.net) French ski school.

Fédération Française de Cyclisme (www.ffc.fr, in French) Founded in 1881, the French Cycling Federation is *the* authority on competitive cycling in France and mountain biking (VTT).

Fédération Française de Vol Libre (http://federation.ffvl.fr, in French) Groups regional clubs specialising in *deltaplane*

(hang-gliding), *parapente* (paragliding) and *le kite-surf* (kitesurfing).

Véloroutes et Voies Vertes (www.af3v.org) A database of 250 signposted *véloroutes* (bike paths) and *voies vertes* (greenways) for cycling and in-line skating.

Business Hours

French business hours are regulated by a maze of regulations, including the 35-hour working week. With the exception of grocery stores, *boulangeries* and florists, businesses close Sunday (and sometimes Monday).

In this book we've only listed business hours where they differ from the following standards:

Banks 9 or 9.30am-1pm & 2-5pm Mon-Fri or Tue-Sat

Bars 7pm to 1am Mon-Sat

Cafes 7 or 8am-10 or 11pm Mon-Sat

Nightclubs 10pm-3, 4 or 5am Thu-Sat

Post Offices 8.30 or 9am-5pm or 6pm Mon-Fri, 8am-noon Sat

Restaurants lunch noon-2.30 or 3pm, dinner 7-10 or 11pm

Shops 9 or 10am-noon & 2-6 or 7pm Mon-Sat

Supermarkets 9am-7pm or 8pm Mon-Sat

Embassies & Consulates

To find a consulate or embassy visit look up *'ambassade'* in France's **Pages Jaunes** (Yellow Pages; www.pagesjaunes.fr, in French).

Gay & Lesbian Travellers

The rainbow flag flies high in France, one of Europe's most liberal when it comes to homosexuality.

Most major gay and lesbian centre organisations are based in Paris. Bordeaux, Lille, Lyon, Toulouse and many other towns also have active communities.

Gay Pride marches are held in major French cities from mid-May to early July.

Online resources:

France Queer Resources Directory (www.france.qrd.org, in French) Gay and lesbian directory.

French Government Tourist Office (http://us.franceguide.com/special-interests/gay-friendly) Information about 'the gay-friendly destination par excellence'.

Gay Travel France (www.gaytravelfrance.com) Gay and lesbian accommodation.

Paris Gay (www.paris-gay.com) Everything about gay Paree.

Holidays

New Year's Day (Jour de l'An) 1 January

Easter Sunday & Monday (Pâques & lundi de Pâques) March/April

May Day (Fête du Travail) 1 May – traditional parades

Victoire 1945 8 May – commemorates the Allied victory in Europe that ended WWII

Ascension Thursday (Ascension) May – celebrated on the 40th day after Easter

Pentecost/Whit Sunday & Whit Monday (Pentecôte & lundi de Pentecôte) Mid-May to mid-June – celebrated on the seventh Sunday after Easter

Bastille Day/National Day (Fête Nationale) 14 July – *the* national holiday

Assumption Day (Assomption) 15 August

All Saints' Day (Toussaint) 1 November

Remembrance Day (L'onze novembre) 11 November – marks the WWI armistice

Christmas (Noël) 25 December

Language Courses

The government site www.diplomatie.gouv.fr (under 'Francophony') and www.europa-pages.com/france list language schools in France. All manner of French language courses are available in Paris and provincial towns and cities; many arrange accommodation.

Some schools you might consider:

Alliance Française (www.alliancefr.org; 101 blvd Raspail, 6e, Paris; Ⓜ St-Placide) Venerable institution for the worldwide promotion of French language and civilisation, with intensive and extensive classes, including literature and business French.

Centre Méditerranéen d'Études Françaises (www.monte-carlo.mc/centremed; chemin des Oliviers, Cap d'Ail) French Riviera school dating to 1952, with an open-air amphitheatre designed by Jean Cocteau overlooking the sparkling blue Med.

Eurocentre d'Amboise (www.eurocentres.com; 9 mail St-Thomas, Amboise) Small, well-organised school in the charming Loire Valley, with branches in La Rochelle and Paris.

Université de Provence (http://sites.univ-provence.fr/wscefee; 29 av Robert Schumann, Aix-en-Provence) A hot choice in lovely Aix.

Legal Matters

French police have wide powers of stop-and-search and can demand proof of identity at any time. Foreigners must be able to prove their legal status in France (eg passport, visa, residency permit).

Money

Credit and debit cards, accepted almost everywhere in France, are convenient, relatively secure and usually offer a better exchange rate than travellers cheques or cash exchanges. Some places (eg 24-hour petrol stations, some autoroute toll machines) only take French-style credit cards with chips and PINs.

Commercial banks charge a €3 to €5 fee per foreign-currency transaction – if they even bother to offer exchange services any more. In Paris and major cities, *bureaux de change* (exchange bureaux) are faster and easier, open longer hours and give better rates than the banks.

For lost cards, call:

Amex (☎01 47 77 72 00)

Diners Club (☎08 10 31 41 59)

MasterCard (☎08 00 90 13 87)

Visa (Carte Bleue; ☎08 00 90 11 79)

Telephone

MOBILE PHONES

French mobile phone numbers begin with ☎06 or ☎07.

France uses GSM 900/1800, compatible with the rest of Europe and Australia but not with the North American GSM 1900 or the totally different system in Japan (though some North Americans have tri-band phones that work here). Buy your own French SIM card (€20 to €30) at ubiquitous outlets run by mobile-phone companies **Bouygues** (www.bouyguestelecom.fr), **Orange** (www.orange.com) and **SFR** (www.sfr.com, in French).

Recharge cards are sold at *tabacs* (tobacco shops) and newsagents; domestic prepaid calls cost about €0.50 per minute.

PHONE CODES

Calling France from abroad Dial your country's international access code, ☎33 (France's country code) and the 10-digit local number *without* the initial 0.

Directory enquiries For France Telecom's *service des renseignements* (directory enquiries) dial ☎11 87 12. For help in English with all France Telecom's services, see www.francetelecom.com or call ☎09 69 36 39 00.

International directory enquiries For numbers outside France, dial ☎11 87 00.

Emergency numbers Can be dialled from public phones without a phonecard (see p397).

Visas

For up-to-date details on visa requirements, visit the **French Foreign Affairs Ministry** (www.diplomatie.gouv.fr).

EU nationals and citizens of Iceland, Norway and Switzerland need only a passport or a national identity card in order to enter France and stay in the country indefinitely. Citizens of Australia, the USA, Canada, Hong Kong, Israel, Japan, Malaysia, New Zealand, Singapore, South Korea

INTERNATIONAL AIRPORTS

AIRPORT	PHONE NUMBER	WEBSITE
Paris	France 39 50	www.aeroportsdeparis.fr
Bordeaux	05 56 34 50 50	www.bordeaux.aeroport.fr
Lille	08 91 67 32 10	www.lille.aeroport.fr
Lyon	08 26 80 08 26	www.lyon.aeroport.fr
Marseille	04 42 14 14 14	www.mrsairport.com
Nantes	02 40 84 80 00	www.nantes.aeroport.fr
Nice	08 20 42 33 33	www.nice.aeroport.fr
Strasbourg	03 88 64 67 67	www.strasbourg.aeroport.fr
Toulouse	08 25 38 00 00	www.toulouse.aeroport.fr

and many Latin American countries do not need visas to visit France as tourists for up to 90 days.

Other people wishing to come to France as tourists have to apply for a **Schengen Visa** (p1319).

Getting There & Away

Air

For a list of airports in France, see the boxed text, p479.

Bus

Eurolines (08 92 89 90 91; www.eurolines.eu), a grouping of 32 long-haul coach operators (including the UK's National Express), links France with cities across Europe and in Morocco and Russia. Discounts are available to people under 26 and over 60. Make advance reservation, especially in July and August.

The standard Paris-London fare is €46 (€57 including high-season supplements) but the trip – including a Channel crossing either by ferry or the Channel Tunnel – can cost as little €15 if you book 45 days ahead.

Car & Motorcycle

A right-hand-drive vehicle brought to France from the UK or Ireland must have deflectors affixed to the headlights to avoid dazzling oncoming traffic.

From the UK, **Eurotunnel shuttle trains** (in UK 08443-35 35 35, in France 08 10 63 03 04; www.eurotunnel.com) whisk bicycles and vehicles from Folkestone through the Channel

INTERNATIONAL FERRY COMPANIES

CONNECTION	FERRY COMPANY	PHONE NUMBER(S)
England–Normandy England–Brittany Ireland–Brittany	Brittany Ferries	in UK 0871-244 0744; in Ireland 021-4277 801; in France 08 25 82 88 28
Ireland–Normandy	Celtic Link Ferries	in Ireland 053-916 2688
Morocco–France	Comanav & Comarit	in Sète (SNCM) 04 67 46 68 00
England–Normandy England–Brittany Channel Islands–Brittany	Condor Ferries	in UK 0845-609 1024; in France 08 25 13 51 35
Tunisia–France	CTN	in Marseille 04 91 91 55 71
Ireland–Normandy Ireland–Brittany	Irish Ferries	in Ireland 0818-300 400; in France 08 10 00 13 57; in Cherbourg 02 33 23 44 44; in Roscoff 02 98 61 17 17
England–Channel Ports England–Normandy	LD Lines	in UK 0844-576 8836; in France 08 25 30 43 04
Channel Islands–Normandy	Manche Îles Express	on Jersey 01534-880 756; on Guernsey 01481-832 059; in France 08 25 13 10 50
England–Channel Ports	Norfolk Line	in UK 0844-847 5042; outside UK +44-208-127 8303; in France 03 28 59 01 01
England–Channel Ports	P&O Ferries	in UK 08716 645 645; in France 08 25 12 01 56
England–Channel Ports	SeaFrance	in UK 0871-423 7119; in France 08 25 82 50 00
Algeria–France Sardinia–France, Tunisia–France	SNCM	in France 32 60; outside France +33 825 88 80 88
England–Normandy	Transmanche Ferries	in UK 0844-576 8836; in France 08 25 30 43 04

Tunnel to Coquelles, 5km southwest of Calais, in 35 minutes.

Train

Rail services link France with virtually every country in Europe. Tickets and information are handled by **Rail Europe** (www.raileurope.com) or, in France, by **SNCF** (☎in France 36 35, from abroad +33 8 92 35 35 35; www.sncf.com).

Eurostar (☎in UK 08432 186 186, in France 08 92 35 35 39; www.eurostar.com) links London St-Pancras to Paris Gare du Nord in 2¼ hours with easy onward connections to destinations all over France. Ski trains connecting England with the French Alps run weekends mid-December to mid-April.

For details on Europe-wide rail passes, see p1329.

Sea

Regular ferries travel to France from Italy, the UK, Channel Islands and Ireland. Several ferry companies ply the waters between Corsica and Italy. For details, see p480.

Getting Around

Air

France's vaunted high-speed train network has made rail travel between some cities (eg from Paris to Lyon and Marseille) faster and easier than flying.

Air France (☎36 54; www.airfrance.com) and its subsidiaries **Brit Air** (☎36 54; www.britair.fr) and **Régional** (☎36 54; www.regional.com) control the lion's share of France's domestic

WEBSITE	PORTS OUTSIDE FRANCE	PORTS IN FRANCE
www.brittany-ferries.co.uk; www.brittanyferries.ie	Cork, Plymouth, Poole, Portsmouth	Caen (Ouistreham), Cherbourg, Roscoff, St-Malo
www.celticlinkferries.com	Rosslare	Cherbourg
www.aferry.to/comanav.htm; www.aferry.to/comarit.htm	Nador, Tangier	Sète
www.condorferries.com	Poole, Portsmouth, Weymouth, Guernsey, Jersey	Cherbourg, St-Malo
www.ctn.com.tn	Tunis	Marseille
www.irishferries.ie; www.shamrock-irlande.com, in French	Rosslare	Cherbourg, Roscoff
www.ldlines.co.uk	Dover, Portsmouth	Boulogne-sur-Mer, Le Havre
www.manche-iles-express.com	Alderney, Guernsey, Jersey	Barneville-Carteret, Diélette, Granville
www.norfolkline.com	Dover	Dunkirk (Loon Plage)
www.poferries.com	Dover	Calais
www.seafrance.com	Dover	Calais
www.sncm.fr	Alger, Annaba, Bejaia, Oran, Porto Torres, Skikda, Tunis	Marseille
www.transmancheferries.com	Newhaven	Dieppe

airline industry. Good deals can be had if you buy your ticket well in advance (at least 42 days ahead for the very best deals) and stay over a Saturday night; tickets can't be changed or reimbursed.

Budget carriers offering flights within France include **easyJet** (www.easyjet.com), **Airlinair** (www.airlinair.com), **Twin Jet** (www.twinjet.net) and **CCM** (www.aircorsica.com).

Bus

You're nearly always better off travelling by train in France. Nevertheless, buses are widely used for short-distance travel within *départements,* especially in rural areas with relatively few train lines.

Bicycle

French train company SNCF does its best to make travelling with a bicycle easy and has a website for cyclists (www.velo.sncf.com, in French).

A growing number of cities have automatic bike rental systems. Otherwise there is usually at least one bike rental shop in town; pay €10 to €20 a day for a mountain bike (VTT) or road bike (VTC). You have to leave ID and/or a deposit (often a credit-card slip).

Car & Motorcycle

Having your own wheels gives you exceptional freedom but can be expensive once you factor in petrol costs and *autoroute* (motorway) tolls. Websites www.viamichelin.com, www.autoroutes.fr and www.mappy.fr can help you work out likely costs for specified routes.

To hire a car you'll need to be aged over 21 and in possession of a valid *permis de conduire* (driving licence) and a credit card. Third-party liability insurance is provided, but collision-damage waivers (CDW) vary; make sure you check the *franchise* (excess) when comparing rates.

Train

France's superb rail network is operated by the state-owned **SNCF** (www.sncf.com); many rural towns not on the SNCF train network are served by SNCF buses. SNCF's flagship trains are the high-speed TGVs.

Before boarding any train, you must validate *(composter)* your ticket by time-stamping it in a *composteur,* one of those yellow posts located on the way to the platform. If you forget (or don't have a ticket for some other reason), find a conductor on the train before they find you – or risk an unwelcome fine.

TGV lines and key stations:

TGV Nord, Thalys & Eurostar These link Paris' Gare du Nord with Lille, Calais, Brussels (Bruxelles-Midi), Amsterdam, Cologne and, via the Channel Tunnel, Ashford, Ebbsfleet and London St Pancras.

TGV Est Européen Connects Paris' Gare de l'Est with Reims, Nancy, Metz, Strasbourg, Zurich and Germany.

TGV Sud-Est & TGV Midi-Méditerranée These lines link Paris' Gare de Lyon with the southeast, including Dijon, Lyon, Geneva, the Alps, Avignon, Marseille and Nice.

TGV Atlantique Sud-Ouest & TGV Atlantique Ouest These link Paris' Gare Montparnasse with western and southwestern France, including Brittany, Tours, Nantes, Bordeaux, Biarritz and Toulouse.

SAMPLE TRAIN FARES

ROUTE	FULL FARE (€)	DURATION (HR)
Amsterdam-Paris	79	3¼
Barcelona-Montpellier	57	4½
Berlin-Paris	238	8
Brussels-Paris	44-64	1½
Frankfurt-Paris	106	4
Geneva-Lyon	25	2
Geneva-Marseille	65	3½
Vienna-Strasbourg	149	9

SNCF TRAIN FARES & DISCOUNTS

The Basics:

Full-fare return travel costs twice as much as a one-way fare; 1st class travel, where still available, costs 20% to 30% extra. Children aged four to 11 pay half price, under fours travel for free.

Ticket prices for many trains are pricier during peak periods. The further in advance you reserve, the lower the fare.

Discount Tickets

» **Prem's** The SNCF's most heavily discounted, use-or-lose tickets, sold online, by phone and at ticket windows/machines a maximum of 90 days and minimum 14 days before you travel.

» **Bons Plans** A grab bag of cheap options for different routes/dates, advertised online under the tab 'Dernière Minute' (Last Minute).

» **iDTGV** Cheap tickets aimed at the iPod generation on advance-purchase TGV travel between about 30 cities; only sold at www.idtgv.com.

Discount Cards

Reductions of 25% to 60% are available with several discount cards (valid for one year):

» **Carte 12-25** (www.12-25-sncf.com in, French; €49) For travellers aged 12 to 25 years.

» **Carte Enfant Plus** (www.enfantplus-sncf.com, in French; €70) For one to four adults travelling with a child aged four to 11 years.

» **Carte Escapades** (www.escapades-sncf.com, in French; €85) Discounts on return journeys of at least 200km that include a Saturday night away or only involve travel on a Saturday or Sunday; for 26 to 59 years.

» **Carte Sénior** (www.senior-sncf.com, in French; €56) Over 60 years.

RAIL PASSES

The **InterRail One Country Pass** (www.interrailnet.com; 3/4/6/8 days €194/209/269/299, 12yr to 25 yr €126/136/175/194), valid in France, entitles residents of Europe who do not live in France to unlimited travel on SNCF trains for three to eight days over a month.

Nonresidents of Europe can purchase a **France Railpass** (www.francerailpass.com), which offers unlimited travel for three days during a one-month period. Full fares are US$239 for three days and US$32 to US$38 for each additional travel day within the same month.

Germany

Includes »

Best Places to Eat

» Bratwursthäusle, Nuremberg (p521)

» Feynsinn, Cologne (p540)

» Wurstküche, Regensburg (p521)

» Konnopke's Imbiss, Berlin (p496)

Best Places to Stay

» Hotel Blauer Bock, Munich (p513)

» Kogge, Hamburg (p550)

» Ostel, Berlin (p495)

» Bremer Backpacker Hostel, Bremen (p545)

Why Go?

Beer or wine? That sums up the German conundrum. One is at the heart of a pilsner-swilling culture, is the very reason for one of the world's great parties (Oktoberfest) and is consumed with pleasure across the land. The other is responsible for gorgeous vine-covered valleys, comes in myriad forms and is enjoyed everywhere, often from cute little green-stemmed glasses.

And the questions about Germany continue. Berlin or Munich? Castle or club? Ski or hike? East or west? BMW or Mercedes? In fact, the answers are simple: both. Why decide? The beauty of Germany is that rather than choosing, you can revel in the contrasts.

Berlin, edgy and vibrant, is a grand capital in a constant state of reinvention. Munich rules Bavaria, the centre of national traditions. Half-timbered villages bring smiles as you wander their cobblestoned and castle-shadowed lanes. Exploring this country and all its facets keeps visitors happy for weeks.

When to Go

Berlin

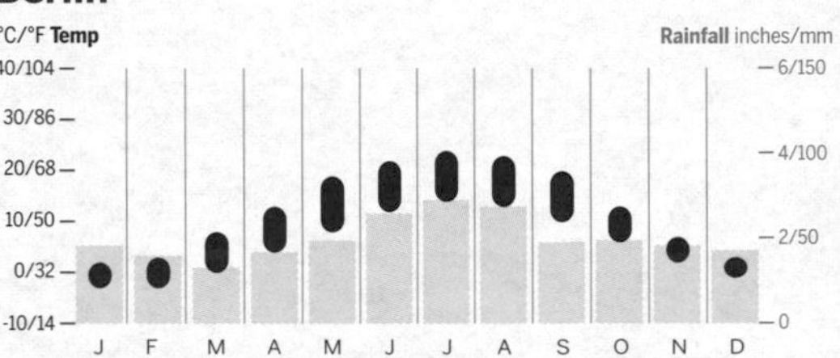

Jun–Aug Warm summer temps cause Germans to shed their clothes; night never seems to come.

Sep Celebrations in the crisp autumn air are found throughout Bavaria.

Dec It's icy, it's cold but you can drink hot wine at Christmas markets across the country.

Connections

At the heart of Europe, Germany's superb railway is well linked to surrounding countries. Freiburg and Stuttgart have services south to Switzerland and Italy, Munich is close to the Czech Republic and to Austria (including Salzburg and Innsbruck), Berlin is close to Poland, Hamburg has frequent services to Denmark, Cologne is good for fast trains to the Netherlands and Belgium (including Brussels for the Eurostar to London), and Frankfurt is the base for high-speed trains to Paris, Strasbourg and other French destinations.

ITINERARIES

One Week

Starting in Berlin, spend three days in and around the city, then head south through the wonderful little Thuringian town of Weimar and the tiny Bavarian town of Bamberg before ending up in Munich.

Two Weeks

Start in Munich for some Bavarian joy, then head up to the goofy castles in Füssen. Take in some of the Bavarian Alps and the fun of Freiburg. Explore the Black Forest, soak up Baden-Baden and settle in for a boat voyage down the Rhine from Mainz. Pop up to Hamburg then south to the old East and Dresden. Finish it all in Berlin.

Essential Food & Drink

» **Sausage** *(Wurst)* More than 1500 types are made countrywide. From sweet, smoky and tiny Nurnbergers to imposing Thüringers to that fast food remedy for the munchies the sliced and drowned currywurst.

» **Mustard** *(Senf)* The perfect accompaniment to sausages, schnitzels and more, German mustards can be hot, laced with horseradish or rich with seeds. Or all three.

» **Bread** *(Brot)* Get Germans talking about bread and often their eyes will water as they describe their favourite type – usually hearty and whole-grained in infinite variations.

» **Cakes** *(Kuchen)* From the confectionery fantasy of the whipped-cream-laden Black Forest cake to all manner of apple-laden, crumb-covered delights, sweet tooths never feel ignored.

» **Beer** *(Bier)* Mostly crisp and clear, the many lagers of the land are easily quaffed, preferably from huge steins. But exceptions exist, such as *Kölsch* in Cologne and *Rauchbier* in Bamberg.

» **Wine** *(Wein)* It's not all sweet and it's not all white; the best is superb and comes from 13 distinct regions.

AT A GLANCE

» **Currency** Euro (€)

» **Language** German

» **Money** ATMs common, cash preferred for small purchases

» **Visas** Schengen rules apply; see p1319

Fast Facts

» **Area** 356,866 sq km

» **Capital** Berlin

» **Country code** ☎49

» **Emergency** ☎112

Exchange Rates

Australia	A$1	€0.74
Canada	C$1	€0.74
Japan	¥100	€0.87
New Zealand	NZ$1	€0.57
UK	UK£1	€1.16
USA	US$1	€0.72

Set Your Budget

» **Budget dorm/private room** €20/60

» **Two-course evening meal** €12

» **Litre of beer** €9

» **Bottle of Rhine wine** €6

» **U-Bahn ticket** €2

Resources

» **Deutschland Portal** (www.deutschland.de)

» **Facts about Germany** (www.tatsachen-ueber-deutschland.de)

» **German National Tourist Office** (www.germany-tourism.de)

» **Online German Course** (www.deutsch-lernen.com)

Germany Highlights

1. Party day and night in **Berlin** (p488); save sleep for somewhere else as there's no time with the clubs, museums and bars
2. Time your journey for Oktoberfest's orgy of suds in **Munich** (p510), or just hang out in a beer garden
3. Go slow in Germany's alluring small towns such as **Bamberg** (p518), with winding lanes, smoked beer (!) and a lack of cliché
4. Compare the soaring peaks of the Dom in **Cologne** (p537) with the towering glasses of the city's famous beer

5 Go cuckoo in the **Black Forest** (p525), discovering its chilly crags and misty peaks

6 Get into the swing of **Dresden** (p502), with a creative culture beyond the restorations

7 Bike around one of the world's great harbours in **Hamburg** (p546)

8 Discover **Regensburg** (p521), Germany's Unesco-recognised ancient gem with traces of Rome and Tuscany around every corner

BERLIN

030 / POP 3.41 MILLION

Something old, something new. Reminders of Berlin's once-divided past sit side-by-side with its united present – Norman Foster's Reichstag dome, Peter Eisenman's Holocaust Memorial and the iconic Brandenburg Gate are all contained within a few blocks of each other. Strolling along Bernauerstrasse near trendy Prenzlauer Berg, you suddenly place your foot on a brick-marked line in the pavement showing where the wall once stood, a past that is rapidly receding.

Renowned for its diversity and tolerance, its alternative culture and night-owl stamina, the best thing about the German capital is the way it reinvents itself and isn't shackled by its mind-numbing history. And the world is catching on – as evidenced by the surge of expats and steady increase in out-of-towners coming to see what all the fuss is about.

In the midst of it all, students rub shoulders with Russian émigrés, fashion boutiques inhabit monumental GDR buildings, Turkish residents live next door to famous DJs and the nightlife has long left the American sector as edgy clubbers watch the sun rise over the neon-lit Universal Music headquarters in the city's east.

In short, all human life is here, and don't expect to get much sleep.

Orientation

The major sights are laid out roughly along an east–west axis going through the Brandenburger Tor (Brandenburg Gate). East of the gate lies Unter den Linden, the Museumsinsel (Museum Island) and the needle-shaped Fernsehturm (TV tower) at Alexanderplatz. Heading west you encounter the Reichstag, Holocaust Memorial, Tiergarten and Siegessäule (Victory Column), plus Potsdamer Platz to the south.

Much of the action now happens in the east – which includes the 'centra' area of Mitte and the districts of Prenzlauer Berg and Friedrichshain. Meanwhile, on the far western side of the Tiergarten, near the Zoo station, lies the Kurfürstendamm, the onetime centre of West Berlin.

Sights

Brandenburg Gate LANDMARK

(Brandenburger Tor; Map p490; Pariser Platz; M S-Bahn Unter den Linden) Finished in 1791 as one of 18 city gates, the neoclassical Brandenburg Gate became an east–west crossing point after the Berlin Wall was built in 1961. A symbol of Berlin's division, it was a place US presidents loved to grandstand. John F Kennedy passed by in 1963. Ronald Reagan appeared in 1987 to appeal to the Russian leader, 'Mr Gorbachev, tear down this wall!'. In 1989 more than 100,000 Germans poured through it as the wall fell.

FREE **Reichstag** HISTORIC BUILDING

(Parliament; Map p490; www.bundestag.de; Platz der Republik 1; 8am-midnight, last admission 10pm; M Bundestag) Just west of the Brandenburg Gate stands this glass-domed building with four national flags fluttering. A fire here in 1933 allowed Hitler to blame the communists and grab power, while the Soviets raised their flag here in 1945 to signal Nazi Germany's defeat. Today the building is once again the German seat of power, but it's the glass cupola added during the 1999 refurbishment that roughly 10,000-plus people a day flock to see. Walking along the internal spiral walkway by British star architect Lord Norman Foster feels like being in a postmodern beehive.

FREE **Holocaust Memorial** MEMORIAL

(Denkmal für die ermordeten Juden Europas; Map p490; www.stiftung-denkmal.de; Cora-Berliner-Strasse 1; field 24hr, information centre 10am-8pm Tue-Sun, last entry 7.15pm Apr-Sep, 10am-7pm Tue-Sun, last entry 6.15pm Oct-Mar; M S-Bahn Unter den Linden) Just south of the Reichstag, this grid of 2711 'stelae' or differently shaped concrete columns is set over 19,000 sq metres of gently undulating ground. The slate-grey expanse of walkways and pillars can be entered from any side, but presents varied sombre perspectives as you move through it. For historical background, there's an excellent underground information centre in the southeast corner of the site.

Unter den Linden HISTORIC AVENUE

Celebrated in literature and lined with lime (or linden) trees, the street Unter den Linden (Map p490) was the fashionable avenue of old Berlin. Today, after decades of communist neglect, it's been rebuilt and regained that status. The thoroughfare stretches east from the Brandenburger Tor to the Museumsinsel, passing shops, embassies, operas, museums and Berlin's revered Humboldt University.

Museumsinsel MUSEUMS

(Museums Island; Map p490; www.smb.museum, www.museumsinsel-berlin.de; adult/concession per museum €10/5, combined ticket for all museums

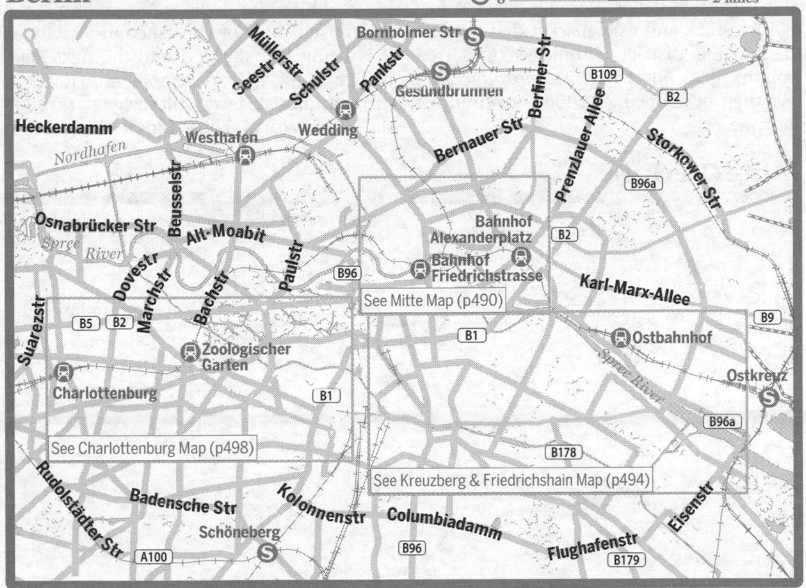

€14/7; ⏲10am-6pm Tue-Sun, to 10pm Thu; Ⓜ S-Bahn Hackescher Markt) Lying along the Spree River, the Museumsinsel contains the **Pergamonmuseum** (Map p490; Am Kupfergraben 5), which is a feast of Mesopotamian, Greek and Roman antiquities looted by archaeologists. The museum takes its name from the Pergamon Altar inside, but the real highlight of the collection is the Ishtar Gate from Babylon.

Meanwhile, the **Alte Nationalgalerie** (Old National Gallery; Map p490; Bodestrasse 1-3) houses 19th-century European sculpture and painting; the **Altes Museum** (Map p490; Am Lustgarten) features classical antiquities but is scheduled for restoration and may be closed in the coming years; and the **Bode Museum** (Map p490; Monbijoubrücke) houses sculpture, Byzantine art and painting from the Middle Ages to the 19th century. The Bode Museum is also up for renovations and parts will be closed in 2011. One of the newest additions was the reopening of the **Neues Museum** (New Museum; Map p490; adult/concession €10/5; ⏲10am-6pm Sun-Wed, to 8pm Thu-Sat), which was reduced to rubble during WWII. It has been fully rebuilt and was reopened in 2009. It houses Queen Nefertiti and other Egyptian artefacts and other artefacts from pre- and early history.

Overlooking the 'island' is the **Berliner Dom** (Berlin Cathedral; Map p490).

Hackescher Höfe HISTORIC AREA

(Map p490; Ⓜ S-Bahn Hackescher Markt) A complex of shops and apartments around eight courtyards, the Hackesche Höfe is commercial and touristy, but it's definitely good fun to wander around the big-name brand shops and smaller boutiques.

Neue Synagogue & Centrum Judaicum SYNAGOGUE

(Map p490; www.cjudaicum.de; Oranienburger Strasse 28-30; adult/concession €3/2; ⏲10am-8pm Sun & Mon, to 6pm Tue-Thu, to 5pm Fri, reduced hr Nov-Apr; Ⓜ S-Bahn Hackescher Markt) Built in 1866, it was Germany's largest synagogue at the time. Now this space doubles as a museum and cultural centre illustrating its history of local Jewish life.

TV Tower LANDMARK

(Fernsehturm; Map p490; www.berlinerfernsehturm.de; adult/concession €10/6.50; ⏲9am-midnight Mar-Oct, from 10am Nov-Feb; Ⓜ U-Bahn & S-Bahn Alexanderplatz) Call it Freudian or call it *Ostalgie* (nostalgia for the communist East or *Ost*), but Berlin's once-mocked socialist 1969 Fernsehturm is fast becoming its most-loved symbol.

Alexanderplatz SQUARE

The Turm dominates Alexanderplatz, a former livestock and wool market that became the low-life district chronicled by Alfred Döblin's 1929 novel *Berlin Alexanderplatz* and then developed as a 1960s communist showpiece.

Even in a city so often described as one big building site, today's Alexanderplatz is an unusual hive of construction activity as it is being transformed into the next Potsdamer Platz-style development. However, its communist past still echoes through the retro **World Time Clock** (Map p490)

Mitte (Berlin)

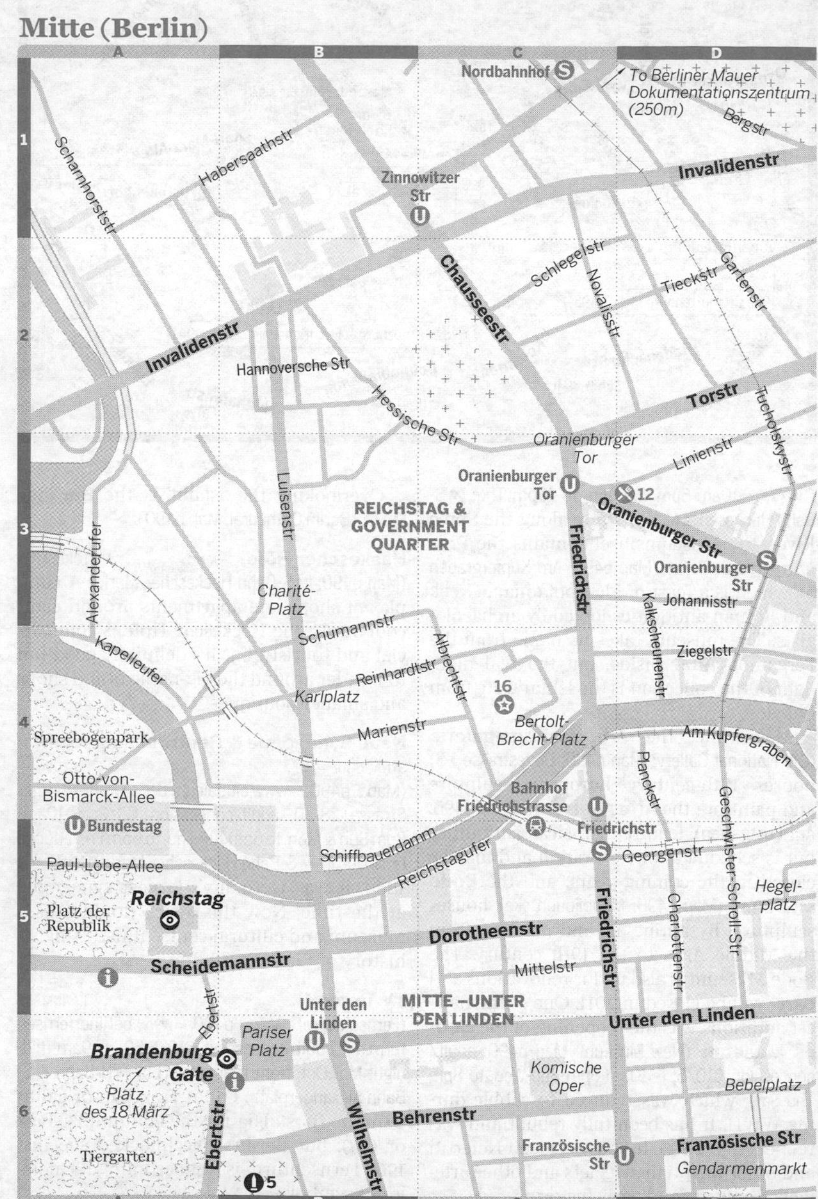

and along the portentous **Karl-Marx-Allee**, which leads east for several kilometres from the square to Friedrichshain.

Tiergarten PARK

(Maps p490 & p498) From the Reichstag, you can see the Tiergarten's **carillon** (John-Foster-Dulles-Allee; 🚌100 or 200) and the **Haus der Kulturen der Welt** (House of World Cultures; John-Foster-Dulles-Allee). The latter was erected during a 1950s building expo and is nicknamed the 'pregnant oyster'.

Further west is the **Siegessäule** (Victory Column; Map p498; 🚌100 or 200), a golden angel

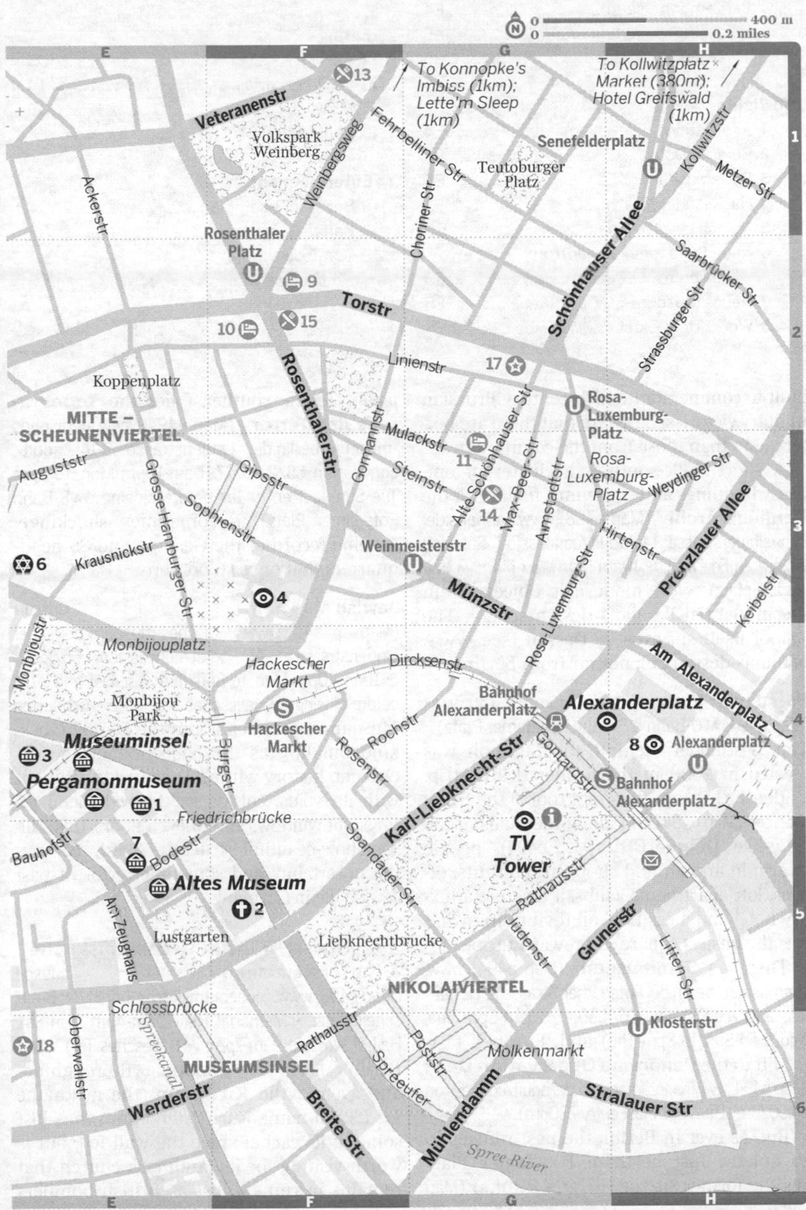

Mitte (Berlin)

Top Sights

	Alexanderplatz	G4
	Altes Museum	E5
	Brandenburg Gate	B6
	Museuminsel	E4
	Pergamonmuseum	E4
	Reichstag	A5
	TV Tower	G5

Sights

1	Alte Nationalgalerie	E4
2	Berliner Dom	F5
3	Bodemuseum	E4
4	Hackesche Höfe	F3
5	Holocaust Memorial	B6
6	Neue Synagogue & Centrum Judaicum	E3
7	Neues Museum	E5
8	World Time Clock	H4

Sleeping

9	Circus Hostel	F2
10	Circus Hotel	F2
11	Wombat's City Hostel	G3

Eating

12	Assel	D3
13	La Foccaceria	F1
14	Monsieur Vuong	G3
15	Sankt Oberholz	F2

Entertainment

16	Berliner Ensemble	C4
17	Kaffee Burger	G2
18	Staatsoper Unter den Linden	E6

built to commemorate 19th-century Prussian military victories. Be aware that there are better views than those from the column's peak.

A short walk south is a cluster of embassy buildings and museums, including the **Bauhaus Archiv** (Map p498; www.bauhaus.de; Klingelhöferstrasse 14; adult/concession Sat-Mon €7/4, Wed-Fri €6/3; 10am-5pm Wed-Mon; M Nollendorf-platz), with modernist objects from the influential Bauhaus design school. The school itself survives in Dessau (see www.bauhaus-dessau.de), not far from Berlin.

Potsdamer Platz LANDMARK

(Map p494; M U-Bahn & S-Bahn Potsdamer Platz) This postmodern temple to Mammon was erected in 2000 in the former death strip. Under the big-top, glass-tent roof of the **Sony Center** (Map p494) and along the malls of the Lego-like **DaimlerCity** (Map p494), people swarm in and around shops, restaurants, offices, loft apartments, clubs, a cinema, a luxury hotel and a casino – all revitalising what was the busiest square in prewar Europe.

There's a **Filmmuseum** (Map p494; www.filmmuseum-berlin.de; Potsdamer Strasse 2, Tiergarten; adult/concession €6/4.50; 10am-6pm Tue, Wed & Fri-Sun, to 8pm Thu) and 'Europe's fastest' lift to the **Panorama Observation Deck** (Map p494; www.panoramapunkt.de; adult/concession €4.50/3; 11am-8pm, last entry 7.30pm).

But, as ever in Berlin, the past refuses to go quietly. Just north of Potsdamer Platz lies the former site of **Hitler's Bunker** (Map p494). To the southeast lies the **Topographie des Terrors** (Map p494; www.juedisches-museum-berlin.de; Lindenstrasse 9-14; adult/concession €5/2.50; 10am-10pm Mon, to 8pm Tue-Sun, last entry 1hr before closing; M S-Bahn Potsdamer Platz), a sometimes shockingly graphic record of the Gestapo and SS headquarters that once stood here.

Jewish Museum MUSEUM

(Map p494; www.juedisches-museum-berlin.de; Lindenstrasse 9-14; adult/concession €5/2.50; 10am-10pm Mon, to 8pm Tue-Sun, last entry 1hr before closing; M Hallesches Tor) The Jüdisches Museum is as much about the Daniel Libeskind building as the collection of Jewish-German history within. Designed to disorient with its 'voids', culs-de-sac, barbed metal fittings, slit windows and uneven floors, this still-somehow-beautiful structure swiftly conveys the uncertainty and sometime terror of past Jewish life in Germany.

TOP CHOICE **Kaiser-Wilhelm-Gedächtniskirche & Kurfürstendamm** CHURCH

(Map p498; www.gedaechtniskirche-berlin.de; Breitscheidplatz; Memorial Hall 10am-4pm Mon-Sat, Hall of Worship 9am-7pm; M Hallesches Tor) West Berlin's legendary shopping thoroughfare and avenue, the **Ku'damm** (the nickname for its full name Kurfürstendamm) has lost some of its cachet since the wall fell, but is worth visiting for its landmark church that remains in ruins – just as British bombers

IF WALLS COULD TALK

Today's remnants of the 155km wall are scattered across the city, but you can follow all or sections of its former path along the 160km-long **Berliner Mauerweg** (Berlin Wall Trail; www.berlin.de/mauer), a signposted walking and cycling path that follows the former border fortifications.

The longest surviving stretch is the **East Side Gallery** (Map p494; www.eastsidegallery.com; Mühlenstrasse; M U-Bahn & S-Bahn Warschauer Strasse) in Friedrichshain. Panels along this 1.3km of graffiti and art include the famous portrait of Soviet leader Brezhnev kissing GDR leader Erich Hönecker.

The sombre **Berliner Mauer Dokumentationszentrum** (Berlin Wall Documentation Centre; off Map p490; www.berliner-mauer-dokumentationszentrum.de; Bernauer Strasse 111; admission free; 10am-6pm Tue-Sun Apr-Oct, to 5pm Nov-Mar; M Bernauersrasse) is a memorial containing a section of the original wall and listening stations featuring old West and East Berlin radio programs as well as eyewitness testimonies.

In Kreuzberg, the famous sign at **Checkpoint Charlie** (Map p494) still boasts 'You are now leaving the American sector'. For a less light-hearted view of the past, visit **Haus am Checkpoint Charlie** (Map p494; www.mauer-museum.com; Friedrichstrasse 43-45; adult/concession €12.50/9.50; 9am-10pm; M Kochstrasse/Stadtmitte). Tales of spectacular escape attempts include through tunnels, in hot-air balloons and even using a one-man submarine.

left it on 22 November 1943 – as an antiwar memorial. Only the broken west tower still stands. In 1961 the modern hall of worship was built adjacent to the church.

Stasi Museum MUSEUM
(www.stasimuseum.de; House 22, Ruschestrasse 103; adult/concession €5/4; 11am-6pm Tue-Fri, 2-6pm Sat & Sun; M Magdalenenstrasse) The one-time secret police headquarters now houses the Stasi Museum. It's largely in German, but worth a visit to see the cunning surveillance devices and communist paraphernalia.

Tours

Guided tours are phenomenally popular; you can choose Third Reich, Wall, bunker, communist, boat or bicycle tours, as well as guided pub crawls. Expect to pay from €15 and up.

New Berlin (www.newberlintours.com) even offers free (yup, free) 3½-hour introductory walking tours. These leave at 10.30am and 12.30pm from the Dunkin' Donuts opposite the Zoologisher Garten train station (Map p498), and 11am and 1pm outside the Starbucks at Pariser Platz near the Brandenburg Gate. Guides are enthusiastic and knowledgeable…and accept tips.

Sleeping

Berlin's independent hostels outdo the **DJH/HI** (www.jugendherberge.de) offerings in the city.

MITTE & PRENZLAUER BERG

Lette'm Sleep HOSTEL €
(off Map p490; 4473 3623; www.backpackers.de; Lettestrasse 7; dm from €11, tw without bathroom from €49, apt from €69; @; M Eberswalder Strasse) Located within stumbling distance of the Prenzlauer Berg nightlife action, this colourful and convenient party hostel is simply groovy, baby, groovy.

Circus Hostel HOSTEL €
(Map p490; 2839 1433; www.circus-hostel.de; Weinbergsweg 1a; dm from €21, s/d €52/72, without bathroom €42/58, 2-/4-person apt €95/150; @; M Rosenthaler Platz) This stalwart is one of the most popular hostels in town, with a great central location and friendly staff. It was thoroughly renovated and the upgraded rooms feature splashes of vibrant colour and modern, Ikea-like furnishings.

Wombat's City Hostel HOSTEL €
(Map p490; 8471 0820; www.wombats-hostels.com; Alte Schönhauser Strasse 2; dm/d €24/65, apt with kitchen €80; @; M Rosa-Luxemburg-Platz) A popular member of the Mitte hostel scene, rooms and dorms (all en suite) are decorated with modern touches and doubles offer long balconies. A hopping lounge and all-you-can-eat breakfast buffet (€3.70) round out the package. Discounts are available from November to February.

Hotel Greifswald HOTEL €
(off Map p490; 4442 7888; www.hotel-greifswald.de; Greifswalderstrasse 211; s/d/tr/apt from

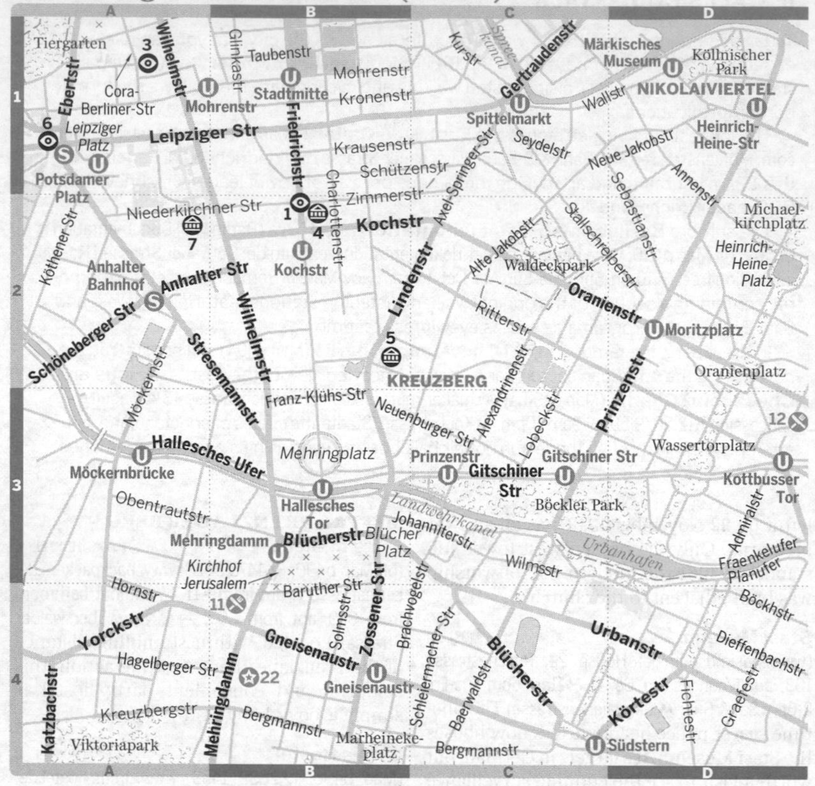

Kreuzberg & Friedrichshain (Berlin)

Sights

1 Checkpoint Charlie ... B2
Daimler City ... (see 6)
2 East Side Gallery ... F2
Filmmuseum ... (see 6)
3 Former Site of Hitler's Bunker ... A1
4 Haus am Checkpoint Charlie ... B2
5 Jewish Museum ... B2
Panorama Observation Deck ... (see 6)
6 Potsdamer Platz ... A1
Sony Center ... (see 6)
7 Topographie des Terrors ... A2

Sleeping

8 Die Fabrik ... G3
9 Ostel ... F1

Eating

10 Bürgeramt Früstücksklub ... H1
11 Curry 36 ... B4
12 Hasir ... D3
13 Nansen ... E4
14 Papaya ... H1
15 Schneeweiss ... H2
16 Türkenmarkt ... E3

Drinking

17 Ankerklause ... E3
18 Hops & Barley ... H1
19 Madame Claude ... F3
20 Süss War Gestern ... H2

Entertainment

21 Berghain/Panoramabar ... G1
22 SchwuZ ... B4
23 Watergate ... G3

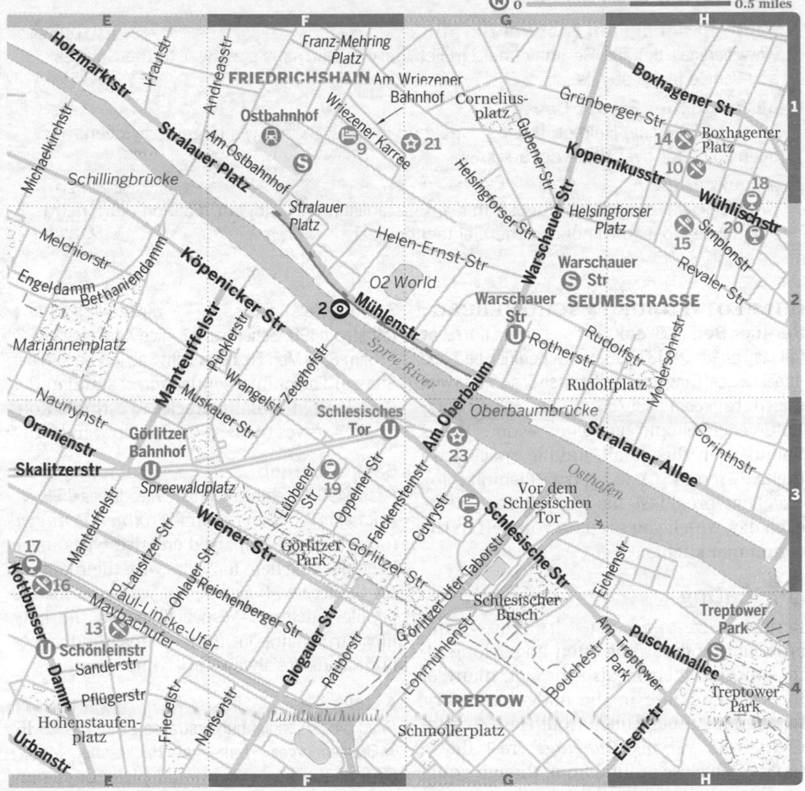

€57.50/69/90/75; @; Senefelder Platz) You'd never guess this informal, quiet hotel set back from the street around a sweet courtyard is regularly home to bands and even rock stars – until you see their photos in the lobby. We love the sumptuous breakfast buffet (€7.50) served until noon.

Circus Hotel HOTEL €€

(Map p490; 2000 3939; www.circus-berlin.de; Rosenthalerstrasse 1; s €70, d from €80, ste €100, apt €115-170; @; Rosenthaler Platz) The fancier younger sister to the Circus Hostel across the intersection, this brand spanking-new hotel has given careful attention to every detail – the result is a retro twist on minimalism, airy rooms, bold-coloured walls and super-shiny wood flooring.

KREUZBERG & FRIEDRICHSHAIN

Ostel HOSTEL €

(Map p494; 2576 8660; www.ostel.eu; Wriezener Karree 5; dm/d €15/56, apt €120; @; U-Bahn & S-Bahn Ostbahnhof) *Ostalgie* – nostalgia for the communist East – is taken to a whole new level at this hostel/hotel with original socialist GDR furnishings and portraits of Honecker and other former socialist leaders. You can even stay in a 'bugged' Stasi Suite. You might think you've entered a surreal time machine – until you access the free wi-fi, that is.

Die Fabrik HOTEL €

(Map p494; 611 7716; www.diefabrik.com; Schlesischestrasse 18; dm €20, s/d/tr/q from €40/54/70/85; @; Schlesisches Tor) A cross between a hostel and a hotel (feels more like the latter), these tidy and simple rooms are a steal. Plenty of spotless shower and toilet facilities are located on each floor and larger doubles come with washbasins and tiny sitting areas – oh, and solar power heats 100% of your hot water in the sunny months (and a smaller percentage in other seasons). Wi-fi is available in the lobby only.

FESTIVALS & EVENTS

» International Film Festival Berlin FILM FESTIVAL
(www.berlinale.de) The Berlinale, held in February, is Germany's answer to the Cannes and Venice film festivals.

» Christopher Street Day GAY EVENT
(www.csd-ber lin.de) Held on the last weekend in June, Germany's largest gay event has been going for over three decades.

» Fuckparade DANCE EVENT
(www.fuckparade.org) Each August, this anti-establishment, antigentrification demonstration dances to its own noncommercial techno beat.

CHARLOTTENBURG & SCHÖNEBERG

Berliner Bed & Breakfast HOTEL €€
(off Map p498; ☎2437 3962; www.berliner-bed-and-breakfast.de; Langenscheidtstrasse 5; s/d/tr/q with shared bathroom €35/55/68/78; Ⓜ Kleistpark) Lofty ceilings and gorgeous wood floors dominate in this small, unique space with themed rooms (Asia, retro, fashionable). Excellent breakfast food is left for guests each day, which you prepare yourself in the communal kitchen.

Eating

Berliners love to eat out – it's relaxed and affordable and patrons often linger long after finishing their meals – in fact, many of the best finds are in the budget category. Restaurants usually open from 11am to midnight, with varying *Ruhetage* (rest days). Cafes often close around 8pm, though equal numbers stay open until 2am or later.

Berlin is a snacker's paradise, with Turkish (your best bet), wurst (sausage), Greek, Italian, and Chinese *Imbiss* (place for quick snacks) stalls throughout the city. Meat eaters should not leave the city without trying Berlin's famous *Currywurst*.

There's also the excellent organic **Kollwitzplatz market** (off Map p490; ⏲9am-4pm Sat & Sun; Ⓜ Senefelderplatz), the relaxed **Winterfeldtplatz farmers market** (Map p498; ⏲Wed & Sat; Ⓜ U-Bahn Nollendorfplatz) and the bustling, ultra-cheap **Türkenmarkt** (Turkish market; Map p494; ⏲noon-6:30pm Tue & Fr; Ⓜ U-Bahn Schönleinstrasse).

MITTE & PRENZLAUER BERG

La Focacceria PIZZA €
(Map p490; Fehrbelliner Strasse 24; slices €1.75; ⏲11am-11pm; Ⓜ Rosenthaler Platz) A character-filled focaccia and pizza joint with an intense local following – perfect for an afternoon snack after a hard day's shopping or sightseeing.

Konnopke's Imbiss WURST SNACK STAND €
(off Map p490; Schönhauser Allee 44a; snacks €2; ⏲6am-8pm Mon-Fri, noon-7pm Sat; Ⓜ Eberswalder Strasse) The quintessential *wurst* stand under the elevated U-Bahn tracks. We think Konnopke's serves the best *Currywurst* in town.

Sankt Oberholz INTERNATIONAL €
(Map p490; Rosenthaler Strasse 72a; dishes €5-8; 📶; Ⓜ Rosenthaler Platz) Berlin's '*Urbanen Pennern*' (officeless, self-employed creative types) have been flocking here for years with their laptops for the free wi-fi access, but we like it for the people-watching – especially from the lofty lifeguard chairs out front. Soups, sandwiches and salads are always satisfying.

Assel GERMAN €€
(Map p490; Oranienburgerstrasse 21; mains €5-16; Ⓜ Oranienburger Strasse or Hackescher Markt) One of the few exceptional picks on a particularly touristy and busy stretch of Mitte. Come for coffee, a bite or a full meal and stretch out in the wooden booths made from old S-Bahn seats. Plus, the toilets are entertaining (you'll see).

Monsieur Vuong ASIAN €€
(Map p490; Alte Schönhauser Strasse 46; mains €7; Ⓜ Weinmeisterstrasse, Rosa-Luxemburg-Platz or Alexanderplatz) Berlin's original designer Asian soup den is trendy, packed and consistently serves amazing Vietnamese fare. Arrive early to avoid queuing.

KREUZBERG & FRIEDRICHSHAIN

Bürgeramt Früstücksklub BURGERS €
(Map p494; Krossenerstrasse 22; burgers €2-4; ⏲from 11am Mon-Fri, from 10am Sat & Sun; Ⓜ Samariterstrasse) A mere 13 types of burgers, including chicken and vegie versions, are cooked up with love and a smile in this wee space – if you can't snag a seat head to the tree-filled square opposite. Hearty breakfast fare is also available.

Hasir TURKISH €
(Map p494; Adalbertstrasse 10; mains €5-10; ⌚24hr; Ⓜ Kottbusser Tor) Local lore says this is the birthplace of Berlin's doner kebab – we haven't seen proof but we do know it tastes fantastic and we can indulge on proper chairs. It's also a fab spot to try simple Turkish fare.

Schneeweiss GERMAN €€
(Map p494; Simplonstrasse 16; day menu €7-10; Ⓜ S-Bahn Warschauer Strasse) Subtly embossed vanilla wallpaper, rectangular glass lights along the long, central table and parquet flooring keep neutral 'Snow White' feeling more après-ski than icy. The vaguely German 'Alpine' food is excellent.

Nansen INTERNATIONAL €€
(off Map p494; Maybachufer 39; mains €10-19; ⌚dinner; Ⓜ Schönlein Strasse) A favourite in this gentrified part of town, here you can dine on seasonal modern German cuisine in a romantic, candlelit space – most menu items are sourced locally.

Curry 36 SAUSAGES €
(Map p494; Mehringdamm 36; snacks €2-6; ⌚9am-4pm Mon-Sat, to 3pm Sun; Ⓜ Mehringdamm) This is Kreuzberg's most popular sausage stand, as evidenced by the daily queues (yes, it really is worth the wait).

Papaya THAI €
(Map p494; Krossener Strasse 11; mains €5-11; Ⓜ Frankfurter Tor) Don't come here for the decor (it's bland) but do come for homemade Thai specialties and it's a prime spot to fill up on quick, satisfying, budget fare before hitting the plethora of bars and clubs on its doorstep.

CHARLOTTENBURG & SCHÖNEBERG

Schwarzes Café INTERNATIONAL €
(Map p498; Kantstrasse 148; dishes €5-10; Ⓜ S-Bahn Zoologischer Garten or Savignyplatz) Founded in 1978, this 24-hour food 'n' booze institution must have seen half of Berlin pass through it (or out in it) at some point. Don't leave without checking out the toilets.

Café Einstein Stammhaus GERMAN €€
(Map p498; Kurfurstenstrasse 58; mains €15-23; ⌚9am-1am; Ⓜ Nollendorfplatz) You'll think you've hopped to another capital at this Viennese coffee house. Choose from schnitzel, strudel and other Austrian fare in the polished, palatial digs.

Drinking

Gemütlichkeit, which roughly translates as 'cosy, warm and friendly, with a decided lack of anything hectic', dominates the upscale bars of the west as well as the hipper, more underground venues in the east. Prenzlauer Berg, the first GDR sector to develop a happening nightlife, still attracts visitors, creative types and gay customers, but as its residents have aged (and produced many, many babies) its nightlife has become more subdued. Clubs and bars in Mitte around Hackescher Markt cater to a cool, slightly older and wealthier crowd. Friedrichshain boasts a young, hipster feel and Kreuzberg remains the alternative hub, becoming grungier as you move east. Charlottenburg and Winterfeldtplatz are fairly upmarket and mature, but liberal.

Bars without food open between 5pm and 8pm and may close as late as 5am (if at all).

Madame Claude BAR
(Map p494; Lübbener Strasse 19; Ⓜ Schlesiches Tor) Kick back with a beer and pretend you've stepped into the pages of *Alice in Wonderland*. Run by a threesome (of course), tables and chairs live on the ceiling and coat hooks are upside down, and the shoes dangling above made us grin like the Cheshire cat. True to Berlin, it's shabby and slightly gritty, with secondhand furniture and a DJ doling out hip tracks.

GAY & LESBIAN BERLIN

Berlin boasts a liberal – no, wild is more like it – gay scene where anything goes. Going strong since the 1920s, Schöneberg is the original gay area, but these days Prenzlauer Berg is the trendiest; Friedrichshain also has a small studenty gay scene. Skim through **Discodamaged** (www.discodamaged.net, in German) for all things gay in Berlin, or **Girl Ports** (www.girlports.com/lesbiantravel/destinations/berlin), a lesbian travel magazine.

SchwuZ (Map p494; www.schwuz.de; Mehringdamm 61; ⌚from 11pm Fri & Sat; Ⓜ Mehringdamm) is one of the longest-running mixed nightclubs; there's a cafe here all week too.

Hafen (Map p498; ☎211 4118; Motzstrasse 19; Ⓜ Nollendorfplatz) is a Schöneberg staple with a consistent party scene. There's also an eclectic quiz night on Monday (in English first Monday of the month).

Charlottenburg (Berlin)

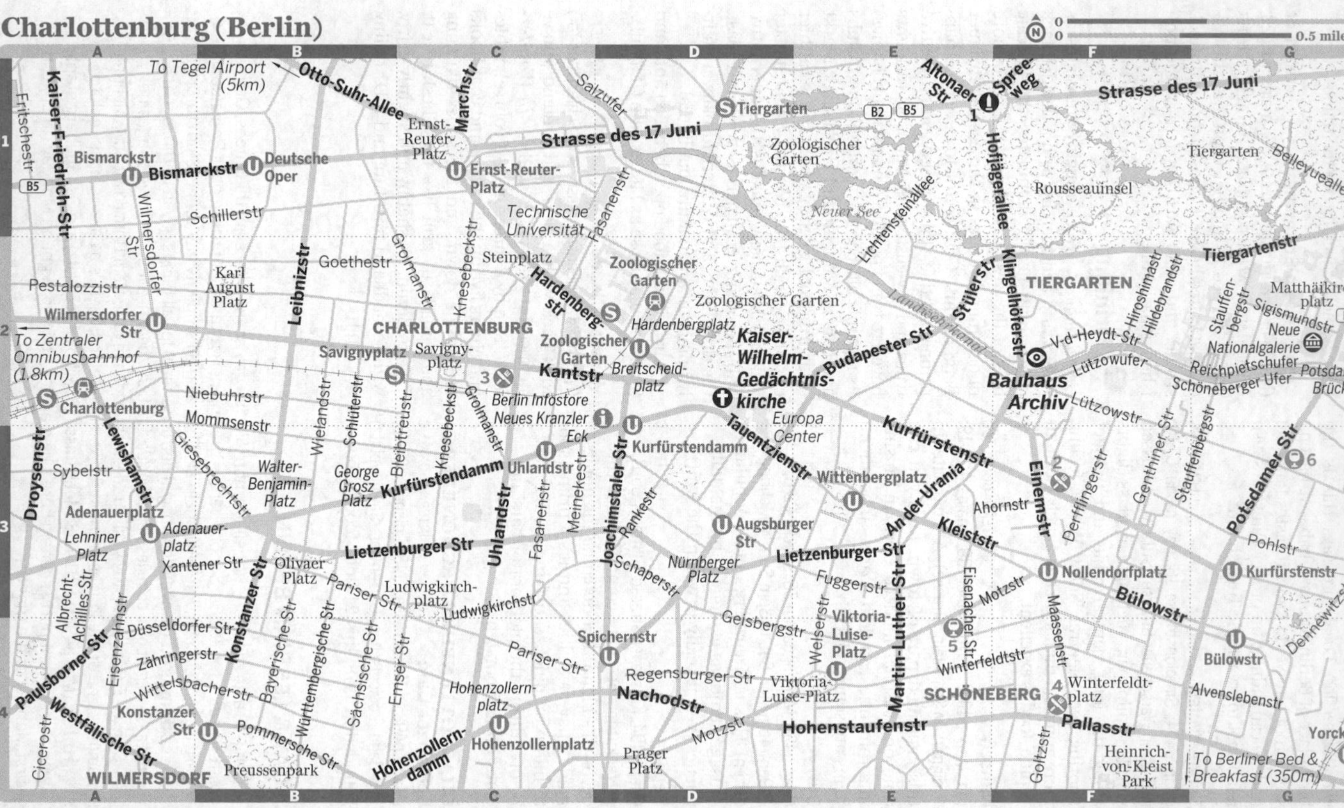

Charlottenburg (Berlin)

Top Sights

Sights

Eating

Drinking

Hops & Barley MICROBREWERY, PUB
(Map p494; Wühlisch Strasse 40; MS-Bahn Warschauer Strasse) Excellent ciders and beers – brewed on site at this convivial microbrewery – pack them in every night. It's set inside a former butcher shop littered with aged-but-refurbushed wood tables and school desks.

Kumpelnest 3000 BAR
(Map p498; Lützowstrasse 23; MKurfürstenstrasse) Once a brothel, always an experience: the Kumpelnest has been famed since the '80s for its wild, inhibition-free nights. Much of the original whorehouse decor remains intact.

Ankerklause BAR
(Map p494; Kottbusser Damm 104; MKottbusser Tor) Slightly kitsch but always a winner, this nautical-themed bar in an old harbourmaster's house is worthy of a brew or two. Thursday it turns into a casual dance floor with music suiting most tastes.

Süss War Gestern BAR
(Yesterday Was Sweet; Map p494; Wülischstrasse 43; MS-Bahn Ostkreuz) Street-art-covered walls, 1970s decorations and comfortable sofas make this outpost worth the trek. Most nights feature a DJ spinning anything from funk to soul to electric music.

Entertainment

Berlin is not only famous for its clubs – its cultural offerings are also renowned. So if you fancy splashing out on a quieter, more refined evening, try one of the following.

Clubbing

Few clubs open before 11pm (and if you arrive before midnight you may be dancing solo) but they stay open well into the early hours – usually sunrise at least. As the scene changes so rapidly, it's always wise to double-check listings magazines or ask locals. Admission charges, when they apply, range from €5 to €20.

Berghain/Panoramabar CLUB
(Map p494; www.berghain.de; Wrienzer Bahnhof; from midnight Thu-Sat; MOstbahnhof) If you only make it to one club in Berlin, this is where you need to go. The upper floor (Panoramabar, aka 'Pannebar') is all about house; the big factory hall below (Berghain) goes hardcore techno. Expect cutting-edge sounds in industrial surrounds.

Kaffee Burger CLUB
(Map p490; 2804 6495; www.kaffeeburger.de; Torstrasse 60; MRosa-Luxemburg-Platz) The original GDR '60s wallpaper is part of the decor at this arty bar, club and music venue in Mitte. Burger hosts popular monthly readings by local (mainly expat) writers in English, but many come here for indie, rock, punk and cult author Wladimir Kaminer's twice-monthly *Russendisko* (Russian disco; www.russendisko.de).

Watergate CLUB
(Map p494; 6128 0394; www.water-gate.de; Falckensteinstrasse 49a; from 11pm Fri & Sat; MSchlesisches Tor) Watch the sun rise over the Spree River through the floor-to-ceiling windows of this fantastic lounge. The music is mainly electro, drum'n'bass and hip hop.

Staatsoper Unter den Linden OPERA HOUSE
(Map p490; information 203 540, tickets 2035 4555; www.staatsoper-berlin.de; Unter den Linden 5-7; MU-Bahn & S-Bahn Unter den Linden) This is the handiest and most prestigious of Berlin's three opera houses, where unsold seats go on sale cheap an hour before curtains-up.

Berliner Ensemble THEATRE
(Map p490; information 284 080, tickets 2840 8155; www.berliner-ensemble.de; Bertolt-Brecht-Platz 1; MFriedrichstrasse) 'Mack the Knife' had its first public airing here, during the *Threepenny Opera's* premiere in 1928. Bertolt Brecht's former theatrical home continues to present his plays.

Information

Internet access is a breeze to find in Berlin – and the entire Sony Center at Potsdamerplatz is a free public hot spot.

Berlin Tourismus (☎250 025; www.berlin-tourist-information.de) Alexanderplatz (Map p490; Alexa Shopping Centre; ⏲10am-6pm); Brandenburger Tor (Map p490; ⏲10am-6pm); Hauptbahnhof/Main train station (Map p490; Ground fl/Europa Platz entrance; ⏲8am-10pm); Reichstag (Map p490; ⏲10am-6pm); Zoologisher Garten station (Map p498; Kurfürstendamm 21; ⏲10am-8pm Mon-Sat, to 6pm Sun)

Berlin Welcome Card (www.berlin-welcomecard.de; 48/72hr €16.90/22.90, incl Potsdam & up to 3 children €18.90/25.90) Free public transport, plus museum and entertainment discounts.

Kassenärztliche Bereitschaftsdienst (Public Physicians' Emergency Service; ☎310 031; www.kvberlin.de, in German) Phone referral service.

Post office (Map p490; Rathausstrasse 5; ⏲8am-7pm Mon-Fri, to 4pm Sat; Ⓜ Alexanderplatz)

Getting There & Away

Air

Berlin has two international airports, reflecting the legacy of the divided city. The larger one is in the northwestern suburb of Tegel (TXL), about 8km from the city centre; the other is in Schönefeld (SXF), about 22km southeast of town.

Berlin will eventually get its own major international airport, as Schönefeld is being expanded into Berlin Brandenburg International (BBI); estimated completion date is 2012. Tegel is due to be decommissioned when BBI fully opens. For information, go to www.berlin-airport.de.

Bus

Berlin is well connected to the rest of Europe by a network of long-distance buses. Most buses arrive at and depart from the **Zentraler Omnibusbahnhof** (ZOB; ☎302 5361; Masurenallee 4-6; Ⓜ Kaiserdamm/Witzleben), opposite the Funkturm radio tower. Tickets are available from travel agencies or at the bus station.

Car

Lifts all over the country can be organised by **ADM Mitfahrzentrale** (ride-share agencies; www.mitfahrzentralen.org, in German) Hardenbergplatz (Map p498; ☎194 240; Hardenbergplatz 14; ⏲9am-8pm Mon-Fri, 10am-2pm Sat, 10am-4pm Sun); Zoologischer Garten station (Map p498; ☎194 40; ⏲9am-8pm Mon-Fri, 10am-6pm Sat & Sun).

Train

Regular long-distance services arrive at the architecturally spectacular Hauptbahnhof (www.berlin-hauptbahnhof.de), with many continuing east to Ostbahnhof. ICE and IC trains leave hourly to every major city in Germany and there are also connections to central Europe. Sample fares include to Leipzig (€36, 1¼ hours), Hamburg (€68, 1½ to two hours), Stralsund (€38 to €46, 2¾ to 3¼ hours) and Prague (€62, 4½ to five hours).

Unfortunately the few lockers available are hidden in the parking garage.

Getting Around

Berlin's public transport system (www.bvg.de) is excellent and a much better choice than driving around the city. One type of ticket is valid on all transport and three tariff zones exist – A, B and C. Unless venturing to Potsdam or the outer suburbs, you'll only need an AB ticket, costing €2.10 for a single, €6.10 for a day pass and €15.40 for a group day pass for up to five people.

Most tickets are available from vending machines in stations, but must be validated before hopping on the train or bus, or as you enter them.

Services operate from 4am until just after midnight on weekdays, with many *Nachtbus* (night bus) services in between. At weekends, they run all night long (except the U4).

AROUND BERLIN

Despite its proximity to Berlin, Brandenburg has suffered from a poor reputation since reunification. Many western Germans still think of Brandenburgers as archetypal Ossis, ambivalent about the demise of the GDR and perhaps even a touch xenophobic. However, even the most sneering Wessi will happily go to Potsdam on a day trip.

Potsdam

☎0331 / POP 150,000

Featuring ornate palaces and manicured gardens dotted around a huge riverside park, the Prussian royal seat of Potsdam is the most popular day trip from Berlin. Elector Friedrich Wilhelm of Brandenburg laid the ground for the town's success when he made it his second residence in the 17th century. But Friedrich II (Frederick the Great) commissioned most of the palaces in the mid-18th century.

In August 1945, the victorious WWII Allies chose nearby Schloss Cecilienhof for the Potsdam Conference, which set the stage for the division of Berlin and Germany into occupation zones.

Potsdam Hauptbahnhof is just southeast of the city centre, across the Havel River. As this is still quite a way (2km) from Park Sanssoucci, you might like to change trains here and transfer to trains for Potsdam Sanssoucci train station.

Sights

Park Sanssouci HISTORIC SITE

At the heart of **Park Sanssouci** (dawn to dusk) lies a celebrated rococo palace, **Schloss Sanssouci** (969 4190; adult/concession Apr-Oct €12/8, Nov-Mar €8/5; 10am-6pm Tue-Sun Apr-Oct, to 5pm Nov-Mar). Built in 1747, it has some glorious interiors. Only 2000 visitors are allowed entry each day (a Unesco rule), so tickets are usually sold by 2.30pm, even in quiet seasons. Tours run by the tourist office guarantee entry.

The late-baroque **Neues Palais** (New Palace; adult/concession €6/5; 10am-6pm Wed-Mon Apr-Oct, to 5pm Nov-Mar) was built in 1769 as the royal family's summer residence. It's one of the most imposing buildings in the park and the one to see if your time is limited.

The **Bildergalerie** (Picture Gallery; adult/concession €2/1.50; 10am-6pm Tue-Sun mid-May–Oct) contains a rich collection of 17th-century paintings by Rubens, Caravaggio and other big names.

Many consider the **Chinesisches Haus** (Chinese House; admission €2; 10am-6pm Tue-Sun mid-May–Oct) to be the pearl of the park. It's a circular pavilion of gilded columns, palm trees and figures of Chinese musicians and animals, built in 1757.

Schloss Cecilienhof/Neuer Garten PALACE

(tours adult/concession €6/5; 9am-6pm Tue-Sun, to 5pm Nov-Mar) When outgoing British prime minister Winston Churchill and his accompanying successor Clement Attlee arrived at this palace in 1945 they must have immediately felt at home. Located in the separate New Garden, northeast of the centre on the bank of the Heiliger See, this is an incongruously English-style country manor in rococo-heavy Potsdam.

Filmpark Babelsberg MUSEUM

(www.filmpark.de; Grossbeerenstrasse; adult/concession €19/16; 10am-6pm Apr-Oct) Germany's **UFA Film Studios** was where Fritz Lang's *Metropolis* was shot and FW Murnau filmed the first Dracula movie, *Nosferatu*. Since a relaunch in 1999, it's helped Berlin regain its film-making crown, with Roman Polanski's *The Pianist* made here, and Quentin Tarantino's *Inglourious Basterds* starring Brad Pitt. The visitor experience includes theme-park rides and a studio tour – the daily stunt show (2pm) is worth catching. The studios are east of the city centre.

Altstadt HISTORIC AREA

The **Brandenburger Tor** (Brandenburg Gate) at the western end of the Old Town on Luisenplatz isn't a patch on the one in Berlin, but it is older, dating from 1770. From here, pedestrian Brandenburger Strasse runs east, providing the town's main eating strip.

Standing out from its surrounds is the pretty **Holländisches Viertel** (Dutch Quarter). Towards the northern end of Friedrich-Ebert-Strasse, it has 134 gabled red-brick houses, built for Dutch workers who came to Potsdam in the 1730s at the invitation of Friedrich Wilhelm I. The homes have been well restored and now house all kinds of interesting galleries, cafes and restaurants.

Tours

Boats belonging to **Weisse Flotte** (www.schiffahrt-in-potsdam.de; Lange Brücke 6; 9.45am-7pm Apr-Oct) cruise the Havel and the lakes around Potsdam, departing regularly from the dock near Lange Brücke, with frequent trips to Wannsee (€9/12 one way/return) and around the castles (€10).

Information

Potsdam tourist office (275 580; www.potsdam tourismus.de; Brandenburger Strasse 3; 9.30am-6pm Mon-Fri, 9.30am-4pm Sat & Sun Apr-Oct, 10am-6pm Mon-Fri, 9.30am-2pm Sat & Sun Nov-Mar) Near the Hauptbahnhof.

Sanssouci Besucherzentrum (969 4202; www.spsg.de; An der Orangerie 1; 8.30am-5pm Mar-Oct, 9am-4pm Nov-Feb) Near the windmill and Schloss Sanssouci.

Getting There & Away

S-Bahn line S7 links central Berlin with Potsdam Hauptbahnhof about every 10 minutes. Some regional (RB/RE) trains from Berlin stop at all three stations in Potsdam. Your ticket must cover Berlin Zones A, B and C (€2.80) to come here.

EASTERN GERMANY

Germany's eastern heartland is for many people (Germans included) the most historically German. Its three states all have their own distinct character. Saxony lives off its reputation based on the momentous history of cities such as Leipzig and Dresden. Thuringia, the self-touted 'green heart' of Germany, entices hordes of visitors to the humanist bastion of Weimar and the state capital Erfurt. Saxony-Anhalt boasts a good

DON'T MISS

SACHSENHAUSEN CONCENTRATION CAMP

In 1936 the Nazis opened a 'model' **concentration camp** (www.gedenkstaette-sachsenhausen.de; admission free; ⌚8.30am-6pm mid-Mar–mid-Oct, to 4pm mid-Oct–mid-Mar) near Oranienburg some 35km north of Berlin. By 1945 about 220,000 prisoners had passed through the gates of Sachsenhausen. About 100,000 people died here. After the war, the Soviets and the communist leaders of the new GDR used the camp for *their* undesirables.

Plan on spending at least two hours. Among the many monuments and museums are **Barracks 38 & 39**, with excellent displays on the camp's history. Maps, brochures, booklets and audio guides in English are available.

The easiest way to get to Sachsenhausen from Berlin is to take the frequent S1 to Oranienburg (€2.80, 50 minutes). The walled camp is a signposted 20-minute walk from Oranienburg station.

swathe of the lovely Harz Mountains (sharing them with Lower Saxony).

Together with Brandenburg, East Berlin and Mecklenburg-Western Pomerania, these states made up the GDR. In the popular tourist towns such as Dresden you'll still easily see vestiges of things past in the monumental – and monumentally ugly – blocks of 1960s buildings around (and sometimes in) the centre.

Any trips south of Berlin should really include stops in this fun and fascinating region.

Dresden

☎0351 / POP 484,000

Proof that there is life after death, Dresden has become one of Germany's most popular attractions, and for good reason. Restorations have returned the city to the glory days when it was famous throughout Europe as 'Florence on the Elbe', owing to the efforts of Italian artists, musicians, actors and master craftsmen who flocked to the court of Augustus the Strong, bestowing countless masterpieces upon the city. Death came suddenly when, shortly before the end of WWII, Allied bombers blasted and incinerated much of the baroque centre, a beautiful jewel-like area dating from the 18th century. More than 25,000 people died, and in bookstores throughout town you can peruse texts showing the destruction (or read about it in Kurt Vonnegut's classic *Slaughterhouse Five*).

Rebuilding began under the communist regime in the 1950s and accelerated greatly after reunification. The city celebrated its 800th anniversary in 2006 and, while much focus is on the restored centre, you should cross the River Elbe to the Neustadt, where edgy new clubs and cafes open every week, joining the scores already there.

Sights

Dresden straddles the Elbe River, with the attraction-studded Altstadt (old town) in the south and the livelier Neustadt to the north.

Frauenkirche CATHEDRAL

(Church of Our Lady; www.frauenkirche-dresden.org; Neumarkt; ⌚10am-6pm) One of Dresden's most beloved icons, the Frauenkirche was rebuilt in time for the city's 800th anniversary celebrations in 2006. Initially constructed between 1726 and 1743 under the direction of baroque architect George Bähr, it was Germany's greatest Protestant church until February 1945, when bombing raids flattened it. The communists decided to leave the rubble as a war memorial; after reunification, calls for reconstruction prevailed, although the paucity of charcoal-tinged original stones shows just how much is new. The surrounding **Neumarkt** is part of a massive redevelopment designed to evoke prewar Dresden.

Semperoper HISTORIC BUILDING

(www.semperoper-erleben.de; Theaterplatz; tours €8; ⌚varies) Designed by Gustav Semper, this neo-Renaissance opera house *is* Dresden. The original building opened in 1841 but burnt down less than three decades later. Rebuilt in 1878, it was pummelled in WWII and reopened in 1985 after the communists invested a fortune restoring it.

Residenzschloss PALACE

(www.skd.museum; Schlossplatz) The Residenzschloss, a massive neo-Renaissance palace, has ongoing restoration projects. Its many features include the **Hausmannsturm** (Servants' Tower; admission €3; ⌚10am-6pm Wed-Mon), which has sobering pictures of the complete WWII destruction.

Grünes Gewölbe
(Green Vault; admission €10; ⏲10am-7pm Wed-Mon) is one of the world's finest collections of precious objects. Buy timed tickets in advance from the office or online.

Fürstenzug
(Procession of Princes; Augustusstrasse) Outside, you'd need a really wide-angle lens to get a shot of Wulhelm Walther's amazing 102m-long tiled mural on the wall of the former Stendehaus (Royal Stables).

Zwinger ART GALLERIES, MUSEUMS
(www.skd.museum; Theaterplatz 1; ⏲10am-6pm Tue-Sun) Dresden's elaborate 1728 fortress, an attraction in its own right with a popular ornamental courtyard, also houses six major museums. The most important is the **Galerie Alte Meister** (admission €10), which features masterpieces including Raphael's *Sistine Madonna*. The **Rüstkammer** (Armoury; admission €3) has a superb collection of ceremonial weapons.

Albertinum MUSEUM
(www.skd.museum; Brühlsche Terrasse; admission €8; ⏲10am-6pm) Massive renovations ended in 2010 and the results are stunning. A light-filled enclosed courtyard welcomes you into this treasure trove of art. Highlights include the **Münzkabinett** collection of antique coins and medals, and the **Skulpturensammlung**, which includes classical and Egyptian works. The **Galerie Neue Meister** has renowned 19th- and 20th-century paintings from leading French and German Impressionists.

Sleeping

Accommodation in Dresden can be very expensive in the high season. Luckily, several good-value budget places can be found in the lively Neustadt.

Lollis Homestay HOSTEL €
(☎810 8458; www.lollishome.de; Görlitzer Strasse 34; dm €13-19, s €30-38, d €40-42; @📶) Dresden's quirkiest hostel has two contenders for Germany's most outlandish dorm – one containing a real Trabant you can bed down in for the night, the other a Giant's Room with oversize furniture that makes guests feel like Tom Thumb. In addition there's free bike rental. Breakfast costs €3.

Hotel Martha Hospiz HOTEL €€
(☎817 60; www.hotel-martha-hospiz.de; Nieritzstrasse 11; r €80-140; 📶) Fifty rooms decked out in Biedermeier style, an attractive winter garden, a sound on-site restaurant with Saxon cooking and local wine make this a very pleasant place to lay your hat. It's all very slick.

Rothenburger Hof HOTEL €€
(☎812 60; www.rothenburger-hof.de; Rothenburger Strasse 15-17; r €75-160, apt €140-180; 📶🏊) This quiet launch pad for Neustadt explorations counts among its assets apartments with kitchenette and balcony, a Moorish-style steam room and a great pool. The included breakfast is lavish.

EV-Ref Gemeinde zu Dresden PENSION €
(☎438 230; www.ev-ref-gem-dresden.de; Brühlscher Garten 4; s/d from €60/75) The name is not a marketer's dream, but this pension is amazing value in a great location – on the river and overlooking the Albertinum. This historic retirement home makes rooms available for travellers whenever a resident has permanently 'checked out'. Rooms have showers and TV and often great views; breakfast is included.

Hostel & Backpacker Kangaroo-Stop HOSTEL €
(☎314 3455; www.kangaroo-stop.de; Erna-Berger-Strasse 8-10; dm/s/d/from €13/29/40; 🚭@📶) Welcoming and low-key, with rooms spread over two buildings: one for backpackers and the other for families. So which will see more immature behaviour? The big breakfast buffet costs €5. Dresden-Neustadt station is nearby.

Eating

It's no problem finding somewhere to eat in the Neustadt, with oodles of cafes and restaurants found along Königstrasse and the streets north of Albertplatz. This is also the centre of Dresden's nightlife. You'll be going until dawn, with dozens of choices.

Off Albertstrasse, the **Neustädter Markthalle** is a gorgeously restored old market hall (enter on Metzer Strasse) with food stalls good for picnics and amazingly cheap *wurst* lunches.

TOP CHOICE **Wenzel Prager Bierstuben** CZECH €€
(Königstrasse 1; mains €7-20; ⏲11am-midnight) This busy beer hall serves up oceans of Czech lager under arched brick ceilings. Always crowded, the menu leans towards traditional meaty mains. The garlic soup is sublime, the cured pork with horseradish a delight.

Raskolnikoff CAFE €
(www.raskolnikoff.de; Böhmische Strasse 34; mains €5-14) This bohemian cafe in a former artists' squat was one of the Neustadt's first post-Wende pubs. The menu is sorted by compass direction (borscht to quiche Lorraine to smoked fish) and there's a sweet little ivy-lined beer garden out back, plus a gallery and pension (rooms €40 to €55) upstairs.

Café Europa CAFE €€
(Königsbrücker Strasse 68; mains €6-15; 24hr; ) Smart open-all-hours Neustadt cafe with newspapers and free internet. Come here to regroup during the early hours.

Drinking

The places listed under Eating above are also good just for a drink.

TOP CHOICE **Café 100** WINE BAR
(Alaunstrasse 100) Off a courtyard. You'll pass hundreds of empty bottles on the way in, a foreshadowing of the lengthy wine list and delights that follow. Candles give the underground space a romantic yet edgy glow. The place to take that someone you met on the train.

Scheunecafé CAFE
(Alaunstrasse 36-40) Set back from the street, this place combines Indian food (mains €7 to €12), a vast beer garden, live music and DJs into a fun and funky stew.

Entertainment

Dresden is synonymous with opera, and performances at the spectacular **Semperoper** (www.semperoper.de; Theaterplatz), opposite the Zwinger, are brilliant. Tickets cost from €10, but they're usually booked out well in advance.

Blue Note JAZZ
(www.jazzdepartment.com; Görlitzer Strasse 2b; to 5am) Small, smoky and smooth, this converted smithy has live jazz almost nightly until 11pm, then turns into a night-owl magnet until the wee hours. The talent is mostly regional.

Strasse E CLUB
(www.strasse-e.de; Werner-Hartmann-Strasse 2) Dresden's most high-octane party zone is in an industrial area between Neustadt and the airport. Half a dozen venues cover the entire sound spectrum, from disco to dark wave, electro to pop. Take tram 7 to Industriegelände.

Information

Dresden City-Card (per 48hr €21) Provides admission to museums, discounted city tours and boats, and free public transport. Buy it at the tourist office.

Dresden Regio-Card (per 72hr €32) Everything offered by the City-Card plus free transport on the entire regional transport network. Valid as far as the Czech border and Meissen.

Tourist office (www.dresden-tourist.de; Kulturpalast, Schlossstrasse; 10am-7pm Mon-Fri, 10am-6pm Sat, 10am-3pm Sun) Also houses the central ticket office.

Getting There & Around

Dresden's **airport** (DRS; www.dresden-airport.de), served by Lufthansa and Air Berlin among others, is 9km north of the city centre, on S-Bahn line 2 (€1.90, 20 minutes).

Dresden is well linked with regular services through the day to Leipzig (€29, 70 minutes), Berlin-Hauptbahnhof by IC/EC train (€36, 2¼ hours) and Frankfurt-am-Main by ICE (€89, 4½ hours).

Dresden's public transport network (www.dvbag.de) charges €1.90 for a single-trip ticket; day tickets cost €5 and can be bought on trams. Trams 3, 7, 8 and 9 provide good links between the Hauptbahnhof, Altstadt and Neustadt.

Around Dresden

MEISSEN

03521 / POP 29,000

Some 27km northwest of Dresden, Meissen is a compact, perfectly preserved old town and the centre of a rich wine-growing region. It makes for a good day trip out of Dresden by train or boat and beguiles with its red-tiled roofs and old Saxon charm.

The **Markt** is framed by the **Rathaus** (1472) and the Gothic **Frauenkirche**, which – fittingly – has a porcelain carillion.

Meissen's medieval fortress, the 15th-century **Albrechtsburg** (www.albrechtsburg-meissen.de; Domplatz 1; admission €8; 10am-6pm Mar-Oct, to 5pm Nov-Feb), crowns a ridge high above the Elbe River and is reached by steep lanes. Augustus the Strong of Saxony created Europe's first porcelain factory here in 1710.

Next door, the towering 13th-century **Albrechtsburg Cathedral** (452 490; Domplatz 7; admission €4; 10am-6pm Mar-Oct, to 4pm Nov-Feb) contains an altarpiece by Lucas Cranach the Elder.

Meissen's porcelain factory is now 1km southwest of the Altstadt in an appropriately beautiful building, the **Porzellan-**

Museum (www.meissen.com; Talstrasse 9; adult €9; ⌚9am-6pm May-Oct, to 5pm Nov-Apr), which dates to 1916.

Information

Tourist office (www.touristinfo-meissen.de; Markt 3; ⌚10am-6pm Mon-Fri, to 4pm Sat & Sun Apr-Oct, 10am-5pm Mon-Fri, to 3pm Sat Nov-Mar)

Getting There & Away

Half-hourly S-Bahn trains run from Dresden's Hauptbahnhof and Neustadt train stations (€5.50, 40 minutes). To visit the porcelain factory, get off at Meissen-Triebischtal (one stop after Meissen).

A more pleasant way to get here is by steamer (between May and September). Boats leave from the **Sächsische Dampfschiffahrt** (☎866 090; www.saechsische-dampfschiffahrt.de) dock in Dresden once daily (€17 return, two hours).

Leipzig

☎0341 / POP 515,000

Leipzig is the busiest city in Saxony, a bustling, more commercial alternative to Dresden. Although it lacks the capital's busload of museums, Leipzig is not weighed down by the past and, like its shopping passages, invites exploration.

Leipzig also has some of the finest classical music and opera in the country, and its art and literary scenes are flourishing. It was once home to Bach, Wagner and Mendelssohn, as well as Goethe, who set a key scene of *Faust* in the cellar of his favourite watering hole. More recently, it earned the sobriquet *Stadt der Helden* (City of Heroes) for its leading role in the 1989 democratic revolution.

Sights

Don't rush from sight to sight – wandering around Leipzig is a pleasure in itself, with many of the blocks around the central Markt crisscrossed by old internal shopping passages, including the classic **Mädlerpassage**.

TOP CHOICE **Stasi Museum** MUSEUM
(www.runde-ecke-leipzig.de; Dittrichring 24; admission free; ⌚10am-6pm) Former headquarters of the East German secret police, the Stasi Museum has exhibits on propaganda, amazingly hokey disguises, surveillance photos and other forms of 'intelligence', all part of the chilling machinations of the GDR's all-out zeal for controlling, manipulating and repressing its own people.

Museum der Bildenden Künste MUSEUM
(Museum of Fine Arts; www.mdbk.de; Grimmaische Strasse 1-7; admission €5; ⌚10am-6pm Tue & Thu-Sun, noon-8pm Wed) Leipzig's finest museum, the Museum der Bildenden Künste, is housed in a stunning glass cube of a building that provides both a dramatic – and echoey – backdrop to its collection, which spans old masters and the latest efforts of local artists.

Bach Museum MUSEUM
(www.bachmuseumleipzig.de; Thomaskirchhof 16; admission €6; ⌚10am-6pm Tue-Sun) Johann Sebastian Bach worked here from 1723 until his death in 1750. The newly revamped collection focuses on the composer's busy life in Leipzig. Multimedia displays allow you to get inside his head as he was composing music. Just across is **Thomaskirche** (Thomaskirchhof 18), where he lead the choir (and was only hired after three others turned the job down).

Alte Spinnerei ART GALLERIES
(www.spinnerei.de; Spinnereistrasse 7; ⌚11am-6pm Tue-Sat) 'Cotton to culture' is the motto at this 19th-century cotton-spinning factory turned artist colony. Around 80 New Leipzig School artists, including Neo Rauch, have their studios in this huge pile of red-brick buildings, alongside designers, architects, goldsmiths and other creative types. Their work is displayed in about 10 galleries, including **Galerie Eigen+Art** (☎960 7886; www.eigen-art.com), internationally renowned for championing young artists. Take the S-1 to Plagwitz.

Sleeping

Leipzig's tourist service offers free booking in private homes near the centre. Average cost is €30 to €50.

Central Globetrotter Hostel HOSTEL €
(☎149 8960; www.globetrotter-leipzig.de; Kurt-Schumacher-Strasse 41; dm €14-18, s/d €28/40; @📶) In a busy location just north of the train station, this 80-room hostel offers bare-bones accommodation, although some rooms boast murals, albeit ones that won't win any scholarships to the Art Academy of Leipzig. Breakfast is €4 extra.

Hotel Markgraf HOTEL €€
(☎303 030; www.markgraf-leipzig.de; Körnerstrasse 36; r €85-100; 📶) This smartly run hotel puts you within staggering distance of the Karl-Liebknecht-Strasse nightlife. Many rooms overlook a pretty park and there's a sauna for relaxing. Take tram 10 or 11 south to Südplatz.

Hotel Kosmos HOTEL €€
(☎233 4422; www.hotel-kosmos.de; Gottschedstrasse 1; s/d from €50/80) Right on a street with burgeoning nightlife, this low-key place in a grand building combines GDR-era furniture with murals in themed rooms. The murals next to the bed in the Marilyn Monroe room may fool the foolhardy.

Also recommended:

Hostel Sleepy Lion HOSTEL €
(☎993 9480; www.hostel-leipzig.de; Käthe-Kollwitz-Strasse 3; dm from €15, s/d €30/45; @🛜) Budget-minded nomads will feel welcome at this low-key hostel, with 60 clean and comfy beds in cheerfully painted rooms with private facilities. Major sights – and bars – are just steps away.

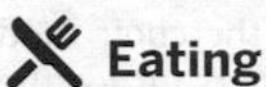

Eating

TOP CHOICE **Auerbachs Keller** GERMAN €€
(☎216 100; www.auerbachs-keller-leipzig.de; Mädlerpassage; mains €14-22) Founded in 1525, Auerbachs Keller is one of Germany's classic restaurants, serving typically hearty fare. Goethe's *Faust – Part I* includes a scene here, in which Mephistopheles and Faust carouse with some students before they ride off on a barrel.

Gosenschenke 'Ohne Bedenken' BEER GARDEN €€
(Menckestrasse 5; mains €6-16) This historic Leipzig institution, backed by the city's prettiest beer garden, is *the* place to sample *Gose,* a local top-fermented beer often served with a shot of liqueur. The menu has a distinctly carnivorous bent. Take tram 12 to Fritz-Seger-Strasse.

Zum Arabischen Coffe Baum CAFE €€
(Kleine Fleischergasse 4; mains €8-15) Leipzig's oldest coffee bar has a staid old restaurant and cafe offering excellent meals over three floors, plus a free coffee museum at the top. Composer Robert Schumann met friends here, and if you ask nicely you can sit at his regular table.

Drinking & Entertainment

Barfussgässchen and Kleine Fleischergasse, to the west of the Markt, form one of Leipzig's two 'pub miles', packed with outdoor tables that fill up the second the weather turns warm. The other is on Gottschedstrasse, a wider cafe strip that's just west of the Altstadt.

TOP CHOICE **Conne Island** LIVE MUSIC
(www.conne-island.de; Koburger Strasse 3) This former squatter's haunt has morphed into the city's top venue for punk, indie, ska, rock and hip-hop gigs. It's in the southern suburb of Connewitz; take tram 9 to Koburger Brücke.

Werk II LIVE MUSIC
(www.werk-2.de; Kochstrasse 132) This large cultural centre in an old factory is great for catching up-and-coming bands, alternative film and theatre or even circus acts. It's also in Connewitz; take tram 9 to Connewitzer Kreuz.

Moritz-Bastei CLUB
(www.moritzbastei.de; Universitätsstrasse 9) One of the best student clubs in Germany, in a spacious cellar below the old city walls. It has live music or DJs most nights and runs films outside in summer.

Information

The Hauptbahnhof contains a modern mall with over 140 shops and (radically for Germany) it is open from 6am to 10pm daily. You'll find good bookshops, a post office, banks and much more.

Leipzig Card (1/3 days €9/19) Free or discounted admission to attractions, plus free travel on public transport. Available from the tourist office and most hotels.

Tourist office (www.leipzig.de; Katharinenstrasse 8; ⏲9.30am-6pm Mon-Fri, to 4pm Sat, to 3pm Sun)

Getting There & Around

Leipzig-Halle airport (LEJ; www.leipzig-halle-airport.de) has regional flights. Ryanair serves tiny **Altenburg airport** (ADC; www.flughafen-altenburg.de), some 53km from Leipzig. There's a shuttle bus (€12, 1¾ hours) timed to coincide with the flights.

Leipzig is an important rail hub and fittingly has a monumental Hauptbahnhof. Regular services include Dresden (€29, 70 minutes), Munich (€87, five hours), Berlin-Hauptbahnhof by ICE (€42, 70 minutes) and Frankfurt (€70, 3½ hours).

Trams (www.lvb.de) are the main public-transport option, with most lines running via the Hauptbahnhof. A single ticket costs €2 and a day card €5.

Erfurt

☎0361 / POP 201,000

Thuringia's capital is a scene-stealing combo of sweeping squares, time-worn alleyways, perky church towers, idyllic river scenery and vintage inns and taverns. Rich merchants founded the university in 1392, allowing students to study common law, rather than religious law. Its most famous graduate was Martin Luther, who studied philosophy here before becoming a monk at the local Augustinian monastery in 1505.

This is a city to stroll. It's a five-minute walk north along Bahnhofstrasse to Anger, the main shopping and business artery. The little Gera River bisects the Altstadt, spilling off into numerous creeks.

Sights

The numerous interesting lanes and alleys in Erfurt's surprisingly large Altstadt make this a fascinating place to explore. Whatever you do, though, you shouldn't miss the massive 13th-century Gothic **Dom St Marien** (Domplatz; ⌚9am-5pm Mon-Fri, to 4.30pm Sat, 2-4pm Sun, reduced hr winter) and **Severikirche**, which dominate the central Domplatz square. The stained glass and elaborate portals make the cathedral one of the most richly ornamented medieval churches in Germany. The Severikirche, meanwhile, boasts the sarcophagus of St Severus.

The eastbound street beside the Rathaus leads to the restored **Krämerbrücke** (1325), a narrow medieval bridge lined with timber-framed shops – it's the only such structure north of the Alps. Further north, on the same side of the river, the **Augustinerkloster** (www.augustinerkloster.de; Augustinerstrasse; tours €5; ⌚tours 10am-5pm Mon-Sat, 11am-3pm Sun), now a nunnery, has a strong pedigree: Martin Luther was a monk here from 1505 to 1511. You can view Luther's cell and an exhibit on the Reformation.

Sleeping & Eating

Look for interesting and trendy restaurants and cafes along Michaelisstrasse and Marbacher Gasse. Try the *Puffbohnenpfanne* (fried broad beans with roast bacon), an Erfurt speciality, or for a quick treat, have a classic *Thuringer Bratwurst* hot off the grill from a **stand** (Schlösserstrasse) near a small waterfall.

Opera Hostel HOSTEL €
(☎6013 1366; www.opera-hostel.de; Walkmühlstrasse 13; dm €14-18, r €40-80; @📶) Run with smiles and aplomb, this upmarket hostel in a historic building scores big with wallet-watching global nomads. You'll sleep like a log in bright, spacious rooms, many with an extra sofa for chilling, and make friends in the communal kitchen and on-site lounge-bar.

Hotel am Kaisersaal HOTEL €€
(☎658 560; www.hotel-am-kaisersaal.de; Futterstrasse 8, r €80 100) The 36 rooms are tip-top and appointed with all expected mod-cons in this highly rated hotel. Request a room facing the yard, though, if street noise disturbs. It's close to the Krämerbrücke.

Zum Goldenen Schwann GERMAN €€
(Michaelisstrasse 9; mains €5-14) It's not so much the unpretentious traditional food that makes this place popular locally, rather the highly rated unfiltered boutique beer. Good for Thuringian cuisine.

Steinhaus GASTRO-PUB €
(Allerheiligenstrasse 20-21; mains €5-10) The ceiling beams may be ancient, but the crowd is intergenerational at this rambling gastro-pub-cum-beer garden in the historic Engelsburg. Dips, baguettes, pasta and gratins should keep your tummy filled and your brain balanced.

Information

Tourist office (www.erfurt-tourismus.de) Benediktsplatz (Benediktsplatz 1; ⌚10am-7pm Mon-Fri, 10am-6pm Sat, 10am-4pm Sun Apr-Dec, 10am-6pm Mon-Sat, 10am-4pm Sun Jan-Mar); Petersberg (⌚11am-6.30pm Apr-Oct, 11am-4pm Nov & Dec)

Getting There & Around

Erfurt's flashy Hauptbahnhof is on a line with frequent services linking Leipzig (€27, one hour) and Weimar (€8, 15 minutes). Hourly ICE/IC services go to Frankfurt (€51, 2¼ hours) and Berlin-Hauptbahnhof (€56, 2½ hours).

Weimar

☎03643 / POP 65,200

The city that was once home to Goethe is not impressive at first glance. There are no vast cathedrals or palaces, nor are there any world-renowned museums. But spend a little time wandering its enchanting old streets and visiting its fascinating little museums and historic houses and soon you will understand the allure. You'll feel the presence of notables such as Luther, Schiller and Liszt, and you'll begin to understand the remarkable cultural accomplishments achieved in Weimar over the centuries. While the city can sometimes feel like a giant museum teeming with tourists, it is one

WORTH A TRIP

EISENACH

Eisenach is home to the Wartburg, the only German castle to be named a Unesco World Heritage site. Composer Johann Sebastian Bach was born here, but he plays second fiddle to the awe-inspiring edifice in stone and half-timber high on the hill.

The **tourist office** (www.eisenach.info; Markt 24; ⏲10am-6pm Mon-Fri, 10am-5pm Sat & Sun) can help you find accommodation if your day trip gets extended.

The **Wartburg** (www.wartburg-eisenach.de; tours €8; ⏲tours 8.30am-5pm Mar-Oct, 9am-3.30pm Nov-Feb), parts of which date from the 11th century, is perched high above the town on a wooded hill. It is said to go back to Count Ludwig der Springer (the Jumper); you'll hear the story of how the castle got its name many times, but listen out for how Ludwig got his peculiar moniker as well.

The castle owes its huge popularity to **Martin Luther**, who went into hiding here from 1521 to 1522 after being excommunicated; during this time he translated the entire New Testament from Greek into German, contributing enormously to the development of the written German language. His modest, wood-panelled **study** is part of the guided tour (available in English), which is the only way to view the interior. The **museum** houses the famous Cranach paintings of Luther and important Christian artefacts from all over Germany. Most of the rooms you'll see here are extravagant 19th-century impressions of medieval life rather than original fittings; the re-imagined Great Hall inspired Richard Wagner's opera *Tannhäuser*. Between Easter and October crowds can be horrendous; arrive before 11am.

Frequent trains run from Erfurt (€12 to €15, 30 to 45 minutes) and most continue on the short distance to Weimar.

of Germany's most fascinating places and should not be missed.

Sights

A good place to begin a tour is in front of the neo-Gothic 1841 **Rathaus** on the Markt. Directly east is the **Cranachhaus**, where painter Lucas Cranach the Elder lived for two years before his death in 1553. Just south is the other extreme of local history, the Nazi-era Hotel Elephant.

Goethe Sites HISTORICAL SITES

The **Goethe Nationalmuseum** (Frauenplan 1; admission €8.50; ⏲9am-6pm Tue-Sun) focuses not so much on the man but his movement, offering a broad overview of German classicism, from its proponents to its patrons. The adjoining **Goethe Haus**, where such works as *Faust* were written, focuses much more on the man himself. He lived here from 1775 until his death in 1832. Goethe's original 1st-floor living quarters are reached via an expansive Italian Renaissance staircase decorated with sculpture and paintings brought back from his travels to Italy.

Goethes Gartenhaus (admission €4.50; ⏲10am-6pm Apr-Oct, to 4pm Nov-Mar) was his beloved retreat and stands in the alluring **Park an der Ilm**.

Bauhaus Museum MUSEUM

(Theaterplatz; admission €5; ⏲10am-6pm) The Bauhaus School and movement were founded here in 1919 by Walter Gropius, who managed to draw artists including Kandinsky, Klee, Feininger and Schlemmer as teachers. The exhibition chronicles the evolution of the group and explains its design innovations, which continue to shape our lives. Once the form is in line with its function, a much grander museum is planned for 2013.

Schlossmuseum MUSEUM

(Burgplatz 4; admission €6; ⏲10am-6pm Tue-Sun Apr-Oct, 10am-4pm Nov-Mar) Housed in the **Stadtschloss**, the former residence of the ducal family of Saxe-Weimar, the museum boasts the Cranach Gallery, several portraits by Albrecht Dürer and collections of Dutch masters and German romanticists. A €90-million restoration project is now in the works.

Sleeping & Eating

The tourist office can help find accommodation, especially at busy times. There are many pensions scattered about the centre, which is where you should stay.

Hotel Anna Amalia HOTEL €€

(☎495 60; www.hotel-anna-amalia.de; Geleitstrasse 8-12; r €60-90, apt €130-180; 📶) The

Mediterranean look, with its nice, fresh colour scheme, exudes feel-good cheer in this family-run hotel near Goetheplatz. For more panache and elbow room, book one of the apartments, which sleep up to four. Good breakfast buffet.

Labyrinth Hostel HOSTEL €
(☎811 822; www.weimar-hostel.com; Goetheplatz 6; dm €13-21, r €30-50; @📶) Loads of imagination has gone into this professionally run hostel with artist-designed rooms. In one double, for example, the bed perches on stacks of books, while another comes with a high-platform wooden bed. Bathrooms are shared and so are the kitchen and the lovely rooftop terrace. Dorm 8 has a balcony.

Jo Hanns BISTRO €€
(Scherfgasse 1; mains €10-20) The food is satisfying but it's the 130 wines from the Saale-Unstrut Region – many served by the glass – that draw people inside the cosy maroon walls or outside on the terrace. Food is inventive, with many specials.

Estragon CAFE €
(Herderplatz 3; meals €4-8; ⏲lunch) There are days when a bowl of steamy soup feels as warm and embracing as a hug from a good friend. This little soup kitchen turns mostly organic ingredients into delicious flavour combos served in three sizes. It shares digs with a small organic supermarket.

Residenz-Café CAFE €€
(Grüner Markt 4; mains €6-16) The 'Resi', one of Weimar's enduring favourites, is a jack of all trades: everyone should find something to their taste here. The Lovers' Breakfast is €20 for two, but the inspired meat and vegetarian dishes may well have you swooning, too.

Entertainment

Studentenclub Kasseturm LIVE MUSIC
(www.kasseturm.de; Goetheplatz 10; ⏲6pm-late) A classic student club, the Kasseturm is a historic round tower with three floors of live music, DJs, cabaret and €2 beers.

ℹ Information

Stiftung Weimarer Klassik (www.weimar-klassik.de) The organisation responsible for Weimar's Unesco monuments and museums has an info-filled website.

Tourist office (www.weimar.de; Markt 10; ⏲9.30am-7pm Mon-Fri, to 4pm Sat & Sun) Discount cards start at €10.

ℹ Getting There & Away

Weimar's Hauptbahnhof is located a 20-minute walk from the city centre. It's on a line with frequent services linking Leipzig (€24, one hour) and Erfurt (€8, 15 minutes). Two-hourly ICE/IC services go to Berlin-Hauptbahnhof (€53, 2¼ hours).

Most buses serve Goetheplatz, on the north-western edge of the Altstadt. Don't have time for the 20-minute walk before the next train? A cab costs €6.

Around Weimar

The museum and memorial at **Buchenwald** (www.buchenwald.de; ⏲9am-6pm Apr-Oct, 9am-4pm Nov-Mar) concentration camp museum are 10km north of Weimar. The contrast between the brutality of the former and the liberal humanism of the latter is hard to comprehend.

Between 1937 and 1945, more than one-fifth of the 250,000 people incarcerated here died. Various parts of the camp have been restored and there is an essential **museum** with excellent exhibits.

After the war, the Soviets turned the tables but continued the brutality by establishing Special Camp No 2, in which 7000 so-called anticommunists and ex-Nazis were literally worked to death.

In Weimar, **Buchenwald Information** (Markt 10; ⏲9.30am-6pm Mon-Fri, to 3pm Sat & Sun) is an excellent resource.

To reach the camp, take bus 6 (€1.80, 15 minutes, hourly).

BAVARIA

Bavaria (Bayern) can seem like every German stereotype rolled into one. Lederhosen, beer halls, oompah bands and romantic castles are just some Bavarian clichés associated with Germany as a whole. But as any Bavarian will tell you, the state thinks of itself as Bavarian first and German second. And as any German outside of Bavaria will tell you, the Bavarian stereotypes aren't representative of the rest of Germany.

Bavaria draws visitors year-round. If you only have time for one part of Germany after Berlin, this is it. Munich, the capital, is the heart and soul. The Bavarian Alps, Nuremberg and the medieval towns on the Romantic Rd are other important attractions.

Munich

☎089 / POP 1.35 MILLION

Pulsing with prosperity and *Gemütlichkeit* (cosiness), Munich (München) revels in its own contradictions. Folklore and age-old traditions exist side by side with sleek BMWs, designer boutiques and high-powered industry. Its museums include world-class collections of artistic masterpieces, and its music and cultural scenes rival Berlin's.

Despite all its sophistication, Munich retains a touch of provincialism that visitors find charming. The people's attitude is one of live-and-let-live – and Müncheners will be the first to admit that their 'metropolis' is little more than a *Weltdorf,* a world village. During Oktoberfest visitors descend on the Bavarian capital in their zillions to raise a glass to this fascinating city.

Munich didn't really achieve prominence until the 19th century, under the guiding hand of King Ludwig I. In the aftermath of WWI, the city became a hotbed of right-wing political ferment. Hitler staged a failed coup attempt here in 1923. WWII brought bombing and more than 6000 civilian deaths. Today it is a growing city with a diversified economy.

Sights

Palaces — PALACES

The huge **Residenz** (Max-Joseph-Platz 3) housed Bavarian rulers from 1385 to 1918 and features more than 500 years of architectural history. Apart from the palace itself, the **Residenzmuseum** (www.residenz-muenchen.de; entrance on Max-Joseph-Platz; admission €6; ⏲9am-6pm Apr–mid-Oct, 10am-5pm mid-Oct–Mar) has an extraordinary array of 100 rooms containing no end of treasures and artworks. In the same building, the **Schatzkammer** (Treasure Chamber; admission €6) exhibits jewels, crowns and ornate gold.

If this doesn't satisfy your passion for palaces, visit **Schloss Nymphenburg** (www.schloesser.bayern.de; admission €5; ⏲9am-6pm Apr–mid-Oct, 10am-4pm mid-Oct–Mar), northwest of the city centre via tram 17 from the main train station (Hauptbahnhof). This was the royal family's equally impressive summer home.

Art galleries — GALLERIES

A veritable treasure house of European masters from the 14th to 18th centuries, the **Alte Pinakothek** (www.pinakothek.de; Barer Strasse 27, enter from Theresienstrasse; admission €7, Sun €1; ⏲10am-8pm Tue, to 6pm Wed-Sun), a stroll northeast of the city, includes highlights such as Dürer's Christ-like *Self Portrait* and his *Four Apostles,* Rogier van der Weyden's *Adoration of the Magi* and Botticelli's *Pietà.*

Immediately north of the Alte Pinakothek, the **Neue Pinakothek** (www.pinakothek.de; Barer Strasse 29, enter from Theresienstrasse; admission €7, Sun €1; ⏲10am-5pm Thu-Mon, to 8pm Wed, closed Tue) contains mainly 19th-century works, including Van Gogh's *Sunflowers,* and sculpture.

One block east of the Alte Pinakothek, the **Pinakothek der Moderne** (www.pinakothek.de; Barer Strasse 40, enter from Theresienstrasse; admisison €10, Sun €1; ⏲10am-6pm Tue, Wed & Fri-Sun, 10am-8pm Thu) displays four collections of modern art and architecture in one suitably arresting building.

Museums — MUSEUMS

An enormous science and technology museum, **Deutches Museum** (www.deutsches-museum.de; Museumsinsel 1; admission €8.50; ⏲9am-5pm) celebrates the achievements of Germans and humans in general. Kids become gleeful as they interact with the exhibits; so do adults. Take the S-Bahn to Isartor.

Tracing the lives of local Jews before, during and after the Holocaust, the **Jüdisches Museum** (www.juedisches-museum.muenchen.de; St-Jakobs-Platz 16; admission €6; ⏲10am-6pm Tue-Sun) offers insight into Jewish history, life and culture in Munich. The Nazi era is dealt with, but the focus is clearly on contemporary Jewish culture.

North of the city, auto-fetishists can thrill to the flashy **BMW Welt** (www.bmw-welt.de; admission €12; ⏲10am-6pm Tue-Sun), adjacent to the BMW headquarters. Take the U3 to Olympiazentrum.

Englischer Garten — PARK

One of the largest city parks in Europe, the Englischer Garten, north of the city centre, is a great place for strolling, especially along the Schwabinger Bach. In summer, nude sunbathing is the rule rather than the exception. It's not unusual for hundreds of naked people to be in the park during a normal business day, with their clothing stacked primly on the grass. If they're not doing this, they're probably drinking merrily at one of the park's **beer gardens**.

Marienplatz & Around — HISTORIC BUILDINGS

The **Marienplatz** is a good starting point for historic buildings. Dominating the square is the towering neo-Gothic **Neues Rathaus**, with its ever-dancing **Glockenspiel** (caril-

DON'T MISS

OKTOBERFEST

Hordes come to Munich for **Oktoberfest** (www.oktoberfest.de; ⏲10am-11.30pm, from 9am Sat & Sun), running the 15 days before the first Sunday in October. Reserve accommodation well ahead and go early in the day so you can grab a seat in one of the hangar-sized beer 'tents'. The action takes place at the Theresienwiese grounds, about a 10-minute walk southwest of the Hauptbahnhof. While there is no entrance fee, those €9 1L steins of beer (called *mass*) add up fast. Although its origins are in the marriage celebrations of Crown Prince Ludwig in 1810, there's nothing regal about this beery bacchanalia now; expect mobs, expect to meet new and drunken friends, expect decorum to vanish as night sets in and you'll have a blast.

A few tips:

» Locals call it *Weisn* (meadow)

» The Hofbräu Festhalle tent is big with tourists

» The Augustiner tent draws traditionalists

» Traditional Oktoberfest beer should be a rich copper colour; order it instead of the tourist-satisfying pale lager

lon), which performs at 11am and noon daily (also at 5pm from March to October), bringing the square to an expectant standstill (note the fate of the Austrian knight...). Two important churches are on this square: the baroque star **St Peterskirche** (Rindermarkt 1; church admission free, tower admission €1.50; ⏲9am-7pm Apr-Oct, to 6pm Nov-Mar) and, behind the Altes Rathaus, the often forgotten but equally important **Heiliggeistkirche** (Tal 77; ⏲7am-6pm).

Head west along shopping street Kaufingerstrasse to the landmark of Munich, the late-Gothic **Frauenkirche** (Church of Our Lady; Frauenplatz 1; ⏲7am-7pm Sat-Wed, 7am-8.30pm Thu, 7am-6pm Fri) with its then-trendy 16th-century twin onion domes. Go inside and join the hordes gazing at the grandeur of the place, or climb the tower for majestic views of Munich.

FREE Dachau HISTORIC SITE
(www.kz-gedenkstaette-dachau.de; Alte-Roemer-strasse 75; ⏲9am-5pm Tue-Sun) The first Nazi concentration camp was Dachau, built in March 1933. Jews, political prisoners, homosexuals and others deemed 'undesirable' by the Third Reich were imprisoned in the camp. More than 200,000 people were sent here; more than 30,000 died at Dachau and countless others died after being transferred to other death camps. An English-language documentary is shown at 11.30am and 3.30pm. Take the S2 (direction Petershausen) to Dachau and then bus 726 to the camp. A Munich XXL day ticket (€7) will cover the trip.

Tours

Mike's Bike Tours BIKE TOURS
(www.mikesbiketours.com; tours from €24) Enjoyable (and leisurely) city cycling tours in English. Tours depart from the archway at the Altes Rathaus on Marienplatz.

Munich Walk Tours WALKING TOURS
(www.munichwalktours.de; tours from €12) Walking tours of the city on topics from Nazis to beer. Meet under the Glockenspiel on Marienplatz.

City Bus 100 BUS
Ordinary city bus that runs from the Hauptbahnhof to the Ostbahnhof via 21 of the city's museums and galleries. This includes all three Pinakothek, the Residenz and the Bayerisches Nationalmuseum.

Sleeping

Munich has no shortage of places to stay – except at Oktoberfest or during some busy summer periods, when the wise (those with a room) will have booked. Many budget and midrange places can be found in the cheerless streets around the train station. If you can, avoid it, as you'll find hotels with more charm and atmosphere elsewhere.

Munich's youth hostels that are DJH and HI affiliated do not accept guests over the age of 26, except group leaders or parents accompanying a child.

Pension Gärtnerplatz HOTEL €€
(☎202 5170; www.pension-gaertnerplatztheater.de; Klenzestrasse 45; r €80-130; 📶) Escape the tourist rabble, or reality altogether, in this

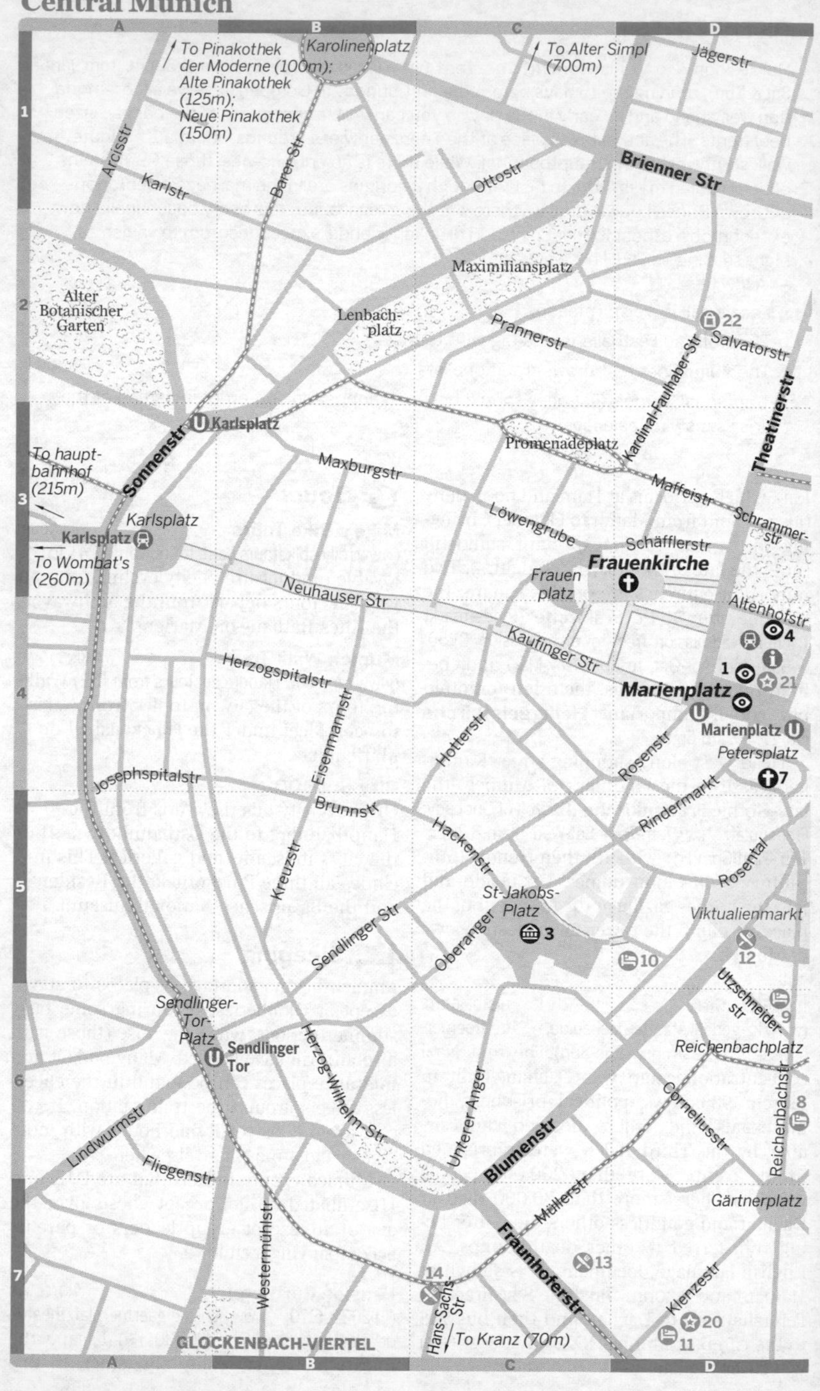

To Pinakothek der Moderne (100m); Alte Pinakothek (125m); Neue Pinakothek (150m)
Karolinenplatz
To Alter Simpl (700m)
Jägerstr
Arcisstr
Karlstr
Barer Str
Ottostr
Brienner Str
Maximiliansplatz
Alter Botanischer Garten
Lenbach-platz
Prannerstr
22
Salvatorstr
Kardinal-Faulhaber-Str
Theatinerstr
Karlsplatz
Promenadeplatz
To haupt-bahnhof (215m)
Sonnenstr
Maxburgstr
Maffeistr
Schrammer-str
Karlsplatz
Karlsplatz
Löwengrube
Schäfflerstr
To Wombat's (260m)
Frauenkirche
Frauen platz
Neuhauser Str
Altenhofstr
4
Kaufinger Str
1
21
Herzogspitalstr
Marienplatz
Marienplatz
Eisenmannstr
Hotterstr
Petersplatz
Rosenstr
7
Josephspitalstr
Rindermarkt
Brunnstr
Hackenstr
Rosental
Kreuzstr
St-Jakobs-Platz
Viktualienmarkt
Sendlinger Str
Oberanger
3
10
12
Utzschneider-str
9
Sendlinger-Tor-Platz
Sendlinger Tor
Herzog-Wilhelm-Str
Reichenbachplatz
Corneliusstr
8
Reichenbachstr
Unterer Anger
Lindwurmstr
Blumenstr
Fliegenstr
Gärtnerplatz
Müllerstr
Fraunhoferstr
Westermühlstr
14
13
Hans-Sachs-Str
Klenzestr
20
11
To Kranz (70m)
GLOCKENBACH-VIERTEL

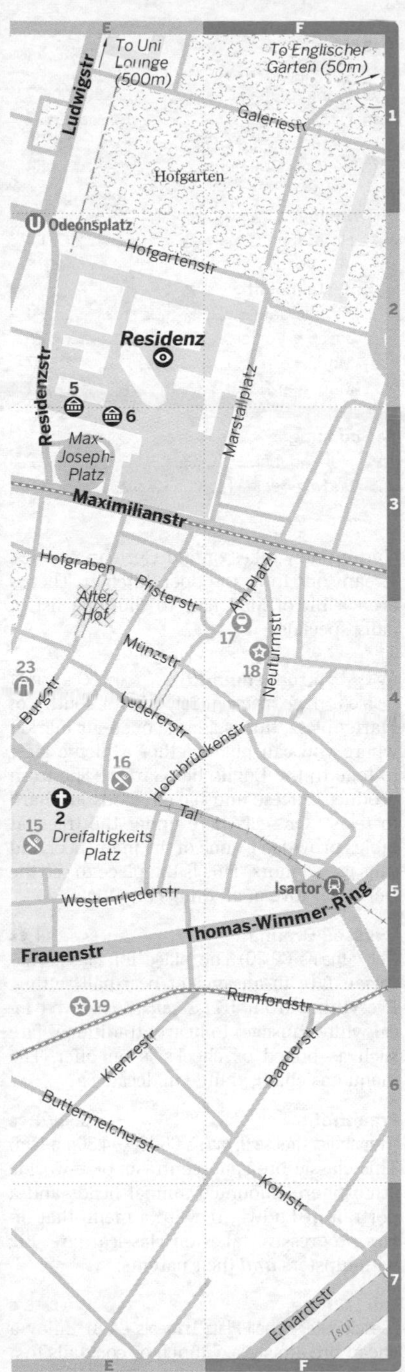

eccentric establishment where rooms are a stylish interpretation of Alpine pomp. The one named 'Sisi' will have you sleeping in a canopy bed guarded by a giant porcelain mastiff. It's well located near trendy cafes and shops.

Deutsche Eiche HOTEL €€
(☎231 1660; www.deutsche-eiche.com; Reichenbachstrasse 13; r incl breakfast €80-160, apt from €200; 📶) Traditionally it's been a gay outpost, but style junkies of all sexual persuasions should enjoy the plushly designed rooms. Cheaper rooms are more utilitarian; near the trendy Gärtnerplatz. Also on the premises: a bathhouse.

Hotel am Viktualienmarkt HOTEL €€
(☎231 1090; www.hotel-am-viktualienmarkt.de; Utzschneiderstrasse 14; r €50-120; 📶) Owners Elke and her daughter Stephanie run this perfectly located property with panache and a sunny attitude. A steep staircase (no lift) leads to rooms, the nicest of which have wooden floors and framed poster art. Book far ahead.

Meininger City Hostel & Hotel HOTEL €
(☎420 956 053; www.meininger-hostels.de; Landsbergerstrasse 20; dm from €18, r from €45; @📶) This hotel-hostel combo scores big points for three reasons: rooftop bar, amenities and service. About 600m west of the Hauptbahnhof, it has 380 beds in 05 cheerful rooms ranging in size from singles to 12-bed dorms. The Augustiner brewery is within stumbling distance.

Wombat's HOTEL €
(☎5998 9180; www.wombats-hostels.com; Senefelderstrasse 1; dm €12-24, r from €70; @📶) Style, comfort and location are hallmarks of this hotel-hostel. You'll sleep well in pine beds with real mattresses (free linen), reading

SPLURGE

A whiff of roasted almonds away from the Viktualienmarkt, tidy **Hotel Blauer Bock** (☎231 780; www.hotelblauerbock.de; Sebastiansplatz 9; s €64-72, r €60-150; 📶) once provided shelter for Benedictine monks and has an ideal location that's the envy of more prestigious abodes. It's comfy, familiar and spacious. Cheaper rooms share bathrooms. The included breakfast buffet offers creative options beyond the norm.

Central Munich

Top Sights

Frauenkirche D3
Marienplatz D4
Residenz E2

Sights

1 Glockenspiel D4
2 Heiliggeistkirche E5
3 Jüdisches Museum C5
4 Neues Rathaus D4
5 Residenzmuseum E2
6 Schatzkammer E3
7 St Peterskirche D4

Sleeping

8 Deutsche Eiche D6
9 Hotel am Viktualienmarkt D6
10 Hotel Blauer Bock D5
11 Pension Gärtnerplatz D7

Eating

12 Der Pschorr D5
13 Fraunhofer C7
14 Nil C7
15 Viktualienmarkt E5
16 Weisses Brauhaus E4

Drinking

17 Hofbräuhaus F4

Entertainment

18 Atomic Café F4
19 Jazzbar Vogler E6
20 Morizz D7
21 München Ticket D4

Shopping

22 Hugendubel D2
23 Ludwig Beck E4

lamps in doubles, and dorms with en-suite bathrooms. Breakfast is an extra €4.

Campingplatz Thalkirchen CAMPING GROUND €
(☎7243 0808; www.camping-muenchen.de; Zentralländstrasse 49; campsites per person/tent €5/4; ⊙mid-Mar-end Oct) To get to this camping ground southwest of the city centre, take the U3 to Thalkirchen and catch bus 135 (about 15 minutes).

Tent CAMPING GROUND €
(☎141 4300; www.the-tent.com; In den Kirschen 30; campsites €5.50 plus per person €5.50, bed in main tent €11; ⊙Jun-Sep) Pads and blankets provided for the bagless; bring your own lock for the lockers. Take tram 17 to the Botanic Gardens then follow the signs to a legendary international party.

Eating

Clusters of restaurants can be found anywhere there's pedestrian life. The streets in and around Gärtnerplatz and Glockenback-Viertel, 600m south of Karlsplatz, are the flavour of the moment. You can always do well in and around Marienplatz and the wonderful Viktualienmarkt.

TOP CHOICE **Der Pschorr** GERMAN €€
(Viktualienmarkt 15; mains €10-18) Shining like a jewel across a square, this modern high-ceilinged restaurant operated by one of the main local brewers is the 21st-century version of a beer hall. Creative dishes, including new takes on old German classics, stream out from the open kitchen. There's even a bit of Med flair to the long list of daily specials.

TOP CHOICE **Viktualienmarkt** OUTDOOR MARKET
(⊙Mon-Fri & morning Sat) Just south of Marienplatz, this is a large open-air market where you can put together a picnic feast to take to the Englischer Garten. The fresh produce, cheese and baked goods are hard to resist. Or relax here under the trees, at tables provided by one of the many beer and sausage vendors. This is the place to see the Germans' love of all things organic.

Weisses Brauhaus BAVARIAN €€
(Tal 7; mains €9-20) The place for classic Bavarian fare in an ancient beer-hall setting. Everything from *Weissewurst* (beloved local white sausage) to hearty traditional fare such as boiled ox cheeks is on offer. The menu has changed little in decades.

Fraunhofer GERMAN €€
(Fraunhoferstrasse 9; mains €6-16; ⊙4.30pm-1am) This classic brewpub contrasts olde-worlde atmosphere (mounted animal heads and a portrait of Ludwig II) with a menu that offers progressive takes on classical fare. Big with hipsters *and* their parents.

Uni Lounge CAFE €
(Geschwister-Scholl-Platz 1; meals €4-8) Enjoy a cheap breakfast, lazy lunch or cocktails to a

soundtrack of high-minded conversation beneath the whitewashed vaulting of this student hang-out. The outdoor seating is ringed by grand university buildings.

Nil CAFE €€

(Hans-Sachs-Strasse 2; meals €8-14; ⏰8am-4am) Right in trendy Glockenbach-Viertel, this hip place draws a straight and gay crowd in the know. Tables outside are packed when the sun shines, inside it's packed all night long.

Kranz CAFE €€

(Hans-Sache-Strasse 12; mains €8-16) A luxe cafe in the heart of the edgy and trendy streets of the Glockenbach-Viertel. Posh desserts beg you to go easy on the organic burgers. Excellent sidewalk tables.

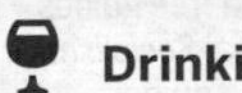

Drinking

Outside of the beer halls and gardens, Munich has no shortage of lively pubs. Schwabing and Glockenbach-Viertel are good places to follow your ears. Many serve food.

Alter Simpl PUB

(Türkenstrasse 57, Maxvorstadt) Thomas Mann and Hermann Hesse used to knock 'em back at this legendary thirst parlour. Alter Simpl is also a good place to satisfy midnight munchies as bar bites are available until one hour before closing time.

Morizz BAR

(Klenzestrasse 43) This mod art deco–style lounge with red leather armchairs and mirrors for posing and preening goes for a more moneyed clientele and even gets the occasional local celebrity drop-in. Packed on weekends.

☆ Entertainment

Munich is one of the cultural capitals of Germany; the publications and websites listed on p516 can guide you to the best events. For tickets, try **München Ticket** (www.muenchenticket.de; Neues Rathaus, Marienplatz).

Kultafabrik CLUBS

(www.kultafabrik.de; Grafingerstrasse 6; ⏰8pm-6am) There're over 25 clubs in this old potato factory that you can sample before you end up mashed or fried. Electro and house beats charge up the crowd at the loungy **apartment 11**, the Asian-themed **Koi** and at **Drei Türme** (www.dreituerme.de), a chic living-room club disguised as a Hollywood castle and lit by a forest of glass-fibre tubes. It's close to the Ostbahnhof station.

Jazzbar Vogler JAZZ

(Rumfordstrasse 17, Gärtnerplatzviertel) This intimate watering hole brings some of Munich's baddest cats to the stage. You never know who'll show up for Monday's blues-jazz-Latin jam session.

BEER HALLS & BEER GARDENS

Beer drinking is not just an integral part of Munich's entertainment scene, it's a reason to visit. Germans drink an average of 130L of the amber liquid each per year, while Munich residents manage much more. Locals will be happy to help ensure that you don't bring down the average.

Beer halls can be vast boozy affairs seating thousands, or much more modest neighbourhood hang-outs. The same goes for beer gardens. Both come in all shapes and sizes. What's common is a certain camaraderie among strangers, huge litre glasses of beer (try putting one of those in your carry-on) and lots of cheap food – the saltier the better. Note that in beer gardens tradition allows you to bring your own food, a boon if you want an alternative to pretzels, sausages and the huge white radishes served with, you guessed it, salt.

On a warm day there's nothing better than sitting and sipping among the greenery at one of the Englischer Garten's classic beer gardens. **Chinesischer Turm** is justifiably popular while the nearby **Hirschau** on the banks of Kleinhesseloher See is less crowded.

TOP CHOICE **Augustiner Bräustuben** (Landsberger Strasse 19) Depending on the wind, an aroma of hops envelops you as you approach this ultra-authentic beer hall inside the actual Augustiner brewery. The Bavarian grub here is superb, especially the *Schweinshaxe* (pork knuckles). Giant black draught horses are stabled behind glass on your way to the loo. It's about 700m west of the Hauptbahnhof.

Hofbräuhaus (Am Platzl 9) The ultimate cliché of Munich beer halls. Tourists arrive by the busload but no one seems to mind that this could be like a theme park such as Disneyland (although the theme park wasn't once home to Hitler's early speeches, like this place was). Wander upstairs for echoes of the past, a small museum and possibly a seat.

GAY & LESBIAN MUNICH

Much of Munich's gay and lesbian nightlife is around **Gärtnerplatz** and the **Glockenback-Viertel**. Any of the nightspots in this area listed earlier (such as Nil and Morizz) will have a mixed crowd.

Our Munich and *Sergej* are monthly guides easily found in this neighbourhood. Another good resource is **Max&Milian** (Ickstattstrasse 2), Munich's best gay bookstore.

The Deutsche Eiche hotel caters to gay and lesbian guests.

Atomic Café CLUB
(www.atomic.de; Neuturmstrasse 5; ⏲10pm-4am, 9pm on concert nights Tue-Sun) This bastion of indie sounds with funky '60s decor is known for bookers with a knack for catching upwardly hopeful bands before their big break.

Shopping

Shoppers converge on **Marienplatz** to buy designer shoes or kitschy souvenirs. Stylish department store **Ludwig Beck** (Marienplatz 11) has something for everyone. Bypass Calvin et al for more unusual European choices. Nearby **Maximilianstrasse** is a fashionable street ideal for window-shopping. Close by, **Hugendubel** (Salvatorplatz 2) is a bookshop crammed with English-language titles.

To truly 'unchain' yourself, though, you should hit the **Gärtnerplatzviertel** and **Glockenbach-Viertel**, bastions of local-designer boutiques and well-edited indie stores. Hans-Sachs-Strasse and **Reichenbachstrasse** are promising. **Maxvorstadt**, especially **Türkenstrasse**, also has an interesting line-up of stores with stuff you won't find on the high street back home.

Information

For late-night shopping and services such as pharmacies and currency exchange, the Hauptbahnhof's multilevel shopping arcades cannot be beaten.

Discount Cards

City Tour Card (www.citytourcard.com; 1/3 days €9.80/18.80) Includes transport and discounts of between 10% and 50% for about 30 attractions. Available at some hotels, MVV (Munich public transport authority) offices and U-Bahn and S-Bahn vending machines.

Medical Services

Bahnhof-Apotheke (☎598 119; Bahnhofplatz 2, Ludwigsvorstadt)

Ärztlicher Bereitschaftsdienst (☎01805-191 212; ⏲24hr) Emergency medical service.

Tourist information

EurAide (☎593 889; www.euraide.de; Hauptbahnhof; ⏲9am-noon & 1-5pm, longer hr in summer) Dispenses savvy travel advice in English; sells and validates rail passes, explains train ticket savings and discounts many tours; staff work in the DB Travel Centre at counter 1.

Tourist office (www.muenchen.de) Hauptbahnhof (Bahnhofplatz 2; ⏲9.30am-6.30pm Mon-Sat, 10am-6pm Sun, longer hr in summer & during holidays); Marienplatz (Neues Rathaus, Marienplatz 8; ⏲10am-8pm Mon-Fri, to 4pm Sat) Be sure to ask for the excellent and free guides *Young and About in Munich, National Socialism in Munich* and various neighbourhood guides.

Websites

www.muenchen-tourist.de Munich's official website.

www.munichfound.com Munich's expat magazine.

www.toytowngermany.com English-language community website with specialised Munich pages; partnered with Berlin's excellent The Local.

Getting There & Away

Air

Munich's sparkling white **airport** (MUC; www.munich-airport.de) is second in importance only to Frankfurt for international and national connections. Flights will take you to all major destinations worldwide.

Bus

Munich has a new **bus station** (ZOB; www.zob-muenchen.de; Arnulfstrasse) that already looks dated. Ticket windows and small waiting areas are on the top floor. It's 500m west of the Hauptbahnhof, at the S-Bahn stop Hackerbrücke. Among the operators here are **Touring** (www.touring.de), which also runs **Europabus** services.

Munich is a stop for the Romantic Road bus; see p518.

Train

Train services to/from Munich are excellent. There are rapid connections at least every two hours to all major cities in Germany, as well as daily trains to other European cities including Paris (€140, six hours), Vienna (€75, four hours) and Zürich (€65, 4¼ hours).

Hourly ICE services head to destinations including Berlin (€113, 5¾ hours), Frankfurt (€89, three hours) and Hamburg (€115, 5½ hours).

Getting Around

To/From the Airport

Munich's international airport is connected by the S8 and the S1 to Marienplatz and the Hauptbahnhof (€9.60). The service takes about 40 minutes and there is a train every 10 minutes from 4am until around 12.30am. The S8 route is slightly faster. For €10.40 you can get a ticket that's good all day.

Taxis make the long haul for at least €60.

Bicycle

Pedal power is popular in relatively flat Munich. **Radius Bike Rental** (www.radiustours.com; Hauptbahnhof near track 32; 10am-6pm May-Sep) rents out two-wheelers from €15 per day. Other tour companies have similar rates.

Public Transport

Munich's excellent public transport network (MVV; www.mvv-muenchen.de) is zone-based, and most places of interest to tourists (except Dachau and the airport) are within the 'blue' inner zone (*Innenraum;* €2.40). MVV tickets are valid for the S-Bahn, U-Bahn, trams and buses, but they must be validated before use. The U-Bahn ceases operating around 12.30am Monday to Friday and 1.30am on Saturday and Sunday, but there are some later buses and S-Bahns. Rail passes are valid exclusively on the S-Bahn.

Kurzstrecke (short rides) cost €1.20 and are good for no more than four stops on buses and trams, and two stops on the U- and S-Bahns. *Tageskarte* (day passes) for the inner zone cost €5.20, while three-day tickets cost €12.80.

Würzburg

0931 / POP 131,000

Nestled among river valleys lined with vineyards, Würzburg beguiles even before you reach the city centre. Three of the four largest wine-growing estates in all of Germany are here and most of the delicate whites produced locally never leave the region. The locals will always reach for a wine glass first – so should you.

Sights

The magnificent, sprawling Unesco-listed **Residenz** (www.residenz-wuerzburg.de; Balthasar-Neumann-Promenade; admission €7; 9am-6pm Apr-Oct, 10am-4pm Oct-Mar), a baroque masterpiece by Neumann, took a generation to build and boasts the world's largest ceiling fresco (graphic artists take note: he didn't need Photoshop); the **Hofgarten** at the back is a beautiful spot.

The interior of the **Dom St Kilian** (museum €5; 10am-7pm Tue-Sun Apr-Oct, to 5pm Tue-Sun Nov-Mar) and the adjacent **Neumünster**, an 11th-century church in the Old Town housing the bones of St Kilian, the patron saint of Würzburg, continue the baroque themes of the Residenz.

Neumann's fortified **Alter Kranen** (old crane), which serviced a dock on the riverbank south of Friedensbrücke, is now the **Haus des Frankenweins** (Kranenkai 1), where you can taste Franconian wines (for around €3 per glass).

The medieval fortress **Marienberg**, across the river on the hill, is reached by crossing the 15th-century stone **Alte Mainbrücke** (old bridge) from the city and walking up Tellstiege, a small alley. It encloses the **Fürstenbau Museum** (355 1753; admission €4; 9am-6pm Tue-Sun Apr-Oct), featuring the Episcopal apartments, and the regional **Mainfränkisches Museum** (Festung Marienberg; admission €4; 10am-5pm Tue-Sun Apr-Oct, to 4pm Tue-Sun Nov-Mar). For a simple thrill, wander the walls enjoying the panoramic views.

Sleeping & Eating

Babelfish Hostel HOSTEL €
(304 0430; www.babelfish-hostel.de; Haugerring 2; dm €17-23, r €45-70; @) This green-powered, independent hostel has moved to new digs in a bank building across from the Hauptbahnhof. Facilities include spotless dorms, rooftop terrace and bike rental (€5 per day).

Hotel Till Eulenspiegel HOTEL €€
(355 840; www.hotel-till-eulenspiegel.de; Sanderstrasse 1a; r €70-120;) Run by the gregarious Johannes, the 18 rooms are comfortable; some have sunny balconies. There's also a small but good *weinstube* (place to enjoy wine in a traditional setting) and a pub serving unusual Bavarian microbrews.

Zum Stachel GERMAN €€
(527 70; www.weinhaus-stachel.de; Gressengasse 1; mains €12-22; closed Sun) There's a restaurant at this 15th-century watering hole, but better yet is to just enjoy a drink on one of its stone balconies overlooking the Romeo-and-Juliet-like Renaissance courtyard.

Weinstuben Juliusspital WEINSTUBE €€
(540 80; Juliuspromenade 19; mains €8-20) This rambling place serves up a long list of wines (especially local whites). You can have a meal or just a drink at one of the many old wooden tables.

WORTH A TRIP

ROMANTIC ROAD

The popular and schmaltzily named Romantic Rd (Romantische Strasse) links a series of picturesque Bavarian towns. It's not actually one road per se, but rather a 353km route chosen to highlight as many quaint towns and cities as possible in western Bavaria.

From north to south it includes the following major stops:

» **Würzburg** Starting point and featuring 18th-century artistic splendour among the vineyards (see p517)

» **Rothenburg ob der Tauber** The medieval walled hub of cutesy picturesque Bavarian touring (p519)

» **Dinkelsbühl** Another medieval walled town replete with moat and watchtowers; a smaller Rothenberg. The town is best reached by bus or car

» **Füssen** The southern end of the route, and the cute and overrun home of mad King Ludwig's castles (p522)

A good first stop is the info-packed website www.romanticroad.de. Also look for the excellent and free large map and route description at tourist offices.

A popular way to tour the Romantic Rd is the **Romantic Road bus** (www.romanticroad coach.de); book online or by phone (☎069 719126-268, 9am to 6pm Monday to Friday).

Starting in Frankfurt in the north and Füssen in the south, a bus runs in each direction each day covering the entire route. However, seeing the entire whack in one day is only for those with unusual fortitude and a love of buses. Stops are brief (17 minutes for Wieskirche, *Schnell!* 35 minutes for Rothenburg, *Schnell!* etc) so you'll want to choose places where you can break the trip for a day (stopovers are allowed). But of course this leads you to decide between a 30-minute visit and a 24-hour one.

Buses depart mid-April to mid-October south from Frankfurt Hauptbahnhof at 8am and north from Füssen at 8am and take 12 hours. The total fare (tickets are bought on board) is a pricey €105. Railpass holders get a paltry 20% discount. You can also just ride for individual segments (eg Rothenberg to Augsburg costs €26), which may be the best use.

Information

The **tourist office** (www.wuerzburg.de; Marktplatz; ⌚10am-6pm Mon-Fri, 10am-2pm Sat & Sun May-Oct, reduced hr & closed Sun other times), in the rococo masterpiece Falkenhaus, runs 90-minute English-language **city walks** (per person €6; ⌚1pm Fri & Sat May-Oct).

Getting There & Away

Würzburg is served by frequent ICE trains from Frankfurt (€33, 70 minutes) and Nuremberg (€33, 69 minutes). It's a major stop for the ICE trains on the Hamburg–Munich line. It is also on the Romantic Rd bus route (€19, 1½ hours to/from Rothenburg). The stop is in front of the train station.

Bamberg

☎0951 / POP 71,000

Off the major tourist routes, Bamberg is celebrated by those in the know. It boasts an amazing and well-preserved collection of 17th- and 18th-century buildings, palaces and churches and its own local style of beer. No wonder it has been recognised by Unesco as a World Heritage site. This is one of the most alluring small towns in Germany.

Bamberg's main appeal is its fine buildings: their sheer number, their jumble of styles and the ambience this creates. Most attractions are spread either side of the Regnitz River, but the colourful **Altes Rathaus** (Obere Brücke) is solidly perched on its own islet. Its lavish murals are among many around town.

The princely ecclesiastical district is centred on Domplatz, where the Romanesque and Gothic **cathedral** (Domplatz; ⌚8am-6pm Apr-Sep, to 5pm Oct-Mar) is the biggest attraction. Across the square, the imposing 17th-century **Neue Residenz** (www.schloesser.bayern.de; Domplatz 8; admission €4; ⌚9am-6pm Apr-Sep, 10am-4pm Oct-May) is filled with treasures and opulent decor.

Above Domplatz is the former Benedictine monastery of St Michael, at the top of Michaelsberg. The **Kirche St Michael**

(Franziskanergasse 2; ⌚9am-6pm) is a must-see for its baroque art.

Sleeping & Eating

Bamberg's unique style of beer is called *Rauchbier*, which literally means smoked beer. Tasting sort of bacony at first, it is a smooth brew that goes down easily. Happily, many of the local breweries also rent rooms.

Backpackers Bamberg HOTEL €
(☎2221 718; www.backpackersbamberg.de; Heiliggrabstrasse 4; dm €15-18, r €40-60;) Newly relocated to a large and accommodating half-timbered building, this hostel is a fine budget choice. It's a five-minute walk from the train station towards the old town. Furnishings are new and the decor has a free-form flair.

TOP CHOICE **Schlenkerla** GERMAN €€
(Dominikanerstrasse 6; mains €8-15; ⌚Wed-Mon) Featuring a warren of rooms decked out with lamps fashioned from antlers, this 16th-century restaurant is famous for tasty Franconian specialities and *Rauchbier* served directly from oak barrels. This should be your one stop if you only have time for one (stop, not beer...).

Klosterbräu GERMAN €
(Obere Mühlbrücke 1-3; mains €6-12) This beautiful half-timbered brewery is Bamberg's oldest. It draws *Stammgäste* (regular local drinkers) and tourists alike who wash down filling slabs of meat and dumplings with its excellent range of ales.

Brauereigasthof Fässla GERMAN €
(☎265 16; www.faessla.de; Obere Königstrasse 19-21; mains €7 to €10) Chairs at the on-site restaurant are embossed with Fässla's cute coat of arms – a gnome rolling a giant beer barrel. Enjoy the light pilsner here, then head upstairs for a snooze (rooms €40 to €70).

Information

Tourist office (www.bamberg.info; Geyerswörthstrasse 3; ⌚9.30am-6pm Mon-Fri, 9.30am-2.30pm Sat & Sun) In the old town.

Getting There & Away

Two trains per hour go to/from both Würzburg (€17, one hour) and Nuremberg (€20, one hour). Bamberg is also served by ICE trains running between Munich (€58, two hours) and Berlin (€74, 3¾ hours) every two hours.

Rothenburg ob der Tauber

☎09861 / POP 12,000

In the Middle Ages, the town fathers of Rothenburg built strong walls to protect the town from siege. Today those same walls are the reason the town is under siege from tourists. Possibly the most stereotypical of all German walled towns, Rothenburg can't help being so cute.

The **Rathaus on Markt** was begun in Gothic style in the 14th century, but completed in Renaissance style. The **tower** (admission €1) gives a majestic view over the town and the Tauber Valley. The **Meistertrunk** scene is re-enacted by the clock figures on the tourist-office building (eight times daily in summer).

The totally uncommercial **Jakobskirche** (Klingengasse 1; admission €2; ⌚9am-5pm) is sober and Gothic. Marvel at the carved *Heilige Blut alter* (Holy Blood altar). Elsewhere, you won't be able to avoid the legion of Christmas shops and other places aimed right at your dowager aunt.

Pension Raidel ☎3115; www.romanticroad.com/raidel; Wenggasse 3; r €25-60) is a half-timbered inn with 500-year-old exposed beams studded with wooden nails, and musical instruments for guests to play. Some rooms share baths.

Altfränkische Weinstube (☎6404; www.altfraenkische-weinstube-rothenburg.de; Am Klosterhof 7; r €60-80;) hides in a quiet side street near the Reichsstadtmuseum and has six atmosphere-laden rooms, all with bathtubs and most with four-poster or canopied beds. The restaurant (open for dinner only) serves up sound regional fare with a dollop of medieval cheer.

There are hourly trains to/from Steinach, a transfer point for service to Würzburg (total journey €13, 70 minutes). Romantic Rd buses pause here for 35 minutes.

Nuremberg

☎0911 / POP 498,000

Nuremberg (Nürnberg) woos visitors with its wonderfully restored medieval Altstadt, its grand castle and its magical Christkindlesmarkt (Christmas market). Thriving traditions also include sizzling *Nürnberger Bratwürste* (finger-sized sausages) and *Lebkuchen* – large, soft gingerbread cookies, traditionally eaten at Christmas time but available here year round.

Nuremberg played a major role during the Nazi years, as documented in Leni Riefenstahl's film *Triumph of the Will* and during the war-crimes trials afterwards. It has done an admirable job of confronting this ugly past with museums and exhibits.

The main artery, the mostly pedestrian Königstrasse, takes you through the old town and its major squares.

Sights

The scenic **Altstadt** is easily covered on foot. On Lorenzer Platz there's the **St Lorenzkirche**, noted for the 15th-century tabernacle that climbs like a vine up a pillar to the vaulted ceiling.

To the north is the bustling **Hauptmarkt**, where the most famous **Christkindlmarkt** in Germany is held from the Friday before Advent to Christmas Eve. The church here is the ornate **Pfarrkirche Unsere Liebe Frau**; the clock's figures go strolling at noon. Near the Rathaus is **St Sebalduskirche** (9.30am-6pm), Nuremberg's oldest church (dating from the 13th century), with the shrine of St Sebaldus.

Kaiserburg CASTLE

(www.schloesser.bayern.de; admission incl museum €6; 9am-6pm Apr-Sep, 10am-4pm Oct-Mar) Climb up Burgstrasse to this enormous 15th-century fortress for good views of the city. The walls spread west to the tunnel-gate of **Tiergärtnertor**, where you can stroll behind the castle to the gardens.

Germanisches Nationalmuseum MUSEUM

(www.gnm.de; Kartäusergasse 1; admission €8; 10am-6pm Tue & Thu-Sun, to 9pm Wed) The most important general museum of German culture in the country, this stunner displays works by German painters and sculptors, an archaeological collection, arms and armour, musical and scientific instruments and, of course, toys.

TOP CHOICE **Nuremberg Trials Memorial** HISTORIC SITE

(www.memorium-nuremberg.de; Bärenschanzstrasse 72; admission €5; 10am-6pm Wed-Mon) From 1945 to 1949 suspected Nazis were tried for war crimes in Nuremberg, which was chosen because it had been the spiritual home of the Third Reich. The courthouse where the trials were held is still in use and is now home to a compelling and comprehensive exhibit about the world's first efforts to prosecute those who commit genocide.

Luitpoldhain HISTORICAL SITE

Nuremberg's role during the Third Reich is well known. The Nazis chose this city as their propaganda centre and for mass rallies, which were held at **Luitpoldhain**, a (never completed) sports complex of megalomaniac proportions. The **Dokumentationzentrum** (www.museen.nuernberg.de; Bayernstrasse 110; admission €5; 9am-6pm Mon-Fri, 10am-6pm Sat & Sun) is in the north wing of the massive unfinished Congress Hall, which would have held 50,000 people for Hitler's spectacles. Its absorbing exhibits trace the rise of Hitler and the Nazis, and the important role Nuremberg played in the mythology. Take tram 9 or 6 to Doku-Zentrum.

Sleeping

Lette'm Sleep HOSTEL €

(992 8128; www.backpackers.de; Frauentormauer 42; dm €16-20, r from €50; @) A backpacker favourite, this independent hostel is just five minutes' walk from the Hauptbahnhof. Private rooms share bathrooms, or you can read to your heart's content in the private facilities of several apartments, which also have kitchens (from €65).

Probst-Garni Hotel HOTEL €€

(203 433; www.hotel-garni-probst.de; Luitpoldstrasse 9; r €60-100) Nuremberg's most reasonably priced pension is squeezed on the 3rd floor of a vintage building. Recent renovations have given the rooms furnishings that are prim and proper. The letters from happy guests are sweet.

DON'T MISS

CHRISTMAS MARKETS

Beginning in late November each year, central squares across Germany – especially those in Bavaria – are transformed into Christmas markets or *Christkindlmarkts* (also known as *Weihnachtsmärkte*). Folks stamp about between the wooden stalls, perusing seasonal trinkets (from treasures to schlock) while warming themselves with tasty *glühwein* (mulled, spiced red wine) and treats such as sausages and potato pancakes. The markets are popular with tourists but locals love 'em too, and bundle themselves up and carouse for hours. Nuremberg's market (www.christkindlesmarkt.de) fills much of the town centre and attracts two million people.

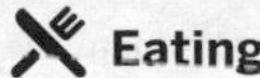

Eating

Don't leave Nuremberg without trying its famous finger-sized grilled sausages. Order 'em by the dozen with *meerrettich* (horseradish) on the side.

TOP CHOICE Bratwursthäusle GERMAN €€
(http://die-nuernberger-bratwurst.de; Rathausplatz 2; meals €6-14; ⏲closed Sun) A local legend and *the* place for flame-grilled and scrumptious local sausages. Get them with *Kartoffelsalat* (potato salad). There are also nice tree-shaded tables outside.

Hütt'n GERMAN €€
(Burgstrasse 19; mains €8-15; ⏲dinner Wed-Mon) Be prepared to queue for a table at this local haunt. The special here is the *ofenfrische Krustenbraten:* roast pork with crackling, dumplings and sauerkraut salad. There's also a near-endless variety of schnapps and beers.

Café am Trödelmarkt CAFE €
(Trödelmarkt 42; dishes €3-5; ⏲9am-6pm) A gorgeous place on a sunny day, this multilevel waterfront cafe overlooks the covered Henkersteg bridge. It's popular for its fresh and tasty continental breakfasts.

Kettensteg BEER GARDEN €
(Maxplatz 35; mains €6-14) Right by the river and with its own suspension bridge to the other side, this beer garden and restaurant is fine on a summer day and cosy in winter. The basic fare is tasty and absorbs lots of beer.

Information

Nürnberg + Fürth Card (€21) Good for two days of unlimited public transport and admissions.

Tourist office (www.tourismus.nuernberg.de) Künstlerhaus (Königstrasse 93; ⏲9am-7pm Mon-Sat, 10am-4pm Sun); Hauptmarkt (Hauptmarkt 18; ⏲9am-6pm Mon-Sat, 10am-4pm Sun)

Getting There & Around

Nuremberg's **airport** (NUE; www.airport-nuernberg.de) is a hub for budget carrier Air Berlin, which has services throughout Germany as well as flights to London. There's frequent service to the airport on the S-2 line (€2, 12 minutes).

The city is also a hub for train services. Sample fares include Berlin-Hauptbahnhof (€89, 4½ hours), Frankfurt (€48, two hours), Munich (€49, one hour) and Stuttgart (€38, 2¼ hours).

Tickets on the bus, tram and U-Bahn system cost €2 each. Day passes are €4.

Regensburg

☎0941 / POP 129,000

On the wide Danube River, student-filled and Unesco-recognised Regensburg has relics of all historic periods as far back as the Romans, yet doesn't have the tourist mobs you'll find in other equally attractive German cities. The centre escaped WWII's carpet bombing and boasts Renaissance towers that could be in Florence mixed with half-timbered charm. Throngs of students keep things from getting too mouldy.

From the main train station, you walk up Maximillianstrasse for 10 minutes to reach the centre.

A veritable miracle of engineering in its time, the **Steinerne Brücke** (Stone Bridge) was cobbled together between 1135 and 1146. For centuries it remained the only solid crossing along the entire Danube.

Lording over Regensburg, **Dom St Peter** (Domplatz; ⏲6.30am-6pm Apr-Oct, to 5pm Nov-Mar) ranks among Bavaria's grandest Gothic cathedrals. The **Altes Rathaus** (admission incl museum €6; ⏲tours in English 3pm Apr-Oct, 2pm Nov, Dec & Mar) was progressively extended from medieval to baroque times and remained the seat of the Reichstag for almost 150 years.

Sleeping & Eating

Atmospheric hotels with modern style can be found scattered through the medieval centre. Hidden around corners you'll find cafes with good wine and boisterous beer gardens.

Hotel Goldenes Kreuz HOTEL €€
(☎558 12; www.hotel-goldeneskreuz.de; Haidplatz 7; r €80-140; 📶) Surely the best deal in town, the nine fairy-tale rooms here each bear the name of a crowned head and are fit for a Kaiser. Huge mirrors, dark antique and Bauhaus furnishings, four-poster beds, chubby exposed beams and parquet flooring produce a stylish opus in leather, wood, crystal and fabric.

TOP CHOICE Wurstküche SAUSAGES €
(☎466 210; Thundorferstrasse 3; meals €7-10; ⏲8am-7pm) The Danube rushes past this little house that's been cooking up the addictive local version of Nuremberg sausages since 1135.

Spitalgarten BEER GARDEN €
(St Katharinenplatz 1; meals €5-10) A veritable thicket of folding chairs and slatted tables by the Danube, this is one of the best places in town for some alfresco quaffing. It claims to have brewed beer (today's Spital) here since

1350, so it probably knows what it's doing by now.

Brook Lane Hostel HOSTEL €
(☎690 0966; www.hostel-regensburg.de; Obere Bachgasse 21; dm €15-20, s/d/apt from €35/45/140; 📶) Regensburg's only backpacker hostel has spanking-new dorms and bathrooms, and its very own food store.

Information

Tourist office (www.regensburg.de; Altes Rathaus; ⏲9am-6pm Mon-Fri, to 4pm Sat & Sun)

Getting There & Away

Regensburg is on the busy train line between Nuremberg (€24, one hour) and Vienna (€75, four hours). There are hourly trains to Munich (€25, 1½ hours).

Füssen

☎08362 / POP 18,000

Close to the Austrian border and the foothills of the Alps, Füssen is primarily visited for the two castles in nearby Schwangau associated with King Ludwig II. It's best seen as a day trip from Munich.

Neuschwanstein & Hohenschwangau Castles CASTLES
The castles provide a fascinating glimpse into the romantic king's state of mind (or lack thereof) and well-developed ego. Hohenschwangau is where Ludwig lived as a child. It's not as cute, even though both castles are 19th-century constructions, but it draws fewer crowds and visits are more relaxed. The adjacent Neuschwanstein is Ludwig's own creation (albeit with the help of a theatrical designer). Although it was unfinished when he died in 1886, there is plenty of evidence of Ludwig's twin obsessions: swans and Wagnerian operas. The sugary pastiche of architectural styles, alternatively overwhelmingly beautiful and just a little too much, reputedly inspired Disney's Fantasyland castle.

Tickets may only be bought from the **ticket centre** (www.ticket-center-hohenschwangau.de; Alpenseestrasse 12, Hohenschwangau; admission €9, incl Schloss Hohenschwangau €17; ⏲tickets 8am-5.30pm Apr-Sep, 9am-3.30pm Oct-Mar). In summer it's worth the €1.80 surcharge each to reserve ahead. To walk to Hohenschwangau takes 20 minutes, while Neuschwanstein is a 45-minute steep hike. Horse-drawn carriages (€6) and shuttle buses (€2) shorten but don't eliminate the hike. The walk between the castles is a piney 45-minute stroll.

Take the bus from Füssen train station (€2, 15 minutes, hourly) or share a taxi (☎7700; €10 for up to four people). Go early to avoid the worst of the rush.

Getting There & Away

Train connections to Munich (€23, two hours) and Augsburg run every hour. Füssen is the start of the Romantic Rd and the **Romantic Road bus** (www.romanticroadcoach.de; ⏲8am daily mid-Apr–mid-Oct) route. Day trips from Munich are widely promoted.

BAVARIAN ALPS

While not quite as high as their sister summits further south in Austria and Switzerland, the Bavarian Alps (Bayerische Alpen) are still standouts, owing to their abrupt rise from the rolling Bavarian foothills. Stretching westward from Germany's southeastern corner to the Allgäu region near Lake Constance, the Alps take in most of the mountainous country fringing the southern border with Austria.

Berchtesgaden

☎08652 / POP 7900

Steeped in myth and legend, the Berchtesgadener Land enjoys a natural beauty so abundant that it's almost preternatural. Framed by six formidable mountain ranges and home to Germany's second-highest mountain, the Watzmann (2713m), the dreamy, fir-lined valleys are filled with gurgling streams and peaceful Alpine villages. Berchtesgaden's history is also indelibly entwined with the Nazi period.

Berchtesgaden town proper is just up the hill from the train station and is rather staid. You might want to make your visit a day trip from Salzburg. There's no need to linger here when there's so much nearby.

Sights & Activities

Dokumentation Obersalzberg MUSEUM
(www.obersalzberg.de; Salzbergstrasse 41, Obersalzberg; adult/student €3/free; ⏲9am-5pm daily Apr-Oct, 10am-3pm Tue-Sun Nov-Apr) In 1933 quiet Obersalzberg (some 3km from Berchtesgaden) became the southern headquarters of Hitler's government, a dark period that's

given the full historical treatment at this at times heartbreaking and compelling museum.

To get there take bus 838 from the 1938-vintage Hauptbahnhof in Berchtesgaden. It's hourly weekdays but infrequent at weekends. A cab costs about €20.

Eagle's Nest HISTORICAL SITE

Berchtesgaden's creepiest – yet impressive – draw is Hitler's retreat atop Mt Kehlstein, a sheer-sided peak at Obersalzberg. Perched at 1834m, the innocent-looking lodge (called Kehlsteinhaus in German) has sweeping views across the mountains and down into the valley where the **Königssee** shimmers. Ironically, Hitler is said to have suffered from vertigo and rarely visited.

Drive or take bus 849 from Dokumentation Obersalzberg to Kehlstein, where you board a special **bus** (www.kehlsteinhaus.de; €16) that drives you up the mountain. It runs between 9am and 4pm, and takes 35 minutes.

Eagle's Nest Tours (649 71; www.eagles-nest-tours.com; Königsseer Strasse 2; adult €48; 1.30pm mid-May–Oct) has four-hour tours in English covering the war years that leave from near the train station.

Information

Tourist office (www.berchtesgaden.de; Königsseer Strasse 2; 8.30am-6pm Mon-Fri, to 5pm Sat, 9am-3pm Sun Apr–mid-Oct, reduced hr other times) Just across the river from the train station.

Getting There & Away

There is an hourly train service to Berchtesgaden from Munich (€30, 2½ hours), which usually requires a change in Frilassing. There are hourly connections to nearby Salzburg in Austria (€10, one hour); bus 840 from the station takes 45 minutes.

BADEN-WÜRTTEMBERG

Most people don't realise it (even as they're enjoying it), but Baden-Württemberg is one of Germany's best tourist regions. For starters, there's the Black Forest – a place on almost every tourist itinerary. Ditto for Heidelberg and its half-timbered charms. Slightly less known but possibly even more worth exploring are the rollicking student town of Freiburg and misty waters of Lake Constance.

Stuttgart

0711 / POP 590,000

Although Stuttgart – with its vine-covered hills – is reputed as staid, the locals surprised many when they rioted over plans to raze the train station in 2010. For tourists, it's another matter: come for the car museums and leave.

Sights

An arms race among the two local car companies has resulted in two glitzy new self-congratulatory museums.

The motor car was first developed by Gottlieb Daimler and Carl Benz at the end of the 19th century. The impressive **Mercedes-Benz Museum** (www.museum-mercedes-benz.com; Mercedesstrasse 100; admission €8; 9am-6pm Tue-Sun) is in the suburb of Bad-Cannstatt; take S-Bahn 1 to Neckarpark. Don't mention Chrysler.

For even faster cars, cruise over to the striking **Porsche Museum** (www.porsche.com; Porscheplatz 1; admission €8; 9am-6pm Tue-Sun); take S-Bahn 6 to Neuwirtshaus, north of the city. No word yet on if they'll be adding a VW wing.

In town and stretching southwest from the Neckar River to the city centre is the **Schlossgarten**, complete with ponds, swans, street entertainers and modern sculptures. At the southern end, the gardens encompass the sprawling baroque **Neues Schloss** and the Renaissance **Altes Schloss**.

Possibly more beautiful than the works within, the **Kunstmuseum Stuttgart** (www.landesmuseum-stuttgart.de; Schillerplatz 6; admission €4.50; 10am-5pm Tue-Sun) glows like a radioactive sugarcube at night. Highlights include works by Otto Dix, Dieter Roth and Willi Baumeister.

Sleeping & Eating

Stuttgart is a great place to sample Swabian specialities such as *Spätzle* (homemade noodles) and *Maultaschen* (a hearty ravioli in broth).

Hotel Unger HOTEL €€

(209 90; www.hotel-unger.de; Kronenstrasse 17; r €90-200;) Right near the Hauptbahnhof, this hotel's corporate feel is offset by its snappy attention to details and comfort. Guests rave about the generous breakfast with smoked fish, fresh fruit and pastries. Floors six and seven have good views.

Basta SWABIAN €€
(Wagnerstrasse 39; mains €10-18) The hum of chatter and herby smells fill this snug Bohnenviertel bistro, which has an intensely loyal following. Each flavour shines through in dishes like wild-garlic *Maultaschen*. Wine lovers have plenty of choice, and the bar is a classy place for a drink even if not dining.

Café Künstlerbund CAFE €
(Schlossplatz 2; mains €7-10) Shelter under the arches facing the park or out in the sunshine at this funky cafe that's part of a large gallery. The drinks menu is huge, as are the choices for breakfast. When the weather gets nasty, duck into the groovy upstairs room.

Hostel Alex 30 HOSTEL €
(838 8950; www.alex30-hostel.de; Alexanderstrasse 30; dm €22, r €35-100; @) Tidy and orderly, near the Bohnenviertel. Take U-Bahn lines 5, 6 or 7 to Olgaeck.

Drinking

Hans-im-Glück Platz, centred on a namesake fountain depicting the caged Grimm fairy-tale character Lucky Hans, is a hub of bars. Club- and lounge-lined Theodor-Heuss-Strasse is thronged with sashaying hipsters. A **beer garden** (Canstatterstr 18) in the Mittlerer Schlossgarten, northeast of the main train station, has beautiful views over the city.

Palast der Republik BAR
(Friedrichstrasse 27) A legendary and tiny pillbox of a bar that pulls a huge crowd of laid-back, genial drinkers. Statuary and stickers abound.

Information

Königstrasse is the spine of central Stuttgart, with most of the major stores and malls.

Stuttcard (from €18) Free museum entry and transport, plus discounts on events, activities and guided tours. Sold at the tourist office and some hotels.

Tourist office (www.stuttgart-tourist.de; Königstrasse 1a; 9am-8pm Mon-Fri, 9am-6pm Sat, 11am-6pm Sun)

Getting There & Around

There are frequent train departures for all major German and many international cities such as Zurich and Paris.

Sample fares for German destinations include Frankfurt (€57, 1¼ hours), Munich (€53, 2¼ hours) and Nuremberg (€38, 2¼ hours).

One-way fares on Stuttgart's public-transport network (www.vvs.de) are €2 in the central zone; a central-zone day pass is €6.

Around Stuttgart

TÜBINGEN

07071 / POP 84,000

Swans set the mood for this hilly, picturesque town, but as the university (founded 1477) has 22,000 students, there's also an appealing edge to it all. On **Marktplatz** is the 1435 **Rathaus** with its ornate baroque facade and astronomical clock. From the Renaissance **Schloss Hohentübingen** (Burgsteig 11) there are fine views over the steep rooftops of the old town.

Stroll up a hill for fine local foods sourced from organic farmers at **Wurstküche** (Am Lustnauer Tor 8; mains €10-16); that sausage you savoured was never fresher.

There's rarely an empty table at **Weinhaus Beck** (Am Markt 1), a convivial wine tavern beside the Rathaus.

There are half-hourly trains between Tübingen and Stuttgart (€12, one hour).

Heidelberg

06221 / 143,000

Heidelberg's baroque old town, lively university atmosphere, excellent pubs and evocative half-ruined castle make it popular with visitors: 3.5 million flock here each year. They are following in the footsteps of the 19th-century romantics, most notably the poet Goethe. Britain's William Turner also loved the city, which inspired him to paint some of his greatest landscapes.

Heidelberg's captivating old town starts to reveal itself after a 15-minute walk that holds very little of interest west of the main train station, along the Kurfürsten-Anlage. Cut to the chase and go direct to the heart of town with bus 32 to Universitätsplatz or bus 33 to Bergbahn – whichever leaves first.

Sights

Heidelberg's imposing red-sandstone **Schloss** (www.schloss-heidelberg.de; admission €5, tours €4; 8am-5.30pm) is one of Germany's finest examples of grand Gothic-Renaissance architecture. The building's half-ruined state actually adds to its romantic appeal. You can take the **funicular railway** (1 way €4; 9am-8pm summer, to 5pm other times) from lower Kornmarkt station, or enjoy a 10-minute walk up steep, stone-laid lanes.

Dominating Universitätsplatz are the 18th century **Alte Universität** and the **Neue Universität**. Nearby **Studentenkarzer** (student jail; Augustinergasse 2; admission €3; ⏲10am-6pm Tue-Sun Apr-Sep, 10am-4pm Tue-Sat Oct-Mar) was used as a jail for misbehaving young scholars from 1778 to 1914. The **Kurpfälzisches Museum** (Palatinate Museum; Hauptstrasse 97; admission €3; ⏲10am-6pm Tue-Sun) contains paintings, sculptures and the jawbone of the 600,000-year-old Heidelberg Man (no word on whether he graduated on time).

A stroll along the **Philosophenweg**, north of the Neckar River, is a welcome respite from Heidelberg's tourist hordes.

Sleeping

Finding any accommodation during Heidelberg's high season can be difficult. Arrive early in the day or book ahead.

Hotel am Kornmarkt HOTEL €€
(☎905 830; www.hotelamkornmarkt.de; Kornmarkt 7; r €40-110) Discreet and understated, this Altstadt favourite has 20 pleasant, well-kept rooms. The pricier rooms have great views of the Kornmarkt, while cheaper ones share spotless hall showers.

Also recommended:

Steffi's Hostel HOSTEL €
(☎0176-2016 2200; www.hostelheidelberg.de; Alte Eppelheimer Strasse 50; dm €20-24, r €45-60; @ wi-fi) Backpackers sing the praises of this hostel, housed in a one-time brick factory near the Hauptbahnhof. Steffi greets guests warmly with bounteous perks.

Sudpfanne HOSTEL €
(☎163 636; www.heidelberger-sudpfanne.de; Hauptstrasse 223; dm €16; wi-fi) Right in the centre of things; the mood is set by the wine-barrel entrance (it's also a cafe).

Eating

Find cheap, fresh food and spicy *wursts* at the centuries-old market on Marktplatz.

Schiller's Café CAFE €
(Heiliggeiststrasse 5; snacks €2-4) Whisper quietly about this half-timbered cafe, housed in one of Heidelberg's oldest buildings, where the film *Schille* was filmed. Hot chocolates with cinnamon, homemade cakes, quiches, and wines are mostly organic.

Brauhaus Vetter GERMAN €€
(Steingasse 9; mains €7-14) A popular brewery that serves up lots of hearty fare to absorb the suds. Groups of six or more can order the brewer's feast, a sausage, pretzels, radishes, meat and cheese smorgasbord.

Café Burkardt CAFE €
(Untere Strasse 27; cakes & snacks €3-8) Full of doily-draped nooks and dark-wood crannies, this nostalgic cafe tempts with Heidelberg's tastiest tarts and cheesecakes. Opt for a table in the courtyard, where Weimar Republic president Friedrich Ebert was born.

Drinking & Entertainment

Two ancient pubs, **Zum Roten Ochsen** (☎209 77; Hauptstrasse 213) and **Zum Sepp'l** (☎230 85; Hauptstrasse 217), are now filled with tourists reliving the uni days they never had.

Cave54 LIVE MUSIC
(www.cave54.de; Krämergasse 2; ⏲Thu-Sun) For live jazz and blues, head to this stone cellar that oozes character. Some nights there's even a DJ.

MaxBar CAFE
(Marktplatz 5t) A French-style cafe with classic views of the Marktplatz. Perfect for a beer or a pastis, it's especially popular on weekend nights. Wave to the Napoleon bust found above the bar.

Information

Heidelberg Card (from €13) Discounts and free admission to many sights.

Tourist office (☎194 33; www.heidelberg-marketing.de) Hauptbahnhof (Willy-Brandt-Platz 1; ⏲9am-7pm Mon-Sat yr-round, 10am-6pm Sun Apr-Nov); Marktplatz (⏲8am-5pm Mon-Fri, 10am-5pm Sat)

Getting There & Around

There are hourly IC trains to/from Frankfurt (€19, one hour) and Stuttgart (€24, 40 minutes). The frequent service to Mannheim (€5, 15 minutes) has connections to cities throughout Germany.

Bismarckplatz is the main public-transport hub. One-way tickets for the excellent bus and tram system (www.vrn.de) are €2.20.

Black Forest

The Black Forest (Schwarzwald) gets its name from its dark canopy of evergreens, though it's also dotted with open slopes and farmland. And while some parts heave with visitors, a 20-minute walk from even

Heidelberg

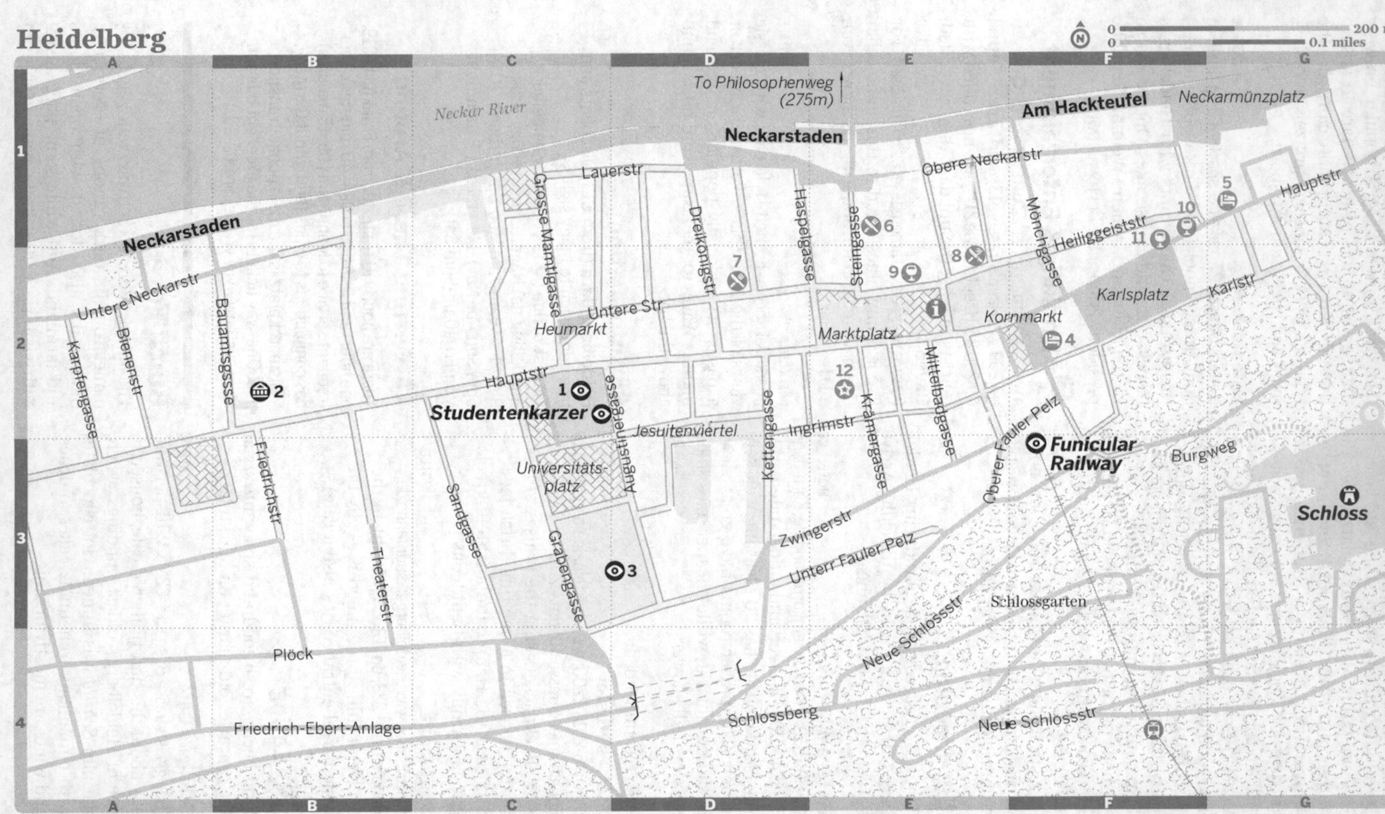
200 m
0.1 miles
A
B
C
D
E
F
G
1
2
3
4
Neckar River
To Philosophenweg (275m)
Am Hackteufel
Neckarmünzplatz
Neckarstaden
Neckarstaden
Lauerstr
Obere Neckarstr
Hauptstr
Untere Neckarstr
Grosse Mamtlgasse
Dreikönigstr
Haspelgasse
Steingasse
Mönchgasse
Heiliggeiststr
Untere Str
Heumarkt
Marktplatz
Kornmarkt
Karlsplatz
Karlstr
Karpfengasse
Bienenstr
Bauamtsgssse
Hauptstr
Studentenkarzer
Augustinergasse
Jesuitenviertel
Kettengasse
Ingrimstr
Krämergasse
Mittelbadgasse
Oberer Fauler Pelz
Funicular Railway
Burgweg
Schloss
Universitäts-platz
Friedrichstr
Sandgasse
Theaterstr
Grabengasse
Zwingerstr
Unterr Fauler Pelz
Schlossgarten
Neue Schlossstr
Plöck
Schlossberg
Neue Schlossstr
Friedrich-Ebert-Anlage
1
2
3
4
5
6
7
8
9
10
11
12

Heidelberg

Top Sights

	Funicular Railway	F3
	Schloss	G3
	Studentenkarzer	C2

Sights

1	Alte Universität	C2
2	Kurpfälzisches Museum	B2
3	Neue Universität	D3

Sleeping

4	Hotel Am Kornmarkt	F2
5	Sudpfanne	G1

Eating

6	Brauhaus Vetter	E1
7	Café Buckardt	D2
8	Schiller's Café	E2

Drinking

9	MaxBar	E2
10	Zum Roten Ochsen	F1
11	Zum Sepp'l	F1

Entertainment

12	Cave54	E2

the most crowded spot will put you in quiet countryside dotted with enormous traditional farmhouses and patrolled by amiable dairy cows. It's not nature wild and remote, but bucolic and picturesque.

The Black Forest is east of the Rhine between Karlsruhe and Basel. It's shaped like a bean, about 160km long and 50km wide. From north to south there are three good bases for your visit: Schiltach, Triberg and Titisee. Each has good train links.

If you have a vehicle, you'll find your visit especially rewarding as you can wander the rolling hills and deep valleys at your will. One of the main tourist roads to take is the Schwarzwald-Hochstrasse (B500), which runs from Baden-Baden to Freudenstadt and from Triberg to Waldshut. And, yes, there are many, many places to buy cuckoo clocks (at €150 or more for a good one, buyers are, well, cuckoo).

Activities

With more than 7000km of marked trails, hiking possibilities during summer are, almost literally, endless. A simple enquiry at any tourist office will yield lots of local options for exploration.

Cross-country skiing is big on all these trails through the winter. For downhill fun, there are runs galore around **Feldberg**.

FREUDENSTADT

07441 / POP 23,000

Freudenstadt is a good base for exploring the northern part of the Black Forest and for hikes into the surrounding countryside. Its most notable feature is a vast **marketplace** that is the largest in the country. The **tourist office** (www.freudenstadt.de; Marktplatz 64; 9am-6pm Mon-Fri, 10am-2pm Sat & Sun May-Oct, shorter hr other times) is good for local hiking ideas.

The Gaiser family extend a warm welcome at **Hotel Adler** (915 20; www.adler-fds.de; Forststrasse 15-17; r €45-95, mains €8-18;), a guest house with comfy, fusty rooms and a terrace. The bistro serves Swabian faves like *Spätzle* (egg noodles).

Hotel Schwanen (915 50; www.schwanen-freudenstadt.de; Forststrasse 6; r €40-110, mains €9-16;) Don't judge this place by its 1970s-style reception, as the rooms have a mod patina (dig the stripes behind the bed). The restaurant is famous for its *Riesenpfannkuchen* (giant pancakes).

From Freudenstadt, hourly trains run south to Schiltach (€7, 30 minutes) and north to the important transfer point of Karlsruhe (€16, 1½ hours). Stuttgart has hourly trains (€16, 1½ hours).

SCHILTACH

07836 / POP 4000

Schiltach is easily the prettiest town in the Black Forest – there is the always underlying roar of the Kinzig and Schiltach Rivers, which meet here. Half-timbered buildings lean at varying angles along the criss-crossing hillside lanes. The **Markt**, the town square, has several tiny museums that cover local history and culture.

There are numerous hotels and restaurants in the compact centre. Choosing a room is an adventure at **Gasthof Sonne** (957 570; Marktplatz 3; www.sonneschiltach.de; r €43-80;). Shall it be a romantic rose-tinged nest or an armour-filled knight's chamber? The restaurant is excellent.

The **tourist office** (www.schiltach.de; Hauptstrasse 5; 10am-5pm Mon-Fri, to 2pm Sat Apr-Oct) can help with accommodation and has a lot of English-language information.

Schiltach is on the train line linking Offenburg (€8, 45 minutes) via Hausach to Freudenstadt (€5, 30 minutes) with hourly services. Change at Hausach for Triberg (€7, 50 minutes).

TRIBERG

☎07722 / POP 5400

Framed by three mountains (hence the name), Triberg has two duelling cuckoo clocks that claim to be the world's largest – it's a close call on these house-sized oddities.

It also has an appealing old centre and plenty of chances to go for a stroll. There's a one-hour walk to a roaring waterfall (and even better hiking beyond) that starts near the **tourist office** (www.triberg.de; Wallfahrtstrasse 4; ⏲10am-5pm).

Kukucksnest (☎869 487; Wallfahrtstrasse 15; r €50-60) has the shop of master woodcarver Gerald Burger. Above is the beautiful nest he has carved for his guests.

The Black Forest cake at **Café Schäfer** (www.cafe-schaefer-triberg.de; Hauptstrasse 33; ⏲9am-6pm, from 11am Sun, closed Wed) is the real deal; they have the original recipe to prove it.

Triberg is midway on the spectacular Karlsruhe (€22, 1½ hours) to Konstanz (€22, 1½ hours) train line. There are hourly services and good connections. Change at Hausach for Schiltach and Freudenstadt. The station is 1.7km from the centre; take any bus to the Markt.

TITISEE

☎07651 / POP 12,000

This iconic glacial **lake** draws no shortage of visitors to the busy village of Titisee. Walking around Titisee and paddle-boating across it are major activities. But if you can, drive into the surrounding rolling meadows to see some of the truly enormous traditional house-barn combos ('Is that the cow or is it your feet?').

The **tourist office** (www.titisee-neustadt.de; Strandbadstrasse 4; ⏲9am-6pm Mon-Fri, 10am-1pm Sat & Sun) can help you arrange a farm stay. The short streets radiating off the lakefront are lined with clock and schlock shops. But fanciers will be in hog heaven with all the **Black Forest ham outlets**. It's time to picnic!

Titisee is linked to Freiburg by frequent train services (€10, 40 minutes). To reach Triberg to the north, there are scenic hourly connections via Neustadt and Donaueschigen (€16, two hours).

Feldberg

The Black Forest **ski season** runs from late December to March. While there is good downhill skiing, the area is more suited to cross-country skiing. The centre for winter sports is around Titisee (the ski jumps are a prominent landmark), with uncrowded downhill ski runs at **Feldberg** (www.liftverbund-feldberg.de; day pass €27) and numerous graded cross-country trails.

In summer you can use the lifts to reach the summit of the shallow-sloped Feldberg (1493m) for a wondrous panorama that stretches to the Alps.

Feldberg is 15km south of Titisee. It can be reached by bus 7300 from Titisee (€4, 12 minutes, hourly) or in season by free ski shuttles.

Freiburg

☎0761 / POP 213,500

Nestled between hills and vineyards, Freiburg im Breisgau is a fun place, thanks to the city's large and thriving university community. There's a sense of fun here best exemplified by the tiny medieval canals *(bächle)* running right down the middle of streets. The monumental 13th-century cathedral is the city's key landmark, but the real attractions are the vibrant cafes, bars and street life, plus the local wines.

Sights

The major sight in Freiburg is the 700-year-old **Münster** (Cathedral; Münsterplatz; tower admission €1.50; ⏲9.30am-5pm Mon-Sat, 1-5pm Sun), a classic example of both high- and late-Gothic architecture that looms over **Münsterplatz**, Freiburg's market square. The bustling **university quarter** is northwest of the **Martinstor** (one of the old city gates).

A fine collection of medieval art, including works by Matthias Grünewald and Cranach plus lavish stained-glass windows are highlights of the **Augustinermuseum** (☎201 2531; Salzstrasse 32; admission €6; ⏲10am-5pm Tue-Sun), which has reopened after a massive refit.

The trip by cable car to the 1286m **Schauinsland peak** (www.bergwelt-schauinsland.de; 1 way/return €8/12; ⏲9am-5pm Jan-Jun, to 6pm Jul-Sep, 9.30am-5pm Oct-Dec) is a quick way to reach the Black Forest highlands. Numerous easy and well-marked trails make the Schauinsland area ideal for day walks. From Freiburg take tram 4 south to Günterstal and then bus 21 to Talstation.

Sleeping

Hotel Schwarzwälder Hof HOTEL €€
(☎380 30; www.schwarzwaelder-hof.eu; Herrenstrasse 43; r €65-110; 📶) This bijou hotel has an unrivalled style-for-euro ratio. Some of the 42 rooms have postcard views of the Altstadt. A wrought-iron staircase has such a

dramatic sweep that you may be tempted to make your entrance twice. Bargain singles share bathrooms.

Hotel Oberkirch HOTEL €€
(☎202 6868; www.hotel-oberkirch.de; Münsterplatz 22; r €95-175; 📶) Our readers sing the praises of this green-shuttered, 250-year-old hotel with the Münster views of a million postcards. The 26 countrified rooms reveal a Laura Ashley love of florals. Enjoy a floral bouquet from the excellent wine selection on offer in the garden.

Black Forest Hostel HOSTEL €
(☎881 7870; www.blackforest-hostel.de; Kartäuserstrasse 33; dm €14-23, s/d €30/50; 🚭@) Freiburg's funkiest budget digs are five minutes' stroll from the centre. Overlooking vineyards, this former factory has been lovingly revamped as a industrial-themed hostel. Bike hire costs €5 per day.

Eating & Drinking

The fragrant smoke around the Münster at lunch isn't incense, it's the smoke from dozens of grills loaded with sausage. On Saturday you can have vegies (and fruit and cheese and...) with your *wurst* when the weekly **produce market** operates. It's one of Germany's best.

Markthalle MARKET €
(Grünwälderstrasse 2; meals €3-8; ⏰7am-8pm) Just when you think you've seen all the stalls here that sell foods from around the world, you round a corner and there're more. Each has a speciality, whether it's South Asian, Italian or simply a bevy of the heartiest soups you could hope to warm by.

Hausbrauerei Feierling BREWERY €€
(Gerberau 46; mains €6-12) Starring one of Freiburg's best beer gardens, this pub serves great vegetarian options and humungous schnitzels with *Brügele* (chipped potatoes). If you drink one too many, take care not to fall in the stream or you may become dinner for the open-jawed *Krokodil*. Huge, fun beer gardens.

Schlappen PUB €
(☎334 94; Löwenstrasse 2; ⏰11am-1am Mon-Thu, to 3am Fri & Sat, 3pm-1am Sun) With its jazz-themed back room and poster-plastered walls, this student watering hole is a perennial fave. Try a *Flammkuche* (tasty, crispy Alsatian pizza), then forget about it with absinthe.

Biergarten Greiffenegg-Schlössle BEER GARDEN €
(Schlossbergring 3; mains €5) Perched above Freiburg, this terrace beer garden is great for watching the sun set over the city's red rooftops. Save your strength for drinking and ride the elevator up, stumble down. The restaurant inside the villa is posh.

Jos Fritz Cafe LOUNGE
(www.josfritzcafe.de; Wilhelmstrasse 15) Down a little alley past the recycling bins, this cafe hosts concerts of alternative bands and events such as political discussions (stir things up with 'Is Merkel too liberal?').

Information

Tourist office (www.freiburg.de; Rathausplatz 2-4; ⏰8am-8pm Mon-Fri, 9.30am-5pm Sat, 10am-noon Sun Jun-Sep, 8am-6pm Mon-Fri, 9.30am-2.30pm Sat, 10am-noon Sun Oct-May) Well stocked with hiking and cycling maps for the region.

Getting There & Around

Freiburg shares **EuroAirport** (www.euroairport.com) with Basel (Switzerland) and Mulhouse (France). It buzzes with low-cost carriers. The **Airport Bus** (www.freiburger-reisedienst.de; per person €20; 55min) runs almost every hour.

Fast trains connect Freiburg to Basel (€23, 45 minutes, hourly) and go north to Frankfurt (€61, two hours, hourly) and beyond.

Cut across the Rhine to France's cute Colmar. Bus 1076 makes the run two to three times daily (€8, 1¼ hours).

Single rides on the efficient local bus and tram system cost €2.20. A 24-hour pass costs €5. Trams depart from the bridge over the train tracks.

Lake Constance

☎07531

Lake Constance (Bodensee) is an oasis in landlocked southern Germany. Even if you never make contact with the water, this giant bulge in the sinewy course of the Rhine can offer a splash of refreshment. There are many historic towns around its periphery, which can be explored by boat or bicycle and on foot. Two good places to start are the namesake Constance, a tidy lake town, and Lindau, a misplaced corner of Bavaria.

Sights & Activities

From medieval **Constance** (get a walking-tour brochure from the tourist office), head across to **Mainau Island** (www.mainau.de; admission €16; ⏲sunrise-sunset), with its baroque castle set in vast and gorgeous gardens with seasonal displays. Take bus 4 (€2, 20 minutes) or a BSB ferry from the harbour behind the station (€6, one hour, hourly).

Connected to the nearby lakeshore by bridges, the key sights of the oh-so-charming island town of **Lindau** all have murals: **Altes Rathaus** (Reichsplatz), the **city theatre** (Barfüsser-platz) and the harbour's **Seepromenade**, with its Bavarian Lion monument and lighthouse.

Other lakeside towns worth a visit include **Meersburg** and **Friedrichshafen**.

A 270km international **bike route** circumnavigates Lake Constance through Germany, Austria and Switzerland, tracing the often-steep shoreline beside vineyards and pebble beaches. You can rent bikes in any town. Popular watery pursuits include sailing and wind-boarding.

A fun way to explore is by **Bodensee-Schiffsbetriebe boats** (BSB; www.bsb-online.com), which, from Easter to late October, call several times a day at the larger towns along the lake; there are discounts for rail-pass holders.

Sleeping & Eating

Lakeside beer gardens and cafes can be found in every town.

Constance

Hotel Barbarossa HOTEL €€
(☎128 990; www.barbarossa-hotel.com; Obermarkt 8-12; r €50-130; 📶) A charming old place that has been carefully restored (although the floors still creak). White walls set off beautiful wooden antiques. The art-deco restaurant (mains €8 to €20) has fine local specialities.

DJH Hostel HOSTEL €
(☎322 60; www.jugendherberge-konstanz.de; Zur Allmannshöhe 18; dm €22) Occupying a water tower, with neat dorms, a bistro and gardens. It's 4km northeast of the Altstadt, served by buses 1 and 4.

Lindau

Alte Post HOTEL €€
(☎934 60; www.alte-post-lindau.de; Fischergasse 3; r €60-140; ⏲closed late Dec-late Mar; 📶) Sitting pretty on cobbled Fischergasse, this 300-year-old coaching inn was once a stop on the Frankfurt–Milan mail run. Well kept, light and spacious, the rooms have chunky pine furnishings and wicker chairs.

Hotel Garni-Brugger HOTEL €€
(☎934 10; www.hotel-garni-brugger.de; Bei der Heidenmauer 11; r €55-100; ⏲closed Dec; 📶) This 18th-century hotel, with 23 bright rooms decked out in floral fabrics and pine, is run by a family that bends over to please. Guests can thaw out in the sauna in winter.

Information

Constance tourist office (www.konstanz.de/tourismus; Bahnhofplatz 43; ⏲9am-6.30pm Mon-Fri, to 4pm Sat, 10am-1pm Sun Apr-Oct, 9.30am-12.30pm & 2-6pm Mon-Fri Nov-Mar) In the train station.

Lindau tourist office (☎260 030; www.lindau.de; Ludwigstrasse 68; ⏲9am-6pm Mon-Fri, 2-6pm Sat & Sun May-Sep, 9am-5pm Mon-Fri Oct-Apr) Opposite the train station.

Getting There & Away

Constance has trains to Offenburg via Triberg in the Black Forest (€29, 2¼ hours, hourly). There are good connections into Switzerland (which is 200m south!), including Zurich (€18, 1¼ hours, hourly).

Lindau has trains to Munich (€38, 2¼ hours, every two hours) and direct to Zurich (€25, four times daily). Trains to nearby Bregenz (€5, nine minutes, two hourly) let you connect to the rest of Austria and Switzerland.

WESTERN GERMANY

The western section of Germany mixes natural beauty with industry. The popular Rhine River offers boat rides amid castles and wineries – what more do you want? The Moselle River offers more of the same but with smaller tourist crowds. Frankfurt is a major transport hub that will suck you in at some point. The northwest, with industrial states like North Rhine-Westphalia, is home to a quarter of Germany's population and little beauty. Beautiful exceptions such as the cities of Cologne and Aachen are *big* exceptions.

Moselle Valley

Exploring the vineyards and wineries of the Moselle (Mosel) Valley is an ideal way to get a taste of German culture and people – and, of course, the wonderful wines. Take the time to slow down and savour a glass or two.

The Moselle is bursting at the seams with historical sites and picturesque towns built along the river below steep rocky cliffs planted with vineyards (they say locals are born with one leg shorter than the other so that they can easily work the vines). It's one of the country's most romantically scenic regions, with stunning views rewarding the intrepid hikers who brave the hilly trails.

Many winemakers have their own small pensions, but accommodation is hard to find in May, on summer weekends or during the local wine harvest (mid-September to mid-October). Note also that much of the region – like the vines themselves – goes into a deep slumber from November to March, albeit after an autumn explosion of colour.

The most scenic part of the Moselle Valley runs 195km northeast from Trier to Koblenz; it's most practical to begin your Moselle Valley trip from one of these places.

Two good information sources for the valley are Koblenz's **tourist office** (www.touristik-koblenz.de; Bahnhofsplatz 7; ⌚9am-6pm Mon-Sat yr-round, plus 10am-6pm Sun Apr-Oct), across from the train station, and Cochem's **tourist office** (www.cochem.de; Endertplatz; ⌚9am-5pm Mon-Sat, 10am-noon Sun, reduced hr in winter), next to the Moselbrücke.

Koblenz is much more transit hub than tourist stop. **Cochem** is a deserving if often crowded stop. For a great view, head up to the **Pinnerkreuz** with the chairlift (€5) on Endertstrasse. The theatrical **Reichsburg Castle** (www.reichsburg-cochem.de; admission €5; ⌚9am-5pm) is just a 15-minute walk up the hill from town.

A great itinerary for the Moselle (good in either direction) would be as follows: by boat Koblenz to Cochem, by train Cochem to Bullay and then by Moselbahn bus to Trier, stopping at any of the little villages along the way that grab you.

You'll find lots of sleeping options in all towns big and small. **Hotel-Pension Garni Villa Tummelchen** (☎910 520; www.villa-tummelchen.com; Schlossstrasse 22; r from €55-80; 📶) is a bit up the hill from Cochem's centre and thus has sweeping Moselle vistas. It's worth an extra couple of euros to get a room with a balcony and a view.

Getting There & Around

Trains fan out in all directions from Koblenz, running up the Moselle to Trier (€20, 1½ hours, hourly) via Cochem.

Moselbahn (www.moselbahn.de) runs eight buses on weekdays (fewer at weekends) between Trier and Bullay (three hours each way), a pretty route following the river's winding course and passing through numerous quaint villages. Buses leave from outside the train stations in Trier and Bullay.

The relaxed way to explore the Moselle in the high season is by boat. From May to early October, **Köln-Düsseldorfer (KD) Line** (www.k-d.com) ferries sail daily between Koblenz and Cochem (€25 one way, 5¼ hours upstream, 4¼ hours downstream). Various smaller ferry companies also operate on the Moselle from various towns. Eurail and German Rail passes are valid for all normal KD Line services, and travel on your birthday is free.

The Moselle is a popular area among cyclists, and for much of the river's course there's a separate 'Moselroute' bike track. Most towns have a rental shop or two; ask at the tourist offices. Many of the Moselbahn buses also carry bikes.

Trier

☎0651 / POP 101,000

Trier is touted as Germany's oldest town and you'll find more Roman ruins here than anywhere else north of the Alps. Its proximity to France can be tasted in its cuisine, while its large student population injects life among the ruins.

Sights

Roman Ruins HISTORIC BUILDINGS

The town's chief landmark is the **Porta Nigra** (admission €3; ⌚9am-6pm Apr-Sep, to 5pm Mar & Oct, to 4pm Nov-Feb), the imposing city gate on the northern edge of the town centre, which dates back to the 2nd century AD.

Additional Roman sites include the **Amphitheater** (Olewigerstrasse; admission €3; ⌚9am-6pm Apr-Sep, to 5pm Mar & Oct, to 4pm Nov-Feb) and the gloomy underground caverns of the **Kaiserthermen** (Im Palastgarten).

Middle Ages Buildings HISTORIC BUILDINGS

Trier's massive (and massively restored) Romanesque **Dom** (www.dominformation.de; Liebfrauenstrasse 12; ⌚6.30am-6pm Apr-Oct, to 5.30pm Nov-Mar) shares a 1600-year history with the nearby and equally impressive **Konstantin Basilika** (☎724 68; Konstantinplatz; ⌚10am-6pm Mon-Fri, noon-6pm Sun Apr-Oct).

Museums MUSEUMS

The **Karl Marx Haus** (www.fes.de/marx; Brückenstrasse 10; admission €3; ⌚10am-6pm daily Apr-Oct, 2-5pm Tue-Sun Nov-Mar) is the suitably modest birthplace of the man. It is a major pilgrimage stop for the growing numbers of mainland Chinese tourists to Europe. The walls are lined with manifestos.

Sleeping & Eating

The narrow and historic **Judengasse**, near the Markt, has several small bars and clubs. There's a cluster of stylish places on **Viehmarktplatz** and another bunch in front of the **Dom**. In summer getting a seat at a cafe can feel like battling a lion.

Hille's Hostel HOSTEL €
(☎710 2785; www.hilles-hostel-trier.de; Gartenfeldstrasse 7; dm €15-19, s/d €41/52; @) The rooms here are furnished with Ikea bunk beds and are set back from the road amid some hardy palms. There's a big kitchen and the chance to ponder the mugs of previous guests that line the walls.

Hotel Pieper HOTEL €€
(☎230 08; www.hotel-pieper-trier.de; Thebäerstrasse 39; r €50-120; wi-fi) An excellent family-run hotel on a residential street with a few neighbourhood cafes, just five minutes from the station. Rooms are comfy and have free wi-fi. Best of all is the bounteous breakfast buffet that includes treats like fresh pineapple.

Walderdorff's CAFE €€
(www.walderdorffs.de; Domfreihof 1a; mains €8-16) A high-concept wine bar and cafe across from the Dom. Score one of the dozens of tables out front or inside in the stylish surrounds. The food is fresh and light; look for salads, sandwiches and many seasonal specials.

Kartoffel Kiste SPUD CAFE €€
(www.kiste-trier.de; Fahrstrasse 13-14; mains €8-16) A local favourite, this place specialises in baked, breaded, soupified and sauce-engulfed potatoes, as well as steaks. There is an extraordinary bronze fountain fronting its many outdoor tables.

Information

Tourist office (www.trier.de; An der Porta Nigra; ⌚9am-6pm Mon-Sat, 10am-5pm Sun May-Oct, reduced hr winter). Located at the Porta Nigra, a 10-minute walk along the Theodor-Heuss-Allee.

Trier-Card (from €9) For discounts and free public transport.

Getting There & Away

Trier has a train service to Koblenz (€20, 1½ hours, hourly) via Bullay and Cochem, as well as to Luxembourg (€16, 50 minutes, hourly).

Rhine Valley – Koblenz to Mainz

A boat trip along the Rhine is on the itinerary of most travellers, as it should be. The section between Koblenz and Mainz offers ever-changing vistas of steep vineyard-covered mountains punctuated by scores of castles. It's really magical. Spring and autumn are the best times to visit; in summer it's overrun and in winter most towns go into hibernation.

Every town along the route offers cute little places to stay or camp, and atmospheric places to drink (wine tasting is hugely popular) and eat.

There are dozens of towns along this prime stretch of the Rhine. Details of some of the more notable follow. All have train and boat services.

Bacharach is a medieval walled village where everyone looks up to the great **Jugendherberge** (☎1266; www.djh.de; dm €19) in a castle. **Boppard** (left bank) features Roman walls and ruins, while **Oberwesel** (left bank) has numerous towers and the walkable walls of a ruined castle.

The towns of **St Goar** and **St Goarshausen** are on opposite sides of the Rhine. St Goar is on the left bank and has one of the most impressive castles on the river: **Burg Rheinfels** (www.st-goar.de; admission €5; ⌚9am-6pm Apr-Oct, 11am-5pm Sat & Sun in good weather Nov-Mar). St Goar's **Jugendherberge** (☎388; www.djh.de; Bismarckweg 17; dm/s/d €18/30/50) is right below the castle. **Hotel Hauser** (☎333; www.hotelhauser.de; Heerstrasse 77; r €50-80) is relaxed like an old easy chair. Large restaurant windows and all 13 rooms overlook the Rhine.

Across the river, just south of St Goarshausen, is the Rhine's most famous sight, the **Loreley Cliff**. Avoid **Rüdesheim**, an overrated and over-visited town of trinkets and hype.

Though the trails here may be a bit more crowded with day-trippers than those along the Moselle, **hiking** along the Rhine is also excellent. The slopes and trails around Bacharach are justly famous.

Getting There & Around

Although Koblenz and Mainz are the best starting point, the Rhine Valley is also easily accessible from Frankfurt on a very long day trip, but it could drive you to drink, as it were.

Each mode of transport on the Rhine has its own advantages and all are equally enjoyable. Try combining several. The **Köln-Düsseldorfer (KD) Line** (www.k-d.com) runs slow and fast boats daily between Koblenz and Mainz (as well as the less-interesting stretch between Cologne and Koblenz). The journey takes about four hours downstream and about 5½ hours upstream (€47, free with rail pass). Boats stop at riverside towns along the way.

Frequent train services operate on both sides of the Rhine River but are more convenient on the left bank. You can travel nonstop on IC/EC trains or travel by slower regional RB or RE services. The ride is amazing; sit on the right heading north and on the left heading south. Note that most stations don't have lockers.

Frankfurt-am-Main

☎069 / POP 645,000

Variously called 'Mainhattan' and 'Bankfurt', Frankfurt is indeed on the Main (pronounced 'mine') River, and, after London, it is Europe's centre of finance. Both sobriquets also refer to the city's soaring skyline of bank-owned skyscrapers.

But while all seems cosmopolitan, it is often just a small town at heart. Streets get quiet in the evenings and the long list of museums is devoid of any really outstanding stars. Then again, it has cute old pubs you would only ever find in a small town. Mind you, when a major trade fair is in town, such as the Frankfurt Book Fair, it feels as jammed as any metropolis.

Frankfurt-am-Main is best enjoyed as a gateway to someplace else rather than a focus of your trip. Note that Frankfurt is often officially referred to as Frankfurt-am-Main, or Frankfurt/Main, since there is another – smaller – Frankfurt (Frankfurt-an-der-Oder) located near the Polish border.

Sights

Get your head up into the clouds atop the **Main Tower** (www.maintower-restaurant.de; Neue Mainzer Strasse 52-58; admission €5; ⌚10am-9pm Apr-Oct, 10am-7pm Nov-Mar, weather permitting), with its open-air viewing platform 200m up. There is also a **cocktail bar** (⌚5.30pm-1am, to 2am Fri & Sat) and restaurant.

Altstadt HISTORIC QUARTER

Frankfurt has room for all its high-rises as about 80% of the old city was wiped off the map by two Allied bombing raids in March 1944. Although postwar reconstruction was subject to the hurried demands of the new age, rebuilding efforts were more thoughtful in the **Römerberg**, the old central area of Frankfurt west of the cathedral, where ersatz 14th- and 15th-century buildings provide a glimpse of the beautiful city this once was.

East of Römerberg is the **Frankfurter Dom** (Domplatz 14; museum admission €3; ⌚church 9am-noon & 2.30-8pm), the coronation site of Holy Roman emperors from 1562 to 1792.

'Few people have the imagination for reality' uttered the ever-pithy Johann Wolfgang von Goethe. Read more of his quotes at the **Goethe-Haus** (www.goethehaus-frankfurt.de; Grosser Hirschgraben 23-25; adult/student €5/2.50; ☎10am-6pm Mon-Sat, 10am-5.30pm Sun), where he was born in 1749.

The Main River flows just south of the Altstadt, with several bridges leading to one of the city's livelier areas, **Sachsenhausen**. Many enjoy summer evenings along the Maan.

Museums MUSEUMS

Frankfurt's museum list is long but a mixed bag. To sample them all, buy a 48-hour **Museumsufer ticket** (adult €15).

North of the cathedral, the excellent **Museum für Moderne Kunst** (www.mmk-frankfurt.de; Domstrasse 10; admission €8; ⌚10am-6pm Tue-Sun, to 8pm Wed) features works of modern art by Joseph Beuys, Claes Oldenburg and many others.

Also on the north bank, the **Jüdisches Museum** (Jewish Museum; www.jewishmuseum.de; Untermainkai 14-15; admission €4; ⌚10am-5pm Tue & Thu-Sun, to 8pm Wed) is housed in the former mansion of the Rothschild family and details the city's rich Jewish life before WWII.

Numerous museums line the south bank of the Main River along the so-called **Museumsufer** (Museum Embankment). Pick of the crop is the **Städel Museum** (www.staedelmuseum.de; Schaumainkai 63; admission €10; ⌚10am-5pm Tue & Fri-Sun, to 9pm Wed & Thu), with a world-class collection of paintings by artists from the Renaissance to the 20th century. A planned expansion may mean that collections shift during construction.

Sleeping

Predictably, most of Frankfurt's budget accommodation is in the grotty Bahnhofsviertel, which surrounds the station. Check a room before committing. The streets between here and the Messe (convention centre) are convenient for early departures. During large trade fairs the town is booked out months in advance and rates soar.

Frankfurt-am-Main

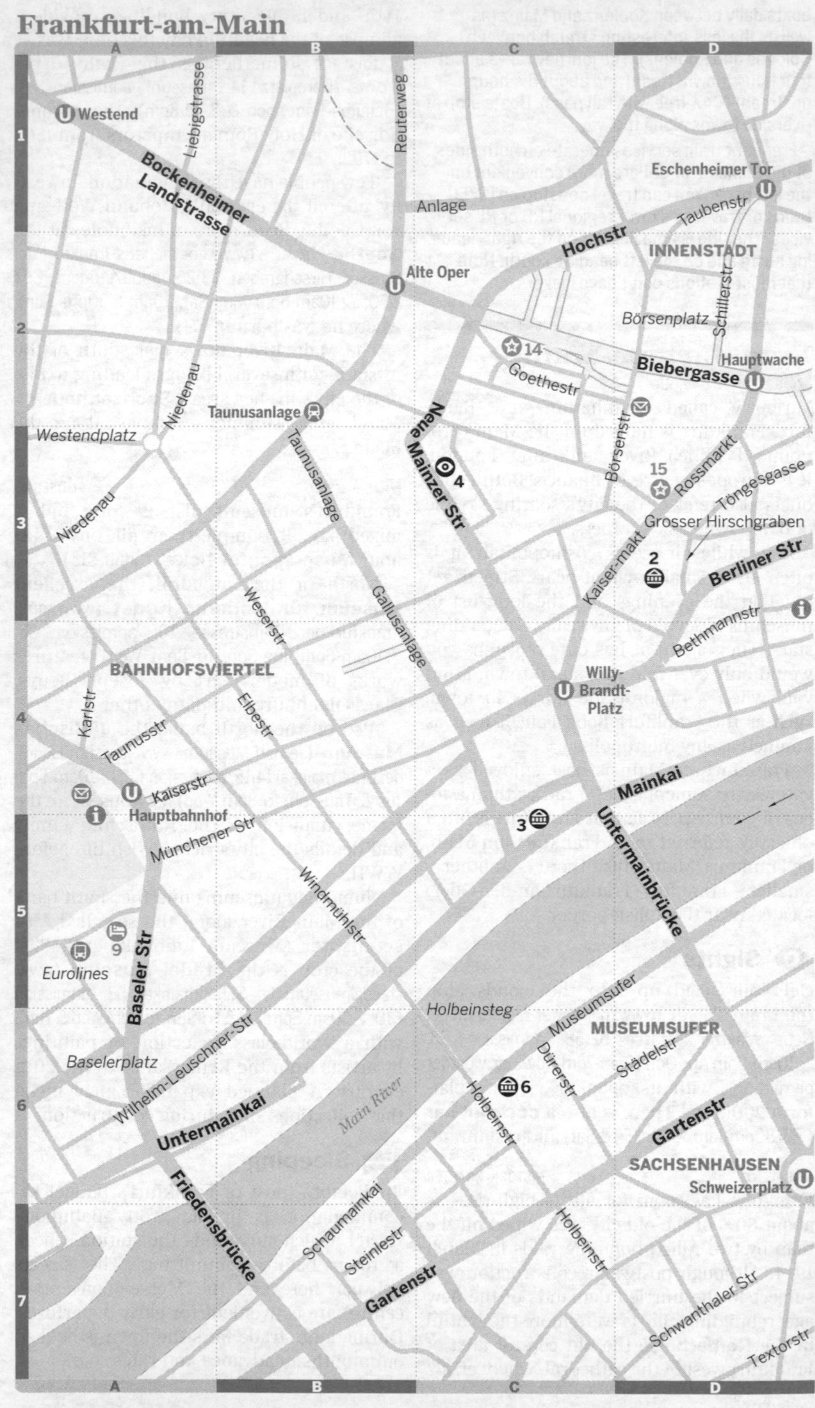

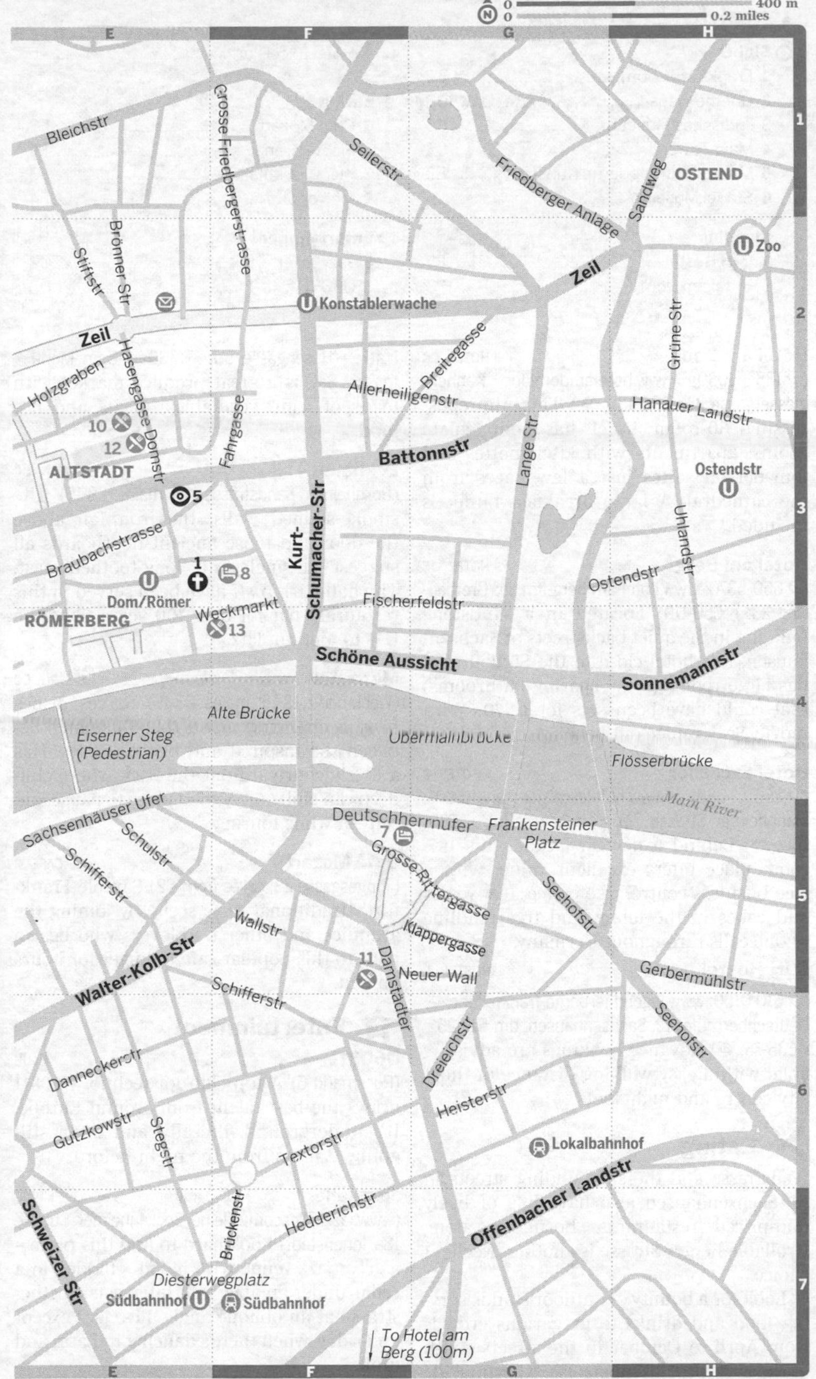
0 400 m
0 0.2 miles
E
F
G
H
1
2
3
4
5
6
7
Bleichstr
Grosse Friedbergerstrasse
Seilerstr
Friedberger Anlage
Sandweg
OSTEND
Zoo
Brönner Str
Stiftstr
Zeil
Konstablerwache
Breitegasse
Grüne Str
Holzgraben
Hasengasse
Allerheiligenstr
Hanauer Landstr
10
12
Domstr
Fahrgasse
Battonnstr
Lange Str
Ostendstr
ALTSTADT
5
Uhlandstr
Braubachstrasse
Kurt-Schumacher-Str
1
8
Ostendstr
Dom/Römer
Weckmarkt
Fischerfeldstr
RÖMERBERG
13
Schöne Aussicht
Sonnemannstr
Alte Brücke
Eiserner Steg (Pedestrian)
Obermainbrücke
Flösserbrücke
Main River
Sachsenhäuser Ufer
Deutschherrnufer
Frankensteiner Platz
7
Schulstr
Grosse Rittergasse
Schifferstr
Seehofstr
Wallstr
Klappergasse
Walter-Kolb-Str
11
Darmstädter
Neuer Wall
Gerbermühlstr
Schifferstr
Seehofstr
Dreieichstr
Danneckerstr
Heisterstr
Gutzkowstr
Stegstr
Lokalbahnhof
Textorstr
Offenbacher Landstr
Schweizer Str
Brückenstr
Hedderichstr
Diesterwegplatz
Südbahnhof
Südbahnhof
To Hotel am Berg (100m)

Frankfurt-am-Main

Sights

1 Frankfurter Dom ... E3
2 Goethe-Haus ... D3
3 Jüdisches Museum ... C5
4 Main Tower ... C3
5 Museum für Moderne Kunst ... E3
6 Städel Museum ... C6

Sleeping

7 DJH Hostel ... F5
8 Hotel am Dom ... F3
9 Hotel Excelsior ... A5

Eating

10 Cafe Mozart ... E3
11 Fichte Kränzi ... F5
12 Kleinmarkthalle ... E3
13 Metropol ... F4

Entertainment

14 Jazzkeller ... C2
15 U60311 ... D3

Hotel am Dom HOTEL €€
(☎138 1030; www.hotelamdom.de; Kannengiessergasse 3; r €90-130; Wi-Fi) This unprepossessing 30-room hotel has immaculate rooms, apartments with kitchenettes and four-person suites just a few paces from the cathedral. A large breakfast buffet is included.

Hotel am Berg HOTEL €€
(☎660 5370; www.hotel-am-berg-ffm.de; Grethenweg 23; r €50-110) Located in a sandstone building in the quiet backstreets of Sachsenhausen, this hotel close to the Südbahnhof has large rooms (some sharing bathrooms) that could have been sets for a '70s porn movie. Seek refuge out back.

Hotel Excelsior HOTEL €
(☎256 080; www.hotelexcelsior-frankfurt.de; Mannheimer Strasse 7-9, Bahnhofsviertel; r €60-100; @) Behind a newish facade, this 197-room place offers excellent value, with a free business centre, free coffee, tea, vegies and cakes in the lobby, and free landline phone calls throughout Germany.

DJH Hostel HOSTEL €
(☎610 0150; www.jugendherberge-frankfurt.de; Deutschherrnufer 12, Sachsenhausen; dm €17-25, r €35-75; @) Advance bookings are advisable; within easy walking distance of the city centre and nightspots.

Eating

Wallstrasse and the surrounding streets in Alt-Sachsenhausen also have lots of lively mid-priced restaurants. Bornheim along strollable Berger Strasse is another excellent choice.

Look for a bounty of outdoor stands serving food and drinks to gregarious crowds from April to October in the streets south of the Zeil. Off Hasenpetrolse, **Kleinmarkthalle** (Hasengasse 5-7; ⌚7.30am-6pm Mon-Fri, to 3pm Sat) is a great produce market with loads of fruit, vegetables, meats and hot food.

Eckhaus GERMAN €€
(Bornheimer Landstrasse 45; mains €8-15) The smoke-stained walls, the iron fan above the door and those ancient floorboards all suggest an inelegant, long-toothed past. The hallmark *rösti* have been served in this restaurant-bar for over 100 years. Take the U-4 to Merianplatz.

Metropol BISTRO €€
(Weckmarkt 13-15; mains €8-16) Serves dishes from a changing menu that fluctuates between the inspired and bistro staples. Has a lovely courtyard out the back where children can chill out. A good place to pause and refresh while touring.

Café Mozart CAFE €
(Töngesgasse 23; cakes from €2) Sample Frankfurt's traditional *torte* scene by joining the grannies and other trad-lovers who beat a path to this popular cafe to linger for hours on end.

Entertainment

U60311 CLUB
(Rossmarkt 6) A top club for techno, U60311 draws the best talent from around Europe. It's underground, literally, and often still going at noon from the night before.

Jazzkeller LIVE MUSIC
(www.jazzkeller.com; Kleine Bockenheimer Strasse 18a, Innenstadt) Look hard to find this place – a great jazz venue with mood – hidden in a cellar under an alley that intersects Goethestrasse at an oblique angle. Live jazz except on Friday, when there's dancing to Latin and funk.

DON'T MISS

APPLE-WINE TAVERNS

Apple-wine taverns are Frankfurt's great local tradition. They serve *Ebbelwoi* (Frankfurt dialect for Apfelwein), an alcoholic apple cider, along with local specialities such as *Handkäse mit Musik* (literally, 'hand-cheese with music'). This is a round cheese soaked in oil and vinegar and topped with onions; your bowel supplies the music. Some good taverns that serve *Ebbelwoi* are situated in Sachsenhausen.

TOP CHOICE **Fichte Kränzi** APPLE WINE €€
(Wallstrasse 5; mains €7-15) Just superb. A smallish place down an alley with a large, shady tree outside. The schnitzels are tops, as is the patter from the waiters.

Apfelwein Solzer APPLE WINE €€
(www.solzer-frankfurt.de; Berger Strasse 260, Bornheim; mains €7-15) Located northeast of the centre in Bornheim, it has wood-panelled walls and a covered courtyard.

Information

Frankfurt Card (1 day/2 days €9/13) Gives 50% off admission to important attractions and unlimited travel on public transport.

Main tourist office (www.frankfurt-tourismus.de) Hauptbahnhof (⏲8am-9pm Mon-Fri, 9am-6pm Sat & Sun); Römer (Römerberg 27; ⏲9.30am-5.30pm Mon-Fri, 10am-4pm Sat & Sun) Northwest corner of the Römerberg square.

Getting There & Away

Air

Germany's largest airport is **Frankfurt airport** (FRA; www.frankfurt-airport.com), a vast labyrinth with connections throughout the world. It's served by most major airlines, although not many budget ones.

Frankfurt-Hahn airport (HHN; www.hahn-airport.de) is 70km west of Frankfurt. Buses from Frankfurt's Hauptbahnhof take about two hours – longer than the flight from London. Given the journey time it's fitting the bus company is called **Bohr** (☎06543-501 90; www.bohr-omnibusse.de; fares €12; hourly).

Bus

Long-distance buses leave from the south side of the Hauptbahnhof, where you'll find **Eurolines** (www.eurolines.eu; Mannheimer Strasse 15), with services to most European destinations.

The **Romantic Rd bus** (www.romanticroadcoach.de) leaves from the south side of the Hauptbahnhof.

Train

The Hauptbahnhof handles more departures and arrivals than any station in Germany. The myriad services include Berlin (€111, four hours), Hamburg (€106, 3½ hours) and Munich (€89, 3¼ hours). For Cologne take the fast (€63, 75 minutes) ICE line or the slower and more scenic line along the Rhine (€41, 2½ hours, hourly).

Many long-distance trains also serve the airport. This station, Fernbahnhof, is 300m beyond the S-Bahn station, which is under Terminal 1.

Getting Around

To/From the Airport

S-Bahn lines S8 and S9 run every 15 minutes between the airport and Frankfurt Hauptbahnhof (€3.80, 11 minutes, 4.15am to 1am), usually continuing via Hauptwache and Konstablerwache. Taxis (about €40) take 30 minutes without traffic jams.

The airport train station has two sections: platforms 1 to 3 (below Terminal 1, hall B) handle S-Bahn connections, while IC and ICE connections are in the long-distance train station (Fern bahnhof) 300m distant.

Public Transport

Tickets for Frankfurt's excellent transport network (RMV; www.traffiq.de) can be purchased from automatic machines at almost any train station or stop. Single tickets cost €2.40 and a 24-hour ticket costs €6 (€9.35 with the airport).

Cologne

☎0221 / POP 1 MILLION

Cologne (Köln) seems almost ridiculously proud to be home to Germany's largest cathedral; the twin-tower shape of its weather-beaten Gothic hulk adorns the strangest souvenirs – from egg cosies and slippers to glassware and expensive jewellery. However, this bustling Rhine-side metropolis has much more to offer than its most recognisable and ubiquitous symbol. As early as the 1st century AD, Colonia Agrippinensis was an important Roman trading settlement.

Today it's one of Germany's most multicultural spots, with a vibrant nightlife only partly fuelled by the local *Kölsch* beer.

The cathedral (Dom) and tourist information office are both on the doorstep of the main train station. The nightlife hubs of the Belgisches Viertel (tram 3, 4 or 5 to Friesenplatz) and the Zülpicher Viertel (tram 8 or 9 to Zülpicher Viertel/Bahnhof Süd) are several kilometres southwest.

Sights & Activities

Dom CATHEDRAL

(www.koelner-dom.de; ⏲6am-7.30pm, no visitors during services) As easy as it is to get church fatigue in Germany, the huge Kölner Dom is one you shouldn't miss. Blackened with age, this gargoyle-festooned Gothic cathedral has a footprint of 12,470 sq metres, with twin spires soaring to 157m. Although its ground stone was laid in 1248, stop-start construction meant it wasn't finished until 1880, as a symbol of Prussia's drive for unification. Just over 60 years later it escaped WWII's heavy night-bombing largely intact.

The interior is dimly lit and moody, while behind the altar lies the most precious reliquary, the **Shrine of the Three Magi** (c 1150–1210). The shrine reputedly contains the bones of the Three Wise Men, brought

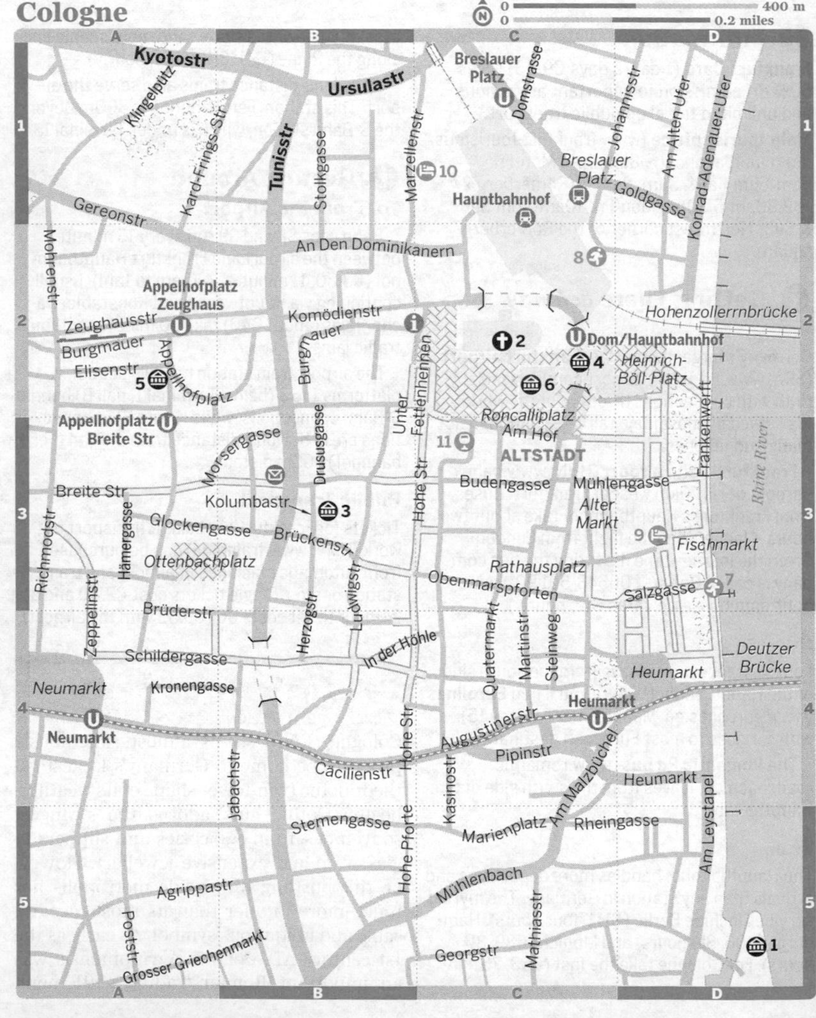

here from Milan in the 12th century. It can be glimpsed through the gates to the inner choir, but for a closer look, take a **guided tour** (adult/concession €6/4; ⏲in English 10.30am & 2.30pm Mon-Sat, 2.30pm Sun).

Alternatively, you can embark on the seriously strenuous endeavour of climbing the 509 steps of the Dom's **south tower** (adult/concession €2.50/1; ⏲9am-6pm May-Sep, to 5pm Oct, Mar & Apr, to 4pm Nov-Feb). You pass the 24-tonne **Peter Bell**, the world's largest working clanger, before emerging at almost 100m to magnificent views.

Museums MUSEUMS, ART GALLERIES
Two prominent museums sit next to the cathedral. The **Römisch-Germanisches Museum** (Roman Germanic Museum; www.museenkoeln.de; Roncalliplatz 4; adult/concession €5/3; ⏲10am-5pm Tue-Sun) displays artefacts from the Roman settlement of Colonia Agrippinensis. The **Museum Ludwig** (www.museenkoeln.de; Bischofsgartenstrasse 1; adult/concession €9/6; ⏲10am-6pm Tue-Sun, to 10pm first Thu of each month) has an astoundingly good collection of pop art, German expressionism and Russian avant-garde painting, as well as photography.

Encased in the ruins of a late-Gothic church, the **Kolumba Museum** (www.kolumba.de; Kolumbastrasse 4; adult/concession €5/3; ⏲noon-5pm Wed-Mon) has a magnificent design by Swiss architect Peter Zumthor. Exhibits span the arc of religious artistry from the early days of Christianity to the present. Coptic textiles, Gothic reliquary and medieval painting are juxtaposed with works by Bauhaus legend Andor Weiniger and edgy room installations.

Cologne's Third Reich history is poignantly documented at the **NS Dokumentationszentrum** (Appellhofplatz 23-25; adult/concession €3.60/1.50; ⏲10am-4pm Tue, Wed & Fri, 10am-6pm Thu, 11am-4pm Sat & Sun). It's in the basement of the building that was the local Gestapo prison, where scores of people were interrogated, tortured and killed.

South along the riverbank is the **Chocolate Museum** (www.schokoladenmuseum.de; Am Schokoladenmuseum 1a; adult/concession €7.50/7; ⏲10am-6pm Tue-Fri, 11am-7pm Sat & Sun), where you nibble on samples while learning the history and process of chocolate-making. Don't miss the 'Cult chocolate' floor.

Tours

Rhine river trips are operated by **KD River Cruises** (www.k-d.com; Frankenwerft 35). Day trips (10am, noon, 2pm and 6pm) cost from €7.20.

Festivals & Events

Held just before Lent in late February or early March, Cologne's **Carnival** (Karneval) rivals Munich's Oktoberfest for exuberance, as people dress in creative costumes and party in the streets. Things kick off the Thursday before the seventh Sunday before Easter and last until Monday *(Rosenmontag)*, when there are formal and informal parades.

Sleeping

Station Hostel for Backpackers HOSTEL €
(☎912 5301; www.hostel-cologne.de; Marzellenstrasse 44-56; dm €17-20, s/d/tr €39/55/75; @📶) You can't get more convenient than this friendly six-floor hostel around the corner from the train station. The rooms could use some sprucing up, but they're perfectly simple and clean. Breakfast costs €3, or you can use the guest kitchen.

Meininger City Hostel & Hotel HOSTEL €
(☎355 332 014; www.meininger-hostels.com; Engelbertstrasse 33-35; dm €17-24, s/d/tr from €43/68/84, breakfast €3.50; @📶) In a former hotel, this charming hostel in the cool Zülpicher Viertel is loaded with retro appeal coupled with modern rooms featuring lockers, reading lamps, a small TV and private bathrooms.

Das Kleine Stapelhäuschen HOTEL €€
(☎272 7777; www.koeln-altstadt.de/stapelhaeuschen; Fischmarkt 1-3; s/d from €45/68; @📶) A small, friendly hotel housed in a historic

Cologne

Sights

1	Chocolate Museum	D5
2	Dom	C2
3	Kolumba Museum	B3
4	Museum Ludwig	C2
5	NS Dokumentationszentrum	A2
6	Römisch-Germanisches Museum	C2

Activities, Courses & Tours

7	KD River Cruises	D3
8	Radstation	C2

Sleeping

9	Das Kleine Staphelhäuschen	D3
10	Station Hostel for Backpackers	C1

Drinking

11	Früh am Dom	C3

12th-century building in the centre of the Old Town just off the riverbank. Exposed beams, antique furnishings and simple but cosy touches give rooms a homey feel.

Pension Jansen HOTEL €€
(☎251 85; www.pensionjansen.de; 2nd fl, Richard Wagner Strasse 18; s €31-45, d €62-65; ⊖) This cute, well-cared-for pension between the Belgisches and Zülpicher Viertels has six individually decorated rooms with cheerful colours and motifs. Details like handmade wreaths hanging on aqua walls – or a big red rose screen-printed on the bed linen – convey a homey atmosphere. Book early.

Eating

Cologne's beer halls serve meals, but the city also overflows with restaurants, especially around the Belgisches and Zülpicher Viertels.

Alcazar PUB FARE €
(Bismarckstrasse 39) The food and atmosphere are both hearty and warming at this old-school, slightly hippie pub in the Belgisches Viertel. The changing menu always has one vegie option.

Feynsinn INTERNATIONAL €€
(Rathenauplatz 7; mains €7-18) The glint of artfully arranged glasses behind the mirrored bar will catch your eye from the street (it's located in a tranquil section of the Zülpicher Viertel), as will the broken-glass chandeliers. Inside under murals, students, creative types and tourists tuck into seasonal cuisine (menu changes weekly) as well as traditional Cologne fare like *Himmel & Aad* (literally 'Heaven & Earth', which is mashed potatoes and apple sauce). The owners have even started to raise their own pigs and cattle.

Weinstube Bacchus INTERNATIONAL €€
(Rathenauplatz 17; ⊙dinner) Dark-wood tables, yellow walls that are lined with paintings by local artists (all pieces are for sale), a seasonal international menu, and an almost exclusively German wine list make this casual wine bar–restaurant in the Zülpicher Viertel popular among the locals.

Drinking & Entertainment

As in Munich, beer reigns supreme here. Local breweries produce a variety called *Kölsch,* which is relatively light and slightly bitter. In the beer halls, it's served in skinny 200mL glasses. You can get food too.

Früh am Dom BEER HALL
(Am Hof 12-14) This three-storey beer hall and restaurant (including cellar bar) is the most central, with black-and-white flooring, copper pans and tiled ovens keeping it real, despite the souvenir shop. It's open for breakfast.

Päffgen BEER HALL
(Friesenstrasse 64-66) Another favourite, this thrumming wood-lined room has its own beer garden. It's not far from the bars of the Belgisches Viertel.

Gebäude 9 CLUB
(Deutz-Mülheimer Strasse 127-129) Once a factory, this is now a Cologne nightlife stalwart spinning drum'n' bass, indie pop, gypsy music and '60s trash to film noir and puppets. It's located about a kilometre east of the Altstadt.

Underground LIVE MUSIC
(Vogelsanger Strasse 200; ⊙Mon & Wed-Sat) This complex combines a pub and two concert halls where indie and alternative rock bands hold forth several times a week. Otherwise it's party time with different music nightly (no cover). There's a beer garden in summer.

Information

Köln Welcome Card (24/48/72hr €9/14/19) Discount card that includes free public transport (including Bonn) and discounted museum admission. Available from the tourist office.

Tourist office (☎2213 0400; www.koelntourismus.de; Unter Fettenhennen 19; ⊙9am-8pm Mon-Sat, 10am-5pm Sun)

Getting There & Away

Air

Cologne-Bonn airport (CGN; www.airport-cgn.de) is growing in importance. There are now direct flights to New York, while budget airlines **germanwings** (www.germanwings.com) and **easyJet** (www.easyjet.com) fly here, among others.

Train

There are frequent RE services operating to Düsseldorf (€11 to €16, 25 to 30 minutes) and Aachen (€13.90, 50 minutes to one hour). Frequent EC, IC, or ICE trains go to Hanover (from €55, 2¾ to three hours), Frankfurt-am-Main (from €39, one to 2¼ hours, three hourly) and Berlin (€104, 4¼ hours, hourly). Frequent Thalys and ICE high-speed services connect Cologne to Brussels (from €45, two hours) and ICE trains go to Amsterdam (from €59, 2½ hours).

Getting Around

Cologne's mix of buses, trams, and U-Bahn and S-Bahn trains is operated by **VRS** (☎01803-504 030; www.vrsinfo.de) in cooperation with Bonn's system.

Short trips (up to four stops) cost €1.60, longer ones €2.40. Day passes are €6.90 for one person and €10.10 for up to five people travelling together.

Cologne is flat and cycle-friendly. Bicycle hire is available next to the main train station at **Radstation** (☎139 7190; www.radstationkoeln.de; Am Hauptbahnhof/Breslauerplatz; per 3hr/1/3/7 days €5/10/20/40; ⏰5.30am-10.30pm Mon-Fri, 6.30am-8pm Sat, 8am-8pm Sun).

Bonn

☎0228 / POP 312,000

Bonn is not only the birthplace of musical genius Ludwig van Beethoven – its brief tenure as capital of West Germany (from 1949) and as the home of German government departments (until 1999) has also left it with an excellent collection of museums.

The **tourist office** (www.bonn-regio.de; Windeckstrasse 1; ⏰9am-6.30pm Mon-Fri, 9am-4pm Sat, 10am-2pm Sun) is a three-minute walk along Poststrasse from the Hauptbahnhof.

Music fans will head straight to the **Beethoven-Haus** (www.beethoven-haus-bonn.de; Bonngasse 24-26; adult/concession €4/3; ⏰10am-6pm Mon-Sat, 11am-6pm Sun Apr-Oct, to 5pm Nov-Mar), where the composer was born in 1770. The house contains memorabilia concerning his life and compositions.

Elsewhere, the **Haus der Geschichte der Bundesrepublik Deutschland** (www.hdg.de; Willy-Brandt-Allee 14; admission free; ⏰9am-7pm Tue-Sun) engagingly presents Germany's postwar history.

From Cologne, it's quicker to take an RE train to Bonn (€6.50, 30 minutes) than a tram (€8.50 day pass, 55 minutes each way). You can get boats here from Cologne.

Düsseldorf

☎0211 / POP 585,000

'D-Town' or 'The City D', as local magazine editors like to call Düsseldorf, is Germany's fashion capital. But that means Jil Sander and Wolfgang Joop rather than cutting-edge streetwear, as you'll soon discover observing fur-clad *Mesdames* with tiny dogs along the ritzy shopping boulevard of the Königsallee.

Indeed, this elegant and wealthy town could feel stiflingly bourgeois if it weren't for its lively old-town pubs, its position on the Rhine, its excellent art galleries and the postmodern architecture of its Mediahafen.

Sights & Activities

Düsseldorf has a lively **Altstadt** filled with enough restaurants and pubs to have earned it the slightly exaggerated title of the 'longest bar in the world'.

What really sets the city apart, however, is the contemporary architecture of its **Mediahafen**. Here, in the city's south, docks have been transformed into an interesting commercial park, most notably including the **Neuer Zollhof**, three typically curved and twisting buildings by Bilbão Guggenheim architect Frank Gehry.

On the street side of the red-brick building, there's a billboard with a map of the entire park. Alternatively, catch the lift 168m up the neighbouring **Rheinturm** (admission €3.50; ⏰10am-11.30pm) for a bird's-eye view.

It's a pleasant stroll between the Mediahafen and the Altstadt along the riverside **Rheinuferpromenade**. Alternatively, you can join the city's elite window-shopping along **Königsallee**, referred to by locals as 'Kö' – Düsseldorf's answer to Rodeo Dr.

Newly reopened in 2010, the **K20** (www.kunstsammlung.de; Grabbeplatz 5; adult/concession €10/5, combination ticket K20 & K21 €17/8.50; ⏰10am-6pm Tue-Fri, 11am-6pm Sat & Sun) museum features a brand-new wing and early-20th-century masters, including an extensive Paul Klee collection.

Sleeping

Jugendgästehaus HOSTEL €
(☎557 310; www.jugendherberge.de; Düsseldorfer Strasse 1; dm/s/tw €25/42/62; @📶) Situated in posh Oberkassel, recent renovations turned this 368-room hostel into a snazzy modern place that feels more like a boutique hotel. All rooms are en suite and breakfast is served in a large, airy space overlooking the Rhine.

Hotel Berial HOTEL €€
(☎490 0490; Gartenstrasse 30; www.hotelberial.de; s/d from €40/60; 🚭@📶) An inviting ambience reigns here, thanks to the friendly staff and the contemporary furnishings. Decor features lots of blue, blond wood, glass bathroom doors and some bright prints. The breakfast buffet is truly gargantuan.

Eating & Drinking

Libanon Express MIDDLE EASTERN €
(Berger Strasse 19-21; cafe snacks & mains €3-14, restaurant mains €10-19) Crammed with mirrors and tiles – and with recommendations stickered on the window – this cafe serves great kebabs, falafel and other Middle Eastern fare.

Ohme Jupp BISTRO €
(Ratinger Strasse 19; ⏲8am-1am) Casual, artsy cafe serving breakfast and seasonal blackboard specials; also a popular after-work drinking den.

Zum Uerige BREW PUB
(Berger Strasse 1) In this noisy, cavernous place, the trademark Uerige Alt beer (a dark and semisweet brew typical of Düsseldorf) flows so quickly that the waiters just carry around trays and give you a glass whenever they spy one empty. They also serve hearty German fare, so it doubles as an excellent place for a bite.

Information

Düsseldorf Welcome Card (24/48/72hr €9/14/19) Discount card offering free public transport and discounted museum admission.
Tourist office (www.duesseldorf-tourismus.de) main office (Immermannstrasse 65b; ⏲9.30am-6.30pm Mon-Sat); Old Town (Marktstrasse/Ecke Rheinstrasse; ⏲10am-6pm).

Getting There & Around

From **Düsseldorf International Airport** (DUS; www.duesseldorf-international.de), trains go directly to other German cities, while frequent S-Bahn services (1 and 7) head to Düsseldorf train station.

Low-cost carrier Ryanair flies to **Niederrhein (Weeze) airport** (NRN; www.flughafen-niederrhein.de). A **shuttle bus** (☎06543-50190; www.bohr-omnibusse.de) to Düsseldorf (€15, 1¼ hours) leaves soon after the planes' scheduled arrivals.

The many train services from Düsseldorf include to Cologne (€10.50 to €16, 25 to 30 minutes), Frankfurt-am-Main (€70, 1½ to 1¾ hours), Hanover (€53, 2½ hours) and Berlin (€97, 4¼ hours).

Most local transport trips within the city cost €2.30; longer trips to the suburbs are €4.50. Day passes are €5.30.

Aachen

☎0241 / POP 247,000

A spa town with a hopping student population and tremendous amounts of character, Aachen has narrow cobbled streets, quirky fountains, shops full of delectable *Printen* (a local biscuit, a bit like gingerbread), and a pretty cathedral, which make for an excellent day trip from Cologne or Düsseldorf or a worthy overnight stop.

Aachen's compact centre is contained within two ring roads roughly tracing the old city walls. The inner ring road, or Grabenring, changes names – most ending in 'graben' – and encloses the old city proper. To get to the tourist office from the Hauptbahnhof, cross Römerstrasse, follow Bahnhofstrasse north and then go left along Theaterstrasse to Kapuzinergraben.

Sights

Old Town & Fountains HISTORIC QUARTER
Next to the tourist office is the **Elisenbrunnen**. Despite its sulphuric 'rotten eggs' smell, you *can* drink it – it's supposedly good for the digestion.

In the far left-hand corner of the park behind the Elisenbrunnen is the **Geldbrunnen**, which represents the circulation of money. The comical figures around the pool clutch their coins or purses while the water is sucked down the central plughole (jokingly known as 'the taxman').

Head east along the top of the park here, towards Forum M, and turn left into Buchkremerstrasse. Soon you'll reach a fountain with a scary-looking creature. This is the mythological **Bahkauv**, rumoured to pounce on those returning late from the pub and demand a piggyback home.

Buchkremerstrasse becomes Büchel. Turn left just past Leo van den Daele restaurant, then right and you'll come to Hühnermarkt, with its **Hühnerdiebbrunnen** (Chicken thief fountain). The hasty thief hasn't noticed one of his stolen chickens is a rooster that is about to unmask him by crowing.

From here, Aachen's main **Markt** is visible just to the northeast. The 14th-century **Rathaus** (adult/concession €2/1; ⏲10am-5pm Mon-Fri, 10am-1pm & 2-5pm Sat & Sun) overlooks the Markt.

Head back down the hill along Krämerstrasse until you come to the **Puppenbrunnen** (puppet fountain), where you're allowed to play with the movable bronze figures.

Dom CATHEDRAL
(Kaiserdom or Münster; www.aachendom.de; ⏲7am-7pm Apr-Oct, to 6pm Nov-Mar) While Cologne's cathedral wows you with size and atmosphere, Aachen's similarly Unesco-list-

ed Dom impresses with its shiny neatness. The small, Byzantine-inspired **octagon** at the building's heart dates from AD 805 but was refurbished in 2003 so its mosaics and marble gleam like new.

The building is significant not just because Charlemagne ordered it built, but also because 30 Holy Roman emperors were crowned here from 936 to 1531.

The brass **chandelier** in the centre was donated by Emperor Friedrich Barbarossa in 1165, while Charlemagne himself lies in the golden **shrine** behind the altar, a centuries-old magnet for pilgrims.

Carolus Thermal Baths BATHS
(www.carolus-thermen.de; Stadtgarten/Passstrasse 79; admission with/without sauna from €22/11; 9am-11pm) The 8th-century Franks were lured to 'Ahha' (water) for its thermal springs. And centuries later the state-of-the-art Carolus Thermen is still reeling them in. The complex is part therapeutic spa and part swimming centre. Don't pay for the sauna; there's a steam room accessible to all. The baths are in the city garden, northeast of the centre.

Sleeping

Hotel Benelux HOTEL €€
(400 030; www.hotel-benelux.de; Franzstrasse 21-23; s €94-109, d €120-154;) This well-run hotel is clean and uncluttered with tasteful art in all its rooms. The rooftop garden with the enclosed gazebo is a bonus.

Jugendgästehaus HOSTEL €
(711 010; www.jugendherberge.de; Maria-Theresia-Allee 260; dm/s/tw €23/37/57; @) This modern DJH outpost sits on a hill overlooking the city, and gets lots of school groups. Take bus 2 to Ronheide.

Eating & Drinking

Aachen's students have their own 'Latin Quarter' along Pontstrasse, with dozens of bars and cheap eats. The street heads northeast off the Markt and runs for nearly a kilometre.

Leo van den Daele INTERNATIONAL €
(Büchel 18) A warren of 17th-century rooms linked by crooked stairs across four merchants' homes, this nationally renowned cafe specialises in gingerbread, or *Printen*. Yet you can also enjoy light meals – soups, sandwiches, quiches and *pastetchen* (vol-au-vents) – among its tiled stoves and antique knick-knacks.

Apollo Kino & Bar BAR, CLUB
(Pontstrasse 141-149) This cavernous basement joint does double duty as an arthouse cinema and a sweaty dance club for the student brigade. Alt-sounds rule on Monday, salsa on Tuesday, but on other nights it could be anything from dancehall to disco, house to power pop.

Information

Tourist office (180 2960/1; www.aachen.de; Atrium Elisenbrunnen, Kapuzinergraben; 9am-6pm Mon-Fri, 9am-2pm Sat, also 10am-2pm Sun Easter-Dec)

Getting There & Around

There are frequent trains to Cologne (€13.90 to €19.50, 30 minutes to one hour) and twice hourly service to Düsseldorf (from €17.20, 70 minutes to 1½ hours). High-speed Thalys and ICE trains pass through regularly to Brussels.

Buses cost €1.50 (trip of a few stops only), €2.20 (regular single) or €6.10 (day pass).

LOWER SAXONY

Lower Saxony (Niedersachsen) likes to make much of its half-timbered towns such as Hamelin. However, the state is also home to the famous Volkswagen car company, and even the business-minded capital, Hanover, has its diversions.

Hanover

0511 / POP 518,000

German comedians like to dismiss Hanover as 'the autobahn exit between Göttingen and Walsrode'. However, the capital of Lower Saxony is really nowhere near that grim. While it's famous for hosting trade fairs, particularly the huge CEBIT computer show in March, it also boasts acres of greenery in the Versailles-like Herrenhäuser Gärten.

Parts of the central Altstadt look medieval, but few are. They're mostly clever fakes built after intense WWII bombing.

Sights

The enormous **Grosser Garten** (Large Garden; admission €3, winter free) is the highlight of the **Herrenhäuser Gärten** (www.herrenhaeuser-gaerten.de; 9am-sunset). It has a small maze, Europe's tallest fountain and a popular beer garden. Check the website in summer for **Wasserspiele**, when fountains are synchronised, and the night-time **Illuminations**. The **Niki de Saint Phalle Grotto** is a magical showcase of the artist's work. She was French – her colourful figures adorn the famous Stravinsky fountain outside Paris's Centre Pompidou – but developed a special relationship with Hanover.

The **Neues Rathaus** was built between 1901 and 1913. Town models in the foyer reveal the extent of WWII devastation. Further east lies the Leine River where, since 1974, **Die Nanas** – three fluorescent-coloured, earth-mama sculptures by de Saint Phalle – have lived. They're best seen on Saturday, when there's a flea market at their feet.

In summer, the **Machsee** (lake) has **ferries** (crossings €3, tours €6) and numerous boats for hire. There's a free public **swimming beach** on the southeastern shore.

Sleeping & Eating

The tourist office only finds private rooms during trade fairs but can arrange hotel bookings year-round for €7.

Jugendherberge HOSTEL €
(131 7674; www.jugendherberge.de; Ferdinand-Wilhelm-Fricke-Weg 1; dm under/over 27yr from €23.90/26.90; @) This large space-lab-looking structure houses a modern hostel with breakfast room and terrace bar overlooking the river in an area that feels more country than city. Take U3 or U7 to Fischerhof, cross the mini, red suspension bridge and turn right.

GästeResidenz PelikanViertel HOTEL €€
(399 90; Pelikanstrasse 11; s €46-69, d €66-89, tr €92-109; @) Upmarket student residence meets budget hotel, this huge complex (located in the former Pelikan fountain-pen factory) has a wide range of Ikea-style rooms, all with kitchenettes. Prices skyrocket during trade-fair periods. Take U3, U7 or U9 to Pelikanstrasse.

Markthalle INTERNATIONAL €
(Karmarschstrasse 49; 7am-8pm Mon-Wed, to 10pm Thu & Fri, to 4pm Sat) This huge covered market of food stalls (sausages, sushi, tapas and more), gourmet delis and standing-only 'bars' is a no-nonsense, atmospheric place for a quick bite. It's also heaving each Friday evening with people proclaiming *Prost!* (Cheers!) to the start of the weekend.

Spandau INTERNATIONAL €€
(1235 7095; Engelbosteler Damm 30; 10am-1am Sun-Wed, 10am-2am Thu-Sat) Retro-'70s Spandau in Hanover's Nordstadt is more like Berlin's Kreuzberg – a place where students from the nearby university and the local Turkish community rub shoulders.

Information

Hannover Tourismus (information 1234 5111, room reservations 1234 555; www.hannover.de; Ernst-August-Platz 8; 9am-6pm Mon-Fri, 9am-2pm Sat, also 9am-2pm Sun Apr-Sep)

Getting There & Around

Hanover's **airport** (HAJ; www.hannover-airport.de) has many connections, including on low-cost carrier **Air Berlin** (www.airberlin.com).

There are frequent IC/ICE train services running to/from Hamburg (€34 to €39, 1¼ to 1½ hours), Berlin (€53 to €58, 1½ to two hours), Cologne (€54 to €61, 2¾ to 3¼ hours) and to Munich (€112, 4¼ to 4¾ hours), among other destinations.

U-Bahn lines from the Hauptbahnhof are boarded in the station's north (follow the signs towards Raschplatz), except the U10 and U17, which are overground trams leaving near the tourist office.

Most visitors only travel in the central 'Hannover' zone. Single tickets are €2.10, day passes €4.10.

Around Hanover

Hanover makes a good jumping-off point for day trips to the beautiful towns of Lower Saxony.

WOLFSBURG

Volkswagen *is* the Lower Saxon town of Wolfsburg – and the huge VW emblem adorning the company's global headquarters (and a factory the size of a small country) won't let you forget it.

The top reason people come here is to experience the theme park called **Autostadt** (Car City; www.autostadt.de; Stadtbrücke; admission €15, entry after 4pm €7; 9am-6pm) is a celebration of all things Volkswagen. Exhibitions run the gamut of automotive design and engineering, the history of the Beetle and the marketing of individual marques including VW itself, Audi, Bentley, Lamborghini, Seat and Skoda.

Frequent train services arrive from Hanover (from €12.90, 30 minutes to one hour) and Berlin (from €34.40, one to 1¼ hours).

WORTH A TRIP

HAMELIN

If you were to believe *The Pied Piper of Hamelin* fairy tale, this quaint, ornate town on the Weser River ought to be devoid of both rats and children. But of course it isn't and in fact is filled with kids buying souvenir plastic rats.

The best way to explore is to follow the **Pied Piper trail** – the line of white rats drawn on the pavements.

The detailed Weser Renaissance style dominates the Altstadt – the **Rattenfängerhaus** (Rat Catcher's House; Osterstrasse 28), from 1602, is perhaps the finest example, with its steep and richly decorated gable. Also not to be missed is the **Hochzeitshaus** (1610–17) at the Markt end of Osterstrasse. The **Rattenfänger Glockenspiel** at the far end chimes daily at 9.35am and 11.35am, while a **carousel of Pied Piper figures** twirls at 1.05pm, 3.35pm and 5.35pm.

Frequent S-Bahn trains (S5) head from Hanover to Hamelin (€10.30, 45 minutes). By car, take the B217 to/from Hanover.

BREMEN

☎0421 / POP 550,000

It's a shame the donkey, dog, cat and rooster in Grimm's *Die Bremerstadmusikanten* (Town Musicians of Bremen) never actually made it here – they would have fallen in love with it. This little city is big on charm, from the statues of the famous fairy-tale characters to the jaw-dropping art-nouveau lane to the impressive Markt. On top of that, the waterfront promenade along the Weser River is a relaxing refuge filled with outdoor cafes, and the student district along Ostertorsteinweg knows it's got a good thing going and leaves little to be desired.

Sights & Activities

Bremen's **Markt** is striking, particularly its gabled **Rathaus**. In front stands a 13m-tall medieval statue of the knight **Roland**, Bremen's protector. On the building's western side, you'll find the **Town Musicians of Bremen** sculpture (1951). The animals are in their most famous pose, scaring the robbers who invaded their house, with the rooster atop the cat, perched on the dog, on the shoulders of the donkey.

Also on the Markt is the **Dom** and its slightly macabre **Bleikeller** (Lead Cellar; adult/concession €1.50/1; ⏱10am-5pm Mon-Fri, 10am-2pm Sat, noon-5pm Sun Apr-Oct). Here, open coffins reveal eight corpses mummified in the dry air underground.

The nearby art-deco alley of **Böttcherstrasse** is unique. Through an arch with a striking golden relief, you enter a world of tall brick houses, shops, galleries, restaurants, a **Glockenspiel** and several (missable) museums.

A maze of narrow, winding alleys, the **Schnoorviertel** was once the fishermen's quarter and then the red-light district. Now its dollhouse-sized cottages are souvenir shops and restaurants.

If you have time, visit **Beck's Brewery** (Am Deich 18-19; tours in German & English €9.50; ⏱2pm & 3.30pm Thu & Fri, 12.30pm, 2pm, 3.30pm & 5pm Sat Jan-Apr, additionally 11am & 12.30pm Thu & Fri, 9.30am & 11am Sat May Dec).

Sleeping

Bremer Backpacker Hostel HOSTEL €
(☎223 8057; www.bremer-backpacker-hostel.de; Emil-Waldmannstrasse 5-6; dm/s/d €17/28/46; @📶) A friendly place five minutes from the train station, here you'll find simply furnished but spotless rooms spread out over several levels (each floor is named after a continent), a full kitchen, a living room and a cheerful courtyard.

DJH Hostel Bremen HOSTEL €
(☎163 820; www.jugendherberge.de; Kalkstrasse 6; dm under/over 27yr €23.50/26.50, s/d €36.50/63; @📶) Looking like a work of art from the exterior, with a yellow and orange Plexiglas facade and slit rectangular windows, this refurbished building looks more like a museum than a hostel. Comfortable dorms are all en suite, there's a bar-breakfast room with huge glass windows overlooking the Weser River, and a rooftop terrace. Take tram 3 or 5 to Am Brill.

Eating

The student quarter in and around Ostertorsteinweg, Das Viertel, is full of restaurants and cafes and has a vaguely bohemian atmosphere. The waterfront promenade, Schlachte, is more expensive and mainstream. The Marktplatz is home to oodles of cheap snack stands.

Piano CAFE, BAR

(☎785 46; Fehrfeld 64) One of the most enduringly popular cafes in the student quarter, Piano is excellent for an evening tipple or a snack from its menu of pizza, pasta, steaks and vegie casseroles. Breakfast can also be enjoyed until 4pm.

Restaurant Flett GERMAN €€

(☎320 995; Böttcherstrasse 3-5) Despite all the tourists who drop in, this is the best place in Bremen to try local specialities such as *Labskaus* (a hash of beef or pork with potatoes, onion and herring) or *Knipp* (fried hash and oats).

Information

Tourist office (☎01805-101030; www.bremen-tour ism.de) Hauptbahnhof (⊙9am-7pm Mon-Fri, 9.30am-6pm Sat & Sun); branch office (Obernstrasse/Liebfrauenkirchhof; ⊙10am-6.30pm Mon-Fri, 10am-4pm Sat & Sun)

Getting There & Around

Flights from **Bremen airport** (BRE; www.airport-bremen.de) include those of low-cost carrier **Air Berlin** (www.airberlin.com) and Ryanair (www.ryanair.com).

Frequent trains go to Hamburg (€20.80 to €28, one hour to 1¼ hours), Hanover (€21 to €30, one hour to 80 minutes) and Cologne (€60, three hours).

Tram 6 leaves the airport frequently, heading to the centre (€2.20, 16 minutes). Other trams cover most of the city. Single bus/tram tickets cost €2.20; a day pass (€5.90 for one adult and two children) is excellent value.

NORTHERN GERMANY

Flat, sparse northwestern Germany features two very different gems. Hamburg might be the country's second-largest city, but its port has also made it the richest. With an outward-looking multicultural population, it features a nightlife and dining-out scene to rival Berlin's.

By contrast, the historic town of Lübeck trades on its absolutely stunning picture-postcard looks.

Hamburg

☎040 / POP 1.77 MILLION

It comes as no surprise that Hamburg is stylishly expanding itself by 40% without batting a eyelid – this is where ambition flows through the ubiquitous waterways and designer-clad residents cycle to their media jobs with a self-assurance unmatched in any other German city. The site of Europe's largest urban-renewal project is a never-ending forest of cranes that are efficiently transforming old city docks into an extension of the city – it all makes you wonder 'What *can't* this city achieve?' Decent weather, that's one thing it can't buy, build or create. But residents are passionately dedicated to their beloved city and will rarely fret about drizzly skies – they just open up their designer umbrellas and get on with it.

Germany's leading port city has always been forward-thinking and liberal. Its dynamism, multiculturalism and hedonistic red-light district, the Reeperbahn, all arise from its maritime history. Joining the Hanseatic League trading bloc in the Middle Ages, Hamburg has been enthusiastically doing business with the rest of the world ever since. In the 1960s it nurtured the musical talent of the Beatles. Nowadays, it's also a media capital and the wealthiest city in Germany.

Sights & Activities

Old Town HISTORIC AREA

Hamburg's medieval **Rathaus** (tours €3; ⊙English-language tours hourly 10.15am-3.15pm Mon-Thu, to 1.15pm Fri, to 5.15pm Sat, to 4.15pm Sun; Ⓜ Rathausmarkt or Jungfernstieg) is one of Europe's most opulent. North of here, you can wander through the **Alsterarkaden**, the Renaissance-style arcades sheltering shops and cafes alongside a canal or 'fleet'.

For many visitors, however, the city's most memorable building is south in the Merchants' District. The 1920s, brown-brick **Chile Haus** (cnr Burchardstrasse & Johanniswall; Ⓜ Mönckebergstrasse or Messberg) is shaped like an ocean liner, with remarkable curved walls meeting in the shape of a ship's bow and staggered balconies that look like decks.

Alster Lakes LAKE

A cruise on the Binnenalster and Aussenalster is one of the best ways to appreciate the elegant side of the city. **ATG Alster-Touristik** (www.alstertouristik.de; 2hr trips €9.50; ⊙Apr-Oct; Ⓜ Jungfernstieg) is a good bet. The

DON'T MISS

LÜNEBURG, THE WOBBLY TOWN

With an off-kilter church steeple, buildings leaning on each other and houses with swollen 'beer-belly' facades, it's as if charming Lüneburg has drunk too much of the Pilsener lager it used to brew.

Of course, the city's wobbly angles and uneven pavements have a more prosaic cause. For centuries until 1980, Lüneburg was a salt-mining town, and as this 'white gold' was extracted from the earth, ground shifts and subsidence knocked many buildings sideways. Inadequate drying of the plaster in the now-swollen facades merely added to this asymmetry.

From the train station, head west into town towards the highly visible, 14th-century **St Johanniskirche**, the 106m-high spire of which leans 2.2m off true.

Continue one block past the Handelskammer and turn right into restaurant-lined Schröderstrasse, which leads to the **Markt**. Admire the square before continuing west along Waagestrasse and down our favourite Lüneburg street, **Auf dem Meere**, en route to the **St Michaeliskirche**.

It's too late now to regain your equilibrium, so head back along Am Flock for the pubs along **Am Stintmarkt** on the bank of the Ilmenau River.

The city is easily reached by train from Hanover (€26, one hour) and Hamburg (€13.20, 30 minutes), making it a good day trip.

company also offers 'fleet' tours and winter tours through the icy waters.

Better yet, hire your own rowboat or canoe. Opposite the Atlantic Hotel you'll find **Segelschule Pieper** (www.segelschule-pieper.de; An der Alster; per hr from €15; ⏲Apr-Oct; Ⓜ Hauptbahnhof).

Speicherstadt & Harbour HISTORIC AREA

The beautiful red-brick, neo-Gothic warehouses lining the Elbe archipelago south of the Altstadt once stored exotic goods from around the world. Now the so-called **Speicherstadt** (Ⓜ Messberg or Baumwall) is a popular sightseeing attraction. It's best appreciated by simply wandering through its streets or taking a Barkassen boat up its canals. **Kapitän Prüsse** (www.kapitaen-pruesse.de; Landungsbrücke No 3; tours from €12.50) offers regular Speicherstadt tours leaving from the port. Other Barkassen operators simply tout for business opposite the archipelago.

Port and Elbe River cruises start in summer at the St Pauli Landungsbrücken. **Hadag** (www.hadag.de; Brücke 2; 1hr harbour trips from €10/5.50) offers some of the best deals and cruises.

Reeperbahn (Red Light District)

(Ⓜ Reeperbahn) No discussion of Hamburg is complete without mentioning St Pauli, home of the Reeperbahn, Europe's biggest red-light district. Sex shops, peep shows, dim bars and strip clubs line the streets, which generally start getting crowded with the masses after 8pm or 9pm. This is also where the notorious **Herbertstrasse** is located (a block-long street lined with brothels that's off-limits to men under 18 and to female visitors of all ages) as well as the **Erotic Art Museum** (www.eroticartmuseum.de; Bernhard-Nocht-Strasse 69; admission €5; ⏲noon-10pm, to midnight Fri & Sat), and the **Condomerie** (www.condomerie.de; Spielbudenplatz 18; ⏲noon-midnight), with its extensive collection of prophylactics and sex toys.

Fischmarkt MARKET

Here's the perfect excuse to stay up all Saturday night. Every Sunday between 5am and 10am, curious tourists join locals of every age and walk of life at the famous Fischmarkt in St Pauli. The market has been running since 1703, and its undisputed stars are the boisterous *Marktschreier* (market criers) who hawk their wares at full volume. Live bands also entertainingly crank out cover versions of ancient German pop songs in the adjoining *Fischauktionshalle* (Fish Auction Hall). Take bus 112 to Hafentreppe.

International Maritime Museum MUSEUM

(www.internationales-maritimes-museum.de; Koreastrasse 1; adult/concession €10/7; ⏲10am-6pm Tue-Wed & Fri-Sun, 10am-8pm Thu; Ⓜ Messberg) Ensconced within Hamburg's new city-within-a-city **HafenCity**, this nine-floor, enormous space examines 3000 years of maritime history through displays of model ships, naval paintings, navigation tools and educational exhibits explaining the seas and its tides and currents. Added bonus: sweeping views of the HafenCity development project greet you at every window.

Hamburger Kunsthalle MUSEUM
(www.hamburger-kunsthalle.de; Glockengiesserwall; adult/concession €8.50/5; ⏲10am-6pm Tue, Wed & Fri-Sun, to 9pm Thu; Ⓜ Hauptbahnhof) An old building houses old masters and 19th-century art, and a white concrete cube known as the Galerie der Gegenwart showcases contemporary German artists, including Rebecca Horn, Georg Baselitz and Gerhard Richter, alongside international stars including David Hockney, Jeff Koons and Barbara Kruger.

Hamburg

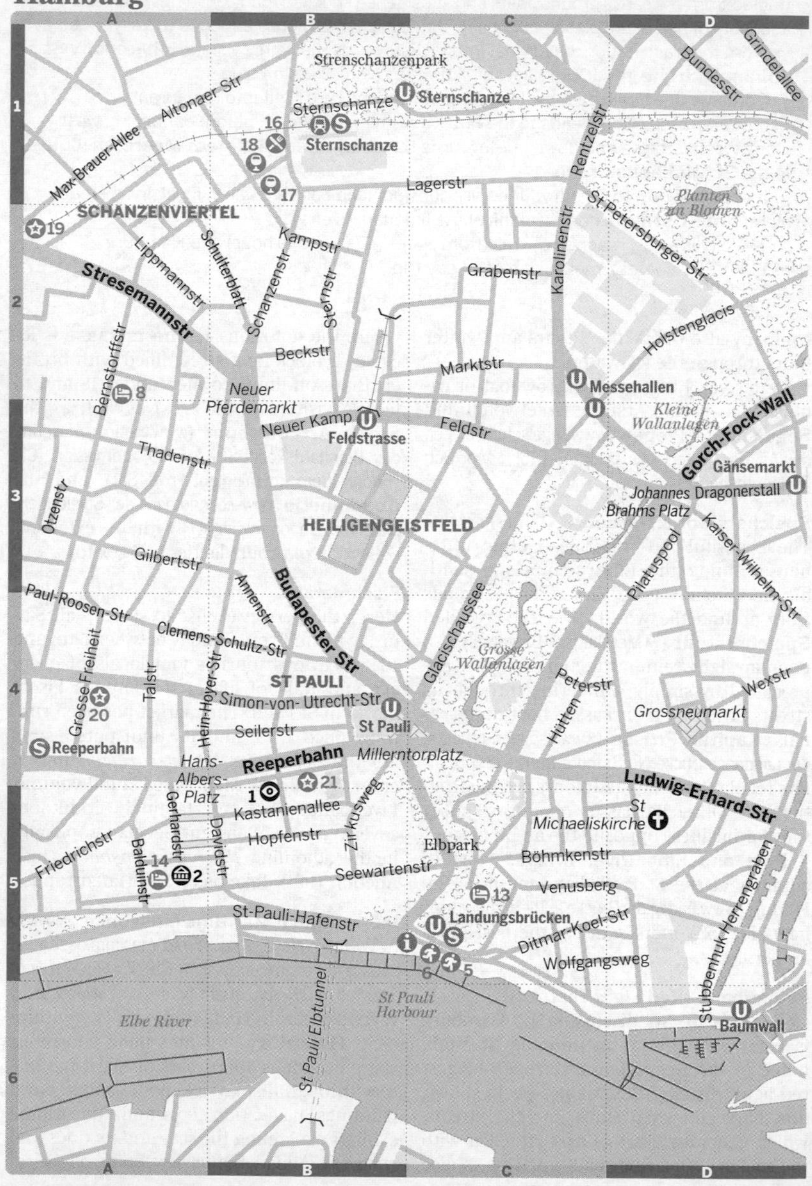

Sleeping

Backpackers St Pauli HOSTEL €

(☎2351 7043; www.backpackers-stpauli.de; Bernstorffstrasse 98; dm €19.50-24, d/tr from €60/75; ; St Pauli) Entered via a bright cafe, this is a great new addition to Hamburg's hostel scene. It has a cool, subterranean maritime-themed lounge containing a small kitchenette, a sunny outdoor terrace, table football, and light-filled rooms (some with private bathrooms) with good-sized lockers.

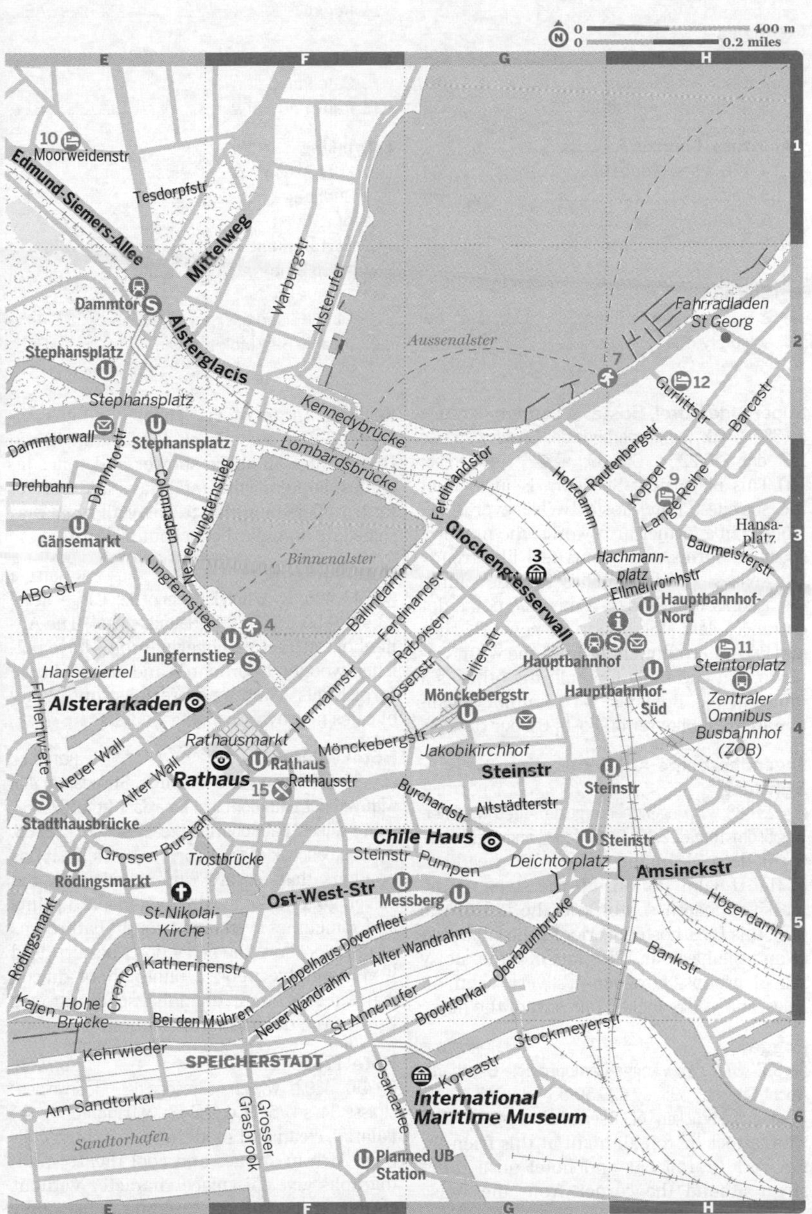

Hamburg

Superbude Hotel, Hostel & Lounge HOSTEL €
(☎380 8780; www.superbude.de; Spaldingstrasse 152; dm €16-22, d €59-89; ⊖@ᯤ; MBerliner Tor) This place near St Georg is just about the snazziest hotel-hostel we've ever seen. Housed in a former printworks, the modern, spacious dorms and rooms feel like trendy loft spaces. Quirky touches include plungers used as wall 'hooks', a metallic polka-dot entrance, slate stone flooring, cowhide rugs and two entertainment rooms (one with Nintendo, Wii and table football; the other is a mini cinema). Breakfast is €7. Laundry facilities are free; bike rental costs €4 per day.

Jugendherberge-Auf dem Stintfang HOSTEL €
(☎313 488; www.jugendherberge.de; Alfred-Wegener-Weg 5; dm from €22.90; ⊖@ᯤ; MLandungsbrücken) Modern, clean and convenient (head out of the U-Bahn station, up the steps to the massive modern complex at the top of the hill), this DJH hostel overlooks the Elbe River and the harbour. With lots of large, noisy school groups, however, it's very keen on rules, and you're locked out part of the day.

Kogge HOTEL €
(☎312 872; www.kogge-hamburg.de; Bernhard-Nocht-Strasse 59; s €29.50-33, d €48.40-55; MLandungsbrücken or Reeperbahn; @ᯤ) We wanna rock 'n' roll all night at this friendly, fun rock 'n' roll bar and hotel on a quiet street around the corner from the noisy Reeperbahn territory. Themed rooms include 'Bollywood', 'Punk Royal' and 'Disco Dream', and all share shower and toilet facilities. Popular with musicians and perfect for travellers planning to party all night and sleep late (standard checkout is 2pm).

Hotel Annenhof HOTEL €
(☎243 426; www.hotelannenhof.de; Lange Reihe 23; s €40-50, d €70-80; MHauptbahnhof) The Annenhof's attractive, cheerful rooms have polished wooden floorboards and clean, simple furnishings. There's no breakfast but plenty of cafes nearby.

Hotel Village HOTEL €€
(☎480 6490; www.hotel-village.de; Steindamm 4; s with/without bathroom incl breakfast from €72/52, d with/without bathroom incl breakfast from €95/68; MHauptbahnhof; @ᯤ) A former bordello, it has boudoirs that feature various mixes of red velvet, gold-flocked wallpaper, leopard prints and sometimes even blue-neon-lit bathrooms or mirrors above the bed – don't be surprised if you stumble upon a photo shoot during your stay. It's a fun, functional space a stone's throw from the main train station.

Hotel Fresena HOTEL €€
(☎410 4892; www.hotelfresena.de; Moorweidenstrasse 34; s €75-99, d €88-13; MDammtor; ⊖@) Palatial, clean and modern rooms, high ceilings, African statues and cool theatre photographs give this place character without clutter. If it's full, the building houses four

other pensions and the friendly staff will help you find a room elsewhere. Breakfast is €9.

Hotel Wedina HOTEL €€
(☎280 8900; www.wedina.de; Gurlittstrasse 23; s/d main bldg incl breakfast from €98/118, other bldg incl breakfast from €108/138; MHauptbahnhof;) You might find a novel instead of a chocolate on your pillow at Wedina, a hotel that's a must for bookworms and literary groupies. Jonathan Franzen, Vladimir Nabokov and JK Rowling are just some of the authors who've stayed and left behind signed books. Young and friendly, the hotel is spread over four buildings, offering a choice of traditional decor in the main red building or modern, urban living in its green, blue and yellow houses. The hotel also offers bike hire (€8 per day).

Eating

The **Schanzenviertel** (MFeldstrasse or Schanzenstern) swarms with cheap eateries; try **Schulterblatt** for Portuguese outlets or **Susanenstrasse** for Asian and Turkish. Be aware that many fish restaurants around the Landungsbrücken are overrated and touristy. St Georg's **Lange Reihe** (MHauptbahnhof) offers many characterful eating spots to suit every budget, and there is a seemingly endless selection of simple but quality, high-value sushi joints all over town.

Café Mimosa INTERNATIONAL €
(Clemens-Schultz-Strasse 87; dishes €5-12; MSt Pauli) A welcome change from the greasy fast-food joints on the nearby Reeperbahn, this gem of a neighbourhood cafe serves delicious pastas, healthy salads, proper coffee and homemade cakes in a theatrical space of stripped floors, bare wooden tables with brass candlesticks and red-and-cream-painted walls. There's a smattering of pavement tables.

frank und frei PUB FARE €
(Schanzenstrasse 93; mains €5-16; MSternschanze) Big, bustling and laid-back restaurant-pub with brick walls, wooden booths, shiny pillars and a stylish curved wood bar, offering simple German fare, salads and pastas. A great place to unwind with a beer, a bite or a full meal.

Café Paris FRENCH €€
(Rathausstrasse 4; mains €10-19; from 9am Mon-Fri, from 10am Sat & Sun; MRathausmarkt) At this stalwart in the city centre, be sure to admire the spectacular maritime-and-industry-themed ceiling murals and tiles. On weekends breakfast is served until 4pm in this bustling French brasserie.

Drinking & Entertainment

Südhang WINE BAR
(www.suedhang-hamburg.de; Susannenstrasse 29; from noon Mon-Sat, from 4pm Sun; MSternschanze) Walk through the shoe store, head up the stairs and enter this friendly wine bar with polished mahogany tables and low-lighting, perched above the neighbourhood hustle.

Tower Bar COCKTAIL BAR
(www.hotel-hafen-hamburg.de; Seewartenstrasse 9; 6pm-1am Mon-Thu, 6pm-2.30am Fri-Sun; MLandungsbrücken, SLandungsbrücken) For a more elegant, mature evening, repair to this 14th-floor eyrie at the Hotel Hafen for unbeatable harbour views.

Fritz Bauch BAR
(Bartelstrasse 6; from 5pm; MSternschanze) A down-to-earth neighbourhood bar in the middle of the Schanzenviertel with yellow and pale-pink walls, wooden arched ceilings, basic, no-nonsense drinks and hopping music.

Meanie Bar/Molotow Club CLUB
(www.molotowclub.com; Spielbudenplatz 5; from 6pm; MReeperbahn) One of the few venues along the Reeperbahn with real local cred, retro Meanie Bar sits above the Molotow Club, where an independent-music scene thrives.

Grosse Freiheit 36/Kaiserkeller LIVE MUSIC
(Grosse Freiheit 36; from 10pm Tue-Sat; MReeperbahn) Wedged between live-sex theatres and peep shows, this is popular for live rock and pop, particularly as the Beatles played in the basement Kaiserkeller.

Astra Stube CLUB
(www.astra-stube.de; Max-Brauer-Allee 200; from 9.30pm Mon-Sat; MSt Pauli) This graffiti-covered red building underneath the train tracks looks totally unpromising, but it's actually a pioneer of Hamburg's underground scene, with DJs playing experimental electro, techno and drum and bass.

Information

Dangers & Annoyances

Although safe, Hamburg contains several red-light districts around the train station and Reeperbahn. The Hansaplatz in St Georg can feel a bit dicey after dark. Fortunately, there's a strong police presence in these areas.

Emergency

Police station Hauptbahnhof (Kirchenallee exit); St Pauli (Davidwache, Spielbudenplatz 31; MReeperbahn)

Tourist Information

Hamburg Tourismus Hauptbahnhof (☎information 3005 1200, hotel bookings 3005 1300; www.hamburg-tourismus.de; Kirchenallee exit; ⏰8am-9pm Mon-Sat, 10am-6pm Sun); Landungsbrücken (btwn piers 4 & 5; ⏰8am-6pm Apr-Oct, 10am-6pm Nov-Mar; Ⓜ Landungsbrücken); airport (☎5075 1010; ⏰6am-11pm) Sells the Hamburg Card (€8.50/19.90/34.90 for one/three/five days) Free public transport and museum discounts.

Getting There & Away

Air

Hamburg's **airport** (HAM; www.flughafen-hamburg.de) has frequent flights to domestic and European cities, including on low-cost carrier **Air Berlin** (www.airberlin.com).

For flights to/from Ryanair's so-called 'Hamburg-Lübeck' airport see p553.

Train

When reading train timetables, remember that there are two main train stations: Hamburg Hauptbahnhof and Hamburg-Altona. There are frequent RE/RB trains to Lübeck (€11.50, 45 minutes), as well as various services to Hanover (from €35, 1¼ to 1½ hours) and Bremen (from €20.90, one to 1¼ hours). In addition there are EC/ICE trains to Berlin (from €65, 1½ to two hours), Cologne (from €78, four hours) and Munich (from €125, 5½ to six hours) as well as EC trains to Copenhagen (from €81, 4¾ hours).

Getting Around

To/From the Airport

The S1 S-Bahn connects the airport directly with the city centre, including the Hauptbahnhof. The journey takes 24 minutes and costs €2.70.

Public Transport

There is an integrated system of buses and U-Bahn and S-Bahn trains. A single journey costs €2.70; day tickets, bought from machines before boarding, cost €6.30, or €5.30 after 9am. From midnight to dawn the night-bus network takes over from the trains, converging on the main metropolitan bus station at Rathausmarkt.

Lübeck

☎0451 / POP 220,900

The two pointed cylindrical towers of Lübeck's Holstentor (gate) greet you upon arrival – if you think they're a tad crooked, you're not seeing things: they lean towards each other across the stepped gable that joins them. Right behind them, the streets are lined with medieval merchants' homes and spired churches forming the city's so-called 'crown'. It's hardly surprising that this 12th-century gem is on Unesco's list of World Heritage sites.

Sights

Holstentor (adult/concession €5/2.50; ⏰10am-6pm Apr-Dec, 11am-5pm Tue-Sun Jan-Mar), the cute city gate, is Lübeck's museum as well as its symbol. It's been under renovation, but should be out of its *trompe l'oeil* wraps by now. The six gabled brick buildings east of the Holstentor are the **Salzspeicher**, once used to store the salt that was pivotal to Lübeck's Hanseatic trade.

Behind these warehouses, the Trave River forms a moat around the old town, and if you do one thing in Lübeck in summer, it should be a boat tour. From April to September, **Maak-Linie** (www.maak-linie.de) and **Quandt-Linie** (www.quandt-linie.de) depart regularly from either side of the Holstentorbrücke. Trips cost €8.

Each of Lübeck's churches offers something different. The shattered bells of the **Marienkirche** (Schüsselbuden 13; admission €1; ⏰10am-6pm Apr-Sep, to 5pm Oct, 10am-4pm Tue-Sun Nov-Mar) still lie on the floor where they fell after a bombing raid. There's also a little devil sculpture outside, with an amusing fairy tale (in English). The tower lift in the **Petrikirche** (Schüsselbuden 13; www.st-petri-luebeck.de; adult/concession €3/2; ⏰9am-9pm Apr-Sep, 10am-7pm Oct-Mar) has superb views.

Have a look at the **Rathaus** before heading to **JG Niederegger** (Breite Strasse 89) opposite. This is Lübeck's mecca of chocolate-coated marzipan, with toothsome sweets and an adjoining cafe.

Lübeck has 90 *Gänge* (walkways) and *Höfe* (courtyards) tucked away behind its main streets, the most famous being the **Füchtingshof** (Glockengiesserstrasse 25; ⏰9am-noon & 3-6pm) and the delightful **Glandorps Gang** (Glockengiesserstrasse 41-51).

Fans of *The Tin Drum* (Die Blechtrommel) shouldn't miss the **Günter Grass-Haus** (www.guenter-grass-haus.de; Glockengiesserstrasse 21; adult/concession €5/2.50; ⏰10am-5pm Apr-Dec, 11am-5pm Jan-Mar), which includes a fine collection of manuscripts and sculptures. Fellow Nobel Prize–winning author Thomas Mann *(Death in Venice)* was born in Lübeck and he's commemorated in the award-winning **Buddenbrookhaus** (www.buddenbrookhaus.de; Mengstrasse 4; adult/concession €5/2.50; ⏰10am-6pm Apr-Dec, 11am-5pm Jan-Mar).

Sleeping

Rucksackhotel HOSTEL €
(☎706 892; www.rucksackhotel-luebeck.de; Kanalstrasse 70; dm €13-15, s €28, d €34-40; @📶) None of the rooms at this 30-bed hostel are en suite, but it has a relaxed atmosphere and good facilities including a well-equipped kitchen, as well as round-the-clock access.

Hotel zur Alten Stadtmauer HOTEL €
(☎737 02; www.hotelstadtmauer.de; An der Mauer 57; s/d with bathroom from €55/65, without bathroom from €37/55; 🚭📶) With pine furniture and splashes of red or yellow, this simple, 25-room hotel is bright and cheerful. The wooden flooring means sound carries, but customers tend to be quieter types. Back rooms overlook the river.

DJH Hostel Altstadt HOSTEL €
(☎702 0399; www.jugendherberge.de; Mengstrasse 33; dm from €19) Standard hostel in the Old Town – it isn't particularly new, but it's cosy and central.

Two very cheap and basic places are **Sleep-Inn** (☎719 20; www.cvjm-luebeck.de; Grosse Petersgrube 11; dm from €14) and the **Hotel Am Dom** (☎399 9430; www.cvjm-luebeck.de; Dankwartsgrube 43; s/d from €37).

Eating

Suppentopf INTERNATIONAL €
(☎400 8136; Fleischerstrasse 36; soups €3.50; ⏰11am-4pm Mon-Fri) It's always bustling here, so join Lübeck's office workers for a stand-up lunch of delicious, often spicy, soup.

Schiffergesellschaft FRISIAN €€
(☎767 76; www.schiffergesellschaft.de; Breite Strasse 2) The fact it's a tourist magnet doesn't detract from this 500-year-old guildhall's thrilling atmosphere. Seafood-heavy Frisian specialities and local beer are the way to go here.

Information

Lübeck's old town is set on an island ringed by the canalised Trave River, a 10-minute walk east of the main train station. Leaving the station, head through the bus station and veer left along Hansestrasse. The tourist office is just across the Puppenbrücke (Doll Bridge), near the Holstentor.

Lübeck Travemünde Tourismus (www.lubeck-tourism.de; Holstentorplatz 1; ⏰9.30am-7pm Mon-Fri, 10am-3pm Sat, 10am-2pm Sun Jun-Sep, 9.30am-6pm Mon-Fri, 10am-3pm Sat Oct-May) City tours; sells discount cards.

Getting There & Away

Lübeck's **airport** (LBC; www.flughafen-luebeck.de) is linked to London by budget carriers Ryanair and easyJet. Synchronised shuttle buses take passengers straight to Hamburg (one way €9, 55 minutes), while scheduled bus 6 (€2.50) serves Lübeck's Hauptbahnhof.

Frequent trains link Lübeck's Hauptbahnhof to Hamburg.

UNDERSTAND GERMANY

History

Events in Germany have often dominated the European stage, but the country itself is a relatively recent invention: for most of its history Germany has been a patchwork of semi-independent principalities and city-states, occupied first by the Roman Empire, then the Holy Roman Empire and finally the Austrian Habsburgs. Perhaps because of this, many Germans retain a strong regional identity, despite the momentous events that have occurred since.

The most significant medieval events in Germany were pan-European in nature. Martin Luther, a monk from Erfurt, brought on the Protestant Reformation with his criticism of the Catholic Church in Wittenberg in 1517, a movement that in turn sparked the Thirty Years' War. Germany became the battlefield of Europe, and only began to regain stability after the Napoleonic Wars, with increasing industrialisation and the rise of the Kingdom of Prussia. In 1866 legendary Prussian 'Iron Chancellor' Otto von Bismarck succeeded in bringing the German states together, largely by force, and a united Germany emerged for the first time in 1871, under Kaiser Wilhelm I.

Germany's rapid growth led to mounting tensions with England, Russia and France, sparking WWI. After Germany's defeat the Weimar Republic was proclaimed, but the new government was hampered by impossible reparation payments. Hyperinflation and economic depression bolstered support for extremist groups, including Adolf Hitler's National Socialists (Nazis).

By 1933, the Nazis had manoeuvred themselves into a position of political dominance: Hitler was appointed chancellor, dissolved parliament and assumed control. In September 1939 he attacked Poland, provoking war with Britain and France. Behind the scenes, concentration camps exterminated an estimated six million Jews and another one million 'enemies of state'. Germany surrendered in May 1945, soon after Hitler's suicide.

After the war, the USA, Britain, France and the Soviet Union divided the country into four occupation zones. In September 1949 the Federal Republic of Germany (FRG) was formed from the three western zones. In response, the communist German Democratic Republic (GDR) was founded in the Soviet zone, with (East) Berlin as its capital. To prevent skilled workers emigrating, the GDR built a wall around West Berlin in 1961, closing its border with the FRG.

For almost 40 years capitalist and socialist Germany coexisted uneasily. In 1989, however, the Peaceful Revolution overtook the reform-shy GDR regime. On 9 November 1989 the Berlin Wall opened, and in 1990 East Germans voted clearly for reunification, which occurred on 3 October 1990.

In recent years the dodgy economy has been the major domestic issue, a situation made worse by global recession. In 2005 Angela Merkel was elected as the first female German chancellor. She was reelected in 2009 but her popularity has waned since as Germany's export-based economy has been battered by global recession. The national mood is glum, especially as German funds are a major part of EU bailouts for Greece, Ireland and others.

Over two decades after reunification, the overall stereotypes of the west and the old east – that the *Wessis* are arrogant while the *Ossis* simply bitch – had become ingrained in German culture. But now both agree on one thing: times used to be better. But many of today's 85 million Germans across the country would agree that times used to be better.

Arts

Historically Germany has always been strong in the arts, with the legacies of such literary, musical, artistic and architectural greats as Goethe, JS Bach, Karl Friedrich Schinkel and Caspar David Friedrich providing a rich vein of inspiration for modern successors like Günter Grass, Arnold Schönberg, Walter Gropius and Paul Klee.

Today the arts still occupy a key place at the heart of German culture. Tradition is scrupulously preserved around the country, but for the new generation of artists experimentation is the way forward. Germany is a hotbed of exciting new architecture, avant-garde art and left-field literature. Above all, the popular-music scene is much more wide-ranging than radio playlists suggest, particularly where electronic dance music is concerned. Berlin and Frankfurt are centres of techno.

Sport

Football (soccer) is the number-one spectator sport in Germany, as in most other European countries. Germany hosted the cup in 2006 in new or rebuilt stadiums all over the country. Although Germany finished third (Italy beat France in the final in Berlin), it was widely praised for hosting a fantastic series of matches, and many Germans took great pride in their time on the world stage.

Germany did one better at Euro 2008, although it lost to Spain in the final in Vienna. Spain again proved troublesome in the 2010 World Cup, beating Germany in the semifinals.

Food

The following price categories for the cost of a main course are used in the listings in this chapter.

€€€ more than €20

€€ €10 to €20

€ less than €10

SURVIVAL GUIDE

Directory A–Z

Accommodation

Germany has all types of places to unpack your suitcase, from hostels, camping grounds and family hotels to chains, business hotels and luxury resorts. Reservations are a good idea, especially if you're travelling in the busy summer season (June to September). Local tourist offices will often go out of their way to find something in your price range.

In this chapter, prices include private bathroom unless otherwise stated and are quoted at high-season rates. Breakfast is not included in rates unless specified. Most rooms are non-smoking.

€€€ more than €150

€€ €80 to €150

€ less than €80

DRINK UP!

Beer is Germany's national beverage and it's both excellent and relatively cheap. Each region and brewery has its own distinctive taste and body.

Some types:

» *Pils* is the crisp pilsener Germany is famous for, often refreshingly and slightly bitter

» *Alt* is darker and more full-bodied

» *Weizenbier* is made with wheat instead of barley malt and served in a tall, 500mL glass; light in colour, it's lovely on a hot day

» *Export* tastes like bland lagers everywhere

» *Bockbier* is often dark and the best is seasonal

» *Helles Bier* is light beer

» *Dunkles Bier* is dark (the best is richly flavoured)

» *Kölsch* is the light, sweet beer of Cologne served in tiny glasses

» *Berliner Weisse* is a low-alcohol wheat beer mixed with woodruff or raspberry syrup

» *Rauchbier* is a Bamberg speciality; smoked to a dark-red colour, it tastes like bacon. Really.

German **wines** are exported around the world, and for good reason. They are inexpensive and typically white, light and intensely fruity. A *Weinschorle* or *Spritzer* is white wine mixed with mineral water. The Rhine and Moselle Valleys are the classic wine-growing regions.

Germany has more than 2000 organised camping grounds, several hundred of which stay open throughout the year. Prices are around €3 to €5 for an adult, plus €3 to €7 for a car and/or tent. Look out for ecologically responsible camping grounds sporting the Green Leaf award from the ADAC motoring association.

Deutsches Jugendherbergswerk (DJH; www.djh.de) coordinates the official Hostelling International (HI) hostels in Germany. Rates in gender-segregated dorms or in family rooms range from €13 to €25 per person, including linen and breakfast. People over 27 are charged an extra €3 or €4.

Indie hostels are more relaxed and can be found in Berlin, Munich, Frankfurt etc.

Business Hours

Banks & government offices 9.30am-4pm Mon-Fri

Bars & cafes 11am-1am

Clubs Mostly 10pm-4am

Post offices 9am-6pm Mon-Fri

Restaurants 10am or 11am-10pm, with a 3-6pm break

Shops 9am-6pm Mon-Sat (also Sun in large cities); many open to 8pm or later on days other than Thu

Discount Cards

Many cities offer discount cards. These cards will usually combine up to three days' free use of public transport with free or reduced admission to major local museums and attractions. They're generally a good deal if you want to fit a lot in; see the Information section under the relevant destination and ask at tourist offices for full details.

Gay & Lesbian Travellers

Overall, Germans are tolerant of gays *(Schwule)* and lesbians *(Lesben)* although, as elsewhere in the world, cities (Berlin!) are more liberal than rural areas, and younger people tend to be more open-minded than older generations. Discrimination is more likely in eastern Germany and in the conservative south, where gays and lesbians tend to keep a lower profile.

Holidays

Germany observes eight religious and three secular holidays nationwide. Shops, banks, government offices and post offices are closed on these days. States with predominantly Catholic populations, such as Bavaria and Baden-Württemberg, also celebrate Epiphany (6 January), Corpus Christi (10 days after Pentecost), Assumption Day (15 August) and All Saints' Day (1 November).

Reformation Day (31 October) is only observed in eastern Germany.

The following are *gesetzliche Feiertage* (public holidays):

Neujahrstag (New Year's Day) 1 January

Ostern (Easter) March/April – Good Friday, Easter Sunday and Easter Monday

Christi Himmelfahrt (Ascension Day) Forty days after Easter.

Maifeiertag/Tag der Arbeit (Labour Day) 1 May

Pfingsten (Whit/Pentecost Sunday and Monday) May/June; 50 days after Easter.

Tag der Deutschen Einheit (Day of German Unity) 3 October

Weihnachtstag (Christmas Day) 25 December

Zweite Weihnachtstag (Boxing Day) 26 December

Legal Matters

By law you must carry some form of photographic identification, such as your passport, national identity card or driving licence. Reporting theft to the police is usually a simple, if occasionally time-consuming, matter.

If driving in Germany, you should carry your driving licence at all times. The permissible blood-alcohol limit is 0.05%; drivers caught exceeding this amount are subject to stiff fines, a confiscated licence and even jail time.

Drinking in public is not illegal, but please be discreet about it.

Illegal drugs are widely available, especially in clubs. Cannabis possession is a criminal offence and punishment may range from a warning to a court appearance. Dealers face far stiffer penalties, as do people caught with any other 'recreational' drugs.

Money

Automatic teller machines can be found outside banks and at train stations.

All major international cards are recognised, and you will find that most hotels, restaurants and major stores accept them (although *not* the Dutch railway). But always check first to avoid, as they say, disappointment. Shops may levy a 5% surcharge (or more) on credit cards to offset the commissions charged by card providers.

The easiest places to change cash in Germany are the banks or foreign-exchange counters at airports and train stations, particularly those of the Reisebank. The main banks in larger cities generally have money-changing machines for after-hours use, although they don't often offer reasonable rates.

TIPPING

Restaurant bills always include a service charge *(Bedienung)*, but most people add 5% or 10% unless the service was truly abhorrent.

» **Maids** €1 per night

» **Bartenders** 5%

» **Taxi drivers** around 10%.

Safe Travel

Although the usual cautions should be taken, theft and other crimes against travellers are relatively rare in Germany. Africans, Asians and southern Europeans may encounter racial prejudice, especially in eastern Germany, where they can be singled out as convenient scapegoats for economic hardship. However, the animosity is usually directed against immigrants, not tourists.

Telephone

German phone numbers consist of an area code followed by the local number, which can be between three and nine digits long. If you're bringing your mobile phone, note that SIM cards in Germany cost from €5.

International access code 00

International directory enquiries 118 34 for an English-speaking operator

National directory enquiries 118 37 for an English-speaking operator; or www.telefonbuch.de

Operator assistance 0180-200 1033

Travellers with Disabilities

Germany is fair at best (but better than much of Europe) for the needs of physically disabled travellers, with access ramps for wheelchairs and/or lifts in some public buildings. Resources include:

Deutsche Bahn Mobility Service Centre (01805-996 633, ext 9 for English operator; www.bahn.de; 8am-8pm Mon-Fri, 8am-4pm Sat) Train access information and help with route planning. The website has useful information in English.

German National Tourism Office (www.deutschland-tourismus.de) Has an entire section (under Travel Tips) about barrier-free travel in Germany.

Natko (www.natko.de) Central clearing house for enquiries about 'tourism without barriers' in Germany.

Getting There & Away

Air

Budget carriers, Lufthansa and international airlines serve numerous German airports from across Europe and the rest of the world. Frankfurt and Munich remain the main hubs however.

Berlin Schönefeld (SXF; www.berlin-airport.de)

Berlin Tegel (TXL; www.berlin-airport.de)

Cologne/Bonn (CGN; www.airport-cgn.de)

Düsseldorf (DUS; www.duesseldorf-international.de)

Frankfurt (FRA; www.frankfurt-airport.de)

Frankfurt-Hahn (HHN; www.hahn-airport.de)

Hamburg (HAM; www.flughafen-hamburg.de)

Munich (MUC; www.munich-airport.de)

Stuttgart (STR; www.stuttgart-airport.com)

For details about individual German airports, including information about getting to and from them, see the listings within the chapter.

Land

BUS

Travelling by bus between Germany and the rest of Europe is cheaper than by train or plane, but journeys will take a lot longer.

Eurolines (www.eurolines.com) is a consortium of national bus companies operating routes throughout the continent. The German affiliate is **Touring** (www.touring.com). Sample one-way fares and travel times include the folowing:

ROUTE	PRICE	DURATION (HR)
Budapest-Frankfurt	€98	13-18
Florence-Munich	€76	9
London-Cologne	£60	13
Paris-Munich	€61	13
Warsaw-Berlin	€58	11

Eurolines has a discounted youth fare for those under 26 that saves you around 10%. Tickets can be purchased throughout Germany at most train stations.

CAR & MOTORCYCLE

Germany is served by an excellent highway system. If you're coming from the UK, the quickest option is the Channel Tunnel. Ferries take longer but are cheaper. You can be in Germany three hours after the ferry docks.

Within Europe, autobahns and highways become jammed on weekends in summer and before and after holidays.

TRAIN

A favourite way to get to Germany from elsewhere in Europe is by train. See p1326 for details on trains in Europe.

Conventional long-distance trains between major German cities and other countries are often called EuroCity (EC) trains. High-speed trains now also link Germany to some other parts of Europe. The main German hubs with the best connections for major European cities include:

Cologne High-speed Thalys trains to France and Belgium (with Eurostar connections from Brussels to London), ICE trains to the Netherlands

Frankfurt ICE trains to Paris

Hamburg Scandinavia

Munich High-speed trains to Paris and Vienna; regular trains to southern and southeastern Europe

Stuttgart High-speed trains to Italy and Switzerland

Often longer international routes are served by at least one day train and sometimes a night train as well.

Sea

Germany's main ferry ports are Kiel, Lübeck and Travemünde in Schleswig-Holstein, and Rostock and Sassnitz (on Rügen Island) in Mecklenburg-Western Pomerania. All have services to Scandinavia and the Baltic states.

Getting Around

Air

There are lots of flights within the country, many by budget carriers such as **Air Berlin** (www.airberlin.com) and **germanwings** (www.germanwings.com) as well as **Lufthansa** (www.lufthansa.de). Note that with check-in and transit times, flying is seldom as efficient and convenient as a fast train.

Bicycle

Simple three-gear bicycles can be hired from around €15/40 per day/week, and more robust mountain bikes from €20/50.

Cycling is allowed on all roads and highways but not on the autobahns. Pavements are often divided into separate sections for pedestrians and cyclists – be warned that these divisions are taken very seriously. Helmets are not compulsory, but wearing one is still a good idea.

Bicycles may be taken on most trains but you must buy a separate *Fahrradkarte* (bicycle ticket). These cost €9 on long-distance trains and €4.50 on regional trains (RB, RE and S-Bahn, valid all day). Bicycles are not allowed on high-speed ICE trains.

Germany's main cycling organisation is the **Allgemeiner Deutscher Fahrrad Club** (ADFC; www.adfc.de).

Boat

Boats are most likely to be used for basic transport when travelling to or between the Frisian Islands, though tours along the Rhine, Elbe and Moselle Rivers are also popular. During summer there are frequent services on Lake Constance but, with the exception of the Constance–Meersburg and the Friedrichshafen–Romanshorn car ferries, these boats are really more tourist crafts than a transport option. From April to October, excursion boats ply lakes and rivers in Germany and can be a lovely way to see the country.

Bus

The bus network in Germany functions primarily in support of the train network. Bus stations or stops are usually located near the train station in any town. Consider using buses when you want to cut across two train lines and avoid long train rides to and from a transfer point. A good example of where to do this is in the Alps, where the best way to follow the peaks is by bus.

However, a few bus lines are vying to lure train passengers with cheap fares – even if comfort and travel times are inferior. These include:

Berlin Linien Bus (www.berlinlinienbus.de) Connects major cities (primarily Berlin, but also Munich, Düsseldorf and Frankfurt) with each other as well as holiday regions such as the Harz and the Bavarian Alps. Express service between Berlin and Hamburg is popular (€9 to €22, 3¼ hours, 12 times daily).

Touring (www.touring.com) is the German affiliate of **Eurolines** (www.eurolines.com). Services include the popular Romantic Rd bus in Bavaria and overnight buses between major cities.

Car & Motorcycle

Cars are impractical in urban areas. Vending machines on many streets sell parking vouchers that must be displayed clearly behind the windscreen. Leaving your car in a central *Parkhaus* (car park) can cost a fortune, as much as €20 per day or more.

Visitors do not need an international driving licence to drive in Germany; bring your licence from home.

AUTOMOBILE ASSOCIATIONS

Germany's main motoring organisation, **ADAC** (Allgemeiner Deutscher Automobil-Club; ☎for roadside assistance 0180-222 2222, if calling from mobile phone 222 222; www.adac.de) offers roadside assistance to members of its affiliates, including British AA, American AAA and Canadian CAA.

HIRE

You usually must be at least 21 years of age to hire a car in Germany. You'll need to show your licence and passport, and make sure you keep the insurance certificate for the vehicle with you at all times.

Rental companies are not always convenient to train stations; check if you plan to pick up a car when you hop off a train. Agencies include:

» **Avis** (☎0180-555 77; www.avis.de)
» **Europcar** (☎0180-580 00; www.europcar.de)
» **Hertz** (☎0180-533 3535; www.hertz.de)
» **Sixt** (☎0180-526 0250; www.sixt.de)

Public Transport

Public transport is excellent within big cities and small towns, and is generally based on buses, *Strassenbahn* (trams), S-Bahn and/or U-Bahn (underground trains). Tickets cover all forms of transit; fares are determined by zones or time travelled, sometimes both. Multiticket strips and day passes are generally available, offering better value than single-ride tickets.

Make certain that you have a ticket when boarding – only buses and some trams let you buy tickets from the driver. In some cases you will have to validate it on the platform or once aboard. Ticket inspections are frequent (especially at night and on holidays) and the fine is a non-negotiable €50 or more.

Train

Operated almost entirely by **Deutsche Bahn** (DB; www.bahn.de), the German train system is the finest in Europe, and is generally the best way to get around the country. There are independent operators, such as ALX, which runs between Munich and Regensburg.

Trains run on an interval system, so wherever you're heading, you can count on a service at least every two hours. Schedules are integrated throughout the country so that connections between trains are time-saving and tight, often only five minutes. Of course this means that when a train is late, connections are missed and you can find yourself stuck waiting for the next train.

CLASSES

It's rarely worth buying a 1st-class ticket on German trains; 2nd class is usually quite comfortable. There's more difference between the train classifications – basically the faster a train travels, the plusher (and more expensive) it is.

Train types in Germany include the following options:

CNL, EN, D These are night trains, although an occasional D may be an extra daytime train.

ICE Sleek InterCityExpress services run at speeds up to 300km/h. The trains are very comfortable and feature cafe cars.

IC/EC Called InterCity or EuroCity, these are the premier conventional trains of DB. When trains are crowded, the open-seating coaches are much more comfortable than the older carriages with compartments.

RE RegionalExpress trains are local trains that make limited stops. They are fairly fast and run at one- or two-hourly intervals.

RB RegionalBahn are the slowest DB trains, not missing a single cow or town.

S-Bahn These suburban trains run frequent services in larger urban areas and rail passes are usually valid. Not to be confused with U-Bahns, which are run by local authorities who don't honour rail passes.

COSTS

Standard DB ticket prices are distance-based. You will usually be sold a ticket for the shortest distance to your destination.

Sample fares for one-way, 2nd-class ICE travel include: Frankfurt to Berlin (€113), Frankfurt to Hamburg (€109) and Frankfurt to Munich (€91).

Regular full-fare tickets are good for four days from the day you tell the agent your journey will begin, and you can make unlimited stopovers along your route during that time. In this chapter train fares given between towns are all undiscounted 2nd class.

Discounts

DB sells Savings Fares that discount the high cost of regular tickets and are sold like airline tickets (ie trains with light loads may have tickets available at a discount, others none). Ask at the ticket counters, use the vending machines or see www.bahn.de. For web purchases, the tickets arrive as email; you then print them out. It's easy.

The following are among the most popular discounts offered by DB (2nd class):

BahnCard 25/50/100 Only worthwhile for extended visits to Germany, these discount cards entitle holders to 25/50/100% off regular fares and cost €57/225/3650.

Dauer-Spezial 'Saver fare' tickets sold at a huge discount on the web.

Savings Fare 25 Round-trip tickets bought three or more days in advance and restricted to specific trains save 25%.

Savings Fare 50 Same conditions as the fare above but also including a Saturday night stay.

Schönes Wochenende 'Happy Weekend' tickets allow unlimited use of RE, RB and S-Bahn trains on a Saturday or Sunday between midnight and 3am the next day, for up to five people travelling together, for €37. They are best suited to weekend day trips from urban areas.

SCHEDULE INFORMATION

The **DB website** (www.bahn.de) is excellent. There is extensive info in English and you can use it to sort out all the discount offers and schemes. In addition it has an excellent schedule feature that works not just for Germany but the rest of Europe.

Telephone information is also available: reservations ☎118 61; toll-free automated timetable ☎0800-150 7090.

TICKETS

Many train stations have a *Reisezentrum* (travel centre) where staff sell tickets and can help you plan an itinerary (ask for an English-speaking agent). Smaller stations may only have a few ticket windows and the smallest ones aren't staffed at all. In this case, you must buy tickets from multilingual vending machines. These are also plentiful at staffed stations and convenient if you don't want to queue at a ticket counter. Both agents and machines accept major credit cards.

During peak periods, a seat reservation (€3.50) on a long-distance train can mean the difference between squatting near the toilet or relaxing in your own seat. Reservations can be made using vending machines or the web.

Buying your ticket on the train carries a surcharge (€3 to €8). Not having a ticket carries a stiff penalty.

TRAIN PASSES

Agencies outside Germany sell **German Rail Passes** for unlimited travel on all DB trains for a number of days during a 30-day period. Sample 2nd-class prices for adults aged 26 and over/under 26 are €188/150 for four days. Given the discounts available, especially on the web, passes may not be good value. Try building an itinerary at the DB website and compare.

Most Eurail and Inter-Rail passes are valid in Germany.

Greece Ελλάδα

Includes »

Best Places to Eat

» Marco Polo Café, Rhodes (p591)

» La Cucina, Corfu (p597)

» Tzitzikas & Mermingas, Athens (p565)

» Fato a Mano, Mykonos (p580)

Best Places to Stay

» Pension Sofi, Naxos (p582)

» Pension Marianna, Nafplio (p572)

» Nassos Guest House, Mithymna (p595)

» Pension Lena, Knossos (p588)

Why Go?

Don't let headline-grabbing financial woes put you off going to Greece. The elements that have made Greece one of the most popular destinations on the planet are still all there, and now is as good a time as any to turn up for some fun in the sun.

That alluring combination of history and hedonism continues to beckon. Within easy reach of magnificent archaeological sites are breathtaking beaches and relaxed tavernas serving everything from ouzo to octopus. Wanderers can island-hop to their heart's content, while party types can enjoy pulsating nightlife in Greece's vibrant modern cities and on islands such as Mykonos, Ios and Santorini. Throw in welcoming locals with an enticing culture and it's easy to see why most visitors head home vowing to come back. Travellers to Greece inevitably end up with a favourite place they long to return to – get out there and find yours.

When to Go

Athens

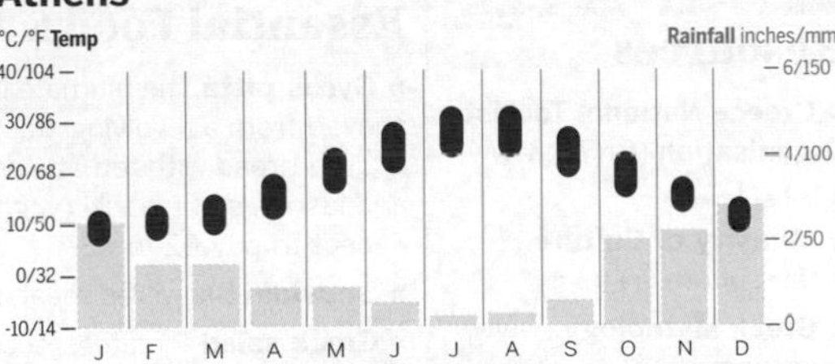

May & Jun Greece opens the shutters in time for Orthodox Easter; the best months to visit.

Jul & Aug Lots happening but be prepared to battle summer crowds, prices and temperatures.

Sep & Oct The season winds down; a relaxing and pleasant time to head to Greece.

AT A GLANCE

- **Currency** Euro (€)
- **Language** Greek
- **Money** ATMs are found all over
- **Visas** Schengen rules apply; see p1319

Fast Facts

- **Area** 131,944 sq km
- **Capital** Athens
- **Country code** ☎30
- **Emergency** Police ☎100

Exchange Rates

Australia	A$1	€0.74
Canada	C$1	€0.74
Japan	¥100	€0.87
New Zealand	NZ$1	€0.56
UK	UK£1	€1.16
USA	US$1	€0.72

Set Your Budget

- **Budget hotel room** €50
- **Two-course evening meal** €20
- **Museum entrance** €5
- **Beer** €2.50
- **Athens metro ticket** €2

Resources

- **Greece National Tourist Organisation** (GNTO; www.gnto.gr)
- **Ministry of Culture** (www.culture.gr)
- **Greek Mythology** (www.theoi.com)
- **Ancient Greece** (www.ancientgreece.com)
- **Greek Ferries** (www.greekferries.gr)

Connections

For those visiting Greece as part of a trip around Europe, there are various exciting options for reaching onward destinations overland or by sea.

There are regular ferry connections between Greece and the Italian ports of Ancona, Bari, Brindisi and Venice. Similarly, there are ferries operating between the Greek islands of Rhodes, Symi, Kos, Samos, Chios and Lesvos and the Aegean coast of Turkey. Island-hopping doesn't have to take you back to Athens.

Overland, it's possible to reach Albania, Bulgaria, Macedonia and Turkey from Greece. If you've got your own wheels, you can drive through border crossings with these four countries. There are bus connections with Albania, Bulgaria and Turkey, and train connections with Bulgaria, Macedonia and Turkey. In summer there are direct train services to Moscow.

ITINERARIES

One Week

Explore Athens' museums and ancient sites on day one before spending a couple of days in the Peloponnese visiting Nafplio, Mycenae and Olympia; ferry to the Cyclades and enjoy Mykonos and spectacular Santorini.

One Month

Give yourself some more time in Athens and the Peloponnese, then visit the Ionians for a few days. Explore the Zagoria villages before travelling back to Athens via Meteora and Delphi. Take a ferry from Piraeus southeast to Mykonos, then island-hop via Santorini to Crete. After exploring Crete, take the ferry northeast to Rhodes, then northwest to Symi, Kos and Samos. Carry on north to Chios, then head on to Lesvos. Take the ferry back to Piraeus when you're out of time or money.

Essential Food & Drink

- **Gyros pitta** The ultimate in cheap eats. Pork or chicken shaved from a revolving stack of sizzling meat is wrapped in pitta bread with tomato, onion, sometimes fried potatoes and lashings of tzatziki (yoghurt, cucumber and garlic). Expect to pay €2 to €3.
- **Souvlaki** Skewered meat, usually pork.
- **Greek salad** Tomatoes, cucumber, red onion, feta and olives.
- **Grilled octopus** All the better with a glass of ouzo.
- **Ouzo** Sipped slowly; this legendary Greek aniseed-flavoured tipple turns a cloudy white when ice and water is added.
- **Raki** Cretan firewater produced from grape skins.
- **Greek coffee** A legacy of Ottoman rule, Greek coffee should be tried at least once by all visitors.

ATHENS ΑΘΗΝΑ

POP 3.2 MILLION

Stroll around Athens and you'll quickly stumble across breathtaking archaeological treasures, reminders of the city's enormous historical influence on Western civilisation. With the makeover that accompanied the 2004 Olympics, Athens presented its cosmopolitan modern side to the world, and with Greece's financial difficulties in 2010 it has revealed its more restive aspect. Though the city still suffers from traffic congestion, pollution and urban sprawl, take the time to look beneath her skin and you will discover a complex metropolis full of vibrant subcultures.

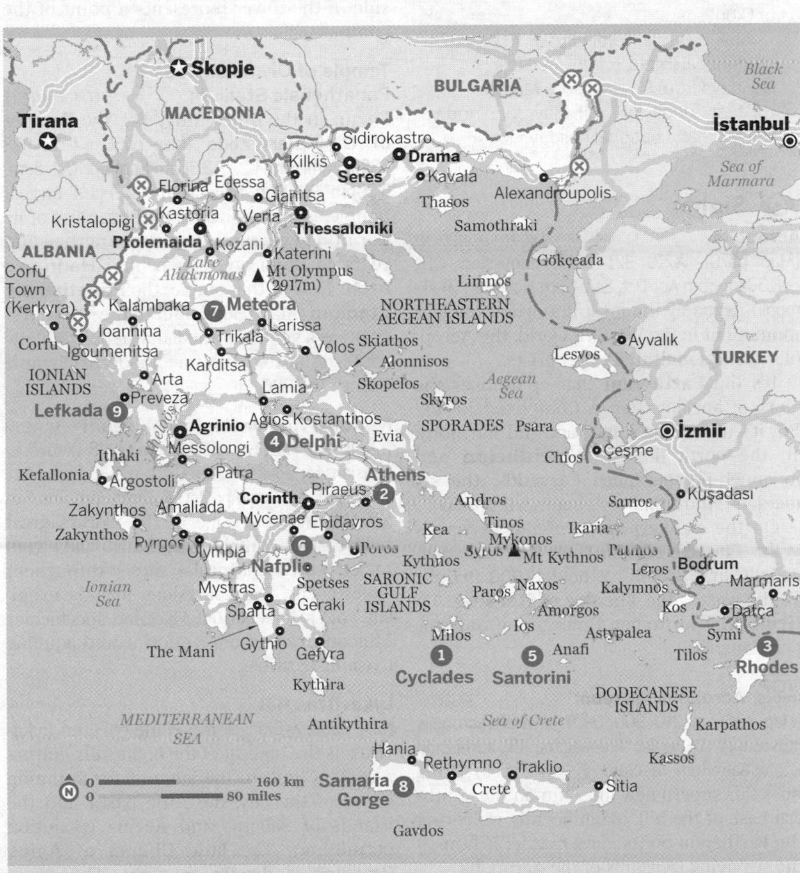

Greece Highlights

1. Island-hop around the **Cyclades** (p604) at your own pace under the Aegean sun
2. Trace the ancient to the modern in **Athens** (p563), from the Acropolis to booming nightclubs
3. Lose yourself within the medieval walls of **Rhodes' Old Town** (p590)
4. Search for the oracle amidst the dazzling ruins of **Delphi** (p574)
5. Stare dumbfounded at the dramatic volcanic caldera of incomparable **Santorini** (p583)
6. Use quaint **Nafplio** (p571) as a base for exploring the back roads and ruins of the Peloponnese
7. Climb russet rock pinnacles to the exquisite monasteries of **Meteora** (p574)
8. Hike through Crete's stupendous **Samaria Gorge** (p589)
9. Sup **ouzo** (p599) while munching on grilled octopus

CHEAPER BY THE HALF-DOZEN

The €12 ticket at the Acropolis (valid for four days) includes entry to the other significant ancient sites: Ancient Agora, Roman Agora, Keramikos, Temple of Olympian Zeus and the Theatre of Dionysos.

Anyone under 19 or with an EU student card gets in free. Also free: Sundays from November to March; the first Sunday of April, May, June and October; and national holidays.

Sights

Acropolis
ANCIENT MONUMENT

(Map p570; ☎210 321 0219; admission €12; ⏲8.30am-8pm Apr-Oct, 8am-5pm Nov-Mar; Ⓜ Akropoli) Arguably the most important ancient monument in the Western world, the Acropolis attracts multitudes of tourists.

It's the **Parthenon** that epitomises the glory of ancient Greece. Completed in 438 BC, it's unsurpassed in grace and harmony. To the north lies the **Erechtheion** and its much-photographed Caryatids, the six maidens who support its southern portico.

On the southern slope of the Acropolis is the **Theatre of Dionysos**. Built between 340 BC and 330 BC, it held 17,000 people. To the west is the **Theatre of Herodes Atticus**, built in Roman times (open only for performances).

TOP CHOICE Acropolis Museum
MUSEUM

(Map p566; ☎210 900 0901; www.theacropolismuseum.gr; Dionysiou Areopagitou 15; admission €5; ⏲8am-8pm Tue-Sun; 📶; Ⓜ Akropoli) Don't miss this superb new museum on the southern base of the hill, magnificently reflecting the Parthenon on its glass facade; it houses the surviving treasures of the Acropolis.

Ancient Agora
ANCIENT MONUMENT

(Map p570; ☎210 321 0185; Adrianou 24; admission €4; ⏲8.30am-8pm Apr-Oct, 8am-5.30pm Nov-Mar; Ⓜ Monastiraki) The Ancient Agora was the marketplace of early Athens and the focal point of civic and social life. The main monuments are the well-preserved **Temple of Hephaestus**, the 11th-century **Church of the Holy Apostles** and the reconstructed **Stoa of Attalos**, which houses the site's excellent museum.

Roman Agora
ANCIENT MONUMENT

(Map p570; ☎210 324 5220; cnr Pelopida & Eolou; admission €2; ⏲8.30am-8pm Apr-Oct, 8am-5.30pm Nov-Mar; Ⓜ Monastiraki) The Romans built their agora just east of the ancient Athenian agora. The wonderful **Tower of the Winds** was built in the 1st century BC by Syrian astronomer Andronicus. Each side of the tower represents a point of the compass.

Temple of Olympian Zeus & Panathenaic Stadium
ANCIENT MONUMENTS

Begun in the 6th century BC, the **Temple of Olympian Zeus** (Map p566; ☎210 922 6330; admission €2; ⏲8.30am-8pm Apr-Oct, 8am-5.30pm Nov-Mar; Ⓜ Akropoli), Greece's largest temple, is impressive for the sheer size of its Corinthian columns. It took more than 700 years to build and sits behind **Hadrian's Arch**. East of the temple, the **Panathenaic Stadium** (Map p566), built in the 4th century BC as a venue for the Panathenaic athletic contests, hosted the first modern Olympic Games in 1896.

National Archaeological Museum
MUSEUM

(☎210 821 7717; www.namuseum.gr; 28 Oktovriou-Patision 44; adult/student €7/3; ⏲1.30-8pm Mon, 8am-8pm Tue-Sun Apr-Oct, 8.30am-3pm Tue-Sun Nov-Mar; Ⓜ Viktoria) One of the world's great museums, it contains significant finds from major archaeological sites throughout Greece. The vast collections include exquisite gold artefacts from Mycenae, spectacular Minoan frescos from Santorini, and aquiline Cycladic figurines.

Lykavittos Hill
PARK

(Map p566; Ⓜ Evangelismos) Pine-covered Lykavittos is the highest of the eight hills dotting Athens. Climb to the summit for stunning views of the city, the Attic basin and the islands of Salamis and Aegina (pollution permitting). The little **Chapel of Agios Giorgios** is floodlit at night. The open-air **Lykavittos Theatre** hosts concerts in summer.

The main path to the summit starts at the top of Loukianou, or take the **funicular railway** (Map p566; return €6; ⏲9am-3am) from the top of Ploutarhou.

National Gardens
PARK

(Map p566; entrances on Leoforos Vasilissis Sofias & Leoforos Vasilissis Amalias, Syntagma; ⏲7am-dusk; Ⓜ Syntagma) A delightful, shady refuge during summer.

FREE ATHENS

A simple wander through the streets of Athens reveals eye candy galore, or you can take in the following free sights:

» National Gardens

» Changing of the Guard

» Monastiraki Flea Market & Sunday Market

» Lykavittos Hill

Parliament & Changing of the Guard CULTURAL RITUAL
In front of the parliament building on **Plateia Syntagmatos** (Syntagma Sq; Map p566) the traditionally costumed *evzones* (guards) of the **Tomb of the Unknown Soldier** change every hour on the hour. On Sunday at 11am, a whole platoon marches down Leoforos Vasilissis Sofias to the tomb, accompanied by a band.

Monastiraki Flea Market MARKET
(Map p570) Enthralling; spreads daily from Plateia Monastirakiou (Monastiraki Sq). The Sunday Market is a bigger version of the Flea Market with stalls in the surrounding streets, especially Ermou.

Festivals & Events

Hellenic Festival CULTURAL EVENT
(210 327 2000; www.greekfestival.gr; box office Panepistimiou 39, Syntagma; 8.30am-4pm Mon-Fri, 9am-2pm Sat; Panepistimio) The city's most important cultural event, this annual festival runs from mid-June to August. International music, dance and theatre fill venues across Athens and Epidavros' ancient theatre.

Sleeping

Book well ahead for July and August.

Athens Style HOSTEL €
(Map p566; 210 322 5010; www.athenstyle.com; Agias Theklas 10, Psyrri; incl breakfast dm €21-25, s/d €51/84, studios €90-124; Monastiraki;) The newest hostel in town is bright and arty, with dorm beds and well-equipped studios. The cool basement lounge has art exhibitions, a pool table and a home cinema; the rooftop bar has Acropolis views.

Marble House Pension HOTEL €
(210 922 8294; www.marblehouse.gr; Zini 35, Koukaki; s/d/tr €39/49/59, d/tr without bathroom €45/55; Syngrou-Fix;) This enduring Athens favourite lies on a quiet cul-de-sac 10 minutes' walk from Plaka. Step through the garden pergola to quiet, spotless rooms.

Tempi Hotel HOTEL €€
(Map p566; 210 321 3175; www.tempihotel.gr; Eolou 29, Monastiraki; d/tr €64/78, s/d without bathroom €43/57; Monastiraki;) No-frills rooms may be tiny, but some have balconies overlooking Plateia Agia Irini. A communal kitchen and nearby markets make it ideal for self-caterers.

Athens Backpackers HOSTEL €
(Map p566; 210 922 4044; www.backpackers.gr; Makri 12, Makrygianni; dm €24-29, studios from €90; Akropoli;) This excellent, popular hostel boasts a rooftop party bar with Acropolis views, a kitchen and daily movies, and the friendly Aussie management hosts (free!) barbecues. Breakfast and nonalcoholic drinks are included; long-term storage, laundry and airport pick-up available.

Student & Travellers' Inn HOSTEL €
(Map p570; 210 324 4808; www.studenttravellersinn.com; Kydathineon 16, Plaka; dm €20-25, d €63, without bathroom €58; Akropoli;) Mixed-sex dorms may be spartan and housekeeping a bit lean, but extras (laundry, left luggage) make up for it.

Eating

In addition to mainstay tavernas, Athens also has bistros and swank eateries. Wear your most stylish togs at night; Athenians dress up to eat out. Eat streets include Mitropoleos, Adrianou and Navarchou Apostoli in Monastiraki, Psyrri, and Gazi near Keramikos metro.

The **fruit and vegetable market** (Map p566) on Athinas, is opposite the **meat market** (Map p566).

TOP CHOICE **Tzitzikas & Mermingas** MEZEDHES €€
(Map p570; Mitropoleos 12-14, Syntagma; mezedhes €6-8; Syntagma) Greek merchandise lines the walls of this cheery, modern *mezedhopoleio*. The great range of delicious and creative *mezedhes* (appetisers; literally 'tastes') draws a bustling local crowd.

Savas SOUVLAKI €
(Map p570; Mitropoleos 86-88, Monastiraki; gyros €2; Monastiraki) This joint, on what becomes one of the city's busiest eat streets late at night, serves enormous grilled-meat plates (€8.50) and the tastiest gyros (pork, beef or chicken) in Athens. Take away or sit down.

Central Athens

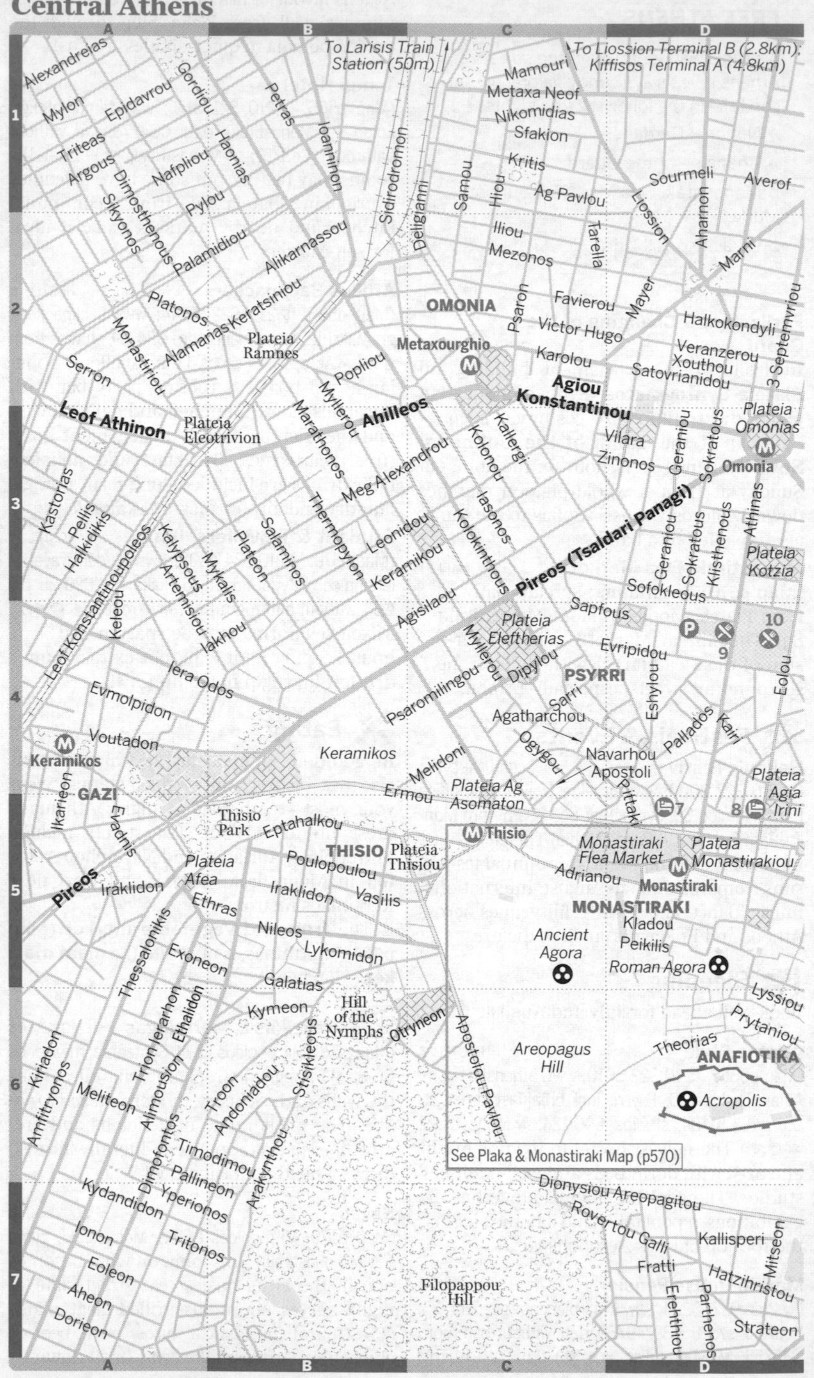

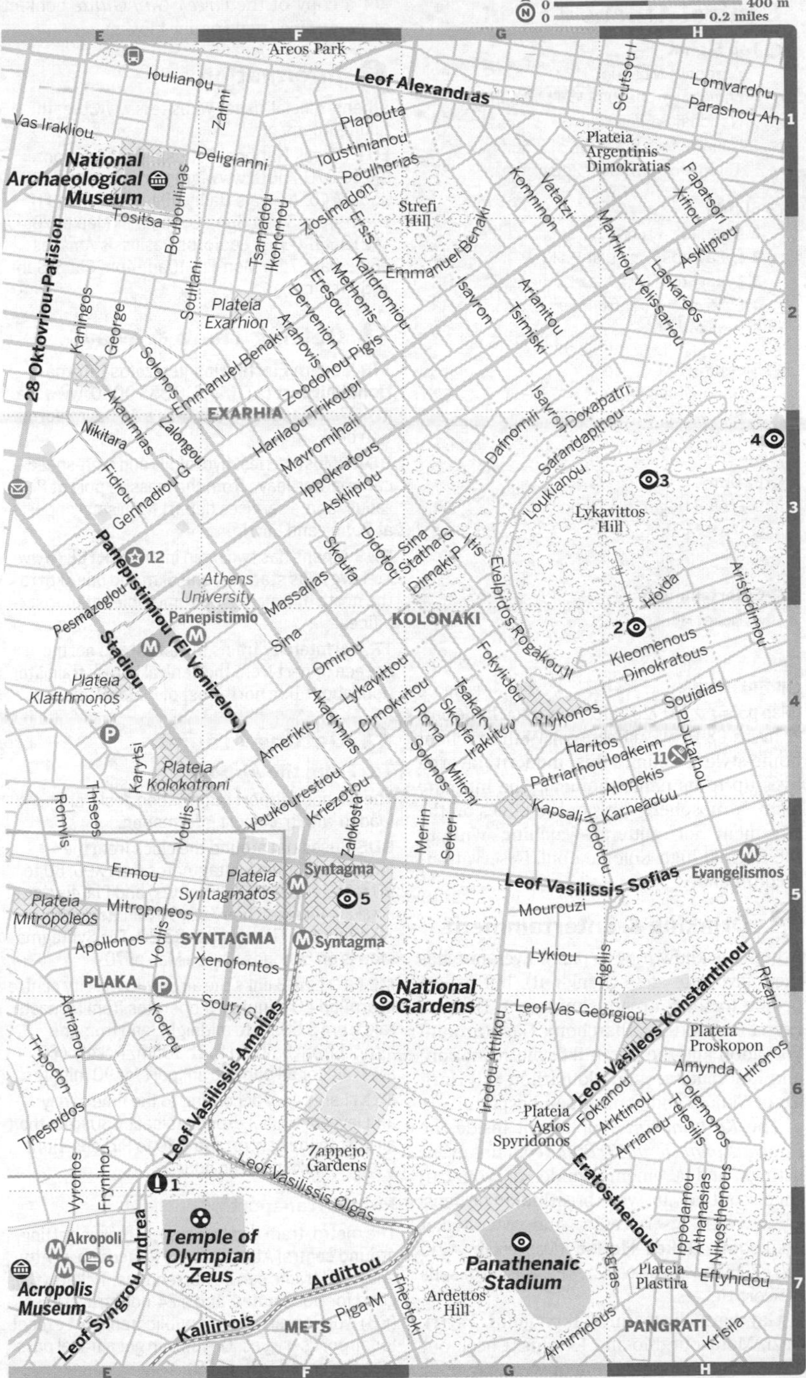
Areos Park
Leof Alexandras
Ioulianou
Zaimi
Vas Irakliou
Plapouta
Ioustinianou
Deligianni
National Archaeological Museum
Poulherias
Tositsa
Bouboulinas
Tsamadou
Ikonomou
Zosimadou
Strefi Hill
Erss
Kallidromiou
Methonis
Eressou
Dervenion
Emmanuel Benaki
Isavron
Arianitou
Tsimiski
Vatatzi
Kominon
Mavrikiou
Velissariou
Laskareos
Asklipiou
Xifiou
Fapatsori
Scutsou I
Lomvardou
Parashou Ah
Plateia Argentinis Dimokratias
28 Oktovriou-Patision
Kaningos
George
Soultani
Plateia Exarhion
Arahovis
Zoodohou Pigis
Solonos
Emmanuel Benaki
Harilaou Trikoupi
Akadimias
Nikitara
EXARHIA
Mavromihail
Ippokratous
Asklipiou
Zalongou
Gennadiou G
Fidiou
Dafnomili
Isavron
Doxapatri
Sarandapihou
Loukianou
Lykavittos Hill
Panepistimiou (El Venizelou)
12
Athens University
Panepistimio
Pesmazoglou
Massalias
Skoufa
Didotou
Sina
Statha G
Dimaki P
Itis
Evelpidos Rogakou II
Hoida
Aristodimou
KOLONAKI
2
3
4
Stadiou
Sina
Omirou
Lykavittou
Dimokritou
Akadimias
Amerikis
Plateia Klafthmonos
Fokylidou
Tsakalof
Skoufa
Irakleitou
Glykonos
Kleomenous
Dinokratous
Souidias
Ploutarhou
Haritos
Patriarhou Ioakeim
Alopekis
11
Karneadou
Kapsali
Irodotou
Roma
Solonos
Milioni
Karytsi
Plateia Kolokotroni
Voukourestiou
Kriezotou
Zalokosta
Merlin
Sekeri
Thiseos
Romvis
Voulis
Ermou
Plateia Syntagmatos
Syntagma
5
Leof Vasilissis Sofias
Evangelismos
Plateia Mitropoleos
Mitropoleos
Mourouzi
Apollonos
Voulis
SYNTAGMA
Syntagma
Xenofontos
Lykiou
Rigilis
PLAKA
National Gardens
Souri G
Leof Vas Georgiou
Leof Vasileos Konstantinou
Rizari
Adrianou
Kodrou
Leof Vasilissis Amalias
Plateia Proskopon
Tripodon
Irodou Attikou
Amynda
Hironos
Thespidos
Plateia Agios Spyridonos
Fokianou
Arktinou
Telesilis
Polemonos
Arrianou
Zappeio Gardens
Leof Vasilissis Olgas
Vyronos
Frynihou
1
Eratosthenous
Ippodamou
Athanasias
Nikosthenous
Temple of Olympian Zeus
Akropoli
6
Leof Syngrou Andrea
Panathenaic Stadium
Agras
Plateia Plastira
Eftyhidou
Acropolis Museum
Arditou
Theotoki
Piga M
Ardettos Hill
METS
Kallirrois
PANGRATI
Arhimidous
Krisila
400 m
0.2 miles
E
F
G
H

Central Athens

Top Sights

Oikeio BISTRO €

(Map p566; ☎210 725 9216; Ploutarhou 15, Kolonaki; mains €8-11; Ⓜ Evangelismos) With excellent home-style cooking, this modern taverna lives up to its name (homey). The intimate bistro atmosphere spills out to tables on the pavement for glitterati-watching without the normal high Kolonaki bill. Reservations recommended.

Drinking & Entertainment

Athenians know how to party. Everyone has their favourite *steki* (hang-out), but expect people to show up after midnight. Head to Psyrri (around Agatharchou), Gazi (around Voutadon and the Keramikos metro station) and Kolonaki (around Ploutarhou and Haritos or Skoufa and Omirou) and explore!

The *Kathimerini* supplement inside the *International Herald Tribune* contains event listings and a cinema guide, or you can check online at www.breathtakingathens.gr, www.ticketservices.gr and www.tickethour.com. **Ticket House** (Map p566; ☎210 360 8366; Panepistimiou 42; Ⓜ Panepistimio) sells concert tickets.

Gay bars cluster in Makrygianni, Psyrri, Gazi, Metaxourghio and Exarhia. Check out www.athensinfoguide.com or www.gay.gr, or get a copy of the *Greek Gay Guide* booklet at *periptera* (newspaper kiosks).

Information

Athens' official visitor website is www.breathtakingathens.gr.

EOT (Greek National Tourism Organisation; ☎210 870 7000; www.gnto.gr) airport (☎210 353 0445; Arrivals Hall; ⊙9am-7pm Mon-Fri, 10am-4pm Sat & Sun); Syntagma (Map p570; ☎210 331 0392; Leoforos Vasilissis Amalias 26; ⊙9am-7pm Mon-Fri, 10am-4pm Sat & Sun; Ⓜ Syntagma)

Getting There & Away

AIR Modern **Eleftherios Venizelos International Airport** (ATH; ☎210 353 0000; www.aia.gr), 27km east of Athens, has a 24-hour information desk.

BOAT Most ferries, hydrofoils and high-speed catamarans leave from the massive port at Piraeus. Some services depart from smaller ports at Rafina and Lavrio.

BUS Athens has two main intercity **KTEL** (www.ktel.org) bus stations, one 5km and one 7km to the north of Omonia. Get timetables at tourist offices.

TRAIN Intercity trains to central and northern Greece depart from the central Larisis train station, about 1km northwest of Plateia Omonias.

Getting Around

To/From the Airport

The 24-hour airport information desks are loaded with transport information.

BUS Buses run around the clock from the airport to Plateia Syntagmatos (bus X95, 60 to 90 minutes, every 30 minutes) and Plateia Karaïskaki in Piraeus (bus X96, 90 minutes, every 20 minutes). Tickets cost €3.20. The Syntagma stop is on Othonos St; see Map p570.

METRO Line 3 links the airport to the city centre in around 40 minutes; it operates from Monastiraki from 5.50am to midnight, and from the airport from 5.30am to 11.30pm. Tickets (€6) are valid for all public transport for 90 minutes.

TAXI Fares vary according to the time of day and level of traffic; expect at least €30 from the airport to the centre, and €40 to Piraeus. Both trips can take up to an hour.

Public Transport

The metro, tram and bus system makes getting around central Athens and to Piraeus easy. Athens' road traffic can be horrendous. Tickets (€1), good for 90 minutes, and a 24-hour travel pass (€3) work on all forms of public transport except for airport services. Or you can get a travel pass (see the boxed text, p569).

TRAVEL PASS

For short-stay visitors, consider the €15 tourist ticket: it's valid for three days of unlimited travel on all of Athens' public transport, including the metro airport service, and the Athens Sightseeing bus.

BUS & TROLLEYBUS Buses and electric trolleybuses operate every 15 minutes from 5am to midnight. Purchase tickets before boarding (from the metro, a bus-ticket booth or a kiosk). Validate as you board.

METRO Trains operate from 5am to midnight, every three minutes during peak periods and every 10 minutes off-peak. Get timetables at www.ametro.gr. Validate tickets as you enter the platforms.

Train

Fast **suburban rail** (☎1110; www.trainose.com) links Athens with the airport, Piraeus, the outer regions and the northern Peloponnese. It connects to the metro at Larisis, Doukissis Plakentias and Nerantziotissa stations, and goes from the airport to Kiato.

AROUND ATHENS

Piraeus Πειραιάς

POP 175,700

The highlights of Greece's main port and ferry hub are the other-worldly rows of ferries, ships and hydrofoils filling its seemingly endless quays. It takes around 30 minutes to get here (10km) from Athens' centre by metro, so there's no reason to stay in bustling Piraeus. The Mikrolimano (Small Harbour), with its cafes and fish restaurants, reveals the city's gentler side.

If you're catching a ferry, give yourself plenty of time; you may be in for a 15- to 20-minute walk to get to the right quay from the metro station. There is free wi-fi around the port. All ferry companies have online timetables and booths on the quays. The main branch of EOT in Athens has a weekly schedule. When buying tickets, confirm the departure point.

To get to Athens' international airport by bus, the X96 Piraeus-Athens Airport Express (€3.20) leaves every 20 minutes from the southwestern corner of Plateia Karaïskaki.

The fastest and most convenient link to Athens is the metro (€1, 30 minutes, every 10 minutes, 5am to midnight), near the ferries.

THE PELOPONNESE ΠΕΛΟΠΟΝΝΗΣΟΣ

The Peloponnese encompasses a breathtaking array of landscapes, villages and ruins. Home to Olympia, birthplace of the Olympic Games; the ancient archaeological sites of magical Epidavros, Mycenae and Corinth; the fairy-tale Byzantine city of Mystras; and ancient Sparta, much Greek history has played out here.

Patra Πάτρα

POP 185,700

Greece's third-largest city, Patra is the principal ferry port for the Ionian Islands and Italy. Despite its 3000-year history, ancient sites and vibrant social life, few travellers linger longer than necessary.

The contemporary buildings of the **Archaeological Museum of Patras** (☎2610 420 645; cnr Amerikis & Patras-Athens National Rd; admission free; ⏲8.30am-3pm Tue-Sun) make up the country's second-largest museum and feature objects from prehistoric to Roman times.

Pension Nikos (☎2610 623 757; cnr Patreos 3 & Agiou Andreou 121; s/d/tr €28/38/45, s/d without bathroom €23/33) is smack in the city centre with spotlessly clean rooms.

Scores of stylish cafes and fast-food eateries lie between Kolokotroni and Ermou; drinking hot spots cluster on Agios Nikolaos and Radinou (off Riga Fereou). Pedestrianised Trion Navarhon is lined with tavernas.

The **tourist office** (☎2610 461 741; www.infocenterpatras.gr; Othonos Amalias 6; ⏲8am-10pm), the best in Greece, has friendly multilingual staff.

Getting There & Away

Ferry schedules vary; the tourist office provides timetables and ticket agencies line the waterfront. Ferries depart for the following islands: Corfu (€30.50, seven hours, one daily), Ithaki (€17.80, four hours, one daily) and Kefallonia (€17.80, 2¾ hours, two daily). For services to Italy, see p602.

The **KTEL Achaia bus station** (☎2610 623 886; cnr Zaimi 2 & Othonos Amalias) services Athens (€17, three hours, half-hourly, via Corinth), Ioannina (€20.90, 4½ hours, two daily), Kalamata (€20, four hours, two daily), Pyrgos (for Olympia; €8.80, two hours, 10 daily) and Thessaloniki (€40, seven hours, four daily).

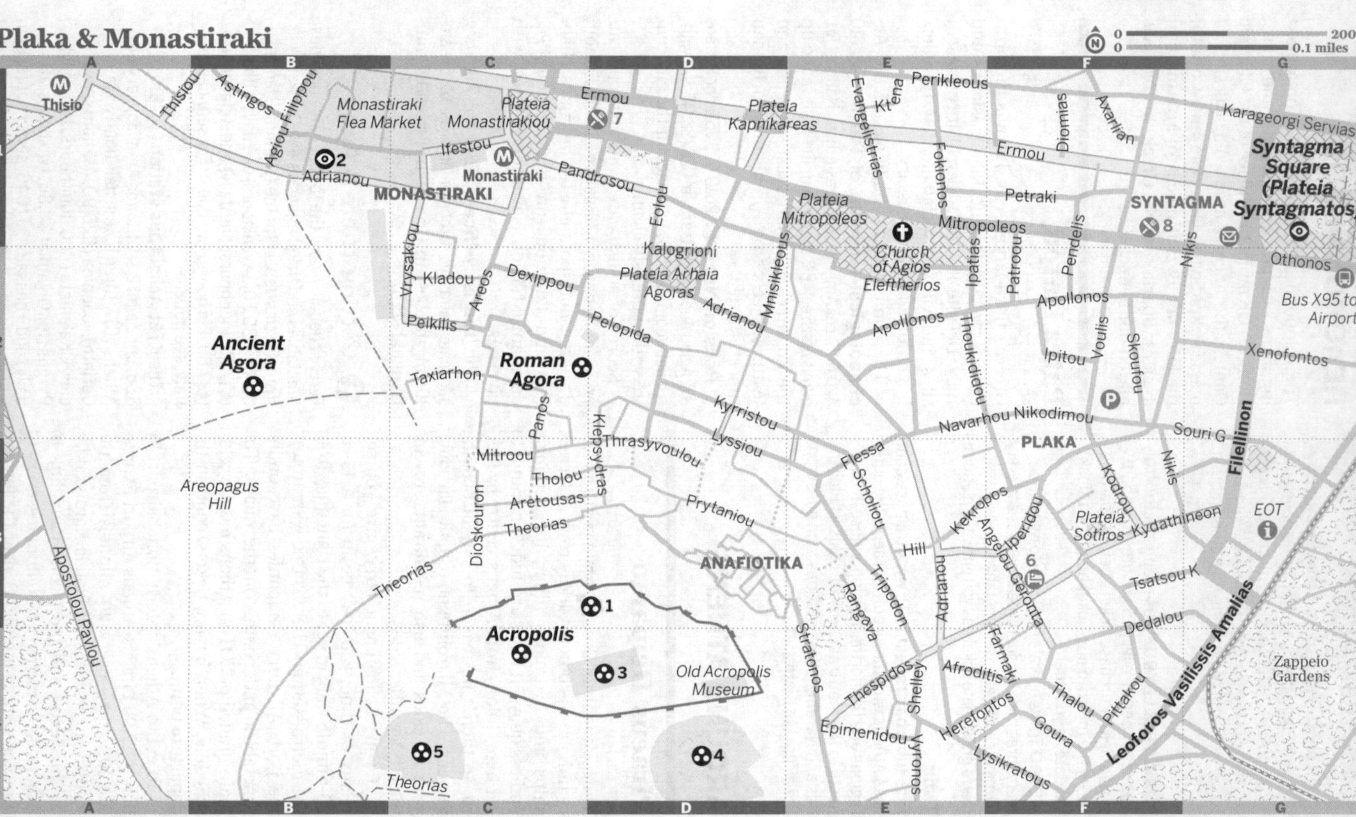
Plaka & Monastiraki
0 200 m
0 0.1 miles
Thisio
Thisiou
Astingos
Agiou Filippou
Monastiraki Flea Market
Plateia Monastirakiou
Ermou
7
Plateia Kapnikareas
Evangelistrias
Kt ena
Perikleous
Diomias
Axarlian
Karageorgi Servias
2
Adrianou
Ifestou
Monastiraki
MONASTIRAKI
Pandrosou
Eolou
Ermou
Fokionos
Petraki
Syntagma Square (Plateia Syntagmatos)
SYNTAGMA
8
Plateia Mitropoleos
Mitropoleos
Church of Agios Eleftherios
Kalogrioni
Plateia Arhaia Agoras
Mnisikleous
Ipatias
Patroou
Pendelis
Nikis
Othonos
Bus X95 to Airport
Vrysakiou
Kladou
Areos
Dexippou
Peikilis
Adrianou
Apollonos
Apollonos
Pelopida
Thoukididou
Ipitou
Voulis
Skoufou
Xenofontos
Ancient Agora
Roman Agora
Taxiarhon
Kyrristou
Navarhou Nikodimou
Souri G
PLAKA
Panos
Klepsydras
Thrasyvoulou
Lyssiou
Flessa
Mitroou
Tholou
Scholiou
Nikis
Kodrou
Filellinon
Areopagus Hill
Aretousas
Prytaniou
Kekropos
Iperidou
Plateia Sotiros
Kydathineon
EOT
Theorias
Dioskouron
Hill
Angelou Geronta
Apostolou Pavlou
Theorias
ANAFIOTIKA
6
Tsatsou K
Tripodon
Adrianou
Rangava
1
Acropolis
Stratonos
Dedalou
Farmaki
3
Old Acropolis Museum
Thespidos
Shelley
Afroditis
Thalou
Pittakou
Zappeio Gardens
Leoforos Vasilissis Amalias
Herefontos
Goura
Epimenidou
Vyronos
Lysikratous
5
4
Theorias

Plaka & Monastiraki

Top Sights

Acropolis C4
Ancient Agora B2
Roman Agora C2
Syntagma Square (Plateia Syntagmatos) G1

Sights

1 Erechtheion D3
2 Monastiraki Flea Market B1
3 Parthenon D4
4 Theatre of Dionysos D4
5 Theatre of Herodes Atticus C4

Sleeping

6 Student & Travellers' Inn F3

Eating

7 Savas D1
8 Tzitzikas & Mermingas F1

Buses to the Ionian Islands, via the port of Kyllini, leave from the **KTEL Lefkada & Zakynthos bus station** (☎2610 220 993; Othonos Amalias 48) or nearby **KTEL Kefallonia bus station** (☎2610 274 938; Othonos Amalias 58).

From the **train station** (☎26106 39108; Othonos Amalias 27), regular/intercity express (IC) services run to Athens' Kiato station (€3.70/6.90, 2½ hours), which connects to suburban rail; Kalamata (€6.60/11.30, five hours); and Pyrgos (for Olympia; €3.70/6.30, 3/1½ hours).

Corinth Κορινθοσ

POP 29,800

Drab, modern Corinth (*ko*-rin-thoss), 6km west of the Corinth Canal, is an uninspiring town; it's better to stay in the village near Ancient Corinth if visiting the ruins.

Buses to Athens (€7.50, 1½ hours, half-hourly) and Ancient Corinth (€1.40, 20 minutes, hourly) leave from the **KTEL Korinthos bus station** (☎27410 75425; Dimocratias 4). Buses to the rest of the Peloponnese leave from the **Corinth Isthmus (Peloponnese) KTEL bus station** (☎27410 83000) on the Peloponnese side of the Corinth Canal.

Trains go to Patra (regular/IC €5.70/8.90) and Athens (14 daily, four of which are IC services). The handy *proastiako* suburban train runs to Athens airport (€10, one hour, eight daily).

Ancient Corinth & Acrocorinth Αρχαια Κορινθοσ & Ακροκορινθοσ

Seven kilometres southwest of Corinth's modern city, the ruins of **Ancient Corinth** (☎27410 31207; site & museum €6; ⏲8am-8pm Apr-Oct, to 3pm Nov-Mar) and its lovely museum lie at the edge of a small village in the midst of fields sweeping to the sea. It was one of ancient Greece's wealthiest cities, but earthquakes and invasions have left only one Greek monument remaining: the imposing **Temple of Apollo**. The rest of the ruins are Roman. **Acrocorinth** (admission free; ⏲8am-3pm), the remains of a citadel built on a massive outcrop of limestone, looms majestically over the site.

The great-value digs at **Tasos Taverna & Rooms** (☎27410 31225; s/d/tr €30/45/55; ❄), 200m from the museum, are spotlessly clean and above an excellent eatery serving Greek classics.

Nafplio Ναυπλιο

POP 14,500

Elegant Venetian houses and neoclassical mansions dripping with crimson bougainvillea cascade down Nafplio's hillside to the azure sea. Vibrant cafes, shops and restaurants fill winding pedestrian streets. Crenulated Palamidi Fortress perches above it all. What's not to love?

Sights

Palamidi Fortress FORTRESS

(☎27520 28036; admission €4; ⏲8am-6.45pm Jun-Aug, to 2.45pm Sep-May) Enjoy spectacular views of the town and surrounding coast from the magnificent hilltop fortress built by the Venetians between 1711 and 1714.

Archaeological Museum MUSEUM

(Plateia Syntagmatos; ⏲8.30am-3pm Tue-Sun; adult/concession €2/1) Fine exhibits include fire middens from 32,000 BC and bronze armour from near Mycenae (12th to 13th centuries BC).

Peloponnese Folklore Foundation Museum MUSEUM

(☎27520 28379; 1 Vas Alexandrou St; admission €4; ⏲9am-2.30pm & 5.30-10.30pm) One of Greece's best small museums, with displays of vibrant regional costumes and rotating exhibitions.

WORTH A TRIP

EPIDAVROS ΕΠΙΔΑΥΡΟΣ

Spectacular World Heritage–listed **Epidavros** (☎27530 22006; admission €6; ⏰8am-7pm Apr-Sep, to 5pm Oct-Mar) was dedicated to Asclepius, god of medicine. Amid pine-covered hills, the magnificent **theatre** is still a venue during the Hellenic Festival (p565), but don't miss the peaceful **Sanctuary of Asclepius**, an ancient spa and healing centre.

For an early-morning visit to the site, stay at **Hotel Avaton** (☎27530 22178; s/d €45/69; ❄), 1km away, at the junction of the road to Kranidi, or go as a day trip from Nafplio (€2.60, 45 minutes, four buses daily).

Sleeping

The Old Town is *the* place to stay but has limited budget options.

Pension Dimitris Bekas PENSION €
(☎27520 24594; Efthimiopoulou 26; s/d/tr €23/29/40) The only good, central budget option. Clean, homey rooms have a top-value location on the slopes of the Akronafplia, and the owner has a killer baseball-cap collection.

Pension Marianna PENSION €€
(☎27520 24256; www.pensionmarianna.gr; Potamianou 9; s/d/tr incl breakfast €70/85/100; ❄📶) Welcoming owners epitomise Greek *filoxenia* (hospitality) and serve delicious organic breakfasts. Up a steep set of stairs, and tucked under the fortress walls, a dizzying array of rooms intermix with sea-view terraces.

Eating

Nafplio's Old Town streets are loaded with standard tavernas; those on Staïkopoulou and those overlooking the port on Bouboulinas get jam-packed on weekends.

Taverna Aeolos TRADITIONAL GREEK €
(☎27520 26828; V Olgas 30; mains €5-13) This boisterous taverna lined with copper pans gets packed with locals sharing generous mixed-grill plates (€8.50). Live music during summer.

Omorfi Poli GREEK, ITALIAN €
(☎27520 29452; Bouboulinas 75; mains €6-16; ⏰dinner) Greek favourites and *mezedhes* (€5) with a slight Italian twist (there's mushroom risotto), plus friendly service and a good wine list.

Information

Kasteli Travel & Tourist Agency (☎27520 29395; 38 Vas Konstantinou; ⏰9am-2pm year-round plus 6-8pm Jun-Sep) Friendly, English-speaking.

Municipal tourist office (☎27520 24444; 25 Martiou; ⏰9am-1pm & 4-8pm) Generally unhelpful. A kiosk in Fillenon Sq offers free headsets for walking tours from 10am to 1pm and 6pm to 8pm.

Getting There & Away

The **KTEL Argolis bus station** (☎27520 27323; Syngrou 8) services Argos (for Peloponnese connections; €1.40, 30 minutes, half-hourly), Athens (via Corinth; €12, 2½ hours, hourly), Epidavros (€2.60, 45 minutes, four daily) and Mycenae (€2.60, one hour, two daily).

Mycenae Μυκήνες

Although settled as early as the 6th millennium BC, **Ancient Mycenae** (☎27510 76585; admission €8; ⏰8am-8pm Jun-Sep, to 6pm Oct, to 3pm Nov-May) was at its most powerful from 1600 to 1200 BC. Mycenae's entrance, the **Lion Gate**, is Europe's oldest monumental sculpture.

Most people visit on day trips from Nafplio. Two buses go daily to Mycenae from Argos (€1.60, 30 minutes) and Nafplio (€2.60, one hour).

Sparta Σπάρτη

POP 14,400

Cheerful, unpretentious modern Sparta (*spar*-tee) is at odds with its ancient Spartan image of discipline and deprivation. Although there's little to see, the town makes a convenient base from which to visit Mystras.

Modern **Hotel Lakonia** (☎27310 28951; www.lakoniahotel.gr; Palaeologou 89; s/d incl breakfast €45/70; ❄📶) maintains comfy, welcoming rooms with spotless bathrooms.

Sparta's **KTEL Lakonias bus station** (☎27310 26441; cnr Lykourgou & Thivronos), on the east edge of town, services Athens via Corinth (€17.60, 3½ hours, eight daily), Gythio (€4, one hour, five daily) and Mystras (€1.40, 30 minutes, 10 daily).

Mystras Μυστράς

Magical **Mystras** (☎27310 83377; adult/student €6/3; ⏰8am-7.30pm Apr-Oct, 8.30am-3pm Nov-Mar) was once the effective capital of the

Byzantine Empire. Ruins of palaces, monasteries and churches, most of them dating from between 1271 and 1460, nestle at the base of the Taÿgetos Mountains.

While only 7km from Sparta, staying in the village nearby allows you to get there early before it heats up. Enjoy exquisite views and a beautiful swimming pool at **Hotel Byzantion** (☎27310 83309; www.byzantionhotel.gr; s/d €45/65; ❄@≋), near the main square.

Camp at **Castle View** (☎27310 83303; www.castleview.gr; campsites per adult/tent/car €6/4/4, 2-person bungalows €30; ⊙Apr-Oct; ≋), about 1km before Mystras village and set in olive trees. Buses will stop outside if you ask.

Gythio Γυθειο

POP 4490

Gythio (*yee*-thih-o) was once the port of ancient Sparta. Now it's an earthy fishing town on the Lakonian Gulf and gateway to the rugged, much more beautiful Mani Peninsula.

Peaceful **Marathonisi islet**, linked to the mainland by a causeway, is said to be ancient Cranae, where Paris (prince of Troy) and Helen (the wife of Menelaus of Sparta) consummated the love affair that sparked the Trojan War.

ANEN Lines (www.anen.gr) has a weekly summertime ferry to Kissamos, Crete (€22, seven hours), via Kythira (€10, 2½ hours).

The **KTEL Lakonia bus station** (☎27330 22228; cnr Vasileos Georgios & Evrikleos), on the square near Hotel Aktion, services Areopoli (€2.40, 30 minutes, four daily), Athens (€21.50, 4½ hours, six daily), the Diros Caves (€3.30, one hour, one daily) and Sparta (€3.90, one hour, four daily).

The Mani Η Μανη

The exquisite Mani completely lives up to its reputation for rugged beauty, abundant wildflowers in spring, and dramatic juxtapositions of sea and the Taÿgetos Mountains (threaded with wonderful walking trails). The Mani occupies the central peninsula of the southern Peloponnese and is divided into two regions: the arid Lakonian (inner) Mani in the south and the verdant Messinian (outer) Mani in the northwest near Kalamata.

LAKONIAN MANI

For centuries the Maniots were a law unto themselves, renowned for their fierce independence and their spectacularly murderous internal feuds. To this day, bizarre tower settlements built as refuges during clan wars dot the rocky slopes of the Lakonian Mani.

Areopoli (population 774), 30km southwest of Gythio and named after Ares, the god of war, is a warren of cobblestone and ancient towers. Enter a dreamlike courtyard to reach the excellent **Pyrgos Kapetanakas** (☎27330 51233; access off Kapetan Matepan; s/d/tr €50/60/80; ❄), in a splendid tower house built by the powerful Kapetanakas family in 1865.

The **bus station** (☎27330 51229; Plateia Athanaton) services Gythio (€2.80, 30 minutes, four daily), Itilo (for the Messinian Mani; €2, 20 minutes, three weekly), Gerolimenas (€3.30, 45 minutes, three daily) and the Diros Caves (€1.40, 15 minutes, one daily).

Eleven kilometres south, the extensive, though touristy **Diros Caves** (☎27330 52222; adult/student €12/7; ⊙8.30am-5.30pm Jun-Sep, to 3pm Oct-May) contain a subterranean river.

MESSINIAN MANI

Stone hamlets dot aquamarine swimming coves and silver olive groves climb the foothills to the snowcapped Taÿgetos Mountains.

The people of the enchanting seaside village of **Kardamyli**, 37km south of Kalamata, know how good they've got it. Sir Patrick Leigh Fermor famously wrote about his rambles here in *Mani: Travels in the Southern Peloponnese*. Trekkers come for the magnificent **Vyros Gorge**. Walks are well organised and colour-coded.

Run by the former housekeeper to Patrick Leigh Fermor, **Lela's Rooms** (☎27210 73541; r €55; ❄) has basic, charming rooms on the sea, while the adjoining Lela's Taverna serves up tasty home-style Greek cuisine (mains €10) under pergolas on the water's edge.

Olympia Koumounakou Rooms (☎27210 73623; s/d €30/35) is basic but clean, and popular with backpackers who like the communal kitchen and courtyard.

Kardamyli is on the main bus route from Itilo to Kalamata (€3.10, one hour) and two to three buses stop daily at the central square.

Olympia Ολυμπια

POP 1000

Tucked alongside the Kladeos River, in fertile delta country, the modern town of Olympia supports the extensive ruins of the same name. The first Olympics were staged here in 776 BC, and every four years thereafter until AD 394 when Emperor Theodosius I banned them.

Ancient Olympia (☎26240 22517; adult/student site €6/3, site & museum €9/5; ⏰8am-8pm Apr-Oct, 8.30am-3pm Nov-Mar) is dominated by the immense, ruined **Temple of Zeus**, to whom the games were dedicated. Don't miss the statue of **Hermes of Praxiteles**, a classical sculpture masterpiece, at the exceptional **Archaeological Museum** (adult/student €6/3; ⏰1.30-8pm Mon, 8am-8pm Tue-Sun Apr-Oct, to 3pm Nov-Mar).

Sparkling clean **Pension Posidon** (☎26240 22567; www.pensionposidon.gr; Stefanopoulou 9; s/d/tr €35/45/60; ❄) offers the best value in the centre. Pitch your tent in the leafy grove at **Camping Diana** (☎26240 22314; campsites per tent/adult €6/8; 🏊), 250m west of town.

Olympia municipal tourist office (☎26240 23100; Praxitelous Kondyli; ⏰9am-3pm Mon-Fri May-Sep) has transport schedules.

Catch buses at the stop on the north end of town. Northbound buses go via Pyrgos (€1.90, 30 minutes), where you connect to buses for Athens, Corinth and Patra. Trains run daily to Pyrgos (€1, 30 minutes), where you can switch for Athens, Corinth and Patra.

CENTRAL GREECE ΚΕΝΤΡΙΚΗ ΕΛΛΑΔΑ

This dramatic landscape of deep gorges, rugged mountains and fertile valleys is home to the magical stone pinnacle-topping monasteries of Meteora and the iconic ruins of ancient Delphi. Established in 1938, **Parnassos National Park** (www.routes.gr), to the north of Delphi, attracts naturalists, hikers and skiers.

Delphi Δελφοί

POP 2800

Modern Delphi and its adjoining ruins hang stunningly on the slopes of Mt Parnassos overlooking the shimmering Gulf of Corinth.

The ancient Greeks regarded Delphi as the centre of the world. **Ancient Delphi** (☎22650 82312; site or museum €6, combined adult/student €9/5, free Sun Nov-Mar; ⏰1.30-7.45pm Mon, 8am-7.45pm Tue-Sun Apr-Oct, 8.30am-2.45pm Nov-Mar) was built as the Sanctuary of Apollo and is one of Greece's most inspiring archaeological sites.

In the town centre, the welcoming **Hotel Hermes** (☎22650 82318; Vasileon Pavlou-Friderikis 27; s/d incl breakfast €45/60; ❄) has spacious rooms sporting balconies with stunning valley views. **Apollon Camping** (☎22650 82762; www.apolloncamping.gr; campsites per person/tent €7.50/4; @📶🏊), 2km west of town, has great facilities, including a restaurant and minimarket.

Six buses a day go to Athens (€13.60, three hours). Take a bus to Lamia (€8.20, two hours, two daily) or Trikala (€13.80, 4½ hours, two daily) to transfer for Meteora.

Meteora Μετέωρα

Meteora (meh-*teh*-o-rah) should be a certified Wonder of the World with its magnificent late-14th-century monasteries perched dramatically atop enormous rocky pinnacles. The tranquil village of **Kastraki**, 2km from Kalambaka, is the best base for visiting.

Meteora's stunning rocks are also a climbing mecca. Licensed mountain guide **Lazaros Botelis** (☎24320 79165, 6948043655; meteora@nolimits.com.gr; Kastraki) can show the way.

Doupiani House (☎24320 75326; www.doupianihouse.com; s/d/tr incl breakfast €40/50/60; ❄@📶) offers a comfy home from which to explore or simply enjoy the panoramic views. **Vrachos Camping** (☎24320 22293; www.campingmeteora.gr; campsites per tent/adult €7/free; 🏊) has great views, excellent facilities and a good taverna, a short stroll from Kastraki.

Local buses shuttle between Kalambaka and Kastraki (€1.90); a bus goes up to the monasteries in the morning. Hourly buses from Kalambaka go to the transport hub of Trikala (€2, 30 minutes), from where buses go to Ioannina (€13.10, three hours, two daily) and Athens (€27, 4½ hours, seven daily). From Kalambaka, express trains run to Athens (regular/IC €14.60/24.30, 5½/4½ hours, two daily of each) and Thessaloniki (€12.10, four hours, three daily).

NORTHERN GREECE ΒΟΡΕΙΑ ΕΛΛΑΔΑ

Northern Greece is stunning, graced as it is with magnificent mountains, thick forests, tranquil lakes and archaeological sites. Most of all, it's easy to get off the beaten track and experience aspects of Greece noticeably different to other mainland areas and the islands.

DON'T MISS

METEORA'S MONASTERIES

While there were once monasteries on all 24 pinnacles, only six are still occupied. Admission is €2 for each monastery and strict dress codes apply (no bare shoulders or knees, and women must wear skirts; borrow a long skirt at the door if you don't have one). Walk the footpaths between monasteries or drive the back road.

Megalou Meteorou (Grand Meteoron; ⊙9am-5pm Wed-Mon Apr-Oct, 9am-4pm Thu-Mon Nov-Mar)

Varlaam (⊙9am-4pm Wed-Mon Apr-Oct, 9am-4pm Thu-Mon Nov-Mar)

Agiou Stefanou (⊙9am-1.30pm & 3.30-5.30pm Tue-Sun Apr-Oct, 9.30am-1pm & 3-5pm Nov-Mar)

Agias Triados (Holy Trinity; ⊙9am-5pm Fri-Wed Apr-Oct, reduced hr Nov-Mar)

Agiou Nikolaou Anapafsa (⊙9am-3.30pm Sat-Thu)

Agias Varvaras Rousanou (⊙9am-6pm Thu-Tue Apr-Oct, reduced hr Nov-Mar)

Thessaloniki Θεσσαλονικη

POP 800,800

Dodge cherry sellers in the street, smell spices in the air and enjoy waterfront breezes in Thessaloniki (thess-ah-lo-*nee*-kih), also known as Salonica. The second city of Byzantium and of modern Greece boasts countless Byzantine churches, a smattering of Roman ruins, engaging museums, shopping to rival Athens, fine restaurants and a lively cafe scene and nightlife.

Sights

Check out the seafront **White Tower** (Lefkos Pyrgos; ☎2310 267 832; admission free; ⊙8am-3pm Tue-Sun) and wander around *hamams* (Turkish baths) and churches like the enormous, 5th-century **Church of Agios Dimitrios** (☎2310 270 008; Agiou Dimitriou 97; ⊙8am-10pm).

The award-winning **Museum of Byzantine Culture** (☎2310 868 570; www.mbp.gr; Leoforos Stratou 2; admission €4; ⊙1.30-8pm Mon, 8am-8pm Tue-Sun) beautifully displays splendid sculptures, mosaics, icons and other intriguing artefacts. The **Archaeological Museum** (☎2310 830 538; Manoli Andronikou 6; admission €6; ⊙8.30am-8pm) showcases prehistoric, ancient Macedonian and Hellenistic finds.

The compelling **Thessaloniki Centre of Contemporary Art** (☎2310 546 683; www.cact.gr; admission free; ⊙11am-7pm Tue-Sun) and hip **Museum of Photography** (☎2310 566 716; www.thmphoto.gr; admission free; ⊙11am-7pm Tue-Sun), beside the port, are worth an hour.

Sleeping

Steep discounts abound during summer; prices rise during conventions.

Hotel Pella HOTEL €
(☎2310 524 221; www.pella-hotel.gr; Ionos Dragoumi 63; s/d €40/50; ❄) Quiet and family run, with spotless rooms.

Hotel Tourist BUSINESS HOTEL €€
(☎2310 270 501; www.touristhotel.gr; Mitropoleos 21; s/d incl breakfast €55/70; ❄@) Spacious rooms in a charming, central, neoclassical building are maintained by friendly staff.

Backpacker's Refuge HOSTEL €
(☎6983433591; backpackers_refuge@hotmail.com; Botsari 84; dm per person €15; 📶) Snug, hostel-like flat with a two-bed and four-bed dorm. Book ahead, as it's frequently full.

Eating & Drinking

Tavernas dot Plateia Athonos; funky bars line Plateia Aristotelous; cafes and bars pack Leoforos Nikis; and Syngrou and Valaoritou streets have newer bars. Head to **Modiano market** for fresh fruit and vegetables.

Zythos TRADITIONAL GREEK €
(☎2310 540 284; Katouni 5; mains €6-12) Popular with locals, this excellent taverna with friendly staff serves up delicious standards, interesting regional specialities, good wines by the glass and beers on tap.

O Arhontis FOOD STAND €
(☎2310 280 202; Ermou 26; mains €5; ⊙11am-5pm) Eat delicious grilled sausages and potatoes off butcher's paper at this popular working-class eatery in Modiano market.

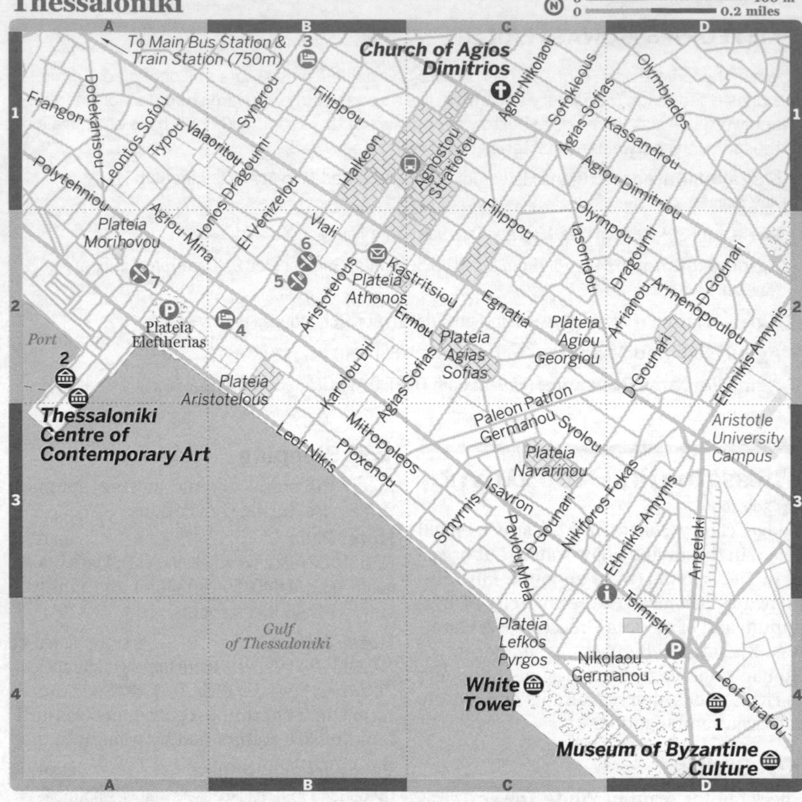

Thessaloniki

Top Sights

Church of Agios Dimitrios C1
Museum of Byzantine Culture D4
Thessaloniki Centre of Contemporary Art A2
White Tower C4

Sights

1 Archaeological Museum D4
2 Museum of Photography A2

Sleeping

3 Hotel Pella.......................................B1
4 Hotel Tourist....................................B2

Eating

5 Modiano Market...............................B2
6 O Arhontis..B2
7 Zythos A2

Information

Office of Tourism Directorate (☎2310 221 100; tour-the@otenet.gr; Tsimiski 136; ⏰8am-8pm Mon-Fri, to 2pm Sat)

Getting There & Away

AIR **Makedonia Airport** (SKG; ☎2310 473 212) is 16km southeast of the centre and served by local bus 78 (€0.60, one hour, from 5am to 10pm). Taxis cost €15 (20 minutes).

BOAT Weekly ferries go to, among others, Limnos (€25, eight hours), Lesvos (€36, 14 hours) and Chios (€37, 19 hours).

BUS The **main bus station** (☎23105 95408; Monastiriou 319) services Athens (€35, 6¼ hours, 10 daily), Ioannina (€28.50, 4¾ hours, six daily) and other destinations.

OSE (☎2310 599 100; Aristotelous 26) runs buses to Sofia (€22, seven hours, two to four times daily) and Tirana (€31, eight hours, twice daily). Buses from the small **KTEL-Asprovalta**

WORTH A TRIP

MT OLYMPUS ΟΛΥΜΠΟΣ ΟΡΟΣ

Just as it did for the ancients, Greece's highest mountain, the cloud-covered lair of the Greek pantheon, fires the visitor's imagination today. The highest of Olympus' eight peaks is Mytikas (2917m), popular with hikers, who use **Litohoro** (elevation 305m), 5km inland from the Athens–Thessaloniki highway, as their base. The main route up takes two days, with a stay overnight at one of the **refuges** (May-Oct). Good protective clothing is essential, even in summer. **EOS** (Greek Alpine Club; 23520 84544; Plateia Kentriki; 9.30am-12.30pm & 6-8pm Mon-Sat Jun-Sep) has information on treks.

The romantic guest house **Xenonas Papanikolaou** (23520 81236; xenpap@otenet.gr; Nikolaou Episkopou Kitrous 1; s/d €45/50;) sits in a flowery garden up in the backstreets, a world away from the tourist crowds.

Olympos Beach Camping (23520 22111; www.olympos-beach.gr; Plaka Litohorou; campsites per adult/tent €7/6, bungalows €45; Apr-Oct) has a funky waterfront lounge and a pleasant beach.

From the **bus station** (23520 81271) 13 buses daily go to Thessaloniki (€8, 1¼ hours) and three to Athens (€28, 5½ hours). Litohoro's **train station**, 9km away, gets 10 daily trains on the Athens–Volos–Thessaloniki line.

station (2310 536 260; Irinis 17) service İstanbul (€45, 9½ hours, two daily).

TRAIN The **train station** (2310 599 421; Monastiriou) services Athens (regular/IC €28/36, 6¾/5½ hours, Seven/10 daily), Alexandroupolis (€13.60, six hours, three daily) and beyond. International trains from Athens (to Belgrade, Sofia, İstanbul etc) stop at Thessaloniki. Get schedules from the **train ticket office** (OSE; 2310 598 120; Aristotelous 18) or the station.

Ioannina Ιωαννινα

POP 61,700

Charming Ioannina (ih-o-*ah*-nih-nah), on the western shore of Lake Pamvotis at the foot of the Pindos Mountains, was a major intellectual centre during Ottoman rule. Today it's a thriving university town with a lively waterfront cafe scene.

Get information at the **EOT** (Greek National Tourism Organisation; 26510 41142; Dodonis 39; 7.30am-2.30pm Mon-Fri) or **EOS** (Greek Alpine Club; 26510 22138; Despotatou Ipirou 2; 7-9pm Mon-Fri).

The narrow stone streets of the evocative **old quarter** (the Kastro) sit on a small peninsula jutting into the lake. Within its impressive fortifications, **Its Kale**, an inner citadel with lovely grounds and lake views, is home to the splendid **Fetiye Cami** (Victory Mosque), built in 1611, and the gemlike **Byzantine Museum** (26510 25989; admission €3; 8am-5pm Tue-Sun).

Filyra (26510 83560; www.hotelfilyra.gr; alley off Andronikou Paleologou 18; r €65;) in the old quarter has five popular self-catering suites that fill up fast. **Limnopoula Camping** (26510 25265; Kanari 10; campsites per tent/adult €4/8; Apr-Oct) is tree-lined and splendidly set on the edge of the lake 2km northwest of town.

From Ioannina there are daily flights to Athens. Slow buses ply the 2km road from the airport into town.

The **bus station** (26510 26286; Georgiou Papandreou) is 300m north of Plateia Dimokratias. Buses service Athens (€35.20, 6½ hours, nine daily), Igoumenitsa (€8.80, 1¼ hours, eight daily), Thessaloniki (€28.50, 4¾ hours, six daily) and Trikala (€13.10, 2¼ hours, two daily).

Zagorohoria & Vikos Gorge Τα Ζαγοροχωρια & Χαραδρα Του Βικου

Do not miss the spectacular Zagori region, with its deep gorges, abundant wildlife, dense forests and snowcapped mountains. Some 46 charming villages, famous for their grey-slate architecture and known collectively as the Zagorohoria, are sprinkled across a large expanse of the Pindos Mountains north of Ioannina. Paved roads wind between these beautifully restored gems, once only connected by stone paths and arching footbridges. Get information on walks from Ioannina's EOT and EOS offices. Book ahead during high season (Christmas, Greek Easter and August); prices plummet in low season.

CYCLADIC CONNECTIONS

For planning purposes, it's worth noting that once the tourist season kicks in, **Hellenic Seaways** (www.hsw.gr) runs daily catamarans up and down the Cyclades, starting from both Piraeus (for Athens) and Iraklio on Crete.

One boat heads south daily from Piraeus to Paros, Naxos, Ios and Santorini, returning along the same route. There's also a daily run from Piraeus to Syros, Tinos and Mykonos.

Heading north from Iraklio (Crete), another catamaran runs to Santorini, Ios, Paros and Mykonos, returning along the same route.

Tiny, carless **Dilofo** makes a peaceful sojourn. Delightful **Monodendri**, known for its special pitta bread, is a popular departure point for hikes through dramatic 12km-long, 900m-deep **Vikos Gorge**, with its sheer limestone walls. Get cosy at quaint **Archontiko Zarkada** (26530 71305; www.monodendri.com; s/d incl breakfast €40/60), one of Greece's best-value small hotels.

There are exquisite inns with attached tavernas in remote (but popular) twin villages **Megalo Papingo** and **Mikro Papingo**. Visit the **WWF's Information Centre** (Mikro Papingo; 10.30am-6pm Fri-Wed) to learn about the area.

In Megalo Papingo, simple **Lakis** (26530 41087; d incl breakfast €65) is a good-value *domatia* (place to stay), taverna and store.

Infrequent buses run from Dilofo (€3.50, three weekly), Monodendri (€3.10, one hour, twice weekly) and the Papingos (€5, two hours, three weekly) to Ioannina.

Igoumenitsa Ηγουμενιτσα

POP 9110

Though tucked beneath verdant hills and lying on the sea, this characterless west-coast port is little more than a ferry hub: keep moving.

If you must stay over, look for *domatia* signs or have a '70s flashback at **Hotel Oscar** (26650 23338; Ag Apostolon 149; s/d €30/40;), across from the Corfu ticket booths.

The **bus station** (26650 22309; Kyprou 29) services Ioannina (€8.20, 2½ hours, nine daily) and Athens (€33, eight hours, five daily).

Several companies operate hourly **ferries to Corfu** (26650 99460; person/car €7/33) between 5am and 10pm, taking 1½ hours, and hydrofoils in summer. International ferries go to the Italian ports of Ancona, Bari, Brindisi and Venice. Ticket agencies line the port.

CYCLADES ΚΥΚΛΑΔΕΣ

The Cyclades (kih-*klah*-dez) are Greek islands to dream about. Named after the rough *kyklos* (circle) they form around the island of Delos, they are rugged outcrops of rock in the azure Aegean Sea, speckled with white cubist buildings and blue-domed Byzantine churches. Throw in sun-blasted golden beaches, more than a dash of hedonism and a fascinating culture, and it's easy to see why many find the Cyclades irresistible.

Mykonos Μυκονοσ

POP 9700

Sophisticated Mykonos glitters happily under the Aegean sun, shamelessly surviving on tourism. The island has something for everyone, with marvellous beaches, romantic sunsets, chic boutiques, excellent restaurants and bars, and its long-held reputation as a mecca for gay travellers.

Sights & Activities

A stroll around **Hora (Mykonos Town)**, shuffling through snaking streets with blinding white walls and balconies of flowers, is a must for any visitor. **Little Venice**, where the sea laps up to the edge of the restaurants and bars, and Mykonos' famous hilltop row of **windmills** should be included in the spots-to-see list. You're bound to run into one of Mykonos' famous resident pelicans on your walk.

The island's most popular beaches are on the southern coast. **Platys Gialos** has wall-to-wall sun lounges, while nudity is not uncommon at **Paradise Beach**, **Super Paradise Beach**, **Agrari Beach** and gay-friendly **Elia Beach**.

Sleeping

Mykonos has two camping areas, both on the south coast. Minibuses from both meet the ferries and buses go regularly into town.

Hotel Lefteris HOTEL **€€**
(22890 27117; www.lefterishotel.gr; 9 Apollonas, Mykonos Town; s/d €95/120, studios €220-260;) Tucked away just up from Taxi Sq, Lefteris

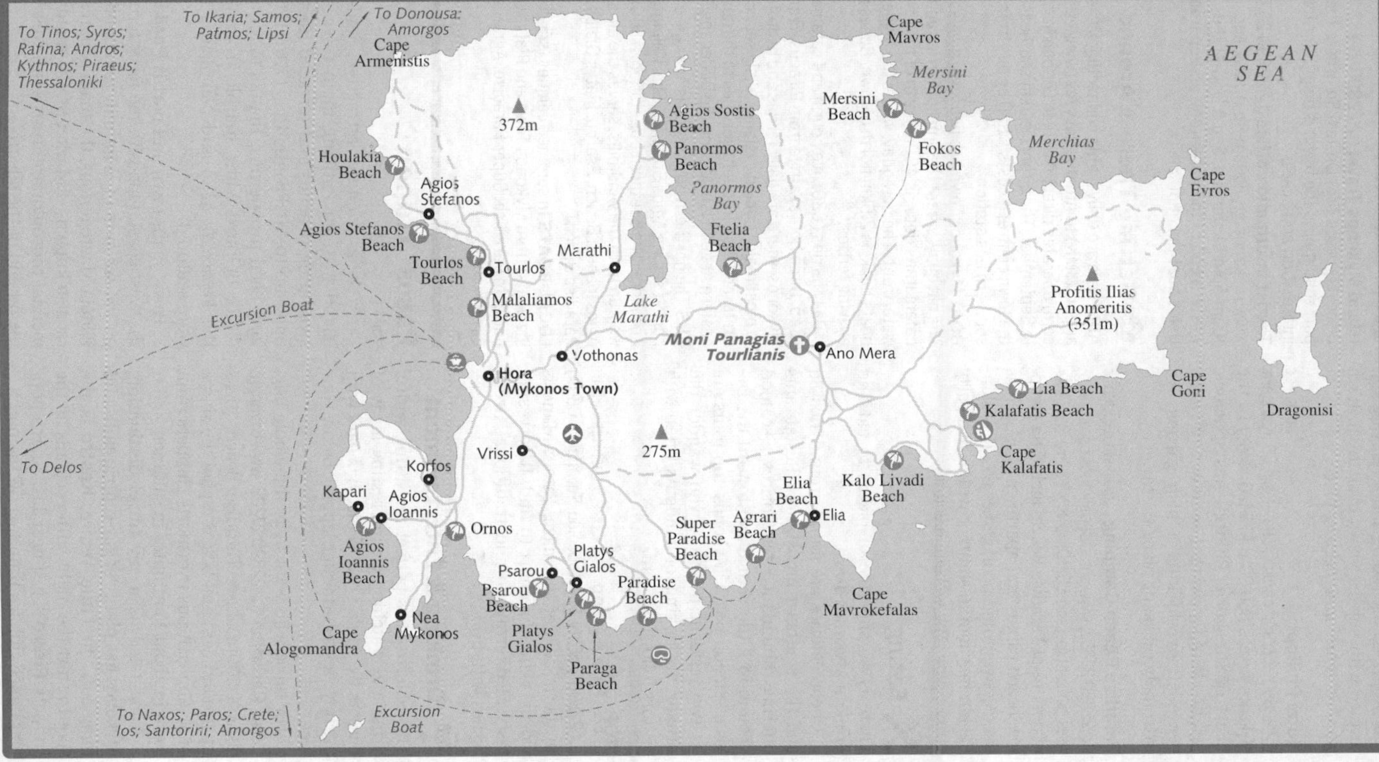
Mykonos
0 5 km
0 3 miles
To Tinos; Syros; Rafina; Andros; Kythnos; Piraeus; Thessaloniki
To Ikaria; Samos; Patmos; Lipsi
To Donousa; Amorgos
Cape Armenistis
Cape Mavros
AEGEAN SEA
Mersini Bay
Mersini Beach
Fokos Beach
Merchias Bay
Cape Evros
372m
Agios Sostis Beach
Panormos Beach
Panormos Bay
Houlakia Beach
Agios Stefanos
Agios Stefanos Beach
Tourlos Beach
Tourlos
Marathi
Ftelia Beach
Malaliamos Beach
Lake Marathi
Excursion Boat
Profitis Ilias Anomeritis (351m)
Moni Panagias Tourlianis
Ano Mera
Vothonas
Hora (Mykonos Town)
Lia Beach
Kalafatis Beach
Cape Gori
Dragonisi
To Delos
Vrissi
275m
Cape Kalafatis
Korfos
Kalo Livadi Beach
Kapari
Agios Ioannis
Elia Beach
Elia
Ornos
Super Paradise Beach
Agrari Beach
Agios Ioannis Beach
Platys Gialos
Psarou
Psarou Beach
Paradise Beach
Cape Mavrokefalas
Nea Mykonos
Cape Alogomandra
Platys Gialos
Paraga Beach
To Naxos; Paros; Crete; Ios; Santorini; Amorgos
Excursion Boat

has bright, comfy rooms and a relaxing sun terrace with superb views over town. It's a good international meeting place.

Hotel Philippi HOTEL €€
(☎22890 22294; chriko@otenet.gr; 25 Kalogera, Mykonos Town; s €60-90, d €75-120; ❄️📶) In the heart of the *hora*, Philippi has spacious, bright, clean rooms that open onto a railed verandah overlooking a lush garden. An extremely pleasant place to stay.

Paradise Beach Camping CAMPING GROUND €
(☎22890 22852; www.paradisemykonos.com; campsites per tent/person €5/10; @🏊) There are lots of options at Paradise Beach, including camping, beach cabins and apartments, as well as bars, a swimming pool, games etc. It is skin-to-skin mayhem in summer with a real party atmosphere. The website has it all.

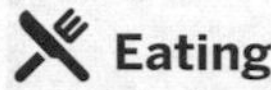

Eating

There is no shortage of places to eat and drink in Mykonos Town.

Cheap eateries are found around Taxi Sq and the southern bus station. Restaurants offering abundant (but pricey) seafood abound in Little Venice and toward the Delos excursion boats. Mykonos' top touts are its two resident pelicans, who wander the restaurants looking for handouts, often with visitors following them.

TOP CHOICE **Fato a Mano** MEDITERRANEAN
(☎22890 26256; Meletopoulou Sq; mains €8-15) In the middle of the maze, Fato a Mano is worth taking the effort to find. It serves up tasty Mediterranean and traditional Greek dishes with pride.

Drinking & Entertainment

The waterfront is perfect for sitting with a drink and watching an interesting array of passers-by, while Little Venice has bars with dreamy views and water lapping below your feet.

For those who want to go the whole hog, **Cavo Paradiso** (☎22890 27205; www.cavoparadiso.gr), 300m above Paradise Beach, picks up around 2am and boasts a pool the shape of Mykonos. A bus transports clubbers from town in about 15 minutes in summer.

Long feted as a gay travel destination, Mykonos has plenty of gay-centric clubs and hang-outs. In Little Venice, **Kastro** is the spot to start the night with cocktails as the sun sets. **Pierro's**, just near Taxi Sq, is a popular dance club for rounding off the night.

Information

Island Mykonos Travel (☎22890 22232; www.discovergreece.org) On Taxi Sq, where the port road meets the town; is helpful for travel information and tickets.

Tourist information office (☎22890 25250; www.mykonos.gr; ⌚9am-9pm Jul & Aug, 10am-5pm Easter-Jun, Sep & Oct) At the western end of the waterfront, just up from the Delos boat ticket office.

Getting There & Around

AIR There are daily flights connecting Mykonos airport (JMK) to Athens. **EasyJet** (www.easyjet.com) operates direct flights to London from May to September. The airport is 3km southeast of the town centre; it costs €1.50 by bus from the southern bus station.

BOAT Mykonos Town has two ferry quays. The old quay, where the smaller ferries and catamarans dock, is 400m north of the town waterfront. The new quay, where the bigger boats dock, is 2.5km north of town. Buses meet arriving ferries.

Daily ferries (€30, five hours) and catamarans (€45, three hours) arrive from Piraeus. From Mykonos, there are daily ferries and hydrofoils to most major Cycladic islands, daily services to Crete, and less-frequent services to the northeastern Aegean Islands and the Dodecanese.

BUS The northern bus station is near the old port. It serves Agios Stefanos, Elia, Kalafatis and Ano Mera. The southern bus station, a 300m walk up from the windmills, serves the airport, Agios Ioannis Beach, Psarou, Platys Gialos and Paradise Beach.

LOCAL BOATS In summer, caiques (small fishing boats) from Mykonos Town and Platys Gialos putter to Paradise, Super Paradise, Agrari and Elia Beaches.

Paros Παροσ

POP 13,000

Paros is a friendly, attractive, laid-back island with an enticing main town, good swimming beaches and terraced hills that build up to Mt Profitis Ilias (770m). It has long been prosperous, thanks to an abundance of pure white marble from which the *Venus de Milo* and Napoleon's tomb were sculpted.

Paros' main town and port is **Parikia**, on the west coast. Opposite the ferry terminal, on the far side of Windmill roundabout, is Plateia Mavrogenous, the main square. Agora, also known as Market St, the main commercial thoroughfare, runs southwest from the far end of the square.

WORTH A TRIP

DELOS ΔΗΛΟΣ

About 6km southwest of Mykonos, the island of **Delos** (22890 22259; sites & museum €5; 9am-3pm Tue-Sun) is the Cyclades' archaeological jewel. The opportunity to clamber among the ruins shouldn't be missed.

According to mythology, Delos was the birthplace of Apollo – the god of light, poetry, music, healing and prophecy. The island flourished as an important religious and commercial centre from the 3rd millennium BC, reaching its apex of power in the 5th century BC.

The climb up **Mt Kynthos** (113m), the island's highest point, is a highlight.

Overnighting on Delos is forbidden. Boats run from Mykonos to Delos (€15 return – not including entrance fee, 30 minutes) between 9am and 1pm. The return boats leave Delos between noon and 3pm.

Sights & Activities

Panagia Ekatontapyliani (22840 21243; 7.30am-9.30pm), known for its beautiful ornate interior, is one of the most impressive churches in the Cyclades, dating from AD 326. Within the church compound, the **Byzantine Museum** (admission €1.50; 9.30am-2pm & 6-9pm) has an interesting collection of icons and other artefacts.

A great option on Paros is to rent a scooter or car at one of the many outlets in Parikia and cruise around the island. There are sealed roads the whole way, and the opportunity to explore villages such as **Naoussa**, **Marpissa** and **Aliki**, and swim at beaches such as **Logaras**, **Punda** and **Golden Beach**.

Sleeping

Rooms Mike ROOMS €
(22840 22856; www.roomsmike.com; s/d/tr €35/45/60) A popular and friendly place, Mike's offers a good location and local advice. There are options of rooms with shared facilities through to fully self-contained units with kitchens. Mike's sign is easy to spot from the quay, away to the left.

Rooms Rena ROOMS €
(22840 22220; www.cycladesnet.gr/rena; Epitropakis; s/d/tr €35/45/60;) The quiet and well-kept rooms here are excellent value. Turn left from the pier then right at the ancient cemetery and follow the signs.

Koula Camping CAMPING GROUND €
(22840 22801; www.campingkoula.gr; campsites per tent/person €4/8; Apr-Oct;) A pleasant, shaded spot behind the beach at the north end of the waterfront.

Eating & Drinking

Budget eating spots are easy to find near Windmill roundabout in Parikia. Head along the waterfront to the west of the ferry quay to find a line-up of restaurants and drinking establishments that gaze out at the setting sun. There are also a number of good eating and drinking options along Market St, which more or less parallels the waterfront.

TOP CHOICE **Ephessus** GREEK
(22840 22520; mains €6-12) On the road back behind Rooms Mike; serves tasty Greek cuisine and has a top reputation with locals.

Information

For information online, visit www.parosweb.com.

Santorineos Travel (22840 24245; bookings@santorineos-travel.gr) On the waterfront near Windmill roundabout; good for ticketing and information.

Getting There & Around

AIR Paros' airport (PAS) has daily connections with Athens. The airport is 8km south of Parikia; it costs €1.50 by bus.

BOAT Parikia is a major ferry hub with daily connections to Piraeus (€30, five hours) and frequent ferries and catamarans to Naxos, Ios, Santorini, Mykonos and Crete. The Dodecanese and the northeastern Aegean Islands are also well serviced from here.

BUS From Parikia there are frequent bus services around the entire island.

Naxos Ναξοσ

POP 18,200

The largest of the Cyclades islands, Naxos could probably survive without tourism –

unlike many of its neighbouring islands. Green and fertile, Naxos produces olives, grapes, figs, citrus fruits, corn and potatoes. **Naxos Town**, on the west coast, is the island's capital and port. The island is well worth taking the time to explore, with its fascinating main town, excellent beaches and striking interior.

Sights & Activities

Behind the waterfront in Naxos Town, narrow alleyways scramble up to the spectacular 13th-century hilltop **kastro**, where the Venetian Catholics lived. The *kastro* looks out over the town and has a well-stocked **archaeological museum** (☎22850 22725; admission €3; ⏰8.30am-3pm Tue-Sun).

The beach of **Agios Georgios** is a 10-minute walk south from the main waterfront. Beyond it, wonderful sandy beaches stretch as far south as **Pyrgaki Beach**. **Agia Anna Beach**, 6km from town, and **Plaka Beach** are lined with accommodation and packed in summer.

A hire car or scooter will help reveal Naxos' dramatic landscape. The **Tragaea region** has tranquil villages, churches atop rocky crags, and huge olive groves. **Filoti**, the largest inland settlement, perches on the slopes of **Mt Zeus** (1004m), the highest peak in the Cyclades. The historic village of **Halki**, one-time centre of Naxian commerce, is well worth a visit.

Sleeping

TOP CHOICE **Pension Sofi** (☎22850 23077; www.pensionsofi.gr; r €30-75; ❄) and **Studios Panos** (☎22850 26078; www.studiospanos.com; Agios Georgios Beach; r €30-60; ❄) are both run by members of the friendly Koufopoulos family. Sofi is in town, while Panos is a 10-minute walk away near Agios Georgios Beach. Prepare yourself to be showered with affection. Guests are met with a glass of family-made wine and rooms are immaculate with bathroom and kitchen. Highly recommended; rates at both places halve out of the high season. Call ahead for a pick-up at the port. Sofi is open year-round; Panos opens from April to October.

On Agia Anna Beach to the south of town, **Camping Maragas** (☎22850 42552; www.maragascamping.gr; campsites €9, d/studio €45/70) has all sorts of options, including camping, rooms and studios, and there is a restaurant and minimarket on site.

Eating & Drinking

Naxos Town's waterfront is lined with eating and drinking establishments. Head into Market St in the Old Town, just down from the ferry quay, to find quality tavernas, such as **Metaximas** (☎22850 26425), serving seafood at its best at reasonable prices.

South of the waterfront, but only a few minutes' walk away, Main Sq is home to plenty of excellent eateries including superlative Tex-Mex at **Picasso Mexican Bistro** (☎22850 25408; mains €5-12).

Information

For information online, visit www.naxos-greece.net.

Naxos Tourist Information Centre (NTIC; ☎22850 25201; ⏰8am-midnight) A privately owned organisation just opposite the port; offers help with accommodation, tours, luggage storage and laundry.

Zas Travel (☎22850 23330; www.zas-travel-naxos.gr; ⏰8am-midnight) Sells ferry tickets opposite the port.

Getting There & Around

AIR Naxos airport (JNX) has daily connections with Athens. The airport is 3km south of town; a taxi costs €15. No buses run out there.

BOAT There are daily ferries (€30, five hours) and catamarans (€45, 3¾ hours) from Naxos to Piraeus, and good ferry and hydrofoil connections to most Cycladic islands and Crete. There are also ferries to Rhodes (€32, 14 hours, twice weekly). The ferry quay is at the northern end of the waterfront, with the bus terminal out front.

BUS Buses travel to most villages regularly from the terminal in front of the port.

Ios Ιος

POP 1900

Ios has long held a reputation as 'Party Island'. There are wall-to-wall bars and nightclubs in 'the village' (Hora) that thump all night, and fantastic fun facilities at Milopotas Beach that entertain all day. You won't leave disappointed if you're there to party.

But there's more to Ios than just hedonistic activities. British poet and novelist Lawrence Durrell thought highly of Ios as a place of poetry and beauty, and there is an enduring claim that Homer was buried on Ios, with his alleged tomb in the north of the island.

Ios' three population centres are close together on the west coast. Ormos is the port, where ferries arrive. Two kilometres inland

and up overlooking the port is Hora, while 2km down from Hora to the southeast is Milopotas Beach.

Sights & Activities

The village has an intrinsic charm with its labyrinth of white-walled streets, and it's very easy to get lost, even if you haven't had one too many.

Milopotas has everything a resort beach could ask for and parties hard. Isolated **Manganari Beach** on the south coast is a beautiful spot, and the drive on Ios' newest sealed road is an experience in itself. More and more roads are being upgraded on the island, and a rental car or scooter is becoming a good option for exploring. **Homer's Tomb** is 12km north of Hora.

A new attraction is **Skarkos** ('The Snail'; admission free; 8.30am-3pm Tue-Sun), an award-winning archaeological triumph for Ios. This Bronze Age settlement crowns a low hill in the plain just to the north of Hora and has had its excavations opened to the public.

Sleeping

TOP CHOICE **Francesco's** ROOMS €
(22860 91223; www.francescos.net; Hora; dm/s/d €15/40/50;) A lively meeting place in the village with superlative views from its terrace bar, legendary Francesco's is convenient for party-going and rates halve out of the high season. The party spirit rules here, especially in the 'giant Jacuzzi'.

Far Out Camping & Beach Club CAMPING GROUND €
(22860 91468; www.faroutclub.com; Milopotas; campsites per person €12, bungalows €10-20, studios €90;) Right on Milopotas Beach, this place has tons of options. Facilities include camping, bungalows and hotel rooms, and its pools are open to the public. Details are on the website. It also has rental cars, quad bikes and scooters.

Eating & Drinking

There are numerous places to get cheap eats such as gyros in the village. Down at Milopotas Beach there's a great bakery and stacks of options for during the day. The restaurants in the village are of a very high standard for later.

Another option is to head down to the port where the taverna serve superb seafood. The port may be filled with visitors in the day, but it's the locals who head there in the evening.

At night, the compact little village erupts with bars. A perennial favourite is **Blue Note** (22860 92271), where happy hour continues all night long!

Information

For information online, visit www.iosgreece.com.

Acteon Travel (22860 91343; www.acteon.gr) Has offices in Ormos, the village and Milopotas, and is helpful.

Getting There & Around

BOAT Ios has daily ferry connections with Piraeus (€31.50, seven hours), and being strategically placed between Mykonos and Santorini there are frequent catamarans and ferries to the major Cycladic islands and Crete.

BUS There are buses every 15 minutes between the port, the village and Milopotas Beach until early morning. Buses head to Manganari Beach in summer (€3 each way).

Santorini (Thira) Σαντορινη (Θηρα)

POP 13,500

Stunning Santorini is unique and should not be missed. The startling sight of the submerged caldera almost encircled by sheer lava-layered cliffs – topped by clifftop towns that look like a dusting of icing sugar – will grab your attention and not let it go. If you turn up in the high season though, be prepared for relentless crowds and commercialism because Santorini survives on tourism.

Fira, the main town, perches on top of the caldera, with the new port of Athinios, where most ferries dock, 10km south by road. The old port of Fira Skala, used by cruise ships and excursion boats, is directly below Fira and accessed by cable car (€4 one way), donkey (€5, up only) or foot (588 steps).

Sights & Activities

FIRA

The stunning caldera views from Fira are unparalleled.

The exceptional **Museum of Prehistoric Thira** (22860 23217; admission €3; 8.30am-8pm Tue-Sun) is two blocks south of the main square. **Megaron Gyzi Museum** (22860 22244; admission €3.50; 10.30am-1pm & 5-8pm Mon-Sat, 10.30am-4.30pm Sun), behind the Catholic cathedral, houses local memorabilia, including photographs of Fira before and after the 1956 earthquake.

AROUND THE ISLAND

At the north of the island, the intriguing village of **Oia** (ee-ah), famed for its postcard sunsets, is less hectic than Fira and a must-visit. Its caldera-facing tavernas are superb spots for brunch. There's a path from Fira to Oia along the top of the caldera that takes three to four hours to walk.

Santorini's black-sand beaches of **Perissa** and **Kamari** sizzle – beach mats are essential.

Of the surrounding islets, only **Thirasia** is inhabited. Visitors can clamber around on volcanic lava on **Nea Kameni** then swim into warm springs in the sea at **Palia Kameni**; there are various boat excursions available to get you there.

Santorini is home to an increasing number of excellent wineries.

TOP CHOICE **Santo Wines** (☎22860 22596; www.santowines.gr; Pyrgos) is a great spot to try the delectable Assyrtico crisp dry white wine while savouring unbelievable views.

Sleeping

Hotel Keti HOTEL €€

(☎22860 22324; www.hotelketi.gr; Agiou Mina, Fira; d/tr €95/120; ❄@) Overlooking the caldera, with views to die for, Hotel Keti has tradi-

Santorini (Thira)

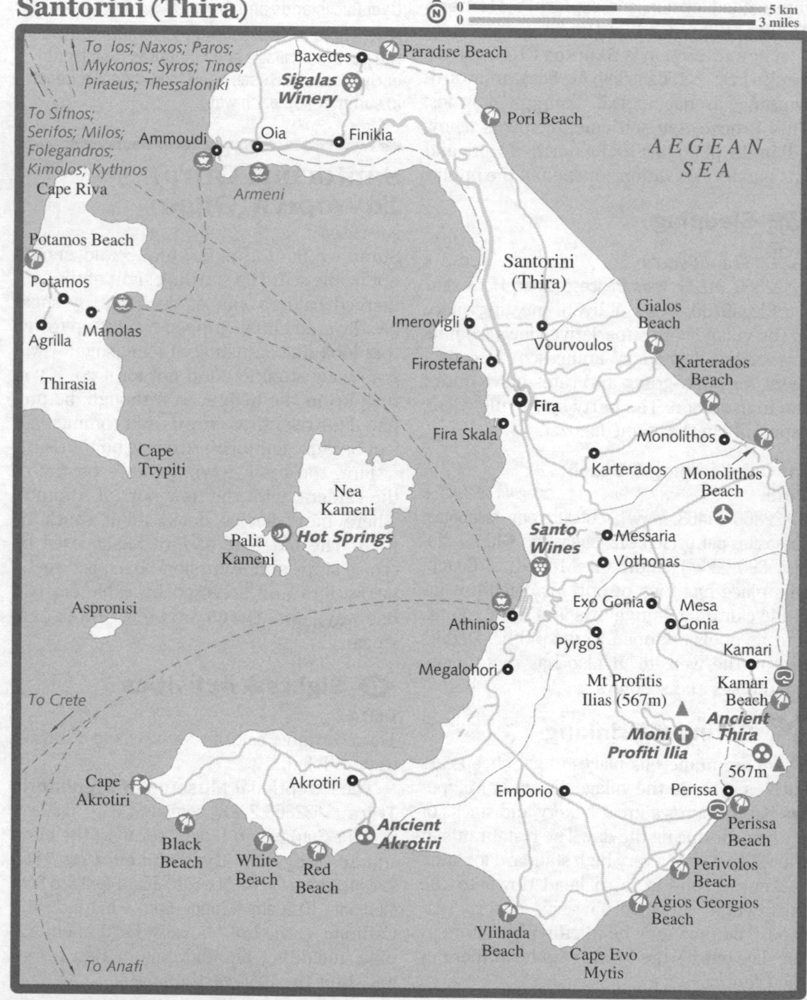

SANTORINI'S BIG BANGS

Santorini's violent volcanic past is visible everywhere, and through the centuries eruptions have regularly changed the shape of the island.

First inhabited around 3000 BC, the island was circular and known as Strongili (Round One). About 1650 BC a massive volcanic explosion – speculated to be the biggest such explosion in recorded history – caused the centre of the island to sink, producing a caldera that the sea quickly filled in. The explosion generated a huge tsunami that is widely believed to have caused the demise of Crete's powerful Minoan culture.

The islet of Palia Kameni appeared in the caldera in 197 BC, while an eruption created the islet of Nea Kameni in 1707. In 1956 a savage earthquake measuring 7.8 on the Richter scale killed scores of people and destroyed most of the houses in Fira and Oia.

One thing is for certain – it isn't over yet. Minor tremors are fairly common. Santorini is incomparable when it comes to a sense of impermanence and precariousness.

tional rooms carved into the cliffs. Some rooms have Jacuzzis. Head down just before Hotel Atlantis and follow the signs.

Pension Petros PENSION €
(☎22860 22573; www.hotelpetros-santorini.gr; Fira; s/d/tr €60/70/85; ❄) Three hundred metres east of the main square, Pension Petros offers decent rooms at good rates, free airport and port transfers, but no caldera views. It's a good budget option, with rates halving outside the high season. The friendly family also has other hotels.

Santorini Camping CAMPING GROUND €
(☎22860 22944; www.santorini camping.gr; Fira; campsites per person €9; @≋) This place, 500m east of Fira's main square, is the cheapest option. There is a restaurant, bar, minimarket and swimming pool, but no caldera views.

Eating & Drinking

Cheap eateries are in abundance around the square in Fira. Prices tend to double at restaurants with caldera views, so don't choose a place to eat solely by the outlook.

Many of the more popular bars and clubs are clustered along Erythrou Stavrou in Fira. Others look out over the caldera; you're often paying for the view, so don't glaze over too early.

Many diners head out to Oia, legendary for its superb sunsets, timing their meal with the setting sun. Good-value tavernas line the waterfronts at the beach resorts of Kamari and Perissa.

Information

For information online, visit www.santorini.net.

Dakoutros Travel (☎22860 22958; www.dakoutrostravel.gr; ⊙8.30am-10pm) Opposite the taxi station in Fira; extremely helpful and good for ticketing.

Getting There & Around

AIR Santorini airport (JTR) has daily connections with Athens, plus seasonal scheduled flights with Iraklio (Crete) and Rhodes. There are also direct flights from Europe; **easyJet** (www.easyjet.com) has flights from London during summer. The airport is 5km southeast

SANTORINI ON A BUDGET

Spectacular Santorini will take your breath away, and if you're on a tight budget, its prices might too. Expect to pay through the nose for caldera views at accommodation and eating establishments in and around Fira.

A budget alternative with the added bonus of a stunning black-sand beach is to head out to Perissa, on the southeast coast, and stay at **Stelios Place** (☎22860 81860; www.steliosplace.com; r €30-80; ❄≋). Stelios is an excellent option one block back from the beach. There's a refreshing pool, very friendly service, and free port and airport transfers. Rates halve out of the high season.

All needs are catered for in Perissa, with bars and restaurants lining the waterfront. **Taverna Lava** (☎22860 81776), at the southern end of the waterfront, is an islandwide favourite with a mouth-watering menu. Head back into the kitchen, see what Yiannis has conjured up for the day, and pick what looks good.

Public buses run regularly into Fira.

of Fira; there are frequent buses (€1.50) and taxis (€12).

BOAT There are daily ferries (€33.50, nine hours) and fast boats (€47, 5¼ hours) to Piraeus; daily connections in summer to Mykonos, Ios, Naxos, Paros and Iraklio (Crete); and ferries to the smaller islands in the Cyclades. Large ferries use Athinios port, where they are met by buses (€2) and taxis.

BUS Buses go frequently to Oia, Kamari, Perissa and Akrotiri from Fira.

CRETE ΚΡΗΤΗ

POP 540,000

Crete is Greece's largest and most southerly island and its size and distance from the rest of Greece gives it the feel of a different country. With its dramatic landscape and unique cultural identity, Crete is a delight to explore.

While Crete's proud, friendly and hospitable people have enthusiastically embraced tourism, they continue to fiercely protect their traditions and culture – and it is the people that remain a major part of the island's appeal.

Cretan Adventures (www.cretanadventures.gr) offers hiking, climbing, canyoning, caving, and even ski touring.

Iraklio Ηρακλειο

POP 131,000

Iraklio (ee-*rah*-klee-oh; often spelt Heraklion), Crete's capital, is a bustling modern city and the fifth-largest in Greece. It has a lively city centre and an excellent archaeological museum, and is close to Knossos, Crete's major visitor attraction.

Iraklio's harbours face north into the Sea of Crete. The old harbour is instantly recognisable as it is protected by the old Venetian fortress. The new harbour is 400m east. Plateia Venizelou, known for its Lion Fountain, is the heart of the city, 400m south of the old harbour up 25 Avgoustou.

Sights

Archaeological Museum MUSEUM

(☎28102 79000; Xanthoudidou 2; adult/student €6/3; ⌚8am-1pm Mon, 8am-8pm Tue-Sun) Iraklio's archaeological museum has an outstanding Minoan collection, second only to that of the national museum in Athens. The museum was under long-term reconstruction at the time of research.

Koules Venetian Fortress FORTRESS

(admission €2; ⌚9am-6pm Tue-Sun) Protecting the old harbour is this impressive fortress, also known as Rocca al Mare, which, like the

Crete

city walls, was built by the Venetians in the 16th century.

FREE **Battle of Crete Museum** MUSEUM
(☎28103 46554; cnr Doukos Beaufort & Hatzidaki; ⏰8am-3pm) This museum chronicles the historic WWII battle with photographs, letters, uniforms and weapons.

Sleeping

Hotel Mirabello HOTEL €
(☎28102 85052; www.mirabello-hotel.gr; Theotokopoulou 20; s/d €35/45; @❄) A pleasant, relaxed budget hotel on a quiet street in the centre of town, this place is run by an ex-sea captain who has travelled the world. A good-value option. Check out the excellent website.

Rent Rooms Hellas ROOMS €
(☎28102 88851; Handakos 24; dm/d/tr without bathroom €12/30/42) A popular budget choice, this place has a lively atmosphere, packed dorms, a rooftop bar and a bargain breakfast (from €3).

Eating & Drinking

There's a congregation of cheap eateries, bars and cafes in the Plateia Venizelou and El Greco Park area. The places around the park are packed at night.

A bustling, colourful market runs all the way along 1866 with a number of reasonably priced tavernas. **Giakoumis Taverna** (☎28102 80277; mains €5-12) is one of the best, offering up Cretan specialties hot off the grill.

Head down towards the old harbour for plenty of seafood options.

Information

For information online, visit www.heraklion-city.gr.

KTEL (www.ktel.org) Runs the buses on Crete; has useful tourist information inside Bus Station A.

Skoutelis Travel (☎28102 80808; www.skoutelis.gr; 25 Avgoustou 20) Between Plateia Venizelou and the old harbour; handles airline and ferry bookings, and rents cars.

Tourist office (☎28102 46299; Xanthoudidou 1; ⏰8.30am-8.30pm Apr-Oct, to 3pm Nov-Mar) Opposite the archaeological museum.

Getting There & Around

AIR There are many flights daily from Iraklio's Nikos Kazantzakis airport (HER) to Athens and, in summer, regular flights to Thessaloniki and Rhodes. **EasyJet** (www.easyjet.com) has scheduled flights to seven destinations across Europe. Summer sees charter flights from all over. The airport is 5km east of town. Bus 1 travels between

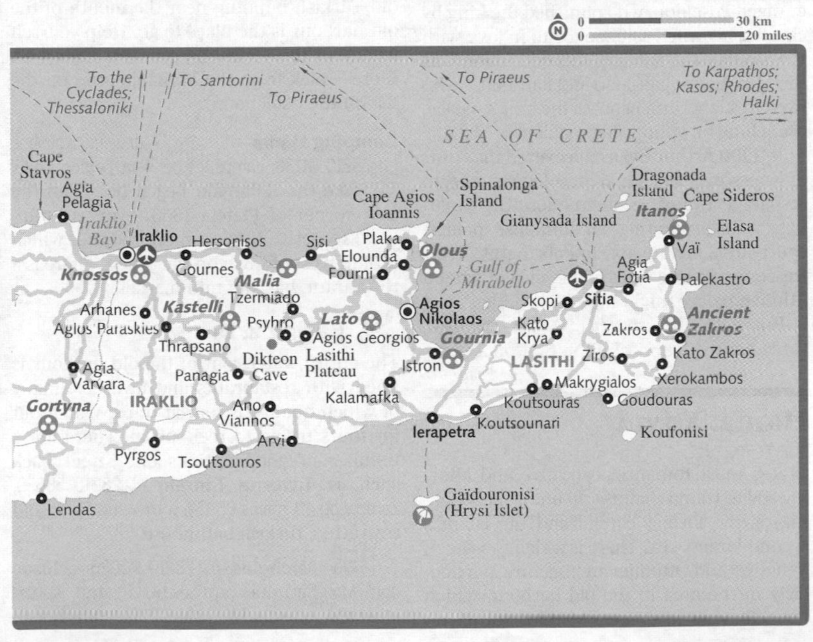

the airport and city centre (€1.20) every 15 minutes from 6am to 1am.

BOAT Daily ferries service Piraeus (€37, seven hours), and catamarans head daily to Santorini and continue on to other Cycladic islands. Twice weekly, ferries sail east to Rhodes (€28, 12 hours) via the Cretan towns of Agios Nikolaos and Sitia, and the islands of Kassos, Karpathos and Halki.

BUS Iraklio has two bus stations. Bus Station A, the main one, is just inland from the new harbour and serves eastern Crete (Agios Nikolaos, Ierapetra, Sitia, Malia and the Lasithi Plateau), as well as Hania and Rethymno.

Bus Station B, 50m beyond the Hania Gate, serves the southern route (Phaestos, Matala and Anogia).

Check out www.ktel.org for long-distance bus information.

Knossos Κνωσσοσ

Five kilometres south of Iraklio, **Knossos** (☎28102 31940; admission €6; ⏲8am-7pm Jun-Oct, to 3pm Nov-May) was the capital of Minoan Crete, and is now the island's major tourist attraction.

Knossos (k-nos-*os*) is the most famous of Crete's Minoan sites and is the inspiration for the myth of the Minotaur. According to legend, King Minos of Knossos was given a magnificent white bull to sacrifice to the god Poseidon, but decided to keep it. This enraged Poseidon, who punished the king by causing his wife Pasiphae to fall in love with the animal. The result of this odd union was the Minotaur – half-man and half-bull – who lived in a labyrinth beneath the king's palace, munching on youths and maidens.

In 1900 Arthur Evans uncovered the ruins of Knossos. Although archaeologists tend to disparage Evans' reconstruction, the buildings – incorporating an immense palace, courtyards, private apartments, baths, lively frescos and more – give a fine idea of what a Minoan palace might have looked like.

Buses to Knossos (€1.30, 20 minutes, three hourly) leave from Bus Station A.

Hania Χανια

POP 53,500

Crete's most romantic, evocative and alluring town, Hania (hahn-*yah;* often spelt Chania) is the former capital and the island's second-largest city. There is a rich mosaic of Venetian and Ottoman architecture, particularly in the area of the old harbour, which lures tourists in droves. Modern Hania retains the exoticism of a city caught between East and West. Hania is an excellent base for exploring nearby idyllic beaches and a spectacular mountainous interior.

Hania's bus station is on Kydonias, two blocks southwest of Plateia 1866, one of the city's main squares. From Plateia 1866, the old harbour is a short walk down Halidon.

Sights

Old Harbour SEA WALL

A stroll around the old harbour is a must for any visitor to Hania. It is worth the 1.5km walk around the sea wall to get to the Venetian **lighthouse** at the entrance to the harbour.

Archaeological Museum MUSEUM

(☎28210 90334; Halidon 30; admission €2; ⏲8.30am-3pm Tue-Sun) The archaeological museum is in a 16th-century Venetian church that the Turks made into a mosque. The building became a movie theatre in 1913 and then was a munitions depot for the Germans during WWII.

Sleeping

TOP CHOICE **Pension Lena** PENSION €

(☎28210 86860; www.lenachania.gr; Ritsou 5; s/d €35/55; ❄) For some real character in where you stay, Lena's *pension* (guest house) in an old Turkish building near the mouth of the old harbour is the place to go. Help yourself to one of the appealing rooms if Lena isn't there – pick from the available ones on the list on the blackboard.

Camping Hania CAMPING GROUND €

(☎28210 31138; campsites per tent/person €4/5; 🏊) Take the Kalamaki Beach bus from the east corner of Plateia 1866 (every 15 minutes) to get to this camping ground, which is 3km west of town on the beach. There is a restaurant, bar and minimarket.

Eating & Drinking

The entire waterfront of the old harbour is lined with restaurants and tavernas, many of which qualify as tourist traps. Watch out for touts trying to reel you in. There are a number of good options one street back such as **Taverna Tamam** (☎28210 58639; Zambeliou 49; mains €5-15), a taverna in an old converted Turkish bathhouse.

TOP CHOICE **Michelas** (☎28210 90026; ⏲10am-4pm Mon-Sat) has authentic Cretan specialities at reasonable prices. This family-run place uses only Cretan ingredients and cooks up a great selection each day that you can peruse, then choose from. Hania's covered **food market**, in a massive cross-shaped building, is worth an inspection and throws up some good eating options.

Café Kriti LIVE MUSIC
(Kalergon 22; 8pm-late) Near the eastern end of the Venetian harbour, is known for its down-to-earth atmosphere and live traditional Cretan music.

Information

For information online, visit www.chania.gr.

Tellus Travel (28210 91500; www.tellustravel.gr; Halidon 108; 8am-11pm)
Schedules and ticketing; rents out cars.

Tourist information office (28210 36155; Kydonias 29; 8am-2.30pm)
Under the Town Hall; is helpful and provides practical information and maps.

Getting There & Away

AIR There are several flights a day between Hania airport (CHQ) and Athens and five flights a week to Thessaloniki. An increasing number of budget airlines are flying directly into Hania; **easyJet** (www.easyjet.com) has flights from London. The airport is 14km east of town on the Akrotiri Peninsula. Taxis to town cost €15; there are few buses.

BOAT Daily ferries sail between Piraeus (€30, nine hours) and the port of Souda, 9km south-east of Hania. There are also increasing numbers of faster boats. Frequent buses (€1.30) and taxis (€10) connect town and Souda.

BUS Frequent buses run along Crete's northern coast to Iraklio (€11, 2¾ hours, half-hourly), Rethymno (€6, one hour, half-hourly) and Kissamos (€4, one hour, 14 daily); buses run less frequently to Paleohora (€6.50, 1¾ hours, four daily), Omalos (€5.90, one hour, three daily) and Hora Sfakion (€6.50, 1½ hours, three daily) from the main bus station on Kydonias.

Samaria Gorge
Φαραγγι Τησ Σαμαριασ

The **Samaria Gorge** (28250 67179; admission €5; 6am-3pm May–mid-Oct) is one of Europe's most spectacular gorges and a superb hike. Hikers should take rugged footwear, food, drinks and sun protection for this strenuous five- to six-hour trek.

You can do the walk as part of an excursion tour, or do it independently by taking the Omalos bus from the main bus station in Hania (€5.90, one hour) to the head of the gorge at Xyloskalo (1230m) at 7.30am, 8.30am and 2pm. It's a 16.7km walk out (all downhill) to Agia Roumeli on the coast, from where you take a boat to Hora Sfakion (€8, 1¼ hours, three daily) and then a bus back to Hania (€6.50, 1½ hours, three daily). You are not allowed to spend the night in the gorge, so you need to complete the walk in a day.

The walk is extremely popular and can get quite crowded, especially in summer. Most walkers have given the gorge a day and are on a rushed trip from Hania and other northern-coast cities. If you've got a bit of time on your hands and decide to do things on your own, there are a couple of excellent options.

One is to take the 2pm bus from Hania and spend the night in the Cretan mountains at 1200m above sea level in **Omalos** (population 30) at the very pleasant **Neos Omalos Hotel** (28210 67269; www.neos-omalos.gr; s/d €20/30). The hotel's restaurant serves excellent Cretan cuisine, local wine by the litre (€6), and they will shuttle you to the start of the gorge track the next morning.

Another option is to leave from Hania in the morning, but let the sprinters go and take your time hiking through this stupendous gorge. When you hit the coast at **Agia Roumeli** (population 125), down a cool beer, take a dip in the refreshing Libyan Sea, savour the tasty Cretan specials at **Faragi Restaurant & Rooms** (28250 91225; mains €4-10; s/d/tr €20/30/35) and stay the night in the tidy rooms above the restaurant. The next day you can take a ferry either west to Sougia or Paleohora, or east to Loutro or Hora Sfakion.

DODECANESE
ΔΩΔΕΚΑΝΗΣΑ

Strung out along the coast of western Turkey, the 12 main islands of the Dodecanese (*dodeca* means twelve) have suffered a turbulent past of invasions and occupations that has endowed them with a fascinating diversity. While Rhodes and Kos, with ease of access, attract throngs of visitors, islands such as Symi, Karpathos and Patmos are well worth the effort to get to.

Rhodes Ροδοσ

POP 98,000

Rhodes (Rodos in Greek) is the largest island in the Dodecanese. According to mythology, the sun god Helios chose Rhodes as his bride and bestowed light, warmth and vegetation upon her. The blessing seems to have paid off, for Rhodes produces more flowers and sunny days than most Greek islands.

Sights & Activities

RHODES TOWN

Rhodes' capital is Rhodes Town (population 56,000), on the northern tip of the island. Its **Old Town**, the largest inhabited medieval town in Europe, is enclosed within massive walls and is a joy to explore. To the north is **New Town**, the commercial centre.

The main port, **Commercial Harbour**, is east of the Old Town, and is where the big interisland ferries dock. Northwest of here is **Mandraki Harbour**, lined with excursion boats and smaller ferries, hydrofoils and catamarans.

AROUND THE ISLAND

The **Acropolis of Lindos** (22440 31258; admission €6; 8.30am-6pm Tue-Sun), 47km from Rhodes Town, is an ancient city spectacularly perched atop a 116m-high rocky outcrop. Below is the town of **Lindos**, a tangle of streets with elaborately decorated 17th-century houses.

The extensive ruins of **Kamiros** (admission €4; 8am-5pm Tue-Sun), an ancient Doric city on the west coast, are well preserved, with the remains of houses, baths, a cemetery and a temple.

Sleeping

Mango Rooms ROOMS €
(22410 24877; www.mango.gr; Plateia Dorieos 3, Old Town; s/d/tr €40/50/60;) A good-value, friendly one-stop shop near the back of the Old Town, Mango has a restaurant, a bar and an internet cafe down below, six well-kept rooms above, and a sun terrace on top.

Hotel International HOTEL €
(22410 24595; diethnes@otenet.gr; 12 Kazouli St, New Town; s/d/tr €45/60/75) In New Town, the International is a friendly family-run operation with immaculately clean and good-value rooms only a few minutes from Rhodes' main town beach. It's a 10-minute stroll to the Old Town, and prices drop by a third out of the high season.

Eating & Drinking

There is food and drink every way you look in Rhodes Town.

Outside the city walls, there are a lot of cheap places in the New Market, at the southern end of Mandraki Harbour. Head further north into New Town for countless restaurants and bars catering to northern European sun worshippers in Rhodes for a good time.

Inside the walls, the Old Town has it all in terms of touts and overpriced tavernas trying to separate less savvy tourists from their euros. The back alleys tend to throw up better quality eateries and prices. Delve into the maze and see what you can come up with.

DON'T MISS

RHODES' OLD TOWN

A wander around Rhodes' World Heritage–listed Old Town is a must. It is reputedly the world's finest surviving example of medieval fortification, with 12m-thick walls. Throngs of visitors pack its busier streets, and eating, sleeping and shopping options abound.

The Knights of St John (see p592) lived in the Knights' Quarter in the northern end of the Old Town.

The cobbled **Odos Ippoton** (Ave of the Knights) is lined with magnificent medieval buildings, the most imposing of which is the **Palace of the Grand Masters** (22410 23359; admission €6; 8.30am-3pm Tue-Sun), which was restored, but never used, as a holiday home for Mussolini.

The 15th-century Knight's Hospital now houses the **archaeological museum** (22410 27657; Plateia Mousiou; admission €3; 8am-4pm Tue-Sun). The splendid building was restored by the Italians and has an impressive collection that includes the ethereal marble statue *Aphrodite of Rhodes*.

The pink-domed **Mosque of Süleyman**, at the top of Sokratous, was built in 1522 to commemorate the Ottoman victory against the knights, then rebuilt in 1808.

You can take a pleasant walk around the imposing walls of the Old Town via the wide and pedestrianised moat walk.

SPLURGE

In a 15th-century building in the Turkish quarter of the Old Town, **Marco Polo Mansion** (☎22410 25562; www.marcopolomansion.gr; Agiou Fanouriou 40, Old Town; d €90-150) is a boutique hotel that's rich in Ottoman-era colours and features in glossy European magazines. Take a look at the rooms online. Attached is the **Marco Polo Café**, one of our top restaurants for Greece. Owner Efi is as tastefully colourful as her mansion and garden restaurant.

Information

For information online, visit www.rodos.gr.

EOT (Greek National Tourism Organisation; ☎22410 35226; cnr Makariou & Papagou, Rhodes Town; ⊙8am-2.45pm Mon-Fri) Has brochures, maps and *Rodos News*, a free English-language newspaper.

Triton Holidays (☎22410 21690; www.tritondmc.gr; Plastira 9, Mandraki, Rhodes Town) In New Town, this place is exceptionally helpful, handling accommodation bookings, ticketing and rental cars. The island-hopping experts, Triton can provide up-to-date advice in these times of constantly changing flight and boat schedules. Email ahead for advice.

Getting There & Away

AIR There are daily flights between Rhodes' Diagoras airport (RHO) and Athens, plus less regular flights to Karpathos, Kassos, Kastellorizo, Thessaloniki, Iraklio (Crete) and Samos. Options are growing. International charter flights swarm in summer, plus budget airlines such as **easyJet** (www.easyjet.com) arrive with scheduled flights.

The airport is on the west coast, 16km southwest of Rhodes Town (25 minutes and €2.20 by bus).

BOAT Rhodes is the main port of the Dodecanese and there is a complex array of departures. There are daily ferries from Rhodes to Piraeus (€53, 13 hours). Most sail via the Dodecanese north of Rhodes, but at least twice a week there is a service via Karpathos, Crete and the Cyclades.

In summer, catamaran services run up and down the Dodecanese daily from Rhodes to Symi, Kos, Kalymnos, Nisyros, Tilos, Patmos and Leros.

There are boats between Rhodes and Marmaris in Turkey (one way/return including port taxes €51/75, 50 minutes). Check www.marmarisinfo.com for up-to-date details.

Getting Around

Rhodes Town has two bus stations a block apart next to the New Market. The **west-side bus station** serves the airport, Kamiros (€4.60, 55 minutes) and the west coast. The **east-side bus station** serves the east coast, Lindos (€4.70, 1½ hours) and the inland's southern villages.

Kos Κωσ

POP 17,900

Captivating Kos, only 5km from the Turkish peninsula of Bodrum, is popular with history buffs as the birthplace of Hippocrates (460–377 BC), the father of medicine. The island also attracts an entirely different crowd – sun-worshipping beach lovers from northern Europe who flock in on charter flights during summer.

Kos Town is based around a circular harbour, protected by the imposing Castle of the Knights, at the eastern end of the island. The ferry quay is north of the castle. Akti Koundourioti is the main drag around the harbourfront.

Sights & Activities

In Kos Town, the focus of the **archaeological museum** (☎22420 28326; Plateia Eleftherias; admission €3; ⊙8am-2.30pm Tue-Sun) is sculpture from excavations around the island.

The **ancient agora**, with the ruins of the **Shrine of Aphrodite** and **Temple of Hercules**, is just off Plateia Eleftherias. North of the agora is the **Hippocrates Plane Tree**, under which the man himself is said to have taught his pupils.

The **Castle of the Knights** (☎22420 27927; admission €4; ⊙8am-2.30pm Tue-Sun), built in the 14th century, protected the knights from the encroaching Ottomans, and was originally separated from town by a moat. That moat is now Finikon, a major street. Entrance to the castle is over the stone bridge behind the Hippocrates tree.

On a pine-clad hill, 4km southwest of Kos Town, stand the extensive ruins of the renowned healing centre of **Asklipieion** (☎22420 28763; adult/student €4/3; ⊙8am-7.30pm Tue-Sun), where Hippocrates practised medicine. Groups of doctors come from all over the world to visit.

THE KNIGHTS OF ST JOHN

Do some island-hopping in the Dodecanese and you'll quickly realise that the Knights of St John left behind a whole lot of castles.

Originally formed as the Knights Hospitaller in Jerusalem in 1080 to provide care for poor and sick pilgrims, the knights relocated to Rhodes (via Cyprus) after the loss of Jerusalem in the First Crusade. In Rhodes, they ousted the ruling Genoese in 1309, built a stack of castles to protect their new home, then set about irking the neighbours by committing acts of piracy against Ottoman shipping. Sultan Süleyman the Magnificent, not a man you'd want to irk, took offence and set about dislodging the knights from their strongholds. Rhodes capitulated in 1523 and the remaining knights relocated to Malta. They set up there as the Sovereign Military Hospitaller of Jerusalem, of Rhodes and of Malta.

If the history is all too much, wander around past the northern end of the harbour to the town **beach**.

Kos Town has recently developed a number of bicycle paths, and renting a bike from one of the many places along the waterfront is a great option for getting around town and seeing the sights.

Sleeping

TOP CHOICE Hotel Afendoulis HOTEL €
(☎22420 25321; www.afendoulishotel.com; Evripilou 1, Kos Town; s/d €35/50; ❄@) In a pleasant, quiet area about 500m south of the ferry quay, this well-kept hotel won't disappoint. Run by the charismatic English-speaking Alexis, it's a great place to relax and enjoy Kos. Port and bus-station transfers are complimentary, and you can get your laundry done here.

Pension Alexis PENSION €
(☎22420 28798; www.pensionalexis.com; Irodotou 9, Kos Town; s/d €25/35; ❄) This highly recommended place has long been a budget favourite with travellers. It has large rooms, some with shared facilities, and a relaxing verandah and garden. You'll get picked up at the port or bus station for free, and there are laundry facilities on site. It's back behind Dolphin roundabout.

Eating & Drinking

Restaurants line the central waterfront of the old harbour, but you might want to hit the backstreets for value. There are plenty of cheap places to eat on the beach to the north of the harbour, and a dozen discos and clubs around the streets of Diakon and Nafklirou, just north of the agora.

TOP CHOICE Stadium Restaurant SEAFOOD
(☎22420 27880; mains €9-16) On the long waterfront 500m southeast of the castle, this place serves succulent seafood at good prices, along with excellent views of Turkey.

Information

For information online, visit www.kosinfo.gr.

Exas Travel (☎22420 28545; www.exas.gr) Near the archaeological museum in the heart of town, to the southwest of the harbour; handles schedules, ticketing and excursions.

Municipal tourist office (☎22420 24460; www.kosinfo.gr; Vasileos Georgiou 1; ⏲8am-2.30pm & 3-10pm Mon-Fri, 9am-2pm Sat) On the waterfront directly south of the port; provides maps and accommodation information.

Getting There & Around

AIR There are daily flights to Athens from Kos' Ippokratis airport (KGS), which is 28km southwest of Kos Town. International charters wing in throughout the summer and **easyJet** (www.easyjet.com) operates scheduled flights from London. Get to/from the airport by bus (€4) or taxi (€25).

BOAT There are frequent ferries from Rhodes to Kos that continue on to Piraeus (€46, 10 hours), as well as ferries heading the opposite way. Daily fast-boat connections head north to Patmos and Samos, and south to Symi and Rhodes.

In summer boats depart daily for Bodrum in Turkey (€34 return, one hour).

BUS There is a good public bus system on Kos, with the bus station on Kleopatras, near the ruins at the back of town.

MINI-TRAIN Next to the tourist office is a blue mini-train for Asklipion (€5 return, hourly) and a green mini-train that does city tours (€4, 20 minutes).

NORTHEASTERN AEGEAN ISLANDS ΤΑ ΝΗΣΙΑ ΤΟΥ ΒΟΡΕΙΟ ΑΝΑΤΟΛΙΚΟ ΑΙΓΑΙΟΥ

These far-flung islands are strewn across the northeastern corner of the Aegean, closer to Turkey than mainland Greece. They harbour unspoilt scenery, welcoming locals and fascinating independent cultures, and remain relatively calm even when other Greek islands are sagging with tourists at the height of summer.

Samos σαμοσ

POP 32,800

A lush mountainous island only 3km from Turkey, Samos has a glorious history as the legendary birthplace of Hera, wife and sister of god-of-all-gods Zeus. Samos was an important centre of Hellenic culture, and the mathematician Pythagoras and storyteller Aesop are among its sons.

Samos has two main ports: Vathy (Samos Town) in the northeast and Pythagorio on the southeast coast. Buses between the two take 25 minutes.

Getting There & Around

AIR There are daily flights to Athens from Samos airport (SMI), 4km west of Pythagorio, plus less regular flights to Iraklio (Crete) and Thessaloniki. Charter flights wing in from Europe in summer.

BOAT A maritime hub, Samos offers daily ferries to Piraeus (€35, 13 hours), plus ferries heading northwest to Chios, west to the Cyclades and south to the Dodecanese. Catamarans head south to Patmos, Leros, Kalymnos and Kos.

There are daily ferries to Kuşadasi (for Ephesus) in Turkey (€35/45 one way/return plus €10 port taxes). Day excursions are also available from April to October. Check with **ITSA Travel** (22730 23605; www.Itsatravelsamos.gr) in Vathy for up-to-date details.

BUS You can get to most of the island's villages and beaches by bus.

VATHY (SAMOS) ΒΑΘΥ ΣΑΜΟΣ

POP 2030

Busy Vathy is an attractive working port town. Most of the action is along Themistokleous Sofouli, the main street that runs along the waterfront. The main square, Plateia Pythagorou, in the middle of the waterfront, is recognisable by its four palm trees and statue of a lion.

The rarely open and hard-to-find **tourist office** (22730 28582; Jun-Sep) is in a side street one block north of the main square. **ITSA Travel** (22730 23605; www.itsatravel.com), opposite the quay, is helpful with travel enquiries, excursions, accommodation and luggage storage. To get to Vathy's bus station, follow the waterfront south and turn left onto Lekati, 250m south of Plateia Pythagorou (just before the police station).

The **archaeological museum** (22730 27469; adult/student €3/2; 8.30am-3pm Tue-Sun), by the municipal gardens, is first rate. The highlight is a 5.5m *kouros* (statue).

TOP CHOICE **Pythagoras Hotel** (22730 28601; www.pythagoras-hotel.com; Kallistratou 12; s/d/tr €20/35/45; @) is a friendly, great-value place with a convivial atmosphere run by English-speaking Stelio. There is a restaurant serving tasty home-cooked meals, a bar, satellite TV and internet access on site. Facing inland, the hotel is 400m to the left of the quay. Call ahead for free pick-up on arrival.

PYTHAGORIO ΠΥΘΑΓΟΡΕΙΟ

POP 1300

Pretty Pythagorio, 25 minutes south of Vathy by bus, is where you'll disembark if you've come by boat from Patmos. It is a small, enticing town with a yacht-lined harbour and a holiday atmosphere.

The cordial **municipal tourist office** (22730 61389; deap5@otenet.gr; 8am-9.30pm) is two blocks from the waterfront on the main street, Lykourgou Logotheti. The bus stop is two blocks further inland on the same street, next to the post office.

The excellent **statue of Pythagoras** and his triangle, on the waterfront opposite the ferry quay, should have you recalling his theorem from your high-school maths days. If not, buy a T-shirt emblazoned with it to remind you.

Ireon (22730 95277; adult/student €4/3; 8.30am-3pm Tue-Sun), the legendary birthplace of the goddess Hera, is about 8km west of Pythagorio. The temple at this World Heritage site was enormous – four times the size of the Parthenon – though only one column remains.

Hotel Alexandra (22730 61429; Metamorfosis Sotiros 22; d €35), not far from the castle, is a friendly place with cosy rooms and an attractive garden.

Lesvos (Mytilini) Λεσβοσ (Μυτιληνη)

POP 93,500

Lesvos, or Mytilini as it is often called, tends to do things in a big way. The third-largest of the Greek Islands, Lesvos produces half the world's ouzo and is home to over 11 million olive trees.

Lesvos has always been a centre of philosophy and artistic achievement, and to this day is a spawning ground for innovative ideas in the arts and politics. An excellent source of information on the island is www.greeknet.com.

The two main towns on the island are the capital of Mytilini on the southeast coast, and attractive Mithymna on the north coast.

Getting There & Away

AIR Written up on flight schedules as Mytilene, Lesvos' Odysseas airport (MJT) has daily connections with Athens, plus flights to Thessaloniki and Iraklio (Crete). The airport is 8km south of Mytilini town; a taxi costs €8.

BOAT In summer there are daily boats to Piraeus (€30, 12 hours) via Chios, and three boats a week to Thessaloniki (€35, 13 hours).

There are four ferries a week to Turkey's Dikeli port (one-way/return €30/45), which serves Ayvalik.

MYTILINI ΜΥΤΙΛΗΝΗ

POP 27,300

The capital and main port, Mytilini is built between two harbours (north and south) with an imposing fortress on the promontory to the east. All ferries dock at the southern harbour, and most of the town's action is around this waterfront. With a large university campus, Mytilini is a lively place year round.

For information online, visit www.lesvos.net. The **tourist office** (☎22510 42512; 6 Aristarhou; ⌚9am-1pm Mon-Fri), 50m up Aristarhou inland from the quay, offers brochures and maps, but its opening hours are limited. On the waterfront, **Zoumboulis Tours** (☎22510 37755; Kountourioti 69) handles flights, boat schedules, ticketing and excursions to Turkey.

Mytilini's excellent neoclassical **archaeological museum** (8 Noemvriou; adult/child €3/2; ⌚8.30am-3pm) has a fascinating collection from Neolithic to Roman times.

A superb place for a stroll or a picnic is the pine forest surrounding Mytilini's impressive **fortress** (adult/student €2/1; ⌚8am-2.30pm Tue-Sun), which was built in early Byzantine times and enlarged by the Turks.

SAPPHO, LESBIANS & LESVOS

Sappho, one of Greece's great ancient poets, was born on Lesvos during the 7th century BC. Most of her work was devoted to love and desire, and the objects of her affection were often female. Because of this, Sappho's name and birthplace have come to be associated with female homosexuality.

These days, Lesvos is visited by many lesbians paying homage to Sappho. The whole island is very gay-friendly, in particular the southwestern beach resort of Skala Eresou, which is built over ancient Eresos, where Sappho was born. The village is well set up to cater to lesbian needs and has a 'Women Together' festival held annually in September. Check out www.sapphotravel.com for details.

There is an excellent statue of Sappho in the main square on the waterfront in Mytilini.

Pension Thalia (☎22510 24640; Kinikiou 1; s/d €25/30) has clean, bright rooms in a large house. It is about a five-minute walk north of the main square, up Ermou, the road that links the south and north harbours. Follow the signs from the corner of Ermou and Adramytiou.

On the waterfront, rooms at **Hotel Sappho** (☎22510 22888; Kountourioti 31; s/d/tr €45/60/70) are simple but clean. It's easy to find, and has the attraction of a 24-hour reception, as ferries into Mytilini tend to arrive at nasty hours.

Mytilini's top spots are a road or two back at the northern end of the harbour. Enjoy a cocktail while watching the mayhem on the waterfront at **Ocean Eleven Bar** (☎22510 27030; Kountourioti 17) before ducking back to **O Diavlos** (☎22510 22020; Ladadika 30) for the best in both local cuisine and art; paintings by local artists line the walls and can be purchased should you get the urge.

Mytilini has two bus stations. For local buses, head along the waterfront to the main square. For long-distance buses, walk 600m from the ferry along the waterfront to El Venizelou and turn right until you reach Agia Irinis park, which is next to the station. There are regular services in summer to Mithymna, Petra, Agiasos, Skala Eresou, Mantamados and Agia Paraskevi.

MITHYMNA ΜΗΘΥΜΝΑ

POP 1500

The gracious, preserved town of Mithymna (known by locals as Molyvos) is 62km north of Mytilini. Cobbled streets canopied by flowering vines wind up the hill below the impressive castle.

From the bus stop, walk straight ahead towards the town for 100m to the helpful **municipal tourist office** (22530 71347; www.mithymna.gr; 8am-9pm Mon-Fri, 9am-7pm Sat & Sun), which has good maps. Some 50m further on, the cobbled main thoroughfare of 17 Noemvriou heads up to the right. Going straight at this point will take you to the colourful fishing port.

The noble **Genoese castle** (admission €2; 8.30am-7pm Tue-Sun) perches above the town like a crown and affords tremendous views out to Turkey. Pebbly **Mithymna Beach** sits below the town and is good for swimming.

Eftalou hot springs (public/private bath per person €3.50/5; public bath 6-8am & 6-10pm, private bath 9am-6pm), 4km from town on the beach, is a superb bathhouse complex with a whitewashed dome and steaming, pebbled pool. There are also private baths where you don't need a bathing suit.

TOP CHOICE **Nassos Guest House** (22530 71432; www.nassosguesthouse.com; Arionis; d €20-35;), in an old Turkish house oozing with character, is an airy, friendly place with shared facilities and a communal kitchen. It's easy to spot as the only blue house below the castle.

Betty's Restaurant (22530 71421; Agora; mains €4-12) has superb home-style Greek food, views and atmosphere in a building that was once a notorious bordello.

Buses to Mithymna (€5) take 1¾ hours from Mytilini, though a rental car is a good option.

AROUND THE ISLAND

Southern Lesvos is dominated by **Mt Olympus** (968m) and the very pretty village of **Agiasos**, which has good artisan workshops making everything from handcrafted furniture to pottery.

Western Lesvos is known for its petrified forest, with petrified wood at least 500,000 years old, and for the gay-friendly town of Skala Eresou, the birthplace of Sappho (see p594).

SPORADES ΣΠΟΡΑΔΕΣ

Scattered to the southeast of the Pelion Peninsula, to which they were joined in prehistoric times, the 11 islands that make up the Sporades group have mountainous terrain and dense vegetation and are surrounded by scintillatingly clear seas. The most popular islands are Skiathos, Skopelos and Alonnisos.

The main ports for the Sporades are Volos and Agios Konstantinos on the mainland.

Skiathos Σκιαθοσ

POP 6150

Lush and green, Skiathos has a beach-resort feel about it. Charter flights bring loads of package tourists, but the island still oozes enjoyment. Skiathos Town and some excellent beaches are on the hospitable south coast, while the north coast is precipitous and less accessible.

Skiathos Town's main thoroughfare is Papadiamanti, named after the 19th-century novelist and short story writer Alexandros Papadiamanti, who was born here. It runs inland opposite the quay.

Sights & Activities

Skiathos has superb beaches, particularly on the south coast. **Koukounaries** is popular with families. A stroll over the headland, **Big Banana Beach** is stunning, but if you want an all-over tan, head a tad further to **Little Banana Beach**, where bathing suits are a rarity.

At the Old Port in Skiathos Town, there are all sorts of offerings in terms of boat excursions – trips to nearby beaches (€10), trips around Skiathos Island (€25), and full-day trips that take in Skopelos, Alonnisos and the marine park (€35).

Sleeping

Pension Pandora ROOMS €

(24270 24357, 69441 37377; www.skiathosinfo.com/accomm/pension-pandora.htm; r €30-70;) Run by the effervescent Georgina, this family-run place is 10 minutes' walk north of the quay. The spotless rooms have TV, kitchen and balcony. Georgina also has two exceptional apartments just off Papadiamanti.

Camping Koukounaries CAMPING GROUND €

(24270 49250; campsites per tent/person €4/10) This camping ground is at beautiful Koukounaries Beach at the southwestern end of the island, 30 minutes by bus from

ECOTOURISM ON THE RISE

In a country not noted for its ecological long-sightedness, locals (especially the fishermen) initially struggled with the idea of the **National Marine Park of Alonnisos** when it was established in 1992 to protect the highly endangered Mediterranean monk seal and to promote the recovery of fish stocks.

These days, though, the people of the Sporades have caught on to the advantages of having such a park on their doorstep. Ecotourism is on the rise, with daily excursions on licensed boats into the park from Skiathos, Skopelos and Alonnisos. Though your odds of seeing the shy monk seal aren't great – it's on the list of the 20 most endangered species worldwide – the chances of cruising among pods of dolphins (striped, bottlenose and common) are high.

town. There are good facilities, a minimarket and a taverna.

Eating & Drinking

Skiathos Town is brimming with eateries. There are seafood options around the old port, and some excellent places up the stairs from there behind the small church, including **Piccolo** (☎24270 22780; mains from €7), which does exquisite pizzas and pastas in a lovely setting, and **1901** (☎69485 26701; mains from €7), a superb fine-dining restaurant with a glowing reputation.

A popular drinking spot is **Kentavros** (☎24270 22980), just off Plateia Papadiamanti. Expect a mellow ambience and a mixture of rock, jazz and blues.

Information

For information online, visit www.skiathosinfo.com.

Heliotropio Travel (☎24270 22430; www.heliotropio.gr) Opposite the ferry quay; handles ticketing and rents cars and scooters.

Tourist information booth (☎24270 23172) At the port but opens irregularly.

Getting There & Around

AIR Along with numerous charter flights from northern Europe, in summer there is a daily flight from Athens to Skiathos. Skiathos airport (JSI) is 2km northeast of Skiathos Town.

BOAT There are frequent daily hydrofoils to and from the mainland ports of Volos (€30, 1¼ hours) and Agios Konstantinos (€33, two hours), as well as cheaper ferries. The hydrofoils head to and from Skopelos (€16, 35 minutes) and Alonnisos (€18, one hour). In summer there is a daily hydrofoil to Thessaloniki (€55, 3½ hours).

BUS Crowded buses ply the south-coast road between Skiathos Town and Koukounaries every 30 minutes between 7.30am and 11pm year round, stopping at all the beaches along the way. The bus stop is at the eastern end of the harbour.

IONIAN ISLANDS ΤΑ ΕΠΤΑΝΗΣΑ

The idyllic cypress- and fir-covered Ionian Islands stretch down the western coast of Greece from Corfu in the north to Kythira, off the southern tip of the Peloponnese. Mountainous, with dramatic cliff-backed beaches, soft light and turquoise water, they're more Italian in feel, offering a contrasting experience to other Greek islands. The most popular islands with visitors, heading north to south, are Corfu, Lefkada, Kefallonia and Zakynthos.

Corfu Κερκυρα

POP 122,700

Many consider Corfu, Kerkyra (*ker*-kihrah) in Greek, to be Greece's most beautiful island – the unfortunate consequence of which is that it's often overrun with crowds.

Getting There & Away

AIR **Ioannis Kapodistrias Airport** (CFU; ☎26610 30180) is 3km from Corfu Town and has flights daily to Athens and a few times weekly to Thessaloniki.

BOAT Ferries go to Igoumenitsa (€7, 1½ hours, hourly) and international ferries stop in Patra (€38, six hours).

BUS Daily buses to Athens (€49, 8½ hours) and Thessaloniki (€45, eight hours) leave from **Avrami long-distance bus station** (☎26610 28927; I Theotoki).

CORFU TOWN

POP 28,700

Built on a promontory and wedged between two fortresses, Corfu's Old Town is a tangle of narrow walking streets through gorgeous Venetian buildings. Explore the winding alleys and surprising plazas in the early morning or late afternoon to avoid the hordes of day trippers seeking souvenirs.

Sights

The **Palaio Frourio** (Old Fortress; ☎26610 48310; adult/concession €4/2; ⏱8.30am-7pm May-Oct, 8.30am-3pm Nov-Apr) stands on an eastern promontory; the **Neo Frourio** (New Fortress) lies to the northwest. The **archaeological museum** (☎26610 30680; Vraïla 5; admission €4; ⏱8.30am-3pm Tue-Sun) houses a collection of finds from Mycenaean to classical times. The richly decorated **Church of Agios Spiridon** (Agios Spiridonos) displays the remains of St Spiridon, paraded through town four times a year.

Sleeping

Accommodation prices fluctuate wildly depending on the season; book ahead.

Hotel Astron HOTEL **€€**
(☎26610 39505; hotel_astron@hol.gr; Donzelot 15, Old Port; s/d €65/70; ❄📶) Recently renovated and some with sea views; light-filled rooms are managed by friendly staff.

Hermes Hotel HOTEL **€**
(☎26610 39268; www.hermes-hotel.gr; Markora 12; s/d/tr €50/60/75; ❄) Completely refurbished, pleasant, well-appointed rooms in the New Town.

Eating

If you're after a bite, cafes and bars line the arcaded Liston.

To Dimarchio ITALIAN, GREEK **€€**
(☎26610 39031; Plateia Dimarchio; mains €8-25) Relax in a luxuriant rose garden on a charming square. Attentive staff serve elegant, inventive dishes, prepared with the freshest ingredients.

La Cucina ITALIAN, CORFIOT **€**
(☎26610 45029; Guilford 17; mains €10-15) Every detail is cared for at this intimate bistro, from the hand-rolled tortelloni to the inventive pizzas and mural-covered walls.

Getting Around

Blue buses (€0.90 to €1.30) for villages near Corfu Town leave from Plateia San Rocco. Services to other destinations leave from Avrami terminal. A taxi from the airport to the centre costs around €15.

AROUND THE ISLAND

The **Corfu Trail** (www.corfutrail.org) traverses the island north to south.

To gain an aerial view of the gorgeous cypress-backed bays around **Paleokastritsa**, the west coast's main resort, go to the quiet village of **Lakones**. Further south, good beaches surround tiny **Agios Gordios**. Backpackers head to low-key **Sunrock** (☎26610 94637; Pelekas Beach; dm/r per person €18/24; @❄) for its full-board hostel and genial atmosphere.

UNDERSTAND GREECE

History

With its strategic position at the crossroads of Europe and Asia, Greece has endured a long and turbulent history. During the Bronze Age (3000–1200 BC in Greece), the advanced Cycladic, Minoan and Mycenaean civilisations flourished. The Mycenaeans were swept aside in the 12th century BC by the warrior-like Dorians, who introduced Greece to the Iron Age. The next 400 years are often referred to as the Dark Ages, a period about which little is known.

By 800 BC, when Homer's *Odyssey* and *Iliad* were first written down, Greece was undergoing a cultural and military revival with the evolution of the city-states, the most powerful of which were Athens and Sparta. Greater Greece (Magna Graecia) was created, with southern Italy as an important component. The unified Greeks repelled the Persians twice, at Marathon (490 BC) and Salamis (480 BC). Victory over Persia was followed by unparalleled growth and prosperity known as the classical (or golden) age.

Pericles commissioned the Parthenon, Sophocles wrote *Oedipus the King* and Socrates taught young Athenians to think. The golden age ended with the Peloponnesian War (431–404 BC), when the militaristic Spartans defeated the Athenians. They failed to notice the expansion of Macedonia under King Philip II, who easily conquered the war-weary city-states.

Philip's ambitions were surpassed by those of his son, Alexander the Great, who marched triumphantly into Asia Minor, Egypt, Persia and what are now parts of Afghanistan and India. In 323 BC he met an untimely death at the age of 33, and his generals divided his empire between themselves.

Roman incursions into Greece began in 205 BC. By 146 BC Greece and Macedonia had become Roman provinces. After the subdivision of the Roman Empire into eastern and western empires in AD 395, Greece became part of the Eastern (Byzantine) Empire, based at Constantinople. In the centuries that followed, Venetians, Franks,

ORIGINAL OLYMPICS

The Olympic tradition emerged around the 11th century BC as a paean to the Greek gods in the form of contests attended initially by notable men – and women – who assembled before the sanctuary priests and swore to uphold solemn oaths. By the 8th century BC attendance had grown to a wide confederacy of city-states, and the festival morphed into a male-only major event lasting five days at the site of Olympia. A ceremonial truce was enforced for the duration of the games. Crowds of spectators lined the tracks, where competitors vied for victory in athletics, chariot races, wrestling and boxing. Three millennia later, while the scale and scope of the games may have expanded considerably, the basic format is essentially unchanged.

Normans, Slavs, Persians, Arabs and, finally, Turks took turns chipping away at the Byzantine Empire.

After the end of the Byzantine Empire in 1453, when Constantinople fell to the Turks, most of Greece became part of the Ottoman Empire. By the 19th century, though, the Ottoman Empire was in decline and the Greeks fought the War of Independence (1821–22). In January 1833, Otho of Bavaria was installed as king until 1862 when he was peacefully ousted and George I, a Danish prince, was chosen as king.

During WWI Greece was allied with France and Britain. Greece fell to Germany in 1941 and resistance movements, polarised into royalist and communist factions, staged a bloody civil war lasting until 1949. This was the trigger for a mass exodus that saw almost one million Greeks head off to places such as Australia, Canada and the USA.

An army coup d'état in 1967 led to a period of appalling brutality, repression and political incompetence. In 1974 the junta attempted to assassinate Cyprus' leader, Archbishop Makarios, prompting Turkey to occupy north Cyprus. The continued Turkish occupation of northern Cyprus remains one of the most contentious issues in Greek politics. The junta had little choice but to hand back power to the people. In 1974 Greece became a republic.

In 1981 Greece entered the European Community (now the EU) as its 10th, smallest and poorest member, and in 2002 adopted the euro; prices have been on the rise ever since. Greece hosted a successful Olympics in 2004 but is still counting the cost.

During the long hot summer of 2007, forest fires threatened Athens and caused untold damage.

Textbooks are being written on Greece's 2010 financial crisis. Simply put, Greece almost fell over from years of over-borrowing and over-spending. Financially crippled and looking likely to drag other failing euro-zone economies down with it, in May 2010 Greece was on the receiving end of a €110 billion bailout package to help right the ship. Time will tell if it stays afloat. Needless to say, austerity measures to help balance the budget were not popular, with citizens angry about cuts in spending, pensions and salaries, along with higher taxes.

People

Greece's population is over 11.1 million, with around one-third living in the greater Athens area and more than two-thirds living in cities – confirming that Greece is now a primarily urban society. Less than 15% live on the islands, the most populous being Crete, Evia and Corfu. Greece has an ageing population and a declining birth rate, with big families a thing of the past. Population growth over the last couple of decades is due to a flood of migrants, both legal and illegal.

About 95% of the Greek population belongs to the Greek Orthodox Church. The remainder are split between the Roman Catholic, Protestant, Evangelist, Jewish and Muslim faiths. While older Greeks and those in rural areas tend to be deeply religious, most young people are decidedly more secular.

The Greek year is centred on the saint's days and festivals of the church calendar. Name days (celebrating your namesake saint) are celebrated more than birthdays. Most people are named after a saint, as are boats, suburbs and train stations.

Orthodox Easter is usually at a different time than Easter celebrated by the Western churches, though it's generally in April/May.

Food & Drinks

This chapter uses the following price ranges for eating options (based on the cost of a main meal):

€€€ more than €40

€€ €15 to €40

€ less than €15

Snacks

Greece has a great range of fast-food options. Foremost among them are gyros and souvlaki. The gyros is a giant skewer laden with seasoned meat that grills slowly as it rotates, the meat being steadily trimmed from the outside. Souvlaki are small cubes of meat cooked on a skewer. Both are served wrapped in pitta bread with salad and lashings of tzatziki (a yoghurt, cucumber and garlic dip). Other snacks are pretzel rings, spanakopita (spinach and cheese pie) and *tyropitta* (cheese pie).

Greece is famous for its appetisers, known as *mezedes* (literally, 'tastes'; meze for short). Standards include tzatziki, *melitzanosalata* (aubergine/eggplant dip), taramasalata (fish-roe dip), dolmadhes (stuffed vine leaves), *fasolia* (beans) and *oktapodi* (octopus). A selection of three or four starters represents a good meal and makes an excellent vegetarian option.

Most Greek desserts are Turkish in origin and are variations on pastry soaked in honey, such as baklava (thin layers of pastry filled with honey and nuts). Delicious Greek yoghurt also makes a great dessert, especially with honey.

Main Dishes

You'll find moussaka (layers of aubergine and mince, topped with béchamel sauce and baked) on every menu, alongside a number of other taverna staples. They include *moschari* (oven-baked veal and potatoes), *keftedes* (meatballs), *stifado* (meat stew), *pastitsio* (baked dish of macaroni with minced meat and béchamel sauce) and *yemista* (either tomatoes or green peppers stuffed with minced meat and rice).

Kalamaria (fried squid) is the most popular (and cheapest) seafood, while *barbouni* (red mullet) and *sifias* (swordfish) tend to be more expensive than meat dishes.

Fortunately for vegetarians, salad is a mainstay of the Greek diet. The most popular is *horiatiki salata,* normally listed on English-language menus as Greek salad. It's a delicious mixed salad comprising cucumbers, red onions, olives, tomatoes and feta. For the full scoop on Greece's legendary feta cheese, check out www.feta.gr.

Drinks

Bottled mineral water is cheap and available everywhere, as are soft drinks and packaged juices.

Mythos, in its distinctive green bottle, and Alfa, are popular Greek beers.

Greece is traditionally a wine-drinking society. An increasingly good range of wines made from traditional grape varieties is available. Wine enthusiasts should take a look at www.allaboutgreekwine.com. Retsina, wine flavoured with pine-tree resin, is a tasty alternative – though an acquired taste for some.

Metaxa, Greece's dominant brandy, is sweet, while if you are offered some raki, make sure to take a small sip first!

'Greek' coffee should be tried at least once. Don't drink the mudlike grounds at the bottom!

Environment

Greece sits at the southern tip of the Balkan Peninsula. Of its 1400 islands, only 169 are inhabited. Around 80% of the land is mountainous, with less than a quarter of the country suitable for agriculture.

The country sits in one of the most seismically active regions in the world – at the meeting point of three continental plates: the Eurasian, African and Arabian. Consequently, Greece has had more than 20,000

THE ART OF OUZO

Ouzo is Greece's most famous but misunderstood tipple. For most Greeks, ouzo has come to embody a way of socialising – best enjoyed during a lazy, extended summer afternoon of seafood *mezedhes* (appetisers) by the beach. Ouzo is sipped slowly and ritually to clean the palate between tastes. It is served in small bottles or *karafakia* (carafes) with water and a bowl of ice cubes, and is commonly drunk on the rocks, diluted with water (it turns a cloudy white). Mixing it with cola is a foreign abomination!

Made from distilled grapes, ouzo is also distilled with residuals from fruit, grains and potatoes, and flavoured with spices, primarily aniseed, giving it that liquorice flavour. The best ouzo is produced on Lesvos, and there are more than 360 brands!

earthquakes in the last 40 years, most of them very minor.

Greece's most visited national parks are Mt Parnitha, north of Athens, and the Samaria Gorge on Crete. The others are Vikos-Aoös and Prespa National Parks in Epiros; Mt Olympus; and Parnassos and Iti National Parks in central Greece. There is also a national marine park off the coast of Alonnisos, and another around the Bay of Laganas area off Zakynthos.

Greece is belatedly becoming environmentally conscious but, regrettably, it's too late for some regions. Deforestation and soil erosion are problems that go back thousands of years, with olive cultivation and goats being the main culprits. Forest fires are also a major problem.

General environmental awareness remains at a depressingly low level, especially where litter is concerned.

SURVIVAL GUIDE

Directory A–Z

Accommodation

Greek accommodation is subject to strict price controls, and by law a notice must be displayed in every room stating the category of the room and the seasonal price.

Price ranges in this chapter are based on the cost of a double room in high season:

€€€ more than €150

€€ €60 to €150

€ less than €60

If you turn up in the shoulder seasons (May and June; September and October) expect to pay significantly less. During the low season (late October to late April) prices can be up to 50% cheaper, but a lot of places, especially on the islands, virtually close their shutters for winter. Websites will usually display these differences in price.

Camping grounds Generally open from April to October; standard facilities include hot showers, kitchens, restaurants and minimarkets – and often a swimming pool. For information, check out **Panhellenic Camping Association** (www.panhellenic-camping-union.gr).

Domatia Greek equivalent of a B&B, minus the breakfast. Don't worry about finding them – owners will find you as they greet ferries and buses, shouting 'room!'

Hostels Found in most major towns and on some islands; check out the **Greek Youth Hostel Organisation** (☎21075 19530; www.athens-yhostel.com).

Hotels Classified as deluxe, or A, B, C, D or E class; ratings seldom seem to have much bearing on the price, which is determined more by season and location.

Mountain refuges Listed in *Greece Mountain Refuges & Ski Centres,* available free of charge at EOT (Greek National Tourism Organisation) and EOS (Greek Alpine Club) offices.

Business Hours

Banks 8am-2.30pm Mon-Thu, 8am-2pm Fri; in cities also 3.30-6.30pm Mon-Fri, 8am-1.30pm Sat

Cafes 10am-midnight

Post offices 7.30am-2pm Mon-Fri; in cities 7.30am-8pm Mon-Fri, 7.30am-2pm Sat

Restaurants 11am-3pm & 7pm-1am (varies greatly)

Street kiosks (periptera) early-late Mon-Sun

Supermarkets 8am-8pm Mon-Fri, 8am-3pm Sat

Gay & Lesbian Travellers

The church plays a significant role in shaping society's views on issues such as sexuality. It is wise to be discreet and to avoid open displays of togetherness. That said, Greece is a popular destination for gay travellers.

HAPHAZARD OPENING HOURS

It's worth noting that for businesses associated with tourists, opening hours can be rather haphazard. In the high season when there are plenty of visitors around, restaurants, cafes, nightclubs and souvenir shops are pretty much open whenever they think they can do good business. If there are few people around, some businesses will simply close early or won't bother opening at all. And in the low season, some places, including some sleeping options, may close up for months at a time.

Athens has a busy gay scene that packs up and heads to the islands for summer. Mykonos has long been famous for its bars, beaches and hedonism. A visit to Eresos on Lesvos has become something of a pilgrimage for lesbians (see p594).

Holidays

New Year's Day 1 January

Epiphany 6 January

First Sunday in Lent February

Greek Independence Day 25 March

Good Friday/Easter Sunday April/May

May Day (Protomagia) 1 May

Feast of the Assumption 15 August

Ohi Day 28 October

Christmas Day 25 December

St Stephen's Day 26 December

Internet Access

Charges for internet access differ wildly (as does the speed of access). Some midrange and most top-end hotels offer some form of internet connection. Laptop-wielding visitors will often be able to connect to wi-fi at hotels and most internet cafes.

Language Courses

For intensive language courses check out the **Athens Centre** (www.athenscentre.gr).

Money

ATMs are everywhere except the smallest villages. Cash is king at street kiosks and small shops, especially in the countryside. Credit cards are generally accepted, but may not be on smaller islands or in small villages. Major currencies can be changed at banks, post offices and currency exchange offices all over the place.

While souvenir shops will generally bargain, prices in other shops are normally clearly marked and non-negotiable; accommodation is nearly always negotiable outside peak season, especially for longer stays. The service charge is included on the bill in restaurants, but it is the custom to 'round up the bill'; same for taxis.

Post

Tahydromia (post offices) are easily identified by the yellow sign outside. Regular post boxes are yellow; red post boxes are for express mail. The postal rate for postcards and airmail letters within the EU is €0.60; to other destinations it's €0.80.

KALIMERA!

Greece is one of those countries where a big smile and some local language can go a long way. If you make an effort, so will the locals. Try these basics on for size – they're likely to be all you'll need, and are best if they come with a smile:

- » ka-li-*me*-ra Good morning
- » *ya*-sas Hello
- » ef-ha-ri-*sto* Thank you
- » pa-ra-ka-*lo* Please/You're welcome
- » *ya*-mas Cheers!

Greece is also one of those countries where it pays not to get upset if things don't go your way. There's no point in getting angry with anyone if the ferry is late (or if it doesn't come at all!). You'll likely be met with a stony face and unhelpful service. Relax. You're in Greece!

Safe Travel

Crime is traditionally low in Greece, but it's on the rise. Watch out for bar scams and spiked drinks *(bombes)*. Be careful of pickpockets on the Athens metro, around Omonia and at the Monastiraki Flea Market.

Telephone

Telephone codes are part of the 10-digit number within Greece. The landline prefix is ☎2 and for mobiles it's ☎6.

The Greek telephone service is maintained by Organismos Tilepikoinonion Ellados, known as OTE (o-*teh*). Public phones are everywhere and all use OTE phonecards; pressing the 'i' button brings up the operating instructions in English. Phonecards are sold at OTE offices and street kiosks. Local calls cost €0.30 for three minutes. Discount-card schemes are available that offer much better value for money.

For directory enquiries within Greece, call ☎131 or ☎132; for international enquiries, call ☎161 or ☎162.

If you have a compatible GSM phone from a country with a global roaming agreement with Greece, you'll be able to use your phone there. There are several mobile service providers; **CosmOTE** (www.cosmote.gr)

has the best coverage. You can purchase a Greek SIM card for around €20.

Toilets

Public toilets are rare, except at airports and bus and train stations. Greek plumbing can't handle toilet paper! Anything larger than a postage stamp will cause a blockage. Put toilet paper, sanitary napkins and tampons in the small bin provided next to every toilet.

Tourist Information

The **Greek National Tourism Organisation** (GNTO; www.gnto.gr) is known as EOT within Greece. There are EOT offices or local tourist offices in almost every town of consequence and on many of the islands. In popular destinations, tourist police can also provide information; contact them if you think you've been ripped off.

Visas

Schengen rules apply. Visitors from most countries don't need a visa for Greece.

Getting There & Away

Air

Most visitors arrive by air, usually into Athens. There are 17 international airports in Greece, but most handle only summer charter flights to the islands. The major international airports are Eleftherios Venizelos Airport (ATH) in Athens, Nikos Kazantzakis Airprot (HER) in Iraklio, Diagoras Airport (RHO) in Rhodes and Macedonia Aiport (SKG) in Thessaloniki.

There's a growing number of scheduled services by budget airlines (eg easyJet flies into Athens, Corfu, Hania, Iraklio, Kos, Mykonos, Rhodes, Santorini, Thessaloniki and Zakynthos).

Greek airlines flying international routes:

Aegean Airlines (A3; www.aegeanair.com)

Olympic Air (OA; www.olympicair.com) Privatised version of former national carrier Olympic Airlines.

Land

BORDER CROSSINGS

You can drive or ride through the following border crossings:

From Albania Kakavia (the main one), 60km northwest of Ioannina; Sagiada, 28km north of Igoumenitsa; Mertziani, 17km west of Konitsa; and Krystallopigi, 14km west of Kotas.

From Bulgaria Promahonas, 109km northeast of Thessaloniki; Ormenio, in northeastern Thrace; and Exohi, 50km north of Drama.

From Macedonia Evzoni, 68km north of Thessaloniki; Niki, 16km north of Florina; and Doïrani, 31km north of Kilkis.

From Turkey Kipi, 43km east of Alexandroupolis; and Kastanies, 139km northeast of Alexandroupolis.

BUS

The **Hellenic Railways Organisation** (OSE; www.ose.gr) operates bus services to the following countries:

Albania An overnight bus between Athens and Tirana (16 hours, daily) via Ioannina and Gjirokastra.

Bulgaria From Athens to Sofia (15 hours, six weekly) and Thessaloniki to Sofia (7½ hours, four daily).

Turkey From Athens to İstanbul (22 hours, six weekly), stopping at Thessaloniki (seven hours) and Alexandroupolis (13 hours).

TRAIN

Trains service the following countries:

Bulgaria Daily between Sofia and Athens (18 hours) via Thessaloniki.

Macedonia Twice daily from Thessaloniki to Skopje (five hours).

Russia Summer-only direct weekly service from Thessaloniki to Moscow (70 hours).

Turkey Daily between İstanbul and Thessaloniki (12 hours).

Sea

Check out ferry routes, schedules and services at www.greekferries.gr.

ALBANIA

From Saranda, **Petrakis Lines** (☎26610 38690; www.ionian-cruises.com) has daily hydrofoils to Corfu (25 minutes).

ITALY

Services run from the following Italian ports:

Ancona In summer, three daily sailings to Patra (20 hours).

Bari Daily sailings to Patra (14½ hours) via Corfu (eight hours) and Kefallonia (14 hours); also daily to Igoumenitsa (11½ hours).

Brindisi Only between April and early October; services to Patra (15 hours), calling at Igoumenitsa.

Venice In summer, up to 12 weekly sailings to Patra (30 hours) via Corfu (25 hours).

TURKEY

Boat services operate between the Greek Islands and Turkey's Aegean coast, from Rhodes to Marmaris, Symi to Datça, Kos to Bodrum, Samos to Kuşadası, Chios to Çeşme and Lesvos to Ayvalık.

Getting Around

Greece has a comprehensive transport system and is easy to get around.

Air

Domestic air travel has been very price competitive of late, and it's sometimes cheaper to fly than take the ferry, especially if you book ahead online. Domestic air carriers:

Aegean Airlines (A3; www.aegeanair.com) The competition, offering newer aircraft and similar prices on popular routes.

Astra Airlines (A2; www.astra-airlines.gr) Based in Thessaloniki; a newcomer flying limited routes.

Athens Airways (ZF; www.athensairways.com) New kid on the block.

Olympic Air (OA; www.olympicair.com) Recently privatised; has the most extensive network.

Sky Express (SHE; www.skyexpress.gr) Based in Iraklio, Crete; mainly flies routes that the big two don't.

Bicycle

Rental bicycles are available at most tourist centres, but generally for pedalling around town rather than for serious riding. Prices range from €10 to €20 per day. For bicycle

Main Ferry Routes

ISLAND-HOPPING

For many, the idea of meandering from island to island by boat in the Greek Islands is the ultimate dream. It's still a lot of fun, but to some extent, not what it used to be. Many of those slow, romantic old ferries you may have seen in the movies have disappeared, replaced by big, modern people-movers.

It's still possible to get away from it all, but it will require some thought – head to smaller islands off the beaten path before the high season kicks in. Every island has a boat service of some sort.

Boat operations are highly seasonal; there's not a lot happening in winter, and services pick up from April. Summer brings the *meltemi*, a strong, dry northerly wind that can blow for days and cause havoc to ferry schedules.

In any season, changes to schedules can take place at the last minute. Be prepared to be flexible. Boats seldom arrive early, but often arrive late. And some don't come at all. Think of it as part of the fun.

Check out www.greekferries.gr for schedules, costs and links to individual boat company websites.

tours, see www.cyclegreece.gr; bicycles are carried for free on ferries.

Boat

Ferries come in all shapes and sizes. Newer high-speed ferries are slashing travel times, but cost much more. 'Classes' on ferries are largely a thing of the past; you have the option of 'deck class', which is the cheapest ticket, or 'cabin class', with air-con cabins. Tickets can be bought at the last minute at the dock, but in the high season, some boats may be full – plan ahead.

High-speed catamarans have become an important part of the island travel scene. They are much less prone to cancellation in rough weather, but fares are generally more expensive than for ferries.

Hydrofoils are a faster alternative to ferries on some routes – they take half the time, but cost twice as much. Most routes will operate only during the high season. Tickets must be bought in advance and there is often seat allocation.

Bus

Long-distance buses are operated by **KTEL** (Koino Tamio Eispraxeon Leoforion; www.ktel.org). Fares are fixed by the government, and service routes can be found on the company's website. The buses are comfortable and generally run on time, and frequent services are offered on all major routes. Tickets are reasonably priced, eg Athens–Volos (€25, five hours) and Athens–Patra (€17, three hours). Tickets should be bought at least an hour in advance to ensure a seat. The vehicles don't have toilets and refreshments, but do stop for a break every couple of hours.

Car & Motorcycle

Your own set of wheels is a great way to explore areas in Greece that are off the beaten track. But be careful – Greece has the highest road-fatality rate in Europe.

The road network has improved dramatically in recent years, but freeway tolls are fairly hefty. Almost all islands are served by car ferries, but they are expensive; costs vary by the size of the vehicle.

The Greek automobile club, **ELPA** (www.elpa.gr), generally offers reciprocal services to members of other national motoring associations. If your vehicle breaks down, dial ☎104.

EU-registered vehicles are allowed free entry into Greece for six months without road taxes being due; a Green Card (international third-party insurance) is all that's required.

HIRE

Rental cars are available just about anywhere in Greece. Check the insurance waivers closely; find out how they can assist in case of a breakdown. High-season weekly rates start at about €280 for the smallest models, dropping to €200 in winter – add tax and extras. The minimum driving age in Greece is 18, but most car-hire firms require a driver of 21 or over.

Mopeds and motorcycles are available for hire everywhere. Regulations stipulate that you need a valid motorcycle licence stating proficiency for the size of motorcycle you wish to rent – from 50cc upwards. Mopeds and 50cc motorcycles range from €10 to €25 per day, 250cc motorcycles from €25 per day. Outside the high season, rates drop considerably. Ensure the bike is in good working order and the brakes work well. Check that your travel insurance covers you for injury resulting from motorcycle accidents.

ROAD RULES

Drive on the right and overtake on the left (not all Greeks do this).

It's compulsory to wear seat belts in the front seats, and in the back if they are fitted. Drink-driving laws are strict; a blood alcohol content of 0.05% incurs a fine of around €150 and over 0.08% is a criminal offence.

Public Transport

All major towns have local bus systems; Athens is the only city with a metro system.

Taxi

Taxis are widely available and reasonably priced. Yellow city cabs are metered; rates double between midnight and 5am. Grey rural taxis do not have meters; settle on a price before you get in. Athens taxi drivers are gifted in their ability to make a little extra with every fare. If you have a complaint, note the cab number and contact the tourist police.

Train

Trains are operated by the **Greek Railways Organisation** (OSE; www.ose.gr). Greece has two main lines: Athens north to Thessaloniki and Alexandroupolis, and Athens to the Peloponnese. There are a number of branch lines (eg Pyrgos–Olympia).

Inter-Rail and Eurail passes are valid; you still need to make a reservation.

Hungary

Includes »

Best Places to Eat

» Köleves, Budapest (p615)

» Bagolyvár, Budapest (p614)

» Az Elefánthoz, Pécs (p622)

» Halászcsárda, Szeged (p623)

Best Places to Stay

» Backpack Guesthouse, Budapest (p611)

» Home-Made Hostel, Budapest (p614)

» Wieden Pension, Sopron (p619)

» Hotel Korona, Szeged (p623)

» Nap Hostel, Pécs (p622)

Why Go?

Where else but Hungary can you laze about in an open-air thermal spa while snow patches glisten around you, then head to a bar where a Romani band yelps while a crazed crowd whacks its boot heels? Or follow that spa visit with a trip to a wine cellar to taste the local vintage alongside arguably Eastern Europe's best, and spiciest, cooking?

If these pursuits don't appeal there are Roman ruins, ancient castles and even the occasional Turkish minaret, holdovers from centuries of Ottoman rule, in cities such as Pécs and Eger. In the countryside you can see storks nesting on street lamps and a sea of blooming apricot trees.

Cosmopolitan Budapest is filled with world-class opera, great clubs, monumental buildings and the mighty Danube River flowing through its centre.

When to Go

Budapest

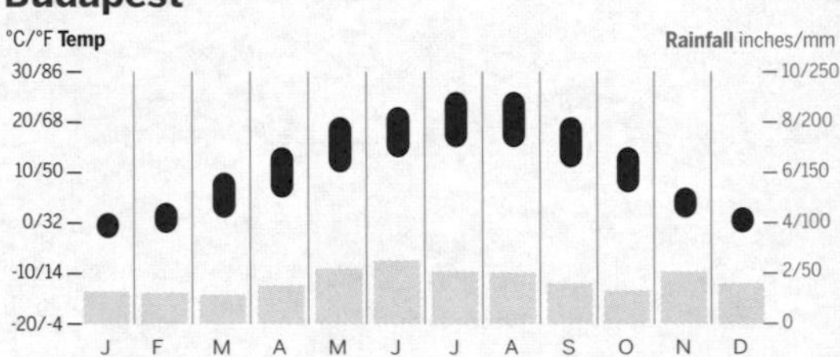

May Spring is in full swing, with generally reliable weather, cool temps and lots of flowers.

Jul & Aug Lots of sunshine; if it's too hot in Budapest, decamp to the countryside or Lake Balaton.

Sep Sunshine, mild temperatures and grape-harvest festivals; may be the best time to visit.

Connections

Hungary's landlocked status ensures plenty of possibilities for onward travel overland. There are direct train connections from Budapest to major cities in all of Hungary's neighbours. International buses head in all directions, including localities across the border in Serbia and Romania. In the warmer months you can take a ferry along the Danube to reach Bratislava or Vienna.

ITINERARIES

One Week

Spend four days in Budapest, checking out the sights, museums and cafes. On your fifth day take a day trip to a Danube Bend town: see the open-air museum in Szentendre or the cathedral at Esztergom. Day six can be spent getting a morning train to Pécs and seeing the lovely Turkish remains, and checking out the many galleries in town.

Two Weeks

If you're here in summer, make sure you spend some time exploring the towns around Lake Balaton, or just chill out on the beach by the side of this popular lake. Siófok is a party town with an Ibiza-style vibe. Alternatively head south to see some of the Great Plain: Szeged is on the Tisza River and Kecskemét is further north.

Essential Food & Drink

» **Gulyás (goulash)** Hungary's signature dish, though here it's served as a soup, not a stew.

» **Pörkölt** This paprika-infused stew is closer to what you imagine as goulash.

» **Galuska** Gnocchi-like dumplings that soak up the sauce in a *pörkölt*.

» **Halászlé** Fish soup made from freshwater fish, tomatoes, green peppers and paprika.

» **Lángos** Street food made from fried dough and topped with cheese and/or sour cream.

» **Wine** Two Hungarian wines are known internationally: the sweet dessert wine Tokaji Aszú and Egri Bikavér (Eger Bull's Blood), a full-bodied red.

» **Pálinka** A strong, firewater-like brandy distilled from fruits.

AT A GLANCE

» **Currency** Hungarian forint (Ft)

» **Language** Hungarian

» **Money** ATMs abundant

» **Visas** Not required for citizens of the EU, USA, Canada, Australia, and New Zealand

Fast Facts

» **Area** 93,000 sq km

» **Capital** Budapest

» **Country code** ☎36

» **Emergency** ☎112

Exchange Rates

Australia	A$1	192Ft
Canada	C$1	191Ft
euro zone	€1	266Ft
Japan	¥100	220Ft
New Zealand	NZ$1	144Ft
UK	UK£1	299Ft
USA	US$1	184Ft

Set Your Budget

» **Budget hotel room** 14,000/9000Ft (Budapest/ outside Budapest)

» **Two-course evening meal** 4000Ft

» **Museum entrance** 800Ft

» **Beer** 450Ft per bottle

Resources

» **Hungarian National Tourism Organisation** (www.hungary.com)

» **Budapest Times** (www.budapesttimes.hu)

» **Caboodle.hu** (www.caboodle.hu) Useful Hungarian news portal.

BUDAPEST

☎1 / POP 1.7 MILLION

Home to almost 20% of the national population, Hungary's capital (*főváros,* or main city) is the nation's administrative, business and cultural centre; everything of importance starts or finishes here.

But it's the beauty of Budapest – both natural and constructed – that makes it stand apart. Straddling a gentle curve in the Danube, the city is flanked by the Buda Hills on the west bank and the beginnings of the Great Plain, in Pest, to the east. Architecturally it is a gem, with enough baroque, neoclassical, eclectic and art-nouveau elements to satisfy anyone.

The city is divided into 23 districts; a Roman numeral before or after the street address indicates the district. The Castle Hill

Hungary Highlights

1 Ease your aching muscles in the warm waters of Budapest's **thermal baths** (p609) and try a spa treatment for good measure

2 Learn about the defiance **Eger** (p624) showed to Turkish invaders and how the city's Bull's Blood wine got its name

3 Chill out in **Szeged** (p622), a relaxed college and party town in the south of the country, in the heart of the Hungarian *puszta* (plain)

4 Absorb the Mediterranean climate and historic architecture of the southern city of **Pécs** (p621), including its intriguing Mosque Church

5 Take a pleasure cruise across (or a dip in) central Europe's largest body of fresh water, **Lake Balaton** (p619)

district in Buda is district I, and the central pedestrian area of Pest is district V.

In recent years Budapest has taken on the role of the region's party town. In the warmer months outdoor beer gardens called *kertek* (gardens) are heaving with party makers, and the world-class Sziget Music Festival in August is a cultural magnet.

Sights & Activities

BUDA

Castle Hill

Surfacing at the M2 metro station of the Socialist-style Moszkva tér, continue left up Várfok utca, or board bus 16A, to reach **Castle Hill** (Várhegy; Map p609), where most of Budapest's remaining medieval buildings are clustered. Castle Hill is high above the glistening Danube, and wandering the old streets and enjoying the city views is part of the attraction, so get off at the first stop after the Vienna Gate and walk.

Matthias Church CHURCH
(Mátyás Templom; Map p609; www.matyas-templom.hu; I Szentháromság tér 2; adult/concession 950/500Ft) Don't miss the gorgeous, neo-Gothic Matthias Church, with a colourful tiled roof and lovely murals inside. Franz Liszt's *Hungarian Coronation Mass* was played here for the first time at the coronation of Franz Joseph and Elizabeth in 1867. Buy tickets to enter the church and the Fishermen's Bastion at ticket counters across from the church entrance.

Fishermen's Bastion MONUMENT
(Halászbástya; Map p609; I Szentháromság tér; adult/concession 500/200Ft) Step across the square, under the gaze of Hungary's first king, immortalised in the equestrian **St Stephen statue** (Szent István szobor; Map p609). Behind the monument, walk along Fishermen's Bastion. The fanciful, neo-Gothic arcade, built on the fortification wall, is prime picture-taking territory, with views of the river and the parliament beyond.

Sikló FUNICULAR RAILWAY
(Map p609; I Szent György tér; 1 way/return 840/1450Ft; ⏲7.30am-10pm, closed 1st & 3rd Mon of month) Tárnok utca runs southeast to Dísz tér; keep going toward the Royal Palace to find the entrance for the Sikló, a funicular railway, to your left. The views from the little capsule, across the Danube and over to Pest, are glorious. The Sikló takes you down the hill to Clark Ádám tér.

Royal Palace PALACE
(Királyi Palota; Map p609) The massive Royal Palace occupies the far end of Castle Hill; inside are the **Hungarian National Gallery** (Nemzeti Galéria; Map p609; www.mng.hu; I Szent György tér 6; adult/concession 900/450Ft) and the **Budapest History Museum** (Budapesti Történeti Múzeum; Map p609; www.btm.hu; I Szent György tér 2; adult/concession 1300/650Ft).

Gellért Hill

Gellért Baths BATHHOUSE
(Gellért Fürdő; Map p612; ☎466 6166; Danubius Hotel Gellért, XI Kelenhegyi út; admission without/with private changing room, 3600/3900Ft; ⏲6am-7pm May-Sep, 6am-7pm Mon-Fri & 6am-5pm Sat & Sun Oct-Apr) Below Gellért Hill is the city's most famous thermal spa, where majestic domes hang above healing waters. This art-nouveau palace has dreamy spas where you can soak for hours while enjoying its elegant and historic architecture.

FREE **Citadella** FORTRESS
(Map p609; www.citadella.hu; ⏲24hr) On Gellért Hill above the baths is the Citadella, built by the Habsburgs after the 1848 revolution to 'defend' the city from further Hungarian insurrection; it was never used as a fortress.

Outside the Centre

Memento Park STATUE PARK
(www.mementopark.hu; XXII Balatoni út 16; adult/concession 1500/1000Ft) In Buda's southwest is Memento Park, a kind of historical dumping ground for socialist statues deemed unsuitable since the early '90s. It's a major tourist attraction and there's a direct bus from Deák tér in Pest at 11am daily, and a second bus at 3pm July and August (adult/concession return 4500/3500Ft, including admission).

PEST

Hősök Tere & Around

Hősök Tere SQUARE
The leafy Andrássy út, Pest's northeastern artery, is the best place to start your sightseeing. From Deák tér, Bajcsy-Zsilinszky becomes Andrássy út, which ends at the wide, tiled Hősök tere (Heroes' Sq). This public space holds a sprawling monument constructed to honour the millennial anniversary (in 1896) of the Magyar conquest of the Carpathian Basin.

Museum of Fine Arts MUSEUM
(Szépmüvészeti Múzeum; www.mfab.hu; XIV Dózsa György út 41; adult/concession 1600/800Ft)

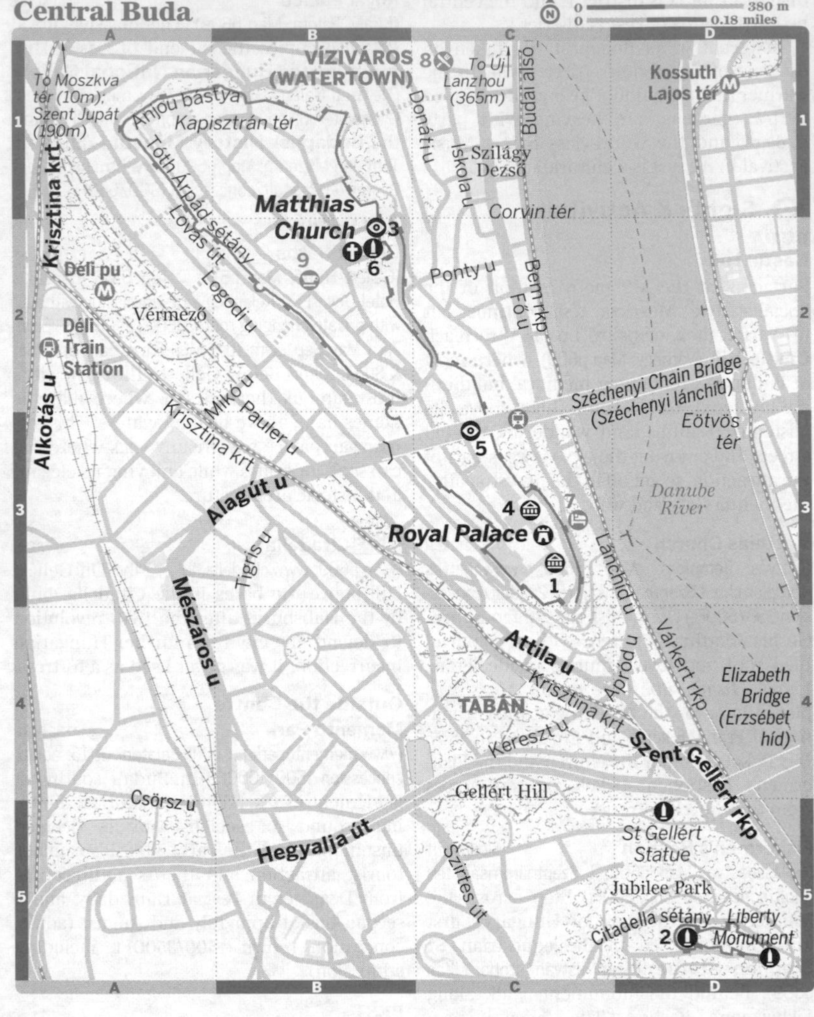

Across the street, the Museum of Fine Arts houses a collection of foreign art, including an impressive number of El Grecos.

FREE City Park PARK

(Városliget; Map p612) Adjacent is the oasis of City Park, which has boating on a small lake in the summer, ice skating in winter and duck feeding year-round. In the park's northern corner is **Széchenyi Baths** (Széchenyi Fürdő; ☎363 3210; XIV Állatkerti út 11; admission with private changing room 3500Ft; ⏲6am-10pm).

Terror House MUSEUM

(Terror Háza; Map p612; www.terrorhaza.hu; VI Andrássy út 60; adult/concession 1800/900Ft; ⏲10am-6pm Tue-Fri, to 7.30pm Sat & Sun) Walk southwest from Hősök tere on Andrássy út to see the old haunt of the dreaded secret police. The museum focuses on the crimes and atrocities committed by Hungary's fascist and Stalinist regimes.

Hungarian State Opera House THEATRE

(Magyar Állami Operaház; Map p612; ☎332 8197; www.operavisit.hu; VI Andrássy út 22; tours adult/concession 2800/1400Ft, mini concert after the

Central Buda

Top Sights
Matthias Church B2
Royal Palace C3

Sights
1 Budapest History Museum....C3
2 Citadella D5
3 Fishermen's Bastion....B2
4 Hungarian National Gallery C3
5 Sikló C3
6 St Stephen Statue B2

Sleeping
7 Lánchíd 19....C3

Eating
8 Édeni Vegan....C1

Drinking
9 Ruszwurm....B2

tour 500Ft; ⏲3pm & 4pm) Further down on Andrássy út, the opulence of the 1884 neo-Renaissance Hungarian State Opera House is a real treat; try to make it to an evening performance here.

Parliament & Around

TOP CHOICE Parliament HISTORIC BUILDING
(Parlament; Map p612; ☎441 4904; www.parlament.hu; V Kossuth Lajos tér 1-3; admission adult/EU citizens/concession 3200/free/1600Ft; ⏲8am-6pm Mon-Fri, 8am-4pm Sat, 8am-2pm Sun) The huge, riverfront Parliament dominates Kossuth Lajos tér. English-language tours are given at 10am, noon and 2pm.

Jewish Quarter

Great Synagogue SYNAGOGUE
(Nagy Zsinagóga; Map p612; VII Dohány utca 2; adult/concession tour 1 3400/2750Ft, tour 2 2750/2050Ft, tour 3 2400/1650Ft; ⏲10am-6.30pm Mon-Thu, to 2pm Fri, to 5.30pm Sun mid-Apr–Oct, 10am-3pm Mon-Thu, to 2pm Fri, to 4pm Sun Nov–mid-Apr) Northeast of the Astoria metro stop is what remains of the Jewish quarter. The twin-towered, 1859 Great Synagogue (or Dohány Synagogue) has a museum with a harrowing exhibit on the Holocaust, and behind the synagogue is the **Memorial of the Hungarian Jewish Martyrs** (Map p612) in the shape of a weeping willow.

Hungarian National Museum MUSEUM
(Magyar Nemzeti Múzeum; Map p612; www.hnm.hu; VIII Múzeum körút 14-16; adult/concession 1100/550Ft) A few blocks south along the *kis körút* (little ring road) is the Hungarian National Museum, with its historic relics, from archaeological finds to coronation regalia. To find the museum from the Great Synagogue, duck under the Astoria metro underpass to cross busy Rákóczi út and walk about 100m.

Festivals & Events

Spring Festival CLASSICAL MUSIC
(www.springfestival.hu) March to April.

Sziget Music Festival INDIE MUSIC FESTIVAL
(www.sziget.hu) On Óbudai hajógyári-sziget (Óbuda Shipbuilding Island), arguably central Europe's premier indie-music fest, from late July to early August.

Hungarian Formula One Grand Prix AUTO RACE
(www.hungaroring.hu) At Mogyoród, 24km northeast of Budapest; usually held in late July or early August.

Budapest International Wine Festival WINE FESTIVAL
(www.winefestival.hu) September.

Sleeping

BUDA

Backpack Guesthouse HOSTEL €
(☎385 8946; www.backpackbudapest.hu; XI Takács Menyhért utca 33; beds in yurt 3000Ft, large/small dm 3800/4500Ft, d 11,000Ft; @) A hippyish, friendly place, though relatively small, with around 40 beds. There's a lush garden in the back with a hammock stretched invitingly between trees. Take bus 7 from Keleti train station to Tétényi út, or tram 18 from Déli train station to Móricz Zsigmond Kőrtér to catch bus 7 to Tétényi út.

Papillon Hotel HOTEL €
(☎212 4750; www.hotelpapillon.hu; II Rózsahegy utca 3/b; s/d/tr/apt from €44/54/69/78; ❄@≋) This small, 20-room hotel in Rózsa-domb has a delightful back garden with a small swimming pool, and some rooms have balconies. There are also four apartments available in the same building, one of which has a lovely roof terrace.

Martos Hostel HOSTEL €
(☎209 4883; http://hotel.martos.bme.hu; XI Sztoczek utca 5-7; s/d/tr/q/apt from 4000/6000/9000/12,000/15,000Ft; @) Primarily student accommodation, Martos is open year-round to all. It's a few minutes' walk from Petőfi Bridge (or take tram 4 or 6).

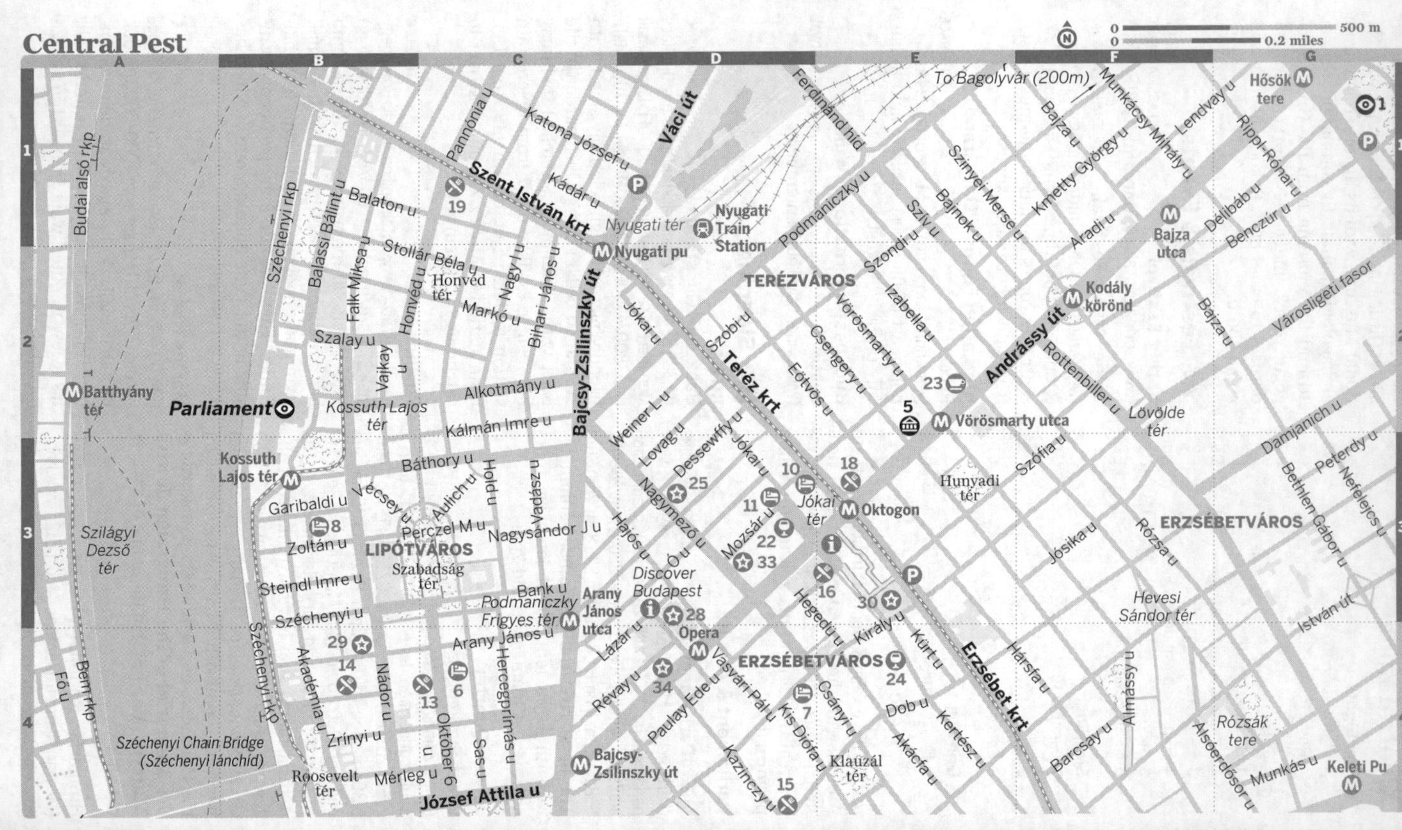
Central Pest
0 500 m
0 0.2 miles
To Bagolyvár (200m)
Hősök tere
Lendvay u
Rippl-Rónai u
Délibáb u
Benczúr u
Városligeti fasor
Munkácsy Mihály u
Bajza utca
Bajza u
Kmetty György u
Aradi u
Kodály körönd
Andrássy út
Rottenbiller u
Lövölde tér
Damjanich u
Peterdy u
Nefelejcs u
Bethlen Gábor u
István út
Keleti Pu
ERZSÉBETVÁROS
Rózsa u
Hevesi Sándor tér
Rózsák tere
Alsóerdősor u
Munkás u
Almássy u
Barcsay u
Szinyei Merse u
Bajnok u
Szív u
Szondi u
Izabella u
Vörösmarty utca
Szófia u
Jósika u
Hunyadi tér
Hársfa u
Erzsébet krt
Kertész u
Akácfa u
Dob u
Kürt u
Király u
Oktogon
Ferdinánd híd
Podmaniczky u
Vörösmarty u
Csengery u
Eötvös u
TERÉZVÁROS
Nyugati Train Station
Nyugati tér
Nyugati pu
Váci út
Szobi u
Teréz krt
Jókai u
Jókai tér
Mozsár u
Dessewffy u
Nagymező u
Lovag u
Weiner L u
Hegedű u
Csányi u
Klauzál tér
Kis Diófa u
Vasvári Pál u
Kazinczy u
Paulay Ede u
Opera
Discover Budapest
Ó u
Hajós u
Lázár u
Révay u
Bajcsy-Zsilinszky út
Szent István krt
Katona József u
Kádár u
Pannónia u
Bihari János u
Nagy I u
Markó u
Alkotmány u
Kálmán Imre u
Vadász u
Nagysándor J u
Hold u
Bank u
Arany János utca
Podmaniczky Frigyes tér
Arany János u
Hercegprímás u
Sas u
Október 6 u
József Attila u
Mérleg u
Roosevelt tér
Zrínyi u
Nádor u
Akadémia u
Széchenyi u
Steindl Imre u
Zoltán u
Garibaldi u
LIPÓTVÁROS
Szabadság tér
Perczel M u
Aulich u
Vécsey u
Báthory u
Kossuth Lajos tér
Honvéd tér
Honvéd u
Stollár Béla u
Balaton u
Vajkay u
Falk Miksa u
Balassi Bálint u
Szalay u
Széchenyi rkp
Parliament
Kossuth Lajos tér
Batthyány tér
Budai alsó rkp
Szilágyi Dezső tér
Bem rkp
Fő u
Széchenyi Chain Bridge (Széchenyi lánchíd)
A
B
C
D
E
F
G
1
2
3
4
5
6
7
8
10
11
13
14
15
16
18
19
22
23
24
25
28
29
30
33
34

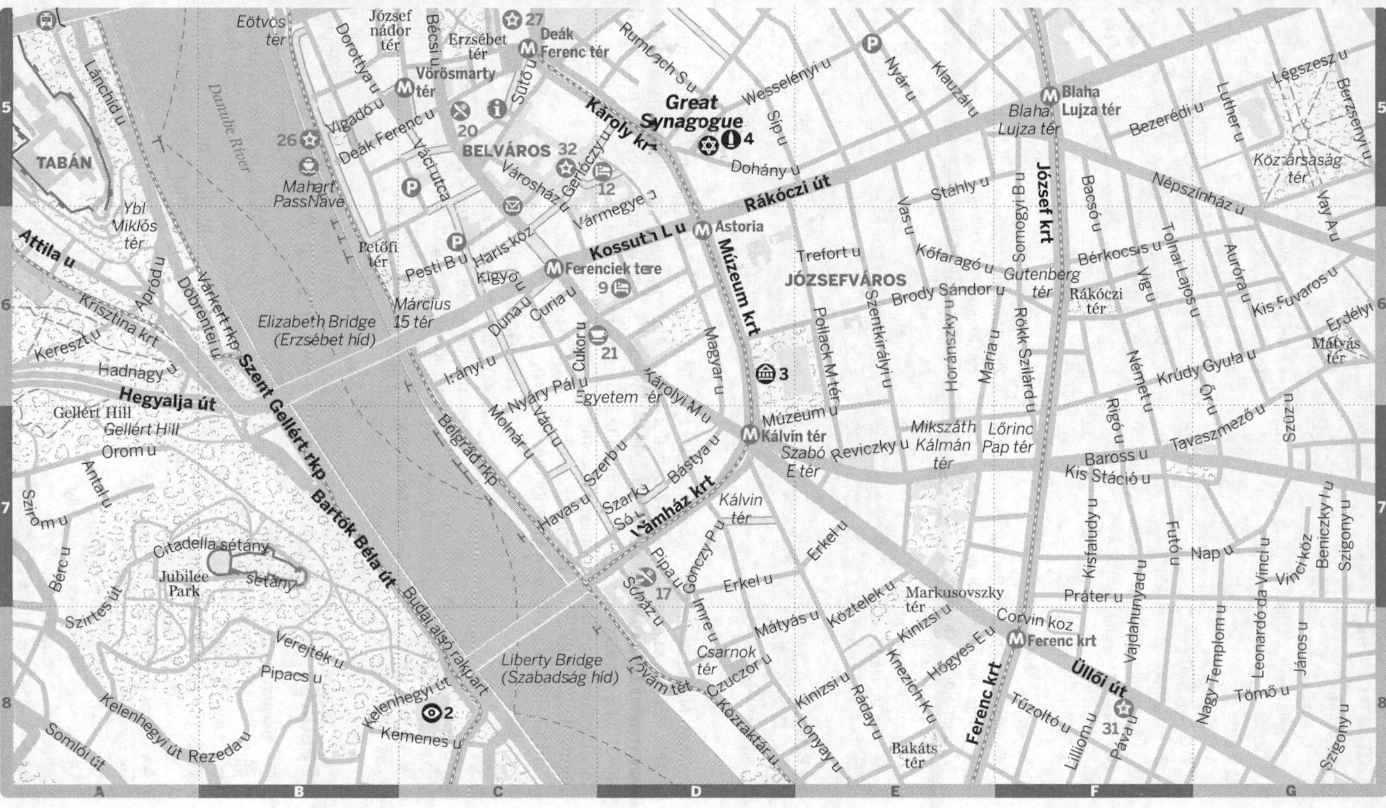
Eötvös tér
József nádor tér
Bécsi u
Erzsébet tér
Deák Ferenc tér
27
Dorottya u
Vörösmarty tér
Sütő u
Rumbach S u
Wesselényi u
Nyár u
Klauzál u
Blaha Lujza tér
Blaha Lujza tér
Légszesz u
Berzsenyi u
Luther u
Bezerédi u
Köztársaság tér
Lánchíd u
Danube River
Vigadó u
Deák Ferenc u
20
Károly krt
Great Synagogue
4
Síp u
TABÁN
26
Mahart PassNave
BELVÁROS
32
Váci utca
Városház u
Gerlóczy u
12
Dohány u
Vármegye u
Rákóczi út
Stáhly u
Vas u
Somogyi B u
József krt
Bacsó u
Népszínház u
Vay A u
Ybl Miklós tér
Attila u
Petőfi tér
Pesti B u
Haris köz
Kígyó u
Kossuth L u
Astoria
Ferenciek tere
9
Múzeum krt
Trefort u
Kőfaragó u
Bérkocsis u
Tolnai Lajos u
Aurora u
JÓZSEFVÁROS
Gutenberg tér
Rákóczi tér
Vig u
Kis Fuvaros u
Apród u
Döbrentei u
Várkert rkp
Krisztina krt
Kereszt u
Március 15 tér
Elizabeth Bridge (Erzsébet híd)
Duna u
Curia u
Cukor u
21
Magyar u
Pollack M tér
Szentkirályi u
Brody Sándor u
Horánszky u
Mária u
Rökk Szilárd u
Német u
Krúdy Gyula u
Őr u
Erdélyi u
Mátyás tér
Hadnagy u
Szent Gellért rkp
Irányi u
Nyáry Pál u
Egyetem tér
Károlyi M u
3
Hegyalja út
Gellért Hill
Gellért Hill
Orom u
Molnár u
Váci u
Múzeum u
Kálvin tér
Mikszáth Kálmán tér
Lőrinc Pap tér
Rigó u
Tavaszmező u
Szűz u
Szabó E tér
Reviczky u
Baross u
Kis Stáció u
Antal u
Belgrád rkp
Szerb u
Bástya u
Havas u
Szarka u
Só u
Vámház krt
Kálvin tér
Szirom u
Bartók Béla út
Erkel u
Kisfaludy u
Futó u
Nap u
Beniczky l u
Szigony u
Citadella sétány
Jubilee Park
sétány
Bérc u
Pipa u
Gönczy P u
Sóház u
17
Erkel u
Vajdahunyad u
Leonardo da Vinci u
Vinci köz
Szirtes út
Imre u
Köztelek u
Markusovszky tér
Práter u
Corvin koz
Ferenc krt
Nagy Templom u
János u
Budai alsó rakpart
Verejték u
Mátyás u
Kinizsi u
Hőgyes E u
Liberty Bridge (Szabadság híd)
Csarnok tér
Czuczor u
Pipacs u
Fővám tér
Knezich K u
Üllői út
Kinizsi u
Ferenc krt
Tömő u
Kelenhegyi út
2
Ráday u
Tűzoltó u
Kelenhegyi út
Rezeda u
Kemenes u
Közraktár u
Lónyay u
Bakáts tér
Lilliom u
31
Páva u
Szigony u
Somlói út
5
6
7
8
A
B
C
D
E
F
G

Central Pest

Top Sights
Great Synagogue ... D5
Parliament ... B2

Sights
1 City Park ... G1
2 Gellért Baths ... C8
3 Hungarian National Museum ... D6
Hungarian State Opera House .... (see 28)
4 Memorial of Hungarian Jewish Martyrs ... D5
5 Terror House ... E2

Sleeping
6 Central Backpack King Hostel ... C4
7 Connection Guest House ... D4
8 Garibaldi Guesthouse ... B3
9 Gingko Hostel ... D6
10 Home-Made Hostel ... D3
11 Medosz Hotel ... D3
12 Red Bus Hostel ... D5

Eating
13 Első Pesti Rétesház ... C4
14 Govinda ... B4
15 Köleves ... D4
16 Menza ... E3
17 Nagycsarnok ... D7
18 Rothschild Supermarket ... E3
19 Szeráj ... C1
20 Vapiano ... C5

Drinking
21 Centrál Kávéház ... D6
22 Kiadó Kocsma ... D3
23 Lukács ... E2
24 Szimpla ... E4

Entertainment
25 Alter Ego ... D3
26 Columbus Jazzklub ... B5
27 Gödör Klub ... C5
28 Hungarian State Opera House ... D3
29 Kalamajka Táncház ... B4
30 Liszt Academy of Music ... E3
31 Mappa Club ... F8
32 Merlin ... C5
33 Symphony Ticket Office ... D3
34 Ticket Express ... D4

Zugligeti Niche Camping CAMPING GROUND €
(☎200 8346; www.campingniche.hu; XII Zugligeti út 101; campsites per person/tent/campervan 1800/1700/3200Ft) An excellent option for mixing a city break with a hiking holiday; the camp is in the Buda Hills at the bottom station of a chairlift. Take bus 158 from Moszkva tér to the terminus.

PEST

Garibaldi Guesthouse B&B €
(Map p612; ☎302 3457; www.garibaldiguesthouse.hu; V Garibaldi utca 5; r from €44, apt per person €25-45) This old building belongs to a gregarious owner who has many apartments available over several floors, as well as private rooms in apartments with shared bathroom and kitchen.

> **SPLURGE**
>
> The boutique **Lánchíd 19** (Map p609; ☎419 1900; www.lanchid19hotel.hu; I Lánchíd utca 19; s/d/ste from €120/140/300; ❄@), facing the Danube, won the European Hotel Design Award for best architecture in 2008. Its facade features changing images derived from the movement of the Danube, and its rooms are equally impressive, containing distinctive artwork and unique chairs designed by art students.

TOP CHOICE **Home-Made Hostel** HOSTEL €
(Map p612; ☎302 2103; www.homemadehostel.com; VI Teréz körút 22; dm/d/q from 3500/12,000/20,000Ft; @) This cosy, extremely welcoming hostel has unique decor, with recycled tables hanging upside down from the ceiling, and old valises serving as lockers. The old-style kitchen is also a blast from the past.

Gingko Hostel HOSTEL €
(Map p612; ☎266 6107; www.gingko.hu; V Szép utca 5; dm/d/tr 3500/11,000/15,000Ft; @) This very green hostel is one of the best kept in town and the fount-of-all-knowledge manager keeps it so clean you could eat off the floor. There are books to share and a positively enormous double giving on to Reáltanoda utca.

TOP CHOICE **Connection Guest House** PENSION €
(Map p612; ☎267 7104; www.connectionguesthouse.com; VII Király utca 41; s/d from €35/50; @) This central, gay-friendly pension above a leafy courtyard attracts a young crowd due to its

proximity to nightlife venues. Three of the seven rooms share bathroom facilities. Excellent, user-friendly hotel website.

Central Backpack King Hostel HOSTEL €
(Map p612; ☎06 30 200 7184; centralbpk@freemail.hu; V Október 6 utca 15; dm/d/tr/q from €12/50/70/80; @) This upbeat place has dorm rooms with between seven and nine beds on one floor, and doubles, triples and quads on another.

Red Bus Hostel HOSTEL €
(Map p612; ☎266 0136; www.redbusbudapest.hu; V Semmelweiss utca 14; dm/s/d/tr 3000/9000/9000/12,500Ft; @) Red Bus is a central and well-managed place, with large and airy dorms as well as five private rooms. It's a quiet spot with a fair number of rules – the full 16 are listed in reception – so don't expect to party here.

Medosz Hotel HOTEL €
(Map p612; ☎374 3001; www.medoszhotel.hu; VI Jókai tér 9; s/d/tr/ste from €49/59/69/89) Well priced for its central location, the Medosz is opposite the restaurants and bars of Liszt Ferenc tér. The rooms are spare but comfortable.

Eating

BUDA

Szent Jupát HUNGARIAN €
(off Map p609; II Dékán utca 3; mains 1700-3600Ft) Late-night choice for solid Hungarian fare, with half-a-dozen vegetarian choices too. It's just north of Moszkva tér and opposite the Fény utca market – enter from II Retek utca 16.

Marcello ITALIAN €
(XI Bartók Béla út 40; mains 2200Ft) Popular with students from the nearby university, this family-owned eatery has good Italian fare at affordable prices.

Édeni Vegan VEGETARIAN €
(Map p609; I Iskola utca 31; mains 900-1200Ft; ⏲8am-9pm Mon-Thu, 8am-6pm Fri, 11am-7pm Sun) Located in a town house just below Castle Hill, this self-service place offers solid but healthy vegan and vegetarian fare.

Új Lanzhou CHINESE €€
(off Map p609; ☎201 9247; II Fő utca 71; mains 1190-3290Ft) Many diners think this is the most authentic Chinese restaurant in Budapest. Make up your own mind while sampling the excellent soups, the relatively large choice of vegetarian dishes and the stylish surrounds.

> **SPLURGE**
>
> Serving imaginatively reworked Hungarian classics, **Bagolyvár** (off Map p612; ☎468 3110, XIV Állatkerti út 2; mains 2850-4250Ft), or the 'Owl's Castle', attracts the Budapest foodie cognoscenti. It's staffed entirely by women – in the kitchen, at table and front of house.

PEST

Stock up on picnic supplies at **Nagycsarnok** (Great Market; Map p612; IX Vámház körút 1-3; ⏲9am-6pm Mon-Sat), a vast historic market built of steel and glass. A nonstop supermarket is the **Rothschild Supermarket** (Map p612; VI Teréz körút 19; ⏲24hr), near Oktogon.

TOP CHOICE **Köleves** HUNGARIAN, JEWISH €€
(Map p612; ☎322 1011; Kazinczy utca 35 & Dob utca 26; mains 1800-3200Ft) Always buzzing, 'Stone Soup' attracts a young crowd with its delicious Hungarian- and Jewish-inspired dishes like catfish stew and noodles.

Menza HUNGARIAN €€
(Map p612; ☎413 1482; VI Liszt Ferenc tér 2; mains 1990-3690Ft) This stylish restaurant takes its name from the Hungarian for a drab school canteen – something it is anything but. It's always packed with diners, who come for its simply but perfectly cooked Hungarian classics with a modern twist. Reservations necessary.

Első Pesti Rétesház BAKERY €
(Map p612; V Október 6 utca 22; strudels 360Ft) The First Strudel House of Pest is just the place to taste this Hungarian pastry filled with apple, cheese, poppy seeds or sour cherries.

Vapiano ITALIAN €
(Map p612; V Bécsi utca 5; mains 1400-2200Ft) A very welcome addition to the food scene is this self-serve pizza and pasta bar, where everything is prepared on site. You'll be in and out in no time, but the taste will pleasantly linger.

Govinda VEGETARIAN €
(Map p612; V Vigyázó Ferenc utca 4; multicourse set menu 1250-1450Ft; ⏲11.30am-8pm Mon-Fri, noon-8pm Sat & Sun) Basement restaurant north-east of the Chain Bridge, serving wholesome salads, soups and desserts as well as daily set menus.

Szeráj KEBABS €
(Map p612; XIII Szent István körút 13; mains 600-1600Ft; ⌚9am-4am Mon-Thu, to 5am Fri & Sat, to 2am Sun) Inexpensive self-service Turkish place for *lahmacun* (or 'Turkish pizza'), falafel and kebabs.

Drinking

Budapest is loaded with pubs and bars and there's enough variation to satisfy all tastes. In summer, the preferred drinking venues are the *kerteks*, outdoor spaces that double as beer gardens and music clubs. The best places to drink are in Pest (Buda's too sleepy to stay up all night), especially along Liszt Ferenc tér and Radáy utca, which have a positively festive feel during the summer.

TOP CHOICE **Szimpla** BAR
(Map p612; VII Kertész utca 48) This distressed-looking, supremely relaxed place remains one of the most popular drinking venues south of Liszt Ferenc tér. There's occasional live music in the evenings.

Kiadó Kocsma PUB
(Map p612; VI Jókai tér 3) The 'Pub for Rent' is a great place for a swift pint and a quick bite (salads and pasta), and is just a stone's throw away from Liszt Ferenc tér.

Centrál Kávéház COFFEE HOUSE
(Map p612; V Károlyi Mihály utca 9; ⌚8am-midnight) One of the finest coffee houses in the city, with high, decorated ceilings, lace curtains, pot plants, elegant coffee cups and professional service.

Lukács CAFE
(Map p612; VI Andrássy út 70) Station yourself where Hungary's dreaded ÁVH secret police once had its HQ.

On the Buda side of the river, drop into popular student pub **Kisrabló** (XI Zenta utca 3) by taking tram 19 or 49 one stop past Danubius Hotel Gellért, or enjoy coffee and cake at **Ruszwurm** (Map p609; I Szentháromság utca 7) on Castle Hill.

Entertainment

The free weekly *Pesti Est* (available at restaurants and clubs) lists live-music acts and guest DJs for clubs, and *Pesti Műsor* lists everything from clubs and films to art exhibits and classical music.

A useful ticket broker with outlets across town is **Ticket Express** (Map p612; ☎030 303 0999; www.tex.hu; VI Andrássy út 18). The **Symphony Ticket Office** (Szimfonikus Jegyiroda; Map p612; ☎302 3841; VI Nagymező utca 19) specialises in classical-music events.

Hungarian State Opera House OPERA
(Map p612; ☎353 0170; www.opera.hu; VI Andrássy út 22) Take in a performance while admiring the incredibly rich interior decoration. The ballet company performs here as well.

Liszt Academy of Music CONCERT HALL
(Map p612; ☎342 0179; VI Liszt Ferenc tér 8) You can hear the musicians practising from outside this magnificent concert hall, which hosts classical-music performances.

Kalamajka Táncház LIVE MUSIC
(Map p612; V Arany János utca 10; ⌚8.30pm-midnight Sat) The Kalamajka is an excellent place to hear authentic Hungarian music, especially on its dance nights, when everyone gets up and takes part.

Nightclubs

Mappa Club CLUB
(Map p612; IX Lilliom utca 41) An arty crowd makes the scene beneath this cultural house and exhibition space, enjoying some of the best DJs in town.

Merlin CLUB
(Map p612; www.merlinbudapest.org; V Gerlóczy utca 4) One of those something-for-everyone places, with everything from jazz and break-beat to techno and house.

Gödör Klub CLUB
(Map p612; V Erzsébet tér) This large underground club offers a mix of folk, world, rock and pop, played to an audience of all ages.

Columbus Jazzklub JAZZ
(Map p612; www.majazz.hu; V Pesti alsó rakpart at Lánchíd bridgehead) Jazz on a boat moored in the Danube, just off the northern end of V Vigadó tér, hosting big-name local and international performers. Music starts at 8pm.

Alter Ego GAY & LESBIAN
(Map p612; www.alteregoclub.hu; VI Dessewffy utca 33) One of the city's leading gay clubs, with a cool crowd (think attitude) and arguably the best dance music.

Information

Discount Cards

Budapest Card (www.budapestinfo.hu; 48/72hr card 6300/7500Ft) offers access to many museums, unlimited public transport and discounts on tours and other services. Buy it at hotels, travel agencies, large metro-station kiosks and tourist offices.

Internet Access

The majority of hostels offer internet access, often free of charge. Among the most accessible internet cafes in Budapest are the following:

Electric Café (VII Dohány utca 37; per hr 200Ft; ⌚9am-midnight) Huge place, very popular with travellers.

Vist@Netcafe (XIII Váci utca 6; per hr 400Ft; ⌚24hr) In Pest. One of the few internet cafes open 24 hours.

Medical Services

FirstMed Centers (☎224 9090; I Hattyú utca 14, 5th fl; ⌚8am-8pm Mon-Fri, 9am-2pm Sat) On call 24/7 for emergencies.

SOS Dent (☎269 6010; VI Király utca 14; ⌚24hr) Dentist.

Teréz Patika (☎311 4439; VI Teréz körút 41; ⌚8am-8pm Mon-Fri, 8am-2pm Sat) Extended-hours pharmacy.

Money

You'll find ATMs everywhere.

K&H Bank (V Váci utca 40) Central.

OTP Bank (V Deák Ferenc utca 7-9) Favourable rates.

Tourist Information

Tourinform main office (☎438 8080; V Sütő utca 2; ⌚8am-8pm); Castle Hill (☎488 0475; I Szentháromság tér; ⌚9am-7pm May-Oct, 10am-6pm Nov-Apr); Liszt Ferenc tér (☎322 4098; VI Liszt Ferenc tér 11; ⌚10am-6pm Mon-Fri)

Travel Agencies

Discover Budapest (☎269 3843; www.discoverbudapest.com; VI Lázár utca 16; ⌚9.30am-6.30pm Mon-Fri, 10am-4pm Sat & Sun) is a one-stop shop for helpful tips and advice, accommodation bookings, internet access and cycling and walking tours.

 Getting There & Away

Air

There is no domestic air service in Hungary. See p628 for international flights.

Boat

In addition to its hydrofoils that travel internationally to Bratislava and Vienna (see p628), **Mahart PassNave** (Map p612; ☎484 4005; www.mahartpassnave.hu; Vigadó tér Pier) ferries depart daily for Szentendre (one way/return 1490/2235Ft, 1½ hours) from May to September, decreasing to weekends only in April and October.

Visegrád (one way/return 2690/3990Ft, one hour) and Esztergom (one way/return 3290/4990Ft, 1½ hours) can be reached by fast hydrofoil from Budapest on weekends between May and September (and also on Friday from June to August).

> **GETTING TO/FROM THE AIRPORT**
>
> The simplest way to get to the centre of town from Ferihegy Airport's Terminal 2 is to take the **airport minibus** (☎296 8555; www.airportshuttle.hu) directly to the place you're staying (one way/return 2990/4990Ft). Buy tickets at clearly marked stands in the arrivals halls.
>
> The cheapest way is to take city bus 200 (320Ft, or 400Ft on the bus), which terminates at the Kőbánya-Kispest metro station. Look for the stop on the footpath between terminals 2A and 2B. From its final stop, take the M3 metro into the city centre. The total cost is 640Ft to 800Ft. Bus 93 runs from Terminal 1 to Kőbánya-Kispest metro station.

Bus

Volánbusz (☎382 0888; www.volanbusz.hu), the national bus line, has an extensive list of destinations from Budapest. All international buses and some buses to/from southern Hungary use **Népliget bus station** (Üllői út 131). **Stadionok bus station** (XIV Hungária körút 48-52) generally serves places to the east of Budapest. Most buses to the northern Danube Bend arrive at and leave from the **Árpád híd bus station** (XIII Róbert Károly körút). All stations are on metro lines, and all are in Pest. If the ticket office is closed, you can buy your ticket on the bus.

Car & Motorcycle

Most big international car-hire chains have branches at the airports. A standard rate is €60 per day with unlimited kilometres. Petrol costs about 340Ft per litre.

Train

The Hungarian State Railways, MÁV, administers the country's extensive rail network. Contact the **MÁV-Start passenger service centre** (☎06 40 494949; www.mav-start.hu) for 24-hour information on domestic train departures and arrivals. The website has a useful timetable (in English) for planning routes. Fares are usually noted for destinations within Hungary.

Buy tickets at one of Budapest's three main train stations. Always confirm your departure station when you buy your tickets, since stations can vary depending on the train.

Keleti train station (Eastern; VIII Kerepesi út 2-4) handles international trains from Vienna and most other points west, plus domestic trains to/from the north and northeast. For some international destinations, as well as domestic ones to/from the northwest and the Danube Bend, head for **Nyugati train station** (Western; Map p612; VI Nyugati tér). For trains bound for Lake Balaton and the south, go to **Déli train station** (Southern; Map p609; I Krisztina körút 37). All train stations are on metro lines.

Getting Around

Public Transport

Public transport is run by **BKV** (☎258 4636; www.bkv.hu). The three underground metro lines (M1 yellow, M2 red, M3 blue) meet at Deák tér in Pest. The HÉV suburban railway runs north from Batthyány tér in Buda. A *turista* transport pass is only good on the HÉV within the city limits (south of the Békásmegyer stop). There's also an extensive network of buses, trams and trolleybuses. Public transport operates from 4.30am until 11.30pm, and 35 night buses run along main roads.

A single ticket for all forms of transport is 320Ft (60 minutes of uninterrupted travel on the same metro, bus, trolleybus or tram line *without* transferring). A transfer ticket (490Ft) is valid for one trip with one validated transfer within 90 minutes. The three-day or seven-day *turista* passes (3850/4600Ft) make things easier, allowing unlimited travel inside the city limits. Keep your ticket or pass handy; the fine for 'riding black' is 6000Ft on the spot.

Taxis

Overcharging is common. Never get into a taxi that does not have a yellow licence plate, the logo of a taxi firm and a posted table of fares.

AROUND BUDAPEST

North of Budapest, the Danube breaks through the Pilis and Börzsöny Hills in a sharp bend before continuing along the Slovak border. The Roman Empire had its northern border here and medieval kings ruled Hungary from majestic palaces overlooking the river at Esztergom and Visegrád.

Szentendre

☎26 / POP 23,500

Once an artists' colony, now a popular day trip from Budapest, pretty little Szentendre (*sen*-ten-dreh) has narrow, winding streets and is a favourite with souvenir shoppers.

The **Tourinform** (☎317 965; szentendre@tourinform.hu; Bercsényi utca 4; ⏲9.30am-4.30pm Mon-Fri year-round, 10am-2pm Sat & Sun mid-Mar–Oct) office hands out maps and info. In 2010 the office moved to this temporary location on a side street just along the Duna korzó.

Outside town is the huge open-air **Ethnographic Museum** (Szabadtéri Néprajzi Múzeum; www.skanzen.hu; Sztaravodai út; adult/concession 1400/700Ft). Walking through reassembled homes and villages from around the country in this *skansen* (village museum), you can see what life was – and sometimes still is – like in rural Hungary. Take the Skansen bus from stand 7 (20 minutes) at the bus station.

The most convenient way to get to Szentendre is to take the commuter HÉV train from Buda's Batthyány tér metro station to the end of the line (one way about 450Ft, 45 minutes, every 10 to 15 minutes). For ferry services from Budapest, see p617.

Visegrád

☎26 / POP 1700

The spectacular vista from the ruins of Visegrád's (*vish*-eh-grahd) 13th-century citadel, high on a hill above a curve in the Danube, is what pulls visitors to this sleepy town. After the 13th-century Mongol invasions, Hungarian kings built the mighty **Visegrád Citadel** (Visegrád Cittadella; adult/concession 1400/700Ft) high on the hilltop. It's a bit of a climb, but the views are well worth it. The **Royal Palace** (Királyi Palota; Fő utca 29; adult/concession 1100/550Ft) stands on the flood plain at the foot of the hills, closer to the centre of town.

Buses arrive from Budapest's Árpád híd bus station (600Ft, 1¼ hours, at least hourly), the Szentendre HÉV station (around 400Ft, 45 minutes, every 45 minutes) and Esztergom (400Ft, 45 minutes, hourly). For ferry services from Budapest, see p617.

Esztergom

☎33 / POP 31,000

It's easy to see the attraction of Esztergom, even from a distance. The city's massive basilica, sitting high above the town and Danube River, is an incredible sight, rising magnificently from its rural setting. The 2nd-century Roman-emperor-to-be Marcus Aurelius wrote his famous *Meditations* while he camped here. Stephen I, founder of the Hungarian state, was born here and crowned at the cathedral, and Esztergom was the royal seat from the 10th to the 13th centuries.

Gran Tours (☎502 001; Széchenyi tér 25) is the best source of information in town.

Hungary's largest church is the **Esztergom Basilica** (Esztergomi Bazilika; www.bazilika-esztergom.hu; Szent István tér 1). At the southern end of the hill is the extensive **Castle Museum** (Vár Múzeum; adult/concession 840/420Ft), with archaeological remnants from the 2nd and 3rd centuries.

Buses run to/from Budapest's Árpád híd bus station (700Ft, 1½ hours) and to/from Visegrád (400Ft, 45 minutes) at least hourly. Trains to Esztergom depart from Budapest's Nyugati train station (1100Ft, 1½ hours, at least hourly). For ferry services from Budapest, see p617.

WESTERN HUNGARY

A visit to this region is a boon for anyone wishing to see remnants of Hungary's Roman legacy, medieval heritage and baroque splendour. Prominent here is vast Lake Balaton (600 sq km), Hungary's inland 'seaside', offering swimming, sailing, sunbathing and fishing during the warmer months.

Sopron

☎99 / POP 59,000

Sopron (*shop*-ron) is an attractive border town with a history that stretches back to Roman times. It boasts well-preserved ruins and a fetching medieval square, bounded by the original town walls. **Tourinform** (☎517 560; sopron@tourinform.hu; Liszt Ferenc utca 1; ⌚9am-6pm daily mid-Jun–Aug, 9am-5pm Mon-Fri, 9am-noon Sat Sep–mid-Jun) offers free internet access and a plethora of tourist information.

Sights

Fő tér PUBLIC SQUARE

Fő tér is the main square in Sopron. At the time of research, much of the square was fenced off as workers were repairing the cobblestones; several attractions, including the massive **Firewatch Tower** (Tűztorony; Fő tér) were closed for repairs. The 60m-high tower rises above the old town's northern gate and is visible from all around. In the centre of Fő tér is the 1701 **Trinity Column** (Szentháromság Ozlop). On the north side of the square are two fabled houses, each holding a pair of **museums** illustrating various aspects of the city's history, from ancient times through the 19th and early-20th centuries. Just off the square, along the town wall, are the small **open-air ruins** (admission free; ⌚24hr), with reconstructed Roman walls and 2nd-century houses dating from the time when Sopron was a tiny Roman outpost known as Scarbantia.

Sleeping & Eating

TOP CHOICE **Wieden Pension** PENSION €

(☎523 222; www.wieden.hu; Sas tér 13; s/d/tr/apt from 7700/10,900/12,900/11,900Ft; @) Sopron's cosiest pension is located in an attractive old town house within easy walking distance of the inner town. The rooms are sparsely furnished but comfortable; the friendly reception staff will go out of their way to make you feel at home.

Vákació Vendégház HOSTEL €

(☎338 502; www.vakacio-vendeghazak.hu; Ady Endre út 31; dm 2800Ft) Cheap lodgings not far west of the town centre. Rooms are clean and furnished with two to 10 beds; bus 10 will drop you off not far from the front door. Phone in advance for reservations; note the reception opens only at 4pm.

Graben HUNGARIAN €

(Várkerület 8; mains 1000-1800Ft) The secluded garden terrace is a welcoming lunch or dinner spot for well-prepared Hungarian dishes, including fresh, lightly baked pike-perch. In winter dine below in a Gothic cellar.

For self-catering supplies, head for **Match** (Várkerület 100; ⌚6.30am-7pm Mon-Fri, 6.30am-3pm Sat) supermarket.

Getting There & Away

There are two buses a day to Budapest (3300Ft, 3¾ hours). Trains run to Budapest's Keleti train station (3500Ft, 2¾ hours, eight daily). You can also travel to Vienna's Meidling station (4200Ft, three hours, up to 15 daily), pending reconstruction of Vienna's Südbahnhof sometime in 2012.

Keszthely

☎83 / POP 21,800

At the western end of Lake Balaton sits Keszthely (*kest*-hey) with its amazing Festetics Palace and popular public beaches. The town centre lies about 1km northwest of (and uphill from) the lake. Summer activity centres on paid-admission beaches, waterfront parks, beer gardens and cafes located near the ferry pier. **Tourinform** (☎314 144; keszthely@tourinform.hu; Kossuth

Lajos utca 28; ⏲9am-8pm Mon-Fri, to 6pm Sat mid-Jun–mid-Sep, 9am-5pm Mon-Fri, to 12.30pm Sat mid-Sep–mid-Jun) has information on the whole Lake Balaton area.

Sights & Activities

Festetics Palace PALACE
(Festetics Kastély; Kastély utca 1; adult/concession 2000/1000Ft) The glimmering white, 100-room Festetics Palace at the northern end of Kossuth Lajos utca was first built in 1745; the wings were extended out from the original building 150 years later. About a dozen rooms in the one-time residence have been turned into a museum.

Lakeside Area LAKE
The lakeside area centres on the long ferry pier. From March to October you can take a one-hour **pleasure cruise** (www.balatonihajozas.hu; ferry pier; adult/concession 1400/600Ft; ⏲11am, 1pm, 3pm & 5pm) on the lake. If you're feeling like a swim, **City Beach** (Városi Strand) is just to the southwest of the ferry pier, near plenty of beer stands and food booths. **Libás Beach** (Libás Strand) is smaller and quieter. It's about 200m northeast of the pier.

Sleeping & Eating

Tourinform can help find private rooms from about 3500Ft per person.

Ambient Hostel HOSTEL €
(☎06 30 460 3536; http://hostel-accommodation.fw.hu; Sopron utca 10; dm/d from 3500/7800Ft; @) A short walk north of the palace is a hostel with basic, cheap dorms, each with its own bathroom. Laundry service is available 3pm to 5pm Monday to Friday. Note reception closes at 9.30pm, so be sure to call ahead if your train or bus gets in later than that.

Castrum Camping CAMPING GROUND €
(☎312 120; www.castrum.eu; Móra Ferenc utca 48; campsites per adult/concession/tent 1400/1000/2000Ft; ⏲Apr-Oct; ≋) North of the stations, this large camping ground is spacious and has a pool.

Lakoma HUNGARIAN €
(Balaton utca 9; mains 1000-2600Ft) Has a good fish selection, grill/roast specialities and a back garden that transforms itself into a leafy dining area in summer.

Getting There & Away

Buses and trains link Keszthely to Budapest. The bus (3300Ft, three hours, seven daily) tends to be faster and cheaper than the train (3500Ft, four hours, six daily). From April to September **Balaton Shipping** (www.balatonihajozas.hu) runs ferries to towns around the lake.

Siófok

☎84 / POP 23,900

Siófok (*shee*-a-folk) is officially known as 'Hungary's summer capital' – unofficially it's 'Hungary's Ibiza'. In July and August nowhere in the country parties as hard or stays up as late as this lakeside resort. Outside the summer months Siófok returns to relative normality.

The bus and train stations are in Millennium Park, just off Fő utca, the main drag. **Tourinform** (☎310 117; tourinform@siofokportal.hu; Fő utca 174-176, inside the Atrium shopping centre; ⏲8am-7pm Mon-Fri, 10am-7pm Sat & Sun mid-Jun–mid-Sep, shorter hr in winter) hands out city maps and can advise on and book rooms in season. Note the office is normally based in the *víztorony* (water tower) but was temporarily relocated here (until end 2011) while the tower undergoes repair.

Sights & Activities

Water Tower MONUMENT
(víztorony; Szabadság tér) The wooden water tower, built in 1912, affords an impressive view. As we were researching this guide the tower was closed for renovation.

Nagy Strand BEACH
(adult/concession 1000/500Ft) 'Big Beach' is centre stage on Petőfi sétány; free concerts are often held here on summer evenings. There are many more managed swimming areas along the lakeshore, which cost around the same as Nagy Strand.

Sleeping & Eating

Prices quoted are for high season in July and August. Tourinform can help find a private room (prices starting around 4000Ft per person).

Hotel Yacht Club BOUTIQUE HOTEL €€
(☎311 161; www.hotel-yachtclub.hu; Vitorlás utca 14; s/d €52/112; ❄@≋) Overlooking the harbour is this excellent hotel with cosy rooms, some of which have balconies overlooking the lake, and a modern wellness centre. Bicycle hire.

Siófok Város College HOSTEL €
(☎312 244; www.siofokvaroskollegiuma.sulinet.hu; Petőfi sétány 1; dm 2700Ft) Close to the ac-

TIHANY

Lake Balaton is not just a party spot. There are many places, especially along the quieter northern shore, where you can get away and enjoy unspoiled nature in relative peace and quiet. One of the loveliest of these is Tihany (tee-hah-nee), a hilly peninsula jutting 5km into the lake. Activity here is centred on the tiny town of the same name, which is home to the celebrated Abbey Church. Contrasting with this are the hills and marshy meadows of the peninsula's nature reserve, which has an isolated, almost wild feel to it.

The peninsula has beaches on both its eastern and western coasts, and a resort complex on its southern tip. However, you can easily shake off the tourist hordes by going hiking. Birdwatchers, bring your binoculars: the trails have abundant avian life. You can reach Tihany by bus from several points along the lake, and passenger ferries sail to and from Siófok from April to September.

tion in central Siófok, it's hard to beat this basic college accommodation for price and location.

Roxy INTERNATIONAL €
(Szabadság tér; mains 1200-3000Ft) Pseudo-rustic restaurant in the commercial centre, attracting diners with a wide range of international dishes and surprisingly imaginative Hungarian mains.

Drinking & Entertainment

Renegade PUB
(Petőfi sétány 9) Wild pub near the beach where table dancing and live music are the main draws.

Palace CLUB
(www.palace.hu; Deák Ferenc utca 2) Popular club. Accessible by free bus that leaves from the Palace cafe along the beach promenade.

Getting There & Away

From April to October passenger ferries run between Siófok and several towns along the lake. Several trains daily run to and from Budapest (2160Ft, two hours).

SOUTHERN HUNGARY

South Hungary is a region of calm with a hint of the Mediterranean, a place to savour life at a slower pace. It's only marginally touched by tourism, and touring through the countryside is like travelling back in time.

Pécs

☎72 / POP 156,000

Blessed with a mild climate, an illustrious past and a number of fine museums and monuments, Pécs (pronounced *paich*) is one of the most pleasant cities to visit in Hungary. Many travellers put it second only to Budapest on their must-see list.

Tourinform (☎213 315; pecs@tourinform.hu; Széchenyi tér 1; 8am-6pm Mon-Fri, 10am-8pm Sat & Sun Jun-Aug, shorter hr out of season) has tonnes of local info, including lists of hotels and museums.

The train station is a little over 1km south of the centre. The bus station is nearby, a few blocks closer to the centre.

Sights

FREE **Mosque Church** CHURCH
(Mecset Templom; Széchenyi tér; 10am-4pm Mon-Sat 11.30am-4pm Sun) The Mosque Church dominates the city's central square. It has no minaret and has been a Christian place of worship for a long time, but the Islamic elements inside, such as the mihrab on the southeastern wall, reveal its original identity.

Modern Hungarian Art Gallery ART GALLERY
(Modern Magyar Képtár; Káplalan utca 4; adult/concession 700/350Ft; noon-4pm Tue-Sun) The excellent Modern Hungarian Art Gallery is next door to the Mosque Church, and here you can get a comprehensive overview of Hungarian art from 1850 till today.

Basilica of St Peter CHURCH
(Szent Péter Bazilika; Dóm tér; adult/concession 800/500Ft; 9am-5pm Mon-Sat, 1-5pm Sun Apr-Oct, 10am-4pm Mon-Sat, 1-4pm Sun Nov-Mar) Continue west to Dóm tér and the walled bishopric complex containing the four-towered Basilica of St Peter. The oldest part of the building is the 11th-century crypt. The 1770 **Bishop's Palace** (Püspöki Palota; adult/concession 1500/700Ft; tours 2pm, 3pm & 4pm Thu late Jun–mid-Sep) stands in front of the cathedral. Also near the square is a 15th-century

barbican *(barbakán)*, the only stone bastion to survive from the old city walls.

Cella Septichora Visitors Centre RUINS
(Janus Pannonius utca; adult/concession 1200/600Ft; ⊙10am-6pm Tue-Sun Apr-Oct, 10am-4pm Tue-Sun Nov-Mar) On the southern side of Dom tér is the Cella Septichora Visitors Centre, which illuminates a series of early-Christian burial sites that have been on Unesco's World Heritage list since 2000. The highlight is the so-called **Jug Mausoleum** (Korsós Sírkamra), a 4th-century Roman tomb whose name comes from a painting of a large drinking vessel with vines.

Synagogue SYNAGOGUE
(zsinagóga; Kossuth tér; adult/concession 500/300Ft; ⊙10am-noon & 12.45-5pm Sun-Fri May-Oct) Pécs' beautifully preserved 1869 synagogue is south of Széchenyi tér.

Sleeping & Eating

Tourinform can help book private rooms at around 4000Ft per person.

TOP CHOICE **Nap Hostel** HOSTEL €
(☎950 684; www.naphostel.com; Király utca 23-25; dm/d from 2500/11,000Ft; @) Clean, friendly hostel with dorms and a double room on the 1st floor of a former bank. There's also a large kitchen. Enter from Szent Mór utca.

Hotel Főnix BOUTIQUE HOTEL €€
(☎311 680; www.fonixhotel.hu; Hunyadi János út 2; s/d 7100/11,300Ft; ❄@) Odd angles and sloping eaves characterise the asymmetrical Hotel Főnix. Rooms are plain and those on the top floor have skylights.

Hotel Diána PENSION €€
(☎328 594; www.hoteldiana.hu; Tímár utca 4/a; s/d/tr from 11,350/16,350/20,350Ft; ❄@) Central pension offers 20 spotless rooms, comfortable kick-off-your-shoes decor and a warm welcome.

TOP CHOICE **Az Elefánthoz** ITALIAN €
(Jókai tér 6; mains 1600-2100Ft) With its welcoming terrace overlooking Jókai tér and quality Italian cuisine, this place is a sure bet for first-rate food in the centre.

Áfium BALKAN €
(Irgalmasok utca 2; mains 1400-1900Ft) With Croatia and Serbia so close, it's a wonder that more restaurants don't offer cuisine from south of the border. Don't miss the bean soup served covered with a top of freshly baked bread. Decently priced set lunches during the week.

Get self-catering supplies at the **Interspar** (Bajcsy-Zsilinszky utca 11; ⊙7am-9pm Mon-Thu & Sat, 7am-10pm Fri, 8am-7pm Sun) supermarket in the basement of the Árkád shopping centre.

Drinking & Entertainment

Pubs, cafes and fast-food eateries line pedestrian-only Király utca. Another good bet is tiny and more intimate Jókai tér.

Korhely PUB
(Boltív köz 2) This popular *csapszék* (tavern) has peanuts on the table, shells on the floor, a half-dozen beers on tap and a sort of 'retro socialist meets Latin American' decor.

Coffein Café CAFE
(Széchenyi tér 9) For the best views across Széchenyi tér to the Mosque Church and Király utca, find a perch at this cool cafe done up in the warmest of colours.

Varázskert OUTDOOR CLUB
(Király utca 65-67; ⊙6pm-3am summer only) Big open-air beer garden and late-hours music club at the far end of Király utca.

Getting There & Away

At least five buses a day connect Pécs with Budapest (3600Ft, 4½ hours), three with Siófok (2480Ft, three hours) and eight with Szeged (3400Ft, 4½ hours). Pécs is on a main rail line to Budapest's Déli train station (4400Ft, three hours, nine daily). One daily train runs from Pécs to Osijek (two hours) in Croatia, with continuing service to Sarajevo (nine hours).

GREAT PLAIN

Like the Outback for Australians or the Old West for Americans, the Great Plain (Nagy Alföld) holds a romantic appeal for Hungarians. Images of cowboys riding across the *puszta* (prairie) are scattered throughout the nation's poetry and painting. Beyond its 'big sky' appeal, the region is also home to cities of graceful architecture, winding rivers and easy-going afternoons.

Szeged

☎62 / POP 170,000

Szeged (*seh*-ged) is a bustling border town with a handful of historic sights that line the embankment along the Tisza River and a clutch of sumptuous art-nouveau town palaces that are in varying states of repair and disrepair. It's also a big university town, which means lots of culture, lots of partying and an active festival scene.

The train station is south of the city centre on Indóház tér; from here, tram 1 takes you along Boldogasszony sugárút into the centre of town. The bus station, on Mars tér, is west of the centre, within easy walking distance via pedestrian-only Mikszáth Kálmán utca. **Tourinform** (☎488 699; http://tip.szegedvaros.hu; Dugonics tér 2; ⏰9am-5pm Mon-Fri, to 1pm Sat) is tucked away in a quiet courtyard off of Kárász.

Sights & Activities

Ferenc Móra Museum MUSEUM
(Móra Ferenc Múzeum; www.mfm.u-szeged.hu; Roosevelt tér 1; adult/concession 700/350Ft) East of Széchenyi tér, the huge, neoclassical Ferenc Móra Museum overlooks the Tisza River. The museum contains a colourful collection of folk art and an exhibit of 7th-century gold work by the Avar, a mysterious people who are thought to have originated somewhere in Central Asia.

TOP CHOICE **New Synagogue** SYNAGOGUE
(Új Zsinagóga; www.zsinagoga.szeged.hu; Gutenberg utca 13; adult/concession 400/300Ft; ⏰10am-noon & 1-5pm Sun-Fri Apr-Sep, 10am-2pm Sun-Fri Oct-Mar) The most beautiful Jewish house of worship in Hungary and still in use.

Pick Salami & Szeged Paprika Museum MUSEUM
(Pick Szalámi és Szegedi Paprika Múzeum; www.pickmuzeum.hu; Felső Tisza-part 10; adult/concession incl salami tasting & paprika sample 880/660Ft; ⏰3-6pm Tue-Sat) Just north of the old town ring road. Two floors of exhibits show traditional methods of salami production.

Sleeping & Eating

Família Panzió PENSION €€
(☎441 122; www.familiapanzio.hu; Szentháromság utca 71; s/d/tr 8400/11,200/14,000Ft; ❄) Family-run guest house with contemporary furnishings in a great old-town building. The reception area may be dim, but rooms have high ceilings and loads of light.

TOP CHOICE **Hotel Korona** BOUTIQUE HOTEL €€
(☎555 787; www.hotelkoronaszeged.hu; Petőfi Sándor sgt 4; s/d 14,000/18,000Ft; ❄) Clean, quiet and close to the action. This well-run mid-range hotel makes for a great splurge option after you've tired of endless shared beds in hostel dorm rooms.

Partfürdő CAMPING GROUND €
(☎430 843; Közép-kikötő sor; campsites per person/tent 990/380Ft, r 5400-6900Ft, bungalows 8,000-12,000Ft; ⏰mid-May–Sep; 🏊) Green, grassy camping ground across the river in New Szeged. Gets crazy during the open-air festival in midsummer.

Halászcsárda HUNGARIAN €€
(☎555 980; Roosevelt tér 14; mains 2200-3600Ft) An institution that knows how to prepare the best fish dish in town – whole roasted pike with garlic, accompanied by pan-fried frog legs and fillet of carp soup.

Taj Mahal INDIAN €
(Gutenberg utca 12; mains 1700-2300Ft) Pleasantly authentic Indian-Pakistani restaurant, just a couple of metres from the New Synagogue.

Agni VEGETARIAN €
(Tisza Lajos körút 76; mains 800-1100Ft) Daily lunch specials round out the menu at this little vegetarian restaurant. Try the substantial paprika-and-mushroom stew with millet. Closed weekends.

Drinking & Entertainment

Szeged's status as a university town means there's a vast array of bars, clubs and other nightspots, especially around Dugonics tér. Nightclub programs are listed in the free *Szegedi Est* magazine.

Jazz Kocsma LIVE MUSIC
(Kálmány Lajos 14; ⏰4pm-2am Mon-Sat) The kind of small, smoky music club no self-

WORTH A TRIP

KECSKEMÉT

A worthwhile destination is the small city of Kecskemét, which lies halfway between Budapest and Szeged along the main rail and road arteries. It's a surprisingly green, pedestrian-friendly city with interesting art-nouveau architecture. **Tourinform** (☎481 065; kecskemet@tourinform.hu; Kossuth tér 1; ⏰8am-7pm Mon-Fri, 10am-8pm Sat & Sun Jul & Aug, 8am-6pm Mon-Fri Sep-Jun) is centrally located on the main square. It can advise on sights, places to stay and outings to the Kiskunsági National Park.

respecting university town would be without. Gets crowded during the school year for live music on Friday and Saturday nights.

Grand Café CAFE
(Deák Ferenc utca 18; ⏲2pm-midnight Mon-Fri, 5pm-2am Sat & Sun) Climb up to the 2nd floor to find this small, trendy cafe-bar with a retro feel. It also holds regular screenings of classic films.

Getting There & Away

Buses run to Pécs (3360Ft, 4¼ hours, seven daily) and to the Serbian city of Subotica up to four times daily. Szeged is on the main rail line to Budapest's Nyugati train station (3000Ft, 2¾ hours, hourly); trains also stop halfway along in Kecskemét (2100Ft, 1¼ hours, hourly). You have to change in Békéscsaba (1600Ft, two hours, half-hourly) to get to Arad in Romania.

NORTHEASTERN HUNGARY

If ever a Hungarian wine were world-famous, it would be Tokay. And this is where it comes from, a region containing micro-climates conducive to wine production. The chain of wooded hills in the northeast constitutes the foothills of the Carpathian Mountains, which stretch along the Hungarian border with Slovakia.

Eger

☎36 / POP 58,300

Filled with wonderfully preserved baroque architecture, Eger (*egg*-air) is a jewel box of a town containing gems aplenty, including wine-tasting opportunities. Eger Bull's Blood (Egri Bikavér) is a world-famous full-bodied red wine produced in the surrounding hills; it took its name from the wine-stained beards of the town's successful defenders against a Turkish attack in 1552. The staff at **Tourinform** (☎517 715; eger@tourinform.hu; Bajcsy-Zsilinszky utca 9; ⏲9am-5pm Mon-Fri, 9am-1pm Sat & Sun mid-Jun–mid-Sep, 9am-5pm Mon-Fri, 9am-1pm Sat mid-Sep–mid-Jun) can supply all the information you need.

The main train station is a 15-minute walk south of town, on Vasút utca, just east of Deák Ferenc utca. The bus station is west of Széchenyi István utca, Eger's main drag. The Valley of Beautiful Women (Szépasszony völgy), where the wine cellars are situated, is about 2km southwest of the centre. You can walk it in about 20 minutes.

Sights & Activities

Eger Castle FORTRESS
(Egri Vár; www.egrivar.hu; Vár 1; adult/concession incl museum 1300/650Ft; ⏲9am-6pm Tue-Sun Apr-Oct, closes earlier in winter) The most striking attraction and the best views of town are at Eger Castle, a huge walled complex at the top of the hill off Dósza tér. First fortified after an early Mongol invasion in the 13th century, the earliest ruins on site are the foundations of St John's Cathedral, built in the 12th century and destroyed by the Turks. The excellent **István Dobó Castle Museum** (Dobó István Vármuzeum), inside the Bishop's Palace (1470) within the castle grounds, explores the history and development of the castle. Other on-site exhibits include the **waxworks** (Panoptikum; adult/concession 450/300Ft) and the **minting exhibit** (Éremverde; adult/concession 400/250Ft).

Minaret MINARET
(Knézich Károly utca; admission 200Ft; ⏲10am-6pm Apr-Oct) A 40m-high minaret, minus the mosque, is allegedly Europe's northernmost remains of the Ottoman invasion in the 16th century. You can climb to the top for a great view of the castle, though the 97 steep steps provide a pretty good workout.

Szépasszony völgy WINE CELLAR
(Valley of the Beautiful Women; off Király utca) To sample Eger's wines visit the extravagantly named Valley of the Beautiful Women, home to dozens of small wine cellars that truck in, store and sell Bull's Blood and other regional red and white wines. Walk the horseshoe-shaped street and stop in front of one that strikes your fancy. Ask (*'megkostolhatok?'*) to taste the wares (around 220Ft per 100mL). If you want wine to go, bring an empty bottle and have it filled for about 500Ft per litre.

Sleeping

Dobó Vendégház BOUTIQUE HOTEL €€
(☎421 407; www.vendeghaz.hu; Dobó utca 19; s/d 9000/13,000Ft) A pleasant guest house a few steps from Eger's main square. The rooms are large and airy, with big wooden beds and fresh cotton linens. Some rooms open onto shared balconies off the back with views toward town.

Bartók Tér Panzió PENSION €
(☎515 556; www.bartokpanzio.com; Bartók Béla tér 8; s/d 6000/9000Ft). Big, cool rooms in summer and the location is convenient to both

WORTH A TRIP

TOKAJ

A worthwhile wine destination is the small village of Tokaj, 43km northeast of Eger, which has long been celebrated for its sweet dessert wines. **Tourinform** (☎552 070; www.tokaj.hu; Serház utca 1; ⊙9am-6pm Mon-Fri, 10am-7pm Sat & Sun Jun-Aug, 9am-5pm Mon-Fri Sep-May) is just off Rákóczi út, and can help with accommodation. Up to 16 trains a day link Tokaj directly to Budapest's Keleti (3750Ft, 2½ hours).

the in-town sights and the wine cellars of the Valley of Beautiful Women.

Tulipán Kemping CAMPING GROUND €
(☎311 542; Szépasszony völgy utca 71; campsites per person/tent 1000/940Ft, bungalows 6000Ft;) Many campsites here are in an open, shadeless field, but you're surrounded by vineyards and stumbling distance from the valley wine cellars.

Eating & Drinking

Palacsintavár CRÊPERIE €
(Dobó István utca 9; mains 1600-1800Ft) Entrée-sized *palacsintak* (crêpelike pancakes) are served with an abundance of fresh vegetables, and range in flavour from Asian to Italian and even local versions that feature hot peppers and chicken livers.

Bikavér Borház BAR €
(Dobó István tér 10) After dinner head to this tastings bar just across from the Senator Ház hotel for a nightcap of some of the region's best wines, served by the glass or the bottle. It also sells bottles to take home.

ℹ Getting There & Away

Buses make the trip from Eger to Kecskemét (2200Ft, 4½ hours, three daily) and Szeged (3500Ft, 5¾ hours, two daily). Up to seven direct trains a day head to Budapest's Keleti train station (2300Ft, 2½ hours).

UNDERSTAND HUNGARY

History

By the 3rd century BC, the Roman Empire had extended its influence far enough to include Pannonia, all of today's Hungary west of the Danube (Transdanubia). By AD 441 the Huns, under Attila and his brother Bleda, had ended Roman rule in the area. However, the Huns' short-lived empire didn't long outlast Attila's death, leaving space for Avars, Franks and Slavs.

Historians usually date the Magyar (Hungarian) conquest to around 896, when Árpád led an alliance of seven tribes in the region. In the year 1000 Hungary's first king and patron saint, Stephen (István), was crowned, marking the foundation of the Hungarian state.

Medieval Hungary was powerful until 1526, when the Turks invaded and occupied lands, including Budapest, for 150 years. After the Turks' expulsion from Buda in 1686, the Austrian Habsburgs annexed the lands that had been under Turkish rule. An 1848 revolt for independence led by Transylvanian princes failed, but unrest eventually led to Hungarian autonomy as half of the Austro-Hungarian Empire in 1867.

After WWI ended, with Hungary on the losing side, the 1920 Trianon Treaty stripped the country of more than two-thirds of its territory. Hungary's ambition to recover its loss drew the nation into WWII on the Axis side. When leftists tried to negotiate a separate peace in 1944, the Germans occupied Hungary and brought the fascist Arrow Cross Party to power. The Arrow Cross immediately began deporting hundreds of thousands of Jews to Auschwitz. By early April 1945, Hungary had been defeated by the Soviet army. In 1947 the communists took control of the government.

On 23 October 1956 anti-Soviet student demonstrations prompted Soviet tanks to move into Budapest and by the end of the fighting, several thousand people had died. Still, Soviet control was not as tight in Hungary as in the Slavic satellite states.

Hungary began moving toward full democracy in 1989. The last Soviet troops left the country in June 1991. Hungary became a member of NATO in 1999 and the EU in 2004.

The painful transition to a market economy resulted in declining living standards initially, but the early years of the 21st century saw astonishing economic growth. The 'Great Recession' in 2008 and 2009 pushed Hungary to the brink of bankruptcy, but by 2010 there were signs the economy was starting to recover.

READING UP

National poetry taught in schools has a huge influence on the Hungarian psyche. The overall mood in the renowned 18th- and 19th-century poems is one of *honfibú*, literally 'patriotic sorrow', which amounts to a penchant for the blues. You can read a sample in the bilingual anthology *The Lost Rider* by Corvina Books. The 2002 Nobel Prize winner, Imre Kertész, writes about the Holocaust and its after-effects in the novels *Fatelessness* and *Kaddish for an Unborn Child*.

People

Just over 93% of Hungary's population of 10.2 million is ethnically Magyar. Non-Magyar minorities include Germans (2.6%), Serbs and other South Slavs (2%), Slovaks (0.8%) and Romanians (0.7%). The number of Roma is officially put at 1.9% of the population (or 193,800 people), though some sources estimate the figure as high as 4%.

Arts

As you will see from the street names in every Hungarian town and city, the country celebrates and reveres its most influential musician, composer and pianist, Franz (or Ferenc) Liszt (1811–86). Béla Bartók (1881–1945) and Zoltán Kodály (1882–1967) made the first systematic study of Hungarian folk music, and both integrated some of their findings into their compositions.

Romani (Gypsy) music, found in restaurants in its schmaltzy form (best avoided), has become a fashionable thing among the young, with Romani bands playing 'the real thing' in trendy bars till the wee hours. Klezmer music (traditional Eastern European Jewish music) has also made a comeback onto the playlists of the young and trendy.

Favourite painters from the 19th century include realist Mihály Munkácsy (1844–1900), the so-called painter of the plains, and Tivadar Kosztka Csontváry (1853–1919). Győző Vásárhelyi (1908–97), who changed his name to Victor Vasarely when he emigrated to Paris, is considered the 'father of op art'. The traditional embroidery, weavings and ceramics of the nation's *népművészet* (folk art) also endure.

Food

Price ranges for meals in Hungary are shown in this chapter as follows:

€€€ more than 3000Ft (5000Ft for Budapest)

€€ 2000Ft to 3000Ft (2500Ft to 5000Ft for Budapest)

€ less than 2000Ft (2500Ft for Budapest)

Environment

Environmental disaster struck Hungary in 2010, when toxic industrial sludge from an aluminium factory in Ajka, in western Hungary, broke through barriers and leached into local rivers.

Initial fears the sludge would contaminate the Danube, however, proved exaggerated and the spill should pose no hazard to visitors. Since the spill there's been a marked improvement in both the public's awareness of environmental issues and the government's dedication to environmental safety.

The country was so sensitive to the spill because water dominates much of Hungary's geography. The Duna (Danube River) divides the Nagy Alföld (Great Plain) in the east from the Dunántúl (Transdanubia) in the west. The Tisza (597km of it in Hungary) is the country's longest river, and historically has been prone to flooding. Hungary has hundreds of small lakes and is riddled with thermal springs. Lake Balaton (600 sq km, 77km long), in the west, is the largest freshwater lake in Europe outside Scandinavia. Hungary's 'mountains' to the north are merely hills, with the country's highest peak being Kékes (1014m) in the Mátra Range.

SURVIVAL GUIDE

Directory A–Z

Accommodation

Price ranges used in this chapter for doubles are as follows.

€€€ more than 15,000Ft (30,000Ft for Budapest)

€€ 10,000Ft to 15,000Ft (15,000Ft to 30,000Ft for Budapest)

€ less than 10,000Ft (15,000Ft for Budapest)

CAMPING

Hungary has more than 400 camping grounds, listed in Tourinform's *Camping Hungary* map/brochure (www.camping.hu).

HOSTELS & STUDENT DORMS

From July to August the cheapest rooms are in vacant student accommodation. Local Tourinform offices can help you locate these. The **Hungarian Youth Hostels Association** (MISZSZ; www.miszsz.hu) keeps a list of year-round hostels throughout Hungary. Having an HI card may get you a 10% discount.

PENSIONS & HOTELS

Quaint, often family-run *panziók* (pensions) are abundant and usually less expensive than hotels. Some hotels *(szállók* or *szállodák)* have less expensive room options, if you're willing to share the bathroom down the hall.

PRIVATE ROOMS

Stick to travel agencies and avoid individuals at train stations in Budapest offering private rooms. Outside Budapest you can look for houses with signs that read *'szoba kiadó'* or the German *'Zimmer frei'*; expect to pay between 3500Ft and 6000Ft per person per night.

Activities

CYCLING

Hungary's flat terrain makes it ideal for cycling. **Velo-Touring** (☎1-319 0571; www.velo-touring.hu) has a great selection of seven-night trips in all regions, from a senior-friendly Danube Bend tour to a bike ride between spas on the Great Plain. Lake Balaton is circled by a long cycling track that takes about four to five days to complete at a leisurely pace.

HIKING & BIRDWATCHING

Hiking enthusiasts may enjoy the trails around Tihany at Lake Balaton, the Bükk Hills north of Eger or the plains at Bugac Puszta south of Kecskemét. Birdwatchers could explore these same paths or take a tour with **Birding Hungary** (www.birdinghungary.com).

SPAS

Hungary has more than 100 thermal baths open to the public. For locations ask Tourinform for the *Spa & Wellness* booklet. For more about Budapest spas check out www.spasbudapest.com.

Business Hours

Banks 9am-5pm Mon-Fri, 9am-noon Sat

Museums 9am or 10am to 5pm or 6pm Tue-Sun

Post offices 8am-6pm Mon-Fri

Restaurants roughly 11am to midnight

Shops 9am-6pm Mon-Fri, stores in shopping centres and in touristed areas open until 8pm. Many stores have shortened hours on Sat, until 2pm or 4pm, with malls open until at least 8pm. Large stores and shopping centres are usually open on Sun from noon until 6pm or 8pm.

Holidays

New Year's Day 1 January

1848 Revolution Day 15 March

Easter Monday March/April

International Labour Day 1 May

Whit Monday May/June

St Stephen's Day 20 August

1956 Remembrance Day 23 October

All Saints' Day 1 November

Christmas holidays 25 to 26 December

Money

The Hungarian forint (Ft) comes in five-, 10-, 20-, 50-, 100- and 200-forint coins, and 500-, 1000-, 2000-, 5000-, 10,000- and 20,000-forint notes. ATMs are everywhere, even in small villages. Tip waiters, hairdressers and taxi drivers approximately 10% of the bill.

Post & Telephone

Postcards and small letters mailed within Europe cost 210Ft. To addresses outside Europe, expect to pay 240Ft.

Hungary's country code is ☎36. To make an outgoing international call, dial ☎00 first. To dial city-to-city (and all mobile phones) within the country, first dial ☎06, then the city code.

The best place to make international calls is from a phone box with a phonecard, which you can buy at news-stands in a variety of denominations.

As with the rest of Europe, Hungarian mobile phones operate on the GSM standard. Compatible handsets will connect automatically with local providers, but watch for high roaming fees, particularly for data downloads.

A cheaper alternative is to purchase a pay-as-you-go SIM card (available at telephone shops and newsagents), which will give you a temporary local number with which to make calls and send text messages.

There are plenty of cafes and other businesses offering free wi-fi connections for customers, meaning that wi-fi enabled smartphones and other devices should work without any problem.

Visas

EU citizens do not need visas to visit Hungary and can stay indefinitely. Citizens of the USA, Canada, Israel, Japan, New Zealand and Australia do not require visas to visit Hungary for stays of up to 90 days. Check with the **Ministry for Foreign Affairs** (www.mfa.gov.hu) for up-to-date information.

Getting There & Away

Air

The vast majority of international flights land at **Ferihegy International Airport** (☎1-296 7000; www.bud.hu) on the outskirts of Budapest. Hungary's national carrier is **Malév Hungarian Airlines** (MA; ☎06 40 212121; www.malev.hu).

Low-cost airlines servicing Hungary include the following:

Air Berlin (AB; www.airberlin.com)

easyJet (EZY; www.easyjet.com)

Germanwings (4U; www.germanwings.com)

Ryanair (FR; www.ryanair.com)

Wizz Air (W6; www.wizzair.com)

Boat

A hydrofoil service on the Danube River between Budapest and Vienna (5½ to 6½ hours) operates daily from late April to early October; passengers can disembark at Bratislava with advance notice. Adult one way/return fares for Vienna are €89/109 and for Bratislava €79/99. Boats leave from the International Ferry Pier (Nemzetközi Hajóállomás), next to the **Mahart PassNave ticket office** (Map p612; ☎1-484 4013; www.mahartpassnave.hu; Belgrád rakpart).

Bus

Most international buses arrive at the Népliget bus station in Budapest. **Eurolines** (www.eurolines.com), in conjunction with its Hungarian affiliate, **Volánbusz** (☎1-382 0888; www.volanbusz.hu), operates a wide network on bus lines that connect Budapest to nearly every country on the continent. Useful international buses include those from Budapest to Vienna (Austria), Bratislava (Slovakia), Subotica (Serbia), Rijeka (Croatia), Prague (Czech Republic) and Sofia (Bulgaria).

Car & Motorcycle

Third-party car insurance is compulsory for driving in Hungary. If your car is registered in the EU, it's assumed you have it. Other motorists must show a Green Card or buy insurance at the border.

Train

The Hungarian State Railways, **MÁV** (☎1-444 4499; www.mav-start.hu) links up with international rail networks in all directions, and its schedule is available online.

EuroCity (EC) and Intercity (IC) trains require a seat reservation and payment of a supplement.

Direct train connections from Budapest include Austria, Slovakia, Romania, Ukraine (continuing to Russia), Croatia, Serbia and Slovenia.

Getting Around

Hungary does not have any scheduled internal flights.

Bus

Domestic buses, run by the **Volán** (www.volan.eu) association of coach operators, cover an extensive nationwide network. Timetables are posted at stations and stops. Some footnotes you could come across include *naponta* (daily), *hétköznap* (weekdays), *munkanapokon* (on work days), *munkaszüneti napok kivételével naponta* (daily except holidays) and *szabad és munkaszüneti napokon* (on Saturday and holidays). A few large bus stations have luggage rooms, but these generally close by 6pm.

Car & Motorcycle

Most of the international car-hire firms have offices in Budapest. In general you must be at least 21 years old and have had your licence for at least a year to hire a car. Note there's a 100% ban on alcohol when you are driving.

Hitching

Hitchhiking is legal except on motorways. However, it is never an entirely safe way to travel and we don't recommend it. **Kenguru** (www.kenguru.hu) is an agency that matches passengers with drivers online.

Local Transport

Public transport is efficient and extensive, with bus and, in many towns, trolleybus services. Budapest and Szeged also have trams, and there's an extensive metro and a suburban commuter railway in Budapest. Purchase tickets at news-stands before travelling and validate them once aboard. Inspectors do check tickets, especially on the metro lines in Budapest.

Train

MÁV (☎06 40 494 949; www.mav-start.hu) operates reliable train services on its 8000km of tracks. Schedules are available online, and computer information kiosks are popping up at rail stations around the country. Second-class domestic train fares range from 150Ft for a journey of less than 5km, to about 4000Ft for a 300km trip. First-class fares are usually 25% more.

IC trains are express trains, the most comfortable and modern. *Gyorsvonat* (fast trains) take longer and use older cars; *személyvonat* (passenger trains) stop at every village along the way. Seat reservations *(helyjegy)* cost extra and are required on IC and some fast trains; these are indicated on the timetable by an 'R' in a box or a circle (a plain 'R' means seat reservations are available but not required).

In all stations a yellow board indicates departures *(indul)* and a white board arrivals *(érkezik)*. Express and fast trains are indicated in red, local trains in black. In some stations, large black-and-white schedules are plastered all over the walls.

InterRail (www.interrailnet.com) and Eurail passes cover Hungary.

Iceland

Includes »

Best Places to Eat

» Fish Company, Reykjavík (p637)

» Indian Mango, Reykjavík (p637)

» Vegamót, Reykjavík (p638)

» Á Næstu Grösum, Reykjavík (p637)

Best Places to Stay

» Reykjavík City Hostel (p636)

» Reykjavík Downtown Hostel (p636)

» Eric the Red Guesthouse, Reykjavík (p636)

» Álfhóll Guesthouse, Reykjavík (p636)

Why Go?

A land of troll-inhabited mountains and black-sand beaches, where calling seabirds are more common than a human voice – it sounds like a fairy tale, but Iceland is only a hop away from mainland Europe. A vast volcanic laboratory, here the earth itself is restless and alive. Admire thundering waterfalls, glittering-white glaciers, geysers, volcanoes and spouting mud pools; and bathe in the Blue Lagoon, the world's biggest natural hotpot. Only the toughest creatures survive: come eye to eye with whales on a boat trip, or horse trek under the midnight sun.

In summer, permanent daylight energises the inhabitants of Iceland's only city, Reykjavík, whose weekend pub crawl *(runtur)* is particularly high-spirited. Fashion and music are woven into the city's fabric: experience both during the Iceland Airwaves festival in October. In winter, with luck, you may see the eerie Northern Lights flickering across the sky.

When to Go

Reykjavík

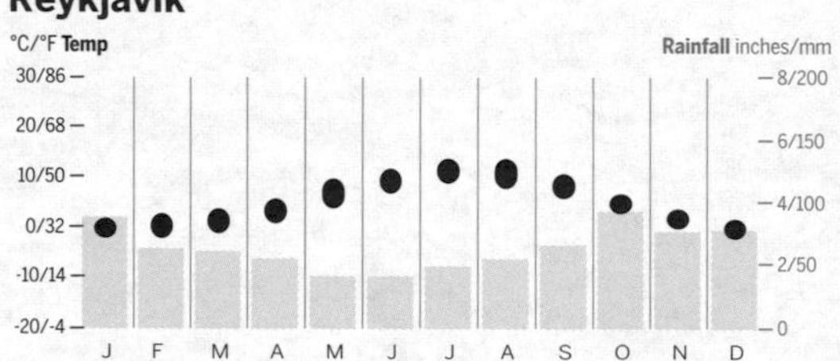

May & Jun Prime birdwatching season happily coincides with the two driest months.

Aug Reykjavík runs at full throttle, culminating in the Culture Night arts festival.

Nov–Apr The best months for the Northern Lights.

Connections

Out on the edge of nothing, Iceland is nevertheless connected by year-round flights from Keflavík airport to European destinations, including Denmark (Copenhagen), Finland (Helsinki), Norway (Bergen, Oslo and Stavanger) and Sweden (Göteborg and Stockholm), as well as France, Germany and the Netherlands.

For a more romantic arrival, take the ferry from Denmark (see p642) to Seyðisfjörður.

ITINERARIES

Three Days

Arrive in Reykjavík on Friday to catch the decadent *runtur*. Sober up in Laugadalur geothermal pool, admire the views from Hallgrímskirkja, then absorb some Viking history at the National Museum. On Sunday, visit Gullfoss, Geysir and Þingvellir on a Golden Circle tour. Stop to soak in the Blue Lagoon on the way home.

Essential Food & Drink

» **Traditional Icelandic dishes** These reflect a nightmarish historical need to eat every last scrap: brave souls might try *svið* (singed sheep's head), *súrsaðir hrútspungar* (pickled ram's testicles) and *hárkarl* (putrefied shark meat), bought from the butcher, fishmonger or old-school workers' canteens. More palatable offerings include *harðfiskur* (dried strips of haddock with butter), *plokkfiskur* (a hearty fish-and-potato gratin) and delicious, yoghurt-like *skyr*.

» **Succulent specialities** Icelandic lamb is among the tastiest on the planet – sheep roam free in the mountains all summer, grazing on sweet grass and wild thyme. Iceland also takes great pride in its fishing industry, and super-fresh fish dishes grace most menus. Pink-footed goose and reindeer meat from the eastern highlands are high-end treats.

» **Whale-meat controversy** Many restaurants serve whale meat: the International Fund for Animal Welfare points out that only 1.1% of Icelanders regularly eat whale, with tourists responsible for consuming a significant proportion of these protected species.

» **Favourite drinks** The traditional alcoholic brew *brennivín* is schnapps made from potatoes and caraway seeds. It's fondly known as *svarti dauði* (black death). Coffee is a national institution.

AT A GLANCE

» **Currency** Icelandic króna (Ikr)

» **Language** Icelandic

» **Money** ATMs everywhere

» **Visas** Not needed for citizens of Australia, Canada, New Zealand, the EU and the USA staying for up to 90 days

Fast Facts

» **Area** 103,000 sq km

» **Capital** Reykjavík

» **Country code** ☎354

» **Emergency** ☎112

Exchange Rates

Australia	A$1	Ikr115
Canada	C$1	Ikr115
euro zone	€1	Ikr161
Japan	¥100	Ikr140
New Zealand	NZ$1	Ikr84
UK	UK£1	Ikr186
USA	US$1	Ikr114

Set Your Budget

» **Budget hotel room** Ikr17,000

» **Two-course evening meal** Ikr4000

» **Museum entrance** free–Ikr1000

» **500mL beer** Ikr800

» **Reykjavík bus ticket** Ikr280

Resources

» **Icelandic Tourist Board** (www.visiticeland.com) With links to regional websites

» **Reykjavík tourist office** (www.visitreykjavik.is)

REYKJAVÍK

POP 117,500

Cute and coffee-fuelled, Iceland's eccentric capital is a tiny city with tremendous soul. You'll find Viking history, state-of-the-art geothermal pools, cosy cafes, stylish bars and a fizzing music scene, all teetering on the brink of the Arctic Circle.

The first settler, Ingólfur Arnarson, landed here in 871, naming the place Reykjavík (Smoky Bay) after steam rising from nearby fissures. Since then, Reykjavík has become a buzzing city while retaining its small-town charm.

Reykjavík's heart lies between Tjörnin (the Pond) and the harbour, with nearly everything else within walking distance.

Sights & Activities

TOP CHOICE **Hallgrímskirkja** CHURCH

(www.hallgrimskirkja.is; Skólavörðuholt; ⏲9am-5pm mid-Aug–mid-Jun, 9am-7pm mid-Jun–mid-Aug) Designed to resemble basalt columns

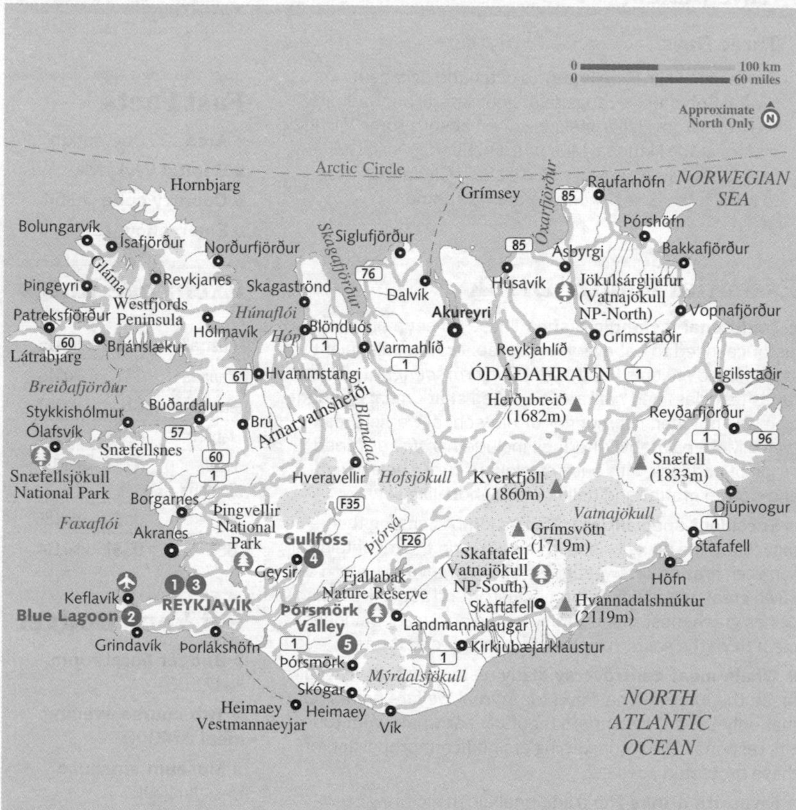

Iceland Highlights

1. Party till dawn on Reykjavík's Friday-night **pub crawl** (p638)
2. Swim through steam clouds at Iceland's world-famous **Blue Lagoon** (p639) spa
3. Come face to face with ocean giants on a **whale-watching trip** (p633)
4. Gullfoss waterfall, the geysers and the nation's birthplace, Þingvellir, on a **Golden Circle bus tour** (p640)
5. Take a wilderness hike in the beautiful **Þórsmörk valley** (p639)

and taking 34 years to construct, this immense concrete church is Reykjavík's most famous building. For unmissable views, take the elevator up the 75m-high **tower** (adults Ikr500).

National Museum MUSEUM
(www.natmus.is; Suðurgata 41; adult/concession Ikr1000/500, admission free Wed; ⏲10am-5pm daily May–mid-Sep, 11am-5pm Tue-Sun mid-Sep–Apr) Award-winning displays on Iceland's culture and history, from Settlement Era swords and silver hoards to items illustrating the country's dramatic leap into the 20th century. The most treasured artefact is a stunning carved 13th-century church door.

TOP CHOICE **Reykjavík 871+/-2** MUSEUM
(Settlement Exhibition; www.reykjavik871.is; Aðalstræti 16; adult Ikr600; ⏲10am-5pm) A unique combination of archaeology, technology and imagination, the city's newest museum is based around a single Viking longhouse. Although it's compact, it's utterly absorbing – go and see!

Laugardalslaug SWIMMING POOL
(Sundlaugavegur 30; adult Ikr360, swimsuit/towel hire Ikr350/350; ⏲6.30am-10.30pm Mon-Fri year-round, 8am-10.30pm Sat & Sun Apr-Sep, to 8pm Oct-Mar) Reykjavík's outdoor swimming pools, heated by volcanic water, are the city's social hubs. The biggest and best is Laugardalslaug, with indoor and outdoor pools, seven Jacuzzi-like 'hotpots' and a five-star health resort next door. It's about 2.5km east of the city centre; take bus 14.

FREE **Nauthólsvík Hot Beach** GEOTHERMAL BEACH
(Ýlströndin; ⏲11am-7pm mid-May–mid-Aug) Bringing the Riviera to Reykjavík, this Blue Flag beach is a dinky crescent of golden sand warmed by 18°C to 20°C geothermal water. It has changing rooms (Ikr200) and boat hire (Ikr600, 4pm to 7pm Wednesday and Thursday). It's about 2.5km south of the city centre; take bus 19.

Elding Whale Watching WHALE WATCHING
(☎555 3565; www.elding.is; adult Ikr8000) Iceland is terrific for whale-spotting, particularly between April and October: minkes often swim right up to the boats. Elding runs three-hour trips from the harbour, also sailing past a puffin breeding ground between mid-May and mid-August.

TOP CHOICE **Volcano Show** FILM
(☎845 9548; vknudsen2000@yahoo.com; Red Rock Cinema, Hellusund 6a; adult Ikr1300) Eccentric eruption-chaser Villi Knudsen screens his footage at the awesome Volcano Show, including rough cuts of the recent Eyjafjallajökull eruptions. One-hour shows in English begin at 11am, 3pm and 8pm in July and August (less frequently outside high season).

Saga Museum & Perlan MUSEUM
(www.sagamuseum.is; adult/concession Ikr1500/1000; ⏲10am-6pm Apr-Sep, noon-5pm Oct-Mar) The excellent Saga Museum brings Iceland's history to life with silicon models and blood-curdling screams. It's inside one of the city's hot-water tanks at **Perlan** (the Pearl), alongside an **artificial geyser** and a 360-degree **viewing deck** with tremendous mountain and city vistas. It's 2km southeast of the city centre; take bus 18 from Lækjartorg.

TOP CHOICE **Þjóðmenningarhúsið** MUSEUM
(www.thjodmenning.is; Hverfisgata 15; adult/concession Ikr400/200, admission free Wed; ⏲11am-5pm) Fans of the Icelandic sagas should head for the excellent Culture House, which offers intelligent displays on the history of these medieval narratives. Darkened rooms contain the actual vellums themselves.

FREE **National Gallery** ART GALLERY
(www.listasafn.is; Fríkirkjuvegur 7; ⏲11am-5pm Tue-Sun) Contains works by Iceland's most renowned artists (mainly from the 19th and 20th centuries) and gives an interesting glimpse into the nation's psyche: surreal mud-purple landscapes and visions of ogresses, giants and dead men walking.

Old Reykjavík ICONIC BUILDINGS
Old Reykjavík evolved around **Tjörnin**, a large central lake filled with hooting water-birds. Near the lake you'll find the **Raðhús** (City Hall; ⏲8am-7pm Mon-Fri, noon-6pm Sat & Sun), containing a cafe and an impressive 3D map of Iceland; the Icelandic parliament **Alþingi** (www.althingi.is; Túngata); and Iceland's small but perfectly proportioned cathedral, the **Dómkirkja** (Lækjargata 14a; ⏲10am-5pm Mon-Fri).

Festivals & Events

Held on a Saturday in mid-August, **Culture Night** is Reykjavík's biggest arts festival, with a grand fireworks finale. The five-day **Iceland Airwaves** (www.icelandairwaves.com)

Central Reykjavík

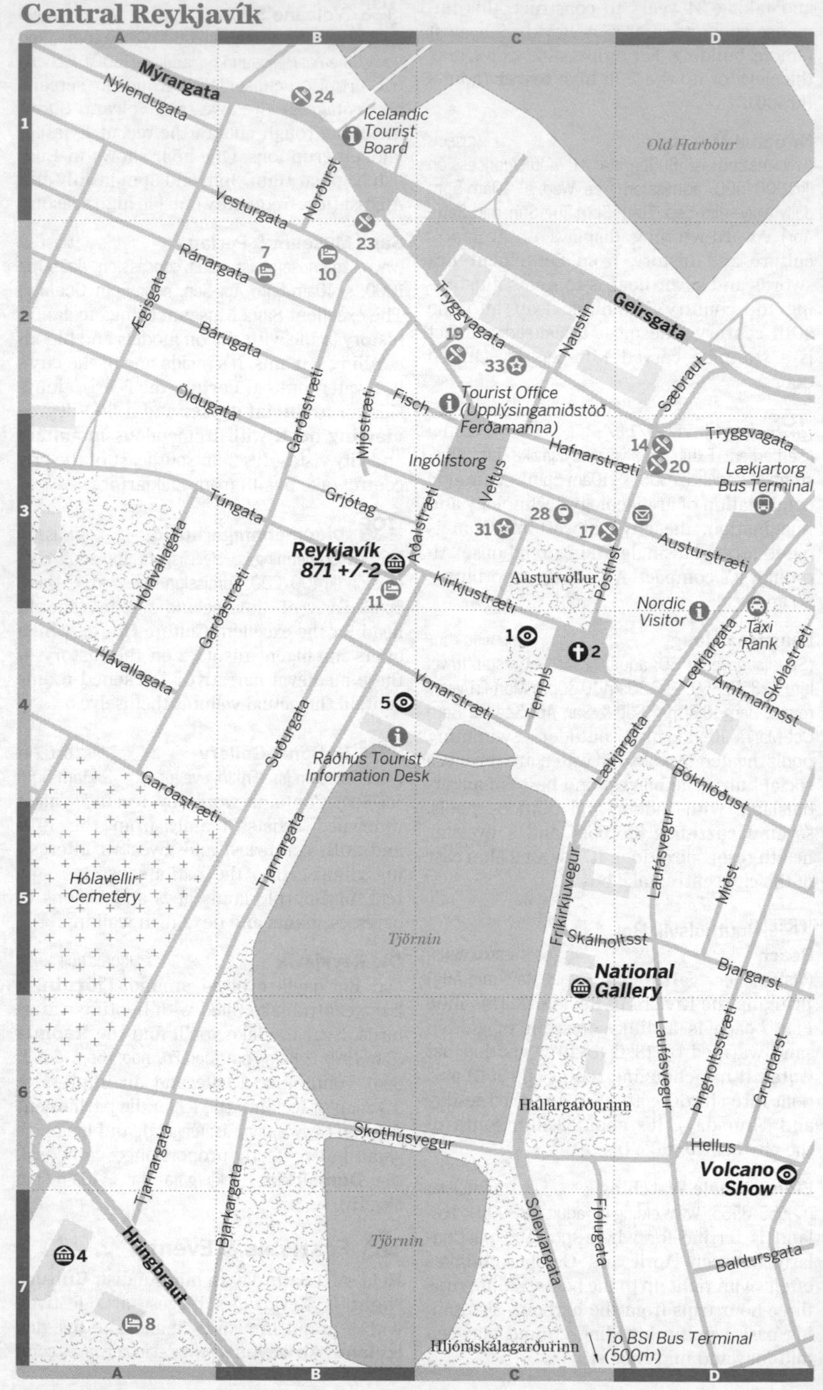

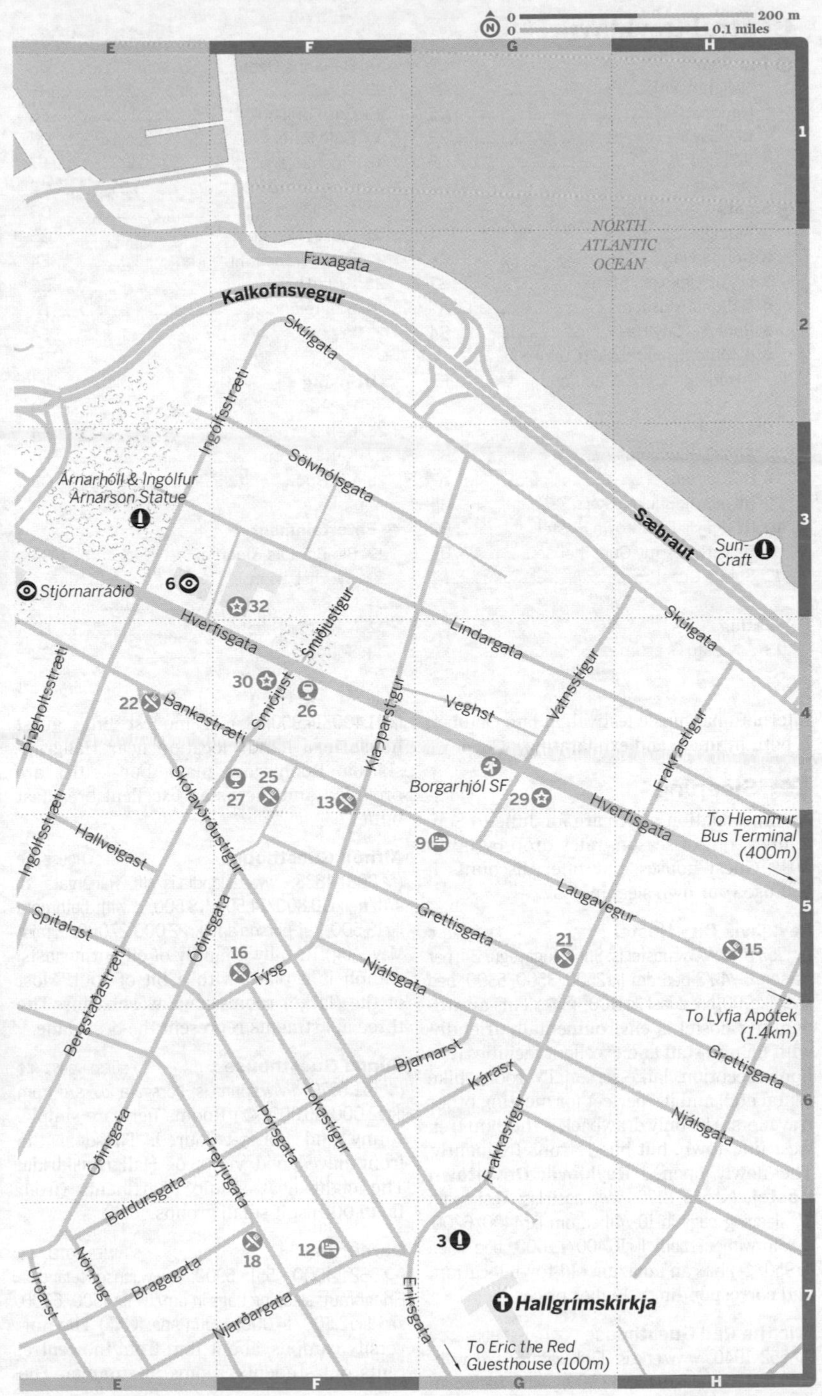

0 200 m
0 0.1 miles
E
F
G
H
1
2
3
4
5
6
7
NORTH ATLANTIC OCEAN
Faxagata
Kalkofnsvegur
Skúlgata
Ingólfsstræti
Sölvhólsgata
Árnarhóll & Ingólfur Árnarson Statue
Sæbraut
Sun-Craft
Stjórnarráðið
6
32
Smiðjustígur
Lindargata
Skúlgata
Hverfisgata
30
Smiðjust
26
22
Bankastræti
Veghst
Vatnsstígur
Frakkastígur
Klapparstígur
Þingholtsstræti
Skólavörðustígur
25
27
13
Borgarhjól SF
29
Hverfisgata
To Hlemmur Bus Terminal (400m)
Ingólfsstræti
Hallveigast
9
Laugavegur
Spitalast
Óðinsgata
Grettisgata
21
15
16
Týsg
Njálsgata
Bergstaðastræti
To Lyfja Apótek (1.4km)
Bjarnarst
Grettisgata
Karast
Lokastígur
Þórsgata
Njálsgata
Óðinsgata
Freyjugata
Frakkastígur
Baldursgata
3
12
18
Nönnug
Bragagata
Urðarst
Njarðargata
Eiriksgata
Hallgrímskirkja
To Eric the Red Guesthouse (100m)

Central Reykjavík

Top Sights
- Hallgrímskirkja G7
- National Gallery C5
- Reykjavík 871 +/-2 .... B3
- Volcano Show D6

Sights
- 1 Alþingi C4
- 2 Dómkirkja C4
- 3 Leifur Eiríksson Statue G7
- 4 National Museum A7
- 5 Raðhús (City Hall) B4
- 6 Þjóðmenningarhúsið (Culture House) E3

Sleeping
- 7 Álfhóll Guesthouse B2
- 8 Garður Inn A7
- 9 Reykjavík Backpackers G5
- 10 Reykjavík Downtown Hostel B2
- 11 Salvation Army Guesthouse B3
- 12 Sunna Guesthouse F7

Eating
- 13 Á Næstu Grösum F4
- 14 Bæjarins Beztu D3
- 15 Bónus H5
- 16 C Is For Cookie F5
- 17 Café Paris C3
- 18 Eldsmiðjan F7
- 19 Fish Company C2
- 20 Hornið D3
- 21 Indian Mango G5
- 22 Kofi Tómasar Frænda E4
- 23 Krua Thai B2
- 24 Sægreifinn B1
- 25 Vegamót F4

Drinking
- Boston .... (see 9)
- 26 Celtic Cross F4
- 27 Kaffibarinn F4
- 28 Vín Búð C3

Entertainment
- 29 Bíó Paradís Cinema G4
- 30 Hverfisbarinn F4
- 31 NASA C3
- 32 National Theatre F3
- 33 Sódóma C2

international music festival, in late October, is both intimate and exhilarating.

Sleeping

Accommodation prices are for June to September; out of season, rates drop by up to 40%. Guest houses may offer discounts if you use your own sleeping bag.

Reykjavík City Hostel HOSTEL €
(☎553 8110; www.hostel.is; Sundlaugavegur 34; per person 6-/4-/2-bed dm Ikr2500/3500/5300, bed linen Ikr900, breakfast Ikr1100; P@) This award-winning hostel is environmentally friendly, with helpful staff and excellent facilities (24-hour reception, large-screen TV room, bike rental etc), and it's perfect for meeting other travellers. The only drawback is the 3km trek west into town, but bus 14 runs frequently. The newly opened **Reykjavík Downtown Hostel** (☎553 8120; www.hostel.is; Vesturgata 17; sleeping bags in 10-/4-bed dm Ikr4400/6200, d with/without bath Ikr16,400/13,000, bed linen Ikr950; @) has an amazing old-town location, and correspondingly higher prices.

Eric the Red Guesthouse GUEST HOUSE €€
(☎552 1940; www.eric.is; Eiríksgata 6; s/d without bathroom Ikr9400/12,900, with bathroom Ikr11,400/14,900; @) A modest little guest house in a handy location near Hallgrímskirkja. Rooms are plain, but kettles are provided and there's an excellent breakfast buffet.

Álfhóll Guesthouse GUEST HOUSE €€
(☎898 1838; www.islandia.is/alf; Ránargata 8; s/d/tr Ikr10,800/14,500/18,500, d with bathroom Ikr18,500, 2-4-person apt Ikr22,000-27,000; ⊙mid-May–Aug) Run by a family of elf enthusiasts, Álfhóll is a place with a bit of soul. Most of the (large) rooms have washbasins. The three apartments represent the best value.

Sunna Guesthouse GUEST HOUSE €€
(☎511 5570; www.sunna.is; Þórsgata 26; s/d from Ikr12,000/15,000; @) Rooms here are simple, sunny and honey-coloured. Those at the front have good views of Hallgrímskirkja. The eight neat studio apartments (from Ikr19,000) suit small groups.

Garður Inn SUMMER HOTEL €€
(☎562 4000, 551 5900; www.innsoficeland.is; Hringbraut; sleeping bags in dm/tw Ikr4500/6000, s/d Ikr12,500/14,000; ⊙Jun-Aug; P@) The university campus, about 1km from the centre, rents out students' rooms in summer. The

SPLURGE

The talk of Reykjavík's dining scene, the atmospheric, gourmet **Fish Company** (Fiskfélagið; ☎552 5300; www.fiskfelagid.is; Vesturgata 2a; mains Ikr4000-6000; ⏲11.30am-2pm & from 6pm daily) serves up an ambitious round-the-world menu. A meal might begin with slow-cooked Spanish serrano, continue with succulent ginger salmon and end with Tahitian coconut cake! Candles and copper lamps cast a cosy glow.

cheapest sleeping-bag accommodation is in 16-person dorms.

Salvation Army Guesthouse HOSTEL €
(☎561 3203; www.herinn.is; Kirkjustræti 2; sleeping bags in dm Ikr3100, s/d/tr/q Ikr7400/10,400/14,400/18,200) The tiny rooms are frills-free, but their location couldn't be better. There's a bustling, backpacker atmosphere, guest kitchen and lounging area.

Reykjavík Backpackers HOSTEL €
(☎578 3700; www.reykjavikbackpackers.com; Laugavegur 28; per person 8-/6-/4-bed dm Ikr3290/3690/3990, deluxe 4-bed dm Ikr4290) A nuts-and-bolts hostel based in a former office block: minuses include small rooms with little storage space; pluses are the great central location and helpful staff. Only 'deluxe' dorm rooms on the 4th floor have kitchen access.

Reykjavík Campsite CAMPING GROUND €
(☎568 6944; www.reykjavikcampsite.is; Sundlaugavegur 32; campsites per person Ikr1100, 2-bed cabins Ikr7500; ⏲mid-May–mid-Sep; @) Reykjavík's well-equipped camping ground gets very busy in summer. It holds 650 people, though, so you'd be unlucky not to find a space. It's 3km east of the city centre; take bus 14.

Eating

Icelandic food (from hot dogs to gourmet dishes) is high quality. Cafes are good for light lunches; restaurants tend to be pricey places for dressed-up evening dining. Most eateries are on Laugavegur, Austurstræti and Ingólfstorg.

Restaurants

Indian Mango INDIAN €€
(☎551 7722; cnr Frakkastígur & Grettisgata; mains Ikr2400-4000; ⏲from 5pm Mon-Sat) A flavoursome experience, Mango focuses on Goan-Icelandic fusion food. Its specialities are *svartfugl* (guillemot) marinaded in Indian spices, and the sweetest, smoothest mango kulfi made with Goan mangoes. Great for vegies.

Á Næstu Grösum VEGETARIAN €
(First Vegetarian; www.anaestugrosum.is; Laugavegur 20b; daily specials Ikr1490; ⏲noon-10pm Mon Sat, 5-10pm Sun) A first-rate vegie restaurant, in a cheerful orange room overlooking Laugavegur, with inventive daily specials. Organic wine and beer are available. There's extra spice on Indian nights (Friday and Saturday).

Hornið ITALIAN €€
(☎551 3340; Hafnarstræti 15; 9-inch pizzas around Ikr2200, mains Ikr2600-4000; ⏲11am-11pm) This bright, easy-going art deco bistro serves large plates of grub. Pizzas are freshly made, the prettily presented pasta meals will set you up for the day and you can sample traditional Icelandic fish dishes.

Sægreifinn SEAFOOD €€
(Geirsgata 9; mains Ikr1500-2500; ⏲11.30am-10pm summer, shorter hr winter) Eccentric Sægreifinn serves fresh seafood in what looks like a 1950s English chip shop...except for the barrel seats and stuffed seal. Specialises in lobster soup and seafood kebabs. Note: whale meat is served here.

Krua Thai THAI €
(www.kruathai.is; Tryggvagata 14; mains Ikr1400-1900; ⏲noon-9.30pm Mon-Sat, 6-9.30pm Sun) Genuine, good-value Thai recipes are served here. A glossy photo-menu shows what you'll get (spicy salads, curries and stir-fries); you order at the counter and tasty, fresh-cooked dishes magically appear.

Cafes

Café Paris BISTRO €€
(Austurstræti 14; snacks Ikr800-2000; ⏲9am-1am) An old favourite, in spite of sometimes-hit-and-miss service. Paris is a prime people-watching spot, particularly in summer when outdoor seating spills onto Austurvöllur square. Start your day with a lazy breakfast and watch the world go by.

C Is For Cookie CAFE €
(Týsgata 8; snacks Ikr500-1000; ⏲9am-8pm Mon-Sat) Seek out central Reykjavík's newest cafe, named in honour of the Cookie Monster, for its cheerful atmosphere, great homemade cakes and pretty lattes. Come for breakfast, or light lunches of salad, soup and grilled sandwiches.

Vegamót BISTRO €€

(www.vegamot.is; Vegamótstígur 4; light meals around Ikr2000; ⏲11am-1am Mon-Thu, 11am-5am Fri & Sat, noon-1am Sun) A clubby place to eat, drink, gossip, see and be seen. The global menu includes Mexican salad, seafood quesadilla and blackened chicken. At night it's packed with fashion-conscious drinkers.

Kofi Tómasar Frænda STUDENT €

(Koffin; Laugavegur 2; snacks around Ikr800; ⏲10am-1am Mon-Thu, 10am-5.30am Fri & Sat, 11am-1am Sun) Subterranean Koffin is a favourite student hang-out. Relax with magazines and a snack (nachos, cakes) and watch people scurrying along Laugavegur. At night, it turns into a candlelit bar with DJs.

Quick Eats & Self-Catering

Bæjarins Beztu HOT-DOG VAN

(Tryggvagata) Icelanders swear by these hot dogs: use the vital sentence, '*Eina með öllu*' ('One with everything').

Eldsmiðjan PIZZA

(☎562 3838; Bragagata 38a; 10-inch pizzas around Ikr1500; ⏲11am-11pm) The wood-fired pizzas are the best in town…no, you didn't imagine the snail topping.

Bónus SUPERMARKET

(Laugavegur 59; ⏲noon-6.30pm Mon-Thu, 10am-7.30pm Fri, 10am-6pm Sat) The cheapest supermarket in town.

Drinking

Reykjavík is renowned for its weekend *runtur,* when hard-working Icelanders buy beer from Vín Búð (state alcohol shop), have a pre-party at home, then hit the town at midnight. Usually the only difference between cafes and bars is the time of day.

Reykjavík is dressy, but there are pub-like places where you can get away with jeans. Things change fast: check the widely distributed English-language newspaper *Grapevine* for up-to-date listings. Minimum drinking age is 20.

Celtic Cross PUB

(Hverfisgata 26) Externally, this place has a macabre air – it's styled as an undertaker's establishment. Inside, it's a cosy Irish pub divided into several snug, wood-lined rooms, with regular live singers and bands.

Kaffibarinn BOHEMIAN BAR

(Bergstaðastræti 1) Damon Albarn of Blur and Gorillaz fame owns part of this trendy bar. It's popular with celebs: at weekends you'll need a famous face or a battering ram to get in.

Boston BOHEMIAN BAR

(Laugavegur 28b) Boston is cool, arty – and easily missed: it's accessed through a doorway on Laugavegur that leads upstairs to a laid-back, candlelit lounge decorated in black wallpaper grown over with silver leaves, and frequented by a nonconformist crowd. Live music/DJs.

☆ Entertainment

Reykjavík's **National Theatre** (☎585 1200, tickets 551 1200; www.leikhusid.is; Hverfisgata 19; admission adult/under 25 Ikr3750/3000; ⏲box office noon-6pm & before evening performances, theatre closed Jul & Aug) puts on around 10 plays, musicals and operas per year. The most central cinema is **Bíó Paradís** (☎412 7711; Hverfisgata 54; Ikr1100). Buy tickets at the box office, or online at http://midi.is/cinema.

Sódóma ROCK VENUE

(☎821 6921; Tryggvagata 22) Opened in 2009, Sódóma is a central bar-club that favours music's rockier end. Its size and brand-new sound system make it a major live-music venue, with gigs from Wednesday to Saturday. (Also famous for its urinals, lined with mugshots of Iceland's former bankers!)

NASA CLUB

(www.nasa.is; Austurvöllur; admission Ikr1000-3500) The biggest nightclub in Reykjavík, NASA is a stripped-pine affair filled with a Prada-clad crowd. It plays chart music and club anthems and is also one of the city's biggest live-music venues.

Hverfisbarinn CLUB

(www.hverfisbarinn.is; Hverfisgata 20) A trendy bar and club with the queues to prove it! It's done out in a cool modern-Scandinavian style, which adds to the spacious feel. Popular with (immaculately dressed) students, who come for live music on Thursday and weekend DJs.

Information

Discount Cards

Reykjavík Welcome Card (24/48/72hr Ikr1500/2000/2500) is available at tourist offices. Gives free entry to galleries, museums and swimming pools, and includes a bus pass.

Internet Access

Aðalbókasafn (Reykjavík City Library; www.borgarbokasafn.is; Tryggvagata 15; per hr Ikr250; ⏲10am-7pm Mon-Thu, 11am-7pm Fri, 1-5pm Sat & Sun)

Medical Services

Dentist on duty (☎575 0505)

Health Centre (☎585 2600; Vesturgata 7) Doctor's appointment for European/non-European visitors Ikr2600/8000.

Landspítali University Hospital (☎543 2000; Fossvogur) Has a 24-hour casualty department; 4km southeast of the city centre.

Lyfja Apótek (☎552 4045; Laugavegur 16; ⏲9am-6pm Mon-Fri, 11am-4pm Sat) Central pharmacy.

Lyfja Apótek (☎533 2300; Lágmúli 5; ⏲7am-1am) Late-night pharmacy, near the Hilton Hotel. Take bus S2, 15, 17 or 19.

Money

The three major Icelandic banks all have branches on Austurstræti and Bankastræti.

Tourist Information

English-language newspaper **Grapevine** (www.grapevine.is), widely distributed, is an irreverent introduction to Reykjavík.

Main tourist office (Upplýsingamiðstöð Ferðamanna; ☎590 1550; www.visitreykjavik.is; Aðalstræti 2; ⏲8.30am-7pm Jun–mid-Sep, 9am-6pm Mon-Fri, 9am-4pm Sat, 9am-2pm Sun mid-Sep–May) There's also a desk at the Raðhús (City Hall).

Getting Around

To/From the Airport

The **Flybus** (☎580 5400; www.re.is) meets all international flights to/from Keflavík airport (hotel/hostel drop-off Ikr2500, 50 minutes). Buy tickets online, or from machines/ticket booth in the airport (credit cards accepted).

Bicycle

Hire bikes from **Borgarhjól SF** (☎551 5653; www.borgarhjol.net; Hverfisgata 50; ⏲8am-6pm Mon-Fri, 10am-2pm Sat) or Reykjavík City Hostel for Ikr4200 per day.

Bus

Straetó (☎540 2700; www.straeto.is) city-bus system runs from 7am to 11pm or midnight (from 10am Sunday), with limited weekend night buses. Central terminals are at **Hlemmur** and **Lækjartorg**; bus stops are marked with the letter 'S'. The fare is Ikr280, with no change given. The Reykjavík Welcome Card includes a bus pass.

Buses to other districts use the **BSÍ bus terminal** (☎562 1011; www.bsi.is; Vatnsmýrarvegur 10; ⏲4.30am-midnight), 1km south of the city centre.

Taxi

Taxis wait outside the bus stations, youth hostels and bars on weekend nights.

» **Borgarbíll** (☎552 2440)

» **BSR** (☎561 0000)

» **Hreyfill-Bæjarleiðir** (☎588 5522)

AROUND REYKJAVÍK

Blue Lagoon

Iceland's most famous attraction is the **Blue Lagoon** (Bláa Lónið; ☎420 8800; www.bluelagoon.is; adult Ikr4500, towel/swimsuit/robe hire Ikr800/800/1450, spa treatments from Ikr2250; ⏲9am-9pm Jun-Aug, 10am-8pm Sep-May), a milky-blue spa set in a massive black lava field, 50km southwest of Reykjavík. The futuristic Svartsengi geothermal plant provides an off-the-planet backdrop, as well as the spa's water – at a perfect 38°C and at Blue Flag standards. Daub yourself in a silica-mud face pack and loll in the hotpots with an ice-blue cocktail – it's so relaxing, you'll never want to leave. The mineral-rich waters dry your hair to straw – wear a bathing cap or bring plenty of hair conditioner.

Between 10am and 6pm daily, there are nine **Reykjavík Excursions** (☎580 5400; www.re.is) buses from the BSÍ bus terminal (or from hotels on request). The Ikr6300 cost includes lagoon admission and return fare to Reykjavík (or onward journey to Keflavík airport).

Þórsmörk

The Woods of Thor is a stunning glacial valley, full of weird rock formations, twisting gorges, a singing cave, mountain flowers and icy streams. Its proximity to Reykjavík (130km) makes it popular in summer, when tents pile up and camping grounds become partyville.

Wild camping is prohibited, but there are three huts – **Þórsmörk–Skagfjörðsskáli** (Ferðafélag Íslands; ☎568 2533; www.fi.is; N 63°40.960, W 19°30.890; sleeping bags in dm Ikr4200), **Básar** (Útivist; ☎562 1000, 893 2910; www.utivist.is; N 63°40.559, W 19°29.014; sleeping bags in dm Ikr2800) and **Húsadalur** (HI Iceland; ☎552 8300, 894 1506; www.hostel.is; N 63°41.350, W 19°33.100; sleeping bags in dm Ikr3100) – which have tent sites (per person Ikr1000) around them. Reservations strongly advised.

From mid-June to mid-September buses run between Reykjavík and Húsadalur (over the hill from Þórsmörk) at 8am daily. A second service runs from mid-June to August at 4pm daily (Ikr5800, 3½ hours).

WORTH A TRIP

THE GOLDEN CIRCLE

Marvel at Iceland's 'big three' destinations – Gullfoss, Geysir and Þingvellir National Park – on one day-long circular tour.

Gullfoss is a spectacular rainbow-tinged double waterfall, which drops 32m before thundering away down a vast rift. Ten kilometres down the road is **Geysir**, after which all spouting hot springs are named. The **Great Geysir**, semiplugged by rubble-throwing tourists in the 1950s, erupts sporadically. Luckily, the ever-reliable **Strokkur** (Butter Churn) is right next door, spouting up to 30m every six minutes.

Þingvellir National Park is Iceland's most important historical location, and a Unesco World Heritage site. The Vikings established the world's first democratic parliament, the Alþing, here in AD 930. They certainly had a sense of drama – Þingvellir is inside an immense rift valley, caused by the separating North American and Eurasian tectonic plates.

The cheapest day trip (Ikr8900) is with **Iceland Excursions** (☎540 1313; www.icelandexcursions.is; Hafnarstræti 20); you're usually collected from your accommodation.

UNDERSTAND ICELAND

History

Iceland's solitude was shattered by the Age of Settlement (AD 871–930), when a wave of Vikings crashed in from Norway. The settlers rejected monarchy in favour of the world's first democratic parliament, the Alþing, established in 930 at Þingvellir (Parliament Plains).

In the early 13th century, violent blood feuds among Icelandic chieftains led to periods of first Norwegian (1262) then Danish (1397) rule. For the next six centuries, Iceland was devastated by a Dark Age of famine, disease and disastrous volcanic eruptions.

Despite never-ending catastrophes, a sense of nationalism slowly grew. By 1874 Iceland had drafted its own constitution. The Republic of Iceland was established on 17 June 1944.

During WWII Iceland serviced British and US troops stationed at Keflavík. The war marked a dramatic leap forward, as subsistence farming gave way to frenzied building and prosperity.

Iceland may have prospered, but its recent apparent wealth was based on high borrowing, and the 2008 global financial crisis hit it especially hard. Only a US$2.1 billion IMF loan saved it from bankruptcy. Jóhanna Sigurðardóttir, Iceland's first female prime minister, applied for EU membership in 2009.

In 2010, the volcano under the glacier Eyjafjallajökull erupted. The resulting 8km-high ash cloud caused the largest air-traffic shutdown since WWII.

People

Most Icelanders are descended from early Scandinavian settlers and their Celtic slaves. Almost half of Iceland's 318,000 inhabitants live in Reykjavík. Icelanders are individualists, with a live-and-let-live attitude and one of the world's highest life expectancies – 79.7 years for men and 83.3 for women! Eight-four percent of the population is Lutheran.

Food

The following prices are for a main course.

€€€ more than Ikr3500

€€ Ikr1500 to 3500

€ less than Ikr1500

Arts

Bloody and powerful, Iceland's 13th-century sagas are its greatest cultural achievement – try *Egils Saga,* about a poet, murderer and grandson of a werewolf. *Independent People,* a blackly humorous novel about early-20th-century Iceland, won its author, Halldór Laxness, the Nobel Prize.

Björk and Sigur Rós are Iceland's most famous musical exports. New sounds surface all the time, spanning the range from quirky troubadours such as Hafdis Huld and Svavar Knútur, to seven-piece indie band Seabear, to electronica (FM Belfast) and the 'distorted metal opera' of Lazyblood. *Screaming Masterpiece* (2005) is an entertaining documentary about Icelandic music.

Environment

Iceland is a young country with an active volcanic zone running southwest to northeast, responsible for all those lava flows, geysers, hot springs and volcanoes.

The only indigenous land mammal is the Arctic fox. Iceland compensates for this shortage with huge numbers of birds and 17 species of whale.

Whaling is an emotional topic. In 2006 Iceland resumed commercial whale hunting: 25 nations issued a formal protest. Many restaurants serve *hval* (whale meat).

SURVIVAL GUIDE

Directory A–Z

Accommodation

All hostels and some guest houses and hotels offer a discount if guests use their own sleeping bags. We have given prices for sleeping-bag accommodation in each review where this service is available. The following price ranges are for a double room.

€€€ more than Ikr19,000

€€ Ikr14,000 to 19,000

€ less than Ikr14,000

Camping is allowed anywhere in Iceland, apart from on private land and in national parks and reserves.

Gistiheimilið (guest houses) range from private homes to purpose-built motels. Many places only open mid-May to August.

Iceland's 36 superb youth hostels are administered by **Hostelling International Iceland** (☎575 6700; www.hostel.is; Borgartún 6, IS-105 Reykjavík). All have hot showers, cooking facilities, sheet hire, luggage storage and sleeping-bag accommodation.

Ferðafélag Íslands (Icelandic Touring Club; ☎568 2533; www.fi.is; Mörkin 6, IS-108 Reykjavík) maintains a system of *sæluhús* (mountain huts).

There are 13 summer-only **Edda Hotels** (☎444 4000; www.hoteledda.is), based in schools or conference centres. Some offer sleeping-bag accommodation in dorms.

Activities

Hiking and mountaineering is stunning all over the country, especially in national parks and nature reserves. July, August and September are the best months for walking. For details contact Ferðafélag Íslands (opposite).

For horse rides, hire sturdy little Icelandic horses at farms and tourist offices countrywide. Two-hour/one-day rides cost about Ikr8000/16,000.

Rafting is best at Varmahlíð in the north. **Arctic Adventures** (☎571 2200; www.rafting.is; ⏲May-Sep) runs an exhilarating six-hour white-water trip (Ikr9800, minimum age 18).

There are daily year-round scuba-diving tours with **Dive.is** (☎663 2858; www.dive.is; 2 dives at Þingvellir Ikr30,000) to Lake Þingvellir, which has astonishing 100m visibility.

Every town has at least one geothermal public pool.

Whale and dolphin watching are best from mid-May to September. Regular sailings depart from Reykjavík, although northern Húsavík is the 'whale-watching capital'.

Business Hours

Banks 9.15am-4pm Mon-Fri

Cafes & Bars 10am-6pm as cafes, then as bars to 1am Mon-Fri, to 3am or 6am at weekends

Post offices 9am-4.30pm Mon-Fri

Restaurants generally close by 10pm

Shops 9am-6pm Mon-Fri, 10am-noon or 4pm Sat, closed Sun

Customs

See www.tollur.is for details of Iceland's customs regulations.

Holidays

The following public holidays are observed in Iceland.

New Year's Day 1 January

Maundy Thursday Thursday before Easter

Good Friday to Easter Monday March/April

First Day of Summer First Thursday after 18 April

Labour Day 1 May

Ascension Day 40 days after Easter

Whit Sunday & Whit Monday 7th Sunday and Monday after Easter

Independence Day 17 June

Shop & Office Workers' Holiday First Monday in August

Christmas Eve 24 December
Christmas Day 25 December
Boxing Day 26 December
New Year's Eve 31 December

Money

ATMs take MasterCard, Visa, Cirrus, Maestro and Electron cards. Icelandic VAT *(söluskattur)* is included in marked prices: spend over Ikr4000 in a shop offering 'Iceland Tax-Free Shopping', and get a tax-refund coupon.

Tipping is not required.

Post

An airmail letter or postcard within Europe costs Ikr 140/165 (economy/priority), and Ikr155/220 outside of Europe.

Telephone

Iceland's international access code is ☎00; it has no area codes. For international directory assistance and reverse-charge (collect) calls, dial ☎1811. Most Icelandic mobile phone numbers begin with 6 or 8.

Visas

Residents of Schengen Agreement countries (see p1319) can enter Iceland with a valid identity card. Citizens of the European Economic Area (EEA), including Ireland and the UK, and the USA and Commonwealth countries can visit without a visa on a valid passport for up to three months. Check the Icelandic Directorate of Immigration's website (www.utl.is) for detailed information on visas, in English.

Getting There & Away

Air

International flights operate out of Keflavík airport (KEF; ☎425 6000, flight times 425 0777; www.keflavikairport.com), 48km west of Reykjavík. Reykjavík domestic airport (REK), in the city centre, is used for flights to Greenland and the Faroe Islands.

Airlines include the following:

Flugfélag Íslands (Air Iceland; NY; ☎570 3030; www.airiceland.is) Flies from Reykjavík to the Faroe Islands, and to Kulusuk and Narsarsuaq (Greenland).

Iceland Express (HW; ☎550 0600; www.icelandexpress.com) Internet-based airline with cheapest flights from Keflavík to London and Copenhagen. New routes from Belfast, Dublin, Edinburgh and the US commenced in summer 2011.

Icelandair (FI; ☎505 0300; www.icelandair.com) Often has equally cheap fares to the UK, the US and Europe.

Boat

Between mid-April and October, the **Smyril Line** (www.smyrilline.com) weekly car ferry *Norröna* sails from Denmark to Seyðisfjörður (eastern Iceland), via Tórshavn (Faroe Islands). Prices and schedules vary; check the website for details.

Getting Around

Air

The domestic flight network is heavily dependent on weather. Iceland's main domestic airline, **Flugfélag Íslands** (Air Iceland; ☎570 3030; www.airiceland.is), offers four-/five-/six-sector air passes (Ikr42,570/48,720/55,770), which must be bought outside the country. There's also a Fly-As-You-Please ticket (Ikr65,240), giving 12 days of unlimited travel. Domestic airport tax (Ikr1180) must be paid on every departure.

Bicycle

Rough roads and wild weather make cycling a challenge! Go prepared, and remember: you can always put your bike on a bus.

In many areas, including Reykjavík, bikes can be hired for around Ikr4000 per day.

Bus

BSÍ (Bifreiðastöð Íslands; ☎562 1011; www.bsi.is; BSÍ bus terminal, Vatnsmýrarvegur 10, Reykjavík) operates long-distance buses and sells money-saving passes. Many buses only run from June to August.

Car & Motorcycle

Renting a vehicle is expensive. The Reykjavík tourist office has details, but booking a car before you arrive is usually cheaper. You must be at least 20 years old to hire a car.

Hitching

In summer hitching is possible in Iceland, but you may have to wait a long time in rural areas.

Ireland

Includes »

Best Places to Eat

- » Farmgate Café, Cork (p657)
- » L'Gueuleton, Dublin (p651)
- » Winding Stair, Dublin (p651)
- » Café Sol, Kilkenny (p656)
- » Vanilla Pod, Killarney (p660)

Best Places to Stay

- » Isaacs Hostel, Dublin (p650)
- » Garnish House, Cork (p659)
- » Kinlay House, Galway (p662)
- » Saddler's House, Derry (p674)

Why Go?

Few countries have an image so plagued by cliché. From shamrocks and shillelaghs to leprechauns and lovable rogues, there's a plethora of platitudes to wade through before you scramble ashore on the real Ireland.

But it's well worth looking beyond the tourist tat, for the Emerald Isle is one of Europe's gems, a scenic extravaganza of lake, mountain, sea and sky. From wind-lashed Donegal to picture-postcard County Cork, there are countless opportunities to get outdoors and explore, whether surfing the beach breaks of Bundoran, cycling the coast of Antrim or hiking the hills of Kerry and Connemara.

There are cultural pleasures too in the land of Joyce and Yeats, U2 and the Undertones. Dublin, Cork and Belfast all have party-on pubs and foot-stomping live-music scenes, while you can enjoy traditional music in the bars of Galway, Doolin and Killarney. So push aside the shamrocks and experience the real Ireland.

When to Go

Dublin

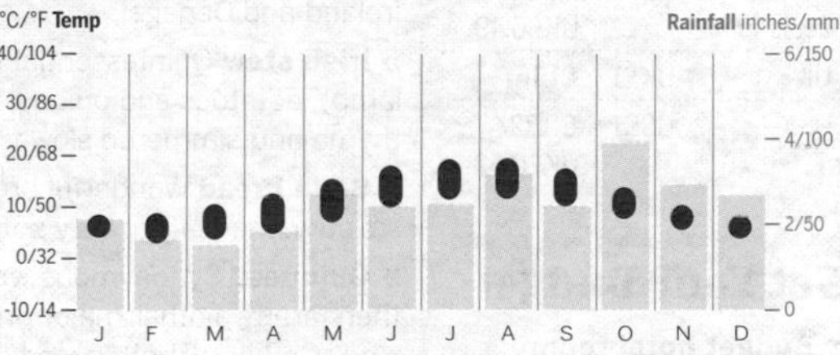

Late Mar Spring is under way, landscape is 40 shades of green, St Patrick's Day beckons.

Jun Best chance of dry weather, long summer evenings, Bloomsday in Dublin.

Sep–Oct Crowds have thinned, autumn colours the countryside, surf's up on the west coast.

AT A GLANCE

» **Currency** Euro (€) in Republic of Ireland, pound (£) in Northern Ireland

» **Languages** English, Irish Gaelic

» **Money** ATMs widespread; credit cards widely accepted

» **Visas** Non-Schengen rules (see p678)

Fast Facts

» **Area** 84,421 sq km

» **Capitals** Dublin (Republic of Ireland), Belfast (Northern Ireland)

» **Country codes** Republic of Ireland ☎353, Northern Ireland ☎44

» **Emergency** ☎112

Exchange Rates

Australia	A$1	€0.74/ UK£0.65
Canada	C$1	€0.74/ UK£0.63
euro zone	€1	€1/ UK£0.87
Japan	¥100	€0.87/ UK£0.76
New Zealand	NZ$1	€0.56/ UK£0.49
UK	UK£1	€1.16/–
USA	US$1	€0.72/ UK£0.62

Set Your Budget

» **Budget hotel room** €60/£75

» **Two-course evening meal** €25/£25

» **Museum entrance** free

» **Pint of beer** €4-€5/£2.50

Connections

Ireland is just about as far west as you can go in Europe – next stop, North America. But the Emerald Isle can serve as a stepping stone between mainland Europe and the UK. Ferry services run from Roscoff and Cherbourg in northern France to Rosslare (near Wexford) in southeast Ireland, from where you can continue your trip from Dublin to Wales, or from Belfast or Larne to Scotland or the Isle of Man. For more info, see p679.

ITINERARIES

One Week

Spend a couple of days in Dublin ambling through the excellent national museums and gorging yourself on Guinness and good company in Temple Bar. Get medieval in Kilkenny before heading on to Cork and discovering why they call it the 'Real Capital'. Meander through lush, idyllic West Cork and take in the friendly spirit and melodious accents of its denizens.

Two Weeks

Follow the one-week itinerary, then make your way from West Cork up to touristy Killarney and the Ring of Kerry on your way to bohemian Galway. Using Galway as your base, go and explore the alluring Aran Islands and the hills of Connemara. Finally, head north to experience the newly optimistic vibe in fast-changing Belfast.

Essential Food & Drink

» **Champ** Northern Irish dish of potatoes mashed with spring onions (scallions).

» **Colcannon** Mashed potato, milk, cabbage and onion fried in butter.

» **Farl** General name for triangular flat bread (often made with mashed potato mixed with flour) common to Northern Ireland and Donegal.

» **Irish stew** Quintessential stew of mutton (preferably lamb), potatoes and onions, flavoured with parsley and thyme and simmered slowly.

» **Soda bread** Wonderful bread, white or brown, sweet or savoury, made from very soft Irish flour and buttermilk.

» **Guinness** Synonymous with stout the world over, but there are two other major producers: Murphy's and Beamish & Crawford, both based in Cork city.

» **Irish whiskey** There are almost 100 different types of Irish whiskey, brewed by only three distilleries – Jameson's, Bushmills and Cooley's. A visit to Ireland reveals a depth of excellence that will make the connoisseur's palate spin, while winning over many new friends to what the Irish call *uisce beatha* (the water of life).

Ireland Highlights

1. Meander through the many museums, pubs and literary haunts of frenetic **Dublin** (p646) and ask a local, 'Where's the *craic* (fun)?'

2. Hang out in bohemian **Galway** (p662), with its hip cafes and live-music venues

3. Hike along the Causeway Coast and clamber across the **Giant's Causeway** (p673)

4. Take a boat trip to the 6th-century monastery perched atop the wild rocky islet of **Skellig Michael** (p661)

5. Sup a pint of Guinness while tapping your toes to a live-music session in a traditional Irish pub

6. Ride a bike through the spectacular lake and mountain scenery of the **Gap of Dunloe** (p660)

7. Discover the industrial history of the city that built the world's most famous ocean liner in **Belfast** (p669)

DUBLIN

☎01 / POP 1.1 MILLION

Sitting in a tapas bar on Great George's St, nursing a Guinness or a hangover (or both), you think about what your favourite experience has been in Dublin so far. Was it drinking in Temple Bar with people from dozens of other countries or was it buying fresh vegies at the Asian food market? Was it admiring the Georgian houses along St Stephen's Green or was it wandering the grounds of Trinity College? You never come to an answer, but you do realise that, just as the waters on the banks of the Liffey River seem to rise every day, so does your affection for this city.

Dublin is on the list of Europe's top 10 most visited cities. Visitors swarm in droves like moths to a light bulb – for the historic museums, top-class attractions and Georgian architecture, while immigrants from Eastern Europe, Asia and Africa set up new lives for their families, adding even more depth and complexity to an already rich cultural tapestry. Add a hard-partying nightlife to this mixture and what you get is a city that's constantly changing, and having a rare ould time as it does so.

Dublin is neatly divided by the Liffey River into the more affluent 'south side' and the less prosperous 'north side'. North of the river are Busáras, the main bus station, and Connolly station, one of the main train stations. Immediately south of the river is the bustling Temple Bar district, Trinity College and, just south of it, the lovely St Stephen's Green. About 2km west is Heuston station, the city's other main train station.

DUBLIN FOR FREE

Dublin is no cheap city, but there are plenty of attractions that won't bust your budget.

» **Trinity College grounds** (p646) Dublin's oldest and most beautiful university.

» **National Museum of Archaeology** (p646) World's finest collection of prehistoric gold artefacts.

» **Chester Beatty Library** (p646) Collection of oriental and religious art.

» **National Gallery** (p647) Irish and European paintings.

» **St Stephen's Green** (Map p648) The city's most picturesque public park.

Sights

Trinity College & Book of Kells MUSEUM

(Map p648; www.bookofkells.ie; College Green; admission to college grounds free, Old Library adult €9; ⌚9.30am-5pm Mon-Sat, vary Sun) Ireland's premier university was founded by Elizabeth I in 1592. Its full name is the University of Dublin, but **Trinity College** is the institution's sole college. Until 1793 the students were all Protestants, but today most of them are Catholic. Women were admitted in 1903.

Student-guided **walking tours** (per person €10) take place twice an hour from 10.45am to 3.40pm Monday to Saturday and 10.45am to 3.15pm Sunday from mid-May to September, departing from inside the main gate on College St. The tour is a good deal since it includes admission to the **Old Library** to see the *Book of Kells*, an elaborately illuminated gospel created by monks on the Scottish isle of Iona around AD 800, and the spectacular **Long Room**, an early-18th-century library lined with marble busts of writers and philosophers.

FREE **National Museum of Archaeology** MUSEUM

(Map p648; www.museum.ie; Kildare St; ⌚10am-5pm Tue-Sat, 2-5pm Sun) Among the highlights of the National Museum's archaeology and history branch are its superb collection of prehistoric gold objects. Other exhibits focus on early Christian art, the Viking period and medieval Ireland.

FREE **Chester Beatty Library** MUSEUM

(Map p652; www.cbl.ie; Dublin Castle; ⌚10am-5pm Mon-Fri, 11am-5pm Sat, 1-5pm Sun, closed Mon Oct-Apr) Bequeathed to the nation by mining engineer Sir Alfred Chester Beatty (1875–1968), this breathtaking collection includes more than 20,000 manuscripts, rare books, miniature paintings, clay tablets, costumes and other objects.

O'Connell Street HISTORIC DISTRICT

Dublin's grandest avenue is dominated by the needle-like **Monument of Light** (Map p648; O'Connell St), better known as 'The Spire', which rises from the spot once occupied by a statue of Admiral Nelson (which disappeared in explosive fashion, thanks to the IRA, in 1966). Soaring 120m into the sky, it is, apparently, the world's tallest sculpture.

Nearby is the 1815 **General Post Office** (GPO; Map p648; O'Connell St; ⌚8am-8pm Mon-

Sat), an important landmark of the 1916 Easter Rising when the Irish Volunteers used it as a base for attacks against the British army. After a fierce battle the GPO was burnt out. Upon surrendering, the leaders of the Irish rebellion and 13 others were taken to Kilmainham Gaol and executed.

Guinness Brewery BREWERY

(off Map p648; www.guinness-storehouse.com; Market St; adult €15; ⌚9.30am-7pm Jul & Aug, to 5pm Sep-Jun) The Guinness Storehouse sits in the malty fug of the mighty Guinness brewery southwest of the city centre. The building is shaped like a pint of Ireland's favourite drink with a bar in the 'head', and the best part of the tour is getting the finest-tasting Guinness of your life for free at the end. Take bus 51B or 78A from Aston Quay, or bus 123 from O'Connell St.

Kilmainham Gaol MUSEUM

(off Map p648; www.heritageireland.com; Inchicore Rd; adult €6; ⌚9.30am-6pm Apr-Sep, 9.30am-5.30pm Mon-Sat, 10am-6pm Sun Oct-Mar) The threatening grey Kilmainham Gaol, 2km west of the city centre, played a key role in Ireland's struggle for independence and was the site of mass executions following the 1916 Easter Rising. Buses 79, 78A and 51B from Aston Quay all pass by here.

FREE **National Gallery** ART GALLERY

(Map p648; www.nationalgallery.ie; West Merrion Sq; admission & guided tours free; ⌚9.30am-5.30pm Mon-Wed, Fri & Sat, to 8.30pm Thu, noon-5.30pm Sun) A magnificent Caravaggio and a breathtaking collection of works by Jack B Yeats – William Butler's younger brother – are the main reasons to visit here. Guided tours are held at 3pm on Saturday and 2pm, 3pm and 4pm on Sunday.

Christ Church Cathedral CATHEDRAL

(Map p648; www.cccdub.ie; Christ Church Pl; adult/concession €6/4; ⌚9am-6pm Jun-Aug, 9.45am-5pm Sep-May) Christ Church is the mother of all of Dublin's cathedrals, a simple wood structure until 1169, when the present church was built. In the southern aisle is a monument to Strongbow, a 12th-century Norman warrior. Note the precariously leaning northern wall (it's been that way since 1562).

Next door, connected to the cathedral by an arched walkway, **Dublinia** (Map p648; www.dublinia.ie; adult €6.95; ⌚10am-5pm Apr-Sep, 11am-4pm Mon-Fri, 10am-4pm Sat & Sun Oct-Mar) is a lively attempt to bring medieval Dublin to life, with models of 10 episodes in Dublin's history. It has wheelchair access.

St Patrick's Cathedral CATHEDRAL

(Map p648; www.stpatrickscathedral.ie; St Patrick's Close; adult €5.50; ⌚9am-6pm Mon-Sat, hr vary Sun Mar-Oct, 9am-5pm Sat, hr vary Sun Nov-Feb, closed during times of worship) There was a church on the site of St Patrick's Cathedral as early as the 5th century, but the present building dates from 1191. St Patrick's choir was part of the first group to perform Handel's *Messiah* in 1742 and you can hear their successors sing the 5.45pm evensong most weeknights.

FREE **Natural History Museum** MUSEUM

(Map p648; www.museum.ie; Merrion St; ⌚10am-5pm Tue-Sat, 2-5pm Sun) Excellent and atmospheric Victorian museum scarcely changed since 1857, when Scottish explorer Dr David Livingstone delivered the opening lecture. Recently reopened after

PORTRAIT OF THE WRITER

Anyone who tells you that James Joyce (1882–1941) is an easy and enjoyable read is a rotten liar and should not be trusted. That said, no-one can doubt that Joyce's dense, often incomprehensible, work revolutionised the way stories are told. Beginning with *A Portrait of the Artist as a Young Man*, Joyce used stream-of-consciousness narratives to wander within a story's timeline, instead of telling it chronologically. Consider him an earlier, more Catholic Quentin Tarantino.

Joyce perfected this technique in his masterpiece, *Ulysses*, which focuses on a day in the life of two Irishmen – one a Catholic, the other a Jew – and in his last major work, *Finnegans Wake*, he went a step further, often using entirely nonsensical terms and disregarding plot completely.

While understanding Joyce's work may be out of the question, understanding his inspirational environment isn't. Next time you see a pub displaying a 'James Joyce Authentic Irish Pub Award' stop in, have a pint, and if anyone asks, tell them that *yer man* James is an easy and enjoyable read.

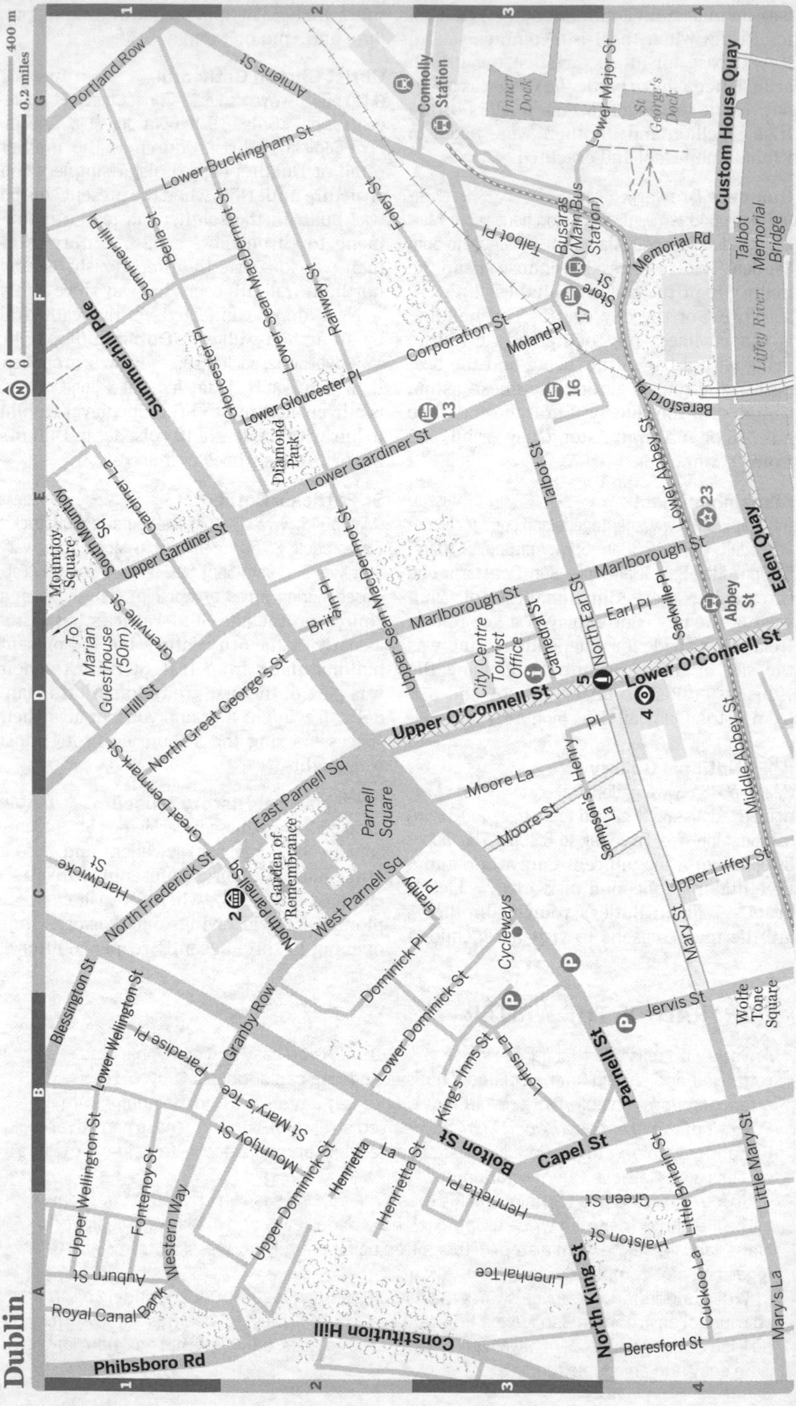

Dublin

0 — 400 m
0 — 0.2 miles

A B C D E F G
1 2 3 4

Portland Row
Amiens St
Connolly Station
Inner Dock
St George's Dock
Lower Major St
Custom House Quay
Lower Buckingham St
Summerhill Pl
Bella St
Lower Sean MacDermot St
Foley St
Talbot Pl
Busaras (Main Bus Station)
Store St
Memorial Rd
Talbot Memorial Bridge
Liffey River
Summerhill Pde
Gloucester Pl
Railway St
Corporation St
Moland Pl
17
16
13
Beresford Pl
Lower Gloucester Pl
Diamond Park
Lower Gardiner St
Talbot St
Lower Abbey St
23
Eden Quay
Gardiner La
Mountjoy Square
South Mountjoy Sq
Upper Gardiner St
Upper Sean MacDermot St
Britain Pl
Marlborough St
Marlborough St
North Earl St
Earl Pl
Sackville Pl
Abbey St
To Marian Guesthouse (50m)
Grenville St
Hill St
North Great George's St
City Centre Tourist Office
Cathedral St
5
Lower O'Connell St
Upper O'Connell St
4
Henry Pl
Middle Abbey St
Great Denmark St
East Parnell Sq
Parnell Square
Moore La
Moore St
Sampson's La
Hardwicke St
North Frederick St
2
Garden of Remembrance
North Parnell Sq
West Parnell Sq
Granby Pl
Cycleways
Upper Liffey St
Mary St
Blessington St
Lower Wellington St
Granby Row
Dominick Pl
Lower Dominick St
Jervis St
Wolfe Tone Square
Paradise Pl
King's Inns St
Loftus La
Parnell St
St Mary's Tce
Mountjoy St
Henrietta La
Henrietta St
Bolton St
Capel St
Little Britain St
Little Mary St
Upper Wellington St
Fontenoy St
Western Way
Upper Dominick St
Henrietta Pl
Green St
Halston St
Auburn St
Linenhal Tce
Cuckoo La
Royal Canal Bank
North King St
Constitution Hill
Phibsboro Rd
Beresford St
Mary's La

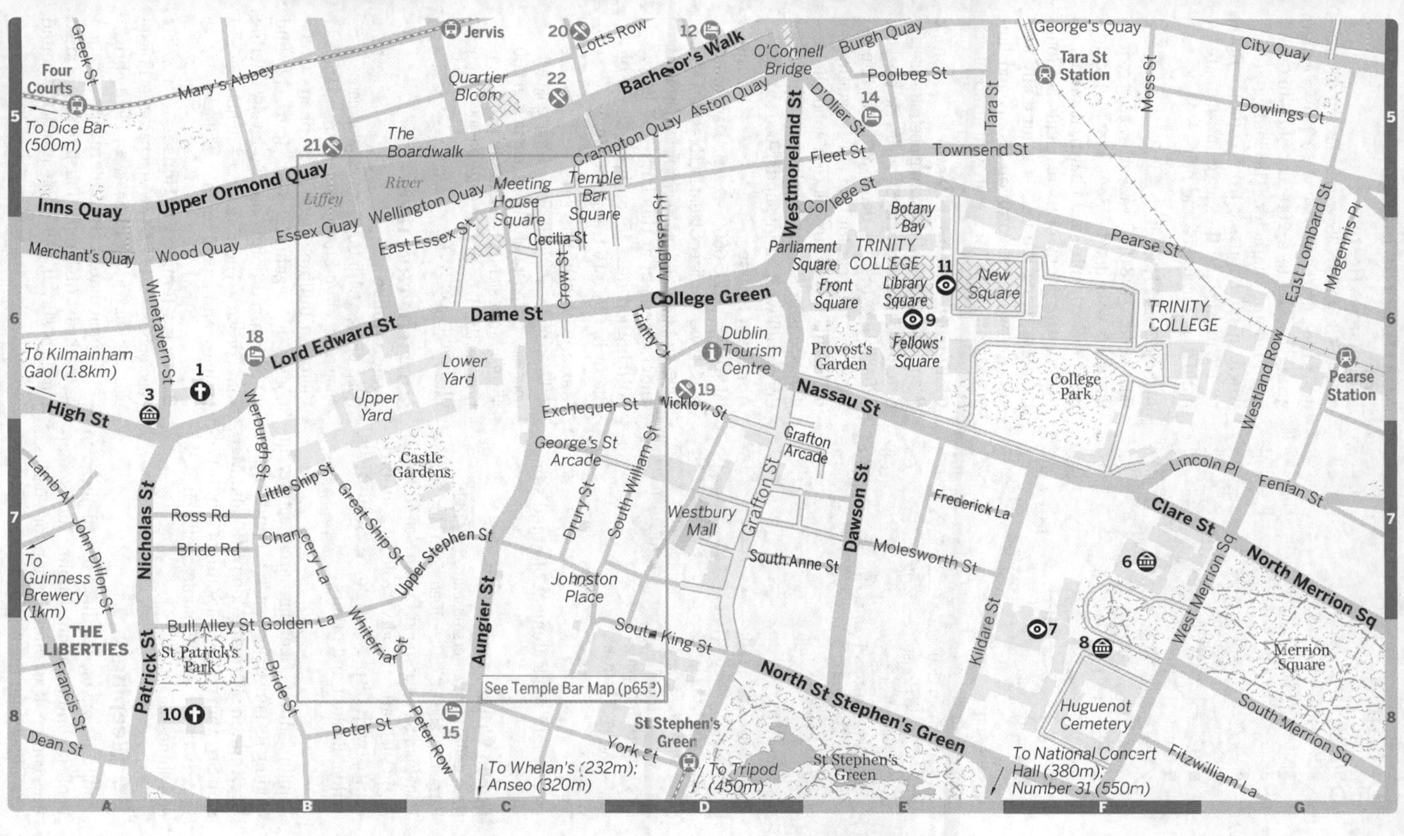

Four Courts
Greek St
To Dice Bar (500m)
Mary's Abbey
Jervis
Lotts Row
Quartier Bloom
Bachelor's Walk
O'Connell Bridge
Burgh Quay
Poolbeg St
George's Quay
Tara St Station
City Quay
Moss St
Dowlings Ct
Tara St
D'Olier St
Aston Quay
Crampton Quay
The Boardwalk
River Liffey
Inns Quay
Upper Ormond Quay
Merchant's Quay
Wood Quay
Essex Quay
Wellington Quay
Meeting House Square
Temple Bar Square
East Essex St
Cecilia St
Crow St
Anglesea St
Westmoreland St
Fleet St
Townsend St
College St
Pearse St
East Lombard St
Magennis Pl
Botany Bay
Parliament Square
TRINITY COLLEGE
Front Square
Library Square
New Square
Fellows' Square
Provost's Garden
TRINITY COLLEGE
College Park
Westland Row
Pearse Station
College Green
Dame St
Lord Edward St
Winetavern St
To Kilmainham Gaol (1.8km)
High St
Dublin Tourism Centre
Trinity St
Wicklow St
Nassau St
Lower Yard
Upper Yard
Exchequer St
George's St Arcade
Castle Gardens
Grafton Arcade
Grafton St
Dawson St
Lincoln Pl
Fenian St
Werburgh St
Little Ship St
Great Ship St
Upper Stephen St
Lamb Al
John Dillon St
To Guinness Brewery (1km)
Nicholas St
Ross Rd
Bride Rd
Chancery La
Drury St
South William St
Westbury Mall
South Anne St
Molesworth St
Frederick La
Clare St
North Merrion Sq
West Merrion Sq
Johnston Place
Aungier St
THE LIBERTIES
Bull Alley St
Golden La
Whitefriar St
South King St
Kildare St
Merrion Square
Patrick St
St Patrick's Park
Bride St
See Temple Bar Map (p652)
North St Stephen's Green
Huguenot Cemetery
South Merrion Sq
Francis St
Dean St
Peter St
Peter Row
St Stephen's Green
York St
St Stephen's Green
To Whelan's (232m); Anseo (320m)
To Tripod (450m)
To National Concert Hall (380m); Number 31 (550m)
Fitzwilliam La

Dublin

Sights

Book of Kells .... (see 9)
1 Christ Church Cathedral A6
2 Dublin Writers Museum C2
3 Dublinia A6
4 General Post Office D4
5 Monument of Light D3
6 National Gallery F7
7 National Museum of Archaeology F8
8 Natural History Museum F8
9 Old Library E6
10 St Patrick's Cathedral A8
11 Trinity College E6

Sleeping

12 Abbey Court Hostel D5
13 Abraham House E3
14 Ashfield House E5
15 Avalon House C8
16 Globetrotters Tourist Hostel F3
17 Isaacs Hostel F3
18 Kinlay House B6

Eating

19 Cornucopia D6
20 Epicurean Food Hall C5
21 Soup Dragon B5
22 Winding Stair C5

Entertainment

23 Abbey Theatre E4

facelift and reinstatement of grand stone staircase.

Dublin Writers Museum MUSEUM
(Map p648; www.writersmuseum.com; 18-19 Parnell Sq; adult €7.50; 10am-5pm Mon-Sat, 11am-5pm Sun year-round, to 6pm Mon-Fri Jun-Aug) Celebrates the city's role as a literary centre, with displays on Joyce, Swift, Yeats, Wilde, Beckett and others.

Dublin's finest Georgian architecture, including its famed doorways, is found around **St Stephen's Green** (Map p648) and **Merrion Sq** (Map p648) just south of Trinity College; both are prime picnic spots when the sun shines.

Sleeping

Dublin is *always* bustling, so call ahead to book accommodation. Dublin Tourism offices can book accommodation for €5 plus a 10% deposit for the first night.

NORTH OF THE LIFFEY

TOP CHOICE **Isaacs Hostel** HOSTEL €
(Map p648; 855 6215; www.isaacs.ie; 2-5 Frenchman's Lane; dm/tw €19/54; @ wi-fi) This popular, grungy hostel in a 200-year-old wine vault has loads of character. The lounge area is where it all happens, from summer BBQs to live music, and the easygoing staff are on hand 24/7 for advice and help.

Abbey Court Hostel HOSTEL €
(Map p648; 878 0700; www.abbey-court.com; 29 Bachelor's Walk; dm/d €18/79; @ wi-fi) What this place lacks in physical charm, it makes up for in *craic*. Many of its residents are long-termers, giving the joint a community feel, and its two large common rooms and fantastic staff make for a convivial atmosphere.

Globetrotters Tourist Hostel HOSTEL €
(Map p648; 878 8088; www.globetrottersdublin.com; 46-48 Lower Gardiner St; dm/tw incl breakfast €20/80; P @) Funky decor and a little patio garden at the rear for that elusive sunny day make this city-centre place a good choice – it has custom-made bunks in a variety of dorms, all with handy, under-bed storage.

Abraham House HOSTEL €
(Map p648; 855 0600; www.abraham-house.ie; 83 Lower Gardiner St; dm incl breakfast €9-20, d incl breakfast €48-60; @ wi-fi) Friendly is an understatement at this large and lively hostel; good rates if you book ahead on the web. Close to train station.

Marian Guesthouse B&B €€
(off Map p648; 874 4129; www.marianguesthouse.ie; 21 Upper Gardiner St; per person €30-45; P) Modest but reasonably priced option in the Upper Gardiner St area (north of the city centre).

SOUTH OF THE LIFFEY

Avalon House HOSTEL €
(Map p648; 475 0001; www.avalon-house.ie; 55 Aungier St; dm/d €18/60; @ wi-fi) This grand old Victorian building near St Stephen's Green houses a megahostel with four-, 12- and 20-bed mixed dorms on two levels, offering some privacy. There's a large kitchen, several lounges, and a pool room.

Barnacles Temple Bar House HOSTEL €
(Map p652; 671 6277; www.barnacles.ie; 19 Temple Lane; dm/d from €15/64; @ wi-fi) Plenty bright and immaculately clean, Barnacles' location in the heart of Temple Bar makes it a great place to stay if you don't mind the sound

of drunken revellers outside your window; rooms at the back are quieter.

Ashfield House HOSTEL €
(Map p648; ☎679 7734; www.ashfieldhouse.ie; 19-20 D'Olier St; dm incl breakfast €9-20, d incl breakfast €48-60; @📶) Housed in a converted church a stone's throw from Temple Bar and O'Connell Bridge, this hostel feels more like a small hotel, with a good range of private en-suite rooms as well as four-, six- and eight-bed dorms.

Kinlay House HOSTEL €
(Map p648; ☎679 6644; www.kinlayhouse.ie; 2-12 Lord Edward St; dm/d from €15/50; @📶) Big, bustling and always busy, this is not a place for shrinking violets.

Gogarty's Temple Bar Hostel HOSTEL €
(Map p652; ☎671 1822; www.gogartys.ie/hostel; 58-59 Fleet St; dm/d from €15/44; 📶) Lively, party-atmosphere hostel right in the middle of the Temple Bar action.

Eating

Despite the downturn, Dubliners' higher-than-average disposable income maintains a fine crop of excellent restaurants, while the city's influx of immigrants has stimulated the market for ethnically diverse eateries.

NORTH OF THE LIFFEY

TOP CHOICE **Winding Stair** IRISH €€€
(Map p648; ☎872 7320; www.winding-stair.com; 40 Ormond Quay; mains €22-27; ⏲noon-3.30pm & 5.30-10.30pm daily) This rustic dining room squeezed above a bookshop serves superb Irish grub, from smoked salmon and wheaten bread to lamb chops with white bean and red onion stew and sticky pear and ginger steam pud. Hugely popular, so book ahead.

Soup Dragon CAFE €
(Map p648; 168 Capel St; mains €5-13; ⏲8am-5.30pm Mon-Fri, 11am-5pm Sat) Eat in or take away one of 12 tasty varieties of homemade soups, including shepherd's pie or spicy vegetable gumbo. Bowls come in three different sizes, and prices include fresh bread and a piece of fruit.

Epicurean Food Hall FOOD HALL €
(Map p648; Lower Liffey St; mains €4-12; ⏲9.30am-5.30pm Mon-Sat) You'll be spoilt for choice in this bustling arcade that houses more than 20 food stalls. The quality can be hit and miss, but good choices include Itsabagel (for bagels), El Corte (for coffee) and Istanbul House (for kebabs).

DUBLIN SPLURGE

The former dwelling of modernist architect Sam Stephenson (1933–2006), **Number 31** (off Map p648; ☎676 5011; www.number31.ie; 31 Leeson Close; s/d/tr from €115/150/225; P📶) still feels like a 1960s designer pad with sunken sitting room, leather sofas, mirrored bar and floor-to-ceiling windows. A hidden oasis of calm, five minutes' walk from St Stephen's Green.

SOUTH OF THE LIFFEY

TOP CHOICE **Gruel** COMFORT €
(Map p652; www.gruel.ie; 68a Dame St; mains €5-15; ⏲7am-9.30pm Mon-Fri, 10.30am-10.30pm Sat & Sun) The best budget eatery in town, whether it's for the superfilling lunchtime roast-in-a-roll – a rotating list of slow-roasted organic meats stuffed into a bap and flavoured with homemade relishes – or the evening menu that includes bangers and mash, shepherds pie, and vegetable tajine.

Queen of Tarts CAFE €
(Map p652; www.queenoftarts.ie; 3-4 Cow's Lane; mains €5-12; ⏲8am-7pm Mon-Fri, 9am-7pm Sat, 10am-7pm Sun) Pocket-sized Queen of Tarts offers a mouth-watering array of savoury tarts and filled focaccias, fruit crumbles, healthy breakfasts and weekend brunch specials. Perfect for breakfast or lunch.

Simon's Place SANDWICHES €
(Map p652; cnr George's St Arcade & South Great George's St; sandwiches €4-5; ⏲9am-5.30pm Mon-Sat) Simon hasn't had to change his menu of doorstop sandwiches and wholesome vegetarian soups since he first opened shop two decades ago – the grub here is as heartening and legendary as he is.

Cornucopia VEGETARIAN €€
(Map p648; www.cornucopia.ie; 19 Wicklow St; mains €8-13; ⏲8.30am-9pm Mon-Fri, 8.30am-8pm Sat, noon-7pm Sun) For those seeking escape from the Irish cholesterol habit, Cornucopia is a popular, mostly vegan cafe turning out scrumptious healthy goodies. There's even a hot vegetarian breakfast as an alternative to muesli.

L'Gueuleton FRENCH €€€
(Map p652; www.lgueuleton.com; 1 Fade St; mains €19-27; ⏲12.30-3pm & 6-10pm Mon-Sat, 1-3pm & 6-9pm Sun) Dubliners just can't get enough

of this restaurant's take on French rustic cuisine, which ranges from slow-roasted pork belly with dauphinoise potatoes to specials such as warm crayfish salad with paprika and flaked almonds. No reservations – queue for a table, or leave your mobile number and they'll text when a table's ready.

Govinda's VEGETARIAN €

(Map p652; www.govindas.ie; 4 Aungier St; mains €7-10; ⏲noon-9pm Mon-Sat) The place is totally vegetarian, with a wholesome mix

Temple Bar

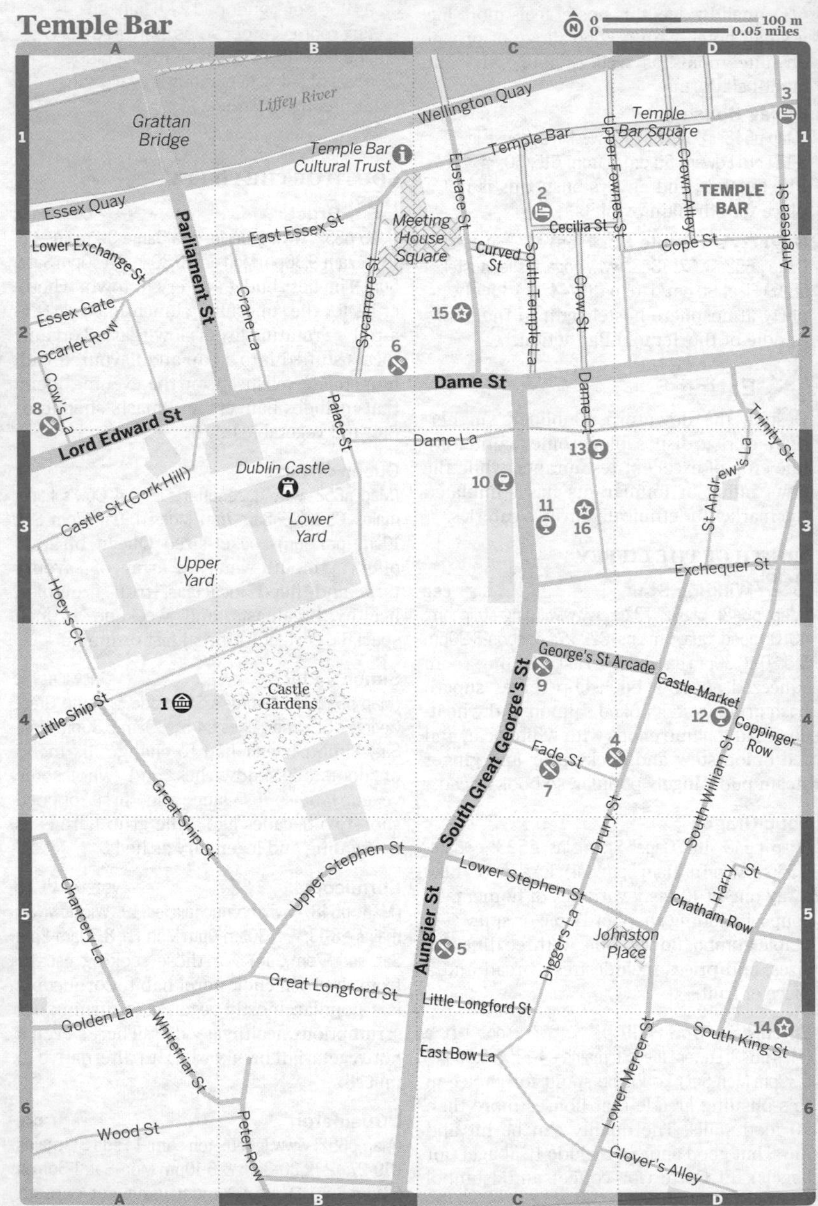

of salads and Indian-influenced hot daily specials.

Asia Market ASIAN MARKET €
(Map p652; 18 Drury St; ⏰10am-7pm) Heaps of fresh produce and stir-fry sauces, in addition to the usual Asian-grocery stand-bys.

Drinking

Temple Bar, Dublin's 'party district', is almost always packed with raucous stag and hen parties, scantily clad girls, and loud guys from Ohio wearing Guinness T-shirts. If you're just looking to get smashed and hook up with someone from another country, there's no better place in Ireland. If that's not your style, there's plenty to enjoy beyond Temple Bar. In fact, most of the best old-fashioned pubs are outside the district.

Grogan's Castle Lounge PUB
(Map p652; www.groganspub.ie; 15 South William St) A city-centre institution, Grogan's has long been a favourite haunt of Dublin's writers and painters, as well as others from the bohemian crowd. Drinks are marginally cheaper in the stone-floored public bar than in the lounge.

Stag's Head PUB
(Map p652; 1 Dame Ct) Built in 1770, and remodelled in 1895, the Stag's Head is possibly the best traditional pub in Dublin (and therefore the world). You may find yourself philosophising in the ecclesiastical atmosphere, as James Joyce once did. Some of the fitters that worked on this pub probably also worked on churches in the area, so the stained-wood-and-polished-brass similarities are no accident.

George BAR
(Map p652; www.thegeorge.ie; 89 South Great George's St) The patriarch of Dublin's gay bars and an excellent cruising venue, the venerable George has club nights Wednesday to Saturday and stand-up comedy on Sunday. Has a reputation for becoming ever more wild and wacky as the night progresses.

Dice Bar BAR
(off Map p648; www.thatsitdublin.com; 79 Queen St; 📶) Co-owned by singer Huey from the band Fun Lovin' Criminals, the Dice Bar looks like something you'd find on New York's Lower East Side.

Anseo BAR
(off Map p648; 28 Lower Camden St) Unpretentious, unaffected and incredibly popular.

Globe BAR
(Map p652; www.globe.ie; 11 South Great George's St; 📶) The granddaddy of the city's hipster bars.

Entertainment

For events, reviews and club listings, check out www.whatsonin.ie/dublin or pick up a copy of the bi-monthly freebie *Event Guide* or the weekly *In Dublin* (www.indublin.ie) available at cafes and hostels. Thursday's *Irish Times* has a pull-out section, 'The Ticket,' that has reviews and listings of all things arty.

Rí Rá CLUB
(Map p652; www.rira.ie; Dame Ct; ⏰Mon-Sat) One of the friendlier clubs in the city centre, Rí Rá is full nearly every night with a diverse crowd who come for the mostly funk music downstairs, or more laid-back lounge tunes and movies upstairs.

Whelan's LIVE MUSIC
(off Map p648; www.whelanslive.com; 25 Wexford St) A Dublin institution, providing a showcase for Irish singer-songwriters and other lo-fi performers.

Temple Bar

Sights
1 Chester Beatty Library ... A4

Sleeping
2 Barnacles Temple Bar House ... C1
3 Gogarty's Temple Bar Hostel ... D1

Eating
4 Asia Market ... C4
5 Govinda's ... C5
6 Gruel ... B2
7 L'Gueuleton ... C4
8 Queen of Tarts ... A2
9 Simon's Place ... C4

Drinking
10 George ... C3
11 Globe ... C3
12 Grogan's Castle Lounge ... D4
13 Stag's Head ... C3

Entertainment
14 Gaiety Theatre ... D6
15 Irish Film Institute (IFI) ... C2
16 Rí Rá ... C3

Gaiety Theatre MUSICALS
(Map p652; www.gaietytheatre.com; South King St) This popular theatre – which famously staged the 1971 Eurovision Song Contest – hosts, among other things, a program of classical concerts, operas and musicals.

National Concert Hall CLASSICAL MUSIC
(off Map p648; www.nch.ie; Earlsfort Tce) Just south of the city centre, Ireland's premier orchestral hall hosts a variety of concerts year-round, including a series of lunch-time concerts from 1.05pm to 2pm on Tuesday from June to August.

Irish Film Institute CINEMA
(IFI; Map p652; www.irishfilm.ie; 6 Eustace St) The fantastic IFI has two screens showing classic and art-house films. Wheelchair access is available.

Abbey Theatre THEATRE
(Map p648; www.abbeytheatre.ie; 26 Lower Abbey St) Ireland's national theatre, putting on new Irish works as well as revivals of Irish classics. Scheduled to move to new location in the Docklands before 2016.

Information

Medical Services

Doctor on Duty (☎453 9333; www.mediserve.ie; ⏰24hr) Request a doctor to come to your accommodation.

Hickey's Pharmacy (☎873 0427; 55 Lower O'Connell St) Open till 10pm every night.

St James Hospital (☎410 3000; www.stjames.ie; James's St) Dublin's main 24-hour accident and emergency department.

Well Woman Clinic (☎872 8051; www.wellwomancentre.ie; 35 Lower Liffey St; ⏰9.30am-7.30pm Mon, Thu & Fri, 8am-7.30pm Tue & Wed, 10am-4pm Sat) Handles women's health issues and can supply contraception.

Tourist Information

All Dublin tourist offices provide walk-in services only – no phone enquiries. For tourist information by phone, call ☎1850 230 330 from within the republic.

City Centre Tourist Office (Map p648; 14 Upper O'Connell St; ⏰9am-5pm Mon-Sat)

Dun Laoghaire Tourist Office (Dun Laoghaire ferry port; ⏰10am-1pm & 2-6pm)

Dublin Tourism Centre (Map p648; www.visitdublin.com; St Andrew's Church, 2 Suffolk St; ⏰9am-5.30pm Mon-Sat, 10.30am-3pm Sun year-round, to 7pm Mon-Sat Jul & Aug) Tourist information for all of Ireland, accommodation bookings, car hire, maps, and tickets for tours, concerts and more. Ask about the **Dublin Pass** (www.dublinpass.ie), which allows entrance into over 30 of Dublin's attractions, as well as tours and special offers.

Northern Ireland Tourist Board (NITB; Map p648; ☎605 7732; www.discovernorthernireland.com) Has a desk in the Dublin Tourism Centre; open same hours.

Temple Bar Cultural Trust (Map p652; ☎677 2255; www.templebar.ie; 12 East Essex St; ⏰9am-5.30pm Mon-Fri, 10am-5.30pm Sat, noon-3pm Sun) Provides free maps, guides and information on sights within the Temple Bar district.

Getting There & Away

Air

Dublin airport (DUB; www.dublinairport.com) About 13km north of the city centre. Ireland's major international gateway, with direct flights from Europe, North America and Asia. Budget airlines including Ryanair and Flybe land here. See p679 for more details.

Boat

There are direct ferries from Holyhead in Wales to **Dublin Port**, 3km northeast of the city centre, and to **Dun Laoghaire**, 13km southeast. Boats also sail direct to Dublin Port from Liverpool and from Douglas, on the Isle of Man. See p679 for more details.

Bus

Busáras (Map p648; www.buseireann.ie; Store St) is Dublin's main bus station, just north of the Liffey. Standard one-way fares from Dublin include:

Belfast (€15, 2½ hours, hourly)

Cork (€13, 4½ hours, six daily)

Galway (€14, 3¾ hours, hourly)

Killarney (€26, three hours, five daily)

The private company **Citylink** (www.citylink.ie) has direct services from Dublin airport to Galway (€15, three hours, 14 daily), with a stop in Dublin city centre.

Train

Iarnród Éireann Travel Centre (☎836 6222, bookings 703 4070; www.irishrail.ie; 35 Lower Abbey St) For travel information and tickets.

Connolly station (Map p648) North of the Liffey; trains to Belfast, Derry, Sligo, other points north and Wexford.

Heuston station South of the Liffey and west of the city centre; trains for Cork, Galway, Killarney, Limerick, and most other points to the south and west.

Regular one-way fares from Dublin include Belfast (from €18, 2¼ hours, up to eight daily), Cork (€20, 2¾ hours, hourly) and Galway (€35, three hours, five daily).

Getting Around

Bicycle

Rates begin around €13/70 a day/week; you'll need a €50 to €200 cash deposit and photo ID.

Cycleways (www.cycleways.com; 185-186 Parnell St)

Neill's Wheels (www.rentabikedublin.com) Various outlets, including Kinlay House and Isaacs Hostel (see Sleeping).

Public Transport

Various public transport **passes** are available from bus and DART stations, tourist offices, post offices and convenience stores; one day's unlimited travel on bus only costs €6 (including Airlink); on bus and tram costs €7.50; and on bus and DART costs €11.

BUS **Dublin Bus** (www.dublinbus.ie) Local buses cost from €1.15 to €2.20 for a single journey. You must pay the exact fare when boarding; drivers don't give change. The **Rambler 1 Day** (€6) ticket allows one day's unlimited travel on buses including Airlink.

TAXI Taxis in Dublin are expensive; flag fall costs €4.10, plus €1.50 per kilometre. For taxi service, call **National Radio Cabs** (☎677 2222).

TRAIN **Dublin Area Rapid Transport** (DART; www.irishrail.ie) Provides quick rail access as far north as Howth and south to Bray; Pearse station is handy for central Dublin.

TRAM **Luas** (www.luas.ie) Tram system runs on two (unconnected) lines; the green line runs from the eastern side of St Stephen's Green southeast to Sandyford, and the red line runs from Tallaght to Connolly station, with stops at Heuston station, the National Museum and Busáras. Single fares range from €1.50 to €2.80 depending on how many zones you travel through.

GETTING INTO DUBLIN

To get to the centre from Busáras, the main bus station, walk west along the river or south to Oliver Plunkett St. Connolly train station, about 1.5km northeast of town, is a little further, but you can easily walk it via MacCurtain St, if you're staying on Wellington Rd. Frequent buses head from the airport (€6, 40 minutes), where there are direct budget flights to major cities all over Europe. Buses run from the Dublin ferry terminal (€2.50, 25 minutes) to Busáras.

AROUND DUBLIN

Brú na Bóinne

☎041

A thousand years older than Stonehenge, the Neolithic necropolis known as Brú na Bóinne (the Boyne Palace) is an extraordinary site. Its tombs date from about 3200 BC, roughly six centuries before Egypt's great pyramids. The complex, including the **Newgrange** and **Knowth** passage tombs, can only be visited on a guided walk run by the **Brú na Bóinne visitor centre** (www.heritageireland.ie; Donore; admission visitor centre only €3, visitor centre & Newgrange €6, visitor centre & Knowth €5; ⏲9am-7pm Jun–mid-Sep, shorter hr rest of yr). At 8.20am during the winter solstice, the rising sun's rays shine directly down Newgrange's passage and illuminate the chamber for a magical 17 minutes. Arrive early in summer as tours tend to fill it up.

Guided day tours from Dublin by **Mary Gibbons** (☎086 355 1355; www.newgrangetours.com; tour incl admission fees €35, student €30 when booked direct; ⏲Mon-Sat) are excellent.

The site is 50km north of Dublin. The easiest transport option is the **Newgrange Shuttlebus** (☎1-800 424 252; www.overthetoptours.com; return €17).

SOUTHEASTERN IRELAND

Kilkenny

☎056 / POP 26,500

Built from black limestone flecked with fossil seashells, Kilkenny is known as 'the marble city'. Its picturesque huddle of medieval lanes, strung between castle and cathedral along the bank of the Nore River, is one of the southeast's biggest tourist draws – the narrow streets are often clogged with tour coaches. But it's worth braving the crowds to soak up the atmosphere of one of Ireland's creative crucibles – Kilkenny is a centre for arts and crafts and home to a host of fine restaurants, cafes, pubs and shops.

Sights

Stronghold of the powerful Butler family, **Kilkenny Castle** (www.kilkennycastle.ie; adult/student incl tour €6/2.50; ⏲9am-5.30pm Jun-Aug, 9.30am-5.30pm Apr-May & Sep, 9.30am-4.30pm Oct-Mar) has a history dating back to 1172, when the legendary Strongbow erected a wooden tower on the site, though much of its present look dates from the 19th century. Highlights of the guided tour include the painted roof beams of the **Long Gallery** and the collection of Victorian antiques. There's an excellent **tearoom** in the former castle kitchens, all white marble and gleaming copper.

The former stables opposite the castle now house the **National Craft Gallery** (www.ccoi.ie; Castle Yard; admission free; ⏲10am-5.30pm Tue-Sat year-round, 11am-5.30pm Sun Apr-Dec) and the **Kilkenny Design Centre** (www.kilkennydesign.com; ⏲10am-7pm Mon-Sat, 11am-7pm Sun), showcases for contemporary Irish crafts.

At the opposite end of town from the castle is **St Canice's Cathedral** (www.stcanicescathedral.ie; adult/concession €4/3; ⏲9am-6pm Mon-Sat, 2-6pm Sun Jun-Aug, shorter hr Sep-May), Ireland's second-largest cathedral, crammed with medieval monuments and tombs.

Festivals

Kilkenny is rightly known as the festival capital of Ireland, with several world-class events throughout the year.

Kilkenny Arts Festival ARTS FESTIVAL
(www.kilkennyarts.ie) Mid-August. The city comes alive with theatre, cinema, music, literature, visual arts, children's events and street spectacles for 10 action-packed days.

Kilkenny Celtic Festival CELTIC FESTIVAL
(www.celticfestival.ie) Late September to early October. A celebration of all things trad Irish, especially the language.

Sleeping

Kilkenny Tourist Hostel HOSTEL €
(☎776 3541; www.kilkennyhostel.ie; 35 Parliament St; dm/tw €17/42; @📶) Centrally located, within a few steps of half a dozen pubs and restaurants, this hostel has a large kitchen and an atmospheric sitting room with sofas and a turf fire.

Rafter Dempsey's B&B €€
(☎772 2970; www.rafterdempseys.ie; 4 Friary St; r €45-130) This place offers basic B&B accommodation in 16 rooms above a simple pub of the same name, just off High St.

Tree Grove Caravan & Camping Park CAMPING GROUND €
(☎777 0302; www.treegrovecamping.com; campsites per tent & 2 adults €15-20; ⏲Mar–mid-Nov) 1.5km south of Kilkenny off the New Ross (R700) road; you can walk into town along a riverside footpath.

Eating

TOP CHOICE **Café Sol** FUSION €€
(☎776 4987; www.cafesolkilkenny.com; William St; mains lunch €9-13, dinner €16-23; ⏲11.30am-9.30pm Mon-Sat, noon-9pm Sun; 📶) The seasonally changing menu at this funky little restaurant lists local sources for most of the produce. The Irish-Mediterranean fusion cuisine, like the bold and edgy artwork on the walls, displays some unexpected combinations – but it works – the place is packed by 1pm, so get in early for lunch. Three-course early-bird menus (€27; 6pm to 7.15pm Sunday to Friday, 5.30pm to 6.15pm Saturday) are great value.

Marble City Bar PUB €€
(66 High St; mains €8-15; ⏲noon-9pm) Usual pub-grub standards such as sausage with mash and fish and chips are raised above the norm here through the use of top-notch ingredients.

Gourmet Store SANDWICHES €
(56 High St; sandwiches €3-4; ⏲9am-6pm Mon-Sat) This classy deli is a good option for picnickers and hostellers.

Drinking & Entertainment

John Cleere's PUB
(22 Parliament St) Cleere's often has good alternative bands – and the occasional poetry reading – in its theatre out back.

Kyteler's Inn PUB
(27 St Kieran's St) The old house of Dame Kyteler (aka the Witch of Kilkenny) is a tourist magnet, but it's an atmospheric pub all the same.

Watergate Theatre THEATRE
(www.watergatetheatre.com; Parliament St) Hosts musical and theatrical productions throughout the year.

Information

Tourist office (☎775 1500; www.kilkennytourism.ie; Rose Inn St; ⏲9am-7pm Mon-Sat, 11am-5pm Sun Jul & Aug, 9.15am-1pm & 2-5pm Mon-Sat Sep-Jun)

Getting There & Away

BUS Buses depart from the train station to Cork (€16, three hours, two daily) and Dublin (€11, 2¼ hours, five daily).

TRAIN McDonagh train station (Dublin Rd) is east of the town centre along John St, next to the MacDonagh Junction shopping mall. Destinations include Dublin Heuston (from €10, 1¾ hours, eight daily) and Galway (€59, four hours, one daily; change at Kildare).

SOUTHWESTERN IRELAND

Cork

021 / POP 119,400

There's a reason the locals call Cork (Corcaigh) the 'Real Capital' or the 'People's Republic of Cork' – something special is going on here. The city has long been dismissive of Dublin and with a burgeoning arts, music and restaurant scene, it's now gaining a cultural reputation to rival the capital's. The flurry of urban renewal that began with the city's stint in 2005 as European Capital of Culture continues apace, with new buildings, bars and arts centres springing up all over town. The best of the city is still happily traditional though – snug pubs with live-music sessions most of the week, excellent local produce in an ever-expanding list of restaurants and a genuinely proud welcome from the locals.

Sights

English Market FOOD MARKET
(www.corkenglishmarket.ie; Princes St & Grand Pde; 8am-6pm Mon-Sat) It could just as easily be called the Victorian Market for its ornate vaulted ceilings and columns, but the English Market is a true gem, no matter what you name it. Scores of vendors sell some of the very best meat, fish, cheese and take-away food in the region. On decent days, take your lunch to nearby Bishop Lucey Park, a popular alfresco eating spot.

Cork City Gaol MUSEUM
(www.corkcitygaol.com; Convent Ave; adult/student €8/7; 9.30am-6pm Mar-Oct, 10am-5pm Nov-Feb) Closed down in 1923, this vast 19th-century prison is now a terrific museum about a terrifying subject. Restored cells, mannequins representing prisoners and guards, and a detailed audio guide bring home the horrors of Victorian prison life.

FREE **Crawford Art Gallery** ART GALLERY
(www.crawfordartgallery.ie; Emmet Pl; 10am-5pm Mon-Sat, to 8pm Thu) The 18th-century Cork Customs House is blended with 21st-century Dutch design in this intruguing gallery, a must-see for anyone who enjoys art and architecture.

FREE **Cork Public Museum** MUSEUM
(www.corkcity.ie; Fitzgerald Park; 11am-5pm Mon-Fri, to 4pm Sat, 3-5pm Sun, closed lunch, closed Sun Oct-Mar) The city museum has a fine collection of artefacts that trace Cork's past from prehistory to the present, including the city's role in the fight for independence.

Sleeping

Brú Bar & Hostel HOSTEL €
(455 9667; www.bruhostel.com; 57 MacCurtain St; dm €17-23, d €50-60; P@) Cork's funkiest hostel also has a popular bar and an internet cafe on the premises. This clean and friendly triple treat can be a rocking good time, especially on the weekends.

Kinlay House Shandon HOSTEL €
(450 8966; www.kinlayhouse.ie; Bob & Joan's Walk; dm €14-19, s/d from €30/48; @) This labyrinthine hostel is in a quiet spot near St Anne's Church in Shandon. It has a fun, laid-back atmosphere; services include bureau de change, laundry and luggage storage. Guests can use the next-door gym at a discount.

Cork International Hostel HOSTEL €
(454 3289; www.corkinternationalhostel.com; 1-2 Redclyffe, Western Rd; dm €13-18, tw €58; P@) The cheerful staff at this bright and busy An Óige hostel do a great job coping with the constant flow of young travellers. It's 2km west of the centre; bus 8 stops outside.

Sheila's Hostel HOSTEL €
(450 5562; www.sheilashostel.ie; 4 Belgrave Pl; dm €14-19, tw €46-54; @) The sauna, cinema room, coffee shop and super-friendly staff make up for the occasionally cramped atmosphere in this always-heaving hostel.

Eating

TOP CHOICE **Farmgate Café** CAFE, BISTRO €€
(www.farmgate.ie; English Market; mains €9-14; 8.30am-10pm Mon-Sat) An unmissable experience at the heart of the English Market, the Farmgate is perched on a balcony overlooking the market below, the source of all that fresh local produce on your plate. Up the stairs and turn left for table service, right for counter service.

Wildways ORGANIC €
(www.wildways.net; 21 Princes St; mains €3-7; 8am-5pm Mon-Fri, 8.30am-4pm Sat) Cork's first organic soup and sandwich bar serves such a variety of delicious and healthy food

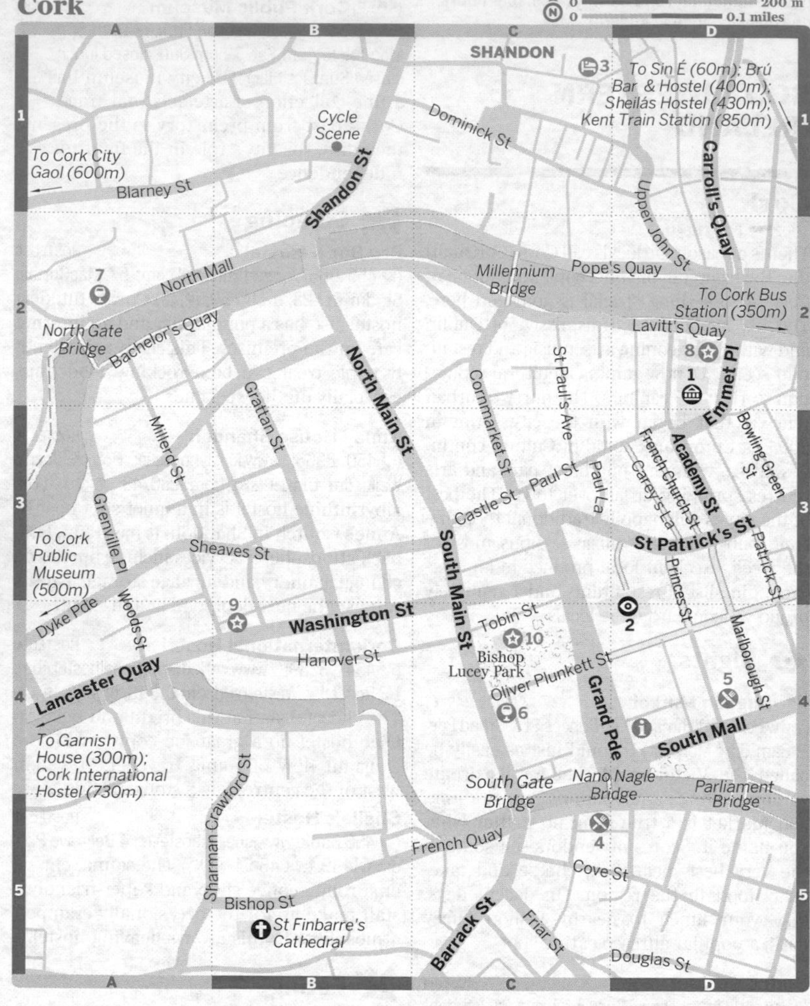

Cork

Sights

1 Crawford Art Gallery D2
2 English Market D4

Sleeping

3 Kinlay House Shandon C1

Eating

Farmgate Café .... (see 2)
4 Quay Co-op C5
5 Wildways D4

Drinking

6 An Spailpín Fánac C4
7 Franciscan Well Brewery A2

Entertainment

8 Cork Opera House D2
Half Moon Theatre .... (see 8)
9 Kino Cinema B4
10 Triskel Arts Centre C4

IRELAND SOUTHWESTERN IRELAND

CORK SPLURGE

With charming rooms (think flowers and fresh fruit), gourmet breakfasts and hosts who are eager to please, **Garnish House** (☎427 5111; www.garnish.ie; Western Rd; s/d from €75/86; P 📶) is possibly the perfect B&B. From the moment you arrive and are greeted with tea and goodies, until the moment you leave, you will experience nothing short of absolute hospitality.

that even the pickiest of eaters can find something scrumptious. If you're around for breakfast, make sure to try the excellent chocolate-chip pancakes.

Quay Co-op VEGETARIAN €
(www.quaycoop.com; 24 Sullivan's Quay; mains €7-11; ⏰9am-9pm Mon-Sat, noon-9pm Sun; 🖉) Flying the flag for alternative Cork, this place offers a range of self-service vegie options, all organic, including big breakfasts and rib-sticking soups and casseroles. It also caters for gluten-, dairy- and wheat-free needs, and is amazingly child-friendly.

Drinking

Cork's pub scene is cracking, easily rivalling Dublin's. Locally brewed Murphy's is the stout of choice here, not Guinness. Check www.corkgigs.com for pubs with live music.

Franciscan Well Brewery MICROBREWERY
(www.franciscanwellbrewery.com; 14 North Mall) The best place to enjoy the beer at this microbrewery is in the enormous beer garden at the back. The pub holds regular beer festivals with other small (and often underappreciated) Irish breweries – check the website for details.

An Spailpín Fánach PUB
(28 Sth Main St) The 'wandering labourer' hosts trad sessions almost nightly.

Sin É PUB
(Coburg St) There are no frills or fuss here – just a comfy, sociable pub long on atmosphere and short on pretension.

Entertainment

Cork's cultural life is generally of a high calibre. To see what's happening, grab *WhazOn?* (www.whazon.com), a free monthly publication available from the tourist office, news agencies, shops, hostels and B&Bs.

Cork Opera House OPERA
(www.corkoperahouse.ie; Emmet Pl) Cork's opera house stages everything from opera and ballet to stand-up and puppet shows. It has wheelchair access.

Half Moon Theatre THEATRE
(www.corkoperahouse.ie; Emmet Pl) Part of Cork Opera House, the Half Moon stages drama, comedy and live music.

Triskel Arts Centre ARTS CENTRE
(www.triskelart.com; Tobin St) Hosts contemporary art, film, theatre, music and photography.

Information

Tourist office (☎425 5100; www.corkkerry.ie; Grand Pde; ⏰9am-6pm Mon-Sat, 10am-5pm Sun Jul & Aug, 9.15am-5pm Mon-Fri, 9.30am-4.30pm Sat Sep-Jun)

Getting There & Around

BIKE **Cycle Scene** (www.cyclescene.ie; 396 Blarney St) Has bikes for hire from €15/80 per day/week.

BOAT **Brittany Ferries** (www.brittany-ferries.com) Has regular sailings from Cork to Roscoff (France). The ferry terminal is at Ringaskiddy, about 15 minutes by car southeast of the city centre along the N28. See p679 for more details.

BUS **Aircoach** (www.aircoach.ie) Provides a direct service to Dublin city and airport from St Patrick Quay (€14, four hours, eight daily). **Cork bus station** (cnr Merchants Quay & Parnell Pl) East of the city centre. Services include Dublin (€13, 4½ hours, six daily), Kilkenny (€19, three hours, three daily) and Killarney (€17, 1¾ hours, hourly).

TRAIN Cork's **Kent train station** (Glanmire Rd Lower) is north of the river and services go to Dublin (€20, 2¾ hours, hourly), Galway (€45, five to six hours, seven daily; two or three changes needed) and Killarney (€26, 1½ to two hours, nine daily).

Around Cork

BLARNEY

☎021

Lying northwest of Cork, the village of Blarney (An Bhlarna) receives a gazillion visitors a year for one sole reason: **Blarney Castle** (www.blarneycastle.ie; adult €10; ⏰9am-6.30pm Mon-Sat, 9am-5.30pm Sun May-Sep, to dusk daily Oct-Apr). If you're not germophobic – there's a greasy mark where millions of lips have been before – you can kiss the castle's legendary **Blarney Stone** and get the 'gift of the gab'.

Buses run regularly from the Cork bus station (€6.20 return, 30 minutes).

Killarney

064 / POP 13,500

Killarney is a well-oiled tourism machine in the middle of sublime scenery. Its manufactured tweeness is renowned – streams of coaches arriving to consume soft-toy shamrocks, and placards on street corners pointing to 'trad' sessions – but it has many charms beyond its proximity to lakes, waterfalls and 1000m-plus peaks. In a town that's been practising the tourism game for over 250 years, competition keeps standards high and visitors on all budgets can expect to find superb restaurants, great pubs and good accommodation.

Sights & Activities

Most of Killarney's attractions are just outside the town. The mountain backdrop is part of **Killarney National Park**, which takes in beautiful Lough Leane, Muckross Lake and Upper Lake. Besides Ross Castle and Muckross House, the park also has much to explore by foot, bike or boat.

In summer the **Gap of Dunloe**, a scenic mountain pass squeezed between Purple Mountain and Carrauntouhill (at 1040m, Ireland's highest peak), is a tourist bottleneck. Rather than join the tourist hordes taking pony-and-trap rides, **O'Connors Tours** (663 0200; www.gapofdunloetours.com; 7 High St, Killarney) can arrange a bus, bike and boat circuit taking in the Gap for around €30.

Sleeping

Book ahead for accommodation from June to August. Hostels often rent out bikes and offer discounted tours. The tourist office books rooms for €5.

Súgán Hostel HOSTEL €
(663 3104; www.suganhostelkillarney.com; Lewis Rd; dm/d €17/40) Resembling a hobbit hole, this homely, alcohol-free hostel has a warm fire and equally warm hosts. The atmosphere is nothing short of familial, which makes leaving a hard task. Bicycle hire is €15 a day.

Killarney Railway Hostel HOSTEL €
(663 5299; www.killarneyhostel.com; Fair Hill; dm €16-19, s/d 45/54; P@) This modern hostel near the train station is about as inviting as hostels get, with en-suite bathrooms, bunks nestling in nooks, and maps and cycling itineraries adorning the walls. Prices include a basic breakfast.

Neptune's Killarney Town Hostel HOSTEL €
(663 5255; www.neptuneshostel.com; Bishop's Lane, New St; dm €16-20, s/d €40/50; @) Neptune's mixed dorms can sleep over 150, but this central hostel feels much smaller thanks to the roaring fire in reception, free internet access, and the staff's unfailing helpfulness.

Rathmore House B&B €€
(663 2829; http://rathmorehousekillarney.com; Rock Rd; s/d €55/85; Mar-Nov; P) There's a real Irish welcome at this long-established, family-run B&B at the entrance to town.

Killarney Flesk Caravan & Camping Park CAMPING GROUND €
(663 1704; www.killarneyfleskcamping.com; Muckross Rd; per car, tent & 2 adults €26, hikers per person €10; mid-Apr–Sep) About 1.5km south of the town centre on the N71 to Kenmare, this camping ground has great views of the mountains.

Eating

TOP CHOICE **Vanilla Pod** MODERN IRISH €€
(662 6559; Old Market Lane; mains €8-13, 4-course dinner €35; 9am-6pm Mon-Sat, 6.30-9.30pm Fri & Sat) This little gem of a place serves a range of locally sourced fresh and organic foods, from eggs Benedict for breakfast to slow-roasted pork belly for dinner. Bakery items can be enjoyed as a treat all day, especially at the tables out front.

Revive Café & Wine Bar CAFE €
(New St; mains €7-9; 9.30am-6pm) This comfortable modern cafe – think chocolate-brown leather armchairs – serves Illy-brand Italian espresso, freshly made sandwiches and delicious, home-baked rhubarb pie.

Jam CAFE €
(77 High St; mains €4-10; 8am-6pm Mon-Sat) This funky little cafe is a healthy pit stop for hot meals, soups, salads, sandwiches, and coffee and cake.

Kathleen's Country Kitchen CAFE €
(New St; breakfast & lunch €5-11; 9am-5.30pm) The place for a breakfast roll, boiled bacon for lunch and no-nonsense service.

Drinking & Entertainment

O'Connor's PUB
(7 High St) O'Connor's is a tiny but hugely popular pub that stages a mix of trad,

stand-up comedy, readings and pub theatre.

Courtney's PUB
(Plunkett St) With a few nice fireplaces, barrels used as tables and nearly everything made from wood, Courtney's offers the ultimate Irish pub atmosphere.

Killarney Grand PUB
(Main St) A great place for authentic music (if you can hear it over the boisterous crowd), the Grand has interesting takes on the traditional thing from 9pm. At 11pm modern bands take over (€6 cover).

Information

Guide Killarney (€5) is a good monthly 'what's on' guide, available at B&Bs, hostels and the tourist office.

Tourist office (663 1633; www.killarney.ie; Beech Rd; 9am-6pm Mon-Sat, 9.15am-1pm & 2-5pm Sun) Busy but efficient; has free map of national park and details of bus services.

Getting There & Around

BIKE O'Sullivan's (www.killarneyrentabike.com; Beech Rd & New St) hires bikes for €15/80 per day/week.

BUS Operating from the train station, Bus Éireann has regular services to Cork (€17, 1¾ hours, hourly), Dublin (€26, three hours, five daily) and Galway (€24, seven hours, six daily) via Limerick.

TAXI Taxis cost roughly €2.65 per kilometre and can be found at the taxi rank on College St.

TRAIN Travelling by train to Cork (€23, 2¼ hours, three daily) or Dublin (€62, six hours, three daily) usually involves changing at Mallow.

The Ring of Kerry

066

The Ring of Kerry, a 179km circuit around the dramatic coastal scenery of the Iveragh Peninsula, is one of Ireland's premier tourist attractions. Most travellers tackle the ring by bus on guided day trips from Killarney, but you could spend days wandering here.

Sights

The **Ballaghbeama Pass** cuts across the peninsula's central highlands and has spectacular views and little traffic, while the shorter **Ring of Skellig**, at the end of the peninsula, has fine views of the Skellig Rocks and is less touristy. You can forgo roads completely by walking the **Kerry Way**, which winds through the Macgillycuddy's Reeks mountains past Carrauntuohill (1040m), Ireland's highest mountain.

Political hero Daniel O'Connell was born near **Cahirciveen**, one of the ring's larger towns. The excellent **Barracks Heritage Centre** (www.theoldbarracks.com; adult/student €4/2; 10am-4.30pm Mon-Fri, 11.30am-4.30pm Sat, 1-5pm Sun Jun-Sep; shorter hr in winter) off Bridge St occupies what was once an intimidating Royal Irish Constabulary (RIC) barracks. Exhibits focus on O'Connell and on the famine's local impact.

South of Cahirciveen the R565 branches west to the 11km-long **Valentia Island**, the jumping-off point for an unforgettable experience: the **Skellig Rocks**, two tiny islands 12km off the coast. The vertiginous climb up uninhabited **Skellig Michael** inspires an awe that monks could have clung to life in the meagre beehive-shaped stone huts that stand on the tiny strip of level land on top.

Calm seas permitting, boats run from spring to late summer from Portmagee, just before the bridge to Valentia, to Skellig Michael. The standard fare is around €45 return. Advance booking is essential; there are half a dozen boat operators, including **Casey's** (947 2437; www.skelligislands.com) and **Sea Quest** (947 6214; www.skelligsrock.com).

Sleeping

There are plenty of hostels and B&Bs along the ring. It's wise to book your next night as you make your way around.

O'Shea's B&B B&B €€
(947 2402; www.osheasbnb.com; Church St, Cahirciveen; s/d €45/70; P) Right in the centre of town, across from the bus stop; a friendly B&B with a nice view.

Skellig Hostel HOSTEL €
(947 9942; www.skellighostel.com; Ballinskelligs; dm/d €15/52; P) This modern building is a little characterless, but the rooms, lounge and dining room are comfortable.

Mannix Point Camping & Caravan Park CAMPING GROUND €
(947 2806; www.campinginkerry.com; Mannix Point; campsites per person €10; Mar-Oct) Regularly wins awards as the best campsite in Ireland; coastal location, sunset views, and campers' lounge with peat fire, musical instruments and resident cats.

Getting There & Around

Bus Éireann runs a daily **Ring of Kerry bus service** from June to mid-September. Buses leave

Killarney at 1.15pm and stop at Killorglin, Glenbeigh, Cahirciveen, Waterville, Caherdaniel and Molls Gap, returning to Killarney at 5.40pm (€18).

Travel agencies and hostels in Killarney offer daily tours of the ring for about €20.

WEST COAST

The Burren

The Burren of northern County Clare is a harsh and haunting landscape of bare rock, softened with a sprinkling of rare wildflowers; *Boireann* is Irish for 'Rocky Country', and the name is no exaggeration. The rugged limestone plateau is littered with ancient dolmens, ring forts, round towers, high crosses and a surprisingly diverse range of flora, while rocky foreshores and splendid cliffs line its coast.

Tim Robinson's excellent *Burren Map & Guide* is available at bookshops or tourist offices. If you're stuck for transport, a number of bus tours leave the Galway tourist office every morning for the Burren and the Cliffs of Moher, including **O'Neachtain Tours** (☎091-553188; www.galway.net/pages/oneachtain-tours). They all cost around €25. **Burren Hill Walks** (☎065-707 7168; http://homepage.eircom.net/~burrenhillwalks) offers half-day guided walks for €15 to €25 per person.

CLIFFS OF MOHER

The towering 200m-high Cliffs of Moher are one of Ireland's most famous features. In summer the cliffs are overrun by day-trippers, so consider staying in nearby Doolin and hiking or biking along the Burren's quiet country lanes, where the views are superb and crowds are never a problem. Be careful along these cliffs, especially in wet or windy weather.

The **Cliffs of Moher tourist centre** (www.cliffsofmoher.ie; adult €6; ⌚8.30am-7.30pm Jun-Aug, 9am-6pm Mar-May, Sep & Oct, 9am-5pm Nov-Feb) has exhibitions about the cliffs and the environment. You can avoid the crowds by visiting after the tourist centre closes.

Galway

☎091 / POP 72,400

Arty and bohemian, Galway (Gaillimh) is legendary around the world for its entertainment scene. Students make up a quarter of the city's population and brightly painted pubs heave with live music on any given night. Cafes spill out onto cobblestone streets filled with a frenzy of fiddles, banjos, guitars and *bodhráns* (hand-held goatskin drums), and jugglers, painters, puppeteers and magicians in outlandish masks enchant passers-by.

Galway's city centre is tightly packed between the east bank of the Corrib River and Eyre Sq. The bus and train stations are within a stone's throw of Eyre Sq.

Sights

Little remains of Galway's old city walls apart from the **Spanish Arch**, which is right beside the river. Nearby **Galway City Museum** (www.galwaycitymuseum.ie; Spanish Pde; admission free; ⌚10am-5pm daily Jun-Sep, 10am-5pm Tue-Sat Oct-May) has exhibits on the city's history from 1800 to 1950, including an iconic Galway Hooker fishing boat, a collection of currachs (boats made from animal hides) and a controversial statue of Galway-born writer and hell-raiser Pádraic O'Conaire (1883–1928), which was previously in Eyre Sq.

Parts of **Lynch's Castle** (Shop St), now a bank, date back to the 14th century. Lynch, so the story goes, was a mayor of Galway in the 15th century who, when his son was condemned for murder, personally acted as hangman. The stone facade that is the **Lynch Memorial Window** (Market St) marks the spot of the deed.

Across the road from the memorial window, in the Bowling Green area, is the **Nora Barnacle House Museum** (8 Bowling Green; admission €3; ⌚10am-5pm mid-May–mid-Sep or by appointment), the former home of the wife and lifelong muse of James Joyce, which displays the couple's letters and photographs.

Festivals

Galway Arts Festival ARTS FESTIVAL
(www.galwayartsfestival.com) Held in July, this is the main event on Galway's calendar.

Galway Oyster Festival OYSTER FESTIVAL
(www.galwayoysterfest.com) Going strong for more than 50 years now, this festival draws thousands of visitors in late September.

Sleeping

Kinlay House HOSTEL €
(☎565244; www.kinlayhouse.ie; Merchant's Rd; dm €16-29, d €54-70; @ wi-fi) The large, modern, wheelchair-accessible Kinlay House is a convenient base, half a block off Eyre Sq. It has clean, spacious rooms and a huge dining-lounge area, which can see all-night revelry.

IRELAND WEST COAST

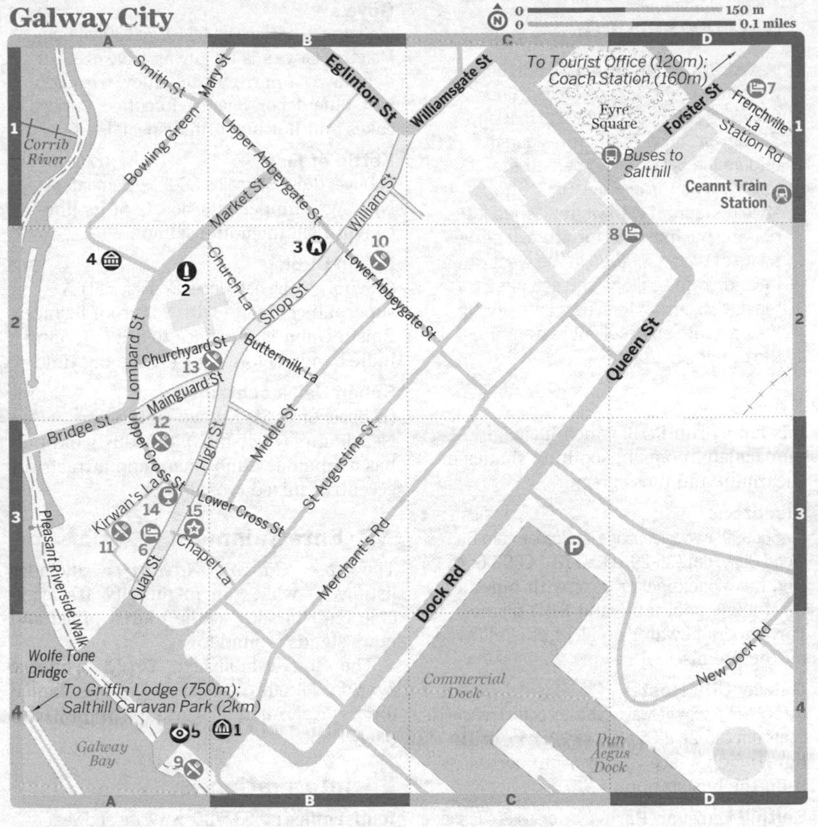

Galway City

Sights

1 Galway City Museum B4
2 Lynch Memorial Window A2
3 Lynch's Castle B2
4 Nora Barnacle House A2
5 Spanish Arch A4

Sleeping

6 Barnacle's Quay Street House A3
7 Galway City Hostel D1
8 Kinlay House D2

Eating

9 Ard Bia & Nimmo's A4
10 Food 4 Thought B2
11 Goya's A3
12 Kettle of Fish A3
13 Tig Cóilí B2

Drinking

14 Séhán Ua Neáchtain A3

Entertainment

15 Druid Theatre A3

You can book discounted bus tours and Aran Islands ferries at reception.

Barnacle's Quay Street House HOSTEL €
(☎568644; www.barnacles.ie; 10 Quay St; dm €10-33, d €60-87; @) Set in a medieval town house with a modern extension, Barnacle's is at the heart of the action, surrounded by all the pubs, cafes and restaurants you came to Galway for.

Griffin Lodge B&B €€
(☎589440; griffinlodge@eircom.net; 3 Father Griffin Pl; s €45-60, d €55-80; P) You'll be welcomed like a long-lost friend at

GALWAY SPLURGE

Ard Bia at Nimmo's (561114; www.ardbia.com; Spanish Arch; mains €17-23; cafe noon-3pm Wed-Fri, 10am-3.30am Sat, noon-7pm Sun, restaurant 6-10pm Tue-Sat), tucked behind the Spanish Arch, is an informal, cottage-style restaurant with whitewashed interior and mismatched furniture. It serves some of the finest food in the west of Ireland, from scallops and sea bass to roast Irish lamb. Open as a cafe during the day, with an excellent restaurant in the evening upstairs.

this family-run B&B, which has eight immaculate rooms in soothing shades of spearmint and moss green.

Sleepzone HOSTEL €
(566999; www.sleepzone.ie; Bóthar nam Ban, Wood Quay; dm €15-29, d €50-78, f €60-96; @) Big, busy backpacker base with bureau de change, pool table and BBQ terrace. Party-goers beware: no alcohol is allowed on the premises.

Galway City Hostel HOSTEL €
(566959; www.galwaycityhostel.com; Frenchville Lane; dm €15-21, d €54-80; @) A no-frills but friendly place to stay, right across from the bus station.

Salthill Caravan Park CAMPING GROUND €
(523972; www.salthillcaravanpark.com; campsites per person €10; Easter-Sep; P) Just west of Salthill, off Salthill Rd, is this scenic spot right on the water. A bus runs into the city centre every half-hour.

Eating & Drinking

Food 4 Thought VEGETARIAN €
(Lower Abbeygate St; mains €6-7; 7.30am-6pm Mon-Fri, 8am-6pm Sat, 11.30am-4pm Sun) Head to this new-age cafe for organic and vegetarian sandwiches, savoury scones, and wholesome dishes such as cashew-nut roast and moussaka made with textured vegetable protein.

Tig Cóilí PUB
(Mainguard St) Two live *céilidh* (traditional Gaelic music and dancing) a day draw the crowds to this authentic fire-engine-red pub, just off High St. It's where musicians go to get drunk or drunks go to become musicians...or something like that.

Goya's CAFE €
(2 Kirwan's Lane; mains €5-10; 9.30am-6pm Mon-Sat) Goya's is a Galway treasure hidden down a narrow back alley, with cool pale-blue decor, Segafredo coffee, superb cakes and hot lunchtime specials.

Kettle of Fish FISH & CHIPS €
(4 Upper Cross St; mains €8-9; 11am-late) A New Age chipper that boasts of its line-caught fish, including salmon.

Róisín Dubh PUB
(www.roisindubh.net; Upper Dominick St) A superpub complete with vast roof terrace, Róisín Dubh is *the* place to see emerging indie bands before they hit the big time.

Séhán Ua Neáchtain PUB
(17 Upper Cross St) Known simply as Neáchtain's (*nock*-tans), this dusty old pub has a fabulous atmosphere and attracts an eccentric, mixed crowd.

Entertainment

The free *Galway Advertiser* includes listings of what's on in the city. It's available on Thursday at the tourist office and news-stands around town.

The long-established **Druid Theatre** (www.druidtheatre.com; Chapel Lane) is famed for its experimental works by young Irish playwrights.

Information

Tourist office (537700; www.irelandwest.ie; Forster St; 9am-5.45pm Jun-Oct, 9am-5.45pm Mon-Sat, 9am-12.45pm Sun Jan-May, Nov & Dec) In summer there can be a long wait to make accommodation bookings.

Getting There & Around

BIKE On Yer Bike (www.onyourbikecycles.com; 40 Prospect Hill) Hires bikes from €12/60 per day/week.

BUS Bus Éireann buses depart from outside the train station. **Citylink** (www.citylink.ie) and **GoBus** (www.gobus.ie) use the **coach station** (cnr Forster St & Fairgreen Rd) a block northeast.

Clifden (€12, 1½ hours, four daily)

Doolin (€14, 1½ hours, seven daily Monday to Saturday in summer, twice on Sunday)

Dublin (€14, 3¾ hours, hourly)

Killarney (€22, 4¾ hours, three daily)

TRAIN Trains run to and from Dublin (€35, three hours, five daily). You can connect with other trains at Athlone.

Aran Islands

099

In the last decade the rocky Aran Islands have become one of Ireland's major attractions. Apart from rugged beauty, the Irish-speaking islands boast some of the country's oldest Christian and pre-Christian ruins.

There are three main islands, all inhabited year-round. Most visitors head for long and narrow **Inishmór** (Inishmore), which is 14.5km by a maximum 4km. The land slopes up from the relatively sheltered northern shores of the island, plummeting on the southern side into the Atlantic. **Inishmaan** and **Inisheer** are much smaller and receive fewer visitors. Though seemingly inhospitable, the islands were actually settled much earlier than the mainland, since agriculture was easier to pursue here than in the forested Ireland of the pre-Christian era.

The islands get crowded at holiday times (St Patrick's Day, Easter) and in July and August, when accommodation is at a premium and advance reservations are advised.

The **tourist office** (61263; www.aranislands.ie; 11am-7pm Jun-Sep, reduced hr rest of year) operates year-round at Kilronan, the arrival point and major village of Inishmór. You can leave your luggage and change money here. Around the corner is a Spar **supermarket** with an **ATM**. The Aran Heritage Centre has **internet access**.

Getting There & Away

AIR Aer Arann (091-593034; www.aerarannislands.ie) flights from Connemara regional airport at Minna, near Inverin, 38km west of Galway, cost €45 return. Flights serve Inishmór at least five times daily (two or three times daily to the other islands) and take less than 10 minutes. A connecting bus from outside Kinlay House in Galway costs €3 one way.

BOAT All three islands are served year-round by **Aran Island Ferries** (www.aranislandferries.com; 4 Forster St, Galway); the trip takes around 40 minutes (adult/child €25/13 return). The boat leaves from Rossaveal, 37km west of Galway – it's an extra €7/4 return to catch an Island Ferries bus from near Kinlay House in Galway. Buses leave 1½ hours before ferry departure times and are scheduled to meet arriving ferries. If you have a car, you can go straight to Rossaveal and leave it in the car park there for free.

Doolin Ferries (www.doolinferries.com) run boats to Inishmór (55 minutes) and Inisheer (40 minutes) from Doolin in County Clare for €40 return (April to September only).

INISHMÓR

The 'Big Island' has four impressive stone forts thought to be 2000 years old. Halfway down the island and about 8km west of Kilronan, semicircular **Dún Aengus** (adult €3; 10am-6pm Mar-Oct, to 4pm Nov-Feb), perched on the edge of the sheer cliffs, is the best known.

About 1.5km north is **Dún Eoghanachta**, while halfway back to Kilronan is **Dún Eochla**; both are smaller, perfectly circular ring forts. Directly south of Kilronan and dramatically perched on a promontory is **Dún Dúchathair**, which is surrounded on three sides by cliffs.

Sleeping & Eating

Kilronan Hostel HOSTEL €
(61255; www.kilronanhostel.com; Kilronan; dm €18-27; @) Perched above Tí Joe Mac's pub, this friendly hostel is just a two-minute walk away from the ferry; staff lend out fishing rods for free and can teach you to play hurling on the beach.

Mainistir House HOSTEL €
(61169; www.mainistirhousearan.com; dm/d €17/50; @) This is a quirky and colourful 60-bed hostel on the main road north of Kilronan. It caters for both backpackers and families. Book ahead for the great-value organic, largely vegetarian buffet dinners (€16; served 8pm to closing in summer, from 7pm in winter).

Man of Aran Cottage B&B €€
(61301; www.manofarancottage.com; s/d €60/90; Mar-Oct) Built for the 1930s film of the same name, this thatched B&B has authentic stone-and-wood interiors with a genuinely homely feel. It also has a **restaurant** (lunch from €6, dinner from €35; lunch & dinner Jun-Sep, dinner Mar-May & Oct) that serves fresh local fish and organic vegies and herbs from the owners' garden (dinner bookings are essential).

INISHMAAN & INISHEER

The least visited of the three islands is Inishmaan (Inis Meáin, or 'Middle Island'), with a jagged coastline of startling cliffs and empty beaches. The main archaeological site is **Dún Chonchúir**, a massive stone fort built on a high point and offering views of the island.

The smallest island, only 8km off the coast from Doolin, is Inisheer (Inis Oírr, or 'Eastern Island'). The 15th-century **O'Brien Castle** (Caislea'n Uí Bhriain) overlooks the beach and harbour.

Connemara

095

With its shimmering black lakes, pale mountains, lonely valleys and more than the occasional rainbow, Connemara in the northwestern corner of County Galway is one of the most gorgeous corners of Ireland. It's prime hillwalking country with plenty of wild terrain, none more so than the **Twelve Bens**, a ridge of rugged mountains that form part of **Connemara National Park** (www.connemaranationalpark.ie).

Connemara's 'capital', **Clifden** (An Clochán), is an appealing Victorian-era country town with an oval of streets offering evocative strolls. Right in the centre of town is **Clifden Town Hostel** (21076; www.clifdentownhostel.com; Market St; dm €17-21, d €44), a cheery IHH hostel set in a cream-coloured house framed by big picture windows.

From Galway, **Lally Tours** (www.lallytours.com) run day-long bus trips through Connemara for around €25 per person.

NORTHWESTERN IRELAND

Sligo

071 / POP 17,900

William Butler Yeats (1865–1939) was born in Dublin and educated in London, but his poetry is infused with the landscapes, history and folklore of his mother's native Sligo (Sligeach). He returned many times and there are plentiful reminders of his presence in this sweet, sleepy town.

The **North West Regional Tourism office** (916 1201; www.sligotourism.ie; Temple St; 9am-5pm Mon-Sat Jun-Aug, 9am-5pm Mon-Fri Sep-May) is just south of the town centre.

In a pretty setting near Hyde Bridge, the Yeats Building houses the **WB Yeats Exhibition** (www.yeats-sligo.com; admission free; 10am-5pm Mon-Fri), which has a video presentation and valuable draft manuscripts; the €2 exhibition catalogue makes a good souvenir of Sligo. The charming **tearoom** (10am-5pm Mon-Sat) has outdoor tables overlooking the river.

In the churchyard at **Drumcliff**, 8km north of Sligo, is the **grave of WB Yeats**. In the 6th century, St Colmcille chose the same location for a monastery – you can still see the stumpy remains of the round tower on the main road nearby. Also in the churchyard is an extraordinary 11th-century **high cross**, carved with intricate biblical scenes. In summer the church shows a 15-minute audiovisual on Yeats and St Colmcille. The island of **Innisfree**, immortalised in Yeats' poem *The Lake Isle of Innisfree,* is in Lough Gill, southeast of Sligo town.

The basic but conveniently located **White House Hostel** (914 5160; Markievicz Rd; dm €15; P) is just north of the town centre. For more comfort head to the excellent **Harbour House** (917 1547; www.harbourhousehostel.com; Finisklin Rd; dm/d €20/50; P), which offers a little budget luxury in the form of colourful en-suite rooms with TV and firm beds.

Osta (Garavogue Weir View, Stephen St; mains €7-10; 8am-7pm Mon-Wed, to 8pm Thu-Sat) is a superb cafe and wine bar with a prime location overlooking the river and outdoor tables in summer. **Fiddler's Creek** (Rockwood Pde; mains €10-25; meals noon-3pm & 5.30-10pm) on the opposite side of the river serves excellent pub grub.

Getting There & Away

BUS Bus Éireann has services to Dublin (€17, four hours, four daily) and Westport (€17, two hours, two daily). The Galway–Sligo–Donegal–Derry service runs three times daily (twice on Sunday); it's €16 and 2½ hours to Galway, and €18 and 2½ hours to Derry.

TRAIN The train station is just west of the town centre along Lord Edward St. There are four or five trains daily to Dublin (€32, 3½ hours).

Bundoran

071 / POP 1700

Surfers from all over the world come to Bundoran (Bun Dobhráin) to seek out some of Europe's best beach breaks. Pass by the tacky arcades, fast-food stalls and souvenir shops in the town centre and head for **Tullan Strand** on the northern edge of town, the focal point of Bundoran's beach scene.

The seasonal **tourist office** (984 1350; Main St; Jun-Sep, hr vary) is opposite the Holyrood Hotel.

Bundoran Surf Co (www.bundoransurfco.com; Main St; 9.30am-7pm) offers surfing lessons for beginners for €30 (three hours, including equipment). Surf and accommodation packages can also be arranged. If you prefer riding a horse to riding a wave, **Donegal Equestrian Centre** (www.donegalequestriancentre.com; Finner Rd) can provide anything from a one-hour beach ride (€30) to a full day's trail ride (€120).

Once the holiday home of Viscount Enniskillen, the 300-year-old building housing the **Homefield Hostel** (☎984 1288; www.homefieldbackpackers.com; Bayview Ave; dm/d from €20/50; P@) now hosts world travellers year-round. A good B&B option is **Bay View** (☎984 1237; cnr Main St & Bayview Ave; s/d €50/70; P), a stately Edwardian town house with a view of the ocean.

Bus Éireann buses stop on Main St. There are direct daily services to Sligo (€9, 45 minutes), Galway (€19, 2¼ hours), Donegal (€7, 40 minutes) and more. Ulsterbus (www.ulsterbus.co.uk) has one daily service Monday to Friday to Belfast via Enniskillen. Feda O'Donnell buses stop two to three times daily, en route to Galway, at the Holyrood Hotel.

DONEGAL BEER FESTIVAL

If you're in Ireland in autumn, make tracks to Donegal town to indulge in its annual **Beer Festival** (www.donegalfestivals.com), a three-day extravaganza of international ales, open-air rock gigs and resoundingly good *craic*. It's held in mid- to late September.

NORTHERN IRELAND

☎028

When you cross from the republic into Northern Ireland you notice a couple of changes: the accent is different, the road signs are in miles, and the prices are in pounds sterling. But there's no border checkpoint, no guards, not even a sign to mark the crossing point – the two countries are in a customs union, so there's no passport control, no customs declarations. All of a sudden, you're in the UK.

Dragged down for decades by the violence and uncertainty of the Troubles, Northern Ireland today is a nation rejuvenated. The 1998 Good Friday Agreement laid the groundwork for peace and raised hopes for the future, and since then the province has seen a huge influx of investment and redevelopment. Belfast has become a happening place with a famously wild nightlife, while Derry is coming into its own as a cool, artistic city, and the stunning Causeway Coast gets more and more visitors each year.

There are still plenty of reminders of the Troubles – notably the 'peace lines' that still divide Belfast – and the passions that have torn Northern Ireland apart over the decades still run deep. But despite occasional setbacks there is an atmosphere of determined optimism.

Belfast

POP 277,000

Once lumped with Beirut, Baghdad and Bosnia as one of the four 'B's for travellers to avoid, Belfast has pulled off a remarkable transformation from bombs-and-bullets pariah to hip-hotels-and-hedonism party town. The city's skyline is in a constant state of flux as redevelopment continues apace. The old shipyards are giving way to the luxury waterfront apartments of the Titanic Quarter, and Victoria Sq, Europe's biggest urban regeneration project, has added a massive city-centre shopping mall to a list of tourist attractions that includes Victorian architecture, a glittering waterfront lined with modern art, foot-stomping music in packed-out pubs and the UK's second-biggest arts festival. The tourists have started to trickle back – get here before it becomes a flood.

The city centre is compact, with the imposing City Hall in Donegall Sq as the central landmark. The principal shopping district is north of the square. North again, around Donegall St and St Anne's Cathedral, is the bohemian Cathedral Quarter.

South of the square, the so-called Golden Mile stretches for 1km along Great Victoria St, Shaftesbury Sq and Botanic Ave to Queen's University and the leafy suburbs of South Belfast; this area has dozens of restaurants and bars and most of the city's budget and midrange accommodation.

Sights

FREE **Ulster Museum** MUSEUM
(www.ulstermuseum.org.uk; Stranmillis Rd; 10am-5pm Tue-Sun) Recently reopened after a major revamp, the Ulster Museum is now one of the north's don't-miss attractions. You could spend several hours browsing the beautifully designed displays, but if you're pressed for time don't miss the following: the **Armada Room**, with artefacts retrieved from the wreck of the Spanish galleon *Girona*; **Takabuti**, a 2500-year-old Egyptian mummy; and the **Bann Disc**, a superb example of Celtic design dating from the Iron Age.

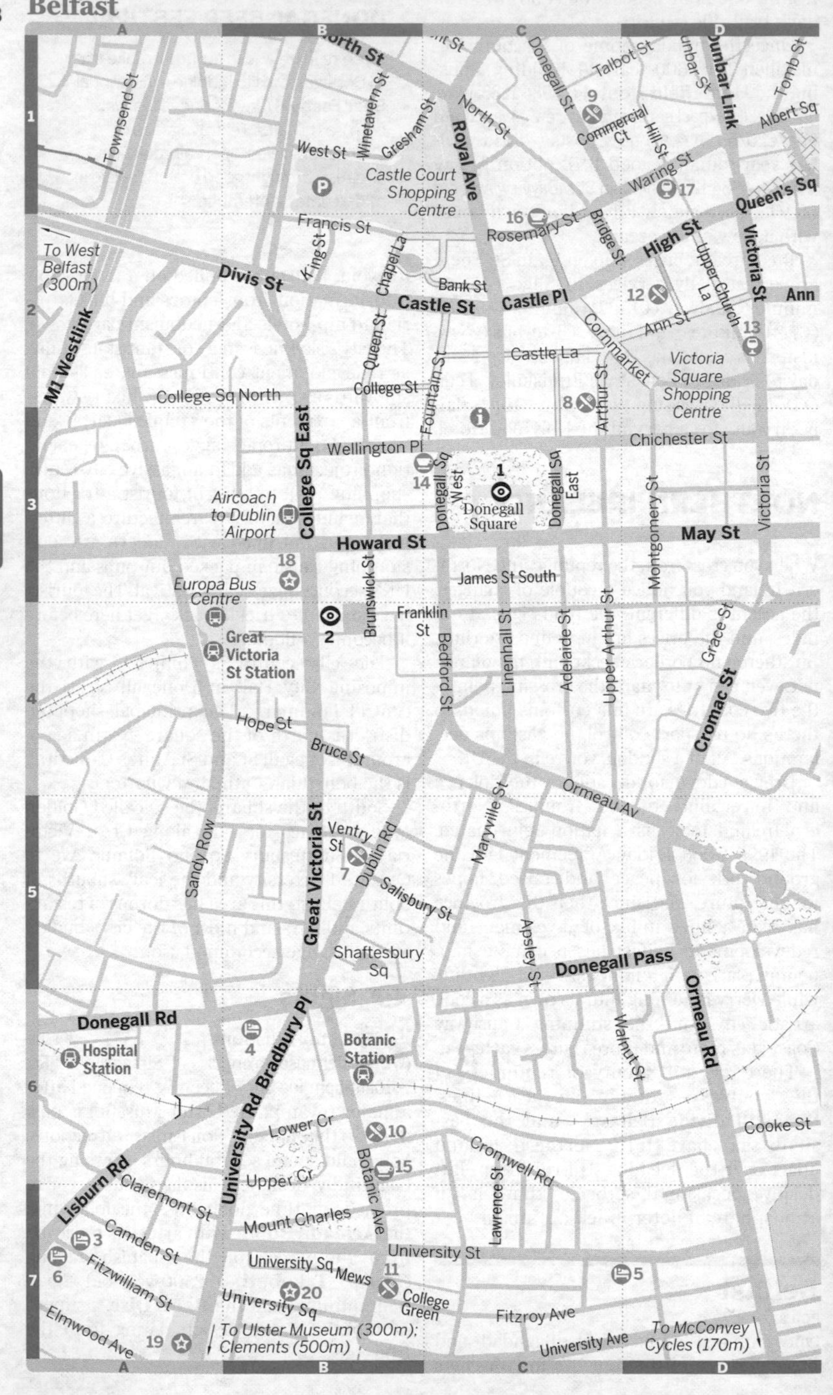
North St
Royal Ave
Donegall St
Talbot St
Dunbar Link
Tomb St
Albert Sq
Townsend St
West St
Winetavern St
Gresham St
Castle Court Shopping Centre
Commercial Ct
Hill St
Waring St
17
Queen's Sq
16
Rosemary St
Francis St
Bridge St
High St
Upper Church La
Victoria St
To West Belfast (300m)
King St
Chapel La
Divis St
Bank St
Castle St
Castle Pl
12
Ann
M1 Westlink
Queen St
Fountain St
Cornmarket
Ann St
13
Castle La
Victoria Square Shopping Centre
College St
College Sq North
Arthur St
8
Wellington Pl
Chichester St
College Sq East
14
Donegall Sq West
1
Donegall Square
Donegall Sq East
Montgomery St
Aircoach to Dublin Airport
Howard St
May St
18
James St South
Europa Bus Centre
Franklin St
Brunswick St
2
Great Victoria St Station
Bedford St
Linenhall St
Adelaide St
Upper Arthur St
Grace St
Cromac St
Hope St
Bruce St
Ormeau Av
Maryville St
Sandy Row
Ventry St
7
Dublin Rd
Salisbury St
Great Victoria St
Shaftesbury Sq
Apsley St
Donegall Pass
Donegall Rd
4
Hospital Station
University Rd
Bradbury Pl
Botanic Station
Walnut St
Ormeau Rd
Lower Cr
10
Cooke St
Cromwell Rd
Botanic Ave
15
Lisburn Rd
Upper Cr
Claremont St
Lawrence St
Mount Charles
3
Camden St
6
University St
University Sq Mews
11
5
Fitzwilliam St
20
University Sq
College Green
Fitzroy Ave
Elmwood Ave
19
To Ulster Museum (300m); Clements (500m)
University Ave
To McConvey Cycles (170m)
A
B
C
D
1
2
3
4
5
6
7

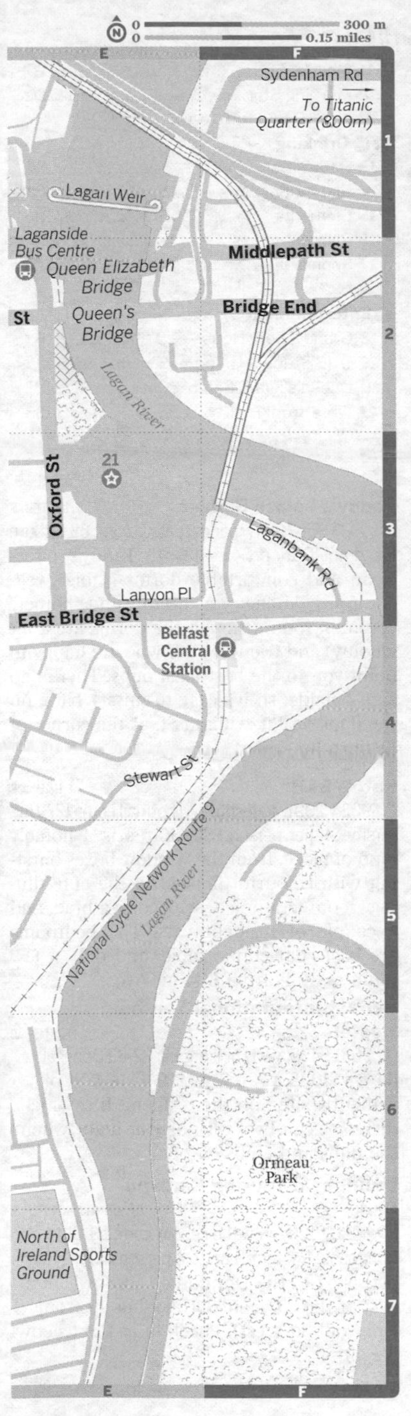

Titanic Quarter HISTORIC DISTRICT

Belfast's **Harland & Wolff shipyards** – whose famous yellow cranes Samson and Goliath dominate the city's eastern skyline – were the birthplace in 1911 of the *Titanic,* the 'unsinkable' ocean liner that struck an iceberg and sank in 1912. At the time of research, construction work had just begun on an 'iconic tourist attraction' rising near the slipway where *Titanic* was built; due to open by 2012 (the centenary of *Titanic's* launch), it will focus on both the ship and also the wider subject of Belfast's maritime heritage.

You can hire a hand-held multimedia device from the Belfast Welcome Centre, which leads you on a self-guided walking tour of the **Titanic Trail** (per device for up to 3hr £8). To get a real feel for the area take the Lagan Boat Company's excellent **Titanic Tour** (www.laganboatcompany.com; adult £10; ⏲12.30pm & 2pm Fri-Mon Mar-Oct, Sat & Sun only Nov & Dec, also 3pm Fri-Mon May-Sep).

West Belfast HISTORIC DISTRICT

The Catholic **Falls Rd** and the Protestant **Shankill Rd** have been battlefronts in Belfast's sectarian conflict since the 1970s. Even so, these areas are now quite safe and well worth visiting, if only to see the famous **murals** expressing local political and religious passions, and the infamous **Peace Line** – a 1km long barrier that divides Catholic and Protestant districts, and which has now been standing longer than the Berlin Wall.

Both **Official Black Taxi Tours** (☎9064 2264; www.belfasttours.com) and **Original Belfast Black Taxi Tours** (☎07751 565359; www.belfasttaxitours.net) offer organised taxi tours of West Belfast, with an even-handed account of the Troubles. They run daily for £8 to £10 per person based on a group of three to six sharing, and pick-up can be arranged.

FREE **Crown Liquor Saloon** HISTORIC BUILDING

(46 Great Victoria St; ⏲11.30am-11pm Mon-Sat, 12.30-10pm Sun) There are not too many historical monuments that you can enjoy while savouring a pint of beer, but Belfast's most famous pub is one. It was built by Patrick Flanagan in 1885 and displays Victorian architecture at its most extravagant.

Ulster Folk & Transport Museums MUSEUM

(www.uftm.org.uk; Cultra, Holywood; adult per museum £6.50, both museums £8; ⏲10am-5pm Tue-Sun Mar-Sep, shorter hr Oct-Feb) The open-air Folk Museum, with reconstructed farmhouses, forges, churches and mills, presents

Belfast

a strong impression of Irish life over the past few hundred years. The Transport Museum contains various Ulster-related vehicles, including a prototype of the DeLorean DMC sports car (of *Back to the Future* fame) and a display on the *Titanic*. The complex is 11km east of town.

FREE **City Hall** HISTORIC BUILDING
(Donegall Sq; guided tours 11am, 2pm & 3pm Mon-Fri, 2pm & 3pm Sat) Reopened after a massive refurbishment, the Renaissance-style City Hall, completed in 1906, is a testament to the city's industrial prosperity.

Festivals

Cathedral Quarter Arts Festival ARTS & MUSIC
(www.cqaf.com) This fantastic festival in early May attracts pioneering writers, comedians, musicians and artists, and presents theatre productions.

Festival at Queen's ARTS
(www.belfastfestival.com) For three weeks in late October/early November, Belfast hosts the second-largest arts festival in the UK, in and around Queen's University.

Sleeping

Arnie's Backpackers HOSTEL £
(9024 2867; www.arniesbackpackers.co.uk; 63 Fitzwilliam St; dm £10-14; @) More cosy than cramped, this small-scale hostel has a relaxed, down-home vibe, and Arnie manages to have a kindly disposition even when faced with an Estonian football fan club who've been drinking vodka for 12 hours straight.

Paddy's Palace Belfast HOSTEL £
(9033 3367; www.paddyspalace.com; 68 Lisburn Rd; dm £10-15, d £45; P @) Paddy's offers clean and comfortable dorms, a big, well-equipped kitchen, a bright and homely common room (though the dorms are a bit gloomy) and friendly staff who are happy to point you to the best local pubs. There's no sign outside, so it's easy to miss – bang on the door on Fitzwilliam St, at the corner of Lisburn Rd.

Kate's B&B B&B ££
(9028 2091; katesbb127@hotmail.com; 127 University St; per person £30) Kate's is a homely kind of place, from the window boxes bursting with colourful flowers to the cute dining room crammed with bric-a-brac and a couple of resident cats. The bedrooms are basic but comfortable, and only a few minutes' walk from Botanic Ave.

Belfast International Youth Hostel HOSTEL £
(9031 5435; www.hini.org.uk; 22-32 Donegall Rd; dm £10-15, s £21-31, tw £29-41; P @) Conveniently sited on the Golden Mile, which means it can be a bit noisy at night when the pubs and clubs empty.

Dundonald Touring Caravan Park CAMPING GROUND £
(9080 9100; www.theicebowl.com; 111 Old Dundonald Rd; tent & up to 4 persons £14; Mar-Oct) Next to the Dundonald Icebowl, 7km east of the city centre (take bus 19 from Donegall Sq West); check in at the Icebowl reception desk.

Eating

Maggie May's CAFE £

(www.maggiemaysbelfast.co.uk; 50 Botanic Ave; mains £3-7; ⌚8am-10.30pm Mon-Sat, 10am-10.30pm Sun) This is a classic little cafe with cosy wooden booths, murals of old Belfast and a host of hungover students wolfing down huge Ulster fries at lunchtime. The all-day breakfast menu runs from tea and toast to eggy bread and maple syrup, while lunch can be soup and a sandwich or steak-and-Guinness pie.

Avoca Cafe CAFE ££

(41 Arthur St; mains £5-12; ⌚9.30am-5pm Mon-Fri, 9am-5pm Sat, 12.30-5pm Sun) Upstairs in the Avoca store, this cafe focuses on healthy rolls, wraps, salads and sandwiches to sit in or take away, as well as offering hot lunch specials such as grilled chicken with Mediterranean vegetables.

Molly's Yard BISTRO ££

(☎9032 2600; www.mollysyard.co.uk; 1 College Green Mews; mains £7-10; ⌚noon-9pm Mon-Thu, noon-6pm Fri & Sat) A restored Victorian stables courtyard is the setting for this cosy bar-bistro with outdoor tables in the yard, a more formal **restaurant** (mains £13-20; ⌚6-9pm Mon-Sat) upstairs, and a seasonal menu focused on fresh local produce. Best to book for dinner.

John Hewitt PUB ££

(www.thejohnhewitt.com; 51 Donegall St; mains £6-9; ⌚meals noon-3pm Mon-Sat) Named for the Belfast poet and socialist, this is a modern pub with a traditional atmosphere and a well-earned reputation for excellent food. The menu changes weekly.

Archana INDIAN ££

(www.archana.co.uk; 53 Dublin Rd; mains £7-10; ⌚noon-2pm & 5pm-midnight Mon-Sat, 5-11pm Sun) Cosy and unpretentious, good range of vegetarian dishes. The *thali* – a platter of three curries – is good value at £17/11 for the meat/vegie version.

Morning Star PUB £

(www.themorningstarbar.com; 17 Pottinger's Entry; mains £5-15; ⌚meals noon-9pm Mon-Sat) Famed for its all-you-can-eat lunch buffet (£5; served noon to 4pm).

Drinking

Bittle's Bar PUB

(103 Victoria St) A cramped and staunchly traditional bar, Bittle's is a 19th-century triangular red-brick building decorated with paintings of Ireland's literary heroes. Pride of place on the back wall is taken by a large canvas depicting Yeats, Joyce, Behan and Beckett at the bar with glasses of Guinness, and Wilde pulling the pints on the other side.

Clements CAFE

(62 Botanic Ave; snacks £2-5; ⌚7.30am-10.30pm) Belfast's home-grown answer to Starbucks. Other branches are located on Donegall Sq West, Rosemary St and Stranmillis Rd.

Spaniard BAR

(www.thespaniardbar.com; 3 Skipper St) Forget 'style': this narrow, crowded bar, which looks as if it's been squeezed into someone's flat, has more atmosphere in one battered sofa than most 'style bars' have in their shiny entirety. Friendly staff, good beer, an eclectic crowd and cool tunes played at a volume that still allows you to talk: bliss.

Entertainment

Whatabout? is a free monthly guide to Belfast events issued by the Belfast Welcome Centre. Another useful guide is *The Big List* (www.the biglist.co.uk).

QUB Student Union CLUB

(www.qubsu-ents.com; Mandela Hall, Queen's Student Union, University Rd) The student union has various bars and music venues hosting club nights, live bands and stand-up comedy. The twice-monthly **Shine** (www.shine.net; admission £22; ⌚ Sat) is one of the city's best club nights.

Queen's Film Theatre CINEMA

(www.queensfilmtheatre.com; 20 University Sq) The QFT is a two-screen art-house cinema, close to the university, and a major venue for the Belfast Film Festival in March.

Waterfront Hall CONCERTS

(www.waterfront.co.uk; Lanyon Pl) The impressive 2235-seat Waterfront is Belfast's flagship concert venue, hosting local, national and international performers from pop stars to symphony orchestras.

Grand Opera House OPERA

(www.goh.co.uk; 2-4 Great Victoria St) This grand old venue plays host to a mixture of opera, popular musicals and comedy shows.

Information

Belfast Welcome Centre (☎9024 6609; www.gotobelfast.com; 47 Donegall Pl; ⌚9am-7pm Mon-Sat, 11am-4pm Sun Jun-Sep, 9am-5.30pm Mon-Sat, 11am-4pm Sun Oct-May; Wi-Fi) Tourist information for all of Ireland, accommodation

GETTING INTO BELFAST

Belfast's two bus stations – Laganside Bus Centre, near the river, and the bigger Europa Bus Centre, next to Great Victoria St train station – are both central, within five minutes' walk of Donegall Sq. Local trains connect Belfast Central (which, ironically, is *not* central) with Great Victoria St station via Botanic station. Most local bus services depart from Donegall Sq, near the City Hall, where there's a ticket and information kiosk.

Airport Express 300 buses link Belfast International airport with the Europa Bus Centre every 30 minutes (£7, 30 minutes). A taxi costs about £25.

booking, left luggage, and internet access for £1 per 20 minutes.

Getting There & Away

Air

George Best Belfast City airport (BHD; www.belfastcityairport.com; Airport Rd) About 6km northeast of the city centre; flights from the UK, Cork and Paris.

Belfast International airport (BFS; www.belfastairport.com) About 30km northwest of the city; flights from Galway, the UK, Europe and New York.

Boat

Ferries to Belfast from Stranraer and Liverpool dock at **Victoria Terminal** (West Bank Rd), 5km north of the city centre; exit the M2 motorway at junction 1. Ferries from the Isle of Man arrive at **Albert Quay** (Serkeley Rd), 2km north of the centre.

Other car ferries to and from Scotland dock at Larne, 30km north of Belfast. For details of ferry services see p679.

Bus

Europa Bus Centre (Great Victoria St) Reached via the Great Northern Mall beside the Europa Hotel. Main terminus for buses to Derry (£10, 1¾ hours, twice hourly), Dublin (£13, three hours, hourly) and destinations in the west and south of Northern Ireland.

Laganside Bus Centre (Oxford St) Near the river. Mainly for buses to County Antrim and eastern County Down.

Aircoach (www.aircoach.ie) Leaves from outside Jury's Hotel on College Sq East, Belfast, for Dublin airport (£12, 2½ hours, hourly).

Train

Belfast has two main train stations: **Great Victoria St** (Great Northern Mall, Great Victoria St), next to the Europa Bus Centre, and **Belfast Central** (East Bridge St), east of the city centre. If you arrive by train at Central Station, your rail ticket entitles you to a free bus ride into the city centre. A local train also connects with Great Victoria St.

Services go to Derry (£11, 2¼ hours, seven or eight daily), Dublin (£28, two hours, eight daily Monday to Saturday, five on Sunday) and Larne Harbour (£6.20, one hour, hourly).

Getting Around

BIKE McConvey Cycles (www.mcconveycycles.com; 182 Ormeau Rd) hires bikes for £15/60 per day/week. Credit-card deposit and photo ID required.

BUS A short trip on a city bus costs £1.40 to £2; a one-day ticket costs £3.50. Most local bus services depart from Donegall Sq, near the City Hall, where there's a ticket kiosk; otherwise, buy a ticket from the driver.

The Causeway Coast

Ireland isn't short of scenic coastlines, but the Causeway Coast between Portstewart and Ballycastle – climaxing in the spectacular rock formations of the Giant's Causeway – is as magnificent as they come.

The **Ulsterbus** (☎9066 6630; www.translink.co.uk) Antrim Coaster (bus 252) links Belfast with Coleraine (£10, four hours, two daily Monday to Saturday) via Larne, the Glens of Antrim, Ballycastle, the Giant's Causeway, Bushmills, Portrush and Portstewart; a Sunday service operates from July to September only.

From June to September the Causeway Rambler (bus 402) links Coleraine and Carrick-a-Rede (£5.50, 40 minutes, four daily) via Bushmills Distillery, the Giant's Causeway, White Park Bay and Ballintoy. The ticket allows unlimited travel in both directions for one day. Bus 172 runs year-round between Ballycastle and Portrush.

There are several hostels along the coast, including the following:

Sheep Island View Hostel HOSTEL £
(☎2076 9391; www.sheepislandview.com; 42a Main St, Ballintoy; campsites/dm £6/14; P@ wi-fi) Offers dorm beds, shared accommodation in the camping barn or a place to pitch a tent. It's on the B15 coast road 1km west of Carrick-a-Rede.

Ballycastle Backpackers HOSTEL £
(☎2076 3612; www.ballycastlebackpackers.net; 4 North St; dm/tw £15/40; P) Near the waterfront and the main bus stop.

Mill Rest Hostel HOSTEL £
(☎2073 1222; 49 Main St; dm/tw £16.50/39; ⊙daily Mar-Oct, Fri-Sun only Nov-Feb; @) Modern hostel, just 4.5km from the Giant's Causeway.

CARRICK-A-REDE ISLAND

The 20m-long **rope bridge** (adult £5.40; ⊙10am-7pm Jun-Aug, to 6pm Mar-May, Sep & Oct, 10.30am-3.30pm Nov & Dec) that connects Carrick-a-Rede Island to the mainland, swaying some 30m above the pounding waves, is a classic test of nerve. The island is the site of a salmon fishery and is a scenic 1.25km walk from the car park. Note that the bridge is closed in high winds.

GIANT'S CAUSEWAY

This spectacular rock formation – Northern Ireland's only Unesco World Heritage site – is one of Ireland's most impressive and atmospheric landscape features. When you first see it you'll understand why the ancients thought it wasn't a natural feature – the vast expanse of regular, closely packed, hexagonal stone columns looks for all the world like the handiwork of giants.

The more prosaic explanation is that the columns are simply contraction cracks caused by a cooling lava flow some 60 million years ago. The phenomenon is explained in an audiovisual (£1) at the **Causeway visitor centre** (☎2073 1855; www.giantscausewaycentre.com; ⊙10am-6pm Jul–Aug, shorter hr rest of yr).

It costs nothing to visit the site, but car parking is an exorbitant £6. It's an easy 10- to 15-minute walk downhill to the causeway itself, but a more interesting approach is to follow the clifftop path northeast for 2km to the Chimney Tops headland, then descend the Shepherd's Steps to the causeway.

Derry

POP 83,700

Derry or Londonderry? The name you use for Northern Ireland's second-largest city can be a political statement, but today most people just call it Derry, whatever their politics. The 'London' prefix was added in 1613 in recognition of the Corporation of London's role in the 'plantation' of Ulster with Protestant settlers.

In the 1960s resentment at the long-running Protestant domination of the city council boiled over in the (Catholic-dominated) civil-rights marches of 1968. In August 1969 fighting between police and local youths in the poor Catholic Bogside district prompted the UK government to send British troops into Derry. In January 1972 'Bloody Sunday' resulted in the deaths of 13 unarmed Catholic civil-rights marchers in Derry at the hands of the British army, an event that marked the beginning of the Troubles in earnest.

Today Derry is as safe to visit as anywhere else in Northern Ireland, while the Bogside and the inner city have been redeveloped. The city's long, dramatic history is still palpable – in the 17th-century city walls, in the captivating Bogside murals – but it's also a laid-back place with a well-founded reputation for musical excellence, from traditional to cutting-edge contemporary, and a lively arts scene that thrives in the city's many innovative venues.

The centre of old Derry is the walled city on the western bank of the River Foyle. The bus station is just outside the walls at its north end; the modern city centre stretches north from here along Strand Rd. The train station is on the east bank of the River Foyle, across Craigavon Bridge, in a district known as the Waterside. The Bogside lies to the west of the walled city.

Sights

Derry's **city walls** (www.derryswalls.com), built between 1613 and 1618, were the last to be constructed in Europe, and are Ireland's only city walls to survive almost intact. They provide a fantastic walk, and offer a grandstand view of the Bogside (itself worth a closer look on foot) and the **People's Gallery**, a series of murals that decorate the gable ends of houses along Rossville St. Painted between 1997 and 2001 by the Bogside Artists, they commemorate key events in the Troubles, including the Battle of the Bogside, Bloody Sunday, and the 1981 hunger strike. The artists now have their own **gallery** (www.bogsideartists.com; cnr Rossville & William Sts; admission free; ⊙9am-6pm daily) and offer guided walking tours of the murals (per person £4).

The **Museum of Free Derry** (☎7136 0880; www.museumoffreederry.org; 55-61 Glenfada Park; adult/concession £3/2; ⊙9am-4.30pm Mon-Fri year-round, 1-4pm Sat Apr-Sep, 1-4pm Sun Jul-Sep), just off Rossville St, chronicles the history of the Bogside, the civil-rights movement and the events of Bloody Sunday.

O'Doherty's Tower, inside the northern corner of the city walls, is home to the **Tower Museum** (☎7137 2411; www.derrycity.gov.uk/museums; adult £4; ⏲10am-5pm Tue-Sat), which traces the story of Derry from the days of St Columbcille to the present, and has an excellent exhibition telling the story of *La Trinidad Valenciera* – a ship of the Spanish Armada which was wrecked at Kinnagoe Bay in Donegal in 1588.

Sleeping

Saddler's House B&B ££

(☎7126 9691; www.thesaddlershouse.com; 36 Great James St; s/d £50/60; wi-fi) Everything about this historic, centrally located Victorian town house is a joy, from the sharp-witted hosts and their bulldog, Bertie, to the elegant rooms with period fireplaces and antique furniture, and the homemade marmalade at breakfast.

Derry City Independent Hostel HOSTEL £

(☎7128 0542; www.derryhostel.com; 44 Great James St; dm/d from £13/36; @wi-fi) Run by experienced backpackers and decorated with souvenirs of their travels around the world, this small, friendly hostel is set in a Georgian town house, just a short walk northwest of the bus station.

Derry Palace Hostel HOSTEL £

(☎7130 9051; www.paddyspalace.com; 1 Woodleigh Tce, Asylum Rd; dm/tw from £13/36; P@wi-fi) Part of the Ireland-wide Paddy's Palace chain, this hostel is central, comfortable and as friendly as they come. There's a sunny garden, a good party atmosphere and the staff regularly organise nights out at local pubs with traditional music.

Eating

Encore Brasserie INTERNATIONAL ££

(☎7137 2492; Millennium Forum, Newmarket St; mains £11-14; ⏲noon-4pm & 5-9pm) Set in the lobby of the city's main cultural venue, the Encore is a stylish little place with friendly, efficient service and a crowd-pleasing menu of perennial favourites, from homemade lasagne to slow-braised lamb shank. All main courses £8 from 8pm to 10pm Friday and Saturday.

Café del Mondo CAFE £

(4 Shipquay St; mains £5; ⏲8.30am-5pm Mon-Sat; wi-fi) A Bohemian cafe that serves excellent fair-trade coffee and a range of healthy lunch dishes, including soups, stews and salads, served with homemade bread.

Café Artisan CAFE £

(18-20 Bishop St Within; mains £3-5; ⏲9.30am-5.30pm Mon-Sat; wi-fi) This cool little cafe serves delicious homemade soups, deli sandwiches, panini and excellent cappuccinos; live jazz on Wednesday evening.

Drinking & Entertainment

Sandino's CAFE, BAR

(www.sandinos.com; 1 Water St) From the posters of Che to the Free Palestine flag, this relaxed cafe-bar exudes a liberal, left-wing vibe. There are live bands on Friday night, DJ sessions on Saturday, and occasional jazz, folk or comedy gigs; check the website for what's on.

Playhouse ARTS CENTRE

(www.derryplayhouse.co.uk; 5-7 Artillery St) Housed in beautifully restored former school buildings with an award-winning modern extension at the rear, this community arts centre stages music, dance and theatre performances by local and international performers.

Nerve Centre ARTS CENTRE

(www.nerve-centre.org.uk; 7-8 Magazine St) A multimedia arts centre for young, local talent in the fields of music and film. It has a performance area, a theatre, an art-house cinema, a bar and a cafe.

Peadar O'Donnell's PUB

(63 Waterloo St) Peadar's goes for traditional music sessions nightly and often in the afternoon on weekends, too.

Information

Derry tourist information centre (☎7137 7577; www.derryvisitor.com; 44 Foyle St; ⏲9am-7pm Mon-Fri, 10am-6pm Sat, 10am-5pm Sun Jul-Sep, closed Sun Mar-Jun & Oct, closed Sat & Sun Nov-Feb) Tourist info for all of Northern Ireland and the republic, as well as Derry. Also internet access (£1 per 20 minutes), currency exchange and accommodation-booking service.

Getting There & Away

BUS The bus station is just northeast of the city walls, on Foyle St. **Ulsterbus** (www.translink.co.uk) service 212, the *Maiden City Flyer*, is the fastest service between Belfast and Derry (£10, 1¾ hours, every half-hour, fewer on Sunday). Bus 234 goes to Coleraine (£6, one hour, five daily Monday to Friday, two Sunday), where you can connect with the 252 Antrim Coaster service (p672). Bus 274 goes from Derry to Dublin (£16, four hours, every two hours).

Bus Éireann (www.buseireann.ie) service 64 runs from Derry to Galway (£18, 5¼ hours, three daily, two on Sunday) via Donegal and Sligo; another four a day terminate at Sligo.

Airporter (www.airporter.co.uk) buses run direct from Derry's Quayside Shopping Centre to Belfast International airport (one way/return £18/28, 1½ hours) and George Best Belfast City airport (one way/return £18/28, two hours) every 90 minutes Monday to Friday, every two hours at weekends.

TRAIN Derry's **Waterside train station** (always referred to as Londonderry in Northern Ireland timetables) lies across the River Foyle from the city centre but is connected to it by a free Rail Link bus. Trains to Belfast (£10, 2¼ hours, seven or eight daily Monday to Saturday, four on Sunday).

GETTING INTO DERRY

A free shuttle bus connects Derry's Waterside train station with the bus station. From there, follow Foyle St towards the Guildhall and edge along the outside of the town walls towards pedestrianised Waterloo Pl. Bear right down Strand Rd; the hostels and B&Bs all have their check-in points on Great James St, off Strand Rd.

UNDERSTAND IRELAND

History

Celtic warriors reached Ireland around 300 BC. Christian monks, including St Patrick, arrived around the 5th century AD, and from the end of the 8th century the rich monasteries were targets of raids by Vikings, who were followed by Anglo-Norman forces in 1169.

Oppression of the Catholic Irish got seriously underway in the 1500s when Henry VIII and his successor Elizabeth I attempted to impose a new Protestant church. Land confiscated from Catholic nobles was given to Protestant settlers from Scotland and England, a policy known as 'the Plantation', sowing the seeds of today's divided Ireland.

By the 18th century, Ireland's Catholics held less than 15% of the land and suffered brutal civil restrictions. Irish movements for civil rights alarmed the Protestant gentry, and in 1800 the Act of Union joined Ireland with Britain.

Successive failures of potato crops between 1845 and 1851 brought about the Great Famine – hundreds of thousands starved while the British and Irish ruling classes profited from inflated food prices. About one million people died from disease or starvation, and another million emigrated.

Moves toward Irish home rule were interrupted by WWI and a bungled uprising in 1916. Though it is now celebrated as a glorious bid for freedom, the Easter Rising was heavy on rhetoric and light on planning on both sides. After the insurrection was put down, a series of trials and executions (15 in all) transformed the ringleaders into martyrs and roused international support for Irish independence.

In the 1918 election, Irish republicans stood under the banner of Sinn Féin (Ourselves Alone) and won a majority of the Irish seats. Ignoring London's Parliament, the newly elected Sinn Féin deputies declared Ireland independent and formed the Dáil Éireann (Irish assembly), led by Eamon de Valera.

The resulting Anglo-Irish War (1919–21) pitted Sinn Féin and its military wing, the Irish Republican Army (IRA), against the British. During this period Michael Collins masterminded the IRA's campaign of violence (while serving as finance minister in the new Dáil). After months of negotiations, he and Arthur Griffith led the delegation that signed the Anglo-Irish Treaty in 1921, giving 26 of Ireland's 32 counties their independence; six largely Protestant counties in Ulster chose to remain part of the UK, as the province of Northern Ireland.

To de Valera and many Irish Catholics, the compromise was a betrayal of republican principles and a brief civil war ensued. A new 1937 constitution abolished fealty to Britain and claimed sovereignty over the six counties of Ulster. In 1948 the Irish government declared the country a republic.

In Northern Ireland, the Protestant majority had systematically excluded Catholics from power. In January 1969 civil-rights marchers walking from Belfast to Derry were attacked by a Protestant mob outside Derry. British troops were sent to Derry and Belfast in August to maintain law and order. The peaceful civil-rights movement foundered and an armed independence struggle began, led by the IRA.

Thus the so-called Troubles thundered through the 1970s and 1980s. Passions exploded in 1972 when 13 unarmed Catholics were shot dead by British troops in Derry on

'Bloody Sunday' (30 January), then again in 1981 when 10 IRA prisoners fasted to death.

In August 1994 a 'permanent cessation of violence' by the IRA was announced, to be matched by a Protestant ceasefire two months later. After setbacks, the peace process regained momentum with the May 1997 victory of Britain's Labour Party, and in July 1997, the IRA declared another ceasefire.

In April 1998 all-party talks produced the Good Friday Agreement, which allowed the people of Northern Ireland to decide their future by majority vote, committed its signatories to 'democratic and peaceful means of resolving differences on political issues', and established a new Northern Ireland Assembly.

The new assembly was beset by divisions from the outset – largely over acts of violence and wrangles about how and when the IRA should 'decommission' its weapons – which resulted in no less than four suspensions, the latest from 2002 until 2007. A deal hammered out between the Democratic Unionist Party and Sinn Féin saw the assembly members finally take their seats in Stormont on 8 May 2007.

Today a cautious optimism prevails and, despite economic recession, occasional flare-ups of sectarian violence, and a renewed bombing campaign by republican splinter groups in Northern Ireland in 2010, the vast majority of people north and south of the border are committed to a peaceful future.

People

Prior to the 1845–51 Great Famine, Ireland's population was around eight million; death and emigration reduced it to around six million, and emigration continued at a high level for the next 100 years. It wasn't until the 1960s that the population began to recover. It is now around 6.2 million overall, with 4.5 million in the Republic of Ireland and 1.7 million in Northern Ireland.

Thanks to the EU and a strong economy, Ireland has seen a modest influx of immigrants, mostly from Eastern Europe, within the past five years. However, the global financial crisis of 2008 hit Ireland's economy hard, especially the once-thriving construction sector, and rising unemployment has seen many recent immigrants heading back home.

Religion has always played a pivotal role in Ireland. About 90% of people in the republic are Roman Catholic, followed by 3% Protestant, 0.1% Jewish and the rest with no professed religious belief. In the north the breakdown is about 53% Protestant and 44% Catholic.

Arts

Literature

The Irish have made an enormous impact on world literature. Important writers include Jonathan Swift, Oscar Wilde, WB Yeats, George Bernard Shaw, James Joyce, Sean O'Casey, Samuel Beckett and Roddy Doyle. The Ulster-born poet Seamus Heaney was awarded the Nobel Prize for Literature in 1995. Earlier Irish Nobel laureates include Shaw (1925), Yeats (1938) and Beckett (1969). Frank McCourt became a world favourite with his autobiographical, Pulitzer Prize-winning *Angela's Ashes*.

Music

Traditional Irish music – played on instruments such as the *bodhrán* (a flat, goatskin drum), *uilleann* (elbow) pipes, flute and fiddle – is an aspect of Irish culture that's impossible to miss. Of the Irish music groups, perhaps the best-known are the Chieftains, the Dubliners and the Pogues. Among popular Irish singers and musicians who have made it on the international stage are Van Morrison, Thin Lizzy, Sinéad O'Connor, Bob Geldof, U2, the Cranberries, the Corrs and Damien Rice.

Food

The following price indicators for main courses are used in this chapter:

€€€ more than €16/£15

€€ €8 to €16/£7 to £15

€ less than €8/£7

Environment

Ireland is divided into 32 counties: 26 in the republic and six in Northern Ireland. The island measures 84,421 sq km (about 83% is the republic) and stretches 486km north to south and 275km east to west. The jagged coastline extends for 5631km. The midlands of Ireland are flat, rich farmland with huge swaths of peat (which is rapidly being depleted for fuel).

Carrauntuohil (1040m) on the Iveragh Peninsula, County Kerry, is the highest mountain on the island. The Shannon River, the longest in Ireland, flows for 259km before emptying into the Atlantic west of Limerick.

Ireland's rivers and lakes are well stocked with fish and the island is home to some three dozen mammal species. The Office of Public Works (OPW) maintains six national parks and 76 nature reserves in the republic; the Department of the Environment owns or leases more than 40 nature reserves in Northern Ireland.

SURVIVAL GUIDE

Directory A–Z

Accommodation

Sleeping listings in this chapter generally state the high-season rate; low-season rates can be 15% to 25% less. Booking ahead is recommended in peak season.

€€€ more than €65/£120

€€ €30 to €65/£50 to £120

€ less than €30/£50

Fáilte Ireland (Irish Tourist Board; www.discoverireland.ie) Will book accommodation for a 10% room deposit and a fee of €5.

Gulliver (www.gulliver.ie) Online booking service for both republic and Northern Ireland; deposit of 10% and a €5 fee is payable.

Northern Ireland Tourist Board (NITB; www.discovernorthernireland.com) Books accommodation at no cost but with a 10% deposit up front.

Commercial camping grounds typically charge €10 to €20 for a tent and two people, and some hostels have space for tents. Unless indicated otherwise, prices given in this chapter for campsites are for a tent plus two people.

Hostels in Ireland can be heavily booked in summer, although there are hundreds of backpacker hostels and about 40 official youth hostels. From June to September most hostels cost from €15 to €20 a night, except for the more expensive hostels in Dublin, Belfast and a few other places. Useful hostel organisations are as follows:

An Óige (www.anoige.ie)

Hostelling International Northern Ireland (HINI; www.hini.org.uk)

Independent Holiday Hostels (IHH; www.hostels-ireland.com)

Independent Hostel Owners in Ireland (IHO; www.independenthostelsireland.com)

Typical B&Bs cost around €20 to €40 per person a night (sharing a double room), though more luxurious B&Bs can cost upwards of €55 per person. Most B&Bs fill up quickly in summer.

Activities

Ireland is great for outdoor activities, and tourist offices have a wide selection of information sheets covering **birdwatching** (County Donegal and County Wexford), **surfing** (great along the west coast), **scuba diving** (West Cork), cycling, fishing, horse riding, sailing, canoeing and many other activities.

Walking is particularly popular, although you must come prepared for wet weather. There are now well over 20 way-marked trails throughout Ireland, one of the most popular being the 132km Wicklow Way.

Business Hours

The standard business hours are generally the same for both the republic and Northern Ireland and are shown below, with any variations noted:

Banks 10am-4pm Mon-Fri (to 5pm Thu)

Post offices Northern Ireland 9am-5.30pm Mon-Fri, 9am-12.30pm Sat; republic 9am-6pm Mon-Fri, 9am-1pm Sat. Smaller post offices may close at lunch and 1 day per week.

Pubs Northern Ireland 11.30am-11pm Mon--Sat, 12.30pm-10pm Sun. Pubs with late licences open until 1am Mon-Sat, and to midnight Sun; republic 10.30am-11.30pm Mon-Thu, 10.30am-12.30am Fri and Sat, noon-11pm Sun. All pubs close Christmas Day and Good Friday.

Restaurants Noon-10.30pm; many close one day of the week.

Shops 9am-5.30pm or 6pm Mon-Sat (until 8pm on Thu and sometimes Fri), noon-6pm Sun (in bigger towns only). Shops in rural towns may close at lunch and 1 day per week.

Festivals & Events

St Patrick's Day A cacophony of parades, fireworks and light shows for three days around 17 March in Dublin; Cork, Armagh and Belfast also have parades.

Dublin International Film Festival April; also a highlight.

Bloomsday In Dublin, Leopold Bloom's Joycean journey around the city is marked by various events on 16 June.

Marching season In Northern Ireland every Orangeman in the country hits the streets on 'the 12th' (of July).

Galway Arts Festival (p662) A great regional cultural event in late July.

Kilkenny Arts Festival Late August.

All-Ireland hurling In Dublin in September.

Gaelic football finals In Dublin in September.

Galway Oyster Festival September.

Belfast Festival At Queen's in November.

Holidays

Public holidays in the republic and/or Northern Ireland:

New Year's Day 1 January

St Patrick's Day 17 March

Easter (Good Friday to Easter Monday inclusive) March/April

May Holiday First Monday in May

Christmas Day 25 December

St Stephen's Day (Boxing Day) 26 December

NORTHERN IRELAND

Spring Bank Holiday Last Monday in May

Orangemen's Day 12 July (following Monday if 12th is at weekend)

August Bank Holiday Last Monday in August

REPUBLIC

June Holiday First Monday in June

August Holiday First Monday in August

October Holiday Last Monday in October

Internet Resources

» **Irish Tourist Board** (www.discoverireland.ie)

» **Northern Ireland Tourism** (www.discovernorthernireland.com)

Money

The republic uses the euro (€), while Northern Ireland uses the British pound sterling (£). Banks offer the best exchange rates; exchange bureaux, open longer, have worse rates and higher commissions. Post offices generally have exchange facilities and open on Saturday morning.

In Northern Ireland several banks issue their own Northern Irish pound notes, which are equivalent to sterling but not readily accepted in Britain. Many hotels, restaurants and shops in the north accept euros.

Fancy hotels and restaurants usually add 10% or 15% service charge on to bills. Simpler places usually don't add service; if you decide to tip, just round up the bill (or add 10% at most). Taxi drivers do not have to be tipped.

Telephone

To call Northern Ireland from the republic, you do not use ☎0044 as for the rest of the UK. Instead, you dial ☎048 and then the local number. To dial the republic from the North, however, use the full international code ☎00353, then the local number.

Local calls from a public phone in the republic cost €0.50 for around three minutes (around €0.60 to a mobile phone). In Northern Ireland a local call costs at least £0.30. Some payphones in the north take euros. Prepaid phonecards work from all payphones.

The mobile (cell) phone network in Ireland runs on the GSM 900/1800 system compatible with the rest of Europe and Australia but not the USA. Mobile numbers in the Republic begin with 085, 086 or 087. A local pay-as-you-go SIM for your mobile will cost from around €10 but may work out free after the standard phone-credit refund.

Visas

Citizens of the EU, Australia, Canada, New Zealand and the US don't need a visa to visit either the republic or Northern Ireland. EU nationals are allowed to stay indefinitely, while other visitors can usually remain for three to six months. UK nationals born in Britain or Northern Ireland don't need a passport to visit the republic but should carry photo identification.

Getting There & Away

Air

There are nonstop flights from Britain, Continental Europe and North America to Dublin, Shannon and Belfast International, and nonstop connections from Britain and Europe to Cork. International departure tax is normally included in the price of your ticket.

International airports in Ireland are as follows:

Belfast City (BHD; www.belfastcityairport.com)

Belfast International (BFS; www.belfast airport.com)

Dublin (DUB; www.dublinairport.com)

Shannon (SNN; www.shannonairport.com)

Sea

There's a wide range of ferry services from Britain and France to Ireland. Prices vary depending on season, time of day, day of the week and length of stay. One-way fares for an adult foot passenger can be as little as £25 but can exceed £75 in summer. For a car plus driver and up to four adult passengers, prices can be £150 to £300.

Keep an eye out for special deals, discounted return fares and other money savers. And plan ahead – some services are booked up months in advance. **Direct Ferries** (www.directferries.co.uk) lists all the available ferry routes and operators.

List of ferry operators:

Brittany Ferries (☎021-427 7801, in France 0825 828 828; www.brittanyferries.com) Once weekly April to October.

Celtic Link Ferries (☎040-238084, in France 02 33 43 23 87; www.celticlinkferries.com) Twice-weekly passenger-only service.

Fastnet Line (☎021-437 8892, in the UK 0844 576 8831; www.fastnetline.com) Three of four sailings a week March to November.

Irish Ferries (☎0818-300 400, in the UK 0870 517 1717, in France 01 56 93 43 40; www.irishferries.com) Holyhead ferries up to four a day year-round, from France to Rosslare three times a week, mid-February to December.

Norfolkline (☎01-819 2999, in the UK 0844 499 0007; www.norfolkline.com) Daily sailings year-round.

P&O Irish Sea (☎01-407 3434, in the UK 0871 66 44 999; www.poirishsea.com) Daily sailings year-round.

Steam Packet (☎1800 805055, in the UK 0870 222 1333; www.steam-packet.com) Ferries operate daily from Easter to September only.

Stena Line (☎01 204 7777, in the UK 08705 707070; www.stenaline.co.uk) Daily sailings year-round.

FERRIES: BRITAIN TO IRELAND

ROUTE	OPERATOR	DURATION	ONE-WAY FARE
Swansea–Cork	Fastnet Line	12hr	£45
Fishguard–Rosslare	Stena Line	3½hr	£25
Pembroke–Rosslare	Irish Ferries	2hr	£30
Holyhead–Dublin	Stena Line, Irish Ferries	3hr	£26
Holyhead–Dublin (fast boat)	Irish Ferries	1¾hr	£30
Holyhead–Dun Laoghaire	Stena Line	1½hr	£40
Liverpool–Dublin	Norfolkline, P&O Irish Sea	8½hr	£25
Liverpool–Belfast	Norfolkline	8½hr	£40
Douglas (Isle of Man)–Dublin	Steam Packet	2¾hr	£40
Douglas (Isle of Man)–Belfast	Steam Packet	2¾hr	£40
Stranraer–Belfast	Stena Line	3hr	£25
Stranraer–Belfast (fast boat)	Stena Line	2hr	£25
Cairnryan–Larne (fast boat)	P&O Irish Sea	1hr	£24
Troon–Larne (fast boat)	P&O Irish Sea	2hr	£24

Ferry services to France are as follows:

Roscoff–Rosslare (Irish Ferries; 17 hours, €150)

Cherbourg–Rosslare (Irish Ferries, Celtic Link; 20 hours, €60)

Roscoff–Cork (Brittany Ferries; 14 hours, €77)

Getting Around

In Ireland public transport can be expensive (particularly trains), infrequent or both. For these reasons having your own transport – car or bicycle – at least for part of your journey – can be a major advantage.

Bicycle

A bike is useful for exploring in rural areas, but beware of traffic on what are often narrow, potholed roads with no space to get out of the way. Note that there is no 'right to roam' as in the UK, and most off-road cycling is technically illegal without the landowner's permission.

Typical bike hire costs are €20 to €25 per day or around €60 to €100 a week. Bags and other equipment can also be hired.

Bicycles can be transported by bus if there is enough room on board; the charge varies. On trains, the cost is €4 to €8 for a one-way journey, but bikes are not allowed on certain routes, including the Dublin Area Rapid Transit (DART).

Raleigh Rent-a-Bike (www.raleigh.ie) has a network of agencies all over Ireland; like many local bike shops, it offers one-way hire for an extra charge.

Bus

The Republic of Ireland's national bus line, **Bus Éireann** (☎01-836 6111; www.buseireann.ie), operates services all over the republic and into Northern Ireland. Fares are much cheaper than train fares. Return trips are usually only slightly more expensive than one-way fares, and special deals (eg same-day returns) are often available. Most intercity buses in Northern Ireland are operated by **Ulsterbus** (☎028-9066 6630; www.translink.co.uk).

Main routes are as follows:

TRAVEL PASSES & DISCOUNTS

International Passes

Eurail Pass Valid for train travel in the Republic of Ireland but not in Northern Ireland 50% discount on Irish Ferries crossings to France.

InterRail Pass 50% discount on train travel within Ireland and on Irish Ferries and Stena Line services.

ISIC Both Bus Éireann and Iarnród Éireann offer discounts to ISIC holders.

Britrail Pass Has an option to add on Ireland for an extra fee. The pass also covers ferry transit.

Ireland-Only Passes

Open Road Pass For bus travel in the republic; €54 for three days' travel out of six consecutive days; €69 (four out of eight days); €129 (eight out of 16 days); or €234 (15 out of 30 days). See www.buseireann.ie.

Irish Rover Bus travel on Bus Éireann (republic) and Ulsterbus (Northern Ireland); €83.50 (for three days' travel out of eight consecutive days), €190 (eight out of 15 days) or €280 (15 out of 30 days). See www.buseireann.ie.

Irish Explorer Rail and bus travel in the republic including DART; €245 for eight days' travel out of 15 consecutive days. See www.buseireann.ie.

Irish Explorer Rail For train-only travel (five days' travel out of 15); €145 within the republic only, €180 including Northern Ireland. Not publicised on the irishrail.ie website at time of research.

Zone 3 iLink Card Replacement for the Freedom of Northern Ireland pass. Smartcard offering unlimited travel on bus and train in Northern Ireland; one day/one week costs £15/55 plus £1.50 on first purchase (can be topped up). See www.translink.co.uk/ilink.

Belfast–Dublin (£13, three hours, seven daily)

Derry–Belfast (£10, 1¾ hours, more than 10 daily)

Derry–Galway (£26, 5¼ hours, four daily)

Dublin–Cork (€12, 4½ hours, six daily)

Dublin–Killarney (€25, six hours, five daily)

Killarney–Galway (€24, four hours, six daily)

Car & Motorcycle

People under 21 cannot hire a car; for most rental companies you must be at least 23 and have had a valid driving licence for one year. Your own local licence is usually sufficient to hire a car for up to three months.

Train

The Republic of Ireland's railway system, **Iarnród Éireann** (www.irishrail.ie), has routes radiating out from Dublin, but there is no direct north–south route along the west coast. Tickets can be twice as expensive as the bus, but travel times may be dramatically reduced. Special fares are often available, and a midweek return ticket sometimes costs just a bit more than the single fare; the flip side is that fares may be significantly higher on Friday and Sunday. Check also for deals on the internet. **Rail Users Ireland** (www.railusers.ie) is more informative than the official website.

Northern Ireland Railways (www.translink.co.uk) has four lines from Belfast, one of which links up with the republic's rail system.

Italy

Includes »

Best Places to Eat

» Pizzeria da Baffetto, Rome (p700)

» Osteria de' Poeti, Bologna (p730)

» L'Osteria di Giovanni, Florence (p739)

» Gelateria I Bastioni (p766)

Best Places to Stay

» Hotel in Pietra, Matera (p757)

» Ca' Angeli, Venice (p722)

» Hostel of the Sun, Naples (p751)

» Beehive, Rome (p698)

Why Go?

The land that has turned its lifestyle into a designer accessory, Italy is one of Europe's great seducers. Ever since the days of the 18th-century Grand Tour, travellers have been falling under its spell and still today it stirs strong emotions. The rush you get when seeing the Colosseum for the first time or cruising down Venice's surreal canals are experiences you'll remember for life.

Of course, Italy is not all about Michelangelo masterpieces and frescoed churches. There's also the food, imitated the world over, and a landscape that boasts beautiful Alpine peaks, stunning coastlines and remote, silent valleys. So if the cities don't do it for you, if their noise, heat and chaos start getting to you – as they get to many locals – change gear and head out to the country for a taste of the sun-kissed slow life.

When to Go

Rome

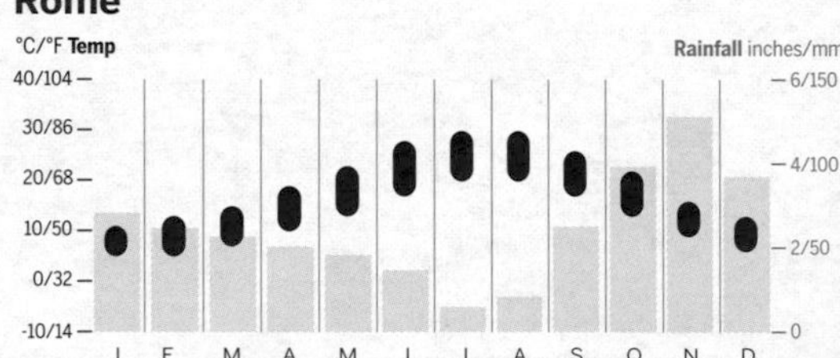

Apr–May Perfect temperatures and Settimana della Cultura (Culture Week).

Jun–Jul Summer means gorgeous beach weather and a packed festival calendar.

Sep–Oct Enjoy the coast without the crowds and tuck into fabulous autumn food.

Connections

Milan and Venice are northern Italy's two main transport hubs. From Milan, trains run to cities across Western Europe, including Barcelona, Paris, Vienna and Zürich. Venice is better placed for Eastern Europe with rail connections to Belgrade, Budapest, Ljubljana and Zagreb. You can also pick up ferries in Venice for Corfu, Igoumenitsa and Patra. Down the east coast, there are ferries from Bari to various Greek ports, as well as to Bar and Dubrovnik. At the other end of the country, Genoa has ferries to Barcelona and Tunis.

ITINERARIES

One Week

A one-week whistle stop tour of Italy is enough to take in some of the country's main cities. After a couple of days exploring Venice's canals, head south to Florence, Italy's great Renaissance city. Two days is not long there but it'll whet your appetite for the artistic and architectural treasures that await in Rome.

Two Weeks

In the second week, continue south for some sea and southern passion. Spend a day dodging traffic in Naples, a day investigating the ruins at Pompeii and a day or two admiring the Amalfi Coast. Then backtrack to Naples for a ferry to Palermo and the gastronomic delights of Sicily. Or maybe Cagliari and Sardinia's magical beaches. You choose.

Essential Food & Drink

» **Pizza** Two varieties: Roman, with a thin crispy base, and Neapolitan, with a higher, more doughy base. The best are always prepared in a wood-fired oven *(forno a legna)*.

» **Gelato** Popular ice-cream flavours include *fragola* (strawberry), *nocciola* (hazelnut) and *stracciatella* (milk with chocolate shavings).

» **Wine** Ranges from big-name reds such as Piedmont's Barolo to light whites from Sardinia and sparkling *prosecco* from the Veneto; sample wine at an enoteca (wine bar).

» **Caffè** Join the locals for a morning cappuccino or post-lunch espresso, both taken standing at a bar.

AT A GLANCE

» **Currency** Euro (€)

» **Language** Italian

» **Money** ATMs widespread; credit cards widely accepted

» **Visas** Schengen visa rules apply; see p1319

Fast Facts

» **Area** 301,340 sq km

» **Capital** Rome

» **Country code** ☎39

» **Emergency** ☎112

Exchange Rates

Australia	A$1	€0.74
Canada	C$1	€0.74
Japan	¥100	€0.87
New Zealand	NZ$1	€0.56
UK	UK£1	€1.16
USA	US$1	€0.72

Set Your Budget

» **Budget hotel room** €55 to €110 (double)

» **Two-course evening meal** pizza meal €10 to €15, otherwise from €20

» **Museum entrance** €6.50 to €15

» **Beer** €2.50 to €5

» **City transport ticket** €1

Resources

» **Italia** (www.italia.it) Inspiration, ideas and planning tips.

» **Italymag** (www.italymag.co.uk) Online mag dedicated to everything Italian.

» **Trenitalia** (www.terroviedellostato.it) Plan your train trips.

» **Lonely Planet** (www.lonelyplanet.com/italy)

Italy Highlights

1. Lap up the *dolce vita* in Italy's mesmerising capital, **Rome** (p685)
2. Take a *vaporetto* ride past grand but crumbling canalside palaces in **Venice** (p718)
3. Marvel at the Medicis' art collection in the Uffizi Gallery, in **Florence** (p736)
4. Hike up the side of an active volcano in the **Aeolian Islands** (p760)
5. Work up an appetite for pizza while exploring the baroque backstreets of **Naples** (p747)
6. Blow your mind on baroque architecture in elegant **Lecce** (p757)
7. Explore imperious **Turin** (p711), so much more than Fiat and factories!
8. Delve into frescoed Etruscan tombs in **Tarquinia** (p707)
9. Enjoy a bike ride and picnic atop the medieval city walls in **Lucca** (p744)

ROME

POP 2.72 MILLION

An epic, monumental metropolis, Rome has been in the spotlight for close on 3000 years. As the showcase centre of the Roman Empire, it was the all-powerful *caput mundi* (capital of the world). Later, as the Renaissance capital of the Catholic world, its name sent shivers of holy terror through believers and infidels alike. Some 500 years on and its name still exerts a powerful hold. Fortunately, the reality is every bit as enticing as the reputation. With its architectural and artistic treasures, its romantic corners and noisy markets, Rome is a city that knows how to impress.

Sights

Most of Rome's sights are concentrated in the area between Stazione Termini and the Vatican. Halfway between the two, the Pantheon and Piazza Navona lie at the heart of the *centro storico* (historic centre). To the southeast, the Colosseum is an obvious landmark.

ADMISSION PRICES

EU citizens aged between 18 and 25 and students from countries with reciprocal arrangements generally qualify for a discount (usually half price) at galleries and museums in Italy. Under 18s and over 65s often get in free. In all cases you'll need proof of identity.

In Rome, the **Roma Pass** (www.romapass.it; 3 days €25) provides free admission to two museums or sites (choose from a list of 38) in Rome, as well as reduced entry to extra sites, unlimited city transport and discounted entry to other exhibitions and events. If you use this for the more expensive sights such as the Colosseum or Musei Capitolini, you will save money.

ANCIENT ROME

Colosseum ROMAN RUINS

(Map p690; ☎06 399 67 700; Piazza del Colosseo; adult/concession incl Roman Forum & Palatino €12/7.50, audio guide €4; ⊙8.30am-1hr before sunset; MColosseo) Rome's iconic monument is a thrilling site. The 50,000 seater Colosseum was ancient Rome's most feared arena and is today one of Italy's top tourist attractions. Queues are inevitable but you can usually avoid them by buying your ticket at the entrance to the Palatino Hill about 250m away at Via di San Gregorio 30. Alternatively, join a walking tour (€4 on top of ticket price) and use the separate ticket line.

Originally known as the Flavian Amphitheatre, the Colosseum was started by Emperor Vespasian in AD 72 and finished by his son Titus in AD 80. It was clad in travertine and covered by a huge canvas awning, held aloft by 240 masts. Inside, tiered seating encircled the sand-covered arena, itself built over underground chambers where animals were caged. Games generally involved gladiators fighting wild animals or each other.

To the west of the Colosseum, the **Arco di Costantino** was built to celebrate Constantine's victory over Maxentius at the battle of Milvian Bridge in AD 312.

Roman Forum ROMAN RUINS

(Map p690; Largo della Salara Vecchia; adult/concession incl Colosseum & Palatino €12/7.50, audio guide €4; ⊙8.30am-1hr before sunset; MColosseo) Now a collection of fascinating, if rather confusing, ruins, the Roman Forum (Foro Romano) was the social, political and commercial hub of the Roman Republic.

As you enter from Largo della Salaria Vecchia, ahead to your left is the **Tempio di Antonino e Faustina**, built by the senate in AD 141 and transformed into a church in the 8th century. To your right, the **Basilica Aemilia**, built in 179 BC, was 100m long with a two-storey porticoed facade lined with shops. At the end of the short path, **Via Sacra** traverses the Forum from northwest to southeast. Opposite the Basilica Aemilia stands the **Tempio di Giulio Cesare**, erected by Augustus in 29 BC on the site where Caesar's body had been burned.

Head right up Via Sacra and you reach the **Curia**, once the meeting place of the Roman senate and later converted into a church. In front is the **Lapis Niger**, a large piece of black marble that purportedly covered Romulus' grave.

At the end of Via Sacra, the **Arco di Settimio Severo** was erected in AD 203 to honour Emperor Septimus Severus and his two sons and celebrate victory over the Parthians. Nearby, the **Millarium Aureum** marked the centre of ancient Rome, from where distances to the city were measured.

Southwest of the arch, eight granite columns are all that remain of the **Tempio di Saturno**, one of ancient Rome's most important temples. Inaugurated in 497 BC, it was later used as the state treasury.

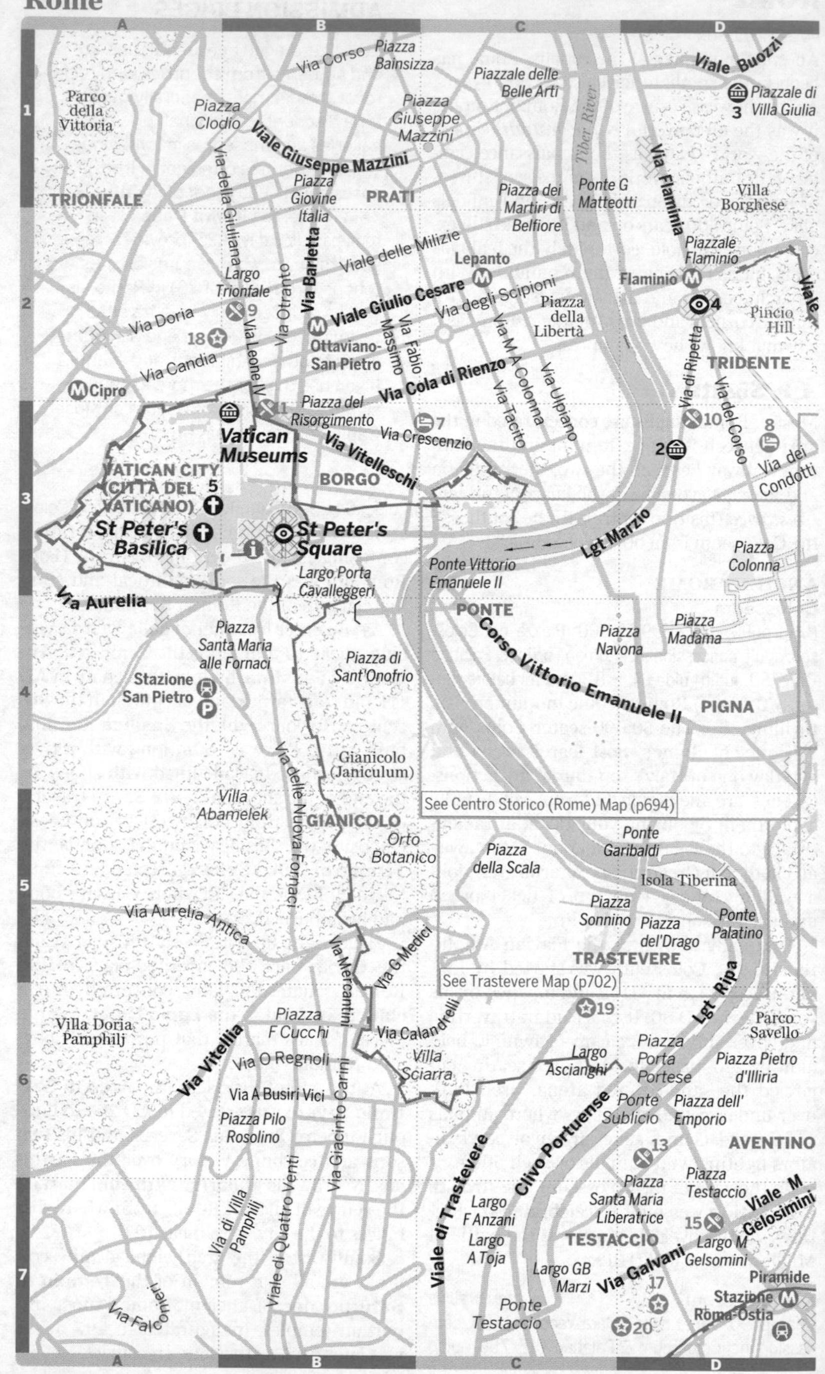

Parco della Vittoria
Piazza Clodio
Via Corso
Piazza Bainsizza
Piazzale delle Belle Arti
Viale Buozzi
Piazzale di Villa Giulia
3
Piazza Giuseppe Mazzini
Viale Giuseppe Mazzini
Tiber River
TRIONFALE
Via della Giuliana
Piazza Giovine Italia
PRATI
Piazza dei Martiri di Belfiore
Ponte G Matteotti
Via Flaminia
Villa Borghese
Viale delle Milizie
Via Barletta
Lepanto
Piazzale Flaminio
Largo Trionfale
Via Otranto
Viale Giulio Cesare
Via degli Scipioni
Flaminio
Viale
9
Via Doria
Piazza della Libertà
4
Pincio Hill
18
Via Leone IV
Ottaviano-San Pietro
Via Fabio Massimo
Via M A Colonna
Via di Ripetta
TRIDENTE
Via Candia
Via Cola di Rienzo
Via Ulpiano
Cipro
Via Tacito
Via del Corso
1
Piazza del Risorgimento
7
10
8
Vatican Museums
Via Crescenzio
Via Vitelleschi
2
Via dei Condotti
VATICAN CITY (CITTÀ DEL VATICANO)
5
BORGO
St Peter's Basilica
St Peter's Square
Lgt Marzio
Piazza Colonna
Ponte Vittorio Emanuele II
Largo Porta Cavalleggeri
Via Aurelia
PONTE
Piazza Santa Maria alle Fornaci
Piazza Navona
Piazza Madama
Corso Vittorio Emanuele II
Piazza di Sant'Onofrio
Stazione San Pietro
PIGNA
Via delle Nuova Fornaci
Gianicolo (Janiculum)
See Centro Storico (Rome) Map (p694)
Villa Abamelek
GIANICOLO
Ponte Garibaldi
Orto Botanico
Piazza della Scala
Isola Tiberina
Via Aurelia Antica
Piazza Sonnino
Piazza del'Drago
Ponte Palatino
Via Mercantini
Via G Medici
TRASTEVERE
See Trastevere Map (p702)
Lgt Ripa
19
Piazza F Cucchi
Villa Doria Pamphilj
Via Vitellia
Via Calandrelli
Parco Savello
Piazza Porta Portese
Via O Regnoli
Villa Sciarra
Largo Ascianghi
Piazza Pietro d'Illiria
Via A Busiri Vici
Via Giacinto Carini
Clivo Portuense
Ponte Sublicio
Piazza dell' Emporio
Piazza Pilo Rosolino
Viale di Trastevere
AVENTINO
13
Piazza Santa Maria Liberatrice
Piazza Testaccio
Viale M Gelosimini
Largo F Anzani
Via di Villa Pamphilj
Viale di Quattro Venti
15
Largo A Toja
TESTACCIO
Largo M Gelsomini
Via Galvani
Largo GB Marzi
17
Piramide
Stazione Roma-Ostia
Via Falconieri
Ponte Testaccio
20

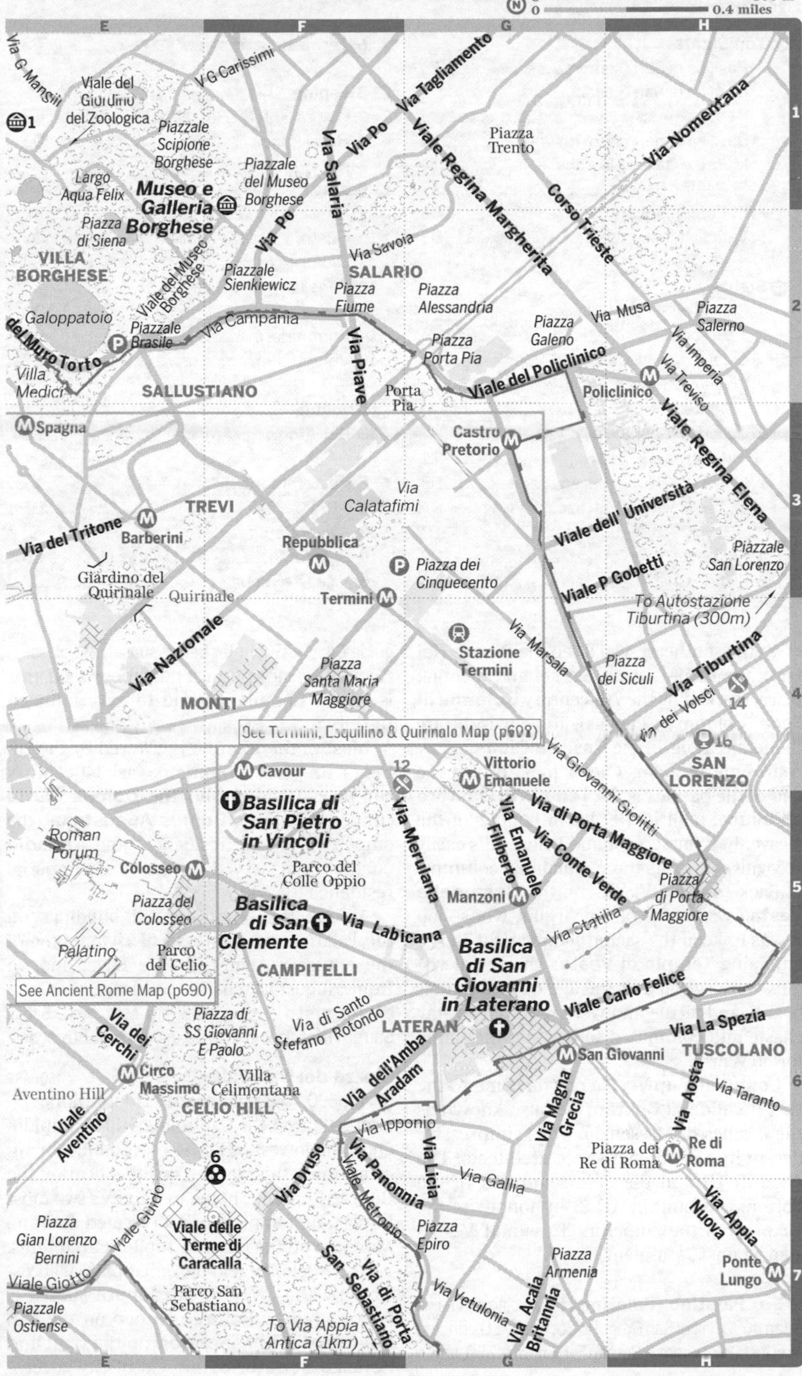
Museo e Galleria Borghese
VILLA BORGHESE
Galoppatoio
Villa Medici
SALLUSTIANO
SALARIO
Via Salaria
Via Po
Via Tagliamento
Viale Regina Margherita
Via Nomentana
Corso Trieste
Piazza Trento
Piazzale Scipione Borghese
Piazzale del Museo Borghese
Largo Aqua Felix
Piazza di Siena
Piazzale Sienkiewicz
Piazza Fiume
Piazza Alessandria
Via Savoia
Via Campania
Piazzale Brasile
Via Piave
Porta Pia
Piazza Porta Pia
Piazza Galeno
Via Musa
Piazza Salerno
Via Imperia
Via Treviso
Viale del Policlinico
Policlinico
Castro Pretorio
Viale Regina Elena
Spagna
TREVI
Via del Tritone
Barberini
Repubblica
Via Calatafimi
Piazza dei Cinquecento
Termini
Viale dell' Università
Viale P Gobetti
Piazzale San Lorenzo
To Autostazione Tiburtina (300m)
Giardino del Quirinale
Quirinale
Via Nazionale
MONTI
Stazione Termini
Via Marsala
Piazza Santa Maria Maggiore
Piazza dei Siculi
Via Tiburtina
Via dei Volsci
14
16
SAN LORENZO
See Termini, Esquilino & Quirinale Map (p698)
Cavour
12
Vittorio Emanuele
Via Giovanni Giolitti
Basilica di San Pietro in Vincoli
Via Merulana
Via Emanuele Filiberto
Via di Porta Maggiore
Via Conte Verde
Roman Forum
Colosseo
Parco del Colle Oppio
Manzoni
Piazza di Porta Maggiore
Piazza del Colosseo
Basilica di San Clemente
Via Labicana
Via Statilia
Palatino
Parco del Celio
CAMPITELLI
Basilica di San Giovanni in Laterano
Viale Carlo Felice
See Ancient Rome Map (p690)
Via dei Cerchi
Piazza di SS Giovanni E Paolo
Via di Santo Stefano Rotondo
LATERAN
Via La Spezia
San Giovanni
TUSCOLANO
Circo Massimo
Villa Celimontana
Aventino Hill
CELIO HILL
Via dell'Amba Aradam
Via Aosta
Via Taranto
Viale Aventino
Via Ipponio
Via Magna Grecia
Piazza dei Re di Roma
Re di Roma
6
Via Druso
Via Panonnia
Viale Metronio
Via Licia
Via Gallia
Via Appia Nuova
Piazza Gian Lorenzo Bernini
Viale Guido
Viale delle Terme di Caracalla
Piazza Epiro
Piazza Armenia
Ponte Lungo
Viale Giotto
Parco San Sebastiano
Via di Porta San Sebastiano
Via Vetulonia
Via Acaia
Britannia
Piazzale Ostiense
To Via Appia Antica (1km)
Via G Mansi
Viale del Giardino del Zoologica
V G Carissimi
Viale del Museo Borghese
del Muro Torto
1
0 800 m
0 0.4 miles

Rome

Top Sights

- Basilica di San Clemente ... F5
- Basilica di San Giovanni in Laterano ... G6
- Basilica di San Pietro in Vincoli ... F5
- Museo e Galleria Borghese ... F1
- St Peter's Basilica ... A3
- St Peter's Square ... B3
- Vatican Museums ... B3

Sights

- Chiesa di Santa Maria dei Miracoli ... (see 4)
- Chiesa di Santa Maria del Popolo ... (see 4)
- Chiesa di Santa Maria in Montesanto ... (see 4)
- 1 Galleria Nazionale d'Arte Moderna ... E1
- 2 Museo dell'Ara Pacis Augustae ... D3
- 3 Museo Nazionale Etrusco di Villa Giulia ... D1
- 4 Piazza del Popolo ... D2
- 5 Sistine Chapel ... A3
- 6 Terme di Caracalla ... F6

Sleeping

- 7 Colors Hotel & Hostel ... C3
- 8 Hotel Panda ... D3

Eating

- 9 Dino e Tony ... B2
- 10 Gusto ... D3
- 11 Old Bridge ... B3
- 12 Panella l'Arte del Pane ... F4
- 13 Pizzeria Remo ... D6
- 14 Pommidoro ... H4
- 15 Volpetti Più ... D7

Drinking

- 16 Bar Arco degli Arunci ... H4

Entertainment

- 17 AKAB ... D7
- 18 Alexanderplatz ... A2
- 19 Big Mama ... C6
- 20 Villaggio Globale ... D7

To the southeast, you'll see the **Piazza del Foro**, the Forum's main market and meeting place, marked by the 7th-century **Colonna di Foca** (Column of Phocus). To your right are the foundations of the **Basilica Giulia**, a law court built by Julius Caesar in 55 BC. At the end of the basilica is the **Tempio di Castore e Polluce**, built in 489 BC in honour of the Heavenly Twins, Castor and Pollux. It is easily recognisable by its three remaining columns.

Back towards Via Sacra, the **Casa delle Vestali** was home of the virgins, whose job it was to keep the sacred flame alight in the adjoining **Tempio di Vesta**. The vestal virgins were selected at the age of 10 for their beauty and virtue and were required to stay chaste and committed to keeping the flame for 30 years.

Continuing up Via Sacra, you come to the vast **Basilica di Costantino**, also known as the Basilica di Massenzio, whose impressive design inspired Renaissance architects. The **Arco di Tito**, at the Colosseum end of the Forum, was built in AD 81 in honour of the victories of the emperors Titus and Vespasian against Jerusalem.

TOP CHOICE **Palatino (Palatine Hill)** ROMAN RUINS

(Map p690; Via di San Gregorio 30; adult/EU concession incl Colosseum & Roman Forum €12/7.50, audio guide €4; 8.30am-1hr before sunset; M Colosseo) Ancient Rome's poshest neighbourhood, this is where Romulus is said to have founded the city in 753 BC.

Most of the Palatine is covered by the ruins of Emperor Domitian's vast 1st-century complex. Divided into the **Domus Flavia** (Imperial Palace), **Domus Augustana** (the emperor's private residence) and a **stadio** (stadium), it served as the main imperial residence for 300 years.

Among the best-preserved buildings on the Palatino are the **Casa di Livia**, home of the emperor Augustus' wife Livia, and, in front, Augustus' separate residence, the **Casa di Augusto** (11am-3.30pm Mon, Wed, Sat & Sun), which boasts some exceptional frescoes.

Piazza del Campidoglio SQUARE

(Map p690; Piazza Venezia) This striking piazza sits atop the Capitoline Hill (Campidoglio), the lowest of Rome's seven hills. In ancient times, this was the spiritual heart of the Roman Republic, home to the city's two most important temples: one dedicated to Juno Moneta and the other to Jupiter Capitolinus.

The Michelangelo-designed piazza, accessible by the graceful **Cordonata** staircase, is bordered by **Palazzo Nuovo** on the left, **Palazzo dei Conservatori** on the right and **Palazzo Senatorio**, the seat of city government since 1143. In the centre, the bronze **statue of Marcus Aurelius** is a copy; the original is in Palazzo Nuovo.

Musei Capitolini ART GALLERY
(Capitoline Museums; Map p690; Piazza del Campidoglio; adult/concession €11/9; ⏲9am-8pm Tue-Sun, last entry 7pm; 🚌Piazza Venezia) Housed in Palazzo Nuovo and Palazzo dei Conservatori, these are the oldest public galleries in the world, dating to 1471. Their collection of classical art, one of Italy's finest, includes the iconic *Lupa capitolina* (She-Wolf), a sculpture of Romulus and Remus sitting under a wolf.

Piazza Venezia SQUARE
Piazza Venezia is dominated by the mountain of white marble that is **Il Vittoriano** (Map p690; 🚌Piazza Venezia), aka the Altare della Patria. Begun in 1885 to commemorate Italian unification and honour Victor Emmanuel II, it incorporates the **tomb of the Unknown Soldier**, as well as the **Museo Centrale del Risorgimento** (admission free; ⏲9.30am-6.30pm), documenting Italian unification. For Rome's best 360-degree views, take the **panoramic lift** (adult/concession €7/3.50; ⏲9.30am-6.30pm Mon-Thu, to 7.30pm Fri-Sun) to the top.

Bocca della Verità OFFBEAT SIGHT
(Map p690; Piazza della Bocca della Verità 18; ⏲10am-5pm; 🚌Via dei Cerchi) A round piece of marble once used as an ancient manhole cover, the Mouth of Truth is one of Rome's great curiosities. According to legend, if you put your hand in the carved mouth and tell a lie, it will bite your hand off. The mouth lives in the portico of the **Chiesa di Santa Maria in Cosmedin**, one of Rome's finest medieval churches.

THE VATICAN

The world's smallest sovereign state, the Vatican (population 830) is the jealous guardian of one of the world's greatest artistic and architectural patrimonies. Covering just 0.44 sq km, this tiny nation is the modern vestige of the Papal States, the papal empire that ruled Rome and much of central Italy for more than a thousand years until Italian unification in 1861. Relations between the papacy and the Italian state remained strained until 1929 when Mussolini and Pope Pius XI signed the Lateran Treaty and formerly established the Vatican State.

St Peter's Basilica CHURCH
(Map p686; St Peter's Sq; admission free; ⏲7am-7pm Apr-Sep, to 6.30pm Oct-Mar; Ⓜ Ottaviano-San Pietro) In a city of churches, none can hold a candle to St Peter's Basilica (Basilica di San Pietro), Italy's biggest, richest and most spectacular church. Built over the spot where St Peter was buried, the first basilica was consecrated by Constantine in the 4th century. In 1503, Bramante designed a new basilica, which took more than 150 years to complete. Michelangelo took over the project in 1547, designing the grand dome, which soars 120m above the altar. The cavernous 187m-long interior contains numerous treasures, including two of Italy's most celebrated masterpieces: Michelangelo's *Pietà*, the only work to carry his signature; and Bernini's 29m baldachin over the high altar.

Entrance to the **dome** (⏲8am-6pm Apr-Sep, 8am-5pm Oct-Mar) is to the right as you climb the stairs to the basilica's atrium. Make the climb on foot (€5) or by lift (€7).

Dress rules and security are stringently enforced at the basilica, so no shorts, miniskirts or sleeveless tops.

FREE THRILLS

Surprisingly, some of Rome's most famous sights are free:

» **All churches** Including St Peter's Basilica

» **Trevi Fountain**

» **Spanish Steps**

» **Pantheon**

» **Bocca della Verità**

» **Vatican Museums** On the last Sunday of the month

St Peter's Square SQUARE
(Map p686; Ⓜ Ottaviano-San Pietro) The Vatican's central piazza, St Peter's Sq (Piazza San Pietro) was designed by Bernini and laid out in the 17th century. It is bound by two semicircular colonnades, each comprising four rows of Doric columns, and in its centre stands an obelisk brought to Rome by Caligula from Heliopolis (in ancient Egypt).

Each Wednesday at 11am, the pope addresses his flock at the Vatican (in July and August in Castel Gandolfo near Rome). For free tickets, download the request form from the Vatican website (www.vatican.va) and fax it to the **Prefettura della Casa Pontificia** (fax 06 698 85 863). Pick them up at the office through the bronze doors under the colonnade to the right of St Peter's.

Ancient Rome

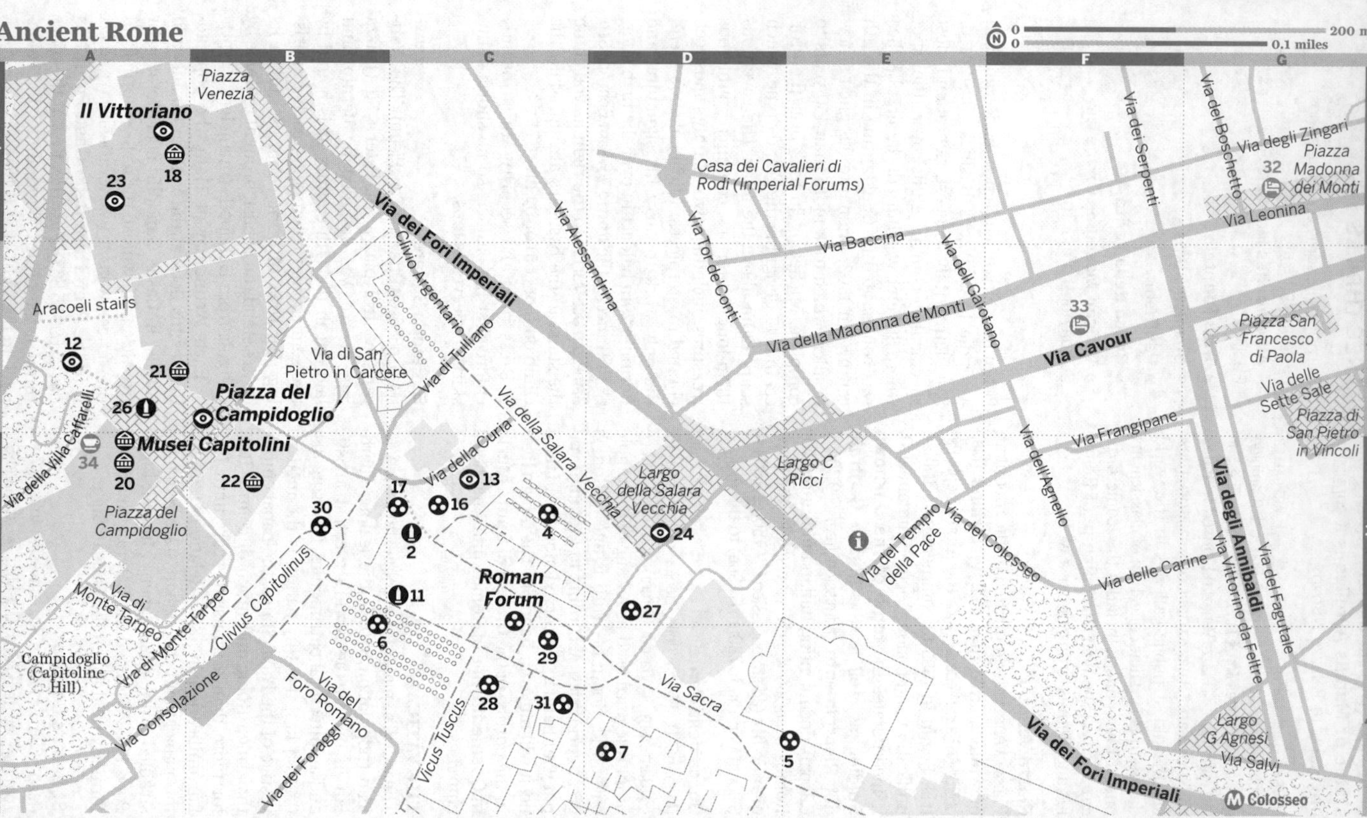

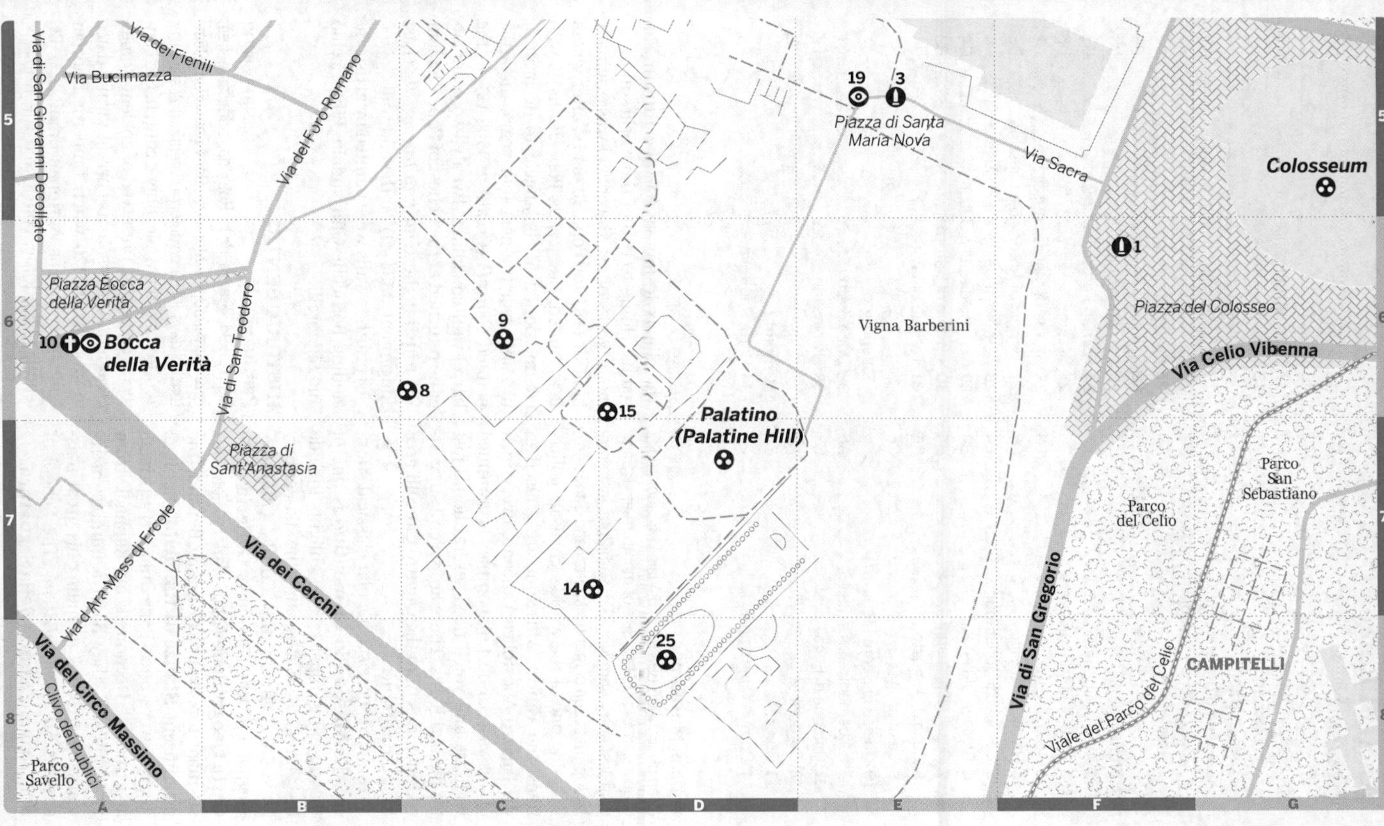
Colosseum
Piazza del Colosseo
Via Celio Vibenna
Parco San Sebastiano
Parco del Celio
CAMPITELLI
Viale del Parco del Celio
Via di San Gregorio
Via Sacra
Piazza di Santa Maria Nova
Vigna Barberini
19
3
1
Palatino (Palatine Hill)
25
15
14
9
8
Via dei Cerchi
Via del Foro Romano
Via di San Teodoro
Piazza di Sant'Anastasia
Bocca della Verità
10
Piazza Bocca della Verità
Via dei Fienili
Via Bucimazza
Via di San Giovanni Decollato
Via d'Ara Mass di Ercole
Via del Circo Massimo
Clivo dei Publici
Parco Savello
A
B
C
D
E
F
G
5
6
7
8

Ancient Rome

Top Sights

Bocca della Verità A6
Colosseum G5
Il Vittoriano A1
Musei Capitolini A3
Palatino (Palatine Hill) D7
Piazza del Campidoglio B2
Roman Forum C3

Sights

1 Arco di Costantino F6
2 Arco di Settimio Severo C3
3 Arco di Tito E5
4 Basilica Aemilia C3
5 Basilica di Constantino E4
6 Basilica Giulia B4
7 Casa delle Vestali D4
8 Casa di Augusto C6
9 Casa di Livia C6
10 Chiesa di Santa Maria in Cosmedin A6
11 Colonna di Foca C3
12 Cordonata A2
13 Curia C3
14 Domus Augustana C7
15 Domus Flavia D6
16 Lapis Niger C3
17 Millarium Aureum C3
18 Museo Centrale del Risorgimento A1
19 Palatino Entrance E5
20 Palazzo dei Conservatori A3
21 Palazzo Nuovo A2
22 Palazzo Senatorio B3
23 Panoramic Lift A1
24 Roman Forum Entrance D3
25 Stadio D8
26 Statue of Marcus Aurelius A2
27 Tempio di Antonino e Faustina D3
28 Tempio di Castore e Polluce C4
29 Tempio di Giulio Cesare C4
30 Tempio di Saturno B3
31 Tempio di Vesta C4

Sleeping

32 Duca d'Alba G1
33 Nicolas Inn F2

Drinking

34 Caffè Capitolino A3

Vatican Museums MUSEUM

(Map p686; ☎06 698 84 676; Viale Vaticano; adult/concession €15/8, last Sun of month free; ⏰9am-6pm, last entry 4pm Mon-Sat, 9am-2pm, last entry 12.30pm last Sun of month; Ⓜ Ottaviano-San Pietro) Boasting one of the world's great art collections, the Vatican Museums are housed in the Palazzo Apostolico Vaticano. Every inch of this vast 5.5-hectare complex is crammed with art, and you'll need several hours just for the highlights. There are several suggested itineraries from the Quattro Cancelli area near the entrance.

Home to some spectacular classical statuary, the **Museo Pio-Clementino** is one of the museums' must-sees. Highlights include the *Apollo Belvedere* and the 1st-century *Laocoön,* both in the Cortile Ottagono. Further on, the 175m-long **Galleria delle Carte Geografiche** (Map Gallery) features 40 huge topographical maps. Beyond, the magnificent **Stanze di Raffaello** (Raphael Rooms) were once Pope Julius II's private apartments. Decorated by Raphael from 1508 onwards, they boast a number of remarkable frescoes, including his great masterpiece *La Scuola d'Atene* (The School of Athens) in the **Stanza della Segnatura**.

Sistine Chapel

The climax to any visit to the Vatican Museums. Home to two of the world's most famous works of art, the chapel was originally built in 1484 for Pope Sixtus IV, after whom it is named, but it was Pope Julius II who commissioned Michelangelo to decorate it in 1508. Over the next four years, the artist painted *Genesis* (Creation; 1508-12) on the barrel-vaulted ceiling. Twenty-two years later he returned at the behest of Pope Clement VII to paint the *Giudizio universale* (Last Judgement; 1534-41) on the end wall.

The other walls were painted by artists including Botticelli, Ghirlandaio, Pinturicchio and Signorelli.

HISTORIC CENTRE

Pantheon ROMAN MONUMENT

(Map p694; Piazza della Rotonda; admission free; ⏰8.30am-7.30pm Mon-Sat, 9am-6pm Sun, 9am-1pm holidays; 🚌 Largo di Torre Argentina) A striking 2000-year-old temple, now a church, the Pantheon is the best preserved of ancient Rome's great monuments. In its current form it dates to around AD 120 when Emperor Hadrian built over Marcus Agrippa's original 27 BC temple. The dome, considered the Romans' most important architectural achievement, was the largest in the world until the 15th century and is still the largest unreinforced concrete dome ever built. Inside, you'll find the tombs of Raphael and kings Vittorio Emanuele II and Umberto I.

Piazza Navona SQUARE

(Map p694; 🚌Corso del Rinascimento) A few blocks west of the Pantheon, Piazza Navona is Rome's great baroque showpiece. Built over the ruins of the 1st-century Stadio di Domiziano (Domitian's Stadium), it is centred on Bernini's 1651 masterpiece, the **Fontana dei Quattro Fiumi** (Fountain of the Four Rivers). For 300 years the piazza was home to Rome's main market and still today it attracts a colourful crowd of street artists, locals, tourists and pigeons.

Campo de' Fiori SQUARE

(Map p694; 🚌Corso Vittorio Emanuele II) Dubbed 'il Campo', Campo de' Fiori is a major focus of Roman life: by day it hosts a noisy market; at night it becomes a vast open-air pub. For centuries this was the site of public executions, and it was here that the philosophising monk Giordano Bruno (the hooded figure in Ettore Ferrari's sinister statue) was burned at the stake in 1600.

Trevi Fountain FOUNTAIN

(Map p698; Ⓜ Barberini) Immortalised by Anita Ekberg's sensual dip in Fellini's *La dolce vita*, the Fontana di Trevi was designed by Nicola Salvi in 1732 and depicts Neptune's chariot being led by Tritons, with sea horses representing the moods of the sea. The custom is to throw a coin into the fountain, thus ensuring your return to Rome. On average about €3000 is chucked away every day.

Spanish Steps MONUMENT

(Map p698; Piazza di Spagna; Ⓜ Spagna) A hangout for flirting adolescents and footsore tourists, **Piazza di Spagna** and the Spanish Steps (Scalinata della Trinità dei Monti) have been a magnet for foreigners since the 18th century. The piazza was named after the Spanish embassy to the Holy See, although the staircase, which was built with French money in 1725, leads to the French church, **Chiesa della Trinità dei Monti**. At the foot of the steps, the fountain of a sinking boat, the **Barcaccia** (1627), is believed to be by Pietro Bernini, father of the more famous Gian Lorenzo. Opposite, **Via dei Condotti** is Rome's poshest shopping strip.

Piazza del Popolo SQUARE

(Map p686; Ⓜ Flaminio) This elegant landmark square was laid out in 1538 at the point of convergence of three roads – Via di Ripetta, Via del Corso and Via del Babuino – at what was then Rome's northern entrance. Guarding its southern approach are the twin 17th-century churches of **Santa Maria dei Miracoli** and **Santa Maria in Montesanto**. On the other side of the square, the **Chiesa di Santa Maria del Popolo** (⊙7am-noon & 4-7pm Mon-Sat, 8am-1.30pm & 4.30-7.30pm Sun) houses two magnificent Caravaggio paintings: the *Conversione di San Paolo* (Conversion of St Paul) and the *Crocifissione di San Pietro* (Crucifixion of St Peter). Rising above the piazza, the **Pincio Hill** affords great views.

Museo dell' Ara Pacis Augustae MUSEUM

(Map p686; Lungotevere in Augusta; adult/concession €6.50/4.50; ⊙9am-7pm Tue-Sun; Ⓜ Flaminio) South of Piazza del Popolo, the Ara Pacis is considered one of the most important works of ancient Roman sculpture. Today, it's controversially housed in a glass pavilion designed by US architect Richard Meier.

VILLA BORGHESE

Just north of the historic centre, Villa Borghese is Rome's best-known park, accessible from Piazzale Flaminio, the Pincio Hill and the top of Via Vittorio Veneto. Bike hire is available at various points, typically costing about €5 per hour.

TOP CHOICE **Museo e Galleria Borghese** ART GALLERY

(Map p686; ☎06 3 28 10; www.galleriaborghese.it; Piazzale del Museo Borghese; adult/concession €8.50/5.25; ⊙8.30am-7.30pm Tue-Sun; 🚌Via Pinciana) Housing the 'queen of all private

QUEUE JUMP AT THE VATICAN MUSEUMS

Here's how to jump the ticket queue – although we can't help with lines for the security checks.

» Book tickets at http://biglietteriamusei.vatican.va/musei/tickets (plus booking fee of €4).

» Time your visit: Wednesday mornings are a good bet as everyone is at the pope's weekly audience at St Peter's; lunchtime is better than the morning; avoid Mondays when many other museums are shut.

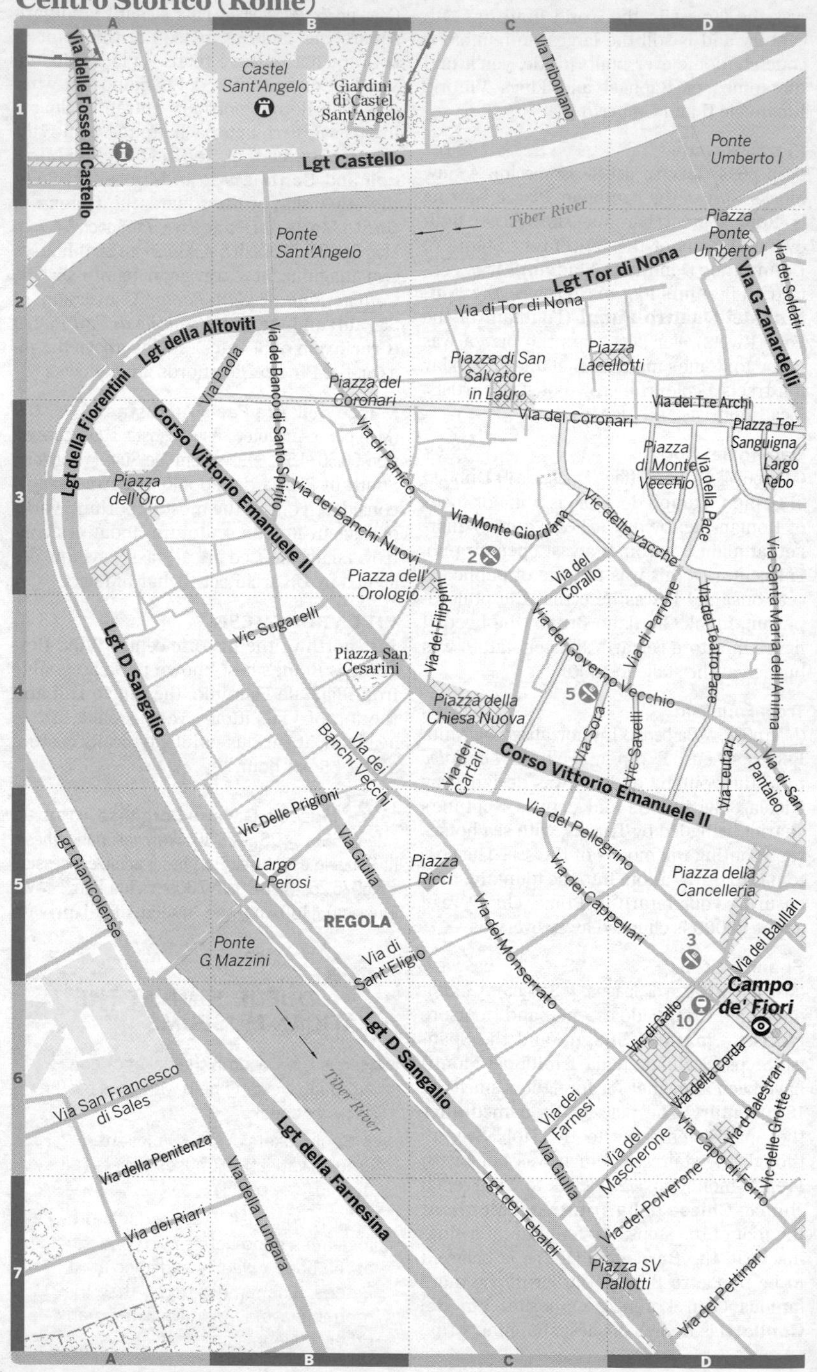
Castel Sant'Angelo
Giardini di Castel Sant'Angelo
Via delle Fosse di Castello
Via Triboniano
Lgt Castello
Ponte Umberto I
Tiber River
Ponte Sant'Angelo
Piazza Ponte Umberto I
Via dei Soldati
Via G Zanardelli
Lgt Tor di Nona
Via di Tor di Nona
Lgt della Altoviti
Lgt dei Fiorentini
Via Paola
Via del Banco di Santo Spirito
Piazza del Coronari
Piazza di San Salvatore in Lauro
Piazza Lacellotti
Via dei Tre Archi
Via dei Coronari
Piazza Tor Sanguigna
Largo Febo
Piazza di Monte Vecchio
Via della Pace
Corso Vittorio Emanuele II
Piazza dell'Oro
Via di Panico
Via dei Banchi Nuovi
Via Monte Giordana
Vic delle Vacche
Via del Corallo
Piazza dell' Orologio
Via dei Filippini
Via Santa Maria dell'Anima
Via di Parione
Via del Teatro Pace
Via del Governo Vecchio
Lgt D Sangalio
Vic Sugarelli
Piazza San Cesarini
Piazza della Chiesa Nuova
Via Sora
Via dei Cartari
Vic Savelli
Via Leutari
Pantaleo
Via di San
Via dei Banchi Vecchi
Vic Delle Prigioni
Via del Pellegrino
Lgt Gianicolense
Largo L Perosi
Via Giulia
Piazza Ricci
Piazza della Cancelleria
Via dei Cappellari
REGOLA
Ponte G Mazzini
Via di Sant'Eligio
Via del Monserrato
Via dei Baullari
Campo de' Fiori
Vic di Gallo
Lgt D Sangalio
Via della Corda
Via d Balestrari
Via San Francesco di Sales
Lgt della Farnesina
Via dei Farnesi
Vic delle Grotte
Via Capo di Ferro
Via della Penitenza
Via della Lungara
Via del Mascherone
Via dei Polverone
Lgt dei Tebaldi
Via dei Riari
Piazza SV Pallotti
Via del Pettinari

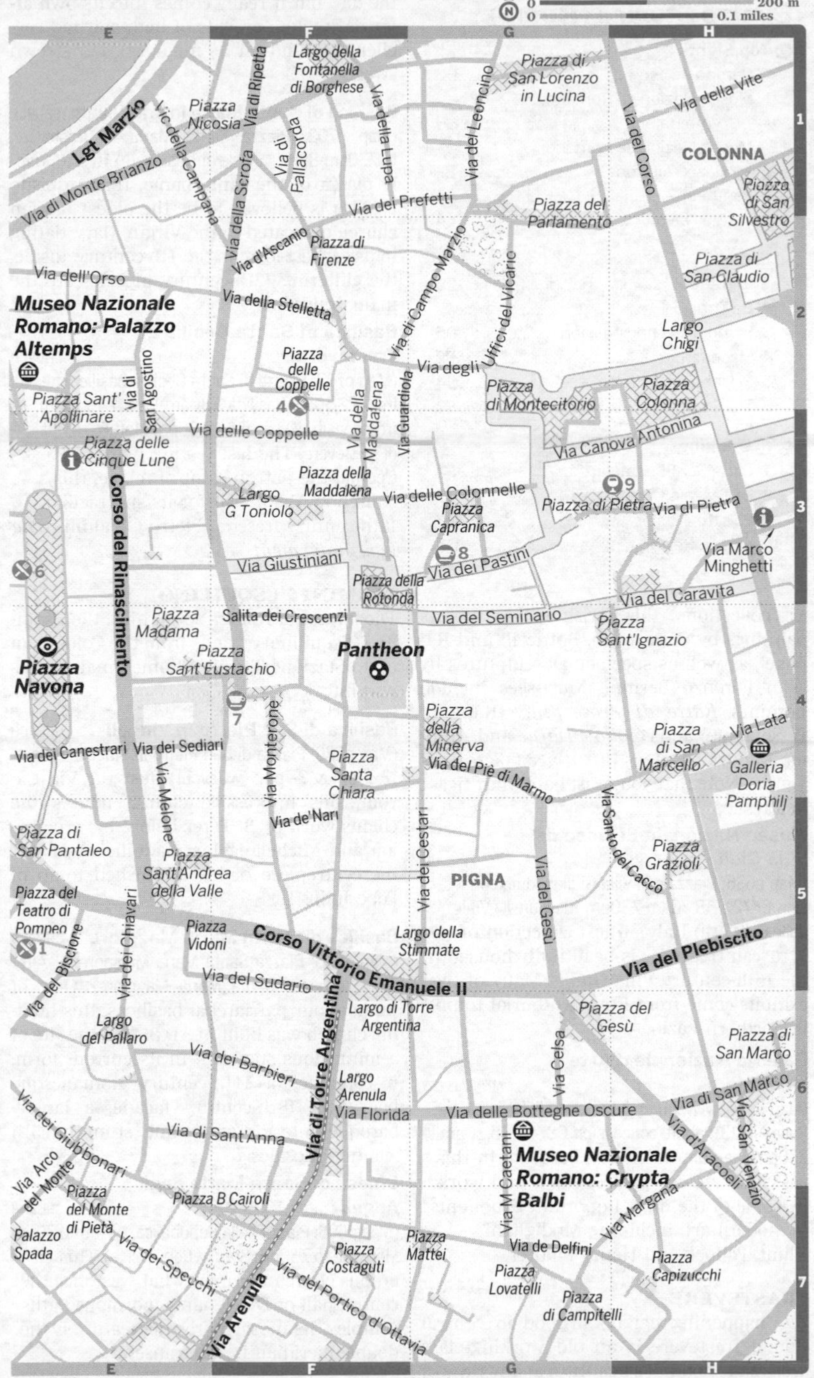

0 200 m
0 0.1 miles
E
F
G
H
1
2
3
4
5
6
7
Largo della Fontanella di Borghese
Piazza di San Lorenzo in Lucina
Via della Vite
Lgt Marzio
Piazza Nicosia
Via di Ripetta
Vic della Campana
Via di Monte Brianzo
Via di Fallacorda
Via della Lupa
Via del Leoncino
Via del Corso
COLONNA
Piazza di San Silvestro
Via dei Prefetti
Piazza del Parlamento
Via della Scrofa
Via d'Ascanio
Piazza di Firenze
Via di Campo Marzio
Uffici del Vicario
Piazza di San Claudio
Via dell'Orso
Via della Stelletta
Museo Nazionale Romano: Palazzo Altemps
Largo Chigi
Via di San Agostino
Piazza delle Coppelle
4
Via degli
Piazza di Montecitorio
Piazza Colonna
Piazza Sant' Apollinare
Via delle Coppelle
Via della Maddalena
Via Guardiola
Via Canova Antonina
Piazza delle Cinque Lune
Corso del Rinascimento
Piazza della Maddalena
Via delle Colonnelle
9
Largo G Toniolo
Piazza Capranica
Piazza di Pietra
Via di Pietra
Via Marco Minghetti
6
Via Giustiniani
8
Via dei Pastini
Piazza della Rotonda
Via del Caravita
Piazza Madama
Salita dei Crescenzi
Via del Seminario
Piazza Sant'Ignazio
Piazza Sant'Eustachio
Pantheon
Piazza Navona
7
Piazza della Minerva
Piazza di San Marcello
Via Lata
Via dei Canestrari
Via dei Sediari
Via Monterone
Piazza Santa Chiara
Via del Piè di Marmo
Galleria Doria Pamphilj
Via Melone
Via de' Nari
Via Santo del Cacco
Piazza di San Pantaleo
Via dei Cestari
Piazza Grazioli
Piazza Sant'Andrea della Valle
PIGNA
Via del Gesù
Piazza del Teatro di Pompeo
1
Via dei Chiavari
Piazza Vidoni
Corso Vittorio Emanuele II
Largo della Stimmate
Via del Plebiscito
Via del Bisclone
Via del Sudario
Via di Torre Argentina
Largo di Torre Argentina
Piazza del Gesù
Largo del Pallaro
Via dei Barbieri
Via Celsa
Piazza di San Marco
Largo Arenula
Via di San Marco
Via dei Giubbonari
Via Florida
Via delle Botteghe Oscure
Via di Sant'Anna
Via San Venanzio
Via d'Aracoeli
Museo Nazionale Romano: Crypta Balbi
Via M Caetani
Via Arco del Monte
Piazza del Monte di Pietà
Piazza B Cairoli
Via Margana
Palazzo Spada
Via dei Specchi
Piazza Costaguti
Piazza Mattei
Via de Delfini
Piazza Capizucchi
Via Arenula
Via del Portico d'Ottavia
Piazza Lovatelli
Piazza di Campitelli

Centro Storico (Rome)

Top Sights

	Campo de' Fiori	D6
	Museo Nazionale Romano: Crypta Balbi	G6
	Museo Nazionale Romano: Palazzo Altemps	E2
	Pantheon	F4
	Piazza Navona	E4
Eating		
1	Baffetto 2	E5
2	Da Tonino	C3
3	Forno di Campo de' Fiori	D5
4	Maccheroni	F2
5	Pizzeria da Baffetto	C4
6	Tre Scalini	E3
Drinking		
7	Caffè Sant'Eustachio	F4
8	La Tazza d'Oro	G3
9	Salotto 42	H3
10	Vineria Reggio	D6

art collections', this lavish gallery boasts paintings by Caravaggio, Botticelli and Raphael, as well as spectacular sculptures by Gian Lorenzo Bernini. Must-sees include Bernini's *Ratto di Proserpina* (Rape of Persephone) and *Apollo e Dafne* and Antonio Canova's *Venere Vincitrice* (Victorious Venus). Note that you must book your ticket in advance.

Museo Nazionale Etrusco di Villa Giulia MUSEUM

(Map p686; Piazzale di Villa Giulia; adult/concession €4/2; 8.30am-7.30pm Tue-Sun; Viale delle Belle Arti) Italy's finest collection of Etruscan treasures is beautifully housed in the 16th-century Villa Giulia. Many of the exhibits come from Etruscan burial tombs in northern Lazio.

Galleria Nazionale d'Arte Moderna ART GALLERY

(Map p686; www.gnam.beniculturali.it; Viale delle Belle Arti 131; adult/concession €8/4; 8.30am-7.30pm Tue-Sun; Viale delle Belle Arti) In this vast *belle époque* palace, you'll find works by some of the most important exponents of modern art, including Modigliani, Klimt, Pollock and Henry Moore.

TRASTEVERE

The happening neighbourhood in central Rome, Trastevere is an old working-class area made good. It's beautiful at any time of the day, but it really comes into its own after dark when crowds of high-spirited revellers descend on its medieval, bar-strewn streets.

Basilica di Santa Maria in Trastevere CHURCH

(Map p702; Piazza Santa Maria in Trastevere; 7.30am-8pm; Viale di Trastevere) In the lovely piazza of the same name, this exquisite basilica is believed to be the oldest Roman church dedicated to the Virgin Mary, dating in its earliest form to the 4th century. Inside, the glittering 12th-century mosaics are the main drawcard.

Basilica di Santa Cecilia in Trastevere CHURCH

(Map p702; Piazza di Santa Cecilia; basilica/fresco free/€2.50; basilica 9.30am-1pm & 4-7.15pm, fresco visits 10.15am & 12.30pm Mon-Fri; Viale di Trastevere) The last resting place of St Cecilia, the patron saint of music, this church merits a visit for its spectacular 13th-century fresco – Pietro Cavallini's *The Last Judgement*.

TERMINI & ESQUILINO

The largest of Rome's seven hills, the Esquilino (Esquiline) extends from the Colosseum up to Stazione Termini, Rome's main transport hub.

Basilica di San Pietro in Vincoli CHURCH

(Map p686; Piazza di San Pietro in Vincoli; 8am-12.30pm & 3-7pm; MCavour) Just off Via Cavour, this impressive church houses the chains worn by St Peter before his crucifixion and Michelangelo's magnificent *Moses*, the centrepiece of his unfinished tomb of Pope Julius II.

Basilica di Santa Maria Maggiore CHURCH

(Map p698; Piazza Santa Maria Maggiore; 7am-7pm; Piazza Santa Maria Maggiore) One of Rome's four patriarchal basilicas, this hulking church was built in AD 352 on the site of a miraculous snowfall. In its current form, it combines a 14th-century Romanesque belfry, an 18th-century facade, a largely baroque interior and some stunning 5th-century mosaics.

Chiesa di Santa Maria degli Angeli CHURCH

(Map p698; Piazza della Repubblica; 7am-6.30pm Mon-Sat, to 7.30pm Sun; MRepubblica) This cavernous church occupies what was once the central hall of Diocletian's enormous baths complex. Its most interesting feature is the double meridian in the transept.

SAN GIOVANNI & CELIO

Basilica di San Giovanni in Laterano CHURCH
(Map p686; Piazza di San Giovanni in Laterano 4; 7am-6.30pm; San Giovanni) For a thousand years, this great white basilica was the most important church in Christendom. Consecrated in AD 324, it was the first Christian basilica to be built in Rome and until the late 14th century was the pope's principal residence.

Basilica di San Clemente CHURCH
(Map p686; Via di San Giovanni in Laterano; admission basilica/excavations free/€5; 9am-12.30pm & 3-6pm Mon-Sat, noon-6pm Sun; Colosseo) This fascinating, multilayered church is just east of the Colosseum. The 12th-century church at street level was built over a 4th-century church that was, in turn, built over a 1st-century Roman house with a temple dedicated to the pagan god Mithras.

Terme di Caracalla ROMAN RUINS
(Map p686; Via delle Terme di Caracalla 52; adult/concession €6/3; 9am-1hr before sunset Tue-Sun, to 2pm Mon; Circo Massimo) The vast ruins of the Terme di Caracalla are an awe-inspiring sight. The 10-hectare baths' complex was inaugurated in AD 217 and included richly decorated pools, gymnasiums, libraries, shops and gardens.

VIA APPIA ANTICA

Known to the ancients as the *regina viarum* (queen of roads), the Appian Way was started in 312 BC and completed 122 years later. It was here that Spartacus and 6000 of his slave rebels were crucified in 71 BC and it's here that you'll find Rome's most celebrated catacombs. These were built as communal burial grounds by the early Christians. Their belief in the Resurrection meant that they couldn't cremate their dead, as was the custom at the time, and Roman law forbade burial within the city walls. Persecution also meant that they needed somewhere hidden to bury their dead.

To get to Via Appia Antica, take Metro Line A to Colli Albani, then bus 660. It's traffic-free on Sunday if you want to walk or cycle it. For information, bike hire or to join a guided tour, head to the **Appia Antica Regional Park Information Point** (06 513 53 16; www.parcoappiaantica.org; Via Appia Antica 58-60; 9.30am-1.30pm & 2-5.30pm; Via Appia Antica).

Catacombs of San Callisto CATACOMBS
(www.catacombe.roma.it; Via Appia Antica 110; adult/concession €8/5; 9am-noon & 2-5pm Thu-Tue, closed Feb; Via Appia Antica) These are Rome's largest, most famous and busiest catacombs. Excavations have so far unearthed the tombs of 16 popes and thousands of early Christians.

Catacombs of San Sebastiano CATACOMBS
(www.catacombe.org; Via Appia Antica 136; adult/concession €8/5; 9am-noon & 2-5pm Mon-Sat, closed mid-Nov–mid-Dec; Via Appia Antica) Extending beneath the Basilica di San Sebastiano, these catacombs provided a safe haven for the remains of St Peter and St Paul during the reign of Vespasian.

Sleeping

There's no point beating around the bush, Rome is expensive. Most of the hostels and budget *pensioni* (guest houses) are in the area around Stazione Termini – the best on the northeast side (take the Via Marsala exit). Always try to book ahead, even if it's just for the first night. You'll find a full list of accommodation options (with prices) at www.060608.it. If you arrive without a booking, there's a hotel **reservation service** (06 699 10 00; booking fee €3; 7am-10pm) next to the tourist office at Termini.

HISTORIC CENTRE & THE VATICAN

Colors Hotel HOSTEL, HOTEL €
(Map p686; 06 687 40 30; www.colorshotel.com; Via Boezio 31; s/d from €30/40; ; Piazza del Risorgimento) Popular with young travellers, this is a friendly, laid-back hotel with 23 brightly painted rooms spread over three floors (no lift though). There are also cheaper rooms with shared bathrooms and, in July and August, six-bed dorms (€18 to €30 per person).

Hotel Panda HOTEL €
(Map p686; 06 678 01 79; www.hotelpanda.it; Via della Croce 35; s €65-80, d €85-110, tr €120-140; ; Spagna) A budget bolthole near the Spanish Steps, the Panda is deservedly popular. Its superb position, attractive high-ceilinged rooms and honest rates ensure a year-round stream of travellers. Air-con costs €6 extra. Cheaper rooms are available with shared bathrooms. Breakfast is extra.

TRASTEVERE

TOP CHOICE **Maria-Rosa Guesthouse** B&B €
(Map p702; 338 770 00 67; www.maria-rosa.it; Via dei Vascellari; s €60-70, d €75-85, q €120-130; ; or Piazza Sonnino) This is a delightful little B&B on the 3rd floor of a

Trastevere townhouse. It's a simple affair with two guestrooms sharing a single bathroom and a small common area, but the sunlight, potted plants and books create a lovely, warm atmosphere.

La Foresteria Orsa Maggiore GUEST HOUSE €
(Map p686; ☎06 689 37 53; www.casainternazionaledelledonne.org; Via San Francesco di Sales 1a; dm €26, s/d €75/110, without bathroom €52/72; @; Piazza Trilussa) This women-only guest house is in a restored 16th-century convent on the edge of Trastevere's buzzing core. Its 13 clean, airy guestrooms are set around an attractive internal garden.

TERMINI & ESQUILINO

Beehive HOSTEL €
(Map p698; ☎06 447 04 553; www.the-beehive.com; Via Marghera 8; dm €20-25, d €70-80; @; MTermini) This is a brilliant boutique hostel run by an environmentally conscious American couple. Beds are in a spotless, eight-person mixed dorm or in one of six double rooms, and breakfast (and Sunday brunch) is served in the hostel's vegetarian cafe.

Welrome PENSION €
(Map p698; ☎06 478 24 343; www.welrome.it; Via Calatafimi 15-19; s €50-100, d €60-110; ; MTermini) This is a lovely, low-key hotel not

Termini, Esquilino & Quirinale (Rome)

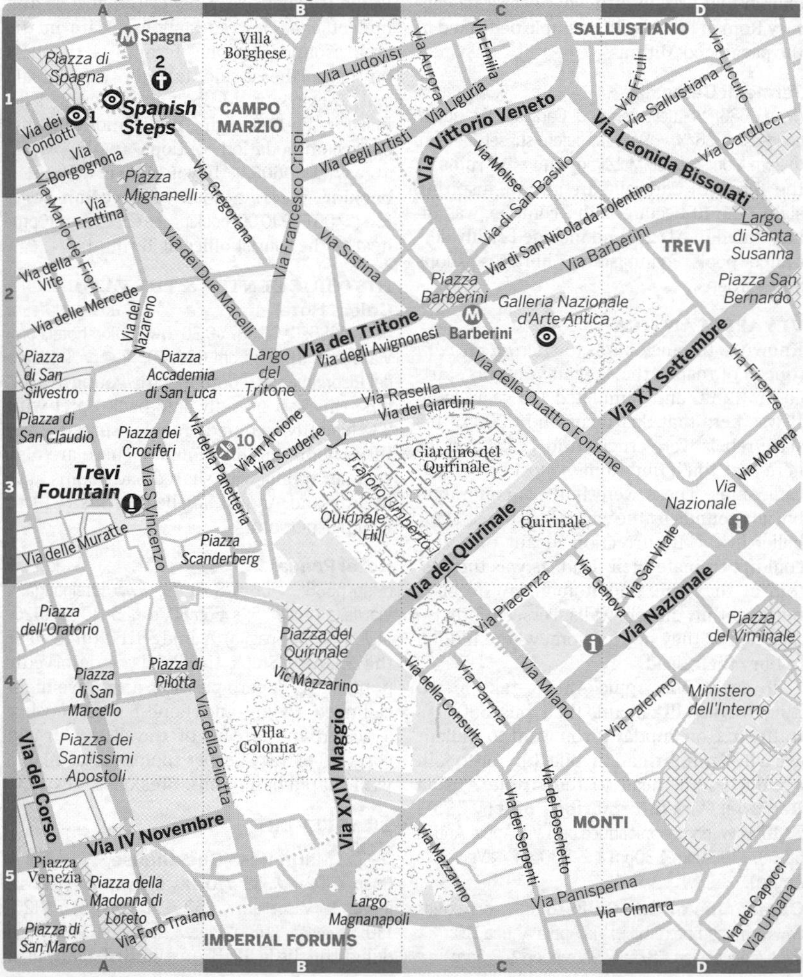

far from Termini. Owner Mary takes great pride in looking after her guests, and her seven rooms provide welcome respite from Rome's relentless streets. Breakfast costs extra.

Funny Palace HOSTEL €
(Map p698; ☎06 447 03 523; www.funnyhostel.com; Via Varese 33; dm €15-25, s €30-70, d €55-100; @; Ⓜ Termini) To find this great little backpacker hostel head for the Splashnet laundry, which doubles as the reception and internet point. Upstairs, the mixed dorms are big and well maintained, and private rooms reveal a simple, homey look. No credit cards.

Alessandro Palace Hostel HOSTEL €
(Map p698; ☎06 44 61 958; www.hostelsalessandro.com; Via Vicenza 42; dm €18-25, d €66-120, tr €58-120; ❄@📶; Ⓜ Termini) A backpacker favourite, this slick hostel offers spick-and-span hotel-style rooms, as well as four- to eight-person dorms. It's run by a friendly international crew, has 24-hour reception and there's a bar with satellite TV. On the other side of Termini, **Alessandro Downtown Hostel** (Map p698; ☎06 443 40 147; Via Cattaneo 23; Ⓜ Termini) offers more of the same.

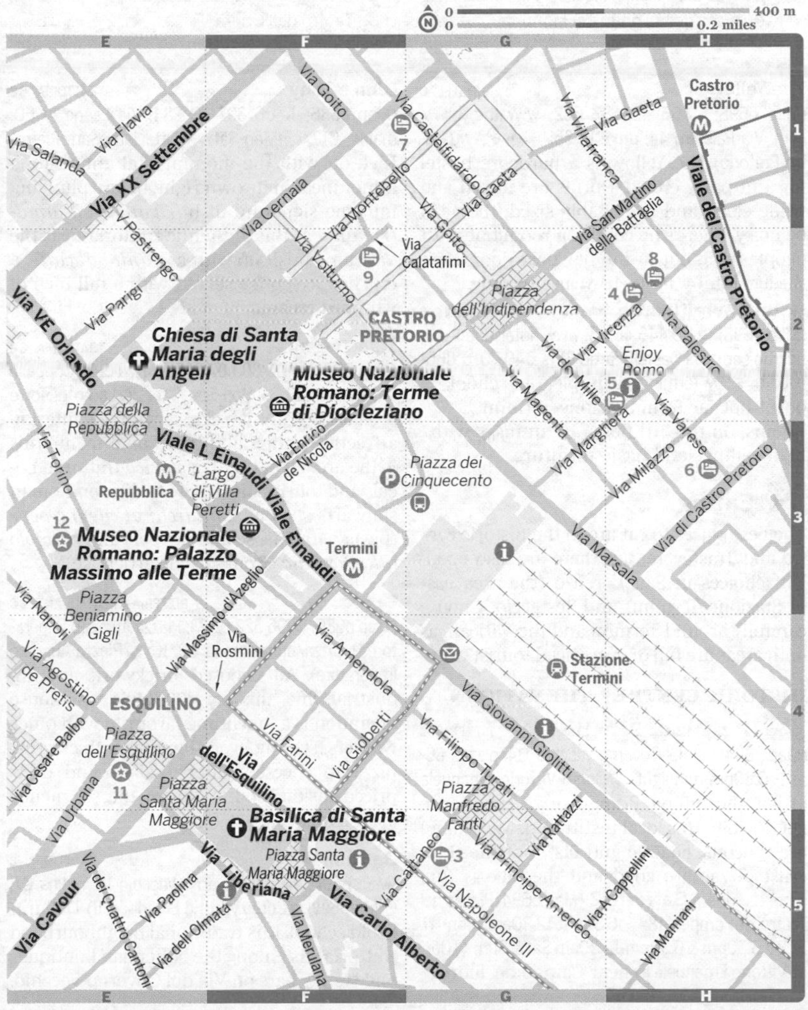

Termini, Esquilino & Quirinale (Rome)

Top Sights

Basilica di Santa Maria Maggiore..........F5
Chiesa di Santa Maria degli Angeli..........E2
Museo Nazionale Romano: Palazzo Massimo alle Terme..........F3
Museo Nazionale Romano: Terme di Diocleziano..........F2
Spanish Steps..........A1
Trevi Fountain..........A3

Sights

1 Barcaccia..........A1
2 Chiesa della Trinità dei Monti..........A1

Sleeping

3 Alessandro Downtown Hostel..........G5
4 Alessandro Palace Hostel..........H2
5 Beehive..........H2
6 Funny Palace..........H3
7 Hotel Castelfidardo..........F1
8 The Yellow..........H2
9 Welrome..........F2

Eating

10 San Crispino..........B3

Entertainment

11 Orbis..........E4
12 Teatro dell'Opera..........E3

The Yellow HOSTEL €
(Map p698; ☎06 493 82 682; www.the-yellow.com; Via Palestro 44; dm €18-35; ❄@📶; MCastro Pretorio) The Yellow is a hardcore hostel for a fit party crowd. Dorms are mixed and while clean and reasonably sized, they can be noisy. There's no common room but most people hang out in the bar next door. Note the age limit – 18- to 40-year olds only.

Hotel Castelfidardo PENSION €
(Map p698; ☎06 446 46 38; www.hotelcastelfidardo.com; Via Castelfidardo 31; s €40-70, d €60-100; ❄📶; MTermini) A simple, old-school outfit not far from Stazione Termini. Rooms, on the 3rd floor, are unfussy with high ceilings and basic furniture.

Eating

The best places to eat are in the historic centre and Trastevere, but there are also excellent choices in San Lorenzo (the area east of Stazione Termini) and Testaccio. Choose carefully around Termini and the Vatican, as both areas are full of overpriced tourist traps.

HISTORIC CENTRE & THE VATICAN

TOP CHOICE **Pizzeria da Baffetto** PIZZERIA €
(Map p694; Via del Governo Vecchio 114; pizzas €6-9; ⌚6.30pm-midnight; 🚌Corso Vittorio Emanuele II) For the full-on Roman pizza experience get down to this local institution. Meals here are raucous, chaotic and fast, but the thin-crust pizzas are good and the vibe is fun. There's also a **Baffetto 2** (Map p694; Piazza del Teatro di Pompeo 18; ⌚6.30pm-12.30am Mon-Fri, 12.30-3.30pm & 6.30pm-12.30am Sat & Sun; 🚌Corso Vittorio Emanuele II) near Campo de' Fiori.

Dino e Tony TRATTORIA €€
(Map p686; ☎06 397 33 284; Via Leone IV 60; mains €12; ⌚Mon-Sat; MOttaviano-San Pietro) Kick off with the monumental antipasto, a minor meal in its own right, before plunging into the signature dish, *rigatoni all' amatriciana*, at this authentic trattoria near the Vatican. Finish up with a *granita di caffè*, a crushed ice coffee served with a full inch of whipped cream.

Maccheroni TRATTORIA €€
(Map p694; ☎06 683 07 895; Piazza delle Coppelle 44; mains €13; ⌚Mon-Sat; 🚌or 🚋Largo di Torre Argentina) With its classic vintage interior, attractive setting and traditional menu, this is the archetypal *centro storico* trattoria. Locals and tourists flock here to dine on Roman stalwarts such as *tonnarelli al cacio e pepe* (pasta with cheese and pepper) and *carciofo alla Romana* (Roman-style artichoke).

Gusto PIZZERIA & RESTAURANT €€
(Map p686; ☎06 322 62 73; Piazza Augusto Imperatore 9; pizza/buffet menu €9/10; 🚌Piazza Augusto Imperatore) All exposed brickwork and industrial chic, this big, '90s-style warehouse operation is a lunchtime favourite with office workers, serving everything from thick-crust pizza to cheese platters, salads and overpriced fusion food. At lunch the set menus are a bargain.

Da Tonino TRATTORIA €
(Map p694; Via del Governo Vecchio 18; mains €7; ⌚Mon-Sat; 🚌Corso Vittorio Emanuele II) Defiantly old school, this traditional neighbourhood trattoria sits among the bohemian boutiques and trendy bars on Via del Governo Vecchio.

MUSEO NAZIONALE ROMANO

Spread over four sites the **Museo Nazionale Romano** houses one of the world's most important collection of classical art and statuary. A combined ticket including each of the sites costs adult/concession €7/3.50 and is valid for three days.

Palazzo Massimo alle Terme MUSEUM
(Map p698; Largo di Villa Peretti 1; 9am-7.45pm Tue-Sun; MTermini) A fabulous museum with amazing frescoes and wall paintings.

Terme di Diocleziano MUSEUM
(Map p698; Via Enrico de Nicola 79; 9am-7.45pm Tue-Sun; MTermini) Housed in the Terme di Diocleziano (Diocletian's Baths), ancient Rome's largest baths complex.

Palazzo Altemps MUSEUM
(Map p694; Piazza Sant'Apollinare 44; 9am-7.45pm Tue-Sun; Corso del Rinascimento) Boasts the best of the museum's classical sculpture.

Crypta Balbi MUSEUM
(Map p694; Via delle Botteghe Oscure 31; 9am-7.45pm Tue-Sun; Largo di Torre Argentina) Set atop an ancient Roman theatre, the Teatro di Balbus (13 BC)

Don't expect frills (or even menus), just tasty Roman cooking served fast and cheap.

Forno di Campo de' Fiori BAKERY €
(Map p694; Campo de' Fiori 22; 7.30am-2.30pm & 4.45-8pm Mon-Sat; Corso Vittorio Emanuele II) This is one of Rome's best bakeries, serving delicious bread, *panini* and straight-from-the-oven pizza *al taglio* (by the slice).

TRASTEVERE

Hostaria dar Buttero TRATTORIA €€
(Map p702; 06 580 05 17; Via della Lungaretta; mains €11; Mon-Sat; or Piazza Sonnino) On Trastevere's main strip, this is a friendly old-school trattoria. The menu lists all the usual pastas, grilled meats and pizzas (evenings only), but the food is well cooked, the atmosphere is convivial and the prices are inviting.

Da Enzo TRATTORIA €
(Map p702; 06 581 83 55; Via dei Vascellari 29; mains €9; Mon-Sat; or Piazza Sonnino) Lunching locals queue for a bowl of hearty pasta at this cheery trattoria in Trastevere's eastern streets. It's not the place for a long, lingering meal but for a no-nonsense *rigatoni alla carbonara* (pasta carbonara) it'll do just fine.

Pizzeria Ivo PIZZERIA €
(Map p702; Via di San Francesco a Ripa 158; pizzas €6; 5.30pm-midnight Wed-Mon; or Viale di Trastevere) A perennially popular pizzeria, Ivo fits the stereotype. With the TV on in the corner and waiters skillfully manoeuvring plates over the noisy hordes, diners chow down on classic thin-crust pizzas.

Forno la Renella BAKERY €
(Map p702; Via del Moro 15-16; 9am-9pm; Piazza Trilussa) Choose from the daily batch of wood-fired pizza, bread and biscuits.

TESTACCIO

Pizzeria Remo PIZZERIA €
(Map p686; Piazza Santa Maria Liberatice 44; pizzas €6; 7.30pm-1am Mon-Sat; or Via Marmorata) This rowdy Testaccio spot is one of the city's most popular pizzerias. Queues are the norm but the large, thin-crust pizzas and delicious *bruschette* (toasted bread drizzled with olive oil and selected toppings) make the wait bearable.

Volpetti Più FOOD STALL €
(Map p686; Via Volta 8; mains €6; Mon-Sat; or Via Marmorata) Next to the ravishing deli of the same name, this upmarket canteen is one of the few places in town where you can sit down and eat well for less than €15. Grab a tray and choose from the sumptuous spread of pizza, pasta, soup, meat, vegetables and fried nibbles.

TERMINI & ESQUILINO

TOP CHOICE **Panella L'Arte del Pane** BAKERY €
(Map p686; Via Merulana 54; pizza slices from €2.50; 8am-midnight Mon-Wed & Fri & Sat, 8am-2pm Thu, 8.30am-2pm Sun; MPiazza Vittorio Emanuele) Not far from the Basilica di Santa Maria Maggiore, this fabulous bakery is a great place for a quick lunch. Pick from the opulent array of sliced pizza, *focaccia,* crepes and *arancini* (fried rice balls), and adjourn to an outdoor table or perch on a stool inside.

Trastevere (Rome)

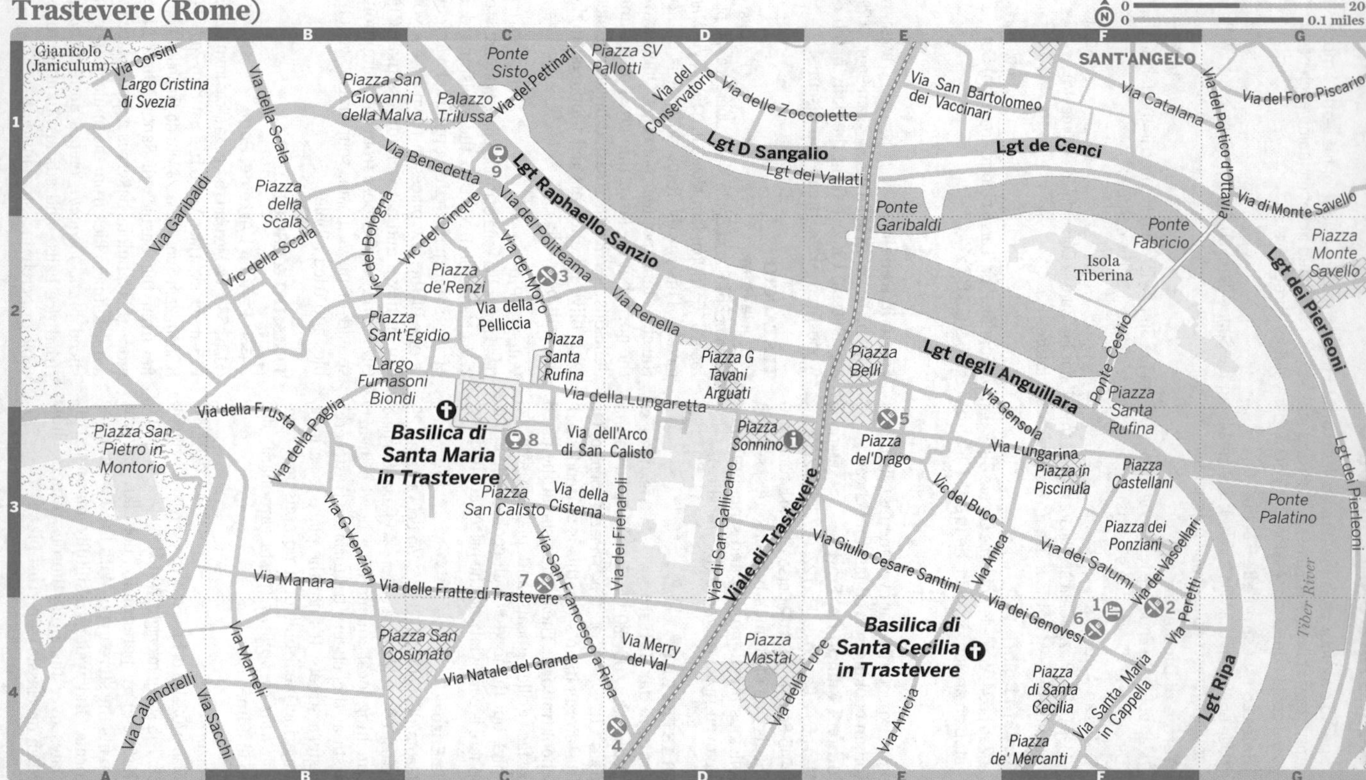

ROME SPLURGE

The rustic **Le Mani in Pasta** (Map p701; ☎06 58 16 017; Via dei Genovesi 37; mains €18; ⏲Tue-Sun; 🚌or 🚋Viale di Trastevere) has an open kitchen that serves up delicious fresh pasta dishes, grilled meats and fresh seafood – try linguine with lobster followed by salt-baked fish. It's a well-known spot so book ahead for dinner.

Pommidoro TRATTORIA €€
(Map p686; ☎06 445 26 92; Piazza dei Sanniti 44; mains €12; ⏲Mon-Sat; 🚌Via Tiburtina) A long-standing favourite in the San Lorenzo area east of Termini, Pommidoro continues to win diners over with its no-fuss traditional food. Celebs sometimes drop by but it remains an unpretentious spot with a laid-back vibe and excellent food.

Drinking

There are hundreds of bars and cafes across the city, with much of the action focused on the *centro storico* – Campo de' Fiori is popular with students and can get messy, while the area around Piazza Navona hosts a more upmarket scene. Over the river, Trastevere is another popular spot with dozens of bars and pubs. To the east of Termini, San Lorenzo is frequented by students and bohemian uptowners.

Trastevere (Rome)

Top Sights
- Basilica di Santa Cecilia in Trastevere E4
- Basilica di Santa Maria in Trastevere C3

Sleeping
1 Maria-Rosa Guesthouse F4

Eating
2 Da Enzo F4
3 Forno la Renella C2
4 Frontoni D4
5 Hostaria dar Buttero E3
6 Le Mani in Pasta F4
7 Pizzeria Ivo C3

Drinking
8 Bar San Calisto C3
9 Freni e Frizioni C1

Freni e Frizioni BAR
(Map p702; www.freniefrizioni.com; Via del Politeama 4-6; ⏲10am-2am; 🚌Piazza Trilussa) A favourite Trastevere hang-out housed in a former garage and spilling out onto a small piazza. The crowd is young and fashionable, the mojitos are great and the aperitif spread is well worth investigating.

Caffè Sant'Eustachio CAFE
(Map p694; Piazza Sant'Eustachio 82; ⏲8.30am-1am; 🚌Corso del Rinascimento) This small unassuming cafe, generally three-deep at the bar, boasts Rome's best coffee. Served sugared and with a layer of froth, the espresso is a smooth, creamy blend with a reassuringly strong caffeine kick.

Salotto 42 BAR
(Map p694; www.salotto42.it; Piazza di Pietra; ⏲10am-2am Tue-Sat, to midnight Sun; 🚌Via del Corso) Run by a Swedish model and her Italian partner, this hip, glamorous lounge bar sports soft sofas, coffee-table books and an excellent *aperitivo* spread.

La Tazza d'Oro CAFE
(Map p694; Via degli Orfani 84-86; ⏲Mon-Sat; 🚌or 🚋Largo di Torre Argentina) A busy, stand-up bar that serves superb espresso and a range of delicious coffee concoctions, such as *granita di caffè,* a crushed-ice coffee with a big dollop of cream.

Vineria Reggio WINE BAR
(Map p694; Campo de'Fiori 15; ⏲8.30am-2am Mon-Sat; 🚌Corso Vittorio Emanuele II) The coolest of the Campo de' Fiori bars, this is a good spot to watch the nightly *campo* circus. It has a small bottle-lined interior and several outside tables.

Bar San Calisto BAR
(Map p702; Piazza San Calisto; ⏲6am-2.30am Mon-Sat; 🚌or 🚋Piazza Sonnino) Intellectuals, bohemians, local alcoholics, foreign students – they all flock to this down-at-heel Trastevere landmark for the cheap prices and laid-back atmosphere.

Bar Arco degli Aurunci BAR
(Map p686; Via degli Aurunci 42; ⏲8am-2am; 🚌Via dei Reti) On a car-free piazza in San Lorenzo, this attractive modern bar is a cool spot for a drink or light meal. Aperitifs are served between 7pm and 9pm.

Entertainment

Rome has a thriving cultural scene, with a year-round calendar of concerts, performances and festivals. Listings guides include

GELATO GALORE

To get the best out of Rome's gelaterie (ice-cream shops) look for the words *'produzione propria'*, meaning 'own production' or 'made on the premises'. Here is a choice of the city's finest:

San Crispino (Map p698; Via della Panetteria 42; MBarberini) Near the Trevi Fountain, it serves natural, seasonal flavours in tubs only.

Old Bridge (Map p686; Via Bastioni di Michelangelo 5; Piazza del Risorgimento) Just right for a pick-me-up after the Vatican Museums.

Tre Scalini (Map p694; Piazza Navona 30; Corso Vittorio Emanuele II) Famous for its *tartufo nero,* a €10 ball of chocolate ice cream filled with chunks of choc and served with cream.

Roma C'è (www.romace.it, in Italian; €1) and *Trova Roma,* a free insert with *La Repubblica* newspaper every Thursday. Both are available at newsstands. Upcoming events are also listed at www.turismoroma.it and www.inromenow.com.

Two good ticket agencies are **Orbis** (Map p698; 06 48 27 403; Piazza dell'Esquilino 37; 9.30am-1pm & 4-7.30pm Mon-Fri, 9.30am-1pm Sat; Via Cavour), which accepts cash payment only, and the online agency **Hello** (800 90 70 80; www.helloticket.it, in Italian).

Classical Music & Opera

Rome's cultural hub and premier concert complex is the **Auditorium Parco della Musica** (06 802 41 281; www.auditorium.com; Viale Pietro de Coubertin 34; Viale Tiziano), which stages everything from classical music concerts to tango exhibitions, book readings and film screenings. The Auditorium is also home to Rome's top orchestra, the **Orchestra dell' Accademia Nazionale di Santa Cecilia** (box office 06 808 20 58; www.santacecilia.it).

Rome's opera season runs from December to June. The main venue is the **Teatro dell'Opera** (Map p698; box office 06 481 60 255; www.operaroma.it; Piazza Beniamino Gigli 7; MRepubblica), which also houses the city's ballet company. In summer, opera is performed outdoors at the Terme di Caracalla.

Clubbing & Live Music

Rome's clubbing scene is centred on Testaccio and the Ostiense area, although you'll also find places in Trastevere and the *centro storico.* You'll need to dress the part to get into the big clubs, which rarely get going much before midnight. Admission is sometimes free but drinks are expensive, typically €10 to €15. Note also that many clubs shut between mid-June and mid-September.

Circolo degli Artisti NIGHTCLUB, LIVE MUSIC
(www.circolodegliartisti.it; Via Casilina Vecchia 42; Tue-Sun; Via Casilina) Out in the Pigneto district southeast of Stazione Termini, this fantastic club is a centre of the city's underground music scene, staging big names and emerging talents.

Alexanderplatz JAZZ CLUB
(Map p686; 06 397 42 171; www.alexanderplatz.it; Via Ostia 9; MOttaviano-San Pietro) Rome's premier jazz joint attracts top international performers and a passionate, knowledgeable crowd. In July the club ups sticks and transfers to the grounds of Villa Celimontana for the summer.

Goa NIGHTCLUB
(Via Libetta 13; Tue-Sun; MGarbatella) Quality international DJs whip the crowd into a frenzy at Rome's top mega-club. Big nights include the Thursday Ultrabeat session, Saturday funky house and the 'Venus Rising' lesbian night every last Sunday of the month.

Villaggio Globale SOCIAL CENTRE
(Map p686; www.vglobale.biz; Lungotevere Testaccio; MPiramide) For a warehouse-party vibe, head to Rome's best-known *centro sociale* (social centre), housed in an ex-slaughterhouse. Live music and DJ sets focus on dancehall, reggae, dubstep and drum'n'bass.

Big Mama BLUES CLUB
(Map p686; 06 581 24 51; www.bigmama.it; Vicolo di San Francesco a Ripa 18; Tue-Sun; or Viale di Trastevere) This Trastevere basement is Rome's self-styled home of blues. It plays host to the world's top blues musicians and stages soul, jazz and funk.

AKAB NIGHTCLUB
(Map p686; www.akabcave.com; Via Monte Testaccio 68-69; Tue-Sat; MPiramide) This is one of the most popular clubs on the Testaccio clubbing strip, with an underground cellar, a chilled garden and a steady supply of house, R&B and techno.

Information

Emergency

Police station (Questura; ☎06 468 61; Via San Vitale 15)

Internet Access

Free wi-fi is now widely available in hostels, B&Bs and hotels across the city. Some also provide laptops/computers for guests' use. You'll find a dwindling number of internet cafes across town.

Medical Services

For emergency treatment, go to the *pronto soccorso* (casualty) section of an *ospedale* (hospital). Pharmacists will serve prescriptions and can provide basic medical advice.

Pharmacy Piazza dei Cinquecento (Piazza dei Cinquecento 49-51; ⏲24hr); Stazione Termini (next to platform 1; ⏲7.30-10.30pm)

Ospedale Santo Spirito (☎06 683 51; Lungotevere in Sassia 1) Near the Vatican; multilingual staff.

Tourist Information

Centro Servizi Pellegrini e Turisti (Map p686; ☎06 698 81 662; St Peter's Sq; ⏲8.30am-6.15pm Mon-Sat) The Vatican's official tourist office.

Enjoy Rome (☎06 445 18 43; www.enjoyrome.com; Via Marghera 8a; ⏲8.30am-7pm Mon-Fri, to 2pm Sat) A private tourist office that arranges tours, airport transfers and hotel reservations.

I Fori di Roma Centro Espositivo Informativo (Map p690; Via dei Fori Imperiali; ⏲9.30am-6.30pm) An information centre dedicated to the Forums.

The Comune di Roma runs a multilingual **tourist information line** (☎06 06 08; ⏲9am-9pm) and information points across the city:

Ciampino Airport (International Arrivals; ⏲9am-6.30pm)

Castel Sant'Angelo (Map p686; Piazza Pia; ⏲9.30am-7pm)

Fiumicino Airport (International Arrivals; ⏲9am-6.30pm)

Piazza delle Cinque Lune (Map p694; ⏲9.30am-7pm) Near Piazza Navona.

Piazza Sonnino (Map p686; ⏲9.30am-7pm) In Trastevere.

Santa Maria Maggiore (Map p686; Via dell'Olmata; ⏲9.30am-7pm) Near the Basilica di Santa Maria Maggiore.

Stazione Termini (⏲8am-8.30pm) In the hall parallel to platform 24.

Via Marco Minghetti (Map p694; ⏲9.30am-7pm) Near the Trevi Fountain.

Via Nazionale (Map p686; ⏲9.30am-7pm) In front of the Palazzo delle Esposizioni.

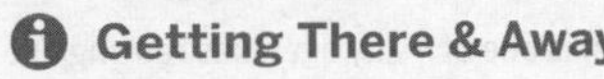

Getting There & Away

Air

Rome's main international airport **Leonardo da Vinci** (FCO; ☎06 6 59 51; www.adr.it), better known as Fiumicino, is 30km west of the city. The much smaller **Ciampino airport** (CIA; ☎06 6 59 51; www.adr.it), 15km southeast of the city centre, serves low-cost carriers including Ryanair and easyJet.

Boat

Rome's port is at Civitavecchia, about 80km north of Rome. The main ferry companies are as follows:

Grimaldi Lines (☎081 464 444; www.grimaldi-lines.com) To/from Barcelona (Spain), Catania (Sicily), Malta, Porto Torres (Sardinia), Trapani (Sicily) and Tunis (Tunisia).

Sardinia Ferries (☎199 400 500; www.corsica-ferries.it) To/from Golfo Aranci (Sardinia).

SNAV (☎076 636 63 66; www.snav.it) To/from Palermo (Sicily) and Olbia (Sardinia).

Tirrenia (☎892 123; www.tirrenia.it) To/from Arbatax, Cagliari and Olbia (all Sardinia).

Bookings can be made at the Termini-based **Agenzia 365** (⏲7am-9pm), at travel agents or online at www.traghettiweb.it. You can also buy directly at the port.

Half-hourly trains depart from Roma Termini to Civitavecchia (€4.50 to €12.50, one hour). On arrival, it's about a 15-minute walk to the port (to your right) as you exit the station.

Bus

Long-distance national and international buses use the **Autostazione Tiburtina** (Piazzale Tiburtina) in front of Stazione Tiburtina. Take metro line B from Termini to Tiburtina.

You can get tickets from the offices next to the bus terminus or at travel agencies. Bus operators:

Interbus (☎091 34 25 25; www.interbus.it, in Italian) To/from Sicily.

Marozzi (☎080 579 01 11; www.marozzivt.it, in Italian) To/from Sorrento, Bari, Matera and Lecce.

SENA (☎0861 199 19 00; www.senabus.it) To/from Siena and Tuscany.

Sulga (☎800 099 661; www.sulga.it, in Italian) To/from Perugia, Assisi and Ravenna.

Car & Motorcycle

Rome is circled by the Grande Raccordo Anulare (GRA) to which all autostradas (motorways) connect, including the main A1 north–south artery (the Autostrada del Sole), and the A12, which connects Rome to Civitavecchia and Fiumicino airport.

Car hire is available at the airport and Stazione Termini. Near Termini, **Bici & Baci** (☎06 482 84 43; www.bicibaci.com; Via del Viminale 5;

⏲8am-7pm) is one of many agencies renting out scooters. Bank on at least €19 per day.

Train

Almost all trains arrive at and depart from **Stazione Termini** (Map p686). There are regular connections to all major Italian cities and many smaller towns. Train information is available from the **Sala Viaggiatori** (⏲6am-midnight) next to platform 1, online at www.ferroviedellostato.it, or, if you speak Italian, by calling ☎89 20 21.

Facilities at Termini include ATMs, tourist information, a post office, an underground shopping mall and **left luggage** (1-5hr €4, 6-12hr per hr €0.60, 13hr & over per hr €0.20; ⏲6am-11.50pm).

Rome's second train station is **Stazione Tiburtina**, on metro line B.

Getting Around

To/From the Airport

FIUMICINO The easiest way to get to/from the airport is by train, but there are also bus services.

Leonardo Express train (€14) Runs from Stazione Termini every 30 minutes between 5.52am and 10.52pm; from the airport between 6.36am and 11.36pm. Journey time is 30 minutes.

FR1 train (€8) To/from Trastevere, Ostiense and Tiburtina stations. Departures from the airport every 15 minutes (hourly on Sunday and public holidays) between 5.57am and 11.27pm, from Tiburtina between 5.05am and 10.33pm.

Cotral bus (www.cotralspa.it; €4.50 or €7 on bus) To/from Stazione Tiburtina via Termini. Eight daily departures including night services from Tiburtina and from the airport. Journey time is 45 minutes to an hour.

SIT bus (www.sitbusshuttle.it; €8) Regular departures from Via Marsala outside Stazione Termini between 5am and 8.30pm, from the airport between 8.30am and 12.30pm. Tickets available on the bus. Journey time is one hour.

Taxi The set fare to/from the city centre is €40, which is valid for up to four passengers with luggage.

CIAMPINO The best option is to take one of the regular bus services into the city. You can also take a bus to Ciampino train station and then pick up a train to Stazione Termini.

Terravision bus (www.terravision.eu; one way/return €4/8) Twice hourly departures to/from Via Marsala outside Stazione Termini. From the airport, services are between 8.15am and 12.15pm, from Via Marsala between 4.30am and 9.20pm. Buy tickets at Terracafè in front of the Via Marsala bus stop. Journey time is 40 minutes.

SIT bus (www.sitbusshuttle.com; one way/return €6/8) Regular departures from Via Marsala outside Stazione Termini between 4.30am and 9.30pm, from the airport between 7.45am and 11.15pm. Tickets available on the bus. Journey time is 45 minutes.

Cotral bus (www.cotralspa.it; one way/return €3.90/6.90) Runs frequent services to/from Ciampino train station (€1.20) where you can connect with trains to Stazione Termini (€1.30).

Taxi The set rate to/from the airport is €30.

Public Transport

Rome's public transport system includes buses, trams, metro and a suburban train network. Tickets are valid for all forms of transport and come in various forms:

Single (BIT; €1) Valid for 75 minutes, during which time you can use as many buses or trams as you like but only go once on the metro.

Daily (BIG; €4) Unlimited travel until midnight of the day of purchase.

3-day (BTI; €11) Unlimited travel for three days.

Weekly (CIS; €16) Unlimited travel for seven days.

Buy tickets at *tabacchi*, newsstands and from vending machines at main bus stops and metro stations. They must be purchased before you start your journey and validated in the yellow machines on buses, at the entrance gates to the metro or at train stations. Ticketless riders risk an on-the-spot €50 fine.

BUSES & TRAMS Run by **ATAC** (☎06 57 003; www.atac.roma.it). The **main bus station** (Map p698; Piazza dei Cinquecento) is in front of Stazione Termini, where there's an **information booth** (⏲7.30am-8pm). Largo di Torre Argentina, Piazza Venezia and Piazza San Silvestro are also important hubs. Buses generally run from about 5.30am until midnight, with limited services throughout the night.

METRO Has two lines, A and B, which both pass through Termini. Take line A for the Trevi Fountain (Barberini), Spanish Steps (Spagna) and Vatican (Ottaviano-San Pietro); and line B for the Colosseum (Colosseo) and Circus Maximus (Circo Massimo). Trains run between 5.30am and 11.30pm (to 1.30am on Friday and Saturday).

Taxi

Official licenced taxis are white with the symbol of Rome on the doors. Always go with the metered fare, never an arranged price (the set fares to/from the airports are exceptions). Official rates are posted in taxis.

You can hail a taxi, but it's often easier to wait at a rank or phone for one. There are major taxi ranks at the airports, Stazione Termini and Largo di Torre Argentina. You can book a taxi by phoning the Comune di Roma's automated **taxi line** (☎06 06 09) or calling a taxi company direct.

La Capitale (☎06 49 94)

Pronto Taxi (☎06 66 45)

Radio Taxi (☎06 35 70)
Samarcanda (☎06 55 51)
Tevere (☎06 41 57)

AROUND ROME

Ostia Antica

An easy day trip from Rome, Ostia Antica is well worth a visit. Ostia was ancient Rome's port, and the clearly discernible ruins of restaurants, laundries, shops, houses and public meeting places give a good impression of what life must once have been like. Ostia was founded in the 4th century BC and thrived until the 5th century, when barbarian invasions and an outbreak of malaria led to its eventual abandonment and slow burial in river silt, thanks to which it has survived so well.

The **ruins** (adult/concession €6.50/3.25; ⏰8.30am-7pm Tue-Sun Apr-Oct, to 6pm Mar, to 5pm Nov, Dec, Jan & Feb) are spread out and you'll need a few hours to do them justice. Highlights include the **Terme di Nettuno** (Baths of Neptune) and adjacent **amphitheatre**, built by Agrippa and later enlarged to hold 3000 people. Behind it, the **Piazzale delle Corporazioni** (Forum of the Corporations) housed Ostia's merchant guilds and is decorated with well-preserved mosaics.

To get to Ostia Antica from Rome take the Ostia Lido train (25 minutes, half-hourly) from Stazione Porta San Paolo next to the Piramide metro station. The journey is covered by standard public transport tickets.

Tivoli

POP 55,630

A Roman resort and playground for the Renaissance rich, hilltop Tivoli is home to two Unesco-listed sites: Villa Adriana and Villa d'Este. Information is available at the **tourist information kiosk** (☎0774 31 35 36; www.tibursuperbum.it; Piazzale delle Nazioni Unite; ⏰9.30am-5.30pm Tue-Sun) near the Cotral bus stop at the top of the hill.

Five kilometres from Tivoli proper, **Villa Adriana** (Hadrian's Villa; adult/concession €6.50/3.25, plus possible €3.50 for exhibition; ⏰9am-1hr before sunset) was Emperor Hadrian's summer residence. One of the largest and most sumptuous villas in the Roman Empire, it was subsequently plundered for building materials, although enough remains to convey its magnificence.

The Renaissance **Villa d'Este** (www.villadestetivoli.info; Piazza Trento; adult/concession €6.50/3.25, plus possible €3.50 for exhibition; ⏰8.30am-1hr before sunset Tue-Sun) was built in the 16th century for Cardinal Ippolito d'Este. But more than the villa, it's the elaborate gardens and their spectacular fountains that draw the crowds.

Tivoli is 30km east of Rome and accessible by Cotral bus (€2, one hour, every 20 minutes) from outside Ponte Mammolo station on metro line B.

To get to Villa Adriana from Tivoli town centre, take CAT bus 4X (€1, 10 minutes, half-hourly) from Largo Garibaldi.

Tarquinia

POP 16,450

Some 90km northwest of Rome, Tarquinia is the pick of Lazio's Etruscan centres. Founded in the 12th century BC, it reached its prime in the 4th century BC when it was a serious rival to Athens. Decline set in a century later and in 204 BC it surrendered to Rome.

The **tourist information office** (☎0766 84 92 82; www.tarquiniaturismo.it; Barriera San Giusto; ⏰9am-1pm & 5-10pm Jul & Aug, shorter afternoon hr rest of year) is just inside the town's medieval gate.

Although the Etruscans were dominant in pre-Roman Italy, little of their culture remains. Much of what scholars know comes from findings in Tarquinia, many of which are displayed at the **Museo Nazionale Tarquiniense** (Piazza Cavour; admission €6, incl necropolis €8; ⏰8.30am-½hr before sunset Tue-Sun). You'll find rooms full of painted friezes, sarcophagi, jewellery and some plates decorated with Etruscan porn.

About 1.5km outside of town is the town's 7th-century BC **necropolis** (Via Ripagretta; admission €6, incl Museo Nazionale Tarquiniense €8; ⏰8.30am-½hr before sunset Tue-Sun). Almost 6000 tombs have been excavated since the first digs in 1489, of which 19 are currently open to the public, including the **Tomba della Caccia e della Pesca**, the richly decorated **Tomba dei Leopardi** and the **Tomba della Fustigazione**, with its erotic depiction of a little friendly S&M.

To get to the necropolis, you can either take bus D (€0.60, nine daily) from outside the tourist office or walk (it takes about 15 minutes).

The easiest way to reach Tarquinia from Rome is to take the Pisa train from Termini

(€6.20, 1¼ hours, eight daily). At Tarquinia station take bus BC (€0.80, every 30 to 50 minutes) to the town centre.

Cerveteri

POP 35,355

With its hilltop *centro storico* and haunting Etruscan tombs, Cerveteri makes a rewarding day trip from Rome. Cerveteri was one of the most important commercial centres in the Mediterranean from the 7th to the 5th century BC, but as Roman power grew so Cerveteri's fortunes faded, and in 358 BC the city was annexed by Rome.

The superhelpful **tourist information point** (☎06 995 52 637; www.etruriaguide.it; Piazza Aldo Moro; ⌚9.30am-12.30pm daily & 5.30-7.30pm Fri & Sat mid-Jun–mid-Sep, 9.30am-12.30pm Mon-Sat mid Sep-mid Jun) provides information on local sights, accommodation and transport.

Cerveteri's Etruscan tombs are concentrated in the Unesco-listed **Necropoli di Banditaccia** (Piazzale Moretti; admission €6, incl museum €8; ⌚9am-1hr before sunset Tue-Sun), just outside the town centre. The tombs are built into grassy *tumoli* (mounds of earth with carved stone bases), laid out in the form of a town. To get to the necropolis take the white shuttle bus G (€0.77) from next to the tourist information point.

Cerveteri is accessible from Rome by Cotral bus (€3.10, 1¼ hours, every 45 minutes) from outside Cornelia station on metro line A.

NORTHERN ITALY

Italy's well-heeled north is an alluring area of historical wealth and natural diversity. Bordered by the northern Alps and boasting some of the country's most spectacular coastline, it also encompasses Italy's largest lowland area, the decidedly nonpicturesque Po Valley. Of the cities it's Venice that hogs the limelight, but in their own way Turin, Genoa and Bologna offer plenty to the open-minded traveller. Verona is one of Italy's most beautiful cities, and the medieval centres of Padua, Ferrara and Ravenna all reward the visitor.

Genoa

POP 611,170

One of the Mediterranean's great ports, Genoa (Genova) is an absorbing city of aristocratic *palazzi*, dark malodorous alleyways, Gothic architecture and industrial sprawl. Birthplace of Christopher Columbus (1451-1506) and home to Europe's second-largest aquarium (the largest is in Valencia), it was once a powerful maritime republic known as La Superba; nowadays it's a fascinating port that's well worth a stopover, particularly as it's the gateway to the magnificent Cinque Terre National Park.

Sights

Central Genoa is squeezed into the area between the city's two main train stations: Stazione Brignole and Stazione Principe, with most sights in the *centro storico* and Porto Antico (Old Port).

Piazza de Ferrari SQUARE

Piazza de Ferrari is Genoa's central square and a good place to start exploring the city. Grandiose and impressive, it's centred on an exuberant fountain and flanked by imposing *palazzi*, including **Teatro Carlo Felice**, the city's historic opera house and **Palazzo Ducale** (www.palazzoducale.genova.it; entrance Piazza Giacomo Matteotti), once the seat of the city's rulers but now used to host major art exhibitions.

Cattedrale di San Lorenzo CHURCH

(Piazza San Lorenzo; ⌚8-11.45am & 3-6.45pm) Genoa's dramatic cathedral is most notable for its black-and-white-striped Italian Gothic facade. It was consecrated in 1118 but the two bell towers and cupola were added in the 16th century.

Acquario di Genova AQUARIUM

(☎010 234 56 78; www.acquariodigenova.it; Ponte Spinola; admission €18; ⌚8.30am-10pm daily Jul & Aug, shorter hr rest of year) The main attraction in Genoa's **Porto Antico** is Europe's second-largest aquarium. Designed by Italian architect Renzo Piano, it houses 5000 animals in six million litres of water.

Musei di Strada Nuovo MUSEUM

(www.museidigenova.it; Via Garibaldi; adult/concession €8/6; ⌚9am-7pm Tue-Fri, from 10am Sat & Sun) Genoa's main museums are in a series of *palazzi* on Via Garibaldi. The three most important, known collectively as the Musei di Strada Nuova, are housed in **Palazzo Bianco** (Via Garibaldi 11), **Palazzo Rosso** (Via Garibaldi 18) and **Palazzo Doria-Tursi** (Via Garibaldi 9). The first two feature works by Flemish, Dutch, Spanish and Italian old masters, while the third displays the personal effects of Niccolò Paganini, Genoa's legendary violinist. Tickets, valid for all three museums, are available from the bookshop in Palazzo Doria-Tursi.

Sleeping

Hotel Bel Soggiorno HOTEL €€
(☎010 54 28 80; www.belsoggiornohotel.com; 2nd fl, Via XX Settembre 19; s €65-110, d €75-135; P ❄ @) Located on Genoa's main shopping strip, this old favourite is an endearing mix of the modern and the antique, with airy, comfortable rooms and modern amenities such as satellite TV and wi-fi.

Ostello di Genova HOSTEL €
(☎010 242 24 57; www.ostellogenova.it; Via Costanzi 120; per person dm/s/d €17/27/25) Genoa's HI hostel is a functional, modern affair, some 2km up from the city centre – take bus 40 from Stazione Principe. Check-in is from 2.30pm to midnight and there's a lockout between 11.30am and 2.30pm.

Albergo Carola PENSION €
(☎010 839 13 40; www.pensionecarola.com; 3rd fl, Via Gropallo 4; s without bathroom €28-35, d €56-70;) Conveniently close to Stazione Brignole, this is a classic old-school *pensione* with simple, well-kept rooms on the 3rd floor of a towering old building. No breakfast.

Eating

Ligurian specialities include *pesto* (a sauce of basil, garlic, pine nuts and Parmesan) served with *trofie* (pasta curls) and focaccia (flat bread made with olive oil). Look out for *friggitore* (stalls selling fritters made with chickpea flour or *baccalà*). There are numerous restaurants and trattorias in the *centro storico*, while the Porto Antico area is good for cheap takeaways.

Regina Margherita RESTAURANT, PIZZERIA €€
(☎010 595 57 53; Piazza della Vittoria 89-103; mains €14, pizzas from €5.50) A bright, modern set-up with a two-floor interior and a small outdoor terrace. It's not in a particularly enticing location – on Piazza della Vittoria – but the food is excellent and the service is friendly and efficient. Speciality of the house is the wood-fired Neapolitan pizza.

Ristorante Pizzeria Piedigrotta RESTAURANT, PIZZERIA €
(☎010 58 05 53; Piazza Savonarola 27; mains €9, pizzas from €5) If you like your pizzas huge, cheap and tasty, you'll love Piedigrotta, a big, bustling outfit on a tree-lined piazza. Enormously popular with locals, it has a welcoming interior and friendly staff.

Osteria San Matteo RESTAURANT €€
(☎010 247 32 82; Piazza San Matteo 4r; mains €12) With its wood-beams and exposed brick walls, this is an inviting *centro storico* osteria. It serves a full menu but pride of place goes to the reasonably priced seafood.

Drinking & Entertainment

Action centres on the *centro storico*, with a number of good bars clustered around Piazza delle Erbe.

Mcafé CAFE
(Piazza Giacomo Matteotti 9; ⊙8am-10pm Mon-Thu, to 1am Fri, 10am-1am Sat & Sun) This swish cafe by the entrance to the Palazzo Ducale is a good place to sip on something cool as you eye up fellow drinkers. Upstairs is a restaurant serving set lunch menus (€12) on weekdays and brunch (€16) weekends.

Storico Lounge Café CAFE
(Piazza de Ferrari 34/36r; ⊙6am-3am) The *aperitivo* buffet here (5pm to 10pm) is a favourite with the city's fashionable set, who congregate at the pavement tables overlooking Teatro Carlo Felice. DJs add to the buzz on Friday and Saturday nights.

Teatro Carlo Felice THEATRE
(☎010 538 12 24; www.carlofelice.it; Passo Eugenio Montale 4) Genoa's historic theatre stages a year-round programme of opera, ballet and classical music. Tickets start at about €25.

Information

Tourist offices (www.turismo.comune.genova.it) Airport (☎010 601 52 47; ⊙9am-1pm & 1.30-5.30pm daily); Antico Porto (⊙10am-7pm); city centre (☎010 860 61 22; Largo Pertini 13; ⊙9.30am-1pm & 2.30-6.30pm daily); Via Garibaldi (☎010 557 29 03; Via Garibaldi 12r; ⊙9.30am-1pm & 2.30-6.30pm daily)

Getting There & Around

Air

Genoa's **Cristoforo Colombo Airport** (GOA; ☎010 60 151; www.airport.genova.it; Sestri Ponente) is 6km west of the city. To get there take the **Volabus** (€6, 30 min, hourly 5.20am-11.20pm) from Stazione Brignole or Stazione Principe. Buy tickets on board or at tourist offices.

Boat

Ferries sail to/from Corsica, Sardinia, Sicily, Spain and Tunisia from the **terminal traghetti** (ferry terminal; www.porto.genova.it; Calata

Chiappella), west of the city centre. Ferry companies are as follows:

Grandi Navi Veloci (☎010 209 45 91; www.gnv.it) To/from Sardinia (Porto Torres from €25, 11 hours; Olbia from €22, nine to 10 hours), Sicily (Palermo from €83, 20 hours), Barcelona (from €81, 18 hours) and Tunis (from €127, 24 hours).

Moby Lines (☎199 30 30 40; www.mobylines.it) To/from Sardinia (Porto Torres from €24, 10 hours).

Tirrenia (☎800 82 40 79; www.tirrenia.it) To/from Sardinia (Porto Torres from €30, 10 hours; Olbia from €30, 9¾ hours; Arbatax from €27, 14½ hours).

Bus

The main bus terminal is on Piazza della Vittoria, south of Stazione Brignole. Book tickets at **Geotravels** (Piazza della Vittoria 57). Local bus 33 runs between Stazione Principe and Stazione Brignole, stopping at Piazza de Ferrari en route.

Train

There are direct trains to Milan (€16.50, 1½ hours, up to 25 daily), Pisa (€16, two hours, up to 15 daily), Rome (€38.50, 5½ hours, nine daily) and Turin (€16, two hours, up to 15 daily). Regional trains to La Spezia service the Cinque Terre (€5.30, two hours, up to 21 daily).

It generally makes little difference whether you leave from Brignole or Principe.

Cinque Terre

Liguria's eastern Riviera boasts some of Italy's most dramatic coastline, the highlight of which is the Unesco-listed **Parco Nazionale delle Cinque Terre** (Cinque Terre National Park) just north of La Spezia. This awesome 18km-long stretch is named after its five tiny villages – Riomaggiore, Manarola, Corniglia, Vernazza and Monterosso.

Summer gets very crowded, so try to come in spring or autumn. You can either visit on a day trip from Genoa or La Spezia or stay overnight in one of the five villages.

Sights & Activities

The Cinque Terre villages are linked by the 9km **Blue Trail** (Sentiero Azzurro), a magnificent, mildly challenging five-hour trail. To walk it, you'll need to buy a **Cinque Terre Card** (adult/concession 1 day €5/2.50, 2 days €8/4), available in all of the park offices. Alternatively, the **Cinque Terre Treno Card** (adult/concession 1 day €8.50/4.30, 2 days €14.70/7.40) covers the walk and provides unlimited train travel between Levanto, just north of the villages, and La Spezia to the south, including all five villages.

The Blue Trail is just one of a network of footpaths and cycle trails that criss-cross the park; details are available from park offices. If water sports are more your thing, you can hire snorkelling gear (€10 per day) and kayaks (single/double €5/10 per hour) at the **Diving Center 5 Terre** (www.5terrediving.it; Via San Giacomo) in Riomaggiore. It also offers a snorkelling boat tour for €18.

Sleeping & Eating

L'Eremo Sul Mare B&B €
(☎346 019 58 80; www.eremosulmare.com; Sentiero Azzurro, Vernazza; r €80-110; ❄) This romantic B&B is beautifully situated on the Blue Trail about 15 minutes' walk from Vernazza train station. It has three rooms, a panoramic sun terrace and a kitchen for guests' use. Cash only.

Ostello 5 Terre HOSTEL €
(☎0187 92 02 15; www.cinqueterre.net/ostello; Via B Riccobaldi 21, Manarola; dm €20-23, d €55-65; ⏲closed Nov-Feb; @) A popular private hostel in Manarola. Beds are in bright six-person single-sex dorms or private rooms with attached bathrooms. Extras include breakfast (€6) and dinner (€18), laundry facilities and sports kit rental. Book at least a week ahead.

Marina Piccola RESTAURANT €€
(☎0187 92 01 03; www.hotelmarinapiccola.com; Via Birolli 120, Manarola; mains €12) Dine on fresh-off-the-boat seafood overlooking the small bay at Manarola. The harbour-side setting is ideal for *zuppa di pesce* (fish soup) or seafood risotto. The adjoining hotel has small but comfortable air-conditioned rooms (single/double €87/115).

Hotel Ca' d'Andrean HOTEL €
(☎0187 92 00 40; www.cadandrean.it; Via Doscovolo 101, Manarola; s €55-72, d €70-100; ❄) An excellent family-run hotel in the upper part of Manarola. No credit cards.

La Cambusa TAKEAWAY €
(Via Renato Birolli 11, Manarola; pizza slice €2.50) A useful spot for snacks and lunchtime pizza.

Information

The park's main **information office** (☎0187 92 06 33; ⏲8am-9.30pm) is to the right as you exit the train station at Riomaggiore; there are other offices in the train stations at Manarola, Corniglia, Vernazza, Monterosso and La Spezia (most open from 8am to 8pm).

Online information is available at www.parconazionale5terre.it and www.cinqueterre.com.

Getting There & Away

Boat

Between July and September, **Golfo Paradiso** (☎0185 77 20 91; www.golfoparadiso.it) operates boat excursions from Genoa's Porto Antico to Vernazza, Monterosso and Riomaggiore. These cost €18 one way, €33 return.

From late March to October, **Consorzio Marittimo Turistico 5 Terre** (☎0187 73 29 87; www.navigazionegolfodeipoeti.it) runs daily ferries between La Spezia and four of the villages (not Corniglia), costing €16 one way including all the stops. Return trips are covered by a daily ticket which costs €23 (weekdays) or €25 (weekends).

Train

Regional trains run from Genoa Brignole to Riomaggiore (€4.80, 1½ to two hours, 20 daily) stopping at each of the Cinque Terre villages. The last train back from Riomaggiore to Genoa is at 11.19pm.

Trains run between La Spezia and Levanto every 20 to 60 minutes between 4.30am and 11.10pm, stopping at all of the villages.

Turin

POP 908,825

Much more than Fiat and smoking factories, Turin (Torino) is a dynamic, cosmopolitan city full of royal *palazzi*, baroque piazzas and world-class museums. If they fail to impress, the thriving cafe culture and vibrant nightlife are sure to win you over. There's also the added interest of the city's occult position. According to believers of magic, Turin is linked to Lyon and Prague by mystical lines of energy to form a so-called 'white magic triangle', and to London and San Francisco by lines of malevolent energy in a 'black magic triangle'.

Sights

Serious sightseers should consider the **Torino & Piedmont Card** (48hr €20), available at tourist offices, which gives free public transport (not the metro) and discounts or entry to 170 museums, monuments and castles.

Piazza Castello SQUARE

Turin's grandest square is **Piazza Castello**, dominated by **Palazzo Madama**, the original seat of the Italian parliament, and the mid-17th-century **Palazzo Reale** (Royal Palace; Piazza Castello; adult/concession €6.50/3.25; ⏲8.30am-7.30pm Tue-Sun), whose **Giardino Reale** (Royal Garden; admission free; ⏲9am-1hr before sunset) was designed in 1697 by Louis le Nôtre, noted for his work at Versailles.

A short walk away, **Piazza San Carlo**, known as Turin's drawing room, is famous for its cafes and twin baroque churches **San Carlo** and **Santa Cristina**.

Cattedrale di San Giovanni Battista CHURCH

(Piazza San Giovanni; ⏲8am-noon & 3-7pm Mon-Sat, from 7am Sun) Turin's 15th-century cathedral houses the famous Shroud of Turin (*Sindone*), supposedly the cloth used to wrap the crucified Christ. A copy is on permanent display in front of the altar while the real thing is kept in a vacuum-sealed box and rarely revealed.

Mole Antonelliana MUSEUM

(Via Montebello 20) Towering 167m over the city skyline, Turin's famous landmark houses the fabulous **Museo Nazionale del Cinema** (www.museocinema.it; adult/concession €7/5; ⏲9am-8pm Tue-Fri & Sun, to 11pm Sat). Don't miss the glass **panoramic lift** (adult/concession €5/3.50; ⏲10am-8pm Tue-Fri & Sun, to 11pm Sat), which whisks you up 85m in 59 seconds. Joint tickets for the museum and lift cost €9/7.

Museo Egizio MUSEUM

(www.museoegizio.it; Via Accademia delle Scienze 6; adult/concession €7.50/3.50; ⏲8.30am-7.30pm Tue-Sun) This fabulous museum boasts the world's most important collection of ancient Egyptian art outside of Cairo and London.

Pinacoteca Giovanni e Marella Agnelli MUSEUM

(www.pinacoteca-agnelli.it; Via Nizza 262; permanent exhibitions €4; ⏲10am-7pm Tue-Sun) A Renzo Piano–designed art gallery in the Lingotto, Fiat's former car factory.

Castello di Rivoli Museo d'Arte Contemporanea MUSEUM

(www.castellodirivoli.org; Piazza Mafalda di Savoia; admission €6.50; ⏲10am-5pm Tue-Thu, 10am-9pm Fri-Sun) A modern art gallery in a castle a few kilometres outside of Turin.

Sleeping & Eating

Hotel Montevecchio HOTEL €

(☎011 562 00 23; www.hotelmontevecchio.com; Via Montevecchio 13; s €45-90, d €60-120; @) Conveniently located about 300m from Porta Nuova train station, this is a friendly, well-run two-star. Rooms come in sunny shades of yellow and there's a long list of extras including wi-fi (€10 per day).

Da Ciro PIZZERIA €

(☎011 531 925; Corso Vinzaglio 17; pizzas from €5.50; ⏲closed Sat lunch & Sun) A favourite of

Juventus footballers – ex-Juve legend Ciro Ferrara is a part-owner – this is a little bit of Naples in the north. Diners pile into the cheery, unpretentious interior to tear into delicious wood-fired pizzas. Booking recommended.

Otto Etre Quarti PIZZERIA & RESTAURANT €€
(☎011 517 63 67; Piazza Solferino 8C; pizzas from €5, mains €12) Claim a table in one of 8¾'s high-ceilinged dining rooms or on the square-side terrace and feast on fab pizzas or tasty pasta dishes such as *paccheri con tonno* (big pasta tubes with tuna).

Alpi Resort Hotel BUSINESS HOTEL €
(☎011 812 96 77; www.hotelalpiresort.it; Via A Bonafous 5; s €54-65, d €69-85; P ❄) A business-like three-star in an excellent location just off Piazza Vittorio Veneto. Its impeccably clean, carpeted rooms are quiet and comfortable, if rather characterless.

Turin has a reputation for magnificent gelato, which you can sample at outlets of **Grom** (⏲11am-midnight Sun-Thu, to 1am Fri & Sat) at Piazza Paleocapa 1d, Via Accademia delle Scienze 4 and Via Garibaldi 11.

Early evening is the time to make for one of the city's cafes and enjoy an *aperitivo* accompanied by a sumptuous buffet (included in the price). The most happening *aperitivo* precinct is Piazza Emanuele Filiberto and environs: try **Pastis** (Piazza Emanuele Filiberto 9) or **I Tre Galli** (Via Sant'Agostino 25; ⏲Mon-Sat). The *aperitivo* drinks cost around €8.

Information

The city's efficient **tourist office** (☎010 53 51 81; www.turismotorino.org; ⏲9am-7pm daily) has branches at Porta Nuova station, Piazza Castello and Via Giuseppe Verdi near the Mole Antonelliana.

Getting There & Around

In Caselle, 16km northwest of the city centre, **Turin Airport** (TRN; ☎011 567 63 61; www.turin-airport.com) serves flights to/from European and national destinations. **Sadem** (☎800 801 600; www.sadem.it, in Italian) runs an airport shuttle (€5.50 or €6 on board, 40 minutes, half-hourly) between the airport and Porta Nuova train station. It operates between 5.15am and 11pm.

Direct trains connect Turin with Florence (€67, three hours, five daily), Genoa (€15, two hours, up to 20 daily), Milan (€14.50, two hours, up to 30 daily) and Rome (€93, 4¼ hours, seven daily).

Milan

POP 1.29 MILLION

Few Italian cities polarise opinion like Milan, Italy's financial and fashion capital. Some people love the cosmopolitan, can-do atmosphere, the vibrant cultural scene and sophisticated shopping; others grumble that it's dirty, ugly and expensive. Certainly, it is not cheap, but in among the urban hustle are some truly great sights – Leonardo da Vinci's *The Last Supper,* the immense Duomo and the world-famous La Scala opera house.

Originally founded by Celtic tribes in the 7th century BC, Milan was conquered by the Romans in 222 BC and developed into a major trading and transport centre. From the 13th century it flourished under the rule of two powerful families, the Visconti and the Sforza.

Sights

Milan's main attractions are concentrated in the area between Piazza del Duomo and Castello Sforzesco. To get to the piazza from Stazione Centrale, take the yellow MM3 underground line.

Duomo CHURCH
(Piazza del Duomo; ⏲7am-7pm) With a capacity of 40,000 people, this is the world's largest Gothic cathedral and the third-largest church in Europe. Commissioned in 1386 to a florid French-Gothic design and finished nearly 600 years later, it's a fairy-tale ensemble of 3400 statues, 135 spires and 155 gargoyles. Climb up to the **roof** (stairs/elevator €5/8; ⏲stairs 9am-5.20pm, lift 9am-9.15pm) for memorable city views.

Teatro alla Scala OPERA HOUSE
(www.teatroallascala.org; Piazza delle Scala; admission €5; ⏲9am-12.30pm & 1.30-5.30pm) The elegant **Galleria Vittorio Emanuele II** shopping arcade leads from Piazza del Duomo through to Milan's legendary opera house. You can peek inside as part of a visit to the theatre's museum providing there are no performances or rehearsals in progress.

The Last Supper (Cenacolo Vinciano) PAINTING
(☎02 928 00 360; www.vivaticket.it; Piazza Santa Maria delle Grazie 2; adult/concession €6.50/3.25 plus booking fee of €1.50; ⏲8.15am-6.45pm Tue-Sun) Milan's most famous tourist attraction, Leonardo da Vinci's mural of *The Last Supper* is in the Cenacolo Vinciano, west of

the city centre. To see it you'll need to book ahead or take a city tour.

Castello Sforzesco CASTLE
(www.milanocastello.it; Piazza Castello 3; admission free; ⏲7am-7pm) This dramatic 15th-century castle was the Renaissance residence of the Sforza dynasty. It now houses the **Musei del Castello** (adult/concession €3/1.50; ⏲9am-5.30pm Tue-Sun), a group of museums dedicated to art, sculpture, furniture, archaeology and music. Entry to the museums is free on Friday between 2pm and 5.30pm and Tuesday to Sunday between 4.30pm and 5.30pm.

Pinacoteca di Brera ART GALLERY
(www.brera.beniculturali.it; Via Brera 28; adult/EU concession €11/8.50; ⏲8.30am-7.15pm Tue-Sun) Art amassed by Napoleon forms the basis for the Pinacoteca's heavyweight collection, which includes Andrea Mantegna's masterpiece, the *Dead Christ*, and Raphael's *Betrothal of the Virgin*.

Sleeping

Accommodation is ridiculously expensive in Milan, particularly when trade fairs are on (which is often). Booking is essential at all times of the year.

Hotel De Albertis HOTEL €€
(☎02 738 34 09; www.hoteldealbertis.it; Via De Albertis 7; s €50-100, d €50-160; @📶) Way out from the centre in a leafy residential street, this small hotel is a welcoming, family-run affair. There are few frills but rooms are clean, comfortable and quiet. Take bus 92 from Stazione Centrale or tram 27 from the Duomo.

Hotel Nuovo HOTEL €€
(☎02 864 64 444; www.hotelnuovomilano.com; Piazza Beccaria 6; r €50-150; ❄📶) In a city where 'cheap' is an ugly word, the Nuovo is a bastion of budget accommodation. Rooms are basic but clean, and the location, just off Corso Vittorio Emanuele II, is a winner. No breakfast.

Ostello Piero Rotta HOSTEL €
(☎02 392 67 095; www.hostelmilan.org; Via Salmoiraghi 1; dm €19.50; 📶) Often used by travelling football fans, Milan's HI hostel is about 10 minutes from the San Siro stadium. Low on atmosphere, it's cheap, clean and well equipped.

Eating & Drinking

There are hundreds of bars and restaurants in Milan, but as a rough guide, the area around the Duomo is full of smart business orientated restaurants, Brera is a fashionable bar haunt and the lively Navigli canal district caters to all tastes. Corso Como and environs is another good area for a stylish drink.

Pizzeria Piccola Ischia PIZZERIA €
(☎02 204 76 13; Via Morgani 7; pizzas €6.50; ⏲closed Wed & lunch Sat & Sun) You might be in the heart of Milan but this bustling, boisterous pizzeria is pure Naples. Everything from the wonderful wood-fired pizza to the fried antipasti and exuberant decor screams of the sunny south. It's hugely popular so expect queues. Also does takeaway.

Premiata Pizzeria PIZZERIA €
(☎02 894 00 648; Via Alzaia Naviglio Grande 2; pizzas €7-12) The ideal spot for a bite in fashionable Navigli. Right on the canal, perennially busy Premiata serves up huge thick-crust pizzas as well as focaccia and a full menu of pastas and mains.

Rinomata GELATERIA €
(☎02 581 13 877; Ripa di Porta Ticinese; ice creams €2.50) If dining in Navigli, skip dessert and grab an ice cream from this historic hole-in-the-wall gelateria. Its fabulous interior features old-fashioned fridges and glass-fronted cabinets filled with cones – and the gelato is good, too.

Zucca in Galleria CAFE €
(Galleria Vittorio Emanuele II 21) Grab a coffee (but skip the overpriced food) at the cafe where Giuseppe Verdi used to drink after performances at the Teatro all Scala.

Entertainment

The opera season at **Teatro alla Scala** (☎02 720 03 744; www.teatroallascala.org; Piazza della Scala) runs from November to July but you can see theatre, ballet and concerts year-round, apart from August. Tickets are available online or from the **box office** (Galleria del Sagrato, Piazza del Duomo; ⏲noon-6pm) beneath Piazza del Duomo. Bank on €26 to €224 for opera and €19 to €138 for ballet performances.

For jazz lovers, **Blue Note** (☎02 690 16 888; www.bluenotemilano.com; Via Borsieri 37; tickets €20-40) stages top international and Italian performers.

A mecca for football fans, the **Stadio Giuseppe Meazza** (Via Piccolomini 5; Ⓜ Lotto) is home to AC Milan and Internazionale. Match tickets (from €23) are available from branches of Banca Intesa (AC Milan) and Banca Popolare di Milano (Inter). To get to the stadium on match days, take the free

Central Milan

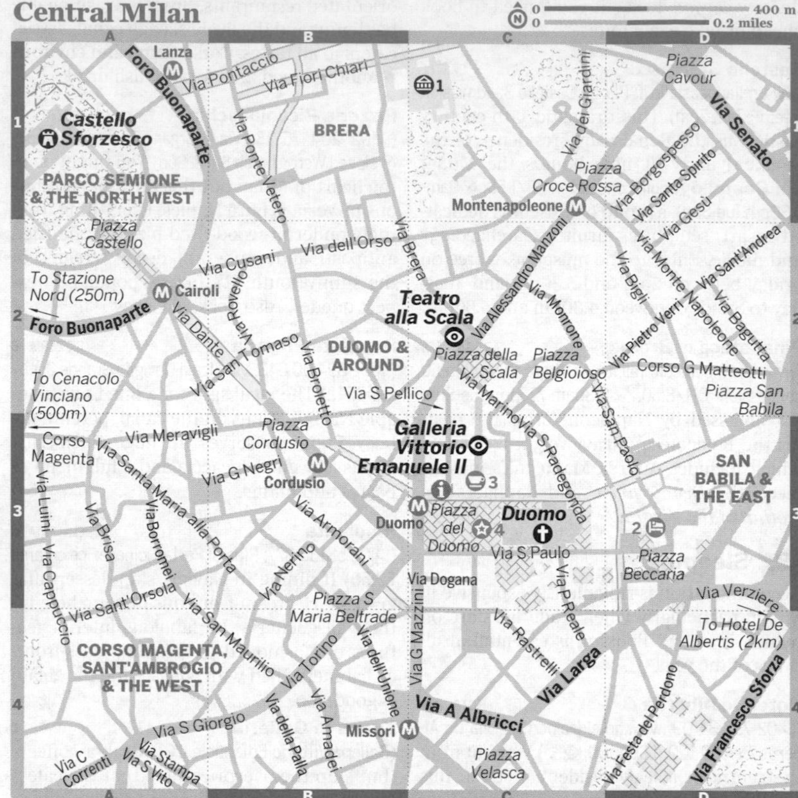

shuttle bus from the Lotto (MM1) metro station.

Information

Pharmacy (☎02 669 07 35; Stazione Centrale; ⏲24hr)

Police station (Questura; ☎02 622 61; Via Fatebenefratelli 11)

Tourist offices (www.visitamilano.it) Piazza del Duomo (☎02 774 04 343; Piazza Duomo 19a; ⏲8.45am-1pm & 2-6pm Mon-Sat, 9am-1pm & 2-5pm Sun); Stazione Centrale (☎02 774 04 318; opposite platform 13; ⏲9am-6pm Mon-Sat, 9am-1pm & 2-5pm Sun) Pick up the free guides *Hello Milano* and *Milanomese*.

Getting There & Away

Air

Most international flights fly into **Malpensa airport** (MXP; ☎02 23 23 23; www.sea-aeroportimilano.it), about 50km northwest of Milan. Domestic and some European flights serve **Linate airport** (LIN; ☎02 23 23 23; www.sea-aeroportimilano.it), about 7km east of the city. Low-cost airlines often use **Orio al Serio airport** (BGY; ☎035 32 63 23; www.sacbo.it), near Bergamo.

Train

Regular daily trains depart **Stazione Centrale** for Bologna (€41, one hour), Florence (€52, 1¾ hours), Rome (€89, 3½ hours), Venice (€30.15, 2½ hours) and other Italian and European cities. Most regional trains stop at Stazione Nord in Piazzale Cadorna. Note that these prices are for the fast Eurostar Alta Velocità services.

Getting Around

To/From the Airport

MALPENSA **Malpensa Shuttle** (www.malpensashuttle.it; adult/concession €7.50/3.75) Buses run to/from Piazza Luigi di Savoia next to Stazione Centrale every 20 minutes between 4.15am and 12.30pm. Buy tickets at Stazione Centrale or the airport. Journey time is 50 minutes.

Central Milan

Top Sights

Sights

Sleeping

Drinking

Entertainment

Malpensa Bus Express (www.autostradale.it; adult/concession €7.50/3.75) To/from Piazza Luigi di Savoia half-hourly between 4.30am and 11pm.The trip takes 50 minutes.

Malpensa Express (www.malpensaexpress.it; adult/concession €11/5.50) Trains from Cadorna underground station half-hourly between 5.57am and 11pm; the 11.27pm run is by bus. Journey time is approximately 35 minutes.

LINATE **Starfly** (www.starfly.net; ticket €4) Buses to/from Piazza Luigi di Savoia half-hourly between 5.40am and 9.30pm. Journey time is 30 minutes. Buy tickets at newsstands or on board.

ATM (www.atm-mi.it; ticket €1) Local bus 73 runs every 10 minutes between 5.35am and 12.35pm from Piazza San Babila.

ORIO AL SERIO **Autostradale** (www.autostradale.it; adult/concession €8.90/4.45) Half-hourly buses to/from Piazza Luigi di Savoia between 4am and 11.30pm. Journey time is one hour.

Bus & Metro

Milan's excellent public transport system is run by **ATM** (www.atm-mi.it). Tickets (€1) are valid for one underground ride or up to 75 minutes travel on city buses and trams. You can buy them at metro stations, *tabacchi* and newsstands.

Verona

POP 265,370

The setting for Shakespeare's *Romeo and Juliet,* Verona is one of Italy's most beautiful and romantic cities. Known as *piccola Roma* (little Rome) for its importance in imperial days, its heyday came in the 13th and 14th centuries under the rule of the Della Scala (aka Scaligeri) family, who built *palazzi* and bridges, were patrons to Giotto, Dante and Petrarch, oppressed their subjects and feuded with everyone else.

Sights & Activities

The **Verona Card** (www.veronacard.it; 1/3 days €10/15) covers city transport and the main monuments. It's available from tourist offices and most sights.

Arena di Verona ROMAN AMPHITHEATRE
(www.arena.it; Piazza Brà; adult/concession €6/4.50; 1.30-7.30pm Mon, 8.30am-7.30pm Tue-Sun Oct-May, 8.30am-3.30pm Jun-Aug) In Piazza Brà, the 1st-century pink marble Arena is the third-largest Roman amphitheatre in existence, with a capacity of 20,000. These days it's most famous as Verona's summer opera house.

Casa di Giulietta MUSEUM
(Via Cappello 23; courtyard free, museum adult/concession €6/4.50; 1.30-7.30pm Mon, 8.30am-7.30pm Tue-Sun) From the Arena, walk along Via Mazzini, Verona's premier shopping strip, to Via Cappello and Juliet's house. Romantic superstition suggests that rubbing the right breast of Juliet's statue will bring you a new lover. Further along the street is **Porta Leoni**, one of the city's Roman gates; the other, **Porta Borsari**, is north of the Arena.

Piazza delle Erbe & Around SQUARE
Set over the city's Roman forum, **Piazza delle Erbe** is lined with sumptuous *palazzi* and filled with touristy market stalls. Through the **Arco della Costa**, **Piazza dei Signori** is flanked by the **Loggia del Consiglio**, the medieval town hall regarded as Verona's finest Renaissance structure, and **Palazzo degli Scaligeri**, the former residence of the Della Scala family.

Sleeping

High-season prices apply during the opera season (late June to the end of August), when it's absolutely essential to book ahead.

Hotel Aurora HOTEL €€
(045 59 47 17; www.hotelaurora.biz; Piazza delle Erbe; s €90-135, d €100-160;) This top-of-the-range two-star has friendly staff and clean and comfortable rooms with an understated decor. The lavish breakfast can be enjoyed on a lovely terrace overlooking Piazza delle Erbe.

Appartamenti L'Ospite APARTMENT €€
(045 803 69 94; www.lospite.com; Via XX Settembre 3; apt for 1 or 2 persons €55-200, for 3 or 4

persons €65-200;) Over the river from the *centro storico,* L'Ospite has six self-contained apartments for up to four people. Simple and bright with fully equipped kitchens, they come with wi-fi and are ideal for longer stays.

Ostello Villa Francescatti HOSTEL €
(045 59 03 60, fax 045 80 09 127; Salita Fontana del Ferro 15; dm €18.50-20, d €37-40; P) This HI hostel is housed in a 16th-century villa set in extensive grounds. To save yourself a steep uphill walk, take bus 73 from the train station (bus 90 on Sunday). There's a strict 11.30pm curfew.

Eating

Boiled meats are a Veronese speciality, as is crisp Soave white wine.

Al Pompiere TRATTORIA €€
(045 803 05 37; http://alpompiere.tv; Vicolo Regina d'Ungheria 5; mains €12-24; Tue-Sat, dinner Mon) There's no secret to the success of this much-loved trattoria – it serves top-notch, seasonally inspired food and has welcoming surroundings. It's particularly noted for its platters of cheese and *salumi* (home-cured meats).

Salumeria G Albertini DELICATESSEN €
(045 803 10 74; www.salumeriaalbertini.it; Corso Sant'Anastasia 41; closed Sun) Albertini has been the place to source picnic provisions ever since 1939. Its range of local artisan meats, cheese and wine will make an alfresco meal by the river or inside the amphitheatre the stuff of which lasting memories are made.

Entertainment

The opera season at the Roman **Arena** (045 800 51 51; www.arena.it; tickets €23-198) runs from late June to the end of August.

Nightlife is centred on the bars and trattorias of Via Sottoriva.

Information

Tourist offices (www.tourism.verona.it) Airport (045 861 91 63; 10am-4pm Mon & Tue, 10am-5pm Wed-Sat); city centre (045 806 86 80; Piazza Brà; 9am-7pm Mon-Sat, 10am-4pm Sun); train station (045 800 08 61; 9am-7pm Mon-Sat, 9am-3pm Sun).

Getting There & Around

AIR Verona Valerio Catullo Airport (VRN; 045 809 56 66; www.aeroportidelgarda.it) is 12km outside the city and accessible by bus from the train station (€4.50, 20 minutes, every 20 minutes between 5.40am and 11.10pm). Ryanair flies to **Brescia airport** (VBS; 030 965 65 99), from where **CGA** (www.cgabrescia.it) shuttle buses (€11, 45 minutes, one daily) connect to Verona's main train station.

BUS From the main bus terminal in front of the train station, AMT bus 72 runs to Piazza Erbe and buses 11, 12 and 13 go to the Arena. Tickets cost €1.10 or €1.20 if purchased on the bus.

TRAIN Verona is directly linked by train to Bologna (€13.50, two hours, six daily), Milan (€17.50, two hours, every 45 minutes), Rome (€64 to €80.50, 4¼ hours, hourly) and Venice (€18.50, 1¼ hours, half-hourly).

VERONA SPLURGE

Established in 1890, **Antica Bottega del Vino** (045 800 45 35; www.bottegavini.it; Via Scudo di Francia 3; mains €15-35; closed Tue) is a wine bar-restaurant that makes one of the essential stops while you're in town. You can enjoy a glass of wine from a mind-boggling array of choices while standing at the bar, or book a table for a meal. The food is rustic and delicious – freshly made *bigoli all'anatra* (pasta with a duck *ragù*), soupy *risotto all'Amarone* (rice cooked with Amarone wine) and a variety of perfectly cooked meat dishes.

Padua

POP 211,940

The lively university city of Padua (Padova) is a fun place to hang out, but what really makes it special are the stunning frescoes in the Cappella degli Scrovegni. From the train station, follow Corso del Popolo and its continuation Corso Garibaldi until you see a park on your left – walk alongside the park, turn left into Via Eremitani and you'll soon come to the *cappella,* which is next to the Chiesa degli Eremitani.

Sights & Activities

The **PadovaCard** (www.padovacard.it; 2/3 days €15/20), available from tourist offices and participating sights, provides free public transport and entry to many sights, including the Cappella degli Scrovegni (plus €1 booking fee).

Cappella degli Scrovegni CHURCH
(☎049 201 00 20; www.cappelladegliscrovegni.it; Piazza Eremitani 8; tickets incl multimedia room & Musei Civici agli Eremitani adult/concession €13/6; ⏲9am-7pm) This medieval chapel is home to Giotto's extraordinary frescoes. The 38 colourful panels (c 1304–06) depicting Christ's life cover the chapel from floor to ceiling. Visits, for which you'll need to book at least 24 hours in advance, are limited to 15 minutes. From March to November (and also over the Christmas week), the Cappella is open until 10pm every day except Monday. Tickets for these evening openings cost adult/concession €8/6.

The picture galleries in the adjacent **Musei Civici agli Eremitani** are home to an impressive collection of paintings and sculptures, including two Giottos.

Basilica di Sant'Antonio CHURCH
(Piazza del Santo; ⏲6.20am-7.45pm Apr-Oct, till 6.45pm Nov-Feb) On the other side of the *centro storic,* Padua's much-loved cathedral is one of Italy's major pilgrimage sights. The big draw is the surprisingly gaudy tomb of St Anthony, the city's patron saint.

Sleeping

Belludi 37 BOUTIQUE HOTEL €€
(☎049 66 56 33; www.belludi37.it; Via Luca Belludi 37; s without bathroom €57-80, d €120-150; ❄P@) Overlooking the Basilica di Sant'Antonio, this sleek boutique hotel offers good-sized rooms and is known for its personal service. It offers tours of the city's markets and *enoteche* (wine bars), as well as bike hire.

Ostello Città di Padova HOSTEL €
(☎049 875 22 19; www.ostellopadova.it; Via Aleardo Aleardi 30; dm from €19; 📶) Padua's HI hostel has an offputting institutional feel and rigid opening hours (7.15am to 9.30am and 4.30pm to 11.30pm). Two-, four-, six- and eight-bed rooms are on offer, some of which have their own bathroom.

Hotel Sant'Antonio HOTEL €
(☎049 875 13 93; www.hotelsantantonio.it; Via San Fermo 118; s €63-69, d €82-94, s without bathroom €39-42; ❄) On the edge of the historic centre, the three-star Sant'Antonio is a safe, if rather staid, option, with quiet, unfussy rooms. Breakfast costs €7 extra.

Eating & Drinking

L'Anfora OSTERIA €€
(☎049 65 66 29; Via dei Sconcin 13; mains €10-15; ⏲closed Sun) A laid-back *osteria* with bare wooden tables and racked wine bottles, L'Anfora's menu changes daily and is full of products and dishes typical of Venice. The nearby **Antica Osteria dal Capo** (☎049 66 31 05; Via degli Obizzi, 2; mains €10-16; ⏲closed Sun all day & lunch Mon) also offers an atmospheric setting and regional menu.

There are a number of stylish *enoteche* in Padua, including **Godenda** (☎049 877 41 92; Via Squarcione, 4; mains €15; ⏲closed Sun all year & Mon in summer), near Piazza dei Signori, and **Enoteca Cortes** (☎049 871 97 97; Riviera Paleocapa 7; mains €16-22; ⏲from 6pm Tue-Sun), to the southwest of the centre.

WORTH A TRIP

MANTUA

The beautiful Unesco-listed town of Mantua (Mantova) is an easy day trip from Verona. Best known as the place where Shakespeare exiled Romeo, it was for centuries (1328–1707) the stronghold of the Gonzaga family, one of Italy's most powerful Renaissance dynasties.

The **tourist office** (☎0376 43 24 32; www.turismo.mantova.it; Piazza Andrea Mantegna 6; ⏲9am-6pm) is close to the city's major attraction, the enormous **Palazzo Ducale** (www.ducalemantova.org; Piazza Sordello; adult/concession €6.50/3.25; ⏲8.30am-7pm Tue-Sun). The highlight of this former seat of the Gonzaga family is its **Camera degli Sposi** (Bridal Chamber), home to extraordinary 15th-century frescoes by Andrea Mantegna. To visit the Camera you need to book ahead of time (☎041 241 18 97).

The best way to get here is by train from Verona (€2.55, 45 minutes).

Information

Tourist offices (www.turismopadova.it) Galleria Pedrocchi (☎049 876 79 27; ⏲9am-1.30pm & 3-7pm Mon-Sat); Piazza Del Santo (☎049 875 30 87; ⏲9am-1.30pm & 3-6pm Mon-Sat, 10am-1pm & 3-6pm Sun Apr-Oct only); train station (☎049 875 20 77; ⏲9am-7pm Mon-Sat, 9am-12.30pm Sun) Pick up the free *Padova Today* magazine.

Getting There & Away

SITA (☎049 820 68 44; www.sitabus.it, in Italian) buses leave from the bus station immediately east of the train station to Venice (€3.55, 45 minutes, hourly) and Marco Polo airport (€3.55, 30 minutes, hourly).

There are regional trains to/from Bologna (€7.45, 1½ hours, hourly), Venice (€2.90, 45 minutes, every 20 minutes) and Verona (€4.95, 1½ hours, hourly).

Venice

POP 270,100

Arriving in Venice (Venezia) is like stepping into a surreal never-never land. Where most cities have car-choked roads and impenetrable one-way systems, Venice has canals, gondolas and *vaporetti* (water buses). But the beauty comes at a price, both for you (Venice is Italy's most expensive city) and for the city itself: Venice's frequently flooded alleyways simply weren't designed for up to 20 million visitors a year.

Surprisingly, though, it's still possible to escape the crowds. Away from Piazza San Marco and the main monuments, there are parts of the city that rarely see many tourists. Make for the back lanes of the Dorsoduro and Castello *sestieri* (districts) for a glimpse of Venice's beguiling and melancholic nature.

History

Venice's origins date to the 5th and 6th centuries, when barbarian invasions forced the Veneto's inhabitants to seek refuge on the lagoon's islands. The city was initially ruled by the Byzantines from Ravenna, but in AD 726 the Venetians elected their first *doge* (duke).

Over successive centuries the Venetian Republic grew into a great merchant power, dominating half the Mediterranean, the Adriatic and the trade routes to the Levant – it was from Venice that Marco Polo set out for China in 1271. Decline began in the 16th century and in 1797 the city authorities opened the gates to Napoleon who, in turn, handed the city over to the Austrians. In 1866 Venice was incorporated into the Kingdom of Italy.

Sights

Venice is not an easy place to navigate and even with a map you're bound to get lost (although that's half the fun of the place). The main area of interest lies between Santa Lucia train station and Piazza San Marco (St Mark's Sq). The signposted path between the two (the nearest Venice has to a main drag) is a good 40- to 50-minute walk. It also helps to know that the city is divided into six districts – Cannaregio, Castello, San Marco, Dorsoduro, San Polo and Santa Croce.

A good way to whet your sightseeing appetite is to take *vaporetto* 1 along the **Grand Canal**, which is lined with rococo Gothic, Moorish and Renaissance palaces. Alight at Piazza San Marco, Venice's most famous sight.

Piazza San Marco SQUARE

Piazza San Marco beautifully encapsulates the splendour of Venice's past and its tourist-fuelled present. Flanked by the arcaded **Procuratie Vecchie** and **Procuratie Nuove**, it's filled for much of the day with tourists, pigeons and policemen. While you're taking it all in, you might see the bronze *Mori* (Moors) strike the bell of the 15th-century **Torre dell'Orologio** (Map p724; clock tower).

But it's to the remarkable **Basilica di San Marco** (Map p724; www.basilicasanmarco.it; Piazza San Marco; admission free; ⌚9.45am-5pm Mon-Sat, 2-5pm Sun Easter-Oct, to 4pm Sun Nov-Easter) that all eyes are drawn. Sporting spangled spires, Byzantine domes, luminous mosaics and lavish marble work, it was originally built to house the remains of St Mark. The original chapel was destroyed by fire in AD 932 and a new basilica was consecrated in its place in 1094. For the next 500 years it was a work in progress as successive *doges* added mosaics and embellishments looted from the East. Behind the main altar is the **Pala d'Oro** (admission €2.50), a stunning gold altarpiece decorated with priceless jewels.

The basilica's 99m freestanding **campanile** (Map p724; bell tower; admission €8; ⌚9am-7pm Easter-Jun & Oct, to 9pm Jul–Sep, 9.30am-3.45pm Nov-Easter) dates from the 10th century, although it suddenly collapsed on 14 July 1902 and had to be rebuilt.

Palazzo Ducale PALACE

(Map p724; Piazzetta di San Marco; admission with Museum Pass or San Marco Museum Plus Ticket; ⌚9am-7pm Apr-Oct, to 6pm Nov-Mar) The official residence of the *doges* from the 9th century and the seat of the Republic's government, Palazzo Ducale also housed Venice's prisons. On the 2nd floor, the massive **Sala del Maggiore Consiglio** is dominated by Tintoretto's *Paradiso* (Paradise), one of the world's largest oil paintings, which measures 22m by 7m.

The **Ponte dei Sospiri** (Map p724; Bridge of Sighs) connects the palace to an additional wing of the city dungeons. It's named after the sighs that prisoners – including Giacomo Casanova – emitted en route from court to cell.

Galleria dell'Accademia ART GALLERY

(Map p724; www.gallerieaccademia.org; Dorsoduro 1050; adult/EU concession €6.50/3.25; ⌚8.15am-

ADMISSION DISCOUNTS

The **Rolling Venice Card** (www.hellovenezia.com; €4) is for visitors aged 14 to 29 years; it offers discounts on food, accommodation, shopping, transport and museums. You can get it at tourist offices and at HelloVenezia booths. You'll need ID.

The **Venice Card Orange** (www.hellovenezia.com; under 30yr 3/7 days €66/87, 30yr & over €73/96) entitles holders to free entry to 12 city museums (including Palazzo Ducale), free entry to the 16 Chorus churches, unlimited use of public transport, limited use of public toilets and reduced admission to various museums and events. It doesn't always represent a saving, so check before buying. It's sold at tourist and HelloVenezia offices.

To visit the museums on Piazza San Marco you'll need to buy either a **Museum Pass** (www.museicivicivenezani.it; adult/EU concession €18/12), which gives entry to the museums on Piazza San Marco and eight other civic museums; or a **San Marco Museum Plus Ticket** (€13/7.50), which gives entry to the San Marco Museums and your choice of one other civic museum. Both are available at participating museums. Discount passes – including an afternoon pass to the museums on Piazza San Marco that costs €10/4.50 – can be purchased in advance at www.veniceconnected.com.

The **Chorus Pass** (www.chorusvenezia.org; adult/concession €10/7) covers admission to 16 of Venice's major churches and is available online or at the churches. Otherwise entry to each church costs €3.

2pm Mon, to 7.15pm Tue-Sun) One of Venice's top galleries, the Galleria dell'Accademia traces the development of Venetian art from the 14th to the 18th century. You'll find works by Bellini, Titian, Carpaccio, Tintoretto, Giorgione and Veronese.

Collezione Peggy Guggenheim ART GALLERY
(Map p724; www.guggenheim-venice.it; Palazzo Venier dei Leoni, Dorsoduro 701; adult/concession €12/7; ⏲10am-6pm Wed-Mon) Housed in the US heiress' former home, this spellbinding collection runs the gamut of modern art with works by, among others, Picasso, Pollock, Braque, Duchamp and Brancusi.

Churches CHURCHES
As in much of Italy, Venice's churches harbour innumerable treasures; unusually, though, you have to pay to get into many of them. See the boxed text, p719.

Scene of the annual Festa del Redentore, the **Chiesa del Santissimo Redentore** (Church of the Redeemer; Map p720; Campo del SS Redentore 194; admission €3, included in Chorus Pass; ⏲10am-5pm Mon-Sat) was built by Palladio to commemorate the end of the Great Plague in 1577.

Guarding the entrance to the Grand Canal, the 17th-century **Chiesa di Santa Maria della Salute** (Map p724; Campo della Salute 1/b; sacristy €2; ⏲9am-noon & 3.30-5.30pm) contains works by Tintoretto and Titian. Arguably the greatest of Venice's artists, Titian's celebrated masterpiece the *Assunta* (Assumption; 1518) hangs above the high altar in the **Basilica di Santa Maria Gloriosa dei Frari** (off Map p724; Campo dei Frari, San Polo 3004; admission €3, included in Chorus Pass; ⏲10am-6pm Mon-Sat, 1-6pm Sun), the same church in which he's buried.

The Lido BEACH
A thin strip of an island about a 15-minute *vaporetto* ride from Venice proper, the Lido hosts the Venice Film Festival and boasts the city's best beach. Be warned, though, that it's almost impossible to find space on the sand in summer. It's accessible by *vaporetti* 1, 2, 8, LN, 51, 52, 61 and 62.

Islands ISLANDS
Murano is the home of Venetian glass. Tour a factory for a behind-the-scenes look at production or visit the **Glass Museum** (Fondamenta Giustinian 8; adult/EU concession €6.50/3; ⏲10am-6pm Apr-Oct, 10am-5pm Thu-Tue Nov-Mar); you'll find it near the Museo *vaporetto* stop. **Burano**, with its cheery pastel-coloured houses, is renowned for its lace. **Torcello**, the republic's original island settlement, was largely abandoned due to malaria and now counts no more than 80 residents. Its not-to-be-missed Byzantine cathedral, **Santa Maria Assunta** (Piazza Torcello; admission €5; ⏲10.30am-6pm Mar-Oct, 10am-5pm Nov-Feb), is Venice's oldest.

Vaporetti 41 and 42 service Murano from the San Zaccaria *vaporetto* stop. *Vaporetto* LN services Murano and Burano from the *vaporetto* stop at Fondamente Nove in the northeast of the city. *Vaporetto* T connects Burano and Torcello.

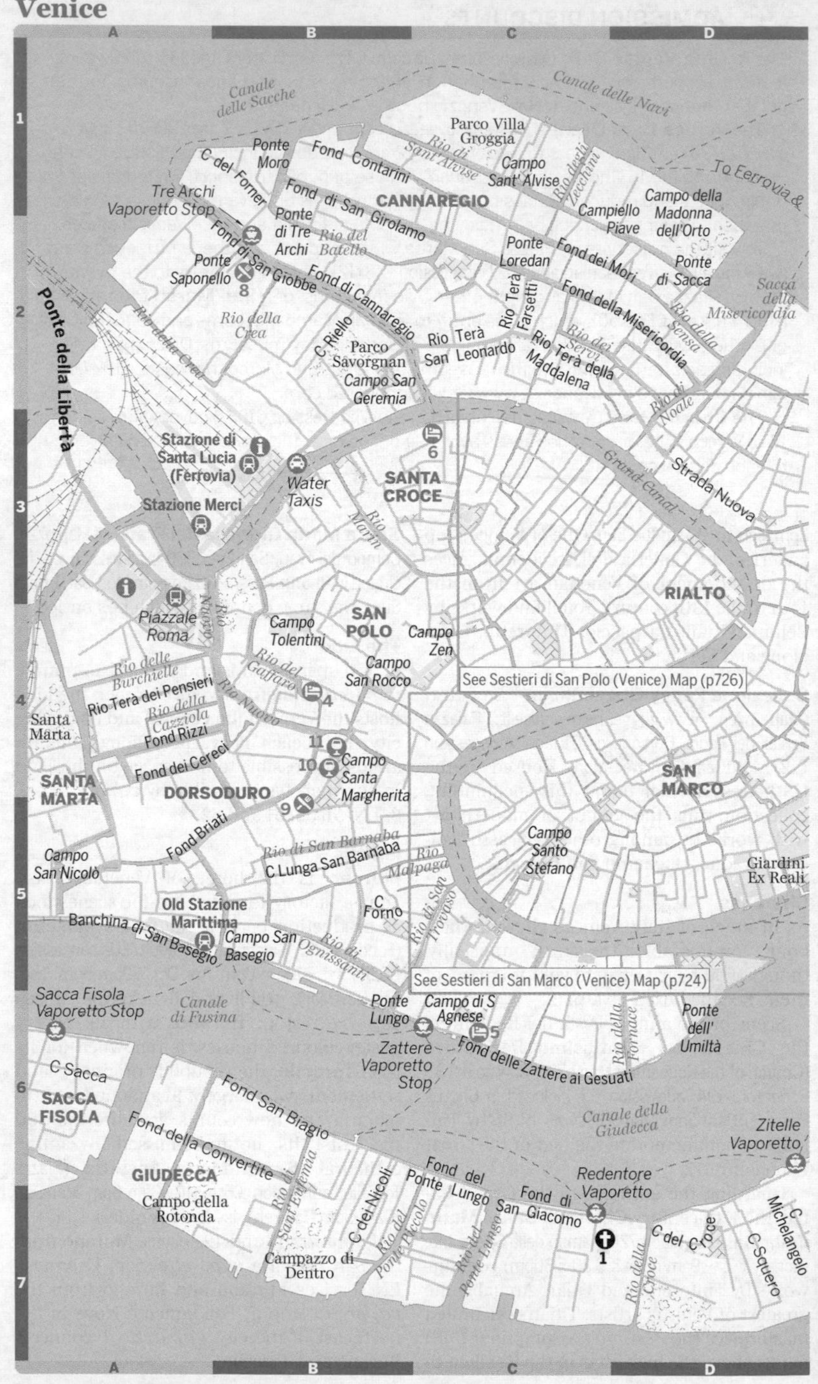
Canale delle Sacche
Canale delle Navi
Parco Villa Groggia
Rio di Sant'Alvise
Campo Sant'Alvise
Rio degli Zecchini
To Ferrovia &
Ponte Moro
Fond Contarini
C del Forner
CANNAREGIO
Tre Archi Vaporetto Stop
Fond di San Girolamo
Campo della Madonna dell'Orto
Campiello Piave
Ponte di Tre Archi
Rio del Batello
Ponte Loredan
Fond dei Mori
Ponte di Sacca
Fond di San Giobbe
Ponte Saponello
Fond di Cannaregio
Rio Terà Farsetti
Fond della Misericordia
Sacca della Misericordia
Rio della Sensa
Ponte della Libertà
Rio della Crea
C Riello
Parco Savorgnan
Rio Terà San Leonardo
Rio dei Servi
Rio Terà della Maddalena
Campo San Geremia
Rio di Noale
Stazione di Santa Lucia (Ferrovia)
Water Taxis
SANTA CROCE
Grand Canal
Strada Nuova
Stazione Merci
Rio Marin
RIALTO
Piazzale Roma
Rio Nuovo
Campo Tolentini
SAN POLO
Campo Zen
Rio delle Burchielle
Rio del Gaffaro
Campo San Rocco
See Sestieri di San Polo (Venice) Map (p726)
Rio Terà dei Pensieri
Rio della Cazziola
Fond Rizzi
Santa Marta
Campo Santa Margherita
Fond dei Cereci
SANTA MARTA
DORSODURO
SAN MARCO
Fond Briati
Rio di San Barnaba
Campo Santo Stefano
Campo San Nicolò
C Lunga San Barnaba
Rio Malpaga
Giardini Ex Reali
Old Stazione Marittima
C Forno
Rio di San Trovaso
Banchina di San Basegio
Campo San Basegio
Rio di Ognissanti
See Sestieri di San Marco (Venice) Map (p724)
Sacca Fisola Vaporetto Stop
Canale di Fusina
Ponte Lungo
Campo di S Agnese
Ponte dell' Umiltà
Zattere Vaporetto Stop
Rio della Fornace
Fond delle Zattere ai Gesuati
C Sacca
SACCA FISOLA
Fond San Biagio
Canale della Giudecca
Zitelle Vaporetto
Fond della Convertite
GIUDECCA
Rio di Sant'Eufemia
Fond del Ponte Lungo
Redentore Vaporetto
Fond di San Giacomo
Campo della Rotonda
C dei Nicoli
Rio del Ponte Piccolo
Rio del Ponte Lungo
C del Croce
C Michelangelo
C Squero
Rio della Croce
Campazzo di Dentro
1
4
5
6
8
9
10
11

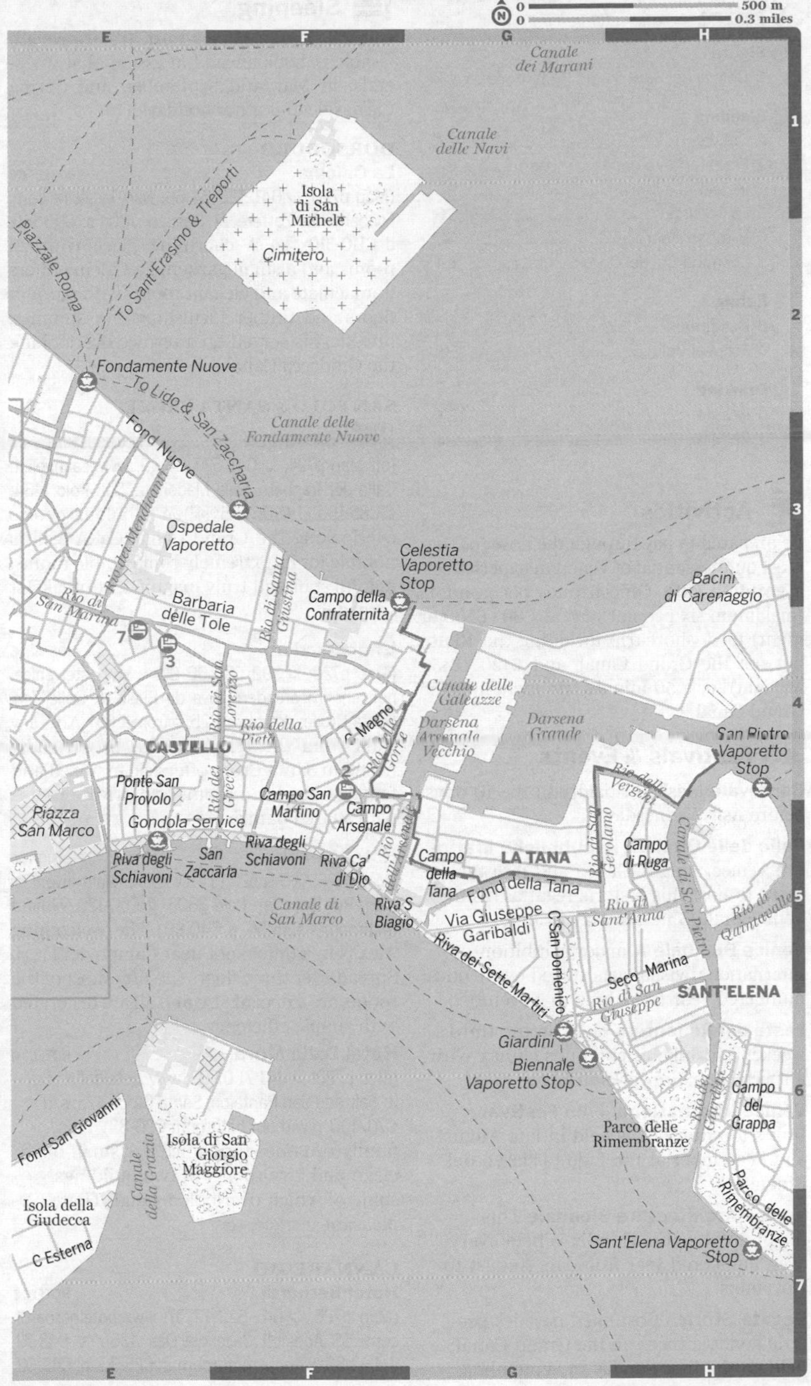

0 500 m
0 0.3 miles
Canale dei Marani
Canale delle Navi
Isola di San Michele
Cimitero
Piazzale Roma
To Sant'Erasmo & Treporti
Fondamente Nuove
To Lido & San Zaccharia
Canale delle Fondamente Nuove
Fond Nuove
Rio dei Mendicanti
Ospedale Vaporetto
Celestia Vaporetto Stop
Campo della Confraternità
Bacini di Carenaggio
Rio di San Marina
Barbaria delle Tole
Rio di Santa Giustina
Rio di San Lorenzo
Canale delle Galeazze
Darsena Arsenale Vecchio
Darsena Grande
Rio della Pietà
C Magno
Rio delle Gorne
CASTELLO
San Pietro Vaporetto Stop
Rio delle Vergini
Ponte San Provolo
Rio dei Greci
Campo San Martino
Campo Arsenale
Piazza San Marco
Gondola Service
Riva degli Schiavoni
San Zaccaria
Riva Ca' di Dio
Rio dell'Arsenale
Campo della Tana
LA TANA
Rio di San Gerolamo
Campo di Ruga
Canale di San Pietro
Fond della Tana
Canale di San Marco
Riva S Biagio
Via Giuseppe Garibaldi
C San Domenico
Rio di Sant'Anna
Rio di Quintavalle
Riva dei Sette Martiri
Seco Marina
Rio di San Giuseppe
SANT'ELENA
Giardini
Biennale Vaporetto Stop
Rio dei Giardini
Campo del Grappa
Parco delle Rimembranze
Fond San Giovanni
Isola di San Giorgio Maggiore
Canale della Grazia
Isola della Giudecca
C Esterna
Sant'Elena Vaporetto Stop

Venice

Sights

1 Chiesa del Santissimo Redentore......C7

Sleeping

2 Ca' Valeri......F4
3 Foresteria Valdese......E4
4 Hotel Della Mora......B4
5 La Calcina......C6
6 L'Imbarcadero......C3
7 Locanda Ca' del Console......E4

Eating

8 Da Marisa......B2
9 Pizza al Volo......B5

Drinking

10 Il Caffè......B4
11 Imagina Café......B4

Activities

Be prepared to pay through the nose for that most quintessential of Venetian experiences, a **gondola ride**. Official rates per gondola (maximum six people) start at €80 (€100 at night) for a short trip including the Rialto but not the Grand Canal, and €120 (€150 at night) for a 50-minute trip including the Grand Canal.

Festivals & Events

Carnevale Masked ribaldry in the 10 days before Ash Wednesday.

Palio delle Quattro Repubbliche Marinare Venice, Amalfi, Genoa and Pisa take turns to host this historic regatta. It's in Venice in 2015 in late May to June.

Venice Biennale A major exhibition of international visual arts staged every odd-numbered year from June to November.

Festa del Redentore Held on the third weekend in July; celebrations climax with a spectacular fireworks display.

Venice International Film Festival Italy's top film fest is held in late August and September at the Lido's Palazzo del Cinema.

Venice Architecture Biennale This major architecture shindig is held every even-numbered year from late August to November.

Regata Storica Costumed parades precede gondola races on the Grand Canal; held on the first Sunday in September.

Sleeping

Ouch! Prices in Venice hurt. It's always advisable to book ahead but essential at weekends, in May and September, and during Carnevale and other holidays.

DORSODURO

La Calcina HOTEL €€

(Map p720; ☎041 520 64 66; www.lacalcina.com; Fondamenta Zattere ai Gesuati 780; s €90-140, d €110-310; ❄) A charming place with 29 rooms and a small garden, La Calcina offers immaculate and elegant rooms with parquet floors and timber furnishings. In summer, breakfast is served on a terrace overlooking the Guidecca Canal.

SAN POLO & SANTA CROCE

TOP CHOICE **Ca' Angeli** BOUTIQUE HOTEL €€

(off Map p724; ☎041 523 24 80; www.caangeli.it; Calle del Tragheto della Madoneta, San Polo 1434; s €85-150, d €105-215; ❄) A fabulous choice overlooking the Grand Canal, Ca' Angeli is notable for its extremely comfortable rooms, helpful staff and truly magnificent breakfast spread.

L'Imbarcadero HOSTEL €

(Map p720; ☎392 584 06 00; www.hostelvenice.net; cnr Imbarcadero Riva de Biasio & Calle Zen, Santa Croce; dm from €25, s from €65) An easy walk from the train station, this friendly hostel in Santa Croce offers clean mixed and female-only dorm rooms and private rooms with shared bathroom.

Hotel Alex PENSION €

(Map p726; ☎041 523 13 41; www.hotelalexinvenice.com; Rio Terá, San Polo 2606; d €60-120, without bathroom s €35-56, d €40-90) The welcoming Alex is in a quiet spot near Campo dei Frari. Spread over three floors (no lift), most of the rooms are a decent size and all are decorated with simple efficiency.

Hotel Dalla Mora HOTEL €

(Map p720; ☎041 71 07 03; www.hoteldallamora.it; Salizada San Pantalon, Santa Croce 42a; s/d €70/100, d without bathroom €80-83) This family-run one-star choice has small but clean and airy rooms in two buildings, some of which overlook a canal. There's a pleasant terrace, too.

CANNAREGIO

Hotel Bernardi HOTEL €

(Map p726; ☎041 522 72 57; www.hotelbernardi.com; SS Apostoli Calle dell'Oca 4366; s €48-72, d €52-85, without bathroom s €25-32, d €45-62;

) Comfortable rooms, hospitable owners and keen prices mean that this top choice is always heavily booked. A recently opened annexe just around the corner (d €57 to €90) offers large rooms with modern bathrooms, free wi-fi and disabled access.

CASTELLO

Foresteria Valdese HOSTEL €
(Map p720; 041 528 67 97; www.foresteriavenezia.it; Centro Culturale P Cavagnis 5170; dm from €30, d from €92;) Run by the Waldensian and Methodist Church and housed in a rambling old mansion close to Piazza San Marco, this hostel is one of the cheapest sleeping options in Venice and is extremely popular. Follow Calle Lunga Santa Maria Formosa from Campo Santa Maria Formosa.

Ca' Valeri B&B €€
(Map p720; 041 241 15 30; www.locandacavaleri.com; Ramo Corazzieri 3845; r €69-169;) The drawcards here are an extremely quiet location and beautifully decorated rooms with excellent bathrooms. The only disappointment is breakfast – you'll be heading to a local cafe as soon as you see what's on offer.

Locanda Ca' del Console B&B €€
(Map p720; 041 523 31 64; www.locandacadelconsole.com; Castello 6217; s €90-110, d €120-180;) This former residence of a 19th century Austrian consul is now an elegant, family-run hotel offering rooms decorated with rugs, richly coloured fabrics and period furniture.

LITORALE DEL CAVALLINO

Marina di Venezia CAMPING GROUND €
(041 530 25 11; www.marinadivenezia.it; Via Montello 6, Punta Sabbioni; per person/tent €9.90/24.30, 4-person bungalow €56-121; mid-Apr–end Sep;) On the coast, this marina camping complex includes a private beach, shops, pools and air-conditioned bungalows. Take the *vaporetto* from Punta Sabbioni to Fondamenta Nuove.

Eating

At Venetian prices you'll be glad of the many affordable snack options. For a sit-down meal, avoid the obvious tourist traps and duck down the side streets.

Venetian specialities include *risi e bisi* (pea soup thickened with rice) and *sarde di saor* (fried sardines marinated in vinegar and onions).

DORSODURO

Grom GELATERIA €
(off Map p724; Campo San Barnaba 2761; gelato from €2.20) Ah, Grom. How do we love thee? Let's count the ways: Colombian extra-dark chocolate, Bronte pistachio, *marron glacé* (glazed chestnut), ricotta and fig... There's another outlet on the Strada Nuova in Cannaregio that only opens between April and September.

Enoteca Ai Artisti WINE BAR €€
(041 523 89 44; www.enotecaartisti.com; Fondamenta della Toletta 1169a; mains €15; closed Sun) This tiny place takes its wine seriously (there's a great choice by the glass) and serves delicious cheeses, *bruschette* (toasts with toppings) and bowls of pasta.

Ristorante La Bitta RESTAURANT €€€
(off Map p724; 041 523 05 31; Calle Lunga San Barnaba 2753a; mains €18-24; closed Sun) The bottle-lined dining room and attractive internal courtyard are a lovely setting in which to enjoy your choice from a small, meat-dominated seasonal menu. No credit cards.

Pizza al Volo PIZZERIA €
(Map p720; Campo Santa Margherita 2944; pizza slices €2-4) In need of a pizza pit-stop? Here's your opportunity. You'll be in the company of a steady stream of interns from the Guggenheim.

SAN POLO & SANTA CROCE

All'Arco WINE BAR €
(Map p726; Calle dell'Arco, San Polo 436; chiceti – bar snacks – €1.50-4; 7.30am-8pm Mon-Sat) Popular with locals, this tiny *osteria* serves delicious *bruschette* and a range of good-quality wine by the glass.

Ae Oche PIZZERIA €
(Map p726; www.aeoche.com; Calle del Tentor, Santa Croce 1552a/b; pizzas €4-9.50) Students adore the Tex-Mex decor and huge pizza list at this bustling place. It's on the main path between the *ferrovia* and San Marco.

Osteria La Zucca WINE BAR, RESTAURANT €€
(Map p726; www.lazucca.it; Calle del Tentor, Santa Croce 1762; mains €10; closed Sun) An unpretentious little restaurant in an out-of-the-way spot, 'The Pumpkin' serves a range of innovative Mediterranean dishes prepared with fresh, seasonal ingredients.

CANNAREGIO

Da Marisa TRATTORIA €€
(Map p720; 041 72 02 11; Fondamenta di San Giobbe 652b; lunch €15 incl wine & coffee, dinner incl wine

Sestieri di San Marco (Venice)

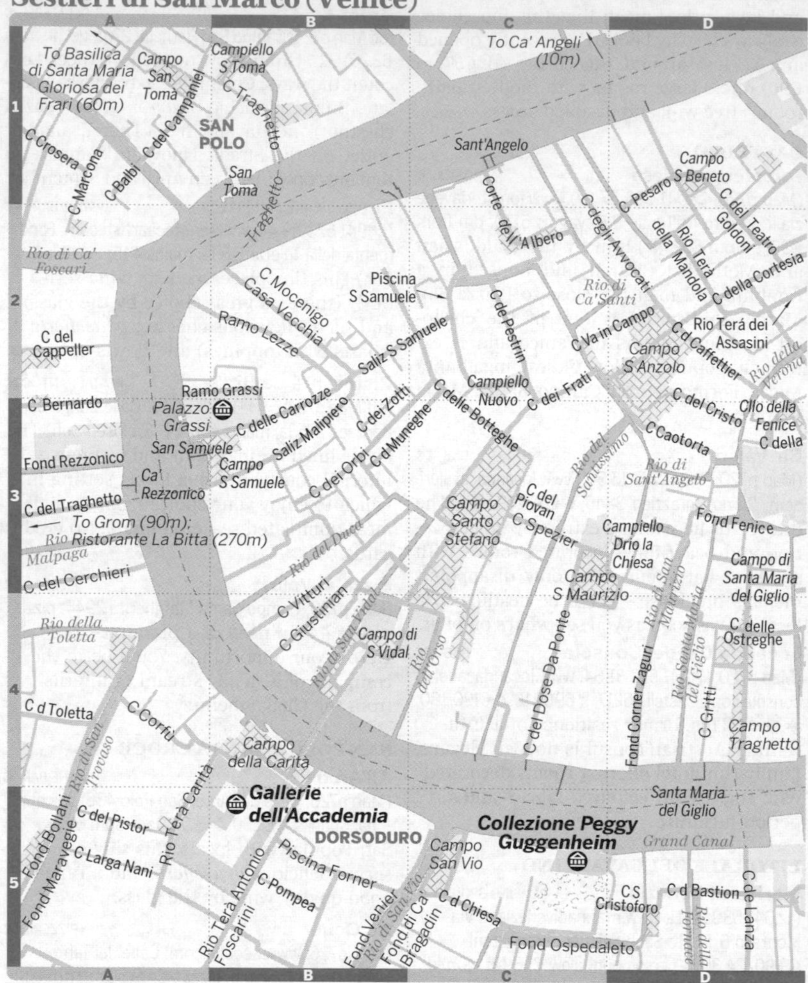

& coffee €35-40; ⏲lunch daily, dinner Tue & Thu-Sat) You can watch the sun setting over the lagoon from the canalside tables here. Local devotees overlook the fact that service can be brusque, meal times are set (noon and 8pm), credit cards aren't accepted and there's no opportunity to vary the excellent daily menu, which is mostly meat but sometimes seafood.

Antica Adelaide BAR, TRATTORIA **€€**
(Map p726; Calle Priuli 3728; mains €10-15) Adelaide has been in the food business as far back as the 18th century. You can pop in for a drink and *cicheti* (bar snacks) or tuck into a hearty bowl of pasta or full meal.

La Cantina WINE BAR **€**
(Map p726; Campo San Felice 3689; chicheti €4-10; ⏲closed Mon, 2 weeks Jul & Aug, 2 weeks Jan) Sit at one of the outdoor tables at this *enoteca* and watch the passing traffic promenade up and down the Strada Nuova. A good choice of wines by the glass and classy *chicheti* make it deservedly popular.

Drinking

Venice harbours hundreds of bars and cafes, but the highest concentration is in the area around Campo Santa Margherita.

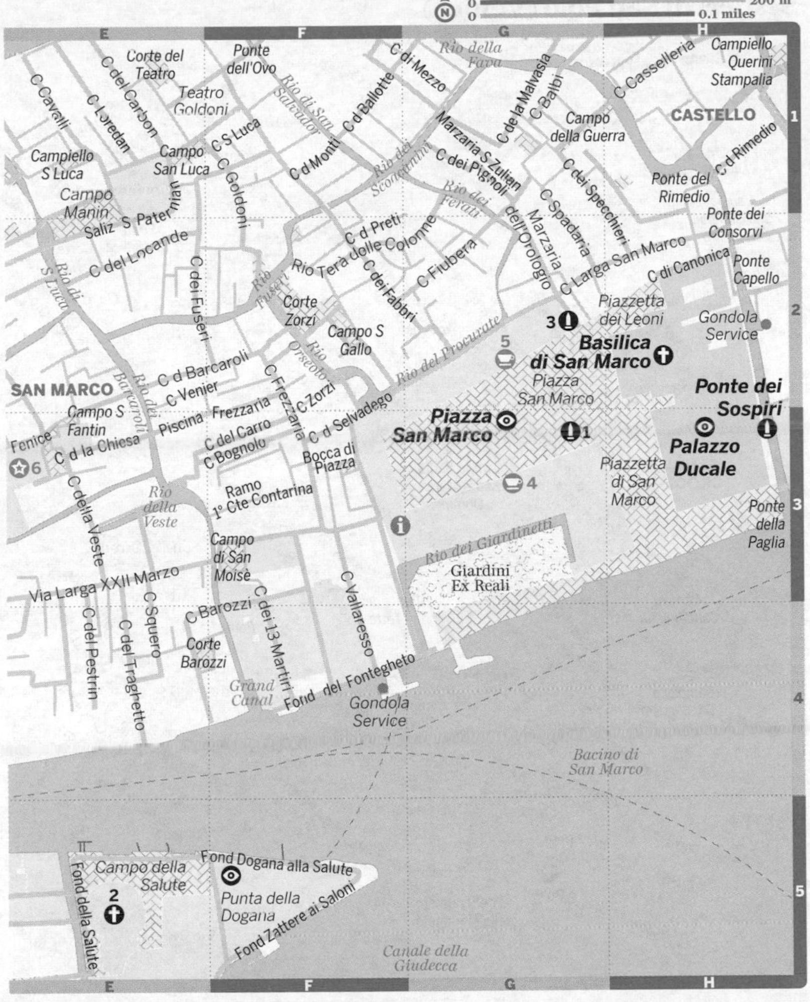

Sestieri di San Marco (Venice)

Top Sights

Basilica di San Marco H2
Collezione Peggy Guggenheim C5
Gallerie dell'Accademia B5
Palazzo Ducale H3
Piazza San Marco G3
Ponte dei Sospiri H3

Sights

1 Campanile G3
2 Chiesa di Santa Maria della Salute E5
3 Torre dell'Orologio G2

Drinking

4 Caffè Florian G3
5 Gran Caffè Quadri G2

Entertainment

6 Gran Teatro La Fenice E3

Sestieri di San Polo (Venice)

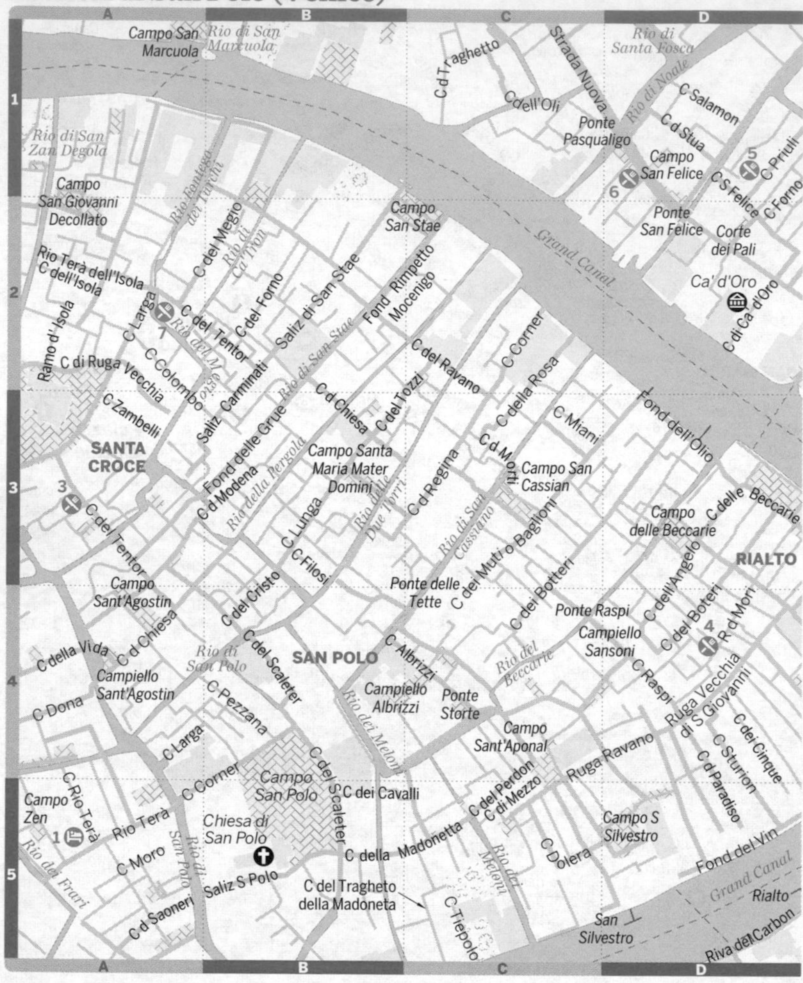

Sestieri di San Polo (Venice)

Sleeping

1 Hotel Alex A5
2 Hotel Bernardi E2

Eating

3 Ae Oche A3
4 All'Arco D4
5 Antica Adelaide D1
6 La Cantina D1
7 Osteria La Zucca A2

Drinking

8 Al Mercà E4
9 Ancorà E4
10 Muro Venezia E3

Al Mercà BAR

(Map p726; Campo Cesare Battisti, San Polo 212-213; ⏲closed Sun) One of the city's best bars, this tiny place serves excellent and keenly priced wines by the glass accompanied by a lavish array of *chicheti* – arrive around 6.30pm for the best choice. No seating, just loads of atmosphere.

Muro Venezia BAR, RESTAURANT

(Map p726; www.murovinoecucina.it; Campo Cesare Battisti, San Polo 222; ⏲closed Sun) The centre of a happening nightlife scene in the market squares of the Rialto, Muro is the watering hole of choice for young locals, who spill out into the square with their drinks.

Ancorà BAR

(Map p726; Fabbriche Vecchie, San Polo; ⏲closed Sun) Enjoy your *apcritivo* with a Grand Canal view while sitting at one of the three outdoor tables on the waterside terrace here.

Caffè Florian CAFE

(Map p724; www.caffeflorian.com; Piazza San Marco 56/59) If you think it's worth paying up to four times the usual price for a coffee, emulate Byron, Goethe and Rousseau and pull up a seat at Piazza San Marco's most famous cafe.

Gran Caffè Quadri CAFE

(Map p724; www.quadrivenice.com; Piazza San Marco 121) Opposite Florian, Caffè Quadri offers more of the same.

Il Caffè BAR

(Map p720; Campo Santa Margherita, Dorsoduro 2963; ⏲closed Sun) Popular with foreign and Italian students, this is one of Venice's historic drinking spots. Known to locals as Caffè Rosso because of its red frontage, it's got outdoor seating and serves a great *spritz* (Venetian cocktail made with *prosecco*, soda water and Aperol or Campari).

Imagina Café CAFE, BAR

(Map p720; www.imaginacafe.it; Campo San Margherita, Dorsoduro 3126; ⏲closed Sun) A constantly changing exhibition programme means that patrons can enjoy art with their *aperitivo* at this hip modern bar.

☆ Entertainment

Tickets for most events in Venice are available from **HelloVenezia ticket outlets** (www.hellovenezia.it; ⏲7am to 10.45pm daily), run by the ACTV transport network. You'll find them in front of the train station and at Piazzale Roma.

Gran Teatro La Fenice (Map p724; ☎for guided tours 041 24 24; www.teatrolafenice.it; Campo San Fantin, San Marco 1977; opera tickets from €20) is one of Italy's most important opera houses.

🛍 Shopping

Classic Venetian gifts include Murano glass, lace from Burano, Carnevale masks and *carta marmorizzata* (marbled paper). There are any number of shops selling these items, but if you want the best deal go to the source. Be warned that genuine Burano lace is expensive; much of the cheaper stuff sold round town is imported from the Far East.

Information

Emergency

Police station (Questura; ☎041 271 55 11; Fondamenta di San Lorenzo, Castello 5053) There's also a small branch at Piazza San Marco 67.

Medical Services

Twenty-four-hour pharmacies are listed in *Un Ospite a Venezia* (A Guest in Venice), a free guide available in many hotels.

Ospedale Civile (Hospital; ☎041 529 41 04; Campo SS Giovanni e Paolo 6777)

Tourist Information

Pick up the free *Shows & Events* guide at tourist offices. It contains comprehensive city listings and a useful public transport map on the inside back cover. The tourist offices also sell a decent city map (€2.50).

Azienda di Promozione Turistica (Venice Tourist Board; central information line ☎041 529 87 11; www.turismovenezia.it) Lido (Gran Viale Santa Maria Elisabetta 6a; ⏲9am-noon & 3-6pm Jun-Sep); Marco Polo airport (Arrivals Hall; ⏲9am-9pm); Piazza San Marco (Map p724; Piazza San Marco 71f; ⏲9am-3.30pm); Piazzale Roma (Map p720; ⏲9.30am-4.30pm Jun-Sep); train station (Map p720; ⏲8am-6.30pm).

Getting There & Away

Air

Most European and domestic flights land at **Marco Polo airport** (VCE; ☎041 260 92 60; www.veniceairport.it), 12km outside Venice. Ryanair flies to **Treviso airport** (TSF; ☎0422 31 51 11; www.trevisoairport.it), about 30km from Venice.

Boat

Minoan Lines (☎210 414 57 00; www.minoan.gr) runs ferries to Corfu (23½ hours), Igoumenitsa (22 hours) and Patra (36 hours) daily in summer and four times per week in winter. Tickets are priced between €54 and €289.

Bus

ACTV (☎041 24 24; www.actv.it) buses service surrounding areas, including Mestre, Padua and Treviso. Tickets and information are available at the bus station in Piazzale Roma.

Train

Venice's Stazione di Santa Lucia is directly linked by regional trains to Ferrara (€6.15, 1½ hours, every two hours), Padua (€2.90, 45 minutes, every 20 minutes) and Verona (€6.35, 1¼ hours, half-hourly). It is easily accessible from Bologna, Milan, Rome and Florence. You can also reach points in Austria, Croatia, France, Germany, Slovenia and Switzerland from here.

Getting Around

To/From the Airport

For travel to/from Marco Polo airport there are various options. **Alilaguna** (www.alilaguna.com) operates four fast-ferry lines between the airport ferry dock and the city (€13, 70 minutes, about every hour); the Rossa (Red) goes to Piazza San Marco and the Oro (Gold) line goes to both Rialto and San Marco. Follow the signs from the arrivals hall to the ferry dock, where there is a ticket office. **ATVO** (☎041 520 55 30; www.atvo.it) runs 'Venezia Express' buses (one way/return €3/5.50, 20 minutes, every half-hour) between the airport and Piazzale Roma, and **ACTV** operates bus 5d (€2.50, 25 minutes, every half-hour).

For Treviso airport, take the ATVO Ryanairbus (€5, 70 minutes, 16 daily) from Piazzale Roma two hours and 10 minutes before your flight departure. The last service is at 7.40pm.

Boat

The city's main mode of public transport is the *vaporetto*. The most useful routes are as follows:

1 From Piazzale Roma to the train station and down the Grand Canal to San Marco and the Lido.

2 From S Zaccaria (near San Marco) to the Lido via Giudecca, Piazzale Roma, the train station and the Rialto.

DM From Piazzale Roma to Murano.

LN From Fondamenta Nuove to S Zaccaria via Murano and Burano.

T Runs between Burano and Torcello.

Tickets, available from ACTV booths at the major *vaporetti* stops, are expensive: €6.50 for a single trip; €16 for 12 hours; €18 for 24 hours; €23 for 36 hours; €28 for two days; €33 for three days; and €50 for seven days. There are significant discounts for holders of the Rolling Venice Card (eg €18 instead of €33 for the three-day ticket) and all tickets are 15% cheaper if you purchase them online in advance of your trip at www.veniceconnected.com.

The poor man's gondola, *traghetti* (€0.50 per crossing) are used by Venetians to cross the Grand Canal where there's no nearby bridge.

Ferrara

POP 134,465

Surrounded by foggy plains, Ferrara is a quiet and well-to-do city that retains much of the austere splendour of its Renaissance heyday, when it was the seat of the powerful Este family (1260–1598). Overshadowed by the menacing Castello Estense, the compact medieval centre is atmospheric and lively.

The **tourist office** (☎0532 29 93 03; www.ferraraterraeacqua.it; ⏲9am-1pm & 2-6pm Mon-

Sat, 9.30am-1pm & 2-5.30pm Sun) is inside Castello Estense.

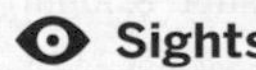

Sights

If you're planning to visit the major monuments, buy a **Museum Card** (adult/concession €17/10), which gives free entry to Palazzo Schifanoia and all municipal museums. They're available from both the Cathedral Museum and Palazzo Schifanoia.

Castello Estense CASTLE
(www.castelloestense.it; Viale Cavour; adult/concession €8/6.50, Lion's Tower extra €2; 9.30am-5.30pm Tue-Sun) Guarding the northern edge of Ferrara's attractive historic centre *(centro storico)*, this stirring castle is quite a sight with its square towers, moat and drawbridges. It was begun by Nicolò II d'Este in 1385 and became the Este family's residence.

Duomo CHURCH
(Piazza Cattedrale; 7.30am-noon & 3-6.30pm Mon-Sat, 7.30am-12.30pm & 3.30-7.30pm Sun) This pink-and-white 12th-century cathedral is most notable for its superb three-tiered marble facade. The upper tier features a graphic Gothic depiction of the Last Judgement.

Palazzo Schifanoia HISTORIC BUILDING
(Via Scandiana 23; adult/concession €6/3; 9am-6pm Tue-Sun) Famous for its frescoes, this Este palace is one of Ferrara's earliest Renaissance buildings. In the **Sala dei Mesi** (Room of the Months), the 15th-century frescoes are considered among the best examples of their type in Italy. Sadly, though, they're not in great condition.

Sleeping & Eating

You won't need to overnight to see Ferrara's sights, but it's a cheap alternative to Bologna and a viable base for Venice.

Hotel de Prati HOTEL €€
(0532 24 19 05; www.hoteldeprati.com; Via Padiglioni 5; s/d €80/120;) A charming three-star on the edge of the *centro storico*. Guest rooms are quietly elegant with wrought-iron bedsteads, high ceilings and classic furniture, while downstairs the yellow-and-orange walls are hung with contemporary art.

Pensione Artisti PENSION €
(0532 76 10 38; Via Vittoria 66; d €60, s/d without bathroom €28/50) Ferrara's best budget option features scrubbed old-fashioned rooms, kitchen facilities, free bikes and an excellent *centro storico* location. The superfriendly owners also ensure a warm welcome. No breakfast.

Ristorante Osteria Balebùste BAR, RESTAURANT €€
(0532 76 35 57; Via Vittoria 44; mains €13; closed Thu) The exposed brick walls and high medieval wood ceiling set the atmospheric backdrop for a relaxed meal of well-presented regional food. Particularly good are the meaty main courses. The adjacent bar also serves an evening *aperitvo*.

Al Brindisi Wine Bar BAR, RESTAURANT €€
(Via Adelardi 11; meals €25-30, set lunch menus from €13; 11am-1am daily) The oldest *osteria* in the world, this atmospheric wine bar dates to 1435 – Titian and Copernicus both drank here. Alongside the substantial wine list there's an extensive menu of traditional pastas, mains and snacks.

Getting There & Around

Ferrara is easy to reach by train. There are regional trains to Bologna (€4, 45 minutes, every 30 to 60 minutes), nearby Ravenna (€5.70, 1¼ hours, 14 daily) and Venice (€6.15, 1½ to two hours, hourly).

From the station take bus 1 or 9 for the historic centre.

Bologna

POP 374,945

Boasting one of the country's great medieval cityscapes, Italy's culinary capital is an attractive, animated city. Its large student population and active gay scene ensure a cosmopolitan vitality, and with hundreds of bars, cafes and trattorias to choose from, you'll soon find somewhere to hang out.

Nicknamed *la rossa* (the red – a political moniker as well as a nod to its colourful buildings), Bologna has long had a reputation for left-wing militancy. Passions have cooled since students faced down tanks in 1977, but the city remains highly political and the university, Europe's oldest, is still a source of student agitation.

Sights

Piazza Maggiore SQUARE
Pedestrianised Piazza Maggiore is Bologna's showpiece square. On the southern flank, the Gothic **Basilica di San Petronio** (Piazza Maggiore; 7.45am-12.30pm & 3-6pm), currently covered in scaffolding, is dedicated to the city's patron saint, Petronius. Its partially complete facade doesn't diminish its status as the

world's fifth-largest basilica. Inside, check out Giovanni da Modena's bizarre *I'Inferno* fresco in the fourth chapel on the left.

To the west is the **Palazzo Comunale** (Town Hall), home to the city's art collection, the **Collezioni Comunali d'Arte** (admission free; ⏰9am-3pm Tue-Fri, 10am-6.30pm Sat & Sun) and the **Museo Morandi** (admission free; ⏰9am-3pm Tue-Fri, 10am-6.30pm Sat & Sun), dedicated to the work of Giorgio Morandi.

Adjacent to the square, **Piazza del Nettuno** is named after the Fontana del Nettuno (Neptune's Fountain), sculpted by Giambologna in 1566 and featuring an impressively muscled Neptune.

Le Due Torri MEDIEVAL TOWERS

Rising above **Piazza di Porta Ravegnana** are Bologna's two leaning towers, Le Due Torri. The taller of the two, the 97m-high **Torre degli Asinelli** (admission €3; ⏰9am-6pm Apr-Oct, to 5pm Nov-Mar), was built between 1109 and 1119 and is now open to the public. Climb the 498 steps for some superb city views. The neighbouring **Torre Garisenda** stands at 48m.

Museo d'Arte Moderna do Bologna MUSEUM

(MAMBO, Museum of Modern Art; www.mambo-bologna.org; Via Don Minzoni 14; admission free; ⏰10am-6pm Tue, Wed & Fri-Sun, to 10pm Thu) An excellent modern art museum housed in a converted bakery.

Sleeping & Eating

Accommodation is expensive (particularly during trade fairs) and can be difficult to find unless you book ahead. The university district northeast of Via Rizzoli harbours hundreds of restaurants, trattorias, takeaways and cafes, while the Quadrilatero district east of Piazza Maggiore is the place for sumptuous deli delights.

Albergo Panorama PENSION €

(☎051 22 18 02; www.hotelpanoramabologna.it; 4th fl, Via Livraghi 1; without bathroom s €40-50, d €60-70; ❄) An easy walk from Piazza Maggiore, this is a friendly old-school *pensione* with simple, spacious rooms, lovely rooftop views and fresh flowers in the hallway. Only cash or Visa credit cards.

Ostello Due Torri & San Sisto 2 HOSTEL €

(☎051 50 18 10; www.ostellodibologna.com; Via Viadagola 5; dm €17, s/d €25/44, without bathroom €23/40; @) Some 6km north of the city centre, Bologna's two HI hostels, barely 100m apart, are modern, functional and cheap. Take bus 93 (Monday to Saturday daytime), 301 (Sunday) or 21b (daily after 8.30pm) from Via Irnerio.

Osteria de' Poeti RESTAURANT €€

(☎051 23 61 66; Via de' Poeti 1b; mains €10; ⏰Tue-Sun) In the cellar of a 14th-century *palazzo*, this atmospheric place is a bastion of old-style service and top-notch regional cuisine. Pasta dishes are driven by what's fresh in the markets, and mains include delicious meat dishes such as succulent roast beef served with rocket and Grana Padano cheese.

Pizzeria Belle Arti PIZZERIA €

(☎051 22 55 81; Via Belle Arti 14; pizzas €5-9, mains €8) This sprawling place near the university serves delicious wood-fired thin-crust pizzas and a full menu of pastas and main courses. You'll find it near the Odeon cinema.

Trattoria Mariposa TRATTORIA €

(☎051 22 56 56; Via Bertiera 12; mains €8; ⏰Mon-Sat) A genial, laid-back trattoria, the Mariposa is good for simple home-made favourites such as tortellini with *ragù* or *burro e salvia* (butter and sage).

Bologna also boasts two superb gelaterie: **Gelateria Stefino** (Via Galleria 49b; ⏰noon-midnight daily) and **La Sorbetteria Castiglione** (Via Castiglione 44; ⏰8am-midnight Tue-Sat, to 11.30pm Mon, to 10.30pm Sun).

Drinking & Clubbing

Bologna's nightlife scene is one of the most vibrant in the country with a huge number of bars, cafes and clubs. Students congregate on and around Piazza Verdi, while the fashionable Quadrilatero district hosts a dressier, more upmarket scene.

Café de Paris CAFE

(Piazza del Francia 1c; ⏰8am-1am Mon-Thu, 8am-late Fri & Sat) Modish bar with daily aperitif between 6pm and 10pm.

Cantina Bentivoglio JAZZ CLUB

(☎051 26 54 16; www.cantinabentivoglio.it; Via Mascarella 4b; ⏰8pm-2am) Bologna's top jazz club. Also a wine bar and restaurant.

La Scuderia BAR

(Piazza Verdi 2; ⏰8am-3am Mon-Fri, 5pm-3am Sat) A popular student bar housed in medieval stables.

Cassero GAY & LESBIAN

(www.cassero.it; Via Don Minzoni 18) Legendary gay and lesbian (but not exclusively) club. Home of Italy's Arcigay movement.

Corto Maltese PUB
(Via Borgo San Pietro 9/2a) Commercial sounds and nightly happy hour at this student pub.

Information

Ospedale Maggiore (Hospital; ☎051 647 81 11; Largo Nigrisoli 2)

Police station (Questura; ☎051 640 11 11; Piazza Galileo 7)

Tourist information (☎051 23 96 60; www.bolognaturismo.info) Airport (⏰9am-7pm); Piazza Maggiore 1 (⏰9am-7pm)

Getting There & Around

Air

European and domestic flights arrive at **Guglielmo Marconi airport** (BLQ; ☎051 647 96 15; www.bologna-airport.it), 6km northwest of the city. An Aerobus shuttle (€5, 30 minutes, every 10 minutes) connects with the main train station.

Bus

National and international coaches depart from the **bus station** (Piazza XX Settembre), southeast of the train station. However, for most Italy destinations the train is a better bet.

Train

Bologna is a major rail hub. From the **central train station** (Piazza delle Medaglie d'Oro), fast Eurostar Alta Velocità (ES AV) trains run to: Florence (€24, 40 minutes, half-hourly), Milan (€41, one hour, hourly), Rome (€58, 2¾ hours, half-hourly) and Venice (€28, 1½ hours, hourly). There are also cheaper, but less regular, trains to Florence (€10.50), Milan (regional trains €13.60, Intercities €23), Rome (€38.50) and Venice (regional trains €9.30, Intercities €16.50).

From the train and bus stations, Via dell'Indipendenza leads to Piazza del Nettuno and Piazza Maggiore, the heart of the city. To get to the centre from the train station take bus A, 25 or 30 (€1).

Ravenna

POP 155,995

Most people visit Ravenna to see its remarkable Unesco-protected mosaics. These relics of the city's golden age as the capital of the Western Roman and Byzantine Empires, are described by Dante in his *Divine Comedy,* much of which was written here. Easily accessible from Bologna, this refined and polished town is easily covered in a day.

Sights

You'll find Ravenna's main mosaics in the 6th-century **Basilica di San Vitale** (Via Fiandrini; ⏰9am-7pm), **Mausoleo di Galla Placidia** (Via Fiandrini; ⏰9am-7pm), **Battistero Neoniano** (Via Battistero; ⏰9am-7pm) and the **Basilica di Sant'Apollinare Nuovo** (Via di Roma; ⏰9am-7pm). These four sites, plus the **Museo Arcivescovile** (Piazza Arcivescovado; ⏰9am-7pm), are covered by a single **ticket** (adult/concession €8.50/7.50), which is available at any of the five sites. Note, however, that in summer there's an extra €2 booking fee for the Mausoleo di Galla Placida. The hours reported here are for April to September; outside of these months they are slightly shorter, typically 9.30am or 10am until 5pm or 5.30pm. Get details at www.ravennamosaici.it.

Five kilometres southeast of the city, the apse mosaic of the **Basilica di Sant'Apollinare in Classe** (Via Romea Sud, Classe; adult/concession €3/1.50; ⏰8.30am-7.30pm Mon-Sat, 1-7.30pm Sun) is another must-see. Take bus 4 (€1) from Piazza Caduti per la Libertà.

Dante spent the last 19 years of his life in Ravenna after he was expelled from Florence. As a perpetual act of penance Florence supplies the oil for the lamp that burns in his **tomb** (Via Dante Alighieri 9; admission free; ⏰9am-7pm).

Eating & Drinking

Ostello Galletti Abbiosi HOSTEL €
(☎0544 313 13; www.galletti.ra.it; Via Roma 140; s €46, d €70-92; ❄📶) In an 18th-century townhouse, this is more a hotel than traditional hostel. With high-ceilinged, spacious rooms, polite service and an enviable location, it's an excellent deal.

Ostello Dante HOSTEL €
(☎0544 42 11 64; www.hostelravenna.com; Via Nicolodi 12; dm/s/d €16/22/44; @📶) Ravenna's friendly and vibrant HI youth hostel is in a modern building about 1km from the train station. Take bus 80 or the red 'Metrobus' A.

Babaleus RESTAURANT, PIZZERIA €
(☎0544 21 64 64; Via Gabbiani 7; pizzas from €4, mains €7; ⏰closed Wed) A relaxed, value-for-money favourite in the historic centre. Pizzas are always a good bet but there's also a full menu of pastas, salads and juicy meat dishes.

Information

Tourist offices (www.turismo.ravenna.it) Classe (☎0544 47 36 61; Via Romea Sud 266, Classe; ⏰9.30am-12.30pm & 3.30-6.30pm); Main office (☎0544 354 04; Via Salara 8/12;

⏲8.30am-7pm Mon-Sat, 10am-6pm Sun); Teodorico (☎0544 45 15 39; Via delle Industrie 14; ⏲9.30am-12.30pm & 3.30-6.30pm) Between October and May hours are slightly shorter; typically closing time is an hour or so earlier.

ℹ Getting There & Around

Regional trains connect the city with Bologna (€6.20, 1½ hours, 14 daily) and Ferrara (€5.70, 1¼ hours, 14 daily).

In town, cycling is popular. The tourist office runs a free bike-hire service to visitors aged 18 or over (take ID).

THE DOLOMITES

A Unesco Natural Heritage site since 2009, the Dolomites stretch across the northern regions of Trentino-Alto Adige and the Veneto. Their stabbing, sawtooth peaks provide some of Italy's most thrilling scenery, as well as superb skiing and hiking.

Facilities are excellent and accommodation is widely available in resorts, ranging from exclusive Cortina d'Ampezzo to more budget-friendly places in the Val Gardena. Ski passes cover either single resorts or a combination of slopes; the most comprehensive is the **Superski Dolomiti pass** (www.dolomitisuperski.com; high season 3/6 days €132/233), which accesses 1220km of runs in 12 valleys.

Hiking opportunities run the gamut from gentle strolls to hardcore mountain treks. Recommended areas include the Alpe di Siusi, a vast plateau above the Val Gardena; the area around Cortina; and Pale di San Martino, accessible from San Martino di Castrozza.

ℹ Information

Area-wide information can be obtained from tourist offices in **Trento** (☎0461 21 60 00; www.apt.trento.it; Via Manci 2; ⏲9am-7pm) and **Bolzano** (☎0471 30 70 00; www.bolzano-bozen.it; Piazza Walther 8; ⏲9am-1pm & 2-7pm Mon-Fri, 9am-2pm Sat). The best online resource is www.dolomiti.org.

ℹ Getting There & Around

Bolzano airport (BZO; ☎0471 25 52 55; www.abd-airport.it) is only served by a couple of European flights. Otherwise the nearest airports are Verona, Bergamo or Innsbruck in Austria, from where trains run south to Bolzano.

The area's excellent bus network is run by **Trentino Trasporti** (☎0461 82 10 00; www.ttesercizio.it) in Trento; **SAD** (☎800 000 471; www.sii.bz.it) in Alto Adige; and **Dolomiti Bus** (www.dolomitibus.it, in Italian) in the Veneto. During winter, most resorts offer 'ski bus' services.

The main towns and the many ski resorts can be reached directly from cities such as Bologna, Florence, Genoa, Milan, Rome and Venice. Information is available from tourist offices and regional bus stations.

Canazei

POP 1865 / ELEV 1460M

One of the best-known resorts in the **Val di Fassa**, Canazei is a great spot for serious skiers. It has 120km of downhill and cross-country runs and is linked to the challenging Sella Ronda ski network. There's even summer skiing on the Marmolada glacier, the stunning 3342m summit of which marks the highest point in the Dolomites.

Spend a cheap night at **Marmolada Camping** (☎0462 60 16 60; www.campingmarmolada.com; Strèda de Parèda 60; per person/tent €10.50/9.50), or contact the **tourist office** (☎0462 60 96 00; www.fassa.com; Piazza Marconi 5; ⏲8.30am-12.30pm & 3-7pm daily) for accommodation lists.

Canazei is served by year-round **Trentino Trasporti** (☎0461 82 10 00; www.ttesercizio.it) buses from Trento (€5.55, 2½ hours) and seasonal services from Bolzano and the Val Gardena.

Val Gardena

Branching northeast off the Val di Fassa, the Val Gardena is a popular skiing area with great facilities and accessible prices. In summer hikers head to the Sella Group and the Alpe di Siusi for rugged, high-altitude treks and to the Vallunga for more accessible walks.

The valley's main towns are Ortisei, Santa Cristina and Selva Gardena, all offering plenty of accommodation and easy access to ski runs. Further information is available online at www.valgardena.it, or from the towns' tourist offices:

Ortisei (☎0471 77 76 00; Via Rezia 1; ⏲8.30am-12.30pm & 2.30-6.30pm Mon-Sat, 10am-noon & 5-6.30pm Sun)

Santa Cristina (☎0471 77 78 00; Via Chemun 9; ⏲8am-noon & 2.30-6.30pm Mon-Sat, 9.30am-noon Sun)

Selva Gardena (☎0471 77 79 00; Via Mëisules 213; ⏰8am-noon & 3-6.30pm Mon-Sat, 9am-noon & 4.30-6.30pm Sun)

The Val Gardena is accessible from Bolzano by year-round **SAD** (☎800 000 471; www.sii.bz.it) buses and from the neighbouring valleys in summer.

San Martino Di Castrozza

ELEV 1450M

At the foot of the imposing **Pale di San Martino**, San Martino di Castrozza acts as a gateway to the **Parco Naturale Paneveggio – Pale di San Martino** (www.parcopan.org). Its **tourist office** (☎0439 76 88 67; www.sanmartino.com; Via Passo Rolle 165; ⏰9am-noon & 3-7pm Mon-Sat, 9.30am-12.30pm Sun) is a mine of useful information.

Trentino Trasporti (☎0461 82 10 00; www.ttesercizio.it) buses run to/from Trento.

CENTRAL ITALY

Encompassing three regions, Tuscany, Umbria and Le Marche, central Italy is a green, hilly area peppered with rural villages and historic towns. Tuscany's fabled rolling landscape has long been considered the embodiment of rural chic and Florence harbours a significant portfolio of the world's Renaissance art collection. But venture off the beaten path and it's still possible to lose yourself down a medieval side street in Umbria and lesser-known Le Marche.

Florence

POP 366,000

One of the most written-about cities in Italy, Florence (Firenze) has a strange effect on visitors. Travellers who normally loathe art galleries queue for hours to get into them, and people with no interest in Renaissance architecture start raving about tiered facades and frescoed apses. But break the spell and you'll find that Florence can be disheartening. Much of the centre has been surrendered to tourism and in summer the heat, pollution and crowds can be stifling. That said, it remains a charismatic city you'd be sorry to miss. The list of its famous sons reads like a Renaissance *Who's Who* – under M alone you'll find Medici, Machiavelli and Michelangelo – and its celebrated cityscape lingers in the memory long after you've left town.

History

Many hold that Florentia was founded around 59 BC, but archaeological evidence suggests an earlier village, possibly established by the Etruscans around 200 BC. A rich merchant city by the 12th century, Florence grew into a powerful city-state under the Medici family, its cultural, artistic and political fecundity culminating in the 15th-century Renaissance.

The Medici were succeeded in the 18th century by the French House of Lorraine, which ruled until 1860 when the city was incorporated into the Kingdom of Italy. From 1865 to 1870, Florence was, in fact, capital of the fledgling kingdom.

During WWII parts of the city were destroyed by bombing, including all of its bridges except for Ponte Vecchio. In 1966 a devastating flood destroyed or severely damaged many important works of art. More recently, in 1993, the Mafia exploded a massive car bomb, killing five people and destroying part of the Uffizi Gallery. The gallery is currently undergoing a long-overdue €60 million renovation that will result in its exhibition space being doubled. It remains open while these works are occurring and the estimated date for their completion is 2013.

Sights & Activities

From Santa Maria Novella train station, it's a 550m walk along Via de' Panzani and Via de' Cerretani to the Duomo. From there, Via Roma leads down to Piazza della Repubblica and Via de' Calzaiuoli connects with Piazza della Signoria. Most major sights are within comfortable walking distance of the Duomo. For the best views in town head up to **Piazzale Michelangelo**, a steep 600m walk from the southern bank of the Arno River.

Piazza del Duomo CATHEDRAL GROUP

One of the world's largest cathedrals, Florence's Gothic **Duomo** (Cathedral; www.duomofirenze.it; ⏰10am-5pm Mon-Wed & Fri, 10am-3.30pm Thu, 10am-4.45pm Sat, to 3.30pm 1st Sat of every month, 1.30-4.45pm Sun) is quite an eyeful. Officially the Cattedrale di Santa Maria del Fiore, it was begun in 1294 by Sienese architect Arnolfo di Cambio and consecrated in 1436. Its most famous feature, the enormous **cupola** (dome; admission €8; ⏰8.30am-6.20pm Mon-Fri, to 5pm Sat), was built by Brunelleschi after his design won a public competition in 1420. The interior is decorated with frescoes by Vasari and Zuccari, and the stained-glass

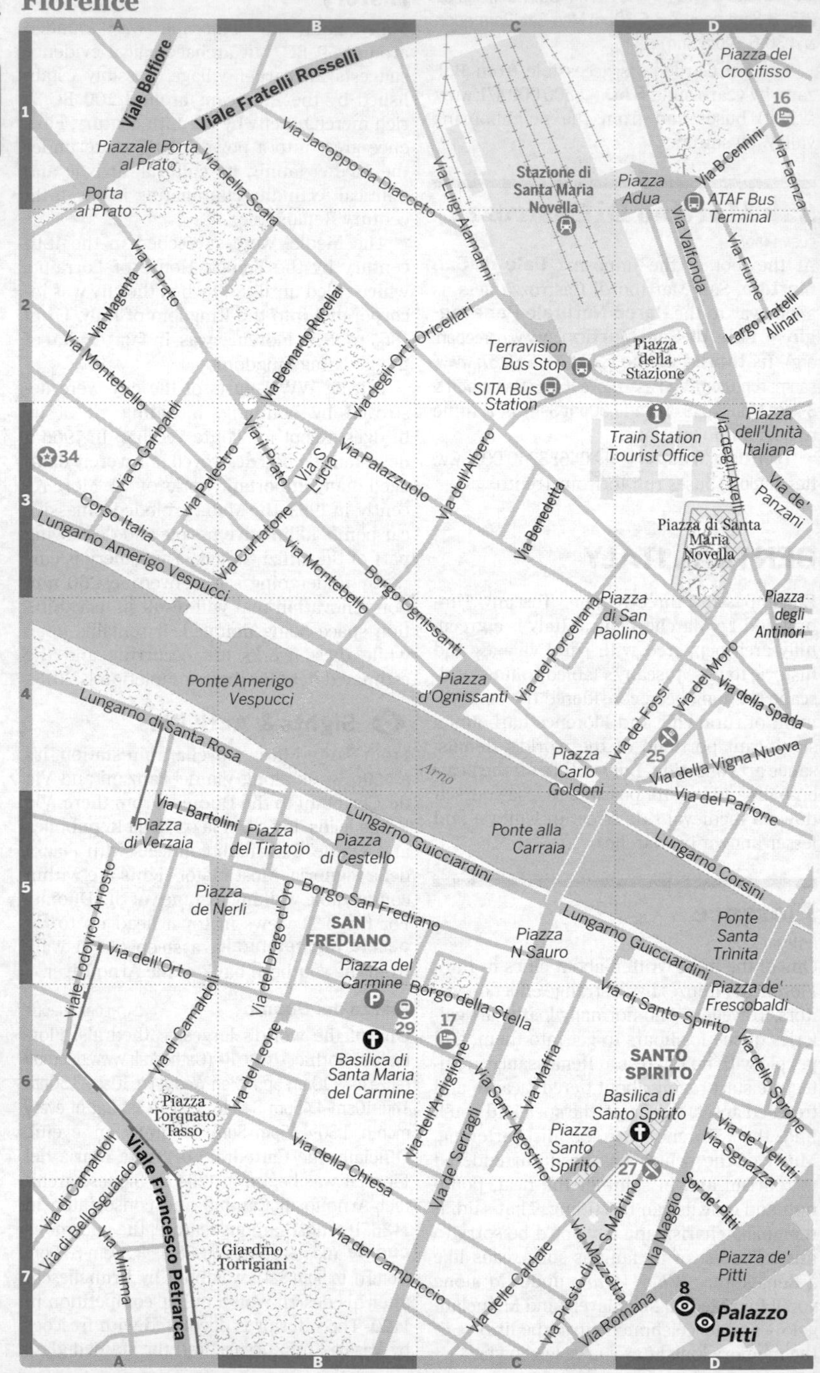
A
B
C
D
1
2
3
4
5
6
7
Viale Belfiore
Viale Fratelli Rosselli
Piazzale Porta al Prato
Porta al Prato
Via della Scala
Via Jacopo da Diacceto
Via Luigi Alamanni
Stazione di Santa Maria Novella
Piazza Adua
Via B Cemini
Via Faenza
ATAF Bus Terminal
Piazza del Crocifisso
16
Via Valfonda
Via Fiume
Largo Fratelli Alinari
Via il Prato
Via Magenta
Via Montebello
Via Bernardo Rucellai
Via degli Orti Oricellari
Terravision Bus Stop
SITA Bus Station
Piazza della Stazione
Train Station Tourist Office
Piazza dell'Unità Italiana
Via degli Avelli
Via de' Panzani
Piazza di Santa Maria Novella
34
Via G Garibaldi
Via Palestro
Via il Prato
Via S Lucia
Via Palazzuolo
Via dell'Albero
Via Benedetta
Corso Italia
Via Curtatone
Via Montebello
Borgo Ognissanti
Lungarno Amerigo Vespucci
Piazza di San Paolino
Piazza degli Antinori
Via del Porcellana
Via del Moro
Via della Spada
Ponte Amerigo Vespucci
Piazza d'Ognissanti
Via de' Fossi
25
Lungarno di Santa Rosa
Piazza Carlo Goldoni
Via della Vigna Nuova
Arno
Via del Parione
Via L Bartolini
Piazza di Verzaia
Piazza del Tiratoio
Piazza di Cestello
Lungarno Guicciardini
Ponte alla Carraia
Lungarno Corsini
Viale Lodovico Ariosto
Piazza de Nerli
Via del Drago d'Oro
Borgo San Frediano
SAN FREDIANO
Lungarno Guicciardini
Ponte Santa Trìnita
Piazza N Sauro
Via dell'Orto
Piazza del Carmine
Borgo della Stella
Via di Santo Spirito
Piazza de' Frescobaldi
Via di Camaldoli
Via del Leone
29
17
Basilica di Santa Maria del Carmine
Via dell'Ardiglione
Via de' Serragli
Via Sant'Agostino
Via Maffia
SANTO SPIRITO
Via dello Sprone
Basilica di Santo Spirito
Piazza Torquato Tasso
Via della Chiesa
Piazza Santo Spirito
27
Via de' Velluti
Via Sguazza
Via di Camaldoli
Via di Bellosguardo
Viale Francesco Petrarca
Via S Martino
Via Maggio
Sor de' Pitti
Via del Campuccio
Via Minima
Giardino Torrigiani
Via delle Caldaie
Via Presto di
Via Mazzetta
Piazza de' Pitti
Via Romana
8
Palazzo Pitti

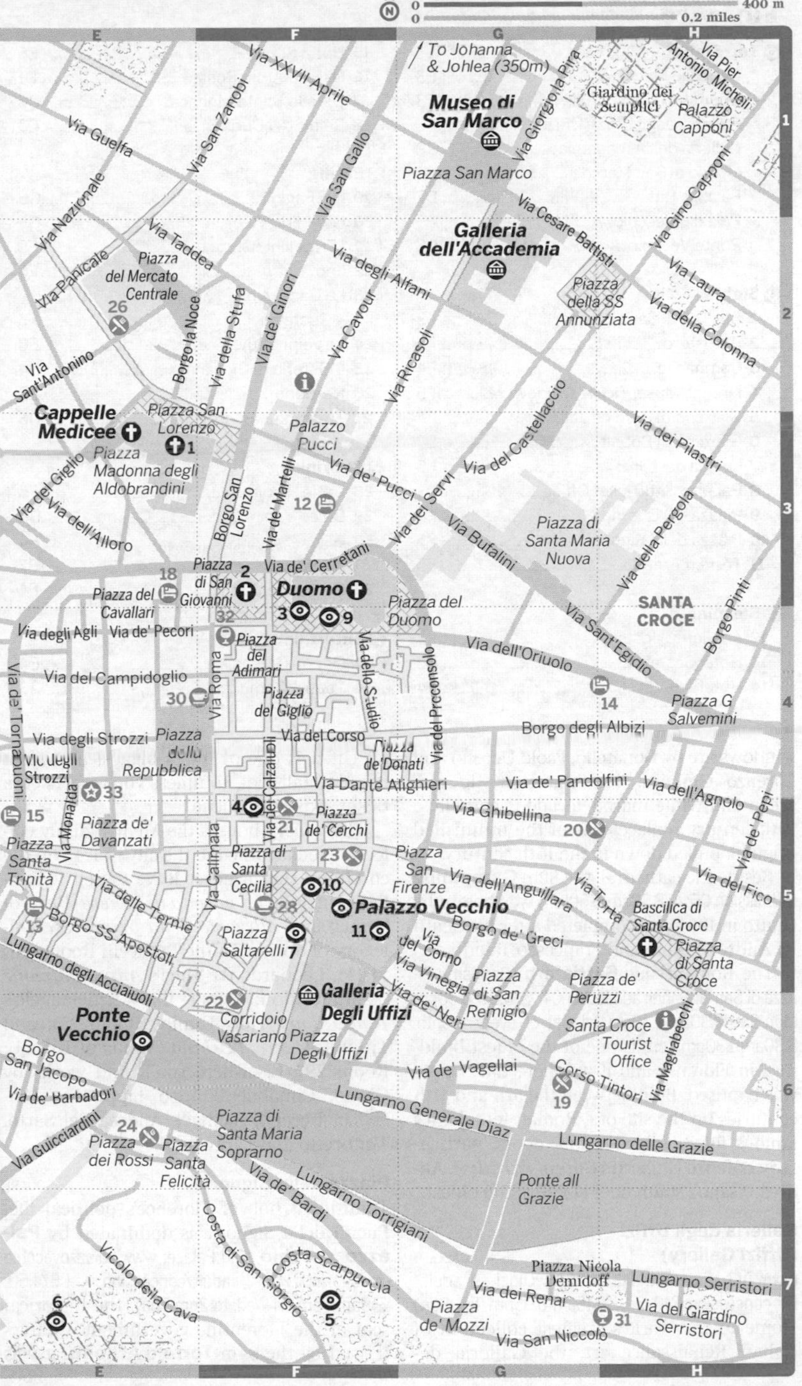
0 400 m
0 0.2 miles
To Johanna & Johlea (350m)
Museo di San Marco
Galleria dell'Accademia
Cappelle Medicee
Duomo
Palazzo Vecchio
Galleria Degli Uffizi
Ponte Vecchio
SANTA CROCE
Basilica di Santa Croce
Santa Croce Tourist Office
Giardino dei Semplici
Palazzo Capponi
Piazza San Marco
Piazza della SS Annunziata
Piazza del Mercato Centrale
Piazza San Lorenzo
Piazza Madonna degli Aldobrandini
Palazzo Pucci
Piazza di Santa Maria Nuova
Piazza di San Giovanni
Piazza del Cavallari
Piazza del Duomo
Piazza del Adimari
Piazza del Giglio
Piazza della Repubblica
Piazza de' Donati
Piazza G Salvemini
Piazza de' Davanzati
Piazza Santa Trinità
Piazza de' Cerchi
Piazza di Santa Cecilia
Piazza San Firenze
Piazza Saltarelli
Piazza di San Remigio
Piazza de' Peruzzi
Piazza di Santa Croce
Corridoio Vasariano
Piazza Degli Uffizi
Piazza di Santa Maria Soprarno
Piazza dei Rossi
Piazza Santa Felicità
Ponte all Grazie
Piazza Nicola Demidoff
Piazza de' Mozzi
Via XXVII Aprile
Via Pier Antonio Micheli
Via Guelfa
Via San Zanobi
Via San Gallo
Via Giorgio la Pira
Via Nazionale
Via Cesare Battisti
Via Gino Capponi
Via Panicale
Via Taddea
Via degli Alfani
Via Laura
Via della Colonna
Borgo la Noce
Via della Stufa
Via de' Ginori
Via Cavour
Via Ricasoli
Via Sant'Antonino
Via del Castellaccio
Via dei Pilastri
Via de' Pucci
Via dei Servi
Via del Giglio
Via dell'Alloro
Borgo San Lorenzo
Via de' Martelli
Via Bufalini
Via della Pergola
Via de' Cerretani
Borgo Pinti
Via Sant'Egidio
Via degli Agli
Via de' Pecori
Via dell'Oriuolo
Via dello Studio
Via del Proconsolo
Via de' Tornabuoni
Via del Campidoglio
Via Roma
Borgo degli Albizi
Via degli Strozzi
Via del Corso
Via Calzaiuoli
Via de' Pandolfini
Via dell'Agnolo
Via Dante Alighieri
Via Monalda
Via Ghibellina
Via de' Pepi
Via Calimala
Via dell'Anguillara
Via del Fico
Via Torta
Via delle Terme
Borgo SS Apostoli
Via del Corno
Borgo de' Greci
Lungarno degli Acciaiuoli
Via Vinegia
Via de' Neri
Via Magliabecchi
Borgo San Jacopo
Via de' Barbadori
Via de' Vagellai
Corso Tintori
Lungarno Generale Diaz
Via Guicciardini
Lungarno delle Grazie
Via de' Bardi
Lungarno Torrigiani
Costa di San Giorgio
Vicolo della Cava
Costa Scarpuccia
Lungarno Serristori
Via dei Renai
Via del Giardino Serristori
Via San Niccolò
1 2 3 4 5 6 7 9 10 11 12 13 14 15 18 19 20 21 22 23 24 26 28 30 31 32 33
E F G H
1 2 3 4 5 6 7

Florence

Top Sights

Cappelle Medicee E3
Duomo F3
Galleria Degli Uffizi (Uffizi Gallery) F6
Galleria dell'Accademia G2
Museo di San Marco G1
Palazzo Pitti D7
Palazzo Vecchio F5
Ponte Vecchio E6

Sights

1 Basilica di San Lorenzo E3
2 Battistero F3
3 Campanile F4
4 Firenze Musei Ticket Window F5
5 Giardino di Bardini F7
6 Giardino di Boboli E7
7 Loggia dei Lanzi F5
8 Palazzo Pitti Ticket Office D7
9 Piazza del Duomo F4
10 Piazza della Signoria F5
11 Torre d'Arnolfo F5

Sleeping

12 Academy Hostel F3
13 Hotel Cestelli E5
14 Hotel Dalí H4
15 Hotel Scoti E5
16 Ostello Archi Rossi D1
17 Ostello Santa Monaca C6
18 Relais del Duomo E3

Eating

19 Del Fagioli G6
20 Gelateria Vivoli G5
21 I Fratellini F5
22 'Ino F6
23 La Canova di Gustavino F5
24 Le volpi e l'uva E6
25 L'Osteria di Giovanni D4
26 Nerbone E2
27 Trattoria La Casalinga D6

Drinking

28 Caffè Rivoire F5
29 Dolce Vita B6
30 Gilli F4
31 Negroni H7
32 Old Stove Duomo F4

Entertainment

33 Odeon Cinehall E4
34 Teatro Comunale A3

windows are by Donatello, Paolo Uccello and Lorenzo Ghiberti. The characteristic red, green and white marble facade is actually a 19th-century replacement of the unfinished original, pulled down in the 16th century.

Beside the cathedral, the 82m **Campanile** (admission €6; 8.30am-6.50pm) was begun by Giotto in 1334 and completed after his death by Andrea Pisano and Francesco Talenti.

The Romanesque **Battistero** (Baptistry; Piazza di San Giovanni; admission €4; 12.15-6.30pm Mon-Sat, 8.30am-1.30pm 1st Sat of every month, 8.30am-1.30pm Sun) is one of the oldest buildings in Florence and it was here that Dante was baptised. Built between the 5th and 11th centuries on the site of a Roman temple, it's famous for its gilded-bronze doors, particularly Lorenzo Ghiberti's *Gate of Paradise*. Andrea Pisano's south door (1336) is the oldest.

Galleria degli Uffizi (Uffizi Gallery) ART GALLERY
(www.uffizi.firenze.it; Piazza degli Uffizi 6; adult/EU concession €10/5; 8.15am-6.05pm Tue-Sun) Home to the world's greatest collection of Italian Renaissance art, the Galleria degli Uffizi is one of Italy's biggest and most popular galleries, so unless you've booked a ticket, expect to queue.

The gallery houses the Medici family collection, bequeathed to the city in 1743 on the condition that it never leave the city. Highlights include *La nascita di Venere* (Birth of Venus) and *Allegoria della primavera* (Allegory of Spring) in the Botticelli Rooms (10 to 14); Leonardo da Vinci's *Annunciazione* (Annunciation; Room 15); Michelangelo's *Tondo doni* (Holy Family; Room 25); and Titian's *Venere d'Urbino* (Venus of Urbino; Room 28). Elsewhere you'll find works by Giotto, Cimabue, Filippo Lippi, Fra' Angelico, Uccello, Raphael, Andrea del Sarto, Tintoretto and Caravaggio.

Piazza della Signoria SQUARE
Traditional hub of Florence's political life, Piazza della Signoria is dominated by **Palazzo Vecchio** (Old Palace; www.palazzovecchio-museoragazzi.it; adult/concession €6/4.50; 9am-7pm Fri-Wed, to 2pm Thu), the historical seat of the Florentine government. Characterised by the 94m **Torre d'Arnolfo**, it was

designed by Arnolfo di Cambio and built between 1298 and 1340.

The statue of *David* outside the *palazzo* is a copy of Michelangelo's original, which stood here until 1873 but is now in the Galleria dell'Accademia. The nearby **Loggia dei Lanzi** (Piazza della Signoria) is an open-air showcase of sculpture from the 14th and 16th centuries – look out for Giambologna's *Rape of the Sabine Women* (c1583) and Agnolo Gaddi's *Seven Virtues* (1384–89).

Ponte Vecchio BRIDGE
Lined with jewellery shops, the 14th-century Ponte Vecchio was originally flanked by butchers' shops, but when the Medici built a corridor through the bridge to link Palazzo Pitti with Palazzo Vecchio, they ordered that the butchers be replaced with goldsmiths.

Palazzo Pitti PALACE
(www.uffizi.firenze.it; Piazza de' Pitti) Built for the Pitti family, great rivals of the Medici, the vast 15th-century Palazzo Pitti was bought by the Medici in 1549 and became their family residence. Today it houses four museums, of which the **Galleria Palatina** (8.15am-6.50pm Tue-Sun) is the most important. Works by Raphael, Filippo Lippi, Titian and Rubens adorn lavishly decorated rooms, culminating in the royal apartments once occupied by members of the House of Savoy. Three other museums – the **Museo degli Argenti** (Silver Museum; 8.15am-7.30pm Jun-Aug, closes earlier rest of year), the **Galleria d'Arte Moderna** (Gallery of Modern Art; 8.15am-6.50pm Tue-Sun) and the **Galleria del Costume** (Costume Gallery; 8.15am-6.50pm Tue-Sun) are located in the palace buildings. Ticketing can be confusing: **ticket one** (adult/EU concession €10/5) gets you into the Galleria del Costume and the Museo degli Argenti, as well as the **Giardino di Boboli** (Boboli Gardens; 8.15am-7.30pm Jun-Aug, earlier closing rest of year) and **Giardino Bardini** (Bardini Gardens; 8.15am-sunset); **ticket two** (adult/EU concession €12/6) gets you into the Galleria Palatina, the royal apartments and the Galleria d'Arte Moderna.

Galleria dell'Accademia MUSEUM
(www.uffizi.firenze.it; Via Ricasoli 60; adult/concession €10/5; 8.15am-6.20pm Tue-Sun) This is where you'll find *David*, arguably the Western world's most famous sculpture. Michelangelo carved the giant figure from a single block of marble, finishing it in 1504 when he was just 29. The gallery also displays paintings by Florentine artists spanning the 13th to 16th centuries.

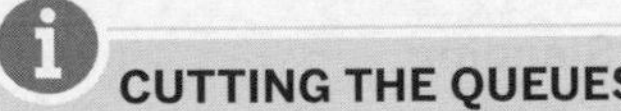

CUTTING THE QUEUES

You'll never avoid queuing in Florence, but by prebooking museum tickets you'll save time. For €4 extra per museum you can book tickets for the Uffizi and Galleria dell'Accademia through **Firenze Musei** (055 29 48 83; www.firenzemusei.it; booking line 8.30am-6.30pm Mon-Fri, to 12.30pm Sat, ticket offices 8.15am-6pm daily). Buy ahead of your visit by booking by telephone or online, or purchase in person from the Firenze Musei desks at the Uffizi, Accademia, Palazzo Pitti or at the **ticket window** (Via dei Calzaiuoli; 10am-5.20pm Mon-Fri, 10am-4.20pm Sat) in the Chiesa di Orsanmichele.

Basilica di San Lorenzo CHURCH
(www.basilicasanlorenzofirenze.com, in Italian; Piazza San Lorenzo; admission €3.50; 10am-5pm Mon-Sat all year, 1.30-5pm Sun Mar-Oct) One of the city's finest examples of Renaissance architecture, this basilica was built by Brunelleschi in the 15th century and includes his **Sagrestia Vecchia** (Old Sacristy), with sculptural decoration by Donatello.

Cappelle Medicee CHURCH
(Medici Chapels; Piazza Madonna degli Aldobrandini; adult/concession €6/3; 8.15am-4pm Tue-Sat, 2nd & 4th Mon & 1st, 3rd & 5th Sun of month) Around the corner from the Basilica di San Lorenzo, at its rear, is the sumptuous Cappelle Medicee, the principal burial place of the Medici grand dukes. Its jewel is the incomplete Sagrestia Nuova, Michelangelo's first architectural effort, which contains some exquisite sculptures.

Festivals & Events

Scoppio del Carro RELIGIOUS CELEBRATION
(Explosion of the Cart) A cart full of fire works is exploded in front of the Duomo on Easter Sunday.

Maggio Musicale Fiorentino MUSIC FESTIVAL
(www.maggiofiorentino.com, in Italian) Italy's longest-running music festival held from April to June.

Festa di San Giovanni RELIGIOUS CELEBRATION
(Feast of St John) Florence's patron saint is celebrated on 24 June with costumed football (soccer) matches on Piazza di Santa Croce and fireworks over Piazzale Michelangelo.

Sleeping

Budget *pensioni* are concentrated around Via della Scala, west of the train station. Look out for off-season website deals – prices often drop by up to 50%.

NORTH OF THE RIVER AMO

Relais del Duomo B&B €
(055 21 01 47; www.relaisdelduomo.it; Piazza dell'Olio 2; s €48-85, d €70-130;) Florentine B&Bs don't come much better than this one. Located in the shadow of the Duomo, it has four light and airy rooms with attractive furnishings and lovely little bathrooms.

Academy Hostel HOSTEL €
(055 23 98 665; www.academyhostel.eu; Via Ricasoli 9; dm €25-38, tw €70-84, s without bathroom €35-45;) The philosophy of this small hostel close to the Duomo is that cheap accommodation shouldn't compromise on comfort. Its dorms (sleeping between three and six) are bright and well set up, with lockers and single beds (no bunks).

Hotel Dalì PENSION €
(055 234 07 06; www.hoteldali.com; Via dell'Oriuolo 17; d €80, s/d without bathroom €40/65; P) An excellent budget hotel with homey, spotless rooms. The location is great and owners Marco and Samanta go out of their way to ensure a pleasant stay.

Johanna & Johlea B&B €
(055 463 32 92; www.johanna.it; Via San Gallo 80; s €70-120, d €80-170;) This highly regarded B&B has more than a dozen tasteful, individually decorated rooms housed in five historic residences. There are also two charming suite apartments (€92 to €280).

Hotel Scoti PENSION €
(055 29 21 28; www.hotelscoti.com; Via de' Tornabuoni 7; s €35-75, d €65-125) On Florence's smartest shopping street, the Scoti is a splendid mix of old-fashioned charm and great value for money. It offers 11 clean and comfortable rooms and an amazing frescoed living room for communal use. Breakfast costs an extra €5.

Hotel Cestelli B&B €
(055 21 42 13; www.hotelcestelli.com; Borgo SS Apostoli 25; d €70-100, s without bathroom €40-60, d €50-80; closed 2 weeks Jan, 3 weeks Aug) Run by Florentine photographer, Alessio and his Japanese partner Asumi, this eight-room hotel is wonderfully located. Though dark, the rooms are attractively furnished, quiet and cool.

Ostello Archi Rossi HOSTEL €
(055 29 08 04; www.hostelarchirossi.com; Via Faenza 94r; dm €21-27, s €40-60, d €60-90; closed 2 weeks Dec;) This busy hostel near Stazione di Santa Maria Novella offers bright dorms with three to nine beds; some are single sex and all have private bathrooms and keyed lockers. Air-conditioning is in private rooms only. The hostel also offers free walking tours.

SOUTH OF THE RIVER AMO

Ostello Santa Monaca HOSTEL €
(Map p734; 055 26 83 38; www.ostello.it; Via Santa Monaca 6; dm €15.50-20.50, d €45-49;) Over the river in a 15th-century convent, this large, popular hostel has a range of mixed and single-sex dorms, as well as smaller double rooms. There's a kitchen, launderette and safe deposits. Curfew is 2am.

Campeggio Michelangelo CAMPING GROUND €
(055 681 19 77; Viale Michelangelo 80; www.ecvacanze.it; per person with tent €10.80; P) Just off Piazzale Michelangelo, this large, well-equipped camping ground is the nearest to the city centre. Take bus 12 from the train station to the piazzale.

Eating

Florence caters well to all budgets. There are hole-in-the-wall sandwich bars, earthy trattorias and some of Italy's top restaurants. Classic Tuscan dishes include *ribollita* (a heavy vegetable soup), *canellini* (white beans) and *bistecca alla Fiorentina* (Florentine steak). Chianti is the local tipple.

NORTH OF THE RIVER AMO

TOP CHOICE **'Ino** SANDWICHES €
(Via dei Georgofili 3r-7r; panini €5-8; 11am-5pm) Short for *panino,* this stylish *paninoteca* (sandwich bar) shop near the Uffizi sources its gourmet ingredients locally and uses them in inventive and delicious ways. A glass of wine is included in the price of every sandwich.

Trattoria Cibrèo (Cibrèino)è TRATTORIA €€
(Viadei Macci 122r; mains €13-16; Tue-Sat, closed Aug) The small dining room here is run with charm and efficiency by a maitre d' who will happily explain the menu and suggest a matching wine. Everything is delicious and exceptionally well priced considering its quality. No reservations and no credit cards.

Del Fagioli TRATTORIA €
(055 24 42 85; Corso Tintori 47r; mains €9-10; Mon-Fri, closed Aug) This Slow Food favou-

FLORENCE SPLURGE

Delicious food, large servings and friendly staff await at **L'Osteria di Giovanni** (☎055 28 48 97; www.osteriadigiovanni.com; Via del Moro 22; mains €18-26; ⏰lunch & dinner Fri-Mon, dinner only Tue-Thu). Giovanni's totally tremendous tavern. It's everything a perfect neighbourhood eatery should be, and then some.

rite near the Basilica di Santa Croce is the archetypical Tuscan trattoria, serving well-priced bean dishes, soups and roasted meats to throngs of appreciative local workers and residents. No credit cards.

La Canova di Gustavino WINE BAR €€
(Via della Condotta 29r; mains €8-12) The rear dining room of this atmospheric *enoteca* is lined with shelves full of Tuscan wine – the perfect accompaniment to a simple bowl of soup, a *bruschetta*, a pasta dish or a hearty main.

I Fratellini SANDWICHES €
(Via dei Cimatori 38r; panini €2.50; ⏰9am-8pm Mon-Sat, closed Fri & Sun 2nd half of Jun & all Aug) I Fratellini is a city institution. Locals flock to its tiny counter for fresh-filled *panini* ready in the twinkle of an eye, which they eat standing in the street.

Gelateria Vivoli GELATERIA €
(Via Isola delle Stinche 7; ⏰7.30am-midnight Tue-Sat, 9am-midnight Sun, closed mid-Aug) Choose a flavour from the huge choice on offer (chocolate with orange is a perennial favourite) and scoff it in the pretty piazza opposite; tubs only.

Nerbone FOOD STALL €
(inside Mercato Centrale, Piazza del Mercato Centrale; panini €3-4, mains €5-6.50; ⏰7am-2pm Mon-Sat) This unpretentious market stall has been serving its rustic dishes to shoppers and stallholders since 1872. It's a great place to try local staples such as *trippa alla fiorentina* (Florentine-style tripe; €6.50) and *panini con bollito* (a boiled beef bun; €3).

SOUTH OF THE RIVER AMO

TOP CHOICE **Le Volpi e l'uva** WINE BAR €
(www.levolpieluva.com; Piazza dei Rossi 1; ⏰11am-9pm Mon-Sat) Near Ponte Vecchio, this intimate *enoteca* has an impressive list of wines by the glass and serves a delectable array of accompanying antipasti, including juicy *prosciutto di Parma*, *lardo*-topped *crostini* and Tuscan cheeses.

Trattoria La Casalinga TRATTORIA €
(Via de'Michelozzi 9r; mains €6-9; ⏰closed Sun) Family run and much loved by locals, this unpretentious and always busy place is one of the city's cheapest trattorias. Brave the queues for hearty and dirt-cheap peasant dishes.

Drinking

Gilli CAFE, BAR
(Piazza della Repubblica 39r; ⏰Wed-Mon) The city's grandest cafe, Gilli has been serving excellent coffee and cakes since 1733. Claiming a table on the piazza is *molto* expensive – we prefer standing at the spacious Liberty-style bar.

Caffè Rivoire CAFE, BAR
(Piazza della Signoria; ⏰closed Mon & 2nd half Jan) Rivoire's terrace has the best view in the city. Settle in for a long *aperitivo* or coffee break – it's worth the high prices.

Old Stove Duomo PUB
(Piazza di San Giovanni 4r) This pub is a magnet for foreign students on holiday, who come here to swill beer and admire the views of the Duomo. Try to snaffle the upstairs balcony table.

Dolce Vita BAR
(www.dolcevitaflorence.com; Piazza del Carmine 6r; ⏰5pm-2am Tue-Sun, closed 2 weeks Aug) A long-standing Oltrarno favourite, 'Sweet Life' serves an *aperitivo* buffet between 7.30pm and 9.30pm, sometimes accompanied by live music.

Negroni BAR
(www.negronibar.com; Via dei Renai 17r; ⏰8am-2am Mon-Sat, from 7pm Sun) The famous Florentine cocktail gives its name to this popular bar in the San Nicolò district. Come here after admiring the sunset over the city from Piazzale Michelangelo.

☆ Entertainment

Florence's definitive monthly listings guide *Firenze Spettacolo* is sold at newsstands (€1.80).

Concerts, opera and dance are performed year-round at the **Teatro Comunale** (☎800 11 22 11; Corso Italia 16), which is also the venue for events organised by the Maggio Musicale Fiorentino.

English-language films are screened at the **Odeon Cinehall** (www.cinehall.it, in Italian; Via Sassetti 1).

Information

Emergency

Police station (Questura; ☎055 497 71; Via Zara 2)

Medical Services

Dr Stephen Kerr (☎055 28 80 55; www.dr-kerr.com; Piazza Mercato Nuovo 1; ⏲3-5pm Mon-Fri)

Emergency Doctor (Guardia Medica; ☎055 233 94 56 north of the Arno, ☎055 21 56 16 south of the Arno)

Tourist Information

Tourist offices (www.firenzeturismo.it) main office (☎055 29 08 32; Via Cavour 1r; ⏲8.30am-6.30pm Mon-Sat, to 1.30pm Sun); airport (☎055 31 58 74; ⏲8.30am-8.30pm); Borgo Santa Croce 29r (☎055 234 04 44; ⏲9am-7pm Mon-Sat, to 2pm Sun Mar-Oct, 9am-5pm Mon-Sat, to 2pm Sun Nov-Feb); Piazza della Stazione 4 (☎055 21 22 45; ⏲8.30am-7pm Mon-Sat, to 2pm Sun)

Getting There & Away

Air

The main airports serving Florence are **Pisa International Galileo Galilei** (PSA; ☎050 84 93 00; www.pisa-airport.com) and Bologna's **Guglielmo Marconi** (BLQ; ☎051 647 96 15; www.bologna-airport.it). There's also a small city airport 5km north of Florence, **Florence Amerigo Vespucci** (FLR; ☎055 306 13 00; www.aeroporto.firenze.it).

Bus

The **SITA bus station** (☎800 37 37 60; www.sitabus.it, in Italian; Via Santa Caterina da Siena 17) is just south of the train station. Buses leave for San Gimignano (€6.25, 1¼ hours, 14 daily) and Siena (€7.10, 1½ hours, every 30 to 60 minutes).

Train

Florence is well connected by train. There are regular services to/from Milan (€16.20, one hour, hourly), Pisa (€5.80, 1¼ hours, every 30 minutes), Rome (€44, 90 minutes, hourly) and Venice (€52, 1¾ hours, 12 daily).

Getting Around

To/From the Airport

Terravision (☎06 321 20 011; www.terravision.eu) runs a bus service between the train station and Pisa International Galileo Galilei airport (€10, 70 minutes, 12 daily). Buy your tickets at the Terravision desk inside Deanna Café, opposite. Otherwise there are regular trains (€5.10, 1½ hours, hourly between 6.37am and 8.37pm).

ATAF (☎800 42 45 00; www.ataf.net) runs a shuttlebus (€5, 25 minutes, half-hourly from 5.30am to 11pm) connecting Florence Amerigo Vespucci airport with the SITA bus station.

Half-hourly trains run between Florence and Bologna Centrale train station (€24, 40 minutes).

Bus

ATAF (☎800 42 45 00; www.ataf.net) buses service the city and environs. The most useful terminal is just outside the train station's eastern exit. Take bus 12 or 13 for Piazzale Michelangelo. Tickets (€1.20, 90 minutes) are sold at *tabacchi* and newsstands – you can also buy a 90-minute ticket on board the bus (€2).

Pisa

POP 87,400

Most people know Pisa as the home of an architectural project gone terribly wrong, but the Leaning Tower is just one of a number of noteworthy sights in this compact and compelling university city.

Pisa's golden age came in the 12th and 13th centuries when it was a maritime power rivalling Genoa and Venice. It was eventually defeated by the Genoese in 1284 and, in 1406, fell to Florence. Under the Medici, the arts and sciences flourished and Galileo Galilei (1564–1642) taught at the university.

Sights & Activities

Pisans claim that the **Campo dei Miracoli** (Field of Miracles) is among the most beautiful squares in the world. Certainly, the immaculate walled lawns provide a gorgeous setting for the Cathedral, Baptistry and Tower; however, few places boast so many tat-waving hawkers. Tickets to the Leaning Tower and Cathedral are sold individually, but for the remaining sights combined tickets are available – €5/6/10 for one/two/five sights. To get to the square from Piazza Sant' Antonio, just west of the train station, is a straightforward 1.5km walk – follow Viale F Crispi north, cross the Arno and continue straight up Via Roma.

Forming the centrepiece of the Campo's Romanesque trio, the candy-striped **Cathedral** (Duomo; admission €2 Mar-Oct, free Nov-Feb; ⏲10am-8pm Apr-Sep, shorter hr rest of year), begun in 1063, has a graceful tiered facade and cavernous interior.

To the west, the cupcake-like **Baptistry** (Battistero; ⏲8am-8pm Apr-Sep, shorter hr rest of year) was started in 1153 and completed by Nicola and Giovanni Pisano in 1260. Inside, note Nicola Pisano's beautiful pulpit.

But it's to the *campanile*, better known as the **Leaning Tower** (Torre Pendente; admis-

WORTH A TRIP

SAN GIMIGNANO

Dubbed the medieval Manhattan, San Gimignano is a tiny hilltop town deep in the Tuscan countryside. A mecca for day trippers from Florence and Siena, it owes its nickname to the 11th-century towers that soar above its pristine *centro storico* (historical cetre). To avoid the worst of the crowds try to visit midweek, preferably in deep winter.

The **tourist office** (0577 94 00 08; www.sangimignano.com; Piazza del Duomo 1; 9am-1pm & 3-7pm Mar-Oct, 9am-1pm & 2-6pm Nov-Feb) is a short walk from Piazza dei Martiri di Montemaggio. On the southern edge of Piazza del Duomo, the **Palazzo Comunale** (Piazza del Duomo; adult/concession €5/4; 9.30am-7pm Mar-Oct, 10am-5.30pm Nov-Feb) houses San Gimignano's art gallery (the Pinacoteca) and tallest tower, the Torre Grossa.

Regular buses link San Gimignano with Florence (€6.50, 1¼ hours, 14 daily), travelling via Poggibonsi, and Siena (€5.50, 1¼ hours, hourly).

sion €15 at ticket office, €17 online; 8.30am-8pm Apr-Sep, shorter hr rest of year), that all eyes are drawn. Bonanno Pisano began building in 1173, but almost immediately his plans came a cropper in a layer of shifting soil. Only three of the tower's seven tiers were completed before it started tilting – continuing at a rate of about 1mm per year. By 1990 the lean had reached 5.5 degrees – a tenth of a degree beyond the critical point established by computer models. Stability was finally ensured in 1998 when a combination of biased weighting and soil drilling forced the tower into a safer position. Today it's almost 4.1m off the perpendicular.

Visits are limited to groups of 10; entry times are staggered and queuing is inevitable. It is wise to book ahead.

Sleeping & Eating

Hotel Francesco HOTEL €
(050 55 54 53; www.hotelfrancesco.com; Via Santa Maria 129; r €60-150;) The best of the hotels lining busy Via Santa Maria (just off Campo dei Miracoli), the small family-run Francesco offers a warm welcome and bright, mod-conned rooms. Breakfast is extra.

Relais Sotto la Torre B&B, HOSTEL €
(050 55 35 59; www.relaisunderthetower.it; Crn Via Santa Maria & Piazza del Duomo; dm €24-25, d €56, without bathroom €52;) In the shadow of the Leaning Tower, this is a cross between a B&B and hostel. Rooms are all clean, but a few have no windows and reception hours are irregular. You're unlikely to find anything better at this price, though.

Ristoro al Vecchio Teatro TRATTORIA €€
(050 20 21 0; Piazza Dante; set menus €25/35, mains €8-12; lunch Mon-Sat, dinner Tue-Sat) Star of the show here are the four-course set menus. These feature local seafood specialities and *castagnaccio,* a sweet chestnut cake that has been known to prompt diners to spontaneous applause.

Il Montino PIZZERIA €
(Vicolo del Monte 1; cecina €2.40, focaccia €2.50; 10.30am-3pm & 5-10pm Mon-Sat) Students and sophisticates alike adore the *cecina* (chickpea pizza) and *spuma* (a sweet, nonalcoholic drink; €1) that are the specialities of this famous pizzeria.

Information

Tourist offices (www.pisaturismo.it) airport (050 50 25 18; 9.30am-11.30pm); city centre (050 4 22 91; Piazza Vittorio Emanuele II 16; 9am-7pm Mon-Sat, to 4pm Sun); Piazza dei Miracoli 334 641 94 08; 9.30am-7.30pm)

Getting There & Away

Pisa International Galileo Galilei airport (PSA; 050 84 93 00; www.pisa-airport.com) is linked to the centre by train (€1.10, five minutes, 15 daily), or by the CPT Linea Rossa bus (www.cpt.pisa.it, in Italian; €1, 10 minutes, every 10 minutes).

Terravision buses depart from the airport to Florence (€10, 70 minutes, 12 daily). **Train SpA** (www.trainspa.it) shuttle buses go to Siena via Empoli (€14, two daily).

Regular trains run to Lucca (€2.40, 30 minutes, every 30-60 minutes), Florence (€5.80, 1¼ hours, every 30 minutes), Rome (€39.50, three hours, nine daily) and Genoa (€16, 2½ hours, eight daily).

Siena

POP 54,160

Siena is one of Italy's most enchanting medieval towns. Its walled centre, a beautifully preserved warren of dark lanes punctuated by Gothic *palazzi,* pretty piazzas and eye-catching churches, has at its centre Piazza del Campo (known as Il Campo), the sloping square that is the venue for the city's famous annual horse race, Il Palio.

According to legend, Siena was founded by the sons of Remus, although it was the Middle Ages that heralded the city's golden age. Between the 13th and 15th centuries, painters of the Sienese School produced significant works of art, and Sts Catherine and Benedict called Siena home.

The centre's main streets – the Banchi di Sopra, Via di Città and Banchi di Sotto – curve around Il Campo.

Sights & Activities

Piazza del Campo SQUARE

Ever since the 14th century, this slanting, shell-shaped piazza has been the city's civic centre. Forming its base, the **Palazzo Pubblico** (Palazzo Comunale) is a magnificent example of Sienese Gothic architecture. Inside, the **Museo Civico** (adult/concession €8/4.50; 10am-6.15pm mid-Mar–Oct, to 4.45pm Nov–mid-Mar) houses some extraordinary frescoes. Soaring above the *palazzo* is the 102m (400-step) **Torre del Mangia** (admission €8; 10am-6.15pm mid-Mar–Oct, to 3.15pm Nov–mid-Mar), which dates from 1297. A combined ticket to the two costs €13 and is only available at the Torre del Mangia ticket office.

Duomo CHURCH

(Piazza del Duomo; admission €3; 10.30am-8pm Mon-Sat, 1.30-6pm Sun Jun-Aug, closes earlier rest of year) Siena's spectacular cathedral is a Gothic masterpiece. Begun in 1196 it was completed in 1215, although work continued well into the 13th century. The striking facade of green, red and white marble was designed by Giovanni Pisano, who also helped his father, Nicola, craft the cathedral's intricate pulpit. Other noteworthy features include Donatello's bronze of St John the Baptist and statues of St Jerome and Mary Magdalene by Bernini.

Siena

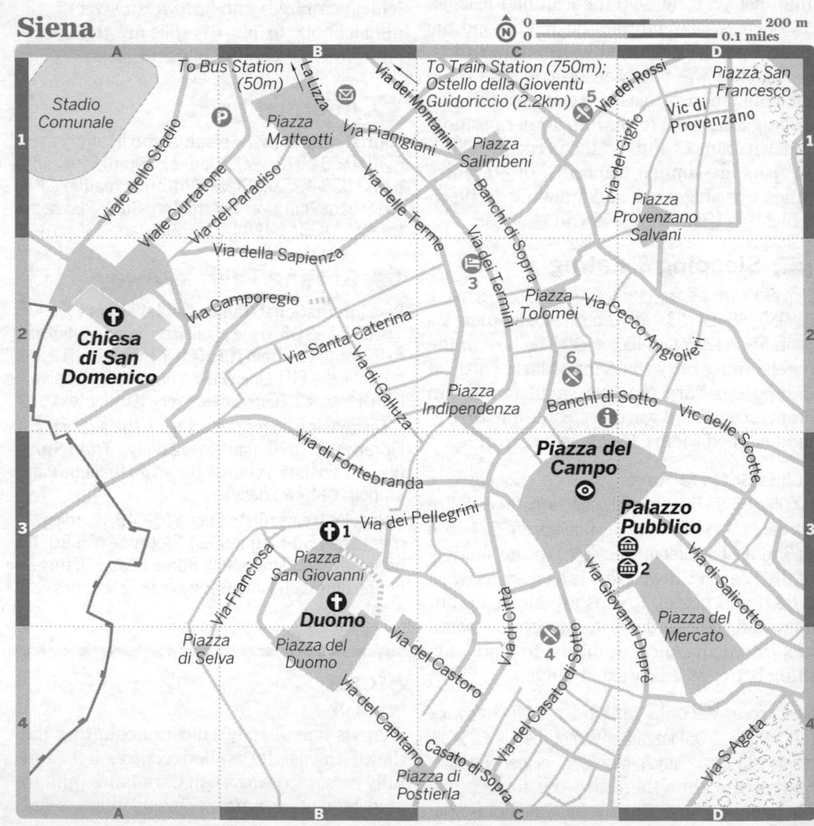

Behind the cathedral and down a flight of stairs, the **Battistero** (Baptistry; admission €3; Piazza San Giovanni; ⏲9.30am-8pm Jun-Aug, shorter hr rest of year) has a Gothic facade and a rich interior of 15th-century frescoes.

A joint ticket for the Duomo, Battistero, Museo dell'Opera, Diocesan Museum, Crypt and Santa Maria della Scala costs €12. See www.operaduomo.siena.it for details.

Chiesa di San Domenico CHURCH
(Piazza San Domenico 1; ⏲7.30am-1pm & 3-6.30pm) On the western edge of the walled city, this is the last resting place of the head and thumb of St Catherine, Siena's patron saint.

Festivals & Events

Siena's great annual event is the **Palio** (2 Jul & 16 Aug), a pageant culminating in a bareback horse race round Il Campo. The city is divided into 17 *contrade* (districts), of which 10 are chosen annually to compete for the *palio* (silk banner). The only rule in the three-lap race is that jockeys can't tug the reins of other horses.

Sleeping

Booking is essential for August and the Palio.

Antica Residenza Cicogna B&B €
(☎347 007 28 88; www.anticaresidenzacicogna.it; Via dei Termini 67; s €75-90, d €85-100; P❄📶) Springless beds, soundproof windows, ornate frescoes, antique furniture and a lavish buffet breakfast make this central option justifiably popular. Reception has limited core hours (8am to 1pm), so arrange your arrival in advance.

Siena

Top Sights

	Chiesa di San Domenico	A2
	Duomo	B3
	Palazzo Pubblico	D3
	Piazza del Campo	C3

Sights

1	Battistero	B3
2	Museo Civico	D3
	Torre del Mangia	(see 2)

Sleeping

3	Antica Residenza Cicogna	C2

Eating

4	Hosteria Il Carroccio	C4
5	L'Osteria	C1
6	Nannini	C2

Ostello della Gioventù Guidoriccio HOSTEL €
(☎0577 522 12; siena@ostellionline.org; Via Fiorentina 89; per person €20; P@) An inconvenient 20-minute bus ride from the town centre, Siena's HI hostel has 46 neat but dark two-bed rooms. Take bus 10 or 15 from Piazza Gramsci or 77 from the train station and tell the driver you're after the *ostello* (hostel).

Siena Colleverde CAMPING GROUND €
(☎0577 33 25 45; www.campingcolleverde.com; Strada di Scacciapensieri 47; per person/tent/car €10.50/6.70/6; 🏊) Some 1.5km from the train station, this panoramic camping ground offers excellent facilities in the hills outside of town. Self-catering bungalows are also available. Take bus 3 from Piazza Gramsci.

Eating

Among many traditional Sienese dishes are *panzanella* (summer salad of soaked bread, basil, onion and tomatoes), *pappardelle con la lepre* (ribbon pasta with hare) and *panforte* (a rich cake of almonds, honey and candied fruit).

Hosteria Il Carroccio TRATTORIA €€
(☎0577 411 65; Via del Casato di Sotto 32; mains €13-25; ⏲Thu-Tue) Recommended by the prestigious Slow Food movement, Il Carroccio specialises in traditional Sienese cooking. Staples include *pici* (thick spaghetti) and succulent *bistecca di chianina alla brace* (grilled steak).

Nannini CAFE €
(24 Via Banchi di Sopra; ⏲7.30am-11pm) Come here for the finest *cenci* (fried sweet pastry), *panforte* and *ricciarelli* (almond biscuits) in town, enjoyed with a cup of excellent coffee.

L'Osteria TRATTORIA €€
(☎0577 28 75 92; Via dei Rossi 79-81; mains €12) Popular with locals and tourists, this no-nonsense trattoria is great for Tuscan classics such as *ribollita* (vegetable stew) and pasta with *sugo di cinghiale* (boar sauce).

Information

Tourist office (☎0577 28 05 51; www.terresiena.it; Piazza del Campo 56; ⏲9am-7pm)

Getting There & Away

Siena is not on a main train line so it's easier to arrive by bus. From the bus station on Piazza Gramsci, **Train SpA** (www.trainspa.it) and SITA buses run to/from Florence (€7.10, 1½ hours, every 30 to 60 minutes), Pisa International Galileo

Galilei airport (€14, two daily) and San Gimignano (€5.50, 1¼ hours, hourly), either direct or via Poggibonsi.

Sena (☎0577 28 32 03; www.sena.it) operates services to/from Rome (€21, three hours, 10 daily).

Both Train SpA and Sena have ticket offices underneath Piazza Gramsci.

Lucca

POP 84,190

Lucca is a love-at-first-sight type of place. Hidden behind monumental Renaissance walls, its historic centre is chock-full of handsome churches, excellent restaurants and tempting *pasticcerie*. Founded by the Etruscans, it became a city-state in the 12th century and stayed that way for 600 years. Most of its streets and monuments date from this period.

Sights

Lucca's 12m-high **city walls** were built around the old city in the 16th and 17th centuries and were once defended by 126 cannons. Today they are crowned by a wide, tree-lined footpath, accessible from Piazzale Verdi or Piazza Santa Maria.

The predominantly Romanesque **Cattedrale di San Martino** (www.museocattedralelucca.it, in Italian; Piazza San Martino; 9.30am-5.45pm Mon-Fri, to 6.45pm Sat, 9am-10.45am & noon-6pm Sun Mar-Oct, shorter hr winter) dates to the 11th century. Inside, there's a magnificent *Last Supper* by Tintoretto.

Sleeping & Eating

Ostello San Frediano HOSTEL €
(☎0583 46 99 57; www.ostellolucca.it; Via della Cavallerizza12; dm €19-21, d €58; P@) Comfort and service levels are high at this HI-affiliated hostel. There are 141 rooms, a bar and a restaurant. Breakfast costs €3.

Forno Giusti BAKERY €
(Via Santa Lucia 20; pizza & filled focaccia €7-16 per kg; 7am-1pm & 4-7.30pm, closed Wed afternoon & Sun) The best way to enjoy a Lucchese lunch is to picnic on the walls, particularly if you buy delectable provisions from this excellent bakery.

La Pecora Nera TRATTORIA €€
(☎0583 46 97 38; Piazza San Francesco 4; mains €9-12; closed Mon, Tue dinner & Sun lunch) The only Lucchese restaurant recommended by Slow Food, La Pecora Nera also scores brownie points for social responsibility, as its profits help fund workshops for young people with Down syndrome.

Information

Tourist offices (☎0583 355 51 00; www.luccatourist.it) Piazza Napoleone (10am-1pm & 2-6pm Mon-Sat); Piazza Santa Maria (9am-7.30pm Apr-Oct, 9am-12.30pm & 3-6.30pm Nov-Mar); Piazza Verdi (9am-7pm). Bike hire is available at the Piazzale Verdi office (per hour €2.50)

Getting There & Away

From the bus station near Piazzale Giuseppe Verdi, **VaiBus** buses run to/from Pisa International Galileo Galilei airport (€3, one hour, hourly Monday to Saturday and every two hours Sunday).

Regional trains run to/from Florence (€5.20, 1½ hours, every 30 to 90 minutes) and Pisa (€2.40, 30 minutes, every 30 to 60 minutes).

Perugia

POP 165,210

The lively student city of Perugia boasts a beautiful medieval centre and sweeping views of the Umbrian landscape. The presence of the University for Foreigners and a year-long calendar of cultural events, climaxing in the July **Umbria Jazz festival** (www.umbriajazz.com), ensure a buzz that's not always apparent in the region's rural hinterland.

Perugia has a bloody past. In the Middle Ages the Baglioni and Oddi families clashed, while later as a papal satellite the city fought with its neighbours. All the while art and culture thrived: Perugino and Raphael, his student, both worked here.

Sights

Perugia's sights are in the historic centre, up the hill from the train and bus stations. From the bus station on Piazza Partigiani *scale mobili* (escalators) go up to Piazza Italia, where local buses terminate. From Piazza Italia, pedestrianised Corso Vannucci runs up to Piazza IV Novembre, the city's focal point.

Flanking Piazza IV Novembre, the austere 14th-century **Duomo** (Cathedral; Piazza IV Novembre; 7.30am-12.30pm & 4-7pm) has an unfinished two-tone facade and, inside, an altarpiece by Signorelli and sculptures by Duccio.

In the centre of the piazza, the stolid Fontana Maggiore was designed by Fra Bevignate and carved by Nicola and Giovanni Pisano between 1275 and 1278.

The 13th-century **Palazzo dei Priori** houses Perugia's best museums, including the **Galleria Nazionale dell'Umbria** (www.gallerianazionaleumbria.it, in Italian; Corso Vannucci 19; adult/EU concession €6.50/3.25; ⌚8.30am-7.30pm Tue-Sun, 9.30am-7.30pm Mon), whose collection contains works by local heroes Perugino and Pinturicchio. Close to the *palazzo,* the impressive **Nobile Collegio del Cambio** (Exchange Hall; Corso Vannucci 25; adult/concession €4.50/2.60; ⌚9am-12.30pm & 2.30-5.30pm Mon-Sat, 9am-1pm Sun, closed Mon pm Nov–mid-Mar) is home to impressive frescoes by Perugino.

The **Perugia Città Museo Card** (adult/EU concession €10/6) gives access to five city museums and is valid for 48 hours.

Courses

The **Università per Stranieri** (University for Foreigners; ☎075 574 61; www.unistrapg.it; Piazza Fortebraccio 4) runs hundreds of courses in language, art, history, music and architecture.

Sleeping

Primavera Mini Hotel PENSION €
(☎075 572 16 57; www.primaveraminihotel.com; Via Vincioli 8; s €42-65, d €65-75; ❄@📶) On the top floor of a 16th-century *palazzo,* this well-run two-star has eight modern rooms that are as clean as they are comfortable. Not all rooms have air-con, and breakfast costs an extra €3 to €6.

Centro Internazionale per la Gioventù HOSTEL €
(☎075 572 28 80; www.ostello.perugia.it; Via Bontempi 13; dm €15; ⌚closed mid-Dec–mid-Jan; @) A private hostel with decent four- to six-bed dorms, a frescoed TV room, a kitchen and great views from the terrace. The lockout (11am to 3.30pm) and 3.30am curfew are strictly enforced. The price doesn't include breakfast.

Albergo Anna PENSION €
(☎075 573 63 04; www.albergoanna.it; Via dei Priori 48; s €30-50, d €50-90) Central and quiet, this homey 4th-floor *pensione* (no lift) is a great bet with lovingly tended rooms, quirky knick-knacks and robust wooden furniture.

Eating & Drinking

Don't leave town without trying Perugia's famous chocolate.

TOP CHOICE **Sandri** CAFE €
(Corso Vannucci 32; ⌚closed Mon) Sandri has been serving exquisite cakes and the best coffee in town since 1860. Sit at tables on the *corso* or stand at the bar and ogle the decadent cakes, pastries and chocolates on offer.

Pizzeria Mediterranea PIZZERIA €
(Piazza Piccinino 11/12; pizzas €4-14; ⌚closed Tue) The wood-fired oven in the middle of the dining room is put to excellent use at this busy pizzeria. You can opt for a simple topping or lash out and order delectable *mozzarella di bufala* (fresh buffalo-milk mozzarella) to go on top for a small surcharge.

Punto di Vista BAR €
(Viale di Indipendenza 2; ⌚closed Mon) The term 'stunning view' is bandied around with gay abandon in Tuscany and Umbria, but here it really does apply. Go for a sunset drink.

Information

City maps are available at the **tourist office** (☎075 573 64 58; www.perugia.umbria2000.it; Piazza Matteotti 18; ⌚8.30am-6.30pm). For information about what's on in town, buy a copy of *Viva Perugia* (€0.80) from a local newsstand.

Getting There & Around

From the bus station on Piazza dei Partigiani, **Sulga** (☎800 09 96 61; www.sulga.it, in Italian) buses depart for Assisi (€3.20, 50 minutes, eight daily), Florence (€10.10, two hours, twice weekly), Naples (€25, 4½ hours, two daily), and Rome's Tiburtina bus station (€16, 2½ hours, two daily) and Leonardo da Vinci airport (€23, 3½ hours, three daily Monday to Saturday, two on Sunday).

Regional trains connect with Rome (€10.60, 3½ hours, 16 daily) and Florence (€10.55, 2¾ hours, 10 daily).

From the train station, take the minimetrò (€1) to the Pincetto stop just below Piazza Matteotti, or bus R, TS or TD (€1, €1.50 if purchased on bus) to Piazza Italia.

Assisi

POP 27,510

Seen from afar, the only clue to Assisi's importance is the imposing form of the Basilica di San Francesco jutting over the hillside. Thanks to St Francis, born here in 1182, this quaint medieval town is a major destination for millions of pilgrims.

Sights & Activities

Dress rules are applied rigidly at the main religious sights, so no shorts, miniskirts, low-cut dresses or tops. To book guided tours (in English) of the Basilica di San Francesco, contact the **information office** (☎075 819 00 84; www.sanfrancescoassisi.org; Piazza San Francesco; ⊙9am-noon & 2-5pm Mon-Sat).

Basilica di San Francesco CHURCH
(Piazza di San Francesco) Assisi's main basilica actually comprises two churches. The **upper church** (⊙8.30am-6.45pm Easter-Nov, to 5.45pm Nov-Easter) was damaged during a severe earthquake in 1997, but has since been restored to its former state. Built between 1230 and 1253 in the Italian Gothic style, it features superb frescoes by Giotto and works by Cimabue and Pietro Cavallini.

Downstairs in the dimly lit **lower church** (⊙6am-6.45pm Easter-Nov, to 5.45pm Nov-Easter), constructed between 1228 and 1230, you'll find a series of colourful frescoes by Simone Martini, Cimabue and Pietro Lorenzetti. The crypt where St Francis is buried is below the church.

Basilica di Santa Chiara CHURCH
(Piazza Santa Chiara; ⊙6.30am-noon & 2-7pm Apr-Oct, to 6pm Nov-Mar) This 13th-century basilica contains the remains of St Clare, friend of St Francis and founder of the Order of Poor Clares.

Sleeping & Eating

You'll need to book ahead during peak times: Easter, August and September, and the Feast of St Francis (3 and 4 October).

Ostello della Pace HOSTEL €
(☎075 81 67 67; www.assisihostel.com; Via Valecchie 177; dm €17-19, r per person €20; @) In a pretty, quiet location between the train station and the Old Town, this family-run HI hostel offers a bar, restaurant, laundry room and bikes for hire.

Trattoria Da Erminio TRATTORIA €
(☎075 81 25 06; www.trattoriadaerminio.it; Via Montecavallo 19; mains €7-11, set menu €16; ⊙closed Thu, Feb & 1st half Jul) Near Piazza Matteotti, Da Ermino is known for its grilled meats, which are prepared on a huge fireplace in the main dining area. In summer, tables on the pretty cobbled street are hot property.

Trattoria Pallotta TRATTORIA €€
(☎075 81 26 49; Vicolo della Volta Pinta 2; mains €8-16, set menus €16-25; ⊙closed Tue) The menu at this brick-vaulted, wood-beamed trattoria is unapologetically local, featuring home-made *strangozzi* (like tagliatelle), roast pigeon and rabbit stew. The same people also run nearby **Hotel Pallotta** (⊙075 81 23 07; www.pallottaassisi.it; Via San Rufino 6; s €35-45, d €58-80; wi-fi), which has bright, value-for-money rooms.

Information

The **tourist office** (☎075 81 25 34; www.assisi.regioneumbria.eu; Piazza del Comune 22; ⊙8am-2pm & 3-6pm Mon-Sat, 10am-1pm Sun) supplies maps, brochures and practical information.

Getting There & Away

It is better to travel to Assisi by bus rather than train, as the train station is 4km from Assisi proper in Santa Maria degli Angeli. Buses arrive at and depart from Piazza Matteotti in the *centro storico*.

Sulga buses connect Assisi with Florence (€12.50, 2½ hours, twice weekly), Perugia (€3.20, 50 minutes, eight daily) and Rome (€18, three hours, one daily).

If you arrive by train, a bus (Linea C; €1, half-hourly) runs between Piazza Matteotti and the station. Regional trains run to Perugia (€2.40, 20 minutes, hourly).

Urbino

POP 15,530

If you visit only one town in Le Marche, make it Urbino. It's a pain to get to, but as you wander its steep, Unesco-protected streets you'll be glad you made the effort. Birthplace of Raphael and Bramante, and a university town since 1564, it's still a bustling centre of culture and learning.

Interest is centred on Urbino's immaculate hilltop *centro storico*. To get there from the bus terminal on Borgo Mercatale, head up Via Mazzini or take the *ascensore* (lift) up to Via Garibaldi (€0.50). The town's grand centrepiece is the Renaissance **Palazzo Ducale** (Piazza Duca Federico; adult/concession €4/2; ⊙8.30am-7.15pm Tue-Sun, to 2pm Mon), completed in 1482. Inside, the **Galleria Nazionale delle Marche** features works by Raphael, Paolo Uccello, della Francesca and Verrocchio.

Sleeping & Eating

Right in the heart of the walled town, **Albergo Italia** (☎0722 27 01; www.albergo-italia-urbino.it; Corso Garibaldi 32; s €48-70, d €75-120; ❄@) has a bland, modern interior offset by helpful staff, a pleasant garden terrace and comfortable rooms.

To dine on earthy regional food, head to **La Trattoria del Leone** (Via Cesare Battisti; mains €10; ⊙dinner daily, lunch Sat & Sun), an unassuming trattoria just off the main square.

Information

Tourist offices (☎0722 26 13; www.urbinoculturaturismo.it) Bus Terminal ⏰9am-6pm Mon-Sat); city centre (Via Puccinoti 35; ⏰9am-7pm) Also useful is www.turismo.pesarourbino.it.

Getting There & Around

The only way to get to Urbino by public transport is by bus. **Adriabus** (☎800 66 43 32; www.adriabus.eu) runs up to 20 daily buses to Pesaro (€2.75 to €3), from where you can catch a train to Bologna and two daily services to Rome (€27, 4¼ hours).

Autolinee Ruocco (☎800 90 15 91; www.viaggiruocco.eu) runs a daily bus to Perugia (€15, 1¾ hours), for which it is essential to book in advance.

SOUTHERN ITALY

A sun-bleached land of spectacular coastlines, windswept hills and proud towns, southern Italy is a robust contrast to the genteel north. Its stunning scenery, graphic ruins and fabulous beaches often go hand in hand with urban sprawl and scruffy coastal development, sometimes in the space of a few kilometres.

Yet for all its troubles, *il mezzogiorno* (the midday sun, as southern Italy is known) has much to offer, specifically the fruitful fusion of architectural, artistic and culinary styles that is the legacy of centuries of foreign dominion.

Naples

POP 963,670

A raucous hell-broth of a city, Naples (Napoli) is loud, anarchic, dirty and edgy. Its Dickensian streets and in-your-face energy leave you disorientated, bewildered and hungry for more. Founded by Greek colonists, it became a thriving Roman city and was later the Bourbon capital of the Kingdom of the Two Sicilies. In the 18th century it was one of Europe's great cities, something you'll readily believe as you marvel at its imperious palaces. Many of Naples finest *palazzi* now house museums and art galleries, the best of which is the Museo Archeologico Nazionale, one of Italy's premier museums and reason enough for a city stopover.

CAMPANIA ARTECARD

The **Campania ArteCard** (☎800 600 601; www.campaniaartecard.it; €12-30) gives free or discounted admission to museums in Naples and the whole region. There are several versions but the most useful is the Napoli e Campi Flegrei card, valid for three days, which includes free public transport, free entrance to three museums and 50% discount for 11 others. Cards are available at participating museums, the internet or through the call centre.

Sights

From Piazza Garibaldi, the city's ugly transport hub outside Stazione Centrale, Corso Umberto I skirts the *centro storico,* which is centred on two parallel roads: Via San Biagio dei Librai (and its continuation Via Benedetto Croce – together known as Spaccanapoli) and Via dei Tribunali. West of the *centro storico,* Via Toledo, Naples' main shopping strip, leads down to the city's grandest square, Piazza del Plebiscito.

Museo Archeologico Nazionale MUSEUM
(http://museoarcheologiconazionale.campaniabeniculturali.it; Piazza Museo Nazionale 19; adult/EU concession €10/5; ⏰9am-7.30pm Wed-Mon) Be sure to visit this museum, home to one of the world's most important collections of Graeco-Roman antiquities. Highlights include the colossal *Toro Farnese* (Farnese Bull), *Ercole* (Hercules) and, on the mezzanine floor, *La Battaglia di Alessandro Contro Dario* (The Battle of Alexander against Darius), one of many awe-inspiring mosaics from Pompeii. On the same floor, the Gabinetto Segreto (Secret Room) boasts some majestic phalluses.

Duomo CHURCH
(Via Duomo; ⏰8am-12.30pm & 4.30-7pm Mon-Sat, 8.30am-1pm & 5-7.30pm Sun). Built in the 13th century, Naples' spiritual heart has a 19th-century neo-Gothic facade and a largely baroque interior. Inside, the holy of holies is the 17th-century Cappella di San Gennaro, containing the head of St Januarius (the city's patron saint) and two vials of his congealed blood. The saint is said to have saved the city from disasters on various occasions.

Piazza del Gesù Nuovo SQUARE
A short walk south of the Museo Archeologico, the Piazza del Gesù Nuovo is flanked by the ashlar facade of the **Chiesa del Gesù Nuovo** (⏰7am-1pm & 4-7.30pm) and the **Basilica di Santa Chiara** (Via Santa Chiara 49; ⏰7.30am-1pm

Central Naples

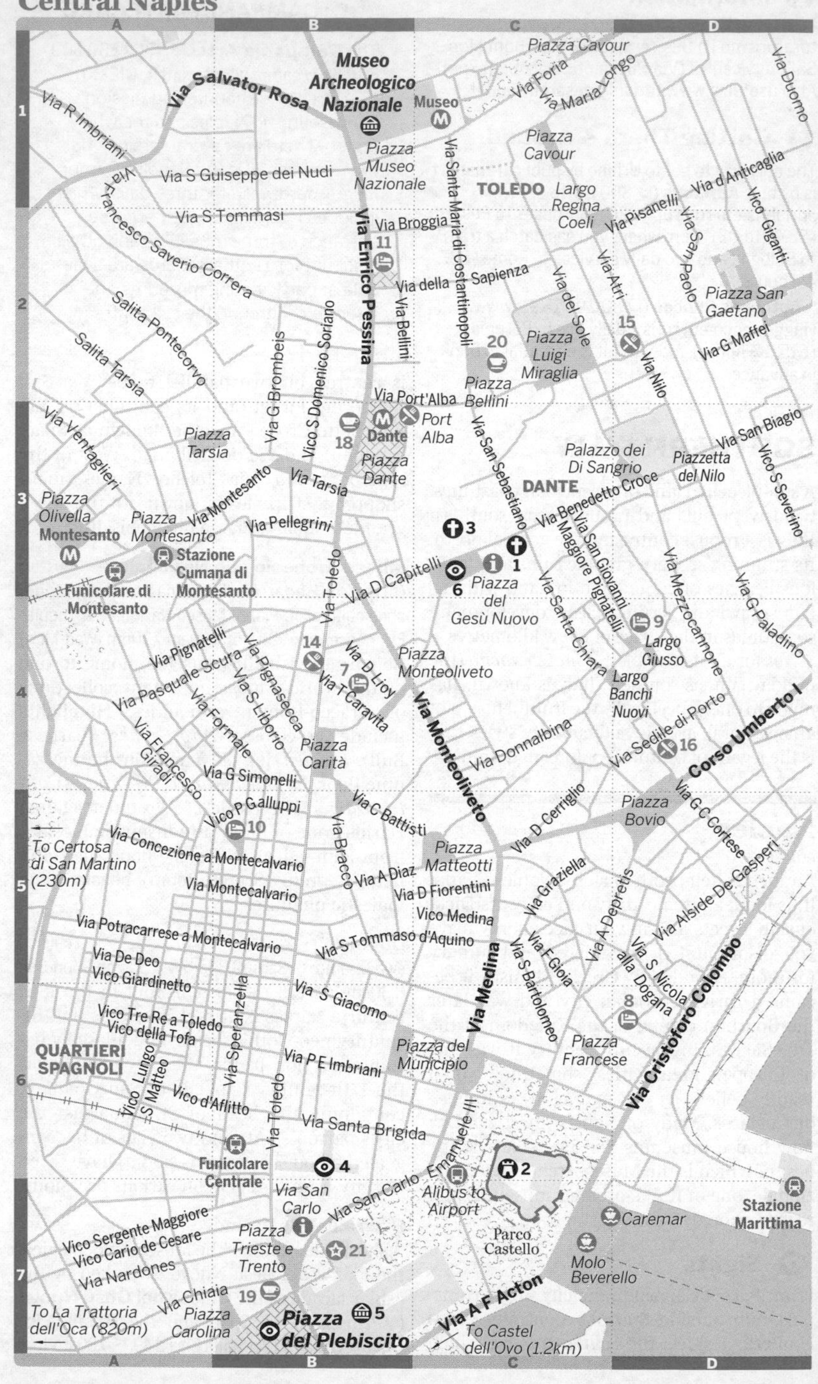

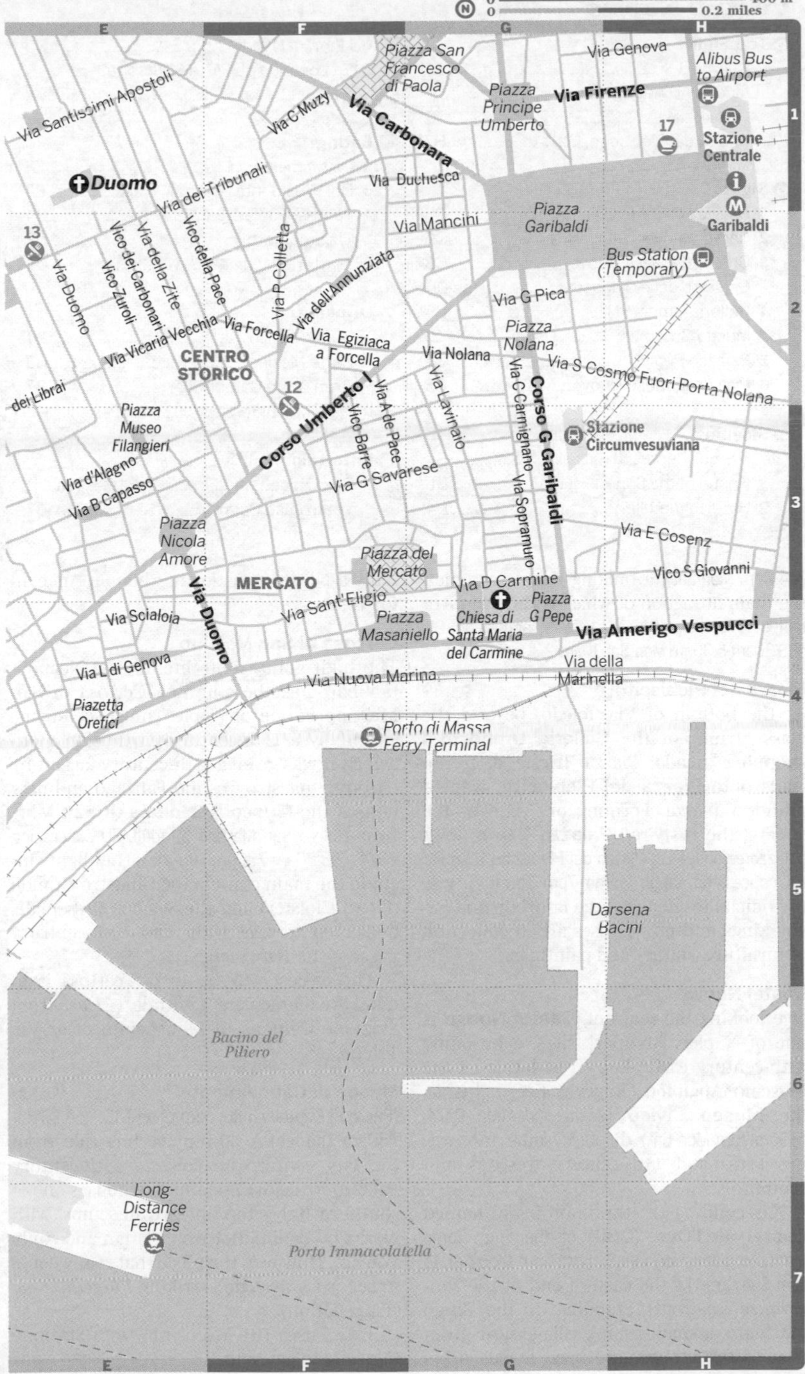
0 400 m
0 0.2 miles
Piazza San Francesco di Paola
Via Genova
Alibus Bus to Airport
Piazza Principe Umberto
Via Firenze
Via Santissimi Apostoli
Via C Muzy
Via Carbonara
17
Stazione Centrale
Duomo
Via dei Tribunali
Via Duchesca
Piazza Garibaldi
Garibaldi
13
Via Mancini
Bus Station (Temporary)
Via Duomo
Vico dei Carbonari
Via della Zite
Vico della Pace
Via P Colletta
Via dell'Annunziata
Vico Zuroli
Via G Pica
Piazza Nolana
Via Vicaria Vecchia
Via Forcella
Via Egiziaca a Forcella
Via Nolana
Via S Cosmo Fuori Porta Nolana
CENTRO STORICO
dei Librai
12
Corso Umberto I
Via A de Pace
Via Lavinaio
Via C Carmignano
Corso G Garibaldi
Stazione Circumvesuviana
Piazza Museo Filangieri
Vico Barre
Via d'Alagno
Via G Savarese
Via B Capasso
Via Sopramuro
Via E Cosenz
Piazza Nicola Amore
Piazza del Mercato
Vico S Giovanni
Via D Carmine
MERCATO
Via Duomo
Piazza G Pepe
Via Sant'Eligio
Via Scialoia
Piazza Masaniello
Chiesa di Santa Maria del Carmine
Via Amerigo Vespucci
Via L di Genova
Via della Marinella
Via Nuova Marina
Piazetta Orefici
Porto di Massa Ferry Terminal
Darsena Bacini
Bacino del Piliero
Long-Distance Ferries
Porto Immacolatella

Central Naples

Top Sights
- Duomo E1
- Museo Archeologico Nazionale B1
- Piazza del Plebiscito B7

Sights
- 1 Basilica di Santa Chiara C3
- 2 Castel Nuovo C6
- 3 Chiesa del Gesù Nuovo C3
- Chiostro delle Clarisse .... (see 1)
- 4 Galleria Umberto I B6
- Museo Civico .... (see 2)
- 5 Palazzo Reale B7
- 6 Piazza del Gesù Nuovo C3

Sleeping
- 7 6 Small Rooms B4
- 8 Hostel of the Sun D6
- 9 Hotel Pignatelli D4
- 10 I Fiori di Napoli B5
- 11 La Locanda dell'Arte & Victoria House B2

Eating
- 12 Da Michele F2
- 13 Del Presidente E2
- 14 Fantasia Gelati B4
- 15 Pizzeria Sorbillo D2
- 16 Trattoria Mangia e Bevi D4

Drinking
- 17 Caffè Mexico H1
- 18 Caffè Mexico B3
- 19 Gran Caffè Gambrinus B7
- 20 Intra Moenia C2

Entertainment
- Box Office .... (see 4)
- 21 Teatro San Carlo B7

& 4-8pm Mon-Sat), a hulking Gothic complex, the main attraction of which is the **Chiostro delle Clarisse** (Nuns' Cloisters; admission €5; ⏲9.30am-5.30pm Mon-Sat, 10am-2.30pm Sun).

Piazza del Plebiscito SQUARE

At the bottom of Via Toledo, beyond the glass atrium of the **Galleria Umberto I** shopping arcade, Piazza Trieste e Trento leads onto **Piazza del Plebiscito**, Naples' grandest piazza. Forming one side of the square, the rusty-red **Palazzo Reale** (www.palazzorealenapoli.it; Piazza del Plebiscito I; adult/EU concession €4/2; ⏲9am-7pm Thu-Tue) was the official residence of the Bourbon and Savoy kings and now houses a rich collection of furniture, statues and paintings.

Castel Nuovo CASTLE

Overlooking the seafront, **Castel Nuovo** is one of Naples' landmark sites, a brooding 13th-century castle known to locals as the Maschio Angioino (Angevin Keep). Inside, the **Museo Civico** (adult/concession €5/4; ⏲9am-7pm Mon-Sat) displays some interesting 14th- and 15th-century frescoes and sculptures.

A second castle, the improbably named **Castel dell'Ovo** (Castle of the Egg; Borgo Marinaro; admission free; ⏲8am-6pm Mon-Sat, to 1pm Sun) marks the eastern end of the *lungomare* (seafront). Standing on the Borgo Marinaro, a small fishing village now given over to restaurants and bars, it was originally a Norman castle and then an Angevin fortress.

Certosa di San Martino MUSEUM

The high point (quite literally) of Neapolitan baroque, the stunning Certosa di San Martino is one of Naples' must-see sights. Originally a 14th-century Carthusian monastery, it was given a 17th-century facelift by baroque maestro Cosimo Fanzago and now houses the **Museo Nazionale di San Martino** (Largo San Martino 5; adult/EU concession €8/4; ⏲8.30am-7.30pm Thu-Tue). Highlights include the main church, the Chiostro Grande (Great Cloister) and the Sezione Presepiale, dedicated to rare 18th- and 19th-century *presepi* (nativity scenes).

The easiest way up to the certosa is to take the Funicolare Centrale (€1.10) from Stazione Cumana di Montesanto, near Via Toledo.

Museo di Capodimonte MUSEUM

(Parco di Capodimonte; admission €10; ⏲8.30am-7.30pm Thu-Tue) A 30-minute bus ride from the city centre, the colossal 18th-century Palazzo Reale di Capodimonte houses one of southern Italy's top fine-art museums, with works by Bellini, Botticelli, Titian and Andy Warhol. However, the piece that many come to see is Caravaggio's striking *Flagellazione* (Flagellation).

Take buses 110, M4 or M5 from Stazione Centrale to get here.

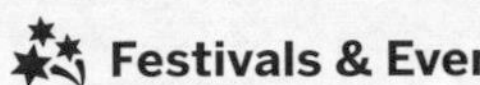

Festivals & Events

The **Festa di San Gennaro** honours the city's patron saint and is held three times a year (first Sunday in May, 19 September and 16 December). Thousands fill the Duomo to witness the saint's blood liquefy, a miracle said to save the city from disaster.

Sleeping

You'll have no problem finding somewhere to stay, though be warned that many places suffer from street noise and double-glazed windows are not common. Most of the budget accommodation is in the ugly area around Stazione Centrale and down near the port.

TOP CHOICE Hostel of the Sun HOSTEL €
(☎081 420 63 93; www.hostelnapoli.com; 7th fl, Via Melisurgo 15; dm €16-20, d €60-70, d without bathroom €50-60; ❄@📶) This award-winning hostel has the lot – great facilities, helpful staff, a shared kitchen for guests' use, and a vibrant colour scheme that extends to the dorms and hotel-quality private rooms on the 5th floor. Just make sure you have €0.05 for the lift.

I Fiori di Napoli B&B €
(☎081 1957 70 83; www.ifioridinapoli.it; 3rd fl, Via Francesco Girardi 92; s/d €40/80, without bathroom €35/60; ❄@📶) This sprawling apartment is run by a friendly multilingual crew who go to a lot of trouble to make guests feel at home. The rooms with bathroom also have air-con and satellite TV, and there's a shared kitchen for guests' use. No lift.

La Locanda dell'Arte & Victoria House B&B €
(☎081 564 46 40; www.bbnapoli.org; Via E Pessina 66; s €45-55, d €60-70; ❄@📶) Spread over two floors in a grand but crumbling *palazzo* near Piazza Dante, the large rooms here have high ceilings, satellite TV and a simple but attractive decor. Excellent value, but remember €0.10 for the lift.

6 Small Rooms HOSTEL €
(☎081 790 13 78; www.6smallrooms.com; Via Diodato Lioy 18; dm €20; @📶) In a dark *centro storico* street, this is a bright hostel with a homey, laid-back atmosphere. Once you've climbed six flights of treacherous stairs, you'll find an inviting living room, a fully equipped kitchen, mixed dorms and three private rooms.

Hotel Pignatelli HOTEL €
(☎081 658 49 50; www.hotelpignatellinapoli.com; Via San Giovanni Maggiore Pignatelli 16; s €40-50, d €70-90) Hidden on the 2nd floor of a historic *palazzo*, this friendly value-for-money hotel offers tasteful rooms decorated with brass beds, terracotta floors and wood-beamed ceilings.

Eating

Pizza was created in Naples and nowhere will you eat it better. There are any number of toppings but locals favour *margherita* (tomato, mozzarella and basil) or *marinara* (tomato, garlic, oregano and olive oil), cooked in a wood-fired oven. Pizzerias serving the 'real thing' have a sign on their door – *la vera pizza napoletana* (the real Neapolitan pizza).

Snacking is popular too. *Misto di frittura* – deep-fried vegetables – are available at takeaways called *friggatorie* all over town. For something sweet try a *sfogliatella* (a flaky pastry filled with cinnamon ricotta).

Pizza

Pizzeria Sorbillo PIZZERIA €
(Via dei Tribunali 32; pizzas from €4; ⊙Mon-Sat) The smartest of the Via dei Tribunali pizzerias, the Sorbillo is hugely popular. So much so that eating here is much like sitting down to a meal in rush hour. The hardworking *pizzaioli* (pizza makers) really know their craft – the pizzas are delicious.

Da Michele PIZZERIA €
(www.damichele.net; Via Cesare Sersale 1/3; pizzas €4-5; ⊙10am-11pm Mon-Sat) The godfather of Neapolitan pizzerias (it opened in 1870), this place near Piazza Garibaldi takes the no-frills ethos to its extremes. It's dingy, old-fashioned and serves only two types of pizza – *margherita* and *marinara*.

Del Presidente PIZZERIA €
(Via dei Tribunali 120/121; pizzas from €4; ⊙closed Sun) This is where British über-chef Heston Blumenthal came when researching pizza for his TV series *In Search of Perfection*, and for good reason. Be prepared for great pizza, crowds and service with attitude.

Not Pizza

La Trattoria dell'Oca TRATTORIA €€
(☎081 41 48 65; Via Santa Teresa a Chiaia 11; mains €12; ⊙closed dinner Sun Oct-May) An intimate, relaxed trattoria serving classic Neapolitan cuisine. Wine bottles and vintage prints line the walls while local seafood dominates the daily-changing menu.

Trattoria Mangia e Bevi TRATTORIA €
(☎081 552 95 46; Via Sedile di Porto 92; meals €10; ⊙lunch Mon-Fri) Students and their

profs squeeze around lively communal tables to chow down on home cooking at rock-bottom prices. Few frills but great for a cheap fill-up.

Fantasia Gelati GELATERIA €
(Via Toledo 381; cones from €2; ⏲7.30am-midnight) It claims to be the '*maesti gelatieri in Napoli*' ('master gelato makers in Naples'), and we thoroughly concur.

Drinking

The city's student drinking scene is around the piazzas and alleyways of the *centro storico*. For a chicer vibe, hit the cobbled lanes of upmarket Chiaia.

Caffè Mexico CAFE
(Piazza Dante 86; ⏲7am-8.30pm Mon-Sat) This retro gem makes the best coffee in the city. There's another branch near Stazione Centrale at Piazza Garibaldi 70.

Gran Caffè Gambrinus CAFE
(Via Chiaia 1-2; ⏲7am-2am) Naples' most venerable cafe features a showy art nouveau interior and a cast of self-conscious drinkers served by smart, waistcoated waiters.

Enoteca Belledonne BAR
(Vico Belledonne a Chiaia 18; ⏲10am-2pm & 7pm-2am Mon, 10am-2pm & 4.30pm-2am Tue-Sat, 7pm-2am Sun;) Exposed brick walls, ambient lighting and bottle-lined shelves set the scene at this much-loved Chiaia wine bar.

Intra Moenia CAFE
(Piazza Bellini 70; ⏲10am-2am) This arty cafe-cum-bookshop is a great place to while away a long summer evening with friends and something cool.

Entertainment

You can buy tickets for most sporting and cultural events at **Box Office** (☎081 551 91 88; www.boxofficenapoli.it; Galleria Umberto I 17).

Opera fans will enjoy an evening at **Teatro San Carlo** (☎box office 081 797 23 31; www.teatrosancarlo.it; Via San Carlo 98; tickets from €25; ⏲box office 10am-7pm Mon-Sat, to 3.30pm Sun), Italy's oldest opera house.

Information

Dangers & Annoyances

Despite Naples' notoriety as a mafia hotspot, the city is pretty safe. That said, travellers should be careful about walking alone late at night near Stazione Centrale and Piazza Dante. Petty crime is also widespread – be vigilant for pickpockets and moped bandits, and never leave anything visible in a parked car.

Other Information

Ospedale Loreto-Mare (Hospital; ☎081 254 27 93; Via Amerigo Vespucci 26)

Police station (Questura; ☎081 794 11 11; Via Medina 75)

Tourist information points (www.inaples.it; ⏲9.30am-1.30pm & 2.30-6pm Mon-Sat, 9am-1.30pm Sun) Piazza del Gesù Nuovo (☎081 551 27 01); Via San Carlo (☎081 40 23 94) All stock *Qui Napoli*, a bilingual monthly publication with useful tourist information.

Getting There & Away

Air

Capodichino airport (NAP; ☎848 88 87 77; www.gesac.it), 7km northeast of the city centre, is southern Italy's main airport. Flights operate to most Italian cities and up to 30 European destinations, as well as New York.

Boat

A fleet of *traghetti* (ferries), *aliscafi* (hydrofoils) and *navi veloci* (fast ships) connect Naples with Sorrento, the bay islands, the Amalfi Coast, Sicily and Sardinia. Hydrofoils leave from Molo Beverello and Megellina; ferries depart from the Porta di Massa ferry terminal.

The major companies:

Alilauro (☎081 497 22 38; www.alilauro.it) To/from Sorrento (€10, 35 minutes).

Caremar (☎081 551 38 82; www.caremar.it, in Italian) To/from Capri (€14.50, 1¼ hours).

Metro del Mare (☎199 600 700; www.metrodelmare.com) To/from Amalfi (€15, 1½ hours), Positano (€14, 55 minutes), Sorrento (€6.50, 45 minutes).

NLG (☎081 552 07 63; www.navlib.it, in Italian) To/from Capri (€16, 30 minutes).

Siremar (☎89 21 23; www.siremar.it, in Italian) To/from Lipari (€50, 10½ hours).

SNAV (☎081 428 55 55; www.snav.it, in Italian) To/from Capri (€16, 45 minutes) and Palermo (€50, 10 hours).

Tirrenia (☎081 89 21 23; www.tirrenia.com) To/from Palermo (€50, 10 hours) and Cagliari (€55, 16¼ hours).

Bus

Most buses leave from Piazza Garibaldi. **SITA** (☎199 73 07 49; www.sitabus.it, in Italian) runs buses to Amalfi (€3.40, two hours, eight daily), Bari (€20, three hours, one daily), Pompeii (€2.40, 40 minutes, hourly), Positano (€3.40, two hours, three daily) and Sorrento (€3.40, one hour 20 minutes, three daily). Buy tickets and catch buses from the terminus near Porto di Massa or from the front of Stazione Centrale.

Miccolis (☎081 200 380; www.miccolis-spa.it, in Italian) serves Lecce (€29, 5½ hours) and Brindisi (€26.60, five hours).

Train

Most trains stop at Stazione Centrale, which incorporates Stazione Garibaldi. There are up to 30 trains daily to Rome (€20.50, 2¼ hours) and some 15 to Salerno (€7, 35 minutes).

The **Circumvesuviana** (☎800 05 39 39; www.vesuviana.it), accessible through Stazione Centrale, operates trains to Sorrento (€3.40, 65 minutes) via Pompeii (€2.40, 35 minutes) and other towns along the coast. There are about 40 trains daily running between 5am and 10.40pm, with reduced services on Sunday.

Getting Around

To/From the Airport

By public transport you can either take the regular **ANM** (☎800 639 525; www.anm.it) bus 3S (€1.10, 30 minutes, half-hourly) from Piazza Garibaldi or the Alibus airport shuttle (€3, 20 minutes, every 20 minutes) from Piazza del Municipio or Stazione Centrale.

Taxi fares are set at €19 to/from the historic centre.

Public Transport

You can travel Naples by bus, metro and funicular. Journeys are covered by the Unico Napoli ticket (www.unicocampania.it), which comes in various forms: the standard ticket, valid for 90 minutes, costs €1.10; a daily pass is €3.10; and a weekend daily ticket is €2.60. Note that these tickets are not valid on the Circumvesuviana train line.

Pompeii

An ancient town frozen in its 2000-year-old death throes, Pompeii (Pompei) was a thriving commercial town until Mt Vesuvius erupted on 24 August AD 79, burying it under a layer of *lapilli* (burning fragments of pumice stone) and killing some 2000 people. The skeletal, Unesco-listed **ruins** (☎081 857 53 47; www.pompeiisites.org; adult/concession €11/5.50, audio guide €6.50; ⏲8.30am-7.30pm Apr-Oct, to 5pm Nov-Mar, last entry 1½hr before closing) provide a remarkable model of a working Roman city. Dotted around the 44-hectare site are a number of creepy body casts, made in the late 19th century by pouring plaster into the hollows left by disintegrated bodies.

Get information from the **tourist office** (☎081 536 32 93; www.pompeiturismo.it; Piazza Porta Marina Inferiore 12; ⏲8am-6pm Mon-Sat, 8.30am-2pm Sun Aug & Sep, shorter hr rest of year) just outside the excavations at Porta Marina.

The easiest way to get to Pompeii is by the Ferrovia Circumvesuviana from Naples (€2.40, 35 minutes, half-hourly) or Sorrento (€1.90, 30 minutes, half-hourly). Get off at Pompeii Scavi-Villa dei Misteri; the Porta Marina entrance is nearby.

Capri

POP 7330

The most visited of the Bay of Naples' islands, Capri is far more interesting than a quick day trip would suggest. Get beyond the glamorous veneer of chichi piazzas and designer boutiques and you'll discover an island of rugged seascapes, desolate Roman ruins and a surprisingly unspoiled rural inland.

The island is easily reached from Naples and Sorrento. Hydrofoils and ferries dock at Marina Grande, from where it's a short funicular ride up to Capri, the main town. A further bus ride takes you up to Anacapri.

Sights & Activities

Capri's single most famous attraction is the **Grotta Azzurra** (Blue Grotto; admission €4; ⏲9am-3pm), a stunning sea cave illuminated by an otherworldly blue light. The best time to visit is in the morning. Boats leave from Marina Grande and the return trip costs €19.50 plus the entrance fee to the grotto; allow a good hour. Note that the grotto isn't visitable when seas are rough or tides are high.

When you're done exploring Capri Town's dinky whitewashed streets, head over to the **Giardini di Augusto** (Gardens of Augustus; admission free; ⏲9am-1hr before sunset) for some breathtaking views. From here **Via Krupp** zigzags vertiginously down to Marina Piccola.

An hour's walk along Via Tiberio, **Villa Jovis** (admission €2; ⏲9am-1hr before sunset) is what's left of Tiberius' main Capri residence. Double back and follow Via Matermània for the **Arco Naturale**, a huge natural rock arch.

Up in Anacapri, **Villa San Michele** (Via Axel Munthe; admission €6; ⏲9am-6pm May-Sep, closes earlier rest of year) boasts some Roman antiquities and beautiful, panoramic gardens. For the best views on the island, take the **seggiovia** (chair lift; one way/return €7/9; ⏲9.30am-5pm Mar-Oct, 10.30am-3pm Nov-Feb) up from Piazza Vittoria to the summit of **Mt Solaro** (589m), Capri's highest point.

Sleeping & Eating

Capri has few genuinely budget sleeping options. Always book ahead.

Hotel La Tosca PENSION €€
(☎081 837 09 89; www.latoscahotel.com; Via Dalmazio Birago 5; s €48-95, d €75-150; ⏲Apr-Oct; ❄📶) La Tosca is one of the island's top budget hotels. With 10 sparkling white rooms, a central location and a roof terrace with panoramic views, it presses all the right buttons.

Hotel Bussola di Hermes HOTEL €€
(☎081 838 20 10; www.bussolahermes.com; Trav La Vigna 14; s €50-110, d €60-150; ❄@) A hospitable outpost on a quiet Anacapri lane, the year-round Bussola offers recently revamped rooms, some with private terraces and sea views.

Trattoria Il Solitario TRATTORIA €
(☎081 837 13 82; Via G Orlandi 96; pizzas from €5, mains €10; ⏲Apr-Oct) Just off Anacapri's main strip, this is a good, honest trattoria serving tasty local food. Sit out the back under the canopy of ivy and lemon trees and choose from a menu of seafood, pizza, pasta and grilled meats.

Verginiello TRATTORIA €
☎081 837 09 44; Via Lo Palazzo 25; mains €10; ⏲closed Nov) Offering straight-up Italian food and great views, this bustling restaurant is as near to a budget diner as you'll get in Capri Town. The atmosphere here is no-frills but the food is filling and of reliable quality.

Information

Information is available online at www.capri.it, www.capritourism.com or from one of the three **tourist offices** Anacapri (☎081 837 15 24; Via G Orlandi 59; ⏲9am-3pm Mon-Sat); Capri Town (☎081 837 06 86; Piazza Umberto I; ⏲8.30am-8.30pm Mon-Sat, 9am-3pm Sun Jun-Sep, 9am-1pm & 3.30-6.45pm Mon-Sat Oct-May); Marina Grande (☎081 837 06 34; ⏲9am-1pm & 3.30-6.45pm Mon-Sat).

Getting There & Around

There are year-round hydrofoils and ferries to Capri from Naples and Sorrento. Timetables and fare details are available online at www.capritourism.com.

From Naples, ferries depart from Porto di Massa and hydrofoils from Molo Beverello and Mergellina. Tickets cost €16 (hydrofoil), €14.50 (fast ferry) and €9.60 (ferry).

From Sorrento, there are more than 25 sailings a day (less in winter). You'll pay €14 for the 20-minute hydrofoil crossing and €9.80 for the 25-minute fast ferry trip.

In summer (mid-April to early October), hydrofoils and ferries connect Capri with Positano (€15.50 to €16.50) and Amalfi (€15 to €17).

On the island, **BUSES** run from Capri Town to/from Marina Grande, Anacapri and Marina Piccola; also from Marina Grande to Anacapri. Single tickets cost €1.40 on all routes, as does the funicular that links Marina Grande with Capri Town in a four-minute trip.

Sorrento

POP 16,590

Overlooking the Bay of Naples and Mt Vesuvius, Sorrento is southern Italy's main package-holiday resort. Despite this, and despite the lack of a decent beach, it's an appealing place whose laid-back charm defies all attempts to swamp it in souvenir tat. There are few must-see sights but the *centro storico* is lively and the town makes a good jumping-off point for the Amalfi Coast, Pompeii and Capri.

Sights & Activities

You'll probably spend most of your time in the *centro storico*, a tight-knit area of narrow streets lined with loud souvenir stores, cafes, churches and restaurants. To the north, the **Villa Comunale park** (entrance free; ⏲8am-midnight summer, 8am-8pm winter) commands grand views over the sea to Mt Vesuvius.

The two main swimming spots are **Marina Piccola** and **Marina Grande**, although neither is especially appealing. Nicer by far is **Bagni Regina Giovanna**, a rocky beach set among the ruins of a Roman villa, 2km west of town. To get there take the SITA bus for Massalubrense.

Sleeping

Ulisse Deluxe Hostel HOSTEL €
(☎081 877 47 53; www.ulissedeluxe.com; Via del Mare 22; dm €18-28, d €28-48; P❄@📶) Masquerading as a three-star hotel, this impeccably run hostel offers smart, modern rooms and dorms (all with bathrooms), access for travellers with disabilities, an internet point (per hour €5) and a wellness centre. Breakfast costs an extra €6.

Casa Astarita B&B €
(☎081 877 49 06; www.casastarita.com; Corso Italia 67; d €70-110; ❄@) The six rooms in this handsome 18th-century building near Piazza Tasso are individually decorated and have all the mod cons you will need.

Nube d'Argento CAMPING GROUND €
(081 878 13 44; www.nubedargento.com; Via del Capo 21; per person/tent/car €11/10/5; Mar-Dec;) A popular camping ground 1km west of the town centre with shady pitches and excellent facilities.

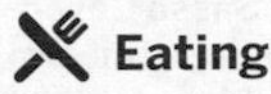

Eating

Pizzeria Da Franco PIZZERIA €
(Corso Italia 265; pizzas €6; 8am-2am) Don't expect frills at this laid-back pizzeria, just queues and the best pizza in town. Grab a spot at one of the rustic wooden tables and tuck into magnificent pizza, served on a metal tray with plastic cutlery.

Inn Bufalito TRATTORIA €
(Vico I Fuoro 21; mains €10; closed Nov-Feb) A bright and breezy mozzarella bar-cum-tavern, this popular spot specialises in fab local produce. Think creamy mozzarella, buffalo meat carpaccio and lovely marinated veggies.

Information

Tourist office (081 807 40 33; www.sorrentotourism.com; Via Luigi de Maio 35; 8.45am-6.15pm Mon-Sat, till 12.45 Sun in Aug) In the Circolo dei Forestieri (Foreigners' Club) in front of the Marina Piccola.

Getting There & Away

Circumvesuviana trains run half-hourly between Sorrento and Naples (€3.40, 65 minutes) via Pompeii (€1.90). Regular SITA buses leave from the train station for the Amalfi Coast, stopping in Positano (€1.40, 50 minutes) and Amalfi (€2.50, 1½ hours).

Sorrento is the main jumping-off point for Capri and ferries and hydrofoils run year-round from Marina Piccola. Tickets cost €14 (hydrofoil) or €9.80 (fast ferry).

Amalfi Coast

Stretching 50km along the southern side of the Sorrentine Peninsula, the Amalfi Coast (Costiera Amalfitana) is a postcard vision of Mediterranean beauty. Against a shimmering blue backdrop, whitewashed villages and terraced lemon groves cling to vertiginous cliffs backed by the craggy Lattari mountains. This Unesco-protected area is one of Italy's top tourist destinations, attracting hundreds of thousands of visitors each year, 70% of them between June and September.

Getting There & Away

Regular SITA buses run from Sorrento to Positano (50 minutes) and Amalfi (1½ hours), and from Salerno to Amalfi (1¼ hours).

Between April and September, **Metrò del Mare** (199 600 700; www.metrodelmare.net) runs boats from Naples to Sorrento (€6.50, 45 minutes), Positano (€14, 55 minutes) and Amalfi (€15, 1½ hours).

Positano

POP 3970

Approaching Positano by boat, you will be greeted by an unforgettable view of colourful, steeply stacked houses packed onto near-vertical green slopes. In town, the main activities are hanging out on the small beach and browsing the expensive boutiques.

The **tourist office** (089 87 50 67; Via del Saracino 4; 8am-2pm & 3.30-8pm Mon-Sat Apr-Oct, 9am-3pm Mon-Fri Nov-Mar) can provide information on walking in the surrounding hills.

Sleeping & Eating

Hostel Brikette HOSTEL €
(089 87 58 57; www.brikette.com; Via Marconi 358; dm €22-27, d €90-110, without bathroom €65-70; Easter-Nov;) Near the bus stop on the coastal road, this hostel is decidedly no-frills with beds in six- to 20-person dorms and modest private rooms, but there's a terrace for drinks and the views are stunning.

Da Costantino TRATTORIA €
(089 87 57 38; Via Montepertuso; pizzas from €6, mains €8; Thu-Tue) About 300m above Hostel Brikette, this is one of the few authentic trattorias in town. Expect honest, down-to-earth Italian grub, including excellent wood-fired pizza, and fabulous views.

Amalfi

POP 5400

An attractive tangle of souvenir shops, dark alleyways and busy piazzas, Amalfi is the coast's main hub. Looming over the central piazza is the town's landmark **Duomo** (Piazza del Duomo; admission 10am-5pm €2.50, 7.30am-10am & 5-7.30pm free; 7.30am-7.30pm), one of the few relics of Amalfi's past as an 11th-century maritime superpower. Between 10am and 5pm, entry is through the adjacent **Chiostro del Paradiso** (Cloisters of Paradise; admission €3; 9am-7.45pm).

Four kilometres west of town, the **Grotta dello Smeraldo** (admission €5; 9am-4pm) is a haunting sea cave. Boat trips from Amalfi cost €10 return.

Get details of these and other activities from the **tourist office** (☎089 87 11 07; www.amalfitouristoffice.it; Corso delle Repubbliche Marinare; ⏰9am-1pm & 4-7pm Mon-Fri, to noon Sat).

Sleeping & Eating

Hotel Lidomare HOTEL €€
(☎089 87 13 32; www.lidomare.it; Largo Duchi Piccolomini 9; s €55-65, d €103-145; ❄ 📶) Housed in a 14th-century building on a petite piazza, the Lidomare is a lovely, family-run hotel. The spacious rooms are full of character with majolica tiles and fine old antiques. Some also have jacuzzis and sea views.

A'Scalinatella Hostel HOSTEL €
(☎089 87 14 92; www.hostelscalinatella.com; Piazza Umberto I 5, Atrani; dm €25-30, d €70-90; @) A 10-minute walk from Amalfi, this popular no-frills operation has four-bed dorms, private rooms and apartments scattered across the village. There's a shared kitchen for guests.

Pizzeria Donna Stella PIZZERIA €
(Salita Rascica 2; pizzas from €6, mains €10; ⏰Tue-Sun) This back-alley pizzeria boasts one of Amalfi's loveliest settings – a delightful summer garden enclosed by jasmine-clad walls. The food is adequate, but nothing to get excited about – pizzas are your best bet.

Matera

POP 60,385

Set atop two rocky gorges, Matera is one of Italy's most remarkable towns. Dotting the ravines are the famous *sassi* (cave dwellings), where up to half the town's population lived until the late 1950s. Ironically, the *sassi* are now Matera's fortune, attracting visitors from all over the world and inspiring Mel Gibson to film *The Passion of the Christ* here.

Get *sassi* maps from the **tourist information kiosk** (Via Ridola; ⏰9am-12.30pm & 3-6pm) near the entrance to Sasso Caveoso. See also www.aptbasilicata.it and www.sassiweb.it.

Sights & Activities

Within Matera there are two *sassi* areas, **Barisano** and **Caveoso**. With a map you can explore them on your own, although you might find an audio guide (€8) from Viaggi Lionetti (Via XX Settembre 9) helpful. There are also plenty of agencies offering tours.

Inhabited since the Paleolithic age, the *sassi* were brought to public attention with the publication of Carlo Levi's book *Cristo si é fermato a Eboli* (Christ Stopped at Eboli; 1954). His description of children begging for quinine to stave off endemic malaria shamed the authorities into action and about 15,000 people were forcibly relocated in the late 1950s. In 1993 the *sassi* were declared a Unesco World Heritage site.

Accessible from Via Ridola, **Sasso Caveoso** is the older and more evocative of the two *sassi*. Highlights include the *chiese rupestre* (rock churches) of **Santa Maria de Idris** and **Santa Lucia alle Malve** (admission free; ⏰9.30am-1.30pm & 4-10pm) with their well-preserved 13th-century Byzantine frescoes.

To see how people lived in the *sassi*, the **Casa-Grotta di Vico Solitario** (off Via Bruno Buozzi; admission €1.50; ⏰9am-8.30pm Jul & Aug, 9.30am-5.30pm rest of yr) has been set up to show a typical cave house of 40 years ago.

Tours

Viaggi Lionetti (☎0835 33 40 33; www.viaggilionetti.com; Via XX Settembre 9) and **Ferula Viaggi** (☎0835 33 65 72; www.ferulaviaggi.it; Via Cappelluti 34) offer guided tours of the *sassi* – about €13 per person for a three-hour tour – as well as excursions into Basilicata.

Sleeping & Eating

Sassi Hotel HOTEL €
(☎0835 33 10 09; www.hotelsassi.it; Via San Giovanni Vecchio 89; s/d €70/90, ste €105-125; ❄) In the Barisano, this friendly *sasso* hotel has a range of rooms in a rambling 18th-century *palazzo*. No two are identical, but the best are bright and spacious with tasteful, modern furniture, terraces and panoramic views.

Le Monacelle HOSTEL, HOTEL €
(☎0835 34 40 97; www.lemonacelle.it; Via Riscatto 9/10; dm/s/d/tr/q €17.60/65/86/105/135; @ 📶) A former monastery near the Duomo, Le Monacelle is a value-for-money hostel-cum-hotel. Rooms are housed in the former cells and retain an air of elegant austerity, while the terrace offers unforgettable *sassi* views.

Il Terrazzino TRATTORIA €
(Vico San Giuseppe 7; tourist menu €18, evening pizza menu €6; ⏰closed Tue) Just off Piazza Vittorio Veneto, this teeming trattoria does a roaring trade in filling, no-nonsense pastas and simple meat dishes. Get into the swing of things with a rustic antipasto of olives, salami and cheese.

For ice cream, the tiny **Idris Dolceria** (Via Bruno Buozzi 62; cones €1.80) serves superb home-made gelato in the Sasso Caveoso.

MATERA SPLURGE

Hotel in Pietra BOUTIQUE HOTEL €€
(☎0835 34 40 40; www.hotelinpietra.it; Via San Giovanni Vecchio 22; s €70, d €110 150; ❄) Housed in a 13th-century church in the Sasso Barisano, this is a fabulously seductive boutique hotel. Everything about the place charms, from the glowing butter-yellow stone walls and soaring arches to the chic minimalist decor and rocky bathrooms. Unforgettable.

Getting There & Away

The best way to reach Matera is by bus. From Rome's Stazione Tiburtina, **Marozzi** (www.marozzivt.it, in Italian) runs three daily buses (€34.50, 4½ to 6½ hours). Matera's bus terminus is north of Piazza Matteotti near the train station.

By train, the **Ferrovie Appulo Lucano** (☎080 572 52 29; www.fal-srl.it) runs hourly services to/from Bari (€4, 1¼ hours).

Bari

POP 325,100

A bustling commercial city, Puglia's capital is best known for its ferry connections. It's not southern Italy's most appealing city but Bari does have a certain rough round-the edges charm and the old town, Bari Vecchia, is worth a quick look. Get the low-down at the **tourist information point** (☎080 990 93 41; www.infopointbari.com; Piazza Aldo Moro; ⌚9am-7pm Mon-Sat, 9am-1pm Sun) in front of the train station.

Bari's most important sight is the **Basilica di San Nicola** (Piazza San Nicola; ⌚7am 8.30pm Mon-Sat, to 10pm Sun), the first great Norman church in the south and the last resting place of St Nicholas, aka Father Christmas.

If you need to stop over, **Hotel Pensione Giulia** (☎080 521 66 30; www.hotelpensionegiulia.it; Via Crisanzio 12; s/d €60/75, without bathroom €50/65; ❄) is an old-fashioned, family-run *pensione*, with clean, basic rooms. For a bite, **Osteria Al Gambero** (☎080 521 60 18; Corso Antonio de Tullio; mains €13; ⌚Mon-Sat) serves fabulous seafood near the port.

Ferries run from Bari to Greece (Corfu, Igoumenitsa, Patra, Keffallonia), Croatia (Split, Dubrovnik) and Montenegro (Bar). Ferry companies have offices at the port, accessible by bus 20 (€0.80) from the train station. You can also get tickets at **Morfimare Travel Agency** (☎080 578 98 11; Corso Antonio de Tullio 36-40) opposite the port.

There are regular trains to/from Rome (from €33.50, four to 6½ hours), Brindisi (from €6.80, one hour 20 minutes) and Lecce (from €8.60, 1½ to two hours), as well as many smaller towns in Puglia.

Lecce

POP 93,600

An urbane university town with a vibrant bar scene and a graceful historic centre, the 'Florence of the South' is well worth a stopover. Its bombastic displays of jaw-dropping baroque architecture (known as *barocco leccese* – Lecce baroque) are one of southern Italy's highlight sights.

Sights

TOP CHOICE **Basilica di Santa Croce** CHURCH
(Via Umberto I; ⌚8am-1pm & 4-9pm) The most celebrated example of Lecce's baroque architecture is this eye-popping basilica. It took a team of 16th- and 17th-century craftsmen more than a 100 years to create the swirling facade that you see today.

A short walk away, **Piazza del Duomo**, Lecce's showpiece square, is yet another orgy of architectural extravagance, much of it down to Giuseppe Zimbalo. He restored the 12th-century **cathedral** (⌚8am-12.30pm & 4-8pm) and fashioned the 68m-high **bell tower**. Facing the cathedral is the 15th-century **Palazzo Vescovile** (Bishop's Palace) and the 17th-century **Seminario**.

Lecce's social and commercial hub, **Piazza Sant'Oronzo** is built round the remains of a 2nd-century **Roman amphitheatre**, once the largest in Puglia.

Sleeping

B&B Centro Storico Prestige B&B €
(☎0832 24 33 53; www.bbprestige-lecce.it; Via S Maria del Paradiso 4; s €50-60, d €70-90, apt €65-90; @📶) This is a cracking little B&B. The irrepressible Renata ushers guests into her lovingly tended 2nd-floor flat where sunlight floods into understated white guest rooms. There's also a ground-floor apartment for four people and a pretty rooftop terrace.

Centro Storico B&B €
(☎0832 24 27 27; www.bedandbreakfast.lecce.it; Via Vignes 2/b; d €70-80, ste €90-100; P❄📶) This characterful hideaway is on the 2nd-floor of a 16th-century *palazzo*. The high-ceilinged

rooms are bright and colourful, decked out with parquet, wrought-iron beds and thoughtful extras. Upstairs, there's a sun terrace.

Eating & Drinking

Alle due Corti RESTAURANT €
(0832 24 22 23; www.alleduecorti.com; Corte dei Giugni 1; mains €9; Mon-Sat) This traditional restaurant is a fine place to get to grips with Salento's gastronomic heritage. The menu, written in dialect, features classics such as *la taieddha* (rice, potatoes and mussels) and *pupette alla sucu* (meatballs in tomato sauce).

Vico Patarnello PIZZERIA, RESTAURANT €
(Vico Mondo Nuovo 2; pizzas €8; 8pm-1.30am Tue-Sun) This popular pizzeria-cum-restaurant is in the backstreets of the historic centre. With outside seating and a modern interior, it's a lovely spot to munch on pizza or pasta dishes such as *linguine all'astice* (thin pasta ribbons with lobster).

Of the city's many bars, the **Caffè Letterario** (Via Paladini 48) is a happening spot, while **Caffè Alvino** (Piazza Sant'Oronzo 30; closed Tue) is the best place for the traditional Leccese pastry, *pasticciotto*.

Information

Tourist office (0832 24 80 92; Corso Vittorio Emanuele 24; 9am-1pm & 4-8pm Mon-Sat mid-Jul–mid-Sep, to 7pm winter)

Ufficio Informazioni Duomo (0832 52 18 77; www.infolecce.it; Piazza del Duomo 2; 9.30am-8pm Mon-Fri, 10am-8pm Sat & Sun) Rents out bikes (per hour/day €3/15) and runs guided tours (per person €7).

Getting There & Away

Lecce is the end of the main southeastern rail line and there are frequent direct trains to/from Bari (€8.60, 1½ to two hours), Brindisi (€2.30, 30 minutes, hourly) and Rome (€62, six hours, seven daily), as well as to points throughout Puglia.

SICILY

The Mediterranean's largest island, Sicily is a hotbed of southern excess. Everything about the place is extreme, from the beauty of its rugged landscape to its hybrid cuisine and flamboyant architecture. Over the centuries Sicily has seen off a catalogue of foreign invaders, from the Phoenicians and ancient Greeks to the Spanish Bourbons and WWII Allies. All have contributed to the island's complex and fascinating cultural landscape.

Getting There & Away

AIR Flights from Italy's mainland cities and a number of European destinations land at Sicily's two main airports: Palermo's **Falcone-Borsellino airport** (PMO; www.gesap.it; 091 702 01 11) and Catania's **Fontanarossa airport** (CTA; 095 723 91 11; www.aeroporo.catania.it).

BOAT Regular car and passenger ferries cross to Sicily (Messina) from Villa San Giovanni in Calabria. The island is also accessible by ferry from Genoa, Livorno, Naples and Cagliari, as well as Malta and Tunisia. The main companies are:

Grandi Navi Veloci (010 209 45 91; www.gnv.it) To Palermo from Genoa, Civitavecchia, Livorno, Tunis and Malta.

Grimaldi Lines (081 49 64 44; www.grimaldi-ferries.com) To Palermo from Tunis and Salerno; to Catania from Genoa, Civitavecchia and Malta.

SNAV (091 601 42 11; www.snav.it) To Palermo from Civitavecchia and Naples.

Tirrenia (892 123; www.tirrenia.it) To Palermo from Naples and Cagliari.

Boat timetables are seasonal; check with a travel agent or online at www.traghettionline.net.

BUS Bus services between Rome and Sicily are operated by **SAIS** (800 21 10 20; www.saisautolinee.it, in Italian), **Interbus** (0935 224 60; www.interbus.it, in Italian) and **Segesta** (091 616 79 19; www.segesta.it in Italian), departing from Rome's Piazza Tiburtina. There are daily buses to Messina (€41, nine hours), Catania (€46, 11 hours), Palermo (€33, 12 hours) and Syracuse (€47, 12 hours).

TRAIN Direct trains run from Florence, Milan, Naples, Reggio di Calabria and Rome to Palermo and Catania. For further information contact **Trenitalia** (89 20 21; www.trenitalia.com).

Palermo

POP 659,440

Still bearing the bruises of its WWII battering, Palermo is a compelling and chaotic city. It takes a little work, but once you've acclimatised to the frenetic streets you'll be rewarded with some of southern Italy's most exotic buildings. In among chaotic street markets and bombed-out *palazzi*, you'll find palaces, castles and churches, as well as some fabulous restaurants and tempting cafes.

Palermo's centre is large but manageable on foot. The main street is Via Maqueda, which runs parallel to Via Roma, the busy road running north from the train station.

Sights

A good starting point is the **Quattro Canti**, a road junction where Palermo's four central districts converge. Nearby, Piazza Pretoria is dominated by the ostentatious **Fontana Pretoria**, whose nude nymphs caused outrage when it was bought from Florence in 1573.

Piazza Bellini SQUARE
Around the corner from the Quattro Canti, Piazza Bellini is home to several eye-catching churches. **La Martorana** (Chiesa di Santa Maria dell'Ammiraglio; donation requested; ⏲8.30am-1pm & 3.30-7pm Mon-Sat, 8.30am-1pm Sun) is celebrated for its 12th-century bell tower and stunning Byzantine mosaics. Next door, the red-domed **Chiesa di San Cataldo** (admission €1.50; ⏲9am-3.30pm Mon-Fri, 9am-12.30pm Sat, 9am-1pm Sun) is of interest more for the Arab-Norman exterior than its surprisingly bare interior.

Palazzo Reale PALACE
(Palazzo dei Normanni; Piazza Indipendenza; admission incl Cappella Palatina adult/concession €8.50/6.50; ⏲8.30am-noon & 2-5pm Mon, Tue, Thu-Sat, 8.30am-12.30pm Sun) This is the theatrical seat of the Sicilian parliament. Downstairs, the 12th-century **Cappella Palatina** (Palatine Chapel; ⏲8.15am-5pm Mon-Sat, 8.15-9.45am & 11.15am-12.15pm Sun) is lavishly decorated with exquisite mosaics. Note that if you visit the chapel on a day when the rest of the *palazzo* is closed, the entry price is reduced to adult/concession €7/5.

Cathedral CHURCH
(Corso Vittorio Emanuele; admission free; ⏲9.30am-5.30pm Mon-Sat, 8am-1.30pm & 4.30-6pm Sun) Palermo's extraordinary cathedral is a visual riot of arches, cupolas and crenellations. Modified many times, it's a superb example of Sicily's unique Arab-Norman architecture.

Teatro Massimo OPERA HOUSE
(☎091 609 08 31; Piazza Giuseppe Verdi; www.teatromassimo.it, in Italian; 25min guided tours adult/concession €5/3, performance tickets €25-125; ⏲tours 10am-2.30pm Tue-Sun) Palermo's neoclassical theatre is supposedly the third-largest 19th-century opera house in Europe after Paris and Vienna. It was used as a backdrop for the closing scene of *The Godfather III*.

Catacombe del Cappuccini CATACOMBS
(Capuchin Catacombs; Piazza Cappuccini 1; admission €3; ⏲9am-noon & 3-5.30pm, closed Sun pm in winter) Southwest of the city centre, these macabre catacombs hold the mummified bodies of some 8000 Palermitans who died between the 17th and 19th centuries.

Sleeping

Al Giardino dell'Allaro B&B €
(☎091 617 69 04; www.giardinodellalloro.it; Vicolo San Carlo 8, ang Via Alloro 78; s €35-50, d €75-85; ❄@) Overlooking a tranquil garden in the Kalsa district, this arty B&B is clean and well maintained. There's a comfortable suite sleeping four, and five simple doubles, most of which overlook the courtyard.

B&B Panormus B&B €
(☎091 617 58 26; www.bbpanormus.com; Via Roma 72; s €25-65, d €40-100; ❄) Keen prices, a charming host and attractive rooms decorated in the Liberty style make this one of the city's most popular B&Bs. Each of the five impeccably clean rooms has its own private bathroom down the passageway.

San Francesco B&B €
(☎091 888 83 91; www.sanfrancescopalermo.it; Via Merlo 30; s €60, d €80-90; ❄) Run by a friendly young couple, the San Francesco has only three rooms but each is atmospheric. The quiet but central location is hard to beat and the breakfast gets rave reviews from guests.

A Casa di Amici HOSTEL €
(☎091 58 48 84; www.acasadiamici.it; Via Volturno 6; dm €20-25, d €66-80, without bathroom s €33-40, d €52-60; ❄@) A friendly, vibrant hostel in a 19th-century *palazzo* behind Teatro Massimo. Rooms are individually themed; all have high ceilings, colourful walls and ethnic decor.

Eating

Traditional yet spicy, Palermo's food marries the island's superb produce with recipes imported by the Arab Saracens in the 9th century. Two specialities to try are *arancini* (deep-fried rice balls) and *cannoli* (pastry tubes filled with ricotta and candied fruit).

Trattoria Il Maestro Del Brodo TRATTORIA €€
(Via Pannieri 7; mains €14; ⏲lunch Tue-Sun, dinner Fri & Sat) A Slow Food–recommended eatery, this no-frills place in the Vucciria offers a sensational antipasto buffet (€5), delicious soups and an array of ultra-fresh seafood.

Pizzeria Biondo PIZZERIA €
(☎091 58 36 62; Via Nicolò Garzilli 27; pizzas €5-12; ⏲dinner Thu-Tue, closed Aug–mid-Sep) This long-standing favourite has managed to hold its

own against the considerable competition posed by the nearby branch of the excellent Fratelli la Bufala chain. Sit in the simple dining room or claim a table on the street to enjoy your choice of pizza from a huge menu.

For an adrenalin-charged food experience, dive into one of Palermo's legendary markets: **Capo** on Via Sant'Agostino or **Il Ballaró** in the Albergheria quarter, off Via Maqueda.

Information

Ospedale Civico (Hospital; ☎091 666 11 11; Via Carmelo Lazzaro)

Police station (Questura; ☎091 21 01 11; Piazza della Vittoria)

Tourist office (☎091 605 83 51; www.palermotourism.com; Piazza Castelnuovo 34; ⏰8.30am-2pm & 2.30-6.30pm Mon-Fri) Offers a few brochures as well as *Agenda Turismo,* containing listings for museums, cultural centres, tour guides and transport companies. There are also **tourist information points** Falcone-Borsellino airport (☎091 59 16 98; ⏰8.30am-7.30pm Mon-Sat), Piazza Bellini, Piazza Castelnuovo, Piazza della Vittoria and Via Cavour (⏰all 9am-1pm & 3-7pm daily).

Getting There & Away

AIR National and international flights arrive at **Falcone-Borsellino airport**, 35km west of Palermo.

BOAT The ferry terminal is northeast of the historic centre off Via Francesco Crispi. Ferries for Cagliari (€51, 14½ hours) and Naples (€50, 10 hours) leave from Molo Vittorio Veneto; for Genoa (€120, 20 hours) from Molo S Lucia.

BUS The main intercity bus station is near Via Paolo Balsamo, east of the train station. Buses serve Agrigento (€8.10, two hours, nine daily), Catania (€14.20, 2½ hours, 13 daily) and Syracuse (€13, 3¼ hours, five daily).

TRAIN Trains leave from the Stazione Centrale for Messina (€11.55, 3¾ hours, hourly) via Milazzo (€10.10, 2½ to 3¼ hours), the jumping-off point for the Aeolian Islands. Long-distance trains go to Naples (€50, 9¼ hours, four daily), Reggio di Calabria (€22.40, 5¾ hours, two daily) and Rome (€61, 11½ hours, seven daily).

Getting Around

To/From the Airport

A half-hourly bus service run by **Prestia e Comandé** (☎091 58 63 51; www.prestiaecomande.it, in Italian) connects the airport with the train station. Tickets for the 50-minute journey cost €5.80 and are available on the bus. There's also the hourly Trinacria Express train service (€5.50, 45 minutes) from Stazione Centrale.

Bus

Walking is the best way to get around Palermo's centre, but if you want to take a bus, most stop outside or near the train station. Tickets cost €1.20 and are valid for 90 minutes.

Aeolian Islands

Rising out of the cobalt blue seas off Sicily's northeastern coast, the Unesco-protected Aeolian Islands (Isole Eolie) have been seducing visitors since Odysses' time. With their wild, windswept mountains, hissing volcanoes and rich waters, they form a beautiful outdoor playground, ideal for divers, sunseekers and sailors.

Lipari is the biggest of the seven islands (Lipari, Salina, Vulcano, Stromboli, Alicudi, Filicudi and Panarea) and the main transport hub. From there you can pick up connections to the other islands, including Vulcano, famous for its therapeutic mud, and Stromboli, whose active volcano supplies spectacular fire shows.

The islands' only **tourist office** (☎090 988 00 95; www.aasteolie.191.it, in Italian; Corso Vittorio Emanuele 202; ⏰8.30am-1.30pm & 4.30-7.30pm Mon-Fri, 8.30am-1.30pm Sat & Sun Jul & Aug) is on Lipari.

Sights & Activities

Lipari ISLAND

You can explore the volcanic history of the islands at the **Museo Archeologico Eoliano** (admission €6; ⏰9am-1pm & 3-7pm Mon-Sat, 9am-1.30pm Sun) in the Spanish Aragon-built **citadel**. For sunbathing, head to Canneto or to Porticello. Snorkelling and diving are popular – contact **Diving Center La Gorgonia** (☎090 981 26 16; www.lagorgoniadiving.it; Salita San Giuseppe; dives from €32) for equipment and guided dives. For tours of the islands, **Da Massimo Dolce Vita Group** (⏰090 981 30 86, 333 298 66 24; www.damassimo.it; Via Maurolico 2) offers various packages, ranging from a €15 tour of Lipari and Vulcano to a €80 summit climb of Stromboli.

Vulcano ISLAND

Vulcano is a malodorous and largely unspoilt island. Most people visit to make the hour-long trek up the **Fossa di Vulcano**, the island's active volcano (€3 for crater entrance), or to wallow in the **Laghetto di Fanghi** mud baths (€2.50 plus €1 for shower).

Stromboli ISLAND

Famous for its spectacular fireworks, Stromboli is the most active volcano in the region. To make the tough seven-hour ascent to the 920m summit you are legally required to hire a guide. At the top you're rewarded with incredible views of the Sciara del Fuoco (Trail of Fire). **Magmatrek** (☎090 986 57 68; www.magmatrek.it) organises afternoon climbs for €28 per person.

Sleeping & Eating

Most accommodation is on Lipari. Try to book ahead as summer is always busy and many places close over the winter.

LIPARI

Don't dismiss outright offers by touts at the port as they're often genuine.

Diana Brown PENSION €

(☎090 981 25 84; www.dianabrown.it; Vico Himera 3; s €30-90, d €40-100; ⊙year-round; ❄) Down a tiny back lane, Diana has comfortable rooms decorated in cheerful summery style. Kettles and fridges are provided and the darker downstairs rooms have a small kitchenette. Breakfast (€5) is served on the solarium.

Pescecane PIZZERIA €

(Via Vittorio Emanuele 223; pizzas from €4.50) One of a number of pizzerias and trattorias on the main strip, this laid-back place serves excellent wood-fired pizzas and typical island food. There's a great antipasto buffet.

VULCANO

Pensione Giara PENSION €€

(☎090 985 22 29; www.pensionelagiara.it; Via Provinciale 18; d €46-144; ⊙Apr-Oct; ❄) Fronted by lemon trees, this is a cheerful, old-school *pensione* on the road from the port to the volcano. It's a modest affair with sunny white rooms and a rooftop terrace affording impressive volcano views.

Ritrovo Remigio BAR €

(Porto di Levante; cannolo €2) Forget the volcanoes, the beaches, the spectacular views. The single most compelling reason to visit Vulcano is to eat a delectable *cannolo* from this otherwise undistinguished bar-gelateria near the port.

STROMBOLI

Casa del Sole GUEST HOUSE €

(☎090 98 63 00; www.casadelstromboli.it; Via Domenico Cincotta; dm €25-35, d €60-100, d without bathroom €50-80; ⊙Mar-Oct) This is a wonderful hacienda style set-up centred on a picturesque courtyard. It has dorms sleeping up to five and private double rooms, as well as a lovely farmhouse kitchen.

Getting There & Around

Ferries and hydrofoils leave for the islands from Milazzo. If arriving in Milazzo by train, you'll need to catch a bus (€0.90) or taxi (€13) to the port, 4km from the station. At the port you'll find ticket offices lined up on Corso dei Mille.

Ustica Lines (☎0923 87 38 13; www.usticalines.it) and **Siremar** (☎892 123; www.siremar.it) run hydrofoils to Vulcano (€14.90, 45 minutes, 17 daily) and on to Lipari (€15.80, one hour). Between June and September departures are almost hourly from 7am to 8pm. Siremar runs cheaper ferries to the same destinations.

From Lipari, there are regular services to Vulcano (ferry/hydrofoil €4.40/5.80, 10/25 minutes), Stromboli (ferry/hydrofoil €12.40/17.80, 1¾/four hours) and the other islands.

Taormina

POP 11,100

Spectacularly perched on a clifftop terrace, Taormina is Sicily's glitziest resort, a sophisticated town with a pristine medieval core and grandstand coastal views. It was made famous by Goethe and DH Lawrence, who both lived here, but in the 9th century it was Sicily's Byzantine capital.

Sights & Activities

The principal pastime in Taormina is wandering the pretty hilltop streets, browsing the shops and eyeing up fellow holidaymakers. Take time to visit the stunning **Teatro Greco** (Via Teatro Greco; adult/concession €6/3; ⊙9am-7pm Mar-Aug, closes earlier rest of year), a noble 3rd-century BC theatre overlooking the sea.

For a swim you'll need to take the **funivia** (cable car; one way/return €2/3; ⊙9am-8.15pm, to 1am summer) down to Taormina's beach, **Lido Mazzarò**, and the tiny **Isola Bella** set in its own picturesque cove.

SAT (⊙0942 2 46 53; www.satgroup.it; Corso Umberto I 73) is one of a number of agencies that organises day trips to Mt Etna, as well as to Syracuse (€45), Palermo and Agrigento (€50).

Sleeping & Eating

Le 4 Fontane B&B €

(☎347 075 06 24; www.le4fontane.it; Corso Umberto 231; s €40-50, d €60-90; ❄) This excellent B&B has three spacious, colourful rooms on the top floor of an old *palazzo* (no lift, though). There's a convenient kitchen and it's perfectly located on Taormina's main drag.

Taormina's Odyssey HOSTEL €
(☎0942 2 45 33; www.taorminaodyssey.com; Via Paternò di Biscari 13; dm from €20, d from €45) Taormina's sole hostel is in a newly constructed building just off Corso Umberto I and features two dorms, four private rooms, a communal kitchen and a large terrace. It's open year-round.

La Piazzetta TRATTORIA €€
(☎094 262 63 17; Via Paladini 5; mains €15-20; ⏲closed Mon winter) Ask locals for a recommendation and many will send you to La Piazzetta. A welcoming family-run outfit with tables on a picturesque square, it serves authentic Sicilian food at honest prices.

Tiramisù PIZZERIA, TRATTORIA €€
(Via Cappuccini 1; mains €18-24, pizzas from €7; ⏲Wed-Mon) Head to this unpretentious place near Porta Messina for a simple pizza and beer or something more elaborate. Round things off with some of its trademark tiramisu.

ℹ Information

The **tourist office** (☎0942 2 32 43; www.gate2taormina.com; Palazzo Corvaja, Corso Umberto I; ⏲8.30am-2pm Mon-Fri & 4-7pm Mon-Thu) has helpful multilingual staff and plenty of practical information.

ℹ Getting There & Away

Taormina is best reached by bus. From the bus terminus on Via Pirandello, Interbus serves Messina (€3.90, 1½ hours, hourly Monday to Saturday, two on Sunday) and **Etna Trasporti** (☎095 53 27 16; www.etnatrasporti.it) connects with Catania's Fontanarossa airport (€5.60, 1½ hours, six daily Monday to Saturday, four on Sunday).

Mt Etna

The dark silhouette of Mt Etna (3330m) broods ominously over the east coast, more or less halfway between Taormina and Catania. One of Europe's highest and most volatile volcanoes, it erupts frequently, spewing out lava and ash from four summit craters and fissures on the mountain's slopes.

By public transport the best way to get there is to take the daily AST bus from Catania. This departs from in front of the main train station at 8.30am (returning at 4.30pm; €5.15 return) and drops you at the Rifugio Sapienza (1923m), where you can pick up the **Funivia dell'Etna** (cable car €28.50, cable car, bus & guide €53; ⏲9am-4.30pm) to 2500m. From there buses courier you up to the official crater zone (2920m). If you want to walk, allow up to four hours for the round trip.

Gruppo Guide Alpine Etna Sud (☎095 791 47 55; www.etnaguide.com) is one of hundreds of outfits offering guided tours, typically involving 4WD transport and a guided trek. These cost from €45 per person for a half-day tour (usually morning or sunset) and about €60 for a full-day tour.

Further Etna information is available from Catania's **tourist office** (☎095 742 55 73; www.comune.catania.it; Via Vittorio Emanuele 172; ⏲8.15am-7.15pm Mon-Fri, 8.15am-12.15pm Sat).

If you want to overnight in Catania, the **Agora Hostel** (☎095 723 30 10; www.agorahostel.com; Piazza Curro 6; dm €17-23, s €30-35, d €45-60; @) is a sociable spot with its own pub and restaurant.

Syracuse

POP 124,100

With its gorgeous *centro storico* and gritty ruins, Syracuse (Siracusa) is a baroque beauty with an ancient past. One of Sicily's most visited cities, it was founded in 734 BC by Corinthian settlers and became the dominant Greek city-state on the Mediterranean, battling the Carthaginians and Etruscans before falling to the Romans in 212 BC.

Sights

Ortygia HISTORIC AREA
Connected to the town by bridge, the island of Ortygia is an atmospheric warren of elaborate baroque *palazzi,* lively piazzas and busy trattorias. Just off Via Roma, the 7th-century **cathedral** (Piazza del Duomo; ⏲8am-6pm) was built over a pre-existing 5th-century BC Greek temple, incorporating most of the original columns in its three-aisled structure. Its sumptuous baroque facade was added in the 18th century.

From the train station, it's just over a 1km walk to Ortygia – take Via Francesco Crispi to Piazzale Marconi and then follow Corso Umberto I down to the bridge. Alternatively, jump on one of the regular shuttle buses which connect Ortygia with the station.

Parco Archeologico della Neapolis ANCIENT SITE (Viale Paradiso; adult/concession €8/4.50, incl Museo Archeologico Paolo Orsi €9; ⌚9am-6pm summer, 9am-3pm Mon-Sat, 9am-1pm Sun winter) Syracuse's main attraction is this extensive archaeological park, home to the city's ancient ruins. Hewn out of solid rock, the 5th-century-BC **Greek theatre** is where Aeschylus premiered many of his tragedies. Nearby, the **Orecchio di Dionisio** is an ear-shaped grotto, whose perfect acoustics allowed Syracuse's tyrant Dionysius to eavesdrop on his prisoners. On the other side of Via Paradiso is the impressive 2nd-century **Roman amphitheatre**.

The park is a 20-minute walk from the train station.

About 500m east of the archaeological zone, the impressive **Museo Archeologico Paolo Orsi** (Viale Teocrito 66/a; adult/concession €8/4, incl Parco Archeologico della Neapolis €9; ⌚9am-6pm daily summer, 9am-3pm Mon-Sat, 9am-1pm Sun winter) houses Sicily's most extensive archaeological collection.

Sleeping & Eating

Lol Hostel HOSTEL € (☎0931 46 50 88; www.lolhostel.com; Via Francesco Crispi 92-96; dm €20-26, d €60-75; ❄@📶) This is a terrific modern hostel near the train station. Accommodation is in mixed and female only dorms or sunny, cheerfully furnished private rooms, all of which have private bathrooms.

Viaggiatori, Viandanti e Sognatori B&B € (☎0931 2 47 81; www.bedandbreakfastsicily.it; Via Roma 156; s €35-50, d €55-65; ❄) Decorated with verve and boasting a prime location in Ortygia, this is Syracuse's best B&B The same family also run the more modest **B&B L'Acanto** (☎0931 46 11 29; www.bebsicilia.it; Via Roma 15; same prices).

Osteria Da Mariano TRATTORIA € (☎0931 6 74 44; Vicolo Zuccalà 9; mains €8; ⌚closed Mon) This bustling place is the very picture of an authentic trattoria. Old-timer waiters squeeze past tightly packed tables dishing out earthy country food to legions of boisterous diners – great stuff.

La Gazza Ladra TRATTORIA € (☎340 060 24 28; Via Cavour 8; mains €12; ⌚Tue-Sun) Hearty, honest fare served in welcoming surroundings at honest prizes. The recipe for success sounds simple, but few manage it as well as this friendly, pocket-sized place.

Information

Tourist offices Municipal tourist office (☎800 555 000; Via Roma 31; ⌚9am-1pm & 2-5.30pm Mon-Fri, 9am-noon Sat); Ortygia tourist office (☎0931 46 42 55; Via Maestranza 33, ⌚8am-2pm & 2.30-5.30pm Mon-Fri, 8am-2pm Sat).

Getting There & Away

BUSES are more convenient than trains, serving the terminus in front of the train station. Both Interbus and **AST** (☎0931 46 48 20; www.aziendasicilianatrasporti.it) run to/from Catania (€5.70, 1¼ hours, hourly Monday to Saturday, six Sunday) and Palermo (€13, 3¼ hours, two daily Monday to Saturday, three Sunday).

TRAINS run to Taormina (€7.95, two hours, 10 daily), Catania (€6.10, 1¼ hours, 10 daily) and Messina (€9.45, 2¾ hours, eight daily).

Agrigento

POP 59,140

Agrigento enjoys fame and notoriety in equal measure – fame for its awe-inspiring Greek temples; notoriety for the rampant *abusivismo* (illegal building) that has overrun the medieval hilltop town. Founded around 581 BC by Greek settlers, Agrigento became an important trading centre under the Romans and Byzantines.

Sights

One of the most compelling archaeological sites in southern Italy, the **Valley of the Temples** is a Unesco-listed complex of temples and walls from the ancient city of Akragas, founded here in 581 BC. The **archaeological park** (adult/EU concession €10/5; ⌚8.30am-7pm) is divided into eastern and western zones. The most spectacular temples are in the eastern zone. First up is the oldest, the **Tempio di Ercole**, built at the end of the 6th century BC and equivalent in size to the Parthenon. Continuing east, the intact **Tempio della Concordia** was transformed into a Christian church in the 6th century; the **Tempio di Giunone** boasts an impressive sacrificial altar.

Over the road in the western zone, the 5th-century BC **Tempio di Giove** originally covered an area of 112m by 56m with 20m-high columns interspersed with *telamoni* (giant male statues), one of which now stands in the **Museo Archeologico** (adult/EU concession €8/4; ⌚9.30am-7pm Tue-Sat, to 1pm Sun & Mon) on the road up to Agrigento.

Take local bus 1, 2 or 3 to the Valley of the Temples from the bus terminus on Piazzale Rosselli.

Sleeping & Eating

B&B Atenea 191 B&B €
(☎0922 59 55 94; www.atenea191.com; Via Atenea 191; s €45-60, d €65-85; ❄) A labour of love for the artist owner, the seven rooms at this welcoming B&B are decorated with original paintings and exuberant floral stencils. Breakfast is served on the rooftop patio.

Campeggio Internazionale San Leone CAMPING GROUND €
(☎0922 41 11 15; www.campingvalledeitempli.com; Viale Emporium 192, San Leone; per person/tent/car €7.50/6/3.50; P@≋) This well-equipped camping ground is on the sea in the small town of San Leone. Take bus 2 from Agrigento train station.

Trattoria Pizzeria Manhattan TRATTORIA, PIZZERIA €
(Salita M Angeli 9; set menu €15-18; ⏲Mon-Sat) Good for straightforward Sicilian cooking, this modest trattoria is halfway up a staircase off Via Ateneo. Help yourself at the buffet antipasto and follow with spaghetti *alla siciliana* (with tomato, aubergine, basil and salty ricotta).

Café Girasole CAFE €
(Via Atenea 68-70; ⏲Mon-Sat) You can prop up the bar or sit on the small terrace at this great little cafe, which is popular with lunching locals and the local *aperitivi* set.

Information

Tourist office (☎800 31 55 55; Piazzale Aldo Moro; ⏲8am-2pm & 3-7pm Mon-Fri, 8am-1pm Sat)

Getting There & Away

The bus is the easiest way to get to/from Agrigento. Cuffaro runs buses to Palermo (€8.10, two hours, nine daily Monday to Saturday, three Sunday) and SAIS services go to Catania and Catania Fontanarossa airport (€12.20, three hours, at least 10 daily).

SARDINIA

Celebrated for its spectacular beaches and VIP resorts, Sardinia is far more than it's made out to be. If you can drag yourself away from the gorgeous coastline and transparent waters, you'll discover a haunting and often spectacular interior of impenetrable granite gorges, forbidding peaks and silent cork forests. Adding a sense of mystery are the 7000 *nuraghi* (circular stone towers) which pepper the landscape, all that's left of Sardinia's prehistoric past.

You can get round Sardinia on public transport, but you'll discover much more with your own wheels.

Getting There & Away

AIR Flights from Italian and European cities serve Sardinia's three main airports: **Elmas** (CAG; ☎070 211 211; www.sogaer.it) in Cagliari; Alghero's **Fertilia** (AHO; ☎079 93 52 82; www.aeroportodialghero.it); and **Olbia Costa Smeralda** (OLB; ☎0789 56 34 44; www.geasar.it).

BOAT Car and passenger ferries sail year-round from various Italian ports, including Civitavecchia, Genoa, Livorno, Naples and Palermo. The major routes and the companies that operate them:

Civitavecchia To/from Olbia (Moby Lines, SNAV, Tirrenia); Cagliari (Tirrenia); and Golfo Aranci (Sardinia Ferries).

Genoa To/from Porto Torres (Grandi Navi Veloci, Tirrenia); Olbia (Grandi Navi Veloci, Moby Lines, Tirrenia); and Arbatax (Tirrenia).

Livorno To/from Olbia (Moby Lines); and Golfo Aranci (Sardinia Ferries).

Naples To/from Cagliari (Tirrenia).

Palermo To/from Cagliari (Tirrenia).

Get up-to-date information and book tickets at www.traghettionline.net.

Cagliari

POP 159,400

Sardinia's capital and largest city, Cagliari rises from the sea in a helter-skelter of golden-hued *palazzi,* domes and facades. Yet for all its splendour, it remains what it always has been – a busy working port with a gritty, down-to-earth atmosphere and a vibrant buzz. With its landmark citadel, great restaurants and popular sandy beach, Cagliari is very much its own city.

The main bus and train stations and port are near Piazza Matteotti, where you'll find the tourist office. The busy seafront road Via Roma connects with Largo Carlo Felice, which heads north to Piazza Yenne, the centre's focal square. Rising above everything is the historic Castello (castle) district.

Sights & Activities

Castello HISTORIC AREA
Housed in what was once Cagliari's arsenal, the **Citadella dei Musei** is the city's main museum complex. Of its four museums,

the most impressive is the **Museo Archeologico Nazionale** (Piazza dell'Arsenale; adult/concession €4/2; ⏰9am-8pm Tue-Sun), whose fascinating prehistoric bronzes provide one of the few clues to the island's mysterious *nuraghic* culture.

At the other end of Castello, past the 13th-century **Cattedrale di Santa Maria** (Piazza Palazzo 4; ⏰6.30am-noon & 4-8pm Mon-Sat, 8am-1pm & 4.30-8.30pm Sun) and its imposing Romanesque pulpits, is **Bastione San Remy** (Piazza Costituzione), a monumental terrace, formerly a strong point in the defensive walls, which commands huge panoramas over the city and distant lagoons.

Anfiteatro Romano ROMAN AMPHITHEATRE
(Viale Sant'Ignazio; adult/concession €4.30/2.80; ⏰9.30am-1.30pm Tue-Sat, 9.30am-1.30pm & 3.30-5.30pm Sun) To the west of the centre, this 2nd-century amphitheatre is the most important Roman monument in Sardinia, a spectacular setting for summer concerts.

Spiaggia di Poetto BEACH
A short bus ride from the centre, Cagliari's vibrant beach boasts inviting blue waters and a happening summer bar scene.

Festivals & Events

The annual **Festival of Sant'Efisio**, a colourful celebration mixing the secular and the religious, is held for four days from 1 May.

Sleeping

Hostel Marina HOSTEL €
(☎070 450 97 09; www.aighostels.com; Piazza San Sepolcro 3; dm/s/d €22/30/60; ❄) This cracking HI hostel is in the thick of the Marina district, not a stone's throw from the seafront. It's housed in a converted 15th-century convent and has spacious, sun-filled single-sex dorms, private rooms and an internal courtyard.

Hotel A&R Bundes Jack PENSION €
(☎070 66 79 70; www.hotelbjvittoria.it; Via Roma 75; s €56-58, d €84-88; ❄) The best budget hotel on the seafront, this is an old-fashioned family-run *pensione*. Rooms, decorated with robust family furniture and sparkling chandeliers, are spacious with high ceilings. Breakfast is not included. No credit cards.

B&B La Marina B&B €
(☎070 67 00 65; www.la-marina.it; Via Porcile 23; s €40, d €70-75; ❄) A good-value B&B. The elderly couple who run the place keep a tight ship and the two white, wood-beamed rooms are pristine.

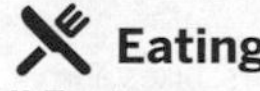

Eating

Il Fantasma PIZZERIA €
(☎070 65 67 49; Via San Domenico 94; pizzas from €6.50; ⏰Mon-Sat) It's quite a trek to this local favourite, but well worth it to chow down on Cagliari's best pizza. If you haven't booked you'll need to arrive early to get a table in the cheerful, brick-lined interior.

Sa Schironada TRATTORIA €
(☎070 451 07 71; Via Baylle 39; set menus €16-30, pizza menu €5-12) This big, barnlike trattoria is great for a cheap fillup. There are various menu options but bear in mind that the antipasto spread is a minor meal in itself with seafood salads, olives, cheese, salamis and stewed snails.

Information

Ospedale Brotzu (Hospital; ☎070 53 91; Via Peretti)

Police station (Questura; ☎070 6 02 71; Via Amat Luigi 9)

Tourist office (☎070 66 92 55; Piazza Matteotti; ⏰8.30am-1.30pm & 2-8pm Mon-Fri, 8am-8pm Sat & Sun)

Getting There & Around

Air

Cagliari's **Elmas airport** (CAG; ☎070 211 211; www.sogaer.it) is 6km northwest of the city. Flights connect with mainland Italy and European destinations. In summer there are additional charter flights. Half-hourly **ARST** (☎800 865 042; www.arst.sardegna.it) buses connect the airport with the bus station on Piazza Matteotti; the 10-minute journey costs €4.

Boat

Cagliari's ferry port is just off Via Roma. **Tirrenia** (☎892 123; www.tirrenia.it; Via dei Ponente 1; ⏰8.30am-12.20pm & 4-6.50pm Mon-Fri, to 6pm Sat, 4-6pm Sun) is the main ferry operator, with year-round services to Civitavecchia (€48 to €58, 16½ hours), Naples (€38 to €44, 16¼ hours) and Palermo (€37 to €44, 14½ hours).

Bus

From the **bus station** (Piazza Matteotti), daily **ARST** (☎800 865 042; www.arst.sardegna.it, in Italian) buses serve Oristano (€6.50, 1½ hours, two daily) and Nuoro (€14.50, 3½ hours, two daily), as well as destinations on the southern coast. Get tickets from the McDonalds on the square. **Turmo Travel** (☎0789 214 87;

www.gruppoturmotravel.com) runs two daily buses to Olbia (€19, 4¼ hours).

Car & Motorcycle

Down by the port, you can rent cars, bikes and scooters from **CIA Rent a Car** (☎070 65 65 03; www.ciarent.it; Via Molo Sant'Agostino 13; car per day from €29).

Train

Trenitalia trains run from the station on Piazza Matteotti to Oristano (€5.95, up to two hours, hourly) and Sassari (€15.75, 4¼ hours, three daily).

Alghero

POP 40,885

A picturesque medieval town, Alghero is the main resort on Sardinia's northwest coast. Surprisingly though, it's not entirely given over to tourism and is still an important fishing port. Interest is centred on the medieval *centro storico* with its robust stone ramparts and tight-knit lanes.

Alghero was founded in the 11th century by the Genovese and later became an important outpost of the Aragonese Catalans. Today, the local dialect is still a form of Catalan and the town retains something of a Spanish atmosphere.

Sights & Activities

Centro Storico HISTORIC CENTRE

Alghero's medieval core is a charming mesh of narrow cobbled alleys hemmed in by Spanish Gothic *palazzi*. Of the various churches, the most interesting is the **Chiesa di San Francesco** (Via Carlo Alberto; ⊙7.30am-noon & 5-8.30pm), with its mix of Romanesque and Gothic styles. A short walk away, the cathedral's **campanile** (bell tower; admission €2; ⊙7pm-9.30pm Tue, Thu & Sat Jul & Aug, 5-8pm Sep, by appointment rest of year) is a fine example of Gothic-Catalan architecture.

Grotte di Nettuno SEA CAVES

(adult/concession €12/6; ⊙9am-7pm Apr-Sep, shorter hr rest of year) From the port you can take a boat trip along the impressive northern coast to **Capo Caccia** and the grandiose **Grotte di Nettuno** cave complex. The cheapest boat is the **Navisarda ferry** (return €14), which departs hourly between 9am and 5pm from June to September, and three times daily between March and May and in October. Allow 2½ hours for the round trip. Cheaper still, you can get a bus to the caves from Via Catalogna (€3.50 return, 50 minutes, three times daily summer, once winter).

Nuraghe di Palmavera PREHISTORIC RUINS

(admission €3; ⊙9am-7pm May-Sep, shorter hr rest of year) Ten kilometres west of Alghero on the road to Porto Conte, this 3500-year-old *nuraghe* village is well worth a visit.

Sleeping

There's plenty of accommodation in Alghero, but you'll need to book between June and September.

Hotel San Francesco HOTEL €

(☎079 98 03 30; www.sanfrancescohotel.com; Via Ambrogio Machin 2; s €52-63, d €82-101; ❄@) This year-round hotel is the only one in Alghero's *centro storico*. Housed in an ex-convent, it has plain, modestly decorated rooms set around a 14th-century cloister.

Camping La Mariposa CAMPING GROUND €

(☎079 95 03 60; www.lamariposa.it; Via Lido 22; per person/tent/car €13/14/6, 4-person bungalows €50-80; ⊙Apr-Oct; @) About 2km north of the centre, this popular camping ground is on the beach amid pine and eucalyptus trees. Alongside the usual facilities (shop, laundry, internet bar, bike hire), there's also an on-site windsurfing centre (www.oceantribe.it).

Hostal de l'Alguer HOSTEL €

(☎079 93 04 78; www.ostelloalghero.com; Via Parenzo 79; dm €18, r per person from €23; P@) A characterless HI hostel near the airport in Fertilia. Although nothing special, it's clean and cheap. Facilities include a laundry and bike hire; meals are available for €10.50.

Eating

Trattoria Maristella TRATTORIA €€

(☎079 97 81 72; Via Fratelli Kennedy 9; mains €11; ⊙closed Sun dinner) Hospitable and unpretentious, this bustling little trattoria serves fresh seafood and classic Sardinian staples such as *culurgiones* (ravioli stuffed with potato, pecorino cheese and mint). It gets very busy in peak periods but service is quick and efficient.

TOP CHOICE **Gelateria I Bastioni** GELATERIA €

(Bastioni Marco Polo 5; cones €1-3, milkshakes €3.50; ⊙Apr-Oct) A hole-in-the-wall gem. Particularly fab are the fresh fruit flavours topped by a generous squirt of whipped cream.

Il Ghiotto CANTEEN €
(Piazza Civica 23; mains €5; ⏲Tue-Sun) A fantastic *tavola calda* (canteen), serving a daily spread of *panini*, pastas, salads and mains.

Cafe Latino CAFF €
(Bastioni Magelllllano 10) A cool bar on the ramparts overlooking the marina.

Information

On the eastern fringe of the *centro storico*, the superhelpful **tourist office** (☎079 97 90 54; www.comune.alghero.ss.it, in Italian; Piazza Porta Terra 9; ⏲8am-8pm Mon-Sat, 10am-1pm Sun) can answer every imaginable question.

Getting There & Away

Alghero's airport **Fertilia** (AHO; ☎079 93 52 82; www.algheroairport.it) is served by a number of low-cost carriers, with connections to mainland Italy and destinations across Europe.

ARST (☎800 86 50 42; www.arst.sardegna.it, in Italian) operates hourly buses (€0.70, 20 minutes) between the airport and the bus terminus on Via Cagliari. **Logudoro Tours** (☎079 28 17 28; www.logudorotours.it) runs two daily buses from the airport to Cagliari (€20, 3½ hours) and vice versa.

WORTH A TRIP

BOSA

As much for the getting there as the town itself, a trip to **Bosa** is well worth your time. The 46km road from Alghero is one of Sardinia's great coastal rides with unforgettable vistas at every turn. Bosa doesn't disappoint either, with its picturesque Old Town rising up from the Temo River.

For the journey, you can rent cars, motorcycles and bikes from **Cicloexpress** (☎079 98 69 50; www.cicloexpress.com; Via Garibaldi, Alghero) for about €75/35/15 per day.

UNDERSTAND ITALY

History

The Etruscans were the first major force to emerge on the Italian peninsula. By the 7th century BC they dominated central Italy, rivalled only by the Greeks from the southern colony of Magna Graecia. Both groups thrived until the 3rd century BC when Rome's rampaging legionnaires crashed in.

Founded in 753 BC – possibly by Romulus, possibly not – Rome became a republic in 509 BC. Expansion followed and by the turn of the millennium it ruled much of Western Europe and the Mediterranean. After Caesar's death in 44 BC, his great-nephew Octavian defeated rivals Mark Antony and Cleopatra and took the top job as Augustus Caesar, the first Roman emperor.

The empire's golden age came in the 2nd century AD but a century later it was in decline. Emperor Constantine legalised Christianity and in AD 330 founded Constantinople in Byzantium, leaving Rome and its Western Empire to invading Germanic barbarians in 476.

The Middle Ages witnessed the development of Italy's powerful city-states, particularly in the centre and north. Of these, it was Florence under the Medici that made the biggest impact, giving rise to the 15th-century Renaissance.

By the early 16th century much of Italy was in foreign hands – the Austrian Habsburgs in the north and the Spanish Bourbons in the south. Not much changed until the mid-19th century when the Risorgimento (unification movement) culminated in the 1861 unification of Italy.

Modern Italy

Italy's brief fascist interlude was a low point. Mussolini gained power in 1925 and in 1940 entered WWII on Germany's side. Defeat ensued and Il Duce was killed by partisans in April 1945.

Italy's postwar era has been largely successful. A founding member of the European Economic Community, it survived a period of domestic terrorism in the 1970s and enjoyed sustained economic growth in the 1980s.

The 1990s heralded a period of crisis as national bribery scandals rocked the nation, paving the way for Silvio Berlusconi's entry into politics. A billionaire media-magnate, Berlusconi has dominated Italian public life since his first foray into politics in 1994. After a short period as prime minister in 1994, he won the elections in 2001, going on to become Italy's longest serving postwar prime minister. In 2008 he returned to the top job after a two-year period in opposition, and, true to form, his third term is proving highly contentious with scandal and controversy never far from the surface.

People

Italy has a population of 60.4 million. Almost half of all Italians live in the industrialised north and almost one in five are over 65. At the other end of the age scale, Italy has one of the world's lowest birth rates.

Traditionally, Italians are very conscious of their regional identity, a phenomenon known as *campanilismo* (literally, an attachment to the local bell tower), and very family orientated. It's not unusual to find three generations living together and even if times are changing, most children stay at home until they marry.

Up to 80% of Italians consider themselves Catholic, although only about one in three regularly attend church. Similarly, the Vatican remains a powerful voice in national debate, but can't find enough priests for its parish churches. Still, first Communions, church weddings and regular feast days remain an integral part of Italian life.

There are no official figures, but it's estimated that there are about 1.3 million Muslims in Italy, making Islam Italy's second religion.

Arts

Literature

Italian literature runs the gamut from Virgil's *Aeneid* to the chilling war stories of Primo Levi and the fantastical tales of Italo Calvino.

Dante, whose *Divina commedia* (Divine Comedy) dates to the early 1300s, was one of three 14th-century greats alongside Petrarch and Giovanni Boccaccio.

Then, in the early 16th century, Machiavelli taught would-be despots how to manipulate power in *Il principe* (The Prince), and 300 years later 19th-century scribe Alessandro Manzoni wrote of star-crossed lovers in *I promessi sposi* (The Betrothed).

Italy's southern regions provide rich literary pickings. Giuseppe Tomasi di Lampedusa depicts Sicily's wary mentality in *Il gattopardo* (The Leopard), a theme that Leonardo Sciascia later returns to in *Il giorno della civetta* (The Day of the Owl), and Carlo Levi denounces southern poverty in *Cristo si é fermato a Eboli* (Christ Stopped at Eboli). More recently, Andrea Camilleri's Sicilian-based Montalbano detective stories have enjoyed great success.

Cinema

Italy has produced some of cinema's most influential filmmakers. In creating the spaghetti western Sergio Leone inspired generations of film-makers, as did horror master Dario Argento and art-house genius Michelangelo Antonioni.

Starting the ball rolling were the post-WWII neo-realists Roberto Rossellini, Vittorio de Sica and Luchino Visconti, who produced classics such as *Ladri di biciclette* (Bicycle Thieves; 1948) and *Roma città aperta* (Rome Open City; 1945). Taking up their mantle, if not their style, Federico Fellini later wowed international audiences with his masterpiece *La dolce vita* (The Sweet Life; 1959).

More recently, Roberto Benigni won an Oscar for *La vita è bella* (Life is Beautiful) in 1999 and Paolo Sorrentino's *Il divo* won the Jury Prize at the 2008 Cannes Film Festival. In the same year, *Gomorra*, Matteo Garrone's film of Roberto Saviano's bestselling book, was awarded the Festival Grand Prix.

Music

Emotional and highly theatrical, opera has always appealed to Italians. Performances of Verdi and Puccini are regularly staged at legendary theatres such as Milan's Teatro alla Scala and Naples' Teatro San Carlo.

Architecture, Painting & Sculpture

Ancient ruins, Renaissance *palazzi* and baroque churches all stand testament to the central role that the arts have played in Italy's past.

Europe's most famous artistic movement, the Renaissance, took off in 15th-century Italy. Under the Medici in Florence and the Roman papacy, Leonardo da Vinci, Michelangelo Buonarrotti and Raphael set new standards of artistic expression.

Controversial and highly influential, Michelangelo Merisi da Caravaggio dominated the late 16th century. His realism contrasted with the exuberant style of the 17th-century baroque rivals Gianlorenzo Bernini and Francesco Borromini.

Signalling a return to classical sobriety, neoclassicism was the rage in the late 18th and early 19th centuries, producing sculptor Canova.

Of Italy's modern artists, Amedeo Modigliani is the most famous. Carrying contemporary Italy's architectural mantle are superstar architects Renzo Piano, the visionary behind Rome's Auditorium, and Rome-born Massimiliano Fuksas.

Food & Drink

Despite the ubiquity of pasta and pizza, Italian cuisine is highly regional. Local specialities abound and regional traditions are proudly maintained, so expect pesto in Genoa, pizza in Naples, and *ragù* (bolognese sauce) in Bologna. It's the same with wine – Piedmont produces Italy's great reds, Barolo, Barbaresco and Dolcetto, while Tuscany is famous for its Chianti, Brunello and white Vernaccia. Italian wines are classified according to strict rules: the top denomination is DOCG *(denominazione di origine controllata e garantita)*, followed by DOC *(denominazione di origine controllata)* and ICG *(indicazione geografica tipica)*; at the bottom of the barrel is *vino da tavola* (table wine).

Eating out is a way of life in Italy and one of its great pleasures. The most basic sit-down eatery is a *tavola calda* (literally 'hot table'), which offers canteen-style food. Pizzerias, the best of which have a *forno a legna* (wood-fired oven), serve the obvious but often a full menu as well. For a full meal you'll want a trattoria or a *ristorante* (restaurant). Restaurants offer more choice and smarter service than trattorias, which are often family-run places serving a basic menu of local dishes.

On the bill expect to be charged for *pane e coperto* (bread and a cover charge). This is standard and is added even if you don't ask for or eat the bread. Typically it ranges from €1 to €4. *Servizio* (service charge) of 10% to 15% might or might not be included; if it's not, tourists are expected to round up the bill or leave 10%.

Throughout this chapter, the following price indicators have been used and apply to the cost of main courses:

€€€ more than €18

€€ €11 to €17

€ less than €11

Environment

Bound by the Adriatic, Ligurian, Tyrrhenian and Ionian Seas, Italy has more than 8000km of coastline. Inland, about 75% of the peninsula is mountainous – the Alps curve 966km round the country's northern border while the Apennines extend 1350km from north to south.

EARTHQUAKES & VOLCANOES

Italy is one of the world's most earthquake-prone countries. A fault line runs through the entire peninsula – from eastern Sicily, up the Apennines and into the northeastern Alps. The country is usually hit by minor quakes several times a year and devastating earthquakes are not uncommon in central and southern Italy. The most recent, measuring 6.3 on the Richter scale, struck the central region of Abruzzo on 6 April 2009, killing 308 people and leaving up to 55,000 homeless.

Italy also has six active volcanoes: Stromboli and Vulcano on the Aeolian Islands; Vesuvius, the Campi Flegrei and the island of Ischia near Naples; and Etna on Sicily. Stromboli and Etna are among the world's most active volcanoes, while Vesuvius has not erupted since 1944.

Italy has 24 national parks, covering about 5% of the country, and more than 400 nature reserves, natural parks and wetlands. It also boasts 45 Unesco World Heritage Sites, more than any other country.

But Italy is not without its environmental problems, of which the worst are air pollution, waste disposal and coastal development.

SURVIVAL GUIDE

Directory A-Z

Accommodation

The bulk of Italy's accommodation is made up of *alberghi* (hotels) and *pensioni*. Other options are youth hostels, camping grounds, B&Bs, *agriturismi* (farm stays), mountain *rifugi* (Alpine refuges), monasteries and villa/apartment rentals.

High-season rates apply at Easter, in summer (mid-June to August) and over the Christmas to New Year period. Peak season in the ski resorts runs from December to March.

Many city-centre hotels offer discounts in August to lure clients from the crowded coast. Conversely, many coastal hotels shut for winter, typically from November to March.

In this chapter prices quoted are the minimum-maximum for rooms with a private bathroom, and unless otherwise stated include breakfast. As a rough guide, reckon on at least €55 for a double room in a budget hotel. The following price indicators apply (for a high-season double):

€€€ €200 and up

€€ €110 to €199

€ under €110

AGRITURISMI

An *agriturismo* (farm stay) is a good option for a country stay, although you will usually need your own transport. Accommodation varies from spartan billets on working farms to palatial suites at luxurious rural retreats. Check out www.agriturist.it or www.agriturismo.com.

B&BS

Quality varies, but the best offer comfort greater than you'd get in a similarly priced hotel room. Online booking services include **Bed & Breakfast Italia** (www.bbitalia.it) and **Cross-pollinate** (www.cross-pollinate.com). Prices are typically €70 to €180 for a double room.

CAMPING

Lists of camping grounds are available from local tourist offices or online at www.campeggi.com, www.camping.it and www.italcamping.it. In high season expect to pay up to €20 per person and a further €25 for a tent pitch. Independent camping is not permitted in many places.

HOSTELS

Official HI-affiliated *ostelli per la gioventù* (youth hostels) are run by the **Italian Youth Hostel Association** (Associazione Italiana Alberghi per la Gioventù; ☎06 487 11 52; www.aighostels.com; Via Cavour 44, Rome). A valid HI card is required for affiliated hostels. You can get this in your home country or directly at hostels.

Additionally, there are many privately run hostels offering dorms and private rooms.

Dorm rates are typically between €15 and €30, with breakfast usually included. Many places also offer dinner for around €10.

MOUNTAIN REFUGES

Italy boasts an extensive network of mountain *rifugi* (refuges). Open from July to September, they offer basic dorm-style accommodation, although some larger ones have double rooms. Reckon on €20 to €30 per person per night with breakfast included. **Club Alpino Italiano** (CAI; www.cai.it) runs many of the refuges.

RELIGIOUS ACCOMMODATION

Basic accommodation is often available in convents and monasteries: see **Chiesa di Santa Susanna** (www.santasusanna.org) for a list of participating institutions throughout the country. You can also try www.monasterystays.com, a specialist online booking service.

Activities

Cycling Tourist offices can provide details on trails and guided rides. The best time is spring. Lonely Planet's *Cycling in Italy* offers practical tips and detailed itineraries.

Hiking & Walking Thousands of kilometres of *sentieri* (marked trails) criss-cross the country. The hiking season is from June to September. Useful websites include www.cai.it and www.parks.it. Lonely Planet's *Walking in Italy* has descriptions of more than 50 walks.

Skiing Italy's ski season runs from December to March. Prices are generally high, particularly in the top Alpine resorts – the Apennines are cheaper. Save money with a *settimana bianca* (literally 'white week') package deal, covering seven days' accommodation, food and ski passes.

Business Hours

In this chapter, opening hours have been provided in the relevant sections when they differ from the following standards:

Banks 8.30am-1.30pm & 3-4.30pm Mon-Fri

Bars & Cafes 7.30am-8pm. Many open earlier and some stay open until the small hours. Pubs often open noon-2am.

Clubs & Discos 10pm-4am

Post offices 8am-7pm Mon-Fri, to 1.15pm Sat. Smaller offices are open 8.30am-2pm Mon-Fri, and to 1pm Sat.

Restaurants noon-3pm & 7.30-11pm or midnight. Most restaurants close one day a week.

Shops 9am-1pm & 3.30-7.30pm Mon-Sat. In larger cities many chain stores and supermarkets open 9am-7.30pm Mon-Sat; some also open Sunday mornings. Food shops are generally closed on Thursday afternoon; some other shops are closed on Monday morning.

Many museums, galleries and archaeological sites operate summer and winter opening hours. Typically, winter hours apply from November to late March or early April.

Gay & Lesbian Travellers

Homosexuality is well tolerated in major cities, but overt displays of affection could attract a negative response, particularly in small towns and in the more conservative south. Italy's main gay and lesbian organisation is **Arcigay** (www.arcigay.it, in Italian), based in Bologna.

Holidays

Most Italians take their annual holiday in August. This means that many businesses and shops close down for at least a part of the month, usually around Ferragosto (15 August). Easter is another busy holiday.

Public holidays are as follows:

New Year's Day (Capodanno) 1 January

Epiphany (Epifania) 6 January

Easter Monday (Pasquetta) March/April

Liberation Day (Giorno delle Liberazione) 25 April

Labour Day (Festa del Lavoro) 1 May

Republic Day (Festa della Repubblica) 2 June

Feast of the Assumption (Ferragosto) 15 August

All Saint's Day (Ognisanti) 1 November

Feast of the Immaculate Conception (Immacolata Concezione) 8 December

Christmas Day (Natale) 25 December

Boxing Day (Festa di Santo Stefano) 26 December

Individual towns also have holidays to celebrate their patron saints:

St Mark (Venice) 25 April

St Janarius (Naples) First Sunday in May, 19 September and 16 December

St John the Baptist (Florence, Genoa and Turin) 24 June

Saints Peter and Paul (Rome) 29 June

St Rosalia (Palermo) 15 July

St Ambrose (Milan) 7 December

Internet Access

Wi-fi is increasingly available and many hotels, hostels, B&Bs and *pensioni* now offer it, either free or for a small charge. Access is also available in internet cafes throughout the country, although many have closed in recent years. Charges are typically around €5 per hour. To use internet points in Italy you must present photo ID.

Money

ATMs, known in Italy as *bancomat,* are widespread. Most credit cards are widely recognised; however, American Express is less common. Remember that many small trattorias, pizzerias and *pensioni* only take cash. Likewise, don't assume that museums and other sights will accept credit cards. If you don't have a PIN, some banks will advance cash over the counter.

If your credit/debit card is lost, stolen or swallowed by an ATM, phone toll-free to block it: **Amex** (☎06 729 00 347); **MasterCard** (☎800 870 866); and **Visa** (☎800 81 90 14).

Post & Telephone

Italy's postal system, **Poste Italiane** (☎80 31 60; www.poste.it), is reasonably reliable. The standard service is *posta prioritaria.* Registered mail is known as *posta raccomandata,* insured mail as *posta assicurato. Francobolli* (stamps) are available at post offices and *tabacchi* (tobacconists).

Area codes are an integral part of all Italian phone numbers and must be dialled even when calling locally. The international access code for Italy is ☎00. To make a reverse-charge (collect) international call, dial ☎170. All operators speak English.

To phone from a public payphone you'll need a *scheda telefonica* from *tabacchi* and newsstands. You'll find cut-price call centres in main cities with good international rates.

MOBILE PHONES

Mobile phone numbers begin with a three-digit prefix such as 330 or 339. Italy uses the GSM 900/1800 network which is compatible with the rest of Europe and Australia, but not with the North American GSM 1900 or the Japanese system (although some GSM 1900/900 phones do work here). If you have a GSM dual- or tri-band cellular phone – or a smart phone – that you can unlock (check with your service provider), you can buy a *prepagato* (prepaid) SIM card in Italy. Companies selling SIM cards include **TIM** (Telecom Italia Mobile; www.tim.it), **Wind** (www.wind.it) and **Vodafone** (www.vodafone.it). All have shops across Italy. You'll need ID to open an account.

Visas

Schengen visa rules apply for entry to Italy. Foreign visitors not staying in a hotel, B&B, hostel etc are supposed to register with the local police within eight days of arrival. A *permesso di soggiorno* (permit to stay) is required by all non-EU nationals who stay in Italy longer than three months. You must apply within eight days of arriving in Italy. Check the exact documentary requirements on www.poliziadistato.it. EU citizens do not require a *permesso di soggiorno.*

Getting There & Away

Getting to Italy is pretty straightforward. It is well served by low-cost carriers and there are plenty of bus, train and ferry routes into the country. Flights, tours and rail tickets can be booked online at lonelyplanet.com/bookings.

Air

There are direct intercontinental flights to/from Rome and Milan. European flights also serve regional airports.

Italy's national carrier is **Alitalia** (www.alitalia.com). The main international airports are as follows:

Leonardo da Vinci (www.adr.it) Italy and Rome's main airport, also known as Fiumicino.

Ciampino (www.adr.it) Rome's second airport. For low-cost European carriers.

Malpensa (www.sea-aeroportimilano.it) Milan's principal airport.

Land

BUS & TRAIN

Eurolines (www.eurolines.com) operates buses from European destinations to Bologna, Florence, Milan, Naples, Rome, Siena, Turin, Verona, Venice and other Italian cities.

International trains connect with various cities, including:

Milan To/from Barcelona, Basel, Geneva, Paris, Vienna and Zürich.

Rome To/from Munich, Paris and Vienna.

Venice To/from Basel, Belgrade, Budapest, Geneva, Ljubljana, Lucerne, Paris, Vienna and Zagreb.

There are also international trains from Bologna, Florence, Genoa, Naples, Turin and Verona. Details are available online at www.ferroviedellostato.it.

In the UK, the **Rail Europe Travel Centre** (www.raileurope.co.uk) can provide fare information on journeys to/from Italy, most of which require a change at Paris. Another excellent online resource is **The Man in Seat Sixty-One** (www.seat61.com), whose Italy page details how to travel from London to Italy.

Eurail and Inter-Rail passes are both valid (assuming you have an option that covers Italy).

BOAT

Ferries serve Italy's main international ferry ports – Ancona, Bari, Brindisi, Genoa and Venice – from Albania, Corsica, Croatia, Greece, Malta, Spain, Tunisia and Turkey. Timetables are seasonal so always check ahead – you'll find details of routes, companies and online booking on **Traghettiweb** (www.traghettiweb.it). Prices quoted in this chapter are for a one-way *poltrona* (reclinable seat).

Holders of Eurail and Inter-Rail passes should check with the ferry company if they are entitled to a discount or free passage.

Getting Around

Bicycle

Tourist offices can generally provide details of designated bike trails and bike hire (bank on at least €10 per day).

Bikes can be taken on regional and international trains carrying the bike logo, but you'll need to pay a supplement (€3.50 on regional trains, €12 on international trains). Bikes can be carried free if dismantled and stored in a bike bag. Bikes generally incur a small supplement on ferries, typically €5 to €10.

Boat

Navi (large ferries) service Sicily and Sardinia; *traghetti* (smaller ferries) and *aliscafi* (hydrofoils) cover the smaller islands. Most long-distance ferries travel overnight.

The main embarkation points for Sardinia are Civitavecchia, Genoa, Livorno and Naples; for Sicily, it's Naples and Villa San Giovanni in Calabria.

The major domestic ferry companies are as follows:

Grandi Navi Veloci (☎010 209 45 91; www.gnv.it)

Moby (☎199 30 30 40; www.mobylines.it)

Sardinia Ferries (☎199 40 05 00; www.corsica-ferries.it)

SNAV (☎081 428 55 55; www.snav.it)

Tirrenia (☎89 21 23; www.tirrenia.it)

Bus

Italy boasts an extensive and largely reliable bus network. Buses are not necessarily cheaper than trains, but in mountainous areas such as Umbria, Sicily and Sardinia they are often the only choice. In larger cities companies have ticket offices or operate through agencies, but in most villages and small towns tickets are sold in bars or on the bus.

Reservations are usually only necessary for high-season long-haul trips.

Car & Motorcycle

All EU driving licences are recognised in Italy. Holders of non-EU licences must get an International Driving Permit (IDP) to accompany their national licence. Many cities have traffic restrictions in their historical centres, although these don't apply to foreign-registered vehicles, mopeds or scooters.

To hire a car you'll require a valid driving licence (plus IDP if necessary) and credit card. Age restrictions vary but generally you'll need to be 21 or over. If driving your own car, carry proof of ownership and an international insurance certificate, known as a Carta Verde (Green Card), available from your insurance company.

Cars use unleaded petrol (*benzina senza piombo*) and diesel (*gasolio*); both are expensive but diesel is slightly cheaper.

Wearing a helmet is compulsory on all two-wheeled vehicles.

Italy's motoring organisation **Automobile Club d'Italia** (ACI; www.aci.it) provides 24-hour roadside assistance (☎803 116).

Train

Many trains are fast, comfortable and relatively cheap. Most services are run by **Trenitalia** (☎89 20 21; www.ferroviedellostato.it). There are several types of train:

Regionale or interregionale (R) Slow local services.

InterCity (IC) Fast trains between major cities.

Eurostar (ES) Similar to Intercity but faster.

Eurostar Alta Velocità (ES AV) High-speed trains operating on the Turin–Milan–Bologna–Florence–Rome–Naples–Salerno line.

Regional trains are the cheapest. InterCity trains require a supplement which is incorporated in the ticket price. If you have a standard ticket and board an InterCity, you will have to pay the difference on board.

Eurostar and Alta Velocità trains require prior reservation. Generally, it's cheaper to buy all local train tickets in Italy.

Train prices quoted in this chapter are for the most common trains on any given route. On some routes that might be a slow Regionale train, on others it could be the fast Alta Velocità Eurostar.

Tickets must be validated – in the yellow machines at the entrance to platforms – before boarding trains.

Kosovo

Includes »

Best Places to Stay & Eat

» Hotel Sara, Pristina (p776)

» Hotel Centrum, Prizren (p778)

» Tiffany, Pristina (p777)

» Renaissance-2, Pristina (p776)

Best Websites

» **Pristina in Your Pocket** (www.inyourpocket.com/city/pristina.html) Downloadable guide also available from bookshops

» **Pristina Insight** (www.prishtinainsight.com) Newspaper run by the Balkan Investigative Reporting Network that gives exactly what its title says

Why Go?

Everyone loves a newborn, and since 2008, when Kosovo declared itself independent, large letters spelling 'NEWBORN' have graced its capital, Pristina. The monument's location – between the secure offices of the United Nations and a shopping mall featuring ubiquitous European chain stores and a sky-clawing crumbling concrete monument – tells all. Kosovo is finding its feet.

Kosovo has delightful mountain-backed towns with hiking opportunities, Ottoman-style ethnographic museums and 13th-century Serbian monasteries, none of which are more than two hours by bus from Pristina; it's possible to visit Decani monastery, barter for goat's cheese in Peja's Turkish-style bazaar and still be back in Pristina in time for dinner.

When to Go

Pristina

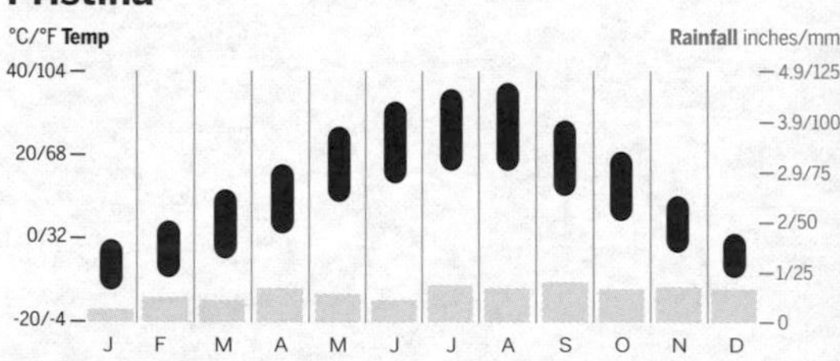

Jul The Ship Film Fest brings short films to Peja.

Aug It's a sweat-free summer as temperatures hover in the mid-20°Cs.

Dec–Apr The skiing's good right until April.

PRISTINA

📞038 / POP 500,000

Pristina manages to mix lazy boulevards with zigzagging Ottoman-style streets, while stamping almost every corner with statues of persons important to Kosovo (Clinton, Mother Theresa, Albright). It has an international vibe (most noticed in its restaurants and bars) and a 'newborn' feel.

Sights

Ethnographic Museum HISTORIC BUILDING

(Rr Iliaz Agushi; admission €2.50; ⏲10am-4pm) Follow the signs to locate this well-kept 'how we lived' Ottoman house.

Kosovo Museum MUSEUM

(Sheshi Adam Jashari; admission €3; ⏲10am-4pm Tue-Sat) A written plea to have antiquities returned from Serbia greets visitors but, while waiting, see modern exhibits upstairs and delicate 6000-year-old statues on the ground floor.

Mosques MOSQUES

Fronting the museum is the 15th-century **Carshi Mosque**. Nearby, the **Sultan Mehmet Fatih Mosque** (the 'Big Mosque') was built by its namesake around 1461, converted to a Catholic church during the Austro-Hungarian era and refurbished again during WWII. **Jashar Pasha Mosque** has

Kosovo Highlights

1. Buy local wine and cheese at the serene 14th-century **Decani monastery** (p778)
2. View the old ottoman-style town of **Prizren** (p778) from the castle above it
3. Smile for the camera in front of new and old buildings in **Pristina** (p775)

Pristina

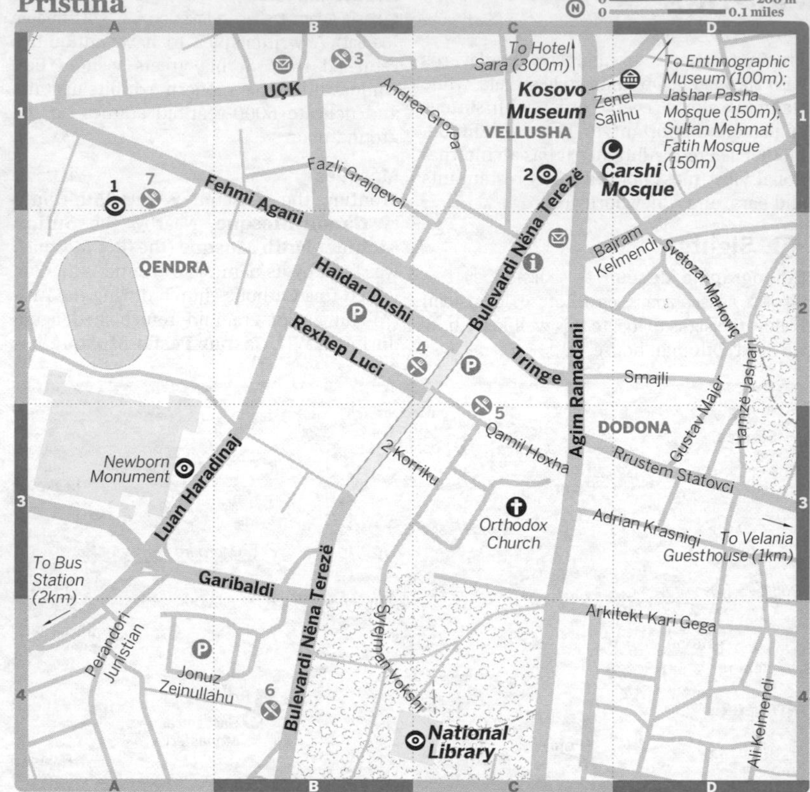

vibrant interiors that exemplify Turkish baroque style.

National Library LIBRARY
(www.biblioteka-ks.org) The National Library, completed in 1982 by Croatian Andrija Mutnjakovic, must be seen to be believed (if you can, think gelatinous eggs wearing armour).

FREE **Independence House of Kosovo** HISTORIC BUILDING
(10am-4pm Mon-Sat) This small house opposite the stadium is devoted to former president Ibrahim Rugova and Kosovo's recent independence movement.

The gates of the government buildings at the northern end of Bul Nëna Terezë bear ghostlike **photos of the missing** – a stark reminder of how recently Pristina was in turmoil.

Sleeping

Hotel Sara HOTEL €€
(236 203; www.hotelsara-medi.com; Rr Maliq Pash Gjinolli; s/d incl breakfast €35/50) Sara's simple, stylish rooms are refreshingly free of clutter, and the welcome is genuine.

Velania Guesthouse PENSION €
(531 742, 044 167 455; http://guesthouse-ks.net/eng/vlersimet.html; Velania 4/34; s/d €15/20; @) This bustling guest house is spread over two buildings in an affluent part of town. The jovial professor who runs it loves a chat and could double as your grandfather.

Eating

Head to **Maxi Supermarket** (Rr Rexhep Luci; 7am-midnight) for groceries.

Renaissance-2 KOSOVAR €€
(044 118 796; meals €15; 6-11pm) Hidden in a lane, this is possibly the classiest all-you-

Pristina

Top Sights

Sights

Eating

can-eat-and-drink restaurant you'll ever find (if you can find it). The starters (baked peppers, divine dips and beans) get usurped by the tender mains (your choice of fish, chicken or beef). Head into the lanes across the road from Radio Kosovo on Boulevardi Nëna Terezë.

Tiffany TRADITIONAL €
(off Fehmi Agani; mains €6; ⊙8am-11pm Mon-Sat, 6-11pm Sun) No menu, no pizza and no pasta (it's official!). Pay up and enjoy the day's grilled special (whatever's fresh that day) and oven baked bread at this restaurant opposite the sports stadium.

de Rada Brasserie TRADITIONAL €
(Rr UÇK 50; mains €7; ⊙8am-midnight Mon-Sat) The sort of place you wish you could afford in Paris. Nibble on calamari in surrounds bursting with olden-day photos.

Pishat KOSOVAR €
(☎245 333; Rr Qamil Hoxha 11; mains €6; ⊙8am-11pm Mon-Sat, noon-11pm Sun) Sample Albanian dishes at this indoor/outdoor spot that is often packed with expats and discerning locals.

WORTH A TRIP

GRAČANICA MONASTERY

Dusty fingers of sunlight pierce the darkness of **Gračanica Monastery** (⊙6am-5pm), completed in 1321 by Serbian King Milutin. Take a Gjilan-bound bus from Pristina (€0.50, 15 minutes, every 30 minutes); the monastery's on your left.

KOSOVO FACTS

» **Area** 10,887 sq km

» **Capital** Pristina

» **Language** Albanian and Serbian

» **Currency** euro (€)

» **Exchange rates** A$1 = €0.72; C$1 = €0.74; ¥100 = €0.87; NZ$1 = €0.56; UK£1 = €1.16; US$1 = €0.72

» **Money** ATMs in larger towns

» **Country code** ☎381

» **Emergency** Police ☎92, ambulance ☎94

» **Visas** Passports are stamped for a 90-day stay on entry; check www.mfa-ks.net for changes

» **Itinerary** Do some fine dining and museum finding in Pristina, then a visit to Gračanica Monastery and a curl through the mountains to Prizren's Ottoman sights

Getting There & Around

There are flights to Pristina from many European cities. Taxis charge €25 for the 18km trip to **Pristina airport** (www.airportpristina.com). The **bus station** (Stacioni I Autobusëve; Rr Lidja e Pejes) is 2km southwest of the centre, off Bul Bil Klinton. Taxis to the centre cost €2. Local taxi trips cost a few euros.

AROUND PRISTINA

Peja (Peć)

☎039 / POP 82,000

Peja is flanked by sites vital to Orthodox Serbians, with a Turkish-style bazaar beating at its heart. Lumbardhi River torrents through town in winter and the surrounding mountains are ripe for hiking in summer.

The **Patriachate of Peć** (☎044 150 755; ⊙9am-6pm) church and monastery is a slice of Serbian Orthodoxy. It's a 10-minute walk from town along the river and is guarded by NATO's Kosovo Force (KFOR); you may need to hand in your passport for the duration of your visit.

Frequent buses head to Pristina (€4, 1½ hours, every 20 minutes).

DON'T MISS

DECANI MONASTERY

This regal **monastery** (Rr Ul St Manastirit, Decani; ⌚11am-1pm & 4-6pm), 15km south of Peja, is one of Kosovo's highlights. Buses go to Decani from Peja (€1, 30 minutes, every 15 minutes) on their way to Gjakovë from Peja. It's a pleasant 2km walk to the monastery from the bus stop. The on-site shop sells delicious monastery-made cheeses and wines.

Sleeping & Eating

Dukagjini Hotel HOTEL €€
(☎429 999; www.hoteldukagjini.com; Sheshi I Dëshmorëve, 2; s/d €30/40; ❄📶) The Dukagjini's rooms have character and a riverside breakfast is included.

Semitronix Centre KOSOVAR €
(Mbretëresha Teutë; meals €4; ⌚7am-11pm) There are sky-high views and good food at this rooftop restaurant.

Prizren

☎029 / POP 70,000

Picturesque Prizren has an Old Town that's worth setting aside a few hours to visit.

Prizren's 15th-century **Ottoman bridge** has been superbly restored. Nearby is **Sinan Pasha Mosque** (1561), which renovations are resurrecting as a central landmark in town. The **Ethnological Museum** (admission €1; ⌚11am-7pm Tue-Sun) is where the Prizren League (for Albanian autonomy) organised itself in 1878. There is naught to see at the 11th-century **Kalaja**, but the 180-degree views over Prizren from this fort are worth the walk.

Stay at stylish and new **Hotel Centrum** (☎230 530; www.centrumprizren.com; Rr Bujtinat 1; s/d/€40/50; 📶).

Regular buses head to Pristina and Peja (€3, 1½ hours).

UNDERSTAND KOSOVO

History

In the 12th century, Kosovo was the heart of the Serbian empire. This Serbian golden age saw construction of many Orthodox churches until the Turkish triumph at the pivotal 1389 Battle of Kosovo ushered in 500 years of Ottoman rule. The number of Serbs fell drastically, and Albanians and Muslims came to dominate the region's ethnic and religious make-up.

In 1989 the autonomy that Kosovo had gained in 1974 was suspended by Slobodan Milošević. Ethnic Albanian leaders declared independence in 1990 and war erupted in 1992.

A US-backed plan to return Kosovo's autonomy was rejected by Serbia in March 1999. After Serbia refused to desist from emptying the province of non-Serbians, NATO unleashed a bombing campaign. In June, Milošević withdrew troops and Kosovo became a UN-NATO protectorate.

UN-sponsored talks on Kosovo's status began in February 2006 and Kosovo's parliament declared Kosovo independent on 17 February 2008. Over 70 countries recognised Kosovo's independence, but Serbia was not one of them. In July 2010 the International Court of Justice ruled that Kosovo's declaration of independence did not violate international law.

People

The population was estimated at 1.8 million in 2010, with 92% Albanian and 8% from other ethnic groups, including Serbs.

Food

The price ranges for the average cost of a main course in an eatery is shown following:

€€€ more than €15

€€ from €5 to €15

€ less than €5

SURVIVAL GUIDE

Directory A-Z

Accommodation

Apart from a few high-standard hotels, expect either midrange hotels or cheap rooms above bars. The price ranges in this chapter for a double room are:

€€€ more than €70

€€ from €30 to €70

€ less than €30

Dangers & Annoyances

Check government travel advisories before travelling to Kosovo. Sporadic violence occurs in North Mitrovica. Unexploded ordnance (UXO) has been cleared from roadsides but seek KFOR advice before venturing off beaten tracks.

Telephone

Vala (www.valamobile.com) and **Zmobile** (www.zmobileonline.com) have SIM cards that are effectively free; the €5 fee includes €5 worth of credit.

Getting There & Away

Kosovo has bus connections to Albania (€10, five hours), Montenegro (€15, seven hours), Macedonia (€5, 1½ hours) and Serbia (€20, six hours).

If you plan to go to Serbia but entered Kosovo via Albania, Macedonia or Montenegro, officials at the Serbian border will deem that you are entering Serbia illegally and you will not be let in.

A daily train links Pristina with Skopje (€4, three hours, 7.10am) in Macedonia.

Getting Around

Buses can be flagged down anywhere and a 1½-hour bus trip in Kosovo will cost you around €4.

The train system operates between Pristina and Peja (€3, 1½ hours, 7.50am and 4.30pm).

Latvia

Includes »

Best Places to Eat

» Istaba, Rīga (p787)

» Meta-Kafe, Rīga (p787)

» Pelmeņi XL, Rīga (p788)

» Ostas Skati, Rīga (p788)

Best Places to Stay

» Hotel Bergs, Rīga (p787)

» Naughty Squirrel, Rīga (p787)

Why Go?

Tucked between Estonia to the north and Lithuania to the south, Latvia is the meat of the Baltic sandwich. We're not implying that the neighbouring nations are slices of white bread, but Latvia is the savoury middle, loaded with colourful fixings. Thick greens take the form of Gauja Valley pines. Onion-domed cathedrals sprout up above local towns. Cheesy Russian pop blares along coastal beaches. And spicy Rīga adds an extra zing as the country's cosmopolitan nexus, unofficial capital of the entire Baltic.

If that doesn't whet your appetite, hear this: the country's under-the-radar profile makes it the perfect pit stop for those seeking something a bit more authentic than the overrun tourist hubs further afield. So, consider altering your Eastern European itinerary and fill up on little Latvia.

When to Go

Riga

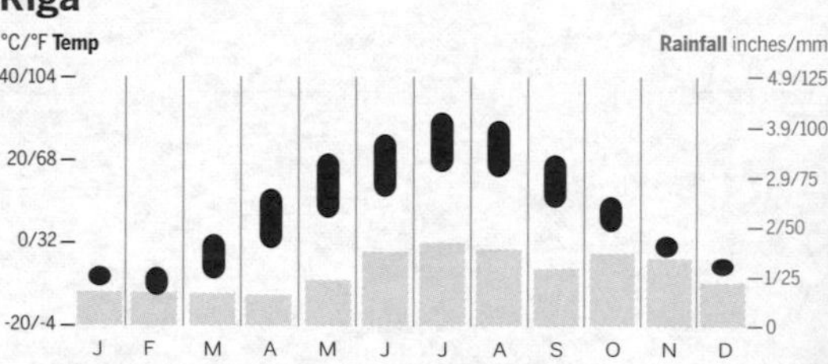

Dec & Jan Fete the holidays in the birthplace of the Christmas tree, and try some bobsledding.

Mid-Jun–Aug After an all-night solstice romp, it's off to the coast for beach lazing

Sep Hanging on to summer, Rīgans sip lattes under heat lamps at the season's last al fresco cafes.

Connections

Latvia is the link in the Baltic chain, making Rīga a convenient connecting point between Tallinn and Vilnius. Long-distance buses and trains also connect the capital to St Petersburg, Moscow and Warsaw, and ferry services shuttle passengers to Sweden and Germany. Rīga is the hub of airBaltic, which offers direct service to over 50 European cities.

ITINERARIES

Three Days

Fill your first two days with a feast of Rīga's architectural eye candy, and spend your third day hiking between Sigulda's castles, sunbathing in scintillating Jūrmala, or snapping photos of Rundāle's opulent palace.

One Week

After a few days in the capital swing by Jūrmala on your way up the horn of Cape Kolka for saunas, sunsets and solitude. Glide through western Latvia, comparing its ultrabucolic townships to Rundāle's majestic grounds, then blaze a trail across eastern Latvia for a rousing trip back in time spiced with adrenalin sports.

Essential Food & Drink

» **Black Balzām** Goethe called it the 'elixir of life'. The 45% proof concoction is a secret recipe of a dozen fairy-tale ingredients, including wormwood and linden blossoms. A shot a day keeps the doctor away, or so say most of Latvia's pensioners. Try mixing it with glass of cola to take off the edge.

» **Mushrooms** Not a sport but a national obsession; mushroom picking takes the country by storm during the first showers of autumn.

» **Alus** For such a tiny nation there's definitely no shortage of *alus* (beer) – each major town has its own brew. You can't go wrong with Užavas (Ventspils' contribution).

» **Smoked fish** Dozens of fish shacks dot the Kurzeme coast – look for the veritable smoke signals rising above the tree line. Grab 'em to go; they make the perfect afternoon snack.

» **Kvass** Single-handedly responsible for the decline of Coca Cola at the turn of the 21st century, Kvass is a beloved beverage made from fermented rye bread. It's surprisingly popular with kids.

AT A GLANCE

» **Currency** lats (Ls)

» **Language** Latvian, Russian

» **Money** ATMs all over Rīga and smaller cities

» **Visas** Schengen rules apply; see p1319

Fast Facts

» **Area** 64,589 sq km

» **Capital** Rīga

» **Country code** ☎371

» **Emergency** ☎112

Exchange Rates

Australia	A$1	0.51Ls
Canada	C$1	0.51Ls
Euro Zone	€1	0.71Ls
Japan	¥100	0.59Ls
New Zealand	NZ$1	0.39Ls
UK	UK£1	0.80Ls
USA	US$1	0.49Ls

Set Your Budget

» **Budget hotel room** 25Ls

» **Two-course evening meal** 10Ls

» **Museum entrance** 1.50Ls

» **Beer** 1.20Ls in a bar or restaurant

» **City transport ticket** 0.70Ls

Resources

» **1188** (www.1188.lv)

» **Latvia Institute** (www.li.lv)

» **Latvia Tourism Development Agency** (www.latviatourism.lv)

Latvia Highlights

1. Click your camera at the menagerie of devilish gargoyles, mythical beasts, praying goddesses and twisting vines that inhabits **Rīga's art nouveau architecture** (p787)
2. Lose yourself in the maze of cobblestones, church spires and gingerbread trim that is **Old Rīga** (p782)
3. Listen to the waves pound the awesomely remote **Cape Kolka** (p791), which crowns the desolate Kurzeme coast
4. Swing through **Sigulda** (p791) on a bungee cord while chronicling its vivid history with stops at rambling Livonian castles
5. Indulge in aristocratic decadence at **Rundāle Palace** (p791)
6. Hobnob with Russian jet-setters in **Jūrmala**'s (p790) swanky spa scene
7. Wander past gritty Soviet tenements and gilded cathedrals in **Liepāja** (p791)

RĪGA

POP 790,000

'The Paris of the North', 'The Second City that Never Sleeps' – everyone's so keen on qualifying Latvia's cosmopolitan capital, but regal Rīga does a hell of a job of holding its own. For starters, the city has the largest and most impressive showing of art nouveau architecture in Europe. Nightmarish gargoyles and praying goddesses adorn over 750 buildings along the stately boulevards radiating out from the city's castle core. The heart of the city – Old Rīga – is a fairy-tale kingdom of winding, wobbly lanes that beat to the sound of clicking stilettos, beer-garden brouhahas and rumbling basement discotheques.

Sights

OLD RĪGA (VECRĪGA)

Touristy Rātslaukums is home to the picture-worthy **Blackheads' House** (Rātslaukums 7; http://nami.riga.lv/mn; admission 2Ls; 10am-5pm Tue-Sun), originally built in 1344 as a veritable fraternity house for the Blackheads guild of unmarried German merchants.

The **Museum of Occupation in Latvia** (www.omf.lv; Latviesu Strēlnieku laukums 1; admission by donation; 11am-6pm) ironically inhabits a Soviet bunker and carefully details Latvia's Soviet and Nazi occupations between 1939 and 1991.

Rīga's skyline centrepiece is Gothic **St Peter's Lutheran Church** (www.peterbaznica.lv; Skārņu iela 19; admission 3Ls; 11am-6pm Tue-Sun). Don't miss the view from the spire.

A colourful row of 18th-century buildings lines **Livu Laukums** – most of which have been turned into beer halls. Check out the **Cat House** (Miestaru iela 10), named for the spooked black cat sitting on the roof.

The centrepiece of expansive Doma Laukums is Rīga's enormous **Dome Cathedral** (www.doms.lv; Doma laukums 1; admission 2Ls; 9am-5pm). Founded in 1211 as the seat of the Rīga diocese, it is still the largest church in the Baltic. The huge, 6768-pipe organ was the world's largest when it was completed in 1884 (it's now the fourth largest).

Verdant Pils Laukums sits at the doorstep of **Rīga Castle** (Pils laukums 3). Originally built as the headquarters for the Livonian Order around 1330, this canary-yellow bastion boasts the **History Museum of Latvia** (admission 2Ls, free Wed; 10am-5pm Tue-Sun) and the **Museum of Foreign Art** (admission 2.50Ls; 11am-5pm Tue-Sun), and is also home to Latvia's president.

The entire north side of Torņa iela is flanked by the custard-coloured **Jacob's Barracks** (Torņa iela 4), now inhabited by cafes. Find **Trokšnu iela** nearby – Old Rīga's narrowest *iela* (street) – and the **Swedish Gate** (Torņu iela 11), which was built in 1698. The cylindrical **Powder Tower** (Smilšu iela 20) dates back to the 14th century and now houses a small war museum.

CENTRAL RĪGA (CENTRS)

Affectionately known as 'Milda', Rīga's **Freedom Monument** (Brīvības bulvāris) was erected in 1935 where a statue of Russian ruler Peter the Great once stood.

DON'T MISS

ART NOUVEAU IN RĪGA

If you ask any Rīgan where to find the city's world-famous art nouveau architecture, you will always get the same answer: 'Look up!' Over 750 buildings in Rīga (more than any other city in Europe) boast this flamboyant and haunting style of decor, and the number continues to grow as myriad restoration projects get under way. Art nouveau is also known as Jugendstil, meaning 'youth style', named after a Munich-based magazine called *Die Jugend*, which popularised the design on its pages.

Art nouveau's early influence was Japanese print art disseminated throughout Western Europe, but as the movement gained momentum the style became more ostentatious and free-form – design schemes started to feature mythical beasts, screaming masks, twisting flora, goddesses and goblins. The turn of the 20th century marked the height of the art nouveau movement, as it swept through every major European city from Porto to Petersburg.

The art nouveau district (known more formally as the Quiet Centre) is anchored around **Alberta iela** (check out 2a, 4 and 13 in particular), but you'll find fine examples all throughout the city. Don't miss the renovated facades of **Strēlnieku 4a** and **Elizabetes 10b** and **33**, then check out the highly informative **Rīga Art Nouveau Centre** (p782).

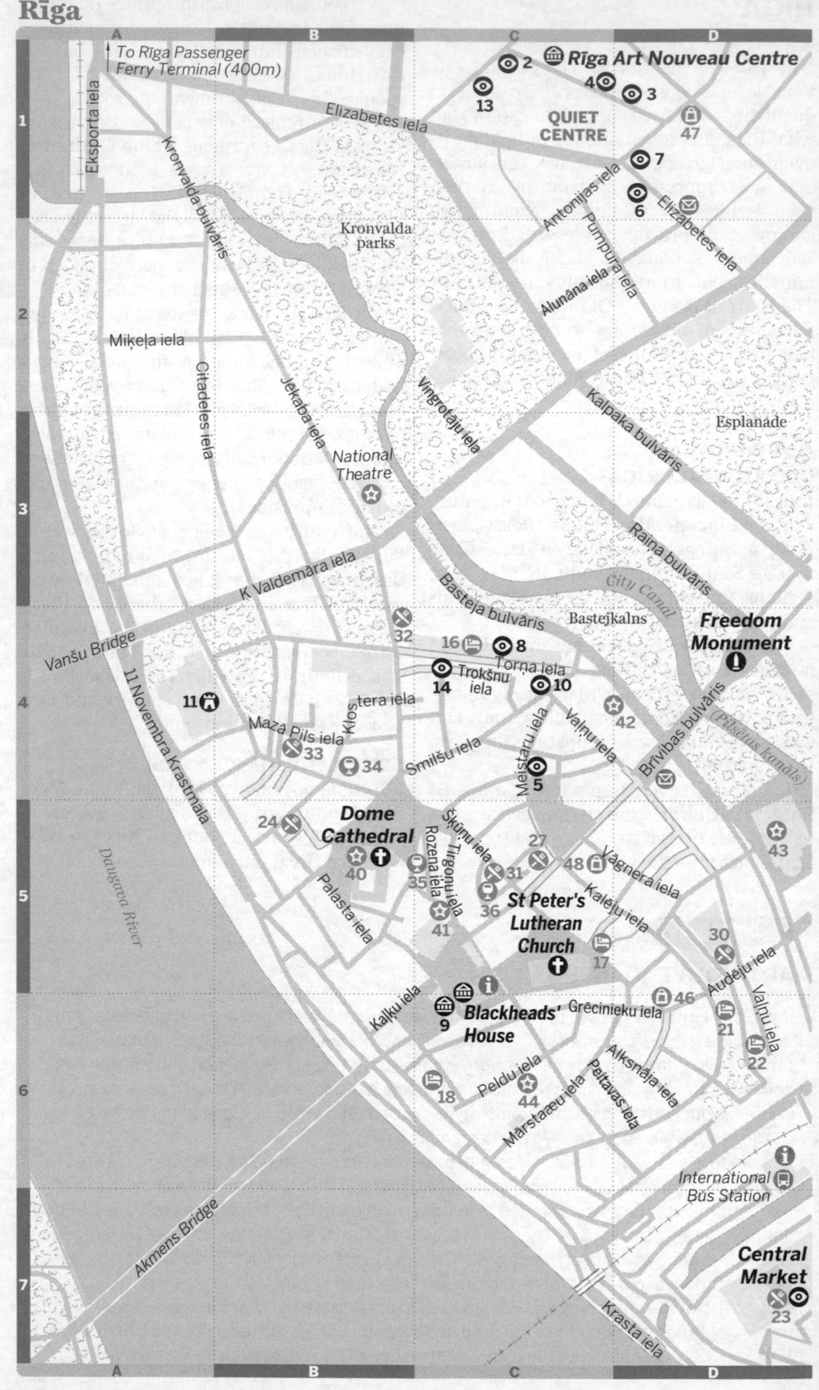
To Rīga Passenger Ferry Terminal (400m)
Rīga Art Nouveau Centre
QUIET CENTRE
Elizabetes iela
Eksporta iela
Kronvalda bulvāris
Kronvalda parks
Antonijas iela
Pumpura iela
Alunāna iela
Miķeļa iela
Citadeles iela
Jēkaba iela
Vingrotāju iela
Kalpaka bulvāris
Esplanade
National Theatre
K Valdemāra iela
Raiņa bulvāris
City Canal
Basteja bulvāris
Bastejkalns
Freedom Monument
Vanšu Bridge
Torņa iela
Trokšņu iela
Klostera iela
11 Novembra Krastmala
Mazā Pils iela
Smilšu iela
Meistaru iela
Vaļņu iela
Brīvības bulvāris
(Pilsētas kanāls)
Dome Cathedral
Šķūņu iela
Rozena iela
Tirgoņu iela
Vāgnera iela
Kalēju iela
St Peter's Lutheran Church
Palasta iela
Daugava River
Audēju iela
Kalķu iela
Blackheads' House
Grēcinieku iela
Alksnāja iela
Peitavas iela
Peldu iela
Mārstaļu iela
International Bus Station
Akmens Bridge
Central Market
Krasta iela

LATVIA

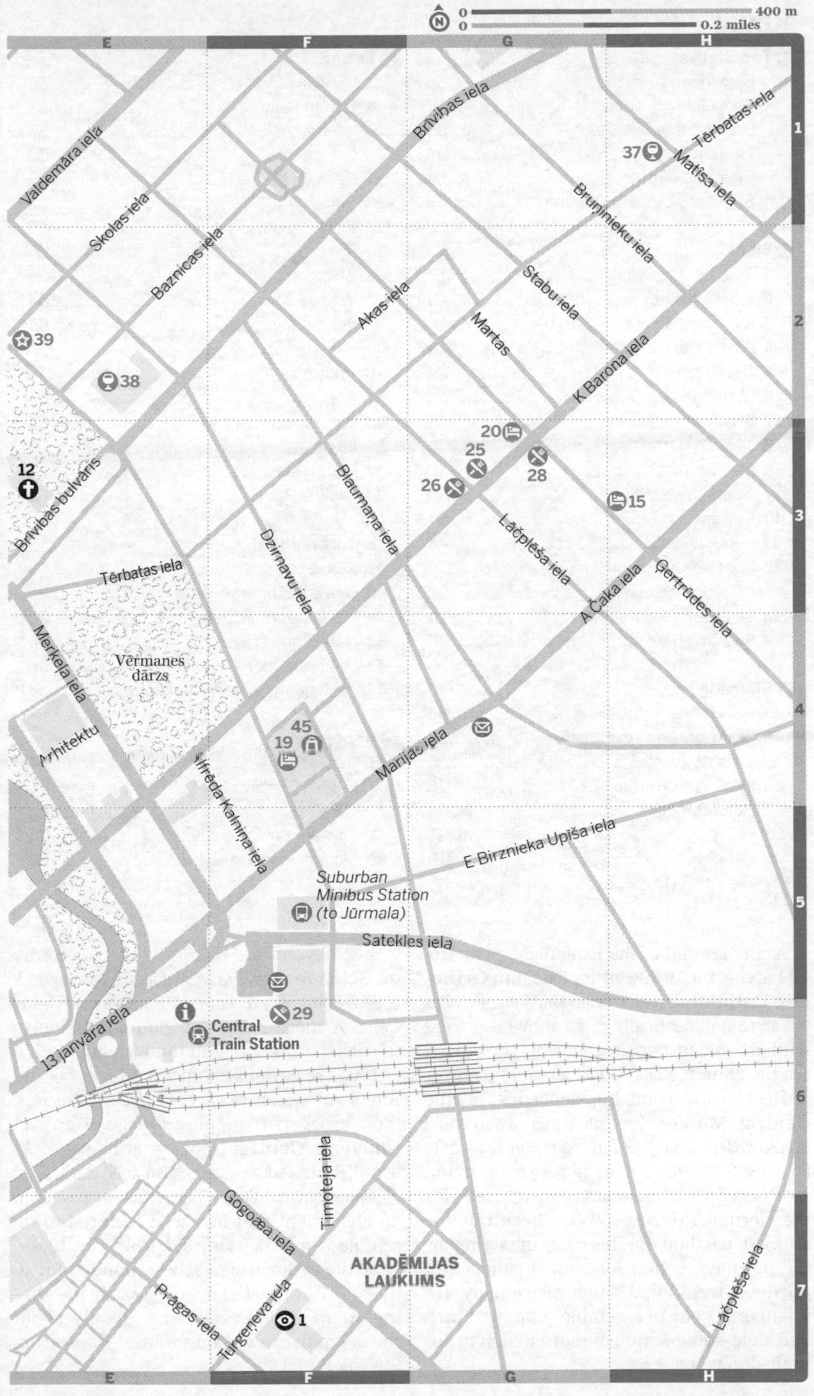
0 400 m
0 0.2 miles
E
F
G
H
1
2
3
4
5
6
7
Brīvības iela
Tērbatas iela
Matīsa iela
Valdemāra iela
Skolas iela
Baznīcas iela
Bruņinieku iela
Stabu iela
Akas iela
Martas
K Barona iela
39
38
37
20
25
28
26
15
12
Brīvības bulvāris
Blaumaņa iela
Dzirnavu iela
Lāčplēša iela
A Čaka iela
Ģertrūdes iela
Tērbatas iela
Merķeļa iela
Vērmanes dārzs
Arhitektu
45
19
Marijas iela
Elfrēda Kalniņa iela
E Birznieka Upīša iela
Suburban Minibus Station (to Jūrmala)
Satekles iela
29
Central Train Station
13 janvāra iela
Timoteja iela
Gogoļa iela
AKADĒMIJAS LAUKUMS
Prāgas iela
Turgeņeva iela
1
Lāčplēša iela

Rīga

Top Sights

	Blackheads' House	C5
	Central Market	D7
	Dome Cathedral	B5
	Freedom Monument	D4
	Rīga Art Nouveau Centre	C1
	St Peter's Lutheran Church	C5

Sights

1	Academy of Science	F7
2	Alberta iela 13	C1
3	Alberta iela 2a	D1
4	Alberta iela 4	C1
5	Cat House	C4
6	Elizabetes iela 10b	D1
7	Elizabetes iela 33	D1
8	Jacob's Barracks	C4
9	Museum of Occupation in Latvia	C6
10	Powder Tower	C4
11	Rīga Castle	A4
12	Russian Orthodox Cathedral	E3
13	Strēlnieku iela 4a	C1
14	Swedish Gate	C4

Sleeping

15	B&B Rīga	H3
16	Blue Cow Barracks	C4
17	Ekes Konventas	C5
18	Friendly Fun Franks	C6
19	Hotel Bergs	F4
20	KB	G3
21	Naughty Squirrel	D6
22	Old Town Hostel	D6

Eating

23	Central Market	D7
24	Dorian Gray	B5
25	Istaba	G3
26	Osīriss	G3
27	Pelmeņi XL	C5
28	Rimi	G3
29	Rimi	F6
30	Rimi	D5
31	Šefpavārs Vilhelms	C5
32	V. Ķuze	B4
33	Vecmeita ar kaki	B4

Drinking

34	Aptieka	B4
35	Cuba Cafe	C5
36	La Belle Epoque	C5
37	Pērle	H1
38	Skyline Bar	E2

Entertainment

39	Club Essential	E2
40	Dome Cathedral	B5
41	Moon Safari	C5
42	Nabaklab	D4
43	National Opera House	D5
44	Pulkvedim Neviens Neraksta	C6

Shopping

45	Berga Bāzars	F4
	Emihla Gustava Shokolahde	(see 45)
	Garage	(see 45)
46	Latvijas Balzāms	D6
47	Madam Bonbon	D1
48	Upe	C5

At the far end of the Esplanade, near Hotel Latvija, the 19th-century **Russian Orthodox Cathedral** (Pareizticīgo katedrāle; Brīvības bulvāris 23) majestically rises above the trees with its gilded cupolas. During the Soviet era the church was used as a planetarium.

Heckle for your huckleberries at the **Central Market** (Centrāl tirgus; www.centraltirgus.lv; Nēgu iela 7; ⏲7am-5pm Sun & Mon, to 6pm Tue-Sat), housed in a series of mammoth Zeppelin hangars constructed for the Germans during WWI. Check out the seafood pavilion for herring, or swing by the produce section for chilled sauerkraut juice – a traditional hangover remedy. It's a fantastic spot to assemble a picnic lunch and ogle some seriously outdated hairdos (hair-don'ts?).

Just beyond the market is the **Academy of Science** (www.lza.lv; Akadēmijas laukums 1; ⏲9am-8pm), also called 'Stalin's Birthday Cake'. A mere 2Ls grants you admission to the observation deck on the 17th floor.

If you're curious about what lurks behind Rīga's imaginative art nouveau facades, then it's worth stopping by the **Rīga Art Nouveau Centre** (www.jugendstils.riga.lv; Alberta iela 12; admission/English tour 2.50/10Ls; ⏲10am-6pm Tue-Sun). The museum sits in an apartment that has been restored to resemble a middle-class flat from the 1920s. Note the geometric frescoes, rounded furniture and original stained glass in the dining room. The website has details about the art nouveau walking routes. Enter from Strēlnieku iela.

Sleeping

Naughty Squirrel HOSTEL €
(☎2646 1248; www.naughtysquirrelbackpackers.com; Kalēju iela 50; dm/d 8/30Ls; @📶) Brilliant slashes of bright paint and cartoon graffiti have breathed new life into the city's capital of backpackerdom, which buzzes as travellers rattle the foosball table and chill out in the TV room. Sign up for regular pub crawls, adrenalin day trips to the countryside, or summer BBQs. The owners also run the excellent **Blue Cow Barracks** (☎2773 6700; www.bluecowbarracks.com; Torņa iela 4-2B; dm/d 10/35Ls; @📶), a smaller and more intimate hostel in the historic Jacob's Barracks on the other side of Old Rīga.

Ekes Konventas HISTORIC HOTEL €€
(☎6735 8393; www.ekeskonvents.lv; Skārņu iela 22; d incl breakfast €57; 📶) This 600-year-old inn oozes wobbly medieval charm from every crooked nook and cranny. Curl up with a book in the adorable stone alcoves on the landing of each storey.

Krišjānis & Ģertrūde B&B €€
(☎6750 6604; www.kg.lv; K Barona iela 39; s/d/tr incl breakfast €35/45/55; @📶) Step off the bustling intersection into this quaint, family-run B&B adorned with still lifes of fruit and flowers. It's best to book ahead since there are only six cosy rooms. Enter from Ģertrudes iela.

Old Town Hostel HOSTEL €
(☎6722 3406; www.rigaoldtownhostel.lv; Valņu iela 43; dm/d 7/30Ls; @📶) The cosy English-style pub on the ground floor doubles as the hostel's hang-out space, and if you can manage to lug your suitcase past the faux bookshelf door and up the twisting staircase, you'll find spacious dorms with chandeliers and plenty of sunlight.

KB B&B €
(☎6731 2323; www.kbhotel.lv; K Barona iela 37; s/d/tr 19/21/23Ls; @📶) This great find in the pinch-a-penny category is located up a rather opulent marble staircase. The rooms are simple but well appointed, and there's a modern communal kitchen.

B&B Rīga APARTMENTS €€
(☎6727 8505; www.bb-riga.lv; Ģertrūdes iela 43; s/d €39/49; @📶) Snug, apartment-style accommodation comes in different configurations (suites with loft bedrooms are particularly charming), scattered throughout a residential block.

Friendly Fun Franks HOSTEL €
(☎2599 0612; www.franks.lv; 11 Novembra Krastmala 29; dm/d from 6/40Ls; @📶) If you want to party, look no further than this bright-orange stag-magnet, where every backpacker is greeted with a hearty hello and a complimentary pint of beer.

Eating

Self-caterers should try the Central Market (p782) or one of the many **Rimi** (www.rimi.lv) branches throughout the city.

TOP CHOICE **Istaba** CAFE €€
(☎6728 1141; K Barona iela 31a; mains 3-10Ls; ⏲Mon-Sat) 'The Room' sits in the rafters above a like-named gallery space adorned with trendsetting bric-a-brac. In summer you can dine on the street-side veranda, though we prefer heading upstairs to grab a seat in the mob of discarded lamps and sofas. There's no set menu – you're subject to the cook's fancy – but it's all about flavourful and filling portions served on mismatched dishware. Reservations are recommended.

Meta-Kafe CAFE €
(www.metakafe.lv; Maskavas iela 12/1; mains 2.90-4.70Ls; 📶) Safely tucked away from those who aren't in the know, this hipster hangout occupies one of the renovated spaces in the newly trendy Spīķeri neighbourhood. Stencil scribbles adorn the spots on the walls that aren't hidden behind shelves of art books. Sip your house wine out the back in the concrete courtyard or join the headphoned loiterers inside as they slurp soups and mess around on their MacBooks.

SPLURGE

A refurbished manor house embellished with Scandi-sleek design, **Hotel Bergs** (☎6777 0900; www.hotelbergs.lv; Elizabetes iela 83/85; ste from €164; P❄@📶) embodies the term 'luxury', from the lobby's mix of sharp lines, rococo portraits and tribal reliefs, to the spacious suites lavished with high-quality monochromatic furnishings worthy of a magazine spread. Our favourite amenity – the 'pillow service' – allows guests to choose from an array of different bed pillows based on material and texture.

Pelmeņi XL FAST FOOD €
(Kaļķu iela 7; dumpling bowls 0.86-2.50Ls; ⊙9am-4am) A Rīga institution for backpackers and undiscerning drunkards, this extra-large cafeteria stays open extra late, serving up huge bowls of *pelmeņi* (Russian-style ravioli stuffed with meat) amid Flintstones-meets-Gaudí decor (you'll see). There's a second location in the central train station.

Ostas Skati GOURMET €€
(☎2000 9045; www.restoransostasskati.lv; Matrožu iela 15; mains 6.50Ls; ⊙8.30am-midnight) Known around town as the 'democratic restaurant' for its recession-proof prices, Ostas Skati sports trendy mood lighting and attractive serving staff. Expertly presented Latvian dishes include Daugava catfish and home-smoked trout. Don't miss the cup of scrumptious curd cream and strawberry jam for dessert – enjoy it on the riverside deck during the summer months.

Aragats GEORGIAN €€
(☎6737 3445; Miera iela 15; mains 4-8Ls; ⊙Tue-Sun) Ignore the plastic shrubbery – this place is all about sampling some killer cuisine from the Caucasus. Start with an appetiser of pickled vegetables – the perfect chaser for your home-brewed *chacha* (Georgian vodka). Then, make nice with the matronly owner as she dices up fresh herbs at your table to mix with the savoury lamb stew. At the end of the meal be a gentleman and pay for the ladies at the table, especially since the women's menus don't have any of the prices listed!

Dorian Gray CAFE €€
(www.doriangray.lv; Mazā Muzeja iela 1; mains 3.60-8Ls) With seating purchased from a car-boot sale, random pillows scattered about and cracked crimson brick crumbling off the walls, Dorian Gray might just be (rather ironically) the least image-obsessed place in town. Down-to-earth wait staff serves curious culinary concoctions throughout the day. Swing by for weekly movie nights and brunch-time screenings of *Ugly Betty*.

V. Ķuze CONFECTIONER €
(www.kuze.lv; Jēkaba iela 20/22; coffee & cake from 1.20Ls) Vilhelms Ķuze was a prominent entrepreneur and chocolatier while Latvia flirted with freedom between the World Wars. When the Soviets barged in he was promptly deported to Siberia, where he met his maker. Today Ķuze Chocolates is up and running once more and this charming cafe-cum-confectioner functions not only as a memoriam to dear Vilhelms, but also as a tribute to the colourful art nouveau era.

LIDO Atpūtas Centrs LATVIAN €
(LIDO Recreation Centre; www.lido.lv; Krasta iela 76; mains 2-6.50Ls) If Latvia and Disney World had a love child it would be the LIDO Atpūtas Centrs – an enormous wooden palace dedicated to the country's coronary-inducing cuisine. Servers dressed like Baltic milkmaids bounce around as patrons hit the rows of buffets for classics like pork tongue and cold beet soup. Take the free bus from Ratslaukums, or tram 3, 7 or 9, and get off at the 'LIDO' stop. There's a handful of miniature LIDO restaurants in the city centre if you can't make it out to the mother ship.

Osīriss CAFE €€
(K Barona iela 31; mains 3-9Ls; ⊙8am-midnight; 📶) Despite Rīga's mercurial cafe culture, Osīriss continues to be a local mainstay. The green faux-marble tabletops haven't changed since the mid-'90s and neither has the clientele: angsty, artsy types scribbling in their Moleskines over a glass of red wine.

Vecmeita ar kaki LATVIAN €€
(The Spinster & Her Cat; Mazā Pils iela 1; mains 3.10-9.90Ls) This cosy spot across from the president's palace specialises in cheap Latvian grub and meaty mains. In warmer weather patrons dine outside on converted sewing-machine tables.

Šefpavārs Vilhelms FAST FOOD €
(Chef William; Šķūņu iela 6; pancake rolls 0.65Ls) Customers of every ilk are constantly queuing for a quick nosh – three blintze-like pancakes smothered in sour cream and jam equals the perfect backpacker's breakfast.

Drinking

If you want to party like a Latvian, assemble a gang of friends and pub crawl your way through the city, stopping at colourful haunts for rounds of shots, belly laughter and, of course, Black Balzāms. On summer evenings nab a spot at one of the city's many beer gardens.

Skyline Bar HOTEL BAR
(Elizabetes iela 55; 📶) A must for every visitor, glitzy Skyline Bar sits on the 26th floor of the Reval Hotel Latvija. The sweeping views are the city's best and the mix of glam spirit-sippers makes for great people watching under the retro purple lighting.

Cuba Cafe BAR
(www.cubacafe.lv; Jaun iela 15; 📶) An authentic mojito and a table overlooking Doma laukums is just what the doctor ordered after a long day of sightseeing. On colder days swig your caipirinha inside amid dangling Cuban flags, wobbly stained-glass lamps and the murmur of trumpet jazz.

Pērle BAR-CAFE
(Tērbatas iela 65) Pērle is where outmoded technology goes to die a stylish rock-star death. It's everything you'd want in a neighbourhood hipster hang-out: discarded Gameboys, racks of vintage tweed, a massacre of mannequin parts and designer lattes…with Baileys. Oh, and everything's for sale. Naturally.

La Belle Epoque BAR
(French Bar; Mazā Jaunavu iela 8) Students flock to this boisterous basement bar to power down its trademark 'apple pie' shots (1Ls). The Renoir mural and kitschy *Moulin Rouge* posters seem to successfully ward off stag parties.

Aptieka BAR
(Pharmacy Bar; Mazā Miesnieku iela 1) Antique apothecary bottles confirm the subtle-but-stylish theme at this popular drinking haunt run by a Latvian-American.

☆ Entertainment

Nightclubs

Nabaklab CLUB
(www.nabaklab.lv; Meierovica bulvaris 12) Imagine if your favourite alternative radio station opened a nightspot that played its signature blend of experimental tunes and electronica. Well, you're in luck – Naba's (93.1FM) club space attracts the city's boho hobos with its DJed beats, vintage clothes racks, art gallery and cheap beer in the quaint Soviet-style den.

Pulkvedim Neviens Neraksta CLUB
(Noone Writes to the Colonel; www.pulkvedis.lv; Peldu iela 26/280) There's no such thing as a dull night at Pulkvedis. The atmosphere is warehouse chic, with pumping '80s tunes on the ground floor and trance beats down below.

Club Essential CLUB
(www.essential.lv; Skolas iela 2) Essential is a spectacle of beautiful people boogying to some of Europe's top DJ talent. Overzealous security aside, this two-storey complex is your safest bet if partying till dawn is your mission.

Moon Safari CLUB
(www.moonsafari.lv; Krāmu iela 2) Beds in the VIP room and a pet snake at the bar? It's all pretty suggestive, but the 2Ls cocktails and colourful karaoke booth lure a young Erasmus crowd for all-night shenanigans.

Performing Arts

National Opera House OPERA
(☎6707 3777; www.opera.lv; Aspazijas bulvāris 3) The pride of Latvia, boasting some of the finest opera in Europe (and for a fraction of the price of other countries). Mikhail Baryshnikov got his start here.

Dome Cathedral LIVE MUSIC
(Doma baznīca; ☎6721 3213; www.doms.lv; Doma laukums 1) Twice-weekly (Wednesday and Saturday evenings) short organ concerts and lengthier Friday night performances are well worth attending.

Shopping

Madam Bonbon ACCESSORIES
(www.madambonbon.lv; Alberta iela 1-7a) Carrie Bradshaw's died and gone to heaven: every surface in this old-school art nouveau apartment features some sort of foot furniture. Squeeze into the stiletto on the baby grand piano, or go for the boot behind the teapot on the kitchen table.

Upe MUSIC
(www.upett.lv; Vāgnera iela 5) Classical Latvian tunes play as customers peruse traditional instruments and CDs of local folk, rock and experimental sounds.

Latvijas Balzāms DRINK
(www.lb.lv; Audēju iela 8) A popular chain of liquor stores selling the trademark Latvian Black Balzām. There are myriad branches around town.

The following shops are located in **Berga Bazārs** (www.bergabazars.lv; Dzirnavu iela 84), a maze of upmarket boutiques orbiting the five-star Hotel Bergs:

Emihla Gustava Shokolahde FOOD & DRINK
(www.sokolade.lv) Latvia's finest chocolate shop doubles as a cafe. The fruit-stuffed truffles are divine, but don't miss the mud-thick hot chocolate.

Garage ART
(www.garage.lv) A gallery and souvenir shop featuring upmarket handicrafts designed by Latvian artists. In the evening it doubles as a wine bar

Information

Internet Access

Every hostel and hotel has some form of internet connection available to guests. Internet cafes are a dying breed in Rīga and they're usually filled with 12-year-old goons blasting cybermonsters. **Elik Kafe** (Merķeļa iela 1; per 30min/1hr 0.45/0.85Ls; ⏲24hr) is convenient to the train station; it has a second location at Kaļķu iela 11.

Media & Websites

Riga in Your Pocket (www.inyourpocket.com/latvia/riga) Handy city guide published every other month. Download a PDF version or pick up a copy at most midrange or top-end hotels (free). The tourist offices and several bookshops also have copies (2Ls).

Riga this Week (www.rigathisweek.lv) An excellent (and free) city guide available at virtually every sleeping option in town. Published every second month.

rigaNOW! (www.bestriga.com) A magazine featuring the city's best spots. Complimentary copies are available at most midrange and top-end hotels. The website has similar info.

Medical Services

ARS (☎6720 1003; www.ars-med.lv; Skola iela 5) has English-speaking doctors; 24-hour consultation available.

Money

There are scores of ATMs scattered around the capital. Withdrawing cash is easier than trying to exchange foreign currencies. **Marika** (Brīvības bulvāris 30) offers 24-hour currency exchange services with reasonable rates; a second location is at Dzirnavu 96.

Post

Those blue storefronts with 'Pasta' written on them aren't Italian restaurants – they're post offices. See www.pasts.lv for more info. The **central post office** (Brīvības bulvaris 32; ⏲7.30am-8pm Mon-Fri, 8am-6pm Sat, 10am-4pm Sun) has international calling and faxing services.

Tourist Information

The **tourist office** (☎6730 7900; www.rigatourism.com; Rātslaukums 6; ⏲9am-6pm) gives out excellent tourists maps and walking-tour brochures. Staff can arrange accommodation and book day trips. Sells concert and opera tickets in summer. Satellite tourism offices can be found at the train station, bus station and airport. Buy the **Rīga Card** (www.rigacard.lv; 24hr card 10Ls), which offers discounts on sights and restaurants, and free rides on public transport.

Getting There & Away

See p794 for details.

Getting Around

To/From the Airport

The airport is about 13km west of the city centre. Take bus 22 (0.70Ls, 30 minutes) into town. AirBaltic runs lime-green vans (3Ls) to several hotels in central Rīga. Taxis to Old Rīga cost 9Ls.

Bicycle

Baltic Bikes (☎6778 8333; www.balticbike.lv; per hr/day 0.70/6Ls) has a handful of stands around Rīga and Jūrmala; simply call the rental service and get the code to unlock your wheels.

Public Transport

Most of Rīga's main tourist attractions are within walking distance of each other, so you might never have to use the city's convoluted transport network. Tickets cost 0.70Ls (0.50Ls if you buy your ticket ahead of time from an automated machine or news stand). A three-day unlimited transport pass can be purchased for 5.70Ls. City transport runs daily from 5.30am to midnight. Some routes have an hourly night service. For Rīga public transport routes and schedules visit www.rigassatiksme.lv.

Taxi

Taxis charge 0.40Ls to 0.50Ls per kilometre and start at 1Ls to 1.50Ls. Insist on having the meter on. Don't pay more than 4Ls for a journey in the city. There are taxi ranks outside the bus and train stations, at the airport and in front of a few major hotels in central Rīga.

AROUND RĪGA

Jūrmala

POP 54,930

Jūrmala's first spa opened in 1838 and since then the area has been known as the 'Baltic Riviera'. The string of seaside townships makes a pleasant day trip from the capital – on summer weekends vehicles clog the roads when jet-setters and holidaying Rīgans flock to the area for some serious fun in the sun.

Treat yourself to some spa action at the **Baltic Beach Hotel** (www.balticbeach.lv; Jūras iela 23/25; day use/massages from 10/35Ls; ⏲8am-10pm) and be sure to check out the colourful collection of **wooden houses** peppered along the pine-studded sand. Four thousand cottages and counting!

Two to three trains and minivans link Rīga (0.95Ls, 30 to 35 minutes) every hour; disembark at Majori station. Motorists driving the 15km into Jūrmala must pay a 1Ls toll per day, even if they are just passing through.

WESTERN LATVIA

Cape Kolka (Kolkasrags)

Enchantingly desolate and hauntingly beautiful, a journey to Cape Kolka feels like a trip to the end of the earth. During Soviet times the entire peninsula was zoned off as a high-security military base. The region's development was subsequently stunted and today the string of desolate coastal villages has a distinct anachronistic feel – as though they've been locked away in a time capsule.

If you plan to stay the night, **Ūši** (☎2947 5692; www.kolka.info; s/d 16/22Ls, camping per person 2.50Ls) has two simple rooms and a spot to pitch tents in the flower-filled garden.

Five daily buses link Rīga and Kolka town (4Ls to 5Ls, 3½ to 4½ hours). The easiest way to reach Cape Kolka, however, is by car.

Liepāja

POP 84,000

The local **tourist office** (☎6348 0808; www.liepaja.lv; Rožu laukums 5; ⏰9am-6pm) calls Liepāja 'the place where wind is born', but we think the city's rough-around-the-edges vibe is undoubtedly the city's biggest draw.

WORTH A TRIP

RUNDĀLE PALACE

A great day trip from Rīga is **Rundāle Palace** (Rundāles pils; ☎6396 2274; www.rundale.net; short/long route 2.50/3.50Ls, photography permit 1Ls; ⏰10am-7pm May-Oct, 10am-5pm Nov-Apr), 75km south of the capital, near the town of Bauska. The architect of this sprawling monument to aristocratic ostentation was the Italian baroque genius Bartolomeo Rastrelli, best known for designing the Winter Palace in St Petersburg. About 40 of the palace's 138 rooms are open to visitors, as are the wonderfully landscaped gardens.

Most tour operators run day trips to the palace (around 20Ls per person), though it's best to rent a car. You can also take a bus from Rīga to Bauska (2Ls, 70 minutes, twice hourly), then switch to one of the nine daily buses (0.35Ls) connecting Bauska to the palace (Pilsrundāle), 12km away.

Start in the Karosta district, 4km north of the city centre, where you'll find a particularly dour collection of **Soviet tenements** mingling with the gilded cupolas of **St Nicholas Orthodox Maritime Cathedral**. Daily multilingual tours lead visitors through **Karosta Prison** (Karostas cietums; ☎2636 9470; www.karostascietums.lv; Invalīdu iela 4; tours 2.50Ls, 2hr shows 5.50Ls, sleepovers 8Ls; ⏰10am-6pm May-Sep, by appointment Oct-Apr), which was used to punish disobedient Soviet soldiers. Masochists can spend the night.

Check out **Hotel Fontaine** (☎6342 0956; www.fontaine.lv; Jūras iela 24; r 15-35Ls; P@🛜), a funky hostelry where the reception doubles as a second-hand knick-knack shop.

For a night out on the town try **Fontaine Palace** (www.fontainepalace.lv; Dzirnavu iela 4), a never-closing rock house luring loads of live acts and crowds of sweaty fanatics.

Buses run to/from Rīga (5.50Ls to 6.50Ls, four hours, every 45 minutes). Liepāja and Rīga are also connected by infrequent trains.

EASTERN LATVIA

Sigulda

POP 10,780

Sigulda is an enchanting little spot with delightful surprises tucked behind every dappled tree. Locals proudly call their pine-peppered town the 'Switzerland of Latvia', but if you're expecting the majesty of a mountainous snowcapped realm, you'll be disappointed. Instead Sigulda mixes its own exciting brew of scenic trails, extreme sports and 800-year-old castles steeped in colourful legends. It's also the gateway to **Gauja National Park** (☎6780 0388; www.gnp.gov.lv; Baznīcas iela 7; ⏰9am-5pm), the country's oldest national park.

Sights & Activities

Start at **Sigulda New Castle** (Pils iela 16), built in the 18th century during the reign of German aristocrats. The **Sigulda Medieval Castle** (Pils iela 18) – now in ruins – around the back, was constructed in 1207 by the Order of the Brethren of the Sword. Take the **cable car** (☎6797 2531; www.bungee.lv; Poruka iela 14; weekday/weekend 2/2.50Ls; ⏰10am-7.30pm Jun-Aug, to 4pm May & Sep) over the scenic river valley to **Krimulda Manor**, currently used as a rehabilitation clinic.

Daredevils can try a 43m **bungee jump** (☎2921 2731; www.bungee.lv; Poruka iela 14; Fri/

weekend jumps 20/25Ls; ⌚6.30pm to last jump Fri-Sun May-Oct) from the moving cable car. Check out the ruins of **Krimulda Medieval Castle** (Krimuldas iela) nearby, then follow the serpentine road to **Gūtmaņa Cave**. Take some time to read the myriad inscriptions carved into the cave walls, then head up to the **Turaida Museum Reserve** (☎6797 1402; www.turaida-muzejs.lv; Turaidas iela 10; admission 3Ls; ⌚10am-6pm May-Oct, to 5pm Nov-Apr) and check out its beautiful medieval castle, erected in the 13th century.

Sigulda's 1200m artificial **bobsled track** (☎6797 3813; bobtrase@lis.lv; Šveices iela 13; rides from 7Ls; ⌚noon-7pm Sat & Sun) was built for the former Soviet bobsleigh team. In winter you can fly down the 16-bend track at 80km/h in a five-person **Vučko tourist bob**, or try the real Olympian experience on the hair-raising **winter bob**. Summer speed fiends can try the wheeled **summer sled**.

The one-of-a-kind **aerodium** (☎2838 4400; www.aerodium.lv; 2min weekday/weekend 15/18Ls; ⌚6-8pm Tue-Fri, noon-8pm Sat & Sun) is a giant wind tunnel propelling participants up into the sky as though they were flying.

Sleeping & Eating

Click on www.sigulda.lv for additional options.

Līvkalns B&B €
(☎6797 0916; www.livkalns.lv; Pēteralas iela; s/d from 15/25Ls) No place is more romantically rustic than this idyllic retreat next to a pond on the forest's edge. The rooms are pine fresh and sit among a campus of adorable thatch-roof manors. The cabin-in-the-woods-style restaurant is fantastic.

Kaķu Māja LATVIAN €
(www.cathouse.lv; Pils iela 8; mains from 2Ls) A restaurant, canteen, bakery and nightclub all rolled into one charming gingerbread house.

Information

Gauja National Park visitors centre (☎6780 0388; www.gnp.gov.lv; Baznīcas iela 7; ⌚9am-5pm) Arranges tours, backcountry camping and other accommodation. Cycle and hiking maps also available.

Tourist office (☎6797 1335; www.sigulda.lv; Raiņa iela 3; ⌚10am-7pm May-Sep, to 5pm Oct-Apr) Has an internet kiosk and mountains of helpful information about activities and accommodation. Ask about the *Sigulda Spiekis* discount card.

Getting There & Around

Buses link Riga and Sigulda every 30 minutes from 7am to 9.30pm (1.80Ls, one hour). Trains run hourly between 7am and 9pm (1.55Ls, 70 minutes). Buses also run between Sigulda and Cēsis (1.40Ls, 45 minutes).

Sigulda's attractions are quite spread out; bus 12 links all of the sights and plies the route seven times daily (more on weekends).

UNDERSTAND LATVIA

History

The first signs of modern man in the region date back to the Stone Age, although Latvians descended from tribes that migrated to the region around 2000 BC.

In 1201 German crusaders conquered Latvia, founded Rīga and started the Knights of the Sword. Rīga became the major city in the German Baltic and joined the Hanseatic League in 1282.

The 15th, 16th and 17th centuries were marked with battles and disputes about how to divvy up what would one day become Latvia. After a 'golden' period of Swedish rule, the Russians conquered the area during the Great Northern War (1700–21) and held the former fiefdom for two centuries.

Out of the post-WWI confusion and turmoil arose an independent Latvian state, declared on 18 November 1918. By the 1930s Latvia had achieved one of the highest standards of living in Europe. Soviet occupation began in 1939; Latvia was occupied by Germany from 1941 to 1945. When WWII ended the Soviets marched back in, claiming to 'save' Latvia from the Nazis.

The country declared independence on 21 August 1991 and on 17 September 1991 Latvia, along with its Baltic brothers, joined the UN. After a game of prime minister roulette and a devastating crash of the country's economy, Latvia finally shook off its antiquated Soviet fetters and, on 1 May 2004, the EU opened its doors to the fledgling nation.

Latvia registered the highest economic growth in the EU from 2004 to 2007, which later proved to be a curse when the national bank imploded during the global financial crisis. The nation is slowly marching back towards stability, but a recent shift in politics might be the prelude to a strengthening trade relationship with Russia rather than the EU.

THE LAND THAT SINGS

Latvians often wax poetic about their country, calling it 'the land that sings'; their canon of traditional tunes is the power source for their indomitable spirit. Latvians (along with their Baltic brothers) literally sang for their freedom from the USSR in a series of dramatic protests known as the 'Singing Revolution' and today the nation holds the **Song and Dance Festival**, which unites thousands of singers from around the world. During the festival, hundreds of Latvia's 1.4 million *dainas* (folk songs) are performed.

In 2003 the Song and Dance Festival was inscribed on Unesco's list of Oral and Intangible Heritage of Humanity masterpieces.

People

Of Latvia's 2.27 million citizens, only 60% are ethnically Latvian. Russians account for 29% and make up the ethnic majority in most major cities, including the capital.

Casual hellos on the street aren't common, but Latvians are a friendly and welcoming bunch. Some will find that there is a bit of guardedness in the culture, but this caution, most likely a response to centuries of foreign rule, has helped preserve the unique language and culture through changing times.

Most Latvians are members of the Lutheran Church, although ancient pagan traditions still influence daily life.

Food & Drink

Price ranges for eateries in this chapter:

€€€ more than 10Ls

€€ from 5Ls to 10Ls

€ less than 5Ls

SURVIVAL GUIDE

Directory A-Z

Accommodation

Dorm beds cost 5Ls to 10Ls. We highly advise booking ahead during summer. Prices listed here are for the high season; rates drop significantly in the colder months. Many of Rīga's hotels publish their rates in euros.

Visit www.hotels.lv for more info. Check out www.camping.lv for details on camping.

In this chapter we've used the following price ranges for accommodation:

€€€ more than 50Ls

€€ from 25Ls to 50Ls

€ less than 25Ls

Business Hours

Standard business hours are 10am to 6pm Monday to Friday and 10am to 5pm Saturday, though many shops tend to stay open until 7pm or later.

Bars 11am or noon-midnight Sun-Thu and around 3am Fri & Sat

Clubs About 11pm-around 6am Wed-Sat; in warmer months open Sun-Tue as well

Restaurants & cafes 11am or noon-11pm

Festivals & Events

Latvians enjoy any excuse to party, especially during summer. Check out www.culture.lv for a yearly listing of festivals and events across the country. Latvia's biggest event, the **Song and Dance Festival**, is held every five years. It was last held in 2008.

Internet Access

Lattelecom (www.lattelecom.lv) has set up wi-fi beacons at every phone booth around the city. To register for a username, call ☎9000 4111, or send an SMS with the word 'WiFi' to ☎1188.

Holidays

The website of the **Latvia Institute** (www.li.lv) has a page of special Latvian remembrance days.

New Year's Day 1 January

Easter in accordance with the Western Church calendar

Labour Day 1 May

Restoration of Independence of the Republic of Latvia 4 May

Mothers' Day second Sunday in May

Whitsunday May or June in accordance with the Western Church

Līgo & Jāņi 23 and 24 June; St John's Day and Summer Solstice festival

National Day 18 November; anniversary of proclamation of Latvian Republic in 1918

Christmas Holiday 24 to 26 December

New Year's Eve 31 December

Money

Latvia's currency, the lats, was introduced in March 1993. The lats (Ls) is divided into 100 santīms. **Latvijas Bankas** (Latvian Bank; www.bank.lv) posts the lats' daily exchange rate on its website. The lats is pegged to the euro in a slow effort to graduate to using the euro.

Post & Telephone

Latvia's official postal service website (www.post.lv) can answer mail-related questions.

Telephone rates are posted on the website of **Lattelecom** (www.lattelecom.lv).

If your mobile phone is GSM900-/1800-compatible, you can purchase a prepaid SIM-card package and top-up credit from any Narvesen superette or Rimi grocery store. The most popular plan is **ZZ by Tele2** (Tele-divi; www.tele2.lv; SIM card 0.99Ls).

Visas

Schengen rules apply. For information on obtaining visas, visit www.mfa.gov.lv/en.

Getting There & Away

Air

Rīga airport (www.riga-airport.com), about 13km southwest of the city centre, houses Latvia's national carrier, **airBaltic** (www.airbaltic.com), which offers direct flights to over 50 destinations within Europe. Check out the airport's website for a detailed list of other carriers.

Boat

Rīga's **passenger ferry terminal** (www.freeportofriga.lv; Eksporta iela 3a), located about 1km downstream (north) of Akmens Bridge, offers service to Stockholm aboard **Tallink** (www.tallink.lv). **DFDS Ferry Lines** (www.lisco.lv) and **Ave Line** (www.aveline.lv; Uriekstes 3) leave from the Vecmīgrāvja cargo terminal (further down the Daugava) for Travemünde (Lübeck), Germany. Service is often suspended in the colder months.

Scandlines (☎6779 6900; www.scandlines.lt) runs ferries twice weekly from Liepāja to Rostock, Germany, and five times weekly from Ventspils to Nynashamn, Sweden (60km from Stockholm). Plans are in the works to run a ferry between Ventspils and Montu on the Estonian island of Saaremaa.

Land

In 2007 Latvia acceded to the Schengen Agreement (p1319), which removed all border control between both Estonia and Lithuania.

BUS

International buses depart from Rīga's **international bus station** (www.autoosta.lv; Prāgas iela 1), located behind the train station. International destinations include Tallinn, Vilnius, Warsaw, St Petersburg and Moscow. Try the following:

Ecolines (☎6721 4512; www.ecolines.net)

Eurolines Lux Express (☎6778 1350; www.luxexpress.eu)

Nordeka (☎6746 4620; www.nordeka.lv)

CAR

Rental cars are allowed to travel around the Baltic at no extra fee. Also see p795.

TRAIN

Rīga's **central train station** (Stacijas laukums) is housed in a conspicuous glass-encased shopping centre near the Central Market. The capital is directly linked by long-distance trains to several destinations, including Moscow (16½ hours) and St Petersburg (13¼ hours). Visit www.ldz.lv for details.

Getting Around

Bus & Train

Buses are more convenient than trains if you're travelling to Kolka, Liepāja or any other destination beyond the capital's suburban rail lines. For timetables, see www.1188.lv.

Most Latvians live in the large suburban ring around Rīga, thus the city's network of commuter rails makes it easy for tourists to reach day-tripping destinations such as Jūrmala and Sigulda.

Car & Motorcycle

Driving is on the right-hand side. Headlights must be on at all times. Ask for *benzene* when looking for a petrol station – *gāze* means air.

Car rentals range from €30 to €60 per day, depending on the type of vehicle and time of year. Companies usually allow you to drive in all three Baltic countries, but not beyond. Some options beyond the usual suspects:

AddCar Rental (☎2658 9674; www.addcarrental.com)

Auto (☎2958 0448; www.carsrent.lv)

EgiCarRent (☎2953 1044; www.egi.lv)

Liechtenstein

Includes »

Best Places

» Schloss Vaduz (p796)

» Fürstensteig, Around Vaduz (p797)

» Adler Vaduz (p796)

» Bergrestaurant Sareiserjoch, Malbun (p798)

Best Known For...

» Postcards stamped by the country's postal service

» Being Europe's fourth-smallest nation

» Being a producer of false teeth

» Being the only country in the world named after the people who purchased it

Why Go?

Liechtenstein makes a fabulous trivia subject – *Did you know it is the sixth smallest country in the world?... That it's still governed by an iron-willed monarch who lives in a Gothic castle on a hill?... Yes, it really is the world's largest producer of false teeth.* It's worth visiting this pocket-sized principality solely for the cocktail-party bragging rights, but keep the operation covert. This theme-park micronation takes its independence seriously and would shudder at the thought of being visited for novelty value alone.

Liechtenstein wows with its stunning natural beauty. Measuring just 25km by 6km, it's barely larger than Manhattan, doesn't have an international airport and is reached by public bus from Switzerland and Austria. Vaduz is not the most soulful place on earth, but if you've come this far – coachloads of day trippers do, simply for the souvenir passport stamp – venture away from the capital. A riot of hiking and cycling trails offering spectacular views of craggy cliffs, quaint villages and lush green forests awaits you.

When to Go

Vaduz

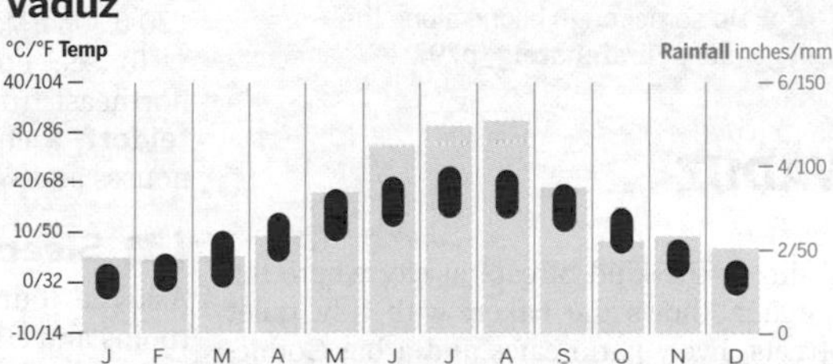

Aug Come on the 15th and celebrate the country's national holiday.

Dec–Mar Pummel down snow-covered pistes at its singular ski resort.

May–Sep Hike to your heart's content, up and away from the busloads of tourists clutching stamps.

Liechtenstein Highlights

1. Snap a picture of the **Schloss Vaduz** with its stunning mountain backdrop (p796)
2. Get a **passport stamp** and send a postcard home (p797)
3. Taste wine at the **Hofkellerei des Fürstens**, the prince's winery (p796)
4. Hit the ski slopes at **Malbun** (p797)
5. Do some tough hiking along the legendary **Fürstensteig** (p797)

VADUZ

POP 5160

Vaduz is the kind of capital city where the butcher knows the baker; with tidy, quiet streets, lively patio cafes and a big Gothic-looking castle on a hill, it feels more like a village than anything else. It's also all most visitors to Liechtenstein see and at times it can feel like its soul has been sold to cater to the whims of tourist hordes that alight for 17 minutes from guided bus tours. Souvenir shops, tax-free luxury-goods stores and cube-shaped concrete buildings dominate the small, somewhat bland town centre.

Sights & Activities

Although **Schloss Vaduz** (Vaduz Castle) is not open to the public, the exterior graces many a photograph and it is worth the climb up the hill. At the top, there's a magnificent vista of Vaduz, with a spectacular mountain backdrop. There's also a network of walking trails along the ridge. For a peek inside the castle grounds, arrive on 15 August, Liechtenstein's **National Day**, when there are magnificent fireworks and the prince invites the entire country over to his place for a glass.

The well-designed **Liechtensteinisches Landesmuseum** (National Museum; ☎239 68 20; www.landesmuseum.li; Städtle 43; adult/concession Sfr8/5, combined with Kunstmuseum Sfr18/8; ⊙10am-5pm Tue & Thu-Sun, to 8pm Wed) provides an interesting romp through the principality's history, from medieval witch trials and burnings to the manufacture of false teeth.

The mainstay of the **Kunstmuseum Liechtenstein** (Art Museum; ☎235 03 00; www.kunstmuseum.li; Städtle 32; adult/concession Sfr12/8, combined with Landesmuseum Sfr18/8; ⊙10am-5pm Tue, Wed & Fri-Sun, to 8pm Thu) is contemporary art, not the prince's collection of old masters, which is in the Liechtenstein Museum in Vienna. The **Post Museum** (☎236 61 05; 1st fl, Städtle 37; admission free; ⊙10am-noon & 1-5pm) showcases all the national stamps issued since 1912.

You must be in a group for a tour at the **Hofkellerei des Fürstens** (www.hofkellerei.li), the prince's vineyard perched north of Vaduz. Independent travellers can visit and indulge in a taste when the **shop** (⊙8am-noon, 1.30-6.30pm Mon-Fri, 9am-1pm Sat) is open.

To see how Vaduz once looked, head northeast from the pedestrian zone to **Mitteldorf**, a charming quarter of traditional houses and verdant gardens.

Sleeping

Ask the tourist office for a list of private rooms and chalets outside Vaduz.

Camping Mittagspitze CAMPING GROUND **€**
(☎392 36 77, 392 23 11; www.campingtriesen.li; campsites per adult/car Sfr9/5, tents Sfr6-8; ⊙year-round; 🏊) A well-equipped ground in a leafy spot with a restaurant, TV lounge, playground and kiosk. Find it 3.5km outside Vaduz, south of Triesen.

YHA Hostel HOSTEL €
(☎232 50 22; www.youthhostel.ch/schaan; Untere Rütigasse 6; dm/s/d Sfr33/57/84; ⊙Mar-Oct) This hostel caters particularly to cyclists and families. Halfway between Schaan and Vaduz, it's within easy walking distance of either. Reception is closed from 10am to 5pm.

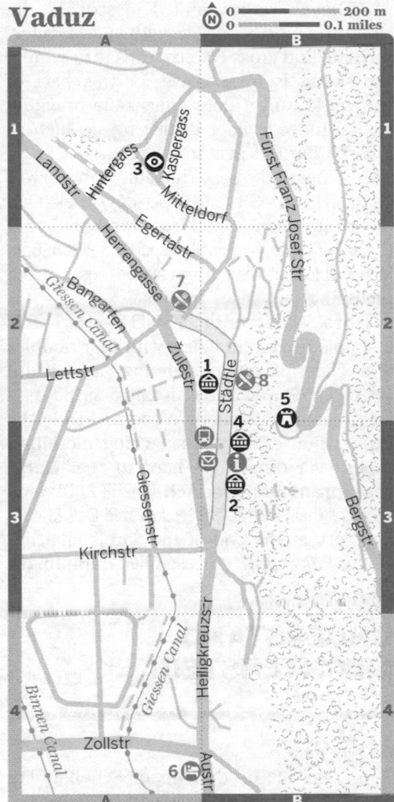

Vaduz

Sights
1 Kunstmuseum Liechtenstein B2
2 Liechtensteinisches Landesmuseum B3
3 Mitteldorf A1
4 Postmuseum B3
5 Schloss Vaduz B2

Sleeping
6 Landgasthof Au A4

Eating
7 Adler Vaduz A2
8 Café Wolf B2
Landgasthof Au ....(see 6)

Landgasthof Au HOTEL €
(☎232 11 17; Austrasse 2; s/d without bathroom Sfr68/110, with bathroom Sfr90/140; P) A couple of bus stops south of Vaduz town centre (about a 10-minute walk), this simple, family-run place is a reasonable budget option. A couple of the bigger doubles have terraces.

Eating

Pedestrian-only Städtle has a clutch of pavement restaurants and cafes.

Café Wolf INTERNATIONAL €€
(Städtle 29) This relaxed cafe and restaurant has pavement tables in summer and a menu that mixes Swiss and international cuisine – anything from pizza to pseudo-Asian dishes.

Adler Vaduz INTERNATIONAL €€
(☎232 21 31; www.adler.li; Herrengasse 2; ⊙Mon-Fri) A pleasant restaurant in the Hotel Adler offering a broad selection, from pasta to *rindsfilet vom grill auf steinpilzrisotto mit trüffel-rotweinsauce nappiert* (beef steak fillet with mushroom risotto and a truffle-and red wine sauce).

Landgasthof Au INTERNATIONAL €€
(☎232 11 17; Austrasse 2; ⊙Wed-Sun) The Landgasthof Au garden restaurant has a good name for its local grub, which ranges from ham omelettes to a couple of vegetarian dishes.

Information

The **Liechtenstein Center** (☎239 63 00; www.tourismus.li; Städtle; ⊙9am-5pm) tourist office sells souvenir passport stamps for Sfr3.

Getting There & Away

See p799.

AROUND VADUZ

Outside Vaduz the air is crisp and clear, with a pungent, sweet aroma of cow dung and flowers. The countryside is dotted with tranquil villages and enticing churches set to a craggy Alps backdrop.

Triesenberg (bus 21 from Vaduz), on a terrace above Vaduz, commands excellent views over the Rhine valley. It has a pretty, onion domed church as well as the

LIECHTENSTEIN FACTS

» **Area** 155 sq km

» **Capital** Vaduz

» **Language** German, although the Swiss-German dialect is the de facto language

» **Currency** Swiss franc (Sfr)

» **Exchange rates** A$1 = Sfr0.95; C$1 = Sfr0.95; €1 = Sfr1.28; ¥100 = Sfr1.13; NZ$1 = Sfr0.69; UK£1 = Sfr1.50; US$1 = Sfr0.92

» **Country code** ☎423

» **Emergency** ☎112, ambulance ☎144, police ☎117

» **Visas** Schengen rules apply, see p1319

» **Hostel bed** Sfr40 to Sfr60

» **One-day/week ski pass** Sfr45/205

» **Itinerary** Snap pics of stunning Schloss Vaduz, then explore the local alpine hiking trails. After, reward your muscles with Swiss or international cuisine at Café Wolf.

Walsermuseum (☎262 19 26; www.triesenberg.li; Jonaboda 2; adult/concession Sfr2/1; ⏲7.45-11.45am & 1.30-5.45pm Mon-Fri, 7.45-11am & 1.30-5pm Sat), devoted to the Walser community, whose members came from Switzerland's Valais in the 13th century.

There are 400km of **hiking trails** in Liechtenstein (see www.wanderwege.llv.li, in German), along with loads of well-marked **cycling routes** (look for signs with a cycling symbol; distances and directions will also be included). The most famous hiking trail is the **Fürstensteig**, a rite of passage for nearly every Liechtensteiner. You must be fit and not suffer from vertigo, as in places the path is narrow, reinforced with rope handholds, and/or falls away to a sheer drop. The hike, up to four hours, begins at the Berggasthaus Gaflei (bus 22 from Triesenberg). Travel light and wear good shoes.

Malbun

POP 32

Welcome to Liechtenstein's one and only ski resort: the 1600m-high resort of Malbun feels – in the nicest possible sense – like the edge of the earth.

The road from Vaduz terminates at Malbun. There is an ATM by the lower bus stop. The **tourist office** (☎263 65 77; www.malbun.li; ⏲9am-noon & 1.30-5pm Mon-Sat, closed mid-Apr–May & Nov–mid-Dec) is on the main street, not far from Hotel Walserhof.

Although rather limited in scope – the runs are mostly novice with a few intermediate and cross-country runs thrown in – the skiing is inexpensive for this part of the world and it does offer some bragging rights. Indeed, older British royals such as Prince Charles learnt to ski here.

A general ski pass (including the Sareis chairlift) costs Sfr45/205 per day/week. One day's equipment rental from **Malbun Sport** (☎263 37 55; www.malbunsport.li; ⏲8am-6pm Mon-Fri, plus Sat & Sun in high season) costs Sfr60, including skis, shoes and poles.

Hotel Walserhof (☎264 43 23; d Sfr140) is a simple mountain house with four doubles and cheerful outdoor dining, and **Kulm** (☎237 27 79; www.hotelkulm.com; d Sfr180) is a solid chalet with modern rooms inside the timber house. For gob-smacking mountain views over dinner, it's hard to beat **Bergrestaurant Sareiserjoch** (☎268 21 01; www.sareis.li; mains Sfr20-35; ⏲Jun–mid-Oct & mid-Dec–Apr), at the end of the Sareis chairlift. Go for *käsknöpfli* (cheese-filled dumplings).

UNDERSTAND LIECHTENSTEIN

History

A merger of the domain of Schellenberg and the county of Vaduz in 1712 by the powerful Liechtenstein family created the country. A principality under the Holy Roman Empire from 1719 to 1806, it achieved full sovereign independence in 1866. A modern constitution was drawn up in 1921, but even today the prince retains the power to dissolve parliament and must approve every act before it becomes law. Prince Franz Josef II was the first ruler to live in the castle above the capital city of Vaduz. He died in 1989 and was succeeded by his son, Prince Hans-Adam II.

In 2003 Hans-Adam won sweeping powers to dismiss the elected government, appoint judges and reject proposed laws. The following year he handed the day-to-day running of the country to his son Alois, although he remains the titular head of state.

Scandal rocked the principality in 2008 when it was discovered that more than 1000 high-flying Germans had evaded tax by depositing large sums of money in trusts run by a Liechtenstein bank partly owned by the princely family. After initially refusing to cooperate with international investigations, Liechtenstein eventually bowed to pressure and began exchanging information.

Low business taxes means around 75,000 firms, many of them so-called 'letter box companies', are registered here – about twice the number of the principality's inhabitants (35,000).

Food

The following price indicators for the cost of a main course are used in this chapter:

€€€ more than Sfr45

€€ from Sfr25 to Sfr44

€ less than Sfr25

SURVIVAL GUIDE

Directory A-Z

Liechtenstein and Switzerland share almost everything, so for more information about Liechtenstein basics, see p1258.

We have used the following price indicators for double-room accommodation for this chapter:

€€€ more than Sfr350

€€ from Sfr125 to Sfr349

€ less than Sfr125

Getting There & Away

The nearest airports are Friedrichshafen (Germany) and Zürich, with train connections to the Swiss border towns of Buchs and Sargans. From each of these towns there are usually three daily buses to Vaduz (Sfr2.40/3.60 from Buchs/Sargans). Buses run every 30 minutes from the Austrian border town of Feldkirch; you sometimes have to change at Schaan to reach Vaduz.

A few Buchs–Feldkirch trains stop at Schaan (bus tickets are valid).

Getting Around

Buses (www.lba.li, in German) are cheap (well, there's not a lot of ground to cover) and reliable and traverse the country. Single fares are Sfr2.40/3.60 for two/three zones. Swiss travel passes are valid on all main routes. Timetables are posted at stops or grab one at the tourist office.

Lithuania

Includes »

Best Places to Eat

» Борщ!, Vilnius (p807)
» Ararat, Klaipėda (p811)
» Senieji Rūsiai, Kaunas (p810)

Best Places to Stay

» Jimmy Jumps House, Vilnius (p806)
» Litinterp Klaipeda, Klaipėda (p811)
» Kauno Arkivyskupijos Svečių Namai, Kaunas (p810)

Why Go?

The Baltic countries have a reputation for their dour ways, but this image fades when you enter rebellious Lithuania, a country blessed with boundless energy and studded with reminders of its turbulent history.

It may be a dot on Europe's map, but that didn't stopped Lithuania from becoming a mighty empire in the 1400s, its territory extending beyond Kursk in the east and all the way to the Black Sea in the south. Even today Lithuanians brim with pride and confidence befitting their mighty heritage.

From the baroque spires and effortless charm of Vilnius' vibrant streets and the ancient ruins of Kernavė to the ghostly sand dunes of the Curonian Spit, and the lakes and forests of the southeast, Lithuania has plenty to offer. More and more travellers are making their way to this tiny country with an earthy vibe, where pagan roots run deep and Catholic passion lives on.

When to Go

Vilnius

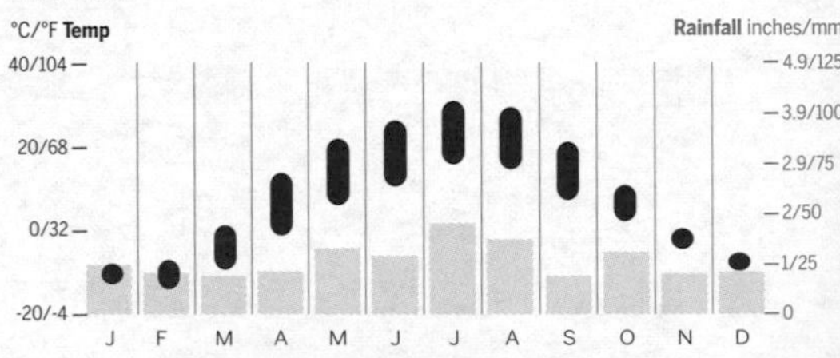

Apr Many top jazz musicians take to the stage in the Kaunas International Jazz Festival.

Jul Take part in boat parades and revelry at the Sea Festival to celebrate Klaipėda's nautical heritage.

Sep Vilnius City Days is a five-day celebration of carnivals, masked parades, music and fashion.

Connections

Buses, trains and ferries provide numerous travel options to Lithuania's neighbouring countries.

Vilnius is a hub for buses to Poland, Latvia, Estonia, Belarus and Russia's Kaliningrad. From Kaunas there are buses to Latvia, Estonia and Kaliningrad, and the latter may also be reached from Klaipėda and the Curonian Spit.

Trains serve Russia, Poland and Belarus from the capital but there are no rail connections to Latvia or Estonia. Sweden and Germany can be reached by ferry from Klaipėda, Lithuania's international port.

ITINERARIES

Three Days

Devote two days to exploring the baroque heart of Vilnius, then day trip to Trakai for its spectacular island castle and the homesteads of the Karaite people, stopping off at Paneriai on the way.

One Week

Spend four nights in Vilnius, with day trips to both Trakai and the Soviet sculpture park near Druskininkai. Travel cross-country to Šiauliai and the Hill of Crosses, then spend two or three days exploring some serious nature on the Curonian Spit. Head back east via Klaipėda and Kaunas.

Essential Food & Drink

» **Potato creations** *Cepelinai* (potato dough zeppelin stuffed with meat, mushrooms or cheese), *bulviniai blynai* (potato pancakes) and *vedarai* (pig intestine stuffed with potato).

» **Beer snacks** Smoked pig ears and *kepta duona* (deep-fried garlicky breadsticks).

» **Beetroot delight** Cold, creamy *šaltibarščiai* (beetroot soup) – a summer speciality.

» **Smoked fish** *Rukytas unguris* (smoked eel) – a Curonian Spit treat.

» **Beer and mead** Šytutys, Utenos and Kalnapilis are top beers; *midus* (mead) is a honey-tinged nobleman's drink.

AT A GLANCE

» **Currency** litas (Lt)

» **Language** Lithuanian

» **Money** ATMs everywhere

» **Visas** Not required for citizens of the EU, Australia, NZ or USA

Fast Facts

» **Area** 65,303 sq km

» **Capital** Vilnius

» **Country code** ☎370

» **Emergency** ☎112

Exchange Rates

Australia	A$1	2.50Lt
Canada	C$1	2.48Lt
Euro Zone	€1	3.45Lt
Japan	¥100	2.85Lt
New Zealand	NZ$1	1.89Lt
UK	UK£1	3.90Lt
USA	US$1	2.38Lt

Set Your Budget

» **Budget hotel room** 180Lt

» **Two-course evening meal** 50Lt

» **Museum entrance** 5Lt

» **Beer** 8Lt for a bottle

» **Bus ticket** 1.20 to 2Lt

Resources

» **In Your Pocket** (www.inyourpocket.com) Extensive, downloadable listings

» **Tourism in Lithuania** (www.tourism.lt) Lithuanian State Tourism Department

» **Museums of Lithuania** (www.muziejai.lt)

» **Litrail** (www.litrail.lt) Train timetable and info

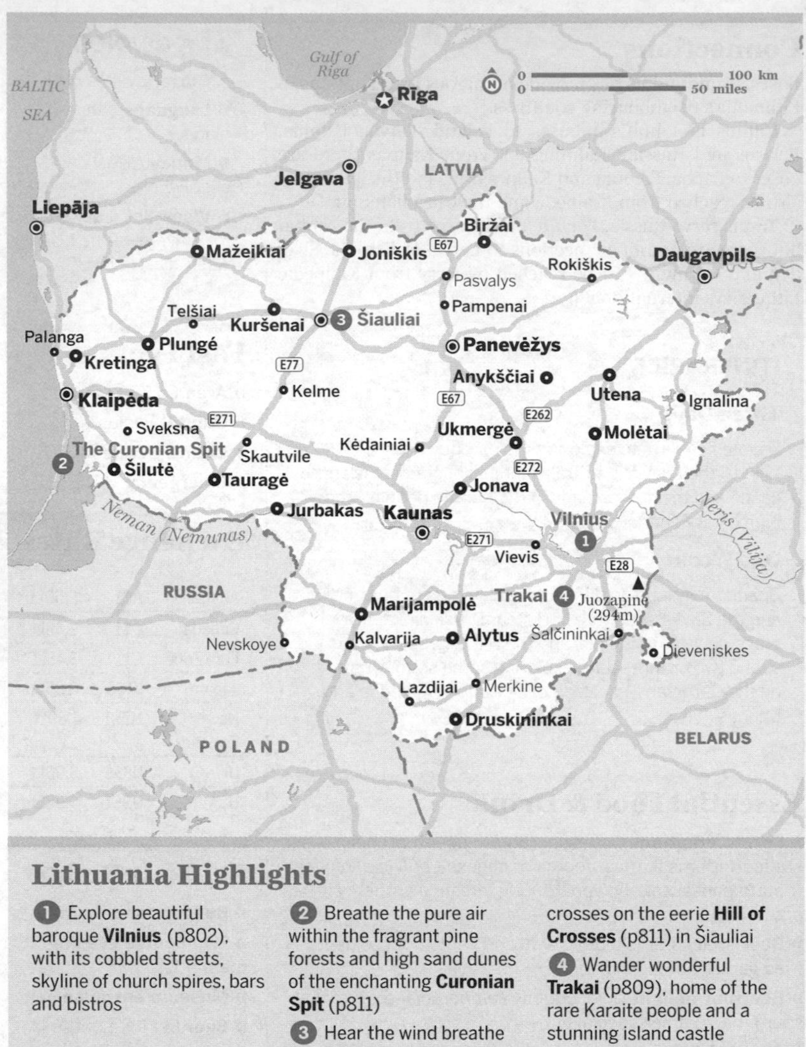

Lithuania Highlights

1 Explore beautiful baroque **Vilnius** (p802), with its cobbled streets, skyline of church spires, bars and bistros

2 Breathe the pure air within the fragrant pine forests and high sand dunes of the enchanting **Curonian Spit** (p811)

3 Hear the wind breathe between the thousands of crosses on the eerie **Hill of Crosses** (p811) in Šiauliai

4 Wander wonderful **Trakai** (p809), home of the rare Karaite people and a stunning island castle

VILNIUS

POP 544,200

Vilnius, the baroque bombshell of the Baltics, is a city of immense allure. As beautiful as it is bizarre, it draws tourists to it with a confident charm and a warm, golden glow that makes one wish for long, midsummer evenings every day of the year.

At its heart is Europe's largest baroque Old Town, so precious that Unesco added it to its World Heritage list in 1994. Its skyline, pierced by (almost) countless Orthodox and Catholic church steeples, appears like a giant bed of nails from the basket of a hot-air balloon. Adding to the intoxicating mix is a combination of cobbled alleys, hilltop views, breakaway states and traditional artists' workshops.

Vilnius feels tiny, but that's a bit deceptive because the suburban sprawl that surrounds Old Town is a fairly typical Soviet-style mess of snarled traffic and concrete.

Sights

CATHEDRAL SQUARE & NEW TOWN

TOP CHOICE **Museum of Genocide Victims** MUSEUM
(www.genocid.lt/muziejus; Aukų gatvė 2a; adult/student 6/3Lt; ⏲10am-6pm Wed-Sat, to 5pm Sun) This building used to be the notorious KGB headquarters and prison from 1940 to 1991. Called the 'KGB Museum' by locals, its detailed, well-presented exhibits deal with the Soviet oppression of the Lithuanian people and the post-WWII Lithuanian resistance movement. However, there is almost no mention of the fact that this was also the Gestapo headquarters between 1941–44, or of its role in the genocide of much of the city's Jewish population.

Cathedral Square HISTORIC AREA
At the base of Gediminas Hill, the square (Katedros aikštė) is dominated by **Vilnius Cathedral** (admission free; ⏲7am-7.30pm, Mass at 8am, 9am, 10am, 11.15am & 6.30pm Sun) and its 57m-tall **belfry**. The first wooden cathedral, built in 1387–88, was in Gothic style, but has been rebuilt many times since. The most important restoration was completed from 1783 to 1801, when the outside was redone in today's classical style. The interior's showpiece is baroque **St Casimir's Chapel**, with frescos depicting the life of St Casimir (Lithuania's patron saint), whose silver coffin lies within.

At the square's eastern end is an **equestrian statue of Gediminas**, built on an ancient pagan site, and behind it stands the **Royal Palace**. Demolished by the Russians in the late 18th century, the palace has been reconstructed and should be open again in 2011.

Gediminas Hill LANDMARK
Vilnius was founded on this 48m-high hill, topped since the 13th century by the oft-rebuilt **Gediminas Tower**. There are amazing views of Old Town from the top of the tower, which houses the **Upper Castle Museum** (admission 5Lt). The tower is reached by **funicular** (3Lt; ⏲10am-7pm), located at the rear of the Museum of Applied Arts.

Museum of Applied Arts MUSEUM
(www.ldm.lt; Arsenalo gatvė 3a; adult/student 6/3Lt; ⏲11am-6pm Tue-Sat, 11am-4pm Sun) The museum, in the old arsenal at the foot of Gediminas Hill, houses exhibitions showcasing 15th- to 19th-century Lithuanian sacred art and the Gothic treasures from Gediminas Castle, which will be displayed in the castle in the future.

National Museum of Lithuania MUSEUM
(www.lnm.lt; Arsenalo gatvė 1; admission 5Lt; ⏲10am-5pm Tue-Sat, 10am-3pm Sun) The displays retell everyday Lithuanian life from the 13th century till WWII.

Gedimino prospektas NOTABLE STREET
The main boulevard of Vilnius' 19th-century New Town heads due west from Cathedral Sq all the way to the silver-domed Orthodox **Church of the Saint Virgin's Apparition** (A Mickevičiaus gatvė 1), 1.75km away. Roughly halfway is Lukiškių aikštė, formerly Lenin Sq.

OLD TOWN & AROUND

Eastern Europe's largest Old Town deserves its Unesco status. The area stretches 1.5km south from Cathedral Sq and the eastern end of Gedimino prospektas.

Pilies gatvė and Vilnius University HISTORIC AREA
Cobbled **Pilies gatvė** – the hub of tourist action and the main entrance to Old Town from Cathedral Sq – buzzes with life. Nearby is Eastern Europe's oldest university, **Vilnius University** (www.vu.lt; Universiteto gatvė 3; admission 5Lt; ⏲9.30am-5.30pm Mon-Sat), featuring 13 courtyards framed by 15th-century buildings and splashed with 300-year-old frescos and **St John's Church** (⏲10am-5pm Mon-Sat), a baroque gem.

TOP FIVE QUIRKY ATTRACTIONS

Vilnius has an undeniable mischievous streak, as the following attest:

» **Frank Zappa memorial** (Kalinausko gatvė 1) The world's first Zappa statue.

» **Angel of Užupis statue** (cnr Užupio & Malūnro gatvė) The trumpet-blowing symbol of Vilnius' strangest neighbourhood.

» **Egg statue** (cnr Šv Stepono & Raugyklos gatvė) This statue was in Užupis' main square until it 'hatched' the Angel of Užupis in 2002.

» **Žaliasis Tiltas (Green Bridge) statues** The communist-era sculptures symbolising youth, labour and military glory.

» **Stebuklas (miracle) tile** (Cathedral Sq) If you stand on this tile square and turn around clockwise, your wish will allegedly come true. But first you must find it!

Central Vilnius

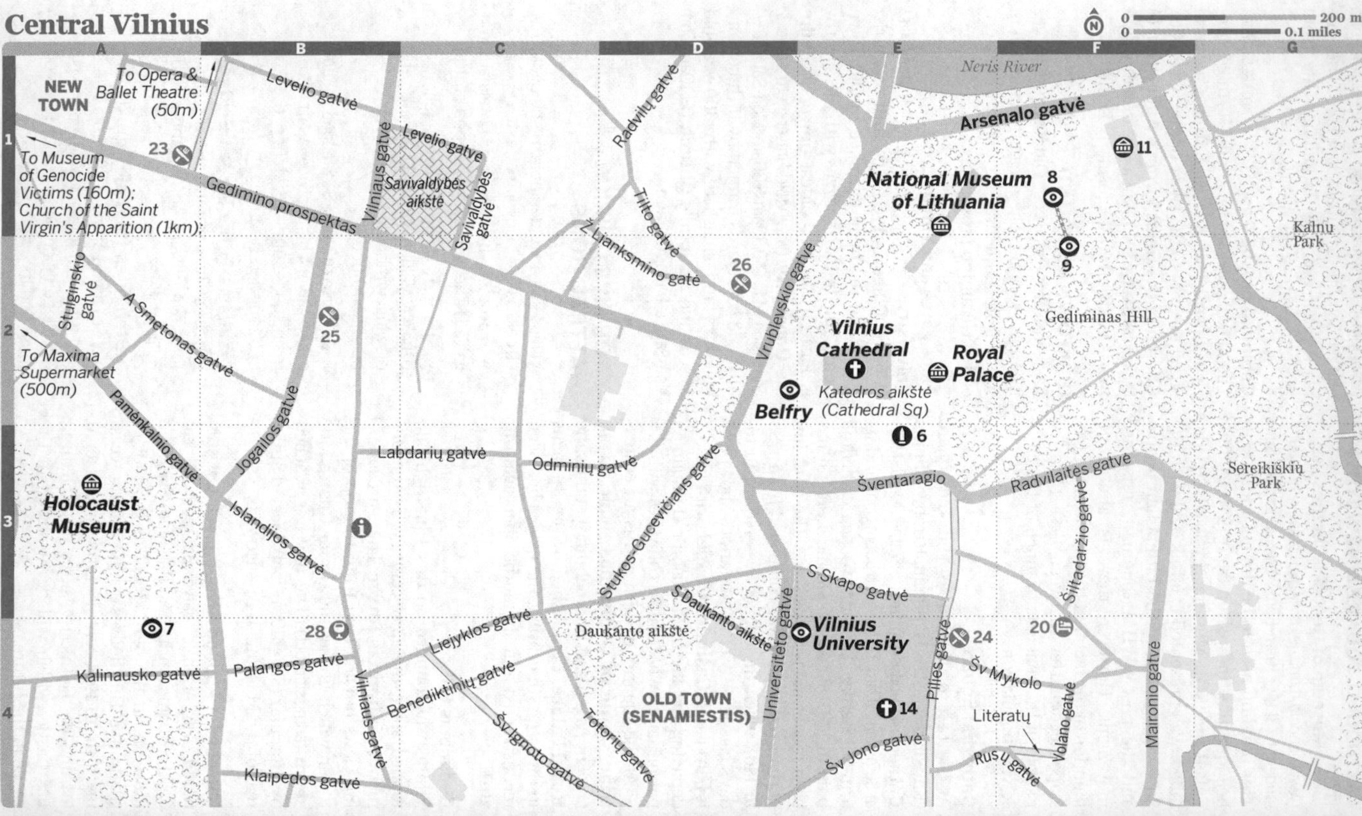

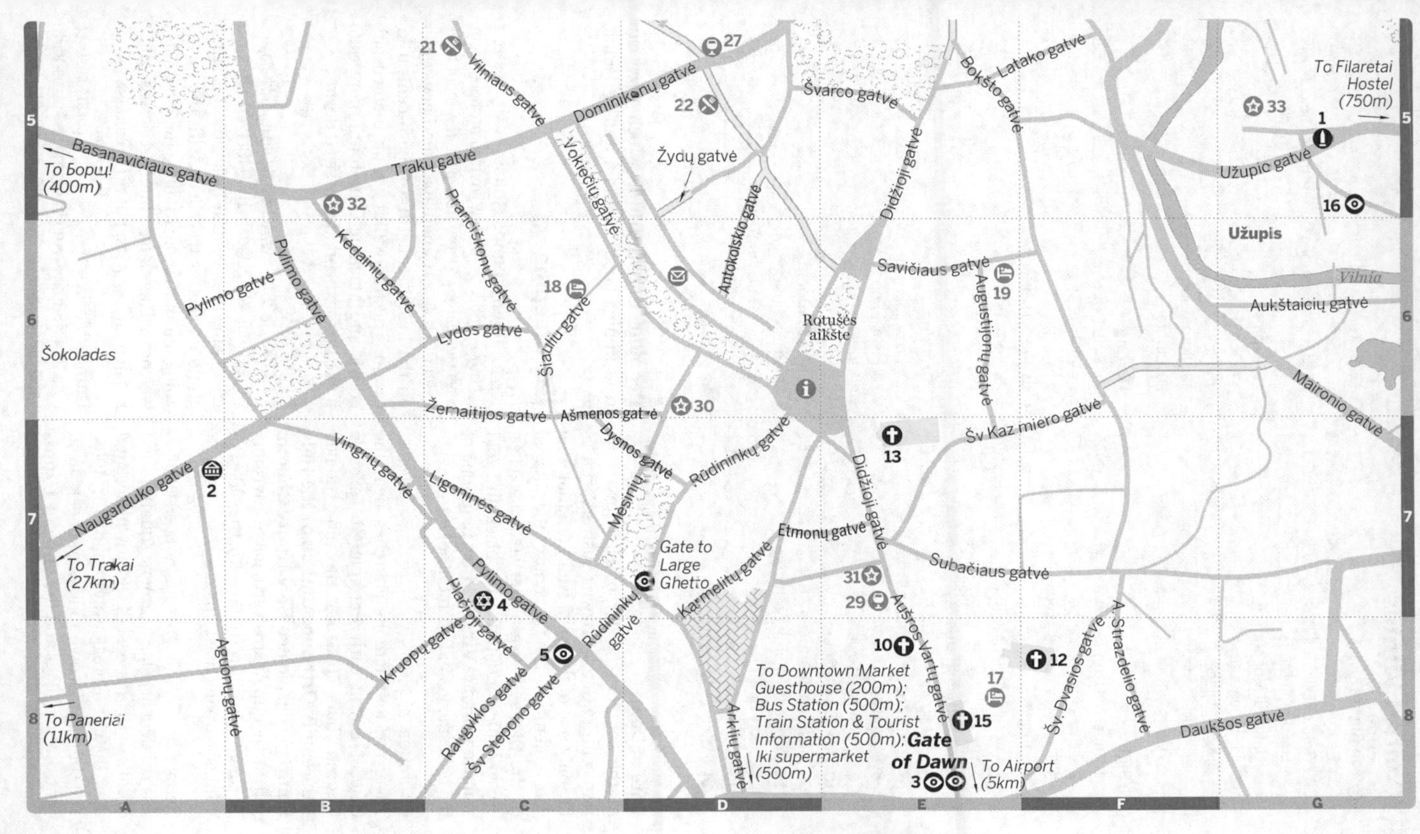
To Бopщ! (400m)
Basanavičiaus gatvė
Trakų gatvė
Vilniaus gatvė
Dominikonų gatvė
Vokiečių gatvė
Žydų gatvė
Antokolskio gatvė
Didžioji gatvė
Švarco gatvė
Bokšto gatvė
Latako gatvė
To Filaretai Hostel (750m)
Užupio gatvė
Užupis
Vilnia
Aukštaicių gatvė
Maironio gatvė
Savičiaus gatvė
Augustijonų gatvė
Rotušės aikštė
Pylimo gatvė
Kedainių gatvė
Pranciškonų gatvė
Šiaulių gatvė
Lydos gatvė
Šokolad*s
Žemaitijos gatvė
Ašmenos gatvė
Dysnos gatvė
Rūdininkų gatvė
Mėsinių
Šv Kaz miero gatvė
Naugarduko gatvė
Vingrių gatvė
Ligonines gatvė
To Trakai (27km)
Gate to Large Ghetto
Etmonų gatvė
Subačiaus gatvė
Karmelitų gatvė
Plačioji gatvė
Kruopų gatvė
Rūdininkų gatvė
Aguonų gatvė
Raugyklos gatvė
Šv Stepono gatvė
Arklių gatvė
Aušros Vartų gatvė
Šv. Dvasios gatvė
A. Strazdelio gatvė
Daukšos gatvė
To Paneriai (11km)
To Downtown Market Guesthouse (200m); Bus Station (500m); Train Station & Tourist Information (500m); Iki supermarket (500m)
Gate of Dawn
To Airport (5km)
A
B
C
D
E
F
G
5
6
7
8
1
2
3
4
5
10
12
13
15
16
17
18
19
21
22
27
29
30
31
32
33

Central Vilnius

Gate of Dawn LANDMARK
At the southern border of Old Town, the 16th-century Gate of Dawn (Aušros Vartai) is the only one of the town wall's original nine gates still intact. The gate houses the **Chapel of the Blessed Virgin Mary** (admission free; 6am-7pm), containing the black-and-gold 'miracle-working' **Virgin Mary icon**, one of the holiest icons in Polish Catholicism.

Churches CHURCHES
There are four famous churches near the Gate of Dawn: early baroque **St Teresa's Church** (built 1635–50); the pink, domed 17th-century **Orthodox Church of the Holy Spirit**; the dilapidated **Holy Trinity Church**; and, further up Aušros Vartų gatvė, ravishing **St Casimir's Church** (1604–15), the oldest of Vilnius' baroque masterpieces.

Užupis NEIGHBOURHOOD
The resident artists, dreamers, squatters and drunks of Užupis, east of Old Town, declared their district a breakaway republic in 1998. The state has its own tongue-in-cheek president, anthem, flags and the 41-point **Užupis Republic Constitution**, which you can read in nine languages on a wall on Paupio gatvė.

Sleeping

TOP CHOICE **Jimmy Jumps House** HOSTEL €
(607 88235; www.jimmyjumpshouse.com; Savičiaus gatvė 12-1; dm from 37Lt, d without bathroom 110Lt; @) Canadian-owned newcomer on the hostel scene in a superb central location. The free walking tour, themed pub crawls and Machine Gun Tours more than make up for the modestly sized dorms.

Hostelgate HOSTEL €
(8-638 32818; www.hostelgate.lt; Mikalojaus gatvė 3; dm 39-42Lt, d/tr 110/140Lt; @) Under a new name, this central little hostel is still a grand choice for travellers, with the owner going out of his way to make the guests feel welcome. There's free internet access, guest kitchen and lockers, but no breakfast.

Domus Maria GUEST HOUSE €€
(5-264 4880; www.domusmaria.lt; Aušros Vartų gatvė 12; s/d/tr/q 250/300/329/369Lt; P@)

This unique guest house within a monastery stays true to its monastic origins with wide-arched corridors and spartan white rooms. The rooms with shared bathrooms are stunning value.

Downtown Market Guesthouse B&B €
(☎8-679 85476; www.downtownmarket.lt; Pylimo gatvė 57; r from 190Lt; 📶) Located next to the central market, this refurbished little guest house has just six individually decorated doubles with private bathroom. The location is very central and the filling breakfast is made from organic produce.

Litinterp B&B €
(☎5-212 3850; www.litinterp.com; Bernardinų gatvė 7-2; s/d/tr with bathroom 100/160/210Lt, without bathroom 80/140/180Lt, apt 280Lt) This bright, clean, and friendly guest house in the heart of Old Town has been the best deal in Vilnius for years.

Filaretai Hostel HOSTEL €
(☎5-215 4627; www.filaretaihostel.lt; Filaretų gatvė 17; dm/s/d 34/70/100Lt; @📶) This chilled-out hostel occupies a quaint old villa in Užupis; take bus 34 from the bus station to the Filaretų stop.

Eating

TOP CHOICE **Борщ!** UKRAINIAN €
(Algirdo gatvė 5-2; mains 11-25Lt) This bright new Ukrainian restaurant combines traditional flavours with a minimum of stodge. Wash down the superb signature borsch and the sweet and savoury *pelmeni* and *vareniki* (dumplings) with the sublime home-made *kvas*, a fermented drink made from black or rye bread.

Forto Dvaras LITHUANIAN €
(Pilies gatvė 16; mains 22-24Lt) Perpetually popular folk-themed restaurant that's in danger of turning its patrons into something visually resembling its signature dish, the *cepelinai*. It's among the best in the city, as are the potato pancakes and the *šaltibarščiai*.

Tres Mexicanos MEXICAN €
(Tilto gatvė 2; mains 18-28Lt) This cheerful little Mexican-run restaurant with a jolly yellow interior packs some proper heat with its authentically spicy enchiladas, tacos and burritos. Best stop for *mole poblano* this side of the Atlantic.

Bistro 18 INTERNATIONAL €€
(Stiklių gatvė 18; mains 20-40Lt) Bistro 18 has plenty going for it: friendly service; minimalist, appealing decor; imaginative, international cuisine; and a lengthy wine menu. At around 26Lt, the lunch menu is a bargain.

Balti Drambliai VEGETARIAN €
(Vilniaus gatvė 41; mains 10-17Lt; 🖉) The White Elephant whips up a vegan and veggie storm, offering pancakes, pizzas, Indian curries and tofu-based dishes to hungry non-meat-eaters. Its cavernous basement hosts reggae and ragga gigs on weekends.

Pizza and pasta often comes cheap in this city. Two worthy options for both are **Čili Pica** (Gedimino prospektas 23; mains 19-35Lt), the ubiquitous pizza chain spread far and wide in Lithuania, and **Pomodoro** (Jogailos gatvė 4; mains 15-22Lt), with its inexpensive, generous portions.

Supermarkets are everywhere: **Iki** (bus station, Sodų gatvė 22) and **Maxima** (Mindaugo gatvė 11; ⏰24hr) are leading chains.

JEWISH VILNIUS

Dubbed by Napoleon as the 'Jerusalem of the north', Vilnius had one of Europe's most prominent Jewish communities until Nazi brutality wiped it out.

The old Jewish quarter lay in the streets west of Didžioji gatvė, including present-day Žydų gatvė (Jews St) and Gaono gatvė, named after Vilnius' most famous Jewish resident, Gaon Elijahu ben Shlomo Zalman (1720–97).

The **Centre for Tolerance** (www.jmuseum.lt; Naugarduko gatvė 10; admission 5Lt; ⏰10am-6pm Mon-Thu, 10am-4pm Fri & Sun), a beautifully restored former Jewish theatre, houses thought-provoking historical displays and occasional art exhibitions. The **Holocaust Museum** (Pamėnkalnio gatvė 12; admission 5Lt; ⏰9am-5pm Mon-Thu, 9am-4pm Fri, 10am-4pm Sun), in the so-called Green House, is a moving museum detailing the horror suffered by Lithuanian Jews in an unedited display of images and letters.

Vilnius' only remaining synagogue, the **Choral Synagogue** (Pylimo gatvė 39; donations welcome; ⏰10am-2pm Sun-Fri), was built in a Moorish style in 1903 and survived only because the Nazis used it as a medical store.

Drinking

Vilnius' party scene centres around clubs in the cold months and outdoor cafes in the summer.

Cozy CAFE
(Dominikonų gatvė 10) The basement DJ club at this welcoming lounge-style cafe-restaurant has all-night soirées on Friday and Saturday and smaller parties on Thursday.

In Vino WINE BAR
(Aušros Vartų gatvė 7) The bar of the moment, with one of the loveliest courtyards in the city. Excellent wines, expensive tapas and a few mains.

Franki Pub PUB
(Vilniaus gatvė 37) Serving up live blues and folk music by night, this intimate, candlelit pub fills up early on weekends.

Entertainment

Stopkė CLUB
(Užupio gatvė 2a) This ramshackle art gallery turns into a live-music space by night, favoured by the alternative and arty crowd. Find it next to the most colourful building in Užupis, by the river.

Pabo Latino CLUB
(www.pabolatino.lt; Trakų gatvė 3) This sultry-red club specialises in live Latin music and strong cocktails against a backdrop of some of the city's most beautiful people.

Brodvėjus LIVE MUSIC
(www.brodvejus.lt; Mėsinių gatvė 4) The place to come for occasionally good live bands and cheesy tunes, or a quieter drink upstairs. Hugely popular with older expats, pretty young things and students.

Opera & Ballet Theatre OPERA
(5-262 0727; www.opera.lt; Vienuolio gatvė 1) Classical productions in a grand, gaudy building near the river.

National Philharmonic CLASSICAL MUSIC
(5-266 5233; www.filharmonija.lt; Aušros Vartų gatvė 5) The country's most renowned orchestras perform here.

Information

Internet Access

A growing number of cafes, restaurants and hotels have free wi-fi zones.

Collegium (Pilies gatvė 22-1; per hr 6Lt; 8am-8pm)

Taškas (Jasinskio gatvė 1/8; per hr 5Lt; 24hr)

Medical Services

Main pharmacy (Gedimino Vaistinė; Gedimino prospektas 27; 8am-10pm Mon-Fri, 10am-5pm Sat &Sun)

Baltic-American Medical & Surgical Clinic (5-234 2020; www.bak.lt; Nemenčinės gatvė 54a; 24hr) English-speaking health centre.

Money

Vilnius is littered with ATMs and banks, most offering currency and travellers-cheque exchange. **Keitykla Exchange** (Parex Bankas; www.keitykla.lt; Geležinkelio gatvė 6; 24hr) has currency exchange with ATM.

Tourist Information

Vilnius tourist information centres (www.vilnius-tourism.lt; 9am-6pm Mon-Fri, 10am-4pm Sat & Sun); town hall (5-262 6470; Didžioji gatvė 31); train station (5-269 2091); Vilniaus gatvė (5-262 9660; Vilniaus gatvė 22) have a wealth of brochures and information. Staff can arrange tours and book accommodation.

Getting There & Away

See p813.

Bus

From Vilnius, departures include Druskininkai (30Lt, two hours, 10 daily), Kaunas (25Lt, 1¾ hours, two to three hourly), Klaipėda (64Lt, four to 5½ hours, 15 daily) and Šiauliai (47Lt, three hours, up to 12 daily).

Train

Suburban trains run from Vilnius to domestic destinations, including Kaunas (15Lt, one to 1¾ hours, up to 17 daily), Klaipėda (51.20Lt, 4½ to five hours, three daily) and Šiauliai (34.80Lt, 2½ hours, three daily).

Getting Around

To/From the Airport

Bus 1 runs between Vilnius International Airport and the train station. A shuttle train service runs every 30 minutes between 6.30am and 7.30pm (2Lt). A taxi from the airport to the city centre should cost around 50Lt.

Bicycle

VeloCity (5-261 2671; www.velo-city.lt; Bernardinų gatvė 10; 10am-7pm) rents bicycles for 10/40Lt per hour/day, provides information on cycling routes and arranges biking tours of the city.

Public Transport

Unless you're heading well out of Old Town, you won't have much need for public transport in Vilnius. Tickets cost 2Lt at news kiosks and 2.50Lt direct from the driver.

Taxi

Taxis officially charge 4Lt per kilometre (more at night) and must have a meter. To avoid rip-offs, order a **taxi** (☎1409, 1411, 1818, no prefix needed), or queue outside the train station.

AROUND VILNIUS

Paneriai

During WWII the Nazis – aided by Lithuanian accomplices – exterminated over 100,000 people, three-quarters of them Jews, at this site in the forest, 10km southwest of central Vilnius. From the entrance a path leads to the small **Paneriai Museum** (Agrastų gatvė 17; ⌚9am-5pm Wed-Sat; admission free) and the grassed-over pits where the Nazis burnt the exhumed bodies of their victims.

There are nearly two dozen trains daily from Vilnius to Paneriai station (2Lt, eight to 11 minutes), from where it's about a 1km walk southwest along Agrastų gatvė to the site.

Trakai

POP 5400

With its red-brick fairy-tale castle, Karaite culture, quaint wooden houses and pretty lakeside location, Trakai is a must-see within easy reach of the capital.

The Karaites are named after the term *kara*, which means 'to study the scriptures' in both Hebrew and Arabic. The sect originated in Baghdad and practises strict adherence to the Torah (rejecting the rabbinic Talmud). Grand Duke of Lithuania Vytautas brought about 380 Karaite families to Trakai from Crimea, in around 1400, to serve as bodyguards. Only 60 Karaites remain in Trakai today and their numbers – about 280 in Lithuania – are dwindling rapidly. This area has protected status as the **Trakai Historical National Park** (www.seniejitrakai.lt).

Trakai's trophy piece is the splendid **Island Castle**, occupying a small island in Lake Galvė. The painstakingly restored, red-brick Gothic castle dates to the late 14th century. Inside the castle's cellars and tower, the **Trakai History Museum** (www.trakaimuziejus.lt; adult/student 12/6Lt; ⌚10am-7pm) traces the history of the castle, with weaponry, coins and interactive displays.

You can sample *kibinai* (meat-stuffed Karaite pastries similar to empanadas) either at **Kibininė** (Karaimų gatvė 65; kibinai 3.80-7Lt) or at **Kybynlar** (Karaimų gatvė 29; mains 18-34Lt).

Up to 10 trains daily (6.20Lt, 35 minutes) travel between Trakai and Vilnius, while the more convenient Alytus-bound buses (5.60Lt, 40 minutes, twice hourly) stop closer to the castle.

WORTH A TRIP

GRŪTO PARKAS

Mildly controversial **Grūto Parkas** (www.grutoparkas.lt; admission 20Lt; ⌚9am-8pm), 125km south of Vilnius, near the spa town of Druskininkai, has been an enormous hit since it opened in 2001. The sprawling grounds, built to resemble a Siberian concentration camp, contain dozens of statues of Soviet heroes, exhibits on Soviet history and loudspeakers bellowing Soviet anthems. The statues once stood confidently in parks or squares across Lithuania.

There are up to 10 buses daily between Druskininkai and Vilnius, and hourly buses to/from Kaunas (both 30Lt, two hours). If going straight to Grūto Parkas, ask to be let off at Grūtas village, then walk the final 1km to the park.

CENTRAL LITHUANIA

Kaunas

POP 352,279

Lithuania's second city has a compact Old Town, a menagerie of artistic and educational museums, and plenty of vibrant, youthful energy provided by its sizeable student population.

Sights

OLD TOWN

In Kaunas' lovely Old Town, most streets lead to Rotušės aikštė (Central Sq), dominated by the 18th-century white, baroque former city hall, now the **Palace of Weddings**. On the northeastern corner of the square, **St Peter & Paul Cathedral** (Vilniaus gatvė 1) owes much to baroque reconstruction, but the early-15th-century Gothic shape of its windows remain. **Maironis' tomb** is outside the south wall of the cathedral.

NEW TOWN

Laisvės alėja, the 1.7km-long pedestrian street lined with bars, shops and restaurants, runs east from Old Town to New Town, dominated by the white, neo-Byzantine **St Michael the Archangel Church**.

TOP CHOICE **Ninth Fort Museum** MUSEUM
(Žemaičių plentas 73; admission 5Lt, catacombs with guide 10Lt; ⊙10am-6pm Wed-Mon) A poignant memorial to 80,000 people murdered by the Nazis, this excellent museum comprises the old WWI fort and a half-bunker/half-church. Displays cover deportations of Lithuanians by the Soviets as well as the fort's other uses. Take bus 23 from Jonavos gatvė to the Forto Muziejus stop, and take the pedestrian crossing under the motorway.

Sugihara House & Foundation MUSEUM
(Vaižganto gatvė 30; admission 10Lt; ⊙10am-5pm Mon-Fri, 11am-4pm Sat & Sun) Just east of New Town, the former home of Chiune Sugihara tells the story of the Japanese consul to Lithuania (1939–40), who saved 6000 lives by issuing transit visas (against orders) to Polish and Lithuanian Jews facing the advancing Nazi terror.

Museum of Devils MUSEUM
(Putvinskio gatvė 64; admission 6Lt; ⊙11am-5pm Tue-Sun) This superb museum contains more than 2000 devil statuettes from the mythologies of countries around the world.

Sleeping

Kauno Arkivyskupijos Svečių Namai B&B €
(☎37-322 597; http://kaunas.lcn.lt/sveciunamai; Rotušės aikštė 21; s/d/tr from 80/120/140Lt; @) This squeaky-clean jewel is enviably located in an old monastery wedged between two ancient churches. Rooms are spartan but spacious and management employs a number of ecofriendly practices; breakfast is not included.

Litinterp B&B €
(☎37-228 718; www.litinterp.com; Gedimino gatvė 28/7; s/d/tr from 120/160/210Lt) Not a lot of character, but rooms are cheap, clean and highly functional, and the staff are superfriendly and knowledgeable about the town.

Eating & Drinking

Senieji Rūsiai LITHUANIAN €€
(Vilniaus gatvė 34; mains 25-50Lt) Easily the tastiest street terrace at which to dine, drink and soak up Old Town. Its candlelit 17th-century cellar has great grilled meats, game dishes and the ubiquitous potato pancakes.

Žalias Ratas LITHUANIAN €
(Laisvės alėja 36b; mains 9-35Lt) Tucked away behind the tourist office is this pseudo-rustic inn where staff don traditional garb and bring piping-hot, belly-filling Lithuanian fare to eager customers.

BO BAR
(Muitinės gatvė 9) The 'Blue Orange' attracts an alternative student set and gets crammed to overflowing on weekends. Its own brew is a tasty but potent offering and there's live music some nights.

Information

Baitukas (www.baitukas.lt; K Donelaičio gatvė 26; per hr 6Lt; ⊙8am-7pm Mon-Fri, 10am-6pm Sat) Internet access.

Tourist office (☎37-323 436; www.kaunastic.lt; Laisvės alėja 36; ⊙9am-6pm Mon-Fri, 10am-6pm Sat, 10am-3pm Sun) Books accommodation, sells maps and guides, and arranges bicycle rental and guided tours of the Old Town.

Getting There & Away

From the **long-distance bus station** (☎37-409 060; Vytauto prospektas 24) buses leave for Vilnius (25Lt, 1¾ hours, up to three per hour), Klaipėda (50Lt, 2¾ hours, up to 18 daily), Šiauliai (35Lt, three hours, up to 18 daily), Rīga (54Lt, five hours, daily) and Tallinn (110Lt, nine hours, daily).

From the **train station** (☎37-221 093; Čiurlionio gatvė 16) there are 17 trains daily to/from Vilnius (12Lt, 1¼ hours) and one to Šiauliai (22.20Lt, 2½ hours).

For details of flights into Kaunas, see p813. The airport is 12km north of the Old Town. Take minibus 120 (2.50Lt) to/from Šv Gertrūdos gatvė (2.50Lt) or bus 29 from the stop on Vytauto prospektas (1.50Lt).

Šiauliai

POP 126,215

Lithuania's fourth-largest city is home to the country's most awe-inspiring sight, the legendary **Hill of Crosses** (Kryžių kalnas). It is a two-hump hillock blanketed by thousands of crosses. The sound of the breeze tinkling through the crosses that appear to grow on the hillock is eerie and unmissable.

Some of the crosses are devotional, others are memorials (many for people deported to

Siberia) and some are finely carved folk-art masterpieces. The crosses were bulldozed by the Soviets, but each night people crept past soldiers and barbed wire to plant yet more, risking their lives or freedom to express their national and spiritual fervour.

This strange place lies 12km north of Šiauliai – 10km north up highway A12, then 2km east from a well-marked turn-off (the sign says 'Kryžių kalnas 2'). You can rent a bike (5Lt per hour) from the **tourist office** (☎41-523 110; www.siauliai.lt/tic; Vilniaus gatvė 213; ⏲9am-6pm Mon-Fri, 10am-4pm Sat) and pedal out here, take a taxi (50Lt) or take a Joniškis-bound bus (2.70Lt, 10 minutes, up to nine daily), getting off at the Domantai stop and walking for 15 minutes.

Šiauliai College Youth Hostel (☎41-523 764; www.jnn.siauliukolegija.lt; Tilžės gatvė 159; s/d/tr 50/70/90Lt; ⊖) takes care of all your lodging needs, with spick-and-span rooms at incredibly low prices, and you'll find restaurants along the pedestrianised Vilniaus gatvė.

To get to Šiauliai take a bus from Vilnius (47Lt, three hours, up to 12 daily), Kaunas (35Lt, three hours, 21 daily), Klaipėda (35Lt, 3½ hours, up to six daily) or Rīga (34Lt, 2½ hours, up to six daily), or a train from Vilnius (35Lt, 2½ hours, three daily).

WESTERN LITHUANIA

Klaipėda

POP 182,716

Gritty Klaipėda is Lithuania's main port city and a gateway to the lush natural beauty of the Curonian Spit. It boasts a fascinating history as the East Prussian city of Memel, and a few buildings from that era still stand. The city celebrates its nautical heritage each July with a flamboyant **Sea Festival**.

The **tourist office** (☎46-412 186; www.klaipedainfo.lt; Turgaus gatvė 7; ⏲9am-7pm Mon-Fri, 10am-4pm Sat & Sun) is exceptionally efficient, selling maps, arranging accommodation, renting bicycles and providing internet access.

Sleeping & Eating

Klaipėda Travellers Hostel (☎46-211 879; www.klaipedahostel.com; Butkų Juzės gatvė 7/4; dm/d 44/88Lt; @📶) is poorly located near the bus station; consider forking out a bit more for the attractive, centrally located **Litinterp Guesthouse** (☎46-410 644; www.litinterp.com; Puodžių gatvė 17; s/d/tr with bathroom 110/180/240Lt, without bathroom 90/160/210Lt; P⊖@📶).

TOP CHOICE **Ararat** (Liepų gatvė 48a; mains 20-30Lt) specialises in superbly flavoured Armenian dishes, while **Pizza Bombola** (H Manto gatvė 1; mains 15-22Lt) serves consistently decent pizzas.

Getting There & Away

There are buses to Klaipėda from Vilnius (64Lt, four to 5½ hours, up to 15 daily), Kaunas (50Lt, 2¾ hours, up to 18 daily) and Šiauliai (35Lt, 3½ hours, five daily).

Trains arrive from Vilnius (51Lt, 4½ to five hours, three daily) and Šiauliai (23Lt, two to three hours, five daily).

The Curonian Spit

POP 3100

This magical sliver of land off the west coast hosts some of the world's most precious sand dunes and a menagerie of elk, deer and avian wildlife. The fragile spit, which Unesco recognised as a World Heritage Site in 2000, is divided roughly evenly between Lithuania and Russia's Kaliningrad region in the south. Lithuania's share is protected as the **Curonian Spit National Park** (www.nerija.lt).

Smiltynė, where the ferries from Klaipėda dock, is jammed on summer weekends with city slickers flocking to its beaches. You're better off heading south to laidback **Juodkrantė**, with its spooky wooden sculpture trail, **Raganų Kalnas** (Witches' Hill), or busier **Nida**, where there are fine guest houses and the unmissable 52m high **Parnidis Dune** with its panoramic views of 'Lithuania's Sahara'.

A flat cycling trail runs through pine forest all the way from Nida to Smiltynė, and you stand a good chance of seeing elk, boar or deer along that path. Don't miss a massive **colony of grey herons and cormorants**, 1km south of Juodkrantė – there's a breathtaking panorama of thousands of nests amid pine trees. There are bicycles for hire in all towns; some allow you to leave your bike in Smiltynė and bus back to Nida.

Litinterp Guesthouse (this page) in Klaipėda can help arrange accommodation, as can the **tourist offices** (www.visitneringa.lt). Private rooms are the cheapest option, going for around 90Lt per room.

Getting There & Away

To get to Smiltynė, board a ferry at the **Old Castle Port** (www.keltas.lt; Žvejų gatvė 8), due west of Klaipėda's Old Town (2.90Lt, 10 minutes, every 30 minutes). Vehicles must use the **New Port** (Nemuno gatvė 8), 2.5km south of the passenger terminal (per car 10Lt, at least hourly).

Buses and microbuses run throughout the day between Smiltynė and Nida (9Lt, one hour, at least six daily) via Juodkrantė.

UNDERSTAND LITHUANIA

History

Lithuania's history is a story of riches to rags and back again. It all started when ancient tribes fanned out across the Baltics to take advantage of the region's amber deposits. In the mid-13th century Aukštaitiai leader Mindaugas unified these tribes to create the Grand Duchy of Lithuania.

The country's golden era was from the 14th to 16th centuries. Vilnius was settled and Lithuania became one of Europe's largest empires. But in the 18th century Lithuania, which had merged with Poland, was carved up by Russia, Austria and Prussia in the partitions of Poland.

Lithuanian nationalists declared independence on 16 February 1918, but Vilnius was seized by Polish troops in 1920 and Kaunas became Lithuania's temporary capital for 19 years. Lithuania's first president, Antanas Smetona, ruled the country with an iron fist during this time.

During WWII the Nazis murdered up to 300,000 people, mostly Jews, in Lithuania – many of them at Paneriai. Between 1944 and 1952, under Soviet rule, 250,000 Lithuanians were killed or deported while armed partisans resisted Soviet rule from the forests.

In the late 1980s Lithuania was the first Soviet state to legalise noncommunist parties, and on 11 March 1990 the new majority party declared independence. Moscow responded by marching troops into Vilnius and in January 1991 Soviet troops stormed key buildings in Vilnius, killing 14 people. The Soviets recognised Lithuanian independence on 6 September 1991 and the first ex-USSR republic was born.

Lithuania joined NATO in April 2004 and entered the EU a month later. The country's enthusiasm for the EU continues unabated but the euro won't be introduced as currency until at least 2014. As with everything, EU membership has its downside: the country's younger generation is leaving in droves for the greener pastures of the UK and Ireland.

People

Easily the most ethnically homogeneous population of the three Baltic countries, Lithuanians account for 85% of the total population of 3,244,000. Poles form 6.3% and Russians 5.1%. The remaining 3.6% comprises various nationalities from Eastern Europe and further afield.

Lithuanians are an outgoing, cheeky bunch, especially compared to reticent Latvia and Estonia. That has led some to call them the 'Spanish of the Baltics'. Others call them the 'Italians of the Baltics', citing their fierce pride – a result of the many brutal attempts to eradicate their culture, and of memories of their long-lost empire.

The last pagan country in Europe, Lithuania is now 70% to 80% Roman Catholic.

Food

Price ranges for dining at eateries used in this chapter are as follows:

€€€ more than 65Lt

€€ from 35Lt to 65Lt

€ less than 35Lt

Environment

Lush forests and more than 4000 lakes mark the landscape of flat Lithuania. Forest covers a third of the country and contains creatures such as wild boar, wolves, deer and elk. However, you're much more likely to spot a stork, as Lithuania has Europe's highest concentration of storks. Come late summer and autumn, mushrooms and wild berries blanket the forest floor, creating a rich food source and a means of income for many rural dwellers who sell them from roadside stores.

For years the environmental hot potato has been the Ignalina Nuclear Power Plant, 120km northeast of Vilnius. One of two reactors similar in design to Chernobyl was closed in December 2004, and the final shutdown of the plant took place in 2009 at a massive cost of €3.2 billion.

SURVIVAL GUIDE

Directory A-Z

Accommodation

Vilnius has a serious room crunch so book ahead in high season. Rooms at coastal locations such as the Curonian Spit fill up months ahead in summer.

High-season prices are around 30% higher than low-season prices; expect to pay 140Lt to 200Lt for a budget double in high season.

Vilnius has numerous youth hostels and budget accommodation is easy to find outside the capital. Many budget guest houses now offer free internet or wi-fi.

Breakfast is included in the price unless stated otherwise.

Price ranges used in this chapter for a double room are as follows:

€€€ more than 450Lt

€€ from 200Lt to 450Lt

€ less than 200Lt

Business Hours

Banks 9am-5pm Mon-Fri

Bars 11am-midnight Sun-Thu, 11am-2am Fri & Sat

Clubs 10pm-5am Thu-Sat

Post offices 8am-8pm Mon-Fri, 10am-9pm Sat, 10am-5pm Sun

Restaurants noon-11pm; later on weekends, especially in cities

Shops 9am or 10am-7pm Mon-Fri; earlier Sat

Holidays

New Year's Day 1 January

Independence Day 16 February; anniversary of 1918 independence declaration

Lithuanian Independence Restoration Day 11 March

Easter Sunday March/April

Easter Monday March/April

International Labour Day 1 May

Mothers Day First Sunday in May

Feast of St John (Midsummer) 24 June

Statehood Day 6 July; commemoration of coronation of Grand Duke Mindaugas

Assumption of Blessed Virgin 15 August

All Saints' Day 1 November

Christmas 25 & 26 December

Money

The Lithuanian litas (the plural is litai; Lt) is divided into 100 centai.

All but the smallest Lithuanian towns have at least one bank with an ATM. Most big banks cash travellers cheques and exchange most major currencies. Credit cards are widely accepted.

A 10% tip in restaurants is appreciated.

Telephone

To call other cities within Lithuania, dial ☎8 followed by the city code and phone number. To make an international call, dial ☎00 before the country code. To call a mobile phone within Lithuania, dial ☎8 followed by the eight-digit number.

Prepaid SIM cards cost 6Lt to 7Lt.

Payphones – increasingly rare given the widespread use of mobiles – only accept phonecards, sold at news stands.

Visas

Citizens from Australia, Canada, Israel, Japan, New Zealand, Switzerland and the US do not require visas if staying for less than 90 days. EU citizens do not require visas and can stay indefinitely, as per the Schengen agreement. For information on other countries and obtaining a visa, visit www.migracija.lt.

Getting There & Away

Air

There are direct flights to Lithuania from a number of European cities, though none from North America. The reliable national airline, **airBaltic** (www.airbaltic.com), runs direct flights between Vilnius and about a dozen Western European destinations.

Vilnius is served by major international carriers, including Aer Lingus, Austrian Airlines, Czech Airlines, Lot, Lufthansa and also SAS.

Kaunas airport (☎37-399 307; www.kaunasair.lt; Savanorių prospektas) is the Ryanair hub with destinations including London, Dublin, Frankfurt, Berlin, Edinburgh as well as Birmingham.

Most international traffic to Lithuania still goes through **Vilnius International Airport** (☎5-273 9305; www.vno.lt; Rodūnė kelias 2). Destinations include London, Dublin, Frankfurt, Moscow, Oslo, Copenhagen and Warsaw.

Boat

From Klaipėda's **International Ferry Port** (Klaipėdos Nafta; ☎46-395 051; Perkėlos gatvė 10), **DFDS Seaways** (☎46-393 600; www.dfdslisco.com; J Janonio gatvė 24) runs passenger ferries to/from Kiel, Germany (from €46, 23 hours, six weekly), Sassnitz, Germany (from €37, 18 hours, three weekly), and Karlshamn, Sweden (from €62, 14 hours, daily).

Bus

The main international bus companies operating in Lithuania, at Vilnius, Kaunas and Klaipėda bus stations, are **Eurolines** (www.eurolines.lt) and **Ecolines** (www.ecolines.net).

Destinations from Vilnius include Rīga (60Lt, 4½ hours, at least four daily), Kaliningrad (65Lt, 7½ hours, daily), Tallinn (116Lt, 10½ hours, up to five daily), Warsaw (59Lt, nine hours, daily), Moscow (156Lt, 16 hours, daily), St Petersburg (153Lt, 16 hours, four daily), and Berlin via Rīga and Tallinn (310Lt, 34 hours, four daily).

Car & Motorcycle

You're looking at a 30-minute to one-hour wait at the two Polish border crossings (Ogrodniki and Budzisko). Lines at the Latvian border are generally nonexistent.

Train

Vilnius is linked by regular direct trains to Moscow (85Lt, 14¾ to 15¾ hours, up to three daily), St Petersburg (from 146Lt, 13½ to 18 hours, twice daily), Kaliningrad (from 84Lt, 6½ to 7½ hours, up to five daily), Minsk (from 74Lt, four to 4½ hours, up to seven daily) and Warsaw (from 130Lt, 8½ hours, one daily).

You'll need a Belarus visa for the Moscow train. For Warsaw, change in Šeštokai.

Getting Around

Bicycle

Lithuania is completely flat and easily explored by bike.

Tourist offices on the Curonian Spit and all the major cities rent bicycles. There are designated cycling lanes in the big cities and along the Curonian Spit.

Information about bike touring in Lithuania is found on **BaltiCCycle** (www.bicycle.lt).

Bus

Timetables for local buses are displayed prominently in most stations. The bus network is extensive, efficient and relatively inexpensive, and covers more destinations than the train network. See **Autobusbilitai** (www.autobusbilietai.lt) for both national and international bus information.

Car & Motorcycle

Modern four-lane highways link Vilnius and Klaipėda (via Kaunas). The speed limit in Lithuania is 50km/h in cities and 90km/h to 110km/h on highways.

The big international rental-car agencies are well represented at Vilnius International Airport. **Rimas** (☎5-277 6213, 8-698-21662) rents older cars at lower rates in Vilnius.

Local Transport

Lithuanian cities are generously covered by networks of buses, trolleybuses and minibuses. A ride costs between 1.20Lt and 2Lt, with a small discount if you buy tickets from a Lietuvos Spauda kiosk. Punch your ticket in one of the punch boxes inside the vehicle or risk a fine.

Train

The efficient train network run by **Lithuanian Railways** (www.litrail.lt) covers the larger cities. Trains are quite frequent, and marginally faster than buses, but also slightly more expensive.

Luxembourg

Includes »

Best Places to Stay

» Hôtel Simoncini, Luxembourg City (p819)

» HI Hostel Remerschen (p822)

Best Castles

» Vianden (p821)

» Bourscheid (p823)

» Larochette (p822)

» Beaufort (p822)

Why Go?

Which European nation, just 84km long, consistently rates amongst the world's three richest countries? Remarkably, the answer is Luxembourg (Luxemburg, Lëtzebuerg). That's quite an achievement for a mostly rural Grand Duchy that suffered wholesale destruction during WWII.

The nation's economic miracle started with steel, but developed with banking – so much so that neighbouring Belgians joke that people only visit to get their money out. That's unfair. Luxembourg's castle villages and attractively forested hills are extremely popular weekend getaways, with lovely forest-shaded hiking trails and well-paved country lanes to keep everything easily accessible. Luxembourg City's Unesco-listed historic core has a fairy-tale quality. And the vineyards of the Moselle Valley keep the population suitably supplied with fine, yet affordable, sparkling wine. Welcome to the good life.

When to Go

Luxembourg City

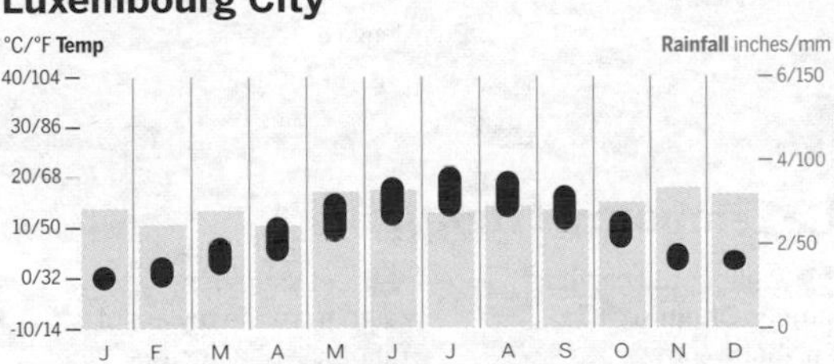

Feb–Mar Bonfires mark the symbolic burning of winter on the first weekend after Carnival.

May–Jun Sprinprozession dancing fills the streets of Echternach on the Tuesday after Whitsun.

Jul, Aug & weekends Luxembourg City's business hotels offer bargain deals, especially online.

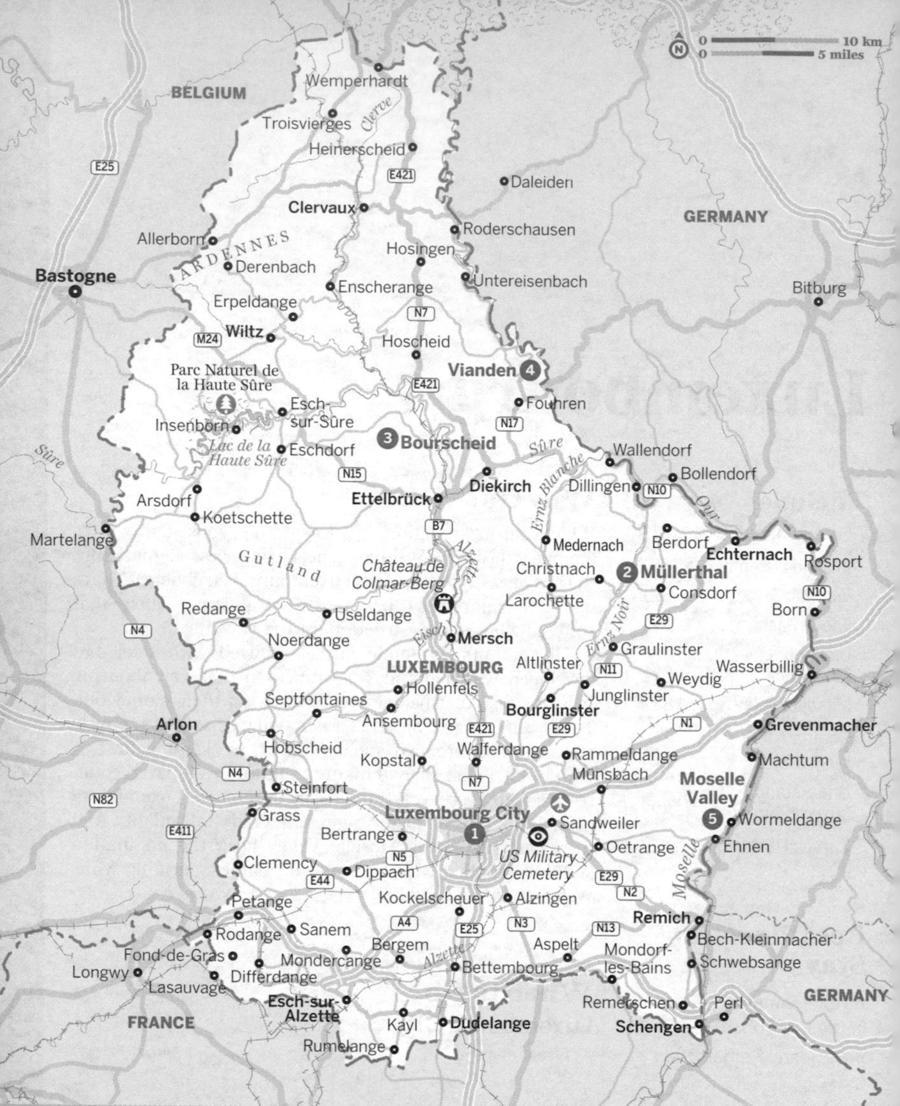

Luxembourg Highlights

1. Wander the capital's famous **Chemin de la Corniche** (p817)

2. Hike into the Tolkienesque woodlands of **Müllerthal** (p822)

3. Let your imagination reign from the towers of quintessential fortress **Château de Bourscheid** (p823)

4. Step back in time and explore **Vianden** (p821), the most evocative of rural Luxembourg's many appealing castle villages

5. Pop the fizz with the sparkling wines of Luxembourg's **Moselle Valley** (p822)

LUXEMBOURG CITY

POP 136,000

Sitting high on a promontory, Luxembourg City's Unesco-listed old town overlooks the deep-cut valleys of the Pétrusse and Alzette rivers. For 1000 years these gorges were the key to the city's defence. Now they provide visitors with spectacular vistas and enclose the interesting old quarters of Clausen, Pfaffenthal and the Grund, conveniently linked to the old-town plateau by an elevator on Plateau du St-Esprit.

Sights

OLD TOWN

The old town's most charming knot of crooked lanes lies behind the impressive royal palace. Directly west is the distinctive **Cathédrale Notre Dame** with its unusually elongated black spires, and **Place Guillaume II**, lined with stately 19th-century buildings. Across the dramatic Pétrusse valley, the distinctively spired 1909 **Spuerkeess** (www.spuerkeess.lu; 1 Place de Metz; ⏲9am-5.30pm Mon-Fri) building houses a little-publicised free **banking museum** and subterranean **Am Tunnel photography gallery** (accessed separately from 16 Rue Ste Zithe, two blocks further south).

> 
>
> **LUXEMBOURG CARD**
>
> The brilliant-value **Luxembourg Card** (www.ont.lu/card-en.html; 1/2/3 days adult €10/17/24, family €20/34/48), marked LC in reviews, allows free admission to most of the Grand Duchy's main attractions and gives unlimited use of public transport nationwide. Buy from tourist offices, museums or certain hotels.

Chemin de la Corniche PROMENADE

Hailed as 'Europe's most beautiful balcony', this pedestrian promenade offers excellent canyon views as it winds along the course of the former city ramparts. Although much was ripped out after 1867, you can still explore the mildly intriguing **Bock Casemates** (Montée de Clausen; admission €3; ⏲10am-5pm Mar-Oct), a honeycomb of damp 18th-century subterranean rock-cut galleries and passages that have housed everything from bakeries to slaughterhouses and garrisons of soldiers.

Palais Grand-Ducal ROYAL PALACE

(17 Rue du Marché-aux Herbes) Photogenically a-twitter with little pointy turrets, this much-extended 1573 palace houses the Grand Duke's office, while Luxembourg's parliament occupies its 1859 annex. In mid-summer, humorous tours (€7), booked via the Luxembourg City tourist office, can get you inside.

Musée d'Histoire de la Ville de Luxembourg MUSEUM

(www.mhvl.lu; 14 Rue du St-Esprit; adult/concession/LC €5/3/free, Thu evening free; ⏲10am-6pm Tue-Sun, to 8pm Thu) This remarkably engrossing and interactive museum hides within a series of 17th-century houses.

MNHA MUSEUM

(Musée National d'Histoire et d'Art; www.mnha.lu; Marché-aux-Poissons; adult/LC €5/free; ⏲10am-6pm Tue-Sun, to 8pm Thu) Startlingly modern for its old-town setting, this impressive museum offers a fascinating, if uneven, coverage of art and history.

KIRCHBERG

Kirchberg is a district of gleaming glass-and-concrete buildings, many hosting EU institutions. Access is on buses 1, 13 or 16 to 'Philharmonie' and various points including the train station and Pl Hamilius.

> **LUXEMBOURG FACTS**
>
> - **Area** 2586 sq km
> - **Capital** Luxembourg City
> - **Language** Lëtzebuergesch, French, German
> - **Currency** Euro (€)
> - **Money** ATMs common in towns but not in villages
> - **Country code** ☎352
> - **Emergency** Ambulance & fire ☎112, police ☎113
> - **Visas** Schengen visa rules apply (see p1319)
> - **Budget hotel double** €85
> - **Two-course evening meal** from €25
> - **Museum entrance** €5 to €9
> - **Itinerary** Visit Luxembourg City during a weekend, when hotel rates are low. Contrast the craggy, ancient heart of the city with its gleaming art galleries and modern museums. Then go wine tasting in the Moselle Valley, hiking around Echternach or castle hunting in rural villages. Finish up at fairy-tale Vianden.

Luxembourg City

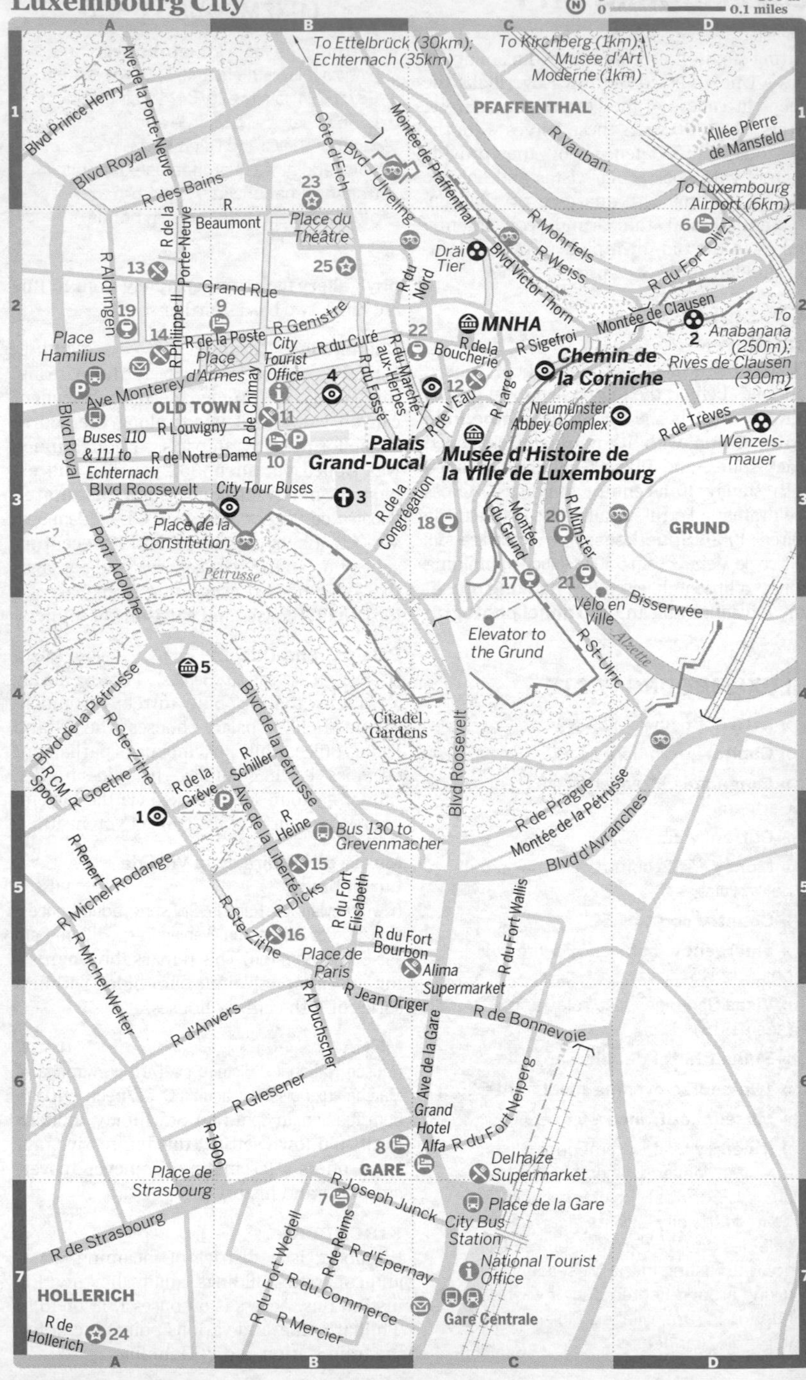

Luxembourg City

Top Sights
- Chemin de la Corniche ... C2
- MNHA ... C2
- Musée d'Histoire de la Ville de Luxembourg ... C3
- Palais Grand-Ducal ... C2

Sights
1. Am Tunnel Photography Gallery ... A5
2. Bock Casemates ... D2
3. Cathédrale Notre Dame ... B3
4. Place Guillaume II ... B2
5. Spuerkeess ... A4

Sleeping
6. Auberge de Jeunesse ... D2
7. Auberge de Reims ... B7
8. Carlton Hôtel ... B6
9. Hôtel Français ... B2
10. Hôtel Simoncini ... B3

Eating
11. Á La Soupe ... B3
12. Am Tiirmschen ... C2
13. Exki ... A2
14. La Table du Pain ... A2
15. La Table du Pain ... B5
16. Restaurant Tibet ... B5

Drinking
17. Café des Artistes ... C3
18. d:qliq ... C3
19. L'Interview ... A2
20. Liquid Café ... C3
21. Scotts ... C3
22. Urban Bar ... C2

Entertainment
23. Cinémathèque ... B1
24. Den Atelier ... A7
25. Secret Garden ... B2

Mudam ART GALLERY
(www.mudam.lu; 3 Parc Dräi Eechelen; adult/concession/LC €5/3/free; ⌚11am-8pm Wed-Fri, 11am-6pm Sat-Mon) Ground-breaking exhibitions in a 2006 architectural icon designed by IM Pei. The building's glass-roofed wings are best admired from the next-door **Fort Thüngen** (Musée Dräi Eechelen; admission free; ⌚10am-4pm Tue-Sun), a 1730 twin-towered remnant of Kirchberg's once-vast complex of Vauban fortifications. To return to the city centre on foot, tunnel through **Fort Obergrünwald**, turn left (easily missed) and descend a long zigzag stairway that emerges near the railway viaduct and youth hostel.

HAMM

US Military Cemetery CEMETERY
(⌚9am-5pm) In this beautifully maintained graveyard near Hamm lie over 5000 US WWII dead, including the audacious General George S Patton Jr, who was instrumental in Luxembourg's 1944 liberation. Take bus 15 from Hôtel Alfa to Käschtewee (15 minutes, every 20 minutes weekdays, variable Saturdays, every 40 minutes Sunday) then walk 10 minutes east.

Sleeping

Luxembourg City's numerous business hotels slash prices at weekends and during July and August when online bargains are commonplace. Around the train station, hotels are generally less expensive but the cheapest (no reservations!) are, not coincidentally, clustered around the tiny red-light district on Rue Junck.

Hôtel Simoncini DESIGN HOTEL €€
(☎22 28 44; www.hotelsimoncini.lu; 6 Rue de Notre Dame; s/d/tr/ste Mon-Fri €135/160/185/200, Sat & Sun €110/120/145/160; @) With a lobby that doubles as a modern-art galley, this brilliantly central hotel has pristine white rooms with occasional touches of colourful retro-cool.

Auberge de Jeunesse HOSTEL €
(☎22 68 89; www.youthhostels.lu; 2 Rue du Fort Olizy; HI members dm/s/d €20/35/52; P ⊖ @ ⓦ) Large modern hostel with plenty of sitting space and a very inexpensive restaurant. It's five minutes' walk steeply down from the 'Plateau Altmünster' bus stop (routes 9, 14). There are alternative HI hostels within an hour's bus ride at Bourglinster (p822), Larochette (p822), and Remerschen (p822).

Hôtel Français HOTEL €€
(☎47 45 34; www.hotelfrancais.lu; 14 Place d'Armes; s/d Mon-Fri €120/140, Sat & Sun €99/125; @) Handily central with 24 presentable, if somewhat small rooms above a popular, supercentral brasserie.

Carlton Hôtel HERITAGE HOTEL €€
(☎29 96 60; www.carlton.lu; 9 Rue de Strasbourg; s/d Mon-Fri €110/125, Sat & Sun €70/85; ⊖ @) Fair-value, modernised rooms in a 1920s

building with stained-glass windows in the foyer.

Auberge de Reims CRASH PAD €
(17 Rue Junck; s/d/tr without bathroom €40/45/50) If saving money is all that counts.

Eating

Around tree-shaded **Place d'Armes** options range from €13 Chinese buffets and fast-food chains to upper-market brasseries stretching down Rue de Chimay. Around **Place de Paris** are several cheaper bar-pizzerias, a sandwich shop, kebab stand and Thai/Chinese eateries with meal deals from €7. For intimate and more original dining options explore the **Ilôt Gourmand** passageways directly behind the palace.

Am Tiirmschen LUXEMBOURGISH €€
(26 27 07 33; www.amtiirmschen.lu; 32 rue de l'Eau, Ilôt Gourmand; mains €15-25; noon-2pm Mon-Fri & 7-10.30pm Tue-Sat) A great pseudo-antique place to sample typical Luxembourg dishes, but there are also French options for those who don't fancy *kniddelen* or smoked pork.

Restaurant Tibet INDIAN/HIMALAYAN €€
(26 48 59; http://tibetrestaurant.com/index.php; 39 Rue St-Zithe; meals €11-16; 11.45am-2pm & 6-11pm) Colourful, incense-scented restaurant offering good-value weekday lunch buffets (€11, prebook). Meal prices include rice.

Anabanana VEGAN €
(www.anabanana.lu; 117 rue de la Tour Jacob; sandwich/lunch/dinner €5/12/18; noon-2pm Tue-Fri & 7-9.45pm Tue-Sat) This colourfully quaint little vegan-fusion restaurant serves a daily-changing fixed dinner. No alcohol; juice €4.50.

Exki ORGANIC FAST-FOOD €
(www.exki.lu; 72 Grand Rue; light meals €3.85-7.15; 7am-7pm Mon-Fri, 8am-6.30pm Sat;) Modern self-service cafe-chain offering wholesome organic food and free wi-fi. Before 11am coffee costs €1.

Á la Soupe SOUP BAR €
(www.alasoupe.net; Rue de Chimay; breakfast €3.50-7, soup €4.50-9; 7am-8.45pm Mon-Sat) Central soup station.

La Table du Pain BAKERY-CAFE €
(www.tabledupain.lu; 7am-6pm Mon-Fri) Ville (19 Ave Monterey); Gare (37 Ave de la Liberté) Convivial neo-rustic bakery-cafes.

Drinking

Rives de Clausen NIGHTLIFE AREA
(www.rivesdeclausen.com) Nine themed bar-resto clubs form the city's liveliest youth scene in the repurposed former Mousel brewery complex. Weekend shuttle buses back to Rue des Bains run until 3.30am.

Urban Bar BAR
(www.urban.lu/urbancity.html; 2 Rue de la Boucherie; noon-1am Sun-Thu, noon-3am Fri & Sat) Hip, crushed-full cafe with waves of '70s-retro foam panelling suggesting a *Star Trek* set.

Liquid Café PUB-CAFE
(www.liquid.lu; 17 Rue Münster; 5pm-1am Mon-Fri, 8pm-1am Sat & Sun) Live jazz Tuesdays, blues gigs Thursdays.

d:qliq BAR-CLUB
(www.dqliq.com; 17 Rue du St-Esprit; 5pm-1am Tue-Thu, 6pm-3am Fri & Sat) DJs and live lesser-known bands in a small, graffiti-chic old-town bar.

Café des Artistes BAR
(22 Montée du Grund; evenings Tue-Sun) Atmospheric cafe, where the piano bursts into life Wednesday to Saturday evenings.

L'Interview CAFE
(Rue Aldringen; 7.30am-1am) Mirrors, wood panelling, great cappuccinos and a pre-party student-aged crowd by night.

Scotts PUB
(Bisserwée; 11am-1am) Outdoor seating perched right above the river.

Entertainment

For listings see www.agendalux.lu, www.luxembourgticket.lu, www.nightlife-mag.lu or www.rave.lu. Note that the country's two biggest rock/pop music venues, **Rockhal** (www.rockhal.lu) and **Kulturfabrik** (www.kulturfabrik.lu), are both a 20-minute train ride away in Esch-sur-Alzette.

Philharmonie CONCERT HALL
(www.philharmonie.lu; 1 Place de l'Europe) Performances range from jazz to classical and opera in what looks like an interstellar space-port.

Cinémathèque CINEMA
(17 Place du Théâtre; adult/concession €3.70/2.40) Great-value art-house offerings.

Secret Garden NIGHTCLUB
(www.secretgarden.lu; 7 Côte d'Eich; cover €10; 10pm-1am Tue, 10pm-3am Wed, 10pm-6am

Thu-Sat) Lively club carved out of old-town houses. Cover includes one drink.

Den Atelier LIVE MUSIC
(www.atelier.lu; 56 Rue de Hollerich) Odd location, decent concerts.

Information

Bibliothèque Municipale (3 Rue Genistre; 10am-7pm Tue-Fri, 10am-6pm Sat). Sign up (with ID) for one hour's free internet. No printing.

Cyber Multimedia (8 Rue de Bonnevoie; internet per hr €2.50; 9am-8pm Mon-Fri, 10am-8pm Sat, 2-8pm Sun)

Luggage lockers (Gare Centrale platform 3; per day €2-4; 6am-9.30pm) Inaccessible at night.

Luxembourg City tourist office (22 28 09; www.lcto.lu; Place Guillaume II; 9am-6pm Mon-Sat, 10am-6pm Sun) Walking tours depart 2pm summer, 1pm winter.

Luxembourg National tourist office (42 82 82 20; www.ont.lu; Gare Centrale concourse; 9.30am-12.30pm & 1-5.30pm) City and national information.

Getting Around

From the train station virtually any bus departing from the platforms to the right as you exit will run to Place Hamilius in the city centre. Or just walk 1.25km straight up Ave de la Gare.

For short hops (under half an hour) use the automated **Velóh** (www.en.veloh.lu; membership per week/year €1/15; 24hr) bike-rental system. Read their regulations carefully. Longer-term hires from **Vélo en Ville** (47 96 23 83; 8 Bisserwée; half-/full-day €12.50/20).

AROUND LUXEMBOURG

Nowhere in Luxembourg is much more than an hour's drive from the capital. Bus connections are efficient even for rural villages.

Vianden

POP 1600

Palace, citadel or fortified cathedral? At first glance it's hard to tell just what it is that towers so grandly above magical little Vianden. In fact it's a vast slate-roofed **castle** (www.castle-vianden.lu; adult/concession/LC €6/4.50/free; 10am-4pm Nov-Feb, 10am-5pm Mar & Oct, 10am-6pm Apr-Sep), entered through a modern exhibition hall and portcullis gate into a vaulted hall full of pikes and armour. Some later rooms are furnished in medieval style.

Grand Rue, Vianden's photogenically cobbled main street, rises 700m to the castle gates from the riverside **tourist office** (83 42 57 1; www.vianden-info.lu; 1a Rue du Vieux Marché; 8am-noon & 1-5pm Mon-Fri, 10am-2pm some weekends). It's lined with several historic buildings, minor museums and family hotels, with several more sleeping and dining options along the riverbanks.

Auberge Aal Veinen (83 43 68; www.hotel-aal-veinen.lu; 114 Grand Rue; s/d €60/80; closed mid-Dec–mid-Jan;) offers eight stylishly refitted guest rooms, seamlessly inserted into an ultra-quaint barrage of ancient wooden beamwork above a cosy medieval **restaurant** (meals €8-27, closed Tue).

The **HI Hostel** (Auberge de Jeunesse; 83 41 77; www.youthhostels.lu; 3 Montée du Château; members dm/s/d €16/28/42;) is close to the castle entrance, so before lugging your bags up the hill be aware that reception is closed between 10am and 5pm.

Lajolla Lounge (www.aubergevianden.lu/en; 35 Rue de la Gare; snacks €7-12, mains €12-24; 10am-10pm), across the main bridge from the tourist office, has an open-air riverside terrace with great castle views.

Bus 570 to/from Diekirch (18 minutes) runs twice hourly on weekdays, less at weekends. It stops briefly beside the bridge.

Echternach

POP 5100

Useful as a Müllerthal hiking base, the ancient town of Echternach has some modest Roman remains, a pretty central square and a gigantic **basilica** (9.30am-6.30pm) that was rebuilt in sombre neo-Romanesque style after suffering merciless WWII bombing. This is Luxembourg's most important religious structure, its crypt housing the sacred relics of its founder, the Northumbrian missionary St-Willibrord (658–739AD).

Between the basilica's main door and the **tourist office** (72 02 30; www.echternach-tourist.lu; Parvis de la Basilique; 9.30am-5.30pm Mon-Fri, daily Jul & Aug), cross a courtyard flanked by reconstructed 18th-century abbey buildings to find the poorly marked entrance to **Musée de l'Abbaye** (adult/LC €3/free; 10am-noon & 2-6pm). Here, amid ancient codex copies in vaulted subterranean cellars that once housed Europe's foremost medieval scriptorium, you can watch a video about Echternach's world famous **dancing**

procession (Sprinprozession), which takes place on the Tuesday after Whitsun.

Hotels and fair-priced street cafes line Rue de la Gare, the pedestrianised street that links the bus station to the main square, Place du Marché, where there's further choice.

Hostellerie de la Basilique (☎72 94 83; www.hotel-basilique.lu; 7 Place du Marché; s/d/tr €94/121/166; ⊙Easter–mid-Nov; ❄@☜) is Echternach's best address, offering 14 tidy rooms with stone-tiled floors and monogrammed linens. Set in a lakeside country park, Echternach's modern **HI Hostel** (Auberge de Jeunesse; ☎72 01 58; echternach@youthhostels.lu; members dm/s €18/29, dinner €9; ⊙reception 8-10am & 5-10pm; P⊖☜) rents mountain bikes (half-/full day €8/15) and features a popular **climbing wall** (guest/nonguest €3.50/6; ⊙7-10pm Tue, Wed, Fri & Sat). To get there from Echternach's main square, head 800m southwest to the fire station (facing the Q8 petrol station) or get off Luxembourg City–Echternach route 110 at bus stop Centre de Secours. Then head 1.2km southeast, in the direction of Rodenhof/Roudenhaff.

Bus 111 takes an alternative route to Luxembourg City (55 minutes, hourly) via Berdorf.

MÜLLERTHAL TRAILS

West of Echternach, well-signposted **forest trails** (www.mullerthal-trail.lu) take hikers through shoulder-wide micro-gorges, across trickling streams with mossy banks and past distinctively eroded sandstone formations. This is hardly Bryce Canyon but quaintness trumps grandeur and one almost expects to meet Asterix and his band around the next rocky pinnacle. There are handily accessible tasters right beside the main road either side of Berdorf village (itself utterly uninteresting). Alternatively try hiking the **E1** (11.7km, four hours), a well-marked circular path that starts up Rue Charly from Echternach bus station and winds through the intriguing **Gorge du Loup**. If this whets your appetite, other Müllerthal trails offer longer alternatives, exploring Luxembourg's misleadingly monikered 'Little Switzerland'. It refers to a patchwork of forests and grassy fields so don't imagine even the vaguest hint of an Alpine peak.

To get to Diekirch, bus 500 is direct. Alternatively take a Larochette-bound bus 414 to Beaufort, visit Beaufort's imposing five-storey **fortress ruin** (www.beaufort.lu; adult/concession/LC €3/2/free, audio guide €3; ⊙9am-6pm Apr-Oct), then continue by getting on bus 502.

Diekirch & Ettelbrück

Of many museums commemorating 1944's Battle of the Ardennes, Diekirch's **Musée National d'Histoire Militaire** (www.mnhm.lu; 110 Rue Bamertal; adult/LC €5/free, WWII veterans free; ⊙10am-6pm Apr–mid-Nov, 2-6pm mid-Nov–Mar) is Luxembourg's most comprehensive and visual, packed full of WWII weaponry, vehicles and numerous well-executed mannequin scenes. It's 10 minutes' walk north of Diekirch's train station. Twice-hourly trains take 40 minutes to Luxembourg City via Ettelbrück (10 minutes), a useful transport hub with bus connections to Bastogne (Belgium).

Bus 100 between Luxembourg City and Diekirch runs via sleepy **Bourglinster** and touristy **Larochette** (www.larochette.eu). Both have HI Hostels and impressive castle ruins.

Moselle Valley

Welcome to wine country. While towns here are nothing special, the Moselle River's steeply rising banks are attractively smothered in the neatly clipped vineyards that produce Luxembourg's balanced Rieslings, fruity Rivaners and excellent *crémants* (sparkling *méthode traditionelle* wines). Taste a selection at the grand **Caves Bernard-Massard** (www.bernard-massard.lu; 8 Rue du Pont; tours from €4; ⊙9.30am-6pm Apr-Oct) in central Grevenmacher where frequent 20-minute winery **tours** are multilingual, spiced with humour and culminate in a genteel sampling cafe. Bus 130 from Rue Heine in Luxembourg City (55 minutes, up to twice hourly) stops outside. Bus 450 continues south through typical wine country to Remich, from where bus 175 returns to Luxembourg City.

Further south at **Remerschen** (on Schengen-bound bus 185 from Luxembourg City) there's a superb new **HI Hostel** (☎26 66 73-1) across the road from an inexpensive wine-tasting bar.

WORTH A TRIP

BOURSCHEID

Château de Bourscheid (www.bourscheid.lu; adult/senior/LC €5/4/free; ⏲9.30am 5.30pm Apr–mid-Oct, 11am-4pm mid-Oct–Mar) is Luxembourg's most evocative castle, a dreamy array of turrets and towers superbly situated on a lonely, rocky bluff amid forested hills. From Ettelbrück take bus 545 (8km) to Bourscheid village, walk 1.8km down to the castle (don't miss the great viewpoint from the caravan park en route). To return, descend 2km further to the N27 road for bus 550 back to Ettelbrück.

UNDERSTAND LUXEMBOURG

History

In 963 Count Sigefroi of Ardennes built a castle on a promontory in the forested heart of Western Europe, the original foundations of what would one day become Luxembourg City. Besieged and rebuilt time and time again, it eventually grew to become one of Europe's strongest fortresses. After Waterloo (1815) Luxembourg was declared a Grand Duchy under the Dutch king. When Belgium declared independence from the Netherlands (1830) it tried to take Luxembourg along but an eventual compromise split the Grand Duchy in half (1839), leaving strategically important Luxembourg City in the Dutch part. In 1867, to defuse political friction between its neighbours, Luxembourg was declared neutral and the bulk of the capital's historic fortifications were dismantled.

Wilhelmina became queen of the Netherlands in 1890. However, Luxembourg's rules of succession demanded a male ruler. This odd quirk resulted in Luxembourg's previously nominal independence becoming reality.

Germany occupied Luxembourg during both world wars. Although liberated in September 1944, the country was devastated three months later during Hitler's last-gasp counter-offensive, the Battle of the Ardennes. After the war, the government became a noted financial centre and tax haven. Luxembourg also became home to several key EU institutions. Today the country enjoys affluence and stability, and has one of Europe's healthiest economies.

People

Luxembourg's population is 492,000. A motto occasionally seen carved in stone walls sums up the people's self-assured character: *Mir wëlle bleiwe wat mir sin* (We want to remain what we are). *Moien* is a handy greeting in Lëtzebuergesch but, day to day, French is more commonly spoken. A third of all Luxembourgers are immigrants.

Food & Drink

Luxembourg's national dish, *judd mat gaardebounen*, is smoked pork-neck in a cream-based sauce with chunks of potato and broad beans. Other specialities include *ferkels-rippchen* (grilled spare ribs), sauerkraut, *traipen* (black pudding), *kuddelfleck* (boiled tripe), *paschtéit* (filled vol-au-vent) and *kachkeis* (cooked cheese). *Kniddelen* (dumplings) are typically gnocchi-style balls served in various sauces but the term can also refer to meatballs. Luxembourg City restaurants also have all kinds of international food.

The Moselle Valley produces fruity white wines and affordable yet high-quality bubbly. Local lager-style beers include Bofferding, Diekirch, Mousel and Simon Pils.

Prices for typical mains are given in our reviews, which use the following ranges:

€€€ more than €20

€€ €10 to €20

€ less than €10

SURVIVAL GUIDE

Directory A-Z

Accommodation

Prices in this chapter are for a midweek double room with bathroom, unless otherwise mentioned. Price indicators are as follows:

€ less than €70

€€ €70 to €200

€€€ more than €200

Camping grounds These are abundant in the central and northern regions.

Holiday house rentals Plentiful for those staying awhile (www.gites.lu).

Hostels Ten HI-affiliated hostels (www.youthhostels.lu) cost from €16 to €21, including breakfast and sheets. HI non-members pay €3 extra.

Hotels Budget hotels are rare but Luxembourg City's business hotels offer serious weekend and summer discounts, especially for online bookings.

Business Hours

Banks 8.30am-4.30pm Mon-Fri, 8.30am-noon Sat

Post offices 9am-5pm Mon-Fri, 9am-noon Sat

Pubs & bars 11am-1am

Restaurants noon-2pm & 7-10.30pm

Shops 9am-6pm Mon-Sat, some close for lunch

Holidays

New Year's Day 1 January

Easter Monday March/April

May Day 1 May

Ascension Day 40th day after Easter

Whit Monday 7th Monday after Easter

National Day 23 June

Assumption 15 August

All Saints' Day 1 November

Christmas Day 25 December

Internet Resources

Dining (www.gastronomie.lu)

FAQs (www.luxembourg.co.uk/faq.html)

Luxembourg City (www.vdl.lu)

Maps of Luxembourg City (www.topographie.lu)

Tourist office (www.ont.lu)

Transport links (www.rail.lu)

Wine (www.ivv.public.lu)

Money

ATMs are common in towns, but not in villages. Despite all the banks, relatively few offer currency exchange. Tipping is not obligatory; service and taxes are included in restaurant prices.

Telephone

It is cheap and easy to purchase a SIM card, which should work in any unlocked mobile phone on the GSM system (global standard except in Japan and North America). Choose between providers **Tango** (www.tango.lu), **LuxGSM** (www.luxgsm.lu) and **Vox** (www.vox.lu).

Getting There & Away

Air

Luxembourg airport (LUX; www.luxairport.lu) is 6km east of the capital by bus 16 (from the train station and Place Hamilius) or bus 9 (via Plateau Altmünster for the youth hostel). **Luxair** (www.luxair.lu) and six other carriers fly to major European destinations. For budget flights, take regular **Flibco** (www.flibco.com) buses from Luxembourg bus/train station to Germany's Frankfurt-Hahn Airport (advance/last-minute €5/17, two hours, hourly via Trier) or Belgium's Charleroi Airport (€5/22, 2½ hours via Arlon).

Bus & Train

Local cross-border buses link Bastogne with Ettelbrück and Luxembourg City with Trier and Saarlouis.

International train services from Luxembourg City include Brussels (€34.60, three hours, 18 daily), Koblenz (direct/changing in Trier €37.40/34.40, 2¼ hours) hourly, Paris (€49 to €94.40, 2¼ hours, five daily TGV with compulsory reservation) and Trier (fast/slow €18.40/15.40, 41/49 minutes, roughly hourly).

Car & Motorcycle

Fuel prices are the lowest in Western Europe so fill her up. The motorway speed limit is 130km/h.

Getting Around

An elegantly simple fare system covers all buses and trains, except services to/from border-crossing points. Either buy a €1.50 *kuurzzäitbilljee* (*billet courte durée*), valid two hours from the time you date-stamp it, or get a €4 *dagesbilljee* (*billet longue durée*), valid until 8am the next morning. Paying aboard a bus is fine but paying aboard a train can attract a €1.50 supplement. For timetables, see www.autobus.lu and www.cfl.lu.

Macedonia
Македонија

Includes »

Best Places to Eat

» Stara Gradska Kuča, Skopje (p829)

» Letna Bavča Kaneo, Ohrid (p833)

» Idadija, Skopje (p830)

Best Places to Stay

» Hotel TCC Plaza, Skopje (p829)

» Villa Dihovo, Bitola (p834)

» Vila Sveta Sofija, Ohrid (p833)

» Chola Guest House, Bitola (p834)

Why Go?

Pound for pound, Macedonia's hard to beat. Part Balkan and part Mediterranean, and offering impressive ancient sites and buzzing modern nightlife, the country packs in much more action, activities and natural beauty than would seem possible for a place its size. Because it's small, getting around is easy and cheap.

In summer, try hiking, mountain biking and climbing in remote mountains, or explore the Old Towns of the capital, Skopje, and Ohrid, noted for its sublime Byzantine churches and an immense lake that's great for swimming.

Still largely undiscovered, Macedonia retains an authenticity somewhat lacking elsewhere in Europe, as visitors will discover among the hospitable, laid-back locals. Agriculture remains vital, as seen by the endless vineyards, watermelon pyramids, hanging red peppers and tobacco plains dotted with storks' nests.

When to Go

Skopje

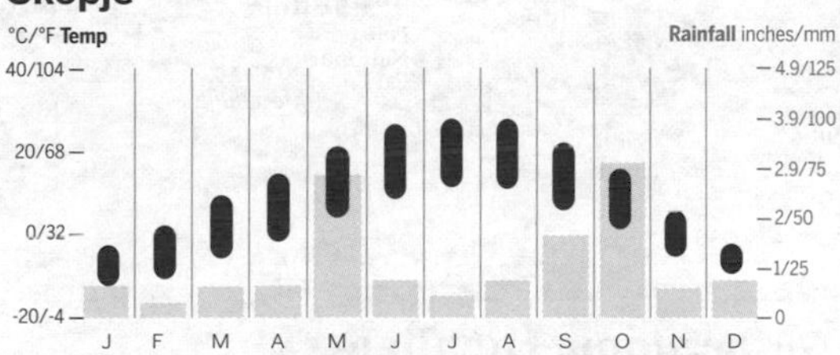

Jun–Aug Enjoy the Ohrid Summer Festival's concerts and nightlife, and dive into Ohrid's lake.

Sep & Oct An Indian summer sees Skopje's Beer Fest, Pivolend, and harvest celebrations.

Dec–Feb Ski mountain getaways and experience Macedonia's idiosyncratic winter carnivals.

Skopje Скопје

☎02 / POP 670,000

Skopje's transformation continues: once a drab, foregone former communist conclusion, it's still concrete, but now adorned with an odd assortment of statues, sculptures and grand buildings. While still thus reserved for experiments in architecture, Skopje's also becoming a livelier place to visit galleries, eat, drink and make merry, as well as boasting numerous historic and cultural attractions to entice visitors.

Confined by the forested Mt Vodno and bisected by the Vardar River, Skopje in winter is enveloped by an all-pervasive fog, symbolic of the conspiratorial overtones of a small Balkan city haunted by foreign diplomats and partisan intrigue. But it also offers Ottoman- and Byzantine-era wonders such as the 15th-century Kameni Most (Stone Bridge), the Čaršija (old Turkish bazaar), the Church of Sveti Spas, with its ornate, hand-carved iconostasis, and the nearby Tvrdina Kale fortress, Skopje's guardian since the 5th century.

Macedonia Highlights

1. Gaze out over Ohrid from the **Church of Sveti Jovan at Kaneo** (p831), immaculately set on a bluff above the lake

2. Unwind in historic **Skopje** (below), combining Ottoman and Byzantine architecture with nightlife

3. Enjoy the old-world ambience of **Bitola** (p833) and visit nearby Pelister National Park

MACEDONIA FACTS

» **Area** 25,713 sq km

» **Capital** Skopje

» **Language** Macedonian

» **Currency** Macedonian denar (MKD)

» **Money** ATMs are widespread in major towns

» **Exchange rates** A$1 = 45.11MKD; C$1 = 44.09MKD; €1 = 61.15MKD; ¥100 = 51.05MKD; NZ$1 = 33.64MKD; UK£1 = 69.32MKD; US$1 = 42.03MKD

» **Country code** ☎389

» **Emergency** Police ☎192; Ambulance ☎194

» **Visas** Not necessary for EU, US, Australian, Canadian or New Zealand citizens

» **Itinerary** Enjoy Skopje's old-town attractions and cafe life for a day, then experience Ohrid's culture, churches and lake for two days

Sights

Ploštad Makedonija MAIN SQUARE

Skopje's main square contains cafes and audacious new statues dedicated to various national heroes, plus smaller works depicting mundane urban life. Cross Dimitrije Čupovski to embrace the cafe life of pedestrianised ul Makedonija.

Čaršija OLD MARKET

From the main square, cross the Vardar River on **Kameni Most** and enter the Čaršija, where Skopje's Ottoman past lingers on in its architecture and largely Muslim Albanian and Turkish population. On the left, the **Church of Sveti Dimitrija** (⊙9am-6pm) is a three-aisled structure dating from 1886.

Behind the church stands the brand-new **Holocaust Memorial Center of the Jews from Macedonia** (www.holocaustfund.org; 11 Mart b.b; admission free; ⊙9am-5pm Tues-Sun), opened in March 2011, that commemorates the all-but-lost Sephardic Jewish culture of Macedonia through educational photos, wall texts, maps and video. During the Holocaust 7148 Macedonian Jews perished.

Across from Sveti Dimitrija, the double domes of the **Daut Paša Baths** (1466), once the Balkans' largest Turkish bath, rise unmistakably. The **City Art Gallery** (Kruševska 1a; admission 100MKD; ⊙9am-3pm Tue-Sun), housed here, displays modern art. Another old-bath-turned-art-gallery is the **Čifte Amam** (Bit Pazarska b.b.; admission 50MKD; ⊙9am-4.45pm Mon-Fri, to 3pm Sat, to 1pm Sun). Further on, the **Museum of Macedonia** (www.musmk.org.mk; Čurčiska 86; admission 50MKD; ⊙9am-5pm Tue-Sun), documenting Neolithic through communist times, contains an ethnographical exhibition, plus ancient jewellery and coins, icons and wood-carved iconostases.

Opposite, archaeological items decorate **Kuršumli An** (1550), once an Ottoman *caravanserai* (inn), now used for concerts and films. The Čaršija ends at **Bit Pazar**, a big, busy vegetable market also purveying household goods.

Back in Čaršija, the **Church of Sveti Spas** (admission 100MKD; ⊙8am-3pm Tue-Sun) is known for its magnificent hand-carved iconostasis. Above it, the 1492 **Mustafa Paša Mosque** (Samoilova bb) is complemented by lawn, garden and fountain. Opposite, **Tvrdina Kale Fortress**, built in the 6th century AD by the Byzantines, offers great views over city and river. Admission is free and it's open during daylight hours.

FINDING YOUR WAY

Many street signs are in Cyrillic. Directions are often given by landmarks because street addresses may be 'bb', meaning *bez broj* (without number).

FREE **Museum of the City of Skopje** MUSEUM

(Mito Hadživasilev Jasmin bb; ⊙9am-3pm Tue-Sat, 9am-1pm Sun) Exhibitions at the city museum include ancient and Byzantine finds from Kale. It's in the old train station; the stone fingers of the station's **clock** were frozen at 5.17am on 27 July 1963, when the earthquake struck.

Skopje

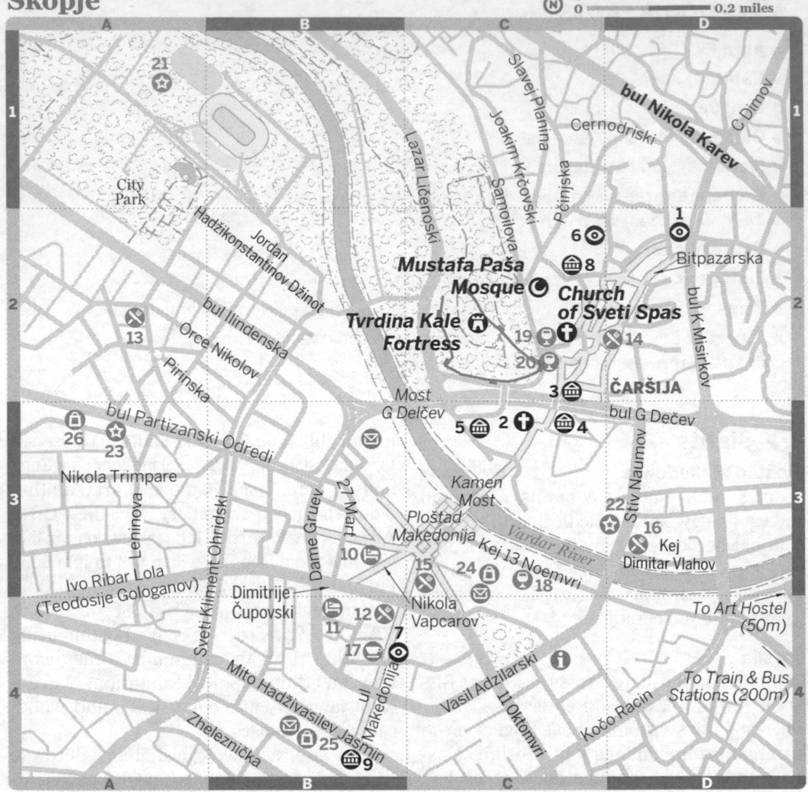

FREE **Memorial House of Mother Teresa** MUSEUM

(www.memorialhouseofmotherteresa.org; ul Makedonija bb; ⌚9am-8pm Mon-Fri, 9am-2pm Sat & Sun) The Memorial House of Mother Teresa displays memorabilia relating to the famed Catholic nun (she was born here in 1910).

Mt Vodno MOUNTAIN

Framing Skopje to the south, **Mt Vodno** is topped by the 66m-high **Millenium Cross**, the world's largest, which is illuminated at night. Further west along Vodno, in the Gorno Nerezi suburb-village, **Sveti Pantelejmon monastery** (1164) has important Byzantine frescoes. Take a taxi (20 minutes, 140MKD).

Festivals & Events

Skopsko Leto CULTURAL FESTIVAL

(www.dku.org.mk) Comprises summertime art exhibitions, performances and concerts.

Pivolend MUSIC, BEER

(www.pivolend.com.mk) Held in September at Kale; features rock acts and DJs, plus numerous beers.

Skopje Jazz Festival JAZZ

(www.skopjejazzfest.com.mk; Maksim Gorki 5) In October; always features a world-renowned artist.

May Opera Evenings OPERA, WORLD MUSIC

In May, this event and **Off-Fest** (www.offest.com.mk; occurs most years, usually in May) combine world music and DJ events.

Sleeping

Art Hostel HOSTEL €

(☎070 233336; www.art-hostel.com.mk; Ante Hadz/vimitkov 5; dm/s/d €12/25/40; ❄@📶)

In its brand-new location only a five-minute walk from the train/bus stations in a little neighborhood along the River Vardar, Art Hostel remains Skopje's most popular

Skopje

choice for backpackers. It has friendly service, free wi-fi, a big common area bar and a great location in easy walking distance of both the train/bus and the city centre. This hostel offers clean but slightly cramped six-bed dorms and small private rooms. Shared bathrooms are clean and new. The relaxed vibe is enhanced by a billiards table and low-lit outdoor balcony with couches.

Hotel Square BUDGET HOTEL €€
(☎3225 090; www.hotelsquare.com.mk; 6th fl, Nikola Vapcarov 2; s/d/tr €45/60/75; ❄@) Well situated high above the action, the Square offers cosy, well-kept modern rooms. The balcony cafe has great views. An optional breakfast (€5 extra) is served in Café Trend below. Look for the signposted business/apartment block off the square.

SPLURGE

Ideal for weary travellers seeking pampering, **Hotel TCC Plaza** (☎3111 807; www.tccplaza.com; Vasil Glavinov 12; s/d/ste €95/115/144) is a central five-star hotel with spacious rooms and suites. The spa centre features a small pool, a fitness centre and massage treatments (from 600MKD).

Hotel Bimbo HOTEL €€
(☎3214 517; www.hotelbimbo.com.mk; 29 Noemvri 63; s/d incl breakfast €40/55; ❄@) Basic but clean rooms, with a cosy breakfast nook, in a residential area near centre.

Eating

Restaurants open until midnight; smoking isn't allowed. *Skara* (grilled meats) is popular, along with international cuisine. For breakfast have *burek* (white cheese, spinach or ground meat in filo pastry) with drinking yoghurt – try it at **Burekdžilnica Rekord** (Dimitrije Čupovski 5; burek 45MKD).

The Čaršija has *kebapčilnici* (beef kebab restaurants) such as **Kebapčilnica Destan** (104 6; kebabs 120MKD); the lurid, less-visited ones can prove unsafe, however. Buy inexpensive fruit and vegetable at open-air markets, like Bit Pazar.

Stara Gradska Kuča MACEDONIAN €€
(Rade Koncar 1; mains 180-250MKD) In the quiet Debar Maalo neighbourhood's *skara* corner,

Idadija has served excellent grills for 80 years.

Idadija SKARA RESTAURANT €€
(Rade Koncar 1; mains 180-250MKD) In the quiet Debar Maalo neighbourhood's *skara* corner, Idadija has served excellent grills for 80 years.

Restaurant Roulette SKARA RESTAURANT €€
(Simeon Kavrakirov 9a; mains 150-250MKD) The best restaurant near the train and bus station, this local favourite on a side street does good grilled meats.

Restaurant Pelister INTERNATIONAL €€
(Ploštad Makedonija; mains 280-350MKD; ⌚7.30am-midnight) It might strike tourists as, well, touristy, but this big square-front place (previously Dal Met Fu) has light pastas, cheerful waitresses and a preening position behind big windows. There's a self-serve salad bar ideal for vegetarians.

Drinking

Cafes and bars open until midnight (1am on weekends). After that, only late-licence nightclubs operate.

Café di Roma CAFE
(ul Makedonija) Skopje's best espresso and a stylish clientele.

La Bodeguito del Medio LATIN BAR
(Kej 13 Noemvri) Known as 'the Cuban', this gregarious riverfront place serves Cuban food and has a long bar lined with carousers and cocktails by night.

Old Town Brewery BEER BAR
(Gradište 1; pint of beer 120-260MKD; ⌚10am-1am Mon-Thu, 10am-3am Fri-Sun) This fun new bar has a good (though pricey) beer selection. In summer, benches spill outside, where bands cover classic rock classics.

Vinoteka Temov WINE BAR
(Gradište 1a; glass of wine 150-350MKD; ⌚9am-midnight Mon-Thu, 9am-1am Fri-Sun) This restored wood building offers candle-lit ambience and a deep wine selection.

☆ Entertainment

Skopje gets international DJs (www.skopjeclubbing.com.mk), when they appear; cover charges run from 250MKD to 500MKD.

Colosseum NIGHTCLUB
(www.colosseum.com.mk) Skopje's biggest, most popular club. It's in the City Park in summer and under the train station in winter.

Element NIGHTCLUB
(www.element.com.mk; City Park) International DJs often appear here.

Universal Hall LIVE MUSIC
(☎3224 158; bul Partizanski Odredi bb; tickets 100-200MKD) Hosts classical, jazz, pop and kids' performances.

Macedonian National Theatre OPERA, BALLET
(☎3114 060; Kej Dimitar Vlahov bb; tickets 100-400MKD) Hosts opera, ballet and classical music.

Kino Milenium CINEMA
(☎3111 111; Gradski Trgovski Centar; tickets 60-120MKD) Skopje's largest cinema, showing Hollywood hits with subtitles.

Shopping

The Čaršija sells jewellery, traditional carpets and clothing, while Bit Pazar sells fruit, vegetables and bric-a-brac. **Gradski Trgovski Centar** (11 Oktomvri) is an open-air mall; **Ramstore** (Mito Hadživasilev Jasmin bb) is more modern.

Information

For updated city info, visit **Skopje Online** (www.skopjeonline.com.mk).

Young Roma beggars along Skopje's square and riverfront can vex; be aware of pickpockets.

City hospital (☎3130 111; 11 Oktomvri 53; ⌚24 hr)

City of Skopje Bureau for Tourism and Information (☎070 812882; www.skopje.mk; Vasil Adzilarski bb; ⌚8.30am-4.30pm Mon-Fri) Skopje's tourism office offers useful info.

Go Macedonia (☎3232 273; www.gomacedonia.com.mk; Trgovski Centar Beverly Hills lok 32, Naroden Front 19) Arranges hiking, cycling, caving and winery tours.

Neuromedica private clinic (☎3133 313; 11 Oktomvri 25; ⌚24hr)

Getting There & Away

Skopje's **bus station** (☎2466 011; bul KJ Pitu) adjoins the **train station** (Zheleznička Stanica; ☎3164 255; bul KJ Pitu). At the former only, English is spoken, and there's an exchange office (both have ATMs). Buses cover international and domestic destinations including Bitola (470MKD, three hours, 12 daily) and Ohrid (520MKD, three hours, 11 daily). In summer, book ahead for Ohrid buses.

Trains serve several domestic destinations; the only international destinations are Serbia, Kosovo and Greece. Bitola (200MKD, four hours, three daily) is the longest domestic rail journey.

Getting Around

Skopje is navigable on foot, and a short trip in a taxi in central Skopje costs 80MKD to 120MKD. City buses cost 25MKD to 35MKD.

Ohrid Охрид

☎046 / POP 55,700

Sublime Ohrid is Macedonia's prime destination, with its atmospheric old quarter with beautiful churches stacked up a graceful hill, all topped by a medieval castle overlooking serene, 34km-long Lake Ohrid, shared by Macedonia (two-thirds) and Albania (one-third). Nearby, mountainous **Galičica National Park** offers pristine nature, while secluded beaches dot the eastern shore.

Ohrid and its beaches are packed from 15 July to 15 August, during the popular summer festival. For more tranquillity, try June or September.

Chris Deliso's *Hidden Macedonia* is an intriguing travelogue about the Ohrid and Prespa lake region.

Sights

Churches usually charge 100MKD admission. On Mondays, museums are closed. The compact Old Town is hemmed in south and west by the lake and by pedestrian mall Sveti Kliment Ohridski in the east.

GORNA PORTA & AROUND

To best navigate Ohrid's sites, work downwards from the Old Town's **Gorna Porta** (Upper Gate), about 80MKD from the centre by taxi.

Inside the gates, turn left to the 13th-century **Church of Sveta Bogorodica Perivlepta** (admission 100MKD; ⏲9am-1pm & 4-8pm), which features vivid biblical frescoes and an **icon gallery** (⏲9am-2pm & 5-8pm Tue-Sun).

Straight on from the Gorna Porta is the impressive **Classical Amphitheatre**. Originally built for theatre, it now hosts the Ohrid Summer Festival.

From Gorna Porta, signs point right to the massive, 10th-century **Car Samoil's Castle** (admission 30MKD; ⏲9am-6pmTue-Sun). Ascend the narrow stairs to the ramparts for fantastic views. Then follow the wooded path down to the **Church of Sveti Kliment i Pantelejmon** (Plaošnik; admission free; ⏲9am-6pm). Originally a 5th-century basilica, it was restored in 2002 according to Byzantine architectural designs. It houses St Kliment's relics, plus original foundations and mosaic under glass floor segments. Across from the church entrance lie 4th-century church foundations, with early Christian mosaics.

BY THE LAKE

The path downhill from Sveti Kliment i Pantelejmon leads to the 13th-century **Church of Sveti Jovan at Kaneo** (admission 50MKD; ⏲9am-6pm), standing on a bluff over the lake. Continuing from here on ul Kočo Racin, you'll pass lovely old houses before a staircase leading to the frescoed, 11th-century **Sveta Sofija Cathedral** (Car Samoil bb; ⏲10am-8pm) lined with columns. Alternatively, from the beach below Kaneo, a new 200m-long walking bridge over the water brings you back to the centre.

Further along Car Samoil, see the architecturally exquisite 1827 **National Museum** (Car Samoil 62; admission 50MKD; ⏲9am-4pm & 7-11pm Tue-Sun). Archaeological finds are displayed at the Robev Residence, and ethnographical ones at the Urania Residence opposite.

Exiting the Old Town on Car Samoil, the pedestrian mall, Sveti Kliment Ohridski, is lined with cafes and shops.

Festivals & Events

Balkan Festival of Folk Dances & Songs FOLK MUSIC

In July, this festival draws regional groups.

Ohrid Summer Festival CLASSICAL

(☎262 304; www.ohridsummer.com.mk) During July and August; features classical and opera concerts, theatre and dance.

Ohrid Swimming Marathon MARATHON

The Sveti Naum–Ohrid swimming marathon (30km) is usually held in August.

Sleeping

Private rooms or apartments (per person €5 to €10) are advertised by the sign *sobi* (rooms) – search, or ask agencies like Sunny Land Tourism or Tourist Bureau Biljana. Since quality varies, shop around.

Villa Lucija RENTED ROOMS €

(☎265 608; www.vilalucija.com.mk; Kosta Abraš 29; s/d/apt €15/25/40; ❄@) Lucija has fantastic Old Town ambience and lovingly decorated, breezy rooms with lake-view balconies.

Stefan Kanevče Rooms RENTED ROOMS €

(☎234 813; apostolanet@yahoo.co.uk; Kočo Racin 47; per person €10) Near Kaneo beach, this atmospheric 19th-century house boasts

Ohrid

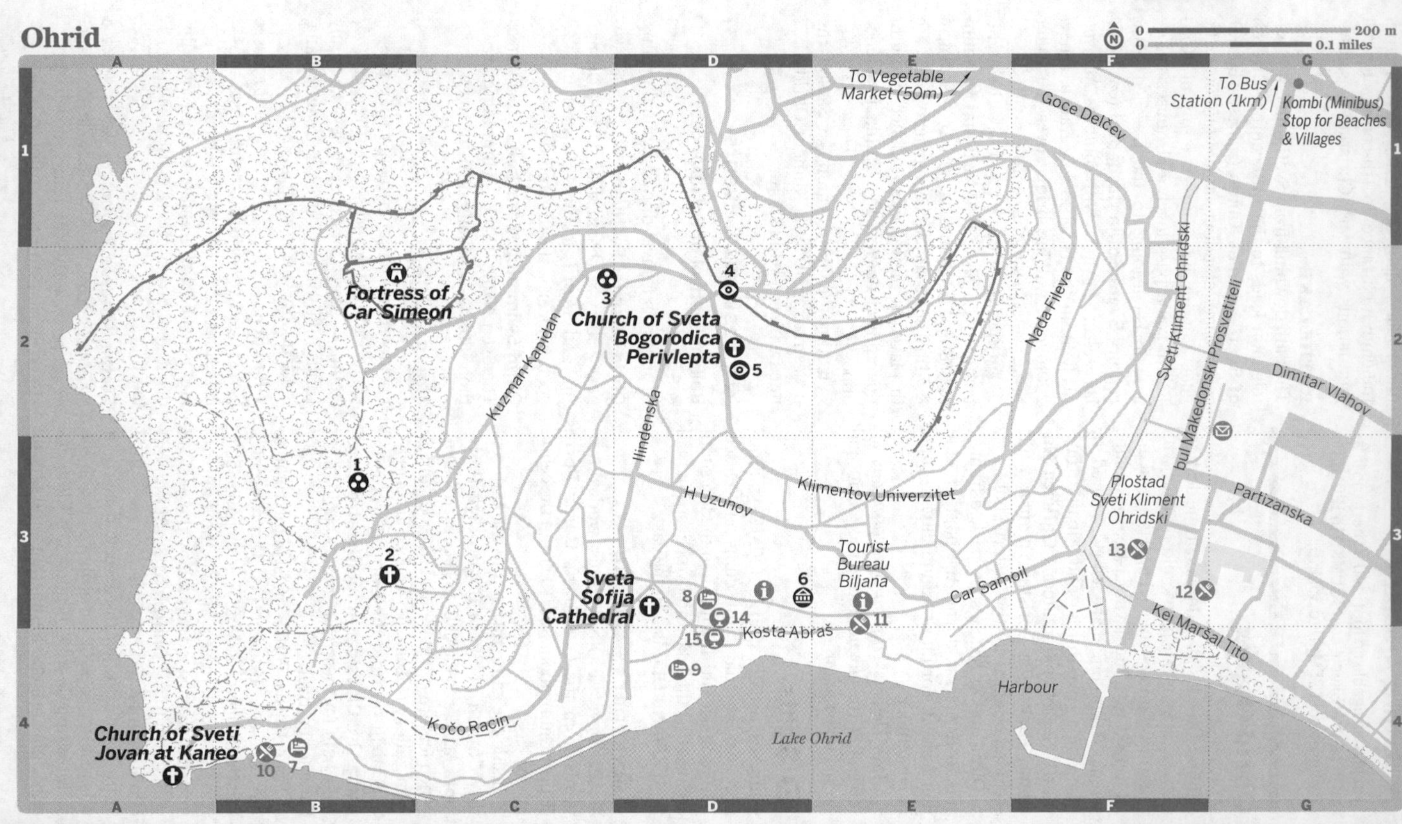
0 200 m
0 0.1 miles
To Vegetable Market (50m)
Goce Delčev
To Bus Station (1km)
Kombi (Minibus) Stop for Beaches & Villages
Fortress of Car Simeon
Church of Sveta Bogorodica Perivlepta
Kuzman Kapidan
Ilindenska
Nada Fileva
Sveti Kliment Ohridski
bul Makedonski Prosvetiteli
Dimitar Vlahov
H Uzunov
Klimentov Univerzitet
Ploštad Sveti Kliment Ohridski
Partizanska
Tourist Bureau Biljana
Car Samoil
Sveta Sofija Cathedral
Kosta Abraš
Kej Maršal Tito
Harbour
Lake Ohrid
Kočo Racin
Church of Sveti Jovan at Kaneo
1
2
3
4
5
6
7
8
9
10
11
12
13
14
15

Ohrid

Top Sights

The Fortress of Car Simeon B2
Church of Sveta Bogorodica Perivlopta D2
Church of Sveti Jovan at Kaneo A4
Sveta Sofija Cathedral D3

Sights

1 4th-Century Church Foundations B3
2 Church of Sveti Kliment i Pantelejmon B3
3 Classical Amphitheatre C2
4 Gorna Porta D2
5 Icon Gallery D2
6 National Museum D3

Sleeping

7 Stefan Kanevče Rooms B4
8 Vila Sveta Sofija D3
9 Villa Lucija D4

Eating

10 Letna Bavča Kaneo B4
11 Pizzeria Leonardo E3
12 Restoran Belvedere F3
13 Tinex Supermarket F3

Drinking

14 Cuba Libre D3
15 Jazz Inn D4

carved wooden ceilings and good hospitality.

Vila Sveta Sofija TRADITIONAL HOTEL €€
(254 370; www.vilasofija.com.mk; Kosta Abraš 64; s/d/ste €35/60/80;) One of Ohrid's most atmospheric and best-known places, Vila Sveta Sofija occupies a restored mansion near the cathedral of Sveta Sofija.

Eating & Drinking

Old Town eateries are good but pricey. Self-caterers have **Tinex supermarket** (bul Makedonski Prosvetiteli) and the **vegetable market** (Sveti Kliment Ohridski).

Letna Bavča Kaneo FISH RESTAURANT €
(Kočo Racin 43) The 'summer terrace' on Kaneo beach, near the church of Sveti Jovan at Kaneo, has tasty and cheap food. A huge fish fry-up of diminutive *plasnica* (lake fish), plus salad, feeds two people for 120MKD. Swim from the dock.

Restaurant Antiko MACEDONIAN €€
(Car Samoil 30; mains 350-600MKD) In an old Ohrid mansion, the famous Antiko has great ambience and pricey but good traditional dishes.

Pizzeria Leonardo PIZZERIA €
(Car Samoil 31; pizzas 200-350MKD) Ohrid's best pizza is served here – it's popular with locals, too.

Restoran Belvedere SKARA RESTAURANT €
(Kej Maršal Tito 2) Does excellent *skara*. The outdoor tables extend under a leafy canopy.

Jazz Inn BAR
(Kosta Abraš 74; 10.30pm-4am) This low-lit, jazzy hipster hang-out gets roaring after midnight.

Cuba Libre BAR
(Kosta Abraš; 10pm-4am) This festive Old Town bar-club is perennially popular.

Information

For information, check out **Ohrid.com** (www.ohrid.com.mk), the municipal website.

Internet Café Inside (Amam Trgovski Centar; per hr 60MKD) In a mall near Ploštad Sveti Kliment Ohridski.

Itna Medicinska Sluzhba (266 217; Dimitar Vlahov bb; 24hr) Accident and emergency clinic.

Sunnyland Tourism (523 008; www.sunnylandtourism.com; Car Samoil; 9am-7pm) Led by local expert Zoran Grozdanovski, Sunnyland finds accommodation and arranges various tours and activities in Ohrid and beyond. It's located by the History Museum.

Tourist Bureau Biljana (070 684 428; www.beyondohrid.com; Car Samoil 38) Offers general information, accommodation assistance, bike rental and outdoor activities.

Getting There & Away

The **bus station** (260 339; 7 Noemvri bb) is 1.5km east of the centre. Buses serve destinations including Skopje.

For Albania, take a bus to Sveti Naum (29km, 110MKD). Cross the border and take a taxi (6km, 300MKD) to Pogradec. Ohrid–Sveti Naum taxis cost 900MKD.

Bitola Битола

047 / POP 95,400

With elegant buildings and beautiful people, elevated Bitola (660m) has a sophistication inherited from its Ottoman days as the 'City of Consuls'. Its colourful 18th- and 19th-century townhouses, Turkish mosques, and cafe culture make it Macedonia's most intriguing and liveable major town. An essential experience is sipping a coffee and people-watching along the pedestrianised Širok Sokak ('Wide Street' in Turkish; still ul Maršal Tito officially).

Sights

Bitola's Ottoman-era attractions include the 16th-century **Yeni Mosque**, **Isak Mosque** and **Yahdar-Kadi Mosque**, all located between the Dragor River and the **Stara Čaršija** (Old Bazaar), where traditional crafts are still practised.

The **Church of Sveti Dimitrij** (11 Oktomvri bb; 7am-6pm) dates from 1830. Bitola's great neoclassical architecture is visible from Širok Sokak's many cafes.

Sleeping

Chola Guest House GUEST HOUSE €
(224 919; www.chola.mk; Stiv Naumov 80; s/d €13/25;) This quiet place in an old mansion has clean, well-kept and pretty rooms, with colourful modern bathrooms. To get here, ask the taxi driver for Video Club Dju (directly opposite the guest house). Free wi-fi.

Via Apartments APARTMENTS €
(075 246261; www.via.mk; Elpida Karamandi 4; s/d €12/24;) These clean, well-designed apartments are located downtown, and have shared kitchen, laundry, lounge and outdoor patio.

Villa Dihovo GUEST HOUSE €€
(070 544744; www.villadihovo.com; Dihovo; pay as you like;) A 10-minute drive east of town in the village of Dihovo, this friendly guest house comprises a restored traditional home with an inviting lawn. It's signposted inside the first long driveway after Dihovo centre's restaurant. The only fixed prices are for the homemade wine, beer and *rakija* (firewater); everything else, room price included, is your choice. It's a great base for local river walks and hikes in Pelister National Park.

Eating & Drinking

El Greko PIZZERIA €
(cnr Maršal Tito & Elipda Karamandi; mains 180-320MKD) This Sokak taverna and pizzeria has great beer-hall ambience.

Basa BAR
(Leninova) A darkly lit, happening bar off Leninova.

Information

Širok Sokak is a wi-fi hot spot, and internet cafes are nearby.

Baloyannis Tours (220 204, 075 207273; Solunska 118; 8am-6pm Mon-Sat) Provides city tours and outdoor adventure trips (with prior notice).

Tourist information centre (241 641; bitola-tourist-info@t-home.mk; Sterio Georgiev 1; 9am-6pm Mon-Sat) Friendly info centre.

Getting There & Away

The **bus station** (231 420; Nikola Tesla) and the **train station** (237 110; Nikola Tesla) are adjacent, about 1km south of centre, near the park. Buses serve Skopje (470MKD, four hours, 12 daily), among other destinations. Trains also serve Skopje (200MKD, three hours, three daily).

For Greece, take a taxi to the border (450MKD), where you can seek a Greek cab; however, some Bitola cab drivers will go to Florina for 3000MKD.

UNDERSTAND MACEDONIA

History

The historical and geographical Macedonia is divided between the Republic of Macedonia, Greece and Bulgaria. The 4th-century BC empire developed by Phillip II and his son, Alexander the Great, spread Macedonian power to India. Their glorious legacy is claimed by both modern-day Macedonians and Greeks, unsurprisingly fuelling enmity and nationalist rhetoric.

In 168 BC, the Romans conquered Macedonia; when Rome split in AD 395, Macedonia was assigned to the Eastern (Byzantine) half. In the 7th century Slavic tribes arrived, and thereafter Macedonia passed between Byzantine, Bulgarian and Serbian rule, before Ottoman Turks conquered in 1389.

In 1913, after the two Balkan Wars, geographical Macedonia was divided between Greece, Bulgaria and Serbia. After WWI, the Serbs incorporated their share (essentially today's Macedonian state) into Royalist Yugoslavia. Assimilation programs were levied against the Macedonian populations in the three newly enlarged states. During WWII, Macedonians largely joined Josip Broz Tito's communist partisans rather than the (then-occupying) Bulgarians.

Tito granted Macedonia republic status within federal Yugoslavia. However, he also nationalised property and imposed communism, altering Macedonia's traditionally rural society. So, while Yugoslavia became relatively prosperous, Macedonia remained its poorest republic.

When Yugoslavia's republics disintegrated violently in the early 1990s, Macedonia alone separated peacefully, in 1992. However, Greece insisted that the new country had no right to the name 'Macedonia', claiming that it implied territorial claims against Greece, which has a similarly named province. Greek pressure meant that Macedonia gained UN admission in 1993 under the 'provisional' title of Former Yugoslav Republic of Macedonia (FYROM). As in other 1990s-era 'transition' countries, oligarchs became established amid shady privatisations and bankrupting of state-owned firms.

Simultaneously, Macedonia's Albanian minority began protesting alleged ill-treatment. During NATO's 1999 Kosovo intervention to defend ethnic Albanians there, Macedonia sheltered 400,000 Kosovar refugees. Nevertheless, Albanian separatists waged war in Macedonian areas bordering Kosovo in early 2001. Hostilities subsided with the internationally brokered Ohrid Framework Agreement in August 2001, granting minorities more rights and political participation.

In December 2005, Macedonia won EU membership candidacy, though NATO membership was quashed in April 2008, when Greece vetoed the invitation, citing its unresolved issue. At the time of writing, the stalemate between Macedonia and Greece remained deadlocked.

People

In the 2004 census the population of 2 million people included Macedonians (66.6%), Albanians (22.7%), Turks (4%), Roma (2.2%), Serbs (2.1%) and others (2.4%). Most Macedonians (and Serbs) are Orthodox Christians, while most Albanians, Turks and Roma are Muslim.

Food

In this chapter the following price indicators apply (for a main meal):

€€€ more than 300MKD

€€ 150MKD to 300MKD

€ less than 150MKD

Arts

Macedonia has many prominent artists. Ethno group Syntesis has performed Macedonian folk music before audiences worldwide, as have classical pianist Simon Trpčevski and opera singer Boris Trajanov.

Toše Proeski, a charismatic pop singer who died tragically in 2007 at the age of 26, remains close to the heart of Macedonians.

Environment

Macedonia's 25,713 sq km is mostly plateau (600m to 900m above sea level), though over 50 mountain peaks top 2500m. The Continental and Mediterranean climate zones converge here, while the Vardar River passes through Skopje en route to the Aegean Sea.

Lakes Ohrid and Prespa, in southwestern Macedonia, are three-million-year-old tectonic lakes; at 300m, Ohrid is the Balkans' deepest and shelters numerous endemic species, including the endangered Ohrid trout. Although fishing this trout is supposedly illegal, restaurants sell it – try one of Macedonia's three other non-endangered trout varieties instead.

SURVIVAL GUIDE

Directory A–Z

Accommodation

City hotels are expensive, though cheaper options are emerging. Affordable, quality private accommodation exists in holiday areas. Monastery dorms are another budget option. Book ahead for summer, Orthodox Christmas (7 January) and Orthodox Easter visits.

The following price indicators apply (for a high-season double room):

€ less than €50

€€ €50 to €80

€€€ more than €80

Activities

Lake Matka, near Skopje, offers great hiking, as do Galičica (near Ohrid) and Pelister (near Bitola) National Parks. Swimming is good in Lake Ohrid.

Business Hours

Banks 7am-5pm Mon-Fri

Businesses 8am-8pm Mon-Fri, 8am-2pm Sat

Cafes 10am-midnight

Post offices 7am-8pm Mon-Fri

Holidays

New Year 1 January

Orthodox Christmas 7 January

Orthodox Easter Week March/April

Labour Day 1 May

SS Cyril and Methodius Day 24 May

Ilinden Day 2 August

Republic Day 8 September

1941 Partisan Day 11 October

Internet Resources

Balkanalysis (www.balkanalysis.com) Politics and current events, covering Macedonia and the Balkans.

Culture in Macedonia (www.culture.in.mk) Cultural info and festival listings.

Exploring Macedonia (www.exploring-macedonia.com) Useful travel website.

Macedonia Loves You (www.macedonialovesyou.eu) Informative, photo-rich site.

Skopje Online (www.skopjeonline.com.mk) Updated city info, plus nightclub listings.

Money

Macedonian denars (MKD) come in 10, 50, 100, 500, 1000 and 5000 notes, and one-, two-, five-, 10- and 50-denar coins. Denars are nonconvertible abroad. Euros are usually accepted. While some hotels quote euro rates, payment in denars is acceptable.

Macedonian exchange offices *(menuvačnici)* work commission-free. ATMs are widespread, except in villages, and using them for cash is the best idea, considering that credit-card fraud, even in well-respected hotels, restaurants and shops, occasionally occurs. Avoid travellers cheques.

Post & Telephone

Mail services to and from Macedonia are efficient. A letter to EU countries or the USA costs from 48MKD.

Internet cafes offer cheap international phone service. Public-telephone cards sold in kiosks or post offices in units of 100 (200MKD), 200 (300MKD), 500 (650MKD) or 1000 (1250MKD) offer good value for domestic calls. Drop the initial zero in city codes and mobile prefixes (the three-digit numbers starting with 07) when calling from abroad.

Visas

Three-month visa-free stays are allowed for passport holders from Australia, Canada, the EU, Iceland, Israel, New Zealand, Norway, Switzerland, Turkey and the USA. Visas are required for most others. Visa fees average US$30/60 for single-/multiple-entry visas. Check www.mfa.gov.mk for updates.

Getting There & Away

Air

Alexander the Great Airport (☎02-3148 651) is 23km from Skopje. Ohrid has little **St Paul the Apostle Airport** (☎046-252 820). See www.airports.com.mk for information. Numerous European airlines serve Skopje, but tickets are pricey. There is no airport bus (printed signs list taxi rates of 1000MKD outside).

Alternatively, fly to Thessaloniki in Greece with a low-budget carrier, and continue by train or bus to Macedonia. Airlines to/from Skopje include the following:

USEFUL BORDER CROSSINGS

Macedonia's 14 border crossings access Albania, Bulgaria, Greece, Kosovo and Serbia.

For Albania, the most used is Kafasan, 12km southwest of Struga on Lake Ohrid (for Tirana). Deve Bair, 90km northeast of Skopje, accesses Sofia, Bulgaria. Thessaloniki, Greece, is reached from the road/rail crossing at Bogorodica/Gevgelija. For Serbia and Kosovo respectively, Tabanovce north of Kumanovo and Blace northwest of Skopje have road/rail transport.

Austrian Airlines (☎02-3248 800; www.austrian.com)

Macedonian Airlines (MAT; ☎02-3292 333; www.mat.com.mk)

SkyWings (☎02-3298 655; www.skywings.info)

Turkish Airlines (☎02-3116 149; www.thy.com)

Bus

From Skopje, buses serve Belgrade (Serbia; 1400MKD, 10 hours, 12 daily), Prishtina (Kosovo; 320MKD, two hours, 12 daily), Sofia (Bulgaria; 1040MKD, 5½ hours, five daily), Thessaloniki (Greece; 1280MKD, four hours, three weekly), Tirana (Albania; 1300MKD, seven hours, two daily), Zagreb (Croatia; 3150MKD, 12 hours, one daily), Ljubljana (Slovenia; 3750MKD, 14 hours, one daily) and İstanbul (Turkey; 2560MKD, 12 hours, five daily), as well as further-flung destinations such as Budapest, Vienna and Stuttgart.

Car & Motorcycle

Green Card insurance is required for entry.

Train

The north–south train line serving Macedonia starts in Thessaloniki, with two daily Thessaloniki–Skopje trains (920MKD, five hours), continuing through Serbia to Belgrade (1300MKD, eight to 10 hours, two daily). Another international line unites Skopje and Prishtina (Kosovo).

For international route timetables, see the **Macedonian Railways** (Makedonski Zheleznici; www.mz.com.mk/patnichki/timetable.htm) website. However, the timetables aren't reliable, and trains are frequently late, so confirm ahead of travel.

Getting Around

Modern and comfortable buses from Skopje travel frequently nationwide; speedier *kombi* (minibuses) are also frequently encountered. Baggage fees (10MKD) are sometimes charged, but bags can usually be carried onboard for free.

Skopje's car rental agencies range from big names to local companies. For emergency car assistance, call ☎196.

Macedonia's trains service limited destinations, the furthest being Gevgelija and Bitola in the south (both trips cost around 200MKD).

Malta

Includes »

Best Places to Eat

» Trabuxu Bistro, Valleta (p840)

» Kitchen, Sliema (p843)

» Mahżen XII, Mdina (p845)

Best Places to Stay

» Asti Guesthouse, Valletta (p840)

» Hotel Valentina, Paceville (p843)

» Point de Vue Guesthouse, Rabat (p844)

» Maria Giovanna Guest-house, Marsalform (p845)

Why Go?

Despite being made up of three tiny islands on the southern edge of Europe, Malta groans under the weight of its rich history and fascinating cultural influences. As a melting pot of Mediterranean culture, Malta merits far deeper exploration than is often given to it by the package crowds whose first priority is hitting the beach.

From ancient stone temples and historic Arabic connections (listen carefully to the local language) to Sicilian-inspired cuisine and an oddly 1950s British atmosphere, Malta will almost certainly surprise you. Valletta and the Three Cities are famed for their grand churches, elegant palaces and honey-coloured limestone fortifications, while nearby Sliema and St Julian's are packed with restaurants and bars. And don't forget little Gozo, a pretty, rural island where the pace of life is that much slower – the perfect chill-out spot.

When To Go

Valletta

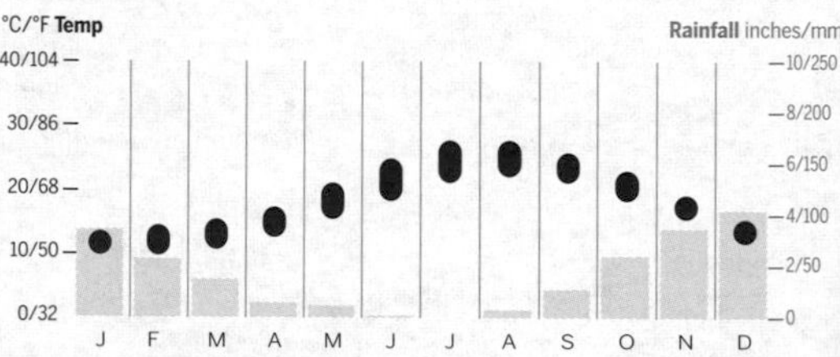

Feb–Mar Pleasant temperatures and spring flowers. Carnival Week brings festivities to Valletta.

Sep–Oct Fewer tourists; perfect sunbathing weather, sea at its warmest and clearest.

Dec Low accommodation prices. Village churches resplendent with fairy lights.

Connections

Malta is well connected to both Sicily and mainland Italy by sea. Catamarans to Pozzallo and Catania in Sicily are the fastest and most frequent connection, while other services link Malta to Palermo, Genoa and Civitavecchia. Ferries operate year-round.

There are frequent flights between Malta and various European destinations, including Sardinia, Larnaca (Cyprus), İstanbul, London, Athens, Dubrovnik and many cities in Italy, France and Spain.

ITINERARIES

Three Days

Start things off in Valletta to get an overview of the country – wander the streets and soak up some of the history. On your second day, head to the Hal Saflieni Hypogeum (you'll need to have booked in advance) before enjoying a seafood meal in St Julian's and the nightlife in Paceville. On the third day visit Mdina and Rabat, then escape to a beach in the northwest.

One Week

As above, then on day four head for gorgeous Gozo. From here you can take a day trip to Comino, find your own beaches and enjoy glorious food in Malta's least-discovered corner.

Essential Food & Drink

» **Ġbejniet** You'll either love or hate this small, hard, white cheese, traditionally made from unpasteurised sheep's or goat's milk. It is dried in baskets and often steeped in olive oil seasoned with salt and crushed black peppercorns.

» **Pastizza** (plural *pastizzi*) This traditional Maltese snack is a small parcel of flaky pastry filled with either ricotta cheese or mushy peas. It's available in most bars or from a *pastizzerija* (usually a hole-in-the-wall takeaway or kiosk).

» **Ftira** Bread baked in a flat disc and traditionally stuffed with a mixture of tomatoes, olives, capers and anchovies.

» **Braġioli** These 'beef olives' are prepared by wrapping a thin slice of beef around a stuffing of breadcrumbs, chopped bacon, hard-boiled egg and parsley, which are then braised in a red-wine sauce.

» **Fenek** (rabbit) The favourite Maltese dish, whether fried in olive oil, roasted, stewed, served with spaghetti or baked in a pie (*fenek bit-tewm u l-inbid* is rabbit cooked in garlic and wine, *fenek moqli* is fried rabbit, *stuffat tal-fenek* is stewed rabbit).

» **Kinnie** You'll see its advertising signs all over Malta – the brand name of a local soft drink flavoured with bitter oranges and aromatic herbs.

AT A GLANCE

» **Currency** euro (€)

» **Language** Malti, English

» **Money** ATMs widespread; credit cards widely accepted

» **Visas** Schengen visa rules apply; see p1319

Fast Facts

» **Area** 316 sq km

» **Capital** Valletta

» **Country code** ☎356

» **Emergency** ☎112

Exchange Rates

Australia	A$1	€0.74
Canada	C$1	€0.74
Japan	¥100	€0.87
New Zealand	NZ$1	€0.56
UK	UK£1	€1.16
USA	US$1	€0.72

Set Your Budget

» **Room in guest house** €16-25 per person

» **Bus trip** €0.50-1.20

» **Cup of coffee** €1.50

» **Day hire of sun lounger** €5

Resources

» **About Malta** (www.aboutmalta.com)

» **Gozo** (www.gozo.com)

» **Malta Tourism Authority** (www.visitmalta.com)

» **StarWeb Malta** (www.starwebmalta.com)

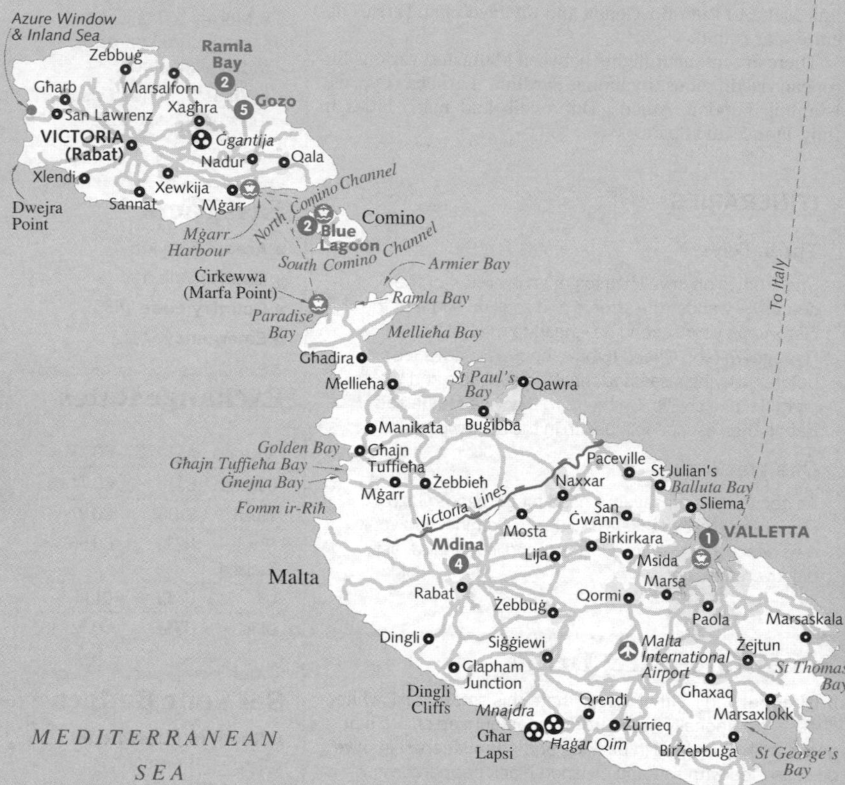

Malta Highlights

1 Immerse yourself in the history and sights of the pint-sized capital **Valletta** (p840)

2 Discover how Malta earned a reputation for beachside holidays at places such as **Ramla Bay** (p845) and **Blue Lagoon** (p845)

3 Toast a patron saint amid an infectious mix of music, food and fireworks at a **festa** (p847)

4 Step back in time in the silent streets of elegant **Mdina** (p844)

5 Take the ferry to **Gozo** (p845) and experience its slower pace or maybe even learn to scuba dive

VALLETTA

POP 7000

The Maltese capital is a stunner. Whereas careless modern development has blighted much of the rest of Malta's coast, Valletta has retained its architectural unity and ancient charm. Activity bustles around Triq ir-Repubbblika and Triq il-Merkanti, but walk the quiet, narrow backstreets to get a feel for everyday life. The city overlooks the impressive Grand Harbour to the southeast and Marsamxett Harbour to the northwest.

Sights

A walk around the massive city walls features spectacular views – be sure to stop at the **Upper Barrakka Gardens** in the southwest for a vista that puts the grand in Grand Harbour.

Check out the breathtaking baroque interior of **St John's Co-Cathedral** (www.stjohnscocathedral.com; Triq ir-Repubblika; adult/student €6/3.50; 9.30am-4.30pm Mon-Fri, to 12.30pm Sat, closed Sun, public holidays & during services), built in the 1570s. Inside is the **Cathedral Museum**, which houses two magnificent works by the Italian painter Caravaggio.

The 16th-century **Grand Master's Palace** (Pjazza San Ġorġ; admission €10; 9am-5pm) is the seat of the Maltese parliament. You can visit the **armoury**, filled with 16th- to 18th-century weapons and suits of armour, and the grand **State Apartments**, decorated with paintings of the Grand Masters and hung with priceless 17th-century Gobelins tapestries.

At the **National Museum of Archaeology** (Triq ir-Repubblika; adult/student €5/3.50; 9am-7pm) you can admire beautiful objects that have been found at Malta's prehistoric sites – check out the intriguing female figurines (the so-called 'fat ladies').

Sleeping

TOP CHOICE **Asti Guesthouse** B&B €

(2123 9506; http://mol.net.mt/asti; 18 Triq Sant'Orsla; per person without bathroom, incl breakfast €17) You'll get a taste of old-school Valletta charm here in a 350-year-old building converted into a guest house that offers the best-value accommodation in town. Asti has a charming host, simple, spacious rooms and spotless shared bathrooms. Breakfast is served in a vaulted dining room under a chandelier.

Coronation Guesthouse B&B €

(2123 7652; 10E Triq M A Vassalli; B&B per person without bathroom , incl breakfast from €16) Friendly, family-run place. All bathrooms are shared.

Midland Guesthouse B&B €

(2123 6024; midlandguesthouse@gmail.com; 255 Triq Sant'Orsla; per person without bathroom, incl breakfast from €18) Well-located place spread over several floors of a large town house; rooms are neat and pleasant.

Eating & Drinking

Cheap and tasty fare can be found at the kiosks beside City Gate bus terminus; Millennium (the first kiosk on your right after you exit City Gate) sells hot *pastizzi* for €0.30 each. There are a couple of low-key bars on Triq Nofs in-Nhar, but if you're after something livelier, head to Paceville (see p843).

TOP CHOICE **Trabuxu Bistro** MALTESE €€

(2122 0357; www.trabuxu.com.mt; 8-9 Triq Nofs in-Nhar; mains €9-16; noon-3pm Mon-Fri, 7pm-midnight Fri & Sat) This cool little bistro, just around the corner from its sister wine bar (p840), serves home-cooked, traditional Maltese dishes using fresh seasonal produce.

Café Jubilee CAFE €

(125 Triq Santa Luċija; mains €4-8; 8am-1am Mon-Thu, 8am-3am Fri & Sat; wi-fi) A feel-good place you can drop into anytime for a breakfast of coffee and *pastizzi*, a lunchtime baguette, or a simple dinner of salad, pasta or risotto. Jubilee is a continental-style bistro; it's also one of the few places where you can eat and drink late.

Trabuxu WINE BAR

(1 Triq id-Dejqa; 7.30pm-late) Things don't come much simpler or much better than this cellar wine bar (the name means 'corkscrew'). Friendly staff are keen to introduce you to Malta's more accomplished wines, which are complemented by a menu of tasty local tapas, cheese and dips. Perfect.

Agius Pastizzerlja BAKERY €

(273 Triq San Pawl; pastries €0.25; 7.30am-5.30pm Mon-Sat) Hole-in-the-wall place serving traditional snacks, including *pastizzi* and other carb-loaded treats.

Wembley Stores SUPERMARKET

(305 Triq ir-Repubblika; 7.45am-7pm Mon-Sat) Stocks a selection of groceries.

Fresh produce market MARKET

(Triq il-Merkanti; 7am-1pm Mon-Sat) Behind the Grand Master's Palace. You can buy fruit and vegetables.

Valletta

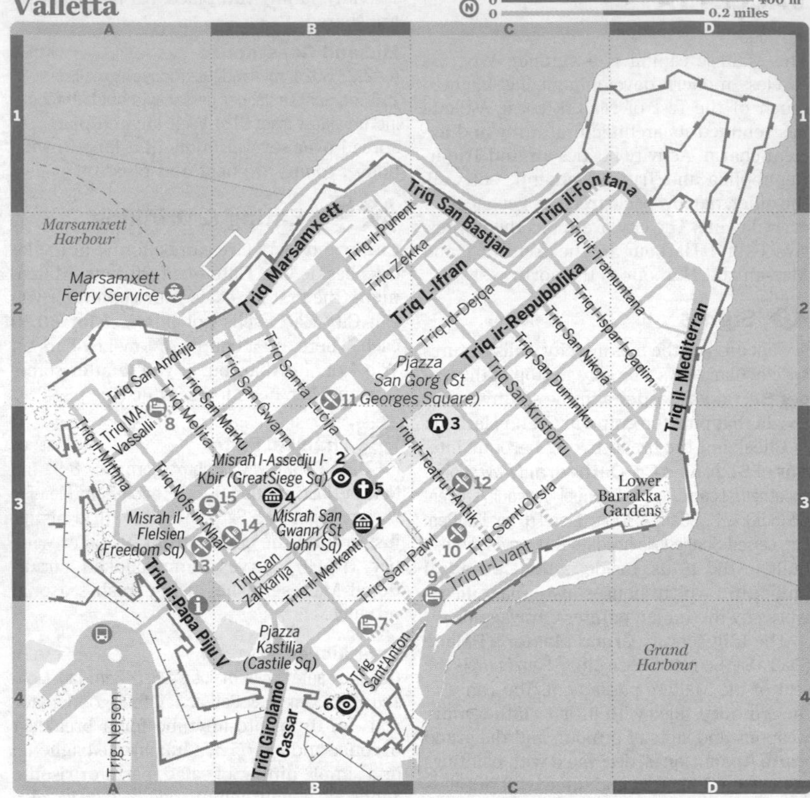

Valletta

Sights

	Armoury	(see 3)
1	Cathedral Museum	B3
2	Entrance to Cathedral & Cathedral Museum	B3
3	Grand Master's Palace	C3
4	National Museum of Archaeology	B3
5	St John's Co-Cathedral	B3
	State Apartments	(see 3)
6	Upper Barrakka Gardens	B4

Sleeping

7	Asti Guesthouse	B4
8	Coronation Guesthouse	A3
9	Midland Guesthouse	C3

Eating

10	Agius Pastizzerija	C3
11	Café Jubilee	B2
12	Fresh Produce Market	C3
13	Trabuxu Bistro	A3
14	Wembley Stores	B3

Drinking

15	Trabuxu	A3

Information

Police station (☎2122 5495; Triq Nofs in-Nhar)

Royal Pharmacy (☎2125 2396; 271 Triq ir-Repubblika) Central pharmacy open during shopping hours.

Tourist office city centre (☎2291 5440; 229 Triq il-Merkanti; ⊙9am-5.15pm Mon-Sat, 9am-12.45pm Sun & public holidays); Valletta

DIY CAPITAL BUS TOUR

Fancy a cheap, quick, DIY bus tour of the capital? Bus 98 is a circular route departing from City Gate every half-hour from 9.30am to 6pm. It does a clockwise loop around the bastions of Valletta and through Floriana, so you can take in harbour views, Fort St Elmo and the start of the Valletta Waterfront area. A complete circuit takes around 20 minutes; the fare is all of €0.93.

Waterfront (☎2122 0633; Pinto Wharf; ⊙8am-5pm daily)

Ziffa (194 Triq id-Dejqa; per 10min €1; ⊙9am-11pm Mon-Sat, 9am-10.30pm Sun) Internet access, wi-fi and good rates for international phone calls.

Getting There & Away

The City Gate **bus terminus** has services to all parts of the island, and there's a convenient ferry service to Sliema (see p848).

AROUND MALTA

Sliema, St Julian's & Paceville

The cool kids of Malta flock to Sliema, St Julian's and Paceville to promenade, eat, drink, shop and play. As well as being a local playground, it's where many tourists base themselves, among the growing number of high-rise hotels, apartment blocks, shops, restaurants, bars and nightclubs.

Sights & Activities

There are good views of Valletta from Triq ix-Xatt (The Strand), even if there's not much to see in Sliema itself. Triq ix-Xatt and Triq it-Torri (Tower Rd) make for a perfect waterfront stroll, with plenty of bars and cafes en route. Beaches in the area are mostly shelves of bare rock; there are better facilities at the private lidos along the coast, which include swimming pools, sun lounges, bars and water sports (admission costs around €5 to €10 per day).

Captain Morgan Cruises (☎2346 3333; www.captainmorgan.com.mt) operates from the waterfront area of Sliema known as 'the Ferries' and has a boat trip for every traveller's taste and budget, including a popular tour of Grand Harbour (€16). Shop around – there are lots of competitors along the waterfront.

Sleeping

TOP CHOICE **Hotel Valentina** HOTEL €€
(☎2138 2232; www.hotelvalentina.com; Triq Schreiber, Paceville; s/d from €82/92; ❄ wifi) Prices at Valentina are shockingly reasonable and the location is fab. There's a boutique feel, but older rooms have a rustic atmosphere while newer ones have clean, contemporary lines and splashes of vivid colour. A bargain, especially in low season.

NSTS Hibernia Residence & Hostel HOSTEL €
(☎2133 3859, 2133 5450; www.nsts.org; Triq Mons G Depiro, Sliema; dm/s/tw €12/57/74; @) This place is perfect for those who are after quality budget accommodation. As well as a TV lounge, internet cafe and rooftop sun terrace, there are single-sex dorms or twin studios with private bathroom and kitchenette. From Valletta take bus 62, 64 or 67 to Balluta Bay and walk 300m up Triq Manwel Dimech; Triq Mons G Depiro is on the left.

Balco Harmony Hostel HOSTEL €
(☎2167 6946; www.balcomalta.com; Triq Cushcieri, Gzira; dm/s/tw €14.50/25/33; wifi) Basic but friendly place a couple of blocks from Sliema waterfront. No permanent reception.

Eating

This area is Malta's gastronomic heartland. Fertile hunting grounds for top dining experiences include Spinola Bay and the sleek Portomaso complex.

TOP CHOICE **Kitchen** MEDITERRANEAN €€€
(☎2131 1112; 210 Triq it-Torri, Sliema; mains €16-23; ⊙lunch Thu-Mon, dinner daily, closed Aug) On a none-too-interesting stretch of the promenade, the Kitchen's owner-chef whips up an exemplary Med-fusion menu in a smart, simple setting. Mouth-watering dishes include white-bean soup with truffle oil, and pan-fried prawns with pea puree; there are also some imaginative vegetarian dishes.

Avenue ITALIAN €€
(Triq Gort, Paceville; mains €7-10; ⊙lunch Mon-Sat, dinner daily) Multicoloured and multiroomed, the Avenue is a quiet escape from Paceville's traffic with a huge pizza and pasta menu,

Murano glass and Venetian masks as decor, and tonnes of outdoor tables. With prices this decent it's no surprise it's enormously popular.

Arkadia Foodstore GROCERY
(Triq il-Knisja, Paceville; ⌚8am-8pm Mon-Sat) Convenient food store.

Tower Foods Supermarket SUPERMARKET
(46 Triq il-Kbira, Sliema; ⌚8am-7.30pm Mon-Sat) Handy supermarket.

Drinking & Entertainment

Paceville is the place for partying, with wall-to-wall bars and clubs, especially around the northern end of Triq San Ġorġ; it's jam-packed on weekends year-round (and nightly in summer).

Muddy Waters BAR
(56 Triq il-Kbira, St Julian's) On Balluta Bay, Muddies has a great jukebox, rock DJs on Friday and Saturday, and live rock bands on Sunday nights, when things can get pretty rowdy and the tables may act as dance floors. It's a favourite of the student crowd.

Havana CLUB
(www.havanamalta.com; Triq San Ġorġ, Paceville; admission free) Six bars and a mixed soundtrack of R&B, soul and commercial favourites keep the crowds happy here. There are lots of students and tourists chatting each other up, but plenty of locals too.

Fuego BAR
(www.fuego.com.mt; Triq Santu Wistin, Paceville; admission free) Get hot and sweaty dancing up a storm at this popular salsa bar – head first to its free salsa-dancing classes (Monday to Wednesday from 8.30pm).

O'Casey's Irish Pub PUB
(Triq Santu Wistin, Paceville) Beneath Hotel Bernard – crowded, lively and well stocked with cold Guinness. It also screens live football games.

Information

MelitaNet (Triq Ball, Paceville; per hr €2; ⌚24hr) Large internet cafe inside Tropicana Hotel. Also offers good-value rates for international calls.

White House (cnr Paceville Ave & Triq Schreiber, Paceville; per 3hr €5; ⌚7am-11pm) Fast internet access with lots of terminals.

WORTH A TRIP

HYPOGEUM

The town of **Paola**, about 4km south of Valletta, is home to the magnificent **Hal Saflieni Hypogeum** (www.heritagemalta.com; Triq iċ-Ċimiterju; admission €25; ⌚tours hourly 9am-4pm), a complex of underground burial chambers thought to date from 3600 to 3000 BC. Excellent 50-minute tours of the complex are available, but the number of visitors has been restricted in order to preserve the fragile Unesco World Heritage Site. Prebooking is therefore absolutely essential (usually a couple of weeks before you wish to visit); tickets are available in person from the Hypogeum and the National Museum of Archaeology in Valletta (p840), or online at www.heritagemalta.org.

Getting There & Away

Buses 62, 64, 66 and 67 run regularly between Valletta and Sliema, St Julian's and Paceville (€0.47). There's also a ferry service between Sliema and Valletta (see p848).

Mdina & Rabat

Elegant, aristocratic Mdina (which is aptly nicknamed the Silent City) is perched on a rocky outcrop in the island's southwest. Fortified for more than 3000 years, it was Malta's old political centre; today visitors can spend hours wandering the quiet, narrow streets. Rabat is the town settlement outside the walls.

Mdina's main square is dominated by **St Paul's Cathedral** (Pjazza San Pawl; adult/student €2.50/1.75; ⌚9.30-4.45pm Mon-Sat, 3-4.45pm Sun), worth visiting for the huge fresco of St Paul's shipwreck.

If you see only one museum in Mdina, make it the **Palazzo Falson** (www.palazzofalson.com; Triq Villegaignon; adult/student €10/5; ⌚10am-5pm Tue-Sun), a beautifully preserved medieval mansion that offers a rare glimpse into the private world behind Mdina's anonymous aristocratic walls.

Sleeping & Eating

Point de Vue Guesthouse B&B €
(☎2145 4117; www.pointdevuemalta.com; 5 Saqqaja, Rabat; per person incl breakfast from €30; @)

This century-old, 12-room guest house is rightly popular thanks to a combination of affordable rates and its position just metres from Mdina's town walls.

TOP CHOICE **Mahżen XII** MALTESE €€
(Triq L-Imhażen; mains €12-15; ⏱noon-3pm Fri-Wed, 7-9pm Wed, Fri & Sat) Tucked into a barrel-vaulted powder magazine in Mdina's western walls (the name means 'Magazine No 12'), this atmospheric little place is a shrine to local produce – much of the food comes from the owner's family farm near Mġarr.

Getting There & Away

From Valletta, take bus 80 or 81 to reach Rabat (€0.54); from Sliema and St Julian's take bus 65 (€1.16). The bus terminus in Rabat is on Is-Saqqajja, 150m south of Mdina's main gate.

GOZO

Malta's little-sister island has a charm all of its own. More relaxed, more rural and home to some stunning scenery, this tiny place should not be missed. Do yourself a favour and spend a few days here, as visiting on a day trip can't really do it justice.

Victoria (Rabat)

Victoria, also known as Rabat, is the chief town of Gozo and sits at the centre of the island, 6km from the ferry terminal at Mġarr. All bus routes originate and finish at the terminus on Triq Putirjal, about 10 minutes' walk from the Citadel.

Pjazza Indipendenza, the main square of Victoria, is a hive of activity, with open-air cafes, craft shops and traders peddling fresh produce.

Above the square rises the **Citadel** (also known as Il-Kastell, or Citadella), a miniature version of Malta's Mdina; a stroll around its battlements offers panoramic views across the island. The **Cathedral of the Assumption** (Misraħ il-Katidral; admission €3; ⏱9am-5pm Mon-Sat) was built between 1697 and 1711. Entrance includes an audio guide.

Call into nearby **Ta'Rikardu** (4 Triq il-Fossos; ⏱10am-6pm) for local produce chock-full of flavour. Order a platter (€10 for two people) and wash it down with Gozitan wine.

Marsalforn

Marsalforn is Gozo's main holiday resort, but it is not an especially lovely town. You can hike eastwards over the hill to Ramla Bay in about 45 minutes, or west to swimming holes and salt pans.

TOP CHOICE **Maria Giovanna Guesthouse** GROCERY
(☎2155 3630; www.gozoguesthouses.com; 41 Triq ir-Rabat; s/d €30/60; @📶) This small, extremely welcoming guest house, just back from the waterfront, retains a loyal clientele who come back again and again, making it the pick of budget accommodation on Gozo. There are 15 rooms, each charmingly decorated in rustic Gozitan style, with private bathrooms; all have balconies, with one exception, and guests are free to use the kitchen.

Marsalforn is a 4km walk from Victoria, or catch bus 21.

Xagħra

Xagħra conforms to the classic Mediterranean image of the tree-lined village square where old men sit and chat in the shade of oleanders. Close by are the megalithic temples of **Ġgantija** (access from Triq L-Imqades; adult/student €8/4, ⏱9am-5pm), dating from 3600 BC. These temples are the oldest free-standing stone structures in the world, predating the pyramids of Egypt by more than 500 years.

It's not far from here to one of Gozo's best beaches. **Ramla Bay** has a beautiful red-sand strand perfect for sunbathing. Follow the signposts from town. Buses 64 and 65 run between Victoria and Xagħra.

COMINO

Tiny Comino, once the hideout of pirates, now hosts boatloads of invaders of the sun-seeking variety. The island's biggest attraction is the photogenic **Blue Lagoon**, a sheltered cove with a white-sand seabed and clear turquoise waters. You can take a boat trip here from many resort areas in Malta and Gozo; hordes of day trippers will put paid to any desert-island fantasies.

The Comino Hotel runs a ferry service from Ċirkewwa in Malta and Mġarr in Gozo (€10 return). Independent water taxis also operate regularly to the island; from Mġarr it's usually €8 return; from Ċirkewwa it's €10 return.

UNDERSTAND MALTA

History

Malta's oldest monuments are the mysterious megalithic temples at Ġgantija on Gozo, and Ħaġar Qim and Mnajdra on the southwest coast of the main island. Built between 3800 and 2500 BC, they're the world's oldest surviving free-standing structures. From around 800 to 218 BC, Malta was colonised by the Phoenicians and Carthaginians, and then became part of the Roman Empire. In AD 60 St Paul was shipwrecked on the island, where, according to folklore, he converted the islanders to Christianity. Arabs arrived in 870 and had a considerable influence on agriculture and language. Then came a succession of Normans, Angevins (French), Aragonese and Castilians (Spanish).

In 1530 the islands were given to the Knights of the Order of St John, a religious crusader organisation founded in Jerusalem. The Knights repelled invading Turks in 1565 and were considered 'saviours of Europe'. Soon afterwards though, the Order declined and surrendered to Napoleon in 1798 without a fight. The British took over in 1800 and began to develop Malta into a major naval base. The new member of the British Empire suffered greatly from bombing during WWII.

In 1947 the devastated island nation was given a measure of self-governance. The country gained independence in 1964 and became a republic in 1974. In 2004 Malta joined the EU, and introduced the euro as its currency in January 2008.

People

Malta, with a population of 410,000, is Europe's most densely populated country. Most live in the satellite towns around Valletta, Sliema and the Grand Harbour; approximately 31,000 live on Gozo, while Comino's permanent population is only four. More than 95% of the population is Maltese-born.

Despite an easy blend of Mediterranean and British culture, there's still a strong feeling of tradition; around 98% of the population is Roman Catholic, businesses are closed on Sunday and abortion and divorce are illegal.

THE MALTESE FESTA

Each village has a *festa* (feast day) honouring its patron saint, and you can't avoid getting caught up in the celebrations. Religious enthusiasm starts in the days leading up to and during the *festa* as families flock to the churches to give thanks. The streets are illuminated and the festivities culminate in a huge procession, complete with fireworks, marching brass bands and a life-sized statue of the patron saint. *Festa* season runs from May to September. But a *festa* isn't the only excuse to throw a party in Malta, and the website www.visitmalta.com/events lists what's on, where and when (including links to *festa* dates and locations).

Food & Drink

Price ranges in this chapter are based on the average cost of a main course in the evening:

€€€ more than €16

€€ €8 to €16

€ less than €8

Environment

The Maltese archipelago consists of three inhabited islands: Malta, Gozo and Comino. They lie in the middle of the Mediterranean, south of Sicily and east of Tunisia. These densely populated islands feature no major hills and little greenery to soften the stony, sun-bleached landscape. There is virtually no surface water and there are no permanent creeks or rivers.

SURVIVAL GUIDE

Directory A-Z

Accommodation

Accommodation is plentiful and the **Malta Tourism Authority** (www.visitmalta.com) can provide listings. There is one camping ground on the Marfa peninsula in the northwest corner of Malta, but its shadeless grounds and remote location render it unappealing. There is a handful of hostels and an array of guest houses that offer great value. Rates are significantly reduced during off-peak periods. The high season is generally June to September, as well as the Christmas–New Year period.

Price ranges in this chapter for double rooms are as follows:

€ less than €50

€€ €50 to €130

€€€ more than €130

Activities

The **Malta Tourism Authority** (www.visitmalta.com) showcases activities available in Malta. Click the 'What to See & Do' pages.

DIVING

Diving conditions are excellent: visibility often exceeds 30m and there's a variety of marine life. The Mediterranean's warm temperatures mean that diving is possible year-round. There are more than 40 diving schools; the majority are members of the **Professional Diving Schools Association** (PDSA; www.pdsa.org.mt). See also www.visitmalta.com/diving-malta for details of dive sites, regulations and operators.

SWIMMING

The best sandy beaches on Malta are Ġnejna Bay, Għajn Tuffieħa Bay and Golden Bay, all in Malta's northwest (bus 47 from Valletta or bus 652 from Sliema); and Mellieħa Bay in the north (bus 44 or 45 from Valletta or bus 645 from Sliema/St Julian's). The best sandy beaches on Gozo are Ramla Bay (bus 42) and Xlendi Bay (bus 87).

There are great rocky swimming spots on Comino (the Blue Lagoon) and in Malta's south (Għar Lapsi). Gozo has some good rocky sites too, including Dwejra in the west.

Business Hours

Banks 8.30am-12.30pm Mon-Fri, 8.30-11.30am Sat, slightly longer hours Jun-Sep

Museums 9am-5pm daily (last entry at 4.30pm); closed on major public holidays

Restaurants noon-3pm & 7-11pm

Shops 9am-1pm & 4-7pm Mon-Sat, closed Sun and public holidays; some stay open all day in summer, especially in tourist areas

Holidays

New Year's Day 1 January

St Paul's Shipwreck 10 February

St Joseph's Day 19 March

Freedom Day 31 March

Good Friday March/April

Labour Day 1 May

Commemoration of 1919 Independence Riots 7 June

Feast of Sts Peter and Paul (L-Imnarja Festival) 29 June

Feast of the Assumption 15 August

Victory Day 8 September

Independence Day 21 September

Feast of the Immaculate Conception 8 December

Republic Day 13 December

Christmas Day 25 December

Money

Malta adopted the euro in January 2008. To avoid stealth price hikes, the cost of all goods is legally required to be listed in the old Maltese lira as well as euros, hence the often bizarre prices for public transport and other state-run services. Banks usually offer better currency exchange rates than hotels. There is a 24-hour exchange bureau and ATMs at the airport and at Valletta's Pinto Wharf. ATMs can be found in most towns.

It's a good idea to round up a taxi fare or restaurant bill to leave a small tip. Shops have fixed prices; hotels and car-hire agencies offer reduced rates in the low and shoulder seasons (October to May).

Telephone

To call Malta from abroad, dial the international access code, ☎356 (Malta's country code), and the eight-digit number (there are no area codes). Local mobile numbers begin with 79 or 99. For overseas enquiries, call ☎1152.

Malta uses the GSM900 mobile phone network which is compatible with the rest of Europe, Australia and New Zealand, but not with the USA and Canada's GSM1900.

Card-operated public telephones are widely available; buy phonecards at kiosks, post offices and souvenir shops.

Visas

Visas are not needed for visits of up to three months by nationals of most Commonwealth countries (excluding South Africa, India and Pakistan), most European countries, the USA and Japan. Full details (and visa application forms) are on the website of Malta's **Ministry of Foreign Affairs** (www.foreign.gov.mt).

Getting There & Away

Malta is well connected to Europe and North Africa. All flights arrive at and depart from **Malta International Airport** (MLA; ☎2124 9600; www.maltairport.com) at Luqa, 8km south of Valletta. The country has regular sea links with Italy. Ferries dock at the Sea Passenger Terminal beside the Valletta Waterfront.

Virtu Ferries (www.virtuferries.com) Malta (☎2206 9022); Catania (☎095-535 711); Pozzallo (☎0932-954 062) offers the fastest Malta–Sicily crossing with its catamaran service from Pozzallo and Catania. The Pozzallo–Malta crossing takes 90 minutes and operates year-round. The return passenger fare on both routes is €147/88 in high/low season.

Grimaldi Ferries (☎2299 5110; www.grimaldi-ferries.com) operates a weekly service year-round from Genoa and Civitavecchia.

Grandi Navi Veloci (GNV; ☎2569 4550; www.gnv.it) operates a Livorno–Palermo–Malta service once a week.

Getting Around

Boat

Malta to Gozo: Gozo Channel (☎2158 0435; www.gozochannel.com) operates car-ferry services between Ċirkewwa (Malta) and Mġarr (Gozo), with crossings every 45 to 75 minutes from 6am to around 8pm (and every two hours throughout the night). The journey takes 25 minutes and the return fare is adult/car (including driver) €4.65/15.70. Bus 45 runs regularly from Valletta to Ċirkewwa to connect with the ferry to Gozo. Bus 25 runs between Victoria and Mġarr on Gozo.

Malta & Gozo to Comino: See p845.

Valletta to Sliema: Marsamxetto ferry service (☎2346 3862) has a five-minute crossing (€0.93) with departures every hour (every half-hour from 10am to 4pm) from 8am to 6pm. Ferries depart from Sliema on the hour and half-hour, and leave from Valletta at quarter past and quarter to the hour.

Bus

Malta and Gozo buses are run by the **Malta Public Transport Association** (ATP; ☎2125 0007/8; www.atp.com.mt). Most of Malta's services originate from the chaotic City Gate terminus, just outside Valletta's fortifications. Fares are cheap – from €0.47 to €1.16 (be sure to have small change for the driver when you board). Services are regular and the more popular routes run till 11pm. Ask at the tourist office for a free timetable.

On Gozo, the bus terminus is in Victoria, just south of Triq ir-Repubblika. Services cost €0.47.

Car & Motorcycle

Malta has low rental rates but you face the aggravation of road rules being ignored, confusingly signposted roads and difficult parking. All the major international car-hire companies are at the airport, and there are dozens of local agencies. Shop around – rates depend on season, length of rental and size and make of car. Daily rates for the smallest vehicles start from around €22.

Taxi

Official taxis are metered but generally expensive. **Wembley Motors** (☎2137 4141) offers a 24-hour service.

Moldova

Includes »

Best Places to Eat

» Carmelo, Chişinău (p851)
» Beer House, Chişinău (p851)
» Kumanek, Tiraspol (p856)
» Celentano, Chişinău (p853)

Best Places to Stay

» Adresa, Chişinău (p851)
» Marisha, Chişinău (p851)
» Chişinău Hostel (p851)

Why Go?

Moldo-who? Travel blogs about Moldova – only vaguely known in Europe, all but anonymous to the rest of the world and consistently ranked near the bottom of the World Database of Happiness – are more often written by melancholy Peace Corps volunteers rather than tipsy revellers enjoying what is arguably the best-value wine drinking (ad)venture on the planet. More sober tourist attractions are few, but outstanding, such as the dramatic and beautiful cave monasteries and the always-petulant breakaway republic of Transdniestr, still plugging along as one of Europe's top (and most notorious) idiosyncratic wonders. Chişinău's unexpectedly superb dining and clubbing options have been known to extend a few visits as well.

Although Moldova is a perpetual contender for the 'Poorest Country in Europe' designation, prices here, particularly for accommodation, can be unexpectedly high.

When to Go

Chişinău

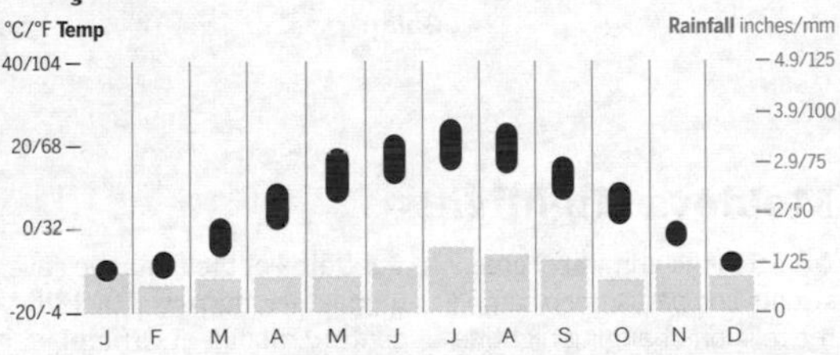

Jun Parks and restaurant terraces fill with recently freed students; markets fill with produce.

Jul High season hits its peak with hiking, wine tours and camping all in full operation.

Oct The Wine Festival, on the second Sunday, is enhanced by a 10-day visa-free interval.

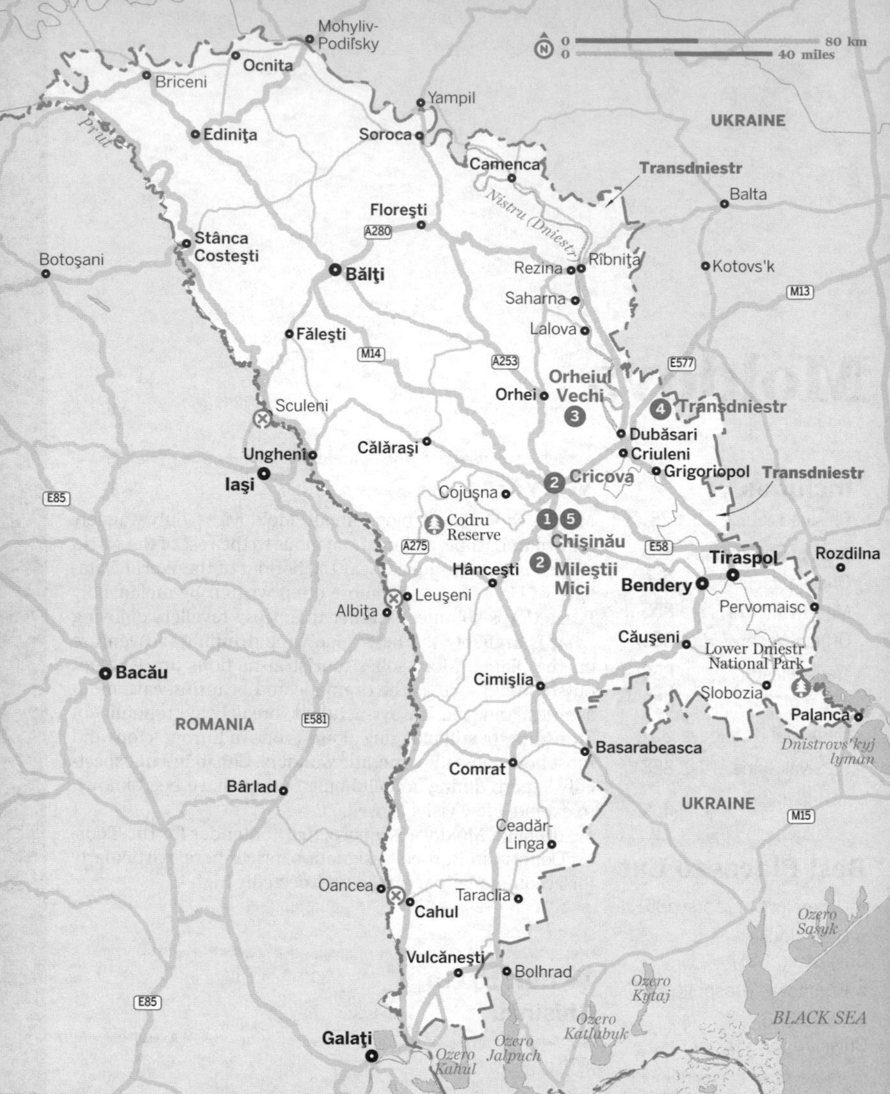

Moldova Highlights

1. Stroll the admirably green streets and parks, then sample the religion-changing nightlife of **Chișinău** (p851)
2. Designate a driver for tours of the world-famous wine cellars at **Mileștii Mici** (p855) and **Cricova** (p855)
3. Detox at the fantastic cave monastery, burrowed by 13th-century monks, at **Orheiul Vechi** (p855)
4. Go *way* off the beaten path in the self-styled 'republic' of **Transdniestr** (p856), a surreal, living homage to the Soviet Union
5. Gorge on the many excellent **dining** (p851) options in Chișinău

CHIŞINĂU

☎22 / POP 785,000

Newly arrived visitors to Moldova, a country routinely found at the bottom of European economic-indicator rankings, may be initially confused when seeing Chişinău's fashionably dressed inhabitants exiting flashy cars, strutting down boutique-lined avenues and talking into state of-the-art mobile phones, as they head to fancy restaurants. Sizeable incoming cash flow from emigrants working abroad accounts for some of this paradoxical affluence, but there's the well-off and then there's the dubiously well-connected – individuals who are above the law and shamelessly conduct themselves as such. While these occasional, disquieting sightings may distract visitors, citizens of this vibrant, good-natured city have long since dismissed such oddities in favour of what really counts: having a good time.

First chronicled in 1420, Chişinău (*kish*-i-now in Moldovan, *kish*-i-nyov in Russian) became a hotbed of anti-Semitism in the early 20th century. Later it was the headquarters of the USSR's southwestern military operations during Soviet rule. Between 1944 and 1990 the city was called Kishinev, its Russian name.

Sights

National Archaeology & History Museum MUSEUM

(www.nationalmuseum.md; Str 31 August 1989 no 121a; admission/camera/video 15/15/40 lei; ⌚10am-6pm Sat-Thu) The grandaddy of Chişinău's museums contains archaeological artefacts from Orheiul Vechi, including Golden Horde coins, Soviet-era weaponry and a huge WWII diorama on the 1st floor.

National Ethnographic & Nature Museum MUSEUM

(Str M Kogălniceanu 82; admission 15 lei; ⌚10am-6pm Tue-Sun) The highlight of this massive exhibition is a life-size reconstruction of a mammoth skeleton, discovered in the Rezine region in 1966. Take an hour to see the museum's pop art, taxidermied animals and exhibits covering geology, botany and zoology.

Pushkin Museum HISTORIC HOUSE

(Str Anton Pann 19; admission 15 lei; ⌚10am-4pm Tue-Sun) Northeast of the central parks, this is where Russian poet Alexander Pushkin (1799–1837) spent his exiled years between 1820 and 1823. It was here that he wrote *The Prisoner of the Caucasus* and other classics. You can step in and view his tiny cottage. An English-language tour costs 50 lei.

Sleeping

Check out **Marisha** (www.marisha.net) and **Adresa** (☎544 392; www.adresa.md; B-dul Negruzzi 1; 1-room apt 395-1100 lei; ⌚24hr) for cheap homestays and apartments in Chişinău.

TOP CHOICE **Chişinău Hostel** HOSTEL €

(☎069-711 918; www.chisinau-hostel.ucoz.com; Str Arborilor 4/5, behind Malldova; dm/d 157/410 lei; 📶@) Moldova's only proper hostel is about a 25-minute walk from the centre. This comfortable, well-run place offers lockers, breakfast, shared kitchen, Wii, laundry (32 lei), and tours to wineries and Transdniestr. A number of maxitaxis stop here from the centre and all stations; ask for 'Malldova' (shopping centre). A taxi ride will cost 35 to 40 lei.

Hotel Turist HOTEL €

(☎220 637; B-dul Renaşterii 13; s 500-700 lei, d 450-560 lei; 📶) For a kitsch blast from the Soviet past, try this place overlooking a giant Soviet memorial to communist youth. The doubles are all unrenovated and spare, but just fine. More expensive rooms have fridges, air-con and balconies. Breafast is 55 lei.

Hotel Zarea HOTEL €€

(☎227 625; Str Anton Pann 4; r 560-700 lei, without bathroom 270-390 lei; ❄) This drab high-rise has dour, smoky rooms that are appropriately priced. Breakfast isn't included. Higher-priced doubles have air-con.

Eating

TOP CHOICE **Carmelo** ITALIAN €€

(Str Veronica Micle 1/1; pasta 80-150 lei, pizzas 75-150 lei) Italian-run, Carmelo serves up excellent pasta dishes and filling, thin-crust pizzas. The *secondi* (meat plates) are special-occasion prices.

TOP CHOICE **Beer House** INTERNATIONAL €€

(B-dul Negruzzi 6/2; mains 68-190 lei) This brewery-restaurant has four delicious home-brewed beers and a superb menu, warming up with chicken wings and peaking at rabbit or chicken grilled in cognac.

Café Vijelios CAFE €

(Str Puşkin 22; mains 10-22 lei) This cafeteria serves surprisingly succulent food priced for the impoverished university crowd.

Central Chişinău

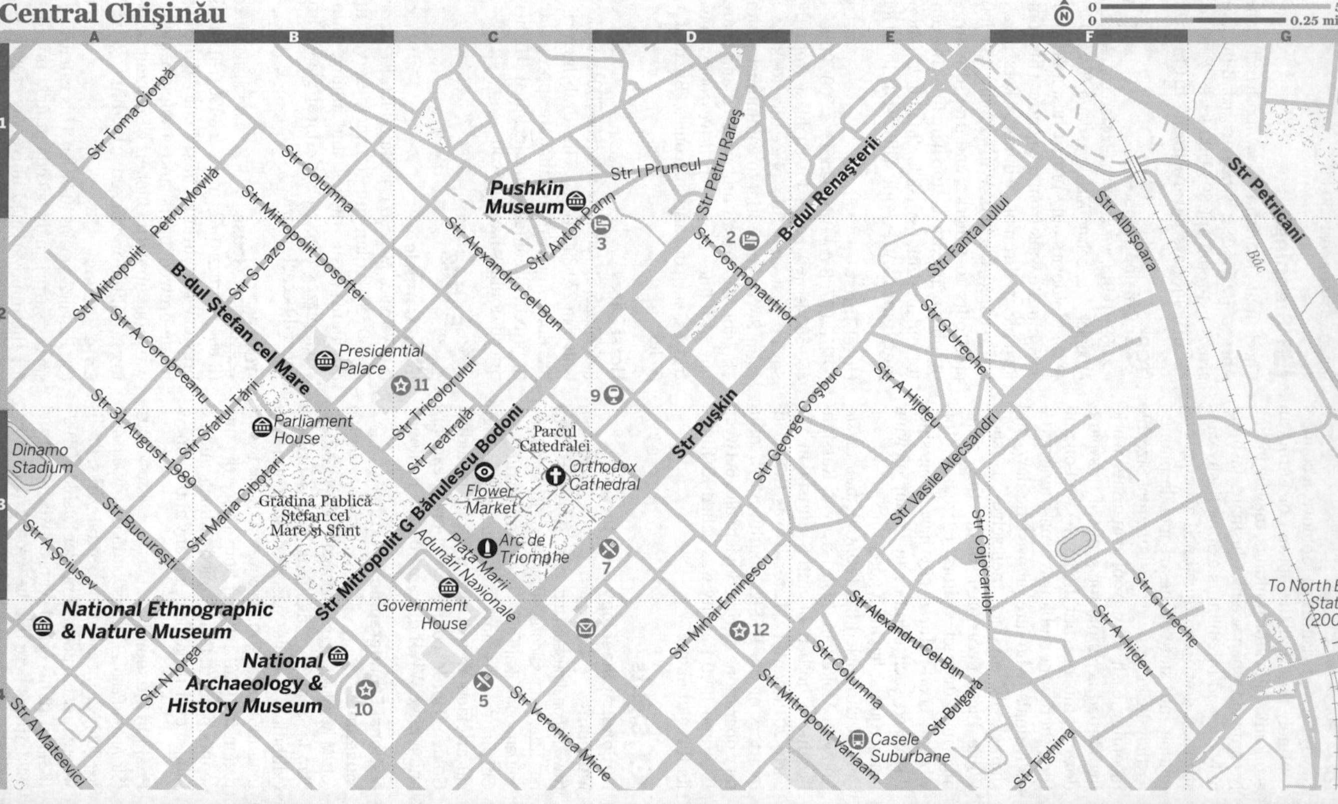

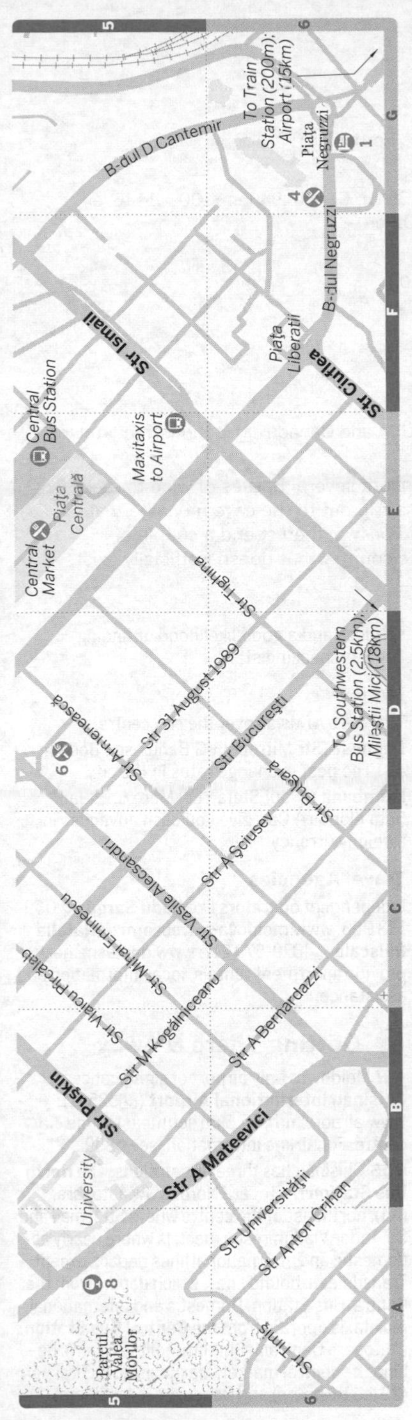

Celentano PIZZA €

(Str Puşkin 30; pizzas 20 lei, plus toppings) Popular for its locally unique build-your-own-pizza offer (our chicken-and-onion pizza was 36 lei). Also does fruit and chocolate shakes.

Drinking

Chişinău Brewery BREWERY

(☎929 243; www.berechisinau.md, in Moldovan; Str Uzinelor 167; ⊙by appointment) Just east of the centre in Ciocana, this brewery offers free, one-hour tours that include a short video and a surprisingly generous tasting.

Robin Pub PUB

(Str Alexandru cel Bun 83; ⊙11am-midnight) A friendly, affordable, local-pub feel reigns in this tastefully decorated hang-out.

Coliba Studenţilor BAR

(Str A Mateevici; ⊙8am-11pm) During the school year the terrace is a good place to bump into eager English speakers.

Entertainment

City Club CLUB

(Str 31 August 1989 121; ⊙10pm-6am) In the alley next to the Licurici Puppet Theatre,

Central Chişinău

Top Sights

National Archaeology & History Museum B4
National Ethnographic & Nature Museum A4
Pushkin Museum C1

Sleeping

1 Adresa G6
2 Hotel Turist D2
3 Hotel Zarea D2

Eating

4 Beer House G6
5 Café Vijelios C4
6 Carmelo D5
7 Celentano D3

Drinking

8 Coliba Studenţilor A5
9 Robin Pub D2

Entertainment

10 City Club B4
11 Opera & Ballet Theatre C2
12 Philharmonic Concert Hall D4

MOLDOVA FACTS

» **Area** 33,851 sq km

» **Capital** Chişinău

» **Language** Moldovan (virtually the same as Romanian)

» **Currency** Moldovan leu (plural lei)

» **Exchange rates** A$1 = 12.35 lei; C$1 = 12.35 lei; €1 = 16.94 lei; ¥100 = 14.16 lei; NZ$1 = 9.15 lei; UK£1 = 19.23 lei; US$1 = 11.91 lei

» **Country code** ☎373

» **Emergency** Police ☎902; ambulance ☎903

» **Money** ATMs abundant in Chişinău

» **Budget hotel room** 500 lei

» **Two-course evening meal** 160 lei

» **Museum entrance** 15 lei

» **Visas** Not required for citizens of the EU, USA and Canada; 'invitations' required for Australians and New Zealanders

» **Itinerary** Arrive in Chişinău – buy and uncork several bottles of wine to fuel partying...erm, civilised wine tasting. Make a trip out to the cave monastery at Orheiul Vechi. Take a tour around a vineyard or two, then spend a couple of memorably surreal days in Transdniestr, the country that doesn't officially exist.

this 2nd-floor club consistently ranks as one of the hippest places in town.

Opera & Ballet Theatre OPERA, BALLET
(B-dul Ştefan cel Mare 152; ⏲box office 10am-2pm & 5-7pm) This venue is home to the esteemed national opera and ballet company. Grab a bite at the Andy's Pizza outside the entrance before the show.

Philharmonic Concert Hall CLASSICAL MUSIC
(Str Mitropolit Varlaam 78) Moldova's National Philharmonic is based here.

Information

Dangers & Annoyances

Travellers are required to have their passports with them at all times. Cheeky police are prone to random checks.

Internet Access

There's free wi-fi in the Cathedral and Ştefan cel Mare Parks.

Internet (Hotel Cosmos, Piaţa Negruzzi 2; per hr 7 lei; ⏲24hr)

Moldtelecom Plaza (cnr B-dul Ştefan cel Mare & Str Ismail) Free wi-fi.

Medical Services

The **US embassy** (☎22-408 300; Str A Mateevici 103) has a list of English-speaking doctors.

Municipal Clinical Emergency Hospital (☎emergency 903, information 248 435; Str Toma Ciorba 1; ⏲24hr) A variety of emergency services and a good likelihood of finding English-speaking staff.

Money

There are ATMs all over the city centre.

Deghest (Str Mitropolit G Bănulescu Bodoni 43) The best exchange rates in the city.

Eximbank (B-dul Ştefan cel Mare 6; ⏲9am-5pm Mon-Fri) Can give you cash advances in foreign currency.

Travel Agencies

Independent operators like **Radu Sargu** (☎069-138 953; www.moldova-travel.com) or **Natalia Raiscaia** (☎079-578 217; www.domasha.net) provide apartment rentals, local information and assistance.

Getting There & Away

AIR Moldova's only airport of significance is **Chişinău International Airport** (☎525 111; www.airport.md), 15.5km southeast of the city centre. For airline information, see p859.

BUS Chişinău has three bus stations. The **North Bus Station** (Autogara Nord; www.autogara.md), northeast of the centre where Str Ismail and Str Tudor Vladimirescu meet, is where nearly all domestic and international lines depart, except Transdniestr-bound lines, which depart from the Central Bus Station. Domestic and international maxitaxis operate from the **Central Bus Station** (Autogara Centrală; Str Mitropolit Varlaam), behind the central market. Maxitaxis go to Tiraspol (29 lei, 1½ hours) and Bendery (25 lei; 1½hrs)

MOLDOVA'S INTERNET RESOURCES

Fest (www.fest.md)

Moldova Azi (www.azi.md)

Moldova.org (www.moldova.org)

Romania & Moldova Travel Guide (www.romaniaandmoldova.com)

Travel Guide Moldova (www.informator.md)

Your Friends in Moldova (www.marisha.net)

every 20 to 35 minutes from 6.30am to 6.30pm, with reduced services until 10pm. There are buses half-hourly from 9.15am to 10pm to Orhei (19 lei), leaving from the 'Casele Suburbane' terminal about 100m west of Central Station. Buses to southern destinations use the **Southwestern Bus Station** (Autogara Sud-vest; cnr Şoseaua Hânceşti & Str Spicului), approximately 2.2km from the city centre, as well as a fleet of minibuses to Iaşi, Romania (110 lei, four hours).

TRAIN International routes departing from Chişinău's **train station** (Aleea Gării), just southeast of Piaţa Negruzii, include three daily trains to Moscow (four-bed sleeper 1275 to 1515 lei, 28 to 32 hours), three daily trains to Kyiv (545 to 670 lei, 14 hours), one each to St Petersburg (1441 lei, 40 hours) and Bucharest (785 lei, 14 hours), and three to Lviv (645 lei, 18 hours), as well as three weekly services to Minsk (743 lei, 25 hours). To get to Budapest, you must change in Bucharest.

Getting Around

TO/FROM THE AIRPORT Maxitaxi 165 departs every 20 minutes from Str Ismail, across from Eximbank near the corner of B-dul Ştefan cel Mare, for the airport (3 lei).

BUS & TROLLEYBUS Route 45 runs from the Central Bus Station to the Southwestern Bus Station, as does maxitaxi 117 from the train station. Bus 1 runs from the train station to B-dul Ştefan cel Mare. Trolleybuses (running by overhead wire) 1, 4, 5, 8, 18 and 22 run to the train station from the city centre. Buses 2, 10 and 16 go to the Southwestern Bus Station. Maxitaxis 176 and 191 go to the North Bus Station from the city centre. Tickets (2 lei for buses and 1 leu for trolleybuses) are sold on board.

TAXI Many taxis do not have meters or prices listed on the door and taxi-stand drivers may occasionally try to rip you off. Ordering a **taxi** (☎1448, 1433, 1422, 1407) is best. If you decide to hop in off the street, agree on a price to your destination before getting in the car.

AROUND CHIŞINĂU

Cricova

Of Moldova's many fine wineries, **Cricova** (☎22-441 204; www.cricova.md; Str Ungureanu 1; ⏲8am-4pm) is arguably the best known. Its underground wine kingdom, 15km north of Chişinău, is one of Europe's biggest. Some 60km worth of the 120km-long underground limestone tunnels – dating from the 15th century – are lined wall-to-wall with bottles.

You must have private transport and advance reservations to get into Cricova or you can arrange for the staff to pick you up in Chişinău. Tours range from 45 minutes to 2½ hours (250 to 1350 lei), with increasing tastings and food as the price climbs.

Mileştii Mici

While Cricova has the hype, **Mileştii Mici** (☎382 333; www.milestii-mici.md; ⏲9am-5pm Mon-Fri, by appointment Sat & Sun) has the goods. Also housed in a limestone mine, these are *the* largest cellars in Europe (more than 200km of tunnels). They were recognised by Guinness World Records in 2005 for having the largest wine collection in the world (1.5 million bottles), though the collection has now surpassed the 2-million-bottle mark.

Two-hour tours cost 250 lei per person; a tour, tasting and lunch costs 500 to 900 lei. Weekday tour groups must have a minimum of four people, though this is negotiable; a Saturday or Sunday tour must have a minimum of 15 people.

Orheiul Vechi

Ten kilometres southeast of Orhei lies Orheiul Vechi (marked on maps as the village of Trebujeni), unquestionably Moldova's most fantastic sight. It's certainly among its most picturesque places.

The **Orheiul Vechi Monastery Complex** (Complexul Muzeistic Orheiul Vechi; ☎235-34 242; admission 15 lei; ⏲9am-6pm Tue-Sun) was carved into a massive limestone cliff in this wild, rocky, remote spot by Orthodox monks in the 13th century.

It's forbidden to wear shorts and women must cover their heads while inside the monastery.

CROSSING THE TRANSDNIESTRAN BORDER

We used to receive frequent reader feedback reporting disturbing high jinks at Transdniestran border crossings, where organised intimidation was used to separate travellers from their money. Though at the time of research it was too early to confidently declare anything, it appeared as if the bribe-factory atmosphere had cooled significantly. It's still a good idea to employ a few precautions, like not carrying ridiculous amounts of cash. Professional-looking cameras or video cameras may still cause some grumbling. For Moldova-Odesa bus journeys, it's still strongly recommended to circumnavigate the region through the southeast village of Palanca.

Entry permit prices and requirements change frequently. At the time of writing, permits were 'officially' 20 Moldovan lei (about 17 Transdniestran rubles or €1.25). For stays of less than 10 hours, you don't need to pay this fee.

If you're staying for more than 24 hours, you'll need to register with **OVIR** (533-55 047; ul Kotovskogo 2a, Tiraspol; 9am-noon Mon, 9am-noon & 1-4pm Tue & Thu, 1-3pm Fri). Registration is free. Outside OVIR business hours go to the **Tiraspol Militia Office** (533-34 169; Roza Luxemburg 66; 24hr), where registration is possible.

TRANSDNIESTR

POP 555,500

The self-declared republic of Transdniestr (Pridnestrovskaia Moldavskaia Respublica, or PMR in Russian), a narrow strip of land covering 3567 sq km on the eastern bank of the Nistru River is, according to them, one of the world's last surviving bastions of communism.

Political jibber-jabber and historical ethnic boundaries notwithstanding, Moldova maintains that Transdniestr was illegally grabbed. With Russia's support, Transdniestr effectively won its 'independence' during a bloody civil war in the early 1990s. A tenuous, bitter truce has ensued ever since.

Travellers will be stunned by this idiosyncratic region that has developed its own currency, police force, army and borders, controlled by Transdniestran border guards. Russian is the predominant language. Transdniestrans boycott the Moldovan independence day and celebrate their own independence day on 2 September.

Rumours and political weirdness aside, visits here can be quite pleasant, and the surreal atmosphere is unforgettable.

Tiraspol

533 / POP 157,000

Tiraspol (from the Greek, meaning 'town on the Nistru'), 70km east of Chişinău, is an open-air museum glorifying all things Soviet. The city was founded in 1792 following Russian domination of the region.

Sights

Tiraspol National United Museum MUSEUM
(ul 25 Oktober 42; admission 25 rubles; 10am-5pm Sun-Fri) The closest thing to a local history museum, it features an exhibit on poet Nikolai Dimitriovich Zelinskogo, who founded the first Soviet school of chemistry. Opposite is the **Presidential Palace**, from which Igor Smirnov rules his mini-empire.

Kvint Factory BRANDY FACTORY
(www.kvint.biz; ul Lenina 38) Since 1897, the Kvint factory has been making some of Moldova's finest brandies. Buy cognac (starting at €2!) either near the front entrance of the plant or at the **Kvint shop** (ul 25 Oktober 84; 24hr).

Sleeping & Eating

You must register if staying more than 24 hours (see the boxed text above).

Stay at Lena's APARTMENT €
(72 536; lena_lozinskiy@inbox.ru; ul pereulok Naberezhnyi 1, apt 79; per person 120-180 rubles) Lena has a cosy two-room apartment with 24-hour hot water and a full kitchen. She can also arrange other rooms or full apartments around Tiraspol.

Hotel Aist HOTEL €€
(73 776; pereulok Naberezhnyi 3; d 250-550 rubles) Despite a derelict exterior, this is a decent hotel. The more expensive rooms have luxuries such as hot water and TV. No breakfast.

Kumanek UKRAINIAN €€
(ul Sverdlova 37; mains 21-89 rubles; 9am-11pm;) Mainly Ukrainian food, though there's a smattering of European dishes as well,

including dumplings, pancakes, fish, pork, mutton, chicken and veal.

7 Fridays CAFE €

(ul 25 Oktober 112; mains 23-66 rubles; ⌚11am-midnight; 📶) A popular cafe serving all manner of meat, salads, soups and, erm, sushi. Menus are Russian-only, but there are pictures to point at.

Information

Central telephone office (ul Karl Marx 149; ⌚8am-8pm) Through the far left door, you can buy phonecards and use internet (per hour 5.50 rubles; from 10am to 10pm). Note that the two sections have separate business hours.

Gasprom Bank (ul 25 Oktober 76; ⌚9.15am-8.30pm Mon-Sat) Changes money. There's an ATM at ul 25 Oktober 85 dispensing Transdniestran rubles.

Internet (ul 25 October 76; per hr 6 rubles; ⌚24hr) Below Gasprom Bank.

Getting There & Away

The train and bus stations are next to each other at the end of ul Lenina.

BUS From Tiraspol there are eight daily buses to Odesa (37.25 rubles, three hours) and one daily to Kyiv (186 rubles, 14 hours). Buses and maxitaxis go to Chişinău (26.70 rubles, 1½ hours) nearly every half-hour from 5.10am to 6.10pm. Trolleybus 19 (1.50 rubles) and quicker maxitaxis 19 and 20 (2.50 rubles) cross the bridge over the Dniestr to Bendery.

TRAIN One daily train goes to Moscow, via Kyiv, leaving promptly at 2.06am (3rd/2nd class 735/1250 rubles, 26 hours). At the time of research, it was reported that normal passenger train service to Chişinău, Odesa, Minsk and St Petersburg, suspended since 2006, would resume shortly.

UNDERSTAND MOLDOVA

History

Moldova today straddles two historic regions divided by the Nistru River. Historic Romanian Bessarabia incorporated the region west of the Nistru, while tsarist Russia governed the territory east of the river (Transdniestr).

Bessarabia, part of the Romanian principality of Moldavia, was annexed in 1812 by the Russian Empire. Anti-Semitism under the Russians was felt in Moldova, with pogroms in 1903 and 1905, and resulted in hundreds being killed or wounded, thousands made homeless and mass Jewish emigration to the Americas.

In 1918, after the October Revolution, Bessarabia declared its independence. Two months later the newly formed Democratic Moldavian Republic united with Romania. Russia never recognised this union.

Then in 1924 the Soviet Union created what came to be known as the Moldavian Autonomous Soviet Socialist Republic (Moldavian ASSR) oblast on the eastern banks of the Nistru River, and incorporated Transdniestr into the Ukrainian Soviet Socialist Republic (SSR). During 1929 the capital was moved to Tiraspol from Balta (in present-day Ukraine).

In June 1940 the Molotov-Ribbentrop Pact meant Soviet troops occupied Romanian Bessarabia and joined it with the southern part.

During 1941 allied Romanian and German troops attacked the Soviet Union. Bessarabia and Transdniestr fell into Romanian hands. Consequently, thousands of Bessarabian Jews were sent to labour camps and then deported to Auschwitz.

In August 1944 the Soviet army reoccupied Transdniestr and Bessarabia. In July 1949, 25,000 ethnic Moldovans (Romanians) were deported to Siberia, followed by another 250,000 from 1950 to 1952.

It wasn't until February 1990 that the first democratic elections to the Supreme Soviet (parliament) were won by the Popular Front. In April 1990 the Moldovan national flag was reinstated – except in Transdniestr. Moldova declared its full independence in August 1991.

Romania's 2007 entrance into the EU transformed the Moldovan border into the EU's eastern frontier, complicating the formerly lenient cross-border traffic.

In April 2009, violent protests broke out after election results showed the Communist Party dubiously retaining its power with 50% of the vote. Police response was severe – 200 people were arrested, with widespread reports of beatings in police stations and prisons.

In early 2010, Moldova's newly elected Western-leaning government, led by Prime Minister Vlad Filat, signed an order to remove nearly 360km of the communist-era barbed wire fence separating Moldova from Romania.

People

Moldovans make up 78.2% of the total population of 4.3 million, Ukrainians constitute 8.4%, Russians 5.8%, Gagauz 4.4%, Bulgarians 1.9%, and other nationalities such as Belarusians, Poles and Roma compose 1.3%.

In Transdniestr, Ukrainians and Russians make up 58% of the region's population; Moldovans make up 34%. It is one of the least urbanised countries in Europe.

Transdniestr and Gagauzia notwithstanding, much of Moldova's culture is Romanian by origin.

Food & Drink

Offering great quality and better prices, Chişinău is an eating and drinking wonderland. Cricova, Mileştii Mici, Cojuşna wineries, among others, offer the most fulfilling and inexpensive wine tours in the world.

Price ranges in this chapter are based on the average cost of a main course:

€€€ more than 170 lei

€€ 100 lei to 170 lei

€ less than 100 lei

Arts

There is a wealth of traditional folk art in Moldova, with carpet-making, pottery, weaving and woodcarving predominating. The country also has prolific modern composers, painters and sculptors.

SURVIVAL GUIDE

Directory A–Z

Accommodation

Chişinău has a good range of hotels. Most towns have small hotels that have survived from communist days. Basic singles or doubles with a shared bathroom cost 420 to 590 lei per room in Chişinău, but outside the capital, rooms will usually be 200 to 340 lei.

Camping grounds *(popas turistic)* are practically nonexistent, but wild camping is allowed anywhere unless otherwise prohibited. Check **Marisha** (www.marisha.net) for a growing list of homestay options.

All prices given in this chapter include breakfast and private bathroom unless otherwise noted. Price ranges are as follows:

€€€ more than 1200 lei

€€ 600 to 1200 lei

€ less than 600 lei

Business Hours

Banks 9am-3pm; many close for an hour around noon

Post offices 8am-7pm Mon-Fri, to 4pm Sat

Restaurants 10am-11pm

Shops 9am or 10am-6pm or 7pm; some close on Sunday

Embassies & Consulates

Romania embassy (☎22-228 126; www.chisinau.mae.ro; Str Bucureşti 66/1); consulate (☎22-237 622; Str Vlaicu Pircalab 39)

Russia (☎22-234 942; www.moldova.mid.ru; B-dul Ştefan cel Mare 153)

Ukraine (☎22-582 151; www.mfa.gov.ua, in Ukrainian; Str V Lupu 17)

Money

We've quoted most prices in this chapter in Moldovan lei to make on-the-ground price references easier. Moldovan lei come in denominations of one, five, 10, 20, 50, 100, 200 and 500. There are coins for one, five, 10, 25 and 50 bani (there are 100 bani in a leu).

Note that the breakaway Transdniestran republic has its own currency, which is useless anywhere else in the world.

Outside Chişinău, ATMs are sparse. It's near impossible to use travellers cheques. Credit cards are widely accepted in larger department stores, hotels and most restaurants in cities and towns. Bring cash for rural travel.

Post & Telephone

From Moldova, it costs 7 to 8.5 lei to send a postcard or letter under 20g to Western Europe, Australia or the USA.

DHL (www.dhl.com) has offices in Chişinău and Tiraspol.

Moldtelecom sells phonecards for domestic calls, available at any telephone centre. International calls require a prepaid card, such as Treitelecom, sold at any Moldpressa newspaper stand.

Mobile phone service in Moldova is provided by Moldcell and the ubiquitous **Orange** (www.orange.md).

Visas

Citizens of the EU, USA, Canada and Japan don't need visas. Australians, New Zealanders and South Africans require an invitation from a company, organisation or individual. The price of a single-/double-entry tourist visa valid for one month is US$40/50 (511/639 lei). Single-/double-entry transit visas valid for 72 hours are US$20/40 (256/511 lei).

Visas can be easily acquired on arrival at Chişinău airport or, if arriving by bus or car from Romania, at three border points: Sculeni (north of Iaşi); Leuşeni (main border when travelling from Bucharest to Chişinău); and Cahul. Visas are not issued at any other border crossings or when entering by train. Citizens of countries requiring an invitation must present the original document (copies/faxes not accepted) at the border if buying a visa there.

Check the website of the **Ministry of Foreign Affairs** (www.mfa.gov.md) for the latest requirements.

Getting There & Away

Air

Moldova's only airport of significance is **Chişinău International Airport** (☎22-525 111; www.airport.md), served by regular flights to/from Amsterdam, Athens, Budapest, Minsk, Moscow, Prague, Rome, Sofia and Vienna.

Air Moldova (9U; ☎22-830 830; www.airmoldova.md; B-dul Negruzzi 10, Chişinău) Has flights between Chişinău and Bucharest five days a week, as well as several cities in Western Europe.

Carpatair (V3; ☎22-549 339; www.carpatair.com) Flies to Timişoara six times weekly.

Moldavian Airlines (2M; ☎22-549 339; www.mdv.md; B-dul Ştefan cel Mare 3, Chişinău) Offers two daily flights to Budapest, from where it has connections to other European destinations.

Land

International connections from Moldova are little better than provincial calibre.

Eurolines (www.eurolines.md) has regular bus routes to Italy, Spain, Germany and Romania. Transiting Transdniestr when going to Odesa (Ukraine) is discouraged.

If coming by car, the Green Card (a routine extension of domestic motor insurance to cover most European countries) is valid in Moldova. Extra insurance can be bought at the borders.

From Chişinău, there are daily trains to Moscow, Kyiv, St Petersburg, Iaşi, Bucharest, Lviv and Minsk. To get to Budapest, you must change in Bucharest.

Getting Around

Bus & Maxitaxi

Moldova has a good network of buses and maxitaxis (a quicker option) running to most towns and villages. Buses from Chişinău to Transdniestr are frequent, but the 'border' crossing has historically been unpredictable; see p856 for details.

Car & Motorcycle

In Chişinău, travel agencies can arrange car hire, but the roads are in poor condition. EU driving licences are accepted here.

The intercity speed limit is 90km/h and in built-up areas 60km/h. For road rescue, dial ☎901. The **Auto Club Asist** (ACM; ☎22-465 543; www.auloclub.md) lists regulations and offers emergency assistance (this is a members-only service).

Taxi

There are official and unofficial taxis that may try to rip you off. You should agree upon a price before getting in the car.

Montenegro Црна Гора

Includes »

Best Places to Stay

» Palazzo Radomiri, Kotor (p864)

» Vila Drago, Sv Stefan (p865)

» Eko-Oaza Suza Evrope, Durmitor NP (p867)

» Euro, Kotor (p864)

Best Free Things

» Kotor's historic lanes (p863)

» Views over Sveti Stefan (p865)

» Velika Plaža, Ulcinj (p865)

» Ostrog Monastery (p866)

» Back road Kotor to Cetinje

Why Go?

Imagine a place with sapphire beaches as spectacular as Croatia's, rugged peaks as dramatic as Switzerland's, canyons nearly as deep as Colorado's, *palazzi* as elegant as Venice's and towns as old as Greece's. Wrap it up in a Mediterranean climate and squish it into an area two-thirds the size of Wales and you start to get a picture of Montenegro.

More adventurous travellers can easily sidestep the peak-season hordes on the coast by heading to the rugged mountains of the north. This is, after all, a country where wolves and bears still lurk in forgotten corners.

Montenegro, Crna Gora, Black Mountain: the name itself conjures up romance and drama. There is plenty of both on offer as you explore this perfumed land, bathed in the scent of wild herbs, conifers and Mediterranean blossoms. Yes, it really is as magical as it sounds.

When To Go

Podgorica

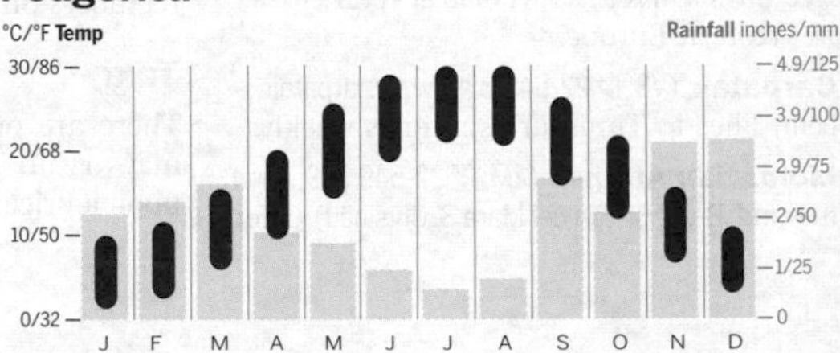

Jun Beat the peak-season rush but enjoy the balmy weather.

Sep Warm water still, but fewer bods to share it with.

Oct The leaves turn golden, making a rich backdrop to walks in the national parks.

Connections

Many travellers make the most of the proximity of Dubrovnik's Čilipi airport to Herceg Novi to tie in a visit to Croatia with a Montenegrin sojourn. At the other end of the coast, Ulcinj is the perfect primer for exploring Albania and is connected by bus to Shkodra. Likewise, Rožaje captures elements of Kosovar culture and is well connected to Peja. A train line and frequent bus connections make a trip to Montenegro's closest cousins in Serbia a breeze. Montenegro shares a longer border with Bosnia and Hercegovina (BiH) than any of its neighbours.

ITINERARIES

Three Days

Base yourself in Kotor and consider day trips to Sveti Stefan, Cetinje and Ostrog Monastery.

One Week

Base yourself in Kotor for two nights and then continue on to Budva. Check out Stari Bar en route to Ulcinj. The following day, double back to Sveti Stefan for your last night on the coast. Head on to Cetinje and Ostrog Monastery en route to Šćepan Polje, where you can stay the night at one of the rafting centres. Go rafting the following morning and then head to Žabljak for a day's hiking in Durmitor National Park.

Essential Food & Drink

» **Njeguški pršut i sir** Smoke-dried ham and cheese from the heartland village of Njeguši.

» **Ajvar** Spicy spread of fried red peppers and eggplant, seasoned with garlic, salt, vinegar and oil.

» **Kajmak** Soft cheese made from the salted cream from boiled milk.

» **Kačamak** Porridge-like mix of cream, cheese, potato and buckwheat or cornflour.

» **Riblja čorba** Fish soup; a staple of the coast.

» **Crni rižoto** Black risotto, coloured with squid ink.

» **Ligne na žaru** Grilled squid, sometimes stuffed (*punjene*) with cheese and smoke-dried ham.

» **Jagnjetina ispod sača** Lamb cooked (often with potatoes) under a metal lid covered with hot coals.

» **Rakija** Domestic brandy, made from nearly anything. The local favourite is grape-based *loza*.

» **Vranac** Local red wine varietal.

» **Krstač** Local white wine varietal.

AT A GLANCE

» **Currency** euro (€)

» **Language** Montenegrin (almost identical to Serbian, Croatian and Bosnian)

» **Money** ATMs in all larger towns

» **Visas** Not required for citizens of most European countries, Australia, New Zealand, Canada and the USA; usually for a stay of up to 90 days

Fast Facts

» **Area** 13,812 sq km

» **Capital** Podgorica

» **Country code** ☎382

» **Emergency** Police ☎122, ambulance ☎124

Exchange Rates

Australia	A$1	€0.74
Canada	C$1	€0.74
Japan	¥100	€0.87
New Zealand	NZ$1	€0.56
UK	UK£1	€1.16
USA	US$1	€0.72

Set Your Budget

» **Budget accommodation** €10-15 per person

» **Two-course evening meal** €8-20

» **Museum entrance** €1-5

» **Nikšićko beer** 330mL €1.50

» **1L petrol** €1.15

Resources

» See p868 for a list of useful websites.

Montenegro Highlights

1. Marvelling at the majesty and exploring the historic towns hemmed in by the limestone cliffs of the **Bay of Kotor** (p863)
2. Driving the vertiginous route from Kotor to the Njegoš Mausoleum at the top of **Lovćen National Park** (p864)
3. Enjoying the iconic island views while lazing on the sands of **Sveti Stefan** (p865)
4. Seeking the spiritual at peaceful **Ostrog Monastery** (p866)
5. Floating through paradise, rafting between the 1km-plus-high walls of the **Tara Canyon** (p866)
6. Discovering glacial lakes on the hiking paths of **Durmitor National Park** (p866)
7. Immersing yourself in Montenegro's culture and history in the old mountain capital, **Cetinje** (p866)

COASTAL MONTENEGRO

Coming from Croatia and entering the mountain-framed folds of the Bay of Kotor, the beauty meter goes off the scale. It doesn't let up when you hit the Adriatic Coast, where you'll find a charismatic set of small settlements, set against clear waters and sandy beaches.

Kotor KOTOP

032 / POP 13,510

Wedged between brooding mountains and a moody corner of the bay, this dramatically beautiful town combines historic grace with happening street culture. Its sturdy ancient walls arch steeply up the slopes behind it. From a distance they're barely discernable from the mountain's grey hide but at night they're spectacularly lit, reflecting in the water to give the town a golden halo. Within those walls lie labyrinthine marbled lanes where churches, boutiques, bars and restaurants on hidden piazzas take you by surprise.

Sights

The old town's most impressive building is the 12th-century **St Tryphon Cathedral** (Trg Sv Tripuna; admission €1.50; 8.30am-7pm).

Kotor Stari Grad (Old Town)

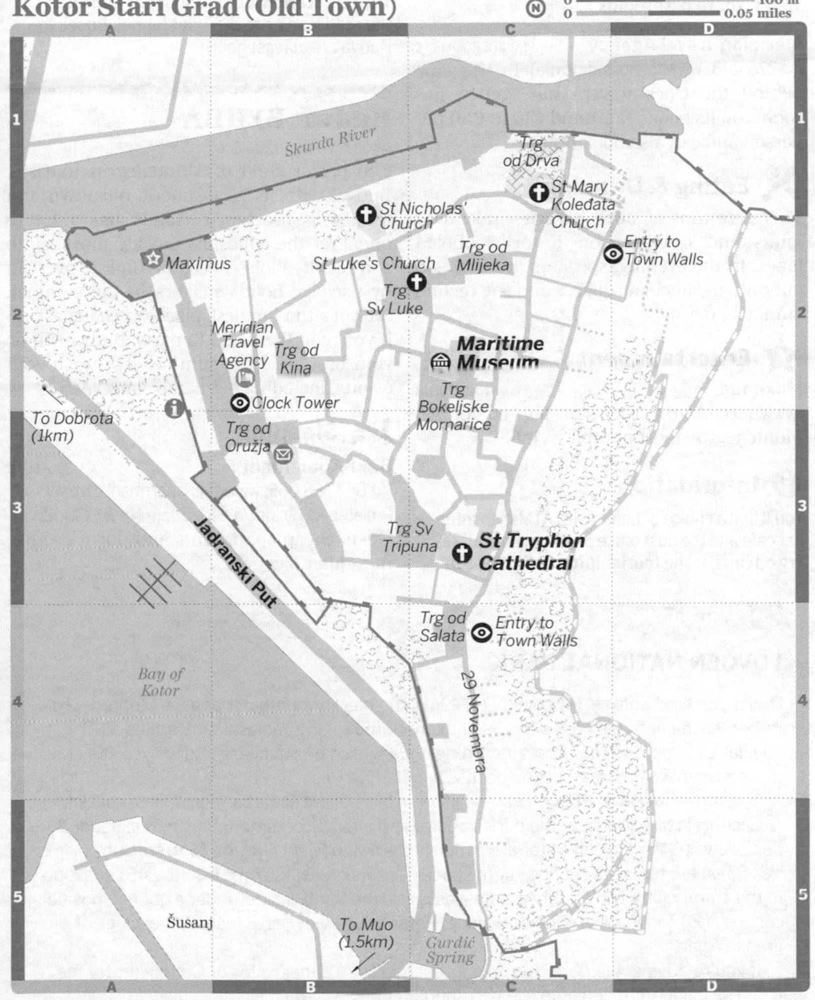

The **Maritime Museum** (Trg Bokeljske Mornarice; adult/child €4/1; ⌚8am-7pm Mon-Sat, 9am-1pm Sun), housed in an early-18th-century palace, celebrates Kotor's proud naval history.

Energetic travellers can make the 280m, 1350-step ascent of the **fortifications** (admission €2).

Sleeping

Euro PENSION €
(☎069-047 712; lemaja1@t-com.me; Muo 33; r per person €20-25; ❄) On the Muo waterfront, this traditional stone building with a small private beach enjoys possibly the best views of Kotor. The top two floors have a scattering of differently configured rooms, some of which share bathrooms.

Meridian Travel Agency PRIVATE ROOMS €
(☎323 448; www.meridiandmc.me) In the lane behind the clock tower, this agency has rooms on its books at around €15 to €30 per person and can also book hotels.

Eating & Drinking

There are tons of small bakeries, takeaway joints and cafe-bars on Kotor's cobbled lanes. In the evening, speakers are dragged out onto the ancient squares and the techno cranked up.

Entertainment

Maximus NIGHTCLUB
(www.discomaximus.com; near Trg od Oružja) Montenegro's most pumping club.

Information

You'll find a choice of banks with ATMs, an internet cafe and the post office on the main square, Trg od Oružja. The **tourist information booth** (www.kotor.travel; ⌚8am-8pm) is outside Vrata od Mora.

SPLURGE

Exquisitely beautiful, the honey-coloured, early-18th-century **Palazzo Radomiri** (☎333 172; www.palazzoradomiri.com; Dobrota; s €60-170, d €80-240; P❄📶🏊; ⌚Mar-Sep) has been transformed into a first-rate boutique hotel. It's worth the lengthy stroll into Kotor.

Getting There & Away

The **bus station** is to the south of town, just off the road leading to the Tivat tunnel. Buses to Budva are at least hourly.

Budva БУДВА

☎033 / POP 10,100

The poster child of Montenegrin tourism, Budva, with its atmospheric old town and numerous beaches, certainly has a lot to offer. Yet the child has quickly moved into a difficult adolescence, becoming overrun by package holidaymakers in the summer. Still, it's the buzziest place on the coast, so if you're in the mood to party, Budva will be your best buddy. In summer it's awash with events, including big-name concerts.

Sleeping

Saki Apartmani HOSTEL €
(☎067-368 065; www.saki-apartmani.com; IV Proleterska bb; dm/d €10/30; P❄📶) Good, clean, cheap apartments and dorm rooms in a quiet location.

WORTH A TRIP

LOVĆEN NATIONAL PARK

Directly behind Kotor is Mt Lovćen (1749m), the black mountain that gave Montenegro its name. The national park's 62.2 sq km are home to 85 species of butterflies, 200 species of birds, and mammals including endangered brown bears and wolves. It's criss-crossed with well-marked hiking paths.

The **national park office** (www.nparkovi.co.me; Ivanova Korita bb; ⌚9am-5pm Apr-Oct, reduced hrs in winter) is near the park's centre and offers accommodation in four-bedded bungalows (€40). Lovćen's star attraction is the magnificent **Njegoš Mausoleum** (admission €3) at the top of its second-highest peak, Jezerski Vrh (1657m). Take the 461 steps up to the entry, where two granite giantesses guard the tomb. Inside, under a golden mosaic canopy, a 28-ton *Vladika* (Bishop-Prince) Petar II Petrović Njegoš rests in the wings of a granite eagle.

If you're driving, the park can be approached from either Kotor or Cetinje (entry fee €2). The back route between the two shouldn't be missed.

Hippo Hostel HOSTEL €
(☎458 348; www.hippohostel.com; IV Proleterska 37; dm €10; P@) Social hostel with an overgrown garden and buzzy atmosphere.

Information

The post office and a cluster of banks are on and around ulica Mediteranska. The **tourist office** (www.budva.travel; Njegošcva bb; 9am-9pm Mon-Sat May-Oct) has brochures on sights and accommodation.

Getting There & Away

The **bus station** (☎456 000; Ivana Milutinovića bb), north of the main highway, has regular services to Kotor (€3, 40 minutes) and Cetinje (€3, 40 minutes).

Sveti Stefan

Impossibly picturesque Sveti Stefan, 5km south of Budva, provides the biggest 'wow' moment on the entire coast. From the 15th century to the 1950s this tiny island, connected to the shore by a narrow isthmus and crammed full of terracotta-roofed dwellings, housed a simple fishing community. Now the entire island is a luxury resort, but you can still enjoy the views from the beaches on either side.

Overlooking it all, **Vila Drago** (☎033-468 177; www.viladrago.com; Slobode 32; r €35-65, high season €60-100; @) offers sublime views, super-comfy pillows and fully stocked bathrooms. Watch the sunset from the grapevine-covered terrace restaurant (mains €5-15) and enjoy local specialities such as roast suckling pig (€15 per kg).

Bar БАР

☎030 / POP 13,800

Dominated by Montenegro's main port, Bar is unlikely to be anyone's highlight but it is a handy transport hub, welcoming trains from Belgrade and ferries from Italy. Accommodation is limited and expensive; if you really must stay here, pick up the private-accommodation brochure from the information centre.

The ruins of impressive **Stari Bar** (adult €1; 8am-8pm) date back over 1000 years and stand on a bluff off the Ulcinj road. A steep, cobbled hill takes you to a short, dark passage through the fortifications, popping you out into what seems to be a huge garden of vine-clad walls, abandoned streets and more than 200 ruins overgrown with grass and wild flowers.

Buses marked Stari Bar depart from the centre of Bar every hour (€1).

Information

Bar's centre, immediately east of the ferry terminal, has a post office, shops and banks. The **tourist information centre** (Obala 13 Jula bb; 8am-8pm Jul & Aug, 8am-4pm Mon-Sat Sep-Jun) has helpful staff with good English, and stocks useful brochures listing sights and private accommodation.

Getting There & Away

The **bus station** and adjacent **train station** are 1km southeast of the centre. Three buses head to Ulcinj (€2.50) daily.

Ulcinj УЛЦИЊ

☎030 / 10,840

If you want a feel for Albania without actually crossing the border, buzzy Ulcinj is the place to go. The population is 72% Albanian and the elegant minarets of numerous mosques give Ulcinj a distinctly Eastern feel. For centuries Ulcinj had a reputation as a pirates' lair but now it's known for its fine beaches, including **Velika Plaža**, which stretches for 12 sandy kilometres.

Sleeping & Eating

Real Estate Travel Agency PRIVATE ROOMS €
(☎421 609; www.realestate-travel.com; Hazif Ali Ulqinaku bb) Obliging, English-speaking staff can help you find private rooms, apartments or hotels. They also rent cars, run tours, organise diving trips and sell maps of Ulcinj.

Restaurant Pizzeria Bazar MONTENEGRIN, PIZZA €
(Hazif Ali Ulqinaku bb; mains €4-10) An upstairs restaurant that's a great idling place when the streets below are heaving with tourists. People watch in comfort as you enjoy a plate of *lignje na žaru* (grilled squid), the restaurant's speciality.

Getting There & Away

The bus station is on the northeastern edge of town, just off Bul Vëllazërit Frashëri. Services head to Bar (€2.50, 30 minutes, three daily), Shkodra (Albania; €6, 1½ hours, two daily) and Pristina (Kosovo; €22.50, eight hours, three daily).

CENTRAL MONTENEGRO

The heart of Montenegro – physically, spiritually and politically – is easily accessed as a day trip from the coast, but it's well deserving of longer exploration. This really is the full Monte: soaring peaks, hidden monasteries, steep river canyons and historic towns. Podgorica, the nation's capital, serves as the transport hub and is worth a day's exploration, although it's elsewhere that your focus should lie.

Cetinje ЦЕТИЊЕ

041 / POP 15,140

Rising from a green vale surrounded by rough, grey mountains, Cetinje is an odd mix of former capital and overgrown village, where single-storey cottages and stately mansions share the same street.

The **National Museum of Montenegro** (9am-5pm) is actually a collection of five museums housed in a clump of important buildings. A combined ticket (adult/child €10/5) will get you into all of them or you can buy individual tickets. Best are the **History Museum** (Novice Cerovića 7; adult/child €4/2) and **Art Museum** (adult/child €4/2), housed in the former parliament (1910). The other three are set around the main square: **King Nikola Museum** (adult/child €5/2.50), **Njegoš Museum** (adult/child €3/1.50) and the **Ethnographic Museum** (adult/child €2/1).

Founded in 1484, **Cetinje Monastery** (8am-6pm) has a spectacular **treasury** (€2; 8am-4pm). It's only open to groups but if you are persuasive enough, appropriately dressed and prepared to wait around, you may be able to get in.

The **bus station** (Trg GolootoČkih Žeta) is two blocks from the main street. Buses leave hourly for Budva (€3).

Durmitor National Park ДУРМИТОР

052 / POP 4900

Magnificent scenery ratchets up to the stupendous in this national park, where ice and water have carved a dramatic landscape from the limestone. Some 18 glacial lakes dot the Durmitor Range, which has 48 peaks over 2000m. From December to March it's a ski resort, while in summer it's popular with hikers and rafters.

WORTH A TRIP

OSTROG MONASTERY

Resting on a cliff 900m above the Zeta valley, gleaming white **Ostrog Monastery** (1665) is a strangely affecting place. Dubbed 'Sv Vasilije's miracle' because no-one seems to understand how it was built, it gives the impression that it has grown out of the very rock. The **guesthouse** (067-405 258; dm €4) offers tidy single-sex dorms. There's no public transport but numerous tour buses head here from the coast (€20).

Activities

Rafting RAFTING

Slicing through the mountains at the northern edge of the national park like they were made from the local soft cheese, the **Tara River** forms a canyon that, at its peak, is 1300m deep. The two-day raft along the river is the country's premier outdoor attraction (May to October only). Most of the day tours from the coast traverse only the last 18km of the river – this is outside the national park and hence avoids hefty fees.

If you've got your own wheels you can save a few bucks by heading directly to Šćepan Polje. **Tara Tour** (069-086 106; www.tara-tour.com) offers an excellent half-day trip (with/without breakfast and lunch €40/30) and has a cute set of wooden chalets with squat toilets and showers in a separate block. Accommodation, three meals and a half-day's rafting costs €55.

Hiking HIKING

Durmitor is one of the best-marked mountain ranges in Europe for hikers (entry fee per day €2). Check the weather forecast, stick to the tracks and prepare for sudden drops in temperature.

Skiing SKIING

The three main ski centres are all accessible from Žabljak: **Savin Kuk** (advanced skiers), **Javorovača** (beginners) and **Mali Štuoc** (suits all levels of experience).

One of the big attractions of skiing here is the cost: day passes are around €15, weekly passes €90 and ski lessons between €10 and €20. You can rent ski and snowboard gear from **Sport Trade** (Vuka Karadžića 7, Žabljak) for €10 per day.

Sleeping

Eko-Oaza Suza Evrope CABINS €
(☎069-444 590; ekooazatara@gmail.com; Dobrilovina; cabin €25-50; P) Situated at the beginning of the arm of the park that stretches along the Tara River, this 'eco oasis' has four comfortable wooden cottages, each sleeping five people.

Autokamp Mlinski Potok Mina CAMPING GROUND €
(☎069-497 625; campsites per person €3, bed €10) With a fabulously hospitable host, there's no escaping the *rakija* shots at this basic camping ground above the national park visitors centre. The owner's house can sleep 12 guests in wood-panelled rooms and he has another house sleeping 11 by the Black Lake.

Information

Durmitor National Park visitor centre (www.nparkovi.co.me; Jovana Cvijića bb; ⌚9am-5pm Mon-Fri) is on the road to the Black Lake, and includes a wonderful micromuseum focusing on the park's flora and fauna. The knowledgeable English-speaking staff sell local craft, maps and hiking guidebooks.

Getting There & Away

The **bus station** is at the southern end of Žabljak on the Nikšić road. Buses head to Belgrade (€18, nine hours, two daily) and Podgorica (€8, 3½ hours, three daily).

UNDERSTAND MONTENEGRO

History

Montenegro's history is one of dogged independence – facing greater forces that have ultimately crashed in failure against its rocky fastness. For 500 years Montenegro retained its independence against the Ottoman Turkish tide that flooded southeast Europe. During this time a distinct identity was born, which distinguished its people from the other Serbian tribes. While the size of its territory waxed and waned, it was always centred on Lovćen, the mountain expanse that contains Cetinje within its foothills. It's from this 'black mountain' that the country takes its name: Crna Gora in the local tongue and Montenegro in Italian.

Following emancipation from the Austrians, who invaded during WWI, Montenegro was incorporated into the first Yugoslavia under the Serbian king. As a reward for its support of the partisans during WWII, Socialist Federal Republic of Yugoslavia president Tito gave Montenegro republic status in the postwar Yugoslav federation. From then on Montenegro was a loyal member of all the Yugoslavian entities, culminating in the loose union of Serbia and Montenegro that came to an end with the vote for independence in May 2006. Montenegro is now fully independent for the first time since 1916.

People

Montenegro's 2003 census revealed a population of 678,000, split into Montenegrins (43%), Serbs (32%), Bosniaks (8%), Albanians (5%) and others (12%). There are large Slavic Muslim and Albanian minorities, mostly in the east. The Bay of Kotor has strong historic links with Croatia's Dalmatian coast.

Montenegrins are closely related to Serbs, with whom they share the same faith, Orthodox Christianity. Montenegrins are on average remarkably tall, making them ideal basketball players.

Food

Price ranges used in this chapter are based on the cheapest main offered:

€€€ more than €10

€€ €5 to €10

€ under €5

Environment

Montenegro has declared itself an 'ecological state' in its constitution, but still faces problems with pollution. Deer, lynx, wolves and brown bears inhabit the mountains, while Lake Skadar (Lake Shkodra) is the biggest bird sanctuary in Europe and one of the Dalmatian pelican's last remaining habitats. There are five national parks (Durmitor, Prokletije, Lovćen, Biogradska Gora and Lake Skadar), and the Bay of Kotor and Durmitor are Unesco-recognised sites.

SURVIVAL GUIDE

Directory A-Z

Accommodation

Prices are very seasonal, peaking in July and August on the coast. The cheapest options are rooms in private houses and apartment rentals. These can be arranged through travel agencies or, in season, you may be approached at the bus stop or see signs hanging outside of houses. Facilities at camping grounds tend to be basic, often with squat toilets and limited water. The national parks have cabin-style accommodation.

An additional tourist tax (less than €2 per night) is added to the rate for all accommodation types. For private accommodation it's sometimes left up to the guest to pay it, but it can be nigh on impossible finding the right authority to pay it to (the procedure varies from area to area). Theoretically you could be asked to provide white accommodation receipt cards (or copies of invoices from hotels) when you leave the country, but in practice this is rarely required.

In this chapter prices quoted are for rooms with a private bathroom, and unless otherwise stated include breakfast. The following price indicators apply (for a high-season double room):

€€€ more than €90

€€ €30 to €90

€ less than €30 per night

Business Hours

Business hours in Montenegro are a relative concept. Even if hours are posted on the doors of museums or shops, don't be surprised if they're not heeded. Reviews don't list opening hours unless they differ from the following:

Banks Usually 8am-5pm Mon-Fri, until noon Sat

Cafe-bars 8am-midnight (later in high season in busy areas)

Restaurants 8am-midnight

Shops 8am or 9am to 8pm or 9pm; often closed in late afternoon

Embassies & Consulates

The following are all in Podgorica, unless otherwise stated:

Albania (☎020-652 796; Zmaj Jovina 30)

BiH (☎020-618 105; Atinska 58)

Croatia Podgorica (☎020-269 760; Vladimira Ćetkovića 2); Kotor (☎032-323 127; Trg od Oružja bb)

Serbia (☎020-667 305; Hercegovačka bb)

Gay & Lesbian Travellers

Although homosexuality was decriminalised in 1977 and discrimination outlawed in 2010, attitudes to homosexuality remain hostile and life for gay people is extremely difficult. Many gay men resort to online connections (try www.gayromeo.com) or take their chances at a handful of cruisy beaches. Lesbians will find it even harder to access the local community.

Holidays

New Year's Day 1 & 2 January

Orthodox Christmas 6, 7 & 8 January

Orthodox Good Friday & Easter Monday April/May

Labour Day 1 May

Independence Day 21 & 22 May

Statehood Day 13 July

Internet Resouces

Black Mountain (www.montenegroholiday.com)

Destination Montenegro (www.destination-montenegro.com)

Montenegro Smiles (www.montenegrosmiles.com)

National Tourist Organisation (www.montenegro.travel)

Visit Montenegro (www.visit-montenegro.com)

Money

Montenegro uses the euro (€). You'll find banks with ATMs in all the main towns, most of which accept Visa, MasterCard, Maestro and Cirrus. Don't rely on restaurants, shops or smaller hotels accepting credit cards.

Tipping isn't expected, although it's common to round up to the nearest euro.

Telephone

The international access prefix is ☎00 or +382 from a mobile phone. Mobile numbers start with 06. Local SIM cards are a good idea if you're planning a longer stay; main providers are T-Mobile, Telenor and M:tel.

Visas

Check www.mip.gov.me/en/index.php/Visas-for-Foreign-Citizens for details about visas.

Women Travellers

Other than a cursory interest shown by men towards solo women travellers, travelling is hassle-free and easy. In Muslim areas some women wear a headscarf but most don't.

Getting There & Away

Air

There are flights from many European cities to Montenegro's two international airports: Tivat and Podgorica. Dubrovnik's Čilipi airport is very close to the border. **Montenegro Airlines** (YM; ☎020-664 411; www.montenegroairlines.com) is the national carrier. Podgorica Airport (www.montenegroairports.com) is 9km south of the city. A shuttle bus (€3) runs between the airport and Trg Republika roughly every 30 minutes. Airport taxis have a standard €15 fare to the centre. From Podgorica you can catch a bus to all of Montenegro's major towns.

Boat

Ferry services connect Montenegro with Italy. Note that cabins cost extra and that cars can be transported.

Azzurra Line (www.azzurraline.com) Has ferries between Bar and Bari (€65, nine hours, weekly in summer) and Kotor and Bari (€65, nine hours, three per week).

Montenegro Lines (☎030-311 164; www.montenegrolines.net) Services from Bar to Bari (€55, nine hours, weekly in summer) and Ancona (€66, 11 hours, twice weekly in summer).

Bus & Train

There's a well-developed bus network linking Montenegro with the major cities of the region.

Montenegro's only working passenger train line starts at Bar and heads into Serbia.

Car & Motorcycle

You'll need an International Driving Permit and a Green Card for your vehicle. A €10 ecotax (valid for one year) is charged on foreign cars entering the country.

Getting Around

The bus network is extensive and reliable. Buses are usually comfortable, air-conditioned and rarely full.

The major European car-hire companies have a presence in various centres but **Meridian Rentacar** (☎033-454 105; www.meridian-rentacar.com), which has offices in Budva, Bar and Podgorica, is a reliable, cheap option.

Hitching, while never entirely safe, is very popular in Montenegro, but take precautions.

Morocco

Includes »

Best Places to Eat

» Outdoor fish grills, Essaouira (p884)

» Café Clock, Fez (p887)

» Earth Café, Marrakesh (p893)

Best Places to Stay

» Dar Nour, Tangier (p874)

» Jnane Mogador, Marrakesh (p891)

» Auberge Restaurant Chez Ali, Draa Valley (p895)

Why Go?

For many travellers, Morocco might just be a short hop away by ferry or by one of the myriad budget airlines from Spain, but it's a much greater distance to travel culturally. The regular certainties of Europe are suddenly swept away by the arrival in full technicolour of Africa and Islam. For the traveller, it's a complete sensory overload.

Atlantic winds blow through cosmopolitan Tangier and Casablanca and the whitewashed coastal gem of Essaouira. The great imperial cities of Marrakesh and Fez have enough surprises hidden in their winding streets to fill a dozen visits.

The High Atlas Mountains seem custom-made for hiking boots, with trails between Berber villages, and North Africa's highest peak to conquer. Or if you prefer someone else to do the walking, saddle up your camel and ride into the Sahara to watch the sun setting over an ocean of sand.

When To Go

Marrakesh

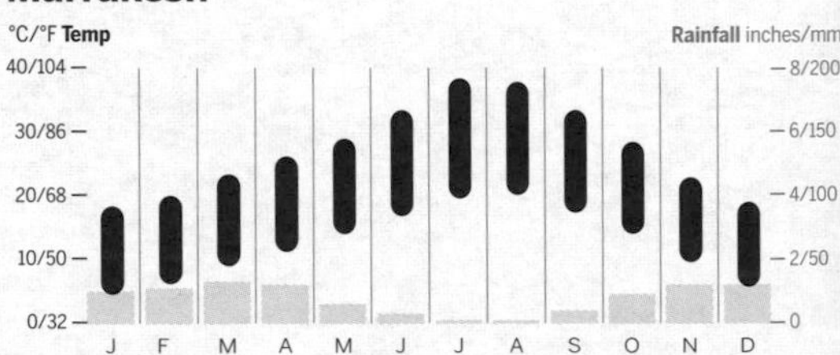

Mar–Jun Spring blooms; it's hot but fresh with a chance of rain. Morocco's at its greenest.

Jul & Aug During Ramadan; many restaurants close during the day and reduced business hours.

Nov–Jan Warm days of winter sun that are perfect for Marrakesh and the south.

Connections

The cheap flight revolution has well and truly arrived in Morocco, and budget airlines link Casablanca, Marrakesh, Fez and Tangier to the major European air hubs (there are plenty of scheduled carriers, but most stick to Casablanca). If you have time, a more enjoyable way of connecting to mainland Europe is by ferry, either zipping across the Straits of Gibraltar from Tangier to Algeciras or Tarifa in Spain, or from Spain's enclaves of Ceuta and Melilla to connect with the Spanish rail network.

ITINERARIES

One Week

From Tangier, make a beeline for Fez and Marrakesh, former imperial cities turned tourist hubs in the Moroccan interior that deserve as much time as you can spare. After that, a detour to artsy Essaouira is a wonderful way to step down a gear after the onslaught of Morocco's most clamorous cities.

Two Weeks

Follow the itinerary above, but en route south stop at chilled-out Chefchaouen, tucked into the Rif Mountains. Meknès is a great detour from Fez, but once into the south past Marrakesh, make time either to head into the High Atlas for mountain hiking (possibly tackling Mt Toubkal, north Africa's highest peak), or saddle up your camel and ride into the great Saharan sand sea at Merzouga or M'Hamid.

Essential Food & Drink

» **Tajine** Slow-cooked stew in a conical-topped earthenware dish. Classic varieties include chicken with olives and lemon, kefta (meatballs), and beef with prunes and almonds.

» **Couscous** Slow-steamed hand-rolled semolina, served with a light broth and meat or vegetables. Usually the centrepiece of a meal.

» **B'stilla** Parcel of layered filo pastry, stuffed with pigeon or chicken, nuts and cinnamon.

» **Khoobz** Traditional Moroccan bread, baked in communal wood-fired ovens.

» **Harira** Classic thick soup with onion, lentil, chickpeas, tomato and lamb.

» **Mint Tea** Morocco's famed 'Berber whiskey': gunpowder tea steeped in bunches of fresh mint and enough sugar to dissolve your teeth.

AT A GLANCE

» **Currency** Moroccan dirham (Dh)

» **Languages** Moroccan Arabic (Darija), French, Berber

» **Money** ATMs widespread; credit cards widely accepted

» **Visas** Schengen rules apply; see p1319

Fast Facts

» **Area** 446,550 sq km

» **Capital** Rabat

» **Country code** ☎212

» **Emergency** ☎190 Police

Exchange Rates

Australia	A$1	Dh8.35
Canada	C$1	Dh8.10
euro zone	€1	Dh11.30
Japan	¥100	Dh9.80
New Zealand	NZ$1	Dh6.50
UK	UK£1	Dh13.03
USA	US$1	Dh7.91

Set Your Budget

» **Budget hotel room** from Dh250

» **Two-course evening meal** Dh70-150

» **Local taxi ride** Dh10

» **Rabat–Marrakesh train (2nd class)** Dh90

Resources

» **The View from Fez** (http://riadzany.blogspot.com) News and what's on

» **Visit Morocco** (www.visitmorocco.com)

» **Al-Bab** (www.al-bab.com/maroc) Handy links

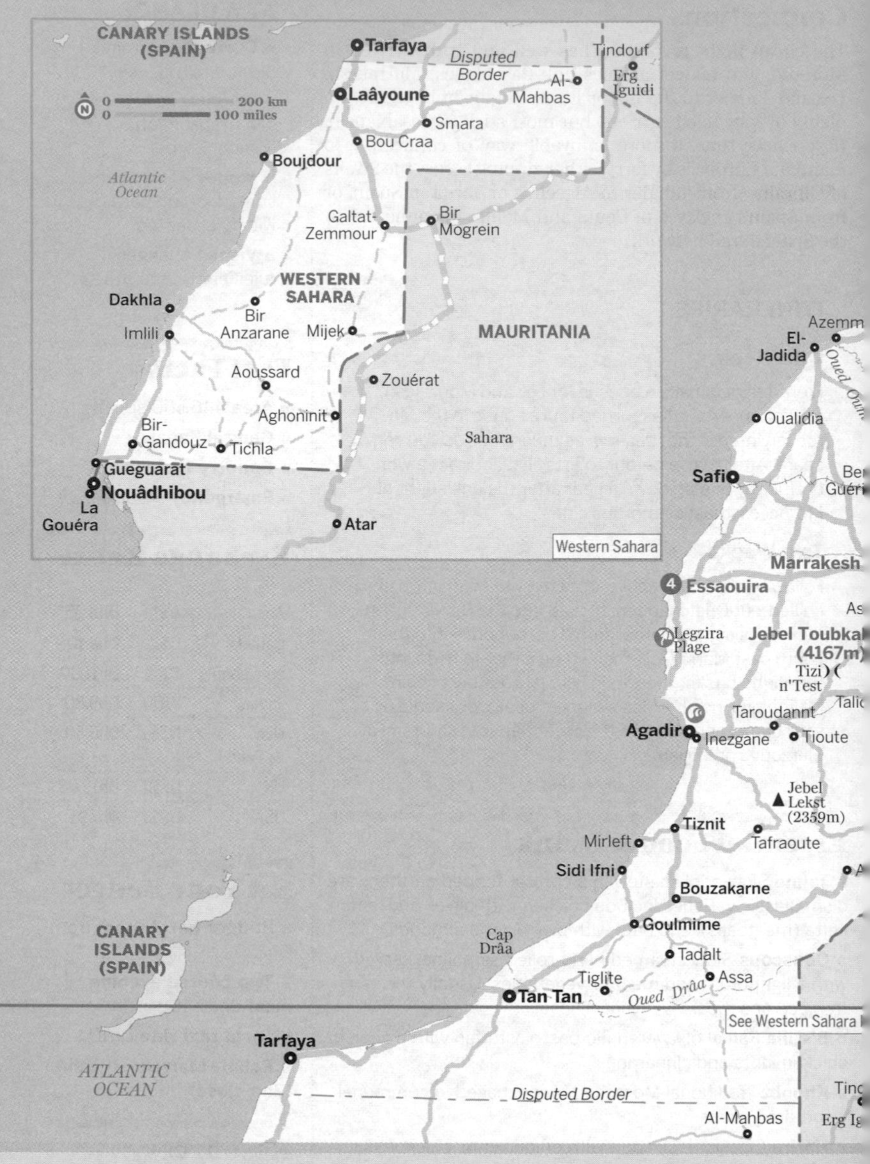

Morocco Highlights

1. Get lost in the alleys of the **Fez medina** (p885), Islam's greatest living medieval city

2. Taste 1001 Nights in the open-air spectacle of the **Djemaa el-Fna square** (p891) in Marrakesh

3. Chill in the Rif Mountains in the dazzling blue town of **Chefchaouen** (p877)

4 Catch the sea breeze in the port town of **Essaouira** (p883), Morocco's hippest resort

5 Admire the mosaics, columns and sweeping landscapes of **Volubilis** (p890), Morocco's foremost ancient ruins

6 Get a natural high by hiking through the High Atlas Mountains to climb **Jebel Toubkal** (p895), North Africa's highest peak

MEDITERRANEAN COAST & THE RIF

Bounded by the red crags of the Rif Mountains and the crashing waves of the Mediterranean, northern Morocco conceals the cosmopolitan hustle of Tangier, the Spanish enclaves of Ceuta and Melilla, the old colonial capital of Tetouan, and the superbly relaxing town of Chefchaouen.

Tangier

POP 650,000

Like the dynamic strait upon which it sits, Tangier is the product of 1001 currents, including Islam, Berber tribes, colonial masters, a highly strategic location, a vibrant port, the Western counterculture and the international jet set. The city has regularly passed between Moroccan and Western control – for half the 20th century it was under the dubious control of an international council, making Tangier a byword for licentious behaviour and dodgy dealings.

Many travellers simply pass through, but if you take it head-on and learn to handle the hustlers, you'll find it a lively, cosmopolitan place with energetic nightlife.

Tangier's small medina climbs up the hill to the northeast of the city, while the ville nouvelle (new town) surrounds it to the west, south and southeast. The large, central square known as the Grand Socco provides the link between the two.

Sights

Kasbah OLD TOWN

On the highest point of Tangier, the kasbah sits behind stout walls. Enter through Bab el-Aassa, to find the **Kasbah Museum** (admission incl Sultan's Gardens Dh10; 9am-12.30pm Wed-Mon, 3-5.30pm Wed, Thu & Sat-Mon), housed in the 17th-century palace of Dar el-Makhzen, and devoted to Moroccan arts. Before leaving, take a stroll around the Andalucian-style **Sultan's Gardens**.

Tangier American Legation Museum MUSEUM

(www.legation.org; 8 Rue d'Amerique; donations appreciated; 10am-1pm & 3-5pm Mon-Fri) An intriguing relic of the international zone with a fascinating collection of memorabilia from the international writers and artists who passed through Tangier.

Musée de la Fondation Lorin MUSEUM

(Rue Touahine; donations appreciated; 11am-1pm & 3.30-7.30pm Sun-Fri) Housed in a former synagogue, the museum has an engaging collection of photographs, posters and prints of Tangier from 1890 to 1960.

Grand Socco SQUARE

Heading uphill, you eventually emerge at the keyhole-shaped gate, Bab Fass, that opens to the renovated plaza of Grand Socco (officially renamed Place du 9 Avril 1947). A short walk up Rue d'Angleterre brings you to one of the more charming oddities of Tangier, the Victorian-era **St Andrew's Church** (services Sun 8.30am, 11am), which has the Lord's Prayer in Arabic above the nave.

Sleeping

Hotel el-Muniria HOTEL €€

(0539 935337; 1 Rue Magellan; s/d Dh200/250, s/d on terrace Dh250/300;) This is your best low-end option in the ville nouvelle, and chock-full of Beat-generation history. French windows and bright, flowery fabrics set it apart, revealing the careful touch of a hands-on family operation.

Hotel de Paris HOTEL €

(0539 931877; 42 Blvd Pasteur; s/d incl breakfast high season Dh350/450) This reliable choice in the heart of the ville nouvelle has a classy, old-world aura in its lobby. Rooms are clean and modern, but those overlooking Blvd Pasteur can get noisy.

TOP CHOICE **Dar Nour** GUEST HOUSE €€

(0662 112724; www.darnour.com; 20 Rue Gourna; d/ste incl breakfast from Dh720/1300;). With no central courtyard, rooms here branch off two winding staircases, creating a maze of rooms and salons, each more romantic than the last. Rooms are stylishly decorated and the roof has an impressive view over the medina.

Hotel Mamora HOTEL €

(0539 934105; 19 Ave Mokhtar Ahardan; s/d with shower Dh60/120, d with toilet Dh200-260) Readers enjoy this hotel near the Petit Socco with its variety of rooms at different rates. It's a bit institutional, but strong value for money. The rooms overlooking the green-tiled roof of the Grande Mosquée are the most picturesque, if you don't mind the muezzin's call.

Eating

In the medina there's a host of cheap eating possibilities around the Petit Socco and the adjacent Ave Mokhtar Ahardan, with rotisserie chicken, sandwiches and brochettes all on offer. In the ville nouvelle, try the streets immediately south of Place de France, which are flush with fast-food outlets, sandwich bars and fish counters.

TOP CHOICE Restaurant Populaire Saveur de Poisson SEAFOOD €€
(☎0539 336326; 2 Escalier Waller; prix fixe Dh150; ⊙lunch & dinner, Sat-Thu; ⊖) This charming seafood restaurant offers excellent set menus in rustic surroundings. The owner serves a four-course meal of fish soup followed by inventive plates of fresh catch and fresh vegetables, washed down with a homemade juice cocktail.

Le Nabab LOCAL €€
(☎0661 442220; 2 Rue al Kadiria; mains Dh80, menu Dh170; ⊙lunch & dinner) A beautifully restored old *fondouq* (caravanserai or inn), all grey *tadelakt* (lime plaster), comfortable seating and swathes of airy pink fabric. Dine around the huge fireplace or in a private alcove. The menu is Moroccan, the welcome friendly and it's licensed.

Anna e Paolo ITALIAN €€
(☎0539 944617; 77 Rue de Prince Heretier; mains from Dh80; ⊙lunch & dinner, Mon-Sat) This is the top Italian bistro in the city, a family-run restaurant with Venetian owners that feels like you have been invited for Sunday dinner. Expect an international crowd and wholesome food including excellent charcuterie and pizzas.

Drinking

Caid's Bar BAR
(El-Minzah Hotel, 85 Rue de la Liberté; wine from Dh20; ⊙10am-midnight) Welcome to Rick's Café – the real-life model for the bar in *Casablanca* in the El-Minzah Hotel is a classy relic of the grand days of international Tangier, and photos of the famous and infamous adorn the walls.

Café Hafa CAFE
(Ave Hadi Mohammed Tazi; ⊙8.30am-11pm Mon-Fri, 8.30am-2am Sat & Sun) You could easily lose an afternoon lazing in this open-air cafe overlooking the strait. Locals hang out here to enjoy a game of backgammon. There's no menu, but scrambled eggs, soup and olives are on offer. It's 750m west of the kasbah.

Entertainment

Tangier's nightlife picks up in summer. Nightclubs cluster near Place de France and line the beach. Cover charges vary and may be rolled into drink prices. **Loft** (☎0673 280927; www.loftclub-tanger.com; Rte de Boubana; ⊙10pm-4am, Thu & Sat) is the premier nightspot. Tangier's gay scene has departed for Marrakesh, but **Finest Pink** (Ave Mohammed VI; ⊙11pm till late) is gay-friendly with lounge, restaurant, tapas bar and disco opposite the Hotel Shahrazad.

Information

Blvds Pasteur and Mohammed V are lined with numerous banks with ATMs and *bureau de change* counters. Blvd Pasteur also has plenty of internet places.

Clinique du Croissant Rouge (Red Cross Clinic; ☎0539 942517; 6 Rue al-Mansour Dahabi)

Espace Net (16 Ave Mexique; per hr Dh5; ⊙9.30am-1am)

Main post office (cnr Rue Quevada & Ave Mohammed V)

ONMT (Délégation Régionale du Tourisme; ☎0539 948050; 29 Blvd Pasteur; ⊙closed Sat & Sun)

Getting There & Away

For ferry options, see p899.

Bus

The **CTM station** is conveniently located beside the port gate. Destinations include Casablanca (Dh130, six hours), Rabat (Dh100, 4½ hours), Marrakesh (Dh230, 10 hours), Fez (Dh110, six hours) and Chefchaouen (Dh40, three hours). Cheaper bus companies operate from the **main bus station** (gare routière; Place Jamia el-Arabia), about 2km south of the city centre.

Taxi

You can hail *grands taxis* (shared taxis) next to the main bus station to Tetouan (Dh30, one hour).

Train

Trains depart from Tanger Ville train station (Dh10 in a local *petit taxi*). One morning and one afternoon service run to Casa-Voyageurs in Casablanca (Dh125, 5½ hours); four trains via Meknès (Dh80, four hours) to Fez (Dh105, five hours), although three involve changing at Sidi Kacem. A night service runs all the way to Marrakesh (Dh205 seat/Dh350 couchette, 12 hours).

Getting Around

Petits taxis (blue with yellow stripe) do standard journeys around town for Dh7 to Dh10. From

Tangier

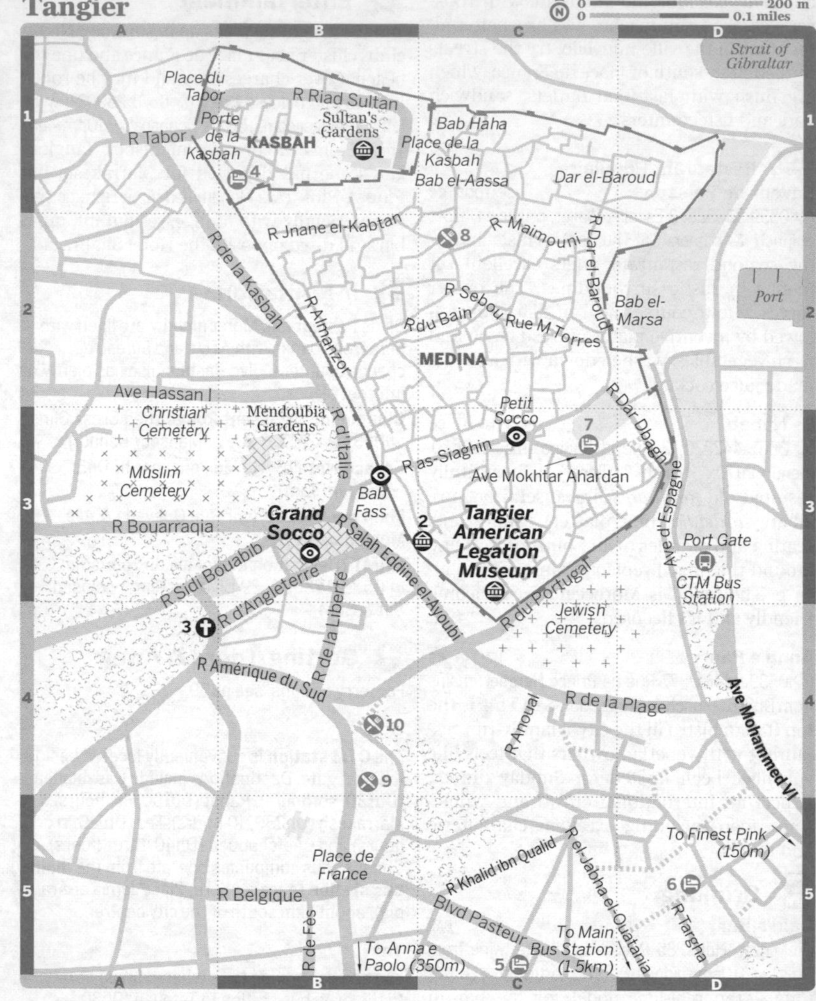

Ibn Batouta airport, 15km southeast of the city, take a cream-coloured *grand taxi* (Dh150).

Tetouan

POP 330,000

Tetouan occupies a striking location at the foot of the Rif Mountains. From 1912 until 1956 it was the capital of the Spanish Protectorate in Morocco. This Hispano-Moorish character is physically reflected in the white buildings and broad boulevards that have recently been restored to their original condition, and also the Unesco World Heritage–listed medina.

If you want to see the sea, the port of Martil is a 15-minute cab ride from Tetouan, as is the classy resort village of M'Diq.

Sights

Medina OLD TOWN

The whitewashed medina (home to some 40 mosques, of which the **Grande Mosqué** and **Saidi Mosque** are the most impressive) opens through its main gate, Bab er-Rouah, onto Place Hassan II, Tetouan's main square. At the opposite end of the medina,

Tangier

Top Sights

Grand Socco B3
Tangier American Legation Museum C3

Sights

1 Kasbah Museum B1
2 Musée de la Fondation Lorin C3
3 St Andrew's Church A4

Sleeping

4 Dar Nour B1
5 Hotel de Paris C5
6 Hotel el-Muniria D5
7 Hotel Mamora C3

Eating

8 Le Nabab C2
9 Restaurant el-Korsan B4
10 Restaurant Populaire Saveur de Poisson B4

Drinking

Caid's Bar .... (see 9)

the **Musée Marocaine** (Musée Ethnographique; admission Dh10; 9am-4pm Mon-Sat) is housed inside the bastion in the town wall.

Artisanal School NOTABLE BUILDING
(admission Dh10; 8.30am-2.30pm Sat-Thu, 8.30-11.30am Fri) Just outside Bab el-Okla is this school offering a fascinating opportunity to see masters teaching apprentices traditional arts, including ornamental woodwork, carved plaster and intricate mosaics.

Sleeping

El Reducto RIAD €€€
(0539 968120; www.riadtetouan.com; 38 Zanqat Zawiya; s incl breakfast Dh400-600, d incl breakfast Dh550-850) This superb house is worth a visit just to see the traditional mosaic tiles with their coppery sheen. The spotless, palatial rooms are truly fantastic (one has a Jacuzzi for two). There's also a licensed restaurant with a Spanish touch to the menu.

Pension Iberia HOTEL €
(0539 963679; 5 Place Moulay el-Mehdi; s/d/tr Dh60/100/150) This is the best budget option, with classic high-ceilinged rooms and shuttered balconies that open out to the Place Moulay el-Mehdi. Bathrooms are shared, and hot showers are an extra Dh10.

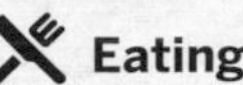

Eating

Snack Taouss FAST FOOD €
(3 Rue 10 Mai; mains from Dh25; lunch & dinner) This snack bar has a Syrian influence and does good falafel and delicious shwarma as well as inexpensive pizzas, salads, *harira* (lentil soup), tajines and more. There's a small seating area upstairs or you can eat on the move.

Restaurant Restinga LOCAL €
(21 Ave Mohammed V; mains from Dh50, beer Dh15; lunch & dinner) The open-air courtyard shaded by a huge tree is this charming restaurant's primary attraction – along with the rare alcohol licence. It's a great place to duck out of the crowded boulevard for local seafood.

Palace Bouhlal LOCAL €€
(0670 85 95 63; 48 Jamaa Kebir; set menu Dh100; lunch) A palace restaurant with plush couches, wall rugs, intimate dining spaces, gurgling fountains and a grand Moorish arch complementing the usual four-course meal. Follow the lane north around the Grande Mosqué and look for signs directing you down a tiny alley.

Information

There are plenty of banks with ATMs along Ave Mohammed V.

BMCE foreign exchange office (Place Moulay el-Mehdi; 10am-2pm & 4-8pm) Change cash and travellers cheques outside regular banking hours.

Main hospital (0539 972430; Martil Rd) About 2km out of town.

Post office (Place Moulay el-Mehdi; 8am-4.30pm Mon-Fri)

Remote Studios (13 Ave Mohammed V; per hr Dh9; 9am-midnight) Internet access.

Getting There & Away

Several bus companies operate from the **bus station** (cnr Rue Sidi Mandri & Rue Moulay Abbas). **CTM** (039 961688) has buses running to the usual array of places, including Casablanca (Dh125, six to seven hours, twice daily) via Rabat (Dh100, 4½ hours), Fez (Dh90, four hours), Marrakesh (Dh235, 11 hours) and many more.

Grands taxis to Martil (Dh5, 15 minutes) leave from Ave Hassan II, southeast of the bus station.

Chefchaouen

POP 45,000

Beautifully situated beneath the raw peaks of the Rif, Chefchaouen (known by its diminutive 'Chaouen') is one of the prettiest towns in Morocco. It's an artsy mountain village that feels like its own world. The old medina is a delight of Moroccan and Andalucian influence with red-tiled roofs, bright blue buildings and narrow lanes converging on a delightful square.

Chefchaouen is split into the medina and the *ciudad nueva,* or new city – a hangover from its occupation by the Spanish. The heart of the medina is Plaza Uta el-Hammam, with its unmistakeable kasbah. The principal route of the *ciudad nueva* is Ave Hassan II. The bus station is a 1km hike southwest of the town centre.

Sights

Plaza Uta el-Hammam TOWN SQUARE

The heart of the medina is the shady, cobbled plaza. This is a peaceful place to relax and watch the world go by, particularly after a long day of exploration. The plaza is dominated by the red-hued walls of the **kasbah** (admission incl museum & gallery Dh10; ⏲9am-1pm & 3-6.30pm Wed-Mon, 9-noon & 3-6.30pm Fri) and the adjacent **Grande Mosqué**, noteworthy for its unusual octagonal minaret. The kasbah is a heavily restored walled fortress that now contains a lovely garden, a small **ethnographic museum** and **art gallery**.

Ras el-Maa WATERFALL

Just beyond the far eastern gate of the medina lie the falls of Ras el-Maa. In season there is a popular cafe on the right, just before the bridge. The sound of the water and the verdant hills just beyond the medina wall provide a sudden, strong dose of nature. Continuing over the bridge, you can walk to the ruined 'Spanish' mosque to take in the views.

Sleeping

TOP CHOICE **Hostal Guernika** GUEST HOUSE €

(☎0539 987434; hostalgernika@hotmail.com; 49 Onssar; d/tr Dh200/300; 📶) This is a warm and charming place, with a very caring and attentive owner, not far from the square. There are several great rooms – large and bright, facing the mountains – but others can be dark. All have showers. The terrace has spectacular views. Reserve in summer, Easter and December.

Dar Terrae GUEST HOUSE €€

(☎0539 98 75 98; www.darterrae.com; Ave Hassan I; s/d/tr incl breakfast Dh290/390/600; 📶) These funky, cheerfully painted rooms are individually decorated and have their own fireplace, and they're hidden up and down a tumble of stairs and odd corners. The Italian owners prepare a fantastic breakfast spread and other meals on request. It's poorly signed – if in doubt ask for the 'Hotel Italiano'.

Hotel Mouritania GUEST HOUSE €

(☎0539 986184; 15 Rue Qadi Alami; s/d Dh60/120; 📶) Rooms are simple here, but staff are helpful, there's a comfy courtyard lounge ideal for meeting other travellers, and the breakfasts (Dh20) are great.

Eating

Plaza café-restaurants LOCAL €

(Plaza Uta el-Hamman; breakfast from Dh20, mains from Dh30;) A popular eating option in Chefchaouen is to choose one of about a dozen on the main square. Menus are virtually identical – continental breakfasts, soups and salads, tajines and seafood – but the food is generally pretty good and the ambience lively.

La Lampe Magique LOCAL €

(Rue Targhi; mains from Dh45, set menu Dh75; ⏲lunch & dinner) This magical place overlooking Plaza Uta el-Hammam serves delicious Moroccan staples in a grand setting. Three bright-blue floors include a laid-back lounge, a more formal dining area and a rooftop terrace. The menu – featuring favourites like lamb tajine with prunes and some great cooked salads – is much better than average, and the ambience is relaxed.

Assaada LOCAL €

(Bab el-Ain; set menu Dh40; ⏲lunch & dinner) This reliable cheapie tries hard to please. Located on both sides of the alley just before Bab el-Ain, it offers the usual menu *complet,* and recommends its 'no-cholesterol' goat *kefta* (meatballs). There's a funky graffiti rooftop terrace that exudes an urban charm but the staircase isn't for the faint-hearted.

Information

Banque Populaire medina (Plaza Uta el-Hammam) ATM; ciudad nueva (Ave Hassan II)

Cyber-Net (Zanqat Sbâa; per hr Dh5; ⏲10am-midnight)

Hospital Mohammed V (☎0539 986228; Ave al-Massira al-Khadra)

Post office (Ave Hassan II)

Getting There & Away

Many bus services from Chefchaouen originate elsewhere and are often full on arrival, so buy your ticket a day in advance if possible. **CTM** (☎039 987669) serves Casablanca (Dh115, eight hours), Rabat (Dh85, six hours), Fez (Dh70, four hours) Tangier (Dh40, three hours) and further destinations.

Grands taxis heading to Tetouan (Dh30, one hour) leave from just below Plaza Mohammed V – change for Tangier or Ceuta.

THE ATLANTIC COAST

Morocco's Atlantic littoral is surprisingly varied, with sweeping beaches and lagoons, and the pretty fishing port of Essaouira. It's also the country's economic motor, centred on the political and business capitals of Rabat and Casablanca.

Rabat

POP 2.5 MILLION

Relaxed and well-kept Rabat is as cosmopolitan as Casablanca, but lacks the frantic pace and grimy feel of its economic big brother. Its elegant tree-lined boulevards and imposing administrative buildings exude an unhurried, diplomatic and hassle-free charm that many travellers grow to like.

The main administrative buildings and many hotels lie just off the city's main thoroughfare, the wide, palm-lined Ave Mohammed V The entrance to the medina is at the northern end of the avenue, while the train station, Rabat Ville, is at the southern end.

Sights

Medina OLD TOWN

Barely 400 years old, Rabat's **medina** is tiny compared to that of Fez or Marrakesh, although it still piques the senses with its rich mixture of spices, carpets, crafts, cheap shoes and bootlegged DVDs.

The **kasbah** sits high up on the bluff overlooking the Oued Bou Regreg and contains within its walls the oldest **mosque** in Rabat, built in the 12th century and restored in the 18th. The kasbah's southern corner is home to the **Andalusian Gardens** (⌚sunrise-sunset), laid out by the French during the colonial period. The centrepiece is the grand 17th-century palace containing the **Musée des Oudaia** (admission Dh10; ⌚9am noon & 3-5pm Oct-Apr, to 6pm May-Sep).

Le Tour Hassan MINARET

Towering above the Oued Bou Regreg is Rabat's most famous landmark, Le Tour Hassan (Hassan Tower). In 1195 the Almohad sultan Yacoub al-Mansour began constructing an enormous minaret, intending to make it the highest in the Islamic world, but he died before the project was completed. At 44m, the carved tower still lords it over the remains of the adjacent mosque.

Mausoleum of Mohammed V MAUSOLEUM

(admission free; ⌚sunrise-sunset) The cool marble mausoleum, built in traditional Moroccan style, lies opposite Le Tour Hassan. The present king's father (the late Hassan II) and grandfather are laid to rest here, surrounded by intensely patterned *zellij* mosaics from floor to ceiling.

Sala Colonia RUINS

Abandoned, crumbling and overgrown with fruit trees and wildflowers, the combined ancient Roman city of Sala Colonia and Merenid necropolis of Chellah (cnr Ave Yacoub al-Mansour & Blvd Moussa ibn Nassair; admission Dh10; ⌚9am-5.30pm) is one of Rabat's most evocative sights. A colony of storks has taken over the ruins, presiding over the site from their treetop nests.

Sleeping

Le Piétri Urban Hotel HOTEL €€

(☎0537 70 78 20; www.lepietri.com; 4 Rue Tobrouk; s/d Dh720/790;) This good-value boutique hotel in a quiet street in a central part of town is modern and chic. The 36 spacious, bright rooms with wooden floors are comfortable, well equipped and decorated in warm colours in a contemporary style. The hotel has an excellent restaurant.

Hôtel Balima HOTEL €€

(☎0537 70 77 55; www.hotel-balima.net; Ave Mohammed V; s/d incl breakfast Dh543/716;) The grand dame of Rabat hotels is showing its age a bit, but still offers newly decorated and comfortable rooms, all immaculately kept and with great views over the city. The glorious shady terrace facing Ave Mohammed V is still the place to meet in Rabat.

Hôtel Dorhmi HOTEL €

(☎0537 72 38 98; 313 Ave Mohammed V; s/d/tr Dh80/130/195, hot shower Dh10) Immaculately kept, very friendly and keenly priced, this family-run hotel is the best of the medina cheapies. The simple rooms are bright and tidy and surround a central courtyard on the 1st floor above the Banque Populaire. Despite being in the hub of things, the Dorhmi (also spelt Doghmi) offers quiet rooms.

Hôtel Splendid HOTEL €
(☎0537 72 32 83; 8 Rue Ghazza; s/d Dh190/230, s/d without bathroom Dh125/160) Slap-bang in the heart of the medina, the spacious, bright rooms with high ceilings, big windows, cheerful colours and simple wooden furniture are set around a pleasant courtyard.

Eating

For quick eating, go to Ave Mohammed V just inside the medina gate, where you'll find hole-in-the-wall joints dishing out tajines, brochettes, salads and chips. There are more fast-food joints around Rue Tanta in the ville nouvelle.

TOP CHOICE **Le Petit Beur – Dar Tajine** LOCAL €€
(☎0537 731322; 8 Rue Damas; mains Dh100; ⏲lunch & dinner Mon-Sat; ⊜) This modest little place is renowned for its excellent food, from succulent tajines and heavenly couscous to one of the best *pastillas* (savoury-sweet chicken or pigeon pies) in town, and it's licensed. At night it fills up quickly, while the waiters double as musicians and play oud music to accompany your meal.

Restaurant el-Bahia LOCAL €
(Ave Hassan II; mains Dh60; ⏲lunch & dinner) Built into the outside of the medina walls and a good spot for people-watching, this laid-back restaurant has the locals lapping up hearty Moroccan fare. Sit on the pavement terrace, in the shaded courtyard or upstairs in the traditional salon.

Information

Numerous banks (with ATMs) are concentrated along Ave Mohammed V.

American bookshop (cnr Rue Moulay Abdelhafid & Rue Boujaad)

Hôpital Ibn Sina/Avicenna (☎037 672871/037 674450 for emergencies; Place Ibn Sina, Agdal)

Internet (Rue Tanta; per hr Dh8; ⏲9am-7.30pm) Next to La Mamma.

Main post office (cnr Rue Soékarno & Ave Mohammed V)

Getting There & Away

Bus & Grands Taxis

Rabat has two bus stations: the main **gare routière**, where most buses depart and arrive, and the **CTM bus station**. Both are about 5km southwest of the centre on the road to Casablanca.

> **SPLURGE**
>
> Sleek, stylish and oozing the charm of an old-world Parisienne brasserie, **Le Grand Comptoir** (☎0537 201514; www.legrandcomptoir.ma; 279 Ave Mohammed V; mains Dh100-160; ⏲lunch & dinner; 📶) is a suave restaurant and lounge bar that woos customers with its chic surroundings and classic French menu. Also good for breakfast or an apéritif.

CTM has eight daily services to Casablanca (Dh35, 1½ hours), seven to Fez (Dh70, 3½ hours), three to Marrakesh (Dh130, five hours), five to Tangier (Dh100, 4½ hours) and one to Tetouan (Dh100, five hours). Arriving by bus from the north, you may pass through central Rabat, so it's worth asking if you can be dropped off in town.

Grands taxis leave for Casablanca (Dh40) from just outside the intercity bus station. Other *grands taxis* leave for Fez (Dh60) Meknès (Dh50) and Salé (Dh5) from a lot off Ave Hassan II behind the Hôtel Bouregreg.

Train

Rabat Ville train station is in the centre of town (not to be confused with Rabat Agdal station west of the city). Trains run every 30 minutes until 10.30pm to Casa-Port train station in Casablanca (Dh35, one hour), with hourly services to Fez (Dh80, 3½ hours, eight daily) via Meknès (Dh65, 2½ hours), Tangier (Dh95, 4½ hours, eight daily) and Marrakesh (Dh120, 4½ hours, nine daily).

Getting Around

Rabat's blue *petits taxis* are plentiful, cheap and quick. A ride around the centre of town will cost about Dh10.

Casablanca

POP 4 MILLION

Many travellers stay in Casablanca just long enough to change planes or catch a train, but Morocco's economic heart offers a unique insight into the country. This sprawling city is home to racing traffic, simmering social problems, wide boulevards, parks and imposing Hispano-Moorish and art deco buildings. Their facades stand in sharp contrast to Casablanca's modernist landmark: the enormous and incredibly ornate Hassan II mosque.

The medina – the oldest part of town – is relatively small and sits close to the port. Nearby is Place des Nations Unies, a large traffic junction that marks the heart of the

Central Casablanca

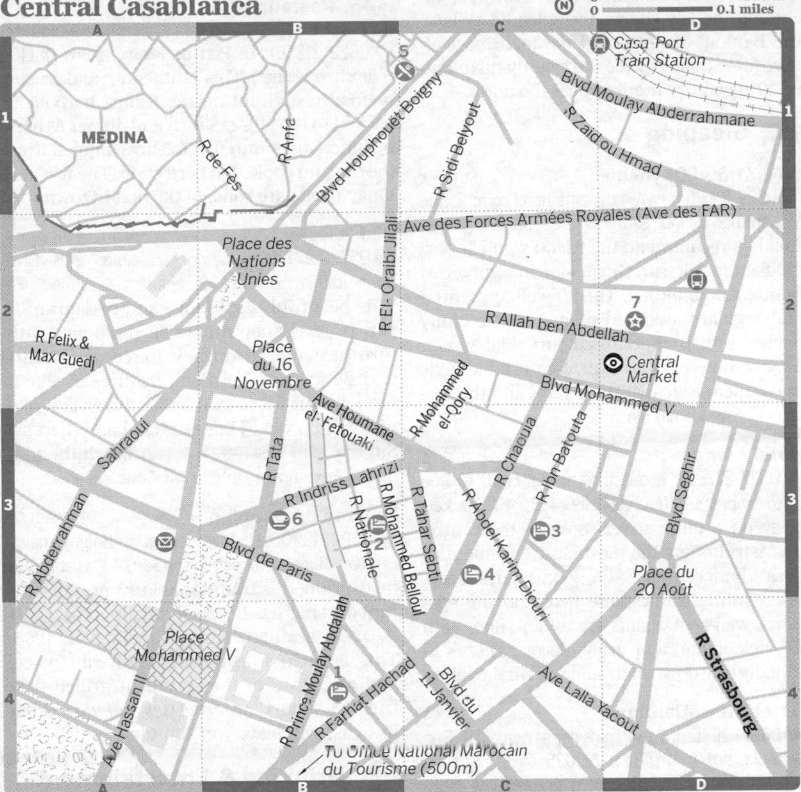

Central Casablanca

Sleeping

1 Hôtel Astrid........B4
2 Hôtel Guynemer........B3
3 Hôtel Maamoura........C3
4 Hôtel Transatlantique........C3

Eating

5 Taverne du Dauphin........C1

Drinking

6 Café Alba........B3

Entertainment

7 La Bodéga........D2

city. The CTM bus station and Casa-Port train station are in the centre of the city. Casa-Voyageurs station is 2km east of the centre and the airport is 30km southeast of town.

Sights

Hassan II Mosque MOSQUE

Rising above the Atlantic northwest of the medina, the Hassan II Mosque is the world's third-largest mosque, built to commemorate the former king's 60th birthday. The mosque rises above the ocean on a rocky outcrop reclaimed from the sea, a vast building that holds 25,000 worshippers and can accommodate a further 80,000 in the courtyards and squares around it. To see the interior of the mosque you must take a **guided tour** (adult/student/child Dh120/60/30; ⌚9am, 10am, 11am & 2pm Sat-Thu; 9am, 10am & 2pm Fri).

Downtown Casablanca ARCHITECTURE

Central Casablanca is full of great art deco and Hispano-Moorish buildings. The best way to take them all in is by strolling in the area around the **Central Market** (Marché Central) and **Place Mohammed V**. The grand square is surrounded by public buildings that were later copied throughout Morocco, including the law courts, the splendid Wilaya, the Bank al-Maghrib and the main post office. After that, explore the slightly dilapidated 19th-century **medina** near the port.

Sleeping

TOP CHOICE **Hôtel Guynemer** HOTEL €
(☎0522 275764; www.guynemerhotel.com; 2 Rue Mohammed Belloul; s/d/tr Dh372/538/626; ❄📶) Readers recommend the friendly and super-efficient family-run Guynemer, in a gorgeous Mauresque building. The 29 well-appointed and regularly updated rooms are tastefully decked out in cheerful colours. Flat-screen TVs, wi-fi access and firm, comfortable beds make them a steal at these rates and the service is way above average.

Hôtel Astrid HOTEL €
(☎0522 277803; hotelastrid@hotmail.com; 12 Rue 6 Novembre; s/d/tr Dh324/386/486; 📶) Tucked away on a quiet street south of the centre, the Astrid offers the most elusive element of Casa's budget hotels – a good night's sleep. There's little traffic noise here and the spacious, well-kept rooms are all en suite, with TV, telephone and frilly decor. There's a friendly cafe downstairs and wi-fi in the lobby.

Hôtel Transatlantique HOTEL €€
(☎0522 294551; www.transatcasa.com; 79 Rue Chaouia; s/d/tr Dh770/925/1025; ❄📶) Set in one of Casa's architectural gems, this 1922 hotel has a snack bar and shady outdoor seating area. Decor in the lobby is over the top, but rooms are comfortable and fairly plain. Avoid the 1st floor, as it gets the brunt of noise from the popular piano bar and nightclub.

Hôtel Maamoura HOTEL €
(☎0522 452967; www.hotelmaamoura.com; 59 Rue Ibn Batouta; s/d/ste Dh430/570/800; ❄📶🏊) This modern hotel offers excellent value for money. The spotless and spacious rooms may lack period detail, but they are very quiet for this central location, tastefully decorated in muted colours and have neat bathrooms. The staff is friendly and helpful.

Eating

Rue Chaouia, opposite the central market, is the best place for a quick bite, with its line of rotisseries, stalls and restaurants serving roast chicken, brochettes and sandwiches.

TOP CHOICE **Restaurant du Port de Pêche** SEAFOOD €€
(☎0522 318561; Le Port de Pêche; mains Dh140; ⏲lunch & dinner) This authentic and rustic seafood restaurant on the fishing harbour is packed to the gills at lunch and dinner as happy diners tuck into fish freshly whipped from the sea and cooked to perfection. The fish and tangy paella are some of the best in town.

Rick's Cafe MEDITERRANEAN €€
(☎0522 274207; www.rickscafe.ma; 248 Blvd Sour Jdid; mains Dh160; ⏲lunch & dinner; 📶) This beautiful bar, lounge and restaurant is run by a former American diplomat, with furniture and fittings inspired by Bogart and Bergman. The menu features excellent French and Moroccan specialities. The pianist will play 'As Time Goes By', and there's a Sunday jam session. You can watch the film again and again on the 1st floor.

Taverne du Dauphin SEAFOOD €€
(☎0522 221200; 115 Blvd Houphouet Boigny; mains Dh140; ⏲lunch & dinner, closed Sun) A Casablanca institution, this traditional Provençal restaurant and bar has been serving up local *fruits de mer* (seafood) since it opened in 1958. This is an old-fashioned family-run place, and one taste of the succulent grilled fish, fried calamari or *crevettes royales* (king prawns) will leave you smitten.

Drinking & Entertainment

Café Alba CAFÉ €
(59-61 Rue Indriss Lahrizi) High ceilings, swish modern furniture, subtle lighting and a hint of elegant colonial times mark this cafe out from the more traditional smoky joints around town. It's hassle-free downtime for women and a great place for watching Casa's up-and-coming.

La Bodéga TAPAS BAR
(129 Rue Allah ben Abdellah) Hip, happening and loved by a mixed-age group of Casablanca's finest, La Bodéga is essentially a tapas bar where the music (everything from Salsa to Arabic pop) is loud and the Rioja (Spanish wine) flows freely. It's a fun place with a lively atmosphere and a packed dance floor after 10pm.

The beachfront suburb of Aïn Diab is the place for late-night drinking and dancing in Casa. Expect to pay at least Dh150 to get in and as much again for drinks. Heavy-set bouncers guard the doors and practise tough crowd control – if you don't look the part, you won't get in. Try **Balcon 33** (33 Blvd de

BUSES FROM CASABLANCA

DESTINATION	COST (DH)	DURATION (HRS)	FREQUENCY
Chefchaouen	125	7	1 daily
Essaouira	145	6	2 with CTM; hourly with private companies
Fez	100	4	8 daily
Marrakesh	90	3½	8 daily
Meknès	90	3½	6 daily
Tangier	145	5½	5 with CTM; regularly with private companies
Tetouan	145	6	5 daily

la Corniche), **Le Carré Rouge** (Hotel Villa Blanca, Blvd de la Corniche; ⏲11.30pm-4am) and **VIP club** (Rue des Dunes).

Information

There are banks – most with ATMS and foreign exchange offices – on almost every street corner in the centre of Casablanca.

Central Market post office (cnr Blvd Mohammed V & Rue Chaouia)

Crédit du Maroc (☎022 477255; 48 Blvd Mohammed V) Separate *bureau de change*.

Gig@net (140 Blvd Mohammed Zerktouni; per hr Dh10; ⏲24hr)

LGnet (81 Blvd Mohammed V; per hr Dh8; ⏲9am-midnight)

Main post office (cnr Blvd de Paris & Ave Hassan II)

Office National Marocain du Tourisme (ONMT; ☎022 271177; 55 Rue Omar Slaoui; ⏲8.30am-4.30pm Mon-Fri)

Polyclinique Atlas (☎0522 27 40 39; 27 Rue Mohammed ben Ali, Quartier Gauthier; ⏲24hr) Off Rue Jean Jaures.

Wafa Cash (15 Rue Indriss Lahrizi; ⏲8am-8pm Mon-Sat) Open longer hours; has an ATM and cashes travellers cheques.

Getting There & Away

Bus

The modern **CTM bus station** (☎022 541010; 23 Rue Léon L'Africain) has daily CTM departures; for details on price and frequency, see the boxed text.

The **Gare Routière Ouled Ziane** (☎022 444470), 4km southeast of the centre, is the bus station for non-CTM services.

Train

All long-distance trains, as well as trains to Mohammed V International Airport, depart from **Casa-Voyageurs train station** (☎022 243818). Destinations include Marrakesh (Dh90, three hours, nine daily), Fez (Dh110, 4½ hours, 18 daily) via Meknès (Dh90, 3½ hours) and Tangier (Dh125, five hours, eight daily).

The **Casa-Port train station** is a few hundred metres northeast of Place des Nations Unies. Trains from here run to Rabat (Dh35, one hour).

Getting Around

The easiest way to get from **Mohammed V International Airport** to Casablanca is by train (2nd class Dh30, 35 minutes); they leave every hour from 6am to midnight from below the ground floor of the airport terminal building. A *grand taxi* between the airport and the city centre costs Dh300.

Expect to pay Dh10 in or near the city centre for a trip in one of the red *petits taxis*.

Essaouira

POP 70,000

Perennially popular Essaouira has long been a favourite on the travellers' trail. It's laid-back and artsy with sea breezes and picture-postcard ramparts, all of which conspire to make a short visit from Marrakesh turn into a stay of several nights. Although it can appear swamped with visitors in the height of summer, when the day trippers get back on the buses there's more than enough space to sigh deeply and just soak up the atmosphere.

Sights & Activities

Medina — WALLED TOWN

Essaouira's Unesco World Heritage–listed 18th-century medina is a prime example of European military architecture in North Africa. The mellow atmosphere, narrow, winding streets lined with colourful shops, whitewashed houses and heavy old wooden doors make it a wonderful place to stroll. The easiest place to access the ramparts is **Skala de la Ville**, the impressive sea bastion built along the cliffs. Down by the harbour, the **Skala du Port** (tower admission Dh10; ⏲8.30am-noon & 2.30-6pm) offers picturesque views over the fishing port and the **Île de Mogador**.

A number of outlets rent water-sports equipment and offer instruction along Essaouira's wide, sandy beach. **Océan Vagabond** (☎0524 783934; www.oceanvagabond.com; ⏲9am-6pm) rents surfboards (three days Dh750) and windsurfing boards (two hours, Dh440) and offers lessons in both as well as kitesurfing. Be aware of strong Atlantic currents.

The **Gnaoua & World Music Festival** (third weekend Jun; www.festival-gnaoua.net) is a four-day musical extravaganza that draws huge crowds.

Sleeping

Hôtel Beau Rivage HOTEL €
(☎0524 475925; www.essaouiranet.com/beaurivage; 14 Place Moulay Hassan; s/d/tr incl breakfast Dh270/390/510; 📶) Readers recommend this friendly hotel in a perfect spot, overlooking the main square. The Beau Rivage has bright, cheerful rooms with modern fittings and spotless bathrooms. Breakfast is served on the charming and quiet roof terrace with views over the port and town.

Lalla Mira GUEST HOUSE €€
(☎0524 475046; 14 Rue d'Algerie; www.lallamira.net; s/d/tr incl breakfast & hammam Dh436/692/860; 📶) This gorgeous little place, the town's first eco-hotel, has simple rooms with ochre *tadelakt* walls, wrought-iron furniture, natural fabrics and solar-powered underfloor heating. The hotel also has a hammam and a restaurant serving organic dishes such as rabbit with peaches and nuts, or goat with argan oil, and a good selection of vegetarian food.

Riad Nakhla RIAD €
(☎/0524 474940; www.essaouiranet.com/riad-nakhla; 2 Rue Agadir; s/d/ste incl breakfast Dh230/360/500; 📶) Riad Nakhla looks like any other budget place from the outside, but inside the weary traveller is met with a beautiful courtyard, with stone columns and a fountain – more what you'd expect from a hotel in a higher price bracket. Bedrooms are simple but comfortable and immaculately kept, with bags of local flavour. Breakfast on the roof terrace with views over the ocean and town. It's an incredible bargain at this price.

Dar Afram B&B €€
(☎0524 785657; www.dar-afram.com; 10 Rue Sidi Magdoul; s Dh250, d Dh400-600) This extremely friendly guest house has simple, spotless rooms with shared bathrooms and a funky vibe. The Aussie-Moroccan owners are musicians and an impromptu session often follows the evening meals shared around a communal table.

Eating

Place Moulay Hassan offers plenty of sandwich stands and cafes for lazy breakfasts and lunches.

TOP CHOICE **Outdoor fish grills** SEAFOOD €
(Place Moulay Hassan; meals Dh40-100) These unpretentious stands at the port end of Place Moulay offer one of the definitive Essaouira experiences. Choose what you want to eat from the colourful displays of freshly caught fish and shellfish at each grill, see it weighed up to arrive at a price and wait for it to be cooked on the spot and served with a pile of bread and salad.

After 5 MEDITERRANEAN €€€
(☎0524 784726; 5 Rue Youssef el-Fassi; mains Dh200; ⏲7-11pm Wed-Mon, noon-3pm Sat & Sun) Deep-purple seating, warm stone arches and giant lampshades dominate this trendy restaurant, which serves well-cooked and original Mediterranean and Moroccan dishes

Taros MEDITERRANEAN €€
(☎0524 476407; 2 Rue du Skala; mains Dh120; ⏲lunch & dinner) At one of the most atmospheric terraces in town, you can dine by candlelight inside or out. There's often live music, too. It's also a good place for afternoon tea or a drink at the bar.

Restaurante Les Alizés LOCAL €€
(☎0524 476819; 26bis Rue de la Skala; mains Dh120; ⏲lunch & dinner) This popular place, run by a charming couple in a 19th-century house, has delicious Moroccan dishes, particularly the couscous with fish and the tajine of *boulettes de sardines* (sardine balls).

Shopping

Essaouira is well known for its woodwork and you can visit the string of **woodcarving workshops** near the Skala de la Ville. The exquisite marquetry work on sale is made from local fragrant thuya wood, unfortunately now endangered. Essaouira also has a reputation as an artists' hub and plenty of galleries around town sell works by local painters.

Information

There are several banks with ATMs around Place Moulay Hassan. There are plentiful internet cafes, most opening from 9am to 11pm and charging Dh8 to Dh10 per hour.

Cyber Les Remparts (12 Rue du Rif)

Délégation du Tourisme (☎024 783532; www.essaouira.com; 10 Rue du Caire; ⏰9am-noon & 3-6.30pm Mon-Fri) Very helpful staff.

Espace Internet (8 bis, Rue du Caire)

Hôpital Sidi Mohammed ben Abdallah (☎024 475716; Blvd de l'Hôpital) Emergencies.

Main post office (Ave el-Mouqawama)

Getting There & Away

The **bus station** is about 400m northeast of the medina, an easy walk during the day but better in a *petit taxi* (Dh10) if you're arriving/leaving late at night. **CTM** has several buses daily for Casablanca (Dh135, six hours), and to Marrakesh (Dh75, 2½ hours) and Agadir (Dh70, three hours). Other companies run cheaper and more frequent buses to the same destinations as well as Taroudannt (Dh70, six hours) and Rabat (Dh90, six hours).

Supratours (☎024 475317) operates from outside the medina and runs coaches to Marrakesh train station (Dh70, 2½ hours, four daily) to connect with trains to Casablanca. Book in advance, particularly in summer.

IMPERIAL CITIES & THE MIDDLE ATLAS

The rolling plains to the north of the Middle Atlas are Morocco's most fertile agricultural region, dotted with olive groves and wheat fields. Several of Morocco's most interesting cities are here, including Fez with its teeming medina, imperial Meknès and the Roman ruins of Volubilis.

Fez

POP 1 MILLION

Marrakesh might be modern Morocco's tourist capital, but 1400-year-old Fez is Morocco's spiritual beating heart. Its medina (Fez el-Bali) is the largest living medieval Islamic city in the world, and the world's largest car-free urban environment. A first visit can be overwhelming, an assault on the eyes, ears and nose through covered bazaars, winding alleys, mosques and workshops, amid people and pack animals, all of which seem to take you out of the 21st century and back to an imagined era of *1001 Arabian Nights*.

Fez can be neatly divided into three distinct parts: Fès el-Bali (the core of the medina; the main entrance is Bab Bou Jeloud) in the east; Fès el-Jdid (containing the *mellah* and Royal Palace) in the centre; and the ville nouvelle, the modern administrative area constructed by the French, to the southwest.

Sights

THE MEDINA (FÈS EL-BALI)

Within the old walls of Fès el-Bali lies an incredible maze of twisting alleys, blind turns and hidden souqs. Navigation can be confusing and getting lost at some stage is a certainty, but this is part of the medina's charm: you never know what discovery lies around the next corner.

Kairaouine Mosque MOSQUE

If Fez is the spiritual capital of Morocco, the Kairaouine Mosque (Map p886) is its true heart. Built in 859 by refugees from Tunisia, and rebuilt in the 12th century, it can accommodate up to 20,000 people at prayer and is Africa's largest mosque. Non-Muslims are forbidden to enter and will have to be content with glimpses of its seemingly endless columns from the gates on Talaa Kebira and Place as-Seffarine.

Medersa Bou Inania ISLAMIC COLLEGE

Located 150m east of Bab Bou Jeloud, the 14th-century Medersa Bou Inania (Map p886; admission Dh10; ⏰9am-6pm, closed during prayers) is the finest of Fez's theological colleges constructed by the Merenids. The *zellij* (tiling), *muqarnas* (plasterwork) and woodcarving are amazingly elaborate and views from the roof are also impressive.

Tanneries CRAFTS

(Map p886; Derb Chouwara, Blida) The tanneries are one of the city's most iconic sights (and smells). It's not possible to get in among the tanning pits themselves, but there are plenty of vantage points from the streets that line them, all occupied (with typical Fassi ingenuity) by leather shops.

Merenid tombs RUINS

(Route de Tour de Fès) North of the medina walls, the tombs are dramatic in their advanced state of ruin. The views over Fez are spectacular and well worth the climb. Look for the black smoke in the southern part of the city, marking the potteries.

FÈS EL-JDID (NEW FEZ)

Dar el-Makhzen PALACE GATES

(Royal Palace; Map p888; Place des Alaouites) Only in a city as old as Fez could you find a district dubbed 'New' because it's only 700 years old. It's home to the Royal Palace, whose entrance at Dar el-Makhzen is a stunning example of modern restoration, but the 80 hectares of palace grounds are not open to the public.

Mellah JEWISH QUARTER

(Map p888) In the 14th century, Fès el-Jdid was a refuge for Jews, thus creating a *mellah* (Jewish quarter). The *mellah*'s southwest corner is home to the fascinating **Jewish Cemetery & Habarim Synagogue** (donations welcomed; 7am-7pm).

Sleeping

MEDINA

Pension Kawtar GUEST HOUSE €

(Map p886; ☎0535 740172; pen sion_kaw@yahoo.fr; Derb Taryana, Talaa Seghira; d Dh300, s/d without bathroom Dh150/250;) Well-signed in an alley off Talaa Seghira, the Kawtar is a friendly Moroccan family-run concern. There are 10 rooms tucked into the place – those on the ground floor are a bit gloomy, but they get better the closer you get to the roof terrace. Great value for the price.

Riad Verus GUEST HOUSE €

(Map p886; ☎0535 574941 www.riadverus.com; 1 Derb Arset Bennis, Batha; dm/d/q Dh280/890/1100;) A relatively new player on the budget scene, this place has rooms configured to give the maximum flexibility for the best budget. Everything is open and airy inside, and the young owners play well to the backpacker crowd with regular live music and iPod docks in the rooms.

Dar Bensouda GUEST HOUSE €€

(Map p886; ☎0535 638939; www.riaddarbensouda.com; 14 Zqaq Labghal, Qettanine; r Dh850-1700;) A converted palace, Dar Bensouda is the most impressive medina restora-

Fez Medina

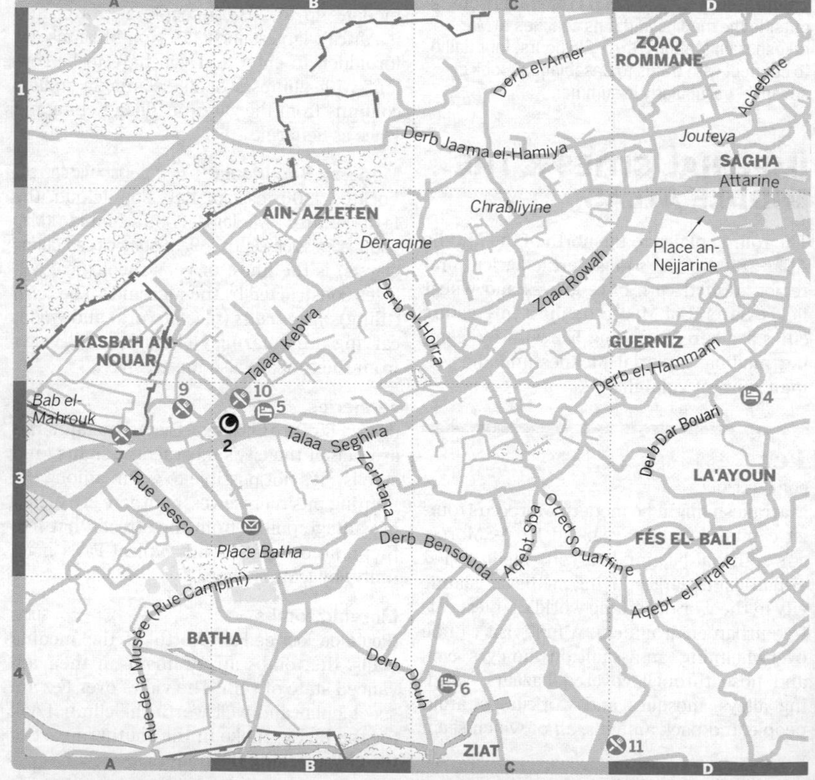

tion project we've seen in a while. Enter into a large column-flanked courtyard and admire the attention to detail here and in the immaculate rooms. Grand without being overwhelming.

Hôtel Central HOTEL €
(Map p888; ☎0535 622333; 50 Rue Brahim Roudani; s/d with shower Dh140/180) A bright and airy budget option just off busy Blvd Mohammed V. All rooms have external toilets, but even those without a shower have their own sinks. It's good value and popular so there are sometimes not enough rooms to go around.

Eating

MEDINA

Bou Jeloud restaurants STREET RESTAURANTS €
(Map p886; Rue Serrajine; mains Dh30-70; ⏲8am-11pm) Walking in from Bab Bou Jeloud to the top of Talaa Seghira, you run the gauntlet of a host of restaurants touting for business. They're all pretty much of a muchness, offering plenty of tajines, couscous, grilled meat and the like. They're also great places to sit and people-watch over a mint tea.

TOP CHOICE **Café Clock** CAFE-RESTAURANT €
(Map p886; ☎035 637855; www.cafeclock.com; Derb el-Mergana, Talaa Kebira; mains Dh55-80; ⏲9am-10pm; 📶) In a restored townhouse, this funky place has a refreshing menu with offerings such as falafel, grilled sandwiches, some interesting vegetarian options, a monstrously large camel burger, and delicious cakes and tarts. Cookery, calligraphy and conversation classes are available, plus there are sunset concerts every Sunday (cover charge around Dh20).

Fès et Gestes GARDEN CAFE €€
(Map p886; ☎0535 638532; 39 Arsat el Hamoumi, Ziat; meals around Dh90; ⏲12-9.30pm, closed Wed) In a bustling medina, this converted French colonial house is a real oasis: step through the gates into its pretty, richly planted garden with trickling fountain and the cares of the day melt away. Ideal for light lunches, full tajine-style dinners, or just a refresing tea or juice to recharge the batteries in the cool green shade.

Chameau Bleu MOROCCAN €€
(Map p886; ☎0535 638991; 1 Derb Tariana; mains Dh55-130; ⏲lunch & dinner) Well-posted just off Talaa Kebira, Chameau Bleu is a converted medina house on several levels, with tables all the way up to the roof terrace. There are tajines aplenty, although we found the grilled meat and fish dishes to be particular

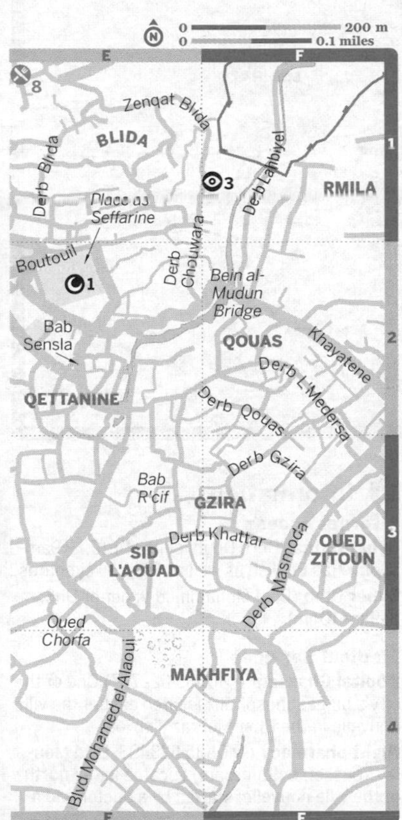

Fez Medina

Sights
1 Kairaouine Mosque E2
2 Medersa Bou Inania B3
3 Tanneries F1

Sleeping
4 Dar Bensouda D3
5 Pension Kawtar B3
6 Riad Verus C4

Eating
7 Bou Jeloud restaurants A3
8 B'sara Stalls E1
9 Café Clock A3
10 Chameau Bleu B3
11 Fès et Gestes D4

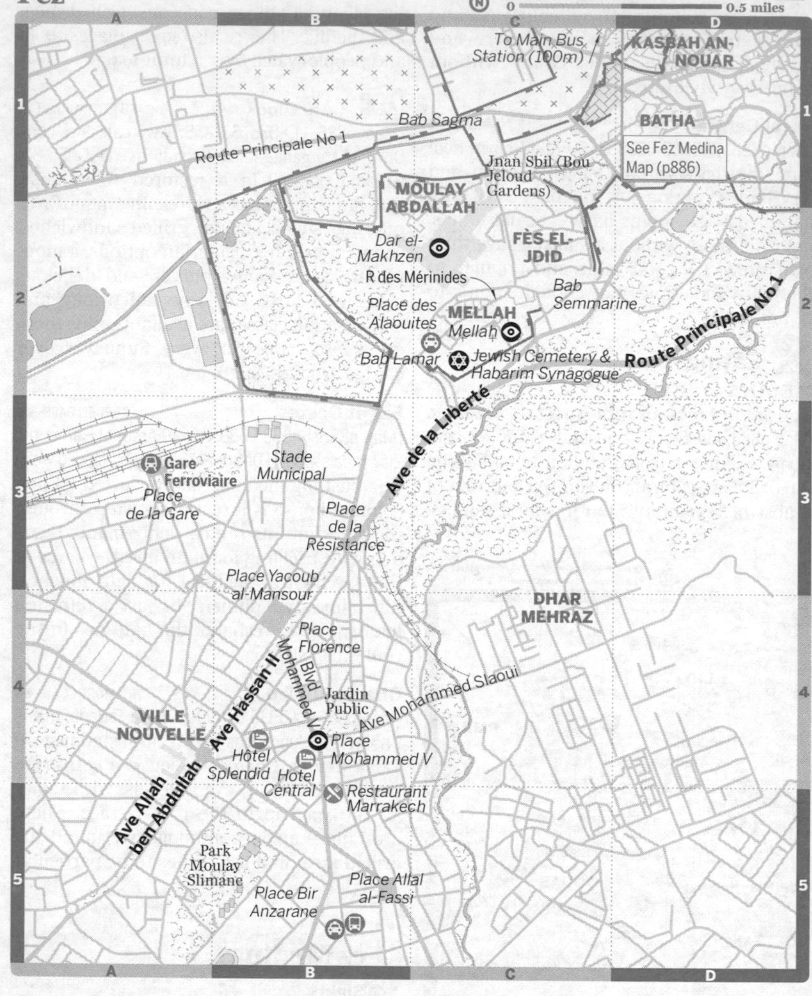

winners; we've also had several good reports about the pasta.

Restaurant Marrakech MOROCCAN €€
(Map p888; ☎035 930876; 11 Rue Omar el-Mokhtar; mains from Dh55; ❄) A charming restaurant that goes from strength to strength behind thick wooden doors. Red *tadelakt* walls and dark furniture, with a cushion-strewn salon at the back, add ambience, while the menu's variety refreshes the palate, with dishes like chicken tajine with apple and olive, or lamb with aubergine and peppers.

Information

Internet access

Cyber Batha (Derb Douh; per hr Dh10; ⏲9am-10pm) Has English as well as French keyboards.

Cyber Club (Blvd Mohammed V; per hr Dh6; ⏲9am-10pm)

Medical Services

Hôpital Ghassani (☎0535 622777) One of the city's biggest hospitals; located east of the ville nouvelle in the Dhar Mehraz district.

Night pharmacy (☎0535 623493; Blvd Moulay Youssef; ⏲9pm-6am) Located in the north of the ville nouvelle; staffed by a doctor and a pharmacist.

BUSES TO/FROM FEZ

DESTINATION	COST (DH)	DURATION (HRS)	FREQUENCY
Casablanca	105	5	7 daily
Chefchaouen	45	4	3 daily
Marrakesh	150	9	2 daily
Rabat	70	3½	7 daily
Tangier	115	6	3 daily
Tetouan	100	5	2 daily

Money

There are plenty of banks (with ATMs) in the ville nouvelle along Blvd Mohammed V. In the medina:

Banque Populaire (Talaa Seghira) ATM and foreign exchange.

Société Générale (Bab Bou Jeloud) ATM and foreign exchange.

Post

Main post office (cnr Ave Hassan II & Blvd Mohammed V)

Post office (Place Batha) In the medina.

Tourist Information

There is no tourist information in the medina.

Tourist Information Office (Syndicat d'Initiative; ☎0535 623460; Place Mohammed V) Not always open, or helpful.

Getting There & Away

Train

The swanky new **train station** (Map p888) is in the ville nouvelle, a 10-minute walk northwest of Place Florence. Trains depart almost hourly between 7am and 5pm for Casablanca (Dh110, 4½ hours), via Rabat (Dh80, 3½ hours) and Meknès (Dh20, one hour), plus there are two overnight trains. Eight trains travel to Marrakesh (Dh195, eight hours) and one goes to Tangier (Dh105, five hours), or four changing at Sidi Kacem.

Bus & Grands Taxis

The main station for **CTM buses** is near Place Atlas in ville nouvelle. CTM runs many daily services to and from Fez; see the boxed text, p889.

Non-CTM buses depart from the **gare routiere** (Map p886) outside Bab el-Mahrouk.

Grands taxis for Meknès (Dh18) and Rabat (Dh60) leave from in front of the main bus station (outside Bab el-Mahrouk) and from near the train station.

Getting Around

Grands taxis from all stands to the airport charge a set fare of Dh120.

Drivers of the red *petits taxis* generally use their meters without any fuss. Expect to pay about Dh9 from the train or CTM station to Bab Bou Jeloud.

Meknès

POP 700,000

Of the four imperial cities, Meknès is the most modest by far. The proximity to Fez rather overshadows Meknès, which receives fewer visitors than it really should. Quieter and smaller than its grand neighbour, it's also more laid back and presents less hassle yet still has all the winding narrow medina streets and fine buildings that it warrants as a one-time home of the Moroccan sultanate. Meknès is the ideal base from which to explore the Roman ruins at Volubilis and the hilltop holy town of Moulay Idriss, two of the country's most significant historic sites.

Sights

The heart of Meknès' medina lies to the north of the main square, Place el-Hedim, with the *mellah* to the west. To the south, Moulay Ismail's **imperial city** opens up through one of the most impressive monumental gateways in all of Morocco, **Bab el-Mansour**. Following the road around to the right, you'll find the grand **Mausoleum of Moulay Ismail** (admission free, donations welcome; ⏱8.30am-noon & 2-6pm Sat-Thu), named for the sultan who made Meknès his capital in the 17th century.

Overlooking Place el-Hedim to the north is the 1882 palace that houses the **Dar Jamaï museum** (Place el-Hedim; admission Dh10; ⏱9am-noon & 3-6.30pm Wed-Mon). Deeper in the medina, opposite the Grand Mosque, the **Medersa Bou Inania** (Rue Najjarine; admission Dh10; ⏱9am-noon & 3-6pm) is typical of the exquisite interior design that distinguishes Merenid monuments.

Sleeping

Maroc Hôtel HOTEL €

(☎0535 530075; 7 Rue Rouamzine; s/d/tr without bathroom Dh100/200/270) A perennially popular shoestring option, the Maroc has kept its standards up over the many years we've been visiting. Friendly and quiet, rooms (with sinks) are simple, and the shared bathrooms are clean. The terrace and courtyard filled with orange trees add to the ambience.

TOP CHOICE **Hôtel Majestic** HOTEL €

(☎0535 522035; 19 Ave Mohammed V; s/d without bathroom Dh159/210, s/d with shower Dh231/322) Open for business since 1937, the Majestic is one of the best deco buildings in Meknès. There's a good mix of rooms (all have sinks), and there's plenty of character to go around from the dark-wood dado to the original deco light fittings. A hard budget option to beat.

TOP CHOICE **Ryad Bahia** GUEST HOUSE €€

(☎0535 554541; www.ryad-bahia.com; Derb Sekkaya, Tiberbarine; r incl breakfast Dh670, ste Dh950-1200; ❄🛜) This charming little riad is just a stone's throw from Place el-Hedim. The main entrance opens onto a courtyard (also hosting a great restaurant), and the whole has an open and airy layout compared to many riads. Rooms are pretty and carefully restored, and the owners (keen travellers themselves) are eager to swap travel stories as well as guide guests in the medina.

Eating

Marhaba Restaurant CANTEEN €

(23 Ave Mohammed V; tajines Dh25; ⏰noon-10pm) We adore this canteen-style place and so does everyone else, judging by how busy it is of an evening. While you can get tajines and the like, do as everyone else does and fill up on a bowl of *harira*, a plate of *makoda* (potato fritters) with bread and hard-boiled eggs – and walk out with change from Dh15. We defy you to eat better for cheaper.

Dar Sultana MOROCCAN €€

(☎0535 535720; Derb Sekkaya, Tiberbarine; mains from Dh70, set menu Dh150) Also going under the name Sweet Sultana, this is a small but charming restaurant in a converted medina house. The tent canopy over the courtyard gives an intimate, even romantic, atmosphere, set off by bright fabrics and walls painted with henna designs. The spread of cooked Moroccan salads is a highlight.

Sandwich stands QUICK EATS €

(Place el-Hedim; sandwiches around Dh30; ⏰7am-10pm) Take your pick of any one of the stands lining Place el-Hedim and sit at the canopied tables to watch the scene as you eat. There are larger meals like tajines, but the sandwiches are usually quick and excellent.

Information

There are plenty of banks with ATMs both in the ville nouvelle (mainly on Ave Hassan II and Ave Mohammed V) and the medina (Rue Sekkakine).

Cyber Bab Mansour (Zankat Accra; per hr Dh6; ⏰9am-midnight)

Hôpital Moulay Ismail (☎035 522805; off Ave des FAR)

Main post office (Place de l'Istiqlal) In the ville nouvelle.

Post office (Rue Dar Smen) In the medina.

Quick Net (28 Rue Emir Abdelkader; per hr Dh6; ⏰9am-10pm)

Getting There & Away

Bus & Grands Taxis

The **CTM bus station** (Ave des FAR) is about 300m east of the junction with Ave Mohammed V. The main bus station lies just outside Bab el-Khemis, west of the medina. CTM departures include: Casablanca (Dh90, 3½ hours, six daily) via Rabat (Dh55, 2½ hours), Marrakesh (Dh160, eight hours, daily) and Tangier (Dh100, five hours, three daily).

The principal *grand taxi* rank is next to the bus station at Bab el-Khemis. There are regular departures to Fez (Dh18, one hour) and Rabat (Dh44, 1½ hours). *Grands taxis* for Moulay Idriss (Dh12, 20 minutes) leave from opposite the Institut Français – the place to organise round trips to Volubilis.

Train

Although Meknès has two train stations, head for the more convenient **El-Amir Abdelkader**. There are plentiful trains to Fez (Dh20, 45 minutes) and Casablanca (Dh90, 3½ hours) via Rabat (Dh59, 2¼ hours), with seven for Marrakesh (Dh174, seven hours) and two for Tangier (Dh80, four hours) – or take a westbound train and change at Sidi Kacem.

Around Meknès

The Roman ruins of **Volubilis** (admission Dh20, parking Dh5, guide Dh140; ⏰8am-sunset) sit in the midst of a fertile plain about 33km north of Meknès. The city is the best-preserved archaeological site in Morocco. One of the country's most important pilgrimage sites, the relaxed, whitewashed town of **Moulay Idriss** is only about 5km from Volubilis. A half-day outing by *grand taxi* from Meknès will cost around Dh350, including a stop at Moulay Idriss.

CENTRAL MOROCCO & THE HIGH ATLAS

Marrakesh is the queen bee of Moroccan tourism, but look beyond it and you'll find great hiking in the dramatic High Atlas, and spectacular valleys and gorges that lead to the vast and empty sands of the Saharan dunes.

Marrakesh

POP 2 MILLION

Marrakesh grew rich on the camel caravans threading their way across the desert, but these days it's cheap flights from Europe bringing tourists to spend their money in the souqs that fill the city's coffers. As many locals have taken the opportunity to move out of the medina into modern housing, foreigners have arrived to transform those houses into stylish magazine-friendly guesthouses.

But Marrakesh's old heart still beats strongly enough, from the time-worn ramparts that ring the city to the nightly spectacle of the Djemaa el-Fna on the edge of the labyrinthine medina.

Like most Moroccan cities, Marrakesh is divided into new and old sections; it's a short taxi ride or a half-hour walk from the centre of the ville nouvelle to Djemaa el-Fna.

Sights

Djemaa el-Fna LANDMARK

The focal point of Marrakesh is Djemaa el-Fna, a huge square in the medina and the backdrop for one of the world's greatest spectacles. Although it can be lively at any hour of the day, Djemaa el-Fna comes into its own at dusk when the curtain goes up on rows of open-air food stalls filling the immediate area with mouth-watering aromas. Jugglers, storytellers, snake charmers, musicians, the occasional acrobat and benign lunatics consume the remaining space, each surrounded by jostling spectators.

Koutoubia Mosque MOSQUE

Dominating the Marrakeshi landscape southwest of Djemaa el-Fna is the 70m-tall minaret of Marrakesh's most famous and most venerated monument, the Koutoubia Mosque. Visible for miles in all directions, it's a classic example of 12th-century Moroccan-Andalucian architecture.

Musée de Marrakech MUSEUM

(www.museedemarrakech.ma; Place ben Youssef; admission Dh40; ⏰9am-6.30pm) Inaugurated in 1997, the Musée de Marrakech is housed in a beautifully restored 19th-century palace, Dar Mnebhi. A combined ticket that also covers **Ali ben Youssef Medersa**, a peaceful place with stunning stucco decoration, costs Dh60. Beside the medersa is **Ali ben Youssef mosque**.

Kasbah OLD TOWN

South of the main medina area is the kasbah, which is home to the most famous of the city's palaces, the now-ruined **Palais el-Badi** (Place des Ferblantiers; admission Dh10; ⏰9am-4.30pm), 'the Incomparable', once reputed to be one of the most beautiful palaces in the world. All that's left are the towering pisé walls taken over by stork nests, and the staggering scale to give an impression of the former splendour. The **Palais de la Bahia** (Rue Riad Zitoun el-Jedid; admission Dh10; ⏰9am-4.30pm), the 'Brilliant', is the perfect antidote to the simplicity of the nearby el-Badi.

Saadian Tombs HISTORICAL SITE

(Rue de la Kasbah; admission Dh10; ⏰9am-4.45pm) Long hidden from intrusive eyes, the area of the Saadian Tombs, alongside the Kasbah Mosque, is home to ornate tombs that are the resting places of Saadian princes.

Jardin Majorelle GARDEN

(☎0524 301852; www.jardinmajorelle.com; cnr Ave Yacoub el-Mansour & Ave Moulay Abdullah; garden Dh30, museum Dh15; ⏰8am-6pm summer, to 5.30pm winter) Marrakesh has more gardens than any other Moroccan city, offering the perfect escape from the hubbub of the souqs and the traffic. The Jardin Majorelle is a sublime mix of art deco buildings and psychedelic desert mirage.

Sleeping

Jnane Mogador RIAD €

(☎0524 426324; www.jnanemogador.com; 116 Derb Sidi Bouloukat, off Rue Riad Zitoun el-Kedim; s/d/tr/q Dh360/480/580/660; @) A 19th-century riad with all the 21st-century guesthouse fixings: prime location, in-house hammam, tea salon, double-decker roof terraces and owner Mohammed's laid-back hospitality. Book well ahead.

Hôtel Central Palace HOTEL €
(☎0524 440235; www.lecentralpalace.com; 59 Derb Sidi Bouloukat; d Dh255-305, with air-con Dh355, d without bathroom Dh155, ste Dh405;❄) Sure it's central, but palatial? Actually, yes. With 40 clean rooms on four floors arranged around a burbling courtyard fountain and a roof terrace lording it over the Djemaa el-Fna, this is the rare example of a stately budget hotel.

Hôtel Toulousain INN €
(☎0524 430033; http://hoteltoulousain.com; 44 Rue Tariq ibn Ziad; s/d Dh180/230-280, s/d without bathroom Dh140/190;📶) An easygoing budget

Marrakesh

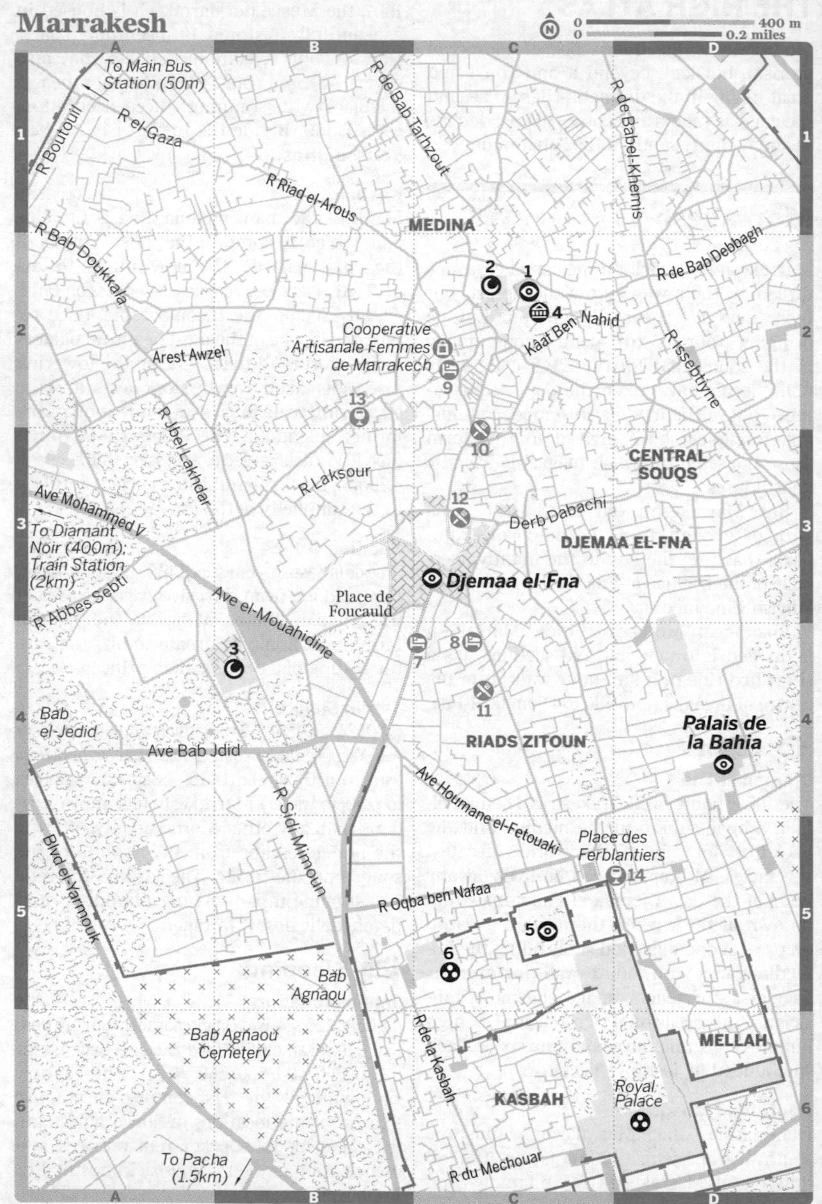

hotel run by a kindly Moroccan-American family in a prime Guéliz location, with tasty restaurants, boutiques, laundry, local travel agency and a literary cafe right at your door. When upstairs rooms get stuffy in summer, guests hang out on patios under banana trees. It's a couple of blocks northwest of Place du 16 Novembre.

Riad Magellan RIAD €€
(☎0661 082042; www.riadmagellan.com; 62 Derb el Hammam, Mouassine; d incl breakfast Dh770-990) The long and winding *derb* (street) leads to your door at this hip hideaway behind the Mouassine Fountain. There's a *tadelakt* hot tub on the terrace, multilingual library in the fireplace salon, and deep-tissue massages to soothe away travel kinks. Antique globes, steamer trunks and rocking chairs add retro flair to sleek *tadelakt* guestrooms generously strewn with rose petals.

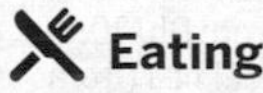

Eating

The cheapest and most exotic places to eat in town remain the food stalls on Djemaa el-Fna, piled high with fresh meats and salads, goats' heads and steaming snails.

Earth Café FUSION, VEGETARIAN €
(☎0661 289402; 2 Derb Zouak, off Rue Riad Zitoun el-Kedim; mains Dh60-80; ⏲11am-11pm; ✎) Now for something completely different: a vegetarian spring roll stuffed with organic spinach, pumpkin, blue cheese and grated carrot with a sesame dressing, right in the heart of the souqs. The Earth Café's sunshine-yellow courtyard is small, but its veg culinary ambitions are great and may make believers out of carnivores.

Haj Mustapha LOCAL €
(East side, Souq Ablueh; meals Dh35-50; ⏲6-10pm) As dusk approaches, several stalls set out paper-sealed crockpots of *tangia* (lamb slow-cooked all day in the ashes of a hammam). This 'bachelor's stew' makes for messy eating, but Haj Mustapha offers the cleanest seating inside a well-scuffed stall. Use bread as your utensil to scoop up *tangia*, sprinkle with cumin and salt, and chase with olives.

Le Chat Qui Rit ITALIAN €€
(☎0524 434311; 92 Rue Yougoslavie; pizzas Dh50-80, set menu Dh150; ⏲7.30-11pm Tue-Sun; ❄) Come here for proper pasta: al dente, tossed with fresh produce and herbs, and drizzled with fruity olive oil. Corsican chef/owner Bernard comes out to ask about everyone's pasta with the delight of a chef who already knows the answer. Seasonal seafood options are a good bet, with fixings just in from the coast daily. It's just north of Ave Hassan II.

Café des Épices CAFE, SANDWICH SHOP €
(☎0254 391770; Place Rahba Kedima; meals Dh25-50; ⏲8am-9pm) Watch the magic happen as you sip freshly squeezed OJ overlooking Rahba Kedima potion-dealers. Salads and sandwiches are fresh and made to order – try the tangy chicken spiked with herbs, nutmeg and olives – and service is surprisingly efficient, given the steep stairs.

Drinking

The number-one spot for a cheap and delicious drink is right on Djemaa el-Fna, where orange juice is freshly squeezed around the clock for just Dh4. Rooftop cafes overlook the square.

Dar Cherifa CAFE
(☎0524 426463; 8 Derb Chorfa Lakbir, near Rue Mouassine; tea/coffee Dh20-25; ⏲noon-7pm) Revive souq-sore eyes at this serene late-15th-century Saadian riad, where tea and saffron coffee are served with contemporary art and literature downstairs or with terrace views upstairs.

Marrakesh

Top Sights
Djemaa el-Fna C3
Palais de la Bahia D4

Sights
1 Ali ben Youssef Medersa C2
2 Ali ben Youssef Mosque C2
3 Koutoubia Mosque B4
4 Musée de Marrakech C2
5 Palais el-Badi C5
6 Saadian Tombs C5

Sleeping
7 Hôtel Central Palace C4
8 Jnane Mogador C4
9 Riad Magellan C2

Eating
10 Café des Épices C3
11 Earth Café C4
12 Haj Mustapha C3

Drinking
13 Dar Cherifa B2
14 Kosybar D5

Kosybar BAR
(☎0524 380324; http://kozibar.tripod.com; 47 Place des Ferblantiers; ⊙noon-1am; ❄) The Marrakesh-meets-Kyoto interiors are full of plush, private nooks, but keep heading upstairs to low-slung canvas sofas and wine by the glass (Dh40 to Dh60) on the rooftop terrace. Enjoy drinks with a side of samba, but skip the cardboard-tasting sushi and stick with bar snacks.

☆ Entertainment

Sleeping is overrated in a city where the nightlife begins around midnight. Most of the hottest clubs are in the Hivernage district of the ville nouvelle. Admissions range from Dh150 to Dh350 including the first drink. Each drink thereafter costs at least Dh50. Dress to impress. Try **Pacha** (www.pachamarrakech.com; Complexe Pacha Marrakech, Blvd Mohammed VI; admission Mon-Wed before/after 10pm free/Dh150, Thu men/women Dh150/free, Sat & Sun Dh200-300;⊙8pm-1am Mon-Thu, 8pm-2am Fri & Sat) or gay-friendly **Diamant Noir** (☎0524 446391; Hôtel Marrakech, cnr Ave Mohammed V & Rue Oum Errabia, Guéliz; admission from Dh150, incl first drink; ⊙10pm-4am).

ℹ Information

Emergency

Ambulance (☎0524 443724)

Brigade Touristique (tourist police; ☎0524 384601; Rue Sidi Mimoun; ⊙24hr)

Internet Access

Internet cafes ringing the Djemaa el-Fna charge Dh8 to Dh12 per hour; just follow signs reading 'c@fe'.

Cyber Café in CyberPark (Ave Mohammed V; per hr Dh10; ⊙9.30am-8pm)

Hassan Internet (☎0524 441989; Immeuble Tazi, 12 Rue Riad el-Moukha; per hr Dh8; ⊙7am-midnight) A bustling place near the Tazi Hotel with 12 terminals.

Medical Services

Pharmacie de l'Unité (☎024 435982; Ave des Nations Unies, Guéliz; ⊙8.30am-11pm)

Polyclinique du Sud (☎0524 447999; cnr Rue de Yougoslavie & Rue Ibn Aicha, Guéliz; ⊙24hr)

Money

There are plenty of ATMs along Rue de Bab Agnaou off the Djemaa el-Fna.

Crédit du Maroc medina (Rue de Bab Agnaou; ⊙8.45am-1pm & 3-6.45pm Mon-Sat); ville nouvelle (215 Ave Mohammed V)

Post

Main post office (☎024 431963; Place du 16 Novembre; ⊙8.30am-2pm Mon-Sat) In the ville nouvelle.

Post office (Rue Bab Agnaou; ⊙8am-noon & 3-6pm Mon-Fri) A convenient branch office in the medina.

Tourist Information

Office National Marocain du Tourisme (ONMT; ☎024 436179; Place Abdel Moumen ben Ali, Guéliz)

ℹ Getting There & Away

Bus

CTM (Rue Abu Bakr Seddik) operates daily buses to Fez (Dh150, 8½ hours) There are also daily services to Agadir (Dh90, four hours, nine daily), Casablanca (Dh85, four hours, three daily) and Essaouira (Dh70, 2½ hours). Other buses arrive and depart from the main **bus station** (Bab Doukkala) just outside the city walls. A number of companies run buses to Fez (from Dh130, 8½ hours, at least six daily) and Meknès (from Dh120, six hours, at least three daily).

Supratours (☎024 435525; Ave Hassan II), next to the train station, operates six daily coaches to Essaouira (Dh70, 2½ hours).

Train

The glitzy **train station** (cnr Ave Hassan II & Blvd Mohammed VI, Guéliz), has trains to Casablanca (Dh90, three hours, nine daily), Rabat (Dh120, four hours), Fez (Dh195, eight hours, eight daily) via Meknès (Dh160, seven hours) and nightly trains to Tangier (Dh205).

ℹ Getting Around

A *petit taxi* to Marrakesh from the airport (6km) should cost no more than Dh70 (Dh100 at night). Alternatively, airport bus 19 runs every 20 minutes from outside the airport carpark to near the Djemaa el-Fna (Dh20). The creamy-beige *petits taxis* around town cost anywhere between Dh8 and Dh20 per journey.

High Atlas Mountains

The highest mountain range in North Africa, the High Atlas runs diagonally across Morocco, from the Atlantic coast northeast of Agadir all the way to northern Algeria, a distance of almost 1000km. In Berber it's called Idraren Draren (Mountain of Mountains) and it's not hard to see why. Flat-roofed, earthen Berber villages cling tenaciously to the valley sides, while irrigated terraced gardens and walnut groves flourish below.

Hiking

The Moroccan tourist office, Office National Marocain du Tourisme (ONMT), publishes the useful booklet *Morocco: Mountain and Desert Tourism* (2005), with lists of guides and other useful information. Treks longer than a couple of days will almost certainly require a guide (Dh300 per day) and pack mule (Dh100).

Drâa Valley

A ribbon of technicoloured *palmeraies* (palm groves), earth-red kasbahs and stunning Berber villages, the Drâa Valley is a special place. The valley eventually seeps out into the sands of the desert, and it once played a key role in controlling the ancient trans-Saharan trade routes that Marrakesh's wealth was built on.

ZAGORA

The iconic 'Tombouktou, 52 jours' (Timbuktu, 52 days) signpost was recently taken down in an inexplicable government beautification scheme, but Zagora's fame as a desert outpost is indelible. Although the town is drab, it has a large market on Wednesday and Sunday selling produce, hardware and livestock, and it is the base for trips to the dunes.

If you don't want to head direct to M'hamid, agencies in Zagora running day and camping trips to the desert include **Caravane Dèsert et Montagne** (☎0524 846898, 066 122312; www.caravanedesertetmontagne.com; 112 Blvd Mohammed V) and **Discovering South Morocco** (☎0524 846115; www.discoveringsouthmorocco.com). Bank on paying around Dh350 per day.

Sleeping & Eating

Auberge Restaurant Chez Ali INN €
(☎0524 846258; www.chez-ali.com; Ave de l'Atlas Zaouiate El Baraka; garden tents per person Dh40, showers Dh10, d half-board Dh360-400; ❄) The welcome here is enthusiastic. Skylit standard rooms upstairs have simple pine furnishings, bathrooms and air-con; tents with pisé walls in the garden sleep four to five and share bathrooms; and 'traditional' rooms have wood-beamed ceilings, mattresses on carpets and shared bathrooms.

All hotels have their own restaurants and will provide set meals (Dh100 to Dh150) to nonguests by prior reservation. Moroccan fare with less flair can be had at cheap, popular restaurants along Blvd Mohammed V.

Getting There & Away

The **CTM bus station** is at the southwestern end of Blvd Mohammed V, and the main bus and *grand taxi* lot is at the northern end. CTM has a daily service to Marrakesh (Dh120) and Casablanca (Dh195). There are also minibuses (Dh25) and *grands taxis* (Dh30) to M'Hamid.

M'HAMID

Once it was a lonesome oasis, but these days M'Hamid is a wallflower no more. The road is flanked with hotels to accommodate travellers lured here by the golden dunes of the Sahara. This one dot on a map actually covers two towns: the M'hamid Jdid is a typical one-street administrative centre with a mosque, a few restaurants, small hotels, craft shops and a Monday market. M'Hamid Bali, the old town, is 3km away across the Oued Drâa. It has an impressive and well-preserved kasbah.

JEBEL TOUBKAL HIKE

One of the most popular trekking routes in the High Atlas is the ascent of Jebel Toubkal (4167m), North Africa's highest peak. The Toubkal area is just two hours' drive south of Marrakesh and is easily accessed by local transport.

The usual starting point is the picturesque village of **Imlil**, 17km from Asni off the Tizi n'Test road between Marrakesh and Agadir. Most trekkers stay overnight in Imlil. There is a *bureau des guides* (guide office) in Imlil, where you should be able to pick up a trained, official guide (with ID cards).

There is plenty of accommodation in Imlil. Try **Hôtel el-Aïne** (☎0524 485625; d incl breakfast with/without bathroom Dh350/300, half-board Dh500/400; 📶) or **Café-Hotel Soleil** (☎0524 485622; www.hotelsoleil.com; d incl breakfast with/without bathroom Dh350/300, half-board Dh500/400; 📶), at the top of the village. Imlil also has shops well stocked with hiking supplies.

Frequent local buses (Dh15, 1½ hours) and *grands taxis* (Dh30, one hour) leave south of Bab er-Rob in Marrakesh to Asni, where you change for the final 17km to Imlil (Dh15 to Dh20, one hour).

M'hamid's star attraction is **Erg Chigaga**, a mind-boggling 40km stretch of golden Saharan dunes that's the equal of Erg Chebbi near Merzouga. It's 56km away – a couple of hours by 4WD or several days by camel. A closer alternative is Erg Lehoudi, but it's in bad need of rubbish collection. **Sahara Services** (☎0661 776766; www.saharaservices.info; Kasbah Sahara Services, M'Hamid) and **Zbar Travel** (☎0668 517280; www.zbartravel.com) are both reliable agencies offering tours – an overnight camel trek should start at about Dh300.

If you're not sleeping with your camel in the desert, **Kasbah Sahara Services** (☎0524 848033; www.hotelmhamid.com; d per person half-board tent/d Dh200/300), 300m on the right after entry to M'Hamid, offers simple but still decent fare.

There's a daily CTM bus at 4.30pm to Zagora (Dh20, two hours), Ouarzazate (Dh60, seven hours), Marrakesh (Dh155, 11 to 13 hours) and Casablanca (Dh220, 15 hours), plus an assortment of private buses, minibuses and *grands taxis*.

UNDERSTAND MOROCCO

History

Most present-day Moroccans are descendents of indigenous tribes that have inhabited the Maghreb hills for thousands of years. When the Romans arrived in the 2nd century BC, they called the locals 'Berbers' (similar to the term 'Barbarian' ascribed to the northern European tribes) because of their incomprehensible tongue.

In the second half of the 7th century, the soldiers of the Prophet Mohammed set forth from the Arabian Peninsula and overwhelmed the peoples of the Middle East. Before long, nearly all Berber tribes were embracing Islam, although local tribes developed their own brand of Islamic Shi'ism, which sparked rebellion against the eastern Arabs.

By 829 local elites had established an Idrissid state dominating all of Morocco, with its capital at Fez. This commenced a cycle of rising and falling dynasties, which included: the Almoravids (1062–1147), who built their capital at Marrakesh; the Almohads (1147–1269), famous for building the Koutoubia Mosque (p891); the Merenids (1269–1465), known for their exquisite mosques and medersas (Qur'anic schools), especially in Fez; the Saadians (1524–1659), responsible for the Palais el-Badi in Marrakesh (p891); and the Alawites (1659 to the present).

France took control in 1912, establishing its capital at Rabat, with Spain holding a token zone in the north of the country. Opposition from Berber mountain tribes was crushed, but political resistance emerged with the development of the Istiqlal (independence) party.

Independence was finally granted in 1956. The Spanish also withdrew, retaining the coastal enclaves of Ceuta and Melilla. Sultan Mohammed V became king, and was succeeded by his son in 1961. Despite moves towards democracy and several coup attempts, Hassan II retained all effective power until his death in 1999. His biggest legacy has been Morocco's occupation and territorial claim of the former Spanish colony of Western Sahara. Western Sahara's legal status is still subject to international dispute.

The new king, Mohammed VI, has adopted a reformist agenda, especially in the area of social policy and women's rights. He has sought to tie Morocco closer to Europe and has overseen a tourism boom and economic liberalisation, but also the backwash of Islamist violence, with a small number of home-grown terrorist attacks.

People

People of Arab-Berber descent make up almost the entire Moroccan population of 32 million, which although still mostly rural, is increasingly urbanised and young to boot – 55% are under 25 years. High growth rates mean that the population is set to double almost every 25 years.

Morocco is a Muslim country. Muslims share their roots with Jews and Christians and respect these groups as *Ahl al-Kteb,* People of the Book. Fundamentalism is mostly discouraged but remains a presence, especially among the urban poor who have enjoyed none of the benefits of economic growth. That said, the popularity of fundamentalism is not as great as Westerners imagine.

Emigration to France, Israel and the USA has reduced Morocco's once robust Jewish community to about 7000 from a high of around 300,000 in 1948.

Environment

Morocco's three ecological zones – coast, mountain and desert – host more than 40 different ecosystems and provide habitat for many endemic species, including the iconic and sociable Barbary macaque (also known as the Barbary ape). Unfortunately, pressure from sprawling urban areas and the encroachment of industrialisation in Morocco's wilderness means that 18 mammal and a dozen bird species are considered endangered.

Pollution, desertification, overgrazing and deforestation are the major environmental issues facing the Moroccan government. The draining of coastal wetlands – which provide important habitats for endangered species – also continues apace to address the rising demand and falling supply of water for irrigation, a problem that becomes increasingly acute with water-hungry tourist developments.

SURVIVAL GUIDE

Directory A-Z

Accommodation

Auberges de jeunesses (youth hostels) operate in Casablanca, Chefchaouen, Fez, Meknès, Rabat and Tangier. Hotels vary dramatically, ranging from dingy dives to gorgeous guest houses and fancy five-stars (the latter mostly in larger cities). Cities that see many tourists also offer wonderful accommodation in the style of a *riad*.

Places to stay are listed by preference and include a private bathroom unless otherwise stated. Prices given are for high season (June to September) and include tax; always check the price you are quoted is TTC (all taxes included).

Advance reservations are highly recommended for all places listed in this chapter, especially in summer.

Price ranges used in this book are as follows, and are for doubles, with the bracketed figures applying for towns and cities that attract large numbers of tourists:

€€€ more than Dh800 (Dh1200)

€€ Dh400 to Dh800 (Dh 600 to Dh 1200)

€ less than Dh400 (Dh 600)

Activities

CAMEL TREKS & DESERT SAFARIS

Exploring the Moroccan Sahara by camel is one of the country's signature activities and one of the most rewarding wilderness experiences, whether done on an overnight excursion or a two-week trek. The most evocative stretches of Saharan sand include the Drâa Valley (p895). Autumn (September to October) and winter (November to early March) are the only seasons worth considering. Prices hover around Dh350 to Dh450 per person per day but vary depending on the number of people, the length of the trek and your negotiating skills.

HAMMAMS

Visiting a *hammam* is a ritual at the centre of Moroccan society and a practical solution for those who don't have hot water at home (or in their hotel). Every town has at least one public *hammam*, and the big cities have fancy spas – both are deep-cleaning and totally relaxing. A visit to a standard *hammam* usually costs Dh20 and extra for a massage.

HIKING

Morocco's mountains offer a variety of year-round hiking possibilities. It's relatively straightforward to arrange guides, porters and mules for a more independent adventure. North Africa's highest peak, Jebel Toubkal (4167m), in the High Atlas (p895), attracts the lion's share of visitors, but great possibilities exist throughout the country, including in the Rif Mountains around Chefchaouen (p877). The Dadès and Todra Gorges in the High Atlas also offer good hiking opportunities. Spring and autumn are the best seasons for hiking.

SURFING & WINDSURFING

Morocco has some great surfing spots. Essaouira (p883) is a centre for windsurfers.

Business Hours

Banks 8.30am-6.30pm Mon-Fri

Post offices 8.30am-4.30pm Mon-Fri

Offices 8.30am-6.30pm Mon-Fri

Eateries noon-3pm & 7-10pm

Bars 4pm-late

Shops 9am-12.30pm & 2.30-8pm Mon-Sat (often closed longer at midday for prayer)

Holidays

All banks, post offices and most shops are shut on the main public holidays:

New Year's Day 1 January

Independence Manifesto 11 January

Labour Day 1 May

Feast of the Throne 30 July

Allegiance of Oued-Eddahab 14 August

Anniversary of the King and People's Revolution 20 August

Young People's Day 21 August

Anniversary of the Green March 6 November

Independence Day 18 November

In addition to secular holidays there are many national and local Islamic holidays and festivals, all tied to the lunar calendar:

Eid al-Adha Marks the end of the Islamic year. Most things shut down for four or five days.

Eid al-Fitr Held at the end of the month-long dawn to dusk Ramadan fast, which is observed by most Muslims. The festivities last four or five days, during which Morocco grinds to a halt.

Moulid an-Nabi (Mouloud) Celebrates the birthday of the Prophet Mohammed.

HOLIDAY	2012	2013	2014
Moulid an-Nabi	5 Feb	25 Jan	14 Jan
Ramadan begins	21 Jul	10 Jul	29 Jun
Eid al-Fitr	19 Aug	8 Aug	28 Jul
Eid al-Adha	26 Oct	15 Oct	4 Oct
New Year begins (year)	16 Nov (1434)	5 Nov (1435)	25 Oct (1436)

Internet Access

Internet access is widely available, efficient and cheap (Dh4 to Dh10 per hour) in internet cafes, usually with pretty impressive connection speeds. One irritant for travellers is the widespread use of French or Arabic (non-qwerty) keyboards.

Most top-end and many midrange hotels offer wi-fi (wi-fi symbol), and it's more or less standard in most *riads* and *maisons d'hôtes*.

Money

The Moroccan currency is the dirham (Dh), which is divided into 100 centimes. It's forbidden to take dirhams out of the country. The Spanish enclaves of Ceuta and Melilla use the euro.

ATMs *(guichets automatiques)* are widespread. Major credit cards are widely accepted in the main tourist centres. Travellers cheques aren't recommended, nor are Australian, Canadian and New Zealand dollars cash.

Tipping and bargaining are integral parts of Moroccan life. Practically any service can warrant a tip, and a few dirham for a service willingly rendered can make your life a lot easier. Tipping between 5% and 10% of a restaurant bill is appropriate.

Post

Post offices are distinguished by the 'PTT' sign or the 'La Poste' logo. You can sometimes buy stamps at *tabacs,* small tobacco and newspaper kiosks. The postal system is fairly reliable, but not terribly fast. It takes about a week for letters to get to European destinations, and two weeks or so to get to Australia and North America.

The parcel office, indicated by the sign '*colis postaux*', is generally in a separate part of the post office building. Take your parcel unwrapped for customs inspection.

Safe Travel

Morocco's era as a hippy paradise is long past. Plenty of *kif* (marijuana) is grown in the Rif Mountains, but drug busts are common and Morocco isn't a good place to investigate prison conditions.

The *brigade touristique* was set up in the principal tourist centres to clamp down on Morocco's notorious *faux guides* and hustlers. Anyone convicted of operating as an unofficial guide faces jail time and/or a huge fine. This has reduced but not eliminated the problem of *faux guides*. You'll still find plenty of these touts hanging around the entrances to medinas and train stations (and even on trains approaching Fez and Marrakesh), and at Tangier port. Remember that their main interest is the commission gained from certain hotels or on articles sold to you in the *souqs*.

If possible, avoid walking alone at night in the medinas of the big cities. Knife-point muggings aren't unknown.

Toilets

Outside midrange and top-end hotels and restaurants, toilets are mostly of the squat variety, feature a tap, hose or container of water for sluicing – the idea being to wash yourself (with your left hand) after performing.

There's often no toilet paper (*papier hygiénique*) so keep a supply with you. Throw the paper in the bin provided

Public toilets are rare outside the major cities. Tip the attendant.

Visas

Most visitors to Morocco do not require visas and are allowed to remain in the country for

90 days on entry. Exceptions to this include nationals of Israel, and most sub-Saharan African countries (including South Africa). Moroccan embassies have been known to insist that you get a visa from your country of origin. Should the standard 90-day stay be insufficient, it is possible (but difficult) to apply at the nearest police headquarters (*Préfecture de Police*) for an extension – it's simpler to leave the country and return. The Spanish enclaves of Ceuta and Melilla have the same visa requirements as mainland Spain.

Women Travellers

Prior to marriage, Moroccan men have little opportunity to meet and get to know women, which is a major reason why Western women receive so much attention.

Foreign women are seen as independent and available. The constant attention is impossible to shake off, no matter what tactic is employed. Be wary but not paranoid – the low-level harassment rarely goes any further.

One benefit for women travelling in Morocco is that, unlike male travellers, you'll have opportunities to meet local women.

Getting There & Away

Air

Morocco's two main international entry points are Mohammed V International Airport 30km southeast of Casablanca and Marrakesh's Ménara airport. Other international airports are in Fez, Tangier and Agadir. For information about Moroccan airports and their facilities, visit the website of **Office National des Aéroports** (www.onda.ma).

Royal Air Maroc (RAM; www.royalairmaroc.com) is Morocco's national carrier, with increasing competition from the budget airlines.

Air Berlin (www.airberlin.com)

Air Europa (www.air-europa.com)

Air France (www.airfrance.com)

Alitalia (www.alitalia.com)

British Airways (www.ba.com)

easyJet (www.easyjet.com)

Iberia (www.iberia.com)

KLM-Royal Dutch Airlines (www.klm.com)

Lufthansa (www.lufthansa.com)

Ryanair (www.ryanair.com)

Bus

The Moroccan bus company **CTM** (www.ctm.co.ma) operates buses from Casablanca and most main cities to European destinations as part of the **Eurolines** (www.eurolines.com) network. Another Moroccan bus service with particularly good links to Spanish networks is **Tramesa** (http://perso.menara.ma/tramesa07, in French).

Sea

Regular ferries run to Europe from several ports along Morocco's Mediterranean coast, of which Tangier is the most popular. Algeciras-Tangier ferries (1½ hours) are hourly in summer. **Direct Ferries** (www.directferries.com) sells tickets for most of the below:

Acciona Transmediterranea, Euroferrys and Ferrimaroc (www.trasmediterranea.es) Almería–Melilla, Almería–Nador, Algeciras–Ceuta, Algeciras–Tangier, Barcelona–Tangier, Málaga–Melilla

Baleària (www.balearia.com) Algeciras–Ceuta, Algeciras–Tangier

Comanav Algeciras–Tangier, Genoa–Tangier, Sète–Nador, Sète–Tangier

Comarit (www.comarit.es, in Spanish) Algeciras–Tangier, Sète–Tangier, Tarifa–Tangier

Getting Around

Air

National carrier **Royal Air Maroc** (RAM; ☎0890 000800; www.royalairmaroc.com) is the main domestic airline, flying from Casablanca to Tangier, Fez, Er-Rachidia, Marrakesh, Essaouira, Agadir and other destinations. For most routes, flying is an expensive and inconvenient option compared to road or rail.

Bus

A dense network of buses operates throughout Morocco, with many private companies competing for business alongside the comfortable and modern coaches of the main national carrier **CTM** (☎in Casablanca 0522 458080).

The **ONCF** (www.oncf.ma, in French) train company runs buses through Supratours to widen its train network, for example running connections from Marrakesh to Essaouira. Morocco's other bus companies are all privately owned and only operate regionally. It's best to book ahead for CTM and

Supratours buses, which are slightly more expensive than those of other companies.

Car & Motorcycle

Taking your own vehicle to Morocco is straightforward. In addition to a vehicle registration document and an International Driving Permit (although many foreign licences, including US and EU ones, are also acceptable), a Green Card is required from the car's insurer. Not all insurers cover Morocco.

Renting a car in Morocco isn't cheap, with prices starting at Dh3000 per day for a basic car. International hire companies are well represented; booking in advance online secures the best deals.

In Morocco you drive on the right-hand side. On a roundabout, give way to traffic entering from the right.

Taxi

Cities and bigger towns have local *petits taxis,* which are a different colour in every city. They are are licensed to carry up to three passengers and are usually metered. Fares increase by 50% after 8pm.

The old Mercedes vehicles you'll see belting along roads and gathered in great flocks near bus stations are *grands taxis.* They link towns to their nearest neighbours. *Grands taxis* take six passengers and leave when full.

Train

Morocco's excellent train network is run by ONCF. There are two lines that carry passengers: from Tangier in the north down to Marrakesh; and from Oujda in the northeast, also to Marrakesh, joining with the Tangier line at the town of Sidi Kacem.

Trains are comfortable, fast and generally preferable to buses. Seats in 2nd-class are more than adequate on any journey. Couchettes are available on the overnight trains between Marrakesh and Tangier.

TRAIN PASSES

Rail Pass This is available for seven/15/30 days (Dh600/1170/2100 for 2nd class, Dh900/1600/3150 for 1st class). Pass prices drop for travellers aged under 26, and again for those under 12.

Carte Fidelité (Dh149) This is for those aged over 26 and gives you 50% reductions on eight return or 16 one-way journeys in a 12-month period.

The Netherlands

Includes »

Best Places to Eat

» Van Dobben, Amsterdam (p907)

» Les Ombrellas, Den Haag (p912)

» De Ballentent, Rotterdam (p916)

» Blauw, Utrecht (p918)

Best Places to Stay

» Hotel Nadia, Amsterdam (p907)

» Hotel Bazar, Rotterdam (p915)

» Stayokay Rotterdam (p915)

» Hotel Holla, Maastricht (p920)

Why Go?

Great Dutch artists Rembrandt, Vermeer and Van Gogh have spanned the centuries and touring the Netherlands you'll see why. Discover clichés such as tulips and windmills or stroll canals in the midst of 17th-century splendour in beautiful small towns such as Leiden and Delft. Of course, enticing Amsterdam's phenomenal and diverse nightlife is world famous, from throbbing clubs to quaint brown cafes.

The locals live on bicycles and you can, too. Almost every train station has a shop to rent a bike and soon you're off on the ubiquitous bike paths heading wherever your mood takes you.

Finally there's the Dutch themselves: warm, friendly and funny. You'll have a hard time being alone in a cafe as someone will soon strike up a conversation, and usually in English. Revel in Amsterdam, don't miss exquisite Maastricht or pulsing Rotterdam, and pick a passel of small towns to add contrast. It's a very big small country.

When to Go

Amsterdam

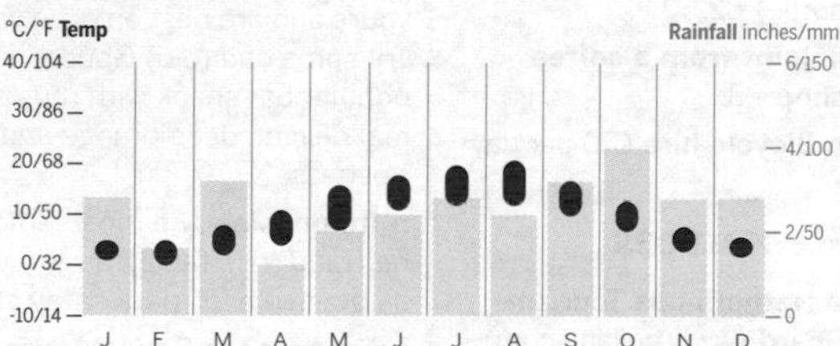

Mar–May The country explodes in colour as billions of bulbs bloom.

Jul Mild summer temperatures and lots of daylight keep you outdoors, cycling and drinking.

Dec–Feb The Dutch passion for ice skating is on display on frozen canals nationwide.

AT A GLANCE

» **Currency** Euro (€)

» **Language** Dutch; English widespread

» **Money** ATMs common; cash preferred for small purchases

» **Visas** Schengen rules apply; see p1319

Fast Facts

» **Area** 41,526 sq km

» **Capital** Amsterdam

» **Country code** ☎31

» **Emergency** ☎112

Exchange Rates

Australia	A$1	€0.74
Canada	C$1	€0.74
Japan	¥100	€0.87
New Zealand	NZ$1	€0.56
UK	UK£1	€1.16
USA	US$1	€0.72

Set Your Budget

» **Budget dorm/double** €20/60

» **Two-course evening meal** €12

» **Heineken** (glass or bottle) €2.50

» **Joint from a coffee shop** €3

» **Bicycle hire** €10 per day

Resources

» **Netherlands Tourism Board** (www.holland.com)

» **Dutch News** (www.dutchnews.nl)

» **Dutch Railways** (www.ns.nl)

» **Windmill Database** (www.molendatabase.com)

Connections

Train connections to neighbouring countries are good. Amsterdam is linked to Cologne (2½ hours), in Germany, and Brussels (1¾ hours on the new Thalys/Fyra high-speed line), in Belgium, where you can connect with Eurostar to London. Maastricht is right on the Belgian and German borders. Connections to Cologne and Brussels take 1½ hours. It would be easy to put together a loop itinerary that includes the wines of the Moselle Valley in Germany and the beers of Belgium.

ITINERARIES

One Week

Spend three days canal-exploring, museum-hopping and cafe-swooping in Amsterdam. Work your way through the ancient towns of the Randstad and the modern vibe of Rotterdam and save a day for the grandeur of Maastricht.

Two Weeks

Allow four days for Amsterdam's many delights, plus a day trip to the old towns of the north such as Edam and a day or two even further north on Texel. Then allow a day each for beautiful Delft, the regal Hague, cute Utrecht and Rotterdam. Finish off with two days in Maastricht.

Essential Food & Drink

» **Vlaamse frites** *Frites* are the iconic French fries smothered in mayonnaise or other gooey sauces; they are the ultimate munchies food.

» **Beer** While big names such as Heineken are ubiquitous, small brewers such as Gulpen, Haarlem's Jopen, Bavaria, Drie Ringen, Leeuw and Utrecht are the best.

» **Gouda** The tastiest varieties have strong, complex flavours and are best enjoyed with a bottle of wine or two. Try some *oud* (old) Gouda, hard and rich in flavour and a popular bar snack with mustard. Oud Amsterdammer is a real delight, deep orange and crumbly with white crystals of ripeness.

» **Indonesian** The most famous dish with colonial roots is *rijsttafel* (rice table), an array of spicy savoury dishes such as braised beef, pork satay and ribs served with white rice.

» **Erwtensoep** Served in winter, a pea soup rich with onions, carrots, smoked sausage and bacon. Ideally a spoon stuck upright in the pot should remain standing.

» **Kroketten** Croquettes are dough balls with various fillings that are crumbed and deep-fried; the variety called *bitterballen* are a popular brown-cafe snack served with mustard. Perfect with beer.

The Netherlands Highlights

1 Stroll canals and soak up beautiful, vibrant and off-beat **Amsterdam** (p904)

2 Immerse yourself in the exhilarating urban vibe and stunning modern architecture of **Rotterdam** (p913)

3 Lose yourself inside the ancient walls and cosmopolitan shops of **Maastricht** (p920)

4 Take a day trip to evocative **Delft** (p912), where Vermeer found his inspiration

5 Wander the beautiful tree-lined boulevards and classy museums of **Den Haag** (p911)

6 Be inspired at **Leiden** (p910), the home of schoolboy Rembrandt; nearby is the springtime explosion of tulips at **Keukenhof Gardens** (p911)

7 Go **bike-crazy** (p925) across the Netherlands

8 Lose a few hours in the atmospheric old confines of a **brown cafe**, the centre of beer-drinking conviviality

AMSTERDAM

020 / POP 747,000

If Amsterdam were a staid place it would still be one of Europe's most beautiful and historic cities, right up there with Venice and Paris. But add the qualities that make it Amsterdam – the funky and mellow bars, the brown cafes full of characters, pervasive irreverence, whiffs of pot and an open-air marketplace for sleaze and sex – and you have a literally intoxicating mix.

Amsterdam has always been a liberal place, ever since the Golden Age, when it led European art and trade. Centuries later, in the 1960s, it again led the pack – this time in the principles of tolerance, with broad-minded views on drugs and same-sex relationships taking centre stage.

Wander the 17th-century streets, tour the iconic canals, stop off to enjoy a masterpiece, discover a funky shop and choose from food from around the world. Walk or ride a bike around the concentric rings of the centre and bask in the many worlds-within-worlds where nothing ever seems the same twice.

From Centraal Station the streets radiate across the network of canals. The Dam is the heart, a 10-minute walk from Centraal Station. Leidseplein, a further 20 minutes' walk, is the centre of (mainstream) Amsterdam nightlife, and Nieuwmarkt is a vast cobblestone square with open-air markets and popular pubs.

Sights & Activities

TOP CHOICE Van Gogh Museum MUSEUM
(www.vangoghmuseum.nl; Paulus Potterstraat 7; admission €14; 10am-6pm Sun-Thu, to 10pm Fri) This outstanding museum houses the world's largest Van Gogh collection. Trace the artist's life from his tentative start though to his Japanese phase, and on to the black cloud that descended over him and his work. There's also works by contemporaries Gauguin, Toulouse-Lautrec, Bernard and Monet.

Rijksmuseum MUSEUM
(www.rijksmuseum.nl; Stadhouderskade 42; admission €12.50; 9am-6pm) The nation's revered museum boasts a collection valued in the billions, but until renovations finish in 2013 (or later) there are only a few masterpieces displayed, including a couple of Vermeers and the crowning glory, Rembrandt's *Night Watch* (1641). On most days crowds make the entire experience unpleasant. The rooms are tight and you'll find mobs snapping pics with abandon. Save one queue by buying your ticket online.

Stedelijk Museum MUSEUM
(www.stedelijkindestad.nl; Museumplein) This fine museum features around 100,000 pieces including impressionist works from Monet, Picasso and Chagall; sculptures from Rodin and Moore; De Stijl landmarks by Mondrian; and pop art from Warhol and Lichtenstein. However, renovations and a new other-

AMSTERDAM NEIGHBOURHOODS

» **City Centre** The not-overly-impressive Royal Palace and the square that puts the dam in Amsterdam anchor the city's oldest quarter.

» **Canal Belt** Created in the 17th century as an upscale neighbourhood, the Canal Belt, especially in the west and south, remains Amsterdam's top district. Wandering here amidst architectural treasures and their reflections on the narrow waters of the Prinsengracht, Keizersgracht and Herengracht can cause days to vanish quicker than some of Amsterdam's more lurid pursuits.

» **Jordaan** Originally a stronghold of the working class, the Jordaan, west of the centre, is now one of the most desirable areas to live in Amsterdam. It's a pastiche of modest 17th- and 18th-century merchants' houses, humble workers' homes and a few modern carbuncles, squashed in a grid of tiny lanes peppered with bite-sized cafes and shops.

» **Red Light District (aka de Wallen)** It retains the power to make your jaw go limp, even if near-naked prostitutes propositioning passers-by from black-lit windows is the oldest Amsterdam cliché. Note that even in the dark heart of the district there are charming shops and cafes where the only thing that vibrates is your mobile phone. The district is bound by Zeedijk, Nieuwmarkt and Kloveniersburgwal in the east; Damstraat, Oude Doelenstraat and Oude Hoogstraat in the south; and Warmoesstraat in the west.

worldly-looking addition mean the museum has closed its doors until at least late 2011.

Vondelpark PARK
(www.vondelpark.nl) Vondelpark is an English-style park with free concerts, ponds, lawns, thickets, winding footpaths and three outdoor cafes.

TOP CHOICE **Anne Frank Huis** HISTORIC BUILDING
(Anne Frank House; ☎556 71 00; www.annefrank.org; Prinsengracht 267; admission €8.50; ⏰9am-9pm mid-Mar–mid-Sep, to 7pm mid-Sep–mid-Mar) The Anne Frank Huis, where Anne wrote her famous diary, lures almost a million visitors annually with its secret annexe, its reconstruction of Anne's melancholy bedroom, and her actual diary, with its sunnily optimistic writing tempered by quiet despair. Look for the photo of Peter Schiff, her 'one true love'. Try going in the early morning or evening when crowds are lightest; book online to avoid long queues.

FREE **Begijnhof** HISTORIC COMPLEX
(www.begijnhofamsterdam.nl; ⏰8am-5pm) To escape from Amsterdam's hubbub, duck into the Begijnhof, an enclosed former convent from the early 14th century. It's an oasis of peace, with tiny houses and postage-stamp gardens around a well-kept courtyard. The Beguines were a Catholic order of unmarried or widowed women who cared for the elderly and lived a religious life without taking monastic vows. The last died in the 1970s.

Museum het Rembrandthuis HISTORIC BUILDING
(Rembrandt House Museum; www.rembrandthuis.nl; Jodenbreestraat 4; admision €10; ⏰10am-5pm) You almost expect to find the master himself at the Museum het Rembrandthuis, the house where Rembrandt van Rijn ran his painting studio only to lose the lot when profligacy set in, enemies swooped, and bankruptcy came knocking. The streets around the house are prime wandering territory: a vibrant mix of old Amsterdam, canals, and quirky shops and cafes.

Heineken Experience BREWERY
(www.heinekenexperience.com; Stadhouderskade 78; admission €15; ⏰11am-7pm) The Heineken Experience is the much-gussied-up reincarnation of the brewer's old brewery tour, featuring multimedia displays, rides and plenty of gift shops. At Amsterdam's most popular attraction, acolytes enjoy samples of the beer, which (like Stella Artois et al) is dismissed as an 'old man's beer' domestically and sold at a premium abroad.

DON'T MISS

ST NICOLAAS BOAT CLUB TOUR

An alternative to the big staid boats bumping around the canals, the small boats of **St Nicolaas Boat Club** (www.amsterdamboatclub.com; suggested donation €10) are piloted by characters as interesting as the passing sights. Have a beer and a smoke and learn about alternative Amsterdam. Departure times vary; sign up at Boom Chicago (p909).

Sleeping

Book ahead for weekends and in summer. Many places cater specifically to party animals, with booze flowing, pot smoking and general mayhem around the clock. Others exude Old World charm. Elevators are rarely found.

Hotel Prinsenhof HOTEL €
(☎623 17 72; www.hotelprinsenhof.com; Prinsengracht 810; s/d without bathroom €49/69, with bathroom €84/89; 📶) Honest value, this 18th-century house features canal views, rooms with mismatched furniture and 'Captain Hook', the electric luggage hoist. The attic quarters provide top views and are most sought-after.

Hotel/Hostel Winston HOTEL, HOSTEL €
(☎623 13 80; www.winston.nl; Warmoesstraat 123; dm €22-42, s €77-100, d €90-120; 📶) With rock-and-roll rooms, an attached nightclub, a beer garden and a smoking deck, this place hops 24/7. Dorms sleep up to eight. Most private rooms are 'art' rooms: local artists were given free rein, with results from sci-fi (robots peering at you) to playful and raunchy.

Hotel Brouwer HOTEL €€
(☎624 63 58; www.hotelbrouwer.nl; Singel 83; r incl breakfast €60-95; 🚭) The eight rooms in this house dating back to 1652 are named for Dutch painters, are simply furnished and boast canal views. There's a mix of Delft-blue tiles and early-20th-century furniture, and a tulip-sized elevator. Credit cards not accepted.

Stadsdoelen Youth Hostel HOSTEL €
(☎624 68 32; www.stayokay.com; Kloveniersburgwal 97; dm €20-28, s €45-60, d €50-80, @📶)

Central Amsterdam

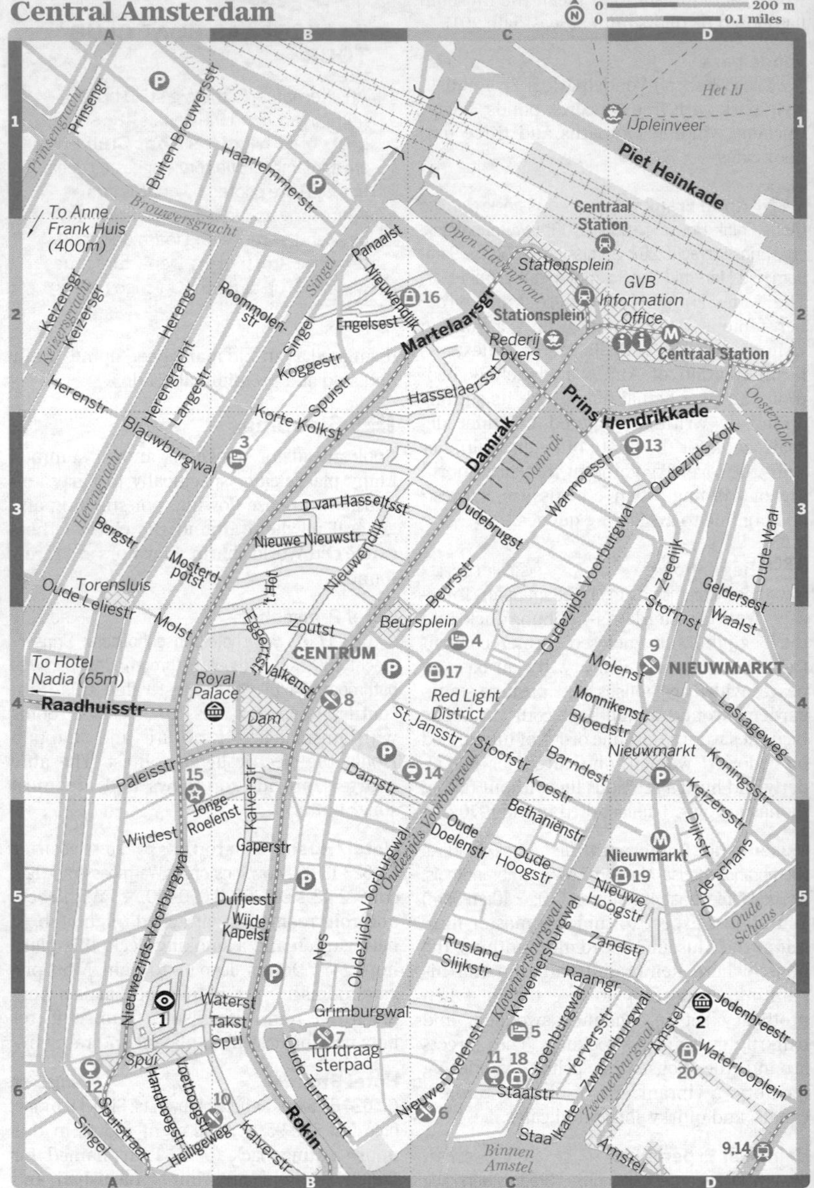

The well-run Stadsdoelen is always bustling with backpackers and offers 11 ultra-clean single-sex and mixed rooms (each with up to 17 beds and free lockers). There's a big TV room, a hopping bar, a pool table and laundry facilities.

International Budget Hostel HOSTEL €
(☎624 27 84; www.internationalbudgethostel.com; Leidsegracht 76; dm €28-32, tw from €70;) The canalside location in a former warehouse is close to nightlife. There's a four-person limit in rooms and a cool mix of backpackers from

Central Amsterdam

Sights

1 Begijnhof ... A6
2 Museum het Rembrandthuis ... D6

Sleeping

3 Hotel Brouwer ... B3
4 Hotel Winston ... C4
5 Stadsdoelen Youth Hostel ... C6

Eating

6 Café de Jaren ... C6
7 Crea ... B6
8 De Bijenkorf ... B4
9 Nam Kee ... D4
10 Vleminckx ... B6

Drinking

11 Doelen ... C6
12 Hoppe ... A6
13 In 't Aepjen ... D3
14 Proeflokaal Fockink ... C4

Entertainment

15 Abraxas ... A4

Shopping

16 Chills & Thrills ... C2
17 Condomerie ... C4
18 Juggle ... C6
19 't Klompenhuisje ... D5
20 Waterlooplein Flea Market ... D6

around the world lounging in the common areas. It's clean and the staff have charm that's greater than the prices.

Eating

Amsterdam abounds in food choices. Happy streets for hunting include Utrechtsestraat, Spuistraat and any of the little streets lining and connecting the west canals, such as Berenstraat.

TOP CHOICE Van Dobben DUTCH €
(Korte Reguliersdwarsstraat 5; mains from €4) Open since the 1940s, the venerable Van Dobben has white tiled walls and white-coated counter staff who specialise in snappy banter. Traditional Dutch fare is the speciality: try the *pekelvlees* (something close to corned beef). You'll also get the best *kroquetten* (croquettes) and pea soup in town.

De Bijenkorf SELF-SERVICE €
(Dam; ⏲11am-7pm) The city's most fashionable department store has a huge snazzy restaurant on the 5th floor with a terrace offering rooftop and steeple views. A dozen stations offer fresh and modern fare.

Pancakes! DUTCH €
(Berenstraat 38; mains from €4) A great place to sample Dutch pancakes amid cool shops along the Western Canals in an atmosphere free of clogs and other kitsch – and there are just as many locals here as tourists.

Tujuh Maret INDONESIAN €€
(Utrechtsestraat 73; mains €14-20) Grab a wicker chair and tuck into spicy Sulawesi-style dishes like dried, fried beef or chicken in red-pepper sauce. *Rijsttafel* is laid out according to spice intensity; *makanan kecil* is a mini-*rijsttafel*.

Nam Kee CHINESE €€
(Zeedijk 113-116; mains €9-20) It won't win any design awards, but Nam Kee is always the most popular Chinese spot in town. The typically long bilingual menu has all the favourites.

Café de Jaren CAFE €€
(Nieuwe Doelenstraat 20; mains €5-12) Watch the Amstel flow by from the balcony and waterside terraces of this soaring, bright, grand cafe. The great reading table has loads of foreign publications for whiling away hours over beers.

Crea CAFE €
(Turfdraagsterpad 17; mains €4-10) Walking along Grimburgwal, you can't help but notice the prime cafe chairs across the canal. They're part of the University of Amsterdam's cultural centre, a laid-back spot that's a superb urban escape.

Vleminckx FRITES €
(Voetboogstraat 31; frites from €2; ⏲11am-6pm) This hole-in-the-wall takeaway place has drawn hordes for its monumental *frites* since 1887. The standard is smothered in mayonnaise, though you can ask for ketchup, peanut sauce or a variety of spicy toppings.

AMSTERDAM SPLURGE

The handsome building housing **Hotel Nadia** (☎620 15 50; www.nadia.nl; Raadhuisstraat 51; r incl breakfast €60-150; @📶) has a precipitous set of stairs, but the energetic staff will tote your luggage up them. Rooms are immaculate and those to the front have great views of the Westerkerk and the Jordaan.

GET UIT & ABOUT

Not sure how to spend your evening? Head to the last-minute-ticket desk at the **Uitburo** (621 13 11; www.aub.nl; 10am-7.30pm Mon-Sat, noon-7.30pm Sun), in the corner of the Stadsschouwburg on the Leidseplein. Comedy, dance, concerts, and even club nights are often available at a significant discount – and handily marked 'LNP' (language no problem) if understanding Dutch isn't vital.

Febo FAST FOOD €
(Leidsestraat 94; snacks from €1.50) Insert a few coins into the machine and live the legend. The *bami* rolls are hot as napalm, the *frikadel* frightening, and the *kaassoufflé* utterly unsoufflélike. But plucking a treat from the automat windows is a drunken Dutch tradition.

Drinking

A particular Amsterdam joy is discovering your own *bruin café* (brown cafe), an especially cosy, atmospheric bar. They are found everywhere, often tucked into the most atmospheric of locations. Many serve food.

TOP CHOICE **Hoppe** BROWN CAFE
(Spuistraat 18) This gritty brown cafe has been luring drinkers for more than 300 years. Journalists, bums, socialites and raconteurs toss back brews amid the ancient wood panelling. Most months the energetic crowd spews out from the dark interior and onto the Spui.

Doelen BROWN CAFE
(Kloveniersburgwal 125) On a busy crossroads between the Amstel and the Red Light District, this cafe dates back to 1895 and looks it: carved wooden goat's head, stained-glass lamps and sand on the floor. During fine weather the tables spill across the street for picture-perfect canal views.

Proeflokaal Fockink BAR
(Pijlsteeg 31; 3-9pm) This wee tasting house (dating from 1679) serves scores of *jenevers* (ginlike liqueur) and liqueurs in an arcade behind Grand Hotel Krasnapolsky. Although there are no seats, it's an intimate place to knock back a taste or two with a friend.

In 't Aepjen BROWN CAFE
(Zeedijk 1) Candles burn even during the day at this bar based in a 15th-century house that is one of two remaining wooden buildings in the city. The name allegedly comes from the bar's role in the 16th and 17th centuries as a crash pad for sailors from the Far East, who often toted *aapjes* (monkeys) with them.

Entertainment

Find out what's on from Thursday's papers or the monthly *Time Out Amsterdam*.

And note that cafes have coffee, but 'coffee shops' are where one buys pot. Smoking regulations mean you can puff pot but not tobacco.

Abraxas COFFEE SHOP
(Jonge Roelensteeg 12; @) The Abraxas management knows what stoners want: mellow music, comfy sofas, rooms with different energy levels, and thick milkshakes. The considerate staff and mellow clientele make this a great place for coffee-shop newbies. Get stoned and send strange emails from the computers.

Rokerij COFFEE SHOP
(Lange Leidsedwarsstraat 41) Behind the black hole of an entrance you'll find Asian decor and candlelight for those tired of the Rastafarian vibe. One of many friendly locations.

Sugar Factory NIGHTCLUB
(www.sugarfactory.nl; Lijnbaansgracht 238) One night it's Balkan beats; another, it's 'wicked jazz sounds' – the Sugar Factory has all kinds of live entertainment. Equally important, the vibe is always welcoming and creative. It's an excellent mid-size space with a smoking lounge upstairs.

Escape NIGHTCLUB
(www.escape.nl; Rembrandtplein 11) Amsterdam's biggest, glitziest club has managed to keep the bass pumping since the '80s. Long lines get longer when a big-name DJ mixes; bouncers are choosy.

Odeon NIGHTCLUB
(www.odeontheater.nl; Singel 460) Set in a skinny canal house, the Odeon has been a creative party spot for decades. Glam but accessible, its club nights are heavy on house and electro.

TOP CHOICE **Paradiso** LIVE MUSIC
(www.paradiso.nl, in Dutch; Weteringschans 6) This converted church has been a premier rock venue since the '60s. Expect interesting dance music; live shows are followed by DJs or club nights.

Melkweg LIVE MUSIC
(www.melkweg.nl; Lijnbaansgracht 234a) The Milky Way – it's housed in a former dairy – must be Amsterdam's coolest club-gallery-cinema-cafe-concert hall. Its vibrant program of events is so full and varied that it's impossible not to find something to go to, from international DJ club nights to live Brazilian jazz.

Boom Chicago COMEDY
(www.boomchicago.nl; Leidseplein 12) Performs English-language stand-up and improv comedy yearround. See it over dinner and a few drinks. Inspiration is culled from Chicago's legendary Second City.

Shopping

The real pleasure of shopping in Amsterdam is tiny shops selling things you'd find nowhere else. Good bets for browsing:

Chills & Thrills HEAD SHOP
(Nieuwendijk 17) You'll find herbal trips, mushrooms, psychoactive cacti, novelty bongs and human-sized alien sculptures.

Condomerie CONDOMS
(Warmoesstraat 141) Puts the 'pro' back in prophylactic: rarely can you shop for a condom in such a tasteful setting and grapple with so many choices.

Several streets on the western canals are dotted with surprising little shops. Try Reestraat and Hartenstraat and the blocks south to Runstraat and Huidenstraat.

Mendo BOOKS, DESIGNER GOODS
(Berenstraat 11) A striking combination of stunning books, art, candy – even umbrellas.

DON'T MISS

AMSTERDAM MARKETS

Albert Cuypmarkt (www.decuyp.nl; Albert Cuypstraat; ⏲10am-5pm Mon-Sat) Amsterdam's largest and busiest market is 100 years old. Food of every description, flowers, souvenirs, clothing, hardware and household goods can be found here.

Waterlooplein Flea Market (Waterlooplein; ⏲9am-5pm Mon-Fri, 8.30am-5.30pm Sat) Amsterdam's most famous flea market: curios, secondhand clothing, music, used footwear, ageing electronic gear, New Age gifts, cheap bicycle parts.

Boekie Woekie BOOKS
(Berenstraat 16) Sells books by artists, whether self-published monographs or illustrated stories handcrafted right down to the paper.

Nieuwmarkt has several eccentric stores. **Juggle** (Staalstraat 3) keeps many balls in the air selling juggling goods. A couple of canals north, **'t Klompenhuisje** (Nieuwe Hoogstraat 9a) has surprisingly comfortable, traditional Dutch *klompen* (clogs).

Information

Centrale Doktersdienst (Central Doctors Service; ☎592 34 34; ⏲24hr) Doctor, dentist or pharmacy referrals.

GWK Travelex (Centraal Station; ⏲8am-10pm Mon-Sat, 9am-10pm Sun) Exchanges travellers cheques and makes hotel reservations; also at Schiphol airport.

I Amsterdam Card (www.iamsterdam.com; per 24/48/72hr €38/48/58) Available at VVV tourist offices and some hotels. Gives admission to most museums, a free canal boat trip, and discounts at shops, attractions and restaurants; includes a transit pass.

Tourist office (VVV; www.vvvamsterdam.nl; Stationsplein 10; ⏲9am-7pm) Maps, guides and transit passes.

Getting There & Away

BUS For details of regional transport in the Netherlands, call the **transport information service** (☎0900 92 92; www.9292ov.nl); it costs €0.70 per minute. Fares and travel durations are covered under towns in the regional sections of this chapter.

Amsterdam has good long-distance bus links with the rest of Europe. **Eurolines** (www.eurolines.nl; Rokin 10) tickets can be bought at its office near the Dam, and at most travel agencies and the NS Reisburo (Netherlands Railways Travel Bureau) in Centraal Station. Departures are from the bus station next to Amstelstation.

TRAIN Amsterdam's main train station is fabled Centraal Station (CS), with service to the rest of the country and major European cities.

Getting Around

TO/FROM THE AIRPORT Trains to Centraal Station leave every few minutes, take 15 to 20 minutes, and cost €4/7 per single/return.

BICYCLE Amsterdam is cycling nirvana: flat and beautiful with dedicated bike paths. About 150,000 bicycles are stolen each year in Amsterdam alone, so always lock up. Rental agencies include the following:

Bike City (www.bikecity.nl; Bloemgracht 68-70; per day/week €14/57) In the Jordaan, and has no advertising on the bikes – you might pass for a local.

Orangebike (www.orangebike.nl; Geldersekade 37; per day/week €10/43) Also offers a range of city tours (from €20).

BOAT Amsterdam's canal boats are a popular way to tour the town but most are actually a bit claustrophobic, with steamed-up glass windows surrounding passengers. Look for a boat with an open seating area.

Rederij Lovers (www.lovers.nl; Prins Hendrikkade 25-27; €13) Runs several routes that stop at major sights allowing you to hop on and off; circuits last about an hour.

PUBLIC TRANSPORT Services – including the iconic trams – are run by local transit authority the GVB; national railway (NS) tickets are not valid on local transport. The GVB has a highly useful **information office** (www.gvb.nl; Stationsplein 10; ⏲7am-9pm Mon-Fri, 8am-9pm Sat & Sun) across the tram tracks from the Centraal Station main entrance. Note that you can avoid the often long lines and buy day passes at the adjoining VVV office.

Public transport in Amsterdam uses the *OV-chipkaart* (p924). Cards for one/two hours cost €2.50/3.50 on trams and buses. A better deal are the unlimited-ride tickets sold by the GVB (from machines and the office), which are good for 24/48/72/96 hours and cost €7/11.50/15.50/19.50.

Night buses take over shortly after midnight when the trams and regular buses stop running.

RANDSTAD

When people think of Holland outside of Amsterdam, they are often really thinking about the Randstad. One of the most densely populated areas on the planet, it stretches from Amsterdam to Rotterdam and features classically Dutch towns and cities, including Leiden, Den Haag and Delft. Most people focus their visit to Holland here, enjoying the peerless cycling network that links the towns amid tulip fields.

Leiden

☎071 / POP 116,800

Leiden is a busy, vibrant town that is a popular day trip from Amsterdam. Claims to fame: it's Rembrandt's birthplace and it's home to the Netherlands' oldest university. Large, dignified 17th-century buildings with tall, almost regal windows line the canals.

Sights

The best way to experience Leiden is by strolling the historic centre, especially along the Rapenburg canal.

Follow the huge steeple to **Pieterskerk** (Pieterskerkhof; ⏲1-4pm), which shines after a grand restoration (a good thing as it's been prone to collapse since it was built in the 14th century). The precinct here is as 'old Leiden' as you'll get and includes the gabled **Latin School** (Schoolstraat), which (before it became a commercial building), from 1616 to 1620, was graced by a pupil named Rembrandt. Across the plaza, look for the **Gravensteen**, which dates to the 13th century and once was a prison. The gallery facing the plaza was where judges watched executions.

The 17th-century **Lakenhal** (Cloth Hall; www.lakenhal.nl; Oude Singel 28-32; admission €7.50; ⏲10am-5pm Tue-Fri, noon-5pm Sat & Sun) has an assortment of works by old masters (including a few Rembrandts) as well as period rooms and temporary exhibits.

Sleeping & Eating

The city-centre canals and narrow old streets have plenty of options, although there's little of interest on the walking route in from the station. The sprawling Saturday **market** along Nieuwe Rijn abounds with fresh fare and flowers.

Hotel Nieuw Minerva HOTEL €€

(☎512 63 58; www.nieuwminerva.nl; Boommarkt 23; r €80-150; @ 📶) The Minerva has a traditional look and a quiet canalside location. Some of the 40 rooms have themed decor. The Rembrandt Room features an old-style walled bed with thick privacy curtains. Stash yourself inside and paint something.

Mangerie de Jonge Koekop BISTRO €€

(Lange Mare 60; mains from €30; ⏲dinner Mon-Sat) Always popular, this bistro has fresh and inventive fare. Dine under the stars at tables outside in summer. Look for the sculpted cow's head on the front, which is as narrow as the first stalk of spring asparagus.

Brasserie het Koetshuis BISTRO €

(Burgsteeg 13; mains from €8) Right in the shadow of De Burcht (an 11th-century citadel), you can sit on the large terrace and ponder the ramparts or huddle inside at a long table in what was once stables. Cafe classics dominate the long and varied menu.

Café l'Esperance BROWN CAFE €

(Kaiserstraat 1; mains €6-12) This brown cafe is long, dark and handsome, all decked out in nostalgic wood panelling and overlooking an evocative bend in the canal. Outside tables buzz with frivolity in summer.

Annie's CAFE €

(Hoogstraat 1a; mains from €8) At the confluence of canals and pedestrian zones, Annie's has a prime water-level location with dozens of tables on a floating pontoon. This classy cafe is good for a drink or a casual meal.

Information

Tourist office (VVV; www.vvvleiden.nl; Stationsweg 41; ⏲8am-6pm Mon-Fri, 10am-4pm Sat, 11am-3pm Sun) Across from the train station; has good maps and historic info.

Getting There & Away

Sample of domestic trains:

Amsterdam €8, 34 minutes, six per hour

Den Haag €3.20, 10 minutes, six per hour

Schiphol airport €5.30, 15 minutes, six per hour

Den Haag (The Hague)

☎070 / POP 486,000

Den Haag, officially known as 's-Gravenhage (Count's Hedge), is the Dutch seat of government (although Amsterdam's the capital). Wide, tree-lined boulevards such as **Lange Voorhout** give Den Haag a suitably regal air to go with its many embassies. Various international courts of justice keep Den Haag in the news, while its museums include one exquisite star.

Sights & Activities

TOP CHOICE **Mauritshuis** ART MUSEUM

(www.mauritshuis.nl; Korte Vijverberg 8; admission €11; ⏲10am-5pm Tue-Sat, 11am-5pm Sun) For a painless introduction to Dutch and Flemish Art 101 visit this small museum in a jewel-box of an old palace. Highlights include the Dutch *Mona Lisa*: Vermeer's *Girl with a Pearl Earring*. Rembrandts include a wistful self-portrait from the year of his death, 1669. Even if you're just passing Den Haag on the train, it's well worth hopping off to visit.

Binnenhof PALACE

(⏲visitor centre 10am-4pm Mon-Sat) The royal palace adjoins the Mauritshuis, surrounded by parliamentary buildings that have long been at the heart of Dutch politics. The central courtyard was once used for executions. A highlight of the complex is the 13th-century Gothic **Ridderzaal** (Knights' Hall).

Grote Kerk CHURCH

(Rond de Grote Kerk 12) Dating from 1450, this modest church has a fine pulpit that was constructed 100 years later. The neighbouring 1565 **old town hall** is a splendid example of Dutch Renaissance architecture.

Gemeentemuseum MUSEUM

(Municipal Museum; Stadhouderslaan 41; www.gemeentemuseum.nl; admission €10; ⏲11am-5pm Tue-Sun) Admirers of De Stijl and Piet Mondrian mustn't miss this Berlage-designed museum. Mondrian's unfinished *Victory Boogie Woogie* takes pride of place (as it should: the museum paid €30 million for it), and there are also a few Picassos and works by some of

SMALL TOWNS & DAY TRIPS

Oodles of cute, small Dutch towns can be reached from Amsterdam in under 1½ hours by train. Here are a few to consider:

» **Alkmaar** is massively touristy, but its cheese ceremony dates back to the 17th century.

» **Deventer** is a sleepy Hanseatic League town with over 1000 16th- and 17th-century buildings.

» **Gouda** is the perfect little Dutch town, replicated in many places across the Netherlands.

» **Haarlem** has cobblestone streets, canals and the excellent Frans Hals Museum.

» **Keukenhof Gardens** (www.keukenhof.nl) shows off millions, maybe billions of tulips in spring, and is close to Leiden.

Get more information at the tourist office across from Amsterdam Centraal Station or online at www.1000dutchdelights.com. For train details to these towns, see www.ns.nl.

the better-known names of the 20th century. Take tram 17 from Den Haag Central Station (CS) and Holland Spoor (HS).

Scheveningen BEACH
(www.scheveningen.nl) On warm days the sands get oversubscribed by mobs of sunseekers but there's commercial relief in a slew of diversions that would warm the cockles of a Blackpool or Atlantic City huckster's heart. Escape the madness on paved bike paths that run for miles through desolate dunes. Trams 1, 9 and 11 heading west serve Scheveningen but it's more pleasantly approached at the end of a 15- to 20-minute (4km) bike ride that will take you past the lush homes of some of Den Haag's well-heeled residents.

Sleeping

Hotel La Ville HOTEL €€
(☎346 36 57; www.hotellaville.nl; Veenkade 5-6; r €45-125; wifi) The 21 rooms here are the best deal close to the centre. Things are basic white but spotless and comfortable; some rooms share bathrooms. Apartments have basic cooking facilities and there's a small cafe.

Stayokay Den Haag HOSTEL €
(☎315 78 88; www.stayokay.com/denhaag; Scheepmakerstraat 27; dm from €23; @) This 220-bed branch of the Stayokay hostel chain has all the usual facilities including a bar, a restaurant, internet and games. It's around 15 minutes' walk from Den Haag HS station.

Eating & Drinking

All those expats on expense accounts support a diverse and thriving cafe culture. The cobbled streets and canals off Denneweg are an excellent place to stroll hungry.

De Zwarte Ruiter CAFE €
(Black Rider; Grote Markt 27; snacks from €4) The Rider faces off with the competing Boterwaag across the Markt like rival Kings of Cool. We call this one the winner, with its terrace and art-deco mezzanine – light-filled, split-level and cavernous – and boisterous crowds of commoners, diplomats and no doubt, the odd international jewel thief.

Café De Oude Mol CAFE €
(Oude Molstraat 61; snacks from €3) Some of the *oude* (old) *National Geographic*s piled in the window actually pre-date the crusty yet genial characters arranged around the bar. Pass through the ivy-covered door and you'll find Den Haag without the pretence.

DEN HAAG SPLURGE

At a confluence of canals in one of the city's most charming districts, **Les Ombrellas** (☎365 87 89; Hooistraat 4; mains €15-30; ⏲lunch Mon-Fri, dinner Mon-Sat) is a long-running favourite that sets up tables across the shady plaza. The tank with live crabs tells you that this is seafood country and the very long menu abounds with choice.

Zebedeüs CAFE €
(Rond de Grote Kerk 8; meals from €7) Built right into the walls of the Grote Kerk, this bright cafe is a day tripper's dream, with huge, fresh sandwiches served all day. Grab one of many tree-shaded tables outside or relax with a coffee and a newspaper at the big tables within.

Information

Tourist office (www.denhaag.com; Hofweg 1; ⏲9.30am-6pm Mon-Fri, 9.30am-5pm Sat, 11am-5pm Sun) Sells tickets for local events and has internet access.

Getting There & Around

TRAINS Most trains start/stop their journeys from Den Haag Centraal Station (CS), but some through trains only stop at Den Haag Holland Spoor (HS) station just south of the centre. Sample domestic trains:

Amsterdam €10, 50 minutes, four per hour
Rotterdam €4.30, 25 minutes, four per hour
Schiphol airport €7.30, 30 minutes, four per hour

TRAMS A useful day pass for local trams costs €6.70 but you have to wait in often long ticket queues at CS and HS.

Delft

☎015 / POP 96,600

Compact, charming and relaxed, Delft may be the perfect Dutch day trip. Founded around 1100, it maintains tangible links to its romantic past despite the pressures of modernisation and tourist hordes. Many of the canalside vistas could be scenes from the *Girl with a Pearl Earring*, the novel about Golden Age painter Johannes Vermeer, which was made into a movie (and partially shot here) in 2003. His *View of Delft* is an enigmatic vision of the town (it hangs in the Mauritshuis in Den Haag). Delft is also famous for its 'delftware', the distinctive blue-and-white pottery originally duplicated from Chinese porcelain by 17th-century artisans.

Sights

The 14th-century **Nieuwe Kerk** (www.nieuwekerk-delft.nl; Markt; adult/child €3.50/1.50; ⏲9am-6pm Mon-Sat Apr-Oct, 11am-4pm Mon-Sat Nov-Mar) houses the crypt of the Dutch royal family and the mausoleum of Willem de Zwijger (William the Silent). The fee includes entrance to the **Oude Kerk** (www.oudekerk-delft.nl; Heilige Geestkerkhof; ⏲9am-6pm Mon-Sat Apr-Oct, 11am-4pm Mon-Sat Nov-Mar) – and vice versa. The latter, 800 years old, is a bizarre sight: its tower leans about 2m from the vertical. Among the tombs inside is Vermeer's. The **town hall** and the **Waag** (weighing house) on the Markt are right out of the 17th century.

Vermeer Centre Delft MUSEUM
(www.vermeerdelft.nl; Voldersgracht 21; admission €7; ⏲10am-5pm) The nonprolific painter (only 35 works are firmly attributed to him) stars at this touristy attraction, which looks at his artistry and life in detail but actually has none of his paintings.

Municipal Museum het Prinsenhof MUSEUM
(www.prinsenhof-delft.nl; St Agathaplein 1; adult/child €7.50/free; ⏲10am-5pm Tue-Sat, 1-5pm Sun) A former convent, this is where William the Silent was assassinated in 1584. The museum displays various objects telling the story of the 80-year war with Spain, as well as 17th-century paintings.

De Candelaer PORCELAIN STUDIO
(www.candelaer.nl; Kerkstraat 13; ⏲9am-5.30pm Mon-Fri, 9am-5pm Sat, plus 9am-5pm Sun Mar-May) Just five artists produce iconic Delftware here. When it's quiet they'll give you a detailed tour of the manufacturing process.

Sleeping & Eating

Quiet Delft would make a good base for exploring much of Holland, with frequent and fast-train services putting towns from Leiden to Rotterdam less than 20 minutes away. The usual array of cafes surround the Markt.

Hotel Coen HOTEL €€
(☎214 59 14; www.hotelcoendelft.nl; Coenderstraat 47; r from €80; @📶) Just behind the train station but removed from the construction, this family-run hotel has 55 beds in a variety of rooms, from budget singles as thin as your wallet to grander doubles.

De Visbanken SEAFOOD STAND €
(Camaretten 2; snacks from €3; ⏲10am-6pm) Someone has been selling fish on this spot since 1342. The present vendors line the display cases in the old open-air pavilion with all manner of fishy things. Enjoy marinated and smoked treats or go for something fried.

Barrique CAFE €€
(Beestenmarkt 33; meals from €8) Just east of the Markt, cafes sprawl across the shady Beestenmarkt. Where pigs were once sold (1449–1972), it is now home to fun-filled consumption – a slick cafe specialises in wine for the beer-weary, tapas and smooth jazz.

Drinking

Locus Publicus PUB
(Brabantse Turfmarkt 67) Glowing from within, this beer cafe has more than 200 beers. It's charming and filled with cheery locals who've quaffed their way through the list.

Getting There & Away

The area around the train station is a vast construction site for years to come as the lines are moved underground. Sample domestic trains:

Amsterdam €11.60, one hour, two per hour
Den Haag €2.50, 12 minutes, four per hour
Rotterdam €3.20, 12 minutes, four per hour

Rotterdam

☎010 / POP 606,000

Rotterdam bursts with energy. Vibrant nightlife, a diverse multi-ethnic community, an intensely interesting maritime tradition and a wealth of top-class museums all make it a must-see part of any visit to Holland, especially if you are passing on the new high-speed trains.

The Netherlands' 'second city', Rotterdam was bombed flat during WWII and spent the following decades rebuilding. You won't find a classic Dutch medieval centre here – it was swept away along with the other rubble and detritus of war. In its place is an architectural aesthetic that's unique in Europe, a progressive perpetual-motion approach to architecture that's clearly a result of the city's postwar, postmodern 'anything goes' philosophy. A fine example of this is the Paul McCarthy statue **Santa with Butt Plug** that the city placed in the main shopping district.

Central Rotterdam

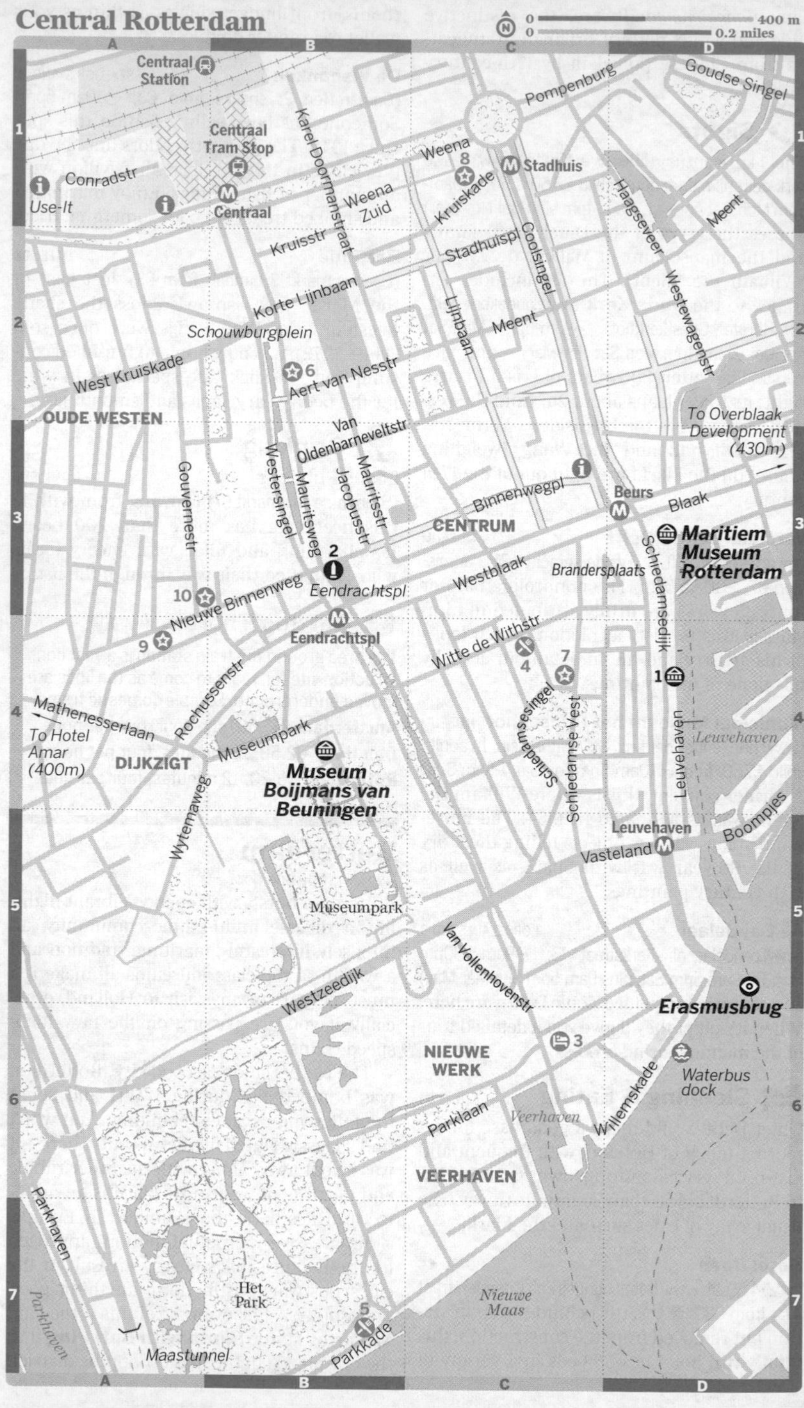

Central Rotterdam

Top Sights
Erasmusbrug....D5
Maritiem Museum Rotterdam....D3
Museum Boijmans van Beuningen....B4

Sights
1 Haven Museum....D4
2 Santa with Butt Plug Statue....B3

Sleeping
Hotel Bazar....(see 4)
3 Room Rotterdam....C6

Eating
4 Bazar....C4
5 De Ballentent....B7

Entertainment
6 De Unie....B2
7 Gay Palace....C4
8 off_corso....C1
9 Pluto....A4
10 Rotown....A3

Sights

Rotterdam is split by the vast Nieuwe Maas shipping channel, which is crossed by a series of tunnels and bridges, notably the fabulously postmodern **Erasmusbrug**.

TOP CHOICE Museum Boijmans van Beuningen MUSEUM
(www.boijmans.nl; Museumpark 18-20; admission €10, Wed free; 11am-5pm Tue-Sun) Museum Boijmans van Beuningen is among Europe's very finest museums and has a permanent collection taking in Dutch and European art (Bosch, Van Eyck, Rembrandt, Tintoretto, Titian and Bruegel's *Tower of Babel*). The surrealist wing features ephemera, paraphernalia and famous works from Dalí, Duchamp, Magritte, Man Ray and more.

Overblaak NOTABLE BUILDING
The Overblaak development (1978–84), designed by Piet Blom, is marked by its pencil-shaped tower and arresting up-ended, cube-shaped apartments. One unit, the **Kijk-Kubus Museum-House** (www.kubuswoning.nl; admission €2.50; 11am-5pm), lets you see what it's like to live at odd angles.

Maritiem Museum Rotterdam MUSEUM
(www.maritiemmuseum.nl; Leuvehaven 1; admission €7.50; 10am-5pm Tue-Sat, 11am-5pm Sun, plus 10am-5pm Mon Jul & Aug) This engaging museum looks at the Netherlands' rich maritime traditions. There's an array of models that any youngster would love to take into the tub, plus more interesting and explanatory displays.

FREE Haven Museum OPEN-AIR MUSEUM
(Leuvehaven 50; visitors centre 10am-5pm Tue-Sun) All manner of old and historic ships are moored in the basin just south of the Maritiem Museum. You can wander the quays around the clock.

Oude Haven HISTORIC AREA
Near the Overblaak development and the Blaak train, metro and tram station is the oldest part of the harbour, dating from the 14th century. Historic boats are moored here and you can often see restorations in progress.

TOP CHOICE Delfshaven HISTORIC AREA
Delfshaven was once the main seaport for the city of Delft and today it's a twee-free piece of Rotterdam's past. A reconstructed 18th-century **windmill** (Voorhaven 210) still grinds flour. Get here on tram 4, which cruises lively Nieuwe Binnenweg.

Sleeping

Hotel Bazar HOTEL €€
(206 51 51; www.hotelbazar.nl; Witte de Withstraat 16; r €70-130) Bazar is deservedly popular for its 27 Middle Eastern, African and South American themed rooms: lush, brocaded curtains, exotically tiled bathrooms and more. Top-floor rooms have balconies and views. Breakfast is spectacular: Turkish breads, international cheeses, yoghurt, pancakes and coffee. The ground-floor cafe is justifiably popular.

Stayokay Rotterdam HOSTEL €
(436 57 63; www.stayokay.com/rotterdam; Overblaak 85-87; dm €17-25, r from €65; ❄@) Those odd angles you see at this hostel may not be to do with what you just smoked: this posh hostel is within the landmark Overblaak development. There are 245 beds in oddly shaped rooms that sleep two to eight. Some have air-con and those on the top floor have cool views.

Hotel Amar HOTEL €
(425 57 95; www.amarhotel.nl; Mathenesserlaan 316; r without bathroom €50-90; @) Small place in a leafy neighbourhood close to Delfshaven, the Museumplein and good nightlife. Rooms are simple and comfy.

Room Rotterdam HOSTEL €
(282 72 77; www.roomrotterdam.nl; Van Vollenhovenstraat 62; dm from €17; @) A popular hostel with 16 dorm rooms, each with two to 10 beds. Each has its own decor, ranging from 'Dutch Delight' to 'Love'.

Eating

Find myriad eating choices in Veerhaven, Witte de Single, Nieuwe Binnenweg and Oude Haven. Historic and appealing, Delfshaven is a vibrant, multi-ethnic neighbourhood with many cafes and bars, especially along the canal near the Oude Kerk.

TOP CHOICE **De Ballentent** DUTCH €
(www.deballentent.nl; Parkkade 1; meals from €5; 9am-11pm) Rotterdam's best waterfront pub-cafe is also a great spot for a meal. Dine on one of two terraces or inside. Mussels, schnitzels and more line the menu but the real speciality here are *bals,* huge homemade meatloafy meatballs.

Bazar MIDDLE EASTERN €€
(Witte de Withstraat 16; mains €7-15) On the ground floor of the inventive Hotel Bazar, this eatery comes up with creative Middle Eastern fusion fare that complements the stylised decor. Dolmades haven't tasted this good any place west of İstanbul.

Het Eethuisje DUTCH €
(Mathenesserdijk 436, Delfshaven; mains €8-10) Traditional Dutch food is served from this little storefront near the canal in Delfshaven. It's utterly tourist-free. Tuck into meaty fare served with rib-sticking starchy sides.

Drinking

De Oude Sluis BROWN CAFE
(Havenstraat 7) The view up the canal from the tables outside this ideal brown cafe goes right out to Delftshaven's windmill. Inside you'll find good beers on tap, including the hoppy Brigand IPA.

Weimar CAFE
(Haringvliet 637) Named for the Hotel Weimar that stood here and was blasted to rubble in 1940, this is one of scores of waterside cafes in Oude Haven. Have a wander and pick one or several, depending on your mood. The Weimar is one of the more gracious.

Entertainment

Rotterdam draws clubbers from across Europe.

Gay Palace NIGHTCLUB
(www.gay-palace.nl; Schiedamsesingel 139) It is Rotterdam's only weekly gay nightclub, with four floors of throbbing gay action – and with different scenes on each floor – to work you into a lather and get you sweaty.

off_corso NIGHTCLUB
(www.off-corso.nl; Kruiskade 22) This is where it's at: bleeding-edge local and international DJs mashing up a high-fibre electronic diet of bleeps 'n' beats. Art displays provide diversions at this prototypical Rotterdam club.

TOP CHOICE **Rotown** LIVE MUSIC
(www.rotown.nl; Nieuwe Binnenweg 17-19) A smooth bar, a dependable live-rock venue, an agreeable outdoor cafe and the anchor of Amsterdam's most interesting street. The musical program features new local talent, established international acts and crossover experiments.

De Unie VENUE
(www.deunie.nu; Mauritsweg 35) Truly cultural, this landmark venue is a vision in white, which provides a blank slate for events from cabaret and accoustic folk to forums about taxation and the middle class.

Pluto COFFEE SHOP
(www.pluto.nl; Nieuwe Binnenweg 54) Space, not the cartoon dog, is the inspiration at this head shop, which sells every kind of pot accessory and the goods to fill them.

Information

The Rotterdam Welcome Card (from €9) offers discounts for sights, hotels and restaurants, and free public transport. Buy it from the tourist office.

Tourist office (www.rotterdam.info) city (Coolsingel 197; 9am-6pm Mon-Sat, 10am-5pm Sun); Groothandelsgebouw (Weena; 9am-5.30pm Mon-Sat, 10am-5pm Sun) Free internet. Pick up the essential *R Zine*. The main (city) branch is located in the City Information Centre, with a good display on architecture since the war and a huge town model. The second location is near the train station in the landmark post-WWII commercial and residential complex Groothandelsgebouw.

Use-It (www.use-it.nl; Schaatsbaan 41-45; 9am-6pm Tue-Sun mid-May–mid-Sep, to 5pm Tue-Sat mid-Sep–mid-May) Off-beat independent tourist organisation all but lost amid the station construction. Books cheap accommodation and publishes the excellent *Simply the Best* budget guide.

Getting There & Away

The area around Rotterdam Centraal Station will be one big construction site until the stunning new train station – set above and below ground – is completed in 2013. Sample trains services:

Amsterdam (high-speed) €21, 40 minutes, two per hour

Amsterdam (via Lieden) €13.30, 65 minutes, five per hour

Brussels (Belgium) €27 to €43, 75 to 107 minutes, one per hour

Schiphol airport €10.70, 47 minutes, three per hour

Utrecht €9.10, 40 minutes, four per hour

Getting Around

Rotterdam's tram, bus and metro services are provided by **RET** (www.ret.nl). Most converge in front of Centraal Station, where there is an **information booth** (⏲6am-11pm Mon-Fri, 8am-11pm Sat & Sun) that also sells tickets. There are other information windows in the major metro stations. Day passes are €6.

Rent bikes from Use-It for €6 per day.

DON'T MISS

BLOWING IN THE WIND

In 1740 a series of windmills were built to drain a polder about 12km southeast of Rotterdam. Today 19 of the Dutch icons survive at **Kinderdijk** (www.kinderdijk.nl), which is a Unesco monument. You can wander the dikes for over 3km amid the spinning sails and visit inside one of the **windmills** (admission €3.50; ⏲9.30am-5.30pm). It's a good bicycle ride; you can rent bikes once there or travel from Rotterdam (16km). Get a map from the tourist office.

A fantastic day trip is by the **Waterbus** (www.waterbus.nl; Willemskade; day pass €11.50). These fast ferries leave every 30 minutes and a connection puts you at Kinderdijk, 1km from the first mill. After the visit, continue by ferry to utterly charming **Dordrecht** and then return to Rotterdam by train.

Utrecht

☎030 / POP 302,000

Utrecht is one of the Netherlands' oldest cities and boasts a beautiful, vibrant, old-world city centre ringed by striking 13th-century canal wharves. The wharves, well below street level, are unique to Utrecht. Canalside streets alongside brim with shops, restaurants and cafes.

Initial impressions may be less auspicious, however. When you step off the train you'll find yourself lost in the maze that is the Hoog Catharijne shopping centre. It's really a nightmare but a vast construction project is transforming the entire area (www.cu2030.nl).

The city's student community of 40,000 is the largest in the country. Saturdays are mad with shoppers and day trippers in from every polder in the region.

Sights

Focus your wanderings on the **Domplein** and south along the tree-lined **Oudegracht**. The tourist office has a good booklet about Utrecht's myriad small museums covering everything from wastewater to old trains.

Domtoren HISTORIC BUILDING

(www.domtoren.nl; Domplein; adult/child €8/4.50; ⏲11am-4pm) The Dom Tower is 112m high, with 465 steps. It's a tough haul to the top but well worth the exertion: the tower gives unbeatable city views. The guided tour in Dutch and English is detailed and gives privileged insight into this beautiful structure. Buy tickets nearby at the tourist office.

Centraal Museum MUSEUM

(www.centraalmuseum.nl; Nicolaaskerkhof 10; admission €9; ⏲11am-5pm Tue-Sun) The Centraal Museum has a wide-ranging collection: applied arts dating back to the 17th century as well as paintings by some of the Utrecht School artists. There's even a 12th-century boat that was dug out of the local mud and a 400-year-old doll's house. There's a surcharge of €3 to tour the house. Admission also includes:

Dick Bruna Huis

(www.dickbrunahuis.nl; Nicolaaskerkhof 10) One of Utrecht's favourite sons, Dick Bruna is the creator of beloved cartoon rabbit Miffy, who takes pride of place here.

Rietveld-Schröderhuis

This Unesco-recognised landmark house is just outside the centre. Built in 1924 by Utrecht architect Gerrit Rietveld, it is a stark example of 'form follows function'.

Sleeping

B&B Utrecht B&B €

(☎065 043 48 84; www.hostelutrecht.nl; Lucas Bolwerk 4; dm from €21, r from €60; @) Straddling the border between hostel and hotel, this spotless inn in an elegant old building has an internal Ikea vibe. Breakfast is free as is use of a huge range of musical instruments. Bikes are available to rent.

Strowis Budget Hostel HOTEL €
(☎238 02 80; www.strowis.nl; Boothstraat 8; dm from €16, r €63; @ 📶) This 17th-century building is near the town centre and has been lovingly restored and converted into a hostel (four- to 14-bed rooms). It has a cosy bar and rents bikes.

Eating & Drinking

When Utrecht groans with visiting mobs you can escape down to the waterside canal piers with a picnic.

TOP CHOICE **Blauw** INDONESIAN €€
(www.restaurantblauw.nl; Springweg 64; set menu from €20; ⏲dinner) Blauw is *the* place for stylish Indonesian food in Utrecht. Young and old alike enjoy spicy, fresh fare amid the stunning red decor that mixes vintage art with hip minimalism.

Café Ledig Erf CAFE €
(Tolsteegbrug 3; mains €6-12) This classy pub overlooks a confluence of canals (and other cafes) at the southern tip of town. The terrace vies with the beer list in offering the most joy. Meals are cheap and filling.

TOP CHOICE **ACU** BAR
(www.acu.nl; Voorstraat 71) Billing itself as a 'political cultural centre', ACU is a classic student dive. It combines bar, disco, lecture hall and more. Argue about whether Trotsky was too conservative while downing organic vegan food.

't Oude Pothuys BROWN CAFE
(Oudegracht 279) Small and dark, this basement pub has nightly music – jam sessions with locals trying their hand at rock and jazz. Enjoy drinks on the totally refurbished canalside pier.

Information

Tourist office (www.utrechtyourway.nl; Domplein 9; ⏲10am-6pm Mon-Fri, 10am-5pm Sat, noon-5pm Sun) Sells maps and tours of the nearby Domtoren.

Getting There & Around

Utrecht is easily walked (once you escape the shopping mall).

The train station is a major connection point and is Holland's busiest. It is on the line linking Amsterdam to Cologne. Sample domestic trains:

Amsterdam €6.70, 30 minutes, four per hour

Maastricht €23.50, two hours, two per hour

Rotterdam €9.10, 40 minutes, four per hour

NORTHERN NETHERLANDS

This region includes independently minded Fryslân province, which used to incorporate regions of the Netherlands, northern Germany and Denmark until it became part of the united Netherlands. Although the Frisian language is similar to Dutch, pronunciation is entirely different.

Groningen

☎050 / POP 185,000

It may be a long way from Amsterdam, but Groningen's a vibrant, youthful city, boasting all you'd expect of a progressive Dutch metropolis – its 20,000-strong student population (the university has been around since 1614) sees to that. There are also the requisite art museums, theatre and classical concerts, as well as gabled houses reflected in silent canals.

Sights

The **Grote Markt** is nothing special. The 16th-century **Martinikerk** (Grote Markt; admission €1; ⏲11am-5pm Mon-Sat mid-Apr–mid-Nov), at the northern corner of the Grote Markt, is eye-catching. Its 96m-high **tower** (admission €3; purchase ticket at tourist office) has sweeping views.

The nearby **Vismarkt** has more intimate charms. Just west, **Aa-kerk** (A-Kerkhof), with parts dating to the 15th century, was a seaman's church, as this was the old harbour area. **Oude Boteringestraat** has a number of appealing buildings dating from the 17th and 18th centuries.

Sleeping

Hotel Garni Friesland HOTEL €
(☎312 13 07; www.hotelfriesland.nl; Kleine Pelsterstraat 4; r €40-100; 📶) The Friesland is bare bones, but it's central and the prices are unbeatable. Service is friendly and amenable, and the 17 rooms are adequate. Some bathrooms are down the hall.

DON'T MISS

HOGE VELUWE NATIONAL PARK

The **Hoge Veluwe** (www.hogeveluwe.nl; admission €8, car €6; ⏲8am-10pm summer, 9am-6pm winter) is the Netherlands' largest national park, a mix of forests and woods, shifting sands and heathery moors, along with red deer, wild boar and mouflon (wild sheep).

It features the world-class **Kröller-Müller Museum** (☎0318-59 12 41; www.kmm.nl; Houtkampweg 6; admission €8; ⏲10am-5pm Tue-Sun), with a superb Van Gogh collection and works by Picasso, Renoir and Manet. You cannot visit the museum without a day ticket for the park.

From Arnhem train station (Utrecht to Arnhem by train: €9.40, 37 minutes, four per hour), take bus 2 (15 minutes, every half-hour) to the Schaarsbergen park entrance (stop: Koningsweg). Various buses run inside the park to the museum.

Eating & Drinking

Groningen has no fixed opening hours for cafes and bars, so party on! The **organic food market** (Vismarkt; ⏲Tue) is a regional favourite for self-catering.

't Feithhuis CAFE €€
(www.restaurant-feithhuis.nl; Martinikerkhof 10; mains €8-16) In a leafy pedestrian quarter just off the Grote Markt, this stylish grand cafe has a wide terrace outside and a stark, woodsy interior. Food ranges from bagels to complex sandwiches and Mediterranean-flavoured mains.

Roezemoes BROWN CAFE
(Gedempte Zuiderdiep 15) You can tell this gem of a brown cafe has been around a while: the bullet holes from the 1672 invasion attempt are a dead giveaway. Come evening, expect to find late-night drinking and the occasional blues band.

De Pintelier BAR
(Kleine Kromme Elleboog 9) Step back to the 1920s at this cosy bar where the selection of beer and *jenevers* reads like an encyclopaedia. Its long wooden bar and thicket of tables are timeless.

Entertainment

Vera NIGHTCLUB
(www.vera-groningen.nl; Oosterstraat 44; ⏲Thu-Sat) Legendary club to see the next big rock act. U2 played to 30-odd people here in the early 1980s, Nirvana later gave a performance to a crowd of 60. Motto: 'club for the international pop underground'.

Information

Tourist office (VVV; www.vvvgroningen.nl; Grote Markt 25; ⏲9am-6pm Mon-Sat, plus 11am-3pm Sun Jun-Aug) Sells excellent walking-tour maps in English (€1.50).

Getting There & Away

Domestic trains include Utrecht (€24.80, two hours, one per hour) and Zwolle (€15.90, 70 minutes, three per hour).

Texel

☎0222 / POP 13,700

Texel (*tes*-sel) is a natural playground of broad white beaches, lush nature reserves, forests and picture-book villages. Some 25km long and 9km wide, it's just 3km off the coast of Noord Holland and makes a superb getaway from the mainland rush. Beauty and isolation are in abundance. The beaches seem to go on forever while inland there's **De Dennen**, a dark and leafy forest. Most villages exude charm, although tourist hub **De Koog** is more redolent with fudge.

Sights & Activities

Duinen van Texel National Park is a patchwork of varied dunescape running along the entire western coast of the island. Salt fens and heath alternate with velvety, grass-covered dunes. Much of the area is a bird sanctuary and is accessible only on foot. Pause at the excellent **Ecomare** (www.ecomare.nl; Ruyslaan 92, De Koog; admission €9; ⏲9am-5pm), a nature centre devoted to the preservation and understanding of Texel's wildlife.

Sleeping

Although Texel has an astounding 46,000 beds, book ahead, especially in July and August. Eating opportunities abound in season.

Bij Jef HOTEL €€
(☎31 96 23; www.bijjef.nl; Herenstraat 34, Den Hoorn; r from €100; 📶) The nine simple, yet stylish, rooms here come with a bath-tub, views of the countryside, and a sun-drenched

balcony. However, the real star is the sumptuous restaurant (set menus from €65) which has an ever-changing menu created from local produce, meats and seafood. Try for a garden table.

't Anker HOTEL €€
(☎31 62 74; www.t-anker.texel.com; Kikkertstraat 24, De Cocksdorp; s/d from €46/90;) This small, family-run hotel is full of charm and cheer, and has basic yet comfy rooms. Its lush garden is an appetiser for the Roggesloot nature reserve close by, and Texel's iconic lighthouse is just a healthy stroll away.

Information

Tourist office (www.texel.net; Emmalaan 66, Den Burg; 9am-5.30pm Mon-Fri, to 5pm Sat) Books rooms; has loads of advice for hikers, bikers and nude sunbathers.

Getting There & Away

Trains from Amsterdam to Den Helder (€13, 75 minutes) are met by a bus that connects with the **car ferry** (www.teso.nl; adult/car return €4/38; 6.30am-9pm), which then makes the crossing in 20 minutes. Local buses criss-cross Texel.

SOUTHERN NETHERLANDS

Actual hills are found along the southern edge of the Netherlands, where Belgium and Germany are within range of a tossed wooden shoe. The not-to-miss-star here is Maastricht.

Maastricht

☎043 / POP 120,000

The Netherlands' other great old city couldn't be further from Amsterdam and the pearls of the Randstad and still be in the country. Granted, Maastricht sits on a little geographic appendage dangling down like an appendix but it is well worth the time to journey here from the northwest (and, from here, you can easily continue on to Belgium or Germany).

Amid the 1650 listed historic buildings, look for Spanish and Roman ruins, French and Belgian twists in the architecture, splendid food and small-town cosmopolitan flair that made Maastricht a natural location for the signing of the namesake treaty, which created the modern EU in 1992.

Sights

Maastricht's delights are scattered along both banks of the Maas. The best approach is to just start strolling. The city's ruins, old fortifications, museums, cafes (and the odd surprise) reward walkers. **Onze Lieve Vrouweplein** is an intimate cafe-filled square named after its church, which still attracts pilgrims. The busy pedestrian **Sint Servaasbrug** dates from the 13th-century and links Maastricht's centre with the Wyck district.

Bonnefantenmuseum MUSEUM
(www.bonnefantenmuseum.nl; Ave Céramique 250; admission €8; 11am-5pm Tue-Sun) This postmodern fantasy features a striking 28m tower that houses various provocative exhibits. The collection combines Flemish masterpieces from the 16th and 17th centuries with modern works.

Vrijthof HISTORIC SQUARE
The large square of Vrijthof is surrounded by lively cafes and cultural institutions. It's dominated by **Sint Servaasbasiliek** (Basilica of St Servatius; admission €2; 10am-5pm Mon-Sat, 12.30-5pm Sun), a pastiche of architecture dating from 1000.

Sint Pietersberg FORT, TUNNELS
(www.maastrichtunderground.nl; admission €5; tour times vary by season) Much of Maastricht is riddled with defensive tunnels dug into the soft sandstone during the many sieges over the centuries, some dating to the Roman times. The best place to see the tunnels is on a tour of Sint Pietersberg, a Roman fort 2km south of Helpoort.

Festivals & Events

Carnaval is celebrated with greater vigour in Maastricht than anywhere else in Europe, save Venice (Italy) and Sitges (Spain). The orgy of partying and carousing begins the Friday before Shrove Tuesday and runs until the last person collapses some time on the following Wednesday.

Sleeping

TOP CHOICE **Hotel Holla** HOTEL €
(☎321 35 23; www.hotelholla.nl; Boschstraat 104-106; r €50-90; @) Located in an elegant 1855 building, the 24 stylish rooms here are well appointed for the price. Adding to the excellent value is the ground-floor cafe, which serves excellent coffee in smart surrounds.

Hotel d'Orangerie HOTEL €€
(☎326 11 11; www.hotel-orangerie.nl; Kleine Gracht 4; r €90-160; 📶) There's a gracious elegance about this hotel in a stately building dating back to 1752. The welcome is genuine. The 22 rooms come in various levels of ornate decor. Take breakfast in the airy courtyard.

Stayokay Maastricht HOSTEL €
(☎750 17 90; www.stayokay.com/maastricht; Maasboulevard 101; dm/r from €20/55; @) A stunner of a hostel with a large terrace right on the Maas; choose from one of the 199 beds in dorms and private rooms. It's just south of the centre in a park.

Eating

Excellent restaurants are even more common than old fortifications in Maastricht.

TOP CHOICE **Gadjah Mas** INDONESIAN €€
(Rechtstraat 42; mains €17-25; ⏲dinner) The Rechtstraat, east of the river, is one of the best streets for dining in Maastricht. This small and lovely Indonesian bistro has a *rijsttafel* that breaks with the clichéd norm. Flavours are bright and spices are not skimped.

Sjieke DUTCH €€
(St Pieterstraat 13; mains €12-25; ⏲dinner) This cosy corner spot turns out traditional Dutch fare, including hearty stews, roasts, fresh fish and more. In summer there's a thicket of tables in the park across the street. Have a red beer and pick out the stars through the trees.

Zondag CAFE €
(www.cafezondag.nl; mains €6-12; Wycker Brugstraat 42) Funky mellow tunes through the day segue to jazzier, harder sounds at night. It's light, airy, beautifully tiled and the food couldn't be fresher. Choose from a huge range of sandwiches and baked goods by day.

Reitz FRITES €
(Markt 75; frites €2) Join the queues at this iconic French-fries stall, which has been serving perfectly scrumptious *frites* under the classic neon sign for decades.

Drinking

TOP CHOICE **Take One** BROWN CAFE
(www.takeonebiercafe.nl, in Dutch; Rechtstraat 28) Cramped and narrow from the outside, this 1930s tavern has well over 100 beers from the most obscure parts of Benelux. It's run by husband-and-wife team Peet Seerden and Méry Willemsen who help you select the beer most appropriate to your tastes.

In den Ouden Vogelstruys PUB
(www.vogelstruys.nl; Vrijthof 15) Overlooking the cathedral across the square is this antique bar, the top choice among many. The entrance has big, old, heavy red curtains, while inside the bar there are big, old, heavy light fittings, and big, old, heavy Trappist beer. (But the local cheese is light and creamy…)

Information

ANWB (Wycker Brugstraat 24; ⏲9.30am-6pm Mon-Fri, to 5pm Sat) Has a tourist office info desk; convenient to the train station.

Tourist office (VVV; www.vvvmaastricht.nl; Kleine Straat 1; ⏲9am-6pm Mon-Sat, plus 11am-3pm Sun May-Oct) In the 15th-century Dinghuis; offers excellent walking-tour brochures.

Getting There & Away

Regular trains link Maastricht to Brussels (€30, 1½ hours) via Liege; with connections to Cologne two hours away (€25). Sample domestic trains:

Amsterdam €26.60, 2½ hours, two per hour

Den Bosch €18.80, 1½ hours, two per hour

Utrecht €23.50, two hours, two per hour

UNDERSTAND THE NETHERLANDS

History

Early Dutch history was bound with Belgium and Luxembourg – the three were known as the Low Countries until the 16th century.

The Netherlands' Golden Age lasted from about 1580 to 1740. The era's wealth was generated by the Dutch East India Company, which travelled to the Far East for spices and other exotic goods, colonised the Cape of Good Hope and Indonesia, and established trading posts throughout Asia.

In 1795 the French invaded. When the occupation ended in 1815, the United Kingdom of the Netherlands – incorporating Belgium and Luxembourg – was the result.

In 1830 the Belgians rebelled and became independent, and Luxembourg followed nine years later.

The Netherlands stayed neutral in WWI and tried to repeat the feat in WWII, only to be invaded by Germany. The country was devastated and most of its Jewish population was murdered.

In 1953 a high spring tide and severe storm breached Zeeland's dikes, drowning 1835 people. A massive engineering project, the Delta Project was built to prevent the tragedy from happening again.

In the 1960s Amsterdam became Europe's radical heart, giving rise to the squatter's movement and the sexual freedom that lingers still. Cannabis was decriminalised in 1976, and in 2003 the Netherlands became the first country in the world to legalise prescriptions of medicinal cannabis.

In 1992 members of the European community assembled in Maastricht to sign the treaty that created the EU.

A year later, the Netherlands regulated doctor-assisted euthanasia, and in 2000 it was legalised under stringent guidelines – again, it was the first country to do so. That year the Netherlands also became the first nation to legalise same-sex marriages.

As the Netherlands has become ever more crowded, immigration has become a political hot potato. In 2002 right-wing politician Pim Fortuyn, an advocate of zero immigration, was shot dead a few days before the Dutch general election.

In 2004 there was another high-profile assassination. Theo van Gogh, an inflammatory right-wing film-maker and columnist, was killed in Amsterdam; the murderer was a Dutch-Moroccan.

The famously tolerant Dutch have moved towards conservatism somewhat in recent years. The notorious coffee shops and legal red light districts are under fire as the populace tires of the antisocial behaviour associated with both – which is often perpetrated by foreigners.

In 2010 elections, no party came close to a majority and months were spent forming a rather tenuous centre-right coalition with Mark Rutte as prime minister.

Meanwhile, Den Haag stays in the news as war-crimes trials move forward for people such as former Bosnian Serb Radovan Karadzic in the city's international courts. Although disappointed by the loss, the country was very proud to see the Orange team reach the 2010 FIFA World Cup finals.

Arts

The Netherlands has spawned a realm of celebrated painters, including Bosch, Rembrandt, Vermeer and Van Gogh. The Dutch are world leaders in modern dance and the Netherlands is home to many orchestras. The Dutch have also won three Best Foreign Language Film Academy Awards.

Rotterdam is an ever-changing festival of modern architecture.

Food & Drink

The Dutch consume almost 17kg of cheese per person per year (nearly two-thirds of it is Gouda). Seafood is found at street stalls, including raw, slightly salted herring cut into bite-sized pieces and served with onion and pickles. Smoked eel and *kibbeling* (deep-fried cod parings) are also popular.

Munchies are squelched around the clock at fast-food joints such as Febo, where deep-fried snacks sing their siren song from behind coin-operated doors.

Lager beer is the staple drink, served cool and topped by a big head of froth. More bars are serving interesting beers from a growing number of small Dutch and Belgian brewers. Look for hoppy Jopen from Haarlem.

Quaff beers at a cosy *bruin café* (brown cafe) – the name comes from smoke stains on the walls, although pretenders make do with brown paint. The best ooze the uniquely Dutch concept of *gezelligheid,* which is one of those words that defies easy translation but which combines cosy, fun and quaint with an overlay of familiarity and good cheer.

Price ranges in this chapter are based on the cost of a main course:

€€€ more than €20

€€ €10 to €20

€ less than €10

SURVIVAL GUIDE

Directory A–Z

Accommodation

Always book accommodation ahead, especially during high season; note that many visitors choose to stay in Amsterdam even if travelling elsewhere. The tourist offices operate booking services; when booking for two, make it clear whether you want two single (twin) beds or a double bed.

Many Dutch hotels have steep, perilous stairs but no lifts, although most top-end and some midrange hotels are exceptions.

Lists of camping grounds are available from the tourist offices. Expect to pay roughly €10 to €20 for two people and a tent overnight, plus €3 to €6 for a car. The camping grounds have plenty of caravan hook-ups.

Stayokay (☎020-501 31 33; www.stayokay.com) is the Dutch hostelling association. A youth hostel card costs €15 at the hostels; nonmembers pay an extra €2.50 per night and after six nights you're a member. The usual HI discounts apply.

In this chapter, prices include private bathrooms unless otherwise stated and are quoted at high-season rates. Breakfast is not included in rates unless specified. Most rooms are nonsmoking.

€€€ more than €150

€€ €80 to €150

€ less than €80

Business Hours

Banks & government offices 9.30am-4pm Mon-Fri

Bars & cafes 11am-1am

Museums Most closed Monday

Nightclubs 10pm-4am

Post offices 9am-6pm Mon-Fri

Restaurants 10am or 11am-10pm, with a 3-6pm break

Shops noon-6pm Mon, 9am-6pm Tue-Sat (also Sun in large cities), to 9pm Thu; supermarkets to 8pm

Discount Cards

Available from the museums themselves, a Museumkaart gives access to 400 museums across the country for €40 (€20 for under 25s).

Holidays

Nieuwjaarsdag New Year's Day

Goede Vrijdag Good Friday

Eerste Paasdag Easter Sunday

Tweede Paasdag Easter Monday

Koninginnedag (Queen's Day) 30 April

Bevrijdingsdag (Liberation Day) 5 May

Hemelvaartsdag Ascension Day

Eerste Pinksterdag Whit Sunday (Pentecost)

Tweede Pinksterdag Whit Monday

Eerste Kerstdag (Christmas Day) 25 December

Tweede Kerstdag (Boxing Day) 26 December

Legal Matters

Drugs are actually illegal in the Netherlands. Possession of soft drugs up to 5g is tolerated but larger amounts can get you jailed. Hard drugs are treated as a serious crime.

Smoking is banned in all public places, including most bars (except for tiny family-run pubs). In a uniquely Dutch solution, you can still smoke pot in coffee shops as long as there's no tobacco mixed in.

Money

ATMs can be found outside banks and at train stations.

All major international cards are recognised, and you will find that most hotels, restaurants and major stores accept them (although *not* the Dutch railway). But always check first to avoid, as they say, disappointment. Shops may levy a 5% surcharge (or more) on credit cards to offset the commissions charged by card providers.

Safe Travel

The Netherlands is a safe country, but be sensible all the same: don't leave valuables in cars and *always* lock your bike. Never buy drugs on the street: you'll get ripped off or mugged and it's illegal. And don't light up joints just anywhere – stick to coffee shops.

Telephone

Most public phones will accept credit cards as well as various phonecards. SIM cards cost from €5.

Country code ☎31

TIPPING

Tipping is not essential as restaurants, hotels, bars etc include a service charge on their bills. A little extra is always welcomed though, and it's an excellent way to compliment the service (if you feel it needs complimenting). The tip can be anything from rounding up to the nearest euro to 10% of the bill.

International access code ☎00

International directory enquiries ☎0900 84 18

National directory enquiries ☎1888

Operator assistance ☎0800 04 10

Getting There & Away

Air

Huge **Schiphol airport** (AMS; www.schiphol.nl) is the Netherlands' main international airport, near Amsterdam (and the Randstad). **Rotterdam airport** (RTM; www.rotterdam-airport.nl) and **Eindhoven Airport** (EIN; www.eindhovenairport.nl) are small, the latter located somewhere out of the way in the south.

Bus

The most extensive European bus network is maintained by **Eurolines** (www.eurolines.com). It offers a variety of passes with prices that vary by time of year.

Busabout (www.busabout.com) is a UK-based budget alternative. It runs coaches on circuits in Continental Europe including one through Amsterdam; passes are available in a variety of flavours.

Car & Motorcycle

You'll need the vehicle's registration papers, third-party insurance and an international driver's permit in addition to your domestic licence. The national auto club, **ANWB** (www.anwb.nl), has offices across the country and will provide info if you can show an auto-club card from your home country.

Sea

There are several companies operating car and passenger ferries between the Netherlands and the UK:

DFDS Seaways (www.dfds.co.uk) Sails between Newcastle and IJmuiden, which is close to Amsterdam.

P&O Ferries (www.poferries.com) Operates an overnight ferry every evening between Hull and Europoort (near Rotterdam).

Stena Line (www.stenaline.co.uk) Sails between Harwich and Hoek van Holland.

Train

The Netherlands has good train links to Germany, Belgium and France. All Eurail, Inter-Rail, Europass and Flexipass tickets are valid on the Dutch national train service, **Nederlandse Spoorwegen** (Netherlands Railway, NS; www.ns.nl). Many international services, including those on the high-speed line to Belgium, are operated under the **Hispeed** (www.nshispeed.nl) and **Fyra** (www.fyra.com) brands. In addition, **Thalys** (www.thalys.com) fast trains serve Brussels (where you can connect to Eurostar) and Paris. Major Dutch train stations have international ticket offices; in peak periods, it's wise to reserve seats in advance.

Finally open (years late and far over budget), the high-speed line from Amsterdam (via Schiphol airport and Rotterdam) speeds travel times to Antwerp (70 minutes), Brussels (1¾ hours) and Paris (three hours).

German ICE high-speed trains run six times a day between Amsterdam and Cologne (2½ hours) via Utrecht. Many continue on to Frankfurt (four hours) via Frankfurt Airport.

Getting Around

Boat

Ferries connect the mainland with the five Frisian Islands, including Texel. Other ferries span the Westerschelde in the south of Zeeland, providing road links to the bit of the Netherlands south of here as well as to Belgium. These are popular with people using the Zeebrugge ferry terminal and run frequently year-round.

Car & Motorcycle

You'll need to show a valid driving licence when hiring a car in the Netherlands, and you must be at least 23 years of age; some firms levy a small surcharge for drivers under 25. Outside Amsterdam, car-hire companies can be in inconvenient locations if you're arriving by train.

Traffic travels on the right and the minimum driving age is 18 for vehicles and 16 for motorcycles. Seat belts are required. Trams always have the right of way and if turning right, bikes have priority.

Speed limits are 50km/h in built-up areas, 80km/h in the country, 100km/h on major through-roads, and 120km/h on freeways (sometimes 100km/h, clearly indicated). The blood-alcohol limit when driving is 0.05%.

Public Transport

National public transport info is available by phone (☎0900 9292) and on the web (www.9292ov.nl).

THE NETHERLANDS BY BIKE

The Netherlands has more than 20,000km of dedicated bike paths *(fietspaden)*, which makes it the most bike-friendly place on the planet. You can criss-cross the country on the motorways of cycling: the **LF routes**. Standing for *landelijke fietsroutes* (long distance routes) but virtually always simply called LF, there are more than 25 routes comprising close to 7000km. All are well marked by distinctive green-and-white signs.

The best overall maps are the widely available Falk/VVV *Fietskaart met Knooppuntennetwerk* (cycling network) maps, a series of 20 that blanket the country in 1:50,000 scale and cost €8. The keys are in English and they are highly detailed and very easy to use. Every bike lane, path and other route is shown, along with distances.

Web Resources

» **http:/holland.cyclingaroundtheworld.nl** Superb English-language site with a vast amount of useful and inspiring information.

» **www.landelijkefietsroutes.nl** Dutch site that lists all the LF routes and gives basic details and an outline of each.

» **http:/fiets.startpagina.nl** Dutch site that lists every conceivable website associated with cycling in the Netherlands.

Bike Rentals

Independent rental shops are available in abundance. Many day trippers avail themselves of the train-station bicycle shops, called **Rijwiel shops** (www.ov-fiets.nl), which are found in more than 100 train stations. Operating long hours (6am to midnight is common), the shops hire out bikes from €6 to €8 per day with discounts by the week. You'll have to show ID and leave a deposit (usually €25 to €100). The shops also usually offer repairs, sell new bikes and have secured bike parking (from €1.10/4.40 per day/week).

On Trains

You may bring your bicycle onto any train as long as there is room; a day pass for bikes (*dagkaart fiets*; €6) is required.

The new universal form of transport payment in the Netherlands, the **OV-chipkaart** (www.ov-chipkaart.nl) is a smartcard that you use in place of cash. Visitors can buy one from vending machines in stations or at ticket windows. Each card stores the value of your payment and deducts the cost of trips as you use it. Refill from machines or ticket windows (although the latter are often thronged).

When you enter and exit a bus, tram or train, you hold the card against a reader at the doors or station gates. The system then calculates your fare and deducts it from the card. Fares for the chip cards are much lower than a ticket bought from the driver or conductor on buses and trams.

You can also buy OV-chipcards that are good for unlimited use for one or more days and this is often the most convenient option if travelling around town.

Train

The train network is run by **Nederlandse Spoorwegen** (NS; www.ns.nl). First-class sections are barely different from the 2nd-class areas, but they are less crowded. Trains are fast and frequent and serve most places of interest. Most train stations have lockers operated by credit cards (average cost €4).

Ticket types:

Enkele reis One-way; you can break your journey along the direct route.

Dagretour Day return; 10% to 15% cheaper than two one-ways.

Weekendretour Weekend return; costs the same as a normal return and is valid from 7pm Friday to 4am Monday.

Dagkaart Day pass; allows unlimited train travel throughout the country. Only good value if you're planning to spend the day on the train.

Norway

Includes »

Best Places to Eat

» Vertshuset Røros (p936)

» Torget Fish Market, Bergen (p941)

» Pingvinen, Bergen (p941)

» Vertshuset Tavern, Trondheim (p948)

» Best Places to Stay

» Skuteviken Gjestehus, Bergen (p940)

» Ellingsens Pensjonat, Oslo (p931)

» Heimly Pensjonat, Flåm (p945)

» Svolvær Sjøhuscamp (p950)

Why Go?

Norway is a once-in-a-lifetime destination and the essence of its appeal is remarkably simple: this is one of the most beautiful countries on earth.

The drama of Norway's natural world is difficult to overstate. Impossibly steep-sided fjords cut gashes deep into the interior. But this is also a land of glaciers, grand and glorious, snaking down from Europe's largest ice fields, and of the primeval appeal of the Arctic.

The counterpoint to so much natural beauty is found in the country's vibrant cultural life. Norwegian cities are cosmopolitan and brimming with architecture that showcases the famous Scandinavian flair for design. At the same time, a busy calendar of festivals, many of international renown, is worth planning your trip around.

Yes, Norway is one of the most expensive countries on earth. But is it worth it? Absolutely. Norway will pay you back with never-to-be-forgotten experiences many times over.

When to Go

Oslo

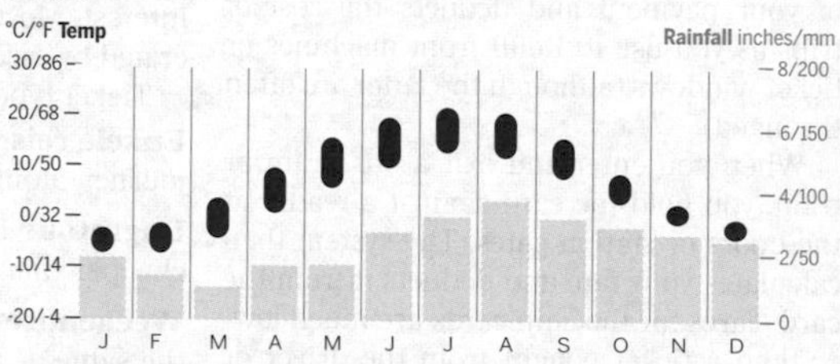

Mid-Jun–mid-Aug Fjords *(probably)* bathed in sunshine and endless days.

Dec–Feb Nature's most spectacular show, the northern lights, and wonderful winter activities.

May–mid-Jun & mid-Aug–Sep Generally fine weather; crowds yet to arrive en masse.

Connections

Trains or buses link Norway with Russia, Sweden and Finland, although for Russia you'll need a visa in your passport before you arrive in Norway. Frequent ferries head to Germany and Denmark from several southern Norwegian ports. Airports in Oslo and Bergen connect Norway to the world, with a handful of international flights to Stavanger, Trondheim and distant Tromsø, way up in the Arctic Circle.

ITINERARIES

One Week

Spend a day in Oslo, then take the Norway in a Nutshell tour to Bergen via Myrdal, Flåm and Nærøyfjord – you'll see the best of Norway's fjord scenery in remarkably little time. Spend two nights in Bergen before travelling, perhaps by Hurtigruten, to Ålesund and then on to Geirangerfjord. At the latter, factor in at least a one-night stay to appreciate the fjord's beauty without the crowds. Return to Oslo.

Two Weeks

Instead of returning to Oslo, head back to Ålesund and take the Hurtigruten along the coast, pausing for two nights in Trondheim. Detour for a night to Røros, before continuing by Hurtigruten to the fishing villages of craggy Lofoten where you should spend a couple of nights; we recommend staying as long as you can in Å. Finally, take the Hurtigruten to Tromsø, the north's most vibrant city, before returning to Oslo.

Essential Food & Drink

» **Reindeer** Grilled or roasted, Scandinavia's iconic species is also its tastiest red meat; you'll find it on menus from Oslo to Svalbard.

» **Elk** Call it what you like (many prefer 'moose'), but this tasty meat usually appears as steaks or burgers.

» **Salmon** World-renowned Norwegian salmon is so popular that you'll eat it for dinner (grilled) or breakfast (smoked).

» **Arctic char** The world's northernmost freshwater fish is a star of northern Norway's seafood-rich menus.

» **Arctic menu** A popular scheme in northern Norway that encourages restaurants to use natural local ingredients; see www.arktiskmeny.no.

» **Fish markets** Often the best (and cheapest) places to eat along the Norwegian coast, with the freshest seafood at fresh-off-the-boat prices.

AT A GLANCE

» **Currency** Kroner (Nkr)

» **Language** Norwegian

» **Money** ATMs everywhere; banks open Mon-Fri

» **Visas** Schengen visa rules apply (see p1319)

Fast Facts

» **Area** 385,155 sq km

» **Capital** Oslo

» **Country code** ☎47

» **Emergency** ☎112

Exchange Rates

Australia	A$1	Nkr5.78
Canada	C$1	Nkr5.73
Euro Zone	€1	Nkr7.90
Japan	¥100	Nkr6.87
New Zealand	NZ$1	Nkr4.22
UK	UK£1	Nkr8.97
USA	US$1	Nkr5.62

Set Your Budget

» **Budget hotel room** up to Nkr750

» **Two-course evening meal** Nkr150-200

» **Beer (glass)** Nkr50-80

» **Oslo bus or tram ticket** Nkr70 (daily pass)

Resources

» **Visit Norway** (www.visitnorway.com) Comprehensive Tourist Board site

» **Fjord Norway** (www.fjordnorway.com) Focused on Norway's star attraction

» **Norway.com** (www.norway.com) Links to tourist information

Norway Highlights

1. Take the ferry from Hellesylt to **Geiranger** (p946) through some of Norway's most spectacular fjord scenery
2. Sleep in a fisherman's *robu* (shanty) on the craggy islands of **Lofoten** (p949)
3. Journey by train from **Oslo** to **Bergen** (p936), arguably Norway's most attractive coastal city
4. Ride the length of Norway's jagged, beautiful northern coast aboard the **Hurtigruten Coastal Ferry** (p956)
5. Draw near to the edge at **Preikestolen** (Pulpit Rock; p945), high above glorious Lysefjord

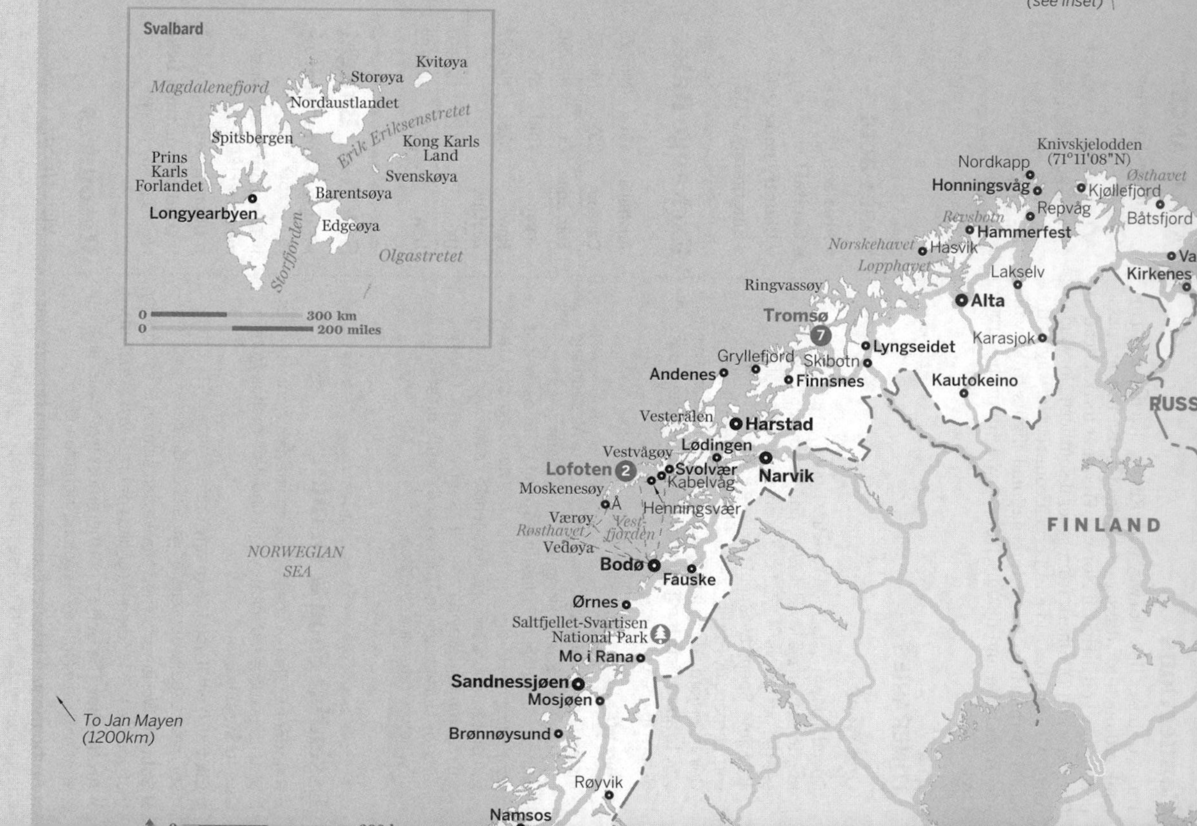

6 Stay overnight in **Røros** (p936), one of Norway's most charming log-built villages

7 Get into the irresistible swing of **Tromsø** (p951), the lively capital of Norway's High Arctic

OSLO

POP 1.42 MILLION

Oslo is home to world-class museums and galleries to rival anywhere else on the European art trail. But Mother Nature has also made her mark and Oslo is fringed with forests, hills and lakes awash in opportunities for hiking, cycling, skiing and boating.

Sights

TOP CHOICE Oslo Opera House NOTABLE BUILDING

(Den Norske Opera & Ballett; www.operaen.no; Kirsten Flagstads Plass 1; admission to foyer free; ⌚foyer 10am-11pm Mon-Fri, 11am-11pm Sat, noon-10pm Sun) The centrepiece of Oslo's ambitious waterfront development is the magnificent new Opera House. Opened in 2008, it resembles a glacier floating in the waters off Oslo.

FREE Nasjonalgalleriet ART GALLERY

(National Gallery; www.nasjonalmuseet.no; Universitetsgata 13; ⌚10am-6pm Tue, Wed & Fri, 10am-7pm Thu, 11am-5pm Sat & Sun) The Nasjonalgalleriet has an impressive collection featuring some of Edvard Munch's best-known works, including *The Scream*. There are also works by Gauguin, Picasso, El Greco, Manet, Degas, Renoir, Matisse, Cézanne and Monet.

Munchmuseet ART GALLERY

(Munch Museum; www.munch.museum.no; Tøyengata 53; admission Nkr75; ⌚10am-6pm Jun-Aug, shorter hours Sep-May) Dedicated to the life work of Norway's most renowned artist, Edvard Munch, this museum contains over 1100 paintings, 4500 watercolours and 18,000 prints that he bequeathed to the city of Oslo.

Bygdøy Peninsula MUSEUMS

The magnificent **Vikingskipshuset** (Viking Ship Museum; www.khm.uio.no; Huk Aveny 35; admission Nkr60; ⌚9am-6pm May-Sep, 11am-4pm Oct-Apr) houses three Viking ships excavated from the Oslofjord region.

Take a look also at the *Kon-Tiki* balsa raft at the **Kon-Tiki Museum** (www.kon-tiki.no; Bygdøynesveien 36; admission Nkr60; ⌚9.30am-5.30pm Jun-Aug, shorter hours Sep-May). Norwegian explorer Thor Heyerdahl sailed from Peru to Polynesia in 1947 on the raft. Also displayed is the papyrus reed boat *Ra II*, used to cross the Atlantic in 1970.

And don't miss the durable *Fram* (1892) at the **Frammuseet** (Polar Ship Fram Museum; www.fram.museum.no; Bygdøynesveien 36; admission Nkr60; ⌚9am-6pm mid-Jun–Aug, shorter hours Sep–mid-Jun), which Roald Amundsen used for the first successful expedition to the South Pole in 1911.

Frognerparken & Vigeland Park PARKS, SCULPTURES

Frognerparken, which has as its centrepiece Vigeland Park, is an extraordinary open-air showcase of work by Norway's best-loved sculptor, Gustav Vigeland, with 212 granite and bronze works.

Akershus CASTLES

King Håkon V began construction of the earthen-walled **Akershus Festning** (Akershus Fortress; admission free; ⌚6am-9pm) in 1299. It's strategically positioned on the eastern side of the harbour; clamber up tree-lined twisting paths for excellent views over Oslofjord.

In the 17th century, Christian IV renovated **Akershus Slott** (Akershus Castle; admission Nkr65; ⌚10am-4pm Mon-Sat, 12.30-4pm Sun May-Aug, shorter hours Sep-Apr, guided tours 11am, 1pm & 3pm Mon-Sat, 1pm & 3pm Sun) into a Renaissance palace, though the front remains decidedly medieval.

Activities

An extensive network of hiking trails leads into Nordmarka from Frognerseteren, at the end of T-bane line 1.

The tourist office has free cycling maps: *Sykkelkart Oslo* traces the bicycle routes throughout the city, and *Idrett og Friluftsliv i Oslo* covers the Oslo hinterland.

NORWAY IN A NUTSHELL

There's no better way to see some of Norway's signature sights in such a short space of time as the popular, self-guided **Norway in a Nutshell** (☎815 68 222; www.norwaynutshell.com), which can be booked at tourist offices or at train stations. From Oslo, the typical route includes a rail trip across Hardangervidda to Myrdal, a descent to Flåm along the dramatic Flåmbanen, a cruise along Nærøyfjord to Gudvangen, a bus to Voss, a connecting train to Bergen for a short visit, then an overnight return train trip to Oslo (including a sleeper compartment); the return tour costs Nkr2165. You can also book one-way tours to Bergen (Nkr1370). There are numerous variations on the theme, with routes also possible from Bergen, Flåm and elsewhere.

Oslo's ski season is roughly from December to March. There are over 2400km of prepared Nordic tracks (1000km in Nordmarka alone), many of them floodlit; easy-access tracks begin right at the T-bane stations Frognerseteren and Sognsvann.

Sleeping

Oslo has plenty of accommodation, including a growing number of small B&Bs, which offer more character than the chain hotels. However, compared to many other parts of Europe, standards are generally fairly low.

TOP CHOICE **Ellingsens Pensjonat** PENSION €
(☎22 60 03 59; www.ellingsenspensjonat.no, in Norwegian; Holtegata 25; s/d without bathroom Nkr400/580, s/d with bathroom Nkr480/670) In a quiet, pleasant neighbourhood, this homey pension offers one of the best deals in the capital. Rooms are bright and airy.

Cochs Pensjonat PENSION €
(☎23 33 24 00; www.cochspensjonat.no; Parkveien 25; s/d without bathroom Nkr480/680, with bathroom from Nkr580/780; 📶) Opened as a guest house for bachelors in the 1920s, the very good value Cochs has sparsely furnished, clean rooms, some of which have kitchenettes.

P-Hotel HOTEL €€
(☎80 04 68 35; www.p-hotels.com; Grensen 19; s/d Nkr795/995; @📶) In addition to offering some of the best prices in central Oslo, the P-Hotel has comfortable if slightly dull rooms with decent bathrooms.

Anker Hostel HOSTEL €
(☎22 99 72 00; www.ankerhostel.no; Storgata 55; 6-/8-bed dm with bathroom from Nkr220/210, s & tw from Nkr580; P@📶) This huge traveller-savvy hostel boasts an international atmosphere, spick-and-span rooms, a laundry, a luggage room, kitchens (some rooms also contain kitchens) and a small bar.

Thon Hotel Spectrum CHAIN HOTEL €€
(☎23 36 27 00; www.thonhotels.com; Brugata 7; s Nkr660-1110, d Nkr925-1375; @📶) Bright purple sofas and equally purple flowers adorn the reception area, and the comfortable and well-priced rooms are noteworthy for their huge windows and fairly small bathrooms.

Oslo Budget Hotel BUDGET HOTEL €
(☎22 41 36 10; www.budgethotel.no; Prinsens gate 6; s Nk500-600, d Nkr600-800; @📶) Don't go expecting any fancy frills, but otherwise this place does what it says on the label and provides cheap, clean and central accommodation that most guests find to their liking.

> **CHEAP STAYS IN THE CITY**
>
> One of the cheaper ways to stay in Oslo is to take a room in one of the city's handful of B&Bs. The tourist office can point you towards some options (but only if you visit in person).
>
> If you're under 26, **Use-It** (☎22 41 51 32; www.use-it.no; Møllergata 3), the Oslo Youth Information Service, will also help with bookings at hostels and private homes; there's no minimum stay and the service is free.

Perminalen Hotel HOSTEL €
(☎23 09 30 81; www.perminalen.no; Øvre Slottsgate 2; dm Nkr370, s/d Nkr620/840; 📶) Perminalen has a barracks feel, but tidy rooms and a central location make up for the sterile, dorm atmosphere. Prices include linen and a simple breakfast.

Eating

Aker Brygge, the old shipyard turned trendy shopping complex west of the main harbour, has a **food court** (⏱11am-10pm) with various eateries and a range of waterside restaurants.

If the weather's nice, the local meal of choice is peel-and-eat shrimp, eaten dockside with a fresh baguette, mayonnaise and just a touch of lemon. In the summer, you can buy shrimp from the **Fisherman's Coop** (Rådhusbrygge 3/4; ⏱7am-5pm Tue-Sat; shrimp per kg Nkr120).

Rust INTERNATIONAL €
(Hegdehaugsveien 22; snacks & light meals Nkr36-60, mains Nkr120-130) On a small side street lined with cafes and restaurants, Rust is bright, colourful and 100% modern Oslo. Good for a quiet cocktail, burgers, hearty salads or tapas late into the night.

Café Skansen MEDITERRANEAN €€
(www.cafeskansen.no, in Norwegian; Rådhusgata 32; pasta & salad mains Nkr90-180) One of the new wave of sophisticated cafes and restaurants currently taking Oslo by storm. As in many such places this one looks south to the Mediterranean for style and taste inspiration.

People & Coffee INTERNATIONAL €
(www.peopleandcoffee.com, in Norwegian; Rådhusgata 21; mains Nkr59-140, lunch specials Nkr139;

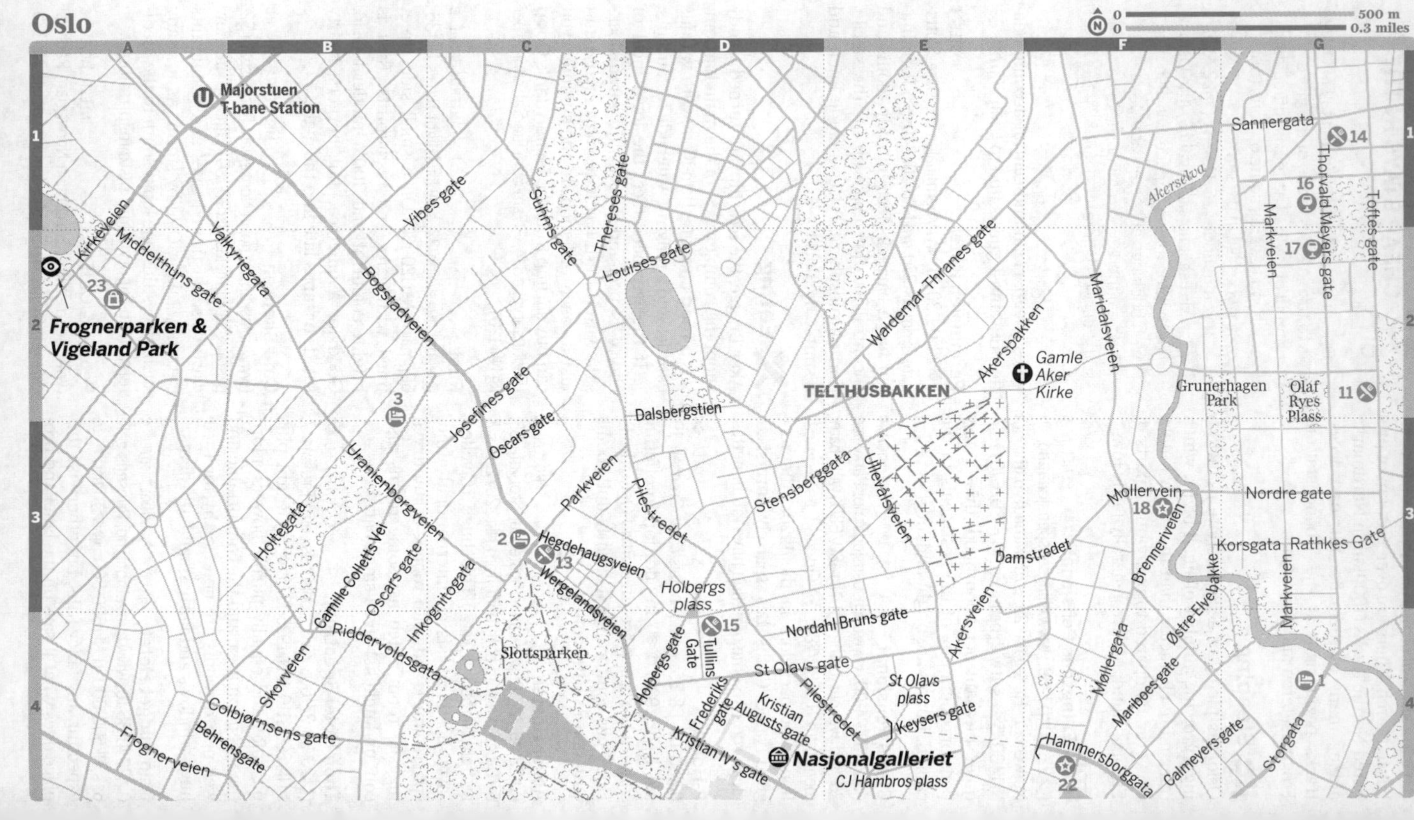
Oslo
500 m
0.3 miles
Majorstuen T-bane Station
Kirkeveien
Middelthuns gate
Valkyriegata
Frognerparken & Vigeland Park
Vibes gate
Bogstadveien
Suhms gate
Thereses gate
Louises gate
Waldemar Thranes gate
Akersbakken
Gamle Aker Kirke
Maridalsveien
Akerselva
Sannergata
Thorvald Meyers gate
Toftes gate
Markveien
Grunerhagen Park
Olaf Ryes Plass
TELTHUSBAKKEN
Dalsbergstien
Josefines gate
Oscars gate
Uranienborgveien
Parkveien
Pilestredet
Stensberggata
Ullevålsveien
Mollervein
Nordre gate
Brenneriveien
Korsgata
Rathkes Gate
Damstredet
Holtegata
Camille Colletts Vei
Oscars gate
Inkognitogata
Hegdehaugsveien
Wergelandsveien
Holbergs plass
Nordahl Bruns gate
Akersveien
Østre Elvebakke
Markveien
Skovveien
Riddervoldsgata
Slottsparken
Holbergs gate
Tullins Gate
St Olavs gate
St Olavs plass
Møllergata
Mariboes gate
Colbjørnsens gate
Behrensgate
Frognerveien
Frederiks gate
Kristian Augusts gate
Pilestredet
Keysers gate
Kristian IV's gate
Nasjonalgalleriet
CJ Hambros plass
Hammersborggata
Calmeyers gate
Storgata

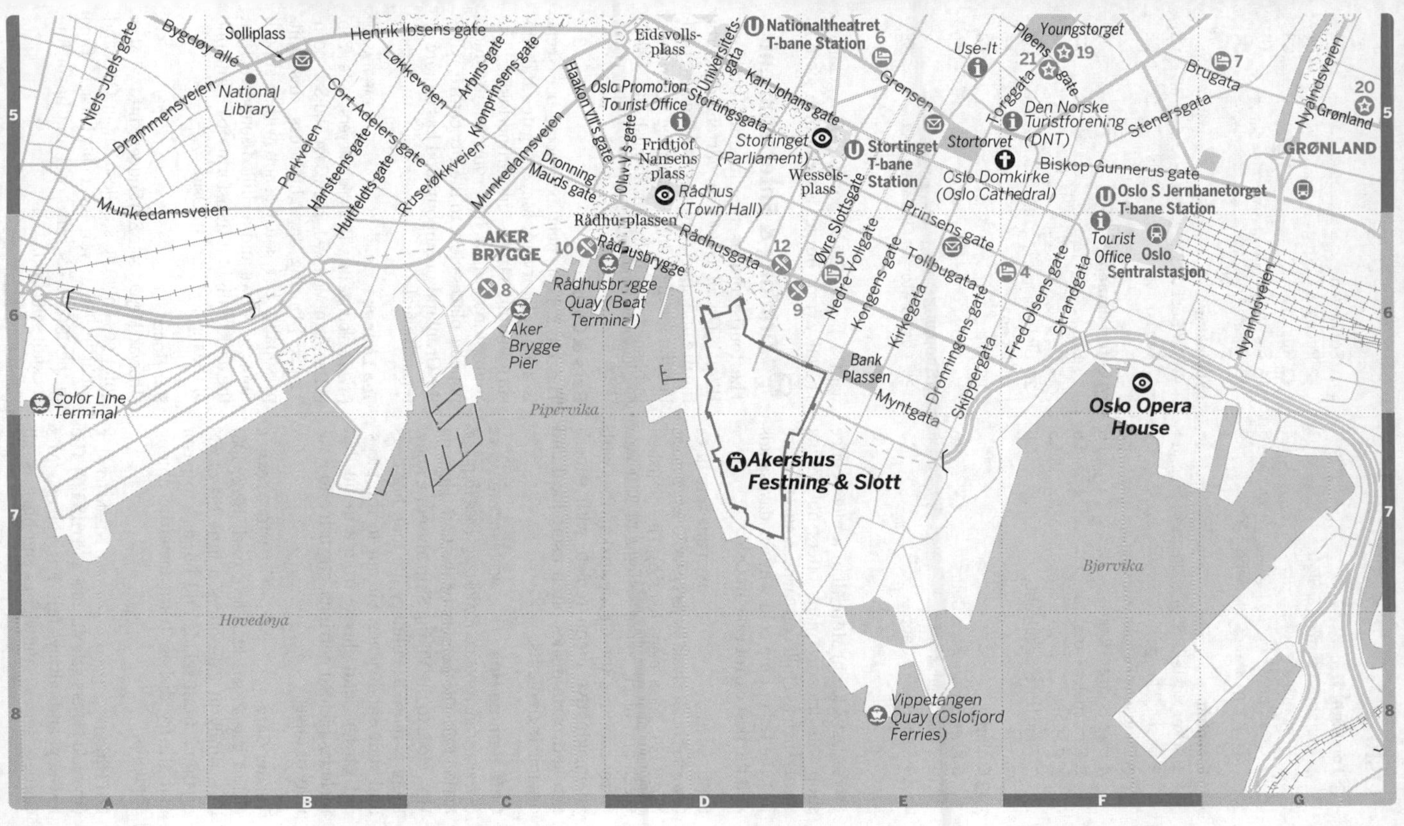
Niels Juels gate
Bygdøy allé
Solliplass
Henrik Ibsens gate
National Library
Drammensveien
Løkkeveien
Arbins gate
Kronprinsens gate
Cort Adelers gate
Parkveien
Hansteens gate
Huitfeldts gate
Ruseløkkveien
Munkedamsveien
Munkedamsveien
Haakon VII's gate
Oslo Promotion Tourist Office
Olav V's gate
Dronning Mauds gate
Fridtjof Nansens plass
Rådhus (Town Hall)
Rådhusplassen
Eidsvolls-plass
Universitets-gata
Stortingsgata
Karl Johans gate
Nationaltheatret T-bane Station
6
Stortinget (Parliament)
Wessels-plass
Stortinget T-bane Station
Grensen
Use-It
Youngstorget
Pløens gate
21
19
Torggata
Den Norske Turistforening (DNT)
Stortorvet
Oslo Domkirke (Oslo Cathedral)
Biskop Gunnerus gate
Brugata
7
Stenersgata
Nyalndsveien
20
Grønland
GRØNLAND
Oslo S Jernbanetorget T-bane Station
Tourist Office
Oslo Sentralstasjon
AKER BRYGGE
10
Rådhusbrygge
Rådhusgata
12
Øvre Slottsgate
5
Nedre Vollgate
Kongens gate
Prinsens gate
Tollbugata
4
Fred Olsens gate
Strandgata
Nyalndsveien
8
Rådhusbrygge Quay (Boat Terminal)
Aker Brygge Pier
9
Kirkegata
Dronningens gate
Skippergata
Bank Plassen
Myntgata
Color Line Terminal
Pipervika
Akershus Festning & Slott
Oslo Opera House
Bjørvika
Hovedøya
Vippetangen Quay (Oslofjord Ferries)
A
B
C
D
E
F
G
5
6
7
8

Oslo

Top Sights

Akershus Festning & Slott ... D7
Nasjonalgalleriet ... D4
Oslo Opera House ... F6
Frognerparken & Vigeland Park ... A2

Sleeping

1 Anker Hostel ... G4
2 Cochs Pensjonat ... C3
3 Ellingsens Pensjonat ... B2
4 Oslo Budget Hotel ... F6
5 Perminalen Hotel ... E6
6 P-Hotel ... E5
7 Thon Hotel Spectrum ... G5

Eating

8 Aker Brygge Food Court ... C6
9 Café Skansen ... D6
10 Fisherman's Coop ... C6
11 Fru Hagen ... G2
12 People & Coffee ... D6
13 Rust ... C3
14 Sult ... G1
15 Tullins Café ... D4

Drinking

16 Bar Boca ... G1
17 Tea Lounge ... G2

Entertainment

18 Blå ... F3
19 Fish Og Vilt ... F5
20 Gloria Flames ... G5
21 Mono ... F5
22 Villa ... F4

Shopping

23 Vestkanttorget Flea Market ... A2

breakfast & lunch) More than a mere coffee shop this friendly place offers hot, filling meals such as chilli con carne, soups that are just the ticket on a cold winter's day, salads and the best carrot cake in Oslo.

Sult MODERN NORWEGIAN €€
(www.sult.no; Thorvald Meyers gate 26; lunch mains Nkr99-139, dinner menu Nkr355) The polished green-and-black colour scheme of Sult perfectly captures the Grünerløkka vibe, with an imaginative menu replete with superb fish and pasta dishes often using local and organic ingredients.

Café Hemma Hos MODERN NORWEGIAN €€
(www.cafehemmahos.no; Fredrikborgsveien 16; mains Nkr165-190) The owners of the Café Hemma Hos, close to the Viking Ship Museum, know there is more to culinary life than hot dogs and stale sandwiches. Sit out in the pleasant gardens and choose from a menu that includes pickled herrings, crayfish and a variety of tapas.

Tullins Café INTERNATIONAL €
(Tullins gate 2; snacks & light meals Nkr69-108) This dimly lit cafe offers a little bit of everything, from salads and burgers to pasta and stir-fry dishes. It's a favourite among students.

Fru Hagen INTERNATIONAL €
(Thorvald Meyers gate 40; mains Nkr118-137) The low-key and always-full Fru Hagen, 'Mrs Garden', serves sandwiches and burgers, all with a healthy side portion of vegetables. The juicy vegie burger is well worth scoffing.

Drinking & Entertainment

The tourist office's free monthly brochure *What's On in Oslo* lists current concerts, theatre and special events, but the best publication for night owls is the free *Streetwise,* published annually in English by Use-It (p935).

Bars & Clubs

The city's best neighbourhood bar scene is along Thorvald Meyers gate and the surrounding streets in Grünerløkka. The Youngstorget area has some of the most popular places close to the city centre, while the Grønland neighbourhood has a more alternative feel.

Tea Lounge BAR, TEASHOP
(www.tealounge.no; Thorvald Meyers gate 33b; 11am-1am Mon-Wed, 11am-3am Thu-Sat, noon-3am Sun) During daylight hours, this split-personality bar is a teashop with a superb range of brews and a chilled soundtrack. In the dark of night it transforms itself into one of the hippest bars in Oslo.

Bar Boca BAR
(Thorvald Meyers gate 30) Squeeze into what is quite possibly the smallest bar in Oslo and you'll find that you have slid back in time to the 1960s. It's retro cool and has a fine cocktail selection.

Fish Og Vilt CLUB
(Pløensgate 1) This bar-club is a popular central spot, with DJs rocking the crowd in the covered backyard and an impressive selection of beers and cocktails. On a Monday night it's the only place worth considering.

The Villa CLUB
(www.thevilla.no; Møllergata 23; ⌚Fri-Sat) With arguably the best sound system in the city, this is a die-hard house and electro music club. It's also open on some Thursdays.

Live Music

Oslo has a thriving live-music scene. Keep your ear to the ground in summer to hear about outdoor concerts at Vigeland Park – a weird-and-wonderful venue.

TOP CHOICE **Blå** JAZZ
(www.blaaoslo.no, in Norwegian; Brenneriveien 9c; cover Nkr100-150) It would be a pity to leave Oslo without checking out Blå, which features on a global list of 100 great jazz clubs compiled by the savvy editors at US jazz magazine *Down Beat*. Sometimes it veers into other musical styles with DJs when there's no live music.

Mono ROCK
(www.cafemono.no, in Norwegian; Pløensgate 4) An upbeat place, Mono is the rock club of choice with the cool and beautiful of Oslo. It's known for booking the best up-and-coming new indie bands.

Gloria Flames ROCK
(www.gloriaflames.no, in Norwegian; Grønland 18) In Grønland, Gloria Flames is a popular rock bar with frequent gigs and a roof-terrace bar during daylight hours.

Shopping

Oslo excels in upmarket shopping and there are many fine shops on Grensen and Karl Johans gate. For art try the galleries on Frognerveien, for exclusive boutiques head to Hegdehaugsveien or Skovveien, and for funky shoes or T-shirts go no further than Grünerløkka.

Vestkanttorget Flea Market FLEA MARKET
(Amaldus Nilsens plass; ⌚10am-4pm Sat) If you're happy with pot luck and sifting through heaps of junk, take a chance here. It's at the plaza that intersects Professor Dahls gate, a block east of Vigeland Park, and it's a more than pleasant way to pass a Saturday morning.

Information

Discount Cards

Oslo Pass (www.visitoslo.com; adult 1/2/3 days Nkr240/340/430)

Emergency

Ambulance (☎113)

Police (☎112, Hammersborggata 10)

Internet Access

Almost all hotels and hostels in Oslo provide wi-fi access (although it's not always free) and some also have computers with Internet for guest use.

Use-It (Møllergata 3; ⌚9am-6pm Mon-Fri, 11am-5pm Sat Jun-Aug, shorter hours Sep-May) Free internet.

Money

There are banks with ATMs throughout the city centre with a particular concentration along Karl Johans gate.

Forex (www.forex.no; Fridtjof Nansens plass 6 & Oslo S; ⌚9am-6pm Mon-Fri) The largest foreign-exchange service in Scandinavia.

Tourist Information

Tourist office (☎81 53 05 55; Jernbanetorget 1, Oslo S; ⌚7am-8pm Mon-Fri, 8am-8pm Sat-Sun May-Sep, 7am-8pm Mon-Fri, 8am-6pm Sat-Sun Oct-Apr)

Use-It (☎24 14 98 20; www.use-it.no; Møllergata 3; ⌚9am-6pm Mon-Fri Jul & Aug, 11am-5pm Mon-Fri Sep-Jun) The exceptionally helpful and savvy Ungdomsinformasjonen (Youth Information Office, better known as Use-It) makes (free) bookings for inexpensive or private accommodation and provides information on anything from current events to hitching possibilities.

Getting There & Away

AIR Most flights land at Oslo's main international airport in **Gardermoen** (www.osl.no), 50km north of the city; it's the country's main international gateway and domestic hub. Oslo Torp, 123km south of the city, and Rygge Airport, 60km southeast of Oslo, are secondary airports.

BUS Long-distance buses arrive and depart from the **Galleri Oslo Bus Terminal** (Schweigaards gate 8, Galleri Oslo); the train and bus stations are linked via an overhead walkway.

TRAIN All trains arrive and depart from Oslo S in the city centre. It has **reservation desks** (⌚6.30am-11pm) and an **information desk** (☎81 50 08 88, press 9 for service in English), that provides details on routes and timetables throughout the country. Major destinations include Stavanger, Bergen, Røros and Trondheim.

Getting Around

TO/FROM GARDERMOEN INTERNATIONAL AIRPORT **Flybussen** (www.flybussen.no) is the airport shuttle to Gardermoen. The trip costs Nkr140/240 one-way/return (valid one month) and takes 40 minutes.

FlyToget (www.flytoget.no) rail services leave Gardermoen airport for Oslo S (Nkr170, 19 minutes) every 10 minutes between 4.18am and midnight. In addition, most northbound **NSB** (www.nsb.no) intercity and local trains stop at Gardermoen (Nkr110, from 26 minutes, hourly but fewer on Saturday).

PUBLIC TRANSPORT Oslo has an efficient public transport system with an extensive network of buses, trams, underground trains (T-bane) and ferries. Tickets for most trips cost Nkr26 if you buy them in advance (at 7-Eleven, Narvesen, Trafikanten) or Nkr40 if you buy them from the driver. A day pass costs Nkr70.

CENTRAL NORWAY

The central region of Norway is strewn with stunning national parks, some of which are traversed by the immensely scenic Oslo–Bergen rail line, including the stark, white snowscape of the Hardangervidda plateau. Røros is one of Norway's prettiest hamlets.

Røros

POP 5580

Røros, a charming Unesco World Heritage Site and former copper-mining town set in a small hollow of stunted forests and bleak fells, is one of Norway's most beautiful villages. Its 80 protected and colourfully painted **log buildings** climb the hillside.

Røros Kirke (Kjerkgata) was closed for renovations when we were there, but is one of Norway's most distinctive Lutheran churches. **Smelthytta** (Malmplassen; adult/student Nkr80/60; ⏲10am-6pm mid-Jun–mid-Aug, shorter hours mid-Aug–mid-Jun), the intriguing mining museum, is housed in an old smelting works. The nearby **slegghaugan** (slag heaps) have lovely views over town, and the tiny turf-roofed **miners' cottages** are charming.

Sleeping & Eating

TOP CHOICE **Erzscheidergården** GUEST HOUSE €€
(☎72 41 11 94; www.erzscheidergaarden.no; Spell Olaveien 6; s/d from Nkr895/1190; 📶) Appealing guest house with 24 wood-panelled rooms.

Frøyas Hus B&B €
(☎92 88 35 30; www.froyashus.no, in Norwegian; Mørkstugata 4; r without bathroom Nkr400-900) Two small, 300-year-old rooms.

Vertshuset Røros HISTORIC HOTEL €€
(☎72 41 93 50; www.vertshusetroros.no, in Norwegian; Kjerkgata 34; s/d from Nkr875/1050, 2-/4-bed apt Nkr1450/2250; 📶) All-wood rooms in a historical 17th-century building. Also the town's best **restaurant** (mains lunch Nkr75-145, dinner Nkr268-345).

Kaffestugu Cafeteria TRADITIONAL NORWEGIAN €
(www.kaffestuggu.no, in Norwegian; Bergmannsgata 18; lunch specials & snacks Nkr59-115, mains Nkr125-245; ⏲10am-9pm Mon-Sat, 11am-6.30pm Sun) Coffee, pastries, snacks and light meals.

Information

Tourist office (☎72 41 00 00; www.roros.no; Peder Hiortsgata 2; ⏲9am-6pm Mon-Sat, 10am-4pm Sun mid-Jun–mid-Aug, 9am-3pm Mon-Fri, 10am-1pm Sat mid-Aug–mid-Jun)

Getting There & Away

BUS There's up to four daily buses to Oslo (Nkr455, six hours).

TRAIN Røros lies on the line between Oslo (from Nkr199, five hours, six daily) and Trondheim (from Nkr199, 2½ hours).

Oslo to Bergen

The Oslo–Bergen railway line, a seven-hour journey past forests and alpine villages, and across the starkly beautiful **Hardangervidda** plateau, is Norway's most scenic (see also boxed text, p930).

Midway between Oslo and Bergen is **Geilo**, a ski centre where you can practically walk off the train and onto a chairlift. From Geilo the train climbs 600m through a tundra-like landscape of high lakes and snowcapped mountains to the tiny village of **Finse**, near the **Hardangerjøkulen** icecap. Finse has year-round **skiing** and summer **hiking trails**. One of Norway's most frequently trodden trails winds from the Finse train station down to the fjord town of **Aurland**, a four-day trek.

BERGEN & THE WESTERN FJORDS

This spectacular region has truly extraordinary scenery. Sognefjorden, Lysefjord and

Geirangerfjord are all variants on the same theme: steep crystalline rock walls dropping with sublime force straight into the sea, often draped with waterfalls, and small farms. Fjærland offers a pair of accessible glaciers. Bergen, a lively city with a 15th-century waterfront, is pleasing to behold, and contains some of Norway's finest nightlife and eateries.

Information on the region is available from **Fjord Norway** (www.fjordnorway.com).

Bergen

POP 256,600

Surrounded by seven hills and seven fjords, Bergen is a beautiful, charming city. With the Unesco World Heritage–listed Bryggen and buzzing Vågen harbour as its centrepiece, Bergen climbs the hillsides with hundreds of timber-clad houses, while cable cars offer stunning views from above. Throw in great museums, friendly locals and a dynamic cultural life and Bergen amply rewards as much time as you can give it.

History

During the 12th and 13th centuries, Bergen was Norway's capital. By the 13th century, the city states of Germany allied themselves into trading leagues, most significantly the Hanseatic League; the sheltered harbour of Bryggen drew the traders in droves. They established their first office here around 1360 and by the early 17th century Bergen was the trading hub of Scandinavia and Norway's most populous city with 15,000 people. In 1899 the Hanseatic League's Bergen offices closed.

Sights

Bryggen HISTORIC AREA

Bryggen, the old medieval quarter whose name means 'The Wharf', consists of timber alleys that offer an intriguing glimpse into the centuries past. The current 58 buildings (25% of the original) cover 13,000 sq metres and date from after a 1702 fire; the building pattern dates back to the 12th century.

Some of Norway's creakiest floors are in the timber building (1704) housing the **Hanseatic Museum** (www.museumvest.no; Finnegårdsgaten 1a; admission high/low-season Nkr50/30; 9am-5pm mid-May–mid-Sep, shorter hours mid-Sep–mid-May), which provides a glimpse of the austere living conditions of Hanseatic merchants. The entry ticket is also valid for **Schøtstuene** (Øvregaten 50), where the Hanseatic fraternity once met for their business meetings and beer guzzling.

FJORD TOURS FROM BERGEN

Fjord Tours (81 56 82 22; www.fjordtours.com) has mastered the art of making the most of limited time with a series of tours into the fjords. Its most popular tour is the year-round **Norway in a Nutshell** (see p934). From May to September, it also runs the 13-hour **Explore Hardangerfjord** (Nkr1320) and **Sognefjord in a Nutshell** (Nkr1150). Fjord Tours also has four-day tours that include Oslo, Sognefjorden, Geiranger and Ålesund (Nkr4410).

Tide Reiser (55 23 87 00; www.tidereiser.no; May-Oct) runs 12-hour **Hardanger Fjord Adventure** tours that include a bus to Norheimsund, and a cruise that takes in Utne, Kinsarvik, Lofthus, Eidfjord and Ulvik (Nkr790).

The site of Bergen's earliest settlement is now **Bryggens Museum** (www.bymuseet.no; Dreggsallmenning 3; admission Nkr60; 10am-4pm mid-May–Aug, shorter hours Sep–mid-May). The 800-year-old foundations unearthed during construction have been incorporated into the exhibits.

Bergen Kunst Museum ART GALLERY

(Bergen Art Museum; www.bergenartmuseum.no; Rasmus Meyers Allé 3, 7 & 9; adult/student Nkr60/40; 11am-5pm mid-May–mid-Sep, 11am-5pm Tue-Sun mid-Sep–mid-May) Three buildings alongside the lake house this superb collection of Norwegian art from the 18th and 19th centuries, including works by Munch and JC Dahl, as well as Picasso, Miró, Rodín, Klee and others.

Bergen Environs FOLK MUSEUM, MANSIONS

The open-air **Gamle Bergen** (www.bymuseet.no; Nyhavnsveien 4, Sandviken; admission Nkr70; hourly tours 10am-5pm early-May–Aug) presents around 40 buildings from the 18th and 19th centuries. It's 4km north of the city centre and can be reached by city buses 20, 23 or 24.

If you want to tour the former lakeside mansion and workshop of composer Edvard Grieg, hop on any bus from platform 19, 20 or 21 of the bus station, get off at Hosbroen and follow the signs to **Troldhaugen** (www.troldhaugen.com; Hop; admission Nkr60; 9am-6pm May-Sep, 10am-4pm Oct-Apr).

Bergen

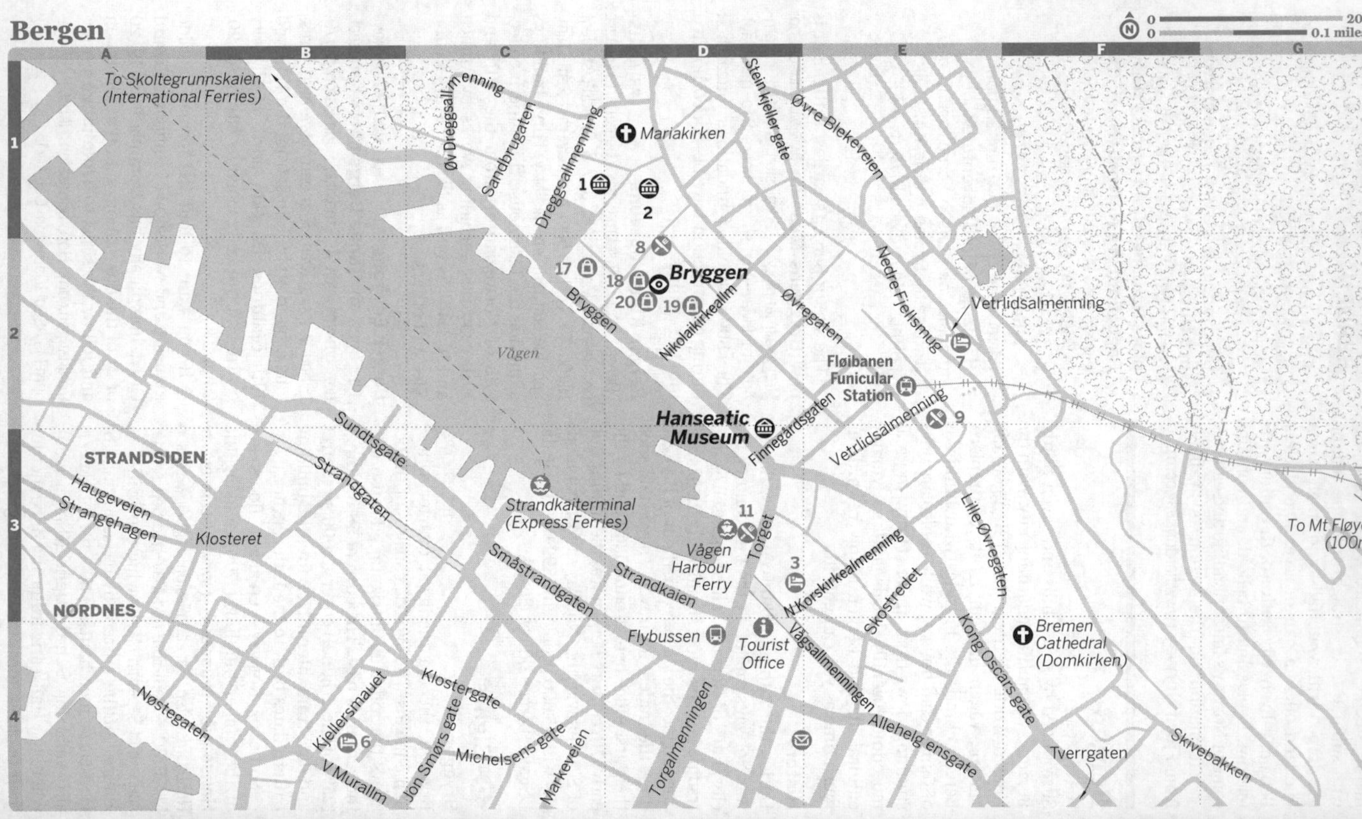
0 200 m
0 0.1 miles
A
B
C
D
E
F
G
1
2
3
4
To Skoltegrunnskaien
(International Ferries)
Øv Dreggsallmenning
Sandbrugaten
Dreggsallmenning
Mariakirken
1
2
Stein kjeller gate
Øvre Blekeveien
8
17
18
Bryggen
20
19
Bryggen
Nikolaikirkeallm
Øvregaten
Nedre Fjellsmug
Vetrlidsalmenning
7
Vågen
Fløibanen
Funicular
Station
Hanseatic
Museum
Finnegårdsgaten
Vetrlidsalmenning
9
Sundtsgate
STRANDSIDEN
Strandgaten
Haugeveien
Strangehagen
Klosteret
Strandkaiterminal
(Express Ferries)
11
Torget
Vågen
Harbour
Ferry
Småstrandgaten
Strandkaien
3
N Korskirkealmenning
Skostredet
Lille Øvregaten
To Mt Fløyen
(100m)
NORDNES
Flybussen
Tourist
Office
Vågsallmenningen
Kong Oscars gate
Bremen
Cathedral
(Domkirken)
Nøstegaten
Kjellersmauet
6
Klostergate
Jon Smørs gate
Michelsens gate
Markeveien
Torgalmenningen
Allehelg ensgate
Tverrgaten
Skivebakken
V Murallm

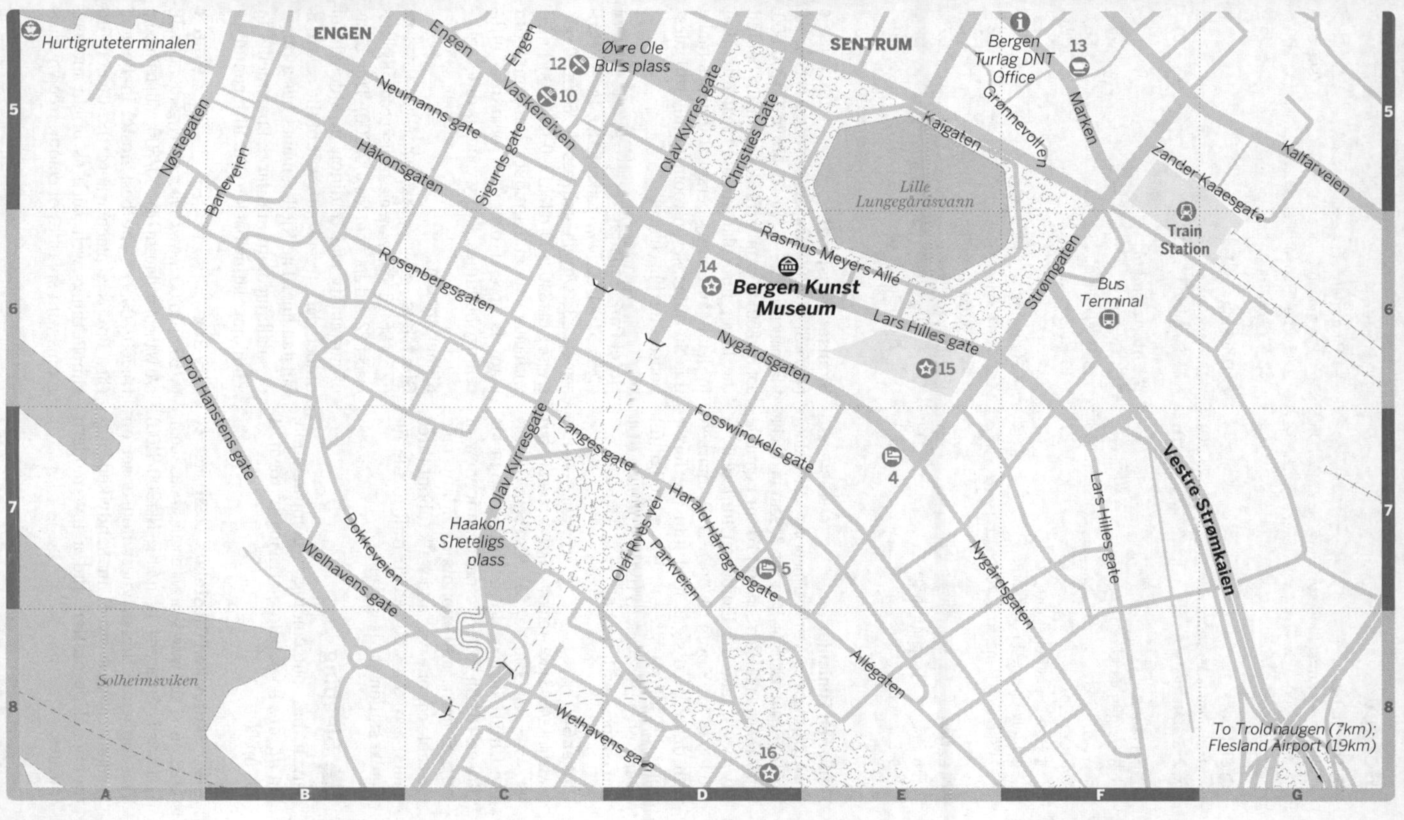

Hurtigruteterminalen
ENGEN
Engen
Engen
Øvre Ole Bulls plass
12
10
SENTRUM
Bergen Turlag DNT Office
13
Neumanns gate
Vaskerelven
Olav Kyrres gate
Christies Gate
Kaigaten
Grønnevollen
Marken
Kalfarveien
Zander Kaaesgate
Nøstegaten
Baneveien
Håkonsgaten
Sigurds gate
Lille Lungegårdsvann
Train Station
Rasmus Meyers Allé
14
Bergen Kunst Museum
Strømgaten
Bus Terminal
Rosenbergsgaten
Lars Hilles gate
Nygårdsgaten
15
Prof Hanstens gate
Olav Kyrresgate
Langes gate
Fosswinckels gate
4
Lars Hilles gate
Vestre Strømkaien
Haakon Sheteligs plass
Dokkeveien
Welhavens gate
Olaf Ryes vei
Parkveien
Harald Hårfagresgate
5
Nygårdsgaten
Allégaten
Solheimsviken
Welhavens gate
16
To Troldhaugen (7km); Flesland Airport (19km)

Bergen

Fløibanen Funicular CABLE CAR, HIKE
(www.floibanen.no; Vetrlidsalmenning 21; return Nkr70; ⏲8am-midnight Mon-Sat & 9am-midnight Sun May-Aug, until 11pm Sep-Apr) For unbeatable city views, take the Fløibanen funicular to the top of Mt Fløyen (320m). Trails marked with dilapidated signs lead into the forest from the hilltop station. For a delightful 40-minute walk back to the city, take trail 4 and connect with trail 6.

Ulriken643 CABLE CAR, HIKE
(www.ulriken643.no; return Nkr145, with bus Nkr245; ⏲9am-9pm May-Sep, 9am-5pm Oct-Apr) The Ulriksbanen cable car to the top of Mt Ulriken (642m) offers a panoramic view of Bergen, fjords and mountains. Many take the cable car one way and walk (about three hours) across a well-beaten trail to the funicular station at Mt Fløyen.

Sleeping

Bergen has outstanding accommodation, but *always* book before arriving in town: it fills up fast.

TOP CHOICE **Skuteviken Gjestehus** GUEST HOUSE €€
(☎93 46 71 63; www.skutevikenguesthouse.com; Skutevikens Smalgang 11; d/attic Nkr900/1100) This authentic timber guest house, set on a small cobbled street in Sandviken, has traditional decoration and a few modern touches.

Skansen Pensjonat GUEST HOUSE €
(☎55 31 90 80; www.skansen-pensjonat.no; Vetrlidsalmenning 29; s Nkr425-475, d Nkr700-800, apt Nkr850) A wonderful location up behind the lower funicular station, real attention to detail, and many personal touches make this charming, seven-room, family-run guest house a terrific choice.

Hotel Park Pension HISTORIC HOTEL €€
(☎55 54 44 00; www.parkhotel.no; Harald Hårfagresgate 35; s/d with Fjord Pass Nkr760/1020, otherwise s Nkr840-1100, d Nkr1090-1350; wi-fi) Filled with character and antiques, this family-run place is spread over two beautiful 19th-century buildings. Every room is different.

Kjellersmauet Gjestehus GUEST HOUSE, APARTMENTS €€
(☎55 96 26 08; www.gjestehuset.com; Kjellersmauet 22; s/d apt from Nkr700/900) This oasis of hospitality and tradition in a delightful timber-clad street southwest of the centre is outstanding. The Kjellersmauet has a range of small, medium and large apartments in a building dating back to the 16th century.

City Box HOSTEL €
(☎55 31 25 00; www.citybox.no; Nygårdsgaten 31; s/d without bathroom Nkr500/600, with bathroom Nkr700/800; wi-fi) The best hostel in Bergen, City Box is a place where the owners do simple things well, such as bright modern rooms with splashes of colour, free wi-fi ac-

cess, a minimalist designer feel without the price tag and friendly young staff.

Bergen Vandrerhjem YMCA HOSTEL €€
(☎55 60 60 55; www.bergenhostel.no; Nedre Korskirkealmenning 4; dm Nkr180-300, d Nkr800-900;) This friendly hostel has that unmistakeable hostel feel, same-sex or mixed dorms, kitchen facilities and a terrific rooftop terrace. Bookings are essential year-round and, unusually, bed linen is included in the price.

Eating

TOP CHOICE Pingvinen BAR-RESTAURANT €
(www.pingvinen.no, in Norwegian; Vaskerelven 14; mains Nkr69-149; ⌚1pm-3am Sun-Fri, noon-3am Sat) Devoted to small-town Norwegian cooking and with an informal atmosphere, Pingvinen is one of our favourite restaurants in Bergen. It's the sort of place where Norwegians come for recipes their mothers and grandparents used to cook.

TOP CHOICE Torget Fish Market FISH MARKET €
(www.torgetibergen.no, in Norwegian; Torget; ⌚7am-7pm daily Jun-Aug, 7am-4pm Mon-Sat Sep-May) For price and atmosphere, it's hard to beat the harbourside fish market. Here you'll find everything from smoked whale meat and salmon to calamari, fish and chips, fish cakes, prawn baguettes, seafood salads, local caviar and, sometimes, nonfishy reindeer and elk.

Bryggen Tracteursted TRADITIONAL RESTAURANT €€€
(☎55 33 69 99; Bryggen; mains lunch Nkr75-135, dinner Nkr285-375; ⌚lunch & dinner May-Sep) Housed in a 1708 building that ranges across the former stables, kitchen and Bergen's only extant *schøtstuene* (dining hall), this fine restaurant does traditional Norwegian dishes that change regularly.

Kafe Kippers INTERNATIONAL €€
(USF; Georgenes Verft 12; mains lunch Nkr65-85, dinner Nkr89-159; ⌚lunch & dinner) Attached to a cultural centre in an old sardine canning factory, this agreeable outdoor terrace has an artsy vibe and serves plentiful lunch dishes, including pastas and salads.

Pygmalion Økocafé ORGANIC CAFE-RESTAURANT €
(Nedre Korskirkealmenning 4; ciabattas Nkr69-89, organic pancakes Nkr79-119, salads Nkr119-149; ⌚11am-11pm) This very cool place has a casual but classy atmosphere and tasty organic food. It's a great place at any time of the day and as good for a snack as something slightly more substantial.

Escalon TAPAS €
(Vetrlidsalmenning 21; tapas Nkr38-108; ⌚3pm-midnight Sun-Fri, 1pm-midnight Sat) Tapas have taken Bergen by storm, but Escalon has been doing it since 1998. The friendly young waiters are happy to make suggestions on wine selection and the tapas are tasty.

Pølse Kiosk SAUSAGE KIOSK €
(Kong Oscars gate 1; hot dogs from Nkr45; ⌚10am-3am) You may have eaten a gutful of Norwegian hot dogs, but this place has *real* sausages (including wild game, reindeer, lamb and chilli), better-than-average sauces and good-sized servings.

Drinking

TOP CHOICE Altona Vinbar WINE BAR
(C Sundtsgate 22; ⌚6pm-12.30am Mon-Thu, 6pm-1.30am Fri & Sat) Our favourite wine bar in town, Altona Vinbar is an intimate warren of softly lit underground rooms that date from the 16th century and it has a huge selection of international wines.

Pingvinen CAFE-BAR
(Vaskerelven 14; ⌚1pm-3am Sun-Fri, noon-3am Sat) As good as a bar as it is as a restaurant, 'Penguin' is laid-back and funky and popular with a friendly thirty-something crowd. It's got all the usual beers, as well as some boutique beers from microbreweries around Norway.

Capello CAFE-BAR
(Marken 16; ⌚noon-5pm Mon-Wed, noon-8pm Thu, noon-1.30am Fri & Sat, noon-7pm Sun) An engaging little place that does smoothies, milkshakes, beer and, on Saturdays, pancakes, Capello is all about 1950s and '60s decor and music downstairs, while upstairs the '70s take over.

Entertainment

Classical Music Concerts

Throughout the year, you'll find classical performances focusing on Bergen's favourite son, composer Edvard Grieg. Venues include the following:

Troldhaugen (www.troldhaugen.com; Hop; adult/student Nkr220/160; ⌚6pm Wed & Sun, 2pm Sat mid-Jul–Sep) Grieg's lakeside mansion and workshop.

SHOPPING IN BRYGGEN

The wooden alleyways of Bryggen have become a haven for artists and craftspeople and there are stunning little shops and boutiques at every turn. Before entering the lanes, start at the waterfront with the Arctic-inspired jewellery of **Juhls' Silver Gallery** (www.juhls.no; Bryggen 39; ⌚9am-10pm Mon-Sat, noon-7pm Sun mid-Jun–Sep, 10am-5pm Mon-Fri, 10am-2pm Sat Oct–mid-Jun). **Per Vigeland** (www.pervigeland.no; Jacobsfjorden, Bryggen; ⌚10am-6pm mid-May–Aug, shorter hours Sep–mid-May) is a local jewellery designer working with silver and gold-plated silver, while **Živa Jelnikar Design** (www.zj-d.com; Jacobsfjorden, Bryggen; ⌚10am-5pm Mon-Fri, 11am-4pm Sat & Sun Jun-Aug, shorter hours Sep-May) is the highly original work of Slovenian designer Živa Jelnikar; both have on-site workshops.

Kvams Flisespikkeri (www.kvams-flisespikkeri.com, in Norwegian; Bredsgården, Bryggen; ⌚9am-6pm mid-May–mid-Sep, shorter hours mid-Sep–mid-May) sells lovely Bryggen-centric paintings, block prints and other artworks. **Læverkstedet** (Jacobsfjorden, Bryggen; ⌚10am-8pm mid-May–mid-Aug, shorter hours mid-Aug–mid-May) is the purveyor of the softest moose leather.

Grieghallen (☎55 21 61 50; www.grieghallen.no; Edvard Griegs plass; ⌚Aug-Jun) Performances by the respected Bergen Philharmonic Orchestra.

Nightclubs & Live Music

Garage ROCK
(www.garage.no; Christies gate 14; ⌚3pm-3am Mon-Sat, 5pm-3am Sun) Garage has taken on an almost mythical quality for rock-music lovers across Europe, with well-known Norwegian and international acts drawn to the cavernous basement.

Hulen ROCK
(www.hulen.no, in Norwegian; Olaf Ryes vei 48; ⌚9pm-3am Thu-Sat mid-Aug–mid-Jun) Going strong since 1968, Hulen is the oldest rock club in northern Europe and it's one of the classic stages for indie rock. Sadly, it closes during summer when many of Bergen's students head off on holidays.

Logen BAR, LIVE MUSIC
(Øvre Ole Bulls plass 6; ⌚6pm-2am Mon-Thu, 6pm-3am Fri & Sat, 8pm-3am Sun) Upstairs from the Wesselstuen Restaurant, Logen is Bergen's antidote to its more famous heavy metal and rock scene. It has a loyal local following for its concerts (Nkr50 to Nkr100) at 9pm on Sunday (jazz or alternative music) and Monday (Voksne Herrers Orkester) from September to May or June.

ℹ Information

Bergen Card (www.visitbergen.com/bergencard; 24/48hr Nkr190/250) Discount card.

Bergen Turlag DNT office (☎55 33 58 10; www.bergen-turlag.no; Tverrgaten 4; ⌚10am-4pm Mon-Wed & Fri, 10am-6pm Thu, 10am-2pm Sat) Maps and information on hiking and hut accommodation throughout western Norway.

Tourist office (☎55 55 20 00; www.visitbergen.com; Vågsallmenningen 1; ⌚8.30am-10pm Jun-Aug, 9am-8pm May & Sep, 9am-4pm Mon-Sat Oct-Apr)

ℹ Getting There & Away

AIR The airport is in Flesland, 19km southwest of central Bergen. Direct flights connect Bergen with major cities in Norway, plus a handful of international destinations.

BOAT The Hurtigruten leaves from the terminal east of Nøstegaten.

Flaggruten (☎53 40 91 20; www.flaggruten.no; Strandkaiterminal) Twice daily services from Sunday to Friday to Stavanger (Nkr750/950), with just one on Saturday.

Fjord1 (☎55 90 70 70; www.fjord1.no; Strandkaiterminalen) At least one daily ferry from Bergen to Sogndal (Nkr570; five hours), with some services going on to Flåm (Nkr665).

BUS Express buses run throughout the Western Fjord region, as well as to Ålesund (Nkr619, 10 hours, one to two daily), Trondheim (Nkr789, 12½ hours, two daily) and Stavanger (Nkr490, 5½ hours, five daily).

TRAIN The spectacular train journey between Bergen and Oslo (Nkr299 to Nkr775, 6½ to eight hours, five daily) runs through the heart of Norway.

ℹ Getting Around

Flybussen (www.flybussen.no) Runs up to four times hourly between the airport, the main bus terminal and opposite the tourist office (one-way/return Nkr90/150, 45 minutes).

Stavanger

POP 123,900

Stavanger's centre is arrayed around a pretty harbour with the quiet streets of the old town climbing up from the water's edge. It's also home to almost two dozen museums. But Stavanger's appeal is as much about atmosphere as architecture. Most nights, especially in summer, the city's waterfront comes alive and can get quite rowdy in the best tradition of oil and port cities. It's an excellent base from which to explore stunning Lysefjord.

Sights

TOP CHOICE **Gamle Stavanger** HISTORIC AREA

Gamle (Old) Stavanger consists of cobblestone walkways passing between rows of late 18th-century whitewashed wooden houses – all 173 of them immaculately kept and adorned with cheerful, well-tended flowerboxes.

TOP CHOICE **Norsk Oljemuseum** MUSEUM

(www.norskolje.museum.no; Kjeringholmen; admission Nkr80; 10am-7pm daily Jun-Aug, 10am-4pm Mon-Sat, 10am-6pm Sun Sep-May) One of Norway's best museums, the Petroleum Museum is filled with high-tech interactive displays, gigantic models and authentic reconstructions.

FREE **Stavanger Domkirke** CHURCH

(Håkon VII's gate; 11am-7pm daily Jun-Aug, 11am-4pm Mon-Sat Sep-May) This beautiful church is an impressive, but understated, medieval stone cathedral dating from approximately 1125. Despite later restoration, it is considered Norway's oldest medieval cathedral still in its original form.

Other Museums MUSEUMS

(www.museumstavanger.no; 11am-4pm mid-Jun–mid-Aug, shorter hours early Jun & late Aug, closed Mon Sep-May) The following museums have combined same-day admission costs of Nkr60 per adult. The main **Stavanger Bymuseum** (Muségata 16) reveals nearly 900 years of Stavanger's history, 'From Ancient Landscape to Oil Town'. More interesting is the **Maritime Museum** (Nedre Strandgate 17), in two restored warehouses. The fascinating **Canning Museum** (Øvre Strandgate 88A) occupies an old sardine cannery.

Sleeping

Book well in advance. This is an oil city and prices can soar on weekdays as business-people arrive, but return to more reasonable levels on weekends – try to plan your visit accordingly. The tourist office website (www.regionstavanger.com) has a list of small B&Bs in and around Stavanger.

TOP CHOICE **Skagen Brygge Hotel** HOTEL €€

(51 85 00 00; www.skagenbryggehotell.no; Skagenkaien 30; s/d Fri & Sat Nkr975/1275, Sun-Thu Nkr1695/1895, daily Jul Nkr1070/1370, with Fjord Pass year-round Nkr880/1260;) This large and supremely comfortable hotel (part of the Fjord Pass network) offers good weekend and summer value from its superb waterside location; ask for a room with harbour view. Free waffles are served from 2pm to 7pm.

Stavanger B&B B&B €€

(51 56 25 00; www.stavangerbedandbreakfast.no; Vikedalsgata 1a; s/d with shared toilet Nkr690/790, with bathroom Nkr790/890;) The simple rooms at this quiet but popular place are tidy and come with satellite TV, shower and a smile from the friendly owners.

Skansen Hotel HOTEL, GUEST HOUSE €€

(51 93 85 00; www.skansenhotel.no; Skansegata 7; guest house s Nkr755-1030, d Nkr970-1190, hotel s Nkr970-1130, d Nkr1110-1290;) This centrally located place, opposite the old customs house, is divided into an older guest house section with simple, comfortable rooms, and newer, larger hotel rooms.

Mosvangen Camping CAMPING GROUND €

(51 53 29 71; www.stavangercamping.no; Tjensvoll 1b; camp sites without/with car Nkr120/170, with caravan or camper Nkr200, huts Nkr450-650; Apr-Sep) During nesting season around Mosvangen lake, campers are treated to almost incessant birdsong amid the green and agreeable surroundings. Take bus 78 or 79 (Nkr32) from opposite the cathedral.

Mosvangen Vandrerhjem HOSTEL €

(51 54 36 36; stavanger.hostel@vandrerhjem.no; Henrik Ibsensgate 19; dm/s/d without bathroom Nkr275/450/525; mid-May–mid-Sep) Stavanger's pleasant and simple lakeside hostel is 3km southwest of the city centre. Take bus 78 or 79 (Nkr32) from opposite the cathedral.

Eating

Le Café Français CAFE €

(Østervåg 30-32; sandwiches & light meals Nkr59-129; 9am-5pm Mon-Wed & Fri, 9am-7pm Thu, 9am-4pm Sat, 11am-5pm Sun) With the widest range of pastries and other sweet goodies in town and pleasant outdoor tables, Le Café Français

WORTH A TRIP

LYSEFJORD

All along the 42km-long Lysefjord (Light Fjord), the granite rock glows with an ethereal, ambient light, even on dull days, all offset by almost-luminous mist. Whether you cruise from Stavanger or hike up to the peerless and precipitous **Preikestolen** (Pulpit Rock; 604m), it's one of Norway's must-sees.

From May to mid-September, five to seven ferries a day run from Stavanger's Fiskespiren Quay to Tau, where the ferries are met by a bus, which runs between the Tau pier and the Preikestolhytta Vandrerhjem. From there, the two-hour trail leads up to Preikestolen. The last bus from Preikestolhytta to Tau leaves at 7.55pm. You can buy tickets at the Stavanger tourist office or Fiskespiren Quay.

Two companies offer three-hour boat cruises from Stavanger to the waters below Preikestolen and back:

Rødne Fjord Cruise (51 89 52 70; www.rodne.no; adult/student Nkr380/280; departures 10.30am & 2.30pm Sun-Fri & 12.30pm Sat Jul & Aug, noon daily May, Jun & Sep, noon Fri-Sun Oct-Apr)

Tide Reiser (51 86 87 88; www.tidereiser.no; adult/student Nkr360/280; departures noon daily late May-late Aug, noon Sat Sep-late May)

is a good place to wind down. It also serves sandwiches, mini quiches and good salads.

NB Sørensen's Damskibsexpedition NORWEGIAN €€
(Skagen 26; mains Nkr125-329; lunch & dinner) One of the better places along the waterfront, this restaurant serves everything from fish to pork ribs, with a seasonal lunch menu that's excellent value.

Emilio's Tapas Bar SPANISH €€
(Sølvberggata 13; tapas Nkr50-190, lunch mains Nkr89-169; lunch & dinner daily, closed Sun Sep-May) This pleasant Spanish tapas bar serves good Iberian food with friendly service that comes at no extra cost.

Kult Kafeen CAFE €
(Sølvberggata 14; sandwiches & salads Nkr120-135; 10am-10pm Mon-Sat, noon-10pm Sun) This cool place has won the affections of families and hip young professionals alike. Well-sized sandwiches and fresh salads are the highpoints, but many people just come for a quiet coffee.

Drinking

Most of the livelier bars are right on the waterfront and cater to a younger crowd with a penchant for loud, energetic music. You'll hear them long before you see them – as the bars are all similar, take your pick.

TOP CHOICE **B.brormann B.bar** COCKTAIL BAR
(Skansegata 7; 4pm-2am) One of Stavanger's coolest bars, where you can actually hear the conversation, this oddly named place with contemporary artworks on the brick walls draws a discerning over-thirties crowd and serves great-value half-litre beers (Nkr63) and award-winning cocktails (Nkr96).

Café Sting CAFE, CLUB
(Valbergjet 3; noon-midnight Mon-Thu, noon-3.30am Fri & Sat, 3pm-midnight Sun) Up the hill but a world away from the harbour clamour, Café Sting is a mellow cafe and a funky cultural space with exhibitions, live jazz whenever the mood takes it, and a weekend nightclub where the DJs keep you on your toes, spinning house, hip hop and soul.

Information

Stavanger Turistforening DNT (51 84 02 00; off Muségata; 10am-4pm Mon-Wed & Fri, 10am-6pm Thu, 10am-2pm Sat) Information on hiking and mountain huts.

Tourist office (51 85 92 00; www.regionstavanger.com; Domkirkeplassen 3; 9am-8pm Jun-Aug, 9am-4pm Mon-Fri, 9am-2pm Sat Sep-May) Local information and advice on Lysefjord and Preikestolen.

Getting There & Around

TO/FROM THE AIRPORT Flybussen (www.flybussen.no) run every half-hour between the bus terminal and the airport at Sola (one-way/return Nkr90/140).

BOAT Flaggruten (518 68 780) runs express passenger catamarans to Bergen (one-way/return Nkr750/950, 4¼ hours, one to four daily). In summer, **Tide Reiser** (www.tidereiser.no; Jun-

Aug) has daily four-hour car ferries with tourist commentary along Lysefjord to Lysebotn (adult/car Nkr210/400) from Fiskepirterminalen.

BUS Nor-Way Bussekspress offers services to Oslo (Nkr795, 9½ hours, up to five daily) and Bergen (Nkr490, 5¾ hours, six daily).

TRAIN Trains run to Oslo (Nkr886, eight hours, up to five daily) via Kristiansand.

Sognefjorden

Sognefjorden, Norway's longest (204km) and deepest (1308m) fjord, cuts a deep slash across the map of western Norway. In places, sheer walls rise more than 1000m above the water while elsewhere a gentler shoreline supports farms, orchards and villages.

Find regional tourist information at www.sognefjord.no.

Getting There & Away

Fjord1 (☎57 75 70 00; www.fjord1.no, in Norwegian) operates an express boat between Bergen and both Flåm (Nkr665, 5½ hours) and Sogndal (570, 4¾ hours), stopping along the way at 10 small towns.

FLÅM

POP 550

A tiny village of orchards and a handful of buildings scenically set at the head of Aurlandsfjorden, Flåm is a jumping-off spot for travellers taking the Gudvangen ferry or the Sognefjorden express boat. Though it sees an amazing 500,000 visitors every summer, walk a few minutes from the centre and you'll experience solitude.

Sights & Activities

Flåmsbana Railway CLASSIC RAIL JOURNEY
(www.flaamsbana.no; one-way/return Nkr240/340) Over the course of 20km, this engineering wonder hauls itself up 864m of altitude gain through 20 tunnels at a gradient of 1:18. This, the world's steepest railway that runs without cable or rack wheels, takes a full 45 minutes to climb to Myrdal, on the bleak, treeless Hardangervidda plateau, past thundering waterfalls. It runs year-round with up to 10 departures daily in summer.

Riding the Rallarvegen BIKE DESCENT
(www.rallarvegen.com) Cyclists can descend the Rallarvegen, the service road originally used by the navvies who constructed the railway, for 83km from Haugastøl (1000m) or an easier 56km from Finse. You can rent bicycles in Haugastøl (two days on weekdays/weekends Nkr480/580, including return transport from Flåm).

Sleeping

Flåm Camping & Youth Hostel HOSTEL, CAMPING GROUND €
(☎57 63 21 21; www.flaam-camping.no; campsites Nkr185-195, dm Nkr200-270, s/d from Nkr330/470, cabins from Nkr685; ⊙May-Sep) In 2010, Hostelling International judged this to be Norway's best hostel and the ninth best in the world. There's a brand new block with en-suite facilities, amenities are impeccable and the welcome couldn't be warmer.

Heimly Pensjonat GUEST HOUSE €€
(☎57 63 23 00; www.heimly.no; s Nkr795-895, d Nkr895-1095, incl breakfast) Overlooking the water on the fringe of the village and away from the port hubbub, this place has straightforward rooms. There's a magnificent view along the fjord from the more expensive ones, and from the small patch of lawn.

Information

Tourist office (☎57 63 33 13; www.alr.no; ⊙8.30am-4pm & 4.30-8pm Jun-Aug, shorter hours Sep-May)

Getting There & Away

FERRY From Flåm, boats head out to towns around Sognefjorden. The most scenic trip from Flåm is the passenger ferry up Nærøyfjord to Gudvangen (one-way/return Nkr255/360). It leaves Flåm at 3.10pm year-round and up to four times daily between May and September. The tourist office sells all ferry tickets.

GUDVANGEN & NÆRØYFJORD

Nærøyfjord, its 17km length a Unesco World Heritage Site, lies between Gudvangen and Flåm. Beside the deep blue fjord (only 250m across at its narrowest point) are towering 1200m-high cliffs, isolated farms and waterfalls plummeting from the heights. It can easily be visited as a day excursion from Flåm or Bergen.

Geirangerfjord

Added to Unesco's World Heritage list in 2005, this king of Norwegian fjords boasts towering, twisting walls that curve inland for 20 narrow kilometres. Along the way abandoned farms cling to the cliffs and breathtakingly high waterfalls drop straight into the sea from forests above.

The cruise by public ferry between Geiranger and Hellesylt is almost too nice to view.

GEIRANGER

POP 250

High mountains with cascading waterfalls and cliff-side farms surround Geiranger, at the head of the crooked Geirangerfjorden. Although the village is quite tiny, it's one of Norway's most-visited spots, but is reasonably serene during the evening when all cruise ships and tour buses have departed.

Sights & Activities

Flydalsjuvet VIEWPOINT

The car park, signposted Flydalsjuvet, about 5km uphill from Geiranger on the Stryn road, offers a great view of the fjord and the green river valley. For the iconic Geiranger photo, drop about 150m down the hill, then descend a slippery and rather indistinct track to the edge.

Dalsnibba VIEWPOINT

For the highest and perhaps most stunning of the many stunning views of the Geiranger valley and fjord, take the 5km toll road (Nkr85 per car) that climbs from the Rv63 to the Dalsnibba lookout (1500m). A bus (return Nkr180) runs three times daily from Geiranger between mid-June and mid-August.

Coastal Odyssey KAYAKING, HIKING

(☎911 18 062; www.coastalodyssey.com) Based at Geiranger Camping, rents sea kayaks (Nkr150/400/750 per hour/half-day/day) and does daily kayaking-with-gentle-hiking trips (Nkr800).

Sleeping & Eating

TOP CHOICE **Villa Utsikten** HOTEL €€€

(☎70 26 96 60; www.villautsikten.no; s Nkr940, d Nkr1340-1600; ⊙May-Sep; @) High on the hill above Geiranger (take Rv63 in the direction of Grotli) the venerable family-owned Utsikten, constructed in 1893, has stunning views over town and fjord.

Geiranger Camping CAMPING GROUND €

(☎70 26 31 20; www.geirangercamping.no; person/site Nkr25/125; ⊙mid-May–mid-Sep; @ 📶) A short walk from the ferry terminal, Geiranger Camping is sliced through by a fast-flowing torrent. Though short on shade it's pleasant and handy for an early-morning ferry getaway.

Laizas CAFE €

(⊙10am-10pm mid-Apr–Sep; @ 📶) At the ferry terminal, just beside the tourist office, the young team at this airy, welcoming place puts on a handful of tasty hot dishes, good salads and snackier items such as focaccia, wraps and sandwiches.

Information

Tourist office (☎70 26 30 99; www.visitalesund-geiranger.com; ⊙9am-6pm mid-May–mid-Sep)

Getting There & Away

BOAT The popular, hugely recommended run between Geiranger and Hellesylt (passenger/car with driver Nkr133/278, adult return Nkr169; one hour) is the most spectacular scheduled ferry route in Norway.

Almost as scenic is the ferry that runs twice daily between Geiranger and Valldal (one-way/return Nkr206/327, 2¼ hours). It runs from mid-June to mid-August.

BUS From mid-June to mid-August two buses daily make the spectacular run over Trollstigen to Åndalsnes (Nkr222, three hours). For Ålesund, change at Linge.

Ålesund

POP 23,000

The coastal town of Ålesund is, for many, just as beautiful as Bergen, if on a smaller scale, and it's far less touristy. Ålesund burned to the ground in 1904 and the amazing rebuilding created a harmonious collection of pastel buildings almost entirely designed in the art-nouveau tradition. All the loveliness is well staged on the end of a peninsula, surrounded by islands, water and hills.

To see the best of Ålesund architecture, pick up the free booklet *On Foot in Ålesund* from the tourist office. For the best views over this scenic town, climb the 418 steps up Aksla hill to the splendid **Kniven viewpoint**.

Ålesund Vandrerhjem (☎70 11 58 30; www.hihostels.no; Parkgata 14; dm/s/d incl breakfast Nkr255/570/790; @ 📶) is the well-run and central HI-affiliated hostel.

Lyst (Kongensgata 12; lunch dishes Nkr75-85, dinner mains Nkr165-295; ⊙10am-11pm) offers good dining within a classic converted art-nouveau building.

Information

Tourist office (☎70 15 76 00; www.visitalesund-geiranger.com; Skaregata 1; ⊙9am-6pm or 7pm daily Jun-Aug, 9am-4pm Mon-Fri Sep-May)

Getting There & Away

AIR There are daily flights to Oslo, Bergen and Trondheim.

BUS One to three daily buses run to Bergen (Nkr610, 9¼ hours).

BOAT The Hurtigruten docks at Skansekaia Terminal.

NORTHERN NORWAY

Highlights of Norway's soulful north include the incredibly steep and jagged Lofoten islands, which erupt vertically out of the ocean; medieval Trondheim, Norway's third-largest city; and lively Tromsø, the world's northernmost university town.

An alternative to land travel is the Hurtigruten coastal ferry (see p956).

Trondheim

POP 170,000

Trondheim, Norway's original capital, is the country's third-largest city. With its wide streets and partly pedestrianised heart, it's a simply lovely city. Fuelled by a large student population, it buzzes with life and has some good cafes and restaurants, and it's rich in museums.

Sights

If you're planning to visit all three sights within the cathedral complex, it's worthwhile purchasing a combined ticket (Nkr100) that gives access to the cathedral, palace museum and crown jewels.

Nidaros Domkirke CHURCH
(www.nidarosdomen.no; Kongsgårdsgata; admission Nkr50; ⏲9am-3pm or 5.30pm Mon-Fri, 9am-2pm Sat, 1-4pm Sun May–mid-Sep, shorter hours mid-Sep–Apr) Nidaros Cathedral is Scandinavia's largest medieval building; the original stone cathedral was built in 1153. Outside, the ornately embellished west wall has statues of biblical characters and Norwegian bishops and kings. Inside, the altar sits over the original grave of St Olav, the Viking king who replaced the Nordic pagan religion with Christianity. In summer, from early June to early August, there are **recitals** (admission free; ⏲1pm Mon-Sat) on the church's magnificent organ and you can climb the cathedral's **tower** for a great view over the city.

Archbishop's Palace MUSEUM
The 12th-century archbishop's residence, commissioned around 1160 and Scandinavia's oldest secular building, is beside the cathedral. In its west wing, Norway's **crown jewels** (admission Nkr70) shimmer and flash. Its **museum** (admission Nkr50; ⏲10am-3pm or 5pm Mon-Sat, noon-4pm Sun May–mid-Sep, shorter hours mid-Sep–Apr) is in the same compound.

Historic Buildings & Neighbourhoods HISTORIC BUILDINGS
Scandinavia's largest wooden palace, the late-baroque **Stiftsgården** (Munkegata 23; admission Nkr60; ⏲10am-4pm Mon-Sat, noon-4pm Sun Jun-late Aug) was completed in 1778 and is now the official royal residence in Trondheim. Admission is by tour only, on the hour.

The picturesque **Gamle Bybro** (Old Town Bridge) originally dates from 1681, but the current wooden structure was built in 1861. From here, enjoy marvellous views over the **Bryggen**, an amazingly intact collection of tall red, yellow, green and orange 18th- and 19th-century warehouses. On the east side of the bridge lies **Bakklandet**, a neighbourhood of cobblestone streets.

The **Sverresborg Trøndelag Folkemuseum** (Sverresborg Allé 13; www.sverresborg.no; admission Nkr85 incl guided tour; ⏲11am-6pm Jun-Aug, 11am-3pm Sep-May), set around the ruins of a medieval castle, is one of Norway's best open-air museums with over 60 period buildings.

Sleeping

Chesterfield Hotel HOTEL €€
(☎73 50 37 50; www.bestwestern.no; Søndre gate 26; s/d from Nkr790/990; @🛜) All 43 rooms at this venerable hotel are spacious. They were decorated and fundamentally renovated, with fresh beds and furniture, in 2006 following a major fire in the adjacent building.

Singsaker Sommerhotel SUMMER HOTEL €
(☎73 89 31 00; http://sommerhotell.singsaker.no; Rogertsgata 1; dm/s/d without bathroom Nkr230/445/685, s/d with bathroom Nkr560/810, all incl breakfast; ⏲mid-Jun–mid-Aug) On a grassy knoll in a quiet residential neighbourhood, this imposing building, usually a student hostel, represents great value. Bus 63 from the train station passes by.

Pensjonat Jarlen GUEST HOUSE €
(☎73 51 32 18; www.jarlen.no; Kongens gate 40; s/d Nkr520/650) There's nothing fancy about this central spot but it does have price, convenience and value for money on its side. All 25 rooms have full bathroom and all except the sole single have a fridge and self-catering facilities.

Flakk Camping CAMPING GROUND €
(☎72 84 39 00; www.flakk-camping.no; car/caravan site Nkr170/200, cabins with outdoor bathroom Nkr400-550; ⏲May-Aug) Sitting right beside

Trondheimfjord, this welcoming camping ground is about 10km from the city centre. Take Rv715 from Trondheim.

Eating

TOP CHOICE Vertshuset Tavern TRADITIONAL NORWEGIAN €€€
(Sverresborg Allé 11; mains Nkr195-295) Once in the heart of Trondheim, this historic (1739) tavern was lifted and transported, every last plank of it, to the Sverresborg Trøndelag Folkemuseum on the outskirts of town. Tuck into its rotating specials of traditional Norwegian fare in one of its 16 tiny rooms.

TOP CHOICE Baklandet Skydsstasjon TRADITIONAL NORWEGIAN €€
(www.skydsstation.no, in Norwegian; Øvre Bakklandet 33; mains Nkr130-245; ⊙noon-1am) Within what began life as an 18th-century coaching inn are several cosy rooms with poky angles and listing floors. On the menu are tasty dishes, including a renowned fish soup.

Ramp BAR, RESTAURANT €
(cnr Strandveien & Gregusgate; mains Nkr85-140; ⊙noon-midnight) Well off the tourist route and patronised by in-the-know locals, alternative Ramp is renowned for its juicy house burgers filled with lamb, beef, fish or chickpeas.

Ravnkloa Fish Market FISH RESTAURANT €
(Munkegata; ⊙10am-5pm Mon-Sat) You can munch on inexpensive fish cakes and other finny fare at this excellent, informal place, which also sells cheeses and other gourmet fare.

Drinking

As a student town, Trondheim offers lots of through-the-night life. The free papers *Natt & Dag* and *Plan B* have listings, mostly in Norwegian. Wharf-side Solsiden (Sunnyside) is Trondheim's trendiest leisure zone.

TOP CHOICE Den Gode Nabo PUB
(☎40 61 88 09; Øvre Bakklandet 66; www.dengodenabo.com, in Norwegian; ⊙1pm-1am) The Good Neighbour, dark and cavernous within and nominated more than once as Norway's best pub, enjoys a prime riverside location; reserve a table on the floating pontoon. It also serves mains (NKr140).

Trondheim Microbryggeri MICROBREWERY
(Prinsens gate 39) This splendid home-brew pub has up to eight of its own brews on tap and good light meals coming from the kitchen. It's a place to linger, nibble and tipple.

Bruk Bar BAR
(Prinsens gate 19; ⊙11am-1.30am) Inside, a stuffed elk head gazes benignly down, candles flicker and designer lamps shed light onto the 30-or-so-year-olds who patronise this welcoming joint. The music is eclectic, but guaranteed loud.

Studentersamfundet STUDENT CENTRE
(Student Centre; Elgesetergate 1) During the academic year, the centre has 10 lively bars, a cinema and frequent live music, while in summer it's mostly a travellers' crash pad.

Entertainment

Dokkhuset CAFE, CULTURAL CENTRE
(Dock House; ⊙11am-1am Mon-Thu, 11am-3am Fri & Sat, 1pm-1am Sun) In a converted former pumping station, this is at once auditorium (where you'll sometimes hear experimental jazz or chamber music), restaurant and cafe-bar.

Frakken CLUB
(Dronningens gate 12; ⊙6pm-3am) This multistorey nightclub and piano bar features both Norwegian and foreign musicians and has live music nightly.

Olavshallen CONCERT HALL
(☎73 99 40 50; Kjøpmannsgaten 44) The home base of the Trondheim Symphony Orchestra, Olavshallen also features international rock and jazz concerts, mostly between September and May.

Information

Tourist office (☎73 80 76 60; www.trondheim.no; Torvet; ⊙8.30am-8pm Mon-Fri, 10am-6pm Sat & Sun late Jun–mid-Aug, shorter hours mid-Aug–late Jun)

Getting There & Away

AIR Værnes airport, 32km east of Trondheim, has both domestic and international flights.

BOAT Trondheim is a major stop on the Hurtigruten coastal ferry route.

BUS The intercity bus terminal (Rutebilstasjon) adjoins Trondheim Sentralstasjon (train station, also known as Trondheim S). **Nor-Way Bussekspress** services run up to three times daily to/from Ålesund (Nkr596, 7 hours) and daily to/from Bergen (Nkr790, 14½ hours).

MIDNIGHT SUN & POLAR NIGHT

TOWN/AREA	LATITUDE	MIDNIGHT SUN	POLAR NIGHT
Bodø	67° 18'	4 Jun–8 Jul	15 Dec–28 Dec
Narvik	68° 26'	27 May–15 Jul	4 Dec–8 Jan
Tromsø	69° 42'	20 May–22 Jul	25 Nov–17 Jan
Hammerfest	70° 40'	16 May–27 Jul	21 Nov–21 Jan
Nordkapp	71° 11'	13 May–29 Jul	18 Nov–24 Jan
Longyearbyen	78° 12'	20 Apr–21 Aug	26 Oct–16 Feb

TRAIN There are two to four trains daily to/from Oslo (Nkr810, 6½ hours), while two head north to Bodø (Nkr982, 9¾ hours).

Getting Around

TO/FROM THE AIRPORT Flybussen (www.flybussen.no) runs to/from the airport (Nkr90, 45 minutes) every 15 minutes from 4am to 9pm (less frequently at weekends). Hourly trains run between Trondheim Sentralstasjon and Værnes (Nkr64, 35 minutes).

BICYCLE Trondheim has a bike-hire scheme (Nkr70 per 24 hours). Pick up a card at the tourist office in return for a refundable deposit of Nkr200, then borrow a bike from any of the 12 cycle stations around town.

Bodø

POP 47,300

Travellers generally use Bodø as a gateway to the Lofoten islands and elsewhere in Nordland. Most get off their boat or train, poke around for a few hours and then get on the first ferry.

Norway's **Norsk Luftfartsmuseum** (Aviation Museum; www.luftfart.museum.no; Olav V gata; admission Nkr95; 10am-6pm) is huge fun to ramble around if you have even a passing interest in flight and aviation history.

If you don't mind being 3km from the centre, **Bodøsjøen Camping** (75 56 36 80; www.bodocamp.no, in Norwegian; Kvernhusveien 1; tent/caravan site Nkr150/200 plus per person Nkr30, cabins without bathroom Nkr250-430, with bathroom Nkr690-840) is well equipped. Buses 12 and 23 stop 250m away. In town, **Skagen Hotel** (75 51 91 00; www.skagen-hotel.no; Nyholmsgata 11; s/d incl breakfast from Nkr725/925;) is attractively decorated and a continent away from chain-hotel clones.

At the docks you can buy inexpensive fresh shrimp. Also quayside, **Løvolds** (75 52 02 61; Tollbugata 9; dishes Nkr105-135, daily special Nkr90-115; 9am-6pm Mon-Fri, 9am-3pm Sat) is Bodø's oldest eating choice, with sandwiches, grills and hearty Norwegian fare.

Information

Backpacker Service (75 65 02 89; backpacker@nfk.no; Sjøgata 15-17; 10am-6pm late Jun–mid-Aug;) Free luggage storage, travel information, internet points, wi-fi, toilets and use of a tandem.

Tourist office (75 54 80 00; www.visitbodo.com; Sjøgata 3; 9am-8pm Mon-Fri, 10am-6pm Sat, noon-8pm Sun mid-May–Aug, 9am-3.30pm Mon-Fri Sep–mid-May)

Getting There & Around

AIR The airport, 2km away, has flights to Svolvær, Trondheim, Tromsø and more. Local buses (Nkr30) marked 'Sentrumsrunden' bring you to town.

BOAT Bodø is a stop on the Hurtigruten coastal ferry. Car ferries sail five to six times daily in summer (less frequently during the rest of the year) between Bodø and Moskenes on Lofoten (car including driver/passenger Nkr568/158, three to 3½ hours).

TRAIN Bodø is the northern terminus of the Norwegian train network, with a service to Trondheim (Nkr982, 10 hours, twice daily).

Lofoten

The Lofoten islands spread their tall, craggy physique against the sky like some spiky sea dragon and you wonder how humans eked out a living in such inhospitable surroundings. The main islands, Austvågøy, Vestvågøy, Flakstadøy and Moskenesøy, are separated from the mainland by Vestfjorden. On each are sheltered bays, sheep pastures and picturesque villages. Check out www.lofoten.info.

SVOLVÆR

POP 4400

A compact town of old wooden buildings and modern concrete blocks, Lofoten's principle town might be two notches less picturesque than its brothers, but it's still a pretty spot from which to base your explorations.

Daredevils like to scale the **Svolværgeita** (Svolvær Goat), a distinctive, two-pronged peak visible from the harbour, and then jump the 1.5m from one horn to the other – a graveyard at the bottom awaits those who miss. For phenomenal views, hikers can ascend the steep path to the base of the Goat and up the slopes behind it.

From the port, several companies offer **boat cruises** (Nkr450) into the constricted confines of nearby Trollfjord, spectacularly steep and narrowing to only 100m.

Sleeping & Eating

TOP CHOICE **Svolvær Sjøhuscamp** SEA HOUSE €
(☎76 07 03 36; www.svolver-sjohuscamp.no; Parkgata 12; d/q Nkr540/800, d with kitchen Nkr690, all without bathroom; 📶) This friendly sea house straddling the water is a convivial, excellent-value place to fetch up and meet fellow travellers.

Svinøya Rorbuer CABINS €€
(☎76 06 99 30; www.svinoya.no; Gunnar Bergs vei 2; 2-/4-bed cabins from Nkr1200/1600) Across a bridge on the islet of Svinøya, site of Svolvær's first settlement, are several cabins, some historic, most contemporary, and all cosy and comfortable.

Norden & Du Verden CAFE, RESTAURANT €€€
(☎76 07 70 99; www.duverden.net) Norden, open daily, has an airy, modern interior and waterfront terrace, serving lunches of salads and sandwiches (around Nkr150) and dinner (mains Nkr265 to Nkr290), where the house speciality is sushi. To the rear, Du Verden, open only for dinner, offers fine gourmet dining (set menus from Nkr435).

Getting There & Away

AIR Svolvær's small airport (4km from town) has flights to Bodø.

BOAT Express boats ply the waters between Svolvær and Bodø (Nkr324, 3½ hours, one daily) and the Hurtigruten stops here.

KABELVÅG

If you got off the boat and thought Svolvær's blend of traditional and modern wasn't cute enough, this pleasing village lies only 5km west and is connected by the E10 and a paved walking trail. Narrow channels lined with old warehouses lead to the circular cobbled *torget* (town square), whose pattern of paving recalls the hulls of small fishing boats, themselves docked nearby.

In central Kabelvåg, **Præstengbrygga** (☎76 07 80 60; Torget; mains around Nkr150) is a friendly pub with an all-wood interior and dockside terracing; it serves sandwiches, pizzas and tasty mains.

HENNINGSVÆR

A delightful 8km shore-side drive southwards from the E10 brings you to the still-active fishing village of Henningsvær, perched at the end of a thin promontory. Its nickname, 'the Venice of Lofoten', may be a tad overblown but it's certainly the lightest, brightest and trendiest place in the archipelago.

Beside the Henningsvær Bryggehotel, the not-for-profit **Ocean Sounds** (☎91 84 20 12; www.ocean-sounds.com; Hjellskjæret; admission Nkr200; ⏲2-6pm Jul–mid-Aug, May-Jun & mid-Aug–Oct on request) has a series of multimedia presentations about cod, whales and other Arctic marine mammals. Or get out and about on a three- to four-hour marine safari in the Zodiac research boat (Nkr800, daily departures, weather permitting).

Lofoten Adventure (☎90 58 14 75; www.lofoten-opplevelser.no) offers sea-eagle safaris (2.30pm, Nkr430, 1½ hours) and snorkelling (11am, Nkr650, two hours) between mid-June and mid-August, and whale safaris (Nkr850, three hours) from November to mid-January.

Information

Tourist office (☎91 24 57 02; www.henningsvar.com; ⏲10am-6pm Mon-Fri, 11am-4pm Sat & Sun mid-Jun–mid-Nov)

Getting There & Away

In summer, bus 510 shuttles between Svolvær (40 minutes), Kabelvåg (35 minutes) and Henningsvær 10 times on weekdays (three services Saturday and Sunday).

LOFOTR VIKING MUSEUM

This 83m-long chieftain's hall, Norway's largest Viking building, has been excavated at Borg, near the centre of Vestvågøy. The **museum** (www.lofotr.no; admission incl guided tour Nkr120; ⏲10am-4pm or 7pm May–mid-Sep) offers an insight into Viking life. The Svolvær-Leknes bus passes the museum's entrance.

Å

Å is a very special place at what feels like the end of the world on the western tip of Lofoten. A preserved fishing village perched on forbidding rocks connected by wooden footbridges, its shoreline is lined with red-painted *rorbuer* (fishing cabins), many of which jut into the sea. Racks of drying cod and picture-postcard scenes occur at almost every turn. Visitors enliven the tiny place in summer, while in winter it's stark, haunting and empty.

Walk to the camping ground at the end of the village for a good hillside view of Værøy island, which lies on the other side of Moskenesstraumen, the swirling maelstrom that inspired the fictional tales of Jules Verne and Edgar Allen Poe.

Sleeping & Eating

Å-Hamna Rorbuer & Vandrerhjem HOSTEL, FISHERMAN'S HUTS €
(☎76 09 12 11; www.lofotenferie.com; hostel s/d/tr/q Nkr300/400/540/720, rorbuer Nkr800-1200) Sleep simple, sleep in more comfort; either way, this is an attractive choice – it has dorms above the Stockfish Museum and in a quiet villa, set in its garden.

Å Rorbuer FISHERMAN'S HUTS €
(☎76 09 11 21; www.lofoten-rorbu.com, in Norwegian; old sea house d/tr/q per person Nkr250, new sea house d incl breakfast Nkr780, rorbuer Nkr1350-2300) Rorbuer accommodation is dispersed throughout Å's historic buildings, the more expensive ones fully equipped and furnished with antiques.

Moskenesstraumen CAMPING GROUND €
(☎76 09 11 48; camping for 1/2/3 persons Nkr90/140/180, caravans Nkr200, 2-/4-bed cabins without bathroom from Nkr450/650, with bathroom Nkr650/750; ⏲Jun-Aug) This wonderful cliff-top camping ground, just south of the village, has flat, grassy pitches between the rocks just big enough for your bivouac. Cabins, too, have great views.

Getting There & Away

FERRY Car ferries sail five to six times daily in summer (less frequently during the rest of the year) between Moskenes (5km north of Å) and Bodø (car including driver/passenger Nkr568/158, 3½ hours).

Tromsø

POP 67,300

Simply put, Tromsø parties. By far the largest town in northern Norway, it's lively with cultural bashes, an animated street scene, a respected university, the hallowed Mack Brewery, and more pubs per capita than any other Norwegian town. Its corona of snow-topped peaks provides arresting scenery, excellent hiking in summer and great skiing and dog-sledding in winter.

Sights

TOP CHOICE **Polaria** ARCTIC INTERPRETIVE CENTRE
(Hjalmar Johansens gate 12; www.polaria.no; admission Nkr100; ⏲10am-7pm) Daringly designed Polaria is an entertaining and informative multimedia introduction to northern Norway and Svalbard. After a lush 14-minute film about the latter (screened every 30 minutes), an Arctic walk leads to a northern lights display, aquariums of cold-water fish and a trio of energetic bearded seals.

Polarmuseet MUSEUM
(Polar Museum; www.polarmuseum.no; Søndre Tollbugata 11; admission Nkr60; ⏲10am-7pm mid-Jun–mid-Aug, 11am-3pm or 5pm mid-Aug–mid-Jun) The 1st floor of this harbourside museum, in a restored early 19th-century customs house, illustrates early polar research, especially the ventures of Nansen and Amundsen.

Arctic Cathedral CHURCH
(www.ishavskatedralen.no; Hans Nilsensvei 41; admission Nkr30; ⏲9am-7pm Mon-Sat, 1-7pm Sun) The 11 arching triangles of the contemporary Arctic Cathedral (1965) suggest glacial crevasses and auroral curtains. The magnificent glowing stained-glass window depicts Christ redescending to earth. Take bus 20 or 24.

Mack Brewery BREWERY
(Mack Ølbryggeri; ☎77 62 45 80; www.olhallen.no; Storgata 5; tours Nkr150; ⏲tours 1pm Mon-Thu) Established in 1877, this venerable institution produces 18 kinds of beer, including the very quaffable Macks Pilsner, Isbjørn, Haakon and several dark beers.

Fjellheisen CABLE CAR
(www.fjellheisen.no; return Nkr100; ⏲10am-1am late May–mid-Aug, 10am-5pm mid-Aug–late May) For a fine view of the city, take the cable car to the top of Mt Storsteinen (421m). Take bus 26 and buy a combination bus/cable car ticket (Nkr135).

Activities

In and around Tromsø there's a whole range of robust activities in the winter twilight, including experiencing the northern lights, cross-country skiing and snowshoeing, reindeer- and dog-sledding, and ice fishing. Ask at the tourist office for details.

Sleeping

Ami Hotel HOTEL €€
(☎77 62 10 00; www.amihotel.no; Skolegata 24; s/d without bathroom Nkr560/820, with bathroom Nkr660/870, all incl breakfast; @) Beside a traffic-free road and park, this is a quiet, friendly, family-owned choice. There's a well-equipped kitchen for self-caterers and a couple of communal lounges.

Rica Ishavshotel HOTEL €€
(☎77 66 64 00; www.rica.no/ishavshotel; Fredrik Langes gate 2; s/d from Nkr995/1195; @) Occupying a prime quayside position, this hotel is immediately recognisable by its tall spire resembling a ship's mast. Of its 180 attractive rooms, 74, including many singles, have superb views of the sound.

Tromsø Camping CAMPING GROUND €
(☎77 63 80 37; www.tromsocamping.no; Tromsdalen; car/caravan sites Nkr205/230, 2-/4-bed cabins Nkr465/570, 4-bed cabins incl bathroom Nkr1470; @) Tent campers enjoy leafy green campsites beside a slow-moving stream. However, bathroom and cooking facilities at this veritable village of cabins are stretched to the limit. Take bus 20 or 24.

Eating

TOP CHOICE **Emmas Under** RESTAURANT €€
(www.emmas.as, in Norwegian; mains Nkr135-165; 11am-10pm Mon-Sat) Intimate and sophisticated, this is one of Tromsø's most popular lunch spots, where mains include northern Norwegian staples such as reindeer fillet, lamb and stockfish. Upstairs is the more formal **Emmas Drømekjøkken** (Emmas Dream Kitchen; ☎77 63 77 30; mains Nkr285-345; dinner Mon-Sat), a highly regarded gourmet restaurant where booking are advised.

TOP CHOICE **Aunegården** CAFE, RESTAURANT €€
(Sjøgata 29; mains Nkr125-260) You can almost lose yourself in this wonderful cafe-cum-restaurant that's all intimate crannies and cubbyholes. It's rich in character and serves excellent salads (from Nkr140), sandwiches (from Nkr105) and mains.

Driv RESTAURANT, BAR €
(www.driv.no; Tollbugata 3; mains Nkr120; noon-6pm mid-Jun–mid-Aug, 2pm-2am mid-Aug–mid-Jun) This student-run converted warehouse serves meaty burgers and great salads. It organises musical and cultural events and has a disco every Saturday.

Drinking & Entertainment

Tromsø enjoys a thriving nightlife, with many arguing that it's the best scene in Norway. On Friday and Saturday, most nightspots stay open to 4am.

Ølhallen Pub PUB
(9am-6pm Mon-Sat) At Mack Brewery's Ølhallen Pub you can sample its fine ales right where they're brewed. Perhaps the world's only, never mind most northerly, watering hole to be closed in the evening, it carries eight varieties on draught.

Verdensteatret CAFE
(Storgata 93b) Norway's oldest film house will satisfy both cinephiles and thirsters after great cafes. The bar is a hip place with free wi-fi and weekend DJs. At other times, the bartender spins from a huge collection of vinyl records.

Blå Rock Café BAR
(Strandgata 14/16; 11.30am-2am) The loudest, most raving place in town has theme evenings, almost 50 brands of beer, occasional live bands and weekend DJs. The music's rock, naturally. Every Monday hour is a happy hour.

Bastard MUSIC, SPORTS BAR
(Strandgata 22; 8pm-2am Mon-Sat, 3-11pm Sun) Bastard (with the stress on the second syllable…) is a cool basement hang-out with low beams and white, furry walls (no polar bears killed during construction). It engages arthouse and underground DJs (Fridays and Saturdays) and bands (up to three times weekly). It also has a faithful following of armchair sporting regulars.

Information

Tourist office (☎77 61 00 00; www.visittromso.no; Kirkegata 2; 9am-7pm Mon-Fri, 10am-6pm Sat & Sun)

Getting There & Away

AIR Tromsø's airport, about 5km from the centre, has domestic and international flights. **Flybuss** (www.flybussen.no) runs between the airport and Rica Ishavshotel (Nkr55, 15 minutes). Alternatively, take city bus 40 or 42 (Nkr26); on arrival, wait for it on the road opposite the airport entrance.

BOAT Tromsø is a major stop on the Hurtigruten coastal ferry route.

BUS The main bus terminal is on Kaigata, beside the Hurtigruten quay. There are at least two daily express buses to/from Narvik (Nkr390, 4¼ hours) and one to/from Alta (Nkr494, 6½ hours).

Nordkapp

POP 3200

Billing itself as the northernmost point in continental Europe, it sucks in visitors by the busload, some 200,000 every year. But it's the view that thrills the most. In reasonable weather, you can gaze down at the wild surf 307m below and watch the mists roll in.

To reach the tip of the continent, by car, by bike, on a bus or walking in, you have to pay a **toll** (Nkr235).

The continent's real northernmost point, **Knivskjelodden** (latitude 71°11'08"N) can't be reached by vehicles, but you can hike 18km return (five hours) to this promontory from a car park 9km south of Nordkapp.

The closest town of any size is **Honningsvåg**, 35km from Nordkapp.

Sleeping & Eating

Northcape Guesthouse GUEST HOUSE €
(☎47 25 50 63; www.northcapeguesthouse.com; Elvebakken 5a; dm Nkr250, d without bathroom Nkr600; ⊙May-Aug) A bright, modern hostel.

Nordkapp Vandrerhjem HOSTEL €€
(☎918 24 156; www.hihostels.no/nordkapp; dm Nkr330, s/d Nkr450/760, incl breakfast; @☎) A 156-bed HI hostel.

Information

Tourist office (☎78 47 70 30; www.nordkapp.no; Fiskeriveien 4b; ⊙8.30am-10pm Mon-Fri, noon-8pm Sat & Sun mid-Jun–mid-Aug, 8.30am-4pm Mon-Fri mid-Aug–mid-Jun) In Honningsvåg.

Getting There & Around

BOAT The Hurtigruten stops in Honningsvåg. Northbound ships stop for 3½ hours, long enough for the ship to offer its passengers a Nordkapp tour. Buses run to/from Alta (Nkr370, four hours, one to two daily).

BUS Between mid-May and late August, local buses (Nkr100, 45 minutes) run daily between Honningsvåg and Nordkapp.

UNDERSTAND NORWAY

History

Norway's greatest impact on world history was during the Viking age, usually dated from the plundering of England's Lindisfarne monastery by Nordic pirates in 793. Over the next century, the Vikings made raids throughout Europe. The Viking leader Harald Hårfagre (Fairhair) unified Norway in 872. Their power ended when Alexander III, King of Scots, defeated a Viking force at the Battle of Largs in 1263.

In 1397 Norway was absorbed into a union with Denmark that lasted over 400 years. Denmark's defeat in the Napoleonic Wars caused it to cede Norway to Sweden in January 1814. Tired of forced unions, on 17 May 1814 a defiant Norway adopted its own constitution. In 1884 a parliamentary government was introduced and a growing nationalist movement eventually led to peaceful secession from Sweden in 1905.

Norway stayed neutral during WWI. It was attacked by the Nazis on 9 April 1940. King Håkon established a government in exile in England and placed most of Norway's merchant fleet under the command of the Allies. Although Norway remained occupied until the end of the war, it had an active resistance movement. The royal family returned in June 1945.

In the late 1960s, oil was discovered in Norway's offshore waters, thereafter transforming Norway from one of Europe's poorest countries to arguably its richest. Norway has been reluctant to forge closer bonds with other European nations, in part due to concerns about the impact on its fishing and small-scale farming industries. During 1994 a national referendum on joining the EU was held and rejected.

People

Norway has 4.7 million people and one of Europe's lowest population densities. Most Norwegians are of Nordic origin and there are about 40,000 Sámi, the indigenous people of Norway's far north. Some Sámi still live a traditional nomadic life, herding reindeer in Finnmark.

Norway has become an increasingly multicultural society in recent years: 11.4% of the population are immigrants or the children of immigrants (compared to 1.5% in 1970).

Food & Drink

In this chapter we show price ranges for main meals as follows:

€€€ more than Nkr200

€€ Nkr125-200

€ under Nkr125

Environment

The Norwegian mainland stretches 2518km from Lindesnes in the south to Nordkapp in the Arctic north. Norway is home to continental Europe's largest icecap (Jostedalsbreen), the world's second- and third-longest fjords (Sognefjorden and Hardangerfjord), Europe's largest and highest plateau (Hardangervidda) and several of the 10 highest waterfalls in the world. Norway's glaciers cover some 2600 sq km (close to 1% of mainland Norwegian territory and 60% of the Svalbard archipelago).

Norway has led many contemporary environmental initiatives. The government has recently declared a goal of making Norway carbon neutral by 2030, largely by purchasing offsets from developing countries.

SURVIVAL GUIDE

Directory A–Z

Accommodation

Price ranges in this chapter relate to a high-season double room with private bathroom and, unless stated otherwise, includes breakfast:

€€€ more than Nkr1400

€€ from Nkr750 to 1400

€ less than Nkr750

CAMPING

Norway has more than 1000 camping grounds. Tent sites ordinarily cost from Nkr90 to Nkr200. Most camping grounds can also rent simple cabins with cooking facilities starting at around Nkr350 for a very basic two- or four-bed bunkhouse. Linen and blankets cost extra (from Nkr50).

For a comprehensive list of Norwegian camping grounds, check out **Norsk Camping** (www.camping.no) and **NAF Camp** (www.nafcamp.no).

DNT & OTHER MOUNTAIN HUTS

Den Norske Turistforening (DNT, Norwegian Mountain Touring Club; ☎22 82 28 22; www.turistforeningen.no; Storgata 7, Oslo) maintains a network of 460 mountain huts or cabins located a day's hike apart along the country's 20,000km of well-marked and well-maintained wilderness hiking routes.

GUEST HOUSES & PENSIONS

Many towns have *pensjonat* (pensions) and *gjestehus* (guest houses). Some are family-run and offer a far more intimate option than the hostel or hotel experience. Prices for a room with a shared bathroom usually start at Nkr450/700 for a single/double.

HOSTELS

Norway has 53 *vandrerhjem* (hostels) affiliated with Hostelling International (HI) and several dozen that are not. Many operate in summer only. Most hostels have private rooms at higher prices. Bring your own sleeping sheet and pillowcase, or hire linen for around Nkr50. Nearly all hostels have kitchens for guests and provide breakfast. The Norwegian hostelling association is **Norske Vandrerhjem** (☎231 24 310; www.hihostels.no).

HOTELS

Norway's hotels are generally modern and excellent. **Fjord Pass** (www.fjordpass.no) is the largest of the hotel passes, costs Nkr120 (valid for two adults and any children under 15) and is available at 170 hotels, guest houses, hostels, cabins and apartments year-round.

Activities

Norway has some of Europe's best **hiking**, including a network of 20,000km of marked trails that range from easy strolls through the green zones around cities to long treks through national parks and wilderness areas. Many of these trails are marked either with cairns or red Ts at 100m or 200m intervals. The hiking season runs roughly from late May to early October, with a much shorter season in the higher mountain areas and the far north.

Den Norske Turistforening (DNT; Norwegian Mountain Touring Club; ☎22 82 28 22; www.turistforeningen.no; Storgata 7, Oslo) is an important resource for anyone heading out on the trail.

Kayaking (summer), **rafting** (summer) and **dog-sledding** (winter) are other popular activities.

Business Hours

Banks 8.15am-3pm Mon-Wed & Fri, 8.15am-5pm Thu

Central post offices 8am-8pm Mon-Fri, 9am-6pm Sat; otherwise 9am-5pm Mon-Fri, 10am-2pm Sat

Restaurants noon-3pm & 6-11pm

Shops 10am-5pm Mon-Wed & Fri, 10am-7pm Thu, 10am-2pm Sat

Holidays

New Year's Day (Nyttårsdag) 1 January

Maundy Thursday (Skjærtorsdag) March/April

Good Friday (Langfredag) March/April

Easter Monday (Annen Påskedag) March/April

Labour Day (Første Mai, Arbeidetsdag) 1 May

Constitution Day (Nasjonaldag) 17 May

Ascension Day (Kristi Himmelfartsdag) May/June, 40th day after Easter

Whit Monday (Annen Pinsedag) May/June, 8th Monday after Easter

Christmas Day (Første Juledag) 25 December

Boxing Day (Annen Juledag) 26 December

Money

ATM machines are ubiquitous and accept most international cards. Don't assume that all banks will change money. Rates at post offices and tourist offices are generally poorer than at banks, but can be convenient outside banking hours. Travellers cheques command a better exchange rate than cash (by about 2%), but attract commissions.

Telephone

Telephone numbers in Norway consist of eight digits, without any area codes. The international access code is ☎00. For directory assistance, call ☎180 (Nkr9 per minute).

There aren't too many places where you can't get GSM mobile access, with coverage for close to 90% of the country. Norwegian SIM cards can be purchased from any 7-Eleven store, Telehust outlet and some Narvesen kiosks. They start from Nkr200, which includes Nkr100 worth of calls.

Three main mobile service providers:

NetCom (www.netcom.no in Norwegian)

Network Norway (www.networknorway.no, in Norwegian)

Telenor Mobil (www.telenor.com)

Tourist Information

Nearly every city and town has its own tourist office, although offices in smaller towns may be open only during peak summer months. Most tourist offices serve as one-stop clearing houses for general information and bookings for accommodation and activities.

Visas

Norway is a member country of the Schengen Convention. Citizens of the USA, Canada, Australia and New Zealand need a valid passport to visit Norway, but do not need a visa for stays of less than three months. Citizens of EU countries and other Scandinavian countries do not require visas.

Getting There & Away

Entering Norway

Crossing most borders into Norway is usually hassle-free; travellers from non-Western countries or those crossing by land into Norway from Russia should expect more rigorous searches.

Air

For a full list of and information on Norwegian airports, visit www.avinor.no. The main international Norwegian airports are: Gardermoen (Oslo), Flesland (Bergen), Sola Airport (Stavanger), Tromsø, Værnes (Trondheim) and Vigra (Ålesund).

Airlines that use Norway as their primary base:

Norwegian (www.norwegian.com) Low-cost airline.

SAS (www.sas.no)

Widerøe (www.wideroe.no) A subsidiary of SAS.

Land

FINLAND

Buses run between northern Norway and northern Finland with most cross-border services operated by the Finnish company **Eskelisen Lapin Linjat** (☎016-342 2160; www.eskelisen-lapinlinjat.com).

RUSSIA

Buses run twice daily between Kirkenes and Murmansk (one-way/return Nkr350/600, five hours). To cross the border you'll need a Russian visa, which must usually be applied for and issued in your country of residence.

SWEDEN

Bus

Swebus Express (☎0200 218 218; www.swebusexpress.se) has the largest (and cheapest) buses between Oslo and Swedish cities. **GoByBus** (www.gobybus.se, in Swedish or Norwegian) is also worth checking out. Frequent services to Oslo include those from Stockholm (from Skr283, eight to 13 hours, around five daily), Gothenburg (Göteborg; from Skr158, 3¾ hours, five daily) and Malmö (from Skr248, eight hours, two to four daily).

Train

Rail services between Sweden and Norway are operated by **Norwegian Railways** (NSB; ☎81 50 08 88; www.nsb.no) or **Swedish Railways** (SJ; ☎in Sweden 0771-75 75 99; www.sj.se). Trains connect Oslo with Göteborg and Stockholm, Narvik with Stockholm and Trondheim with Östersund.

Sea

DENMARK

Color Line (☎Denmark 99 56 19 77, Norway 22 94 42 00; www.colorline.com) Up to 14 weekly departures from Hirtshals to Kristiansand (from €39, 2¼ to 3¼ hours) and Larvik (from €49.50, 3¾ hours).

DFDS Seaways (☎Denmark 33 42 30 00, Norway 21 62 13 40; www.dfdsseaways.com) From Copenhagen to Oslo (from €112, 16½ hours, seven weekly).

Fjord Line (☎Denmark 97 96 30 00, Norway 51 46 40 99; www.fjordline.com) From Hirtshals to Bergen (from €30, 19½ hours, three weekly), Kristiansand (from €39, 2¼ to 3¼ hours, up to 14 weekly) and Stavanger (from €72, 12 hours, four weekly).

Stena Line (☎Norway 02010; www.stenaline.no) From Fredrikshavn to Oslo (from €29, 12 hours, seven weekly).

GERMANY & SWEDEN

Color Line (☎Germany 0431-7300 300, Norway 81 00 08 11, Sweden 0526-62000; www.colorline.com) also connects Norway with Germany (from Kiel to Oslo; from €174.50, 20 hours, seven weekly) and Sweden (from Strömstad to Sandefjord; from €22, 2½ hours, up to 20 weekly). Check the website for different fare and accommodation types.

Getting Around

Norway has an extremely efficient public transport system. The handy *NSB Togruter*, available free at most train stations, details train timetables and includes information on connecting buses.

Train lines reach as far north as Bodø (you can also reach Narvik by rail from Sweden); further north you're limited to buses and ferries.

Air

Three main airlines fly domestic routes:

Norwegian (www.norwegian.com)

SAS (www.sas.no)

Widerøe (www.wideroe.no)

Bicycle

Given Norway's great distances, hilly terrain and narrow roads, only serious cyclists engage in extensive cycle touring, but those who do, rave about the experience. Buses, express ferries and nonexpress trains carry bikes for various additional fees (around Nkr120), but express trains don't allow them at all.

Boat

An extensive network of ferries and express boats links Norway's offshore islands, coastal towns and fjord districts.

Norway's legendary **Hurtigruten coastal ferry** (☎81 00 30 30; www.hurtigruten.com) is one of the most popular ways to explore Norway. Year in, year out, one of 11 Hurtigruten ferries heads north from Bergen every night of the year, pulling into 35 ports on its six-day journey to Kirkenes, where it

MAJOR INTERNATIONAL TRAIN ROUTES

FROM	TO	FARE	DURATION	FREQUENCY
Gothenburg (Göteborg)	Oslo	Nkr199-484	4hr	up to 3 daily
Stockholm	Oslo	from Skr314	6-7½hr	up to 3 daily
Stockholm	Narvik	from Skr782	18-20hr	1-2 daily
Malmö	Oslo	from Skr401	7½hr	1 daily

then turns around and heads back south. The return journey takes 11 days and covers a distance of 5200km. In agreeable weather (which is by no means guaranteed) the fjord and mountain scenery along the way is nothing short of spectacular.

Onboard, meals are served in the dining room and you can buy snacks and light meals in the cafeteria.

Bus

Nor-Way Bussekspress (☎815 44 444; www.nor-way.no), the main carrier, has routes connecting every main city. Considerably cheaper (although running along fewer routes) are buses operated by **Lavpriseksspressen** (☎67 98 04 80; www.lavprisekspressen.no, in Norwegian), which sells tickets over the internet.

Car & Motorcycle

The **Road User Information Centre** (☎175) tells you the latest road conditions throughout Norway. For 24-hour breakdown assistance call ☎08505. The national automobile association is **Norges Automobil-Forbund** (NAF; ☎92 60 85 05; www.naf.no).

Major international car-rental agencies operate in Norway, but hire is costly and geared mainly to the business traveller. Walk-in rates for a compact car with 200km per day free typically costs Nkr1000 per day (including VAT); insurance starts at Nkr60 per day extra. Short-term visitors may hire a car with only their home country's driving licence.

ROAD RULES

The legal age for driving a car is 18 years; for motorcycles and scooters it is 16 to 21 years (depending on the motorcycle's power); a licence is required. Motorcycles may not be parked on the pavement (footpath).

The use of dipped headlights (including on motorcycles) is required at all times. Speed limits are 80km/h on the open road, but pass a house or place of business and the limit drops to 70km/h or even 60km/h. Through villages limits range from 50km/h to 60km/h and, in residential areas, they're 30km/h.

The blood-alcohol limit is 0.02%.

Train

Norwegian State Railways (Norges Statsbaner; NSB; ☎81 50 08 88, press 9 for English; www.nsb.no) operates an excellent, though limited, system of lines connecting Oslo with Stavanger (via Kristiansand), Bergen, Åndalsnes, Trondheim, Fauske, Røros and Bodø.

MINIPRIS – A TRAVELLER'S BEST FRIEND

On every long-distance train route, for every departure, **Norwegian State Railways** (www.nsb.no) sets aside a limited number of tickets known as *minipris*. Those who book the earliest can get just about any route for just Nkr199. Once those are exhausted, the next batch of *minipris* tickets goes for Nkr299 and so on. These tickets can only be bought over the internet or in ticket-vending machines at train stations. Remember that *minipris* tickets may only be purchased in advance (minimum one day), and reservations are non-refundable and cannot be changed once purchased.

Poland

Includes »

Best Places to Eat

» Sketch, Warsaw (p964)

» Momo, Kraków (p970)

» Magia, Lublin (p973)

» Bazylia, Wrocław (p977)

» Gospoda Pod Modrym Fartuchem, Toruń (p984)

Best Places to Stay

» Castle Inn, Warsaw (p963)

» Mama's Hostel, Kraków (p969)

» Hotel Patio, Wrocław (p977)

» Dom Zachariasza Zappio, Gdańsk (p982)

» Green Hostel, Toruń (p984)

Why Go?

If they were handing out prizes for 'most eventful history', Poland would be sure to get a medal. The nation has spent centuries at the pointy end of history, grappling with war and invasion. Nothing, however, has succeeded in suppressing the Poles' strong cultural identity. As a result, centres such as bustling Warsaw and cultured Kraków exude a sophisticated energy that's a heady mix of old and new.

Away from the cities, Poland is a diverse land, from its beaches to its magnificent mountains. Everywhere in between are towns and cities dotted with ruined castles, picturesque squares and historic churches.

Although prices are slowly rising as its economy gathers momentum, Poland is still good value for travellers. As the Polish people work on combining their national identity with their place in Europe, it's a fascinating time to visit this beautiful country.

When to Go

Warsaw

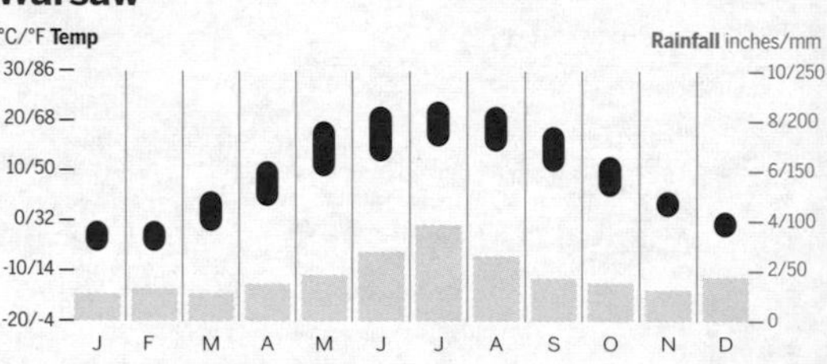

May–Jun Indulge as Poland's restaurants serve dishes starring fresh asparagus.

Jul–Aug Hit the beaches on Poland's long, sandy Baltic coast

Sep Go walking in the beautiful Tatra Mountains, bedding down in a cosy hikers' refuge

Connections

Due to its central position, Poland offers plenty of possibilities for onward travel. The country is well connected by train: there are direct connections to Berlin from both Warsaw (via Poznań) and Kraków; to Prague from Warsaw and Kraków; and to Kyiv from Warsaw and Kraków (via Przemyśl and Lviv). Trains also link Warsaw to Minsk and Moscow, and Gdańsk to Kaliningrad. International buses head in all directions, including eastward to the Baltic States, Belarus and Ukraine. From southern Zakopane it's easy to hop to Slovakia via bus, or even minibus. And from the Baltic coast ports of Gdańsk and Gydnia, ferries head to various ports in Scandinavia.

ITINERARIES

One Week

Spend a day exploring Warsaw with a stroll round the Old Town and a stop at the Warsaw Rising Museum. The next day, head to Kraków for three days, visiting the Old Town, Wawel Castle, the former Jewish district of Kazimierz and Wieliczka. Take a sobering day trip to Oświęcim, then head on to Zakopane for two days.

Two Weeks

Follow the above itinerary, then on the eighth day travel to Wrocław for two days. Progress north to Gothic Toruń for two days, then onward to Gdańsk for three days, exploring its Main Town and taking a day trip to the magnificent castle at Malbork.

Essential Food & Drink

» **Soups** Hearty examples include *żurek* (sour soup with sausage and hard-boiled egg) and *barszcz* (red beetroot soup).

» **Stomach-filling dishes** Extinguish hunger pangs with *bigos* (a thick sauerkraut and meat stew), *pierogi* (dumplings stuffed with various fillings), or *placki ziemniaczane* (potato pancakes often topped with a meaty sauce).

» **Beer** Good, cold and inexpensive, and often served in colourful beer gardens.

» **Vodka** Try it plain, or ask for *myśliwska* (flavoured with juniper berries), *wiśniówka* (with cherries) or *żubrówka* (flavoured with bison grass from the Białowieża Forest).

» **Something sweet** *Szarlotka* (apple cake with cream), or the weighty *sernik* (baked cheesecake).

AT A GLANCE

» **Currency** Złoty

» **Language** Polish

» **Money** ATMs are everywhere

» **Visas** Schengen rules apply; see p1319

Fast Facts

» **Area** 312,685 sq km

» **Capital** Warsaw

» **Country code** ☎48

» **Emergency** ☎112

Exchange Rates

Australia	A$1	2.80zł
Canada	C$1	2.75zł
Euro Zone	€1	3.94zł
Japan	¥100	3.37zł
New Zealand	NZ$1	2.20zł
UK	UK£1	4.42zł
USA	US$1	2.70zł

Set Your Budget

» **Budget hotel room** 150zł

» **Two-course evening meal** 50zł

» **Museum entrance** 10zł

» **Beer** 6-9zł

» **City transport ticket** 2.50zł

Resources

» **Official tourism site** (www.poland.travel)

» **News and website directory** (www.poland.pl)

» **Comprehensive government portal** (www.poland.gov.pl)

Poland Highlights

1 Experience the beauty and history of Kraków's **Wawel Castle** (p966)

2 Hunt for gnome statues in the Old Town of **Wrocław** (p976)

3 Remember the victims of Nazi genocide at former extermination camp **Auschwitz-Birkenau** (Oświęcim, p971)

4 Soak up the cosmopolitan vibe of **Gdańsk** (p980)

5 Enjoy the skiing or hiking life at **Zakopane** (p974)

6 Discover the tragic wartime history of **Warsaw** (p961) at the Warsaw Rising Museum

WARSAW

POP 1.7 MILLION

Warsaw (Warszawa in Polish, var-*shah*-va) may not be the prettiest of Poland's cities, but this bustling business centre is home to a dazzling array of dining and nightlife options.

It's true that the city can be hard work, its traffic-choked streets lined with uninspiring, massive concrete buildings. But look at Warsaw with a historic perspective – as a city that's survived everything fate could throw at it – and you'll see the capital in an entirely new light.

When you factor in its entertainment options, the beauty of its reconstructed Old Town and Royal Way, and the history represented by its former Jewish district and the Warsaw Rising Museum, what emerges is a complex city that well repays a visit.

Sights & Activities

The area west of the Vistula River includes the city centre and the historic Old Town, superbly rebuilt from its foundations after the destruction of WWII. Almost all tourist attractions and facilities are located in this zone.

OLD TOWN

Castle Square HISTORIC SQUARE

(Plac Zamkowy) This is the main gateway to the Old Town. Within the square stands the **Monument to Sigismund III Vasa**, who moved the capital of Poland from Kraków to Warsaw in 1596.

Royal Castle CASTLE

(Plac Zamkowy 4; adult/concession 22/14zł; ⏲10am-4pm Mon-Sat, 11am-4pm Sun, closed Mon Oct-Apr) The highlight of this massive 13th-century castle's sumptuously decorated rooms is the Senators' Antechamber, where landscapes of 18th-century Warsaw by Bernardo Bellotto (Canaletto's nephew) are on show.

Historical Museum of Warsaw MUSEUM

(www.mhw.pl; Rynek Starego Miasta 42; adult/concession 8/4zł, Sun free; ⏲11am-6pm Tue & Thu, 10am-3.30pm Wed & Fri, 10.30am-4.30pm Sat & Sun) Off the magnificent **Old Town Market Square** (Rynek Starego Miasta) is this museum. At noon it shows an English-language film depicting the wartime destruction of the city (6zł).

Barbican FORTIFICATION

Northwest of the Old Town Market Sq along ul Nowomiejska is the Barbican, an imposing fortified section of the medieval city walls.

Marie Skłodowska-Curie Museum MUSEUM

(ul Freta 16; adult/concession 10/5zł; ⏲10am-4pm Tue-Sat, 10am-3pm Sun) North along ul Freta are these unexciting displays about the great lady, who, along with husband Pierre, laid the foundations for radiography, nuclear physics and cancer therapy.

Monument to the Warsaw Rising MONUMENT

(cnr ul Długa & ul Miodowa) West of the Old Town, this striking set of statuary honours the heroic Polish revolt against German rule in 1944.

ROYAL WAY (SZLAK KRÓLEWSKI)

This 4km route connects the Old Town with the modern city centre; it's served by bus 180.

St Anne's Church CHURCH

(ul Krakowskie Przedmieście 68; ⏲11am-8pm) Just south of the Royal Castle, this ornate 15th-century church has impressive views from its **tower** (adult/concession 3/2zł; ⏲11am-8pm May-Oct).

Museum of Caricature MUSEUM

(www.muzeumkarykatury.pl; ul Kozia 11; adult/concession 5/3zł, Sat free; ⏲11am-6pm Tue-Sun) Quirky museum exhibiting numerous original works by Polish and foreign caricaturists, created from the 18th century onwards.

Saxon Gardens GARDENS

West of the Royal Way are these attractive gardens, at whose entrance stands the small but poignant **Tomb of the Unknown Soldier**. The ceremonial changing of the guard takes place at noon on Sunday.

Church of the Holy Cross CHURCH

(ul Krakowskie Przedmieście 3; ⏲dawn-dusk) Chopin's heart is preserved in the second pillar on the left-hand side of the main nave of this 17th-century church. It was brought from Paris, where he died of tuberculosis aged only 39.

Chopin Museum MUSEUM

(ul Okólnik 1; adult/concession 22/13zł, Tue free; ⏲noon-8pm Tue-Sun) To learn more about Poland's most renowned composer, head along ul Tamka to this institution devoted to his life and work. On show are letters, handwritten musical scores and the great man's last piano.

National Museum MUSEUM

(www.mnw.art.pl; Al Jerozolimskie 3; adult/concession 12/7zł, incl temporary exhibitions 17/10zł, Sat

Central Warsaw

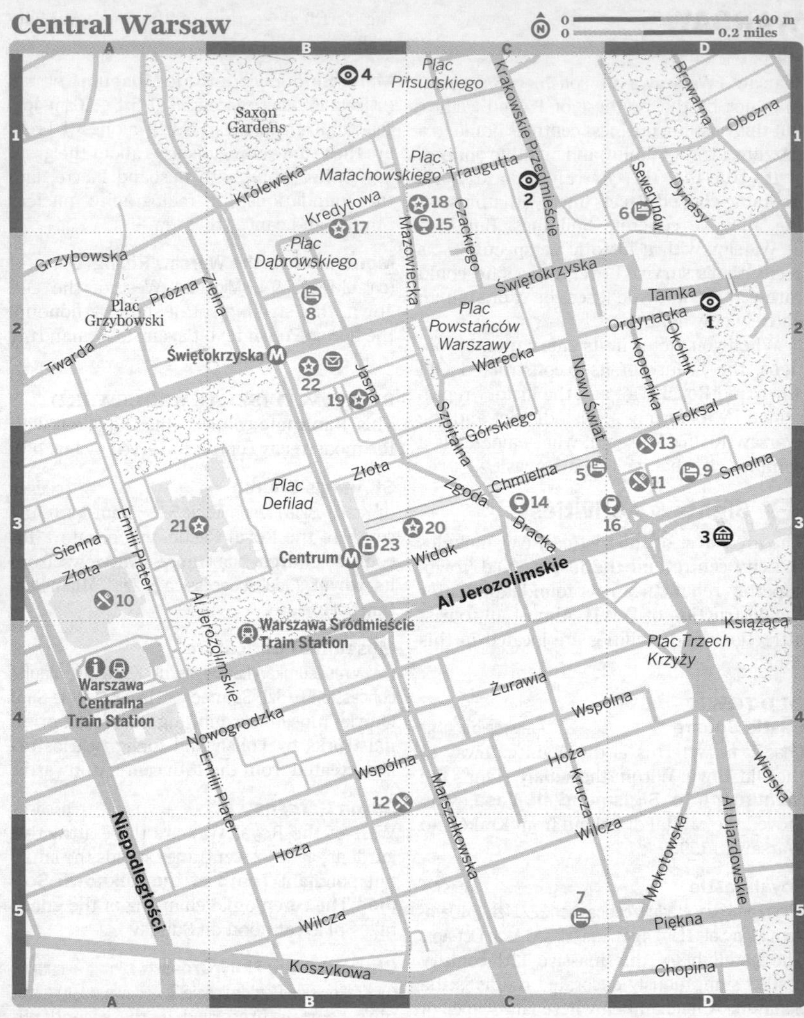

free; ⏲10am-4pm Tue-Thu, noon-9pm Fri, noon-6pm Sat & Sun) Contains Greek and Egyptian antiquities, Coptic frescoes, medieval woodcarvings and paintings; look out for the surrealistic fantasies of Jacek Malczewski.

WEST OF THE CITY CENTRE

TOP CHOICE Warsaw Rising Museum MUSEUM
(ul Grzybowska 79; adult/concession 7/5zł, Sun free; ⏲8am-6pm Mon, Wed & Fri, 8am-8pm Thu, 10am-6pm Sat & Sun) Commemorates Warsaw's insurrection against its Nazi occupiers in 1944, which ended in the destruction of much of the city and its population. The moving story of the Rising is retold via photographs, exhibits and audiovisual displays, with captions in English. Catch tram 8, 22 or 24 west from Al Jerozolimskie.

The suburbs northwest of the Palace of Culture & Science were once predominantly inhabited by Jewish Poles.

Ghetto Heroes Monument MONUMENT
(cnr ul Anielewicza & ul Zamenhofa) This monument to the Jewish ghetto established here by the Nazis remembers its victims via pictorial plaques.

Central Warsaw

Sights
1 Chopin Museum ... D2
2 Church of the Holy Cross ... C1
3 National Museum ... D3
4 Tomb of the Unknown Soldier ... B1

Sleeping
5 Apartments Apart ... C3
6 Hostel Helvetia ... D1
7 Nathan's Villa Hostel ... C5
8 Oki Doki Hostel ... B2
9 Smolna Youth Hostel ... D3

Eating
10 Albert Supermarket ... A3
11 Cô Tú ... D3
12 Green Way ... B4
13 Sketch ... D3

Drinking
14 Między Nami ... C3
15 Paparazzi ... C1
16 Sense ... D3

Entertainment
17 El Presidente ... B1
18 Enklawa ... C1
19 Filharmonia Narodowa ... B2
20 Kino Atlantic ... C3
21 Kinoteka ... A3
22 Underground Music Café ... B2

Shopping
23 Wars & Sawa ... B3

FREE **Pawiak Prison Museum** MUSEUM
(ul Dzielna 24/26; 10am-4pm Wed-Sun) Once a Gestapo prison during the Nazi occupation, this institution now contains moving exhibits, including letters and other personal items.

Jewish Cemetery CEMETERY
(ul Okopowa 49/51; admission 4zł; 10am-5pm Mon-Thu, 9am-1pm Fri, 11am-4pm Sun) Founded in 1806, Europe's largest Jewish resting place has more than 100,000 gravestones. Visitors must wear a head-covering to enter, and it's accessible from the Old Town on bus 180, heading north from ul Nowy Świat.

Festivals & Events

Mozart Festival MUSIC
(www.operakameralna.pl) June/July.

Warsaw Summer Jazz Days MUSIC
(www.adamiakjazz.pl) July.

Street Art Festival PERFORMING ARTS
(www.sztukaulicy.pl) July.

Warsaw Autumn International Festival of Contemporary Music MUSIC
(www.warsaw-autumn.art.pl) September.

Warsaw Film Festival FILM
(www.wff.pl) October.

Sleeping

Warsaw is the most expensive city in Poland for accommodation, though there are several reasonably priced hostels around town.

TOP CHOICE **Castle Inn** HOTEL €€
(22 425 0100; www.castleinn.eu; ul Świętojańska 2; s/d from 235/265zł) Progress up the stairs to the striking purple decor and shiny tiles of this Old Town hotel, situated in a 17th-century tenement house. All rooms overlook either Castle Sq or St John's Cathedral, and come in a range of playful styles.

Oki Doki Hostel HOSTEL €
(22 828 0122; www.okidoki.pl; Plac Dąbrowskiego 3; dm 37-73zł, s/d 132/220zł) Each dorm is decorated thematically using the brightest paints available; try the communist (red with a big image of Lenin). The hostel also has a bar, a free washing machine and a kitchen, and hires out bikes (27zł per day).

Nathan's Villa Hostel HOSTEL €
(22 622 2946; www.nathansvilla.com; ul Piękna 24/26; dm 45-70zł, r 170-200zł) Nathan's sunlit courtyard leads to well-organised dorms and comfortable private rooms. The kitchen is well set up, and there's a laundry, a book exchange and games to while away rainy days.

Apartments Apart APARTMENTS €€
(22 351 2250; www.apartmentsapart.com; ul Nowy Świat 29/3; apt from €75) Agency offering a range of apartments dotted through the Old Town and the city centre. Most include a washing machine in addition to a kitchen. Check online first, as last-minute web specials can be great value.

Hotel Premiere Classe HOTEL €€
(☎22 624 0800; www.premiere-classe-warszawa.pl, in Polish; ul Towarowa 2; r 189zł) Rooms are small but bright, and neatly set up with modern furnishings. Guests can use the restaurants, bars and fitness centre in the neighbouring sister hotels.

Hostel Helvetia HOSTEL €
(☎22 826 7108; www.hostel-helvetia.pl; ul Kopernika 36/40; dm 45-57zł, r 160-220zł) Bright hostel with an attractive combined lounge and kitchen. Dorms have lockers available, and there's one small women-only dorm. Bike hire is 25zł per day. Enter from the street behind, ul Sewerynów.

Hostel Kanonia HOSTEL €
(☎22 635 0676; www.kanonia.pl; ul Jezuicka 2; dm 45zł, s/d 190/220zł) Housed in a historic building in the heart of the Old Town. Some rooms have picturesque views onto the cobblestone streets, and there's a dining room with basic kitchen facilities.

Smolna Youth Hostel HOSTEL €
(☎22 827 8952; www.hostelsmolna30.pl; ul Smolna 30; dm 40zł, s/d 70/130zł) Very central and popular, though there's a midnight curfew (2am in July and August) and reception is closed between 10am and 4pm. Note that guests are separated into dorms according to gender, and reception is up four flights of stairs.

Camping 123 CAMPING GROUND €
(☎22 823 3748; www.astur.waw.pl; ul Bitwy Warszawskiej 1920r 15/17; campsites per person/tent 14/14zł, cabins s/d 41/70zł;) Set in extensive grounds near the Dworzec Zachodnia bus station. The cabins are available from mid-April to mid-October, and there's a tennis court nearby.

Eating

Warsaw's eateries cover diverse cuisines and price ranges; a good selection can be found in the Old Town and around ul Nowy Świat.

Self-caterers can buy groceries at the **Albert Supermarket** (ul Złota 59) in the Złote Tarasy shopping centre behind Warszawa Centralna train station; and **ML Delikatesy** (ul Piwna 47) in the Old Town.

TOP CHOICE **Sketch** INTERNATIONAL €€
(☎60 276 2764; ul Foksal 19; mains 16-48zł; noon-1am) Shiny bright restaurant and bar serving baguettes, salads, pasta and grilled dishes. At weekends the joint throws a 'before party' with DJs in its upstairs room from 10pm.

Bar Mleczny Pod Barbakanem CAFETERIA €
(ul Mostowa 27/29; mains 4-9zł; 8am-5pm Mon-Fri, 9am-5pm Sat & Sun) This popular former milk bar that survived the fall of the Iron Curtain continues to serve cheap, unpretentious food.

Cô tú ASIAN €
(Hadlowo-Usługowe 21; mains 13-19zł; 10am-9pm Mon-Fri, 11am-7pm Sat & Sun) The wok at this simple Asian diner never rests, cooking up seafood, vegetable, beef, chicken and pork dishes. Duck through the archway at Nowy Świat 26 to find it.

Green Way VEGETARIAN €
(☎22 696 9321; ul Hoża 54; mains 8-15zł; 10am-8pm Mon-Fri, 11am-7pm Sat & Sun) Slicker than the usual outlets of this chain, with a cafe ambience and a good outdoor dining zone. Take your pick of the international menu, which includes goulash, curry, samosas and enchiladas.

Gospoda Pod Kogutem POLISH €€
(☎22 635 8282; ul Freta 50; mains 17-40zł) Cosy eatery at the top of the New Town, presenting quality versions of Polish classics in a soothing dark green interior. Eat outside in summer. If you're game, try pig's trotters 'the Polish way'.

Drinking

There's no shortage of good bars and clubs in Warsaw. Explore ul Mazowiecka, ul Sienkiewicza and the area around ul Nowy Świat for more action.

TOP CHOICE **Sense** BAR
(ul Nowy Świat 19; noon-late) Modern venue with a mellow atmosphere and an extensive wine and cocktail list. Try ginger rose vodka, the house speciality. There's also an impressive food menu.

Paparazzi BAR
(ul Mazowiecka 12) One of Warsaw's flashest venues, where you can sip a bewildering array of cocktails under big photos of Hollywood stars. It's big and roomy, with comfortable seating around the central bar.

Między Nami CAFE, BAR
(ul Bracka 20) A mix of bar, restaurant and cafe, 'Between You and Me' attracts a trendy set with its designer furniture, whitewashed walls, and excellent vegetarian menu.

Entertainment

To discover what's on, check out the *Visitor* and the cheeky but comprehensive *Warsaw*

SPLURGE

Attractive, old-fashioned **Restauracja Przy Zamku** (☎22 831 0259; Plac Zamkowy 15; mains 39-85zł) has hunting trophies on the walls and attentive, white-aproned waiters. The top-notch Polish menu includes fish and game and a bewildering array of starters – try the excellent hare pâté served with cranberry sauce.

in Your Pocket (5zł), available from tourist offices or online (www.inyourpocket.com/poland/warsaw).

Teatr Ateneum (☎22 625 2421; www.teatrateneum.pl, in Polish; ul Jaracza 2) leans towards contemporary Polish-language theatre productions, while **Teatr Wielki** (☎22 692 0200; www.teatrwielki.pl; Plac Teatralny 1) hosts opera and ballet. **Filharmonia Narodowa** (☎22 551 7111; www.filharmonia.pl; ul Jasna 5) is the venue for classical music concerts.

Free jazz concerts happen in the Old Town Market Sq on Saturday at 7pm in July and August.

Catch a film at the central **Kino Atlantic** (ul Chmielna 33), or **Kinoteka** (Plac Defilad 1) within the Palace of Culture & Science.

Clubbing

Enklawa CLUB
(www.enklawa.com, in Polish; ul Mazowiecka 12; ⌚9pm-4am Tue-Sat) Funky space with comfy plush seating, two bars and plenty of room to dance. Wednesday night is 'old school' night, with music from the '70s to the '90s.

El Presidente CLUB
(www.elpresidente.pl; ul Kredytowa 9; ⌚8pm-10pm Mon-Thu, 8pm-late Fri & Sat, noon-10pm Sun) Slickly decorated dance space with an illuminated gold bar contrasting with the black interior. Patrons are dressed to impress.

Underground Music Café CLUB
(www.under.pl, in Polish; ul Marszałkowska 126/134) Students and backpackers love this basement club for its cheap beer, dark lighting and diverse music. Enter via the staircase facing McDonald's.

Shopping

Wars & Sawa (ul Marszałowska 104/122) is a sprawling modern shopping mall in the city centre.

There are also plentiful antique, arts and crafts shops around the Old Town Market Sq, so brandish your credit card and explore.

Information

Internet Access

Verso Internet (ul Freta 17; ⌚8am-8pm Mon-Fri, 9am-5pm Sat, 10am-4pm Sun) Enter from the rear, off ul Świętojerska.

Warsaw Point Gallery (Złote Tarasy, ul Złota 59; ⌚9am-10pm) Pay at the information desk of this shopping mall.

Medical Services

Apteka Grabowskiego (Warszawa Centralna; ⌚24hr) Nonstop pharmacy at the train station.

Hospital of the Ministry of Internal Affairs & Administration (☎22 508 2000; ul Wołoska 137)

Tourist Information

Each tourist office provides free city maps and booklets (look out for *Warsaw in Short* and the *Visitor*), and helps book hotel rooms.

Tourist office (☎22 19431; www.warsawtour.pl) Old Town (Rynek Starego Miasta 19; ⌚9am-9pm May-Sep, 9am-7pm Oct-Apr); Okęcie airport (⌚8am-8pm May-Sep, 8am-7pm Oct-Apr); main hall of Warszawa Centralna train station (⌚8am-8pm May-Sep, 8am-7pm Oct-Apr)

Warsaw Tourist Information Centre (☎22 635 1881; www.wcit.waw.pl; pl Zamkowy 1/13; ⌚9am-6pm Mon-Fri, 10am-6pm Sat & Sun)

Warsaw Tourist Card (www.warsawcard.com; 1/3 days 35/65zł) Free or discounted access to museums, public transport and some theatres, sports centres and restaurants. Available from tourist offices.

Getting There & Away

Air

Frederic Chopin Airport (www.lotnisko-chopina.pl) is more commonly called Okęcie airport. Flights can be booked at the **LOT office** (☎0801 703 703; Al Jerozolimskie 65/79).

Bus 175 travels via Warszawa Centralna train station and ul Nowy Świat, terminating at Plac Piłsudskiego, about a 500m walk from Castle Sq in the Old Town. If you arrive in the wee hours, night bus N32 links the airport with Warszawa Centralna train station every 30 minutes. The taxi fare between the airport and the city centre is from 40zł to 45zł.

Bus

Warsaw has two major bus terminals for PKS buses. **Dworzec Zachodnia** (Western Bus Station; www.pksbilety.pl; Al Jerozolimskie 144) handles domestic buses heading south, north and west of the capital, including nine daily to Częstochowa (41zł, 3½ hours), 13 to Gdańsk (53zł, six hours), seven to Kraków (48zł, six hours), 15 to Toruń (42zł, four hours), five to Wrocław (54zł, seven hours) and five to Zakopane (60zł, eight hours).

Dworzec Stadion (Stadium Bus Station; www.pksbilety.pl; ul Sokola 1) handles domestic buses to the east and southeast, including 16 daily to Lublin (23zł, three hours) and three to Zamość (35zł, 4¾ hours).

International buses depart from and arrive at Dworzec Zachodnia or, occasionally, outside Warszawa Centralna.

Train

The train station that most travellers will use is **Warszawa Centralna** (Warsaw Central; Al Jerozolimskie 54). However, it's not always where trains start or finish, so make sure you get on or off promptly.

Getting Around

Public Transport

The standard ticket (2.80zł) is valid for one ride only on a bus, tram or metro train travelling anywhere in the city. Warsaw is the only place in Poland where holders of International Student Identity Cards (ISIC) get a public-transport discount (48%).

Tickets are also available for 60/90 minutes (4/6zł), one day (9zł), three days (16zł), one week (32zł) and one month (78zł). Buy tickets from kiosks (including those marked RUCH) before boarding, and validate them on board.

Taxi

Taxis are a quick and easy way to get around. Beware of unauthorised 'Mafia' taxis parked in front of top-end hotels, at the airport, outside Warszawa Centralna train station and in the vicinity of most tourist sights. To avoid them, always look for a cab with signage on its roof bearing the company's name and phone number.

MAŁOPOLSKA

Małopolska (literally 'lesser Poland') is a beautiful area, within which the visitor can spot plentiful remnants of traditional life amid green farmland and historic cities. The region covers a large swath of southeastern Poland, from the former royal capital, Kraków, to the eastern Lublin Uplands.

Kraków

POP 755,000

While many Polish cities are centred on an attractive Old Town, none can compare with Kraków for sheer effortless beauty. Miraculously escaping from destruction in WWII, the city seems to have led a lucky existence. As it was the royal capital of Poland until 1596, Kraków is packed with attractive historic buildings and streetscapes. The city's centrepiece is the stunning Wawel Castle and Cathedral.

Just outside the Old Town lies Kazimierz, the former Jewish quarter, its silent synagogues reflecting the tragedy of the recent past. The district's tiny streets and low-rise architecture make it an interesting place to explore.

Sights & Activities

OLD TOWN

Main Market Square HISTORIC SQUARE

(Rynek Główny) This vast square is the focus of the Old Town, and is Europe's largest medieval town square (200m by 200m). Climb its most prominent feature, the 15th-century **town hall tower** (adult/concession 7/5zł; ⌚10.30am-6pm May-Oct).

Cloth Hall MARKET

At the centre of the square is this 16th-century Renaissance building (known in Polish as the Sukiennice), which houses a large souvenir market. Here you can enter **Rynek Underground** (www.podziemiarynku.com; adult/concession 13/10zł, Mon free; ⌚10am-8pm Wed-Mon, 10am-4pm Tue), a fascinating new attraction beneath the market square, consisting of an underground route through medieval market stalls and other long-forgotten chambers. The experience is enhanced by holograms and other audiovisual wizardry.

St Mary's Church CHURCH

(Rynek Główny 4; adult/concession 6/4zł; ⌚11.30am-6pm Mon-Sat, 2-6pm Sun) This 14th-century place of worship fills the northeastern corner of the square. The huge main altarpiece by Wit Stwosz (Veit Stoss in German) of Nuremberg is the finest Gothic sculpture in Poland, and is opened ceremoniously each day at 11.50am.

Every hour a *hejnał* (bugle call) is played from the highest tower of the church, breaking off abruptly to commemorate the moment when the throat of a 13th-century trumpeter was pierced by a Tatar arrow. Between May and August you can climb the **tower** (adult/concession 5/3zł).

Collegium Maius HISTORIC UNIVERSITY

(ul Jagiellońska 15; adult/concession 12/6zł; ⌚10am-2.20pm Mon-Fri, 10am-1.20pm Sat) Guided tours of Poland's oldest surviving university building run half-hourly; there's usually a couple in English, at 11am and 1pm. Even if you don't go on a tour, check out the magnificent arcaded courtyard.

Historical Museum of Kraków MUSEUM
(www.mhk.pl; Rynek Główny 35; adult/concession 8/6zł, Sat free; ⌚10am-5pm Tue-Sun) On the northwest corner of the Rynek, this institution contains paintings, documents and oddments relating to the city.

Florian Gate FORTIFICATION
This 14th-century gate is a tourism hot spot, with crowds, buskers, and artists selling their work along the remnant section of the old city walls. Beyond it is the **Barbican** (adult/concession 6/4zł; ⌚10.30am-6pm Apr-Oct), a defensive bastion built in 1498.

Czartoryski Museum ART MUSEUM
(ul Św. Jana 19) Near the Florian Gate, this museum features an impressive collection of weaponry and European art. At the time of research it was undergoing a major renovation, expected to take until 2012.

Historic Churches CHURCHES
South of the square is the 17th-century Jesuit **Church of SS Peter & Paul** (ul Grodzka 64; ⌚dawn-dusk), Poland's first baroque church. Nearby, the Romanesque 11th-century **Church of St Andrew** (ul Grodzka 56; ⌚9am-6pm Mon-Fri) was the only building in Kraków to withstand the Tatars' attack of 1241.

WAWEL HILL

South of the Old Town, this prominent mount is crowned with a castle containing a cathedral, both of which are enduring symbols of Poland.

Wawel Castle CASTLE
(☎12 422 5155; www.wawel.krakow.pl; grounds admission free; ⌚6am-dusk) You can choose from several attractions within this magnificent structure, each requiring a separate ticket.

Most popular are the splendid **State Rooms** (adult/concession 17/10zł, Sun free Nov-Mar; ⌚9.30am-5pm Tue-Fri, 11am-6pm Sat & Sun Apr-Oct, 10am-4pm Tue-Sun Nov-Mar) and **Royal Private Apartments** (adult/concession 24/18zł; ⌚9.30am-5pm Tue-Fri, 11am-6pm Sat & Sun Apr-Oct, 9.30am-4pm Tue-Sat Nov-Mar). Entry to the latter is only allowed on a guided tour; you may have to accompany a Polish-language tour if it's the only one remaining for the day. To hire a guide who speaks English or other languages, contact the on-site **guides office** (☎12 422 1697).

The 14th-century **Wawel Cathedral** (www.katedra-wawelska.pl; admission free; ⌚9am-5pm Mon-Sat, 12.30-5pm Sun) was the coronation and burial place of Polish royalty for four centuries. Within is the **Cathedral Museum** (adult/concession 12/7zł; ⌚10am-3pm Tue-Sun), the **Royal Tombs**; and the **bell tower** of the golden-domed **Sigismund Chapel** (1539), which contains the country's largest bell (11 tonnes).

Other attractions within the castle grounds include the **Museum of Oriental Art** (adult/concession 8/5zł; ⌚9.30am-5pm Tue-Fri, 11am-6pm Sat & Sun Apr-Oct, 9.30am-4pm Tue-Sat Nov-Mar); the **Crown Treasury & Armoury** (adult/concession 15/8zł, Mon free; ⌚9.30am-5pm Tue-Fri, 11am-6pm Sat & Sun Apr-Oct, 9.30am-4pm Tue-Sun Nov-Mar); the **Lost Wawel** (adult/concession 8/5zł, Mon free Apr-Oct, Sun free Nov-Mar; ⌚9.30am-1pm Mon, 9.30am-5pm Tue-Fri, 11am-6pm Sat & Sun Apr-Oct, 9.30am-4pm Tue-Sat, 10am-4pm Sun Nov-Mar), and the atmospheric **Dragon's Den** (admission 3zł; ⌚10am-5pm Apr-Oct). Go here last, as this cave's exit leads out onto the riverbank.

KAZIMIERZ & PODGÓRZE

Founded by King Kazimierz the Great in 1335, Kazimierz was originally an independent town which became a Jewish district. Its community was devastated in the Holocaust. If you want to learn more, **Jarden Tourist Agency** (☎12 421 71 66; www.jarden.pl; ul Szeroka 2; tours 60zł) runs tours.

Jewish Museum MUSEUM
(ul Szeroka 24; adult/concession 8/6zł, Mon free; ⌚10am-2pm Mon, 10am-5pm Tue-Sun Apr-Oct, 10am-2pm Mon, 9am-4pm Wed-Sun Nov-Mar) This museum with exhibitions on Jewish traditions is housed in the 15th-century **Old Synagogue**, the oldest in Poland.

Galicia Jewish Museum MUSEUM
(www.galiciajewishmuseum.org; ul Dajwór 18; adult/concession 15/8zł; ⌚10am-6pm) Fine photographic exhibition depicts modern-day traces of southeastern Poland's once thriving Jewish community.

TOP CHOICE **Schindler's Factory** MUSEUM
(www.mhk.pl; ul Lipowa 4; adult/concession 15/13zł; ⌚10am-2pm Mon, 10am-6pm Tue-Sun) Impressive new facility covering the Nazi occupation of Kraków in WWII, housed in the former enamel factory of Oskar Schindler, immortalised in Steven Spielberg's haunting film *Schindler's List*.

Kraków – Old Town & Wawel

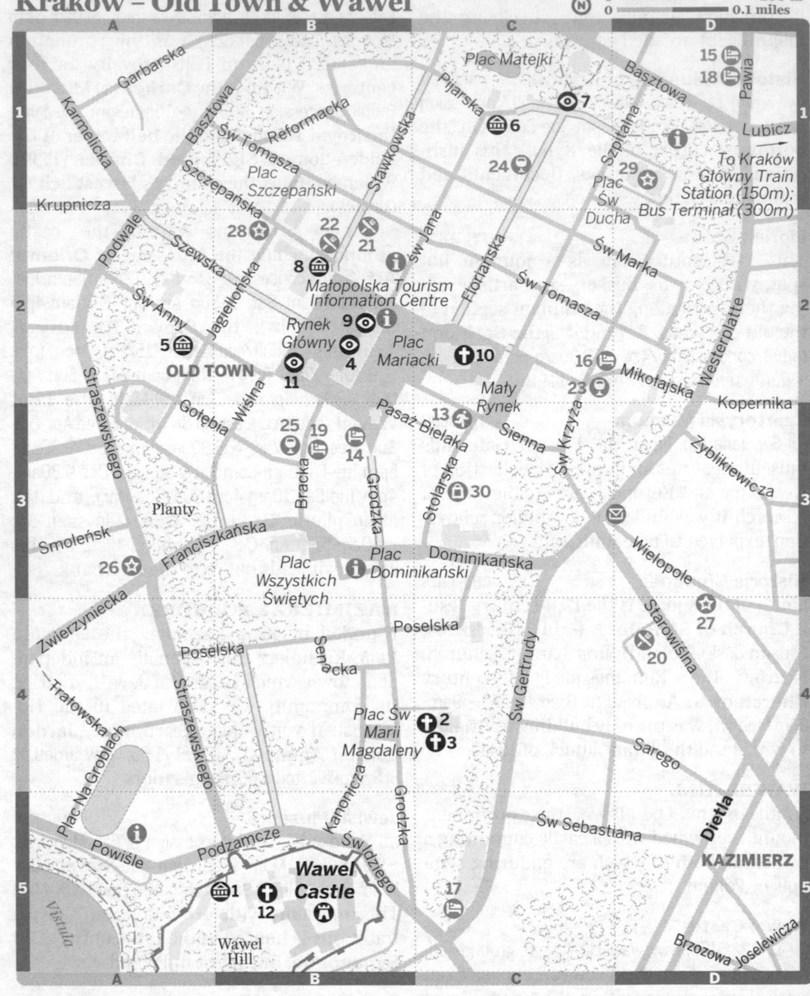

Activities

English Language Club SOCIAL GROUP
(ul Sienna 5; admission 2zł; ⏰6-8pm Wed) Just south of St Mary's, this social group has met weekly since the dying days of communism. Its meetings are a fun way to meet a mixed bunch of Poles, expats and tourists.

Festivals & Events

Organ Music Festival MUSIC
March.

Krakow International Film Festival FILM
(www.kff.com.pl) May/June.

Jewish Culture Festival JEWISH
(www.jewishfestival.pl) June/July.

International Festival of Street Theatre STREET FESTIVAL
July.

Summer Jazz Festival JAZZ
(www.cracjazz.com) July/August.

Sleeping

Kraków is unquestionably Poland's major tourist destination, with prices to match. An agency offering decent private rooms is **Jordan Tourist Information & Accommo-**

Kraków – Old Town & Wawel

Top Sights
Wawel Castle B5

Sights
1 Cathedral Museum B5
2 Church of SS Peter & Paul C4
3 Church of St Andrew C4
4 Cloth Hall B2
5 Collegium Maius A2
6 Czartoryski Museum C1
7 Florian Gate C1
8 Historical Museum of Kraków B2
9 Rynek Underground B2
10 St Mary's Church C2
11 Town Hall Tower B2
12 Wawel Cathedral B5

Activities, Courses & Tours
13 English Language Club C3

Sleeping
14 Cracow Hostel B3
15 Greg & Tom Hostel D1
16 Hotel Amadeus C2
17 Hotel Royal C5
18 Jordan Tourist Information & Accomodation Centre D1
19 Mama's Hostel B3

Eating
20 Il Calzone D4
21 Metropolitan B2
22 Restauracja pod Gruszką B2

Drinking
23 Paparazzi C2
24 Piwnica Pod Złotą Pipą C1
25 Rdza B3

Entertainment
26 Filharmonia Krakowska A3
27 Łubu-Dubu D4
28 Stary Teatr B2
29 Teatr im Słowackiego D1

Shopping
30 Galeria Plakatu C3
Souvenir Market .... (see 4)

dation Centre (☎12 422 6091; www.jordan.pl; ul Pawia 8; s/d from 130/150zł; ⏰8am-6pm Mon-Fri, 9am-2pm Sat).

TOP CHOICE **Mama's Hostel** HOSTEL €
(☎12 429 5940; www.mamashostel.com.pl; ul Bracka 4; dm 50-60zł, d 180zł) Centrally located red-and-orange lodgings with a beautiful sunlit lounge overlooking a courtyard, with the aroma of freshly roasted coffee drifting up from a cafe below. There's a washing machine on site.

Nathan's Villa Hostel HOSTEL €
(☎12 422 3545; www.nathansvilla.com; ul Św. Agnieszki 1; dm from 45zł, d 180zł) Comfy rooms and a friendly atmosphere make this place a big hit with backpackers, along with its cellar bar, mini-cinema, beer garden and pool table.

Hotel Abel HOTEL €€
(☎12 411 8736; www.hotelabel.pl; ul Józefa 30; s/d 170/200zł) Reflecting the character of Kazimierz, this hotel has a distinctive personality, evident in its polished wooden staircase, arched brickwork and age-worn tiles.

Tournet Pokoje Gościnne HOTEL €€
(☎12 292 0088; www.accommodation.krakow.pl; ul Miodowa 7; s/d from 150/200zł) This is a neat pension in Kazimierz, offering simple but comfortable and quiet rooms with compact bathrooms.

Greg & Tom Hostel HOSTEL €
(☎12 422 4100; www.gregtomhostel.com; ul Pawia 12; dm 50zł, d from 130zł) This well-run hostel is spread over two locations; the private rooms are a 10-minute walk away on ul Warszawska. Laundry facilities are included.

Cracow Hostel HOSTEL €
(☎12 429 1106; www.cracowhostel.com; Rynek Główny 18; dm 40-85zł, d 170zł) This place is perched high above the Main Market Sq, and has an amazing view of St Mary's Church. There's also a kitchen and a washing machine.

Good Bye Lenin Hostel HOSTEL €
(☎12 421 2030; www.goodbyelenin.com; ul Joselewicza 23; dm 35zł, d 140zł) Comically decorated communist-themed hostel, with numerous common spaces including a basement bar with a pool table. There's a washing machine, and one female-only dorm.

Hotel Royal HOTEL €€
(☎12 421 3500; www.hotelewam.pl; ul Św. Gertrudy 26-29; s/d from 220/320zł) Impressive art nouveau edifice below Wawel Castle. It's split

SPLURGE

Everything about **Hotel Amadeus** (☎12 429 6070; www.hotel-amadeus.pl; ul Mikołajska 20; s/d €130/150) screams 'class' – or rather, speaks it softly in a well-modulated tone. Rooms are tastefully furnished, and there's a sauna, a fitness centre and an accomplished restaurant. While hanging around the foyer, you can check out photos of famous guests.

into two sections: the higher-priced rooms are cosy, and preferable to the fairly basic rooms at the back.

Camping Smok CAMPING GROUND €
(☎12 429 8300; www.smok.krakow.pl; ul Kamedulska 18; campsites per person/tent 22/15zł, r 120-200zł) This camping ground is small, quiet and located 4km west of the Old Town. To get here from Kraków Główny train station, take tram 1, 2 or 6 to the end of the line in Zwierzyniec (destination marked 'Salwator') and change for any westbound bus (except bus 100).

Eating

Kraków is a food lover's paradise, packed with restaurants serving a wide range of international cuisines. There's a **supermarket** within the Galeria Krakowska shopping mall, next to the train station.

TOP CHOICE **Momo** VEGETARIAN €
(☎60 968 5775; ul Dietla 49; mains 8-17zł; ⏰11am-8pm) Vegans will cross the doorstep of this Kazimierz restaurant with relief – the majority of the menu is completely animal-free. The Tibetan dumplings are a treat worth ordering.

Restauracja Pod Gruszką POLISH €€
(☎12 346 5704; ul Szczepańska 1; mains 12-59zł; ⏰noon-midnight) A favourite haunt of writers and artists, with elaborate old-fashioned decor. The menu covers a range of Polish dishes, the most distinctive being the soups served within small bread loaves.

Il Calzone ITALIAN €€
(☎12 429 5141; ul Starowiślna 15a; mains 15-44zł; ⏰noon-11pm Mon-Thu) This pleasant slice of Italy is a well-kept secret, tucked away in a quiet nook set back from the street.

Ariel JEWISH €€
(☎12 421 7920; ul Szeroka 18; mains 11-51zł) Atmospheric Jewish restaurant packed with old-fashioned timber furniture, serving a range of kosher dishes. There's often live music here at night.

Metropolitan INTERNATIONAL €€
(☎12 421 9803; ul Sławkowska 3; mains 16-69zł; ⏰7.30am-midnight Mon-Sat, 7.30am-10pm Sun) Attached to Hotel Saski, this is a great place for breakfast. It also serves pasta, grills and steaks.

Drinking

There are hundreds of pubs and bars in Kraków's Old Town, many housed in ancient vaulted cellars. Kazimierz also has a lively bar scene, centred on Plac Nowy and its surrounding streets.

Paparazzi BAR
(ul Mikołajska 9; ⏰11am-1am Mon-Fri, 4pm-4am Sat & Sun) Bright, modern place, with photos of celebrities covering the walls and a diverse drinks menu. There's also inexpensive bar food.

Singer BAR
(ul Estery 20; ⏰9am-4am Sun-Thu, 9am-5am Fri & Sat) Laid-back Kazimierz hang-out with a moody candlelit interior. Alternatively, sit outside and converse over a sewing machine affixed to the table.

Piwnica Pod Złotą Pipą PUB
(ul Floriańska 30; ⏰noon-midnight) Less claustrophobic than other cellar bars, with lots of tables for eating or drinking. Decent bar food and international beers on tap.

TOP CHOICE **Alchemia** BAR, CLUB
(ul Estery 5; ⏰9am-3am) This Kazimierz venue exudes a shabby-is-the-new-cool look with rough-hewn wooden benches and candlelit tables. It hosts regular live music gigs and theatrical events.

Entertainment

The monthly Polish-English booklet *Karnet* (4zł) lists almost every event in the city.

Clubbing

Łubu-Dubu CLUB
(ul Wielopole 15; ⏰7pm-late) The name of this grungy upstairs joint (*woo*boo-*doo*boo) is as funky as its '70s decor. DJs spin old-school tracks, and a series of rooms creates spaces for talking or dancing as the mood strikes.

Rdza CLUB

(www.rdza.pl; ul Bracka 3/5; 7pm-late) Basement club with Polish house music bouncing off exposed brick walls and comfy sofas. Guest DJs start spinning at 9pm.

Arts

Stary Teatr THEATRE

(12 422 4040; www.stary-teatr.pl, in Polish; ul Jagiellońska 5) Offers quality theatre.

Teatr im Słowackiego OPERA, THEATRE

(12 422 4022; Plac Św Ducha 1) Built in 1893, this theatre focuses on Polish classics and large productions.

Filharmonia Krakowska CLASSICAL MUSIC

(12 422 9477; www.filharmonia.krakow.pl; ul Zwierzyniecka 1) Concerts are usually held on Friday and Saturday.

Kino Sztuka CINEMA

(cnr ul Św. Tomasza & ul Św. Jana) Central cinema in eccentric arty premises.

Shopping

The place to start (or perhaps end) your Kraków shopping is at the large **souvenir market** within the Cloth Hall. Fascinating examples of Polish poster art can be purchased at **Galeria Plakatu** (12 421 2640; www.cracowpostergallery.com; ul Stolarska 8; 11am-6pm Mon-Fri, 11am-2pm Sat).

Information

Internet Access

Greenland Internet Café (ul Floriańska 30; per hr 4zł; 9am-midnight)

Klub Garinet (ul Floriańska 18; per hr 4zł; 9am-10pm)

Tourist Information

Two free magazines, *Welcome to Cracow & Małopolska* and *Visitor: Kraków & Zakopane*, are available at tourist offices. The useful *Kraków in Your Pocket* booklet (5zł) can also be downloaded for free (www.inyourpocket.com/poland/krakow).

Kraków Tourist Card (www.krakowcard.com; 2/3 days 50/65zł) Available from tourist offices, the card includes travel on public transport and entry to many museums.

Tourist office ul S'w. Jana (12 421 7787; www.karnet.krakow.pl; ul Św. Jana 2; 10am-6pm); Cloth Hall (12 433 7310; Rynek Główny 1; 9am-7pm May-Sep, 9am-5pm Oct-Apr); northeastern Old Town (12 432 0110; ul Szpitalna 25; 9am-7pm May-Sep, 9am-5pm Oct-Apr); southern Old Town (12 616 1886; Plac Wszystkich Świętych 2; 9am-7pm May-Sep, 9am-5pm Oct-Apr); Wawel Hill (ul Powiśle 11; 9am-7pm); Kazimierz (12 422 0471; ul Józefa 7; 9am-5pm)

Getting There & Away

The **John Paul II International Airport** (www.lotnisko-balice.pl) is accessible by train (8zł, 17 minutes, half-hourly) from Kraków Główny station.

LOT flies between Kraków and Warsaw several times a day, and there are daily flights via Jet Air to Poznań and Gdańsk. Budget operators connect Kraków to various European cities, including an array of destinations across Britain and Ireland.

The modern main **bus terminal** (ul Bosacka 18) is conveniently located on the other side of the main train station from the Old Town, but its services are of limited interest.

Kraków Główny train station (Plac Dworcowy), on the northeastern outskirts of the Old Town, handles all international trains and most domestic rail services. Each day from Kraków, 20 trains head to Warsaw, most of them fast Express InterCity services (110zł, 2½ hours). There are also 17 trains daily to Wrocław (48zł, 4¾ hours), 10 to Częstochowa (33zł, 2¼ hours), 14 to Poznań (56zł, 7½ hours), eight to Toruń (58zł, eight hours), nine to Zakopane (35zł, 3½ hours) and two to Lublin (53zł, 4¾ hours). The 10 services to Gdynia via Gdańsk are evenly split between five TLK trains (68zł, 13 hours) and five much faster Express InterCity services (129zł, nine hours).

Oświęcim

POP 40,800

Few place names have more impact than **Auschwitz**, which is seared into public consciousness as the location of history's most extensive experiment in genocide. Every year hundreds of thousands visit Oświęcim (osh-*fyen*-cheem) to learn about the infamous Nazi death camp's history, and to pay respect to the dead.

Established within disused army barracks in 1940, Auschwitz was expanded into the largest centre for the extermination of European Jews. Two more camps were subsequently established nearby: Birkenau (Brzezinka), also known as Auschwitz II, and Monowitz (Monowice). In the course of their operation, between one and 1.5 million people were murdered in these death factories.

Many of Auschwitz's original buildings remain, serving as a bleak document of the camp's history. A dozen surviving prison blocks house sections of the **State Museum Auschwitz-Birkenau** (☎33 844 8100; www.auschwitz.org.pl; admission free; ⏰8am-7pm Jun-Aug, 8am-6pm May & Sep, 8am-5pm Apr & Oct, 8am-4pm Mar & Nov, 8am-3pm Dec-Feb).

The murder of huge numbers of Jews and other inmates took place at **Birkenau** (admission free; ⏰8am-7pm Jun-Aug, 8am-6pm May & Sep, 8am-5pm Apr & Oct, 8am-4pm Mar & Nov, 8am-3pm Dec-Feb). Although much of the camp was destroyed by retreating Nazis, the size of the place provides some idea of the scale of this heinous crime.

English-language **tours** (adult/concession 39/30zł, 3½ hours) of Auschwitz and Birkenau leave at 10am, 11am, 1pm and 3pm daily. Between May and October it's compulsory to join a tour if you arrive between 10am and 3pm. About every half-hour, the cinema in the visitors centre at the entrance to Auschwitz shows a 15-minute documentary **film** (adult/concession 3.50/2.50zł) about the liberation of the camp by Soviet troops on 27 January 1945.

Some basic explanations in Polish, English and Hebrew are provided on site, but you'll understand more if you buy the *Auschwitz Birkenau Guide Book* (translated into about 15 languages) from the visitors centre.

Getting There & Away

Buses run approximately hourly from the bus station in Kraków to Oświęcim (11zł, 1½ hours), either passing by or terminating at the museum.

Every half-hour from 11.30am to 4.30pm between 15 April and 31 October, free buses run between the visitors centres at Auschwitz and Birkenau (operating to 5.30pm in May and September, and to 6.30pm from June to August). Otherwise, follow the signs for an easy 3km walk between both places.

Lublin

POP 350,000

If the crowds are becoming too much in Kraków, you could do worse than jump on a train to Lublin. This attractive eastern city has many of the same attractions – a beautiful Old Town, a castle, good bars and restaurants – but is less visited by international tourists.

It's also remembered for an important moment in Polish history: in 1569 the Lublin Union was signed here, uniting Poland and Lithuania. Today its beautifully preserved Old Town is an attractive blend of Gothic, Renaissance and baroque architecture.

Sights

Lublin Castle CASTLE

A substantial fortification that was constructed in the 14th century, then rebuilt as a prison in the 1820s. During the Nazi occupation, more than 100,000 people passed through its doors before being deported to the death camps. Its major occupant is now the **Lublin Museum** (www.zamek-lublin.pl; ul Zamkowa 9; adult/concession 7.50/5.50zł; ⏰9am-4pm Wed-Sat, 9am-5pm Sun).

Underground Route WALKING TOUR

(Rynek 1; adult/concession 10/7zł; ⏰10am-4pm) This 280m trail winds its way through connected cellars beneath the Old Town. Entry is from the neoclassical **Old Town Hall** in the **Market Square** (Rynek in Polish) at approximately two-hourly intervals.

Historical Museum of Lublin MUSEUM

(Plac Łokietka 3; adult/concession 3.50/2.50zł; ⏰9am-4pm Wed-Sat, 9am-5pm Sun) Situated within the 14th-century **Kraków Gate**, this institution displays documents and photos relating the city's history.

Archdiocesan Museum MUSEUM

(Plac Katedralny; adult/concession 7/5zł; ⏰10am-2.30pm Tue-Fri, 10am-5pm Sat & Sun) This museum of sacred art also offers expansive views of the Old Town, as it's housed within the lofty **Trinitarian Tower** (1819).

Cathedral CHURCH

(Plac Katedralny; ⏰dawn-dusk) Near the Trinitarian Tower is this 16th-century place of worship and its impressive baroque frescos. The painting of the Virgin Mary is said to have shed tears in 1949.

FREE **Majdanek State Museum** MEMORIAL

(www.majdanek.pl; ⏰9am-4pm) About 4km southeast of the Old Town is this former Nazi death camp where some 235,000 people, including more than 100,000 Jews, were massacred. Barracks, guard towers and barbed-wire fences remain in place; even more chilling are the crematorium and gas chambers.

Trolleybus 156 and bus 23 leave from a stop near the Bank Pekao on ul Królewska, to the entrance of Majdanek.

Sleeping

Hostel Lublin HOSTEL €

(☎79 288 8632; www.hostellublin.pl; ul Lubartowska 60; dm 40zł, r 95zł) The city's first modern hostel contains neat, tidy dorms, a basic kitchenette and a cosy lounge. Take trolleybus 156 or 160 north from the Old Town.

Dom Nauczyciela HOTEL €€
(☎81 533 8285; www.lublin.oupis.pl/hotel; ul Akademicka 4; s/d from 134/162zł) Value-packed accommodation in the heart of the university quarter, west of the Old Town. Rooms have old-fashioned decor but are clean, with good bathrooms.

Youth Hostel HOSTEL €
(☎81 533 0628; ul Długosza 6; dm 32zł, d 72zł) Simple rooms are decorated with potted plants, and there's a kitchen and a pleasant courtyard area. It's 100m up a poorly marked lane off ul Długosza.

Lubelskie Samorządowe Centrum Doskonalenia Nauczycieli HOSTEL €
(☎81 532 9241; www.lscdn.pl; ul Dominikańska 5; dm 52zł) This place is in an atmospheric Old Town building, and has rooms with between two and five beds.

Camping Marina CAMPING GROUND €
(☎81 745 6910; www.graf-marina.pl, in Polish; ul Krężnicka 6; per tent 16zł, cabins from 70zł) Lublin's only camping ground is serenely located on a lake about 8km south of the Old Town. To get there, take bus 25 from the stop on the main road east of the train station.

Eating & Drinking

There's a **supermarket** located near the bus terminal.

TOP CHOICE **Magia** INTERNATIONAL €€
(☎81 532 3041; ul Grodzka 2; mains 20-65zł; ⊙noon-midnight) Charming, relaxed restaurant with a large outdoor courtyard. Dishes range from tiger shrimps and snails to deer and duck, with every sort of pizza, pasta and pancake between.

Biesy POLISH €€
(☎81 532 1648; Rynek 18; mains 12-47zł) Atmospheric cellar eatery whose tasty speciality is large pizza-like baked tarts with a variety of toppings.

Pizzeria Acerna PIZZA €
(☎81 532 4531; Rynek 2; mains 10-35zł) Popular eatery on the main square, serving cheap pizzas and pasta in dazzling variations.

Caram'bola Pub PUB
(ul Kościuszki 8; ⊙10am-late Mon-Fri, noon-late Sat & Sun) Pleasant place for a beer or two, with inexpensive bar food.

Information

Net Box (ul Krakowskie Przedmieście 52; per hr 5zł; ⊙9am-9pm Mon-Fri, 10am-8pm Sat, 2-6pm Sun) Internet access in a courtyard off the street.

Tourist office (☎81 532 4412; www.loit.lublin.pl; ul Jezuicka 1/3; ⊙9am-7pm Mon-Fri, 10am-5pm Sat, 10am-4pm Sun May-Sep, 9am-5pm Mon-Fri, 10am-4pm Sat Oct-Apr) Lots of free brochures, including the city walking-route guide *Tourist Routes of Lublin*.

Getting There & Away

From the **bus terminal** (Al Tysiąclecia), opposite the castle, services head to Kraków (42zł, 5½ hours, five daily), Zakopane (56zł, nine hours, four daily), Zamość (16zł, two hours, hourly) and Warsaw (30zł, three hours, at least hourly). Private minibuses also head to various destinations, including Zamość (12zł, 1½ hours, half-hourly), from the minibus station north of the bus terminal.

The **train station** (Plac Dworcowy) is 1.2km south of the Old Town and accessible by bus 1 or 13. Services go to Warsaw (37zł, 2½ hours) and Kraków (53zł, 4¾ hours).

Zamość

POP 66,500

While most Polish cities date from the Middle Ages, Zamość (*zah*-moshch) is pure Renaissance. It was founded in 1580 by nobleman Jan Zamoyski and designed by an Italian architect, and was intended to become a prosperous trading settlement. The splendid architecture of Zamość's Old Town escaped destruction in WWII, and was added to Unesco's World Heritage list in 1992.

Sights

Great Market Square HISTORIC SQUARE
This impressive Italianate Renaissance square (Rynek Wielki in Polish) is the heart of Zamość's attractive Old Town. It's dominated by the lofty, pink **town hall** and surrounded by colourful arcaded burghers' houses, many adorned with elegant designs. The **Museum of Zamość** (ul Ormiańska 30; adult/concession 6/3zł; ⊙9am-4pm Tue-Sun) is based in two of the loveliest buildings on the square.

Cathedral CHURCH
Southwest of the square is the mighty 16th-century **cathedral** (ul Kolegiacka; ⊙dawn-dusk), whose **belfry** (admission 2zł; ⊙May-Sep) can be climbed. In the grounds, the **Sacral Museum** (admission 2zł; ⊙10am-4pm Mon-Fri, 10am-1pm Sat & Sun May-Sep, 10am-1pm Sun Oct-Apr) features various robes, paintings and sculptures.

Synagogue SYNAGOGUE
(ul Pereca 14) Before WWII, Jewish citizens accounted for 45% of the town's population. The most significant Jewish architectural relic is this Renaissance place of worship. At the time of research it was under renovation, being converted into a cultural centre and Jewish museum.

Bastion FORTIFICATION
(ul Łukasińskiego) On the eastern edge of the Old Town is the best surviving bastion from the original city walls. You can take a **tour** (adult/child 5/3zł; ⏲8am-6pm) through the renovated fortifications; tickets must be bought from the tourist office in the Great Market Sq.

Sleeping & Eating

For self-caterers, there's the handy **Lux mini-supermarket** (ul Grodzka 16; ⏲7am-8pm Mon-Sat, 8am-6pm Sun).

Hotel Arkadia HOTEL €€
(☎84 638 6507; www.arkadia.zamosc.pl; Rynek Wielki 9; s/d from 140/160zł) This shabby but charming hotel right on the market square also offers a pool table and restaurant.

Hotel Renesans HOTEL €€
(☎84 639 2001; www.hotelrenesans.pl; ul Grecka 6; s/d from 156/222zł) It's ironic that a hotel named after the Renaissance is housed in the Old Town's ugliest building. However, it's central and the rooms are surprisingly pleasant.

Camping Duet CAMPING GROUND €
(☎84 639 2499; ul Królowej Jadwigi 14; s/d 75/90zł;) West of the Old Town is this set of bungalows, with tennis courts and a restaurant. Larger bungalows sleep up to six.

Pokoje Gościnne OSiR HOSTEL €
(☎84 677 5460; ul Królowej Jadwigi 8; dm 24zł, s/d/tr 90/125/150zł) Located in a sprawling sporting complex, a 15-minute walk west of the Old Town. Rooms are plainly furnished, clean and comfortable.

Restauracja Muzealna POLISH €€
(☎84 638 7300; ul Ormiańska Ormianska 30; mains 14-27zł; ⏲11am-10pm Mon-Sat, 11am-9pm Sun) Subterranean restaurant serving a better class of Polish cuisine at reasonable prices, with a well-stocked bar.

Bar Asia POLISH €
(ul Staszica 10; mains 5-9zł; ⏲8am-5pm Mon-Fri, 8am-4pm Sat) Old-style *bar mleczny* dishes up cheap and tasty Polish food in a minimally decorated space.

Information

K@fejka Internetowa (Rynek Wielki 10; per hr 3zł; ⏲9am-5pm Mon-Fri, 10am-2pm Sat) Internet access.

Tourist office (☎84 639 2292; Rynek Wielki 13; ⏲8am-6pm Mon-Fri, 10am-5pm Sat & Sun May-Sep, 8am-5pm Mon-Fri, 9am-2pm Sat Oct-Apr)

Getting There & Away

The **bus terminal** (ul Hrubieszowska) is 2km east of the Old Town and reached by city buses 0 and 3. Daily buses go to Kraków (44zł, seven hours, four daily), Warsaw (35zł, 4¾ hours, three daily) and Lublin (16zł, two hours, hourly).

Quicker and cheaper are the minibuses that travel every 30 minutes between Lublin and Zamość (12zł, 1½ hours). They leave from the **minibus station** opposite the bus terminal in Zamość and from a corner north of the bus terminal in Lublin.

CARPATHIAN MOUNTAINS

The Carpathians (Karpaty) stretch from the southern border with Slovakia into Ukraine, and their wooded hills and snowy mountains are a beacon for hikers, skiers and cyclists. The most popular destination here is the mountain resort town of Zakopane.

Zakopane

POP 27,300

Zakopane is Poland's major winter sports centre, located at the foot of the Tatra Mountains. It may resemble a tourist trap, with its overcommercialised, overpriced exterior, but it has a relaxed, laid-back vibe that makes it a great place to chill out for a few days, even if you don't want to ski or hike.

Mt Gubałówka (1120m) offers excellent views over the Tatras. The **funicular** (adult/concession 1-way 10/8zł, return 15/12zł; ⏲8am-10pm Jul & Aug, 8.30am-6pm Apr-Jun & Sep, 8.30am-6pm Oct & Nov) covers the 1388m-long route in less than five minutes, climbing 300m from the funicular station just north of ul Krupówki.

Sleeping

Accommodation prices fluctuate considerably between low season and high season (the latter includes December to February, and July to August). Always book in advance.

Some travel agencies in Zakopane can arrange private rooms. Expect a double room

WORTH A TRIP

CZĘSTOCHOWA

It's not every day you get to meet a miracle worker. However, in the pilgrimage town of Częstochowa, 114km northwest of Kraków, you can come face to face with the **Black Madonna**. Since the 15th century, this religious portrait has been credited with miracles, from the summoning forth of spring water to the protection of the monastery during the Swedish sieges of the 1650s. In addition to the holy painting, the graceful Jasna Góra monastery houses three museums. Częstochowa has regular train connections with Warsaw, Kraków, Zakopane and Wrocław.

to cost about 80zł in the peak season in the town centre, and about 60zł for somewhere further out.

Locals offering private rooms may approach you at the bus or train stations; alternatively, just look out for signs posted in front of private homes – *noclegi* and *pokoje* both mean 'rooms available'.

Carlton HOTEL €€
(☎18 201 4415; www.carlton.pl; ul Grunwaldzka 11; s/d/tr 100/200/300zł) Good-value pension in a grand old house. There's an impressive shared balcony overlooking the road, and a big, comfy lounge lined with potted plants.

Youth Hostel Szarotka HOSTEL €
(☎18 201 3618; www.szarotkaptsm.republika.pl; ul Nowotarska 45; dm 40zł, d 100zł) This friendly, homely place is packed during the high season. There's a kitchen and washing machine on site. It's on a noisy road about a 10-minute walk from the town centre.

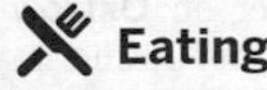

Eating

The main street, ul Krupówki, is lined with all sorts of eateries.

Pstrąg Górski SEAFOOD €€
(☎18 206 4613; ul Krupówki 6; mains 15-30zł; ⏲9am-10pm) This eatery, done up in traditional style and overlooking a narrow stream, serves some of the freshest trout, salmon and sea fish in town.

Stek Chałupa POLISH €€
(☎18 201 5918; ul Krupówki 33; mains 12-32zł; ⏲8am-midnight) Big, friendly barn of a place, with homely decor and waitresses in traditional garb. The menu features meat dishes, particularly steaks, though there are vegetarian choices among the salads and *pierogi*.

Information

Centrum Przewodnictwa Tatrzańskiego (Tatra Guide Centre; ☎18 206 37 99; ul Chałubińskiego 42a; ⏲9am-3pm) Arranges English-speaking mountain guides.

Tourist office (☎18 201 2211) bus station (ul Kościuszki 17; ⏲9am-5pm daily Jul & Aug, 9am-5pm Mon-Fri Sep-Jun); town (ul Kościeliska 7; ⏲9am-5pm daily Jul & Aug, 9am-5pm Mon-Fri Sep-Jun)

Widmo (ul Galicy 6; per hr 5zł; ⏲7.30am-midnight Mon-Fri, 9am-midnight Sat & Sun) Internet access.

Getting There & Away

From the **bus terminal** (ul Chramcówki), PKS buses run to Kraków every 45 to 60 minutes (18zł, two hours). Private companies Trans Frej and Szwagropol also run Kraków-bound buses (18zł) at the same frequency.

Two daily buses head to Poprad in Slovakia (18zł). Otherwise, catch a bus/minibus heading to Lake Morskie Oko and on to Polana Palenica. Get off at Łysa Polana, cross the Slovakian border on foot and catch an onward bus from there.

The **train station** (ul Chramcówki) has nine daily services to Kraków (35zł, 3½ hours), two to Częstochowa (48zł, 5½ hours), four to Lublin (56zł, nine hours), two to Gdynia via Gdańsk (70zł, 16 hours), one to Poznań (60zł, 11½ hours) and four to Warsaw (58zł, 8½ hours).

Tatra Mountains

The Tatras, 100km south of Kraków, form the highest range of the Carpathian Mountains, stretching across the Polish–Slovakian border. A quarter is in Poland and is mostly part of the Tatra National Park (about 212 sq km).

The **cable car** (www.pkl.pl; adult/concession return 42/32zł; ⏲7am-9pm Jul & Aug, 7.30am-5pm Apr-Jun, Sep & Oct, 8am-4pm Nov) trip from Kuźnice (2km south of Zakopane) to the summit of Mt Kasprowy Wierch (1985m) is a classic tourist experience. At the end of the trip, you can get off and stand with one foot in Poland and the other in Slovakia. Another popular destination is the emerald-green **Lake Morskie Oko** (Eye of the Sea), among the loveliest in the Tatras.

If you're doing any hiking in the Tatras, get a copy of the *Tatrzański Park Narodowy* map (1:25,000), which shows all the hiking trails in the area.

Zakopane boasts four major ski areas, and **Mt Kasprowy Wierch** and **Mt Gubałówka** offer the best conditions and most challenging slopes. The ski season extends until early May.

Camping isn't allowed, but **PTTK** (Polish Tourist Country Lovers Society; www.pttk.pl) maintains several mountain refuges and hostels, which provide simple accommodation. Check availability with the **PTTK office** (☎18 201 2429; ul Krupówki 12) in Zakopane.

SILESIA

Silesia (Śląsk, *shlonsk,* in Polish) is a fascinating mix of landscapes. Though the industrial zone around Katowice has limited attraction for visitors, beautiful Wrocław is a historic city with lively nightlife, and the Sudeten Mountains draw hikers and other nature lovers.

Wrocław

POP 632,000

When citizens of beautiful Kraków enthusiastically encourage you to visit Wrocław (*vrots*-wahf), you know you're onto something good. The city's beautiful Old Town is a gracious mix of Gothic and baroque styles, and its large student population ensures a healthy number of restaurants, bars and nightclubs.

Wrocław has been traded back and forth between various rulers over the centuries, having begun life in the year 1000. Upon its return to Poland from Germany in 1945, Wrocław was a shell of its former self, having sustained massive damage in WWII. Sensitive restoration has since returned the historic centre to its former splendour.

Sights

City Dwellers' Art Museum MUSEUM
(adult/concession 7/5zł; ⌚10am-5pm Tue-Sat, 10am-6pm Sun) The beautiful 14th-century **town hall** on the southern side of the attractive **Market Square** (Rynek) has stately rooms housing exhibits on the art of gold and the stories of famous Wrocław inhabitants.

Jaś i Małgosia HISTORIC HOUSES
(ul Św. Mikołaja) In the northwestern corner of the square are these two attractive small houses linked by a baroque gate. They're a couple better known to English speakers as Hansel and Gretel.

TOP CHOICE **Gnomes of Wrocław** STATUES
See if you can spot the diminutive statue of a gnome at ground level, just to the west of the Jaś i Małgosia houses; he's one of over 150 scattered through the city. You can buy a gnome map (5zł) from the tourist office.

Church of St Elizabeth CHURCH
(ul Elżbiety 1; admission 5zł; ⌚9am-6pm Mon-Fri, 11am-5pm Sat, 1-5pm Sun) Behind houses and gnome is this monumental 14th-century church with its 83m-high **tower**, which can be climbed for city views.

Panorama of Racławicka MONUMENTAL ARTWORK
(www.panoramaraclawicka.pl; ul Purkyniego 11; adult/concession 20/15zł; ⌚9am-5pm Tue-Sun May-Oct, 9am-4pm Tue-Sun Nov-Apr) Wrocław's major tourist attraction is this giant 360-degree painting of the 1794 Battle of Racławice, in which the Polish peasant army, led by Tadeusz Kościuszko, defeated Russian forces intent on partitioning Poland. It's an immense 114m long and 15m high.

Obligatory tours (with audio in English and other languages) run every 30 minutes between 9am and 4.30pm from April to November, and 10am and 3pm from December to March. The ticket also allows entry to the National Museum on the same day.

National Museum ART GALLERY
(www.mnwr.art.pl; Plac Powstańców Warszawy 5; adult/concession 15/10zł, Sat free; ⌚10am-4pm Wed-Fri & Sun, 10am-6pm Sat) Near the Panorama, this museum exhibits Silesian medieval art, and a fine collection of modern Polish painting.

Cathedral of St John the Baptist CHURCH
(Plac Katedralny; ⌚10am-6pm Mon-Sat, except during services) Across the river on **Ostrów Tumski** (Cathedral Island) is this Gothic cathedral, with a unique lift to whisk you to the top of its **tower** (adult/concession 5/4zł).

Botanical Gardens GARDENS
(ul Sienkiewicza 23; adult/concession 7/5zł; ⌚8am-6pm Apr-Oct) North of the cathedral are these charming gardens, where you can chill out among the chestnut trees and tulips.

Passage SCULPTURE
(cnr of ul Świdnicka & ul Piłsudskiego) This fascinating artwork depicts a group of pedestrians being swallowed by the pavement, only to re-emerge on the other side of the street.

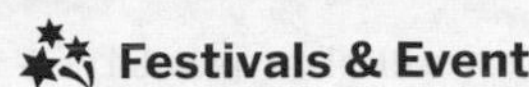

Festivals & Events

Jazz on the Odra International Festival MUSIC
(www.jnofestival.pl) February/March.

Castle Party MUSIC
(www.castleparty.com) July/August.

Wratislavia Cantans MUSIC
(www.wratislaviacantans.pl) September.

Sleeping

TOP CHOICE **Hotel Patio** HOTEL €€
(☎71 375 0400; www.hotelpatio.pl; ul Kiełbaśnicza 24; s/d from 249/279zł; ❄) Pleasant lodgings housed within two buildings linked by a covered sunlit courtyard. The breakfast spread is spectacular.

Hostel Babel HOSTEL €
(☎71 342 0250; www.babelhostel.pl; ul Kołłątaja 16; dm from 45zł, d 140zł) A tatty old staircase leads up to pleasant budget accommodation, and guests have free access to a kitchen and washing machine. There's a DVD player for rainy days.

Nathan's Villa Hostel HOSTEL €
(☎71 344 1095; www.nathansvilla.com; ul Świdnicka 13; dm from 40zł, r from 150zł) Comfortable 96-bed accommodation just 150m south of the Rynek. It sometimes hosts noisy Polish school groups, so check before you check in.

Hotel Zaułek HOTEL €€
(☎71 341 0046; www.hotelzaulek.pl; ul Garbary 11; s/d from 260/330zł) Run by the university, this guest house has a dozen homely rooms. The 1pm checkout is a plus for heavy sleepers. Breakfast is an additional 12zł.

Hotel Europejski HOTEL €€
(☎71 772 1000; www.silfor.pl; ul Piłsudskiego 88; s/d 179/219zł) Smart business hotel with clean, bright rooms, and handy for the train station. Breakfast is an extra 25zł.

MDK Youth Hostel HOSTEL €
(☎71 343 8856; www.mdk.kopernik.wroclaw.pl; ul Kołłątaja 20; dm/d from 27/72zł) Not far from the train station is this basic hostel located in a grand mustard-coloured building. It's almost always full, so book ahead.

Eating & Drinking

TOP CHOICE **Bazylia** CAFETERIA €
(Plac Uniwersytecki; mains per 100g 2.15zł; ⊙8am-7pm) Inexpensive and bustling modern take on the classic *bar mleczny,* in a curved space with huge plate-glass windows. The menu has a lot of Polish standards, and a decent range of salads and other vegetable dishes.

Bar Wegetariański Vega VEGETARIAN €
(☎71 344 3934; Rynek 1/2; mains 5-7zł; ⊙8am-7pm Mon-Fri, 9am-5pm Sat & Sun) Cheap cafeteria in the centre of the Rynek, offering vegie dishes and a good choice of soups and crepes. Upstairs there's a vegan section, open from noon.

Mexico Bar MEXICAN €€
(☎60 090 4577; ul Rzeźnicza 34; mains 16-35zł; ⊙11am-midnight) Compact, warmly lit restaurant featuring sombreros and a chandelier made of beer bottles. Book at least two days ahead for a table on weekends.

Pub Guinness PUB
(Plac Solny 5; ⊙noon-2am) A lively, fairly authentic Irish pub. The ground-floor bar buzzes with student and traveller groups getting together, and there's a restaurant and beer cellar as well.

PRL BAR, CLUB
(Rynek Ratusz 10; ⊙noon-late) The dictatorship of the proletariat is alive and well in this venue inspired by communist nostalgia.

Entertainment

Check out the (free and in English) bimonthly *Visitor* for details of what's on in this important cultural centre.

Teatr Polski THEATRE
(☎71 316 0777; www.teatrpolski.wroc.pl, in Polish; ul Zapolskiej 3) Stages classic Polish and foreign drama.

Filharmonia CLASSICAL MUSIC
(☎71 342 2001; www.filharmonia.wroclaw.pl; ul Piłsudskiego 19) Classical music concerts, mostly on Friday and Saturday nights.

Information

Tourist office (☎71 344 3111; www.wroclaw-info.pl; Rynek 14; ⊙9am-9pm Apr-Oct, 9am-7pm Nov-Mar)

W Sercu Miasta (ul Przejście Żelaźnicie 4; per hr 5zł; ⊙10am-11pm Mon-Fri, 10am-9pm Sat, noon-11pm Sun) Internet access down a laneway in the middle of Rynek.

Getting There & Away

From **Copernicus Airport** (www.airport.wroclaw.pl), LOT flies between Wrocław and Warsaw, Brussels, Frankfurt and Munich. Tickets can be purchased at the **LOT office** (☎801 703 703;

ul Piłsudskiego 36). Jet Air also links Wrocław to Gdańsk.

Various budget carriers connect Wrocław with other European cities, including British and Irish destinations. Consult the airport's website for details and schedules. The half-hourly bus 406 and night bus 249 link the airport with Wrocław Główny train station.

If you're travelling to/from Wrocław at the weekend by bus or train, you'll be in competition with thousands of itinerant university students, so book your ticket as early as possible.

The **bus terminal** (ul Sucha 11) is south of the main train station, and offers five daily buses to Warsaw (44zł, seven hours). For most other travel, however, the train is more convenient.

From **Wrocław Główny train station** (ul Piłsudskiego 105), trains to Kraków (48zł, 4¾ hours) depart every one or two hours, with similarly frequent services to Warsaw (118zł, 5½ hours). Wrocław is also linked by train to Poznań (37zł, 2½ hours, at least hourly), Częstochowa (37zł, three hours, four daily) and Toruń (51zł, five hours, two daily).

WIELKOPOLSKA

Wielkopolska (Greater Poland) is the region in which Poland came to life in the Middle Ages. As a result of this ancient eminence, its cities and towns are full of historic and cultural attractions. The region's historic significance didn't save it from international conflict, however, and it became part of Prussia in 1793. The battles of WWII later caused widespread destruction throughout the area, though Poznań has since been restored to its prominent economic role.

Poznań

POP 556,000

No one could accuse Poznań of being too sleepy. Between its regular trade fairs, student population and visiting travellers, it's a vibrant city with a wide choice of attractions. There's a beautiful Old Town at its centre, with a number of interesting museums and a range of lively bars, clubs and restaurants. The surrounding countryside is also good for cycling and hiking.

Sights

Historical Museum of Poznań MUSEUM
(adult/concession 5.50/3.50zł, Sat free; ⌚9am-3pm Tue-Thu, noon-9pm Fri, 11am-6pm Sat & Sun) Located within the Renaissance **town hall** on the bustling **Old Market Square** (Stary Rynek), this museum displays splendid period interiors. If you're outside the building at noon, look up. Every midday two mechanical metal goats above its clock butt their horns together 12 times.

Franciscan Church CHURCH
(ul Franciszkańska 2; ⌚8am-8pm) This 17th-century church, one block west of the square, has an ornate baroque interior, complete with wall paintings and rich stucco work.

National Museum: Paintings & Sculpture Gallery MUSEUM
(Al Marcinkowskiego 9; adult/concession 10/6zł, Sat free; ⌚9am-3pm Tue-Thu, noon-9pm Fri, 11am-6pm Sat & Sun) This museum branch displays mainly 19th- and 20th-century Polish paintings.

Monument to the Victims of June 1956 MUSEUM
(Plac Mickiewicza) Emotive memorial to the dead and injured of the massive 1956 strike by the city's industrial workers, which was crushed by tanks. It's in a park west of the prominent Kaiserhof building.

Museum of Poznań June 1956 MUSEUM
(ul Św. Marcin 80/82; adult/concession 4/2zł, Sat free; ⌚9am-5pm Tue-Fri, 10am-4pm Sat & Sun) In the Zamek Cultural Centre within the Kaiserhof, there's more detail to be uncovered of the 1956 strike.

Palm House GREENHOUSE
(ul Matejki 18; adult/concession 5.50/4zł; ⌚9am-5pm Tue-Sat, 9am-6pm Sun) This huge greenhouse (built in 1910) contains 17,000 species of tropical and subtropical plants. It's located in Park Wilsona, 1km southwest of the train station.

Lake Malta LAKE
Some 1.6km east of the Old Town is this body of water, a favourite weekend destination for Poles.

A fun way to visit the lake is to take tram 4, 8 or 17 from Plac Wielkopolski to the Rondo Śródka stop on the other side of Ostrów Tumski. From the nearby terminus, you can catch a miniature train along the **Malta Park Railway** (ul Jana Pawła II; adult/concession 5/3.50zł; ⌚10am-6.30pm Apr-Oct), which follows the lake's shore to the **New Zoo** (ul Krańcowa 81; adult/concession 11/7zł; ⌚9am-7pm Apr-Sep, 9am-4pm Oct-Mar).

Festivals & Events

Poznań Jazz Fair March.

St John's Fair Cultural festival in June.

Malta International Theatre Festival (www.malta-festival.pl) June.

Sleeping

During Poznań's regular trade fairs (January, June, September, October), accommodation rates increase dramatically. A room may also be difficult to find, so it pays to book ahead; accommodation agency **Biuro Zakwaterowania Przemysław** (☎61 866 3560; www.przemyslaw.com.pl; ul Głogowska 16; s/d from 60/90zł, apt from 180zł; ⏲8am-6pm Mon-Fri, 10am-2pm Sat) can help. Prices given here are for outside trade fair periods.

Rezydencja Solei HOTEL €€
(☎61 855 7351; www.hotel-solei.pl; ul Szewska 2; s/d 199/299zł) Temptingly close to the Old Market Sq, this tiny hotel offers small but cosy rooms. The attic suite is amazingly large and can accommodate up to four people.

Frolic Goats Hostel HOSTEL €
(☎61 852 4411; www.frolicgoatshostel.com; ul Wrocławska 16/6; dm from 50zł, d 170zł) Hostel named after the feisty goats who fight above the town hall clock. There's a washing machine on the premises, bike hire is available for 30zł per day, and room rates are unaffected by trade fairs. Enter from ul Jaskółcza.

Hotel Rzymski HOTEL €€
(☎61 852 8121; www.hotelrzymski.pl; Al Marcinkowskiego 22; s/d from 250/310zł) Offers the regular amenities of three-star comfort, and overlooks Plac Wolności. Rooms aren't quite as grand as the elegant facade suggests, but they're a decent size.

Hotel Lech HOTEL €€
(☎61 853 0151; www.hotel-lech.poznan.pl; ul Św. Marcin 74; s/d 200/295zł) Hotel Lech has standard three-star decor, but rooms are relatively spacious and the bathrooms are modern. Flash your ISIC card for a discount.

Mini Hotelik HOTEL €
(☎61 633 1416; Al Niepodległości 8a; s/d from 65/129zł) Like it says on the label, this is a small place between the train station and the Old Town. It's basic but clean, and some rooms share a bathroom. Enter from ul Taylora.

Youth Hostel No 3 HOSTEL €
(☎61 866 4040; ul Berwińskiego 2/3; dm 35zł) Cheap lodgings about a 15-minute walk southwest of the train station along ul Głogowska, adjacent to Park Wilsona. It's a basic 'no frills' option, but fills up fast with students and school groups. There's a 10pm curfew.

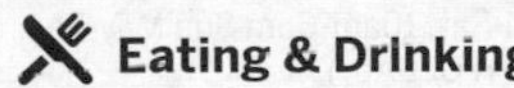

Eating & Drinking

Tapas Bar SPANISH €€
(☎61 852 8532; Stary Rynek 60; mains 18-72zł; ⏲noon-midnight) Atmospheric place dishing up authentic tapas and Spanish wine, in a room lined with Mediterranean-themed bric-a-brac. Most tapas dishes cost 18zł to 22zł, so forget the mains and share with friends.

Gospoda Pod Koziołkami POLISH €€
(☎61 851 7868; Stary Rynek 95; mains 12-27zł; ⏲11am-10pm) Homely bistro within Gothic arches. The menu is crammed with tasty Polish standards, including some distinctive Wielkopolska specialties.

Bar Caritas CAFETERIA €
(☎61 852 5130; Plac Wolności 1; mains 6-12zł; ⏲8am-7pm Mon-Fri, 10am-5pm Sat, noon-5pm Sun) Cheap and convenient milk bar with many variants of *naleśniki* (crepes) on the menu. Lunchtimes get crowded, so be prepared to share a table.

Sioux AMERICAN €€
(☎61 851 6286; Stary Rynek 93; mains 24-100zł; ⏲noon-11pm) 'Western'-themed place, complete with waiters dressed as cowboys. Bizarrely named dishes such as 'Scoundrels in Uniforms from Fort Knox' (chicken legs) are on the menu, along with lots of steaks, ribs, grills and enchiladas.

Proletaryat BAR
(ul Wrocławska 9; ⏲1pm-2am Mon-Sat, 3pm-2am Sun) Communist nostalgia bar with an obligatory bust of Lenin in the window. Play 'spot the communist leader' while sipping a boutique beer from the Czarnków Brewery.

Czarna Owca CLUB
(ul Jaskółcza 13; ⏲noon-2am Mon-Fri, 5pm-2am Sat) Literally 'Black Sheep', this popular club has nightly DJs playing a mix of genres including R&B, house, rock, Latin, soul and funk.

Entertainment

Teatr Wielki THEATRE
(☎61 659 0280; www.opera.poznan.pl; ul Fredry 9) Opera and ballet.

Filharmonia CLASSICAL MUSIC
(☎61 853 6935; www.filharmonia.poznan.pl; ul Św. Marcin 81) Classical concerts at least weekly.

Information

Tourist office (☎61 852 6156; Stary Rynek 59; ⊙9am-8pm Mon-Sat, 10am-6pm Sun May-Sep, 10am-6pm Mon-Fri Oct-Apr)

Tunel (Poznań Główny train station; per hr 5zł; ⊙24hr) Internet access beneath the train station concourse.

Getting There & Away

From **Poznań airport** (www.airport-poznan.com.pl), LOT flies regularly to Warsaw, Frankfurt and Munich. Tickets are available from the **LOT office** (☎0801 703 703; airport) or from **Orbis Travel** (☎61 851 2000; Al Marcinkowskiego 21). There are also five domestic flights a week via Jet Air to each of Kraków and Gdańsk. A vast array of other European cities are serviced by budget airlines, including London, Dublin and Copenhagen. Check the airport's website for schedules. The airport is accessible by buses 48, 59 and L, and by night bus 242.

The **bus terminal** (ul Towarowa 17) is located about 600m east of the train station. However, most destinations can be reached more comfortably and frequently by train. The busy **Poznań Główny train station** (ul Dworcowa 1) offers services to Kraków (56zł, 7½ hours, 14 daily), Gdańsk and Gdynia (53zł, six hours, eight daily), Toruń (25zł, two hours, eight daily), Wrocław (37zł, 2½ hours, at least hourly) and Warsaw (51zł, 3½ hours, at least hourly).

POMERANIA

Pomerania (Pomorze in Polish) is an attractive region with diverse drawcards, from beautiful beaches to architecturally pleasing cities. The historic port city of Gdańsk is situated at the region's eastern extreme, while the attractive Gothic city of Toruń lies inland.

Gdańsk

POP 456,000

From Gdańsk's lively riverside waterfront to the Renaissance splendour of its charming narrow streets, there's plenty to like about this coastal city.

After being tussled over by Germans and Poles for centuries, Gdańsk suffered immense damage in WWII. In the 1980s it achieved international fame as the home of the Solidarity trade union, whose rise helped precipitate the fall of communism in Europe.

Sights

MAIN TOWN

Royal Way HISTORIC ROUTE

The historic parade route of Polish kings runs from the western **Upland Gate** (built in the 1770s), onward through the **Foregate** (which once housed a torture chamber) and **Golden Gate** (1614), and east to the Renaissance **Green Gate** (1568). Along the way it passes through beautiful **ul Długa** (Long Street) and **Długi Targ** (Long Market).

Amber Museum MUSEUM

(www.mhmg.gda.pl/bursztyn; Foregate; adult/concession 10/5zł, Tue free; ⊙10am-2.30pm Tue, 10am-3.30pm Wed-Sat, 11am-3.30pm Sun) Within the Foregate, you can marvel at the history of so-called 'Baltic gold'.

Historical Museum of Gdańsk MUSEUM

(ul Długa 47; adult/concession 10/5zł, Tue free; ⊙10am-3pm Tue, 10am-4pm Wed-Sat, 11am-4pm Sun) Inside the towering Gothic **town hall** is this institution depicting photos of old Gdańsk, and the damage caused to the city during WWII.

Neptune's Fountain FOUNTAIN

Legend says this decorative fountain (1633) once gushed forth *goldwasser*, the iconic Gdańsk liqueur. Also note the nearby **Golden House** (1618), which has a strikingly rich facade.

St Mary's Church CHURCH

(⊙8.30am-6pm, except during services) Stroll along picturesque **ul Mariacka** to this gigantic 14th-century place of worship. Little figures troop out at noon from its 14m-high astronomical clock, adorned with zodiacal signs. You can climb the 405 steps of the **tower** (adult/concession 5/3zł).

Central Maritime Museum MUSEUM

(ul Ołowianka 9-13; 1 section adult/concession 8/5zł, all sections 18/10zł; ⊙10am-4pm) On the waterfront is the 15th-century **Gdańsk Crane**, part of this maritime history museum. Its branch on the east bank of the Motława River offers a fascinating insight into Gdańsk's seafaring past, including the **Sołdek Museum Ship**.

OLD TOWN

TOP CHOICE **Roads to Freedom Exhibition** MUSEUM

(ul Wały Piastowskie 24; adult/concession 6/4zł; ⊙10am-4pm Tue-Sun) This excellent museum charts the decline and fall of Polish com-

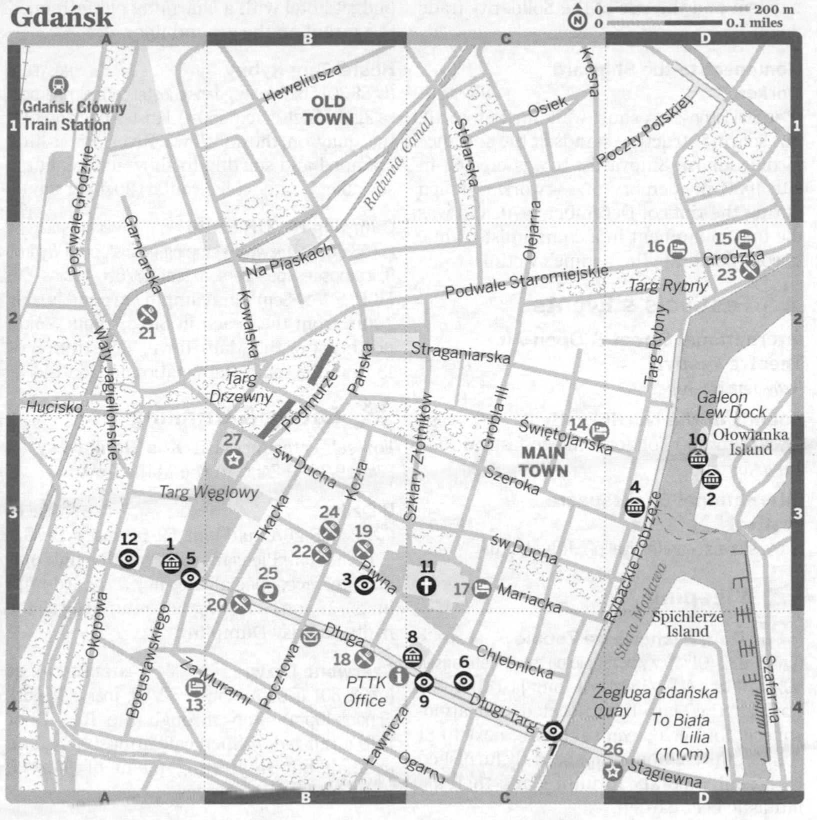

Gdańsk

Sights

1 Amber Museum A3
2 Central Maritime Museum D3
Foregate .... (see 1)
3 Free City of Danzig Historical Zone B3
4 Gdańsk Crane D3
5 Golden Gate A3
6 Golden House C4
7 Green Gate C4
8 Historical Museum of Gdańsk C4
9 Neptune's Fountain C4
10 Sołdek Museum Ship D3
11 St Mary's Church C3
Town Hall .... (see 8)
12 Upland Gate A3

Sleeping

13 Dom Harcerza A4
14 Dom Zachariasza Zappio C3
15 Happy Seven Hostel D2
16 Hostel Targ Rybny D2
17 Kamienica Gotyk C3

Eating

18 Bar Mleczny Neptun B4
19 Czerwone Drzwi B3
20 Green Way B3
21 Green Way A2
22 Kos Delikatesy B3
23 Przystań Gdańska D2
24 U Dzika B3

Drinking

25 Café Ferber B3

Entertainment

26 Miasto Aniołow D4
27 Teatr Wybrzeże B3

munism and the rise of the Solidarity trade union.

Monument to the Shipyard Workers MONUMENT
(Plac Solidarności) A short walk further north, this soaring structure stands at the entrance to the Gdańsk Shipyards. It was erected in late 1980 in memory of 44 workers killed during the riots of December 1970, and was the first monument in a communist regime to commemorate the regime's victims.

Festivals & Events

International Street & Open-Air Theatre Festival THEATRE
(www.feta.pl) July.

Sounds of the North Festival MUSIC
(www.nck.org.pl) Folkloric music festival in July/August.

International Shakespeare Festival THEATRE
(www.shakespearefestival.pl) July/August.

Sleeping

TOP CHOICE **Dom Zachariasza Zappio** HOSTEL €
(☎58 322 0174; www.zappio.pl; ul Świętojańska 49; dm 45zł, s/d 92/158zł) At long last there's a hostel in the Main Town, located in an atmospheric former convent building next to St John's Church. Rooms are brightly furnished with contemporary furniture, and there's a fantastic beer garden.

Kamienica Gotyk HOTEL €€
(☎60 284 4535; www.gotykhouse.eu; ul Mariacka 1; s/d 280/310zł) This Gothic guest house claims to be Gdańsk's oldest residence. Inside, the rooms are compact but neat, with clean bathrooms.

Happy Seven Hostel HOSTEL €
(☎58 320 8601; www.happyseven.com; ul Grodzka 16; dm from 45zł, d 150zł) New hostel in which each dorm has a light-hearted theme, including the 'Travel' dorm plastered with maps and the soothing green 'Jungle' dorm.

Apartments Poland APARTMENTS €€
(☎58 346 9864; www.apartmentpoland.com; apt €30-70) An agency with a number of renovated properties. Be aware of the additional electricity charge when checking out, based on a meter reading.

Dom Harcerza HOTEL €
(☎58 301 3621; www.domharcerza.pl; ul Za Murami 2/10; dm 39zł, s/d from 75/140zł) Well-located budget hotel with a charming old-fashioned restaurant on the ground floor.

Hostel Targ Rybny HOSTEL €
(☎58 301 5627; www.gdanskhostel.com.pl; ul Grodzka 21; dm 55zł, d from 150zł) Hostel overlooking the quay on the Motława River. It's a little cramped and starting to show its age, but is sociable. It offers bike rental (20zł per day).

Camping Nr 218 Stogi CAMPING GROUND €
(☎58 307 3915; www.kemping-gdansk.pl; ul Wydmy 9; campsites per person/tent 13/6zł, cabins 60-130zł; ⏰May-Sep) This camping ground is only 200m from the beach in Stogi, about 5.5km northeast of the Main Town. Take tram 8 or 13 from the main train station in Gdańsk.

Eating & Drinking

For self-catering, visit **Kos Delikatesy** (ul Piwna 9/10; ⏰24hr) in the Main Town.

U Dzika POLISH €€
(☎58 305 2676; ul Piwna 59/61; mains 15-39zł; ⏰11am-10pm) Pleasant eatery with a nice outdoor terrace, specialising in *pierogi* (dumplings). If you're feeling adventurous, try the fruity Fantasy Dumplings.

Czerwone Drzwi INTERNATIONAL €€
(☎58 301 5764; ul Piwna 52/53; mains 18-65zł; ⏰noon-10pm) Step through the Red Door into a relaxed, refined cafe atmosphere, and a small but interesting menu of *pierogi*, pasta and Polish classics.

Bar Mleczny Neptun CAFETERIA €
(ul Długa 33/34; mains 2-13zł; ⏰7.30am-7pm Mon-Fri, 10am-6pm Sat & Sun) This joint is a cut above your run-of-the-mill milk bar, with potted plants, lace curtains, decorative tiling and old lamps for decor.

Green Way VEGETARIAN €
(☎58 301 4121; ul Garncarska 4/6; mains 4-12zł; ⏰10am-8pm Mon-Fri, noon-7pm Sat & Sun) Serves everything from soy cutlets to Mexican goulash in an unfussy green-and-orange space. There's another, more central, branch at ul Długa 11.

Przystań Gdańska POLISH €€
(☎58 301 1922; ul Wartka 5; mains 15-32zł) An atmospheric place to enjoy outdoor seafood dining, with a view along the river to the Gdańsk Crane.

Café Ferber CAFE, BAR
(ul Długa 77/78; ⏰9.30am-late) It's startling to step straight from Gdańsk's historic main

street into this very modern cafe-bar. Partake of breakfast, well-made coffee, international wines and cocktails here.

☆ Entertainment

Miasto Aniołów CLUB
(www.miastoaniolow.com.pl, in Polish; ul Chmielna 26) Late-night revellers can hit this club's spacious dance floor, crash in the chill-out area, or hang around the atmospheric deck overlooking the Motława River. Nightly DJs play disco and other dance-oriented sounds.

State Baltic Opera Theatre OPERA
(☎58 763 4912; www.operabaltycka.pl; Al Zwycięstwa 15) In the suburb of Wrzeszcz, not far from the train station at Gdańsk Politechnika.

Teatr Wybrzeże THEATRE
(☎58 301 1328; www.teatrwybrzeze.pl, in Polish; ul Św. Ducha 2) Next to the Arsenal is the main city theatre, presenting Polish and foreign classics.

Information

Jazz 'n' Java (ul Tkacka 17/18; per hr 6zł; ⏲10am-10pm) Internet access.

PTTK office (☎58 301 1343; www.pttk-gdansk.pl; ul Długa 45; ⏲10am-6pm Mon-Fri, 8.30am-4.30pm Sat & Sun) Tourist office opposite the town hall.

Getting There & Away

Air

From **Lech Wałęsa airport** (www.airport.gdansk.pl), LOT flies to Warsaw, Frankfurt and Munich. Tickets can be bought at the **LOT office** (☎801 703 703; ul Wały Jagiellońskie 2/4). Gdańsk is also connected to a plethora of other European cities, including London, Dublin and Copenhagen. Check the airport's website for schedules. The airport is accessible by bus 210 or night bus N3 from Gdańsk Główny train station.

Bus

The **bus terminal** (ul 3 Maja 12) is behind the main train station. Useful services include nine daily buses to Warsaw (52zł, six hours).

Train

The city's main train station, **Gdańsk Główny** (ul Podwale Grodzkie 1), is conveniently located on the western outskirts of the Old Town. Most long-distance trains start or finish at Gdynia, so make sure you get on/off quickly here.

Each day 10 trains (mainly Express InterCity services) head to Warsaw (114zł, 5½ hours). There are also trains to Malbork (16zł, 1¼ hours, at least hourly), Kraków (129zł, eight hours, 10 daily), Poznań (51zł, 4¾ hours, seven daily), Toruń (39zł, four hours, 11 daily) and Lublin (63zł, nine hours, two daily).

> WORTH A TRIP
>
> **MALBORK CASTLE**
>
> The magnificent **Malbork Castle** makes a great day trip from Gdańsk. It's the largest Gothic castle in Europe, and was once known as Marienburg, headquarters of the medieval Teutonic Knights. Its sinister form looms over the relatively small town and the Nogat River – grab a sneak preview by looking to the right as your train crosses the river. Trains run regularly from Gdańsk Głowny station (1¼ hours). Once you get to Malbork station, turn right, cross the highway and follow ul Kościuszki to the castle. Compulsory tours are usually in Polish but come with an audio tour in English. There are places to eat at the castle and in the town.

Toruń

POP 206,000

The first thing that strikes you about Toruń, south of Gdańsk, is its massive red-brick churches, looking more like fortresses than places of worship. The city is a pleasant place to spend a few days, offering a nice balance between a relaxing slow pace and engaging entertainment diversions.

Toruń is also famous as the birthplace of Nicolaus Copernicus, who revolutionised the field of astronomy in 1543 by asserting that the earth travelled around the sun.

Toruń was fortunate to escape major damage in WWII, and as a result is the best-preserved Gothic town in Poland.

Sights

Old Town Market Square HISTORIC SQUARE
The starting point for any exploration of Toruń is this central square (Rynek Staromiejski in Polish). It's the focal point of the Old Town, lined by elegant facades and dominated by the massive 14th-century **Old Town Hall**.

In front of the town hall is an elegant **statue** of Copernicus. Look for other interesting items of statuary dotted around the square.

Regional Museum MUSEUM
(www.muzeum.torun.pl; Rynek Staromiejski 1; adult/concession 10/6zł; ⌚10am-6pm Tue-Sun May-Sep, 10am-4pm Tue-Sun Oct-Apr) Within the town hall, this institution features a fine collection of 19th- and 20th-century Polish art, along with medieval stained glass and religious paintings. Climb the 40m-high **tower** (adult/concession 10/6zł; ⌚10am-4pm Tue-Sun Apr, 10am-8pm Tue-Sun May-Sep) for great views.

House of Copernicus MUSEUM
(ul Kopernika 15/17; adult/concession 10/7zł; ⌚10am-6pm Tue-Sun May-Sep, 10am-4pm Tue-Sun Oct-Apr) It's thought that in 1473 Copernicus was born in the brick Gothic house that now contains this fairly dull museum, presenting replicas of the great astronomer's instruments.

More engaging, if overpriced, is the museum's short **audiovisual presentation** (adult/concession 12/7zł) regarding Copernicus' life in Toruń; and the extravagantly titled **World of Toruń's Gingerbread** (adult/concession 10/6zł). A combined ticket to any two of the three attractions costs 18/11zł.

Cathedral of SS John the Baptist & John the Evangelist CHURCH
(ul Żeglarska; adult/concession 3/2zł; ⌚9am-5.30pm Mon-Sat, 2-5.30pm Sun Apr-Oct) One block south of the square is this mighty 13th-century place of worship with its massive **tower** (adult/concession 6/4zl) and bell.

Teutonic Knights' Castle Ruins RUINS
(ul Przedzamcze; adult/concession 6/4zł, Mon free; ⌚10am-6pm Mar-Oct, 10am-4pm Nov-Feb) East of the remnants of the old city walls are the ruins of the Teutonic Castle, destroyed in 1454 by angry townsfolk protesting against the knights' oppressive regime.

Far Eastern Art Museum ART GALLERY
(Rynek Staromiejski 35; adult/concession 7/4zł, Wed free; ⌚10am-6pm Tue-Sun May-Sep, 10am-4pm Tue-Sun Oct-Apr) The richly decorated, 15th-century **House Under the Star** contains this collection of art from Asia.

Sleeping

TOP CHOICE **Green Hostel** HOSTEL €
(☎56 561 4000; www.greenhostel.eu; ul Małe Garbary 10; s/d 50/100zł) This hostel without dorms boasts shiny rooms, a kitchen and a pleasant lounge. A great option for the price.

Hotel Pod Czarną Różą HOTEL €€
(☎56 621 9637; www.hotelczarnaroza.pl; ul Rabiańska 11; s/d 170/210zł) Spread between a historic inn and a newer wing facing the river. Some doubles come with small but functional kitchens.

Orange Hostel HOSTEL €
(☎56 652 0033; www.hostelorange.pl; ul Prosta 19; dm 30zł, s/d 50/90zł) International backpacker hostel in a handy location. Its decor is bright and cheerful, and its kitchen is an impressive place to practise the gentle art of self-catering.

Hotel Pod Orłem HOTEL €€
(☎56 622 5024; www.hotel.torun.pl; ul Mostowa 17; s/d from 130/165zł) This hotel is great value, though the rooms are smallish. The foyer and corridors are fun with their jumble of framed pop-art images and old photos.

Camping Nr 33 Tramp CAMPING GROUND €
(☎56 654 7187; www.mosir.torun.pl; ul Kujawska 14; campsites per person 9zł, tents 6-12zł, s/d from 50/65zł; ⌚May-Sep) There's a choice of cabins or hotel-style rooms at this camping ground, a five-minute walk west of the main train station.

Eating & Drinking

TOP CHOICE **Gospoda Pod Modrym Fartuchem** POLISH, INDIAN €€
(☎56 622 2626; Rynek Nowomiejski 8; mains 16-30zł; ⌚10am-10pm) This pleasant, unpretentious 15th-century pub on the New Town Sq has been visited by Polish kings and Napoleon. Polish dishes are joined by an array of Indian food, including a good vegetarian selection.

Bar Mleczny Pod Arkadami CAFETERIA €
(ul Różana 1; mains 1-9zł; ⌚9am-7pm Mon-Fri, 11am-6pm Sat & Sun) Classic milk bar just off the Old Town Market Sq. Its takeaway window serves a range of tasty *zapiekanki* (toasted rolls with cheese, mushrooms and ketchup) and sweet waffles.

Parmis MIDDLE EASTERN €
(☎56 621 0607; ul Mostowa 7; mains 8-23zł; ⌚noon-midnight) A splash of Middle Eastern cuisine in northern Poland, serving kebabs, soups, salads and pizzas.

Manekin POLISH €
(☎56 621 0504; Rynek Staromiejski 16; mains 8-15zł) Vaguely Wild West decor adorns this inexpensive central restaurant. It offers a va-

riety of filled pancakes, including vegetarian options.

Tantra BAR
(ul Ślusarska 5; ⌚5pm-late) Astonishingly decorated bar done out in an Indian and Tibetan theme. Sit on the cushion-strewn divans, order a drink from the long list, and meditate on the infinite.

Koci Ogon CLUB
(ul Rabiańska 17; ⌚5pm-2am Sun-Thu, 5pm-4am Fri & Sat) Lively cellar club with rock DJs most nights from 9pm.

☆ Entertainment

Nasze Kino CINEMA
(www.naszekino.pl, in Polish; ul Podmurna 14) Cool arthouse cinema within part of the old city wall.

Teatr im Horzycy THEATRE
(☎56 622 5222; Plac Teatralny 1) The main stage for theatre performances.

Dwór Artusa CLASSICAL MUSIC
(☎56 655 4929; Rynek Staromiejski 6) This place often presents classical music.

ℹ Information

Ksero Uniwerek (ul Franciszkańska 5; per hr 3zł; ⌚8am-7pm Mon-Fri, 9am-4pm Sat) Internet access.

Tourist office (☎56 621 0931; www.it.torun.pl; Rynek Staromiejski 25; ⌚9am-4pm Mon & Sat, 9am-6pm Tue-Fri, 10am-2pm Sun) Hires out handheld mp3 players with English-language audio tours of the city (10zł per four hours).

ℹ Getting There & Away

The **bus terminal** (ul Dąbrowskiego) is about 1km north of the Old Town, but most places can be reached more efficiently by train.

The main **Toruń Główny train station** (Al Podgórska) is on the opposite side of the Vistula River and linked to the Old Town by buses 22 and 27. Some trains stop and finish at the more convenient **Toruń Miasto train station** (Plac 18 Stycznia), about 500m east of the New Town.

From Toruń Główny there are trains to Poznań (25zł, two hours, eight daily), Gdańsk and Gdynia (39zł, four hours, 11 daily), Kraków (58zł, eight hours, eight daily), Wrocław (51zł, five hours, two daily) and Warsaw (48zł, three hours, 10 daily). There are also eight daily trains to Malbork (21zł, three hours), including three operated by private company **Arriva** (www.arriva.pl).

WARMIA & MASURIA

Great Masurian Lakes

The dominant feature of Warmia and Masuria is its beautiful postglacial landscape dominated by thousands of lakes. The largest lake is **Lake Śniardwy** (110 sq km). About 200km of canals connect these bodies of water, so the area is a prime destination for yachties and canoeists, as well as those who prefer to hike, fish and mountain-bike.

The detailed *Wielkie Jeziora Mazurskie* map (1:100,000) is essential for anyone exploring the region by water or hiking trail. The *Warmia i Mazury* map (1:300,000), available at regional tourist offices, is perfect for more general use.

Mikołajki (mee-ko-*wahy*-kee) is a picturesque base for exploring the lakes. The **tourist office** (☎87 421 6850; www.mikolajki.pl; Plac Wolności 3; ⌚10am-6pm Jun-Aug, 10am-6pm Mon-Sat May & Sep) is in the town centre. From the bus terminal, next to the bridge at Plac Kościelny, two buses go to Olsztyn each day (16zł, two hours), from where you can connect to major cities. Buses also head to Giżycko (11zł, one hour, hourly) and Warsaw (41zł, five hours, two daily).

The remains of Hitler's wartime headquarters, called the **Wolf's Lair** ('Wolfsschanze' in German), is a local bus ride from Kętrzyn (reached via Giżycko or Olsztyn), about 30km north of Mikołajki. In 1944 a group of high-ranking German officers tried to assassinate Hitler here. Although the explosion killed and wounded several people, Hitler suffered only minor injuries. Those involved in the plot were subsequently executed. These dramatic events were reprised in the 2008 Tom Cruise movie *Valkyrie*. To reach the eerie ruins of the complex, catch one of several daily PKS buses (5zł, 15 minutes) from Kętrzyn to Węgorzewo (via Radzieje, not Srokowo) and get off at the entrance.

UNDERSTAND POLAND

History

Poland's history started in the early Middle Ages with the Polanians (People of the Plains). Mieszko I, Duke of the Polanians, adopted Christianity in 966 and embarked on a successful campaign of conquest.

Encroachment from Germanic peoples led to the relocation of the royal capital from Poznań to Kraków in 1038. The kingdom prospered under Kazimierz III 'the Great' (1333–70), and in 1569 Poland and Lithuania were united as the largest state in Europe, stretching from the Baltic to the Black Sea.

The 18th century was a period of disaster and decline. Russia, Prussia and Austria repeatedly divided Polish territory between them; by 1795 Poland had vanished from the map of Europe. Finally, upon the end of WWI the old imperial powers dissolved, and a sovereign Polish state was restored.

On 1 September 1939, a Nazi blitzkrieg rained down from the west; soon after, the Soviets invaded Poland from the east. The Germans then used Poland as a base for invading the Soviet Union. By the time the Nazi regime was finally ousted at the end of WWII, six million Poles had died, including the country's three million Jews, who were brutally annihilated in death camps.

After WWII, Poland endured four decades of Soviet-dominated communist rule. Finally, in 1990 Solidarity leader Lech Wałęsa became Poland's first democratically elected postwar president. The postcommunist transition brought radical changes, but within a decade Poland had rebuilt the foundations of a market economy. Poland joined the EU in May 2004.

In the 2007 parliamentary elections, Poles decisively rejected the eccentric Eurosceptic policies of the government headed by the identical-twin Kaczyński brothers, president Lech and prime minister Jarosław. The new Civic Platform government of prime minister Donald Tusk began steering a pro-business, pro-EU course.

In April 2010, President Kaczyński was killed in an air crash during an attempted landing at Smolensk, Russia. The Polish public was stunned by the tragedy, and campaigning for the ensuing election was subdued. In July 2010 Tusk's party ally Bronisław Komorowski was elected as president.

People

Due to Nazi genocide and the forced resettlements that followed WWII, Poland became an ethnically homogeneous country. Some 98% of the 38 million population are ethnic Poles.

Poles are friendly and polite but not overly formal. The way of life in large urban centres increasingly resembles Western styles and manners. In the countryside, however, a more conservative culture dominates, with traditional gender roles, and strong religious convictions and family ties.

Outside the big towns, knowledge of foreign languages is limited.

READING UP

God's Playground: A History of Poland, by Norman Davies, offers an in-depth analysis of Polish history, and his *Rising '44* vividly covers the wartime Warsaw Rising. Also check out Timothy Garton Ash's *The Polish Revolution: Solidarity 1980-82*. *Jews in Poland*, by Iwo Cyprian Pogonowski, is a comprehensive work.

Arts

Poland has inherited a rich literary tradition dating from the 15th century, though its modern voice was shaped during the long period of foreign occupation in the 19th century.

At the turn of the 20th century, the avant-garde 'Young Poland' movement in art and literature developed in Kraków. Among its most notable representatives were the writer Stanisław Wyspiański (1869–1907).

The most famous Polish musician was undoubtedly Frédéric Chopin (1810–49), whose music displays the melancholy and nostalgia that became hallmarks of the national style. Present-day Polish musicians you might catch live in concert include the controversial Doda (pop singer), Feel (pop-rock band), Łzy (pop-rock band), Indios Bravos (reggae band) and Kasia Cerekwicka (pop singer).

Poland's most renowned painter was Jan Matejko (1838–93), whose monumental historical paintings hang in galleries throughout the country.

Poland has produced several world-famous film directors including Roman Polański, who directed hits such as *Rosemary's Baby* and *Chinatown*, and Krzysztof Kieślowski, best known for the *Three Colours* trilogy.

Food

In this chapter, price ranges for main dishes are indicated as follows:

€€€ more than 25zł

€€ 10zł to 25zł

€ less than 10zł

SURVIVAL GUIDE

Directory A–Z

Accommodation

Unless otherwise noted, rooms have private bathrooms and the indicative rate is for a double room including breakfast.

€€€ more than 350zł

€€ 150zł to 350zł

€ less than 150zł

CAMPING GROUNDS & MOUNTAIN REFUGES

Poland has hundreds of camping grounds, and many offer good-value cabins and bungalows. Most open May to September, but some only open their gates between June and August. A good online resource is the **Polish Camping and Caravanning Federation** (www.pfcc.eu).

PTTK (www.pttk.pl) runs a chain of mountain refuges *(schroniska górskie)* for hikers. The more-isolated refuges are obliged to accept everyone, so can be crowded in the high season. Refuges are normally open all year, but confirm with the nearest PTTK office.

PRIVATE ROOMS, HOSTELS & HOTELS

Some destinations have agencies – usually called a *biuro zakwaterowania* or *biuro kwater prywatnych* – which arrange accommodation in private homes. Rooms cost about 80/110zł for singles/doubles. During high season, home owners also directly approach tourists, and private homes in smaller resorts and villages have signs outside their gates or doors offering a *pokoje* (room) or *noclegi* (lodging).

Older-style youth hostels *(schroniska młodzieżowe)* are run by the **Polish Youth Hostels Association** (www.ptsm.org.pl). Some of these only open in July and August; the year-round hostels have more facilities. These hostels are open to all, with no age limit. Curfews are common.

Privately run hostels operate in the main cities, geared towards international backpackers. They offer more modern facilities, though prices are higher. These hostels usually offer free use of washing machines, in response to the absence of laundromats in Poland. A dorm bed can cost anything from 25zł to 75zł per person per night. Double rooms, if available, cost from about 150zł.

Hotel prices often vary according to season, and discounted weekend rates are often available.

Two reliable websites for arranging accommodation over the internet: www.poland4u.com and www.hotelspoland.com.

Activities

Hikers can enjoy marked trails across the Tatra and Sudeten Mountains, and the Great Masurian Lakes district. Trails are easy to follow, and detailed maps are available from most larger bookshops. Poland is fairly flat and ideal for cyclists. Zakopane will delight skiers from December to March.

Business Hours

Banks 8am-5pm Mon-Fri, sometimes 8am-2pm Sat

Cafes & restaurants 11am-11pm

Shops 10am-6pm Mon-Fri, 10am-2pm Sat

Nightclubs 9pm-late

Dangers & Annoyances

Poland is relatively safe, but be alert for pickpockets around major train stations, such as Warszawa Centralna. Robberies have been a problem on night trains, especially on international routes. Try to share a compartment with other people if possible.

Smoking is common in most public places, especially pubs and restaurants.

Gay & Lesbian Travellers

Overt homophobia from state officials has declined in recent years; though with the Church remaining influential in social matters, gay acceptance in Poland is still a work in progress. As a result, the Polish gay and lesbian scene is fairly discreet.

Warsaw and Kraków are the best places to find bars and clubs. A good source of information on gay Warsaw and Kraków is online at www.gayguide.net.

Holidays

Poland's public holidays:

New Year's Day 1 January

Easter Sunday March or April

Easter Monday March or April

State Holiday 1 May

Constitution Day 3 May

Pentecost Sunday Seventh Sunday after Easter

Corpus Christi Ninth Thursday after Easter

Assumption Day 15 August

All Saints' Day 1 November

Independence Day 11 November

Christmas 25 and 26 December

Internet Access

Internet access is near-universal in Polish accommodation. As a result, individual accommodation with internet access has not been denoted as such in this chapter.

In the unlikely event that your lodgings are offline, you'll likely find an internet cafe nearby; expect to pay between 3zł and 5zł per hour.

Money

Poland's currency is the złoty (*zwo*-ti), abbreviated to zł. The złoty is divided into 100 groszy, abbreviated as gr.

ATMs *(bankomats)* and foreign exchange offices – called *kantors* – are common in all sizeable towns. Banks without an ATM might give cash advances over the counter on credit cards, which are widely accepted.

Tipping isn't common in Poland, but feel free to leave 10% extra for waiters or taxi drivers if you've had good service.

Telephone

Phone numbers throughout Poland have nine digits, with no area codes. To call from abroad, dial the country code ☎48, then the local number. The international access code for overseas calls from Poland is ☎00.

Most public telephones use magnetic phonecards, available at post offices and kiosks in units of 15 (9zł), 30 (15zł) and 60 (24zł).

Poland's three mobile telephone providers are Orange, Era and Plus GSM. Prepaid accounts are cheap by Western European standards, and are easy to set up at local offices of these companies.

Visas

EU citizens do not need visas to visit Poland and can stay indefinitely. Citizens of Australia, Canada, Israel, New Zealand, Switzerland and the USA can stay in Poland up to 90 days without a visa. Other nationals should check the website of the Ministry of Foreign Affairs, www.msz.gov.pl.

Note that, since Poland's entry into the Schengen zone of European countries in December 2007, the 90-day visa-free entry period has been extended to cover travel through all the Schengen countries in total.

These embassies in Warsaw may be useful in organising visas for onward travel:

Belarus (☎22 742 0710; www.belembassy.org/poland; ul Wiertnicza 58)

Russia (☎22 849 5111; http://warsaw.rusembassy.org; ul Belwederska 49)

Ukraine (☎22 622 4797; www.ukraine-emb.pl; Al Szucha 7)

Getting There & Away

Border Crossings

Since Poland joined the Schengen zone, the only border-crossing formalities are with the following:

Belarus Terespol and Kuźnica Białostocka

Russia Gronowo and Bezledy

Ukraine Medyka, Hrebenne and Dorohusk

Air

The majority of international flights to Poland arrive at Warsaw's Okęcie airport, while other well-serviced airports include Kraków, Gdańsk, Poznań and Wrocław.

The national carrier **LOT** (☎0801 703 703, from mobile 22 19572; www.lot.com) flies to major European cities, and to some North American cities during the summer months.

A vast array of budget carriers fly into Poland from airports across Europe, including a range of regional airports in Britain and Ireland. For more information on low-cost airlines, see p1321.

Boat

Any travel agency in Scandinavia will sell tickets for the following services. In Warsaw, enquire at **Orbis Travel** (☎22 827 7265; ul Bracka 16) or its branches in other cities.

Polferries (www.polferries.pl) Operates daily between Gdańsk and Nynäshamn (19 hours) in Sweden.

Stena Line (www.stenaline.com) Sails between Gdynia and Karlskrona (10½ hours, twice daily) in Sweden.

Bus & Train

International bus services are cheaper than trains, but not as comfortable or fast. From Warsaw, **Eurolines Polska** (www.eurolinespol

ska.pl) operates a huge number of buses to destinations throughout Europe.

Domestic trains in Poland are significantly cheaper than international services, so you'll save money if you buy a ticket to a Polish border destination, then take a local train.

Car & Motorcycle

To drive a car into Poland, EU citizens need their driving licence, while other nationalities must obtain an International Driving Permit in their home country. Vehicle registration papers and liability insurance are also required.

Getting Around

Bus

Buses can be useful on short routes and through the southern mountains, but usually trains are quicker and more comfortable, and private minibuses are quicker and more direct.

Most buses are operated by the state bus company PKS, which provides two kinds of service from its bus terminals *(dworzec autobusowy PKS):* ordinary buses (marked in black on timetables) and fast buses (marked in red), which ignore minor stops.

Tickets for buses are usually bought at the terminal but sometimes are purchased from drivers.

Car & Motorcycle

Major international car-rental companies such as **Avis** (www.avis.pl), **Hertz** (www.hertz.pl) and **Europcar** (www.europcar.com.pl) have offices in larger cities and at airports. Prices are comparable to rental in Western Europe.

Car theft is a problem in Poland, so consider paying for guarded parking.

Train

Trains will be your main means of transport, especially for long distances. They are cheap, reliable and rarely overcrowded.

Express InterCity trains only stop at major cities and are the fastest way to travel by rail. They require seat reservations.

The older but cheaper **TLK trains** *(pociąg TLK)* are slower but will likely be the type of train you most often catch. TLK trains do not normally require seat reservations, except at peak times.

InterRegio trains run services between adjoining regions of Poland, and often operate less frequently at weekends.

At the bottom of the hierarchy, slow **passenger trains** (*pociąg osobowy*) stop by every tree at the side of the track that could be imagined to be a station, and are best used only for short trips. Seats on slow trains cannot be reserved.

Most trains offer two classes: 2nd *(druga klasa)* and 1st *(pierwsza klasa),* which is 50% more expensive.

Portugal

Includes »

Best Places to Eat

» Antiga Confeitaria de Belém, Lisbon (p998)

» Café Ingles, Silves (p1005)

» A Grade, Porto (p1011)

» Taberna do Valentim, Viana do Castelo (p1016)

Best Places to Stay

» Alfama Patio Hostel, Lisbon (p997)

» Oasis Lisboa (p997)

» Pensão-Restaurante Flôr de Coimbra, Coimbra (p1008)

Why Go?

Medieval castles, frozen-in-time villages, captivating cities and golden-sand beaches: the Portugal experience can mean many things. History, great food and wine, idyllic scenery, and blazing nightlife are just the beginning.

Portugal's capital, Lisbon, and its northern rival, Porto, are gems among the urban streetscapes of Europe. Both are magical places for the wanderer, with picturesque river views, rattling trams and atmospheric lanes that hide boutiques, stylish lounges and a vibrant mix of restaurants, fado clubs and open-air cafes.

Outside the cities, Portugal's landscape unfolds in all its variegated beauty. Here you can overnight in converted hilltop fortresses fronting age-old vineyards, hike amid granite peaks or explore historic villages of the little-visited hinterland. Over 800km of coast offers more outdoor enticements. You can gaze out over dramatic end-of-the-world cliffs, surf stellar breaks or laze peacefully on sandy islands fronting calm blue seas.

When to Go

Lisbon

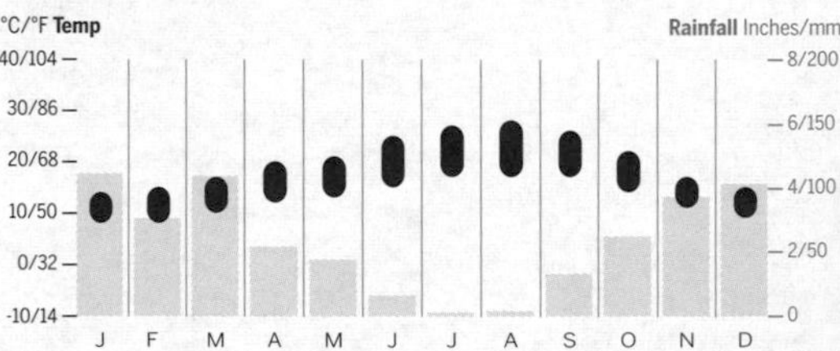

Apr–May Pleasant sunny days and blooming wildflowers set the stage for outdoor activities.

Jun–Aug Summer is lovely and lively with a packed festival calendar and steamy beach days.

Late-Sep–Oct Magical, crisp mornings and sunny days; prices dip and crowds disperse.

Connections

Travelling overland from Portugal entails a trip through Spain. Good places to cross the (invisible) border include the ferry crossing from Vila Real de Santo António in the Algarve to Ayamonte (Spain), with onward connections to Seville. There is one daily train from Elvas to Badajoz (Spain) and a train service from Valença do Minho in the north to Santiago de Compostela (Spain).

ITINERARIES

One Week

Devote three days to Lisbon, including a night of fado in the Alfama, bar-hopping in Bairro Alto, and Unesco-gazing and pastry-eating in Belém. Spend a day taking in the wooded wonderland of Sintra, before continuing to Porto, gateway to the magical wine-growing region of the Douro Valley. Wind up your week in the picturesque lanes of Coimbra, Portugal's own Cambridge.

Two Weeks

On week two, stroll the historic lanes of Évora and visit the nearby megaliths. Take in magical hilltop castle towns such as Monsaraz before hitting the Algarve. Travel along the coast, visiting the pretty beach-surrounded towns of Tavira, Faro, Lagos and Sagres. End the grand tour back in alluring Lisbon.

Essential Food & Drink

» **Seafood** Char-grilled *lulas* (squid), *polvo* (octopus) and *sardinhas* (sardines); *cataplana* (seafood cooked in a copper pot) and *caldeirada* (fish stew).

» **Cod for all seasons** Portuguese have dozens of ways to prepare *bacalhau* (salted cod). Try *bacalhau a brás* (grated cod fried with potatoes and eggs), *bacalhau espiritual* (cod soufflé) or *bacalhau com natas* (baked cod with cream and grated cheese).

» **Field and fowl** *Porco preto* (sweet 'black' pork), *leitão* (roast suckling pig), *cabrito assado* (roast kid), *arroz de pato* (duck risotto).

» **Port and red wines** Port and red wines from the Douro Valley, *alvarinho* and *vinho verde* (crisp, semi-sparkling wine) from the Minho and great, little-known reds from the Altentejo and the Beiras.

» **Pastries** The *pastel de nata* (custard tart) is legendary, especially in Belém. Other delicacies: *travesseiros* (almond and egg pastries) and *queijadas* (mini-cheese pastries).

AT A GLANCE

» **Currency** Euro (€)

» **Language** Portuguese

» **Money** ATMs widespread

» **Visas** Schengen rules apply; see p1319

Fast Facts

» **Area** 91,470 sq km

» **Capital** Lisbon

» **Country code** ☎351

» **Emergency** ☎119

Exchange Rates

Australia	A$1	€0.74
Canada	C$1	€0.74
Japan	¥100	€0.87
New Zealand	NZ$1	€0.56
UK	UK£1	€1.16
USA	US$1	€0.72

Set Your Budget

» **Budget hotel room** €40

» **Two-course evening meal** €10-16

» **Museum entrance** €4-6

» **Bottle of Sagres beer** €2-3

» **Lisbon metro ticket** €0.80

Resources

» **Portugal Tourism** (www.visitportugal.com) Portugal's official tourism site with upcoming events

» **ViniPortugal** (www.viniportugal.pt) Covers wine regions, grape varieties and wine routes

Portugal Highlights

1. Follow the sound of fado spilling from the lamplit lanes of the Alfama, an enchanting old-world neighbourhood in the heart of **Lisbon** (p993)
2. Take in the laid-back charms of **Tavira** (p1004), before hitting some of the Algarve's prettiest beaches
3. Catch live music in **Coimbra** (p1008), a festive university town with a stunning medieval centre
4. Explore the wooded hills of **Sintra** (p1001), studded with fairy-tale-like palaces, villas and gardens
5. Conquer the trails of the ruggedly scenic **Parque Nacional da Peneda-Gerês** (p1017)
6. Enjoy heady beach days in **Lagos** (p1004), a surf-loving town with a vibrant drinking and dining scene
7. Explore the Unesco World Heritage–listed centre of **Porto** (p1010), sampling velvety ports at riverside wine lodges

Lisbon

POP 580,000

Spread across steep hillsides that overlook the Rio Tejo, Lisbon has captivated visitors for centuries. Windswept vistas at breathtaking heights reveal the city in all its beauty: Roman and Moorish ruins, white-domed cathedrals and grand plazas lined with sun-drenched cafes. But the real delight of discovery is delving into the narrow cobblestone lanes.

As bright yellow trams clatter through curvy tree-lined streets, Lisboêtas stroll through lamplit old quarters, much as they've done for centuries. Gossip is exchanged over fresh bread and wine at tiny patio restaurants as fado (traditional melancholic Portuguese music) singers perform in the background. In other parts of town, Lisbon reveals her youthful alter ego at stylish dining rooms and lounges, late-night street parties, riverside nightspots and boutiques selling all things classic and cutting-edge.

Just outside Lisbon, there's more to explore: enchanting woodlands, gorgeous beaches and seaside villages – all ripe for discovery.

Sights

Valid for free admission to 28 museums, plus unlimited travel on the city's transport network, the **Lisbon Card** represents good value. Pick it up at any Lisbon tourist office or information kiosk. The 24-/48-/72-hour versions cost €17/27/34.

ALFAMA

Alfama is Lisbon's Moorish time capsule: a medinalike district of tangled alleys, hidden palm-shaded squares and narrow terracotta-roofed houses that tumble down to the glittering Tejo. The terrace at **Largo das Portas do Sol** provides a splendid view over the neighbourhood. To get there, follow the tram tracks 200m past the Sé (cathedral).

Castelo de São Jorge CASTLE RUINS

(Admission €7; ⏲9am-9pm) Dating from Visigothic times, the Castelo de São Jorge sits high above the city with stunning views of the city and river. Inside the Ulysses Tower, a camera obscura offers a unique 360-degree angle on Lisbon, with demos every half-hour.

Museu do Fado MUSEUM

(Largo do Chafariz de Dentro; admission €3; ⏲10am-6pm Tue-Sun) This engaging museum provides vibrant audiovisual coverage of the history of fado from its working-class roots to international stardom.

FREE LISBOA

Aside from the Castelo de São Jorge, all the Lisbon sights listed in this chapter have free entrance on Sundays from 10am to 2pm. For a free cultural fix on other days, make for Belém's **Museu Colecção Berardo** (p996) for great art exhibits, **Museu do Teatro Romano** (Roman Theatre Museum; Pátio do Aljube 5; ⏲10am-1pm & 2-6pm Tue-Sun) for Roman ruins, and the fortress-like **Sé** (cathedral), built in 1150 on the site of a mosque. For more Roman ruins, take a free tour of the **Núcleo Arqueológico** (Rua dos Correiros 9; ⏲10am-5pm Mon-Sat), which contains a web of tunnels hidden under the Baixa. The new **Museu de Design e da Moda** (Rua Augusta 24; ⏲10am-8pm Tue-Sun) exhibits eye-catching furniture, industrial design and couture dating from the 1930s to the present.

SALDANHA

Museu Calouste Gulbenkian MUSEUM

(Avenida de Berna 45; admission €4; ⏲10am-6pm Tue-Sun) This celebrated museum showcases an epic collection of Eastern and Western art: Egyptian mummy masks, Mesopotamian urns, Qing porcelain and paintings by Rembrandt, Renoir and Monet.

Centro de Arte Moderna MUSEUM

(Modern Art Centre; Rua Dr Nicaulau de Bettencourt; admission €4; ⏲10am-6pm Tue-Sun) In a sculpture-dotted garden alongside Museu Calouste Gulbenkian, the modern art museum contains a stellar collection of 20th-century Portuguese art.

BELÉM

This quarter, 6km west of Rossio, reflects Portugal's Golden Age and is home to several iconic sights. Belém also prepares some of the country's best *pastéis de nata* (custard tarts).

To reach Belém, hop aboard tram 15 from Praça da Figueira or Praça do Comércio.

Mosteiro dos Jerónimos MONASTERY

(Praça do Império; admission €6; ⏲10am-6pm Tue-Sun) Dating from 1496, this Unesco World

Central Lisbon

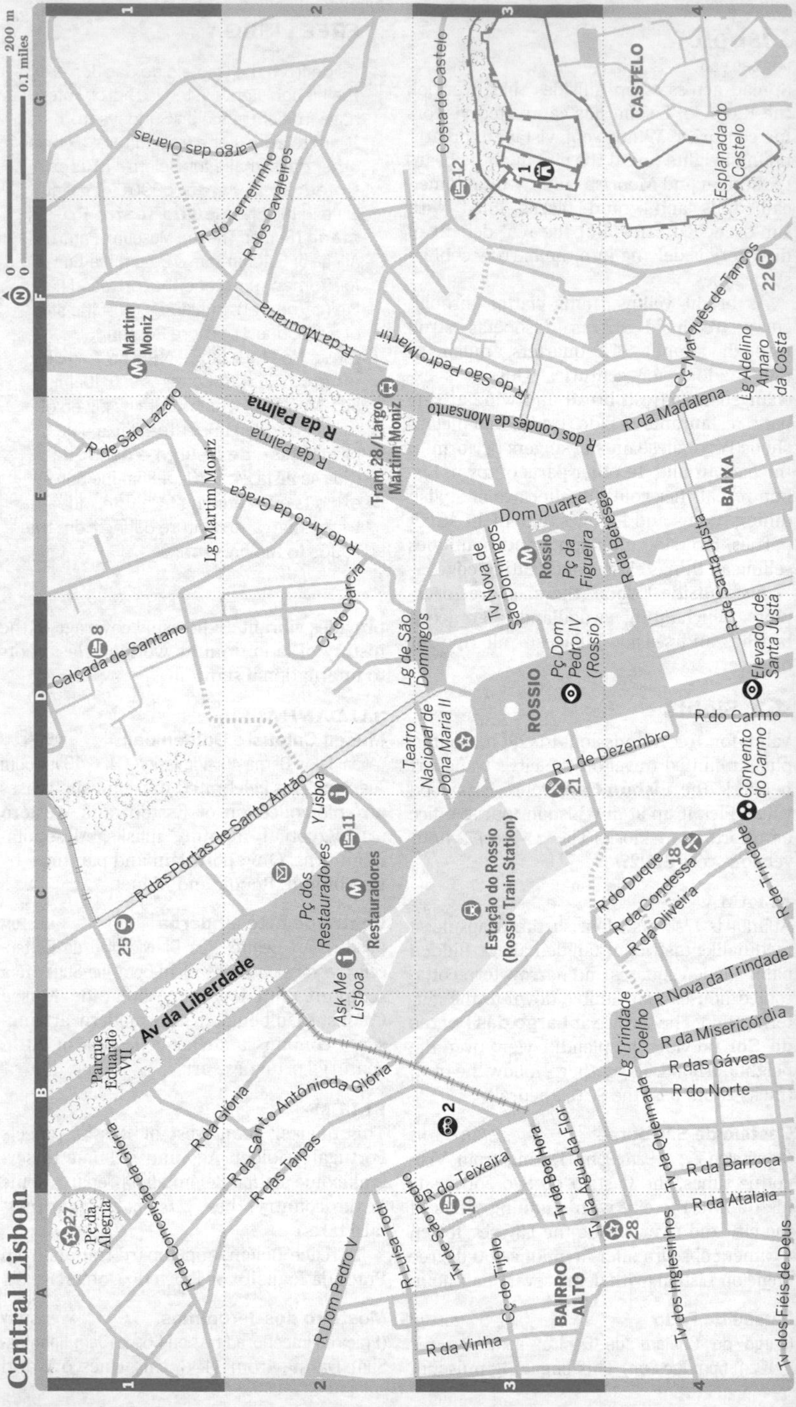

0 200 m
0 0.1 miles

A B C D E F G
1 2 3 4

Pç da Alegria
27
Parque Eduardo VII
Av da Liberdade
25
R das Portas de Santo Antão
Calçada de Santano
8
R de São Lazaro
Martim Moniz
Largo das Olarias
R da Conceição da Glória
R da Glória
R da Santo Antóniod a Glória
R das Taipas
Lg Martim Moniz
R do Terreirinho
R dos Cavaleiros
R Dom Pedro V
Pç dos Restauradores
Ask Me Lisboa
Restauradores
11
Y Lisboa
Cç do Garcia
R do Arco da Graça
R da Palma
R da Palma
R da Mouraria
Tram 28/Largo Martim Moniz
R Luísa Todi
Tv de São Pedro
R do Teixeira
10
2
R da Vinha
Cç do Tijolo
Teatro Nacional de Dona Maria II
Lg de São Domingos
R do São Pedro Martir
Costa do Castelo
12
Estação do Rossio (Rossio Train Station)
Tv Nova de São Domingos
Dom Duarte
R dos Condes de Monsanto
1
BAIRRO ALTO
Tv da Boa Hora
Tv da Água da Flor
21
R 1 de Dezembro
ROSSIO
Pç Dom Pedro IV (Rossio)
Rossio
Pç da Figueira
28
Lg Trindade Coelho
R do Duque
R da Condessa
R da Oliveira
18
R da Betesga
CASTELO
Tv dos Inglesinhos
Tv da Queimada
R Nova da Trindade
R da Misericórdia
R das Gáveas
R do Norte
R da Barroca
R da Atalaia
R do Carmo
R de Santa Justa
BAIXA
R da Madalena
Cç Marquês de Tancos
Esplanada do Castelo
Tv dos Fiéis de Deus
R da Trindade
Convento do Carmo
Elevador de Santa Justa
Lg Adelino Amaro da Costa
22

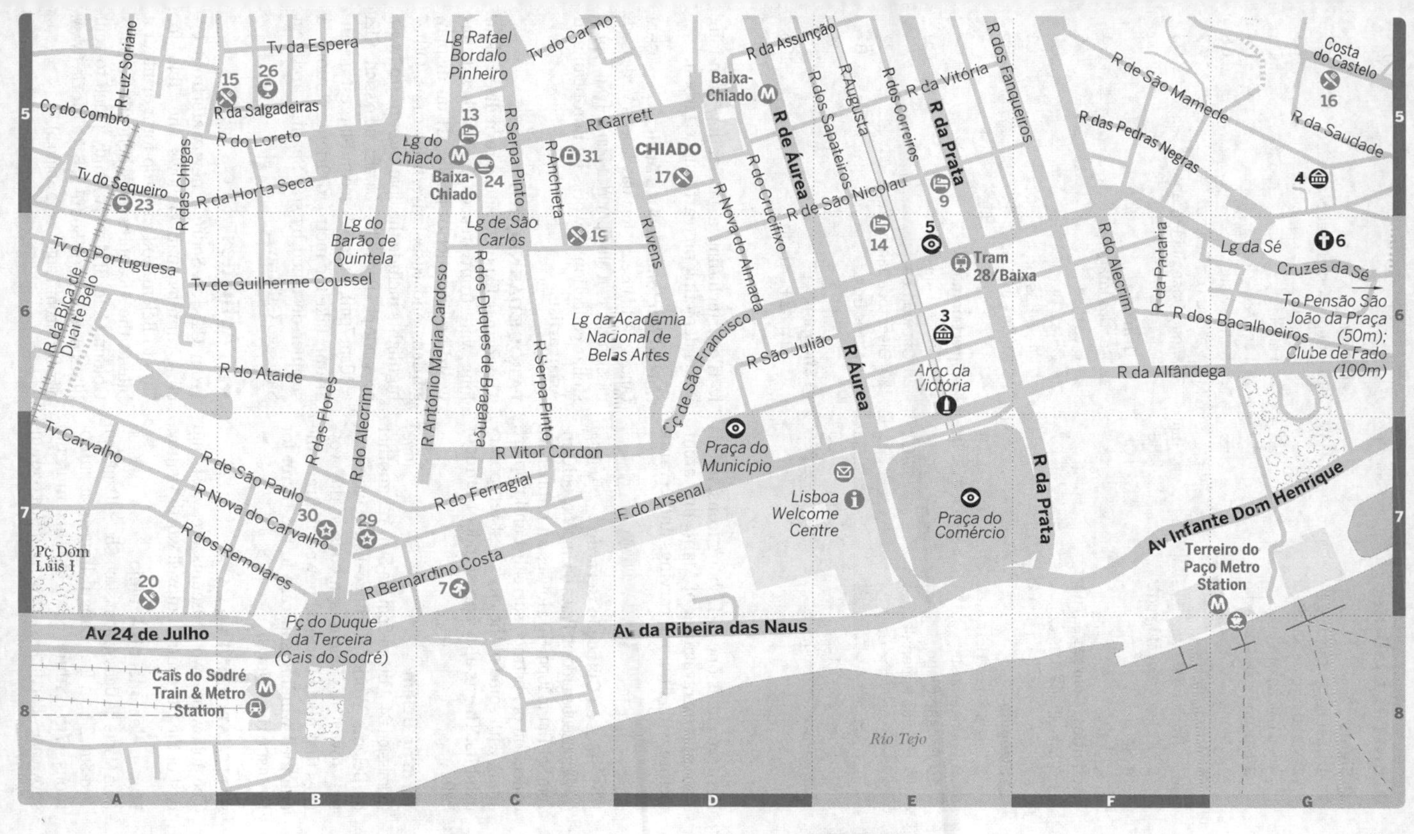
R Luz Soriano
Tv da Espera
15
26
R da Salgadeiras
Cç do Combro
R do Loreto
R das Chigas
Tv do Sequeiro
23
R da Horta Seca
Lg Rafael Bordalo Pinheiro
Tv do Carmo
13
Lg do Chiado
Baixa-Chiado
24
R Serpa Pinto
R Anchieta
31
R Garrett
CHIADO
17
Baixa-Chiado
R da Assunção
R de Áurea
R dos Sapateiros
R Augusta
R dos Correiros
R da Vitória
R da Prata
R dos Fanqueiros
R de São Mamede
R das Pedras Negras
Costa do Castelo
16
R da Saudade
4
6
Lg da Sé
Cruzes da Sé
To Pensão São João da Praça (50m); Clube de Fado (100m)
R dos Bacalhoeiros
R da Padaria
R do Alecrim
R da Alfândega
Tv do Portuguesa
Lg do Barão de Quintela
Tv de Guilherme Coussel
Lg de São Carlos
15
R Ivens
R do Crucifixo
R Nova do Almada
R de São Nicolau
9
14
5
Tram 28/Baixa
3
R da Bica de Duarte Belo
R do Ataide
R António Maria Cardoso
R dos Duques de Bragança
R Serpa Pinto
Lg da Academia Nacional de Belas Artes
Cç de São Francisco
R São Julião
R Áurea
Arco da Victória
Tv Carvalho
R das Flores
R do Alecrim
R Vitor Cordon
Praça do Município
R de São Paulo
R Nova do Carvalho
R dos Remolares
30
29
R do Ferragial
R do Arsenal
Lisboa Welcome Centre
Praça do Comércio
R da Prata
Av Infante Dom Henrique
Terreiro do Paço Metro Station
Pç Dom Luís I
20
R Bernardino Costa
7
Av 24 de Julho
Pç do Duque da Terceira (Cais do Sodré)
Av da Ribeira das Naus
Cais do Sodré Train & Metro Station
Rio Tejo
A
B
C
D
E
F
G
5
6
7
8

Central Lisbon

Sights

1 Castelo de São Jorge G3
2 Miradouro de São Pedro de Alcântara B3
3 Museu de Design e da Moda E6
4 Museu do Teatro Romano G5
5 Núcleo Arqueológico E6
6 Sé G6

Activities, Courses & Tours

7 Bike Iberia C7

Sleeping

8 Lavra Guest House D1
9 Lounge Hostel E5
10 Pensão Globo A3
11 Pensão Imperial C2
12 Pensão Ninho das Águias G3
13 Poets Hostel C5
14 Travellers House E6

Eating

15 Antigo Primeiro de Maio B5
16 Chapitô G5
17 Fábulas D5
18 Faca & Garfo C4
19 Kaffee Haus C6
20 Mercado da Ribeira A7
21 Pingo Doce Supermarket D3

Drinking

22 Bar das Imagens F4
23 Bicaense A5
24 Café a Brasileira C5
25 Crew Hassan C1
26 Maria Caxuxa B5

Entertainment

27 Cabaret Maxime A1
28 Catacumbas A4
29 Discoteca Jamaica B7
30 Music Box B7

Shopping

31 Livraria Bertrand C5

Heritage site is one of Lisbon's icons, and is a soaring extravaganza of Manueline architecture with stunning carvings and ceramic tiles.

FREE **Museu Colecção Berardo** MUSEUM
(www.museuberardo.pt; Praça do Império; 10am-7pm Sat-Thu, to 10pm Fri) Houses an impressive collection of abstract, surrealist and pop art, along with some of the city's best temporary exhibits. There's also a great indoor-outdoor cafe.

Torre de Belém TOWER
(admission €4; 10am-5pm Tue-Sun) Yet another of Belém's World Heritage–listed wonders, the Tower of Belém symbolises the voyages that made Portugal powerful. Brave the cramped winding staircase to the turret for fantastic river views.

SANTA APOLÓNIA & LAPA

The following two museums are west and east of the city centre, but well worth visiting.

Museu Nacional do Azulejo MUSEUM
(Rua Madre de Deus 4; admission €5; 10am-6pm Wed-Sun, 2-6pm Tue) Languishing in a sumptuous 17th-century convent, this museum showcases Portugal's artful *azulejos* (ceramic tiles), including a fascinating 36m-long panel depicting pre-earthquake Lisbon.

Museu Nacional de Arte Antiga MUSEUM
(Ancient Art Museum; Rua das Janelas Verdes; admission €5; 10am-6pm Wed-Sun, 2-6pm Tue) A stellar collection of works by European and Asian artists.

PARQUE DAS NAÇÕES

The former Expo '98 site, a revitalised 2km-long waterfront area in the northeast, has weird and wonderful public art on display, gardens and casual riverfront cafes. Other highlights include the epic **Oceanário** (www.oceanario.pt; Doca dos Olivais; admission €12; 10am-7pm), Europe's second-largest oceanarium. Take the metro to Oriente station – a stunner designed by star Spanish architect Santiago Calatrava.

Activities

From Caís do Sodré a new waterfront cycling/running path follows the Tejo for 7km to Belém. You can stop for a drink or a bite at the Alcântara dock beneath the faux Golden Gate Bridge. A handy place to rent bikes near Cais do Sodré is **Bike Iberia** (www.bikeiberia.com; Largo Corpo Santo 5).

Festivals & Events

The **Festa do Santo António** (Festival of Saint Anthony), from 12 to 13 June, is the culmination of the three-week **Festas de Lisboa**, with processions and dozens of street parties – liveliest in Alfama.

Sleeping

Lisbon has inexpensive *pensões* (guest houses) and style-conscious backpacker digs. For atmosphere, go to Alfama; for a great central location, book in Baixa; for nightlife, check into Bairro Alto.

TOP CHOICE **Alfama Patio Hostel** HOSTEL €€
(☎218 883 127; www.flashhostel.com; Escola Gerais 3; dm/d from €17/60; @☎) In the heart of the Alfama, this place attracts a cool, laid-back crowd. There are loads of activities (pub crawls, day trips to the beach), plus barbecues on the garden-like patio.

Oasis Lisboa HOSTEL €
(☎213 478 044; www.oasislisboa.com; Rua de Santa Catarina 24; dm incl breakfast €20; @☎) The self-defined backpacker mansion offers wood-floored dorms, a sleek lounge and kitchen, and a rooftop terrace with river views.

Poets Hostel HOSTEL €
(☎213 461 058; www.lisbonpoetshostel.com; 5th fl, Rua Nova da Trindade 2; dm €21; @☎) The 17th-century town house has been lovingly reincarnated as a charming hostel with high-ceilinged dorms plus a relaxed lounge with beanbags.

Lounge Hostel HOSTEL €€
(Map p994; ☎213 462 061; www.lisbonloungehostel.com; Rua de São Nicolau 41; dm/d incl breakfast €20/60; @) These ultrahip Baixa digs have a party vibe. Bed down in immaculate dorms and meet like-minded travellers in the hip lounge.

Lisbon Dreams GUEST HOUSE €€
(☎213 872 393; www.lisbondreamsguesthouse.com; Rua Rodrigo da Fonseca 29; s/d/tr without bathroom incl breakfast €40/60/75; @☎) Charming guest house with bright modern rooms and high-end mattresses. Bathrooms are shared, but spotless.

Travellers House HOSTEL €
(☎210 115 922; http://travellershouse.com; Rua Augusta 89; dm from €22; @) This superfriendly hostel is set in a converted 250-year-old house and offers cosy dorms, a retro lounge with beanbags, an internet corner and a communal kitchen.

Pensão Imperial GUEST HOUSE €
(☎213 420 166; Praça dos Restauradores 78; s/d €25/40) Cheery Imperial has a terrific location over the main square. The rooms, with simple wooden furniture and high ceilings, are nothing flash, but some have flower-draped balconies overlooking the *praça*.

Pensão Ninho das Águias GUEST HOUSE €
(☎218 854 070; Costa do Castelo 74; s/d/tr without bathroom €30/40/60) It isn't called 'eagle's nest' for nothing: this guest house has a Rapunzelesque turret affording magical 360-degree views over Lisbon. Book ahead.

Pensão Globo GUEST HOUSE €
(☎213 462 279; www.pensaoglobo-lisbon.com; Rua do Teixeira 37; r from €50) Offers 16 tidy, individually decorated rooms – from scarlet ones with postage stamp–sized courtyards to lime-green and leafy jobs.

Pensão São João da Praça GUEST HOUSE €
(☎218 862 591; 2nd fl, Rua de São João da Praça 97; d with/without bathroom €50/35) So close to the *Sé* you can almost touch the gargoyles, this 19th-century guest house has a pick-and-mix of clean, sunny rooms; the best have river-facing verandas.

Lavra Guesthouse GUEST HOUSE €
(☎218 820 000; www.lavra.pt; Calçada de Santana 182; s/d from €40/50; ☎) Set in a former convent, the Lavra Guesthouse has a range of rooms, from basic quarters facing onto an inner courtyard, to brighter rooms with wood floors and tiny balconies.

Eating

New-generation chefs at the stove, first-rate ingredients and a generous pinch of world spice have put the Portuguese capital back on the gastro map.

The city's best food market is **Mercado da Ribeira** (Av da 24 de Julho; ⏰5am-2pm Mon-Sat), near Cais do Sodré station. A good central supermarket is **Pingo Doce** (Rua de Dezembro 73; ⏰9am-9pm).

ALFAMA

TOP CHOICE **Santo António de Alfama** PORTUGUESE €€
(☎218 881 328; Beco de Saõ Miguel 7; mains €13-16; ⏰lunch & dinner) With a lovely front courtyard, this bistro is one of the Alfama's stars, with tasty appetisers such as roasted

HEAVENLY VIEWS

Lisbon's *miradouros* (viewpoints) provide memorable settings to take in the panorama. Some have outdoor cafes attached.

» **Largo das Portas do Sol** With a stylish bar and cafe.

» **Miradouro de Santa Luzia** Trickling fountain, bougainvillea and *azulejos* depicting the 1147 Siege of Lisbon.

» **Miradouro da Graça** A pine-fringed square that's perfect for sundowners.

» **Miradouro da Senhora do Monte** The highest lookout, with memorable castle views.

» **Miradouro de São Pedro de Alcântara** (Map p994) Drinks and sweeping views on the edge of Bairro Alto.

eggplant with yoghurt, as well as filling Portuguese mains.

Chapitô CONTEMPORARY €€
(Map p994; ☎218 867 334; Costa do Castelo 7; tapas €4-5, mains €10-17; ⏰7.30pm-2am Mon-Fri, noon-2am Sat & Sun) Chapitô's tree-filled courtyard hums with arty types tucking into tapas or barbecued steaks. Zebra and giraffe prints glam up the top-floor restaurant, which affords mesmerising views over Lisbon.

Pois Café CAFE €€
(Rua de São João da Praça 93; mains €5-12; ⏰11am-8pm Tue-Sun) Boasting a laid-back boho vibe, Pois Café has creative salads, sandwiches and tangy juices. Its sofas invite lazy afternoons spent reading novels and sipping coffee.

CHIADO, BAIRRO ALTO & PRÍNCIPE REAL

Antigo Primeiro de Maio PORTUGUESE €€
(Rua da Atalaia 8; mains €10-12; ⏰dinner Mon-Sat, lunch Mon-Fri) Always packed, this small festive tasca (tavern) serves excellent traditional Portuguese dishes, amid tiled walls, a garrulous crowd and harried but friendly waiters.

Kaffee Haus CAFE & RESTAURANT €
(Rua Anchieta 3; mains €6-10; ⏰11am-midnight Tue-Thu, 11am-2am Fri & Sat, 11am-8pm Sun) Overlooking a peaceful corner of the Chiado, this cool but unpretentious cafe has daily chalkboard specials – big salads, tasty schnitzels, strudels, cakes and more.

Faca & Garfo PORTUGUESE €
(Rua da Condessa 2; mains €6-8; ⏰lunch & dinner Mon-Sat) The sweet *azulejo*-filled Faca & Garfo serves carefully prepared Portuguese recipes at reasonable prices. Try the authentic *alheira de mirandela* (chicken sausage) or the *bife à casa* (steak with cream and port wine sauce).

 **Terra** VEGETARIAN €€
(Rua da Palmeira 15; buffet €15; ⏰lunch Sat & Sun, dinner Tue-Sun) Terra is famed for its superb vegetarian buffet (including vegan options) of salads, kebabs and curries, plus organic wines and juices. A fountain gurgles in the tree-shaded courtyard, lit by twinkling lights after dark.

GREATER LISBON

Zé Varunca PORTUGUESE €€
(Rua de São José 54; mains €10-13; ⏰lunch & dinner Mon-Sat) This charming, rustically decorated restaurant specialises in Alentejo cooking, serving up regional favourites such as roast pork with clam sauce and *migas de bacalhau* (a bread-based dish cooked with cod).

Antiga Confeitaria de Belém PATISSERIE €
(Rua de Belém 86-88) A classically tiled and elegant cafe with probably the best *pastéis de nata* on earth. Delicious!

🍷 Drinking

All-night street parties in Bairro Alto, sunset drinks from high Alfama terraces, and sumptuous art deco cafes scattered about Chiado – Lisbon has enticing options for imbibers.

Bars & Lounges

Cinco Lounge LOUNGE
(Rua Ruben António Leitão 17; ⏰9pm-2am Tue-Sat) Take an award-winning London-born mixologist, add a candlelit, gold-kissed setting and give it a funky twist and you have Cinco Lounge. Come for the laid-back scene and legendary cocktails.

Pavilhão Chinês LOUNGE
(Rua Dom Pedro V 89-91) An old curiosity shop of a bar with oil paintings and model spitfires dangling from the ceiling, and cabinets brimming with glittering Venetian masks and Action Men. Play pool or bag a comfy armchair with port or beer in hand.

Meninos do Rio OUTDOOR BAR
(Rua da Cintura do Porto de Lisboa, Armação 255; ⏰12.30pm-1am Sun-Thu, to 4am Fri & Sat) Perched on the river's edge, Meninos do Rio has palm

trees, wooden decks, reggae-playing DJs and tropical cocktails, making it a fine spot for a sundowner.

Bicaense BAR
(Rua da Bica de Duarte Belo 42a) Indie kids have a soft spot for this chilled Santa Catarina haunt, kitted out with retro radios, projectors and squishy beanbags. DJs spin house to the preclubbing crowd and the back room stages occasional gigs.

Maria Caxuxa BAR
(Rua Barroca 6; ⌚8am-2am) Maria Caxuxa has effortless style, its several rooms decked with giant mixers, azulejo-lined walls and 1950s armchairs and sofas, as funk-laden jazz plays overhead.

Bar das Imagens BAR
(Calçada Marquês de Tancos 1; ⌚11am-2am Tue-Sat, 3-11pm Sun) With a terrace affording vertigo-inducing views over the city, this cheery bar serves potent Cuba libres and other well-prepared cocktails.

Noobai Café CAFE-BAR
(Miradouro de Santa Catarina; ⌚noon-midnight) Lisbon's best-kept secret is next to Miradouro de Santa Catarina, with a laid-back vibe, jazzy beats and magnificent views from the terrace.

Crew Hassan BAR-CAFE
(Rua das Portas de Santo Antão 159; @) Alternative types dig Crew Hassan's graffiti, threadbare sofas, cheap vegie fare and free internet. Its line-up spans films, gigs, exhibitions and DJs playing music from reggae to minimalist techno.

Cafes

Fábulas CAFE
(Calçada Nova de São Francisco 14; mains €6-10; ⌚10am-midnight Mon-Sat, 10am-8pm Sun; @) Stone walls, low lighting and twisting corridors do indeed conjure a *fábula* (storybook fable). Sink into a comfy couch with coffee or wine, or nosh on salads, pasta, burritos, crepes and daily specials.

Café a Brasileira CAFE
(☎213 469 547; Rua Garrett 120; ⌚8am-2am) A historic watering hole for Lisbon's 19th-century greats, with warm wooden innards and a busy counter serving daytime coffees and pints at night.

☆ Entertainment

For event listings, grab a copy of the free monthly *Follow Me Lisboa* from tourist offices or check www.visitlisboa.com. If you speak Portuguese, check out **Time Out Lisboa** (http://timeout.sapo.pt), **Guia da Noite** (www.guiadanoite.com) and **Agenda Cultural Lisboa** (www.lisboacultural.pt).

Nightclubs

Cover charges for nightclubs vary from €5 to €20.

Lux NIGHTCLUB
(www.luxfragil.com; Av Infante Dom Henrique) Lisbon's ice-cool, must-see club, Lux is run by ex-Frágil maestro Marcel Reis and part-owned by John Malkovich. Lux hosts big-name DJs and has a fine roof terrace overlooking the Tejo.

Music Box NIGHTCLUB
(Rua Nova do Carvalho 24; www.musicboxlisboa.com) Under the brick arches on Rua Nova do Carvalho lies one of Lisbon's hottest clubs. Music Box hosts loud and sweaty club nights with music shifting from electro to rock, plus ear-splitting gigs by rising bands.

Incógnito NIGHTCLUB
(Rua Poiais de São Bento 37) No-sign, pint-sized Incógnito offers an alternative vibe and DJs thrashing out indie rock and electro-pop. Sweat it out with a fun crowd on the tiny basement dance floor, or breathe more easily in the loft bar upstairs.

Discoteca Jamaica NIGHTCLUB
(Rua Nova do Carvalho; ⌚11pm-4am) Gay and straight, black and white, young and old – everyone has a soft spot for this offbeat club. It gets going around 2am at weekends with DJs pumping out reggae, hip hop and retro tunes.

Cabaret Maxime NIGHTCLUB
(www.cabaret-maxime.com; Praça da Alegria 58) Young Lisboetas flock to this former strip club for DJ nights of old-school tunes, or loud, sweaty gigs of established and upcoming local bands.

LX Factory ART SPACE, CLUB
(www.lxfactory.com; Rua Rodrigues de Faria 103) Lisbon's new hub of creativity hosts a dynamic menu of events from live concerts and film screenings to fashion shows and art exhibitions. Weekend nights see parties with a dance- and art-loving crowd.

Live Music

Onda Jazz Bar JAZZ
(www.ondajazz.com; Arco de Jesus 7) This vaulted cellar features a menu of mainstream

PORTUGUESE SOUL

Infused by Moorish song and the ditties of homesick sailors, bluesy bittersweet fado encapsulates the Lisbon psyche like nothing else. The uniquely Portuguese style was born in the Alfama – still the best place in Lisbon to hear it live. Minimum consumption charges range from €15 to €25 per person.

On a good night, walking into **A Baîuca** (☎218 867 284; Rua de São Miguel 20; ⏰dinner Thu-Mon) is like gatecrashing a family party. It's a special place with *fado vadio*, where locals take a turn and spectators hiss if anyone dares to chat during the singing.

Clube de Fado (☎218 852 704; www.clube-de-fado.com; Rua de São João da Praça; ⏰9pm-2.30am Mon-Sat) hosts the cream of the fado crop in vaulted, dimly lit surrounds. Big-name *fadistas* perform here alongside celebrated guitarists.

A magical place to hear fado, tiny **Mesa de Frades** (☎917 029 436; www.mesadefrades.com; Rua dos Remédios 139a; admission minimum €15; ⏰dinner Wed-Mon) used to be a chapel. It's decorated with exquisite *azulejos* (ceramic tiles) and has just a handful of tables.

jazz, plus the more eclectic beats of bands hailing from Brazil and Africa.

Catacumbas JAZZ

(Travessa da Água da Flor 43) Moodily lit and festooned with portraits of legends like Miles Davis, this den is jam-packed when it hosts live jazz on Thursday nights.

Gay & Lesbian Venues

Lisbon has a relaxed yet flourishing gay scene. Visit www.gaylisbon4u.com for more listings.

Bar 106 BAR

(www.bar106.com; Rua de São Marçal 106) Young and fun with an upbeat, preclubbing vibe and themed party nights.

Finalmente NIGHTCLUB

(Rua da Palmeira 38) This popular club has a tiny dance floor, nightly drag shows and wall-to-wall crowds.

Trumps NIGHTCLUB

(www.trumps.pt; Rua da Imprensa Nacional 104B) Lisbon's hottest gay club with cruisy corners and a sizeable dance floor.

Cinemas

Lisbon has dozens of cinemas, including the grand **São Jorge** (Av da Liberdade 175) and **Cinemateca Portuguesa** (National Film Theatre; www.cinemateca.pt; Rua Barata Salgueiro 39) for arthouse fare.

Sport

Lisbon's football teams are Benfica, Belenenses and Sporting. Euro 2004 led to the upgrading of the 65,000-seat Estádio da Luz and the construction of the new 54,000-seat Estádio Nacional. Bullfights are staged on Thursdays from May to October at **Campo Pequeno** (Av da República; tickets €10-75). Tickets for both sports are available at **ABEP ticket kiosk** (☎213 475 824; Praça dos Restauradores).

Information

Bookshop

Livraria Bertrand (Map p994; Rua Garrett 73) Bertrand has excellent selections amid 18th-century charm.

Emergency

Tourist police post (Map p994; ☎213 421 634; Palácio Foz, Praça dos Restauradores; ⏰24hr)

Internet Access

Sans laptop, head to the following (€2 to €3 per hour):

Cyber Bica (Rua dos Duques de Bragança; ⏰11am-midnight Mon-Fri)

Web Café (Rua do Diário de Notícias 126; ⏰7pm-2am)

Medical Services

British Hospital (☎217 213 400; Rua Tomás da Fonseca) English-speaking staff and doctors.

Money

Cota Câmbios (Rossio 41) Offers a good exchange rate.

Telephone

Portugal Telecom (Rossio 68; ⏰8am-11pm)

Tourist Information

Ask Me Lisboa (www.askmelisboa.com; Praça dos Restauradores; ⏰9am-8pm) The largest and most helpful tourist office. Can book accommodation or reserve rental cars.

Y Lisboa (www.askmelisboa.com; Praça dos Restauradores; ⏰9am-8pm)

Lisboa Welcome Centre (www.visitlisboa.com; Praça do Comércio; ⏰9am-6pm)

Information kiosks Located at Rua Augusta (near Rua Conceição; ⊙10am-1pm & 2-6pm), Santa Apolónia (inside train station; ⊙8am-1pm Tue-Sat), Belém (Largo dos Jernónimos; ⊙10am-1pm & 2-6pm Tue-Sat) and the airport (⊙7am-midnight).

Getting There & Away

Air

Around 6km north of the centre, the **Aeroporto de Lisboa** (☎218 413 500; www.ana.pt) operates direct flights to many European cities.

Bus

Lisbon's long-distance bus terminal is **Sete Rios** (Rua das Laranjeiras), conveniently linked to both Jardim Zoológico metro station and Sete Rios train station. The big carriers, **Rede Expressos** (☎213 581 460; www.rede-expressos.pt) and **Eva** (☎213 581 466; www.eva-bus.com), run frequent services to almost every major town.

The other major terminal is **Gare do Oriente** (at Oriente metro and train station), concentrating on services to the north and to Spain. The biggest companies operating from here are **Renex** (☎218 956 836; www.renex.pt) and the Spanish operator **Avanza** (☎218 940 250; www.avanzabus.com).

Train

Santa Apolónia station is the terminus for northern and central Portugal. You can catch trains from Santa Apolónia to Gare do Oriente train station, which has departures to the Algarve and international destinations. **Cais do Sodré** station is for Belém, Cascais and Estoril. **Rossio** station is the terminal to Sintra via Queluz.

For fares and schedules visit www.cp.pt.

Getting Around

To/From the Airport

The AeroBus (91) runs every 20 minutes from 7.45am to 8.15pm, taking 30 to 45 minutes between the airport and Cais do Sodré; buy your ticket (€3.50) on the bus. A taxi into town is about €10 to €14.

Public Transport

A 24-hour Bilhete Carris/Metro (€3.75) gives unlimited travel on all buses, trams, metros and funiculars. Pick it up from Carris kiosks and metro stations.

BUS & TRAM Buses and trams generally run from 6am to 1am. A single ticket costs €1.40 on board or €0.81 if you buy a refillable *Viva Viagem* card (€0.50), available at Carris offices (there's one in Praça da Figueira) and in metro stations.

Don't leave the city without riding **tram 28** from Largo Martim Moniz through the narrow streets of the Alfama; **tram 12** goes from Praça da Figueira out to Belém.

FERRY Car, bicycle and passenger ferries leave frequently from the Cais do Sodré ferry terminal to Cacilhas (€0.81, 10 minutes).

METRO The **metro** (www.metrolisboa.pt; 1-zone/2-zone s €0.85/1.15; ⊙6.30am-1am) is useful for hops across town and to the Parque das Nações. Buy tickets from metro ticket machines, which have English-language menus.

AROUND LISBON

Sintra

POP 26,400

Lord Byron called this hilltop town a 'glorious Eden' and, although best appreciated at dusk when the coach tours have left, it *is* a magnificent place. Less than an hour west of Lisbon, Sintra was the traditional summer retreat of Portugal's kings. Today it's a fairytale setting of stunning palaces and manors surrounded by rolling green countryside.

Sights & Activities

Although the whole town resembles a historical theme park, there are several compulsory eye-catching sights. Most are free or discounted with the Lisboa Card.

TOP CHOICE **Quinta da Regaleira** VILLA
(www.regaleira.pt; Rua Barbosa du Bocage; admission €6; ⊙10am-8pm) Exploring this neo-Manueline manor and gardens is like delving into another world. The villa has ferociously carved fireplaces, frescos and Venetian glass mosaics with wild mythological and Knights Templar symbols. The playful gardens hide fountains, grottoes, lakes and underground caverns. All routes seem to lead to the 30m-deep initiation well, **Poço Iniciáto**, with mysterious hollowed-out underground galleries lit by fairy lights.

Palácio Nacional de Sintra PALACE
(Largo Rainha Dona Amélia; admission €7; ⊙10am-5.30pm Thu-Tue) The whimsical interior of Sintra's iconic twin-chimney palace is a mix of Moorish and Manueline styles, with arabesque courtyards, barley-twist columns and stunning 15th- and 16th-century geometric *azulejos*.

Castelo dos Mouros CASTLE
(admission €6; ⊙10am-8pm) An energetic, 3km greenery-flanked hike from the centre, the 8th-century ruined ramparts of this castle provide fine views.

Palácio Nacional da Pena PALACE

(admission €8; ⏲10am-7pm) This exuberantly kitsch palace is a further 20min walk from the Castelo dos Mouros, and is an architectural extravaganza crammed with curious treasures.

FREE **Museu de Arte Moderna** MUSEUM

(www.berardocollection.com; Avenida Heliodoro Salgado; ⏲10am-6pm Tue-Sun) This first-rate museum hosts rotating exhibitions covering the entire modern-art spectrum, from pop art to surrealism and expressionism.

Monserrate Park GARDENS

(www.parquesdesintra.pt; admission €6; ⏲9.30am-8pm) Wild and rambling Monserrate Park is a 30-hectare wooded garden bristling with exotic foliage. A manicured lawn sweeps up to the whimsical, 19th-century Moorish-inspired **palácio** (⏲10am-1pm & 2-6.30pm). The park is 3.5km west of Sintra.

Sleeping & Eating

Monte da Lua GUESTHOUSE €

(☎219 241 029; Av Dr Miguel Bombarda 51; d €35-40) Opposite the train station, this quiet marshmallow-pink villa offers clean but dowdy rooms with blue carpeting and floral or plaid details; the best overlook the wooded valley at the back.

Casa de Hóspedes Dona Maria da Parreirinha GUESTHOUSE €

(☎219 232 490; Rua João de Deus 12-14; d €45-55) A short walk from the train station, this small, homely guest house has old-fashioned but spotless rooms, with big windows, darkwood furnishings and floral fabrics.

Tulhas PORTUGUESE €€

(Rua Gil Vicente 4; mains €9-14; ⏲closed Wed) Renowned for its *bacalhau com natas* (shredded cod with cream and potato), Tulhas is set in a dark, tiled converted grain warehouse, with twisted chandeliers and a relaxed atmosphere.

Saudade CAFE €

(Av Dr Miguel Bombardo 8; snacks €2-4; ⏲8am-10pm Tue-Sun) This elegant former bakery makes a fine spot for pastries or lighter fare.

Information

The Sintra train station is a 1.5km scenic walk northeast of the centre. Sintra's bus station, and another train station, are a further 1km east in the new-town district of Portela de Sintra. Frequent shuttle buses run to the historic centre.

The **tourist office** (www.cm-sintra.pt; Praça da República 23) has useful maps and can help with accommodation. There's also an **information booth** in the train station.

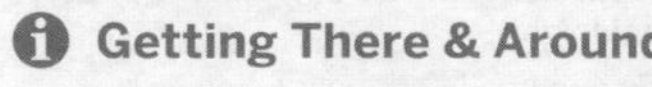

Getting There & Around

Train services (€1.80, 40 minutes) run every 15 minutes between Sintra and Lisbon's Rossio station. Buses run regularly between Sintra and Cascais (€3.50, one hour).

A handy bus for accessing the castle is the hop-on hop-off Scotturb bus 434 (€4.60), which runs from the train station via Sintra-Vila to Castelo dos Mouros (10 minutes), Palácio da Pena (15 minutes) and back.

Cascais

POP 33,400

Cascais is a crowded summer seaside resort with elegant buildings, an atmospheric old town, and a happy abundance of bars and restaurants.

The **tourist office** (www.visiteestoril.com; Rua Visconde de Luz 14) can provide maps and accommodation lists.

Sights & Activities

Cascais' three sandy bays – **Praia da Conceição**, **Praia da Rainha** and **Praia da Ribeira** – are great for a sunbake or a tingly Atlantic dip, but attract crowds in summer.

Sintra's stellar new attraction, the **Casa das Histórias Paula Rego** (www.casadashistoriaspaularego.com; Av da República 300; admission free; ⏲10am-8pm) showcases the evocative, twisted fairy-tale like paintings of Paula Rego, one of Portugal's finest living artists.

Nearby, the picturesque gardens of **Parque Marechal Carmona** (Avenida Rei Humberto II) house the **Museu Condes de Castro Guimarães** (admission €2; ⏲10am-5pm Tue-Sun), a whimsical early-19th-century mansion, complete with castle turrets and an Arabic cloister.

Estoril is a somewhat faded resort 2km east of Cascais with a popular sandy beach and Europe's largest **casino** (www.casino-estoril.pt).

The sea roars into the coast at **Boca do Inferno** (Hell's Mouth), 2km west of Cascais. Spectacular **Cabo da Roca**, Europe's westernmost point, is 16km from Cascais and Sintra and is served by buses from both towns.

A **bicycle path** runs the entire 9km stretch from Cascais to lovely Guincho beach. **Free bikes** are available from Largo da Estação near the train station (bring ID).

Sleeping & Eating

Cascais Beach Hostel HOSTEL €
(☎309 906 421; www.cascaisbeachhostel.com; Rua da Vista Alegre 10; dm/d €20/50; @📶❄) Central to Cascais' beaches and nightlife, this hostel has wood-floored rooms, a lounge, communal kitchen and a pool.

Agarre o Momento HOSTEL €
(☎214 064 532; www.agarreomomento.com; Rua Joaquim Ereira 458; dm/d from €20/40; @📶) Ten minutes' walk north of the station, this backpackers' offers clean, airy dorms, plus other perks such as a garden, free wi-fi, shared kitchen and bike rental.

Apeadeiro SEAFOOD €€
(Av Vasco da Gama 252; mains €7-12; ⏰lunch & dinner) With chequered tablecloths, big windows and walls hung with fishing nets, Apeadeiro is known for its superb chargrilled fish – the shrimp piri-piri is delicious.

Getting There & Around

Trains run frequently to Cascais, via Estoril (€1.80, 40 minutes), from Cais do Sodré station in Lisbon.

THE ALGARVE

Love it or loathe it, it's easy to see the allure of the Algarve: breathtaking cliffs, golden sands, scalloped bays and long sandy islands. Although overdevelopment has blighted parts of the coast, head inland and you'll find lovely Portuguese countryside once again. Highlights include the pretty riverside town of Tavira and windswept, historic Sagres. Underrated Faro is the regional capital.

You can travel the Algarve via the train line running from Lagos to the Spanish border; local tourist offices have timetables.

Faro

POP 58,000

Faro is an attractive seaside town and makes a good place from which to explore the rest of this coastal strip. It has an attractive marina, well-maintained parks and plazas and a historic Old Town full of pedestrian lanes and outdoor cafes.

The bus and train terminals are on Av da República just north of the marina. Go online at **Café Aliança** (Rua Dr Francisco Gomes; ⏰8am-10pm Mon-Sat). The central **tourist office** (www.visitalgarve.pt; Rua da Misericórdia 8) has informative leaflets and maps.

Sights & Activities

The small picturesque **Cidade Velha** (Old Town) is an intriguing place to wander, with its winding, peaceful cobbled streets and squares. The palm-clad **waterfront** has pleasant kick-back cafes. Faro's beach, **Praia de Faro** (Ilha de Faro), is 6km southwest of town; take bus 16 from opposite the bus station. Less crowded is unspoilt **Ilha Deserta**, reachable by ferry (five departures daily from May to September) for €5 one way.

Sleeping & Eating

Residencial Dandy GUEST HOUSE €€
(☎289 824 791; Rua Filipe Alistão 62; s without bathroom €35, d with/without bathroom from €55/40) The best rooms of the eclectic Dandy have antique furniture, high ceilings and wrought-iron balconies. Smaller, tile-floored rooms are in the back.

Pensão Residencial Central GUEST HOUSE €€
(☎289 807 291; Largo do Bispo 12; s/d €40/50-55) The eight rooms in this small place are cool and tiled and vary in size. Those rooms with balconies overlook the pretty square.

Pousada da Juventude HOSTEL €
(☎289 826 521; www.pousadasjuventude.pt; Rua da Polícia de Segurança Públioa 1; dm/d from €14/32) Adjoining a small park, this hostel offers basic, clean rooms with no frills but it is a good ultrabudget option.

Adega Nova PORTUGUESE €€
(Rua Francisco Barreto 24; mains €6-16; ⏰lunch & dinner) This long-time favourite serves tasty meat and fish dishes amid country charm.

Gengibre e Canela VEGETARIAN €
(Travessa da Mota 10; buffet €7.50; ⏰lunch Mon-Sat) Give the tastebuds a break from meat and fish dishes, and head to this Zen-like vegetarian restaurant.

Getting There & Away

The airport is 6km from the centre. Buses 14 and 16 (€1.65) run into town until 9pm. A taxi costs about €12 from the airport to the town centre. From May to September, five ferries a day run from to/from Ilha Deserta (www.ilha-deserta.com; €5 one way).

To Lisbon, there are six daily express buses (€19, four hours) and five daily trains (€21, four hours), plus frequent bus and train connections to other coastal towns.

Tavira

POP 12,600

Set on either side of the meandering Rio Gilão, Tavira is a charming town. The ruins of a hilltop castle, an old Roman bridge and a smattering of Gothic and Renaissance churches are among the historic attractions. The **tourist office** (Rua da Galeria 9) can help with accommodation and the **câmara municipal** (town hall; Praça da Republica; ⏲9am-8pm Mon-Fri, 10am-1pm Sat) provides free internet access.

Sights & Activities

One of the town's 30-plus churches, the 16th-century **Igreja da Misericórdia** (Rua da Galeria) is among the most striking in the Algarve. Tavira's ruined **castle** (Rua da Liberdade; admission free; ⏲10am-5pm) dominates the town. Nearby, the 16th-century **Palácio da Galeria** (☎281 320 540; Calçada da Galeria; admission €2; ⏲10am-noon & 3-6.30pm Tue-Sat) holds occasional exhibitions.

Ilha da Tavira is an island beach connected to the mainland by a ferry at Quatro Águas. Walk the 2km or take the (summer only) bus from the bus station.

Enjoy pedal power with a rented bike from **Casa Abilio** (Rua João Vaz Corte Real 23). Rent kayaks for a paddle along the river at **Sport Nautica** (Rua Jacques Pessoa 26).

Sleeping & Eating

Pensão Residencial Lagôas GUEST HOUSE €
(☎281 322 252; Rua Almirante Cândido dos Reis 24; s/d from €20/30) A long-standing favourite, friendly Lagôas has small (some cramped), spotless rooms. There's a plant-filled courtyard and good terrace views.

Ilha de Tavira CAMPING GROUND €
(☎281 321 709; www.campingtavira.com; sites per 1/2 people incl tent €11/16; ⏲May-Oct) Tavira's nearest campsite has a great location on the Ilha de Tavira.

Pensão Residencial Almirante GUEST HOUSE €
(☎281 322 163; Rua Almirante Cândido dos Reis 51; d €30) One block from the river, this cosy family house is full of clutter, but its six rooms are spacious and charmingly old-fashioned.

Restaurante Bica SEAFOOD €€
(Rua Almirante Cândido dos Reis 24; mains €7-16) Deservedly popular, Bica serves splendid food, such as fresh grilled fish, which diners enjoy with inexpensive but decent Borba wine.

Getting There & Away

Some 15 trains and six express buses run daily between Faro and Tavira (€3.20, one hour).

Lagos

POP 17,500

In summer the pretty fishing port of Lagos has a party vibe; its picturesque cobbled streets and pretty nearby beaches pack with revellers and sun seekers. The municipal **tourist office** (www.visitalgarve.pt; Praça Gil Eanes) is in the centre of town. Sip coffee while emailing at **Café Gélibar** (Rua Lançarote de Freitas 43; per hr €3; ⏲9am-10pm; @).

Sights & Activities

The beach scene includes **Meia Praia**, a vast strip to the east; **Praia da Luz** to the west; and the smaller **Praia do Pinhão**.

Blue Ocean (☎964 665 667; www.blue-ocean-divers.de) organises diving, kayaking and snorkelling safaris. On the promenade, fishermen offer motorboat jaunts to nearby grottoes. **Kayak Adventures** (www.kayakadventures-lagos.com) offers kayaking trips from Batata Beach.

Sleeping & Eating

Pensão Marazul GUEST HOUSE €
(☎282 770 230; www.pensaomarazul.com; Rua 25 de Abril 13; s/d from €40/50; @ wi-fi) Draws a good mix of foreign travellers to its small but cheerfully painted rooms – and the best rooms offer sea views.

Pensão Caravela GUEST HOUSE €
(☎282 763 361; Rua 25 de Abril 16; s €25, d €30-35) In the central pedestrian zone, Caravela hasn't been renovated in years but 'keeps on keeping on'. Some of the ageing rooms have their own rickety showers, but none have toilets.

Pousada da Juventude HOSTEL €
(☎282 761 970; www.pousadasjuventude.pt; Rua Lançarote de Freitas 50; dm €16, d with/without bathroom €43/35; @) One of Portugal's best, this well-run hostel is a great place to meet other travellers.

TOP CHOICE **A Forja** PORTUGUESE €€
(Rua dos Ferreiros 17; mains €7-15; ⏲lunch & dinner Sun-Fri) This buzzing place pulls in the crowds for its hearty, top-quality traditional food. Plates of the day are always reliable, as are the fish dishes.

Casa Rosa CAFE €
(Rua do Ferrador 22; mains €3-7; ⌚9am-midnight) Backpacker-favourite Casa Rosa serves up simple, great-value mains such as vegie stir-fry, chilli con carne and fajitas. The friendly owner serves up drinks at the bar.

Getting There & Away

Bus and train services depart frequently for other Algarve towns, and around eight times daily to Lisbon (€20, 4¼ hours).

Silves

POP 10,800

The one-time capital of Moorish Algarve, Silves is a pretty town of jumbled orange rooftops scattered above the banks of the Rio Arade. Clamber around the ramparts of its fairy-tale **castle** for superb views.

Silves train station is 2km from town with a connecting bus.

Residencial Ponte Romana (☎282 443 275; s/d €20/35) has an ace location beside a Roman bridge with views of the castle and surrounding orchards. Rooms are comfortable, and there's a welcoming bar-restaurant downstairs.

Café Ingles (mains €7-14), below the castle, is a funky, English-owned place serving up vegetarian dishes, homemade soups and wood-fired pizza, plus live music at weekends.

Eight trains run daily from Lagos (€2.15, 35 minutes), and are met by local buses. Four to seven buses run daily to Albufeira (€3.75, 40 minutes).

Sagres

POP 1940

The small, elongated village of Sagres has an end-of-the-world feel with its sea-carved cliffs and empty, wind-whipped fortress high above the ocean. There is a central **tourist office** (Rua Comandante Matoso; ⌚Tue-Sat).

The **fort** (admission €3; ⌚10am-8.30pm) offers breathtaking views over the seaside cliffs; according to legend, this is where Henry the Navigator established his navigation school and primed the early Portuguese explorers.

Visit Europe's southwestern-most point, the **Cabo de São Vicente** (Cape St Vincent), 6km to the west. A solitary lighthouse stands on this barren cape (there's one bus on weekdays).

This coast is ideal for surfing; hire windsurfing gear at sand-dune fringed **Praia do Martinhal**. You can sign up for surfing lessons, hire bikes and arrange canoe trips with **Sagres Natura** (www.sagresnatura.com; Rua São Vicente). **Divers Cape** (☎965 559 073; www.diverscape.com; Porto da Balereira) organises diving trips.

Orbitur Sagres (☎282 624 371; campsite per person/tent €3.50/4), 2km from town, is off the Cabo de São Vicente road. **Casa do Cabo de Santa Maria** (☎282 624 722; casacabosantamaria@sapo.pt; Rua Patrão António Faustino; r from €50) has nicely furnished rooms. **Dromedário** (Rua Comandante Matoso) has good food and ambience and creative cocktails.

Frequent daily buses run from Lagos (€3.50, 50 minutes).

CENTRAL PORTUGAL

The vast centre of Portugal is a rugged swath of rolling hillsides, whitewashed villages, olive groves and cork fields. Richly historic, it is scattered with prehistoric remains and medieval castles. It's also home to one of Portugal's most architecturally intriguing towns, Évora, as well as several spectacular walled villages. There are fine local wines and plenty of outdoor exploring in the dramatic Beiras region.

Évora

POP 56,500

Évora is an enchanting place to delve into the past. Inside 14th-century walls, narrow, winding lanes lead to a striking medieval cathedral, a Roman temple, and a picturesque town square. These old-fashioned good looks are the backdrop to a lively student town surrounded by wineries and dramatic countryside.

Sights & Activities

Évora's cathedral, **Sé** (Largo do Marquês de Marialva; admission €2-5; ⌚9am-noon & 2-5pm), has fabulous cloisters and a museum jam-packed with ecclesiastical treasures.

The **Templo Romano** (Temple of Diana; Largo do Conde de Vila Flor) was once part of the Roman Forum; it's a heady slice of drama right in town.

Capela dos Ossos (Praça 1 de Maio; admission €2; ⌚9am-1pm & 2.30-6pm) provides a real *Addams Family* day out. This ghoulish Chapel of Bones is constructed from the bones and skulls of several thousand people.

Sleeping

Casa dos Teles GUEST HOUSE €
(266 702 453; Rua Romão Ramalho 27; d €30-40;) These nine mostly light and airy rooms are a good value; quieter rooms at the back overlook a courtyard.

Residencial Policarpo GUEST HOUSE €€
(266 702 424; www.pensaopolicarpo.com; Rua da Freiria de Baixo 16; d with/without bathroom €57/35; @) This former 16th-century home is charming and atmospheric, if somewhat faded. The rooms are decorated with a mix of carved wooden and traditionally hand-painted Alentejan furniture.

Parque de Campismo CAMPING GROUND €
(266 705 190; www.orbitur.pt; adult/tent/car €5.40/6.10/5.30) Flat, grassy and tree-shaded, Orbitur's well-equipped campsite is 2km southwest of town. Bus 41 (€1.20) goes close by.

Eating & Drinking

Snack-Bar Restaurante A Choupana PORTUGUESE €€
(Rua dos Mercadores 18; mains €5-13; lunch & dinner Mon-Sat) A festive, tiled place favoured by locals for tasty, good-value daily mains (including generous half-serves).

Évora

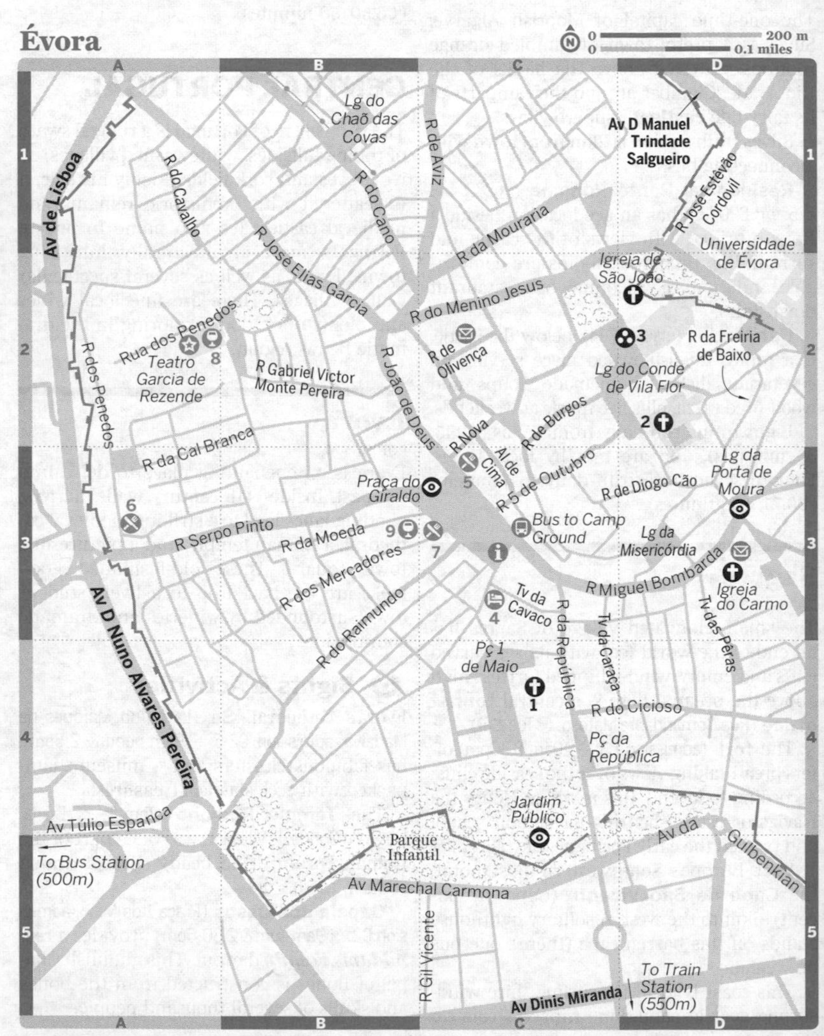

Dom Joaquim PORTUGUESE €€
(☎266 731 105; Rua dos Penedos 6; mains €11-13; ⊙lunch & dinner Thu-Tue) Amid stone walls and modern artwork, Dom Joaquim serves excellent traditional cuisine including meats (game and succulent, fall-off-the bone oven lamb) and seafood dishes.

Café Arcada CAFE-RESTAURANT €
(Praça do Giraldo 10; meals €7-10; ⊙breakfast, lunch & dinner) An Évora institution, serving up coffee, crêpes and cakes, with outdoor tables on the plaza.

Bar do Teatro BAR
(Praça Joaquim António de Aguiar; ⊙8pm-2am) This small, inviting bar has high ceilings and old-world decor with a friendly mixed crowd.

Oficin@Bar BAR
(Rua da Moeda 27; ⊙8pm-2am Mon-Sat) Attracting all ages, this is a small, relaxed bar with jazz and blues playing in the background.

Information

The train station is 1km southeast of the centre. The bus station is 500m west of the centre.

The **tourist office** (Praça do Giraldo 73) has an excellent city map. Log on for free at the **town hall** (Praça de Sertório; ⊙9am-12.30pm & 2-5pm Mon-Fri; @).

Getting There & Away

Évora has six to 12 buses daily to Lisbon (€12, two hours) and three to Faro (€16, five hours), departing from the station off Av São Sebastião (700m southwest of the centre). Three daily trains run from Lisbon (€11, 2½ hours).

Évora

Sights

1 Capela dos Ossos ... C4
2 Sé ... D2
3 Templo Romano ... D2

Sleeping

4 Casa dos Teles ... C3

Eating

5 Café Arcada ... C3
6 Dom Joaquim ... A3
7 Snack-Bar Restaurante A Choupana ... C3

Drinking

8 Bar do Teatro ... A2
9 Oficin@Bar ... B3

Monsaraz

In a dizzy setting, high above the plain, this walled village has a moody medieval feel and magnificent views. The **tourist office** (Praça Dom Nuno Álvares) can advise on accommodation. Eat before 8pm as the town tucks up early to bed.

The **Museu de Arte Sacra** (Plaça Dom Nuno Álvares; admission €1.80; ⊙10am-6pm) has a good display of religious artefacts; the 15th-century fresco here is quite superb. Situated 3km north of town is **Menhir of Outeiro**, one of the tallest megalithic monuments ever discovered.

There are several places to stay in town, including the friendly **Casa Paroquial** (☎266 557 181; Rua Direita 4; s/d/tr €35/40/70) with whitewashed walls and heavy wooden furniture.

Up to four daily buses connect Monsaraz with Reguengos de Monsaraz (€3, 35 minutes, Monday to Friday), with connections to Évora.

Óbidos

POP 3100

This exquisite walled village was a wedding gift from Dom Dinis to his wife Dona Isabel (beats a fondue set), and its historic centre is a delightful place to wander. Highlights include the **Igreja de Santa Maria** (Church of Saint Mary; Rua Direita), with fine *azulejos,* and views from the town walls. The helpful **tourist office** (Rua Direita) is just outside Porta da Vila, the town's main entrance gate. There's free web-surfing at **Espaço Internet** (Rua Direita 107).

Óbido Sol (☎262 959 188; Rua Direita 40; d €40-50) is a neatly kept old town house, with comfortable rooms surrounding a snug living room.

There are direct buses to Óbidos Monday to Friday from Lisbon (€7, 70 minutes) or via Caldas da Rainha, 10 minutes away.

Nazaré & Around

POP 16,000

With a warren of narrow cobbled lanes running down to a wide cliff-backed beach, Nazaré is Estremadura region's most picturesque coastal resort. The town centre is jammed with seafood restaurants, bars and local women in traditional dress hawking rooms for rent. The **tourist office** is at the end of Av da República.

Beaches are the main attraction here; swimmers should be wary of dangerous currents. Climb or take the funicular to cliff-top **Sítio** with its cluster of fishermen's cottages and technicolour views.

Two of Portugal's big-time architectural masterpieces are close by. Follow the signs to **Alcobaça** where, right in the centre of town, is the immense **Mosteiro de Santa Maria de Alcobaça** (admission €6; ⏲9am-7pm) dating from 1178; don't miss the colossal former kitchen.

Batalha's massive **Mosteiro de Santa Maria de Vitória** (admission €6; ⏲9am-6pm), dating from 1388, is among the supreme achievements of Manueline architecture.

Uphill a few blocks from the beach in Nazaré, **Vila Conde Fidalgo** (☎262 552 361; http://vilaturisticacondefidalgo.blogspot.com; Avenida da Independência Nacional 21a; d from €45) is a pretty complex built around a series of flower-filled courtyards. Rooms all have kitchenettes.

The popular family tavern **A Tasquinha** (Rua Adrião Batalha 54; mains €6.50-10; ⏲Tue-Sun) serves high-quality seafood at reasonable prices.

Nazaré has numerous bus connections to Lisbon (€9.50, two hours). There are several buses daily to Alcobaça (€2.20, 20 minutes).

Tomar

POP 16,000

A charming town straddling a river, Tomar is the famed home of the Knights Templar; check out their headquarters, the outstanding monastery **Convento de Cristo** (admission €6; ⏲9am-6pm Jun-Sep). Other rarities include a magnificent 17th-century **Aqueduto de Pegões** (aqueduct) and a medieval **synagogue** (Rua Dr Joaquim Jacinto 73; admission free; ⏲10am-7pm Tue-Sun). The town is backed by the dense greenery of the **Mata Nacional dos Sete Montes** (Seven Hills National Forest). Tomar's **tourist office** (Av Dr Cândido Madureira) dispenses town and forest maps.

Tomar's most atmospheric budget choice, **Residencial União** (☎249 323 161; www.hotel-ami.com/hotel/uniao; Rua Serpa Pinto 94; s/d €25/38; 📶) features large rooms with antique furniture and fixtures.

Tomar's best-known restaurant, **Bela Vista** (Rua Fonte do Choupo 6; mains €6-11) serves traditional plates (like roast kid) and has a riverside terrace.

Frequent buses and trains run to Lisbon (€8.35, two hours).

Coimbra

POP 101,000

Coimbra is a dynamic yet comfortably lived-in city, with a student life centred on the magnificent 13th-century university. Aesthetically eclectic, there are elegant shopping streets, ancient stone walls and backstreet alleys with hidden *tascas* (taverns) and fado bars.

Coimbra's annual highlight is **Queima das Fitas**, a boozy week of revelry when students celebrate the end of the academic year (beginning the first Thursday in May).

Sight & Activities

Igreja de Santa Cruz CHURCH
(Praça 8 de Maio; admission €2.50; ⏲9am-noon & 2-5pm Mon-Sat) Has a fabulous ornate pulpit and medieval royal tombs. Located at the bottom of the hill in the Old Town, the monastery can be reached via the elevator (one way €1.60) by the market.

Velha Universidade UNIVERSITY
(Old University; admission €7; ⏲10am-noon & 2-5pm) Unmissable in its grandeur. You can visit the library with its gorgeous book-lined hallways and the Manueline chapel dating back to 1517.

O Pioneiro do Mondego KAYAKING
(www.opioneirodomondego.com) Rents out kayaks for paddling the Rio Mondego between Penacova and Torres de Mondego, an 18km trip costing €20 per person.

Sleeping

Pensão-Restaurante Flôr de Coimbra GUEST HOUSE €€
(☎239 823 865; flordecoimbrahr.com.sapo.pt; Rua do Poço 5; d with/without bathroom €60/35; 📶) This once-grand 19th-century home with its own restaurant (mains €10-12) offers loads of character in a great location.

Pensão Residencial Larbelo GUEST HOUSE €
(☎239 829 092; residencialarbelo@sapo.pt; Largo da Portagem 33; s/d €30/40; ❄) Larbelo is bang in the centre and boasts high-ceilinged rooms with wooden floors and modern furnishings. Front rooms open onto scenic Largo da Portagem.

Grande Hostel de Coimbra HOSTEL €
(☎239 108 212; www.grandehostelcoimbra.com; Rua Antero Quental 196; dm/d €18/40; @📶) You won't find a hostel more laid back than this and it's hard to beat the location in a grand, century-old townhouse near the nightlife of Coimbra's university campus.

Eating

Head to the lanes west of Praça do Comércio, especially Rua das Azeiteiras, for cheap eats. Self-caterers should stop by the modern **Mercado Municipal Dom Pedro V** (Rua Olímpio Nicolau Rui Fernandes; ⌚Mon-Sat) for fruit, vegetables and more.

Restaurante Zé Manel PORTUGUESE €
(Beco do Forno 12; mains €7-9; ⌚lunch & dinner Mon-Fri, lunch Sat) Great food, huge servings and a zany atmosphere with walls papered with diners' comments, cartoons and poems.

Restaurante Zé Neto PORTUGUESE €
(Rua das Azeiteiras 8; mains €6-10; ⌚lunch & dinner Mon-Sat) This marvellous family-run place specialises in homemade Portuguese standards.

Italia ITALIAN €€
(Parque Dr Manuel de Braga; mains €8-15; ⌚noon-midnight) Expand your midriff at this excellent Italian restaurant on the riverfront.

Drinking

Café Santa Cruz CAFE
(Praça 8 de Maio; ⌚Mon-Sat) A former chapel that has been resurrected into one of Portugal's most atmospheric cafes.

Galeria Bar Santa Clara BAR, CAFE
(Rua António Augusto Gonçalves 67; ⌚2pm-2am Sun-Thu, 2pm-3am Fri & Sat) Arty tearoom by day and chilled-out bar at night with a series of sunny rooms and a riverfront terrace.

Bar Quebra Costas BAR
(www.quebra.eu; Rua Quebra Costas 45-49; ⌚Mon-Sat) This Coimbra classic has a sunny cobblestoned terrace, an artsy interior and chilled tunes.

Feitoconceito BAR
(Rua Alexandre Herculano 16A; ⌚Mon-Sat) Entered through the Tabacaria Pavão downstairs, this hip little hideaway near Praça da República woos a student-heavy crowd with cheap cocktails and regular DJ sets.

Via Latina DANCE CLUB
(Rua Almeida Garrett 1; ⌚Tue-Sat) Students swear by the DJs at this simple, sweaty dance club.

Entertainment

Coimbra-style fado is more cerebral than the Lisbon variety, and its adherents are staunchly protective. Catch it live at **Á Capella** (www.acapella.com.pt; Rua Corpo de Deus; admission €10; ⌚10pm-2am), housed in a fabulous 14th-century former chapel.

WORTH A TRIP

ROMAN RUINS

Conimbriga, 16km south of Coimbra, is the site of the well-preserved ruins of a **Roman town** (⌚9am-8pm), including mosaic floors, elaborate baths and trickling fountains. It's a fascinating place to explore, with a good **museum** (admission €4; ⌚10am-6pm Tue-Sun) that describes the once-flourishing and later-abandoned town. There's a sunny cafe on site. Frequent buses run to Condeixa, 2km from the site; there are also two direct buses (€2.15) from Coimbra.

Information

For town info, visit the **tourist office** (www.turismodecoimbra.pt; Praça da Porta Férrea).

Espaço Internet (Praça 8 de Maio 37; ⌚10am-8pm) has free internet access.

Getting There & Away

At least a dozen buses and as many trains run daily from Lisbon (€12, 2½ hours) and Porto (€11, 1½ hours), plus buses from Faro and Évora, via Lisbon. The main train stations are Coimbra B, 2km northwest of the centre, and central Coimbra A. Most long-distance trains call at Coimbra B. The bus station (Av Fernão Magalhães) is about 400m northeast of the centre.

Luso & the Buçaco Forest

POP 2000

This sylvan region harbours a lush forest of century-old trees surrounded by countryside dappled with heather, wildflowers and leafy ferns. There's even a fairy-tale **palace** here, a 1907 neo-Manueline extravagance, where visitors can dine or stay overnight. Buçaco was chosen as a retreat by 16th-century monks and surrounds the lovely spa town of Luso.

The **tourist office** (Avenida Emídio Navarro 136; ⌚Mon-Sat) has maps and leaflets about the forest and trails. The **Maloclinic Spa** (www.maloclinicspa.com; Rua Álvaro Castelões) offers a range of treatments.

Just above the town, **Casa de Hóspedes Familiar** (☎231 939 612; paulcoelho@sapo.pt; Rua Ernesto Navarro 34; d/tr €35/45) is a homey late-Victorian-style country house with simple cosy rooms, some with little verandahs and views.

Palace Hotel do Buçaco (☎231 937 970; www.palacehoteldobussaco.com; Mata Nacional do Buçaco; d from €150; ❄) provides the fairy-tale overnight in an ostentatious palace complete with gargoyles, ornamental garden and turrets. The elegant restaurant offers seven-course meals from €35.

Buses to/from Coimbra (€3.20, 45 minutes) run four times daily each weekday and twice daily on weekends. IR trains run four times daily from Coimbra B to Luso/Buçaco station (€1.80, 25 minutes).

Serra da Estrela

The forested Serra da Estrela has a raw natural beauty and offers some of the country's best hiking. This is Portugal's highest mainland mountain range (1993m), and the source of its two great rivers: Mondego and Zêzere. The town of **Manteigas** makes a good base for hiking and exploring the area. The **main park office** (☎275 980 060; pnse@icn.pt; Rua 1 de Maio 2; Manteigas; ⏲Mon-Fri) provides details of popular walks in the Parque Natural de Serra da Estrela; additional offices are at Seia, Gouveia and Guarda.

Sleeping

TOP CHOICE **Quinta das Cegonhas** CAMPING GROUND, ROOMS €€
(☎238 745 886; www.cegonhas.com; Nabainhos; sites per adult/tent/car €4.20/4.10/3, d/apt from €58/65; @🛜🏊) This restored Dutch-owned 17th-century *quinta* (country estate) 6km northeast of Gouveia has terraced tent sites and several private rooms and self-catering apartments. Meals available by arrangement.

TOP CHOICE **Residencial Santos** HOTEL €
(☎271 205 400; www.residencialsantos.com; Rua Tenente Valadim 14, Guarda; s/d/tr/q €30/45/55/65; 🛜) Santos is warmly recommended for its spotless, newly furnished rooms, good prices, generous breakfasts and welcoming staff.

Pousada da Juventude HOSTEL €
(☎275 335 375; penhas@movijovem.pt; dm/d from €10/28) Located 10km above Covilhã, this first-rate mountaintop hostel is a good excursion base, providing meals and kitchen facilities.

Covão da Ametade CAMPING GROUND €
(campsite €1; ⏲Jul–mid-Sep) This idyllic, barebones camping ground has striking panoramas and is tucked away in the mountains surrounding Manteigas. It's signposted at a hairpin bend 12km west of Manteigas along the N338.

Getting There & Around

Two regular weekday buses connect Manteigas with Guarda, from which there are onward services to Coimbra and Lisbon. Several buses run daily from Coimbra along the park's perimeter to Seia, Gouveia, Guarda or Covilhã.

NORTHERN PORTUGAL

Beneath Spanish Galicia, northern Portugal is a land of lush river valleys, sparkling coastline, granite peaks and virgin forests. This region is also gluttony for wine-lovers: it's the home of refreshing *vinho verde* wine and ancient vineyards along the dramatic Rio Douro. Gateway to the north is Porto, a beguiling riverside city blending both medieval and modern attractions. Smaller towns and villages also offer cultural allure, from majestic Braga, the country's religious heart, to the seaside beauty Viana do Castelo.

Porto

POP 300,000

At the mouth of the Rio Douro, the hilly city of Porto presents a jumble of styles, eras and attitudes: narrow medieval alleyways, extravagant baroque churches, prim squares, and wide boulevards lined with beaux-arts edifices. A lively city with chatter in the air and a tangible sense of history, Porto's old-world river-frontage district is a World Heritage site. Across the water twinkle the neon signs of Vila Nova de Gaia, the headquarters of the major port manufacturers.

The Porto centre is small enough to cover mainly by foot. The city clings to the north bank of the Douro, which is spanned by five bridges to Vila Nova de Gaia.

Sights & Activities

Head for the **Ribeira** (riverside) district for an atmospheric stroll and check out the gritty local bars, superb restaurants and river cruises.

Torre dos Clérigos (Rua dos Clérigos; admission €2; ⏲10am-noon & 2.30-7pm) is atop 225 steep steps but rewards those who make it to the top with the best panorama of the city.

Dominating Porto is the **Sé** (Terreiro da Sé; cloisters €3; ⏲9am-12.30pm & 2.30-7pm). The cathedral is worth a visit for its mixture of architectural styles and vast ornate interior.

Within the verdant gardens west of the city, the arrestingly minimalist **Museu de Arte Contemporânea** (Musuem of Modern Art; www.serralves.pt; Rua Dom João de Castro 210; admission €5; 10am-7pm Tue-Sun) features works by contemporary Portuguese artists.

Museu do Vinho do Porto (Port Wine Museum; Rua de Monchique 45; admission €2; 11am-7pm Tue-Sun) traces the history of wine- and port-making with an informative short film, models and exhibits. Tastings available.

Porto's best art museum, the **Soares dos Reis National Museum** (Rua Dom Manuel II 44; admission €6; 10am-6pm Wed-Sun, 2-6pm Tue) exhibits Portuguese painting and sculpture masterpieces from the 19th and 20th centuries.

Many of the port-wine lodges in Vila Nova de Gaia offer daily tours and tastings, including **Taylor's** (www.taylor.pt; Rua do Choupelo 250; admission free; 10am-6pm Mon-Fri) and **Graham's** (www.grahamsportlodge.com; Rua Rei Ramiro 514; admission €3; 9:30am-6pm Mon-Fri).

A few kilometres west of the city centre, the seaside suburb of **Foz do Douro** is a prime destination on hot summer weekends. It has a long beach promenade and a scattering of ocean-fronting bars and restaurants.

Festivals & Events

Porto's biggest festival is the **Festa de São João** (St John's Festival) from 20 to 24 June, with processions, live music and merrymaking across town. Other good picks are a week-long **international folk festival** in late July/early August and a late-August rock fest, **Noites Ritual Rock** (www.noitesritual.com).

Sleeping

Pensão Astória GUEST HOUSE €
(222 008 175; Rua Arnaldo Gama 56; r €25-35) In an austere but elegant town house above the Rio Douro, this spotless place has old-world charm; several rooms have superb views. Reservations recommended.

Porto Downtown Hostel HOSTEL €
(222 018 094; www.portodowntownhostel.com; Praça Guilherme Gomes Fernandes 66; dm/d from €15/36;) This popular hostel has large sunlit dorms with new beds, and common areas with shag rugs and beanbag chairs strewn about.

Pousada da Juventude HOSTEL €
(226 177 257; www.pousadasjuventude.pt; Rua Paulo da Gama 551; dm/d from €15/35; @) In a bright, modern building on bluffs above the Rio Douro, the crown jewel of Portugal's hostels offers basic but handsome doubles with sweeping views of the river, as well as clean, well-maintained dorms. It's 4km from central Porto.

Pensão Cristal GUEST HOUSE €
(222 002 100; www.pensaocristal.com; Rua Galeria de Paris 48; s/d €35/45;) Pensão Cristal has narrow, artwork-lined corridors and cosy rooms with wood furnishings. It sits on a romantic street that can get rowdy on weekends when the nearby galleries and bars get rolling.

Pensão Duas Nações GUEST HOUSE €
(222 081 616; www.duasnacoes.com.pt; Praça Guilherme Gomes Fernandes 59; s/d/tr from €15/26/38; @) A backpacker favourite with walls washed in bright primary colours and comfortable, clean rooms.

Eating

TOP CHOICE **A Grade** PORTUGUESE €€
(223 321 130; Rua da Saoicolau 9; mains €10-20; lunch & dinner Mon-Sat) Both a humble family operation and a masterwork of traditional fare, with standouts like baked octopus in butter and wine, roast veal and grilled seafood casseroles. Reservations recommended.

Churrasqueira do Infante PORTUGUESE €
(Rua Monzinho da Silveira 20; mains €5-6; lunch & dinner Mon-Sat) Popular with locals and for good reason. Their *platos do dia* (dishes of the day) are filling and fresh. If they have it, get the grilled *robalo* (a type of fish) – it falls off the bone.

Cafeteria Pintainho SEAFOOD €
(Mercado do Bolhão, Barraca 36; mains €5-7; breakfast & lunch Mon-Sat) A cheap and cheerful fish grill in the heart of Porto's romantic market. No frills here, just the freshest of fish salted, grilled and squeezed with lemon.

Pedro dos Frangos GRILL €
(Rua do Bonjardim 219; mains €4-7; noon-7pm Wed-Mon) *Frango no espeto* (spit-roasted chicken) is the name of the game at this extremely popular and inexpensive grill.

Nakité VEGETARIAN €
(Rua do Breiner 396; mains €6-9; breakfast, lunch & dinner) This pleasant vegetarian restaurant with patio seating has satisfying daily specials featuring tofu, seitan and tempeh paired nicely with goat cheese, shiitake mushrooms and other fresh ingredients.

Porto

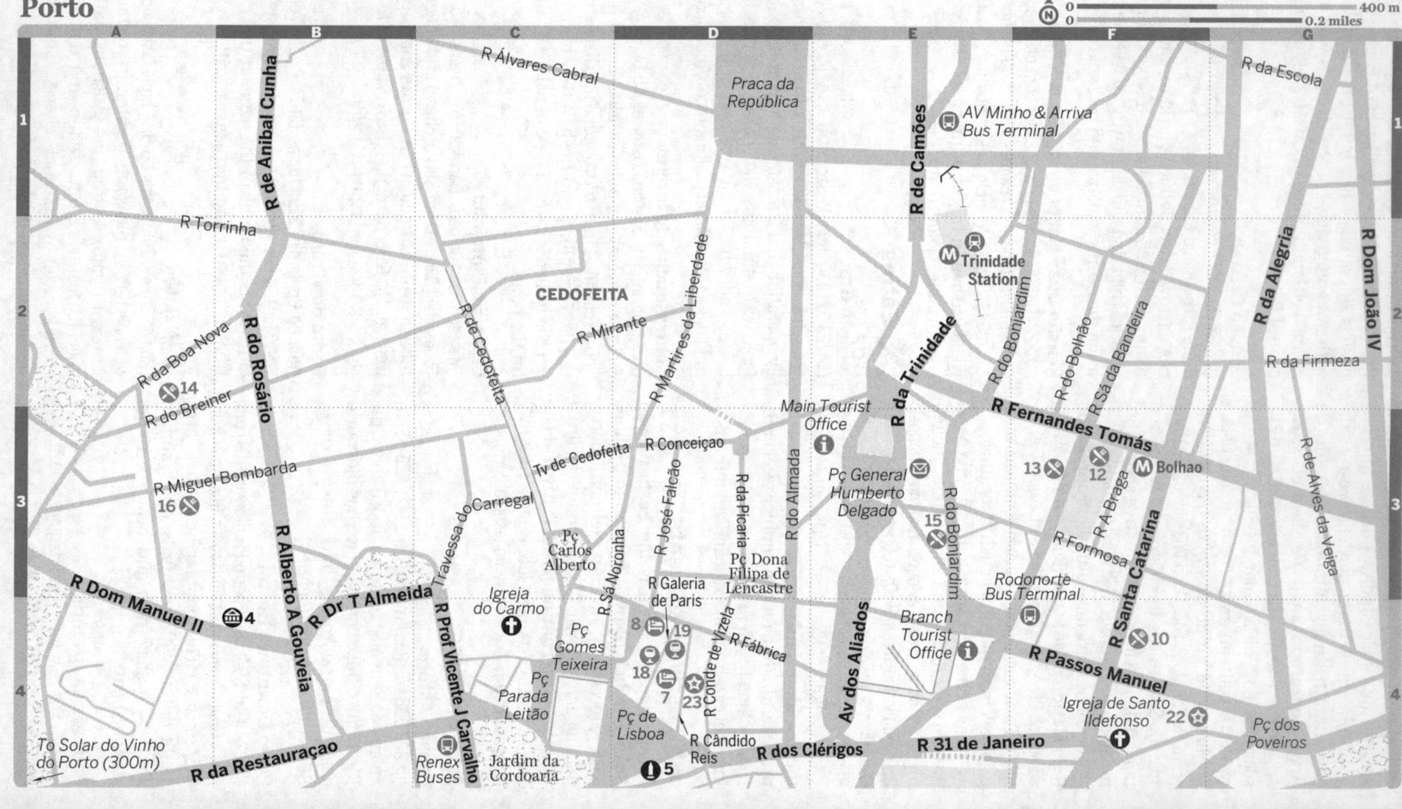
0 400 m
0 0.2 miles
A
B
C
D
E
F
G
1
2
3
4
R Álvares Cabral
Praca da República
R de Camões
AV Minho & Arriva Bus Terminal
R da Escola
R de Anibal Cunha
R Torrinha
Trinidade Station
CEDOFEITA
R Dom João IV
R da Alegria
R Mirante
R Martires da Liberdade
R de Cedofeita
R da Trinidade
R do Bonjardim
R do Bolhão
R Sá da Bandeira
R da Firmeza
R da Boa Nova
R do Rosário
14
R do Breiner
Main Tourist Office
R Fernandes Tomás
R de Alves da Veiga
R Conceiçao
Tv de Cedofeita
R Miguel Bombarda
16
R da Picaria
R do Almada
Pç General Humberto Delgado
13
12
Bolhao
R A Braga
Travessa do Carregal
R José Falcão
15
R do Bonjardim
R Formosa
R Santa Catarina
Pç Carlos Alberto
R Sá Noronha
Pç Dona Filipa de Lencastre
Rodonorte Bus Terminal
R Alberto A Gouveia
R Dom Manuel II
4
R Dr T Almeida
R Prof Vicente J Carvalho
Igreja do Carmo
R Galeria de Paris
8
19
Pç Gomes Teixeira
18
7
23
R Conde de Vizela
R Fábrica
Av dos Aliados
Branch Tourist Office
10
R Passos Manuel
Pç Parada Leitão
Pç de Lisboa
R Cândido Reis
Igreja de Santo Ildefonso
22
Pç dos Poveiros
To Solar do Vinho do Porto (300m)
R da Restauraçao
Renex Buses
Jardim da Cordoaria
5
R dos Clérigos
R 31 de Janeiro

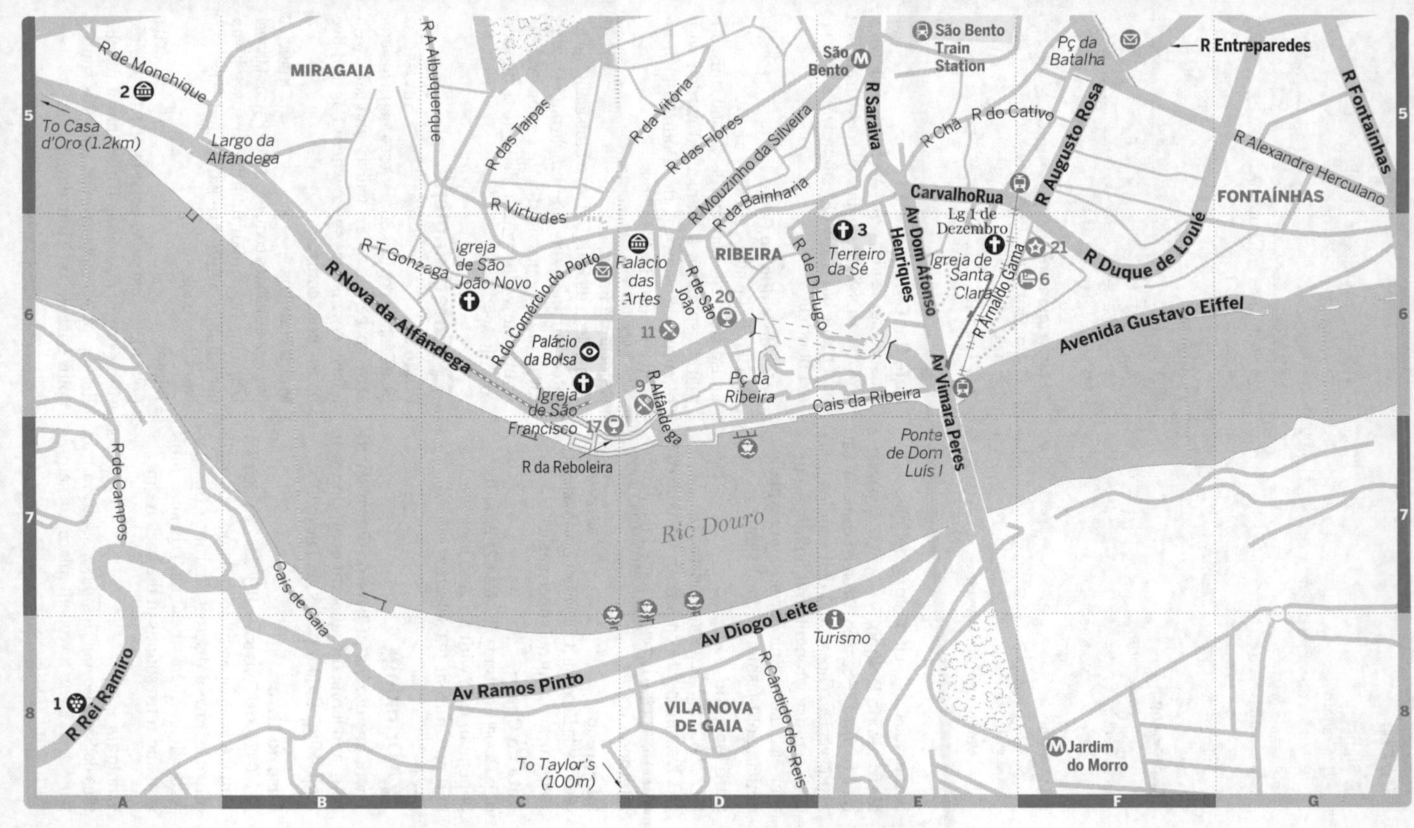
R de Monchique
2
MIRAGAIA
R A Albuquerque
To Casa d'Oro (1.2km)
Largo da Alfândega
R das Taipas
R da Vitória
R das Flores
R Mouzinho da Silveira
R da Bainharia
São Bento
São Bento Train Station
R Saraiva
Pç da Batalha
R Entreparedes
R Fontainhas
R Chã
R do Cativo
R Augusto Rosa
R Alexandre Herculano
FONTAÍNHAS
CarvalhoRua
Lg 1 de Dezembro
R Duque de Loulé
R Virtudes
R T Gonzaga
Igreja de São João Novo
R do Comércio do Porto
Falacio das Artes
RIBEIRA
R de D Hugo
3
Terreiro da Sé
Av Dom Afonso Henriques
Igreja de Santa Clara
R Arnaldo Gama
21
6
R de São João
20
11
R Nova da Alfândega
Palácio da Bolsa
Igreja de São Francisco
17
9
R Alfândega
Pç da Ribeira
Cais da Ribeira
Av Vimara Peres
Avenida Gustavo Eiffel
Ponte de Dom Luís I
R da Reboleira
R de Campos
Rio Douro
Cais de Gaia
Av Diogo Leite
Turismo
Av Ramos Pinto
R Cândido dos Reis
VILA NOVA DE GAIA
1
R Rei Ramiro
To Taylor's (100m)
Jardim do Morro

Porto

Sights

1 Graham's A8
2 Museu do Vinho do Porto A5
3 Sé E6
4 Soares dos Reis National Museum B4
5 Torre dos Clérigos D4

Sleeping

6 Pensão Astória F6
7 Pensão Cristal D4
8 Pensão Duas Nações D4

Eating

9 A Grade D6
10 Café Majestic F4
Cafeteria Pintainho .... (see 12)
11 Churrasqueira do Infante D6
12 Mercado do Bolhão F3
13 Minipreço F3
14 Nakité A2
15 Pedro dos Frangos E3
16 Rota do Chá A3

Drinking

17 Café Bar O Cais C7
18 Casa do Livro D4
19 Galeria de Paris D4
20 Vinologia D6

Entertainment

21 Hot Five Jazz & Blues Club F6
22 Maus Hábitos F4
23 Plano B D4

Some cafes and self-catering options:

Mercado do Bolhão MARKET €
(Rua Formosa; 8am-5pm Mon-Fri, 8am-1pm Sat) Fruit, vegies, cheese and deli goodies in a 19th-century wrought-iron building. Further east along Rua Formosa are equally enticing old-fashioned food shops.

Café Majestic CAFE €
(222 003 887; Rua Santa Catarina 112; 9.30am-midnight Mon-Sat) An art-nouveau extravagance where old souls linger over afternoon tea.

Minipreço SUPERMARKET €
(Rua Sá da Bandeira 355; 9am-8pm Mon-Sat) A well-stocked central supermarket.

Rota do Chá CAFE €
(Rua Miguel Bombarda 457; tea €2) Proudly bohemian cafe with a rustic back garden and magnificent tea selection.

Drinking

There are dozens of bars on Praça da Ribeira and along the adjacent quay. On warm nights the outdoor tables get packed.

Casa do Livro BAR
(Rua Galeria de Paris 85; 11.30am-2am Mon-Sat) Vintage wallpaper, gilded mirrors and walls of books give a discreet charm to this perfectly lit bar. On weekends DJs spin funk, soul and retro sounds in the back room.

Vinologia PORT BAR
(Rua de São João 46) This oaky, subterranean wine bar is an excellent place to sample Porto's fine quaffs.

Café Bar O Cais BAR
(Rua Fonte Taurina 2A) A loyal following crowds this funky, classic rock drenched basement bar with old stone walls and vinyl booths.

Solar do Vinho do Porto PORT BAR
(Rua Entre Quintas 220) In a 19th-century house near the Palácio de Cristal, this upmarket spot has a manicured garden with picturesque views of the Douro and hundreds of ports by the glass.

Galeria de Paris BAR-CAFE
(Rua Galeria de Paris 56) A whimsically decorated bar (and daytime lunch buffet), with toys, old phones and other memorabilia lining the walls, which shake to a hip-hop soundtrack.

Entertainment

Plano B GALLERY, BAR
(Rua Cândido dos Reis 30; closed Aug) This creative space has an art gallery and cafe, with a cosy downstairs space where DJs and live bands hold court.

Maus Habitos NIGHTCLUB
(www.maushabitos.com; 4th fl, Rua Passos Manuel 178) This bohemian multiroom space hosts art exhibits, while live bands and DJs work the back stage.

Triplex CLUB
(www.triplex.com.pt; Av Boavista 911) In a pink, three-storey mansion, Triplex has a regular line-up of '80s, electronica and '60s sounds (plus karaoke on Thursdays).

Hot Five Jazz & Blues Club JAZZ
(www.hotfive.eu; Largo Actor Dias 51; ⌚10pm-3am Wed-Sun) Hosts live jazz and blues as well as the acoustic, folk and all-out jam sessions.

Casa da Música CONCERT HALL
(www.casadamusica.com; Av da Boavista 604) Porto's magnificent Rem Koolhaas-designed concert hall hosts an eclectic range of musical fare; there's a 1st-floor cafe-bar and a top-notch restaurant on the 7th floor.

Information

Branch tourist office (Rua Infante Dom Henrique 63) Small but helpful office.

Main post office (Praça General Humberto Delgado) Across from the main tourist office.

Main tourist office (www.portoturismo.pt; Rua Clube dos Fenianos 25) Opposite the *câmara municipal*.

On web (Praça General Humberto Delgado 291; per hr €1.80; ⌚10am-2am Mon-Sat, 3pm-2am Sun) Internet access.

Santo António Hospital (☎222 077 500; Largo Prof Abel Salazar) Has English-speaking staff.

Getting There & Away

Air

Porto is connected by daily flights from Lisbon and London, with direct links to numerous European cities.

Bus

Porto has many private bus companies leaving from different terminals; the main tourist office can help. In general, for Lisbon (€18) and the Algarve the choice is **Renex** (www.renex.pt; Campo Mártires de Pátria 37) or **Rede Expressos** (www.rede-expressos.pt; Rua Alexandre Herculano 370).

Several companies operate from or near Praceto Régulo Magauanha, off Rua Dr Alfredo Magalhães: **Transdev-Norte** goes to Braga (€5); **AV Minho** to Viana do Castelo (€7).

Train

Porto is a northern Portugal rail hub with three stations. Most international trains, and all intercity links, start at Campanhã, 2km east of the centre. Inter regional and regional services depart from Campanhã or the central **São Bento station** (Praça Almeida Garrett). Frequent local trains connect these two.

At São Bento station you can book tickets to any other destination.

Getting Around

To/From the Airport

The metro's 'violet' line provides handy service to the airport. A one-way ride to the centre costs €1.50 and takes about 45 minutes. A daytime taxi costs €20 to €25 to/from the centre.

Public Transport

Save money on transport, by purchasing a refillable Andante Card (€0.50), valid for transport on buses, metro, funicular and tram. Bus tickets are cheapest from STCP kiosks or newsagents (€1.80 return within Porto). Tickets bought on the bus are one-way €1.50. There's also a €5 day pass available.

METRO Porto's metro (www.metrodoporto.pt) currently comprises four metropolitan lines that all converge at the Trinidade stop. Tickets cost €1.50 for a single ride, and €1 with an Andante card.

TRAM Porto has three antique trams that trundle around town. The most scenic line, 1E, travels along the Douro towards the Foz district.

Along the Douro

Portugal's best-known river flows through the country's rural heartland. In the upper reaches, port-wine grapes are grown on steep terraced hills punctuated by remote stone villages and, in spring, by splashes of dazzling white almond blossom.

The Douro River is navigable right across Portugal. Highly recommended is the train journey from Porto to Pinhão (€9, 2½ hours, five trains daily), the last 70km clinging to the river's edge; trains continue to Pocinho (from Porto €10.65, 3½ hours). **Porto Tours** (☎222 000 073; www.portotours.com; Torre Medieval, Calçada Pedro Pitões 15), situated next to Porto's cathedral, can arrange tours and idyllic Douro cruises. Cyclists and drivers can choose river-hugging roads along either bank, and visit wineries along the way (check out www.rvp.pt for an extensive list of wineries open to visitors). You can also overnight in scenic wine lodges among the vineyards.

Viana do Castelo

POP 15,600

The jewel of the Costa Verde (Green Coast), Viana do Castelo has both an appealing medieval centre and lovely beaches just outside the city. In addition to its natural beauty, Viana do Castelo whips up some excellent seafood and hosts some magnificent traditional festivals, including the spectacular **Festa de Nossa Senhora da Agonia** in August. The **tourist office** (Rua Hospital Velho) is handily located in the old centre.

Sights & Activities

The stately heart of town is Praça da República, with its delicate fountain and grandiose buildings, including the 16th-century **Misericórdia**, a former almshouse.

Atop Santa Luzia Hill, the **Templo do Sagrado Coração de Jesus** (Temple of the Sacred Heart of Jesus; 258 823 173; admission free; 8am-7pm Apr-Sep) offers a grand panorama across the river. It's a steep 2km climb; you can also catch a ride on the newly restored **funicular railway** (one-way/return €2/3).

Viana's enormous arcing beach, **Praia do Cabedelo**, is one of the Minho's best, with little development to spoil its charm. It's across the river from town, best reached by ferry (one-way €1.20, hourly 9am to 6pm) from the pier south of Largo 5 de Outubro.

Sleeping

Hospedaria Senhora do Carmo GUEST HOUSE €
(258 825 118; batistaesilva@sapo.pt; Rua Grande 72; r with/without bathroom €30/17) Clean, bright rooms have parquet floors, fresh paint and a warm welcome. It's in a four-storey walk-up hidden above a small newsstand and is one of Viana's best-value spots.

Pousada da Juventude HOSTEL €
(258 838 458; www.pousadasjuventude.pt; Rua da Lima; dm/d from 14/32; @) The exterior may need a paint job, but the interiors of this Carrilho Graça–designed hostel overlooking the marina are decked out nicely. It's 1km from the centre.

Pousada da Juventude Gil Eannes HOSTEL €
(258 847 169; www.pousadasjuventude.pt; Gil Eannes; dm from €10;) Sleep in the bowels of a huge, creaky hospital ship where men were stitched up and underwent emergency dentistry. The floating hostel scores well for novelty, but has few amenities.

Orbitur CAMPING GROUND €
(258 322 167; www.orbitur.pt; Praia do Cabedelo; campsites per person/tent/car €5/6/5;) Nestled on the inland side of lovely sand dunes, this shady site is within walking distance of the ferry pier, and also has two- to six-person bungalows (€24 to €75).

Eating & Drinking

TOP CHOICE **Taberna do Valentim** SEAFOOD €€
(Rua Monsignor Daniel Machado 180; mains €12-16; Mon-Sat) In the old fishermen's neighbourhood, this fantastic seafood restaurant serves grilled fish by the kilo and rich seafood stews – *arroz de tamboril* (monkfish rice) and *caldeirada* (fish stew).

Restaurante Santos PORTUGUESE €
(Rua dos Poveiros 48; mains €5-8; lunch & dinner) The scent of freshly grilled chicken and the sound of laughter pour out of this backstreet pink casa. Stop in for €5 lunch specials.

Dolce Vianna ITALIAN €
(Rua do Poço 44; mains €6-9; lunch & dinner) This pleasant local favourite cooks up thin-crust, cheese-heavy pizzas in a wood-burning oven.

Getting There & Away

Five to 10 trains go daily to Porto (€5-8, two hours). There are also buses to Porto (€6.50, 2¼ hours) and Braga (€4, 1½ hours).

Braga

POP 133,000

Braga boasts a superb array of churches, their splendid baroque facades looming above the old plazas and narrow lanes of the historic centre. Lively cafes, trim little boutiques and some excellent restaurants add to the appeal.

Sights & Activities

In the centre of Braga is the **Sé** (Rua Dom Paio Mendes; admission free; 8.30am-6.30pm), one of Portugal's most extraordinary cathedrals, with roots dating back 1000 years. Within the cathedral you can also visit the **treasury** (admission €2) and **choir** (admission €2).

At Bom Jesus do Monte, a hilltop pilgrimage site 5km from Braga, is an extraordinary stairway, the **Escadaria do Bom Jesus**, with allegorical fountains, chapels and a superb view. City bus 2 (€1.30) runs frequently from Braga to the site.

It's an easy day trip to **Guimarães** with its medieval town centre and a palace of the dukes of Bragança. It's also a short jaunt to **Barcelos**, a town famed for its enormous Thursday market.

Sleeping

TOP CHOICE **Casa Santa Zita** GUEST HOUSE €
(253 618 331; Rua São João 20; s/d from €25/40) This impeccably kept pilgrim's lodge (look for the small tile reading 'Sta Zita') has bright, spotless rooms and an air of palpable serenity. Midnight curfew.

Pousada da Juventude HOSTEL €
(253 616 163; www.pousadasjuventude.pt; Rua de Santa Margarida 6; dm/d €10/25; @) Braga's

rather institutional but lively youth hostel (with pool table), 700m northeast of the *turismo,* has frill-free, eight-bed dorms with high ceilings and huge windows.

Residencial dos Terceiros GUEST HOUSE €
(☎253 270 466; www.terceiros.com; Rua dos Capelistas 85; r €25-45; 📶) On a quiet pedestrian street near Praça da República, there are great deals on recently repainted and updated rooms overlooking a small square.

Eating & Drinking

Churrasqueira da Sé GRILL €
(Rua do Paio Mendes 25; mains €4; ⊙lunch & dinner) This churrasqueria serves chicken or ribs grilled to perfection and smothered in spicy barbecue sauce, with fries made to order.

Livraria Café CAFE €
(Avenida Central 118; mains €4-6; ⊙9am-7.30pm Mon-Sat) Tucked inside the bookshop Centésima Página, this cafe serves tasty quiches, salads and desserts. Outdoor tables are in the pleasantly rustic garden.

Anjo Verde VEGETARIAN €
(Largo da Praça Velha 21; mains €6-9; ⊙lunch & dinner Mon-Sat) Braga's vegetarian offering serves up generous, elegantly presented plates in a lovely, airy dining room.

Taperia Palatu SPANISH, PORTUGUESE €€
(☎253 279 772; Rua Dom Afonso Henriques 35; mains €8-12; ⊙lunch & dinner Mon-Sat) A Spanish/ Portuguese couple serves up delectable Spanish tapas and classic Portuguese dishes in a pleasantly minimalist dining room or out in the airy courtyard.

Information

Arriving at the train station, it's a 15-minute walk to the old town via Rua Andrado Corvo. The main bus station is a 10-minute walk north of town. The **tourist office** (www.cm-braga.pt; Praça da República 1) can help with accommodation and maps.

Getting There & Away

Trains arrive from Porto (€2.20, hourly, one hour), Coimbra (€19, 2¼ hours, five to seven daily) and Lisbon (€31, four hours, two to four daily). Daily bus services link Braga to Porto (€4.50, 1¼ hours) and Lisbon (€19, five hours). Car hire is available at **AVIC** (☎253 203 910; Rua Gabriel Pereira de Castro 28; ⊙Mon-Fri), with prices starting at €35 per day.

Parque Nacional da Peneda-Gerês

Spread across four impressive granite massifs, this vast park encompasses boulder-strewn peaks, precipitous valleys, gorse-clad moorlands and forests of oak and pine. It also shelters more than 100 granite villages that, in many ways, have changed little since Portugal's founding in the 12th century. For nature lovers the stunning scenery is unmatched in Portugal for camping, hiking and other outdoor adventures. The park's main centre is at at the sleepy, hot-spring village of Vila do Gerês (also called Caldas do Gerês and simply Gerês – though Campo do Gerês is another town altogether).

Activities

Hiking

There are trails and footpaths through the park, including some between villages with accommodation. Leaflets detailing these are available from the park offices.

Day hikes around Vila do Gerês are popular. An adventurous option is the old Roman road from Mata do Albergaria (10km up-valley from Vila do Gerês), past the **Vilarinho das Furnas** reservoir to Campo do Gerês. More distant destinations include **Ermida** and **Cabril**, both with simple accommodation.

Cycling & Horse Riding

Mountain bikes can be hired in Campo do Gerês (15km northeast of Vila do Gerês) from **Equi Campo** (☎253 357 022, www.equicampo.com; per hr/day €5/18; ⊙10am-7pm). Guides here also lead horse-riding trips, hikes and combination hiking/climbing/ abseiling excursions.

Water Sports

Rio Caldo, 8km south of Vila do Gerês, is the base for water sports on the Caniçada reservoir. English-run **AML** (Água Montanha e Lazer; ☎965 000 917; www.aguamontanha.com; Lugar de Paredes) rents kayaks, pedal boats, rowing boats and small motorboats. It also organises kayaking trips along the Albufeira de Salamonde.

Sleeping & Eating

Vila do Gerês has plenty of *pensões* (hostels), though many are block-booked by spa patients in summer.

TOP CHOICE Hotel de Peneda BOUTIQUE HOTEL €€
(251 460 040; www.hotelpeneda.com; Lugar da Peneda; r €40-75;) Set in the Serra da Peneda in the northern reaches of the park, this mountain lodge has a waterfall backdrop, a gushing creek beneath and ultra-cosy rooms with blonde-wood floors and views of quaint Peneda village across the ravine. The restaurant is decent.

Parque Campismo de Cerdeira CAMPING GROUND €
(253 351 005; www.parquecerdeira.com; campsites per person/tent/car €5/4/5; bungalows €50-65;) In Campo de Gerês, this place has oak-shaded sites, ecofriendly bungalows, laundry, pool, minimarket and a particularly good restaurant.

Pousada da Juventude de Vilarinho das Furnas HOSTEL €
(253 351 339; www.pousadasjuventude.pt; dm/bungalows €13/50; @) Campo's woodland hostel began life as a temporary dam-workers' camp and now offers a spotless selection of spartan dormitories, simply furnished doubles (with bathrooms) and roomier bungalows with kitchen units.

Pensão Central Jardim GUEST HOUSE €
(253 391 132; Av Manuel F Costa 141; s/d €40/50) A great option in Vila do Gerês, this stone building overlooks swaying oaks and a cascading stream. Spacious rooms, warm service and central location make it a winner.

Information

The head park office is **Adere-PG** (258 452 250;www.adere-pg.pt; Mon-Fri) in Ponte de Barca. Obtain park information and reserve cottages and other park accommodation through them. Other Adere-PG stations are at Mezio and Lamas de Mouro.

Gerês' **tourist office** (253 391 133; fax 253 391 282; closed Thu) can provide information on activities and accommodation.

Getting Around

Because of the lack of transport within the park, it's good to have your own wheels. You can rent cars in Braga.

Getting There & Away

From Braga, at least five coaches run daily to Rio Caldo and Vila do Gerês, and three to Campo do Gerês (fewer at weekends). Because of the lack of transport within the park, it's a good place to have your own wheels. You can rent a vehicle in Braga.

UNDERSTAND PORTUGAL

History

The early history of this nation of 10.8 million was one of occupation, stretching back to 700 BC when the Celts arrived on the Iberian Peninsula, followed by Phoenicians, Greeks, Romans, Visigoths, Moors and Christians.

The Moors ruled southern Portugal for over 400 years, and some scholars describe that time as a golden age. The Arabs introduced new crops (bananas, rice, coconuts, corn and sugar cane) and opened schools and set about campaigns to achieve mass literacy (in Arabic of course), as well as the teaching of mathematics, geography and history. Muslims, Christians and Jews all peacefully coexisted.

The 15th century marked a golden era in Portuguese history, when Portuguese explorers helped transform the small kingdom into a great imperial power. Henry the Navigator (1394–1460) played a pivotal role in establishing Portugal's maritime dominance. As governor of the Algarve, he assembled the very best sailors, map-makers, shipbuilders, instrument-makers and astronomers.

Bartolomeu Dias' 1488 journey around Africa's southern tip was followed by Vasco da Gama's epic voyage in 1497–98 when he reached Southern India, and in 1500 when Cabral discovered Brazil. With gold and slaves from Africa and spices from the East, Portugal was soon rolling in riches. As its explorers reached Timor, China and eventually Japan, Portugal cemented its power with garrison ports and trading posts.

The Salazar Years

In 1908 King Carlos and his oldest son were assassinated in Lisbon. Two years later Portugal became a republic, which set the stage for an enormous power struggle. Another coup in 1926 brought forth new names and faces, most significantly António de Oliveira Salazar, a finance minister who would rise up through the ranks to become prime minister – a post he would hold for 36 years.

Salazar hastily enforced his 'New State' – a republic that was nationalistic, Catholic, authoritarian and essentially repressive. All political parties were banned except for the loyalist National Union, which ran the show, and the National Assembly. Strikes were banned and propaganda, censorship and brute force kept society in order. The new secret police, Polícia Internacional e de Defesa do Estado (PIDE), inspired terror and suppressed opposition by imprisonment and torture. The only good news was a dramatic economic turnaround, with surging industrial growth through the 1950s and 1960s.

Decolonisation finally brought the Salazarist era to a close. Independence movements in Portugal's African colonies led to costly and unpopular military interventions. In 1974, military officers reluctant to continue fighting bloody colonial wars staged a nearly bloodless coup – later nicknamed the Revolution of the Carnations (after victorious soldiers stuck carnations in their rifle barrels). Carnations are still a national symbol of freedom.

Arts

The best-known form of Portuguese music is *fado* (literally 'fate'), the melancholic, nostalgic songs said to have originated from troubadour and African slave songs. The late Amália Rodrigues was the Edith Piaf of Portuguese fado. Today it is Mariza who has captured the public's imagination with her extraordinary voice and fresh contemporary image. Lisbon's Alfama district has plenty of fado houses where you can hear the good stuff.

Unique to Portugal is Manueline architecture, named after its patron, King Manuel I (1495–1521). It symbolises that era's zest for discovery and is hugely flamboyant with spiralling columns and elaborate ornamentation.

The most striking Portuguese visual art is the stunning painted *azulejo* tiles, covering everything from houses to churches.

Food

The following price indicators for a meal are used in this chapter:

€€€ more than €14

€€ €9 to €14

€ less than €9

SURVIVAL GUIDE

Directory A-Z

Accommodation

Most tourist offices have lists of accommodation to suit all budgets, and can help with reservations.

Camping is always the cheapest option, although some camping grounds close out of season. The multilingual, annually updated *Roteiro Campista* (www.roteiro-campista.pt; €6), sold in larger bookshops, lists Portugal's camping grounds.

The most common types of guest house are the *residencial* and the *pensão,* which are usually family-owned and comfortable; many have cheaper rooms with shared bathroom.

Portugal has dozens of *pousadas da juventude* (youth hostels; www.pousadasjuventude.pt) within the Hostelling International (HI) system, plus many flashy new private hostels, particularly in Lisbon.

Another cheaper option is a *quarto particular* (private room); ask at tourist offices.

Pousadas are pricey government-run guest houses in former castles, monasteries or palaces; see www.pousadas.pt for listings.

In this chapter, prices are listed at high-season rates for a double room, and generally do not include breakfast.

€€€ more than €100

€€ from €50 to €100

€ less than €50

Activities

Off-road cycling and bike trips are growing in popularity in Portugal; good starting points are Tavira in the Algarve, Sintra and Setúbal in central Portugal and Parque Nacional da Peneda-Gerês in the north.

Fine country hikes are found in Parque Nacional da Peneda-Gerês, Serra da Estrela. The ambitious can follow the 240km walking trail Via Algarviana (www.algarviana.org) across southern Portugal.

Popular water sports include surfing, windsurfing, canoeing, rafting and water-skiing.

Business Hours

Restaurants noon-3pm & 7-10pm

Cafes 9am-7pm

Shops 9.30am-noon & 2-7pm Mon-Fri, 10am-1pm Sat

Bars 7pm-2am

Nightclubs 11pm-4am Thu-Sat

Malls 10am-10pm

Banks 8.30am-3pm Mon-Fri

Post offices 8.30am-4pm Mon-Fri

Holidays

New Year's Day 1 January

Carnival Shrove Tuesday February/March

Good Friday and the following Saturday March/April

Liberty Day 25 April (commemorating the 1975 revolution)

Labour Day 1 May

Corpus Christi May/June (the ninth Thursday after Easter)

Portugal Day 10 June

Feast of the Assumption 15 August

Republic Day 5 October

All Saints' Day 1 November

Independence Day 1 December (celebrating independence from Spain in 1640)

Immaculate Conception 8 December

Christmas Day 25 December

Money

There are numerous banks with ATMs located throughout Portugal. Credit cards are accepted in midrange and top-end hotels, restaurants and shops.

Telephone

Portugal's country code is ☎351. There are no regional area codes. Mobile phone numbers within Portugal have nine digits and begin with ☎9.

For general information dial ☎118, and for reverse-charge (collect) calls dial ☎120.

Phonecards are the most reliable and cheapest way of making a phone call from a telephone booth. They are sold at post offices, newsagents and tobacconists in denominations of €5 and €10.

Portugal uses the GSM 900/1800 frequency like the rest of Europe, the UK and Australia. If your phone is unlocked and on this frequency, you can purchase a prepaid SIM card for under €10. The main carriers with nationwide coverage are Vodafone, Optimus and TMN.

Getting There & Away

Air

TAP (www.tap.pt) is Portugal's international flag carrier as well as its main domestic airline. Portugal's main airports:

Lisbon (☎218 413 500; www.ana-aeroportos.pt)

Porto (☎229 432 400; www.ana-aeroportos.pt)

Faro (☎289 800 800; www.ana-aeroportos.pt)

Bus

Eurolines (www.eurolines.com) services from the UK and France cross to Portugal via northwest Spain. Other international companies are Alsa, Avanza, Damas and Eva.

Train

The most popular train link from Spain is on the Sud Express, operated by **Renfe** (www.renfe.com; one-way from €59), which has a nightly sleeper service between Madrid and Lisbon. Badajoz (Spain)–Elvas–Lisbon is slow (five hours, €25) and there is only one regional service daily, but the scenery is stunning. Coming from Galicia, in the northwest of Spain, travellers can go from Vigo to Valença do Minho (Portugal) and continue on to Porto.

From France, there's a Lisbon service via Irún (Spain) that takes around 20 hours (one-way ticket from €136) from Paris. From Paris, contact **SNCF** (www.sncf.com).

Getting Around

Bicycle

Mountain biking is a great way to explore the country although, given the recklessness of some Portuguese drivers, it can be dangerous. For short jaunts, some towns have bike-rental outfits (around €10 a day). Bicycles can be taken free on most trains as accompanied baggage.

Bus

A host of small private bus operators, most amalgamated into regional companies, run a dense network of services across the country. Among the largest companies are **Rede Expressos** (www.rede-expressos.pt), **Rodonorte** (www.rodonorte.pt) and the Algarve line **Eva** (www.eva-bus.com).

BUSES TO PORTUGAL

FROM	TO	VIA	DURATION	COST	COMPANY
Madrid	Porto	Guarda	8½ hrs	€50	Eurolines
Madrid	Lisbon	Évora	8 hrs	€50	Eurolines, Avanza & Alsa
Barcelona	Lisbon	Évora	18 hrs	€100	Eurolines
Madrid	Lisbon	Évora	8 hrs	€45	Eurolines
Seville	Lisbon	Évora	7 hrs	€48	Eurolines, Alsa, Eva & Damas
Seville	Faro	Huelva	4½ hrs	€20	Eva and Damas

Classes and discounts:

Expressos Comfortable, fast buses between major cities

Rápidas Quick regional buses

Carreiras Marked CR, slow, stopping at every crossroad

An under-26 student card should get you a small discount, at least on the long-distance services.

Car & Motorcycle

Automóvel Clube de Portugal (ACP; ☎213 180 100; www.acp.pt) has a reciprocal arrangement with many of the better-known foreign automobile clubs, including AA and RAC. ACP provides medical, legal and breakdown assistance. The 24-hour emergency help number is ☎707 509 510.

To hire a car in Portugal you must generally be at least 25. To hire a scooter of up to 50cc you must be 18-plus with a driving licence. For more powerful motorbikes you must have a driving licence covering these vehicles from your home country.

Speed limits for cars and motorcycles are 50km/h in cities and public centres, 90km/h on normal roads and 120km/h on motorways. Motorcyclists and passengers must wear helmets, and motorcycles must always have headlights on. Using a mobile phone while driving could result in a fine.

Drink-driving laws are strict with a maximum legal blood-alcohol level of 0.05%.

Local Transport

Lisbon and Porto have speedy, convenient metros; pick up route maps from the respective tourist offices.

Taxis are plentiful and fairly inexpensive, but don't miss the trams in Lisbon and Porto, or the funiculars and lifts of Lisbon.

Train

Caminhos de Ferro Portugueses (www.cp.pt) is the statewide train network and is generally efficient.

There are three main types of long-distance service. Note that international services are marked IN on timetables.

Regional trains (R) Slow, stop everywhere

Interregional (IR) Reasonably fast trains

Intercidade (IC) Also called rápido express trains

Alfa Pendular Deluxe, marginally faster and much pricier service than IC trains.

Romania

Includes »

Best Places to Eat

» Felinarul Café, Sibiu (p1035)

» Restaurant Transylvania, Braşov (p1031)

» Sale e Pepe, Bucharest (p1028)

» Casa cu Flori, Timişoara (p1038)

Best Places to Stay

» Butterfly Villa Hostel, Bucharest (p1025)

» Felinarul Hostel, Sibiu (p1035)

» Bed & Breakfast Kula, Sighişoara (p1034)

» Retro Hostel, Cluj-Napoca (p1036)

Why Go?

Romania's rapid urban evolution has had little effect on its singularly beautiful, beguilingly simple and utterly fascinating rural landscape, where aesthetically stirring handploughed fields, sheep-instigated traffic jams, and homemade plum brandy still endure. The Carpathian Mountains offer relatively uncrowded hiking, cycling and skiing. Transylvania's Saxon towns are time-warp strolling grounds for Gothic architecture, Austro-Hungarian legacy and Vlad 'Ţepeş' Dracula shtick. Unesco-listed painted monasteries dot Southern Bucovina. And, for the record, the big cities are a blast too.

The antics of an infinitesimal number of con artists have birthed exaggerated stories about Romanians, but in truth you're far less likely to be the victim of crime here than in much of Western Europe. Instead, enjoy the friendliness of a new generation with no vivid memories of Nicolae Ceauşescu.

When to Go

Bucharest

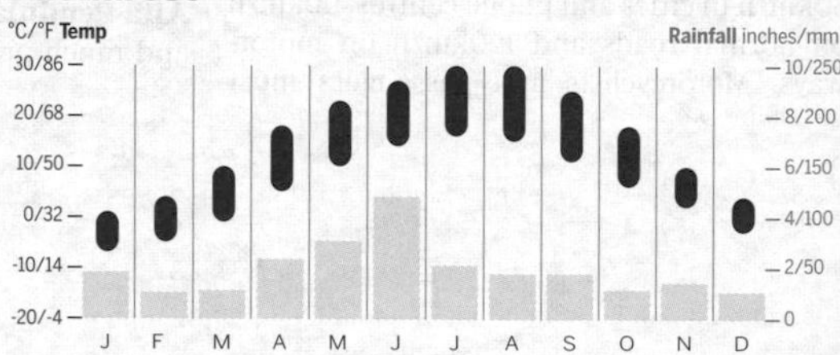

May Some of the best festivals: Sibiu Jazz, Transylvania Film Festival and Bucharest Carnival.

Jun Mountain hiking starts in mid-June, roughly when the Transfăgărăşan Road opens.

Aug Folk festivals: National Romanian, Hora de la Prislop, and Fundata's Mountain Festival.

Connections

Trains, buses and maxitaxis swarm around every available border crossing.

Trains depart Bucharest heading for destinations including Sofia (Bulgaria), Budapest (Hungary), Chişinău (Moldova), İstanbul (Turkey), Belgrade (Serbia), Kyiv (Ukraine), Minsk (Belarus) and Moscow (Russia) – the last three via Suceava. Bucharest also has long-haul buses to Western European destinations, and a daily maxitaxi service to Sofia.

Budapest can be easily reached by bus or train from Oradea, Timişoara and Cluj-Napoca.

Suceava has one daily bus to Chernivtsi (Ukraine), as well as Chişinău, though entering Moldova is easier from Iaşi. Timişoara buses go to countries all over Western Europe, including Spain, Italy and Sweden. Nearly every major city has a bus service to İstanbul.

ITINERARIES

One Week

Spend a day viewing the parts of Bucharest that survived Ceauşescu, then catch the train to Braşov, Transylvania's main event, for castles, activities and beers at sidewalk cafes. Spend a day in Sighişoara's medieval citadel, then train back to Bucharest or on to Budapest (Hungary).

Two Weeks

Arrive in Bucharest (by plane) or Timişoara (by train), then head into Transylvania, devoting a day or two each to Braşov, Sighişoara and Sibiu. Tour Southern Bucovina's painted monasteries, then continue to Kyiv (Ukraine), Chişinău (Moldova) or return to Bucharest.

Essential Food & Drink

» **Mămăligă** Essentially cornmeal mush that's boiled or fried, sometimes topped with sour cream and/or cheese

» **Ciorbă** This soup is a mainstay of the Romanian diet and a powerful hangover remedy

» **Muşchi de vacă/porc/miel** Cutlet of beef/pork/lamb

» **Piept de pui** Chicken breast

» **Wine** Among the best Romanian wines are Cotnari, Murfatlar, Odobeşti, Târnave and Valea Călugărească

» **Ţuică** A once-filtered clear brandy made from fermented fruit (the tastiest and most popular is plum *ţuică*), usually 30 proof. *Palincă* is similar, only it's filtered twice and is usually around 60 proof.

AT A GLANCE

» **Currency** Romanian leu (plural lei)

» **Language** Romanian

» **Money** ATMs abundant

» **Visas** Not required for citizens of the EU, USA, Canada, Australia and New Zealand

Fast Facts

» **Area** 237,500 sq km

» **Capital** Bucharest

» **Country code** ☎40

» **Emergency** ☎112

Exchange Rates

Australia	A$1	3.01 lei
Canada	C$1	3.01 lei
euro zone	€1	4.11 lei
Japan	¥100	3.44 lei
New Zealand	NZ$1	2.23 lei
UK	UK£1	4.67 lei
USA	US$1	2.89 lei

Set Your Budget

» **Budget double hotel room** 100–150 lei

» **Two-course evening meal** 20 lei

» **Museum entrance** 6 lei

» **Bottle of beer** 4 lei

» **City transport ticket** 1.5–3 lei

Resources

» **Romania National Tourism Office** (www.romaniatourism.com)

» **Romania and Moldova Travel Guide** (www.romaniaandmoldova.com)

» **Vivid** (www.vivid.ro)

BUCHAREST

POP 2.1 MILLION

Many Romanians slam it, some travellers depart shell-shocked after a couple of days, but Bucharest is an intriguing and evolving mix of eras. Wide boulevards with century-old villas mingle with (deviously hidden) 18th-century monasteries, unsightly communist-built housing blocks and statement-making government headquarters. The country's top museums are here, and there's plenty of green parks providing escape from the repellent effects of newly available personal car loans. Ongoing development and gentrification of the crumbling historic centre has resulted in a popular entertainment district.

Sights

CEAUŞESCU'S BUCHAREST

Strangely inspired by trips to Pyongyang and Beijing in the 1980s, Nicolae Ceauşescu had an entire suburb of historic buildings smashed to create **B-dul Unirii**, Romania's 'Champs-Élysées', a chaotic, fountain-lined

Romania Highlights

1 Ascend castles, mountains and castles on top of mountains using the Gothic, medieval town of **Braşov** (p1031) as a base

2 Follow the Unesco World Heritage conga line of painted monasteries in **Southern Bucovina** (p1039)

3 Soak in **Sibiu** (p1034), the beautifully restored Saxon town and 2007 European Capital of Culture

4 Explore the medieval citadel of **Sighişoara** (p1033), Dracula's birthplace

5 Trace the heroic 1989 revolution to tenacious **Timişoara** (p1037)

3.2km boulevard – deliberately pipping Paris' by a resounding 6m.

Palace of Parliament HISTORIC BUILDING
(Palatul Parlamentului; ☎021-311 3611; B-dul Naţiunile Unite; adult/student 25 lei/free; ⏰10am-3.45pm) Anchoring B-dul Unirii is the mother of all white elephants, the Palace of Parliament, the world's second-largest administrative building (after the US Pentagon). Built in 1984 (and still unfinished), the building's 12 storeys and 3100 rooms cover 330,000 sq metres and cost an estimated €3.3 billion. The hourly 45-minute tours are the only way to see a handful of the opulent marble rooms; enter from the north side. Tour reservations are required. Call one or two days in advance or try between 9am and 9.30am for a same-day spot. Passports or international IDs are required to enter.

HISTORIC QUARTER & PIAŢA REVOLUŢIEI

National History Museum MUSEUM
(Muzeul National de Istorie a Romaniei; www.mnir.ro; Calea Victoriei 12; adult/student 8/2 lei; ⏰10am-6pm Wed-Sun) Despite ongoing renovations, this museum is worth seeing for the dismantled replica of the 2nd-century 40m Trajan's Column; its 2500 characters retell the Dacian Wars against Rome. There's also a gold-crammed treasury.

Stavropoleos Church CHURCH
(Str Stavropoleos) On a street meaning 'town of the cross', the church dates from 1724 and is one of Bucharest's most atmospheric.

Old Princely Court RUINS
(Curtea Veche; Str Franceza 21-23; admission 3 lei; ⏰10am-5pm) The heart of the historic centre is the busted-up Old Princely Court from the 15th century with a Vlad Ţepeş statue out front. The nearby **Hanul lui Manuc** inn (1808), built to shelter and feed travelling merchants, has fallen into serious neglect.

Revolution Sites HISTORIC SITES
The scene of Ceauşescu's infamous final public appearance on 21 December 1989 was on the balcony of the former **Central Committee of the Communist Party building**. The crowds cried 'down with Ceauşescu' as the leader tried vainly to make his last speech. The **building shell** (cnr Str Dl Dobrescu & Str Boteanu) is all that remains of the former home of the hated secret police after it was destroyed by protestors in 1989.

National Art Museum ART GALLERY
(Muzeul Naţional de Artă; www.mnar.arts.ro; Calea Victoriei 49-53; combination ticket 15 lei, Romanian or European collection 10 lei, 1st Wed of month free; ⏰11am-7pm Wed-Sun) Housed in the early-19th-century Royal Palace, this is a super multipart museum with Romanian art, European art (Rembrandt, Rodin) and pieces from the Romanian treasury.

NORTHERN BUCHAREST

Museum of the Romanian Peasant MUSEUM
(Muzeul Tăranului Român; Şos Kiseleff 3; adult/student 6/1.50 lei; ⏰10am-6pm Tue-Sun) Handmade cards personalise enlightening rural exhibits, such as a full 19th-century home and a heartbreakingly sweet room devoted to grandmas.

National Village Museum MUSEUM
(Muzeul Naţional al Satului; www.muzeul-satului.ro; Şos Kiseleff 28-30; adult/student 6/3 lei; ⏰9am-7pm Tue-Sun, to 5pm Mon) Accessed from Şos Kiseleff, this is a terrific open-air collection of homesteads, churches, mills and windmills that have been relocated from rural Romania.

Herăstrău Park PARK
Hugging the chain of lakes that stripe northern Bucharest.

Sleeping

TOP CHOICE **Butterfly Villa Hostel** HOSTEL €
(☎021-314 7595; www.villabutterfly.com; Str Stirbei Voda 96; dm 50-54 lei, d 116 lei; ❄@📶) One of Bucharest's best hostels, run by a German-Romanian couple. There are lounge-y spaces, a kitchen and a small courtyard to kick back in. It's about a 15-minute walk from the train station.

Midland Youth Hostel 2 HOSTEL €
(☎021-314 5323; www.themidlandhostel.com; Str Biserica Amzei 22; dm 50-60 lei; @📶) Reasonably central and very spacious, micro-bathrooms notwithstanding. Amenities include TV room, kitchen, free internet and wi-fi, lockers, laundry (5 lei) and bike rental.

Hotel Carpaţi HOTEL €€
(☎021-315 0140; www.hotelcarpatibucuresti.ro; Str Matei Millo 16; s/d without bathroom 128/180 lei, d with bathroom 240 lei; 📶) This popular option has 40 recently renovated rooms – some rather tiny and creaky – and a great breakfast (included in the price) served with a little pomp in the Paris-style lobby lounge.

Central Bucharest

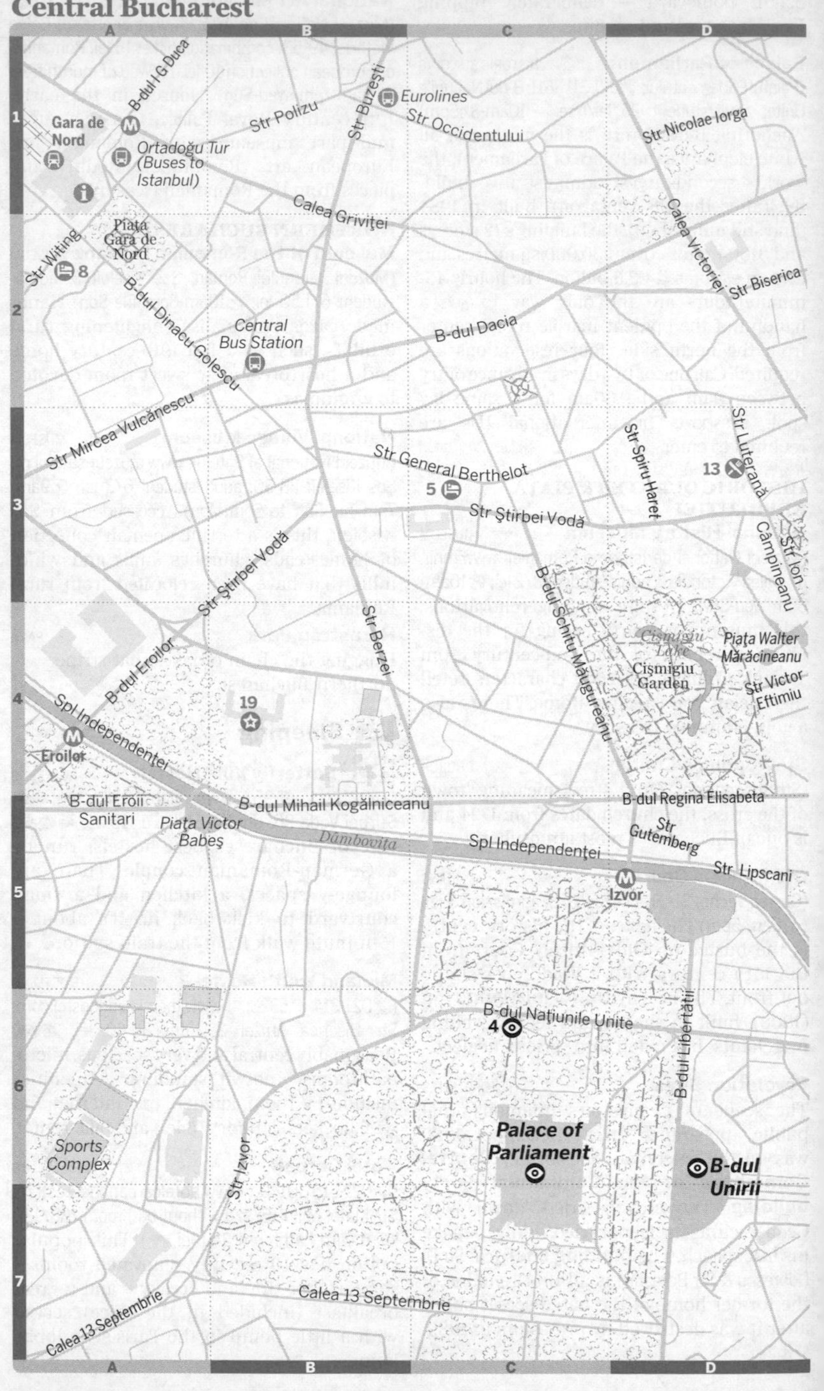

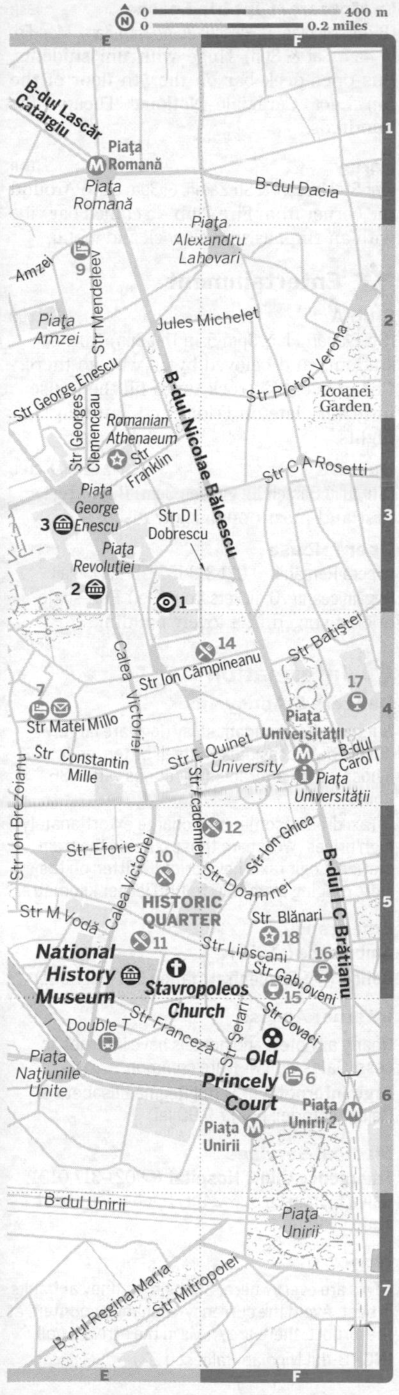

Central Hostel HOSTEL €€
(☎021-610 2214; www.centralhostel.ro; Str Salcâmilor 2; dm/d from 55/160 lei; @ 📶) A converted villa in a quiet neighbourhood east of the centre has clean rooms with new beds, a kitchen, a laundry (8 lei), lockers and patio seating under a vine shade.

Funky Chicken HOSTEL €
(☎021-312 1425; www.funkychickenhostel.com; Str Gen Berthelot 63; dm 40-45 lei; 📶) Near Cişmigiu Garden, this bare-bones, pleasant, hostel occupies a historic home on a shady street. No breakfast, but there's a kitchen.

Hotel Das President HOTEL €€
(☎021-311 0535; www.daspresident.ro; B-dul Dinacu Golescu 29; s/d without bathroom 90/150,

Central Bucharest

Top Sights
- B-dul Unirii D6
- National History Museum E5
- Old Princely Court F6
- Palace of Parliament C6
- Stavropoleos Church E5

Sights
1. Central Committee of the Communist Party Building E3
2. National Art Museum (Gallery of European Art) E3
3. National Art Museum (Gallery of Romanian Art) E3
4. Palace of Parliament Entry C6

Sleeping
5. Funky Chicken C3
6. Hanul lui Manuc F6
7. Hotel Carpaţi E4
8. Hotel Das President A2
9. Midland Youth Hostel 2 .... E2

Eating
10. Bistro Vilacrosse E5
11. Caru' cu Bere E5
12. Crama Blanduziei F5
13. Sale e Pepe D3
14. Snack Attack! F4

Drinking
15. Fire Club F5
16. Harley F5
17. La Motoare/Lăptăria Enache F4

Entertainment
18. Club A F5
19. Opera House B4

s/d with bathroom 110/170 lei;) Nothing special, though it's ideal for a sleep during a train layover or before an early departure. Rooms are small and basic, as are the beds, though there's a tiny balcony and TV.

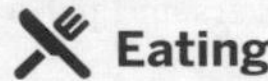

Eating

Sale e Pepe ITALIAN €€
(Str Luterană 3; pizzas 8-29 lei; 10am-midnight Mon-Fri, 3pm-midnight Sat & Sun) This tiny pizza and pasta place specialises in crunchy thin-crust pizzas and, for once in Romania, they're not undercooked. Breakfast is available, too.

Caru' cu Bere ROMANIAN €€€
(www.carucubere.ro; Str Stavropoleos 3-5; mains 15-60 lei;) Bucharest's oldest beer house continues to draw in a strong local crowd. The colourful belle époque interior and stained-glass windows dazzle, as does the mixed sausage platter (for two).

Burebista GRILL €€€
(Calea Moşilor 195; mains 11-60 lei; noon-midnight) The rustic Burebista endeavours to grill every meat on the continent, including hare, quail, pheasant, duck, wild boar and 'bear with mustard sauce'. Excellent salads, too.

Crama Blanduziei ROMANIAN €€
(Str Academiei 2; mains 20-30 lei; 11am-11pm) Great location just on the fringe of Lipscani, with a traditional dining room and a more relaxed terrace. The three-course lunch menu (20 lei) is a good deal.

Bistro Vilacrosse BISTRO €€
(Pasajul Macca/Vilacrosse; mains 14-20 lei) The small Vilacrosse borrows its style heavily from Parisian side streets, and the food and service are great. Try the wine-splattered Transylvanian pork fillet on a bed of (French!) fries and roasted cabbage.

Snack Attack! QUICK EATS €
(Str Ion Câmpineanu 10; sandwiches 8 lei; 7.30am-8pm Mon-Fri, to 2pm Sat) Fresh, cheap takeaway panini and salads (including hummus and tabouli with tortillas).

Drinking

Bucharest's bar scene is liveliest in the Str Lipscani area.

Fire Club BAR
(Str Gabroveni 12) Groups of students crouch on stools around small tables with bottles of Tuborg in hand. Rock and punk shows are staged in the basement.

La Motoare/Lăptăria Enache BAR
(B-dul Nicolae Bălcescu 2; 2pm-3am Mon-Fri, to 4am Sat & Sun) Huge with uni students, this open-deck bar on the 5th floor of the Ion Luca Caragiale National Theatre fits hundreds.

Harley BAR
(cnr Str Lipscani & Str Zarafi; 3pm-3am) Around the corner from Fire Club – a chilled bar vibe with an emphasis on alt rock and metal.

Entertainment

Club A CLUB
(Str Blănari 14; 9pm-5am Thu-Sun) Run by students and beloved by all who go there. Cheap beer and rock tunes fill the house until very late on Friday and Saturday nights.

Queen's GAY & LESBIAN CLUB
(Str Juliu Barach 13; noon-3am) Bucharest's first and most popular gay disco.

Opera House OPERA
(Opera Română; 021-313 1857; B-dul Mihail Kogălniceanu 70; tickets from 8 lei) Full-scale operas staged in a lovely building.

Information

Dangers & Annoyances

Bucharest's abundant stray dogs are largely docile, but occasionally bite. If bitten, go to a hospital for antirabies injections within 36 hours.

Taxi drivers sometimes charge extortionately high prices. Worst are those outside the train station. Legit taxis have prices written on the side, ranging from 1.30 to 1.50 lei per kilometre.

Emergency

Ambulance (973)

Police (955, central station 021-311 2021)

Internet Access

Nearly all hotels and hostels have internet access. Cafes with wi-fi are common.

Argo Internet (cnr B-dul Regina Elisabeta & Calea Victoriei; per hr 5.90 lei)

Medical Services

Emergency Clinic Hospital (021-317 0121; Calea Floreasca 8; 24hr) Bucharest's best state hospital.

Money

ATMs are everywhere. Changing money at banks is best. Avoid the currency-exchange counters at the airport; there are ATMs in the arrivals hall.

ING (B-dul Nicolae Bălcescu 22)

Telephone

RomTelecomm cards (from 10 lei) are available at news-stands. Most phone booths are neglected, but still work. You'll have no problem finding a shop selling Orange or Vodaphone SIM cards for your mobile phone.

Tourist Information

Info Tourist Point (www.infotourist.ro) Gara de Nord (☎0371-155 063; ⊙9am-9pm); Piaţa Universităţii Underpass (⊙9am-6pm Mon-Fri, 10am-1pm Sat) Bucharest now has two tourist information offices, offering maps, brochures and multilingual assistance.

Wasteels (☎021-317 0370; www.wasteels.ro; ⊙8am-7pm Mon-Fri) On the left side of the exit hallway of the train station, Wasteels can help with train reservations and rent cars.

 Getting There & Away

Air

Romania's national airline is **Tarom** (Transporturile Aeriene Române; www.tarom.ro); airport ☎021-317 4444; city centre ☎021-337 0400, Spl Independenţei 17; ⊙8.30am-7.30pm Mon-Fri, 9am-2pm Sat).

Henri Coandă airport (formerly Otopeni; ☎021-204 1000; www.otp-airport.ro; Şos Bucureşti-Ploieşti), 18km north of Bucharest, is where most international flights arrive. There are **information desks** (☎021-204 1220; ⊙24hr) in both terminals.

Domestic, charter and a few budget airlines use **Băneasa airport** (☎021-232 0020; www.baneasa.aero; Şos Bucureşti-Ploieşti 40), 8km north of the centre.

Bus

DOMESTIC Bucharest's bus system is frankly a mess, scarred by ever-changing departure locations, companies and schedules. Check www.cdy.ro or ask your hotel to help with the latest.

The most popular routes are the maxitaxis to Braşov (30 lei, 2½ hours), which stop in Sinaia (26 lei), Buşteni and Predeal on the way. Some continue on to Sighişoara (54 lei, five hours). **C&I** (☎021-256 8039; Str Ritmului 35) runs these services from its office 3.25km east of Piaţa Romana. From metro station Piaţa Iancului, go south for one block on Şoseaua Mihei Bravu (toward Maxbet Casino) and right on B-dul Ferdinand. It's up two blocks on the left. Buses 69 and 85 go there from Gara de Nord.

INTERNATIONAL The biggest names in international buses are **Eurolines** (☎021-316 3661; www.eurolines.ro; Str Buzeşti 44; ⊙24hr) and **Atlassib** (www.atlassib.ro), which link many Western European destinations with Bucharest.

Double T (☎021-313 3642; Calea Victoriei 2) has a daily service to Ruse (Bulgaria; 43 lei, 2½ hours) leaving at 3.50pm, which continues to Pleven and Sofia (107 lei, eight hours).

There are several options to İstanbul leaving from around Gara de Nord, including **Ortadoğu Tur** (☎021-318 7538; Str Gara de Nord 6-8) and **Toros** (☎021-233 1898; Calea Griviţei 134-136). The 12-hour trip costs about 200 lei one-way.

Car & Motorcycle

Major car-hire agencies can be found at the Henri Coandă International Airport arrivals hall. Cheapest are **D&V** (☎021-201 4611, 0788-998 877; www.dvtouring.ro) and **Autonom** (www.autonom.com), offering Daewoo Matiz for 72 lei per day if you hire for over a week.

Train

Gara de Nord (☎021-319 9539; Piaţa Gara de Nord 1) is the central station for national and international trains. Call ☎021-9521 or ☎021-9522 for reservations. Left luggage, located in the hallway leading to the front exit, is 3 lei and 6 lei for small and large bags.

Tickets can also be purchased at the **Agenţia de Voiaj CFR** (www.cfr.ro; Str Domnita Anastasia 10-14; ⊙7.30am-7.30pm Mon-Fri, 9am-1.30pm Sat). **Wasteels** (☎021-317 0370; www.wasteels.ro; ⊙8am-7pm Mon-Fri), on the left side of the exit hallway of the train station, can help out too.

Check the latest train schedules on www.cfr.ro or the reliable German site www.bahn.de.

Daily international services include three trains to Budapest (180 lei, 13 to 15 hours), two to Sofia (130 lei, 11 hours) and one train each to Belgrade (130 lei, 12 hours), Chişinău (113 lei, 12 hours) and İstanbul (240 lei, 20 hours).

A sample of direct daily services within Romania:

BRAŞOV (42 lei, 2½ hours, frequent)
CLUJ-NAPOCA (78 lei, 7½ hours, seven daily)
SIBIU (49 lei, 7 hours, three daily)
SIGHIŞOARA (43 lei, 5½ hours, frequent)
TIMIŞOARA (68 lei, 8½ hours, six daily)

 Getting Around

To/From the Airport

BUS To get to Henri Coandă (Otopeni) or Băneasa airports, take bus 783 from the city centre, departing every 15 minutes between 5.37am and 11.23pm (every half-hour at weekends) from Piaţas Unirii and Victoriei and every *piaţa* in between. The Piaţa Unirii stop is on the south side. Buy a ticket, valid for a round trip or two people one-way, for 7 lei at any **RATB** (Régie Autonome de Transport de Bucureşti; www.ratb.ro) bus-ticket booth near a bus stop. Once onboard, stamp the ticket.

TAXI Taking a reputable taxi from the centre to Henri Coandă should cost no more than 40 to 65 lei. Fly Taxi and others monopolise airport transfers to the centre for a staggering 3.5 lei per kilometre. Alternatively, walk down to the 'departures' doors and jump into a regular taxi arriving from the city as it drops people off.

TRAIN Train service to Henri Coandă leaves hourly, at 10 past the hour, from Gara de Nord from 5am to 11pm. The journey (6 lei, 45 minutes) includes a short shuttle-bus ride from the train terminus to the airport.

Public Transport

You can buy tickets (1.30 lei) for buses, trams and trolleybuses at any **RATB** (www.ratb.ro) street kiosk, marked 'casa de bilete' or simply 'bilete'. Punch your ticket on-board or risk an on-the-spot fine.

Bucharest's metro (two-ride/10-ride tickets 2.50/8 lei) runs frequently between 5.30am and 11.30pm.

The taxis outside Gara de Nord are not recommended. Call for a reputable company, such as **Cobalcescu** (☎021-9451), **CrisTaxi** (☎021-9461) and **Taxi Sprint** (☎021-9495).

TRANSYLVANIA

After a century of being name-checked in literature and cinema, the word 'Transylvania' enjoys instant, worldwide recognition. The mere mention of it conjures waves of imagery: mind-bending mountains, Gothic castles, fortified churches, dusty peasant villages, spooky moonlight and a role-call of bloodthirsty, shape-shifting creatures with wicked overbites.

Unexplained puncture-wounds to the neck notwithstanding, Transylvania is all those things and more. There's hiking in the Bucegi and Făgăraş Mountains, cited as being second only to Switzerland, valleys with Saxon towns, fortified churches, Bran and Peleş Castles, and yes, Dracula's face will stare back at you from coffee mugs and T-shirts.

Sinaia

POP 14,600

Sinaia is set amid an exquisite, fir-clad scrap of the towering Bucegi Mountains, offering ski runs and hiking trails for year-round fun. It developed into a major resort after King Carol I selected the area for his summer residence in 1870 and built the sinfully lavish Peleş Castle, now one of Romania's primary tourist destinations.

From the train station, climb up the stairway across the street to busy B-dul Carol I. The cable car is to the left and the palace uphill to the right.

Romania's new monarchy debuted in a blaze of pomp with **Peleş Castle** (compulsory tours 20 lei; ⌚11am-5pm Tue, 9am-4.15pm Wed-Sun). King Carol I's vision of fairy-tale turrets rising above acres of green meadows and grand reception halls with heavy woodcarved ceilings and gilded pieces is still awe-inspiring a century later. Worthwhile tours take in the 1st floor only – note the ground-breaking central vacuuming system. About 100m uphill is Queen Marie's less fussy art-nouveau-style home, the **Pelişor Palace** (compulsory tours 10 lei; ⌚9am-5pm Wed-Sun).

Sleeping & Eating

Travel agencies can help find rooms in *pensiunes* (guest houses) and villas in the area. There are a few fast-food stands and pizza places along B-dul Carol I.

Hotel Caraiman HOTEL €€
(☎0244-313 551; B-dul Carol I 4; palace@rdslink.ro; s/d/apt 155/205/260 lei; 📶) Of all the faded-glory century-old hotels, this 1881 red-and-white Caraiman is less royal ball and more rustic and laid-back.

Hotel Economat HOTEL €€
(☎0244-311 153; www.apps.ro; Aleea Peleşului 2; s/d from 90/180 lei) Just outside the Peleş gate, this hotel has decent rooms in a setting lovely enough that first-time visitors have been known to mistake it for the castle!

Irish House INTERNATIONAL €€
(www.irishhouse.ro; B-dul Carol I nr 80; mains 17-32 lei) There's Guinness on tap (9 lei) and Irish dishes on offer, including an 'Irish Breakfast' (11 lei), but this place fills for its good Romanian food and pizzas.

Information

Banks are along B-dul Carol I.

Central post office (B-dul Carol I 3; ⌚7am-8pm Mon-Fri, 8am-1pm Sat)

Dracula's Land (☎0244-311 441; mihneasutu@yahoo.com; B-dul Carol I nr 14; ⌚9am-5pm) Signed simply 'Tourist Office', with chummy blokes that find villa rooms or arrange guides.

Salvamont (☎0244-313 131, nationwide 0-SALVAMONT; www.salvamont.org, in Romanian; Primărie, B-dul Carol I) Voluntary mountain-rescue organisation; inside the tourist information centre and at Cota 2000 chairlift station.

Tourist information office (☎0244-315 656; www.info-sinaia.ro; B-dul Carol I 47; ⌚8.30am-4.30pm Mon-Fri) Lots of information, brochures and maps, but it can't book rooms.

Getting There & Away

TRAIN Sinaia is on the Bucharest–Braşov train line – 126km from the former and 45km from the latter – so jumping on a train to Bucharest (27 lei, 1½ hours) or Braşov (12 lei, one hour) is a cinch.

BUSES and maxitaxis run every 45 minutes between roughly 6am and 10pm from the train station to Bucharest (24 lei) and Braşov (9 lei).

Braşov

POP 278,000

Braşov is Romania's ground-zero tourist destination for very good reason. Ringed by perfect mountains and verdant hills, the city is adorned with baroque facades, bohemian outdoor cafes, the lovely Piaţa Sfatului and agreeable locals. Innumerable day trips can be launched from here: hiking or skiing in the Bucegi Mountains, visiting castles in Bran, Râşnov and Sinaia, and more.

Sights

Though Braşov is sorely lacking in decent museums, drifting through its medieval glory is arresting enough.

Piaţa Sfatului MAIN SQUARE

A good starting point for a walk is central Piaţa Sfatului, where prisoners were once tortured in the gold **Council House** (Casa Sfatului), which dates from 1420. The building also houses the good tourist information centre and the unmemorable **Braşov Historical Museum** (adult/student 7/1.50 lei; ⏲10am-6pm summer, 9am-5pm winter, closed Mon).

Black Church CHURCH

(Biserica Neagră; admission 6 lei; ⏲10am-5pm Mon-Sat) Looming from the south, the Gothic Black Church, built between 1384 and 1477, gained its name after a 1689 fire blackened its walls. Inside the church you can view apse statues moved from outside and 120 fabulous Turkish rugs. Recitals (6 lei) are held in summer on the 4000-pipe organ.

Mt Tâmpa MOUNTAIN

You can't miss the 'Braşov' sign that looks over town from Mt Tâmpa. To reach it, take the **Tâmpa cable car** (Telecabina; one-way/return 10/20 lei; ⏲9.30am-5pm Tue-Sun). A couple of blocks west is the cobblestone **Stradă Sforii**, one of Europe's narrowest 'streets'.

Black Tower & White Tower VIEWPOINTS

Good vantage points of the city from the west side are at the Black Tower (Turnul Neagru) and White Tower (Turnul Alba) – both rather white actually – reached on a creekside promenade alongside the city's original walls. A side road leads to the promenade from about 200m south of the Black Church.

Sleeping

Two hostels are south of the centre, near Piaţa Unirii, and reached by bus 51 from the train station.

Kismet Dao Villa HOSTEL €

(☎0268-514 296; www.kismetdao.ro; Str Democratiei 2b; dm/d 43/130 lei; @📶) This four-floor villa offers a DVD library, playful staff and one free beer or soda to get your evening started. Walk through the left side of Piaţa Unirii, about 600m south of Schei Gate, past St Nicholas' Cathedral, heading uphill, then right on Str Democratiei.

Casa Kermany PENSION €

(☎0368-436 068; Str Nicolae Bălcescu 26; s/d/apt 130/140/160; 📶) A central and good-value place, with smallish rooms, decent beds and an inner courtyard that insulates from the street noise.

Rolling Stone Hostel HOSTEL €

(☎0268-513 965; www.rollingstone.ro; Str Piatra Mare 2a; dm 35-50 lei, r from 118 lei; @📶) Run by the high-energy Bolea family, the Stone is a homey, friendly place. Walk through Piaţa Unirii, past Casa Româneasca restaurant (on the right side), continue for one short block then turn right on Str Piatra Mare.

Hotel Postăvarul HOTEL €

(☎0268-477 448; Str Republicii 62; s/d 60/80 lei; 📶) Despite a 1910 German design, the gloriously faded grandeur of this place completes, by accident, the stereotypical vision of a 'Transylvanian hotel'. But rooms are vacuumed daily and have private toilets; shared showers are down the hall.

Eating & Drinking

Restaurant Transylvania ROMANIAN €

(Str Castelului 106; mains 6-38 lei) Probably the best value and most comprehensively delicious Romanian fare in town. *Ciorbăs* (soups) start at 3 lei and a litre of house wine is only 16 lei.

Bistro de l'Arte BISTRO €€

(www.bistrodelarte.ro; Piaţa Enescu 11; mains 12-28 lei) On the ground floor of a cosy 15th-century building, the Bistro serves small meals – sandwiches, fish, spaghetti – and breakfasts.

Casa Româneasca ROMANIAN €€
(Piaţa Unirii; mains 12-26 lei) This *casa* serves tasty *sarmalute cu mamaliguta* (boiled beef rolled with veggies and cabbage; 15 lei).

Spar SUPERMARKET
(Str Nicolae Bălcescu; ⌚24hr) A fully stocked supermarket next to the indoor-outdoor fruit and vegetable market.

Deane's Irish Pub & Grill PUB
(Str Republicii 19) The smoky pub checklist has been painstakingly filled here, including live music, a proper pub menu and a darts room.

Information

You'll find numerous ATMs, banks and exchange offices on and around Str Republicii and B-dul Eroilor.

Active Travel (☎0268-477 112; www.activetravel.ro; Str Republicii 50; ⌚10am-6pm Mon-Fri, 10am-1pm Sat) Leads hiking, mountain biking and cultural tours. Also rents bikes (3/24 hours 25/50 lei).

County Hospital (☎0268-333 666; Calea Bucureşti 25-27; ⌚24hr) Northwest of the centre.

Iulian Cozma (☎0744-327 686; www.mountainguide.ro) Guides multiday hiking and skiing trips in southern Transylvania.

Braşov

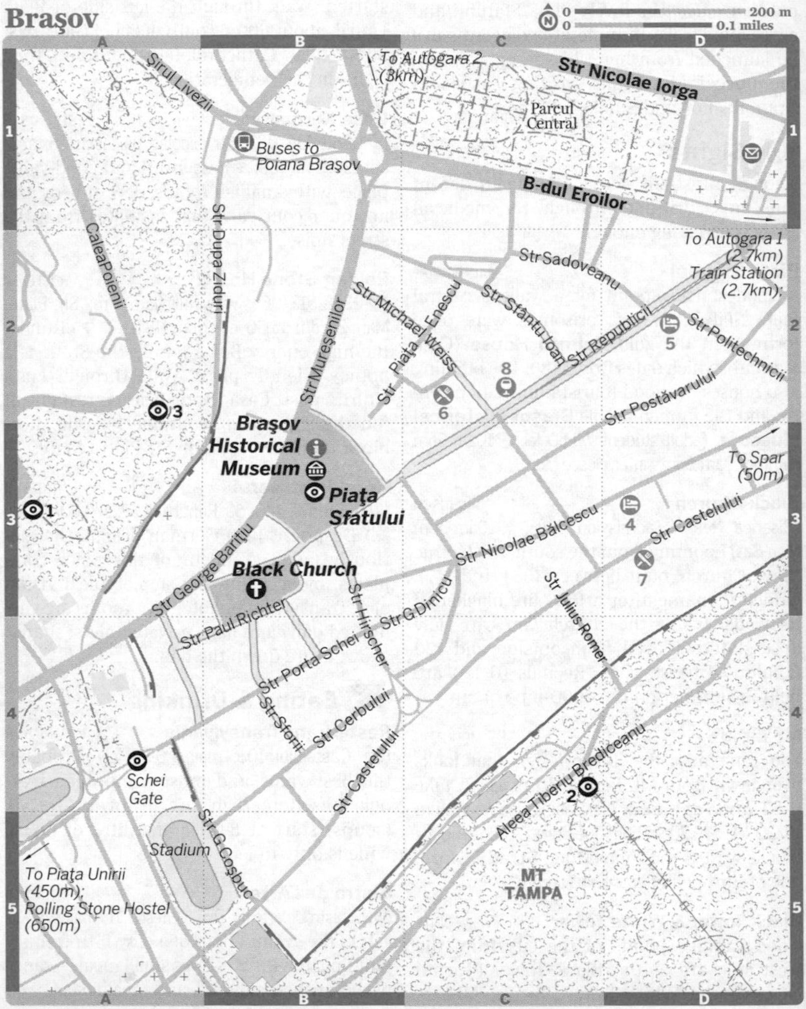

0 200 m
0 0.1 miles
Str Nicolae Iorga
To Autogara 2 (3km)
Parcul Central
Şirul Livezii
Buses to Poiana Braşov
B-dul Eroilor
To Autogara 1 (2.7km); Train Station (2.7km)
Str Dupa Ziduri
Calea Poienii
Str Sadoveanu
Str Mureşenilor
Str Michael Weiss
Str Enescu
Str Piaţa Enescu
Str Sfântu Ioan
Str Republicii
Str Politechnicii
Str Postăvarului
Braşov Historical Museum
Piaţa Sfatului
To Spar (50m)
Str Nicolae Bălcescu
Str Castelului
Black Church
Str George Bariţiu
Str Paul Richter
Str G Dimicu
Str Hirscher
Str Julius Romer
Str Porta Schei
Str Sforii
Str Cerbului
Str Castelului
Schei Gate
Str G Coşbuc
Stadium
Aleea Tiberiu Brediceanu
MT TÂMPA
To Piaţa Unirii (450m); Rolling Stone Hostel (650m)

Tibi (Str Gheorghe Bariţiu 8; per hr 2.40 lei) Internet access.

Tourist information office (www.brasovcity.ro; Piaţa Sfatului 30; ⌚9am-5pm) The English speaking staff offer free brochures and help book rooms.

Getting There & Around

BUS Braşov has a few bus stations – Autogara 1, next to the train station, is the most active. It has hourly services along the Târgu Mureş–Sighişoara–Braşov–Buşteni–Bucharest route.

Autogara 2 (Bartolomeu; Str Avram Iancu 114), 1km west of the train station, sends half-hourly buses to Râşnov (2.50 lei, 25 minutes) and Bran (4 lei, 40 minutes) from roughly 6.30am to 11.30pm. Take bus 12 to/from the centre (leaving from the roundabout just north of the station).

CAR Autonom (☎0268-415 250; www.autonom.com) usually has the best car-hire prices (Daewoo Matiz from 120 lei per day, with discounts for long-term rentals).

TRAIN The train station is 3km northeast of the city centre. Advance tickets are sold at the **Agenţia de Voiaj CFR** (Str 15 de Noiembre 43; ⌚8am-7.30pm Mon-Fri). Left luggage is 7 lei per day. From the station, take bus 51 to the centre.

Daily service includes hourly runs to Bucharest (42 lei, 3½ hours), a dozen to Sighişoara (36 lei, 2½ hours), two to Sibiu (50 lei, four hours) and 10 to Cluj-Napoca (65 lei, six hours). International links include three daily trains to Budapest, Hungary (seat/sleeper 150/200 lei, 14 hours).

Braşov

Top Sights

	Black Church	B3
	Braşov Historical Museum	B3
	Piaţa Sfatului	B3
Sights		
1	Black Tower	A3
2	Tâmpa Cable Car	C4
3	White Tower	A2
Sleeping		
4	Casa Kermany	D3
5	Hotel Postăvarul	D2
Eating		
6	Bistro de l'Arte	C2
7	Restaurant Transylvania	D3
Drinking		
8	Deane's Irish Pub & Grill	C2

Bran & Râşnov

The atmospheric **Bran Castle** (www.brancastlemuseum.ro; adult/student 12/6 lei; ⌚9am-7pm Tue-Sun, noon-7pm Mon May-Sep, 9am-5pm Tue-Sun Oct-Apr), 30km south of Braşov, dates from 1378. Though Vlad Ţepeş only dropped by once in the 15th century (maybe), it's hard to skip this so-called 'Dracula's castle'.

Râşnov, 12km toward Braşov, offers the tempting ruins of the 13th-century **Râşnov fortress** (Cetatea Râşnov; admission 10 lei; ⌚9am-8pm May-Oct, to 6pm Nov-Apr).

Pensiunea Stefi (☎0721-303 009; www.hotelstefi-ro.com; Piaţa Unirii 5; r 90 lei; @📶) is a five-room guest house with a sauna, a fitness centre and a wading pool; breakfast costs 14 lei. **Vila Bran** (☎0268-236 866; www.vilabran.ro; Str Principală 238; r 120-140 lei; 📶) is unflinchingly touristy, but the view of the hills is worth it; no breakfast.

See the Braşov section for information on transport.

Sighişoara

POP 32,300

Where Vlad 'Ţepeş' Dracula first scampered about, when skewered Turks were just a twinkle in his eye, Sighişoara is a dreamy, compact, medieval citadel town. Brightly coloured, 500-year old townhouses border hilly cobblestone streets, church bells clang atmospherically in the early hours, and overloaded tour buses jockey for parking space.

Sights

Blink and you'll miss the tiny sign announcing that you can visit the History Museum, the Collection of Medieval Arms and the Torture Room Museum for a combination ticket price of 17 lei.

The renovated **Casa Dracula** (Str Cositorarilor 5), now a restaurant, serving 4 lei glasses of wine in the moody dining room, is where Vlad Ţepeş reputedly lived until the age of four.

Citadel Complex MUSEUMS

Sighişoara's primary sights are clustered in the compact, delightfully medieval citadel – perched on a hillock and fortified with a 14th-century wall. Entering the citadel, you pass under the massive **clock tower** (Turnul cu Ceas), dating from 1280. Inside is the great **History Museum** (Piaţa Muzeului 1; admission 10 lei; ⌚9am-5.30pm Tue-Fri, 10am-

5.30pm Sat & Sun), with small rooms off the steps winding up to the 7th-floor lookout.

The small, dark **Torture Room Museum** (adult/student 4/1 lei; ⌚9am-5.30pm Tue-Fri, 10am-5.30pm Sat & Sun) shows how fingers were smashed and prisoners burned with coals. The **Collection of Medieval Arms** (adult/student 6/1.50 lei; ⌚9am-5.30pm Tue-Fri, 10am-5.30pm Sat & Sun) has four rooms with medieval helmets, shields, crossbows and maces.

Sleeping

TOP CHOICE Bed & Breakfast Kula PENSION €
(☎0265-777 907; Str Tâmplarilor 40; r per person 65 lei; @) Run by a heart-warmingly kind family, this 400-year-old home in the citadel has large rooms with classic ceramic wood-fire heaters.

Nathan's Villa HOSTEL €
(☎0265-772 546; www.nathansvilla.com; Str Libertăţii 8; dm 43-50 lei; @ wi-fi) This popular choice is efficiently run and often has the best nightlife in town. It's about 500m west of the train station. Open from March to December.

Burg Hostel HOSTEL €
(☎0265-778 489; www.burghostel.ro; Str Bastionului 4-6; dm 40 lei, s/d without bathroom 70/90 lei, with bathroom 80/95 lei; wi-fi) This slightly sterile hostel has functional rooms with various bed counts. Breakfast is 12 lei.

Gia Hostel HOSTEL €
(☎0722-490 003; www.hotelgia.ro; Str Libertăţii 41; dm/r from 35/95 lei; @ wi-fi) Backing onto the train line, about 300m west of the station, these rooms recently enjoyed a complete and thoughtful redecoration.

Eating

Rustic ROMANIAN €
(Str 1 Decembrie 1918 nr 7; mains 6-20 lei; ⌚8am-midnight Mon-Sat, noon-midnight Sun) This wood-and-brick 'man's man' bar-restaurant is down the hill from the citadel. The *ciorbă ţaraneasca de porc* (countryside pork soup) will erase the hangover acquired at Nathan's Villa. Eggs served all day.

Information

The bus and train stations are about a 15-minute walk north of the (visible) citadel. Banca Transilvania has an ATM in the citadel.

Café International & Family Centre (☎0265-777 844; Piaţa Cetăţii 8; internet per hr 5 lei; ⌚8am-8pm Mon-Sat Jun-Sep, 1-7pm Mon-Sat Oct-May; wi-fi) Internet access and tourist office (in summer only).

Tourist information office (☎0265-770 415; Str O Goga; ⌚10am-4pm Mon-Fri, 9am-1pm Sat) Can book beds.

Getting There & Away

TRAIN A dozen trains daily connect Sighişoara with Braşov (28 lei, two hours), 10 of which continue on to Bucharest (43 lei, 4½ hours). Five daily trains go to Cluj-Napoca (39 lei, 3½ hours). Three daily trains go to Budapest (138 lei, nine hours).

BUS Next to the train station on Str Libertăţii, the bus station sends four daily buses to Sibiu (14 lei, 2½ hours).

Sibiu

POP 154,500

Crumbling, car-rattling old Sibiu, despite being the capital and most culturally active of the Transylvanian Saxon towns, was frequently overshadowed by Braşov, Sighişoara and Cluj-Napoca. Then the EU designated it as a 'Capital of Culture' for 2007. Now freshly scrubbed, painted and cobblestoned, the pedestrian areas are frame-worthy from any angle and every third building has been declared a historic monument. Some locals liked the old Sibiu better, falling roof tiles, ankle-twisting cobblestones and all, but there's no arguing that new Sibiu is a beaut.

The adjacent bus and train stations are near the centre of town. Exit the station and stroll up Str General Magheru four blocks to Piaţa Mare, the historic centre.

Sibiu's **International Astra Film Festival** is held in May.

Sights

The expansive Piaţa Mare was the very centre of the old walled city. It's worth walking along the 16th-century **city walls** and watchtowers, southeast of Piaţa Mare.

A combination ticket for the History, Brukenthal and Pharmacy Museums and others is adult/student 30/7.5 lei.

To the east of the city is the spectacular **Transfăgăraşan Road** that winds its way south to Piteşti.

History Museum MUSEUM
(Str Mitropoliei 2; admission 17 lei; ⌚10am-5pm) Serious coin went into these swanky new displays, starting at the Palaeolithic age and sweeping through all the epochs.

Brukenthal Museum ART GALLERY
(www.brukenthalmuseum.ro; Piaţa Mare 5; adult/student 12/3 lei; ⌚10am-6pm) This is likely the

oldest and finest art gallery in Romania, with excellent collections of 16th- and 17th-century Flemish, Italian, Dutch, French, Austrian and Romanian paintings, including a giant painting of Sibiu from 1808.

Biserica Evanghelică CHURCH
(Evangelical Church; Pieţa Huet) The Gothic Biserica Evanghelică, built from 1300 to 1520, is undergoing renovations until 2015. You can climb the **church tower** (admission 3 lei); ask for entry at the Casa Luxemburg travel agency (p1035).

Museum of Traditional Folk Civilisation OUTDOOR MUSEUM
(Muzeul Civilizaţiei Populare Tradiţionale Astra; Calea Răşinarilor 14; admission 15 lei; ⏲10am-6pm Tue-Sun, to 8pm in good weather) Sibiu's highlight is an open-air museum 5km from the centre with more than 120 traditional dwellings, mills and churches brought from around the country. Trolleybus 1 from the train station goes there (get off at the last stop and keep walking; it's less than 1km).

Sleeping

TOP CHOICE **Felinarul Hostel** HOSTEL €
(☎0269-235 260; www.felinarulhostelsibiu.ro; Str Felinarul 8; dm/d without bathroom 50/100 lei; @📶) Setting the bar for boutique hostels everywhere, this friendly 14-bed sanctuary is roughly mid way between the train station and the centre.

Flying Time Hostel HOSTEL €
(☎0369-730 179; www.sibiuhostel.ro; Str Gheorghe Lazar 6; dm/d from 42/130 lei; @📶) In an 18th-century building designed to stay naturally cool, there's great beds, a flowery inner courtyard cafe and a pub with live music.

Happy Day Pension PENSION €
(☎0269-234 985; www.pensiuneahappyday.ro, in Romanian; Str Lungă 2; s/d 100/125 lei; 📶) A 10-minute walk northwest of the centre, with perks like a full English breakfast (included), this place shapes up as an excellent budget option.

Eating

TOP CHOICE **Felinarul Café** INTERNATIONAL €€
(Str Felinarul 8; mains 7-25 lei; ⏲cafe noon-midnight Tue-Sat, kitchen noon-3pm & 5pm-11pm Tue-Sat) The rotating menu includes chicken in green curry, extravagant salads, shark, buffalo wings and what is probably the best cheeseburger in Eastern Europe.

Grand Plaza ROMANIAN €
(Str 9 Mai 60; mains 9-20 lei) Just around the corner from Felinarul Hostel, this place serves no-nonsense Romanian cuisine at great prices. The *ciolan de porc cu iahnie de fasole* (smoked knuckle of pork with beans; 15 lei) is quite the spectacle.

Pizzeria La Reggina PIZZA €€
(Piaţa Mica 8; pizzas 7-25 lei) Not to be confused with Go In next door, this place wins for both sheer variety and quality.

Drinking

Piaţa Mică is Sibiu's drinking headquarters.

Music Club BAR
(Piaţa Mică 23) Order cocktails (12 to 15 lei) using buttons on the tables. There's live music every Thursday and on other random nights.

Information

ATMs are located all over the centre.

Banca Comercială Română (Str Nicolae Bălcescu 11) Gives cash advances.

Casa Luxemburg (☎0269-216 854; www.kultours.ro; Piaţa Mică 16) Travel agent offering city tours, day trips and a free Sibiu map.

Tourist information office (☎0269-208 913; www.sibiu.ro; Piaţa Mare 2; ⏲9am-5pm Mon-Fri, to 1pm Sat & Sun) On the ground floor of the new city hall.

Getting There & Around

Air

Blue Air (www.blueair-web.com) Flies to Madrid, London and Stuttgart.

Carpatair (☎0269-229 161; www.carpatair.com) At the airport; flies to Germany and Italy via Timişoara.

Sibiu airport (☎0269-229 161; Sos Alba Iulia 73) is 5km west of the centre. Trolleybus 8 runs between the airport and the train station.

Tarom (☎0269-211 157; www.tarom.ro; Str Nicolae Bălcescu 10; ⏲9am-12.30pm & 1.30-7pm Mon-Fri, 9am-1pm Sat) Has daily flights to Bucharest (from 222 lei one-way).

Bus & Train

The **bus station** (Piaţa 1 Decembrie 1918) is opposite the train station. Services include Braşov (20 lei, 2½ hours, two daily), Bucharest (48 lei, 5½ hours, three to four daily) and Timişoara (45 lei, six hours, two daily).

There are four daily trains to Bucharest (49 lei, six to eight hours) and three to Timişoara (47 lei, 6½ hours). Buy tickets at the station or the **Agenţia de Voiaj CFR** (Str Nicolae Bălcescu 6; ⏲7am-8pm Mon-Fri). Trolleybus 1 connects the train station with the centre, but it's only a 450m walk.

Cluj-Napoca

POP 306,000

Aka 'Club-Napoca', this city isn't as picturesque as its Saxon neighbours, but it's famed for its dozens of cavernous, unsnooty discos filled with agreeable students. Even outside the clubs, Cluj is one of Romania's most energised and welcoming cities.

Sights

Pharmaceutical Museum MUSEUM
(Str Regele Ferdinand 1; admission 5.20 lei; ⏲10am-4pm Mon, Tue Wed & Fri, noon-6pm Thu) This small three-room museum features ground mummy dust, 18th-century aphrodisiacs and medieval alchemy symbols.

St Michael's Church CHURCH
This vast 14th-century church with a neo-Gothic tower (1859) dominates Piaţa Unirii. Outside is a huge **equestrian statue** (1902) of the famous Hungarian king Matthias Corvinus (r 1458–90), who was born here.

National Art Museum ART GALLERY
(Piaţa Unirii 30; admission 4 lei; ⏲10am-5pm Wed-Sun) Housed inside the baroque Banffy Palace (1791).

National History Museum of Transylvania MUSEUM
(Str Constantin Daicoviciu 1; admission 6 lei) Just off lovely Piaţa Muzeului and filled with ancient tombs and Roman pieces. It's undergoing major renovation.

Citadel FORTRESS
For an overall view of Cluj-Napoca, climb up the 1715 citadel *(cetatea)*, northwest of the centre.

Courses

Access LANGUAGE
(☎0264-420 476; www.access.ro; Str Ţebei 21, 3rd fl; ⏲10am-6pm Mon & Thu, 2-8pm Tue-Wed, 2-6pm Fri) Offers Romanian language courses.

Sleeping

TOP CHOICE **Retro Hostel** HOSTEL €
(☎0264-450 452; www.retro.ro; Str Potaissa 13; dm/s/d/tr from 44/85/125/180 lei; @📶) On a quiet lane amid 16th-century citadel wall fragments, the Retro is one of Romania's best hostels. Breakfast is 14 lei.

Transylvania Hostel HOSTEL €€
(☎0264-443 266; www.transylvaniahostel.com; Str Iuliu Maniu 26; dm 47-65 lei, d 170 lei; 📶@🚭) This centrally located place has all the next-gen hostel attributes: PCs, wi-fi, home theatre, game room with ping pong and large self-cater kitchen.

Vila Eunicia HOTEL €
(☎0264-594 067; www.vilaeunicia.ro, in Romanian; Str Emile Zola 2; s/d 100/150 lei; ❄📶) Furniture is a bit dated in some rooms, and beds are firm, but it doesn't get much more central than this 10-room option. Breakfast (20 lei) is delivered to your room. Get a rear-facing room.

Eating

Pizzeria New Croco PIZZA €€
(www.newcroco.ro; Str V. Babeş 12; pizzas 11-34 lei) Great woodfire pizza. To get here go south on Str Gheorghe Bilascu, then turn right on Str Ion Creangă. It's on the right after about 150m.

Hotel Agape CAFETERIA €
(Str Iuliu Maniu 6; mains 7 lei) Has a Romanian-style, glass-roofed cafeteria on the ground floor.

Central Market MARKET
A bustling indoor market, behind the Complex Commercial shopping centre, which also houses supermarket **Oncos**.

Drinking & Entertainment

Janis CLUB
(www.janis.ro; B-dul Eroilor 5; ⏲9pm-6am) Standard club nights with DJs and general bedlam are jazzed up with frequent theme nights.

L'Atelier Café BAR
(Str Memorandumului 9, 1st fl; 📶) Furniture made of cardboard, doors for tables and pumping indie music can be found in this eccentric, hip place.

Information

Most cafes have free wi-fi.

Banca Comercială Română (Str Gheorghe Bariţiu 10-12) Gives cash advances.

Blade Net (Str Iuliu Maniu 17; per hr 2.40 lei) Internet access.

Green Mountain Holidays (☎0744-637 227; www.greenmountainholidays.ro) Terrific eco-tourism agency providing trips in the Apuseni Mountains.

Pan Travel (☎0264-420 516; www.pantravel.ro; Str Grozavescu 13; ⏲9am-5pm Mon-Fri)

WORTH A TRIP

SOUTHERN BUCOVINA

The painted churches of Southern Bucovina are among the greatest artistic monuments of Europe – in 1993 they were collectively designated a Unesco World Heritage Site. Erected at a time when northern Moldavia was threatened by Turkish invaders, the Orthodox monasteries were surrounded by strong defensive walls. Biblical stories were portrayed on the church walls in colourful pictures possibly for mere aesthetics or so illiterate worshippers could better understand the stories, but more likely in reaction to encroaching Protestantism from Western Europe. The exteriors of many of the churches are covered with these magnificent 16th-century frescos. Remarkably, most of the intense colours have been preserved despite five centuries of punishing weather.

Bucovina's monasteries are generally open from 9am to 5pm or 6pm daily. The monasteries of **Voroneţ**, **Humor** and **Moldoviţa** provide a representative sample of what Bucovina has to offer. The gateway to the painted churches is **Suceava**. **Gura Humorului**, a small logging town 37km west of Suceava, is an alternative base from which to visit some of the monasteries, but transport connections are weak.

Getting to Suceava, six trains run daily from Bucharest (78 lei, seven hours) and five from Cluj-Napoca (47 lei, 6½ hours).

Books accommodation, offers car rental (from 108 lei per day) and arranges trips to Maramureş in northern Romania, Europe's last thriving peasant settlement.

Tourist information office (☎0264-452 244; www.primariaclujnapoca.ro, in Romanian; B-dul Eroilor 6-8; ⏲8.30am-5pm Mon-Fri, 10am-5pm Sat) Maps and information on events, restaurants and accommodation.

Getting There & Around

AIR Tarom has two to five direct flights daily to Bucharest (one-way/return from 250/400 lei). Tickets can be bought at the airport (8km east of town, reached by bus 8) or in town at **Tarom** (☎0264-432 669; www.tarom.ro; Piaţa Mihai Viteazul 11; ⏲8am-8pm Mon-Fri, 9am-2pm Sat). Budget carrier **Wizz Air** (www.wizzair.com) flies to London, Paris, Rome, Barcelona and more.

BUS Bus services from Autogara 2 (Autogara Beta), 350m northwest of the train station (take the overpass), include Braşov (40 lei, five hours, one daily), Bucharest (58 lei, 7½ hours, three daily), Budapest (80 lei, several daily) and Sibiu (28 lei, 3½ hours, eight daily). There is no Autogara 1.

CAR **Autonom** (☎0264-590 588; www.autonom.ro; Str Victor Babes 10) offers Dacias and Matiz starting at 108 lei per day.

TRAIN The train station is 1.5km north of the central Piaţa Unirii, reached by tram 101 down Str Horea. The **Agenţia de Voiaj CFR** (☎0264-432 001; Piaţa Mihai Viteazul 20; ⏲8am-8pm Mon-Fri, 9am-1.30pm Sat) sells advance tickets. Sample fares for *accelerat* trains include Braşov (46 lei, four hours), Bucharest (57 lei, 7½ hours), Budapest (117 lei, five hours) and Timişoara (49 lei, seven hours).

CRIŞANA & BANAT

Until 1918, the areas of Crişana (north of the Mureş river) and Banat (to the south) were governed jointly with Vojvodina (Serbia) and Hungary's Great Plain. This legacy can still be appreciated in spirit and in the weathered Habsburg architecture in Oradea, Arad and Timişoara, the latter still brimming with pride after lighting the fuse that ignited the 1989 revolution.

Timişoara

POP 312,000

Tenacious Timişoara stunned the world – not to mention the Ceauşescus – as the birthplace of the 1989 revolution. Beaming residents refer to it as 'Primul Oraş Liber' (First Free Town). A charming Mediterranean air pervades here, accentuated by regal Habsburg buildings and a thriving cultural and sports scene.

Sights

Piaţas MAIN SQUARES

Begging to be photographed with your widest lens is **Piaţa Victoriei**, a beautiful pedestrian mall with shops and cafes. The **National Theatre & Opera House** (Teatrul Naţional şi Opera Română; Str Mărăşeşti 2) sits at its head. **Piaţa Libertăţii** and the **Primăria Veche** (Old Town Hall; 1734) lie north. Further north still is **Piaţa Unirii**, featuring a baroque 1754 Roman Catholic Cathedral and the 1754 Serbian Orthodox Cathedral.

Banat History Museum MUSEUM
(Muzeul Banatului; Piaţa Huniade 1; adult/student 2/1 lei; ⏲10am-4pm) Housed in the 15th-century **Huniades Palace**, the Banat History Museum has displays on natural history, geology, armour, weapons, archaeology, ceramics, tools and scale-model countryside shelters.

Sleeping & Eating

TOP CHOICE **Pension Casa Leone** PENSION €
(☎0256-292 621; www.casaleone.ro; B-dul Eroilor 67; s/d/tr 120/140/180 lei; @📶) This lovely 16-room pension offers exceptional service and individually decorated rooms. Take tram 8 from the train station and alight at the Deliblata station, or call ahead to arrange transport.

Youth Hostel HOSTEL €
(☎0256-490 469; djt.timis@yahoo.com; P-ta Huniade 3; per person under/over 35 50/70 lei) An institutional but ideally located youth hostel run by the county's youth department, situated just a block off Piaţa Victoriei. The entrance is on Str M Eminescu. No breakfast.

Camping International CAMPING GROUND €
(☎0256-208 925; campinginternational@yahoo.com; Aleea Pădurea Verde 6; campsites per tent 20 lei, chalets s/d/q 92/126/220 lei) Nestled in the Green Wood forest on the opposite side of town from the train station. Catch trolleybus 11 to the end of the line; the bus stops less than 50m from the camping ground.

Hotel Cina Banatul HOTEL €
(☎0256-490 130; B-dul Republicii 3-5; s/d 120/140 lei) Still the best-value pad in the centre, with clean, modern rooms.

Casa cu Flori ROMANIAN €€
(Str Alba Julia 1; mains 18-28 lei) Excellent high-end Romanian cooking at moderate prices.

Java Coffee House COFFEE SHOP €
(Str Pacha 6; ⏲24hr) A dark, cosy coffee shop. Hot sandwiches (7 lei) are available across the street at Java Snack House.

Entertainment

Cinema Timiş CINEMA
(Piaţa Victoriei 7; tickets 6 lei) Movies are screened in their original language.

National Theatre & Opera House OPERA
(Teatrul Naţional şi Opera Română; Str Mărăşeşti 2) Highly regarded classic opera productions.

Information

Info Centru Turistic (☎0256-437 973; www.timisoara-info.ro; Str Alba Iulia 2) Assists with accommodation and trains, and provides maps.

Telephone office (Str N Lenau; ⏲9am-6pm Mon-Fri, to 1pm Sat; @📶) Has fax facilities, plus free internet.

Volksbank (Str Piatra Craiului 2)

Getting There & Away

AIR The airport is 12km east of the centre. Timişoara is the hub of **Carpatair** (www.carpatair.ro), with direct service to key Romanian cities and international destinations. **Tarom** (☎0256-200 003; www.tarom.ro; B-dul Revoluţiei 1989 3-5; ⏲8am-8pm Mon-Fri, 9am-2pm Sat) has daily flights to Bucharest (starting at 241 lei) and several weekly international flights.

BUS The **autogara** (B-dul Maniu Iuliu 54) is beside the Idsefin Market, three blocks from the train station (3.5km southwest of the centre). Buses run to Sibiu (43 lei, six hours, two daily) among other destinations.

International buses leave from the East Bus Station, outside the Eastern Train Station. **Atlassib** (☎0256-226 486; www.atlassib.ro) goes to Rome (340 lei) and Barcelona (382 lei). **Eurolines** (☎0256-288 132; www.eurolines.ro) goes to Budapest (200 lei, three weekly) among other places. **Murat** (☎0744-144 326, no English) goes to İstanbul every Monday (250 lei).

TRAIN Confusingly, **Gara Timişoara-Nord** (Str Gării 2), the Northern Train Station, is 3km west of the centre. From there, trains run to Bucharest (90 lei, 8½ hours), Cluj-Napoca (49 lei, six to seven hours), Budapest (105 lei) and Belgrade (60 lei). Purchase advance tickets from the **Agenţia de Voiaj CFR** (cnr Str Măcieşilor & Str V Babeş; ⏲7am-8pm Mon-Fri).

UNDERSTAND ROMANIA

History

Ancient Romania was inhabited by Thracian tribes, also known as Dacians. From the 7th century BC the Greeks established trading colonies along the Black Sea, and the Romans conquered the area in AD 105–106.

From the 10th century the Magyars expanded into Transylvania, and by the 13th century all of Transylvania was under the Hungarian crown.

Prince Vlad, ruler of Wallachia in 1448 and again from 1456 to 1462 and 1476 to 1477, gained the name Ţepeş (Impaler) after the punishment he used against enemies – driving a wooden stake through the victim's backbone without touching any vital nerve, ensuring at least 48 hours of suffering before death. He was called 'Dracula', meaning 'son of the dragon', after his father, Vlad Dracul.

After the Russian defeat in the Crimean War (1853–56) Romanian nationalism grew, and in 1859 Alexandru Ioan Cuza was elected to the thrones of Moldavia and Wallachia, creating a national state, which took the name Romania in 1862.

In 1916 Romania entered WWI on the Allied side. As Romania began losing land in WWII, General Ion Antonescu imposed a fascist dictatorship and joined Hitler, sending 400,000 Romanian Jews and 36,000 Roma to grisly deaths at Auschwitz and other camps. But in 1944 Romania changed sides, declaring war on Nazi Germany. In 1947 the monarchy was abolished and the Romanian People's Republic proclaimed.

In 1960 Romania adopted an independent foreign policy under two leaders, Gheorghe Gheorghiu-Dej (leader from 1952 to 1965) and his protégé Nicolae Ceauşescu (1965 to 1989). Ceauşescu's domestic policy was chaotic and megalomaniacal – famously exported food to finance his schemes while citizens starved.

On 15 December 1989 ethnic-Hungarian Father Lászlo Tökés publicly condemned the dictator, prompting the Reformed Church of Romania to remove him from his post. Civil unrest quickly spread and Ceauşescu dispatched troops to crush the rebellion. On 21 December in Bucharest, an address by Ceauşescu was cut short by booing demonstrators, who were crushed by police gunfire and armoured cars. The following morning thousands more took to the streets. By the next day Ceauşescu and his wife were arrested. On 25 December they were executed by firing squad.

In 1990 Romania held its first democratic elections, but internal disagreements hampered economic reform.

Romania joined the Council of Europe in 1993 and NATO in 2002. Chumming up with the USA, Romania allowed Iraq-bound military to set up bases and granted lucrative construction projects to US companies – something some EU members weren't happy with. At the last minute, the EU granted Romania membership in 2007 – though Brussels warned it will continue to monitor progress in fighting corruption and organised crime. Romania has since been threatened with EU sanctions after reviews in both 2007 and 2008 cited a lack of progress. In 2009, though minor progress had been noted, they were again reproached for lack of momentum.

People

Romanians make up 89% of the population of 22 million; Hungarians are the next largest ethnic group (7%), followed by Roma (2%), and smaller populations of Ukrainians, Germans, Russians and Turks. Germans and Hungarians live almost exclusively in Transylvania, while Ukrainians and Russians live mainly near the Danube Delta, and Turks mainly live along the Black Sea coast.

The government estimates that only 400,000 Roma live in Romania, although other sources estimate between 1.5 and 2.5 million.

Food

In this chapter, the following price indicators apply (for a main meal):

€€€ more than 25 lei

€€ 15 to 25 lei

€ less than 15 lei

Arts

Romania has a strong tradition of rural crafts, music and dance. Religious icon painting was widely practised, particularly between the 17th and 19th centuries.

Artist Nicolae Grigorescu (1838–1907) is known for adapting impressionism to Romanian peasant themes. Sculptor Constantin Brancusi (1876–1957) was a central figure of the modernist movement and one of the early pioneers of abstractionism.

The so-called 'Romanian Wave' in cinema is red hot and showing no signs of abating. Director Cristian Mungiu won the Cannes Film Festival's top prize in 2007 with *4 Months, 3 Weeks and 2 Days,* a disturbing tale of illegal abortion in communist-era Romania, while the late Cristian Nemescu's film *California Dreamin'* also took honours. More recent buzz-worthy films include a rare Romanian comedy *Tales from the Golden Age* (2009) by Cristian Mungiu, *Police, Adjective* by Corneliu Porumboiu, *Aurora* (2010) by Cristi Puiu and Radu Muntean's *Tuesday, After Christmas* (2010).

Environment

Romania is made up of three main geographical regions. The mighty Carpathian Mountains form the shape of a scythe sweeping down through the country's centre from Ukraine and then curling northwards. East of the mountains are low-lying plains that end at the Black Sea and Europe's second-largest delta region, where the Danube spills into the Black Sea.

Romania has nearly 600 protected areas, including 13 national parks, three biosphere reserves and one World Natural Heritage Site (the Danube Delta), totalling over 1.2 million hectares.

Rural Romania has thriving wildlife pop ulations in its parks and mountains, including lynxes, foxes, wolves, bears and badgers.

SURVIVAL GUIDE

Directory A–Z

Accommodation

Prices for Romanian accommodation dipped notably in 2010, to lure travellers back during the recession. It's impossible to say how long these discounts will last.

Budget permitting, aim for *pensiunes*, which are often lovingly run, costing 100 to 150 lei (€25 to €35) per person. The best resources are www.ruraltourism.ro and **Antrec** (National Association of Rural, Ecological & Cultural Tourism; www.antrec.ro).

Budget double rooms are 150 lei (€35) or less. Hostels cost 45 to 60 lei (€11 to €14) for a dorm bed; private rooms (usually with shared bathroom) 85 to 130 lei (€20 to €30). **Youth Hostels Romania** (www.hihostels-romania.ro) has information on HI hostels.

In-town camping is often in less-than-ideal locations, and conditions are sometimes shoddy. In most mountain areas there's a network of cabanas (cabins or chalets) with restaurants and dorms.

All prices given in this chapter include breakfast and private bathroom unless otherwise noted.

Price ranges used for accommodation are as follows:

€€€ more than 300 lei

€€ 150 to 300 lei

€ less than 150 lei

Activities

Most outdoor fun is related to Romania's Carpathian Mountains, which stripe the country impressively. Emergency rescue is provided by **Salvamont** (☎0-SALVAMONT; www.salvamont.org, in Romanian), a voluntary mountain-rescue organisation with 21 stations countrywide.

Hiking is the number one activity, with the most popular places being the Bucegi and Făgăraş Mountains.

Mountain biking has taken off in recent years, though some roads can be hair-raising to ride along as traffic zooms by.

Ski and **snowboard** centres are popular, but ski runs tend to be fewer (and costlier) than on many Bulgarian slopes. Sinaia and Poiana Braşov are the most popular ski areas.

Business Hours

Banks 9am-5pm Mon-Fri, 9am-noon Sat

Restaurants 10am-midnight

Holidays

New Year 1 & 2 January

Catholic & Orthodox Easter Mondays March/April

Labour Day 1 May

Romanian National Day 1 December

Christmas 25 & 26 December

Money

In Romania the only legal tender is the leu (plural lei; abbreviated 'RON'). Notes come in denominations of one, five, 10, 50, 100, 200 and 500 – try to avoid the 200s and 500s as they're difficult to spend outside hotels. Coins come in one, five, 10, 20 and 50. People sometimes still quote prices in old lei (discontinued in 2007, and sporting an extra four zeros), giving hapless travellers sticker-shock.

We've quoted most prices in this chapter in Romanian lei to make on-the-ground price references easier.

ATMs are everywhere. Moneychangers are ubiquitous (avoid changers with bodyguard goons), but you should change currency at banks whenever possible. Cashing travellers cheques is becoming increasingly difficult.

Credit cards won't get you anywhere in rural areas, but they're widely accepted in larger department stores, hotels and most restaurants in cities and towns. Some banks give cash advances on credit cards.

Post & Telephone

The postal system is reliable, if slow.

You must use area codes when dialling landline numbers in Romania, even if you're just down the road. This goes for nonemergency three- and four-digit short numbers as well. Emergency numbers are still only three digits.

Phonecards (10 lei) can be purchased at news-stands and used in phone booths for domestic or international calls.

Mobile-phone numbers are 10 digits, beginning with ☎07. European mobile phones with roaming work in Romania; otherwise you can get a Romanian number from Orange or Vodaphone. The SIM card costs about 18 lei including credit; domestic calls are about 0.35 to 0.50 lei per minute.

Dial ☎971 for an international operator.

Visas

Your passport's validity must extend to at least six months beyond the date you enter the country in order to obtain a visa.

Citizens of the USA, Canada, Australia, New Zealand, Japan and many other countries may travel visa-free for 90 days in Romania. EU citizens, obviously, may stay indefinitely. As visa requirements change frequently, check with the **Ministry of Foreign Affairs** (www.mae.ro) before departure.

Romania issues two types of visas to tourists: transit or single-entry. Transit visas (for those from countries other than the ones mentioned above) are for stays of no longer than five days, and cannot be bought at the border.

Make sure you check your visa requirements for Serbia, Hungary, Bulgaria and Ukraine if you plan to cross those borders. If you are taking the Bucharest–St Petersburg train, particularly if you're Australian or New Zealander, you'll need Ukrainian and Belarusian transit visas on top of the Russian visa.

Getting There & Away

Air

Tarom (Transporturile Aeriene Române; www.tarom.ro) is Romania's state airline. National airline **Carpatair** (☎0256-300 900; www.carpatair.com) uses Timişoara as its hub.

Most international flights land at Bucharest's **Henri Coandă airport** (formerly Otopeni; ☎021-204 1000; www.otp-airport.ro), though Wizz Air uses **Băneasa Airport** (www.baneasa.aero; ☎021-232 0020).

Some international flights – with direct services to Paris, London, Amsterdam, Germany, Italy, Greece, Budapest and other destinations in Eastern Europe – originate from Timişoara, Cluj-Napoca, Sibiu and Târgu Mureş.

Budget airlines flying into the country include the following:

Blue Air (☎021-208 8686; www.smartflying.ro)

easyJet (www.easyjet.com)

German Wings (☎0903 760 101; www.germanwings.com)

RyanAir (www.ryanair.com)

Wizz Air (☎403 6440 2000; www.wizzair.com)

Bus

Romania is well linked by bus lines to central and Western Europe as well as Turkey. While not as comfortable as the train, buses tend to be faster, though not always cheaper.

Many companies offer daily buses to Budapest and İstanbul from cities throughout Romania. **Eurolines** (www.eurolines.ro) goes to Germany, Paris and Rome among others.

Car & Motorcycle

The best advice here is to ensure your documents (ID, insurance, registration and visas, if required) are in order before crossing into Romania. The Green Card (a routine extension of domestic motor insurance to cover most European countries) is valid in Romania. Extra insurance can be bought at the borders.

Expect long queues at Romanian checkpoints, particularly on weekends.

Train

International train tickets are sold at train stations and CFR (Romanian State Railways) offices in town. International tickets must be bought at least two hours prior to departure.

Those travelling on an Inter-Rail or Eurail pass still need to make seat reservations (13 to 17 lei, or 65 lei if using a couchette) on express trains within Romania, but cheap train prices hardly justify the cost of using a rail pass here. If you already have a ticket, you may be able to make reservations at the station an hour before departure, though it's preferable to do so at a CFR office at least one day in advance.

Getting Around

Air

State-owned **Tarom** (www.tarom.ro) is Romania's main carrier. **Carpatair** (www.carpatair.com) runs domestic routes from its hub in Timişoara.

Bicycle

Cyclists have become a more frequent sight in Romania, but rental is not that widespread. A good place to rent a bike is Sinaia.

Bus

A mix of buses, microbuses and maxitaxis combine to form the seriously disorganised Romanian bus system. Finding updated information can be tough without local help. The website www.autogari.ro gives a snapshot of domestic and international bus schedules, but is by no means comprehensive. Generally it's easier to plan train travel.

Car & Motorcycle

Even if you're on a budget, it's well worth splitting the costs of a car to see the countryside; it's sometimes as low as 120 lei (€28) per day for short-term rental or 75 lei (€18) per day for long-term rental. **Autonom** (www.autonom.com) is a reliable and inexpensive agency with offices around the country.

Factor in a lot of extra time when driving (road construction is booming), and get a road map from city bookstores or petrol stations.

Your country's driving licence will be recognised here. There is a 0% blood-alcohol tolerance limit. Seatbelts are compulsory. Headlights need to be turned on when driving on any major roads, day or night.

Speed limits are 90km/h on major roads and 50km/h inside highway villages and towns unless otherwise noted.

Local Transport

Buses, trams and trolleybuses provide transport within most towns and cities in Romania, although many are crowded. They usually run from about 5am to midnight, but services can get thin on the ground after 7pm in more remote areas. Purchase tickets at street kiosks marked 'bilete' or 'casă de bilete' before boarding, and validate them once on-board.

In many rural parts, the only vehicle that passes will be horse-powered. Bucharest is the only city in Romania to boast a metro system.

Train

The punctual **Căile Ferate Române** (CFR; Romanian State Railways; www.cfr.ro) provides service to most cities, towns and larger villages in the country.

The cheapest trains are local *personal* trains. *Accelerat* trains are faster, and *rapid* faster still, hence a tad more expensive and less crowded. Seat reservations are obligatory and automatic when you buy your ticket; pricier intercity trains are the most comfortable.

Sosire means 'arrivals' and *plecare* is 'departures'. *Linia* means 'platform'.

Sleepers *(vagon de dormit)* are available between Bucharest and Arad, Cluj-Napoca, Oradea, Suceava and Timişoara.

Russia Россия

Includes »

Best Places to Eat

» Volkonsky, Moscow (p1051)

» Stolovaya 57, Moscow (p1051)

» Stolle, Moscow & St Petersburg (p1051 & p1058)

» St-Leninsbar, St Petersburg (p1057)

» Croissant Café, Kaliningrad (p1062)

Best Places to Stay

» Home From Home Hostel, Moscow (p1050)

» Artel Hotel, Moscow (p1051)

» Hostel Ligovsky 74, St Petersburg (p1057)

» Stony Island Hotel, St Petersburg (p1057)

» Villa Severin, Kaliningrad (p1062)

Why Go?

Could there be a more iconic image of Eastern Europe than the awe-inspiring architectural ensemble of Moscow's Red Sq? Russia's brash, exciting and economically powerful capital is a must on any trip to the region.

St Petersburg, on the Baltic coast, also shouldn't be missed. The former imperial capital is still Russia's most beautiful and alluring city with its colourful and often crumbling Italianate mansions, wending canals and enormous Neva River.

Emulating the tourist-friendly nature of its Baltic neighbours is little Kaliningrad, wedged between Poland and Lithuania on the Baltic Sea. It's a fascinating destination, combining all the best elements of its enormous mother, and deserves more visitors.

Visa red tape deters many travellers from visiting Russia – don't let it keep you from experiencing the incredible things to see and do in the European part of the world's largest country.

When to Go

Moscow

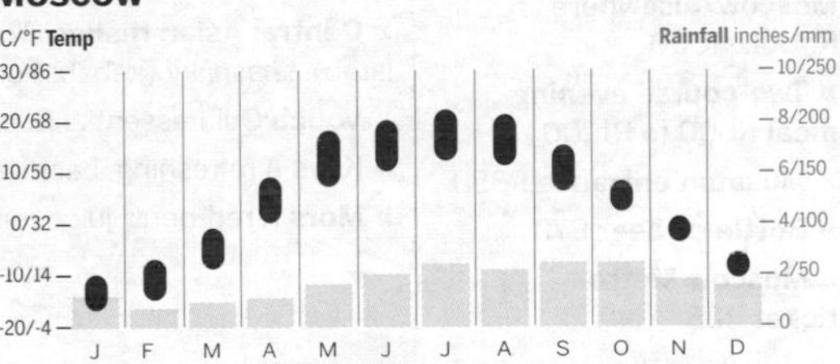

9 May Big military parades and a public holiday mark the end of WWII.

Jun–Jul Party all night during St Petersburg's White Nights; bask on Kaliningrad's beaches.

Dec–Jan Arts festivals and snow make Moscow and St Petersburg magical.

AT A GLANCE

» **Currency** Rouble (R)

» **Language** Russian

» **Money** Plenty of ATMs in easy to find locations, most accepting foreign cards

» **Visas** Required by all – apply at least a month before travel. For details, see p1065.

Fast Facts

» **Area** 16,995,800 sq km

» **Capital** Moscow

» **Country code** ☎7

» **Emergency** ☎112; ambulance ☎03; police ☎02

Exchange Rates

Australia	A$1	R29.95
Canada	C$1	R28.83
euro zone	€1	R40.12
Japan	¥100	R34.75
New Zealand	NZ$1	R23.01
UK	UK£1	R46.30
USA	US$1	R28.16

Set Your Budget

» **Budget hotel room Moscow/elsewhere** R3000/1000

» **Two-course evening meal** R600 to R1200

» **Museum entrance** R350

» **Bottle of beer** R70

» **Moscow Metro ticket** R26

Resources

» **Visit Russia** (www.visitrussia.org.uk)

» **Moscow Expat Site** (www.expat.ru)

Connections

Bordering Belarus, Estonia, Latvia, Lithuania, Poland and Ukraine, Russia has excellent train and bus connections with the rest of Europe. Routes connecting Kaliningrad with St Petersburg will take you through the Baltic countries, while trains between Kaliningrad and Moscow head through Belarus. Trains from Kharkiv in Ukraine transit via Kursk, Oryol and Tula to terminate in Moscow.

ITINERARIES

Two Days

In Moscow Tour Red Sq and the Kremlin. Admire art old and new at the State Tretyakov Gallery, the Pushkin Museum of Fine Art and Garazh.

In St Petersburg Wander up Nevsky Pr, see Palace Sq and the mighty Neva River, then tour the magnificent collection of the Hermitage. Visit St Peter & Paul Fortress, the Church of the Saviour on Spilled Blood and the wonderful Russian Museum.

In Kaliningrad Admire the reconstructed Gothic cathedral, then wander along the river to the excellent World Ocean Museum. The Amber Museum is also impressive. Explore the sand dunes and forests of the Kurshskaya Kosa National Park.

Essential Food & Drink

» **Soups** Such as the lemony meat *solyanka* or the hearty fish *ukha*.

» **Bliny** Pancakes with *ikra* (caviar) or *tvorog* (cottage cheese).

» **Salads** A wide variety usually slathered in mayonnaise, including the chopped potato one called *olivier*.

» **Pelmeni** Dumplings stuffed with meat and eaten with sour cream and vinegar.

» **Central Asian dishes** *Plov* (fried rice with vegetables and lamb), *shashliky* (kebabs) or *lagman* (noodles).

» **Vodka** Quintessential Russian tipple.

» **Kvas** A refreshing, beerlike drink.

» **Mors** A red-berry juice mix.

Russia Highlights

1. Be awe-inspired by the massive scale and riches of **Moscow** (p1046), Russia's brash, energetic capital

2. Savour the imperial past in elegant **St Petersburg** (p1053), a city of colourful and often crumbling Italianate mansions, wending canals and the enormous Neva River

3. Use **Kaliningrad** (p1059) city as a base for discovering this tiny, separate piece of Russia that aims to emulate its Baltic neighbours for friendliness

4. Kick back on the pristine beaches of the **Kurshskaya Kosa National Park** (p1061) or go in search of its 'dancing forest'

MOSCOW МОСКВА

POP 10 MILLION

Intimidating in its scale, but also exciting and unforgettable, Moscow is many things to many people, a place that inspires extreme passion or loathing. History, power and wild capitalism hang in the air, alongside an explosion of creative energy throwing up edgy art galleries and a dynamic restaurant, bar and nightlife scene with something for everyone. Tchaikovsky and Chekhov are well represented at the city's theatres, but you can also see world premiers by up-and-coming composers and choreographers. Although much of its architectural heritage has been destroyed, the sturdy stone walls of the Kremlin continue to occupy the founding site of Moscow, and remains of the Soviet state are scattered all around the city.

The medieval centre of the city, the Kremlin, is a triangle on the northern bank of the Moscow River. The modern city centre radiates around it – the main streets being Tverskaya ul and ul Novy Arbat. The eight-lane highway known as the 'garden ring' encloses Moscow's central district.

Sights

Kremlin MUSEUM

(☎495-202 3776; www.kreml.ru; adult/student R350/100; ⌚9.30am-4pm Fri-Wed; MAleksandrovsky Sad) The apex of Russian political power and once the centre of the Orthodox Church, the Kremlin is the kernel not only of Moscow but of the whole country. It's from here that autocratic tsars, communist dictators and democratic presidents have done their best – and worst – for Russia.

Occupying a roughly triangular plot of land covering Borovitsky Hill on the north bank of the Moscow River, the Kremlin is enclosed by high walls 2.25km long, with Red Sq outside the east wall. The best views of the complex are from Sofiyskaya nab across the river.

Before entering the Kremlin, deposit bags at the **left-luggage office** (per bag R60; ⌚9am-6.30pm Fri-Wed), beneath the Kutafya Tower near the main ticket office in the Alexandrovsky Garden, just off Manezhnaya pl. The entrance ticket covers admission to all five church-museums and the Patriarch's Palace. It does not include the Armoury, the Diamond Fund Exhibition or exhibits in the Ivan the Great Bell Tower. You can buy tickets for all those places here, too.

Photography is not permitted inside the Armoury or any of the buildings on Sobornaya pl (Cathedral Sq). Visitors wearing shorts will be refused entry.

Southwest Buildings

From the Kutafya Tower, which forms the main visitors entrance, walk up the ramp and pass through the Kremlin walls beneath the **Trinity Gate Tower** (Troitskaya Bashnya). The lane to the right (south) passes the 17th-century **Poteshny Palace** (Poteshny Dvorets), where Stalin lived. The horribly out of place glass-and-concrete **State Kremlin Palace** (Kremlyovksy Dvorets Syezdov) houses a concert and ballet auditorium, where many Western pop stars play when they are in Moscow.

Armoury & Diamond Fund

In the Kremlin's southwestern corner is the **Armoury** (adult/student R700/200; ⌚entry 10am, noon, 2.30pm & 4.30pm), a numbingly opulent collection of treasures accumulated over time by the Russian state and church. Tickets specify entry times. Highlights include Fabergé eggs and cartloads of royal regalia.

If the Armoury doesn't sate your diamond lust, there are more in the separate **Diamond Fund Exhibition** (Vystavka Almaznogo Fonda; ☎495-629 2036; admission R500; ⌚10am-1pm & 2-5pm Fri-Wed), in the same building. The lavish collection includes the largest sapphire in the world.

Sobornaya Ploshchad

On the northern side of Sobornaya pl, with five golden helmet domes and four semicircular gables facing the square, is the **Assumption Cathedral** (Uspensky Sobor), built between 1475 and 1479. As the focal church of prerevolutionary Russia, it's the burial place of most heads of the Russian Orthodox Church from the 1320s to 1700.

The delicate little single-domed church beside the west door of the Assumption Cathedral is the **Church of the Deposition of the Robe** (Tserkov Rizopolozheniya), built between 1484 and 1486 by masons from Pskov.

With its two golden domes rising above the eastern side of Sobornaya pl, the 16th-century **Ivan the Great Bell Tower** (Kolokolnya Ivana Velikogo) is the Kremlin's tallest structure. Beside the bell tower stands the **Tsar Bell**, a 202-tonne monster that cracked before it ever rang. North of the bell tower is the mammoth **Tsar Cannon**, cast in 1586 but never shot.

The 1508 **Archangel Cathedral** (Arkhangelsky Sobor), at the square's southeastern corner, was for centuries the coronation, wedding and burial church of tsars. The tombs of all of Russia's rulers from the 1320s to the 1690s are here bar one (Boris Godunov, who was buried at Sergiev Posad).

Finally, the **Annunciation Cathedral** (Blagoveshchensky Sobor), at the southwest corner of Sobornaya pl and dating from 1489, contains the celebrated icons of master painter Theophanes the Greek. He probably painted the six icons at the right-hand end of the diesis row, the biggest of the six tiers of the iconostasis. *Archangel Michael* (the third icon from the left on the diesis row) and the adjacent *St Peter* are ascribed to Russian master Andrei Rublev.

Red Square SQUARE

Entering massively impressive Red Sq (or Krasnaya pl) through the **Resurrection Gate** (Voskresenskiye Vorota), you'll emerge with a superb view of the magnificently flamboyant **St Basil's Cathedral** (Sobor Vasilia Blazhennogo; ☎495-698 3304; adult/student R100/50; ⏰11am-5pm Wed-Mon; Ⓜ Pl Revolyutsii) on the far side. This ultimate symbol of Russia was created between 1555 and 1561 (replacing an existing church on the site) to celebrate the capture of Kazan by Ivan the Terrible. Built over the grave of the barefoot holy fool Vasily (Basil) the Blessed, who predicted Ivan's damnation, its design is the culmination of a wholly Russian style that had been developed through the building of wooden churches. Go inside to see the stark medieval wall paintings.

FREE **Lenin's Mausoleum** (☎495-623 5527; ⏰10am-1pm Tue-Thu, Sat & Sun; Ⓜ Pl Revolyutsii) is found at the square's northwestern corner. The embalmed Soviet leader remains as he has been since 1924 (apart from a retreat to Siberia during WWII). Before joining the queue, drop your camera at the left-luggage office in the State History Museum, as you will not be allowed to take it with you. After trooping past the embalmed, oddly waxy figure, emerge from his red and black stone tomb and inspect where Stalin, Brezhnev and many of communism's other heavy hitters are buried along the Kremlin wall.

The **State History Museum** (☎495-692 3731; www.shm.ru; adult/student R250/60, ⏰10am-6pm Tue-Sat, 11am-8pm Sun; Ⓜ Okhotny Ryad) has an enormous collection covering the whole Russian empire from the Stone Age onward. The building, dating from the late 19th century, is itself an attraction – each room is in the style of a different period or region.

State Tretyakov Gallery ART GALLERY

(☎499-238 1378; Lavrushinsky per 10; adult/student R300/180; ⏰10am-6.30pm Tue-Sun; Ⓜ Tretyakovskaya) Nothing short of spectacular, the State Tretyakov Gallery holds the world's best collection of Russian icons and an outstanding collection of other prerevolutionary Russian art.

New Tretyakov & Art Muzeon ART GALLERY

(☎499-238 1378; Krymsky val; adult/student R300/180; ⏰10am-6.30pm Tue-Sun; Ⓜ Oktyabrsakaya) The New Tretyakov is the premier venue for 20th-century Russian art and shouldn't be missed. Besides the plethora of socialist realism, the exhibits showcase key works by avant-garde artists such as Kazimir Malevich, Vasily Kandinsky, Marc Chagall, Natalia Goncharova and Lyubov Popova.

Beside the gallery is the open-air sculpture park **Art Muzeon** (☎499-238 3396; ul Krymsky val 10; admission R100; ⏰9am-9pm; Ⓜ Park Kultury). What started as a collection of Soviet statues put out to pasture when they were ripped from their pedestals post-1991 has now been joined by fascinating and diverse contemporary work.

Zurab Tsereteli's monumental but controversial **Peter the Great statue** (Bersenevskaya nab; Ⓜ Polyanka) stands on the river bank overlooking the park.

Pushkin Museum of Fine Arts ART GALLERY

(☎495-697 7998; www.museum.ru/gmii; ul Volkhonka 12; adult/student R300/150; ⏰10am-6pm Tue-Sun; Ⓜ Kropotkinskaya) Moscow's premier foreign-art museum displays a broad selection of European works, mostly appropriated from private collections after the revolution. They include Dutch and Flemish masterpieces from the 17th century, several Rembrandt portraits, and the Ancient Civilisation exhibits, which include the impressive Treasures of Troy.

The Pushkin's amazing collection of Impressionist and post-Impressionist paintings are found next door at the **Gallery of European & American Art of the 19th & 20th Centuries** (☎495-697 1546; ul Volkhonka 14; adult/student R300/150; ⏰10am-6pm Tue-Sun, to 8pm Thu; Ⓜ Kropotkinskaya).

FREE **Garazh Centre for Contemporary Culture** ART GALLERY

(☎495-645 0520; www.garageccc.com; ul Obraztsova 19a; ⏰11am-9pm Mon-Thu, to 10pm Fri-Sun; Ⓜ Savyolvskaya) A handsomely renovated bus depot, designed by constructivist

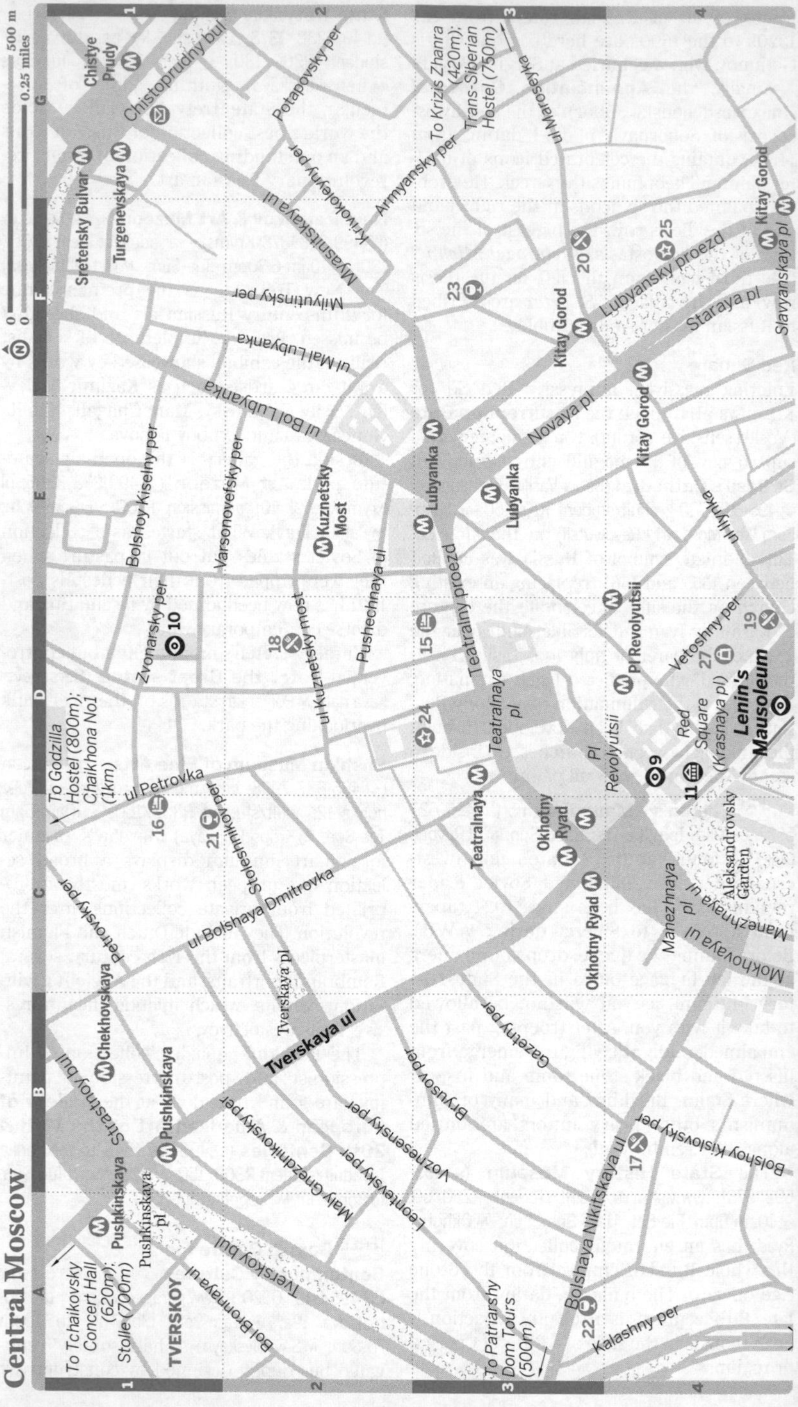

Central Moscow

0 500 m
0 0.25 miles

To Tchaikovsky Concert Hall (620m); Stolle (700m)
Pushkinskaya
Strastnoy bul
Chekhovskaya
Petrovsky per
To Godzilla Hostel (800m); Chaikhona No1 (1km)
Sretensky Bulvar
Chistye Prudy
Turgenevskaya
Chistoprudny bul
Pushkinskaya pl
Pushkinskaya
TVERSKOY
ul Petrovka
16
Zvonarsky per
10
Bolshoy Kiselny per
21
Bol Bronnaya ul
Tverskoy bul
Maly Gnezdnikovsky per
Tverskaya ul
Tverskaya pl
ul Bolshaya Dmitrovka
Stoleshnikov per
Varsonovefsky per
18
ul Kuznetsky most
Kuznetsky Most
ul Bol Lubyanka
ul Mal Lubyanka
Milyutinsky per
Myasnitskaya ul
Krivokoleyny per
Potapovsky per
Leontevsky per
Voznesensky per
Pushechnaya ul
Armyansky per
Bryusov per
24
15
Lubyanka
Teatralny proezd
To Krizis Zhanra (420m); Trans-Siberian Hostel (750m)
23
Teatralnaya
Teatralnaya pl
Lubyanka
To Patriarshy Dom Tours (500m)
Gazetny per
Okhotny Ryad
Novaya pl
ul Maroseyka
Kitay Gorod
20
22
Bolshaya Nikitskaya ul
Okhotny Ryad
Pl Revolyutsii
Pl Revolyutsii
Kitay Gorod
Kalashny per
17
9
Manezhnaya pl
11
Red Square (Krasnaya pl)
Vetoshny per
Lubyansky proezd
25
27
ul Ilyinka
Staraya pl
Bolshoy Kislovsky per
Mokhovaya ul
Manezhnaya ul
Aleksandrovsky Garden
Lenin's Mausoleum
19
Kitay Gorod
Slavyanskaya pl

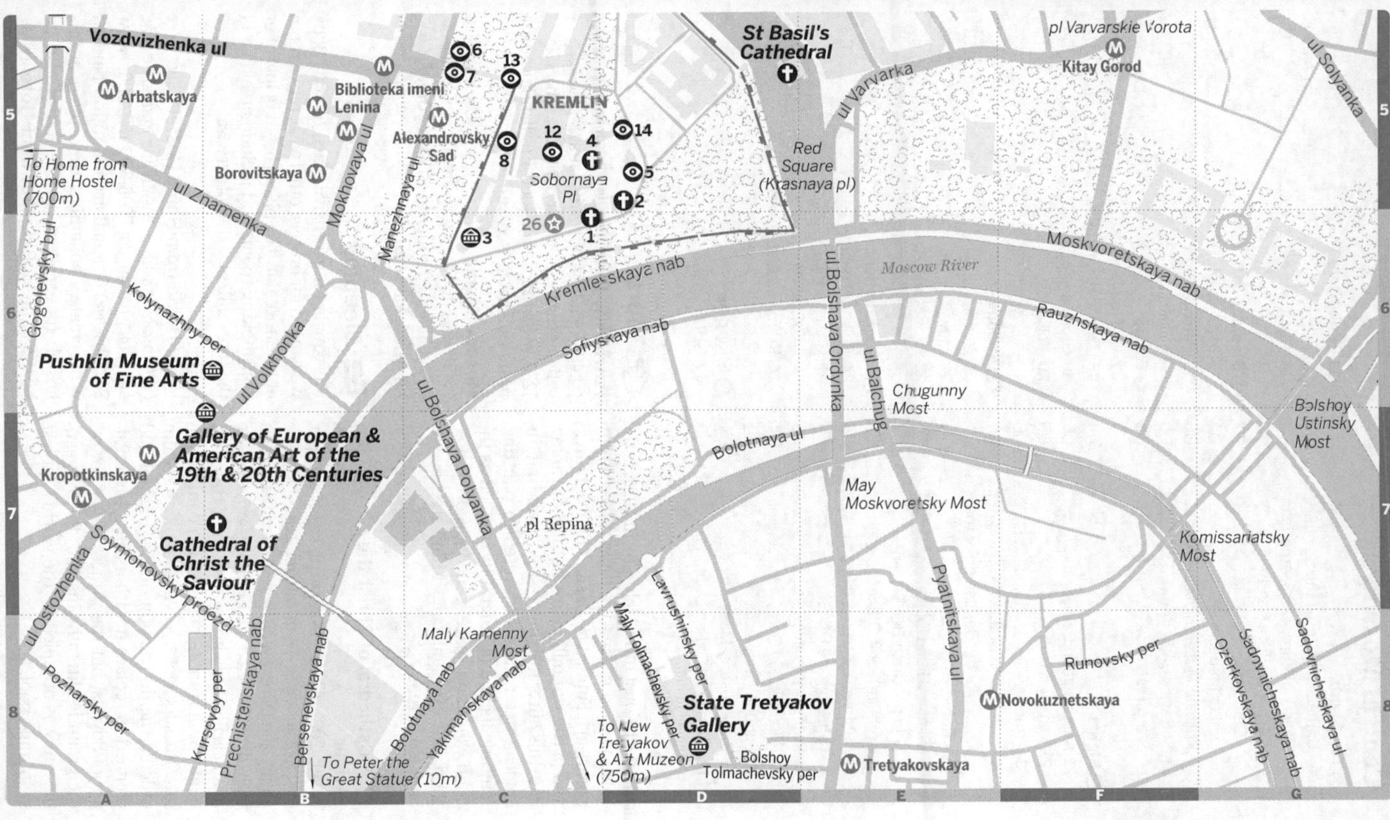
Vozdvizhenka ul
Arbatskaya
Biblioteka imeni Lenina
Alexandrovsky Sad
Borovitskaya
To Home from Home Hostel (700m)
ul Znamenka
Mokhovaya ul
Manezhnaya ul
KREMLIN
Sobornaya Pl
St Basil's Cathedral
Red Square (Krasnaya pl)
pl Varvarskie Vorota
Kitay Gorod
ul Varvarka
ul Solyanka
Moskvoretskaya nab
Moscow River
Kremlevskaya nab
Sofiyskaya nab
Rauzhskaya nab
ul Bolshaya Ordynka
ul Balchug
Chugunny Most
Bolshoy Ustinsky Most
Gogolevsky bul
Kolymazhny per
ul Volkhonka
Pushkin Museum of Fine Arts
Gallery of European & American Art of the 19th & 20th Centuries
Kropotkinskaya
Cathedral of Christ the Saviour
Soymonovsky proezd
ul Ostozhenka
Pozharsky per
Kursovoy per
Prechistenskaya nab
Bersenevskaya nab
To Peter the Great Statue (10m)
Bolotnaya nab
Yakimanskaya nab
Maly Kamenny Most
ul Bolshaya Polyanka
pl Repina
Bolotnaya ul
May Moskvoretsky Most
Komissariatsky Most
Maly Tolmachevsky per
Lavrushinsky per
State Tretyakov Gallery
To New Tretyakov & Art Muzeon (750m)
Bolshoy Tolmachevsky per
Tretyakovskaya
Pyatnitskaya ul
Novokuznetskaya
Runovsky per
Ozerkovskaya nab
Sadovnicheskaya nab
Sadovnicheskaya ul
1
2
3
4
5
6
7
8
12
13
14
26
A
B
C
D
E
F
G
5
6
7
8

Central Moscow

Top Sights

Cathedral of Christ the Saviour B7
Gallery of European & American Art of the 19th & 20th Centuries B7
Lenin's Mausoleum D4
Pushkin Museum of Fine Arts B6
St Basil's Cathedral D5
State Tretyakov Gallery D8

Sights

1 Annunciation Cathedral C6
2 Archangel Cathedral D5
3 Armoury C6
4 Assumption Cathedral C5
Church of the Deposition of the Robe .... (see 4)
Diamond Fund Exhibition .... (see 3)
5 Ivan the Great Bell Tower D5
6 Kremlin Ticket Office C5
7 Kutafya Tower C5
Left-Luggage Office .... (see 7)
8 Poteshny Palace C5
9 Resurrection Gate D4
10 Sanduny Baths D1
11 State History Museum D4
12 State Kremlin Palace C5
13 Trinity Gate Tower C5
Tsar Bell .... (see 5)
14 Tsar Cannon D5

Sleeping

15 Artel Hotel D3
16 Petrovka Loft C1

Eating

17 Coffee Mania B4
18 Jagannath D2
19 Stolovaya 57 .... D4
20 Volkonsky F3

Drinking

21 Gogol C1
22 Mayak A3
23 Propaganda F3

Entertainment

24 Bolshoi Theatre D3
25 Chinese Pilot Dzhao-Da F4
26 Kremlin Ballet Theatre C6

Shopping

27 GUM D4

architect Konstantin Melnikov in 1927, is the location for a fascinating foray into contemporary art. Funded by Dasha Zukova, heiress and partner of billionaire Roman Abramovich, this aircraft-hanger-sized building includes three galleries (devoted to painting, multimedia and photography) as well as the main exhibition space, a media room, bookshop and excellent cafe. Many free events are held here.

FREE Cathedral of Christ the Saviour CHURCH
(☎495-202 4734; www.xxc.ru; ⏲10am-5pm; MKropotkinskaya) Dominating the skyline along the Moscow River, this gargantuan cathedral, finished in 1997, sits on the site of an earlier and similar church of the same name, built from 1839 to 1883 to commemorate Russia's victory over Napoleon. Stalin ordered the destruction of the original and planned to replace it with a 315m-high 'Palace of Soviets', but the project never got off the ground – literally. Instead, for 50 years the site was occupied by the world's largest swimming pool.

Tours

Patriarshy Dom Tours SPECIALIST TOURS
(☎495-795 0927; http://russiatravel-pdtours.netfirms.com; Vspolny per 6, Moscow school No 1239; MBarrikadnaya) Good English-language tours on specialised subjects.

Moscow Mania WALKING TOURS
(☎916-992 4644; www.mosmania.com; from R300) Themed itineraries with young, knowledgeable guides.

Sleeping

Moscow is an expensive place to stay. Book well ahead for hostels; otherwise, rent a room or an entire flat. The places listed below offer nonsmoking rooms and include breakfast in the rates unless stated otherwise.

TOP CHOICE Home from Home Hostel HOSTEL €
(☎495-229 8018; www.home-fromhome.com; Apt 9, ul Arbat 49; dm R700-800, d R2000; @; MSmolenskaya) Original art and mural-painted walls create a bohemian atmosphere at this hostel. Its excellent private rooms also go by the name of **Bulgakov Mini-Hotel** (www.

bulgakovhotel.com). Enter the courtyard from Plotnikov per and look for entrance No 2.

TOP CHOICE **Artel Hotel** HOTEL €€
(495-626 9008; www.artelhotel.ru; Bldg 3, 3 Teatralny pr 3; s/d from R3100/3400; M Lubyanka) Wacky art abounds in this creative space where each room is a unique design – the cheapest are tiny, though. Downstairs is the equally funky restaurant/bar/club/theatre space **Masterskaya** (www.mstrsk.ru).

Godzillas Hostel HOSTEL €
(495-699 4223; www.godzillashostel.com; Bolshoy Karetny per 6; dm/d/tr R868/2100/2883; @; M Tsvetnoy bul) Moscow's biggest and most professionally run hostel, with 90 beds over four floors. Rooms are spacious, light filled and painted in different colours. There are also three kitchens and a comfy lounge with satellite TV.

Trans-Siberian Hostel HOSTEL €
(495-916 2030; www.tshostel.com; Barashevsky per 12; dm R630-700, d R1750; @; M Kitay-Gorod) Snag one of the two double rooms in this tiny train-themed hostel and you're getting one of the capital's best bargains. Staff are superfriendly and there's a good kitchen-lounge to hang out in.

Petrovka Loft HOTEL €€
(495-626 2210; www.petrovkaloft.com; 17/2 Petrovka ul; r from R3500) Enter the courtyard and go straight ahead to find the entrance to this 10-room top-floor hotel on the left. None of the rooms are en suite but everything is stylish and clean.

Eating

TOP CHOICE **Volkonsky** BAKERY €
(www.wolkonsky.com; meals R300-500; 8am-11pm) Kitay-Gorod (ul Maroseyka 4/2; M Kitay-Gorod); Volkonsky Tverskoy (Bolshaya Sadovaya ul 2/46; M Mayakovskaya) The queue often runs out the door as loyal patrons wait their turn for the city's best fresh-baked breads, pastries and pies.

TOP CHOICE **Stolovaya 57** RUSSIAN €
(3rd fl, GUM, Red Sq; 10am-10pm; M Okhotny Ryad) This place offers a nostalgic re-creation of dining in post-Stalinist Russia. The food is good – and cheap for such a fancy store.

Stolle RUSSIAN €
(www.stolle.ru; meals R200-600; 8am-10pm) Khamovniki (Malaya Pirogovskaya ul 16; M Sportivnaya); Tverskoy (Bolshaya Sadovaya ul 8/1; M Mayakovskaya) The selection of sweet and savoury pies sit on the counter, fresh from the oven. It may be difficult to decide (mushroom or meat? apricot or apple?), but you really can't go wrong.

Coffee Mania CAFE €€
(www.coffeemania.ru; Bolshaya Nikitskaya ul 13; meals R600-800; 24hr; M Okhotny Ryad) The friendly, informal cafe is beloved for its homemade soups, fresh-squeezed juices and steaming cappuccinos, not to mention its summer terrace overlooking the leafy courtyard of the conservatory.

Jagannath VEGETARIAN €
(http://jagannath.ru; Kuznetsky most 11; meals R300-500; 10am-11pm; ; M Kuznetsky Most) Long-running self-serve cafe and shop. Its Indian-theme decor is more New Agey than ethnic

> **FLAT RENTAL AGENCIES**
>
> The following online agencies offer good deals, some from as low as R770 (€18.50) per night:
>
> » www.cheap-moscow.com
>
> » www.hofa.ru
>
> » www.moscowapartments.net

Drinking & Entertainment

The line between cafe, bar and club in Moscow is hazy. The same place can morph from somewhere to have a quiet morning coffee to a hedonistic venue for cocktail-swilling late-night frolics. At in places you'll have to brave 'face control' but, on the whole, Moscow nightlife is becoming more democratic, especially at the following.

Mayak CAFE, BAR
(www.clubmayak.ru; Bolshaya Nikitskaya ul 19; meals R600-800; M Okhotny Ryad) Named for the Mayakovsky Theatre downstairs, this is more cafe than club. It still attracts actors, artists and writers, who come to see friendly faces, eat filling European fare and drink into the night.

Gogol CAFE, BAR
(www.gogolclubs.ru; Stoleshnikov per 11; cover R350; 24hr, concerts 9pm or 10pm Thu-Sat; M Chekhovskaya) Fun, informal and affordable (so surprising on swanky Stoleshnikov!),

Gogol is great for food, drinks and music. In summer the action moves out to the courtyard, where the gigantic tent is styled like an old-fashioned street scene.

Chaikhona No 1 CAFE, BAR
(www.chaihona.com; ⏲noon to last customer) Gorky Park (Ⓜ Frunzenskaya); Hermitage Gardens (Ⓜ Chekhovskaya) This cool Uzbek lounge and cafe is housed in an inviting, exotic tent laid with oriental rugs and plush pillows. There's *plov* and *shashlyk* on the menu.

Propaganda CAFE, CLUB
(www.propagandamoscow.com; Bolshoy Zlatoustinsky per 7; ⏲noon-6am; Ⓜ Kitay-Gorod) This longtime favourite features exposed-brick walls and pipe ceilings. It's a cafe by day (meals R500 to R700), but at night they clear the dance floor and let the DJ do his stuff. Sunday is gay night.

Krizis Zhanra CAFE, CLUB
(www.kriziszhanra.ru; ul Pokrovka 16/16; ⏲concerts 9pm daily, 11pm Fri & Sat; Ⓜ Chistye Prudy) Everybody has something good to say about Krizis and what's not to love? Good cheap food, copious drinks and rockin' music every night, all of which inspires the gathered to get their groove on.

Check **Gay.Ru** (www.gay.ru) for gay-friendly listings. Gravitate toward the **Hermitage Gardens** (Ⓜ Pushkinskaya Tverskaya) or the **Aleksandrovsky Garden** (Ⓜ Okhotny Ryad) during the summer months for relaxed beer drinking amid the greenery.

✩ Entertainment

To find out what's on, see the weekly magazine *element,* the entertainment section in Thursday's *Moscow Times,* and the bimonthly edition of *Moscow in Your Pocket.* For major concerts, the main venues are the Olimpiisky Sports Complex (Ⓜ Tsvetnoy Bulvar) and the Kremlin Palace (p1046).

Bolshoi Theatre BALLET, OPERA
(☎495-250 7317; www.bolshoi.ru; Teatralnaya pl 1; tickets R200-5000; Ⓜ Teatralnaya) An evening at the Bolshoi is one of Moscow's most romantic options. Both the ballet and opera companies perform a range of Russian and foreign works. Productions take place both on the main stage, now back in operation after a multiyear renovation, and the smaller New Stage (Novaya Stsena).

Kremlin Ballet Theatre BALLET
(☎495-928 5232; www.kremlin-gkd.ru; ul Vozdvizhenka 1; Ⓜ Alexandrovsky Sad) The Bolshoi does not have a monopoly on ballet in Moscow. Leading dancers also appear with the Kremlin Ballet, which performs in the State Kremlin Palace (inside the Kremlin).

Tchaikovsky Concert Hall CLASSICAL MUSIC
(☎495-232 0400; www.meloman.ru; Triumfalnaya pl 4/31; tickets R100-1000; Ⓜ Mayakovskaya) This venue is home to the State Symphony Orchestra, which specialises in the music of its namesake composer and other Russian classics.

Chinese Pilot Dzhao-Da LIVE MUSIC
(☎495-623 2896; www.jao-da.ru; Lubyansky pr 25; cover R300-500; ⏲concerts 10pm Thu, 11pm Fri & Sat; Ⓜ Kitay-Gorod) This relaxed basement dive hosts lots of different kinds of bands from around Europe and Russia, so check out the website in advance. Often has free concerts on Monday night.

Shopping

Ul Arbat (Ⓜ Arbatskaya or Smolenskaya), about 1km west of the Kremlin, has always been a tourist attraction and is littered with souvenir shops and stalls.

GUM MALL
(☎495-788 4343; www.gum.ru; Krasnaya pl 3; ⏲10am-10pm; Ⓜ Pl Revolyutsii) Elegant heritage building on Red Sq, packed with designer labels and good souvenir shops, including the glam grocery Gastronom No 1.

Izmaylovo Market SOUVENIRS
(www.kremlin-izmailovo.com; Izmaylovskoye shosse; ⏲9am-6pm Sat & Sun; Ⓜ Partizanskaya) Sprawling area packed with art, handmade crafts, antiques, Soviet paraphernalia and just about anything you might want for a souvenir. Also has a kitsch mock Kremlin (great for photos!) and tasty *shashlyk* (kebab) stands.

ℹ Information

American Medical Center (☎495-933 7700; www.amcenter.ru; Grokholsky per 1; Ⓜ Pr Mira) Offers 24-hour emergency service, consultations and a full range of medical specialists, including paediatricians, dentists and on-site pharmacy.

Central Telegraph (Tverskaya ul 7; ⏲post 8am-10pm, telephone 24hr; Ⓜ Okhotny Ryad) This convenient office offers telephone, fax and internet services.

element (www.elementmoscow.ru) Weekly newsprint magazine with restaurant reviews and concert and art exhibition listings; look out for its quarterly restaurant guide.

Main post office (Myasnitskaya ul 26; ⏱8am-8pm Mon-Fri, 9am-7pm Sat & Sun; Ⓜ Chistye Prudy)

Maria Travel Agency (☎495-775 8226; www.maria-travel.com; ul Maroseyka 13; Ⓜ Kitay-Gorod) Offers visa support, apartment rental and some local tours, including to the Golden Ring.

Moscow in Your Pocket (www.inyourpocket.com) Good bi-monthly booklet of listings and features available in major hotels and hostels.

Moscow Times (www.themoscowtimes.com) Best of the locally published English-language newspapers.

Time Online (www.timeonline.ru; per hr R70-100; ⏱24hr) Komsomolskaya (Komsomolskaya pl 3; Ⓜ Komsomolskaya); Okhotny Ryad (Ⓜ Okhotny Ryad) Offers copy and photo services, as well as over 100 zippy computers and free wi-fi.

Unifest Travel (☎495-234 6555; www.unifest.ru; Komsomolsky pr 13; Ⓜ Park Kultury) About 500m south of the metro station is this on-the-ball travel company offering rail and air tickets, visa support etc.

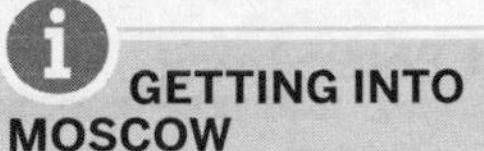

GETTING INTO MOSCOW

All airports are accessible by **Aeroexpress** (www.aeroexpress.ru). These convenient train services leave from different stations depending on the airport they serve. If you have a lot of luggage and you wish to take a taxi, it is highly recommended to book in advance to take advantage of fixed rates offered by most companies (usually R1000 to R1500 to/from any airport).

Getting Around

Metro

The **Moscow metro** (www.mosmetro.ru) is the easiest, quickest and cheapest way of getting around Moscow. Stations are marked outside by 'M' signs. Magnetic tickets (R26) are sold at ticket booths. Save time by buying a multiple-ride ticket (5/10/20 rides R125/240/460).

Taxi

See p1067 for information on hailing unofficial taxis. Expect to pay R200 to R300 for a ride around the city centre. To book a taxi try **Taxi Blues** (☎495-243 4919; www.the-taxi.ru) or **Woman Taxi** (Zhenskoye Taksi; ☎495-662 0033; www.womantaxi.ru), offering female drivers and child car seats.

ST PETERSBURG САНКТ ПЕТЕРБУРГ

☎812 / POP 4.6 MILLION

Elegant, enchanting and hedonistic, Russia's one-time capital is a fascinating hybrid of traditional Russia and contemporary Europe, where one moment you can be sniffing incense inside a mosaic-covered Orthodox church, the next grooving on the dance floor of an underground club or posing at a contemporary art event in a renovated bakery. Above all, the city is a visual delight. The Neva River and surrounding canals reflect unbroken facades of handsome 18th- and 19th-century buildings, housing a spellbinding collection of cultural storehouses, culminating in the incomparable Hermitage.

St Petersburg is spread out across many different islands, some real and some created through the construction of canals. The central street is Nevsky Pr, which extends for some 4km from the Alexander Nevsky Monastery (Lavra Alexandra Nevskogo) to the Hermitage.

Sights

Hermitage & Dvortsovaya Ploshchad — MUSEUM

(www.hermitagemuseum.org; Dvortsovaya pl 2; adult R400, student & under 17yr free; ⏱10.30am-6pm Tue-Sat, to 5pm Sun; Ⓜ Nevsky Pr) Mainly set in the magnificent Winter Palace, the State Hermitage is stacked with treasures, ranging from Egyptian mummies and Scythian gold to early-20th-century European art by Matisse and Picasso.

The museum can be very busy on the first Thursday of the month, when admission is free for all, and throughout the summer. Either go late in the day when the lines are likely to be shorter or book your ticket online through the Hermitage's website.

The museum's main entrance is from **Dvortsovaya ploshchad** (Palace Sq), one of the city's most impressive and historic spaces. Stand back to admire the palace and the central 47.5m **Alexander Column**, named after Alexander I and commemorating the 1812 victory over Napoleon.

Church of the Saviour on Spilled Blood — CHURCH

(www.cathedral.ru; Konyushennaya pl; adult/student R320/170; ⏱11am-7pm Thu-Tue Oct-Apr, 10am-8pm Thu-Tue May-Sep; Ⓜ Nevsky Pr) This

Central St Petersburg

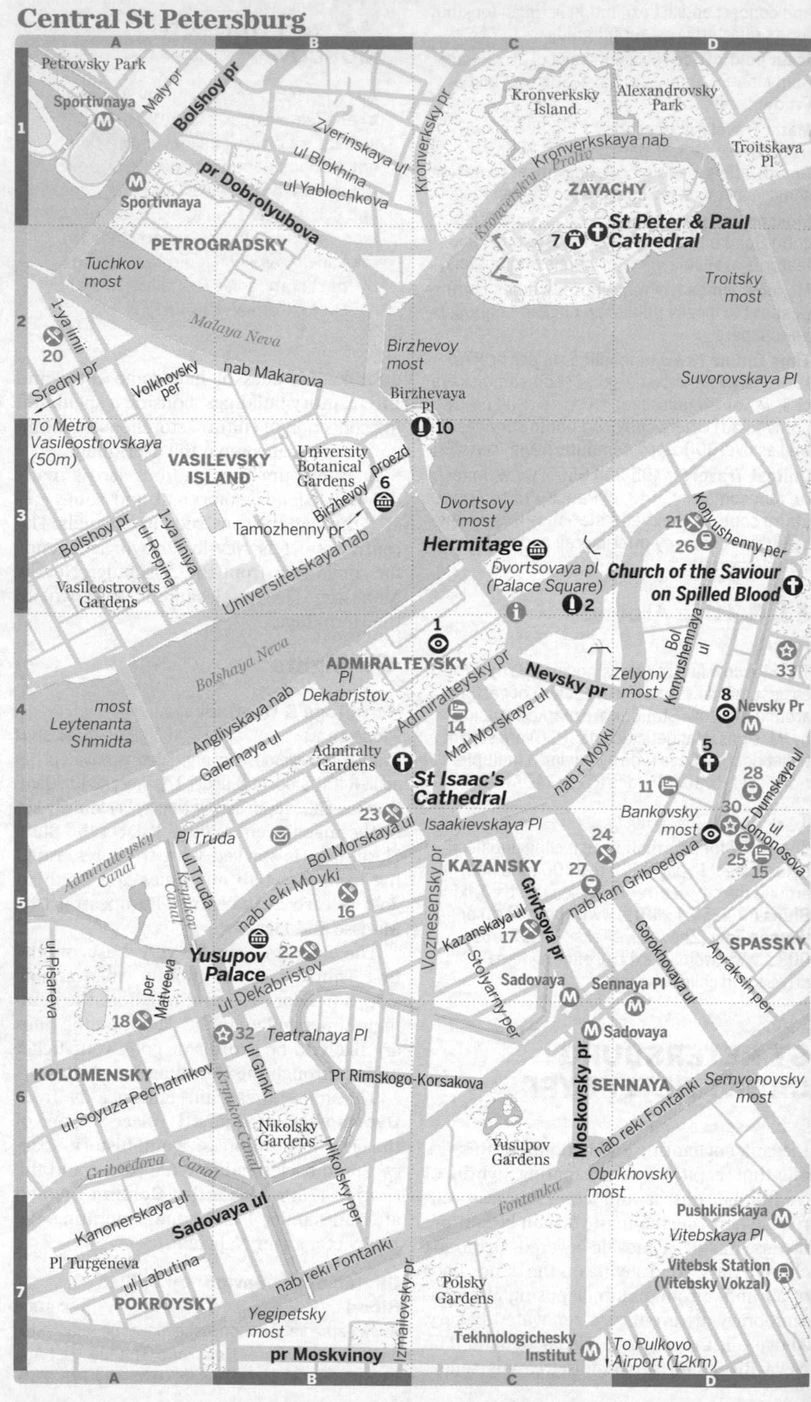

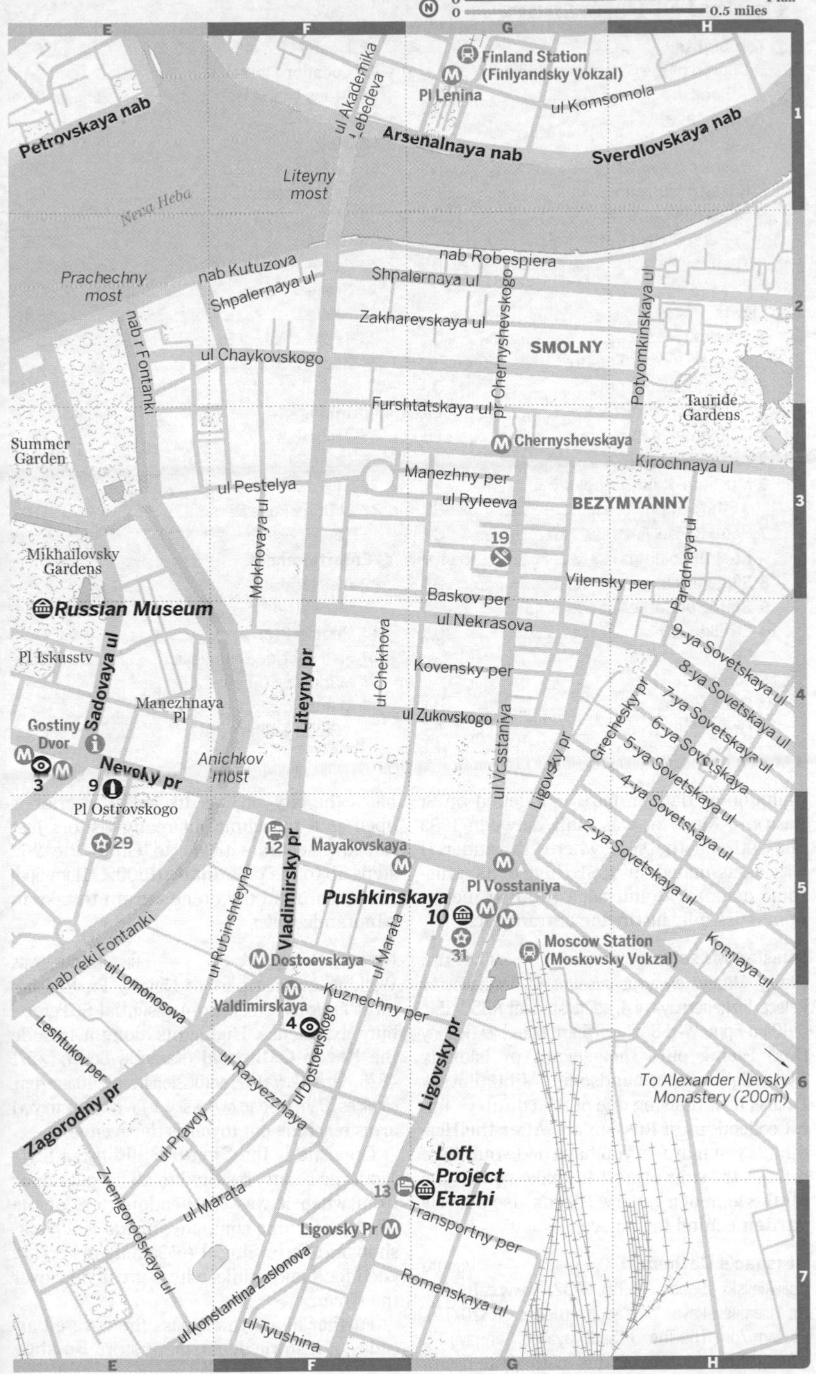

0 1 km
0 0.5 miles
E
F
G
H
1
2
3
4
5
6
7
Finland Station
(Finlyandsky Vokzal)
Pl Lenina
ul Komsomola
ul Akademika Lebedeva
Petrovskaya nab
Arsenalnaya nab
Sverdlovskaya nab
Liteyny most
Neva Heba
nab Robespiera
Prachechny most
nab Kutuzova
Shpalernaya ul
Zakharevskaya ul
SMOLNY
Potyomkinskaya ul
pr Chernyshevskogo
nab r Fontanki
ul Chaykovskogo
Furshtatskaya ul
Tauride Gardens
Chernyshevskaya
Summer Garden
Kirochnaya ul
Manezhny per
ul Pestelya
ul Ryleeva
BEZYMYANNY
Mokhovaya ul
Paradnaya ul
Mikhailovsky Gardens
Vilensky per
Russian Museum
Baskov per
ul Nekrasova
Pl Iskusstv
Sadovaya ul
ul Chekhova
Kovensky per
Liteyny pr
9-ya Sovetskaya ul
8-ya Sovetskaya ul
7-ya Sovetskaya ul
6-ya Sovetskaya
5-ya Sovetskaya ul
4-ya Sovetskaya ul
2-ya Sovetskaya ul
Manezhnaya Pl
ul Zukovskogo
ul Vosstaniya
Ligovsky pr
Grechesky pr
Gostiny Dvor
Nevsky pr
Anichkov most
Pl Ostrovskogo
Mayakovskaya
Vladimirsky pr
ul Rubinshteyna
Pushkinskaya
Pl Vosstaniya
Moscow Station
(Moskovsky Vokzal)
Konnaya ul
nab reki Fontanki
Dostoevskaya
ul Marata
ul Lomonosova
Valdimirskaya
Kuznechny per
Leshtukov per
ul Razyezzhaya
ul Dostoevskogo
Ligovsky pr
To Alexander Nevsky Monastery (200m)
Zagorodny pr
ul Pravdy
Loft Project Etazhi
Zvenigorodskaya ul
ul Marata
Ligovsky Pr
Transportny per
Romenskaya ul
ul Konstantina Zaslonova
ul Tyushina
3
9
29
12
10
31
4
19
13

Central St Petersburg

Top Sights

Church of the Saviour on Spilled Blood D3
Hermitage C3
Loft Project Etazhi G7
Pushkinskaya 10 .... G5
Russian Museum E4
St Isaac's Cathedral B4
St Peter & Paul Cathedral C2
Yusupov Palace B5

Sights

1 Admiralty C4
Aleksandrinsky Theatre .... (see 29)
2 Alexander Column C3
3 Bolshoy Gostiny Dvor E4
4 Coachmen's Banya F6
5 Kazan Cathedral D4
6 Museum of Anthropology & Ethnography B3
7 Peter & Paul Fortress C2
Rostral Columns .... (see 10)
8 Singer Building D4
9 Statue of Catherine the Great E4
10 Strelka C3

Sleeping

11 Cuba Hostel D4
12 Hostel Life F5
13 Hostel Ligovsky 74 .... F7
14 Location Hostel C4
15 Stony Island Hotel D5

Eating

16 Café Idiot B5
17 St-Leninsbar C5
18 Stolle A6
19 Stolle G3
20 Stolle A2
21 Stolle D3
22 Stolle B5
23 Teplo B5
24 Zoom Café C5

Drinking

25 Atelierbar D5
26 Other Side D3
27 Stirka C5
28 ul Dumskaya Bars D4

Entertainment

29 Aleksandrinsky Theatre E5
30 Central Station D5
31 Fish Fabrique Nouvelle G5
32 Mariinsky Theatre B6
33 Mikhaylovsky Opera & Ballet Theatre D4

multidomed dazzler, partly modelled on St Basil's in Moscow, was built between 1883 and 1907 on the spot where Alexander II was assassinated in 1881 (hence its gruesome name). The interior's 7000 sq metres of mosaics fully justify the entrance fee.

Russian Museum ART GALLERY
(Russy Muzey; www.rusmuseum.ru; Mikhailovsky Palace, Inzhenernaya ul 4; adult/student R350/150; ⏲10am-6pm Wed-Sun, to 5pm Mon; Ⓜ Gostiny Dvor) Facing onto the elegant pl Iskusstv (Arts Sq) is the handsome Mikhailovsky Palace, now housing one of the country's finest collections of Russian art. After the Hermitage you may feel you have had your fill of art, but try your utmost to make some time for this gem of a gallery. There's also a lovely **garden** behind the palace.

St Isaac's Cathedral MUSEUM
(Isaakievsky Sobor; ☎315 9732; www.cathedral.ru; Isaakievskaya pl; adult/student R320/170; ⏲11am-7pm Thu-Tue; Ⓜ Sadovaya or Sennaya Pl) The golden dome of this cathedral dominates the city skyline. Its lavish interior is open as a museum, but many visitors just buy the separate ticket to climb the 262 steps up to the **colonnade** (R100; ⏲11am-6pm Thu-Tue) around the dome's drum to take in panoramic views.

Nevsky Prospekt HISTORIC BUILDINGS
Walking at least part of Nevsky Pr, Russia's most famous street, is an essential St Petersburg experience. Highlights along it include the **Kazan Cathedral** (Kazansky Sobor; ☎571 4826; Kazanskaya pl 2; admission free; ⏲10am-7pm, services 10am & 6pm; Ⓜ Nevsky pr) with its curved arms reaching out towards the avenue.

Opposite is the **Singer Building**, a Style Moderne beauty restored to all its splendour from when it was the headquarters of the sewing-machine company; inside is a bookshop and **Café Singer** (⏲9am-11pm) serving good food and drinks with a great view over the street.

Further along you'll pass the covered arcades of historic department store **Bolshoy**

Gostiny Dvor (www.bgd.ru; Nevsky pr 35; MGostiny Dvor), a Rastrelli creation (1757–85). An enormous **statue of Catherine the Great** stands at the centre of Ploshchad Ostrovskogo, commonly referred to as the Catherine Gardens; at the southern end of the gardens is **Aleksandrinsky**, where Chekhov's *The Seagull* premiered in 1896.

Yusupov Palace MUSEUM
(☎314 9883; www.yusupov-palace.ru; nab reki Moyki 94; adult/student R500/380; ⏲11am-5pm; MSadovaya or Sennaya Pl) In a city of glittering palaces, the dazzling interiors of the Yuspov more than hold their own. Best known as the place where Rasputin met his untimely end, the palace sports a series of richly decorated rooms culminating in a gilded jewel box of a theatre, where performances are still held.

Peter & Paul Fortress HISTORIC BUILDINGS
(Petropavlovskaya krepost; www.spbmuseum.ru; ⏲grounds 6am-10am, exhibitions 11am-6pm Thu-Mon, to 5pm Tue; MGorkovskaya) Founded in 1703 as the original military fortress for the new city, the Peter & Paul Fortress was mainly used as a political prison up to 1917. It's also home to the **St Peter & Paul Cathedral** (adult/student R200/90), with its landmark needle-thin spire and magnificent baroque interior. All Russia's tsars since Peter the Great have been buried here.

Individual tickets are needed for each of the fortress's attractions so the best deal is the **combined entry ticket** (adult/student R350/170; valid 2 days) allowing access to most of the exhibitions on the island.

Museum of Anthropology & Ethnography MUSEUM
(Kunstkamera; www.kunstkamera.ru; Tamozhenny per; adult/student R250/150; ⏲11am-6pm Tue-Sun; MVasileostrovskaya) Crowds still flock to see Peter the Great's ghoulish collection of monstrosities, notably preserved freaks, two-headed foetuses and odd body parts. The anthropological and ethnographic displays from around the world are pretty interesting, too.

Strelka MONUMENTS
Sweeping city views can be had from Vasilevsky Island's eastern 'nose', known as the Strelka. The two **Rostral Columns** on the point, studded with ships' prows, were oil-fired navigation beacons in the 1800s; on some holidays, such as Victory Day, gas torches are still lit on them.

Sleeping

Room prices are at a premium between May and September. Outside this period, rates can drop up by up to 30% on those quoted here. For homestays and flat rentals try **HOFA** (☎911-766 5464; www.hofa.ru) as well as **City Realty** and **Ost-West Kontaktservice** (for details of both of these see p1058).

TOP CHOICE **Hostel Ligovsky 74** HOSTEL €
(☎329 1274; www.hostel74.ru; Ligovsky pr 74; dm/tw/designer r R600/1500/2500; @; MLigovsky pr) You'll find this happening hostel within **Loft Project Etazhi** (www.loftprojectetagi.ru) a contemporary art space on the site of a former bakery. The dorms beds are OK but it's the three fab design rooms, all en suite, that are the standouts.

TOP CHOICE **Stony Island Hotel** HOTEL €€
(☎740 1588; www.stonyisland.ru; ul Lomonosova 1; d or tw incl breakfast from R4500; @; MNevsky Pr/Gostiny Dvor) Exposed-brick walls and chic contemporary furnishings give this super-central hotel the design edge.

Cuba Hostel HOSTEL €
(☎921 7115; www.cubahostel.ru; Kazanskaya ul 5; dm/tw R490/1250; @; MNevsky Pr) Cool Cuba presses all the right buttons in terms of atmosphere, friendliness, price and location. Each of the dorms is painted a different colour and arty design is used throughout.

Location Hostel HOSTEL €
(☎490 6429; www.location-hostel.ru; Admiralteisky pr 8; dm/tw incl breakfast from R600/1400; @; MNevsky pr) So chic they even have Philippe Starck chairs in their well-equipped kitchen! The grand stairwell acts as a photo exhibition space.

Hostel Life HOSTEL €
(☎318 1808; http://hostel-life.ru; Nevsky pr 47; dm/tw from R700/2200; @; MMaykovskaya) Totally modern, this big, colourfully decorated hostel with a large lounge and kitchen is accessed from Zagorodny pr.

Eating

St Petersburg offers a broad range of quality restaurants and cafés serving many different cuisines.

TOP CHOICE **St-Leninsbar** RUSSIAN €
(Grivtsova per 7; ⏲noon-midnight; MSadovaya or Sennaya Pl) This tiny cheeky homage to

Lenin is a great place to sample well-executed classics of Russian cuisine at socialist prices. Its placemats also provide a lesson on how to drink vodka.

Stolle RUSSIAN €
(www.stolle.ru; pies R60-100; ⌚8am-10pm); Konyushennaya per (Konyushennaya per 1/6; Ⓜ Nevsky Pr); ul Dekabristov 19 (ul Dekabristov 19; Ⓜ Sadovaya or Sennaya Pl); ul Dekabristov 33 (ul Dekabristov 33; Ⓜ Sadovaya or Sennaya Pl); ul Vosstaniya (ul Vosstaniya 32; Ⓜ Chernyshevskaya); Vasilevsky Island (1-ya linii 50; Ⓜ Vasileostrovskaya) We can't get enough of Stolle's traditional Russian savoury and sweet pies. It's easy to make a meal of it with soups and other dishes that can be ordered at the counter.

Zoom Café RUSSIAN, EUROPEAN €
(www.cafezoom.ru; Gorokhovaya ul 22; mains R200-400; ⊖; Ⓜ Nevsky Pr) Popular, relaxed hang-out with regularly changing art exhibitions. Serves unfussy tasty European and Russian food.

Café Idiot RUSSIAN, VEGETARIAN €€
(☎315 1675; nab reki Moyki 82; meals R400; ⌚11am-1am; Ⓜ Sennaya Pl; ⊖) This long-running cafe charms with its prerevolutionary atmosphere. It's ideal for a nightcap or late supper.

Drinking

The strip of dive bars along ul Dumskaya, near Nevsky Pr metro station, including Dacha, Fidel and Belgrad, get packed with youthful revellers who spill onto the streets from midnight to dawn.

Atelierbar BAR, CAFE
(www.atelierbar.ru; ul Lomonosova 1; ⌚9am-6am; Ⓜ Gostiny Dvor) Attitude free, shabby chic and youthful – just what you'd expect from the groovesters behind Cuba Hostel. During the day it's a cafe on the ground floor; late at night is when the bar-club on the two upper floors cranks up.

Other Side BAR, LIVE MUSIC
(www.theotherside.ru; Bolshaya Konyushennaya ul 1; ⌚noon to last customer; Ⓜ Nevsky Pr) Check the website for info about concerts (always Saturday night, but sometimes other days too), at this gastrobar, which serves decent food (mains R200 to R500). Most people turn up to enjoy the several beers on tap.

Stirka CAFE, BAR
(☎314 5371; Kazanskaya ul 26; ⌚11am-1am Sun-Thu, to 4am Fri & Sat; Ⓜ Sadovaya or Sennaya Pl) Hipsters' hang-out where you can play chess or listen to the DJ while also doing your laundry – what a good idea! A 5kg wash costs R150; the dryer R100; and a mug of excellent Vasileostrovskoe beer R120.

Entertainment

Check out Friday's edition of the *St Petersburg Times* for the latest listings.

Mariinsky Theatre OPERA, BALLET
(☎326 4141; www.mariinsky.ru; Teatralnaya pl 1; ⌚11am-7pm box office; Ⓜ Sadovaya or Sennaya Pl) Home to the world-famous Kirov Ballet and Opera Company. A visit here is a must, if only to wallow in the sparkling glory of the interior. Book online either for the theatre or the acoustically splendid new **Mariinsky Concert Hall** (ul Pisareva 20) nearby.

Mikhailovsky Opera & Ballet Theatre OPERA, BALLET
(☎585 4305; www.mikhailovsky.ru; pl Iskusstv 1; Ⓜ Nevsky Pr) Challenging the Mariinksy in terms of the standards and range of its performances is this equally historic and beautifully restored theatre.

Fish Fabrique Nouvelle LIVE MUSIC
(http://vkontakte.ru/club250531; Ligovsky pr 53; cover R100-150; ⌚3pm-late; Ⓜ Pl Vosstaniya) The new project of the legendary bar set in **Pushkinskaya 10** (www.p-10.ru) a complex that's the focus of the city's avant-garde art scene. Rock and alternative music concerts happen in the original small hall and this larger space.

Central Station GAY & LESBIAN
(www.centralstation.ru; ul Lomonosova 1/28; cover after midnight R100-300; ⌚6pm-6am; Ⓜ Gostiny Dvor) The city's main gay club, with two dance floors, several bars, a cafe and souvenir shop. Check out **Excess** (www.xs.gay.ru) for the latest on gay-friendly bars and clubs.

Information

American Medical Clinic (☎740 2090; www.amclinic.ru; nab reki Moyki 78; Ⓜ Sadovaya)

Cafemax (www.cafemax.ru; Nevsky pr 90/92; per hr R40; ⌚24hr; Ⓜ Mayakovskaya) Wi-fi available here. Also has a branch in the Hermitage.

Central post office (www.spbpost.ru; Pochtamtskaya ul 9; ⌚24 hr; Ⓜ Sadovaya or Sennaya Pl) Worth visiting just to admire its elegant Style Moderne (art deco) interior. The express mail service EMS Garantpost is available here.

City Realty (☎570 6342; www.cityrealtyrussia.com; Muchnoy per 2; Ⓜ Nevsky Pr) Reliable

GETTING INTO ST PETERSBURG

From Moskovskaya metro station, bus 39 runs to Pulkovo-1, the domestic air terminal, and bus 13 runs to Pulkovo-2, the international terminal. There are also plenty of *marshrutky* (minibuses). The trip takes about 15 minutes and costs just R16 to R22. Or you can take the buses and *marshrutky* K3 all the way from the airport to Sennaya pl in the city centre or K39 to pl Vosstaniya (R35). Buses stop directly outside each of the terminals. By taxi it's around R600 to get to the city (R400 is the price from the city to the airport). Most taxi drivers will request more from foreigners, so be prepared to haggle or take the bus.

agency that can arrange all types of accommodation, transport tickets and visas.

City Tourist Information Centre (www.visit-petersburg.ru) main office (982 8253; Sadovaya ul 14/52; 10am-7pm Mon-Fri, noon-6pm Sat; M Gostiny Dvor); Hermitage booth (Dvortsovaya pl 12; 10am-7pm daily; M Nevsky Pr); Pulkovo-1 and -2 air terminals (10am-7pm Mon-Fri)

Ost-West Kontaktservice (327 3416; www.ostwest.com; Nevsky pr 100; 10am-6pm Mon-Fri; M Pl Vosstaniya) The multilingual staff here can find you an apartment to rent and organise tours and tickets.

St Petersburg in Your Pocket (www.inyourpocket.com) Monthly listings booklet with useful up-to-date information and short features.

St Petersburg Times (www.sptimes.ru) Published Tuesday and Friday, this plucky little newspaper has been fearlessly telling it like it really is for over 15 years.

Getting Around

The **metro** (single ride/10 trips in a week R22/185; 5.30am-midnight) is usually the quickest way around the city. *Zhetony* (tokens) and credit-loaded cards can be bought from booths in the stations.

Marshrutky (minibuses) are faster than the regular buses and trolleybuses. Costs vary with the route, but the average fare is R20 and fares are displayed prominently inside each van.

To book a taxi call either **Ladybird** (900 0504; www.ladybird-taxi.ru), which has women drivers and child car seats, or **Peterburgskoe taksi 068** (068-324 7777; www.taxi068.spb.ru).

KALININGRAD REGION КАЛИНИНГРАДСКАЯ ОБЛАСТЬ

POP 955,300

Sandwiched between Poland to the south and Lithuania to the east and north, and with 148km of Baltic coastline to the west, the Kaliningrad region is a Russian exclave that's intimately attached to the motherland yet also a world apart. In this 'Little Russia' – only 15,100 sq km – you'll find plenty of fine hotels and restaurants, a youthful outlook plus all the traditions of the big parent, wrapped up in a manageable package of beautiful countryside, splendid beaches and fascinating historical sights.

Kaliningrad КАЛИНИНГРАД

4012 / POP 423,000

This fascinating, affluent city is an excellent introduction to Russia's most liberal region. Interesting museums and historical sights sprout in between the shiny new shopping centres and a multitude of leafy parks that soften vast swaths of brutal Soviet architecture.

Founded as a Teutonic fort in 1255, Königsberg joined the Hanseatic League in 1340, and from 1457 to 1618 was the residence of the grand masters of the Teutonic order and their successors, the dukes of Prussia. The first king of Prussia, Frederick I, was crowned here in 1701. For the next couple of centuries the city flourished, producing citizens such as the philosopher Immanuel Kant (1724–1804).

Old photos attest that Königsberg was once an architectural gem equal to Prague or Kraków. The combined destruction of WWII and the Soviet decades put an end to all that. However, there are lovely prewar residential suburbs that evoke the Prussian past.

Leninsky pr, a north–south avenue, is the city's main artery, running over 3km from the bus and main train station, Yuzhny vokzal (South Station), to Severny vokzal (North Station). About halfway it crosses the Pregolya River and passes the cathedral, the city's major landmark. The city's modern heart is further north, around pl Pobedy.

Kaliningrad

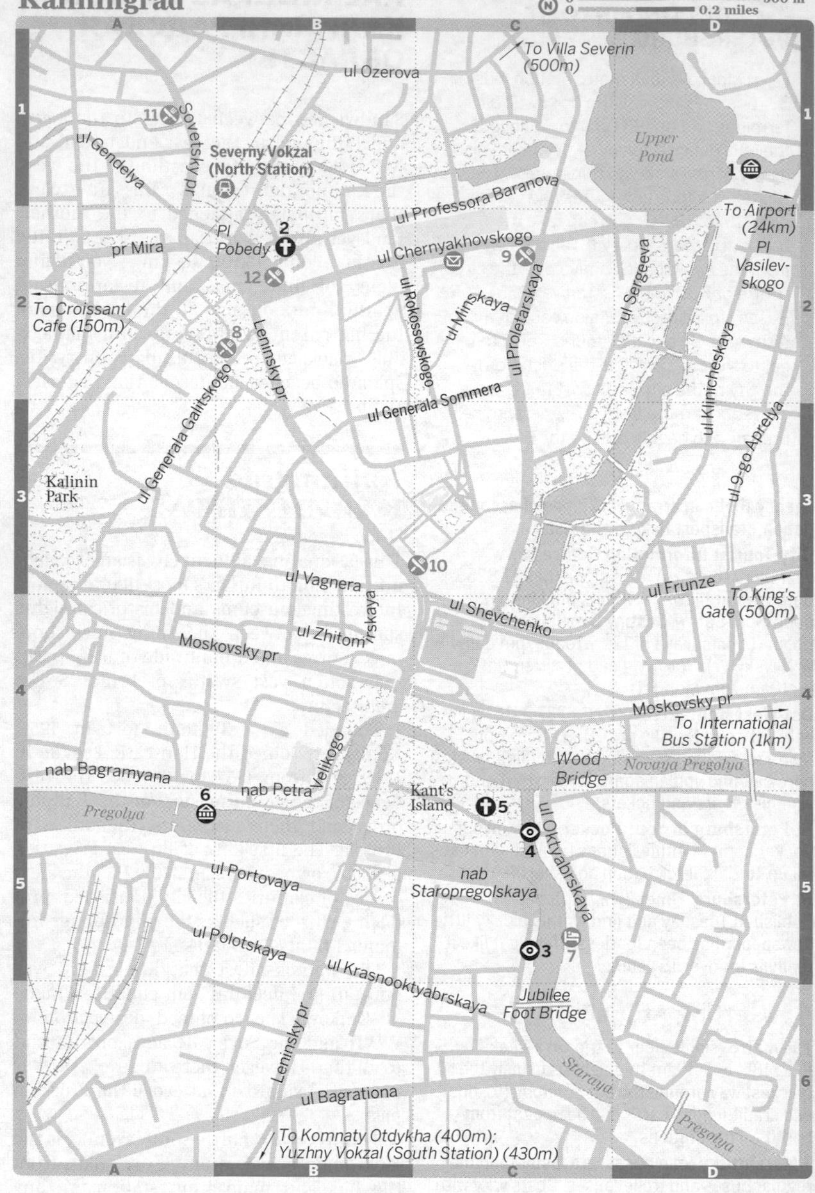

Sights

Kaliningrad Cathedral CHURCH
(631 705; www.sobor-kaliningrad.ru; adult/student R100/50; 9am-5pm) The geographical and spiritual heart of old Königsberg, this Gothic cathedral founded in 1333 was almost destroyed during WWII. Restoration began in 1992 and the showpiece main hall, with fabulous vaulted ceilings, now serves as a concert hall. Upstairs a museum has displays of old Königsberg, objects from archaeologi-

Kaliningrad

Sights

Sleeping

Eating

cal digs and a shrine to Immanuel Kant, who was born, studied and died in Königsberg.

East of the cathedral, the **Honey Bridge**, the oldest of the city's bridges, leads to the half-timber riverside development known as **Fish Village** (Ribnaya Derevnya). Disneyland-ish it may be, but this collection of hotels, shops, cafes and restaurants is a laudable attempt to reprise some of the city's destroyed architectural heritage.

World Ocean Museum MUSEUM
(☎340 244; www.world-ocean.ru; nab Petra Velikogo 1; adult/student R250/170, individual vessels R80/40; ⏰10am-6pm Wed-Sun) Along the river west of the cathedral is this fascinating museum, where you can learn about sea and space exploration aboard a B-413 submarine and two giant Soviet research ships.

Amber Museum MUSEUM
(www.ambermuseum.ru; pl Marshala Vasilevskogo 1; adult/student R180/130; ⏰10am-6pm Tue-Sun) On the edge of the Prud Verkny (Upper Pond), this museum has some 6000 examples of amber artworks, the most impressive being from the Soviet period. Exhibits include enormous pieces of jewellery containing prehistoric insects suspended within, and a four-panelled amber and ivory chalice depicting Columbus, the *Niña*, the *Pinta* and the *Santa Maria*.

City Fortifications & Gates HISTORIC BUILDINGS
The Amber Museum is housed in the attractive **Dohna Tower**, a bastion of the city's old defensive ring. Remnants of the fortifications and gates remain scattered around the city, including the impressively renovated **King's Gate** (ul Frunze 112; adult/student R80/40; ⏰11am-6pm Wed-Sun), housing a small museum with models of old Königsberg and exhibits on the personalities who shaped the region's history.

Ploshchad Pobedy SQUARE
Ploshchad Pobedy, the modern heart of Kaliningrad, is the site of several shopping centres and the Russo-Byzantine-style **Cathedral of Christ the Saviour** (Kafedralny Sobor Khrista Spasitelya), built in 2006, its gold domes visible from many points in the city.

Extending west of the square is pr Mira, a pleasant, shop-lined artery leading to bustling Central Park (Tsentralny Park). Walks through the linden-scented, tree-lined old German neighbourhood of Amalienau around here is the best way to experience old Königsberg.

Sleeping

Budget accommodation is thin on the ground.

WORTH A TRIP

KURSHSKAYA KOSA NATIONAL PARK

Tall, windswept sand dunes and dense pine forests teeming with wildlife lie along the 98km-long Curonian Spit, a Unesco World Heritage site that divides the tranquil Curonian Lagoon from the Baltic Sea. The 50km of the spit that lies in Russian territory is protected within the **Kurshskaya Kosa National Park** (www.kurshskayakosa.ru; admission per person R30, per car R200) and it's a fascinating place to explore or to relax on pristine beaches. Highlights include the spectacular views of the dunes from raised platforms at **Vistota Efa** (42km mark) and the **Dancing Forest** (Tantsuyushchiy Les; 37km mark) where wind-sculpted pines do indeed appear to be frozen mid-boogie.

Four buses a day from Kaliningrad (via Zelenogradsk) head up the Spit en route to Klaipėda in Lithuania. For more flexibility rent a car or arrange a tour in either Kaliningrad or Zelenogradsk, from where a car and driver for half a day should cost around R1500.

TOP CHOICE Villa Severin PENSION €€
(☎365 373; www.villa-severin.ru; ul Leningradskaya 9a; s/d from R1600/1850; ❄@) There's a very homely atmosphere at this pretty villa, set back from the Prud Verkny, with 10 comfortably furnished rooms including one simple student room (R1000 without breakfast). It also has a small sauna and cafe.

Skipper Hotel HOTEL €€
(Gastinitsa Shkiperskaya; ☎592 000; www.skipperhotel.ru; ul Oktyabrskaya 4A; r from R2500; ❄) Cute hotel with rooms with wood furnishings and river views. Attached is the pricey seafood restaurant Langust; breakfast is taken in a cafe in the nearby lighthouse.

Komnaty Otdykha HOTEL €
(☎586 447; pl Kalinina; s/d R950/1500) These resting rooms inside the Yuzhny vokzal (South Station) have been very nicely renovated into en-suite accommodation. The women in charge are friendly and justifiably proud of their small hotel. To find it, turn right down the corridor after the ticket hall and walk up to the 3rd floor.

Eating & Drinking

TOP CHOICE Croissant Café BAKERY, CAFE €
(pr Mira 23; meals R100; ⏲9am-11pm Sun-Thu, 24hr Fri & Sat) A chic baked-goods heaven. Indulge in flaky pastries, quiches, muffins, biscuits and cakes, as well as omelettes and bliny for breakfast. There are also branches in the Evropa mall as well at Leninksy pr 63 and ul Proletarskaya 79.

TOP CHOICE Kmel RUSSIAN, MICROBREWERY €
(☎593 377; Clover City Centre mall, pl Pobedy 10; meals R350-500; ⏲10am-2am) Four types of good beer are brewed at this appealing multilevel gastropub overlooking pl Pobedy. They're served alongside an interesting range of Russian and Siberian dishes including unusual ingredients such as reindeer and *omul*, a fish from Lake Baikal.

GETTING INTO KALININGRAD

Take bus 144 from Khrabrovo airport to the bus station (R30, 30 minutes, hourly) next to the Yuzhny vokzal (South Train Station). A taxi to/from the airport is R300 with **Taxi Kaliningrad** (☎585 858; www.taxi-kaliningrad.ru).

Don Chento PIZZA €
(Sovetsky pr 9-11; meals R200-300) No need to endure depressing Soviet-throwback *stolovye* (canteens) for budget meals when you can dig in at the self-serve salad bar or pick a slice of pizza at this stylish chain with several branches across the city.

Information

Baltma Tours (☎931 931; www.baltma.ru; pr Mira 94, 4th fl & Klover, Pobedy Sq) The efficient, multilingual staff here can arrange visas, accommodation and an array of local excursions.

King's Castle (☎350 782; www.kaliningradinfo.ru; Hotel Kaliningrad, Leninsky pr 81; ⏲8am-8pm Mon-Fri, 9am-4pm Sat) A private agency that offers tours of the city and to the Kurshskaya Kosa.

Königsberg.ru (www.konigsberg.ru) Web-based tour agency through which you can arrange visas, including the useful 72-hour express visa.

Official tourism site (http://en.tourismkaliningrad.ru)

Post office (ul Kosmonavta Leonova 22; ⏲9am-8pm Mon-Fri, 10am-6pm Sat & Sun) About 600m north of pr Mira.

Getting There & Away

There are three border crossings from Poland and four from Lithuania.

BUS **Yuzhny bus station** (ul Zheleznodorozhnaya 7) is the departure point for international services run by **Ecolines** (☎656 501; www.ecolines.net) to Warsaw and several German cities. The **international bus station** (Moskovsky pr 184) has services to:

Klaipėda (R300, four hours, two daily)
Rīga (R737, nine hours, two daily)
Tallinn (R1332, 14 hours, daily)
Vilnius (R716, eight hours, daily)
Warsaw (R750, nine hours, daily)

TRAIN Kaliningrad's two stations are **Severny vokzal** (North Station) and the larger **Yuzhny vokzal** (South Station). All long-distance and many local trains go from Yuzhny vokzal, passing through but not always stopping at Severny vokzal. Note that *all* trains in Kaliningrad, including local ones, run on Moscow time, so if a train is scheduled to depart at 10am it will leave at 9am Kaliningrad time.

Destinations serviced include:

Berlin (R4400, 14 hours, May-Oct daily)
Moscow (R2600-2900, 23 hours, three daily)
St Petersburg (R2800, 26 hours, daily)
Vilnius (R1600, six hours, four daily)

UNDERSTAND RUSSIA

History

Russia has its cultural origins in Kyivan Rus, the kingdom located in what is today Ukraine and Belarus. From here the Slavs expanded into modern European Russia. It was during the Romanov dynasty (1613–1917) that Russia began to develop into the vast nation it is today: territorial expansion from the 17th to 19th centuries saw the country gobble up Siberia, the Arctic, the Russian Far East, Central Asia and the Caucasus. Peter the Great set up a navy and built a new capital, St Petersburg, in 1703. Catherine the Great continued Peter's progressive policies to create a world power by the mid-18th century.

Nicholas II's refusal to countenance serious political and societal change precipitated the 1917 revolution. What began as a liberal revolution was hijacked later the same year in a coup led by the Bolsheviks under Lenin, which resulted in the setting up of the world's first communist state.

Under Communist Party rule (1917–91) Russia became a superpower, having created the Union of Soviet Socialist Republics (USSR) and absorbing some 14 neighbouring states between 1922 and 1945. The terror of Stalin, the reforms of Khrushchev and the stagnation during the Brezhnev era finally led to Mikhail Gorbachev's period of reform known as *perestroika* in 1985. Within six years the USSR had collapsed alongside communism and reformer Boris Yeltsin led Russia into a new world of cutthroat capitalism.

On New Year's Eve 1999, Yeltsin resigned in favour of Vladimir Putin, a steely-faced ex-KGB officer and then prime minister. Putin's policy of steering a careful course between reform and centralisation (plus an economy booming off the back of oil and gas exports) made him popular. But his tightening of control over the media and ruthlessness with political opponents, as well as Russia's brutal clampdown on the independence movement in Chechnya, caused concern among liberals.

Having served his two-term limit as president, Putin was succeeded in March 2008 by heir apparent Dmitry Medvedev. The financial crisis later the same year dented the bank balances of Russia's richest, but oil and gas revenues continue to generate great wealth for the country. In October 2010, when Medvedev sacked Yuri Luzhkov, Moscow's mayor of 18 years, some interpreted it as a move by the president to secure his power base in the run-up to the March 2012 elections. However, Putin has not ruled out that he won't stand again for a second round in the top job.

People

Russia has a population of 141.1 million people. While the vast majority you meet will describe themselves as Russian, ethnic homogeneity is far from that simple. Over the centuries Russia has absorbed people from a huge number of nationalities including the Mongols, the Tatars, Siberian peoples, Ukrainians, Jews and Caucasians. Soviet rulers did their best to mould a common culture but differences in ways of life do exist.

At the individual level, Russians have a reputation for being dour, depressed and unfriendly. In fact, most Russians are anything but, yet find constant smiling indicative of idiocy, and ridicule pointless displays of happiness commonly seen in Western culture. And even though some Russians can be unfriendly – even downright rude – when you first meet them, their warmth as soon as the ice is broken is quite astounding. Just keep working at it.

Arts

Russian literature is one of the world's greatest: the 19th-century poet Alexander Pushkin is the national bard, while other greats include Mikhail Lermontov, Leo Tolstoy, Anton Chekhov and Fyodor Dostoyevsky. Russia's musical heritage is equally illustrious: Tchaikovsky, Prokofiev and Shostakovich have all had a huge influence on the development of modern classical music.

Food

Budget ranges for Moscow and St. Petersburg for eateries are as follows:

€€€ more than R1500

€€ R600 to R1500

€ less than R600

Environment

European Russia is characterised by flat fields and forests. You can take the train from one city to the other and barely pass a hill or a valley. However, the Kaliningrad region sports half of the sandy Kurshskaya Kosa (Curonian Spit), the Curonian Lagoon and the world's largest supply of amber.

The disastrous environmental legacy of communism is enormous. As well as both Moscow and St Petersburg being polluted from traffic and heavy industry, the countryside is frequently blighted by factories and other industrial plants. Environmental consciousness remains relatively low, although things are slowly changing with the emergence of a small but vocal Russian environmental movement.

For more details on Russia's environmental problems see **Greenpeace Russia** (www.greenpeace.org/russia/en) and **World Wide Fund for Nature in Russia** (www.wwf.ru/eng).

SURVIVAL GUIDE

Directory A–Z

Accommodation

Both Moscow and St Petersburg have a number of well-established and reliable hostels, although they are significantly more expensive than in most other countries (budget around R750 per night). Hotel rooms start from about R500, although these are invariably shabby Soviet relics; R1000 to R1500 is a more realistic minimum. Booking ahead is always advised.

Budget ranges for Moscow and St Petersburg are as follows:

€€€ more than R10,000

€€ R3000 to R10,000

€ less than R3000

Ranges for the rest of the country:

€€€ more than R4000

€€ R1500 to R4000

€ less than R1500

Activities

Taking a traditional Russian *banya* is a must. These wet saunas are a social hub and a fantastic experience for any visitor to Russia. Leave your inhibitions at home and be prepared for a beating with birch twigs (far more pleasant than it sounds). Russians swear there's no better way of getting clean – ask at your hostel or hotel for the nearest public *banya* where entry can be as low as R100.

In Moscow try the luxurious **Sanduny Baths** (www.sanduny.ru; Neglinnaya ul 14; private room per hr from R1300, general admission per 2hr R600-800; ⌚8am-10pm; Ⓜ Kuznetsky Most) and in St Petersburg the traditional **Coachmen's Banya** (Yaskiye Bani; www.yamskie.ru; ul Dostoevskogo 9; admission R150-500; ⌚men 8am-10.30pm Mon & Wed-Sun, women 8am-10.30pm daily; Ⓜ Vladimirskaya).

Business Hours

Banks 8am or 9am-5pm or 6pm Mon-Fri

Offices 8am or 9am-5pm or 6pm Mon-Fri

Restaurants Noon-11am; many are in fact virtually 24-hour establishments

Embassies & Consulates

In Your Pocket (www.inyourpocket.com) guides to Moscow and St Petersburg list foreign embassies and consulates in those cities.

Holidays

New Year's Day 1 January

Russian Orthodox Christmas Day 7 January

Defender of the Fatherland Day 23 February

International Women's Day 8 March

International Labour Day/Spring Festival 1 May

Victory Day (1945) 9 May

Russian Independence Day When the Russian republic of the USSR proclaimed its sovereignty in June 1991; 12 June

Unity Day 4 November

Many businesses are also closed from 1 to 7 January. Another widely celebrated holiday is Easter Monday.

Money

The Russian currency is the rouble, written as 'рубль' and abbreviated as 'ру' or 'р'. There are 100 kopecks in a rouble and these come in coin denominations of one (rarely seen), five, 10 and 50. Also issued in coins, roubles come in amounts of one, two, five and 10, with banknotes in values of 10, 50, 100, 500, 1000 and 5000 roubles.

You can use all major credit and debit cards in ATMs, and in good restaurants and hotels. It's possible to exchange travellers cheques, although at a price. Euro or US-dollar cash is the best to bring and should be in pristine condition. Most major currencies can be exchanged at change booths all over any town in Russia. Look for the sign *obmen valyut*.

Post

The Russian post service **Potcha Rossia** (www.russianpost.ru) gets an unfair rap. Postcards, letters and parcels sent abroad usually arrive within a couple of weeks, but there are occasional lapses.

Safe Travel

While the situation has improved slowly, many police officers and other uniformed officials are on the make – some are not much better than the people they are employed to protect the public from. If you feel you are being unfairly treated or if the police try to make you go somewhere with them, pull out your mobile phone and threaten to call your embassy *('ya pozvonyu svoyu posolstvu')*. This will usually be sufficient to make them leave you alone. However, if they still want you to go somewhere, it's best to call your embassy immediately.

Sadly, racism is a problem in Russia. Be vigilant on the streets around Hitler's birthday (20 April), when bands of right-wing thugs have been known to roam around spoiling for a fight with anyone who doesn't look Russian. It's a sure thing that if you look like a foreigner you'll be targeted with suspicion by many (the police, in particular) at any time of year. Although far from a daily occurrence, Moscow and St Petersburg have all seen violent attacks on non-Russians, particularly people from the Caucasus. If you stick to the main tourist areas and stay aware of what's going on around you, you should be fine.

Telephone

The international code for Russia is ☎7. The international access code from land lines in Russia is ☎8, followed by 10 after the second tone, followed by the country code. From mobile phones, just dial + before the country code to place an international call. To call a mobile phone (typically 10-digit numbers starting with 9) from a land line or vice versa dial ☎8 plus the number.

At the time of research, Moscow had two area codes: ☎495 and ☎499. Over the next few years many ☎495 numbers will change to the ☎499 code (with a slight change of number in several cases). It's easy to buy pay-as-you-go SIM cards for your mobile phone at high-street shops across Russia. Note: it's best to buy separate ones for Moscow, St Petersburg and Kaliningrad if you want to avoid expensive roaming charges.

Visas

Everyone needs a visa to visit Russia – allow yourself at least a month before you travel to secure one. For most travellers a tourist visa, valid for 30 days from the date of entry, will be fine. The process has three stages – invitation, application and registration.

INVITATION

To obtain a visa, you first need an invitation. Hotels and hostels will usually issue anyone staying with them an invitation (or 'visa support') free or for a small fee (typically around €20 to €30). Visa invitation fees are similar if you apply via a travel agent or online through the following:

Express to Russia (www.expresstorussia.com)

Visa Able (www.visaable.com)

Way to Russia (http://waytorussia.net)

Zierer Visa Services (☎1-866 788 1100; www.zvs.com)

APPLICATION

Invitation in hand, you can then apply for a visa at any Russian embassy. Costs vary – anything from €35 to €350 – depending on the type of visa applied for and how quickly you need it. Rather frustratingly, Russian embassies are practically laws unto themselves, each with different fees and slightly different application rules. Avoid potential hassles by checking well in advance what these rules might be.

We highly recommended applying for your visa in your home country rather than on the road. Indeed, the rule is that you're supposed to do this, although we know from experience that some embassies and consulates can be more flexible than others.

REGISTRATION

On arrival, you should fill out an immigration card – a long, white form issued by passport control; often these are given out in advance on your flight. You surrender one half of the form immediately to the passport control, while the other you keep for the duration of your stay and give up only on exiting Russia. Take good care of this as you'll need it for registration and could face problems while travelling in Russia – and certainly will on leaving – if you cannot produce it.

You must register your visa within three working days of arrival. If you're staying at a hotel, the receptionist should be able to do this for you for free or a small fee (typically R600 to R1000). Once registered, you should receive a separate slip of paper confirming the dates you'll be staying at that particular hotel. Keep this safe – that's the document that any police who stop you will need to see.

If staying in a homestay or rental apartment, you'll either need to pay a travel agency (anything from R1000 to R3200) to register your visa for you (most agencies will do this through a hotel) or make arrangements with the landlord or a friend to register you through the post office. See http://waytorussia.net/RussianVisa/Registration.html for how this can be done, as well as a downloadable form that needs to be submitted at post offices.

Getting There & Away

Air

Moscow's **Sheremetyevo-2** (SVO; ☎495-232 6565; http://svo.aero) and the much more congenial **Domodedovo** (DME; ☎495-933 6666; www.domodedovo.ru) airports host the bulk of Russia's international flights. There are also many daily international services to St Petersburg's **Pulkovo-2** (LED; ☎812-704 3444; www.pulkovoairport.ru/eng) airport and Kaliningrad's **Khrabrovo airport** (☎459 426).

Airlines flying into Russia include the following. Phone numbers are given for the Moscow office, where applicable.

Aeroflot Russian International Airlines (☎495-223 5555; www.aeroflot.ru)

Air Berlin (☎800 555 0737; www.airberlin.com)

British Airways (☎495-363 2525; www.britishairways.com)

Finnair (☎495-933 0056; www.finnair.com)

Lufthansa (☎495-980 9999; www.lufthansa.com)

Rossiya (☎495-995 2025; http://eng.pulkovo.ru/en)

SAS (☎495-775 4747; www.flysas.com)

S7 Airlines (☎495-777 9999; www.s7.ru)

Transaero Airlines (☎495-788 8080; www.transaero.com)

Bus

There are regular buses from St Petersburg to Helsinki, Finland (from €40; eight hours, four to six daily). A couple of operations are **Ardis Finnord** (☎314 8951; Italiyanskaya ul 37; Ⓜ Gostiny Dvor) which runs two buses daily, and **Sovavto** (☎702 2550; www.sovavto.ru; Vitebsky pr 3; Ⓜ Moskovskie Vorota) with daily departures to Helsinki and Turku (11 hours).

Euroline (www.luxexpress.eu; from R950, 7½ hr, 7 daily) buses from St Petersburg's **Baltisky vokzal** (Baltic Station; Ⓜ Baltiyskaya) provide connections to Tallinn.

From Moscow – considering distances – it's far better to take the train to neighbouring countries.

Sea

Linking Helsinki and St Petersburg three times a week is the Finnish ferry **St Peter Line** (☎322 6699; www.stpeterline.com); coming from Helsinki passengers are allowed to stay in St Petersburg visa-free for up to 72 hours. **DFDS** (www.dfds.com) also runs a weekly ferry connecting St Petersburg with Kiel in Germany via Karlshamn in Sweden.

Trans-Exim (☎660 468; www.transexim.ru; ul Suvorova 45) runs weekly car ferries between Baltiysk and Ust-Luga, 150km west of St Petersburg.

Train

There are excellent daily connections between both Moscow and St Petersburg and many European cities, even as far afield as Paris. The overnight trains between St Petersburg and Moscow run daily and tickets start at around R1000. For up-to-date schedules, see **Poezda.net** (www.poezda.net).

Getting Around

Bus

For short trips from major cities the bus can be faster than the train and often with more frequent services. There's almost no need to reserve a seat and, in most places, it's impossible anyway. Just arrive a good 30 minutes to one hour before the departure is scheduled and buy a ticket.

Car & Motorcycle

Poor roads, reckless drivers and rapacious traffic cops make driving in Russia an unappetising prospect. Thankfully, public trans-

UNOFFICIAL TAXIS

In Russia few people think twice about flagging down any car to request a ride. A fare is negotiated for the journey and off you go. However, proceed with caution if you are alone and/or it's late at night as there are occasional stories of violent attacks on passengers. There are plenty of official taxis now that charge reasonable rates: numbers and websites for these are listed in the transport sections for Moscow and St Petersburg.

port is very good. However, if you do drive in Russia, you must have a valid International Driving Permit, your passport and insurance documentation for your vehicle.

Train

Russian Railways (www.eng.rzd.ru/wps/portal/rzdeng/fp) long-distance services need to be booked at least 24 hours in advance. The cheapest tickets are for *Platskartny* (3rd class) compartments which have open bunk accommodation. *Kupeyny* (coupé; 2nd class) carriages contain four fold-down beds per compartment. Prices between Moscow and St Petersburg in 3rd class begin at R1000.

You'll need to present your passport (or a photocopy) to buy tickets. At stations, queues can be very long and slow moving. Instead use one of the generally queue-free service centres that exist in all big train stations, or a travel agency – at either you'll typically pay a surcharge of around R200 per ticket. Hostels can also usually book tickets for you and have them delivered for a small fee.

Serbia Србија

Includes »

Best Places to Eat

» ?, Belgrade (p1075)
» Dačo, Belgrade (p1075)
» Ravel, Subotica (p1080)
» Kod Lipa, Novi Sad (p1079)

Best Places to Stay

» Green Studio Hostel, Belgrade (p1074)
» Arka Barka, Belgrade (p1074)
» Downtown, Novi Sad (p1079)

Why Go?

Warm, welcoming and a hell of a lot of fun; everything you never heard about Serbia is true. Exuding a feisty mix of élan and *inat* (a Serbian trait of rebellious defiance), this country doesn't do 'mild': its capital, Belgrade, is one of the world's wildest party destinations, the northern town of Novi Sad hosts the rocking EXIT Festival, and even its hospitality is emphatic – expect to be greeted with *rakija* (strong distilled spirit most commonly made from plums) and a hearty three-kiss hello.

While political correctness here is about as commonplace as a nonsmoking bar, Serbia is nevertheless a cultural crucible: art-nouveau Subotica revels in its proximity to Hungary, minaret-studded Novi Pazar nudges some of the most sacred sites in Serbian Orthodoxy, and in mountainous Zlatibor ancient traditions coexist with après-ski bling. Forget what you think you know about Serbia: come and say *'zdravo'* (hello)...or better yet, *'živeli'* (cheers)!

When to Go

Belgrade

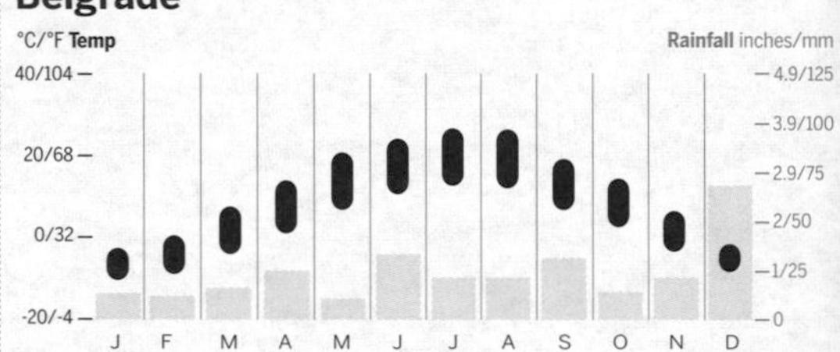

Apr Watch winter melt away with a scenic ride on the nostalgic Šargan 8 railway.

Jul–Aug Rock out at Novi Sad's Exit Festival and go trumpet-wild at Guča.

Dec–Mar Head south to Zlatibor for some alpine adventure.

Connections

Serbia is landlocked by accessible neighbours. From the northern town of Subotica, you can travel over the Hungarian border and onwards to Budapest. The town of Vršac is only 10km from the Romanian border, and the Bulgarian border is 45 minutes from the small town of Pirot. When things are calm on the Kosovo border, €7 and three hours get you from Novi Pazar to Pristina. The Zlatibor region stretches to Bosnia & Hercegovina, allowing travellers with wheels the opportunity to take a day trip to the bridge on the River Drina.

The whole of Eastern Europe feels accessible from Belgrade: Bucharest, Budapest, Moscow, Sofia and Zagreb are a train ride away, and regular buses serve destinations including Banja Luka, Ljubljana, Sarajevo and Split.

ITINERARIES

One Week

Revel in three days of cultural and culinary exploration in Belgrade, with at least one night hitting the capital's legendary nightspots. Carry on to Novi Sad for day trips to Fruška Gora and Sremski Karlovci.

Two Weeks

Follow the above then head north to treat your eyes to the art-nouveau architecture of Subotica, before slicing south to Zlatibor en route to Ottoman-influenced Novi Pazar.

Essential Food & Drink

» **Kajmak** Like a saltier clotted cream, this dairy delight is lashed on to everything from plain bread to burgers.

» **Grill** *Ćevapčići* (skinless sausage) and *pljeskavica* (head-sized spicy hamburger) make it very easy to be a carnivore in Serbia.

» **Burek** This flaky meat, cheese or vegetable pie is eaten with yoghurt as a breakfast belly-filler or an anytime snack.

» **Žito** Tuck into this dessert of crushed wheat and walnuts, or try *palačinke* (crepes) loaded with jam or hazelnut spread.

» **Rakija** A distilled spirit most commonly made from plums. Treat with caution: this ain't your grandpa's brandy.

AT A GLANCE

» **Currency** Dinar (DIN)

» **Language** Serbian

» **Money** ATMs in all main and mid-sized towns

» **Visas** Not required for most visitors; see p1082

Fast Facts

» **Area** 77,474 sq km

» **Capital** Belgrade

» **Country code** ☎038

» **Emergency** Police ☎92; Ambulance ☎94

Exchange Rates

Australia	A$1	74.68DIN
Canada	C$1	74.68DIN
euro zone	€1	102.38DIN
Japan	¥100	85.66DIN
New Zealand	NZ$1	55.31DIN
UK	UK£1	116.23DIN
USA	US$1	71.99DIN

Set Your Budget

» **Budget hotel room** 2000DIN

» **Two-course evening meal** 1000DIN

» **Museum entrance** 100DIN

» **Bottle of beer** 100DIN

» **City transport ticket** 80DIN

Resources

» **National Tourism Organisation of Serbia** (www.serbia.travel)

» **Serbia Travel Club** (www.serbiatravelers.org)

Serbia Highlights

1. Marvel at Belgrade's mighty **Kalemegdan Citadel** (p1071)
2. Witness the laid-back town of **Novi Sad** (p1077) as it morphs into the State of Exit every July
3. Goggle at the art-nouveau treasures of **Subotica** (p1080)
4. Ponder the cultural fusions of Turkish-toned **Novi Pazar** (p1077)
5. Steel your eardrums (and liver) at Guča's **Dragačevo Trumpet Assembly** (p1076)
6. Ski, hike or just ramble in the magical villages of **Zlatibor** (p1077)

BELGRADE БЕОГРАД

011 / POP 1.76 MILLION

Outspoken, adventurous, proud and audacious: Belgrade is by no means a 'pretty' capital, but its gritty exuberance makes it one of the most happening cities in all of Europe. It's here where the Sava River meets the Danube (Dunav) River, where old-world culture gives way to new-world nightlife.

Grandiose coffee houses, sidewalk ice creameries and smoky dens all find rightful place along Knez Mihailova, a lively pedestrian boulevard flanked by historical buildings all the way to the ancient Kalemegdan Citadel, crown of the city. Deeper in Belgrade's bowels, museums guard the country's heritage.

'Belgrade' literally translates as 'White City', but Serbia's colourful capital is red hot.

Sights

Kalemegdan Citadel FORTRESS

Some 115 battles have been fought over imposing Kalemegdan. Fortifications began in Celtic times; much of what stands today is 18th-century Austro-Hungarian and Turkish reconstructions.

Entering from Knez Mihailova brings you to the Upper Citadel. Through Stambol Gate, built by the Turks around 1750, you'll find yourself in the firing line of canons and tanks; welcome to the **Military Museum** (www.muzej.mod.gov.rs; admission 100DIN; 10am-5pm Tue-Sun), presenting the military history of the former Yugoslavia up to the 1999 NATO bombings.

National Museum MUSEUM

(www.narodnimuzej.rs; Trg Republike 1A) At the other end of Knez Mihailova is Trg Republike (Republic Sq), a meeting point and outdoor exhibition space. On the square is the National Museum, which will hopefully reopen soon.

Palace of Princess Ljubica PALACE

(Kneza Sime Markovića 8; admission 100DIN; 10am-5pm Tue, Wed & Fri, noon-8pm Thu, 10am-2pm Sat & Sun) A Balkan-style palace built in 1831 for the wife of Prince Miloš. Take coffee with 'the princess' each Saturday from noon (250DIN) as she leads you through privileged 19th-century life.

Ethnographic Museum MUSEUM

(www.etnografskimuzej.rs; Studentski Trg 13; adult/student 150/60DIN; 10am-5pm Tue-Sat, 9am-2pm Sun) This museum features traditional costumes, working utensils and folksy mountain-village interiors.

Gallery of Frescoes ART GALLERY

(www.narodnimuzej.rs; Cara Uroša 20; admission 100DIN; 10am-5pm Tue, Wed & Fri, noon-8pm Thu & Sat, 10am-2pm Sun) The gallery features full-size replicas (and the odd original) of Byzantine Serbian church art, right down to the last scratch.

Skadarska HISTORIC AREA

Skadarska (or Skadarlija) is Belgrade's answer to Paris' Montmartre. This cobblestoned strip was the bohemian heartland at the turn of the 20th century; local artistes and raffish types still gather in its legion of cute restaurants and cafes.

Nikola Tesla Museum MUSEUM

(www.tesla-museum.org; Krunska 51; admission 300DIN; 10am-6pm Tue-Fri, 10am-3pm Sat & Sun) Release your inner nerd at one of Belgrade's best museums with some wondrously sci-fi-ish interactive elements. Admission includes a guided tour in English.

Museum of Automobiles MUSEUM

(Majke Jevrosime 30; admission 100DIN; 11am-7pm) A compelling collection of cars and motorcycles, including Maršal Tito's '57 Cadillac convertible.

Sveti Marko Church CHURCH

(Bulevar Kralja Aleksandra 17) This five-domed church houses priceless Serbian icons and the tomb of Emperor Dušan 'The Mighty' (1308–55).

Sveti Sava CHURCH

(www.hramsvetogsave.com, in Serbian; Svetog Save) Sveti Sava is the world's biggest Orthodox church and is built on the site where the Turks apparently burnt relics of St Sava (founder of the independent Serbian Orthodox church). Work on the interior continues today.

Maršal Tito's Grave HISTORIC GRAVE

(Kuća Cveća, House of Flowers; www.mij.rs; Bulevar Mira; admission 200DIN; 10am-4pm Tue-Sun) A visit to Tito's mausoleum is obligatory. Also on display are gifts from political leaders and the voguish set of the era. Take trolleybus 40 or 41 at the south end of Parliament on Kneza Miloša. It's the second stop after it turns into Bulevar Mira. Admission includes entry to the Museum of Yugoslav History.

Ada Ciganlija BEACH

(www.adaciganlija.rs) In summertime, join the hordes of sea-starved locals (up to 250,000 a day) at this man-made island on the Sava. Take bus 53 or 56 from Zeleni Venac.

Central Belgrade

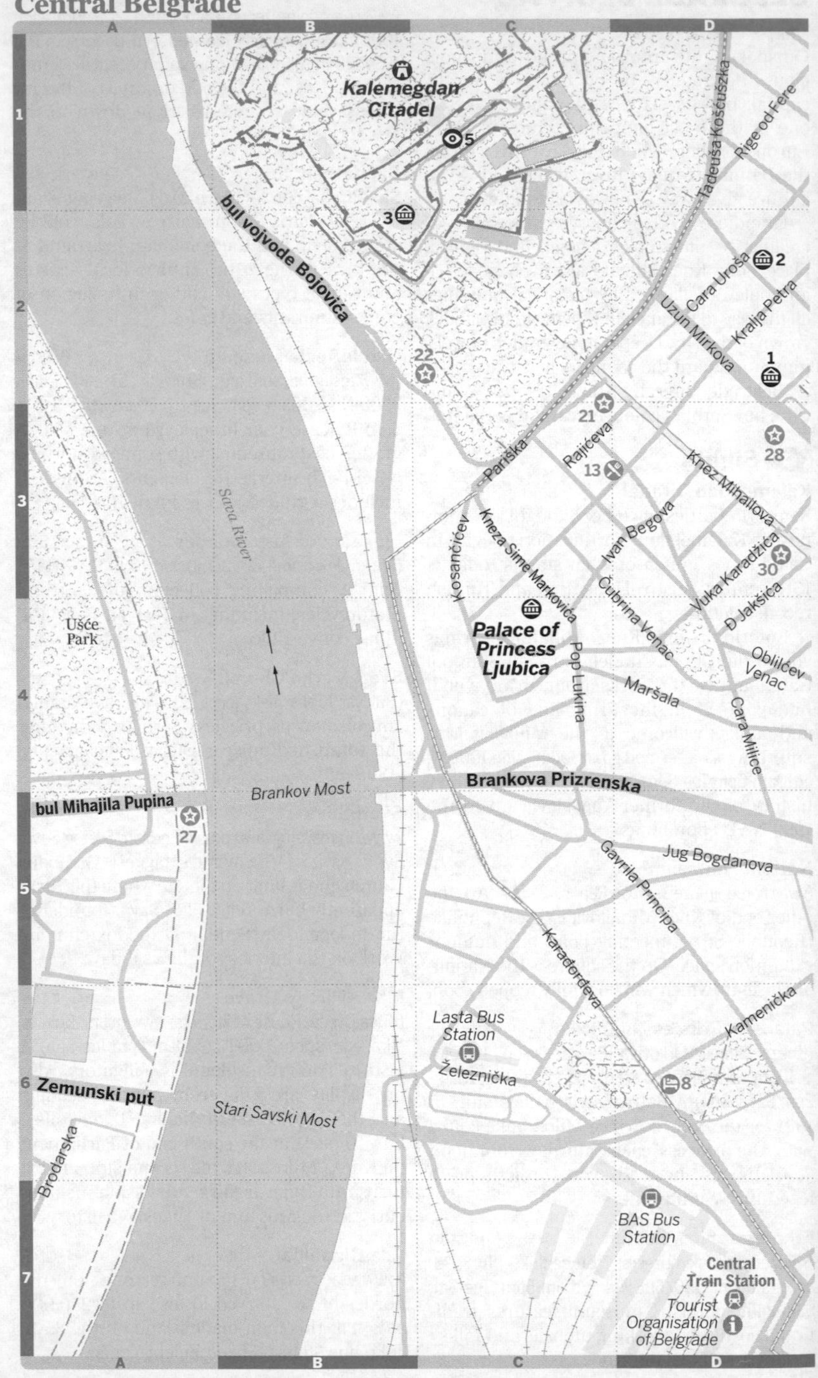

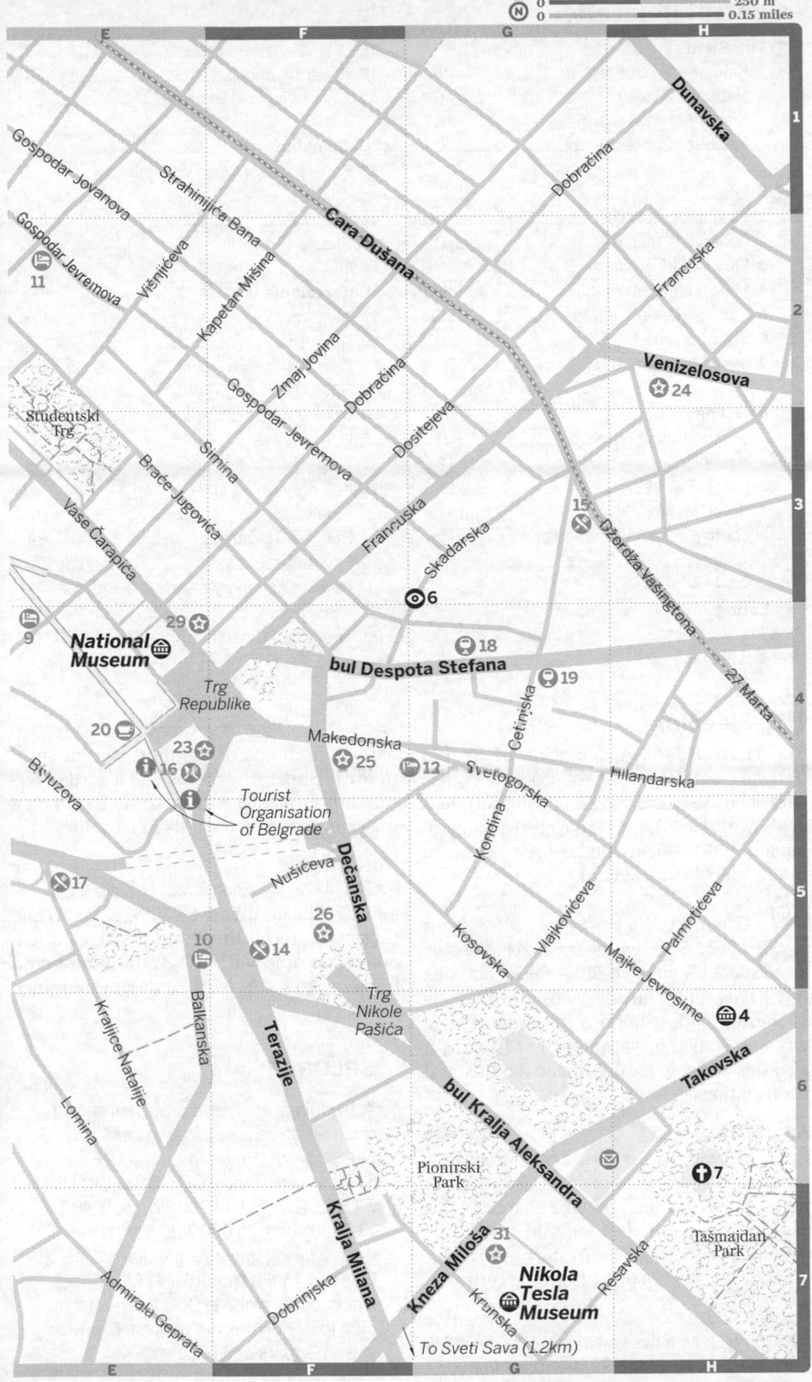
0 250 m
0 0.15 miles
Dunavska
Dobračina
Cara Dušana
Gospodar Jovanova
Strahinjića Bana
Gospodar Jevremova
Višnjićeva
Kapetan Mišina
Francuska
Venizelosova
Zmaj Jovina
Dobračina
Gospodar Jevremova
Dositejeva
Studentski Trg
Simina
Braće Jugovića
Vase Čarapića
Francuska
Skadarska
Džordža Vašingtona
National Museum
bul Despota Stefana
Trg Republike
27 Marta
Cetinjska
Makedonska
Svetogorska
Hilandarska
Tourist Organisation of Belgrade
Kondina
Nušićeva
Dečanska
Vlajkovićeva
Palmotićeva
Kosovska
Majke Jevrosime
Trg Nikole Pašića
Balkanska
Terazije
Kraljice Natalije
Takovska
bul Kralja Aleksandra
Lomina
Pionirski Park
Kralja Milana
Kneza Miloša
Tašmajdan Park
Resavska
Nikola Tesla Museum
Krunska
Dobrinjska
Admirala Geprata
To Sveti Sava (1.2km)

Central Belgrade

Top Sights
Kalemegdan Citadel B1
National Museum E4
Nikola Tesla Museum G7
Palace of Princess Ljubica C4

Sights
1 Ethnographic Museum D2
2 Gallery of Frescoes D2
3 Military Museum B2
4 Museum of Automobiles H6
5 Stambol Gate C1
6 Starodarska G3
7 Sveti Marko Church H6

Sleeping
8 Green Studio Hostel D6
9 Hostel 360 .... E4
10 Hotel Moskva E5
11 Hotel Royal E2
12 Youth Hostel Association of Serbia G4

Eating
13 ? D3
14 Biblioteka F5
15 Dva Jelena G3
16 Pekara Toma E4
17 Zeleni Venac Market E5

Drinking
18 Federal Association of Globe Trotters G4
19 Pub Brod G4
20 Russian Tsar E4

Entertainment
21 Akademija C3
22 Andergraund C2
23 Bilet Servis E4
24 Bitef Art Cafe H2
25 Dom Omladine F4
26 Dom Sindikata F5
27 Freestyler A5
28 Kolarčev University Concert Hall D3
29 National Theatre E4
Povetarac .... (see 27)
30 Serbian Academy of Arts & Sciences D3
31 Tuckwood Cineplex G7

Sleeping

The **Youth Hostel Association of Serbia** (Ferijalni Savez Beograd; 324 8550; www.serbia-hostels.org; Makedonska 22/2; 9am-5pm) does deals with local hotels. You need HI membership (500/700DIN under/over 26) or an international student card.

TOP CHOICE **Green Studio Hostel** HOSTEL €
(637 562 357; www.greenstudiohostel.com; Karađorđeva 69; dm from €10, r €9-30, apt €40;) This sunny surprise goes down as one of the top budget options in Serbia. Clean, airy and staffed by your new best friends, it also has a handy location near the bus and train stations.

Arka Barka HOSTEL €
(0649253507; www.arkabarka.net; Nikole Tesle bb; dm €15;) Bobbing off Ušće Park a mere stagger from Danube barges, this 'floating house' offers rooms in 'wake-up!' colours, party nights and fresh river breezes. Walk or take bus 15 or 84 from the centre.

Hostel 360 HOSTEL €
(328 4523; www.threesixtyhostel.com; Knez Mihailova 21; dm/s/tw/d €15/29/44/50, apt from €75;) Hostel 360 peers down at Knez Mihailova from one of the most central spots in town. Super-tidy rooms and a garden terrace are surpassed only by spirited staff on a mission to immerse guests in local life.

Hotel Royal HOTEL €€
(263 4222; www.hotelroyal.rs; Kralja Petra 56; s 4280-4815DIN, d 5136-6313DIN; @) While those who recall the Royal's days as a legendary cheapie will baulk at the almost doubling of rates, this is still a decent midrange

SPLURGE

Art-nouveau icon and proud symbol of the best of Belgrade, the majestic **Hotel Moskva** (Hotel Moscow; 011-268 6255; www.hotelmoskva.rs; Balkanska 1; s 7725-12,420DIN, d 14,000DIN, ste 14,490-18,000DIN, apt 25,000DIN;) has been wowing guests – including Albert Einstein, Indira Gandhi and Alfred Hitchcock – since 1906. Laden with ye olde glamour, this is the place to write your memoirs at a big old desk.

option. Rooms are basic, but this (very) central choice disarms with character and buzz.

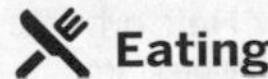

Eating

TOP CHOICE ? SERBIAN €

(Znak Pitanja, Kralja Petra 6; meals 450-600DIN) Belgrade's oldest *kafana* (cafe) has been attracting the artsy set since 1823 with dishes like lamb under the iron pan. The '?' is courtesy of a dispute with the adjacent church, which objected to the tavern's plans of naming itself in relation to a house of God ('By the Cathedral').

Dačo SERBIAN €€

(☎278 1009; www.kafanadaco.com; Patrisa Lumumbe 49; meals 500-1150DIN; ⏰noon-midnight Tue-Sun) Eating here is like visiting the Serbian granny you never knew you had: the walls are cluttered with homey bits and bobs, checked tablecloths adorn rickety tables, and chooks strut around in the garden. Reservations recommended.

Dva Jelena SERBIAN €€

(Two Deer; www.dvajelena.com; Skadarska 32; meals 400-900DIN; ⏰11am-1am) A local icon, Dva Jelena has been dishing up hearty fare for over 180 years. Rustic, homespun and with the obligatory violin serenades, it ticks all the Skadarska boxes.

Biblioteka INTERNATIONAL €€

(Terazije 27; meals 300-900DIN; ⏰7am-midnight) Buzzing outside and aptly library-ambient inside, Biblioteka is popular with locals for its extensive breakfast menu, served until 1pm.

Pekara Toma BAKERY €

(Kolarčeva 10; snacks 50-200DIN; ⏰24hr) Cheap bakeries abound near Trg Republike. This is a favourite for fresh pizzas, sandwiches and salads.

Zeleni Venac Market MARKET €

(cnr Brankova Prizrenska & Kraljice Natalije; ⏰6am-7pm) Forage for DIY food.

Drinking

TOP CHOICE Kafana Pavle Korčagin TAVERN

(☎240 1980; Ćirila i Metodija 2a; ⏰8pm-1am) Raise a glass to Tito at this festive *kafana*. Lined with communist memorabilia, this table-thumping throwback fills up nightly; reserve in advance.

Federal Association of Globe Trotters BAR

(www.usp-aur.rs; Bulevar Despota Stefana 7/1; ⏰1pm-midnight Mon-Fri, 3pm-late Sat & Sun; wi-fi) Through the big black gate and down into the basement lies one of Belgrade's coolest hang-outs. Miscellaneous oddities clamour for wall space while an equally motley clientele yak over cocktails.

Pub Brod BAR

(Bulevar Despota Stefana 36; ⏰noon-4am) This congenial student hang-out thumbs its nose at dress codes, Top 40 and nouveau-Belgrade bling. Small and smoky inside; in summertime, indie music pumps over a whooping sidewalk sprawl.

Russian Tsar CAFE

(Ruski Car; www.ruskicar.net; cnr Knez Mihailova & Obilićev Venac) Whisking up decadent cakes and Russian treats since 1890, this gold-trimmed parlour is one of Belgrade's most popular rendezvous.

☆ Entertainment

Nightclubs

Belgrade has a reputation as one of the world's top party cities, with a wild club scene limited only by imagination and hours in the day. Ask a local for the latest hotspot.

CLUBS

Andergraund CLUB

(Pariška 1a) Leader of the pack in a city renowned for partying hard, Andergraund has spaces on a tiered terrace on the citadel walls, but most of it is underneath in catacombs where sweaty crowds gyrate.

Akademija LIVE MUSIC

(www.akademija.net; Rajićeva 10) Akademija has been king of Belgrade's underground scene (literally: it's in a basement) for over 20 years. Alternative crowds rock this cult institution every night, especially on Thursdays and Saturdays.

Bitef Art Cafe LIVE MUSIC

(www.bitefartcafe.rs; Skver Mire Trailović 1; ⏰7pm-4am) There's something for everyone at this delightful hotchpotch of a cafe-club. Funk, soul and jazz get a good airing, as do rock and classical. Karaoke competitions pack in the punters.

RIVER BARS & CLUBS

Adjacent to Hotel Jugoslavija in Novi Belgrade is a 1km-long strip of some 20 party barges. Most are closed in winter. Get there with bus 15 or 84 from Zeleni Venac or 68, 603 or 701 from Trg Republike.

GO WILD IN GUČA

On the surface, the **Dragačevo Trumpet Assembly**, an annual gathering of brass musicians, sounds nerdily endearing. But it's actually the most boisterous music festival in all of Europe, if not the world.

Known simply as 'Guča' after the western Serbian village which has hosted it each August since 1961, the four-day festival is hedonism at its most rambunctious: tens of thousands of beer-and-brass-addled visitors do a wild *kolos* (dance) through the streets, gorging on spit-meat and slapping dinar on the sweaty foreheads of roaming performers. The music itself is relentless and frenzy-fast.

Guča is an easy three- to four-hour bus ride from Belgrade (several depart daily); it's also a straightforward journey with your own (or rented) wheels. Festival promoters can help with transport arrangements: see www.guca.rs for more.

Blaywatch BARGE
(midnight-late) This throbbing place gets crowded and dress codes may be enforced (sneakers bad on boys, skimpy good on girls). The crowd is a mix of local 'beautiful people' and foreigners, all occupied with each other and the turbofolk tunes.

Acapulco BARGE
(www.acapulco.co.rs; noon-late) Where blinged-up boys come to flaunt their (new) money and she-accessories. Low turbofolk threshold? Start swimming.

On the western bank of the Sava River is a 1.5km strip of floating bars, restaurants and discos known as 'splavs'. Most are only open in summer. **Freestyler** (www.splavfree.rs; Brodarska bb; 11pm-5am Tue-Sun) has been a symbol of splav saturnalia for years. For something different, try the **Povetarac** (www.povetarac.com; Brodarska bb; midnight-late, 8pm-late in winter), a rusting cargo ship drawing an indie crowd.

Performing Arts

For concert and theatre tickets go to **Bilet Servis** (303 3311; www.biletservis.co.rs; Trg Republike 5; 9am-9pm Mon-Fri, 9am-3pm Sat).

National Theatre THEATRE
(262 0946; www.narodnopozoriste.co.rs; Trg Republike; box office 10am-2pm Tue-Sun) During winter, the National Theatre stages operas, dramas and ballets.

Kolarčev University Concert Hall LIVE MUSIC
(630 550; www.kolarac.co.rs; Studentski Trg 5; box office 10am-noon & 6-8pm) See the Belgrade Philharmonica here.

Dom Omladine LIVE MUSIC, THEATRE
(324 8202; www.domomladine.org; Makedonska 22; box office 10am-8pm Mon-Fri, 3-8pm Sat) Hosts a range of mostly youth-based cultural events.

Serbian Academy of Arts & Sciences LIVE MUSIC
(202 7200; www.sanu.ac.rs; Knez Mihailova 35; concerts from 6pm Mon & Thu Oct-Jun) Free concerts and exhibitions.

Sava Centar LIVE MUSIC
(220 6060; www.savacentar.com; Milentija Popovića 9, Novi Beograd; box office 10am-8pm Mon-Fri, 10am-3pm & hourly before event Sat) For larger shows and visiting stars.

Belgrade Arena LIVE MUSIC
(Beogradska Arena; 220 2222; www.arenabeograd.com; Bulevar Arsenija Ĉarnojevića 58, Novi Beograd; 10am-8pm Mon-Fri, 10am-3pm Sat) Also for larger shows and visiting stars.

Cinemas

For Hollywood blockbusters in English or with English subtitles, try:

Tuckwood Cineplex CINEMA
(323 6517; www.tuck.rs; Kneza Miloša 7; adult/student 300/250DIN)

Dom Sindikata CINEMA
(323 4224; www.ds.co.rs; Trg Nikole Pašića 5; adult/student 300/250DIN)

INFORMATION

Internet Resources

Belgrade City (www.beograd.rs)

Belgrade in Your Pocket (www.inyourpocket.com/serbia/belgrade)

Belgraded (www.belgraded.com)

Tourist Information

Tourist Organisation of Belgrade (www.tob.co.rs); central train station (361 2732; 8am-8pm Mon-Fri, 8am-4pm Sat & Sun); Knez Mihailova 6 (328 1859; 9am-9pm Mon-Sat); Nikola Tesla Airport (209 7828; 9am-9pm Mon-Sun); Terazije Underpass (263 5622; 9am-8pm Mon-Fri, 9am-4pm Sat & Sun) Helpful folk with a raft of brochures, city maps and all the other info you could need.

WORTH A TRIP

NOVI PAZAR

Novi Pazar is the cultural heartland of the southern Sandžak region, with a mostly Muslim population. Its winding streets and Ottoman skyline make this town delightfully disorienting: it feels more Turkish than some parts of İstanbul. Amazingly, some of Serbia's most revered Orthodox monasteries are just a cab ride away.

Getting There & Away

BUS Belgrade has two adjacent bus stations: **BAS** (263 6299; www.bas.rs; Železnička 4) serves the region, while **Lasta** (334 8555; www.lasta.rs; Železnička 2) deals with destinations around Belgrade. Services include Subotica (1300DIN, three hours), Novi Sad (700DIN, one hour) and Novi Pazar (1200DIN, three hours) for Kosovo.

TRAIN Frequent trains go to Novi Sad (288DIN, 1½ hours) and Subotica (560DIN, three hours) from the central train station.

Getting Around

TO/FROM THE AIRPORT Nikola Tesla Airport is 18km from Belgrade. The JAT bus that connects the airport with the JAT bus terminal via the railway station wasn't running at the time of research; see www.beg.aero for updates. Otherwise, bus 72 connects the airport with Zeleni Venac (65 to 100DIN, half-hourly from 5.20am to midnight from airport and 4.40am to 11.40pm from town); the cheapest tickets are purchased from newsstands.

Avoid the airport taxi shark pit: ask the tourist office in the arrivals hall to call a cab for you. A taxi from the airport to Knez Mihailova should be around 1150DIN.

BUS Bus tickets are 42DIN from street kiosks or 80DIN from the driver.

TAXI Only hail distinctly labelled cabs, or get a local to call one for you. A 5km trip costs around 415DIN.

TRAM Tram 2 connects Kalemegdan Citadel with Trg Slavija, bus stations and the central train station.

VOJVODINA ВОЈВОДИНА

Home to more than 25 ethnic groups, six official languages and the best of Hungarian and Serbian traditions, Vojvodina's pancake plains mask a rich diversity. Novi Sad hosts the Exit Festival, while charming Subotica is an oasis of art-nouveau delights. For more information, visit www.vojvodinaonline.com.

Novi Sad Нови Сад

021 / POP 350,000

As convivial as a *rakija* toast – and at times just as carousing – Novi Sad is a chipper town with none of the stress of the big smoke. Locals sprawl in outdoor cafes and laneway bars pack out nightly, while Petrovaradin Citadel keeps a stern eye on proceedings.

Sights

Petrovaradin Citadel FORTRESS

Towering over the river on a 40m-high volcanic slab, this mighty sconce is aptly nicknamed 'Gibraltar on the Danube'. Built with slave labour between 1692 and 1780, the citadel's dungeons have held prisoners including Karađorđe (leader of the first uprising against the Turks) and Tito... albeit not at the same time.

Within the citadel walls, the **museum** (admission 100DIN; 9am-5pm Tue-Sun) offers insight, sans English explanations, into the site's history.

WORTH A TRIP

ZLATIBOR

Zlatibor is a special region of rolling plains, traditions and hospitality.

Quirky adventures await in Mokra Gora village. **Drvengrad** (Küstendorf; 31-800 686; www.mecavnik.info; Mećavnik hill; admission 180DIN; 9am-9pm) was built in 2002 by director Emir Kusturica for his film *Life is a Miracle*. Take Bruce Lee St past the church for prime panoramas.

The twisty-turny **Šargan 8 railway** (31-510 288; www.serbianrailways.com; 2½hr trip 500DIN; 10.30am & 1.25pm Apr-Sep, 8am & 4.10pm when required) tourist train was once part of a narrow-gauge railway linking Belgrade with Sarajevo and Dubrovnik.

Reach these sights via bus from Užice or through **Zlatibor Tours** (031-845 957; Tržni centar bus station; 8am-9pm).

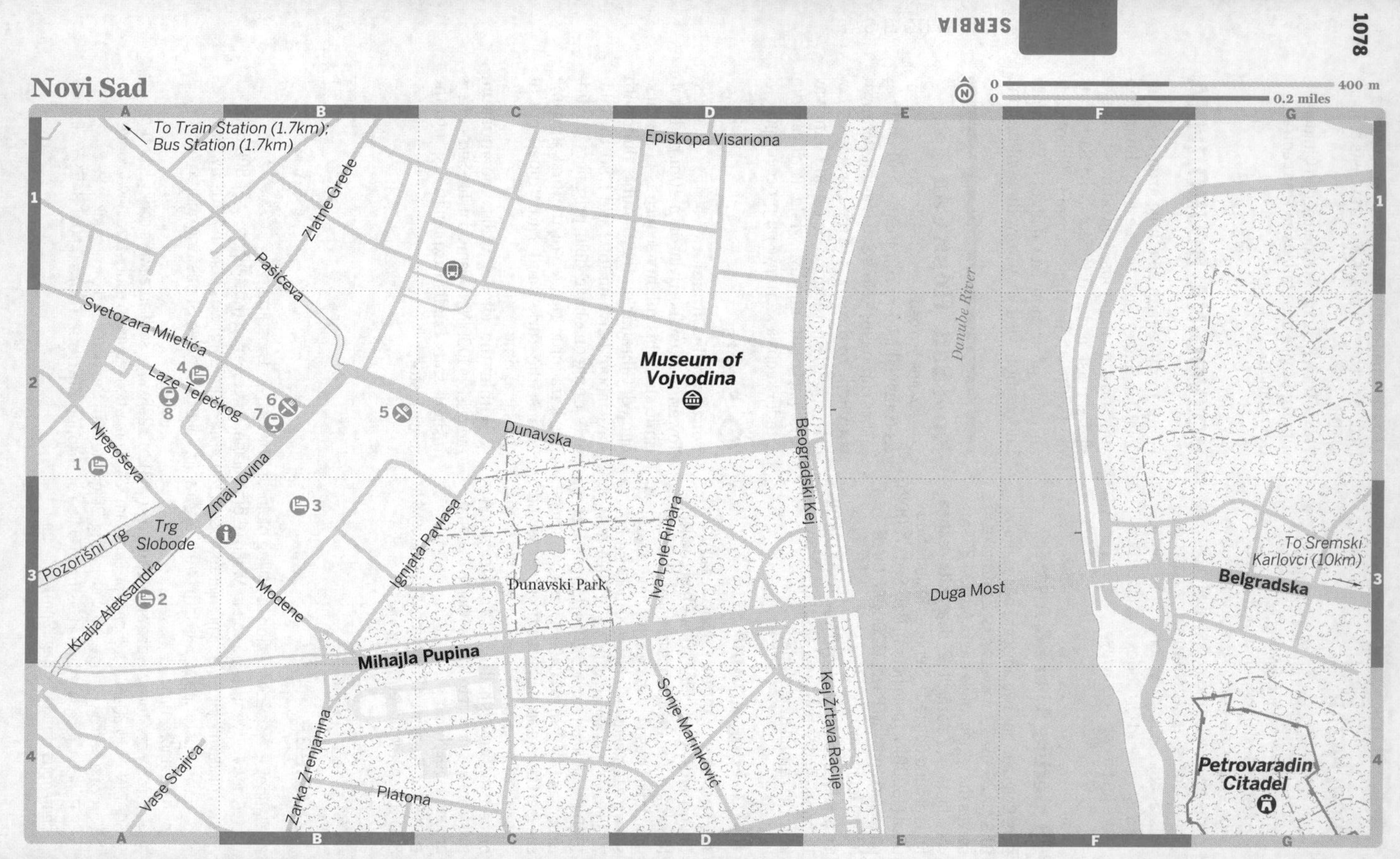
Novi Sad
0
0
400 m
0.2 miles
To Train Station (1.7km);
Bus Station (1.7km)
Episkopa Visariona
Zlatne Grede
Pašićeva
Svetozara Miletića
Laze Telečkog
Museum of Vojvodina
Dunavska
Danube River
Njegoševa
Zmaj Jovina
Trg Slobode
Pozorišni Trg
Kralja Aleksandra
Modene
Ignjata Pavlasa
Dunavski Park
Iva Lole Ribara
Beogradski Kej
Duga Most
To Sremski Karlovci (10km)
Belgradska
Mihajla Pupina
Sonje Marinković
Kej Žrtava Racije
Zarka Zrenjanina
Platona
Vase Stajića
Petrovaradin Citadel
1
2
3
4
5
6
7
8

Novi Sad

Top Sights

Museum of Vojvodina D2
Petrovaradin Citadel G4

Sleeping

1 Downtown A2
2 Hotel Vojvodina A3
3 Hotel Zenit B3
4 Lazin Hostel A2

Eating

5 Evropa B2
6 Kod Lipa B2

Drinking

7 Atrium B2
8 Cuba Libre A2
London Underground Club .... (see 8)

Museum of Vojvodina MUSEUM
(Muzej Vojvodine; www.muzejvojvodine.org.rs; Dunavska 35-7; admission 100DIN; 9am-5pm Tue-Sun) This museum houses historical, archaeological and ethnological exhibits. Building 35 covers Vojvodinian history from Palaeolithic times to the late 19th century. Building 37 takes the story to 1945.

Sleeping

TOP CHOICE **Downtown** HOSTEL €
(69 139 7708; www.hostelnovisad.com; Njegoševa 2; dm from €9, tw €18; @) Super-friendly staff and an in-the-thick-of-it location make this rambunctious, slightly ramshackle hostel a Novi Sad experience in itself.

Hotel Vojvodina HISTORIC HOTEL €€
(622 122; Trg Slobode 2; s/d from 3500/5000DIN) Reeking of communist-era retro, Novi Sad's oldest hotel (1854) isn't as slick as others but its location overlooking the town square is unbeatable.

Lazin Hostel HOSTEL €
(63 443 703; www.lazinhostel.org; Laze Telečkog 10; dm €11-13, d & tw €15; @) Party people will appreciate this spotless, sociable place, just a few seconds' stumble from bars galore.

Hotel Zenit HOTEL €€
(66 21 444; www.hotelzenit.co.rs; Zmaj Jovina 8; s/d 4715/6530DIN, apt 10,030-15,190DIN;) With its modern glass-fronted facade, the timber-bedecked interior of the Zenit is a cosy surprise. Personal service and a central location add to the charm.

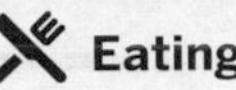

Eating

TOP CHOICE **Kod Lipa** SERBIAN €
(Svetozara Miletića 7; meals from 300DIN; 7am-11pm Mon-Fri, 7am-1am Sat & Sun) This down-home eatery has been dishing up old-school ambience alongside traditional Vojvodinian fare since the 19th century.

Bubi Grill GRILL €
(Dimitrija Tucovića 3; pljeskavica from 160DIN; 24hr) Lap up the greasy goodness at this grill – renowned as the best in town – near the football stadium.

Evropa BAKERY €
(Dunavska 6; cakes 100DIN) Lapse into a sugar coma.

Drinking

Laze Telečkog is lined with bars to suit every whim. Squeeze into the frenetic **London Underground Club** (Laze Telečkog 15; 8am-3am) or sidle next door to **Cuba Libre** (Laze Telečkog 13) and stake your spot on the dance floor. The infinitely more calm **Atrium** (Laze Telečkog 2) serves drinks in a civilised (faux) library.

Information

Tourist information centre (661 7343; www.turizamns.rs; Modene 1; 7.30am-8pm Mon-Fri, 9am-5pm Sat) Has loads of information in English.

Getting There & Away

Frequent trains leave the **train station** (Bulevar Jaše Tomića 4) for Belgrade (490DIN, 1½ hours) and Subotica (390DIN, 1½ hours).

The **bus station** (information counter 6am-11pm) next door has regular departures to Belgrade (605DIN, one hour, every 10 minutes) and Subotica (830DIN, 1½ hours).

ENTERING THE STATE OF EXIT

Home to the epic **EXIT Festival** (www.exitfest.org), the Petrovaradin Fortress in Novi Sad is stormed by thousands of revellers each July. The first festival in 2000 lasted 100 days and galvanised a generation of young Serbs against the Milošević regime, who 'exited' himself just weeks after the event. The festival has been attended in recent years by the likes of Faith No More, Chemical Brothers, Missy Elliot and Kraftwerk, plus an annual tally of over 150,000 merrymakers.

Subotica Суботица

☎024 / POP 148,400

Sugarspun art-nouveau marvels, a laid-back populace and a delicious sprinkling of Serbian and Hungarian flavours make this quaint town a worthy day trip or en-route stopover.

Sights

Town Hall HISTORIC BUILDING

(Trg Republike) Built in 1910, this behemoth of a building is a curious mix of art nouveau and something Gaudí may have had a dab at. Its elaborate council chambers are not to be missed.

Modern Art Gallery HISTORIC BUILDING

(www.likovnisusret.com; Park Ferenca Rajhla 5; admission 50DIN; ⏲8am-6pm Mon-Fri, 9am-noon Sat) One of the most sumptuous buildings in Serbia, it's a vibrant flourish of mosaics, ceramic tiles, floral patterns and stained glass.

City Museum MUSEUM

(www.gradskimuzej.subotica.rs; Trg Sinagoge 3; admission 100DIN; ⏲10am-8pm Tue-Sat) This eclectic museum holds exhibitions in an art-nouveau residence designed by Budapest's Vago brothers.

Synagogue SYNAGOGUE

Subotica's first art-nouveau building remains shuttered as long-awaited renovations have failed to materialise. Grasp its former glory from the footpath.

Sleeping

Hostel Incognito HOSTEL €

(☎559 254; www.hostel-subotica.com; Hugo Badalića 3; s/d/tr/apt 1000/1800/2400/7000DIN; 📶) Run by brothers Darko and Zoran, this basic but clean hostel is a couple minutes' walk from all the Subotica sights. Reception is in the restaurant downstairs.

Hostel Bosa Milećević HOSTEL €

(☎548 290; Marije Vojnić Tošinice 7; per person 820DIN) Cheapie tucked well away behind the Ekonomski Fakultet (Faculty of Economics) at Segedinski put 9-11.

Eating

TOP CHOICE **Ravel** CAFE €

(Nušićeva 2; cakes 60-150DIN; ⏲9am-10pm Mon-Sat, 11am-10pm Sun) Dainty cake nibbles and twee tea-taking is the name of the game at this adorable art-nouveau classic.

> WORTH A TRIP
>
> **FRUŠKA GORA & SREMSKI KARLOVCI ФРУШКА ГОРА & СРЕМСКИ КАРЛОВЦИ**
>
> Fruška Gora is an 80km stretch of rolling hills where monastic life has continued for centuries. Thirty-five monasteries were built here between the 15th and 18th centuries to safeguard Serbian culture and religion from the Turks; 16 remain.
>
> The town of Sremski Karlovci is littered with stunning structures such as the **Orthodox cathedral** (1758–62), baroque **Four Lions fountain** and the **Chapel of Peace** (where Turks and Austrians signed the 1699 Peace Treaty).
>
> Visit the tourist offices in Novi Sad or log on to www.karlovci.org.rs.

Boss Caffe INTERNATIONAL €

(www.bosscaffe.com; Matije Korvina 7-8) Boss' offerings include tacos (240DIN to 455DIN) and pizza with sour cream (405DIN to 455DIN). It's directly behind the Modern Art Gallery.

Information

Tourist information centre (☎670 350; www.visitsubotica.rs; ⏲8am-8pm Mon-Fri, 9am-noon Sat & Sun) In the town hall.

Getting There & Away

From Subotica's **train station** (Bose Milećević bb), there are frequent trains to Belgrade (560DIN, 3½ hours) which stop at Novi Sad (400DIN, 1½ hours).

The **bus station** (Senćanski put 3) has hourly buses to Novi Sad (800DIN, two hours) and Belgrade (1200DIN, 3½ hours).

UNDERSTAND SERBIA

History

The region's original Illyrian inhabitants were augmented by Celts and Slavs in the 6th century AD. The assignation of Serbia to the Byzantine Empire in AD 395, and the conversion of the population to Orthodoxy in 879, wedded Serbia to Eastern Europe.

The Ottoman Turks defeated Serbia at the pivotal 1389 Battle of Kosovo; independence from Turkish rule wasn't achieved until 1815.

After WWI, Serbia joined Croatia, Slovenia, Vojvodina and Macedonia to form Yugoslavia, which during WWII was partitioned between Germany, Italy, Hungary and Bulgaria. Tito, a Communist Partisan resistance leader, became leader of the Federal Republic of Yugoslavia in 1945, of which Serbia became a republic.

By 1986 Serbian nationalists were espousing a 'Greater Serbia', an ideology that would encompass Serbs from all republics into one state. Appropriated by Serbia's Communist Party leader Slobodan Milošević, the doctrine was fuelled by claims of the genocide of Serbs by Kosovar Albanians, leading to the abolishment of self-rule in Kosovo in 1990. Inflamed by Serbia's mounting authoritarianism and territorial claims, Croatia, Slovenia, Bosnia & Hercegovina and Macedonia seceded from the federation, sparking a series of violent conflicts known collectively as the Yugoslav Wars.

Bitter, bloody and monstrously complex, the wars – Slovenia's Ten-Day War, the Croatian War of Independence and the Bosnian War – were fought not just between breakaway forces and the majority-Serb Yugoslav Army, but along fractious ethnic and religious lines as well. Atrocities were committed on all sides: perhaps the most stunning display of savagery came with the Srebrenica massacre, Europe's largest mass murder since WWII in which 8000 Bosnian men and boys were killed under orders of Republika Srpska Army (RSA) commander Ratko Mladić and RS president Radovan Karadžić. Allegations of rape camps, ethnic cleansing and other barbarisms under Milošević's leadership saw Serbia assume the role of international pariah.

Violence erupted in Kosovo in 1998, and the flight of thousands of Kosovar Albanians into Macedonia and Albania galvanised NATO into action. Serbian forces withdrew after air strikes.

In 2001 Milošević was defeated in presidential elections and forced from office by a popular uprising. He was extradited to the international war crimes tribunal in the Hague, where he died in March 2006.

In 2006, 55% of Montenegrins voted for independence from Serbia, which was formally declared the following month. Kosovo declared independence in 2008, which Serbia deemed illegal. In May 2008 President Boris Tadić won 102 seats in Serbia's parliament, reaffirming Serbia's pro-European future. Fractures remain over Kosovo. In May 2011, fugitive Ratko Mladić was tracked down after 16 years in hiding; he was arrested and sent to Den Haag to be tried by the International Court of Justice.

People

The last census revealed a population of 7.3 million, which is comprised of Serbs (83%), Hungarians (3.9%), Bosniaks (1.8%), Roma (1.4%), Yogoslavs (1%) and others (8.9%). Serbs aren't famous for their warmth but they should be.

Food

Price ranges in this chapter are based on the cost of a main course:

€€€ more than 1000DIN (€10)

€€ 600DIN to 1000DIN (€6 to €10)

€ less than 600DIN (€6)

SURVIVAL GUIDE

Directory A–Z

Accommodation

More hostels are opening in Serbia all the time; try **Hostel World** (www.hostelworld.com) for bookings. Private rooms and apartments can be organised through tourist offices. 'Wild' camping is possible outside national parks.

Price ranges in this chapter are based on the cost of a double room in high season:

€€€ more than €75 (7000DIN)

€€ €30 to €75 (3000DIN to 7000DIN)

€ less than €30 (3000DIN)

Business Hours

Banks 8am or 9am-5pm Mon-Fri, 8am-2pm Sat

Bars 8am-3am

Restaurants 8am-midnight or 1am

Shops 8am-6pm Mon-Fri; some to early afternoon Sat

Embassies & Consulates

A complete list of embassies and consulates in Serbia, as well as Serbian embassies around the world, is available at www.mfa.gov.rs/worldframe.htm.

Money

Serbia retains the dinar though payment for accommodation in euros is commonplace. Exchange offices are recognisable by 'Menjačnica' signs.

Post & Telephone

Parcels should be taken unsealed to the main post office for inspection.

Phonecards can be bought in post offices and tobacco kiosks for 300DIN (local cards) and 600DIN (international cards). Halo Plus cards allow for longer calls.

SIM cards can be purchased at branches for around 200DIN, and recharge cards at supermarkets and kiosks.

Visas

Tourist visas for stays of less than 90 days aren't required by citizens of most EU countries, Australia, New Zealand, Canada and the USA.

Officially, all visitors must register with the police. Hotels and hostels will do this for you but if you're camping or staying in a private home, you are expected to register at the local police station within 24 hours of arrival. Unofficially? This is rarely enforced, but being unable to produce registration documents upon leaving Serbia could result in a fine.

Getting There & Away

Air

Belgrade's **Nikola Tesla Airport** (☎011-209 4444, 0648485402, 063255066; www.beg.aero) handles routes to and from most European countries.

Land

Serbia does not acknowledge crossing points into Kosovo as international border crossings; it may not be possible to enter from Kosovo unless you first entered Kosovo from Serbia.

Buses travel as far north as Sweden and as far east as Turkey.

People driving into the country need International Driving Permits and vehicles need Green Card insurance.

Daily train services from Belgrade include the following: Bucharest (2800DIN, 14 hours), Budapest (1590DIN, seven hours), İstanbul (4525DIN, 26 hours), Ljubljana (2327DIN, 10 hours), Moscow (8405DIN, 50 hours), Munich (12,102DIN, 17 hours), Sofia (2000DIN, 11 hours), Thessaloniki (3160DIN, 16 hours), Vienna (6516DIN, 11 hours) and Zagreb (1990DIN, seven hours). See www.serbianrailways.com for more.

Getting Around

Bicycle paths are improving in larger cities such as Belgrade and Novi Sad. Vojvodina is relatively flat, but main roads make for dull days.

Bus services are extensive, though outside major hubs connections can be sporadic. Reservations are only worthwhile for international buses and during festivals.

Major car hire companies are ubiquitous. Small-car hire typically costs €40 to €50 per day. The **Automobile & Motorcycle Association of Serbia** (Auto-Moto Savez Srbije; ☎011-333 1100; www.amss.org.rs; Ruzveltova 18, Belgrade) provides **roadside assistance** (☎987).

Serbian Railways (☎011-361 4811; www.serbianrailways.com) serves Novi Sad, Subotica and Niš from Belgrade.

Slovakia

Includes »

Best Places to Eat

» Bratislavský Meštiansky Pivovar, Bratislava (p1087)

» Kolkovna. Bratislava (p1087)

» Reštaurácia Bašta, Trenčín (p1091)

Best Places to Stay

» Ginger Monkey Hostel, Belá Tatras (p1094)

» Hostel Blues, Bratislava (p1087)

» Grand Hotel Kempinski, High Tatras (p1087)

» Penzión Tatra, High Tatras (p1093)

Why Go?

Ancient castle ruins, traditional villages and mountainous national parks: visiting Slovakia is about experiencing a place where age-old folkways and nature still hold sway. In this compact country you can hike an alpine peak one day and see nail-less wooden churches in a village museum the next. The small capital of Bratislava is abuzz with development. It's not as cheap as it once was, but the rabbit-warren Old Town centre is well worth a day or two of cafe-hopping.

Just make sure you also venture east. Prices fall dramatically in the countryside, where fortresses tower over cities and well-preserved medieval towns nestle below the rocky peaks of the High Tatra mountains – great for hiking. Here there's plenty to see and eat on a shoestring. So, pull up a heaping plate of *bryndzové halušky* (sheep's cheese dumplings) with a glass of *slivovica* (firewater-like plum brandy) and drink a toast for us – *nazdravie*!

When to Go

Bratislava

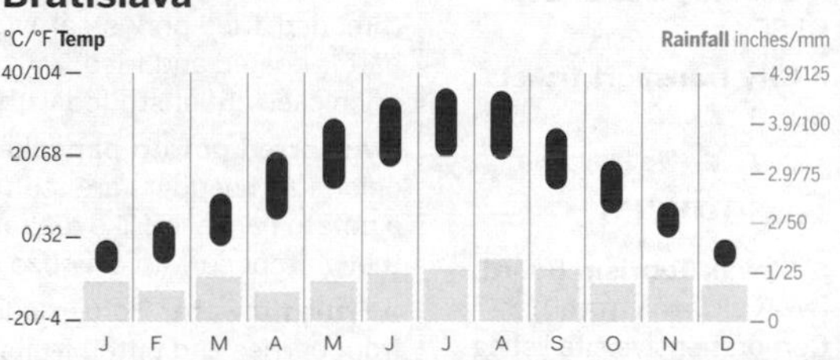

May & late Sep Few crowds, temperate weather; shoulder-season travel is a breeze.

Jul & Aug Festivals abound, High Tatras hiking trails are open; just book lodging ahead.

Jan & Feb Peak ski season in the mountains, but many sights closed.

AT A GLANCE

» **Currency** euro (€)

» **Language** Slovak

» **Money** ATMs widely available in cities

» **Visas** Not required for most visitors staying less than 90 days

Fast Facts

» **Area** 49,035 sq km

» **Capital** Bratislava

» **Country code** ☎421

» **Emergency** ☎112

Exchange Rates

Australia	A$1	€0.73
Canada	C$1	€0.73
Japan	¥100	€0.84
New Zealand	NZ$1	€0.54
UK	UK£1	€1.14
USA	US$1	€0.70

Set Your Budget

» **Budget hotel room** €30–60

» **Two-course evening meal** €15

» **Museum entrance** €3

» **500mL glass of beer** €1.50

» **City transport ticket** €0.70

Resources

» **Slovak Tourism Board** (www.slovakia.travel) Comprehensive site listing attractions and lodging.

» **What's On Slovakia** (www.whatsonslovakia.com) Monthly event tips.

» **Slovakia Document Store** (www.panorama.sk)

Connections

Though few airlines fly into Slovakia itself, Bratislava is just 60km from the well-connected Vienna International Airport. By train from Bratislava, Budapest (three hours) and Prague (five hours) are super easy to reach. Travelling further east, buses become your best bet. Connect to Zakopane (Poland; two hours) from Poprad, and to Uzhhorod (Ukraine; 2½ hours) through Košice.

ITINERARIES

Three Days

Two nights in Bratislava is enough time to wander the Old Town streets, see a museum or two, and stop at a new river-park restaurant. The third day is best spent on a castle excursion, either to Devín or Trenčín. Alternatively, spend all three days hiking in the rocky High Tatras mountains, staying central in the Starý Smokovec resort town or in more off-beat Ždiar in the Belá Tatras.

One Week

After a couple of days in the capital and western Slovakia, go east. Spend at least four nights in and around the Tatras so you can hike to a mountain hut and take day trips to the must-see Spiš Castle ruins and medieval Levoča. Then, the last night or two, continue on to Bardejov to see a complete Renaissance town square, icon art and the neighbouring folk village and wooden churches.

Essential Food & Drink

» **Sheep's cheese and more sheep's cheese** *Bryndza* (sharp, soft and spreadable); *oštiepok* (solid and ball-shaped); *korbačik* ('little whips' or long, smoked strands); *žinčica* (a traditional sheep's whey drink, like sour milk).

» **Schnitzel by any other name** *Vyprážaný bravčový rezeň* (breaded, fried pork steak); *Černohorský rezeň* (potato batter-coated and fried, with cheese); *gordon blu* (fried pork or chicken cutlet stuffed with ham and cheese).

» **Assorted potato pancakes** Various sautéed meats, onions and peppers are stuffed *v zemiakovej placke* (in a potato pancake), like *diabolské soté* (devil's sautée), or they're topped with *bryndza* cheese and sour cream.

» **Fruit firewater** Homemade or store-bought liquor, made from berries and pitted fruits, such as *borovička* (from juniper) and *slivovica* (from plums).

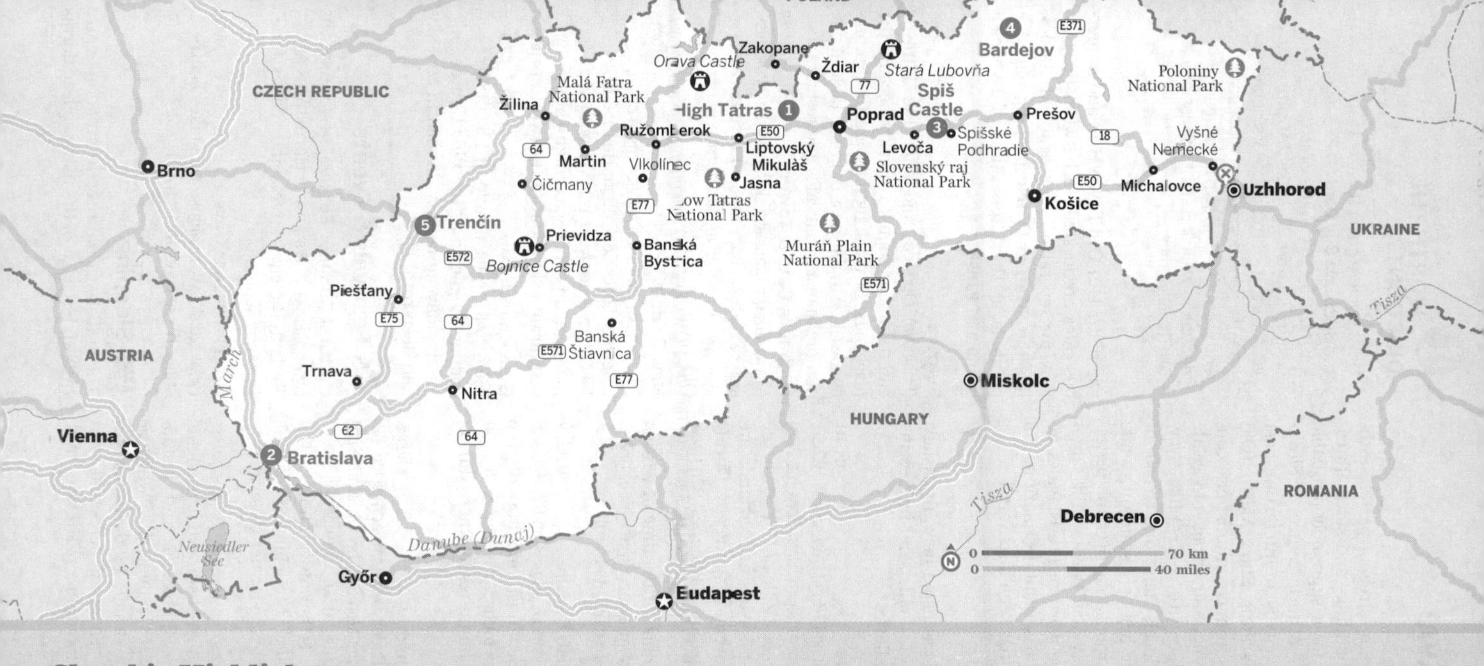

Slovakia Highlights

1. Hike between fully-catered mountain huts in one of Europe's most affordable alpine mountain ranges, the **High Tatras** (p1092)
2. Linger over drinks at the myriad sidewalk and riverfront cafes in Old Town **Bratislava** (p1086)
3. Wander among the 4-hectare ruins of **Spiš Castle** (p1095), among the largest in Europe
4. Gaze on Renaissance splendour and ancient icons in **Bardejov** (p1096)
5. Tour **Trenčín Castle** (p1091) by torchlight, as medieval actors bring the place to life

BRATISLAVA

☎02 / POP 428,800

Narrow pedestrian streets, pastel 18th-century rococo buildings and sidewalk cafes galore make for a supremely strollable – if minuscule – historic centre to Slovakia's capital. The city is an interesting host of contrasts: charming Starý Mesto (Old Town) lies across from communist-era, concrete-block housing, and an age-old castle shares the skyline with a UFO-like 'New Bridge'. Trendy locals hang out riverfront at the latest chic bar or restaurant, while European tour groups take over the pedestrian lanes. A few stag parties still target the town, but, be warned, Bratislava is no longer a bargain-basement destination. You could say 'Blava' has been discovered.

Sights

In addition to those listed here, Bratislava has a number of small, semi-interesting museums and galleries.

Bratislava Castle CASTLE
(www.snm.sk; grounds free, museum €2.50; ⏲grounds 9am-9pm, museum 10am-6pm Tue-Sun) Lording over the west side of Old Town, the castle's winding ramparts and grounds are great for a walk overlooking the city. During the Turkish occupation of Budapest, this was the seat of Hungarian royalty. Years-long renovations are ongoing. At the time of writing only a temporary museum space was open; history and culture exhibits to follow.

Museum of Jewish Culture MUSEUM
(www.snm.sk; Židovská 17; admission €7; ⏲11am-5pm Sun-Fri) The most moving of the excellent exhibits focuses on a large Jewish community and buildings lost here during and after WWII.

St Martin's Cathedral CHURCH
(Dóm sv Martina; Rudnayovo nám; admission €2; ⏲9-11.30am & 1-5pm Mon-Sat, 1.30-4.30pm Sun) Eleven Austro-Hungarian monarchs were crowned in this 14th-century church. The busy motorway almost touching St Martin's follows the moat of the former city walls.

Pedestrian Plazas SQUARES
Two Old Town squares stand out as sights unto themselves. Embassies and restaurants line **Hviezdoslavovo nám**, which is dominated by the ornate, 1866 **Slovak National Theatre**. There's a perpetual craft fair beside the fountain on **Hlavné nám**, where the 1421 **Old Town Hall** and numerous cafes are located. In between the two, look for several oft-photographed statues, like the **'Man at Work'** peeping out of a manhole at the intersection of Rybárska brána and Panská.

Eurovea NEIGHBOURHOOD
(Pribinova) Opened mid-2010, the Eurovea entertainment complex quickly became the place to be. Stroll along the waterfront promenades, laze in the grass or grab a table at one of more than a dozen cafes and restaurants.

Michael's Gate & Tower TOWER
(www.muzeum.bratislava.sk; Michalská 24; admission €2; ⏲10am-6pm Tue-Sun) Five narrow storeys of medieval weaponry; superior Old Town overlook.

New Bridge TOWER
(Nový most; www.u-f-o.sk; Viedenská cesta; observation deck €8; ⏲10am-11pm) A 1972, UFO-like modernist marvel with viewing platform, an over-hyped nightclub and a restaurant asking out-of-this-world prices.

Blue Church CHURCH
(Bezručova 2; ⏲dawn-dusk) St Elizabeth's, commonly known as the Blue Church, is an art-nouveau fantasy dressed in cool sky and deep royal blue.

> **WORTH THE DISCOUNT?**
>
> Unless you're going to take a tour, the **Bratislava City Card** (1/2/3 days €10/12/15), sold at the Bratislava Culture & Information Centre, probably isn't worth it. The card covers public transport and discounted museum entry, but the Old Town is compact enough to walk and sight admissions are usually cheap.

Festivals & Events

Cultural Summer Festival PERFORMANCE ARTS
(www.bkis.sk) Plays and performances come to the city's streets and venues June through September.

Bratislava Jazz Days MUSIC
(www.bjd.sk) World-class jazz takes centre stage three days in October.

Sleeping

The Bratislava Culture & Information Centre (p1090) has a list of the many college dorms

DON'T MISS

DEVÍN CASTLE

To see a historically complete fortress outfitted as in olden days, travel 8km outside the capital to **Devín Castle** (www.muzeum.bratislava.sk; Muranská; adult €3; ⏲10am-5pm Tue-Fri, to 6pm Sat & Sun), once the military plaything of 9th-century warlord Prince Rastislav. Most castle remains date from the 11th to 19th centuries. Peer at the older bits that have been unearthed and tour a reconstructed palace museum. Catch bus 29 to Devín beneath the New Bridge (Nový Most).

open to all in summer (from €10 a night). Unless noted otherwise, hostels listed here have free wi-fi, kitchens, laundries, and beer and wine for sale.

TOP CHOICE Hostel Blues HOSTEL €
(☎0905204020; www.hostelblues.sk; Špitálska 2; dm €15-20, d €52-63; ⊖@📶) Friendly, professional staff not only help you plan your days, they offer free city sightseeing tours. The coffee-house-like communal space, which occasionally hosts concerts, adds to the urban apartment-living feel. Choose from five- to 10-bed, single-sex or mixed dorms, or those with double bunk beds(!).

Downtown Backpackers HOSTEL €
(☎5464 1191; www.backpackers.sk; Panenská 31; dm €13-20, d €45-60; ⊖@📶) Bratislava's first hostel is still a boozy (you enter through the bar), bohemian classic. Red brick walls and tapestries add character to this place, as does the fact you have to walk through some dorm rooms to get to others.

Penzión Virgo PENSION €€
(☎3300 6262; www.penzionvirgo.sk; Panenská 14; s/d €65/78; ⊖@) Arranged around a courtyard, each exterior-access room feels light and airy despite dark wood floors and baroque-accent wallpaper. Sip an espresso with the breakfast buffet (€5), or cook for yourself in an apartment (€100).

Hotel-Penzión Arcus PENSION €€
(☎5557 2522; www.hotelarcus.sk; Moskovská 5; s/d incl breakfast €65/100; ⊖📶) Because this family-run place was once an apartment building, the 13 rooms are quite varied (some with balcony, some with courtyard views). Flowery synthetic linens seem a bit outdated but bathrooms are new and sparkly white.

City Hostel HOTEL €
(☎5263 6041; www.cityhostel.sk; Obchodná 38; s/d €40/60; @) More hotel than hostel, with cubicle-like singles and doubles that have private bathrooms and TV.

A1 Hostel HOSTEL €
(☎0944280288; www.a1hostelbratislava.com; Heydukova 1; dm/d €15/40; ⊖📶) Little more than a super-clean, three-room flat; A1 offers quiet and camaraderie – but no kitchen.

Patio Hostel HOSTEL €
(☎5292 5797; www.patiohostel.com; Špitálska 35; dm €23-28; ⊖@) Much like a college dorm (100 beds); tiny kitchenettes on various floors.

Eating

Most restaurants offer incredibly reasonable daily set menus (€4 to €9) from 11am until 2pm. Student-oriented cheap eats line Obchodná street.

TOP CHOICE Kolkovna CZECH, SLOVAK €€
(☎2091 5280; Eurovea, Pribinova 8; mains €7-12; ⏲11am-midnight) Our top choice for al-fresco dining at Eurovea. Hearty portions of braised and roast meats highlight the menu here, but there is lighter fare to go with your tank-imported draught Pilsner beer (no bottles means no preservatives). Weekend reservations are essential.

Bratislavský Meštiansky Pivovar SLOVAK €€
(☎0944512265; Drevená 8; mains €6-12, ⏲11am-midnight Sun-Thu, to 1am Fri & Sat) Bratislava's only microbrewery also serves some of the city's most creative Slovak cooking. Crowds fill the room beneath the vaulted ceilings; reservations are a good idea.

SPLURGE

If you plan to indulge at Eurovea's riverfront bars and restaurants, staying on-site at the **Sheraton Bratislava** (☎02-3535 0000; www.sheratonbratislava.com; Eurovea, Pribinova 12; r €150-240; P❄@📶🏊) can be a worthy splurge. It's one of Blava's newest properties, and the modern rooms have all the latest luxuries. Watch for weekend specials.

Central Bratislava

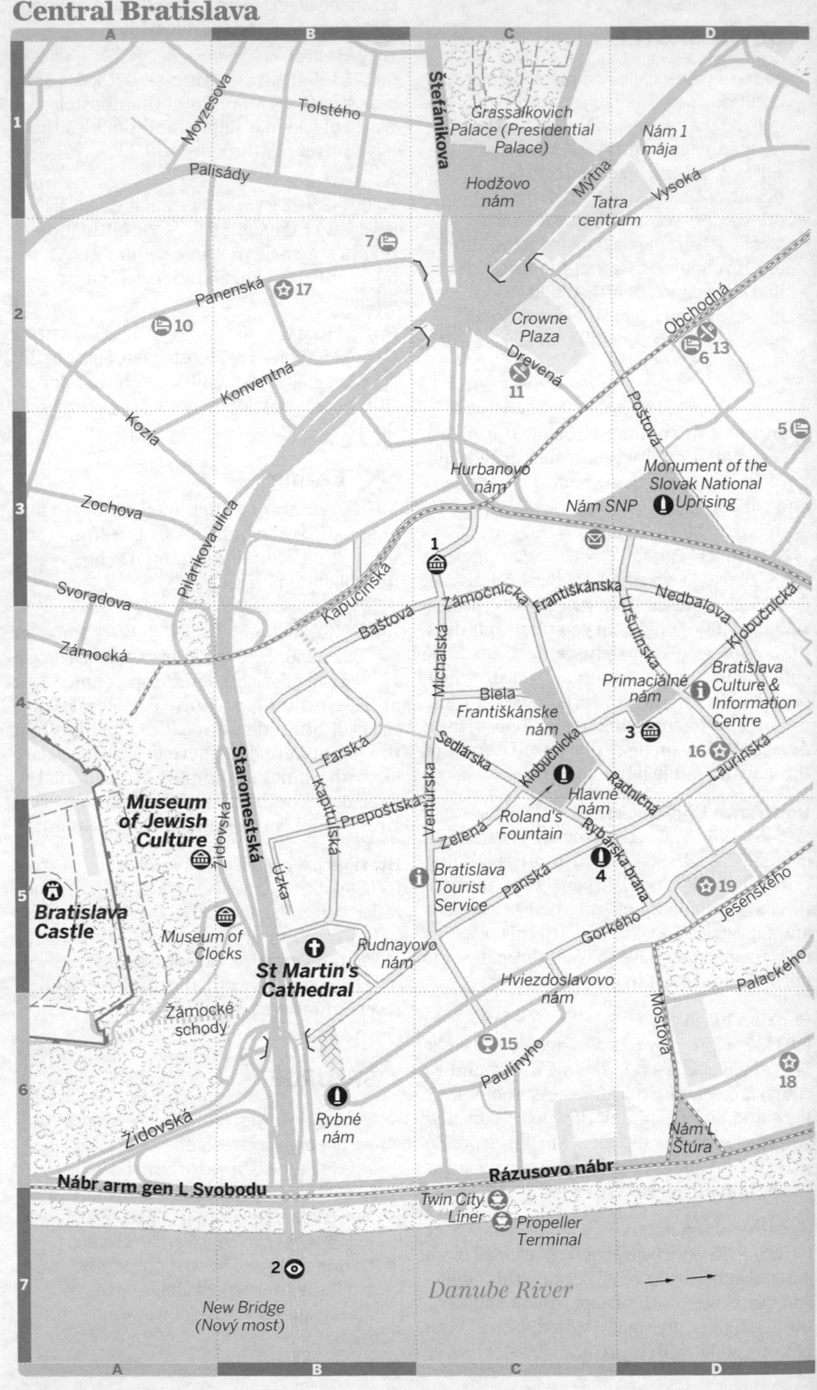

Divný Janko SLOVAK €

(Jozefská 2; mains €3-6) Get your fix of tasty fried pork and chicken steaks – stuffed with pineapple, sausage, you name it – at this locally popular little hang-out. Salads available, too.

Slovak Pub SLOVAK €€

(Obchodná 62; mains €5-10; ⏲10am-midnight Mon-Thu, 10am-1am Fri & Sat, noon-midnight Sun) Serving every national dish you can think of, in historically themed rooms. Popular with students, and firmly on the tourist trail.

Činska Panda CHINESE €€

(Vysoká 39; mains €5-8) Authentic Chinese-run restaurant with solid vegetarian options and huge set lunches.

Tesco SUPERMARKET €

(Kamenné nám 1; ⏲8am-9pm Mon-Fri, 9am-7pm Sat & Sun) Big basement supermarket for self-catering.

Central Bratislava

Top Sights

Bratislava Castle ... A5
Museum of Jewish Culture ... A5
St Martin's Cathedral ... B5

Sights

1 Michael's Gate & Tower ... C3
2 New Bridge ... B7
3 Primate's Palace ... D4
4 Man at Work Statue ... C5

Sleeping

5 A1 Hostel ... D3
6 City Hostel ... D2
7 Downtown Backpackers ... B2
8 Hostel Blues ... F2
9 Patio Hostel ... F2
10 Penzión Virgo ... A2

Eating

11 Bratislavský Meštiansky Pivovar ... C2
12 Činska Panda ... E1
13 Slovak Pub ... D2
14 Tesco ... F3

Drinking

15 Sky Bar ... C6

Entertainment

16 Aligator Rock Pub ... D4
17 Apollon Club ... B2
18 Nu Spirit ... D6
19 Slovak National Theatre - Historic SND ... D5

Drinking

Old Town's pedestrian streets are crammed with places to drink, especially around Hviezdoslavovo (look for names like Verne, Bar 17 and Slang Pub). Some bouncers have become unfriendly towards rowdy blokes, but you shouldn't have any trouble if you don't start any. The pubs listed in the Eating section are also good places to imbibe. The backpacker-oriented **Bratislava Pub Crawl** (www.befreetours.sk; Rock OK, Šafárikovo nám 4; tickets €13; 9.30pm Tue-Sat) visits four different bars and clubs in one night.

Sky Bar BAR
(Hviezdoslavovo nám 7) Upscale Old Town bar with amazing 7th-storey views. Think trendy.

Entertainment

Nightclubs

Nu Spirit CLUB
(Medená 16; 10am-4am Mon-Fri, 5pm-4am Sat & Sun) Hip underground club dabbling in all the soulful sounds on weekends; quiet enough for conversation weekdays.

Aligator Rock Pub CLUB
(Laurinská 7; 5pm-3am Mon-Sat) Live performances at this cellar club run the gamut from Pink Floyd covers to harder-core rock; packed even on work nights.

Apollon Club CLUB
(www.apollon-gay-club.sk; Panenská 24; 6pm-3am Mon-Thu, 8pm-5am Fri & Sat, 8pm-1am Sun) *The* gay disco in town has two bars and three stages.

Performing Arts & Sport

Slovak National Theatre THEATRE
(SND; www.snd.sk) Enjoy opera, ballet and concerts on a budget (€15 to €30 per seat; discount for students with ID) among the gilt decorations of the landmark **Historic SND** (Hviezdoslavovo nám; booking office cnr Jesenského & Komenského; 8am-5.30pm Mon-Fri, 9am-1pm Sat) or at the modern **New SND** (Pribinova 17; 9am-5pm Mon- Fri), which contains a cafe. While its building is under indefinite reconstruction, the **Slovak Philharmonic** (www.filharmonia.sk) also plays here.

HC Slovan ICE HOCKEY
Bratislava's hallowed ice-hockey team plays at the **Ondrej Nepela Stadium** (Odbojárov 9), which underwent a €40-million upgrade for the 2011 Ice Hockey World Championships. Buy tickets online at www.ticketportal.sk.

Information

Emergency

Main police station (159; Gundulićova 10)

Internet Access

Hlavné and Hviezdoslavovo squares are free wi-fi zones.

Klar-i-net (Klariská 4; per 30min €2; 10am-10pm Mon-Fri, 3-10pm Sat & Sun) Numerous well-equipped terminals; office services and beverages available.

Internet Resources

Bratislava City Guide (www.bratislava-city.sk)

Visit Bratislava (www.visit.bratislava.sk)

Media

Slovak Spectator (www.slovakspectator.sk) English-language weekly newspaper with current affairs and event listings.

Medical Services

Poliklinika Ruzinov (4823 4113; Ružinovská 10) Hospital and 24-hour pharmacy.

Money

The Old Town has a plethora of banks and ATMs, with several convenient branches on Poštova and around Kamenné nám. Bus, plane and train stations all have ATMs.

Tourist Information

Bratislava Culture & Information Centre (BKIS; 16 186; www.bkis.sk; Klobučnícka 2; 9am-6pm Mon-Fri, 9am-3pm Sat, 10am-3pm Sun) Brusque, official city office. Small city guide available from behind the counter.

Bratislava Tourist Service (BTS; 2070 7501; www.bratislava-info.sk; Ventúrska 9; 10am-8pm) Tiny space, lots of souvenirs, but more helpful staff and longer hours.

Getting There & Away

Check bus and train timetables at www.cp.atlas.sk.

Air

Airport Bratislava (BTS; www.airportbratislava.sk; Ivanská cesta) is 9km northeast of the city centre. Keep in mind that Vienna's much busier airport, **Vienna International Airport** (VIE; Schwechat; www.viennaairport.com), is only 60km west, with regular bus connections.

Danube Wings (V5; www.danubewings.eu) has weekday flights connecting with Košice. For international airlines, see p1098.

Boat

From April through October you can cruise to Vienna (€17, 1½ hours) and Budapest (€79, four hours) with **Slovak Shipping & Ports** (5293 2226; www.lod.sk; Hydrofoil Terminal, Fajnorova nábr 2). **Twin City Liner** (0903610716; www.twincityliner.com;

Propeller Terminal, Rázusovo nábr) runs similar but more frequent trips to Vienna only.

Bus

The **main bus station** (Autobusová stanica, AS; Mlynské Nivy; www.sad.sk) is 1.5km east of the Old Town; locals call it 'Mlynské Nivy' (for the street name). Direct destinations include cities throughout Slovakia and Europe, but the train is usually comparably priced and more convenient.

Eurolines (☎5556 7349; www.slovaklines.sk) and **Eurobus** (☎0972250305; www.eurobus.sk) serve international routes. Sample direct international services:

BUDAPEST (€14, 2½ to four hours, eight daily)
LONDON (€81, 23 hours, one daily)
PRAGUE (€16, 4¼ hours, four daily)
VIENNA (€8, 1¼ hours, 12 daily)

Train

The **main train station** (Hlavná stanica; www.slovakrail.sk; Predštanicné nám) is 1km north of centre. Sample international IC/EC services:

BUDAPEST (€14, 2¾ hours, five daily)
MOSCOW (€110, 37 hours, daily)
PRAGUE (€24, 4¼ hours, six daily)
VIENNA (€10, one hour, hourly)
WARSAW (€58, 10½ hours, nightly)

Sample domestic services:

KOŠICE (€19, 5½ hours, four daily)
POPRAD (€16, four hours, four daily)
TRENČÍN (€9, 1½ hours, three daily)
ŽILINA (€11, 2½ hours, four daily)

Getting Around

To/From the Airport

A shuttle bus runs hourly from Bratislava airport to the main bus station (€1) weekdays from 9am to 6.50pm. City bus 61 links the airport with the main train station (20 minutes). Standing taxis (over)charge about €20 to town; be sure to ask price before you get in.

A regular bus (€9, one hour) connects Vienna airport with the Bratislava bus station.

Public Transport

Bratislava has an extensive tram, bus and trolleybus network, though the Old Town is so small you won't often need it. **Dopravný Podnik Bratislava** (DPB; www.dpb.sk; Hodžovo nám; ⏲6am-7pm Mon-Fri), the public transport company office, is in the underground passage beneath Hodžovo square.

Tickets cost €0.25/0.70/1.40 for 10/60/90 minutes; buy them at news-stands and validate on board (or risk a €50 fine). One-/two-/three-/seven-day passes cost €3.50/6.50/8/12; buy them at the DPB office and validate on board.

Important lines:

Tram 13 Main train station to Nám L Štúra
Bus 93 Main train station to Hodžovo nám
Bus 206 Main bus station to Hodžovo nám
Bus 210 Main bus station to main train station

WESTERN & CENTRAL SLOVAKIA

Trenčín

☎032 / POP 60,000

What's not to like about a place with a mighty clifftop castle, pretty Renaissance buildings and a lively university population? Roman legionnaires were the first tourists to arrive, establishing a garrison outpost here in the 2nd century. From the bus and train stations walk west through the city park and under the highway past the Tatra Hotel, where a street bears left uphill to **Mierové nám**, one of several contiguous pedestrian squares.

The town's highlight, reconstructed **Trenčín Castle** (www.muzeumtn.sk; admission €5; ⏲9am-5.30pm), dates from around the 15th century. You can wander the ramparts after paying admission, but visiting the palace rooms requires taking a 75-minute tour (included in admission). Minstrels and sword fighters bring medieval times to life during night tours in July and August. Carved in the rock below the castle is a Roman inscription from AD 179 that recalls the 2nd Legion's victory over the Germanic Kvad tribes. To see it you have to ask at the reception inside the **Hotel Tatra** (Gen MR Štefánika 2).

Staying over? **Penzión pri Parku** (☎0902979814; www.penzionpriparku.sk; Kragujevackých hrdinov 7; s/d €25/33; wi-fi) has spiffy, mod rooms in a Victorian near both the train and bus stations. **Penzión Svorad** (☎743 03 22; www.svorad-trencin.sk; Palackého 4; dm €19-26; no smoking) is a dormlike hostel in a grammar school. Neat little log cabins surround a small tent area on the island in the middle of the Vah River at **Autocamping na Ostrove** (☎7434 013; www.slovanet.sk/camping; Ostrov; campsites from €6, bungalows €14).

Numerous cafes, perfect for a drink or a nibble, line the town's pedestrian plazas. Chicken and risotto dishes at the **Cinema Movie Club Restaurant** (Palackého 33; mains €5-7; wi-fi) are quite popular with students, but the real steal is the weekday set menu lunch. On the island, **Reštaurácia Bašta**

WORTH A TRIP

SLOVAKIA'S NATIONAL PARKS

Slovakia has several national parks that encompass lower, forested mountains worth a visit. Sentinel-like formations stand watch at the entrance to hiker-friendly **Vratna Valley** (www.vratna.sk), the heart of **Malá Fatra National Park**. In **Slovenský raj National Park** (www.slovenskyraj.sk), ladders, chain assists and other technical aids make the challenging, narrow gorges and waterfalls accessible to those seeking a challenge.

(Ostrove Zamarovce; mains €5-15; 24hr) has some of the freshest, cooked-to-order Slovak classics we've tasted: pork stuffed with spicy *klobasa*, *bryndza* (sheep's cheese) cream soup... For nightlife, check out **Steps Bar** (Sládkovičova 4-6), which has cafe tables downstairs and a dance floor up.

Slovakia's largest music festival, **Bazant Pohoda Festival** (www.pohodafestival.sk), rocks the whole town one weekend in July. Find out more at the exceptionally helpful **Cultural Information Centre** (6504 294; www.visittrencin.sk; Sládkovičova 1; 9am-6pm Mon-Fri, 8am-4pm Sat). There are several banks and ATMs on Mierové nám.

Four IC trains from Bratislava (€9, 1½ hours) continue on from here to Poprad (€14, 2¾ hours) via Žilina (€8, one hour).

EASTERN SLOVAKIA

Alpine peaks, old towns and even older castles: eastern Slovakia's mountains are a must-see for anyone visiting the country.

High Tatras

052

Pristine snowfields, ultramarine mountain lakes, crashing waterfalls: the photo opportunities at upper elevations in the High Tatras (Vysoké Tatry) might get you fantasising about a career with *National Geographic*. The tallest range in the Carpathian Mountains contains more than 25 peaks that measure above 2500m. But at a compact 25km wide by 78km long, this isn't the Alps. Thank goodness, since prices here are comparatively low. (Hint: if you really want to save money, check out the Belá Tatras to the east.) A comprehensive network of tourist trails and ski tows, lifts and runs covers the range. Since 1949 most of the area has been part of Tatra National Park. Upper trails are officially closed when snow lingers from November to mid-June. August and September are the best months for high-altitude hiking; July can be rainy.

Three main resort towns string out mid-elevation, where traditionally thick pine forests took a beating in a serious wind storm but meadows and small trees are making a comeback. Starý Smokovec, a 20th-century resort town, is roughly central, with peaceful Tatranská Lomnica 11km east and overdeveloped lakeside Štrbské pleso 16km west. Poprad is the closest city, 14km below Smokovec.

Activities

More than 600km of hiking trails criss-cross the range and lead up to some peaks, with mountain huts to stop at along the way. Year-round, an extremely popular **gondola** (www.vt.sk; return €13; 8.30am-7pm Jul & Aug, to 4pm Sep-Jun) links Tatranská Lomnica with the bustling fun park and winter ski areas of **Skalnaté pleso** (1751m). The smaller **cable car** (www.vt.sk; return €20; 8.30am-5.30pm Jul & Aug, to 3.30pm Sep-Jun) that continues up from there to the precipitous 2634m summit of **Lomnický štít** is a don't-miss experience. With relatively little elevation change you can also hike three hours west of Skalnaté Pleso along a segment of the **Magistrála Trail**, past Zamkovského mountain hut, to **Hrebienok** (1280m). There a **funicular railway** (www.vt.sk; return €7; 7am-7pm Jul & Aug, 8am-5pm Sep-Jun) will shuttle you back down to Starý Smokovec and public transport.

Štrbské pleso also has several good day-hike options, including a three-hour return tromp up to **Popradské pleso** (1494m), an idyllic lake and chalet. Its year-round **chairlift** (www.parksnow.sk; return €7.50; 8am-3.30pm) leads to other hikes and ski runs.

Sleeping

A *chata* (mountain hut) along the upper-altitude trails may be anything from a hiker's shack to a full-service chalet. Some food is always available. For private rooms in Tatranská Lomnica and lower villages, booking online is recommended (www.tatry.sk and www.tanap.sk/homes.html). Hotel prices drop by at least a third from October to December and March through May.

STARÝ SMOKOVEC & AROUND

TOP CHOICE Penzión Tatra PENSION €

(☎0903650802; www.tatraski.sk; Starý Smokovec 66; s/d incl breakfast €25/50; @☎) Colourful modern rooms fill the super-central 1900s alpinesque building above the train station. Have your breakfast in the large common room or out on the terrace.

Pension Vesna PENSION €

(☎4422 774; www.penzionvesna.sk; Nový Smokovec 69; s/d €30/54) Family run and friendly. The seven rooms in this simple guest house are all spacious; some have three beds and a separate living area.

Bilíkova chata MOUNTAIN HUT €

(☎4422 439; www.bilikovachata.sk; Hrebienok; s/d without bathroom €25/50) Log chalet five minutes from the upper terminus of the funicular station; has private rooms and a full restaurant.

Zbojnícka chata MOUNTAIN HUT €

(☎0903638000; www.zbojnickachata.sk; dm incl breakfast €15) One 16-bed dorm and small kitchen; more than four hours' hike from Hrebienok.

TATRANSKÁ LOMNICA & AROUND

Penzión Encian PENSION €€

(☎4467 520; www.tatry.sk/encian; s/d €33/66) Steep roofs, overflowing flower boxes and a small restaurant hearth give Encian an appropriate mountain appeal. No genuine nonsmoking rooms; mercurial owner.

Hotel & Intercamp Tatranec CAMPING GROUND €

(☎4467 092; www.hoteltatranec.com; Tatranská Lomnica 202; campsites €6-9, r €40, cabins €60) The area's largest camping ground has ageing six-person cabins, motel and restaurant, around an open tent field. It's north of the 'T Lomnica zast' stop on the train line to Studený Potok.

Rijo Camping CAMPING GROUND €

(☎4467 493; www.rijocamping.eu; Stará Lesná 52; campsites €5-7.50; ⊙May-Sep) Pine trees shade much of this small, tent-only site; 1km north of Stará Lesná bus stop.

TOP CHOICE Zamkovského chata MOUNTAIN HUT €

(☎4422 636; www.zamka.sk; per person €15-20) Atmospheric wood chalet with four-bed bunk rooms and restaurant; midway between Skalnaté pleso and Hrebienok.

Chata pri Zelenom plese MOUNTAIN HUT €

(☎4467 420; www.zelenepleso.sk; dm €15) Fifty-bed lakeside lodging at 1540m; about 2½ hours' hike east of Skalnaté pleso, en route to the Belá Tatras.

> **SPLURGE**
>
> Most of Štrbské pleso is overdeveloped and overpriced. But if you're going to splash out, the lakefront **Grand Hotel Kempinski** (☎3262 222; www.kempinski-hightatras.com; Kupelna 6; r €199-300; ❄@≋) is far and away the swankiest Tatra accommodation, with evening turndown service, heated marble bathroom floors and incredible lake views.

Eating & Drinking

The three main villages are close enough to eat in one and sleep in another; each has a *potraviny* (grocery store).

TOP CHOICE Reštaurácia Svišť SLOVAK €€

(Nový Smokovec 30; mains €5-11) From hearty dumplings to beef fillet with a wine reduction, this stylish Slovak restaurant does it all well – and surprisingly reasonably.

Pizzeria La Montanara ITALIAN €

(Starý Smokovec 22; mains €4-7) A local favourite, La Montanara serves good pies, pastas, soups and vegetables. It's above a grocery store on the eastern edge of town.

Samoobslužná Reštaurácia SLOVAK €

(Hotel Toliar, Štrbské pleso 21; mains €2-6; ⊙7am-10pm) Self-service cafeteria with one-dish meals (goulash, chicken stir-fry etc) and vegetarian options.

Reštaurácia Stará Mama SLOVAK €€

(Shopping centre Sintra, Tatranská Lomnica; mains €5-12) A rustic fave; think substantial soups and homemade *pirohy* (half-moon-shaped dumplings served with sheep's cheese and bacon).

Tatry Pub PUB

(Tatra Komplex, Starý Smokovec; ⊙3pm-1am Sun-Thu, 3pm-3am Fri & Sat; ☎) The official watering hole of the Mountain Guide Club is a lively place to drink, with a full schedule of dart tournaments, concerts and the like.

Information

All three villages have ATMs and internet cafes. Note that information offices do not book rooms, but they do hand out a brochure listing some – not all – accommodations.

Tatra Information Office Starý Smokovec (TIK; ☎4423 440; www.tatry.sk; Starý Smokovec 23; ⊙8am-8pm Mon-Fri, to 1pm Sat) Largest area info office, with the most brochures.

TIK Štrbské pleso (☎4492 391; Štrbské Pleso; ⊙8am-4pm) Provides good trail info especially; up hill north from Hotel Toliar.

TIK Tatranská Lomnica (☎4468 118; Cesta Slobody; ⊙10am-6pm Mon-Fri, 9am-1pm Sat) Has the most helpful staff; opposite Penzión Encian on the main street.

Getting There & Around

To reach the Tatras by public transport you'll need to transfer in Poprad. From there a narrow-gauge electric train makes numerous stops in the resort towns along the main road; buses go to smaller downhill villages as well. Either way, to get between Štrbské pleso and Tatranská Lomnica, you have to change in Starý Smokovec. Check schedules at www.cp.atlas.sk.

BUS Buses run from Poprad to Starý Smokovec (€0.85, 20 minutes, half-hourly), Tatranská Lomnica (€1.10, 30 minutes, hourly) and Štrbské pleso (€1.60, one hour, every 45 minutes), and from Tatranská Lomnica to Ždiar (€1, 25 minutes, eight daily).

TRAIN During daylight hours, electric trains (TEZ) run at least every two hours. You can buy individual TEZ tickets at stations, and block tickets (one to three per trip) additionally at tourist offices. Validate all on-board. Services run from Poprad to Starý Smokovec (€0.70, 25 minutes), Tatranská Lomnica (€0.80, 25 minutes) and Štrbské pleso (€1.30, 1¼ hours); they also run from Štrbské pleso to Starý Smokovec (€1, 40 minutes) and Starý Smokovec to Tatranská Lomnica (€0.60, 10 minutes).

Belá Tatras

☎052

Travel east over the High Tatras mountain ridges and you start to hear Slovak spoken with a Polish accent. The Goral folk culture and wooden cottages give tiny Ždiar, the main settlement in the Belá Tatras (Belianské Tatry), a rustic, laid-back quality that the larger resort villages lack. From here it's an easy day trip or journey on to Poland; heck, you can walk there.

Several hiking trails lead off from the rural village lined with decorated timber cottages. The tiny **Ždiar House Museum** (Ždiarsky dom; admission €3; ⊙10am-4pm Tue-Sun) showcases colourful local folk costumes and has a restaurant attached.

TOP CHOICE **Ginger Monkey Hostel** (☎4498 084; www.gingermonkey.eu; Ždiar 294; dm/d €13/30; @📶) offers crushing mountain views from a comfy old Goral-style house. Hot tea at any hour, a laundry, a full kitchen with free breakfast, and hosts who are good fun make it clear that the world-travelling owners have picked up a tip or two along the way. A communal dinner may be served (by donation) or at weekends the whole group may go to one of several local eateries in the extended one-street village.

For more, check with **PLP Shop** (☎0903642492; www.zdiar.sk; Ždiar 333; ⊙9am-noon & 3-6pm), an info office with souvenirs, bicycle rental and internet use.

Bus is the mode of transport in the Belá Tatras. Poland's open EU border is only 14km north of Ždiar. For Slovak schedules, visit www.cp.atlas.sk; for Polish, www.strama.eu. Direct connections include Poprad (€1, one hour, 11 daily), Starý Smokovec (€1.60, 40 minutes, 11 daily), Tatranská Lomnica (€1, 30 minutes, 21 daily) and Zakopane (Poland; €2.50, 50 minutes, two daily).

Poprad

☎052 / POP 55,200

Poprad is an important transport transfer point for the High Tatras. Otherwise, it's known mainly for its giant thermal water park, **Aqua City** (☎7851 222; www.aquacitypoprad.sk; Športová 1397; day pass from €18; ⊙9am-9pm).

At the time of writing, **Poprad-Tatry International Airport** (☎7763 875; www.airport-poprad.sk; Na Letisko 100) receives no regular flights, but look for that to change.

Buses are best from here to Levoča (€1.60, 30 minutes, hourly), Bardejov (€4.50, 2¼ hours, four daily) and Zakopane (Poland; €5, two hours, two daily).

Four daily IC, and more 'Fast' trains, take you to Bratislava (€16, four hours), Trenčín (€14, 2¾ hours) and Košice (€5, 1½ hours).

Levoča

☎053 / POP 14,700

So this is what Slovakia looked like in the 14th century... Fairly complete medieval walls still protect the age-old centre from onslaught and, so far, international chain stores have been held at bay. **Nám Majstra Pavla**, Levoča's main square, is chock-a-block with superb Gothic and Renaissance buildings, a few of which contain small museums. The **tourist information**

office (☎4513 763; www.levoca.sk; Nám Majstra Pavla 58; ⏲9am-noon & 12.30-4pm) has a handy free photocopied map, which you have to request. The spindles-and-spires **Church of St Jacob** (Chrám sv Jakuba; Nám Majstra Pavla; admission €3; ⏲by tour 11am-4pm Mon, 8.30am-4pm Tue-Sat, 1-4pm Sun), and its 16m-high carved wooden altar (1517) carved by renowned Master Pavol of Levoča, are the pride of the town. Purchase tickets at the Municipal Weights House opposite the north door. Next to the Gothic **town hall** *(radnica)*, also centre square, stands a 16th-century **cage of shame** for naughty boys and girls.

Two- to four-bed rooms in the hostel-like guest house **Oáza** (☎4514 511; www.ubytovanieoaza.sk; Nová 65; dm incl breakfast €10) surround a central, shared garden, complete with chickens. **Hotel Arkáda** (☎4512 372; www.arkada.sk; Nám Majstra Pavla 26; s/d €36/52; @ 📶) has uninspired Old Town rooms, but an atmospheric cellar restaurant. **Reštaurácia Slovenka** (☎4512 339; Nám Majstra Pavla 66; mains €3-7) is the best place in town to get homemade, traditional Slovak sheep's-cheese dishes.

Bus travel is most practical here. The local bus stop at Nám Štefana Kluberta is closer to town than the main station, which is 1km southeast of centre. Buses run to Spiš Castle/Spišské Podhradie (€1, 20 minutes, 11 daily), Košice (€4.50, two hours, five daily) and Poprad (€1.60, 30 minutes, hourly, transfer to the High Tatras or the main train line).

Spišské Podhradie

☎053 / POP 3830

The 4-hectare ruins of Unesco World Heritage site **Spiš Castle** (www.spisskemuzeum.com; admission €4.50; ⏲9am-7pm May-Oct) are eerie enough. Just imagine how imposing the fortress complex crowning the ridge on the eastern side of Spišské Podhradie was in full form. Historic chronicles first mention Spiš Castle in 1209, and the central residential tower, at the highest elevation, is thought to date from that time. Few structures are whole, but there's a **cistern**, a **Romanesque palace** that contains the very small museum, and the **chapel** adjacent to it. Opt for the excellent, legend-filled English-language audio.

A kilometre west of Spišské Podhradie is the still-active **Spiš Chapter** (Spišská Kapitula 1; admission €1; ⏲10am-noon & 1-5pm Mon-Sat), a 13th-century Catholic complex and church encircled by a 16th-century wall.

MORE CASTLES TO CONQUER

If you like Spiš Castle, you'll love that there are dozens more castles to conquer around Slovakia. Numerous local books and maps list them, or you can look online at www.castles.sk. Heck, you could just buy a detailed map, locate a castle-ruin symbol and start hiking. Fortress remains litter hillside public trails above rivers. A few more complete castles to look for:

» **Bojnice** (www.bojnice.sk) Central, near Prievidza

» **Orava** (www.oravamuzeum.sk) North, above Ružomberok

» **Stará Lubovňa** (www.muzeumsl.sk) East of the Tatras

Buses connect with Levoča (€1, 20 minutes) and Poprad (€2.50, 50 minutes) about hourly, making this an easy full-day trip from Levoča or the Tatras. Buses stop 1km west of the castle and 1km east of Spiš Chapter in the village centre.

Košice

☎055 / POP 235,300

An eclectic mix of ancient to art-nouveau architecture makes Slovakia's second city eminently agreeable. Though industry rings the city's outskirts today (US Steel is the town's main employer), the Old Town heart is alive and well. Locals are constantly out and about on the long, garden- and fountain-filled pedestrian square, Hlavná, which contains most of the town's sights and restaurants.

The dark and brooding 14th-century **Cathedral of St Elizabeth** (Dóm sv Alžbety, Hlavná; church free, tower €1; ⏲1-3pm Mon, 9am-5pm Tue-Fri, 9am-1pm Sat) wins the prize for sight most likely to grace your Košice postcard home. Explore the medieval defence chambers and waterways in the excavations of the **Lower Gate Underground Museum** (Hlavná; admission €1; ⏲10am-6pm Tue-Sun), discovered during city building work in 1996.

For cheap sleeps, the **City Information Centre** (☎6258 888; www.kosice.sk; Hlavná 59; ⏲9am-6pm Mon-Fri, 9am-1pm Sat, 1-5pm Sun Jun-Sep, closed Sun Oct-May) lists student dorms open in summer; otherwise, **K2** (☎6255 948; Štúrova 32; s/d without bathroom €16/27) is a faded but well-located worker hostel. You'll find more charm at **Penzión Slovakia** (☎7289 820; www.penzionslovakia.sk; Orliá 6; s/d €45/55; ❄📶), a small city guest house, and more design-driven style at **Chrysso Penzión** (☎6230 450; www.penzionchrysso.sk; Zvonárska 3; s/d/apt €58/68/78; ❄📶).

Hlavná has cafes and pubs aplenty. **Karczma Mlyn** (Hlavná 82; mains €3-8) is good for a pint and heaping portions of hearty traditional Slovak fare. **Cafe Napoli** (Hlavná 82; mains €4-11) serves tasty wood-fired pizzas and has a lengthy cocktail list. Look, too, for sandwich and ice-cream shops, plus a **Tesco** (Hlavná 69) grocery store for self-catering.

Košice International Airport (KSC; www.airportkosice.sk) is 6km southeast of the centre (via bus 23). **Danube Wings** (V5; www.danubewings.eu) operates two daily flights to Bratislava, on weekdays only.

The adjacent bus and train stations are an easy five minutes' walk east of the Old Town; follow Mlynské to Hlavná.

Buses are most efficient for Levoča (€4.50, two hours, five daily), Bardejov (€4, two hours, 12 daily) and Uzhhorod (Ukraine; €7, two to three hours, three daily).

Direct trains run to Poprad (€5, 1½ hours, four IC trains daily), Bratislava (€19, four IC trains daily), Miskolc (Hungary; €5, 1¼ hours, two daily), Lviv (Ukraine; €32, 22½ hours, nightly) and Moscow (€85, 36 hours, nightly).

Bardejov

☎054 / POP 33,400

All steep roofs and flat fronts, pastel hues and paint-and-plaster details, Bardejov's 15th-century Gothic-Renaissance town square has been enthusiastically well preserved (Unesco thinks so, too). The **Tourist Information Centre** (☎4723 013; www.bardejov.sk; Radničné nám 21; ⌚9am-5.30pm Mon-Fri, 11.30am-3.30pm Sat & Sun, closed Sat & Sun Oct-Apr) provides free, walking-tour-like maps of the main square, which has a few small museums. The excellent **Icon Exposition** (Expozícia ikony; Radničné nám 27; adult/concession €2/1; ⌚8am-noon & 12.30-4pm Tue-Sun) boasts more than 130 dazzling icons (16th to 19th centuries), which shed light on the region's eastern Christian religions. Nearby **Bardejovské Kúpele** (www.bardejovske-kupele.sk), 3km north, is a leafy spa town with an excellent rustic village museum and wooden churches (see opposite).

Bunk out near the old fortified walls at **Penzión Hradby** (☎0918349229; www.penzion-hradby.sk; Stöcklova 8; s/d/tr €20/28/40; 📶); rooms share a fully equipped kitchen. Grilled meat platters at **La Bello** (Radničné nám 50; mains €4-11) are quite the bargain.

No trains connect directly with Bardejov, but buses make the run to/from Košice (€4, 1¾ hours, 12 daily), Poprad (€4.50, 2¼ hours, five daily) and beyond.

UNDERSTAND SLOVAKIA

History

Slavic tribes wandered west into what would become Slovakia around the 5th century; by the 9th, the territory was part of the short-lived Great Moravian Empire. Subsequently the Magyars (Hungarians) moved in next door and laid claim to the whole territory for the next 800 or so years.

In the 19th century Slovak intellectuals cultivated ties with the Czechs, and after WWI took the nation into the united Czechoslovakia. The day before Hitler's troops invaded Czech territory in March 1939, a fascist puppet state set up the first independent Slovakia as a German ally. It was not a populist move, however, and in August 1944 Slovak partisans instigated the ill-fated Slovak National Uprising (Slovenské Národné Povstanie, or SNP), inspiring countless future street names.

After 1948, power was centralised in Prague until the 1989 Velvet Revolution brought down the curtain on communism. Vladimír Mečiar and the Movement for a Democratic Slovakia (HZDS) brought to power a zealous nationalism. Without ref-

WOODEN CHURCHES

Look, no nails. A handful of Slovakia's mostly Greek Catholic (Uniate) and Orthodox hand-hewn wooden churches, constructed using wood joinery, are among the more recent Slovak additions to Unesco's World Heritage list. The best place to see them is outside Bardejov in Bardejovské Kúpele's village museum. But other examples (often locked) are located in small eastern villages. For a full list, check out **Wooden Architecture in Prešovsky Kraj** (www.po-kraj.sk/en/presov-region/remains/wooden-architecture/).

AN ICE-HOCKEY OBSESSION

Wander into any bar or restaurant during puck-pushing season (September to April) and 12 large men and an ice rink will never be far from the TV screen. Stoking the obsessive fires is the fact that Slovakia hosted the IIHF World Championships in the spring of 2011.

erendum, but peacefully, the Czechoslovak federation dissolved on 1 January 1993. Slovakia became an independent nation and the balance of power shifted from left to right and back again. In May 2004, the country entered NATO and the EU, and in January 2009 adopted the euro as its official currency. Bratislava and the High Tatras were the first areas to bounce back from the subsequent global economic downturn and investment once again pours in.

People

A deeply religious (84% of the population of 5.5 million claim religious affiliation, 80% of which are Catholic) and familial people, Slovaks have strong social ties and a deep sense of folk traditions. Young people are generally warm and open, often speaking English, but there can be a reserve about the older generations. If you're able to break through (asking for help often works), the shell cracks to reveal amazing generosity and hospitality.

Folk Arts

Traditional folk arts, crafts, music and dance continue to flourish in Slovakia. Úľuv is the national artisan collective, with stores all over the country. Watch for the colourful costumes and upbeat folk music (punctuated by stomps and squeals) featured at the frequent summer festivals nationwide.

Food

Price ranges in this chapter are based on the cost of a main course:

€€€ more than €12

€€ €6 to €12

€ less than €6

Environment

A hilly, forested country for the most part, Slovakia straddles the northwestern end of the Carpathian Mountains. Not to be missed is High Tatras (Vysoké Tatry) National Park, a rocky alpine range that seems to rise out of nowhere. National parks and protected areas comprise 20% of the territory and the entire country is laced with a network of trails. With such great scenery it's not surprising that most Slovaks spend their weekends outdoors. You will doubtless run into a backpack-toting Slovak wherever you walk in nature.

SURVIVAL GUIDE

Directory A–Z

Accommodation

Backpacker-style, service-loaded hostels (from €10 to €20 per bed) are numerous in Bratislava, but almost non-existent elsewhere (besides Ždiar in the Belá Tatras). Pensions are reasonably priced and numerous outside the capital. University dorms are open to all lodgers in July and August; enquire at local tourist offices.

Camping grounds often have older facilities, fields for tents and small bungalows. A full list of camping grounds is available at www.slovakia.travel. Camping wild is prohibited.

In this chapter we've quoted main-season rates (May to September); prices rise during Christmas and Easter holidays and drop 10% to 50% from October to April. Price ranges used in this chapter are as follows:

€€€ more than €150

€€ €60 to €150

€ less than €60

Business Hours

Most museums and castles are closed on Monday, and tourist attractions outside the capital may only open from May to September.

Banks 8am-5pm Mon-Thu, to 4pm Fri

Bars noon-midnight or 1am

Clubs 4pm-4am Wed-Sun

Post offices 8am-7pm Mon-Fri, to 11am Sat

Restaurants 11am-10pm

Shops 9am-5pm Mon-Fri, 9am-noon Sat; department stores have longer hours

Gay & Lesbian Travellers

Homosexuality has been legal in Slovakia since the 1960s, but this is a conservative, mostly Catholic country. A GLBT scene only really exists in Bratislava, and it's super small. Check out www.gay.sk.

Money

Since January 2009, Slovakia's currency has been the euro. It was formerly the Slovak crown (Slovenská koruna; Sk).

ATMs are common, even in smaller towns. Credit cards are accepted at most hotels, some restaurants and train stations (only if you announce ahead that you plan to pay by card).

Telephone

When calling from abroad, drop the initial 0 from the area code; in country, include it. To dial out internationally from Slovakia, dial ☎00.

Slovakia uses the GSM (900/1800MHz) and 3G UMTS mobile-phone networks, operated by Orange, T-Mobile and O2.

Tourist Information

Association of Information Centres of Slovakia (AICES; ☎16 186; www.aices.sk) Extensive network of city information centres.

Slovak Tourist Board (www.slovakia.travel) Online only.

Visas

No visas are required for EU citizens. Visa-free stays of up to 90 days are available for visitors from Australia, New Zealand, Canada, Japan and the US. Visas are required for South African nationals, among others. For a full visa list, see www.mzv.sk (under 'Ministry' and then 'Travel').

Getting There & Away

Air

Bratislava's intra-European airport is small. Vienna (Austria), 60km west, is the nearest major transcontinental air hub. Airlines operating in Slovakia:

Austrian Airlines (OS; www.aua.com) Connects Košice with Vienna.

Czech Airlines (OK; www.czechairlines.com) Links Prague with Bratislava and Košice.

Danube Wings (V5; www.danubewings.eu) Connects Bratislava with Basel (Switzerland); has summer flights to Italian and Croatian holiday destinations.

Lot Airlines (WAW; www.lot.com) Flies four days a week between Bratislava and Warsaw.

Ryanair (FR; www.ryanair.com) Connects Bratislava with numerous destinations all across the UK and Italy, plus coastal Spain, Paris, Brussels and Stockholm.

Land

There are no border posts between Slovakia and fellow EU Schengen member states, Czech Republic, Hungary, Poland and Austria. This makes checks at the Ukrainian crossing all the more strident.

BUS & TRAIN

Local buses connect Poprad and Ždiar with Zakopane (Poland). International bus lines **Eurobus** (www.eurobus.sk) and **Eurolines** (www.slovaklines.sk) head across Europe from Bratislava and east to Ukraine from Košice.

International and domestic train schedules can be found at www.cp.atlas.sk. Trains run directly from Bratislava to Austria, Czech Republic, Poland and Hungary, and from Košice to Czech Republic, Poland, Ukraine and Russia.

CAR & MOTORCYCLE

Private vehicles heading into Slovakia must have registration papers, Green Card (third-party liability) insurance, nationality stickers, first-aid kits and warning triangles.

River

Hydrofoils connect Vienna and Budapest with Bratislava, from April through October.

Getting Around

Checking nationwide bus, train and plane schedules is easiest at www.cp.atlas.sk.

Air

Danube Wings (V5; www.danubewings.eu) provides the only domestic air service, weekdays between Bratislava and Košice.

Bicycle

Roads are often narrow and in towns cobblestones and tram tracks can be a dangerous combination. Theft is a problem, so a lock is a must. The cost of transporting a bicycle by rail is usually 10% of the train ticket, but not all trains have bicycle compartments.

Bus & Train

Slovenská autobusová doprava (SAD; www.sad.sk) operates a comprehensive national bus network, comparable to train prices; it's most useful in the mountains.

Rail is the main way to get around Slovakia, and **Slovak Republic Railways** (Železnice Slovenskej republiky; www.zsr.sk) provides an efficient national service. Information listed in this chapter is for the quickest, Intercity and Eurocity (IC/EC) trains. Rychlík (R), or 'Fast' trains take longer but run more frequently and cost less. Osobný (Ob) trains stop in every tiny village.

Car & Motorcycle

Foreign driving licences with photo are valid in Slovakia. Toll stickers (*nálepka;* available at petrol stations) are required on all green-signed motorways, and hefty fines are levied for not having them. City parking restrictions are eagerly enforced; buy a ticket from a machine, attendant or newsagent.

Local Transport

Towns have extensive bus and tram networks (no metros) that run from 4.30am to 11.30pm. Tickets can be purchased at news agents and from machines; validate on board or risk serious fines.

Slovenia

Includes »

Best Places to Eat

» Špajza, Llubljana (p1106)

» Gostilna Pri Planincu, Bled (p1109)

» Pri Mari, Piran (p1114)

Best Places to Stay

» Celica Hostel, Llubljana (p1103)

» Traveller's Haven, Bled (p1109)

» Alibi Hostels, Piran (p1113)

Why Go?

It's a pint-sized place, no doubt about that. But 'good things come in small packages', and never was that old chestnut more appropriate than in describing Slovenia (Slovenija). Slovenia has been dubbed a lot of different things by its PR machine – 'Europe in Miniature', the 'Sunny Side of the Alps', the 'Green Piece of Europe' – and they're all true. From beaches, snow-capped mountains and hills awash in grape vines to Gothic churches and baroque palaces, Slovenia has everything.

Its incredible mixture of climates brings warm Mediterranean breezes up to the foothills of the Alps, where it can snow in summer. And with well over half of its total area covered in forest, Slovenia really is one of the 'greenest' countries in the world. In recent years, it has taken on the role of Europe's activities playground.

When To Go

Ljubljana

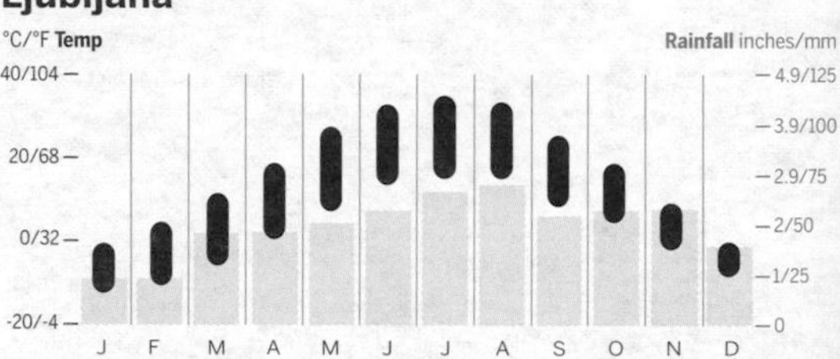

Apr–Jun Spring is a great time to be in the lowlands and the flower-carpeted valleys of Gorenjska.

Sep This is the month made for everything – still warm enough to swim and tailor-made for hiking.

Dec–Mar Everyone (and their grandmother) dons their skis in this winter sport–mad country.

Connections

Border formalities with Slovenia's three European Union neighbours – Italy, Austria and Hungary – are nonexistent and all are accessible by train and (less frequently) bus. Venice can also be reached by boat from the coast. Expect a somewhat closer inspection of your documents when travelling to/from non-EU Croatia.

ITINERARIES

One Week

Spend a couple of days in Ljubljana, then head north to unwind in Bled or Bohinj beside idyllic mountain lakes. Take a bus or drive over the hair-raising Vršič Pass into the valley of the vivid blue Soča River and take part in some adventure sports in Bovec before returning to Ljubljana.

Two Weeks

Another week will allow you to see just about everything in this chapter: all of the above as well as the Karst caves at Škocjan and Postojna and the Venetian ports of Koper and Piran on the Adriatic.

Essential Food & Drink

» **Pršut** Air-dried, thinly sliced ham from the Karst region, not unlike Italian prosciutto.

» **Žlikrofi** Ravioli-like parcels filled with cheese, bacon and chives.

» **Žganci** The Slovenian stodge of choice – groats made from barley or corn but usually *ajda* (buckwheat).

» **Potica** A kind of nut roll eaten at teatime or as a dessert.

» **Wine** Distinctively Slovenian tipples include peppery red Teran from the Karst region and Malvazija, a straw-colour white wine from the coast.

AT A GLANCE

» **Currency** Euro

» **Language** Slovene

» **Money** ATMs are everywhere

» **Visas** Schengen rules apply; see p1319

Fast Facts

» **Area** 20,273 sq km

» **Capital** Ljubljana

» **Country code** ☎386

» **Emergency** ambulance/fire ☎112; police ☎113

Exchange Rates

Australia	A$1	€0.72
Canada	C$1	€0.74
Japan	¥100	€0.87
New Zealand	NZ$1	€0.56
UK	UK£1	€1.16
USA	US$1	€0.72

Set Your Budget

» **Budget hotel room** €40

» **Two-course evening meal** €20

» **Museum entrance** €3

» **Bottle of beer in shop/bar** €1/3

» **100km by train/bus** €6.03/9.20

Resources

» **E-uprava** (http://e-uprava.gov.si) Official portal with info and many links

» **Slovenia Times** (www.sloveniatimes.com) Press agency's biweekly magazine

» **Slovenian Landmarks** (www.burger.si)

LJUBLJANA

☎01 / POP 257,675

Charming Ljubljana has a perfectly formed Old Town, a vibrant street-cafe culture and a large student community. Add some excellent museums and galleries, atmospheric bars and varied, accessible nightlife and the Slovenian capital can sometimes feel like a mini-Prague or a Lilliputian Kraków.

Prešernov trg, on the left bank of the Ljubljanica River, is the heart of Ljubljana. Just across Triple Bridge below Castle Hill is the Old Town.

Sights

Delightfully sprinkled with cafes, **Mestni trg**, **Stari trg** and **Gornji trg** wend picturesquely beneath a bluff crowned by **Ljubljana Castle** (☎306 4293; www.ljubljanafestival.si;

Slovenia Highlights

1. Experience the architecture, hilltop castle, green spaces and cafe life of **Ljubljana** (p1102), Slovenia's beloved capital
2. Wax romantic in picture-postcard **Bled** (p1108), with a lake, an island and a castle as a backdrop
3. Get into the outdoors at **Bovec** (p1112), one of the country's major outdoor-activities centres
4. Explore the karst caves at **Škocjan** (p1112), with scenes straight out of Jules Verne's *A Journey to the Centre of the Earth*
5. Swoon at the wonderful Venetian architecture in the romantic port of **Piran** (p1113)

admission free; ⌚9am-11pm summer, 10am-9pm winter). Up here the best views are from the 19th-century **watchtower** (admission €5; ⌚9am-9pm summer, 10am-6pm winter). The fastest way to reach the castle is via the **funicular** (return ticket €3; ⌚9am-11pm summer, 10am-9pm winter) from Krekov trg.

Ljubljana's main square, **Prešernov trg**, showcases the salmon-pink **Franciscan Church of the Annunciation** (1660), the **Prešeren Monument** (1905) to the nation's favourite poet, France Prešeren, and **Triple Bridge**, a work by prolific architect Jože Plečnik.

East of the bridge is the **Central Market**, the frescoed **Cathedral of St Nicholas** (Dolničarjeva ul 1; ⌚10am-noon & 3-6pm), dating from the early 18th century, and the much loved **Dragon Bridge**, whose guardian dragons are city mascots.

The grand main building of **Ljubljana University** (Kongresni trg 12) was erected as a ducal palace in 1902. The more restrained **Philharmonic Hall** (Kongresni trg 10) dates from 1898 and is home to the Slovenian Philharmonic Orchestra.

West of main Slovenska c is the impressive **National Gallery** (☎241 54 18; www.ng-slo.si; Prešernova c 24 & Cankarjeva c 20; admission €7; ⌚10am-6pm Tue-Sun) and **National Museum of Slovenia** (☎241 44 00; www.nms.si; Prešernova c 20; admission €3; ⌚10am-6pm Fri-Wed, 10am-8pm Thu), the latter in an elegant 1888 building. Admission to each is free on the first Sunday of the month.

Sleeping

The TIC (p1108) has comprehensive details of **private rooms** (from s/d €30/50) and **apartments** (from d/q €55/80), though only a handful are central.

TOP CHOICE Celica Hostel HOSTEL €€
(☎230 97 00; www.hostelcelica.com; Metelkova ul 8; dm €17-21, s/d/tr cell €53/56/66, 3- to 5-bed r per person €21-26, 7-bed r per person €19-23; @📶) This stylishly former prison (1882) in Metelkova has 20 'cells', complete with their original bars, nine rooms and apartments with three to seven beds and a popular 12-bed dorm. The ground floor is home to three cafes and a gallery.

Penzion Pod Lipo PENSION €€
(☎031-809 893; www.penzion-podlipo.com; Borštnikov trg 3; d/tr/q €64/75/100; @) Atop a venerable old *gostilna* (inn), this 10-room place offers excellent value right in the centre. We love the communal kitchen, the sunny, east-facing terrace and the computer in each room.

SPLURGE

Ljubljana's original boutique hotel, **Antiq Hotel** (☎421 35 60; www.antiqhotel.si; Gornji trg 3; s €61-133, d €77-168; @) has 16 spacious rooms and apartments in the Old Town and a multilevel back garden. The decor is kitsch with a smirk, and there are fabulous little touches throughout. The two cheapest rooms (Nos 2 and 9) have their own bathrooms (but they're in the corridor).

Zeppelin Hostel HOSTEL €
(☎051-637 436; www.zeppelinhostel.com; 2nd fl, Slovenska c 47; dm €18-24, d €49-60; @📶) Located in a historic building, this hostel with three large and bright dorm rooms (four to eight beds) and three doubles (one with en suite) is run by an affable Slovenian–Spanish couple.

H2O HOSTEL €
(☎041-662 266; info@simbol.si; Petkovškovo nabrežje 47; dm/d/q €17/50/68; @📶) On the Ljubljanica, this hostel with six rooms each with a kitchen wraps around a tiny courtyard. One room has views of the castle.

Alibi Hostel HOSTEL €
(☎251 12 44; www.alibi.si; Cankarjevo nabrežje 27; dm €15-18, d €40-50; @📶) This well-situated 106-bed hostel right on the Ljubljanica has brightly painted, airy dorm rooms with four to eight wooden bunks and a dozen doubles.

Ljubljana Resort CAMPING GROUND €
(☎568 39 13; www.ljubljanaresort.si; Dunajska c 270; campsite per person €7.50-13.50; @🏊) It's got a pretty grandiose name, but wait till you see the facilities at this attractive six-hectare camping ground and resort 5km north of the centre (bus 6 or 11).

Eating

Handy supermarkets include a **Mercator** (Slovenska c 55; ⌚7am-9pm) southwest of the stations and the enormous **Maximarket** (basement, Trg Republike 1; ⌚9am-9pm Mon-Fri, 8am-5pm Sat). The colourful **open-air market** (Pogačarjev trg & Vodnikov trg; ⌚6am-6pm Mon-Fri, to 4pm Sat summer, 6am-4pm Mon-Sat winter) is north and east of the cathedral.

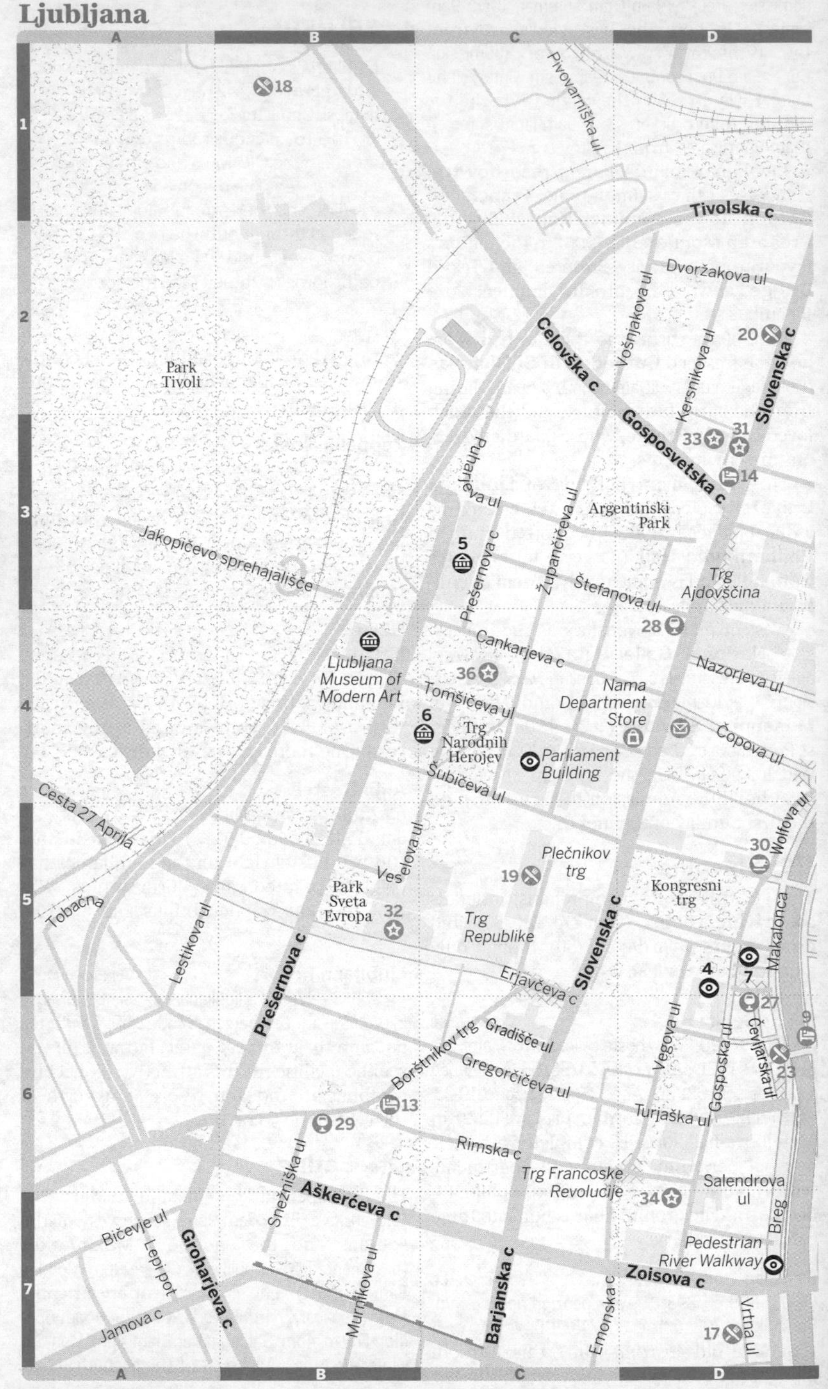
Pivovarniška ul
Tivolska c
Dvoržakova ul
Vošnjakova ul
Kersnikova ul
Slovenska c
Celovška c
Gosposvetska c
Park Tivoli
Puharjeva ul
Argentinski Park
Župančičeva ul
Prešernova c
Jakopičevo sprehajališče
Štefanova ul
Trg Ajdovščina
Ljubljana Museum of Modern Art
Cankarjeva c
Nazorjeva ul
Tomšičeva ul
Nama Department Store
Trg Narodnih Herojev
Parliament Building
Čopova ul
Šubičeva ul
Cesta 27 Aprila
Wolfova ul
Veselova ul
Plečnikov trg
Kongresni trg
Tobačna
Park Sveta Evropa
Trg Republike
Lestikova ul
Makalonca
Erjavčeva c
Prešernova c
Slovenska c
Vegova ul
Gosposka ul
Čevljarska ul
Borštnikov trg
Gradišče ul
Gregorčičeva ul
Turjaška ul
Rimska c
Snežniška ul
Trg Francoske Revolucije
Salendrova ul
Aškerčeva c
Bičevje ul
Lepi pot
Groharjeva c
Breg
Pedestrian River Walkway
Zoisova c
Murnikova ul
Barjanska c
Emonska c
Jamova c
Vrtna ul
SLOVENIA LJUBLJANA

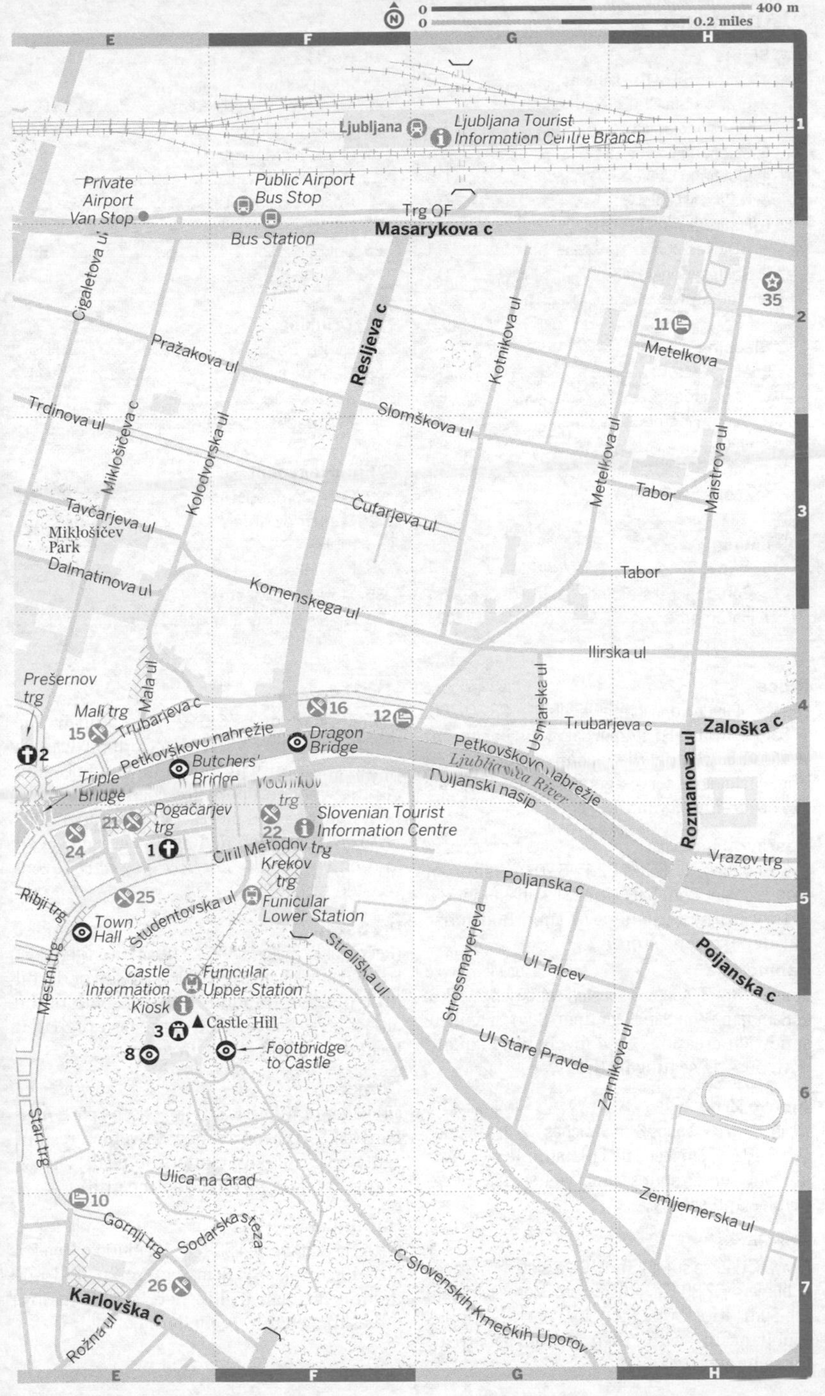
0 400 m
0 0.2 miles
Ljubljana
Ljubljana Tourist Information Centre Branch
Private Airport Van Stop
Public Airport Bus Stop
Bus Station
Trg OF
Masarykova c
Cigaletova ul
Resljeva c
Kotnikova ul
35
11
Metelkova
Pražakova ul
Trdinova ul
Slomškova ul
Miklošičeva c
Kolodvorska ul
Metelkova ul
Maistrova ul
Tabor
Tavčarjeva ul
Čufarjeva ul
Miklošičev Park
Dalmatinova ul
Komenskega ul
Tabor
Ilirska ul
Prešernov trg
Mala ul
Mali trg
Trubarjeva c
16
12
Usnjarska ul
Trubarjeva c
Zaloška c
15
2
Petkovškovo nabrežje
Dragon Bridge
Butchers' Bridge
Petkovškovo nabrežje
Ljubljanica River
Poljanski nasip
Rozmanova ul
Triple Bridge
Vodnikov trg
Pogačarjev trg
21
22
Slovenian Tourist Information Centre
24
1
Ciril Metodov trg
Krekov trg
Vrazov trg
Poljanska c
25
Ribji trg
Študentovska ul
Funicular Lower Station
Town Hall
Streliška ul
Strossmayerjeva
Ul Talcev
Poljanska c
Mestni trg
Castle Information Kiosk
Funicular Upper Station
3
Castle Hill
8
Footbridge to Castle
Ul Stare Pravde
Zarnikova ul
Stari trg
Ulica na Grad
10
Zemljemerska ul
Gornji trg
Sodarska steza
26
C Slovenskih Kmečkih Uporov
Karlovška c
Rožna ul
E
F
G
H
1
2
3
4
5
6
7

Ljubljana

Sights

1 Cathedral of St Nicholas ... E5
2 Franciscan Church of the Annunciation ... E4
3 Ljubljana Castle ... E6
4 Ljubljana University ... D5
5 National Gallery ... C3
6 National Museum of Slovenia ... C4
7 Philharmonic Hall ... D5
8 Watchtower ... E6

Sleeping

9 Alibi Hostel ... D6
10 Antiq Hotel ... E7
11 Celica Hostel ... H2
12 H2O ... F4
13 Penzion Pod Lipo ... B6
14 Zeppelin Hostel ... D3

Eating

15 Ajdovo Zrno ... E4
16 Čompa ... F4
17 Harambaša ... D7
18 Hot Horse ... B1
19 Maximarket ... C5
20 Mercator Supermarket ... D2
21 Open-air Market ... E5
22 Open-air Market ... F5
23 Paninoteka ... D6
Restavracija 2000 ... (see 19)
24 Ribca ... E5
25 Sokol ... E5
26 Špajza ... E7

Drinking

27 Dvorni Bar ... D6
28 Nebotičnik ... D4
29 Žmavc ... B6
30 Zvezda ... D5

Entertainment

31 Cafe Compañeros ... D3
32 Cankarjev Dom ... B5
33 Klub K4 ... D3
34 Križanke ... D7
35 Metelkova Mesto ... H2
36 Opera House ... C4

Ribca SEAFOOD €
(Adamič-Lundrovo nabrežje 1; dishes €3.30-7.60; 8am-4pm Mon-Fri, to 2pm Sat) This basement seafood bar below the Plečnik Colonnade in Pogačarjev trg serves generous set lunches (€7.50) to hungry market-goers.

Restavracija 2000 SELF-SERVICE €
(Trg Republike 1; dishes €2.15-3.70; 9am-7pm Mon-Fri, 9am-3pm Sat) Upbeat self-service eatery in the basement of the Maximarket department store.

Paninoteka SANDWICH BAR €
(Jurčičev trg 3; soups & toasted sandwiches €3-6; 8am-1am Mon-Sat, 9am-11pm Sun) Healthy sandwich creations on a lovely little square with outside seating by the river.

Ajdovo Zrno VEGETARIAN €
(Trubarjeva c 7; soups & sandwiches €2-4, set lunch €6; 10am-7pm Mon-Fri) This simple vegetarian cafe serves soups, sandwiches, fried vegetables and salads.

Hot Horse BURGERS €
(www.hot-horse.si; Park Tivoli, Celovška c 25; snacks & burgers €2.80-6; 10am-6am Mon, 9am-6am Tue-Sun) Kiosk in the city park supplies Ljubljančani with their favourite treat: horse burgers.

TOP CHOICE **Špajza** SLOVENIAN €€
(Gornji trg 28; mains €15-22; noon-11pm) The 'Pantry' is a nicely decorated rabbit warren of a restaurant with rough-hewn tables and chairs, wooden floors, frescoed ceilings and nostalgic bits and pieces. Try the stupendous *žlikrofi* (pasta stuffed with cheese, bacon and chives) or the *kozliček iz pečiče* (oven-roasted kid).

Pri Škofu SLOVENIAN €€
(Rečna ul 8; mains €8-22; 10am-midnight Mon-Fri, noon-midnight Sat & Sun) This wonderful little place in tranquil Krakovo, south of the city centre, serves some of the best prepared local dishes and salads in town.

Čompa SLOVENIAN €€
(Trubarjeva c 40; mains €10-18; noon-3pm & 7pm-1am Mon-Sat) Favourite new Slovenian restaurant serves massive platters of meats, cheese and vegetables *na žaru* (on the grill).

Harambaša BALKAN €
(Vrtna ul 8; dishes €4.50-6; 10am-10pm Mon-Fri, noon-10pm Sat, noon-6pm Sun) You'll find authentic Bosnian dishes here served at low tables in a charming modern cottage.

Sokol SLOVENIAN €
(Ciril Metodov trg 18; mains €7-20; ⏲7am-11pm Mon-Sat, 10am-11pm Sun) In an old vaulted house, traditional Slovenian food is served by costumed waiters.

Drinking

Central Ljubljana has a concentration of inviting cafes and bars.

Žmavc CAFE-BAR
(Rimska c 21; ⏲7.30am-1am Mon-Fri, from 10am Sat, from 6pm Sun) Super-popular student hang-out west of Slovenska c, with manga comic-strip scenes and graffiti decorating the walls.

Zvezda CAFE
(Kongresni trg 4 or Wolfova ul 14; ⏲7am-11pm Mon-Sat, 10am-8pm Sun) The 'Star' is celebrated for its shop-made cakes, especially *skutina pečena*, an eggy cheesecake.

Nebotičnik CAFE-BAR
(12th fl, Štefanova ul 1; ⏲8am-3am) This cafe-bar with its breathtaking terrace atop Ljubljana's famed Art Deco 'Skyscraper' (1933) has spectacular views.

Dvorni Bar WINE BAR
(Dvorni trg 2; ⏲8am-1am Mon-Sat, 9am-midnight Sun) This wine bar stocks more than 100 varieties and is an excellent place to taste Slovenian vintages.

Sax Pub PUB
(Eipprova ul 7; ⏲noon-1am Mon, 10am-1am Tue-Sat, 4-10pm Sun) Over two decades in Trnovo, the colourful Sax has live or canned jazz depending on the day of the week and time of year.

☆ Entertainment

The free bimonthly **Ljubljana in Your Pocket** (www.inyourpocket.com) is your best source of information though **Ljubljana.info** (www.ljubljana.info) has listings as well.

Nightclubs

Metelkova Mesto CLUBS
(www.metelkova.org; Masarykova c 24) 'Metelkova Town', an ex-army garrison taken over by squatters after independence, contains a number of idiosyncratic clubs, bars and art spaces that generally come to life after midnight, daily in summer and at weekends the rest of the year. Venues come in and go out; try to wade though the website or just stroll over and have a look yourself. It's just behind the Celica Hostel.

Cafe Compañeros CLUB
(Slovenska c 51; ⏲11am-5am) Raucous studenty hang-out with a lounge and terrace bar on the ground floor and a wild and crazy club with live music below.

Klub K4 CLUB
(www.klubk4.org; Kersnikova ul 4; ⏲10pm-2am Tue, 11pm-4am Wed & Thu, 11pm-6am Fri & Sat, 10pm-4am Sun) This evergreen venue in the basement of the student union features rave-electronic music Fridays and Saturdays and a popular gay and lesbian night on Sundays.

Performing Arts

Cankarjev Dom LIVE MUSIC
(☎241 71 00, box office 241 72 99; www.cd-cc.si; Prešernova c 10) Ljubljana's premier cultural centre, with two large auditoriums (the Gallus Hall has perfect acoustics) and a dozen smaller performance spaces.

Križanke LIVE MUSIC
(☎241 60 00, box office 241 60 26; www.festival-lj.si; Trg Francoske Revolucije 1-2) A former 18th-century monastic complex that hosts concerts during the Ljubljana Festival as well as other events.

Opera House OPERA, DANCE
(☎241 17 40, box office 241 17 66; www.opera.si; Župančičeva ul 1) Opera and ballet are performed at the renovated and extended neo-Renaissance Opera House (1882).

ℹ Information

Discount Card

Urbana-Ljubljana Tourist Card (www.visitljubljana.si/en/ljubljana-and-more/ljubljana-tourist-card) This excellent-value card, available for 24/48/72 hours (€23/30/35) from tourist offices, offers free admission to museums and galleries, walking and boat tours and unlimited city bus travel.

Internet Access

Internet is available at virtually every hostel and hotel as well as the STIC (per half-hour €1) and the following:

Cyber Cafe Xplorer (☎430 19 91; Petkovškovo nabrežje 23; per 30min/hr €2.50/4; ⏲10am-10pm Mon-Fri, 2-10pm Sat & Sun) Wi-fi and cheap international phone calls too.

Portal.si Internet (☎234 46 00; Trg OF 4; per hr €4.20; ⏲5.30am-10.30pm Sun-Fri, 5am-10pm Sat) In the bus station (get user code from window No 4).

STA Travel Café (☎439 16 90; 1st fl, Trg Ajdovščina 1; per 20min €1; ⏲8am-midnight Mon-Sat) Part of a travel agency.

Left Luggage

Bus station (Trg OF 4; per day €2; ⌚5.30am-10.30pm Sun-Fri, 5am-10pm Sat) Window No 3.

Train station (Trg OF 6; per day €2-3; ⌚24hr) Coin lockers on platform No 1.

Medical Services

Health Centre Ljubljana (www.zd-lj.si; ☎472 37 00; Metelkova ul 9; ⌚7.30am-7pm) For nonemergencies.

University Medical Centre Ljubljana (☎522 50 50; www3.kclj.si; Zaloška c 2; ⌚24hr) Has accident and emergeny services.

Money

There's a row of ATMs outside the main city tourist information centre (TIC) office. At the train station you'll find a **bureau de change** (⌚7am-8pm) changing cash (no commission) but not travellers cheques.

Tourist Information

Kod & Kam (☎600 50 80; www.kod-kam.si; Miklošičeva c 34; ⌚8am-7pm Mon-Fri, to 1pm Sat) Map specialists.

Tourist Information Centre Ljubljana (TIC) Old Town (☎306 12 15; www.visitljubljana.si; Kresija Bldg, Stritarjeva ul; ⌚8am-9pm Jun-Sep, to 7pm Oct-May); train station (☎433 94 75; Trg OF 6; ⌚8am-10pm Jun-Sep, 10am-7pm Mon-Fri, 8am-3pm Sat Oct-May)

Slovenia Tourist Information Centre (STIC) (☎306 45 76; www.slovenia.info; Krekov trg 10; ⌚8am-9pm Jun-Sep, to 7pm Oct-May) Internet and bicycle hire also available.

Getting There & Away

The bus and train stations are 800m northeast of Prešernov trg up Miklošičeva cesta. Ljubljana's Jože Pučnik Airport is 27km north of the city at Brnik near Kranj.

Bus

Ljubljana's **bus station** (☎234 46 00, information 090-934 230; www.ap-ljubljana.si; Trg OF 4; ⌚5.30am-10.30pm Sun-Fri, 5am-10pm Sat) has multilingual info-phones. Frequent buses serve Bohinj (€8.70, 2¼ hours) via Bled (€6.30, 1¼ hours). Most buses to Piran (€12, 2½ hours, up to five daily) go via Koper (€11.10, 1¾ to 2½ hours) and Postojna (€6, one hour). There's also a service to Maribor (€12.40, three hours).

Train

The **train station** (☎291 33 32; www.slo-zeleznice.si; Trg OF 6; ⌚5am-10pm) has services to Koper (€10, 2½ hours, up to five times daily). Alternatively you can take one of the more frequent Sežana-bound trains and change at Divača (€6.85, 1½ hours). For international services, see p1117.

Getting Around

The cheapest way to/from Ljubljana's **Jože Pučnik Airport** (LJU; ☎04-206 19 81; www.lju-airport.si) at Brnik is by city bus (€4.10, 45 minutes) from stop 28 at the bus station. These run at 5.20am and hourly from 6.10am to 8.10pm Monday to Friday; on weekends there's a bus at 6.10am and then one every two hours from 9.10am to 7.10pm. A **shuttle van** (☎040-771 771, 051-321 414; www.airport-shuttle.si) also links the bus station (€5) or your hotel (€9) with the airport (30 minutes) up to 11 times daily between 5.10am and 10.30pm.

Ljubljana has an excellent network of city buses but you'll need them only if you're staying out of town. The flat fare (€0.80) is paid with a stored-value magnetic **Urbana Card** (www.jh-lj.si/urbana) purchased at newsstands, tourist offices or at the **LPP Information Centre** (☎430 51 75; Slovenska c 56; ⌚7am-7pm Mon-Fri) for €2; credit can then be added.

Ljubljana Bike (per 2hr/day €1/5; ⌚8am-7pm or 9pm Apr-Oct) has two-wheelers available from various locations around the city, including the STIC and opposite the Antiq Hotel.

JULIAN ALPS

The Julian Alps – named in honour of Caesar himself – form Slovenia's dramatic northwest frontier with Italy. **Triglav National Park**, established in 1924, includes almost all of the alps lying within Slovenia. The centrepiece of the park is, of course, triple-peaked Mt Triglav (2864m), Slovenia's highest mountain. Along with an abundance of fauna and flora, the area offers a wide range of adventure sports.

Bled

☎04 / POP 5460

With its emerald-green lake, picture-postcard church on a tiny island, medieval castle clinging to a rocky cliff and some of the country's highest peaks as backdrops, Bled seems to have been designed by the very god of tourism. It's a small and convenient base from which to explore the mountains.

Sights

On its own romantic tiny island is the baroque **Church of the Assumption** (⌚9am-dusk). Reach it by piloted **gondola** (€12) on a trip that lasts 1½ hours. Row-yourself **boats** for up to four people cost €1 to €15 per hour.

Perched atop a 100m-cliff, **Bled Castle** (www.blejski-grad.si; Grajska c 25; admission €7;

⏰8am-8pm summer, to 6pm winter) is the perfect backdrop to the lake. A footpath leads up from behind the Bledec Hostel.

Activities

The 6km stroll around the lake shouldn't take more than a couple of hours, including the short climb to the **Osojnica viewing point**. An easy walk is to **Vintgar Gorge** (admission €4; ⏰8am-7pm mid-May–Oct), 4.5km to the northwest. In summer, a bus (one-way/return €3.50/6.30) leaves the bus station daily for Vintgar at 10am, returning at 12.30pm.

For something more adrenalin-inducing, ask **3glav adventures** (☎041-683 184; www.3glav-adventures.com; Ljubljanska c 1; ⏰9am-7pm Apr-Oct) about their rafting or kayaking trips (€25 to €55) and other activities.

Sleeping

Private rooms are available though Kompas (p1109), with singles/doubles starting at €24/38.

Traveller's Haven HOSTEL **€**
(☎041-396 545; www.travellers-haven.si; Riklijeva c 1; dm/d €19/48; @) This uberpopular hostel in a converted old villa has half a dozen rooms with between two and six beds, a great kitchen, laundry, free bikes and a chilled vibe.

Bledec Hostel HOSTEL **€**
(☎574 52 50; www.youth-hostel-bledec.si; Grajska c 17; dm €18-20, d €48-52; @📶) Well-organised HI-affiliated hostel in the shadow of the castle has dorms with four to eight beds and attached bathrooms, a bar and an inexpensive restaurant.

Vila Gorenka PENSION **€**
(☎574 47 22, 040-958 624; http://freeweb.siol.net/mz2; Želeška c 9; per person €17-25; @) This budget establishment has 10 double rooms with washbasins – toilets and showers are shared – in a charming old two-storey villa dating back to 1909. Some rooms have wooden balconies facing out onto the lake.

Camping Bled CAMPING GROUND **€**
(☎575 20 00; www.camping-bled.com; Kidričeva c 10c; campsite per person €8.50-12.50, huts d €30-40; @📶) This popular 6.5-hectare site fills a small valley at the western end of the lake. The all-natural A-frame huts on a terrace above the site are a delight.

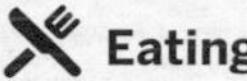

Eating

You'll find a **Mercator** (Ljubljanska c 4; ⏰7am-8pm Mon-Sat, 8am-noon Sun) supermarket at the eastern end of Bled Shopping Centre. There's a smaller **Mercator** (Prešernova c 48; ⏰7am-8pm Mon-Sat, 8am-4pm Sun) close to the hostels.

Ostarija Peglez'n SEAFOOD **€€**
(C Svobode 19a; mains €8.50-27; ⏰noon-midnight) The most colourful restaurant in Bled, the 'Iron Inn' has attractively retro decor and some of the best fish dishes in town.

Gostilna Pri Planincu SLOVENIAN, BALKAN **€€**
(Grajska c 8; mains €7-22; ⏰10am-10pm) 'At the Mountaineers' is a homey pub-restaurant just down the hill from the hostels, with Slovenian mains and grilled Balkan specialities.

Pizzeria Rustika PIZZA **€**
(Riklijeva c 13; pizza €5.70-9.50; ⏰noon-11pm) A marble-roll down the hill from the hostels, Rustika has its own wood-burning oven plus an outside terrace.

Slaščičarna Šmon CAFE **€**
(Grajska c 3; ⏰7.30am-10pm) This is the place for Bled's sweet of choice: *kremna rezina* (€2.40), a layer of vanilla custard topped with whipped cream and sandwiched neatly between two layers of flaky pastry.

Information

A Propos Bar (Bled Shopping Centre, Ljubljanska c 4; per 15/60min €1.25/4.20; ⏰8am-midnight Sun-Thu, to 1am Fri & Sat) Internet access.

Gorenjska Banka (C Svobode 15) Just north of the Park Hotel.

Kompas (☎572 75 00; www.kompas-bled.si; Bled Shopping Centre, Ljubljanska c 4; ⏰8am-7pm Mon-Sat, 8am-noon & 4-7pm Sun) Private rooms and bicycle rentals.

Tourist Information Centre Bled (☎574 11 22; www.bled.si; C Svobode 10; ⏰8am-9pm Mon-Sat, 10am-6pm Sun Jul & Aug, less hours rest of the year) Free internet access for 15 minutes, then €2.50/4 per 30/60 minutes.

Getting There & Around

Buses to Bohinj (€3.60, 40 minutes) and Ljubljana (€6.30, 1¼ hours) depart hourly from the **central bus station**. Trains to Bohinjska Bistrica (€1.70, 20 minutes, eight daily) and Nova Gorica (€5.90, 1¾ hours, eight daily) use **Bled Jezero train station**, which is 2km west of the centre. Trains for Ljubljana (€4.50 to €6.10, 45 minutes to one hour) use **Lesce-Bled train station**, 4km to the east.

Bled

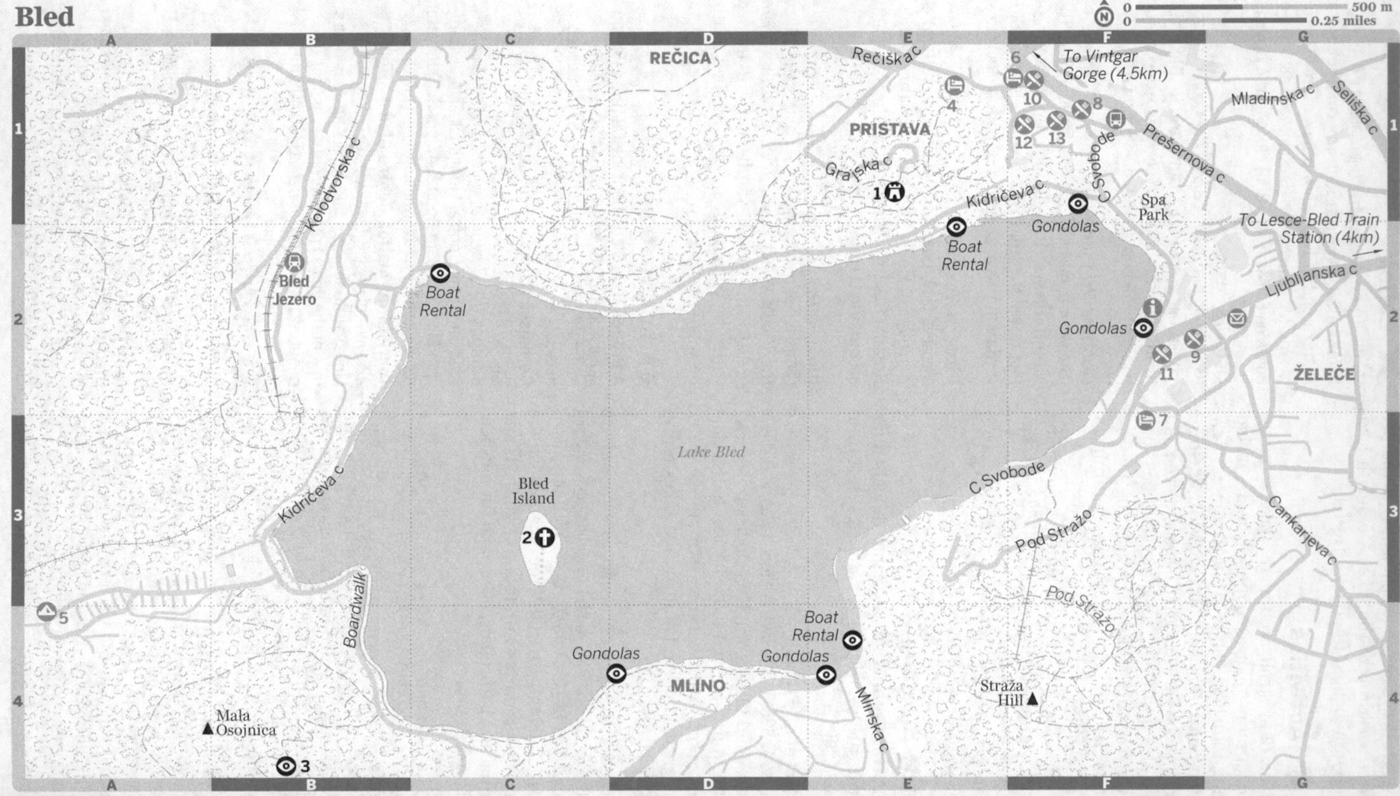
0 500 m
0 0.25 miles
RECICA
PRISTAVA
Rečiška c
To Vintgar Gorge (4.5km)
Mladinska c
Seliška c
Prešernova c
C Svobode
Grajska c
Kidričeva c
Spa Park
To Lesce-Bled Train Station (4km)
Ljubljanska c
Kolodvorska c
Bled Jezero
Boat Rental
Gondolas
Lake Bled
Bled Island
ŽELEČE
C Svobode
Pod Stražo
Cankarjeva c
Kidričeva c
Boardwalk
MLINO
Mlinska c
Straža Hill
Mala Osojnica
1
2
3
4
5
6
7
8
9
10
11
12
13

Bled

Sights

1 Bled Castle....E1
2 Church of the Assumption....C3
3 Osojnica Viewing Point....B4

Sleeping

4 Bledec Hostel....E1
5 Camping Bled....A4
6 Traveller's Haven....F1
7 Vila Gorenka....F3

Eating

8 Gostilna Pri Planincu....F1
9 Mercator Supermarket....F2
10 Mercator Supermarket....F1
11 Ostarija Peglez'n....F2
12 Pizzeria Rustika....F1
13 Slaščičarna Šmon....F1

Bohinj

04 / POP 5275

Bohinj, with its larger and much less developed glacial lake, is 26km to the southwest and a world apart from Bled. Mt Triglav is visible from here and there are activities galore – from kayaking and mountain biking to trekking up Triglav via one of the southern approaches.

Bohinjska Bistrica, the area's largest village, is 6km east of the lake but only useful for its train station. The main tourist hub on the lake is **Ribčev Laz** at the eastern end, with a supermarket, post office with an ATM and a **tourist office** (574 60 10; www.bohinj-info.com; Ribčev Laz 48; 8am-8pm Mon-Sat, to 6pm Sun summer, 8am-6pm Mon-Sat, 9am-3pm Sun winter).

Sights & Activities

Central **Alpinsport** (572 34 86, 041-596 079; www.alpinsport.si; Ribčev Laz 53; 9am or 10am-6pm or 8pm) organises a range of activities, and hires out kayaks, canoes, bikes (per hour/day €4/13.50) and other equipment from a kiosk near the stone bridge. Next door is the delightful **Church of St John the Baptist** (10am-noon & 4-7pm summer), which contains splendid 15th- and 16th-century frescoes.

The nearby village of **Stara Fužina** has an appealing little **Alpine Dairy Museum** (577 01 56; Stara Fužine 181; admission €2.50; 11am-7pm Tue-Sun Jul & Aug, 10am-noon & 4-6pm Tue-Sun Jan-Jun, Sep & Oct). Just 2km east is **Studor**, a village famed for its *kozolci* and *toplarji*, Slovenia's unique single and double hayracks.

Sleeping

The tourist office can help arrange accommodation in **private rooms** (€13 to 15 per person) and **apartments** (€42.50 to €48.50 for a double, €75 to €86 for a queen).

Penzion Gasperin PENSION €
(059-920 382, 041-540 805; www.bohinj.si/gasperin; Ribčev Laz 36a; per person €25-35; @) This spotless chalet-style guest house with 23 rooms is 350m east of the tourist office and run by a friendly British/Slovenian couple.

Hostel Pod Voglom HOSTEL €
(572 34 61; www.hostel-podvoglom.com; Ribčev Laz 60; dm €17-19, r per person €23-26, r per person without bathroom €20-22; @) This budget hostel, 3km west of the centre, has 122 beds in 46 somewhat frayed rooms in two buildings. The hostel building has doubles, triples and dormitory accommodation with up to four beds and shared facilities; rooms in the Rodica Annexe, with between one and four beds, have an en suite.

Camp Zlatorog CAMPING GROUND €
(572 30 64; www.hoteli-bohinj.si/en; Ukanc 2; per person €7-19, tent/campervan €11/23; May-Sep) This pine-shaded 2.5 hectare camping ground accommodating 500 guests is at the lake's western end, 4.5km from Ribčev Laz.

Getting There & Around

Buses run from Ukanc ('Bohinj Zlatorog' on most schedules) to Ljubljana (€8.70, 2¼ hours, hourly) via Ribčev Laz, Bohinjska Bistrica and Bled (€4.10, 50 minutes), with six extra buses daily between Ukanc and Bohinjska Bistrica (€2.30, 20 minutes). From Bohinjska Bistrica, passenger trains to Nova Gorica (€5.20, 1¼ hours, up to nine daily) make use of a century-old tunnel under the mountains that provides the only direct option for reaching the Soča Valley.

SOČA VALLEY

The Soča Valley region is defined by the 96km-long Soča River, coloured a deep, almost artificial turquoise. The valley has more than its share of historical sights, most of them related to one of the costliest battles of WWI, but the majority of visitors are here for adventure sports.

Bovec

☎05 / POP 1818

The best alpine views are at Bovec, which lies in the shadow of Mt Kanin, Slovenia's highest ski resort. The compact village square, Trg Golobarskih Žrtev, has everything you need, including the **Tourist Information Centre Bovec** (TIC; ☎389 64 44; www.bovec.si; Trg Golobarskih Žrtev 8; ⌚8.30am-8.30pm summer, 9am-6pm winter) and a half-dozen adrenalin-raising adventure-sports companies, including the top three: **Bovec Rafting Team** (☎388 61 28, 041-338 308; www.bovec-rafting-team.com), **Soča Rafting** (☎389 62 00, 041-724 472; www.socarafting.si) and **Top Extreme** (☎041-620 636; www.top.si).

The TIC has a list of **private rooms** (per person €15 to €30). Camping facilities are generally better in nearby Kobarid but **Kamp Polovnik** (☎388 60 07; www.kamp-polovnik.com; Ledina 8; campsite per person €6.50-7.50; ⌚Apr–mid-Oct;), about 500m southeast of the centre, is more convenient. **Martinov Hram** (☎388 62 14; www.martinov-hram.si; Trg Golobarskih Žrtev 27; s €33-48, d €54-70;) is a central guest house just 100m east of the centre with a dozen nicely furnished rooms and an excellent restaurant.

Getting There & Away

Buses to Nova Gorica (€7.50, two hours, up to five a day) go via Tolmin (€3.10, 30 minutes). A service to Kranjska Gora (€6.70, 2¼ hours) via Vršič Pass departs five times daily (six at the weekend) from late June to early September.

KARST & COAST

Slovenia's short coast (47km) is not renowned for its fine beaches, though the southernmost resort of **Portorož** has some decent ones. Koper and Piran, two important towns full of Venetian Gothic architecture, are the main drawcards here. En route from Ljubljana or the Soča Valley, you'll cross the Karst, a huge limestone plateau and a land of olives, ruby-red Teran wine, *pršut* (air-dried ham) and deep caves.

Postojna & Škocjan Caves

☎05

Just under 2km northwest of the town of Postojna (population 8910), **Postojna Cave** (☎700 01 00; www.postojnska-jama.si; Jamska c 30; admission €20; ⌚tours hourly 9am-6pm summer, 3 or 4 times from 10am daily winter) is home to the endemic *Proteus anguinus*, eyeless salamanders nicknamed 'human fish'. The cave is filled with endless stalagmites, stalactites and almost as many tourists. Visits (lasting 1½ hours) involve an underground train ride as well as a 1.7km walk with gradients but no steps. Dress warmly or rent a shawl as it's only 8°C to 10°C down there.

The quieter and more remote **Škocjan Caves** (☎708 21 10; www.park-skocjanske-jame.si; Škocjan 2; admission €14; ⌚tours hourly 10am-5pm Jun-Sep, 10am, 1pm & 3.30pm Apr, May & Oct, 10am & 1pm Mon-Sat, 10am, 1pm & 3pm Sun Nov-Mar) are 5km southeast of Divača (population 1325). A van meets incoming trains at 10am, 11.04am, 2pm and 3.10pm and will transport those with bus or train tickets to the caves for free. Otherwise there is a large map indicating the walking route posted outside the station.

Sleeping & Eating

Kompas Postojna PRIVATE ROOMS €
(☎721 14 80; www.kompas-postojna.si; Titov trg 2a; per person r €17-24; ⌚8am-7pm Mon-Fri, 9am-1pm Sat summer, 8am-5pm Mon-Fri, 9am-1pm Sat winter) Private rooms in town and down on the farm.

Hotel Sport HOTEL, HOSTEL €€
(☎720 22 44; www.sport-hotel.si; Kolodvorska c 1; dm €25, s/d from €55/70; P@) In Postojna, the Sport offers reasonable value for money, with 37 spic-and-span rooms, including five with nine hostels beds each. There's a kitchen with small eating area. It's 300m north of the centre.

Gostilna Malovec PENSION €
(☎763 12 25; Kraška c 30a; s/d €32/48) In Divača, you'll find half a dozen basic but renovated rooms in a building beside a popular traditional **restaurant** (mains €5-15; ⌚8am to 10pm) and a flashy 20-room hotel next door.

Getting There & Around

Buses from Ljubljana to Koper, Piran and Nova Gorica all stop in Postojna (€6, one hour, half-hourly) and Divača (€7.90, 1½ hours, half-hourly). The train is good for Divača (€6.85, 1½ hours, hourly) but less useful for Postojna.

Koper

☎05 / POP 24,830

Coastal Slovenia's largest town, Koper (Italian: Capodistria) at first appears to be a workaday city that scarcely gives tourism a second thought. Yet its medieval core is delightfully quiet and far less overrun than its ritzy cousin Piran, 18km down the coast.

The **Tourist Information Centre Koper** (☎664 64 03; www.koper.si; Titov trg 3; ⌚9am-8pm Jul & Aug, 9am-5pm Sep-Jun) is within the restored Renaissance **Praetorian Palace** (admission free), which also houses an old pharmacy and elaborate ceremonial hall. Opposite, the 15th-century **City Tower** (admission €2; ⌚9am-2pm & 4-9pm) can be climbed (204 steps). The **Koper Regional Museum** (☎663 35 70; www.pmk-kp.si; Kidričeva ul 19; admission €2/1.50; ⌚9am-7pm Tue-Fri, to 1pm Sat & Sun) inside the Belgramoni-Tacco Palace has an Italianate sculpture garden.

Sleeping & Eating

Museum Hostel HOSTEL, APARTMENTS €
(☎626 18 70, 041-504 466; bozic.doris@siol.net; Mladinska ul 7 & Kidričeva ul 34; per person €20-25; wi-fi) This excellent-value place is more a series of bright apartments with modern kitchens and bathrooms than a hostel. Reception is at the little Museum Bife, a cafe-bar at Muzejski trg 6.

Motel Port HOSTEL €
(☎611 75 44; www.motel-port.si; Ankaranska c 7; dm €22, s €36/49.50; ⌚Jul-Aug; @ wi-fi) On the 2nd floor of a shopping centre southeast of the Old Town, this student house open to visitors in summer only has 30 rooms, some of them with en suite and air-conditioned and others dorm rooms with four to six beds.

Istrska Klet Slavček ISTRIAN, SLOVENIAN €
(Župančičeva ul 39; dishes €3-12; ⌚7am-10pm Mon-Fri) The 'Istrian Cellar' below an 18th-century palace is one of the most colourful places for a meal in Koper's Old Town. Filling set lunches go for less than €8.

Getting There & Away

Buses run to Piran (€2.70.10, 30 minutes) every 20 minutes on weekdays and every 40 minutes on weekends. Up to five buses daily head for Ljubljana (€11.10, 1¾ to 2½ hours), though the six daily trains (€8.50 to €10, 2¼ hours) are more comfortable.

Piran

☎05 / POP 4515

Picturesque Piran (Pirano in Italian) sits on the tip of a narrow peninsula, the westernmost point of Slovenian Istria. Piran Bay and Portorož (population 2900), Slovenia's largest beach resort, lie to the south. Piran's Old Town is a gem of Venetian Gothic architecture and full of picturesque narrow streets.

The **Sergej Mašera Maritime Museum** (www.pommuz-pi.si; Cankarjevo nabrežje 3; admission €3.50; ⌚9am-noon & 5-9pm Tue-Sun summer, 9am-5pm Tue-Sun winter) and the renovated **Aquarium Piran** (☎673 25 72; www.aquarium piran.com; Kidričevo nabrežje 4; admission €7; ⌚9am-7pm summer, to 5pm winter) are on opposite sides of the harbour south of central Tartinijev trg, where you'll find the **Tourist Information Center Piran** (☎673 02 20, 673 44 40; www.portoroz.si; Tartinijev trg 2; ⌚9am-8pm summer, 9am-5pm winter).

The town is dominated by the **Cathedral of St George** (Adamičeva ul 2), whose soaring **bell tower** (1609) was modelled on the campanile of St Mark's Cathedral in Venice. The nearby **Minorite monastery** (Bolniška ul 30) has a delightful cloister.

Sleeping

The **Maona Tourist Agency** (☎673 45 20; www.maona.si; Cankarjevo nabrežje 7; ⌚9am-8pm Mon-Sat, 10am-1pm & 5-7pm Sun) rents private rooms (singles €18 to €31.50, doubles €26 to €48).

Kamp Fiesa CAMPING GROUND €
(☎674 62 30; autocamp.fiesa@siol.net; admission €12; ⌚May-Sep) The closest camping ground to Piran is at Fiesa, 4km by road but less than 1km by coastal trail east from the Cathedral of St George. It's tiny and crowded but right on the beach.

Alibi B11 HOSTEL €
(☎031-363 666; www.alibi.si; Bonifacijeva ul 11; per person €20-22; ⌚Apr-Dec; @ wi-fi) The flagship of the Alibi stable – there are two more and an apartment within spitting distance – is not their nicest property. It has mostly doubles in eight rooms over four floors, with a roof terrace on the top of this ancient townhouse. Reception for all three hostels is here and there's a washing machine.

Val Hostel HOSTEL €
(☎673 25 55; www.hostel-val.com; Gregorčičeva ul 38a; per person €22-27; @ wi-fi) This central, partially renovated hostel has 20 rooms, with two to four beds in each, shared bathroom, kitchen and washing machine. It's a great favourite with backpackers.

SPLURGE

Piran's most romantic accommodation option, **Max Piran** (☎673 34 36, 041-692 928; www.maxpiran.com; Ul IX Korpusa 26; d €60-70; @📶) has just six rooms – each bearing a woman's name rather than a number – in a delightful coral-coloured 18th-century townhouse. It's a short walk from the cathedral and the views from on high are spectacular.

Eating

There's a small **Mercator** (Levstikova ul 5; ⏰7am-8pm Mon-Sat, 8am-noon Sun) supermarket in the Old Town.

Flora PIZZA €
(☎673 12 58; Prešernovo nabrežje 26; pizza €4-8; ⏰10am-1am summer, 10am-10pm winter) The terrace of this simple pizzeria east of the Punta lighthouse has uninterrupted views of the Adriatic.

Pri Mari MEDITERRANEAN, SLOVENIAN €€
(☎673 47 35, 041-616 488; Dantejeva ul 17; mains €8.50-16; ⏰noon-11pm Tue-Sun summer, noon-10pm Tue-Sat, noon-6pm Sun winter) Run by an Italian-Slovenian couple, this welcoming restaurant south of the bus station serves the most inventive Mediterranean and Slovenian dishes in town. Be sure to book ahead.

Galeb SEAFOOD €
(Pusterla ul 5; mains €8-11; ⏰11am-4pm & 6pm-11pm or midnight Wed-Mon) This excellent family-run restaurant with seafront seating is east of the Punta lighthouse.

Getting There & Away

From the bus station, buses run every 20 to 30 minutes to Koper (€2.70, 30 minutes) via Izola. Five buses head for Trieste, Italy (€10, 1¾ hours) between 6.45am and 6.55pm Monday to Saturday. Between three and five daily buses go to Ljubljana (€12, 2½ to three hours) via Divača and Postojna.

UNDERSTAND SLOVENIA

History

Slovenes played a key role in the development of democracy. By the early 7th century their Slavic forebears had founded the Duchy of Carantania (now Karnburg in Austria), where ruling dukes were elected by ennobled commoners. This model was noted by Thomas Jefferson when drafting the American Declaration of Independence in 1776.

Austria controlled Slovenia almost uninterrupted from the 14th century until 1918. After some of the most ferocious fighting in WWI, western Slovenia was handed over to Italy as Austro-Hungarian postwar reparations, and northern Carinthia voted to stay within Austria. The rest of Slovenia joined fellow south Slavs in forming the Kingdom of Serbs, Croats and Slovenes, later Yugoslavia.

Nazi occupation in WWII was for the most part resisted by Slovenian partisans, though the anti-partisan Slovenian Domobranci (Home Guards) threw their support behind the Germans after Italy surrendered. The war ended with Slovenia regaining the Italian-held areas from Piran to Bovec but losing Trst (Trieste) and Gorica (Gorizia).

Small Slovenia was a major economic powerhouse in Yugoslavia, producing up to

WORTH A TRIP

EASTERN SLOVENIA

Slovenia's second city and European Capital of Culture in 2012, **Maribor** (population 87,300) has no unmissable sights but oozes with charm thanks to its delightful (but tiny) Old Town. Pedestrianised central streets buzz with cafes and student life, and in late June/early July the riverside Lent district hosts a major arts festival (p1116). The **Tourist Information Centre Maribor** (☎234 66 11; www.maribor-pohorje.si; Partinzanska c 6a; ⏰9am-7pm Mon-Fri, to 6pm Sat & Sun) has a list of places to stay, but for budget accommodation try the **Lollipop Hostel** (☎040-243 160; lollipophostel@yahoo.com; Maistrova ul 17; dm €20; @), a short distance from the train station. From Ljubljana reach Maribor by bus (€12.40, three hours, 141km, two to four a day) or by much more frequent train (€8.50, 2½ hours).

Consider a quick bus trip to picture-postcard **Ptuj**, which is just down the road by bus from Maribor (€3.60, 45 minutes, departs hourly).

20% of the GDP. By the 1980s the federation was becoming increasingly Serb-dominated and, after free elections, Slovenia broke away from Yugoslavia on 25 June 1991. A 10-day war that left 66 people dead followed; Yugoslavia swiftly signed a truce in order to concentrate on regaining control of coastal Croatia instead. Slovenia was admitted to the UN in 1992 and joined the EU in 2004. It adopted the euro as its national currency three years later.

People

The population of Slovenia (just under two millions) is largely homogeneous. Just over 83% are ethnic Slovenes, with the remainder being Croats, Serbians, Bosnians and Roma; there are also small enclaves of Italians and Hungarians. Slovenes are ethnically Slavic, typically hardworking, multilingual and extrovert. Just under 58% are Roman Catholic.

Closely related to Croatian and Serbian, the Slovene language *(slovenščina)* is written in the Roman alphabet. On toilets an 'M' *(Moški)* indicates 'men' and 'Ž' *(Ženske)* is 'women'. Virtually everyone in Slovenia speaks at least one other language (usually English, German or Italian).

Arts

Slovenia's most beloved writer is the Romantic poet France Prešeren (1800–49), whose lyric poetry helped to raise Slovenian national consciousness.

Many of Ljubljana's most characteristic architectural features were added by the ubertalented Jože Plečnik (1872–1957).

Slovenia's vibrant music scene embraces rave, techno, jazz, punk, thrash-metal and *chansons* (eg torch songs from Vita Mavrič); the most popular local rock group is Siddharta. There's also a folk-music revival: listen for the groups Katice and Katalena and the vocalist Brina.

Food

Price ranges for restaurants listed in this book are indicated by the following:

€€€ more than €20

€€ from €10 to €20

€ below €10

Environment

Slovenia is amazingly green; indeed, about 58% of its total surface area is covered in forest. Triglav National Park is particularly rich in native flowering plants. Among endemic fauna is a blind salamander called *Proteus anguinus*, which lives deep in karst caves and can survive for years without eating.

SURVIVAL GUIDE

Directory A-Z

Accommodation

A tourist tax – routinely from €1 per person per day – is usually not included in the quoted price of accommodation in this guide. Price ranges for a double listed in this chapter are indicated by the following:

€€€ more than €100

€€ €50 to €100

€ less than €50

Unless otherwise indicated, rooms include en-suite toilet and bath or shower and breakfast.

Camping grounds generally charge per person. Most sites close between mid-October and mid-April.

Slovenia has an ever-growing stable of hostels. Throughout the country there are student dorms moonlighting as hostels in July and August.

Tourist information offices can help you access private rooms, apartments and tourist farms, or they can recommend private agencies that will. Be aware that there are usually surcharges of 30% to 50% on stays of fewer than three nights.

Activities

Skiing is a national passion, with slopes particularly crowded over the Christmas holidays and early in February. See www.slovenia.info/skiing for details.

Hiking is extremely popular, with around 8250km of waymarked mountain trails and 174 mountain huts. Check out the website of the **Alpine Association of Slovenia** (www.pzs.si).

Bovec is a magnet for fans of extreme sports, notably paragliding and canyoning. The nearby Soča River offers Slovenia's best white-water rafting. The Sava River at Bohinj is a great base for fly-fishing.

Mountain bikes are available for rent from travel agencies at Bled, Bohinj, Bovec and Postojna.

Business Hours

Usual business hours in Slovenia include the following:

Banks 8am or 8.30am to 5pm Mon to Fri (often closed from noon or 12.30pm to 2pm or 3pm), 8am to noon or 1pm Sat.

Main post offices 8am to 7pm Mon to Fri, 8am to noon or 1pm Sat.

Restaurants From 10am or 11am to 10pm or 11pm daily.

Shops 10am to 6pm Mon to Fri, to 1pm on Saturday; a handful of grocery stores open Sun.

Supermarkets from 8am to 7pm on Mon to Fri and to 1pm Sat.

Festivals & Events

Major cultural and sporting events are listed under 'Upcoming Events' on the home page of the of the **Slovenian Tourist Board** (www.slovenia.info) website and in the STB's comprehensive *Calendar of Major Events in Slovenia*. The most important and/or colourful include the following:

Kurentovanje (www.kurentovanje.net) A 'rite of spring' celebrated in Ptuj for 10 days leading up to Shrove Tuesday (February or early March).

Festival Lent (http://lent.slovenija.net) A two-week extravaganza of folklore and culture in Maribor's Old Town in late June/early July.

Ljubljana Festival (www.ljubljanafestival.si) The nation's premier cultural event (music, theatre and dance) held from early July to late August.

Cows' Ball (www.bohinj.si) A zany weekend of folk dance and music at Bohinj in September, marking the return of the cows from their high pastures to the valleys.

Gay & Lesbian Travellers

Slovenia has no sodomy laws. A national gay rights law bans discrimination in employment and other areas on the basis of sexual preference, and homosexuals are allowed in the military. Outside Ljubljana, however, there is little evidence of a gay presence, much less a lifestyle.

Roza Klub (☎01-430 47 40; Kersnikova ul 4) in Ljubljana is made up of the gay and lesbian branches of **ŠKUC** (www.skuc.org), which stands for Študentski Kulturni Center (Student Cultural Centre) but is no longer student-orientated as such.

A more or less monthly publication called **Narobe** (Upside Down; www.narobe.si) is in Slovene only, though you might be able to glean something from the listings.

Holidays

Slovenia celebrates the following holidays:

New Year 1 & 2 January

Prešeren Day (Slovenian Culture Day) 8 February

Easter March/April

Insurrection Day 27 April

Labour Days 1 & 2 May

National Day 25 June

Assumption Day 15 August

Reformation Day 31 October

All Saints' Day 1 November

Christmas Day 25 December

Independence Day 26 December

Internet Access

Virtually every hostel and hotel has internet access – a computer for guests' use (free or for a nominal fee), wi-fi, or both. Most cities and towns have at least one cyber cafe but they usually only have a handful of terminals.

Internet Resources

The website of the **Slovenian Tourist Board** (www.slovenia.info) is tremendously useful, as is that of **Mat'Kurja** (www.matkurja.com), a directory of Slovenian web resources.

Money

The official currency is the euro. Exchanging cash is simple at banks, major post offices, travel agencies and *menjalnice* (bureaux de change), although many of the last don't accept travellers cheques. Major credit and debit cards are accepted almost everywhere, and ATMs are ubiquitous.

Post & Telephone

Local mail costs €0.33 for up to 20g, while an international airmail stamp costs €0.49. Poste restante is free; address it to and pick it up from the main post office at Slovenska c 32, 1101 Ljubljana.

Public telephones require a phonecard *(telefonska kartica* or *telekartica)*, available at post offices and some newsstands. The cheapest card (€3, 25 units) gives about 20 minutes' calling time to other European countries; the highest value is €14.60 with 300 units. Local SIM cards with €5 credit are available from **SiMobil** (www.simobil.si), **Mobitel** (www.mobitel.si) and **Tušmobil** (www.tusmobil.si). Mobile numbers in Slovenia are identified by the prefix 030 and 040 (SiMobil), 031, 041, 051 and 071 (Mobitel) and 070 (Tušmobil).

Tourist Information

The Ljubljana-based **Slovenian Tourist Board** (☎01-589 85 50; www.slovenia.info; Dimičeva ul 13) has dozens of tourist information centres (TICs) in Slovenia, and seven branches abroad. See 'STB Representative Offices Abroad' on its website for details.

Visas

Border formalities with Slovenia's three fellow European Union neighbours – Italy, Austria and Hungary – are now virtually nonexistent. However, as a member state that forms part of the EU's external frontier, Slovenia must implement the strict Schengen border rules, so expect a somewhat closer inspection of your documents - national ID (for EU citizens) or passport and, in some cases, visa when travelling to/from Croatia. Holders of EU and Swiss passports can enter using a national identity card.

Those who do require visas (including South Africans) can get them for up to 90 days at any Slovenian embassy or consulate – see the website of the **Ministry of Foreign Affairs** (www.mzz.gov.si) for a full listing. Visas cost €35 and you'll need confirmation of a hotel booking plus one photo, and you may have to show a return or onward ticket.

Getting There & Away

Air

Slovenia's national airline, **Adria Airways** (☎080 13 00, 01-369 10 10; www.adria-airways.com) flies to some 30 European cities. Discount airline **easyJet** (www.easyjet.com) has daily nonstop flights to Ljubljana from London's Stansted airport.

Boat

Venezia Lines (☎05-674 71 61; www.venezialines.com) catamarans sail to Venice from Piran (one way €45-55, return €64-69, 2¼ hours) at 8.30am on Wednesday from May to September. The **Prince of Venice** (☎05-617 80 00; www.kompas-online.net) catamaran from nearby Izola also serves Venice (€50 to €70, 2½ hours) between one and three times a week mid-April to September. **Trieste Lines** (www.triestelines.it) ferries run between Piran and Trieste (one-way/return €8.50/15.70) daily during the same period.

Bus

International bus services from Ljubljana include: Belgrade (€35, 7¾ hours, three daily); Frankfurt (€86, 14 hours, 6.30pm daily) via Munich (€44, 6¾ hours); Pula (€22, 4½ hours, 5pm Mon & Fri, 9.30am Sat & Sun) via Poreč (€21, three hours) and Rovinj (€21, 2½ hours); Trieste (€11.60, 2¼ hours, 5.10am daily and 6.35am Monday to Saturday); and Venice-Mestre (€25, five hours, three daily).

Train

Ljubljana Vienna trains (€63.20, 6¼ hours, one direct, four via Maribor daily) via Graz (€31.20, 3½ hours) are expensive, although Spar Schiene fares go as low as €29 on certain trains at certain times.

Three trains depart Ljubljana daily for Munich (€72, six hours). The 11.50pm departure has sleeping carriages available.

A Venice train (one-way/return €25/40, four hours) via Sežana departs at 2.28am. But it's cheaper to go first to Nova Gorica (€8.50, 3½ hours, five daily), cross over on foot to the train station in Gorizia and then take an Italian train to Venice (about €9, 2½ hours).

For Zagreb (€13.40, 2½ hours) there are seven trains daily via Zidani Most. Two trains from the capital at 6.20am and 2.53pm serve Rijeka (€13.80, 2½ hours) via Postojna.

Getting Around

Bus & Train

Ljubljana bus station (☎234 46 00, information 090-934 230; www.ap-ljubljana.si) is your best source of information on long-distance domestic bus travel. Book long-distance buses ahead of time, especially when travelling on Friday afternoon. If your bag has to go in the luggage compartment below the bus, it will cost €1.50 extra.

Buy tickets on **Slovenian Railways** (Slovenske Železnice; ☎01-291 33 32; www.slo-zeleznice.si) before boarding or you'll incur a €2.50 supplement charge. Be aware that EuroCity (EC) and InterCity (IC) trains carry a surcharge of €1.60 while InterCity Slovenia ones cost €9.50/6.30 in 1st/2nd class. Unusually, trains in Slovenia are usually cheaper than buses.

Car & Bicycle

Rates for car hire usually start at €40/210 per day/week, including unlimited mileage and insurance.

You must keep your headlights illuminated throughout the day. Your vehicle must display a *vinjeta* (road-toll sticker; per week/month €15/30) on the windscreen; a rental car will already have one. Further information is available from the **Automobile Association of Slovenia** (☎01-530 52 00; www.amzs.si).

Bicycle rental places are generally concentrated in the more popular tourist areas such as Ljubljana, Bled, Bovec and Piran though a fair few cycle shops and repair places hire them out as well.

Hitching

Hitchhiking is fairly common and legal everywhere in Slovenia except on motorways and a few major highways. But it's never totally safe and Lonely Planet doesn't recommend it.

Spain

Includes »

Best Places to Eat

» Arzak, San Sebastián (p1162)

» Mercado de San Miguel, Madrid (p1131)

» La Pepica, Valencia (p1167)

» Restaurante La Troya, Trujillo (p1186)

Best Places to Stay

» La Flor de al-Andalus, Mérida (p1188)

» Cat's Hostel, Madrid (p1127)

» Pensión Bellas Artes, San Sebastián (p1161)

» Posada de San José, Cuenca (p1146)

Why Go?

Passionate, sophisticated and devoted to living the good life, Spain is at once a stereotype come to life and a country more diverse than you ever imagined.

Spanish landscapes stir the soul, from the jagged Pyrenees and wildly beautiful cliffs of the Atlantic northwest to charming Mediterranean coves, while astonishing architecture spans the ages at seemingly every turn. Spain's cities march to a beguiling beat, rushing headlong into the 21st century even as timeless villages serve as beautiful signposts to Old Spain. And then there's one of Europe's most celebrated (and varied) gastronomic scenes.

But above all, Spain lives very much in the present. Perhaps you'll sense it along a crowded post-midnight street when all the world has come out to play. Or maybe that moment will come when a flamenco performer touches something deep in your soul. Whenever it happens, you'll find yourself nodding in recognition: *this* is Spain.

When to Go

Madrid

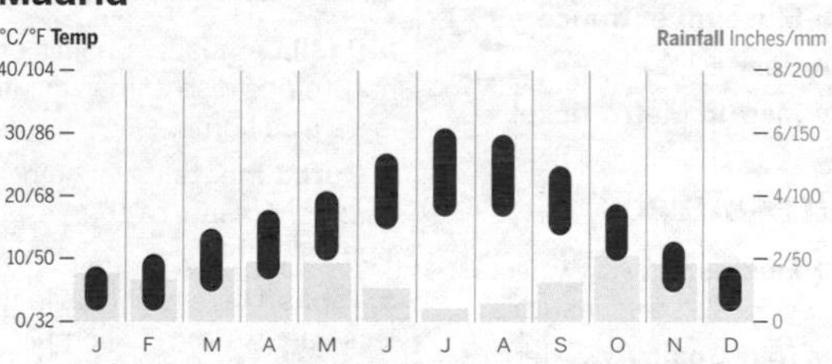

Jun–Sep The weather's warm and Spaniards head for the coast, but quiet corners still abound.

Mar–Apr Wildflowers, Easter processions and mercifully mild temperatures in the south.

May & Sep Mild and often balmy weather but without the crowds of high summer.

AT A GLANCE

» **Currency** Euro (€1)

» **Languages** Spanish (Castellano), Catalan, Basque, Galician (Gallego)

» **Money** ATMs are everywhere

» **Visas** Schengen visa rules apply (see p1319)

Fast Facts

» **Area** 504,782 sq km

» **Capital** Madrid

» **Country code** ☎34

» **Emergency** ☎112

Exchange Rates

Australia	A$1	€0.74
Canada	C$1	€0.74
Japan	¥100	€0.87
New Zealand	NZ$1	€0.56
UK	UK£1	€1.16
USA	US$1	€0.72

Set Your Budget

» **Budget hotel room** up to €60

» **Two-course evening meal** €25-35

» **Museum entrance** €6-10

» **Beer** €2-3

» **Madrid Metro ticket** €9

Resources

» **Fiestas.net** (www.fiestas.net) Fiestas and festivals

» **Tour Spain** (www.tourspain.org) Useful for culture and food, with links to hotels and transport

» **Turespaña** (www.spain.info) Spanish tourist office

Connections

Spanish airports are among Europe's best connected, while the typical overland route leads many travellers from France over the Pyrenees into Spain. Rather than taking the main road/rail route along the Mediterranean coast (or between Biarritz and San Sebastián), you could follow lesser-known, pretty routes over the mountains. There's nothing to stop you carrying on to Portugal. Numerous roads and the Madrid–Lisbon rail line connect the two countries.

The most obvious sea journeys lead across the Strait of Gibraltar to Morocco. The most common routes connect Algeciras or Tarifa with Tangier, from where there's plenty of transport deeper into Morocco. Car ferries also connect Barcelona with Italian (and occasionally Moroccan) ports. For more transport details, turn to p1195.

ITINERARIES

One Week

Marvel at Barcelona's art nouveau–influenced Modernista architecture and seaside style before taking the train to San Sebastián, with a stop in Zaragoza on the way. Head on to Bilbao for the Guggenheim Museum and end the trip living it up on Madrid's legendary night scene.

One Month

Take the high-speed train from Madrid to stunning Seville, before moving on to picture-perfect Cádiz, Granada and Córdoba. Take the train back to Madrid, from where you can check out Toledo, Salamanca and Segovia. Make east for the coast and Valencia, detour northwest into the postcard-perfect villages of Aragón and the Pyrenees, and then travel east into Catalonia, spending time in Tarragona before reaching Barcelona. Take a plane or boat for the Balearic Islands, from where you can get a flight home.

Essential Food & Drink

» **Paella** Arguably Spain's premier culinary export, this signature rice dish comes in infinite varieties, although Valencia is its true home.

» **Cured meats** Wafer-thin slices of delicious chorizo, *lomo*, *salchichón* and, of course, *jamón serrano* appear on most Spanish tables.

» **Tapas** There is genius in these bite-sized morsels of endless variety, from uncomplicated samples of Spanish staples to gastronomic innovation in its purest form.

» **Olive oil** Spain is the world's largest producer of olive oil. Subject to strict quality controls, Spanish *aceite de oliva* is many meals' perfect accompaniment.

» **Wine** Spain has the largest area (1.2 million hectares) of wine cultivation in the world. La Rioja and Ribera del Duero are the best-known wine-growing regions.

MADRID

POP 3.6 MILLION

No city on earth is more alive than Madrid, a beguiling place where the sheer energy carries a simple message: this city knows how to live. Explore the old streets of the centre, relax in the plazas, soak up the culture in its excellent art museums and take at least one night to experience the city's legendary nightlife.

Established as a Moorish garrison in 854, Madrid was little more than a muddy, mediocre village when King Felipe II declared it Spain's capital in 1561. Despite being home to generations of nobles, the city was a squalid grid of unpaved alleys and dirty buildings until the 18th century, when King Carlos III turned his attention to public works. With 175,000 inhabitants under Carlos' rule, Madrid had become Europe's fifth-largest capital.

When Spain's dictator, General Franco, died in 1975, the city exploded with creativity and life, giving Madrileños the party-hard reputation they still cherish. Terrorist bombs rocked Madrid in March 2004, just before national elections, and killed 191 commuters on four trains.

Sights & Activities

Get under the city's skin by walking its streets, sipping coffee and beer in its plazas and relaxing in its parks. Madrid de los Austrias, the maze of mostly 15th- and 16th-century streets that surround Plaza Mayor, is the city's oldest district. Tapas-crazy La Latina, alternative Chueca, bar-riddled Huertas and Malasaña, and chic Salamanca are other districts that reward exploration.

Build in time for three of Europe's top art collections at the Prado, Reina Sofía and Thyssen-Bornemisza museums, as well as a visit to the Palacio Real.

Museo del Prado ART GALLERY

(Map p1128; www.museodelprado.es; Paseo del Prado; adult/student €8/4, free 6-8pm Tue-Sat & 5-8pm Sun; 9am-8pm Tue-Sun; M Banco de España) Spain's premier art museum, the Prado is a seemingly endless parade of priceless works from Spain and beyond. The collection is roughly divided into eight major collections: Spanish paintings (1100–1850), Flemish paintings (1430–1700), Italian paintings (1300–1800), French paintings (1600–1800), German paintings (1450–1800), sculptures, decorative arts, and drawings and prints. There is generous coverage of Spanish greats, including Goya, Velázquez and El Greco. Other masters on show include Peter Paul Rubens, Pieter Bruegel, Rembrandt, Anton Van Dyck, Dürer, Rafael, Tiziano (Titian), Tintoretto, Sorolla, Gainsborough, Fra Angelico and Tiepolo.

Museo Thyssen-Bornemisza ART GALLERY

(Map p1128; www.museothyssen.org; Paseo del Prado 8; adult/student €8/5.50; 10am-7pm Tue-Sun; M Banco de España) Almost opposite the Prado, the Museo Thyssen-Bornemisza is an outstanding collection of international masterpieces. Begin your visit on the 2nd floor, where you'll start with medieval art, and make your way down to modern works on the ground level, passing paintings by Titian, El Greco, Rubens, Rembrandt, Anton van Dyck, Canaletto, Cézanne, Monet, Sisley, Renoir, Pissarro, Degas, Constable, Van Gogh, Miró, Modigliani, Matisse, Picasso, Gris, Pollock, Dalí, Kandinsky, Toulouse-Lautrec, Lichtenstein and many others on the way.

Centro de Arte Reina Sofía ART GALLERY

(Map p1124; www.museoreinasofia.es; Calle de Santa Isabel 52; adult/concession €6/free, free Sun, 7-9pm Mon & Wed-Fri, 2.30-9pm Sat; 10am-9pm Mon & Wed-Sat, 10am-2.30pm Sun; M Atocha) A stunning collection of mainly Spanish modern art, the Centro de Arte Reina Sofía is home to Picasso's *Guernica* – his protest against the German bombing of the Basque town of Guernica during the Spanish Civil War in 1937 – in addition to important works by surrealist Salvador Dalí and abstract paintings by the Catalan artist Joan Miró.

Caixa Forum CONTEMPORARY ART & MULTIMEDIA CENTRE

(Map p1128; www.fundacio.lacaixa.es; Paseo del Prado 36; admission free; 10am-8pm; M Atocha) The Caixa Forum, opened in 2008, seems to hover above the ground. On one wall is the *jardín colgante* (hanging garden), a lush vertical wall of greenery almost four storeys high. Inside are four floors used to hold top-quality art and multimedia exhibitions.

Palacio Real ROYAL PALACE

(Map p1124; www.patrimonionacional.es; Calle de Bailén; adult/concession €10/3.50, adult without guided tour €8, EU citizens free Wed; 9am-6pm Mon-Sat, 9am-3pm Sun & holidays; M Ópera) When the 16th-century Alcázar that formerly stood on this spot went up in flames on Christmas Eve 1734, King Felipe V ordered construction of a new palace on the same ground. The opulent Palacio Real was finished in 1755 and Carlos III moved in during 1764. Still used

Spain Highlights

1 Explore the **Alhambra** (p1179), an exquisite Islamic palace complex in Granada

2 Visit Gaudí's singular work in progress, Barcelona's **La Sagrada Família** (p1147), a cathedral that truly defies imagination

3 Wander amid the horseshoe arches of Córdoba's **Mezquita** (p1177), close to perfection wrought in stone

4 Eat your way through **San Sebastián** (p1161), a gourmand's paradise with an idyllic setting

5 Join the pilgrims making their way to the magnificent **Santiago de Compostela** (p1165)

6 Soak up the scent of orange blossom, admire the architecture and surrender to the party atmosphere in sunny **Seville** (p1173)

7 Discover the impossibly beautiful Mediterranean beaches and coves of **Menorca** (p1172)

8 Spend your days in some of Europe's best art galleries, and nights amid its best nightlife in **Madrid** (p1121)

9 Be carried away by the soulful strains of live **flamenco** (p1190)

Bordeaux
FRANCE
Avignon
Nîmes
Montpellier
Toulouse
BASQUE COUNTRY
San Sebastián
Irún
NAVARRA
Golfe de Beauduc
Vitoria
Pamplona
Perpignan
Miranda de Ebro
Jaca
Andorra la Vella
ANDORRA
Logroño
Calahorra
Figueres
Huesca
CATALONIA
Girona
Fornells
Costa Brava
AP68
A9
Manresa
Soria
Tossa de Mar
Lleida
Zaragoza
AP2
Barcelona
Sitges
CASTILLA Y LEÓN
Tarragona
ARAGÓN
A23
AP7
Guadalajara
Alcalá de Henares
Teruel
Ciutadella de Menorca
Menorca
Cuenca
Mao
Mallorca
Inca
Artà
A3
Sagunto
Manacor
VALENCIA
Valencia
Palma de Mallorca
Alginet
Manzanares
Albacete
Ibiza
Balearic Islands
AP7
Denia
Valdepeñas
Benidorm
Alicante
Elche
Cieza
Costa Blanca
Murcia
MURCIA
MEDITERRANEAN SEA
A7
A91
Cartagena
Guadix
Mojácar
Costa Cálida
Almería
Adra
Cabo de Gata
Costa De Almería
ALGERIA
0 300 km
0 150 miles

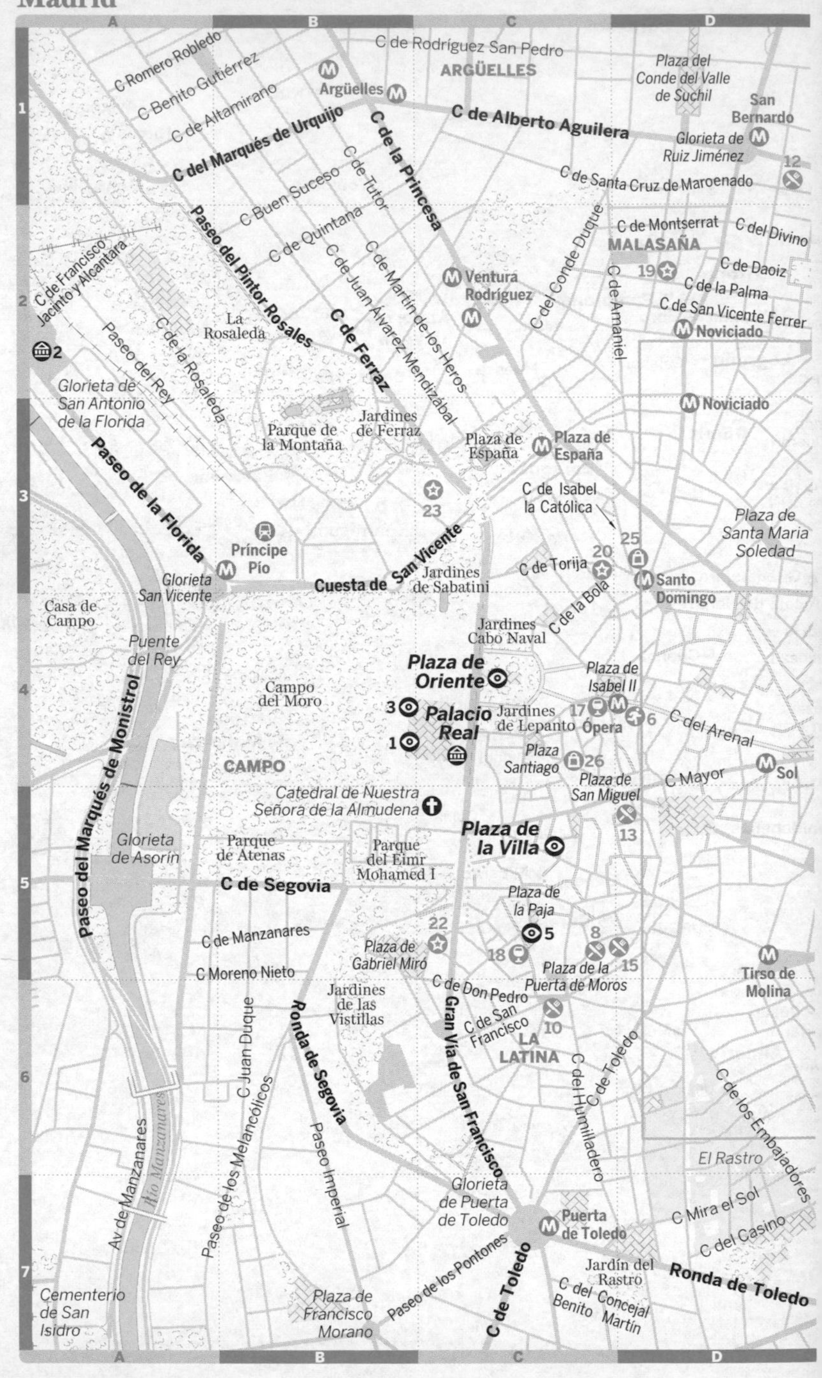
ARGÜELLES
C de Rodríguez San Pedro
Argüelles
C Romero Robledo
C Benito Gutiérrez
C de Altamirano
C del Marqués de Urquijo
C de la Princesa
C de Alberto Aguilera
Plaza del Conde del Valle de Súchil
San Bernardo
Glorieta de Ruiz Jiménez
C de Santa Cruz de Maroenado
C Buen Suceso
C de Tutor
C de Quintana
Paseo del Pintor Rosales
C de Juan Álvarez Mendizábal
C de Martín de los Heros
C de Ferraz
C del Conde Duque
C de Montserrat
C del Divino
MALASAÑA
C de Daoiz
C de la Palma
C de San Vicente Ferrer
C de Amaniel
Ventura Rodríguez
Noviciado
C de Francisco Jacinto y Alcantara
La Rosaleda
C de la Rosaleda
Paseo del Rey
Glorieta de San Antonio de la Florida
Parque de la Montaña
Jardines de Ferraz
Plaza de España
Paseo de la Florida
C de Isabel la Católica
Plaza de Santa Maria Soledad
Príncipe Pío
Glorieta San Vicente
Cuesta de San Vicente
Jardines de Sabatini
C de Torija
C de la Bola
Santo Domingo
Casa de Campo
Puente del Rey
Jardines Cabo Naval
Plaza de Oriente
Plaza de Isabel II
Campo del Moro
Palacio Real
Jardines de Lepanto
Ópera
C del Arenal
Paseo del Marqués de Monistrol
CAMPO
Plaza Santiago
Plaza de San Miguel
C Mayor
Sol
Catedral de Nuestra Señora de la Almudena
Plaza de la Villa
Glorieta de Asorín
Parque de Atenas
Parque del Emir Mohamed I
C de Segovia
Plaza de la Paja
C de Manzanares
Plaza de Gabriel Miró
C Moreno Nieto
Plaza de la Puerta de Moros
Tirso de Molina
Jardines de las Vistillas
C de Don Pedro
C de San Francisco
LA LATINA
Ronda de Segovia
Gran Vía de San Francisco
C Juan Duque
C de Toledo
C del Humilladero
C de los Embajadores
Paseo de los Melancólicos
Paseo Imperial
Río Manzanares
Av de Manzanares
El Rastro
Glorieta de Puerta de Toledo
Puerta de Toledo
C Mira el Sol
C del Casino
Paseo de los Pontones
Jardín del Rastro
Ronda de Toledo
C del Concejal Benito Martín
Cementerio de San Isidro
Plaza de Francisco Morano
C de Toledo

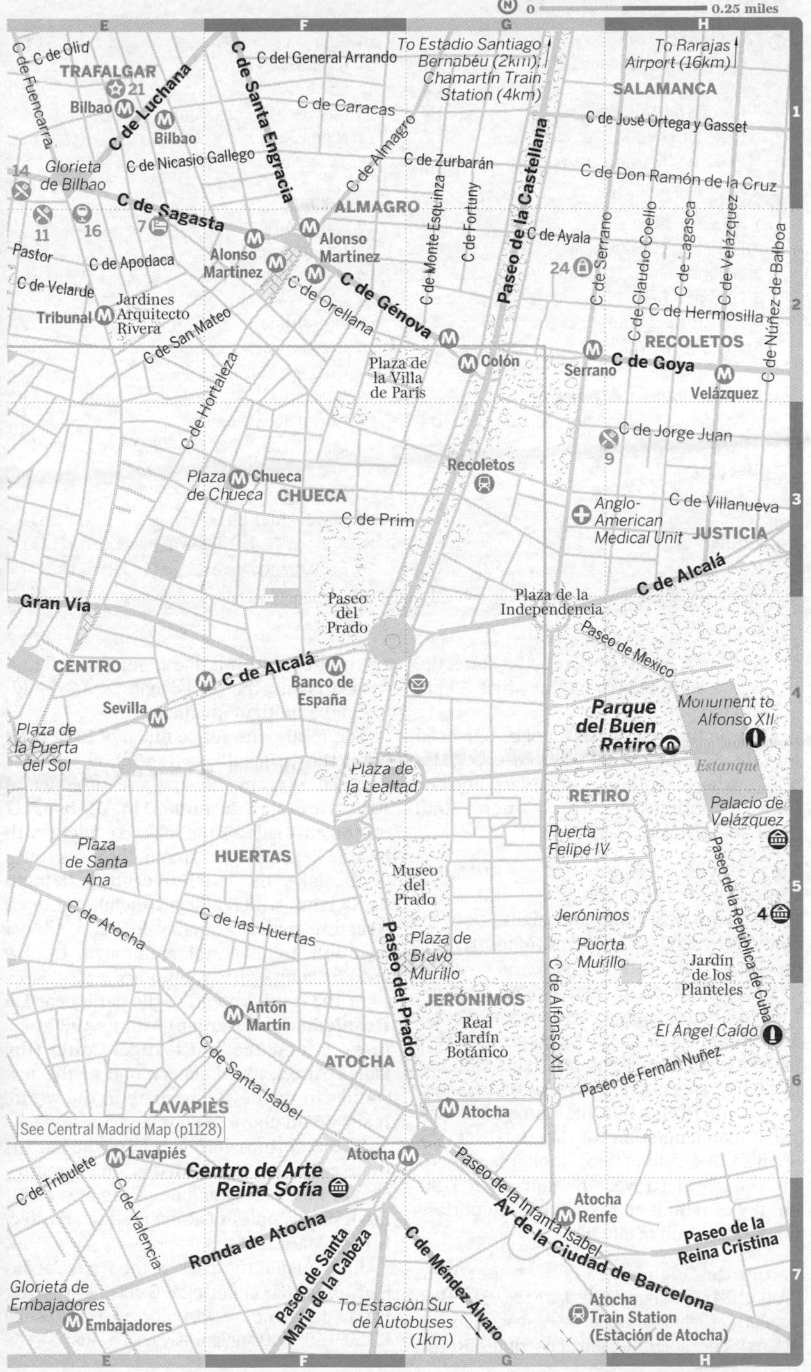

TRAFALGAR
SALAMANCA
ALMAGRO
RECOLETOS
CHUECA
JUSTICIA
CENTRO
RETIRO
HUERTAS
JERÓNIMOS
ATOCHA
LAVAPIÈS
To Estadio Santiago Bernabéu (2km); Chamartín Train Station (4km)
To Barajas Airport (16km)
C de Luchana
C de Santa Engracia
C del General Arrando
C de Caracas
C de Almagro
C de Zurbarán
C de José Ortega y Gasset
C de Don Ramón de la Cruz
C de Sagasta
C de Génova
Paseo de la Castellana
C de Goya
Colón
Plaza de la Villa de París
Plaza de Chueca
Recoletos
Anglo-American Medical Unit
C de Alcalá
Gran Vía
Plaza de la Independencia
Paseo de Mexico
Parque del Buen Retiro
Monument to Alfonso XII
Estanque
Palacio de Velázquez
Plaza de la Puerta del Sol
Banco de España
Plaza de la Lealtad
Museo del Prado
Paseo del Prado
Real Jardín Botánico
Atocha
Centro de Arte Reina Sofía
Ronda de Atocha
Paseo de la Infanta Isabel
Av de la Ciudad de Barcelona
Paseo de la Reina Cristina
Atocha Train Station (Estación de Atocha)
To Estación Sur de Autobuses (1km)
Glorieta de Embajadores
Embajadores
See Central Madrid Map (p1128)
0 500 m
0 0.25 miles

Madrid

Top Sights
- Centro de Arte Reina Sofía ... F7
- Palacio Real ... C4
- Parque del Buen Retiro ... H4
- Plaza de la Villa ... C5
- Plaza de Oriente ... C4

Sights
- 1 Armería Real ... B4
- 2 Ermita de San Antonio de la Florida ... A2
- 3 Farmacia Real ... B4
- 4 Palacio de Cristal ... H5
- 5 Plaza de la Paja ... C5

Activities, Courses & Tours
- 6 Academia Madrid Plus ... D4

Sleeping
- 7 Albergue Juvenil ... E2

Eating
- 8 Almendro 13 ... C5
- 9 Biotza ... H3
- 10 Juanalaloca ... C6
- 11 La Isla del Tesoro ... E2
- 12 La Musa ... D1
- 13 Mercado de San Miguel ... D5
- 14 Nina ... E1
- 15 Txacolina ... D5

Drinking
- 16 Café Comercial ... E2
- 17 Café del Real ... C4
- 18 Delic ... C5

Entertainment
- 19 Café La Palma ... D2
- 20 Charada ... C3
- 21 Clamores ... E1
- 22 Corral de la Morería ... C5
- 23 Las Tablas ... C3

Shopping
- 24 Agatha Ruiz de la Prada ... G2
- 25 Antigua Casa Talavera ... D3
- 26 El Flamenco Vive ... C4

for important events of pomp and state, the palace has 2800-plus rooms, of which 50 are open to the public.

Outside the main palace, poke your head into the **Farmacia Real** (Royal Pharmacy; Map p1124), where apothecary-style jars line the shelves. Continue on to the **Armería Real** (Royal Armoury; Map p1124).

Plaza Mayor PUBLIC SQUARE

Ringed with cafes and restaurants, and packed with people day and night, the 17th-century arcaded Plaza Mayor (Map p1128) is an elegant and bustling square.

Designed in 1619 by Juan Gómez de Mora, the plaza's first public ceremony was the beatification of San Isidro Labrador, Madrid's patron saint. Thereafter, bullfights watched by 50,000 spectators were a recurring spectacle until 1878, while the autos-da-fé (the ritual condemnation of heretics) of the Spanish Inquisition also took place here. Fire largely destroyed the square in 1790, but it was rebuilt and became an important market and hub of city life.

Parque del Buen Retiro PUBLIC GARDENS

(Map p1124; 6am-midnight May-Sep, 6am-11pm Oct-Apr; M Retiro, Príncipe de Vergara, Ibiza or Atocha) The splendid gardens of El Retiro are littered with marble monuments, landscaped lawns, the occasional elegant building and abundant greenery.

The focal point for so much of El Retiro's life is the artificial lake *(estanque)*, which is watched over by the massive ornamental structure of the **Monument to Alfonso XII** on the east side of the lake, complete with marble lions. Hidden among the trees south of the lake, the late-19th-century **Palacio de Cristal**, a magnificent metal and glass structure that is arguably El Retiro's most beautiful architectural monument, is now used for temporary exhibitions.

At the southern end of the park, near **La Rosaleda** (Rose Garden) with its 4000-plus roses, is a statue of **El Ángel Caído** (the Fallen Angel, aka Lucifer), one of the few statues to the devil anywhere in the world. It sits 666m above sea level...

In the northeastern corner of the park is the **Ermita de San Isidro**, a small country chapel noteworthy as one of the few, albeit modest, examples of Romanesque architecture in Madrid.

Just outside the park is the **Real Jardín Botánico** (Royal Botanical Garden; Map p1128; Plaza de Bravo Murillo 2; adult/concession €2.50/1.25; 10am-9pm May-Aug; M Atocha).

Other Sights SIGHTS

The frescoed ceilings of the **Ermita de San Antonio de la Florida** (Map p1124; Glorieta de San Antonio de la Florida 5; admission free; ⌚9.30am-8pm Tue-Fri, 10am-2pm Sat & Sun, varied hr Jul & Aug; Ⓜ Príncipe Pío) are one of Madrid's most surprising secrets. In the southern of the two small chapels you can see Goya's work in its original setting, rendered in 1798. The painter is buried in front of the altar.

The somewhat fusty **Real Academia de Bellas Artes de San Fernando** (Map p1128; http://rabasf.insde.es, in Spanish; Calle de Alcalá 13; adult/student €3/1.50; ⌚9am-5pm Tue-Sat, 9am-2.30pm Sun & Mon Sep-Jun, varied hr Jul & Aug; Ⓜ Sevilla) offers a broad collection of old and modern masters, including works by Zurbarán, El Greco, Rubens, Tintoretto, Goya, Sorolla and Juan Gris.

Madrid also has some lovely public squares, among them **Plaza de Oriente** (Map p1124; Ⓜ Ópera), **Plaza de la Villa** (Map p1124; Ⓜ Ópera or Sol), **Plaza de la Paja** (Map p1124; Ⓜ La Latina) and **Plaza de Santa Ana** (Map p1128; Ⓜ Sol, Sevilla or Antón Martín).

Festivals & Events

Madrid's social calendar is packed with festivals and special events. Major holidays and festivals include the following:

Fiesta de San Isidro CITY FESTIVAL

Street parties, parades, bullfights and other fun events honour Madrid's patron saint on and around 15 May.

Suma Flamenca FLAMENCO

A soul-filled flamenco festival that draws some of the biggest names in the genre to the Teatros del Canal in May or June.

Veranos de la Villa SUMMER FESTIVAL

Madrid's town hall stages a series of cultural events, shows and exhibitions, known as Summers in the City, in July and August.

Sleeping

Where you decide to stay will play an important role in your experience of Madrid. Los Austrias, Sol and Centro put you in the heart of the busy downtown area, while La Latina (the best *barrio* for tapas), Lavapiés and Huertas (good for nightlife) are ideal for those who love Madrid nights and don't want to stagger too far to get back to their hotel. You don't have to be gay to stay in Chueca, but you'll love it if you are, while Malasaña is another inner-city *barrio* with great restaurants and bars.

LOS AUSTRIAS, SOL & CENTRO

TOP CHOICE **Cat's Hostel** HOSTEL €

(Map p1128; ☎91 369 28 07; www.catshostel.com; Calle de Cañizares 6; dm/d from €15/42; ❄@; Ⓜ Antón Martín) Forming part of a 17th-century palace, the internal courtyard here is Madrid's finest – lavish Andalucian tilework surrounded on four sides by an open balcony. There's a super-cool basement bar with free internet connections and fiestas, often with live music.

Hostal Madrid HOSTAL & APARTMENTS €

(Map p1128; ☎91 522 00 60; www.hostal-madrid.info; 2nd fl, Calle de Esparteros 6; s €40-60, d €50-78, apt €60-150; Ⓜ Sol) The 19 excellent apartments here range in size from 33 sq metres to 200 sq metres and each has a fully equipped kitchen, its own sitting area, bathroom and, in some, an expansive terrace with good rooftop views. The double *hostal* rooms are comfortable and well-sized and the service is extremely friendly.

Mad Hostel HOSTEL €

(Map p1128; ☎91 506 48 40; www.madhostel.com; Calle de Cabeza 24; dm from €15; ❄@; Ⓜ Antón Martín) From the same people who brought you Cat's Hostel, the Mad Hostel is less distinguished architecturally but a similar deal. The 1st-floor courtyard – with retractable roof – is a wonderful place to chill, while the four- to eight-bed rooms are smallish but new and clean. There's a small rooftop gym equipped with state-of-the-art equipment.

Hotel Plaza Mayor HOTEL €€

(Map p1128; ☎91 360 06 06; www.h-plazamayor.com; Calle de Atocha 2; s/d from €50/60; ❄; Ⓜ Sol or Tirso de Molina) Stylish decor, charming original elements of a 150-year-old building and helpful staff are selling points here. The rooms are attractive, some with a light colour scheme and wrought-iron furniture. The attic rooms have great views.

Los Amigos Sol Backpackers' Hostel HOSTEL €

(Map p1128; ☎91 559 24 72; www.losamigoshostel.com; 4th fl, Calle de Arenal 26; dm incl breakfast €17-20; @; Ⓜ Ópera or Sol) If you arrive in Madrid keen for company, this could be the place for you – lots of students stay here, the staff are savvy (and speak English) and there are

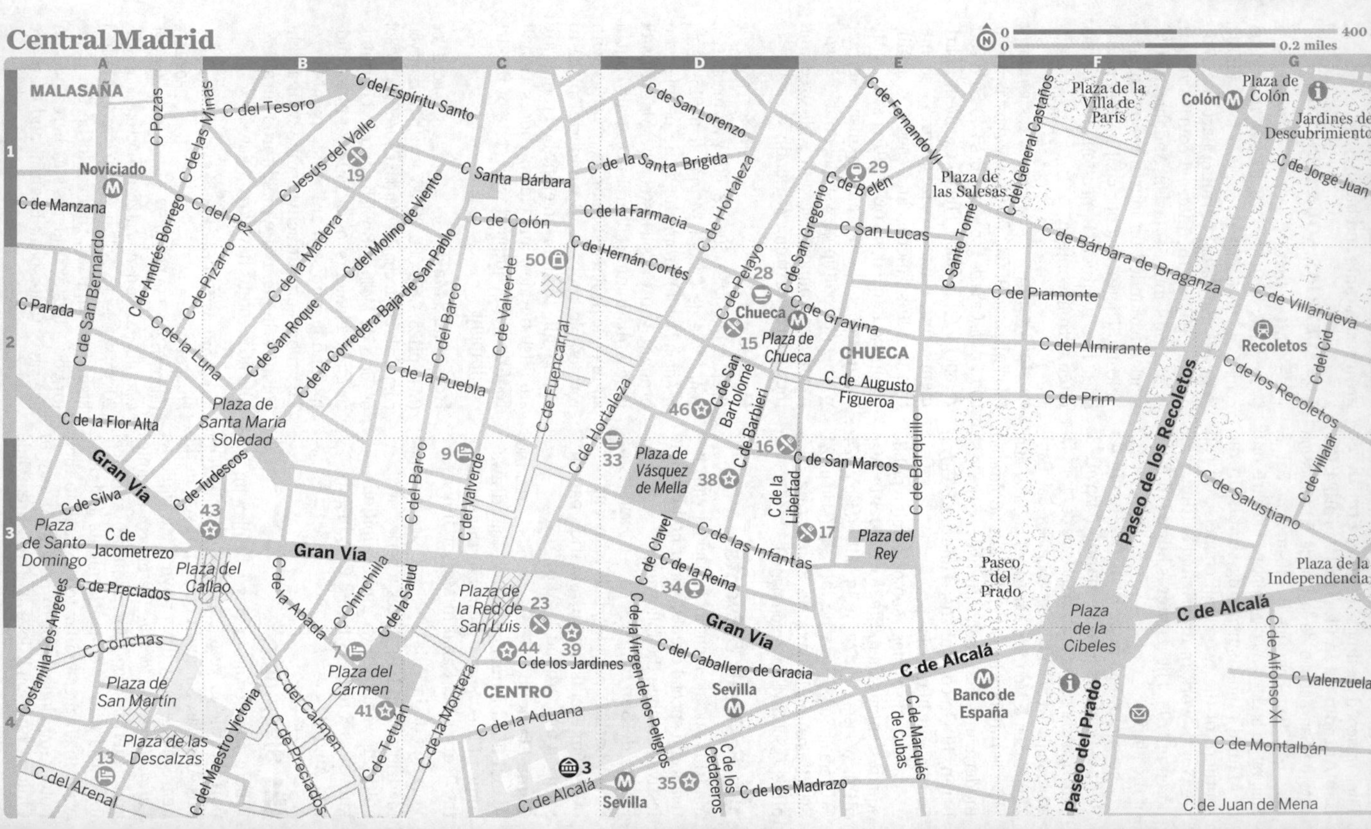
Central Madrid
0.2 miles
400 m
MALASAÑA
CHUECA
CENTRO
Paseo de los Recoletos
Paseo del Prado
C de Alcalá
Gran Vía
Plaza de Colón
Colón
Jardines de Descubrimiento
Recoletos
Plaza de la Independencia
Plaza de la Cibeles
Banco de España
Plaza de la Villa de París
Plaza de las Salesas
Paseo del Prado
Plaza del Rey
Plaza de Chueca
Chueca
Plaza de Vásquez de Mella
Sevilla
Plaza de la Red de San Luis
Plaza del Carmen
Plaza del Callao
Plaza de Santa María Soledad
Plaza de Santo Domingo
Plaza de San Martín
Plaza de las Descalzas
Noviciado
C de Jorge Juan
C de Villanueva
C del Cid
C de Villalar
C de los Recoletos
C de Salustiano
C Valenzuela
C de Alfonso XI
C de Montalbán
C de Juan de Mena
C de Bárbara de Braganza
C de Piamonte
C del Almirante
C de Prim
C del General Castaños
C de Fernando VI
C Santo Tomé
C San Lucas
C de Belén
C de San Gregorio
C de Gravina
C de Augusto Figueroa
C de Barquillo
C de San Marcos
C de Marqués de Cubas
C de la Libertad
C de las Infantas
C de Pelayo
C de Hortaleza
C de San Bartolomé
C de Barbieri
C de la Reina
C de Clavel
C del Caballero de Gracia
C de los Madrazo
C de los Cedaceros
C de la Virgen de los Peligros
C de San Lorenzo
C de la Santa Brígida
C de la Farmacia
C de Hernán Cortés
C de Fuencarral
C de los Jardines
C de la Aduana
C Santa Bárbara
C de Colón
C de Valverde
C del Valverde
C del Barco
C de la Montera
C del Espíritu Santo
C del Molino de Viento
C de la Corredera Baja de San Pablo
C de la Puebla
C de la Salud
C Chinchilla
C de Tetuán
C Jesús del Valle
C de la Madera
C de San Roque
C de la Abada
C del Carmen
C de Preciados
C del Tesoro
C del Pez
C de Pizarro
C de la Luna
C de Tudescos
C del Maestro Victoria
C de las Minas
C Pozas
C de Andrés Borrego
C de San Bernardo
C de la Flor Alta
C de Silva
C de Jacometrezo
C Conchas
C del Arenal
Costanilla Los Ángeles
C de Manzana
C Parada

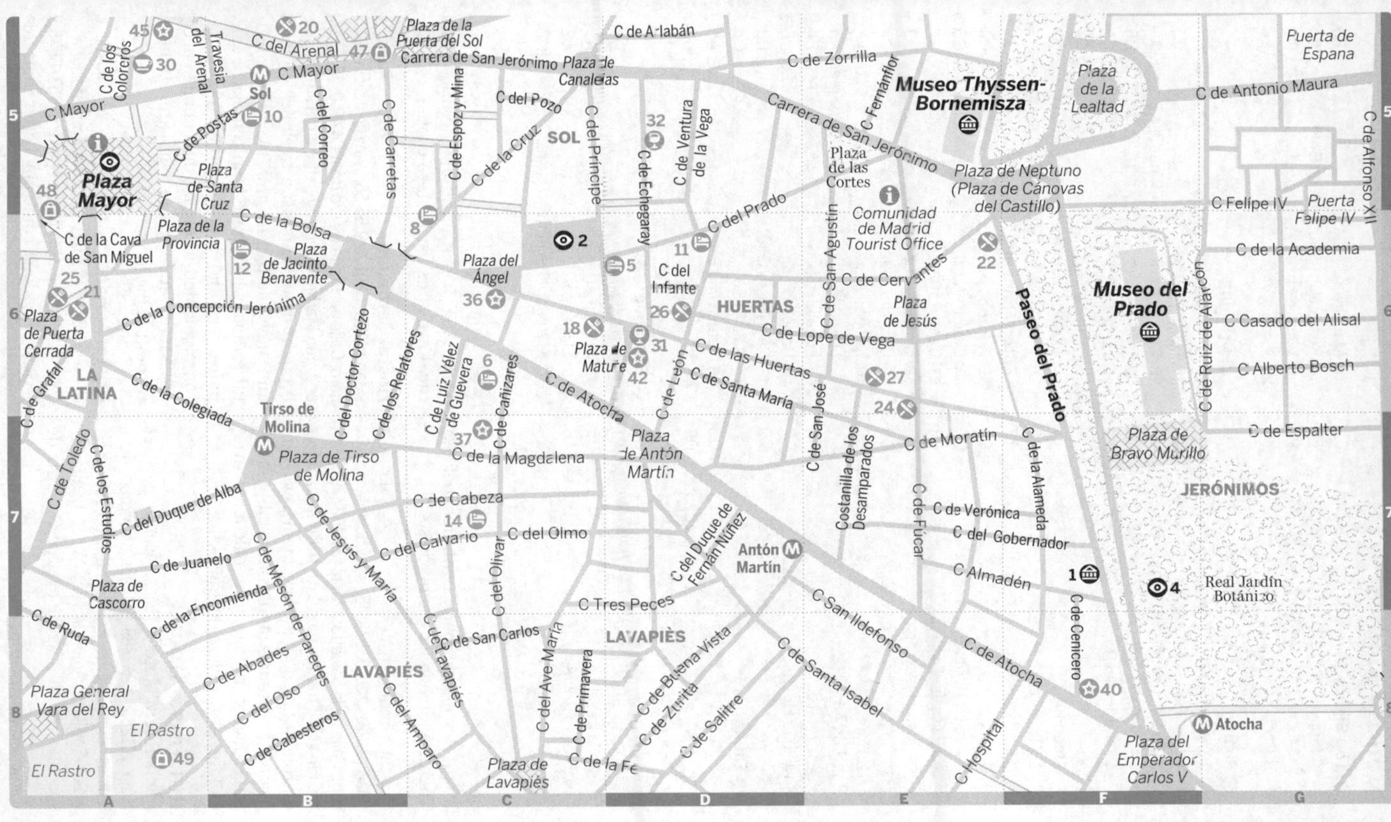
Plaza Mayor
C Mayor
C de los Coloreros
Travesía del Arenal
C del Arenal
Sol
Plaza de la Puerta del Sol
Carrera de San Jerónimo
Plaza de Canalejas
C de A-labán
C de Zorrilla
C Fernánflor
Museo Thyssen-Bornemisza
Plaza de la Lealtad
C de Antonio Maura
Puerta de Espana
C de Alfonso XII
C de Postas
C del Correo
C de Carretas
C de Espoz y Mina
C del Pozo
C de la Cruz
SOL
C del Príncipe
C de Echegaray
C de Ventura de la Vega
Plaza de las Cortes
Plaza de Neptuno (Plaza de Cánovas del Castillo)
C Felipe IV
Puerta Felipe IV
Plaza de Santa Cruz
C de la Cava de San Miguel
Plaza de la Provincia
C de la Bolsa
Plaza de Jacinto Benavente
Plaza del Ángel
C del Prado
C de San Agustín
Comunidad de Madrid Tourist Office
C de la Academia
C del Infante
HUERTAS
C de Cervantes
Museo del Prado
C de Ruiz de Alarcón
C Casado del Alisal
Plaza de Puerta Cerrada
C de la Concepción Jerónima
Plaza de Jesús
C de Lope de Vega
Paseo del Prado
Plaza de Matute
C de las Huertas
C Alberto Bosch
C de Grafal
LA LATINA
C de la Colegiada
C del Doctor Cortezo
C de los Relatores
C de Luiz Vélez de Guevera
C de Cañizares
C de Atocha
C de León
C de Santa María
C de San José
Costanilla de los Desamparados
C de Moratín
C de la Alameda
Plaza de Bravo Murillo
C de Espalter
Tirso de Molina
Plaza de Tirso de Molina
C de la Magdalena
Plaza de Antón Martín
C de Toledo
C de los Estudios
C del Duque de Alba
C de Cabeza
C de Jesús y María
C de Fúcar
C de Verónica
JERÓNIMOS
C del Calvario
C del Olmo
C del Gobernador
C de Juanelo
C de Mesón de Paredes
C del Olivar
C del Duque de Fernán Núñez
Antón Martín
C Almadén
Real Jardín Botánico
Plaza de Cascorro
C de la Encomienda
C Tres Peces
C San Ildefonso
C de Cenicero
C de Ruda
C de San Carlos
C de Lavapiés
C del Ave María
LAVAPIÈS
C de Atocha
C de Abades
LAVAPIÉS
C de Primavera
C de Buena Vista
C de Santa Isabel
Plaza General Vara del Rey
C del Oso
C del Amparo
C de Zurita
C de Salitre
C Hospital
Atocha
El Rastro
C de Cabesteros
Plaza de Lavapiés
C de la Fe
Plaza del Emperador Carlos V
A
B
C
D
E
F
G
5
6
7
8
1
2
4
5
6
8
10
11
12
14
18
20
21
22
24
25
26
27
30
31
32
36
37
40
42
45
47
48
49

Central Madrid

Top Sights
- Museo del Prado ... F6
- Museo Thyssen-Bornemisza ... E5
- Plaza Mayor ... A5

Sights
1 Caixa Forum ... F7
2 Plaza de Santa Ana ... C6
3 Real Academia de Bellas Artes de San Fernando ... C4
4 Real Jardín Botánico ... F7

Sleeping
5 Alicia Room Mate ... D6
6 Cat's Hostel ... C6
7 Hostal Acapulco ... B4
8 Hostal Adriano ... C6
9 Hostal La Zona ... C3
10 Hostal Madrid ... B5
11 Hostal Sardinero ... D6
12 Hotel Plaza Mayor ... B6
13 Los Amigos Sol Backpackers' Hostel ... A4
14 Mad Hostel ... C7

Eating
15 Baco y Beto ... D2
16 Bazaar ... D3
17 Bocaito ... E3
18 Casa Alberto ... C6
19 Casa Julio ... B1
20 Casa Labra ... B5
21 Casa Revuelta ... A6
22 Estado Puro ... E6
23 La Gloria de Montera ... C3
24 Maceiras ... E6
25 Restaurante Sobrino de Botín ... A6
26 Vinos González ... D6
27 Viva La Vida ... E6

Drinking
28 Café Acuarela ... D2
29 Café Belén ... E1
30 Chocolatería de San Ginés ... A5
31 El Imperfecto ... D6
32 La Venencia ... D5
33 Mamá Inés ... D3
34 Museo Chicote ... D3

Entertainment
35 Adraba ... D4
36 Café Central ... C6
37 Casa Patas ... C7
38 Club 54 Studio ... D3
39 Costello Café & Niteclub ... C4
40 Kapital ... F8
Liquid Madrid ... (see 38)
41 Localidades Galicia ... B4
42 Popular ... D6
43 Sala Bash/Ohm ... B3
44 Sala El Sol ... C4
45 Teatro Joy Eslava ... A5
46 Why Not? ... D2

Shopping
47 Casa de Diego ... B5
48 El Arco Artesanía ... A5
49 El Rastro ... A8
50 Mercado de Fuencarral ... C2

bright dorm-style rooms (with free lockers). There's a kitchen for use by guests.

Hostal Acapulco HOSTAL €
(Map p1128; ☎91 531 19 45; www.hostalacapulco.com; Calle de la Salud 13; s/d/tr €52/62/79; ❄📶; Ⓜ Gran Vía) This immaculate little *hostal* has marble floors, double-glazed windows, renovated bathrooms and comfortable beds. Street-facing rooms have balconies overlooking sunny Plaza del Carmen.

HUERTAS & ATOCHA

Alicia Room Mate BOUTIQUE HOTEL €€
(Map p1128; ☎91 389 60 95; www.room-matehoteles.com; Calle del Prado 2; d €105-165; ❄📶; Ⓜ Sol, Sevilla or Antón Martín) With beautiful, spacious rooms, Alicia overlooks Plaza de Santa Ana. It has an ultramodern look and the downstairs bar is oh-so-cool.

Hostal Sardinero HOSTAL €
(Map p1128; ☎91 429 57 56; www.hostalsardinero.com; Calle del Prado 16; s/d from €42/50; ❄; Ⓜ Sol or Antón Martín) A change of owners here has brought more than just a fresh lick of paint and new mattresses and TVs. The cheerful rooms, which have high ceilings, a safe, hairdryers and renovated bathrooms, are complemented nicely by the equally cheerful Nieves and Jimmy, who are attentive without being in your face.

Hostal Adriano HOSTAL €
(Map p1128; ☎91 521 13 39; www.hostaladriano.com; 4th fl, Calle de la Cruz 26; s/d/tr €53/65/85; Ⓜ Sol) They don't come any better than this

bright and cheerful *hostal* wedged in the streets that mark the boundary between Sol and Huertas. Most rooms are well sized and each has its own colour scheme.

MALASAÑA & CHUECA

Hostal La Zona HOSTEL €
(Map p1128; ☎91 521 99 04; www.hostallazona.com; 1st fl, Calle de Valverde 7; s/d/tr €50/60/85; ❄📶; Ⓜ Gran Vía) Catering primarily to a gay clientele, the stylish Hostal La Zona has exposed brickwork, wooden pillars and a subtle colour scheme. Other highlights include free internet, helpful staff and air-con/heating in every room.

Albergue Juvenil HOSTEL €
(Map p1124; ☎91 593 96 88; www.ajmadrid.es; Calle de Mejía Lequerica 21; dm €19-25; ❄📶; Ⓜ Bilbao or Alonso Martínez) The Albergue's dorms are spotless, no dorm houses more than six beds (and each has its own bathroom), and facilities include a pool table, gym, wheelchair access, free internet, laundry and a TV/DVD room.

Eating

Madrid is a focal point of cooking from around the country and is particularly attached to seafood; despite not having a sea, Madrid has the world's second-largest fish market (after Tokyo's).

From the chaotic tapas bars of La Latina to countless neighbourhood favourites, you'll have no trouble tracking down specialities such as *cochinillo asado* (roast suckling pig) or *cocido madrileño* (a hearty stew made of chickpeas and meats).

LOS AUSTRIAS, SOL & CENTRO

TOP CHOICE **Mercado de San Miguel** TAPAS, DELICATESSEN €€
(Map p1124; www.casinodemadrid.es; Plaza de San Miguel; meals €15-35; ⏲10am-midnight Sun-Wed, 10am-2am Thu-Sat; Ⓜ Sol) One of Madrid's oldest and most beautiful markets, the Mercado de San Miguel has undergone a stunning major renovation. Within the early-20th-century glass walls, the market has become an inviting space strewn with tables (difficult to nab) where you can enjoy the freshest food or a drink.

Restaurante Sobrino de Botín ROAST MEATS, TRADITIONAL SPANISH €€
(Map p1128; ☎91 366 42 17; www.botin.es; Calle de los Cuchilleros 17; meals €40-45; Ⓜ La Latina or Sol) It's not every day that you can eat in the oldest restaurant in the world (1725). The secret of its staying power is fine *cochinillo* (suckling pig; €22.90) and *cordero asado* (roast lamb; €22.90) cooked in wood-fired ovens. Eating in the vaulted cellar is a treat.

La Gloria de Montera TRADITIONAL SPANISH, FUSION €€
(Map p1128; Calle del Caballero de Gracia 10; meals €25-30; Ⓜ Gran Vía) Minimalist style, tasty Mediterranean dishes and great prices mean that you'll probably have to wait in line (no reservations taken) to eat here.

LA LATINA & LAVAPIÉS

This area is best known for its tapas bars. See the boxed text, p1132, for more.

TOP CHOICE **Viva La Vida** VEGETARIAN BUFFET €
(Map p1128; www.vivalavida.vg; Costanilla de San Andrés 16; vegetarian buffet per 100g €2.10; ⏲noon-midnight; Ⓜ La Latina) This organic food shop has as its centrepiece an enticing vegetarian buffet with hot and cold food that's always filled with flavour. On the cusp of Plaza de la Paja, it's a great place at any time of the day, especially outside normal Spanish eating hours.

HUERTAS & ATOCHA

TOP CHOICE **Vinos Gonzalez** TAPAS, DELICATESSEN €€
(Map p1128; Calle de León 12; meals €20-25; ⏲9am-midnight Tue-Thu, 9am-1am Fri & Sat; Ⓜ Antón Martín) Ever dreamed of a deli where you could choose a tasty morsel and sit down to eat it right there? Well, here you can. On offer are a tempting array of cheeses, cured meats and other typically Spanish delicacies.

TOP CHOICE **Casa Alberto** TRADITIONAL SPANISH €€
(Map p1128; ☎91 429 93 56; www.casaalberto.es, in Spanish; Calle de las Huertas 18; meals €25-30; ⏲noon-1.30am Tue-Sat, noon-4pm Sun; Ⓜ Antón Martín) One of the most atmospheric old *tabernas* of Madrid, Casa Alberto has been around since 1827. The secret to its staying power is vermouth on tap, excellent tapas and fine sit-down meals; *rabo de toro* (bull's tail) is a good order.

Maceiras GALICIAN €€
(Map p1128; Calle de las Huertas 66; meals €20-30; Ⓜ Antón Martín) Galician tapas (think octopus, green peppers etc) never tasted so good as in this agreeably rustic bar down the bottom of the Huertas hill, especially when washed down with a crisp white Ribeiro.

A TAPAS TOUR OF MADRID

Madrid's home of tapas is La Latina, especially along Calle de la Cava Baja and surrounding streets. **Almendro 13** (Map p1124; Calle del Almendro 13; meals €15-20; Ⓜ La Latina) is famous for quality rather than decor. Down on Calle de la Cava Baja, **Txacolina** (Map p1124; Calle de la Cava Baja 26; meals €15-20; ⏲lunch & dinner Sat, dinner Mon & Wed-Fri; Ⓜ La Latina) does some of the biggest *pintxos* (Basque tapas) you'll find. Not far away, **Juanalaloca** (Map p1124; Plaza de la Puerta de Moros 4; meals €25-35; ⏲lunch & dinner Tue-Sun, dinner Mon; Ⓜ La Latina) does a magnificent *tortilla de patatas* (potato and onion omelette).

In the centre, for *bacalao* (cod) the historic **Casa Labra** (Map p1128; Calle de Tetuán 11; meals €15-20; ⏲11am-3.30pm & 6-11pm; Ⓜ Sol) and **Casa Revuelta** (Map p1128; Calle de Latoneros 3; meals €15-20; ⏲10.30am-4pm & 7-11pm Mon & Wed-Sat, 10.30am-4pm Sun, closed Aug; Ⓜ La Latina or Sol) have no peers.

Along the Paseo del Prado, there's super-cool **Estado Puro** (Map p1128; www.tapasenestadopuro.com, in Spanish; Plaza de Cánovas del Castillo 4; tapas €1.95-9.50; ⏲11am-1am Tue-Sat, 11am-4pm Sun; Ⓜ Banco de España or Atocha), with gourmet tapas inspired by Catalonia's world-famous El Bulli restaurant. In Salamanca **Biotza** (Map p1124; Calle de Claudio Coello 27; ⏲9am-midnight Mon-Thu, 9am-1am Fri & Sat; Ⓜ Serrano) offers creative Basque *pintxos*.

In Chueca don't miss **Bocaito** (Map p1128; Calle de la Libertad 4-6; meals €20-25; ⏲lunch & dinner Mon-Fri, dinner Sat; Ⓜ Chueca), a purveyor of Andalucian *jamón* (ham) and seafood. **Casa Julio** (Map p1128; Calle de la Madera 37; meals €10-15; ⏲lunch & dinner Mon-Sat; Ⓜ Tribunal) does Madrid's best *croquetas*. Another brilliant choice is **Baco y Beto** (Map p1128; www.bacoybeto.com, in Spanish; Calle de Pelayo 24; meals €20-25; ⏲lunch & dinner Fri & Sat, dinner Mon-Thu; Ⓜ Chueca).

MALASAÑA & CHUECA

TOP CHOICE **La Musa** SPANISH FUSION €€
(Map p1124; www.lamusa.com.es; Calle de Manuela Malasaña 18; meals €25-30; ⏲9am-1.30am Sun-Thu, 9am-2.30am Fri & Sat; Ⓜ San Bernardo) Snug yet loud, a favourite of Madrid's hip young crowd yet utterly unpretentious, La Musa is all about designer decor, lounge music on the sound system and food (breakfast, lunch or dinner) that is always fun and filled with flavour. The menu is divided into three types of tapas – hot, cold and BBQ.

TOP CHOICE **Bazaar** NOUVELLE SPANISH CUISINE €€
(Map p1128; www.restaurantbazaar.com; Calle de la Libertad 21; meals €20-25; Ⓜ Chueca) Bazaar's popularity among the well-heeled and often famous shows no sign of abating. Its pristine white interior design with theatre lighting may draw a crowd that looks like it stepped out of the pages of *Hola!* magazine, but the food is extremely well priced and innovative. It doesn't take reservations.

Nina MEDITERRANEAN FUSION €€
(Map p1124; ☎91 591 00 46; Calle de Manuela Malasaña 10; meals €30-40; Ⓜ Bilbao) Sophisticated, intimate and wildly popular, Nina has an extensive menu (available in English) of nouvelle Mediterranean cuisine that doesn't miss a trick. We like the decor, all exposed brick and subtle lighting, and we love just about everything on the menu, but we adore the honey-and-sobrasada-glazed grilled ostrich steak with a salmon and raspberry crust.

La Isla del Tesoro VEGETARIAN €€
(Map p1124; ☎91 593 14 40; www.isladeltesoro.net; Calle de Manuela Malasaña 3; meals €30-40; Ⓜ Bilbao) La Isla del Tesoro is loaded with quirky charm – the dining area is like someone's fantasy of a secret garden come to life. The cooking is assured and wide-ranging in its influences; the jungle burger is typical in a menu that's full of surprises.

Drinking

Madrid lives life on its streets and plazas. Bar-hopping is a pastime enjoyed by young and old alike. If you're after the more traditional, with tiled walls and flamenco tunes, head to Huertas. For gay-friendly drinking, Chueca is the place. Malasaña caters to a grungy, funky crowd, while La Latina has friendly bars that guarantee atmosphere most nights. In summer, terrace bars pop up all over the city.

The bulk of Madrid bars open to 2am Sunday to Thursday, and to 3am or 3.30am Friday and Saturday.

TOP CHOICE **Museo Chicote** COCKTAIL BAR

(Map p1128; www.museo-chicote.com; Gran Vía 12; 6pm-3am Mon-Thu, 6pm-3.30am Fri & Sat; M Gran Vía) The founder of this Madrid landmark is said to have invented more than 100 cocktails, which the likes of Hemingway, Ava Gardner, Grace Kelly, Sophia Loren and Frank Sinatra all enjoyed at one time or another. It's at its best after midnight when a lounge atmosphere takes over, couples cuddle on the curved benches and some of the city's best DJs do their stuff.

TOP CHOICE **Café Comercial** LITERARY CAFE

(Map p1124; Glorieta de Bilbao 7; 7.30am-midnight Mon, 7.30am-1am Tue-Thu, 7.30am-2am Fri, 8.30am-2am Sat, 9am-midnight Sun; M Bilbao) This glorious old Madrid cafe proudly fights a rearguard action against progress with heavy leather seats, abundant marble and old-style waiters. As close as Madrid came to the intellectual cafes of Paris' Left Bank, Café Comercial now has a clientele that has broadened to include just about anyone.

TOP CHOICE **La Venencia** SHERRY BAR

(Map p1128; Calle de Echegaray 7; 1-3.30pm & 7.30pm-1.30am; M Sol) This is how sherry bars should be – old-world, drinks poured straight from the dusty wooden barrels and none of the frenetic activity for which Huertas is famous. La Venencia is a *barrio* classic, with fine sherry from Sanlúcar and *manzanilla* from Jerez.

Café Belén CHILL-OUT BAR

(Map p1128; Calle de Belén 5; 3.30pm-3am; M Chueca) Café Belén is cool in all the right places – lounge and chill-out music, dim lighting, a great range of drinks (the mojitos are especially good) and a low-key crowd that's the height of casual sophistication.

Delic BAR-CAFÉ

(Map p1124; Costanilla de San Andrés 14; 11am-2am Sun & Tue-Thu, 7pm-2am Mon, 11am-2.30am Fri & Sat; M La Latina) We could go on for hours about this long-standing cafe-bar, but we'll reduce it to its most basic elements: nursing an exceptionally good mojito (€8) or three on a warm summer's evening at Delic's outdoor tables on one of Madrid's prettiest plazas is one of life's great pleasures.

Café del Real BAR-CAFE

(Map p1124; Plaza de Isabel II 2; 9am-1am Mon Thu, 9am-3am Fri & Sat; M Ópera) One of the nicest bar-cafes in central Madrid, this place serves a rich variety of creative coffees and a few cocktails to a soundtrack of chill-out music. The best seats are upstairs, where the low ceilings, wooden beams and leather chairs make a great place to pass an afternoon.

El Imperfecto BAR

(Map p1128; Plaza de Matute 2; 3pm-2am Sun-Thu, 3pm-3am Fri & Sat; M Antón Martín) Its name notwithstanding, the Imperfect One is our ideal Huertas bar, with live jazz most Tuesdays at 9pm and a drinks menu as long as a saxophone, ranging from cocktails (€6.50) and spirits to milkshakes, teas and creative coffees.

MADRID'S FAVOURITE POST-CLUBBING MUNCHIES

Join the sugar-searching throngs who end the night at the mythic **Chocolatería de San Ginés** (Map p1128; Pasadizo de San Ginés 5; 9.30am-7am Mon-Fri, 9am-7am Sat & Sun; M Sol), famous for its freshly fried *churros* (fried sticks of dough) and syrupy hot chocolate.

Entertainment

The **Guía del Ocio** (www.guiadelocio.com, in Spanish; magazine €1) is the city's classic weekly listings magazine. Also good are **Metropoli** (www.abc.es/metropoli, in Spanish) and **On Madrid** (www.elpais.com, in Spanish), respectively *ABC's* and *El País'* Friday listings supplements.

Nightclubs

No *barrio* is without a decent club or disco, but the most popular dance spots are in the centre. Don't expect dance clubs or *discotecas* (nightclubs) to get going until after 1am at the earliest. Standard entry fee is €10, which usually includes the first drink, although megaclubs and swankier places charge a few euros more.

Teatro Joy Eslava CLUB

(Map p1128; www.joy-eslava.com; Calle del Arenal 11; admission €12-15; 11.30pm-6am; M Sol) The only things guaranteed at this grand old Madrid dance club (housed in a 19th-century theatre) are a crowd and the fact that it will be open. (The club claims to have opened every single day for the past 29 years.) The music and the crowd are a mixed bag, but queues are long and invariably include locals and tourists, and even the occasional *famoso*.

GAY & LESBIAN MADRID

The heartbeat of gay Madrid is the inner-city *barrio* of Chueca, where Madrid didn't just come out of the closet, but ripped the doors off in the process.

A good place to get the low-down is the laid-back **Mamá Inés** (Map p1128; www.mamaines.com, in Spanish; Calle de Hortaleza 22; ⊙10am-2am Sun-Thu, 10am-3am Fri & Sat; Ⓜ Gran Vía or Chueca). **Café Acuarela** (Map p1128; Calle de Gravina 10; ⊙11am-2am Sun-Thu, 11am-3am Fri & Sat; Ⓜ Chueca) is another dimly lit centrepiece of gay Madrid.

Two of the most popular Chueca nightspots are **Club 54 Studio** (Map p1128; www.studio54madrid.com, in Spanish; Calle de Barbieri 7; ⊙11.30pm-3.30am Thu-Sat; Ⓜ Chueca), modelled on the famous New York club Studio 54, and **Liquid Madrid** (Map p1128; www.liquid.es; Calle de Barbieri 7; ⊙9am-3am Mon-Thu, 9am-3.30am Fri & Sat; Ⓜ Chueca). **Why Not?** (Map p1128; Calle de San Bartolomé 7; admission €10; ⊙10.30pm-6am; Ⓜ Chueca) is a place where nothing's left to the imagination. Another club popular with a predominantly gay crowd is **Sala Bash/Ohm** (Map p1128; Plaza del Callao 4; ⊙midnight-6am Fri & Sat; Ⓜ Callao).

Charada CLUB

(Map p1124; www.charadaclubdebaile.com, in Spanish; Calle de la Bola 13; admission €10-15; ⊙midnight-6am Thu-Sat; Ⓜ Santo Domingo) Charada took the Madrid nightlife scene by storm in 2009 and has never looked back. Its decor is New York chic (with no hint of its former existence as a brothel), the cocktails are highly original, the clientele is well-heeled and often famous and it's the home turntable for some of the best house DJs in town.

Adraba CLUB

(Map p1128; www.fsmgroup.es, in Spanish; Calle de Alcalá 20; admission €15-18; ⊙midnight-6am Wed-Sun; Ⓜ Sevilla) This historic nightclub finally reopened to much fanfare in 2010 and has rapidly re-established itself as one of the city's best. The designer decor is stunning, there are five nights of dancing and the crowd's sophisticated. Whatever the night, the resident DJs are among the best in Madrid.

Kapital CLUB

(Map p1128; www.grupo-kapital.com, in Spanish; Calle de Atocha 125; admission €20; ⊙6-10pm & midnight-6am Thu-Sun; Ⓜ Atocha) One of the most famous megaclubs in Madrid, this massive seven-storey nightclub has something for everyone: from cocktail bars and dance music to karaoke, salsa, hip-hop and more chilled spaces for R&B and soul, as well as a section devoted to 'Made in Spain' music.

Live Music

Other genres of live music are also well catered for.

Many of flamenco's top names perform in Madrid, making it an excellent place to see interpretations of the art.

Corral de la Morería FLAMENCO

(Map p1124; ☎91 365 84 46; www.corraldelamoreria.com; Calle de la Morería 17; admission €27-37; ⊙8.30pm-2.30am, shows 10pm & midnight Sun-Fri, 7pm, 10pm & midnight Sat; Ⓜ Ópera) This is one of the most prestigious flamenco stages in Madrid, with 50 years as a leading venue and top performers most nights. The stage area has a rustic feel and tables are pushed up close. We'd steer clear of the overpriced restaurant, but the performances have a far higher price to quality ratio.

Las Tablas FLAMENCO

(Map p1124; ☎91 542 05 20; www.lastablasmadrid.com; Plaza de España 9; admission €24; ⊙shows 10.30pm Sun-Thu, 8pm & 10pm Fri & Sat; Ⓜ Plaza de España) Las Tablas has quickly earned a reputation for quality flamenco. Most nights you'll see a classic flamenco show, with plenty of throaty singing and soul-baring dancing. Antonia Moya and Marisol Navarro, leading lights in the flamenco world, are regular performers.

Casa Patas FLAMENCO

(Map p1128; ☎91 369 04 96; www.casapatas.com, in Spanish; Calle de Cañizares 10; admission €30-35; ⊙shows 10.30pm Mon-Thu, 9pm & midnight Fri & Sat; Ⓜ Antón Martín or Tirso de Molina) One of the top flamenco stages in Madrid, this *tablao* always offers unimpeachable quality.

Café Central JAZZ CLUB

(Map p1128; ☎91 369 41 43; www.cafecentralmadrid.com, in Spanish; Plaza del Angel 10; admission €10-15; ⊙1pm-2.30am Sun-Thu, 1.30pm-3.30am Fri & Sat; Ⓜ Antón Martín or Sol) This art-deco bar has consistently been voted one of the best jazz venues in the world by leading jazz magazines, and with almost 9000 gigs under its belt, it rarely misses a beat. Shows start at 10pm and tickets go on sale an hour before the set starts.

FREE Populart JAZZ CLUB

(Map p1128; www.populart.es, in Spanish; Calle de las Huertas 22; ⌚6pm-2.30am Sun-Thu, 6pm-3.30am Fri & Sat; Ⓜ Antón Martín or Sol) One of Madrid's classic jazz clubs, this place offers a low-key atmosphere and top-quality music – mostly jazz, but with occasional blues, swing and even flamenco thrown into the mix. Shows start at 10.15pm, but if you want a seat get here early.

Costello Café & Niteclub CLUB, LIVE MUSIC

(Map p1128; www.costelloclub.com; Calle del Caballero de Gracia 10; admission €5-10; ⌚6pm-1am Sun-Wed, 6pm-2.30am Thu-Sat; Ⓜ Gran Vía) Very cool. Costello Café & Niteclub is smooth-as-silk ambience wedded with an innovative mix of pop, rock and fusion in Warholesque surrounds. There's live music every night of the week (except Sunday) at 9.30pm, with resident and visiting DJs until closing time from Thursday to Saturday.

Sala El Sol LIVE MUSIC

(Map p1128; www.elsolmad.com, in Spanish; Calle de los Jardines 3; admission €8-25; ⌚11pm-5.30am Tue-Sat Jul-Sep; Ⓜ Gran Vía) Madrid institutions don't come any more beloved than Sala El Sol. It opened in 1979 and quickly established itself as a leading stage for all the icons of the era. The music rocks and rolls and usually resurrects the '70s and '80s, while soul and funk also get a run.

Café La Palma LIVE MUSIC

(Map p1124; ☎91 522 50 31; www.cafelapalma.com, in Spanish; Calle de la Palma 62; admission free-€12; ⌚4.30pm-3am Sun-Thu, 4.30pm-3.30am Fri & Sat; Ⓜ Noviciado) It's amazing how much variety Café La Palma has packed into its labyrinth of rooms. Live shows featuring hot local bands are held at the back, while DJs mix up the front. You might find live music other nights, but there are always two shows at 10pm and midnight from Thursday to Saturday.

Clamores LIVE MUSIC

(Map p1124; ☎91 445 79 38; www.clamores.es, in Spanish; Calle de Alburquerque 14; admission €5-15; ⌚6pm-3am; Ⓜ Bilbao) This one-time classic jazz cafe has morphed into one of the most diverse live-music stages in Madrid. Jazz is still a staple, but world music, flamenco, soul fusion, singer-songwriter, pop and rock all make regular appearances. Live shows can begin as early as 9pm.

Sport

Get tickets to football matches and bullfights from box offices or through agents such as **Localidades Galicia** (Map p1128; ☎91 531 91 31; www.bullfightticketsmadrid.com; Plaza del Carmen 1; ⌚9.30am-1pm & 4.30-7pm Mon-Sat, 9.30am-1pm Sun; Ⓜ Sol).

Estadio Santiago Bernabéu FOOTBALL STADIUM

(off Map p1124; www.realmadrid.com; Avenida de Concha Espina 1; tours €15; ⌚10am-7pm Mon-Sat, 10.30am-6.30pm Sun; Ⓜ Santiago Bernabéu) The mythic Real Madrid plays at this stadium. Fans can visit the stadium and take an interesting tour through the presidential box, dressing room and field. The all-important phone number for booking game tickets (which you later pick up at Gate 42) is ☎902 32 43 24, which only works if you're calling from within Spain.

Plaza de Toros Las Ventas BULLFIGHTING

(☎91 356 22 00; www.las-ventas.com, in Spanish; Calle de Alcalá 237; tours €7; ⌚tours 10am-2pm; Ⓜ Ventas) Some of Spain's top *toreros* swing their capes in Plaza de Toros Las Ventas. Fights are held every Sunday afternoon from mid-May through October. Get tickets (from €5 standing in the sun) at the plaza box office, Localidades Galicia (p1135), or from official ticket agents on Calle Victoria close to the Plaza de la Puerta del Sol. For excellent tours of the bullring in English and Spanish, contact **Tauro Tour** (☎91 556 92 37; gregorio@trazopublicidad.es; 4th fl, Paseo de la Castellana 115).

Shopping

Salamanca is the home of upmarket fashions, with chic boutiques lining up to showcase the best that Spanish and international designers have to offer. Some of it spills over into Chueca, but Malasaña is Salamanca's true alter ego, home to fashion that's as funky as it is offbeat. Central Madrid – Sol, Huertas or La Latina – offers plenty of individual surprises.

Antigua Casa Talavera TRADITIONAL CERAMICS

(Map p1124; Calle de Isabel la Católica 2; ⌚10am-1.30pm & 5-8pm Mon-Fri, 10am-1.30pm Sat; Ⓜ Santo Domingo) The extraordinary tiled facade of this wonderful old shop conceals an Aladdin's Cave of ceramics from all over Spain. This is not the mass-produced stuff aimed at the tourist market, but comes from the small family potters of Andalucía and Toledo.

El Arco Artesanía CONTEMPORARY SOUVENIRS

(Map p1128; Plaza Mayor 9; ⌚11am-9pm; Ⓜ Sol or La Latina) This original shop in the southwestern corner of Plaza Mayor sells an outstanding array of homemade designer souvenirs, from stone and glasswork to jewellery and home fittings.

El Flamenco Vive FLAMENCO
(Map p1124; www.elflamencovive.es; Calle Conde de Lemos 7; ⏲10am-2pm & 5-9pm Mon-Sat; Ⓜ Ópera) This temple to flamenco has it all, from guitars, songbooks and well-priced CDs, to polka-dotted dancing costumes, shoes, colourful plastic jewellery and literature about flamenco.

Casa de Diego SPANISH FANS, CANES & UMBRELLAS
(Map p1128; www.casadediego.com; Plaza de la Puerta del Sol 12; ⏲9.30am-8pm Mon-Sat; Ⓜ Sol) This classic shop has been around since 1858, selling and repairing Spanish fans, shawls, umbrellas and canes. Service is old-style and the staff occasionally grumpy, but the fans are works of antique art.

El Rastro FLEA MARKET
(Map p1128; Calle de la Ribera de Curtidores; ⏲8am-3pm Sun; Ⓜ La Latina, Puerta de Toledo or Tirso de Molina) A Sunday morning at El Rastro, Europe's largest flea market, is a Madrid institution. You could easily spend an entire morning inching your way down the Calle de la Ribera de Curtidores and through the maze of streets that hosts El Rastro. For every 10 pieces of junk, there's a real gem (a lost masterpiece, an Underwood typewriter) waiting to be found. A word of warning: pickpockets love El Rastro as much as everyone else.

Agatha Ruiz de la Prada CLOTHING
(Map p1124; www.agatharuizdelaprada.com; Calle de Serrano 27; ⏲10am-8.30pm Mon-Sat; Ⓜ Serrano) This boutique has to be seen to be believed, with pinks, yellows and oranges at every turn. It's fun and exuberant but it's not just for kids: it's also serious and highly original fashion. Agatha Ruiz de la Prada is one of the enduring icons of 1980s Madrid.

Mercado de Fuencarral CLOTHING
(Map p1128; www.mdf.es, in Spanish; Calle de Fuencarral 45; ⏲11am-9pm Mon-Sat; Ⓜ Tribunal) Madrid's home of alternative club-cool is still going strong, revelling in its reverse snobbery. With shops like Fuck, Ugly Shop and Black Kiss, it's funky, grungy and filled to the rafters with torn T-shirts and more black leather and silver studs than you'll ever need.

ℹ Information

Dangers & Annoyances

Madrid is a generally safe city, although you should, as in most European cities, be wary of pickpockets in the city centre, on the Metro and around major tourist sights.

Prostitution along Calle de la Montera and in the Casa del Campo park means that you need to exercise extra caution in these areas.

Discount Cards

The **Madrid Card** (☎91 360 47 72; www.madridcard.com; 1/2/3 days €47/60/74) includes free entry to more than 40 museums in and around Madrid and discounts on public transport. The cheaper version (€31/35/39 for 1/2/3 days) covers just cultural sights.

Emergency

Emergency (☎112)

Policía Nacional (☎091)

Servicio de Atención al Turista Extranjero (Foreign Tourist Assistance Service; ☎91 548 85 37, 91 548 80 08; www.esmadrid.com/satemadrid; Calle de Leganitos 19; ⏲9am-10pm; Ⓜ Plaza de España or Santo Domingo).

Internet Access

In the downtown area, your best options are the following:

Café Comercial (Map p1124; Glorieta de Bilbao 7; per 50 min €1; ⏲7.30am-midnight Mon, 7.30am-1am Tue-Thu, 7.30am-2am Fri, 8.30am-2am Sat, 9am-midnight Sun; Ⓜ Bilbao) One of Madrid's grandest old cafes, with internet upstairs.

Centro de Turismo de Madrid (www.esmadrid.com; Plaza Mayor 27; ⏲9.30am-8.30pm; Ⓜ Sol) Free internet for up to 15 minutes at its branch on Plaza Mayor, or free and unlimited access at the Plaza de Colón branch.

Medical Services

Anglo-American Medical Unit (Unidad Medica; ☎91 435 18 23; www.unidadmedica.com; Calle del Conde de Aranda 1; ⏲9am-8pm Mon-Fri, 10am-1pm Sat for emergencies; Ⓜ Retiro) Private clinic with Spanish- and English-speaking staff. Consultations cost around €125.

Farmacia Mayor (☎91 366; Calle Mayor 13; ⏲24hr; Ⓜ Sol)

Money

Like all Spanish cities, Madrid is fairly crawling with bank branches equipped with ATMs. As a rule, exchange bureaux have longer hours but worse rates and steeper commissions.

Post

Main post office (www.correos.es; Plaza de la Cibeles; ⏲8.30am-9.30pm Mon-Fri, 8.30am-2pm Sat; Ⓜ Banco de España)

Tourist Information

Centro de Turismo de Madrid (www.esmadrid.com; Plaza Mayor 27; ⏲9.30am-8.30pm; Ⓜ Sol) Excellent city tourist office with a smaller office underneath Plaza de Colón and information points at Plaza de la Cibeles, Plaza de Callao, outside the Centro de Arte Reina Sofía and at the T4 terminal at Barajas airport.

Regional tourist office (www.turismomadrid.es; Calle del Duque de Medinaceli 2; ⏲8am-8pm Mon-Sat, 9am-2pm Sun; Ⓜ Banco de España) Further offices at Barajas airport (T1 and T4) and Chamartín and Atocha train stations.

Getting There & Away

Air

Madrid's international Barajas airport (MAD), 15km northeast of the city, is a busy place, with flights coming in from all over Europe and beyond. See p1193 for more information.

Bus

Estación Sur de Autobuses (off Map p1124; ☎91 468 42 00; www.estaciondeautobuses.com, in Spanish; Calle de Méndez Álvaro 83; Ⓜ Méndez Álvaro), just south of the M-30 ring road, is the city's principal bus station. It serves most destinations to the south and many in other parts of the country. Major bus companies include **ALSA** (☎902 422 242; www.alsa.es) and **Avanzabus** (☎902 020 052; www.avanzabus.com).

Train

Madrid is served by two main train stations. The bigger of the two is **Puerta de Atocha** (Ⓜ Atocha Renfe), at the southern end of the city centre. **Chamartín train station** (Ⓜ Chamartín) lies in the north of the city. For bookings, contact **Renfe** (☎902 24 02 02; www.renfe.es) at either station.

High-speed Tren de Alta Velocidad Española (AVE) services connect Madrid with Seville (via Córdoba), Valladolid (via Segovia), Toledo, Valencia, Málaga and Barcelona (via Zaragoza and Tarragona).

Getting Around

To/From the Airport

Metro (www.metromadrid.es, in Spanish; entrances in T2 and T4) Line 8 to the Nuevos Ministerios transport interchange connects with lines 10 and 6. It operates from 6.05am to 2am. A single ticket costs €1 (10-ride Metrobús ticket €9); there's an additional €1 supplement if you're travelling to/from the airport.

A new 24-hour bus service between Plaza de la Cibeles and the airport was due to start soon after this book went to print.

AeroCITY (☎91 747 75 70; www.aerocity.com; per person €5-19) is a private minibus service that takes you door-to-door between central Madrid and the airport.

A taxi to the city centre will cost you around €25 (up to €35 from T4); in addition to what the meter reads, you pay a €5.50 airport supplement.

Public Transport

Madrid's **Metro** (www.metromadrid.es) is extensive and well-maintained. A single ride costs €1 and a 10-ride ticket is €9.30. The Metro runs from 6am until 2am.

The bus system is also good; contact **EMT** (www.emtmadrid.es) for more information.

CASTILLA Y LEÓN

Spain's Castilian heartland, Castilla y León is littered with hilltop towns sporting magnificent Gothic cathedrals, monumental city walls as well as many mouth-watering restaurants.

Ávila

POP 56,855

Ávila's old city, surrounded by imposing city walls with eight stupendous gates, 88 watchtowers and more than 2500 turrets, is one of the best preserved medieval bastions in all Spain. The city is known as the birthplace of Santa Teresa, a mystical writer and reformer of the Carmelite order.

Sights

Don't even *think* of leaving town without enjoying the walk along the top of Ávila's 12th-century **murallas** (walls; ☎920 21 13 87; adult €4; ⏲10am-8pm Tue-Sun). The two access points are at **Puerta del Alcázar** and **Puerta de los Leales**, which allow walks of 300m and 1200m respectively.

Embedded into the eastern city walls, the splendid 12th-century **cathedral** (Plaza de la Catedral; admission €4; ⏲10am-7pm Mon-Fri, 10am-8pm Sat, noon-6pm Sun) was the first Gothic-style church built in Spain. It boasts rich walnut choir stalls and a long, narrow central nave that makes the soaring ceilings seem all the more majestic.

The **Convento de Santa Teresa** (admission free; ⏲8.45am-1.30pm & 3.30-9pm Tue-Sun) was built in 1636 at the birthplace of 16th-century mystic and ascetic Santa Teresa.

Sleeping

Hostal San Juan BUDGET HOTEL €
(☎920 25 14 75; www.hostalsanjuan.es; Calle de los Comuneros de Castilla 3; s/d €30/48; 📶) With warm tones throughout, Hostal San Juan is pleasant, friendly and close to everything in Ávila. The recent addition of a small fitness room, complete with exercise machines, is a real one-off in this budget category.

Hostal Arco San Vicente BUDGET HOTEL €€
(☎920 22 24 98; www.arcosanvicente.com; Calle de López Núñez 6; s/d €55/65; P 📶) This gleaming *hostal* has small blue-carpeted rooms with pale paintwork and wrought-iron bedheads. The location, just inside Puerta de San Vicente, and the parking (€10), are additional perks.

Eating & Drinking

Ávila is famous for its *chuleton de Ávila* (T-bone steak) and *judías del barco de Ávila* (white beans, often with chorizo, in a thick sauce).

Hostería Las Cancelas SOPHISTICATED REGIONAL €€
(☎920 21 22 49; www.lascancelas.com; Calle de la Cruz Vieja 6; meals €30-40; ⏲lunch & dinner Feb-Dec) Part of the hotel of the same name, this courtyard restaurant occupies a delightful interior patio dating back to the 15th century. Renowned for being a mainstay of Ávila cuisine, traditional meals are prepared with a salutary attention to detail. Reservations recommended.

Posada de la Fruta TRADITIONAL CASTILIAN €
(www.posadadelafruta.com, in Spanish; Plaza de Pedro Dávila 8; meals €10-15) Simple, tasty meals can be had in a light-filled, covered courtyard, while the traditional *comedor* (dining room) caters to a conservative palate.

TOP CHOICE **La Bodeguita de San Segundo** WINE BAR
(www.vinoavila.com, in Spanish; Calle de San Segundo 19; ⏲11am-midnight Thu-Tue) Situated in the 16th-century Casa de la Misericordia, this superb wine bar is standing room only most nights and more tranquil in the quieter afternoon hours.

Information

Centro de Recepción de Visitantes (tourist office; ☎902 10 21 21; www.avilaturismo.com; Avenida de Madrid 39; ⏲8am-8pm)

Regional tourist office (☎920 21 13 87; www.turismocastillayleon.com; Calle San Segundo 17; ⏲9am-8pm Sun-Thu, 9am-9pm Fri & Sat).

Getting There & Away

BUS From Ávila's bus station, there are frequent services to Segovia (€5.45, 55 minutes) and Salamanca (€6.76, 1½ hours).

TRAIN More than 30 trains run daily to Madrid (from €8.25, 1¼ to two hours). There are also services to Salamanca (€9.65, one to 1½ hours, nine daily).

Salamanca

POP 155,619

Whether floodlit at night or bathed in midday sun, Salamanca is a dream destination. This is a city of rare architectural splendour, awash with golden sandstone overlaid with Latin inscriptions in ochre, and with an extraordinary virtuosity of plateresque and Renaissance styles. But this is also Castilla's liveliest city; home to a massive Spanish and international student population, who throng the streets at night and provide the city with so much youth and vitality.

Sights & Activities

TOP CHOICE **Plaza Mayor** MAIN SQUARE
This harmonious plaza was completed in 1755 to a design by Alberto Churriguera, one of the clan behind, at times, an overblown variant of the baroque style that bears their name.

FREE **Catedral Nueva & Catedral Vieja** CATHEDRALS
The **Catedral Nueva** (New Cathedral; Plaza de Anaya; ⏲9am-8pm), completed in 1733, is a late-Gothic masterpiece that took 220 years to build. Its magnificent Renaissance doorways stand out. For fine views over Salamanca, head to the southwestern corner of the cathedral facade and the **Puerta de la Torre** (Ieronimus; Plaza de Juan XXIII; admission €3.25; ⏲10am-7.15pm). The largely Romanesque **Catedral Vieja** (Old Cathedral; admission €4.75; ⏲10am-7.30pm) is a 12th-century temple with a stunning 15th-century altarpiece that has 53 panels depicting scenes from the life of Christ and Mary, topped by a representation of the Last Judgement. The entrance is inside the Catedral Nueva.

Universidad Civil UNIVERSITY
(Calle de los Libreros; adult/student €4/2, Mon morning free; ⏲9.30am-1pm & 4-7pm Mon-Fri,

Salamanca

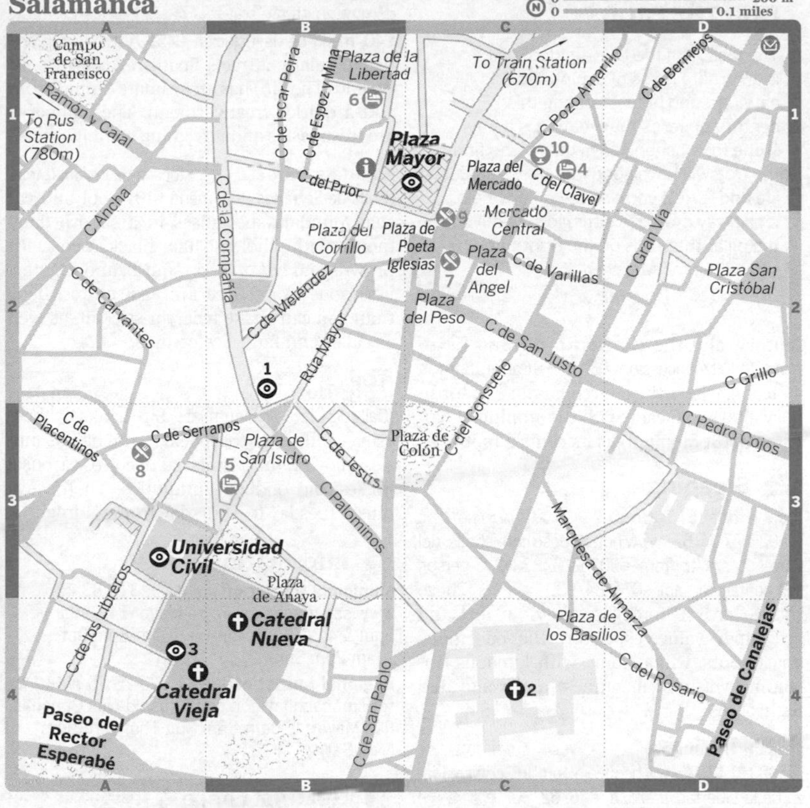

Salamanca

Top Sights

Catedral Nueva ... B4
Catedral Vieja ... A4
Plaza Mayor ... C1
Universidad Civil ... A3

Sights

1 Casa de las Conchas ... B2
2 Convento de San Esteban ... C4
3 Puerta de la Torre ... A4

Sleeping

4 Aparthotel El Toboso ... C1
5 Hostal Catedral ... B3
6 Hostal Concejo ... B1

Eating

7 El Pecado ... C2
8 Mandala Café ... A3
9 Mesón Cervantes ... C2

Drinking

10 Tío Vivo ... C1

9.30am-1pm & 4-6.30pm Sat, 10am-1pm Sun) The university is a tapestry in sandstone, bursting with images of mythical heroes, religious scenes and coats of arms. You can visit the old classrooms and one of the oldest university libraries in Europe.

Other Buildings NOTABLE BUILDINGS

Among the other stand-out buildings are the glorious **Casa de las Conchas** (Calle de la Compañia 2; admission free; 9am-9pm Mon-Fri, 9am-2pm & 4-7pm Sat, 10am-2pm & 4-7pm Sun), a city symbol since it was built in the 15th

FIND THE FROG

The facade of the Universidad Civil is an ornate mass of sculptures and carvings, and hidden among this 16th-century plateresque creation is a tiny stone frog. Legend says those who find the frog will have good luck in studies, life and love. If you don't want any help, look away now...it's sitting on a skull on the pillar that runs up the right-hand side of the facade.

century, and the **Convento de San Esteban** (adult/concession €3/2; ⏲10am-1.15pm & 4-7.15pm), where the church has an extraordinary altarlike facade with the stoning of San Esteban (St Stephen) as its central motif.

Sleeping

Aparthotel El Toboso APARTMENT HOTEL €
(☎923 27 14 62; www.hoteltoboso.com; Calle del Clavel 7; s/d/tr from €30/52/82, 3-/4-/5-person self-contained apt €76/84/93; ❄📶) These rooms have a homey, spare-room feel and are super value, especially the enormous apartments, which come with kitchens (including washing machines) and renovated bathrooms.

Hostal Concejo SMALL HOTEL €€
(☎923 21 47 37; www.hconcejo.com, in Spanish; Plaza de la Libertad 1; s/d/tr €45/62/80; P❄@📶) A cut above the average *hostal*, the stylish Concejo has polished-wood floors, tasteful furnishings and a superb central location.

Hostal Catedral BUDGET HOTEL €
(☎923 27 06 14; Rúa Mayor 46; s/d €30/48; ❄) Just across from the cathedrals, this pleasing *hostal* has just six extremely pretty, clean-as-a-whistle, bright bedrooms with showers. All look out onto the street or cathedral, which is a real bonus, as is the motherly owner, who treats her visitors as honoured guests.

Eating & Drinking

Mesón Cervantes TRADITIONAL CASTILIAN €
(Plaza Mayor 15; meals €15-20; ⏲10am-midnight) A great place where you can eat at the outdoor tables on the plaza, but the dark wooden beams and atmospheric buzz of the Spanish crowd on the 1st floor should be experienced at least once. The food's a mix of salads and *raciones* (large tapas plate).

El Pecado MODERN CREATIVE €€
(☎923 26 65 58; Plaza de Poeta Iglesias 12; meals €40, menú de degustación €45) A trendy place that regularly attracts Spanish celebrities, El Pecado (The Sin) has an intimate dining room and a quirky, creative menu. The hallmarks are fresh tastes and intriguing combinations.

Mandala Café MODERN MEDITERRANEAN €
(Calle de Serranos 9-11; menú €10) Cool and casual Mandala specialises in a superb daily menu with choices like black rice with prawns and *calamares* (squid), and vegetarian moussaka. There are also more salads than you can shake a carrot stick at, as well as cakes and fancy ice creams.

TOP CHOICE **Tío Vivo** MUSIC BAR
(Calle del Clavel 3; ⏲4pm-late) Sip drinks by flickering candlelight to a background of '80s music, enjoying the whimsical decor of carousel horses and oddball antiquities. There's live music Tuesday to Thursday from midnight.

Information

Municipal tourist office (☎923 21 83 42; www.salamanca.es; Plaza Mayor 14; ⏲9am-2pm & 4.30-8pm Mon-Fri, 10am-8pm Sat, 10am-2pm Sun)

Regional tourist office (☎923 26 85 71; www.turismocastillayleon.com; Casa de las Conchas, Rúa Mayor; ⏲9am-8pm Sun-Thu, 9am-9pm Fri & Sat)

Getting There & Away

BUS Buses run from the **bus station** (Avenida de Filiberto Villalobos 71-85) to Madrid (regular/express €14.80/21.90, 3/2½ hours, hourly), Ávila (€6.76, 1½ hours, one to four daily) and Segovia (€10.96, 2¾ hours, two daily).

TRAIN Up to eight trains depart daily for Madrid's Chamartín station (€19.10, 2½ hours) via Ávila (€9.65, one hour). The train station is 600m beyond Plaza de España.

Segovia

POP 56,100

Unesco World Heritage–listed Segovia has a stunning monument to Roman grandeur, a castle said to have inspired Walt Disney and is a city of warm terracotta and sandstone hues set amid the rolling hills of Castilla.

Sights

TOP CHOICE **El Acueducto** ROMAN AQUEDUCT
El Acueducto, an 894m-long engineering wonder that looks like an enormous comb

of stone blocks plunged into the lower end of old Segovia, is the obvious starting point of a tour of town. This Roman aqueduct is 28m high and was built without a drop of mortar – just good old Roman know-how.

TOP CHOICE **Alcázar** CASTLE
(www.alcazardesegovia.com; Plaza de la Reina Victoria Eugenia; adult/concession €4/3, tower €2, EU citizens 3rd Tue of month free; ⌚10am-7pm Apr-Sep) The fortified and fairy-tale Alcázar is perched dramatically on the edge of Segovia. Roman foundations are buried somewhere underneath the splendour, but what we see today is a 13th-century structure that burned down in 1862 and was subsequently rebuilt. Inside is a collection of armour and military gear, but even better are the ornate interiors of the reception rooms and the 360-degree views from the **Torre de Juan II**.

Catedral CATHEDRAL
(Plaza Mayor; adult/concession €3/2, free 9.30am-1.15pm Sun; ⌚9.30am-6.30pm) In the heart of town is the resplendent late-Gothic Catedral, which was started in 1525 and completed a mere 200 years later. The Cristo del Consuelo chapel houses a magnificent Romanesque doorway preserved from the original church that burned down.

Sleeping & Eating

Hostal Fornos HOSTAL €
(☎921 46 01 98; www.hostalfornos.com, in Spanish; Calle de la Infanta Isabel 13; s/d €41/55; ❄) This tidy little *hostal* is a cut above most places in this price category. It has a cheerful air and rooms with a fresh white-linen-and-wicker-chair look. Some are larger than others, but the value is unbeatable.

Natura – La Hostería HOSTAL €€
(☎921 46 67 10; www.naturadesegovia.com, in Spanish; Calle de Colón 5-7; r €60; ❄📶) An eclectic choice a few streets back from Plaza Mayor. The owner obviously has a penchant for Dalí prints and the rooms have plenty of character, with chunky wooden furnishings and bright paintwork.

The main food speciality here is *cochinillo asado* (roast suckling pig).

Restaurante El Fogón Sefardí SEPHARDIC €€
(☎921 46 62 50; www.lacasamudejar.com; Calle de Isabel La Católica 8; meals €30-40) One of the most original places in town, serving Sephardic cuisine in a restaurant with an intimate patio or in a splendid dining hall with original, 15th-century Mudéjar flourishes.

Casa Duque GRILLED MEATS €€
(☎921 46 24 87; www.restauranteduque.es; Calle de Cervantes 12; menús del día €21-40, meals €25-35) They've been serving *cochinillo asado* here since the 1890s. For the uninitiated, try the *menú segoviano* (€31), which includes *cochinillo*, or the *menú gastronómico* (€40). Downstairs is the informal *cueva* (cave), where you can get tapas and full-bodied *cazuelas* (stews).

Information

Centro de Recepción de Visitantes (tourist office; www.turismodesegovia.com; Plaza del Azoguejo 1; ⌚10am-7pm Sun-Fri, 10am-8pm Sat)

Getting There & Away

BUS Buses travel to Madrid (€6.70, 1½ hours, every half-hour), Ávila (€5.45, 1¼ hours, five daily) and Salamanca (€10.96, 2¾ hours, two daily).

TRAIN Up to nine normal trains run daily from Madrid to Segovia (€6.50, two hours), leaving you at the main train station 2.5km from the aqueduct. The faster option is the high-speed AVE (€9.90, 35 minutes), which deposits you at the newer Segovia-Guiomar station, 5km from the aqueduct.

León

POP 135,100

León's stand-out attraction is its cathedral, one of the most beautiful in Spain. By day, this pretty city rewards long exploratory strolls. By night, the city's large student population floods into the narrow streets and plazas of the picturesque old quarter, the Barrio Húmedo.

Sights

TOP CHOICE **Catedral** CATHEDRAL
(www.catedraldeleon.org, in Spanish; ⌚8.30am-1.30pm & 4-8pm Mon-Sat, 8.30am-2.30pm & 5-8pm Sun) With its soaring towers, flying buttresses and breathtaking interior, the 13th-century cathedral is the city's spiritual heart. The extraordinary facade has a radiant rose window, three richly sculpted doorways and two muscular towers. Inside, a remarkable gallery of 128 *vidrieras* (stained-glass windows) with a surface of 1800 sq metres awaits, but mere numbers cannot convey the ethereal quality of light permeating this cathedral.

Real Basílica de San Isidoro ROMANESQUE CHURCH
Older even than the cathedral, the Real Basílica de San Isidoro provides a stunning Romanesque counterpoint to the former's Gothic strains. The attached **Panteón Real** (admission €4, free Thu afternoon; ⌚10am-1.30pm & 4-6.30pm Mon-Sat, 10am-1.30pm Sun) houses some of Spain's finest Romanesque frescos.

Barrio Gótico HISTORIC QUARTER
On the fringes of León's old town (also known as the Barrio Gótico), Plaza de San Marcelo is home to the **ayuntamiento** (City Hall), which occupies a charmingly compact Renaissance-era palace. The Renaissance theme continues in the form of the splendid **Palacio de los Guzmanes** (1560). Next door is Antoni Gaudí's sober contribution to León's skyline, the castlelike, neo-Gothic **Casa de Botines** (1893).

Down the hill, the delightful **Plaza de Santa María del Camino** feels like a cobblestone Castilian village square. At the northeastern end of the old town is the beautiful and time-worn 17th-century **Plaza Mayor**.

Sleeping & Eating

TOP CHOICE **Hostal San Martín** HISTORIC HOTEL €
(☎987 87 51 87; www.sanmartinhostales.com; 2nd fl, Plaza de Torres de Omaña 1; s without bathroom €20, s/d/tr with bathroom €31/43/55) In a splendid central position, this recently overhauled 18th-century building has light, airy rooms painted in candy colours with small terraces.

La Parrilla del Humedo TRADITIONAL TAPAS €
(Calle Azabacheria 6; raciones €7-13) This place is always packed with euro-economising *leonéses*, here for the remarkably good house wine and accompanying, good-size tapas; both for the bargain basement price of €1.50. Head for the dining room out back for heartier portions of local dishes.

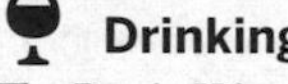

Drinking

The Barrio Húmedo's night-time epicentre is Plaza de San Martín – prise open the door of any bar here or in the surrounding streets (especially Calle de Juan de Arfe and Calle de la Misericordia), inch your way to the bar and you're unlikely to want to leave until closing time.

Information

Tourist office (☎987 23 70 82; www.turismo castillayleon.com; Calle el Cid 2; ⌚9am-8pm)

Getting There & Away

BUS Buses travel to Madrid (€22, 3½ hours) and Burgos (€14.10, 3¾ hours).

TRAIN There are train services to Burgos (from €20.10, two hours), Oviedo (from €18.80, two hours), Madrid (from €28.30, 4¼ hours) and Barcelona (from €68.40, nine hours).

Burgos

POP 174,100

The legendary warrior El Cid was born just outside Burgos and is buried in its magnificent cathedral. The grey-stone architecture, fortifying cuisine and a climate of extremes can lend Burgos a chilly edge, but below the spartan surface lies vibrant nightlife, good restaurants and, when the sun's shining, pretty streetscapes.

Sights

TOP CHOICE **Catedral** CATHEDRAL
(Plaza del Rey Fernando; admission €5; ⌚9.30am-6.30pm) The Unesco World Heritage–listed cathedral is a masterpiece. It had humble origins as a modest Romanesque church, but work began on a grander scale in 1221. Remarkably, within 40 years most of the French Gothic structure that you see today had been completed.

Monasterio de las Huelgas MONASTERY
(guided tours adult/concession €5/2.50, free Wed; ⌚10am-1pm & 3.45-5.30pm Tue-Sat, 10.30am-2pm Sun) A 30-minute walk west of the city centre, on the southern bank of Río Arlanzón, this monastery was once among the most prominent in Spain. This veritable royal pantheon contains the tombs of numerous kings and queens, as well as a spectacular gilded Renaissance altar.

Sleeping & Eating

Hotel Jacobeo SMALL HOTEL €
(☎947 26 01 02; www.hoteljacobeo.com; Calle de San Juan 24; s/d incl breakfast €47/58; ⊜❄☜) This stylish small hotel has gleaming rooms of burgundy-and-whitewashed walls, terracotta tiles and parquet floors. Bathrooms are well equipped, if on the small side.

TOP CHOICE **Cervecería Morito** TRADITIONAL TAPAS €
(Calle de la Sombrerería 27; tapas €3, raciones €5-7) The undisputed king of Burgos tapas bars is always crowded. A typical order is *alpargata* (lashings of cured ham with bread,

tomato and olive oil) or *calamares fritos* (fried calamari).

Information

Municipal tourist office (☎947 28 88 74; www.aytoburgos.es, in Spanish; Plaza del Rey Fernando 2; ⏲10am-2pm & 4.30-7.30pm Mon-Fri, 10am-1.30pm & 4-7.30pm Sat & Sun)

Getting There & Away

BUS There are bus services to Madrid (€16.25, 2¾ hours), Bilbao (€11.86, two hours) and León (€14.10, 3¾ hours).

TRAIN Trains run to Madrid (from €25.60, four hours, up to seven daily), Bilbao (from €18.70, three hours, five daily), León (from €20.10, two hours, four daily) and Salamanca (from €20.90, 2½ hours, three daily).

CASTILLA-LA MANCHA

Known as the stomping ground of Don Quiote and Sancho Panza, Castilla-La Mancha conjures up images of lonely windmills, medieval castles and bleak, treeless plains. The characters of Miguel de Cervantes provide the literary context, but the richly historic cities of Toledo and Cuenca are the most compelling reasons to visit.

Toledo

POP 82,291

Toledo is Spain's equivalent of a downsized Rome. Commanding a hill rising above the Tajo River, it's crammed with monuments that attest to the waves of conquerors and communities – Roman, Visigoth, Jewish, Muslim and Christian – who have called the city home during its turbulent history. It's one of the country's major tourist attractions.

Sights

TOP CHOICE **Catedral de Toledo** CATHEDRAL
(Plaza del Ayuntamiento; admission €7; ⏲10.30am-6.30pm Mon-Sat, 2-6.30pm Sun) Toledo's cathedral dominates the skyline, reflecting the city's historical significance as the heart of Catholic Spain. Within its hefty stone walls there are stained-glass windows, tombs of kings and art in the sacristy by the likes of El Greco, Zurbarán, Crespi, Titian, Rubens and Velázquez. Behind the main altar lies a mesmerising piece of 18th-century Churrigueresque baroque, the **Transparente**. Look out for the extravagant **Custodia de Arfe**, by the celebrated 16th-century goldsmith Enrique de Arfe.

Jewish Quarter SYNAGOGUES
Toledo's former *judería* (Jewish quarter) was once home to 11 synagogues. The magnificent 14th-century **Sinagoga del Tránsito** (www.museosefardi.net, in Spanish; Calle Samuel Leví; admission €2.40, audio guide €3; ⏲10am-9pm Tue-Sat, 10am-2pm Sun) now houses the **Museo Sefardi** (⏲same hrs). The more modest **Sinagoga de Santa María La Blanca** (Calle de los Reyes Católicos 4; admission €2.30; ⏲10am-6pm) is characterised by delicate horseshoe arches.

San Juan de los Reyes FRANCISCAN MONASTERY
(Calle San Juan de los Reyes 2; admission €2.30; ⏲10am-6pm) North of the synagogues lies the early-17th-century Franciscan monastery and church of San Juan de los Reyes, notable for its delightful cloisters.

FREE **Museo de Santa Cruz** CITY MUSEUM
(Calle de Cervantes 3; ⏲10am-6.30pm Mon-Sat, 10am-2pm Sun) Just off the Plaza de Zocodover, the 16th-century Museo de Santa Cruz is a beguiling combination of Gothic and Spanish Renaissance styles. The ground-level gallery contains a number of El Grecos, a painting *(Cristo Crucificado)* attributed to Goya, and the wonderful 15th-century *Tapestry of the Astrolabes*.

Sleeping

Accommodation is often full, especially from Easter to September. Most people visit on a day trip from Madrid.

TOP CHOICE **Casa de Cisneros** BOUTIQUE HOTEL €€
(☎925 22 88 28; www.hostal-casa-de-cisneros.com; Calle del Cardenal Cisneros; s/d €50/80; ⊖❄📶) Across from the cathedral, this seductive hotel is built on the site of an 11th-century Islamic palace, parts of which can be spied via a glass porthole in the lobby floor. In comparison, this building is a 16th-century youngster with pretty stone-and-wood-beamed rooms and voguish private bathrooms.

Hostal Santo Tomé BUDGET HOTEL €
(☎925 22 17 12; www.hostalsantotome.com; Calle de Santo Tomé 13; s/d €42/55; P❄) This good-value *hostal*, above a souvenir shop, has larger-than-most rooms with light wood floors and furniture, plus bathrooms with

Toledo

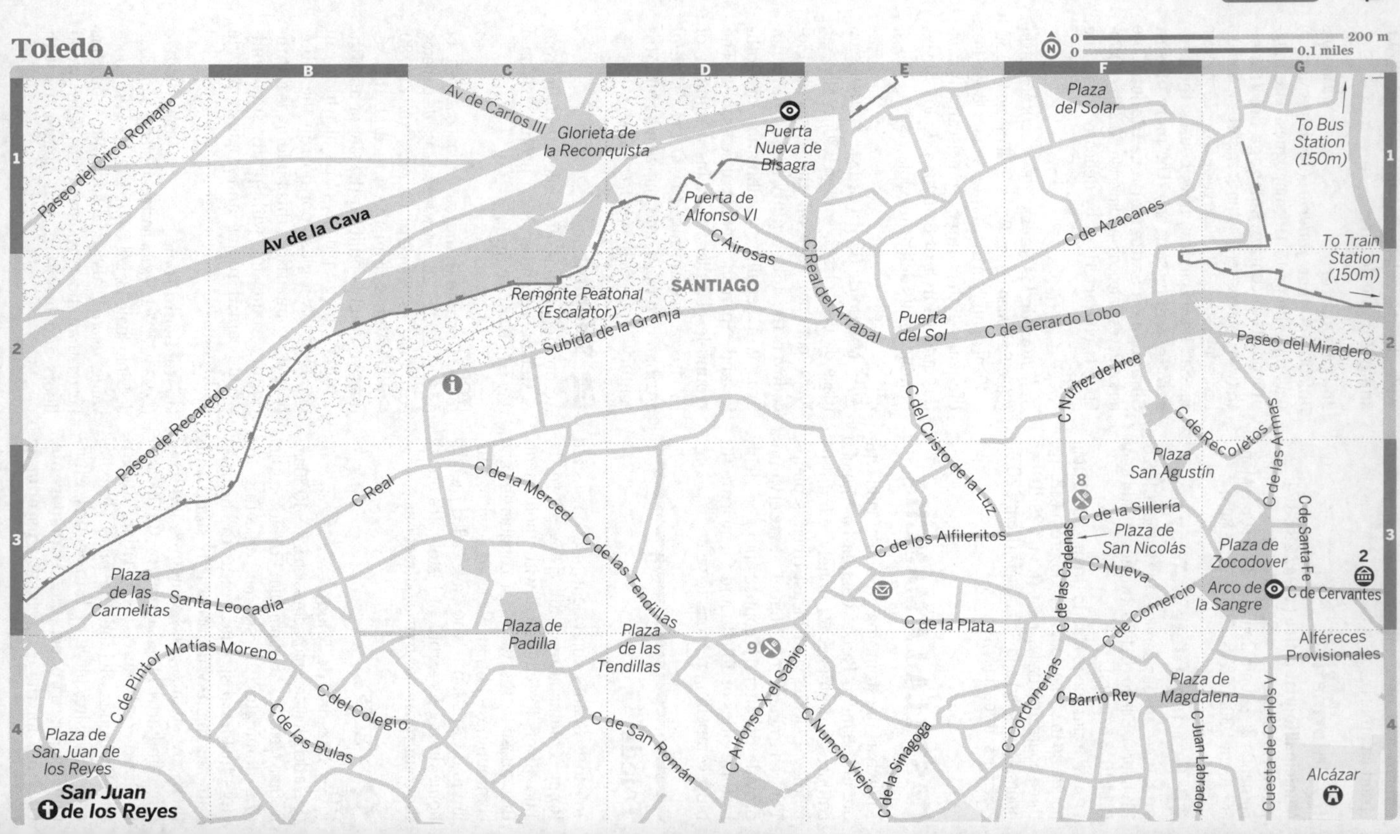
0 200 m
0 0.1 miles
A
B
C
D
E
F
G
1
2
3
4
Paseo del Circo Romano
Av de Carlos III
Glorieta de la Reconquista
Puerta Nueva de Bisagra
Puerta de Alfonso VI
C Airosas
Av de la Cava
Remonte Peatonal (Escalator)
SANTIAGO
Subida de la Granja
C Real del Arrabal
Puerta del Sol
C de Gerardo Lobo
Plaza del Solar
C de Azacanes
To Bus Station (150m)
To Train Station (150m)
Paseo del Miradero
Paseo de Recaredo
C Núñez de Arce
C del Cristo de la Luz
C de Recoletos
Plaza San Agustín
C de las Armas
C Real
C de la Merced
C de las Tendillas
8
C de la Sillería
Plaza de San Nicolás
C Nueva
C de las Cadenas
C de los Alfileritos
Plaza de Zocodover
C de Santa Fe
2
Arco de la Sangre
C de Cervantes
C de Comercio
C de la Plata
Plaza de las Carmelitas
Santa Leocadia
Plaza de Padilla
Plaza de las Tendillas
9
C Alfonso X el Sabio
C Nuncio Viejo
C de la Sinagoga
C Cordonerías
C Barrio Rey
Plaza de Magdalena
C Juan Labrador
Cuesta de Carlos V
Alféreces Provisionales
Alcázar
C de Pintor Matías Moreno
C del Colegio
C de las Bulas
C de San Román
Plaza de San Juan de los Reyes
San Juan de los Reyes

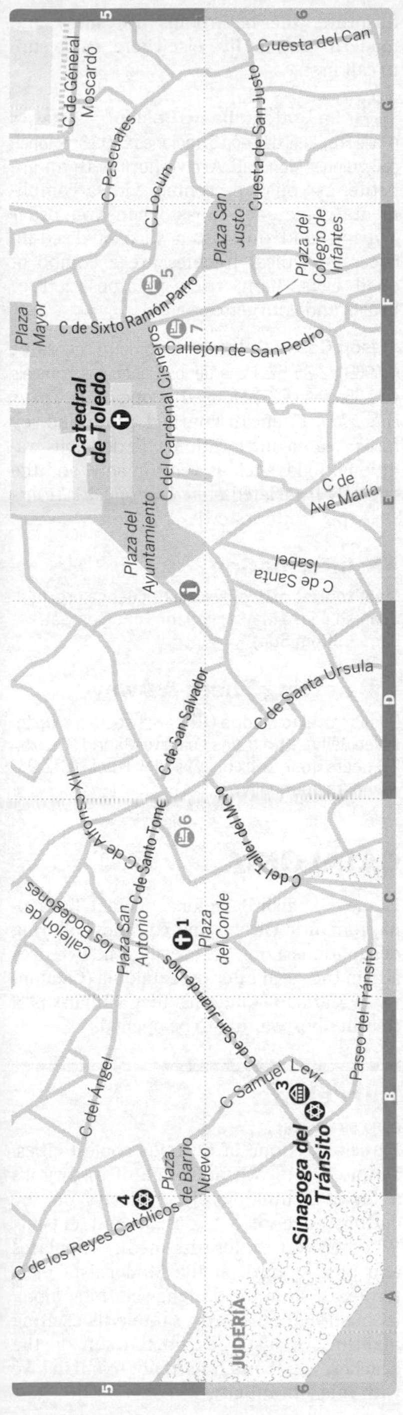

five-star attitude offering extras such as shoe polish and hairdryers.

La Posada de Manolo BOUTIQUE HOTEL **€€**
(☎925 28 22 50; www.laposadademanolo.com; Calle de Sixto Ramón Parro 8; s/d incl breakfast €42/66; ❄📶) This memorable hotel has themed each floor with furnishings and decor reflecting one of the three cultures of Toledo: Christian, Islamic and Jewish.

Eating

La Abadía SPANISH **€€**
(www.abadiatoledo.com; Plaza de San Nicolás 3; meals €25-30) In a former 16th-century palace, this atmospheric bar and restaurant has arches, niches and subtle lighting spread over a warren of brick-and-stone-clad rooms. The menu includes lightweight dishes like *verduras a la parrilla* (grilled fresh vegetables) – perfect for small appetites.

Palacios HOME-STYLE TRADITIONAL **€**
(Calle Alfonso X el Sabio 3; menú €13.90, meals €14-18) An unpretentious place where stained glass, beams and efficient old-fashioned service combine with traditional no-nonsense cuisine. Hungry? Try a gut-busting bowl of traditional *judías con perdiz* (white beans with partridge) for starters.

Information

Main tourist office (☎925 25 40 30; www.toledoturismo.com; Plaza del Ayuntamiento; ⌚10.30am-2.30pm Mon, 10.30am-2.30pm & 4.30-7pm Tue-Sun)

Toledo

Top Sights
Catedral de Toledo E5
San Juan de los Reyes A4
Sinagoga del Tránsito B6

Sights
1 Iglesia de Santo Tomé C5
2 Museo de Santa Cruz G3
3 Museo Sefardi B6
4 Sinagoga de Santa María La Blanca A5

Sleeping
5 Casa de Cisneros F5
6 Hostal Santo Tomé C5
7 La Posada de Manolo F5

Eating
8 La Abadía F3
9 Palacios D4

Getting There & Away

For most major destinations, you'll need to backtrack to Madrid.

BUS There are buses to Madrid (from €5.25, one to 1½ hours) every half-hour from 6am to 10pm daily (fewer on Sunday). There are also services on weekdays and Sunday to Cuenca (€11.40, 2¼ hours).

TRAIN The high-speed AVE service runs almost hourly to Madrid (€9.90, 30 minutes).

Cuenca

POP 53,000

A World Heritage Site, Cuenca is one of Spain's most memorable small cities, with its old centre a stage set of evocative medieval buildings. Most emblematic are the *casas colgadas* (hanging houses).

Sights

Casas Colgadas HANGING HOUSES

Cuenca's *casas colgadas* jut out precariously over the steep defile of Río Huécar. Dating from the 16th century, the houses with their layers of wooden balconies seem to emerge from the rock as if an extension of the cliffs. One of the finest restored examples now houses the **Museo de Arte Abstracto Español** (Museum of Abstract Art; www.march.es; admission €3; 11am-2pm & 4-6pm Tue-Fri, 11am-2pm & 4-8pm Sat, 11am-2.30pm Sun), an impressive contemporary-art museum. For the best views of the *casas colgadas,* cross the **Puente de San Pablo** footbridge, or walk to the **mirador** at the northernmost tip of the old town.

Sleeping & Eating

TOP CHOICE **Posada de San José** HISTORIC HOTEL €€

(969 21 13 00; www.posadasanjose.com; Ronda de Julián Romero 4; s/d without bathroom €30/43, d without/with views €82/94) This 17th-century former choir school retains an extraordinary monastic charm with its labyrinth of rooms, crumbling portal, uneven floors and original tiles. The cheaper rooms are in the former priests' cells, while the more costly doubles combine homey comfort with sumptuous old-word charm.

Hostal San Pedro HOSTAL €€

(969 23 45 43, 628 407601; www.hostalsanpedro.es; Calle San Pedro 34; s/d €35/60) At this well-priced and well-positioned *hostal,* rooms have butter-coloured paintwork, wrought-iron bedheads and rustic wood furniture; the bathrooms are shiny and modern. Owners live elsewhere, so be sure to call first.

TOP CHOICE **La Bodeguilla de Basilio** TAPAS €

(Calle Fray Luis de León 3; raciones €10-13; lunch daily, dinner Mon-Sat) Arrive here with an appetite, as you're presented with a complimentary plate of tapas when you order a drink, and not just a slice of dried-up cheese – typical freebies are a combo of quail eggs, ham, fried potatoes, lettuce hearts and courgettes.

Mesón Casas Colgadas TRADITIONAL SPANISH €€

(969 22 35 52; Calle de los Canónigos 3; meals €25-35, menú €27) Housed in one of the *casas colgadas,* Cuenca's gourmet pride and joy fuses an amazing location with delicious traditional food, such as venison stew and the quaintly translated *boned little pork hands stew* (pig trotters stew!).

Information

Main tourist office (www.aytocuenca.org, in Spanish; Plaza Mayor; 9am-9pm Mon-Sat, 9am-2.30pm Sun)

Getting There & Away

Buses travel to Madrid (€13.48, two hours, up to seven daily), with trains going to Madrid (€11.75, 2½ hours, four to six daily) and Valencia (€12.95, 3¼ hours, four daily).

CATALONIA

Home to stylish Barcelona, ancient Tarragona, romantic Girona and countless alluring destinations along the coast, in the Pyrenees and in the rural interior, Catalonia (Catalunya in Catalan, Cataluña in Castilian) is a treasure box waiting to be opened.

Barcelona

POP 1.59 MILLION

Barcelona is one of Europe's coolest cities. Despite some two millennia of history it's a forward-thinking place, always on the cutting edge of art, design and cuisine. Whether you explore its medieval palaces and plazas, gawk at the Modernista masterpieces, shop for designer clothing along its bustling boulevards, sample its exciting nightlife, or just soak up the sun on the beaches, you'll find it hard not to fall in love with this vibrant city.

Sights & Activities

La Rambla PEDESTRIAN BOULEVARD

Spain's most famous boulevard, the part-pedestrianised La Rambla, explodes with life. Stretching from **Plaça de Catalunya** to the waterfront, it's lined with street artists, news stands and vendors selling everything from mice to magnolias.

The colourful **Mercat de la Boquería** (Map p1152; La Rambla; 8am-8pm Mon-Sat; M Liceu), a fresh-food market with a Modernista entrance, is one of La Rambla's highlights. Nearby, stop for a tour of the **Gran Teatre del Liceu** (Map p1152; 93 485 99 14; www.liceubarcelona.com; Rambla dels Caputxins 51-59; admission with/without guide €8.70/4; guided tours 10am, unguided visits 11.30am, noon, 12.30pm & 1pm; M Liceu), the city's fabulous opera house.

Also stop at **Plaça Reial** (Map p1152), a grand 19th-century square surrounded by arcades lined with restaurants and bars.

Barri Gòtic GOTHIC QUARTER

Barcelona's Gothic **Catedral** (Map p1152; Plaça de la Seu; admission free, special visits free-€5; 8am-12.45pm & 5.15-8pm, special visits 1-5pm Mon-Sat, 2-5pm Sun & holidays; M Jaume I) was built atop the ruins of an 11th-century Romanesque church.

Not far from the cathedral is pretty Plaça del Rei and the fascinating **Museu d'Història de Barcelona** (Map p1152; www.museuhistoria.bcn.cat; Carrer del Veguer; adult/senior & student €7/5, from 4pm 1st Sat of month & from 3pm Sun free; 10am-8pm Tue-Sat, 10am-8pm Sun, 10am-3pm holidays; M Jaume I), where you can visit a 4000-sq-metre excavated site of Roman Barcelona under the plaza.

El Raval ALTERNATIVE DISTRICT

To the west of La Rambla is El Raval, a once-seedy, now-funky area overflowing with cool bars and shops. Visit the **Museu d'Art Contemporani de Barcelona** (Macba; Map p1152; 93 412 08 10; www.macba.cat; Plaça dels Àngels 1; adult/concession €7.50/6; 11am-8pm Mon & Wed, 11am-midnight Thu & Fri, 10am-8pm Sat, 10am-3pm Sun & holidays; M Universitat), with an impressive collection of contemporary art.

The best example of Romanesque architecture in the city, **Església de Sant Pau** (Map p1152; Carrer de Sant Pau 101; admission free; cloister 10am-1pm & 4-7pm Mon-Sat; M Parallel) has a dainty little cloister.

La Ribera NEIGHBOURHOOD

A series of palaces where wealthy merchants lived now house the **Museu Picasso** (Map p1152; www.museupicasso.bcn.es; Carrer de Montcada 15-23; adult/student €9/6, temporary exhibitions €5.80/2.90, free 3-8pm Sun & all day 1st Sun of month; 10am-8pm Tue-Sun & holidays; M Jaume I), home to more than 3000 Picassos, most from early in the artist's career. This is one of the most visited museums in the country, so expect queues.

The heart of the neighbourhood is the elegant **Església de Santa Maria del Mar** (Map p1152; Plaça de Santa Maria del Mar; admission free; 9am-1.30pm & 4.30-8pm; M Jaume I), a stunning example of Catalan Gothic and arguably the city's most elegant church.

The opulent **Palau de la Música Catalana** (Map p1148; www.palaumusica.org; Carrer de Sant Francesc de Paula 2; adult/student & EU senior €12/10; 50min tours every hr 10am-6pm Easter & Aug, 10am-3.30pm Sep-Jul; M Urquinaona) is one of the city's most delightful Modernista works. Designed by Lluís Domènech i Montaner in 1905, it hosts concerts regularly.

Nearby, **Mercat de Santa Caterina** (Map p1152; www.mercatsantacaterina.net, in Catalan; Avinguda de Francesc Cambó 16; 7.30am-2pm Mon, 7.30am-3.30pm Tue, Wed & Sat, 7.30am-8.30pm Thu & Fri; M Jaume I), with its loopily pastel-coloured wavy roof, is a temple to fine foods designed by the adventurous Catalan architect Enric Miralles.

Waterfront WATERFRONT DISTRICT

Barcelona has two major ports, **Port Vell** (Old Port) at the base of La Rambla, and **Port Olímpic** (Olympic Port) 1.5km up the coast. Between the two ports sits the one-time factory workers' and fishermen's quarter, **La Barceloneta**. It retains a delightfully scruffy edge and abounds with crowded seafood eateries.

Barcelona boasts 4km of city *platjas* (beaches), beginning with the gritty **Platja de la Barceloneta** and continuing north-east, beyond Port Olímpic, with a series of cleaner, more attractive strands. All get packed in summer.

L'Eixample NEIGHBOURHOOD

Modernisme, the Catalan version of art nouveau, transformed Barcelona's cityscape in the early 20th century. Modernisme's star architect was the eccentric Antoni Gaudí (1852–1926), a devout Catholic whose work is full of references to nature and Christianity.

TOP CHOICE **La Sagrada Família** (Expiatory Temple of the Holy Family; Map p1148; www.sagradafamilia.org; Carrer de Mallorca 401; adult/senior & student €12/10; 9am-8pm Apr-Sep, 9am-6pm Oct-Mar; M Sagrada Família) is Gaudí's

Barcelona

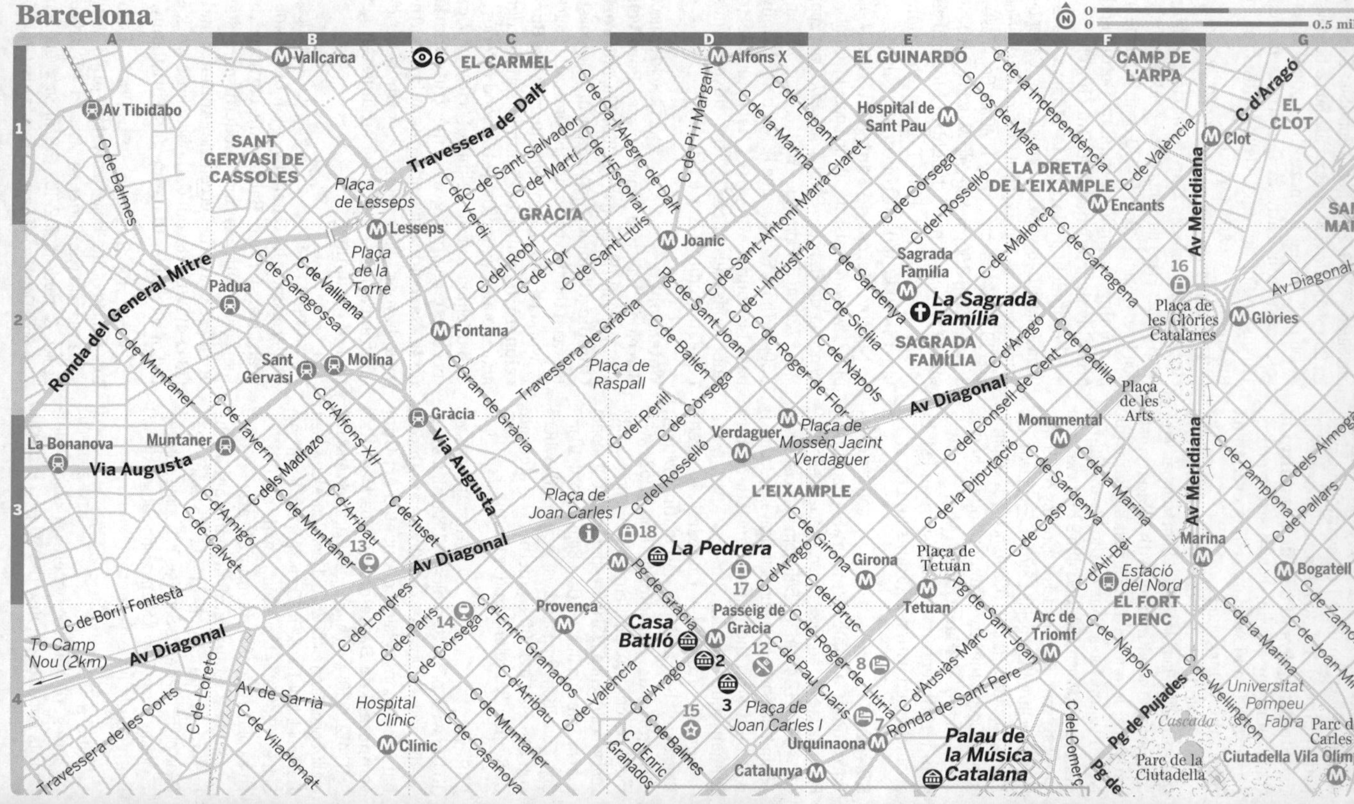
0 1 km
0 0.5 miles
A
B
C
D
E
F
G
1
2
3
4
Vallcarca
6
EL CARMEL
Alfons X
EL GUINARDÓ
CAMP DE L'ARPA
C d'Aragó
EL CLOT
Clot
Av Tibidabo
C de Balmes
SANT GERVASI DE CASSOLES
Travessera de Dalt
Plaça de Lesseps
C de Verdi
C de Sant Salvador
C de Martí
C de l'Escorial
C de Ca l'Alegre de Dalt
C de Pi i Margall
C de la Marina
C de Lepant
C de Sant Antoni Maria Claret
Hospital de Sant Pau
C Dos de Maig
C de la Independència
LA DRETA DE L'EIXAMPLE
C de València
Encants
Av Meridiana
SANT MARTÍ
Lesseps
GRÀCIA
Joanic
C de Còrsega
C del Rosselló
C de Mallorca
C de Cartagena
16
Av Diagonal
Plaça de les Glòries Catalanes
Glòries
Ronda del General Mitre
Pàdua
C de Saragossa
C de Vallirana
Plaça de la Torre
C del Robí
C de l'Or
C de Sant Lluís
Pg de Sant Joan
C de l'Indústria
C de Sardenya
Sagrada Família
La Sagrada Família
C de Sicília
C de Roger de Flor
C de Nàpols
SAGRADA FAMÍLIA
C d'Aragó
C de Padilla
Fontana
Travessera de Gràcia
C de Bailèn
Plaça de Raspall
C de Muntaner
Sant Gervasi
Molina
C d'Alfons XII
C Gran de Gràcia
Gràcia
C del Perill
C de Còrsega
Av Diagonal
C del Consell de Cent
Monumental
Plaça de les Arts
C de Tavern
La Bonanova
Muntaner
Via Augusta
C dels Madrazo
Verdaguer
Plaça de Mossèn Jacint Verdaguer
C de la Diputació
C de Sardenya
C de la Marina
C de Pamplona
C dels Almogàvers
C d'Amigó
C de Calvet
C de Muntaner
C d'Aribau
C de Tuset
Plaça de Joan Carles I
C del Rosselló
L'EIXAMPLE
C de Casp
C de Pallars
13
18
La Pedrera
C de Girona
Girona
Plaça de Tetuan
C d'Alí Bei
Marina
Bogatell
Pg de Gràcia
17
C d'Aragó
C del Bruc
Tetuan
Estació del Nord
EL FORT PIENC
C de Bori i Fontestà
C de Londres
14
C de París
C d'Enric Granados
Provença
Casa Batlló
Passeig de Gràcia
C de Roger de Llúria
Pg de Sant Joan
Arc de Triomf
C de Nàpols
C de la Marina
C de Zamora
To Camp Nou (2km)
Av Diagonal
C de Loreto
Av de Sarrià
C de Còrsega
2
12
C de Pau Claris
8
C d'Ausiàs Marc
C de Wellington
C de Joan Miró
C de Viladomat
Hospital Clínic
C d'Aribau
C de València
3
Plaça de Joan Carles I
Ronda de Sant Pere
Pg de Pujades
Universitat Pompeu Fabra
Travessera de les Corts
C de Casanova
C de Muntaner
15
C de Balmes
C d'Enric Granados
7
Cascada
Parc de Carles I
Clínic
Urquinaona
Catalunya
Palau de la Música Catalana
C del Comerç
Pg de
Parc de la Ciutadella
Ciutadella Vila Olímpica

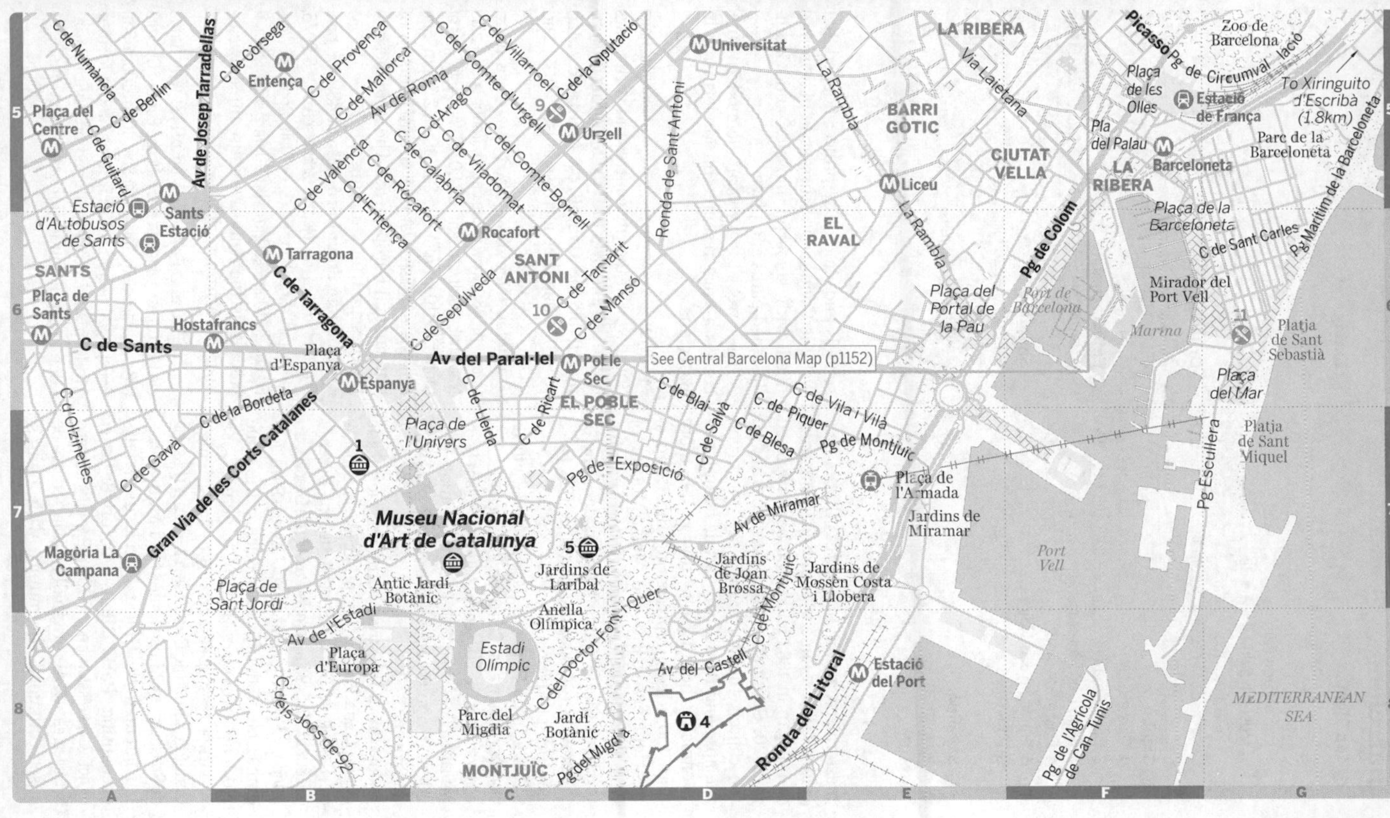
C de Numància
C de Berlin
Plaça del Centre
C de Guitard
Av de Josep Tarradellas
C de Còrsega
Entença
C de Provença
C de Mallorca
Av de Roma
C del Comte d'Urgell
C de Villarroel
C de la Diputació
C d'Aragó
C de València
C de Calàbria
C de Viladomat
C del Comte Borrell
Urgell
9
C de Rocafort
C d'Entença
Rocafort
Estació d'Autobusos de Sants
Sants Estació
Tarragona
SANTS
Plaça de Sants
C de Tarragona
SANT ANTONI
C de Tamarit
C de Sepúlveda
10
C de Mansó
Hostafrancs
C de Sants
Plaça d'Espanya
Av del Paral·lel
Poble Sec
Espanya
C d'Olzinelles
C de la Bordeta
C de Lleida
C de Ricart
EL POBLE SEC
Plaça de l'Univers
C de Gavà
Gran Via de les Corts Catalanes
1
Pg de l'Exposició
Museu Nacional d'Art de Catalunya
5
Magòria La Campana
Antic Jardí Botànic
Jardins de Laribal
Plaça de Sant Jordi
Av de l'Estadi
Anella Olímpica
Plaça d'Europa
Estadi Olímpic
C del Doctor Font i Quer
C dels Jocs de 92
Parc del Migdia
Jardí Botànic
MONTJUÏC
Pg del Migdia
4
Universitat
Ronda de Sant Antoni
La Rambla
LA RIBERA
Via Laietana
BARRI GÒTIC
CIUTAT VELLA
Liceu
EL RAVAL
Pg de Colom
Plaça del Portal de la Pau
Port de Barcelona
See Central Barcelona Map (p1152)
C de Blai
C de Salvà
C de Piquer
C de Vila i Vilà
C de Blesa
Pg de Montjuïc
Plaça de l'Armada
Av de Miramar
Jardins de Miramar
Jardins de Joan Brossa
C de Montjuïc
Jardins de Mossèn Costa i Llobera
Av del Castell
Ronda del Litoral
Estació del Port
Port Vell
Pg de l'Agrícola
de Can Tunis
Picasso
Pg de Circumval·lació
Zoo de Barcelona
To Xiringuito d'Escribà (1.8km)
Plaça de les Olles
Estació de França
Pla del Palau
Barceloneta
Parc de la Barceloneta
LA RIBERA
Plaça de la Barceloneta
C de Sant Carles
Pg Marítim de la Barceloneta
Mirador del Port Vell
Marina
11
Platja de Sant Sebastià
Plaça del Mar
Pg Escullera
Platja de Sant Miquel
MEDITERRANEAN SEA
A
B
C
D
E
F
G
5
6
7
8

Barcelona

Top Sights
Casa Batlló D4
La Pedrera D3
La Sagrada Família E2
Museu Nacional d'Art de Catalunya C7
Palau de la Música Catalana E4

Sights
1 CaixaForum B7
2 Casa Amatller D4
3 Casa Lleó Morera D4
4 Castell de Montjuïc D8
5 Fundació Joan Miró C7
6 Park Güell C1

Sleeping
7 Hostal Goya E4
8 Hotel Constanza E4

Eating
9 Amaltea C5
10 Inopia C6
11 Suquet de l'Almirall G6
12 Tapaç 24 .... D4

Drinking
13 Berlin B3
14 Dry Martini C4

Entertainment
15 Arena Madre D4

Shopping
16 Els Encants Vells F2
17 Joan Murrià D3
18 Vinçon D3

masterpiece, a work in progress that is Barcelona's most famous building. Construction began in 1882 and could be completed in 2020. Gaudí spent 40 years working on the church, though he only saw the crypt, the apse and the nativity facade completed. Eventually there'll be 18 towers, all more than 100m high, representing the 12 apostles, four evangelists and Mary, Mother of God, plus the tallest tower (170m) standing for Jesus Christ. Climb high inside some of the towers (or take the elevator, €2) for a new perspective.

Gaudí's **La Pedrera** (Map p1148; www.fundaciocaixacatalunya.es; Carrer de Provença 261-265; adult/student & EU senior €10/6; ⏲9am-8pm; Ⓜ Diagonal) is his best-known secular creation. It ripples around the corner of Carrer de Provença.

Just down the street is the unique facade of the **Casa Batlló** (Map p1148; www.casabatllo.es; Passeig de Gràcia 43; adult/student & senior €17.80/14.25; ⏲9am-8pm; Ⓜ Passeig de Gràcia), an allegory for the legend of St George (Sant Jordi in Catalan) the dragon slayer. On the same block are two other Modernista gems, **Casa Amatller** (Passeig de Gràcia 41) by Josep Puig i Cadafalch and the **Casa Lleó Morera** (Passeig de Gràcia 35) by Lluís Domènech i Montaner.

High up in the Gràcia district sits Gaudí's enchanting **Park Güell** (Map p1148; Carrer d'Olot 7; admission free; ⏲10am-9pm; Ⓜ Lesseps or Vallcarca, 🚌24), originally designed to be a self-contained community with houses, schools and shops. The project flopped, but we're left with a Dr Seuss–style playground filled with colourful mosaics and Gaudí-designed paths and plazas.

The website www.rutadelmodernisme.com is a great resource on Modernisme in Barcelona.

Montjuïc NEIGHBOURHOOD

Southwest of the city centre, and with views out to sea and over the city, Montjuïc is dominated by the **Castell de Montjuïc** (Map p1148), a one-time fortress. Buses 50, 55 and 61 all head up here.

Museu Nacional d'Art de Catalunya (Map p1148; www.mnac.cat; Mirador del Palau Nacional; adult/student €8.50/6, free 1st Sun of month; ⏲10am-7pm Tue-Sat, 10am-2.30pm Sun & holidays; Ⓜ Espanya) is a broad panoply of Catalan and European art. The Romanesque frescoes are truly stunning.

Fundació Joan Miró (Map p1148; www.bcn.fjmiro.es; Plaça de Neptu; adult/senior €8.50/6, temporary exhibitions €4/3; ⏲10am-8pm Tue, Wed, Fri & Sat, 10am-9.30pm Thu, 10am-2.30pm Sun & holidays) is the definitive museum showcasing Joan Miró's works.

FREE **CaixaForum** (Map p1148; www.fundacio.lacaixa.es; Avinguda de Francesc Ferrer i Guàrdia 6-8; ⏲10am-8pm Tue-Fri & Sun, 10am-10pm Sat; Ⓜ Espanya) is housed in a remarkable former Modernista factory designed by Puig i Cadafalch and puts on major art exhibitions.

Festivals & Events

Festes de la Mercè CULTURE
(www.bcn.cat/merce) The city's biggest party, with four days of concerts, dancing, *castellers* (human-castle builders) and fireworks. Held around 24 September.

Dia de Sant Joan MIDSUMMER
The evening before 24 June is a colourful midsummer celebration with bonfires and fireworks.

Sleeping

Numerous private apartment-rental companies operate in Barcelona. These can often be a better deal than staying in a hotel. Start your search at **Aparteasy** (☎93 451 67 66; www.aparteasy.com), **Barcelona On Line** (☎902 887 017, 93 343 79 93; www.barcelona-on-line.es) and **Rent a Flat in Barcelona** (☎93 342 73 00; www.rentaflatinbarcelona.com).

Hostal Gat Raval HOSTAL €€
(Map p1152; ☎93 481 66 70; www.gataccommodation.com; Carrer de Joaquín Costa 44; d €82, s/d without bathroom €58/74; ❄@☎; MUniversitat) There's a pea-green and lemon-lime colour scheme in this hip, young, 2nd-floor, hostel-style lodging deep in El Raval. Rooms are pleasant, secure and each is behind a green door, but only some have private bathroom.

Hostal Goya HOSTAL €€
(Map p1148; ☎93 302 25 65; www.hostalgoya.com; Carrer de Pau Claris 74; s €70, d €96-113; ❄; MPasseig de Gràcia) The Goya is a gem of a spot on the chichi side of l'Eixample and a short stroll from Plaça de Catalunya. Rooms have parquet floors and a light colour scheme that varies from room to room. In the bathrooms, the original mosaic floors have largely been retained, combined with contemporary design features.

TOP CHOICE **Hotel Banys Orientals** BOUTIQUE HOTEL €€
(Map p1152; ☎93 268 84 60; www.hotelbanysorientals.com; Carrer de l'Argenteria 37; s/d €93/107; ❄@; MJaume I) Cool blues and aquamarines combine with dark-hued parquet floors to lend this boutique beauty an understated charm. All rooms – admittedly on the small side but impeccably presented – look onto the street or back lanes.

Pensió 2000 PENSIÓN €
(Map p1152; ☎93 310 74 66; www.pensio2000.com; Carrer de Sant Pere més Alt 6; s/d €52/65, without bathroom €35/45; @; MUrquinaona) Sitting in front of the Modernista chocolate box that is the Palau de la Música Catalana (p1155), this cheerful *pensión,* with its seven canary-yellow rooms, is a conveniently placed option. Two rooms (the pick) have their own bathroom. You can also take time out on the little terrace.

Alberg Hostel Itaca HOSTEL €
(Map p1152; ☎93 301 97 51; www.itacahostel.com; Carrer de Ripoll 21; dm €14-20, d €55; @☎; MJaume I) A bright, quiet hostel near La Catedral, Itaca has spacious dorms (sleeping six, eight or 12 people) with parquet floors, spring colours and a couple of doubles with private bathrooms.

Hostal Campi HOSTAL €
(Map p1152; ☎93 301 35 45; www.hostalcampi.com; Carrer de la Canuda 4; d €67, s/d without bathroom €34/57; MCatalunya) An excellent bottom-end deal. The best rooms are the doubles with their own loo and shower. Although basic, they are extremely roomy and bright.

Hotel Constanza BOUTIQUE HOTEL €€
(Map p1148; ☎93 270 19 10; www.hotelconstanzabarcelona.com; Carrer del Bruc 33; s/d €110/130; ❄@; MGirona or Urquinaona) Constanza is a boutique belle that has stolen the heart of many a visitor to Barcelona. Even smaller singles are made to feel special with broad mirrors and strong colours (reds and yellows, with black furniture). Suites and studios are further options. The terrace is a nice spot to relax for a while, looking over the rooftops of the l'Eixample.

Eating

Although Barcelona has a reputation as a hot spot of 'new Spanish cuisine', you'll still find local eateries serving up time-honoured local grub, from squid-ink *fideuà* (a satisfying paellalike noodle dish) to pig trotters, rabbit with snails, and *butifarra* (a tasty local sausage).

LA RAMBLA & BARRI GÒTIC

Skip the overpriced traps along La Rambla and get into the winding lanes of the Barri Gòtic.

Agut CATALAN €€
(Map p1152; ☎93 315 17 09; Carrer d'En Gignàs 16; meals €35; ⊙lunch Tue-Sun, dinner Tue-Sat; ⊖; MJaume 1) Contemporary paintings set a contrast with the fine traditional Catalan dishes offered in this timeless restaurant. You might start with something like the

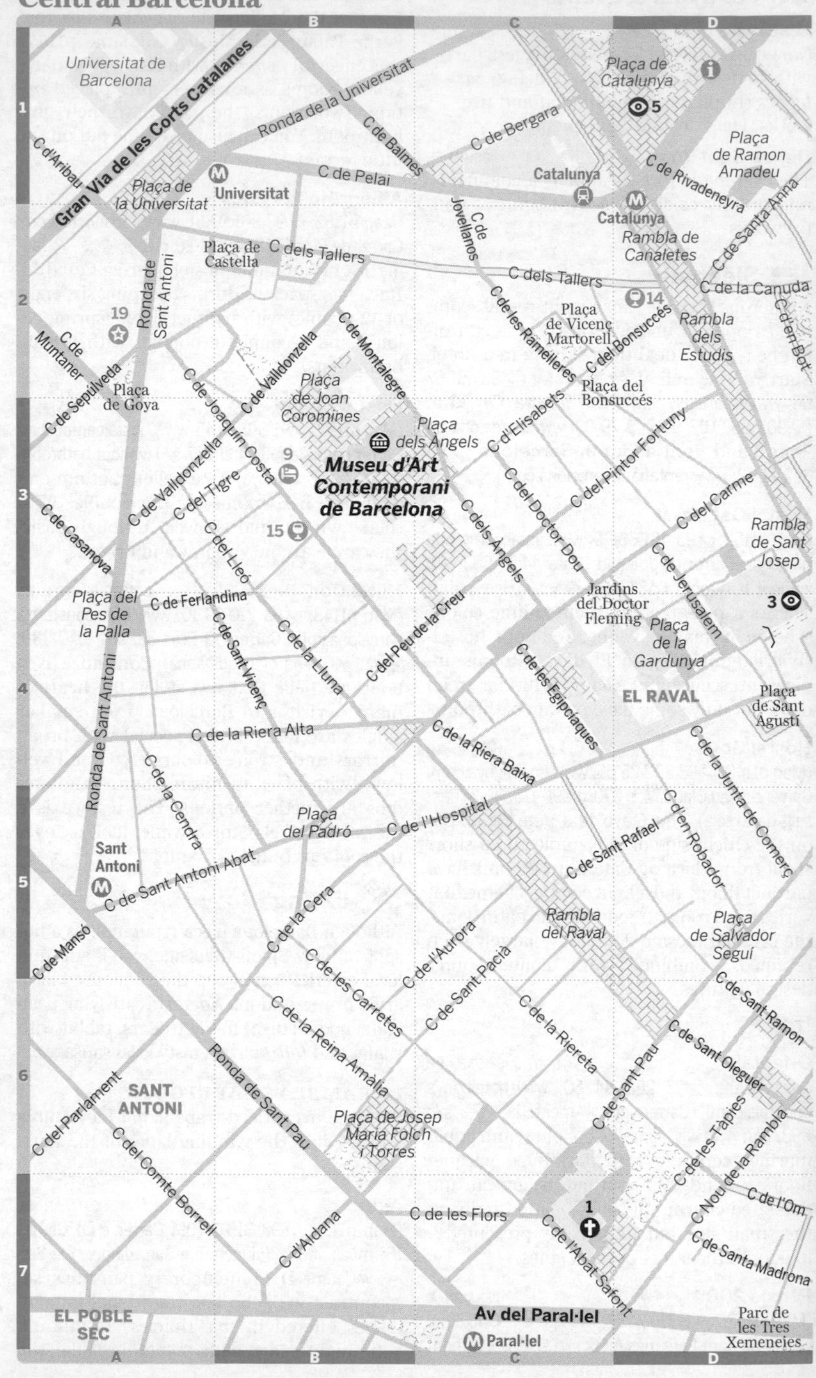
A
B
C
D
1
2
3
4
5
6
7
Universitat de Barcelona
Gran Via de les Corts Catalanes
Ronda de la Universitat
C de Balmes
C de Bergara
Plaça de Catalunya
5
Plaça de Ramon Amadeu
C d'Aribau
Plaça de la Universitat
Universitat
C de Pelai
Catalunya
Catalunya
C de Rivadeneyra
C de Santa Anna
C de Jovellanos
Rambla de Canaletes
Plaça de Castella
C dels Tallers
C dels Tallers
Ronda de Sant Antoni
14
C de la Canuda
19
C de Muntaner
C de Montalegre
C de les Ramelleres
Plaça de Vicenç Martorell
C del Bonsuccés
Rambla dels Estudis
C d'en Bot
C de Valldonzella
Plaça de Joan Coromines
Plaça del Bonsuccés
C de Sepúlveda
Plaça de Goya
C de Joaquín Costa
Plaça dels Àngels
C d'Elisabets
C del Pintor Fortuny
9
Museu d'Art Contemporani de Barcelona
C de Valldonzella
C del Tigre
C del Doctor Dou
C de Casanova
15
C dels Àngels
C del Carme
Rambla de Sant Josep
C del Lleó
C de Jerusalem
Jardins del Doctor Fleming
3
Plaça del Pes de la Palla
C de Ferlandina
C de Sant Vicenç
C de la Lluna
C del Peu de la Creu
Plaça de la Gardunya
C de les Egipcíaques
EL RAVAL
Plaça de Sant Agustí
Ronda de Sant Antoni
C de la Riera Alta
C de la Riera Baixa
C de la Junta de Comerç
C de la Cendra
Plaça del Padró
C de l'Hospital
C d'en Robador
Sant Antoni
C de Sant Antoni Abat
C de Sant Rafael
C de Mansó
C de la Cera
Rambla del Raval
Plaça de Salvador Seguí
C de l'Aurora
C de les Carretes
C de Sant Pacià
C de Sant Ramon
C de la Riereta
C de la Reina Amàlia
C de Sant Oleguer
Ronda de Sant Pau
C de Sant Pau
C del Parlament
SANT ANTONI
Plaça de Josep Maria Folch i Torres
C de les Tàpies
C del Comte Borrell
C Nou de la Rambla
C de l'Om
1
C de les Flors
C d'Aldana
C de l'Abat Safont
C de Santa Madrona
EL POBLE SEC
Av del Paral·lel
Paral·lel
Parc de les Tres Xemeneies
A
B
C
D

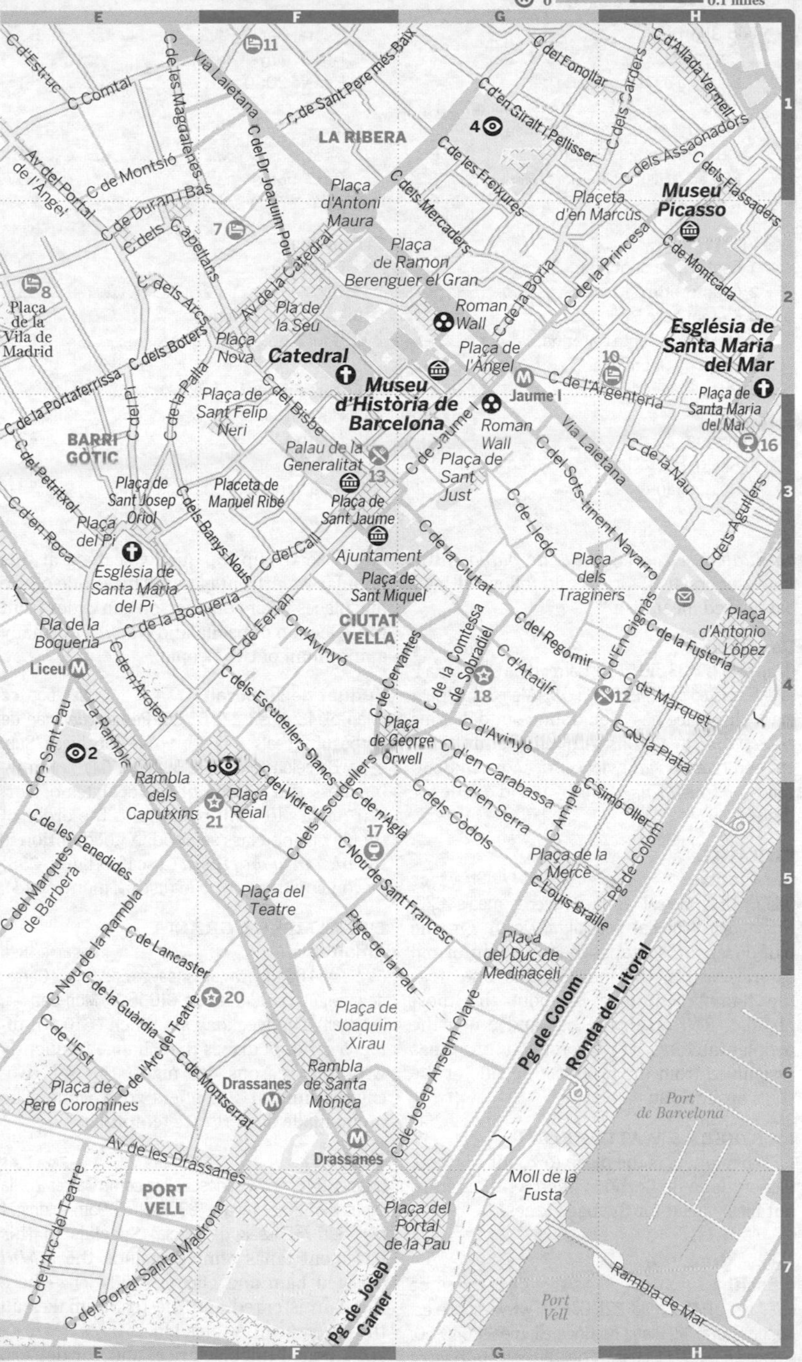
0 200 m
0 0.1 miles
LA RIBERA
BARRI GÒTIC
CIUTAT VELLA
PORT VELL
Catedral
Museu d'Història de Barcelona
Museu Picasso
Església de Santa Maria del Mar
Església de Santa Maria del Pi
Roman Wall
Roman Wall
Palau de la Generalitat
Ajuntament
Plaça d'Antoni Maura
Plaça de Ramon Berenguer el Gran
Pla de la Seu
Plaça Nova
Plaça de Sant Felip Neri
Plaça de l'Àngel
Plaça de Sant Just
Plaça de Sant Jaume
Plaça de Sant Miquel
Placeta de Manuel Ribé
Plaça de Sant Josep Oriol
Plaça del Pi
Plaça de la Vila de Madrid
Pla de la Boqueria
Plaça de George Orwell
Plaça dels Traginers
Plaça d'Antonio López
Plaça de Santa Maria del Mar
Placeta d'en Marcús
Plaça Reial
Rambla dels Caputxins
Plaça del Teatre
Plaça de la Mercè
Plaça del Duc de Medinaceli
Plaça de Joaquim Xirau
Rambla de Santa Mònica
Plaça de Pere Coromines
Plaça del Portal de la Pau
Moll de la Fusta
Port de Barcelona
Port Vell
Jaume I
Liceu
Drassanes
Drassanes
Via Laietana
C d'Estruc
C Comtal
C de les Magdalenes
C de Sant Pere més Baix
C del Fonollar
C dels Carders
C d'Allada Vermell
C d'en Giralt i Pellisser
C dels Assaonadors
C dels Flassaders
C de les Freixures
C dels Mercaders
C del Dr Joaquim Pou
Av del Portal de l'Àngel
C de Montsió
C de Duran i Bas
C dels Capellans
C dels Arcs
Av de la Catedral
C de la Princesa
C de Montcada
C de la Bòria
C de l'Argenteria
C dels Boters
C de la Portaferrissa
C del Pi
C de la Palla
C del Bisbe
C de Jaume I
C del Sots-tinent Navarro
C de la Nau
C dels Agullers
C del Petritxol
C d'en Roca
C dels Banys Nous
C del Call
C de Lledó
C de la Ciutat
C de la Boqueria
C de Ferran
C d'Avinyó
C de la Comtessa de Sobradiel
C del Regomir
C d'Ataülf
C d'En Gignàs
C de la Fusteria
C de Marquet
C de la Plata
C de n'Aroles
C dels Escudellers Blancs
C de Cervantes
C d'Avinyó
C d'en Carabassa
C d'en Serra
C Ample
C Simó Oller
C de Sant Pau
La Rambla
C del Vidre
C dels Escudellers
C de n'Aglà
C dels Còdols
C Nou de Sant Francesc
C Louis Braille
Pg de Colom
C de les Penedides
C del Marquès de Barberà
C Nou de la Rambla
C de Lancaster
Ptge de la Pau
C de la Guàrdia
C de l'Arc del Teatre
C de l'Est
C de Montserrat
C de Josep Anselm Clavé
Pg de Colom
Ronda del Litoral
Av de les Drassanes
C de l'Arc del Teatre
C del Portal Santa Madrona
Pg de Josep Carner
Rambla de Mar
E F G H
1 2 3 4 5 6 7

Central Barcelona

Top Sights
Catedral ... F2
Església de Santa Maria del Mar ... H2
Museu d'Art Contemporani de Barcelona ... B3
Museu d'Història de Barcelona ... G2
Museu Picasso ... H2

Sights
1 Església de Sant Pau ... C7
2 Gran Teatre del Liceu ... E4
3 Mercat de la Boqueria ... D4
4 Mercat de Santa Caterina ... G1
5 Plaça de Catalunya ... D1
6 Plaça Reial ... F4

Sleeping
7 Alberg Hostal Itaca ... F2
8 Hostal Campi ... E2
9 Hostal Gat Raval ... B3
10 Hotel Banys Oriental ... H2
11 Pensió 2000 ... F1

Eating
12 Agut ... H4
Bar Pinotxo ... (see 3)
13 Can Conesa ... F3

Drinking
14 Boadas ... D2
15 Casa Almirall ... B3
16 La Vinya Del Senyor ... H3
17 Soul Club ... F5

Entertainment
18 Harlem Jazz Club ... G4
19 Metro ... A2
20 Moog ... F6
21 Sala Tarantos ... F5

bouillabaisse con cigalitas de playa (little seawater crayfish) for €11 and follow with an oak-grilled meat dish.

Can Conesa SNACKS €
(Map p1152; ☎93 310 57 95; Carrer de la Llibreteria 1; rolls & toasted sandwiches €3-5; ⊙Mon-Sat; Ⓜ Jaume I) This place has been doling out delicious *entrepans* (bread rolls with filling), frankfurters and toasted sandwiches for more than 50 years – *barcelonins* swear by it and queue for them.

EL RAVAL

Bar Pinotxo TAPAS €€
(Map p1152; Mercat de la Boqueria; meals €20; ⊙6am-5pm Mon-Sat Sep-Jul; Ⓜ Liceu) Of the half-dozen or so tapas bars and informal eateries within the market, this one near the Rambla entrance is about the most popular. Roll up to the bar and enjoy the people-watching as you munch on tapas assembled from the products on sale at the stalls around you.

LA RIBERA & WATERFRONT

La Barceloneta is the place to go for seafood. Passeig Joan de Borbó is lined with eateries, but locals head for the back lanes.

TOP CHOICE **Xiringuito d'Escribà** SEAFOOD & RICE DISHES €€
(off Map p1148; ☎93 221 07 29; www.escriba.es; Ronda Litoral 42, Platja de Bogatell; meals €40-50; ⊙lunch daily; Ⓜ Llacuna) The Barcelona pastry family serves up top-quality seafood at this popular waterfront eatery. This is one of the few places where one person can order from the selection of paella and *fideuá* (normally a minimum of two people).

Suquet de l'Almirall SEAFOOD €€
(Map p1148; ☎93 221 62 33; Passeig de Joan de Borbó 65; meals €45-50; ⊙Tue-Sat, lunch Sun; ⊖; Ⓜ Barceloneta or 🚌17, 39, 57 or 64) A family business run by one of the acolytes of Ferran Adrià's El Bulli restaurant, the order of the day is top-class seafood. A good option is the *pica pica marinera* (a seafood mix, €38) or you could opt for the tasting menu (€44).

L'EIXAMPLE & GRÀCIA

Amaltea VEGETARIAN €
(☎93 454 86 13; www.amalteaygovinda.com; Carrer de la Diputació 164; meals €10-15; ⊙Mon-Sat; ⊖; Ⓜ Urgell) The weekday set lunch (€10.50) offers a series of dishes that change frequently with the seasons. At night, the set two-course dinner (€15) offers good value. The home-made desserts are tempting.

Tapaç 24 TAPAS €€
(Map p1148; www.carlesabellan.com; Carrer de la Diputació 269; meals €30-35; ⊙9am-midnight Mon-Sat; Ⓜ Passeig de Gràcia) Specials in this basement tapas temple include the *bikini* (toasted ham and cheese sandwich – here the ham is cured and the truffle makes all the difference!), a thick black *arròs negre de sípia* (squid-ink black rice) and, for dessert,

xocolata amb pa, sal i oli (delicious balls of chocolate in olive oil with a touch of salt and wafer).

Inopia TAPAS €€
(Map p1148; 93 424 52 31; Carrer de Tamarit 104; meals €25-30; dinner Tue-Sat, lunch Sat; Rocafort) Albert Adrià, brother of star chef Ferran, has his hands full with this constantly busy gourmet-tapas temple. Select a *pintxo de cuixa de pollastre a l'ast* (chunk of rotisserie chicken thigh) or the lightly fried, tempura-style vegetables. Wash down with house red or Moritz beer.

Drinking

The city abounds with daytime cafes, laid-back lounges and lively night-time bars. Closing time is generally 2am Sunday to Thursday and 3am on Friday and Saturday.

EL RAVAL

Boadas COCKTAIL BAR
(Map p1152; Carrer dels Tallers 1; noon-2am Mon-Thu, noon-3am Fri & Sat; Catalunya) Inside the unprepossessing entrance is one of the city's oldest cocktail bars (famed for its daiquiris). The bow-tied waiters have been serving up their poison since 1933; Joan Miró and Hemingway tippled here.

Casa Almirall BAR
(Map p1152; Carrer de Joaquín Costa 33; 5.30pm-2.30am Sun-Thu, 7pm-3am Fri & Sat; Universitat) In business since the 1860s, this unchanged corner bar is dark and intriguing, with Modernista decor and a mixed clientele. There are some great original pieces in here, like the marble counter.

LA RIBERA

La Vinya del Senyor WINE BAR
(Map p1152; Plaça de Santa Maria del Mar 5; noon-1am Tue-Sun; Jaume I) The wine list is as long as *War and Peace*, and the terrace lies in the shadow of Santa Maria del Mar. You can crowd inside the tiny wine bar itself or take a bottle upstairs.

L'EIXAMPLE & GRÀCIA

Berlin BAR
(Map p1148; Carrer de Muntaner 240; 10am-2am Mon-Wed, 10am-2.30am Thu, 10pm-3am Fri & Sat; Diagonal or Hospital Clínic) This elegant corner bar attracts waves of night animals starting up for a long night. In warmer weather you can sit outside on the footpath, or head downstairs into the basement if the bar's too crowded.

Dry Martini COCKTAIL BAR
(Map p1148; 93 217 50 72; www.drymartinibcn.com; Carrer del Consell de Cent 247; 5pm-3am; FGC Provença) Well-dressed waiters serve up the best dry martini in town, or whatever else your heart desires, in this classic cocktail lounge. Sink into a leather lounge and nurse a huge G&T.

Entertainment

To keep up with what's on, pick up a copy of the weekly listings magazine *Guía del Ocio* (€1) from news stands.

Nightclubs

Entry can cost from nothing to €20 (one drink usually included).

TOP CHOICE **Terrrazza** CLUB
(www.laterrrazza.com; Avinguda de Francesc Ferrer i Guàrdia; admission €10-20; midnight-5am Thu, midnight-6am Fri & Sat; Espanya) One of the city's top summertime dance locations, Terrazza attracts squadrons of the beautiful people, locals and foreigners alike, for a full-on night of music and cocktails partly under the stars inside the Poble Espanyol complex.

TOP CHOICE **Soul Club** DANCE BAR
(Map p1152; Carrer Nou de Sant Francesc 7; 10pm-2.30am Mon-Thu, 10pm-3am Fri & Sat, 8pm-2.30am Sun; Drassanes) Each night the DJs change the musical theme, which ranges from deep funk to Latin grooves. The tiny front bar is for drinking and chatting (get in early for a stool or the sole lounge). Out back is where the dancing is done.

Moog CLUB
(Map p1152; www.masimas.com/moog; Carrer de l'Arc del Teatre 3; admission €10; midnight-5am; Drassanes) This fun, minuscule club is a downtown hit. In the main downstairs dance area, DJs dish out house, techno and electro, while upstairs you can groove to indie and occasional classic pop.

Gay & Lesbian Venues

The gay and lesbian scene is concentrated in the blocks around Carrers de Muntaner and Consell de Cent (dubbed Gayxample). Here you'll find ambience every night of the week in the bars, discos and drag clubs.

Party hard at classic gay discos such as **Arena Madre** (Map p1148; www.arenadisco.com in Spanish; Carrer de Balmes 32; Universitat) and **Metro** (Map p1152; www.metrodiscobcn.com; Carrer de Sepúlveda 185; 1am-5am Mon,

NO MORE BULLS?

On 28 July 2010, Catalonia became the first region in mainland Spain to ban bullfighting (the Canary Islands voted to make bullfighting illegal in 1991). The vote, which came as a result of a 180,000-strong petition, follows moves by 23 municipalities (including Barcelona) who have declared themselves to be anti-bullfighting cities in recent years. With Catalonia never the strongest bastion of bullfighting tradition, and with Spain's major national political parties opposing Catalonia's ban, the chances of other Spanish regions following suit seem remote. However, other factors do pose a significant (albeit longer-term) threat to bullfighting. Recent surveys have found that around 50% of Spaniards oppose bullfighting, with the figures much higher among younger Spaniards. The recent global economic crisis has also taken its toll – there was a 50% drop in the number of bullfights in 2009, with many small towns forced to cancel their annual fiestas.

midnight-5am Sun & Tue-Thu, midnight-6am Fri & Sat; MUniversitat).

Sport

FC Barcelona (Barça for aficionados) has one of the best stadiums in Europe – the 99,000-capacity **Camp Nou** (off Map p1148; 902 189 900; Carrer d'Aristides Maillol; box office 9am-1.30pm & 3.30-6pm Mon-Fri; MPalau Reial or Collblanc) in the west of the city. Tickets for national-league games are available at the stadium, by phone or online (www.fcbarcelona.com). For the latter two options, nonmembers must book 15 days before the match.

Live Music

TOP CHOICE **Harlem Jazz Club** MUSIC BAR
(Map p1152; www.harlemjazzclub.es; Carrer de la Comtessa de Sobradiel 8; admission up to €10; 8pm-4am Tue-Thu & Sun, 8pm-5am Fri & Sat; MDrassanes) This narrow, smoky, old-town dive is one of the best spots in town for jazz.

Sala Tarantos MUSIC BAR
(Map p1152; 93 319 17 89; www.masimas.net; Plaça Reial 17; admission from €7; performances 8.30pm, 9.30pm & 10.30pm daily; MLiceu) This basement locale is the stage for some of the best flamenco to pass through Barcelona.

Shopping

Most mainstream fashion stores are along a shopping 'axis' that runs from Plaça de Catalunya along Passeig de Gràcia, then left (west) along Avinguda Diagonal.

The El Born area in La Ribera is awash with tiny boutiques, especially those purveying young, fun fashion. There are plenty of shops scattered throughout the Barri Gòtic (stroll Carrer d'Avinyò and Carrer de Portaferrissa). For secondhand stuff, head for El Raval, especially Carrer de la Riera Baixa.

Joan Murrià FOOD & DRINK
(Map p1148; www.murria.cat; Carrer de Roger de Llúria 85; MPasseig de Gràcia) Ramon Casas designed the Modernista shopfront ads for this delicious delicatessen, where the shelves groan under the weight of speciality food from around Catalonia and beyond.

Els Encants Vells FLEA MARKET
(The Old Charms; Map p1148; www.encantsbcn.com, in Catalan; Plaça de les Glòries Catalanes; 7am-6pm Mon, Wed, Fri & Sat; MGlòries) Bargain hunters love this free-for-all flea market.

Vinçon HOMEWARES
(Map p1148; www.vincon.com; Passeig de Gràcia 96; 10am-8.30pm Mon-Sat; MDiagonal) Vinçon has the slickest designs in furniture and household goods, local and imported.

Information

Dangers & Annoyances

Purse snatching and pickpocketing are major problems, especially around Plaça de Catalunya, La Rambla and Plaça Reial.

Emergency

Tourists who want to report thefts need to go to the Catalan police, known as the **Mossos d'Esquadra** (088; Carrer Nou de la Rambla 80), or the **Guàrdia Urbana** (Local Police; 092; La Rambla 43).

Emergency number (112)

Medical Services

Call 010 to find the nearest late-opening duty pharmacy.

Farmàcia Clapés (93 301 28 43; La Rambla 98; MLiceu)

Hospital Clínic i Provincial (93 227 54 00; Carrer de Villarroel 170; MHospital Clínic)

Money

Banks (with ATMs) and foreign-exchange offices abound in Barcelona. **Interchange** (Rambla dels Caputxins 74; ⏲9am-11pm; ⓂLiceu) represents American Express.

Tourist Information

Oficina d'Informació de Turisme de Barcelona Main Branch (☎93 285 38 32; www.barcelonaturisme.com; Plaça de Catalunya 17-S underground; ⏲9am-9pm); Aeroport del Prat (Terminal 1 arrivals, Terminal 2B arrivals hall, Terminal 2A arrivals hall; ⏲9am-9pm); Estació Sants (⏲8am-8pm late Jun-late Sep, 8am-8pm Mon-Fri, 8am-2pm Sat, Sun & holidays Oct-May; ⓂSants Estació); town hall (Carrer de la Ciutat 2; ⏲9am-8pm Mon-Fri, 10am-8pm Sat, 10am-2pm Sun & holidays; ⓂJaume I)

Regional tourist office (☎93 238 80 91, from outside Catalonia 902 400 012; www.gencat.net/probert; Passeig de Gràcia 107; ⏲10am-7pm Mon-Sat, 10am-2.30pm Sun; ⓂDiagonal)

Getting There & Away

Air

Barcelona's airport, **El Prat de Llobregat** (☎902 404 704; www.aena.es), is 12km southwest of the city centre. Barcelona is a big international and domestic destination, with direct flights from North America as well as many European cities.

Boat

Regular passenger and vehicular ferries to/from the Balearic Islands, operated by **Acciona Trasmediterranea** (☎902 454 645; www.trasmediterranea.es), dock along both sides of the Moll de Barcelona wharf in Port Vell; see p1193 for further information.

The Grimaldi group's **Grandi Navi Veloci** (☎in Italy 010 209 4591; www1.gnv.it; ⓂDrassanes) runs high-speed, thrice-weekly luxury ferries between Barcelona and Genoa, while **Grimaldi Ferries** (☎902 531 333, in Italy 081 496444; www.grimaldi-lines.com) operates similar services to Civitavecchia (near Rome), Livorno (Tuscany) and Porto Torres (northwest Sardinia).

Bus

The main terminal for most domestic and international buses is the **Estació del Nord** (Map p1148; ☎902 303 222; www.barcelonanord.com; Carrer d'Ali Bei 80; ⓂArc de Triomf). ALSA goes to Madrid (€28.18, eight hours, up to 16 daily), Valencia (€25.34, 4½ to 6½ hours, up to 14 daily) and many other destinations.

Eurolines (www.eurolines.com) offers international services from Estació del Nord and **Estació d'Autobusos de Sants** (Carrer de Viriat), which is next to Estació Sants Barcelona.

Train

Virtually all trains travelling to and from destinations within Spain stop at **Estació Sants** (ⓂSants-Estació). High-speed trains to Madrid, via Lleida and Zaragoza take as little as two hours 40 minutes; prices vary wildly. Other trains run to Valencia (€38.50 to €43.10, three to 4½ hours, 15 daily) and Burgos (from €49, six to seven hours, four daily).

There are also international connections with French cities from the same station.

Getting Around

To/From the Airport

The **A1 Aerobús** (☎93 415 60 20) runs from Terminal 1 to Plaça de Catalunya (€5, 30 to 40 minutes) from 6.05am to 1.05am. A2 Aerobús does the same run from Terminal 2, from 6am to 12.30am. Buy tickets on the bus.

Renfe's R2 Nord train line runs between the airport and Passeig de Gràcia (via Estació Sants) in central Barcelona (about 35 minutes). Tickets cost €3, unless you have a T-10 multitrip public-transport ticket, which costs less.

A taxi to/from the centre, about a half-hour ride depending on traffic, costs around €20 to €25.

Public Transport

Barcelona's metro system spreads its tentacles around the city in such a way that most places of interest are within a 10-minute walk of a station. Buses and suburban trains are needed only for a few destinations. A single metro, bus or suburban train ride costs €1.40, but a T-1 ticket, valid for 10 rides, costs €7.85.

Girona

POP 92,200

A tight huddle of ancient arcaded houses, grand churches, climbing cobbled streets and medieval baths, all enclosed by defensive walls and a lazy river, constitutes a powerful reason for visiting north Catalonia's largest city, Girona (Castilian: Gerona).

The billowing baroque facade of the **cathedral** stands at the head of a majestic flight of steps rising from Plaça de la Catedral. Repeatedly rebuilt and altered down the centuries, it has Europe's widest Gothic nave (23m). Girona's ancient Jewish quarter, the **Call**, was centred on Carrer de la Força.

Bed & Breakfast Bells Oficis (☎972 22 81 70; www.bellsoficis.com; Carrer dels Germans Busquets 2; r incl breakfast €35-85; ❄📶) has six desirable rooms, while **Gro Hostel Girona** (☎972 31 20 45; www.equity-point.com; Plaça Catalunya 23; dm incl breakfast with/without bathroom

DALÍ'S CATALONIA

A short train ride north of Girona, Figueres is home to the zany **Teatre-Museu Dalí** (www.salvador-dali.org; Plaça de Gala i Salvador Dalí 5; admission €11; ⏲9am-8pm Jul-Sep, 9.30am-6pm Tue-Sun Mar-Jun & Oct, 10.30am-6pm Tue-Sun Nov-Feb), housed in a 19th-century theatre converted by Salvador Dalí (who was born here). It's full of surprises, tricks and illusions, and contains a substantial portion of his life's work.

Dalí fans will want to travel south to visit the equally kooky **Castell de Púbol** (☎972 48 86 55; www.salvador-dali.org; admission €7; ⏲10am-8pm, closed Jan–mid-Mar & Mon outside high season) at La Pera, 22km northwest of Palafrugell, and his summer getaway at Port Lligat (1.25km from Cadaqués), the **Casa Museu Dalí** (☎972 25 10 15; www.salvador-dali.org; admission €10; ⏲by advance reservation only).

from €20/18; ❄@📶) is a great-value, colourful and friendly hostel.

La Terra (Carrer Ballestenes 23; menus €6.90) serves home-made burgers, quiches and cakes. **L'Alqueria** (☎972221882; www.restaurantalqueria.com; Carrer Ginesta 8; mains €15-20; ⏲closed Sun & Tue night & all day Mon), a smart new restaurant, serves the finest *arrós negre* (rice cooked in cuttlefish ink) and *arrós a la Catalan* in the city.

Information

Tourist office (☎872 97 59 75; www.girona.cat; Joan Maragall 2; ⏲8am-8pm Mon-Fri, 8am-2pm & 4-8pm Sat, 9am-2pm Sun)

Getting There & Away

AIR Girona-Costa Brava airport, 11km south of the centre, is Ryanair's Spanish hub.

TRAIN There are train services to Figueres (€10.50 to €13.70, 30 to 40 minutes, 20 daily) and Barcelona (from €14.90, 1½ hours, 20 daily).

Tarragona

POP 134,160

Barcelona's senior in Roman times, and a lesser medieval city, Tarragona is a provincial sort of place with some outstanding attractions: Catalonia's finest Roman ruins, a magnificent medieval cathedral in a pretty old town and some decent beaches.

Most places of interest are about 400m northeast of the train station. Note that high-speed trains stop at a different station, about 11km north of the centre.

Sights & Activities

Museu d'Història de Tarragona ROMAN RUINS
(www.museutgn.com; admission per site €3, incl all MHT elements €10; ⏲9am-9pm Mon-Sat, 9am-3pm Sun Easter-Oct, shorter hrs rest of year) Four separate Roman sites (which, since 2000, have constituted a Unesco World Heritage site) make up this museum. Start with the **Pretori i Circ Romans** (Plaça del Rei), which includes part of the vaults of the Roman circus. Near the beach is the crown jewel of Tarragona's Roman sites, the well-preserved **Amfiteatre Romà** (Plaça d'Arce Ochotorena). Southeast of Carrer de Lleida are remains of the **Fòrum Romà** (Carrer del Cardenal Cervantes), dominated by several imposing columns. The **Passeig Arqueològic** is a peaceful walk around part of the perimeter of the old town.

Museu Nacional Arqueològic de Tarragona MUSEUM
(www.mnat.es; Plaça del Rei 5; admission €2.40; ⏲10am-8pm Tue-Sat, 10am-2pm Sun & holidays Jun-Sep, shorter hrs rest of year) This carefully presented museum gives further insight into Roman Tarraco.

Catedral CATHEDRAL
(Pla de la Seu; admission €3.80; ⏲10am-7pm Mon-Sat) Sitting grandly at the top of the old town, Tarragona's cathedral combines Romanesque and Gothic features, as typified by the main facade on Pla de la Seu.

Sleeping & Eating

Look for tapas bars and inexpensive cafes on the Plaça de la Font. The Moll de Pescadors (Fishermens' Wharf) is the place to go for seafood restaurants.

Pensió Forum PENSION €
(☎977 23 1718; Plaça de la Font 37; s/d €26/38) The small but oh-so-colourful rooms at this helpful pension perch above a restaurant and overlook the main square – views of which can be enjoyed from one of the rooms with a balcony.

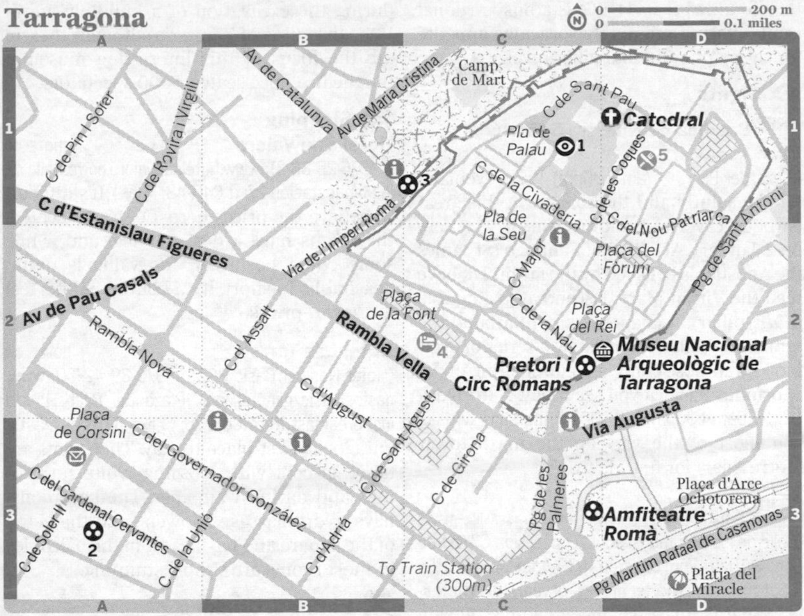

Tarragona

Tarragona

Aq MODERN REGIONAL €
(☎977 21 59 54; Carrer de les Coques 7; mains €15, menú del día from €18; ⏲Tue-Sat) This is a bubbly designer haunt with stark colour contrasts (black, lemon and cream linen), slick lines and intriguing plays on traditional cooking.

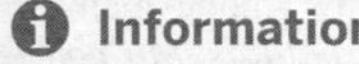

Information

Tourist office (☎977 25 07 95; www.tarragonaturisme.cat; Carrer Major 39; ⏲10am-8pm Mon-Sat, 10am-2pm Sun Jul-Oct, 10am-2pm & 4-7pm Mon-Sat Nov-Jun)

Getting There & Away

BUS There are buses to Barcelona, Valencia, Zaragoza, Madrid, Alicante, Pamplona, the main Andalucian cities, Andorra and the north coast.

TRAIN At least 16 regional trains per day run to/from Barcelona's Passeig de Gràcia (1½ hours, €13.60 to €20) via Sants.

ARAGÓN, BASQUE COUNTRY & NAVARRA

This northeast area of Spain is brimming with fascinating destinations: the arid hills and proud history of Aragón; the lush coastline and gourmet delights of the Basque Country (País Vasco); and the wine country and famous festivals of Navarra.

Aragón

ZARAGOZA

POP 624,700 / ELEV 200M

Sitting on the banks of the mighty Ebro River, Zaragoza (a contraction of Caesaraugusta, the name the Romans gave to the city when they founded it in 14 BC) is a busy regional capital with a seemingly voracious appetite for eating out and late-night revelry.

Sights

FREE Basílica de Nuestra Señora del Pilar CHURCH

(Plaza del Pilar; 7am-8.30pm) Brace yourself for the saintly and the solemn in this great baroque cavern of Catholicism. It was here on 2 January AD 40, that Santiago (St James the Apostle) is believed by the faithful to have seen the Virgin Mary descend atop a marble *pilar* (pillar). A chapel was built around the remaining pillar, followed by a series of ever-more-grandiose churches, culminating in the enormous basilica you see today. A **lift** (adult €2; 10am-1.30pm & 4-6.30pm Tue-Sun) whisks you most of the way up the north tower (Torre Pilar) for fine views.

TOP CHOICE Aljafería ISLAMIC PALACE

(Calle de los Diputados; adult/concession €3/1, free Sun; 10am-2pm Sat-Wed, 4.30-8pm Mon-Wed, Fri & Sat Jul & Aug, shorter hrs rest of year) La Aljafería is Spain's finest Islamic-era edifice outside Andalucía. It's not in the league of Granada's Alhambra or Córdoba's Mezquita, but it's nonetheless a glorious monument. The Aljafería was built as a pleasure palace for Zaragoza's Islamic rulers, chiefly in the 11th century. After the city passed into Christian hands in 1118, Zaragoza's Christian rulers made alterations.

La Seo CATHEDRAL

(Plaza de la Seo; admission €4; 10am-6pm Tue-Fri, 10am-2pm & 3-6pm Sat, 10-11.30am & 2.30-6pm Sun Jun-Sep) La Seo may lack the fame of the Basílica de Nuestra Señora del Pilar, but its interior is easily its architectural superior. Built between the 12th and 17th centuries, it displays a fabulous spread of architectural styles from Romanesque to baroque.

Museo Del Foro de Caesaraugusta ROMAN MUSEUM

(Plaza de la Seo 2; admission €2.50; 9am-8.30pm Tue-Sat, 10am-2pm Sun Jun-Sep, shorter hrs rest of year) The trapezoid building on Plaza de la Seo is the entrance to an excellent reconstruction of part of Roman Caesaraugusta's forum, now well below ground level.

Museo del Teatro de Caesaraugusta ROMAN THEATRE & MUSEUM

(Calle de San Jorge 12; admission €3.50; 9am-8.30pm Tue-Sat, 9am-1.30pm Sun) Discovered during the excavation of a building site in 1972, the ruins of Zaragoza's Roman theatre are the focus of this interesting museum; the theatre once seated 6000 spectators.

Sleeping

Hotel San Valero HOTEL €

(976 29 86 21; www.hotelsanvalero.com; Calle de la Manifestación 27; d €40-48;) It's difficult to believe the prices here. Centrally located, the rooms have a designer feel and, while some could be larger, the value is unimpeachable. In short, it's a boutique-hotel feel for *hostal* prices.

Hotel Las Torres HOTEL €€

(Hotel Nastasi Basic ZGZ; 976 39 42 50; www.nastasibasiczgzhotel.com; Plaza del Pilar 11; s/d incl breakfast from €65/75;) This is easily Zaragoza's best place to stay. The rooms are designer-cool with dazzling white furnishings and daring wallpaper. The bathrooms have hydromassage showers, and the views of the square and basilica from the balconies in most rooms are simply stunning.

Eating & Drinking

Zaragoza has some terrific tapas bars, with dozens of places on or close to Plaza de Santa Marta and towards the southern end of Calle Heroísmo. Otherwise the narrow streets of El Tubo, north of Plaza de España, are tapas central.

Calle del Temple, southwest of Plaza del Pilar, is the spiritual home of Zaragoza's roaring nightlife. This is where the city's students head to drink. There are more bars lined up along this street than anywhere else in Aragón.

TOP CHOICE Casa Pascualillo TAPAS BAR €

(Calle de la Libertad 5; meals €15-25; lunch daily, dinner Tue-Sat) The bar here groans under the weight of every tapas variety imaginable, with seafood and meat in abundance; the house speciality is El Pascualillo, a 'small' *bocadillo* of *jamón*, mushrooms and onion.

El Rincón de Aragón ARAGONESE €€

(976 20 11 63; Calle de Santiago 3-5; meals €20-35) There's no time for unnecessary elaborations here – the decor is basic and the food stripped down to its essence – but the eating is top-notch and ideal for finding out why people get excited about Aragonese cooking. One house speciality among many is the *ternasco asado con patatas a la pobre* (roasted suckling lamb ribs with 'poor man's potatoes').

Information

Municipal tourist office (976 20 12 00; www.zaragozaturismo.es; Plaza del Pilar; 9am-9pm mid-Jun–mid-Oct, 10am-8pm mid-Oct–mid-Jun)

Getting There & Away

AIR The **Zaragoza-Sanjurjo airport** (976 71 23 00) has domestic and international flights.

BUS There are buses to Madrid (from €14.47, 3¾ hours) and Barcelona (€13.71, 3¾ hours).

TRAIN High-speed AVE services depart almost hourly to Madrid (€58.20, 1½ hours, approximately 10 daily) and Barcelona (€63.70, from 1½ hours).

AROUND ARAGÓN

In Aragón's south, little-visited **Teruel** is home to some stunning Mudéjar architecture. Nearby, **Albarracín** is one of Spain's most beautiful villages.

In the north, the Pyrenees dominate and the **Parque Nacional de Ordesa y Monte Perdido** is excellent for hiking; the pretty village of **Torla** is the gateway. South of the hamlet of **La Besurta** is the great Maladeta massif, a superb challenge for experienced climbers. This forbidding line of icy peaks, with glaciers suspended from the higher crests, culminates in **Aneto** (3404m), the highest peak in the Pyrenees. Another enchanting base for exploration in the region is **Aínsa**, a hilltop village of stone houses.

In Aragón's northwest, **Sos del Rey Católico** is another gorgeous stone village draped along a ridge.

Basque Country

SAN SEBASTIÁN

POP 183,300

Stylish San Sebastián (Donostia in Basque) has the air of an upscale resort, complete with an idyllic location on the shell-shaped Bahía de la Concha. The natural setting – crystalline waters, a flawless beach, green hills on all sides – is captivating. But this is one of Spain's true culinary capitals, with more Michelin stars per capita than anywhere else on earth.

Sights & Activities

Beaches & Isla de Santa Clara BEACHES

Fulfilling almost every idea of how a perfect city beach should be formed, **Playa de la Concha** and its westerly extension, **Playa de Ondarreta**, are easily among the best city beaches in Europe. Less popular, but just as showy, **Playa de Gros**, east of Río Urumea, is the city's main surf beach.

Museo Chillida Leku OPEN-AIR MUSEUM

(www.museochillidaleku.com; admission €8.50; 10.30am-8pm Mon-Sat, 10.30am-3pm Sun Jul & Aug, shorter hrs rest of yr) This open-air museum, south of San Sebastián, is the most engaging museum in rural Basque Country. Amid the beech, oak and magnolia trees, you'll find 40 sculptures of granite and iron created by the renowned Basque sculptor Eduardo Chillida.

To get here, take the G2 bus (€1.35) for Hernani from Calle de Okendo in San Sebastián and get off at Zabalaga.

Aquarium AQUARIUM

(www.aquariumss.com; Paseo del Muelle 34; admission €12; 10am-9pm daily Jul & Aug, 10am-8pm Mon-Fri, 10am-9pm Sat & Sun Apr-Jun & Sep, shorter hrs rest of yr) In the city's excellent aquarium, the highlights are the deep-ocean and coral-reef exhibits and the long tunnel, around which swim monsters of the deep.

Monte Igueldo LOOKOUT

The views from the summit of Monte Igueldo, just west of town, will make you feel like a circling hawk staring over the vast panorama of the Bahía de la Concha and the surrounding coastline and mountains. The best way to get there is via the old-world **funicular railway** (return €2.60; 10am-10pm mid-Jul–Aug, shorter hrs rest of yr).

Sleeping

TOP CHOICE **Pensión Bellas Artes** BOUTIQUE HOTEL €€

(943 47 49 05; www.pension-bellasartes.com; Calle de Urbieta 64; s/d from €75/95;) To call this magnificent place a mere *pensión* is to do it something of a disservice. Its spacious rooms (some with glassed-in balconies) with exposed stone walls and excellent bathrooms should be the envy of many a more expensive hotel.

Pensión Aida BOUTIQUE HOTEL €€

(943 32 78 00; www.pensionesconencanto.com; Calle de Iztueta 9; s/d €59/82, studios €145; @) The rooms here are bright and bold, full of exposed stone, and everything smells fresh and clean. The communal area, stuffed with soft sofas and mountains of information, is a big plus.

Pensión Amaiur Ostatua PENSION €

(943 42 96 54; www.pensionamaiur.com; Calle de 31 de Agosto 44; s without bathroom €40-45, d without bathroom €50-65; @) Sprawling over three floors of an old town house, this

SAN SEBASTIÁN SPLURGE

With three shining Michelin stars, acclaimed chef Juan Mari Arzak takes some beating when it comes to *nueva cocina vasca* and his gourmet restaurant **Arzak** (☎943 27 84 65; www.arzak.info; Avenida Alcalde Jose Elosegui 273; meals around €150; ⏲closed last 2 weeks Jun & all Nov) is, not surprisingly, considered one of the best places to eat in Spain. Reservations, well in advance, are obligatory. The restaurant is about 1.5km east of San Sebastián.

excellent *pensión* continues to improve. The rooms, all of which share bathrooms, are fairly small but have had a great deal of thought put into them.

Pensión Altair BOUTIQUE PENSIÓN €
(☎943 29 31 33; www.pension-altair.com; Calle Padre Larroca 3; s/d €60/84; ❄@📶) This brand new *pensión* might well be the future of the San Sebastián accommodation scene: a beautifully restored town house with unusual arched windows and spacious, minimalist rooms. Reception is closed between 1.30pm and 5pm.

✖ Eating

San Sebastián is paradise for food lovers. Considered the birthplace of *nueva cocina española,* this area is home to some of the country's top chefs. Yet not all the good food is pricey. Head to the Parte Vieja for San Sebastián's *pintxos* (Basque-style tapas). Expect to pay €2.50 to €3.50 for a *pintxo* and *txakoli.*

TOP CHOICE **La Cuchara de San Telmo** TAPAS €
(Calle de 31 de Agosto 28) This unfussy, hidden-away (and hard to find) bar offers miniature *nueva cocina vasca* (new Basque cuisine) from a supremely creative kitchen, where chefs Alex Montiel and Iñaki Gulin conjure up innovative delights.

Astelana TAPAS €
(Calle de Iñigo 1) The *pintxos* draped across the counter in this bar, tucked into the corner of Plaza de la Constitución, stand out as some of the best in the city. Many of them are a fusion of Basque and Asian inspirations, but the best of all are perhaps the foie gras–based treats.

Restaurante Alberto SEAFOOD €
(☎943 42 88 84; Calle de 31 de Agosto 19; menus €14; ⏲closed Tue) A charming old seafood restaurant with a fishmonger-style window display of the day's catch. It's small, dark and friendly, but much of the fish is sold by the kilogram so bring a friend.

La Mejíllonera TAPAS €
(Calle del Puerto 15) If you thought mussels came only with garlic sauce, come here and discover mussels (from €3) by the thousands in all their glorious forms. Mussels not for you? Opt for the calamari and *patatas bravas.* We promise you won't regret it.

ℹ Information

Oficina de Turismo (☎943 48 11 66; www.sansebastianturismo.com; Alameda de Blvd 8; ⏲9am-8pm Mon-Sat, 10am-7pm Sun Jun-Sep, 9am-1.30pm & 3.30-7pm Mon-Thu, 9.30am-7pm Fri & Sat, 10am-2pm Sun Oct-May)

ℹ Getting There & Away

BUS There are buses to Bilbao (€7.06 to €14, one hour), Bilbao Airport (€15.40, 1¼ hours), Biarritz (France; €8.50, 1¼ hours), Madrid (from €31.99, five hours) and Pamplona (€6.88, one hour).

TRAIN The main **Renfe train station** (Paseo de Francia) is just across Río Urumea. There are regular services to Madrid (from €52.60, five hours) and Barcelona (from €36.90, eight hours). There's only one direct train to Paris, but there are plenty more from the Spanish/French border town of Irun (or sometimes Hendaye; €1.80, 25 minutes), which is also served by **Eusko Tren/Ferrocarril Vasco** (www.euskotren.es, in Spanish and Basque).

BILBAO

POP 354,200

The commercial hub of the Basque Country, Bilbao (Bilbo in Basque) is best known for the magnificent Guggenheim Museum. An architectural masterpiece by Frank Gehry, the museum was the catalyst of a turnaround that saw Bilbao transformed from an industrial port city into a vibrant cultural centre. After visiting this must-see temple to modern art, spend time exploring Bilbao's Casco Viejo (Old Quarter), a grid of elegant streets dotted with shops, cafes, *pintxos* bars and several small but worthy museums.

👁 Sights

TOP CHOICE **Museo Guggenheim** ART GALLERY
(www.guggenheim-bilbao.es; Avenida Abandoibarra 2; admission €13; ⏲10am-8pm daily Jul & Aug, 10am-8pm Tue-Sun Sep-Jun) Opened in 1997, Bilbao's Museo Guggenheim lifted modern

architecture and Bilbao into the 21st century – with sensation. The Guggenheim may be more famous for its architecture than its content, but Canadian architect Frank Gehry's inspired use of flowing canopies, cliffs, promontories, ship shapes, towers and flying fins is irresistible. The permanent exhibition of sculptures, including mazes of metal, fill the ground floor, but the world-class temporary exhibitions are the stars of the show – check the website for what's on.

Museo de Bellas Artes ART GALLERY
(Fine Arts Museum; www.museobilbao.com; Plaza del Museo 2; admission €6, free Wed; ⏲10am-8pm Tue-Sun) Bilbao's Museo de Bellas Artes has three main subcollections: classical art, with works by Murillo, Zurbarán, El Greco, Goya and van Dyck; contemporary art, featuring works by Gauguin, Francis Bacon and Anthony Caro; and Basque art, with the works of the great sculptors Jorge de Oteiza and Eduardo Chillida.

Casco Viejo OLD TOWN
The compact Casco Viejo, Bilbao's atmospheric old quarter, is full of charming streets, boisterous bars and plenty of quirky and independent shops. At the heart of the Casco are Bilbao's original 'seven streets', Las Siete Calles, which date from the 1400s.

Euskal Museoa (Museo Vasco) MUSEUM
(Museum of Basque Archaeology, Ethnography & History; www.euskal-museoa.org; Plaza Miguel Unamuno 4; admission €3, free Thu; ⏲11am-5pm Tue-Sat, 11am-2pm Sun) This museum is probably the most complete museum of Basque culture and history in all of the Basque regions.

Sleeping

The Bilbao tourism authority has a useful **reservations department** (☎902 877 298; www.bilbaoreservas.com) for accommodation.

TOP CHOICE Pensión Iturrienea Ostatua BOUTIQUE HOTEL €€
(☎944 16 15 00; www.iturrieneaostatua.com; Calle de Santa María 14; d/tr €66/80; 📶) Easily the most eccentric hotel in Bilbao, it's part farmyard, part old-fashioned toyshop and a work of art in its own right. Try to get a double room on the 1st floor (singles don't come with quite as many frills and ribbons).

Hostal Begoña BOUTIQUE HOTEL €€
(☎944 23 01 34; www.hostalbegona.com; Calle de la Amistad 2; s/d from €54/62; @📶) Begoña speaks for itself with colourful rooms decorated with modern artworks, all with funky tiled bathrooms and wrought-iron beds.

Eating

TOP CHOICE Rio-Oja BASQUE €
(☎944 15 08 71; Calle de Perro 4; mains €9-12) An institution that shouldn't be missed. It specialises in light Basque seafood and heavy inland fare, but to most foreigners the sheep brains and squid floating in pools of its own ink are the makings of a culinary adventure story they'll be recounting for years.

Café Iruña BASQUE €
(☎944 23 70 21; cnr Calles de Colón de Larreátegui & Berástegui; menú del día €13.50) Moorish style and a century of gossip are the defining characteristics of this grand old dame. It's the perfect place to indulge in a bit of people-watching and, while you're at it, you might as well also indulge in a meal or, in the evening, some *pinchos morunos* (spicy kebabs with bread; €2.20).

Information

Tourist office (☎944 79 57 60; www.bilbao.net/bilbaoturismo; Plaza del Ensanche 11; ⏲9am-2pm & 4-7.30pm Mon-Fri) Other branches at the Teatro Arriaga, Museo Guggenheim and airport.

Getting There & Away

TRAIN Madrid (from €48.60, six hours, two daily) and Barcelona (€62.30, six hours, two daily) are serviced from the Abando train station. Slow **FEVE** (www.feve.es) trains run from Concordia station next door west into Cantabria and Asturias.

BUS Buses run to Madrid (€27.17, 4¾ hours), Barcelona (€41.90, seven hours), Pamplona (€13.40, two hours) and Santander (from €6.71, 1¼ hours).

Navarra

PAMPLONA

POP 195,800

Immortalised by Ernest Hemingway in *The Sun Also Rises,* the pre-Pyrenean city of Pamplona (Iruña in Basque) is home to the wild Sanfermines (aka Encierro or Running of the Bulls) festival but is also an extremely walkable city that's managed to mix the charm of old plazas and buildings with modern shops and a lively nightlife.

SURVIVING SANFERMINES

The **Sanfermines festival** is held on 6 to 14 July, when Pamplona is overrun with thrill seekers, curious onlookers and, oh yeah, bulls. The Encierro (Running of the Bulls) begins at 8am daily, when bulls are let loose from the Coralillos Santo Domingo. The 825m race lasts just three minutes, so don't be late. The safest place to watch the Encierro is on TV. If that's too tame for you, try to sweet talk your way onto a balcony, or book a room in a hotel with views, and be prepared to pay for the privilege.

Sights

Cathedral CATHEDRAL
(Calle Dormitalería; guided tours €4.40; 10am-7pm Mon-Fri, 10am-2pm Sat mid-Jul–mid-Sep, closed for lunch rest of year) Pamplona's main cathedral stands on a rise just inside the city ramparts, amid a dark thicket of narrow streets. The real joys are the vast interior and the Gothic cloister, where there is marvellous delicacy in the stonework.

Ciudadela & Parks PARK
(Avenida del Ejército) The walls and bulwarks of the grand fortified citadel, the star-shaped Ciudadela, lurk amid the verdant grass and trees in what is now a charming park, the portal to three more parks that unfold to the north and lend the city a lovely green escape.

Museo Oteiza MUSEUM
(www.museooteiza.org; Calle de la Cuesta 7; admission €4, free Fri; 11am-7pm Tue-Sat, 11am-3pm Sun Jun-Sep) Around 9km northeast of Pamplona, in the town of Alzuza, this impressive museum contains almost 3000 pieces by the renowned Navarran sculptor Jorge Oteiza.

Sleeping

Hotel Puerta del Camino BOUTIQUE HOTEL €€
(948 22 66 88; www.hotelpuertadelcamino.com; Calle dos de Mayo 4; s/d €69/81; P❄@) A very stylish new hotel inside a converted convent beside the northern gates to the old city. The functional rooms have clean, modern lines and it's positioned in one of the prettier, and quieter, parts of town.

Habitaciones Mendi PENSION €
(948 22 52 97; Calle de las Navas de Tolosa 9; s/d €30/45) Full of the spirits of Pamplona past, this charming little guest house is a real find. Creaky, wobbly, wooden staircases and equally creaky, chintzy rooms make it just like being at your gran's, and the woman running it will cluck over you as if she were your gran.

Eating & Drinking

Central streets such as Calle San Nicolás and Calle Estafeta are lined with tapas bars, many of which morph into nightspots on weekends.

Baserri BASQUE €
(948 22 20 21; Calle de San Nicolás 32; menú del día €14) This place has won so many *pintxo* awards that we could fill this entire book listing them. As you'd expect from such a certificate-studded bar, the *pintxos* are superb but sadly the full meals play something of a second fiddle in comparison.

Mesón Pirineo BASQUE €
(948 22 20 45; Calle de la Estafeta 41; mains €12-16) There's nothing fancy and modern about this place; it's just old Navarran style and superb *pintxos* all the way.

Café Iruña HISTORIC CAFE
(Plaza del Castillo 44) Opened on the eve of Sanfermines in 1888, Café Iruña's dominant position, powerful sense of history and frilly belle-époque decor make this by far the most famous and popular watering hole in the city.

Information

Tourist office (848 42 04 20; www.turismo.navarra.es; Calle de Esclava 1; 9am-8pm Mon-Sat, 9am-2pm Sun)

Getting There & Away

BUS Buses travel to Bilbao (€13.40, two hours), San Sebastián (€6.88, one hour) and elsewhere.

TRAIN There are train services to Madrid (€56, three hours, four daily) and San Sebastián (from €20.40, two hours, two daily).

CANTABRIA, ASTURIAS & GALICIA

With a landscape reminiscent of parts of the British Isles, 'Green Spain' offers great walks in national parks, seafood feasts in sophisticated towns and oodles of opportunities to plunge into the ice-cold waters of the Bay of Biscay.

Cantabria

SANTILLANA DEL MAR

Some 34km west of the regional capital, Santander, **Santillana del Mar** (www.santillanadelmar.com) is a bijou medieval village and the obvious overnight base for visiting the country's finest prehistoric art, in the **Cueva de Altamira**, 2km southwest of Santillana del Mar. Though it is off-limits to all but the scientific community, since 2001 the **Museo Altamira** (http://museodealtamira.mcu.es; adult/under-18, EU senior or student €3/free, Sun & from 2.30pm Sat free; 9.30am-8pm Tue-Sat, 9.30am-3pm Sun & holidays) has allowed all comers to view the inspired, 14,500-year-old depictions of bison, horses and other beasts (or rather, their replicas) in a full-size, dazzling re-creation of the cave's most interesting chamber, the Sala de Polícromos (Polychrome Hall).

Buses run three to four times a day from Santander to Santilla del Mar.

WORTH A TRIP

PICOS DE EUROPA

These jagged mountains straddling Asturias, Cantabria and northeast Castilla y León amount to some of the finest walking country in Spain. They comprise three limestone massifs (the highest peak rising to 2648m). The 647-sq-km **Parque Nacional de los Picos de Europa** covers all three massifs and is Spain's second-biggest national park. Check out www.picosdeeuropa.com (in Spanish).

There are numerous places to stay and eat all over the mountains. Getting here and around by bus can be slow going but the Picos are accessible from Santander and Oviedo (the latter is easier) by bus.

Santiago de Compostela

POP 79,000

The supposed burial place of St James (Santiago), Santiago de Compostela is a bewitching city. Christian pilgrims journeying along the Camino de Santiago often end up mute with wonder on entering its medieval centre.

Sights

Catedral de Santiago de Compostela CATHEDRAL

(www.catedraldesantiago.es; Praza do Obradoiro; 7am-9pm) The grand heart of Santiago, the cathedral soars above the city centre in a splendid jumble of moss-covered spires and statues. Though Galicia's grandest monument was built piecemeal through the centuries, its beauty is only enhanced by the mix of Romanesque, baroque and Gothic flourishes. For an unforgettable bird's-eye view of the city, take the **cathedral rooftop tour** (981 55 29 85; www.santiagoturismo.com; adult €10; 10am-2pm & 4-8pm).

Museo da Catedral MUSEUM

(Cathedral Museum; www.catedraldesantiago.es; Praza do Obradoiro; adult/senior, student & pilgrim €5/3; 10am-2pm & 4-8pm, closed Sun afternoon) The many-roomed Museo da Catedral, entered to the right of the Obradoiro facade, spreads over four floors and includes the cathedral's large 16th-century, Gothic/plateresque cloister, Maestro Mateo's original stone choir and tapestries.

Around the Cathedral PLAZAS

The cathedral is surrounded by handsome plazas that invite you to wander through them. The grand **Praza do Obradoiro** (Workshop Plaza), to which most arriving Camino pilgrims instinctively find their way, earned its name from the stonemasons' workshops set up here while the cathedral was being built. At its northern end, the Renaissance **Hostal dos Reis Católicos** was built in the early 16th century. Today it shelters well-off travellers instead, as a luxurious *parador*. Along the western side of the square is the elegant 18th-century **Pazo de Raxoi**, now the city hall.

Around the corner, **Praza das Praterías** (Silversmiths' Sq) is marked with the **Fuente de los Caballos** (1829) fountain, with the cathedral's south facade at the top of the steps. Curiously, the **Casa do Cabildo**, facing it on the lower side of the square, is no more than a 3m-deep facade, erected in 1758 to embellish the plaza.

Sleeping & Eating

Meiga Backpackers HOSTEL €

(981 57 08 46; www.meiga-backpackers.es; Rúa dos Basquiños 67; dm incl breakfast €17-18;) Clean, colourful, friendly and handily placed between the bus station and city centre, Meiga has spacious bunk dorms, a kitchen, a garden and no curfew. It's the only place you need consider if you're on the budget backpacking

trail – unless you want a private room, in which case **Meiga Backpackers Pension** (981 59 64 01; www.meiga-backpackers.es; Rúa da República del Salvador 32; d €36-42;), in the new town, could fit the bill nicely.

Hostal Alameda HOSTAL €
(981 58 81 00; www.alameda32.com, in Spanish; Rúa de San Clemente 32; s/d €41/54, without bathroom €25/34;) Great value, with good-sized, recently decorated rooms, this *hostal,* run by a friendly family, sits opposite the Alameda park on the edge of the old town.

Casa Rosalía TAPAS, RACIONES €
(Rúa do Franco 10; raciones €4-16) With a more contemporary style than other nearby bars, Rosalía draws crowds for tapas and *raciones* like scallop-and-monkfish brochette or Galician cheese salad. A selection of tempting snacks (€1.10 to €1.60) is ranged along the bar.

Information

City tourist office (981 55 51 29; www.santiagoturismo.com; Rúa do Vilar 63; 9am-9pm)

Regional tourist office (981 58 40 81, 902 332010; www.turgalicia.es; Rúa do Vilar 30-32; 10am-8pm Mon-Fri, 11am-2pm & 5-7pm Sat, 11am-2pm Sun)

Getting There & Around

AIR Flights from various Spanish and European destinations land at **Lavacolla airport** (981 54 75 00). Up to 36 Empresa Freire buses (€1.80) run daily between Lavacolla airport and Rúa do Doutor Teixeiro, in the new town southwest of Praza de Galicia.

BUS Castromil-Monbus runs from the **bus station** (981 54 24 16; www.tussa.org, in Spanish; Praza de Camilo Díaz Baliño) to destinations throughout Galicia. ALSA has services to Oviedo (€26 to €43, 4¾ to 5½ hours), San Sebastián (€58, 12½ to 13½ hours), León (€23 to €27, six hours) and Madrid (€42 to €60, eight to 9¾ hours). ALSA also has direct daily services to Porto (€29, three hours) and Lisbon (€50, seven to nine hours).

TRAIN From the **train station** (Avenida de Lugo), regional trains run up and down the coast, while a daytime Talgo and an overnight Trenhotel head to Madrid (€49.50, nine hours).

VALENCIA

A warm climate, an abundance of seaside resorts, and interesting cities make this area of Spain a popular destination. The beaches of the Costa Blanca (White Coast) draw most of the visitors, but venture beyond the shore to get a real feel for the region.

Valencia

POP 814,200

Valencia, where paella first simmered over a wood fire, is a vibrant, friendly, slightly chaotic place. It has two outstanding fine-arts museums, an accessible old quarter, Europe's newest cultural and scientific complex and one of Spain's most exciting nightlife scenes.

Sights & Activities

TOP CHOICE **Ciudad de las Artes y las Ciencias** SCIENCE CENTRE
(reservations 902 10 00 31; www.cac.es; combined ticket for all 3 attractions €31.50) The aesthetically stunning City of Arts and Sciences occupies a massive 350,000-sq-metre swath of the old Turia riverbed. It's mostly the work of stellar local architect, the world-renowned Santiago Calatrava. The complex includes the **Oceanogràfic** (admission €24; 10am-6pm or 8pm), a stunning aquarium; **Hemisfèric** (admission €7.50), a planetarium and IMAX cinema; **Museo de las Ciencias Príncipe Felipe** (admission €7.50; 10am-7pm or 9pm), an interactive science museum; and the extraordinary **Palau de les Arts Reina Sofía** (www.lesarts.com; Autovía a El Saler) concert hall. Take bus 35 from Plaza del Ayuntamiento or bus 95 from Torres de Serranos or Plaza de América.

Barrio del Carmen HISTORIC DISTRICT
You'll see Valencia's best face by simply wandering around the Barrio del Carmen. Valencia's Romanesque-Gothic-baroque-Renaissance **catedral** (admission incl audio guide €4; 10am-5.30pm or 6.30pm Mon-Sat, 2-5.30pm Sun) is a compendium of centuries of architectural history and home to the Capilla del Santo Cáliz, a chapel said to contain the Holy Grail (the chalice Christ supposedly used in the last supper). Climb the 207 stairs of the **Micalet (or Miguelete) bell tower** (adult €2; 10am-7pm) for sweeping city views.

Plaza del Mercado HISTORIC PLAZA
Over on Plaza del Mercado, two emblematic buildings, each a masterpiece of its era, face each other. **La Lonja** (10am-2pm & 4.30-8.30pm Mon-Sat, 10am-3pm Sun) is a splendid late-15th-century building, and Unesco World Heritage site and was originally Valencia's silk and commodity exchange. Valencia's Modernista covered market, the

BURN BABY BURN

In mid-March, Valencia hosts one of Europe's wildest street parties: **Las Fallas de San José** (www.fallas.es, in Spanish). For one week (12 to 19 March), the city is engulfed by an anarchic swirl of fireworks, music, festive bonfires and all-night partying. On the final night, giant *ninots* (effigies), many of political and social personages, are torched in the main plaza.

If you're not in Valencia then, see the *ninots* saved from the flames by popular vote at the **Museo Fallero** (Plaza Monteolivete 4; admission €2; ⌚10am-2pm & 4.30-8pm Tue-Sat, 10am-3pm Sun).

Mercado Central (⌚7.30am-2.30pm Mon-Sat), recently scrubbed and glowing as new, was constructed in 1928. With over 900 stalls, it's a swirl of smells, movement and colour.

FREE **Museo de Bellas Artes** FINE ARTS MUSEUM
(Calle San Pío V 9; ⌚10am-8pm Tue-Sun) Bright and spacious, the Museo de Bellas Artes ranks among Spain's best. Highlights include works by El Greco, Goya, Velázquez, Murillo, Ribalta and artists such as Sorolla and Pinazo of the Valencian Impressionist school.

Beaches BEACHES
Playa de la Malvarrosa runs into **Playa de las Arenas**. Each is bordered by the **Paseo Marítimo** promenade and a string of restaurants. **Playa El Salér**, 10km south, is backed by shady pine woods.

Sleeping

TOP CHOICE **Ad Hoc** HOTEL €€
(☎96 391 91 40; www.adhochoteles.com; Calle Boix 4; s €65-101, d €76-125; ❄📶) Friendly, welcoming Ad Hoc offers comfort and charm deep within the old quarter. The late-19th-century building has been restored to its former splendour with great sensitivity.

Hostal Antigua Morellana HOSTAL €
(☎96 391 57 73; www.hostalam.com; Calle En Bou 2; s €45-55, d €55-65; ❄) The friendly, family-run 18-room Hostal Antigua Morellana is tucked away near the central market. Occupying a renovated 18th-century *posada* (where wealthier merchants could spend the night), it has cosy, good-sized rooms, most with balconies.

Pensión París PENSIÓN €
(☎96 352 67 66; www.pensionparis.com; 1st & 3rd fl, Calle Salvá 12; basic s/d/tr €23/34/50, d/tr with shower €40/54, d with bathroom €42) Welcoming, with spotless rooms – most with corridor bathrooms, some with en-suite facilities – this family-run option on a quiet street is the antithesis of the crowded, pack-'em-in hostel.

Eating

At weekends, locals in their hundreds head for Las Arenas, just north of the port, where a long line of restaurants overlooking the beach serve up authentic paella in a three-course meal costing around €15.

TOP CHOICE **La Pepica** SEAFOOD €€
(☎96 371 03 66; Paseo Neptuno 6; meals around €25; ⌚lunch daily, dinner Mon-Sat) More expensive than its competitors, La Pepica is renowned for its rice dishes and seafood. Here Ernest Hemingway, among many other luminaries, once strutted. Between courses, browse through the photos and tributes that plaster the walls.

Bar Pilar TAPAS €
(☎96 391 04 97; Calle del Moro Zeit 13; ⌚noon-midnight daily) Cramped, earthy Bar Pilar is great for hearty tapas and *clóchinas*, small, juicy local mussels, available between May and August. For the rest of the year, it serves *mejillones*, altogether fatter if less tasty. Ask for an *entero*, a platterful in a spicy broth that you scoop up with a spare shell.

Drinking

The Barrio del Carmen, the university area (around Avenidas de Aragón and Blasco Ibáñez), the area around the Mercado de Abastos and, in summer, the new port area and Malvarrosa are all jumping with bars and clubs.

Sant Jaume CAFE BAR
A converted pharmacy, its 1st floor is made up all quiet crannies and poky passageways

Cafe-Bar Negrito CAFE BAR
(Plaza del Negrito) Recently redesigned, it traditionally attracts a more left-wing, intellectual clientele.

Café Lisboa CAFE BAR
(Plaza del Doctor Collado 9) Another lively, student-oriented bar with a large, street-side terrace.

Café Infanta CAFE BAR
(Plaza Tossal 3) The interior is a clutter of cinema memorabilia, while its external terrace is great for people-watching.

Café de las Horas COCKTAIL BAR
(Calle Conde de Almodóvar 1) Offers high baroque, tapestries, music of all genres, candelabras and a long list of exotic cocktails.

Information

Regional tourist office (96 398 64 22; www.comunitatvalenciana.com; Calle Paz 48; 9am-8pm Mon-Sat, 10am-2pm Sun)

Turismo Valencia (VLC) tourist office (96 315 39 31; www.turisvalencia.es; Plaza de la Reina 19; 9am-7pm Mon-Sat, 10am-2pm Sun)

Getting There & Away

AIR Valencia's **Aeropuerto de Manises** (96 159 85 00) is 10km west of the city centre. It's served by metro lines 3 and 5. Budget flights serve major European destinations.

BOAT **Acciona Trasmediterránea** (www.acciona-trasmediterranea.es) operates car and passenger ferries to Ibiza, Mallorca and Menorca.

BUS Valencia's **bus station** (96 346 62 66) is beside the riverbed on Avenida Menéndez Pidal. **Avanza** (www.avanzabus.com) operates hourly bus services to/from Madrid (€18 to €27, four hours). **ALSA** (www.alsa.es) has numerous buses to/from Barcelona (€26 to €30, 4½ hours) and Alicante (€21, 2½ hours), most passing by Benidorm (€14.50, 1¾ hours).

TRAIN From Valencia's Estación del Norte, major destinations include Madrid (from €50, 1½ hours, 13 to 17 daily), Alicante (€29, 1¾ hours, eight daily) and Barcelona (€39 to €43, three to 3½ hours, at least 12 daily).

Alicante

POP 334,750

With its elegant, palm-lined boulevards, lively nightlife scene and easy-to-access beaches, Alicante (Alacant in Valenciano) is an all-in-one Spanish city. The city is at its most charming at night, when tapas bars and taverns in El Barrio (Old Quarter) come alive.

Sights & Activities

TOP CHOICE **Castillo de Santa Bárbara** CASTLE
(10am-10pm) There are sweeping views over the city from this 16th-century castle, which will soon house **MUSA** (Museo de la Ciudad de Alicante), a new museum recounting the history of the city. A lift/elevator, reached by a footbridge opposite Playa del Postiguet, rises through the bowels of the mountain.

TOP CHOICE **MACA (Museo de Arte Contémporaneo de Alicante)** ART GALLERY
(Plaza Sta María 3; admission free; 10am-8pm Tue-Sat, to 2pm Sun) This splendid museum has an excellent collection of 20th-century Spanish art, including works by Dalí, Miró, Chillida, Sempere, Tàpies and Picasso.

Beaches BEACHES
Immediately north of the port is the sandy beach of **Playa del Postiguet**. **Playa de San Juan**, easily reached by tram, is larger and usually less crowded.

Sleeping

TOP CHOICE **Hostal Les Monges Palace** HOSTAL €
(96 521 50 46; www.lesmonges.es; Calle San Agustín 4; s €30-44, d €45-59;) This agreeably quirky place is a treasure with its winding corridors, tiles, mosaics and antique furniture. Each room is individually decorated and reception couldn't be more welcoming.

Guest House Antonio BOUTIQUE HOSTAL €
(650 718353; www.guesthousealicante.com; Calle Segura 20; s €35-40, d €45-50;) Here's a magnificent budget choice. Each of the eight large, tastefully decorated rooms has a safe, full-size fridge and free beverage-making facilities. The five apartments (€70 to €80), two with their own patio, are exceptional value.

Eating & Drinking

The old quarter around Catedral de San Nicolás is wall-to-wall bars. Down by the harbour, the Paseo del Puerto, tranquil by day, is a double-decker line of bars, cafes and night-time discos.

TOP CHOICE **Piripi** VALENCIAN €€
(96 522 79 40; Avenida Oscar Esplá 30; mains €12-26) This highly regarded restaurant is strong on rice, seafood and fish, which arrives fresh and daily from the wholesale markets of Denia and Santa Pola. There's a huge variety of tapas and a *valenciano* speciality that changes daily.

El Trellat MODERN CREATIVE €
(965 20 62 75; Calle de Capitán Segarra 19; lunch menús €10, dinner menús €10-25; lunch Mon-Sat, dinner Fri & Sat) Beside the covered market,

this small, friendly place does exceptionally creative, flexible *menús:* first course a serve-yourself buffet, then an ample choice of inventive mains.

Information

The **municipal tourist office** (www.alicanteturismo.com) has branches at the bus and train stations.

Getting There & Away

AIR Alicante's El Altet airport, gateway to the Costa Blanca, is around 12km southwest of the centre. It's served by budget airlines, charters and scheduled flights from all over Europe.

BUS There are bus services to Madrid (€27.50, 5¼ hours, at least 10 daily) and Valencia (€21, 2½ hours, 10 daily).

TRAIN Destinations from the main **Renfe Estación de Madrid** (Avenida de Salamanca) include Barcelona (€55, five hours, eight daily), Madrid (€45, 3¾ hours, seven daily) and Valencia (€29, 1¾ hours, seven daily).

BALEARIC ISLANDS

POP 1.07 MILLION

The Balearic Islands (Illes Balears in Catalan) adorn the glittering Mediterranean off Spain's eastern coastline. Beach tourism destinations par excellence, each of the four islands has a quite distinct identity and all have managed to retain much of their individual character and beauty. All boast beaches second-to-none in the Med but each offers reasons for exploring inland too.

Check out websites such as www.illesbalears.es, www.platgesdebalears.com and www.balearsculturaltour.com.

Getting There & Away

AIR In summer, charter and regular flights converge on Palma de Mallorca and Ibiza from all over Europe. Major operators from the Spanish mainland include **Iberia** (www.iberia.com), **Air Europa** (www.aireuropa.com), **Spanair** (www.spanair.com), **Air Berlin** (www.airberlin.com) and **Vueling** (www.vueling.com).

BOAT Compare prices and look for deals at **Direct Ferries** (www.directferries.es). The following ferries serve the Balearic Islands, usually from Barcelona, Valencia or Denia:

Acciona Trasmediterránea (☎902 454 645; www.trasmediterranea.es)

Baleària (☎902 160 180; www.balearia.com)

Cala Ratjada Tours (☎902 100 444; www.calaratjadatours.es, in Spanish)

Iscomar (☎902 119 128; www.iscomar.com)

Mallorca

The sunny, ochre hues of the medieval heart of Palma de Mallorca (pop 401,300), the archipelago's capital, make a great introduction to the islands. The northwest coast, dominated by the Serra de Tramuntana mountain range, is a beautiful region of olive groves, pine forests and ochre villages, with a spectacularly rugged coastline. Most of Mallorca's best **beaches** are on the north and east coasts and, although many have been swallowed up by tourist developments, you can still find the occasional exception. There is also a scattering of fine beaches along the south coast.

Getting Around

BUS Most of the island is accessible by bus from Palma. All buses depart from or near the **bus station** (Carrer d'Eusebi Estada).

TRAIN Two train lines run from Plaça d'Espanya in Palma de Mallorca. The popular old train runs to Sóller and is a pretty ride. A standard train line runs inland to Inca (€1.80, 40 minutes, every half-hour), where the line splits with a branch to Sa Pobla (€2.40, one hour, hourly) and another to Manacor (€2.40, 1¼ hours, hourly).

PALMA DE MALLORCA

Sights & Activities

TOP CHOICE **Cathedral** CHURCH

(La Seu; Carrer del Palau Reial 9; admission €4; ⏲10am-5.15pm Mon-Fri, 10am-2.15pm Sat) This awesome structure, completed in 1601, is predominantly Gothic, apart from the main facade (replaced after an earthquake in 1851) and parts of the interior. The front altar's centrepiece, a light, twisting wrought-iron sculpture suspended from the ceiling, is one of Gaudí's more eccentric creations. For once Gaudí is upstaged by the island's top contemporary artist, Miquel Barceló, who reworked the **Capella del Santíssim i Sant Pere**, at the head of the south aisle, in a dream-fantasy, swirling ceramic rendition of the miracle of the loaves and fishes.

Palau de l'Almudaina PALACE

(Carrer del Palau Reial s/n; admission €3.20, audio guide €2.50; ⏲10am-5.45pm Mon-Fri, 10am-1.15pm Sat) Originally an Islamic fort, this mighty construction was converted into a residence for the Mallorcan monarchs at the end of the 13th century. It consists of a series of cavernous and austere stone-walled rooms, a chapel with a rare Romanesque entrance, and upstairs royal apartments adorned with Flemish tapestries and period furniture.

Es Baluard (Museu d'Art Modern i Contemporani) CONTEMPORARY ART MUSEUM
(www.esbaluard.org; Porta de Santa Catalina 10; admission €6, temporary exhibitions €4; 10am-8pm or 9pm Tue-Sun) This 21st-century concrete complex nests within Palma's grand Renaissance-era seaward fortifications.

Palau March CONTEMPORARY ART MUSEUM
(www.fundacionbmarch.es; Carrer de Palau Reial 18; admission €3.60; 10am-6pm Mon-Fri, 10am-2pm Sat) This house, palatial by any definition, contains sculptures by 20th-century greats such as Henry Moore, Auguste Rodin, Barbara Hepworth and Eduardo Chillida, which grace the outdoor terrace. Within is a set of Salvador Dalí prints.

FREE **Museu d'Art Espanyol Contemporani** CONTEMPORARY ART MUSEUM
(Museu Fundació Juan March; www.march.es/arte/palma; Carrer de Sant Miquel 11; 10am-6.30pm Mon-Fri, 10.30am-2pm Sat) On permanent display within this 18th-century mansion are some 70 pieces that together constitute a veritable who's who of mostly 20th-century artists, including Picasso, Miró, Juan Gris (of cubism fame), Dalí and the sculptor Julio González.

Sleeping & Eating

Hotel Born HISTORIC HOTEL €€
(971 71 29 42; www.hotelborn.com; Carrer de Sant Jaume 3; s incl breakfast €52, d incl breakfast €76-97;) A superb place in the heart of the city, this hotel is in an 18th-century palace. Rooms combine elegance and history with all mod cons. The best have an engaging view onto the palm-shaded patio.

Hostal Corona CLASSIC HOTEL €
(971 73 19 35; www.hostal-corona.com; Carrer de Josep Villalonga 22; s €30, d €45-60) With its palm trees and cornucopia of plants, the generous courtyard garden of this little hotel (the house was once a private villa) has a faraway feel. Rooms are simple, with timber furnishings and old tiled floors.

Bon Lloc VEGETARIAN €
(971 71 86 17; www.bonllocrestaurant.com, in Spanish; Carrer Sant Feliu 7; menús €13.50; lunch Mon-Sat) This 100% vegetarian place, where all produce is organic, is light, open and airy. There are no agonising decisions – just a satisfying, take-it-or-leave-it four-course *menú*. It's hugely popular so ring to reserve.

13% TAPAS €
(971 42 51 87; www.13porciento.com; Carrer Sant Feliu 13A; meals around €15) At the quieter end of the old town, this L-shaped barn of a place is both wine and tapas bar. Most items are organic and there's plenty of choice for vegetarians. Wines are displayed on racks and all can be purchased (both bar and take-away prices are quoted so you know exactly the mark-up).

Drinking & Entertainment

The old quarter is the city's most vibrant nightlife zone. Particularly along the narrow streets between Plaça de la Reina and Plaça de la Drassana, you'll find an enormous selection of bars, pubs and bodegas. According to a much-flouted law, bars should shut by 1am Sunday to Thursday (3am Friday and Saturday).

Vamos 365 (www.vamosmallorca365.com), a monthly freebie, has its finger on Palma's night-time pulse.

Information

Consell de Mallorca tourist office (971 71 22 16; www.infomallorca.net; Plaça de la Reina 2; 8am-8pm Mon-Fri, 9am-2pm Sat)

Municipal tourist office (902 102365; 9am-8pm Mon-Sat) main office (Casal Solleric, Passeig d'es Born 27); branch office (train station)

AROUND MALLORCA

Mallorca's northwestern coast is a world away from the high-rise tourism on the other side of the island. Dominated by the Serra de Tramuntana, it's a beautiful region of olive groves, pine forests and small villages with shuttered stone buildings.

Sóller is a good place to base yourself for hiking, and the nearby village of **Fornalutx** is one of the prettiest on Mallorca.

From Sóller, it's a 10km walk to the beautiful hilltop village of **Deià** (www.deia.info), where Robert Graves, poet and author of *I Claudius*, lived for most of his life. From the village, you can scramble down to the small shingle beach of **Cala de Deià**. Further east, **Pollença** and **Artà** are attractive inland towns. Nice beaches include those at **Cala Sant Vicenç**, **Cala Mondragó** and around **Cala Llombards**.

The Consell de Mallorca tourist office in Palma (p1170) can supply information on rural and other accommodation around the island.

Ibiza

Ibiza (Eivissa in Catalan) is an island of extremes. Its formidable party reputation is completely justified, with some of the world's greatest clubs attracting hedonists from the world over. The interior and northeast of the island, however, are another world: peaceful country drives, hilly green territory, a sprinkling of mostly laid-back beaches and coves and some wonderful inland accommodation and eateries.

IBIZA CITY

Sights & Activities

Ibiza City's port area of **Sa Penya** is crammed with funky and trashy clothing boutiques and arty-crafty market stalls. From here, you can wander up into **D'Alt Vila**, the atmospheric old walled town.

Ramparts CITY WALLS

A ramp leads from Plaça de sa Font in Sa Penya up to the 1585 **Portal de ses Taules** gateway, the main entrance. The walls consist of seven artillery bastions joined by thick protective walls up to 22m in height. You can walk the entire perimeter of these impressive Renaissance-era walls.

Catedral CATHEDRAL

Ibiza's cathedral elegantly combines several styles: the original 14th-century structure is Catalan Gothic but the sacristy was added in 1592 and a major baroque renovation took place in the 18th century.

Sleeping & Eating

Many of Ibiza City's hotels and *hostales* are closed in the low season and heavily booked between April and October. Make sure you book ahead.

Hostal La Marina HOSTAL €€

(971 31 01 72; www.hostal-lamarina.com; Carrer de Barcelona 7; r €68-125;) Looking onto both the waterfront and bar-lined Carrer de Barcelona, this mid-19th-century building has all sorts of brightly coloured rooms. A handful of singles and some doubles look onto the street (with the predictable noise problem), with pricier doubles and attics with terraces and panoramic port and/or town views.

Casa de Huéspedes Navarro BUDGET HOTEL €

(971 31 07 71; Carrer de sa Creu 20; s/d without bathroom €28/55; May-Oct) Right in the thick of things, this simple option has eight rooms at the top of a long flight of stairs. The front rooms have harbour views, interior ones are quite dark (but cool in summer) and there's a sunny rooftop terrace. Bathrooms are shared but spotless.

TOP CHOICE **Comidas Bar San Juan** MEDITERRANEAN €

(971 31 16 03; Carrer de Guillem de Montgri 8; meals €15-20; Mon-Sat) A family-run operation with two small dining rooms, this simple eatery offers outstanding value, with fish dishes for around €10 and many small mains for €6 or less. It doesn't take reservations so arrive early.

Drinking

Sa Penya is the nightlife centre. Dozens of bars keep the port area jumping. Alternatively, various bars at Platja d'En Bossa combine sounds, sand, sea and sangria.

Discobus (www.discobus.es; €3; midnight-6am Jun-Sep) runs around the major discos, bars and hotels in Ibiza City, Platja d'en Bossa, Sant Rafel, Es Canar, Santa Eulària and Sant Antoni.

CLUBBING IN IBIZA

In summer (late May to the end of September) the west of the island is a continuous party from sunset to sunrise and back again. In 2009 the International Dance Music Awards ranked two Ibiza clubs, Pacha and Space, among its worldwide top five.

The clubs operate nightly from around 1am to 6am and each has something different. Theme nights, fancy-dress parties and foam parties (where you are half-drowned in the stuff) are regular features. Admission can cost anything from €25 to €60.

The best include **Amnesia** (www.amnesia.es; early Jun-Sep), located 4km north of Ibiza City on the road to Sant Rafel; **Es Paradis** (www.esparadis.com; Carrer de Salvador Espriu 2, Sant Antoni; mid-May–Sep) in Sant Antoni de Portmany; **Pacha** (www.pacha.com; nightly Jun-Sep, Fri & Sat Oct-May), on the north side of Ibiza port; **Privilege** (www.privilegeibiza.com), 5km north of Ibiza City on the road to Sant Rafel; and **Space** (www.spaceibiza.com; Jun–mid-Oct).

A good website is **Ibiza Spotlight** (www.ibiza-spotlight.com).

Information

Tourist office (www.ibiza.travel) Main office (☎971 30 19 00; Passeig de Vara de Rei 1; ⌚9am-8pm Mon-Fri, 9am-7pm Sat); D'Alt Vila office (☎971 39 92 32; Carrer Major 2; ⌚9am-8pm Mon-Sat, 9am-3pm Sun)

AROUND IBIZA

Ibiza has numerous unspoiled and relatively undeveloped beaches. **Cala de Boix**, on the northeast coast, is the only black-sand beach on the island, while further north are the lovely beaches of **S'Aigua Blanca**.

On the north coast near Portinatx, **Cala Xarraca** is in a picturesque, secluded bay, and near Port de Sant Miquel is the attractive **Cala Benirrás**.

In the southwest **Cala d'Hort** has a spectacular setting overlooking two rugged rock islets, Es Verda and Es Verdranell.

The best thing about rowdy **Sant Antoni**, the island's second-biggest town, is heading to the small rock-and-sand strip on the north shore to join hundreds of others for sunset drinks at a string of chilled bars. The best-known remains **Café del Mar** (⌚4pm-1am), our favourite.

Check out rural accommodation at www.ibizaruralvillas.com and www.casasrurales ibiza.com (in Spanish). For more standard accommodation start at www.ibizahotels guide.com.

Menorca

Renowned for its pristine beaches and archaeological sites, tranquil Menorca was declared a Biosphere Reserve by Unesco in 1993. The capital, Maó, is known as Mahón in Castilian.

Sights & Activities

Maó absorbs most of the tourist traffic. North of Maó, a drive across a lunar landscape leads to the lighthouse at **Cap de Faváritx**. South of the cape stretch some fine sandy bays and beaches, including **Cala Presili** and **Platja d'en Tortuga**, reachable on foot.

Ciutadella, with its smaller harbour and historic buildings, has a more distinctly Spanish feel to it and is the more attractive of the two towns. A narrow country road leads south of Ciutadella (follow the 'Platges' sign from the *ronda,* or ring road) and then forks twice to reach some of the island's loveliest beaches: (from west to east) **Arenal de Son Saura**, **Cala en Turqueta**, **Es Talaier**, **Cala Macarelleta** and **Cala Macarella**. As with most beaches, you'll need your own transport.

In the centre of the island, the 357m-high **Monte Toro** has great views.

On the northern coast, the picturesque town of **Fornells** is on a large bay popular with windsurfers.

Sleeping

Many accommodation options on the island are closed between November and April. The following are both in Ciutadella.

Hotel Gèminis HOTEL €€
(☎971 38 46 44; www.hotelgeminismenorca.com; Carrer de Josepa Rossinyol 4; s/d €65/96; ❄📶🏊) A friendly, stylish, two-star place on a Ciutadella backstreet, this graceful, three-storey, rose-and-white lodging offers comfortable, if somewhat neutral, rooms just a short walk from the city centre.

Hostal-Residencia Oasis BUDGET HOTEL €
(☎971 38 21 97; Carrer de Sant Isidre 33; s/d €35/45) Run by a delightful elderly couple, this quiet place is close to the heart of the old quarter. Rooms, mostly with bathroom, are set beside a spacious garden courtyard. Their furnishings, though still trim, are from deep into the last century.

Eating & Drinking

The ports in both Maó and Ciutadella are lined with bars and restaurants.

El Varadero SEAFOOD €
(☎971 35 20 74; Moll de Llevant 4, Maó; mains €11.50-17; ⌚Easter-Nov) With such a splendid vista from the harbourside terrace, it must be tempting to simply sit on your laurels. But El Varadero doesn't. There's a range of tempting rice dishes and a short, select choice of fish and meat mains.

TOP CHOICE **Cas Ferrer de Sa Font** MENORCAN €€
(☎971 48 07 84; www.casferrer.com; Carrer del Portal de Sa Font 16, Ciutadella; meals €35; ⌚Tue-Sun) Nowhere on the island will you find more authentic Menorcan cuisine, based upon meats and vegetables from the owner's organic farm. Dine on the delightful interior patio of this charming 18th-century building or inside, below beams and soft curves, in what was once a blacksmith's forge.

Information

The **tourist office** (☎971 38 26 93; Plaça de la Catedral 5; ⌚8.30am-3pm & 5-9pm) is in Ciutadella.

ANDALUCÍA

Images of Andalucía are so potent, so quintessentially Spanish that it's sometimes difficult not to feel a sense of déjà vu. It's almost as if you've already been there in your dreams: a solemn Easter parade, an ebullient spring festival, exotic nights in the Alhambra. In the stark light of day the picture is no less compelling.

Seville

POP 703,000

A sexy, gutsy and gorgeous city, Seville is home to two of Spain's most colourful festivals, fascinating and distinctive *barrios* and a local population that lives life to the fullest. A fiery place (as you'll soon see in its packed and noisy tapas bars), it is also hot climatewise – avoid July and August!

Sights & Activities

Cathedral & La Giralda CHURCH

(adult/concession €8/2; ⌚11am-5.30pm Mon-Sat, 2.30-6.30pm Sun Sep-Jun, 9.30am-4.30pm Mon-Sat, 2.30-6.30pm Sun Jul & Aug) After Seville fell to the Christians in 1248 its main mosque was used as a church until 1401, when it was knocked down to make way for what would become one of the world's largest cathedrals and an icon of Gothic architecture. Over 90m high, the perfectly proportioned and exquisitely decorated La Giralda was the minaret of the mosque that stood on the site before the cathedral. The views from the summit are exceptional.

Alcázar CASTLE

(adult/senior & student €7.50/free; ⌚9.30am-7pm Apr-Sep, to 6pm Oct-Mar) Seville's Alcázar, a royal residence for many centuries, was founded in 913 as a Muslim fortress. The Alcázar has been expanded and rebuilt many times in its 11 centuries of existence. The Catholic Monarchs, Fernando and Isabel, set up court here in the 1480s as they prepared for the conquest of Granada. Later rulers created the Alcázar's lovely gardens. The Alcázar's highlights include exquisitely adorned patios and the showpiece **Palacio de Don Pedro**.

Barrio de Santa Cruz JEWISH QUARTER

Seville's medieval *judería* (Jewish quarter), east of the cathedral and Alcázar, is today a tangle of atmospheric, winding streets and lovely plant-decked plazas perfumed with orange blossom. Among its most characteristic plazas is **Plaza de Santa Cruz**, which gives the *barrio* its name. **Plaza de Doña Elvira** is another romantic perch, especially in the evening.

Museo del Baile Flamenco MUSEUM

(www.museoflamenco.com; Calle Manuel Rojas Marcos 3; admission €10; ⌚9.30am-7pm daily) The brainchild of Sevillana flamenco dancer Cristina Hoyos, this is Seville's newest museum, spread over three floors of an 18th-century palace, although it's more than a little overpriced.

Parque de María Luisa PARK

(⌚8am-10pm) A large area south of the tobacco factory was transformed for Seville's 1929 international fair, the Exposición Iberoamericana, when architects adorned it with fantastical buildings, many of them harking back to Seville's past glory or imitating the native styles of Spain's former colonies. In its midst is the large Parque de María Luisa, a living expression of Seville's Moorish and Christian past.

Festivals & Events

The first of Seville's two great festivals is **Semana Santa**, the week leading up to Easter Sunday. Throughout the week, thousands of members of religious brotherhoods parade in penitents' garb with tall, pointed *capirotes* (hoods) accompanying sacred images through the city, while huge crowds look on.

The **Feria de Abril**, a week in late April, is a welcome release after this solemnity: the festivities involve six days of music, dancing, horse riding and traditional dress, plus daily bullfights.

The city also stages Spain's largest flamenco festival, the month-long **Bienal de Flamenco**. It's held in September in even-numbered years.

Sleeping

Hotel Amadeus HOTEL €€

(☎954 50 14 43; www.hotelamadeussevilla.com; Calle Farnesio 6; s/d €85/95; P❄📶) This musician family converted its 18th-century mansion into a stylish hotel with 14 elegant rooms of which Mozart would have been proud.

Hotel Puerta de Sevilla HOTEL €€

(☎954 98 72 70; www.hotelpuertadesevilla.com; Calle Puerta de la Carne 2; s/d €66/86; P❄@📶) This small, shiny hotel has a great location, azulejos tiles, flower-pattern textiles and wrought-iron beds, all for one star.

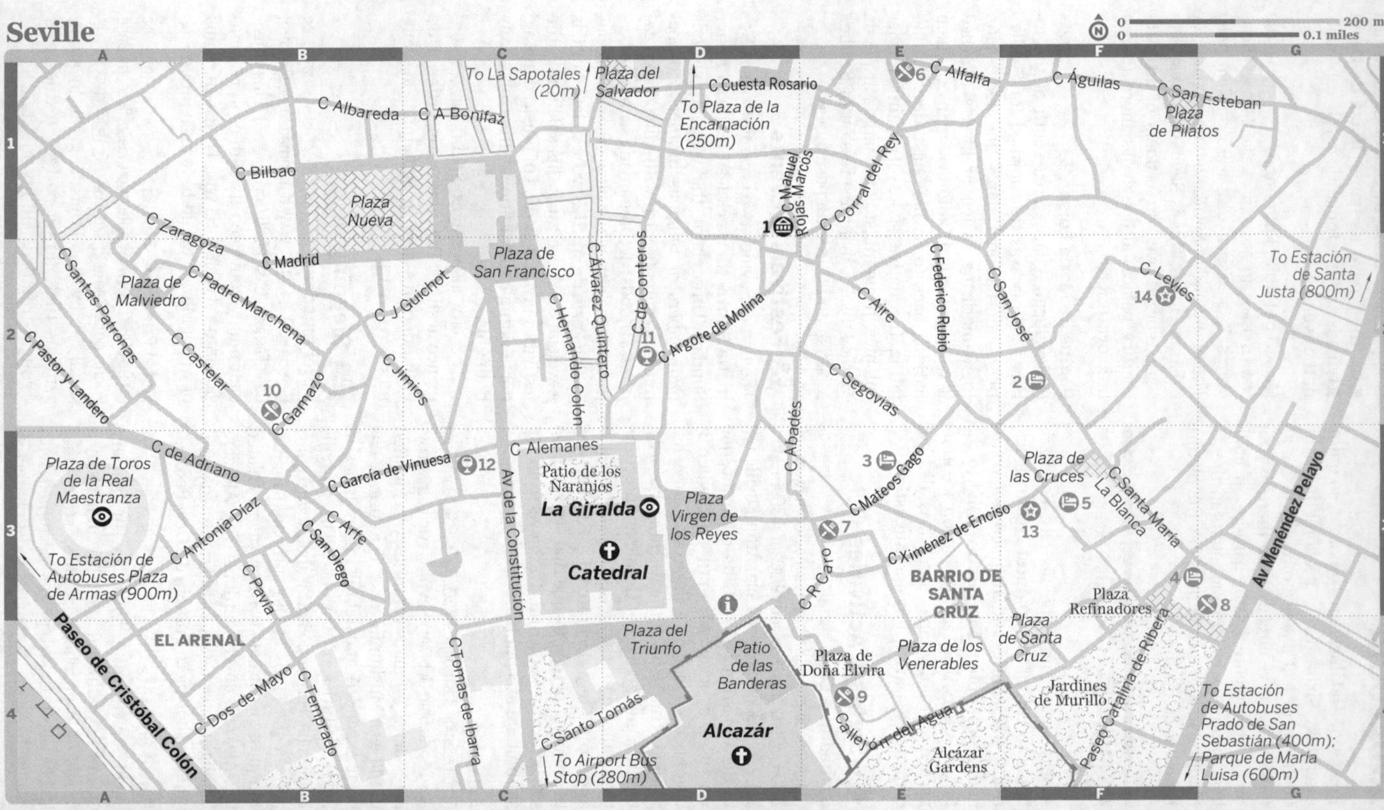
Seville
0 200 m
0 0.1 miles
To La Sapotales (20m)
Plaza del Salvador
C Cuesta Rosario
To Plaza de la Encarnación (250m)
C Alfalfa
C Águilas
C San Esteban
Plaza de Pilatos
C Albareda
C A Bonifaz
C Bilbao
Plaza Nueva
C Manuel Rojas Marcos
C Corral del Rey
C Zaragoza
C Madrid
Plaza de San Francisco
C Álvarez Quintero
C de Conteros
C Federico Rubio
C San José
C Leyíes
To Estación de Santa Justa (800m)
Plaza de Malviedro
C Santas Patronas
C Padre Marchena
C J Guichot
C Hernando Colón
C Argote de Molina
C Aire
C Pastor y Landero
C Castelar
C Jimios
C Gamazo
C Segovias
C Abadés
C de Adriano
C Alemanes
C García de Vinuesa
Plaza de Toros de la Real Maestranza
Patio de los Naranjos
La Giralda
Catedral
Plaza Virgen de los Reyes
C Mateos Gago
Plaza de las Cruces
C Santa María La Blanca
Av Menéndez Pelayo
C Antonia Díaz
C Arfe
C San Diego
Av de la Constitución
C R Caro
C Ximénez de Enciso
To Estación de Autobuses Plaza de Armas (900m)
C Pavía
BARRIO DE SANTA CRUZ
Plaza Refinadores
Plaza de Santa Cruz
Paseo de Cristóbal Colón
EL ARENAL
Plaza del Triunfo
Patio de las Banderas
Plaza de Doña Elvira
Plaza de los Venerables
Jardines de Murillo
Paseo Catalina de Ribera
C Dos de Mayo
C Temprado
C Tomas de Ibarra
C Santo Tomás
Alcazár
Callejón del Agua
Alcázar Gardens
To Airport Bus Stop (280m)
To Estación de Autobuses Prado de San Sebastián (400m); Parque de María Luisa (600m)

Seville

Top Sights

Sights

Sleeping

Eating

Drinking

Entertainment

Pensión San Pancracio HOTEL €
(☎954 41 31 04; Plaza de las Cruces 9; d with bathroom €50, s/d without bathroom €25/35) An ideal budget option in Santa Cruz, this old, rambling family house has plenty of different room choices (all cheap) and a pleasant flower-bedizened patio-lobby.

Hotel Goya HOTEL €€
(☎954 21 11 70; www.hotelgoyasevilla.com; Calle Mateos Gago 31; s/d €40/60; ❄@📶) The gleaming Goya is more popular than ever. Book ahead.

Oasis Backpackers' Hostel HOSTEL €
(☎954 29 37 77; www.oasissevilla.com; Plaza de la Encarnación 29; dm/d incl breakfast €15/50; ❄@📶🏊) Seville's offbeat, buzzing backpacker central offers 24-hour free internet access. The new location is in Plaza Encarnación, a narrow street behind the Church of the Anunciación, to the north of the city centre. Each dorm bed has a personal safe and there is a small rooftop pool.

Eating

TOP CHOICE **Catalina** TAPAS €
(Paseo Catalina de Ribera 4; raciones €10) If your view of tapas is 'glorified bar snacks', then your ideas could be blown out of the water here with a creative mix of just about every ingredient known to Iberian cooking.

Bodega Santa Cruz TAPAS €
(Calle Mateos Gago; tapas €1.50-2) Forever crowded and with a mountain of paper on the floor, this place is usually standing-room only with tapas and drinks enjoyed al fresco as you dodge the marching army of tourists squeezing through Santa Cruz's narrow streets.

Extraverde TAPAS €
(☎954 21 84 17; Plaza de Doña Elvira 8; tapas €2.50-4; ⏲10.30am-11.30pm) New on the scene, Extraverde is a unique bar-shop specialising in Andalucian products such as olive oil, cheese and wine. You can taste free samples standing up, or sit down inside and order a full tapa.

Mesón Cinco Jotas TAPAS €
(Calle Castelar 1; tapas/media raciones €3.80/9.45) Try some of the best *jamón* in town here and move on to the *solomillo ibérico* (Iberian pork sirloin) in sweet Pedro Ximénez wine for the peak of porcine flavour.

Bar Alfalfa TAPAS €
(cnr Calles Alfalfa & Candilejo; tapas €2-3) It's amazing how many people, hams, wine bottles and other knick-knacks you can stuff into such a small space. No matter; order through the window when the going gets crowded.

Drinking

Antigüedades BAR
(Calle Argote de Molina 40) Blending mellow beats with offbeat decor, the tiled window seats with a view of the busy street are the best place to nurse your drink.

Casa Morales BAR
(Garcia de Vinuesa 11) Founded in 1850, not much has changed in this defiantly old-world bar, with charming anachronisms wherever you look. Towering clay *tinajas* (wine storage jars) carry the chalked-up tapas choices of the day.

Café Central BAR
(Alameda de Hércules 64) One of the oldest and most popular bars along the street, Central

has yellow bar lights, wooden flea-market chairs and a massive crowd that gathers at weekends. It's about 1.2km north of the city centre.

Entertainment

Seville is arguably Spain's flamenco capital and you're most likely to catch a spontaneous atmosphere (of unpredictable quality) in one of the bars staging regular nights of flamenco with no admission fee. *Soleares,* Flamenco's truest *cante jondo* (the original musical form from which flamenco derived; literally 'deep song') was first concocted in Triana; head here to find some of the more authentic clubs.

TOP CHOICE La Carbonería FLAMENCO BAR
(Calle Levíes 18; admission free; ⏲about 8pm-4am) During the day there is no indication that this happening place is anything but a large garage. But come after 8pm and the converted coal yard in the Barrio de Santa Cruz reveals two large bars and nightly live flamenco (11pm and midnight) for no extra charge.

Casa de la Memoria de Al-Andalus FLAMENCO TABLAO
(☎954 56 06 70; Calle Ximénez de Enciso 28; tickets €15; ⏲9pm) This place in Santa Cruz is probably the most intimate and authentic nightly *tablao* (flamenco show), offering a wide variety of flamenco styles in a room of shifting shadows. Space is limited to 100, so reserve tickets in advance.

Casa Anselma FLAMENCO BAR
(Pagés de Corro 49; ⏲from midnight Mon-Sat) If you can squeeze in past the foreboding form of Anselma (a celebrated Triana flamenco dancer) at the door you'll quickly realise that anything can happen in here. Casa Anselma (beware: there's no sign, just a doorway embellished with azulejos tiles) is the antithesis of a tourist flamenco *tablao,* with cheek-to-jowl crowds, thick cigarette smoke, zero amplification and spontaneous outbreaks of dexterous dancing. Pure magic. It's about 800m west of the city centre.

Information

Discover Sevilla (www.discoversevilla.com)
Explore Seville (www.exploreseville.com)
Regional tourist office Avenida de la Constitución 21 (⏲9am-7pm Mon-Fri, 10am-2pm & 3-7pm Sat, 10am-2pm Sun, closed holidays); Estación Santa Justa (⏲9am-8pm Mon-Fri, 10am-2pm Sat & Sun, closed holidays)
Seville Tourism (www.turismo.sevilla.org)
Turismo Sevilla (www.turismosevilla.org; Plaza del Triunfo 1; ⏲10.30am-7pm Mon-Fri)

Getting There & Away

AIR Domestic and international flights land at Seville's Aeropuerto San Pablo, 7km from the city centre.

BUS From the **Estación de Autobuses Prado de San Sebastián** (Plaza San Sebastián), there are 12 or more buses daily to/from Cádiz (€11.50, 1¾ hours), Córdoba (€10, two hours), Granada (€19, 3½ hours), Ronda (€11, 2½ hours, five or more daily) and Málaga (€15.75, 2¾ hours).

From the **Estación de Autobuses Plaza de Armas** (Avenida del Cristo de la Expiración), destinations include Madrid (€18.65, six hours, 14 daily), Mérida (€13, three hours, 12 daily), Cáceres (€15, four hours, six daily) and Portugal.

TRAIN The modern, efficient **Estación de Santa Justa** (Avenida Kansas City) is 1.5km northeast of the city centre. There's also a city-centre **Renfe ticket office** (Calle Zaragoza 29).

Twenty or more superfast AVE trains, reaching speeds of 280km/h, whiz daily to/from Madrid (€80.70, 2½ hours). Other destinations include Barcelona (€61 to €88, 10½ to 13 hours, three daily; AVE €130, 6½ hours, one daily), Cádiz (€12.75, 1¾ hours, 13 daily), Córdoba (€16 to €32, 40 minutes to 1½ hours, 21 or more daily), Granada (€24, three hours, four daily), Málaga (€19.10 to €36.40, 2½ hours, five daily) and Mérida (€14, five hours, one daily).

Getting Around

Los Amarillos (www.losamarillos.es) runs buses between the airport and the Ave del Cid (€2.20 to €2.50, at 15 and 45 minutes past the hour), near the San Sebastión bus station. A taxi costs about €20.

Buses run by Seville's urban transport authority **Tussam** (www.tussam.es, in Spanish), C1, C2, C3 and C4, do useful circular routes linking the main transport terminals and the city centre.

Tussam's **Tranvia** (www.tussam.es, in Spanish), the city's sleek tram service, was launched in 2007. Individual rides cost €1.20, or you can buy a Bono (travel pass offering five rides for €5) from many newspaper stands and tobacconists.

Córdoba

POP 302,000

Córdoba was once one of the most enlightened Islamic cities on earth and enough remains to place it in the contemporary top three of Andalucian draws. The centrepiece is the gigantic and exquisitely rendered

Mezquita. Surrounding it is an intricate web of winding streets, geranium-sprouting flower boxes and cool, intimate patios that are at their most beguiling in late spring.

Sights & Activities

TOP CHOICE **Mezquita** CHURCH, MOSQUE
(admission €8, 8.30-10am Mon-Sat free; ⌚10am-7pm Mon-Sat Apr-Oct, 9-10.45am & 1.30-6.30pm Sun year-round) Founded in 785, Córdoba's gigantic mosque is a wonderful architectural hybrid with delicate horseshoe arches, making this unlike anywhere else in Spain. Once inside you can see straight ahead to the **mihrab**, the prayer niche in a mosque's *qibla* (the wall indicating the direction of Mecca) that was the focus of prayer. The first 12 transverse aisles inside the entrance, a forest of pillars and arches, comprise the original 8th-century mosque.

Judería NEIGHBOURHOOD
The medieval *judería*, extending northwest from the Mezquita almost to Avenida del Gran Capitán, is today a maze of narrow streets and whitewashed buildings with flowery window boxes. The beautiful little 14th-century **Sinagoga** (Calle de los Judíos 20; admission adult/EU citizen €0.30/free; ⌚9.30am-2pm & 3.30-5.30pm Tue-Sat, to 1.30pm Sun & holidays) is one of only three surviving medieval synagogues in Spain and the only one in Andalucía.

Alcázar de los Reyes Cristianos CASTLE
(Campo Santo de Los Mártires s/n; adult/student €4/2, Fri free; ⌚10am-2pm & 5.30-7.30pm Tue-Sat, 9.30am-2.30pm Sun & holidays) Just southwest of the Mezquita, the Alcázar, or Castle of the Christian Monarchs, began as a palace and fort for Alfonso X in the 13th century. From 1490 to 1821 the Inquisition operated from here. Today its gardens are among the most beautiful in Andalucía.

Hammam Baños Árabes ARAB BATHHOUSE
(☎957 48 47 46; www.hammamspain.com/cordoba; Calle Corregidor Luis de la Cerda 51; bath/bath & massage €26/33; ⌚2hr sessions at 10am, noon, 2pm, 4pm, 6pm, 8pm & 10pm) Follow the lead of the medieval Cordobans and dip your toe in the beautifully renovated Arab baths, where you can enjoy an aromatherapy massage, with tea, hookah and Arabic sweets in the cafe later.

Medina Azahara ISLAMIC RUINS
(Madinat al-Zahra; adult/EU citizen €1.50/free; ⌚10am-6.30pm Tue-Sat, to 8.30pm May–mid-Sep, to 2pm Sun) Even in the cicada-shrill heat and stillness of a summer afternoon, the Medina Azahara whispers of the power and vision of its founder, Abd ar-Rahman III. The self-proclaimed caliph began the construction of a magnificent new capital 8km west of Córdoba around 936, and took up full residence around 945. It was destroyed in the 11th century and just 10% of the site has been excavated. A taxi costs €37 for the return trip, with one hour to view the site, or you can book a three-hour coach tour for €6.50 to €10 through many Córdoba hotels.

Sleeping

TOP CHOICE **Hotel Hacienda Posada de Vallina** HOTEL €€
(☎957 49 87 50; www.hhposadadevallinacordoba.com; Corregidor Luís de la Cerda 83; s/d €50/70; P❄@📶) In an enviable nook on the quiet side of the Mezquita (the building actually predates it), this cleverly renovated hotel uses portraits and period furniture to enhance a plush and modern interior. The rooms make you feel comfortable but in-period (ie medieval Córdoba). Columbus allegedly once stayed here.

Hostal La Fuente HOTEL €
(☎957 48 78 27; www.hostallafuente.com; Calle San Fernando 51; s/d €35/50; ❄@📶) A journeyman hotel, though in Córdoba this means you get an airy patio, azulejos tiles, exposed brick and interesting architectural details. The rooms are clean and comfortable and the staff quietly helpful.

Hostal El Reposo de Bagdad HOTEL €
(☎957 20 28 54; Calle Fernández Ruano 11; s/d €30/45) Hidden in a tiny street in the *judería*, this 200-year-old house feels thrillingly Moorish. The rooms are simple but clean.

Eating & Drinking

TOP CHOICE **Taberna San Miguel El Pisto** TAPAS €
(Plaza San Miguel 1; tapas €3, media-raciones €5-10; ⌚closed Sun & Aug) Stand aside, Seville. Fine wine, great atmosphere, professional old-school waiters, zero pretension and a clamorous yet handsome decor make El Pisto (The Barrel) a Cordoban and Andalucian tapas classic.

Taberna Salinas TAPAS €
(Calle Tundidores 3; tapas/raciones €2.50/8; ⌚closed Sun & Aug) Dating back to 1879, this large patio restaurant fills up fast. Try the

Córdoba

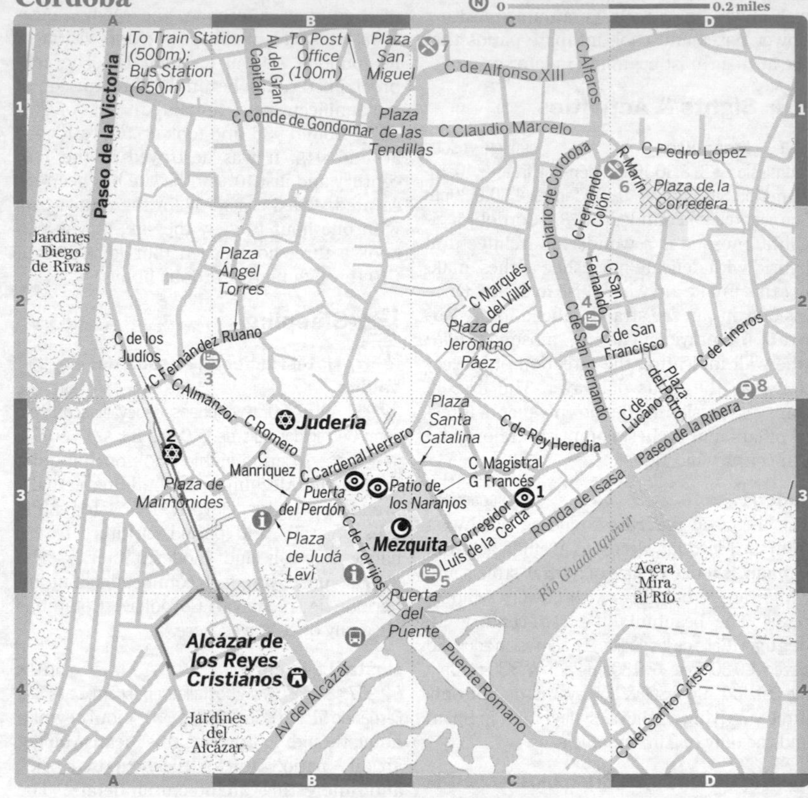

Córdoba

Top Sights
- Alcázar de los Reyes Cristianos B4
- Judería B3
- Mezquita B3

Sights
- 1 Hammam Baños Árabes C3
- 2 Sinagoga A3

Sleeping
- 3 Hostal El Reposo de Bagdad A2
- 4 Hostal La Fuente C2
- 5 Hotel Hacienda Posada de Vallina C3

Eating
- 6 Taberna Salinas D1
- 7 Taberna San Miguel El Pisto C1

Drinking
- 8 Amapola D2

delicious aubergines with honey, or potatoes with garlic. The tavern side is quieter in the early evening and the friendly bar staff will fill your glass with local Montilla whenever you look thirsty.

Amapola BAR
(Paseo de la Ribera 9; ⏲9am-3pm Mon-Fri, 5pm-4am Sat & Sun) This is where the young and beautiful lounge on green leather sofas and consume elaborate cocktails. DJs spin until the small hours.

Information

Municipal tourist office (Plaza de Judá Levi; ⌚8.30am-2.30pm Mon-Fri)

Regional tourist office (☎957 35 51 79; Calle de Torrijos 10; ⌚9am-7.30pm Mon-Fri, 9.30am-3pm Sat, Sun & holidays)

Getting There & Away

BUS The **bus station** (Glorieta de las Tres Culturas) is 1km northwest of Plaza de las Tendillas. Destinations include Seville (€10.36, 1¾ hours, six daily), Granada (€12.52, 2½ hours, seven daily) and Málaga (€12.75, 2¾ hours, five daily).

TRAIN From Córdoba's **train station** (Avenida de América) destinations include Seville (€10.60 to €32.10, 40 minutes to 1½ hours, 23 or more daily), Madrid (€52 to €66.30, 1¾ to 6¼ hours, 23 or more daily), Málaga (€21 to €39.60, one hour to 2½ hours, nine daily) and Barcelona (€59.40 to €133, 10½ hours, four daily).

Granada

POP 300,000

Granada's eight centuries as a Muslim capital are symbolised in its keynote emblem, the remarkable Alhambra, one of the most graceful architectural achievements in the Muslim world. Islam was never completely expunged here and today it seems more present than ever in the shops, restaurants, tearooms and mosque of a growing North African community in and around the maze of the Albayzín. The tapas bars fill to bursting with hungry and thirsty revellers, while flamenco dives resound to the heart-wrenching tones of the south.

Sights & Activities

Alhambra ISLAMIC PALACE

(☎902 441221; advance ticket purchase www.alhambra-patronato.es; adult/EU senior/EU student €12/9/9, Generalife only €6; ⌚8.30am-8pm mid-Mar–Oct, to 6pm Nov–mid-Mar) The mighty Alhambra is breathtaking. Much has been written about its fortress, palace, patios and gardens, but nothing can really prepare you for seeing the real thing.

The **Alcazaba**, the Alhambra's fortress, dates from the 11th to the 13th centuries. There are spectacular views from the tops of its towers. The **Palacio Nazaríes** (Nasrid Palace), built for Granada's Muslim rulers in their 13th- to 15th-century heyday, is the centrepiece of the Alhambra. The **Generalife** (Palace Gardens) is a great spot to relax and contemplate the complex from a little distance.

The Palacio Nazaríes is also open for **night visits** (⌚10pm-11.30pm Tue-Sat Mar-Oct, 8pm-9.30pm Fri & Sat Nov-Feb). Book for night visits the same way as for day visits.

Other Attractions OTHER SIGHTS

Exploring the narrow, hilly streets of the **Albayzín**, the old Moorish quarter across the river from the Alhambra, is the perfect complement to the Alhambra. The cobblestone streets are lined with gorgeous *cármenes* (large mansions with walled gardens; from the Arabic *karm* for garden). It survived as the Muslim quarter for several decades after the Christian conquest in 1492. Head uphill to reach the **Mirador de San Nicolás**, a viewpoint with great vistas and a relaxed scene.

It's also well worth exploring the streets and lanes surrounding Plaza Bib-Rambla, and visiting the **Capilla Real** (www.capillarealgranada.com; Calle Oficios; admission €3.50; ⌚10.30am-1.30pm & 4-7.30pm Mon-Sat, 11am-1.30pm & 4-7pm Sun Apr-Oct), where Fernando and Isabel, the Christian monarchs on the throne when Spain conquered Granada in 1492, are buried.

ALHAMBRA TICKETS

Up to 6600 tickets to the Alhambra are available for each day. About one-third of these are sold at the ticket office on the day, but they sell out early and you need to start queuing by 7am to be reasonably sure of getting one. It's highly advisable to book in advance (€1 extra per ticket). You can book up to a year ahead in two ways:

» **Alhambra Advance Booking** (☎in Spain 902 88 80 01, from outside Spain 0034 934 92 37 50; ⌚8am-9pm)

» **Servicaixa** (www.servicaixa.com). Online booking in Spanish and English. You can also buy tickets in advance from **Servicaixa cash machines** (⌚8am-7pm Mar-Oct, 8am-5pm Nov-Feb), but only in the Alhambra grounds.

Next door to the chapel is Granada's **Catedral** (admission €3.50; ⏲10.45am-1.30pm & 4-8pm Mon-Sat, 4-8pm Sun), which dates from the early 16th century.

Sleeping

Hotel Casa del Capitel Nazarí HISTORIC HOTEL €€
(☎958 21 52 60; www.hotelcasacapitel.com; Cuesta Aceituneros 6; s/d €88/110; ❄@📶) Albayzín magic in a 1503 Renaissance palace, which is as much architectural history lesson as plush hotel. Rooms have Moroccan inflections and the courtyard hosts art exhibits.

Hostal Molinos HOTEL €
(☎958 22 73 67; www.hotelmolinos.es; Calle Molinos 12; s/d/tr €29/32/45; 📶) Don't let the 'narrowest hotel in the world' moniker put you off (and yes, it actually is – and has a certificate from the *Guinness Book of Records* to prove it), there's plenty of breathing space in Molino's nine rooms, and warm hospitality in its information-stacked lobby. Situated at the foot of the Realejo, it makes an economical central option.

Oasis Backpackers' Hostel HOSTEL €
(☎958 21 58 48; www.oasisgranada.com; Placeta Correo Viejo 3; dm/d €18/40; ❄@📶) Bohemian digs in a bohemian quarter, Oasis is seconds away from the *teterías* (tearooms) and bars on Calle Elvira. There's free internet access, a rooftop terrace and personal safes. As backpacker hostels go, it's a gem.

Eating

Granada is one of the last bastions of that fantastic practice of free tapas with every drink, and some have an international flavour. The labyrinthine Albayzín holds a wealth of eateries tucked away in the narrow streets. Calle Calderería Nueva is a fascinating muddle of *teterías* and Arabic-influenced takeaways.

Granada

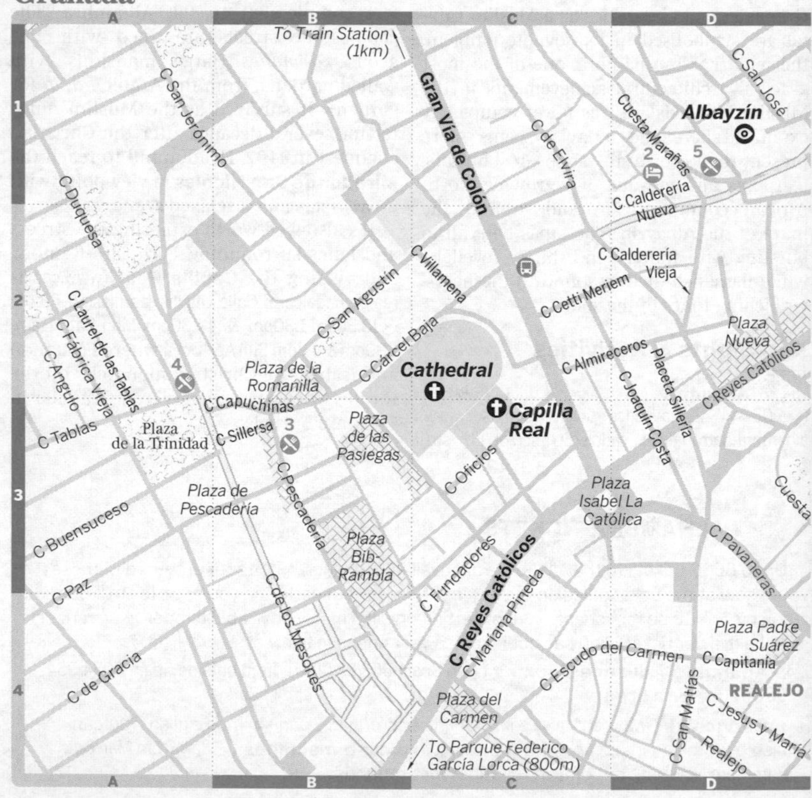

TOP CHOICE **Restaurante Arrayanes** MOROCCAN **€**
(☎958 22 84 01; Cuesta Marañas 4; mains €8.50-19; ⊙from 8pm) The best Moroccan food in a city known for its Moorish throwbacks? Recline on lavish seating, try the fruity tagine casseroles and make your decision. No alcohol.

Reca TAPAS **€**
(Plaza de la Trinidad; raciones €8; ⊙closed Tue) A tapas classic rightly famous for its *salmorejo* (thicker version of gazpacho) and its all-through-the-afternoon food service.

Oliver SEAFOOD **€**
(Calle Pescadería 12; mains €12-18; ⊙closed Sun) Sandwiched in between Plazas Bib-Rambla and Trinidad, this is a favourite lunchtime office-worker stop, revered for its fried fish.

☆ Entertainment

The excellent monthly *Guía de Granada* (€1), available from kiosks, lists entertainment venues and tapas bars.

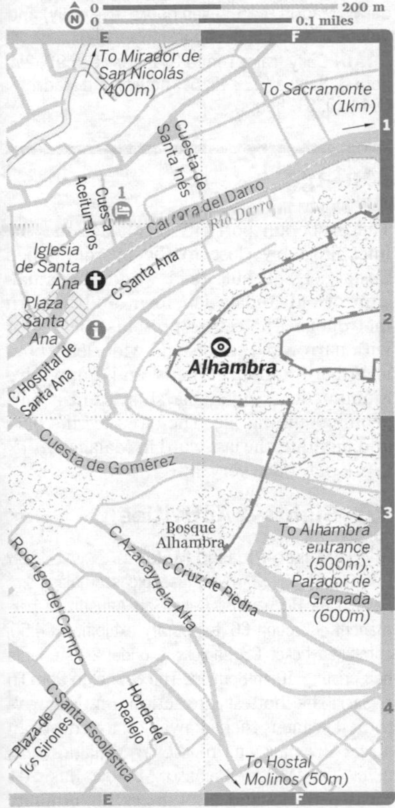

Situated above and to the northwest of the city centre, and offering panoramic views over the Alhambra, the Sacromonte is Granada's centuries-old *gitano* (Roma people) quarter. The Sacromonte caves harbour touristy flamenco haunts, for which you can prebook through hotels and travel agencies, some of which offer free transport. Try the Friday or Saturday midnight shows at **Los Tarantos** (☎day 958 22 45 25, night 958 22 24 92; Camino del Sacromonte 9; admission €24) for a lively experience.

Peña de la Platería FLAMENCO CLUB
(Placeta de Toqueros 7) Buried deep in the Albayzín warren, this is a genuine aficionados' club with a large outdoor patio. Dramatic 9.30pm performances take place on Thursday or Saturday in an adjacent room and cost €12.

ℹ Information

Municipal tourist office (www.granadatur.com; Calle Almona del Campillo 2; ⊙9am-7pm Mon-Fri, to 6pm Sat, 10am-2pm Sun & holidays)

ℹ Getting There & Away

AIR Destinations from Granada's airport include Madrid, Barcelona, Milan and Bologna.

BUS Granada's **bus station** (Carretera de Jaén) is 3km northwest of the city centre. **Alsina Graells** (☎902 42 22 42; www.alsa.es) runs to Córdoba (€12.52, 2¾ hours, nine daily), Seville (€19.32, three hours, eight daily), Málaga (€9.75, 1½ hours, 16 daily) and Madrid (€16.30, five to six hours, 10 to 13 daily).

TRAIN The **train station** (Avenida de Andaluces) is 1.5km west of the centre. Trains run to/from Seville (€23.85, three hours, four daily), Almería (€15.90, 2¼ hours, four daily), Ronda (€13.50, three hours, three daily), Algeciras (€20.10, 4½ hours, three daily), Madrid

Granada

Top Sights

Sleeping

Eating

(€66.80, four to five hours, one to two daily), Valencia (€50.60, 7½ to eight hours, one daily) and Barcelona (€62.10, 12 hours, one daily).

Costa de Almería

The coast east of Almería in eastern Andalucía is perhaps the last section of Spain's Mediterranean coast where you can have a beach to yourself. This is Spain's sunniest region – even in late March it can be warm enough to strip off and take in the rays.

Sights & Activities

The **Alcazaba** (Calle Almanzor s/n; adult/EU citizen €1.50/free; 9am-8.30pm Tue-Sun Apr-Oct, 9am-6.30pm Tue-Sun Nov-Mar), an enormous 10th-century Muslim fortress, is the highlight of Almería city.

The best thing about the region is the wonderful coastline and semidesert scenery of the **Cabo de Gata** promontory. Along the 50km coast from El Cabo de Gata village to Agua Amarga, some of the most beautiful and empty beaches on the Mediterranean alternate with precipitous cliffs and scattered villages. The main village is laid-back **San José**, with excellent beaches nearby, such as **Playa de los Genoveses** and **Playa de Mónsul**.

Sleeping & Eating

Almería City

TOP CHOICE **Hotel Costasol** HOTEL €
(950 23 40 11; www.hotelcostasol.com; Paseo de Almería 58; r €54; P ❄ @ ≈) It's amazing what some red colour accents and a clean, simple but funky refurb can do. Factor in the sleek reception, enormous bathrooms, spacious communal areas and stylish basement restaurant and you won't find a better hotel for this price in Andalucía.

Hotel Torreluz HOTEL €€
(950 23 43 99; www.torreluz.com; Plaza de las Flores 2 & 3; s/d 2-star €39/64, 3-star €56/74; P ❄ ≈) Burnt-plum-coloured walls, comfortable beds and good prices make this one of Almería's best-value places to stay.

Cabo de Gata

Sanctuario San José HOTEL €€
(902 87 73 88; www.elsantuariosanjose.es; Camino de Calahiguera 9; s/d €64/79; mains €15-24; P ❄) This refurbished 28-room, brilliant-white hotel offers minimal yet friendly design with attractive lounging and dining terraces.

Restaurante Mediterraneo SEAFOOD €
(950 38 00 93; Puerto Deportivo de San José; mains €10-22) Last stop in a run of similarly good seafood restaurants near the marina, this one has particularly friendly staff and a less frantic atmosphere than some of its neighbours.

Information

The **regional tourist office** (950 27 43 55; Parque de Nicolás Salmerón; 9am-7pm Mon-Fri, 10am-2pm Sat & Sun) is in Almería city.

Getting There & Away

AIR Almería **airport** (950 21 37 00), 10km east of the city centre, receives flights from several European countries, as well as Barcelona, Madrid and Melilla.

BOAT Daily sailings to/from Melilla, Nador (Morocco) and Ghazaouet (Algeria). The tourist office has details.

BUS Destinations served from Almería's **bus station** (950 26 20 98) include Granada (€13.45, 2¼ hours, 10 daily), Málaga (€16, 3¼ hours, 10 daily), Murcia (€17.25, 2½ hours, 10 daily), Madrid (€25, seven hours, five daily) and Valencia (€35.65, 8½ hours, five daily).

TRAIN Daily trains run to Granada (€15.90, 2¼ hours), Seville (€38.15, 5½ hours) and Madrid (€44.10, 6¾ hours).

Málaga

POP 720,000

The exuberant port city of Málaga may be uncomfortably close to the overdeveloped Costa del Sol, but it's a wonderful amalgam of old Andalucian town and modern metropolis. The centre presents the visitor with narrow old streets and wide, leafy boulevards, beautiful gardens and impressive monuments, fashionable shops and a burgeoning cultural life. The city's terrific bars and nightlife, the last word in Málaga *joie de vivre,* stay open very late.

Sights & Activities

TOP CHOICE **Museo Picasso Málaga** ART GALLERY
(902 44 33 77; www.museopicassomalaga.org; Palacio de Buenavista, Calle San Agustín 8; permanent collection €6, temporary exhibition €4.50, combined ticket €8, seniors & under-26 students half-price; 10am-8pm Tue-Thu & Sun, to 9pm Fri & Sat) The hottest attraction on Málaga's tourist scene is tucked away on a pedestrian street in what was medieval Málaga's *judería.* The Museo Picasso Málaga has 204 Picasso works and also stages high-quality

temporary exhibitions on Picasso themes. The Picasso paintings, drawings, engravings, sculptures and ceramics on show (many never previously on public display) span almost every phase and influence of the artist's colourful career. Picasso was born in Málaga in 1881 but moved to northern Spain with his family when he was nine.

Cathedral CHURCH
(Calle Molina Lario, entrance Calle Císter; admission €3.50; ⏲10am-5.30pm Mon-Fri, to 5pm Sat, closed Sun & holidays) Preserved rather magnificently, like an unfinished Beethoven symphony, Málaga's cathedral was begun in the 16th century on the former site of the main mosque and was never properly completed.

Alcazaba CASTLE
(Calle Alcazabilla; admission €2.10, incl Castillo de Gibralfaro €3.40; ⏲9.30am-8pm Tue-Sun Apr-Oct) At the lower, western end of the Gibralfaro hill, the wheelchair-accessible Alcazaba was the palace-fortress of Málaga's Muslim governors, dating from 1057. The brick path winds uphill, interspersed with arches and stone walls and is refreshingly cool in summer.

Castillo de Gibralfaro CASTLE
(admission €2.10; ⏲9am-9pm Apr-Sep, to 6pm Oct-Mar) Above the Alcazaba rises the older Castillo de Gibralfaro, built by Abd ar-Rahman I, the 8th-century Cordoban emir, and rebuilt in the 14th and 15th centuries. Nothing much remains of the castle's interior, but the walkway around the ramparts affords exhilarating views.

Beaches BEACHES
Sandy city beaches stretch several kilometres in each direction from the port. **Playa de la Malagueta**, handy to the city centre, has some excellent bars and restaurants close by. **Playa de Pedregalejo** and **Playa del Palo**, about 4km east of the centre, are popular and reachable by bus 11 from Paseo del Parque.

Sleeping

El Riad Andaluz HOTEL €€
(☎952 21 36 40; www.elriadandaluz.com; Calle Hinestrosa 24; s/d €70/86; ❄@📶) Colourful and exotic, this gorgeous restored monastery in the Centro Historico offers eight rooms with Moroccan decor set around an atmospheric patio, with tea and coffee on tap all day.

Hotel Carlos V HOTEL €
(☎952 21 51 20; www.hotel-carlosvmalaga.com; Calle Císter 10; s/d €36/59; P❄@) Close to the cathedral and Picasso Museum, the Carlos V is enduringly popular. Renovated in 2008, bathrooms sparkle in their new uniform of cream-and-white tiles. Excellent standard for the price and helpful staff make this hotel a winner.

Hostal Derby HOSTAL €
(☎952 22 13 01; Calle San Juan de Dios 1, 4th fl; s/d €36/48; @) A friendly, well-run and good-value *hostal* with spacious rooms and big windows, some overlooking the harbour.

Eating

Most of the best eating places are sandwiched in the narrow streets between Calle Marqués de Larios and the cathedral.

La Rebaná TAPAS €
(Calle Molina Lario 5; tapas €4.20-8.50, raciones €7-11.50) A great, noisy tapas bar near the Picasso Museum and the cathedral. Dark wood, tall windows and exposed-brick walls create a modern, minimal but laid-back space. Try the foie gras with salted nougat for a unique tapa.

Café Lepanto CAFE & SNACKS €
(Calle Marqués de Larios 7) An old-world Italianite coffee and ice-cream bar that serves as Málaga's top *confitería,* Lepanto is insanely popular, probably because most of its sweets and pastries are highly addictive. Enjoy them in the art-nouveau-embellished interior being served by athletic waiters in waistcoats.

Drinking & Entertainment

On weekend nights the web of narrow old streets north of Plaza de la Constitución comes alive. Look for bars around Plaza de la Merced, Plaza Mitjana and Plaza de Uncibay.

Information

Municipal tourist office (www.malagaturismo.com) Plaza de la Marina (⏲9am-8pm Mar-Sep, 9am-6pm Oct-Feb); Casita del Jardinero (Avenida de Cervantes 1; ⏲9am-8pm Mar-Sep, 9am-6pm Oct-Feb)

Getting There & Away

AIR Málaga's busy **airport** (☎952 04 88 38) is Andalucía's main international gateway. Trains run about every half-hour to Málaga-Renfe (€2, 11 minutes) and Málaga-Centro stations.

BUS Málaga's **bus station** (Paseo de los Tilos) is 1km southwest of the city centre. Frequent buses go to Seville (€16, 2½ hours), Granada (€9.75, 1½ to two hours) and Córdoba (€12.50, 2½ hours).

TRAIN The main station, **Málaga-Renfe** (Explanada de la Estación), is around the corner from the bus station. The superfast AVE service runs to Madrid (€76.40 to €85, 2½ hours, six daily). Trains also go to Córdoba (€21 to €44, one hour, 10 daily), Seville (€19.10 to €36.40, two to 2½ hours, five daily) and Barcelona (€62.70 to €138, 6½ to 13 hours, two daily).

Cádiz

POP 128,600

Cádiz, widely considered the oldest continuously inhabited settlement in Europe, is crammed onto the head of a promontory like an overcrowded ocean liner. Columbus sailed from here on his second and fourth voyages, and after his success in the Americas, Cádiz grew into Spain's richest and most cosmopolitan city in the 18th century. The best time to visit is during the February *carnaval* (carnival), which rivals Rios for its outrageous exuberance.

Sights & Activities

The yellow-domed, 18th-century **Catedral** (Plaza de la Catedral; adult/student €5/3; 10am-6.30pm Mon-Sat, 1.30-6.30pm Sun) is the city's most striking landmark. From a separate entrance on Plaza de la Catedral, climb to the top of the **Torre de Poniente** (Western Tower; adult/senior €4/3; 10am-6pm, to 8pm 15 Jun-15 Sep) for marvellous vistas.

You can also get your bearings by climbing up the baroque **Torre Tavira** (Calle Marqués del Real Tesoro 10; adult/student €4/3.30; 10am-6pm, to 8pm 15 Jun-15 Sep), the highest of Cádiz's old watchtowers, featuring sweeping views of the city.

The **Museo de Cádiz** (Plaza de Mina; EU citizen/other free/€1.50; 2.30-8.30pm Tue, 9am-8.30pm Wed-Sat, 9.30am-2.30pm Sun) has a magnificent collection of archaeological remains, as well as an excellent fine-art collection. The city's lively **central market** (Plaza de las Flores) is on the site of a former Phoenician temple.

The broad, sandy **Playa de la Victoria**, a lovely Atlantic beach, stretches about 4km along the peninsula from its beginning, 1.5km beyond the Puertas de Tierra. Bus 1 'Plaza España-Cortadura' from Plaza de España will get you there.

Sleeping & Eating

TOP CHOICE **Hotel Argantonio** HOTEL €€

(956 21 16 40; www.hotelargantonio.com; Calle Argantonio 3; s/d incl breakfast €90/107;) A very attractive small new hotel in the old city with an appealing Mudéjar accent to its decor. Staff are welcoming, and the rooms are comfortable, with wi-fi access and flat-screen TVs.

Casa Caracol HOSTEL €

(956 26 11 66; www.caracolcasa.com; Calle Suárez de Salazar 4; dm/hammocks incl breakfast €16/10;) Casa Caracol is the only backpacker hostel in the old town. Friendly, as only Cádiz can be, it has bunk dorms for four and eight, a communal kitchen and a roof terrace with hammocks. Green initiatives include recycling, water efficiency and plans for solar panels.

El Aljibe TAPAS €

(www.pablogrosso.com; Calle Plocia 25; tapas €2-3.50, mains €10-15) *Gaditano* chef Pablo Grosso concocts delicious combinations of the traditional and the adventurous. Try the pheasant breast stuffed with dates and the *solomillo ibérico* (Iberian pork sirloin) with Emmental cheese, ham and piquant peppers. You can enjoy his creations as tapas in the stone-walled downstairs bar.

Information

Municipal tourist office (Paseo de Canalejas s/n; 8.30am-6pm Mon-Fri, 9am-5pm Sat & Sun)

Getting There & Away

BUS There are daily bus service to Seville (€11, 1¾ hours, 10 daily), Tarifa (€8.46, two hours, five daily), Málaga (€20, four hours, six daily), and Granada (€28, five hours, four daily).

TRAIN Trains travel to Seville (€12.75, two hours), Córdoba (€23.85 to €38.20, three hours) and Madrid (€70, five hours). High-speed AVE services to Madrid are slated for 2012.

Tarifa

POP 17,700

Windy, laid-back Tarifa is so close to Africa that you can almost hear the call to prayer issuing from Morocco's minarets. The town is a bohemian haven of cafes and crumbling Moorish ruins. There's also a lively windsurfing and kitesurfing scene.

Sights

A wander round the old town's narrow streets, of mainly Islamic origin, is an appetiser for Morocco. The Mudéjar **Puerta de Jerez** was built after the Reconquista. The **Mirador El Estrecho**, atop part of the castle walls, has spectacular views across to Africa, only 14km away. The 10th-century **Castillo**

de Guzmán (Calle Guzmán El Bueno; admission €2; ⊙11am-4pm) is also worth a wander; tickets must be bought at the tourist office.

Of the beaches, spectacular **Playa de los Lances** stretches northwest for 10km to the huge sand dune at **Ensenada de Valdevaqueros**.

Activities

KITESURFING & WINDSURFING

Tarifa now has around 30 kitesurfing and windsurfing schools, many of them with offices or shops along Calle Batalla del Salado or on Calle Mar Adriático. Most rent equipment and run classes.

WHALE WATCHING

The Strait of Gibraltar is a top site for viewing whales and dolphins. Killer whales visit in July and August, huge sperm and fin whales lurk here from spring to autumn, and pilot whales and three types of dolphin stay all year. **Firmm** (☎956 62 70 08; www.firmm.org; Calle Pedro Cortés 4; ⊙Mar-Oct) runs daily two- to 2½-hour boat trips to observe these marine mammals.

Sleeping & Eating

Hostal Africa HOTEL €€
(☎956 68 02 20; Calle María Antonia Toledo 12; s with/without bathroom €50/35, d with/without bathroom €65/50; ⊙closed 24 Dec-31 Jan) The well-travelled owners of this revamped house know just what travellers need. Rooms are attractive and there's an expansive terrace with wonderful views. Short-term storage for boards, bicycles and baggage available.

Melting Pot HOSTEL €
(☎956 68 29 06; www.meltingpothostels.com; Calle Turriano Gracil 5; dm/d incl breakfast €25/55; @☎) The Melting Pot is a friendly, well-equipped hostel just off the Alameda. The five dorms, for five to eight people, have bunks and there's one for women only. A good kitchen adjoins the cosy bar-lounge, and all guests get their own keys.

Chilimoso ARABIC €
(☎956 68 50 92; Calle Peso 6; dishes €4-6) This tiny place serves tasty vegan and vegetarian food with oriental leanings. Try the falafel with hummus, tzatziki and salad.

Information

Tourist office (☎956 68 09 93; www.ayto tarifa.com, in Spanish; Paseo de la Alameda; ⊙10am-2pm daily, 4-6pm Mon-Fri Oct-May, 6-8pm Mon-Fri Jun-Sep)

Getting There & Away

BUS Comes (☎956 68 40 38; Calle Batalla del Salado 13) runs daily buses to Cádiz (€8.45, 1¾ hours), Algeciras (€2, 30 minutes), La Línea de la Concepción (for Gibraltar; €3.83, 45 minutes), Seville (€17.05, three hours) and Málaga (€12.75, two hours).

BOAT FRS (☎956 68 18 30; www.frs.es; Estación Marítima) runs fast ferries between Tarifa and Tangier (passenger/car/motorcycle €37/93/31, 35 minutes, eight daily).

EXTREMADURA

A sparsely populated stretch of vast skies and open plains, Extremadura is far enough from most beaten tourist trails to give you a genuine sense of exploration.

Trujillo

POP 9822

With its medieval architecture, leafy courtyards, fruit gardens, churches and convents, Trujillo truly is one of the most captivating small towns in Spain. It can't be much bigger now than it was in 1529, when its most famous son, Francisco Pizarro, set off with his three brothers for an expedition that culminated in the bloody conquest of the Incan empire.

Sights

Plaza Mayor MAIN SQUARE
A large equestrian **Pizarro statue** by American Charles Rumsey looks down over the spectacular Plaza Mayor. Overlooking the Plaza Mayor from the northeast corner is the 16th-century **Iglesia de San Martín** (admission €1.40; ⊙10am-2pm & 4-7pm), with delicate Gothic ceiling tracing, stunning stained-glass windows and a grand organ (climb up to the choir loft for the best view).

Upper Town NEIGHBOURHOOD
The 900m of walls circling the upper town date from Muslim times and it was here the newly settled noble families built their mansions and churches after the Reconquista.

The 13th-century **Iglesia de Santa María la Mayor** (admission €1.40; ⊙10am-2pm & 4-7pm) has a mainly Gothic nave and a Romanesque tower that you can ascend (all 106 steps) for fabulous views.

WORTH A TRIP

GIBRALTAR

The British colony of Gibraltar (population 28,000) is like 1960s Britain on a sunny day, with bobbies, double-decker buses and fried-egg-and-chip-style eateries. In British hands since 1713, it was the starting point for the Muslim conquest of Iberia 1000 years earlier. Spain has never fully accepted UK control of the territory but, for the moment at least, talk of joint sovereignty seems to have gone cold.

The large **Upper Rock Nature Reserve** (admission incl attractions £10, vehicle £2, pedestrian excl attractions £0.50; 9.30am-7.15pm, last entry 6.45pm), covering most of the upper rock, has spectacular views. The rock's most famous inhabitants are its colony of Barbary macaques, the only wild primates in Europe. Other attractions include **St Michael's Cave**, a large natural grotto renowned for its stalagmites and stalactites, and the **Great Siege Tunnels**, a series of galleries hewn from the rock by the British during the Great Siege by the Spaniards (1779–83) to provide new gun emplacements.

Dolphin watching is an option from April to September. Most boats go from Watergardens Quay or adjacent Marina Bay. The trips last about 1½ hours and cost around £20 per adult.

Easyjet (www.easyjet.com) flies about 15 times weekly from London Gatwick, **British Airways** (www.britishairways.com) operates seven weekly flights from London Heathrow and **Monarch Airlines** (www.flymonarch.com) flies daily to/from London Luton and thrice weekly to/from Manchester.

La Línea de la Concepción bus station is only a five-minute walk from the Spanish border.

At the top of the hill Trujillo's **castle** (admission €1.40; 10am-2pm & 4-7pm) of 10th-century Muslim origin, later strengthened by the Christians, is impressive. Patrol the battlements for magnificent 360-degree sweeping views.

Sleeping & Eating

TOP CHOICE **Posada Dos Orillas** POSADA €€
(927 65 90 79; www.dosorillas.com; Calle de Cambrones 6; d Sun-Thu €69-90, Fri & Sat €80-107;) The rooms here replicate Spanish colonial taste; those in the older wing bear the names of the 'seven Trujillos' of Extremadura and the Americas. It has a pleasant courtyard restaurant.

El Mirador de las Monjas HOSTERÍA €€
(927 65 92 23; www.elmiradordelasmonjas.com, in Spanish; Plaza de Santiago 2; s/d incl breakfast Mon-Thu €50/60, Fri-Sun €60/70;) High in the old town, this contemporary six-room *hostería* has large, minimalist rooms with clean lines and stylish bathrooms.

TOP CHOICE **Restaurante La Troya** TRADITIONAL SPANISH €
(927 32 13 64; Plaza Mayor 10; set menú €15) Mention Trujillo to anyone in Spain and chances are that they'll have heard of La Troya – the restaurant is an *extremeño* institution. You will be directed to one of several dining areas and there be presented with plates of tortilla, chorizo, cheese and salad, followed by a three-course menu (with truly gargantuan portions), including wine and water.

Information

Tourist office (927 32 26 77; www.trujillo.es, in Spanish; Plaza Mayor s/n; 10am-2pm & 4-7pm Oct-May, 10am-2pm & 5-8pm Jun-Sep)

Getting There & Away

The **bus station** (927 32 12 02; Avenida de Miajadas) is 500m south of Plaza Mayor. There are services to/from Madrid (€19.34 to €31.40, three to 4¼ hours, five daily), Cáceres (€4.19, 40 minutes, eight daily) and Mérida (€8.15, 1½ hours, three daily).

Cáceres

POP 89,100

Cáceres' *ciudad monumental* (old town), built in the 15th and 16th centuries, is perfectly preserved. The town's action centres on Plaza Mayor, at the foot of the old town, and busy Avenida de España, a short distance south.

Sights

Plaza de Santa María PUBLIC SQUARE
Enter the *ciudad monumental* from Plaza Mayor through the 18th-century **Arco de la**

Estrella, built this wide for the passage of carriages. The **Concatedral de Santa María** (Plaza de Santa María; admission €1; ⏲9.30am-2pm & 5.30-8.30pm Mon-Sat, 9.30-11.50am & 5.30-7.15pm Sun May-Sep), a 15th-century Gothic cathedral, creates an impressive opening scene. Climb the **bell tower** (adult €1) for stunning views.

Also on the plaza are the **Palacio Episcopal** (Bishop's Palace), the **Palacio de Mayoralgo** and the **Palacio de Ovando**, all in 16th-century Renaissance style. Heading back through Arco de la Estrella, you can climb the 12th-century **Torre de Bujaco** (Plaza Mayor; adult €2; ⏲10am-2pm & 5.30-8.30pm Mon-Sat, 10am-2pm Sun Apr-Sep, 10am-2pm & 4.30-7.30pm Mon-Sat, 10am-2pm Sun Oct-Mar) for good stork's-eye views of the Plaza Mayor.

Plaza de San Mateo & Plaza de las Veletas PUBLIC SQUARES

From Plaza de San Jorge, Cuesta de la Compañía climbs to Plaza de San Mateo and the **Iglesia de San Mateo**, traditionally the church of the land-owning nobility and built on the site of the town's Islamic mosque.

Below the square is the excellent **Museo de Cáceres** (Plaza de las Veletas 1; admission/EU citizens €1.20/free; ⏲9am-2.30pm & 5-8.15pm Tue-Sat, 10.15am-2.30pm Sun) in a 16th-century mansion built over an evocative 12th-century *aljibe* (cistern), the only surviving element of Cáceres' Muslim castle. It has an impressive archaeological section and an excellent fine-arts display (open only in the mornings), with works by Picasso, Miró, Tapiès and other renowned Spanish painters and sculptors.

Sleeping & Eating

Hotel Casa Don Fernando HOTEL €€

(☎927 21 42 79; www.casadonfernando.com; Plaza Mayor 30; d €60-140; P ❄ ᯤ) Arguably the classiest midrange choice in Cáceres, this boutique hotel sits on Plaza Mayor, directly opposite the Arco de la Estrella. Spread over four floors, there are rooms on each floor with plaza views and the designer rooms and bathrooms are tastefully chic. Parking costs €9.

Hotel Iberia HOTEL €€

(☎927 24 76 34; www.iberiahotel.com; Calle de los Pintores 2; s/d €46/60; ❄) Located in an 18th-century former palace just off Plaza Mayor, this friendly and family-run 36-room hotel has public areas that look like an old-world museum piece, decorated with antique furnishings. The rooms are more subdued with parquet floors, cream walls and pale-grey tiled bathrooms.

Mesón El Asador TRADITIONAL EXTREMEÑO €€

(☎927 22 38 37; Calle de Moret 34; raciones €6-8, meals €20-30, set menus €15-26; ⏲Mon-Sat) Enter the dining room and you get the picture right away: one wall is covered with hung hams. It's often packed to the rafters with locals, not least because you won't taste better roast pork (or lamb) in town. Its bar also serves *bocadillos* (bread rolls with filling) and a wide range of *raciones*, while the *menú especial* (€26) is terrific value.

Information

Municipal tourist office (☎927 25 58 00; Calle de los Olmos 3; ⏲10am-2pm & 4.30-7.30pm or 5.30-8.30pm)

Getting There & Away

BUS Buses travel to Trujillo (€4.19, 40 minutes, eight daily) and Mérida (€5.35, 50 minutes, two to four daily).

TRAIN There are train services to Madrid (€25.80 to €38.50, four hours) and Mérida (from €4.30, one hour).

Mérida

POP 74,900

Once the biggest city in Roman Spain, Mérida is home to more ruins of that age than anywhere else in the country and is a wonderful spot to spend a few archaeologically inclined days.

Sights

Roman Remains RUINS

The **Teatro Romano** (Calle Alvarez S de Buruaga; admission €8; ⏲9.30am-7.30pm Jun-Sep, 9.30am-1.45pm & 4-6.15pm Oct-May), built around 15 BC to seat 6000 spectators and set in lovely gardens, has a dramatic and well-preserved two-tier backdrop of Corinthian stone columns; the stage's facade *(scaenae frons)* was inaugurated in AD 105. The theatre hosts performances during the Festival del Teatro Clásico in summer. The adjoining **Anfiteatro**, opened in 8 BC for gladiatorial contests, had a capacity of 14,000.

Los Columbarios (Calle del Ensanche s/n; admission €4; ⏲9.30am-1.45pm & 5-7.15pm Jun-Sep, 9.30am-1.45pm & 4-6.15pm Oct-May) is a Roman funeral site. A footpath connects it with the **Casa del Mitreo** (Calle Oviedo s/n; admission €4; ⏲9.30am-1.45pm & 5-7.15pm Jun-Sep, 9.30am-1.45pm & 4-6.15pm Oct-May), a 2nd-century Roman house with several intricate mosaics and a well-preserved fresco.

Don't miss the extraordinarily powerful spectacle of the **Puente Romano** over the Río Guadiana, which at 792m in length, with 60 granite arches, is one of the longest bridges built by the Romans.

The **Templo de Diana** (Calle de Sagasta) stood in the municipal forum, where the city government was based. The restored **Pórtico del Foro**, the municipal forum's portico, is just along the road.

Museo Nacional de Arte Romano MUSEUM
(http://museoarteromano.mcu.es; Calle de José Ramón Mélida; adult/EU seniors & students €3/free; ⌚9.30am-3.30pm & 5.30-8.30pm Tue-Sun Jul-Sep, shorter hr rest of yr) On no account miss this fabulous museum, which has a superb collection of statues, mosaics, frescos, coins and other Roman artefacts. Designed by the architect Rafael Moneo, the soaring brick structure makes a remarkable home for the collection.

Sleeping & Eating

TOP CHOICE **La Flor de al-Andalus** HOSTEL €
(☎924 31 33 56; www.laflordeal-andalus.es, in Spanish; Avenida de Extremadura 6; s/d €33/45; ❄📶) If only all *hostales* were this good. Opened in May 2010 and describing itself as a 'boutique *hostal*', La Flor de al-Andalus has beautifully decorated rooms in an Andalucian style. The buffet breakfast costs just €3.

TOP CHOICE **Hotel Adealba** HOTEL €€
(☎924 38 83 08; www.hoteladealba.com; Calle Romero Leal 18; d incl breakfast from €96; P⊖❄📶) Opened in 2009, this stunning hotel occupies a 19th-century town house close to the Templo de Diana and does so with a classy, contemporary look. The designer rooms have strong, contrasting colours and there's a pillow menu. Parking costs €12.

Convivium TAPAS & TRADITIONAL SPANISH €
(Calle de Sagasta 21; tortillinas €1, meals €15-20) Head straight for the pretty patio with tables set under a large lemon tree at this informal place where the speciality is *tortillinas* (mini-omelettes with fillings such as cod, salami, spinach, aubergines and prawns). Its *tortillina*, gazpacho and drink for €2.50 has to be Mérida's best deal.

Information

Municipal tourist office (☎924 33 07 22; www.merida.es, in Spanish; Paseo de José Álvarez Sáenz de Buruaga s/n; ⌚9.30am-2pm & 5-7.30pm)

Getting There & Away

BUS There are buses to Seville (€13.10, 2½ hours, five daily), Cáceres (€5.35, 50 minutes, two to four daily), Trujillo (€8.15, 1¼ hours, three daily) and Madrid (€22.15 to €27, four to five hours, eight daily).

TRAIN Trains run to Madrid (€31.80 to €36.30, 4½ to 6½ hours, five daily), Cáceres (from €4.30, one hour, six daily) and Seville (€14.10, four hours, one daily).

UNDERSTAND SPAIN

History

North Africans settled on the Iberian peninsula from around 8000 BC and, in the millennia that followed, Celtic tribes, Phoenician merchants, Greeks and Carthaginians trickled in. The Romans arrived in the 3rd century BC but by AD 410 they had been replaced by the Christian Visigoths. Three hundred years later, Muslim Berbers and Arabs from North Africa took over most of the peninsula.

The 8th century saw the beginning of the Christian Reconquista. By the mid-13th century, the Christians had taken most of the peninsula. In 1469, the kingdoms of Castile and Aragón were united by the marriage of Isabel, princess of Castile, and Fernando, heir to Aragón's throne. Known as the Catholic Monarchs, they united Spain and laid the foundations for the Spanish golden age. They also expelled and executed thousands of Jews and other non-Christians under the dark cloud of the Inquisition. In 1492, the Reconquista was completed when the last Muslim ruler of Granada surrendered to them.

That same year, Christopher Columbus stumbled on the Bahamas and claimed the Americas for Spain. This sparked a period of exploration and exploitation that yielded Spain enormous wealth, while destroying the ancient American empires. Spain's downfall began soon after. It would culminate with the disastrous Spanish-American War of 1898, which marked the end of the Spanish empire.

During the Spanish Civil War (1936–39) the Nationalists, led by General Francisco Franco, received heavy military support from Nazi Germany and fascist Italy, while the elected Republican government received support only from the Soviet Union and the International Brigades, made up of volunteer foreign leftists. By 1939 Franco had won and an estimated 350,000 Spaniards had died. Franco's 35-year dictatorship began with Spain isolated and crippled by recession. It wasn't until the 1950s and '60s that the country began to recover.

Franco died in 1975, having named Juan Carlos his successor. King Juan Carlos I is widely credited with having overseen Spain's transition from dictatorship to democracy. The first elections were held in 1977 and a new constitution was drafted in 1978. Spain joined the European Community in 1986.

The forward-thinking Spain of today is led by the Socialist Party of Spain (PSOE), under President José Luís Rodríguez Zapatero. Zapatero was elected in 2004, just days after the 11 March terrorist attacks in Madrid. He made waves immediately by withdrawing Spanish troops from Iraq. Under Zapatero, gay marriage was legalised and a massive amnesty legalised the presence of hundreds of thousands of illegal immigrants. Zapatero's attempts to reach a peace deal with ETA Basque terrorists, however, ended in failure.

Shortly after his re-election in March 2008, Zapatero was confronted with an economy that came juddering to a halt after years of enviable growth. Unemployment exploded from 8.3% to 11.3% in the 12 months to October 2008 and now sits stubbornly close to 20%. As the recession began to bite, Zapatero pushed through a law on 'historic memory' that provoked sharp debate. Aimed at investigating the crimes and executions of the Franco years, it represented the first official attempt to deal with the country's dictatorial past.

People

Spain has a population of 46 million, descended from the many peoples who have settled here over the millennia, among them Iberians, Celts, Romans, Jews, Visigoths, Berbers, Arabs and 20th-century immigrants from across the globe. Each region proudly preserves its own unique culture, and some – Catalonia and the Basque Country in particular – display a fiercely independent spirit. Spain's immigrant population has grown from 2% to 12% of the population in the last 15 years.

Only about 20% of Spaniards are regular churchgoers, but Catholicism is deeply ingrained in the culture. As the writer Unamuno said, 'Here in Spain we are all Catholics, even the atheists'. The Church, which was a strong supporter of Franco's rule, retains a powerful public voice in national debates. The Socialist government's raft of social reforms set the government at odds with conservative Spanish clerics, and drew tens of thousands of Catholic protesters onto the streets.

Food & Drink

Reset your stomach's clock in Spain unless you want to eat alone, with other tourists or, in some cases, not at all.

Most Spaniards start the day with a light *desayuno* (breakfast), perhaps coffee with a *tostada* (piece of toast) or *pastel/bollo* (pastry), although they might stop in a bar later for a mid-morning *bocadillo* (baguette). *La comida* (lunch) is usually the main meal of the day, eaten between about 2pm and 4pm. The *cena* (evening meal) is usually lighter and most locals won't sit down for it before 9pm. The further south you go, the later start times tend to be – anything from 10pm to midnight!

Throughout this chapter, each place to eat is accompanied by one of the following symbols (the price relates to a three-course meal per person with house wine):

€€€ more than €50

€€ €20 to €50

€ less than €20

Staples & Specialities

The variety in Spanish cuisines is quite extraordinary and each region has its own styles and specialities. One of the most characteristic dishes, from the Valencia region, is paella – rice, seafood, the odd vegetable and often chicken or meat, all simmered together and traditionally coloured yellow with saffron.

Many would argue that tapas are Spain's greatest culinary gift to the world, not least because the possibilities are endless: anything can be a tapa. For tapas, the cities of Andalucía are usually (but not always) bastions of tradition, while the undoubted king of tapas destinations is San Sebastián, where they call tapas '*pintxos*'. It all comes together in Madrid (see the boxed text, p1132).

Drinks

Vino (wine) comes *blanco* (white), *tinto* (red) or *rosado* (rosé). Exciting wine regions include Penedès, Priorat, Ribera del Duero and La Rioja. There are also many regional specialities, such as *jerez* (sherry) in Jerez de la Frontera and *cava* (a sparkling wine) in Catalonia. Sangria, a sweet punch made of red wine, fruit and spirits, is a summer drink and especially popular with tourists. *Tinto*

JAMÓN – A PRIMER

Spanish *jamón* (ham) is, unlike Italian prosciutto, bold, deep red and well marbled with buttery fat. Like wine and olive oil, Spanish *jamón* is subject to a strict series of classifications. *Jamón serrano* refers to *jamón* made from white-coated pigs introduced to Spain in the 1950s. Once salted and semidried by the cold, dry winds of the Spanish sierra, most now go through a similar process of curing and drying in a climate-controlled shed for around a year. *Jamón serrano* accounts for approximately 90% of cured ham in Spain.

Jamón ibérico – more expensive and generally regarded as the elite of Spanish hams – comes from a black-coated pig indigenous to the Iberian peninsula and descended from the wild boar. If the pig gains at least 50% of its body weight during the acorn-eating season, it can be classified as *jamón ibérico de bellota,* the most sought-after designation.

de verano, a kind of wine shandy, is a summer alternative.

Agua del grifo (tap water) is usually safe to drink.

Where to Eat & Drink

Bars and cafes are open all day (see p1192 for detailed hours), serving coffees, pastries, *bocadillos* and usually tapas (which generally cost from €1.50 to €4). You can also order *raciones,* a large-sized serving of these snacks.

Spaniards like to eat out, and restaurants (which come in different styles and with different names such as *taberna, mesón, tasca* and *restaurante*) abound even in small towns. At lunchtime, most places offer a *menú del día* – a fixed-price lunch menu and the traveller's best friend. For €8 to €12 you typically get three courses, bread and a drink. The *plato combinado* (combined plate) is a cousin of the *menú* and usually includes a meat dish with some vegetables.

As of 1 January 2011, all bars and restaurants are smoke-free.

Arts

Cinema

Modern Spanish cinema's best-known director is Pedro Almodóvar, whose humorous, cutting-edge films are often set amid the great explosion of drugs and creativity that occurred in Madrid in the 1980s. His *Todo Sobre Mi Madre* (All About My Mother; 1999) and *Habla Con Ella* (Talk to Her; 2002) are both Oscar winners, while *Volver* (2006) is his most acclaimed recent work.

Alejandro Amenábar, the young Chilean-born director of *Abre los Ojos* (Open Your Eyes; 1997), *The Others* (2001) and the Oscar-winning *Mar Adentro* (The Sea Inside; 2004), is Almodóvar's main competition for Spain's 'best director' title. The latter film's star, Javier Bardem, won the Oscar for Best Supporting Actor in the Coen brothers' disturbing *No Country for Old Men* in 2008.

Woody Allen set his *Vicky Cristina Barcelona* (2008), a light romantic comedy, largely in Barcelona; the Madrid-born actress Penélope Cruz won an Oscar for Best Supporting Actress for her role in the film.

Painting

The giants of Spain's golden age (around 1550–1650) were Toledo-based El Greco (originally from Crete) and Diego Velázquez, considered Spain's best painter by greats such as Picasso and Dalí. El Greco and Velázquez are well represented in Madrid's Museo del Prado, as is the genius of the 18th and 19th centuries, Francisco Goya.

Catalonia was the powerhouse of early-20th-century Spanish art, claiming the hugely prolific Pablo Picasso (although born in Málaga, Andalucía), the colourful symbolist Joan Miró and surrealist Salvador Dalí. To get inside the latter's world, head for Figueres or the Castell de Púbol. The two major museums dedicated to Picasso's work are the Museu Picasso in Barcelona and the Museo Picasso Málaga, while his signature *Guernica* and other works are found in Madrid's Centro de Arte Reina Sofía. The Reina Sofía also has works by Miró, as does the Fundació Joan Miró.

Important artists of the late 20th century include the Basque sculptor Eduardo Chillida; his Museu Chillida Leku is south of San Sebastián.

Flamenco

Most musical historians speculate that flamenco probably dates back to a fusion of songs brought to Spain by the *gitanos*

(Roma people or gypsies), with music and verses from North Africa crossing into medieval Muslim Andalucía. Flamenco as we now know it first took recognisable form in the 18th and early 19th centuries among *gitanos* in western Andalucía. Suitably, for a place considered the cradle of the genre, the Seville–Jerez de la Frontera–Cádiz axis is still considered the flamenco heartland and it's here, purists believe, that you must go for the most authentic flamenco experience.

Environment

Spain faces some of the most pressing environmental issues of our time. Drought, massive overdevelopment of its coastline, overexploitation of scarce water resources by tourist projects and intensive agriculture, and spiralling emissions of greenhouse gases are all major concerns. It's a slightly more nuanced picture than first appears – Spain is a leading player in the wind-power industry, it has locked away around 40,000 sq km of protected areas, including 14 national parks, and its system of public transport is outstanding. But the apparent absence of any meaningful political will to tackle these issues is storing up problems for future generations.

SURVIVAL GUIDE

Directory A-Z

Accommodation

In this chapter, budget options include everything from dorm-style youth hostels to family-style *pensiones* and slightly better-heeled *hostales*. At the upper end of this category you'll find rooms with air-con and private bathrooms. Midrange *hostales* and hotels are more comfortable and most offer standard hotel services.

Throughout this chapter, each place to stay is accompanied by one of the following symbols (the price relates to a double room with private bathroom):

€€€ more than €120 (€200 for Madrid and Barcelona)

€€ €60 to €120 (€70 to €200 for Madrid and Barcelona)

€ less than €60 (€70 for Madrid and Barcelona)

The price of any type of accommodation varies with the season, and accommodation prices listed in this chapter are a guide only. As a rule we've given high-season prices.

CAMPING

Spain has around 1000 officially graded *campings* (camping grounds) and they vary greatly in service, cleanliness and style. Camping grounds usually charge per person, per tent and per vehicle – typically €5 to €9 for each. Many camping grounds close from around October to Easter.

Useful websites include the following:

Campings Online (www.campingsonline.com/espana) Booking service.

Campinguía (www.campinguia.com) Contains comments (mostly in Spanish) and links.

Guía Camping (www.guiacampingfecc.com) Online version of the annual *Guía Camping* (€13.60), which is available in bookshops around the country.

HOTELS, HOSTALES & PENSIONES

Most options fall into the categories of hotels (one to five stars, full amenities), *hostales* (high-end guest houses with private

FLAMENCO – THE ESSENTIAL ELEMENTS

A flamenco singer is known as a *cantaor* (male) or *cantaora* (female); a dancer is a *bailaor/a*. Most of the songs and dances are performed to a blood-rush of guitar from the *tocaor/a* (flamenco guitarist). Percussion is provided by tapping feet, clapping hands and sometimes castanets. Flamenco *coplas* (songs) come in many different types, from the anguished *soleá* or the intensely despairing *siguiriya* to the livelier *alegría* or the upbeat *bulería*. The first flamenco was *cante jondo* (deep song), an anguished instrument of expression for a group on the margins of society. *Jondura* (depth) is still the essence of pure flamenco.

The traditional flamenco costume – shawl, fan and long, frilly *bata de cola* (tail gown) for women, flat Cordoban hats and tight black trousers for men – dates from Andalucian fashions in the late 19th century.

bathroom; one to three stars) or *pensiones* (guest houses, usually with shared bathroom; one to three stars).

YOUTH HOSTELS

Albergues juveniles (youth hostels) are cheap places to stay, especially for lone travellers. Expect to pay from €15 to €28 per night, depending on location, age and season. Spain's Hostelling International (HI) organisation, **Red Española de Albergues Juveniles** (REAJ; www.reaj.com), has around 250 youth hostels throughout Spain. Official hostels require HI membership (you can buy a membership card at virtually all hostels) and many have curfews.

Activities

HIKING

Spain is a trekker's paradise. Read about some of the best treks in the country in Lonely Planet's *Walking in Spain*. Useful for hiking, especially in the Pyrenees, are maps by Editorial Alpina. Buy them at bookshops, sports shops and sometimes at petrol stations near hiking areas.

Throughout Spain, you'll come across GR (Grandes Recorridos, or long distance) trails. These are indicated with red-and-white markers. The Camino de Santiago (St James' Way, with several branches) is perhaps Spain's best-known long-distance walk.

SKIING

Skiing is cheaper but less varied than in much of the rest of Europe. The season runs from December to mid-April. The best resorts are in the Pyrenees, especially in northwest Catalonia and Aragón. The Sierra Nevada in Andalucía offers the most southerly skiing in Western Europe.

SURFING, WINDSURFING & KITESURFING

The Basque Country has good surf spots, including San Sebastián, Zarautz and the legendary left at Mundaka. Tarifa, with its long beaches and ceaseless wind, is generally considered to be the windsurfing capital of Europe. It's also a top spot for kitesurfing.

Business Hours

Reviews in this guidebook only list business hours if they differ from the following standards:

Banks 8.30am-2pm Mon-Fri; some also open 4-7pm Thu and 9am-1pm Sat

Central post offices 8.30am-9.30pm Mon-Fri, 8.30am-2pm Sat

Nightclubs midnight or 1am to 5am or 6am

Restaurants lunch 1-4pm, dinner 8.30pm-midnight or later

Shops 10am-2pm & 4.30-7.30pm or 5-8pm; big supermarkets and department stores generally open 10am-10pm Mon-Sat

Holidays

National holidays are as follows:

Año Nuevo (New Year's Day) 1 January

Viernes Santo (Good Friday) March/April

Fiesta del Trabajo (Labour Day) 1 May

La Asunción (Feast of the Assumption) 15 August

Fiesta Nacional de España (National Day) 12 October

La Inmaculada Concepción (Feast of the Immaculate Conception) 8 December

Navidad (Christmas) 25 December

Regional governments set five holidays and local councils two more. Common dates include the following:

Epifanía (Epiphany) or **Día de los Reyes Magos (Three Kings' Day)** 6 January

Día de San José (St Joseph's Day) 19 March

Jueves Santo (Good Thursday) March/April. Not observed in Catalonia and Valencia.

Corpus Christi The Thursday after the eighth Sunday after Easter Sunday.

Día de San Juan Bautista (Feast of St John the Baptist) 24 June

Día de Santiago Apóstol (Feast of St James the Apostle) 25 July

Día de Todos los Santos (All Saints Day) 1 November

Día de la Constitución (Constitution Day) 6 December

Internet Access

Wi-fi is increasingly available at most hotels and in some cafes, restaurants and airports; it's generally (but not always) free.

Good internet cafes that last the distance are increasingly hard to find; ask at the local tourist office. Prices per hour range from €1.50 to €3.

Language Courses

Among the more popular places to learn Spanish are Barcelona, Granada, Madrid, Salamanca and Seville.

The **Escuela Oficial de Idiomas** (EOI; www.eeooiinet.com, in Spanish) is a nationwide language institution where you can learn Spanish and other local languages. On the website's opening page, hit 'Centros' under 'Comunidad' and then 'Centros en la Red' to get to a list of schools.

Maps

Some of the best maps for travellers are by Michelin, which produces the 1:1,000,000 *Spain Portugal* map and six 1:400,000 regional maps covering the whole country. Also good are the GeoCenter maps published by Germany's RV Verlag.

Money

Cajeros automáticos (ATMs) are everywhere. Credit and debit cards can be used to pay for most purchases. You'll often be asked to show your passport or some other form of identification.

Most banks and exchange offices will exchange travellers cheques in major foreign currencies. Banks offer the best rates; take your passport.

Menu prices include a service charge, but most people also leave some small change as a tip.

Safe Travel

Most visitors to Spain never feel remotely threatened, but a sufficient number have unpleasant experiences to warrant an alert. The main thing to be wary of is petty theft (which may, of course, not seem so petty if your passport, cash, travellers cheques, credit card and camera go missing).

Stay alert and you can avoid most thievery techniques. Barcelona, Madrid and Seville are the worst offenders, as are popular beaches in summer (never leave belongings unattended).

Telephone

Blue public payphones are common and fairly easy to use. They accept coins, phonecards and, in some cases, credit cards. Phonecards come in €6 and €12 denominations and are sold at post offices as well as tobacconists.

International reverse-charge (collect) calls are simple to make: dial ☎900 99 followed by the appropriate code. For example: ☎900 99 00 61 for Australia, ☎900 99 00 44 for the UK, ☎900 99 00 11 (AT&T) for the USA etc.

All Spanish mobile-phone companies (Telefónica's MoviStar, Orange and Vodafone) offer *prepagado* (prepaid) accounts for mobiles. The SIM card costs from €50, which includes some prepaid phone time.

PHONE CODES

All phone numbers in Spain are nine digits and you just dial that nine-digit number. Numbers starting with 900 are national toll-free numbers, while those starting 901 to 905 come with varying costs; most can only be dialled from within Spain.

English-speaking international operator ☎1008 (for calls within Europe) or ☎1005 (rest of the world)

International access code ☎00

Spain country code ☎34

Tourist Information

Most towns and large villages of any interest have a helpful *oficina de turismo* (tourist office), where you can get maps and brochures. **Turespaña** (www.spain.info, www.tourspain.es), the country's national tourism body, presents a variety of general information and links on the entire country in its web pages.

Visas

Spain is a member country of the Schengen Agreement. Citizens of the 27 EU member states and Switzerland can travel to Spain with their national identity card alone. If such countries do not issue ID cards – as in the UK – travellers must carry a full valid passport. Citizens of the USA, Canada, Australia and New Zealand need a valid passport, but do not need a visa for stays of less than three months.

Getting There & Away

Entering the Country

Immigration and customs checks usually involve a minimum of fuss, although there are exceptions. Your vehicle could be searched on arrival from Morocco; they're looking for controlled substances. Expect long delays at these borders, especially in summer.

The tiny principality of Andorra is not in the EU, so border controls (and rigorous customs checks for contraband) remain in place.

Air

Flights from all over Europe, including numerous budget airlines, serve main Spanish airports. All of Spain's airports share the user-friendly website and flight-information telephone number of **Aena** (902 404 704; www.aena.es), the national airports authority. For more information on each airport on Aena's website, choose English and click on the drop-down menu of airports. Each airport's page has details on practical information (such as parking and public transport) and a full list of (and links to) airlines using that airport.

Madrid's Aeropuerto de Barajas is Spain's busiest (and Europe's fourth-busiest) airport. Other major airports include Barcelona's Aeroport del Prat (BCN) and the airports of Palma de Mallorca (PMI), Málaga (AGP), Alicante (ALC), Girona (GRO), Valencia (VLC), Ibiza (IBZ), Seville (SVQ), Bilbao (BIO) and Zaragoza (ZAZ).

For information on the main budget airlines operating across Europe, see p1322.

Land

Spain shares land borders with France, Portugal and Andorra.

Apart from shorter cross-border services, **Eurolines** (www.eurolines.com) is the main operator of international bus services to Spain from most of Western Europe and Morocco.

ANDORRA

Regular buses connect Andorra with Barcelona (including winter ski buses and direct services to the airport) and other destinations in Spain (including Madrid) and France.

FRANCE

Bus

Eurolines (www.eurolines.fr) heads to Spain from Paris and more than 20 other French cities and towns. It connects with Madrid (17¾ hours), Barcelona (14¾ hours) and many other destinations.

Train

There are plans for a high-speed rail link between Madrid and Paris by 2012. In the meantime, the major cross-border services are as follows:

Paris-Austerlitz–Madrid-Chamartín (chair/sleeper class €166/194, 13½ hours, one daily) *Trenhotel Francisco de Goya* runs via Orléans, Blois, Poitiers, Vitoria, Burgos and Valladolid.

Paris-Austerlitz–Barcelona Estacio de Franca (sleeper class €188, 12 hours, one daily) *Trenhotel Joan Miró* runs via Orléans, Limoges, Figueres and Girona.

Montpellier–Valencia (from €82, 7¾ to 9¾ hours, twice daily) Talgo service along the Mediterranean coast via Girona, Barcelona and Tarragona.

PORTUGAL

Bus

Avanza (in Spain & Portugal 902 02 09 99; www.avanzabus.com) runs two daily buses between Lisbon and Madrid (€55.25, 7½ to nine hours). Other bus services run north via Porto to Tui, Santiago de Compostela and A Coruña in Galicia, while local buses cross the border from towns such as Huelva in Andalucía, Badajoz in Extremadura and Ourense in Galicia.

Train

From Portugal, the main line runs from Lisbon across Extremadura to Madrid.

Lisbon–Madrid (chair/sleeper class €58/83, 10½ hours, one daily)

Lisbon–Irún (chair/sleeper class €68/96, 14½ hours, one daily)

Sea

Ferries run to mainland Spain regularly from the Canary Islands, Italy, North Africa (Algeria, Morocco and the Spanish enclaves of Ceuta and Melilla) and the UK. Most services are run by the Spanish national ferry company, **Acciona Trasmediterránea** (902 45 46 45; www.trasmediterranea.es). You can take vehicles on the following routes.

ALGERIA

Almería–Ghazaouet (eight hours, four weekly)

Almería–Oran (eight hours, two weekly)

ITALY

Barcelona–Genoa (18 hours, three weekly)

Barcelona–Civitavecchia (20½ hours, six to seven weekly)

Barcelona–Livorno (Tuscany) (19½ hours, three weekly)

Barcelona–Porto Torres (Sardinia) (12 hours, one daily)

MOROCCO

In addition to the following, there are also ferries to the Spanish enclaves of Melilla (from Almería and Málaga) and Ceuta (from Algeciras).

Tangier–Algeciras (70 minutes, up to eight daily)

Tangier–Barcelona (24 hours, weekly)

Tangier–Tarifa (35 minutes, up to eight daily)

Nador–Almería (five to eight hours, up to three daily)

UK

From mid-March to mid-November, **Brittany Ferries** (0871 244 0744; www.brittany-ferries.co.uk) runs the following services.

Plymouth–Santander (24 to 35 hours, weekly)

Portsmouth–Santander (24 to 35 hours, three weekly)

Getting Around

Students and seniors are eligible for discounts of 30% to 50% on most transport.

Air

Domestic Spanish routes are operated by the following:

Air Berlin (www.airberlin.com)

Air Europa (www.aireuropa.com)

easyJet (www.easyjet.com)

Iberia (www.iberia.es)

Ryanair (www.ryanair.com)

Spanair (www.spanair.com)

Vueling (www.vueling.com)

Boat

Regular ferries connect the Spanish mainland with the Balearic Islands. For more details see p1169.

Bus

Spain's bus network is operated by countless independent companies and reaches into the most remote towns and villages. Many towns and cities have one main bus station, where most buses arrive and depart. The best-known national company, under whose umbrella many smaller companies operate, is **Alsa** (902 42 22 42; www.alsa.es).

It is not necessary, and often not possible, to make advance reservations for local bus journeys. It is, however, a good idea to turn up at least 30 minutes before the bus leaves to guarantee a seat. For longer trips, you can and should buy your ticket in advance.

Car & Motorcycle

All EU member states' driving licences are recognised. Other foreign licences should be accompanied by an International Driving Permit. These are available from automobile clubs in your country and valid for 12 months.

Spain's roads vary enormously but are generally good. Fastest are the *autopistas;* on some, you have to pay hefty tolls. Minor routes can be slow going but are usually more scenic. Trying to find a parking spot in larger towns and cities can be a nightmare. *Grúas* (tow trucks) can and will tow your car. The cost of bailing out a car can be €200 or more.

Spanish cities do not have US-style parking meters at every spot. Instead, if you park in a blue or green zone, you obtain a ticket from a street-side meter, which may be a block away. Display the ticket on the dash.

Petrol stations are easy to find along highways and *autopistas*.

Spain's automobile association is **Real Automóvil Club de España** (RACE; 902 404 545; www.race.es, in Spanish).

HIRE

To rent a car in Spain you have to have a licence, be aged 21 or over and have a credit or debit card. Rates vary widely from place to place. The best deals tend to be in major tourist areas, including airports. Prices are especially competitive in the Balearic Islands. Expect a compact car to cost around €30 and up per day.

ROAD RULES

Drive on the right

Blood-alcohol limit 0.05%

Legal driving age (car) 18

Legal driving age (motorcycle and scooter) 16 (80cc and over) or 14 (50cc and under). A licence is required.

Motorcyclists Must use headlights at all times and wear a helmet if riding a bike of 125cc or more.

Speed limits In built-up areas, 50km/h (and in some cases, such as inner-city Barcelona, 30km/h), which increases to 100km/h on major roads and up to 120km/h on *autovías* and *autopistas* (toll-free and tolled dual-lane highways, respectively).

Train

Renfe (☎902 240 202; www.renfe.es) is the national railway company. Trains are mostly modern and comfortable, and late arrivals are the exception. The high-speed network is in constant expansion.

You can buy tickets and make reservations online, at stations, at travel agencies displaying the Renfe logo and in Renfe offices in many city centres.

Rail passes are valid for all long-distance Renfe trains, but InterRail users have to pay supplements on Talgo, InterCity and AVE trains. All pass holders making reservations pay a small fee.

Among Spain's numerous types of trains are the following:

Alaris, Altaria, Alvia, Arco, Avant Long-distance intermediate-speed services.

Euromed Similar to AVE trains; it connects Barcelona with Valencia and Alicante.

Talgo, Intercity Slower long-distance trains.

Tren de Alta Velocidad Española (AVE) High-speed trains that link Madrid with Barcelona, Burgos, Córdoba, Cuenca, Huesca, Lerida, Málaga, Seville, Valencia, Valladolid and Zaragoza. There is also a Barcelona–Seville service. In coming years Madrid–Cádiz and Madrid–Bilbao trains should come on line.

Trenhotel Overnight trains with sleeper berths.

CLASSES & COSTS

All long-distance trains have 2nd and 1st classes, known as *turista* and *preferente* respectively. The latter is 20% to 40% more expensive.

Fares vary enormously depending on the service (faster trains cost considerably more) and, in the case of some high-speed services such as the AVE, on the time and day of travel.

Buying a return ticket often gives you a 10% to 20% discount on the fare. Students and people up to 25 years of age with a Euro<26 Card (Carnet Joven in Spain) are entitled to 20% to 25% off most ticket prices.

Eurail and InterRail passes that include Spain are available.

Sweden

Includes »

Best Places to Eat

» Chokladkoppen, Stockholm (p1205)

» Hötorgshallen, Stockholm (p1205)

» Vurma, Stockholm (p1208)

Best Places to Stay

» STF Vandrarhem Gärdet, Stockholm (p1204)

» Hotel Flora, Göteborg (p1219)

» STF Vandrarhem Malmö City (p1215)

Why Go?

As progressive and civilised as it may be, Sweden is a wild place. Its scenery ranges from barren moonscapes and impenetrable forests in the far north to sunny beaches and lush farmland further south. Its short summers and long winters mean that people cling to every last speck of sunshine on a late August evening – crayfish parties on seaside decks can stretch into the wee hours. In winter locals rely on candlelight and *glögg* to warm their spirits. But lovers of the outdoors will thrive here in any season: winter sees skiing and dog-sledding while the warmer months invite long hikes, swimming and sunbathing, canoeing, cycling, you name it – if it's fun and can be done outdoors, you'll find it here. For less rugged types, there's always shopping and nightclub hopping. And in most Swedish cities you'll find top-notch museums dedicated to local and national history, art and culture.

When to Go

Stockholm

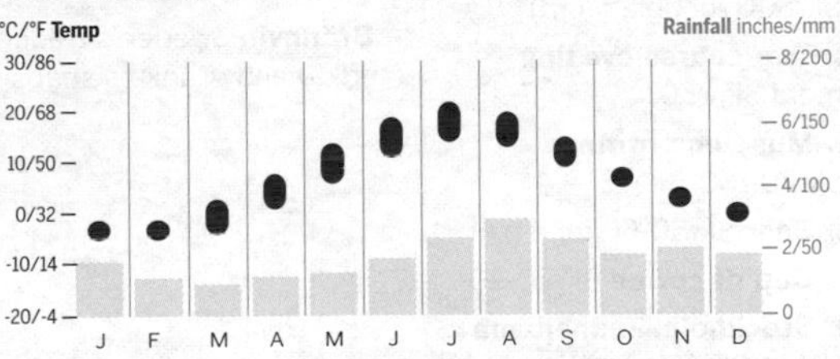

Jun–Aug Sweden's summers are short but intense, and hotel prices drop.

Sep & Oct Nothing's open, but the countryside is stunning in autumn.

Dec–Feb Winter sports and the Northern Lights keep Norrland towns buzzing.

AT A GLANCE

Currency *krona* (Skr)

Language Swedish, plus minority languages Romani, Finnish, Yiddish, Meänkieli (Finnish dialects) and Sami (three languages)

Money ATMs found all over

Visas Schengen rules apply; seep1319

Fast Facts

» **Area** 449,964 sq km

» **Capital** Stockholm

» **Country code** ☎46

» **Emergency** ☎112

Exchange Rates

Australia	A$1	Skr 6.59
Canada	C$1	Skr 6.32
euro zone	€1	Skr 9.03
Japan	¥100	Skr 7.75
New Zealand	NZ$1	Skr 5.10
UK	UK£1	Skr 10.15
USA	US$1	Skr 6.19

Set Your Budget

» **Budget hotel room** from Skr800 (double room)

» **Two-course evening meal** Skr250

» **Museum entrance** Skr70-100

» **Beer** Skr50-60 for a pint

» **Cup of coffee** Skr20-30

» **Stockholm Tunnelbana ticket** Skr30 (single-trip)

Resources

» See internet resources, p1226

Connections

Getting to the rest of Scandinavia and further into Europe from Sweden is easy. From Stockholm there are train and bus connections to London or Berlin as well as to Denmark, Finland and Norway. Ferries are another option, with frequent connections between many Swedish ports and the rest of Europe. Airports in Stockholm and Göteborg connect Sweden with the rest of the world.

ITINERARIES

One Week

Spend three days exploring Stockholm and Uppsala, and two days in and around Göteborg before continuing south to the dynamic cities of Malmö and Lund. Alternatively, explore the Stockholm region more thoroughly, including a couple of days in the archipelago, before heading to Uppsala.

Two Weeks

As above, but include a trip northwards to Östersund, then further up toward Kiruna to check out the world-famous Ice Hotel. Outdoorsy types will find plenty to do here in winter, but in summer you may opt to cycle around Gotland instead.

Essential Food & Drink

» **Köttbullar och potatis** Meatballs and mashed potatoes, served with *lingonsylt* (lingonberry jam)

» **Gravlax** Cured salmon

» **Sill and strömming** Herring, eaten smoked, fried or pickled and often accompanied by capers, mustard and onion; beware the pungent *surströmming* (fermented Baltic herring)

» **Toast skagen** Toast with bleak roe, crème fraiche and chopped red onion

» **Brännvin** Sweden's trademark spirit, also called aquavit (vodka) and drunk as *snaps*

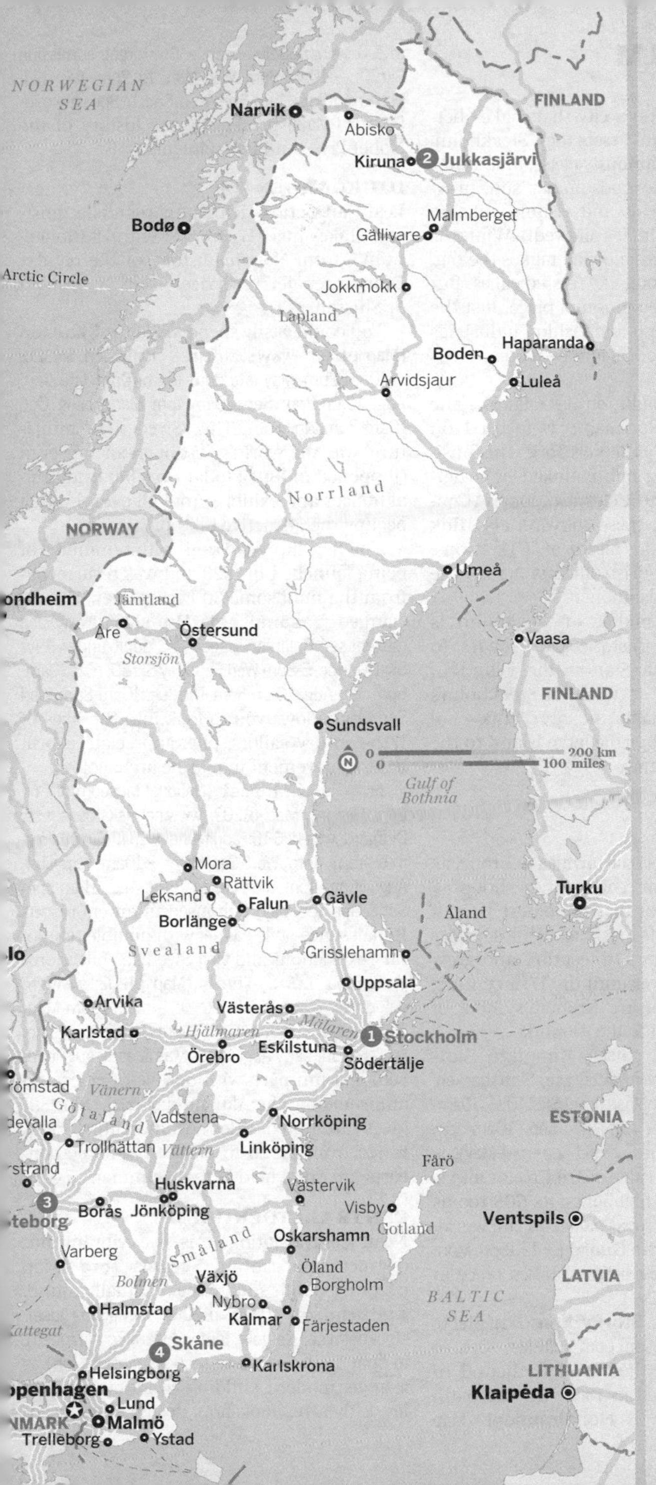

Sweden Highlights

1. Touring the urban waterways, exploring top-notch museums and wandering the labyrinthine Old Town of **Stockholm** (p1200)
2. Hiking through wild landscapes, seeing herds of reindeer, absorbing Sami culture and sleeping in the world-famous Ice Hotel at **Jukkasjärvi** (p1223) in Lappland
3. Digging into the art, fashion and originality that make Sweden's 'second city' of **Göteborg** (p1218) first-rate
4. Admiring the picturesque farmsteads and cosmopolitan cities that dot the green fields of **Skåne** (p1214) in southern Sweden

STOCKHOLM

08 / POP 802,600

It's hard to imagine a city that makes better use of its natural assets than Stockholm. The capital city's famously clean, blue water sparkles under the midsummer sun, practically begging locals and visitors alike to take a dip (go ahead, it's allowed!). Winter is equally beautiful, as snowfall makes the big, square buildings look like frosted cakes. But the city is far from a museum piece. Just the opposite – its design and fashion industries race to be cutting edge, and its food scene is intensely hip.

Stockholm is built on 14 islands. The modern centre (Norrmalm) is focused on the square known as Sergels Torg. This business and shopping hub is linked by a network of subways to Centralstationen (Central train station); these subways also link with the *tunnelbana* (metro, or 'T') stations. The large, busy tourist office is across the street from Centralstationen.

Smack in the middle of Stockholm is Gamla Stan, the historic Old Town. To the east of Gamla Stan is the island of Djurgården, home to many of Stockholm's museums. Södermalm, the city's funky, bohemian area, inhabits the large island to the south of Gamla Stan.

Sights

GAMLA STAN

Once you get over the armies of tourists wielding ice-cream cones and shopping bags, you'll discover that the oldest part of Stockholm is also its most beautiful. The city emerged here in the 13th century and grew with Sweden's power until the 17th century, when the castle of Tre Kronor, symbol of that power, burned to the ground.

The 'new' royal palace, **Kungliga Slottet** (Map p1206; www.royalcourt.se; Slottsbacken; admission Skr100, combined ticket Skr140; 10am-4pm mid-late May & early–mid-Sep, 10am-5pm Jun-Aug, noon-3pm Tue-Sun mid-Sep–mid-May), is constructed on the ruins of Tre Kronor and is one of Stockholm's highlights. Its 608 rooms make it the largest royal palace in the world. The **Changing of the Guard** (12.15pm Mon-Sat, 1.15pm Sun & public holidays) takes place in the outer courtyard.

Near the palace, **Storkyrkan** (Map p1206; admission Skr25; 9am-6pm mid-May–Oct, to 4pm rest of year) is the Royal Cathedral of Sweden, consecrated in 1306. On the main square, Stortorget, is **Nobelmuseet** (Map p1206; www.nobelmuseet.se; Stortorget; admission Skr70; 10am-5pm Wed-Mon, to 8pm Tue mid-May–mid-Sep, 11am-5pm Wed-Sun, to 8pm Tue mid-Sep–mid-May), presenting the history of the Nobel Prize and its recipients.

DJURGÅRDEN

Leafy, attraction-rich Djurgården is a must-see. Take bus 47 from Centralstationen, tram 7 from Norrmalmstorg, or the regular Djurgården ferry services from Nybroplan or Slussen.

You could easily spend all day at **Skansen** (Map p1202; www.skansen.se; admission Skr120; 10am-8pm May-late Jun, 10am-10pm late Jun-Aug, 10am-8pm Sep, 10am-4pm Mar, Apr & Oct, 10am-3pm Nov-Feb). This 'Sweden in miniature' was the world's first open-air museum (it opened in 1891); today over 150 traditional houses and exhibits from all over Sweden occupy the attractive hilltop.

The flagship *Vasa* sank within minutes of being launched in 1628 and was resurrected from the mud some 300 years later. The acclaimed **Vasamuseet** (Map p1202; www.vasamuseet.se; Galärvarvsvägen 14; adult/under 19yr Skr110/free, 5-8pm Wed Sep-May Skr80; 8.30am-6pm Jun-Aug, 10am-5pm Thu-Tue, 10am-8pm Wed Sep-May) allows you to look into the lives of 17th-century sailors, plus appreciate a brilliant achievement in marine archaeology.

Nordiska Museet (National Museum of Cultural History; Map p1202; www.nordiskamuseet.se; Djurgårdsvägen 6-16; adult/under 19yr Skr80/free, free from 4pm Wed Sep-May; 10am-5pm Jun-Aug, 10am-4pm Mon-Fri, to 8pm Wed, 11am-5pm Sat & Sun Sep-May) is housed in an enormous Renaissance-style castle, with notable temporary exhibitions and vast Swedish collections.

Gröna Lund Tivoli (Map p1202; www.gronalund.com; admission Skr90; noon-10pm Mon-Sat, to 8pm Sun Jun, 11am-10pm Sun-Thu, to 11pm Fri & Sat Jul-early Aug, varies May & early Aug–mid-Sep) is a fun park with dozens of rides and amusements; the Åkband day pass (Skr289) gives unlimited rides, or individual rides range from Skr20 to Skr60. Big-name concerts are often held here in summer.

CENTRAL STOCKHOLM

Near Centralstationen is the vibrant but distinctly unbeautiful **Sergels Torg** (Map p1206), a public square that's actually round. **Kulturhuset** (Map p1206; www.kulturhuset.stockholm.se; Sergels Torg; 11am-7pm Mon-Fri, to 5pm Sat & Sun, some sections closed Mon) is a huge, modern building containing galleries, a theatre, bookshop, design store, reading room, cafes, a comics library and a craft room for teens.

Not far away is the beloved public park **Kungsträdgården** (Map p1206), where locals gather in all weather. There's an outdoor stage, winter ice-skating rink, cafes and kiosks.

Sweden's largest art museum, the excellent **Nationalmuseum** (Map p1206; www.nationalmuseum.se; Södra Blasieholmshamnen; adult/under 19yr Skr120/free; ⌚11am-5pm Wed-Sun, to 8pm Tue Jun-Aug, 11am-5pm Wed-Sun, to 8pm Tue & Thu Sep-May) houses the national collection of painting, sculpture, drawings, decorative arts and graphics from the Middle Ages to the present.

The main national historical collection is at the enthralling **Historiska Museet** (Museum of National Antiquities; Map p1202; www.historiska.se; Narvavägen 13; adult/under 19yr Skr70/free; ⌚11am-5pm, 11am-8pm Thu Oct-Apr, 10am-5pm May-Sep). Displays cover prehistoric, Viking and medieval archaeology and culture, and the incredible Gold Room's rare treasures include a seven-ringed gold collar.

OTHER AREAS

Across the bridge in **Skeppsholmen** (Map p1206), by the Nationalmuseum, are more museums, including the sleek, impressive **Moderna Museet** (Map p1206; www.modernamuseet.se; Exercisplan 4; adult/under 19yr Skr100/free; ⌚10am-8pm Tue, 10am-6pm Wed-Sun), which boasts a world-class collection of modern art, sculpture, photography and installations, temporary exhibitions and an outdoor sculpture garden. The adjoining **Arkitekturmuseet** (Museum of Architecture; Map p1206; www.arkitekturmuseet.se; Exercisplan 4; adult/under 19yr Skr50/free, 4-6pm Fri free; ⌚10am-8pm Tue, 10am-6pm Wed-Sun) has a permanent exhibition spanning 1000 years of Swedish architecture.

The main visitor sight in **Kungsholmen** (Map p1206) is the landmark **Stadshuset** (City Hall; Map p1206; Hantverkargatan 1; admission by tour only Skr80; tours in English ⌚10am, 11am, noon, 2pm, 3pm & 4pm Jun-Aug, 10am, noon & 2pm rest of year), resembling a large church, with two internal courtyards. Inside are the mosaic-lined Gyllene Salen (Golden Hall), Prins Eugen's own fresco re-creation of the lake view from the gallery, and the Blå Hallen (Blue Hall), where the annual Nobel Prize banquet is held. The **tower** (admission Skr30; ⌚9am-5pm Jun-Aug, 9am-4pm May & Sep) offers stellar views and a great thigh workout.

Södermalm (Map p1206) is Stockholm's most striking neighbourhood, where artistic and alternative types hang out – if you're looking for, say, an all-ages vegan punk club, this is the place. For gorgeous views over Stockholm from the island's northern cliffs (called the Söder Heights), head to **Katarinahissen** (Slussen; Map p1206; admission Skr10), an old lift that goes up from Slussen. Wooden stairs also snake up the hillside.

Activities

From Djurgårdsbron's **Sjöcafe** (Map p1202; ☎660 57 57; canoes per hr/day Skr80/300; ⌚9am-9pm mid-Apr–mid-Sep), next to the bridge leading to Djurgården, you can rent bikes, inline skates, kayaks, canoes, rowboats and pedalboats. Opposite, floating resto-bar **Strandbryggan** (Map p1202; www.strandbryggan.se; Strandvägskajen 27) rents sailing and motorboats from April to September. Sailing boats cost around Skr500 per hour, and all boats can be rented for a day, weekend or week.

Festivals & Events

Smaka På Stockholm FOOD

(www.smakapastockholm.se) Taste samples from some of Stockholm's top kitchens and watch cooking duels at this fest in Kungsträdgården in the first week of June each year.

Stockholm Jazz Festival JAZZ

(late Jul; www.stockholmjazz.com) Held on the island of Skeppsholmen, this internationally known jazz fest in late July brings artists from all over; evening jam sessions at famed Stockholm jazz club Fasching are a highlight.

Sleeping

Most hotels give steep discounts on weekends and in summer (mid-June to mid-August), up to 50% off. Stockholm has several HI-affiliated STF hostels, as well as SVIF and independent hostels (no membership cards required). Many have options for single, double or family rooms. Many hostels have breakfast available, usually for an additional Skr65 to Skr80. Sheets are almost always required; if you don't have your own, you'll need to rent them (around Skr50).

TOP CHOICE **Vandrarhem af Chapman** HOSTEL €

(Map p1206; ☎463 22 66; www.stfchapman.com; dm/d from Skr215/530; @) The legendary af Chapman is a storied vessel that has done plenty of travelling of its own. It's now well anchored in a superb, quiet location, sway-

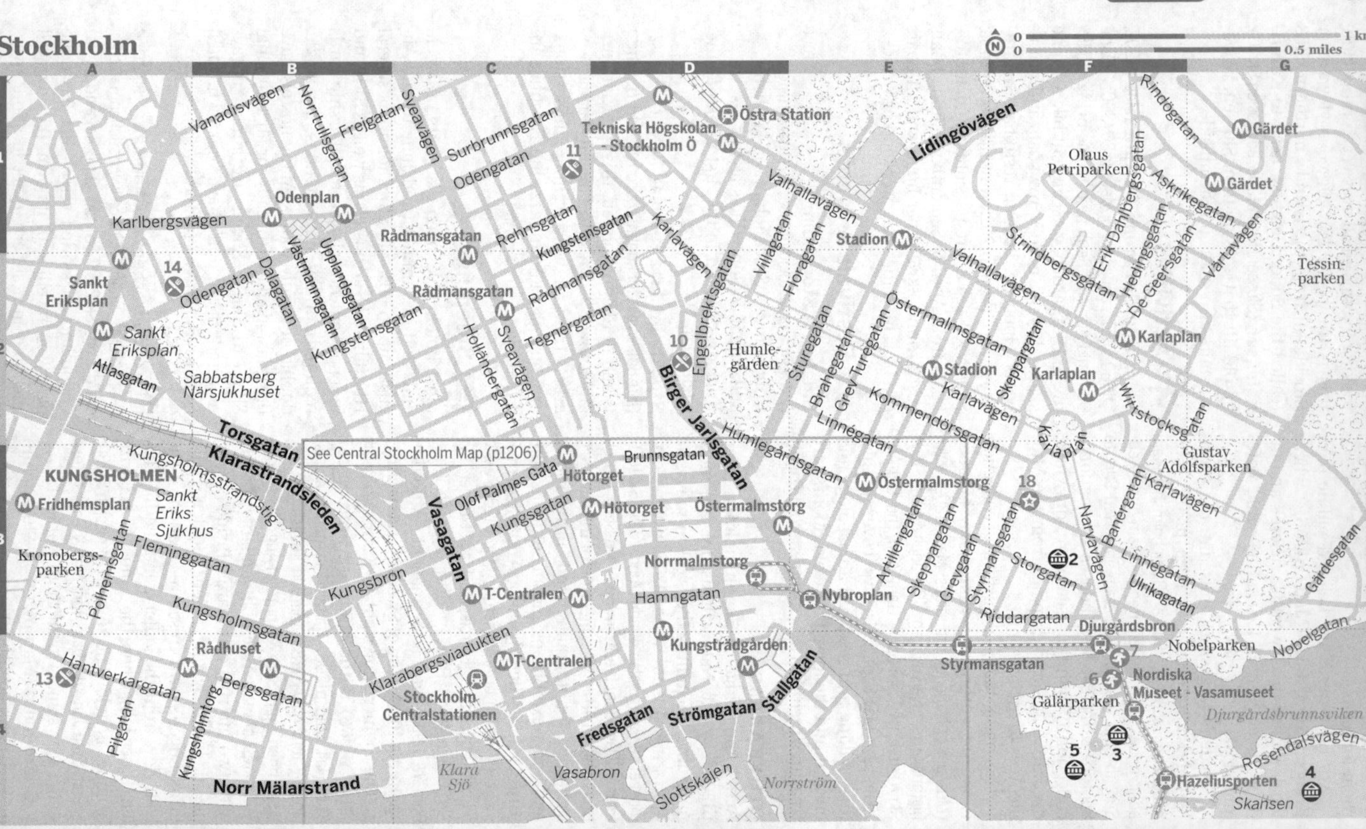
Stockholm
0.5 miles
1 km
A
B
C
D
E
F
G
1
2
3
4
Vanadisvägen
Norrtullsgatan
Frejgatan
Sveavägen
Surbrunnsgatan
Odengatan
Tekniska Högskolan - Stockholm Ö
Östra Station
Lidingövägen
Rindögatan
Gärdet
Olaus Petriparken
Askrikegatan
Gärdet
Odenplan
Karlbergsvägen
Rådmansgatan
Rehnsgatan
Kungstensgatan
Karlavägen
Valhallavägen
Stadion
Erik Dahlbergsgatan
Hedinsgatan
De Geersgatan
Värtavägen
Tessinparken
Sankt Eriksplan
Odengatan
Dalagatan
Västmannagatan
Upplandsgatan
Rådmansgatan
Villagatan
Floragatan
Strindbergsgatan
Valhallavägen
Östermalmsgatan
Karlaplan
Sankt Eriksplan
Atlasgatan
Sabbatsberg Närsjukhuset
Kungstensgatan
Holländergatan
Sveavägen
Tegnérgatan
Engelbrektsgatan
Humlegården
Sturegatan
Brahegatan
Grev Turegatan
Stadion
Skeppargatan
Karlaplan
Birger Jarlsgatan
Kommendörsgatan
Karlavägen
Wittstocksgatan
Linnégatan
Karlaplan
Torsgatan
Klarastrandsleden
Kungsholmsstrandstig
See Central Stockholm Map (p1206)
Brunnsgatan
Humlegårdsgatan
Östermalmstorg
Gustav Adolfsparken
KUNGSHOLMEN
Fridhemsplan
Sankt Eriks Sjukhus
Olof Palmes Gata
Hötorget
Vasagatan
Kungsgatan
Hötorget
Östermalmstorg
Karlavägen
Banérgatan
Narvavägen
Kronobergsparken
Polhemsgatan
Fleminggatan
Norrmalmstorg
Artillerigatan
Skeppargatan
Grevgatan
Styrmansgatan
Storgatan
Linnégatan
Ulrikagatan
Gärdesgatan
Kungsbron
T-Centralen
Hamngatan
Nybroplan
Riddargatan
Djurgårdsbron
Nobelparken
Nobelgatan
Kungsholmsgatan
Rådhuset
Klarabergsviadukten
T-Centralen
Kungsträdgården
Styrmansgatan
Nordiska Museet - Vasamuseet
Hantverkargatan
Bergsgatan
Stockholm Centralstationen
Galärparken
Djurgårdsbrunnsviken
Stallgatan
Strömgatan
Fredsgatan
Pilgatan
Kungsholmtorg
Norr Mälarstrand
Klara Sjö
Vasabron
Slottskajen
Norrström
Rosendalsvägen
Hazeliusporten
Skansen
2
3
4
5
6
7
10
11
13
14
18

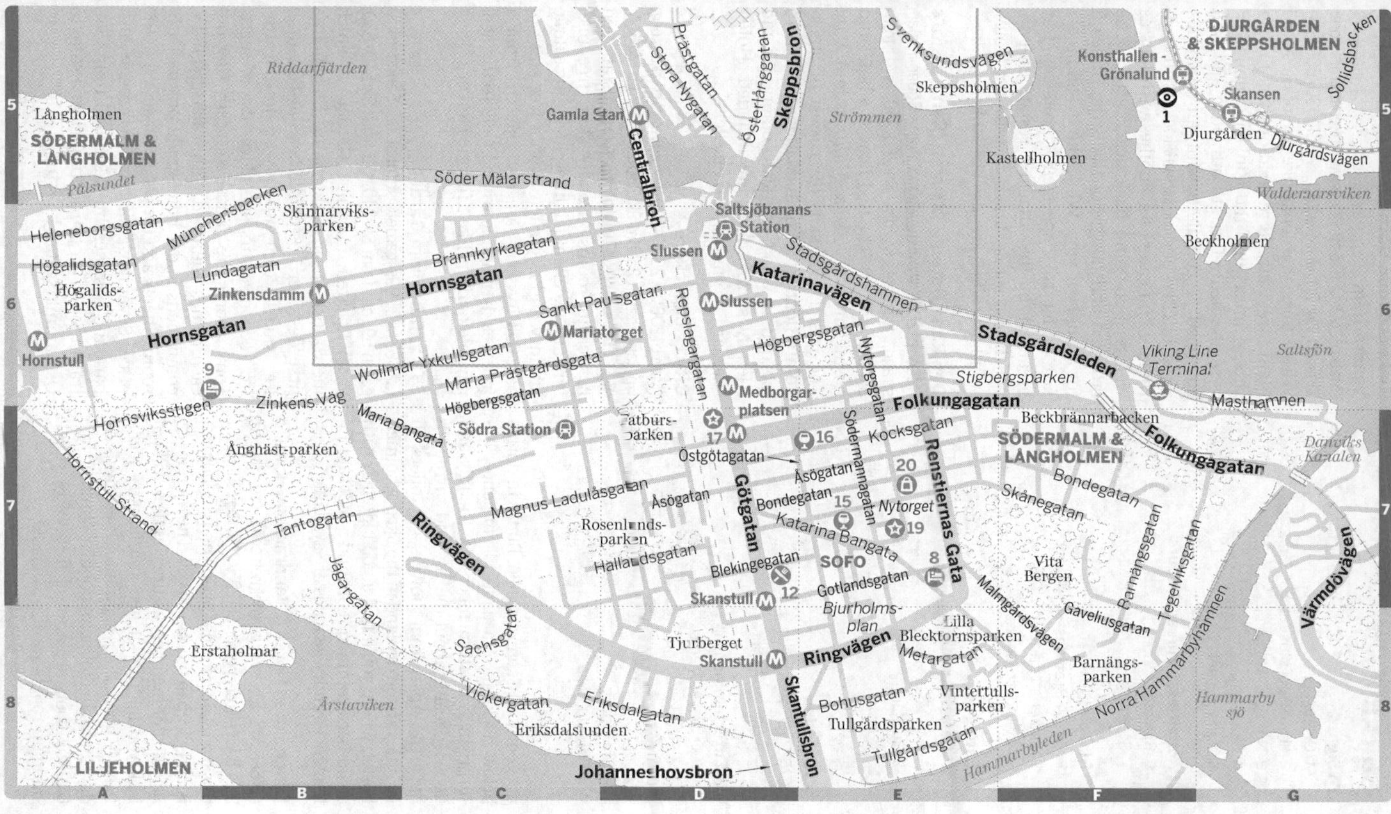
DJURGÅRDEN & SKEPPSHOLMEN
Konsthallen - Grönalund
Skansen
Sollidsbacken
1
Djurgården
Djurgårdsvägen
Svenksundsvägen
Skeppsholmen
Kastellholmen
Strömmen
Waldemarsviken
Beckholmen
Riddarfjärden
Långholmen
SÖDERMALM & LÅNGHOLMEN
Pålsundet
Gamla Stan
Centralbron
Prästgatan
Stora Nygatan
Österlånggatan
Skeppsbron
Söder Mälarstrand
Saltsjöbanans Station
Slussen
Stadsgårdshamnen
Katarinavägen
Stadsgårdsleden
Viking Line Terminal
Saltsjön
Masthamnen
Stigbergsparken
Beckbrännarbacken
Folkungagatan
SÖDERMALM & LÅNGHOLMEN
Danviks Kanalen
Värmdövägen
Helenеborgsgatan
Münchensbacken
Skinnarviksparken
Högalidsgatan
Lundagatan
Högalidsparken
Zinkensdamm
Brännkyrkagatan
Hornsgatan
Hornstull
Sankt Paulsgatan
Mariatorget
Repslagargatan
Högbergsgatan
Nytorgsgatan
Wollmar Yxkullsgatan
Maria Prästgårdsgata
Högbergsgatan
9
Hornsviksstigen
Zinkens Väg
Maria Bangata
Södra Station
Medborgarplatsen
Fatbursparken
17
16
Kocksgatan
Södermannagatan
Renstiernas Gata
Östgötagatan
Åsögatan
20
Bondegatan
Skånegatan
Änghäst-parken
Hornstull Strand
Magnus Ladulåsgatan
Åsögatan
15
Nytorget
19
Katarina Bangata
Götgatan
Tantogatan
Ringvägen
Rosenlundsparken
Hallandsgatan
Blekingegatan
SOFO
8
Vita Bergen
Barnängsgatan
Tegelviksgatan
Jägargatan
Skanstull
12
Gotlandsgatan
Bjurholmsplan
Malmgårdsvägen
Gaveliusgatan
Lilla Blecktornsparken
Erstaholmar
Sachsgatan
Tjurberget
Ringvägen
Metargatan
Barnängsparken
Norra Hammarbyhamnen
Hammarby sjö
Årstaviken
Vickergatan
Eriksdalsgatan
Eriksdalslunden
Skantullsbron
Bohusgatan
Vintertullsparken
Tullgårdsparken
Tullgårdsgatan
Hammarbyleden
LILJEHOLMEN
Johanneshovsbron
A
B
C
D
E
F
G
5
6
7
8

Stockholm

Sights

1 Gröna Lund Tivoli F5
2 Historiska Museet F3
3 Nordiska Museet F4
4 Skansen G4
5 Vasamuseet F4

Activities, Courses & Tours

6 Sjöcafé F4
7 Strandbryggan F4

Sleeping

8 Bed & Breakfast 4 Trappor E7
9 Zinkensdamm Hotell & Vandrarhem B6

Eating

10 Café Saturnus D2
11 Caffé Nero C1
12 Pelikan D7
13 Vurma A4
14 Vurma A2

Drinking

15 Pet Sounds Bar E7
16 Soldaten Svejk E7

Entertainment

17 Debaser Medis D7
18 Elverket F3
19 Roxy E7

Shopping

20 Tjallamalla E7

ing gently off Skeppsholmen. Bunks in dorms below decks have a nautical ambience, unsurprisingly. Staff members are friendly and knowledgeable about the city and surrounding areas. Apart from showers and toilets, all facilities are on dry land in the Skeppsholmen hostel, where you'll find a good kitchen with a laid-back common room and a separate TV lounge. Laundry facilities are available.

Långholmen Hotell & Vandrarhem HOSTEL €
(☎668 05 10; www.langholmen.com; dm Skr240, 2-/4-bed cells per person Skr295/240; @) Guests at this hostel, in a former prison on Långholmen island, sleep in bunks in a cell. The friendly, efficient staff members assure you they will not lock you in. The kitchen and laundry facilities are good, the restaurant serves meals all day, and Långholmen's popular summertime bathing spots are a towel flick away. Hotel-standard rooms are also available.

Zinkensdamm Hotell & Vandrarhem HOSTEL €
(Map p1202; ☎616 81 00; www.zinkensdamm.com; Zinkens väg 20; dm Skr230, s/d Skr430/600; @) With a foyer that looks like one of those old Main Street facade re-creations you find in cheesy museums, the Zinkensdamm STF is unabashedly fun. It's attractive and well equipped – complete with an ubersleek guest kitchen and personal lockers in each room – and caters for families with kids as well as pub-going backpackers. It can be crowded and noisy, but that's the trade-off for an upbeat vibe. While the hostel breakfast buffet isn't spectacular, you can buy breakfast in the attached restaurant-pub, which also serves lunch and dinner. Hotel-standard rooms are also available.

Den Röda Båten – Mälaren/Ran HOSTEL €
(Map p1206; www.theredboat.com; Söder Mälarstrand, Kajplats 6; dm Skr260-290, s/d from Skr480/620; @) 'The Red Boat' is a hotel and hostel on two vessels, *Mälaren* and *Ran*. The hostel section is the cosiest of Stockholm's floating accommodations, thanks to lots of dark wood, nautical memorabilia and friendly staff. Linens are included. Hotel-standard rooms are also excellent.

City Backpackers HOSTEL €
(Map p1206; ☎20 69 20; www.citybackpackers.org; Upplandsgatan 2a; dm Skr230-280, d from Skr650; @) The closest hostel to Centralstationen has clean rooms, friendly staff, free bike hire and excellent facilities, including sauna, laundry and a kitchen (with a free stash of pasta). City tours are also offered, from a free weekly neighbourhood walk to themed, payable options like 'Historic Horror'.

STF Vandrarhem Gärdet HOSTEL €
(☎463 22 99; gardet@stfturist.se; Sandhamnsgatan 59; dm from Skr340, s/d from Skr540/680; @ wi-fi) Located in quiet Gärdet, a quick metro ride from Östermalm, Stockholm's first 'designer hostel' ditches low-cost drab for smart, contemporary rooms featuring red pin chairs and clever use of space. Some rooms are almost comically tiny, but each comes equipped with a flatscreen TV, comfy beds and a hotel-grade private bathroom. Sheets and towels are included in the price. Several walking trails through lush parkland pass nearby. Take bus 1 from Centralstationen (or Gärdet tunnelbana stop) to Östhammarsgatan bus stop.

Bed & Breakfast 4 Trappor B&B €€
(Map p1202; ☎642 3104, 0735-69 38 64; www.4trappor.se; Gotlandsgatan 78; apt s/d Skr725/850, with breakfast Skr800/1000) For elegant slumming, it's hard to beat this sassy, urbane apartment, complete with cosy, floorboarded bedroom (maximum two guests), modern bathroom and well-equipped kitchen (espresso machine included!). Breakfast is served in the wonderful owners' next-door apartment, and the SoFo address means easy access to Stockholm's coolest shops and hangouts. There's a two-night minimum stay and a discounted rate for stays of more than five nights. It's a huge hit, so book months ahead.

Eating

The sheer number of dining choices in Stockholm means it's usually possible to fill your belly without emptying your wallet. Don't miss coffee and cake in an old-fashioned *konditori* (bakery cafe) or a visit to one of the dizzying market halls.

Look out for the daily lunch special called *dagens rätt* or *dagens lunch* at a fixed price (usually Skr65 to Skr75) between 11.30am and 2pm. For a quick, inexpensive snack, try a *grillad korv med bröd* – grilled hot dog on a bun (Skr15 to Skr25, available from countless stands and carts).

A handy central supermarket is **Hemköp** (Map p1206; Klarabergsgatan 50; ⏲7am-9pm Mon-Fri, 10am-9pm Sat & Sun), beneath Åhléns department store. Other reliable and ubiquitous supermarket chains include ICA and Konsum.

Chokladkoppen CAFE €
(Map p1206; Stortorget; cakes and snacks Skr30-70) Arguably Stockholm's best-loved cafe, hole-in-the-wall Chokladkoppen sits slap bang on the Old Town's enchanting main square. It's a gay-friendly spot, with cute, gym-fit waiters, a look-at-me summer terrace, and yummy grub like broccoli and blue cheese pie and scrumptious cakes.

Hermitage CAFE €€
(Map p1206; Stora Nygatan 11; lunch Skr90; ⏲closed Sun) Don't let the '80s-style coffee-shop decor put you off; herbivores love Hermitage for its simple, tasty vegetarian nosh. Salad, home-made bread, tea and coffee are included in the price of a main.

Vetekatten CAFE €
(Map p1206; Kungsgatan 55; snacks from Skr35; ⏲7.30am-8pm Mon-Fri, 9.30am-5pm Sat, noon-5pm Sun) A cardamom-scented labyrinth of cosy nooks, antique furnishings and oil paintings, Vetekatten is not so much a cafe as an institution.

Caffé Nero CAFE €
(Map p1202; Roslagsgatan 4; coffee & pastries from Skr35; ⏲7am-10pm Mon-Fri, 8am-10pm Sat, 8am-6pm Sun) Architect Tadao Ando would approve of the brutal concrete interiors at this Vasastan hang-out where local hipsters down mighty coffees, grappa shots, salubrious panini and Italian home cooking, from sublime veal meatballs to a tiramisu.

Hötorgshallen FOOD HALL €€
(Map p1206; Hötorget; ⏲10am-6pm Mon-Thu, 10am-6.30pm Fri, 10am-4pm Sat, 10am-6pm Mon-Fri, 10am-3pm Sat Jun & Jul) Below Filmstaden cinema, multicultural Hötorgshallen sells everything from fresh Nordic seafood to fluffy hummus and fragrant teas. Squeeze into galley-themed dining nook **Kajsas Fiskrestaurang** for soulful *fisksoppa* (fish stew) with mussels and aioli.

Östermalms Saluhall SWEDISH €€
(Map p1206; Östermalmstorg; ⏲9.30am-6pm Mon-Thu, until 6.30pm Fri & 4pm Sat) Stockholm's historic market spoils tastebuds with fresh fish, seafood and meat, as well as fruits, vegetables and hard-to-find cheeses. In addition to the market, it's full of small eateries serving everything from sushi to pasta. The building itself is a Stockholm landmark, designed as a Romanesque cathedral of food in 1885.

Café Saturnus CAFE €
(Eriksbergsgatan 6; baguettes from Skr35; ⏲7am-8pm Mon-Fri, 9am-7pm Sat & Sun) For velvety caffe latte, Gallic-inspired baguettes and perfect pastries, saunter into this casually chic bakery-cafe. Sporting a stunning mosaic floor, it's a fabulous spot to flick through the paper while devouring Stockholm's finest (and notoriously gigantic) cinnamon buns.

Nystekt Strömming FAST FOOD €
(Map p1206; Södermalmstorg; combo plates Skr35-65; ⏲10am-6pm Mon-Fri, 11am-4pm Sat & Sun) Pick up some authentically Swedish fast food – fried *(stekt)* herring – at this humble cart outside the metro station at Slussen. The strömming burger makes a great snack on the go, and the full dinner combos are excellent if you want something more substantial.

Pelikan SWEDISH €€
(Map p1202; Blekingegatan 40; mains Skr80-180; ⏲dinner daily & lunch Sat & Sun) Lofty ceilings, wood panelling and no-nonsense waiters

Central Stockholm

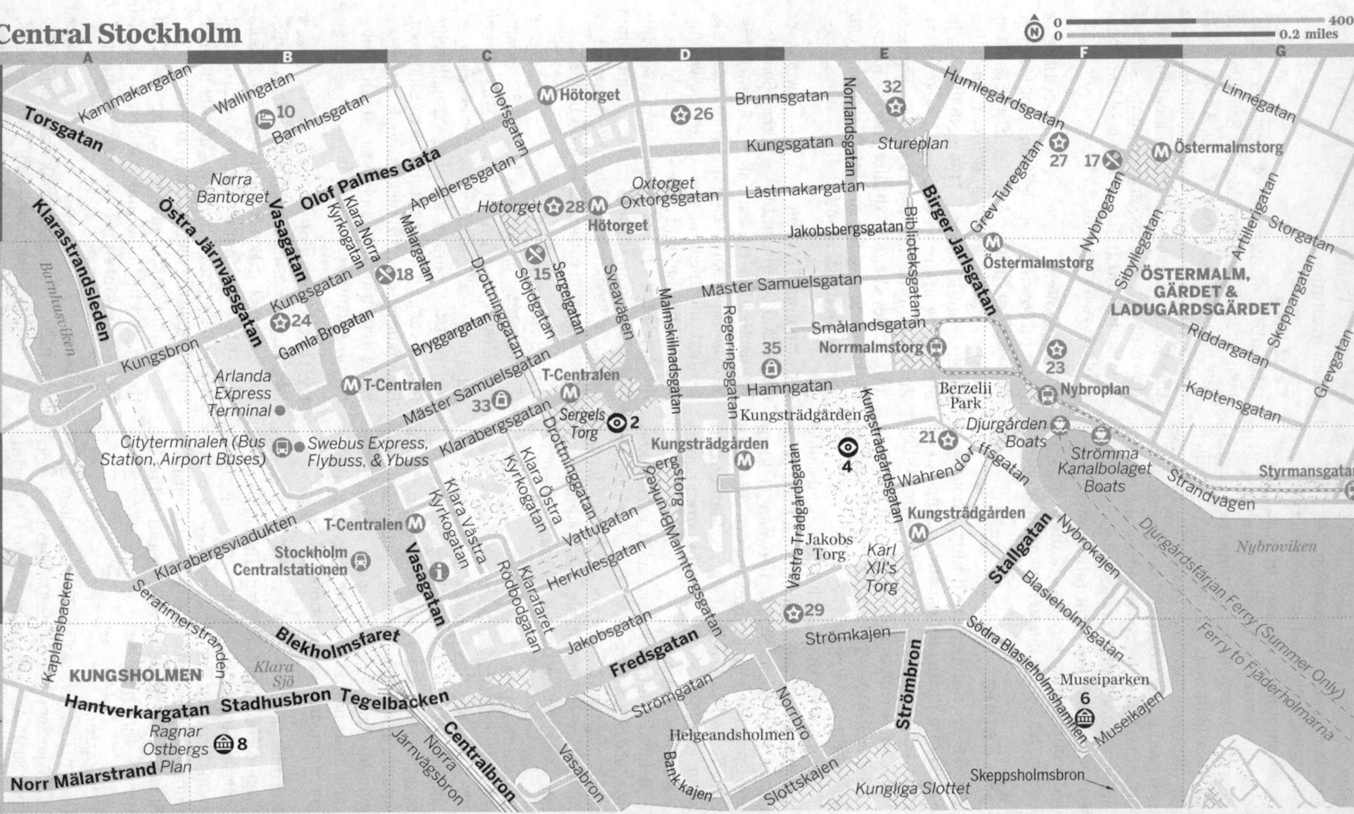

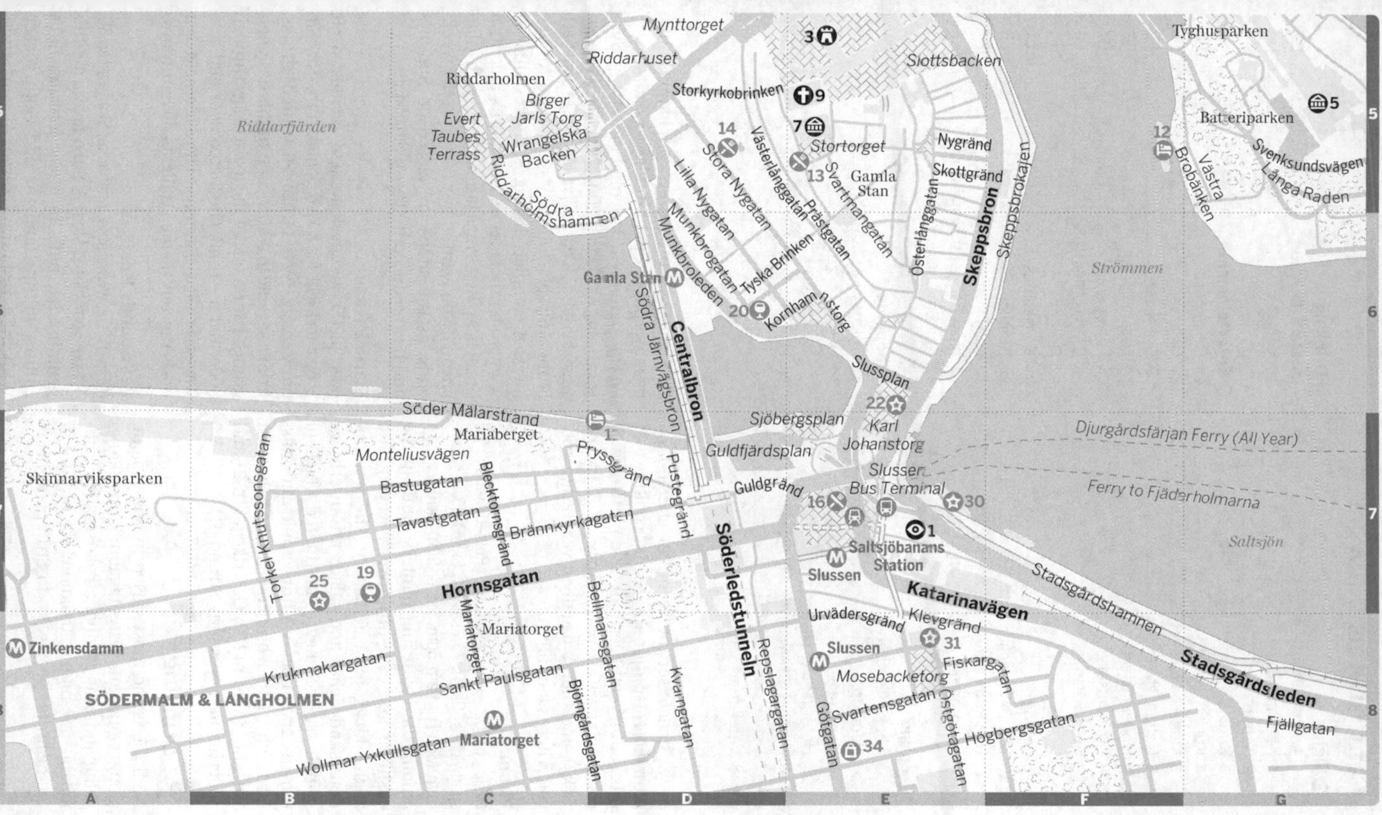
Mynttorget
Riddarhuset
Slottsbacken
Tyghusparken
Riddarholmen
Birger Jarls Torg
Evert Taubes Terrass
Wrangelska Backen
Riddarfjärden
Södra Riddarholmshamnen
Storkyrkobrinken
Batteriparken
Stortorget
Nygränd
Skottgränd
Gamla Stan
Stora Nygatan
Västerlånggatan
Svartmangatan
Prästgatan
Lilla Nygatan
Munkbrogatan
Munkbroleden
Tyska Brinken
Österlånggatan
Skeppsbron
Skeppsbrokajen
Västra Brobänken
Svenksundsvägen
Långa Raden
Strömmen
Gamla Stan
Södra Järnvägsbron
Centralbron
Kornhamnstorg
Slussplan
Söder Mälarstrand
Mariaberget
Sjöbergsplan
Karl Johanstorg
Guldfjärdsplan
Djurgårdsfärjan Ferry (All Year)
Monteliusvägen
Pryssgränd
Pustegränd
Skinnarviksparken
Bastugatan
Blecktornsgränd
Guldgränd
Slussen
Bus Terminal
Ferry to Fjäderholmarna
Tavastgatan
Brännkyrkagatan
Söderledstunneln
Saltsjöbanans Station
Saltsjön
Torkel Knutssonsgatan
Hornsgatan
Slussen
Katarinavägen
Stadsgårdshamnen
Mariatorget
Bellmansgatan
Urvädersgränd
Klevgränd
Zinkensdamm
Slussen
Stadsgårdsleden
Krukmakargatan
Sankt Paulsgatan
Repslagargatan
Fiskargatan
Mosebacketorg
SÖDERMALM & LÅNGHOLMEN
Björngårdsgatan
Kvarngatan
Götgatan
Svartensgatan
Östgötagatan
Fjällgatan
Högbergsgatan
Wollmar Yxkullsgatan
Mariatorget

Central Stockholm

Sights

	Arkitekturmuseet	(see 5)
1	Katarinahissen	E7
2	Kulturhuset	D2
3	Kungliga Slottet (Royal Palace)	E5
4	Kungsträdgården	E3
5	Moderna Museet	G5
6	National Museum	F4
7	Nobelmuseet	E5
8	Stadshuset	B4
9	Storkyrkan	E5

Sleeping

10	City Backpackers	B1
11	Den Röda Båten - Mälaren/Ran	D7
12	Vandrarhem af Chapman	F5

Eating

13	Chokladkoppen	E5
	Hemköp	(see 33)
14	Hermitage	D5
15	Hötorgshallen	C2
16	Nystekt Strömming	E7
17	Östermalms Saluhall	F1
18	Vetekatten	B2

Drinking

19	Marie Laveau	B7
20	Torget	D6

Entertainment

21	Berns Salonger	E3
22	Debaser	E6
23	Dramaten	F2
24	Fasching	B2
25	Folkoperan	B7
26	Glenn Miller Café	D1
27	Grodan	F1
28	Konserthuset	C1
29	Kungliga Operan	E3
30	Lady Patricia	E7
31	Mosebacke Etablissement	E8
32	Spy Bar	E1

Shopping

33	Åhléns	C2
34	DesignTorget	E8
	DesignTorget	(see 2)
35	NK Department Store	D2

in waistcoats set the scene for classic *husmanskost* (traditional home cooking) at this century-old beer hall. The herring-and-cheese platters are particularly good (try the 'SOS'), and there's usually a vegetarian special. There's a minimum age of 23.

Vurma CAFE €
(Map p1202; www.vurma.se; Polhemsgatan 15; sandwiches Skr45-75, salads Skr70-85, 8am-6pm Mon-Fri, 9am-6pm Sat & Sun) Squeeze in among the chattering punters, fluff up the cushions and eavesdrop over a vegan latte at this kitsch-hip cafe-bakery. The scrumptious sandwiches and salads are utterly inspired; try the chevre, marinated chicken, tomato, cucumber, walnuts, apple and mustard salad. Other branches include those in Vasastan (Map p1202, Gästrikegatan 2) and Södermalm (Bergsunds Strand 31).

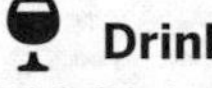

Drinking

Nightlife is the most varied in Södermalm, along Götgatan, Östgötagatan and Skånegatan and near Medborgarplatsen. For fashionable late-night bars and clubs brimful of the beautiful people, go to Stureplan. Beers are cheapest during after-work happy hours, usually 4pm to 6pm Monday to Friday.

The state-owned alcohol monopoly, **Systembolaget** (Map p1206; 796 98 10; Regeringsgatan 44; 10am to 7pm Mon-Fri, to 3pm Sat), is the only place to buy real booze to take away. A complete listing is given online at www.systembolaget.se, but there's a central branch at Regeringsgatan. Be sure to plan ahead if you want to buy booze on the weekends, as the shops are closed on Sundays and have reduced hours on Saturdays.

Marie Laveau BAR
(Map p1206; www.marielaveau.se; Hornsgatan 66; 5pm-midnight Tue & Wed, 5pm-3am Thu-Sat) Sip on vaguely New Orleans-flavoured drinks, from a sazerac to a hurricane, at this designer-grunge bar on one of the main drags through Södermalm – think chequered floor and subway-style tiled columns. The basement bar hosts raucous theme DJ nights on Saturdays.

Pet Sounds Bar BAR
(Map p1202; www.petsoundsbar.se; Skånegatan 80; from 5pm, closed Mon) A SoFo favourite, this jamming bar pulls in music journos, indie culture vultures and the odd Goth rocker. While the restaurant serves decent Italo-

French grub, the real fun happens in the basement. Head down for a mixed bag of live bands, release parties and DJ sets.

Soldaten Svejk PUB
(Map p1202; www.svejk.se; Östgötagatan 35; ⏲from 5pm) In this crowded, amber-windowed, wooden-floored pub, decorated with heraldic shields, regulars pine for Prague with great Czech beer, including the massively popular Staropramen, on tap. Line your stomach with simple, solid Czech meals (Skr102 to Skr185); the smoked cheese is sublime. Head in early or prepare to queue for a table.

☆ Entertainment

Clubbing

Stockholm is home to some mighty clubs, with DJ royalty regularly on the decks. You'll find the slickest spots in Östermalm, near Stureplan. Expect an entry charge of Skr100 to Skr200 at the trendiest venues. Södermalm offers a more varied scene, with club nights spanning local indie to salsa.

Spy Bar CLUB
(Map p1206; www.thespybar.com; Birger Jarlsgatan 20; ⏲10pm-5am Wed-Sat) Set in a turn-of-the-century flat (spot the tiled stoves), this party stalwart pulls in a 20- and 30-something media crowd, as well as the odd American heiress (yes, Paris partied here). Expect three bars with electro, rock and hip-hop beats.

Berns Salonger CLUB
(Map p1206; www.berns.se; Berzelii Park; ⏲bar/nightclub 11pm-4am Thu-Sat, midnight-5am Thu-Sat) A Stockholm institution since 1862, this glitzy entertainment palace remains one of the city's hottest party spots. While the gorgeous ballroom hosts some brilliant live-music gigs, the best of Berns' bars is the intimate basement bar/club **2.35:1**, packed with cool creative types, top-notch DJs and projected arthouse images.

Grodan CLUB
(Map p1206; www.grodannattklubb.se; Grev Turegatan 16; ⏲10pm-3am Fri & Sat) At street level it's a packed bar and mock-baroque restaurant. Down in the cellar, A-list DJ talent from Stockholm, London and beyond spin the vinyl, pumping out house and electro tracks for sweat-soaked clubbers.

Gay & Lesbian Venues

For club listings and events, pick up a free copy of street-press magazine *QX*, found at many clubs, stores and cafes around town. Its website (www.qx.se) is more frequently updated. *QX* also produces the free, handy Gay Stockholm Map.

Torget GAY & LESBIAN
(Map p1206; www.torgetbaren.com; Mälartorget 13) Gamla Stan's premier gay bar has eye-candy staff, mock-baroque touches and a civilised salon vibe.

Roxy GAY & LESBIAN
(Map p1202; www.roxysofo.se; Nytorget 6; ⏲from 5pm) Chic resto-bar popular with lipstick lesbians, publishing types and SoFo's creative set.

Lady Patricia GAY & LESBIAN
(Map p1206; ☎743 05 70; Stadsgårdskajen 152; ⏲Sun) This perennial Sunday-night favourite has a superb seafood restaurant, two crowded dancefloors, drag shows and a pop-loving crowd, all on board a docked yacht.

Theatre & Dance

Dramaten THEATRE
(Map p1206; ☎667 06 80; www.dramaten.se; Nybroplan) The Royal Theatre stages a range of plays in a sublime Art Nouveau environment. Dramaten's experimental stage **Elverket** (Map p1202; Linnégatan 69) pushes all the boundaries with some edgier offerings that are performed within a converted power station.

Folkoperan THEATRE
(Map p1206; ☎616 07 50; www.folkoperan.se; Hornsgatan 72) Folkoperan gives opera a thoroughly modern overhaul with its intimate, cutting-edge and sometimes controversial productions. Those under 26 enjoy half-price tickets.

Live Music

Debaser INDIE ROCK
(Map p1206; www.debaser.se, in Swedish; Karl Johanstorg 1, Slussen; ⏲7pm-1am, to 3am club nights Sun-Thu, 8pm-3am Fri & Sat) The king of rock clubs hides away under the Slussen interchange. Emerging or bigger-name acts play most nights, while the killer club nights span anything from rock-steady to punk and electronica. One metro stop further south, **Debaser Medis** (Map p1202; Medborgarplatsen 8) is its sprawling sister venue, with three floors rocking to live acts and DJ-spun tunes.

Mosebacke Etablissement LIVE MUSIC
(Map p1206; www.mosebacke.se, in Swedish; Mosebacketorg 3; ⏲to 11pm Mon & Tue, to 1am Wed & Sun, to 2am Thu-Sat) Eclectic theatre and club nights aside, this historic culture palace hosts a mixed line-up of live music. Tunes span

anything from homegrown pop to antipodean rock. The outdoor terrace combines dazzling city views with a thumping summer bar.

Operran OPERA

(Map p1206; 791 44 00; www.operan.se; Operahuset, Gustav Adolfs Torg) The Royal Opera is the place to go for thunderous tenors, sparkling sopranos and classical ballet. It also has some bargain tickets in seats with poor views for as little as Skr40, and occasional lunchtime concerts for Skr180 (including light lunch).

Konserthuset CLASSICAL

(Map p1206; 50 66 77 88; www.konserthuset.se; Hötorget) Head here for classical concerts and other musical marvels, including the Royal Philharmonic Orchestra.

For jazz and blues, try the intimate, snob-proof **Glenn Miller Café** (Map p1206; 10 03 22; Brunnsgatan 21) or the reliable **Fasching** (Map p1206; www.fasching.se; Kungsgatan 63).

Shopping

A design and fashion hub, Stockholm offers shoppers everything from top-name boutiques to the tiniest second-hand shops. Good local buys include edgy streetwear, designer home decor and clever gadgets, and edible treats such as cloudberry jam, pickled herring and bottles of *glögg* (spiced wine). Södermalm's 'SoFo' district (the streets south of Folkungagatan) is your best bet for home-grown fashion, while Östermalm is the place for high-end names such as Marc Jacobs and Gucci.

For all-in-one retail therapy, scour department store giant **Åhléns** (Map p1206; Klarabergsgatan 50) or its upmarket rival **NK** (Map p1206; Hamngatan 12-18).

DesignTorget GIFTS & GADGETS

Götgatan (Map p1206; Götgatan 31, Södermalm; (Map p1206; 10am-7pm Mon-Fri, 10am-5pm Sat, noon-5pm Sun); Sergels Torg (Map p1206; Basement, Kulturhuset, Sergels Torg B; 10am-7pm Mon-Fri, 10am-6pm Sat, 11am-5pm Sun) If you love good design but don't own a gold Amex, head to this chain, which sells the work of emerging designers alongside established denizens. There are several branches around the city.

Tjallamalla CLOTHING

(Map p1202; www.tjallamalla.com; Bondegatan 46; noon-6pm Mon-Fri, noon-4pm Sat) Raid the racks at this fashion icon for rookie designers such as Hot Sissy, Papagaio and organic Malmö streetwear label Kärleksgatan. Graduates from Stockholm's prestigious Beckmans College of Design School sometimes sell their collections here on commission.

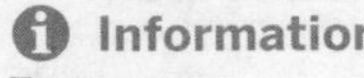

Information

Emergency

24-hour medical advice (32 01 00)

24-hour police stations Kungsholmen (401 00 00; Kungsholmsgatan 37, Kungsholmen); Södermalm (401 03 00; Torkel Knutssonsgatan 20, Södermalm)

Internet Access

Most hostels and many hotels have a computer with internet access for guests, and nearly all also offer wi-fi access in rooms (usually free, but sometimes for a fee of up to Skr120 per 24hr). Wi-fi is also widely available in coffee shops and bars and in Centralstationen. Those without their own computer have more limited options, but the ubiquitous Sidewalk Express terminals are handy.

Sidewalk Express (www.sidewalkexpress.se; per hr Skr19) Rows of computer monitors and tall red ticket machines mark out these self-service internet stations. They're found at various locations, including Cityterminalen, Centralstationen, Arlanda airport, and numerous 7-Eleven locations around town.

Left Luggage

There are three sizes of **left-luggage box** (per 24hr Skr50-120) at Centralstationen. Similar facilities exist at the neighbouring bus station and at major ferry terminals.

Medical Services

Apoteket CW Scheele (454 81 30; Klarabergsgatan 64) A 24-hour pharmacy.

CityAkuten (412 29 00; Apelbergsgatan 48; 8am-8pm) Emergency health and dental care.

Södersjukhuset (616 10 00; Ringvägen 52) The most central hospital.

Money

ATMs are plentiful, with a few at Centralstationen; expect queues.

The exchange company Forex has more than a dozen branches in the capital and charges Skr15 per travellers' cheque.

Forex Bank (10 49 90; Vasagatan 16; 9am-7pm Mon-Fri, 10am-5pm Sat, noon-4pm Sun)

Tourist Information

Tourist office (Map p1206; 508 28 508; www.stockholmtown.se; Vasagatan 14; 9am-6pm Mon-Fri, 10am-5pm Sat, 10am-4pm Sun mid-Sep–Apr, 9am-7pm Mon-Fri, 10am-5pm Sat, 10am-4pm Sun May–mid-Sep) Just across the street from the Centralstationen. There's a Forex currency-exchange counter next door.

TOURIST DISCOUNT CARDS & INFO

Planning ahead will help you make the most of your time and money in Sweden. Shoestring travellers should find the following resources useful:

» **Stockholm a la Carte** (☎663 00 80; www.destination-stockholm.com; from Skr465) Discount hotel-and-sightseeing packages; can be booked online. It's available weekends year-round and throughout the summer.

» **Stockholm Card** (www.stockholmtown.com; 24/48/72/120hr Skr395/525/625/895) Available from tourist offices, camping grounds, hostels, hotels, and Storstockholms Lokaltrafik (SL) public transport centres, the card gives free entry to about 75 attractions (including Skansen), free city parking in metered spaces, free sightseeing by boat and free travel on public transport (including the lift, Katarinahissen, but excluding local ferries and airport buses).

Websites

» **www.stockholmtown.com** Excellent tourist information in English (and many other languages).

» **www.thelocal.se** News and features about Sweden, written locally, in English.

» **www.visit-stockholm.com** A helpful source for travellers, with nearly 500 pages of information on sights, food, accommodation, shopping and getting out of town.

Getting There & Away

Air

Stockholm's main airport, **Arlanda** (ARN; ☎797 60 00), is 45km north of the city centre. **Bromma airport** (BMA; ☎797 68 74), 8km west of Stockholm, is a minor airport used for some domestic flights. Two airports are used by some low-cost carriers and sometimes labelled as 'Stockholm', despite being a fair distance from the capital: **Skavsta airport** (NYO; ☎0155-28 04 00) is 100km south of Stockholm, near Nyköping; and **Västerås airport** (VST; ☎021-80 56 00) is near the town of Västerås, about 105km northwest of Stockholm.

Bus

Cityterminalen (Map p1206; www.cityterminalen.com) The main bus station, connected to Centralstationen. The ticket counter (open 7am to 6pm) sells tickets for several bus companies, including Flygbussarna (airport coaches), Swebus Express, Svenska Buss, Eurolines and Ybuss.

Swebus Express (☎0771-21 82 18; www.swebusexpress.com; 2nd level, Cityterminalen) runs daily to destinations including Malmö (9¼ hours), Göteborg (seven hours) and Oslo (eight hours). There are also direct runs to Uppsala (one hour) and Västerås (1¾ hours).

Ybuss (☎020 033 44 44; www.ybuss.se; Cityterminalen) runs services to the northern towns of Sundsvall, Östersund and Umeå.

Train

Stockholm is the centre for SJ's national services. Direct trains to/from Copenhagen, Oslo, Storlien (for Trondheim) and Narvik arrive and depart from **Centralstationen**, as do the SL *pendeltåg* (commuter) services that operate within Stockholm county.

Getting Around

To/From the Airports

The **Arlanda Express** (Map p1206; ☎020-22 22 24; tickets from Skr240) train from Centralstationen takes 20 minutes to reach Arlanda; trains run every 10 to 15 minutes from about 5am to 12.30am. The same trip in a taxi costs around Skr450.

The cheaper option is the **Flygbuss** service between Arlanda airport and Cityterminalen. Buses leave every 10 or 15 minutes (Skr119, 40 minutes). Tickets can be purchased on arrival at the Flygbuss counter at Arlanda airport's main terminal. From either Skavsta airport or Vasteras airport to Stockholm (one way/return Skr139/249, one hour 20 minutes).

Bicycle

Stockholm has an extensive network of bicycle paths, and top day trips include Djurgården; a loop going from Gamla Stan to Södermalm, Långholmen and Kungsholmen (on lakeside paths); and Drottningholm.

Boat

Djurgårdsfärjan city ferry services connect Gröna Lund Tivoli on Djurgården with Nybroplan and Slussen as frequently as every 10 minutes in summer (less frequently in the low season); a single trip costs Skr30 (free with the SL transport passes).

FARES IN STOCKHOLM

The **Stockholm Card** covers travel on all SL trains and buses in greater Stockholm. There are also 24-hour (Skr100) and 72-hour (Skr200) SL Tourist Cards; the latter is especially good value if you use the third afternoon for transport to either end of the county – you can reach the ferry terminals in Grisslehamn, Kapellskär or Nynäshamn, as well as all of the archipelago harbours. If you want to explore the county in more detail, get yourself a 30-day SL pass.

On Stockholm's public transport system the minimum fare costs two coupons, and each additional zone costs another coupon (up to five coupons for four or five zones). Coupons cost Skr30 each, but it's better value (and handier) to buy strips of 16 tickets for Skr180. Coupons are stamped at the start of a journey and are good for two hours. Travelling without a valid ticket can lead to a fine of Skr600 or more. Coupons, tickets and passes can be bought at metro stations, Pressbyrån kiosks, SL train stations and SL information offices. Some bus stops now have ticket-vending machines, but plan ahead, as tickets cannot be bought on buses.

Public Transport

Storstockholms Lokaltrafik (SL; www.sl.se) runs all tunnelbana (T or T-bana) metro trains, local trains and buses within the entire Stockholm county. There is an SL information office in the basement concourse at **Centralstationen** (6.30am-11.15pm Mon-Sat, 7am-11.15pm Sun) and another near the Sergels Torg entrance (open until 6.30pm weekdays, 5pm weekends), which issues timetables and sells the SL Tourist Card and Stockholm Card. You can also call 600 10 00 for schedule and travel information.

AROUND STOCKHOLM

Many Stockholmers will tell you that their favourite way to spend a day off in their city is to get out on the water with an archipelago tour, whether overnight or just for the day.

Stockholm Archipelago

08

The website **Stockholmtown** (www.stockholmtown.com) has a large section devoted to the archipelago and its 24,000 islands.

Visit Skärgården (10 02 22; www.visitskargarden.se; Kajplats 18, Strandvägen; 9am-5pm Mon-Fri, 10am-4pm Sat, 11am-4pm Sun), a waterside information centre, can advise on (and book) accommodation and tours.

The biggest boat operator is **Waxholmsbolaget** (679 58 30; www.waxholmsbolaget.se). Timetables and information are available from its offices outside the Grand Hotel in Stockholm, at the harbour in Vaxholm and online. The Båtluffarkortet pass (Skr420 for five days) gives you unlimited boat rides plus a handy map with suggested itineraries.

Each island has its own character, and while many can be visited on a day trip, staying overnight is recommended. **Finnhamn** has excellent swimming spots. **Vandrarhem Finnhamn** (54 24 62 12; info@finnhamn.se; dm Skr260; @) is an STF hostel in a large wooden villa, with boat hire available. It's the largest hostel in the archipelago. Advance booking is essential.

A cycling paradise in the southern archipelago, **Utö** has it all: sublime sandy beaches, lush fairy-tale forests, sleepy farms and abundant birdlife. Reception for the **STF hostel** (dm Skr325; Sep-May) is at the nearby **Utö Värdshus** (50 42 03 00; receptionen@utovardshus.se; 2-person chalets incl breakfast per person from Skr995), whose **restaurant** (lunch Skr89-125, mains around Skr215; closed Jan) is ranked among the best in the archipelago.

Uppsala

018 / POP 182,000

Drenched in history but never stifled by the past, Uppsala has the party vibe of a university town to balance out its atmosphere of weighty cultural significance. It's a good combination, one that makes the town both fun and functional.

On the edge of the city is Gamla (Old) Uppsala, the original site of the town, once a flourishing 6th-century religious centre where humans made sacrifices to the Norse gods and home to an ancient burial ground.

The **tourist office** (727 48 00; www.uppsalatourism.se; Fyristorg 8; 10am-6pm Mon-Fri, 10am-3pm Sat, also noon-4pm Sun mid-Jun–mid-Aug) is near the cathedral; pick up the *Walk-*

ing Tour of Uppsala leaflet, and *What's On Uppsala* for event listings.

Sights & Activities

Uppsala began at the three great grave mounds at **Gamla Uppsala** (admission free; 24hr), 4km north of the modern city and well signposted (bus 2 from Stora Torget). The mounds are said to be the graves of pre-Viking kings and lie in a cemetery with about 300 smaller mounds and a great heathen temple. **Gamla Uppsala Museum** (23 93 00; admission Skr60; 11am-5pm May-Aug, noon-3pm Wed, Sat & Sun Sep–mid-Dec & Jan–Apr) contains finds from the cremation mounds, a poignant mix of charred and melted beads, bones and buckles.

Originally constructed by Gustav Vasa in the mid-16th century, **Uppsala Slott** (Castle; www.uppsalaslott.se; admission by guided tour only Skr80; tours in English at 12.45pm & 2.45pm Mon-Fri, 12.45 & 3.15pm Sat & Sun Jun–Aug) features the state hall where kings were enthroned and a queen abdicated. Wander the **Botanic Gardens** (Villavägen 6-8; admission free; 7am-9pm May-Sep, 7am-7pm Oct-Apr) below the castle hill, originally laid out by Carl von Linné (Linnaeus).

A wonder cabinet of wonder cabinets, the **Museum Gustavianum** (www.gustavianum.uu.se; Akademigatan 3; admission Skr40; 11am-4pm Tue-Sun) rewards appreciation of the weird and well organised. The shelves in the pleasantly musty building hold case after case of obsolete tools and preserved oddities: stuffed birds, astrolabes, alligator mummies, exotic stones and dried sea creatures. Don't miss the anatomical theatre tucked inside the dome.

Sleeping & Eating

Uppsala Vandrarhem HOSTEL €
(10 00 08; www.uppsalavandrarhem.se; Kvarntorget 3; dm/s/d from Skr190/400/500; @) A 10-minute walk from the city centre, Uppsala Vandrarhem is an ultra-tidy STF hostel built around an interior courtyard reminiscent of a gym or swimming hall. Rooms are modern and in good shape (although dorms suffer from traffic and level-crossing noise). A breakfast buffet is available, and there's a nearby supermarket for self-caterers.

Ofvandahls CAFE €
(Sysslomansgatan 3-5; cakes & snacks Skr40) Something of an Uppsala institution, this classy *konditori* dates back to the 19th century and is a cut above your average coffee-and-bun shop. It's been endorsed by no less a personage than the king, and radiates old-world charm; somehow those faded red-striped awnings just get cuter every year.

Eko Caféet CAFE €€
(Drottninggatan 5; mains Skr89) This funky little place with retro and mismatched furniture serves some of the best (and least expensive!) coffee in town. It does Italian-style wholefood, turns into a tapas bar on Wednesday to Saturday evenings, and frequently hosts live jazz/folk, as well as changing art exhibits and general studenty goings-on. Things quiet down somewhat in the summer, when it just opens for lunch Monday to Friday.

Getting There & Around

The **Flygbuss** (bus 801) departs at least twice an hour around the clock for nearby Arlanda airport (one way Skr100, 45 minutes); it leaves from outside the Uppsala Central Station.

Swebus Express (0200-21 82 18; www.swebusexpress.se) runs regular direct services to destinations including Stockholm (Skr57, one hour, at least hourly) and Västerås (Skr122 to Skr222, 3½ hours, six daily).

There are frequent **SJ** (www.sj.se) trains to/from Stockholm (Skr30 to Skr70, 40 minutes) and Östersund (Skr436 to Skr595, five hours, at least two daily) and other destinations.

Upplands Lokaltrafik (0771-14 14 14; www.ul.se) runs traffic within the city and county. City buses leave from Stora Torget and the surrounding streets. Tickets for unlimited travel for 90 minutes cost from Skr30.

GOTLAND

0498 / POP 57,400

Gorgeous Gotland has much to brag about: a Unesco-lauded capital, truffle-sprinkled woods, A-list dining hot spots, talented artisans, and more hours of sunshine than anywhere else in Sweden. It's also one of the country's richest historical regions, with around 100 medieval churches and countless prehistoric sites, from stone-ship settings and burial mounds to hilltop fortress remains.

Getting There & Away

Destination Gotland (0771-22 33 00; www.destinationgotland.se) operates year-round ferries between Visby and both Nynäshamn and Oskarshamn; departures from Nynäshamn are one to five times daily (about three hours), and from Oskarshamn, there are one or two daily departures in either direction (three to four hours).

Regular one-way adult tickets for the ferry cost between Skr152 and Skr499, but from mid-June to mid-August there is a more complicated fare system; some overnight, evening and early-morning sailings in the middle of the week have cheaper fares.

Getting Around

In Visby, hire bikes from Skr100 per 24 hours at **Gotlands Cykeluthyrning** (☎21 41 33), behind the tourist office (on the harbour).

Kollektiv Trafiken (☎21 41 12) runs buses via most villages to all corners of the island. A one-way ticket will cost no more than Skr68 (bicycles cost an additional Skr40); monthly tickets are Skr675.

Visby

☎0498 / POP 22,300

The port town of Visby is medieval eye candy and enough to warrant a trip to Gotland all by itself. A Unesco World Heritage site, Visby swarms with holidaymakers in the summer, and from mid-June to mid-August cars are banned in the old town. For many, the highlight of the season is the costumes, performances, crafts, markets and re-enactments of **Medeltidsveckan** (Medieval Week; www.medeltidsveckan.com), held during the first or second week of August. Finding accommodation during this time is almost impossible unless you've booked ahead.

The **tourist office** (☎20 17 00; www.gotland.info; Skeppsbron 4-6; ⏲8am-7pm in summer, 8am-4pm Mon-Fri rest of year) is at the harbour.

Set aside enough time to stroll the perimeter (3.5km) along the **13th-century wall** with its 40 towers. The ruins of 10 medieval churches are all within the town walls and contrast with the old but sound **cathedral**, north of Stortorget. **Gotlands Fornsal** (www.lansmuseetgotland.se; Strandgatan 14; admission Skr80; ⏲10am-6pm Fri-Wed, to 7pm Thu Jun–mid-Sep, noon-4pm Tue-Sun mid-Sep–May) is one of the largest and best regional museums in Sweden, with a notable collection of runestones and early grave findings.

Sleeping

Moderately priced accommodation in and around Visby is in demand; book well in advance.

Fängelse Vandrarhem HOSTEL €
(☎20 60 50; www.visbyfangelse.se; Skeppsbron 1; dm/s/d from Skr200/350/450) As hard to get into as it once was to get out of, this hostel offers beds year-round in the small converted cells of an old prison. It's in a handy location, between the ferry dock and the harbour restaurants, and there's a cute terrace bar in summer. Reserve well in advance and call ahead before arriving to ensure someone can let you in.

Gotlands Resor APARTMENTS, COTTAGES €€
(☎20 12 60; www.gotlandsresor.se; Färjeleden 3; cottages from Skr780) This travel agency, in Hamnhotellet, books stylish, fully equipped cottages in eastern and northern Gotland, as well as apartments in the Visby area. Bookings for the summer should be made around six months in advance. The agency also organises bike hire (per day from Skr70) and rents camping equipment.

Eating & Drinking

Sitting in cafes and bars facing the harbour or town square seems to be the chief pastime in Visby, and the choices are legion (although much more limited outside of the summer season). Self-caterers will find a handy **ICA supermarket** (Stora Torget; ⏲8am-8pm Mon-Sat, 10am-8pm Sun) right on the main square; larger options are outside Österport gate.

Skafferiet SWEDISH €€
(Adelsgatan 38; quiches Skr69, lunch special Skr95) This old-school Swedish cafe, with its low ceilings, stubby candles, rough-hewn wood tables and copper saucepans on the walls, is equally good for lingering over coffee or a quick, convenient lunch of the quiche-and-salad variety. Staff are adorable and cheery.

Cafe Amalia CAFE €
(Hästgatan 3; pastries Skr35, lunch mains Skr65-85) This friendly hang-out is sweet and spacious, with big people-watching windows, good music, breakfast served all day and possibly the best coffee in Sweden. Pasta bowls and sandwiches are huge and satisfying; try a cold salmon and gorgonzola panini. Sweets are all home-made.

SOUTHERN SWEDEN

Sweden's southernmost county, Skåne (Scania) was Danish property until 1658 and still flaunts its differences. You can detect them in the strong dialect *(skånska)*, the half-timbered houses and in Skåne's hybrid flag: a Swedish yellow cross on a red Danish background.

Malmö

040 / POP 280,900

Once dismissed as crime-prone and tatty, Sweden's third-largest city has rebranded itself as progressive and downright cool. It's no coincidence that two of Stockholm's hippest icons – rock club Debaser and fashion-forward boutique Tjallamalla – have come to town.

Sights & Activities

The cobblestone streets and appealing buildings around **Lilla Torg** are restored parts of the late-medieval town. The houses are now galleries, boutiques and restaurants.

The main museums of Malmö are based in and around **Malmöhus** (www.malmo.se/museer; Malmöhusvägen; combined admission Skr40; 10am-4pm Jun-Aug, noon-4pm Sep-May). You can walk through the royal apartments, see the **Stadsmuseum** with its city-centric collection, and see works by important Swedish artists like John Bauer and Sigrid Hjerten at the **Konstmuseum**. There's also an **aquarium** and **Naturmuseum**.

Moderna Museet Malmö (www.modernamuseet.se; Gasverksgatan 22; admission Skr50; 11am-6pm Tue-Sun, 11am-9pm Wed), the southern outpost of Stockholm's modern art museum, is currently home to several favourites from the larger museum, by major players such as Robert Rauschenberg, Öyvind Fahlström and Niki de Saint Phalle.

Sleeping

Private rooms or apartments from Skr395 per person are available through **City Room** (795 94; www.cityroom.se); bedsheets and towels cost an additional Skr100 per set. The agency has no office address but can be reached by phone on weekdays from 9am to noon. Otherwise, contact the tourist office.

STF Vandrarhem Malmö City HOSTEL €
(611 62 20; malmo.city@stfturist.se; Rönngatan 1; dm Skr190, s/d from Skr390/460; @) This huge hostel has spotless, brand-new facilities, and several rooms include TV and private bathrooms. There's a big kitchen, spacious dining room, TV lounge, and very helpful staff, and most sights are within easy walking distance.

Bosses Gästvåningar HOSTEL €
(32 62 50; www.bosses.nu; Södra Förstadsgatan 110B; s/d/tr/q from Skr375/525/625/850; @) The quiet, clean rooms in this central SVIF hostel are like those of a budget hotel, with proper beds, TV and shared bathrooms. Service is helpful and it's close to Möllevångstorget and opposite the town hospital (follow the signs for 'Sjukhuset' if arriving by car).

Eating & Drinking

Malmö isn't short on dining experiences, whether it's vegan grub in a grungy hangout or designer supping on contemporary Nordic flavours. One surefire strategy is to try whichever kebab stand in Möllevångstorget has the longest line. For atmosphere and conviviality, head to the restaurant-bars on Lilla Torg: **Victors**, **Moosehead** and **Mello Yello** are all great spots with varied menus (from Thai to Tex-Mex), affable service and alfresco seating (complete with heaters and blankets in cold weather).

Solde CAFE €
(Regementsgatan 3; panini from Skr45; 7.15am-6.30pm Mon-Fri, 9am-4pm Sat) Malmö's coolest cafe is a grit-chic combo of concrete bar, white-tiled walls, art exhibitions and indie-hip regulars. The owner is an award-winning barista; watch him in action over lip-smacking Italian panini, biscotti and *cornetti* (croissants).

Glassfabriken CAFE €
(Kristianstadsgatan 16; mains Skr50; 11am-8pm, closed Mon) Easy to miss, this grungy, arty, alcohol-free hang-out serves cheap, tasty grub such as vegan salads, ciabatta and freshly baked cakes; locals like the weekend brunch (Skr45). Play boardgames over mango milkshakes, check out the local art on display or catch the occasional music or theatre gig. It's two blocks northeast of Möllevångstorget.

Krua Thai THAI €€
(Möllevångstorget 14; mains Skr79-115; 11am-3pm Mon, 11am-3pm & 5-10pm Tue-Fri, 1-10pm Sat, 2-10pm Sun) Anchoring one corner of the buzzing Möllevångstorget is this authentic, long-standing Thai joint, a reliable if less than thrilling choice. The family also run a central **takeaway** (Södergatan 22; 2 dish combo Skr60) with longer hours.

Information

Forex (Centralstationen; 7am-9pm) Currency exchange.

Malmö Card The discount card covers free bus transport, street parking, entry to several museums and discounts at other attractions and on sightseeing tours; Skr130/160 for one/two days. Buy it at the tourist office.

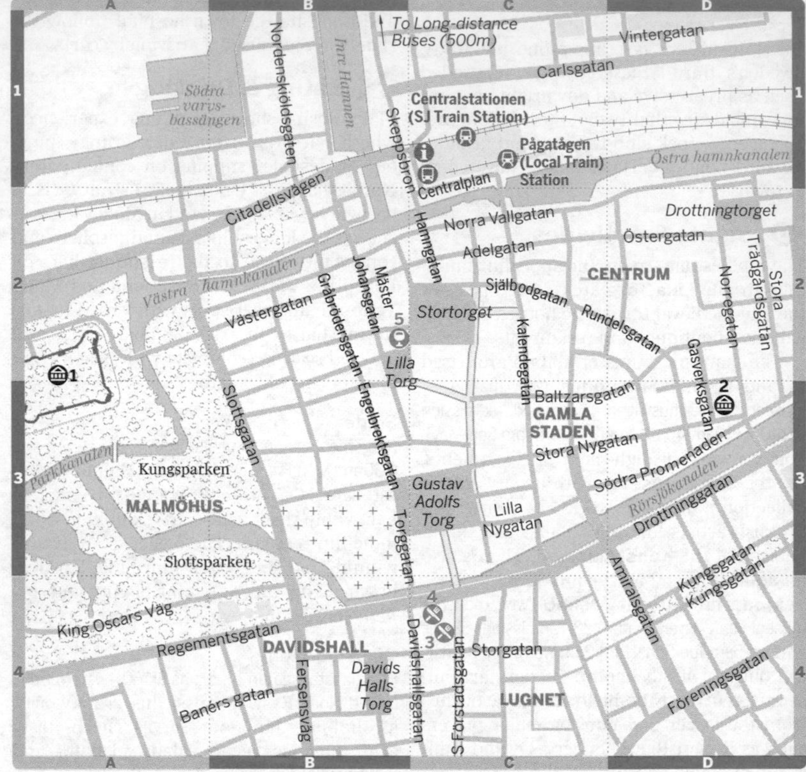

Skånegården (☎20 96 00; www.skane.com; Stortorget 9, SE-21122 Malmö; ⏲9am-8pm Mon-Fri, 9am-4pm Sat & Sun mid-Jun–mid-Aug, shorter hr rest of yr, closed Sun Oct-early Jun) Tourist office, on the E20, 800m from the Öresund bridge tollgate that's designed for motorists entering from Denmark.

Tourist office (☎34 12 00; www.malmo.se; ⏲9am-7pm Mon-Fri, 10am-4pm Sat & Sun mid-Jun–early Sep, shorter hr rest of the year) Inside Centralstationen (train station); has free internet and a hotel-booking service (with fee).

Getting There & Away

Sturup airport (☎613 10 00; www.malmoairport.se) is situated 33km southeast of Malmö. **SAS** (☎0770-72 77 27; www.sas.se) has up to 11 nonstop flights to Stockholm Arlanda daily. **Malmö Aviation** (☎0771-55 00 10; www.malmoaviation.se) flies several times daily to Stockholm Bromma airport.

Trains run directly from Malmö to Copenhagen's main airport (Skr95, 35 minutes, every 20 minutes), which has a much wider flight selection.

There are two bus terminals with daily departures to Swedish and European destinations. **Travelshop** (Malmö Buss & Resecenter; ☎33 05 70; www.travelshop.se; Skeppsbron 10), north of the train station by the harbour, services (and sells tickets for) several companies, including **Swebus Express** (☎0771-21 82 18; www.swebusexpress.com), which runs two to four times daily to Stockholm (Skr400 to Skr600, 8½ hours) and up to 10 times daily to Göteborg (Skr268, three to four hours); five continue to Oslo (Skr445, eight hours).

The second long-distance bus terminal, **Öresundsterminalen** (☎59 09 00; Terminalgatan 10) is reached via bus 35 from Centralstationen to Arlöv (Skr16; 30 minutes). From here, **Svenska Buss** (☎0771-67 67 67; www.svenskabuss.se) runs a service to Stockholm (Skr370, 11 hours), four times weekly.

Malmö

Sights

	Aquarium	(see 1)
	Konstmuseum	(see 1)
1	Malmöhus	A2
2	Moderna Museet Malmö	D3
	Museer	(see 1)
	Naturmuseum	(see 1)

Eating

3	Krua Thai Takeaway	C4
4	Solde	C4

Drinking

	Mello Yello	(see 5)
	Moosehead	(see 5)
5	Victors	B2

GoByBus (☎0771-15 15 15; www.gobybus.se, in Swedish) has six buses on the Copenhagen–Malmö–Göteborg route per day, with a couple originating from Berlin and continuing on to Oslo.

Lund

☎046 / POP 105,300

Centred round a striking cathedral, Lund is a soulful blend of leafy parks, medieval abodes and coffee-sipping bookworms. Like most university hubs, however, it loses some of its buzz during the summer, when students head home for the holidays.

The **tourist office** (☎35 50 40; www.lund.se; Kyrkogatan 11; ⊙10am-7pm Mon-Fri, 10am-3pm Sat, 11am-3pm Sun mid-Jun–Aug, 10am-5pm Mon-Fri, 10am-3pm Sat May–mid-Jun & Sep, 10am-5pm Mon-Fri Oct-Apr) is opposite the cathedral.

Construction on Lund's Romanesque **Domkyrka** (cathedral) began about 1100, when Lund became Europe's largest archbishopric. The cathedral is magnificent: visit at noon or 3pm (1pm and 3pm weekends and holidays) when the astronomical clock strikes up *In Dulci Jubilo*.

Sleeping & Eating

STF Vandrarhem Lund Tåget HOSTEL €
(☎14 28 20; www.trainhostel.com; Vävaregatan 22; dm Skr160) This quirky hostel is based in old railway carriages in parkland behind the station. The triple bunks and tiny rooms are OK if you're cosying up with loved ones, but a little claustrophobic with strangers. Less novel are the hot-water vending machines in the showers (have a few Skr1 coins handy). Reception is open for check-in from 5pm to 8pm, and reservations are recommended.

Hotel Ahlström HOTEL €€
(☎211 01 74; www.hotellahlstrom.se; Skomakaregatan 3; s/d without bathroom Skr670/850, d Skr1100) Lund's oldest hotel is friendly and affordable, and on a quiet, central street. Rooms have parquet floors, cool white walls and washbasins (most have shared bathroom). Breakfast is brought to your door.

Ebbas Skafferi CAFE €
(Bytaregatan 5; main Skr65; ⊙9am-7pm Mon-Fri, to 6pm Sat & Sun) Ebbas is the perfect cafe: think warm wooden tables, green plants and flowers, odd bits of artwork, a laidback courtyard, and scrumptious coffee, teas, and tasty grub like hearty risotto and moreish cheesecake.

Getting There & Away

It's 15 minutes from Lund to Malmö by train, with frequent local Pågatågen (commuter train) departures (Skr39). Some trains continue to Copenhagen (Skr125, one hour). Other direct services run from Malmö. All long-distance trains from Stockholm or Göteborg to Malmö stop in Lund. Buses leave from outside the train station.

Helsingborg

☎042 / POP 125,000

At its heart, Helsingborg is a sparkly showcase of rejuvenated waterfront, metro-glam restaurants, lively cobbled streets and lofty castle ruins. With Denmark looking on from a mere 4km across the Öresund, its flouncy, turreted buildings feel like a brazen statement.

The **tourist office** (☎10 43 50; www.helsingborg.se; Rådhuset, Stortorget; ⊙9am-8pm Mon-Fri, 9am-5pm Sat 10am-3pm Sun mid-Jun–Aug, shorter hr & closed Sun rest of yr) can help with inquiries.

First Stop Sweden (☎10 41 30; www.firststopsweden.com; Bredgatan 2; ⊙9am-8pm Mon-Fri, 9am-5pm Sat & Sun late Jun–mid-Aug, shorter hr rest of yr, closed Sat & Sun Sep-early May), near the car-ferry ticket booths, dispenses tourist information on the whole country and has an X-Change currency exchange counter.

You can access the square medieval tower **Kärnan** (admission Skr20; ⏲10am-6pm Jun-Aug, closed Mon rest of year) from steps near the tourist office. The tower is all that remains of a 14th-century castle; the view from the top (34m) overlooks Öresund to the Danish heartland.

Sleeping & Eating

Helsingborgs Vandrarhem HOSTEL €
(☎14 58 50; www.hbgturist.com; Järnvägsgatan 39; dm from Skr195, s/d Skr395/595; 📶) Despite the somewhat anonymous vibe, this central hostel offers clean, comfortable rooms located about 200m from Knutpunkten. Reception is open between 3pm and 6pm.

Villa Thalassa HOSTEL €
(☎38 06 60; www.villathalassa.com; Dag Hammarskjöldsväg; dm from Skr200, 2-/3-bed r Skr595/795) This SVIF option is a lovely early 20th-century villa situated in beautiful gardens. Hostel accommodation is in huts, but the hotel-standard rooms are a cut above if your budget will stretch. The villa lies 3km north of central Helsingborg in the Pålsjö area. Bus 219 stops 500m short, at the Pålsjöbaden bus stop.

Ebbas Fik CAFE €
(Bruksgatan 20; sandwiches Skr25-75; ⏲9am-6pm Mon-Fri, 9am-4pm Sat; 📶) It's still 1955 at this kitsch-tastic retro cafe, complete with jukebox, retro petrol pump and hamburgers made to Elvis' recipe. The extensive cafe menu also includes (huge) sandwiches, baked potatoes and crazy cakes and buns.

Getting There & Away

The main transport centre is Knutpunkten; the underground platforms serve SJ trains bound for Stockholm, Göteborg, Copenhagen and Oslo, plus regional trains. At ground level and a little south, but still inside the same complex, is the bus terminal. Daily long-distance services run to destinations including Göteborg and Oslo.

Knutpunkten is the terminal for frequent ferries to Denmark and Oslo.

Göteborg (Gothenburg)

☎031 / POP 493,600

Often caught in Stockholm's shadow, gregarious Göteborg (Gothenburg in English) socks a mighty punch of its own. Some of the country's finest talent hails from its streets, including music icons José González and Soundtrack of Our Lives. Ornate architecture lines its tram-rattled streets, grit-hip cafes hum with bonhomie. West of Kungsportsavenyn (dubbed the 'Champs Élysées' in brochures and a 'tourist trap' by locals), the Haga and Linné districts buzz with creativity. A must-see is Scandinavia's amusement-park heavyweight.

Sights

Liseberg (www.liseberg.se; tickets from Skr80, annual pass Skr195; ⏲to 10pm or 11pm most days May-Aug, to 9pm or 10pm during Christmas period) fun park is dominated by its spaceport-like tower. The ride to the top, some 83m above the ground, climaxes in a spinning dance and a breathtaking view of the city. Leave your stomach at the gate. Each ride costs between one and four coupons (Skr20 each) per go, but more economical passes are available in various configurations, depending on your ambitions and endurance. The opening hours for the park are complex – check the website. To get there, take tram 4 or 5, and enter from Örgrytevägen or Getebergsled.

By Liseberg is the striking **Universeum** (www.universeum.se; Södra Vägen 50; admission Skr155; ⏲10am-6pm), a huge and impressive 'science discovery centre' featuring everything from rainforests to a shark tank.

The **Stadsmuseum** (☎61 27 70; Östindiska huset, Norra Hamngatan 12; adult/under 25yr Skr40/free; ⏲10am-5pm May-Aug, 10am-5pm Tue-Sun, to 8pm Wed rest of year) has archaeological, local and historical collections, including Sweden's only original Viking ship.

The main art collections are at **Konstmuseet** (www.konstmuseum.goteborg.se; Götaplatsen; adult/under 25yr Skr40/free, during special exhibitions adult Skr60; ⏲11am-6pm Tue & Thu, 11am-9pm Wed, 11am-5pm Fri-Sun), with impressive collections of Nordic and European masters (notable for works by Rubens, Van Gogh, Rembrandt and Picasso) and touring exhibitions.

The excellent **Röhsska Museet** (www.designmuseum.se; Vasagatan 37; adult/under 20yr Skr40/free; ⏲noon-8pm Tue, noon-5pm Wed-Fri, 11am-5pm Sat & Sun) covers modern Scandinavian design and decorative arts.

There are some lovely green oases in the city, including **Trädgårdsföreningen** (Nya Allén; admission mid-Apr–mid-Sep Skr15, other times free; ⏲7am-6pm Mon-Fri, 9am-6pm Sat & Sun), laid out in 1842 and home to a couple of pretty cafes, a rosarium and a **palm house**.

Sleeping

STF Vandrarhem Slottsskogen HOSTEL €
(☎42 65 20; www.sov.nu; Vegagatan 21; dm Skr215, s/d Skr360/440; @) Unlike many Swedish hostels, big, friendly Slottsskogen is a cracking place for meeting other travellers. For a small extra payment there's access to a laundry, sauna and sun bed, and the buffet breakfast (Skr65) is brilliant. Parking spaces can be booked for a fee. Reception is closed between noon and 2pm. Take tram 1 or 6 to Olivedalsgatan.

Masthuggsterrassens Vandrarhem HOSTEL €
(☎42 48 20; www.mastenvandrarhem.com; Masthuggsterrassen 10h; dm/d Skr195/500; @) If you're after a good night's sleep, try this clean, quiet, well-run place, whose long hallways are plastered with vintage film posters. Facilities include three lounges, three kitchens and a little library (mostly Swedish books), and it's handy if you're catching an early ferry to Denmark. Take tram 3, 9 or 11 to Masthuggstorget and follow the signs up the hill.

Kvibergs Vandrarhem & Stugby HOSTEL, CAMPING GROUND €
(☎43 50 55; www.vandrarhem.com; Kvibergsvägen 5; d/tr/q Skr490/600/720; @) This sterling SVIF hostel, a few kilometres northeast of the city centre (tram 6, 7 or 11), boasts super amenities, including flatscreen TVs, sauna, sun beds, laundry, table tennis, two kitchens and two lounges. There are no dorms; you rent out the entire room. Hotel-style rooms and cabins are also available. Rates drop in low season.

Hotel Flora BOUTIQUE HOTEL €€
(☎13 86 16; www.hotelflora.se; Grönsakstorget 2; s/d Skr1395/1695; @) An extreme makeover took Flora from frumpy to fabulous, with uberslick rooms flaunting black-and-white interiors, designer chairs, flatscreen TVs and sparkling bathrooms. Top-floor rooms have air-con, several rooms offer river views and the chic split-level courtyard is perfect for sophisticated chilling.

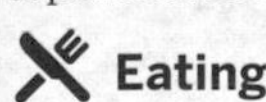

Eating

Kungsportsavenyn is lined with restaurants, cafes and bars (although prices here can be higher than in other parts of town). Vasagatan is close to the student heartland and has excellent cafes. Linnégatan (close to most of the hostels) has more good options.

Alexandras SOUP €
(☎711 23 81; Kungstorget; soups and pastas Skr40) Located in the central Saluhallen, this famous Greek soup kitchen dishes out excellent hearty soups and pastas, particularly welcoming on a chilly day.

Andrum VEGETARIAN €
(☎13 85 04; Östra Hamngatan 19; large plate Skr70; ⏲11am-9pm Mon-Fri, noon-8pm Sat & Sun) Vegetarians love this casual, meat-free spot with its value for money, all-day lunch buffet. It's simple, tasty, wholesome stuff, and cheerfully recommended.

Bar Doppio CAFE €
(☎42 56 66; Linnégatan; breakfast packets Skr50-80; ⏲7am-6.30pm Mon-Fri, 8am-5pm Sat & Sun) More class-A caffeine awaits at this Scandi-cool cafe, where regulars keep track of their tabs on a giant blackboard. The tiny space has a great neighbourhood vibe and fresh grub like home-made muesli, soup, focaccia and fruit smoothies.

Publik GASTROPUB €€
(☎14 65 20; Andra Långgatan 20; lunch Skr75, mains Skr100-145; ⏲11.30am-1am Mon-Sat) Arguably Göteborg's coolest hang-out (think grit-chic interiors, local art exhibitions, DJ-spun tunes and creative indie crowds), this cafe-bar hybrid also serves brilliant, great-value grub like goat cheese-stuffed eggplant with red pesto potatoes. The well-priced house wine is perfectly drinkable and there's a backyard courtyard for fine-weather lounging.

Drinking

Lokal BAR
(Kyrkogatan 11; ⏲4pm-1am Mon-Sat) Awarded best bar in Göteborg and run by the team from Publik, this cool hang-out pulls everyone from artists and media types to the odd punk rocker. The drinks are inspired (think kiwi and ginger daiquiris), the pick-and-mix menu brims with fusion flavours, and music spans soul, jazz and electro. Best of all, staff donate 10% of their tips to a Cambodian orphanage.

Sjöbaren PUB
(Haga Nygata 25; ⏲11am-midnight) One of the few old-school pubs in Göteborg, this friendly but unfussy nautical-themed place in Haga often has what look to be real fishermen smoking outside the front door. Beer pours out of a copper diving helmet, and the menu covers the full range of seafood.

Entertainment

Clubs in Göteborg have varying minimum-age limits, ranging from 18 to 25, and many may charge admission depending on the night. Check the websites for details on how to get there.

Röda Sten CLUB

(www.rodasten.com; Röda Sten 1; Fri & Sat) Paging Berlin with its post-industrial look, this power station-turned-art gallery cranks up the party vibe with a variety of pan-European DJs, live music and club nights on Fridays and Saturdays. Check the website for

Göteborg

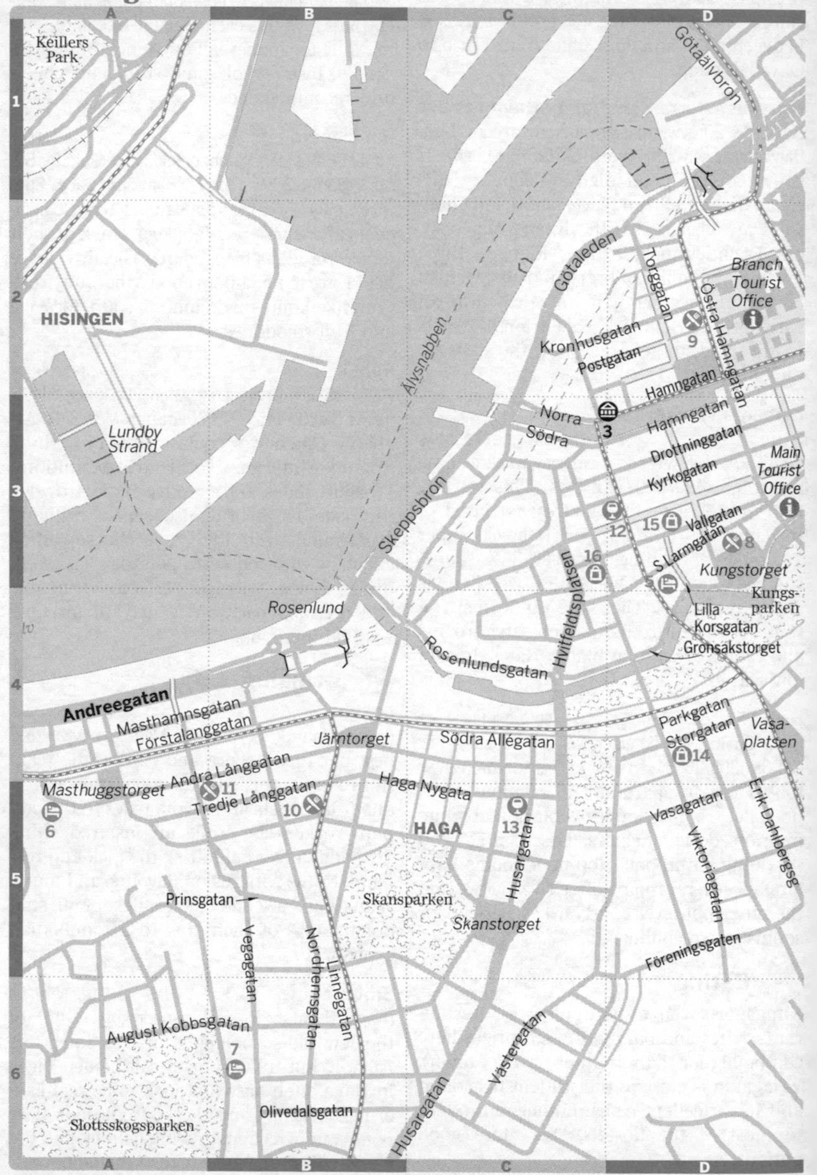

a schedule. There's also a restaurant known for its fish soup.

Nefertiti CLUB

(☎711 15 33; Hvitfeldtsplatsen 6) A Göteborg institution, this effortlessly cool venue is famous for its smooth live jazz, blues and world music, usually followed by kicking club nights spanning from techno, deep house and soul to hip hop and funk. Times vary, so check the website (www.nefertite.se).

Shopping

DesignTorget DESIGN

(Vallgatan 14) Cool, affordable design objects from both established and up-and-coming Scandi talent.

Prickig Katt CLOTHING

(Magasinsgatan 17; ⊙closed Sun) The 'Spotted Cat' sports retro-clad staff, idiosyncratic fashion from Dutch, Danish and home-grown labels, as well as kitschy wares and out-there handmade millinery and bling.

DEM Collective CLOTHING

(Storgatan 11; ⊙closed Sun) Head to this bite-size boutique for Scandi cool, fair-trade threads. Completely organic, designs are minimalist, street-smart and supremely comfortable.

Information

Göteborg Pass (Skr245 for 24hr, Skr390 for 48hr) Gives free entry to Liseberg and some city attractions, city tours and public transport. Collect it at tourist offices, hotels and hostels.

Göteborg

Sights

1 Konstmuseet F5
2 Röhsska Museet E4
3 Stadsmuseum D3
4 Trädgårdsföreningen E3

Sleeping

5 Hotel Flora D3
6 Masthuggsterrassens Vandrarhem A5
7 STF Vandrarhem Slottsskogen B6

Eating

8 Alexandras D3
9 Andrum D2
10 Bar Doppio B5
11 Publik B5

Drinking

12 Lokal D3
13 Sjöbaren C5

Shopping

14 DEM Collective D4
15 DesignTorget D3
16 Prickig Katt C3

Östra Sjukhuset (☎343 40 00) Large hospital near tram terminus 1, northeast of town.

Tourist offices (☎61 25 00; www.goteborg.com) branch tourist office (Nordstan complex; ⏲10am-6pm Mon-Fri, 10am-6pm Sat, noon-5pm Sun); main tourist office (Kungsportsplatsen 2; ⏲9.30am-8pm mid-Jun–mid-Aug, 9am-5pm Mon-Fri, 10am-2pm Sat Sep-Apr, 9.30am-6pm Mon-Fri, 10am-2pm Sat & Sun May–mid-Jun & end Aug)

Getting There & Away

Air

Twenty-five kilometres east of the city, **Landvetter airport** (GOT; ☎94 10 00) has services to many European cities. **Gothenburg City airport** (GSE; ☎92 60 60; www.goteborgcityairport.se) is a minor airport 10km northwest of the city centre, used by Ryanair.

Boat

Göteborg is a major entry point for ferries, with several terminals including Fredrikshaven and Kiel. For full details see p1228.

Bus

The modern bus station, Nils Ericson Terminalen, is next to Centralstationen. Eurolines and Swebus Express share an office here.

Swebus Express (☎0771-21 82 18; www.swebusexpress.com) has an office at the bus station and operates frequent buses to most major towns. Services to Stockholm (Skr260, seven hours) run five to seven times daily. Other direct destinations include Copenhagen (Skr179, four to five hours), Helsingborg (Skr113, three hours), Oslo (Skr173, four hours) and Malmö (Skr131, three hours).

Svenska Buss (☎0771-67 67 67; www.svenskabuss.se) has daily departures for Stockholm (Skr430, 7½ hours).

As always, prices are lower for advanced bookings, especially for Swebus Express and GoByBus.

Train

Centralstationen serves SJ and regional trains, with direct trains to Malmö, Copenhagen, Oslo and Stockholm, plus other destinations in the southern half of Sweden. Direct train services to Stockholm depart approximately hourly (Skr600 to Skr1200, three to five hours).

Getting Around

Buses, trams and ferries run by **Västtrafik** (☎0771-41 43 00; www.vasttrafik.se) make up the city's public transport system; there are Västtrafik information booths selling tickets and giving out timetables inside **Nils Ericson Terminalen** (⏲6am-10pm Mon-Fri, 9am-10pm Sat, 9am-7pm Sun), in front of the train station on **Drottningtorget** (⏲6am-8pm Mon-Fri, 8am-8pm Sat & Sun) and at **Brunnsparken** (⏲7am-7pm Mon-Fri, 9am-6pm Sat).

Holders of the Göteborg Pass travel free, including on late-night transport. Otherwise a city transport ticket costs adult/child Skr25/19 (Skr50 on late-night transport). A 24-hour Dagkort (day pass) for the whole city area costs Skr65, or Skr130 for 72 hours.

The easiest way to cover lengthy distances in Göteborg is by tram. Lines, numbered 1 to 13, converge near Brunnsparken (a block from the train station).

NORTHERN SWEDEN

Norrland is remote enough that travellers here aren't likely to see much of the tour-bus crowd – or, for that matter, anyone else. Reindeer outnumber cars on the roads, and much of the landscape consists of deep green forest. It's a paradise for nature lovers who enjoy hiking, skiing and other outdoor activities.

Östersund

☎063 / POP 58,400

This pleasant town by Lake Storsjön, in whose chilly waters is said to lurk a rarely sighted monster, has good budget accommodation and is a relaxed and scenic place and an excellent gateway town for further explorations of Norrland. The **tourist office** (☎14 40 01; www.turist.ostersund.se; Rådhusgatan 44; ⏲9am-5pm Mon-Thu, 10am-3pm Fri-Sun) is opposite the town hall; it has free internet access.

Don't miss **Jamtli** (www.jamtli.com; admission mid-Jun–Aug Skr110, rest of year Skr60; ⏲11am-5pm), 1km north of the town centre. It combines an open-air museum park (à la Skansen in Stockholm) with a first-rate regional culture museum. Take bus 2.

An offshoot of Färgfabriken in Stockholm, **Färgfabriken Norr** (www.fargfabrikennorr.se; Byggnad 33, Infanterigatan 30; admission free; ⏲noon-4pm Thu-Sun during exhibitions) is a huge art space across E14 from Jamtli. Take bus 14 or 8.

Other attractions lie on the adjacent island of Frösön, reached by road or footbridge from the middle of Östersund.

Sleeping & Eating

STF Vandrarhem Jamtli HOSTEL €
(☎12 20 60; vandrarhemmet@jamtli.com; Museiplan; dm Skr150, s/d from Skr245/300) Right inside the gates of Jamtli museum park is this comfortable hostel, housed in a low, barnlike wooden

building with a huge kitchen. Dorms are in two- to five-bed rooms, and facilities are all top-notch. Reservations are recommended.

Volos GREEK-SWEDISH €€
(Prästgatan 38; daily lunch Skr79, mains Skr159-179; ⏲11am-9pm, until midnight Sat & Sun & Jul–Aug) This upscale Greek restaurant emphasizes locally produced, organic ingredients, including beef from Jämtland, potatoes from Härjedalen and char from nearby Landö Lake, served in traditional Jämtland style.

Getting There & Away

Bus 63 runs northeast to Umeå (six hours, two to four daily).

SJ trains run from Stockholm (from Skr607, six hours). Trains also go to Trondheim in Norway.

Umeå

☎090 / POP 112,000

With the vibrant feel of a college town (it has around 30,000 students), Umeå is a welcome outpost of urbanity in the barren north. It's one of the fastest-growing towns in Sweden and an agreeable place to hang out, wind down or stock up for an outdoor adventure. The **tourist office** (☎16 16 16; www.visitumea.se; Renmarkstorget 15) is central.

Gammlia (☎1/ 18 00; admission free, ⏲10am-5pm mid-Jun–mid-Aug, 10am-4pm Tue-Fri, noon-4pm Sat, noon-5pm Sun rest of year), a cluster of museums 1km east of the town centre, includes the cultural/historical exhibits and Sami collections of the regional **Västerbottens Museum**.

STF Vandrarhem Umeå (☎77 16 50; www.umeavandrarhem.com; Västra Esplanaden 10; dm Skr160, s/d from Skr260/320; @ 📶) has tiny but comfortable rooms and is one of the few youth hostels in the region actually occupied by young people.

The long-distance bus station is opposite the train station on Järnvägsallén, just north of the town centre. Umeå is the main centre for **Länstrafiken Västerbotten** (☎020-91 00 19), the regional bus network. Direct buses run to Mo i Rana in Norway; other daily destinations include Östersund.

Kiruna

☎0980 / POP 23,500

A few years back, it became clear that years of iron-ore extraction was sucking the stability out of the bedrock underneath Kiruna. In 2007 the town voted to shift itself a few kilometres northwest; plans are to move the railway and about 450 homes by 2013, with the rest of the town centre to follow gradually.

Every winter at **Jukkasjärvi**, 18km east of Kiruna, the amazing **Ice Hotel** (www.icehotel.com) is built from hundreds of tonnes of ice from the frozen local river. This custom-built 'igloo' has a chapel and a bar – you can drink from a glass made of ice – and ice-sculpture exhibitions. It also has 50 'hotel rooms' outfitted with reindeer skins and sleeping bags.

Near the church in Jukkasjärvi is **Gárdi** (adult/child Skr60/30; ⏲tours 10am-6pm mid-Jun–mid-Aug), a reindeer yard that you can tour with a Sami guide to learn about reindeer farming and Sami culture. Regular bus 501 runs between Kiruna and Jukkasjärvi (Skr29, 30 minutes, several daily).

The **tourist office** (☎188 80; www.lappland.se; in Folkets Hus, Lars Janssonsgatan 17; ⏲8.30am-9pm Mon-Fri, 8.30am-6pm Sat & Sun Jun-Aug, Mon-Sat rest of year), on the main square, has computers for internet access (Skr20 per hr) and can book mine tours and accommodation.

Sleeping & Eating

Rådhusbyn Ripan Hotell & Camping CAMPING GROUND, HOTEL €
(☎630 00; www.ripan.se; Campingvägen 5; campsites/s/d from Skr135/1450/1610, cabins from Skr995; @) In the northern part of town, this is a large and well-equipped camping ground with hotel rooms and chalets in addition to its caravan sites and campsites. Ask about the organised walk to Samegården, the museum of Sami culture (Skr450, 1pm Fridays), and other activities.

SVIF Yellow House HOSTEL €
(☎137 50; www.yellowhouse.nu; Hantverkaregatan 25; dm/s/d Skr170/350/440) The hostel also has budget hotel rooms; the excellent facilities include a sauna, kitchen and laundry, a TV in each room, and a nice, quiet enclosed garden.

Café Safari CAFE €
(Geologsgatan 4; sandwiches Skr35, ⏲until 9pm Thu-Sat) This is the nicest cafe in town, a long skinny room with good French-press coffee, cakes and light meals such as sandwiches, quiche and baked potatoes.

Getting There & Away

The small **airport** (KRN; ☎680 00), 9km east of town, has flights to/from Stockholm.

Regional buses in this vast region are operated by **Länstrafiken Norrbotten** (☎020-47 00 47) from the bus station on Hjalmar Lundbohmsvägen, opposite the town hall. Buses serve all major settlements.

UNDERSTAND SWEDEN

History

The Viking Age was getting under way by the 9th century; Vikings made their mark in Russia, as well as trading with (and pillaging) Byzantine territories. Along with pagan gods, the aristocrats and their chosen kings (many from Denmark as a result of the Union of Kalmar in 1397) reigned. A century of Swedish nationalist grumblings erupted in rebellion under the young nobleman Gustaf Vasa, who was crowned Gustaf I in 1523. In 1809 a constitutional amendment divided legislative powers between king and parliament.

By 1900 almost one in four Swedes lived in cities and the level of industry was increasing. In this environment the working class was radicalised. Sweden declared itself neutral at the outbreak of WWI. The Social Democrats, in power since 1932, introduced a welfare state after the war.

The 1950s and '60s saw a rapid rise in the standard of living for ordinary Swedes. But the world recession of the early 1990s led to massive devaluation of the Swedish krona. Their economy and national confidence shaken, Swedes voted to join the EU, effective on 1 January 1995. But a 2003 referendum on whether Sweden should adopt the euro resulted in a 'no' vote.

In 2006, the long-entrenched Social Democrats lost their leadership position in parliament. The centre-right Alliance Party won the election, with new Prime Minister Fredrik Reinfeldt campaigning on a 'work first' platform.

The global economic crisis again affected Sweden in 2008; that year the Swedish krona dropped to its weakest level since 2002. As ever, economic tensions fed social anxieties. An annual survey about ethnic diversity, conducted by Uppsala University researchers, indicated twice as many Swedes had an 'extremely negative' attitude toward racial diversity in 2008 than in 2005. (Researchers added, however, that Sweden is still well ahead of the rest of Europe in terms of encouraging diversity.)

People

Around nine million people call Sweden home, making it Scandinavia's most populous country. Most live in the urban centres of Stockholm, Göteborg and Malmö – only 12% of the population lives in Norrland, which takes up two-thirds of the country's geographical area.

There are about 17,000 Sami (the indigenous people of Scandinavia, sometimes called Lapps) in Sweden, largely concentrated in the north. More than 17% of Sweden's population are foreign-born. Most immigrants have come from other European countries, including Russia, the former Yugoslavia, Poland and Greece. The largest non-European ethnic group consists of Assyrian/Syriac people. Communities that have come from Chile and Somalia also have a sizeable presence, and there are around 45,000 Roma.

Sweden's overall approach to family life is in line with its socially progressive tendencies. The extensive state-mandated maternity/paternity leave is shared equally between parents. Gay and lesbian couples have the same rights as heterosexual married couples under Swedish law.

Some 87% of the Swedish population is Lutheran, although only about 10% regularly attend church services.

At first, Sweden might not seem so distinct from its Scandinavian neighbours. However, attentive visitors will notice a tone here that hints at many things: depth of feeling, awareness of doom, absence of sentimentality, strength of principle, avoidance of conflict, a sombre conviction that certain things simply matter. Swedish culture, from design to literature and cinema, favours a weighty sense of drama blended with gallows humour and stark aesthetics.

Arts

Sweden's 19th-century artistic highlights include the warm art nouveau oil paintings of Carl Larsson (1853–1919), the nudes and portraits of Anders Zorn (1860–1920), August Strindberg's violently moody seascapes and the nature paintings of Bruno Liljefors (1860–1939). Carl Milles (1875–1955) is Sweden's greatest sculptor, once employed as Rodin's assistant.

Well-known Swedish writers include the poet Carl Michael Bellman (1740–95), playwright August Strindberg (1849–1912) and children's writer Astrid Lindgren (1907–2002). Vilhelm Moberg (1898–1973) won international acclaim with *Utvandrarna* (The Emigrants; 1949) and *Nybyggarna* (The Settlers; 1956).

Swedish cinema is inextricably linked with the name of Ingmar Bergman. His deeply contemplative films *(The Seventh Seal, Through a Glass Darkly, Persona)* explore alienation, the absence of god, the meaning of life, the certainty of death and other light-hearted themes. Recently, Trollhättan and Ystad have become filmmaking centres, thanks to younger directors like Lukas Moodysson, whose *Lilja 4-Ever, Fucking Åmål* and *Tillsammans* have all been hits.

Any survey of Swedish music must at least mention ABBA, the iconic, dubiously outfitted winners of the 1974 Eurovision Song Contest (with 'Waterloo'). More current Swedish successes are pop icon Robyn, indie melody-makers Peter Björn & John, and the exquisitely mellow José González, whose cover of The Knife's track 'Heartbeats' catapulted the Göteborg native to international stardom.

Sweden is a living gallery of inspired design, from Jonas Bohlin 'Tutu lamps' to Tom Hedquist milk cartons. Aesthetic prowess also fuels Sweden's thriving fashion scene. Since the late 1990s, local designers have aroused global admiration: Madonna dons Patrik Söderstam trousers, and Acne Jeans sell like hotcakes at LA's hip Fred Segal. In fact, Sweden now exports more fashion than pop.

Food

Restaurants in this chapter have been categorised by the price of an average main course, as follows:

€€€ more than Skr185

€€ Skr75 to Skr185

€ less than Skr75

Environment

Sweden covers an area of 449,964 sq km, and its maximum north–south extent is 1574km. Flat and open Skåne in the south is similar to Denmark, but further north the landscape is hillier and heavily forested. The coastline is notable for its small fjords and skerries.

Nature-loving Swedes led Europe in setting up national parks in the early 20th century; there are now 29 in Sweden.

Ecological consciousness in Sweden is very high. Swedes are fervent believers in sorting and recycling household waste (paper, glass, plastic etc) – you'll be expected to do the same in hostels and camping grounds.

SURVIVAL GUIDE

Directory A–Z

Accommodation

Our Sleeping entries are listed according to the price of a standard double room with private bathroom in high season (June to August). The following price ranges apply to listings:

€€€ more than Skr1600

€€ Skr800 to Skr1600

€ less than Skr800

CABINS & CAMPING

Daily rates for *stugor* (cabins and chalets, often found at camping grounds or in the countryside) offer good value for small groups, and range in both facilities and price (Skr350 to Skr800). Check www.stuga.nu for details.

Sweden has hundreds of camping grounds, most open from May through August. Prices vary, from Skr200 for a basic camp site to Skr350 for the highest standards. Most camping grounds have kitchens and laundry facilities. Visit www.camping.se for more information.

HOSTELS

Sweden has nearly 500 *vandrarhem* (hostels). Some 315 hostels are affiliated with **Svenska Turistföreningen** (STF; ☎08-463 21 00; www.svenskaturistforeningen.se), part of Hostelling International (HI). Holders of HI membership cards pay the same rates as STF members. Nonmembers can pay Skr50 extra (Skr100 at some mountain lodges), or join up at hostels. In this book we quote prices at STF hostels for members.

Around 190 hostels belong to **Sveriges Vandrarhem i Förening** (SVIF; ☎0413-55 34 50; www.svif.se). No membership is required and rates are similar to those of STF hostels. Pick up the free guide at tourist offices or SVIF hostels.

Reception hours are often limited, so be sure to make arrangements for getting in when you book.

HOTELS

There are few budget hotels in Sweden, but even upscale hotels provide good-value weekend and summer (mid-June to mid-August) rates, often up to 50% off regular prices, and many offer substantial discounts for early or online booking. All prices listed in this chapter are regular prices.

Activities

Swedes are huge nature lovers and are active year-round, on bike paths, forest jogging tracks, rivers and lakes, mountain trails, and the snow and ice.

The right of public access to the countryside (called *allemansrätten*) means that in Sweden, by law, you're allowed to walk, boat, ski or swim on private land as long as you stay at least 70m from houses and keep out of gardens, fenced areas and cultivated land. You can camp for more than one night in the same place, and fires may be set where safe (not on bare rocks) with fallen wood. Cars may not be driven across open land or on private roads. Close all gates. Do not disturb farm animals or reindeer.

HIKING

Hiking is popular everywhere in Sweden and the mountain challenge of the northern national parks is compelling. These parks are rarely snow free, however, and the jewel, Sarek, is for experienced hikers only. Good equipment is vital.

For information on organised group walks and STF mountain huts, which are placed at intervals averaging about 20km along popular trails like Kungsleden, near Kiruna, contact **STF** (☎08-463 21 00; www.svenskaturistforeningen.se).

SKIING

Cross-country (Nordic) skiing opportunities vary depending on snow and temperatures, but the northwest usually has plenty of snow from December to April (but not a lot of daylight in December and January). Practically all town areas (except the far south) have marked skiing tracks, often illuminated. For resort reviews in English, visit www.goski.com and www.thealps.com.

Business Hours

Bars 5pm-1am

Restaurants lunch 11.30am-2pm, dinner 6-10pm. Many close Sun or Mon.

Shops 9am-6pm Mon-Fri, to 1pm Sat

Public Holidays

Many businesses close early the day before and all day after official public holidays, including the following:

Nyårsdag (New Year's Day) 1 January

Trettondedag Jul (Epiphany) 6 January

Långfredag, Påsk, Annandag Påsk (Good Friday, Easter Sunday & Monday) March/April

Första Maj (Labour Day) 1 May

Kristi Himmelsfärds dag (Ascension Day) May/June

Pingst, Annandag Pingst (Whit Sunday and Monday) Late May or early June

Midsommardag (Midsummer's Day) First Saturday after 21 June

Alla Helgons dag (All Saints' Day) Saturday, late October or early November

Juldag (Christmas Day) 25 December

Annandag Jul (Boxing Day) 26 December

Internet Access

Most hotels have wi-fi connections, and some have laptops you can borrow. Hostels and tourist offices frequently have at least one internet-enabled computer available for use, occasionally with a fee of Skr10 to Skr25 per hour.

Nearly all public libraries offer free internet access, but often the timeslots are booked for days in advance by locals.

Internet cafes typically charge around Skr1 per online minute, or Skr50 per hour. Wi-fi is almost universal at coffeeshops, train stations, bars, cafes and hotels, although often there's a fee for access.

Internet Resources

» **Visit Sweden** (www.visitsweden.com)
» **The Local** (www.thelocal.se)
» **Smorgasbord** (www.sverigeturism.se/smorgasbord)
» **Swedish Institute** (www.si.se/English)
» **Introduction to the Sami People** (http://boreale.konto.itv.se/samieng.htm)

Money

ATMs are everywhere and easy to find. The Swedish krona (plural: kronor), usually called 'crown' by Swedes speaking English, is denoted Skr (or SEK in Sweden) and divided into 100 öre. Coins are 50 öre (obsolete) and one, five and 10 kronor, and notes are 20, 50, 100, 500 and 1000 kronor.

TAXES & REFUNDS

At shops that display the 'Tax Free Shopping' sign, non-EU citizens making single purchases of goods exceeding Skr200 are eligible for a VAT refund of up to 17.5% of the purchase price. Ask at tourist offices about tax-free shopping through Global Refund, or call ☎545-284 40 for more information.

Telephone

Most Swedes own a mobile phone, so there aren't many public phones and even fewer coin phones; all public telephones take Telia phonecards (Skr50 or Skr120 for 50 or 120 units), available at Pressbyrå shops.

Visas

Citizens of EU countries can enter Sweden with a passport or a national identification card (passports are recommended) and stay up to three months. Nationals of Nordic countries (Denmark, Norway, Finland and Iceland) can stay and work indefinitely, but nationals of other countries require residence permits *(uppehållstillstånd)* for stays of between three months and five years; there is no fee for this permit for EU citizens.

Citizens of Australia, New Zealand, Canada and the USA can enter and stay in Sweden without a visa for up to 90 days. Sweden is part of the Schengen zone and nationals of participating countries don't need visas for up to 90 days. Australian and New Zealand passport holders aged 18 to 30 can qualify for a one-year working-holiday visa.

Citizens of South Africa and many other African, Asian and some Eastern European countries require tourist visas for entry. These are only available in advance from Swedish embassies (allow two months); there's a nonrefundable application fee of Skr550 for most applicants.

Getting There & Away

Air

Arlanda airport (☎08-797 60 00; www.lfv.se) The major international airport, north of Stockholm.

Landvetter airport (GOT; ☎031-94 10 00) In Göteborg.

Sturup airport (MMX; ☎040-613 10 00) In Malmö.

SAS (☎0770-72 77 27; www.scandinavian.net) The national carrier.

Budget airlines that fly to Sweden include:

Skyways (www.skyways.se)

easyJet (www.easyjet.com)

Ryanair (www.ryanair.com)

Blue1 (www.blue1.com)

Land

Long-distance bus operator **Eurolines** (☎031-10 02 40; www.eurolines.com) the has an office inside the bus terminals in Sweden's three largest cities: Stockholm, Göteborg and Malmö. Full schedules and fares are listed on the website.

TO/FROM CONTINENTAL EUROPE

Eurolines services run between Sweden and several European cities. The Göteborg to London service (Skr1319, 30 hours, one to four times weekly) goes via Malmö, Copenhagen, Hamburg and Amsterdam or Brussels. There are also services from Göteborg to Berlin (Skr709, 17 hours, three weekly).

TO/FROM DENMARK

Eurolines runs buses between Stockholm and Copenhagen (Dkr285, nine hours, at least three per week), and between Göteborg and Copenhagen (Dkr205, 4½ hours, daily). **Swebus Express** (☎0200-21 82 18; www.swebusexpress.se) and **GoByBus** (☎0771-15 15 15; www.gobybus.se, in Swedish) both run regular buses on the same routes, and have discount fares for travel from Monday to Thursday. All companies offer student and youth (under 26) discounts.

Öresund trains operated by **Skånetrafiken** (www.skanetrafiken.se) run every 20 minutes from 6am to midnight (and once an hour thereafter) between Copenhagen and Malmö (one way Skr105, 35 minutes) via the bridge. The trains usually stop at Copenhagen airport.

TO/FROM FINLAND

Frequent bus services run from Haparanda to Tornio (Skr15, 10 minutes). **Tapanis Buss** (☎0922-129 55; www.tapanis.se, in Swedish) runs express coaches from Stockholm to Tornio via Haparanda twice a week (Skr570, 15 hours).

TO/FROM NORWAY

GoByBus runs from Stockholm to Oslo (Skr425, 7½ hours, five times daily), and from Göteborg to Oslo (Skr265, four hours, seven daily). Swebus Express has the same routes with similar prices.

In the north, buses run once daily from Umeå to Mo i Rana (eight hours) and from Skellefteå to Bodø (nine hours, daily except Saturday); for details, contact **Länstrafiken i Västerbotten** (☎0771-10 01 10; www.tabussen.nu) and **Länstrafiken i Norrbotten** (☎0771-10 01 10; www.ltnbd.se), respectively.

Trains run daily between Stockholm and Oslo (Skr500 to Skr700, six to seven hours), and there's a night train from Stockholm to Narvik (Skr810, about 20 hours). You can also travel from Helsingborg to Oslo (Skr750, seven hours), via Göteborg. X2000 high-speed trains are more expensive.

Sea

TO/FROM DENMARK

Helsingør to Helsingborg

This is the quickest route and has frequent ferries (crossing time around 20 minutes).

HH-Ferries (☎042-19 80 00; www.hhferries.se) A 24-hour service. Pedestrian/car and up to nine passengers Skr30/385.

Scandlines (☎042-18 63 00; www.scandlines.se) Similar service and prices to HH-Ferries.

Göteborg to Fredrikshavn

Stena Line (☎031-704 00 00; www.stenaline.se) Three-hour crossing. Up to six ferries daily. Pedestrian/car and five passengers/bicycle Skr195/1535/375.

Stena Line (Express) Two-hour crossing. Up to three ferries daily. Pedestrian/car and five passengers/bicycle Skr300/1795/400.

Varberg to Grenå

Stena Line (☎031-704 00 00; www.stenaline.se) Four-hour crossing. Three or four daily. Pedestrian/car and five passengers/bicycle Skr195/1535/285.

Ystad to Rønne

BornholmsTrafikken (☎0411-55 87 00; www.bornholmstrafikken.dk) Conventional (1½ hours) and fast (80 minutes) services, two to nine times daily. Pedestrian/car and five passengers/bicycle from €24/141/26.

TO/FROM EASTERN EUROPE

To/from Estonia, **Tallink** (☎08-666 6001; www.tallink.ee, in Estonian) runs the Stockholm–Tallinn and Kapellskär–Paldiski routes.

Scandlines (☎08-5206 02 90; www.scandlines.dk) operates Ventspils to Nynäshamn ferries around five times per week.

To/from Lithuania, **Lisco Line** (☎0454-33680; www.lisco.lt) operates daily between Karlshamn and Klaipėda.

To/from Poland, **Polferries** (☎040-121700; www.polferries.se) and **Unity Line** (☎0411-556900; www.unityline.pl) have daily Ystad–Swinoujscie crossings. Polferries also runs Nynäshamn-Gdańsk. **Stena Line** (☎031-704 0000; www.stenaline.se) sails Karlskrona–Gdynia.

TO/FROM FINLAND

Helsinki is called Helsingfors in Swedish, and Turku is Åbo.

Stockholm to Helsinki and Stockholm to Turku ferries run daily throughout the year via the Åland Islands (exempt from the abolition of duty-free within the EU, making them a popular outing for Swedes). These ferries have minimum age limits; check before you travel.

Stockholm to Helsinki

Silja Line (☎08-22 21 40; www.silja.com) Around 15 hours. Ticket and cabin berth from about €130.

Viking Line (☎08-452 40 00; www.vikingline.fi) Operates the same routes with slightly cheaper prices (from €100).

Stockholm to Turku

RG Line (☎090-18 52 00; www.rgline.com) Runs the Umeå–Vaasa and Sundsvall–Vaasa routes.

Silja Line (☎08-22 21 40; www.silja.com) 11 hours. Deck place €11, cabins from €45; prices are higher for evening trips. From September to early May, ferries also depart from Kapellskär (90km northeast of Stockholm); connecting buses operated by Silja Line are included in the full-price fare.

Viking Line (☎08-452 40 00; www.vikingline.fi) Operates the same routes with slightly cheaper prices. In high season it offers passage from both Stockholm and Kapellskär.

Stockholm to Åland Islands (Mariehamn)

Besides the Silja Line and Viking Line routes above, two companies offer foot passenger-only overnight cruises. Prices quoted are for return trips.

Ånedin-Linjen (☎08-456 22 00; www.anedinlinjen.se, in Swedish) Six hours, daily. Couchette Skr115, berth from Skr355.

Birka Cruises (☎08-702 72 00; www.birkacruises.com) A 22-hour round-trip. One or two daily. Berth from Skr480. Prices include supper and breakfast.

Eckerö Linjen (☎0175-258 00; www.eckerolinjen.fi) Runs to the Åland Islands from Grisslehamn.

TO/FROM GERMANY

Trelleborg to Sassnitz

Scandlines (☎042-18 61 00; www.scandlines.se) A 3¾-hour trip. Two to five times daily. Pedestrian/car and up to nine passengers/passenger with bicycle Skr145/1050/210. A fuel surcharge of Skr50 to Skr80 may be added.

Trelleborg to Rostock

Scandlines (☎042-18 61 00; www.scandlines.se) Six hours (night crossing 7½ hours). Two or three daily. Pedestrian/car and up to nine passengers/passenger with bicycle Skr210/1160/245. A fuel surcharge of Skr50 to Skr80 may be added.

TT-Line (☎0410-562 00; www.ttline.com) Operates the same as Scandlines, with similar prices.

Trelleborg to Travemünde

TT-Line (☎0410-562 00; www.ttline.com) Seven hours. Two to five daily. Car and up to five passengers from Skr1350, Skr50 surcharge for bicycles. Berths are compulsory on night crossings.

Göteborg to Kiel

Stena Line (☎031-704 00 00; www.stenaline.se) 14 hours. One crossing nightly. Pedestrian/car and up to five passengers from Skr520/1390. Rates are flexible depending on how early you book and which cabin level you choose.

TO/FROM NORWAY

There's a daily overnight **DFDS Seaways** (☎031-65 06 80; www.dfdsseaways.com) ferry between Copenhagen and Oslo (from €120 per passenger), via Helsingborg. Passenger fares between Helsingborg and Oslo (14 hours) cost from Skr1100, and cars Skr475, but the journey can't be booked online; you'll need to call. DFDS also sails from Göteborg to Kristiansand (Norway), three days a week (from seven hours); contact them for prices.

A **Color Line** (☎0526-620 00; www.colorline.com) ferry between Strömstad (Sweden) and Sandefjord (Norway) sails two to six times daily (2½ hours) year-round. Tickets cost from Nkr180 (rail passes get 50% discount).

Getting Around

Air

Sweden's internal flight operators and their destinations include the following:

Malmö Aviation (TF; ☎040-660 29 00; www.malmoaviation.se; hub Stockholm Bromma) Göteborg, Stockholm and Umeå.

SAS (☎0770-72 77 27; www.flysas.com) Göteborg, Kiruna, Malmö, Stockholm, Umeå, Visby, plus many other regional destinations throughout Sweden.

Skyways (☎0771-95 95 00; www.skyways.se) Göteborg, Stockholm, Visby, plus many other regional destinations throughout Sweden.

Bicycle

Skåne and Gotland are ideal for cycling. The best season is May to September in the south, and July and August in the north. You'll find bike-hire outlets and dedicated paths in most major towns.

Boat

An extensive boat network serves the Stockholm archipelago, and boat services on Lake Mälaren, west of Stockholm, are busy in summer. Regular ferries from Nynäshamn and Oskarshamn serve Gotland and, in summer, many small islands off the coast.

Bus

Swebus Express (☎0200-21 82 18; www.swebusexpress.se) has the largest network of express buses, but they only serve the southern half of the country (as far north as Mora in Dalarna). **Svenska Buss** (☎0771-67 67 67; www.svenskabuss.se) and **GoByBus** (☎0771-15 15 15; www.gobybus.se, in Swedish), formerly Säfflebussen, also connect many southern towns and cities with Stockholm; prices are often slightly cheaper than Swebus Express, but services are less frequent.

North of Gävle, regular connections with Stockholm are provided by several smaller operators, including **Ybuss** (☎0771-33 44 44; www.ybuss.se), which has services to Sundsvall, Östersund and Umeå.

You don't have to reserve a seat on Swebus Express services. Generally, tickets purchased online or for travel between Monday and Thursday are cheaper. Students should ask about discounts.

Car & Motorcycle

International car-hire chains start at around Skr800 per day for smaller models, but shop around, as weekend or summer packages may be offered at discount rates. All the major firms (eg Avis, Hertz, Europcar) have offices in major cities. If bringing your own car, you'll need vehicle registration documents.

The Swedish national motoring association is **Motormännens Riksförbund** (☎020-21 11 11, 08-690 38 00; www.motormannen.se; Sveavägen 159, SE-10435 Stockholm).

Train

Sweden has an extensive and reliable railway network, and trains are certainly faster than buses. Many destinations in the northern half of the country, however, cannot be reached by train alone, and Inlandsbanan, the historic train line through Norrland, runs only during summer.

Sveriges Järnväg (SJ; ☎0771-75 75 75; www.sj.se) National network covering most main lines, especially in the southern part of the country. Its X2000 fast trains run at speeds of up to 200km/h.

Tågkompaniet (☎0771-44 41 11; www.tagkompaniet.se, in Swedish) Operates excellent overnight trains from Göteborg and Stockholm north to destinations including Kiruna.

Inlandsbanan (☎0771-53 53 53; www.inlandsbanan.se) Slow and scenic 1300km route from Kristinehamn to Gällivare, one of the great rail journeys in Scandinavia. It takes seven hours from Mora to Östersund (Skr414) and 15 hours from Östersund to Gällivare (Skr962). A pass allows two weeks' unlimited travel for Skr1595.

COSTS

Travel on the super-fast X2000 services is much pricier than on 'normal' trains. Full-price 2nd-class tickets for longer journeys cost about twice as much as equivalent bus trips, but there are various discounts available, especially for booking a week or so in advance *(förköpsbiljet)*, online or at the last minute. Students (with a Swedish CSN or SFS student card if aged over 26), and people aged under 26 get a steep discount on the standard adult fare.

X2000 tickets include a seat reservation. All SJ ticket prices are reduced in summer, from late June to mid-August. Most SJ trains don't allow bicycles to be taken onto trains (they have to be sent as freight), but those in southern Sweden (especially Skåne) do; check when you book your ticket.

TRAIN PASSES

The Sweden Rail Pass, Eurodomino tickets and international passes, such as Inter-Rail and Eurail, are accepted on SJ services and most regional trains.

The **Eurail Scandinavia Pass** (www.eurail.com) entitles you to unlimited 2nd-class rail travel in Denmark, Finland, Norway and Sweden; it is available for four, five, six, eight or 10 days of travel within a two-month period (prices start from youth/adult US$235/315). X2000 trains require all rail-pass holders to pay a supplement of Skr65 (including the obligatory seat reservation). The pass also provides free travel on some buses, Scandlines' Helsingør to Helsingborg route, and 20% to 50% discounts on other selected ferry routes.

Switzerland

Includes »

Best Places to Eat

» Druck Punkt, Basel (p1257)
» Lötschberg AOC, Bern (p1243)
» Al Lido, Lugano (p1245)

Best Places to Stay

» Pension für Dich, Zürich (p1250)
» Hôme St-Pierre, Geneva (p1237)
» Mountain Hostel, Gimmelwald (p1255)

Why Go?

What giddy romance Zermatt, St Moritz and other glitterati-encrusted names evoke. This is *Sonderfall Schweiz* ('special case Switzerland'), a privileged neutral country set apart from others, proudly idiosyncratic, insular and unique. Blessed with gargantuan cultural diversity, its four official languages alone say it all.

The Swiss don't do half-measures: Zürich, their most gregarious urban centre, has cutting-edge art, legendary nightlife and one of the world's highest living standards. The national passion for sweat, stamina and clingy Lycra takes 65-year-olds across 2500m-high mountain passes for Sunday strolls, sees giggly three-year-olds skiing rings around grown-ups, prompts locals done with 'ordinary' marathons to sprint backwards up mountains – all in the name of fun.

Join tourists comparing memories of Bern's chocolate-box architecture, the Matterhorn, the thundering Rheinfall et al, but understand that Switzerland is a place so outrageously beautiful it simply has to be seen to be believed.

When to Go

Geneva

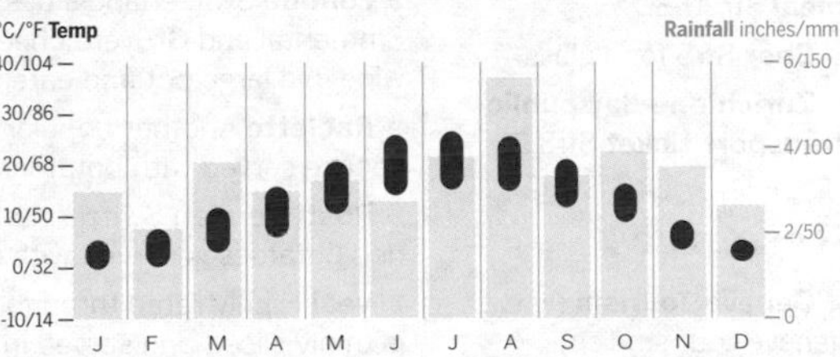

Dec–early Apr Carve through powder and drink glühwein at an Alpine resort.

Aug Celebrate Swiss National Day on 1 August and witness Swiss national pride in full force.

May–Sep Hike in the shadow of the Matterhorn and be wowed by its mesmerising presence.

AT A GLANCE

» **Currency** Swiss franc (Sfr)

» **Language** French, German, Italian, Romansch

» **Money** ATMs are readily available

» **Visas** Schengen rules apply; see p1319

Fast Facts

» **Area** 41,285 sq km

» **Capital** Bern

» **Country code** ☎41

» **Emergency** ☎117

Exchange Rates

Australia	A$1	Sfr0.94
Canada	C$1	Sfr0.95
euro zone	€1	Sfr1.28
Japan	¥100	Sfr1.13
New Zealand	NZ$1	Sfr0.69
UK	UK£1	Sfr1.50
USA	US$1	Sfr0.92

Set Your Budget

» **Budget hotel room** Sfr80-100

» **Two-course evening meal** Sfr20-30

» **Beer** Sfr5 for a glass

» **Zurich one-day public transport ticket** Sfr8.20

Resources

» **Geneva Tourism** (www.geneve-tourisme.ch)

» **Swiss Tourism Board** (www.myswitzerland.com) Links to all regional and city tourism board sites

» **Swissinfo.ch** (www.swissinfo.ch) Swiss news

Connections

Landlocked between France, Germany, Austria, Liechtenstein and Italy, Switzerland's a doddle to move on from. Geneva city buses run as far as the French border (a couple cross into France, continuing along the southern shore of Lake Geneva) and there are plenty of direct train connections from Geneva to Paris, as well as Hamburg, Milan and Barcelona. New rail lines mean it's now only 3½ hours from Paris to Geneva.

Cosmopolitan Zürich enjoys many international rail connections, including daily trains to/from Stuttgart, Munich and Innsbruck. In northern Switzerland, Basel is a major European rail hub, with separate train stations serving France and Germany. Then, of course, there is Italy, a mere hop and a skip from Locarno in Italianate Ticino.

ITINERARIES

One Week

Start in vibrant Zürich. Shop famous Bahnhofstrasse and hit the bars of Züri-West. Next, head to the Jungfrau region to explore some kick-ass (think James Bond racing an avalanche down a sheer, snowy rock face) Alpine scenery. Take a pit stop in beautiful Lucerne before finishing up in the capital, Bern.

Two Weeks

As above, then head west for French immersion lessons. Check out Geneva's Jet d'Eau (aka 140km tall skyrocketing bolt of water) and head to Montreux to get a dose of lakeside style flanked by alpine peaks in the Swiss Riviera Zip to Zermatt or across to St Moritz to frolic in snow or green meadows then loop east to taste the Italian side of Switzerland.

Essential Food & Drink

» **Fondue** Switzerland's best-known dish, in which melted Emmental and Gruyère cheese are combined with white wine in a large pot and eaten with bread cubes.

» **Raclette** Another popular artery-hardener of melted cheese served with potatoes.

» **Rösti** German Switzerland's national dish of fried shredded potatoes is served with everything.

» **Veal** Highly rated throughout the country; in Zürich veal is thinly sliced and served in a cream sauce *(gschnetzeltes kalbsfleisch)*.

» **Bündnerfleisch** Dried beef, smoked and thinly sliced.

» **Wurst** Like their northern neighbours, the Swiss also munch on a wide variety of sausages.

LAKE GENEVA REGION

Western Europe's biggest lake stretches like a liquid mirror between French-speaking Switzerland (north) and France (south). Known as Lake Geneva by most or Lac Léman to Francophones, the Swiss shore cossets palm-tree-studded Riviera resorts and emerald vines marching uphill.

Geneva

POP 185,700

Supersleek, slick and cosmopolitan, Geneva (Genève in French, Genf in German) is a rare breed of city. It's one of Europe's priciest. Its people chatter in every language under the sun (184 nationalities comprise 45% of the city's population) and it's constantly thought of as the Swiss capital, which it isn't. Still, Switzerland's second-largest city, superbly strung around the sparkling shores of Europe's largest Alpine lake houses the world – the UN, International Red Cross, International Labour Organization, World Health Organization. All in all, 200-odd international governmental and nongovernmental organisations help prop up the overload of banks, jewellers and chocolate shops for which Geneva is known. Strolling manicured city parks, sailing the lake and skiing in the Alps are weekend pursuits.

Sights & Activities

LEFT BANK (RIVE GAUCHE)

Geneva's best-known landmark (spot it from the plane) is the 140m-high **Jet d'Eau**. At any one time seven tonnes of water shoot into the air with incredible force – 200km/h, 1360 horsepower – to create a sky-high plume kissed by a rainbow on sunny days.

Other sights include the **Flower Clock** (Horloge Fleurie), crafted from 6500 flowers, in the **Jardin Anglais** (Quai du Général-Guisan); and **Île Rousseau**, an island pierced by a statue honouring the thinker born on the old town's main street at Grand Rue 40, which is now a museum. Nearby is the part-Romanesque, part-Gothic **Cathédrale St Pierre**, where Protestant John Calvin preached from 1536 to 1564; trace his life in the **International Museum of the Reformation** (022 310 24 31; www.musee-reforme.ch; Rue du Cloître 4; adult/concession Sfr10/7; 10am-5pm Tue-Sun).

RIGHT BANK (RIVE DROITE)

At the art deco **Palais des Nations** (022 907 48 96; Ave de la Paix 14; tours Sfr10; 10am-noon & 2-4pm Apr-Jun & Sep-Oct, 10am-5pm Jul & Aug, 10am-noon & 2-4pm Mon-Fri Nov-Mar), the European arm of the UN, see where decisions about world affairs are made on the hour-long tour (bring your passport). Don't miss its gardens and the towering grey titanium monument donated by the USSR to commemorate the conquest of space.

The **International Red Cross & Red Crescent Museum** (022 748 95 25; www.micr.org; Ave de la Paix 17; admission free; 10am-5pm Wed-Mon) is a compelling multimedia trawl through atrocities perpetuated by humanity.

Flowers, art installations and soul-stirring views of Mont Blanc on clear days make the northern lakeshore promenade a pleasure to walk: pass hip **Bains des Pâquis** (022 732 29 74; www.bains-des-paquis.ch; Quai du Mont-Blanc 30; 9am-8pm mid-Apr–mid-Sep) where Genevans have frolicked in the sun since 1872. Further north, peacock-studded lawns ensnare the **Jardin Botanique** (admission free; 8am-7.30pm Apr–Oct, 9.30am-5pm Nov-Mar).

The web was born 8km west of the city centre at the **European Organisation for Nuclear Research** (CERN; 022 767 84 84; visits-service@cern.ch; free guided tour by advance reservation; tours 10.30am Mon-Sat), a laboratory for research into particle physics funded by 20 nations. Book tours one month in advance and bring your passport. Take tram 14 or 16 to Avanchet, then bus 56.

FREE THRILLS

Bags of fabulous things to see and do in Geneva don't cost a cent. Our favourite freebies:

» Dashing like mad under the iconic **Jet d'Eau** (p1233)

» Getting lost in the **old town**

» Commiserating over the dark side of humanity at the **International Red Cross & Red Crescent Museum** (p1233)

» Hobnobbing with big-bang scientists at the **European Organisation for Nuclear Research** (p1233)

» Going green in the **Jardin Botanique** (p1233)

» Flopping on the beach on the **Bains de Pâquis** (p1233)

» **Pedalling** (p1238) along the lake into France or towards Lausanne

Switzerland Highlights

1 Hit the hip bars of **Zürich** (p1247) and relax the next day with a stroll along the city's sublime lake

2 Be wowed by the Eiger's monstrous north face on a ride to the 'top of Europe', 3471m **Jungfraujoch** (p1255)

3 Get wet with a fountain dash beneath Geneva's **Jet d'Eau** (p1233) or a soak in a white-chocolate bath

4 Be surprised by Swiss capital **Bern** (p1242): think medieval charm, folkloric fountains and a pulsating party scene

5 Gape at the iconic Matterhorn and wander around the car-free Alpine village of **Zermatt** (p1240)

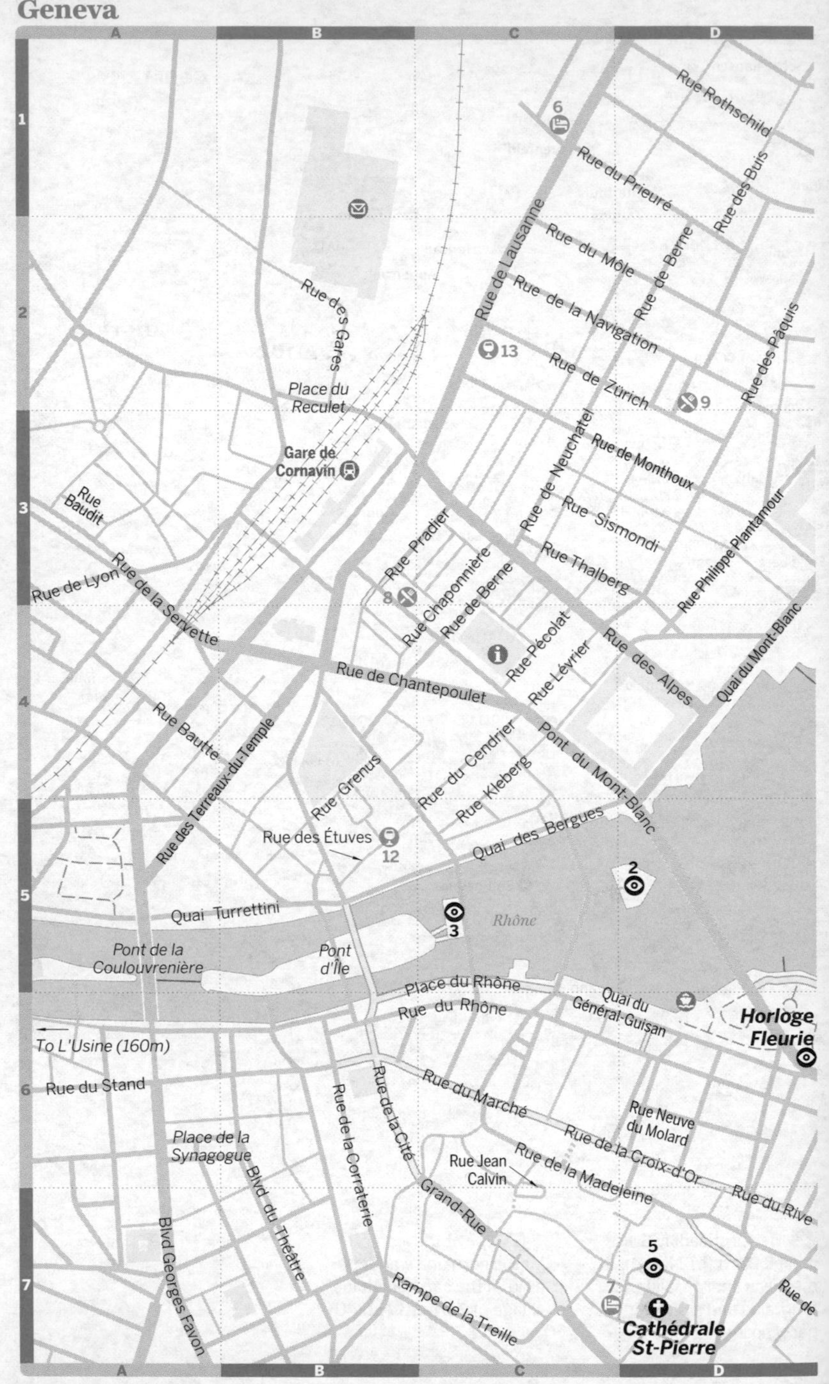

Rue Rothschild
Rue du Prieuré
Rue des Buis
Rue de Lausanne
Rue du Môle
Rue de Berne
Rue de la Navigation
Rue des Gares
Rue de Zürich
Rue des Pâquis
Place du Reculet
Gare de Cornavin
Rue de Monthoux
Rue de Neuchatel
Rue Baudit
Rue Sismondi
Rue Philippe Plantamour
Rue Pradier
Rue Thalberg
Rue de Lyon
Rue de la Servette
Rue Chaponnière
Rue de Berne
Quai du Mont-Blanc
Rue Pécolat
Rue des Alpes
Rue Lévrier
Rue de Chantepoulet
Rue Bautte
Rue du Cendrier
Pont du Mont-Blanc
Rue des Terreaux-du-Temple
Rue Grenus
Rue Kleberg
Quai des Bergues
Rue des Étuves
Quai Turrettini
Rhône
Pont de la Coulouvrenière
Pont d'Île
Place du Rhône
Rue du Rhône
Quai du Général-Guisan
Horloge Fleurie
To L'Usine (160m)
Rue du Stand
Rue de la Cité
Rue de la Corraterie
Rue du Marché
Rue Neuve du Molard
Place de la Synagogue
Blvd du Théâtre
Rue de la Croix-d'Or
Rue Jean Calvin
Rue de la Madeleine
Rue du Rive
Grand-Rue
Blvd Georges Favon
Rampe de la Treille
Rue de
Cathédrale St-Pierre

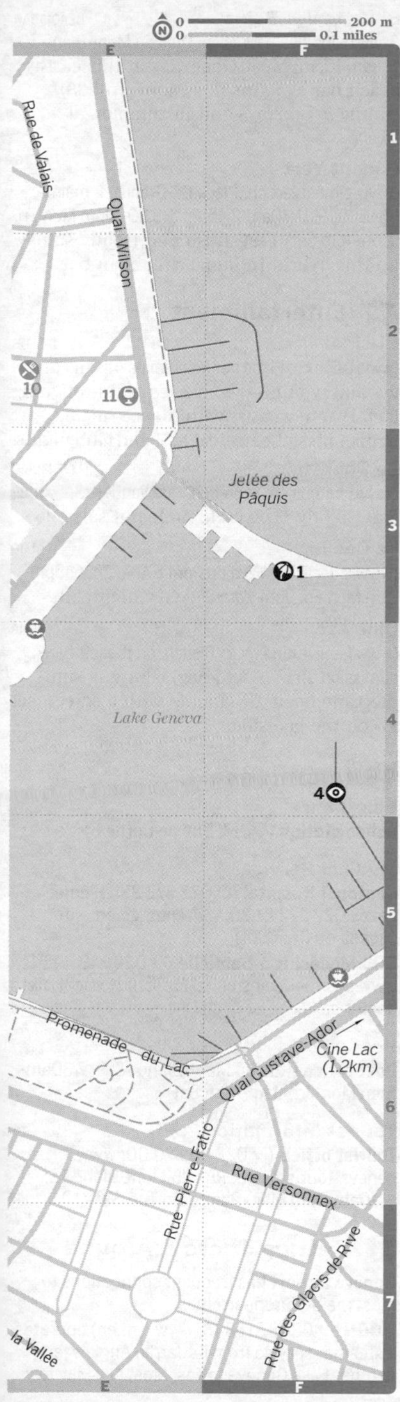

Festivals & Events

The historical festival **L'Escalade**, held in Geneva on 11 December, celebrates deliverance from would-be conquerors.

Sleeping

When checking in, ask for your free public transport ticket, covering unlimited bus travel for the duration of your hotel stay.

Hôme St-Pierre HOSTEL €
(022 310 37 07; www.homestpierre.ch; Cour St-Pierre 4; dm Sfr31, s/d with washbasin Sfr48/72; reception 9am-noon & 4-8pm Mon-Sat, 9am-noon Sun; @) This boarding house was founded by the German Lutheran Church in 1874. Women are its primary clientele – just six dorm beds are up for grabs for six lucky guys – and the rooftop terrace that crowns the place is magical.

City Hostel HOSTEL €
(022 901 15 00; www.cityhostel.ch; Rue de Ferrier 2; dm from Sfr32, s/d from Sfr61; reception 7.30am-noon & 1pm-midnight; P@) Spanking-clean is the trademark of this organised hostel, where two-bed dorms give travellers a chance to double up cheaply. Rates include

Geneva

Top Sights
- Cathédrale St-Pierre ... D7
- Flower Clock ... D6

Sights
1. Bains des Pâquis ... F3
2. Île Rousseau ... D5
3. Information de la Ville de Genève ... C5
4. Jet d'Eau ... F4
5. International Museum of the Reformation ... D7

Sleeping
6. City Hostel ... C1
7. Hôme St-Pierre ... C7

Eating
8. Café de Paris ... B3
9. Les 5 Portes ... D2
10. Mikado ... E2

Drinking
- Buvette des Bains ... (see 1)
11. Paillote ... E2
12. Piment Vert ... B5
13. Scandale ... C2

sheets, towels and use of the kitchen, TV room and a free locker.

Auberge de Jeunesse HOSTEL €
(☎022 732 62 60; www.yh-geneva.ch; Rue Rothschild 28-30; dm Sfr29, d from Sfr85; ⊙reception 6.30-10am & 2pm-1am Jun-Sep, 6.30-10am & 4pm-midnight Oct-May; @) Dorms max out at 12 beds.

Eating

In the old town, terrace cafes and restaurants crowd Geneva's oldest square, medieval Place du Bourg-de-Four. Rue de Fribourg, Rue de Neuchâtel, Rue de Berne and the northern end of Rue des Alpes are loaded with kebab, falafel and other quick-eat joints.

Café de Paris FRENCH €
(rue du Mont Blanc 26; salad, steak & chips Sfr40; ⊙11am-11pm daily) A memorable dining experience since 1930. Everyone goes for the same thing here: green salad, beef steak with a killer-calorie herb and butter sauce and as many fries as you can handle.

Mikado JAPANESE €
(Rue de l'Ancien Port 9; sushi Sfr2.50, mains Sfr6.50; ⊙10am-6.30pm Tue-Fri, 10am-6pm Sat) If you want authentic, quick and tasty fast food served on a red lacquered tray, then this Japanese delicatessen will hit the spot.

Les 5 Portes FRENCH €
(☎022 731 84 38; Rue de Zürich 5; mains Sfr16-22; ⊙9am-2am Mon-Fri, 11am-2am Sat, 11am-8pm Sun) The Five Doors is a fashionable Pâquis port of call that embraces every mood and moment.

Drinking

Pâquis, the district between the train station and lake, is particularly well endowed with bars. In summer the **paillote** (Quai du Mont-Blanc 30; ⊙to midnight), with wooden tables inches from the water, gets crammed.

Scandale BAR
(Rue de Lausanne 24; ⊙11am-2am Tue-Fri, 5pm-2am Sat) Retro 1950s furnishings in a cavernous interior with comfy sofas ensures this lounge bar is never empty. Happenings include art exhibitions, Saturday night DJs and bands.

La Plage BAR
(Rue Vautier 19; ⊙11am-1am Mon-Thu, 10am-2am Fri & Sat, 5pm-1am Sun) With bare wood tables, checked lino floor, green-wood shutters and tables outside, 'the Beach' in Carouge is a timeless drinking hole.

Buvette des Bains BEACH BAR
(www.bains-des-paquis.ch; Quai du Mont-Blanc 30; ⊙8am-10pm) Meet Genevans at this earthy beach bar at Bains des Pâquis (p1233). Dining is on trays and in summer, al fresco.

Piment Vert BAR
(www.pimentvert.ch; Place De-Grenus 4; mains Sfr15-19; ⊙11.30am-2.45pm & 5.30-10pm Mon-Fri, noon-4pm Sat) Fast, fresh and trendy sums up this hybrid Indian–Sri Lankan bar.

☆ Entertainment

L'Usine CLUB
(www.usine.ch; Place des Volontaires 4) This grungy and youthful converted gold-roughing factory entertains with dance nights, art happenings, theatre, cabaret and club nights.

Le Chat Noir LIVE MUSIC
(www.chatnoir.ch, in French; Rue Vautier 13; ⊙Tue-Sat) Nightly jazz, rock, funk and salsa gigs.

Le Déclic CLUB
(www.ledeclic.ch; Blvd du Pont d'Arve 28; ⊙5pm-2am Mon-Fri, 9pm-2am Sat) Gay nightclub.

Ciné Lac CINEMA
(www.geneve.cine.ch, in French; on the left bank; admission Sfr17; ⊙Jul & Aug) Glorious summertime open-air cinema with a screen set up on the lakeside.

Information

Emergency

Police station (☎117; Rue de Berne 6)

Medical Services

Cantonal Hospital (☎022 372 33 11, emergency 022 372 81 20; www.hug-ge.ch; Rue Micheli du Crest 24)

SOS Médecins à Domicile (☎022 748 49 50; www.sos-medecins.ch, in French) Home/hotel doctor calls.

Post

Post office (Rue du Mont-Blanc 18; ⊙7.30am-6pm Mon-Fri, 9am-4pm Sat)

Tourist Information

Tourist office (☎022 909 70 00; www.geneve-tourisme.ch; Rue du Mont-Blanc 18; ⊙10am-6pm Mon, 9am-6pm Tue-Sat)

Getting There & Around

Geneva airport has frequent connections to most major European cities.

CGN (☎0848 811 848; www.cgn.ch) operates a steamer service from its Jardin Anglais jetty to other Lake Geneva towns. Most sail May to

September, including those to/from Lausanne (Sfr37.60, 3½ hours).

International buses depart from the **bus station** (☎0900 320 320, 022 732 02 30; www.coach-station.com; Place Dorcière).

Train connections include Lausanne (Sfr20.60, 40 minutes), Bern (Sfr46, 1¾ hours), Zürich (Sfr80, 2¾ hours), Paris (Sfr127, 3½ hours), Hamburg (Sfr276, 9½ hours), Milan (Sfr97, 4½ hours) and Barcelona (Sfr125, 10 hours).

Pick up a bike (per day/weekend Sfr12/20) at **Genève Roule** (☎022 740 13 43; www.geneveroule.ch; Place de Montbrillant 17; ⊙8am-6pm Mon-Sat) or its seasonal Jetée des Pâquis pick-up point. May to October, borrow a bike carrying publicity for free.

Public transport is excellent. A day pass costs Sfr7.

Lausanne

POP 125,890

In a fabulous location overlooking Lake Geneva, Lausanne is an enchanting beauty with several distinct personalities: the former fishing village, Ouchy, with its summer, beach-resort feel; Place St-François, with stylish, cobblestone shopping streets; and Flon, a warehouse district of bars, galleries and boutiques. One of the country's grandest Gothic cathedrals dominates Lausanne's medieval centre.

The **tourist office** (☎021 613 73 21; www.lausanne-tourisme.ch; Place de la Navigation 4; ⊙9am-6pm Oct-Mar, to 8pm Apr-Sep) adjoins Ouchy metro station.

Sights

TOP CHOICE Musée de l'Art Brut MUSEUM

(www.artbrut.ch; Ave des Bergières 11-13; adult/student Sfr10/5, 1st Sat of month free; ⊙11am-6pm Tue-Sun Sep-Jun, 11am-6pm daily Jul & Aug) With its fascinating amalgam of 15,000 works of art created by psychiatric patients, eccentrics and incarcerated criminals, this is Switzerland's most alluring museum.

Another must is the Gothic **Cathédrale de Notre Dame** (⊙7am-7pm Mon-Fri, 8am-7pm Sat & Sun Apr-Aug, 7am-5.30pm Sep-Mar).

Sleeping

Hotel guests get a Lausanne Transport Card covering unlimited public transport.

Lausanne GuestHouse GUEST HOUSE €€

(☎021 601 80 00; www.lausanne-guesthouse.ch; Chemin des Épinettes 4; dm/s/d Sfr36/96/125, s/d with shared bathroom Sfr86/105; P⊖@📶) An attractive mansion converted into quality backpacker accommodation near the train station. Many rooms have lake views and some of the building's energy is solar.

Camping de Vidy CAMPING GROUND €

(☎021 622 50 00; www.campinglausannevidy.ch; Chemin du Camping 3; campsites per adult/tent Sfr8.50/from €12) This camping ground is on the lake, just to the west of the Vidy sports complex. Sites are well maintained and it's popular with families in summer. Get off bus 2 at Bois de Vaux.

Eating & Drinking

Lausanne is one of Switzerland's busier night-time cities. Look for the handy free listings booklet **What's Up** (www.whatsupmag.ch) in bars.

Café de Grancy INTERNATIONAL €

(☎021 616 86 66; www.cafedegrancy.ch; Ave du Rond Point 1; mains Sfr18-36; ⊙8am-midnight Mon, Wed & Thu, 8am-1am Fri, 10am-1am Sat, 10am-midnight Sun; 📶) An old-time bar resurrected with flair by young entrepreneurs, this spot is a hip hang-out with floppy lounges, weekend brunch and a tempting restaurant out back.

XIIIeme Siècle PUB

(Rue Cité-Devant 10; ⊙10pm-4am Tue-Sat) In a grand medieval setting with stone vaults and huge timber beams, this cosy stalwart is a great place for a beer or six and boasts a laid-back, convivial atmosphere.

Bar Tabac BAR

(Rue Beau Séjour 7; ⊙7am-9pm Mon-Wed, 7am-1am Thu & Fri, 9am-2am Sat, 9am-3pm Sun) Squeaky timber floors lend warmth, and punters engage in animated chat around the bar at this spruced corner tavern of old.

Le Bleu Lézard BAR

(www.bleu-lezard.ch; Rue Enning 10; ⊙7am-1am Mon-Thu, 7am-2am Fri, 8am-2am Sat, 9.30am-1am Sun; 📶) An oldie but a goodie, this corner bar-eatery cooks up Sunday brunch, a chatty atmosphere and a club-styled dance floor in the cellar.

Getting There & Around

There are trains to Geneva (Sfr20.60, 33 to 51 minutes, up to six hourly), Geneva airport (Sfr25, 42 to 58 minutes, up to four hourly) and Bern (Sfr31, 70 minutes, one or two hourly). For boat services, see p1239.

Montreux

POP 24,600

In 1971 Frank Zappa was doing his thing in the casino in Montreux when the building caught fire, casting a pall of smoke over Lake Geneva and inspiring the members of Deep Purple to pen their classic rock number *Smoke on the Water*.

It wasn't anything new – this Swiss Riviera showpiece has inspired writers, artists and musicians for centuries, and it's easy to see why: Montreux boasts stunning Alps views, tidy rows of pastel buildings and Switzerland's most extraordinary castle, 11th-century **Château de Chillon** (021 966 89 10; www.chillon.ch; Ave de Chillon 21; adult/student Sfr12/10; 9am-6pm Apr-Sep, 9.30am-5pm Mar & Oct, 10am-4pm Nov-Feb), a 45-minute walk from Montreux, or a shorter ride on trolley bus 1 (Sfr2.30).

Crowds throng to the two-week **Montreux Jazz Festival** (www.montreuxjazz.com) in early July. Free concerts take place daily, but big-name gigs cost Sfr40 to Sfr100.

On the waterfront, **Auberge de Jeunesse** (021 963 49 34; Passage de l'Auberge 8, Territet; dm from Sfr35; mid-Feb–mid-Nov; @) is a chirpy hostel 30 minutes' walk along the lake (clockwise) from the tourist office (or take the local train to Territet or bus 1).

Café du Grütli (Rue du Grand Chêne 8; mains Sfr18-32) is a cheerful little eatery hidden in the old town that provides good home cooking.

There are trains to Geneva (Sfr28, 70 minutes, hourly) and Lausanne (Sfr10.20, 25 minutes, three hourly).

VALAIS

Matterhorn country: an intoxicating land that seduces the toughest of critics with its endless panoramic vistas. A century ago farmers in this earthy part of southern Switzerland didn't have two francs to rub together. Today celebrities sip Sfr10,000 champagne cocktails from ice-carved goblets in this jet-set land with an outdoors so extraordinary it never goes out of fashion. Switzerland's 10 highest mountains, all over 4000m, are here.

Zermatt

POP 5830

The Matterhorn – that unfathomable monolith synonymous with Switzerland that one simply can't quite stop looking at. And it's right here in Zermatt, an indisputable skiing, mountaineering and hiking hotspot (and car-free to boot!).

The **tourist office** (027 966 81 00; www.zermatt.ch; Bahnhofplatz 5; 8.30am-6pm Mon-Sat, 8.30am-noon & 1.30-6pm Sun mid-Jun–Sep, 8.30am-noon & 1.30-6pm Mon-Sat, 9.30am-noon & 4-6pm Sun rest of year) has useful information.

Sights & Activities

A walk in the **cemetery** is a sobering experience for any would-be mountaineer, as numerous monuments tell of untimely deaths on Monte Rosa and the Matterhorn.

On 13 July 1865 Edward Whymper led the first successful ascent of the Matterhorn. The climb took 32 hours but the descent was marred by tragedy when four team members crashed to their deaths in a 1200m fall down the north face. See the infamous rope that

WORTH A TRIP

ZEN OUT IN GRYON & LEYSIN

Trek off the beaten track to lap up Swiss Alpine charm in untouched **Gryon** (1130m), with great meadow hiking trails and **Chalet Martin** (024 498 33 21; www.gryon.com; dm/d from Sfr25/70; P @), a Swiss-Australian-run hostel that travellers give rave reviews. The vibe is laid-back and the place organises dozens of activities – paragliding, skiing and chocolate tasting included. Take a train from Lausanne to Bex (Sfr17.40, 40 minutes, hourly) then the cogwheel train to Gryon (Sfr6.20, 30 minutes, hourly). The hostel is a five-minute signposted walk from the train stop.

Equally Zen is **Leysin**, a hub for skiers, boarders and hikers who can't sing the praises highly enough of **Hiking Sheep** (024 494 35 35; www.hikingsheep.com; dm/d Sfr30/80; P ❄ @). The tall, art deco house has a kitchen, great communal facilities, a pine-forested backyard and breathtaking views from its balconies. Find it a two-minute walk from the Leysin-Grand Hôtel train station. Ride the cogwheel train from Aigle (Sfr10.80, 30 minutes, hourly), in turn linked by train to Lausanne (Sfr14.80, 30 minutes, hourly).

WORTH A TRIP

NEUCHÂTEL

Its old-town sandstone elegance, the airy Gallic nonchalance of its cafe life and the lively lakeside air that breezes along the shoreline of its glittering lake, make Neuchâtel disarmingly charming. The small university town, complete with its own spirited *comune libre* (free commune), is compact enough to discover on foot, while the French spoken here is said be Switzerland's purest. Not just that: Neuchâtel's town observatory gives the official time-check for all of Switzerland.

The pedestrian zone and Place Pury (the local bus hub) are about 1km from the train station; walk down the hill along Ave de la Gare. The lakeside **tourist office** (☎032 889 68 90; www.neuchateltourism.ch; Hôtel des Postes, Pl du Port; ⏲9am-noon & 1.30-5.30pm Mon-Fri, 9am-noon Sat Sep-Jun, 9am-6.30pm Mon-Fri, 9am-4pm Sat, 10am-2pm Sun Jul & Aug) adjoins the post office.

The 15th-century **Chateau de Neuchâtel** (☎032 889 60 00; guided tours free; ⏲10am-noon & 2-4pm Mon-Sat, 2-4pm Sun Apr-Sep) and the adjoining **Collegiate Church** are the centrepieces of the old town. The striking cenotaph of 15 statues dates from 1372. Scale the nearby **prison tower** (☎032 717 71 02; Rue Jehanne de Hochberg 5; admission Sfr1; ⏲8am-6pm Apr-Sep) for broad views of town and lake.

Visit the **Musée d'Art et d'Histoire** (☎032 717 79 25; www.mahn.ch, in French; Esplanade Léopold Robert 1; admission Sfr8, Wed free; ⏲11am-6pm Tue-Sun) to see beloved 18th-century clockwork figures.

Trains serve Geneva (Sfr38, 70 minutes, hourly), Bern (Sfr18.20, 35 minutes, hourly) and other destinations.

broke in the **Matterhorn Museum** (☎027 967 41 00; www.matterhornmuseum.ch; Kirchplatz; adult/student Sfr10/8; ⏲11am-6pm mid-Dec–Sep, 2-6pm Oct, closed Nov–mid-Dec).

Views from the cable cars are uniformly breathtaking, as is the cogwheel train to 3000m **Gornergrat** (Sfr38 one way, 35 to 45 minutes, two to three per hour). Sit on the right-hand side to gawp at the Matterhorn. Alternatively, hike from Zermatt to Gornergrat in five hours.

Zermatt is cruising heaven, with long red runs, a scattering of blues for ski virgins and knuckle-whitening blacks for experts. Free buses shuttle skiers between the three ski areas, **Rothorn**, **Stockhorn** and **Klein Matterhorn**. Snowboarders make for Klein Matterhorn's freestyle park and half-pipe, while mogul fans go wild over Stockhorn. Klein Matterhorn is topped by Europe's highest cable-car station (3820m), providing access to Europe's highest skiing and Switzerland's most extensive summer skiing. A day pass for all ski lifts in Zermatt costs Sfr67/57 per adult/student, or Sfr75/64 (including Cervinia).

Find the ski school and mountain guides office inside the **Alpin Center** (☎027 966 24 60; www.alpincenter-zermatt.ch; Bahnhofstrasse 58; ⏲8.30am-noon & 3-7pm mid-Nov–Apr & Jul-Sep).

Sleeping

Many places close between seasons.

Berggasthaus Trift HOSTEL €
(☎079 408 70 20; dm/d with half-board Sfr66/152; ⏲Jul-Sep) It's a trudge to this 2337m-high mountain hut but the hike is outstanding. The Alpine haven is run by Hugo (a whiz on the alphorn) and Fabienne, who serve treats such as home-cured beef and oven-warm apple tart on the terrace. Get the camera ready for when the sun sets over Monte Rosa.

Zermatt SYHA Hostel HOSTEL €
(☎027 967 23 20; Staldenweg 5; dm/d from Sfr48/110; @) Question: how many hostels have the Matterhorn peeking through the window in the morning? Answer: one. And if that doesn't convince you, the modern dorms, sunny terrace and first-rate facilities should.

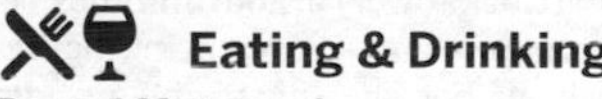

Eating & Drinking

Bayard Metzgerei SWISS €
(Bahnhofstrasse 9; ⏲noon-6.30pm Jul-Sep, 4-6.30pm Dec-Mar) Follow your nose to this butcher's grill for to-go bratwurst, chicken and other carnivorous bites.

Papperla Pub PUB
(Steinmattstrasse 34; ⏲11am-11.30pm; wi-fi) Rammed with sloshed skiers, this pub blends pulsating music with lethal Jägermeister

bombs and good vibes. Squeeze in, slam shots, then shuffle downstairs to Schneewittchen club (open to 4am) for more of the same.

Hennu Stall BAR

(Klein Matterhorn; ⌚2-7pm) Last one down to this snow-bound 'chicken run' is a rotten egg. Hennu is the wildest après-ski shack on Klein Matterhorn. A 1m-long 'ski' of shots will make you cluck all the way down to Zermatt.

Getting There & Around

Trains depart roughly every 20 minutes from Brig (Sfr35, 1½ hours), stopping at Visp en route. Zermatt is also the starting point of the *Glacier Express* to Graubünden, one of the world's most spectacular train rides.

Motorists must park at Täsch (Sfr13.50 per day) and train (Sfr7.60, 12 minutes) it up to Zermatt.

BERN

POP 123,400

One of the planet's most underrated capitals, Bern is fabulous. With the genteel, old soul of a Renaissance man and the heart of a high-flying 21st-century gal, this riverside city is both medieval and modern. The 15th-century old town is gorgeous enough to sweep you off your feet and make you forget the century (it's definitely worthy of its Unesco World Heritage protection order). But edgy vintage boutiques, artsy-intellectual bars and Renzo Piano's futuristic art museum crammed with Paul Klee pieces slam you firmly back into the present.

Bern takes on a carnival atmosphere for the unique **Onion Market**, held on the fourth Monday of November.

Sights

Medieval Bern's **old town,** with 6km of covered arcades and cellar shops/bars descending from the streets, is the sandstone city's prime attraction. Join the crowds around the **Zytglogge** (clock tower) at four minutes before the hour to watch its revolving figures twirl; snack on hot chestnuts; and wander between decorative **fountains** (1545) depicting historical and folkloric characters...and a giant snacking on children at the **Kindlifresserbrunnen** on Kornhausplatz.

The dizzying climb up the lofty spire – Switzerland's tallest – of the 15th-century Gothic **münster** (cathedral; audio guide Sfr5, tower admission Sfr4; ⌚10am-5pm Tue-Sat, 11.30am-5pm Sun Easter-Nov, 10am-noon & 2-4pm Tue-Fri, to 5pm Sat, 11.30am-2pm Sun rest of year, tower closes 30 min earlier) is worth the 344-step hike.

The world's most famous scientist developed his theory of relativity in 1905 at what's now the **Einstein Museum** (☎031 312 00 91; www.einstein-bern.ch; Kramgasse 49; adult/student Sfr6/4.50; ⌚10am-7pm Mon-Fri, to 4pm Sat Feb-Dec), housed in the humble apartment where Einstein lived while working as a clerk in the local patent office.

Bern was founded in 1191 by Berchtold V and named for the unfortunate bear (*bärn* in local dialect) that was his first hunting victim. The bear remains the city's heraldic mascot, hence the **Bärengraben** (bear pit; www.baerenpark-bern.ch, in German; ⌚9.30am-5pm). Since 2009 the bears have lived in a new, spacious, riverside park. Beware: don't feed the bears anything random, but do buy a paper cone of fresh fruit (Sfr3).

Paul Klee Centre MUSEUM

(☎031 359 01 01; www.zpk.org; Monument in Fruchtland 3; admission Sfr18, audio guides Sfr5; ⌚10am-5pm Tue-Sun) Bern's Guggenheim, the fabulous Zentrum Paul Klee is an eye-catching 150m-long building designed by Renzo Piano 3km east of town. Inside the three-peak structure, the middle 'hill' showcases 4000 rotating works from Klee's prodigious and often playful career. Interactive computer displays built into the seating mean you can get the low-down on all the Swiss-born artist's major pieces and audio guides take visitors on one-hour musical tours of his work. In the grounds a walk through fields will take you past a stream of sculptures, including some contemporary works by artists such as Yoko Ono and Sol LeWitt. To get here take bus 12.

Houses of Parliament HISTORIC BUILDINGS

(☎031 332 85 22; www.parliament.ch; Bundesplatz; admission free; ⌚hourly tours 9am-4pm Mon-Sat) The 1902 Bundeshäuser, home of the Swiss Federal Assembly, are impressively ornate, with a huge, 214-bulb chandelier. Tours are offered when the parliament is in recess; otherwise watch from the public gallery. Bring your passport.

Sleeping

Hotel Landhaus HOTEL €

(☎031 331 41 66; www.landhausbern.ch; Altenbergstrasse 4; dm from Sfr33, d with/without bathroom from Sfr160/120; P⊖@) Backed by the grassy slope of a city park and fronted by the river and old-town spires, this historic hotel oozes character. Its soulful ground-floor restaurant is a tad bohemian and draws a staunchly local crowd.

Hotel Glocke Backpackers Bern HOSTEL €
(☎031 37 71; www.bernbackpackers.com; Rathausgasse 75; dm Sfr34-45; ⏲reception 8-11am & 3-10pm;) Its old-town location makes this many backpackers' first choice, although street noise might irritate light sleepers.

YHA Hostel HOSTEL €
(☎031 326 11 11; www.youthhostel.ch/bern; Weihergasse 4; dm from Sfr33; ⏲reception 7am-noon & 2pm-midnight;) In a pretty location set across from the river, this well-organised hostel sports clean dorms and a leafy terrace with red seating and ping-pong table. Free bike rental May to October (Sfr20 deposit).

Eating

Lötschberg AOC SWISS €€
(☎031 311 34 55; Zeughausgasse 16; mains Sfr14-28) Take an all-Swiss wine and beer list, add cheese specialities from the Valais (including fondue and raclette, of course), decorate it with circular, wooden wine racks mounted on cheerful yellow walls, add chequered tablecloths and you have one of the most dynamic Swiss restaurants in the country. This popular, casual spot, favoured by locals and visitors alike, manages to retain exceptional Swiss fare without the kitsch. It's as great for a bite and a glass of wine as it is for a full sit-down meal. Bonus: all wines can be bought to take-away.

Terrasse & Casa ITALIAN €€
(☎031 350 50 01; www.schwellenmaetteli.ch; Damaziquai 11; mains Sfr29-44; ⏲Terrasse 9am-11.30pm Mon-Sat, 9am-10pm Sun, Casa lunch & dinner Tue-Fri, 11.45am-11.30pm Sat & Sun) Dubbed 'Bern's Riviera', this twinset of classy hangouts on the Aare is an experience. Terrasse is a glass shoebox with wooden decking over the water and sun-loungers overlooking a weir, and Casa cooks Italian food in a country-styled, timber-framed house.

Drinking & Entertainment

For an earthy drink with old-generation locals, prop up the marble-topped bar inside Markthalle (p1245).

Sous le Pont BAR
(www.souslepont.ch; Neubrückstrasse 8; ⏲11.30am-2.30pm & 6pm-2.30am Tue-Thu, 11.30am-2.30pm & 7pm-2am Fri, 7pm-2.30am Sat) Delve into the grungy underground scene around the station in the bar of the semichaotic alternative-arts centre Reitschule. Find it in an old stone, graffiti-covered building – an old riding school built in 1897 – by the railway bridge.

Silo Bar BAR
(www.silobar.ch, in German; Mühlenplatz 11; ⏲10pm-3.30am Thu-Sat) By the water in the hip Matte quarter, Bern's monumental 19th-century corn house throbs with mainstream hits and a lively, predominantly student, set – *the* place to drink, dance and party.

Wasserwerk CLUB
(www.wasserwerkclub.ch; Wasserwerkgasse 5; ⏲10pm-late Thu-Sat) Bern's main techno venue with bar, club and occasional live music.

Information

Bern Tourismus (☎031 328 12 12; www.berninfo.com; Bahnhoftplatz; ⏲9am-8.30pm Jun-Sep, 9am-6.30pm Mon-Sat, 10am-5pm Sun Oct-May) Street-level floor of the train station. City tours, free hotel bookings, internet access (Sfr12 per hour).

BernCard (per 24/48/72hr Sfr20/31/38) Discount card providing admission to permanent collections at 27 museums, free public transport and city-tour discounts.

TOP PICKS: CHEAP EATS

This student-busy city has some fab low-priced options, oozing atmosphere and even a table thrown in for a highly affordable price.

» **Markthalle** (Bubenbergplatz 9; ⏲6.30am-11.30pm Mon-Wed, 6.30am-12.30am Thu & Fri, 7.30am-12.30am Sat) With a buzzing atmosphere and quick-snack action, this covered market arcade is jam-packed with eateries from around the world. Curries, vegetarian, food, wok stir-fries, *bruschette*, noodles, pizza, south Indian, Turkish, Middle Eastern... you name it, it's here. Eat standing at bars or around plastic tables.

» **Tibits** (Bahnhofplatz 10; ⏲6.30am-11.30pm Mon-Wed, 6.30am-midnight Thu-Sat, 8am-11pm Sun) This vegetarian buffet restaurant inside the train station is just the ticket for a quick healthy meal any size, any time of day. Serve yourself, get it weighed and pay accordingly.

Bern

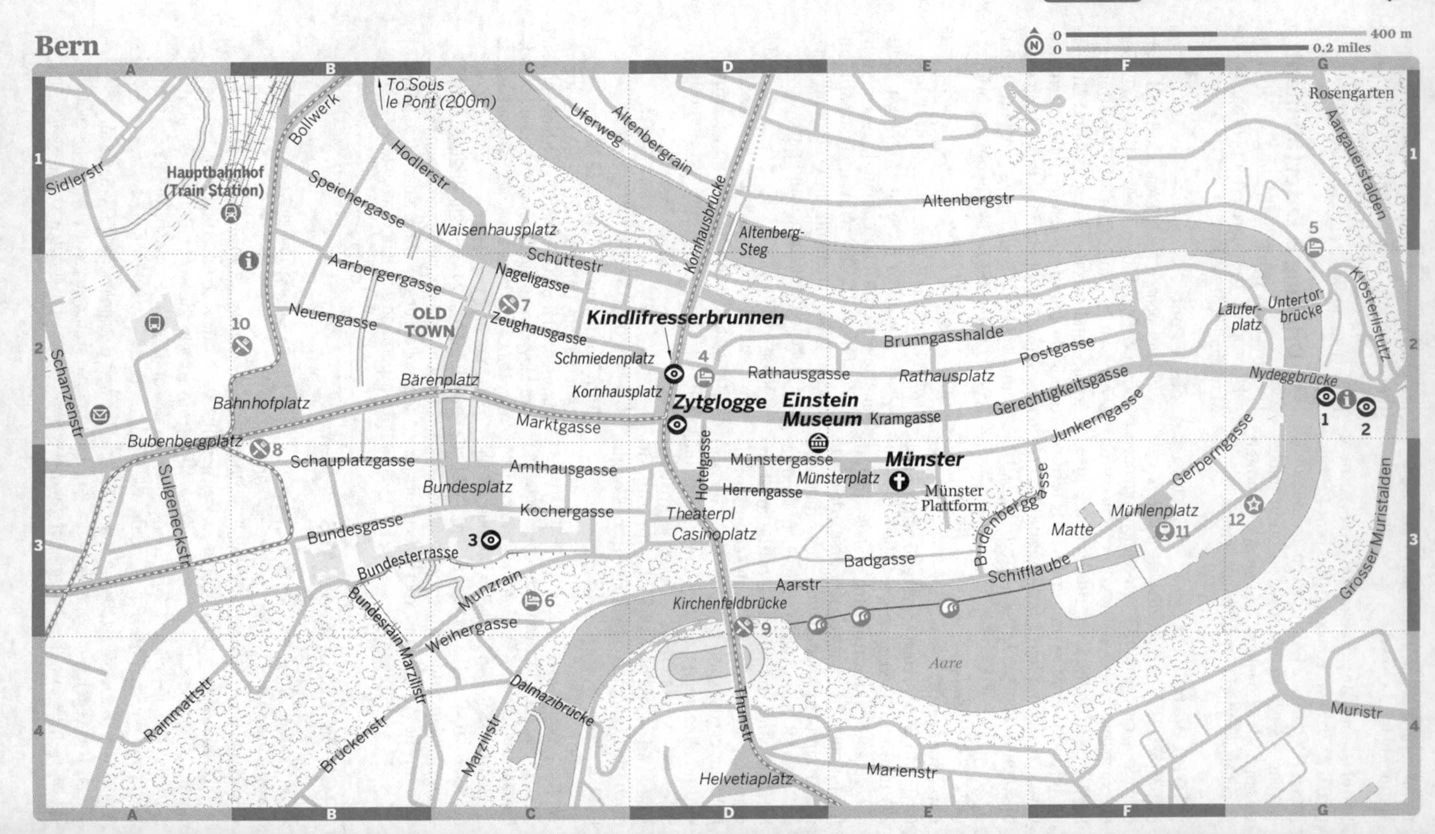
0
0
400 m
0.2 miles
To Sous
le Pont (200m)
Rosengarten
Aargauerstalden
Sidlerstr
Hauptbahnhof
(Train Station)
Bollwerk
Hodlerstr
Uferweg
Altenbergrain
Speichergasse
Kornhausbrücke
Altenbergstr
Waisenhausplatz
Altenberg-
Steg
Schüttestr
Aarbergergasse
Nageligasse
Klösterlistutz
Neuengasse
OLD
TOWN
Zeughausgasse
Kindlifresserbrunnen
Läufer-
platz
Untertor-
brücke
Brunngasshalde
Schanzenstr
Schmiedenplatz
Postgasse
Bärenplatz
Rathausgasse
Rathausplatz
Nydeggbrücke
Kornhausplatz
Gerechtigkeitsgasse
Bahnhofplatz
Zytglogge
Einstein
Museum
Kramgasse
Junkerngasse
Marktgasse
Bubenbergplatz
Hotelgasse
Gerberngasse
Schauplatzgasse
Münstergasse
Münster
Sulgeneckstr
Amthausgasse
Münsterplatz
Bundesplatz
Herrengasse
Münster
Plattform
Grosser Muristalden
Badenberggasse
Kochergasse
Theaterpl
Mühlenplatz
Bundesgasse
Matte
Casinoplatz
Bundesterrasse
Badgasse
Schifflaube
Munzrain
Aarstr
Kirchenfeldbrücke
Bundesrain Marzilistr
Weihergasse
Aare
Dalmazibrücke
Thunstr
Muristr
Rainmattstr
Brückenstr
Marzilistr
Marienstr
Helvetiaplatz
1
2
3
4
5
6
7
8
9
10
11
12
A
B
C
D
E
F
G

Bern

Top Sights

Einstein Museum ... D3
Kindlifresserbrunnen ... D2
Münster ... E3
Zytglogge ... D2

Sights

1 Bärengraben ... G2
2 Bern Show ... G2
3 Houses of Parliament ... C3

Sleeping

4 Hotel Glocke Backpackers Bern ... D2
5 Hotel Landhaus ... G1
6 SYHA Hostel ... C3

Eating

7 Lötschberg AOC ... C2
8 Markthalle ... B3
9 Terrasse & Casa ... D3
10 Tibits ... B2

Drinking

11 Silo Bar ... F3

Entertainment

12 Wasserwerk ... G3

Post office (Schanzenstrasse 4; 7.30am-9pm Mon-Fri, 8am-4pm Sat, 4-9pm Sun)

Tourist office (031 328 12 12; Bärengraben; 9am-6pm Jun-Sep, 10am-4pm Mar-May & Oct, 11am-4pm Nov-Feb) Tourist office by the old bear pits.

Getting There & Around

Hourly trains connect to most Swiss towns, including Geneva (Sfr46, 1¾ hours), Basel (Sfr37, 70 minutes) and Zürich (Sfr46, one hour).

Walk around or hop on a bus or tram; tickets cost Sfr2/3.80 for six stops/single journey within zones 1 and 2.

Cycle, skateboard or nip around on a microscooter with **Bern Rollt** (079 277 28 57; www.bernrollt.ch; train station; first four hours free, then Sfr1 per hour).

TICINO

Heidi never mentioned this Switzerland: the summer air is rich and hot, and the peacock-proud posers propel their scooters in and out of traffic – Italian weather, Italian style and, yes, Italian ice cream, Italian pizza, Italian architecture and Italian language.

South of the Alps, Ticino (Tessin in German and French) fuses Swiss cool with Italian passion, as evidenced by a lusty love for Italian comfort food and full-bodied wines balanced by a respect for rules and regulations.

Locarno

POP 15,600

A rambling red enclave of Mediterranean piazzas and arcades on the northern shore of Lake Maggiore, Locarno enjoys more sunshine than any other Swiss town.

Five minutes' walk west of the train station is its heart, Piazza Grande, and **tourist office** (091 791 00 91; www.maggiore.ch; Largo Zorzi 1; 9am-6pm Mon-Fri, 10am-6pm Sat, 10am-1.30pm & 2.30-5pm Sun mid-Mar–Oct, 9.30am-noon & 1.30-5pm Mon-Fri, 10am-noon & 1.30-5pm Sat Nov–mid-Mar).

The formidable **Madonna del Sasso**, with its panoramic views of the lake and town, features a church with 15th-century paintings and a small museum.

In August 150,000-odd film buffs hit town for the two-week **International Film Festival** (www.pardo.ch). Cinemas are used during the day but at night films are shown in the open air on a giant screen in the Piazza Grande.

Camping Delta (091 751 60 81; www.campingdelta.com; Via Respini 7; camp sites Sfr48-59 plus per adult/student Sfr20/17, Mar-Oct), brilliantly located between the shores of Lago Maggiore and the Maggia River, is ab fab.

Rooms at **Vecchia Locarno** (091 751 65 02; www.hotel-vecchia-locarno.ch; Via della Motta 10; s/d Sfr58/110) are gathered around a sunny internal courtyard, evoking a Mediterranean mood. Digs are simple but comfy; bathrooms are shared.

Lake Maggiore has a great range of fresh tasty fish, including *persico* (perch) and *corigone* (whitefish).

A huge hit with night owls, **Bar Sport** (Via della Posta 4; 8am-1am Mon-Fri, 10am-1am Sat, 2pm-1am Sun) is a rough-and-tumble bar with a red-walled dance space out the back and a beer garden. A few other bars are nearby.

There are trains to/from Brig (Sfr51, 2½ hours, hourly).

Lugano

POP 51,900

There is a distinct snappiness in the air in Switzerland's southernmost tourist town, where visitors unravel the spaghetti maze of cobblestone streets while locals toil behind counters – this is the country's third most important banking centre.

A sophisticated slice of Italian life with colourful markets, upmarket shops, interlocking piazza and lakeside parks, lucky Lugano lounges on Lake Lugano's northern shore, at the feet of Mts San Salvatore and Bré. It's a superb base for lake trips, water sports and hillside hikes.

The **tourist office** (☎091 913 32 32; www.lugano-tourism.ch; Riva Giocondo Albertolli; ⌚9am-7pm Mon-Fri, 9am-5pm Sat, 10am-5pm Sun Apr-Oct, 9am-noon & 2-5.30pm Mon-Fri, 10am-12.30pm & 1.30-5pm Sat Nov-Mar) also runs a booth at the train station (open 2pm to 7pm Monday to Saturday), a 10-minute walk uphill from the old town.

Wander the porticoed lanes woven around the busy main square, Piazza della Riforma; pop into Romanesque **Chiesa di Santa Maria degli Angioli** (Piazza Luini) with two frescoes by Bernardino Luini; and chomp on chocolate at the **Museo del Cioccolato Alprose** (☎091 611 88 88; www.alprose.ch; Via Rompada 36, Caslano; adult Sfr3; ⌚9am-5.30pm Mon-Fri, 9am-4.30pm Sat & Sun).

The **SYHA hostel** (☎091 966 27 28; www.luganoyouthhostel.ch; Via Cantonale 13, Savosa; dm/s/d Sfr29/70/98; ⌚mid-Mar–Oct;), housed in Villa Savosa, is one of Switzerland's more enticing youth hostels. To get there take bus 5 to Crocifisso.

For pizza or overpriced pasta, any of the places around Piazza della Riforma are pleasant and lively enough. Lugano's lakeside beach restaurant **Al Lido** (☎091 971 55 00; Viale Castagnola; snacks Sfr9-15, mains Sfr19-32; ⌚brunch 11am-6pm, dinner Wed-Sat) is hot for Sunday brunch and on Wednesday evenings, with DJ thrown in. Local Lugano beauties crowd around the long, orange-lit bar in **Soho Café** (Corso Pestalozzi 3) where chilled music creates a pleasant buzz.

Postal buses run to/from St Moritz (Sfr69, four hours, daily late June to mid-October and late December to early January). Reserve at the **bus station** (☎091 807 85 20; Via Serafino Balestra) or train-station information office.

GRAUBÜNDEN

Don't be fooled by Graubünden's diminutive size on a map. This is topographic origami at its finest. Unfold the rippled landscape to find an outdoor adventurer's paradise, riddled with walking trails, lakes and downhill ski slopes – including superswanky St Moritz and backpacker mecca Flims-Laax. Linguistically wired to flick from Italian to German to Romansch, locals keep you on your toes, too.

St Moritz

POP 5070

Switzerland's original winter wonderland and the cradle of Alpine tourism, St Moritz (San Murezzan in Romansch) has been luring royals, the filthy rich and moneyed wannabes since 1864. With its smugly perfect lake, aloof mountains and Gucci set propping up the bars, the town looks a million dollars…and is – in the shape of a superb carving on Corviglia (2486m), hairy black Diavolezza runs and endless hiking trails when the powder melts. See www.engadin.stmoritz.ch for the complete low-down.

The **tourist office** (☎081 837 33 33; www.stmoritz.ch; Via Maistra 12; ⌚9am-6.30pm Mon-Fri, 9am-noon & 1.30-6pm Sat, 4-6pm Sun) is in St Moritz Dorf, above the train station.

Budget beds are gold-dust-rare in St Moritz, but you'll find one at **Jugendherberge St Moritz** (☎081 836 61 11; www.youthhostel.ch/st.moritz; Stille Via Surpunt 60; dm/d Sfr55/140; @), edging the forest. The four-bed dorms and doubles are quiet and clean. There's a kiosk, games room and laundromat.

English-styled **Bobby's Pub** (Via dal Bagn 50a) and **Roo Bar** (Via Traunter Plazzas 7) are hot watering holes.

The **Palm Express postal bus** (☎058 386 31 66) runs to/from Lugano (Sfr69, four hours, daily summer, Friday, Saturday and Sunday winter); advance reservations are obligatory.

Flims-Laax

They say if the snow isn't falling anywhere else, you'll surely find some around Flims-Laax. These two towns, along with tiny Falera, 20km west of Chur, form a single ski area known as the Weisses Arena (White Arena), with 220km of slopes catering for all levels. Laax, in particular, is known as a mecca for snowboarders, who spice up the local nightlife, too. The resort is barely two hours by train and bus (less by car) from Zürich airport.

The main **tourist office** (☎081 920 92 00; www.flims.com (summer), www.laax.com (winter); Via Nova; ⌚8am-6pm Mon-Fri, to noon Sat mid-Jun–mid-Aug, 8am-5pm Mon-Sat mid-Dec–mid-Apr) is in Flims-Dorf.

Mostly, intermediate and easy ski slopes peak at 3000m, although there are some 45km of more-challenging runs. A one-day ski pass (Sfr62 plus Sfr5 for KeyCard to access lifts) also covers ski buses.

Laax was the first Swiss resort to allow snowboarders to use the lifts back in 1985, and remains a mecca for boarders, with two huge half-pipes (one said to be the biggest in the world) and a freestyle park huddled around the unfortunately named Crap Sogn Gion peak. The season starts in late October on the glacier and, depending on snowfalls, in mid-December elsewhere.

In summer try river rafting on a turbulent 17km stretch of the Vorderrhein between Ilanz and Reichenau. It will take you through the **Rheinschlucht** (Rhine Gorge), aka Switzerland's Grand Canyon. **Swissraft** (☎081 911 52 50; www.swissraft.ch; half-/full day Sfr109/160) runs rafting expeditions.

Sleep? Dream on. It may resemble an oversized Rubik's cube, but **Riders Palace** (☎081 927 97 00; www.riderspalace.ch; Laax Murschetg; dm Sfr32-62, d Sfr185-285; Wi-Fi) is a curious slice of designer cool with bare concrete walls and fluorescent lighting. Choose between basic five-bed dorms, slick rooms with Philippe Starck tubs, or hi-tech suites complete with PlayStation and Dolby surround. Find it 200m from the Laax lifts.

Titillate taste buds with the raw funk of **La Vacca** (☎081 927 99 62; Plaun Station, Laax-Murschetg lifts; mains Sfr40-70), a tepee where cowhide-draped chairs surround an open fire and the menu (think bison steak paired with full-bodied Argentine wine) is as exciting as the design.

After a day pounding powder, you can slam shots, check email and shimmy in your snow boots at **Crap Bar** (Laax-Murschetg lifts).

Postal buses run to Flims hourly from Chur (Sfr12.80 to Flims-Dorf, 30 minutes).

ZÜRICH

POP 365,400

Zürich used to be Europe's best-kept secret. Conservative bankers and perfect, medieval landmarks stood at the forefront, with no hint that a city as cool and hip as Berlin or Amsterdam lurked within this financial centre's impeccably clean streets. But somewhere between ranking as the top city in the world for quality of life seven years running, hosting Europe's largest street party and erecting a flagship store made entirely of 16 stacked shipping containers, the secret got out, and the international press starting catching on and writing about the real Zürich: a cool, stylish and surprising city.

Eat a traditional wurst while pondering a swim in the postcard-perfect lake dotted with majestic swans, sip a cocktail atop an ancient tower with a view of the Alps or go clubbing in a former powdered milk warehouse. Switzerland's biggest city and finance centre is also the hippest. Here, Berlin grunge meets swish posh, where fashion fiends flock to drink and club.

Sights

Elegant **Bahnhofstrasse** is simply perfect for window-shopping and affluent-Züricher watching. On Sunday it seems as if all of Zürich takes an afternoon stroll around the lake: odd human traffic jam aside, it's worth the cultural experience.

The 13th-century **Fraumünster** (cathedral; Münsterplatz; ⌚9am-6pm May-Sep, 10am-5pm Oct-Apr) has some of the world's most distinctive stained-glass windows, while the 13th-century tower of **St Peterskirche** (St Peter's Church; St-Peterhofstatt; ⌚8am-6pm Mon-Fri, 8am-4pm Sat, 11am-5pm Sun) has Europe's largest clock face (8.7m in diameter).

Exhibitions at Zürich's **Museum für Gestaltung** (Design Museum; ☎043 446 67 67; www.museum-gestaltung.ch; Ausstellungstrasse 60; adult/student Sfr9/6; ⌚10am-8pm Tue-Thu, to 5pm Fri-Sun) are impressive and wide-ranging – anything from Bollywood to photographic short stories.

GREEN DETOUR TO MARS

When the urban action gets too much, take a green breather with a half-day trip to Mars – or at least along the two-hour walking trail poetically known as **Planetenweg** ('Planetary Path'). From Zürich take the train (line S10) to Uetliberg (23 minutes, departures every 30 minutes), from where the planetary trail winds along the mountain ridge to Felsenegg. En route, scale models of the planets are interspersed with fabulous lake views. At Felsenegg, a cable car descends every 10 minutes to Adliswill, from where frequent trains return to Zürich (line S4, 16 minutes). Buy the Sfr15.80 Albis-Netzkarte, which gets you to Uetliberg and back, including unlimited travel downtown.

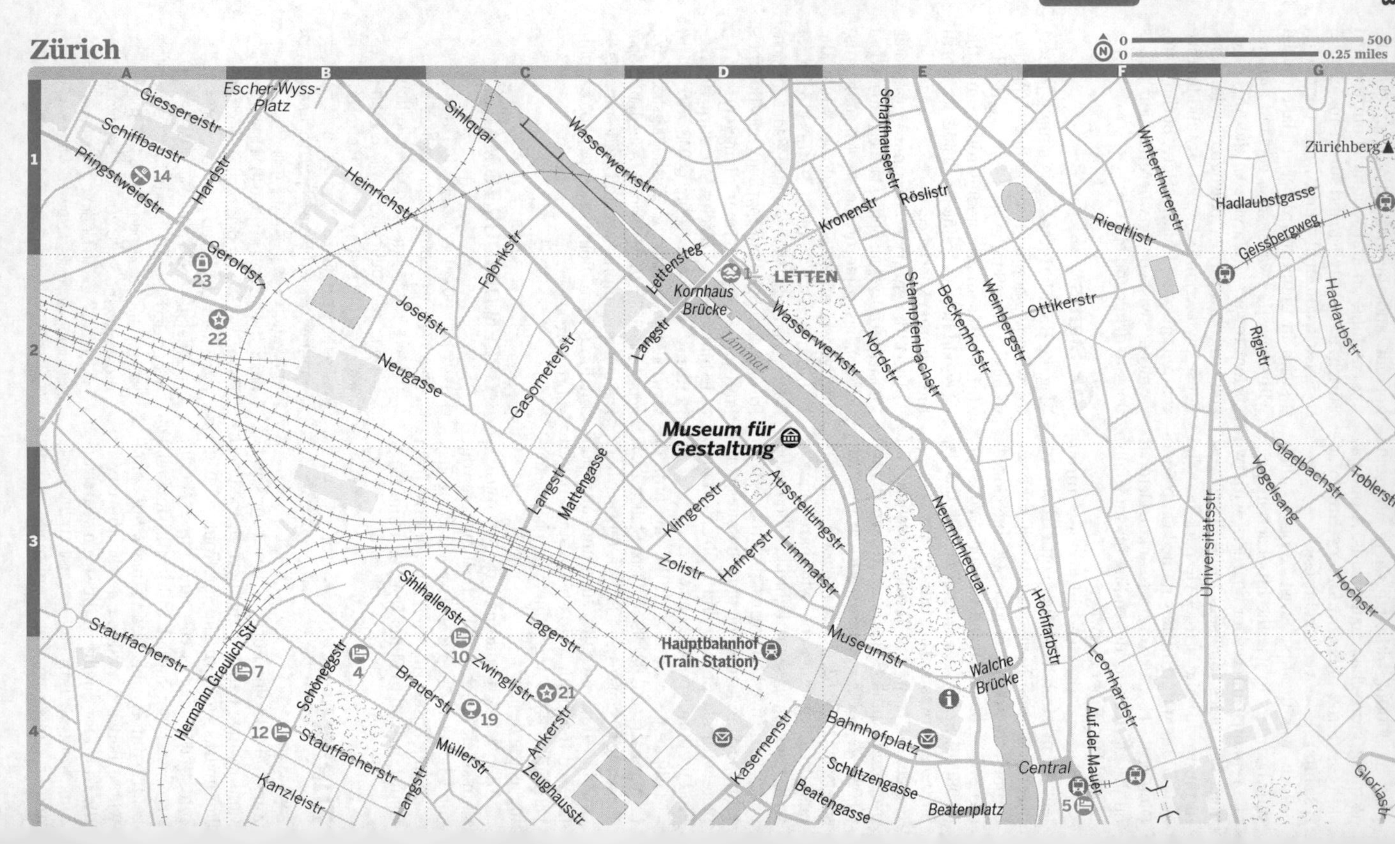
Zürich
0
0
500 m
0.25 miles
A
B
C
D
E
F
G
1
2
3
4
Escher-Wyss-Platz
Giessereistr
Schiffbaustr
Pfingstweidstr
14
Hardstr
Geroldstr
23
22
Sihlquai
Wasserwerkstr
Heinrichstr
Fabrikstr
Josefstr
Neugasse
Gasometerstr
Schaffhauserstr
Röslistr
Kronenstr
Lettensteg
Kornhaus Brücke
1
LETTEN
Langstr
Limmat
Wasserwerkstr
Nordstr
Stampfenbachstr
Beckenhofstr
Weinbergstr
Ottikerstr
Winterthurerstr
Riedtlistr
Zürichberg
Hadlaubstgasse
Geissbergweg
Hadlaubstr
Rigistr
Museum für Gestaltung
Langstr
Mattengasse
Klingenstr
Ausstellungsstr
Zolistr
Hafnerstr
Limmatstr
Neumühlequai
Gladbachstr
Vogelsang
Toblerstr
Universitätsstr
Hochstr
Hochfarbstr
Stauffacherstr
Hermann Greulich Str
7
Schöneggstr
4
Sihlhallenstr
10
Lagerstr
Zwinglistr
21
Brauerstr
19
12
Stauffacherstr
Müllerstr
Ankerstr
Kanzleistr
Langstr
Zeughausstr
Hauptbahnhof (Train Station)
Museumstr
Walche Brücke
Leonhardstr
Kasernenstr
Bahnhofplatz
Schützengasse
Beatengasse
Beatenplatz
Central
Auf der Mauer
5
Gloriastr

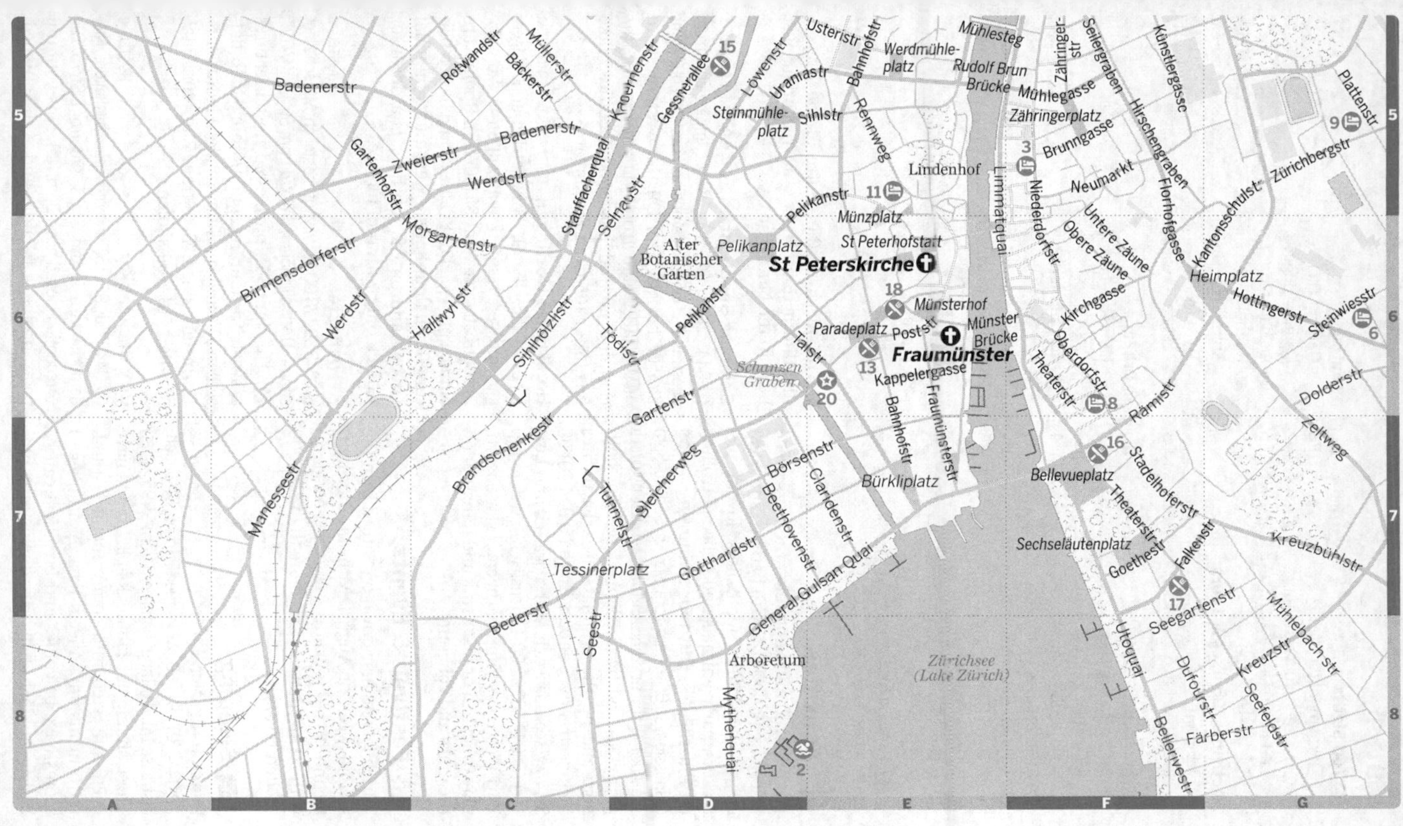
5
6
7
8
A
B
C
D
E
F
G
Badenerstr
Rotwandstr
Müllerstr
Bäckerstr
Badenerstr
Kasernenstr
Gessnerallee
15
Löwenstr
Usteristr
Uraniastr
Bahnhofstr
Werdmühle-platz
Mühlesteg
Rudolf Brun Brücke
Zähringer-str
Seilergraben
Künstlergasse
Plattenstr
9
Zürichbergstr
Mühlegasse
Zähringerplatz
Brunngasse
3
Hirschengraben
Steinmühle-platz
Sihlstr
Rennweg
Lindenhof
Zweierstr
Gartenhofstr
Werdstr
Stauffacherquai
Selnaustr
Pelikanstr
11
Münzplatz
Limmatquai
Niederdorfstr
Neumarkt
Kantonsschulstr
Florhofgasse
Untere Zäune
Obere Zäune
Morgartenstr
Alter Botanischer Garten
Pelikanplatz
St Peterhofstatt
St Peterskirche
Heimplatz
Birmensdorferstr
18
Münsterhof
Kirchgasse
Hottingerstr
Steinwiesstr
6
Werdstr
Hallwylstr
Sihlhölzlistr
Tödistr
Pelikanstr
Paradeplatz
Poststr
Münster Brücke
Fraumünster
Talstr
13
Kappelergasse
Oberdorfstr
Schanzen Graben
20
Theaterstr
8
Rämistr
Dolderstr
Gartenstr
Fraumünsterstr
Bahnhofstr
Zeltweg
Brandschenkestr
Börsenstr
16
Bleicherweg
Claridenstr
Bürkliplatz
Bellevueplatz
Stadelhoferstr
Manessestr
Tunnelstr
Beethovenstr
Theaterstr
Sechseläutenplatz
Kreuzbühlstr
Tessinerplatz
Gotthardstr
General Guisan Quai
Goethestr
Falkenstr
17
Bederstr
Seegartenstr
Mühlebach str
Seestr
Utoquai
Arboretum
Zürichsee (Lake Zürich)
Dufourstr
Kreuzstr
Mythenquai
Seefeldstr
Bellerivestr
Färberstr
2

Zürich

Activities

From May to mid-September the city's green lakeshore parks buzz with bathers, sun seekers, in-line skaters, footballers, lovers, picnickers, party animals and police patrolling on rollerblades. **Outdoor swimming areas** (admission Sfr6; 9am-7pm May & Sep, to 8pm Jun-Aug) – think rectangular wooden piers partly covered by pavilion – are open both here and up the Limmat River. Favourites include trendy **Seebad Enge** (044 201 38 89; www.seebadenge.ch; Mythenquai 95) and **Letten** (044 362 92 00; Lettensteg 10), where hip Züri-Westers swim, barbecue, skateboard, play volleyball or just drink and hang-out on the grass and concrete.

Festivals & Events

Zürich lets its hair down on Saturday in the second week of August with an enormous techno **street parade** (www.street-parade.ch) with 30 lovemobiles and more than 500,000 excited ravers.

Sleeping

Pension für Dich PENSION €€
(044 317 91 60; www.fuerdich.ch; Stauffacherstrasse 141; d without bathroom from Sfr95;) These simple but fabulous apartments have been converted into comfy rooms – think retro furnishings meets Ikea. A number of rooms have balconies and breakfast can be had for a steal at its cafe downstairs, plus you're smack in the centre of the Kreis 4 nightlife action. There's no reception, just head to the bar in the cafe.

Camping Seebucht CAMPING GROUND €
(044 482 16 12; www.camping-zurich.ch; Seestrasse 559; campsites per adult/tent Sfr7.50/11; May-Sep) On the western shore of the lake, 4km from the city centre, this camping ground has good facilities. Take bus 161 or 165 from Bürkliplatz.

Hotel Foyer Hottingen HOTEL €
(044 256 19 19; www.hotel-foyer-hottingen.ch; Hottingerstrasse 31; dm from Sfr45, s/d with/without bathroom from Sfr130/115) Rooms are clinical but excellent value. Some have a balcony. Each floor has showers and communal kitchen and on the top floor is a dorm for women only with roof terrace.

SYHA hostel HOSTEL €
(043 399 78 00; www.youthhostel.ch; Mütschellenstrasse 114, Wollishofen; dm/s/d from Sfr42/107/127; @) This bulbous, purple-red hostel features a swish 24-hour reception/dining hall, flat-screen TVs and sparkling modern bathrooms. Dorms are small. Take tram 7 to Morgental, or S-Bahn to Wollishofen.

City Backpacker HOSTEL €
(044 251 90 15; www.city-backpacker.ch; Niederdorfstrasse 5; dm Sfr35, s/d from Sfr75/115; reception closed noon-3pm; @) This youthful party hostel is friendly and well-equipped,

if a trifle cramped. Overcome the claustrophobia in summer by hanging out on the roof terrace – the best spot in Zürich to wind down at sunset with a few cold beers.

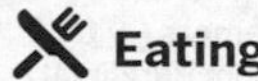

Eating

Cheap eats abound around the train station, especially in the underground Shopville. Niederdorfstrasse has a string of snack bars offering pizza, kebabs and Asian food.

Zeughauskeller SWISS €€
(044 211 26 90; www.zeughauskeller.ch; Bahnhofstrasse 28a; mains Sfr18-35; 11.30am-11pm) The menu at this huge, atmospheric beer hall – set inside a former armoury (look for the shields and various protective antiques hanging from the walls) – offers 20 different kinds of sausages in eight languages, as well as numerous other Swiss specialities, both carnivorous and vegetarian. It's a local institution and well-loved by the lunch crowd, so expect queues during the week between noon and 2pm.

Cafe Für Dich CAFE €
(Stauffacherstrasse 141; snacks Sfr5-9; 6pm-midnight Mon, 9am-midnight Tue-Sun) This laid-back cafe in Kreis 4 could easily be in San Francisco or Brooklyn, with its no-nonsense come-and-hang-out vibe. Occasional one-man-band live music and poetry readings keep the atmosphere serious but fun, and it's a fab spot to grab a tea, single malt, local beer or a small snack (olives, quiches) throughout the day and eve.

les halles INTERNATIONAL €€
(044 273 11 25; www.les-halles.ch; Pfingstweidstrasse 6; mains Sfr22-31; 11am-midnight Mon-Wed, to 1am Thu-Sat) One of several chirpy bar-restaurants in revamped factory buildings, this is the best place in town to tuck into *Moules mit Frites* (mussels and fries). Hang at the bustling bar and shop at the market.

Reithalle INTERNATIONAL €€
(044 212 07 66; www.restaurant-reithalle.ch; Gessnerallee 8; mains Sfr22-35; lunch Mon-Fri, dinner daily) Fancy dining in stables in a former barracks complex? The walls at this boisterous, convivial spot are still lined with the cavalry horses' feeding and drinking troughs. Cuisine is copious Swiss and international, and tables are cleared at 11.30pm, when the place morphs into a dance club.

Café Sprüngli SWISS €
(www.spruengli.ch; Bahnhofstrasse 21; mains Sfr9-15; 7am-6.30pm Mon-Fri, 8am-6pm Sat, 9.30am-5.30pm Sun) Indulge in cakes, chocolate and coffee at this epicentre of sweet Switzerland, in business since 1836. You can have a light lunch too but whatever you do, don't fail to check out the chocolate shop heaven around the corner on Paradeplatz.

Tibits by Hiltl INTERNATIONAL €
(www.tibits.ch; Seefeldstrasse 2; meals per 100g Sfr3.80, mains from roughly Sfr10; 6.30am-midnight Mon-Fri, 8am-midnight Sat, 9am-midnight Sun) Tibits is where with-it, health-conscious Zürichers eat light. Think tasty vegetarian buffet, fresh fruit juices, coffees and cake – take your pick and pay at the counter.

Sternen Grill SWISS €
(Bellevueplatz/Theatrestrasse 22; snacks from Sfr6; 11.30am-midnight) This is the city's most famous – and busiest – sausage stand; just follow the crowds streaming in for a tasty greasefest.

ONCE A TRUCK TARPAULIN, NOW A BAG

Freitag (043-3669520; Geroldstrasse 17; 11am-7:30pm Mon-Fri, 11am-5pm Sat), run by two ambitious Swiss dudes, proves everything can have a second life. Choose an industrial-looking messenger bag, travelling tote or women's purse made from 100% recycled materials (truck tarps, seat belts etc) in this flagship store housed in a 26m-high stack of retired shipping containers in Züri-West. Even if you can't afford the pricey bags, hike up to the al fresco viewing platform in the top container.

Drinking & Entertainment

Drinking options congregate in the happening Kreis 4 and Kreis 5 districts, together known as Züri-West. Langstrasse, behind the station, is a minor red-light district – safe to wander but you might be offered drugs or sex – with loads of popular bars humming in side streets. May to September the trendy water bars at the lake baths are hot places to hang barefooted. Clubbers should dress well and be prepared to cough up Sfr15 to Sfr30 admission.

Longstreet Bar BAR
(www.longstreetbar.ch; Langstrasse 92; 8pm-3am Tue-Thu, to 4am Fri & Sat, to 2am Sun) Run

by the guy seemingly behind half of Zürich's nightlife, this purple-felt-lined one-time cabaret is now a throbbing music bar with DJs. Count the thousands of light bulbs.

Liquid CLUB
(www.liquid-bar.ch; Zwinglistrasse 12; 5pm-1am Mon-Thu, 5pm-3am Fri, 7pm-3am Sat) With its striped wallpaper and plastic chairs moulded in the shape of boiled eggs broken in half, this is kitsch at its best – a hip backdrop for lounge-oriented music nights.

Supermarket CLUB
(www.supermarket.li; Geroldstrasse 17; 11pm-late Thu-Sat) Looking like an innocent little house, Supermarket boasts three cosy lounge bars around the dance floor, a covered rear courtyard and an interesting roster of DJs playing house. The crowd is mid-20s.

Alte Börse CLUB
(www.alteboerse.com; Bleicherweg 5; 10pm-late Thu-Sat) Hundreds of dance fanatics cram in to this recently opened club, in a respectable town-centre building, for intense electronic sessions with DJs from all over the world. It also gets in occasional live acts.

Information

Bellevue Apotheke (☎044 266 62 22; Theaterstrasse 14; 24hr) Chemist.

Police station (☎044 216 71 11; Bahnhofquai 3)

Quanta (☎044 260 72 66; Limmatquai 94; per hr Sfr10; 9am-midnight) Internet access.

University Hospital (☎044 255 11 11/21 11; Rämistrasse 100) Casualty.

Zürich Tourism (☎044 215 40 00, hotel reservations 044 215 40 40; www.zuerich.com; train station; 8am-8.30pm Mon-Sat, 8.30am-6.30pm Sun May-Oct; 8.30am-7pm Mon-Sat, 9am-6.30pm Sun Nov-Apr)

ZürichCard (24/72hr Sfr17/24) Available from the tourist office and airport train station; provides free public transport, free museum admission and more.

Getting There & Away

Zürich airport (☎043 816 22 11; www.zurich-airport.com), 10km north of the centre, is a small international hub with two terminals.

Daily trains serve Stuttgart (Sfr76, three hours), Munich (Sfr104, 4½ hours), Innsbruck (Sfr79, four hours) and many other international destinations. There are direct departures to most major Swiss towns, including Lucerne (Sfr23, 46 to 50 minutes), Bern (Sfr46, 57 minutes) and Basel (Sfr31, 55 minutes).

Getting Around

There is a comprehensive bus, tram and S-Bahn service. Short trips under five stops are Sfr2.40 and a 24-hour pass for the centre is Sfr7.80.

From April to October **lake steamers** (☎044 487 13 33; www.zsg.ch) depart from Bürkliplatz.

City bikes (www.zuerirollt.ch) can be picked up at **Velogate** (train station; 8am-9.30pm) for free if you bring the bike back after six hours or pay Sfr5 per day.

CENTRAL SWITZERLAND & BERNER OBERLAND

This region should come with a health warning: may cause trembling at the north face of Eiger, uncontrollable bouts of euphoria at the foot of Jungfrau, 007 delusions at Schilthorn and A-list fever in Gstaad. Indeed the landscape here is such that electric-green spruce forests, mountains so big they'll swallow you up, surreal china-blue skies, swirling glaciers and turquoise lakes seem hallucinatory.

Lucerne

POP 59,500

Recipe for a gorgeous Swiss city: take a cobalt lake ringed by mountains of myth, add a medieval old town and sprinkle with covered bridges, sunny plazas, candy-coloured houses and waterfront promenades. Lucerne is bright, beautiful and has been Little Miss Popular since the 19th century.

Don't miss the old town with its medieval ramparts and towers, 15th-century buildings with painted facades, and its famous bridges: **Kapellbrücke** (Chapel Bridge; 1333), destroyed in part by a spectacular 1993 fire and subsequently rebuilt (fire damage is still obvious on the 17th-century pictorial panels under the roof); and the **Spreuerbrücke** (Spreuer Bridge), with darker but better-preserved *Dance of Death* panels.

Lucerne's blockbuster cultural attraction is the **Sammlung Rosengart** (☎041 220 16 60; www.rosengart.ch; Pilatusstrasse 10; adult/student Sfr18/16; 10am-6pm Apr-Oct, 11am-5pm Nov-Mar), studded with masterpieces by Cézanne, Klee, Kandinsky, Miró, Matisse and Monet. Some 200 photographs capturing the last years of Picasso's life complement the main collection.

Lucerne's boisterous six-day **Fasnacht** party kicks off on 'Dirty Thursday' with the emergence of the character 'Fritschi' from the town hall, and moves through raucous celebrations climaxing on Mardi Gras (Fat Tuesday). June's Yodelling Festival, **Jodlerfest Luzern**, is a classic Alpine shindig comprising 12,000 yodellers, alphorn players and flag throwers.

Sleeping

Backpackers Lucerne HOSTEL €
(041 360 04 20; www.backpackerslucerne.ch; Alpenquai 42; dm/d Sfr33/74; reception 7-10am & 4-11pm;) Travellers love the vibe here at what's quite possibly backpacker heaven with its lake-facing balconies, art-slung walls and soulful lounge. Find it a 15-minute walk southeast of the train station.

SYHA hostel HOSTEL €
(041 420 88 00; www.youthhostel.ch/luzern; Sedelstrasse 12; dm/d Sfr35/84; check in 2pm-midnight in summer, from 4pm in winter;) Modern, well-run and clean, with value-for-money meals available throughout the day. Take bus 18 from the train station to Jugendherberge.

Self-caterers head to Hertensteinstrasse where cheap eats are plentiful.

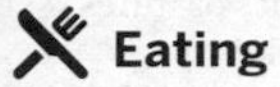

Eating

Jazzkantine ITALIAN €
(041 410 73 73; Grabenstrasse 8; mains Sfr16-24) With its stainless-steel bar, sturdy wooden tables and chalkboard menus, Jazzkantine is an arty haunt. Go for tasty *bruschette* or more ambitious dishes like penne vodka. Saturday-night gigs follow weeknight jazz workshops.

Schützengarten INTERNATIONAL €
(041 240 01 10; Bruchstrasse 20; mains Sfr18-47) As well as a cracking sense of humour, Schützengarten has smiley service, wood-panelled surrounds, appetising vegetarian and vegan dishes and organic wine. Sit on the vine-strewn terrace in summer.

Getting There & Away

Destinations served by hourly trains include Zürich (Sfr23, one hour), Interlaken (Sfr33.40, two hours) and Bern (Sfr35, 1½ hours).

Interlaken

POP 5310

Catering to backpackers like nowhere else in the country, Interlaken is often the main Swiss destination for budget travellers. It is also a mecca for thrill seekers, and many a traveller leaves with a much lighter wallet after blowing mind-boggling amounts of cash on a range of white-knuckle, high-adrenalin sports. Most are not disappointed.

Activities

Some say leaping from an aeroplane over the Swiss Alps is a life-changing experience. Others argue that canyoning is, while some swear by night sledding or zorbing (Sfr95), the latest craze where you're strapped inside a giant plastic ball and flung down a hill. Whatever your adventure-sport taste, you'll find it in Interlaken.

Other options include rock climbing (Sfr90), rafting or canyoning (Sfr110), bungee jumping (Sfr130), skydiving (Sfr430), paragliding (Sfr160) and hang-gliding (Sfr195). Most excursions are without incident, but there's always a small risk and it's wise to ask about safety records and procedures.

Major operators:

Alpin Center (033 823 55 23; www.alpincenter.ch; Hauptstrasse 16)

Alpinraft (033 823 41 00; www.alpinraft.ch; Hauptstrasse 7)

Outdoor Interlaken (033 826 77 19; www.outdoor-interlaken.ch; Hauptstrasse 15)

Swissraft (033 821 66 55; www.swissraft-activity.ch; Obere Jungfraustrasse 72)

If you don't have loads of money, check out the myriad hiking trails in the area – the views are amazing and free.

Sleeping

RiverLodge & Camping TCS CAMPING GROUND €
(033 822 44 34; Brienzstrasse 24; camp sites per adult/tent/car Sfr10/9/4, dm/s/d Sfr28/64/88; May–mid-Oct;) Facing the Aare River and handy for Interlaken Ost train station, this camping ground and hostel duo offers 1st-class facilities, including a kitchen, laundry and wi-fi. Rent bikes and kayaks here.

Balmer's Herberge HOSTEL €
(033 822 19 61; www.balmers.ch; Hauptstrasse 23; dm from Sfr29, s/d Sfr45/78;) Adrenalin junkies hail Balmer's for its fun frat-house vibe. These party-mad digs offer beer-garden happy hours, wrap lunches, a pumping bar with DJs, and chill-out hammocks for nursing your hangover.

Schlaf im Stroh FARM STAY €
(033 822 04 31; www.uelisi.ch; Lanzenen 30; May-Sep;) Our readers have been singing the praises of this friendly farm for

years. Bring your sleeping bag to snooze in the straw and wake up to a hearty breakfast. Kids adore the resident cats, goats and rabbits. It's 15 minutes' walk from Interlaken Ost station, along the Aare River (upstream). Note: the farm will be closed to visitors during 2011 due to maintenance, but the owners swear they will reopen the barn doors to farm stays again in 2012 – check the website.

Backpackers Villa Sonnenhof HOSTEL € (☎033 826 71 71; www.villa.ch; Alpenstrasse 16; dm/d Sfr38/100, Jungfrau view extra Sfr5; ⊙reception 7am-11pm; @📶) While most Interlaken hostels are charged with more energy than a Duracell bunny, this homely place recharges your batteries. The olive-fronted villa exudes Victorian flair with stucco and vintage steamer trunks, immaculate dorms, a well-equipped kitchen and leafy garden.

Eating & Drinking

Am Marktplatz is scattered with bakeries and bistros that have alfresco seating. The bars at Balmer's and Funny Farm are easily the liveliest drinking holes for revved-up 20-somethings.

Sandwich Bar SWISS € (Rosenstrasse 5; snacks Sfr4-9; ⊙7.30am-7pm Mon-Fri, 8am-5pm Sat) This snack bar is an untouristy gem. Choose your bread and get creative with fillings. Our favourite is *Bündnerfleisch* (air-dried meat), sundried tomatoes and parmesan. Otherwise try soups, salads and locally made ice cream.

Goldener Anker INTERNATIONAL € (☎033 822 16 72; www.anker.ch, in German; Marktgasse 57; mains Sfr18-40) This beamed restaurant, locals whisper in your ear, is the best in town. Globetrotters include everything from sizzling fajitas to red snapper and ostrich steaks. There are live bands.

Information

Most of Interlaken lies between its two train stations, Interlaken Ost and West. The main shopping street, Höheweg, runs between the stations and you can walk from one to the other in 20 minutes.

Near Interlaken West is **Interlaken Tourismus** (☎033 826 53 00; www.interlakentourism.ch; Höheweg 37; ⊙8am-7pm Mon-Fri, 8am-5pm Sat, 10am-noon & 5-7pm Sun Jul–mid-Sep, 8am-noon & 1.30-6pm Mon-Fri, 9am-noon Sat rest of year).

Getting There & Away

Trains to Grindelwald (Sfr10.20, 40 minutes, hourly), Lauterbrunnen (Sfr7, 20 minutes, hourly) and Lucerne (Sfr30, two hours, hourly) depart from Interlaken Ost. Trains to Brig (Sfr41, 1½ hours, hourly) and Montreux via Bern or Visp (Sfr57 to Sfr67, 2¼ hours, hourly) leave from either Interlaken West or Ost.

Jungfrau Region

This is where your heart skips a beat. Presided over by glacier-encrusted monoliths Eiger, Mönch and Jungfrau (Ogre, Monk and Virgin), the scenery stirs the soul and strains the neck muscles. A magnet for skiers and boarders, a one-day ski pass costs Sfr59. Come summer, walk and walk and walk.

GRINDELWALD

POP 3815

Skiers and hikers cottoned onto the charms of this simple farming village, nestled in a valley under the north face of the Eiger, in the late 19th century, making it one of Switzerland's oldest resorts. Think archetypal Alpine chalets and verdant pastures set against an Oscar-worthy backdrop.

Grindelwald tourist office (☎033 854 12 12; www.grindelwald.ch; Dorfstrasse; ⊙8am-noon & 1.30-6pm Mon-Fri, 9am-noon & 1.30-5pm Sat & Sun summer & winter, 8am-noon & 1.30-5pm Mon-Fri, 9am-noon Sat rest of year) is at the Sportzentrum, 200m from the train station.

First is the main skiing area, with runs stretching from Oberjoch at 2486m to the village at 1050m. In summer ride Europe's longest **cable car** (☎033 854 80 80; www.maennlichen.ch; one way/return Sfr 31/51) from Grindelwald-Grund to Männlichen to revel in extraordinary views and soul-rousing hikes.

The cosy wooden chalet housing the excellent **SYHA hostel** (☎033 853 10 09; www.youthhostel.ch/grindelwald; Terrassenweg; dm Sfr33-40, d with/without bathroom Sfr108/80; ⊙reception 7.30-10am & 4-10pm; @) is perched high on a hill with magnificent views. Avoid the 20-minute slog from the train station by taking the Terrassenweg-bound bus to the Gaggi Säge stop.

Near the Männlichen cable-car station, **Mountain Hostel** (☎033 854 38 38; www.mountainhostel.ch; dm Sfr38-44, d Sfr92-102; P) is a good base for sports junkies. Cyclists are especially welcomed. Rates include free ice skating and swimming nearby.

Hourly trains link Grindelwald with Interlaken Ost (Sfr10.20, 40 minutes).

SLEEP SUSTAINABLY

Perched above Grindelwald village, eco-friendly chalet **Naturfreundehaus** (☎033 853 13 33; www.naturfreundehaeuser.ch; Terrassenweg; dm/s/d Sfr36/46/72; ⏰closed low season; P), whose name suitably translates as the House of Friends of Nature, is a green gem. Most folk have a cat or dog as family pet; Vreni and Heinz have Mono, a six-year-old trout. Creaking floors lead up to cute pine-panelled rooms, including a shoebox single – Switzerland's smallest, so they say. Try an Eiger coffee with amaretto or a home-made mint cordial in the quirky cafe downstairs. The garden has wonderful views to Eiger and Wetterhorn.

GIMMELWALD

POP 118

Decades ago an anonymous backpacker scribbled these words in the Mountain Hostel's guest book: 'If heaven isn't what it's cracked up to be, send me back to Gimmelwald'. Enough said. When the sun is out in Gimmelwald, the place will take your breath away.

Surrounding hiking trails include one down from Mürren (30 to 40 minutes) and one up from Stechelberg (1¼ hours). Cable cars are also an option (Mürren or Stechelberg Sfr5.60).

After a long summer hike, bed down at **Pension Zum Berggeist** (☎033 855 17 30; dm/d Sfr17/45), a dead-simple rustic place with bargain rooms, priceless views and sandwiches sold by the centimetre. Book all kinds of activities here, including skydiving and llama trekking.

Otherwise there's backpacking legend **Mountain Hostel** (☎033 855 17 04; www.mountainhostel.com; dm Sfr22-25; ⏰reception 8.30am-noon & 6-11pm Apr-Nov; @📶). A soak in its outdoor whirlpool with stunning views hits the spot every time.

MÜRREN

POP 438

Arrive on a clear evening when the sun hangs low on the horizon, and you'll think you've died and gone to heaven. Car-free Mürren *is* storybook Switzerland.

The **tourist office** (☎033 856 86 86; www.wengen-muerren.ch; ⏰8.30am-7pm Mon-Sat, to 8pm Thu, to 6pm Sun high season, 8.30am-7pm Mon-Sat, to 5pm Sun shoulder seasons, 8.30am-noon & 1-5pm Mon-Fri low season) is in the sports centre.

Sleeping options include **Eiger Guesthouse** (☎033 856 54 60; www.eigerguesthouse.com; dm Sfr42-70, d with/without bathroom from Sfr165/120; @📶), by the train station, with a downstairs pub serving tasty grub.

Tham's (☎033 856 01 10; mains Sfr18-30; ⏰dinner) serves Asian food cooked by a former five-star chef who's literally taken to the hills to escape.

SCHILTHORN

There's a tremendous 360-degree panorama from the 2970m **Schilthorn** (www.schilthorn.ch). On a clear day you can see from Titlis to Mont Blanc and across to the German Black Forest. This is where some scenes from *On Her Majesty's Secret Service* were shot in the 1960s, as the fairly tacky **Touristorama** below the Piz Gloria revolving restaurant reminds you.

Buy a Sfr116 excursion trip, a combination train and cable car trip, (Half-Fare Card and Eurail Pass 50% off, Swiss Pass 65% off) going to Lauterbrunnen, Grütschalp, Mürren, Schilthorn and returning through Stechelberg to Interlaken. A return from Lauterbrunnen (via Grütschalp) and Mürren costs about Sfr100, as does the return journey via the Stechelberg cable car.

JUNGFRAUJOCH

Sure, the world wants to see Jungfraujoch (3454m) and, yes, tickets are expensive, but don't let that stop you. It's a once-in-a-lifetime trip. There's a reason why two million people a year visit this, Europe's highest train station.

Clear, good weather is essential for the trip; check www.jungfrau.ch or call ☎033 828 79 31, and don't forget warm clothing, sunglasses and sunscreen. Up top, when you tire of the view (is this possible?), dash downhill on a snow disc (free), zip across the frozen plateau on a flying fox (Sfr20), enjoy a bit of tame skiing or boarding (Sfr33), drive a team of Greenland dogs (from Sfr45) or do your best Tiger-Woods-in-moon-boots impersonation with a round of glacier golf. It isn't cheap at Sfr10 a shot, but get a hole-in-one and you win the Sfr100,000 jackpot (which, mysteriously, nobody has yet won).

From Interlaken Ost the journey time is 2½ hours (Sfr177.80 return, Swiss Pass/Eurail Sfr133, cheaper early morning tickets available).

KIRSCH & KISSES

It's just melted cheese and bread, right? Wrong. You'll encounter two variations of fondue dominate most menus: *moitié-moitié*, a mix of vacherin and Gruyère cheeses (a slightly nutty concoction) or pure *vacherin* (smooth and creamy). In both versions the finely grated cheese is added to a *caquelon* (a special ceramic pot) with a clove of garlic rubbed along its sides. White wine and a touch of Kirsch (cherry schnapps) are added carefully until the cheese reaches an ideal consistency – not too thin, not too thick. Then you begin dipping bread into the mixture.

A common error frequently made by foreigners is to drink beer with the dish – this is a bad idea. Beer simply sits on top of the cheese in your stomach, resulting in an unpleasant (and often sleepless) night holding your belly. Do as the locals do and drink hot tea or wine or, better yet, dip the cubes of bread into Kirsch before hitting the cheese. But make sure you stir carefully, unless you have a crush on one of your dinner companions, that is: by Swiss tradition, if you lose your bread in the pot you must kiss the person seated on your left.

NORTHERN SWITZERLAND

This region is left off most people's Switzerland itineraries – precisely why you should add it to yours! It's known for industry and commerce, but it has a healthy dose of grazing cows, green rolling hills, tiny rural towns and water (in the form of Lake Constance and the Rhine River on the German border).

Basel

POP 165,100

Strangely, given its northerly location, Basel (Bâle) has some of Switzerland's hottest weather. And indeed, as the mercury rises, the city sheds its notorious reserve and cuts loose as locals bob along the Rhine (Rhein) River, cool off in fountains, whiz around on scooters and dine and drink on overcrowded pavements. It could almost be Italy, not the border with France and Germany.

The **tourist office** (☎061 268 68 68; www.basel.com; Stadt-Casino, Barfüsserplatz, Steinenberg 14; ⊙8.30am-6.30pm Mon-Fri, 9am-5pm Sat, 9am-4pm Sun) has all the bumf on Basel's many art galleries.

Sights & Activities

With its cobbled streets, fountains (check the wacky one by Swiss sculptor Jean Tinguely on Theaterplatz) and medieval churches, the old town is wonderful to wander. In Marktplatz enjoy the rust-coloured **Rathaus** (town hall), with frescoed courtyard. Southeast, the 12th-century **cathedral** is another highlight.

Art lovers ogle at Switzerland's largest art collection inside the **Kunstmuseum** (Museum of Fine Arts; ☎061 206 62 62; www.kunstmuseumbasel.ch; St Alban-Graben 16; adult/student Sfr12/5, first Sun of month free; ⊙10am-5pm Tue-Sun).

But the art space to really knock your socks off is the **Fondation Beyeler** (☎061 645 97 00; www.beyeler.com; Baselstrasse 101, Riehen; adult/student Sfr23/12; ⊙10am-6pm, to 8pm Wed). Of all the private Swiss collections made public, former art dealers Hildy and Ernst Beyeler's treasure chest of Miró and Max Ernst sculptures, tribal figures from Oceania, 19th- and 20th-century Picassos and Rothkos etc is the most remarkable. To get to the low, light-filled, open-plan building by leading Italian architect Renzo Piano, ride tram 6 to Riehen.

In summer, join the locals swim in the Rhine – it's spectacular, popular and free.

Sleeping

When you check in, remember to ask for your mobility ticket entitling you to free public transport.

Basel Backpack HOSTEL €
(☎061 333 00 37; www.baselbackpack.ch; Dornacherstrasse 192; dm/s/d Sfr33/80/100; ⊖@ᯤ) Converted from a factory, this independent hostel has colour-coded eight-bed dorms and sedate doubles.

SYHA Basel City Youth Hostel HOSTEL €
(☎061 365 99 60; www.youthhostel.ch/basel.city; Pfeffingerstasse 8; dm/s/d Sfr36/80/96; ⊙reception 7am-noon & 3-11pm; @) In former post-office buildings across from the train station, this hostel touts rooms with up to four

beds and space aplenty – including a summertime interior courtyard to hang out in.

Eating & Drinking

For a quick, cheap bite on the run, the daily **market** on Marktplatz has tasty bratwurst (Sfr5) and delicious breads (up to Sfr10). Steinenvorstadt has countless fast-food outlets, cafes and restaurants, and Barfüsserplatz teems with teens and 20-somethings on the weekends. A whiff of grunge floats around Kleinbasel (the area around Rheingasse and Utengasse) with a few bars and a red-light zone to lend it an edge.

Acqua ITALIAN €€

(☎061 564 66 66; www.acquabasilea.ch; Binningerstrasse 14; dishes Sfr15-42; ⊙lunch Tue-Fri, dinner Tue-Sat) For a glam post-industrial experience, head to these converted waterworks. Cuisine is mainly Tuscan and Basel's beautiful people drink in the attached lounge bar. There is also a summer terrace.

Druck Punkt INTERNATIONAL €

(St Johanns Vorstadt 19; set menus Sfr17.50 & 22.50; ⊙Mon-Fri) This converted print shop makes an unpretentious bistro, with chalky walls and heavy wooden tables.

Getting There & Around

EuroAirport (☎061 325 31 11; www.euroairport.com), 5km north in France, serves Basel (as well as Mulhouse, France and Freiburg, Germany).

Basel is a major European rail hub with two main train stations, the Swiss-French SBB (south bank) and the BBF (north bank) for trains to/from Germany. Destinations include Paris (Sfr91, 3¾ hours, five nonstop trains daily), Frankfurt (Sfr133, three hours, daily), Hamburg (Sfr214, 6½ to 7½ hours, daily), Geneva (Sfr69, 2¾ hours, twice hourly) and Zürich (Sfr31, 55 minutes to 1¼ hours, twice hourly).

If you're not staying in town, bus and tram tickets cost Sfr1.90/3/8 for up to four stops/central zone/day pass.

UNDERSTAND SWITZERLAND

History

In 1291 the forest communities of Uri, Schwyz and Nidwalden formed an alliance – the origin of the Swiss Confederation. The Swiss began seizing more land, but finally overreached themselves. Defeated by a superior force of French and Venetians in 1798, they declared neutrality.

Following Napoleon's defeat at Waterloo, Switzerland gained full independence. In 1848 the Swiss agreed upon a new federal constitution.

The Swiss carefully guarded their neutrality during the world wars, and emerged with a thriving commercial, financial and industrial base. Zürich developed as an international banking centre, and international bodies set up their headquarters in Geneva. However, an independent commission of historians has confirmed that tens of thousands of Jewish refugees were refused entry at Switzerland's border during WWII and left to face their fate in Nazi Germany. Swiss banks were accused of banking Nazi plunder and the savings of Holocaust victims during WWII. After years of recriminations and a threatened lawsuit, two Swiss banks made a settlement of US$1.25 billion to Holocaust victims' families in 1998.

Switzerland's *annus horribilus* was 2001: the national airline Swissair collapsed, a canyoning accident in the Bernese Oberland killed 21 tourists, and an unprecedented gun massacre in the Zug parliament and fatal fire in the Gotthard Tunnel prompted intense soul searching. Switzerland became the 190th member of the UN in 2002 and in 2005 it joined Europe's Schengen passport-free travel zone.

Switzerland's privileged banking sector was not immune to the global financial crisis. Its two largest banks, UBS and Crédit Suisse, both admitted heavy losses in 2008, prompting the government to wade in with a US$60-billion bail-out package for UBS.

People

Living quietly with your neighbours is a national obsession and there are strict rules about noise levels. Good manners infuse the national psyche and politeness is the cornerstone of all social intercourse. Always shake hands when being introduced to a Swiss, and kiss on both cheeks to greet and say goodbye to friends. Don't forget to greet shopkeepers when entering shops.

The population in 2010 numbered 7,866,500. Of the four national languages, German speakers account for around 64% of the population, French 19%, Italian 8% and Romansch under 1%. Around 20% of the country's residents are non-Swiss citizens.

Food

Price indicators in this chapter are based on the cost of a main course:

€€€ more than Sfr40

€€ Sfr 20 to Sfr39

€ less than Sfr20

Environment

Mountains make up 70% of Switzerland's 41,285 sq km. The Dufourspitze (4634m) in the Monte Rosa Massif is the highest point, but the Toblerone-shaped Matterhorn (4478m) is way more famous.

The St Gotthard Mountains in central Switzerland are the source of many lakes and rivers, including the Rhine and the Rhône. The Jura Mountains straddle the border with France, and peak at around 1700m.

The ibex with its huge curved ridged horns is the most distinctive Alpine animal. Spot some of the 12,000 remaining in the country's only national park, the 169-sq-km Swiss National Park.

The Swiss are environmentally friendly: citizens produce less than 400kg of waste each per year (half the figure for the USA), are diligent recyclers and are fans of public transport.

The most pressing topic is not so much how to be ecological – several Swiss mountain resorts already burn clean energy. Rather, it is what can be done to keep ski resorts sustainable as the globe warms. Switzerland's 1800 glaciers cover 2000 sq km but are melting rapidly.

SURVIVAL GUIDE

Directory A-Z

Accommodation

Switzerland has HI-affiliated hostels (see www.youthhostel.ch), where nonmembers pay an additional 'guest fee' of Sfr6; and independent hostels, which can be more charismatic. Alpine chalets and rural farmhouses offering hostel-style accommodation can be found through **Naturfreundehaus** (Friends of Nature; www.nfhouse.org). A dorm bed costs between Sfr30 and Sfr40, including sheets (sleeping bags have long been banished from Swiss hostels for fear of bed bugs).

Our price ranges refer to double rooms with a private bathroom. Quoted rates are for high season, which in mountain resorts is July to August, Christmas and also mid-February to Easter.

€€€ more than Sfr325

€€ Sfr 200 to Sfr324

€ less than Sfr 200

Useful websites:

Aventure sur la paille/Schlaf im Stroh (www.abenteuer-stroh.ch) Camp on straw in a hay barn. This is a novel experience that's unique to Switzerland.

BnB (www.bnb.ch) Bed and breakfasts, budget to palatial.

Camping & Caravanning in Switzerland (www.camping-switzerland.ch) Swiss Camping Association.

MySwitzerland.com (www.myswitzerland.com) Great resource for tracking down all types of accommodation, including bunkers, igloos and so on.

Rural Tourism (www.tourisme-rural.ch) Rural sleeps.

Swiss Backpackers (www.swissbackpackers.ch) Private hostel group.

Swiss Holidays Farms (www.bauernhof-ferien.ch) Farm accommodation, including camping.

Swiss Youth Hostels (SYHA; www.youthhostel.ch)

Activities

There are dozens of ski resorts throughout Switzerland. Equipment hire is available at resorts, and ski passes allow unlimited use of mountain transport.

There's no better way to enjoy the spectacular scenery than to walk through it. There is 50,000km of designated paths. Yellow trail signs make it difficult to get lost, and each gives an average walking time to the next destination. Slightly more strenuous mountain paths have white-red-white markers. You can waterski, sail and windsurf on most lakes, and there are over 350 lake beaches. Rafting is possible on many Alpine rivers, including the Rhine and the Rhône.

Bungee jumping, paragliding, canyoning and other high-adrenalin sports are available throughout Switzerland, especially in the Interlaken area.

Business Hours

Usual business hours in Switzerland:

Banks 8.30am-4.30pm Mon-Fri, with some local variations

Post offices 7.30am-noon & 2-6.30pm Mon-Fri, 7.30-11am Sat

Restaurants noon-2pm & 6-10pm

Shops 8am-6.30pm Mon-Fri, with 90min or 2hr break at noon

Embassies & Consulates

For a comprehensive list of embassies in Switzerland and Swiss embassies abroad, see www.eda.admin.ch.

Festivals & Events

Find more events than we could possibly list on www.switzerland.com.

Fasnacht A lively spring carnival of wild parties and parades is celebrated countrywide in February, with particular enthusiasm in Basel and Lucerne.

Combats de Reines March to October, the lower Valais stages traditional cow fights.

National Day Fireworks mark the country's National Day on 1 August.

Vintage Festivals Early October, down a couple in wine-growing regions like Neuchâtel and Lugano.

Holidays

New Year's Day 1 January

Easter March/April; Good Friday, Easter Sunday and Monday

Ascension Day 40th day after Easter

Whit Sunday & Monday 7th week after Easter

National Day 1 August

Christmas Day 25 December

St Stephen's Day 26 December

Internet Access

Surfing in internet cafes is expensive (Sfr5 to Sfr15 per hour) and sometimes limited; you often can't open attachments. Public wireless access points are at major airports, 30-odd train stations and more and more hostels, hotels and cafes. Most cost around Sfr4 per hour on top of provider charges; track Swisscom's 1200 hot spots online at www.swisscom.ch.

Money

Swiss francs (Sfr, written CHF locally) are divided into 100 centimes (called *rappen* in German-speaking Switzerland). All major travellers cheques and credit cards are accepted. Virtually all train stations have money-exchange facilities open daily.

Post & Telephone

Postcards and letters to Europe cost Sfr1.30/1.20 priority/economy; to elsewhere they cost Sfr1.80/1.40.

The country telephone code for Switzerland is ☎41. Area codes don't exist in Switzerland. Numbers for a particular city or town share the same three-digit prefix (eg Bern 031, Geneva 022) but numbers must always be dialled in full, even when calling from next door.

Mobile numbers start with 079. To find a phone number in Switzerland check the **digital phone book** (http://tel.local.ch/en), dial ☎1812 to speak to a machine or ☎1811 for a real person.

Prepaid local SIM cards (Sfr30 to Sfr100) are available from the three network operators: **Orange** (www.orange.ch), **Sunrise** (www.sunrise.ch) and **Swisscom Mobile** (www.swisscom.ch). You'll need your passport when you buy.

National telephone provider **Swisscom** (http://fr.swisscom.ch) operates the world's densest network of public phone booths (coin- and card-operated). Minimum charge for a call is Sfr0.50 and phones accept euro coins too.

Save money by buying a prepaid Swisscom card worth Sfr10, Sfr20, Sfr50 and Sfr100. Or look for prepaid cards from rival operators such as **Mobile Zone** (www.mobilezone.ch, in German, French & Italian).

Visas

Visas are not required for passport holders from the EU, USA, Canada, Australia, New Zealand, South Africa, Norway and Iceland (see p1319).

Getting There & Away

Air

Zürich (www.zurich-airport.com) and **Geneva** (www.gva.ch) are the two busiest international airports, served by dozens of international airlines. In addition loads of budget operators serve Switzerland:

Air Berlin (AB; www.airberlin.com)

Air Transat (TS; www.airtransat.com)

Baboo (F7; www.flybaboo.com)
bmibaby (WW; www.bmibaby.com)
easyJet (EZS/EZY; www.easyjet.com)
Flybe (BE; www.flybe.com)
germanwings (4U; www.germanwings.com)
Helvetic (2L; www.helvetic.com)
Jet2.com (LS; www.jet2.com)
Ryanair (FR; www.ryanair.com)
Transavia.com (HV; www.transavia.com)

Car & Motorcycle

Roads into Switzerland are good. Some minor Alpine passes are closed November to May; check with the local tourist offices. To use Swiss motorways buy a **vignette** (www.vignette.ch); it costs Sfr40, is valid for one year and must be stuck on your windscreen.

Train

Switzerland is a train-travel hub. Zürich is the busiest international terminus with two direct day trains and a night train to Vienna (book separate women-only compartments in advance) and plenty of German connections. Several daily trains run to Paris from Geneva, Lausanne, Bern and Basel. Most connections to/from Italy pass through Milan.

Getting Around

Bicycle

Hire wheels from many train stations (see www.rent-a-bike.ch; Sfr33 per day) and return to any station with a rental office. Bikes can be transported on most trains; station-rented bikes travel free (maximum five bikes per train), otherwise buy a bike pass (Sfr15 per day). Bern, Geneva and Zürich offer free bike loans from their train stations.

Bus & Train

Yellow postal buses supplement the rail network, linking towns to the more inaccessible regions in the mountains. Services are regular; departures tie in with train arrivals. Check www.postbus.ch.

Trains are clean, reliable, frequent and as fast as the terrain allows. Major stations are connected by hourly departures, but services stop from around midnight to 6am. For train information surf **Swiss Federal Railways** (www.sbb.ch/en).

Prices are high but travel passes make them affordable. They are available online at www.swisstravelsystem.ch.

The **Swiss Pass** (www.swisstravelsystem.ch) allows unlimited travel on almost every train, boat and bus service in the country, and on trams and buses in 38 towns. Reductions of 50% apply on funiculars, cable cars and private railways, such as Jungfrau Railways. These passes are available for four days (Sfr260), eight days (Sfr376), 15 days (Sfr455), 22 days (Sfr525) and one month (Sfr578); prices are for 2nd-class tickets. If you are under 26, buy the **Swiss Youth Pass** equivalent, 25% cheaper in each instance. The **Swiss Flexi Pass** allows free, unlimited trips for three to six days within a month and costs Sfr249 to Sfr397 (2nd class). With either pass, two people travelling together get 15% off. Passes also allow you free admission to all Swiss museums, making them an even better bargain.

The **Swiss Card** allows a free return journey from your arrival point to any destination in Switzerland, 50% off rail, boat and bus excursions, and reductions on mountain railways. It costs Sfr182 (2nd class) or Sfr255 (1st class) and it is valid for a month. The **Half-Fare Card** is a similar deal, minus the free return trip. It costs Sfr99 for one month.

Car & Motorcycle

The **Swiss Touring Club** (www.tcs.ch) is affiliated with Britain's AA. Prebook for the best deals on car hire; competitive rates are often found on **Auto Europe** (www.autoeurope.com).

Switzerland is tough on drink driving; if your blood-alcohol level is over 0.05% you face a large fine or imprisonment.

Turkey

Includes »

Best Places to Eat

- » Cooking Alaturka, İstanbul (p1271)
- » Sakız, İzmir (p1275)
- » Fish Market (p1277)
- » Kahvaltı Sokak, Van (p1287)

Best Places to Stay

- » Marmara Guesthouse İstanbul (p1267)
- » Odyssey Guesthouse, Bergama (p1274)
- » Jimmy's Place, Selçuk (p1276)
- » Şaban Tree Houses, Olympos (p1281)

Why Go?

While many Turks see their country as European, Turkey packs in as many towering minarets and spice-trading bazaars as its Middle Eastern neighbours. The country has absorbed Europe's modernism, as well as Asia's culture and tradition. Travellers can enjoy suberb historical hot spots, mountain outposts and caravanserai-loads of the exotic, while not foregoing comfy beds and transport.

Cappadocia (Kapadokya), a dreamscape dotted with fairy chimneys, is unlike anywhere else on the planet. Likewise, spots such as Mt Nemrut, littered with giant stone heads, and Olympos, where Lycian ruins peek from the undergrowth, are quintessentially Turkish mixtures of natural splendour and ancient remains.

The beaches and mountains offer enough activities to impress the fussiest Ottoman sultan. Worldy pleasures include historic hotels, meze to savour on panoramic terraces and, of course, Turkey's famous kebaps.

When To Go

Ankara

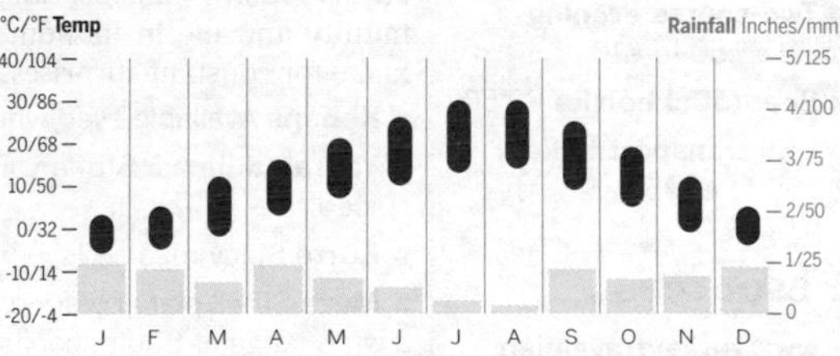

Apr–May Spring sunshine without summer crowds; tulips bloom in İstanbul.

Sep–Oct The crowds thin; autumn is perfect for walking and diving in the southwest.

Dec–Jan Brave the cold to ski, celebrate New Year and see Cappadocia in the snow.

AT A GLANCE

» **Currency** Turkish lira

» **Language** Turkish, Kurdish

» **Money** ATMS widespread; credit cards accepted in cities and tourist areas

» **Visas** Issued on arrival; see p1291

Fast Facts

» **Area** 779,452 sq km

» **Capital** Ankara

» **Country code** ☎90

» **Emergency** Ambulance ☎112, police ☎155

Exchange Rates

Australia	A$1	TL1.72
Canada	C$1	TL1.64
euro zone	€1	TL2.30
Japan	¥100	TL1.98
New Zealand	NZ$1	TL1.32
UK	UK£1	TL2.64
USA	US$1	TL1.60

Set Your Budget

» **Budget hotel room** Up to €37.50

» **Two-course evening meal** €7.50 to €10

» **Beer (50cl bottle)** €2.50

» **City transport ticket** €0.50 to €1.75

Resources

» **www.turkeytravelplanner.com** Useful travel info

» **www.hurriyetdailynews.com** Turkish news in English

» **www.mymerhaba.com** Information for expats and travellers

Connections

İstanbul is well connected to Europe. Buses leave the *otogar* (bus station) for countries including Austria, Bulgaria, Germany, Greece, Macedonia, Romania and Slovenia, but trains and ferries are more romantic.

The most useful daily trains are the *Bosfor/Balkan Express* to Bucharest (Romania; with connections including Budapest, Hungary) via Dimitrovgrad (Bulgaria; with connections including Sofia, Bulgaria, and Belgrade, Serbia); and the *Dostluk/Filia Express* to Thessaloniki (Greece; with connections to Athens). A suggested train route from London to İstanbul is the three-night journey via Paris, Munich, Budapest and Bucharest; see www.seat61.com/turkey for more information and other routes.

Ferries connect Turkey's Aegean and Mediterranean coasts with the Greek Islands, Northern Cyprus and Italy; İstanbul with Ukraine; and Trabzon on the Black Sea coast with Russia.

See p1291 for more information.

INTINERARIES

One Week

Devote two or three days to magical İstanbul, then head down the Aegean coast, via the Gallipoli battlefields or Pergamum (Bergama), to marvel at the ruins of Ephesus.

Two Weeks

From Ephesus, head inland to Pamukkale's shiny travertine formations, then return to the coast at laid-back Kaş and travel along the Mediterranean to Roman-Ottoman Antalya, checking out Olympos' tree houses en route. With more time, or by skipping some of the above spots, work in a detour on the way back to İstanbul, to Cappadocia's surreal valleys and fairy chimneys.

Essential Food & Drink

Turkish food is taken seriously and is a celebration of community and life in its home country. Regional differences make for constant surprises.

» **Kebaps** Available everywhere and swooningly succulent

» **Yaprak dolması** Stuffed vine leaves filled with subtly spiced rice

» **Köfte** Spicy meatballs

» **Meze** Small plates of food, including dips, vegetables and a wide range of traditional fish and meat dishes

» **Lahmacun** Arabic pizza

» **Gözleme** Thin savoury crepes

» **Mantı** Turkish ravioli

» **Börek** Filled pastries

» **Rakı** Fiery, highly alcoholic aniseed drink best accompanied by meze

İSTANBUL

0212 / POP 13 MILLION

Some ancient cities are the sum of their monuments. But others, such as İstanbul, factor a lot more into the equation. Here, you can visit Byzantine churches and Ottoman mosques in the morning, shop in chic boutiques during the afternoon and party at glamorous nightclubs through the night. In the space of a few minutes, you can hear the evocative strains of the call to prayer issuing from the Old City's minarets, the sonorous horn of a commuter ferry crossing between Europe and Asia, and the strident cries of a street hawker selling fresh seasonal produce. This marvellous metropolis is an exercise in sensory seduction like no other.

The Bosphorus strait, between the Black Sea and the Sea of Marmara, divides Europe from Asia. On its western shore, European İstanbul is further divided by the Golden Horn (Haliç) into Old İstanbul in the southwest and Beyoğlu in the northeast.

Overlooked by the Galata Tower, the Galata Bridge (Galata Köprüsü) spans the Golden Horn between Eminönü, north of Sultanahmet in Old İstanbul, and Karaköy. Ferries depart from Eminönü and Karaköy for the Asian shore.

Beyoğlu, uphill from Karaköy, was once the 'new', or 'European', city. The Tünel funicular railway links Karaköy to the bottom of Beyoğlu's pedestrianised main street, İstiklal Caddesi. At the top of İstiklal, Taksim Sq is the heart of 'modern' İstanbul, and home to luxury hotels and airline offices.

History

Late in the 2nd century AD, the Roman Empire conquered the small city-state of Byzantium, which was renamed Constantinople in AD 330 after Emperor Constantine moved his capital there. The city walls kept out barbarians for centuries while the western part of the Roman Empire collapsed. When the city fell for the first time in 1204, it was ransacked by the loot-hungry Europeans of the misguided Fourth Crusade.

İstanbul regained its former glory only after 1453, when it was captured by Mehmet the Conqueror and made the capital of the Ottoman Empire. During the glittering reign of Süleyman the Magnificent (1520–66) the city was graced with many beautiful new buildings, and managed to retain much of its charm even during the empire's long decline.

Occupied by Allied forces after WWI, the city came to be regarded as the decadent playpen of the sultans, and when the Turkish Republic was proclaimed in 1923, Ankara became the new capital. Nevertheless, İstanbul remains a commercial, cultural and financial centre, and is still Turkey's number one city in all but name.

Sights & Activities

OLD İSTANBUL

The Sultanahmet area is 'Old İstanbul', a Unesco-designated World Heritage site packed with so many wonderful sights you could spend weeks here.

Aya Sofya (Church of Holy Wisdom) MUSEUM

(Map p1266; 522 0989; Aya Sofya Meydanı, Sultanahmet; admission TL20, official guide (45min) TL30-50; 9am-6pm Tue-Sun May-Oct, till 4pm Nov-Apr, upper gallery closes 15-30min earlier) No doubt you will gasp at the overblown splendour of Aya Sofya, one of world's most glorious buildings. Completed in AD 537, as part of Emperor Justinian's effort to restore the greatness of the Roman Empire, it reigned as the grandest church in Christendom until the Conquest in 1453.

Supported by 40 decorated ribs, its dome was constructed of special hollow bricks made in Rhodes from a unique, light, porous clay. These rest on huge pillars concealed in the interior walls, which creates an impression inside the building that the dome hovers unsupported.

Blue Mosque MOSQUE

(Sultan Ahmet Camii; Map p1266; Hippodrome, Sultanahmet; closed during prayer times) Just southwest of the Aya Sofya, Sultan Ahmet I's mosque (built between 1606 and 1616)

FREE THRILLS

İstanbul is such a richly cultural city that just wandering its streets and markets, marvelling at the mosques and smelling the kebaps, is a great way to a get a taste of the place. At these spots you can amble for free:

» **İstiklal Caddesi** (p1267)
» **Grand Bazaar** (p1266)
» **Blue Mosque** (p1263)
» **Spice Bazaar** (p1269)
» **Divan Yolu Caddesi** (Map p1266)
» **Hippodrome** (Map p1266)

Turkey Highlights

1. Uncover **İstanbul** (p1263), the glorious one-time Ottoman and Byzantine capital and one of the world's truly great cities
2. Sleep in fairy chimneys and explore underground cities in jaw-droppingly bizarre and beautiful **Cappadocia** (p1285)
3. Imagine the tourists streaming down the Curetes Way are wearing togas in **Ephesus** (p1275), one of the greatest surviving Greco-Roman cities
4. Hike through the Mediterranean countryside on a section of the 500km **Lycian Way** (p1290)

5 Explore Turkey's exotic east at **Mt Nemrut** (**Nemrut Dağı**; p1287), where decapitated stone heads litter a king's burial mound

6 Cruise over a sunken Lycian city at Kekova Island from **Kaş** (p1280), one of many blue voyages offered at Aegean and Mediterranean harbours

7 Wander the Roman-Ottoman old quarter of **Antalya** (p1281), a stylish Mediterranean hub located on both the 'Turquoise Coast' and the 'Turkish Riviera'

is a voluptuous architectural feat, light and delicate compared with its squat, ancient neighbour. The graceful exterior is notable for its six slender minarets and cascade of domes and half-domes; the interior is luminous blue, an effect created by stained-glass windows and tens of thousands of tiles.

Topkapı Palace PALACE

(Topkapı Sarayı; Map p1266; ☎512 0480; www.topkapisarayi.gov.tr/eng; Babıhümayun Caddesi; admission palace/harem TL20/15; ⏲9am-6pm, harem closes 5pm) One of İstanbul's most iconic monuments, the opulent Topkapı Palace witnessed centuries of royal intrigue. Mehmet started work on the palace shortly after the Conquest in 1453, and Ottoman sultans lived in this rarefied environment until the 19th century. It consists of four massive courtyards (the third and fourth were only open to the royal family, VIPs and palace staff) and a series of imperial buildings. Make sure you visit the mind-blowing **harem**, the palace's most famous sight, and the **treasury**, which features an incredible collection of precious objects.

Grand Bazaar BAZAAR

(Kapalı Çarşı; Map p1266; ⏲8.30am-7.30pm Mon-Sat) Just north of Divan Yolu is Turkey's most mind-boggling bazaar, a labyrinthine medieval shopping mall with 2000-plus shops selling everything from carpets to *nazar boncuk* ('evil eye' beads and pendants), including silverware, jewellery, antiques and belly-dancing costumes. It's a fun place to wander around and get lost – which you almost certainly will!

Basilica Cistern HISTORIC BUILDING

(Map p1266; ☎522 1259; Yerebatan Caddesi 13; admission TL10; ⏲9am-7.30pm) Across the tram lines from Aya Sofya is the entrance to this majestic, refreshingly cool underground chamber, built by Justinian in AD 532. This vast, atmospheric, column-filled cistern stored up to 80,000 cubic metres of water for the Great Palace and surrounding buildings.

İstanbul Archaeology Museums MUSEUM (Map p1266; ☎520 7740; Osman Hamdi Bey Yokuşu, Gülhane; admission TL10; ⏲9am-6pm Tue-Sun May–Sep, to 4pm Oct–Apr) Downhill from the Topkapı Palace, this superb museum complex is a must-see for anyone interested in the Middle East's ancient past. The main building houses an outstanding collection of classical statuary, including the magnificent sarcophagi from the Royal Necropolis at Side in Lebanon. On the same site, the **Museum of the Ancient Orient**, houses Hittite and other pre-Islamic archaeological finds.

BEYOĞLU & THE BOSPHORUS

Beyoğlu, the heart of modern İstanbul, is ground zero for galleries, cafes and boutiques, with hip new restaurants opening almost nightly, and enough bars to quench a dedicated drinker's thirst. It's a showcase of cosmopolitan Turkey at its best – miss Beyoğlu and you haven't seen İstanbul.

Climbing from Tünel Sq to Taksim Sq, **İstiklal Caddesi** (Independence Ave; Map p1268), known in the late 19th century as the Grand Rue de Péra, carries the life of the modern city up and down its lively promenade. A stroll along its length is a must – or take the quaint **antique tram**.

Don't leave İstanbul without exploring the Bosphorus on one of the boats departing from Eminönü (Map p1266). Private **excursion boats** cruise to Anadolu Hisarı (at the northern end of the Bosphoros) and back, without stopping (TL10, 90 minutes). İDO's much-loved **Public Bosphorus Excursion Ferry** (www.ido.com.tr; Boğaz İskelesi; one way/return TL15/25; ⏲10.30am, plus noon & 1.30pm mid-Apr–Oct, 7.15pm Sat mid-Jun–early Aug) travels to Anadolu Kavağı (the turnaround point, 90 minutes away), stopping at various points en route. The shores are sprinkled with sights, including the monumental Dolmabahçe Palace, the majestic Bosphorus Bridge, lavish *yalıs* (waterfront wooden summer residences), numerous mosques and affluent suburbs on the hills above the strait.

Tours

İstanbul Walks (Map p1268; ☎292 2874; www.istanbulwalks.net; 5th fl, İstiklal Caddesi 53, Beyoğlu; walking tours adult/student & seniors €20/16) offers guided walking tours including the excellent Grand Bazaar tour.

Sleeping

Before confirming bookings, ask if the hotel will give you a discount for cash payment and whether there are discounts for extended stays. A pick-up from the airport is often included if you stay more than three nights. Book ahead from May to September.

SULTANAHMET & AROUND

Sultanahmet has the most budget and midrange options. Many have stunning views from their roof terraces, and are close to the old city's sights.

TOP CHOICE **Marmara Guesthouse** PENSION €€ (Map p1266; ☎638 3638; www.marmaraguesthouse.com; Terbıyık Sokak 15, Cankurtaran; s/d from €35/45; ❄@) Charming manager Elif and family go out of their way to make guests feel welcome. Rooms have comfortable beds with feather doonas, double-glazed windows and safes. There's a vine-covered terrace and a light-filled breakfast room.

Osman Han Hotel HOTEL €€ (Map p1266; ☎458 7702; www.osmanhanhotel.com; Çetinkaya Sokak 1, Cankurtaran; s/d €45/75; ❄@) The seven en-suite rooms have minibar, tea/coffee facilities, satellite TV and rainshower/anti-stress showerheads. The pretty breakfast room and terrace have wonderful views.

Hanedan Hotel HOTEL €€ (Map p1266; ☎516 4869; www.hanedanhotel.com; Adliye Sokak 3, Cankurtaran; s €30-40, d €40-60; ❄@) Rooms have pale lemon walls, polished wooden floors, white-marble bathrooms and firm beds with crisp white linen. There's a terrace and the family rooms (from €70), one with a sea view, are spacious and well priced.

BEYOĞLU & AROUND

İstanbul Apartments APARTMENT €€ (Map p1268; ☎249 5065; www.istanbulapt.com; Tel Sokak 27, Taksim; apts per night €70-120; ❄@) On a quiet side street off İstiklal Caddesi, these two- to six-person apartments each have a

SPLURGE

The fabulous US-run **Hotel Empress Zoe** (Map p1266; ☎518 2504; www.emzoe.com; Adliye Sokak 10, Cankurtaran; s/d/ste from €80/120/140; ❄) is a boutique hotel with individually decorated rooms, a gorgeous flower-filled garden where breakfast is served, and a rooftop lounge-terrace for sundowners.

Sultanahmet & Bazaar District

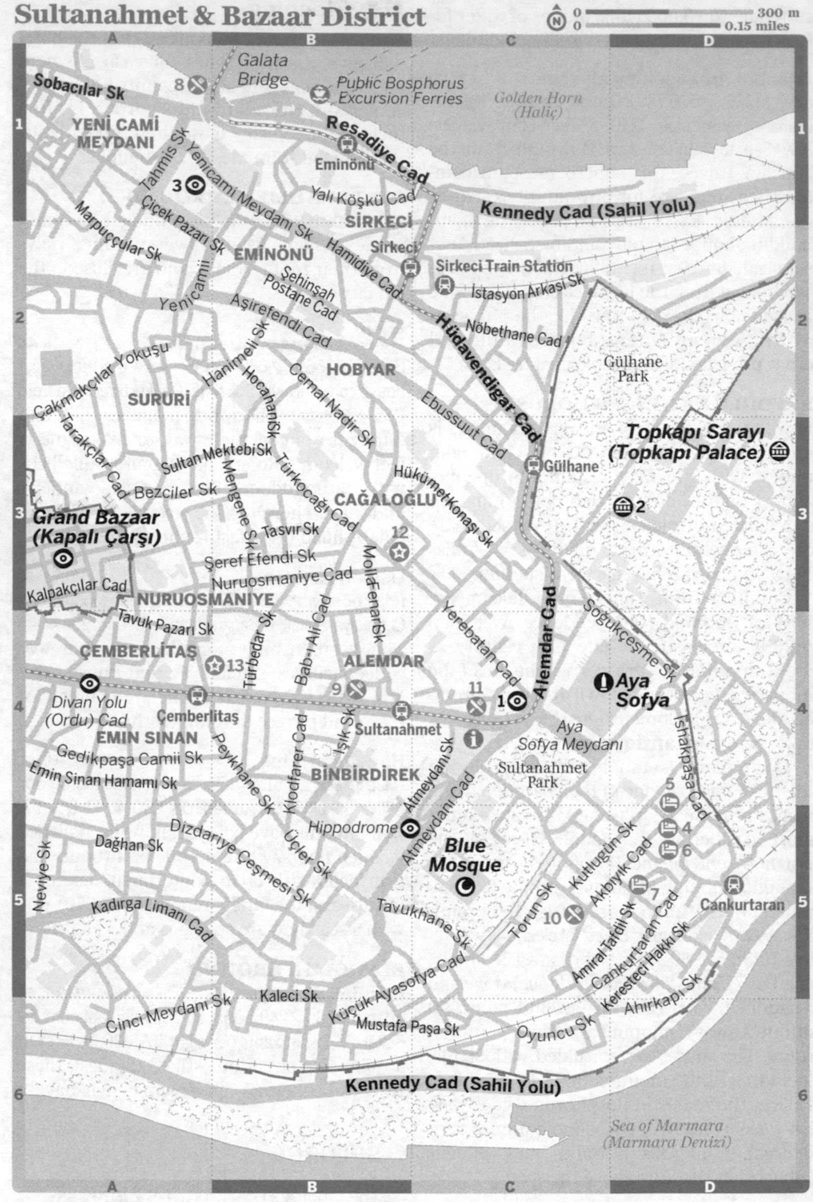

small lounge with well-equipped kitchenette, couch, dining table and satellite TV, plus one or two bedrooms with comfortable beds and good-sized bathrooms. Antique rugs, objets d'art, paintings and textiles feature, along with a communal washing machine and dryer.

World House Hostel HOSTEL €
(Map p1268; ☎293 5520; www.worldhouseistanbul.com; Galipdede Caddesi 117; dm €10-14, d €50; @) This hostel near the Galata Tower is small,

Sultanahmet & Bazaar District

Top Sights

	Aya Sofya	C4
	Blue Mosque	C5
	Grand Bazaar (Kapalı Çarşı)	A3
	Topkapı Sarayı (Topkapı Palace)	D3

Sights

1	Basilica Cistern	C4
2	İstanbul Archaeological Museums	D3
3	Spice Bazaar (Mısır Carşısı)	A1

Sleeping

4	Hanedan Hotel	D5
5	Hotel Empress Zoe	D4
6	Marmara Guesthouse	D5
7	Osman Han Hotel	D5

Eating

8	Balık Ekmek (Fish Kebap) Boats	A1
9	Çiğdem Pastanesi	B4
10	Cooking Alaturka	C5
	Spice Bazaar (Mısır Carşısı)	(see 3)
11	Tarihi Sultanahmet Köftecisi Selim Usta	C4

Entertainment

12	Cağaloğlu Hamamı	B3
13	Çemberlitaş Hamamı	B4

friendly and calm; it's close to Beyoğlu's nightlife, but also conducive to a decent night's kip. The four- to 14-bed dorms are clean and light and there's a cheerful ground-floor cafe.

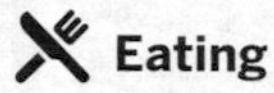

Eating

Teeming with affordable fast-food joints, cafes and restaurants, İstanbul is a food-lover's paradise.

Head to Divan Yolu Caddesi (Map p1266) and the streets off İstiklal Caddesi (Map p1268) for cheap kebaps and street food. The locals eat in Beyoğlu (Map p1268), which has more atmosphere.

The **Spice Bazaar** (Mısır Çarşısı; Map p1266) is good for nuts, honeycomb, dried fruit, figs and Turkish delight

Avoid the rip-off eateries near the accommodation and bars on Akbıyık Caddesi in Cankurtan (Map p1266).

İstanbul Eats (http://istanbuleats.com) is a local foodie website.

Çiğdem Pastanesi CAFE €
(Map p1266; Divan Yolu Caddesi 62a) Serving locals since 1961, Çiğdem's *ay çöreği* (pastry with a walnut, sultana and spice filling) is the perfect accompaniment to a cappuccino; *su böreği* (white-cheese-and-parsley *börek*) goes well with tea or fresh juice.

Tarihi Sultanahmet Köftecisi Selim Usta KÖFTECI €
(Map p1266; Divan Yolu Caddesi 12; köfte, beans & salad €8) Locals flock here to snack on the signature *köfte,* served with white beans, pickled chillies and salad.

Karaköy Lokantası TAVERN €€
(Map p1268; ☎292 4455; Kemankeş Caddesi 37; meals €3.50-8; closed Sun) The tasty food is well priced, the tiled interior attractive and the service friendly and efficient. It functions as a *lokanta* (eatery serving ready-made food) during the day, and at night morphs into a popular, slightly pricier *meyhane* (tavern).

FISH KEBAP

The cheapest way to enjoy fresh fish in İstanbul is a *balık ekmek* (fish kebap; €2). On bobbing boats tied to the quay at the Eminönü end of the Galata Bridge (Map p1266), cookers are loaded with fish fillets, which are crammed into quarter loaves of fresh bread and eaten on dry land.

Drinking & Entertainment

Sultanahmet's bar scene is concentrated on Akbıyık Caddesi, catering to the denizens of the surrounding hostels. Dedicated bar- and club-goers should seek out the byways of Beyoğlu, where there are popular bar precincts on and around **Balo** and **Sofyalı Sokaks** (Map p1268). The latter is also good for *meyhanes,* crammed with raucous crowds guzzling rakı, meze and fish and carousing to *fasıl* (a local form of gypsy music).

To check out the city's vistas, don your finest threads and head to Beyoğlu's ultra-cool rooftop bars, such as **360** (Map p1268; www.360istanbul.com; 8th fl, İstiklal Caddesi 311) and the slightly more casual **5 Kat** (Map p1268; www.5kat.com; 5th fl, Soğancı Sokak 7; 10am-1.30am).

Beyoğlu & Around

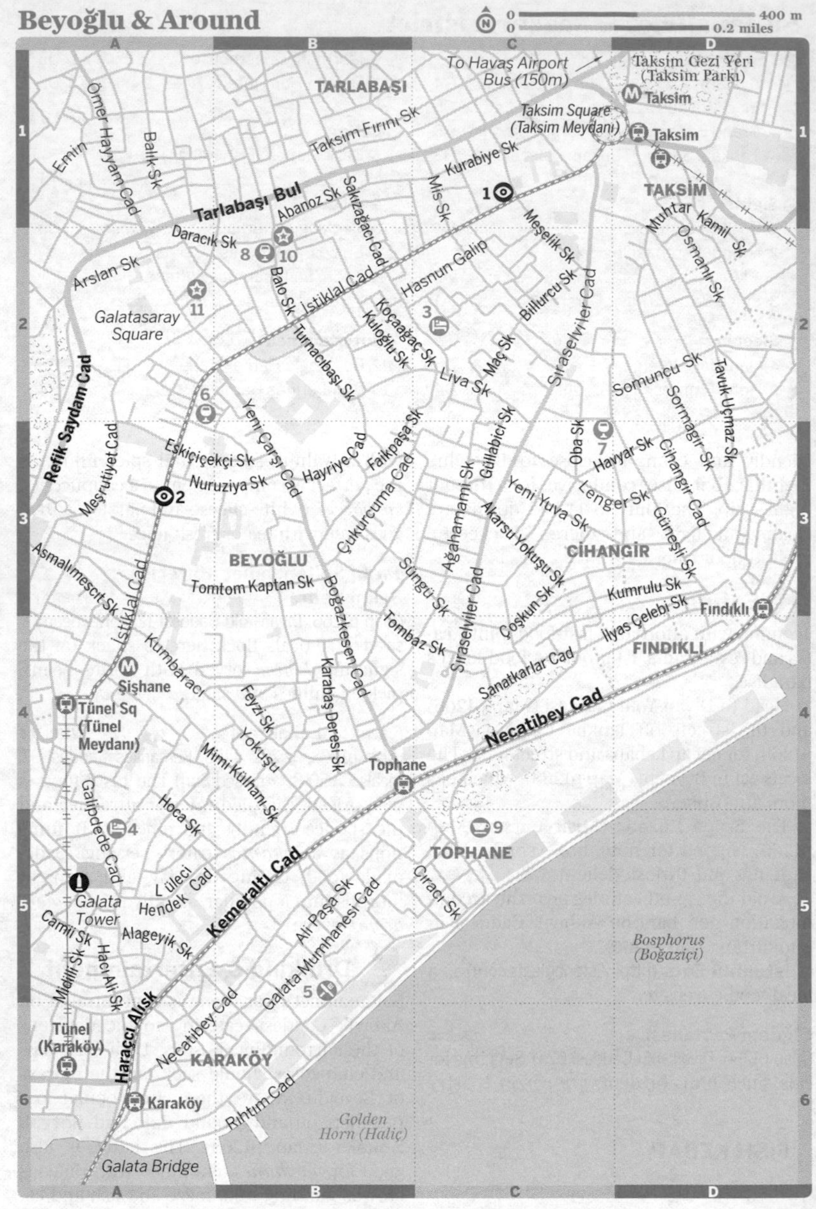

Drinks are expensive, but worth it for the extraordinary views.

Be aware that Beyoğlu can be seedy. Avoid the neighbourhood of Tarlabaşı and ignore 'friendly' locals who try to lure you into trouble with promises of free drinks etc (see also p1290).

Tophane Nargileh CAFE

(Map p1268; off Necatibey Caddesi; 24hr) Follow the smell of apple tobacco to this atmospheric

Beyoğlu & Around

Sights
1 İstanbul Walks C1
2 İstiklal Caddesi A3

Sleeping
3 Istanbul Apartments C2
4 World House Hostel A5

Eating
5 Karaköy Lokantası B5

Drinking
6 360 .... A2
7 5 Kat C3
8 Papillon B2
9 Tophane Nargileh C5

Entertainment
10 Araf B2
11 Ghetto A2

row of *nargileh* (water pipe) cafes opposite the Tophane tram stop. It's always packed with teetotallers, and is a fabulous place to come after a meal.

Papillon BAR
(Map p1268; 4th fl, Balo Sokak 31) This laid-back top-floor hangout is scattered with beanbags, pot plants, mirrorballs and psychedelic decor. The drinks are cheap, too. Head down Balo Sokak past the Irish pub, and take the steps on the left just before the 'Balo' and 'Haydar Rock Bar' signs; it gets going after 10pm.

Nightclubs

Araf CLUB
(Map p1268; 5th fl, Balo Sokak 32) Popular among English teachers and Turkish-language students for the in-house gypsy band and cheap beer.

Ghetto CLUB
(Map p1268; Kalyoncu Kulluk Caddesi 10) Has bold postmodern decor and an interesting musical program featuring local and international acts.

> **EATING SPLURGE**
>
> A little haven in the midst of the carpet-selling frenzy, **Cooking Alaturka** (Map p1266; 458 5919; www.cookingalaturka.com; Akbiyik Caddesi 72a; set meal €25; lunch Mon-Sat, dinner by reservation Mon-Sat), run by a Dutch-born foodie, serves a set four-course menu that changes daily according to what's in season.

Hammams

Sultanahmet's atmospheric Ottoman *hammams* (Turkish baths) are pricey and touristy, but worth visiting nonetheless.

Cağaloğlu Hamamı (Map p1266; Yerebatan Caddesi 34; bath, scrub & massage €39-49; 8am-10pm men, to 8pm women)

Çemberlitaş Hamamı (Map p1266; Vezir Hanı Caddesi 8; bath, scrub & soap massage €27.50; 6am-midnight)

Information

Emergency

Tourist Police (527 4503; Yerebatan Caddesi 6, Sultanahmet)

Internet Access

Wi-fi is widespread, and hotels and hostels often offer a computer with internet access. There are internet cafes throughout İstanbul.

Medical Services

American Hospital (Amerikan Hastanesi; 444 3777; Güzelbahçe Sokak 20, Nişantaşı; 24hr)
German Hospital (Alman Hastanesi; 293 2150; Sıraselviler Caddesi 119, Taksim; 24hr)

Money

ATMs and exchange offices are widespread. The exchange rates offered at the airport are usually as good as those offered in town.

Telephone

İstanbul has two area codes: 0212 for the European side, 0216 for the Asian zone. All numbers here use the 0212 code unless otherwise indicated.

Tourist Information

Tourist offices are found in several locations.
Atatürk International Airport (International arrivals; 24hr)
Sultanahmet (518 8754; 8.30am-5pm) At the northeast end of the Hippodrome.

Travel Agencies

Both of these go to the Gallipoli Peninsula (see p1272) among other destinations.
Fez Travel (www.feztravel.com) Also operates the Fez Bus (see p1292).
Trooper Tours (www.troopertours.com)

Getting There & Away

Air

Atatürk International Airport (465 5555; www.ataturkairport.com) Long-haul flights

GETTING INTO TOWN

To travel between central İstanbul and the airports:

» **Airport Shuttle** (www.istanbulairportshuttle.com; €10) Seven per day between the airports and Sultanahmet/Taksim. Book ahead and allow lots of time before your flight.

» **Havaş Airport Bus** (☎444 0487; www.havas.com.tr; 40min) Half-hourly buses connect Cumhuriyet Caddesi near Taksim Sq with Atatürk (TL10, 40 minutes) and Sabıha Gökçen (TL13, one hour), leaving Atatürk from 4am until 1am and Sabıha Gökçen from 4am to midnight and thereafter when flights land.

» **LRT** (Light Rail Transport; 50min to Sultanahmet, 85min to Taksim Sq) From Atatürk arrivals, follow the 'Rapid Transit' signs to the station and travel to Zeytinburnu, then connect with the tram to Sultanahmet and Beyoğlu.

» **Taxi** From Atatürk/Sabıha Gökçen to the centre should cost around TL35/90; more if there's heavy traffic.

generally touch down here, 23km west of Sultanahmet.

Sabiha Gökçen International Airport (☎0216-585 5000; www.sgairport.com) Some 50km east of Sultanahmet, on the Asian side of the city, and popular with cut-price European carriers.

Boat

The main dock for ferries across the Sea of Marmara to Yalova, Bursa and Bandırma departs from Yenikapı Fast Ferry Port (Map p1265), southwest of Sultanahmet.

Bus

At Esenler, about 10km northwest of Sultanahmet, the Big İstanbul Bus Station is a monster, with buses leaving for all parts of Turkey and beyond. Excluding holiday periods, you can usually turn up, do some shopping around and be on your way within the hour.

Many bus companies offer a *servis* (free shuttle bus) to/from the *otogar*; alternatively, you can get here on the tram and LRT (Light Rail Transport), changing at Aksaray.

Train

The station for Edirne and Europe is Sirkeci (Map p1266). The twice-daily *Dostluk/Filia Express* to/from Thessaloniki (Greece; 1st/2nd class from TL52/78; 13 hours) was not running at the time of writing. The overnight *Bosfor/Balkan Express* crosses Bulgaria to/from Bucharest (Romania; see p1262).

On the Asian shore, Haydarpaşa (off Map p1265) is the terminus for trains to Anatolia (see p1293 for services), Syria and Iran. Several daily express trains run to Ankara (seat/sleeper TL23/80, eight hours), but the coast is not well served. Ferries cross between Haydarpaşa and the European side.

ℹ Getting Around

Public transport tickets in İstanbul generally cost TL1.75.

Boat

The most scenic and enjoyable way to cross İstanbul is by **İDO** (www.ido.com.tr) ferry. The main ferry docks are at the mouth of the Golden Horn (Map p1266; Eminönü, Sirkeci and Karaköy) and at Beşiktaş, a few kilometres northeast of the Galata Bridge, near Dolmabahçe Palace.

Bus

İstanbul's efficient bus system has major stations at Taksim Sq, Beşiktaş, Aksaray, Rüstempaşa-Eminönü, Kadıköy and Üsküdar, with most services running between 6.30am and 11.30pm. You must have a ticket before boarding; stock up at the white booths near major stops, and at some shops.

Funicular Railway

The 19th-century Tünel funicular system (Map p1268) climbs from Karaköy to Tünel Sq, the bottom of İstiklal Caddesi (every 10 minutes, 7.30am to 9pm).

A new funicular railway (Map p1268) climbs from the Bosphorus shore and tram stop at Kabataş to Taksim Sq (every three minutes).

LRT

A light rail transport service connects Aksaray with the airport, stopping at 16 stations, including the *otogar*, along the way. It operates from 5.40am to 1.40am.

Taxi

İstanbul is full of yellow taxis, all of them with meters; do not let drivers insist on a fixed rate. From Sultanahmet to Taksim Sq costs around €6.

Tram

The *tramvay* (tramway) runs between Zeytinburnu and Kabataş via Aksaray, Sultanahmet, Sirkeci, Eminönü and Karaköy (every five minutes or so, 6am to midnight), connecting to the LRT and both funicular railways.

BUS ARRIVALS

If you're arriving from Anatolia, rather than travelling all the way to the Big İstanbul Bus Station, it's quicker to get out at the smaller **Harem Otogar** (Map p1265; ☎0216-333 3763), north of Haydarpaşa Train Station on the Asian shore, and take the ferry to Sirkeci/Eminönü.

AEGEAN COAST

Turkey's Aegean coast can convincingly claim more ancient ruins per square kilometre than any other region in the world. Here you'll see the famous ruins of Troy, Ephesus and Pergamum (Bergama), and you can contemplate the devastation of war at the Gallipoli battlefields. The area isn't as scenic as the Med, but it doesn't have as many resort developments either, particularly in the north.

Gallipoli (Gelibolu)

To generations of Turks, Australians and New Zealanders, the battle for the Dardanelles was one of the most poignant chapters in WWI. On 25 April 1915 the first Anzac (Australia and New Zealand Army Corps), British and Indian troops landed on the Gallipoli peninsula, hoping for a quick victory against Turkish defences. However, strategic blunders turned the operation into a protracted stalemate, and after nine months of horrendous casualties the Allied forces withdrew.

Mustafa Kemal, later Atatürk, was responsible for the defence of Gallipoli, and his success is commemorated in Turkey on 18 March. The big draw for many foreign travellers is Anzac Day (25 April), when a dawn service attended by thousands commemorates the anniversary of the Allied landings.

The scenic peninsula is now a national park, scattered with moving memorials to the dead of the various nations that fought here. The best way to see the sights is on an afternoon minibus tour from Eceabat with **Crowded House Tours** (☎0286-814 1565; www.crowdedhousegallipoli.com) or **TJs Tours** (☎0286-814 3121; www.anzacgallipolitours.com). If you're not pressed for time and don't mind walking, you can catch a *dolmuş* (minibus; €1.25) or taxi from Eceabat to the **Kabatepe Information Centre & Museum**, 750m from the bottom of the road up to the main battlefields.

Eceabat, on the Thracian (European) side of the strait, has accommodation and restaurants. **Hotel Crowded House** (☎0286-814 1565; www.crowdedhousegallipoli.com; Hüseyin Avni Sokak 4; dm/s/d TL15/45/60; ❄@) is a gem of a backpackers with comfortable, spick-and-span rooms and dorms, plus a bar.

Hourly car ferries cross the strait between Eceabat and Çanakkale (from €1, 25 minutes), and hourly buses run to/from İstanbul (€19, five hours).

Çanakkale

☎0286 / POP 86,600

The liveliest settlement on the Dardanelles, this sprawling harbour town would be worth a visit for its sights, nightlife and overall vibe even if it didn't lie opposite the Gallipoli Peninsula. A good base for visiting Troy, it's a popular destination for weekending Turks; during the summer, try to visit midweek.

Sights

A park in the military zone at the southern end of the quay houses the **Military Museum** (admission TL4; ⏱9am-5pm Tue, Wed & Fri-Sun), alongside an **Ottoman castle** and a replica of the **Nusrat minelayer.**

Just over 2km south of the ferry pier, on the road to Troy, the **Archaeological Museum** (admission TL5; ⏱8am-5pm) displays artefacts from Troy and Assos.

Sleeping & Eating

Çanakkale has hotels to suit all pockets, except around Anzac Day (25 April), when prices skyrocket and you should book months in advance.

Stalls along the waterfront sell corn on the cob, mussels and other simple items. Head to Fetvane and Matbaa Sokaks for bars and soak-up-the-Efes eateries.

Efes Hotel PENSION €
(☎217 3256; www.efeshotelcanakkale.com; Fetvane Sokak 5; s/d TL40/50, breakfast TL5; ❄) Good for couples and lone women, the friendly Efes has a female touch, with cheerful rooms, small balconies and a fountain in the back garden.

Yellow Rose Pension HOSTEL €
(☎217 3343; www.yellowrose.4mg.com; Aslan Abla Sokak 5; dm/s/d/tr/q TL20/30/50/70/90; P@) This hostel on a quiet, central street has a lounge with a monumental TV, and small

rooms and dorms. The tiled floors and smell of disinfectant are rather spartan, but there's a kitchen.

Anafartalar Kebap KEBAPÇI €€
(☎214 9112; Kayserili Ahmet Paşa Caddesi 40; mains TL10) Quieter and better value than the nearby waterfront fish restaurants, serving excellent pide and *İskender* kebap.

Information

Araz Internet (Fetvane Sokak 21; per hr €0.75; ⌚9am-midnight)

Tourist office (☎217 1187; ⌚8am-7pm Jun-Sep, 8.30am-5.30pm Oct-May) Near the ferry pier.

Getting There & Away

Ferries run to Eceabat (see p1273). There are regular buses to/from İstanbul (TL35, six hours), İzmir (TL35, six hours) and Bandırma (TL20, 2½ hours).

Troy (Truva)

Of all Turkey's ancient sites, the remains of the great city of Troy are in fact among the least impressive. You'll have to work hard to imagine the fateful day when the Greeks tricked the Trojans by hiding soldiers inside a wooden horse. Still, it's an important site for history buffs and fans of Homer's *Iliad* – and the wooden horse is fun.

To get the most out of a visit to the **ruins** (☎0286-283 0536; admission TL15; ⌚8.30am-7pm May–15 Sep, to 5pm 16 Sep–end Apr) it's worth hiring a guide (€50, 1½ hours). Enquire at the ticket booth or nearby Hotel Hisarlık, or contact **Mustafa Askin** (www.thetroyguide.com). The souvenir stalls and on-site shop sell illustrated guidebooks.

Companies offering Gallipoli tours (p1272) also offer morning trips to Troy (around €30 per person).

From Çanakkale, *dolmuşes* (shared taxis) to Troy ticket booth (€2, 35 minutes) leave every half-hour (less frequently at weekends) from the northern end of the bridge over the Sarı River. Returning, they leave on the hour.

Bergama

☎0232 / POP 58,200

This workaday market town has become a major stop on the tourist trail because of its proximity to the remarkable ruins of Pergamum, site of ancient Rome's preeminent medical centre. During Pergamum's heyday (between Alexander the Great and the Roman domination of Asia Minor) it was one of the Middle East's richest and most powerful small kingdoms.

The **tourist office** (☎631 2851; Hükümet Konağı, Cumhuriyet Caddesi; ⌚8.30am-noon & 1-5.30pm) is on the main street, just north of the Archaeology Museum.

Pergamum's **Acropolis** (admission TL20; ⌚8.30am-5.30pm), a windswept hilltop site 5km from the Red Basilica (and linked by a new cable car), is impressive even by Turkey's standards, with its commanding location and spectacular sloping amphitheatre.

The **Asclepion** (Temple of Asclepios; admission/parking TL15/3; ⌚8.30am-5.30pm), 3km uphill from the centre, was a famous medical centre. Galen's work here in the 2nd century was the basis for Western medicine well into the 16th century.

In Bergama, the **Red Basilica** (admission TL5; ⌚8.30am-5.30pm) is the imposing remains of a 2nd-century temple to the Egyptian gods Serapis, Isis and Harpocrates.

In the **Archaeology Museum** (Cumhuriyet Caddesi; admission TL5; ⌚8.30am-5.30pm Tue-Sun), look out for the statues from Pergamum.

In a converted 180-year-old house with views of the Red Basilica, the **Odyssey Guesthouse** (☎631 3501; www.odysseyguesthouse.com; Abacıhan Sokak 13; dm TL15, s/d from TL35/40, without bathroom from TL25/35, breakfast TL7) is full of crannies, corners and character, with a rooftop terrace and kitchenette.

Hourly buses run to İzmir (€5, two hours) and Ayvalık (€3.75, 1¼ hours).

İzmir

☎0232 / POP 2.7 MILLION

Though you will soon fall for Alsancak's studenty nightlife, shopping in the bazaar and catching ferries along the *kordon* (seafront), İzmir can take some getting used to. Certainly nowhere else in the region prepares you for the sheer size, sprawl and intensity of Turkey's third-largest city. The wide, pleasant seafront esplanade is one of İzmir's main attractions, providing plenty of eating, drinking and sunset-watching opportunities.

Inland, the ruins of the 2nd-century Roman **agora** (admission TL3; ⌚8.30am-5.30pm) are just southeast of the chaotic, atmospheric **Kemeraltı Bazaar**. The wide plaza **Konak Meydanı** is İzmir's centrepiece, with a late Ottoman **clock tower** in ornate late-Ottoman style.

Sleeping & Eating

There are plenty of budget and midrange hotels around the bazaar and Basmane train station. East of the station, 1368 Sokak is good for budget options.

For fresh fruit and veg, freshly baked bread and delicious savoury pastries, head for the canopied market, just off Anafartalar Caddesi. In Alsancak's eateries and bars, you lose the *kordon*'s sea views (and high prices) but gain on atmosphere; head to the lanes linking Cumhuriyet Bulvarı and Kıbrıs Şehitleri Caddesi.

Konak Saray Hotel BOUTIQUE HOTEL €€
(483 7755; www.konaksarayhotel.com; Anafartalar Caddesi 635; s/d TL60/90;) A hit with readers, occupying a restored Ottoman house with a top-floor restaurant. Its small, modern rooms have minibars, plasma-screen TVs and soundproofing against bazaar noise.

TOP CHOICE **Sakız** MODERN TURKISH €€
(484 1103; Şehıt Nevresbey Bulvarı 9a; mains €6-11; noon-2pm & 7.30-10pm Mon-Sat) With a wooden terrace, Sakız serves fresh meze, including *balık kokoreç* (fish intestines), and unusual mains. For lunch, choose between 35 vegetarian dishes (10 on Saturday).

Information

Banks, ATMs, internet cafes and wi-fi networks are found throughout the centre

Tourist office (483 5117; 1344 Sokak 2)

Getting There & Around

The bus companies' ticket offices mostly cluster on Dokuz Eylül Meydanı. They usually provide a *servis* to/from İzmir's mammoth *otogar*, 6.5km from the centre. Frequent buses serve destinations including Selçuk (TL8, one hour) and Bodrum (TL25, 3¼ hours).

Most intercity train services arrive at Basmane station, although Alsancak is being vamped up. Services run to Ankara (TL27, 15 hours, two daily) and Bandırma (TL17, six hours). Some Bandırma trains link with the ferry to/from İstanbul.

The pleasantest way to get around İzmir is by **ferry** (TL3). Roughly half-hourly services link piers including Konak, Pasaport and Alsancak.

Selçuk

0232 / POP 27,300

Selçuk boasts the remains of one of the Seven Wonders of the Ancient World, an excellent museum, a fine basilica, a stork nest-studded aqueduct and, right on the town's doorstep, Ephesus. However, it remains a quiet place, acting as a weigh station for the throngs of passers through.

The western side of Atatürk Caddesi, northwest of Ephesus Museum, is the quieter part of town and contains many *pensions;* the eastern side holds the *otogar* and plenty of shops and restaurants. The **tourist office** (www.selcuk.gov.tr; 8am-noon & 1-5pm summer, Mon-Fri winter) is opposite the museum.

Sights & Activities

Ephesus ANCIENT RUINS
(admission/parking TL20/3; 8am-6.30pm May-Oct, to 4.30pm Nov-Apr) Even if you're not an architecture buff, you can't help but be dazzled by the sheer beauty of these ruins. Once the capital of the Roman province of Asia, Ephesus is the best-preserved classical city in the eastern Mediterranean.

Wandering down Curetes Way, the former main street, you'll see the well-preserved (or restored) remains of structures such as the Temple of Hadrian, terraced houses (where the rich folk lived) and the Trajan Fountain. The real photo ops, though, are at the Great Theatre, which could hold 25,000 people, and at the monumental Library of Celsus, which stored 12,000 scrolls in niches around its walls.

The mediocre audioguide is not recommended; nor are the 'guides' loitering at the entrances. Organise a guide in advance. Ephesus is 3km west of Selçuk; the last part of the journey is an uphill climb along an unshaded stretch of highway. *Dolmuşes* from Selçuk frequently pass the Ephesus turn-off, a 20-minute walk from the lower gate.

FREE **Temple of Artemis** ANCIENT RUINS
(admission free; 8am-5pm, to 7pm May-Sep) At the western end of Selçuk, one enormous pillar remains of what was once the largest temple to Artemis, eclipsing the Parthenon at Athens and becoming one of the Seven Wonders of the Ancient World.

Ephesus Museum MUSEUM
(Uğur Mumcu Sevgi Yolu Caddesi; admission TL5; 8.30am-6.30pm summer, to 4.30pm winter) The main attraction in Selçuk, with a striking collection of artefacts including the effigy of Priapus, the Phallic God.

Basilica of St John HISTORIC BUILDING
(Ayasuluk Hill; admission TL5; 8.30am-6.30pm summer, to 4.30pm winter) Emperor Justinian built this 6th-century basilica on the site

WORTH A TRIP

PAMUKKALE

East of Selçuk, Pamukkale's gleaming white **travertines** (admission TL20; ⏲daylight), calcite shelves with pools cascading down the plateau edge, are a World Heritage Site. Next to this fragile wonder, you can tour the magnificent ruins of the Roman city of **Hierapolis**, an ancient spa resort with a theatre, colonnaded street, latrine building and necropolis.

You can bathe amid sunken columns at Hierapolis' **Antique Pool** (admission TL25; ⏲9am-7pm) and visit the **Hierapolis Archaeology Museum** (admission TL3; ⏲9am-12.30pm & 1.30-7pm Tue-Sun).

One of several budget *pensions* in the village, **Melrose Hotel** (☎272 2250; www.melroseresidence.com; Vali Vekfi Ertürk Caddesi 8; s/d TL50/60; ❄@≋) offers cheery pastel rooms and hearty dinners.

Buses connect local hub Denizli with Selçuk (TL18, three hours) and İzmir (TL20, four hours). Buses run between Denizli and Pamukkale every 15 minutes (TL2, 30 minutes).

where it was believed St John had been buried.

Sleeping & Eating

Competition between Selçuk's many *pensions* is intense, keeping standards of service and value high.

Most *pensions* offer home-cooked dinners at reasonable prices. Behind the *otogar*, the Saturday **market** is a great place to stock up for a picnic.

TOP CHOICE **Jimmy's Place** HOTEL €
(☎892 1982; www.jimmysplaceephesus.com; 1016 Sokak 19; d/ste from €30/70; ❄@≋) Near the *otogar*, inviting Jimmy's has five spacious floors of neat rooms. Staff are eager to please, offering gut-busting breakfasts and extras including an informative travel service.

Homeros Pension PENSION €
(☎892 3995; www.homerospension.com; 1048 Sokak 3; s/d/tr TL45/70/105; ❄@) On a quiet alley, Homeros' two houses are imprinted with the quirky character of the welcoming, kind-hearted owner. Traditional-style furniture mixes with hanging textiles and the roof terraces have good views.

Selçuk Köftecisi KÖFTECI €
(Şahabettin Dede Caddesi; mains TL6-9) This family-run spot has been churning out meatballs since 1959. It's highly recommended despite being monopolised by tour groups.

Getting There & Away

Frequent *dolmuşes* run to Kuşadası (TL4, 30 minutes). Bus services include İzmir (TL8, one hour, every 40 minutes in summer). If you ask in advance, you can usually be dropped at the junction of the road to Adnan Menderes Airport (a 2km walk or TL10 taxi from the airport).

Kuşadasi

☎0256 / POP 54,660

The fourth busiest cruise port in the entire Mediterranean, this former fishing village offers a decent, if oft-crowded, beach, and some of the coast's headiest nightlife.

The stone **castle** on the island in the harbour, connected to the mainland by a causeway, makes a pleasant stroll. Kuşadası is also a convenient base for visiting the ancient cities of **Priene**, **Miletus** and **Didyma** (admission to each TL3, tour €50).

Pensions and business hotels are found in the centre, with resorts on the bays extending north and south. Following a refurbishment, central **Hotel Ilayda** (☎614 3807; www.hotelilayda.com; Atatürk Bulvarı 46; s/d TL70/120; ❄@) is unbeatable with its good restaurant and record-low price tag. **Atlantique Holiday Club** (☎633 1320; www.atlantiqueclub.com; Karaova Mevkii Sahil Setileri; full board per person from TL70, ❄@≋), 7km south of the centre, offers seaside resort facilities and buffet meals – at backpacker prices.

The cheapest eating options are inland in the old quarter, Kaleiçi. **Avlu** (☎614 7995; Cephane Sokak 15; mains TL5-8) is worth seeking out, offering first-class mama-cooked meals.

Situated near the entrance of Bar St, **Köftecı Ali** (Arsanlar Caddesi 14; mains TL5; summer 24 hr) does some terrific spicy wrapped pide kebaps.

Barlar Sokak (Bar St) is chock-a-block with Irish-theme pubs. Locals prefer Kaleiçi's bars and clubs in stone houses and courtyards.

Dolmuşes leave from the central Adnan Menderes Bulvarı and the *otogar*, out on the bypass road. In summer, afternoon buses go to Bodrum (TL20, 2½ hours); in winter, take a *dolmuş* to Söke (TL4). Frequent *dolmuşes* run to Selçuk (TL4, 30 minutes) via the Ephesus turn-off.

From April to October boats depart daily to Samos, Greece (one-way/same-day return €30/35).

Bodrum

0252 / POP 39,320

The beating heart of a holiday-happy peninsula, Bodrum is a famously posh paradise where sun-kissed travellers dance the breezy summer nights away. With laws restricting the height of its buildings, the town has a nice architectural uniformity; the idyllic whitewashed houses with their bright-blue trim call out to tourists' cameras. Even when the clubs are bumpin' there's something rather refined about the town.

Sights & Activities

The conspicuous **Castle of St Peter** (admission TL5; 9am-noon & 1-5pm Tue-Sun), built in 1437 by the Knights Hospitaller, houses attractions including the **Museum of Underwater Archaeology**, arguably the most important museum of its kind in the world.

Boats moored on Neyzen Tevfik Caddesi run **day trips** (Western Bay; around TL24) to nearby spots including **Karaada** (Black Island), where hot springs gush out of a cave and produce supposedly curative orange mud.

Sleeping & Eating

With shuttles linking Bodrum to the rest of the peninsula, it's worth checking out hotels on the other bays. The town centre is dominated by cheap, usually lacklustre *pensions*, with better but pricier options on the hills. The closer you stay to the sea, the noisier it is at night.

Around the Eastern Bay, you'll find filling food after a night at the adjacent nightspots. The **fruit market** (Cevat Şakir Caddesi) offers healthy snacks during the day.

Mars Otel PENSION €€
(316 6559; www.marsotel.com; Turgutreis Caddesi, İmbat Çikmazi 29; s/d €30/40;) Located a five-minute walk from the sea, Mars is a mini-resort with a pool, lounge chairs, small bar and friendly staff. Free *otogar* and port transfers are offered.

Otel Atrium RESORT €€
(316 3926; www.atriumbodrum.com; Fabrika Sokak 21; s/d half board from TL80/110;) For little more than *pension* prices, the popular Atrium offers luscious gardens and an informal resort atmosphere, with a sociable pool area and friendly staff.

TOP CHOICE **Fish Market** SEAFOOD €€
(Cevat Şakir Caddesi; fish/meze TL20/from TL4; dinner Mon-Sat) Order drinks and mezes, then select your catch at the fishmongers (avoid the cheap farm fish), which the restaurant will cook for an extra TL4. Book in advance.

Drinking & Entertainment

Dr Alim Bey Caddesi and Cumhuriyet Caddesi function as Bodrum's waterfront 'Bar Street'. Under the looming castle turrets, decades-old **Hadigari** (1025 Sokak 2; 7pm-5am) is Bodrum's oldest bar.

Kitschy **Halıkarnas** (www.halikarnas.com.tr; Cumhuriyet Caddesi 178; admission weekday/weekend TL35/40; 10pm-5am summer) and the floating **Marine Club Catamaran** (www.clubcatamaran.com; Dr Alimbey Caddesi; admission weekday/weekend TL35/40; 10pm-4am mid-May–Sep) are famous nightclubs.

Information

Head to Cevat Şakir Caddesi for the PTT (post office) and ATMs.

Tourist office (Kale Meydanı; 8am-6pm Mon-Fri, daily in summer)

Getting There & Away

Boat

For tickets and the latest times, contact the **Bodrum Ferryboat Association** (www.bodrumferryboat.com; Kale Caddesi Cümrük Alanı 22).

DATÇA (one-way/return €12.50/20, two hours) Daily ferries from mid-June to September; three weekly from April to mid-June and in October.

KOS (one-way or same-day return €28, one hour) Daily ferries.

RHODES (one-way or same-day return €60, 2¼ hours) From June to September, two weekly hydrofoils.

Bus

There are at least two daily buses to destinations including: İzmir (TL25, 3½ hours), Kuşadası (TL20, 2½ hours) and Marmaris (TL18, three hours).

MEDITERRANEAN COAST

The western Mediterranean coastline, known as the 'Turquoise Coast', is a region of endless azure sea lined with sandy beaches and backed by mountains rising up to almost 3000m. Add to that ancient ruins strewn through the aromatic scrub and pine forests, and a sophisticated menu of activities. The most dramatic way to see this stretch of coastline is aboard a *gület* (traditional wooden yacht) or on a section of the 500km-long Lycian Way.

Marmaris

0252 / POP 40,000

A popular resort town that swells to over 200,000 people during the summer, in-your-face Marmaris is Mediterranean Turkey's answer to Spain's tacky Costa del Sol. Bar Street offers unparalleled decadence and boats can whisk you around the bay or along the coast. Lord Nelson organised his fleet in the stunning natural harbour before attacking the French at Abukir in 1798.

Sights & Tours

The small **castle** (admission TL3; 8am-noon & 1-5pm Tue-Sun) houses an archaeology museum and offers lovely views.

Not far south, the deeply indented Datça and Bozburun Peninsulas, reached by *dolmuş* or boat, hide azure bays backed by pine-covered mountains and gorgeous fishing villages.

Between May and October, '*dolmuş* boats' offer day tours of Marmaris Bay, its islands and beaches (about TL25 to TL30 per person). Check carefully exactly what you'll get before committing.

Overnight, two- and three-day excursions often take in **Dalyan** and the ruins of **Kaunos**; you can charter longer, more serious trips to **Datça** and the ruins at **Knidos**, or along the Bozburun Peninsula.

Sleeping & Eating

Marmaris is geared towards package groups, so good-value independent sleeping options are rare. Hedonists should join the fun on Bar Street (39 Sokak), where there are regular foam parties.

Maltepe Pansiyon PENSION €€
(412 1629, 0532 346 4244; www.maltepepansiyon.com; 66 Sokak 9; s/d TL30/60;) A shady garden and kitchen are among the attractions at this long-time backpacker favourite.

Özcan Pansiyon PENSION €€
(412 7761; ozcanpansitonmarmaris@hotmail.com; 66 Sokak 17; s/d TL35/60;) Resembling an old apartment block, with a pleasant garden terrace and, in some rooms, balconies and en-suite bathrooms.

İdil Mantı Evi BAR €€
(39 Sokak 140; meze TL5-6, mains TL8-20; 4pm-5am) A great spot on Bar St for night nibbles.

Alin's Cafe and Restaurant FAMILY RESTAURANT €€
(36 Sokak 23; mains TL5.90-14.90; 8am-12.30am) This chain is full of Turkish families feasting on healthy grills, burgers and spuds.

Information

Mavi Internet (26 Sokak 8; per hr TL2; 9am-11pm)

Tourist office (412 1035; İskele Meydanı 2; 8am-noon & 1-5pm Mon-Fri, daily Jun–mid-Sep) Right below the castle; but unhelpful.

Getting There & Away

Boat

From mid-April to October, catamarans sail daily to Rhodes (one-way/same-day return from €43/45, 50 minutes). Buy tickets from Marmaris agencies at least one day in advance.

Bus

The *otogar* is 3km north of the centre, and there are ticket offices around the Tansaş Shopping Centre. Bus services include Bodrum (TL18, 3¼ hours, at least every two hours) and Fethiye (TL16, three hours, half-hourly) via Ortaca (for Dalyan; TL10, 1½ hours).

Dalyan

0252 / POP 3000

Dalyan is a laid-back riverside community with a farming pedigree and a growing penchant for package tourism. It makes an excellent base for exploring the surrounding fertile waterways, in particular **Lake Köyceğiz** and the turtle-nesting grounds at unspoilt **İztuzu Beach**.

The main activity here is boating out of town. The **Dalyan Kooperatifi** (0541-505 0777) is recommended; its standard tour (about TL30 including lunch) takes in the **Sultaniye hot springs and mud baths** on the lake shores, the ruins of **Kaunos** (admission TL8; 8.30am-5.30pm) and **İztuzu Beach**.

Happy Caretta (284 2109; www.happycaretta.com; Kaunos Sokak 26; s/d TL100/150;)

has a magical garden and simple but stylish rooms. **Dalyan Camping** (☎284 5316; Maraş Caddesi 144; per tent/caravan TL10/20, large/small bungalows per person TL20/25; ⏰Apr-Oct) is centrally located by the river. The pinewood bungalows are simple and clean.

Restaurants vary greatly in quality, so be selective. **Kösk** (Maraş Caddesi; mains TL10-14; ⏰8am-11pm) is Dalyan's busiest eatery, thanks to its home-style meze and grills.

From Cumhuriyet Meydanı near the mosque, minibuses frequently run to Ortaca *otogar* (TL3), for buses to locations including Dalaman (TL4, 15 minutes).

Fethiye

☎0252 / POP 74,000

In 1958 an earthquake levelled the old harbour city of Fethiye, sparing only the ancient remains of Telmessos (400 BC). Today, Fethiye is once again a prosperous and proud hub of the western Mediterannean. Its natural harbour, tucked away in the southern reaches of a broad bay scattered with pretty islands, is perhaps the region's finest.

The **tourist office** (☎614 1527; İskele Meydanı; ⏰8am-noon & 1-5pm Mon-Fri) is opposite the marina.

Sights & Activities

Dolmuşes run southeast to the beautiful **Saklıkent Gorge** and Lycian ruins dotting the countryside, including **Tlos** and **Pınara**.

Telmessos — RUINS

In central Fethiye, little remains of the city of Telmessos other than a **Roman theatre** and **Lycian sarcophagi**. The cliffs hold several rock-cut tombs, including the Ionic **Tomb of Amyntas** (admission TL8; ⏰8am-5pm). **Fethiye Museum** (505 Sokak; admission TL5; ⏰8.30am-5pm Tue-Sun) has small statues and votive stones from Telmessos and other Lycian sites.

Boat trips — CRUISE

Numerous trips are offered by a number of local operators, including the 12-Island Tour (per person TL25), the Butterfly Valley tour (TL25) via Ölüdeniz, the Saklıkent Gorge tour (TL45) and the Dalyan Tour (TL25). See also the boxed text, below.

Kayaköy — HISTORIC AREA

(admission TL8; ⏰8.30am-6pm) *Dolmuşes* run to this nearby open-air museum, an evocative Ottoman Greek 'ghost town' abandoned after the population exchange of 1923.

Ölüdeniz — WATER SPORTS

A little further south from Kayaköy, Ölüdeniz (Dead Sea) has a sheltered lagoon and a long spit of sandy beach, although its charms have become a package-holiday curse. Popular activities are **paragliding** and **parasailing**.

Butterfly Valley — NATURE

You may prefer to take a shuttle boat/cruise (one-way/return TL15/20) from Ölüdeniz to this beautiful valley, where laid-back accommodation options are found as well as nearby Faralya and Kabak.

Lycian Way — WALK

Fethiye is at the western end of this superb **walking trail** (see p1289), which passes Ölüdeniz.

BLUE CRUISE

Fethiye is the hub of Turkey's cruising scene, and the most popular route is the 'Blue Voyage' (*Mavi Yolculuk*) to Olympos: a four-day, three-night journey on a *gület* (traditional wooden yacht) that attracts young party animals. Boats usually call in at Ölüdeniz and Butterfly Valley and stop at Kaş, Kalkan and Kekova, with the final night at Gökkaya Bay opposite the eastern end of Kekova. A less common (but some say prettier) route is between Marmaris and Fethiye.

Depending on the season the price is €135 to €185 per person (food and water should be included). Make sure you shop around – there are many shoddy operators working the waters and wallets. Recommended operators include **Before Lunch Cruises** (☎0535 636 0076; www.beforelunch.com), **Ocean Turizm & Travel Agency** (☎0252-612 4807; www.oceantravelagency.com) and **Olympos Yachting** (☎0242-892 1145; www.olymposyachting.com).

For more-ambitious trips you can charter the whole boat yourself, with or without crew, and set off wherever your fancy takes you. Fethiye and Marmaris (p1278) are both good starting points.

Sleeping & Eating

Most accommodation is up the hill behind the marina in Karagözler or further west. Many *pensions* organise transport from the *otogar*.

Fethiye's enormous canalside Tuesday **market** takes place between Atatürk Caddesi and Pürşabey Caddesi next to the stadium.

Night spots are mostly on Hamam Sokak in the old town, and along Dispanser Caddesi south of the Martyrs' Monument.

Yildirim Guest House HOSTEL, PENSION €
(☎614 4627; www.yildirimguesthouse.com; Fevzi Çakmak Caddesi 37; dm/s/d/tr TL25/35/70/105; ❄@) Shipshape Yildirim has four- to six-bed dorms and spotless rooms, some facing the harbour. Excursions, laundry and dinner are offered.

Ferah Pension HOSTEL, PENSION €
(☎614 2816; www.ferahpension.com; Ortdu Caddesi 23; dm/s/d TL20/30/50; ❄@≋) 'Monica's place' has a leafy, glass-enclosed lobby terrace and little pool, with paintings and 'sexy dinners' by the owner.

Paşa Kebab KEBAPÇI €€
(Çarşı Caddesi 42; meze, pide, kebaps & pizza TL4-13.50; ⏰9am-1am) Considered locally to offer Fethiye's best kebaps, including the gigantic Paşa Special (beef, tomato and cheese).

Recep's Place SEAFOOD €€
(☎614 8297; Hal ve Pazar Yeri 51; mains TL10-20; ⏰10am-midnight) Buy some fish from the fishmongers (per kilo TL18 to TL25) and get it cooked at one of the restaurants opposite. Recep's charges TL5 for the service, with accompanying sauce, green salad, garlic bread, fruit and coffee.

Getting There & Away

Boat

Catamarans sail to Rhodes (one-way/same-day return €58/65, 1½ hours) between mid-April and October.

Bus & Dolmuş

Fethiye's *otogar* is 2.5km east of the centre, with services to Antalya (inland route TL18, four hours; coastal route TL25, 7½ hours), Kaş (TL12, 2½ hours) and Olympos (TL22, five hours).

From the stops near the mosque, minibuses run to local destinations including Ölüdeniz (TL4, 25 minutes)

Patara

☎0242 / POP 945

Patara's superb 20km of white sand, Turkey's longest uninterrupted beach, is a nesting ground for sea turtles. The extensive, overgrown **ruins** (admission incl beach TL5; ⏰9am-5pm) include a triple-arched triumphal gate and a necropolis containing Lycian tombs.

Nearby are two Unesco World Heritage Sites: **Letoön** (admission TL5; ⏰8.30am-5.30pm), which has excellent mosaics and a Hellenistic theatre; and impressive **Xanthos** (admission TL3; ⏰9am-5pm), with a Roman theatre and Lycian pillar tombs.

Patara's amenities are in Gelemiş village, 2km south of the highway turn-off and 1.5km from the ruins. Offering a free shuttle to the beach, **Flower Pension** (☎843 5164; www.pataraflowerpension.com; s/d/apt from TL20/40/50; ❄@) has simple, airy rooms with balconies overlooking a garden.

Buses on the Fethiye–Kaş route drop you on the highway 4km from the village. From here hourly *dolmuşes* run to the village. In season, minibuses run from the beach through the village to local destinations.

Kaş

☎0242 / POP 5929

Kaş ('cash') may not sport the region's finest beach culture, but this yachties' haven has a wonderfully mellow atmosphere. The surrounding area is ideal for day trips by sea or scooter, and a plethora of adventure sports are offered, including some excellent wreck diving.

Apart from enjoying the small pebble **beaches**, you can walk a few hundred metres to the well-preserved Hellenistic theatre. Lycian **rock tombs** are cut into the cliffs above town, and it's well worth climbing the hilly street to the east of the main square to the **Lion Tomb**, a Lycian sarcophagus.

The most popular **boat trip** (€25) is to **Kekova Island** and **Üçağız**, passing submerged Lycian ruins. Other activities, organised by local operators such as **Bougainville Travel** (☎836 3737; www.bougainville-turkey.com; İbrahim Selin Sokak 10), include scuba-diving, paragliding, mountain biking, canyoning, sea-kayaking and canoeing. Kayaking over the sunken ruins alongside Kekova Island is suitable for all fitness levels.

Sleeping

Most accommodation is west and northwest of the centre along the waterfront and up the hill around the Yeni Cami (New Mosque).

Santosa Pension PENSION €
(☎836 1714; www.santosapension.com; Recep Bilgin Sokak 4; s/d TL45/70; ❄@) The floral rooms at this clean, quiet and cheap backpacker hangout are simple but excellent value.

Kaş Camping CAMPING GROUND €
(☎836 1050; www.kaskamping.com; Hastane Caddesi 3; campsite TL20, standard/deluxe bungalow TL55/140; ❄@) Located on a rocky outcrop 800m west of town, this popular site with a lively terrace bar is 100m from the sea. Deluxe bungalows have bathrooms and air conditioning.

Eating & Drinking

Southeast of the main square are some excellent restaurants, especially around Sandıkçı Sokak. A Friday **market** takes place along the old Kalkan road. **2000 Restaurant** (Atatürk Bulvarı 1; dishes TL3-4; ⏱24hr) Serves a superb *dürüm* (kebap wrapped in pitta).

There is a good choice of atmospheric drinking holes. Try **Hi-Jazz Bar** (Zümrüt Sokak 3) or, on the harbour, the hip **Echo Cafe & Bar** (Limanı Sokak).

Information

Computer World (per hr €1; ⏱9am-11pm) Opposite the PTT.

Tourist office (☎836 1238; ⏱8am-noon & 1-5pm Mon-Fri) On the main square.

Getting There & Away

There are *dolmuşes* at least every hour to:

ANTALYA (€8, 3½ hours)

FETHIYE (€6, 2½ hours) Change here for Ankara or İzmir.

OLYMPOS (€7.50, 2½ hours)

PATARA (€4, 45 minutes)

Olympos

☎0242

Long beloved of hippies, ancient **Olympos** (admission TL3; ⏱9am-6pm) was once an important Lycian city; now it's a fantastically wild, abandoned place where ruins appear undiscovered among the vines and flowering trees. The deep, shaded valley containing the ruins runs to the **beach**.

According to legend, the **Chimaera** (Yanartaş; admission TL3.50), a cluster of natural flames on the slopes of Mt Olympos, was the hot breath of a monster. At night the 20 or 30 main flames are visible at sea. To find the Chimaera, 7km from Olympos, follow the hillside signs from Çıralı (*pensions* and agencies offer lifts/tours for TL5/15).

Sleeping & Eating

The 'tree house' camps, which line the track along the valley down to the ruins, have long been the stuff of travel legend. Most include breakfast and dinner in the price. Be extra attentive to personal hygiene and food while staying here; every year some travellers get ill. The huge influx of summer visitors can overwhelm the camps' capacity for proper waste disposal.

TOP CHOICE **Şaban Tree Houses** CAMPING GROUND, PENSION €
(☎892 1265; www.sabanpansion.com; dm/tree house/en-suite bungalow TL25/35/45; ❄@) Şaban is not a party place, and instead offers tranquillity, space and great home cooking.

Kadır's Yörük Top Treehouse CAMPING GROUND, PENSION €
(☎892 1250; www.kadirstreehouses.com; dm/en-suite bungalow from TL15/40; ❄@) Kadir's started the arboreal action, and it's still fun: the Bull Bar is the valley's liveliest and there's an activities centre.

Getting There & Away

Buses and minibuses plying the Fethiye–Antalya road will stop near the Olympos junction. From there, minibuses serve Olympos (TL6). They can take a while to fill up between October to April, but most accommodation will pick you up if you ask in advance.

Antalya

☎0242 / POP 956,000

The gateway to the 'Turkish Riviera', Antalya is generating a buzz among culture-vultures. Situated directly on the Gulf of Antalya (Antalya Körfezi), the largest city on Turkey's Mediterranean coast is both stylishly modern and classically beautiful. It boasts the creatively preserved Roman-Ottoman quarter of Kaleiçi, a splendid Roman harbour and superb ruins in the surrounding Beydağları (Bey Mountains).

Sights & Activities

Kaleiçi HISTORIC AREA
Heading downhill from the old stone **clock tower** in the main square, called **Kale Kapısı** (Fortress Gate), you'll pass Antalya's symbol, the **Yivli Minare**. The fluted 13th-century Seljuk minaret stands above a restored whirling dervish monastery and a gallery.

The monumental **Hadrian's Gate** (Hadriyanüs Kapısı; off Atatürk Caddesi) was erected for the Roman emperor's visit to Antalya (130 BC).

The **Suna & İnan Kiraç Kaleiçi Museum** (Kocatepe Sokak 25; admission TL3; ⏲9am-noon & 1-6pm Thu-Tue) is an ethnography museum in a restored Ottoman mansion and Greek Orthodox church.

The **Kesik Minare** (Truncated Minaret) is a stump of a tower on the site of a ruined Roman temple.

Karaalioğlu Parkı is one of the cliffside vantage points giving stunning views over the beautiful **marina** and soaring Beydağları.

Antalya Museum MUSEUM
(Konyaaltı Caddesi 1; admission TL15; ⏲9am-5.30pm Tue-Sun) About 2km west of the centre and accessible on the tram, Antalya's comprehensive city museum houses spectacular finds from Lycian and Pamphylian cities, and statues of Olympian gods, most found at nearby Perge.

Sleeping & Eating

In Kaleiçi, signs point the way to some of Turkey's best guest houses.

Many cafes and eateries are found around the harbour. For cheap eating, cross Atatürk Caddesi to the commercial district.

White Garden Pansiyon PENSION €
(☎241 9115; www.whitegardenpansion.com; Hesapçı Geçidi 9; s/d TL35/45; ❄@☒) Metin's *pension* combines tidiness and class beyond its price level with impeccable service, in a charmingly restored building and courtyard.

Sabah Pansiyon PENSION €
(☎247 5345; www.sabahpansiyon.8m.com; Hesapçı Sokak 60; dm/s/d from TL20/30/40; ❄@) Long a budget stalwart, rooms here vary greatly so ask to see a couple. The shaded courtyard is perfect for meeting other travellers.

Can Can Pide ve Kebap Salonu KEBAPÇI €
(Arık Caddesi 4/A; pide TL3-4, dürüm TL5-6; ⏲9am-11pm Mon-Sat) Fantastic *çorba,* pide and Adana *dürüm* (beef kebap rolled in pitta) at bargain prices; opposite the Plaza Cinema.

Information

Rıhtım Cafe (per hr €0.50; ⏲9am-midnight) Internet access in a *nargileh* cafe north of Cumhuriyet Meydanı.

Tourist Office (☎241 1747; Anafatlar Caddesi 31, Seleker; ⏲8am-6pm Mon-Fri)

Getting There & Away

The *otogar* is 4km north of the centre; the blue-and-white Terminal Otobusu 93 runs to the centre every 20 minutes or so. Regular buses serve Göreme/Ürgüp (TL40, nine hours) and Konya (TL25, five hours).

From opposite the Sheraton Voyager Antalya Hotel, west of the centre's services go to Kaş (TL16, 3½ hours) and Olympos (TL13, 1½ hours).

CENTRAL ANATOLIA

On central Turkey's hazy plains, the sense of history is so pervasive that the average kebap chef can remind you that the Romans preceded the Seljuks. This is, after all, the region where the whirling dervishes first swirled, Atatürk began his revolution, Alexander the Great cut the Gordian Knot, King Midas turned everything to gold, and Julius Caesar uttered his famous line, *'Veni, vidi, vici'* (I came, I saw, I conquered).

Ankara

☎0312 / POP 4.5 MILLION

İstanbullus may quip that the best view in Ankara is the train home, but the Turkish capital has more substance than its reputation as a staid administrative centre suggests. The capital established by Atatürk boasts two of the country's most important sights, and a few neighbourhoods with some charm: the hilltop *hisar* (citadel); the chic Kavaklıdere district; and Kızılay, one of Turkey's hippest urban quarters.

Sights & Activities

Anatolian Civilisations Museum MUSEUM
(☎324 3160; Gözcü Sokak 2; admission TL15; ⏲8.30am-5pm) Provides the perfect introduction to the complex weave of Turkey's chequered ancient past, with artefacts cherry-picked from just about every signifi-

cant archaeological site in Anatolia. While you're here, explore the side streets inside the nearby thick Byzantine walls of the **citadel**.

FREE **Anıt Kabir** MONUMENT
(admission free; ⏲9am-4pm) Pay your respects to the founder of modern Turkey and observe the Turks' enduring reverence for Atatürk at his monumental mausoleum, 2km west of Kızılay.

Roman baths RUINS
(admission TL3; ⏲8.30am-12.30pm & 1.30-5.30pm) About 400m north of Ulus Meydanı, these sprawling remains date back to the 3rd century. Southeast of the baths, you'll find more Roman ruins, including the **Column of Julian** (AD 363) in a square ringed by government buildings.

Ethnography Museum MUSEUM
(Talat Paşa Bulvarı; admission TL3; ⏲8.30am-12.30pm & 1.30-5.30pm) If you have any energy left for museums, this one is worth a look, as is the neighbouring **Painting & Sculpture Museum** (admission free; ⏲9am-noon & 1-5pm).

Sleeping

Most budget accommodation is in Ulus, which is handy for the Anatolian Civilisations Museum. A revamp will hopefully spruce up the slightly seedy area.

Hotel Oğultürk HOTEL €
(☎309 2900; www.ogulturk.com; Rüzgarlı Eşdost Sokak 6; s/d/tr TL50/60/70; ❄) Just off Rüzgarlı Sokak, the Oğultürk is one of central Ulus' smarter options. It's professionally managed and is a good option for lone women.

Otel Mithat HOTEL €
(☎311 5410; www.otelmithat.com.tr; Tavus Sokak 2; s/d/tr €23/33/43; wi-fi) Rooms are miniscule, but the wi-fi is lightning fast, and the breakfast is super-sized.

Eating & Drinking

Most Ulus options are cheap and basic. **Ulus Hali food market** sells provisions from oversized chilli peppers to jars of honey. For more choice, head to the pedestrian zone north of Ziya Gökalp Caddesi in Kızılay.

Fast and friendly, **Urfalı Kebap** (Karanfil Sokak 69, Kızılay; mains TL5-10), one of Ankara's best kebap restaurants, attracts diners from students to three-generation families.

Kızılay is also great for a night out, with buzzing hangouts such as **Qube Bar** (Bayındır Sokak 16B) and **Le Man Kültür** (Konur Sokak 8a-b; ⏲10am-11pm).

Information

There are many internet cafes in Ulus and Kızılay, particularly around Ulus Meydanı and Karanfıl Sokak.

Tourist office (☎310 8789/231 5572; Gazi Mustafa Kemal Bulvarı; ⏲9am-5pm Mon-Fri, 10am-5pm Sat) Opposite the train station.

Getting There & Around

AIRPORT Half-hourly Havaş shuttle buses depart from Gate B at 19 May Stadium (€5, 45 minutes). They may leave sooner if they fill up, so get there early.

BUS Ankara's huge *otogar* (AŞTİ), linked to Kızılay and Ulus by underground trains, dispatches passengers across the country all day and night. You can often turn up, buy a ticket and be on your way in less than an hour.

TRAIN Services between İstanbul and Ankara are the best in the country, and an even faster rail link is set to open imminently. Fast trains also continue to Konya.

Konya

☎0332 / POP 762,000

Turkey's equivalent of the 'Bible Belt', conservative Konya treads a delicate path between its historical significance as the home town of the whirling dervish orders and a bastion of Seljuk culture on the one hand, and its modern importance as an economic boom town on the other.

If you are crossing the surrounding plains, say from the coast to Cappadocia, bear in mind that the turquoise-domed Mevlâna Museum is one of Turkey's finest and most characteristic sights.

The centre stretches from Alaaddin Tepesi, the hill topped by the Seljuk Alaaddin Camii, along Mevlâna Caddesi to the Mevlâna Museum.

Sights & Activities

The centre is dotted with imposing Seljuk buildings, some housing museums. Highlights include the **İnce Minare Medresesi** (Seminary of the Slender Minaret) and **Sırçalı Medrese** (Glass Seminary).

Mevlâna Museum HISTORICAL BUILDING, MUSEUM
(admission €1; ⏲9am-6.30pm Tue-Sun, 10am-6pm Mon) Join the pilgrims at this wonderful

Ankara

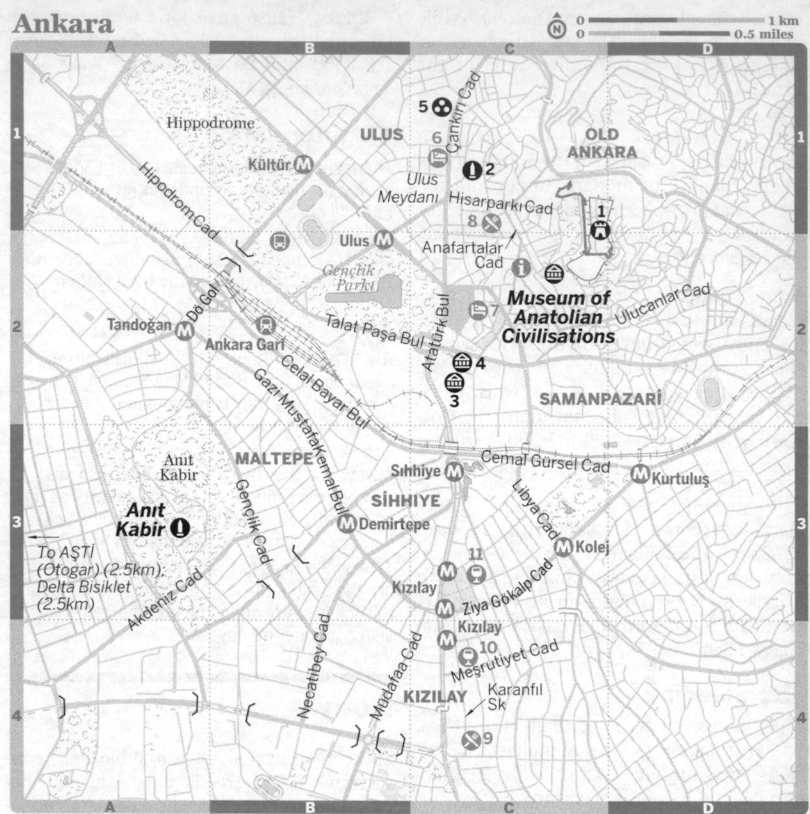

museum-cum-shrine at the eastern end of Mevlâna Caddesi, where the turban-topped tombs of eminent dervishes include that of Mevlâna (Our Guide) himself: the great mystic philosopher Celaleddin Rumi (1207–73). The former lodge of the whirling dervishes, it is crowned by a brilliant turquoise-tiled dome – one of Turkey's most distinctive sights.

Sleeping & Eating

Ulusan Otel HOTEL €
(☎351 5004; Çarşi PTT Arkasi 4; s/d from TL40/70) Behind the post office is this spotless little hotel, with graceful management, hearty breakfasts and palatial shared bathrooms.

Mevlâna Sema Otel HOTEL €
(☎350 4623; www.semaotel.com; Mevlâna Caddesi 67; s/d/tr TL50/75/100; ❄) The Mevlâna Sema has a great position, some swanky decor and comfortable, beige rooms. Rooms at the rear are quieter.

Gülbahçesı Konya Mutfağı TURKISH €
(☎351 0768; Gülbahçe Sokak 3; mains TL4-8; ⏲8am-10pm) Restaurants around the Mevlâna Museum and tourist office have great views, but their food is not recommended – with this exception, which stages occasional *sema* performances.

Information

Elma Net (Çinili Sokak 14; per hr €0.50; ⏲10am-11pm) One of the web cafes around Alaaddin Tepesi.

Tourist office (☎353 4020; Mevlâna Caddesi 21; ⏲8.30am-5.30pm Mon-Sat)

Getting There & Away

Express trains link Konya with İstanbul, with a direct, high-speed link to/from Ankara scheduled to open in 2011.

From the *otogar,* 7km north of the centre and accessible by tram from Alaaddin Tepesi, regular buses serve destinations including Ankara

Ankara

(TL20, four hours), İstanbul (TL45, 11½ hours) and Kayseri (TL25, four hours).

CAPPADOCIA

In extraordinary Cappadocia, Central Anatolia's mountain-fringed plains give way to a land of fairy chimneys and underground cities. The fairy chimneys – rock columns, pyramids, mushrooms and even a few resembling camels – were formed, alongside the valleys of cascading white cliffs, when Erciyes Daği (Mt Erciyes) erupted. The intervening millennia added to the remarkable Cappadocian canvas, with Byzantines carving cave churches and subterranean complexes to house thousands.

Göreme

0384 / POP 6350

Göreme is the archetypal travellers' utopia: a beatific village where the surreal surroundings spread a fat smile on everyone's face. Beneath the honeycomb cliffs, the locals live in fairy chimneys – or, increasingly, run hotels in them. Gazing at the wavy valleys in the distance, with their hiking trails, panoramic viewpoints and rock-cut churches, is best accompanied by meze on one of Göreme's panoramic terraces.

Sights & Activities

A World Heritage Site, **Göreme Open-Air Museum** (admission TL15; 8am-5pm) is Cappadocia's finest collection of rock-hewn cave churches. The churches are tiny, so avoid weekends and try to nip in between the tour groups (early morning, midday and late afternoon are busy). The fresco filled **Karanlık Kilise** (Dark Church; admission TL8) is worth the extra charge; across the road from the main entrance, the **Tokalı Kilise** (Buckle Church), with an underground chapel and fabulous frescos, is included in the entrance fee.

Tours

Göreme is the main base for tours of Cappadocia's most popular sites (one-day trips about TL70). Tours usually start at a lookout point with a view across the valleys, then continue to locations such as Ihlara Valley (see p1285), a pottery in Avanos, the rock formations in Devrent Valley, Uçhisar's **rock citadel** (admission TL3; 8am-8.15pm), and one of the fascinating underground cities at **Kaymaklı** (admission TL15; 8am-5pm, last admission 4.30pm) and **Derinkuyu** (admission TL15; 8am-5pm, last admission 4.30pm). Many companies also offer trips further afield, for example to eastern Turkey. We recommend the following:

Yama Tours (271 2508; www.yamatours.com; Müze Caddesi 2) Also offers three-day trips to Mt Nemrut (see p1287).

Middle Earth Travel (271 2559; www.middleearthtravel.com; Cevizler Sokak 20) The adventure-travel specialist offers one-day to one-week climbing and trekking expeditions.

Kapadokya Balloons (271 2442; www.kapadokyaballoons.com; Adnan Menderes Caddesi, Göreme) Well-respected hot-air balloon company offering dawn flights from €175 (one hour).

Sleeping

Competition keeps prices low in Göreme. Between October and May, pack warm clothes as *pensions* may delay using the heating, and phone to check your choice is open.

TOP CHOICE **Kelebek Hotel & Cave Pension** CAVE HOTEL €€
(271 2531; www.kelebekhotel.com; Yavuz Sokak 31; fairy chimney s/d from €28/35;) Local guru Ali Yavuz leads a charming team at the village's original boutique hotel. The *pension* spreads over two gorgeous stone houses with

WORTH A TRIP

IHLARA VALLEY

A beautiful canyon full of greenery and Byzantine rock-cut churches, **Ihlara Valley** (admission TL5; ⌚8am-6.30pm) is an excellent, and popular, spot for a walk. Footpaths follow the river for 13km between Ihlara village and **Selime Monastery** (⌚dawn-dusk).

The easiest way to see the valley is on a day tour (see p1285), which allows a few hours for a one-way walk through the stretch of the gorge with most churches. To get there by bus, you must change in Nevşehir and Aksaray, making it tricky to get there and back from Göreme and complete the walk in a day.

If you want to walk the whole valley – and it's definitely worth the effort – there are modest *pensions* in Ihlara village and Selime, and a *pension* and riverside camping grounds halfway along the valley in Belisırma. All close between December and March.

Ten *dolmuşes* a day travel down the valley from Aksaray; to travel in the opposite direction, you have to catch a taxi.

fairy chimney protruding skyward and a stunning terrace.

Köse Pension HOSTEL €
(☎271 2294; www.kosepension.com; Ragıp Üner Caddesi; dm TL15, r TL25-90;) Following a refurbishment, this Scottish-Turkish family affair remains a winner for families and independent folk. The spotless rooms feature brilliant bathrooms, bright linens and comfortable beds, and the TL15 three-course Turkish feast is great value.

Flintstones Cave HOSTEL €
(☎271 2555; www.theflintstonescavehotel.com; dm/s/d from TL10/20/40; @) Göreme's premium budget joint has a spacious new wing with Jacuzzi rooms, and a huge bar with pool table and noticeboard. Dorms include a five-bedder with communal areas and private bathroom.

Kaya Camping Caravaning CAMPING GROUND €
(☎343 3100; kayacamping@www.com; camp sites TL15; @) This impressive camping ground is 2.5km from the centre, uphill from Göreme Open-Air Museum. Set among fields and trees, it has magnificent views and top-notch facilities.

Eating

There is a strip of cafes on the quiet side of the dry canal, away from the busy main road.

Nazar Börek TURKISH €
(☎271 2441; Müze Caddesi; mains TL7) Munch on simple yet delicious meals, including *gözleme* and *börek* such as *sosyete böreği* (stuffed spiral pastries served with yoghurt and tomato sauce), in the canal-side chill-out area.

Dibek ANATOLIAN €
(☎271 2209; Hakkı Paşa Meydanı 1; mains TL10-18; ⌚9am-11pm) This family restaurant in a 475-year-old building still churns out homemade wine. The best dish is *testi kebap* (kebap slow-cooked in a terracotta pot, broken at the table to serve). Book at least three hours ahead to try this.

Information

Mor-tel Telekom (Roma Kalesi Arkası; per hr TL2; ⌚9am-midnight) For internet and international calls.
Tourist information booth (Otogar)

Getting There & Away

Air

There are airports in Kayseri (see p1286) and Nevşehır (Turkish Airlines flies to/from İstanbul four times a week). Accommodation options can organise transfers.

Bus

When you purchase your ticket to Cappadocia, make sure it clearly states your final destination. The bus company should provide a free *servis* from transport hub Nevşehır to the surrounding villages. Nevşehır is notorious; if you get stuck, do *not* book a tour, and phone your accommodation for a pick-up or get the hourly bus. Daily services from Göreme:

ANKARA (€12.50, 4½ hours)
ANTALYA (€17.50, nine hours)
İSTANBUL (€20, 12 hours)
KONYA (€10, three hours)

Kayseri

☎0352 / POP 1.2 MILLION

Mixing Seljuk tombs, mosques and modern developments, Kayseri is both central Turkey's most Islamic city after Konya and one of the economic powerhouses nicknamed the 'Anatolian tigers'. It lacks central Cappadocia's charms, but if you are passing through this transport hub, it's worth taking a look at a Turkish boomtown with a strong sense of its own history.

Now acting as an overflow valve for the nearby bazaar, the basalt-walled Seljuk **citadel** is Kayseri's centrepiece. Across the Ottoman **kapalı çarşı** (vaulted bazaar), the **Ulu Cami** (Great Mosque) has one of Anatolia's first brick minarets. The Ottoman-style **Kurşunlu Cami** (Lead-Domed Mosque) is one of the sights in the parks across Park Caddesi. **Güpgüpoğlu Konağı**, a wonderful 18th-century Ottoman stone mansion, houses an interesting **Ethnographic Museum** (admission TL3; 8am-5pm Tue-Sun).

Beyond the dark reception and institutional corridors at **Hotel Sur** (222 4367; Talas Caddesi 12; s/d/tr TL40/60/75), rooms are bright and comfortable and some overlook the city walls. Flashy business hotel **Grand Ülger** (323 8303; www.grandulgerhotel.com; Osman Kavuncu Caddesi 55; s/d TL50/90;) has comfortable rooms and a decent restaurant.

Turkish Airlines and Onur Air fly to/from İstanbul daily; Sun Express flies to/from İzmir twice a week. Kayseri has many bus services, including to Göreme (TL10, 1½ hours) and Malatya (TL25, five hours). There are trains to destinations including Ankara, İstanbul, Kars, Malatya and Tatvan.

EASTERN TURKEY

Like a challenge? Eastern Turkey – vast, remote and culturally very Middle Eastern – is the toughest part of Turkey to travel in but definitely the most exotic, and certainly the part that feels least affected by mass tourism. Winter here can be bitterly cold and snowy.

Fighting between the Turkish military and the PKK (Kurdistan Workers' Party) separatist group has simmered down in south eastern Turkey, but find out the current situation before travelling in the region.

Mt Nemrut National Park

Two thousand years ago, a meglomaniac Commagene king erected his own memorial sanctuary on Mt Nemrut (Nemrut Dağı; 2150m), the centrepiece of today's stunning **national park** (admission TL6.50; dawn-dusk). The fallen heads of the gigantic decorative statues of gods and kings, toppled by earthquakes, form one of the country's most enduring images.

There are several bases for visiting Mt Nemrut. To the northwest is **Malatya**, where the **tourist office** (0422 323 2942) organises daily minibus tours (TL100, minimum two people, May to September/October), with a night at Güneş Hotel below the summit and visits to the heads at sunset and sunrise. Alternatively, visiting from **Kahta** is a good option as you can see the sights on the south side, but be wary as Kahta has a reputation as a rip-off town. **Mehmet Akbaba** (0535 295 4445; akbabamehmet@hotmail.com) and Hotel Nemrut-based **Nemrut Tours** (0416 725 6881) offer informative English-speaking guides.

Taking a two-day tour from **Cappadocia** (see p1285) is a tedious drive; if you have enough time and money, a three-day tour is better.

In high summer the most pleasant places to stay, especially if you have your own transport, are the camping grounds, village *pensions* and hotels on the southern slopes of the mountain. The pretty village of **Karadut**, 12km from the summit, has a few small eateries.

Van

0432 / POP 391,000

On the southeastern shore of vast Lake Van, the easygoing city of the same name boasts a hilltop **castle** (admission TL3, 9am-dusk), overlooking the foundations of **Eski Van** (the old city) and a fabulous **museum** (admission TL3; 8am-noon & 1-5pm Tue-Sun), but the 10th-century **Armenian church** on Akdamar Island is the star attraction. Its biblical reliefs are jaw-dropping, not to mention its location 3km out on Lake Van, a vast expanse of water ringed by snowcapped mountains. The island is a day trip from Van by minibus and boat.

Otel Bahar (215 5748; Ordu Caddesi 20; s/d TL25/50) is one of Van's best cheapies, with simple rooms featuring clean bathrooms and compact balconies.
Around the corner, try Van's famous *kahvaltı* (breakfast; about TL15), featuring local speciality *otlu peynir* (cheese mixed with a tangy herb), on '**Kahvaltı Sokak**' (pedestrianised Eski Sümerbank Sokak).

For Kars, the scenic route is seen from *dolmuşes* via Doğubayazıt and Iğdır, but catching the bus via Erzurum (TL50, 10 hours total) is easier.

Frequent buses go to Diyarbakır (TL35, seven hours), from where you can continue to Kahta (for Mt Nemrut National Park).

The twice-weekly *Vangölü Ekspresi* train from İstanbul and Ankara meets the ferry from Van in Tatvan.

Kars

☎0474 / POP 78,500

The medieval fortress and fine old Russian houses are well worth a look, but most people come to the setting of Orhan Pamuk's novel *Snow* to visit the dramatic ruins of **Ani** (admission TL5; ⏰8.30am-5pm), 45km east of the city. Formerly the capital of the Armenian kingdom, Ani was completely deserted in 1239 after a Mongol invasion. The ghost city, with its lightning-cleaved **Church of the Redeemer**, now lies amid undulating grass overlooking the Armenian border. The site exudes an eerie ambience that is simply unforgettable.

Kars' secure **Güngören Hotel** (☎212 6767; Millet Sokak; s/d TL40/70) offers spacious rooms, well-scrubbed bathrooms, good rates and a copious breakfast.

There are daily buses to locations including Ankara (TL50, 16 hours) and Van (TL35, six hours). Trains go to Kayseri.

Transport to Ani is sparse; take a taxi minibus (about €17.50 with a minimum of six passengers) organised by Kars' **tourist office** (☎212 6817, 0532-226 3966; Lise Caddesi; ⏰8am-noon & 1-5pm Mon-Fri) or a taxi (from €45).

UNDERSTAND TURKEY

History

The greatest early Anatolian civilisation was the Hittites, who were a force to be reckoned with from 2000 to 1200 BC. After the collapse of the Hittite empire, Anatolia splintered and did not reunite until the Greco-Roman period.

In AD 330 the Roman emperor Constantine founded an imperial city at Byzantium. Renamed Constantinople, it became the capital of the Eastern Roman Empire and was the Byzantine Empire's heart for a thousand years. However, invasion by the Seljuk Turks heavily reduced the empire's territory, and Constantinople was sacked during the Fourth Crusade (1202–04). The Byzantines regained the ravaged city in 1261.

In 1453 Constantinople fell to the Ottoman sultan Mehmet II (the Conqueror) and was renamed İstanbul. A century later, under Süleyman the Magnificent, the Ottoman Empire reached its zenith, spreading deep into Europe, Asia and North Africa.

By the 20th century European nationalism was widespread, and the Turks emerged from WWI stripped of their last non-Turkish provinces. Most of Anatolia was set to be divided among the victorious Europeans, leaving the Turks with virtually nothing.

At this low point, Mustafa Kemal (later Atatürk), the father of modern Turkey, took over. Under his rule, the Turks won their War of Independence (1919–23), repelling the Greeks at Smyrna (İzmir), and founded a new secular Turkish republic. The still-venerated Atatürk's modernising reforms actually had many casualties. 'Ghost villages', vacated but never reoccupied, were created in the population exchange, in which Greek-speaking people from Anatolia were shipped to Greece, while Muslim residents of Greece were transferred to Turkey.

Following Atatürk's death in 1938, Turkey experienced considerable political turbulence; no fewer than 60 different governments have held office since independence. The army became a key force in national politics, stepping in roughly once a decade to restore national order. The occupation and division of Cyprus became the major issue of the 1970s, and the reigning political and economic chaos prompted a military coup in 1980. A brief period of progress followed the elections in 1983, under Turgut Özal.

During the late 1980s and '90s, Turkey was wracked by conflict with the Kurdistan Workers' Party (PKK), who were fighting for the creation of a Kurdish state in the southeast.

In February 2001 the Turkish economy collapsed spectacularly, and the events of 9/11 hit the previously resilient tourist sector. The International Monetary Fund (IMF) pumped in funds to refloat the economy, and with the 2002 landslide election of the Justice and Development Party (AKP), things started to look up for the country. So far Prime Minister Recep Tayyip Erdoğan's regime has proved moderate and has trodden a skilful path through Turkey's minefield of vested interests. However, many Turks are wary of the party's pro-Islamic leanings.

The AKP's opponents mounted a legal campaign in 2008 to close down the ruling party for 'nonsecular activities'; political meltdown was averted when the Constitutional Court ruled against the closure.

Accession talks with the EU began in October 2005; the resulting concessions and development have fostered a growing optimism. Turkey currently has one of the world's most bullish economies and the AKP's constitutional reform will hopefully herald greater democracy. However, many critics fear the reform will be a blow to secularism, and many of the country's old tensions remain. Sporadic bombings by Kurdish separatists throughout Turkey – including in İstanbul (in 2008 and 2010) and coastal tourist resorts – and skirmishes in southeastern Anatolia persist.

People

Turkey's population of 77.8 million consists predominantly of Turks, with a large Kurdish minority (about 15 million) and much smaller groups of Laz, Hemşin, Arabs, Jews, Greeks and Armenians. Arab influence is strongest in the Antakya (Hatay) area bordering Syria. southeastern Turkey is solidly Kurdish.

Republican Turkey has predominantly adopted a Westernised lifestyle, at least on the surface. In smaller towns and villages, particularly in the east, you will encounter more conservative people.

Turkey is 99% Muslim, about 80% Sunni, with Shiites and Alevis mainly in the east. The country espouses a more relaxed version of Islam than many Middle Eastern nations. Many men drink alcohol and many women uncover their heads (although almost no one touches pork).

Food

The price ranges used in this book are based on the cost of a main course (prices in İstanbul are at the high ends of these brackets):

€€€ More than TL20 (€8.75)

€€ from TL10 to TL20 (€4.50 to €8.75)

€ Less than TL10 (€4.50)

Environment

The Dardanelles, Sea of Marmara and Bosphorus strait divide Turkey between Asia and Europe. Eastern Thrace (European Turkey) makes up 3% of the total land area; the remaining 97% is Anatolia, a vast plateau rising far eastward towards the Caucasus Mountains.

Turkey has 8300km of coastline, much of it dedicated to tourism on the Aegean and Mediterranean coasts – which have mild, rainy winters and hot, dry summers. The Anatolian plateau can be boiling in summer and freezing in winter. The Black Sea coast is mild and humid in summer, and chilly and wet in winter.

Mountainous eastern Turkey is icy cold and snowy in winter, and only pleasantly warm during high summer. The southeastern parts are dry and mild in winter and baking hot during summer.

The ferry and train are the best low-emission ways to get to and around Turkey.

SURVIVAL GUIDE

Directory A–Z

Accommodation

The rates quoted in this chapter are for high season (May to September) and include tax (KDV) and, unless otherwise mentioned, breakfast.

The price ranges used are based on the cost of a double room with private bathroom, and breakfast included:

€€€ More than TL175 (€76)

€€ from TL75 to TL175 (€32 to €76)

€ Less than TL75 (€32)

Camping grounds are mostly found along the coasts and in tourist regions. *Pensions* and hostels will often let you camp on their grounds for a small fee.

There are a few Hostelling International members in Turkey and plenty of hostels in touristy destinations, where dorm beds usually cost about TL15 to TL20 per night.

Most tourist areas offer cosy, family-run *pensions,* where a good, clean single or double costs around TL40 or TL70. *Pensions* generally represent better value than hotels; the cheapest hotels, which charge around TL25 for a single, are mostly used by working-class Turkish men, and are not suitable for solo women.

Virtually nowhere in Turkey is far from a mosque; light sleepers might want to bring earplugs for the early-morning call to prayer.

Activities

Hiking and trekking are highly recommended; options include the national parks and two 500km-long waymarked trails, the **Lycian Way** (Fethiye to Antalya) and St Paul Trail (Perge to Lake Eğirdir). The website www.trekkinginturkey.com has details on the above trails and others, including Western Anatolia's new Evliya Çelebi Way for trekkers and horse riders.

The Lycian Way is particularly wild and beautiful on the coast around Uçağız (east of Kaş) and in the hills around Bezirgan and Sidek (east of Kalkan).

Water and wind sports from diving to paragliding are available on the Aegean and Mediterranean. Those who wish to relax can take an extended *gület* (traditional wooden yacht) trip, or soak in the *hammam*.

Skiing and snowboarding are becoming more popular, with slopes at Uludağ, near Bursa, and Mt Erciyes, above Kayserı. The biggest and most renowned resort is Palandöken (near Erzurum) and the most scenic is Sarıkamış (near Kars).

Business Hours

The following experience some seasonal variations; for example, during the holy month of Ramazan (which currently falls during the summer), the working day gets shortened. Most museums close on Monday.

Banks & post offices 8.30am to noon and 1.30pm to 5pm Mon-Fri

Restaurants 8am to 11am, noon to 4pm, 6pm to 10pm

Bars 4pm to late

Nightclubs 9pm to late

Shops 9am to 6pm Mon to Fri (longer in tourist areas and big cities – including weekend opening)

Embassies & Consulates

Foreign embassies are in Ankara but many countries also have consulates in İstanbul and elsewhere. For more information and contact details of diplomatic missions in Turkey, visit http://tinyurl.com/6ywt8a.

Holidays

New Year's Day 1 January

National Sovereignty & Children's Day 23 April

Youth & Sports Day 19 May

Victory Day 30 August

Republic Day 28 to 29 October

Turkey also celebrates the main Islamic holidays, the most important of which are **Şeker Bayramı** (18 to 20 August in 2012), marking the end of the holy month of **Ramazan**; and about two months later, **Kurban Bayramı** (25 to 29 October in 2012). Due to the fact that these holidays are celebrated according to the Muslim lunar calendar, they take place around 11 days earlier every year.

Internet Access

Internet cafes are widespread. Most accommodation options offer free wi-fi, as do many other businesses. We have used the internet icon (@) where an accommodation option provides a computer with internet access for guest use. In Eating and Drinking reviews, we have used the wi-fi icon (wi-fi) where the business has a network.

Money

Turkey's currency, the Türk Lirası (Turkish Lira; TL), replaced the Yeni Türk Lirası (New Turkish Lira; YTL) in January 2009.

The Turkish Lira comes in notes of five, 10, 20, 50 and 100, and coins of one, five, 10, 25 and 50 kuruş and one lira.

CASH & CREDIT CARDS

Euros and US dollars are the most readily accepted foreign currencies, and the easiest to change. Many exchange offices and banks will change other major currencies such as UK pounds and Japanese yen.

Visa and MasterCard are widely accepted by hotels, shops and restaurants, although not by *pensions* and local restaurants outside main tourist areas. You can also get cash advances on these cards. Amex is more commonly accepted in top-end establishments.

TIPPING & BARGAINING

Round up metered taxi fares and leave waiters and masseurs around 10% to 15% of the bill. Check a *servis ücreti* (service charge) hasn't been automatically added to restaurant bills.

Hotel prices are sometimes negotiable, and you should always bargain for souvenirs.

Post

The Turkish postal service is known as the PTT. *Postanes* (post offices) are indicated by blue-on-yellow 'PTT' signs.

Safe Travel

Although Turkey is in no way a dangerous country to visit, it's always wise to be a little cautious, especially if you're travelling alone. Be wary of pickpockets in buses, markets and other crowded places. Keep an eye out for anyone lurking near ATMs.

Turks are fast drivers and pedestrians should give way to cars and trucks in all situations – and be ready to dive out of the way.

In İstanbul single male visitors are sometimes lured to bars by new Turkish 'friends', then made to pay an outrageous bill. Drugging is also a risk. Be a tad wary who you befriend, especially when you're new to the country.

Travelling in most of Kurdish southeastern Anatolia is safe, but you should check travel advisories before setting off. Sporadic bombings, linked to Kurdish separatist groups, target affluent areas frequented by tourists, including a suicide-bomb attack in İstanbul's Taksim Sq in 2010.

Telephone

Türk Telekom (www.telekom.gov.tr) has a monopoly on phone services, and service is efficient if costly.

If you're only going to make one call, look for signs saying *köntörlü telefon*, where the cost of your call is metered.

Public telephones require phone cards. The cheapest option for international calls is with cards such as IPC, available at post offices.

If you set up a roaming facility with your home network, most mobiles can connect to Turkcell (the most comprehensive network), Vodafone and Avea. To buy a Turkcell SIM card (TL25 to TL35), you need to show your passport and ensure the seller phones your details through to Turkcell.

Visas

Nationals of countries including Denmark, Finland, France, Germany, Israel, Italy, Japan, New Zealand, Sweden and Switzerland don't need a visa to visit Turkey for up to 90 days.

Nationals of countries including Australia, Austria, Belgium, Canada, Ireland, the Netherlands, Norway, Portugal, Spain, the UK and the USA need a visa, but it is just a sticker bought on arrival at the airport or border post.

Your passport must be valid for at least six months from the date you enter the country. Depending on your nationality, the standard visa usually allows for multiple entries.

The cost varies. At the time of writing, Australians and US citizens paid US$20 (or €15), Canadians US$60 (or €45) and British citizens UK£10 (or €15 or US$20).

Customs officers expect to be paid in one of these currencies, often in hard cash. They now accept credit and debit card at major entrance points such as İstanbul's Atatürk International Airport. No photos are required. See the **Ministry of Foreign Affairs** (www.mfa.gov.tr) for the latest information.

RESPECTING MUSLIM SENSIBILITIES

Women should keep their legs, upper arms and neckline covered, except on the beach. In mosques, women should cover their heads and shoulders, and everyone should cover their legs and remove their shoes. Do not eat or drink in the street during Ramazan, and have patience with waiters and other locals who are probably fasting.

Women Travellers

Things may be changing but Turkish society is still basically segregated by gender, especially once you get away from the big cities and tourist resorts. Although younger Turks are questioning the old ways and women hold positions of authority (there has even been a female prime minister), foreign women can find themselves being harassed. It's mostly just catcalls and dubious remarks, but serious assaults do occasionally occur.

Travelling with companions usually improves matters and it's worth remembering that Turkish women ignore men who speak to them in the street. Dressing appropriately will also reduce unwanted attention. In eastern Anatolia, keep your dealings with men formal and polite, not friendly.

Getting There & Away

Air

The cheapest fares for Turkey are usually to İstanbul's **Atatürk International Airport** (www.ataturkairport.com), 23km west of Sultanahmet, and **Sabiha Gökçen International Airport** (www.sgairport.com), 50km east of Sultanahmet on the Asian side of the city.

FERRIES FROM TURKEY

ROUTE	FREQUENCY	DURATION	FARE (ONE WAY/ RETURN)	COMPANY
Ayvalık–Lesvos, Greece	Mon-Sat May-Sep; three times weekly Oct-May	1½ hours	€40/50, car €60/70	Jale Tour (www.jaletour.com)
Çeşme–Chios, Greece	daily mid-May-mid-Sep; twice weekly Sep-May	1½ hours	€25/40, car €70/120	Ertürk (www.erturk.com.tr)
Çeşme–Ancona, Italy	weekly May-Sep	60 hours	one-way €215 to €505, car €260	Marmara Lines (www.marmaralines.com)
Datça–Rhodes	Sat May-Sep	45 minutes	€45/90	Knidos Yachting (www.knidosyachting.com)
Datça–Simi, Greece	Hydrofoil Sat May-Sep; *gület* on demand	Hydrofoil 15 minutes, *gület* 70 minutes	Hydrofoil €30/60; *gület* one-way €60	Knidos Yachting (www.knidosyachting.com)
İstanbul–Sevastapol, Ukraine	weekly	32 hours	return from €185	Sudostroyenie
Kaş–Meis (Kastellorizo), Greece	daily	20 minutes	single or same-day return €20	Meis Express (www.meisexpress.com)
Marmaris–Rhodes	twice daily Apr-Oct, twice weekly Nov-Mar	50 minutes to two hours	from €43/45; car from €95/120	Yeşil Marmaris Travel & Yachting (www.yesilmarmaris.com)
Trabzon–Sochi, Russia	weekly	12 hours	one-way €65	Apollonia II & Princess Victoria Lines

You can also get cheap flights in summer to Antalya, İzmir, Bodrum and Dalaman.

İstanbul is connected to most major European cities by Turkey's national carrier, **Turkish Airlines** (www.thy.com), its budget subsidiary **Sun Express** (www.sunexpress.com), its Turkish competitor **Pegasus Airlines** (www.flypgs.com) and European carriers including **easyJet** (www.easyjet.com).

If you're planning a two- or three-week trip, it's worth enquiring about charter flights, and looking at flight and accommodation packages if you intend to stay on the coast.

In addition to the above, the following offer cheap flights to and around Turkey:

Anadolu Jet (www.anadolujet.com)

Atlasjet (www.atlastjet.com)

British Airways (www.ba.com)

Condor (www.catchafly-t.com)

Corendon (www.corendon.com)

Germanwings (www.germanwings.com)

Just the Flight (www.justtheflight.co.uk)

Onur Air (www.onurair.com.tr)

Thomson Airways (www.thomsonfly.com)

Land

Austria, Bulgaria, Germany, Greece, Macedonia and Romania have the most direct buses to İstanbul; if you're travelling from other countries, you'll likely have to catch a connecting bus.

The Turkish companies **Varan Turizm** (www.varan.com.tr), **Metro Turizm** (www.metroturizm.com.tr) and **Öz Batu** (http://ozbatuturizm.com) operate on the above routes. Sample one-way journeys to/from İstanbul: Berlin (€140, 36 hours); and Sofia in Bulgaria (€25, 10 hours).

See p1262 and p1293 for details of trains between İstanbul and Europe. Also check out **Turkish State Railways** (www.tcdd.gov.tr).

Sea

Departure times change between seasons, with fewer ferries generally running in the winter. **Ferrylines** (www.ferrylines.com) is a good starting point for information.

Getting Around

Bicycle

Riding a bike is a great way of exploring, especially in touristy areas, where you can hire bikes from *pensions* and rental outfits. Road surfaces are acceptable, if a bit rough, though Turkey's notorious road-hog drivers are a hazard.

Bus

Turkish buses go almost everywhere, cheaply, frequently, comfortably and free of smoke. Kamil Koç, Metro Turizm, Ulusoy and Varan Turizm are the better companies, offering greater speed and comfort for slightly higher fares (plus better safety records than many rivals).

A town's *otogar* (bus station) is often outside the centre, but bus companies should offer a *servis* (free shuttle bus) to/from the centre.

Local routes are usually operated by midibuses or *dolmuşes* (minibuses), which might run to a timetable or set off when full.

Fez Bus (www.feztravel.com) is a hop-on, hop-off bus service linking the main resorts of the Aegean and the Mediterranean with İstanbul.

Car & Motorcycle

Turkey has some of the world's most expensive fuel prices (over TL3 per litre) and highest motor-vehicle-accident rates.

An international driving permit (IDP) is handy, but not obligatory.

Turkish car-hire rates are similar to those in Europe.

Türkiye Turing ve Otomobil Kurumu (Turkish Touring & Automobile Association; www.turing.org.tr)

Economy Car Rentals (www.economycarrentals.com) Good rates.

Hitching

Although we don't recommend hitching *(otostop)*, short hitches are not uncommon in Turkey – for example to get from the highway to an archaeological site.

Face the traffic, hold your arm out towards the road, and wave it up and down as if bouncing a basketball.

Many drivers expect payment; commercial vehicles are most likely to pick you up. Women should never hitchhike alone.

Train

Train travel is comfortable; most services have air-con now and sleepers on long routes. Although most people still opt for buses as train journey times can be long, the system is being overhauled and a few fast lines (such as İstanbul–Ankara) are in service.

The train network covers the country fairly well, with the notable exception of along the coastlines.

Useful routes include İstanbul–Ankara, İstanbul–İzmir (including ferry), İzmir–Ankara and Konya–Ankara (opening in 2011).

Long-distance, overnight destinations from İstanbul include Adana, Kars, Konya and Tatvan (Lake Van). Check out **The Man in Seat 61** (www.seat61.com/turkey2) and **Turkish State Railways** (www.tcdd.gov.tr).

Ukraine Україна

Includes »

Best Places to Eat

» Masonic Restaurant, Lviv (p1302)

» Dim Lehend, Lviv (p1302)

» Varenichnaya #1, Kyiv (p1298)

» Kyivska Perepichka, Kyiv (p1298)

Best Places to Stay

» Kosmonaut Hostel, Lviv (p1302)

» Central Station Hostel, Kyiv (p1298)

» Chillout Hostel, Kyiv (p1298)

Why Go?

Big, diverse and largely undiscovered, Ukraine is one of Europe's last genuine travel frontiers, a poor nation rich in colour-splashed tradition, warm-hearted people and off-the-map travel experiences.

'Ukraine' means 'land on the edge', an apt title for this slab of Eurasia in more ways than one. This is the Slavic hinterland on Europe's periphery, but it's also a country creeping toward the edge of change and modernity. One look at its renovated city centres, its resurfaced roads and the infrastructure erected for the 2012 UEFA European Football Championship is enough to see that after two decades of independence, Ukraine is edging toward where it aspires to be, despite the failure of the 2004 Orange Revolution.

Kyiv and Lviv are the main draws but wherever you head, Ukraine is great budget travel territory thanks to the devaluation of the local currency, the hryvnya, in 2008.

When to Go

Kyiv

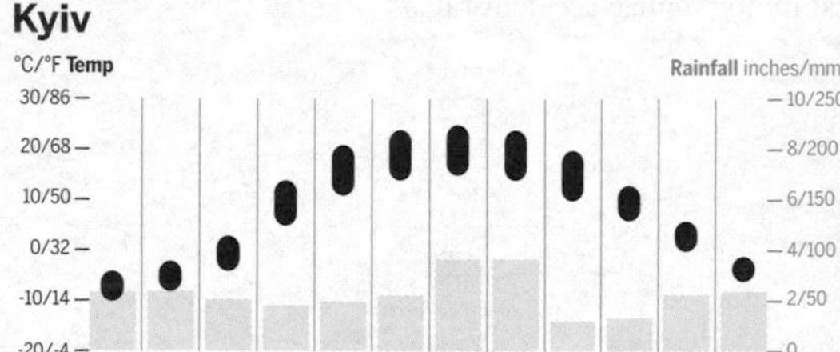

Jan Plunge starkers into the nippy Dnipro river during Kyiv's Epiphany celebrations.

May Take a Sunday-morning stroll through Lviv's centre with church music around you.

Sep Get back to the grind at Lviv's famous coffee festival.

Connections

Ukraine is well linked to its neighbours, particularly Russia and Belarus, with whom it shares the former Soviet rail system. Kyiv is connected by bus or train to Moscow, St Petersburg, Minsk, Warsaw and Budapest, as well as other Eastern European capitals. Odesa is the hub for travelling to Moldova, with several daily buses to Chişinău (some going via Tiraspol); the city also has ferries to Bulgaria, Georgia and Turkey though the service is erratic. From Uzhhorod it's a short journey to the international mainline into Europe at Chop, connecting Ukraine with Slovakia and Hungary. Lviv, the biggest city, is close to the Polish border and an ever increasing number of travellers are taking budget flights to Poland then crossing the border to Lviv by bus or train. It's also possible to take no-frills flights to Budapest and Bratislava and continue to Ukraine from there by train.

ITINERARIES

Two Days

A couple of days are just enough to 'do' Kyiv, starting at its stellar attraction, the Caves Monastery. Follow this with a hike up arty Andriyivsky Uzviz, for a taste of prewar Ukraine before plunging into the beeswax-perfumed Byzantine interior of Unesco-listed St Sophia's Church.

Five Days

Having seen the sights in Kyiv, hop aboard a slow night train to Lviv, Ukraine's most central-European city complete with bean-scented coffee houses, Gothic and Baroque churches and trundling trams.

Essential Food & Drink

» **Borshch** Ukrainian national soup made with beetroot, pork fat and herbs; there's also an aromatic 'green' variety, based on sorrel

» **Kasha** Sometimes translated as porridge, but usually turns out to be buckwheat drenched in milk and served for breakfast

» **Khlib** Bread is often used in religious ceremonies and on special occasions; visitors are traditionally greeted with bread and salt

» **Salo** Basically raw pig fat, cut into slices and eaten with bread or added to soups and other dishes; look out for the 'Ukrainian Snickers bar' – *salo* in chocolate

» **Varenyky** Ukrainian dumplings; similar to Polish *pierogi* – pasta pockets filled with everything from mashed potato to sour cherries

» **Vodka** Also known in Ukraine as *horilka;* accompanies every celebration, red-letter day and get-together in copious amounts

AT A GLANCE

» **Currency** Hryvnya (uah)

» **Language** Ukrainian, Russian

» **Money** ATMs widespread; credit cards accepted at most hotels but only upmarket restaurants

» **Visas** Generally not needed for stays of up to 90 days but Australians and New Zealanders need visas (see p1305)

Fast Facts

» **Area** 603,550 sq km

» **Capital** Kyiv

» **Country code** ☎380

» **Emergency** ☎112

Exchange Rates

Australia	A$1	8.17uah
Canada	C$1	8.12uah
euro zone	€1	11.22uah
Japan	¥100	9.79uah
New Zealand	NZ$1	5.99uah
UK	UK£1	12.77uah
USA	US$1	7.97uah

Set Your Budget

» **Budget hotel room** 200uah

» **Two-course evening meal** 60uah

» **Museum admission** 5 to 15uah

» **0.5L beer** 10 to 20uah

Resources

» See Internet Resources, p1305.

Ukraine Highlights

1. Inspect Kyiv's collection of mummified monks by candlelight at the **Caves Monastery** (p1298)
2. Take a hike up **Andriyivsky Uzviz** (p1298), Kyiv's most atmospheric street
3. Do a spot of cobble-surfing in **Lviv's historical centre** (p1299), packed with churches, museums and eccentric restaurants

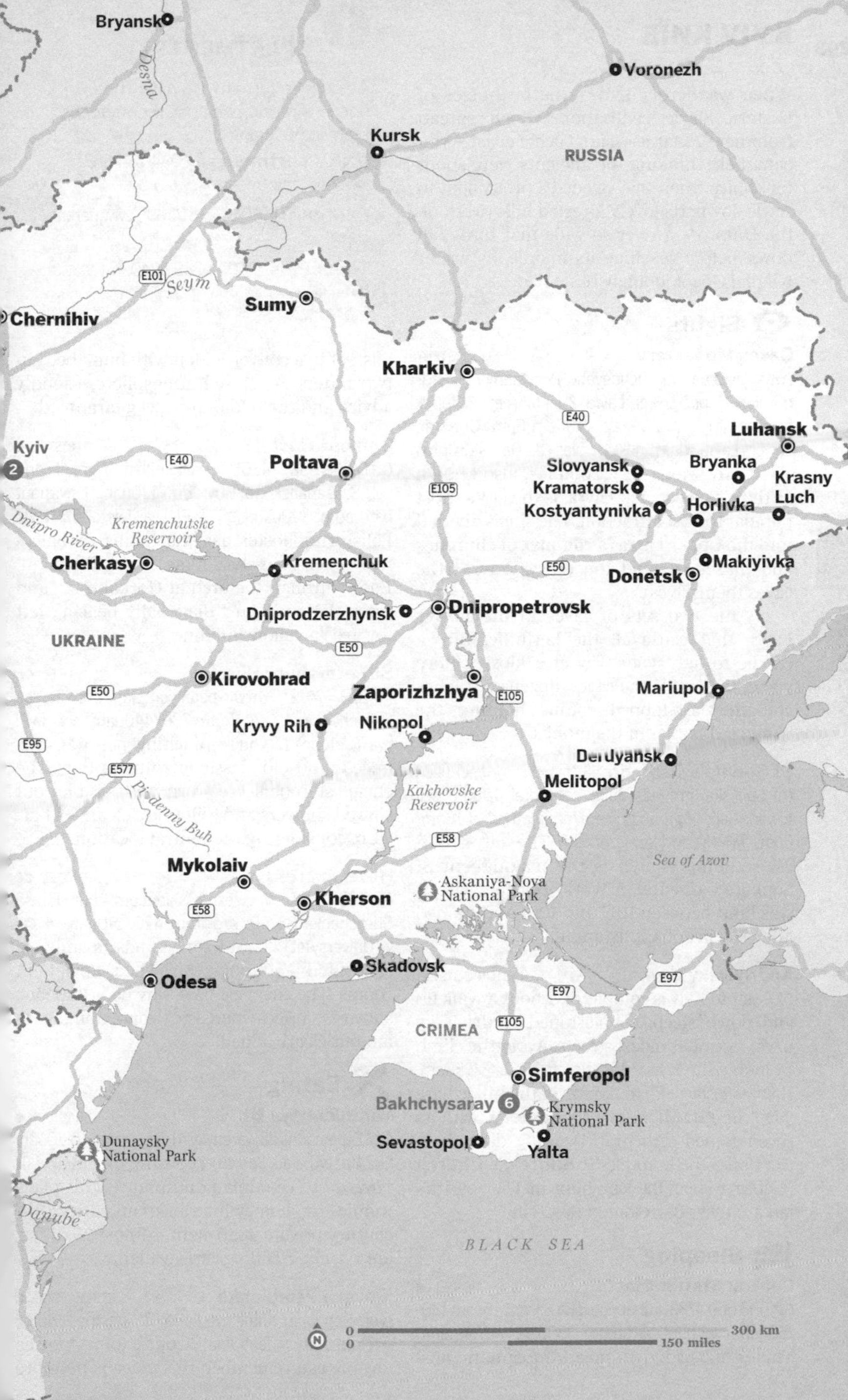

Bryansk
Desna
Voronezh
Kursk
RUSSIA
E101
Seym
Sumy
Chernihiv
Kharkiv
E40
Luhansk
Kyiv
2
E40
Poltava
Slovyansk
Bryanka
Krasny
Luch
Kramatorsk
E105
Kostyantynivka
Horlivka
Dnipro River
Kremenchutske
Reservoir
Cherkasy
Kremenchuk
Makiyivka
E50
Donetsk
Dniprodzerzhynsk
Dnipropetrovsk
UKRAINE
E50
Kirovohrad
Mariupol
E50
Zaporizhzhya
E105
Kryvy Rih
Nikopol
E95
Berdyansk
E577
Melitopol
Pidenny Buh
Kakhovske
Reservoir
E58
Sea of Azov
Mykolaiv
Askaniya-Nova
National Park
Kherson
E58
Skadovsk
Odesa
E97
E97
E105
CRIMEA
Simferopol
Bakhchysaray
6
Krymsky
National Park
Sevastopol
Yalta
Dunaysky
National Park
Danube
BLACK SEA
0
300 km
0
150 miles

KYIV КИЇВ

044 / POP 2.7 MILLION

When wandering Kyiv – the birthplace of Eastern Slavic civilisation, which spread from here as far as Asia's Pacific coast – you can't help thinking the ancients were spoilt for choice when they needed a pretty spot to settle down. Its lovely forested hills overlook the Dnipro – a river so wide that birds fall down before reaching its middle, as writer Nikolai Gogol jokingly remarked.

APARTMENTS

A budget alternative to a Kyiv hotel or hostel is renting an apartment: prices start at 500uah.

UKR Apartments (044-234 5637; www.ukr-apartments.kiev.ua)

Rentguru (044-228 7509; www.uarent.com)

Teren Plus (044-289 3949; www.teren.kiev.ua)

Sights

Caves Monastery MONASTERY
(www.lavra.ua; vul Sichnevoho Povstannya 21; admission Upper/Lower Lavra 20uah/free; Upper Lavra 9am-7pm Apr-Sep, 9.30am-6pm Oct-Mar, Lower Lavra dawn-dusk, caves 8.30am-4.30pm) The Caves Monastery Complex, also known as the Kyiv-Pechersk Lavra, is the city's most popular tourist attraction. The site is divided into the Upper Lavra (a complex of churches and museums) and the Lower Lavra (the caves themselves).

It's the two sets of caves in the Lower Lavra that cause all the kerfuffle. Buy a candle to light your way at a kiosk before you enter. Inside the caves, dozens of niches contain glass-topped coffins holding the blanketed bodies of the monks.

St Sophia's Cathedral CHURCH
(pl Sofiyska; grounds 3uah, cathedral 40uah, bell tower 8uah; grounds 9am-7pm, cathedral 10am-6pm; M Maydan Nezalezhnosti) The city's oldest standing church is the magnificent St Sophia's Cathedral. A World Heritage site, it was built between 1017 and 1031 and named after Hagia Sofia in İstanbul.

Andriyivsky Uzviz HISTORIC STREET
No visit to Kyiv is complete without a walk up and down steep, cobblestoned Andriyivsky uzviz, one of its oldest streets. Avoid the climb by taking the **funicular** (tickets 2uah; 6.30am-11pm; M Poshtova Pl) to the top of the hill, where you'll find **St Michael's Monastery**, with its seven-domed cathedral. Heading down, you can't miss the baroque **St Andrew's Church** (10am-6.30pm Thu-Tue), built in 1754 by Italian architect Bartolomeo Rastrelli.

Sleeping

Central Station Hostel HOSTEL €
(098 669 4783; vul Gogolivska 25, apt 15; dm 130-150uah, r without bathroom 350uah; M Vokzalna) This is one of Kyiv's most atmospheric hostels, set in a converted flat with bunk beds in two rooms. A relaxed atmosphere, friendly advice and the odd pub crawl guaranteed.

Chillout Hostel HOSTEL €
(093 332 4306; chillouthostel@gmail.com; vul Saksahanskoho 30v; dm 130uah, r without bathroom 390uah; ; M Pl Lva Tolstoho) This Polish-run hostel has the bonus of balconies with Thai-style mats for chilling out. Enter through the arch at Gorkoho 22, and cross the courtyard diagonally bearing left towards a yellow building.

St Petersburg Hotel HOTEL €€
(279 7472; www.s-peter.com.ua; bul Tarasa Shevchenka 4; s/d from 280/440uah; ; M Pl Lva Tolstoho) If you're pinching pennies, this once-grand old classic is a fine option. The cheapest rooms are worn and simple, but shared showers and toilets are clean – a bargain, considering the central location.

Hotel Express HOTEL €€
(503 3045; www.expresskiev.com; bul Tarasa Shevchenka 38/40; s/d from 420/510uah; @; M Universytet) The Express has a mix of renovated and non-refurbished Soviet-era rooms. The cheapest have tiny beds and lack showers. Prices increase proportionally as amenities are added.

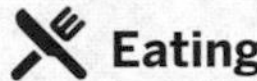

Eating

Varenichnaya #1 UKRAINIAN €
(vul Esplanadna 28; varenyky 41uah, mains 40-70uah; 24hr; M Palats Sportu) Focusing on cheap-ish *varenyky* (Ukrainian dumplings), this place mimics the homey interior of an early 20th-century private apartment. Almost 25 different *varenyky* fillings are available.

Kyivska Perepichka STREET FOOD €
(vul Bohdana Khmelnytskoho 3; pastries 4uah; 11am-9pm; M Teatralna) Around for as long as anyone can remember, this place is no more

than a window issuing sausages in fried dough – but it's an essential Kyiv experience.

Svytlytsa FRENCH, UKRAINIAN €€
(Andriyivsky uzviz 136; mains 60uah; Ⓜ Poshtova pl, Kontraktova pl) This ex-Soviet cafe in a wooden house reinvented itself as a French crêperie, though it keeps serving inexpensive Ukrainian fare. Yacht-themed decor and Russian pop music contribute to the overall schizophrenia.

Krym CRIMEAN TATAR €
(prov Tarasa Shevchenka 1; dishes 23-35uah; Ⓜ Maydan Nezalezhnosti) This dirt-cheap Crimean Tatar basement restaurant spills right out onto maydan Nezalezhnosti in summer. Central Asian favourites plus reasonably priced beer.

Bulochna Yaroslavna PIE CANTEEN €
(vul Yaroslaviv Val 13; pies 3-5uah; ⏲9am-10pm Ⓜ Zoloti Vorota) If a true Kyivite gives you a tour of the city, we'll bet that sooner or later you'll end up munching on a meat- or jam-filled pie and drinking cocoa at a stand-up table here.

Drinking

Palata No.6 BAR
(Ward No.6; vul Vorovskoho 31a; Ⓜ Universytet) This well-hidden dive bar is named after Anton Chekhov's tale about life in a madhouse. White-robed waiters nurse you with excellent steaks and use giant syringes to squirt vodka into your glass.

Kaffa COFFEE HOUSE
(prov Tarasa Shevchenka 3; Ⓜ Maydan Nezalezhnosti) Long-standing Kaffa still serves the most heart-pumping coffees and teas from all over the world. Pots are sufficient for two or three punters.

Repriza CAFE
(vul Bohdana Khmelnytskoho 40/25; Ⓜ Zoloti Vorota) Serves great coffee and delectable sandwiches, pastries and cakes.

Entertainment

Art Club 44 LIVE MUSIC
(www.club44.com.ua; vul Khreshchatyk 44; ⏲10am-2am; Ⓜ Teatralna) With its jazz nights on Tuesdays, Balkan parties on Thursdays and an occasional gig over the weekend, this venue remains a beacon for more sophisticated night creatures.

Xlib CLUB
(www.xlib.com.ua; vul Frunze 12; cover 50-100uah; Ⓜ Kontraktova Ploscha) Decidedly anti glamorous, this hard-to-find place cooks a finely crafted acoustic stew for the iPod generation.

Information

American Medical Center (☎emergency hotline 907 600; http://amcenters.com; vul Berdychivska 1; ⏲24hr; Ⓜ Lukyanivska) English-speaking doctors.

C-Club (Metrograd mall, lowest level; per hr 15uah; ⏲9am-8am) Internet cafe.

Central post office (vul Khreshchatyk 22; internet per hr 12uah; ⏲internet 24hr; Ⓜ Maydan Nezalezhnosti)

Getting There & Away

AIR Most flights use **Boryspil International Airport** (☎490 4777; www.airport-borispol.kiev.ua), about 35km east of the city.

BUS The **Central Bus Station** (pl Moskovska 3) is one stop from Lybidska metro station on trolleybus 4 or 11. **Autolux** (☎451 8628; www.autolux.com.ua) and **Gunsel** (☎525 4505; www.gunsel.com.ua) run the fastest and most comfortable long-distance buses; they have frequent trips to most regional centres.

TRAIN Lviv is served by daytime express trains (100uah, 6½ hours, one or two daily except Mondays), as well as several overnight trains (165uah, nine to 11 hours) from the modern **train station** (pl Vokzalna 2; Ⓜ Vokzalna).

Getting Around

TO/FROM THE AIRPORT Polit/Atass buses run to/from Boryspil airport (25uah, 45 minutes to one hour). Bus 322 (marked 'Політ') departs from behind the train station's South Terminal.

PUBLIC TRANSPORT The metro runs between 6am and midnight. Blue-green plastic tokens *(zhetony)* are sold at windows and dispensers at station entrances. Tickets (1.50uah) for buses, trolleybuses and trams are sold at kiosks or by drivers/conductors.

LVIV ЛЬВІВ

☎032 (7-DIGIT NOS), ☎0322 (6-DIGIT NOS) / POP 735,000

Mysterious, architecturally lovely but retaining a whiff of Sovietness, Lviv boasts that it's Ukraine's least Soviet city. It may have a point. The city's Unesco World Heritage–listed centre was built like a rich layer-cake of neoclassical architecture upon rococo, baroque, Renaissance and Gothic styles. There's nary a concrete Soviet apartment block in sight (in the centre, at least), and it has a deep-rooted coffee-house culture that is oh-so central European.

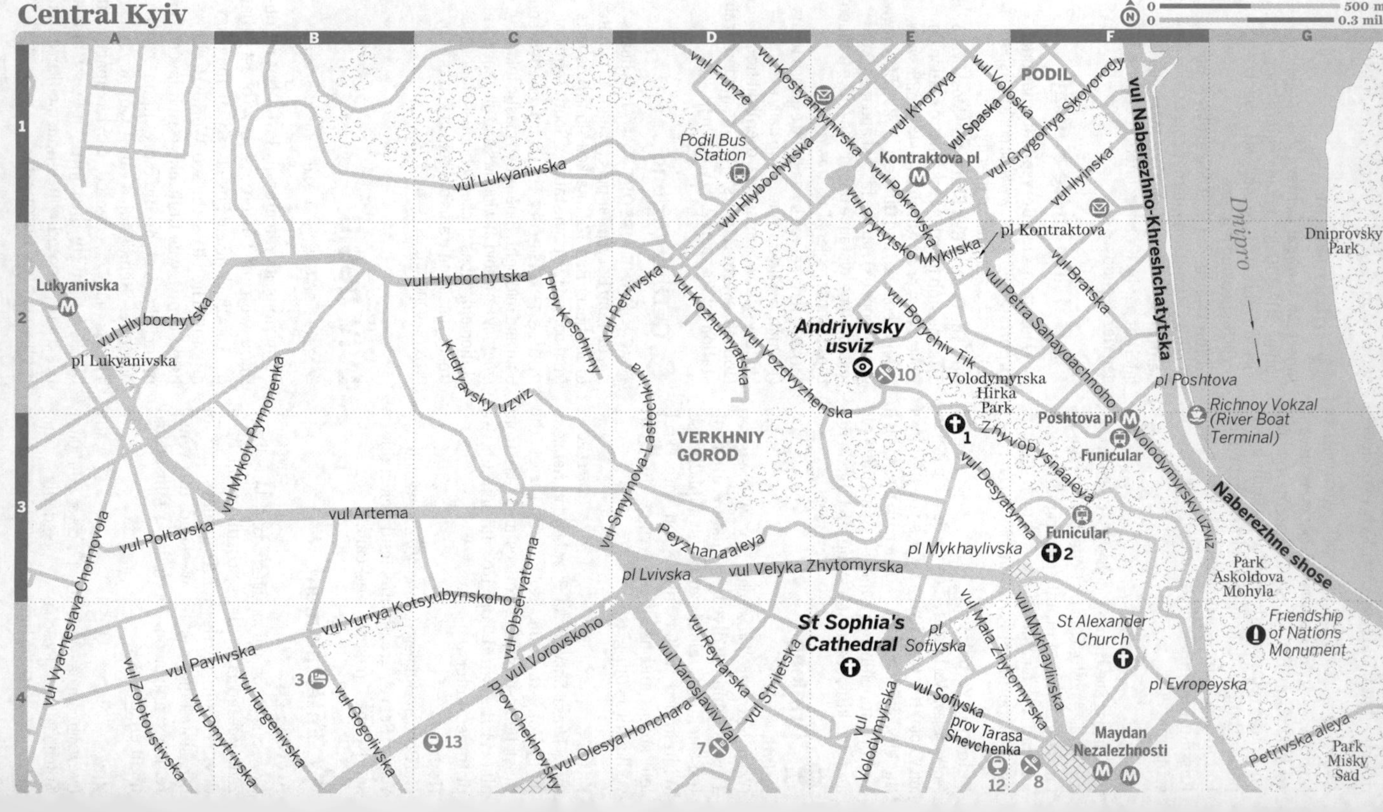
Central Kyiv
500 m
0.3 miles
A
B
C
D
E
F
G
1
2
3
4
vul Frunze
vul Kostyantynivska
vul Khoryva
vul Voloska
vul Spaska
PODIL
vul Grygoriya Skovorody
vul Naberezhno-Khreshchatytska
Dnipro
Dniprovsky Park
Podil Bus Station
Kontraktova pl
vul Ilyinska
vul Lukyanivska
vul Hlybochytska
vul Pokrovska
vul Prytytsko Mykilska
pl Kontraktova
vul Bratska
vul Hlybochytska
prov Kosohirny
vul Petrivska
vul Kozhumyatska
vul Borychiv Tik
vul Petra Sahaydachnoho
Lukyanivska
vul Hlybochytska
pl Lukyanivska
Andriyivsky usviz
10
Kudryavsky uzviz
vul Smyrnova-Lastochkina
vul Vozdvyzhenska
Volodymyrska Hirka Park
pl Poshtova
Richnoy Vokzal (River Boat Terminal)
Poshtova pl
1
Zhyvopysnaaleya
Funicular
vul Mykoly Pymonenka
VERKHNIY GOROD
vul Desyatynna
Volodymyrsky uzviz
Naberezhne shose
vul Artema
Funicular
vul Poltavska
Peyzhanaaleya
pl Mykhaylivska
2
Park Askoldova Mohyla
pl Lvivska
vul Velyka Zhytomyrska
vul Vyacheslava Chornovola
vul Yuriya Kotsyubynskoho
vul Observatorna
St Sophia's Cathedral
pl Sofiyska
vul Mala Zhytomyrska
vul Mykhaylivska
St Alexander Church
Friendship of Nations Monument
vul Pavlivska
vul Vorovskoho
vul Reytarska
vul Striletska
3
vul Yaroslaviv Val
pl Evropeyska
vul Zolotoustivska
vul Dmytrivska
vul Turgenivska
vul Gogolivska
prov Chekhovsky
vul Olesya Honchara
vul Volodymyrska
vul Sofiyska
prov Tarasa Shevchenka
Maydan Nezalezhnosti
Petrivska aleya
Park Misky Sad
13
7
12
8

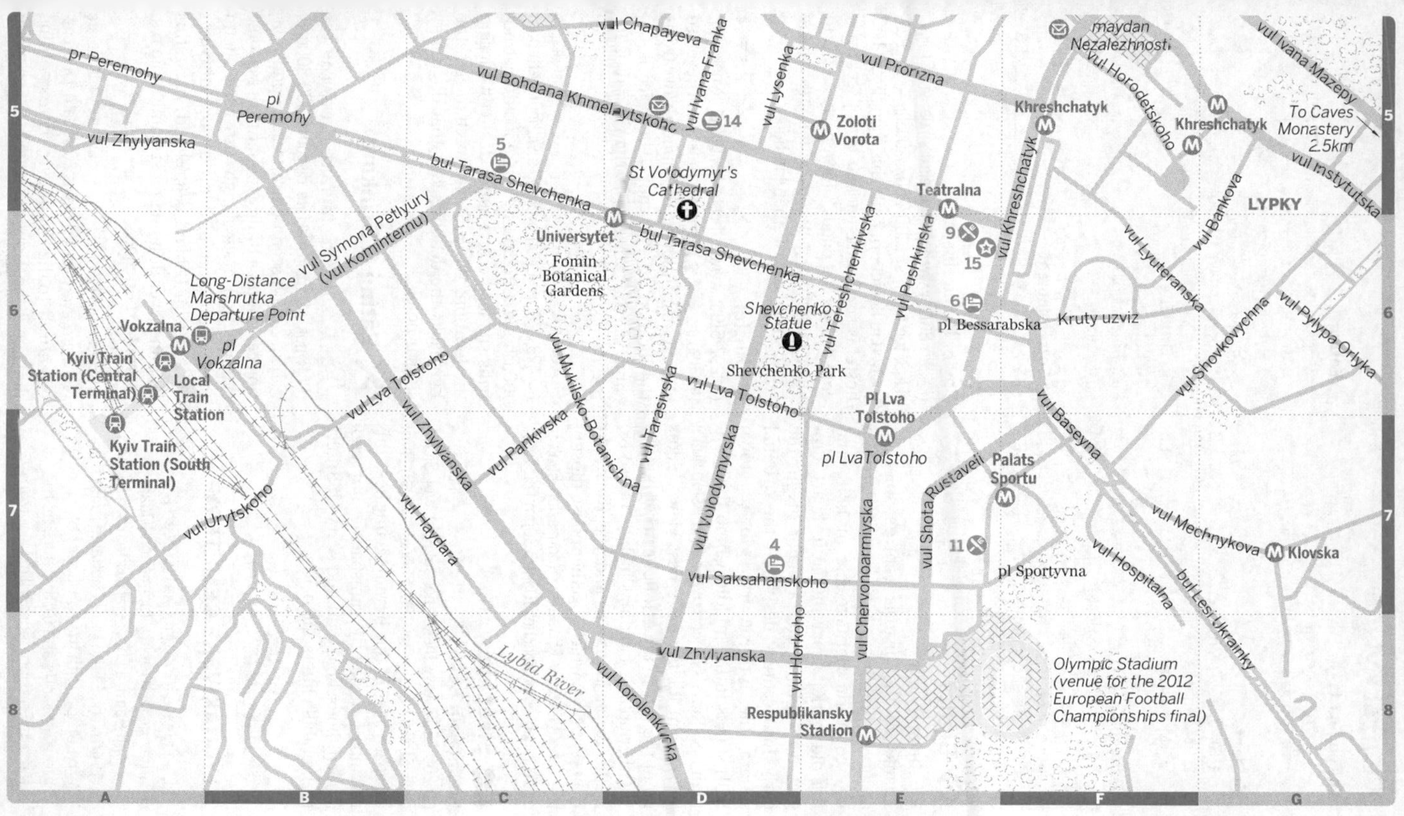
A
B
C
D
E
F
G
5
6
7
8
pr Peremohy
vul Chapayeva
vul Bohdana Khmelnytskoho
vul Ivana Franka
14
vul Lysenka
vul Prorizna
maydan Nezalezhnosti
vul Horodetskoho
vul Ivana Mazepy
To Caves Monastery 2.5km
Khreshchatyk
Khreshchatyk
Zoloti Vorota
pl Peremohy
vul Zhylyanska
5
bul Tarasa Shevchenka
St Volodymyr's Cathedral
Teatralna
vul Khreshchatyk
vul Bankova
LYPKY
vul Instytutska
vul Symona Petlyury (vul Kominternu)
Universytet
bul Tarasa Shevchenka
9
15
vul Lyuteranska
Fomin Botanical Gardens
vul Pushkinska
vul Tereshchenkivska
Long-Distance Marshrutka Departure Point
6
Kruty uzviz
Shevchenko Statue
pl Bessarabska
vul Shovkovychna
vul Pylypa Orlyka
Vokzalna
pl Vokzalna
Kyiv Train Station (Central Terminal)
Local Train Station
vul Lva Tolstoho
vul Mykilsko-Botanichna
vul Tarasivska
Shevchenko Park
vul Lva Tolstoho
Pl Lva Tolstoho
vul Zhylyanska
vul Pankivska
pl Lva Tolstoho
vul Baseyna
Kyiv Train Station (South Terminal)
vul Volodymyrska
vul Shota Rustaveli
Palats Sportu
vul Urytskoho
vul Haydara
vul Chervonoarmiyska
vul Mechnykova
Klovska
4
11
vul Hospitalna
vul Saksahanskoho
pl Sportyvna
bul Lesi Ukrainky
vul Zhylyanska
vul Horkoho
Lybid River
vul Korolenkivska
Olympic Stadium (venue for the 2012 European Football Championships final)
Respublikansky Stadion

Central Kyiv

Sights

Ploshcha Rynok SQUARE

Thanks to the historic centre's splendid array of buildings, Lviv was declared a Unesco World Heritage site in 1998, and this old market square lies at its heart. Progressively rebuilt after a major fire in the early 16th century destroyed the original square, the 19th-century **ratusha** (town hall) stands in the middle. Climb the 65m-high neo-Renaissance **tower** (admission 5uah; 9am-6pm) for the city's best views. Signs point the way to the 4th-floor ticket booth.

Other notable buildings include house No 2, the **Black Mansion**, and the **Kornyakt House** at No 6, which together house most of the **Lviv History Museum** (admission 5uah to each branch; all branches 10am-5.30pm Thu-Tue).

Sleeping

Kosmonaut Hostel HOSTEL €

(260 1602; www.thekosmonaut.com; vul Sichovykh Striltsiv 8; dm/tw 100/250uah;) Not as space-age as the branding implies, this resembles a slightly ramshackle but cool student household. Fun and scary USSR-era memorabilia litters the place.

DON'T MISS

LYCHAKIVSKE CEMETERY

Don't leave town until you've seen this amazing **cemetery** (admission 10uah; 9am-6pm), a short tram ride from the centre. This is the Père Lachaise of Eastern Europe, with the same sort of overgrown grounds and Gothic aura as the famous Parisian necropolis. Take tram 7.

Soviet Home Hostel HOSTEL €

(225 8611; www.homehostels.com.ua; vul Drukarska 3, top fl; dm/s/d 100/280/320uah;) Festooned in Soviet-era junk, this friendly, 20-bed hostel is small-scale enough to not feel overcrowded yet big enough for a party crowd to form. Dorms are generous with not too many bunks and there's a small kitchen.

Art Hostel HOSTEL €

(297 5195; www.arthostel.lviv.ua; pl Rynok 3/4; dm 85uah;) Bright, messy and ever so slightly institutional; the main drawcard is the location on Pl Rynok. The price is the same whether you stay in the six-bed or 10-bed dorms.

Hotel Lviv HOTEL €

(423 270; pr Chornovola 7; s without bathroom 100uah, s/d 200/250uah) You're looking at no-frills singles here, a super deal considering the location. While Soviet in character, the Lviv lacks the deal-breakers that dog many similar hotels.

Eating & Drinking

TOP CHOICE **Masonic Restaurant** UKRAINIAN €€€

(Pl Rynok 14; mains before discount 300-800uah; 11am-2am) A secret entrance, an odd initiation ceremony, a dining room full of Masonic symbols and a shockingly expensive menu (make sure you pick up a 90% discount card at Dim Lehend beforehand) make this Ukraine's weirdest and most unmissable restaurant experience.

Dim Lehend LVIV-THEMED €€

(vul Staroyevreyska 48; mains 20-75uah) Dedicated entirely to the city of Lviv, there's nothing dim about the 'House of Legends'. The menu pamphlet you receive at the door is more a map used to explore the five floors of Lviv-themed paraphernalia. The coffee and desserts are central European bliss.

Dzyga CAFE €€
(vul Virmenska 35; 9am-11.30pm) This cafe-cum-art gallery has a relaxed vibe and is particularly popular with bohemian, alternative types. Organises many events in and around Lviv.

Puzata Khata CAFE €
(vul Sichovykh Striltsiv 12; mains from 10uah; 8am-11pm) This super-sized version of Ukraine's number-one restaurant chain stands out for its classy, Hutsul-themed interior and pure Ukrainian-rock soundtrack.

Pyrizhky PIE CANTEEN €
(vul Slovatskoho 4; pyrizhky 3-5uah) This simple canteen has been serving budget *pyrizhky* (pies/turnovers) to students, and now budget travellers, for over 50 years.

Information

Central post office (vul Slovatskoho 1)

Chorna Medea (vul Petra Doroshenka 50; per hr 6uah; 24hr) Internet cafe.

Tourist Information Centre (254 6079; www.visitlviv.net; Ratusha, pl Rynok 1; 10am-7pm Mon-Fri, to 6pm Sat, to 5pm Sun)

Getting There & Away

AIR Lviv's new **airport** (www.airport.lviv.ua) is 9km west of the centre. Take trolleybus 9 to the university or *marshrutka* 95 to the centre. Book flights to Kyiv (four daily) through **Kiy Avia** (272 7818; www.kiyavia.com; vul Hnyatuka 20-22).

BUS The inconveniently located **main bus station** (vul Stryska) is 8km south of the centre. Take trolleybus 5.

TRAIN Lviv's train station is 2km west of the centre. Take trams 1 and 9 to/from the centre. Kyiv is served by daytime express (100uah, 6½ hours, daily except Tuesday) and overnight trains. Book at the station or the **train ticket office** (vul Hnatyuka 20; 8am-2pm & 3-8pm Mon-Sat, to 6pm Sun).

UNDERSTAND UKRAINE

History

Before the 13th century, Ukraine was yanked back and forth by raiders from the East such as the Huns and Mongols before settling in the hands of Russian princes. By the 15th century, groups of fierce warriors calling themselves Cossacks fought anyone who encroached upon their borders or belief system (Orthodoxy).

Ukraine was a founding member of the USSR in 1922. In 1932 and 1933, Stalin engineered a famine, killing millions in Ukraine. In WWII, an estimated six million Ukrainians perished.

The country was the scene of the world's worst nuclear accident when the Chornobyl atomic power station exploded in April 1986.

Ukraine declared independence from the USSR in August 1991, and Leonid Kuchma led the country during the late '90s and early noughties. Kuchma's close ally Viktor Yanukovych ran in the 2004 presidential elections, challenged by Viktor Yushchenko, an opposition leader allegedly poisoned a week before the poll.

In a run-off between the two, Yanukovych was declared winner amid allegations of vote-rigging. Suspecting foul play, the Ukrainian population came out en masse throughout the winter of 2004, gathering on Kyiv's maydan Nezalezhnosti with tents and orange flags. This so-called 'Orange Revolution' forced a repeat run-off on 26 December, which Yushchenko won.

Between 2005 and 2010 the blond-braided Yulia Tymoshenko, a weak president Yushchenko and a resurgent Viktor Yanukovych engaged in an absurd political soap opera featuring snap elections, fisticuffs in parliament and musical chairs in the prime minister's office. Russia turned off the gas at opportune moments. The upshot was disillusionment with the Orange Revolution among the population and Viktor Yanukovych's victory in the April 2010 presidential elections.

People

Having endured centuries of many different foreign rulers, Ukrainians are a long-suffering people. They're nothing if not survivors; historically they've had to be, but after suffering a kind of identity theft during centuries of Russian rule in particular, this ancient nation that 'suddenly' emerged some 20 years ago is starting to forge a new personality.

This is a religious and superstitious society, in which traditional gender roles and strong family and community ties still bind. It's a culture where people are sometimes friendly and more generous than they can really afford to be. Paradoxically, it's also one in which remnants of Soviet mentality remain, with many people leading a kind of double life – snarling, elbowing Homo Sovieticus outside of the home but generous, hospitable Europeans around their kitchen tables.

Despite centuries of invasion and settlement, most people describe themselves as Ukrainians and, hence, of Slavic origin. According to the last census (2001) of the country's 45 million people, 78% are ethnically Ukrainian, while 17% describe their ethnicity as Russian.

Broadly speaking, Russian-speaking Easterners look toward Russia, while Ukrainian-speaking Westerners look toward a future in Europe.

Food & Drink

'*Borshch* and bread – that's our food.' With this national saying, Ukrainians admit theirs is a cuisine of comfort, full of hearty, mild dishes designed for fierce winters rather than one of gastronomic zing. See p1295 for descriptions of traditional dishes.

Ukraine produces some very quaffable beers. Chernihivske, Lvivske, Slavutych and Obolon are the most popular brands. The best wines still come from neighbouring Moldova. The biggest name in Ukrainian vodka is **Nemiroff** (www.nemiroff.ua).

Restaurant (ресторан) and cafe (кафе) sound similar in English and Ukrainian when pronounced. A *stolova* (столова) is a self-service canteen. Price ranges used in this chapter for eateries are as follows:

€€€ more than 150uah

€€ 50uah to 150uah

€ less than 50uah

SURVIVAL GUIDE

Directory A–Z

Accommodation

Although the traveller's single biggest expense in Ukraine, accommodation is more affordable than it once was thanks to the 2008 devaluation of the hryvnya.

Ukraine has a bewildering array of hotel and room types. At the bottom are Soviet-era budget crash pads for as little as 50uah, at the top 'six-star' overpriced luxury in OTT surroundings. Everything in between can be very hit-and-miss and there are no national standards to follow.

Kyiv and Lviv have a healthy gaggle of backpacker digs. **Hostelling Ukraine International** (www.hihostels.com.ua) gathers together all of Ukraine's hostels under one site. Hospitality clubs such as www.couchsurfing.com and www.hospitalityclub.org have thousands of Ukrainian members offering homestays.

Accommodation price ranges used in this chapter for a high-season double room with bathroom, not including breakfast:

€€€ more than 800uah

€€ 400uah to 800uah

€ less than 400uah

Business Hours

Business hours can be hard to pin down in Ukraine. Lunch breaks are common, Sunday closing rare.

Banks & offices 9am-5pm or 10am-6pm

Shops 9am-6pm, big-city shops to 8pm or 9pm

Sights 9am-5pm or 6pm, closed at least one day a week

Restaurants noon-11pm

Embassies & Consulates

The following are all in Kyiv.

Australia (☎044-235 7586; Apt 11, vul Kominternu 18; Ⓜ Vokzalna)

Belarus (☎044-537 5200; vul Mykhayla Kotsyubynskoho 3; Ⓜ Universytet)

Canada (☎044-590 3100; www.canadainternational.gc.ca/ukraine; Yaroslaviv Val 31; Ⓜ Zoloti Vorota)

Moldova (☎044-521 2279; www.ucraina.mfa.md; vul Sichnevoho Povstannya 6; Ⓜ Arsenalna)

Russia (☎044-244 0961; www.embrus.org.ua; pr Vozdukhoflotsky 27; Ⓜ Vokzalna); consulate (☎044-284 6816; vul Kutuzova 8; Ⓜ Pecherska)

UK (☎044-490 3660; http://ukinukraine.fco.gov.uk/en; vul Desyatynna 9; Ⓜ Maydan Nezalezhnosti); consulate (☎044-494 3418; Artyom Centre, vul Hlybochytska 4; Ⓜ Lukyanivska)

USA (☎044-490 0000; http://kyiv.usembassy.gov; vul Yuriya Kotsyubynskoho 10; Ⓜ Lukyanivska); consulate (☎044-207 7071; vul Mykoly Pymonenka 6; Ⓜ Lukyanivska)

Holidays

New Year's Day 1 January

Orthodox Christmas 7 January

International Women's Day 8 March

Orthodox Easter (Paskha) April

Labour Day 1–2 May

Victory Day (1945) 9 May

Constitution Day 28 June

Independence Day (1991) 24 August

Internet Resources

» **Brama** (www.brama.com) Most useful gateway site

» **Infoukes** (www.infoukes.com) Ukrainian-Canadian pages featuring online maps and visitor tips

» **Ukraine.com** (www.ukraine.com) Up-to-date news and heaps of information

» **Encyclopedia of Ukraine** (www.encyclopediaofukraine.com) One of the largest sources of info on Ukraine

Money

Coins come in denominations of one, five, 10, 25 and 50 kopecks, plus the rare one hryvnya. Notes come in one, two, five, 10, 20, 50, 100, 200 and 500 hryvnya.

US dollar (post-1990 issue only), euro and Russian rouble notes (in pristine condition) are the easiest currencies to exchange. Credit cards are increasingly accepted but Ukraine remains primarily a cash economy.

Telephone

Ukraine recently simplified the way numbers are dialled, banishing Soviet-era prefixes and dialling tones for good. All numbers now start with ☎0.

Ukraine's country code is ☎380. To call Kyiv from London, dial ☎00 38 044 and the subscriber number. To call internationally, dial ☎0, wait for a second tone, then dial zero again, followed by the country code, city code and number.

If you intend making a few calls from your mobile, it's more economical to get a prepaid SIM card locally. European GSM phones usually work in Ukraine.

Visas

Visa-free stays of up to 90 days are available to citizens of the EU, Canada, USA, Iceland, Japan, Norway, Switzerland, Andorra, Liechtenstein, Monaco, San Marino, South Korea and the Vatican.

Visas are required for citizens of most other countries.

Getting There & Away

The majority of visitors fly to Ukraine – generally to Kyiv. However, low-cost flights to neighbouring countries mean a growing number of travellers enter the country overland. Passports must be valid for at least one month beyond travellers' intended departure from Ukraine.

Air

Low-cost airlines have struggled to find their way into Ukraine, but the situation is likely to change once Lviv's new terminal is built. Airports include the following:

Boryspil International Airport (KBP; www.airport-borispol.kiev.ua) Kyiv's main airport.

Lviv International Airport (LWO; www.airport.lviv.ua)

Bus & Train

Buses are best for short hops of up to three hours between towns. Services are frequent and cheap.

Both Kyiv and Lviv are well connected to major cities by train in both Eastern and Western Europe.

Car & Motorcycle

To bring your own vehicle into the country, you'll need original registration papers (no photocopies) and a 'Green Card' International Motor Insurance Certificate.

Getting Around

Air

Domestic airlines **AeroSvit** (www.aerosvit.ua) and **Dniproavia** (www.dniproavia.com) code-share four flights daily between Kyiv and Lviv.

Bus & Train

Buses run between Kyiv and Lviv (50uah to 90uah, nine hours, four daily).

An express daytime train (100uah, 6½ hours, daily except Tuesday) and at least 10 regular trains per day, many overnight (165uah, nine to 11 hours), run between Lviv and Kyiv.

Survival Guide

Europe Directory A-Z

Accommodation

Europe offers the fullest possible range of budget accommodation, from camping grounds, hostels and student dormitories to private rooms, guest houses and cheap hotels. Plus there are more novel options, such as farm stays and couch surfing. In this guide we've listed reviews by author preference.

Unless otherwise stated in individual reviews or in country directories, all hotels and hostels in this book include a private bathroom and do not include breakfast.

Categories

Accommodation options in this book generally range from no stars to two stars, with the occasional smarter 'splurge' option. The very cheapest options are dorms or hostels with shared bathrooms and toilets, while at the upper end there are self-contained rooms with en suite facilities, TV and free wi-fi.

Price Icons

Each sleeping option has an indicative price category next to it (from **€** to **€€€**) – these correspond to the price of the room relative to that country's price breakdown.

Reservations

During peak holiday periods, particularly Easter, summer and Christmas – and any time of year in popular destinations such as London, Paris and Rome – it's wise to book ahead. Most places can now be reserved online. In general, always try to book directly with the establishment; this means you're paying just for your room, with no surcharge going to a middleman as occurs with many hostel-booking websites.

Seasons

Rates in this guide are for high season; rates often drop outside the high season by as much as 50%.

High season in ski resorts is usually between Christmas and New Year and around the February–March winter holidays.

B&Bs & Guest Houses

Guest houses (*pension, Gasthaus, chambre d'hôte* etc) and B&Bs offer greater comfort than hostels for a marginally higher price. Most are simple affairs, sometimes still with shared bathroom facilities.

In private rooms with a local family, or in a small guest house, you benefit from greater contact with locals. You'll still have privacy and autonomy, but remember you won't be able to bring the party back to your place.

In some destinations, particularly in Eastern Europe, locals wait in train stations touting rented rooms. Just be sure such accommodation isn't in a far-flung suburb that requires an expensive taxi ride to and from town. Also check that both parties are clear on price beforehand, and remember that in these cases it's unwise to leave valuables in your room when you go out.

Many B&Bs (bed and breakfasts) in the UK and Ireland aren't budget accommodation at all. Even the lowliest tend to have midrange prices and a new generation of 'designer' B&Bs are positively top end.

Camping

Camping is the cheapest accommodation option. It's newly trendy in parts of Europe, such as the UK (albeit with designer tents, ecotents and Airstream caravans; see, for example, www.coolcamping.co.uk). In other countries, such as the Czech Republic, Germany, the Netherlands and Poland, it has never gone out of fashion.

BOOK YOUR STAY ONLINE

For more reviews by Lonely Planet authors, check out hotels.lonelyplanet.com/. You'll find independent reviews, as well as recommendations on the best places to stay. Best of all, you can book online.

In large European cities, most camping grounds are some distance from the centre, so you'll need your own transport. As few budget travellers have that, this book lists easily accessible camping grounds only, or includes sites where it's common for travellers to bed down en masse under the stars (for example, on some Greek islands).

National tourist offices provide lists of camping grounds, and camping organisation contacts are also listed in some individual country directories of this book. At designated grounds, there will usually be a charge per tent or site, per person and per vehicle. In busy areas, in busy seasons, it's sometimes necessary to book.

Camping other than at designated grounds is difficult in Western Europe, because it's hard to find a suitably private spot.

Camping is also illegal without the permission of the local authorities (the police or local council office) or the landowner. Don't be shy about asking; you might be pleasantly surprised.

In some countries, such as Austria, the UK, France and Germany, free camping is illegal on all but private land, and in Greece it's illegal altogether but not enforced. This doesn't prevent hikers from occasionally pitching their tent, and you'll usually get away with it if you have a small tent, are discreet, stay just one or two nights, decamp during the day and don't light a fire or leave rubbish. At worst, you'll be woken by the police and asked to move on.

In Eastern Europe, free camping is more widespread.

Homestays & Farmstays

You needn't volunteer on a farm to sleep on it. In Switzerland and Germany, there's the opportunity for ordinary tourists to sleep in barns or 'hay hotels'. It saves you money and is a great experience. For further details, visit **Abenteuer im Stroh** (www.abenteuer-stroh.ch) and **Hay Hotels** (www.heuhotel.de, in German). When their cows are out to pasture in summer, or even after they've been brought in for the winter come early October, farmers charge travellers a small amount to sleep on straw in their hay barns or lofts (listening to the jangle of cow or goat bells beneath your head). Farmers provide cotton undersheets (to avoid straw pricks) and woolly blankets for extra warmth, but guests need their own sleeping bag and torch.

Hostels

Hostels in Europe vary enormously from veritable backpacker palaces to real dumps. We've tried to ensure we don't include any of the latter, but expect there to be a variation in standards across the region.

HI Hostels, ie ones affiliated to **Hostelling International** (www.hihostels.com), offer the cheapest (secure) roof over your head in Europe and you don't have to be particularly young to use them. Only southern German hostels enforce a strict age limit of 26 years. That said, if you're over 26 you'll frequently pay a small surcharge (usually about €3) to stay in an official hostel.

Most HI hostels have dorm rooms sleeping four to five people, although larger ones do exist. Hostel rules vary per facility and country, but some ask that guests vacate the rooms for cleaning purposes or impose a curfew. Most offer a complimentary breakfast, although the quality of this varies.

You need to be a YHA or HI member to use HI-affiliated hostels, but nonmembers can stay by paying an extra charge of a few euros, which will then be set against future membership. After sufficient nights (usually six), you automatically become a member. To join, ask at any hostel or contact your national hostelling office, which you'll find on the HI website, where you can also make online bookings.

There are also many private hostelling organisations in Europe and hundreds of unaffiliated backpacker hostels. Private hostels have fewer rules (eg no curfew, no daytime lockout), more self-catering kitchens and fewer large, noisy school groups. However, while HI hostels must meet minimum safety and cleanliness standards, facilities vary greatly in private hostels. Dorms in many private hostels can be mixed sex. If you aren't happy to share mixed dorms, be sure to ask when you book.

Hotels

Hotels are usually the most expensive accommodation option, though at their lower end there is little to differentiate them from guest houses or even hostels.

Be careful when choosing inexpensive hotels around bus and train station areas. They can be convenient for late-night or early-morning arrivals and departures, but some hotels are unofficial brothels or just downright sleazy places where things go missing in the night.

If you can, check the room beforehand and make sure you're clear on price and what it covers.

Discounts for longer stays are usually possible and hotel owners in southern Europe *might* be open to a little bargaining if times are slack. In many countries it's common for business hotels (usually more than two stars) to slash their rates by up to 40% on Friday and Saturday nights.

University Accommodation

Some university towns rent out their student accommodation during the holiday periods. This is a popular practice in France, the UK and many Eastern European countries (see individual country chapters for more details). University accommodation will sometimes be in single rooms (although it's more commonly in doubles or triples) and might have cooking facilities. For details inquire at individual colleges or universities, at student information offices or local tourist offices.

Books

Europe has inspired a huge amount of writing, though little that covers the entire complex continent. Here are a few exceptions that make for great background reading.

» In *Neither Here nor There: Travels in Europe*, Bill Bryson retraces his youthful 1970s European tour some 20 years later as an older, less agile, more sober adult.

» Tim Moore reaches further back into history with *Continental Drifter*. Here, he muses on the origins of the 17th-century European Grand Tour, by which well-to-do young Englishmen sought to educate themselves – all the while re-creating it himself, sleeping rough in a vintage Rolls Royce and (crumpled) velvet suit.

» Peter Moore (no relation to Tim) makes life even more difficult for himself in *The Wrong Way Home*. The 'wrong way' turns out to be without a plane journey, from London to Sydney. Although the travelogue naturally ventures into Asia and Europe.

» For something perhaps more akin to your own experience, try *Rite of Passage: Tales of Backpacking 'round Europe*. Edited by Lisa Johnson, it's a group of stories by young travellers conquering the continent for the first time. From crowded hostels to heated flings, this book taps into the seemingly insignificant events that fuel lifelong memories.

» Classic European travel tales come from two leading authors. In *A Tramp Abroad*, Mark Twain chronicles, with his usual wit, a 15-month 'walking tour' (by train and coach) through central Europe and the Alps in the 19th century. Patrick Leigh Fermor's *A Time of Gifts* is widely regarded as a masterpiece of travel literature. Writing in 1977, Fermor looks back on the time when, as a teenager in 1934, he walked from the Hoek van Holland to Constantinople (present-day İstanbul), relying on the kindness of strangers to house and feed him. This book takes him as far as Hungary, where another book, *Between the Woods and the Water*, takes over.

STAY FOR FREE

Wish you had mates all over Europe so you could crash on their sofas when you were travelling? Don't we all? Luckily, with the phenomenon of online hospitality clubs, you can make it a reality. **Couch Surfing** (www.couchsurfing.com) is the perfect example, linking travellers with hundreds of thousands of global residents who'll let you occupy their couch or spare room – and sometimes show you around town – all cost-free. Couch Surfing is unusual in not insisting you return the favour by hosting other travellers at some point; it's entirely up to you.

Similar schemes, such as **Global Freeloaders** (www.globalfreeloaders.com) and **Hospitality Club** (www.hospitalityclub.org), tend to be stricter on that, although both are happy for you to first enjoy others' hospitality before reciprocating.

If you're worried about how safe this is, there are many security measures in place, with members verified and vouched for by others, and we've not heard any bad stories. However, at the very least, always let friends and family know where you're staying and carry your mobile phone with you.

Female travellers might want to investigate the women-only, membership-based **5W** (www.womenwelcomewomen.org.uk).

Business Hours

In most of Europe businesses are open 9am to 6pm Monday to Friday, and 9am to 1pm or 5pm on Saturday. In smaller towns there may be a one- to two-hour closure for lunch. Some shops close on Sunday. Businesses also close on national holidays and local feast days.

Banks have the shortest opening times, often closing between 3pm and 5pm, and occasionally even shutting for lunch. They only open on weekdays.

Restaurants typically open around noon until midnight and bars open around 6pm. Museums usually close on Monday or (less commonly) on Tuesday.

Customs Regulations

The European Union (EU) has a two-tier customs system: one for goods bought duty-free for importation to or exportation from the EU, and one for goods bought in another EU country where taxes and duties have already been paid.

» Entering or leaving the EU, you are allowed to carry duty-free: 200 cigarettes, 50 cigars or 250g of tobacco; 2L of still wine plus 1L of spirits over 22% alcohol or another 2L of wine (sparkling or otherwise); 50g of perfume, 250cc of eau de toilette.

» Travelling from one EU country to another, the duty-paid limits are: 800 cigarettes, 200 cigars, 1kg of tobacco, 10L of spirits, 20L of fortified wine, 90L of wine (of which not more than 60L is sparkling) and 110L of beer.

» Non-EU countries often have different regulations and many countries forbid the exportation of antiquities and cultural treasures; see individual country chapters.

Discount Cards

Camping Cards

The Camping Card International (CCI; formerly the Camping Carnet) is camping ground ID that can be used instead of a passport when checking into a camping ground and includes third-party insurance. Many camping grounds offer a small discount if you sign in with one. CCIs are issued by automobile associations, camping federations and, sometimes, at camping grounds.

Rail Passes

If you plan to visit more than a few countries, or one or two countries in-depth, you might save money with a rail pass; see p1329.

Student Cards

The **International Student Travel Confederation** (ISTC; www.istc.org) issues three cards for students, teachers and under-26s, offering thousands of worldwide discounts on transport, museum entry, youth hostels and even some restaurants. These cards are: the International Student Identity Card (ISIC), the International Teacher Identity Card (ITIC) and the International Youth Travel Card (IYTC). You can check the full list of discounts and where to apply for the cards on the ISTC website. Issuing offices include **STA Travel** (www.statravel.com).

For under-26s, there's also a specific European card, the **Euro<26** (www.euro26.org). Many countries have raised the age limit for this card to 30.

Electricity

Europe generally runs on 220V, 50Hz AC, but there are exceptions. The UK runs on 230/240V AC, and some old buildings in Italy and Spain have 125V (or even 110V in Spain). The Continent is moving towards a 230V standard. If your home country has a vastly different voltage you will need a transformer for delicate and important appliances.

The UK and Ireland use chunky, three-pin square plugs. Most of the Continent uses the 'europlug' with two round pins. Greece, Italy and Switzerland use a third round pin in a way that the two-pin plug usually – but not always in Italy and Switzerland – fits. The important thing is to buy an adapter before leaving home; those on sale in Europe generally go the other way.

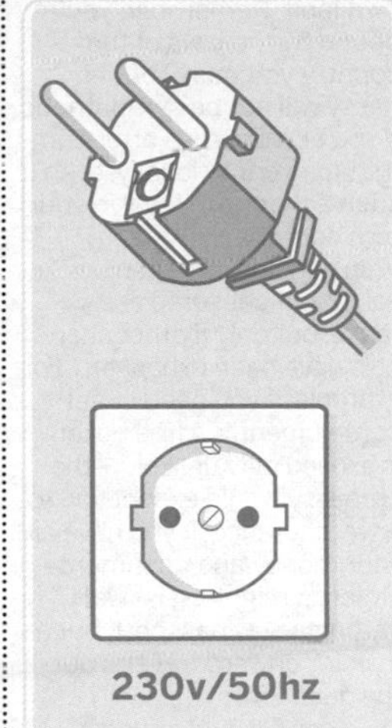

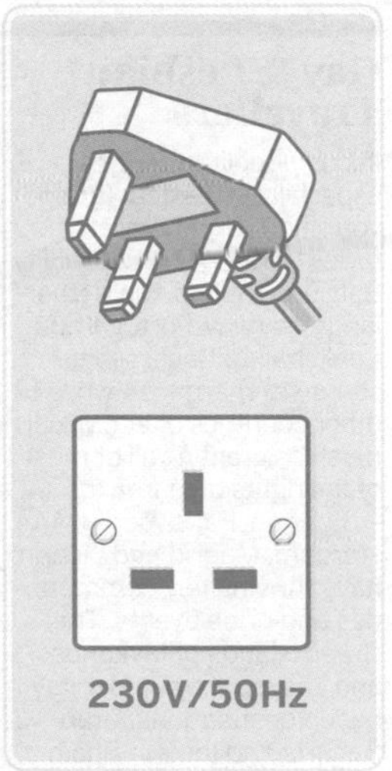

Embassies & Consulates

It's important to realise what your own embassy can and can't do to help you if you get into trouble. Generally speaking, it won't be much help in emergencies if the trouble you're in is remotely your own fault. Remember, you're bound by the laws of the country you're in. Your embassy will not be sympathetic if you end up in jail after committing a crime locally, even if such actions are legal in your own country.

In genuine emergencies you might get some assistance, but only if other channels have been exhausted. For example, if you need to get home urgently, a free ticket is exceedingly unlikely – the embassy would expect you to have insurance. If you have all your money and documents stolen, it might assist with getting a new passport, but a loan for onward travel is out of the question.

See individual country chapters for contact information for foreign embassies in Europe.

Gay & Lesbian Travellers

In cosmopolitan centres, especially in Western Europe, you'll find very liberal attitudes towards homosexuality. Belgium, Iceland, the Netherlands, Norway, Portugal and Spain have all legalised full same-sex marriages, while 13 other countries offer civil partnerships granting all or most of the rights of marriage.

London, Paris, Berlin, Amsterdam, Madrid and Lisbon have thriving gay communities and pride events. The Greek islands of Mykonos and Lesvos are popular gay beach destinations. Gran Canaria and Ibiza in Spain are big centres for both gay clubbing and beach holidays.

Eastern Europe tends to be far less progressive, though even in Russia and Belarus, where gay rights are in their infancy, there are still accessibly open gay scenes.

Outside the big cities, attitudes become more conservative and discretion is advised, particularly in Morocco, Turkey and most parts of Eastern Europe. There is an absolute dearth of good gay-travel websites, making it far better to consult websites specific to the country to which you're travelling. See the individual country directories for these, where available. Also see individual country chapters for gay and lesbian venues.

Health

Good, sometimes excellent, health care is readily available in Western Europe and, for minor illnesses, pharmacists can give valuable advice and sell over-the-counter medication. They can also advise when specialised help is required and point you in the right direction. The standard of dental care is usually good.

While the situation in Eastern Europe is improving all the time since the EU accession of many countries, quality medical care is not always readily available outside of major cities, but embassies, consulates and five-star hotels can usually recommend doctors or clinics.

No jabs are necessary for Europe. However, the World Health Organization (WHO) recommends that all travellers should be covered for diphtheria, tetanus, measles, mumps, rubella and polio, regardless of their destination. Since most vaccines don't produce immunity until at least two weeks after they're given, visit a physician at least six weeks before departure.

Tap water is generally safe to drink in large parts of Western Europe. However, bottled water is recommended in most parts of Eastern Europe, and is a must in some countries, including Russia (particularly St Petersburg) and Ukraine, where giardia can be a problem. Do not drink water from rivers or lakes as it may contain bacteria or viruses.

Condoms are widely available in Europe; however, emergency contraception may not be, so take the necessary precautions. The **International Planned Parent Federation** (www.ippf.org) can advise about the availability of contraception in different countries. When buying condoms, look for a European CE mark, which means they have passed quality tests.

Insurance

It's foolhardy to travel without insurance to cover theft, loss and medical problems. There's a wide variety of policies, so check the small print.

FURTHER HEALTH INFORMATION

There is a wealth of travel-health advice on the internet. The **World Health Organization** (www.who.int/ith/en) also publishes a superb book called *International Travel and Health,* which is revised annually and is available online at no cost. Another useful website is **MD Travel Health** (www.mdtravelhealth.com), which provides travel health recommendations for every country; updated daily.

It's usually a good idea to consult your government's website before departure, if one is available:

» **Australia** (www.smartraveller.gov.au)
» **Canada** (www.travelhealth.gc.ca)
» **UK** (www.dh.gov.uk)
» **USA** (www.cdc.gov/travel)

Some policies specifically exclude 'dangerous activities', which can include scuba diving, motorcycling, winter sports, adventure sports or even hiking. Some pay doctors or hospitals directly, but most require you to pay upfront, save the documentation and claim later. Some policies also ask you to call back (reverse charges) to a centre in your home country, where an immediate assessment of your problem is made.

Check that the policy covers ambulances or an emergency flight home.

The policies handled by STA Travel and other student travel agencies are usually good value. In the UK, the website **Money Supermarket** (www.moneysupermarket.com) does an automated comparison of 450 partner policies and comes up with the best for your needs.

Worldwide travel insurance is available online at www.lonelyplanet.com/bookings/insurance.do. You can buy, extend and claim online anytime – even if you're already on the road.

USEFUL WEB RESOURCES

Blue Flag (www.blueflag.org) Eco label for sustainably developed beaches and marinas.

Budget Traveller's Guide to Sleeping in Airports (www.sleepinginairports.net) Funny and useful resource for backpackers flying stand-by.

Currency Conversions (www.xe.com) Up-to-the-second exchange rates for hundreds of currencies.

Guide for Europe (www.guideforeurope.com) With a handy hostel review page posted by visitors.

Hostelworld (www.hostelworld.com) Also handy for other travellers' views on hostels.

Lonely Planet (www.lonelyplanet.com/thorntree) On Lonely Planet's message board you can usually get your travel questions answered by fellow travellers in a matter of hours.

Money Saving Expert (www.moneysavingexpert.com) Excellent tips on the best UK travel insurance, mobile phones and bank cards to use abroad. The Flight-checker facility shows the latest cheap flights available.

The Man in Seat 61 (www.seat61.com) A professional-standard personal website, dedicated to rail travel across Europe.

Internet Access

Internet access varies enormously across Europe. In most places, you'll be able to find wireless (wi-fi, also called WLAN in some countries), although whether it's free varies greatly.

Throughout this book, where the wi-fi icon (📶) appears, it means that the establishment offers free wi-fi that you can access immediately, or by asking for the access code from staff.

Bringing a laptop, smartphone or iPad is a great way to stay in touch on the road. If you don't have a device that connects to the internet, you'll be limited to the fast-declining number of internet cafes or the increasingly rare number of hotels and hostels that offer a guest terminal for emailing.

Most hotels and hostels now offer free wi-fi, as do many restaurants and cafes. At airports it is rarely free and you'll have to register with a credit card or buy an access card.

Access is generally straightforward, although a few tips are in order. If you can't find the @ symbol on a keyboard, try Alt Gr + 2, or Alt Gr + Q. Watch out for German and some Balkans keyboards, which reverse the Z and the Y positions. Using a French keyboard is an art unto itself.

Where necessary in relevant countries, click on the language prompt in the bottom right-hand corner of the screen or hit Ctrl + Shift to switch between the Cyrillic and Latin alphabets.

Legal Matters

Most European police are friendly and helpful, especially if you have been a victim of a crime. In most countries you are required by law to prove your identity if asked by police (although make sure they really are police), so always carry your passport, or an identity card, or at least a photocopy of either document.

You can generally purchase alcohol (beer and wine) from between 16 and 18 (usually 18 for spirits), but if in doubt, ask. Although you can drive at 17 or 18, you might not be able to hire a car until you reach 25 years of age.

Cigarette smoking bans have been progressively introduced across Europe since 2004. Countries that now prohibit smoking in bars and restaurants include Austria, Croatia, Estonia, Finland, France, Greece, Hungary, Iceland, Ireland, Italy, Malta, the Netherlands, Norway, Sweden, Turkey and the UK. Many other countries will be passing similar laws in the near future, so with such change afoot, ask before lighting up.

Drugs are often quite openly available in Europe, but that doesn't mean they're legal. The Netherlands is most famed for its liberal attitudes, with 'coffee shops' openly selling cannabis. Yet this once famously relaxed drugs culture has been challenged in recent years, with local mayors objecting to 'drug tourism' and closing down coffee shops – particularly in Rotterdam and border towns.

Elsewhere in the Netherlands possession of cannabis is only decriminalised not legalised (apart from its medicinal use). Don't take this relaxed attitude as an invitation to buy harder drugs; if you get caught, you'll be punished. Since 2008 magic mushrooms have been banned in the Netherlands.

Equally, in Belgium, the possession of up to 5g of cannabis is legal, but selling the drug isn't, so if you get caught at the point of sale, you could be in trouble.

In Portugal, the possession of *all* drugs has been decriminalised. Once again, however, selling is illegal.

Britain downgraded cannabis from a Class B to Class C drug several years back, but in 2009 it reverted to Class B status, meaning that if you're caught you may face arrest. Anyone caught smoking in public or in front of children is very likely to be arrested.

Switzerland has gone the other way. It was moving towards decriminalisation and then had a last-minute legal about-face. Some people still smoke pot openly, but if police decide to enforce the law, you'll face a fine of up to Sfr400 just for possession of cannabis.

Spain and Italy have also tightened their cannabis laws in recent years, so make sure you're careful there, too.

Getting caught with drugs in other parts of Europe, particularly countries such as Turkey and Morocco, can lead to imprisonment.

If in any doubt, err on the side of caution. For your own safety, don't even think about taking drugs across international bordc ers.

Maps

Good maps are easy to find in Europe and in good bookshops beforehand.

Road atlases are essential if you're driving or cycling. Leading brands are **Freytag & Berndt** (www.freytagberndt.com), **Hallwag**, **Kümmerly + Frey** (www.kuemmerly-frey.ch) and **Michelin** (www.michelin.com). Maps published by European automobile associations, such as Britain's **AA** (www.theaa.com) and Germany's **ADAC** (www.adac.de, in German), are usually excellent and sometimes free if membership of your local association gives you reciprocal rights. Tourist offices are another good source for (usually free and fairly basic) maps.

Money

A common currency, the euro, is used in 17 EU states: Austria, Belgium, Cyprus, France, Finland, Germany, Greece, Ireland, Italy, Luxembourg, Malta, the Netherlands, Portugal, Slovakia, Slovenia and Spain. Three further non-EU states, Andorra, Kosovo and Montenegro, also use the euro and more countries are scheduled to join in the coming decade.

The euro is made up of 100 cents, and notes come in denominations of €5, €10, €20, €50, €100, €200 and €500 euros, though any notes above 50 are rarely used on a daily basis. Coins come in 1c, 2c, 5c, 10c, 20c, 50c, €1 and €2.

Denmark, the UK and Sweden have held out against adopting the euro for political reasons, while non-EU nations, such as Albania, Belarus, Iceland, Norway, Russia, Switzerland and Ukraine, also have their own currencies. See individual country chapters for details.

For security and flexibility, diversify your source of funds. Carry an ATM card, credit card, cash and possibly travellers cheques.

Set up an internet banking account before you leave home, so you can track your spending. However, be sure to log off properly whenever you use these services from a public computer.

ATMs

Every country in this book has international ATMs that allow you to withdraw cash directly from your home account, and this is the most common way European travellers now access their money. However, you should always have a back-up option, as some readers have reported glitches with ATMs in individual countries, even when their card worked elsewhere in Europe. In some remote areas, ATMs might be scarce, too.

Much of Western Europe now uses a chip-and-pin system for added security. You will have problems if you don't have a four-digit PIN number and might have difficulties if your card doesn't have a metallic chip. Check with your bank.

If your card is rejected, try again in a few hours' time. Make sure you bring your bank's phone number and, if your card fails again, call them. Also be aware that some banks automatically block foreign transactions until they are able to call the cardholder and confirm they are abroad.

When you withdraw money from an ATM, the amounts are converted and dispensed in local currency. However, there will be fees. If you're uncertain, ask your bank to explain.

Finally, always cover the keypad when entering your PIN and make sure there are no unusual devices attached to the machine, which can copy your card's details or cause it to stick in the machine. If your card disappears and the screen goes blank before you've even entered your PIN, don't enter it – especially if a 'helpful' bystander tells you to do so. If you can't retrieve your card, call your bank's emergency number, if you can, before leaving the ATM.

Cash

Nothing beats cash for convenience…or risk. If you lose it, it's gone forever and very few travel insurers will come to your rescue. Those that do will limit the amount to somewhere around €300. It's still a good idea, though, to bring some local currency in cash, if only to cover yourself until you get to an exchange facility or find an ATM. The equivalent of €100 or €150 should usually be enough. Some extra cash in an easily exchanged currency is also a good idea, especially in Eastern Europe.

Credit Cards

Credit cards are handy for major purchases, such as air or rail tickets, and offer a lifeline in certain emergencies. Visa and MasterCard/Eurocard are more widely accepted in Europe than Amex and Diners Club; Visa (sometimes called Carte Bleue) is particularly strong in France and Spain.

There are, however, regional differences in the general acceptability of credit cards. In the UK, for example, you can usually flash your plastic in the most humble of budget restaurants; in Germany it's rare for restaurants to take credit cards. Cards are not widely accepted off the beaten track.

To reduce the risk of fraud, always keep your card in view when making transactions; for example, in restaurants that do accept cards, pay as you leave, following your card to the till. Keep transaction records and either check your statements when you return home, or check your account online while still on the road.

Letting your credit-card company know roughly where you're going lessens the chance of fraud – or of your bank cutting off the card when it sees (your) unusual spending.

Debit Cards

Ticket machines in many European train stations and other places such as car parks or city-bike stands (eg in Vienna) frequently accept Maestro debit cards, sometimes exclusively. So it's always worthwhile having a Maestro-compatible debit card, which differs from a credit card in deducting money straight from your bank account. Check with your bank or MasterCard (Maestro's parent) for compatibility.

Exchanging Money

In general, euros, US dollars and UK pounds are the easiest currencies to exchange in Europe. The major European currencies are fully convertible, but you may have trouble exchanging some lesser-known ones at small banks.

The importation or exportation of certain currencies (eg Moroccan dirham) is restricted or banned, so try to get rid of any local currency before you leave such countries. Get rid of Scottish pounds before leaving the UK; nobody outside Britain will touch them.

Most airports, central train stations, big hotels and many border posts have banking facilities outside regular business hours, at times on a 24-hour basis. Post offices in Europe often perform banking tasks, tend to open longer hours and outnumber banks in remote places. While they always exchange cash, they might baulk at handling travellers cheques not in the local currency.

The best exchange rates are usually at banks. *Bureaux de change* usually – but not always – offer worse rates or charge higher commissions. Hotels and airports are almost always the worst places to change money.

International Transfers

International bank transfers are good for secure one-off movements of large amounts of money, but they might take three to five days and there will be a fee (about £25 in the UK, for example). Be sure to specify the name of the bank, plus the sort code and address of the branch where you'd like to pick up your money.

In an emergency it's quicker and easier to have money wired via an **Amex** (www.americanexpress.com) office, **Western Union** (www.westernunion.com) or **MoneyGram** (www.moneygram.com). All are quite costly.

Taxes & Refunds

Sales tax applies to many goods and services in Europe. Depending on the country and the product, it will add between 10% and 20% to the price of goods. Luckily, when non-EU residents spend more than a certain amount (around €75) they can usually reclaim that tax when leaving the country.

Making a tax-back claim is straightforward. First, make sure the shop offers duty-free sales (often a sign will be displayed reading 'Tax-Free Shopping'). When making your purchase, ask the shop attendant for a tax-refund voucher, filled in with the correct amount and the date. This can be used to claim a refund directly at international airports, or stamped at ferry ports or border crossings and mailed back for a refund.

None of this applies to EU residents. Even an American citizen living in London is not entitled to rebate on items bought in Paris. Conversely, an EU passport holder living in New York is.

Tipping & Bargaining

Tipping has become more complicated, with 'service charges' increasingly added to bills. In theory this means you're not obliged to tip. In practice that money often doesn't go to the server and they might make it clear they still expect a gratuity. Don't pay twice. If the service charge is optional, remove it from the bill and pay a tip. If the service charge is not optional, don't tip.

Generally, waiters in Western Europe tend to be paid decent wages. For more details on tipping, see the individual country chapters.

Bargaining is common in Turkey and Morocco; see those chapters for more information.

Travellers Cheques

As travellers cheques have been overtaken in popularity by international ATMs, it's become more difficult to find places that cash them. Certainly in parts of the former Soviet Union, only a few banks handle them, and the process can be quite bureaucratic and costly.

That said, having a few cheques is a good back-up. If they're stolen you can claim a refund, provided you have a record of cheque numbers, but it's vital to store these numbers away from the cheques themselves.

Amex and Thomas Cook are reliable brands of travellers cheques, while cheques in US dollars, euros or British pounds are the easiest to cash. When changing them ask about fees and commissions as well as the exchange rate.

Western Union

If everything goes horribly wrong – your money, travellers cheques and credit cards are all stolen – don't despair. While it's a terrible (and highly unusual) situation, a friend or relative back home will be able to wire money to you anywhere in Europe via Western Union (WU). The sender is given a code that they communicate to you, then you take the code to the nearest office, along with your passport, to receive your cash.

We don't list WU representatives in this guide as there are literally thousands of them; just look for the distinctive yellow-and-black sign.

Photography & DVDs

Film is available in Europe, but most travellers shoot digital these days. So for the majority, the most important thing is to have enough memory to store pictures. Memory cards of up to 8GB are available, but if you do run out, some internet cafes will burn CDs.

DVDs each have a regional code (1 for North America, 2 for Europe and South Africa and 3 for Australasia). If you buy a disc in Europe, check that the code corresponds with your machine at home, or look for international discs coded 0. Additionally, you will have to check your DVD player is universally compatible and the TV systems work together too (which is NTSC in the USA and Japan, but PAL in Europe and Australasia). The upshot of all this is that while DVDs bought in Europe frequently won't play on your TV back home, they will probably work on your computer. Universal players are more common in Europe, so DVDs brought here from elsewhere will probably (but not necessarily) work.

Post

From major European centres, airmail typically takes about five days to North America and about a week to Australasian destinations, although mail from such countries as Albania or Russia is much slower. See the individual country chapter for local costs.

Poste restante services, where friends and family can write to you care of main post offices, are still offered, but email has rendered these largely obsolete. Courier services such as **DHL** (www.dhl.com) are best for essential deliveries.

Safe Travel

Travelling in Europe is usually very safe. Violent crime is rare; the main threats facing travellers are pickpockets, petty thieves and scam artists. Specific country perils are covered in the Dangers & Annoyances sections of individual chapters. The following outlines a range of general guidelines.

Discrimination

Divergent views about immigration, plus a small rump of anachronistic attitudes, mean that, in some parts of Europe, travellers of African, Arab or Asian descent might encounter unpleasant attitudes that are unrelated to them personally. In rural areas travellers whose skin colour marks them out as foreigners might experience unwanted attention. Some travellers have reported negative encounters because locals mistook them for Roma.

Attitudes vary from country to country. People tend to be more accepting in cities than in the country. Race is also less of an issue in Western Europe than in parts of the former Eastern Bloc. For example, there has been a spate of fatal racist attacks in St Petersburg and other parts of Russia in recent years.

Druggings

Although rare, some drugging of travellers does occur in Europe. Travellers are especially vulnerable on trains and buses where a new 'friend' may offer you food or a drink that will knock you out, giving them time to fleece you of your belongings.

Gassings have also been reported on a handful of overnight international trains. The usual scenario involves the release of a sleep-inducing gas into a sleeping compartment in the night. The best protection is to lock the door of your compartment (use your own lock if there isn't one) and to lock your bags to luggage racks, preferably with a sturdy combination cable.

If you can help it, never sleep alone in a train compartment.

Pickpockets & Thieves

Theft is definitely a problem in parts of Europe and you also have to be aware of other travellers.

» Don't store valuables in train-station lockers or luggage-storage counters and be careful about people who offer to help you operate a locker. Also be vigilant if someone offers to carry your luggage: they might carry it away altogether.

» Don't leave valuables lying around in your car, on train seats or in your room. When going out, don't flaunt cameras, iPods and other expensive electronic goods.

» Carry a small daypack, as shoulder bags are an open invitation for snatch thieves and, for extra peace of mind, use small zipper locks on your packs.

» Pickpockets are most active in dense crowds, especially in busy train stations and on public transport during peak hours. Be careful in these situations.

» Spread valuables, cash and cards around your body or in different bags. Some travellers walk around with €100 in their shoe; others put €50 in their aspirin bottle.

» A money belt with your essentials (passport, cash, credit cards, airline tickets) is usually a good idea. However, so you needn't delve into it in public, carry a wallet with a day's worth of cash.

» A dummy wallet, with fake 'credit' cards (eg library cards or video store cards) is also a good ploy.

» Having your passport stolen is less of a disaster if you've recorded the number and issue date or, even better, photocopied the relevant data pages. You can also scan them and email them to yourself.

» Also record the serial numbers of travellers cheques and carry photocopies of your credit cards, airline tickets and other travel documents.

» If you do lose your passport, notify the police immediately to get a statement, and contact your nearest consulate.

If this all sounds a lot to absorb, remember it's basically common sense, and rest assured there's no need to fret about theft constantly. Just be sensible with your possessions.

Scams

Most scams involve distracting you – either by kids running up to you, someone asking for directions or spilling something on you – while another person steals your wallet. Be alert in such situations.

In some countries, especially in Eastern Europe, you may encounter people claiming to be from the tourist police, the special police, the super-secret police, whatever. Unless they're wearing a uniform and have good reason for accosting you (eg you're robbing a bank), treat their claims with suspicion.

One common scam runs like this: someone asks you to change money. You say no, and seconds later an 'undercover' police officer 'arrests' the moneychanger. The officer then asks to check your passport and money, in case it's counterfeit. Something then goes missing or is confiscated when the 'undercover officer' handles your valuables.

Another swindle involves someone dropping a wad of money near you. Someone else picks it up and asks if it's yours. The first person then says they had twice that and requests you open your wallet to prove you don't have the other half. At this point, a 'policeman' turns up, and the scenario proceeds as per the moneychanging scam.

Needless to say, never show your passport or cash to anyone on the street. Simply walk away. If someone flashes a badge, offer to accompany them to the nearest police station.

Unrest & Terrorism

Civil unrest and terrorist bombings are rare in Europe, but they do occur. Attacks by ETA (the Basque separatist group in Spain and France) and attacks by Muslim extremists in the UK, Spain and Russia have all occurred in recent years. All you can do is keep an eye on the news and avoid areas where any flare up seems likely.

Telephone

Travel is made infinitely easier with a mobile phone you can use on the road. If your phone is European, it's often perfectly feasible to use it on roaming throughout the continent.

If you're coming from outside Europe, it's usually worth buying a prepaid local SIM in one European country. Even if you're not staying there long, calls across Europe will still be cheaper if they're not routed via your home country and the prepaid card will enable you to keep a limit on your spending. In several countries you need your passport to buy a SIM card.

In order to be able to use other SIM cards in your phone, your handset will have needed to be unblocked by your home provider.

Europe uses the GSM 900 network, which also covers Australia and New Zealand, but is not compatible with the North American GSM 1900 or the totally different system in Japan. However,

EMERGENCY NUMBERS

The phone number ☎112 can be dialled for emergencies in all EU states. See the individual country chapters for country-specific emergency numbers.

some North American GSM 1900/900 phones do work here. If you have a GSM phone, check with your service provider about using it in Europe. You'll need international roaming, but this usually costs nothing to enable.

See individual country chapters for information on country-specific calling codes, phonecards and mobile phone networks.

You can call abroad from almost any phone box in Europe. Public telephones accepting phonecards (available from post offices, telephone centres, newsstands or retail outlets) are virtually the norm now; in some countries, eg France, coin-operated phones are almost impossible to find.

Without a phonecard, you can ring from a telephone booth inside a post office or telephone centre and settle your bill at the counter. Reverse-charge (collect) calls are often possible, but not always. From many countries, however, the Country Direct system lets you phone home by billing the long-distance carrier you use at home. These numbers can often be dialled from public phones without even inserting a phonecard.

Time

Europe is divided up into four time zones. From west to east these are:

» **UTC** (Britain, Iceland, Ireland, Portugal) GMT (GMT+1 in summer

» **CET** (the majority of European countries) GMT+1 (GMT+2 in summer)

» **EET** (Greece, Turkey, Bulgaria, Romania, Moldova, Ukraine, Belarus, Lithuania, Latvia, Estonia, Kaliningrad, Finland) GMT+2 (GMT+3 in summer)

» **MSK** (Russia) GMT+3 (GMT+4 in summer)

At 9am in Britain it's 1am (GMT/UTC minus eight hours) on the US west coast, 4am (GMT/UTC minus five hours) on the US east coast, 10am in Paris and Prague, 11am in Athens, midday in Moscow and 7pm (GMT/UTC plus 10 hours) in Sydney.

In most European countries, clocks are put forward one hour for daylight-saving time on the last Sunday in March, and turned back again on the last Sunday in October.

Toilets

Many public toilets in Europe require a small fee either deposited in a box or given to the attendant. Forget horror stories about having to squat – sit-down toilets are the rule in the vast majority of places. Squat toilets can still be found in rural areas, although they are definitely a dying breed.

Public-toilet provision remains very changeable from city to city. If you can't find one, simply drop into a hotel or restaurant and ask to use theirs.

Tourist Information

Unless otherwise indicated in individual country chapters, tourist offices are common and widespread. Only in emerging tourist destinations might you have problems locating them. See individual country chapters for more information.

Travellers with Disabilities

Cobbled medieval streets, 'classic' hotels, congested inner cities and underground metro systems make Europe a tricky destination for people with mobility impairments. However, the train facilities are good and some destinations boast new tram services or lifts to platforms. The following websites can help with specific details.

Accessible Europe (www.accessibleurope.com) Specialist European tours with van transport. Prices start from as little as €240 for four days.

Lonely Planet (www.lonelyplanet.com/thorntree) Share experiences on the Travellers With Disabilities branch of the Thorn Tree message board.

Mobility International Schweiz (www.mis-ch.ch) Good site listing 'barrier-free' destinations in Switzerland and abroad, plus wheelchair-accessible hotels in Switzerland. Sadly it's only partly in English; address English emails to info@mis-ch.ch.

Mobility International USA (www.miusa.org) Publishes guides and advises travellers with disabilities on mobility issues.

Royal Association for Disability & Rehabilitation (www.radar.org.uk) Publishes a comprehensive annual guide, *Holidays in Britain & Ireland – A Guide for Disabled People*.

Society for the Advancement of Travelers with Handicaps (www.sath.org) Reams of information for travellers with disabilities.

Visas

Citizens of the USA, Canada, Australia, New Zealand and the UK need only a valid passport to enter nearly all countries in Europe, includng the entire EU. Two Eastern European countries, Belarus and Russia, require a prearranged visa before arrival and even an 'invitation' from (or booking with) a tour operator or hotel. In addition Australians and New Zealanders need a visa for both Ukraine and Moldova. See the respective country chapters for specific information on travel visas and, because regulations can change, double-check with the relevant embassy or consulate before travelling.

Several types of visa exist, including tourist, transit and business permits. Transit visas are usually cheaper than tourist or business visas but they allow a very short stay (one to five days) and can be difficult to extend.

If you require a visa, remember it has a 'use-by' date and you'll be refused entry afterwards. In some cases it's easier to get visas as you go along, rather than arranging them all beforehand. Carry spare passport photos (you may need from one to four every time you apply for a visa).

Visas to neighbouring countries are usually issued immediately by consulates in Eastern Europe, although some may levy a 50% to 100% surcharge for 'express service'. When regulations are confusing (say in Belarus or Russia) it's more simple and safer to obtain a visa before leaving home. Visas are often cheaper in your own country anyway.

Consulates are generally open weekday mornings (if there's both an embassy and a consulate, you want the consulate).

Volunteering

If you want to spend more time living and working in Europe rather than simply travelling around it, a short-term volunteer project might seem a good idea, say, teaching English in Poland or building a school in Turkey. However, most voluntary organisations levy high charges for airfares, food, lodging and recruitment (from about €250 to €800 per week), making such work impractical for most shoestringers. One exception is **WWOOF International** (www.wwoof.org), which helps link volunteers with organic farms in Germany, Slovenia, Czech Republic, Denmark, the UK, Austria and Switzerland. A small membership fee is required to join the national chapter but in exchange for your labour you'll receive free lodging and food.

Weights & Measures

The metric system is used throughout Europe. In Britain, however, nonmetric equivalents are common (distances continue to be

THE SCHENGEN AREA

Twenty-five European countries are signatories to the Schengen Agreement, which has effectively dismantled internal border controls between them. The countries in question are Austria, Belgium, Czech Republic, Denmark, Estonia, Finland, France, Germany, Greece, Iceland, Italy, Hungary, Latvia, Lithuania, Luxembourg, Malta, the Netherlands, Norway, Poland, Portugal, Slovenia, Slovakia, Spain, Sweden and Switzerland.

Citizens of the US, Australia, New Zealand, Canada and the UK only need a valid passport to enter these countries. However, other nationals, including South Africans, can apply for a single visa – a Schengen visa – when travelling throughout this region.

Non-EU visitors (with or without a Schengen visa) should expect to be questioned, however perfunctorily, when entering the region. However, later travel within the zone is much like a domestic trip, with no border controls.

If you need a Schengen visa, you must apply at the consulate or embassy of the country that's your main destination, or your point of entry. You may then stay up to a maximum of 90 days in the entire Schengen area within a six-month period. Once your visa has expired, you must leave the zone and may only re-enter after three months abroad.

If you're a citizen of the US, Australia, New Zealand or Canada, you may stay visa-free a total of 90 days, during six months, within the *entire* Schengen region. Shop around when choosing your point of entry, as visa prices may differ from country to country.

If you're planning a longer trip, you need to inquire personally as to whether you need a visa or visas. Your country might have bilateral agreements with individual Schengen countries allowing you to stay there longer than 90 days without a visa. However, you will need to talk directly to the relevant embassies or consulates.

While the UK and Ireland are not part of the Schengen area, their citizens can stay indefinitely in other EU countries, only needing paperwork if they want to work long term or take up residency.

given in miles and beer is sold in pints, not litres)

Women Travellers

Women might attract unwanted attention in rural Spain and southern Italy, especially Sicily, where many men view whistling and catcalling as flattery. Conservative dress can help to deter lascivious gazes and wolf whistles; dark sunglasses help avoid unwanted eye contact.

Marriage is highly respected in southern Europe, and a wedding ring can help, along with talk about 'my husband'. Hitchhiking alone is not recommended anywhere.

Female readers have reported assaults at Turkish hotels with shared bathrooms, so women travelling to Turkey might want to consider a more expensive room with private bathroom.

Journeywoman (www.journeywoman.com) maintains an online newsletter about solo female travels all over the world.

Working

Working in Europe is not always straightforward. EU citizens are allowed to work in any other EU country, but there can still be tiresome paperwork to complete. Other nationalities require special work permits that can be almost impossible to arrange, especially for temporary work. However, that doesn't prevent enterprising travellers from topping up their funds by working in the hotel or restaurant trades at beach or ski resorts, or teaching a little English – and they don't always have to do this illegally. The UK, for example, issues special 'working holiday' visas to Commonwealth citizens who are aged between 17 and 30, valid for 12 months' work during two years (see www.ukvisas.gov.uk). Your national student-exchange organisation might be able to arrange temporary work permits to several countries.

If you have a grandparent or parent who was born in an EU country, you may have certain rights of residency or citizenship. Ask that country's embassy about dual citizenship and work permits. With citizenship, also ask about any obligations, such as military service and residency. Beware that your home country may not recognise dual citizenship.

Seasonal Work

Work Your Way Around the World by Susan Griffith gives practical advice, as does *Summer Jobs Abroad*, edited by David Woodworth.

Remember, if you find a temporary job, the pay might be less than that offered to locals. Typical tourist jobs (picking grapes in France, working at a bar in Greece) often come with board and lodging, and the pay is essentially pocket money, but you'll have a good time partying with other travellers.

Busking is fairly common in major European cities such as Amsterdam and Paris. However, it's illegal in some parts of Switzerland and Austria. Even in Belgium and Germany, where it has been tolerated in the past, crackdowns are not unknown. Some other cities, including London, require permits and security checks. Make sure you talk to other buskers first.

Starting points include the following:

EuroJobs (www.eurojobs.com) Links to hundreds of organisations looking to employ both non-Europeans (with the correct work permits) and Europeans.

Jobs in the Alps (www.jobs-in-the-alps.com) Mainly service jobs, eg chambermaids, bar staff and porters. Some linguistic skills required.

Natives (www.natives.co.uk) Summer and winter resort jobs, and various tips.

Picking Jobs (www.pickingjobs.com) Includes some tourism jobs.

Season Workers (www.seasonworkers.com) Best for ski-resort work and summer jobs, although it also has some English-teaching jobs.

Teaching English

Although teaching English is an option, most schools prefer a bachelor's degree and a TEFL (Teaching English as a Foreign Language) certificate.

It is easier to find TEFL jobs in Eastern Europe than in Western Europe. The **British Council** (www.britishcouncil.org) can provide advice about training and job searches. Alternatively, try the big schools such as **Berlitz** (www.berlitz.com) and **Wall Street Institute International** (www.wallstreetinstitute.com).

Transport in Europe

GETTING THERE & AWAY

Arriving from beyond the Continent is nearly always done by plane these days. While a few hardy souls do still arrive overland from Asia and the Middle East, or from North Africa by ferry, they are the small minority. This section covers all means of transport for getting to Europe from the rest of the world.

Flights, tours and rail tickets can be booked online at www.lonelyplanet.com/travel_services.

Entering Europe

All countries require travellers to have a valid passport, preferably with at least six months between the time of departure and the passport's expiry date.

EU travellers from countries that issue national identity cards are increasingly using these to travel within the EU, although it's impossible to use these as the sole travel documents outside of the EU.

Visas are another consideration. Some countries require some nationalities to buy a document allowing entry between certain dates. Specifically, Belarus and Russia require all nationalities to obtain visas, while Aussie and Kiwi travellers also need visas to enter Moldova and Ukraine. Other nationalities may have additional requirements; see p1318 or the individual country directories for details.

Air

Airports & Airlines

If travelling from another continent, your air ticket to Europe will be your single biggest expense. To save money, it's best to travel off-season. This means, if possible, avoid mid-June to early September, Easter, Christmas and school holidays.

Regardless of your ultimate destination, it's sometimes better to pick a recognised transport 'hub' as your initial port of entry, where high traffic volumes help keep prices down. The busiest, and therefore most obvious, airports are London, Frankfurt, Paris and Rome. Sometimes tickets to Amsterdam, Athens, Barcelona, Berlin, Madrid, Shannon and Vienna are worth checking out.

Long-haul airfares to Eastern Europe are rarely a bargain; you're usually better flying to a Western European hub and taking an onward budget airline flight or train.

Most of the aforementioned gateway cities are also well serviced by low-cost carriers that fly to other parts of Europe. Many low-cost airlines are included in the individual country chapters, but some of the major ones are:

Air Berlin (www.airberlin.com) Hubs in Germany; service across Europe.

easyJet (www.easyjet.com)

CLIMATE CHANGE & TRAVEL

Every form of transport that relies on carbon-based fuel generates CO^2, the main cause of human-induced climate change. Modern travel is dependent on aeroplanes, which might use less fuel per person than most cars but travel much greater distances. The altitude at which aircraft emit gases (including CO^2) and particles also contributes to their climate change impact. Many websites offer 'carbon calculators' that allow people to estimate the carbon emissions generated by their journey and, for those who wish to do so, to offset the impact of the greenhouse gases emitted with contributions to portfolios of climate-friendly initiatives throughout the world. Lonely Planet offsets the carbon footprint of all staff and author travel.

Flies to major airports across Europe.

Germanwings (www.germanwings.com) Hubs in Germany; service across Europe.

Ryanair (www.ryanair.com) Flies to scores of destinations across Europe, but confirm your destination airport is not a deserted airfield out in the sticks.

Tickets

Buying tickets to and within Europe is easily done online. However, checking a host of airline websites can soon become tedious and confusing, which is where the convenience of flight booking websites is unmatched. Lonely Planet's flight search engine compares lots of different flight websites to find you the best deal, see www.lonelyplanet.com/bookings/flights.do.

Some useful websites:

Ebookers (www.ebookers.com)

Expedia (www.expedia.com)

Kayak (www.kayak.com)

Opodo (www.opodo.com)

Orbitz (www.orbitz.com)

Skyscanner (www.skyscanner.com)

Travelocity (www.travelocity.com)

Land

It's possible to reach Europe by various different train routes from Asia. Most commonly used is the Trans-Siberian Railway, that connects Moscow to Siberia, the Russian Far East, Mongolia, China and North Korea.

It is also possible to reach Moscow from several Central Asian states and İstanbul from Iran, Jordan and Syria. See www.seat61.com for more information about these adventurous routes.

Sea

There are numerous ferry routes between Europe and Africa. For details on services within Europe, including the English Channel and the Baltic and North Seas, see p1322, as well as the individual country chapters.

Ferry routes between Africa and Europe, include links from Spain to Morocco, Italy and Malta to Tunisia, France to Morocco and France to Tunisia. Check out www.traghettionline.net for comprehensive information on all Mediterranean ferries. There are also ferries between Greece and Israel via Cyprus. Ferries are often filled to capacity in summer, especially to and from Tunisia, so book well in advance if you're taking a vehicle across.

Passenger freighters (typically carrying up to 12 passengers) aren't nearly as competitively priced as airlines. Journeys also take a long time. However, if you've got your heart set on a transatlantic journey, **Travltips Cruise & Freighter** (www.travltips.com) has a downloadable freighter directory.

GETTING AROUND

Travel within the EU, whether by air, rail or car, was made easier by the Schengen Agreement, which abolished border controls between most member states (see p1323).

In most European countries, the train is the best option for internal transport. Check the websites of national rail systems as they often offer fare specials and national passes that are significantly cheaper than point-to-point tickets.

Air

Airlines

In recent years low-cost carriers have revolutionised European transport and now it's often cheaper (to the great chagrin the environmentally conscious) to take a flight than a train journey for long-distance European trips. Most budget airlines have a similar pricing system – namely that ticket prices rise with the number of seats sold on each flight, so book as early as possible to get a decent fare.

Some low-cost carriers – Ryanair being the prime example – have made a habit of flying to smaller, less convenient airports on the outskirts of their destination city, or even to the airports of nearby cities, so check before you book.

Departure and other taxes (often including extortionate booking fees, fees checking in a piece of hold luggage and other surcharges) soon add up and are included in the final price of your ticket by the end of the online booking process – usually a lot more than you were hoping to pay!

In the face of competition from low-cost airlines, many national carriers have decided to drop their prices and/or offer special deals. Some, such as British Airways, have even adopted the low-cost model of online booking, where the customer can opt to buy just a one-way flight, or can piece together their own return journey from two one-way legs. For details of national airlines, see individual country chapters.

For a comprehensive overview of which low-cost carriers fly to or from which European cities, check out the excellent flycheapo.com. Some low-cost carriers:

» **Air Berlin** (www.airberlin.com) Well-respected German outfit. Flies to central airports around the world, but book early for good prices.

» **BMIBaby** (www.bmibaby.com) Cheap flights leaving from regional UK cities to Belgium, Czech Republic, France, Germany, Italy, Poland, Portugal, Spain and Switzerland.

» **easyJet** (www.easyjet.com) Flies to a large number of central airports. Main hubs are in London, Paris, Madrid and Basel, but also has point-to-point services between continental cities.

» **Flybe** (www.flybe.com) Cheap flights from regional UK cities within the UK and across Western Europe; much loved by business travellers.

» **German Wings** (www.germanwings.com) Another reputable German budget airline with a huge number of flights to all corners of the Continent. Main hubs are Cologne-Bonn, Berlin Schönfeld and Stuttgart. Unusually, it has cheap flights to Russia.

» **Ryanair** (www.ryanair.com) Ryanair's sheer number of routes is extraordinary. With nonreclining seats, incessant advertising throughout flights and tight legroom, you'll just have to grin and bear it to get a good price – which, with all due credit – is all too often!

» **Wizz Air** (W6; www.wizzair.com) This recommended Hungarian operator has numerous bases in Poland as well as Budapest and London, and a vast array of flights across Europe. Wizz has the best links to Ukraine and Bulgaria from Western Europe.

Air Passes

Various travel agencies and airlines offer air passes for non-European citizens. Check with your travel agent for current promotions.

The **Europe By Air Flight Pass** (www.europebyair.com) costs from US$99 per flight for hundreds of European cities. The most economical routes would be long hops from one region of Europe to another, such as St Petersburg to London, rather than shorter routes serviced by low-cost carriers.

Scandinavian Airline's **Visit Scandinavia/Europe Air Pass** (☎08-797 0000 in Sweden; www.flysas.com) connects visitors to Scandinavian cities for US$60 to US$168 per flight.

Bicycle

Much of Europe is ideally suited to cycling. In the northwest, the flat terrain ensures that bicycles are a popular form of everyday transport, though headwinds often spoil the fun. In the rest of the region, hills and mountains can make for tough going, but this is offset by the dense concentration of things to see.

Cycling is a great way to explore many of the Mediterranean islands. Popular cycling areas include the Belgian Ardennes, the west of Ireland, the upper reaches of the Danube in southern Germany and anywhere in northern Switzerland, Denmark or the south of France. Exploring the small villages of Turkey and Eastern Europe also provides up-close access to remoter areas.

A primary consideration on a cycling trip is to travel light, but you should take a few tools and spare parts, including a puncture-repair kit and an extra inner tube. Panniers are essential to balance your possessions on either side of the bike frame. The wearing of helmets is not compulsory but is certainly advised.

Michelin maps indicate scenic routes, which can help you plan good cycling itineraries. Seasoned cyclists can average 80km a day, but it depends on what you're carrying and your level of fitness.

Useful contacts and websites in English:

» **Cyclists' Touring Club** (CTC; ☎0844 736 8450; www.ctc.org.uk, www.cyclingholidays.org) The national cycling association of the UK runs organised trips to Continental Europe.

» **Veloland European Cyclists' Federation** (www.ecf.com) Has details of 'EuroVelo', the European cycle network of 12 pan-European cycle routes, plus tips for other tours.

» **Veloland Schweiz** (www.cycling-in-switzerland.ch) Details of Swiss national routes and more.

Rental & Purchase

It is easy to hire bikes throughout most of Europe on an hourly, half-day, daily or weekly basis. Many Western European train stations have bike-rental counters. It is sometimes possible to return the bike at a different outlet so you don't have to retrace your route. See individual country chapters for more details.

There are plenty of places to buy bikes in Europe (shops sell new and secondhand bicycles, or you can check local papers for private vendors), but you'll need a specialist bicycle shop for a bike capable of withstanding a European trip. Cycling is very popular in the Netherlands and Germany, and those countries are good places to pick up a well-equipped touring bicycle.

European prices are quite high (certainly higher than in North America), however non-European residents should be able to claim back value-added tax (VAT) on the purchase.

Transporting a Bicycle

For major cycling trips, it's best to have a bike you're familiar with, so consider bringing your own rather than buying on arrival. If coming from outside Europe, ask about the airline's policy on transporting bikes before purchasing your ticket.

From the UK to the Continent, Eurostar (the train service through the Channel Tunnel) charges £30 to send a bike as registered luggage on its routes. You can also transport your bicycle with you on Eurotunnel through the Channel Tunnel. With a bit of tinkering and dismantling (eg removing wheels), you might be able to get your bike into a bag or sack and take it on a train as hand luggage.

Alternatively, the **European Bike Express** (www.bike-express.co.uk) is a coach service based in the UK where cyclists can travel with their bicycles to various cycling destinations on the Continent.

Once on the Continent, you can put your feet up on the train if you get tired of pedalling or simply want to skip a boring section. On slower trains, bikes can usually be transported as luggage, subject to a small supplementary fee. Some cyclists have reported that Italian and French train attendants have refused bikes on slow trains, so be prepared for regulations to be interpreted differently by officious staff.

Fast trains can rarely accommodate bikes; they might need to be sent as registered luggage and may end up on a different train from the one you take. This is often the case in France and Spain.

Boat

Several different ferry companies compete on the main ferry routes, resulting in a comprehensive but complicated service. The same ferry company can have a host of different prices for the same route, depending on the time of day or year, validity of the ticket and length of your vehicle. Vehicle tickets usually include the driver and often up to five passengers free of charge.

It's worth planning (and booking) ahead where possible as there may be special reductions on off-peak crossings and advance-purchase tickets. On English Channel routes, apart from one-day or short-term excursion returns, there is little price advantage in buying a return ticket versus two singles.

Rail-pass holders are entitled to discounts or free travel on some lines. Food on ferries is often expensive (and lousy), so it is worth bringing your own. Also be aware that if you take your vehicle on board, you are usually denied access to it during the voyage.

Lake and river ferry services operate in many countries, Austria and Switzerland being just two. Some are very scenic. For more details, see the individual country chapters.

From the UK & Ireland

Britain is well connected with Western Europe by ferry. Check out www.ferrybooker.com for information.

» **P&O Ferries** (www.poferries.com) is one of the world's main ferry companies. Ferries sail from England to France (Dover-Calais), to the Netherlands (Hull-Rotterdam), to Belgium (Hull-Zeebrugge) and to Ireland (Liverpool-Dublin), among many other routes.

» **Brittany Ferries** (www.brittany-ferries.co.uk) operates services from England to France or Spain. You can also go by ferry from Ireland to France.

From Ireland it's also possible to travel directly to mainland Europe with **Irish Ferries** (www.irishferries.com) and **Brittany Ferries** (www.brittany-ferries.co.uk) on their routes to Roscoff and Cherbourg from Rosslare and Cork in Ireland.

Northern Europe & Scandinavia

Northern German port towns such as Lübeck and Rostock are well connected by ferry to Norway, Denmark, Sweden, Finland, the UK and the Baltic countries. The Faroe Islands-based **Smyril Line** (www.smyrilline.com) connects Iceland to Denmark via the Faroe Islands. For the full range of options visit:

» **Color Line** (www.colorline.com)

» **Finnlines** (www.finnlines.de)

» **Finnlines-Nordölink** (www.nordoe-link.com)

» **Lisco** (www.lisco-baltic-service.de)

» **Scandlines** (www.scandlines.de)

» **Stena Line** (www.stenaline.de)

» **TT-Line** (www.ttline.de)

Mediterranean Ferries

Blue Star Ferries (www.bluestarferries.com) and **Hellenic Mediterranean** (www.hml.it, in Italian) travel from Italy (Ancona, Brindisi or Bari) to Greece (Corfu, Igoumenitsa and Patras).

The Greek Islands are connected to the mainland and each other by a spider web of routes; see p604 for more information.

Bus

International Buses

Buses are often cheaper than trains, sometimes substantially so, but also tend to be slower and less comfortable. While they are generally more expensive and take much longer than low-cost airlines (a double whammy), they do cover many routes low-cost airlines don't.

In Portugal, Greece, parts of Spain and Turkey, buses are often a better option than trains.

Europe's biggest organisation of international buses operates under the name **Eurolines** (www.eurolines.com). The various national companies that create this group can be accessed through this website. The group's network covers cities as far afield as Edinburgh, Stockholm, Rīga, Bucharest, Rome and Madrid. A **Eurolines Pass** (www.eurolines-pass.com) is offered for extensive travel, allowing passengers to visit a choice 43 cities in 18 countries over 15 or 30 days. In the high season (mid-June to mid-September) the pass costs €290/345 for those aged under 26, or €375/455 for those 26 and over. It's cheaper in other periods.

Another popular option is **Busabout** (www.busabout.com), whose buses do three

EUROPE'S BORDER CROSSINGS

Border formalities have been relaxed in most of the EU, but still exist in all their original bureaucratic glory in parts of Eastern Europe.

In line with the Schengen Agreement, there are officially no passport controls at the borders between Austria, Belgium, Czech Republic, Denmark, Estonia, Finland, France, Germany, Greece, Iceland, Italy, Hungary, Latvia, Lithuania, Luxembourg, Malta, the Netherlands, Norway, Poland, Portugal, Slovakia, Slovenia, Spain, Sweden and Switzerland. Sometimes, however, there are spot checks on trains crossing borders, so always have your passport. The UK, which is an EU country but a nonsignatory to Schengen, maintains border controls over traffic from other EU countries (except Ireland, with which it shares an open border), although there are no customs control.

Most borders in Eastern Europe will be crossed via train, where border guards board the train and go through the compartments checking passengers' papers. It is rare to get hit up for bribes, but occasionally in Belarus or Moldova you may face a difficulty that can only be overcome with a 'fine'. Travelling between Turkey and Bulgaria typically requires a change of trains and is subject to a lengthy border procedure.

interconnected circuits around Europe, stopping at major cities. You can 'hop off' at any scheduled stop, then 'hop on' a later bus. Buses are often oversubscribed, so book each sector to avoid being stranded. It departs every two days from April to the end of October. The circuits cover most countries in Continental Western Europe, plus the Czech Republic. Myriad other options are available as well.

Another company offering a similar service is **Eastern Trekker** (www.easterntrekker.com), which covers Eastern Europe and offers everything from Dracula-themed castle tours of Romania to an eight-day sailing tour of Croatia.

National Buses

Domestic buses provide a viable alternative to trains in most countries. Again, they are usually slightly cheaper and somewhat slower. Buses are generally best for shorter hops, such as getting around cities and reaching remote villages and they are often the only option in mountainous regions.

Reservations are rarely necessary. On many city buses you usually buy your ticket in advance from a kiosk or machine and validate it on entering the bus. See the individual country chapters for more details on local buses.

Car & Motorcycle

Travelling with your own vehicle gives flexibility and is the best way to reach remote places. However, the independence does sometimes isolate you from local life. Also, cars can be a target for theft and are often impractical in city centres, where traffic jams, parking problems and getting thoroughly lost can make it well worth ditching your vehicle and using public transport. Various car-carrying trains can help you avoid long, tiring drives.

Campervan

One popular way to tour Europe is for a group of three or four people to band together and buy or rent a campervan. London is the usual embarkation point. Look at the advertisements in London's free magazine **TNT** (www.tntmagazine.com) if you wish to form or join a group. *TNT* is also a good source for purchasing a van, as is **Loot** (www.loot.com).

Some secondhand dealers offer a 'buy-back' scheme for when you return from the Continent, but we've heard stories that some dealers don't fully honour their refund commitments. Buying and reselling privately should be more advantageous if you have time. In the UK, **Downunder Insurance** (www.duinsure.com) offers a campervan policy.

Campervans usually feature a fixed high-top or elevating roof and two to five bunk beds. Apart from the essential camping gas cooker, you may get a sink, fridge and built-in cupboards. Prices vary considerably, and it's worth getting advice from a mechanic to determine whether you're being offered a fair price. Once on the road you should be able to keep budgets lower than backpackers using trains, but don't forget to set money aside for emergency repairs.

The main advantage of going by campervan is flexibility; with transport, eating and sleeping requirements all taken care of in one unit, you are tied to nobody's timetable but your own. It's also easier to set up at night than if you rely on a car and tent.

A disadvantage of campervans is that you are in a confined space for much of the time. Four adults in a small van can soon get on each other's nerves, particularly if the group has been formed at short notice. You might also miss out on experiences in the world outside your van. Other negatives are that vans are not very manoeuvrable around town, and you'll often have to leave your gear unattended inside (many people bolt extra locks onto the van). Fuel costs also soon add up.

Fuel

Fuel prices can vary enormously (though fuel is always more expensive than in North America or Australia). Refuelling in Luxembourg, Gibraltar or Andorra is about 30% cheaper than in neighbouring countries. The Netherlands, France and Italy have Europe's most expensive petrol. Greece, Spain and (surprisingly) Switzerland have reasonable prices. The Baltic and Eastern European countries are cheaper still.

Unleaded petrol only is available throughout much of Europe, but not always in Romania, Albania, Slovakia, Serbia or Montenegro. Diesel is usually cheaper, though the difference is marginal in Britain, Ireland and Switzerland.

Ireland's Automobile Association maintains a webpage of European fuel prices at www.aaireland.ie/petrolprices.

Leasing

Leasing a vehicle involves fewer hassles than purchasing and can work out much cheaper than hiring for longer than 17 days. This program is limited to certain types of new cars, including Renault and Peugeot, but you save money because leasing is exempt from VAT, and inclusive insurance plans are cheaper than daily insurance rates.

Leasing is also open to people as young as 18 years old. To lease a vehicle your permanent address must be outside the EU. In the USA, contact **Renault Eurodrive** (www.renaultusa.com) for more information.

Motorcycle Touring

Europe is made for motorcycle touring, with quality winding roads, stunning scenery and an active motorcycling scene. Just make sure your wet-weather motorcycling gear is up to scratch.

Rider and passenger crash helmets are compulsory everywhere in Europe. Austria, Belgium, France, Germany, Luxembourg, Portugal and Spain also require that motorcyclists use headlights during the day; in other countries it is recommended.

On ferries, motorcyclists rarely have to book ahead as they can generally be squeezed on board.

Take note of the local custom about parking motorcycles on pavements (sidewalks). Though this is illegal in some countries, the police often turn a blind eye provided the vehicle doesn't obstruct pedestrians. Don't try to park your bike on the pavement in Britain, however.

Preparations

Always carry proof of ownership of your vehicle (Vehicle Registration Document for British-registered cars) when touring Europe. An EU driving licence is acceptable for those driving throughout Europe. If you have any other type of licence, you should obtain an International Driving Permit (IDP) from your motoring organisation. Check what type of licence is required in your destination prior to departure.

Third-party motor insurance is compulsory. Most UK policies automatically provide this for EU countries. Get your insurer to issue a Green Card (which may cost extra), an internationally recognised proof of insurance, and check that it lists all the countries you intend to visit. You'll need this in the event of an accident outside the country where the vehicle is insured.

Also ask your insurer for a European Accident Statement form, which can simplify things if worst comes to worst. Never sign statements that you can't read or understand – insist on a translation and sign that only if it's acceptable.

For non-EU countries, check the requirements with your insurer. Travellers from the UK can obtain additional advice and information from the **Association of British Insurers** (www.abi.org.uk).

Take out a European motoring assistance policy. Non-Europeans might find it cheaper to arrange international coverage with their national motoring organisation before leaving home. Ask your motoring organisation for details about the free services offered by affiliated organisations around Europe.

Every vehicle that travels across an international border should display a sticker indicating its country of registration. A warning triangle, to be used in the event of breakdown, is compulsory almost everywhere.

Some recommended accessories include a first-aid kit (compulsory in Austria, Slovenia, Croatia, Serbia, Montenegro and Greece), a spare bulb kit (compulsory in Spain), a reflective jacket for every person in the car (compulsory in France, Italy and Spain) and a fire extinguisher (compulsory in Greece and Turkey).

Residents of the UK should contact the **RAC** (www.rac.co.uk) or the **AA** (www.theaa.com) for more information. In the USA, contact **AAA** (www.aaa.com).

Purchase

The purchase of vehicles in some European countries is illegal for non-nationals or non-EU residents. Britain is probably the best place to buy; second-hand prices are good and, whether buying privately or from a dealer, the absence of language difficulties will help you establish exactly what you are getting and what guarantees you can expect if you break down.

However, bear in mind that British cars have steering wheels on the right-hand side. If you wish to have left-hand drive and can afford to buy a new car, prices are generally reasonable in Greece, France, Germany, Belgium, Luxembourg and the Netherlands.

Paperwork can be tricky wherever you buy, and many countries have compulsory roadworthiness checks on older vehicles.

Rental

Renting a car is ideal for people who will need cars for 16 days or less. Anything more, it's better to lease. Big international rental firms will give you reliable service and good vehicles. Usually you will have the option of returning the car to a different outlet at the end of the rental period, but inquire about extra charges for this.

Book early for the lowest rates and make sure you compare rates in different cities. Prices in some cities are cheaper than in others. Taxes range from 15% to 20% and surcharges apply if rented from an airport.

One operator worth bearing in mind if you're renting a car in the UK, France, Greece, Ireland, Italy, Portugal, Spain or Switzerland is **Easycar** (www.easycar.com) which has rentals starting at rock-bottom rates. Otherwise, check the sites of the following major operators, where you can make reservations online:

» **Alamo** (www.alamo.com)
» **Avis** (www.avis.com)
» **Budget** (www.budget.com)
» **Europcar** (www.europcar.com)
» **Hertz** (www.hertz.com)

Note that if you rent a car in the EU you might not be able to take it outside the EU, and if you rent the car outside the EU, you will only be able to drive within the EU for eight days. Ask at the rental agencies for other such regulations.

If you want to rent a car and haven't booked ahead, look for national or local firms, which can often undercut the big companies by up to 40%. Nevertheless, you need to be wary of dodgy operations that take your money and point you towards some clapped-out wreck, or where the rental agreement is bad news if you have an accident or the car is stolen. Read before you sign.

No matter where you rent, make sure you understand what is included in the price (unlimited or paid kilometres, tax, injury insurance, collision damage waiver etc) and what your liabilities are. We recommend taking the collision damage waiver, though you can probably skip the injury insurance if you and your passengers have decent travel insurance. Ask in advance if you can drive a rented car across borders from a country where hire prices are low to another where they're high.

The minimum rental age is usually 21 years and sometimes 25, and you'll need a credit card and to have held your licence for at least a year.

Motorcycle and moped rental is common in some countries, such as Italy, Spain, Greece and southern France. Sadly, it's also common for inexperienced riders to leap on rented bikes and very quickly fall off them again, leaving a layer or two of skin on the road in the process.

Road Conditions & Road Rules

Conditions and types of roads vary across Europe. The fastest routes are generally four- or six-lane highways known locally as motorways, autoroutes, *autostrade*, *autobahnen* etc. These tend to skirt cities and plough through the countryside in straight lines, often avoiding the most scenic bits.

Some highways incur tolls, which are often quite hefty (especially in Italy, France and Spain), but there will always be an alternative route. Motorways and other primary routes are generally in good condition.

Road surfaces on minor routes are unreliable in some countries (eg Greece, Albania, Romania, Ireland, Morocco, Russia and Ukraine), although normally they will be more than adequate. These roads are narrower and progress is generally much slower. However, to compensate for this, you can expect much better scenery and plenty of interesting villages along the way.

Except in Britain, Ireland, Malta and Cyprus, you should drive on the right. Vehicles brought to the Continent from any of these locales should have their headlights adjusted to avoid blinding oncoming traffic (a simple solution on older headlight lenses is to cover up a triangular section of the lens with tape). Priority is often given to traffic approaching from the right in countries that drive on the right-hand side.

Speed limits vary from country to country. You may be surprised at the apparent disregard for traffic regulations in some places (particularly in Italy and Greece), but as a visitor it is always best to be cautious. Many driving infringements are subject to an on-the-spot fine. Always ask for a receipt.

European drink-driving laws are particularly strict. The blood-alcohol concentration (BAC) limit when driving is usually between 0.05% and 0.08%, but in certain areas (such as Gibraltar and some Eastern European countries such as Bulgaria and Belarus) it can be zero.

Hitching

Hitching is never entirely safe and we cannot recommend it. Travellers who decide to hitch should understand that they are taking a small but potentially serious risk. It will be safer if they travel in pairs and let someone know where they plan to go.

A man and woman travelling together is probably the best combination. A woman hitching on her own is taking a larger than normal risk.

Hitching in Western Europe can be simultaneously the most rewarding and yet frustrating way of getting around. You get to meet and interact with local people and can have unplanned detours that may yield unexpected highlights off the beaten track. But you might get stuck on the side of the road to nowhere with nowhere (or nowhere cheap) to stay.

Don't try to hitch from city centres; take public transport to the suburban exit routes. Hitching is usually illegal on highways – stand on the slip roads, or approach drivers at petrol stations and truck stops.

Look presentable and cheerful, and make a cardboard sign indicating your intended destination in the local language. Never hitch where drivers can't stop in good time or without causing an obstruction. At dusk, give up and stay the night.

It is sometimes possible to arrange a lift in advance: scan student notice boards in colleges, or check out www.rideshare.co.uk or www.drive2day.de.

Local Transport

High-density populations mean European towns and cities have excellent local-transport systems, often encompassing trams as well as buses and metro/subway/underground rail networks.

Be sure to remove your pack on public transport and hold it in front of you to avoid battering your neighbour and deter pickpockets. Also give up your seat to the elderly, infirm or pregnant women.

Most travellers will find areas of interest in European cities can be easily traversed by foot or bicycle. In Greece and Italy, travellers sometimes rent mopeds and motorcycles for scooting around a city or island.

HITCHING FOR CASH

In parts of Eastern Europe including Russia, Ukraine and Turkey, traditional hitchhiking is rarely practised. Instead, anyone with a car can be a taxi and it's quite usual to see locals stick their hands out (palm down) on the street, looking to hitch a lift. The difference with hitching here, however, is that you pay for the privilege. You will need to speak the local language (or at least know the numbers) to discuss your destination and negotiate a price.

Taxi

Taxis in Europe are metered and rates are usually high. There might also be supplements for things such as luggage, time of day, location of pick-up and extra passengers.

Good bus, rail and underground-railway networks often render taxis unnecessary, but if you need one in a hurry, they can be found idling near train stations or outside big hotels. Lower fares make taxis more viable in some countries, such as Spain, Greece, Portugal and Turkey.

See the boxed text, above, detailing the situation in some Eastern European countries.

Train

Comfortable, frequent and reliable, trains are *the* way of getting around Europe. Indeed, it's safe to say that Europe has some of the most efficient and comprehensive train services in the world, particularly in Switzerland, Austria and Germany. Trains are a great way to meet people, see the countryside, get into the heart of cities and to scribble furiously into that sacred journal.

If you plan to travel extensively by train, it is worth obtaining the *Thomas Cook European Timetable*, giving a comprehensive listing of train schedules and indicating where supplementary fares apply or where reservations are necessary. It's available from **Thomas Cook** (www.thomascookpublishing.com) outlets and online.

Many state railways have interactive websites publishing their timetables and fares, including www.bahn.de (Germany) and www.sbb.ch (Switzerland), which both have pages in English. The **Eurail** (www.eurail.com) website links to more than 20 national train companies in Europe.

The very comprehensive, privately run website **The Man in Seat 61** (www.seat61.com) is a gem, while the US-based **Budget Europe Travel Service** (www.budgeteuropetravel.com) can also help with tips.

Paris, Milan and Vienna are important hubs for international train connections. See the relevant city sections for details. Note that European trains sometimes split en route to service two destinations, so even if you're on the right train, make sure you're also in the correct carriage.

A train journey to almost every station in Europe can be booked via **Rail Europe** (www.raileurope.co.uk), which also sells InterRail and other passes; see p1327.

Note that train travel is often much more expensive than air travel in Europe, especially since the advent of the low-cost airlines. But aside from being infinitely more pleasurable, it's also far more environmentally friendly than taking flights.

Express Trains

Europeans are unlikely to catch a plane between London and Paris or Brussels.

That's because those routes are served by the high-speed passenger train service **Eurostar** (www.eurostar.com).

Eurostar links London's St Pancras International station, via the Channel Tunnel, with Paris' Gare du Nord (2¼ hours, up to 25 a day) and Brussels' international terminal (one hour 50 minutes, up to 12 a day). Some trains also stop at Lille and Calais in France. The train stations at St Pancras International, Paris and Brussels are all much more central than the cities' airports. So, overall, the journey takes as little time as the equivalent flight, with less hassle.

Eurostar in London also sells tickets onward to some Continental destinations, although its list is much less comprehensive than Rail Europe's. Holders of Eurail and InterRail passes are offered discounts on some Eurostar services; check when booking.

Within Europe, express trains are identified by the symbols 'EC' (EuroCity) or 'IC' (InterCity). The French TGV, Spanish AVE and German ICE trains are even faster, reaching up to 300km/h. Supplementary fares can apply on fast trains (which you often have to pay when travelling on a rail pass), and it is a good idea (sometimes obligatory) to reserve seats at peak times and on certain lines. The same applies for branded express trains, such as the Thalys (between Paris and Brussels, Bruges, Amsterdam and Cologne), and the Eurostar Italia (between Rome and Naples, Florence, Milan and Venice).

If you don't have a seat reservation, you can still obtain a seat that doesn't have a reservation ticket attached to it. Check which destination a seat is reserved for – you might be able to sit in it until the person boards the train.

International Rail Passes

If you're covering lots of ground, you should get a rail pass. But do some price comparisons of point-to-point ticket charges and rail passes beforehand to make absolutely sure you'll break even. Also shop around for rail-pass prices as they do vary between outlets. When weighing up options, look into cheap deals that include advance-purchase reductions, one-off promotions or special circular-route tickets, particularly over the internet.

Normal point-to-point tickets are valid for two months, and you can make as many stops as you like en route; make your intentions known when purchasing, and inform train conductors how far you're going before they punch your ticket.

Supplementary charges (eg for some express and overnight trains) and seat reservation fees (mandatory on some trains, a good idea on others) are not covered by rail passes. Always ask. Note that European rail passes also give reductions on Eurostar through the Channel Tunnel and on certain ferries.

Pass-holders must always carry their passport with them for identification purposes. The railways' policy is that passes cannot be replaced or refunded if lost or stolen. However, with some sales outlets (ie www.raileurope.co.uk) you can buy insurance that will reimburse you for any days not used at the point a pass is stolen.

NON-EUROPEAN RESIDENTS

Eurail Passes

Eurail (www.eurail.com) passes vary in what they cover depending on how often you plan to travel and what areas you wish to travel in. They can be bought only by residents of non-European countries and should be purchased before arriving in Europe.

The inaccurately named 'Global Pass' covers 22 countries, namely Austria (including Liechtenstein), Belgium, Bulgaria, Croatia, Czech Republic, Denmark, Finland, France, Germany, Greece, Hungary, Ireland, Italy, Luxembourg, the Netherlands, Norway, Portugal, Romania, Slovenia, Spain, Sweden and Switzerland.

While the pass is valid on some private train lines in the region, if you plan to travel extensively in Switzerland, be warned that the many private rail networks and cable cars, especially in the Jungfrau region around Interlaken, don't give Eurail discounts. A Swiss Pass or Half-Fare Card (see p1260) might be an alternative or necessary addition.

You can use the Global Pass on some Italy–Greece, Denmark–Sweden, Germany–Sweden and Sweden–Finland ferries. Reductions are given on some other ferry routes and on river/lake steamer services in various countries.

For those under 26 years of age, a continuous Eurail Youth pass will cost €345/445/547/772/952 for 15 days/21 days/one month/two months/three months. Holders of youth passes must travel in 2nd-class compartments. Those aged 26 and over must purchase the full-fare Eurail pass. This costs €529/683/841/1188/1464 for the periods outlined above. However, this full-fare pass entitles you to travel 1st class.

Many permutations of the pass are available. With a Selectpass you nominate three, four or five countries in which you wish to travel, and then buy a pass allowing five, six, eight, 10 or 15 travel days in a two-month period. Prices start at €218/334 per youth/adult. The five- and six-day passes offer an attractive price break, but as the Selectpass continues up its pricing ladder, the continuous pass becomes better value.

A range of more than 15 Eurail Regional Passes covering two or three countries is also offered, but you might want to ensure that they are good value given your travel plans. Similarly, there are now Eurail National Passes for just one country at a time.

Two to five people travelling together can get a Saver version of all Eurail passes for a 15% to 25% discount.

EUROPEAN RESIDENTS

Rail Europe (www.raileurope.co.uk) sells **InterRail** (www.interrail.net) passes to European residents for unlimited 2nd- and 3rd-class rail travel through 30 European and North African countries (excluding the pass-holder's country of residence). To qualify as a resident in this sense, you must have lived in a European country for six months.

InterRail Global Passes for five days of travel in 10 days cost £169/259 for under 26 years/26 and over; 10 days travel in 22 days costs £249/369; and a one-month continuous global pass with unlimited travel is £409/619.

While an InterRail pass will get you further than a Eurail pass along the private rail networks of Switzerland's Jungfrau region (near Interlaken), its benefits are limited. A Swiss Pass or Half-Fare Card (see p1260) might be a necessary addition if you plan to travel extensively in that region.

For a small fee, European residents can buy a Railplus Card, entitling the holder to a 25% discount on international train journeys. In most countries, it's sold only to those aged 60 and over. However, some national rail networks may make the Railplus Card available to young people or other travellers. It is available from counters in main train stations.

ALL NATIONALITIES

Several other passes are available, especially if you're interested in travelling in the Continent's east. For purchase of and further information about the following passes, contact **Rail Europe** (www.raileurope.co.uk, www.raileurope.com) in your home country.

France Railpass

This **pass** (www.francerailpass.com) offers unlimited travel for three days during a one-month period. Full fares are US$239 for three days and US$32 to US$38 for each additional travel day within the same month-long period, depending on how many days you buy.

Eastern Europe Passes

One pass is the European East Pass, which provides five days of travel over a month in Austria, Czech Republic, Hungary, Poland and Slovakia for US$307/214 for 1st/2nd class.

Meanwhile, a Balkans Flexipass provides five to 15 days of 1st-class train travel in a month throughout Bulgaria, Greece, Macedonia, Montenegro, Romania, Serbia and Turkey, starting at US$156/260 per youth (under 26)/adult.

National Rail Passes

As well as the national rail passes offered by Rail Europe, national rail operators might offer their own passes, or at least a discount card, offering substantial reductions on tickets purchased (eg the Bahn Card in Germany or the Half-Fare Card in Switzerland).

Link to individual train operator sites via www.raileurope.co.uk to check. Such discount cards are usually only worth it if you're staying in the country a while and doing a lot of travelling.

Overnight Trains

On overnight trains, you can use your sleeping hours to cover territory and save money you'd otherwise use on accommodation.

There are usually two types of sleeping accommodation: dozing off upright in your seat or stretching out in a sleeper. Again, reservations are advisable, as sleeping options are allocated on a first-come, first-served basis. Couchette bunks are comfortable enough, if lacking in privacy. There are four per compartment in 1st class, six in 2nd class.

Sleepers are the most comfortable option, offering beds for one or two passengers in 1st class, or two or three passengers in 2nd class. Charges vary depending upon the journey, but they are significantly more costly than couchettes.

In the former Soviet Union countries explored in this guide, the most common options are either 2nd-class *kupeyny* compartments – which have four bunks – or the cheaper *platskartny*, which are open-plan compartments with reserved bunks. This 3rd-class equivalent is not great for those who value privacy, and theft might be a problem.

Other options include the very basic bench seats in *obshchiy* (*zahalney* in Ukrainian) class and 1st-class, two-person sleeping carriages (*myagki* in Russian). In Ukrainian, this last option is known as *spalney*, but is usually abbreviated to CB in Cyrillic (pronounced *es-ve*). First class is not available on every Russian or Ukrainian train.

Most long-distance trains have a dining (buffet) car or an attendant who wheels a snack trolley through carriages. Prices tend to be steep, though – you're much better off packing a picnic before boarding the train.

Security

Stories sometimes surface about passengers being gassed or drugged and then robbed, but bag snatching is much more of a worry.

Sensible security measures include always keeping your bags in sight (especially at stations), chaining them to the luggage rack, locking compartment doors overnight and sleeping in compartments with other people.

Bear in mind, however, that horror stories are very rare.

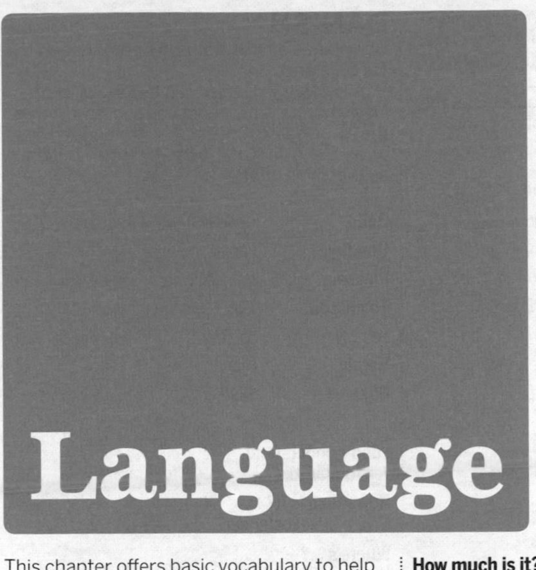

Language

WANT MORE?

For in-depth language information and handy phrases, check out Lonely Planet's *Europe Phrasebook*. You'll find it at **shop.lonelyplanet.com**, or you can buy Lonely Planet's iPhone phrasebooks at the Apple App Store.

This chapter offers basic vocabulary to help you get around Europe. If you read our coloured pronunciation guides as if they were English, you'll be understood just fine.

Note that, in our pronunciation guides, the stressed syllables are indicated with italics. Also, kh and gh represent a throaty sound (as in the Scottish *loch*) wherever they appear in this chapter.

ALBANIAN

There are two main dialects of Albanian – Tosk (spoken in southern Albania, Greece, Italy and Turkey) and Gheg (spoken in northern Albania, Kosovo and the surrounding areas of Serbia, Montenegro and Macedonia). Tosk is the official language of Albania and is also used in this chapter.

Note that ew is pronounced as ee with rounded lips, uh as the 'a' in 'ago', dh as the 'th' in 'that', dz as the 'ds' in 'adds', and zh as the 's' in 'pleasure'. Also, ll and rr are pronounced stronger than when they are written as single letters.

Hello.	*Tungjatjeta.*	toon·dya·*tye*·ta
Goodbye.	*Mirupafshim.*	mee·roo·*paf*·sheem
Please.	*Ju lutem.*	yoo *loo*·tem
Thank you.	*Faleminderit.*	fa·le·meen·*de*·reet
Yes./No.	*Po./Jo.*	po/yo
Help!	*Ndihmë!*	*ndeeh*·muh
Cheers!	*Gëzuar!*	guh·*zoo*·ar

I don't understand.
Unë nuk kuptoj. — oo·nuh nook koop·*toy*

How much is it?
Sa kushton? — sa koosh·*ton*

Where's ...?
Ku është ...? — koo *uhsh*·tuh ...

Where are the toilets?
Ku janë banjat? — koo *ya*·nuh *ba*·nyat

BULGARIAN

Note that uh is pronounced as the 'a' in 'ago' and zh as the 's' in 'pleasure'.

Hello.	Здравейте.	zdra·*vey*·te
Goodbye.	Довиждане.	do·*veezh*·da·ne
Please.	Моля.	*mol*·ya
Thank you.	Благодаря.	bla·go·dar·*ya*
Yes./No.	Да./Не.	da/ne
Help!	Помощ!	*po*·mosht
Cheers!	Наздраве!	na·*zdra*·ve

I don't understand.
Не разбирам. — ne raz·*bee*·ram

How much is it?
Колко струва? — *kol*·ko *stroo*·va

Where's ...?
Къде се намира ...? — kuh·*de* se na·*mee*·ra ...

Where are the toilets?
Къде има тоалетни? — kuh·*de* ee·ma to·a·*let*·nee

CROATIAN & SERBIAN

Linguists commonly refer to the varieties spoken in Croatia, Serbia, Bosnia-Hercegovina, Montenegro and Kosovo with the umbrella term 'Serbo-Croatian', while acknowledging dialectical differences between them. In this chapter, we've indicated significant differences between Croatian and Serbian with (C) and (S) respectively.

Note that r is rolled, zh is pronounced as the 's' in 'pleasure', and the apostrophe (') indicates a slight y sound.

Hello.	*Bog.* (C)	bog
	Zdravo. (S)	*zdra*·vo
Goodbye.	*Zbogom.*	*zbo*·gom
Please.	*Molim.*	*mo*·lim
Thank you.	*Hvala.*	*hva*·la
Yes./No.	*Da./Ne.*	da/ne
Help!	*Upomoć!*	*u*·po·moch
Cheers!	*Živjeli!*	*zhi*·vye·li

I don't understand.
Ja ne razumijem. ya ne ra·*zu*·mi·yem

How much is it?
Koliko stoji/ košta? (C/S) ko·*li*·ko *sto*·yi/ *kosh*·ta

Where's ...?
Gdje je ...? gdye ye ...

Where are the toilets?
Gdje se nalaze zahodi/toaleti? (C/S) gdye se *na*·la·ze *za*·ho·di/to·a·*le*·ti

CZECH

An accent mark over a vowel in written Czech indicates it's pronounced as a long sound.

Note that air is pronounced as in 'hair', aw as in 'law', oh as the 'o' in 'note', ow as in 'how', uh as the 'a' in 'ago', kh as in the Scottish *loch*, and zh as the 's' in 'pleasure'. Also, r is rolled in Czech and the apostrophe (') indicates a slight y sound.

Hello.	*Ahoj.*	*uh*·hoy
Goodbye.	*Na shledanou.*	*nuh*·skhle·duh·noh
Please.	*Prosím.*	*pro*·seem
Thank you.	*Děkuji.*	*dye*·ku·yi
Yes.	*Ano.*	*uh*·no
No.	*Ne.*	ne
Help!	*Pomoc!*	*po*·mots
Cheers!	*Na zdraví!*	nuh *zdruh*·vee

I don't understand.
Nerozumím. *ne*·ro·zu·meem

How much is it?
Kolik to stojí? *ko*·lik to *sto*·yee

Where's ...?
Kde je ...? gde ye ...

Where are the toilets?
Kde jsou toalety? gde ysoh *to*·uh·le·ti

DANISH

Danish has official status in Denmark and the Faroe Islands.

All vowels in Danish can be long or short. Note that aw is pronounced as in 'saw', eu as the 'u' in 'nurse', ew as 'ee' with rounded lips, oh as the 'o' in 'note', ow as in 'how', and dh as the 'th' in 'that'.

Hello.	*Goddag.*	go·*da*
Goodbye.	*Farvel.*	faar·*vel*
Please.	*Vær så venlig.*	ver saw *ven*·lee
Thank you.	*Tak.*	taak
Yes./No.	*Ja./Nej.*	ya/nai
Help!	*Hjælp!*	yelp
Cheers!	*Skål!*	skawl

I don't understand.
Jeg forstår ikke. yai for·*stawr* *i*·ke

How much is it?
Hvor meget koster det? vor *maa*·yet *kos*·ta dey

Where's ...?
Hvor er ...? vor ir ...

Where's the toilet?
Hvor er toilettet? vor ir toy·*le*·tet

DUTCH

Dutch is spoken in The Netherlands as well as in the northern half of Belgium (Flanders) and in parts of the Belgian capital, Brussels.

Hello.	*Dag.*	dakh
Goodbye.	*Dag.*	dakh
Please.	*Alstublieft.*	al·stew·*bleeft*
Thank you.	*Dank u.*	dangk ew
Yes.	*Ja.*	yaa
No.	*Nee.*	ney
Help!	*Help!*	help
Cheers!	*Proost!*	prohst

I don't understand.
Ik begrijp het niet. ik buh·*khreyp* huht neet

How much is it?
Hoeveel kost het? hoo·*veyl* kost huht

Where's ...?
Waar is ...? waar is ...

Where are the toilets?
Waar zijn de toiletten? waar zeyn duh twa·*le*·tuhn

ESTONIAN

Double vowels in written Estonian indicate they are pronounced as long sounds.

Note that air is pronounced as in 'hair', aw as in 'law', ea as in 'ear', eu as in 'nurse', ew as ee with rounded lips, oh as the 'o' in 'note', ow as in 'how', uh as the 'a' in 'ago', kh as in the Scottish *loch*, and zh as the 's' in 'pleasure'.

Hello.	*Tere.*	*te*·re
Goodbye.	*Nägemist.*	*nair*·ge·mist
Please.	*Palun.*	*pa*·lun
Thank you.	*Tänan.*	*tair*·nan
Yes./No.	*Jaa./Ei.*	yaa/ay
Help!	*Appi!*	*ap*·pi
Cheers!	*Terviseks!*	*tair*·vi·seks

I don't understand.
Ma ei saa aru. — ma ay saa *a*·ru

How much is it?
Kui palju see maksab? — *ku*·i *pal*·yu sey *mak*·sab

Where's ...?
Kus on ...? — kus on ...

Where are the toilets?
Kus on WC? — kus on *ve*·se

FINNISH

In Finnish, double consonants are held longer than their single equivalents. Note that eu is pronounced as the 'u' in 'nurse', ew as 'ee' with rounded lips, oh as the 'o' in 'note', ow as in 'how', and uh as the 'u' in 'run'.

Hello.	*Hei.*	hay
Goodbye.	*Näkemiin.*	*na*·ke·meen
Please.	*Ole hyvä.*	o·le *hew*·va
Thank you.	*Kiitos.*	*kee*·tos
Yes./No.	*Kyllä./Ei.*	*kewl*·la/ay
Help!	*Apua!*	*uh*·pu·uh
Cheers!	*Kippis!*	*kip*·pis

I don't understand.
En ymmärrä. — en *ewm*·mar·ra

How much is it?
Mitä se maksaa? — *mi*·ta se *muhk*·saa

Where's ...?
Missä on ...? — *mis*·sa on ...

Where are the toilets?
Missä on vessa? — *mis*·sa on *ves*·suh

FRENCH

French is spoken in France, Switzerland, Luxembourg, the southern half of Belgium (Wallonia) and in parts of its capital, Brussels.

The r sound is a throaty one and there are nasal vowels (pronounced as if you're trying to force the sound through your nose) which are indicated in our guides with o or u followed by an almost inaudible nasal consonant sound m, n or ng. Syllables in French words are, for the most part, equally stressed.

Hello.	*Bonjour.*	bon·zhoor
Goodbye.	*Au revoir.*	o·rer·vwa
Please.	*S'il vous plaît.*	seel voo play
Thank you.	*Merci.*	mair·see
Yes./No.	*Oui./Non.*	wee/non
Help!	*Au secours!*	o skoor
Cheers!	*Santé!*	son·tay

I don't understand.
Je ne comprends pas. — zher ner kom·pron pa

How much is it?
C'est combien? — say kom·byun

Where's ...?
Où est ...? — oo ay ...

Where are the toilets?
Où sont les toilettes? — oo son ley twa·let

GERMAN

German has official status in Germany, Austria, Liechtenstein, Switzerland, Luxembourg and Belgium.

Hello.		
(in general)	*Guten Tag.*	*goo*·ten taak
(Austria)	*Servus.*	*zer*·vus
(Switzerland)	*Grüezi.*	*grew*·e·tsi
Goodbye.	*Auf Wiedersehen.*	owf *vee*·der·zey·en
Please.	*Bitte.*	*bi*·te
Thank you.	*Danke.*	*dang*·ke
Yes./No.	*Ja./Nein.*	yaa/nain
Help!	*Hilfe!*	*hil*·fe
Cheers!	*Prost!*	prawst

I don't understand.
Ich verstehe nicht. — ikh fer·*shtey*·e nikht

How much is it?
Wie viel kostet das? — vee feel *kos*·tet das

Where's ...?
Wo ist ...? — vaw ist ...

Where are the toilets?
Wo ist die Toilette? — vo ist dee to·a·*le*·te

GREEK

Greek is the language of mainland Greece and its islands, as well as a co-official language of Cyprus.

Hello.	Γεια σου.	yia su
Goodbye.	Αντίο.	a·*di*·o
Please.	Παρακαλώ.	pa·ra·ka·*lo*
Thank you.	Ευχαριστώ.	ef·kha·ri·*sto*
Yes./No.	Ναι./Όχι.	ne/*o*·hi

Help!	Βοήθεια!	vo·*i*·thia
Cheers!	Στην υγειά μας!	stin i·*yia* mas

I don't understand.
Δεν καταλαβαίνω. dhen ka·ta·la·*ve*·no
How much is it?
Πόσο κάνει; *po*·so *ka*·ni
Where's ...?
Που είναι ...; pu *i*·ne ...
Where are the toilets?
Που είναι η τουαλέτα; pu *i*·ne i tu·a·*le*·ta

HUNGARIAN

A symbol over a vowel in written Hungarian indicates it's pronounced as a long sound. Double consonants should be drawn out a little longer than in English.

Note that aw is pronounced as in 'law', eu as in 'nurse', ew as 'ee' with rounded lips, and zh as the 's' in 'pleasure'. Also, r is rolled in Hungarian and the apostrophe (') indicates a slight y sound.

Hello. (to one person)
Szervusz. *ser*·vus
Hello. (to more than one person)
Szervusztok. *ser*·vus·tawk

Goodbye.	*Viszlát.*	*vis*·lat
Please.	*Kérem.* (pol) *Kérlek.* (inf)	*key*·rem *keyr*·lek
Thank you.	*Köszönöm.*	*keu*·seu·neum
Yes.	*Igen.*	*i*·gen
No.	*Nem.*	nem
Help!	*Segítség!*	*she*·geet·sheyg

Cheers! (to one person)
Egészségedre! e·geys·shey·ged·re
Cheers! (to more than one person)
Egészségetekre! e·geys·shey·ge·tek·re
I don't understand.
Nem értem. nem *eyr*·tem
How much is it?
Mennyibe kerül? *men'*·nyi·be *ke*·rewl
Where's ...?
Hol van a ...? hawl von o ...
Where are the toilets?
Hol a vécé? hawl o *vey*·tsey

ICELANDIC

In Icelandic, double consonants are pronounced long. Note that eu is pronounced as the 'u' in 'nurse', oh as the 'o' in 'note', ow as in 'how', öy as the '-er y-' in 'her year' (without the 'r'), dh as the 'th' in 'that', and kh as the 'ch' in the Scottish *loch*.

Hello.	*Halló.*	*ha*·loh
Goodbye.	*Bless.*	bles
Please.	*Takk.*	tak
Thank you.	*Takk fyrir.*	tak *fi*·rir
Yes.	*Já.*	yow
No.	*Nei.*	nay
Help!	*Hjálp!*	hyowlp
Cheers!	*Skál!*	skowl

I don't understand.
Ég skil ekki. yekh skil *e*·ki
How much is it?
Hvað kostar þetta? kvadh *kos*·tar *the*·ta
Where's ...?
Hvar er ...? kvar er ...
Where are the toilets?
Hvar er snyrtingin? kvar er *snir*·tin·gin

ITALIAN

The language of Italy also has official status – and is spoken – in Switzerland.

Hello.	*Buongiorno.*	bwon·*jor*·no
Goodbye.	*Arrivederci.*	a·ree·ve·*der*·chee
Please.	*Per favore.*	per fa·*vo*·re
Thank you.	*Grazie.*	*gra*·tsye
Yes./No.	*Sì./No.*	see/no
Help!	*Aiuto!*	ai·*yoo*·to
Cheers!	*Salute!*	sa·*loo*·te

I don't understand.
Non capisco. non ka·*pee*·sko
How much is it?
Quant'è? kwan·*te*
Where's ... ?
Dov'è ... ? do·ve ...
Where are the toilets?
Dove sono i gabinetti? do·ve so·no ee ga·bee·*ne*·tee

LATVIAN

A line over a vowel in written Latvian indicates it's pronounced as a long sound.

Note that air is pronounced as in 'hair', aw as in 'law', ea as in 'ear', ow as in 'how', wa as in 'water', dz as the 'ds' in 'adds', and zh as the 's' in 'pleasure'. The apostrophe (') indicates a slight y sound.

Hello.	*Sveiks.*	svayks
Goodbye.	*Atā.*	*a*·taa
Please.	*Lūdzu.*	*loo*·dzu
Thank you.	*Paldies.*	*pal*·deas

Yes./No.	*Jā./Nē.*	yaa/nair
Help!	*Palīgā!*	*pa*·lee·gaa
Cheers!	*Priekā!*	*prea*·kaa

I don't understand.
Es nesaprotu. es *ne*·*sa*·prwa·tu

How much is it?
Cik maksā? tsik mak·*saa*

Where's ...?
Kur ir ...? kur ir ...

Where are the toilets?
Kur ir tualetes? kur ir *tu*·a·le·tes

LITHUANIAN

Symbols on vowels in written Lithuanian indicate they are pronounced as long sounds.

Note that aw is pronounced as in 'law', ea as in 'ear', ow as in 'how', wa as in 'water', dz as the 'ds' in 'adds', and zh as the 's' in 'pleasure'.

Hello.	*Sveiki.*	svay·*ki*
Goodbye.	*Viso gero.*	*vi*·so *ge*·ro
Please.	*Prašau.*	pra·*show*
Thank you.	*Ačiū.*	*aa*·choo
Yes./No.	*Taip./Ne.*	taip/ne
Help!	*Padėkit!*	pa·*dey*·kit
Cheers!	*Į sveikatą!*	ee svay·*kaa*·taa

I don't understand.
Aš nesuprantu. ash ne·su·pran·*tu*

How much is it?
Kiek kainuoja? keak kain·*wo*·ya

Where's ...?
Kur yra ...? kur ee·ra ...

Where are the toilets?
Kur yra tualetai? kur ee·*ra* tu·a·*le*·tai

MACEDONIAN

Note that dz is pronounced as the 'ds' in 'adds', zh as the 's' in 'pleasure', and that r is a rolled sound.

Hello.	Здраво.	*zdra*·vo
Goodbye.	До гледање.	do *gle*·da·nye
Please.	Молам.	*mo*·lam
Thank you.	Благодарам.	bla·*go*·da·ram
Yes./No.	Да./Не.	da/ne
Help!	Помош!	*po*·mosh
Cheers!	На здравје!	na *zdrav*·ye

I don't understand.
Јас не разбирам. yas ne *raz*·bi·ram

How much is it?
Колку чини тоа? *kol*·ku *chi*·ni *to*·a

Where's ...?
Каде е ...? *ka*·de e ...

Where are the toilets?
Каде се тоалетите? *ka*·de se to·a·*le*·ti·te

MOROCCAN ARABIC

In this section we've represented the Arabic phrases with the Roman alphabet using a simplified pronunciation system. .

Note that ay is pronounced as in 'day', ai as in 'aisle', ow as in 'how', dh as the 'th' in 'this', kh as the 'ch' in the Scottish *loch*, gh is a throaty sound like the French 'r', h is a strongly whispered 'h' and q is a strong, throaty 'k' sound.

Hello.	es salaam alaykum (polite)
	wa alaykum salaam (response)
Goodbye.	bessalama/m'a ssalama
Please.	'afak/'afik/'afakum (said to man/woman/ more than one person)
Thank you.	shukran
Yes./No.	eeyeh/lay
Help!	'teqnee!
Cheers!	bsaha!
I don't understand	mafhemtsh
How much is it?	bshhal?
Where's ...?	feen kayn ...?
Where are the toilets?	feen kayn lbeet lma?

NORWEGIAN

There are two official written forms of Norwegian, *Bokmål* and *Nynorsk*. They are actually quite similar and understood by all speakers. It's estimated that around 85% speakers of Norwegian use *Bokmål* and about 15% use *Nynorsk*. In this section only *Bokmål* is used.

Each vowel can be either long or short. Generally, they're long when followed by one consonant and short when followed by two or more consonants. Note that aw is pronounced as in 'law', eu as the 'u' in 'nurse', ew as 'ee' with pursed lips, and ow as in 'how'.

Hello.	*God dag.*	go·*daag*
Goodbye.	*Ha det.*	*haa*·de
Please.	*Vær så snill.*	veyr saw snil
Thank you.	*Takk.*	tak
Yes./No.	*Ja./Nei.*	yaa/ney
Help!	*Hjelp!*	yelp
Cheers!	*Skål!*	skawl

I don't understand.
Jeg forstår ikke. yai fawr·*stawr* i·key

How much is it?
Hvor mye koster det? vor *mew*·e kaws·ter de

Where's ...?
Hvor er ...? vor ayr ...

Where are the toilets?
Hvor er toalettene? vor eyr to·aa·*le*·te·ne

POLISH

Polish vowels are generally pronounced short. Nasal vowels are pronounced as though you're trying to force the air through your nose, and are indicated with n or m following the vowel.

Note that ow is pronounced as in 'how', kh as in the Scottish *loch*, and zh as the 's' in 'pleasure'. Also, r is rolled in Polish and the apostrophe (') indicates a slight y sound.

Hello.	*Cześć.*	cheshch
Goodbye.	*Do widzenia.*	do vee·*dze*·nya
Please.	*Proszę.*	*pro*·she
Thank you.	*Dziękuję.*	jyen·*koo*·ye
Yes.	*Tak.*	tak
No.	*Nie.*	nye
Help!	*Na pomoc!*	na *po*·mots
Cheers!	*Na zdrowie!*	na *zdro*·vye

I don't understand.
Nie rozumiem. nye ro·*zoo*·myem

How much is it?
Ile to kosztuje? ee·le to kosh·*too*·ye

Where's ...?
Gdzie jest ...? gjye yest ...

Where are the toilets?
Gdzie są toalety? gjye som to·a·*le*·ti

PORTUGUESE

Most vowel sounds in Portugal's language have a nasal version (ie pronounced as if you're trying to force the sound through your nose), which is indicated in our pronunciation guides with ng after the vowel.

Hello.	*Olá.*	o·*laa*
Goodbye.	*Adeus.*	a·de·*oosh*
Please.	*Por favor.*	poor fa·*vor*
Thank you.	*Obrigado.* (m)	o·bree·*gaa*·doo
	Obrigada. (f)	o·bree·*gaa*·da
Yes.	*Sim.*	seeng
No.	*Não.*	nowng
Help!	*Socorro!*	soo·*ko*·rroo
Cheers!	*Saúde!*	sa·*oo*·de

I don't understand.
Não entendo. nowng eng·*teng*·doo

How much is it?
Quanto custa? *kwang*·too *koosh*·ta

Where's ...?
Onde é ...? *ong*·de e ...

Where are the toilets?
Onde é a casa de banho? *ong*·de e a *kaa*·za de *ba*·nyoo

ROMANIAN

Romanian is the official language of Romania and Moldova (where it's called Moldovan).

Note that ew is pronounced as 'ee' with rounded lips, oh as the 'o' in 'note', ow as in 'how', uh as the 'a' in 'ago', and zh as the 's' in 'pleasure'. The apostrophe (') indicates a very short, unstressed i (almost silent). The sounds y and w generally act as semivowels.

Hello.	*Bună ziua.*	*boo*·nuh *zee*·wa
Goodbye.	*La revedere.*	la re·ve·*de*·re
Please.	*Vă rog.*	vuh rog
Thank you.	*Mulţumesc.*	mool·tsoo·*mesk*
Yes./No.	*Da./Nu.*	da/noo
Help!	*Ajutor!*	a·zhoo·*tor*
Cheers!	*Noroc!*	no·*rok*

I don't understand.
Eu nu înţeleg. ye·oo noo ewn·tse·*leg*

How much is it?
Cât costă? kewt *kos*·tuh

Where's ...?
Unde este ...? *oon*·de *yes*·te ...

Where are the toilets?
Unde este o toaletă? oon·*de yes*·te o to·a·*le*·tuh

RUSSIAN

Note that kh is pronounced as in the Scottish *loch* and zh as the 's' in 'pleasure'. Also, r is rolled in Russian and the apostrophe (') indicates a slight y sound.

Hello.	Здравствуйте.	*zdrast*·vuyt·ye
Goodbye.	До свидания.	da svee·*dan*·ya
Please.	Пожалуйста.	pa·*zhal*·sta
Thank you.	Спасибо	spa·*see*·ba
Yes.	Да.	da
No.	Нет.	nyet
Help!	Помогите!	pa·ma·*gee*·tye
Cheers!	Пей до дна!	pyey da dna

I don't understand.
Я не понимаю. ya nye pa·nee·*ma*·yu

How much is it?
Сколько стоит? *skol'·ka sto·eet*

Where's ...?
Где (здесь) ...? gdye (zdyes') ...

Where are the toilets?
Где здесь туалет? gdye zdyes' tu·al·*yet*

SLOVAK

An accent mark over a vowel in written Slovak indicates it's pronounced as a long sound.

Note that air is pronounced as in 'hair', aw as in 'law', oh as the 'o' in 'note', ow as in 'how', uh as the 'a' in 'ago', dz as the 'ds' in 'adds', kh as in the Scottish *loch,* and zh as the 's' in 'pleasure'. The apostrophe (') indicates a slight y sound.

Hello.	*Dobrý deň.*	*do*·bree dyen'
Goodbye.	*Do videnia.*	do *vi*·dye·ni·yuh
Please.	*Prosím.*	*pro*·seem
Thank you.	*Ďakujem*	*dyuh*·ku·yem
Yes./No.	*Áno./Nie.*	*a*·no/*ni*·ye
Help!	*Pomoc!*	*po*·mots
Cheers!	*Nazdravie!*	*nuhz*·druh·vi·ye

I don't understand.
Nerozumiem. *nye*·ro·zu·myem

How much is it?
Koľko to stojí? *kol'*·ko to *sto*·yee

Where's ...?
Kde je ...? kdye ye ...

Where are the toilets?
Kde sú tu záchody? kdye soo tu *za*·kho·di

SLOVENE

We've used the symbols oh (as the 'o' in 'note') and ow (as in 'how') to help you pronounce vowels followed by the letters *l* and *v* in written Slovene – at the end of a syllable these combinations produce a sound similar to the 'w' in English.

Note also that uh is pronounced as the 'a' in 'ago', zh as the 's' in 'pleasure', r is rolled, and the apostrophe (') indicates a slight y sound.

Hello.	*Zdravo.*	*zdra*·vo
Goodbye.	*Na svidenje.*	na *svee*·den·ye
Please.	*Prosim.*	*pro*·seem
Thank you.	*Hvala.*	*hva*·la
Yes./No.	*Da./Ne.*	da/ne
Help!	*Na pomoč!*	na po·*moch*
Cheers!	*Na zdravje!*	na *zdrav*·ye

I don't understand.
Ne razumem. ne ra·*zoo*·mem

How much is it?
Koliko stane? *ko*·lee·ko *sta*·ne

Where's ...?
Kje je ...? kye ye ...

Where are the toilets?
Kje je stranišče? kye ye stra·*neesh*·che

SPANISH

Spanish is the main language of Spain. Note that the th sound is pronounced 'with a lisp'.

Hello.	*Hola.*	*o*·la
Goodbye.	*Adiós.*	a·*dyos*
Yes./No.	*Sí./No.*	see/no
Please.	*Por favor.*	por fa·*vor*
Thank you.	*Gracias.*	*gra*·thyas
Help!	*¡Socorro!*	so·*ko*·ro
Cheers!	*¡Salud!*	sa·*loo*

I don't understand.
Yo no entiendo. yo no en·*tyen*·do

How much is it?
¿Cuánto cuesta? *kwan*·to *kwes*·ta

Where's ...?
¿Dónde está ...? *don*·de es·*ta* ...

Where are the toilets?
¿Dónde están los servicios? *don*·de es·*tan* los ser·*vee*·thyos

SWEDISH

Swedish is the national language of Sweden and it also has official status in Finland.

Swedish vowel sounds can be either short or long – generally the stressed vowels are long, except when they are followed by double consonants. Note that aw is pronounced as in 'saw', air as in 'hair', eu as the 'u' in 'nurse', ew as 'ee' with rounded lips, oh as the 'o' in 'note', and fh is a breathy sound pronounced with rounded lips, like saying 'f' and 'w' at the same time.

Hello.	*Hej.*	hey
Goodbye.	*Hej då.*	hey daw
Please.	*Tack.*	tak
Thank you.	*Tack.*	tak
Yes./No.	*Ja./Nej.*	yaa/ney
Help!	*Hjälp!*	yelp
Cheers!	*Skål!*	skawl

I don't understand.
Jag förstår inte. yaa feur·*shtawr* in·te

How much is it?
Hur mycket kostar det? hoor *mew*·ke *kos*·tar de

Where's ...?
Var finns det ...? var finns de ...

Where are the toilets?
Var är toaletten? var air toh·aa·*le*·ten

TURKISH

Turkish is the official language in Turkey and the northern part of Cyprus.

Double vowels are pronounced twice. Note that eu is pronounced as the 'u' in 'nurse', ew as 'ee' with rounded lips, uh as the 'a' in 'ago', zh as the 's' in 'pleasure', r is always rolled and v is a little softer than in English.

Hello.	*Merhaba.*	*mer*·ha·ba
Goodbye.	*Hoşçakal.* (by person leaving)	hosh·*cha*·kal
	Güle güle. (by person staying)	gew·*le* gew·*le*
Please.	*Lütfen.*	*lewt*·fen
Thank you.	*Teşekkür ederim.*	te·shek·*kewr* e·*de*·reem
Yes./No.	*Evet./Hayır.*	e·*vet*/*ha*·yuhr
Help!	*İmdat!*	*eem*·dat
Cheers!	*Şerefe!*	she·re·*fe*

I don't understand.
Anlamıyorum. an·*la*·muh·yo·room

How much is it?
Ne kadar? ne ka·*dar*

Where's ...?
... nerede? ... *ne*·re·de

Where are the toilets?
Tuvaletler nerede? too·va·let·*ler* *ne*·re·de

UKRAINIAN

Vowels in unstressed syllables are generally pronounced shorter and weaker than they are in stressed syllables. Note that kh is pronounced as in the Scottish *loch* and zh as the 's' in 'pleasure'. The apostrophe (') indicates a slight y sound.

Hello.	Добрий день.	*do*·bry den'
Goodbye.	До побачення.	do po·*ba*·chen·nya
Please.	Прошу.	*pro*·shu
Thank you.	Дякую.	*dya*·ku·yu
Yes.	Так.	tak
No.	Ні.	ni
Help!	Допоможіть!	do·po·mo·*zhit'*
Cheers!	Будьмо!	*bud'*·mo

I don't understand.
Я не розумію. ya ne ro·zu·*mi*·yu

How much is it?
Скільки це він/вона коштує? (m/f) *skil'*·ki tse vin/vo·*na* *ko*·shtu·ye

Where's ...?
Де ...? de ...

Where are the toilets?
Де туалети? de tu·a·le·ti

behind the scenes

SEND US YOUR FEEDBACK

We love to hear from readers – your comments keep us on our toes and help make our books better. Our well-oiled team reads every word on what you loved or loathed about this book. Although we cannot reply individually to postal submissions, we always guarantee that your feedback goes straight to the appropriate authors, in time for the next edition. Each person who sends us information is thanked in the next edition – and the most useful submissions are rewarded with a free book.

Visit **lonelyplanet.com/contact** to submit your updates and suggestions or to ask for help. Our award-winning website also features inspirational travel stories, news and discussions.

Note: We may edit, reproduce and incorporate your comments in Lonely Planet products such as guidebooks, websites and digital products, so let us know if you don't want your comments reproduced or your name acknowledged. For a copy of our privacy policy visit lonelyplanet.com/privacy.

OUR READERS

Many thanks to the travellers who used the last edition and wrote to us with helpful hints, useful advice and interesting anecdotes:

Jessica Boyle, Thais Chalencon, Miraya Engelage, Madeleine Gasparinatos, Sara Knight, Evan M Morrison, Erhard Rathmayr, Cat Ryan, Amanda Schellenberg, Michael Schmid, Barney Smith, Keith Stanton, Nicole Stirling, Anbjørg Tovsrud, Emily Turner, Willem Vlotman, Aaron Williams, Kate Zappa

AUTHOR THANKS

Tom Masters

An enormous thanks to my hugely talented and hard-working co-authors on this book, whose passion for new discovery and getting the facts right made them, as always, such a pleasure to work with. Thanks especially to Jo Potts, Joe Bindloss, Imogen Bannister and all the in-house teams at Lonely Planet. In Belarus a big thank you to Leonid, Anna, Sasha and Alyona in Minsk, to Vera and Nina in Brest and the kind employees of the Chagall Museum in Vitebsk for their help on a particularly difficult day.

Brett Atkinson

Thanks to my Czech friends and drinking partners who again conspired to make a globetrotting Kiwi feel right at home. Special thanks to Greg and Francie in Olomouc, and at Lonely Planet, thanks to Jo Potts for the editorial support, and to coordinating author Tom Masters and the cartographer team for bringing the whole shebang together. Finally, love and special thanks to Carol and to Mum and Dad.

Carolyn Bain

Big Baltic hugs to friends who shared with me the pleasure of their company on parts of this trip, especially Graham Harris, Brandon Presser and Tallinn's finest tea-meister, Steve Kokker. I am again indebted to Steve for his friendship, kindness and immense local wisdom. Thanks to others who helped out with tips and company around the country, including Geli Lillemaa, Sirli Kalep and Andrew Meek.

James Bainbridge

A hearty *çok teşekkür* to everyone who helped me in İstanbul and around Turkey: Selcuk Akgul, Yener and friends, Leyla Tabrizi, Funda Dagli, Pat, Ekrem and the Kelebek posse in Göreme, Ece in İzmir, Ziya, Bill and the gang in Eceabat, Melek Anne and Café Pena in Edirne, Lütfi et al in Behramkale, Annette in Ayvalık, Mustafa in Bergama and Talat in Alaçatı. Thanks to Jen for teaching me backgammon, and to Leigh-Robin for coming on the adventure.

Mark Baker

On the ground in Hungary, my gratitude goes out to the helpful people at Tourinform and to my friend in Pécs, Krisztina Koncz, who introduced me to Villány's wonderful wines and even took the day off to show me around Szeged. Thanks also to my LP commissioning editors Jo Potts and Anna Tyler for choosing me as an author and cheerfully answering questions as they arose. A special thanks to coordinating author Tom Masters for his patience and calm.

Cristian Bonetto

On the ground, an epic 'Tak' to Søren Rose, Rune RK, Tue Hesselberg Foged, Toke Lykkeberg, Jens Martin Skibsted, Trine Wackerhaus, René Redzepi, Rasmus Kofoed, Aaron Giles and Julie Sanders. Thanks also to the many locals who offered time, tips and humour along the way. At Lonely Planet, many thanks to Jo Potts, Anna Tyler, Imogen Bannister, Sally Schafer, Darren O'Connell, Laura Stansfeld, Tom Masters and Herman So.

Paul Clammer

Thanks to my fellow Lonely Planet authors on Morocco: James Bainbridge, Helen Ranger and Alison Bing. *Shukran* to all my Fassi 'family' – you know who you are.

Kerry Christiani

Special thanks go to my husband Andy for being with me every step of the way on this book. I'd also like to thank all the tourism professionals who made the road to research silky smooth, especially Sabine Günterseder (Upper Austria Tourism), Monika Reichel (Salzburg Information) and Nicholas Boekdrukker (Innsbruck Tourism). At Lonely Planet, thanks go to Jo Potts, Tom Masters and Herman So.

Jayne D'Arcy

Thanks to fellow travellers Peter van der Brugghen and Marja Exterkate, familiar faces Mario Qytyku and Scott Logan, colleagues Carolyn Bain and Peter Dragičević and Lawrence and Mia Marzouk in Kosovo. Thanks to Tawan Sierek for the laughs during my third(!) visit to Butrint, to my dearest partner Sharik Billington for making sure young Miles was fed, watered and schooled until we were all together again, and to Miles. You guys rock.

Chris Deliso

Researching this book was generally a breeze but I should extend my appreciation to Petar and family in Dihovo and Zoran Grozdanovski in Ohrid. Coordinating author Tom Masters and Lonely Planet's editors Jo Potts and Anna Tyler, the ever-helpful Imogen Bannister, and Herman So and his map-making team also deserve a hearty thanks.

Marc Di Duca

When researching in Ukraine, you're never short of people bending over backwards to help you along the way. Firstly, a huge thanks to Ukraine expert Greg Bloom for all his support and a mammoth дякую to my Kyiv parents-in-law Mykola and Vira for taking care of son Taras while I was on the road. Big thanks also go to Markiyan, Yarema and Ihor in Lviv and to my wife Tanya, for all the days we spend apart.

Peter Dragičević

Thanks to Hayley Wright, Jack Delf and Amy Watson for helpful tips and contacts. Special thanks to Michael Woodhouse for finding Belgrade's campest accommodation and generally making the first week of research so enjoyable.

Lisa Dunford

My most heartfelt thanks go to my dear friends Saša, Fero, Šimon and Sara Petriska, Edita and Anton Augustin. It means so much to me being a part of your 'family.' I appreciate the hospitality and guidance of everyone along the road, including Andrea Sarkany, Miro, Vera & Jan Zachar, Jennifer Josifek, and Jess McMurray.

Mark Elliot

A million *mercis* to my beloved wife, Danielle Systermans, and to all our Benelux friends who have taught me so much over the years. Many thanks to Jan van Akker, David de Graef, Valerie De Kerpel, Lesley Devos, Guy Jacobs, Ludovic Desmet, Rémi Durand, Wieland de Hoon, Hans Rossel, Matthieu Segard and Brandon Noble. Endless thanks to my unbeatable family back in England whose love and inspiration gave me the joy and freedom to live and learn.

David Else

As always, massive appreciation goes to my wife Corinne, for joining me on many of my research trips around Britain, and for not minding when I locked myself away for 12 hours at a time to write this book – and for bringing coffee when it got nearer 18 hours. Thanks also to Tom and the other authors that worked with me on this book, to the helpful team of commissioning editors at LP London, and of course to the production editors and cartographers at LP Melbourne that brought this book to final fruition.

Steve Fallon

Thanks to Tatjana Radovič and Petra Stušek at the Ljubljana Tourist Board and Lucija Jager at the Slovenian Tourist Board. Slovenian Railways' Marino Fakin, Tone Plankar at the Ljubljana bus station and Tomaž Škofic of Adria Airways helped with transport. As always, my efforts here are dedicated to my partner, Michael Rothschild.

Duncan Garwood

Grazie to all the friends and family who helped me out on this job – Lorenzo, Viviana, Pino, Andrea, Luigi, Sonia, Giacomo, Antonello and Dora. Thanks also to fellow LP scribe Virginia Maxwell and to tourist office staff: Daniela Pinna (Cagliari), Tiziana (Cala Gonone), Patrizia (Alghero), Ilaria Lucentini (Cerveteri), Caterina Gucciardo (Mantua), Chiara De Angelis (Urbino), Laura Longa (Bari), the ladies at Genoa, and Mikaela Bandini (Matera). As always, a huge hug to Lidia, Ben and Nick.

Anthony Ham

In eight years of living in Madrid and during four extended stays in Norway, I have been welcomed and assisted by too many people to name and whose lives and stories have become a treasured part of the fabric of my own. It was my great fortune a week after arriving in Madrid to meet my wife and soulmate, Marina, who has made this city a true place of the heart. And to my daughters, Carlota and Valentina: truly you are Madrid's greatest gift of all.

Anna Kaminski

Many thanks to everyone who helped me on my Lithuania journey, including all of the too-numerous-to-mention-individually tourist office and Litinterp staff. A special thank you to Mikael for the late, late Vilnius nights, to Gintaras for his insider tips on Kaunas, to Justas and Milda for the memorable Klaipėda dinner, and to Luisė and Juozas for the smoked eel and boundless hospitality in Nida, yet again.

Craig McLachlan

A hearty thanks to all those who helped me out on the road, but most of all to my exceptionally beautiful wife Yuriko who let me know when I'd had enough Mythos each day! – and who also limited my daily intake of gyros pitta.

Anja Mutić

Hvala mama, for your home cooking and contagious laughter. *Gracias* to the Barcelona family. *Obrigada*, Hoji, for always being there. A huge *hvala* to my friends in Croatia who gave me endless contacts and recommendations. Lidija, you're always full of great ideas! Special thanks to Viviana Vukelić and her team at HTZ. A thank you also goes to Tom Masters for his flexibility. Finally, to the inspiring memory of my late father who travels with me still.

Becky Ohlsen

Becky Ohlsen would like to thank her fellow authors, especially Tom Masters for putting it all together, as well as Matt and Lindy in Tärnaby and Peter Kvarnestam and family in Skåne for their generous hospitality and entertainment.

Fran Parnell

A huge thank you to everyone who helped during the research and writing of the Iceland chapter of this book. This includes all the tourist-office, museum and activity-guide staff, particularly Auður from Reykjavík TI, Svanhvít at BSÍ, Svala at Air Iceland and Erlendur at Strýtan Divecenter. It's always fun catching up with Jón Trausti Sigurðarson at Grapevine. On a personal note, I am very grateful to the people who helped when my car fell to pieces on a mountain pass, especially Dagur from Sixt. And thanks to Kristján for being a calm presence before the marathon.

Leif Pettersen

In Romania, a hearty thanks goes to Monica Zavoianu in Suceava, Iulian Cozma in Braşov, Duncan Crombie and Josephine Postema in Sibiu, the folks at Retro Hostel in Cluj and Craig Turp in Bucharest. In Moldova I'm indebted to Rali Roesing, Sandy and Andy Smith, Josh Boissevain and, as always, Marisha Waters and Vitalie Eremia. And general gratitude to anyone who forced their *ţuică* into my hands. Unsurprisingly, I don't remember any of your names.

Brandon Presser

Paldies first and foremost to my pal Aleks Karlsons for his help and hospitality. Thanks also to Richard Baerug and Karlis Celms. Hey Emma: 'what? you don't like thank yous?' In LP-land, props to the savvy production staff, Jo Potts, Anna Tyler, Imogen Bannister, Herman So, and my talented co-authors – especially CA Tom Masters, and hostess-with-the-mostest, the illustrious Carolyn Bain.

Josephine Quintero

Josephine would like to thank all the helpful folk in the various tourist offices, in particular Alexis Christodoulides from the CTO in Larnaka. She would also like to thank Athina Papadoupoulou from the Nicosia Masterplan Office for her invaluable contribution. Thanks too, to Duncan Garwood for his continued support, as well as all those involved in the title from the Lonely Planet London- and Melbourne-based offices.

Tim Richards

As always, I'm indebted to the staff of Poland's tourist offices and railway company PKP. Much love to my Polish friends, Ewa, Magda, Gosia and Andrzej. Thanks to Wrocław artist Tomasz Moczek, with whom I spent a pleasant sunny hour drinking beer while talking about gnomes; and to Belarusian sailor Aleksandr, who kept me company on a train journey to Białystok. Hi also to Ania and Jaime, who I met via Twitter and shared a drink with in Lublin. Cheers!

Simon Richmond

In Moscow, *bolshoi spasibo* to Mirjana Vesentin for her hospitality and company on my culinary travels around the city. Leonid Ragozin was also a great help as was Roxane Chatounovski. As always, Sasha and Andrey were fabulous hosts in St Petersburg where I also must thank Peter and Valery for their company and input.

Miles Roddis

Lots of thanks to Ingrid, who skied the slopes, rode the moguls and chipped in with valuable après-ski advice as I scurried my way around this tiny land. Major thank-yous as well to particularly helpful tourist office staff Carolina (Andorra la Vella), Eva (Ordino) and Aret, Sonia and Ingrid (Canillo).

Caroline Sieg

Thanks to my parents for instilling in me a lifelong zest for travel. Thanks *mucho* to Lucy Monie for giving me this gig and *merci viel mal* to all my friends – old and new – for wining and dining with me across the country. And last but not least, thanks to Jules and Thresher, for all those memories that never go out of style.

Tamara Sheward

Alas, it's impossible to attempt to thank everyone here, so to be brutally specific, *hvala* and *živeli* to: Nevenka and Bane Šuvakov, Lazar Pašćanović, Benn and Olya, the good folk at Downtown Novi Sad (wrenched-out tooth notwithstanding), the Green Studio girls, Yellowbed kitchen-party people, Mick Muck, Cath Lanigan, David Collins and Tony Jackson for getting me in this fine mess to begin with, and the exceptionally patient and sage Brandon Presser. *Dušan, hvala na svemu moj divan durak.*

Regis St Louis

Big thanks to CA maestro Tom Masters and *Portugal* co-authors Kate, Gregor and Adam, who proved a stellar team to work with. In Portugal, I'd like to thank João for deep insight into Lisboa, Paolo for the enlightening Castelo walk and the memorable meals, Bruno for the radical UMM experience, and the many locals who shared tips along the way. As always *beijos* to Cassandra and daughters Magdalena and Genevieve for their support.

Andy Symington

Particular thanks for proofreading and Finnish support go to Riika Åkerlind, and to my family for their encouragement. I am indebted to numerous helpful people that I met along the way, particularly in tourist offices, and owe thanks to many Finnish friends for kindnesses and hospitality.

Ryan Ver Berkmoes

In Germany, Angela Cullen was a dear as always and I'm happy to see she still prefers Harry over a chihuahua. It was good to get back on track with Alan Wissenburg. Thanks to Birgit Borowski and Dr Eva Missler in Stuttgart. And thanks to Claudia Stehle as always for taking me to the dark depths of the BF. Samuel L Bronkowitz gets a nod as does Erin, the Kona-Denny's girl.

Richard Watkins

Many thanks to Martin Nedelchev in Sofia for the dinner and perhaps too much rakia. Thanks also go to all the girls at Zig Zag Holidays and the staff at Odysseia-In for their assistance in Sofia. I'd also like to thank the helpful staff at tourist offices in Burgas and Plovdiv.

Nicola Williams

Kudos to the exceptional commitment, creativity and cooperation of the *France* 9 team of authors whose prose I cut and manicured to create the France chapter of this guide. *Un grand merci* to Parisians Laure Chouillou and Sophie Maisonnier; and at home *bisous* to Matthias and our three wonderfully travel-happy children, Niko (9), Mischa (6) and Kaya (10 months).

Neil Wilson

Thanks to the friendly and helpful staff who worked at the tourist offices all over Ireland (and also in Malta), and to all those folk in pubs and on the road who offered their advice and recommendations.

ACKNOWLEDGMENTS

Climate map data adapted from Peel MC, Finlayson BL & McMahon TA (2007) 'Updated World Map of the Köppen-Geiger Climate Classification', Hydrology and Earth System Sciences, 11, 163344.
Cover photographs: Anders Blomqvist, Tony Burns, Grant Dixon, John Elk III, David Else, Lee Foster, Lou Jones, Rachel Lewis, Oliver Strewe. Many of the images in this guide are available for licensing from Lonely Planet Images: www.lonelyplanetimages.com.

THIS BOOK

lany people have helped to reate this 7th edition of Lonely lanet's *Europe on a shoestring* uidebook, which is part of onely Planet's Europe series. ther titles in this series include *'estern Europe*, *Mediterranean urope*, *Central Europe*, *Scandi-avia* and *Eastern Europe*. Lonely anet also publishes phrase-ooks for these regions. This uidebook was commissioned Lonely Planet's London office, d produced by the following:

ommissioning Editor Potts

Coordinating Editor Evan Jones

Coordinating Cartographer Valentina Kremenchutskaya

Coordinating Layout Designer Jacqui Saunders

Managing Editors Kirsten Rawlings, Tasmin Waby McNaughtan

Managing Cartographer Amanda Sierp

Managing Layout Designer Jane Hart

Assisting Editors Sarah Bailey, Andrew Bain, Jessica Crouch, Craig Kilburn, Sonya Mithen, Catherine Naghten, Kristin Odijk, Chris Pitts, Matty Soccio, Sophie Splatt, Gabbi Stefanos, Jeannette Wall, Kate Whitfield

Assisting Cartographers Csanad Csutoros, Eve Kelly, Jennifer Johnson, Katalin Dadi-Racz, Tom Webster

Cover Research Mazzy Princep

Internal Image Research Aude Vauconsant

Language Content Branislava Vladisavljevic

Thanks to Helen Christinis, Brigitte Ellemor, Chris Girdler, Lisa Knights, John Mazzocchi, Anna Metcalfe, Susan Paterson, John Taufa, Juan Winata

NOTES

index

000 Map pages
000 Photo pages

000 Map pages
000 Photo pages

G

H

000 Map pages
000 Photo pages

000 Map pages
000 Photo pages

M

000 Map pages
000 Photo pages

Q

R

000 Map pages
000 Photo pages

S

V

000 Map pages
000 Photo pages

W

X

Y

Z

Þ

how to use this book

These symbols will help you find the listings you want:

- Sights
- Activities
- Courses
- Tours
- Festivals & Events
- Sleeping
- Eating
- Drinking
- Entertainment
- Shopping
- Information/ Transport

These symbols give you the vital information for each listing:

- Telephone Numbers
- Opening Hours
- Parking
- Nonsmoking
- Air-Conditioning
- Internet Access
- Wi-Fi Access
- Swimming Pool
- Vegetarian Selection
- English-Language Menu
- Family-Friendly
- Pet-Friendly
- Bus
- Ferry
- Metro
- Subway
- London Tube
- Tram
- Train

Reviews are organised by author preference.

Look out for these icons:

- TOP CHOICE — Our author's recommendation
- FREE — No payment required
- A green or sustainable option

Our authors have nominated these places as demonstrating a strong commitment to sustainability – for example by supporting local communities and producers, operating in an environmentally friendly way, or supporting conservation projects.

Map Legend

Sights

- Beach
- Buddhist
- Castle
- Christian
- Hindu
- Islamic
- Jewish
- Monument
- Museum/Gallery
- Ruin
- Winery/Vineyard
- Zoo
- Other Sight

Activities, Courses & Tours

- Diving/Snorkelling
- Canoeing/Kayaking
- Skiing
- Surfing
- Swimming/Pool
- Walking
- Windsurfing
- Other Activity/ Course/Tour

Sleeping

- Sleeping
- Camping

Eating

- Eating

Drinking

- Drinking
- Cafe

Entertainment

- Entertainment

Shopping

- Shopping

Information

- Post Office
- Tourist Information

Transport

- Airport
- Border Crossing
- Bus
- Cable Car/ Funicular
- Cycling
- Ferry
- Metro
- Monorail
- Parking
- S-Bahn
- Taxi
- Train/Railway
- Tram
- Tube Station
- U-Bahn
- Other Transport

Routes

- Tollway
- Freeway
- Primary
- Secondary
- Tertiary
- Lane
- Unsealed Road
- Plaza/Mall
- Steps
- Tunnel
- Pedestrian Overpass
- Walking Tour
- Walking Tour Detour
- Path

Boundaries

- International
- State/Province
- Disputed
- Regional/Suburb
- Marine Park
- Cliff
- Wall

Population

- Capital (National)
- Capital (State/Province)
- City/Large Town
- Town/Village

Geographic

- Hut/Shelter
- Lighthouse
- Lookout
- Mountain/Volcano
- Oasis
- Park
- Pass
- Picnic Area
- Waterfall

Hydrography

- River/Creek
- Intermittent River
- Swamp/Mangrove
- Reef
- Canal
- Water
- Dry/Salt/ Intermittent Lake
- Glacier

Areas

- Beach/Desert
- Cemetery (Christian)
- Cemetery (Other)
- Park/Forest
- Sportsground
- Sight (Building)
- Top Sight (Building)

Nicola Williams

France Independent travel writer and editorial consultant Nicola Williams has lived in France and written about it for more than a decade. From her hillside house on the southern shore of Lake Geneva, it's a quick and easy hop to the French Alps (call her a ski fiend...), Paris (... art buff), southern France (... foodie and wine lover). Paris this time around meant stylish apartment living in the heart of St-Germain des Prés, aided and abetted by husband extraordinaire Matthias and three small tri-lingual kids with ant in their pants. Nicola has worked on numerous Lonely Planet titles, including *France, Discover France, Paris, Provence & the Côte d'Azur* and *The Loire*. She blogs at tripalong.wordpress.com and tweets@Tripalong.

Read more about Nicola at:
lonelyplanet.com/members/nicolawilliams

Neil Wilson

Ireland, Malta Neil's first experiences of Ireland were a sailing trip to Kinsale in 1990 and a tour of Northern Ireland's Antrim coast in 1994. Since then he has returned regularly for holidays, hiking trips and guidebook research – this time round he finally climbed Carrauntoohil, Ireland's highest peak. Neil is a full-time travel writer based in Edinburgh, Scotland, and has written around 50 guidebooks, including working on the last four editions of Lonely Planet's *Ireland* guide.

Read more about Neil at:
lonelyplanet.com/members/neilwilson

Tamara Sheward

Serbia After years of freelance travel writing, rock'n'roll journalism and insalubrious authordom, Tamara leapt at the chance to join the Lonely Planet ranks in 2009 as presenter of LPTV's *Roads Less Travelled: Cambodia* documentary. Taking on the decidedly less leech-infested Serbia for this book was a natural fit for a half-Russian Australian girl with a penchant for Cyrillic, *ćevapĉići* and home-made spirits, although getting trapped in a derelict Tito-era lift did test pan-Slavic relations somewhat. As befitting someone who believes that mayonnaise, sour cream and cheese does a salad make, Tamara has extensively travelled in and written about the Balkans, the Caucasus and Russia, and will continue to do so, as soon as the brain cells she lost at Guĉa are rejuvenated.

Caroline Sieg

Switzerland, Liechtenstein Half-Swiss, half-American, Caroline's relationship with Switzerland began when she and her family first moved to Lucerne at age five. Several moves back and forth across the Atlantic ended when she resided in Zurich throughout high-school and beyond, including working a season in a ski resort in the Valais. These days, Caroline heads to Switzerland as often as possible – to ski, indulge in cheese and chocolate or to simply meander along Lake Zürich.

Read more about Caroline at:
lonelyplanet.com/members/carolinesieg

Regis St Louis

Portugal Regis' long-time admiration for wine, rugged coastlines and melancholic music made him easy prey for Portugal. He has travelled extensively across the country – most recently fêting Lisbon's favourite saint at the Festa de Santo Antonio, exploring gorgeous beaches in the Parque Natural da Arrábida and eating too many *pasteis de nata* (including six in one day – oops). Regis is the coordinating author of Lonely Planet *Portugal*, and his travel essays have appeared in newspapers, in-flight magazines and online. He lives in Brooklyn, New York.

Read more about Regis at:
lonelyplanet.com/members/regisstlouis

Andy Symington

Finland Andy first visited Finland many years ago more or less by accident, and walking on frozen lakes with the midday sun low in the sky made a quick and deep impression on him, even as fingers froze in the -30°C temperatures. Since then they can't keep him away, fuelled by a love of huskies, saunas, Finnish mustard, moody Suomi rock and metal, but above all, of Finnish people and their beautiful country.

Read more about Andy at:
lonelyplanet.com/members/andysymington

Ryan Ver Berkmoes

Germany, Netherlands Ryan Ver Berkmoes once lived in Germany. Three years in Frankfurt during which time he edited a magazine until he got a chance for a new career: with Lonely Planet. One of his first jobs was working on the Germany chapter of the 4th edition of this very book. Later he worked on the 1st edition of LP's *The Netherlands*, a country where they pronounce his name better than he can. He continues to write about both. These days he lives in Portland, Oregon. Follow him at ryanverberkmoes.com. He tweets at @ryanvb.

Read more about Ryan at:
lonelyplanet.com/members/ryanverberkmoes

Richard Watkins

Bulgaria Richard studied ancient history at Oxford, and his first job after university was teaching conversational English to college students in Sofia. He tried teaching for a while in Singapore, but found travelling much more fun, and he has returned to Bulgaria several times since, discovering something new each time. Richard has contributed to various guidebooks, newspapers and websites, and has written for Lonely Planet since 2003. His previous titles include two editions of Lonely Planet *Bulgaria* as well as *Poland, Best of Krakow, Eastern Europe* and *Italy*.

Leif Pettersen

Moldova, Romania In 2003, after nine years of feigning interest in electronic payments for the US Federal Reserve System, Leif Pettersen – from Minneapolis, Minnesota – was 'Kramered' into being a homeless, shameless, godless freelance travel writer by an unbalanced friend. Leif's weakness for beauty first brought him to Romania in 2004, where he's since lived and/or traveled for two cumulative years. He's repeatedly visited every notable patch of grass in Romania and Moldova, making dear friends, except for Romania's Neo-Nazi Party who publicly denounced him in 2008, calling him a 'slimeball' and 'human piece of garbage'. (True story.) Leif writes an almost award-winning, 'slightly caustic' blog, where he dishes on travel writing, Romania, Italy's woeful internet and his remarkable-gift-for-hyphenation at KillingBatteries.com.

Brandon Presser

Latvia His wanderlust bigger than his wallet, Brandon earned his backpacker stripes after an epic overland adventure from Morocco to Finland. He then joined the glamourous ranks of eternal nomadism as a fulltime travel writer, and has since contributed to over 20 Lonely Planet titles. He co-authored *Estonia, Latvia & Lithuania* and was delighted to return to the Baltic where he put his Harvard art history degree to good use while checking out Rīga's surplus of evocative art nouveau architecture.

Josephine Quintero

Cyprus Josephine has visited Cyprus many times and finds the island fascinating, as well as experiencing a real affinity with the Cypriots from both sides of the Green Line. Highlights during this trip were visiting the incredible frescoed Byzantine churches in the Republic and a moonlit stroll around the north's Kyrenia harbour; a quintessential Mediterranean resort. Josephine also re-discovered the irresistible appeal of the traditional meze, especially when washed down with local Cypriot wine from one of the growing number of wineries in the Troodos.

Read more about Josephine at:
lonelyplanet.com/members/josephinequintero

Tim Richards

Poland Tim taught English in Kraków in 1994-95, after a two-year teaching stint in Egypt. He was fascinated by the post-communism transition affecting every aspect of Polish life, and by surviving remnants of the Cold War days. He's since returned to Poland repeatedly for Lonely Planet, deepening his relationship with this beautiful, complex country. When he's not on the road for Lonely Planet, Tim is a freelance journalist living in Melbourne, Australia. You can see more of his writing at www.iwriter.com.au.

Simon Richmond

Russia After studying Russian history and politics at university, Simon's first visit to the country was in 1994 when he wandered goggle eyed around gorgeous St Petersburg, and peeked at Lenin's mummified corpse in Red Square. He's since travelled the breadth of the nation from Kamchatka in the far east to Kaliningrad in the far west, stopping off at many points between. An award-winning writer and photographer, Simon is the co-author of the first and subsequent editions of Lonely Planet's *Trans-Siberian Railway* as well as editions 3, 4 and 5 of *Russia*. Read more about his travels in the country for this edition of *Europe on a shoestring* on his blog at www.simonrichmond.com.

Read more about Simon at:
lonelyplanet.com/members/simonrichmond

Miles Roddis

Andorra Living in Valencia, on Spain's Mediterranean coast, Miles loses count of the times he's nipped up to Andorra for a skiing weekend or a summertime camping and walking break – though never, ever to shop. He has written or contributed to more than 50 Lonely Planet titles, including guides, both general and walking, to Spain and France, Andorra's immediate neighbours.

Read more about Miles at:
lonelyplanet.com/members/serranoham

Duncan Garwood

Italy Since moving to Italy in 1997, Duncan has travelled the length and breadth of the country numerous times, contributing to a raft of Lonely Planet Italy titles as well as newspapers and magazines. Each trip throws up special memories and this time it was a perfect beach moment in Sardinia – driving down a rough dirt track to find a deserted strip of sand lapped by limpid aquamarine waters. He currently lives in the Alban hills just outside of Rome.

Read more about Duncan at:
lonelyplanet.com/members/duncangarwood

Anthony Ham

Norway, Spain In 2002 Anthony arrived in Madrid on a one-way ticket, has called the city home ever since and now lives with his *madrileña* wife and two daughters overlooking their favourite plaza in the city. He has written or co-written more than 50 guidebooks for Lonely Planet, including *Spain, Madrid* and *Norway,* and writes regularly on both countries for newspapers and magazines around the world. Researching this guide allowed him to rediscover his home city afresh and revisit one of his true passions, the Arctic North.

Read more about Anthony at:
lonelyplanet.com/members/anthony_ham

Anna Kaminski

Lithuania Many thanks to everyone who helped me on my Lithuania journey, including all of the too-numerous-to-mention-individually tourist office and Litinterp staff. A special thank you to Mikael for the late, late Vilnius nights, to Gintaras for his insider tips on Kaunas, to Justas and Milda for the memorable Klaipeda dinner, and to Luisė and Juozas for the smoked eel and boundless hospitality in Nida, yet again.

Craig McLachlan

Greece Craig has researched the Greek Islands for the last four editions of Lonely Planet's Europe guidebooks. He is also a regular visitor to Greece as a tour leader, guiding mainly hiking groups in the mountains and gorges of Crete and around the Cyclades. He's even taken a group of Japanese doctors to Kos to see the birthplace of Hippocrates. A Kiwi, Craig spends the southern hemisphere summer running an outdoor adventure company in Queenstown before heading north for the winter as a 'freelance anything'. He is also a karate instructor and Japanese interpreter. Check out his website at www.craigmclachlan.com.

Read more about Craig at:
lonelyplanet.com/members/craigmclachlan

Anja Mutić

Croatia It's been more than 18 years since Anja left her native Croatia. The journey took her to several countries before she made New York City her base 11 years ago. But the roots are a'calling. She's been returning to Croatia frequently for work and play, intent on discovering a new place on every visit. On her last trip, she loved exploring Hvar's lavender-dotted interior. Anja blogs about her travels at www.everthenomad.com.

Read more about Anja at:
lonelyplanet.com/members/anjamutic

Becky Ohlsen

Sweden Becky has traveled in Sweden since age two and is constantly amazed at the fact that no matter how often she visits, she still finds things she's never seen before, whether it's an underground cafe in Södermalm or a Viking-era stone ship hidden away in the forest. Becky's favorite things about Sweden include fried herring and saffron ice cream (not together), the art of John Bauer, the diaries of August Strindberg, the films of Ingmar Bergman, the hiking trails of Norrland, and the little red huts scattered everywhere. She has also written about England and the Pacific Northwest for Lonely Planet. Becky lives in Portland, Oregon.

Fran Parnell

Iceland Fran updated the Iceland chapter. Her passion for Scandinavia began while studying for a masters degree in Anglo-Saxon, Norse and Celtic. A strange university slideshow, featuring sublime Icelandic mountains and a matter-of-fact man who'd literally dug his own grave, awakened a fascination with Iceland that has just kept on growing. Fran returns to the country as often as possible, and always finds something new to appreciate. This year, she ran the Reykjavík Marathon for the first time, and would recommend the experience to everyone! Fran has worked on other Lonely Planet guides to Scandinavia, including *Scandinavia, Iceland, Sweden, Denmark* and *Reykjavík.*

Marc Di Duca

Ukraine Driven by an urge to discover Eastern Europe's wilder side, Marc first hit Kyiv one dark, snow-flecked night in early 1998. Several prolonged stints, countless near misses with Kyiv's metro doors and many bottles of *horilka* later, he still never misses a chance to fine-tune his Russian while exploring far-flung corners of this immense land. An established travel author, Marc has penned guides to Moscow and Lake Baikal, as well as working on Lonely Planet's *Trans-Siberian Railway* and *Russia* books.

Read more about Marc Di Duca at:
lonelyplanet.com/members/madidu

Peter Dragičević

Montenegro Among the two dozen or so Lonely Planet books that Peter's co-written are the first ever *Montenegro* country guide, *Western Balkans* and the two previous editions of this title. While it was family ties that first drew him to the Balkans, it's the history, natural beauty, convoluted politics, cheap *rakija* and intriguing people that keep bringing him back. This trip's highlight was a particularly dramatic trek through the clouds to the Njegoš monument on the top of Mt Lovćen.

Lisa Dunford

Slovakia A fascination with Europe has gripped Lisa since childhood, probably because her grandfather emigrated from the Carpathian mountains that were a part of Hungary, then Czechoslovakia and now are in the Ukraine. She studied in Budapest junior year at university and, post graduation, worked for the Agency for International Development at the US embassy in Bratislava. While living in Slovakia, Lisa danced with the country as it became an independent nation, learned the language and made life-long friends. She returns often as a freelance writer. Lisa has contributed to numerous books for Lonely Planet, including *Czech & Slovak Republics, Hungary* and *Central Europe*.

Mark Elliot

Belgium, Bosnia & Hercegovia, Luxembourg In 1995, a chance encounter at a Turkmenistan camel market saw British-born author Mark Elliott tumble into the arms of his Belgian bride-to-be. He followed her home and is now well into a second decade living in the Benelux, still revelling in the crazy carnivals, fabulous festivals, classic castles and brilliant beer cafes that make this area one of the world's most underestimated destinations. Mark was only 11 when his family first dragged him to Sarajevo and stood him in the now defunct concrete footsteps of Gavrilo Princip. Fortunately no Austro-Hungarian emperors were passing at the time. He has since visited virtually every corner of BiH supping fine Hercegovinian wines with master vintners, talking philosophy with Serb monks and Sufi mystics and drinking more Bosnian coffee than any healthy stomach should be subjected to.

David Else

Britain David is a professional travel writer and author of more than 40 guidebooks, including numerous editions of Lonely Planet's guides to *Great Britain, England* and *Walking in Britain*. His knowledge comes from a lifetime of travel around the country – often on foot – a passion dating from university years, when heading for the hills was always more attractive than visiting the library. Originally from London, David has lived in Yorkshire, Wales and Derbyshire, and is currently based on the southern edge of the Cotswolds.

Read more about David at:
lonelyplanet.com/members/davidelse

Steve Fallon

Slovenia Steve has been travelling to Slovenia since the early 1990s, when most everyone but the Slovenes had never heard of the place. Never mind, it was his own private Idaho for over a decade. Though *on še govori slovensko kot jamski človek* (he still speaks Slovene like a caveman), Steve considers part of his soul to be Slovenian and returns as often as he can for a glimpse of the Julian Alps in the sun, a dribble of *bučno olje* and a dose of the dual.

Mark Baker

Hungary Mark first came to Eastern Europe in the mid-'80s as a grad student in International Affairs. Those were the dark days of the dying communist regimes, yet even then he was hooked by the region's quirky history, beauty and cheap booze. He's lived in Prague for the better part of 20 years, and is a frequent traveller throughout the region (and now has a special fondness for Hungary). After working as a fulltime journalist for The Economist Group and Radio Free Europe, he's found permanent employment as a freelance travel writer and is co-author of Lonely Planet's *Prague* and *Romania*, among other titles.

Cristian Bonetto

Denmark A weakness for svelte design, adventurous chefs and cycle-toned bodies first drew Cristian Bonetto to Denmark. Years later, the Australian-born writer is no less impressed by the country's progressive green policies and high quota of perfect cheekbones. Indeed, Denmark's effortless cool continues to inspire this one-time soap scribe, whose musings on travel and popular culture have appeared in Australian, British and Italian publications. When Cristian isn't hunting down Denmark's best *kanelsneggle* ('cinnamon snail'), you're likely to find him scouring Sweden, Italy and New York for decent espresso, cheap chic and the perfect shot to post on Facebook.

Kerry Christiani

Austria Born in Essex, Kerry now lives in the Black Forest, Germany. Ever since her first encounter with real snow in the Tyrolean Alps, she has been travelling back to those incredible mountains. On her second visit for Lonely Planet she discovered the truth about the von Trapps in Salzburg, sweated out a rare heatwave in the Alps and climbed (almost) every mountain. In so doing, she fell in love with the little country and its great outdoors all over again. Kerry's incurable wanderlust has taken her to six continents, inspiring numerous articles and some 20 guidebooks, including Lonely Planet *Austria, Germany, Switzerland* and *France*.

Read more about Kerry at:
lonelyplanet.com/members/kerrychristiani

Paul Clammer

Morocco As a student, Paul had his first solo backpacking experience when he took a bus from his Cambridgeshire home all the way to Casablanca. After an interlude where he trained and worked as a molecular biologist, he returned to work as a tour guide, trekking in the Atlas and trying not to lose passengers in the Fez medina. The increasing number of budget-airline routes from the UK to Morocco is one of his favourite recent travel innovations, allowing him to continue to hop over to Morocco on a regular basis.

Read more about Paul at:
lonelyplanet.com/members/paulclammer

Jayne D'Arcy

Albania & Kosovo Counting Albania's highlights every two years for the past six has led Jayne to the startling conclusion that Albania resembles a robust child's growth chart. Taking advantage of the growth are cyclists in remote corners, hikers turning the 'Accursed Mountains' into a 'must-hike' and backpacker hostels opening in the hottest spots. When she's not taking photos of vintage folding bikes in Albania, Jayne also writes about the southern hemisphere (*South East Asia on a shoestring* and *Australia*) and rides her own vintage folding bike around Melbourne, Australia.

Chris Deliso

Macedonia US travel writer and journalist Chris Deliso (www.chrisdeliso.com) has been exploring widely in the Balkans ever since finishing a master's in Byzantine History at Oxford University, back in 1999. He's lived in Greece, Turkey and, for the most part, Macedonia – a country that still continues to surprise him on a daily basis. In researching the present guide, Chris checked out new nightspots in Skopje's revitalised old town, gazed out from beatific mountaintop monasteries, and hopped boulders while fending off freshwater crabs in Macedonia's rushing rivers. Chris has contributed to several other Lonely Planet guidebooks, including *Greece, Bulgaria* and *Western Balkans*.

Read more about Chris at:
lonelyplanet.com/members/chrisdeliso

OUR STORY

A beat-up old car, a few dollars in the pocket and a sense of adventure. In 1972 that's all Tony and Maureen Wheeler needed for the trip of a lifetime – across Europe and Asia overland to Australia. It took several months, and at the end – broke but inspired – they sat at their kitchen table writing and stapling together their first travel guide, *Across Asia on the Cheap*. Within a week they'd sold 1500 copies. Lonely Planet was born.

Today, Lonely Planet has offices in Melbourne, London and Oakland, with more than 600 staff and writers. We share Tony's belief that 'a great guidebook should do three things: inform, educate and amuse'.

OUR WRITERS

Tom Masters

Co-ordinating Author, Belarus An inveterate traveller since childhood, Tom has backpacked, trained, flown, walked and driven through all corners of Europe over the past three decades. Having lived in London, Paris, St Petersburg and Berlin, he feels more European than English these days. When not travelling through police states and avoiding arrest from shadowy security services, Tom can usually be found in the bars and cafes of East Berlin. You can find him online at www.tommasters.net.

Read more about Tom at: lonelyplanet.com/members/tommasters

Brett Atkinson

Czech Republic Brett Atkinson has been travelling to Eastern Europe for more than 20 years, honeymooning in Bosnia, Croatia and Hungary, writing about the legacy of the communist era, and enjoying more than a few local beers. For his fourth extended research trip to the Czech Republic, he dived into Prague's emerging visual arts scene, trekked the spectacular valleys of the Bohemian Switzerland region, and continued to marvel at sunsets above Prague Castle. When he's not on the road for Lonely Planet, Brett's at home in Auckland, planning his next overseas sojourn with wife Carol. He's contributed to more than 20 Lonely Planet titles, and travelled to more than 60 countries. See www.brett-atkinson.net for details of his latest writing and travels.

Carolyn Bain

Estonia Melbourne-based Carolyn studied European history and languages and has lived and studied in a few Euro hotspots, from London to rural Denmark to St Petersburg. Lonely Planet has given her licence to further investigate great pockets of the continent – Greece, Malta, Sweden, Denmark, the Baltics – and there's still a huge buzz to be had in crossing the Arctic Circle or swimming in the Med in December, all in the name of work. For this book she returned to the northeast, where Estonia combines the best of Eastern Europe and Scandinavia and delivers something heartwarmingly unique.

James Bainbridge

Turkey Coordinating two editions of Lonely Planet's *Turkey* took James from Aegean islands to the Anatolian plateau. He also spent most of 2010 living in İstanbul – trendy Cihangir to be exact – and learning to love suffixes on a Turkish course. Originally from England, he now lives in Cape Town (Turkey, give my South African girlfriend a visa next time!) and writes about Africa, the Middle East and Europe for worldwide publications. His other Lonely Planet credits include the previous edition of this guide and, most recently, coordinating *Morocco*. You can find links to travel articles by James at the Lonely Planet website.

Read more about James at: lonelyplanet.com/members/james_bains

OVER PAGE MORE WRITERS

Published by Lonely Planet Publications Pty Ltd
ABN 36 005 607 983
7th edition – Oct 2011
ISBN 978 1 74179 676 6

10 9 8 7 6 5 4 3 2 1
Printed in Singapore